Say it in Spanish
Say it in English, but ...
Say exactly what you mean.

This is just what this newly revised bilingual dictionary allows you to do. When you look for a word in Spanish or English, you will find equivalents and *also* distinguishing labels that separate various meanings according to context, enabling you to pick the word that means exactly what you intend. Entries include derivatives, phrases, idiomatic expressions, and pronunciations in the International Phonetic Alphabet. Completely updated to reflect current usage in both English and Spanish, *The New World Spanish/English-English/Spanish Dictionary* makes it possible for you to use the language *as native speakers do.*

Cariño

Dígalo en español
Dígalo en inglés, pero ...
Diga exactamente lo que Vd. intenta.

Esto es justamente lo que este diccionario bilingue nuevamente revisado hace posible. Cuando busca una palabra en español o en inglés, encuentra sus equivalentes inscritos y *además* signos clasificantes de significación, a fin de que pueda escoger la palabra que dé a entender lo más exactamente lo que Vd. intenta. Se incluye bajo la palabra clave derivados, frases y modismos, y pronunciaciones en Alfabeto Fonético Internacional. Completamente puesto al día de modo de manifestar el uso corriente en inglés así como en español. EL DICCIONARIO NEW WORLD ESPAÑOL/INGLÉS-INGLÉS/ESPAÑOL le permite usar el idioma *como lo usan los nativos.*

THE NEW WORLD
SPANISH/ENGLISH
ENGLISH/SPANISH
DICTIONARY

SECOND EDITION

Salvatore Ramondino
EDITOR

A SIGNET BOOK

SIGNET
Published by New American Library, a division of Penguin Group (USA) Inc., 375 Hudson Street, New York, New York 10014, USA
Penguin Group (Canada), 10 Alcorn Avenue, Toronto, Ontario M4V 3B2, Canada (a division of Pearson Penguin Canada Inc.)
Penguin Books Ltd., 80 Strand, London WC2R 0RL, England
Penguin Ireland, 25 St. Stephen's Green, Dublin 2, Ireland (a division of Penguin Books Ltd.)
Penguin Group (Australia), 250 Camberwell Road, Camberwell, Victoria 3124, Australia (a division of Pearson Australia Group Pty. Ltd.)
Penguin Books India Pvt. Ltd., 11 Community Centre, Panchsheel Park, New Delhi - 110 017, India
Penguin Group (NZ), cnr Airborne and Rosedale Roads, Albany, Auckland 1310, New Zealand (a division of Pearson New Zealand Ltd.)
Penguin Books (South Africa) (Pty.) Ltd., 24 Sturdee Avenue, Rosebank, Johannesburg 2196, South Africa

Penguin Books Ltd., Registered Offices: 80 Strand, London WC2R 0RL, England

First published by Signet, an imprint of New American Library,
a division of Penguin Group (USA) Inc.

First Printing, May 1969
First Printing (Second Edition), August 1996
30 29 28 27 26 25 24 23 22 21 20

Copyright © Penguin Group (USA) Inc., 1969, 1996
All rights reserved

 REGISTERED TRADEMARK—MARCA REGISTRADA

Printed in the United States of America

CONTENTS

ÍNDICE GENERAL

PREFACE TO THE SECOND EDITION

The editors here present, for the many users of our first edition, and to introduce to new users of this second edition, a completely revised, expanded, and updated work. New features include: (1) an augmented selection of more than 3,000 useful words, terms, and phrases; (2) prefixes and suffixes in both languages have been collected together in separate lists; (3) in the Spanish-English section, irregular inflections of verbs have been referred by an appropriate number to the list of Spanish Model Verbs; (4) a more thorough treatment of English verbal inflections in appropriate lists; (5) a large selection of geographical names in English and Spanish; (6) inclusion of contemporary computer terms, as well as scientific and commercial terms, and terms in other fields that have grown significantly in the years since the first edition was published.

INTRODUCTION

In the treatment of Spanish words, virtually all existing bilingual dictionaries have relied on the highly conservative lexicons of the Spanish language. They do little more than translate, literally, the definitions of each Spanish word as given in the standard Spanish dictionaries, without giving the user of the bilingual dictionary any indication of the relative importance or usefulness of the various senses with their English equivalents.

In an effort to improve on this method, and in order to convey the living substance of the Spanish language to the English-speaking user, the editors of this dictionary have consulted representative writers and speakers of Spanish in all areas. The Spanish-speaking user, for his part, will find exact, usable, and current equivalents in English of the elements of his own language.

All the most important and useful words in both languages, and *only* the most important and useful, have been selected for inclusion. Common prefixes, suffixes, and combining elements are included, with equivalents, if they exist, or with an explanation in the opposite language of the meaning and use of the element, or both. The most distinctive and frequently used idiomatic and colloquial expressions have been rendered in the opposite language by usable equivalents on the same level of usage and as far as possible conveying the same flavor. Slang and colloquial terms are included when important and in common usage and are defined by standard terms unless an exact equivalent at the same level of usage exists. Classical Spanish and English terms are covered. All words used in definitions in one section of the dictionary appear as entries in the other section.

Throughout this dictionary the empasis is on usage in the Western Hemisphere. American English usage and spellings are preferred; British and dialectal forms and meanings are included only if they are widely known in the United States, and pronunciation follows best usage in regions where there is no marked perculiarity in speech and in normal conversation rather than in formal speech.

Similarly, Americanisms in Spanish—i.e., words and phrases customary in Latin America and in Spanish-speaking sections of the U.S. Southwest and Far West—receive special attention, and the standards of pronunciation, spelling, and usage prevailing in the Spanish-speaking countries of the New World are given prominence.

Currency and practicality are the qualities that students and travelers alike demand in a foreign-language dictionary and these they will be sure to find here.

In this dictionary each main entry is composed of two or more of the following elements, explained here in the order in which they may be expected to appear.

1. The *main* entry is printed in boldface type and may be a simple or compound word or a phrase. Variant spellings commonly used are also in boldface type.

2. The *pronunciation* follows the entry word in parentheses. All entries are pronounced, with the exception of compound words or phrases whose elements are pronounced as main entries elsewhere in the dictionary. If a variant spelling is pronounced the same as the main entry, only one pronunciation is given; if the variant spelling and the main entry have different pronunciations, each is pronounced separately. Symbols used in the pronunciations are explained on pages 511–517.

3. *Parts of speech.* All words, simple or compound, are identified as to part of speech; phrases are not so identified. If a

word is used as more than one part of speech, each part of speech is defined separately. Part-of-speech labels are combined only in cases in which the entry word and the word or words used to define it are the same in more than one part of speech.

4. In the English-Spanish section, *inflected forms* of irregular verbs, irregular plurals of nouns, and irregular comparative forms of adjectives are given in boldface type within brackets. Regular inflections are shown only when a word has both irregular and regular forms that are commonly used. In some cases inflected forms of irregular verbs are not given, but another verb is referred to as a model. In the Spanish-English section, inflected forms of irregular verbs are referred to by an appropriate number to the list of Model Spanish Verbs. Pronunciation of inflected forms is given unless the form is listed as a main entry.

5. *Definitions.* Each distinct meaning of a word is separately numbered and defined. Numbers are used only to separate distinct meanings, or denotations, of a word. Within each numbered definition there may be two or more words or phrases used to define the word in that meaning. These are separated by semicolons, indicating that they differ only in *connotation*—that is, in nuance of meaning—but have in general the same *denotation.* A word may also be defined by reference to a main entry that is a synonym.

6. *Labels,* in italics, furnish information of a special sort concerning the word being defined. They may indicate its currency of usage (*archaic, historical,* etc.), standard of usage (*colloq., slang,* etc.), special geographical area of usage (*Amer., Brit., W.I.,* etc.), or special field of usage (*law, med., math.,* etc.).

7. In the *English-Spanish section,* each distinct sense of an English word is identified by a *label* in parentheses. This label (the "contextual gist" label) is a concise identification of the specific sense in which the word is being rendered by the Spanish equivalent. This contextual gist label may be supplemented or replaced by a special field label (see 6, above).

8. *Qualifying word or phrase.* A definition may be complemented by a word or phrase to clarify its meaning. If the word or phrase can be used with the definition to form a semantic unit, it is printed in roman type in parentheses; if it cannot, it is printed in italic type in parentheses.

9. *Subsidiary entries* appear in boldface type following the last defined part of speech. They may be:

a. *inflected forms* of main entry words that have senses that differ from those of the principal form;

b. *variant forms,* including common variant spellings, and synonymous forms based on the same or related stems;

c. *derivatives,* i.e., words formed on the same stem as the main entry, but with distinctive form and meaning. Derivatives are pronounced only when the elements used to form them are not separately listed in this dictionary;

d. *idiomatic phrases,* i.e., phrases formed of the principal word, whether that word is a main entry or a subsidiary entry, plus one or more other elements (usually adverbs or object nouns).

PREFACIO A LA SEGUNDA EDICIÓN

Los Redactores les presentan ahora, a los numerosos lectores de nuestra primera edición, y para los que consiguen nuevamente esta segunda edición, una obra completamente revisada, anumentada y puesta al día. Sus innovaciones comprenden: (1) aumentada compilación de más de 3,000 palabras, términos y modismos útiles; (2) prefijos y sufijos en ambos idiomas vienen extraídos de los vocabularios generales y presentados todos juntos en listas separadas; (3) en la parte española-inglesa, las inflexiones de los verbos irregulares están recopiladas en listas separadas, con llamada numérica a la lista de Verbos Modelos del Español; (4) tratamiento más comprensivo de las inflexiones verbales del inglés en listas separadas; (5) amplia selección de nombres geográficos con equivalentes en inglés y en español; (6) agregación de términos corrientes de informática, de ciencia y de comercio, así como de otros ramos que han manifestado tan notable aumentación durante los años transcurridos desde la aparición de la primera edición.

INTRODUCCIÓN

En cuanto al idioma español, todos los diccionarios bilingües existentes han tomado como fuente los léxicos castellanos más conservadores. Hacen poco más que traducir literalmente cada palabra. No dan al que consulta el diccionario ninguna indicación de la relativa importancia o utilidad que ofrece el conocimiento de las varias acepciones de una palabra con su equivalente en inglés.

Con el objeto de mejorar este método y el de transmitir la substancia viva de la lengua española a la persona de habla inglesa que utiliza esta obra, los redactores de este diccionario han consultado a escritores y nacionales de todas las regiones de habla española, representativos de las mismas. A su vez, la persona de habla española encontrará traducciones fieles, de uso práctico y frecuente, que corresponden a los elementos de su propio idioma.

Las palabras más importantes y útiles de ambas lenguas, y *sólo* las más importantes y útiles, han sido seleccionadas para su inclusión. Se incluyen, igualmente, los prefijos, sufijos y elementos comunes que se usan para formar palabras. Siempre que sea posible, se da un equivalente exacto en el otro idioma. En caso contrario, se ofrece una explicación sobre su significado y uso. En ocasiones figuran ambas cosas. Las expresiones idiomáticas y familiares más características y más frecuentes se han traducido de modo que revelan un uso similar en ambas lenguas y un mismo sabor idiomático, de ser posible. Los vulgarismos y giros familiares se incluyen cuando son importantes y de uso común, con su correspondiente explicación, a menos que exista una traducción exacta de la expresión. Los vocablos clásicos de ambos idiomas aparecen en esta obra. Todas las palabras que se emplean en una definición aparecen como vocablos en la otra sección.

En este diccionario se da mayor énfasis al uso del idioma en el Hemisferio Occidental. La ortografía y el uso de inglés de los Estados Unidos tienen carácter preferente al de Inglaterra. Las expresiones británicas y los regionalismos se incluyen sólo cuando son ampliamente conocidos en los Estados Unidos. La pronunciación que se ofrece es la del mejor uso en las regiones donde no hay marcadas peculiaridades de pronunciación, y refleja una dicción conversacional más que clásica.

De igual modo, los americanismos de la lengua española—es decir, palabras y frases de uso común en Hispanoamérica y en regiones de habla española del Suroeste y Oeste de los Estados Unidos—reciben una atención especial, dándosele una mayor importancia a la pronunciación, ortografía y uso del idioma en los países de habla española del Nuevo Mundo.

Tanto el estudiante como el viajero buscan en un diccionario bilingüe las palabras de uso corriente y práctico. Esto hallarán aquí con toda seguridad.

En este diccionario, cada artículo o palabra se compone de dos o más de los siguientes elementos, que se explican a continuación en el orden en que aparecen.

1. Cada *artículo* figura en negrilla y puede ser una palabra simple, una palabra compuesta o una frase. Las variantes ortográficas de uso frecuente se dan también en negrilla.

2. La *pronunciación* sigue, entre paréntesis, a cada artículo. Se exceptúan aquellas palabras compuestas o frases cuyos elementos componentes y su correspondiente pronunciación aparezcan como artículo principal en el lugar que les corresponde. Si la variante ortográfica se pronuncia de igual modo, se indica la pronunciación una sola vez; si cambia la pronunciación se ofrecen ambas. Los símbolos fonéticos se explican en las páginas 1266–1269.

3. *Partes de la oración.* El oficio que desempeña en la oración cada palabra, simple o compuesta, aparece indicado. No así en el caso de frases. Si una palabra desempeña diversos oficios, se define cada uno separadamente, a menos que la definición sea idéntica, en cuyo caso aparecen combinados los oficios en un mismo rótulo.

4. *Accidentes gramaticales.* En la parte inglesa-española, terminaciones irregulares de los verbos, plurales irregulares de los nombres y adjetivos comparativos irregulares aparecen en negrilla dento de corchetes. Las inflexiones regulares aparecen sólo cuando una palabra se usa comúnmente en ambas formas, regular e irregular. La pronunciación de estas variantes se da siempre, a menos que la misma aparezca como artículo principal en el lugar que le corresponde. En la parte española inglesa, las inflexiones verbales de las differentes clases de verbos están recopiladas en listas separadas, con llamada numérica a la lista de Verbos Modelos del Español.

5. *Definiciones.* Los distintos significados de cada palabra se numeran y definen separadamente. Se usan los números

solamente para separar los distintos significados o denotaciones de una palabra. En cada definición numerada puede haber dos o más palabras o frases, separadas por punto y coma, que se emplean para definir el artículo con ese significado. Esto indica que difieren solamente en la *connotación*—esto es, matices del significado—pero que tienen en general la misma *denotación*. También puede definirse una palabra refiriéndola a un sinónimo ya definido.

6. *Rótulos.* Palabras en bastardilla, dentro de paréntesis, ofrecen información especial relacionada con el vocablo definido. Pueden indicar frecuencia del uso (*arcaico, histórico,* etc.), clase de uso (*familiar, vulgar, ofensivo,* etc.), uso regional (*Estados Unidos, Inglaterra, Antillas,* etc.) o ámbito especial del uso (*derecho, medicina, matemáticas,* etc.). Una lista de estos rótulos, con las abreviaturas usadas en este diccionario, aparece en la página xiii.

7. En el texto inglés-español, cada variación del sentido de una palabra inglesa tiene su *rótulo* en paréntesis. Este rótulo ("esencia del contexto") muestra precisamente el sentido especial de su equivalente en español. Este rótulo puede tener adición o ser sustituido por el rótulo de una área especial (véase supra, 6).

8. *Palabra o frase explicativa.* Puede complementarse una defición con una palabra o frase que aclare su significado. Si la aclaración forma una unidad semántica con la definición, aparece aquélla entre paréntesis, con letra de tipo romano; en caso contrario aparece en bastardilla.

9. Los *artículos secundarios* figuran en negrilla después de la última definición del artículo principal en el oficio que desempeña como parte de la oración. Estos artículos pueden ser:

a. *accidentes* de palabras variables en su flexión, cuyo significado difiere del principal después del cambio;

b. *variantes,* incluyendo las ortográficas, y sinónimos que se basan en la misma raíz;

c. *derivados,* esto es, palabras que tienen la misma raíz que el artículo principal, pero distinta forma y significado. Su pronunciación aparece sólo en el caso de que sus componentes no figuren en otra parte de este diccionario;

d. *expresiones idiomáticas,* esto es, frases que se forman de la palabra principal, ya sea artículo principal o secundario, con la adición de uno o más elementos (generalmente adverbios o complementos).

LABELS AND ABBREVIATIONS USED IN THE DICTIONARY

LOS ROTULOS Y ABREVIATURAS USADOS EN EL DICCIONARIO

abbr., abr.	abbreviation	abreviatura
acc., ac.	accusative	acusativo
A.D., A.C.	Anno Domini	Año de Cristo
adj.	adjective; adjectival	adjetivo; adjetival
adv.	adverb; adverbial	adverbio; adverbial
aero.	aeronautics	aeronáutica
agric.	agriculture	agricultura
alg., álg.	algebra	álgebra
alt.	alternate	alternativo
A.M.	ante meridiem	antemeridiano; por la mañana
Amer., amer.	American	americano
anat.	anatomy	anatomía
Ant.	West Indies	Antillas
archaeol., arqueol.	archaeology	arqueología
archit., arquit.	architecture	arquitectura
Arg.	Argentina	Argentina
arith., aritm.	arithmetic	aritmética
art.	article	artículo
astrol.	astrology	astrología
astron.	astronomy	astronomía
auto.	automotive	automotor; automóvil
aux.	auxiliary	auxiliar
B.C.	before Christ	antes de Cristo
biol.	biology	biología
bot.	botany	botánica
Brit., brit.	British	británico
C.A.	Central America	Centroamérica; América Central
cap.	capital; capitalized	mayúscula
carp.	carpentry	carpintería
chem.	chemistry	química
cir.	surgery	cirugía
colloq.	colloquial	familiar
comm., com.	commerce; commercial	comercio; comercial
comp.	comparative	comparativo
comput.	computer science; computers	computación; computadoras
cond.	conditional	condicional
conj.	conjunction	conjunción
contr.	contraction	contracción
dat.	dative	dativo
def.	definite	definido

dem.	demonstrative	demostrativo
dent.	dentistry	odontología
der.	law	derecho
derog., desp.	derogatory	despectivo
dial.	dialect; dialectal	dialecto; dialectal
dim.	diminutive	diminutivo
dir.	direct	directo
eccles., ecles.	ecclesiastical	eclesiástico
econ.	economics	economía
educ.	education	educación
EE.UU.	United States	Estados Unidos
elect.	electricity; electronics	electricidad; electrónica
Eng.	English	inglés
eng.	engineering	ingeniería
entom.	entomology	entomología
esc.	sculpture	escultura
Esp.	Spain	España
esp.	especially	especialmente
españ.	Spanish	español
etc.	et cetera	etcétera
exc.	except	excepto
fam.	colloq.	familiar
farm.	pharmacology	farmacología
fem., f.	feminine	femenino
ferr.	railroads; railroading	ferrovías; ferroviario
fig.	figurative	figurativo
filos.	philosophy	filosofía
fin.	finance; financial	finanzas; financiero
1st, 1º	first	primero
fisiol.	physiology	fisiología
fol.	followed	seguido
fonét.	phonetics	fonética
fotog.	photography	fotografía
fut.	future	futuro
gen.	genitive	genitivo
geog.	geography	geografía
geol.	geology	geología
geom.	geometry	geometría
ger.	gerund	gerundio
gram.	grammar; grammatical	gramática; gramático
her.	heraldry	heráldica
hist.	history; historical	historia; histórico
hortic.	horticulture	horticultura
ichthy., ictiol.	ichthyology	ictiología
impers.	impersonal	impersonal
impf.	imperfect	imperfecto
impr.	printing	imprenta
impv.	imperative	imperativo
ind.	indicative	indicativo
indecl.	indeclinable	indeclinable
indef.	indefinite	indefinido
indir.	indirect	indirecto
infl.	inflection	inflexión
ing.	English	inglés

ingen.	engineering	ingeniería
interj.	interjection.	interjección
interr.	interrogative	interrogativo
intr.	intransitive	intransitivo; neutro
irreg.	irregular	irregular
jer.	slang	jerga; jerigonza
law	law	derecho
l.c.	lower case	minúscula
ling.	linguistics	lingüística
lit.	literal; literally	literal; literalmente
marc.reg.	trade name	marca registrada
masc., m.	masculine	masculino
med.	medicine	medicina
metall., metal.	metallurgy	metalurgia
meteorol.	meteorology	meteorología
Mex., Méx.	Mexico	México
mfg.	manufacturing	fabricación
mil.	military	militar
minús.	lower case	minúscula
mus., mús.	music	música
myth., mitol.	mythology	mitología
naut., náut.	nautical	náutico
neg.	negative	negativo
n.f.	feminine noun	nombre femenino
n.m.	masculine noun	nombre masculino
nom.	nominative	nominativo
obj.	object; objective	objeto; objetivo
odontol.	dentistry	odontología
opt., ópt.	optics	óptica
ornith., ornit.	ornithology	ornitología
p.	participle	participio
paint.	painting	pintura
pathol, patol.	pathology	patología
perf.	perfect	perfecto
pers.	person; personal	persona; personal
pert.	pertaining	perteneciente
pharm.	pharmacology	farmacología
philos.	philosophy	filosofía
phonet.	phonetics	fonética
photog.	photography	fotografía
physiol.	physiology	fisiología
pint.	painting	pintura
pl.	plural	plural
plupf.	pluperfect	pluscuamperfecto
P.M.	post meridiem	postmeridiano; por la tarde
poet., poét	poetic	poético
polit. polít.	politics; political	política; político
poss., pos.	possessive	posesivo
p.p.	past participle	participio pasivo
pref.	prefix	prefijo
prep.	preposition	preposición
pres.	present	presente
pret.	preterit	pretérito

print.	printing	imprenta
pron.	pronoun	pronombre
prov.	provincial	provincial
pr.p., p.pr.	present participle	participio presente o activo
Prot., prot.	Protestant	protestante; evangélico
psychol., psicol.	psychology	psicología
p.t.	past tense	pretérito
quím.	chemistry	química
refl.	reflexive	reflexivo
reg.	regular	regular
rel.	relative	relativo
relig.	religion	religión
rhet., ret.	rhetoric	retórica
R.R.	railroads; railroading	ferrovías; ferroviario
S.A.	South America	Sudamérica
sculp.	sculpture	escultura
2nd, 2⁰	second	segundo
seg.	followed	seguido
seismol., sismol.	seismology	sismología
sing.	singular	singular
Sp.	Spain	España
Span.	Spanish	español
St., Ste., S., Sto., Sta.	Saint	San; Santo; Santa
subj., suj.	subject	sujeto
subjv.	subjunctive	subjuntivo
suf.	suffix	sufijo
superl.	superlative	superlativo
surg.	surgery	cirugía
technol., tecnol.	technology	tecnología
teleg.	telegraphy	telegrafía
theat., teat.	theater	teatro
theol., teol.	theology	teología
3rd, 3⁰	third	tercero
tipog.	typography	tipografía
T.N.	trade name	marca registrada
TV	television	televisión
typog.	typography	tipografía
U.S.	United States	Estados Unidos
usu.	usually	usualmente
v.	verb	verbo
v.a.	active or transitive verb	verbo activo o transitivo
Venez.	Venezuela	Venezuela
var.	variant	variante
vet.	veterinary medicine	veterinaria
v.i., v.n.	intransitive verb	verbo intransitivo o neutro
voc.	vocative	vocativo
v.r.	reflexive verb	verbo reflexivo
v.t. v.a.	transitive verb	verbo transitivo o activo
vulg.	vulgar; vulgarism	vulgar; vulgarismo
zoöl., zool.	zoölogy	zoología
=	equals	equivalente a

A

A, a (a) *n.f.* first letter of the Spanish alphabet.

a (a) *prep.* **1,** to; toward. **2,** at; in; on; upon. **3,** by; near. **4,** of; for. **5,** with. **6,** against; next to. **7,** according to. **8,** used before the direct object when it denotes a person or the name of a place: *Vimos a Juan ayer,* We saw John yesterday. *Visitamos a Londres el año pasado,* We visited London last year.

abacería (a·βa·θe'ri·a; -se'ri·a) *n.f.* grocery. —**abacero** (-'θe·ro; -'se·ro) *n.m.* grocer.

ábaco ('a·βa·ko) *n.m.* abacus.

abad (a'βað) *n.m.* abbot. —**abadesa** (-'ðe·sa) *n.f.* abbess. —**abadía** (-'ði·a) *n.f.* abbey.

abadejo (a·βa'ðe·xo) *n.m.*, *ichthy.* ling.

abajo (a'βa·xo) *adv.* **1,** down; below. **2,** downstairs, —*interj.* down with....! —**boca abajo,** face down; upside down. —**hasta abajo,** all the way down; to the bottom. —**para** *or* **hacia abajo,** down; downwards. —**por abajo,** under; below; underneath.

abalanzar (a·βa·lan'θar; -'sar) *v.t.* [*infl.:* **rezar, 10**] **1,** to balance; weigh. **2,** to hurl. —**abalanzarse,** *v.r.* **1,** to rush headlong. **2,** *Amer.* to pounce; spring.

abalear (a·βa·le'ar) *v.t., Amer.* to riddle with bullets; rain bullets on.

abalorio (a·βa'lo·rjo) *n.m.* **1,** bead; glass bead. **2,** ornament made of beads; trinket.

abanderado (a·βan·de'ra·ðo) *n.m.* standard-bearer.

abanderar (a·βan·de'rar) *v.t.* to register (a ship) under a flag.

abanderizar (a·βan·de·ri'θar; -'sar) *v.t.* [*infl.:* **rezar, 10**] to cause to take sides; split into factions. —**abanderizarse,** *v.r.* to take sides.

abandonado (a·βan·do'na·ðo) *adj.* **1,** abandoned; forsaken. **2,** careless; slovenly.

abandonar (a·βan·do'nar) *v.t.* to abandon. —*v.i., chess* to resign. —**abandonarse,** *v.r.* **1,** to give oneself up (to); abandon oneself (to). **2,** to become careless or slovenly.

abandono (a·βan'do·no) *n.m.* **1,** abandon. **2,** carelessness; slovenli-

ness. **3,** abandonment; forsaken condition.

abanico (a·βa'ni·ko) *n.m.* fan. —**abanicar** (-ni'kar) *v.t.* [*infl.:* **tocar, 7**] to fan.

abaratar (a·βa·ra'tar) *v.t.* to cheapen. —**abaratarse,** *v.r.* to fall in price; become cheap or cheaper.

abarcar (a·βar'kar) *v.t.* [*infl.:* **tocar, 7**] to encompass; embrace; take in.

abarrancar (a·βa·rran'kar) *v.t.* [*infl.:* **tocar, 7**] to run into a ditch. —*v.i.* to run aground. —**abarrancarse,** *v.r.* **1,** to run into a ditch. **2,** to run aground. **3,** to get into a jam.

abarrotar (a·βa·rro'tar) *v.t.* **1,** to stuff; cram. **2,** *Amer.* to glut; flood (the market).

abarrotes (a·βa'rro·tes) *n.m.pl., Amer.* groceries. —**abarrotero,** *n.m., Amer.* grocer. —**tienda de abarrotes,** *Amer.* grocery.

abastecer (a·βas·te'θer; -'ser) *v.t.* [*infl.:* **conocer, 13**] to supply. —**abastecedor,** *adj.* supplying. —*n.m.* supplier.

abastecimiento (a·βas·te·θi·'mjen·to; -si'mjen·to) *n.m.* **1,** supply; supplying. **2,** *pl.* supplies.

abasto (a'βas·to) *n.m.* **1,** supply. **2,** *pl.* supplies; provisions. —**dar abasto,** to supply enough; give enough.

abatanar (a·βa·ta'nar) *v.t.* to full (cloth).

abate (a'βa·te) *n.m.* abbot.

abatir (a·βa'tir) *v.t.* **1,** to bring down; fell. **2,** to discourage; dishearten. —*v.i.* to diminish; abate. —**abatirse,** *v.r.* to lose spirit; become depressed or discouraged. —**abatido,** *adj.* dejected; crestfallen. —**abatimiento,** *n.m.* depression; dejection.

abdicar (aβ·ði'kar) *v.t. & i.* [*infl.:* **tocar, 7**] to abdicate. —**abdicación,** *n.f.* abdication.

abdomen (aβ'ðo·men) *n.m.* abdomen. —**abdominal** (-mi'nal) *adj.* abdominal.

abecé (a·βe'θe; -'se) *n.m.* **1,** alphabet; abc's. **2,** rudiments (*pl.*).

abecedario (a·βe·θe'ða·rjo; a·βe·se-) *n.m.* **1,** alphabet. **2,** spelling primer.

abedul (a·βe'ðul) *n.m.* birch.

abeja (a'βe·xa) *n.f.* bee. —**abeja maestra** *or* **reina**, queen bee. —**abeja obrera**, worker bee. —**abejar**, *n.m.* beehive; apiary.

abejarrón (a·βe·xa'rron) *also*, **abejorro** (-'xo·rro) *n.m.* bumblebee.

abejera (a·βe'xe·ra) *n.f.* apiary.

abejero (a·βe'xe·ro) *n.m.* bee-keeper. —*adj.* bee *(attrib.)*

abejón (a·βe'xon) *n.m.* 1, drone. 2, bumblebee.

aberración (a·βe·rra'θjon; -'sjon) *n.f.* 1, aberration; mental disturbance. 2, *opt.; astron.* aberration; deviation.

aberrugado (a·βe·rru'ɣa·ðo) *adj.* = averrugado.

abertura (a·βer'tu·ra) *n.f.* opening; aperture.

abeto (a'βe·to) *n.m.* fir. —**abeto rojo**, spruce.

abierto (a'βjer·to) *v., p.p. of* abrir. —*adj.* 1, open. 2, frank; sincere.

abigarrado (a·βi·ɣa'rra·ðo) *adj.* motley; variegated; speckled.

abismado (a·βis'ma·ðo) *adj.* 1, dejected. 2, absorbed, engrossed. 3, *Amer.* astonished; flabbergasted.

abismarse (a·βis'mar·se) *v.r.* 1, to grieve deeply. 2, to be absorbed or engrossed.

abismo (a'βis·mo) *n.m.* abyss; chasm. —**abismal** (-'mal) *adj.* abysmal. —**abismar**, *v.t.* to overwhelm; dishearten.

abjurar (aβ·xu'rar) *v.t.* to abjure; renounce. —**abjuración**, *n.f.* abjuration; renunciation. —**abjurar de**, to abjure; renounce.

ablandar (a·βlan'dar) *v.t.* to soften. —**ablandarse**, *v.r.* to relent. —**ablandador**, *n.m.* softener. —**ablandamiento**, *n.m.* softening.

ablativo (a·βla'ti·βo) *n.m.* ablative case.

abnegar (aβ·ne'ɣar) *v.t.* [*infl.:* pagar, 8] to abnegate; renounce. —**abnegarse**, *v.r.* to devote or dedicate oneself. —**abnegación**, *n.f.* abnegation; renunciation. —**abnegado**, *adj.* self-effacing.

abobamiento (a·βo·βa'mjen·to) *n.m.* 1, silliness; stupidity. 2, stupefaction; shock.

abobarse (a·βo'βar·se) *v.r.* to become silly. —**abobado**, *adj.* silly-looking; stupid-looking.

abocar (a·βo'kar) *v.t.* [*infl.:* tocar, 7] 1, to face; come to grips with. 2, to seize with the mouth. 3, to pour; decant. —**abocarse**, *v.r.* to meet; come together; come face to face.

abochornar (a·βo·tʃor'nar) *v.t.* to make blush; to shame; to embarrass. —**abochornado**, *adj.* embarrassed.

abofetear (a·βo·fe·te'ar) *v.t.* 1, to slap in the face. 2, to insult.

abogado (a·βo'ɣa·ðo) *n.m.* lawyer; attorney. —**abogacía** (-'θi·a; -'si·a) *n.f.* legal profession.

abogar (a·βo'ɣar) *v.i.* [*infl.:* pagar, 8] 1, to plead. 2, to intercede. —**abogar contra**, to argue against; oppose. —**abogar por**, to advocate; support.

abolengo (a·βo'len·go) *n.m.* ancestry; heritage.

abolición (a·βo·li'θjon; -'sjon) *n.f.* abolition; abolishment. —**abolicionismo**, *n.m.* abolitionism. —**abolicionista**, *adj. & n.m. & f.* abolitionist.

abolir (a·βo'lir) *v.t., defective (used only in tenses with terminations beginning with* i*)* to abolish.

abolsarse (a·βol'sar·se) *v.r.* to bag; become baggy. —**abolsado**, *adj.* baggy; puffed.

abollar (a·βo'ʎar; -'jar) *v.t.* to dent. —**abolladura**, *n.f.* dent.

abollonar (a·βo·ʎo'nar; -jo'nar) *v.t.* to emboss. —**abollonadura**, *n.f.* embossing; embossment.

abombar (a·βom'bar) *v.t.* 1, to cause to bulge or swell; make convex. 2, *Amer., colloq.* to cause to smell bad; stink up. —**abombarse**, *v.r., Amer., colloq.* to smell bad; smell spoiled or rotten.

abominable (a·βo·mi'na·βle) *adj.* abominable. —**abominación**, *n.f.* abomination.

abominar (a·βo·mi'nar) *v.t.* to abominate; condemn. —**abominar de**, to detest; abhor. —**abominar contra**, to rail at or against.

abonar (a·βo'nar) *v.t.* 1, to credit. 2, to fertilize. 3, to pay. —**abonarse**, *v.r.* to subscribe. —**abonable**, *adj.* payable; due. —**abonado**, *n.m.* subscriber. —**abonador**, *n.m.* guarantor.

abonaré (a·βo·na're) *n.m.* promissory note; I.O.U.

abono (a'βo·no) *n.m.* 1, subscription. 2, fertilizer; manure. 3, surety. 4, *comm.* credit; receipt. 5, season ticket. 6, commutation ticket. 7, contribution. 8, payment.

aboque (a'βo·ke) v., pres.subjve. of abocar.

aboqué (a·βo'ke) v., 1st pers.sing. pret. of abocar.

abordar (a·βor'ðar) v.t. 1, to board (a ship). 2, to approach; accost. 3, to bring up; broach. —**abordaje**, n.m., naut. boarding.

aborígenes (a·βo'ri·xe·nes) n.m. & f.pl. natives; aborigines. —**aborigen** (-'ri·xen) adj. aboriginal. —n.m. & f.sing. aborigine.

aborrascarse (a·βo·rras'kar·se) v.r. [infl.: tocar, 7] to become stormy.

aborrecer (a·βo·rre'θer; -'ser) v.t. [infl.: conocer, 13] to abhor. —**aborrecible**, adj. abhorrent. —**aborrecimiento**, n.m. abhorrence.

abortar (a·βor'tar) v.t. & i. to abort. —v.i. to miscarry. —**abortivo** (-'ti·βo) adj. abortive.

aborto (a'βor·to) n.m. 1, abortion. 2, miscarriage.

abotagar (a·βo·ta'γar) v.t. [infl.: pagar, 8] to bloat; cause to be or feel bloated. —**abotagarse**, v.r. to be or feel bloated. —**abotagamiento**, n.m. bloated feeling.

abotonar (a·βo·to'nar) v.t. to button.

abovedar (a·βo·βe'ðar) v.t. to vault; arch. —**abovedado**, adj. vaulted.

abra ('a·βra) n.f. 1, gorge. 2, cove.

abracadabra (a·βra·ka'ða·βra) n.m. abracadabra.

abracadabrante (a·βra·ka·ða·'βran·te) adj. 1, riotous; boisterous. 2, puzzling.

abrasar (a·βra'sar) v.t. to burn. —**abrasarse**, v.r. to get burned; feel too much heat. —**abrasador**, adj. extremely hot.

abrasión (a·βra'sjon) n.f. abrasion.

abrasivo (a·βra'si·βo) adj. & n.m. abrasive.

abrazadera (a·βra·θa'ðe·ra; a·βra·sa-) n.f. clamp; cleat.

abrazar (a·βra'θar; -'sar) v.t. [infl.: rezar, 10] 1, to embrace; clasp; hug. 2, to include; comprise. 3, to take up; follow; adopt.

abrazo (a'βra·θo; -so) n.m. embrace; hug.

abrelatas (a·βre'la·tas) n.m.sing. & pl. can opener.

abrevadero (a·βre·βa'ðe·ro) n.m. watering place for cattle; trough.

abrevar (a·βre'βar) v.t. 1, to water (cattle). 2, to soak; drench.

abreviar (a·βre'βjar) v.t. to shorten; abridge; abbreviate. —**abreviación**, n.f. shortening; abridgement. —**abreviadamente**, n.f. briefly; summarily.

abreviatura (a·βre·βja'tu·ra) n.f. abbreviation.

abridor (a·βri'ðor) n.m. opener. —adj. opening.

abrigar (a·βri'γar) v.t. & i. [infl.: pagar, 8] 1, to shelter. 2, to protect from cold; keep (one) warm. 3, to harbor; cherish; hold. —**abrigarse**, v.r. to keep warm; cover oneself.

abrigo (a'βri·γo) n.m. 1, overcoat; wrap. 2, shelter; protection. 3, naut. harbor; haven. —**al abrigo de**, sheltered or protected from or by; in the lee of. —**de abrigo**, warm; that keeps warm.

abril (a'βril) n.m. April.

abrillantar (a·βri·ʎan'tar; -jan·'tar) v.t. to brighten.

abrir (a'βrir) v.t. [p.p. abierto] 1, to open, 2, to whet (the appetite). —**abrirse**, v.r. 1, to open. 2, to open up; come out of one's shell. —**abrir paso**, to clear the way.

abrochar (a·βro'tʃar) v.t. to hook; fasten; button.

abrogar (a·βro'γar) v.t. [infl.: pagar, 8] to abrogate. —**abrogación**, n.f. abrogation.

abrojo (a'βro·xo) n.m. thistle.

abrumar (a·βru'mar) v.t. to overwhelm. —**abrumarse**, v.r. to become hazy or foggy. —**abrumador**, adj. overwhelming; crushing; oppressive.

abrupto (a'βrup·to) adj. rugged; steep; abrupt.

abrutado (a·βru'ta·ðo) adj. brutish.

absceso (aβs'θe·so; aβ'se·so) n.m. abscess; small tumor; boil.

abscisa (aβs'θi·sa; aβ'si·sa) n.f. abscissa.

absentismo (aβ·sen'tis·mo) n.m. absenteeism. —**absentista**, n.m. & f. absentee owner.

ábside ('aβ·si·ðe) n.m. apse.

absintio (aβ'sin·tjo) n.m. absinthe.

absolución (aβ·so·lu'θjon; -'sjon) n.f. 1, absolution. 2, acquittal.

absoluto (aβ·so'lu·to) adj. absolute; complete. —**absolutismo**, n.m. absolutism. —**en absoluto**, 1, not at all. 2, absolutely.

absolutorio (aβ·so·lu'to·rjo) *adj.*
acquitting; absolving.

absolver (aβ·sol'βer) *v.t.* [*infl.*:
mover, 30; *p.p.* **absuelto**] to absolve; acquit.

absorbencia (aβ·sor'βen·θja;
-sja) *n.f.* 1, absorption. 2, absorbency.

absorbente (aβ·sor'βen·te) *adj.* 1,
absorbing. 2, absorptive. —*adj.* &
n.m. absorbent.

absorber (aβ·sor'βer) *v.t.* to absorb.

absorción (aβ·sor'θjon; -'sjon) *n.f.*
absorption.

absorto (aβ'sor·to) *adj.* absorbed;
engrossed.

abstemio (aβs'te·mjo) *adj.* abstemious.

abstención (aβs·ten'θjon; -'sjon)
n.f. abstention.

abstenerse (aβs·te'ner·se) *v.r.*
[*infl.*: tener, 65] to abstain.

abstinencia (aβs·ti'nen·θja; -sja)
n.f. abstinence. —**abstinente,** *adj.*
abstinent; abstentious. —*n.m.* & *f.*
abstainer.

abstracción (aβs·trak'θjon;
-'sjon) *n.f.* 1, abstraction. 2, preoccupation.

abstracto (aβs'trak·to) *adj.* & *n.m.*
abstract.

abstraer (aβs·tra·er) *v.t.* [*infl.*:
traer, 67] to abstract. —**abstraerse,**
v.r. to become absorbed or abstracted.

abstraído (aβs·tra'i·ðo) *adj.* 1, absentminded. 2, aloof.

abstruso (aβs'tru·so) *adj.* abstruse.

absuelto (aβ'swel·to) *v., p.p.* of
absolver.

absuelva (aβ'swel·βa) *v., pres.*
subjve. of **absolver.**

absuelvo (aβ'swel·βo) *v., pres.*
ind. of **absolver.**

absurdo (aβ'sur·ðo) *adj.* absurd.
—*n.m.* [*also,* **absurdidad,** *n.f.*] absurdity.

abuelo (a'βwe·lo) *n.m.* grandfather;
pl. grandparents; forefathers.
—**abuela,** *n.f.* grandmother.

abultar (a·βul'tar) *v.i.* 1, to bulge.
2, to bulk large. —*v.t.* 1, to cause to
bulge; make bulky. 2, to exaggerate;
magnify. —**abultado,** *adj.* bulky.

abundamiento (a·βun·da'mjento) *n.m., in* **a mayor abundamiento,** furthermore; and what is
more . . .

abundancia (a·βun'dan·θja; -sja)

n.f. abundance; plenty. —**abundante,** *adj.* abundant; plentiful.

abundar (a·βun'dar) *v.i.* to
abound.

aburguesarse (a·βur·ɣe'sar·se)
v.r. to acquire bourgeois attitudes.

aburrir (a·βu'rrir) *v.t.* to bore.
—**aburrirse,** *v.r.* to be bored.
—**aburrido,** *adj.* wearying; boring. —**aburrimiento,** *n.m.* tediousness; boredom.

abusador (a·βu·sa'ðor) *adj.* bullying. —*n.m.* bully.

abusar (a·βu'sar) *v.i., usu.fol. by*
de, 1, to abuse. 2, to use in excess;
overindulge in. 3, to take advantage
of.

abusivo (a·βu'si·βo) *adj.* 1, abusive. 2, *Amer.* bullying. —*n.m.,*
Amer. bully.

abuso (a'βu·so) *n.m.* abuse.

abyecto (aβ'jek·to) *adj.* abject;
vile. —**abyección** (-jek'θjon; -'sjon)
n.f. abjectness; servility.

acá (a'ka) *adv.* here; over here.
—**por acá,** through here; this way.

acabado (a·ka'βa·ðo) *adj.* 1, finished; complete. 2, faultless. 3,
emaciated. —*n.m.* 1, finish; polish.
2, finishing touch.

acaballadero (a·ka·βa·ʎa'ðe·ro;
-ja'ðe·ro) *n.m.* stud farm.

acabar (a·ka'βar) *v.t.* & *i.* to finish;
end. —**acabar con,** to finish; finish
off or with; make an end of.
—**acabar de,** to have just: *Acaba*
de salir, He has just gone out.
—**acabar por,** to end up by or in;
end by doing; do finally.

acabóse (a·ka'βo·se) *n.m., colloq.*
the end; the limit; the last straw.

acacia (a'ka·θja; -sja) *n.f.* acacia.

academia (a·ka'ðe·mja) *n.f.* 1, private school. 2, academy.

académico (a·ka'ðe·mi·ko) *adj.*
academic. —*n.m.* 1, academician. 2,
professor; teacher.

acaecer (a·ka·e'θer; -'ser) *v.impers.*
[*infl.*: conocer, 13] to happen;
come to pass. —**acaecimiento,** *n.m.*
event.

acalambrarse (a·ka·lam'brar-
se) *v.r.* to have cramps; become
cramped.

acalenturarse (a·ka·len·tu'rar-
se) *v.r.* to become feverish.

acalorado (a·ka·lo'ra·ðo) *adj.* 1,
heated; hot. 2, angry; excited.

acalorar (a·ka·lo'rar) *v.t.* 1, to
warm; cause to feel warm or hot. 2,
to inflame; excite. —**acalora-**

miento, *also,* **acaloro** (-'lo·ro) *n.m.* heat; ardor.

callar (a·ka'ʎar; -'jar) *v.t.* **1,** to quiet; silence. **2,** to assuage.

campar (a·kam'par) *v.i.* to encamp; camp.

canalar (a·ka·na'lar) *v.t.* to flute; groove.

cantilado (a·kan·ti'la·ðo) *n.m.* cliff. —*adj.* steep.

canto (a'kan·to) *n.m.* acanthus.

cantonar (a·kan·to'nar) *v.t.* to quarter (troops). —**acantonamiento,** *n.m.* cantonment.

caparar (a·ka·pa'rar) *v.t.* to monopolize; hoard; corner. —**acaparador,** *n.m.* monopolizer; hoarder. —**acaparamiento,** *n.m.* hoarding.

caracolado (a·ka·ra·ko'la·ðo) *adj.* spiral.

caramelado (a·ka·ra·me'la·ðo) *adj.* **1,** sugary; sugared. **2,** *colloq.* mawkish; sentimental.

caramelar (a·ka·ra·me'lar) *v.t.* **1,** to caramelize. **2,** to sugar-coat. —**acaramelarse,** *v.r.* **1,** to caramelize. **2,** *fig., colloq.* to become sweet; put on sweetness.

cariciar (a·ka·ri'θjar; -'sjar) *v.t.* to caress. —**acariciador,** *adj.* caressing.

caro ('a·ka·ro) *n.m.* mite.

carrear (a·ka·rre'ar) *v.t.* **1,** to cart; transport. **2,** to cause; bring on. —**acarreador,** *n.m.* carrier. —*adj.* transporting; used for transport. —**acarreo** (-'rre·o) *also,* **acarramiento,** *n.m.* cartage.

caso (a'ka·so) *adv.* perhaps; maybe. —*n.m.* chance; eventuality. —**al acaso,** aimlessly. —**por si acaso,** just in case.

catar (a·ka'tar) *v.t.* to comply with; respect; obey. —**acatamiento,** *also,* **acato** (a'ka·to) *n.m.* compliance; respect. —**darse acato de,** to realize; take account of.

catarrarse (a·ka·ta'rrar·se) *v.r.* to catch cold.

caudalar (a·kau·ða'lar) *v.t.* **1,** to acquire; to accumulate. **2,** to hoard (wealth). —**acaudalado,** *adj.* wealthy.

caudillar (a·kau·ði'ʎar; -'jar) *v.t.* to command; to lead; to head. —**acaudillamiento,** *n.m.* lead; command.

cceder (ak·θe'ðer; ak·se-) *v.i.* to accede; agree; acquiesce.

ccesible (ak·θe'si·βle; ak·se-)

adj. accessible. —**accesibilidad,** *n.f.* accessibility.

accesión (ak·θe'sjon; ak·se-) *n.f.* accession.

acceso (ak'θe·so; ak'se-) *n.m.* **1,** access. **2,** outburst; fit. **3,** *med.* attack; seizure.

accesorio (ak·θe·'so·rjo; ak'se-) *adj. & n.m.* accessory. —**accesoria,** *n.f.* outbuilding.

accidentado (ak·θi·ðen'ta·ðo; ak·si-) *adj.* rough; uneven. —*n.m.* accident casualty.

accidente (ak·θi'ðen·te; ak·si-) *n.m.* accident. —**accidental,** *adj.* accidental. —**accidentarse,** *v.r.* to suffer an accident.

acción (ak'θjon; -'sjon) *n.f.* **1,** action; act. **2,** *fin.* share. **3,** lawsuit. —**accionar,** *v.i.* to gesticulate. —*v.t.* to drive; to operate. —**accionista,** *n.m.* stockholder. —**acción de gracias,** thanksgiving.

acebo (a'θe·βo; a'se-) *n.m* holly.

acece (a'θe·θe; a'se·se) *v., pres. subjve. of* **acezar.**

acecé (a·θe'θe; a·se'se) *v., 1st pers.sing. pret. of* **acezar.**

acechar (a·θe'tʃar; a·se-) *v.t.* to watch; keep an eye on. —*v.i.* to lie in wait; lurk. —**acecho** (a'θe·tʃo; a'se-) *n.m., also,* **acechanza,** *n.f.* watch; watching.

acedera (a·θe'ðə·ra; a·se-) *n.f.* sorrel. —**acedera menor,** oxalis.

acedía (a·θe'ði·a; a·se-) *n.f.* heartburn.

acedo (a'θe·ðo; a'se-) *adj.* sour; acid.

aceitar (a·θei'tar; a·sei-) *v.t.* to oil; lubricate. —**aceitado,** *n.m.* oiling; lubrication.

aceite (a'θei·te; a'sei-) *n.m.* oil. —**aceitoso,** *adj.* oily.

aceitera (a·θei'te·ra; a·sei-) *n.f.* **1,** oil can. **2,** oil cup.

aceitillo (a·θei'ti·ʎo; a·sei'ti·jo) *n.m.* satinwood.

aceituna (a·θei'tu·na; a·sei-) *n.f.* olive. —**aceitunado,** *adj.* olive-colored. —**aceituno,** *n.m.* olive tree.

acelerar (a·θe·le'rar; a·se-) *v.t. & i.* to accelerate. —**aceleración,** *n.f.* acceleration. —**aceleradamente,** *adv.* hastily. —**acelerador,** *n.m.* accelerator. —*adj.* accelerating.

acelga (a'θel·ɣa; a'sel·-) *n.f.* chard.

acémila (a'θe·mi·la; a'se-) *n.f.* pack mule.

acemita (a·θe'mi·ta; a·se-) *n.f.* bran bread.

acendrado (a·θen'dra·ðo; a·sen-) *adj.* pure; concentrated.

acento (a'θen·to; a'sen-) *n.m.* accent.

acentuar (a·θen'twar; a·sen-) *v.t.* [*infl.:* **continuar, 23**] **1,** to accent. **2,** to accentuate; emphasize. —**acentuación,** *n.f.* accentuation.

acepción (a·θep'θjon; a·sep'sjon) *n.f., gram.* meaning; acceptation.

acepillar (a·θe·pi'ʎar; a·se·pi'jar) *v.t.* = **cepillar.**

aceptar (a·θep'tar; a·sep-) *v.t.* **1,** to accept. **2,** *comm.* to honor. —**aceptabilidad,** *n.f.* acceptability. —**aceptable,** *adj.* acceptable. —**aceptación,** *n.f.* acceptance.

acequia (a'θe·kja; a'se-) *n.f.* ditch, esp. irrigation ditch.

acera (a'θe·ra; a'se-) *n.f.* sidewalk.

acerar (a·θe'rar; a·se-) *v.t.* **1,** to edge with steel. **2,** to pave. **3,** *fig.* to strengthen. —**acerarse,** *v.r.* to take courage. —**acerado,** *adj.* steely.

acerbo (a'θer·βo; a'ser-) *adj.* tart; bitter. —**acerbidad,** *n.f.* acerbity; bitterness.

acerca de (a'θer·ka·θe; a'ser-) about; concerning; with regard to.

acercamiento (a·θer·ka'mjen·to; a·ser-) *n.m.* **1,** approach. **2,** rapprochement.

acercar (a·θer'kar; a·ser-) *v.t.* [*infl.:* **tocar, 7**] to bring near; draw up. —**acercarse,** *v.r.* to come near; approach.

acero (a'θe·ro; -'se·ro) *n.m.* steel. —**aceros,** *n.m.pl.* temper; mettle. —**acero al carbono,** carbon steel. —**acero de herramientas,** tool steel. —**acero inoxidable,** stainless steel. —**acero de aleación,** alloy steel.

acerolo (a·θe'ro·lo; a·se-) *n.m.* hawthorn. —**acerola,** *n.f.* hawthorn berry.

acérrimo (a'θe·rri·mo; a'se-) *adj., superl.* of **acre.**

acerro (a'θe·rro; a'se-) *n.m.* **1,** heap. **2,** *law* common property.

acertado (a·θer'ta·ðo; a·ser-) *adj.* right; apt; well-considered.

acertar (a·θer'tar; a·ser-) *v.t. & i.* [*infl.:* **pensar, 27**] to hit; hit upon; guess correctly. —**acertar a, 1,** to succeed in. **2,** to happen to. —**acertar con,** to happen upon; come across.

acertijo (a·θer'ti·xo; a·ser-) *n.m.* riddle.

acetanilida (a·θe·ta·ni'li·ða; a·se-) *n.f.* acetanilide.

acetato (a·θe'ta·to; a·se-) *n.m.* acetate.

acético (a'θe·ti·ko; a'se-) *adj.* acetic.

acetileno (a·θe·ti'le·no; a·se-) *n.m.* acetylene.

acetona (a·θe'to·na; a·se-) *n.f.* acetone.

acezar (a·θe'θar; a·se'sar) *v.i.* [*infl.* **rezar, 10**] to pant; gasp.

aciago (a'θja·yo; a'sja-) *adj.* fateful; disastrous.

aciano (a'θja·no; a'sja-) *n.m.* cornflower.

acíbar (a'θi·βar; a'si-) *n.m.* **1,** áloe. **2,** *fig.* bitterness.

acicalar (a·θi·ka'lar; a·si-) *v.t.* to adorn; to embellish. —**acicalarse,** *v.r.* to dress up. —**acicalamiento,** *n.m.* embellishment.

acicate (a·θi'ka·te; a·si-) *n.m.* **1,** spur. **2,** incentive. —**acicatear,** *v.t. Amer.* to spur; prod.

ácido ('a·θi·ðo; 'a·si-) *adj. & n.m.* acid. —**acidez,** *n.f.* acidity.

acierte (a'θjer·te; -'sjer·te) *v., pres. subjve.* of **acertar.**

acierto (a'θjer·to; -'sjer·to) *n.m.* **1,** dexterity; ability. **2,** success. **3,** appropriateness.

acierto (a'θjer·to; -'sjer·to) *pres.ind.* of **acertar.**

acimut (a·θi'mut; a·si-) *n.m.* [*pl.* **acimuts** (-'muts)] azimuth.

aclamar (a·kla'mar) *v.t.* to acclaim. —**aclamación,** *n.f.* acclamation.

aclarar (a·kla'rar) *v.t.* **1,** to clear. **2,** to explain. **3,** to thin. **4,** to rinse. —*v.i.* to become clear. —**aclaración,** *n.f.* explanation. —**aclarado,** *also,* **aclaratorio,** *adj.* explanatory.

aclimatar (a·kli·ma'tar) *v.t.* to acclimate; acclimatize. —**aclimatación,** *n.f.* acclimation; acclimatization.

acné (ak'ne) *n.f.* acne.

acobardar (a·ko·βar'ðar) *v.t.* to intimidate. —**acobardarse,** *v.r.* to become frightened; to turn tail.

acodado (a·ko'ða·ðo) *adj.* elbow-shaped; bent in the form of an elbow.

acodarse (a·ko'ðar·se) *v.r.* to rest on one's elbow; to lean.

acodillar (a·ko·ði'ʎar; -'jar) *v.t.* to bend in the form of an elbow.

acogedor (a·ko·xe'ðor) *adj.* 1, sheltering. 2, kind; hospitable.

acoger (a·ko'xer) *v.t.* [*infl.:* coger, 15] 1, to receive; greet. 2, to harbor; shelter. —**acogerse,** *v.r.* to take refuge.

acogida (a·ko'xi·ða) *n.f.* reception; greeting; welcome. *Also,* **acogimiento** (-'mjen·to) *n.m.*

acogotar (a·ko·γo'tar) *v.t.* 1, to kill with a blow in the nape. 2, *colloq.* to strangle. 3, *colloq.* to grab by the nape of the neck.

acolchar (a·kol'tʃar) *v.t.* 1, to quilt. 2, to pad; put padding in.

acólito (a'ko·li·to) *also,* **acolitado** (-'ta·ðo) *n.m.* altar boy; acolyte.

acombar (a·kom'bar) *v.t.* = combar.

acomedirse (a·ko·me'ðir·se) *v.r., Amer.* [*infl.:* pedir, 33] to volunteer.

acometer (a·ko·me'ter) *v.t.* 1, to attack. 2, to undertake. —**acometedor,** *adj.* enterprising. —**acometividad** (-ti·βi'ðað) *n.f.* aggressiveness.

acometida (a·ko·me'ti·ða) *n.f., also,* **acometimiento,** *n.m.* 1, attack. 2, service connection (of wires, pipes, etc.).

acomodar (a·ko·mo'ðar) *v.t.* 1, to accommodate. 2, to place; put; locate. 3, to arrange. 4, to lodge. 5, to usher. —**acomodarse,** *v.r.* 1, to make oneself comfortable. 2, to adapt oneself. —**acomodable,** *adj.* adaptable. —**acomodamiento,** *n.m., also,* **acomodación,** *n.f.* accommodation. —**acomodadizo,** *also,* **acomodaticio,** *adj.* accommodating. —**acomodado,** *adj.* well-to-do. —**acomodador,** *n.m.* theater usher.

acomodo (a·ko'mo·ðo) *n.m.* 1, job; position. 2, convenience. 3, accommodations. 4, space; room (to contain something). 5, solution; arrangement.

acompañamiento (a·kom·pa·ɲa'mjen·to) *n.m.* 1, accompaniment. 2, retinue. 3, *theat.* extras (*pl.*).

acompañar (a·kom·pa'ɲar) *v.t.* 1, to accompany. 2, to keep (someone) company; be company for. 3, to go well with; agree with. —**acompañador,** *n.m.* accompanist. —**acompañante,** *n.m.* [*fem.* -ta] companion; escort.

acompasado (a·kom·pa'sa·ðo) *adj.* 1, rhythmic; regular. 2, deliberate; measured.

acomplejado (a·kom·ple'xa·ðo) *adj.* having a mental complex.

aconchar (a·kon'tʃar) *v.t.* 1, to cup, as the hands. 2, to shelter. —**aconcharse,** *v.r., S.A.* to form a deposit; settle.

acondicionar (a·kon·di·θjo'nar; -sjo'nar) *v.t.* 1, to condition. 2, to arrange. —**acondicionador,** *n.m.* conditioner. —**acondicionador de aire,** air conditioner. —**acondicionamiento,** *n.m.* conditioning. —**aire acondicionado,** air conditioning. —**con aire acondicionado,** air conditioned.

acongojar (a·kon·go'xar) *v.t.* to afflict; grieve.

acónito (a'ko·ni·to) *n.m.* aconite.

aconsejar (a·kon·se'xar) *v.t.* to advise; to counsel. —**aconsejable,** *also,* **aconsejado,** *adj.* advisable. —**aconsejador,** *n.m.* = consejero.

acontecer (a·kon·te'θer; -'ser) *v.impers.* [*infl.:* conocer, 13] to happen. —**acontecimiento,** *n.m.* happening; event.

acopiar (a·ko'pjar) *v.t.* to gather; store; amass. —**acopio** (a'ko·pjo) *n.m.* amassing; gathering; collection.

acoplar (a·ko'plar) *v.t.* 1, to couple; hitch; join. 2, to reconcile. —**acoplarse a,** to join; join with; hitch onto. —**acoplado,** *n.m.* coupled vehicle; trailer. —**acoplamiento,** *n.m., also,* **acopladura,** *n.f.* coupling.

acoquinar (a·ko·ki'nar) *v.t., colloq.* = amedrentar.

acoralado (a·ko·ra'la·ðo) *adj.* coral (*color*).

acorazar (a·ko·ra'θar; -'sar) *v.t.* [*infl.:* rezar, 10] to armor; cover with armor. —**acorazado,** *adj.* armored; ironclad. —*n.m.* battleship.

acorazonado (a·ko·ra·θo'na·ðo; -so'na·ðo) *adj.* heartshaped.

acordar (a·kor'ðar) *v.t.* [*infl.:* acostar, 28] 1, to resolve. 2, to agree upon; settle upon. 3, to recall; remind. —**acordarse,** *v.r.* to remember. —**si mal no me acuerdo,** if my memory serves me.

acorde (a'kor·ðe) *n.m., music* chord. —*adj. & adv.* agreed; in accord.

acordeón (a·kor·ðe'on) *n.m.* accordion. —**acordeonista,** *n.m. & f.* accordionist.

acordonar (a·kor·ðo'nar) *v.t.* 1, to

lace (shoes). **2,** to mill (coins). **3,** to put a cordon around.

acornear (a·kor·ne'ar) *v.t.* to gore; pierce with a horn. *Also,* **cornear.**

acorralar (a·ko·rra'lar) *v.t.* **1,** to corral (animals). **2,** to corner (an opponent).

acorrucarse (a·ko·rru'kar·se) *v.r.* = **acurrucarse.**

acortar (a·kor'tar) *v.t.* to shorten. **—acortarse,** *v.r.* to draw back; be bashful. **—acortar la marcha,** to slow down.

acosar (a·ko'sar) *v.t.* to pursue relentlessly; to harass. **—acosador,** *n.m.* pursuer. **—acosamiento,** *n.m.* relentless persecution.

acostar (a·kos'tar) *v.t.* [*infl.:* 28] **1,** to put to bed. **2,** to lay flat. **—acostarse,** *v.r.* to go to bed; lie down.

acostumbrar (a·kos·tum'brar) *v.t.* to accustom. **—***v.i., fol. by inf.* to be in the habit of; to be used to. **—acostumbrado,** *adj.* accustomed.

acotación (a·ko·ta'θjon; -'sjon) *n.f.* **1,** elevation mark. **2,** marginal note; annotation.

acotar (a·ko'tar) *v.t.* **1,** to mark off. **2,** to annotate.

acotillo (a·ko'ti·ʎo; -jo) *n.m.* sledgehammer.

acre ('a·kre) *adj.* acrid; bitter. **—***n.m.* acre.

acrecencia (a·kre'θen·θja; -'sen·sja) *n.f.* accretion; accrual; increase.

acrecentar (a·kre·θen'tar; -sen'tar) *v.t.* [*infl.:* **pensar,** 27] to increase. **—acrecentamiento,** *n.m.* increase.

acrecer (a·kre'θer; -'ser) *v.t.* [*infl.:* **conocer,** 13] = **acrecentar.**

acreción (a·kre'θjon; -'sjon) *n.f.* accretion.

acreditar (a·kre·ði'tar) *v.t.* to accredit. **—acreditarse,** *v.r.* to acquire reputation. **—acreditación,** *n.f.* accreditation; (security) clearance. **—acreditado,** *adj.* accredited; reputable.

acreedor (a·kre·e'ðor) *n.m.* creditor. **—***adj.* deserving. **—acreedor hipotecario,** mortgagee.

acribillar (a·kri·βi'ʎar; -'jar) *v.t.* to riddle. **—acribillado a balazos,** riddled with bullets.

acrílico (a'kri·li·ko) *adj. & n.m.* acrylic.

acriminar (a·kri·mi'nar) *v.t.* to accuse; incriminate. **—acriminación,** *n.f.* accusation; incrimination.

acrimonia (a·kri'mo·nja) *n.f.* acrimony. **—acrimonioso,** *adj.* acrimonious.

acriollarse (a·krjo'ʎar·se; -'jar·se) *v.r., Amer.* to adopt Latin American customs.

acrisolar (a·kri·so'lar) *v.t.* to purify; refine. **—acrisolado,** *adj.* pure; spotless.

acritud (a·kri'tuð) *n.f.* acridity; acridness.

acróbata (a'kro·βa·ta) *n.m. & f.* acrobat. **—acrobacia** (-'βa·θja; -sja) *n.f.* acrobatics. **—acrobático** (-'βa·ti·ko) *adj.* acrobatic. **—acrobatismo** (-'tis·mo) *n.m.* acrobatics.

acta ('ak·ta) *n.f.* **1,** record of proceedings. **2,** official certificate. **—acta notarial,** affidavit.

actínico (ak'ti·ni·ko) *adj.* actinic.

actinio (ak'ti·njo) *n.m.* actinium.

actinón (ak·ti'non) *n.m.* actinon.

actitud (ak·ti'tuð) *n.f.* attitude.

activar (ak·ti'βar) *v.t.* to activate. **—activación,** *n.f.* activation; promotion. **—activador,** *n.m.* activator.

actividad (ak·ti·βi'ðað) *n.f.* **1,** activity. **2,** activeness.

activo (ak'ti·βo) *adj.* **1,** active. **2,** *gram.* transitive. **—***n.m.* assets (*pl.*).

acto ('ak·to) *n.m.* **1,** act. **2,** *theat.* act. **3,** public ceremony. **4,** *law.* **—acto seguido,** immediately afterward. **—en el acto,** at once.

actor (ak'tor) *n.m.* **1,** actor. **2,** *law* [*fem.* **actora**] plaintiff. **—actriz** (-'triθ; -'tris) *n.f.* actress.

actuación (ak·twa'θjon; -'sjon) *n.f.* **1,** actuation. **2,** conduct; behavior. **3,** performance; acting of a role. **4,** legal proceedings.

actual (ak'twal) *adj.* actual; present. **—actualidad,** *n.f.* present time. **—actualmente,** *adv.* at present.

actualizar (ak·twa·li'θar; -'sar) *v.t.* [*infl.:* **rezar,** 10] to bring up to date.

actuar (ak'twar) *v.t. & i.* [*infl.:* **continuar,** 23] to act. **—***v.t.* to actuate.

actuario (ak'twa·rjo) *n.m.* **1,** actuary. **2,** court recorder. **—actuarial** (-'rjal) *adj.* actuarial.

acuarela (a·kwa're·la) *n.f.* water color. **—acuarelista,** *n.m. & f.* water-color painter.

acuario (a'kwa·rjo) *n.m.* **1,** aquarium. **2,** *cap., astron.* Aquarius.

acuartelar (a·kwar·te'lar) *v.t.* to

quarter; to billet. —**acuartela-miento**, *n.m.* quartering; billeting.

acuático (a·kwa·ti·ko) *adj.* aquatic.

acuatinta (a·kwa'tin·ta) *n.f.* aquatint.

acucia (a'ku·θja; -sja) *n.f.* **1**, zeal; diligence. **2**, keen desire. **3**, acuteness (of pain).

acuciar (a·ku'θjar; -'sjar) *v.t.* **1**, to urge. **2**, to desire greatly; be eager for. —**acuciamiento**, *n.m.* urging.

acucioso (a·ku'θjo·so; -'sjo·so) *adj.* greatly desirous; eager.

acuclillarse (a·ku·kli'ʎar·se; -'jar·se) *v.r.* to squat.

acuchillar (a·ku·tʃi'ʎar; -'jar) *v.t.* to knife; stab to death; cut. —**acuchillarse**, *v.r.* to fight with knives.

acudir (a·ku'ðir) *v.i.* **1**, to betake oneself, **2**, to respond (to a call); come to one's aid. **3**, to resort; have recourse,

acueducto (a·kwe'ðuk·to) *n.m.* aqueduct.

ácueo ('a·kwe·o) *adj.* aqueous. —**humor ácueo**, aqueous humor.

acuerde (a'kwer·ðe) *v., pres. subjve.* of **acordar**.

acuerdo (a'kwer·ðo) *v., pres.ind.* of **acordar**. —*n.m.* **1**, agreement. **2**, resolution. —**de acuerdo**, in accord; in agreement. —**de común acuerdo**, with one accord. —**hacerle acuerdo a uno**, to remind one; bring to one's mind.

acueste (a'kwes·te) *v., pres.subjve.* of **acostar**.

acuesto (a'kwes·to) *v., pres.ind.* of **acostar**.

acullá (a·ku'ʎa; -'ja) *adv.* there; over there.

acumen (a'ku·men) *n.m.* acumen.

acumular (a·ku·mu'lar) *v.t.* to accumulate; to amass. —**acumula-ción**, *n.f.* accumulation. —**acumulador**, *n.m.* storage battery. —*adj.* accumulative.

acunar (a·ku'nar) *v.t.* to cradle.

acuñación (a·ku·ɲa'θjon; -'sjon) *n.f.* **1**, coinage. **2**, wedging. **3**, die stamping.

acuñar (a·ku'ɲar) *v.t.* **1**, to coin; mint. **2**, to wedge. **3**, to die-stamp.

acuoso (a'kwo·so) *adj.* watery; aqueous. —**acuosidad**, *n.f.* wateriness.

acurrucarse (a·ku·rru'kar·se) *also,* **acorrucarse** (a·ko-) *v.r.* [*infl.:*

tocar, 7] **1**, to huddle; huddle up. **2**, to crouch.

acusar (a·ku'sar) *v.t.* **1**, to accuse. **2**, to indict. **3**, to acknowledge (receipt). **4**, *cards* to declare; meld. —**acusación**, *n.f.* accusation; indictment. —**acusado**, *n.m.* accused; defendant. —*adj.* well attested. —**acusador**, *n.m.* accuser; prosecutor. —*adj.* accusing.

acusativo (a·ku·sa'ti·βo) *adj. & n.m.*, accusative case.

acuse (a'ku·se) *n.m.* **1**, acknowledgment (of receipt). **2**, winning card.

acusón (a·ku'son) *n.m.*, *colloq.* tattletale. *Also, Amer.,* **acusete** (-'se·te).

acústica (a'kus·ti·ka) *n.f.* acoustics (*pl.*). —**acústico**, *adj.* acoustic.

achacar (a·tʃa'kar) *v.t.* [*infl.:* **tocar**, 7] to impute.

achacoso (a·tʃa'ko·so) *adj.* sickly; ailing.

achaflanar (a·tʃa·fla'nar) *v.t.* to bevel; chamfer.

achampañado (a·tʃam·pa'ɲa·ðo) *adj.* champagne-like.

achantarse (a·tʃan'tar·se) *v.r.*, *colloq.* to cringe; cower.

achaparrado (a·tʃa·pa'rra·ðo) *adj.* squat; stubby.

achaque (a'tʃa·ke) *n.m.* **1**, chronic ailment. **2**, pretext; excuse. **3**, *usu.pl.* matters; affairs.

achatar (a·tʃa'tar) *v.t.* to flatten.

achicar (a·tʃi'kar) *v.t.* [*infl.:* **tocar**, 7] **1**, to diminish; shorten. **2**, *naut.* to bail out. —**achicarse**, *v.r.* to humble oneself; efface oneself. —**achicador**, *n.m.* bailing scoop.

achicoria (a·tʃi'ko·rja) *n.f.* chicory.

achicharrar (a·tʃi·tʃa'rrar) *v.t.* **1**, to scorch. **2**, to overcook. **3**, *colloq.* to bedevil.

achinado (a·tʃi'na·ðo) *adj.*, *Amer.* having Mongoloid features.

achispar (a·tʃis'par) *v.t.*, *colloq.* to make tipsy. —**achispado**, *adj.*, *colloq.* tipsy.

achocolatado (a·tʃo·ko·la'ta·ðo) *adj.* chocolate-colored.

achulado (a·tʃu'la·ðo) *adj.*, *colloq.* rough; rowdy.

adagio (a'ða·xjo) *n.m.* **1**, adage. **2**, *mus.* adagio.

adalid (a·ða'lið) *n.m.* chieftain; leader.

adamado (a·ða'ma·ðo) *adj.* **1**, womanish; feminine. **2**, garish.

adamascado (a·ða·mas'ka·ðo) *adj.* damask.

adán (a'ðan) *n.m.* **1,** ragged fellow. **2,** lazybones. **3,** *cap.* Adam.

adaptar (a·ðap'tar) *v.t.* to adapt; to fit; to accustom. —**adaptable,** *adj.* adaptable. —**adaptación,** *n.f.* adaptation. —**adaptador,** *n.m.* adapter.

adarga (a'ðar·ya) *n.f.* leather shield.

adarme (a'ðar·me) *n.m.* speck; bit.

adecentar (a·ðe·θen'tar; -sen'tar) *v.t.* to make decent (in appearance).

adecuado (a·ðe'kwa·ðo) *adj.* **1,** adequate. **2,** appropriate; apt.

adefesio (a·ðe'fe·sjo) *n.m., colloq.* **1,** *usu.pl.* nonsense *(sing.);* absurdity *(sing.).* **2,** ridiculous attire; ludicrous spectacle; sight.

adehala (a·ðe'a·la) *n.f.* **1,** gratuity, bonus. **2,** perquisite.

adelantado (a·ðe·lan'ta·ðo) *adj.* **1,** advanced; precocious. **2,** fast, as a clock. —**por adelantado,** in advance.

adelantar (a·ðe·lan'tar) *v.t. & i.* **1,** to advance. **2,** to gain. **3,** to accelerate. **4,** to anticipate. —**adelantarse,** *v.r.* to move ahead; gain the lead. —**adelantamiento,** *n.m.* advancement.

adelante (a·ðe'lan·te) *adv.* ahead; forward. —*interj.* **1,** forward! **2,** come in! **3,** go on!; go ahead! —**de aquí en adelante,** henceforth; hereafter. —**más adelante, 1,** later. **2,** further on; further ahead.

adelanto (a·ðe'lan·to) *n.m.* **1,** progress. **2,** *comm.* advance payment. **3,** advancement *(of a time schedule, clock, etc.).*

adelfa (a'ðel·fa) *n.f.* oleander.

adelgazar (a·ðel·ya'θar; -'sar) *v.t.* [*infl.:* rezar, 10] to make thin; to taper; to slenderize. —*v.i.* to grow slender; become thin.

ademán (a·ðe'man) *n.m.* **1,** gesture. **2,** attitude. —**ademanes,** *n.m.pl.* manners. —**hacer ademán de,** to make as if to.

además (a·ðe'mas) *adv.* furthermore; besides. —**además de,** besides; in addition to.

adenoide (a·ðe'noi·ðe) *n.f.* adenoid. —**adenoideo** (-'ðe·o) *adj.* adenoidal.

adentrarse (a·ðen'trar·se) *v.r.* **1,** to enter; penetrate. **2,** to trespass; encroach.

adentro (a'ðen·tro) *adv.* inside; within.

adepto (a'ðep·to) *adj.* **1,** adept. **2,** initiated. —*n.m.* follower; adherent.

aderezamiento (a·ðe·re·θa-'mjen·to; -sa'mjen·to) *n.m.* **1,** embellishment. **2,** seasoning. **3,** starch; gum, etc. used for stiffening.

aderezar (a·ðe·re'θar; -'sar) *v.* [*infl.:* rezar, 10] to embellish. **2,** to season; prepare (food). **3,** to clean; repair. **4,** to patch up; gloss over.

aderezo (a·ðe're·θo; -so) *n.m.* **1,** dressing. **2,** seasoning. **3,** size *(for stiffening).* **4,** embellishment. **5,** set of jewels.

adestrar (a·ðes'trar) *v.t.* [*infl.:* pensar, 27] = adiestrar.

adeudar (a·ðeu'ðar) *v.t.* **1,** to owe. **2,** *comm.* to debit; to charge.

adherir (a·ðe'rir) *v.t.* [*infl.:* sentir, 31] to stick; make adhere. —**adherirse,** *v.r.* **1,** to adhere. **2,** *fol. by* a, to embrace (a point of view). —**adherencia,** *n.f.* adherence. —**adherente,** *n.m.* follower; adherent. —*adj.* adhering.

adhesión (a·ðe'sjon) *n.m.* **1,** adhesion. **2,** cohesion. —**adhesivo** (-'si·βo) *adj. & n.m.* adhesive.

adición (a·ði'θjon; -'sjon) *n.f.* addition. —**adicional,** *adj.* additional. —**adicionar,** *v.t.* to add to; augment.

adicto (a'ðik·to) *adj.* addicted. —*n.m.* **1,** addict. **2,** follower. **3,** habitué.

adiestrar (a·ðjes'trar) *also,* adestrar, *v.t.* to train; instruct; drill. —**adiestrador,** *n.m.* trainer; instructor. —**adiestramiento,** *n.m.* training.

adinerado (a·ði·ne'ra·ðo) *adj.* wealthy.

adiós (a'ðjos) *interj.* good-bye; farewell. —*n.m.* farewell; adieu *(pl.).*

adiposo (a·ði'po·so) *adj.* **1,** adipose. **2,** fat; obese. —**adiposis,** *n.* obesity.

aditamento (a·ði·ta'men·to) *n.m.* attachment; addition; accessory.

aditicio (a·ði'ti·θjo; -sjo) *adj.* added; additional.

aditivo (a·ði'ti·βo) *adj. & n.m.* additive.

adivinar (a·ði·βi'nar) *v.t.* **1,** to predict. **2,** to guess; divine. **3,** to solve (a riddle). —**adivinación,** *n.f.* prediction; divination. —**adivinanza,** *n.f.* riddle. —**adivin**

(-'βi·no), **adivinador**, *n.m.* forecaster; soothsayer; fortuneteller.

adjetivo (að·xe'ti·βo) *adj.* & *n.m.* adjective. —**adjetival**, *adj.* adjectival.

adjudicar (að·xu·ði'kar) *v.t.* [*infl.*: **tocar**, 7] to adjudicate; award. —**adjudicación**, *n.f.* adjudication; judgment.

adjuntar (að·xun'tar) *v.t., Amer.* to enclose; include.

adjunto (að'xun·to) *adj.* **1**, attached. **2**, adjunct. **3**, enclosed (*in a communication*). —*n.m.* **1**, attachment; addition. **2**, adjunct. **3**, *law* appurtenance.

adminículo (að·mi'ni·ku·lo) *n.m.* accessory item.

administración (að·mi·nis·tra·'θjon; -'sjon) *n.f.* **1**, administration. **2**, manager's office. —**por administración**, by or under the management or the government; officially.

administrar (að·mi·nis'trar) *v.t.* to administer. —**administrador**, *n.m.* administrator. —**administradora**, *n.f.* administratrix. —**administrativo**, *adj.* administrative.

admiración (að·mi·ra'θjon; -'sjon) *n.f.* **1**, admiration; wonder. **2**, [*also*, **punto de admiración**] exclamation point.

admirar (að·mi'rar) *v.t.* to admire. —**admirarse**, *v.r.* to wonder; to be amazed. —**admirable**, *adj.* admirable. —**admirador**, *n.m.* admirer. —**admirativo**, *adj.* admiring.

admisible (að·mi'si·βle) *adj.* admissible.

admisión (að·mi'sjon) *n.f.* **1**, admission. **2**, acceptance.

admitir (að·mi'tir) *v.t.* **1**, to admit. **2**, accept.

admonición (að·mo·ni'θjon; -'sjon) *n.f.* = **amonestación**.

adobar (a·ðo'βar) *v.t.* to dress; prepare (food). —**adobado**, *adj.* dressed; prepared. —*n.m.* pickled meat. —**adobo** (a'ðo·βo) *n.m.* dressing for cooking or pickling.

adobe (a·ðo·βe) *n.m.* adobe.

adoctrinar (a·ðok·tri'nar) *v.t.* to indoctrinate. —**adoctrinamiento**, *n.m.* indoctrination.

adolecer (a·ðo·le'θer; -'ser) *v.i.* [*infl.*; **conocer**, 13] to become ill. —**adolecer de**, to suffer from; be afflicted with.

adolescencia (a·ðo·les'θen·θja; -le'sen·sja) *n.f.* adolescence.

—**adolescente**, *adj.* & *n.m.* & *f.* adolescent.

adolorido (a·ðo·lo'ri·ðo) *also*, **adolorado** (-'ra·ðo) *adj.* = **dolorido**.

adonde (a'ðon·de) *adv.* where; to which place; whither.

adondequiera (a·ðon·de'kje·ra) *adv.* anywhere; wherever; whithersoever.

adopción (a·ðop'θjon; -'sjon) *n.f.* adoption.

adoptar (a·ðop'tar) *v.t.* to adopt. —**adoptable**, *adj.* adoptable. —**adoptador**, *n.m.* adopter.

adoptivo (a·ðop'ti·βo) *adj.* adoptive.

adoquín (a·ðo'kin) *n.m.* cobblestone. —**adoquinado**, *adj.* paved with cobblestones; cobbled.

adorar (a·ðo'rar) *v.t.* to adore. —**adorable**, *adj.* adorable. —**adoración**, *n.f.* adoration.

adormecer (a·ðor·me'θer; -'ser) *v.i.* [*infl.*: **conocer**, 13] to lull; make drowsy; put to sleep. —**adormecerse**, *v.r.* to become sleepy; grow numb. —**adormecimiento**, *n.m.* drowsiness; sleepiness; numbness.

adormidera (a·ðor·mi'ðe·ra) *n.f.* poppy.

adormilarse (a·ðor·mi'lar·se) *v.r.* to drowse; doze.

adornar (a·ðor'nar) *v.t.* to adorn. —**adorno** (a'ðor·no) *n.m.* adornment.

adosar (a·ðo'sar) *v.t.* to lean (something) against (another); place (something) close to or up against (another).

adquirir (að·ki'rir) *v.t.* [*infl.*: **34**] to acquire.

adquisición (að·ki·si'θjon; -'sjon) *n.f.* acquisition. —**adquisitivo** (-'ti·βo) *adj.* of or pert. to acquisition; serving to acquire. —**poder adquisitivo**, purchasing power.

adrede (a'ðre·ðe) *adv.* purposely; intentionally.

adrenalina (a·ðre·na'li·na) *n.f.* adrenaline.

adscribir (aðs·kri'βir) *v.t.* [*p.p.* **adscrito** (-to) *also*, **adscripto** (-'krip·to)] **1**, to ascribe; attribute. **2**, to allot; assign.

adscripción (aðs·krip'θjon; -'sjon) *n.f.* **1**, ascription; attribution. **2**, allotment; assignment.

adsorber (að·sor'βer) *v.t.* to adsorb. —**adsorción** (-'θjon; -'sjon) *n.f.* adsorption. **—adsorptivo** (-sorp'ti·βo) *adj.* adsorptive.

aduana (a·'ðwa·na) *n.f.* custom house. **—aduanal, aduanero,** *adj.* of or pert. to customs. **—aduanero,** *n.m.* customs officer.

aducir (a·ðu·'θir; -'sir) *v.t.* [*infl.:* **conducir,** 40] to adduce.

adueñarse (a·ðwe·'ɲar·se) *v.r., fol.* by **de,** to seize; take possession of.

adular (a·ðu'lar) *v.t.* to flatter. **—adulación,** *n.f.* flattery. **—adulador,** *n.m.* flatterer.

adularia (a·ðu·la·rja) *n.f.* moonstone.

adulón (a·ðu'lon) *n.m.* [*fem.* **-ona**] gross flatterer.

adulterar (a·ðul·te'rar) *v.t.* to adulterate. **—adulterante,** *adj. & n.m. & f.* adulterant. **—adulteración,** *n.f.* adulteration.

adulterino (a·ðul·te·ri'no) *adj.* adulterous.

adulterio (a·ðul'te·rjo) *n.m.* adultery.

adúltero (a'ðul·te·ro) *adj.* adulterous. **—n.m.** adulterer. **—adúltera,** *n.f.* adulteress.

adulto (a'ðul·to) *adj. & n.m.* adult.

adusto (a'ðus·to) *adj.* grim; forbidding. **—adustez,** *n.f.* grimness.

aduzca (a'ðuθ·ka; -'ðus·ka) *v., pres.subjve.* of **aducir.**

aduzco (a'ðuθ·ko; -'ðus·ko) *v., 1st pers.sing. pres.ind.* of **aducir.**

advenedizo (að·βe·ne'ði·θo; -so) *adj. & n.m.* **1,** alien. **2,** immigrant. **3,** upstart; parvenu.

advenimiento (að·βe·ni'mjen·to) *n.m.* **1,** advent; arrival. **2,** accession.

adventicio (að·βen'ti·θjo; -sjo) *adj.* extraneous.

adventista (að·βen'tis·ta) *adj. & n.m. & f.* Adventist.

adverbio (að'βer·βjo) *n.m.* adverb. **—adverbial,** *adj.* adverbial.

adversario (að·βer'sa·rjo) *n.m.* adversary; foe; opponent.

adverso (að'βer·so) *adj.* adverse. **—adversidad,** *n.f.* adversity.

advertir (að·βer'tir) *v.t.* [*infl.:* **sentir,** 31] **1,** to notice. **2,** to warn; advise. **—advertencia,** *n.f.* admonition; warning. **—advertidamente,** *adv.* knowingly. **—advertido,** *adj.* alert; capable.

Adviento (að'βjen·to) *n.m.* Advent.

adyacente (að·ja'θen·te; -'sen·te) *adj.* adjacent.

aeración (a·e·ra'θjon; -'sjon) *n.* aeration.

aéreo (a'e·re·o) *adj.* **1,** aerial; airborne. **2,** aeronautic. **3,** *fig.* fantastic.

aeróbico (a·e·ro·βi·ko) *adj.* aerobic. **—aerobio** (-βjo) *n.m.* aerobic microorganism; aerobe.

aerodinámica (a·e·ro·ði'na·mi·ka) *n.f.* aerodynamics (pl.). **—aerodinámico,** *adj.* aerodynamic. **—de forma aerodinámica,** streamlined.

aerofotografía (a·e·ro·fo·to·ɣra'fi·a) *n.f.* **1,** aerial photograph, **2,** aerial photography.

aerograma (a·e·ro'ɣra·ma) *n.m.* radiograma.

aerolínea (a·e·ro'li·ne·a) *n.f.* airline.

aerolito (a·e·ro'li·to) *n.m.* meteorite.

aeromozo (a·e·ro'mo·θo; -so) *n.m., Amer.* (*fem.* **-oza**) flight attendant; steward (-ess).

aeroplano (a·e·ro'pla·no) *n.m.* airplane.

aeropostal (a·e·ro·pos'tal) *adj.* of or by air mail.

aeropuerto (a·e·ro'pwer·to) *n.m.* airport.

aerosol (a'e·ro·sol) *n.m.* aerosol.

aerospacial (a·e·ro·spa'θja; -'sjal) *adj.* aerospace (*attrib.*).

aerostación (a·e·ros·ta'θjon; -'sjon) *n.f.* ballooning; balloon navigation.

aerostática (a·e·ros'ta·ti·ka) *n.* aerostatics. **—aerostático,** *adj.* aerostatic.

aeróstato (a·e'ros·ta·to) *n.m.* aerostat.

aerovía (a·e·ro'βi·a) *n.f.* airway.

afable (a'fa·βle) *adj.* affable; agreeable. **—afabilidad,** *n.f.* affability; geniality.

afamado (a·fa'ma·ðo) *adj.* renowned; famous.

afán (a'fan) *n.m.* **1,** eagerness; zeal. **2,** toil.

afanar (a·fa'nar) *v.t.* to trouble; bother. **—afanarse,** *v.r.* **1,** to strive; toil. **2,** to be perturbed.

afanoso (a·fa'no·so) *adj.* **1,** laborious; painful. **2,** eager. **3,** perturbed; anxious.

afear (a·fe'ar) *v.t.* to deface; to make ugly.

afección (a·fek'θjon; -'sjon) *n.f.* affection.

afectar (a·fek'tar) *v.t.* to affect

—**afectarse,** *v.r.* to feel; to be moved. —**afectación,** *n.f.* affectation. —**afectado,** *adj.* affected.
afectivo (a·fek'ti·βo) *adj.* **1,** affective. **2,** sensitive. —**afectividad,** *n.f.* sensitivity; sensibility.
afecto (a'fek·to) *n.m.* affection. —*adj.* fond.
afectuoso (a·fek'two·so) *adj.* affectionate. —**afectuosidad,** *n.f.* affectionateness.
afeitar (a·fei'tar) *v.t.* **1,** to shave. **2,** to smooth. —**afeitada,** *n.f., Amer.* shave. —**afeitadora,** *n.f.* electric shaver.
afeite (a'fei·te) *n.m., usu.pl.* cosmetics; makeup.
afelio (a'fe·ljo) *n.m.* aphelion.
afelpado (a·fel'pa·ðo) *adj.* velvety; plushy.
afeminado (a·fe·mi'na·ðo) *adj.* effeminate. —*n.m.* effeminate man. —**afeminación,** *n.f.;* **afeminamiento,** *n.m.* effeminacy. —**afeminar,** *v.t.* to make effeminate.
aferramiento (a·fe·rra'mjen·to) *n.m.* **1,** grasping. **2,** obstinacy.
aferrar (a·fe'rrar) *v.t. & i.* [*infl.:* **pensar, 27**] **1,** to grip; hold. **2,** to moor; anchor. —**aferrarse,** *v.r.* to cling; hold fast.
afestonado (a·fes·to'na·ðo) *adj.* festooned.
afianzamiento (a·fjan·θa'mjen·to; -sa'mjen·to) *n.m.* **1,** security. **2,** support.
afianzar (a·fjan'θar; -'sar) *v.t.* [*infl.:* **rezar, 10**] **1,** to make fast; secure. **2,** to give security for, guarantee. **3,** to place firmly; set in place. **4,** to support; uphold; strengthen.
afición (a·fi'θjon; -'sjon) *n.f.* **1,** fondness; inclination. **2,** avocation; hobby.
aficionado (a·fi·θjo'na·ðo; -sjo·'na·ðo) *n.m.* [*fem.* **-da**] amateur; devotee; fan. —**aficionado a,** fond of; addicted to.
aficionar (a·fi·θjo'nar) *v.t.* to attract. —**aficionarse a, 1,** to take an interest in; become a fan of. **2,** to become fond of.
afiche (a'fi·tʃe) *n.m.* **1,** *Amer.* notice; poster; bill. **2,** *motion pictures* publicity still.
áfido ('a·fi·ðo) *n.m.* aphid.
afiebrarse (a·fje'βrar·se) *v.r., Amer.* to become feverish; have fever.
afijo (a'fi·xo) *n.m.* affix. —*adj.* affixed.

afilar (a·fi'lar) *v.t.* to sharpen. —**afilado,** *adj.* sharp; keen. —**afilador,** *n.m.* grinder *(person)*; sharpener *(tool)*.
afiliar (a·fi'ljar) *v.t.* to affiliate. —**afiliarse a,** to affiliate with. —**afiliación,** *n.f.* affiliation.
afiligranar (a·fi·li·ɣra'nar) *v.t.* to filigree. —**afiligranado,** *adj.* filigree *(attrib.)*.
afín (a'fin) *adj.* similar; related. —*n.m. & f.* relative by marriage.
afinación (a·fi·na'θjon; -'sjon) *n.f.* **1,** perfection; refinement. **2,** tuning.
afinado (a·fi'na·ðo) *adj.* **1,** refined. **2,** well-tuned; in tune.
afinar (a·fi'nar) *v.t.* **1,** to perfect; refine. **2,** to tune. **3,** to sharpen; make more acute. —*v.i.* to play *or* sing in tune. —**afinador,** *n.m.* piano tuner.
afincarse (a·fin'kar·se) *v.r.* [*infl.:* **tocar, 7**] to get a foothold.
afinidad (a·fi·ni'ðað) *n.f.* **1,** affinity. **2,** relationship by marriage.
afirmado (a·fir'ma·ðo) *n.m.* roadbed.
afirmar (a·fir'mar) *v.t.* **1,** to affirm; declare. **2,** to strengthen; prop up. **3,** to set or place firmly. —**afirmarse,** *v.r.* to steady oneself. —**afirmación,** *n.f.* affirmation; assertion. —**afirmativo,** *adj. & n.m.* affirmative. —**afirmativa,** *n.f.* affirmation; consent.
aflicción (a·flik'θjon; -'sjon) *n.f.* affliction. —**aflictivo** (-'ti·βo) *adj.* afflicting; distressing.
afligir (a·fli'xir) *v.t.* [*infl.:* **coger, 15**]; *p.p.* **aflicto** (-'flik·to)] to afflict. —**afligirse,** *v.r.* to grieve.
aflojar (a·flo'xar) *v.t.* **1,** to loosen; slacken. **2,** *colloq.* to hand over; loosen up with, as money. **3,** *colloq.* to let go with; strike with. —*v.i.* to abate. —**aflojamiento,** *n.m.* loosening; slackening.
aflorar (a·flo'rar) *v.i.* to come to the surface; appear; crop up. —**afloramiento,** *n.m.* outcrop.
afluir (a'fluir) *v.i.* [*infl.:* **huir, 26**] **1,** to come together. **2,** to flow (into). —**afluencia,** *n.f.* affluence. —**afluente,** *adj.* affluent. —*n.m.* tributary.
afónico (a'fo·ni·ko) *adj.* hoarse; speechless.
aforador (a·fo·ra'ðor) *n.m.* **1,** appraiser. **2,** gauger.
aforar (a·fo'rar) *v.t.* [*infl.:* **acostar,**

28] **1,** to appraise. **2,** to measure; gauge.

aforismo (a-fo'ris-mo) *n.m.* aphorism. —**aforístico,** *adj.* aphoristic.

aforo (a'fo-ro) *n.m.* **1,** appraisal. **2,** gauging. **3,** seating capacity.

afortunado (a-for-tu'na-ðo) *adj.* fortunate; lucky.

afrancesar (a-fran-θe'sar; -se'sar) *v.t.* to Gallicize; to Frenchify.

afrecho (a'fre-tʃo) *n.m.* bran.

afrenta (a'fren-ta) *n.f.* affront. —**afrentar,** *v.t.* to affront. —**afrentoso,** *adj.* insulting.

africano (a-fri'ka-no) *adj. & n.m.* African.

afrodisíaco (a-fro-ði'si-a-ko) *adj. & n.m.* aphrodisiac.

afrontar (a-fron'tar) *v.t.* **1,** to confront; put face to face. **2,** to face; be situated opposite. **3,** to face up to; brave.

aftoso (af'to-so) *adj., in* **fiebre aftosa,** hoof-and-mouth disease.

afuera (a'fwe-ra) *adv.* **1,** out; outside. **2,** away. —*interj.* one side! make way! —**afueras,** *n.f.pl.* outskirts.

agachada (a-ɣa'tʃa-ða) *n.f.* **1,** trick; stratagem. **2,** ducking of the head or body.

agachadiza (a-ɣa-tʃa'ði-θa; -sa) *n.f.* snipe.

agachar (a-ɣa'tʃar) *v.t.* to bow down; bend. —**agacharse,** *v.r.* **1,** to bend down; crouch; stoop. **2,** *fig.* to bow one's head; submit.

agalla (a'ɣa-ʎa; -ja) *n.f.* **1,** *bot.* gallnut. **2,** *ichthy.* gill. **3,** *vet.* windgall. **4,** *pl., colloq.* tonsils. —**tener agallas,** *colloq.* **1,** to have guts. **2,** *Amer.* to be greedy.

agangrenarse (a-ɣan-gre'nar-se) *v.r.* = **gangrenarse.**

ágape ('a-ɣa-pe) *n.m.* banquet.

agarrada (a-ɣa'rra-ða) *n.f., colloq.* wrangle; hassle.

agarradera (a-ɣa-rra'ðe-ra) *n.f., also,* **agarradero** (-ro) *n.m.* handle; holder.

agarrado (a-ɣa'rra-ðo) *adj., colloq.* stingy.

agarrar (a-ɣa'rrar) *v.t.* **1,** to grasp; seize. **2,** to catch, as an illness. —*v.i.* **1,** to take root. **2,** to take; take hold. —**agarrarse,** *v.r.* **1,** to hold on; catch hold, **2,** to fight; wrangle. —**agarrarse de,** to resort to; use as a pretext or excuse.

agarrón (a-ɣa'rron) *n.m., Amer., colloq.* **1,** tug; yank. **2,** = **agarrada.**

agarrotar (a-ɣa-rro'tar) *v.t.* **1,** to strangle. **2,** to bind tightly with ropes. —**agarrotarse,** *v.r.* **1,** *mech.* to seize, as a bearing. **2,** to stiffen, as a muscle.

agasajar (a-ɣa-sa'xar) *v.t.* to entertain; regale. —**agasajador,** *adj.* obliging; attentive.

agasajo (a-ɣa'sa-xo) *n.m.* **1,** regalement. **2,** party favor; treat.

ágata ('a-ɣa-ta) *n.f.* agate.

agave (a'ɣa-βe) *n.m.* agave.

agazaparse (a-ɣa-θa'par-se; a-ɣa-sa-) *v.r.* to crouch.

agencia (a'xen-θja; -sja) *n.f.* agency. —**agencia de colocaciones,** employment agency.

agenciar (a-xen'θjar; -'sjar) *v.t.* to promote; manage to bring about. —**agenciarse,** *v.r., colloq.* to manage; get along.

agenda (a'xen-da) *n.f.* **1,** agenda. **2,** memorandum.

agente (a'xen-te) *n.m.* agent. —**agente de policía,** policeman. —**agente** *or* **corredor de aduana,** customs broker.

agigantar (a-xi-ɣan'tar) *v.t.* to exaggerate; build up; magnify. —**agigantado,** *adj.* enormous. —**a pasos agigantados,** by leaps and bounds.

ágil ('a-xil) *adj.* agile. —**agilidad,** *n.f.* agility.

agio ('a-xjo) *n.m.* speculation. —**agiotaje** (-'ta-xe) *n.m.* illicit speculation. —**agiotista** (-'tis-ta) *n.m. & f.* speculator.

agitador (a-xi-ta'ðor) *adj.* agitating. —*n.m.* **1,** agitator. **2,** stirring rod.

agitanado (a-xi-ta'na-ðo) *adj.* gypsylike.

agitar (a-xi'tar) *v.t.* to agitate; shake; stir. —**agitarse,** *v.r.* to become excited; become disturbed. —**agitación,** *n.f.* agitation; excitement.

aglomerar (a-ɣlo-me'rar) *v.t.* to agglomerate. —**aglomeración,** *n.f.* agglomeration; crowd. —**aglomerante,** *n.m.* = **aglutinante.**

aglutinar (a-ɣlu-ti'nar) *v.t.* to agglutinate; bind together. —**aglutinación,** *n.f.* agglutination. —**aglutinante,** *adj. & n.m.* agglutinant.

agnosticismo (aɣ-nos-ti'θis-mo; -'sis-mo) *n.m.* agnosticism. —**agnóstico** (-'nos-ti-ko) *adj. & n.m.* agnostic.

agobiar (a·ɣo'βjar) v.t. to over-whelm; weigh down. —**agobiante,** adj. exhausting. —**agobio** (a'ɣo·βjo) n.m. burden; anguish.

agolpar (a·ɣol'par) v.t. to crowd; jam. —**agolparse,** v.r. to rush; rush together.

agonía (a·ɣo'ni·a) n.f. agony.

agónico (a'ɣo·ni·ko) adj. **1,** of death; death (attrib.). **2,** agonizing.

agonizar (a·ɣo·ni'θar; -'sar) v.i. [infl.: rezar, 10] **1,** to agonize; suffer. **2,** to be dying. —**agonizante,** adj. dying. —n.m. & f. dying person.

agorero (a·ɣo're·ro) adj. **1,** ill-omened. **2,** foreboding; foretelling. —n.m. augur; soothsayer.

agostar (a·ɣos'tar) v.t. to wither; parch. —**agostarse,** v.r. to wither away; fade away.

agosto (a·ɣos·to) n.m. August. —**hacer su agosto,** to make a fortune; strike it rich.

agotar (a·ɣo'tar) v.t. to exhaust; to drain. — ɪgotadu, adj. **1,** exhausted. **2,** out of print. **3,** sold out. —**agotador,** adj. exhausting. —**agotamiento,** n.m. exhaustion.

agraciar (a·ɣra'θjar; -'sjar) v.t. to favor; reward. —**agraciado,** adj. favored; charming.

agradable (a·ɣra'ða·βle) adj. pleasant; agreeable.

agradar (a·ɣra'ðar) v.t. to please. —v.i. to be pleasing. —**agradarse de,** to be pleased at.

agradecer (a·ɣra·ðe'θer; -'ser) v.t. [infl.: conocer, 13] **1,** to show gratitude to (someone); thank (someone). **2,** to be thankful for (something). —**agradecido,** adj. grateful. —**agradecimiento,** n.m. gratitude.

agrado (a'gra·ðo) n.m. liking; pleasure. —**de mi agrado,** to my liking.

agrandar (a·ɣran'dar) v.t. to enlarge. —**agrandamiento,** n.m. enlargement.

agrario (a'ɣra·rjo) adj. agrarian.

agravar (a·ɣra'βar) v.t. to aggravate; make worse. —**agravador,** adj. aggravating. —**agravamiento,** n.m., also, **agravación,** n.f. aggravation.

agraviar (a·ɣra'βjar) v.t. to wrong; offend. —**agraviarse,** v.r. to take offense. —**agraviarse de,** to be offended with (someone). —**agraviarse por,** to take offense at (something). —**agraviante,** adj. offending; offensive.

agravio (a'ɣra·βjo) n.m. insult; offense; affront. —**agravioso,** adj. offensive; insulting.

agredir (a·ɣre'ðir) v.t. defective (used only in tenses with termina-tions beginning with i) to assault; attack.

agregado (a·ɣre'ɣa·ðo) n.m. **1,** aggregate. **2,** supernumerary. **3,** attaché; assistant. **4,** addition; something added or attached.

agregar (a·ɣre'ɣar) v.t. [infl.: pagar, 8] to add; to annex. —**agregarse,** v.r. to join; to attach oneself. —**agregación,** n.f. aggregation.

agremiar (a·ɣre'mjar) v.t. to unionize. —**agremiarse,** v.r. to join a union. —**agremiación,** n.f. unionization.

agresión (a·ɣre'sjon) n.f. aggression.

agresivo (a·ɣre'si·βo) adj. aggressive. —**agresividad,** n.f. aggressiveness

agresor (a·ɣre'sor) n.m. aggressor. —adj. aggressive.

agreste (a'ɣres·te) adj. rustic; uncouth.

agriar (a'ɣrjar) v.t. to sour. —**agriarse,** v.r. to turn sour.

agrícola (a'ɣri·ko·la) adj. agricultural.

agricultor (a·ɣri·kul'tor) n.m. agriculturist; farmer.

agricultura (a·ɣri·kul'tu·ra) n.f. agriculture.

agridulce (a·ɣri'ðul·θe; -se) adj. & n.m. bittersweet.

agrietarse (a·ɣrje'tar·se) v.r. to crack; become filled with cracks.

agrimensura (a·ɣri·men'su·ra) n.f. land surveying. —**agrimensor,** n.m. surveyor.

agrio ('a·ɣrjo) adj. **1,** sour; acid. **2,** fig. rude; rough; harsh.

agronomía (a·ɣro·no'mi·a) n.f. agronomy. —**agronómico** (-'no·mi·ko) adj. agronomical. —**agrónomo** (a'ɣro·no·mo) n.m. agronomist.

agropecuario (a·ɣro·pe'kwa·rjo) adj. pert. to agriculture and cattle-raising.

agrumar (a·ɣru'mar) v.t. to curdle; clot.

agrupar (a·ɣru'par) v.t. to group. —**agruparse,** v.r. to form a group; gather. —**agrupación,** n.f. grouping; group; cluster. Also, **agrupamiento,** n.m.

agrura (a'ɣru·ra) *n.f.* sourness; sour taste.

agua ('a·ɣwa) *n.f.* **1,** water. **2,** rain. **3,** luster of precious stones. **4,** slope (of a roof). **—agua bendita,** holy water. **—agua de coco,** coconut milk. **—agua de colonia,** cologne; toilet water. **—agua de Seltz,** soda water. **—agua dulce,** fresh water. **—agua fuerte,** nitric acid. **—agua oxigenada,** hydrogen peroxide. **—agua salobre** or **salada,** salt water. **—aguas jurisdiccionales,** territorial waters. **—ahogarse en poca agua,** to worry unnecessarily. **—estar con el agua al cuello,** to be in deep water. **—estar entre dos aguas,** to be on the fence. **—hacer agua,** to leak. **—¡hombre al agua!,** man overboard!

aguacate (a·ɣwa'ka·te) *n.m.* avocado; alligator pear.

aguacero (a·ɣwa'θe·ro; -'se·ro) *n.m.* downpour.

aguachento (a·ɣwa'tʃen·to) *adj., Amer.* = **aguado.**

aguada (a'ɣwa·ða) *n.f.* waterhole; source of water, esp. for men and livestock.

aguadero (a·ɣwa'ðe·ro) *n.m.* waterhole; drinking place, as for wild animals.

aguadija (a·ɣwa'ði·xa) *n.f.* water, as in a blister, sore, etc.

aguado (a'ɣwa·ðo) *adj.* **1,** mushy; bland. **2,** watery; thin.

aguador (a·ɣwa'ðor) *n.m.* water carrier.

aguafiestas (a·ɣwa'fjes·tas) *n.m. & f.sing. & pl., colloq.* killjoy; wet blanket.

aguafuerte (a·ɣwa'fwer·te) *n.f.* **1,** [*also,* **agua fuerte**] nitric acid. **2,** etching. **—grabar al aguafuerte,** to etch.

aguamala (a·ɣwa'ma·la) *n.f.* = **medusa.**

aguamarina (a·ɣwa·ma'ri·na) *n.f.* aquamarine.

aguamiel (a·ɣwa'mjel) *n.f.* mead.

aguantar (a·ɣwan'tar) *v.t.* **1,** to bear; endure; tolerate. **2,** to hold on to. **3,** to hold back; contain; restrain. **—v.i.** to hold out. **—aguantarse,** *v.r.* to restrain oneself.

aguante (a'ɣwan·te) *n.m.* endurance; fortitude.

aguar (a'ɣwar) *v.t.* **1,** to dilute with water. **2,** *colloq.,* to spoil (a party). **—aguarse,** *v.r.* **1,** to become diluted. **2,** to become filled with water.

aguardar (a·ɣwar'ðar) *v.t.* to await; wait for. **—v.i.** to wait.

aguardentoso (a·ɣwar·ðen'to·so) *adj.* hoarse; raucous.

aguardiente (a·ɣwar'ðjen·te) *n.m.* raw brandy. **—aguardiente de caña,** raw rum.

aguarrás (a·ɣwa'rras) *n.m.* turpentine.

aguazal (a·ɣwa'θal; -'sal) *n.m.* large puddle; pool.

aguce (a'ɣu·θe; -se) *v., pres. subjve. of* **aguzar.**

agucé (a·ɣu'θe; -'se) *v., 1st pers. sing. pret. of* **aguzar.**

agudeza (a·ɣu'ðe·θa; -sa) *n.f.* **1,** sharpness. **2,** *fig.* witticism.

agudizar (a·ɣu·ði'θar; -'sar) *v.t.* [*infl.:* **rezar,** 10] **1,** to sharpen; make more acute. **2,** to aggravate; make worse.

agudo (a'ɣu·ðo) *adj.* **1,** sharp; acute. **2,** high-pitched. **3,** *gram.* accented on the last syllable.

agüero (a'ɣwe·ro) *n.m.* **1,** augury; omen. **2,** *Amer.* augur; soothsayer.

aguerrido (a·ɣe'rri·ðo) *adj.* **1,** combat-hardened. **2,** brave; valiant.

aguijada (a·ɣi'xa·ða) *n.f.* goad.

aguijar (a·ɣi'xar) *v.t.* to goad.

aguijón (a·ɣi'xon) *n.m.* **1,** goad, **2,** sting. **—aguijonear** (-ne'ar) *v.t.* to prick; goad.

águila ('a·ɣi·la) *n.f.* eagle.

aguileño (a·ɣi'le·ɲo) *adj.* aquiline. **—aguileña,** *n.f.* columbine.

aguilera (a·ɣi'le·ra) *n.f.* eagle's nest; eyrie.

aguilón (a·ɣi'lon) *n.m.* **1,** boom of a crane. **2,** peak of a roof or gable. **3,** large eagle.

aguilucho (a·ɣi'lu·tʃo) *n.m.* eaglet.

aguinaldo (a·ɣi'nal·do) *n.m.* Christmas or New Year gift.

aguja (a'ɣu·xa) *n.f.* **1,** needle. **2,** hand (of a clock); pointer. **3,** compass. **4,** steeple; spire. **5,** *R.R., usu. pl.* switch. **6,** firing pin. **7,** sailfish. **—agujazo,** *n.m.* pinprick.

agujero (a·ɣu'xe·ro) *n.m.* hole. **—agujerear,** *v.t.* to make holes in; perforate.

aguzar (a·ɣu'θar; -'sar) *v.t.* [*infl.:* **rezar,** 10] to sharpen.

¡ah! (a) *interj.* ah!

ahí (a'i) *adv.* there. **—de ahí,** thence. **—de ahí que,** hence; therefore. **—por ahí,** around there; thereabouts.

ahijar (a·i'xar) *v.t.* to adopt; father. **—v.i.** to breed; sprout. **—ahijada,** *n.f.* goddaughter; protégée. **—ahijado,** *n.m.* godchild; protégé.

ahincar (a·in'kar) *v.t.* [*infl.:* **tocar,** 7] to insist upon; urge. **—v.r.** to hurry; make haste. **—ahincado,** *adj.* earnest; zealous.

ahinco (a'in·ko) *n.m.* eagerness; insistence.

ahitar (ai'tar) *v.t.* to satiate. **—ahíto** (a'i·to) *n.m.* indigestion. **—adj.** gorged.

ahogar (a·o'yar) *v.t.* [*infl.:* **pagar,** 8] to drown; smother; throttle. **—ahogarse,** *v.r.* **1,** to drown. **2,** to feel suffocated.

ahogo (a'o·yo) *n.m.* **1,** suffocation. **2,** *fig.* oppression.

ahondar (a·on'dar) *v.t.* **1,** to deepen. **2,** to delve into.

ahora (a'o·ra) *adv.* **1,** now. **2,** just now; a little while ago. **3,** soon. **—ahora bien,** now and then. **—ahora mismo,** right now; at once. **—ahora que,** nevertheless. **—por ahora,** for the time being.

ahorcar (a·or'kar) *v.t.* [*infl.:* **tocar,** 7] to hang (a person). **—ahorcadura,** *n.f.* hanging.

ahorita (a·o'ri·ta) *adv., colloq.* **1,** just now; a little while ago. **2,** right away; soon.

ahorquillar (a·or·ki'ʎar; -'jar) *v.t.* & *i.* to fork. **—ahorquillarse,** *v.r.* to be or become forked. **—ahorquillado,** *adj.* forked.

ahorrar (a·o'rrar) *v.t.* & *i.* to save; economize. **—ahorrador,** *adj.* thrifty. **—ahorrativo** (-'ti·βo) *adj.* frugal; stingy.

ahorro (a'o·rro) *n.m.* **1,** thrift. **2,** saving. **3,** *pl.* savings.

ahuecar (a·we'kar) *v.t.* [*infl.:* **tocar,** 7] **1,** to make hollow; hollow out. **2,** to deepen; make throaty, as the voice. **3,** to cup, as the hands.

ahumar (a·u'mar) *v.t.* to smoke; cure with smoke. **—v.i.** to give off smoke. **—ahumarse,** *v.r.* **1,** to become smoky (*in taste or appearance*). **2,** *colloq.* to get drunk. **—ahumado,** *adj.* smoked.

ahuyentar (au·jen'tar) *v.t.* **1,** to frighten away. **2,** to banish or dismiss (a thought, grief, etc.). **3,** to overcome (an emotion). **—ahuyentarse,** *v.r.* to flee; take flight.

airar (ai'rar) *v.t.* to make angry.

—airarse, *v.r.* to become angry. **—airado,** *adj.* angry.

aire ('ai·re) *n.m.* **1,** air. **2,** wind; breeze. **3,** song. **4,** aspect. **—aire libre,** outdoors. **—azotar el aire,** to work in vain. **—tener** *or* **darse un aire a otro,** to look like someone else. **—palabras al aire,** idle talk.

aire acondicionado air conditioning.

aireado (ai·re'a·ðo) *adj.* airy.

airear (ai·re'ar) *v.t.* to air; ventilate. **—airearse,** *v.r.* **1,** to take the air. **2,** to catch cold. **—aireación,** *n.f.* ventilation.

airón (ai'ron) *n.m.* egret.

airoso (ai'ro·so) *adj.* **1,** graceful. **2,** successful. **—salir airoso,** to come through with flying colors; win.

aislacionismo (ais·la·θjo'nis·mo; -sjo'nis·mo) *n.m.* isolationism. **—aislacionista,** *n.m. & f.* isolationist.

aislado (ais'la·ðo) *adj.* **1,** isolated. **2,** insulated.

aislador (ais·la'ðor) *n.m.* insulator. **—adj.** **1,** isolating. **2,** insulating.

aislamiento (ais·la'mjen·to) *n.m.* **1,** isolation. **2,** insulation.

aislar (ais'lar) *v.t.* [*infl.:* **enviar,** 22] **1,** to isolate. **2,** to insulate. **—aislarse,** *v.r.* to seclude oneself; keep to oneself.

¡ajá! (a'xa) *interj.* aha!

ajar (a'xar) *v.t.* **1,** to muss; rumple. **2,** to fade; wilt; wither. **3,** to wear out by use.

ajedrea (a·xe'ðre·a) *n.f., bot.* savory.

ajedrez (a·xe'ðreθ; -'ðres) *n.m.* chess. **—ajedrecista** (-'θis·ta; -'sis·ta) *n.m. & f.* chess player. **—ajedrezado,** *adj.* checkered; checked.

ajenjo (a'xen·xo) *n.m.* absinthe.

ajeno (a'xe·no) *adj.* **1,** of or belonging to another; another's. **2,** extraneous; foreign; alien. **3,** other; different. **—ajeno de sí,** detached; aloof. **—estar ajeno de,** to be unaware of.

ajetrearse (a·xe·tre'ar·se) *v.r.* to busy oneself; hustle about. **—ajetreo** (-'tre·o) *n.m.* bustle; agitation.

ají (a'xi) *n.m.* **1,** chili; red pepper. **2,** sweet pepper.

ajiaco (a'xja·ko) *n.m., Amer.* a stew of meat and local vegetables.

ajo ('a·xo) *n.m.* garlic. **—echar ajos,** *colloq.* to talk obscenely.

—**revolver el ajo,** *colloq.* to stir up a row.

ajonjolí (a·xon·xo'li) *n.m.* sesame.

ajorca (a'xor·ka) *n.f.* bangle.

ajuar (a'xwar) *n.m.* **1,** furnishings, esp. for the home. **2,** trousseau. **3,** layette.

ajustador (a·xus·ta'ðor) *n.m.* **1,** corselet. **2,** *Amer.* brassiere. **3,** *mech.* assembler; fitter.

ajustar (a·xus'tar) *v.t.* **1,** to adjust. **2,** to fit; fit together. **3,** to settle. **4,** to tighten. —*v.i.* to fit. —**ajustarse,** *v.r.* to conform; comply. —**ajustado,** *adj.* close-fitting; tight.

ajuste (a'xus·te) *n.m.* **1,** agreement. **2,** adjustment. **3,** fit. **4,** arrangement.

ajusticiar (a·xus·ti'θjar; -'sjar) *v.t.* to execute; put to death.

al (al) *contr. of* **a + el.**

ala (a'la) *n.f.* **1,** wing. **2,** brim (of a hat). **3,** *mil.* flank. **4,** propeller blade. **5,** *pl., fig.* airs; swagger. —**ahuecar el ala,** *colloq.* to beat it.

Alá (a'la) *n.m.* Allah.

alabar (a·la'βar) *v.t.* to praise; glorify. —**alabarse,** *v.r.* to praise oneself; brag. —**alabanza,** *n.f.* praise.

alabarda (a·la'βar·ða) *n.f.* halberd. —**alabardero,** *n.m.* halberdier.

alabastro (a·la'βas·tro) *n.m.* alabaster. —**alabastrino,** *adj.* of or like alabaster.

alacena (a·la'θe·na; -'se·na) *n.f.* cupboard.

alacrán (a·la'kran) *n.m.* scorpion.

alacridad (a·la·kri'ðað) *n.f.* alacrity.

alada (a'la·ða) *n.f.* beat or flutter of wings.

alado (a'la·ðo) *adj.* winged.

alamar (a·la'mar) *n.m.* frog (*ornamental fastening*).

alambicar (a·lam·bi'kar) *v.t.* [*infl.:* **tocar, 7**] **1,** to distill. **2,** to overrefine; complicate.

alambique (a·lam'bi·ke) *n.m.* still.

alambrada (a·lam'bra·ða) *n.f., mil.* wire entanglement.

alambrado (a·lam'bra·ðo) *n.m.* **1,** wire fence. **2,** wiring; wires (*pl.*) —*adj.* fenced with wires.

alambre (a'lam·bre) *n.m.* wire. —**alambrera** (-'bre·ra) *n.f.* wire screen; wire cover.

alameda (a·la'me·ða) *n.f.* **1,** mall. **2,** boulevard. **3,** poplar grove.

álamo ('a·la·mo) *n.m.* poplar. —**álamo temblón,** aspen.

alano (a'la·no) *n.m.* mastiff.

alarde (a'lar·ðe) *n.m.* **1,** ostentation; display. **2,** *mil.* review; show of force. —**hacer alarde,** *also,* **alardear,** *v.i.* to show off; boast.

alargar (a·lar'yar) *v.t.* [*infl.:* **pagar, 8**] to lengthen; to prolong. —**alargarse,** *v.r.* to become longer; to last longer. —**alargamiento,** *n.m.* lengthening.

alarido (a·la'ri·ðo) *n.m.* howl; yell.

alarma (a'lar·ma) *n.f.* alarm. —**alarmar,** *v.t.* to alarm. —**alarmarse,** *v.r.* to be alarmed; take alarm. —**alarmista,** *n.m. & f.* alarmist.

alazán (a·la'θan; -'san) *adj.* sorrel; reddish-brown. —*n.m.* sorrel (*horse*).

alba ('al·βa) *n.f.* dawn.

albacea (al·βa'θe·a; -'se·a) *n.m.* executor. —*n.f.* executrix. —**albaceazgo,** *n.m.* executorship.

albacora (al·βa'ko·ra) *n.f.* albacore.

albahaca (al·βa'a·ka) *n.f.* sweet basil.

albañal (al·βa'ɲal) *n.m.* sewer.

albañil (al·βa'ɲil) *n.m.* bricklayer; mason. —**albañilería,** *n.f.* masonry.

albarda (al'βar·ða) *n.f.* packsaddle.

albardilla (al·βar'ði·ʎa; -ja) *n.f.* **1,** small packsaddle. **2,** *archit.* cope; coping.

albaricoque (al·βa·ri'ko·ke) *n.m.* apricot. —**albaricoquero** (-'ke·ro) *n.m.* apricot tree.

albatros (al'βa·tros) *n.m.* albatross.

albayalde (al·βa'jal·de) ·*n.m.* white lead.

albedrío (al·βe'ðri·o) *n.m.* will; free will.

albéitar (al'βei·tar) *n.m.* veterinarian.

alberca (al'βer·ka) *n.f.* **1,** cistern. **2,** *Mex.* swimming pool.

albérchigo (al'βer·tʃi·yo) *n.m.* **1,** clingstone (peach). **2,** tree producing this fruit.

albergar (al·βer'yar) *v.t.* [*infl.:* **pagar, 8**] to harbor; shelter.

albergue (al'βer·ye) *n.m.* **1,** shelter; lodging; inn. **2,** lair.

albero (al'βe·ro) *n.m.* dishtowel.

albino (al'βi·no) *adj. & n.m.* albino. —**albinismo** (-'nis·mo) *n.m.* albinism.

albo ('al·βo) *adj., poet.* white.

albóndiga (al'βon·di·ya) *n.f.* meatball; fishball.

albondigón (al·βon·di'γon) *n.m.* hamburger.

albor (al'βor) *n.m.* **1,** *usu.pl.* beginning. **2,** dawn. **3,** *poet.* whiteness.

alborada (al·βo'ra·ða) *n.f.* **1,** dawn. **2,** morning song. **3,** reveille.

alborear (al·βo·re'ar) *v.i.* to dawn.

albornoz (al·βor'noθ; -'nos) *n.m.* **1,** burnoose, **2,** terry cloth. **3,** bathrobe *(of terry cloth)*.

alborotar (al·βo·ro'tar) *v.t.* to excite; arouse; agitate. —*v.i.* to make noise; cause a disturbance; riot. —**alborotarse,** *v.r.* **1,** to get excited. **2,** to riot. **3,** *(of the sea)* to become rough. —**alborotadizo,** *adj.* excitable; restless. —**alborotado,** *adj.* rash; rough *(of the sea)*.

alboroto (al·βo'ro·to) *n.m.* disturbance; tumult; riot.

alborozo (al·βo'ro·θo; -so) *n.m.* joy; exultation. —**alborozar,** *v.t.* [*infl.:* **rezar, 10**] to cheer; fill with joy.

albricias (al'βri·θjas; -sjas) *n.f.pl.* good news. —*interj.* congratulations!

álbum ('al·βum) *n.m.* album.

albumen (al'βu·men) *n.m.* albumen.

albúmina (al'βu·mi·na) *n.f.* albumin.

albur (al'βur) *n.m.* chance; risk. —**correr un albur,** to take a chance.

alca ('al·ka) *n.f.* auk.

alcachofa (al·ka't∫o·fa) *n.f.* artichoke. *Also, Sp.* **alcacil** (-'θil; -'sil) *n.m.*

alcahueta (al·ka'we·ta) *n.f.* **1,** bawd; procuress. **2,** *fem. of* **alcahuete.**

alcahuete (al·ka'we·te) *n.m.* **1,** procurer; pander. **2,** *colloq.* go-between. **3,** *colloq.* meddler. **4,** *colloq.* gossip.

alcahuetear (al·ka·we·te'ar) *v.t.* **1,** to procure. **2,** to pander to. —*v.i.* **1,** to pander. **2,** *colloq.* to act as go-between.

alcahuetería (al·ka·we·te'ri·a) *n.f.* **1,** pandering; procuring. **2,** chicanery. **3,** malicious gossip.

alcaide (al'kai·ðe) *n.m.* warden.

alcalde (al'kal·de) *n.m.* **1,** mayor. **2,** justice of the peace.

alcaldesa (al·kal'de·sa) *n.f.* **1,** mayor's wife. **2,** mayoress.

alcaldía (al·kal'di·a) *n.f.* **1,** mayoralty. **2,** mayor's office. **3,** city hall.

álcali ('al·ka·li) *n.m.* alkali.

—**alcalinidad,** *n.f.* alkalinity.

—**alcalino,** *adj.* alkaline.

alcalizar (al·ka·li'θar; -'sar) *v.t.* [*infl.:* **rezar, 10**] to alkalize. —**alcalización,** *n.f.* alkalization.

alcaloide (al·ka'loi·ðe) *n.m.* alkaloid.

alcance (al'kan·θe; -se) *n.m.* **1,** reach; scope; range *(of a gun)*. **2,** *comm.* balance due. **3,** *usu.pl.* capacity; capability. **4,** import; significance. **5,** latest news. —**al alcance de,** within reach of. —**dar alcance a,** to overtake.

alcancía (al·kan'θi·a; -'si·a) *n.f.* **1,** child's bank; piggy bank. **2,** *Amer.* poorbox.

alcanfor (al·kan'for) *n.m.* camphor. —**alcanforado,** *adj.* camphorated. —**alcanforero,** *n.m.* camphor tree.

alcantarilla (al·kan·ta'ri·ʎa; -ja) *n.f.* **1,** culvert. **2,** sewer. —**alcantarillado,** *n.m.* sewerage; sewer system.

alcanzado (al·kan'θa·ðo; -sa·ðo) *adj.* needy; in financial straits.

alcanzar (al·kan'θar; -'sar) *v.t.* [*infl.:* **rezar, 10**] **1,** to overtake. **2,** to reach. **3,** to attain. **4,** to manage; succeed in doing. **5,** to reach for; get. —*v.i.* **1,** to reach. **2,** to be sufficient.

alcaparra (al·ka'pa·rra) *n.f.* **1,** caper bush. **2,** caper.

alcaravea (al·ka·ra'βe·a) *n.f.* caraway.

alcatraz (al·ka'traθ; -'tras) *n.m.* pelican.

alcaudón (al·kau'ðon) *n.m.* shrike.

alcayata (al·ka'ja·ta) *n.f.* hook; spike.

alcázar (al'ka·θar; -sar) *n.m.* **1,** royal palace; castle. **2,** *naut.* quarterdeck. **3,** fortress.

alce ('al·θe; -se) *n.m.* **1,** moose; elk. **2,** *cards* raise. **3,** *cards* cut.

alce ('al·θe; -se) *v., pres.subjve. of* **alzar.**

alcé (al'θe; -'se) *v., 1st pers.sing. pret. of* **alzar.**

alcista (al'θis·ta; -'sis·ta) *n.m. & f., fin.* bull. —*adj.* bullish.

alcoba (al'ko·βa) *n.f.* **1,** bedroom. **2,** alcove.

alcohol (al'kol) *n.m.* alcohol. —**alcohólico,** *adj. & n.m.* alcoholic. —**alcoholismo,** *n.m.* alcoholism.

Alcorán (al·ko'ran) *n.m.* (the) Koran.

alcornoque (al·kor'no·ke) *n.m.* **1,** cork tree. **2,** blockhead.

alcurnia (al'kur·nja) *n.f.* lineage; ancestry.

alcuza (al'ku·θa; -sa) *n.f.* oil can.

aldaba (al'da·βa) *n.f.* **1,** door knocker. **2,** hasp. —**aldabilla,** *n.f.* latch.

aldea (al'de·a) *n.f.* village; hamlet. —**aldeano,** *n.m.* villager. —*adj.* & *n.m.* rustic; hick.

aldehido (al·de'i·ðo) *n.m.* aldehyde. ·

aldehuela (al·de'we·la) *n.f.* tiny village; hamlet.

alderredor (al·de·rre'ðor) *adv.* = alrededor.

¡ale! ('a·le) *interj.* let's go! get moving!

alear (a·le'ar) *v.t.* to alloy. —**aleación,** *n.f.* alloy.

aleccionar (a·lek·θjo'nar; -sjo'nar) *v.t.* to brief; coach; instruct.

aledaño (a·le'ða·ɲo) *adj.* bordering; outlying. —*n.m., usu. pl.* **1,** environs; outskirts. **2,** limits.

alegación (a·le·ɣa'θjon; -'sjon) *n.f.* allegation.

alegar (a·le'ɣar) *v.t.* [*infl.:* pagar, 8] **1,** to allege. **2,** to invoke; cite. **3,** to argue; plead. —*v.i., Amer.* to quarrel; dispute.

alegato (a·le'ɣa·to) *n.m.* **1,** *law* brief; plea. **2,** argument; reasoning. **3,** *Amer.* dispute; quarrel.

alegoría (a·le·ɣo'ri·a) *n.f.* allegory. —**alegórico** (-'ɣo·ri·ko) *adj.* allegoric.

alegrar (a·le'ɣrar) *v.t.* **1,** to gladden; enliven. **2,** *fig.* to brighten. —**alegrarse,** *v.r.* **1,** to rejoice; to be glad. **2,** *colloq.* to get tipsy.

alegre (a·le·ɣre) *adj.* **1,** gay. **2,** *colloq.* tipsy.

alegría (a·le'ɣri·a) *n.f.* gaiety; cheer.

alegro (a·le'ɣro) *n.m.* & *adj., mus.* allegro.

alegrón (a·le'ɣron) *n.m., colloq.* thrill.

alejamiento (a·le·xa'mjen·to) *n.m.* **1,** drawing apart. **2,** *fig.* estrangement.

alejar (a·le'xar) *v.t.* **1,** to separate; estrange. **2,** to put further apart. —**alejarse,** *v.r.* to draw away.

alelar (a·le'lar) *v.t.* to daze. —**alelado,** *adj.* dazed; aghast.

alelí (a·le'li) *n.m.* = alhelí.

aleluya (a·le'lu·ja) *n.f.* & *interj.*

hallelujah; alleluia. —**aleluyas,** *n.f.pl.* doggerel.

alemán (a·le'man) *adj.* & *n.m.* German.

alentado (a·len'ta·ðo) *adj.* **1,** courageous; spirited. **2,** hardy; resistant. **3,** presumptuous.

alentar (a·len'tar) *v.t.* [*infl.:* pensar, 27] to encourage; cheer. —**alentada,** *n.f.* long breath. —**alentador,** *adj.* encouraging; cheering.

alerce (a'ler·θe; -se) *n.m.* larch.

alergia (a'ler·xja) *n.f.* allergy. —**alergeno** (-'xe·no) *n.m.* allergen. —**alérgico** (-xi·ko) *adj.* allergic.

alero (a'le·ro) *n.m.* eaves (*pl.*).

alerón (a·le'ron) *n.m.* aileron.

alerta (a'ler·ta) *adv.* on the alert. —*interj.* look out!; watch out! —*n.m.* alarm; alert. —**alertar,** *v.t.* to alert.

alerto (a'ler·to) *adj.* alert.

alesna (a'les·na) *n.f.* awl.

aleta (a'le·ta) *n.f.* **1,** small wing. **2,** fin. **3,** blade (of a propeller or blower). —**aletazo,** *n.m.* flap (with a wing).

aletargado (a·le·tar'ɣa·ðo) *adj.* lethargic. —**aletargarse,** *v.r.* to become lethargic.

aletear (a·le·te'ar) *v.i.* to flutter. —**aleteo** (-'te·o) *n.m.* fluttering.

aleve (a'le·βe) *adj.* = alevoso.

alevosía (a·le·βo'si·a) *n.f.* perfidy; treachery. —**alevoso,** *adj.* treacherous; perfidious.

alfa ('al·fa) *n.f.* alpha.

alfabetizar (al·fa·βe·ti'θar; -'sar) *v.t.* [*infl.:* rezar, 10] **1,** to alphabetize. **2,** to make literate.

alfabeto (al·fa'βe·to) *n.m.* alphabet. —**alfabético** (-'βe·ti·ko) *adj.* alphabetical.

alfajor (al·fa'xor) *n.m.* a name given to various types of pastry, usu. with a cream or honey filling.

alfalfa (al'fal·fa) *n.f.* alfalfa. —**alfalfar,** *n.m.* alfalfa field.

alfanje (al'fan·xe) *n.m.* cutlass.

alfanumérico (al·fa·nu'me·ri·co) *adj.* alphanumeric.

alfarda (al'far·ða) *n.f.* joist; light beam.

alfarería (al·fa·re'ri·a) *n.f.* **1,** pottery. **2,** potter's shop. —**alfarero,** *n.m.* potter.

alfeñicarse (al·fe·ɲi'kar·se) *v.r.* [*infl.:* tocar, 7] **1,** to become thin. **2,** to be or become squeamish.

alfeñique (al·fe'ɲi·ke) *n.m.* **1,** sugar paste. **2,** thin, gaunt person. **3,** squeamishness.

alférez (al'fe·reθ; -res) *n.m.* **1,** *naut.* ensign. **2,** *mil.* second lieutenant. —**alférez de navío,** naval lieutenant.

alfil (al'fil) *n.m. chess* bishop.

alfiler (al·fi'ler) *n.m.* **1,** common pin. **2,** brooch. —**alfileres,** *n.m.pl.* pin money. —**de veinticinco alfileres; con todos sus alfileres,** *colloq.* in one's best bib and tucker.

alfilerazo (al·fi·le'ra·θo; -so) *n.m.* pinprick.

alfiletero (al·fi·le'te·ro) *n.m.* pincushion.

alfombra (al'fom·bra) *n.f.* carpet; rug. —**alfombrado,** *n.m.* carpeting. —**alfombrar,** *v.t.* to carpet.

alfombrilla (al·fom'bri·ʎa; -ja) *n.f.* **1,** small rug; mat. **2,** German measles.

alfóncigo (al'fon·θi·ɣo; -si·yo) *n.m.* pistachio.

alforfón (al·for'fon) *n.m.* buckwheat.

alforja (al'for·xa) *n.f.* **1,** *usu.pl.* saddlebag. **2,** knapsack. **3,** provisions for a journey. —**pasarse a la otra alforja,** *Amer.* to overstep one's bounds.

alforza (al'for·θa; -sa) *n.f.* hem; tuck. —**alforzar,** *v.t.* [*infl.:* **rezar,** 10] to tuck.

alga (al'ɣa) *n.f.* alga; seaweed.

algarabía (al·ɣa·ra'βi·a) *n.f.* **1,** jargon; gibberish. **2,** *colloq.* uproar.

algarroba (al·ɣa'rro·βa) *n.f.* carob bean; St.-John's-bread.

algarrobo (al·ɣa'rro·βo) *n.m.,* *also,* **algarrobera** (-'βe·ra) *n.f.* carob tree.

algazara (al·ɣa'θa·ra; -'sa·ra) *n.f.* din; uproar.

álgebra ('al·xe·βra) *n.f.* algebra. —**algebraico** (-'βrai·ko) *adj.* algebraic.

algo ('al·ɣo) *indef.pron.* something. —*adv.* somewhat; rather. —**algo es algo,** every little bit counts. —**algo por el estilo,** something of the sort. —**tener en algo,** to value.

algodón (al·ɣo'ðon) *n.m.* **1,** cotton. **2,** cotton plant. —**algodonal,** *n.m.* cotton plantation. —**algodonar,** *v.t.* to stuff with cotton. —**algodonoso,** *adj.* cottony. —**algodón en rama,** raw cotton.

algodonero (al·ɣo·ðo'ne·ro) *adj.* of or pert. to cotton. —*n.m.* **1,** cotton plant. **2,** cotton trader.

algoritmo (al·ɣo'rit·mo) *n.m.* algorithm. —**algorítmico,** *adj.* algorithmic. —**lenguaje algorítmico,** ALGOL.

alguacil (al·ɣwa'θil; -'sil) *n.m.* bailiff; constable.

alguien ('al·ɣjen) *indef. pron.* someone; anyone.

algún (al'ɣun) *adj.* = **alguno** *before a masc. noun.*

alguno (al'ɣu·no) *adj.* some; any; —*pron.* someone; something. —**alguna que otra vez,** once in a while. —**alguno que otro,** a few.

alhaja (a'la·xa) *n.f.* **1,** jewel; gem. **2,** *colloq., ironic* sly one; fine one. —**alhajar,** *v.t.* to bejewel.

alharaca (a·la'ra·ka) *n.f., usu.pl.* fuss; ado; ballyhoo. —**alharaquiento** (-'kjen·to) fussy; overdemonstrative.

alhelí *also,* **alelí** (a·le'li) *n.m.* gillyflower.

alheña (a'le·ɲa) *n.f.* henna. —**alheñar,** *v.t.* to henna.

alianza (a'ljan·θa; -sa) *n.f.* **1,** alliance. **2,** wedding ring.

aliarse (a'ljar·se) *v.r.* [*infl.:* **enviar,** 22] to ally (oneself); become allied. —**aliado,** *adj.* allied. —*n.m.* ally.

alias ('a·ljas) *n.m. & adv.* alias.

alibí (a·li'βi) *n.m.* alibi.

alicaído (a·li·ka'i·ðo) *adj., colloq.* crestfallen; downhearted.

alicates (a·li'ka·tes) *n.m.pl.* pliers.

aliciente (a·li'θjen·te; -'sjen·te) *n.m.* incentive; inducement.

alienable (a·lje'na·βle) *adj.* alienable.

alienación (a·lje·na'θjon; -'sjon) *n.f., law; med.* alienation.

alienar (a·lje'nar) *v.t.* **1,** to drive (one) insane. **2,** *law* to transfer (property). —**alienación,** *n.f.* **1,** insanity. **2,** transfer (of property). —**alienado,** *adj.* insane; mentally deranged.

alienista (a·lje'nis·ta) *n.m. & f.* alienist.

aliento (a'ljen·to) *n.m.* **1,** breath. **2,** encouragement. **3,** courage.

aligerar (a·li·xe'rar) *v.t.* **1,** to lighten. **2,** to ease; mitigate. —*v.i., colloq.* to hurry; hasten. —**aligerar el paso,** to hurry.

alijar (a·li'xar) *v.t.* **1,** to unload; lighten. **2,** to gin (cotton). —**alijadora,** *n.f.* cotton gin.

alijo (a'li·xo) *n.m.* **1,** smuggling. **2,** contraband.

alimaña (a·li'ma·ɲa) *n.f.* animal pest; varmint.

alimentar (a·li·men'tar) *v.t.* 1, to feed; nourish. 2, *fig.* to foster; encourage. —**alimentarse**, *v.r.* to feed oneself. —**alimentación**, *n.f.* feeding; nourishment. —**alimentario**, *adj.* alimentary.

alimenticio (a·li·men'ti·θjo; -sjo) *adj.* 1, nourishing; nutritious. 2, alimentary.

alimento (a·li'men·to) *n.m.* 1, nourishment; food. 2, *pl.* allowance; pension; alimony.

alindar (a·lin'dar) *v.t.* 1, to mark off; limit. 2, to adorn; beautify. —*v.i.* to be contiguous or adjacent.

alinear (a·li·ne'ar) *v.t.* to align. —**alinearse**, *v.r.* to line up; fall into line. —**alineación**, *n.f., also,* **alineamiento**, *n.m.* alignment.

aliñar (a·li'ɲar) *v.t.* 1, to dress or season (food). 2, to adorn. —**aliño** (a'li·ɲo) *n.m.* seasoning; dressing.

alisar (a·li'sar) *v.t.* to smooth.

alisios (a'li·sjos) *n.m.pl.* trade winds.

aliso (a'li·so) *n.m., bot.* alder.

alistamiento (a·lis·ta'mjen·to) *n.m.* 1, listing. 2, enlistment; recruitment.

alistar (a·lis'tar) *v.t.* 1, to make ready; prepare. 2, to list; enter in a list. 3, *mil.* to induct. —**alistarse**, *v.r.* to enlist.

aliteración (a·li·te·ra'θjon; -'sjon) *n.f.* alliteration. —**aliterado** (-'ra·ðo) *adj.* alliterative.

aliviar (a·li'βjar) *v.t.* to relieve; mitigate. —**aliviarse**, *v.r.* to be soothed or relieved. —**alivio** (a'li·βjo) *n.m.* relief.

aljaba (al'xa·βa) *n.f.* quiver (*for arrows*).

aljibe (al'xi·βe) *n.m.* 1, cistern. 2, *naut.* water tender.

alma ('al·ma) *n.f.* 1, soul. 2, core. 3, web (*of a beam*). 4, *fig.* spirit; heart. 5, bore (*of a gun*). —**alma de Dios**, simple soul. —**caérsele el alma a los pies**, to be deeply disappointed. —**volverle a uno el alma al cuerpo**, to recover, as from fear.

almacén (al·ma'θen; -'sen) *n.m.* 1, warehouse. 2, wholesale store. 3, department store. 4, *Amer.* general store. —**almacén de víveres**, grocery.

almacenar (al·ma·θe'nar; -se-'nar) *v.t.* to store. —**almacenaje**, *n.m.* storage.

almacenero (al·ma·θe'ne·ro; -se-'ne·ro) *n.m., S.A.* storekeeper.

almacenista (al·ma·θe'nis·ta; -se'nis·ta) *n.m. & f.* 1, wholesale merchant. 2, *Amer.* salesperson in a wholesale store. 3, *Amer.* storekeeper.

almácigo (al'ma·θi·ɣo; -si·ɣo) *n.m.* mastic tree. —**almáciga**, *n.f.* mastic.

almadía (al·ma'ði·a) *n.f.* raft.

almagre (al'ma·ɣre) *n.m.* red ocher.

almanaque (al·ma'na·ke) *n.m.* almanac; calendar.

almeja (al'me·xa) *n.f.* clam.

almena (al'me·na) *n.f.* battlement.

almenado (al·me'na·ðo) *adj.* crenelated; embattled. —*n.m.* [*also,* **almenaje**] battlements.

almendra (al'men·dra) *n.f.* almond. —**almendro**, *n.m.* almond tree.

almendrado (al·men'dra·ðo) *adj.* almond-shaped. —*n.m.* macaroon.

almiar (al'mjar) *n.m.* haystack; hayrick.

almíbar (al'mi·βar) *n.m.* sugar syrup.

almibarar (al·mi·βa'rar) *v.t.* to candy; sugar-coat.

almidón (al·mi'ðon) *n.m.* starch. —**almidonar**, *v.t.* to starch.

almidonado (al·mi·ðo'na·ðo) *adj.* 1, starched. 2, *fig.* stiff; dressed with affectation.

alminar (al·mi'nar) *n.m.* minaret.

almirante (al·mi'ran·te) *n.m.* admiral. —**almiranta**, *n.f.* viceadmiral's ship. —**almirantazgo**, *n.m.* admiralty.

almizcle (al'miθ·kle; -'mis·kle) *n.m.* musk. —**almizcleño**, *adj.* musky.

almizclero (al·miθ'kle·ro; al·mis-) *n.m.* musk deer. —*adj.* 1, musky. 2, musk (*attrib.*) —**almizclera**, *n.f.* [*also,* **rata almizclera**] muskrat.

almohada (al·mo'a·ða) *n.f.* pillow. —**consultar** (algo) **con la almohada**, to sleep on it.

almohadilla (al·mo·a'ði·ʎa; -ja) *n.f.* 1, small pillow. 2, cushion. 3, pad.

almohadón (al·mo·a'ðon) *n.m.* cushion.

almohaza (al·mo'a·θa; -sa) *n.f.* currycomb. —**almohazador**, *n.m.* groom. —**almohazar**, *v.t.* to curry.

almoneda (al·mo'ne·ða) *n.f.* **1**, public auction. **2**, clearance sale. —**almonedear,** *v.t.* to auction.

almorranas (al·mo'rra·nas) *n.f.pl.* hemorrhoids; piles.

almorzar (al·mor'θar; -'sar) *v.i.* [*infl.*: **acostar, 28; rezar, 10**] to lunch. —*v.t.* to eat for lunch.

almuédano (al'mwe·ða·no) *n.m.* muezzin. *Also,* **almuecín** (-'θin; -'sin).

almuerzo (al'mwer·θo; -so) *n.m.* lunch.

¡aló! (a'lo) *interj.* hello *(on the telephone)*.

alocar (a·lo'kar) *v.t.* [*infl.*: **tocar, 7**] to drive mad. —**alocado,** *adj.* reckless; wild.

alocución (a·lo·ku'θjon; -'sjon) *n.f.* brief speech; talk.

áloe ('a·lo·e) *n.m.* **1**, aloe. **2**, aloes.

aloja (a'lo·xa) *n.f.* mead.

alojamiento (a·lo·xa'mjen·to) *n.m.* **1**, lodging. **2**, *mil.* quarters.

alojar (a·lo'xar) *v.t.* **1**, to lodge. **2**, to station (troops). — **alojarse,** *v.r.* to take lodgings.

alón (a'lon) *n.m.* plucked wing of a bird.

alondra (a'lon·dra) *n.f., ornith.* lark.

alopatía (a·lo·pa'ti·a) *n.f.* allopathy. —**alopático** (-'pa·ti·ko) *adj.* allopathic.

alotropía (a·lo·tro'pi·a) *n.f.* allotropy. —**alotrópico** (-'tro·pi·ko) *adj.* allotropic. —**alótropo** (a'lo·tro·po) *n.m.* allotrope.

alpaca (al'pa·ka) *n.f.* alpaca.

alpargata (al·par'ya·ta) *n.f.* a sandal with hemp sole.

alpinismo (al·pi'nis·mo) *n.m.* alpinism; mountain-climbing. —**alpinista,** *n.m.* & *f.* alpinist; mountain-climber.

alpino (al'pi·no) *adj.* alpine. *Also,* **alpestre** (al'pes·tre).

alpiste (al'pis·te) *n.m.* canary seed. —**dejar a uno alpiste,** to disappoint; leave out (of plans, etc.).

alquería (al·ke'ri·a) *n.f.* farmhouse.

alquiladizo (al·ki·la'ði·θo; -so) *n.m., derog.* hireling.

alquilar (al·ki'lar) *v.t.* to let; rent; hire. —**de alquiler,** for rent or hire.

alquimia (al'ki·mja) *n.f.* alchemy.

—**alquimista** (-'mis·ta) *n.m.* & *f.* alchemist.

alquitrán (al·ki'tran) *n.m.* tar; coal tar. —**alquitranar,** *v.t.* to tar.

alrededor (al·re·ðe'ðor) *adv.* around. —**alrededores,** *n.m.pl.* environs. —**alrededor de,** around, about.

alta ('al·ta) *n.f.* **1**, discharge, esp. from a hospital. **2**, enrollment. —**dar de alta,** to discharge, esp. from a hospital. —**darse de alta,** to join (an organization).

altamente (al·ta'men·te) *adv.* highly.

altanería (al·ta·ne'ri·a) *n.f.* haughtiness; arrogance. —**altanero** (-'ne·ro) haughty; arrogant.

altar (al'tar) *n.m.* altar.

altavoz (al·ta'βoθ; -'βos) *n.m.* loudspeaker.

altea (al'te·a) *n.f.* marsh mallow.

alteración (al·te·ra'θjon; -'sjon) *n.f.* **1**, alteration; change. **2**, disturbance; agitation.

alterar (al·te'rar) *v.t.* **1**, to alter. **2**, to disturb; upset. —**alterarse,** *v.r.* to become upset; become irritated.

altercar (al·ter'kar) *v.i.* [*infl.*: tocar, **7**] to wrangle; altercate. —**altercado,** *n.m., also,* **altercación,** *n.f.* wrangle; altercation.

alternador (al·ter·na'ðor) *n.m.* alternator.

alternar (al·ter'nar) *v.t.* & *i.* to alternate. —**alternarse,** *v.r.* to take turns. —**alternar con, 1**, to associate with. **2**, to compete with.

alternativa (al·ter·na'ti·βa) *n.f.* **1**, alternative. **2**, *sports* initiation of a bullfighter. **3**, *pl., colloq.* ups and downs. —**alternativo,** *adj.* **1**, alternate. **2**, alternating.

alterno (al'ter·no) *adj.* **1**, alternate. **2**, alternating.

alteza (al'te·θa; -sa) *n.f.* Highness.

altibajos (al·ti'βa·xos) *n.m.pl.* ups and downs.

altillo (al'ti·ʎo; -jo) *n.m.* **1**, hillock. **2**, *S.A.* attic.

altímetro (al'ti·me·tro) *n.m.,* altimeter.

altiplano (al·ti'pla·no) *n.m., also* **altiplanicie** (-'ni·θje; -sje) *n.f.* high plateau.

altísimo (al'ti·si·mo) *adj. superl. of* **alto.** —*n.m., cap.* Most High; God.

altisonante (al·ti·so'nan·te) *adj.* high-sounding; highflown. —**altisonancia,** *n.f.* highflown language.

altísono (al'ti·so·no) *adj.* high-sounding.

altitud (al·ti'tuð) *n.f.* altitude.

altivo (al'ti·βo) *adj.* haughty; proud. —**altivez** (-'βeθ; -'βes) *n.f.* haughtiness; pride.

alto ('al·to) *adj.* **1,** high; tall. **2,** loud. —*n.m.* **1,** height. **2,** *pl., Amer.* top floor. **3,** *Amer.* pile; bunch. —*adj. & n.m., mus.* alto. —*adv.* **1,** high. **2,** loud; loudly. —**altas horas,** late hours. —**pasar por alto,** to overlook.

alto ('al·to) *n.m.* halt. —*interj.* halt! —**hacer alto,** to stop; halt.

altocúmulo (al·to'ku·mu·lo) *n.m., meteorol.* altocumulus.

altoparlante (al·to·par'lan·te) *n.m., Amer.* loudspeaker.

altozano (al·to'θa·no; -'sa·no) *n.m.* **1,** hillock. **2,** elevation; high place.

altruísmo (al·tru'is·mo) *n.m.* altruism. —**altruísta,** *n.m. & f.* altruist. —*adj* altruistic.

altura (al'tu·ra) *n.f.* **1,** height. **2,** *often pl.* stage; point; level. **3,** latitude. —**estar a la altura de,** to measure up to; be equal to.

alucinar (a·lu·θi'nar; -si'nar) *v.t.* **1,** to delude. **2,** to fascinate. —**alucinarse,** *v.r.* to delude oneself. —**alucinación,** *n.f.* hallucination. —**alucinatorio** (-'na·to·ri·o) *adj.* hallucinatory. —**alucinogénico** (-no'xe·ni·ko) *adj.* hallucinogenic.

alud (a'luð) *n.m.* avalanche.

aludir (a·lu'ðir) *v.i.* to allude.

alumbramiento (a·lum·bra·'mjen·to) *n.m.* **1,** childbirth. **2,** lighting.

alumbrar (a·lum'brar) *v.t.* **1,** to light. **2,** *fig.* to enlighten. —*v.i.* to give birth. —**alumbrarse,** *v.r.* **1,** to light one's way. **2,** *slang* to get tipsy. —**alumbrado,** *adj.* lighted; lit. —*n.m.* lighting system.

alumbre (a'lum·bre) *n.m.* alum.

alúmina (a'lu·mi·na) *n.f.* alumina.

aluminio (a·lu'mi·njo) *n.m.* aluminum.

alumna (a'lum·na) *n.f.* pupil.

alumnado (a·lum'na·ðo) *n.m.* **1,** student body. **2,** boarding school.

alumno (a'lum·no) *n.m.* pupil.

alunizar (a·lu·ni'θar; -'sar) *v.i.* [*infl.:* rezar, 10] to land on the moon. —**alunizaje** (-'θa·xe; -'sa·xe) *n.m.* lunar landing.

alusión (a·lu'sjon) *n.f.* allusion. —**alusivo** (-'si·βo) *adj.* allusive.

aluvión (a·lu'βjon) *n.m.* **1,** alluvium. **2,** freshet. —**aluvial,** *adj.* alluvial.

alvéolo (al'βe·o·lo) *n.m.* alveolus. —**alveolar,** *adj.* alveolar.

alza ('al·θa; -sa) *n.f.* **1,** rise. **2,** rear sight (*of a firearm*). **3,** *print.* overlay. —**jugar al alza,** to buy on margin.

alzada (al'θa·ða; al'sa-) *n.f.* **1,** height (*of a horse*). **2,** *law* appeal. **3,** *archit.* front elevation.

alzado (al'θa·ðo; al'sa-) *adj.* **1,** insurgent. **2,** *Amer.* haughty; proud. **3,** *Amer.* in heat; in rut. **4,** *Amer.* gone wild, as an animal.

alzamiento (al·θa'mjen·to; al·sa-) *n.m.* **1,** rise in prices. **2,** overbid. **3,** rebellion.

alzar (al'θar; -'sar) *v.t.* [*infl.:* rezar, 10] **1,** to raise; lift. **2,** to erect. **3,** to elevate (the Host). **4,** to cut (cards). —**alzarse,** *v.r.* **1,** to rise in revolt. **2,** to make a fraudulent bankruptcy. **3,** to abscond. —**alzar el codo,** to drink heavily. —**alzar el vuelo,** to take flight.

allá (a'ʎa; a'ja) *adv.* **1,** there; yonder; far away. **2,** long ago. —**allá él (ella; Vd.),** that's his (her, your) concern. —**allá voy,** I'm coming. —**el más allá,** the beyond. —**más allá,** farther.

allanamiento (a·ʎa·na'mjen·to; a·ja-) *n.m.* **1,** razing; leveling. **2,** acquiescence. **3,** incursion; irruption. —**allanamiento de morada,** housebreaking.

allanar (a·ʎa'nar; a·ja-) *v.t.* **1,** to raze; to level. **2,** to overcome (a difficulty). —*v.r.* to acquiesce. —**allanar el camino,** to pave the way.

allegar (a·ʎe'ɣar) *v.t. & i.* [*infl.:* pagar, 8] to approach; draw near; gather. —**allegarse,** *v.r.* to become close or intimate. —**allegado,** *adj.* close; related. —*n.m.* supporter; adherent.

allende (a'ʎen·de; a'jen-) *adv. & prep.* beyond. —**allende los mares,** overseas; abroad.

allí (a'ʎi; -'ji) *adv.* there; right there. —**por allí,** that way; through there.

ama ('a·ma) *n.f.* **1,** mistress (of a household). **2,** owner; landlady. —**ama de leche** (*or de cría o de teta*) wet nurse. —**ama de llaves,** housekeeper. —**ama seca,** governess; nanny.

amable (a'ma·βle) *adj.* amiable;

kind; good. —**amabilidad**, *n.f.* amiability; kindness; goodness.

amachado (a·ma'tʃa·ðo) *adj.* **1**, manly; virile. **2**, *(of a woman)* mannish.

amachetear (a·ma·tʃe·te'ar) *v.t.* = machetear.

amado (a'ma·ðo) *adj.* & *n.m.* beloved.

amaestrar (a·ma·es'trar) *v.t.* **1**, to train. **2**, to tame; break (a horse). —**amaestrado**, *adj.* trained.

amagar (a·ma'yar) *v.t.* & *i.* [*infl.:* **pagar, 8**] **1**, to feint. **2**, to threaten. **3**, to feign.

amago (a'ma·yo) *n.m.* **1**, feint. **2**, indication; sign. **3**, threat.

amainar (a·mai'nar) *v.i.* to subside. —*v.t.* to take in; lower (sails).

amalgama (a·mal'ya·ma) *n.f.* amalgam. —**amalgamación**, *n.f.* amalgamation. —**amalgamar**, *v.t.* to amalgamate.

amamantar (a·ma·man'tar) *v.t.* to suckle.

amanecer (a·ma·ne'θer; -'ser) *v.i.* [*infl.:* **conocer, 13**] **1**, to dawn. **2**, to arrive or appear at dawn. —*n.m.* dawn.

amanecida (a·ma·ne'θi·ða; -'si·ða) *n.f.* daybreak; dawn.

amanerarse (a·ma·ne'rar·se) *v.r.* to adopt mannerisms or affectations. —**amanerado**, *adj.* affected; artificial. —**amaneramiento**, *n.m.* affectation; mannerism.

amansar (a·man'sar) *v.t.* to tame.

amante (a'man·te) *n.m.* lover. —*n.f.* mistress. —*adj.* loving.

amanuense (a·ma'nwen·se) *n.m.* & *f.* amanuensis.

amañado (a·ma'ɲa·ðo) *adj.* **1**, clever; cunning. **2**, contrived; spurious. **3**, inured; habituated.

amañarse (a·ma'ɲar·se) *v.r.* **1**, to contrive. **2**, to become inured or habituated.

amaño (a'ma·ɲo) *n.m.* **1**, cleverness; cunning. **2**, *pl.* tools; instruments. **3**, *often pl.* machinations; intrigue.

amapola (a·ma'po·la) *n.f.* poppy.

amar (a'mar) *v.t.* & *i.* [*infl.:* **1**] to love. —**amarse**, *v.r.* to love each other; be in love.

amaranto (a·ma'ran·to) *n.m.* amaranth.

amargar (a·mar'yar) *v.t.* [*infl.:* **pagar, 8**] to make bitter. —**amargarse**, *v.r.* to become bitter. —**amargado**, *adj.* embittered.

amargo (a'mar·yo) *adj.* bitter. —*n.m.* bitterness. —**amargos**, *n.m. pl.* bitters.

amargor (a·mar'yor) *n.m.* **1**, bitterness. **2**, sorrow. *Also,* **amargura** (-'yu·ra) *n.f.*

amarilis (a·ma'ri·lis) *n.f.* amaryllis.

amarillear (a·ma·ri·ʎe'ar; -je'ar) *v.t.* to color yellow. —*v.i.* to yellow; become yellow.

amarillo (a·ma'ri·ʎo; -jo) *adj.* yellow. —**amarillento**, *adj.* yellowish.

amarra (a'ma·rra) *n.f.* **1**, tie; fastening. **2**, *naut.* hawser; cable; *pl.* moorings.

amarradero (a·ma·rra'ðe·ro) *n.m.* **1**, hitching post. **2**, *naut.* mooring; dock; berth.

amarrar (a·ma'rrar) *v.t.* **1**, to fasten; tie; bind. **2**, *also intr.* to moor.

amarre (a'ma·rre) *n.m.* **1**, fastening; binding. **2**, mooring. **3**, moorage.

amarrete (a·ma'rre·te) *adj., Amer.* tight; stingy. —*n.m.* tightwad.

amartillar (a·mar·ti'ʎar; -'jar) *v.t.* **1**, to hammer. **2**, to cock (a gun).

amasar (a·ma'sar) *v.t.* **1**, to knead. **2**, to amass. **3**, to concoct.

amasijo (a·ma'si·xo) *n.m.* **1**, dough. **2**, kneading. **3**, mess; hodgepodge. **4**, plot; intrigue.

amatista (a·ma'tis·ta) *n.f.* amethyst.

amatorio (a·ma'to·rjo) *adj.* amatory.

amazacotado (a·ma·θa·ko'ta·ðo; a·ma·sa-) *adj.* **1**, thick; heavy; lumpy. **2**, clumsy *(as of style)*; heavy-handed.

amazona (a·ma'θo·na; -'so·na) *n.f.* **1**, amazon. **2**, horsewoman; equestrienne. **3**, woman's riding habit.

ambages (am'ba·xes) *n.m.pl.* circumlocution; ambiguity. —**sin ambages**, to the point.

ámbar ('am·bar) *n.m.* amber. —**ambarino**, *adj.* amber. —**ámbar gris**, ambergris.

ambas ('am·bas) *adj., fem of* **ambos**.

ambición (am·bi'θjon; -'sjon) *n.f.* ambition. —**ambicionar**, *v.t.* to covet; aspire to. —**ambicioso** (-'θjo·so; -'sjo·so) *adj.* ambitious; greedy.

ambidextro (am·bi'ðeks·tro) *adj.* ambidextrous.

ambiente (am'bjen·te) *n.m.* atmosphere; surroundings; environment.

—*adj.* [*also,* **ambiental**] surrounding; environmental.

ambiguo (am'bi·ɣwo) *adj.* ambiguous. —**ambigüedad** (-ɣwe'ðað) *n.f.* ambiguity.

ámbito ('am·bi·to) *n.m.* ambit; limits; confines.

ambivalente (am·bi·βa'len·te) *adj.* ambivalent. —**ambivalencia,** *n.f.* ambivalence.

amblar (am'blar) *v.i.* to pace; amble (*as a horse*).

ambo ('am·bo) *n.m.,* in *lotto,* a pair of numbers.

ambos ('am·bos) *adj.m.pl.* [*fem.* **ambas**] both.

ambrosía (am·bro'si·a) *n.f.* **1,** ambrosia. **2,** *bot.* ragweed.

ambulancia (am·bu'lan·θja; -sja) *n.f.* **1,** ambulance. **2,** *mil.* field hospital.

ambular (am·bu'lar) *v.i.* to wander. —**ambulante,** *adj.* roving. —**vendedor ambulante,** peddler.

ambulatorio (am·bu·la'to·rjo) *adj.* ambulatory.

ameba (a'me·βa) *n.f.* ameba. *Also,* **amiba.**

amedrentar (a·me·ðren'tar) *v.t.* to intimidate; frighten. —**amedrentarse,** *v.r.* to become frightened.

amén (a'men) *n.m., adv. & interj.* amen. —**amén de,** besides.

amenaza (a·me'na·θa; -sa) *n.f.* threat; menace.

amenazar (a·me·na'θar; -'sar) *v.t. & i.* [*infl.:* **rezar, 10**] to threaten. —**amenazante, amenazador,** *adj.* threatening; impending.

amenguar (a·men'gwar) *v.t.* [*infl.:* **averiguar, 9**] to diminish; lessen.

ameno (a'me·no) *adj.* pleasing; agreeable. —**amenidad,** *n.f.* amenity. —**amenizar** (-ni'θar; -'sar) *v.t.* [*infl.:* **rezar, 10**] to make pleasant.

amento (a'men·to) *n.m.* ament; catkin.

americana (a·me·ri'ka·na) *n.f.* man's jacket.

americanizar (a·me·ri·ka·ni·'θar -'sar) *v.t.* [*infl.:* **rezar, 10**] to Americanize. —**americanización,** *n.f.* Americanization.

americano (a·me·ri'ka·no) *adj.* American. —*n.m.* **1,** American. **2,** Latin-American. —**americanismo,** *n.m.* Americanism. —**americanista,** *n.m. & f.* student of American languages and cultures.

americio (a·me'ri·θjo; -sjo) *n.m.*

americium. *Also,* **américo** (a'me·ri·ko).

amerizar (a·me·ri'θar; -'sar) *v.t.* [*infl.:* **rezar, 10**] to land (an aircraft) on the water.

ametralladora (a·me·tra·ʎa'ðo·ra; -ja'ðo·ra) *n.f.* machine gun. —**ametrallador** (-'ðor) *n.m.* machine gunner. —**ametrallar** (-'ʎar; -'jar) *v.t.* to machine-gun.

amianto (a'mjan·to) *n.m.* asbestos.

amiba (a'mi·βa) *n.f.* = **ameba.**

amígdala (a'miɣ·ða·la) *n.f.* tonsil. —**amigdalitis,** *n.f.* tonsillitis.

amigo (a'mi·ɣo) *n.m.* friend; boy friend. —*adj.* friendly. —**amiga,** *n.f.* friend; girl friend. —**amigable,** *adj.* friendly. —**amigote** (-'ɣo·te) *n.m.* pal; chum. —**pie de amigo,** prop; support. —**ser amigo de,** to be fond of; take to; be inclined to.

amilanar (a·mi·la'nar) *v.t.* to cow. —**amilanarse,** *v.r.* to be cowed; shrink in fright.

amillarar (a·mi·ʎa'rar; -ja'rar) *v.t.* to assess. —**amillaramiento,** *n.m.* assessment.

aminoácido (a·mi·no'a·θi·ðo; -si·ðo) *n.m.* amino acid.

aminorar (a·mi·no'rar) *v.t.* to diminish; lessen.

amir (a'mir) *n.m.* emir.

amistad (a·mis'tað) *n.f.* **1,** friendship. **2,** friend. —**trabar amistad,** to strike up a friendship.

amistar (a·mis·'tar) *v.t.* to reconcile; restore to friendship. —*v.i.* [*also,* **amistarse,** *v.r.*] to be reconciled; resume friendly relations.

amistoso (a·mis'to·so) *adj.* friendly; amicable.

amnesia (am'ne·sja) *n.f.* amnesia. —**amnésico** (-si·ko) *adj. & n.m.* amnesic; amnesiac.

amnistía (am·nis'ti·a) *n.f.* amnesty. —**amnistiar** (-'tjar) *v.t.* [*infl.:* **enviar, 22**] to grant amnesty; pardon.

amo ('a·mo) *n.m.* **1,** master. **2,** head of a family or household. **3,** owner; landlord.

amoblar (a·mo'βlar) *v.t.* [*infl.:* **acostar, 28**] = **amueblar.**

amodorrarse (a·mo·ðo'rrar·se) *v.r.* to become drowsy. —**amodorrar,** *v.t.* to make drowsy. —**amodorrado,** *adj.* drowsy; sleepy.

amohinar (a·mo·i'nar) *v.t.* to annoy; discomfit.

amolar (a·mo'lar) *v.t.* [*infl.:*

acostar, 28] 1, to grind; sharpen. **2,** *colloq.* to bother; annoy. —**amoladera,** *n.f.* grinder; grindstone. —**amolador,** *n.m.* grinder; one who grinds or sharpens. —*adj., colloq.* bothersome; annoying. —**amoladura,** *n.f.* grinding; sharpening. —**amoladuras,** *n.f.pl.* grit.

amoldar (a·mol'dar) *v.t.* to mold; fashion. —**amoldarse,** *v.r.* to adapt or adjust oneself.

amonestar (a·mo·nes'tar) *v.t.* to admonish. —**amonestación,** *n.f.* admonition. —**correr las amonestaciones,** to publish marriage banns.

amoníaco (a·mo'ni·a·ko) *n.m.* ammonia.

amonio (a'mo·njo) *n.m.* ammonium.

amoniuro (a·mo'nju·ro) *n.m.* ammoniate.

amontonar (a·mon·to'nar) *v.t.* to heap; accumulate. —**amontonarse,** *v.r.* to crowd together. —**amontonamiento,** *n.m.* accumulation; gathering.

amor (a'mor) *n.m.* love. —**amores,** *n.m.pl.* love affair. —**amor patrio,** patriotism. —**amor propio,** pride; self-esteem.

amoral (a·mo'ral) *adj.* amoral. —**amoralidad,** *n.f.* amorality.

amoratado (a·mo·ra'ta·ðo) *adj.* livid; black and blue.

amoratarse (a·mo·ra'tar·se) *v.r.* **1,** to turn blue or purple, as with cold. **2,** to become black and blue, as from a blow.

amorcillo (a·mor'θi·ʎo; -'si·jo) *n.m.* **1,** flirtation. **2,** cupid figure.

amordazar (a·mor·ða'θar; -'sar) *v.t.* [*infl.* rezar, 10] to gag; muzzle.

amorfo (a'mor·fo) *adj.* amorphous; vague; shapeless.

amorío (a·mo'ri·o) *n.m., colloq.* flirtation; infatuation; love affair.

amoroso (a·mo'ro·so) *adj.* amorous.

amorrar (a·mo'rrar) *v.i.* [*also,* **amorrarse,** *v.r.*] *colloq.* to sulk.

amortajar (a·mor·ta'xar) *v.t.* to enshroud.

amortiguador (a·mor·ti·gwa·'ðor) *adj.* cushioning; softening; muffling. —*n.m.* **1,** shock absorber. **2,** muffler.

amortiguar (a·mor·ti'gwar) *v.t.* [*infl.:* averiguar, 9] **1,** to deaden; cushion; soften. **2,** to muffle. **3,** to dim (lights). —**amortiguamiento,**

n.m., also, **amortiguación,** *n.f.* cushioning; softening.

amortizar (a·mor·ti'θar; -'sar) *v.t.* [*infl.:* **rezar, 10**] to amortize; redeem. —**amortización,** *n.f.* amortization.

amoscarse (a·mos'kar·se) *v.r.* [*infl.:* tocar, 7] **1,** to be or become annoyed. **2,** *Amer.* to blush; be embarrassed.

amostazar (a·mos·ta'θar; -'sar) *v.t., colloq.* [*infl.:* rezar, 10] to irritate; annoy.

amotinado (a·mo·ti'na·ðo) *adj.* mutinous; rebellious. —*n.m.* mutineer; rebel.

amotinar (a·mo·ti'nar) *v.t.* to incite to mutiny or riot. —**amotinarse,** *v.r.* to mutiny; rebel; riot. —**amotinamiento,** *n.m.* mutiny; riot.

amparar (am·pa'rar) *v.t.* to protect; shelter; help. —**ampararse,** *v.r.* to find protection. —**amparo** (am'pa·ro) *n.m.* shelter; protection.

amperímetro (am·pe'ri·me·tro) *n.m.* ammeter.

amperio (am'pe·rjo) *n.m.* ampere. —**amperaje** (-'ra·xe) *n.m.* amperage.

ampliar (am'pljar) *v.t.* [*infl.:* enviar, 22] to amplify; broaden; extend; enlarge. —**ampliación,** *n.f.* extension; enlargement.

amplificar (am·pli·fi'kar) *v.t.* [*infl.:* tocar, 7] to amplify. —**amplificación,** *n.f.* amplification. —**amplificador,** *n.m.* amplifier. —*adj.* amplifying.

amplio ('am·pljo) *adj.* **1,** broad. **2,** ample. **3,** generous; openhanded. **4,** broadminded.

amplitud (am·pli'tuð) *n.f.* **1,** breadth. **2,** amplitude.

ampolla (am'po·ʎa; -ja) *n.f.* **1,** blister. **2,** decanter; cruet. —**ampollar,** *v.t.* to blister. —**ampollarse,** *v.r.* to become blistered.

ampolleta (am·po'ʎe·ta; -'je·ta) *n.f.* **1,** ampoule. **2,** hourglass. **3,** small vial.

ampuloso (am·pu'lo·so) *adj.* bombastic; wordy.

amputar (am·pu'tar) *v.t.* to amputate. —**amputación,** *n.f.* amputation.

amuchachado (a·mu·tʃa'tʃa·ðo) *adj.* childish.

amueblar (a·mwe'βlar) *v.t.* to furnish.

amuele (a'mwe·le) v., pres.subjve. of amolar.

amuelo (a'mwe·lo) v., pres.ind. of amolar.

amujerado (a·mu·xe'ra·ðo) adj. effeminate.

amulatado (a·mu·la'ta·ðo) adj. like a mulatto; having mulatto features.

amuleto (a·mu'le·to) n.m. amulet.

amura (a'mu·ra) n.f., naut. 1, tack of a sail. 2, grommet. 3, forepart of a ship; bow.

amurallar (a·mu·ra'ʎar; -'jar) v.t. to wall; surround with a wall.

amurrarse (a·mu'rrar·se) v.r., Amer. to become glum or downcast.

ana ('a·na) n.f. ell (measure).

anabolismo (a·na·βo'lis·mo) n.m. anabolism. —**anabólico** (-'βo·li·ko) adj. anabolic.

anacardo (a·na'kar·ðo) n.m. cashew.

anaconda (a·na'kon·da) n.f. anaconda.

anacoreta (a·na·ko're·ta) n.m. & f. hermit; anchorite.

anacronismo (a·na·kro'nis·mo) n.m. anachronism. —**anacrónico** (-'kro·ni·ko) adj. anachronistic.

ánade ('a·na·ðe) n.m. 1, duck. 2, any ducklike bird.

anadear (a·na·ðe'ar) v.i. to waddle. —**anadeo** (-'ðe·o) n.m. waddle.

anadeja (a·na'ðe·xa) n.f. duckling. Also, **anadino** (-'ði·no) n.m. [fem. -na].

anaerobio (a·na·e'ro·βjo) adj. anaerobic. —n.m. anaerobe.

anafe (a'na·fe) n.m. brazier.

anagrama (a·na'ɣra·ma) n.m. anagram.

anal (a'nal) adj. anal.

anales (a'na·les) n.m.pl. annals.

analfabeto (a·nal·fa'βe·to) adj. & n.m. illiterate. —**analfabetismo**, n.m. illiteracy.

analgesia (a·nal'xe·sja) n.f. analgesia. —**analgésico** (-si·ko) adj. & n.m. analgesic.

análisis (a'na·li·sis) n.m. or f. 1, analysis. 2, gram. parsing.

analista (a·na'lis·ta) n.m. & f. 1, analyst. 2, annalist.

analítico (a·na'li·ti·ko) adj. analytic; analytical.

analizar (a·na·li'θar; -'sar) v.t. [infl.: rezar, 10] 1, to analyze. 2, gram. to parse.

analogía (a·na·lo'xi·a) n.f. analogy. —**analógico** (-'lo·xi·ko) adj.

analogical. —**análogo** (a'na·lo·ɣo) adj. analogous.

anamorfosis (a·na·mor'fo·sis) n.f.sing. & pl. anamorphosis.

ananás (a·na'nas) also, **ananá**, n.f. pineapple.

anapesto (a·na'pes·to) n.m. anapest. —**anapéstico**, adj. anapestic.

anaquel (a·na'kel) n.m. shelf.

anaranjado (a·na·ran'xa·ðo) adj. orange-colored. —n.m. orange color.

anarquía (a·nar'ki·a) n.f. anarchy. —**anárquico** (a'nar·ki·ko) adj. anarchic; anarchical.

anarquismo (a·nar'kis·mo) n.m. anarchism. —**anarquista**, n.m. & f. anarchist. —adj. anarchistic.

anatema (a·na'te·ma) n.f. anathema. —**anatematizar** (-ti'θar; -'sar) v.t. [infl.: rezar, 10] to anathematize.

anatomía (a·na·to'mi·a) n.f. 1, anatomy. 2, dissection. —**anatómico** (-'to·mi·ko) adj. anatomical. —**anatomista**, n.m. & f. anatomist.

anatomizar (a·na·to·mi'θar; -'sar) v.t. [infl.: rezar, 10] to anatomize; dissect.

anca ('an·ka) n.f. 1, buttock; rump. 2, haunch; croup. —**ancas de rana**, frogs' legs.

ancestral (an·θes'tral; an·ses-) adj. ancestral.

anciano (an'θja·no; an'sja-) adj. aged; old. —n.m. old man. —**anciana**, n.f. old woman. —**ancianidad**, n.f. old age.

ancla ('an·kla) n.f. anchor.

ancladero (an·kla'ðe·ro) n.m. anchorage; anchoring place.

anclaje (an'kla·xe) n.m. 1, anchoring. 2, anchorage; anchoring place. 3, fee paid for anchorage.

anclar (an'klar) v.i. 1, to anchor; cast anchor. 2, to ride at anchor.

anclote (an'klo·te) n.m. kedge; kedge anchor.

áncora (an'ko·ra) n.f. = ancla.

ancho ('an·tʃo) adj. 1, wide; broad. 2, ample; spacious. —n.m. width; breadth. —**a sus anchas**, at one's ease; at one's leisure.

anchoa (an'tʃo·a) n.f. anchovy. Also, **anchova** (-βa).

anchura (an'tʃu·ra) n.f. 1, width; breadth. 2, looseness; freedom. —**anchuroso**, adj. wide; spacious.

andadas (an'da·ðas) n.f.pl. tracks (of animals). —**andada**, n.f.sing., Amer. long walk; ramble. —**volver**

a las andadas, to go back to one's old tricks; fall back into old habits.

andaderas (an·da'ðe·ras) *n.f.pl.* child's walker.

andado (an'da·ðo) *adj.* well-trodden; well-worn.

andador (an·da'ðor) *n.m.* **1,** fast mover. **2,** walker (for a child or invalid). **—andadores,** *n.m.pl.* leading strings.

andadura (an·da'ðu·ra) *n.f.* **1,** pacing. **2,** gait. **3,** amble; walk.

andamio (an'da·mjo) *n.m.* work platform; scaffold. **—andamiaje,** *n.m., also,* **andamiada,** *n.f.* scaffolding.

andanada (an·da·na·ða) *n.f.* **1,** *naut.* broadside. **2,** grandstand. **3,** *colloq.* tirade.

andante (an'dan·te) *adv.* & *n.m., mus.* andante. **—adj.** walking. **—caballero andante,** knight errant.

andanza (an'dan·θa; -sa) *n.f.* **1,** happening; occurrence. **2,** fortune; luck.

andar (an'dar) *v.i.* [*infl.:* 35] **1,** to walk. **2,** to move; go. **3,** to get along; fare. **4,** to function; run. **5,** to go about. **6,** *fol. by* **con** *or* **en,** to indulge in; engage in. **7,** to pass; elapse (*of time*). **8,** to be (*in a specified state or activity):* **andar en pecado,** to be (or live) in sin. **9,** to continue; keep on. **—v.t.** to go or walk (a certain way or distance). **—n.m.** walk; gait; pace. **—andarse,** *v.r.* **1,** to pass; elapse (*of time*). **2,** to go on; continue. **3,** to go off; go away. **4,** to go about. **—¡ándale!** ('an·da·le) *interj., Amer.* get on!; move! **—¡andando!,** *interj.* get on!; go on! **—andando el tiempo,** in the course of time. **—a todo andar,** at full speed.

andariego (an·da'rje·ɣo) *adj.* restless; roving.

andarivel (an·da·ri'βel) *n.m.* **1,** ferry cable. **2,** *colloq.* contraption; makeshift.

andas ('an·das) *n.f.pl.* **1,** stretcher; litter. **2,** bier, esp. one with carrying poles. **3,** portable platform used in processions. **—en andas,** in triumph.

andén (an'den) *n.m.* **1,** station platform. **2,** walk.

andino (an'di·no) *adj.* Andean.

andrajo (an'dra·xo) *n.m.* **1,** rag; tatter. **2,** *fig.* despicable person.

andrógino (an'dro·xi·no) *adj.* androgynous; hermaphroditic.

androide (an'droi·ðe) *n.m.* & *f.* android.

andullo (an'du·ʎo; -jo) *n.m.* **1,** plug tobacco. **2,** rolled tobacco leaf. **3,** *Amer.* any large leaf used as a wrapper.

andurrial (an·du'rrjal) *n.m., usu. pl.* **1,** byway; lonely road. **2,** out-of-the-way place.

anduve (an'du·βe) *v., pret. of* **andar.**

anea (a'ne·a) *n.f.* cattail; bulrush. *Also,* **enea** (e'ne·a).

aneblar (a·ne'βlar) *v.t.* [*infl.:* **pensar,** 27] to cloud; becloud. **—aneblarse,** *v.r.* to cloud over; become cloudy.

anécdota (a'nek·ðo·ta) *n.f.* anecdote. **—anecdótico,** *adj.* anecdotal.

anegar (a·ne'ɣar) *v.t.* [*infl.:* **pagar,** 8] **1,** to flood. **2,** to drown. **—anegación,** *n.f., also,* **anegamiento,** *n.m.* flooding. **—anegadizo,** *adj.* subject to frequent flooding.

anejar (a·ne'xar) *v.t.* to join; annex. **—anejo** (a'ne·xo) *adj.* annexed, attached. **—n.m.** annex; appendix.

anemia (a'ne·mja) *n.f.* anemia. **—anémico** (-mi·ko) *adj.* & *n.m.* anemic.

anemómetro (a·ne'mo·me·tro) *n.m.* anemometer.

anémona (a'ne·mo·na) *also,* **anémone,** *n.f.* anemone.

aneroide (a·ne'roi·ðe) *adj.* aneroid. **—n.m.** aneroid barometer.

anestesia (a·nes'te·sja) *n.f.* anesthesia. **—anestesiar** (-'sjar) *v.t.* to anesthetize. **—anestésico** (-'te·si·ko) *n.m.* & *adj.* anesthetic. **—anestesista** (-te'sis·ta) *n.m.* & *f.* anesthetist.

aneurisma (a·neu'ris·ma) *n.m.* or *f.* aneurysm.

anexar (a·nek'sar) *v.t.* to annex. **—anexión** (-'sjon) *n.f.* annexation. **anexo** (a'nek·so) *adj.* annexed; attached. **—n.m.** annex.

anfetamina (an·fe·ta'mi·na) *n.f.* amphetamine.

anfibio (an'fi·βjo) *adj.* amphibious. **—n.m.** amphibian.

anfiteatro (an·fi·te'a·tro) *n.m.* amphitheater.

anfitrión (an·fi'trjon) *n.m.* host. **—anfitriona** (-'trjo·na) *n.f.* hostess.

ánfora ('an·fo·ra) *n.f.* amphora; urn; *Mex.* ballot box.

angarillas (an·ga·ri'ʎas; -jas)

n.f.pl. **1,** panniers. **2,** cruets; cruet stand. **3,** stretcher.

ángel ('an·xel) *n.m.* angel.

angelical (an·xe·li'kal) *adj.* angelic; angelical. *Also,* **angélico** (an'xe·li·ko).

angina (an'xi·na) *n.f.* angina. —**angina de pecho,** angina pectoris.

anglicanismo (an·gli·ka'nis·mo) *n.m.* Anglicanism. —**anglicano** (-'ka·no) *adj. & n.m.* Anglican.

anglicismo (an·gli'θis·mo; -'sis·mo) *n.m.* Anglicism.

anglicización (an·gli·θi·θa'θjon; -si·sa'sjon) *n.f.* Anglicization.

anglo ('an·glo) *adj.* Anglian. —*n.m.* Angle.

Anglo ('an·glo) *adj. & n.m.* or *f.* Anglo; Anglo-American.

angloamericano (an·glo·a·me·ri'ka·no) *adj. & n.m.* Anglo-American.

anglófilo (an'glo·fi·lo) *adj. & n.m.* Anglophile.

anglófobo (an'glo·fo·βo) *adj. & n.m.* Anglophobe. —**anglofobia** (an·glo'fo·βja) *n.f.* Anglophobia.

anglosajón (an·glo·sa'xon) *adj. & n.m.* Anglo-Saxon.

angostar (an·gos'tar) *v.t.* to narrow; make narrow.

angosto (an·gos'to) *adj.* narrow. —**angostura,** *n.f.* **1,** narrowness. **2,** narrow passage. **3,** narrows; strait. **4,** bitters.

anguila (an'gi·la) *n.f.* **1,** eel. **2,** *pl., naut.* ways.

angula (an'gu·la) *n.f.* young eel.

angular (an·gu'lar) *adj.* angular. —**piedra angular,** cornerstone.

ángulo ('an·gu·lo) *n.m.* angle; corner.

anguloso (an·gu'lo·so) *adj.* angular; sharp. —**angulosidad,** *n.f.* angularity.

angurria (an'gu·rrja) *n.f., Amer.* greed; hoggishness; gluttony. —**angurriento,** *adj., Amer., colloq.* greedy; grasping; hoggish.

angustia (an'gus·tja) *n.f.* anguish; affliction; distress. —**angustiar,** *v.t.* to distress; anguish. —**angustiarse,** *v.r.* to torment oneself. —**angustioso,** *adj.* painful; anguished.

anhelar (a·ne'lar) *v.t.* to crave; to long for. —**anhelo** (a'ne·lo) *n.m.* yearning; longing; eagerness. —**anheloso,** *adj.* anxious; eager.

anidar (a·ni·'ðar) *v.i.* **1,** to nest. **2,** to nestle. —*v.t.* to nestle; shelter.

anieble (a'nje·βle) *v., pres.subjve. of* **aneblar.**

anieblo (a'nje·βlo) *v., pres.ind. of* **aneblar.**

anilina (a·ni'li·na) *n.f.* aniline.

anilla (a'ni·ʎa; -ja) *n.f.* **1,** ring; hoop. **2,** curtain ring. **3,** ring fastener.

anillo (a'ni·ʎo; -jo) *n.m.* ring.

ánima ('a·ni·ma) *n.f.* **1,** soul; spirit. **2,** *usu.pl.* souls in purgatory.

animación (a·ni·ma'θjon; -'sjon) *n.f.* animation; liveliness.

animado (a·ni'ma·ðo) *adj.* **1,** animate. **2,** animated; lively.

animador (a·ni·ma'ðor) *adj.* animating; enlivening. —*n.m.* master of ceremonies.

animadversión (a·ni·mað·βer·'sjon) *n.f.* animadversion.

animal (a·ni'mal) *n.m. & adj.* animal. —**animalada,** *n.f., colloq.* stupidity. —**animalidad,** *n.f.* animality. —**animalote,** *n.m.* large animal.

animar (a·ni'mar) *v.t.* **1,** to encourage. **2,** to enliven. **3,** to revive. —**animarse,** *v.r.* to be encouraged; to take heart.

anímico (a'ni·mi·ko) *adj.* psychic; spiritual.

animismo (a'ni'mis·mo) *n.m.* animism. —**animista,** *adj.* animistic. —*n.m. & f.* animist.

ánimo ('a·ni·mo) *n.m.* spirit; courage. —¡**ánimo!** *interj.* cheer up! —**animoso,** *adj.* spirited.

animosidad (a·ni·mo·si'ðað) *n.f.* animosity.

aniñado (a·ni'ɲa·ðo) *adj.* childish.

anión (a·ni'on) *n.m.* anion.

aniquilar (a·ni·ki'lar) *v.t.* to annihilate. —**aniquilarse,** *v.r.* to be destroyed; to be ruined. —**aniquilación,** *n.f., also,* **aniquilamiento,** *n.m.* annihilation.

anís (a'nis) *n.m.* **1,** anise. **2,** aniseed. **3,** anisette.

anisado (a·ni'sa·ðo) *adj.* anise-flavored. —*n.m.* [*also,* **anisete** (-'se·te)] anisette.

aniversario (a·ni·βer'sa·rjo) *adj. & n.m.* anniversary.

ano ('a·no) *n.m.* anus.

anoche (a'no·tʃe) *adv.* last night.

anochecer (a·no·tʃe'θer; -'ser) *v.i.* [*infl.:* **conocer,** 13] **1,** to grow dark. **2,** to be or arrive at nightfall. —*n.m.* nightfall. —**anochecida,** *n.f.* dusk; nightfall.

anodino (a·no'ði·no) *adj. & n.m.*

anodyne. —*adj.*, *colloq.* insignificant; insipid.

ánodo ('a·no·ðo) *n.m.* anode.

anofeles (a·no'fe·les) *n.m. sing. & pl.* anopheles.

anomalía (a·no·ma'li·a) *n.f.* anomaly. —**anómalo** (a'no·ma·lo) *adj.* anomalous; extraordinary.

anón (a'non) *n.m., also,* **anona,** *n.f.* custard apple (*tree and fruit*).

anonadar (a·no·na'ðar) *v.t.* to overwhelm. —**anonadarse,** *v.r.* to be completely discouraged. —**anonadación,** *n.f.* discouragement; dejection.

anonimato (a·no·ni'ma·to) *n.m.* anonymity.

anónimo (a'no·ni·mo) *adj.* anonymous. —*n.m.* **1,** anonymous letter. **2,** anonymity. —**sociedad anónima,** corporation.

anormal (a·nor'mal) *adj.* abnormal. —*n.m. & f.* abnormal person. —**anormalidad,** *n.f.* abnormality.

anotación (a·no·ta'θjon; -'sjon) *n.f.* **1,** annotation; written comment. **2,** score. **3,** note.

anotador (a·no·ta'ðor) *n.m.* **1,** annotator; commentator. **2,** scorer.

anotar (a·no'tar) *v.t.* **1,** to make notes on; comment on. **2,** to score.

anquilosarse (an·ki·lo'sar·se) *v.r.* **1,** to become stiff in the joints. **2,** to grow creaky with age. —**anquilosamiento,** *n.m.* stiffening; paralysis.

ánsar ('an·sar) *n.m.* wild goose.

ansarino (an·sa'ri·no) *n.m.* gosling.

ansia ('an·sja) *n.f.* **1,** anxiety. **2,** yearning. **3,** *pl.* nausea. —**ansiar,** *v.t.* to desire earnestly; long for. —**ansiedad,** *n.f.* anxiety. —**ansioso,** *adj.* anxious.

anta ('an·ta) *n.f.* elk; moose.

antagónico (an·ta'yo·ni·ko) *adj.* antagonistic.

antagonista (an·ta·yo'nis·ta) *n.m. & f.* antagonist. —**antagonismo,** *n.m.* antagonism.

antagonizar (an·ta·yo·ni'θar; -'sar) *v.t.* [*infl.*: **rezar, 10**] to antagonize.

antaño (an'ta·ɲo) *adv.* formerly; in olden times. —**de antaño,** of old; of yore.

antártico (an'tar·ti·ko) *adj.* antarctic. —**Antártica,** *n.f.* Antarctica.

ante ('an·te) *n.m.* elk.

ante ('an·te) *prep.* **1,** in the presence of; before. **2,** in comparison with. **3,** over; above; in preference to. **4,** ahead of; in front of.

anteanoche (an·te·a'no·tʃe) *adv.* night before last.

anteayer (an·te·a'jer) *adv.* day before yesterday.

antebrazo (an·te'βra·θo; -so) *n.m.* forearm.

antecámara (an·te'ka·ma·ra) *n.f.* anteroom; lobby.

antecedente (an·te·θe'ðen·te; -se'ðen·te) *adj. & n.m.* antecedent. —**antecedentes,** *n.m.pl.* **1,** forefathers, **2,** past history; record.

anteceder (an·te·θe'ðer; -se'ðer) *v.t. & i.* to precede.

antecesor (an·te·θe'sor; -se'sor) *n.m.* **1,** predecessor. **2,** ancestor.

antedata (an·te'ða·ta) *n.f.* antedate. —**antedatar,** *v.t.* to antedate.

antedicho (an·te'ði·tʃo) *adj.* aforesaid.

antediluviano (an·te·ði·lu'βja·no) *adj.* antediluvian. *Also,* **antidiluviano.**

antelación (an·te·la'θjon; -'sjon) *n.f.* anticipation. —**con antelación,** in advance; beforehand.

antemano (an·te'ma·no) *adv., usu.* **de antemano,** previously; beforehand.

antemeridiano (an·te·me·ri'ðja·no) *adj.* in the forenoon; A.M.

antena (an'te·na) *n.f.* antenna.

antenoche (an·te'no·tʃe) *adv.* = anteanoche.

anteojera (an·te·o'xe·ra) *n.f.* **1,** spectacle case. **2,** *usu.pl.* blinkers.

anteojo (an·te'o·xo) *n.m.* **1,** spyglass; telescope. **2,** sight (*of instruments*). **3,** eyeglass. —**anteojos,** *n.m.pl.* **1,** binoculars. **2,** spectacles.

antepasado (an·te·pa'sa·ðo) *n.m., usu.pl.* ancestor. —*adj.* previous to the last; before the last.

antepecho (an·te'pe·tʃo) *n.m.* **1,** parapet. **2,** railing. **3,** sill.

antepenúltimo (an·te·pe'nul·ti·mo) *adj.* antepenultimate. —*n.m.* [*also,* **antepenúltima,** *n.f.*] antepenult.

anteponer (an·te·po'ner) *v.t.* [*infl.*: **poner, 54**] **1,** to put before. **2,** to prefer. —**anteponerse,** *v.r.* to push oneself ahead. —**anteponerse a,** to overcome.

anteproyecto (an·te·pro'jek·to) *n.m.* preliminary design or draft.

antepuesto (an·te'pwes·to) *v.,*

p.p. of **anteponer.** —*adj.* aforementioned.

antera (an'te·ra) *n.f.* anther.

anterior (an·te'rjor) *adj.* preceding; former; anterior. —**anterioridad,** *n.f.* priority. —**con anterioridad,** previously.

antes ('an·tes) *adv.* **1,** formerly. **2,** rather; better; preferably. —*conj., fol. by* **de, que** *or* **de que,** before. —*adj.* previous; preceding. —**cuanto antes,** as soon as possible.

antesala (an·te'sa·la) *n.f.* anteroom; sitting room.

antiácido (an'tja·θi·ðo; -si·ðo) *adj. & n.m.* antacid.

antiaéreo (an·tja'e·re·o) *adj.* antiaircraft.

antialcalino (an·tjal·ka'li·no) *n.m.* antalkali.

antiamericano (an·tja·me·ri·'ka·no) *adj.* un-American.

antibiótico (an·ti'βjo·ti·ko) *adj. & n.m.* antibiotic.

anticipación (an·ti·θi·pa'θjon; -si·pa'sjon) *n.f.* **1,** anticipation. **2,** advance. —**con anticipación,** in advance.

anticipar (an·ti·θi'par; -si'par) *v.t.* **1,** to advance (a date). **2,** to advance (money). **3,** to forestall. **4,** to anticipate; act ahead of. —**anticiparse,** *v.r.* to act or occur early or prematurely. —**anticiparse a, 1,** to anticipate; act ahead of. **2,** to hurry to; be in a rush to. —**anticipadamente,** *adv.* beforehand. —**anticipante,** *adj.* anticipatory. —**por anticipado,** in advance.

anticipo (an·ti'θi·po; -'si·po) *n.m.* **1,** anticipation. **2,** advance; advance payment.

anticlerical (an·ti·kle·ri'kal) *adj.* anticlerical.

anticlímax (an·ti'kli·maks) *n.m.* anticlimax.

anticonceptivo (an·ti·kon·sep 'ti·βo) *adj. & n.m.* contraceptive.

anticongelante (an·ti·kon·xe 'lan·te) *n.m.* **1,** antifreeze. **2,** deicer.

anticonstitucional *adj.* unconstitutional.

anticristiano (an·ti·kris'tja·no) *adj.* unchristian.

Anticristo (an·ti'kris·to) *n.m.* Antichrist.

anticuar (an·ti'kwar) *v.t.* to outdate. —**anticuarse,** *v.r.* to become outdated. —**anticuado,** *adj.* outdated; antiquated; obsolete.

anticuario (an·ti'kwa·rjo) *adj.* antiquarian. —*n.m.* **1,** antiquary; antiquarian. **2,** antique dealer or collector.

anticuerpo (an·ti'kwer·po) *n.m.* antibody.

antidemocrático (an·ti·ðe·mo·'kra·ti·ko) *adj.* undemocratic.

antidetonante (an·ti·ðe·to·'nan·te) *adj. & n.m.* antiknock.

antídoto (an'ti·ðo·to) *n.m.* antidote.

antieconómico (an·tje·ko'no·mi·ko) *adj.* uneconomical; wasteful.

antier (an'tjer) *adv.* = **anteayer.**

antifaz (an·ti'faθ; -'fas) *n.m.* mask.

antífona (an'ti·fo·na) *n.f.* **1,** antiphon. **2,** anthem.

antigás (an·ti'yas) *adj.* protecting against gas. —**máscara antigás,** gas mask.

antigualla (an·ti'ywa·ʎa; -ja) *n.f.* **1,** old story; old hat. **2,** antique; relic; museum piece.

antigüedad (an·ti·ywe'ðað) *n.f.* **1,** antiquity. **2,** seniority. **3,** *pl.* antics. **4,** *pl.* antiques.

antiguo (an'ti·ywo) *adj.* ancient; old. —**antiguamente,** *adv.* formerly; long ago.

antihigiénico (an·ti·i'xje·ni·ko) *adj.* unhygienic; unsanitary.

antílope (an'ti·lo·pe) *n.m.* antelope.

antimateria (an·ti·ma'te·rja) *n.f.* antimatter.

antimonio (an·ti'mo·njo) *n.m.* antimony.

antimonopolio (an·ti·mo·no·'po·ljo) *adj.indecl.* antitrust.

antipapa (an·ti'pa·pa) *n.m.* antipope.

antiparras (an·ti'pa·rras) *n.f.pl., colloq.* = **anteojos.**

antipatía (an·ti·pa'ti·a) *n.f.* antipathy; dislike. —**antipático** (-'pa·ti·ko) *adj.* antipathetic; disagreeable.

antipatriótico (an·ti·pa'trjo·ti·ko) *adj.* unpatriotic.

antípoda (an'ti·po·ða) *n.m.* antipode. —*adj. m. & f.* antipodal.

antiprohibicionista (an·ti·pro·i·βi·θjo'nis·ta; -sjo'nis·ta) *adj. & n.m. & f.* (one) opposed to prohibition; wet.

antiquísimo (an·ti'ki·si·mo) *adj., superl. of* **antiguo.**

antisemita (an·ti·se'mi·ta) *n.m. & f.* anti-Semite. —**antisemítico,** *adj.* anti-Semitic. —**antisemitismo,** *n.m.* anti-Semitism.

antisepsia (an·ti'sep·sja) *n.f.* antisepsis. —**antiséptico** (-ti·ko) *adj. & n.m.* antiseptic.

antisocial (an·ti·so'θjal; -'sjal) *adj.* antisocial.

antitanque (an·ti'tan·ke) *adj.* antitank.

antítesis (an'ti·te·sis) *n.f.* antithesis. —**antitético** (-'te·ti·ko) *adj.* antithetical; opposing.

antitoxina (an·ti·tok'si·na) *n.f.* antitoxin. —**antitóxico** (-'tok·si·ko) *adj.* antitoxic.

antojo (an'to·xo) *n.m.* whim. —**antojadizo** (-xa'ði·θo; -so), *adj.* capricious. —**antojarse,** *v.r. impers.* to come to one's whim or fancy.

antología (an·to·lo'xi·a) *n.f.* anthology.

antónimo (an'to·ni·mo) *n.m.* antonym. —*adj.* antonymous; opposite. —**antonimia** (an·to'ni·mja) *n.f.* antonymy.

antorcha (an'tor·tʃa) *n.f.* torch.

antracita (an·tra'θi·ta; -'si·ta) *n.f.* anthracite.

ántrax ('an·traks) *n.m.* anthrax.

antro ('an·tro) *n.m.* den; lair.

antropófago (an·tro'po·fa·ɣo) *n.m.* cannibal. —*adj.* cannibalistic.

antropoide (an·tro'poi·ðe) *adj. & n.m. & f.* anthropoid. *Also,* **antropoideo** (-'ðe·o) *adj. & n.m.*

antropología (an·tro·po·lo'xi·a) *n.f.* anthropology. —**antropológico** (-'lo·xi·ko) *adj.* anthropological. —**antropólogo** (-'po·lo·ɣo) *n.m.* anthropologist.

antropomórfico (an·tro·po'mor·fi·ko) *adj.* anthropomorphic. —**antropomorfismo** (-mor'fis·mo) *n.m.* anthropomorphism.

anual (a'nwal) *adj.* annual; yearly. —**anualidad,** *n.f.* annuity; yearly rent.

anuario (a'nwa·rjo) *n.m.* yearbook.

anublar (a·nu'βlar) *v.t.* to cloud up; darken. —**anublarse,** *v.r.* **1,** to become cloudy. **2,** *fig.* to wither away.

anudar (a·nu'ðar) *v.t.* **1,** to knot; fasten with a knot. **2,** to tie in; relate.

anular (a·nu'lar) *adj.* circular. —**dedo anular** ring finger.

anular (a·nu'lar) *v.t.* **1,** to nullify; void; annul. **2,** to incapacitate; render powerless. —**anulación,** *n.f.,* **anulamiento,** *n.m.* annulment.

anunciante (a·nun'θjan·te; -'sjan·te) *n.m. & f., also,* **anuncia-** dor, *n.m.* **1,** announcer. **2,** advertiser. —*adj.* **1,** announcing. **2,** advertising.

anunciar (a·nun'θjar; -'sjar) *v.t.* **1,** to announce. **2,** to advertise. —**anunciación,** *n.f.* annunciation.

anuncio (a'nun·θjo; -sjo) *n.m.* **1,** advertisement. **2,** notice; announcement. **3,** poster; sign.

anverso (an'βer·so) *adj. & n.m.* obverse.

anzuelo (an'θwe·lo; an'swe-) *n.m.* **1,** fishhook. **2,** *fig.* lure; enticement.

añadir (a·ɲa'ðir) *v.t.* to add. —**añadidura,** *n.f.* increment; addition.

añagaza (a·ɲa'ɣa·θa; -sa) *n.f.* trick; chicanery.

añejo (a'ɲe·xo) *adj.* aged, as wine. —**añejarse,** *v.r.* to age, as wine.

añicos (a'ɲi·kos) *n.m.pl.* fragments. —**hacer añicos,** to break into small bits.

añil (a'ɲil) *n.m.* indigo; anil.

año ('a·ɲo) *n.m.* year. —**año bisiesto,** leap year. —**año económico,** fiscal year. —**año en curso,** current year. —**entrado en años,** well along in years. —**tener . . . años,** to be . . . years old.

añojo (a'ɲo·xo) *n.m.* yearling.

añorar (a·ɲo'rar) *v.t.* to recall with nostalgia; yearn for. —**añoranza,** *n.f.* nostalgia; yearning.

añoso (a'ɲo·so) *adj.* aged; old.

aojar (a·o'xar) *v.t.* **1,** to jinx; hoodoo; give the evil eye. **2,** to eye; ogle. —**aojo** (a'o·xo) *n.m.* evil eye; jinx; hoodoo.

aorta (a'or·ta) *n.f.* aorta.

aovado (a·o'βa·ðo) *adj.* egg-shaped.

apabullar (a·pa·βu'ʎar; -'jar) *v.t., colloq.* **1,** to crush. **2,** to squelch.

apacentar (a·pa·θen'tar; -sen·'tar) *v.t.* [*infl.:* **pensar, 27**] to graze; pasture. —**apacentadero,** *n.m.* pasture.

apacibilidad (a·pa·θi·βi·li'ðað; a·pa·si-) *n.f.* **1,** peacefulness. **2,** peaceableness.

apacible (a·pa'θi·βle; -'si·βle) *adj.* **1,** peaceful; quiet. **2,** peaceable.

apaciguar (a·pa·θi'ɣwar; -si'ɣwar) *v.t.* [*infl.:* **averiguar, 9**] to appease; pacify. —**apaciguarse,** *v.r.* to calm down. —**apaciguador,** *adj.* calming; pacifying. —*n.m.*[*fem.* -**dora**] appeaser. —**apaciguamiento,** *n.m.* calming down; appeasement.

apache (a'pa·tʃe) *n.m.* **1,** Apache. **2,** *slang* thug.

apachurrar (a·pa·tʃu'rrar) *v.t.,* *Amer. colloq.* = **despachurrar.**

apadrinar (a·pa·ði'nar) *v.t.* **1,** to sponsor; favor. **2,** to second (*in a duel*). **3,** to act as best man or godfather to.

apagado (a·pa'ɣa·ðo) *adj.* **1,** dull (*of colors*). **2,** extinct (*of a volcano*). **3,** *fig.* unassuming; self-effacing.

apagar (a·pa'ɣar) *v.t.* [*infl.:* **pagar,** 8] **1,** to extinguish; quench. **2,** to put out; turn off. **3,** to deaden; muffle; mute. **4,** to dull or soften (colors) **5,** to slake (lime). —**apagarse,** *v.r.* to go out; die out; go off.

apagón (a·pa'ɣon) *n.m.* black-out. —**apagón parcial,** brownout.

apalabrar (a·pa·la'βrar) *v.t.* to confer on; discuss. —**apalabrarse,** *v.r.* to agree; reach an agreement.

apalear (a·pa·le'ar) *v.t.* **1,** to beat; cudgel. **2,** to thresh.

apandillarse (a·pan·di'ʎar·se; -'jar·se) *v.r.* to band together.

apañar (a·pa'ɲar) *v.t.* **1,** to grasp; seize. **2,** to dress; deck out. **3,** to cloak; conceal. **4,** to abet. **5,** *colloq.* to steal; filch. —**apañarse,** *v.r., colloq.* to contrive; scheme.

aparador (a·pa·ra'ðor) *n.m.* sideboard; cupboard.

aparato (a·pa'ra·to) *n.m.* **1,** apparatus. **2,** machine. **3,** device; gadget. **4,** show; ostentation.

aparatoso (a·pa·ra·to·so) *adj.* **1,** showy. **2,** exaggerated.

aparcar (a·par'kar) *v.t., Amer.* [*infl.:* **tocar,** 7] to park. —**aparcamiento,** *n.m.* parking.

aparcería (a·par·θe'ri·a; -se'ri·a) *n.f.* **1,** partnership; sharecropping.

aparcero (a·par'θe·ro; -'se·ro) *n.m.* **1,** partner; associate. **2,** sharecropper.

aparear (a·pa·re'ar) *v.t.* to couple; match. —**aparearse,** *v.r.* to be paired; form a pair. —**apareamiento,** *n.m.* coupling; matching.

aparecer (a·pa·re'θer; -'ser) *v.i.* [*infl.:* **conocer,** 13] to appear. —**aparecerse,** *v.r.* to show up. —**aparecido,** *n.m.* ghost.

aparejar (a·pa·re'xar) *v.t.* **1,** to prepare. **2,** to rig. **3,** to harness. **4,** *Amer.* to pair. **5,** *painting* to prime; size. —**aparejarse,** *v.r.* to equip oneself; get ready.

aparejo (a·pa're·xo) *n.m.* **1,** preparation. **2,** harness; rigging; tackle. **3,** sizing; priming. **4,** gear; equipment.

aparentar (a·pa·ren'tar) *v.t.* to feign; pretend. —**aparenta treinta años,** he (she) seems to be about thirty.

aparente (a·pa'ren·te) *adj.* **1,** apparent. **2,** feigned. **3,** suitable. **4,** conspicuous.

aparición (a·pa·ri'θjon; -'sjon) *n.f.* **1,** appearance. **2,** apparition.

apariencia (a·pa'rjen·θja; -sja) *n.f.* appearance.

aparragarse (a·pa·rra'ɣar·se) *v.r., Amer.* [*infl.:* **pagar,** 8] **1,** to nestle. **2,** to flatten oneself; crouch.

apartadero (a·par·ta'ðe·ro) *n.m., R.R.* siding.

apartadizo (a·par·ta'ði·θo; -so) *adj.* unsociable. —*n.m.* **1,** screened-off room. **2,** recluse.

apartado (a·par'ta·do) *adj.* distant; secluded. —*n.m.* post office box.

apartamiento (a·par·ta'mjen·to) *also,* **apartamento** (-'men·to) *n.m.* **1,** apartment. **2,** retiring place.

apartar (a·par'tar) *v.t.* **1,** to separate; set aside. **2,** to push aside; push away. —**apartarse,** *v.r.* **1,** to withdraw. **2,** to stand aside.

aparte (a'par·te) *adv.* **1,** apart; aside. **2,** elsewhere. —*n.m.* **1,** *theat.* aside. **2,** new paragraph. **3,** side remark. —*adj.* separate.

apartidar (a·par·ti'ðar) *v.t.* **1,** to back; support; side with. **2,** to win the support of. —**apartidarse,** *v.r.* to side; take sides.

apasionamiento (a·pa·sjo·na·'mjen·to) *n.m.* **1,** passion. **2,** vehemence.

apasionar (a·pa·sjo'nar) *v.t.* **1,** to inspire passion in; impassion. **2,** to captivate. —**apasionarse,** *v.r.* to become impassioned. —**apasionado,** *adj.* passionate; impassioned. —**apasionante,** *adj.* captivating; gripping.

apatía (a·pa'ti·a) *n.f.* apathy. —**apático** (a'pa·ti·ko) *adj.* apathetic.

apeadero (a·pe·a'ðe·ro) *n.m.* whistle stop.

apear (a·pe'ar) *v.t.* to help to dismount. —**apearse,** *v.r.* to get down or off; dismount; alight. —**apearse del burro,** to admit one's error. —**apearse por la cola** (*or* **las orejas**), to go off on a tangent.

apechugar (a·pe·tʃu'ɣar) *v.i.* [*infl.:* **pagar,** 8] to push with the chest; breast one's way. —*v.t., Amer.* to grab off; snatch. —**ape-**

chugar con, to do or bear reluctantly; resign oneself to.

apedrear (a·pe·ðre'ar) *v.t.* to stone.

apego (a'pe·ɣo) *n.m.* attachment. —**apegarse** (-'ɣar·se) *v.t.* [*infl.:* **pagar, 8**] to become attached.

apelar (a·pe'lar) *v.i.* **1,** *law* to appeal. **2,** to relate; refer; have reference. —**apelación,** *n.f., law* appeal.

apelativo (a·pe·la'ti·βo) *adj.* & *n.m.* appellative. —*n.m.* name; appellation.

apelmazar (a·pel·ma'θar; '-sar) *v.t.* [*infl.:* **rezar, 10**] **1,** to thicken; make lumpy. **2,** to tighten; compress.

apelotonar (a·pe·lo·to'nar) *v.t.* to gather; mass together. —**apelotonarse,** *v.r.* to cluster.

apellidar (a·pe·ʎi'ðar; -ji'ðar) *v.t.* to name; call by a name. —**apellidarse,** *v.r.* to have for a surname.

apellido (a·pe'ʎi·ðo; -'ji·ðo) *n.m.* **1,** surname; family name. **2,** nickname. —**apellido de soltera,** maiden name.

apenar (a·pe'nar) *v.t.* to grieve; cause pain. —**apenarse,** *v.r.* to grieve.

apenas (a'pe·nas) *adv.* **1,** scarcely; hardly. **2,** with difficulty. —*conj.* as soon as.

apendectomía (a·pen·dek·to·'mi·a) *n.f.* appendectomy.

apéndice (a'pen·di·θe; -se) *n.m.* **1,** appendix. **2,** appendage.

apendicitis (a·pen·di'θi·tis; -'si·tis) *n.f.* appendicitis.

aperar (a·pe'rar) *v.t.* **1,** to construct or repair (wagons, farm equipment, etc.). **2,** *Amer.* to harness. —**aperador,** *n.m.* wheelwright.

apercibimiento (a·per·θi·βi·'mjen·to; a·per·si-) *n.m.* **1,** preparation. **2,** warning. **3,** perception.

apercibir (a·per·θi'βir; -si'βir) *v.t.* **1,** to prepare. **2,** to warn. **3,** to perceive. —**apercibirse,** *v.r.* to get ready.

apergaminado (a·per·ɣa·mi·'na·ðo) *adj.* like parchment; dried up; yellowed.

aperitivo (a·pe·ri'ti·βo) *n.m.* appetizer; aperitif.

aperlado (a·per'la·ðo) *adj.* pearly.

apero (a'pe·ro) *n.m., usu.pl.* **1,** farm implements. **2,** set of tools. **3,** *Amer.* harness; riding gear.

apertura (a·per'tu·ra) *n.f.* **1,** aperture; opening. **2,** beginning.

apesadumbrar (a·pe·sa·ðum·'brar) *v.t.* to distress. —**apesadumbrarse,** *v.r.* to grieve. —**apesadumbrado,** *adj.* grieved; distressed.

apestar (a·pes'tar) *v.i.* & *t.* **1,** to stink; smell. **2,** *colloq.* to pester. —**apestarse,** *v.r.* to suffer a plague or blight. —**apestoso** (-'to·so) *adj.* stinking.

apetecer (a·pe·te'θer; -'ser) *v.t.* [*infl.:* **conocer, 13**] to crave; desire. —**apetecible,** *adj.* desirable.

apetencia (a·pe'ten·θja; -sja) *n.f.* appetite; desire.

apetito (a·pe'ti·to) *n.m.* appetite. —**apetitoso,** *adj.* appetizing; tasty; savory. —**abrir el apetito,** to whet the appetite.

apiadar (a·pja'ðar) *v.t.* to move to pity. —**apiadarse,** *v.r., fol. by* **de,** to have pity on.

ápice ('a·pi·θe; -se) *n.m.* **1,** apex. **2,** iota; jot. **3,** crux.

apícola (a'pi·ko·la) *adj.* of or pert. to beekeeping.

apicultura (a·pi·kul'tu·ra) *n.f.* beekeeping. —**apicultor** (-'tor) *n.m.* beekeeper.

apilar (a·pi'lar) *v.t.* to pile up.

apiñar (a·pi'ɲar) *v.t.* to jam; squeeze; press. —**apiñarse,** *v.r.* to crowd together; crowd up. —**apiñamiento,** *n.m.* crowd; press; jam.

apio ('a·pjo) *n.m.* celery.

apisonar (a·pi·so'nar) *v.t.* to tamp; ram down.

aplacar (a·pla'kar) *v.t.* [*infl.:* **tocar, 7**] to placate; calm down. —**aplacarse,** *v.r.* to subside. —**aplacamiento,** *n.m.* placation.

aplanar (a·pla'nar) *v.t.* to flatten; level. —**aplanarse,** *v.r.* to become discouraged. —**aplanadora** (-'ðo·ra) *n.f.* steamroller.

aplastar (a·plas'tar) *v.t.* to flatten; crush. —**aplastarse,** *v.r.* to become flat. —**aplastante,** *adj.* crushing; *fig.* dumfounding.

aplaudir (a·plau'ðir) *v.t.* to applaud. —**aplauso** (a'plau·so) *n.m.* applause.

aplazamiento (a·pla·θa'mjen·to; a·pla·sa-) *n.m.* **1,** postponement. **2,** adjournment.

aplazar (a·pla'θar; -'sar) *v.t.* [*infl.:* **rezar, 10**] **1,** to postpone. **2,** to adjourn. **3,** *Amer.* to fail (a student); hold back from promotion.

aplicable (a·pli·ka·βle) *adj.* applicable. —**aplicabilidad,** *n.f.* applicability.

aplicación (a·pli·ka'θjon; -'sjon) *n.f.* **1,** application. **2,** devotion to study.

aplicado (a·pli'ka·ðo) *adj.* **1,** applied. **2,** studious.

aplicar (a·pli'kar) *v.t.* [*infl.:* **tocar, 7**] **1,** to apply. **2,** to assign; place. **3,** to attribute; impute. **4,** *law* to adjudge. —**aplicarse,** *v.r.* **1,** to apply; be applicable. **2,** to apply oneself; devote oneself.

aplomar (a·plo'mar) *v.t.* to plumb; make plumb. —**aplomarse,** *v.r.* to collapse.

aplomo (a'plo·mo) *n.m.* aplomb; poise. —**aplomado,** *adj.* poised.

Apocalipsis (a·po·ka'lip·sis) *n.m.* Apocalypse. —**apocalíptico** (-'lip·ti·ko) *adj.* apocalyptic.

apocar (a·po'kar) *v.t.* [*infl.:* **tocar, 7**] **1,** to restrict; limit. **2,** to reduce; make smaller. **3,** to belittle. —**apocarse,** *v.r.* **1,** to humble oneself. **2,** to wilt; cringe. —**apocado,** *adj.* diffident; shy. —**apocamiento,** *n.m.* diffidence; shyness.

apocopar (a·po·ko'par) *v.t.* to apocopate; elide. —**apócope** (a'po·ko·pe) *n.m.* apocope; elision.

apócrifo (a'po·kri·fo) *adj.* apocryphal. —**libros apócrifos,** Apocrypha.

apodar (a·po'ðar) *v.t.* to nickname.

apoderar (a·po·ðe'rar) *v.t.* to grant power of attorney to. —**apoderarse,** *v.r.*, *fol. by* **de,** to seize; take possession of. —**apoderado,** *n.m.* proxy; holder of power of attorney.

apodo (a'po·ðo) *n.m.* nickname.

apogeo (a·po'xe·o) *n.m.* **1,** *astron.* apogee. **2,** *fig.* height (of fame, power, etc.).

apolillarse (a·po·li'ʎar·se; -'jar·se) *v.r.* to become motheaten. —**apolillado,** *adj.* motheaten.

apolítico (a·po'li·ti·ko) *adj.* nonpolitical.

apología (a·po·lo'xi·a) *n.f.* **1,** apology. **2,** defense. **3,** eulogy. —**apologético** (-'xe·ti·ko) *adj.* apologetic. —**apologista** (-'xis·ta) *n.m.* & *f.* apologist.

apologizar (a·po·lo·xi'θar; -'sar) *v.t.* [*infl.:* **rezar, 10**] to defend. —*v.i.* to apologize; make a formal defense.

apoltronarse (a·pol·tro'nar·se) *v.r.* **1,** to become lazy. **2,** to sprawl; lounge.

apoplejía (a·po·ple'xi·a) *n.f.* apoplexy. —**apoplético** (-'ple·ti·ko) *adj.* apoplectic.

aporrear (a·po·rre'ar) *v.t.* to beat; cudgel. —**aporreo** (-'rre·o) *n.m.* beating.

aportar (a·por'tar) *v.t.* to contribute (one's share). —*v.i.* to make port; arrive. —**aportación,** *n.f.*, *also,* **aporte** (a'por·te) *n.m.* contribution.

aportillar (a·por·ti'ʎar; -'jar) *v.t.* **1,** to open a hole in; breach. **2,** to break up; break apart.

aposento (a·po'sen·to) *n.m.* room. —**aposentar,** *v.r.* to lodge.

aposición (a·po·si'θjon; -'sjon) *n.f.* apposition.

apostar (a·pos'tar) *v.t.* [*infl.:* **acostar, 28**] **1,** to bet. **2,** to station. —**apostarse,** *v.r.* to station oneself. —**apostadero,** *n.m.* military post; naval station.

apostatar (a·pos·ta'tar) *v.i.* to apostatize. —**apostasía** (-'si·a) *n.f.* apostasy. —**apóstata** (a'pos·ta·ta) *n.m.* & *f.* apostate.

apostilla (a·pos'ti·ya; -ja) *n.f.* marginal note. —**apostillar,** *v.t.* to make marginal notes in or on.

apóstol (a'pos·tol) *n.m.* apostle. —**apostolado,** *n.m.* apostolate. —**apostólico** (-'to·li·ko) *adj.* apostolic.

apostrofar (a·pos·tro'far) *v.t.* **1,** *rhet.* to apostrophize. **2,** to insult.

apóstrofe (a'pos·tro·fe) *n.m. or f.* **1,** *rhet.* apostrophe, **2,** *usu.masc.* invective; insult.

apóstrofo (a'pos·tro·fo) *n.m., gram.* apostrophe (').

apostura (a·pos'tu·ra) *n.f.* **1,** handsomeness; grace; neatness. **2,** look; aspect.

apotecario (a·po·te'ka·rjo) *n.m.* apothecary; pharmacist.

apoteosis (a·po·te'o·sis) *n.f.* apotheosis. —**apoteósico** (-'o·si·ko) *adj.* glorifying; glorious.

apoyar (a·po'jar) *v.t.* **1,** to lean; rest. **2,** to support. **3,** to favor; sponsor. **4,** to base (an argument, opinion, etc.). —**apoyarse,** *v.r.* **1,** to lean; rest. **2,** to base oneself.

apoyo (a'po·jo) *n.m.* **1,** prop; support. **2,** patronage; protection.

apreciable (a·pre'θja·βle; -'sja·βle) *adj.* **1,** valuable. **2,** estimable.

apreciar (a·pre'θjar; -'sjar) *v.t.* **1,** to esteem. **2,** to appraise; estimate. —**apreciación,** *n.f.* estimate; judgment.

aprecio (a'preˑθjo; -sjo) *n.m.* **1**, esteem. **2**, appraisal.

aprehender (aˑpreˑen'der; aˑpren'der) *v.t.* to apprehend. —**aprehensión** (-'sjon) *n.f.* apprehension. —**aprehensivo** (-'siˑβo) *adj.* apprehensive. —**aprehensor** (-'sor) *n.m.* one who arrests; arresting officer.

apremiar (aˑpre'mjar) *v.t.* to urge; compel. —**apremiante,** *adj.* urgent; pressing.

apremio (a'preˑmjo) *n.m.* **1**, compulsion. **2**, judicial order.

aprender (aˑpren'der) *v.t. & i.* to learn. —**aprender de memoria,** to learn by heart; to memorize.

aprendiz (aˑpren'diθ; -'dis) *n.m. & f.* apprentice. —**aprendizaje,** *n.m.* apprenticeship.

aprensión (aˑpren'sjon) *n.f.* fear; scruple. —**aprensivo** (-'siˑβo) *adj.* apprehensive.

apresar (aˑpre'sar) *v.t.* to seize.

aprestar (aˑpres'tar) *v.t.* **1**, to prepare. **2**, to size (cloth).

apresto (a'presˑto) *n.m.* **1**, preparation. **2**, size (*for cloth*).

apresurar (aˑpreˑsu'rar) *v.t.* to hasten. — **apresurarse,** *v.r.* to make haste. —**apresurado,** *adj.* hasty. —**apresuramiento,** *n.m.* haste; hastiness.

apretado (aˑpre'taˑðo) *adj.* **1**, tight. **2**, risky; allowing little margin. **3**, difficult. **4**, urgent.

apretar (aˑpre'tar) *v.t.* [*infl.:* **pensar, 27**] **1**, to tighten; squeeze; clench. **2**, *fig.* to press; harass. —*v.i.* **1**, to worsen; get worse. **2**, to be too tight; pinch. —**apretar el paso,** to hurry.

apretazón (aˑpreˑta'θon; -'son) *n.m., Amer.* congestion; jam.

apretón (aˑpre'ton) *n.m.* squeeze; sudden pressure. —**apretón de manos,** handshake; handclasp.

apretujar (aˑpreˑtu'xar) *v.t., colloq.* to squeeze or press tight.

apretura (aˑpre'tuˑra) *n.f.* **1**, crush; press. **2**, = **aprieto.**

aprieto (a'prjeˑto) *n.m.* **1**, predicament; tight spot. **2**, = **apretura.**

aprisa (a'priˑsa) *adv.* swiftly.

aprisco (a'prisˑko) *n.m.* fold; sheepfold.

aprisionar (aˑpriˑsjo'nar) *v.t.* **1**, to imprison; confine. **2**, to seize; hold.

aprobar (aˑpro'βar) *v.t.* [*infl.:* **acostar, 28**] **1**, to approve. **2**, to pass; give a passing mark to.

—**aprobación.** *n.f* approval.
—**aprobado,** *n.m.* passing mark.
—**aprobatorio,** *adj.* approving.

aprontar (aˑpron'tar) *v.t.* **1**, to ready; make ready with. **2**, to prompt; prepare (a person). **3**, to hand over promptly. —**apronte** (a'pronˑte) *n.m.,* sports workout.

apropiar (aˑpro'pjar) *v.t.* **1**, to adapt. **2**, to take possession of. —**apropiarse,** *v.r., usu.fol. by* **de,** to appropriate. —**apropiación,** *n.f.* appropriation. —**apropiado,** *adj.* appropriate.

apropincuarse (aˑproˑpin'kwarse) *v.r., colloq.* = **acercarse.**

aprovechable (aˑproˑβe'tʃaˑβle) *adj.* **1**, usable. **2**, available.

aprovechado (aˑproˑβe'tʃaˑðo) *adj.* **1**, industrious; studious. **2**, self-seeking.

aprovechamiento (aˑproˑβetʃa'mjenˑto) *n.m.* **1**, utilization; use; exploitation. **2**, profit; advantage. **3**, improvement; progress.

aprovechar (aˑproˑβe'tʃar) *v.t.* **1**, to make use of. **2**, to aid; avail. —*v.i.* to make progress. —**aprovecharse,** *v.r., usu.fol. by* **de,** to take advantage (of); benefit (from).

aprovisionar (aˑproˑβiˑsjo'nar) *v.t.* to supply; provide.

aproximación (aˑprokˑsiˑma'θjon; -'sjon) *n.f.* **1**, approximation. **2**, consolation prize.

aproximado (aˑprokˑsi'maˑðo) *adj.* approximate; close. —**aproximadamente,** *adv.* approximately; nearly.

aproximar (aˑprokˑsi'mar) *v.t.* **1**, to approach. **2**, to estimate. —**aproximarse,** *v.r.* to draw near; approach. —**aproximarse a,** to approximate; be almost or close to.

apto ('apˑto) *adj.* apt. —**aptitud,** *n.f.* aptitude.

apuesta (a'pwesˑta) *n.f.* bet; wager.

apuesto (a'pwesˑto) *adj.* handsome; elegant.

apuntación (aˑpunˑta'θjon; -'sjon) *n.f.* **1**, annotation. **2**, memorandum. **3**, musical notation.

apuntador (aˑpunˑta'ðor) *n.m.* [*fem.* -**dora**] **1**, *theat.* prompter. **2**, *mil.* pointer; gunner.

apuntalar (aˑpunˑta'lar) *v.t.* **1**, to prop up; shore. **2**, to give support to; help.

apuntar (aˑpun'tar) *v.t.* **1**, to aim; point. **2**, to make a note of. **3**, to prompt. **4,** *cards* to bet; stake. —*v.i.* to begin to show or appear.

apunte (a'pun·te) *n.m.* **1,** annotation; memorandum. **2,** examination mark. **3,** stake.

apuñalar (a·pu·ɲa'lar) *v.t.* to stab.

apurado (a·pu·ra·ðo) *adj.* **1,** needy. **2,** pressed; hurried. **3,** drained. **4,** risky; perilous.

apurar (a·pu'rar) *v.t.* **1,** to press; hurry. **2,** to drain. —**apurarse,** *v.r.* **1,** to worry; be concerned. **2,** *Amer.* to hurry; make haste.

apuro (a'pu·ro) *n.m.* **1,** predicament. **2,** need; distress. **3,** *Amer.* haste.

aquejar (a·ke'xar) *v.t.* to ail; pain.

aquel (a'kel) *dem.adj.masc.* [*fem.* **aquella** (a·ke·ʎa, -ja); *pl.* **aquellos** (-ʎos; -jos), **aquellas** (-ʎas; -jas)] **1,** that; that one; *pl.* those. **2,** former.

aquél (a'kel) *dem. pron. masc.* [*fem.* **aquélla** (a·ke·ʎa, -ja); *pl.* **aquéllos** (-ʎos, -jos), **aquéllas** (-ʎas, -jas)] **1,** that; that one; *pl.* those. **2,** the former.

aquello (a'ke·ʎo; -jo) *dem.pron. neut.* that; that matter.

aquende (a'ken·de) *adv.* hither.

aquerenciarse (a·ke·ren'θjar·se; -'sjar·se) *v.r.* (*with* **a**) to become fond of.

aquí (a'ki) *adv.* here; hither. —**de aquí en adelante,** henceforth. —**de aquí que,** hence; consequently. —**hasta aquí,** hitherto. —**por aquí,** this way.

aquiescencia (a·kjes'θen·θja; -kje'sen·sja) *n.f.* acquiescence.

aquietar (a·kje'tar) *v.t.* to quiet; calm. —**aquietarse,** *v.r.* to calm down.

aquilatar (a·ki·la'tar) *v.t.* **1,** to assay. **2,** to judge; evaluate.

aquilino (a·ki'li·no) *adj., poet.* = **aguileño.**

aquilón (a·ki'lon) *n.m.* **1,** north. **2,** north wind.

ara ('a·ra) *n.f.* **1,** altar, esp. sacrificial altar. **2,** communion table.

árabe ('a·ra·βe) *adj. & n.m. & f.* Arabian; Arab. —*adj. & n.m.* Arabic (*language*).

arabesco (a·ra'βes·ko) *n.m.* arabesque.

arábico (a'ra·βi·ko) *adj.* Arabic; Arabian.

arábigo (a'ra·βi·ɣo) *adj.* Arabic; Arabian. —*n.m.* Arabic (*language*).

arable (a'ra·βle) *adj.* arable.

arácnido (a'rak·ni·ðo) *n.m., zoöl.* arachnid.

arado (a'ra·ðo) *n.m.* **1,** plow. **2,** plowing.

arameo (a·ra'me·o) *adj. & n.m.* Aramaic.

arancel (a·ran'θel; -'sel) *n.m.* tariff. —**derechos arancelarios,** customs duties.

arándano (a'ran·da·no) *n.m.* bilberry; whortleberry. —**arándano agrio,** cranberry.

arandela (a·ran'de·la) *n.f.* **1,** *mech.* washer. **2,** drip bowl of a candlestick.

araña (a'ra·ɲa) *n.f.* **1,** spider. **2,** chandelier. —**tela de araña,** spider web.

arañar (a·ra'ɲar) *v.t.* to scratch. —**arañazo** (-'ɲa·θo; -so) *also,* **arañón,** **araño** (a'ra·ɲo) *n.m.* scratch.

arar (a'rar) *v.t.* to plow.

arbitrar (ar·βi'trar) *v.t. &i.* **1,** to arbitrate. **2,** to referee; umpire. **3,** to contrive. —**arbitrador,** *n.m.* arbitrator. —**arbitraje,** *n.m.* **1,** arbitration. **2,** arbitrage.

arbitrario (ar·βi'tra·rjo) *adj.* arbitrary. —**arbitrariedad,** *n.f.* arbitrariness.

arbitrio (ar'βi·trjo) *n.m.* **1,** free will. **2,** judgment. **3,** tax, esp. municipal.

árbitro ('ar·βi·tro) *n.m.* **1,** arbiter; judge. **2,** referee; umpire. **3,** arbitrator.

árbol ('ar·βol) *n.m.* **1,** tree. **2,** *mech.* arbor; shaft. **3,** *naut.* mast.

arbolado (ar·βo'la·ðo) *adj.* wooded; grown with trees. —*n.m.* wooded area; wood.

arboladura (ar·βo·la'ðu·ra) *n.f., naut.* masts and spars.

arboleda (ar·βo'le·ða) *n.f.* grove; wood.

arbóreo (ar'βo·re·o) *adj.* arboreal.

arboreto (ar·βo're·to) *n.m.* arboretum.

arbusto (ar'βus·to) *n.m.* shrub.

arca ('ar·ka) *n.f.* **1,** chest; coffer. **2,** strongbox; vault. **3,** ark. —**arca de agua,** water tower.

arcabuz (ar·ka'βuθ; -'βus) *n.m.* [*pl.* **-buces**] harquebus.

arcada (ar'ka·ða) *n.f.* **1,** arcade. **2,** retching.

arcaico (ar'kai·ko) *adj.* archaic. —**arcaísmo** (-ka'is·mo) *n.m.* archaism.

arcángel (ar'kan·xel) *n.m.* archangel.

arcano (ar'ka·no) *adj.* hidden; secret. —*n.m.* secret.

arce ('ar·θe; -se) *n.m.* maple tree.

arcediano (ar·θe'ðja·no; ar·se-) *n.m.* archdeacon.

arcilla (ar'θi·ʎa; -'si·ja) *n.f.* clay. —**arcilloso,** *adj.* clayey.

arcipreste (ar·θi'pres·te; ar·si-) *n.m.* archpriest.

arco ('ar·ko) *n.m.* **1,** bow. **2,** arc. **3,** arch. **4,** hoop. —**arco iris,** rainbow.

archidiácono (ar·tʃi'ðja·ko·no) *n.m.* = arcediano.

archidiócesis (ar·tʃi'ðjo·θe·sis; -se·sis) *n.f.* archdiocese.

archiduque (ar·tʃi'ðu·ke) *n.m.* archduke. —**archiducado,** *n.m.* archduchy. —**archiducal,** *adj.* archducal. —**archiduquesa,** *n.f.* archduchess.

archipiélago (ar·tʃi'pje·la·ɣo) *n.m* archipelago.

archivador (ar·tʃi·βa'ðor) *n.m.* filing cabinet or case.

archivo (ar'tʃi·βo) *n.m.* file; archives. —**archivar,** *v.t.* to file. —**archivero,** *n.m.* archivist.

ardentísimo (ar·ðen'ti·si·mo) *adj., superl. of* **ardiente.**

arder (ar'ðer) *v.i.* **1,** to burn; blaze. **2,** to rage. **3,** to yearn. **4,** *Amer.* to itch; chafe.

ardid (ar'ðið) *n.m.* stratagem.

ardiente (ar'ðjen·te) *adj.* ardent.

ardilla (ar'ði·ʎa; -ja) *n.f.* squirrel. —**ardilla listada; ardilla norteamericana,** chipmunk.

ardimiento (ar·ði'mjen·to) *n.m.* courage; daring.

ardite (ar'ði·te) *n.m.* an ancient Spanish coin of little value. —**no valer un ardite,** not to be worth a tinker's dam.

ardor (ar'ðor) *n.m.* **1,** ardor; heat. **2,** courage; valor. —**ardoroso,** *adj.* fiery.

arduo ('ar·ðwo) *adj.* arduous. —**arduidad,** *n.f.* arduousness.

área ('a·re·a) *n.f.* **1,** area; region. **2,** are.

arena (a're·na) *n.f.* **1,** sand. **2,** arena. —**arena movediza,** quicksand.

arenal (a·re'nal) *n.m.* **1,** sandy terrain; desert. **2,** quicksand.

arenga (a'ren·ga) *n.f.* harangue.

arengar (a·ren'gar) *v.t. & i.* [*infl.:* **pagar, 8**] to harangue.

arenisca (a·re'nis·ka) *n.f.* sandstone.

arenoso (a·re'no·so) *also,* **arenisco** (-'ni·sko) *adj.* sandy.

arenque (a'ren·ke) *n.m.* herring.

arete (a're·te) *n.m.* earring.

argamasa (ar·ɣa'ma·sa) *n.f.* mortar. —**argamasar,** *v.t.* **1,** to mix (mortar). **2,** to join with mortar.

argentar (ar·xen'tar) *v.t.* to silver; trim with silver.

argentino (ar·xen'ti·no) *adj.* **1,** [*also, poet.,* **argentado** (-'ta·ðo), **argénteo** (-'xen·te·o)] silvery. **2,** Argentine; Argentinian. —*n.m.* Argentine.

argentoso (ar·xen'to·so) *adj.* mixed with silver.

Argirol (ar·xi'rol) *n.m., T.N.* Argyrol.

argo ('ar·ɣo) *n.m.* argon. *Also,* **argón.**

argolla (ar'ɣo·ʎa; -ja) *n.f.* **1,** metal ring or band. **2,** *Amer.* engagement or wedding band. **3,** croquet (*game*).

argón (ar'ɣon) *n.m.* argon.

argonauta (ar·ɣo'nau·ta) *n.m.* **1,** *cap., myth.* Argonaut. **2,** *ichthy.* argonaut; paper nautilus.

argot (ar'ɣo) *n.m.* [*pl.* **argots** (ar'ɣo)] argot; jargon.

argucia (ar'ɣu·θja; -sja) *n.f.* sophistry.

argüir (ar'ɣwir) *v.t. & i.* [*infl.:* **huir, 26**] to argue.

argumentar (ar·ɣu·men'tar) *v.t.* to deduce; infer. —*v.i.* to argue; —**argumentación,** *n.f.* argument; argumentation. —**argumentador,** *adj.* argumentative. —*n.m.* arguer. —**argumentativo,** *adj.* argumentative.

argumento (ar·ɣu'men·to) *n.m.* **1,** argument. **2,** plot (*of a play, novel, etc.*).

aria ('a·rja) *n.f.* aria.

árido ('a·ri·ðo) *adj.* arid. —**aridez,** *n.f.* aridity.

Aries ('a·rjes) *n.m.* Aries.

ariete (a'rje·te) *n.m.* battering ram. —**ariete hidráulico,** hydraulic ram.

ario ('a·rjo). *adj. & n.m.* Aryan.

arisco (a'ris·ko) *adj.* untamed; rough.

arista (a'ris·ta) *n.f.* **1,** awn. **2,** edge; ridge; rib.

aristocracia (a·ris·to'kra·θja; -sja) *n.f.* aristocracy. —**aristócrata** (-'to·kra·ta) *n.m. & f.* aristocrat.

—**aristocrático** (-'kra·ti·ko) *adj.* aristocratic.

aritmética (a·rit'me·ti·ka) *n.f.* arithmetic. —**aritmético,** *adj.* arithmetical. —*n.m.* arithmetician.

arlequín (ar·le'kin) *n.m.* harlequin. —**arlequinada,** *n.f.* buffoonery; harlequinade.

arma ('ar·ma) *n.f.* weapon. —**armas,** *n.f.pl.* **1,** arms. **2,** military profession. **3,** coat of arms. —**alzarse en armas,** to rebel. —**arma blanca,** steel weapon. —**arma de fuego,** firearm. —**de armas tomar,** easily aroused; ready to fight. —**maestro de armas,** fencing master. —**pasar por las armas,** to execute. —**rendir las armas,** to surrender. —**sobre las armas,** under arms.

armada (ar'ma·ða) *n.f.* navy; fleet.

armadía (ar·ma'ði·a) *n.f.* raft.

armadillo (ar·ma'ði·ʎo; -jo) *n.m.* armadillo.

armado (ar'ma·ðo) *adj.* **1,** armed. **2,** reinforced. —*n.m.* assembly; mounting.

armador (ar·ma'ðor) *n.m.* **1,** assembler; rigger. **2,** *naut.* outfitter.

armadura (ar·ma'ðu·ra) *n.f.* **1,** armor. **2,** armature; framework. **3,** *elect.* armature.

armamento (ar·ma'men·to) *n.m.* **1,** armament. **2,** *naut.* fitting out.

armar (ar'mar) *v.t.* **1,** to arm. **2,** to load (a weapon). **3,** *carp.* to assemble. **4,** *mech.* to mount; rig up. **5,** *naut.* to equip; fit out. **6,** *colloq.* to start (a noisy action). —**armarse,** *v.r.* **1,** to arm; arm oneself. **2,** *Amer., colloq.* to strike it rich. —**armar caballero,** to knight.

armario (ar'ma·rjo) *n.m.* wardrobe; cabinet.

armatoste (ar·ma'tos·te) *n.m.* clumsy person or thing; hulk.

armazón (ar·ma'θon; -'son) *n.f.* framework; frame. —*n.m.* skeleton.

armella (ar'me·ʎa; -ja) *n.f.* screweye.

armería (ar·me'ri·a) *n.f.* **1,** armory. **2,** gunsmith's trade or shop. **3,** arms collection; arms museum.

armero (ar'me·ro) *n.m.* **1,** gunsmith. **2,** keeper of arms. **3,** rifle rack.

armiño (ar'mi·ɲo) *n.m.* ermine.

armisticio (ar·mis'ti·θjo; -sjo) *n.m.* armistice.

armonía (ar·mo'ni·a) *n.f.* **1,** har-

mony. **2,** harmoniousness. **3,** harmonics.

armónica (ar'mo·ni·ka) *n.f.* harmonica.

armónico (ar'mo·ni·ko) *adj. & n.m.* harmonic.

armonioso (ar·mo'njo·so) *adj.* harmonious.

armonizar (ar·mo·ni'θar; -'sar) *v.t. & i.* [*infl.:* **rezar, 10**] to harmonize.

arnés (ar'nes) *n.m.* coat of mail. —**arneses,** *n.m.pl.* harness.

árnica ('ar·ni·ka) *n.f.* arnica.

aro ('a·ro) *n.m.* **1,** hoop; large ring. **2,** croquet wicket. —**aro de émbolo,** piston ring. —**entrar por el aro,** to be forced to submit.

aroma (a'ro·ma) *n.m.* aroma.

aromático (a·ro'ma·ti·ko) *adj.* aromatic. —**sales aromáticas,** smelling salts.

aromatizar (a·ro·ma·ti'θar; -'sar) *v.t.* [*infl.:* **rezar, 10**] to perfume. —**aromatizador,** *n.m.* atomizer.

arpa ('ar·pa) *n.f.* harp.

arpeo (ar'pe·o) *n.* grapple; grappling iron.

arpía (ar'pi·a) *n.f.* harpy; shrew.

arpillera (ar·pi'ʎe·ra; -'je·ra) *n.f.* = **harpillera.**

arpista (ar'pis·ta) *n.m. & f.* harpist.

arpón (ar'pon) *n.m.* harpoon. —**arponear** (-ne'ar) *also,* **arponar** (-'nar) *v.t.* to harpoon.

arponero (ar·po'ne·ro) *n.m.* **1,** harpooner. **2,** harpoon maker.

arqueada (ar·ke'a·ða) *n.f.* **1,** retch; retching. **2,** *mus.* bowing.

arquear (ar·ke'ar) *v.t.* to arch; bend; bow. —*v.i.* to retch.

arqueo (ar'ke·o) *n.m.* **1,** arching; bending. **2,** inventory, esp. of cash.

arqueología (ar·ke·o·lo'xi·a) *n.f.* archaeology. —**arqueológico** (-'lo·xi·ko) *adj.* archaeological. —**arqueólogo** (-'o·lo·ɣo) *n.m.* archaeologist.

arquero (ar'ke·ro) *n.m.* **1,** archer. **2,** bow maker. **3,** *sports* goalkeeper.

arquetipo (ar·ke'ti·po) *n.m.* archetype.

arquidiócesis (ar·ki-) *n.f.* = **archidiócesis.**

arquitectura (ar·ki·tek'tu·ra) *n.f.* architecture. —**arquitecto** (-'tek·to) *n.m.* architect. —**arquitectónico** (-'to·ni·ko) *adj.* architectural.

arrabal (a·rra'βal) *n.m.* **1,** suburb; outskirts. **2,** poor quarter; slum. **3,** *Amer.* slum dwelling; tenement.

arrabalero (a·rra·βa'le·ro) *adj.* **1,** suburban; of the outskirts. **2,** slum (*attrib.*). **3,** ill-bred. —*n.m.* **1,** slum dweller. **2,** roughneck; rowdy.

arracimar (a·rra·θi'mar; -si'mar) *v.t.* to cluster; bunch. —**arracimarse,** *v.r.* to form in a cluster. —**arracimado,** *adj.* clustered; bunched.

arraigar (a·rrai'γar) *v.i.* [*infl.:* **pagar, 8**] to take root. —**arraigarse,** *v.r.* to settle; become established. —**arraigado,** *adj.* deep-rooted.

arraigo (a'rrai·γo) *n.m.* **1,** settling; taking root. **2,** property; real estate.

arrancada (a·rran'ka·δa) *n.f.* **1,** start; takeoff. **2,** spurt; burst of speed.

arrancado (a·rran'ka·δo) *adj., slang* broke; penniless.

arrancar (a·rran'kar) *v.t.* [*infl.:* **tocar, 7**] **1,** to uproot. **2,** to pull out. **3,** to tear off or away. **4,** to force out; eject; heave (a sigh). —*v.i.* to start; take off. —**arrancar de,** to spring from; stem from.

arranchar (a·rran'tʃar) *v.t., Amer.* to snatch; grab. —*v.i., Amer. colloq.* to live (with someone); cohabit.

arranque (a'rran·ke) *n.m.* **1,** start; starting. **2,** outburst. **3,** sudden impulse; fit. **4,** *mech.* starter.

arras ('a·rras) *n.f.pl.* traditional gift of thirteen coins given by the bridegroom to the bride.

arrasar (a·rra'sar) *v.t.* **1,** to raze; level. **2,** to fill; cause to brim over. —*v.i.* [*also,* **arrasarse,** *v.r.*] to clear up, as the sky.

arrastrar (a·rras'trar) *v.t.* to drag; haul. —*v.i.* to play trumps. —**arrastrarse,** *v.r.* **1,** to crawl. **2,** *fig.* to cringe; fawn. —**arrastrado,** *adj.* miserable. —*n.m.* knave; miscreant.

arrastre (a'rras·tre) *n.m.* **1,** drayage; haulage. **2,** dragging; hauling. **3,** *Amer.* drag; pull. **4,** *cards* trump lead.

arrayán (a·rra'jan) *n.m.* myrtle.

¡arre! ('a·rre) *interj.* gee up!; giddap!

arrear (a·rre'ar) *v.t.* **1,** to drive (animals). **2,** to deal (a blow, insult, etc.). **3,** *Amer.* to rustle (livestock).

arrebatar (a·rre·βa'tar) *v.t.* **1,** to snatch. **2,** to captivate. —**arrebatarse,** *v.r.* to be carried away emotionally. —**arrebatado,** *adj.* rash; violent; *slang* crazy.

—**arrebatador,** *adj.* captivating; stirring.

arrebato (a·rre'βa·to) *n.m.* **1,** paroxysm; rage. **2,** rapture.

arrebol (a·rre'βol) *n.m.* **1,** red or rosy tinge. **2,** rouge. —**arreboles,** *n.m.pl.* [*also,* **arrebolada,** *n.f.sing.*] red clouds. —**arrebolarse,** *v.r.* to redden; turn red.

arrebujar (a·rre·βu'xar) *v.t.* to cover up; bundle up; muffle.

arreciar (a·rre'θjar; -'sjar) *v.i.* to rage; become more intense.

arrecife (a·rre'θi·fe; -'si·fe) *n.m.* reef. —**arrecife de arena,** sand bar.

arredrarse (a·rre'δrar·se) *v.r.* to shrink; draw back, as in fright.

arreglar (a·rre'γlar) *v.t.* **1,** to arrange. **2,** to settle; adjust. **3,** to repair; fix. **4,** to tidy; put in order. —**arreglarse,** *v.r.* **1,** to conform. **2,** to agree; reach an agreement. —**arreglárselas,** *colloq.* to get along; manage.

arreglo (a'rre·γlo) *n.m.* **1,** settlement; compromise. **2,** arrangement; order. **3,** putting in order; tidying. **4,** repair. —**con arreglo a,** in accordance with; according to.

arrellanarse (a·rre·ʎa'nar·se; -ja'nar·se) *v.r.* to lounge; loll; sprawl.

arremangar (a·rre·man'gar) *v.t.* [*infl.:* **pagar, 8**] to roll or tuck up (one's sleeves, trousers, skirts, etc.).

arremeter (a·rre·me'ter) *v.i.* to attack. —**arremetida,** *n.f.* attack.

arremolinarse (a·rre·mo·li'nar·se) *v.r.* to spin; whirl; eddy.

arrendador (a·rren·da'δor) *n.m.* **1,** lessor. **2,** tenant.

arrendajo (a·rren·da·xo) *n.m.* jay bird.

arrendamiento (a·rren·da·'mjen·to) *n.m.* **1,** rent; lease. **2,** rental.

arrendar (a·rren'dar) *v.t.* [*infl.:* **pensar, 27**] **1,** to rent. **2,** to lease. **3,** to hitch up (horses).

arrendatario (a·rren·da'ta·rjo) *adj.* **1,** renting. **2,** leasing. — *n.m.* **1,** tenant. **2,** lessee.

arreos (a'rre·os) *n.m.pl.* harness. —*adv.* uninterruptedly.

arrepentirse (a·rre·pen'tir·se) *v.r.* [*infl.:* **sentir, 31**] to repent. —**arrepentido,** *adj.* repentant. —**arrepentimiento,** *n.m.* repentance.

arrestar (a·rres'tar) *v.t.* to arrest.

arresto (a'rres·to) *n.m.* arrest.

arriar (a'rrjar) *v.t.,* [*infl.:* enviar, 22] to lower. —**arriar las velas,** to take in sail. —**arriar la bandera,** to strike the colors. —**arriar un cabo,** to pay out a rope.

arriba (a'rri·βa) *adv.* **1,** above; up; on high. **2,** upstairs. —**arriba de,** upwards of (*in expressions of quantity*). —**boca arriba,** face up; right side up. —**de arriba abajo,** from head to foot; from top to bottom. —**hasta arriba,** all the way up; to the top. —**para** *or* **hacia arriba,** up; upwards.

arribar (a·rri'βar) *v.i.* to arrive. —**arribo** (a'rri·βo) *n.m., also,* **arribada,** *n.f.* arrival.

arriende (a'rrjen·de) *v., pres. subjve.* of **arrendar.**

arriendo (a'rrjen·do) *n.m.* = **arrendamiento,** —*v., pres.ind.* of **arrendar.**

arriero (a'rrje·ro) *n.m.* muleteer; teamster.

arriesgado (a·rrjes'ɣa·do) *adj.* **1,** risky. **2,** reckless.

arriesgar (a·rrjes'ɣar) *v.t.* [*infl.:* pagar, 8] to risk. —**arriesgarse,** *v.r., colloq.* to take a chance.

arrimar (a·rri'mar) *v.t.* to bring close; to place near. —**arrimarse,** *v.r.* to draw near. —**arrimarse a, 1,** to get close to. **2,** to seek the protection of.

arrinconado (a·rrin·ko'na·ðo) *adj.* **1,** shelved; put aside; neglected. **2,** secluded; remote. **3,** cornered.

arrinconar (a·rrin·ko'nar) *v.t.* **1,** to place in a corner. **2,** to corner. **3,** to shelve; put aside. —**arrinconarse,** *v.r.* to seclude oneself.

arriscarse (a·rris'kar·se) *v.r.* [*infl.:* tocar, 7] to become angry; flare up. —**arriscado,** *adj.* conceited.

arritmia (a'rrit·mja) *n.f.* **1,** lack of rhythm. **2,** *pathol.* arrhythmia.

arroba (a'rro·βa) *n.f.* **1,** a Spanish unit of weight of about 25 pounds. **2,** a Spanish liquid measure varying by region and the weight of the liquid.

arrobar (a·rro'βar) *v.t.* to entrance. —**arrobo** (a'rro·βo) *also,* **arrobamiento,** *n.m.* ecstasy.

arrocero (a·rro'θe·ro; -'se·ro) *n.m.* rice grower. —*adj.* of or pert. to rice.

arrodillarse (a·rro·ðiʎar·se; -'jar·se) *v.r.* to kneel.

arrogancia (a·rro'ɣan·θja; -sja) *n.f.* **1,** arrogance. **2,** gallantry.

arrogante (a·rro'ɣan·te) *adj.* **1,** arrogant. **2,** gallant.

arrogarse (a·rro'ɣar·se) *v.r.* [*infl.:* pagar, 8] to arrogate to oneself; usurp. —**arrogación,** *n.f.* arrogation.

arrojadizo (a·rro·xa'ði·θo; -so) *adj.* for throwing or hurling, as a weapon.

arrojado (a·rro'xa·ðo) *adj.* reckless; bold. —**arrojo** (a'rro·xo) *n.m.* boldness; recklessness.

arrojar (a·rro'xar) *v.t.* **1,** to throw. **2,** to cast out. **3,** to shed; give off. **4,** to show (balance or numerical result). —**arrojarse,** *v.r.* to rush; throw oneself. —*v.i.* to vomit.

arrollar (a·rro'ʎar; -'jar) *v.t.* **1,** to overwhelm. **2,** to run over. **3,** to sweep away.

arropar (a·rro'par) *v.t.* to clothe; cover. —**arroparse,** *v.r.* to clothe or cover oneself.

arrostrar (a·rros'trar) *v.t.* to brave; face.

arroyo (a'rro·jo) *n.m.* **1,** brook. **2,** gutter.

arroz (a'rroθ; a'rros) *n.m.* rice. —**arrozal,** *n.m.* rice field.

arruga (a'rru·ɣa) *n.f.* wrinkle.

arrugar (a·rru'ɣar) *v.t.* [*infl.:* pagar, 8] to wrinkle. —**arrugar la frente** *or* **el entrecejo,** to frown.

arruinar (a·rrwi'nar) *v.t.* to ruin. —**arruinador,** *adj.* ruinous.

arrullar (a·rru'ʎar; -'jar) *v.t.* **1,** to coo to. **2,** to whisper or murmur to; say sweet nothings to. **3,** to lull.

arrullo (a'rru·ʎo; -jo) *n.m.* **1,** coo; cooing. **2,** whisper; murmur. **3,** lullaby.

arrumaco (a·rru'ma·ko) *n.m., usu.pl., colloq.* show of affection.

arrumar (a·rru'mar) *v.t.* to stow (cargo). —**arrumarse,** *v.r., naut.* to become overcast. —**arrumaje,** *n.m.* stowage.

arrumbar (a·rrum'bar) *v.t.* to put aside; shelve.

arrurruz (a·rru'rruθ; -'rrus) *n.m.* arrowroot.

arsenal (ar·se'nal) *n.m.* **1,** shipyard. **2,** arsenal. **3,** *fig.* store; storehouse.

arsénico (ar'se·ni·ko) *n.m.* arsenic. —**arsenical,** *adj.* arsenical.

arte ('ar·te) *n.m. or f.* art. —**artes y oficios,** arts and crafts. —**bellas**

artes, fine arts. **—no tener arte ni parte en,** to have nothing to do with.

artefacto (ar·te'fak·to) *n.m.* **1,** artifact. **2,** device; gadget.

artejo (ar'te·xo) *n.m.* joint; segment.

artemisa (ar·te'mi·sa) *n.f.* sagebrush. *Also,* **artemisia** (-sja).

arteria (ar'te·rja) *n.f.* artery. **—arterial** (-'rjal) *adj.* arterial.

artería (ar·te'ri·a) *n.f.* trickery; chicanery.

arteriosclerosis (ar·te·rjos·kle·'ro·sis) *n.f.* arteriosclerosis.

artero (ar'te·ro) *adj.* sly; underhanded; artful.

artesa (ar'te·sa) *n.f.* trough; kneading trough.

artesanía (ar·te·sa'ni·a) *n.f.* **1,** craftsmanship. **2,** = **artesanado. 3,** handicraft.

artesano (ar·te'sa·no) *n.m.* artisan; craftsman. **—artesanado,** *n.m.* artisans or craftsmen collectively.

artesiano (ar·te'sja·no) *adj.* artesian.

ártico ('ar·ti·ko) *adj.* arctic. **—n.m.,** *cap.* Arctic Ocean.

articulación (ar·ti·ku·la'θjon; -'sjon) *n.f.* **1,** joint. **2,** articulation.

articulado (ar·ti·ku'la·ðo) *adj.* **1,** articulated; jointed. **2,** articulate.

articular (ar·ti·ku'lar) *v.t.* to articulate.

articulista (ar·ti·ku'lis·ta) *n.m.* & *f.* feature writer; columnist.

artículo (ar'ti·ku·lo) *n.m.* article. **—artículo de comercio,** commodity. **—artículo de fondo,** editorial. **—artículo de primera necesidad,** basic commodity.

artífice (ar'ti·fi·θe; -se) *n.m.* & *f.* **1,** artist; craftsman (or craftswoman). **2,** artificer.

artificial (ar·ti·fi'θjal; -'sjal) *adj.* artificial. **—artificialidad,** *n.f.* artificiality.

artificio (ar·ti'fi'θjo; -sjo) *n.m.* **1,** skill; craftsmanship. **2,** artifice; device. **—artificioso,** *adj.* artful; contrived.

artilugio (ar·ti'lu·xjo) *n.m.* **1,** low trick. **2,** contraption. **3,** gimmick.

artillado (ar·ti'ʎa·ðo; -'ja·ðo) *n.m.* complement of guns or artillery.

artillar (ar·ti'ʎar; -'jar) *v.t.* to arm with guns or artillery.

artillería (ar·ti·ʎe'ri·a; ar·ti·je-) *n.f.* **1,** artillery. **2,** gunnery.

—artillería de campaña, field artillery.

artillero (ar·ti'ʎe·ro; -'je·ro) *n.m.* **1,** gunner. **2,** artilleryman.

artimaña (ar·ti'ma·ɲa) *n.f.* trap; snare; trick.

artista (ar'tis·ta) *n.m.* & *f.* artist. **—artístico,** *adj.* artistic.

artritis (ar'tri·tis) *n.f.* arthritis. **—artrítico,** *adj.* arthritic.

artrópodo (ar'tro·po·ðo) *n.m.* arthropod.

arveja (ar'βe·xa) *n.f.* **1,** vetch. **2,** *Amer.* pea.

arzobispo (ar·θo'βis·po; ar·so-) *n.m.* archbishop. **—arzobispado,** *n.m.* archbishopric. **—arzobispal,** *adj.* archiepiscopal.

as (as) *n.m.* ace.

asa ('a·sa) *n.f.* handle. **—en asas,** akimbo.

asado (a'sa·ðo) *n.m.* roast. **—adj.** roasted. **—asador,** *n.m.* spit; roaster.

asaetear (a·sa·e·te'ar) *v.t.* **1,** to shoot with an arrow; rain arrows upon. **2,** to harass; importune.

asafétida (a·sa'fe·ti·ða) *n.f.* asafetida.

asalariado (a·sa·la'rja·ðo) *adj.* salaried; paid. **—n.m.** paid worker; salaried employee.

asaltar (a·sal'tar) *v.t.* to assault. **—asaltador, asaltante,** *n.m.* assailant. **—adj.** assailing.

asalto (a'sal·to) *n.m.* **1,** assault. **2,** *fencing* bout. **3,** *boxing* round. **4,** *Amer.* surprise party. **—por asalto,** by storm.

asamblea (a·sam'ble·a) *n.f.* assembly. **—asambleísta** (-'is·ta) *n.m.* & *f.* assemblyman or assemblywoman.

asar (a'sar) *v.t.* to roast. **—asarse,** *v.r.* to feel extremely hot.

asaz (a'saθ; a'sas) *adv.* very; extremely; exceedingly.

asbesto (as'βes·to) *n.m.* asbestos.

ascalonia (as·ka'lo·nja) *n.f.* shallot. *Also,* **escalonia** (es-).

ascáride (as'ka·ri·ðe) *n.m.* roundworm.

ascendencia (as·θen'den·θja; a·sen'den·sja) *n.f.* **1,** ancestry. **2,** ascendancy; influence. **—ascendente,** *adj.* ascending; rising; ascendant.

ascender (as·θen'der; a·sen-) *v.t.* [*infl.:* perder, 29] to promote; advance in grade or rank. **—v.i. 1,** to ascend; climb. **2,** to be promoted or advanced. **—ascender a,** to come to; amount to.

ascendiente (as·θen'djen·te; a·sen-) *n.m.* & *f.* ancestor. —*n.m.* ascendancy; influence. —*adj.* = **ascendente**.

ascensión (as·θen'sjon; a·sen-) *n.f.* **1**, ascent; ascension. **2**, elevation; exaltation. **3**, *cap., relig.* Ascension. —**ascensionista**, *n.m.* & *f.* balloonist.

ascenso (as'θen·so; a'sen-) *n.m.* **1**, promotion; rise. **2**, career step or grade.

ascensor (as·θen'sor; a·sen-) *n.m.* elevator.

asceta (as'θe·ta; a'se-) *n.m.* & *f.* ascetic.

ascético (as'θe·ti·ko; a'se-) *adj.* ascetic. —**ascetismo**, *n.m.* asceticism.

asco ('as·ko) *n.m.* repugnance. —**estar hecho un asco**, to be dirty; to be slovenly.

ascua ('as·kwa) *n.f.* ember —**estar en** *or* **sobre ascuas**, *colloq.* to be on pins and needles.

asear (a·se'ar) *v.t.* to clean; tidy. —**aseado**, *adj.* clean; tidy.

asechar (a·se'tʃar) *v.t.* to ambush; waylay. —**asechanza**, *n.f.* trap; snare.

asediar (a·se'ðjar) *v.t.* to besiege. —**asedio** (a·se·ðjo) *n.m.* siege.

asegurar (a·se·ɣu'rar) *v.t.* **1**, to secure; make fast. **2**, to assure. **3**, to insure.

asemejar (a·se·me'xar) *v.t.* **1**, to make alike. **2**, to liken; compare. —*v.i.* [*also,* **asemejarse**, *v.r.*] to be alike; have a likeness or resemblance.

asenso (a'sen·so) *n.m.* **1**, assent. **2**, credence; belief.

asentada (a·sen'ta·ða) *n.f.* sitting. —**de una asentada**, at one sitting.

asentaderas (a·sen·ta'ðe·ras) *n.f.pl., colloq.* buttocks.

asentado (a·sen'ta·ðo) *adj.* **1**, seated; situated. **2**, stable; permanent. **3**, tranquil.

asentar (a·sen'tar) *v.t.* [*infl.:* **pensar, 27**] **1**, to put; set; place. **2**, to flatten; tamp. **3**, to affirm; assert. **4**, to go well with; agree with. **5**, to consolidate. **6**, to note down; record. **7**, to deliver; deal (a blow). **8**, *slang* to sit (someone) down. —*v.i.* **1**, to be becoming. **2**, to agree; go well. —**asentarse**, *v.r.* **1**, to settle; become settled. **2**, to become firm. **3**, to lie heavy, as food.

asentir (a·sen'tir) *v.i.* [*infl.:* **sentir,** **31**] to assent. —**asentimiento**, *n.m.* assent.

aseo (a'se·o) *n.m.* **1**, cleanliness; neatness. **2**, cleaning.

asepsia (a'sep·sja) *n.f.* asepsis. —**aséptico** (a'sep·ti·ko) *adj.* aseptic.

asequible (a·se'ki·βle) *adj.* **1**, attainable. **2**, obtainable. **3**, *(of persons)* approachable.

aserción (a·ser'θjon; -'sjon) *n.f.* assertion.

aserrar (a·se'rrar) *v.t.* [*infl.:* **pensar, 27**] to saw. —**aserradero**, *n.m.* sawmill. —**aserrado**, *adj.* serrated. —**aserrador**, *n.m.* sawyer. —**aserradura**, *n.f.* cut; *pl.* sawdust.

aserrín (a·se'rrin) *n.m.* sawdust.

aserruchar (a·se·rru'tʃar) *v.t., Amer.* to saw, esp. with a handsaw.

aserto (a'ser·to) *n.m.* assertion. —**asertivo** (-'ti·βo) *adj.* assertive.

asesinar (a·se·si'nar) *v.t.* to assassinate. —**asesinato**, *n.m.* assassination.

asesino (a·se'si·no) *n.m.* assassin. —*adj.* murderous.

asesor (a·se'sor) *n.m.* adviser; consultant.

asesorar (a·se·so'rar) *v.t.* to advise. —**asesorarse**, *v.r.* to take advice; seek counsel. —**asesoramiento** *n.m.* **1**, counseling; advising. **2**, counsel, advice.

asestar (a·ses'tar) *v.t.* **1**, to aim; direct. **2**, to deal (a blow). **3**, to hurl; fire (a shot).

aseverar (a·se·βe'rar) *v.t.* to affirm; assert. —**aseveración**, *n.f.* positive statement; assertion. —**aseveradamente**, *adv.* positively.

aseverativo (a·se·βe·ra'ti·βo) *adj.* **1**, assertive; affirmative. **2**, declarative case.

asexual (a·sek'swal) *adj.* asexual.

asfalto (as'fal·to) *n.m.* asphalt. —**asfaltar**, *v.t.* to pave with asphalt.

asfixia (as'fik·sja) *n.f.* asphyxia; suffocation. —**asfixiar**, *v.t.* to asphyxiate.

asfódelo (as'fo·ðe·lo) *n.m.* asphodel.

asga ('as·ɣa) *v., pres.subjve.* of **asir**.

asgo ('as·ɣo) *v., 1st pers.sing. pres.ind.* of **asir**.

así (a'si) *adv.* so; thus. —*conj.* though; although. —**así así**, so-so, *also* **así asá**. —**así como**, **1**, just as. **2**, as well as. **3**, as soon as. —**así.... como**, both.... and; not only.... but also. —**así como así;**

así que así, anyway; anyhow. —**así no más,** *Amer., colloq.* so-so. —**así que, 1,** so that. **2,** as soon as. —**así sea,** would that it be (*or* were) so. —**así y todo,** nevertheless.

asiático (a'sja·ti·ko) *adj. & n.m.* Asiatic; Asian. —**lujo asiático,** Oriental splendor.

asidero (a·si'ðe·ro) *n.m.* **1,** grip; handle. **2,** pretext.

asiduo (a'si·ðwo) *adj.* assiduous. —*n.m.* habitué. —**asiduidad,** *n.f.* assiduity.

asienta (a'sjen·ta) *v.* **1,** *pres. subjve. of* **asentir. 2,** *pres.ind. 3rd pers.sing. of* **asentar.**

asiente (a'sjen·te) *v., pres.subjve. of* **asentar.**

asiento (a'sjen·to) *n.m.* **1,** seat. **2,** sediment. **3,** *comm.* entry. **4,** settling (*of a building*). **5,** *fig.* good judgment; stability. —*v.* **1,** *pres.ind. of* **asentar. 2,** *pres.ind. of* **asentir.**

asierre (a'sje·rre) *v.t., 1st pers. sing. pres.subjve. of* **aserrar.**

asierro (a'sje·rro) *v.t., pres. ind. of* **aserrar.**

asignación (a·siɣ·na'θjon; -'sjon) *n.f.* **1,** assignment. **2,** salary; allowance.

asignar (a·siɣ'nar) *v.t.* to assign.

asignatario (a·siɣ·na'ta·rjo) *n.m., law, Amer.* trustee; legatee.

asignatura (a·siɣ·na'tu·ra) *n.f.* academic subject.

asilado (a·si'la·ðo) *n.m.* **1,** inmate (*of an asylum, home, etc.*). **2,** refugee.

asilar (a·si'lar) *v.t.* **1,** to shelter; give asylum to. **2,** to place in a home or asylum.

asilo (a'si·lo) *n.m.* asylum; refuge.

asimetría (a·si·me'tri·a) *n.f.* asymmetry. —**asimétrico** (-'me·tri·ko) *adj.* asymmetrical.

asimilar (a·si·mi'lar) *v.t. & i.* to assimilate. —**asimilarse,** *v.r.* to be or become alike. —**asimilación,** *n.f.* assimilation.

asimismo (a·si'mis·mo) *adv.* likewise; also; exactly.

asir (a'sir) *v.t.* [*infl.:* 36] to grasp; seize. —**asirse,** *v.r.* to take hold. —**asirse a,** to catch at; hold on to. —**asirse de,** to seize (as an opportunity); take advantage of.

asirio (a'si·rjo) *adj. & n.m.* Assyrian.

asistencia (a·sis'ten·θja; -sja) *n.f.*

1, assistance; aid. **2,** attendance. **3,** *pl.* subsistence; support.

asistenta (a·sis'ten·ta) *n.f.* **1,** female assistant. **2,** day maid.

asistente (a·sis'ten·te) *n.m.* **1,** assistant; helper; *mil.* orderly. **2,** attendant.

asistir (a·sis'tir) *v.t.* **1,** to assist; aid. **2,** to attend; stand by. **3,** to serve; minister to. —*v.i.* **1,** to be present. **2,** *cards* to follow suit.

asma ('as·ma) *n.f.* asthma. —**asmático** (-'ma·ti·ko) *adj. & n.m.* asthmatic.

asnada (as'na·ða) *n.f.* asininity.

asnería (as·ne'ri·a) *n.f.* **1,** drove of asses. **2,** asininity.

asno ('as·no) *n.m.* ass; donkey. —**asnal,** *adj.* asinine; of or pert. to asses.

asociación (a·so·θja'θjon; -sja·'sjon) *n.f.* **1,** association. **2,** partnership.

asociado (a·so'θja·ðo; -'sja·ðo) *adj.* **1,** associated. **2,** associate. —*n.m.* member; associate.

asociar (a·so'θjar; -'sjar) *v.t.* **1,** to associate. **2,** to attach; join. **3,** to take into membership or partnership. —**asociarse,** *v.r.* **1,** to associate; consort. **2,** to associate oneself; become a member or partner. **3,** to form a partnership or association. —**asociarse a** *or* **con,** to join.

asolar (a·so'lar) *v.t.* **1,** [*infl.:* acostar, 28] to raze; devastate. **2,** [*regularly inflected*] to burn up; parch (vegetation). —**asolador,** *adj.* devastating. —**asolamiento,** *n.m.* devastation.

asoleada (a·so·le'a·ða) *n.f., Amer.* **1,** sunning; sunbath. **2,** sunstroke.

asolear (a·so·le'ar) *v.t.* to sun. —**asoleado,** *adj.* sunny.

asomar (a·so'mar) *v.t.* to show; to allow to be seen. —*v.i.* to begin to appear. —**asomarse,** *v.r.* **1,** to lean out. **2,** to show oneself; to look out.

asombrar (a·som'brar) *v.t.* to amaze. —**asombrarse,** *v.r.* to be amazed. —**asombrador** *adj.* [*fem.* **-dora**] amazing.

asombro (a'som·bro) *n.m.* amazement. —**asombroso,** *adj.* amazing.

asomo (a'so·mo) *n.m.* sign; indication. —**ni por asomo,** not by a long shot; by no means.

asonancia (a·so'nan·θja; -sja) *n.f.* assonance. —**asonante,** *adj.* assonant.

aspa ('as·pa) n.f. **1,** X-shaped cross. **2,** arm of a windmill.

aspaventar (as·pa·βen'tar) v.t. [infl.: pensar, 27] to frighten.

aspaventero (as·pa·βen'te·ro) adj. excitable; fussy. —n.m. demonstrative person; ham actor; ham.

aspaviento (as·pa'βjen·to) n.m. fuss.

aspecto (as'pek·to) n.m. aspect; countenance; appearance.

asperilla (as·pe'ri·ʎa; -ja) n.f. woodruff.

áspero ('as·pe·ro) adj. **1,** rough; harsh. **2,** fig. sharp; sour. **3,** severe. —**aspereza,** n.f. roughness; harshness.

aspersión (as·per'sjon) n.f. sprinkling; aspersion.

áspid ('as·piδ) n.f. asp.

aspiración (as·pi·ra'θjon; -'sjon) n.f. **1,** inhalation. **2,** aspiration. **3,** suction.

aspirar (as·pi'rar) v.t. & i. **1,** to inhale. **2,** to aspirate. **3,** to vacuum. **4,** to aspire; covet. —**aspiradora,** n.f., also, **aspirador,** n.m. vacuum cleaner. —**aspirante,** n.m. & f. aspirant; candidate. —**bomba aspirante,** vacuum pump.

aspirina (as·pi'ri·na) n.f. aspirin.

asquear (as·ke'ar) v.t. to consider with disgust. —v.i. to feel nauseated.

asqueroso (as·ke'ro·so) adj. **1,** filthy. **2,** loathsome; disgusting. **3,** easily disgusted; squeamish. **4,** nauseated. —**asquerosidad,** n.f. filth; filthiness.

asta ('as·ta) n.f. **1,** shaft; handle. **2,** lance; pike; spear. **3,** flagpole. **4,** antler; horn. —**a media asta,** at half mast.

astacio (as'ta·θjo; -sjo) n.m. astatine.

áster ('as·ter) n.f. aster.

asterisco (as·te'ris·ko) n.m. asterisk.

asteroide (as·te'roi·δe) n.m. asteroid.

astigmático (as·tiɣ'ma·ti·ko) adj. astigmatic.

astigmatismo (as·tiɣ·ma'tis·mo) n.m. astigmatism.

astil (as'til) n.m. **1,** shaft (of an arrow or feather). **2,** beam (of a balance).

astilla (as'ti·ʎa; -ja) n.f. splinter. —**astillar,** v.t. to splinter.

astillero (as·ti'ʎe·ro; -'je·ro) n.m. **1,** shipyard. **2,** lumberyard.

astral (as'tral) adj. astral.

astringir (as·trin'xir) v.t. [infl.: coger, 15] to astringe. —**astringencia,** n.f. astringency. —**astringente,** adj. & n.m. astringent.

astro ('as·tro) n.m. **1,** heavenly body; star. **2,** fig. male star.

astrofísica (as·tro'fi·si·ka) n.f. astrophysics. —**astrofísico,** adj. astrophysical. —n.m. astrophysicist.

astrología (as·tro·lo'xi·a) n.f. astrology. —**astrológico** (-'lo·xi·ko) adj. astrological. —**astrólogo** (as'tro·lo·ɣo) n.m. astrologer.

astronauta (as·tro'nau·ta) n.m. & f. astronaut. —**astronáutica** (-'nau·ti·ka) n.f. astronautics.

astronave (as·tro'na·βe) n.f. spaceship; spacecraft.

astronomía (as·tro·no'mi·a) n.f. astronomy. —**astronómico** (-'no·mi·ko) adj. astronomical. —**astrónomo** (as'tro·no·mo) n.m. astronomer.

astucia (as'tu·θja; -sja) n.f. **1,** astuteness. **2,** ruse.

astuto (as'tu·to) adj. astute; sly.

asuele (a'swe·le) v., 1st. pers. pres.subjve. of **asolar.**

asuelo (a'swe·lo) v., 1st pers. pres.ind. of **asolar.**

asueto (a'swe·to) n.m. vacation; holiday.

asumir (a·su'mir) v.t. to assume; take upon oneself.

asunción (a·sun'θjon; -'sjon) n.f. **1,** assumption. **2,** elevation (to a high office). **3,** cap., relig. Assumption.

asunto (a'sun·to) n.m. subject matter; affair; business.

asustar (a·sus'tar) v.t. to frighten. —**asustarse,** v.r. to be frightened. —**asustadizo,** adj. easily frightened.

atabal (a·ta'βal) n.m. kettledrum.

atacar (a·ta'kar) v.t. [infl.: tocar, 7] **1,** to attack. **2,** to fasten.

atadero (a·ta'δe·ro) n.m. **1,** place or means of attachment. **2,** hitching post.

atado (a'ta·δo) n.m. bundle.

atadura (a·ta'δu·ra) n.f. **1,** tying; fastening. **2,** rope; cord. **3,** knot. **4,** fig. bond; tie.

atajar (a·ta'xar) v.t. **1,** to intercept. **2,** to restrain. —v.i. to take a shortcut.

atajo (a'ta·xo) n.m. shortcut.

atalaya (a·ta'la·ja) *n.f.* watch-tower.

atañer (a·ta'ɲer) *v.t.* [*infl.*: **tañer,** 20] to concern.

ataque (a'ta·ke) *n.m.* attack.

atar (a'tar) *v.t.* to tie. —**atarse,** *v.r., fig.* to tie oneself in knots; to be confused. —**atar cabos,** to put two and two together.

atarantar (a·ta·ran'tar) *v.t.* to confuse, bewilder. —**atarantado,** *adj., colloq.* restless; nervous; impulsive.

atardecer (a·tar·ðe'θer; -'ser) *n.m.* late afternoon; dusk. —*v.i.* [*infl.*: **conocer,** 13] to grow dark.

atarear (a·ta·re'ar) *v.t.* to assign work to. —**atarearse,** *v.r.* to be busy; busy oneself. —**atareado,** *adj.* busy.

atarugar (a·ta·ru'ɣar) *v.t.* [*infl.*: **pagar,** 8] to wedge; stuff; plug. —**atarugarse,** *v.r.* **1,** to choke. **2,** to stumble (in speaking). —**atarugamiento,** *n.m.* stuffing; choking.

atascadero (a·tas·ka'ðe·ro) *n.m.* **1,** mudhole. **2,** obstruction.

atascar (a·tas'kar) *v.t.* [*infl.*: **tocar,** 7] **1,** to clog; choke. **2,** to plug; stop up. **3,** to obstruct; impede. —**atascarse,** *v.r.* to bog down.

atasco (a'tas·ko) *n.m.* **1,** obstacle; impediment. **2,** clog; jam; obstruction.

ataúd (a·ta'uð) *n.m.* coffin.

ataviar (a·ta'βjar) *v.t.* [*infl.*: **enviar,** 22] to deck out. —**ataviarse,** *v.r.* to dress up.

atávico (a'ta·βi·ko) *adj.* atavistic.

atavío (a·ta'βi·o) *n.m.* dress; attire. —**atavíos,** *n.m.pl.* finery.

atavismo (a·ta'βis·mo) *n.m.* atavism.

ataxia (a'tak·sja) *n.f.* ataxia. —**ataxia locomotriz,** locomotor ataxia.

atece (a'te·θe; -se) *v., pres.subjve.* of **atezar.**

atecé (a·te'θe; -'se) *v., 1st pers. sing. pret.* of **atezar.**

ateísmo (a·te'is·mo) *n.m.* atheism. —**ateísta,** *n.m. & f.* atheist. —*adj.* [*also,* **ateístico**] atheistic.

atemorizar (a·te·mo·ri'θar; -'sar) *v.t.* [*infl.*: **rezar,** 10] to intimidate. —**atemorizarse,** *v.r.* to become frightened.

atención (a·ten'θjon; -'sjon) *n.f.* **1,** attention. **2,** *usu.pl.* courtesy. —**¡atención!** *interj.* attention!; look out! —**en atención a,** in view of; considering. —**prestar atención,** to pay attention.

atender (a·ten'der) *v.t. & i.* [*infl.*: **perder,** 29] **1,** to pay attention (to); attend (to). **2,** to assist; take care (of). **3,** to show courtesy (to).

ateneo (a·te'ne·o) *n.m.* club, esp. literary or artistic.

atenerse (a·te'ner·se) *v.r.* [*infl.*: **tener,** 65] *usu.fol. by* **a,** to abide (by); go (by); rely (on).

atenio (a'te·njo) *n.m.* athenium.

atenta (a'ten·ta) *n.f.* favor *(letter)* **atentamente,** *adv.* sincerely yours.

atentado (a·ten'ta·ðo) *n.m.* **1,** attempt; attack. **2,** abuse of authority. **3,** crime; offense, esp. against authority.

atentar (a·ten'tar) *v.t.* [*infl.*: **pensar,** 27] to attempt, as a crime. —**atentar a** *or* **contra,** to make an attempt on.

atento (a'ten·to) *adj.* **1,** attentive. **2,** courteous. —**atento a,** in view of; considering.

atenuación (a·te·nwa'θjon; -'sjon) *n.f.* **1,** attenuation. **2,** extenuation.

atenuar (a·te'nwar) *v.t.* [*infl.*: **continuar,** 23] **1,** to attenuate. **2,** to extenuate. —**atenuante,** *adj.* extenuating. —*n.m.* extenuating circumstance.

ateo (a'te·o) *n.m.* atheist. —*adj.* atheistic.

aterciopelado (a·ter·θjo·pe'la·ðo; a·ter·sjo-) *adj.* velvety.

aterirse (a·te'rir·se) *v.r., defective* (*used only in tenses with terminations beginning with* i) to become numb or stiff with cold.

aterrador (a·te·rra'ðor) *adj.* terrifying; appalling.

aterrar (a·te'rrar) *v.* [*infl.*: **pensar,** 27] —*v.t.* to pull down; demolish. —*v.i.* = **aterrizar.** —**aterrarse,** *v.r., naut.* to stand inshore. *This verb is regular in the following senses:* —*v.t.* to terrify. —**aterrarse,** *v.r.* to be appalled.

aterrizar (a·te·rri'θar; -'sar) *v.i., aero.* [*infl.*: **rezar,** 10] to land. —**aterrizaje,** *n.m.* landing. —**aterrizaje forzoso,** forced landing. —**pista de aterrizaje,** landing strip.

aterrorizar (a·te·rro·ri'θar; -'sar) *v.t.* [*infl.*: **rezar,** 10] to terrify. —**aterrorizarse,** *v.r.* to become terrified.

atesorar (a·te·so'rar) *v.t.* **1,** to hoard; treasure. **2,** to possess (good qualities).

atestar (a'tes·tar) *v.t.* **1**, [*infl.:* pensar, 27*] to cram; fill up; jam. **2**, [*regularly inflected*] to attest. —**atestación**, *n.f.* attestation.

atestiguar (a·tes·ti'ɣwar) *v.t.* [*infl.:* averiguar, 9*] to witness; attest to. —**atestiguación**, *n.f., also,* **atestiguamiento**, *n.m.* testimony; deposition.

atezado (a·te'θa·ðo; -'sa·ðo) *adj.* **1**, tan; tanned; swarthy. **2**, smooth; silken, as the skin.

atezar (a·te'θar; -'sar) *v.t.* [*infl.:* rezar, 10*] **1**, to tan; darken. **2**, to make smooth.

atiborrar (a·ti·βo'rrar) *v.t.* **1**, to stuff; cram. **2**, to gorge; glut.

atice (a'ti·θe; -se) *v., pres.subjve.* of **atizar**.

aticé (a·ti'θe; -'se) *v., 1st pers.sing. pret.* of **atizar**.

ático ('a·ti·ko) *n.m.* attic. —*adj.* **1**, Attic. **2**, elegant; classic.

atienda (a'tjen·da) *v., pres.subjve. of* **atender**.

atiendo (a'tjen·do) *v., pres.ind. of* **atender**.

atiene (a'tje·ne) *v.r., 3rd pers. sing. pres.ind. of* **atenerse**.

atiente (a'tjen·te) *v., pres.subjve. of* **atentar**.

atiento (a'tjen·to) *v., 1st pers. sing. pres.ind. of* **atentar**.

atierre (a'tje·rre) *v., pres.subjve. of* **aterrar**.

atierro (a'tje·rro) *v., 1st pers. sing. pres.ind. of* **aterrar**.

atiesar (a'tje·sar) *v.,* **1**, to stiffen. **2**, to tense.

atieste (a'tjes·te) *v., pres.subjve. of* **atestar**.

atiesto (a'tjes·to) *v., 1st pers. sing. pres.ind. of* **atestar**.

atigrado (a·ti'ɣra·ðo) *adj.* spotted.

atildado (a·til'da·ðo) *adj.* neat; fastidious; nice.

atinadamente (a·ti·na·ða'men·te) *adv.* **1**, wisely. **2**, pertinently.

atinar (a·ti'nar) *v.i.* to guess correctly; *slang* to hit the mark. —**atinar a**, to succeed in.

atirantar (a·ti·ran'tar) *v.t.* **1**, to tighten. **2**, to brace, make secure.

atisbar (a·tis'βar) *v.t.* to watch; spy on. —**atisbo** (a'tis·βo) *n.m.* glimpse. —**al atisbo**, on the watch.

¡atiza! (a'ti·θa; -sa) *interj.* my goodness!

atizar (a·ti'θar; -'sar) *v.t.* [*infl.:* rezar, 10*] **1**, to stir up; poke (a fire). **2**, *fig.* to rouse. **3**, *colloq.* to

deal (a blow, kick, etc.) —**atizador**, *n.m.* poker; fire iron.

atlántico (at'lan·ti·ko) *adj.* Atlantic. —*n.m., cap.* Atlantic Ocean.

atlas ('at·las) *n.m.* atlas.

atleta (at'le·ta) *n.m. & f.* athlete. —**atlético**, *adj.* athletic. —**atletismo**, *n.m.* athletics.

atmósfera (at'mos·fe·ra) *n.f.* atmosphere. —**atmosférico** (-'fe·ri·ko) *adj.* atmospheric.

atolón (a·to'lon) *n.m.* atoll.

atolondrado (a·to·lon'dra·ðo) *adj.* giddy; harebrained. —**atolondramiento**, *n.m.* giddiness.

atolondrar (a·to·lon'drar) *v.t.* to bewilder. —**atolondrarse**, *v.r.* to become confused or bewildered.

atolladero (a·to·ʎa'ðe·ro; a·to·ja-) *n.m.* **1**, mudhole. **2**, *colloq.* impasse.

atollarse (a·to'ʎar·se; -'jar·se) *v.r.* to get stuck; bog down.

atómico (a'to·mi·ko) *adj.* atomic.

atomizar (a·to·mi'θar; -'sar) *v.t.* [*infl.:* rezar, 10*] to spray; atomize. —**atomización**, *n.f.* spray. —**atomizador**, *n.m.* atomizer.

átomo ('a·to·mo) *n.m.* atom.

atonal (a·to'nal) *adj.* atonal. —**atonalidad**, *n.f.* atonality.

atónito (a'to·ni·to) *adj.* astonished.

atontar (a·ton'tar) *v.t.* to stun. —**atontarse**, *v.r.* **1**, to become stupid. **2**, to be stunned. —**atontadamente**, *adv.* foolishly. —**atontado**, *adj.* stunned; groggy.

atorar (a·to'rar) *v.t.* to choke; plug; clog. —**atorarse**, *v.r.* to choke; become plugged or clogged.

atormentar (a·tor·men'tar) *v.t.* to torment; torture. —**atormentarse**, *v.r.* to distress oneself. —**atormentador**, *n.m.* tormentor. —*adj.* tormenting.

atornillar (a·tor·ni'ʎar; -'jar) *v.t.* to screw. —**atornillador**, *n.m.* screwdriver.

atorrante (a·to'rran·te) *n.m., Amer.* tramp; bum.

atosigar (a·to·si'ɣar) *v.t.* [*infl.:* pagar, 8*] **1**, to poison. **2**, to harry; press.

atóxico (a'tok·si·ko) *adj.* nontoxic.

atrabilis (a·tra'βi·lis) *n.m.* **1**, black bile. **2**, ill humor. —**atrabiliario** (a·tra·βi'lja·rjo) *adj.* **1**, atrabilious. **2**, *colloq.* ill-tempered.

atracadero (a·tra·ka'ðe·ro) *n.m.* dock; landing.

atracar (a·tra'kar) *v.t.* [*infl.:* tocar, 7*] **1**, to gorge. **2**, to hold up; rob. **3**, to swindle. **4,** *colloq.* to place or hold against. —*v.i.* to dock; berth. —**atracarse,** *v.r.* to gorge; stuff oneself. —**atracarse a,** *colloq.* to get close to; hug.

atracción (a·trak'θjon; -'sjon) *n.f.* **1,** attraction. **2,** amusement.

atraco (a'tra·ko) *n.m.* holdup; swindle.

atracón (a·tra'kon) *n.m.* overeating; gorging. —**darse un atracón,** to gorge oneself.

atractivo (a·trak'ti·βo) *adj.* attractive. — *n.m.* **1,** attraction. **2,** attractiveness.

atraer (a·tra'er) *v.t.* [*infl.:* traer, 67] to attract.

atragantarse (a·tra·ɣan'tar·se) *v.r.* to choke; gag.

atrancar (a·tran'kar) *v.t.* [*infl.:* tocar, 7] = **trancar.** —**trancarse,** *v.r., Amer.* to be stubborn or opinionated.

atrapar (a·tra'par) *v.t.* to catch; trap.

atraque (a'tra·ke) *v., pres.subjve. of* **atracar.**

atraqué (a·tra'ke) *v., 1st pers. sing. pret. of* **atracar.**

atrás (a'tras) *adv.* back; behind; ago. —¡**atrás!** *interj.* back!

atrasado (a·tra'sa·ðo) *adj.* **1,** late. **2,** in arrears. **3,** backward. **4,** slow, as a clock. **5,** retarded. —**número atrasado,** back number.

atrasar (a·tra'sar) *v.t.* **1,** to retard. **2,** to set back (hands of a clock). —**atrasarse,** *v.r.* **1,** to lag behind; be late. **2,** to be slow, as a clock.

atraso (a'tra·so) *n.m.* **1,** tardiness. **2,** delay; lag. **3,** backwardness. **4,** *pl.* arrears. **5,** mental retardation.

atravesado (a·tra·βe'sa·ðo) *adj.* **1,** crosswise. **2,** somewhat crosseyed. **3,** crossbred; hybrid; mongrel. **4,** ill-natured.

atravesar (a·tra·βe'sar) *v.t.* [*infl.:* pensar, 27] **1,** to cross. **2,** to pierce. **3,** to lay across. —**atravesarse,** *v.r.* to interfere; get in the way.

atrayente (a·tra'jen·te) *adj.* attractive.

atreverse (a·tre'βer·se) *v.r.* to venture; dare. —**atrevido,** *adj.* bold; impudent. —**atrevimiento,** *n.m.* audacity; impudence.

atribución (a·tri·βu'θjon; -'sjon) *n.f.* **1,** attribution. **2,** *usu.pl.* prerogatives; powers.

atribuir (a·tri·βu'ir) *v.t.* [*infl.:*

huir, 26] to attribute. —**atribuible,** *adj.* attributable.

atribular (a·tri·βu'lar) *v.t.* to pain; grieve. —**atribularse,** *v.r.* to suffer pain or grief.

atributo (a·tri'βu·to) *n.m.* attribute. —**atributivo,** *adj.* attributive.

atril (a'tril) *n.m.* **1,** lectern. **2,** music stand.

atrincherar (a·trin·tʃe'rar) *v.t.* to entrench. —**atrincherarse,** *v.r.* to entrench oneself; take cover, as in trenches. —**atrincheramiento,** *n.m.* entrenchment.

atrio ('a·trjo) *n.m.* entrance hall; inner court; atrium.

atrocidad (a·tro·θi'ðað; -si'ðað) *n.f.* **1,** atrocity. **2,** *colloq.* enormity. —¡**qué atrocidad!,** how terrible!

atrofia (a'tro·fja) *n.f.* atrophy. —**atrofiarse,** *v.r.* to atrophy.

atronar (a·tro'nar) *v.t.* [*infl.:* acostar, 28] **1,** to deafen. **2,** to discomfit; rattle. —**atronado,** *adj.* reckless; harebrained; scatterbrained. —**atronador,** *adj.* deafening; thunderous.

atropellar (a·tro·pe'ʎar; -'jar) *v.t.* **1,** to run over; trample. **2,** *fig.* to ride roughshod over. —**atropellarse,** *v.r.* to stumble over oneself in haste. —**atropellado,** *adj.* precipitate.

atropello (a·tro'pe·ʎo; -jo) *n.m.* **1,** trampling; a running or being run over. **2,** *fig.* abuse; outrage. *Also* **atropellamiento.**

atropina (a·tro'pi·na) *n.f.* atropine.

atroz (a'troθ; a'tros) *adj.* atrocious outrageous.

atún (a'tun) *n.m.* tuna.

aturdido (a·tur'ði·ðo) *adj.* scatterbrained.

aturdir (a·tur'ðir) *v.t.* to stun; bewilder. —**aturdirse,** *v.r.* to be stunned or bewildered. —**aturdimiento,** *n.m.* bewilderment.

aturrullar (a·tu·ru'ʎar; -'jar) *also* **aturullar** (a·tu·rru–) *v.t.* to confuse; flurry; fluster. —**aturullamiento,** *n.m.* confusion; flurry; fluster.

audacia (au'ða·θja; -sja) *n.f.* audacity.

audaz (au'ðaθ; -'ðas) *adj.* audacious.

audible (au'ði·βle) *adj.* audible.

audición (au·ði'θjon; -'sjon) *n.f.* **1,** audition. **2,** radio performance. **3,** musical program; recital.

audiencia (au'ðjen·θja; -sja) *n.f.*

1, audience; hearing. **2,** *law* district court. **3,** court building. **—dar audiencia,** to grant a hearing.

audífono (au'ði·fo·no) *n.m.* **1,** hearing aid; audiphone. **2,** = **auricular.**

audiovisual (au·djo·βi'swal) *adj.* audiovisual.

auditivo (au·ði'ti·βo) *adj.* auditory.

auditor (au·ði'tor) *n.m.* **1,** *law* judge advocate. **2,** *Amer.* auditor.

auditorio (au·ði'to·rjo) *n.m.* audience.

auge ('au·xe) *n.m.* **1,** culmination. **2,** *colloq.* increment.

augur (au'yur) *n.m.* augur.

augurar (au·yu'rar) *v.t.* to augur. **—augurio** (-'yu·rjo) *n.m.* augury.

augusto (au'yus·to) *adj.* august.

aula ('au·la) *n.f.* **1,** classroom. **2,** lecture hall. **3,** *poet.* palace.

aulaga (au'la·ya) *n.f.* furze.

aullar (a·u'ʎar; -'jar) *v.i.* [*infl.:* **continuar, 23**] to howl.

aullido (au'ʎi·ðo; -'ji·ðo) *n.m.* howl.

aumentación (au·men·ta'θjon; -'sjon) *n.f.* **1,** augmentation; increase. **2,** *rhet.* climax.

aumentar (au·men'tar) *v.t.* to augment; increase. **—aumentativo,** *n.m. & adj., gram.* augmentative.

aumento (au'men·to) *n.m.* **1,** augmentation; increase. **2,** enlargement. **3,** promotion. **4,** *gram.* augment.

aun (aun) *adv.* even. **—aun así,** even so. **—aun cuando,** even though; although. **—ni aun,** not even.

aún (a'un) *adv.* **1,** yet; still. **2,** also; furthermore.

aunque (a'un·ke; 'aun·ke) *conj.* although.

aura ('au·ra) *n.f.* **1,** aura. **2,** *poet.* breeze; breath. **3,** popular acclaim. **4,** *ornith.* turkey buzzard.

áureo ('au·re·o) *adj.* of gold; golden.

aureola (au·re'o·la) *also,* **auréola** (au're-) *n.f.* halo.

aureomicina (au·re·o·mi'θi·na; -'si·na) *n.f.* aureomycin.

aurícula (au'ri·ku·la) *n.f.* auricle (*of the heart*).

auricular (au·ri·ku'lar) *adj., anat.* auricular. **—n.m.** telephone receiver; headphone.

aurífero (au'ri·fe·ro) *adj.* auriferous.

auriga (au'ri·ya) *n.m.* charioteer.

aurora (au'ro·ra) *n.f.* dawn; aurora. **—aurora austral,** aurora australis. **—aurora boreal,** aurora borealis.

auscultar (aus·kul'tar) *v.t.* to auscultate. **—auscultación,** *n.f.* auscultation.

ausencia (au'sen·θja; -sja) *n.f.* absence.

ausentar (au·sen'tar) *v.t.* to drive away; cause to depart. **—ausentarse,** *v.r.* to absent oneself; leave.

ausente (au'sen·te) *adj.* **1,** absent. **2,** missing. **—n.m.** & *f.* **1,** absentee. **2,** missing person. **—ausentismo,** *n.m.* = **absentismo.**

auspicio (aus'pi·θjo; -sjo) *n.m.* **1,** omen. **2,** patronage. **—auspicios,** *n.m.pl.* auspices. **—auspiciar,** *v.t., Amer.* to sponsor. **—auspicioso,** *adj., Amer.* auspicious.

austero (aus'te·ro) *adj.* austere. **—austeridad,** *n.f.* austerity.

austral (aus'tral) *adj.* southern; austral. **—n.m.** former monetary unit of Argentina.

austro ('aus·tro) *n.m.* **1,** south wind. **2,** south.

autarquía (au·tar'ki·a) *n.f.* **1,** autarchy. **2,** autarky.

autárquico (au'tar·ki·ko) *adj.* **1,** autarchic; autarchical. **2,** autarkic; autarkical.

autenticar (au·ten·ti'kar) *v.t.* [*infl.:* **tocar, 7**] to authenticate. **—autenticación,** *n.f.* authentication.

auténtico (au'ten·ti·ko) *adj.* authentic. **—autenticidad** (-θi'ðað; -si'ðað) *n.f.* authenticity.

autista (au'ti·sta) *adj.* autistic. **—autismo,** *n.m.* autism.

auto ('au·to) *n.m.* **1,** writ; judicial act. **2,** *colloq.,* auto; automobile. **3,** short play.

autoadhesivo (au·to·a·ðe'si·βo) *adj.* self-adhesive.

autobiografía (au·tc·βjo·yra-'fi·a) *n.f.* autobiography. **—autobiográfico** (-'yra·fi·ko) *adj.* autobiographical.

autobús (au·to'βus) *n.m.* omnibus; bus.

autocamión (au·to·ka'mjon) *n.m.* truck.

autocar (au·to'kar) *n.m.* bus; motorcoach.

autocargador (au·to·kar·ya'ðor) *adj.* self-loading.

autocracia (au·to'kra·θja; -sja) *n.f.* autocracy. **—autócrata** (-'to-

kra·ta) *n.m. & f.* autocrat. —**auto-crático** (-'kra·ti·ko) *adj.* autocratic.
autocrítica (au·to'kri·ti·ka) *n.f.* self-criticism.
autóctono (au'tok·to·no) *adj.* native; aboriginal.
autodestrucción *n.f.* self-destruction.
autodeterminación *n.f.* self-determination.
autodidacto (au·to·ði'ðak·to) *adj.* self-educated; self-taught.
autodisciplina *n.f.* self-discipline.
autógrafo (au'to·ɣra·fo) *n.m.* autograph.
autómata (au'to·ma·ta) *n.m.* automaton.
automático (au·to'ma·ti·ko) *adj.* automatic.
automatizar (au·to·ma·ti'θar; -'sar) *v.t.* [*infl.:* rezar, 10] to automate. —**automatización**, *n.f.* automation.
automotor (au·to·mo'tor) *adj.* 1, automotive. 2, self-propelled. —*n.m.* railway motor coach.
automotriz (au·to·mo'triθ; -'tris) *adj.fem.* [*pl.* -**trices** (-'tri·θes; -ses)] self-propelled.
automóvil (au·to'mo·βil) *adj. & n.m.* automobile. —**automovilismo**, *n.m.* motoring. —**automovilista**, *n.m. & f.* motoring devotee; motorist. —**automovilístico**, *adj.* automobile (*attrib.*).
autonomía (au·to·no'mi·a) *n.f.* autonomy. —**autónomo** (au'to·no·mo) *adj.* autonomous.
autonómico (au·to'no·mi·ko) *adj.* autonomic.
autopista (au·to'pis·ta) *n.f.* turnpike; parkway.
autopropulsado (au·to·pro·pul'sa·ðo) *adj.* self-propelled.
autopsia (au'top·sja) *n.f.* autopsy.
autor (au'tor) *n.* author. —**autora** (-'to·ra) *n.f.* authoress.
autoridad (au·to·ri'ðað) *n.f.* authority.
autoritario (au·to·ri'ta·rjo) *adj.* authoritative. —*adj. & n.m.* authoritarian.
autorizado (au·to·ri'θa·ðo; -'sa·ðo) *adj.* 1, authorized. 2, authoritative.
autorizar (au·to·ri'θar; -'sar) *v.t.* [*infl.:* rezar, 10] to authorize. —**autorización**, *n.f.* authorization.
autorretrato (au·to·rre'tra·to) *n.m.* self-portrait.

autorriel (au·to'rrjel) *n.m.* = **autovía**.
autoservicio *n.m.* self-service.
autostop (au·to'stop) *n.m.* hitch-hiking. —**hacer autostop**, to hitchhike.
autosugestión *n.f.* autosuggestion.
autovía (au·to'βi·a) *n.m.* or *f.* railway motor coach.
autumnal (au·tum'nal) *adj.* autumnal.
auxiliar (au·ksi'ljar) *v.t.* to aid; assist. —*adj.* auxiliary. —*n.m. & f.* aid; assistant; auxiliary.
auxilio (au'ksi·ljo) *n.m.* assistance. —¡**auxilio!**, *interj.* help! —**prestar auxilio**, to aid.
aval (a'βal) *n.m.* 1, endorsement; countersignature. 2, affidavit. —**avalar**, *v.t.* to vouch for, esp. by an affidavit.
avalancha (a·βa'lan·tʃa) *n.f.* avalanche.
avalorar (a·βa·lo'rar) *v.t.* to evaluate.
avaluar (a·βa'lwar) *v.t.* = **valuar**. —**avaluación**, *n.f.*, *also*, **avalúo** (-'lu·o) *n.m.* = **valuación**.
avanzar (a·βan'θar; -'sar) *v.t. & i.* [*infl.:* rezar, 10] to advance. —**avance**, *n.m.* 1, advance. 2, preview. —**avanzada**, *n.f.* vanguard; outpost.
avaricia (a·βa'ri·θja; -sja) *n.f.* avarice. —**avaricioso**, *adj.* avaricious.
avariento (a·βa'rjen·to) *adj.* avaricious; miserly. —*n.m.* miser. *Also*, **avaro** (a'βa·ro) *adj. & n.m.*
avasallar (a·βa·sa'ʎar; -'jar) *v.t.* to subject; enslave. —**avasallarse**, *v.r.* 1, to submit. 2, to become a vassal.
ave ('a·βe) *n.f.* bird. —**ave de corral**, domestic or barnyard fowl. —**ave cantora**, songbird. —**ave de paso**, bird of passage. —**ave de rapiña**, bird of prey.
avecinarse (a·βe·θi'nar·se; a·βe·si-) *v.r.* to approach.
avecindarse (a·βe·θin'dar·se; a·βe·sin-) *v.r.* to settle; take up residence.
avechucho (a·βe'tʃu·tʃo) *n.m.* 1, ugly bird. 2, *colloq.* queer duck; odd bird.
avefría (a·βe'fri·a) *n.f.* plover.
avejentarse (a·βe·xen'tar·se) *v.r.* to age prematurely.
avellana (a·βe'ʎa·na; -'ja·na) *n.f.* filbert; hazelnut. —**avellanar**, *n.m. also*, **avellanedo**, *n.m.* **avella-**

neda, *n.f.* hazel grove. **—avellano,** *n.m.* hazel.

avellanar (a·βe·ʎa'nar; -ja'nar) *v.t.* to countersink. **—avellanador,** *n.m.* countersink *(tool).*

avemaría (a·βe·ma'ri·a) *n.f.* Hail Mary. **—¡Ave María!,** *interj.* Good Heavens! **—en un avemaría,** in a jiffy.

avena (a'βe·na) *n.f.* oats.

avenencia (a·βe'nen·θja; -sja) *n.f.* agreement; understanding.

avenida (a·βe'ni·ða) *n.f.* **1,** avenue. **2,** flood; flash flood.

avenir (a·βe'nir) *v.t.* [*infl.:* **venir, 69**] reconcile. **—avenirse,** *v.r.* to agree; compromise.

aventadura (a·βen·ta'ðu·ra) *n.f., vet.* windgall.

aventajar (a·βen·ta'xar) *v.t.* **1,** to give preference or advantage to. **2,** to surpass; excel. **—aventajarse,** *v.r.* **1,** to gain preference or advantage. **2,** to excel. **—aventajado,** *adj.* outstanding.

aventar (a·βen'tar) *v.t.* [*infl.:* **pensar, 27**] **1,** to winnow. **2,** *colloq.* to throw out; eject (a person). **3,** *Amer., colloq.* to throw; hurl. **—aventarse,** *v.r.* **1,** to swell. **2,** *colloq.* to escape. **—aventamiento,** *n.m.* winnowing. **—aventón** (-'ton) *n.m., Amer., colloq.* shove; push.

aventura (a·βen'tu·ra) *n.f.* **1,** adventure. **2,** venture. **—aventurado,** *adj.* venturesome; risky. **—aventurar,** *v.t.* to venture. **—aventurarse,** *v.r.* to risk oneself; *colloq.* to take a chance. **—aventurero,** *n.m.* adventurer. **—aventurera,** *n.f.* adventuress.

avergonzar (a·βer·ɣon'θar; -'sar) *v.t.* [*infl.:* **acostar, 28; rezar, 10**] to shame. **—avergonzarse,** *v.r.* to be ashamed.

avería (a·βe'ri·a) *n.f.* **1,** damage. **2,** defect; imperfection. **—averiar,** *v.t.* [*infl.:* **enviar, 22**] to damage. **—averiarse,** *v.r.* to suffer damage.

averiguación (a·βe·ri·ɣwa'θjon; -'sjon) *n.f.* **1,** ascertainment. **2,** inquiry; investigation.

averiguar (a·βe·ri'ɣwar) *v.t.* [*infl.:* **9**] to ascertain.

averno (a·βe'ri·no) *n.m.* hell; Hades.

averrugarse (a·βe·rru'ɣar·se) *v.r.* [*infl.:* **pagar, 8**] to become warty. **—averrugado,** *adj.* warty.

aversión (a·βer'sjon) *n.f.* aversion.

avestruz (a·βes'truθ; -'trus) *n.m.* ostrich.

avetoro (a·βe'to·ro) *n.m.* bittern. *Also,* **ave toro.**

avezado (a·βe'θa·ðo; -'sa·ðo) *adj.* **1,** inured; accustomed. **2,** experienced; well versed.

aviación (a·βja'θjon; -'sjon) *n.f.* **1,** aviation. **2,** air force.

aviador (a·βja'ðor) *n.m.* aviator **—aviatriz** (-'triθ; -'tris) [*pl.* **-trices** (-'tri·θes; -ses)] *also,* **aviadora,** *n.f.* aviatrix.

aviar (a'βjar) *v.t.* [*infl.:* **enviar, 22**] **1,** to get ready; prepare. **2,** *colloq.* to equip; fit out. **—aviado,** *adj., colloq.* in a quandary; in a tight spot.

avidez (a·βi'ðeθ; -'ðes) *n.f.* avidity **—ávido** ('a·βi·ðo) *adj.* avid.

aviente (a'βjen·te) *v., pres.subjve.* of **aventar.**

aviento (a'βjen·to) *v., pres.ind. of* **aventar.**

avieso (a'βje·so) *adj.* perverse; evil-minded.

avillanar (a·βi·ʎa'nar; -ja'nar) *v.t.* to debase. **—avillanarse,** *v.r.* to degenerate. **—avillanado,** *adj.* vile.

avinagrado (a·βi·na'ɣra·ðo) *adj.* **1,** sour; vinegary. **2,** *colloq.* bad-tempered.

avión (a'βjon) *n.m.* airplane **—avión de caza,** pursuit plane. **—avión de propulsión** (*or* **reacción) a chorro,** jet plane.

avíos (a'βi·os) *n.m.pl.* equipment.

avisar (a·βi'sar) *v.t.* to inform; announce; advise. **—avisado,** *adj.* judicious.

aviso (a'βi·so) *n.m.* **1,** warning. **2,** notice; advertisement. **3,** sign; poster. **—sobre aviso,** on notice; alerted.

avispa (a'βis·pa) *n.f.* **1,** wasp. **2,** clever person. **—avispado,** *adj.* clever; sharp. **—avispar,** *v.t.* to stir up; rouse.

avispero (a·βis'pe·ro) *n.m.* **1,** wasp's nest. **2,** swarm of wasps. **3,** *colloq.* hornet's nest; touchy matter.

avispón (a·βis'pon) *n.m.* hornet.

avistar (a·βis'tar) *v.t.* to sight; catch sight of. **—avistarse,** *v.r.* to have an interview.

avivar (a·βi'βar) *v.t.* to enliven; inflame.

avizor (a·βi'θor; -'sor) *adj.* watchful. **—n.m.** watcher. **—avizorar,** *v.t.* to watch.

axial (a'ksjal) *adj.* axial.

axila (a'ksi·la) *n.f.* armpit.

axioma (a'ksjo·ma) *n.m.* axiom.
—**axiomático** (-'ma·ti·ko) *adj.* axiomatic.

axis ('ak·sis) *n.m.sing. &. pl., anat.* axis.

¡ay! (ai) *interj.* alas!; ouch! —**¡ay de mí!**, woe is me!

aya ('a·ja) *n.f.* governess.

ayer (a'jer) *adv. & n.m.* yesterday.

ayo ('a·jo) *n.m.* tutor; preceptor.

ayuda (a'ju·ða) *n.m.* help. —**ayuda de cámara**, valet.

ayudante (a·ju'ðan·te) *n.m.* **1,** helper. **2,** *mil.* aide; adjutant.

ayudar (a·ju'ðar) *v.t. & i.* to help.

ayunar (a·ju'nar) *v.i.* to fast. —**ayunador**, *n.m.* one who fasts.

ayuno (a'ju·no) *adj.* fasting. —*n.m.* fast; fasting. —**en ayunas**, on an empty stomach. —**en ayunas de; ayuno de**, abysmally ignorant of. —**quedarse en ayunas**, *colloq.* to miss the point.

ayuntamiento (a·jun·ta'mjen·to) *n.m.* **1,** municipal government. **2,** city hall. **3,** union; coupling.

azabache (a·θa'βa·tʃe; a·sa-) *n.m.* **1,** jet *(mineral).* **2,** jet-black color. —**azabachado**, *adj.* jet; of or like jet; jet-black.

azada (a'θa·ða; a'sa-) *n.f.* hoe. —**azadón**, *n.m.* large curved hoe. —**azadonar**, *v.t. & i.* to hoe.

azafata (a·θa'fa·ta; a·sa-) *n.f.* **1,** lady in waiting. **2,** hostess; stewardess.

azafate (a·θa'fa·te; a·sa-) *n.m.* tray; server.

azafrán (a·θa'fran; a·sa-) *n.m.* saffron.

azagaya (a·θa'ya·ja; a·sa-) *n.f.* javelin.

azahar (a·θa'ar; a·sa-) *n.m.* citrus blossom.

azalea (a·θa'le·a; a·sa-) *n.f.* azalea.

azar (a'θar; a'sar) *n.m.* hazard; chance. —**al azar**, at random.

azaroso (a·θa'ro·so; a·sa-) *adj.* **1,** hazardous. **2,** unfortunate.

azimut (a·θi'mut; a·si-) *n.m.* = **acimut.**

ázimo ('a·θi·mo; 'a·si-) *adj.* unleavened.

ázoe ('a·θo·e; -so·e) *n.m.* nitrogen. —**azoado**, *adj.* = **nitrogenado.** —**azoato**, *n.m.* = **nitrato.**

azogue (a'θo·ɣe; a'so-) *n.m.* mercury. —**azogar**, *v.t.* [*infl.:* **pagar, 8**] to coat with mercury; to silver (a mirror). —**ser un azogue**, *colloq.* to be restless.

azoico (a'θoi·ko; a'soi-) *adj.* **1,** *chem.* = **nítrico. 2,** *geol.* azoic.

azor (a'θor; a'sor) *n.m.* goshawk.

azorar (a·θo'rar; a·so-) *v.t.* **1,** to confound; abash. **2,** to excite; rouse.

azotar (a·θo'tar; a·so-) *v.t.* to beat; lash; whip. —**azotaina** (-'tai·na) *n.f., colloq.* spanking; whipping. —**azotazo** (-'ta·θo; -so) *n.m.* blow with a whip or rod; spank.

azote (a'θo·te; a'so-) *n.m.* **1,** whip; rod; scourge. **2,** whipping; beating.

azotea (a·θo'te·a; a·so-) *n.f.* flat roof.

azteca (aθ'te·ka; as-) *adj. & n.m. & f.* Aztec.

azúcar (a'θu·kar; a'su-) *n.m. or f.* sugar. —**azucarado**, *adj.* sugary. —**azucarar**, *v.t.* to sweeten. —**azucararse**, *v.r., Amer.* to crystallize. —**azucarera**, *n.f.* sugar bowl. —**azucarero**, *adj.* pert. to sugar. —*n.m.* sugar producer. —**azúcar blanca**, refined sugar. —**azúcar cande**, rock candy. —**azúcar negra, morena** *or* **prieta**, brown sugar.

azucena (a·θu'θe·na; a·su'se-) *n.f.* white lily.

azuela (a'θwe·la; a'swe-) *n.f.* adz.

azufaifo (a·θu'fai·fo; a·su-) *n.m.* jujube *(tree).* —**azufaifa**, *n.f.* jujube *(fruit).*

azufre (a'θu·fre; a'su-) *n.m.* sulfur. —**azufrado**, *adj.* sulfured; sulfurated; sulfurous. —*n.m.* sulfuring. —**azufrar**, *v.t.* to sulfur; sulfurate. —**azufrera**, *n.f.* sulfur mine.

azul (a'θul; -'sul) *adj. & n.m.* blue. —**azulado**, *adj.* bluish; blue.

azular (a·θu'lar; a·su-) *v.t.* to blue; color or dye blue. —**azularse**, *v.r.* to turn blue.

azulejo (a·θu'le·xo; a·su-) *n.m.* glazed tile. —**azulejar**, *v.t.* to tile.

azulino (a·θu'li·no; a·su-) *adj.* bluish.

azur (a'θur; a'sur) *adj. & n.m.* azure.

azuzar (a·θu'θar; -su'sar) *v.t.* [*infl.:* **rezar, 10**] **1,** to sick; set (dogs) on. **2,** *fig.* to incite.

B

B, b (be) *n.f.* 2nd letter of the Spanish alphabet.

baba ('ba·βa) *n.f.* drivel; slaver; slime. **—babaza,** *n.f.* slime.

babear (ba·βe'ar) *v.i.* to drivel; slaver; drool. **—babeo** (-'βe·o) *n.m.* driveling; drooling.

babel (ba'βel) *n.m. or f.* **1,** babel; bedlam; confusion. **2,** *cap.* Babel.

babero (ba'βe·ro) *n.m.* bib.

Babia ('ba·βja) *n.f.* a mountain district of León. **—estar en Babia,** *colloq.* to be absentminded; to be forgetful.

babilonia (ba·βi'lo·nja) *n.f.* **1,** babel; confusion. **2,** *cap.* Babylonia; Babylon. **—babilonio,** *adj. & n.m.* Babylonian.

babilónico (ba·βi'lo·ni·ko) *adj.* **1,** Babylonian. **2,** sumptuous; magnificent.

babor (ba'βor) *n.m.,* *naut.* port; larboard.

babosa (ba'βo·sa) *n.f.,* *zoöl.* slug.

babosear (ba·βo·se'ar) *v.t.* to drivel; slaver.

baboso (ba'βo·so) *adj.* slippery.

babucha (ba'βu·tʃa) *n.f.* slipper.

babuino (ba'βwi·no) *n.m.* baboon.

baca ('ba·ka) *n.f.* top of a bus, stagecoach, etc., covered with canvas or leather, used for passengers or baggage; also, the cover itself.

bacalao (ba·ka'la·o) *also,* **bacallao** (-'ʎa·o; -'ja·o) *n.m.* **1,** codfish. **2,** *colloq.* skinny person.

bacanal (ba·ka'nal) *n.f.* bacchanal. **—adj.** bacchanalian. **—bacanales,** *n.f.pl.* bacchanalia.

bacará (ba·ka'ra) *n.m.* baccarat.

baceta (ba'θe·ta; -'se·ta) *n.f., cards* widow.

bacía (ba'θi·a; -'si·a) *n.f.* metal basin; shaving dish.

bacilo (ba'θi·lo; -'si·lo) *n.m.* bacillus.

bacín (ba'θin; -'sin) *n.m.* **1,** chamber pot. **2,** beggar's bowl. *Also,* **bacineta, bacinica, bacinilla.**

bacteria (bak'te·rja) *n.f.* bacterium. **—bacterias,** *n.f.pl.* bacteria. **—bacteriano** (-'rja·no), *also,* **bacterial** (-'rjal), **bactérico** (-'te·ri·ko) *adj.* bacterial.

bacteriología (bak·te·rjo·lo'xi·a) *n.f.* bacteriology. **—bacteriológico**

(-'lo·xi·ko) *adj.* bacteriological. **—bacteriólogo** (-'rjo·lo·ɣo) *n.m.* bacteriologist.

báculo ('ba·ku·lo) *n.m.* **1,** stick; staff. **2,** *fig.* support; aid.

bache ('ba·tʃe) *n.m.* rut; pothole.

bachiller (ba·tʃi'ʎer; -'jer) *n.m.* **1,** recipient of a college degree; bachelor. **2,** prattler; chatterbox. **—bachillerato,** *n.m.* baccalaureate.

bada ('ba·ða) *n.f.* = **rinoceronte.**

badajada (ba·ða'xa·ða) *n.f.* **1,** stroke of a bell. **2,** foolish talk; nonsense.

badajo (ba'ða·xo) *n.m.* **1,** clapper of a bell. **2,** *colloq.* prattler.

badán (ba'ðan) *n.m.* trunk of a plant or animal.

badana (ba'ða·na) *n.f.* dressed sheepskin. **—zurrarle a uno la badana,** *colloq.* to tan someone's hide; give a dressing-down.

badén (ba'ðen) *n.m.* natural drainage ditch; gully.

badulaque (ba·ðu'la·ke) *n.m.* fool; sap.

bagaje (ba'ɣa·xe) *n.m.* **1,** beast of burden. **2,** *mil.* baggage.

bagasa (ba'ɣa·sa) *n.f.* **1,** prostitute. **2,** baggage.

bagatela (ba·ɣa'te·la) *n.f.* bagatelle; trifle.

bagazo (ba'ɣa·θo; -so) *n.m.* bagasse.

bagre ('ba·ɣre) *n.m.,* *Amer.* a kind of catfish.

bagual (ba'ɣwal) *adj., Amer.* wild; untamed.

¡bah! (ba) *interj.* bah!

bahía (ba'i·a) *n.f.* bay; harbor.

bahuno (ba'u·no) *also,* **bajuno** (-'xu·no) *adj.* depraved; vile.

bailar (bai'lar) *v.i. & t.* **1,** to dance. **2,** to spin. **—bailador** (-'ðor) *n.m.* dancer. **—bailarín** (-'rin) *n.m.* [*fem.* **-ina**] dancer.

baile ('bai·le) *n.m.* dance; ball; ballet.

bailía (bai'li·a) *n.f.* bailiwick.

bailotear (bai·lo·te'ar) *v.i.* to hop about, as in dancing. **—bailoteo** (-'te·o) *n.m.* dancing; hopping.

baja ('ba·xa) *n.f.* **1,** fall (in price); diminution. **2,** *mil.* casualty. **—dar de baja,** *mil.* to report as missing, or as a casualty. **—darse de baja,** to resign.

bajá (ba'xa) *n.m.* pasha.

bajada (ba·xa·da) *n.f.* slope; descent.

bajamar (ba·xa'mar) *n.f.* low tide.

bajamente (ba·xa'men·te) *adv.* basely; meanly.

bajar (ba'xar) *v.i.* to descend; alight. **—v.t.** to lower; reduce. **—bajarse,** *v.r.* 1, to descend; alight. 2, to grovel.

bajareque (ba·xa're·ke) *n.m., Cuba* hovel; shack.

bajel (ba'xel) *n.m.* boat; vessel.

bajero (ba'xe·ro) *adj.* lower; under; placed or used below or under.

bajete (ba'xe·te) *n.m.* short person; shorty.

bajeza (ba'xe·θa; -sa) *n.f.* baseness; meanness.

bajío (ba'xi·o) *n.m.* 1, shoal; sand bank. 2, *Amer.* lowland.

bajista (ba'xis·ta) *n.m., fin.* bear.

bajo ('ba·xo) *adj.* 1, short; low. 2, soft; not loud. 3, *mus.* bass. 4, shallow. 5, base; mean; vulgar. **—n.m.** 1, deep place. 2, shoal. 3, *mus.* bass. **—prep.** beneath; under. **—adv.** 1, below. 2, softly.

bajón (ba'xon) *n.m.* 1, bassoon. 2, bassoonist. **—bajonista,** *n.m. & f.* bassoonist.

bajorrelieve (ba·xo·rre'lje·βe) *n.m.* bas-relief.

bala ('ba·la) *n.f.* 1, bullet; shot. 2, bale.

balada (ba'la·ða) *n.f.* ballad.

baladí (ba·la'ði) *adj.* trivial; worthless.

baladrar (ba·la'ðrar) *v.i.* to shout; cry. **—baladro** (-'la·ðro) *n.m.* shout; howl.

baladronear (ba·la·ðro·ne'ar) *v.i. & t.* 1, to boast. 2, to bluff; bully. **—baladrón,** *n.m.* boaster; bully. **—baladronada,** *n.f.* boast; bluff.

bálago ('ba·la·ɣo) *n.m.* 1, grain stalk; straw. 2, [*also,* **balaguero** (-'ɣe·ro)] haystack.

balance (ba'lan·θe; -se) *n.m.* 1, oscillation. 2, equilibrium. 3, *comm.* balance; balance sheet. 4, *naut.; aero.* roll. **—balance comercial,** balance of trade.

balancear (ba·lan·θe'ar; -se'ar) *v.i.* 1, to roll; sway. 2, to waver. 3, to teeter; seesaw. **—v.t.** to balance. **—balanceo** (-'θe·o; -'se·o) *n.m.* balancing; wavering.

balancín (ba·lan'θin; -'sin) *n.m.* 1,

crossbeam; balance beam. 2, outrigger *(of a canoe).* 3, seesaw. 4, whiffletree. 5, balancing pole.

balandra (ba'lan·dra) *n.f.* sloop. **—balandro,** *n.m.* small sloop; fishing boat.

balandrán (ba·lan'dran) *n.m.* cassock.

bálano ('ba·la·no) *also,* **balano** (-'la·no) *n.m., anat.* glans.

balanza (ba'lan·θa; -sa) *n.f.* scale; balance. **—balanza de comercio,** balance of trade.

balar (ba'lar) *v.i.* to bleat.

balasto (ba'las·to) *n.m., R.R.* ballast.

balaustre (ba'laus·tre) *n.m.* baluster. **—balaustrada,** *n.f.* balustrade.

balazo (ba'la·θo; -so) *n.m.* 1, shot. 2, bullet wound.

balboa (bal'βo·a) *n.m.* monetary unit of Panama; balboa.

balbucear (bal·βu·θe'ar; -se'ar) *v.i.* to babble; prattle. **—balbucencia,** *n.f.* babbling; prattling. **balbucco** (-'θe·o; -'se·o) *n.m.* babble; prattle.

balbucir (bal·βu'θir; -'sir) *v.i., defective (used only in tenses with terminations beginning with i)* = **balbucear.**

balcánico (bal'ka·ni·ko) *adj.* Balkan. **—los Balcanes,** the Balkans.

balcón (bal'kon) *n.m.* 1, balcony. 2, railing.

baldaquín (bal·da'kin) *n.m.* canopy.

baldar (bal'dar) *v.t.* 1, to cripple. 2, to bother. 3, *cards* to trump. **—baldarse,** *v.r.* 1, to become crippled. 2, to be exhausted.

balde ('bal·de) *n.m.* bucket; pail. **—de balde,** *adv.* gratis; free. **—en balde,** in vain.

baldear (bal·de'ar) *v.i.* to flush or drench with pails of water.

baldío (bal'di·o) *adj.* untilled; uncultivated.

baldón (bal'don) *n.m.* 1, affront; insult. 2, blot; stain; stigma. **—baldonar,** *v.t.* to insult; affront.

baldosa (bal'do·sa) *n.f.* 1, flat paving stone. 2, floor tile. **—baldosado** (-'sa·ðo) *n.m.* tile pavement; tile flooring. **—baldosar** (-'sar) *v.t.* to tile; pave with tile.

baleo (ba'le·o) *n.m.* round rug or mat.

balido (ba'li·ðo) *n.m.* bleat; bleating.

balín (ba'lin) *n.m.* small bore bullet; pellet. —**balines,** *n.m.pl.* buckshot.

balística (ba'lis·ti·ka) *n.f.* ballistics. —**balístico,** *adj.* ballistic.

baliza (ba'li·θa; -sa) *n.f.* **1,** signal buoy. **2,** *aero.* beacon.

balneario (bal·ne'a·rjo) *n.m.* spa; watering place. —*adj.* of or for baths or bathing.

balompié (ba·lom'pje) *n.m.* football; soccer.

balón (ba'lon) *n.m.* **1,** large ball; balloon. **2,** football. **3,** bale.

baloncesto (ba·lon'θes·to; -'ses·to) *n.m.* basketball.

balonmano (ˌba·lon'ma·no) *n.m.* handball.

balota (ba'lo·ta) *n.f.* ballot. —**balotar,** *v.i.* to ballot; vote.

balsa ('bal·sa) *n.f.* **1,** raft; barge. **2,** pond; pool. **3,** *bot.* balsa. —**balsear,** *v.t.* to cross on raft or ferry.

balsámico (bal'sa·mi·ko) *adj.* **1,** balmy; fragrant. **2,** soothing; healing.

bálsamo ('bal·sa·mo) *n.m.* balsam; balm.

báltico ('bal·ti·ko) *adj.* Baltic. —*n.m., cap.* Baltic.

baluarte (ba'lwar·te) *n.m.* bastion; bulwark.

ballena (ba'ʎe·na; ba'je-) *n.f.* **1,** whale. **2,** whalebone; corset stay. **3,** baleen. —**ballenato,** *n.m.* young whale. —**ballenero,** *n.m.* whaler. —*adj.* of or pert. to whaling.

ballesta (ba'ʎes·ta; -'jes·ta) *n.f.* **1,** crossbow. **2,** carriage spring; auto spring.

ballet (ba'le) *n.m.* [*pl.* **ballets** (ba'le)] ballet.

ballueca (ba'ʎwe·ka; -'jwe·ka) *n.f.* wild oats.

bambalina (bam·ba'li·na) *n.f., theat.* flies.

bambolear (bam·bo·le'ar) *v.i., also,* **bambolearse,** *v.r.* to reel; stagger; sway. —**bamboleo** (-'le·o) *n.m.* reeling; staggering.

bambú (bam'bu) *n.m.* [*pl.* **-búes**] bamboo.

banal (ba'nal) *adj.* banal; trivial. —**banalidad,** *n.f.* banality.

banana (ba'na·na) *n.f.* banana. —**bananal,** *n.m.* banana plantation. —**bananero,** *adj.* of or pert. to bananas. —*n.m.* banana tree.

banano (ba'na·no) *n.m.* **1,** banana. **2,** banana tree.

banasta (ba'nas·ta) *n.f.* large basket.

banca ('ban·ka) *n.f.* **1,** bench. **2,** banking. **3,** bank (*in games*). —**bancario** (-'ka·rjo) *adj.* of or pert. to banking.

bancarrota (ban·ka'rro·ta) *n.f.* bankruptcy. —**hacer bancarrota,** to go into bankruptcy.

banco ('ban·ko) *n.m.* **1,** bench; seat. **2,** bank. **3,** shoal; sandbar. **4,** *geol.* stratum. **5,** school of fish. —**banco de datos,** data bank.

banda ('ban·da) *n.f.* **1,** sash; ribbon; scarf. **2,** band; gang. **3,** edge; border. **4,** *mus.* band.

bandada (ban'da·ða) *n.f.* **1,** covey; flock of birds. **2,** *colloq.* flock of people. **3,** school (*of fish*).

bandazo (ban'da·θo; -so) *n.m., chiefly naut.* lurch; roll.

bandeado (ban·de'a·ðo) *adj.* striped.

bandeja (ban·de·xa) *n.f.* tray.

bandera (ban·de·ra) *n.f.* banner; flag; standard.

bandería (ban·de·ri·a) *n.f.* band; faction.

banderilla (ban·de·ri·ʎa; -ja) *n.f.* banderilla. —**banderillero,** *n.m.* banderillero.

banderín (ban·de·rin) *n.m.* signal flag. —**banderín de enganche,** recruiting post.

banderola (ban·de·ro·la) *n.f.* **1,** streamer; pennant. **2,** signal flag.

bandido (ban'di·ðo) *n.m.* bandit; outlaw. —**bandidaje** (-'ða·xe) *n.m.* banditry.

bando ('ban·do) *n.m.* **1,** decree; edict. **2,** faction; party.

bandola (ban'do·la) *n.f.* mandolin.

bandolera (ban·do'le·ra) *n.f.* **1,** bandoleer. **2,** female bandit. —**bandolerismo,** *n.m.* brigandage. —**bandolero,** *n.m.* brigand; highwayman.

bandurria (ban'du·rrja) *n.f.* a twelve-stringed instrument of the lute family; bandurria.

baniano (ba'nja·no) *n.m.* banyan.

banjo ('ban·xo) *n.m.* banjo. —**banjoísta,** *n.m. & f.* banjoist.

banquero (ban'ke·ro) *n.m.* **1,** banker. **2,** card dealer.

banqueta (ban'ke·ta) *n.f.* **1,** footstool; stool. **2,** *Mex.* sidewalk.

banquete (ban'ke·te) *n.m.* banquet; feast. —**banquetear,** *v.t. & i.* to banquet.

banquillo (ban'ki·ʎo; -jo) *n.m.* small stool.

bañadera (ba·ɲa'ðe·ra) *n.f., Amer.* bathtub.

bañador (ba·ɲa'ðor) *n.m.* swim suit.

bañar (ba'ɲar) *v.t.* **1,** to bathe; wash. **2,** to dip. **3,** to coat. —**bañarse,** *v.r.* to bathe.

bañera (ba'ɲe·ra) *n.f.* bathtub.

bañista (ba'ɲis·ta) *n.m. & f.* bather.

baño ('ba·ɲo) *n.m.* **1,** bath; bathing. **2,** bathroom. **3,** covering; coating. —**baño de María,** double boiler.

baptista (bap'tis·ta) *adj & n.m. & f.* = **bautista.**

baptisterio (bap·tis'te·rjo) *n.m.* baptistery.

baquelita *also,* **bakelita,** **bakelita** (ba·ke·'li·ta) *n.f.* bakelite.

baqueta (ba'ke·ta) *n.f.* **1,** ramrod. **2,** drumstick. **3,** gauntlet. —**correr baquetas; pasar por baquetas,** to run the gauntlet. —**tratar a (la) baqueta,** to treat with scorn.

baquetear (ba·ke·te'ar) *v.t.* **1,** to beat; put through the gauntlet. **2,** to annoy. —**baqueteado,** *adj.* inured; accustomed.

baquiano (ba'kja·no) *n.m.* guide. —*adj.* experienced; skillful.

bar (bar) *n.m.* bar; taproom.

barahunda (ba·ra'un·da) *n.f.* = **baraúnda.**

baraja (ba'ra·xa) *n.f.* pack of cards.

barajar (ba·ra'xar) *v.t.* **1,** to shuffle (cards). **2,** to mix. —*v.i.* to quarrel.

barajón (ba·ra'xon) *n.m.* snowshoe.

baranda (ba'ran·da) *n.f.* railing; rail.

barandal (ba·ran'dal) *n.m.* **1,** railing. **2,** banister.

barandilla (ba·ran·di·ʎa; -ja) *n.f.* **1,** railing. **2,** balustrade.

barata (ba'ra·ta) *n.f.* **1,** barter. **2,** *Amer.* bargain sale. —**baratear,** *v.t.* to sell cheaply.

baratería (ba·ra·te'ri·a) *n.f., law* **1,** fraud. **2,** barratry.

baratijas (ba·ra'ti·xas) *n.f.pl.* trinkets; novelties.

baratillo (ba·ra'ti·ʎo; -jo) *n.m.* **1,** secondhand goods. **2,** secondhand shop; bargain counter. **3,** bargain sale.

barato (ba'ra·to) *adj.* cheap; low-priced. —*n.m.* bargain sale. —*adv.* cheaply.

baraúnda *also,* **barahunda** (ba·ra'un·da) *n.f.* noise; tumult; turmoil.

barba ('bar·βa) *n.f.* **1,** chin. **2,** beard. **3,** *pl.* fine roots; fibers. **4,**

wattle *(of birds).* —**barbado,** *adj.* bearded; barbed.

barbacoa (bar·βa'ko·a) *n.f., Amer.* barbecue.

barbárico (bar'βa·ri·ko) *adj.* barbaric.

barbaridad (bar·βa·ri'ðað) *n.f.* **1,** barbarity; brutality. **2,** rashness; rudeness. **3,** enormity.

barbarie (bar'βa·rje) *n.f.* savagery; brutality; incivility.

bárbaro ('bar·βa·ro) *adj.* **1,** barbarous; savage; crude. **2,** *colloq.* huge. —*n.m.* barbarian. —**barbarismo,** *n.m.* barbarism.

barbechar (bar·βe'tʃar) *v.t.* to fallow. —**barbechera** (-'tʃe·ra) *n.f.* fallowing; fallowing season. —**barbecho** (-'βe·tʃo) *n.m.* fallow.

barbería (bar·βe'ri·a) *n.f.* barber shop. —**barbero** (-'βe·ro) *n.m.* barber. —**barberil** (-'ril) *adj.* tonsorial.

barbilla (bar'βi·ʎa; -ja) *n.f.* **1,** point of the chin. **2,** *ichthy.* barb; barbel.

barbiturato (bar·βi·tu'ra·to) *n.m.* barbiturate. —**barbitúrico** (-'tu·ri·ko) *adj.* barbituric.

barbotar (bar·βo'tar) *also,* **barbotear** (-te'ar) *v.t. & i.* to mutter; mumble. —**barboteo** (-'te·o) *n.m.* muttering; mumbling.

barbudo (ba'βu·ðo) *adj.* long-bearded.

barbulla (bar'βu·ʎa; -ja) *n.f., colloq.* hullabaloo. —**barbullar** (-'ʎar; -'jar) *v.i.* to prattle; chatter noisily. —**barbullón** (-'ʎon; -'jon) *adj.* loudmouthed. —*n.m.* [*fem.* -**ona**] loudmouth.

barca ('bar·ka) *n.f.* small boat; launch. —**barcaza** (-'ka·θa; -sa) *n.f.* barge; lighter.

barcarola (bar·ka'ro·la) *n.f.* barcarole.

barcia ('bar·θja; -sja) *n.f.* chaff.

barcino (bar'θi·no; -'si·no) *adj. (of animals)* white with brown or reddish spots.

barco ('bar·ko) *n.m.* boat; ship.

bardo ('bar·ðo) *n.m.* bard.

bario ('ba·rjo) *n.m.* barium.

barítono (ba'ri·to·no) *adj. & n.m.* baritone.

barlovento (bar·lo'βen·to) *n.m., naut.* windward.

barniz (bar'niθ; -'nis) *n.m.* **1,** varnish. **2,** gloss; glaze. **3,** face paint. **4,** printer's ink.

barnizar (bar·ni'θar; -'sar) *v.t.*

[*infl.:* **rezar,** 10] **1,** to varnish. **2,** to glaze. **3,** to shine; polish.

barómetro (ba'ro·me·tro) *n.m.* barometer. —**barométrico,** *adj.* barometric.

barón (ba'ron) *n.m.* baron. —**baronesa,** *n.f.* baroness. —**baronía,** *n.f.* barony.

barquero (bar'ke·ro) *n.m.* boatman.

barqueta (bar'ke·ta) *n.f.* small boat.

barquichuelo (bar·ki·tʃwe·lo) *n.m.* small boat.

barquilla (bar'ki·ʎa; -ja) *n.f.* **1,** small boat. **2,** *naut.* log. **3,** wafer mold. **4,** *aero.* control car; gondola.

barquillero (bar·ki'ʎe·ro; -'je·ro) *n.m.* **1,** wafer mold. **2,** waffle iron.

barquillo (bar'ki·ʎo; -jo) *n.m.* **1,** wafer. **2,** wafer cone. **3,** waffle.

barquín (bar'kin) *n.m.* bellows.

barquinazo (bar·ki'na·θo; -so) *n.m.* jolting, swaying or upset of a boat or vehicle.

barra ('ba·rra) *n.f.* **1,** bar; rod; beam; lever. **2,** sandbar. **3,** ingot.

barrabás (ba·rra'βas) *n.m.* fiend; devil. —**barrabasada,** *n.f.* fiendishness; fiendish act.

barraca (ba'rra·ka) *n.f.* **1,** barrack; cabin. **2,** *Amer.* warehouse. —**barracón,** *n.m.* **1,** large barrack or cabin. **2,** stall; booth.

barracuda (ba·rra'ku·ða) *n.f.* barracuda.

barrado (ba'rra·ðo) *adj. (of cloth)* ribbed; corded.

barranca (ba'rran·ka) *n.f.* ravine; gorge; cleft.

barranco (ba'rran·ko) *n.m.* **1,** cliff; precipice. **2,** *fig.* obstacle; difficulty. **3,** = **barranca.**

barrancoso (ba·rran'ko·so) *adj.* **1,** uneven; rough. **2,** steep; precipitous.

barrar (ba'rrar) *v.t.* to daub; smear.

barredera (ba·rre'ðe·ra) *n.f.* sweeper *(person or tool).*

barredor (ba·rre'dor) *n.m.* [*fem.* -**dora**] street sweeper. —**barredora eléctrica,** vacuum cleaner.

barredura (ba·rre'ðu·ra) *n.f.* sweeping. —**barreduras,** *n.f.pl.* sweepings.

barreminas (ba·rre'mi·nas) *n.m. sing. & pl.* mine sweeper.

barrena (ba'rre·na) *n.f.* **1,** borer; drill; auger. **2,** *aero.* tailspin.

barrenar (ba·rre'nar) *v.t.* **1,** to drill; bore. **2,** to scuttle (a ship). **3,**

fig. to foil; thwart. **4,** to infringe; violate.

barrendero (ba·rren'de·ro) *n.m.* [*fem.* -**ra**] sweeper.

barrenillo (ba·rre'ni·ʎo; -jo) *n.m., entom.* borer.

barreno (ba'rre·no) *n.m.* **1,** large drill or borer. **2,** drilled or bored hole. **3,** blast hole.

barreño (ba'rre·ɲo) *n.m.* earthen pan; dishpan. *Also,* **barreña,** *n.f.*

barrer (ba'rrer) *v.t.* to sweep.

barrera (ba'rre·ra) *n.f.* barrier; barricade; fence.

barreta (ba'rre·ta) *n.f.* **1,** small bar. **2,** shoe lining.

barriada (ba'rrja·ða) *n.f.* = **barrio.**

barrica (ba'rri·ka) *n.f.* cask.

barricada (ba·rri'ka·ða) *n.f.* barricade.

barrido (ba'rri·ðo) *n.m.* sweep; sweeping.

barriga (ba'rri·ya) *n.f.* belly; bulge. —**barrigón** (-'ɣon), **barrigudo** (-'ɣu·ðo) *adj.* pot-bellied.

barril (ba'rril) *n.m.* barrel; cask. —**barrilero,** *n.m.* cooper.

barrilete (ba·rri'le·te) *n.m.* **1,** keg. **2,** clamp.

barrilla (ba'rri·ʎa; -ja) *n.f.* **1,** saltwort. **2,** soda ash.

barrillo (ba'rri·ʎo; -jo) *n.m.* pimple.

barrio ('ba·rrjo) *n.m.* **1,** ward; precinct; district; quarter. **2,** suburb. —**barrio bajo,** slum. —**el otro barrio,** *colloq.* the other world.

barrizal (ba·rri'θal; -'sal) *n.m.* mire; mud pit.

barro ('ba·rro) *n.m.* **1,** clay; mud; mire. **2,** earthenware. **3,** pimple. —**barro cocido,** terra cotta.

barroco (ba'rro·ko) *adj & n.m.* baroque.

barroso (ba'rro·so) *adj.* **1,** muddy. **2,** pimply.

barrote (ba'rro·te) *n.m.* **1,** iron bar; rod. **2,** brace.

barrumbada (ba·rrum'ba·ða) *n.f.* **1,** boastfulness. **2,** extravagance.

barruntar (ba·rrun'tar) *v.t.* **1,** to foresee. **2,** to conjecture.

barrunto (ba'rrun·to) *n.m.* **1,** foreboding. **2,** conjecture.

bartola (bar'to·la) *n.f., in a la bartola,** *colloq.* in a carefree way; carelessly.

bártulos ('bar·tu·los) *n.m.pl.* **1,** belongings; tools. **2,** business. —**liar los bártulos,** *colloq.* to pack up. —**preparar los bártulos,** *colloq.* to get set.

baruca (ba'ru·ka) *n.f., colloq.* artifice; trickery.

barullo (ba'ru·ʎo; -jo) *n.m.* tumult; confusion.

barzón (bar'θon;--'son) *n.m.* 1, idle stroll; wandering. 2, ring of a yoke.

basa ('ba·sa) *n.f.* 1, pedestal; base. 2, foundation; basis.

basal (ba'sal) *adj.* basal; basic.

basalto (ba'sal·to) *n.m.* basalt.

basar (ba'sar) *v.t.* 1, to base; found. 2, to support; secure. —**basarse en,** to rely on.

basca ('bas·ka) *n.f.* nausea; queasiness.

báscula ('bas·ku·la) *n.f.* platform scale.

base ('ba·se) *n.f.* 1, base. 2, basis. 3, foot. —**básico** ('ba·si·ko) *adj.* basic.

basílica (ba'si·li·ka) *n.f.* basilica.

basilisco (ba·si'lis·ko) *n.m.* basilisk.

basquear (bas·ke'ar) *v.i.* to be nauseated.

básquetbol ('bas·ket·βol) *n.m.* basketball.

basta ('bas·ta) *n.f.* basting; basting stitch.

¡basta! ('bas·ta) *interj.* enough!

bastante (bas'tan·te) *adj.* sufficient; enough. —*adv.* 1, enough. 2, rather.

bastar (bas'tar) *v.i.* to suffice; to be enough.

bastardear (bas·tar·ðe'ar) *v.t. & i.* to degenerate; bastardize.

bastardía (bas·tar'ði·a) *n.f.* 1, bastardy. 2, meanness; depravity.

bastardillo (bas·tar'ði·ʎo; -jo) *adj., print.* italic. —**bastardillas,** *n.f.pl.* italics.

bastardo (bas·tar·ðo) *n.m. & adj.* bastard.

baste ('bas·te) *n.m.* 1, basting. 2, saddle pad. —**bastear,** *v.t.* to baste; tack.

bastidor (bas·ti'ðor) *n.m.* 1, frame. 2, window sash. 3, stretcher for hand embroidery. 4, *paint.* canvas stretcher. 5, *theat.* wing. —**entre bastidores,** behind the scenes.

bastilla (bas'ti·ʎa; -ja) *n.f.* hem. —**bastillar,** *v.t.* to hem.

bastimento (bas·ti'men·to) *n.m.* 1, provisions; supplies. 2, vessel; ship.

bastión (bas'tjon) *n.m.* bastion; bulwark. —**bastionado,** *adj.* fortified.

basto ('bas·to) *adj.* coarse; rude. —*n.m.* 1, packsaddle. 2, *cards* club *(in the Spanish deck).* 3, basting; basting stitch.

bastón (bas'ton) *n.m.* cane; stick; staff. —**bastonada,** *n.f., also,* **bastonazo,** *n.m.* blow with a cane or stick. —**bastón de mando,** baton; staff of office.

bastoncillo (bas·ton'θi·ʎo; -'si·jo) *n.m.* 1, small cane or stick. 2, narrow trimming lace.

bastonera (bas·to'ne·ra) *n.f.* cane stand; umbrella stand.

basura (ba'su·ra) *n.f.* sweepings *(pl.);* trash; refuse.

basurero (ba·su're·ro) *n.m.* 1, garbage collector; street cleaner. 2, trash can. 3, garbage dump; refuse heap.

bata ('ba·ta) *n.f.* robe; housecoat; bathrobe.

batacazo (ba·ta'ka·θo; -so) *n.m.* thud.

batahola (ba·ta'o·la) *n.f., colloq.* bustle; clatter.

batalla (ba'ta·ʎa; -ja) *n.f.* battle; combat; struggle. —**batallador** (-'ðor) *n.m.* warrior; combatant. —*adj.* battling; fighting. —**batallar,** *v.i.* to fight; struggle.

batallón (ba·ta'ʎon; -'jon) *n.m.* battalion.

batán (ba'tan) *n.m.* fulling mill. —**batanar,** *v.t.* to full (cloth). —**batanero,** *n.m.* fuller.

batanear (ba·ta·ne'ar) *v.t., colloq.* to beat; thrash.

bataola (ba·ta'o·la) *n.f.* = **batahola.**

batata (ba'ta·ta) *n.f.* sweet potato.

batayola (ba·ta'jo·la) *n.f., naut.* rail.

bate ('ba·te) *n.m.* baseball bat.

batea (ba'te·a) *n.f.* 1, tray; trough. 2, *Amer.* washtub. 3, flat-bottomed boat; punt. 4, *R.R.* flatcar.

batear (ba·te'ar) *v.t. & i., baseball* to bat. —**bateador** (-'ðor) *n.m.* batter.

bateo (ba'te·o) *n.m., baseball* batting.

batería (ba·te'ri·a) *n.f.* 1, *elect.; mil.; baseball* battery. 2, kitchenware. 3, *mus.* percussion section; drums. 4, *theat.* footlights.

batey (ba'tei) *n.m., Cuba* sugar mill.

batida (ba·ti·ða) *n.f.* **1,** beating (for game). **2,** search; reconnoitering.

batido (ba·ti·ðo) *adj.* beaten, as a path. —*n.m.* **1,** batter. **2,** beaten whites or yolks of eggs. **3,** milk-shake.

batidor (ba·ti'ðor) *adj.* beating. —*n.m.* **1,** beater *(person or tool).* **2,** scout.

batiente (ba'tjen·te) *n.m.* **1,** jamb; doorpost. **2,** leaf of a double door.

batín (ba'tin) *n.m.* smoking jacket.

batintín (ba·tin'tin) *n.m.* gong.

batir (ba'tir) *v.t.* **1,** to beat; strike; pound. **2,** to raze; demolish. **3,** to mix; stir. **4,** to defeat. **5,** to reconnoiter. **6,** to strike (camp). —**batirse,** *v.r.* to fight.

batiscafo (ba·tis'ka·fo) *n.m.* bathyscaphe.

batisfera (ba·tis'fe·ra) *n.f.* bathysphere.

batista (ba'tis·ta) *n.f.* batiste.

baturrillo (ba·tu'rri·ʎo; -jo) *n.m.* hodgepodge; medley.

batuta (ba'tu·ta) baton.

baudio ('bau·ðjo) *n.m.,* comput. baud.

baúl (ba'ul) *n.m.* trunk.

bauprés (bau'pres) *n.m.* bowsprit.

bautismo (bau'tis·mo) *n.m.* baptism; christening. —**bautismal** *adj.* baptismal.

bautista (bau'tis·ta) *n.m.* baptizer. —*adj.* & *n.m.* & *f.* Baptist.

bautisterio (bau·tis'te·rjo) *n.m.* baptistery.

bautizar (bau·ti'θar; -'sar) *v.t.* [*infl.:* **rezar,** 10] to baptize; christen.

bautizo (bau'ti·θo; -so) *n.m.* christening; baptism.

bauxita (bau'ksi·ta) *n.f.* bauxite.

baya ('ba·ja) *n.f.* berry.

bayeta (ba'je·ta) *n.f.* **1,** baize. **2,** mop; swab.

bayetón (ba·je'ton) *n.m.* **1,** shaggy wool cloth, used for coats. **2,** Amer. a kind of long poncho.

bayo ('ba·jo) *adj.* bay. —*n.m.* bay *(horse).*

bayoneta (ba·jo'ne·ta) *n.f.* bayonet. —**bayonetazo,** *n.m.* bayonet thrust or wound.

baza ('ba·θa; -sa) *n.f.* cards trick. —**no dejar meter baza,** *colloq.* to monopolize the conversation. —**meter baza,** *colloq.* to butt in.

bazar (ba'θar; -'sar) *n.m.* bazaar; market.

bazo ('ba·θo; -so) *n.m.* spleen. —*adj.* yellowish brown.

bazofia (ba'θo·fja; ba'so-) *n.f.* offal; refuse.

bazucar (ba·θu'kar; ba·su-) [*infl.:* **tocar,** 7] *also,* **bazuquear** (-ke'ar) *v.t.* to stir; shake (liquids). —**bazuqueo** (-'ke·o) *n.m.* stirring; shaking.

beata (be'a·ta) *adj.* & *n., fem.* of **beato.** —*n.f.* lay sister.

beatificar (be·a·ti·fi'kar) *v.t.* [*infl.:* **tocar,** 7] to beatify. —**beatificación,** *n.f.* beatification.

beatífico (be·a'ti·fi·ko) *adj.* beatific.

beatísimo (be·a'ti·si·mo) *adj.* most holy.

beatitud (be·a·ti'tuð) *n.f.* **1,** beatitude. **2,** *cap., eccles.* a title of the Pope.

beato (be'a·to) *adj.* **1,** blessed; beatified. **2,** pious; devout. **3,** prudish; bigoted. —*n.m.* **1,** devout person. **2,** prude; bigot. —**beatón,** *n.m.* [*fem.* **-ona**] bigot; hypocrite.

bebé (be'βe) *n.m.* baby.

bebedero (be·βe'ðe·ro) *n.m.* drinking trough.

bebedizo (be·βe'ði·θo; -so) *n.m.* potion; philter.

beber (be'βer) *v.t.* & *i.* to drink. —*n.m* drink; drinking. —**bebedor** (-'ðor) *n.m.* tippler; drunkard. —**bebible,** *adj., colloq.* barely drinkable. —**bebida** (-'βi·ða) *n.f.* drink; beverage. —**bebido** (-ðo) *adj.* tipsy.

beca ('be·ka) *n.f.* scholarship; fellowship. —**becario** (-'ka·rjo) *also, Amer.* **becado** (-'ka·ðo) *n.m.* holder of a scholarship; fellow.

becerra (be'θe·rra; be'se-) *n.f.* **1,** yearling calf. **2,** *bot.* snapdragon.

becerril (be·θe'rril; be·se-) *adj.* of or pert. to a calf.

becerro (be'θe·rro; be'se-) *n.m.* **1,** yearling calf. **2,** calfskin.

becuadro (be'kwa·ðro) *n.m., mus.* natural sign.

bedel (be'ðel) *n.m.* beadle. —**bedelía** (-'li·a) *n.f.* beadleship.

beduino (be'ðwi·no) *adj.* & *n.m.* Bedouin. —*n.m.* barbarian.

befa ('be·fa) *n.f.* derision; scoff. —**befar,** *v.t.* to scoff at; mock.

befo ('be·fo) *adj.* **1,** thick-lipped. **2,** knock-kneed. —*n.m.* **1,** lip *(of some animals).* **2,** a long-tailed monkey.

begonia (be'γo·nja) *n.f.* begonia.

behaviorismo (be·a·βjo'ris·mo) *n.m.* behaviorism. —**behaviorista,**

adj. & n.m. & f. behaviorist. —*adj.* behavioristic.

behemot (be·e'mot) *n.m., Bib.* behemoth.

béisbol ('beis·βol) *n.m.* baseball. —**beisbolero, beisbolista,** *n.m.* baseball player.

bejín (be'xin) *n.m., bot.* puffball.

bejuco (be'xu·ko) *n.m.* rattan; reed. —**bejucal,** *n.m.* an area where reeds grow.

beldad (bel'dað) *n.f.* 1, beauty. 2, beautiful woman.

Belén (be'len) *n.m.* 1, Bethlehem. 2, *l.c.* crèche. 3, *l.c.* confusion; bedlam.

beleño (be'le·ɲo) *n.m.* henbane.

belfo ('bel·fo) *adj.* thick-lipped. —*n.m.* lip *(of some animals).*

belga ('bel·ɣa) *adj. & n.m. & f.* Belgian.

belicismo (be·li'θis·mo; -'sis·mo) *n.m.* militarism. —**belicista,** *adj.* militaristic.

bélico ('be·li·ko) *adj.* 1, of or pert. to war. 2, warlike; martial. —**belicosidad** (-si'ðað) *n.f.* bellicosity. —**belicoso** (-'ko·so) *adj.* bellicose.

beligerancia (be·li·ɣe'ran·θja; -sja) *n.f.* belligerence; belligerency. —**beligerante,** *adj. & n.m. & f.* belligerent.

bellaco (be'ʎa·ko; be'ja-) *adj.* cunning; vile. —*n.m.* villain; rogue. —**bellacada** (-'ka·ða) *n.f.* villainous act. —**bellaquear** (-ke'ar) *v.i.* to cheat; to play roguish tricks. —**bellaquería** (-ke'ri·a) *n.f.* roguery; cunning; vile act or expression.

belladona (be·ʎa'ðo·na; be·ja-) *n.f.* belladonna.

belleza (be'ʎe·θa; -'je·sa) *n.f.* 1, beauty. 2, beautiful woman.

bello ('be·ʎo; -jo) *adj.* fair; beautiful. —**bellas artes,** fine arts.

bellota (be'ʎo·ta; be'jo-) *n.f.* acorn.

bemol (be'mol) *adj. & n.m., mus.* flat. —**tener bemoles,** *colloq.* to be very difficult; be hard to take.

bencedrina (ben·θe'ðri·na; ben·se-) *n.f.* benzedrine.

benceno (ben'θe·no; -'se·no) *n.m.* benzene.

bencina (ben'θi·na; -'si·na) *n.f.* benzine.

bendecir (ben·de'θir; -'sir) *v.t.* [*infl.:* 37] to bless. —**bendición,** *n.f.* blessing; benediction. —**bendito,** *adj.* blessed. —*n.m.* simple soul.

benedictino (be·ne·ðik'ti·no) *adj. & n.m.* Benedictine.

benefactor (be·ne·fak'tor) *n.m.* benefactor.

beneficencia (be·ne·fi'θen·θja; -'sen·sja) *n.f.* beneficence; welfare.

beneficiado (be·ne·fi'θja·ðo; -'sja·ðo) *n.m.* 1, person benefited or receiving benefits. 2, *eccles.* beneficiary.

beneficiar (be·ne·fi'θjar; -'sjar) *v.t.* 1, to benefit. 2, to improve. 3, to cultivate (land). 4, to exploit (natural resources). 5, to work (a mine). 6, to process (ores). 7, *Amer.* to slaughter (cattle). —*v.i. [also,* **beneficiarse,** *v.r.*] to profit; gain; benefit.

beneficiario (be·ne·fi'θja·rjo; -'sja·rjo) *n.m.* beneficiary.

beneficio (be·ne'fi·θjo; -sjo) *n.m.* 1, benefit; utility; profit. 2, *eccles.* benefice. —**beneficioso,** *adj.* beneficial; profitable.

benéfico (be'ne·fi·ko) *adj.* beneficial; beneficent; benevolent.

benemérito (be·ne'me·ri·to) *adj.* worthy; deserving.

beneplácito (be·ne'pla·θi·to; -si·to) *n.m.* approval; sanction.

benevolencia (be·ne·βo'len·θja; -sja) *n.f.* benevolence. —**benévolo** (be'ne·βo·lo) *adj.* benevolent.

bengala (ben'ga·la) *n.f.* flare; signal flare.

benigno (be'niɣ·no) *adj.* benign; gentle; mild. —**benignidad** (-ni·'ðað) *n.f.* kindness; mildness.

benjuí (ben'xwi) *n.m.* benzoin.

benzoato (ben·θo'a·to; ben·so-) *n.m.* benzoate. —**benzoico** (-'θoi·ko; -'soi·ko) *adj.* benzoic. —**benzol** (-'θol; -'sol) *n.m.* benzol.

beodo (be'o·ðo) *adj.* drunk. —*n.m.* drunkard. —**beodez** (-'ðeθ; -'ðes) *n.f.* drunkenness.

berbiquí (ber·βi'ki) *n.m.* drill brace.

bereber (be·re'βer) *also,* **berberí** (ber·βe'ri) *adj. & n.m. & f.* Berber.

berenjena (be·ren'xe·na) *n.f.* eggplant. —**berenjenal** (be·ren·xe'nal) *n.m.* 1, eggplant patch. 2, *colloq.* mess; predicament.

bergante (ber'ɣan·te) *n.m.* rascal. —**bergantín** (ber·ɣan'tin) *n.m.* brigantine.

beriberi (be·ri'βe·ri) *n.m.* beriberi.

berilio (be'ri·ljo) *n.m.* beryllium.

berilo (be'ri·lo) *n.m.* beryl.

berkelio (ber'ke·ljo) *n.m.* berkelium.

berlina (ber'li·na) *n.f.* closed carriage; coupé.

bermejo (ber'me·xo) *adj.* bright red; vermillion. —**bermejizo** (-'xi·θo; -so) *adj.* reddish. —**bermejón** (-'xon) *adj.* reddish. —**bermellón** (-'ʎon; -'jon) *n.m.* vermillion.

berrear (be·rre'ar) *v.i.* to bellow; scream. —**berrido** (-'rri·ðo) *n.m.* bellow; scream.

berrinche (be'rrin·tʃe) *n.m., colloq.* rage; tantrum.

berro ('be·rro) *n.m.* watercress. —**berrizal** (-rri'θal; -'sal) *n.m.* watercress bed.

berza ('ber·θa; -sa) *n.f.* cabbage. —**berzal** (-'θal; -'sal) *n.m.* cabbage patch.

besar (be'sar) *v.t.* to kiss.

beso ('be·so) *n.m.* kiss.

bestia ('bes·tja) *n.f.* beast. —*n.m. & f.* dunce; dimwit. —*adj.* stupid. —**bestia de carga,** beast of burden.

bestial (bes'tjal) *adj.* bestial; brutish. —**bestialidad,** *n.f.* bestiality; brutishness.

besucar (be·su'kar) *v.t. colloq.* [*infl.:* **tocar,** 7] = besuquear.

besucón (be·su'kon) *adj. colloq.* much given to kissing. —*n.m. colloq.* [*fem.* -**ona**] a person much given to kissing.

besugo (be'su·ɣo) *n.m.* sea bream.

besuquear (be·su·ke'ar) *v.t. colloq.* to kiss repeatedly or excessively. —**besuqueo** (-'ke·o) *n.m., colloq.* repeated kissing.

beta ('be·ta) *n.f.* **1,** piece of string or thread; tape. **2,** beta.

betarraga (be·ta'rra·ɣa) *also,* **betarrata** (-'rra·ta) *n.f.* **betabel,** *n.m., Mex.* beet.

betel (be'tel) *n.m.* betel.

betún (be'tun) *n.m.* **1,** pitch; bitumen. **2,** shoe polish. **3,** *Mex.* frosting, icing.

betunar (be·tu'nar) *v.t.* **1,** to pitch; tar. **2,** to polish (shoes). **3,** to blacken.

bezo ('be·θo; -so) *n.m.* **1,** blubber lip. **2,** proud flesh.

biberón (bi·βe'ron) *n.m.* nursing bottle.

Biblia ('bi·βlja) *n.f.* Bible. —**bíblico** ('bi·βli·ko) *adj.* Biblical.

bibliófilo (bi'βljo·fi·lo) *n.m.* bibliophile.

bibliografía (bi·βljo·ɣra'fi·a) *n.f.* bibliography. —**bibliográfico** (-'ɣra·fi·ko) *adj.* bibliographical.

bibliomanía (bi·βljo·ma'ni·a)

n.f. bibliomania. —**bibliómane** (bi'βljo·ma·no) *n.m.* bibliomaniac.

biblioteca (bi·βljo'te·ka) *n.f.* **1,** li brary. **2,** bookcase. —**bibliotecario** *n.m.* librarian.

bicameral (bi·ka·me'ral) *adj.* bi cameral.

bicarbonato (bi·kar·βo'na·to *n.m.* bicarbonate.

bicentenario (bi·θen·te'na·rjo bi·sen-) *adj. & n.m.* bicentennial.

bíceps ('bi·θeps; -seps) *n.m.* biceps

bicicleta (bi·θi'kle·ta; bi·si-) *n.f* bicycle.

biciclo (bi'θi·klo; bi'si-) *n.m.* earl form of bicycle with large fron wheel; velocipede.

bicimoto (bi·θi'mo·to; bi·si-) *n.f* motorbike.

bicloruro (bi·klo'ru·ro) *n.m.* bi chloride.

bicoca (bi'ko·ka) *n.f.* trifle; baga telle.

bicolor (bi·ko'lor) *adj.* bicolor bicolored.

bicornio (bi'kor·njo) *n.m.* two cornered hat.

bicúspide (bi'kus·pi·ðe) *adj.* bi cuspid.

bichero (bi'tʃe·ro) *n.m.* boat hook.

bicho ('bi·tʃo) *n.m.* **1,** insect; ver min. **2,** *colloq.* despicable person —**bicharraco** (-tʃa'rra·ko) *n.m colloq.* repulsive animal or person.

biela ('bje·la) *n.f.* connecting rod.

bieldo ('bjel·do) *n.m., also,* **bielda** *n.f.* **1,** pitchfork. **2,** winnowing fork. **3,** wooden rake.

bien (bjen) *adv.* **1,** well; properly right. **2,** all right; fine. **3,** much very; fully. **4,** indeed. **5,** willing ly; readily. —**ahora bien,** now then. —**bien que,** although. —**má bien,** rather; somewhat. —**po bien,** willingly. —**si bien,** while though. —*n.m.* good; welfare; bene fit; sake. —**bienes,** *n.m.pl.* wealth —**bienes dotales,** dowry. —**biene gananciales,** community property —**bienes muebles,** chattels —**bienes raíces** *or* **inmuebles,** rea estate.

bienal (bje'nal) *adj.* biennial.

bienamado (bjen·a'ma·ðo) *adj* dearly beloved.

bienandante (bjen·an'dan·te) *adj* happy; prosperous. —**bienandanza** *n.f.* happiness; prosperity.

bienaventurado (bjen·a·βen tu'ra·ðo) *adj.* blessed.

bienaventuranza (bjen·a·βen

tu·ran·θa; -sa) *n.f.* bliss; beatitude; *cap., usu.pl.* Beatitudes.

bienestar (bjen·es'tar) *n.m.* well-being; welfare.

bienfortunado (bjen·for·tu'na·ðo) *adj.* fortunate; lucky.

bienhablado (bjen·a'βla·ðo) *adj.* well-spoken.

bienhadado (bjen·a'ða·ðo) *adj.* fortunate; lucky.

bienhechor (bjen·e'tʃor) *n.m.* benefactor.

bienintencionado (bjen·in·ten·θjo'na·ðo; -sjo'na·ðo) *adj.* well-meaning.

bienio ('bje·njo) *n.m.* biennium.

bienmesabe (bjen·me'sa·βe) *n.m.* meringue batter.

bienoliente (bjen·o'ljen·te) *adj.* pleasant-smelling; fragrant.

bienquerencia (bjen·ke'ren·θja; -sja) *n.f.* **1,** affection. **2,** goodwill.

bienquerer (bjen·ke'rer) *v.t.* [*infl.:* **querer, 55**] **1,** to be fond of. **2,** to wish (someone) well.

bienqueriente (bjen·ke'rjen·te) *adj.* **1,** affectionate; fond. **2,** well-adjusted.

bienquistar (bjen·kis'tar) *v.t.* to reconcile.

bienquisto (bjen'kis·to) *adj.* respected; esteemed.

bienvenida (bjen·βe'ni·ða) *n.f.* welcome. —**bienvenido,** *adj.* welcome. —**dar la bienvenida a,** to welcome.

bifocal (bi·fo'kal) *adj.* bifocal.

biftec (bif'tek) *also,* **bistec** (bis'tek) **bisté** (-'te) *n.m.* beefsteak.

bifurcación (bi·fur·ka'θjon; -'sjon) *n.f.* **1,** bifurcation. **2,** fork (*of a road*). **3,** junction.

bifurcarse (bi·fur'kar·se) *v.r.* [*infl.:* **tocar, 7**] to bifurcate; fork; branch off. —**bifurcado,** *adj.* bifurcate(d); forked; branched.

bigamia (bi'ɣa·mja) *n.f.* bigamy.

bígamo ('bi·ɣa·mo) *adj.* bigamous. —*n.m.* [*fem.* **-ma**] bigamist.

bigardo (bi·ɣar·ðo) *adj.* dissolute; licentious. —**bigardía** (-'ði·a) *n.f.* dissoluteness; licentiousness.

bigornia (bi'ɣor·nja) *n.f.* anvil.

bigote (bi'ɣo·te) *n.m.* mustache. —**bigotudo** (-'tu·ðo) *adj.* heavy-mustached.

bigotera (bi·ɣo'te·ra) *n.f.* bow compass.

bilabial (bi·la·βjal) *adj. & n.f.* bilabial.

bilateral (bi·la·te'ral) *adj.* bilateral.

bilingüe (bi'lin·gwe) *adj.* bilingual. —**bilingüismo** (-'gwis·mo) *n.m.* bilingualism.

bilis ('bi·lis) *n.f.* bile; gall. —**bilioso,** (-'ljo·so) *adj.* bilious. —**biliosidad,** *n.f.* biliousness.

billar (bi'ʎar; -'jar) *n.m.* **1,** billiards. **2,** billiard table. —**billar automático** *or* **romano,** pinball.

billete (bi'ʎe·te; bi'je-) *n.m.* **1,** ticket. **2,** bill; note; banknote. —**medio billete,** half-fare; half-price ticket.

billetera (bi·ʎe'te·ra; bi·je-) *n.f.,* *Amer.* wallet; billfold.

billón (bi'ʎon; -'jon) *n.m.* a million million; *U.S.* trillion; *Brit.* billion. —**billonario,** *n.m.* billionaire. —**billonésimo,** *n.m. & adj.* million millionth; *U.S.* trillionth; *Brit.* billionth.

bimensual (bi·men'swal) *adj.* twice monthly; semimonthly.

bimestral (bi·mes'tral) *adj.* bi-monthly.

bimestre (bi'mes·tre) *adj.* bi-monthly. —*n.m.* **1,** a period of two months. **2,** bimonthly payment.

binar (bi'nar) *v.t.* to plow the ground for the second time. —**binador** (-'ðor) *n.m.* weeder; hoe.

binario (bi'na·rjo) *adj.* binary.

binocular (bi·no·ku'lar) *adj.* binocular. —**binóculo** (-'no·ku·lo) *n.m.* **1,** binoculars. **2,** pince-nez.

binomio (bi'no·mjo) *n.m.* binomial. —**binómico** (-'no·mi·ko) *adj.* binomial.

binza ('bin·θa; -sa) *n.f.* thin membrane.

biografía (bjo·ɣra'fi·a) *n.f.* biography. —**biografiar** (-'fjar) *v.t.* [*infl.:* **enviar, 22**] to write a biography of. —**biográfico** (-'ɣra·fi·ko) *adj.* biographical. —**biógrafo** ('bjo·ɣra·fo) *n.m.* biographer.

biología (bjo·lo'xi·a) *n.f.* biology. —**biológico** (-'lo·xi·ko) *adj.* biological. —**biólogo** ('bjo·lo·ɣo) *n.m.* biologist.

biombo ('bjom·bo) *n.m.* folding screen.

biopsia (bi'op·sja) *n.f.* biopsy.

bioquímica (bi·o'ki·mi·ka) *n.f.* biochemistry. —**bioquímico,** *adj.* biochemical. —*n.m.* biochemist.

biosfera (bi·os'fe·ra) *n.f.* biosphere.

bióxido (bi'ok·si·ðo) *n.m.* dioxide.

bipartito (bi'par·ti·to) *adj.* [*also*, -ido] bipartite.

bípede ('bi·pe·ðe) *adj.* biped. —**bípedo** (-ðo) *adj. & n.m.* biped.

biplano (bi'pla·no) *n.m.* biplane.

birimbao (bi·rim'ba·o) *n.m.* jew's-harp.

birlar (bir'lar) *v.t.*, *colloq.* **1**, to snatch away; rob; swindle. **2**, to fell with one blow or shot. —**birlador**, *n.m.* swindler.

birlocha (bir'lo·tʃa) *n.f.* paper kite.

birlocho (bir'lo·tʃo) *n.m.* buggy; surrey.

birreta (bi'rre·ta) *n.f.* biretta.

birrete (bi'rre·te) *n.m.* **1**, biretta. **2**, academic cap; mortarboard.

birretina (bi·rre'ti·na) *n.f.* grenadier's cap; hussar's cap; busby.

bis (bis) *adv.* twice; repeated. —*interj.* encore!

bisabuelo (bis·a'βwe·lo) *n.m.* great-grandfather. —**bisabuela**, *n.f.* great-grandmother.

bisagra (bi'sa·ɣra) *n.f.* hinge.

bisbisar (bis·βi'sar) *v.i. & t.*, *colloq.* to mumble; mutter. —**bisbiseo** (-'se·o) *n.m.*, *colloq.* mumbling; muttering.

bisecar (bi·se'kar) *v.t.* [*infl.:* **tocar, 7**] to bisect. —**bisección** (-sek'θjon; -'sjon) *n.f.* bisection.

bisector (bi·sek'tor) *adj.* [*fem.* **-triz**] bisecting. —**bisectriz** [*pl.* **-trices**] *n.f.* bisector; bisectrix.

bisel (bi'sel) *n.m.* bevel. —**biselado**, *adj.* beveled. —*n.m.* beveling. —**biselar**, *v.t.* to bevel.

bisemanal (bi·se·ma'nal) *adj.* twice weekly.

bisexual (bi·sek'swal) *adj. & n.m. & f.* bisexual.

bisiesto (bi'sjes·to) *adj.* bissextile. —**año bisiesto**, leap year.

bismuto (bis'mu·to) *n.m.* bismuth.

bisnieto (bis'nje·to) *also*, **biznieto**, *n.m.* great-grandson. —**bisnieta**, **biznieta**, *n.f.* great-granddaughter.

bisojo (bi'so·xo) *adj.* squint-eyed. —*n.m.* squinter.

bisonte (bi'son·te) *n.m.* bison.

bisoño (bi'so·ɲo) *adj.* inexperienced. —*n.m.* novice; rookie. —**bisoñada**, *n.f.* blunder.

bistec (bis'tek) *also*, **bisté** (-'te) *n.m.* beefsteak.

bisturí (bis·tu'ri) *n.m.* scalpel.

bisulco (bi'sul·ko) *adj.* cloven-hoofed.

bitácora (bi'ta·ko·ra) *n.f.*, *naut.* binnacle.

bitio ('bi·tjo) *n.m.*, *comput.* bit.

bitoque (bi'to·ke) *n.m.* **1**, bung; stopper. **2**, *Amer.* faucet; tap.

bituminoso (bi·tu·mi'no·so) *adj.* bituminous.

bivalente (bi·βa'len·te) *adj.* bivalent. —**bivalencia**, *n.f.* bivalence.

bivalvo (bi'βal·βo) *adj. & n.m.* bivalve.

bizantino (bi·θan'ti·no; bi·san-) *adj. & n.m.* Byzantine.

bizarro (bi'θa·rro; bi'sa-) *adj.* brave; gallant. —**bizarría**, *n.f.* gallantry; courage.

bizcar (biθ'kar; bis-) *v.t.* [*infl.:* **tocar, 7**] to wink (the eye). —*v.i.* to squint.

bizco ('biθ·ko; 'bis-) *adj.* cross-eyed; squint-eyed.

bizcocho (biθ'ko·tʃo; bis-) *n.m.* biscuit; cookie; cake. —**bizcochuelo** (-'tʃwe·lo) *n.m.* small biscuit.

bizma ('biθ·ma; 'bis-) *n.f.* poultice. —**bizmar**, *v.t.* to poultice.

biznieta (biθ'nje·ta; bis-) *n.f.* = **bisnieta**.

biznieto (biθ'nje·to; bis-) *n.m.* = **bisnieto**.

bizquear (biθ·ke'ar; bis-) *v.i.*, *colloq.* to squint.

blanca ('blan·ka) *n.f.*, *in* **estar sin blanca**, *also*, **no tener blanca**, *colloq.* to be penniless; be flat broke.

blancazo (blan'ka·θo; -so) *adj.*, *colloq.* whitish.

blanco ('blan·ko) *adj.* **1**, white. **2**, blank. **3**, fair; light-complexioned. —*n.m.* **1**, white person. **2**, white color. **3**, target. **4**, blank. —**blancor** (-'kor) *n.m.*, **blancura** ('ku·ra) *n.f.* whiteness. —**blancuzco** (-'kuθ·ko; -'kus·ko) *adj.* whitish.

blandeador (blan·de·a'ðor) *adj.* **1**, softening. **2**, persuading.

blandear (blan·de'ar) *v.t.* **1**, to soften. **2**, to brandish. **3**, to persuade.

blandir (blan'dir) *v.t.* to brandish; swing; flourish.

blando ('blan·do) *adj.* **1**, bland; soft; pliant. **2**, weak; delicate.

blandura (blan'du·ra) *n.f.* **1**, softness; gentleness. **2**, blandishment; flattery.

blanquear (blan·ke'ar) *v.t.* **1**, to whiten; bleach. **2**, to clean. **3**, to whitewash. **4**, to blanch. —*v.i.* to blanch; apple; pale. —**blanqueador**, *n.m.* [*fem.* **-dora**] whitener. —*adj.* whitening. —**blanqueadura**, *n.f.* = **blanqueo**.

blanquecer (blan·ke'θer; -'ser) *v.t.* [*infl.:* **conocer, 13**] **1**, to whiten; bleach. **2**, to blanch.

blanquecino (blan·ke'θi·no; -'si·no) *adj.* whitish.

blanqueo (blan'ke·o) *n.m.* whitening; bleaching.

blanquillo (blan'ki·ʎo; -jo) *adj.* whitish. —*n.m., Mex.* egg.

blasfemar (blas·fe'mar) *v.i.* to blaspheme; curse. —**blasfemador, blasfemante,** *n.m.* blasphemer. —*adj.* blaspheming; blasphemous. —**blasfemia** (-'fe·mja) *n.f.* blasphemy. —**blasfemo** (-'fe·mo) *adj.* blasphemous. —*n.m.* blasphemer.

blasón (bla'son) *n.m.* **1,** blazon; coat of arms. **2,** blazonry; heraldry. **3,** honor; glory.

blasonar (bla·so'nar) *v.t.* to blazon. —*v.i.* to boast. —**blasonador** (-na'ðor) *adj.* boasting. —**blasonería** (-ne'ri·a) *n.f.* boasting.

bledo ('ble·ðo) *n.m.* wild amaranth. —**no importarle un bledo,** *colloq.* not to care at all. —**no valer un bledo,** *colloq.* to be worthless.

blindado (blin'da·ðo) *adj.* armored; protected. —**blindaje** (-'da·xe) *n.m.* armor; armor plate; shield. —**blindar** (-'dar) *v.t.* to armor; shield.

bloc (blok) *n.m.* **1,** bloc. **2,** notebook.

blondo ('blon·do) *adj.* blond.

bloque ('blo·ke) *n.m.* block.

bloquear (blo·ke'ar) *v.t.* to block; blockade. —**bloqueo** ('ke·o) *n.m.* blockade.

blusa ('blu·sa) *n.f.* blouse. —**blusón** (blu'son) *n.m.* long blouse; smock.

boa ('bo·a) *n.f.* **1,** *zoöl.* boa. **2,** *(neckpiece)* boa.

boato (bo'a·to) *n.m.* pomp; ostentation.

bobada (bo'βa·ða) *n.f.* = **bobería**.

bobalicón (bo·βa·li'kon) *n.m.* & *adj.* = **bobo**.

bobear (bo·βe'ar) *v.i.* to talk or act foolishly.

bobería (bo·βe'ri·a) *n.f.* foolishness; nonsense.

bobina (bo'βi·na) *n.f.* bobbin; spool; reel; coil.

bobo ('bo·βo) *adj.* foolish; silly. —*n.m.* fool; simpleton; booby.

boca ('bo·ka) *n.f.* mouth; opening; orifice; entrance. —**boca abajo,**

face downward. —**boca arriba,** face upward. —**boca de agua** *or* **riego,** hydrant. —**a pedir de boca,** according to one's wish. —**no decir esta boca es mía,** not to utter a word.

bocacalle (bo·ka'ka·ʎe; -je) *n.f.* street intersection.

bocacaz (bo·ka'kaθ; -'kas) *n.m.* spillway; sluice.

bocací (bo·ka'θi; -'si) *n.m.* buckram.

bocadillo (bo·ka'ði·ʎo; -jo) *n.m.* **1,** morsel; tidbit. **2,** sandwich.

bocado (bo'ka·ðo) *n.m.* **1,** mouthful. **2,** morsel. **3,** bite. **4,** bridle bit.

bocallave (bo·ka'ʎa·βe; -'ja·βe) *n.f.* keyhole.

bocamanga (bo·ka'man·ga) *n.f.* cuff *(of a sleeve)*.

bocanada (bo·ka'na·ða) *n.f.* **1,** mouthful. **2,** puff *(of smoke)*.

bocaza (bo'ka·θa; -sa) *n.f.* big mouth. —*n.m. & f., colloq.* blabbermouth.

boceto (bo'θe·to; bo'se-) *n.m.* sketch; outline; drawing. —**bocetar,** *v.t.* to sketch.

bocina (bo'θi·na; bo'si-) *n.f.* horn; trumpet; megaphone. —**bocinar,** *v.i.* to blow a horn.

bocio ('bo·θjo; -sjo) *n.m.* goiter.

bocoy (bo'koi) *n.m.* hogshead.

bocha ('bo·tʃa) *n.f.* bowling ball. —**bochas,** *n.f.pl.* the game of bowls.

boche ('bo·tʃe) *n.m.* **1,** = **bochas. 2,** *Venez.; W.I.* slight; rebuff. —**dar boche a,** to slight; rebuff.

bochinche (bo'tʃin·tʃe) *n.m.* tumult; uproar. —**bochinchero,** *n.m.* rowdy person.

bochista (bo'tʃis·ta) *n.m. & f.* bowler.

bochorno (bo'tʃor·no) *n.m.* **1,** hot breeze. **2,** embarrassment; shame.

bochornoso (bo·tʃor'no·so) *adj.* **1,** embarrassing. **2,** sultry.

boda ('bo·ða) *n.f.* wedding; nuptials.

bodega (bo'ðe·ɣa) *n.f.* **1,** wine cellar. **2,** storeroom; warehouse. **3,** ship's hold. **4,** *Amer.* grocery.

bodegón (bo·ðe'yon) *n.m.* **1,** cheap restaurant. **2,** *paint.* still life.

bodeguero (bo·ðe'ye·ro) *n.m.* **1,** owner or keeper of a wine cellar. **2,** *Amer.* grocer.

bodoque (bo'ðo·ke) *n.m.* **1,** lump; bump; bulge. **2,** bundle; package. **3,**

lummox; lug. **4,** *Amer.* bump or swelling on the head or body.

bóer ('bo·er) *adj. & n.m. & f.* Boer.

bofes ('bo·fes) *n.m.pl.* lungs *(of an animal).* —**echar los bofes,** to work very hard; slave.

bofetada (bo·fe'ta·ða) *n.f.* slap in the face.

bofetón (bo·fe'ton) *n.m.* hard slap; buffet.

bofo ('bo·fo) *adj.* = **fofo.**

boga ('bo·ɣa) *n.f.* vogue; fashion. —**estar en** *or* **de boga,** to be fashionable.

bogar (bo'ɣar) *v.i.* [*infl.:* **pagar, 8**] **1,** to row. **2,** to sail.

bohardilla (bo·ar'ði·ʎa; -ja) *n.f.* = **buhardilla.**

bohemio (bo'e·mjo) *adj. & n.m.* Bohemian; bohemian.

bohío (bo'i·o) *n.m., Amer.* rustic dwelling; shack; hut.

boicot (boi'kot) *n.m.* boycott. —**boicotear** (-te'ar) *v.t.* to boycott; picket. —**boicoteo** (-'te·o) *n.m.* boycotting.

boina ('boi·na) *n.f.* beret; flat round cap.

boj (box) *n.m., bot.* box; boxwood.

bola ('bo·la) *n.f.* **1,** ball; sphere. **2,** *Amer.* bowling. **3,** *colloq.* lie; hoax. **4,** *Amer., colloq.* brawl. **5,** *cards* slam. **6,** shoe polish. **7,** *Mex.* shoeshine.

bolchevique (bol·tʃe'βi·ke) *adj. & n.m. & f.* Bolshevik; Bolshevist. —**bolchevismo** (-'βis·mo), **bolcheviquismo** (-βi'kis·mo) *n.m.* Bolshevism.

boleadoras (bo·le·a'ðo·ras) *n.f. pl., Arg.* a lariat with balls attached, used by gauchos; bolas.

bolear (bo·le'ar) *v.t.* **1,** to bowl. **2,** to throw balls. **3,** *Arg.* to throw bolas. —*v.t.* **1,** to blackball. **2,** to confuse. **3,** to deceive. **4,** *Mex.* to shine (shoes).

boleo (bo'le·o) *n.m.* **1,** bowling. **2,** bowling green.

bolera (bo'le·ra) *n.f.* bowling alley.

bolero (bo'le·ro) *n.m.* **1,** bolero *(dance; jacket).* **2,** truant. **3,** liar. —*adj.* **1,** truant. **2,** lying; deceitful.

boleta (bo'le·ta) *n.f.* **1,** admission ticket; pass. **2,** pay slip. **3,** *Amer.* ballot. —**boletería** (-te'ri·a) *n.f., Amer.* box office.

boletín (bo·le'tin) *n.m.* **1,** bulletin. **2,** pay slip. **3,** admission ticket.

boleto (bo'le·to) *n.m., Amer.* ticket.

boliche (bo'li·tʃe) *n.m.* **1,** small

bowling ball. **2,** bowling. **3,** bowling alley. **4,** small dragnet. **5,** *colloq.* gambling house.

bólido ('bo·li·ðo) *n.m.* shooting star; meteor.

bolígrafo (bo'li·ɣra·fo) *n.m.* ballpoint pen.

bolita (bo'li·ta) *n.f.* small ball; marble.

bolívar (bo'li·βar) *n.m.* monetary unit of Venezuela; bolivar.

boliviano (bo·li'βja·no) *adj. & n.m.* Bolivian. —*n.m.* monetary unit of Bolivia; boliviano.

bolo ('bo·lo) *n.m.* **1,** ninepin; tenpin. **2,** dunce; dull person. **3,** bolo knife. **4,** *cards* slam. —**bolos,** *n.m. pl.* bowls; bowling.

boloña (bo'lo·ɲa) *n.f.* bologna.

bolsa ('bol·sa) *n.f.* **1,** purse; bag; pouch. **2,** stock exchange. **3,** *anat.* bursa.

bolsear (bol·se'ar) *v.t., Amer.* to pick the pocket of.

bolsillo (bol'si·ʎo; -jo) *n.m.* **1,** pocket. **2,** small purse; pocketbook.

bolsín (bol'sin) *n.m., fin.* curb exchange.

bolsista (bol'sis·ta) *n.m. & f.* stockbroker.

bolso ('bol·so) *n.m.* change purse; money bag.

bollo ('bo·ʎo; -jo) *n.m.* **1,** small loaf; roll; muffin; brioche. **2,** dent; bump. **3,** *Amer.* loaf of bread. **4,** *Amer.* tamale. **5,** *Amer., colloq.* trouble; perplexity.

bomba ('bom·ba) *n.f.* **1,** pump. **2,** fire engine. **3,** bomb; bombshell. **4,** lie; fib. **5,** drunken spree. —**bomba aspirante,** suction pump. —**pasarlo bomba,** to revel; go on a spree.

bombacho (bom'ba·tʃo) *adj.* loose-fitting *(of breeches).* —**bombachas,** *n.f.pl., Amer.* knickers.

bombardear (bom·bar·ðe'ar) *v.t.* to bombard; bomb. —**bombardeo** (-'ðe·o) *n.m.* bombardment. —**bombardero** (-'ðe·ro) *n.m.* bomber; bombardier.

bombástico (bom'bas·ti·ko) *adj.* bombastic.

bombazo (bom'ba·θo; -so) *n.m.* **1,** bomb burst. **2,** bomb damage.

bombear (bom·be'ar) *v.t.* **1,** to pump. **2,** to bomb.

bombeo (bom'be·o) *n.m.* **1,** bombing. **2,** *Amer.* pumping. **3,** bulge; swelling.

bombero (bom'be·ro) *n.m.* fireman.

bombilla (bom'bi·ʎa; -ja) *n.f. also, Amer.*, **bombita,** *n.f.*, **bombillo,** *n.m.* light bulb.

bombo ('bom·bo) *n.m.* **1,** bass drum. **2,** revolving drum. **3,** barge; lighter. **4,** ballyhoo. —*adj.* **1,** lukewarm. **2,** slightly spoiled *(of food).* **3,** astonished. —**darse bombo,** to put on airs.

bombón (bom'bon) *n.m.* **1,** bonbon; sweet; candy. **2,** handsome man or woman. —**bombonera** (-'ne·ra) *n.f.* candy dish or box.

bombona (bon'bo·na) *n.f.* carboy.

bonachón (bo·na'tʃon) *adj., colloq.* kind; good-natured.

bonancible (bo·nan'θi·βle; -'si·βle) *adj.* calm; fair *(of weather).*

bonanza (bo'nan·θa; -sa) *n.f.* **1,** bonanza. **2,** fair weather.

bondad (bon'dað) *n.f.* goodness; kindness. —**bondadoso,** *adj.* kind; good.

bonete (bo'ne·te) *n.m.* bonnet; cap.

bongó (bon'go) *n.m.* bongo drum.

boniato (bo'nja·to) *n.m.* = **buniato.**

bonificación (bo·ni·fi·ka'θjon; -'sjon) *n.f.* **1,** bonus. **2,** allowance; discount. **3,** improvement.

bonísimo (bo'ni·si·mo) *adj., superl. of* **bueno.**

bonitamente (bo·ni·ta'men·te) *adv.* **1,** prettily; neatly. **2,** slowly; gradually.

bonito (bo'ni·to) *adj.* pretty; neat. —*n.m., ichthy.* bonito.

bono ('bo·no) *n.m.* **1,** bond. **2,** certificate; voucher. **3,** bonus.

boñiga (bo'ɲi·ɣa) *n.f.* cow dung; manure.

boquear (bo·ke'ar) *v.i.* **1,** to gape. **2,** to gasp. **3,** to expire; to be dying. —**boqueada,** *n.f.* gasp, gape.

boquerón (bo·ke'ron) *n.m.* **1,** wide opening. **2,** fresh anchovy.

boquete (bo'ke·te) *n.m.* gap; narrow opening.

boquiabierto (bo·ki·a'βjer·to) *adj.* open-mouthed; astonished.

boquilla (bo'ki·ʎa; -ja) *n.f.* **1,** small opening. **2,** mouthpiece. **3,** nozzle. **4,** cigarette tip or holder.

borato (bo'ra·to) *n.m.* borate. —**boratado** (-'ta·ðo) *adj.* borated.

bórax ('bo·raks) *n.m.* borax.

borbollar (bor·bo'ʎar; -'jar) *also,* **borbollear** (-ʎe'ar; -je'ar) *v.i.* to bubble out; boil up; gush out.

borbollón (bor·bo'ʎon; -'jon) *n.m.* spurt; bubbling; boiling; gushing of water. —**a borbollones,** impetuously; precipitately.

Borbón (bor'βon) *n.m., hist.* Bourbon.

borbor (bor'βor) *n.m.* bubbling.

borbotar (bor·βo'tar) *v.i.* to gush out; boil over.

borbotón (bor·βo'ton) *n.m.* = **borbollón.**

borceguí (bor·θe'ɣi; bor·se-) *n.m.* **1,** buskin. **2,** half boot.

borda ('bor·ða) *n.f.* **1,** cottage; hut. **2,** *naut.* gunwale.

bordada (bor'ða·ða) *n.f., naut.* tack; tacking. —**dar bordadas,** to tack back and forth.

bordar (bor'ðar) *v.t.* to embroider. —**bordado,** *adj.* embroidered. —*n.m.* embroidery. —**bordador** (-'ðor) *n.m.* embroiderer. —**bordadura** (-'ðu·ra) *n.f.* embroidery.

borde ('bor·ðe) *n.m.* **1,** border; edge; brim. **2,** hem; fringe. **3,** *naut.* board.

bordear (bor·ðe'ar) *v.t.* **1,** to border; trim. **2,** to skirt. —*v.t., naut.* to tack. —**bordeo** (-'ðe·o) *n.m., naut.* tacking.

bordo ('bor·ðo) *n.m., naut.* **1,** board; side of a ship. **2,** tack. —**a bordo,** on board; aboard.

bordón (bor'ðon) *n.m.* **1,** staff; support. **2,** *mus.* refrain; burden. **3,** *mus.* bass string.

boreal (bo·re'al) *adj.* boreal; northern.

borgoña (bor'ɣo·ɲa) *n.m.* Burgundy *(wine).*

bórico ('bo·ri·ko) *adj.* boric. —**ácido bórico,** boric acid.

borinqueño (bo·rin'ke·ɲo) *also,* **boricua** (bo'ri·kwa) *adj. & n.m.* Puerto Rican. —**Borinquen** (bo·'rin·ken) *n.f.* Puerto Rico.

borla ('bor·la) *n.f.* **1,** tassel. **2,** doctor's cap. **3,** doctor's degree. —**tomar la borla,** to take a doctor's degree.

borne ('bor·ne) *n.m.* **1,** tip of a lance or spear. **2,** *elect.* terminal.

bornear (bor·ne'ar) *v.t.* to twist; turn; bend. —**bornearse,** *v.r.* to warp; bulge. —**borneo** (-'ne·o) *n.m.* turning; winding; swinging about.

boro ('bo·ro) *n.m.* boron.

borona (bo'ro·na) *n.f.* **1,** millet. **2,** Indian cornbread.

borra ('bo·rra) *n.f.* **1,** yearling ewe. **2,** cotton or wool waste. **3,** *colloq.* trash; rubbish. **4,** *colloq.* idle talk. **5,** borax.

borracho (bo'rra·tʃo) *adj.* drunk.
—**borrachera** (-'tʃe·ra) *n.f.* drunkenness; revelry. —**borrachez**
(-'tʃeθ; -'tʃes) *n.f.* intoxication
—**borrachín** (-'tʃin) *n.m., colloq.*
drunkard. —*adj., colloq.* tipsy.
—**borrachón** (-'tʃon) *n.m.* drunkard.

borrador (bo·rra'ðor) *n.m.* 1,
rough draft; sketch. 2, *Amer.* eraser.
—**libro borrador,** blotter.

borradura (bo·rra'ðu·ra) *n.f.* erasure.

borrajear (bo·rra·xe'ar) *v.t. & i.* 1,
to scribble. 2, to doodle.

borrar (bo'rrar) *v.t.* to erase; blot;
blur; obliterate.

borrasca (bo'rras·ka) *n.f.* 1, storm;
squall. 2, *colloq.* spree; orgy.
—**borrascoso,** *adj.* stormy.

borregada (bo·rre'ɣa·ða) *n.f.* 1,
flock of sheep. 2, *colloq.* silly action; foolishness.

borrego (bo'rre·ɣo) *n.m.* 1, yearling lamb. 2, *colloq.* dunce.

borrica (bo'rri·ka) *n.f.* 1, she-ass.
2, *colloq.* stupid woman.

borricada (bo·rri'ka·ða) *n.f.* 1,
drove of asses. 2, foolish action.

bórrico (bo'rri·ko) *n.m.* 1, donkey;
ass. 2, sawhorse. 3, *colloq.* simpleton. —**borricón** (-'kon) *n.m.,
colloq.* plodder.

borrón (bo'rron) *n.m.* blotch; blot;
blur. —**borronear** (-ne'ar) *v.t.* to
blotch; scribble; sketch.

borroso (bo'rro·so) *adj.* blurred;
blurry.

borrumbada (bo·rrum'ba·ða) *n.f.*
= **barrumbada.**

boruca (bo'ru·ka) *n.f., colloq.*
noise; racket.

borujo (bo'ru·xo) *n.m.* small lump.
—**borujón** (-'xon) *n.m.* lump;
bump.

boscaje (bos'ka·xe) *n.m.* 1, wood;
thicket. 2, *paint.* woodland scene.

bosque ('bos·ke) *n.m.* forest;
woods. —**boscoso** (bos'ko·so) *adj.*
wooded; forested.

bosquejo (bos'ke·xo) *n.m.* sketch;
outline. —**bosquejar** (-'xar) *v.t.* to
sketch; outline.

bosta ('bos·ta) *n.f.* manure; dung.

bostezar (bos·te'θar; -'sar) *v.i.*
[*infl.:* **rezar, 10**] to yawn; gape.
—**bostezo** (-'te·θo; -so) *n.m.* yawn;
gape.

bota ('bo·ta) *n.f.* 1, boot. 2, wineskin. 3, butt; cask. 4, a liquid

measure equal to 516 liters or 125
gallons.

botadura (bo·ta'ðu·ra) *n.f.* launching; christening (*of a ship*).

botalón (bo·ta'lon) *n.m., naut.*
boom.

botánica (bo'ta·ni·ka) *n.f.* 1, botany. 2, *Amer.* health food store; herb
shop. —**botánico,** *adj.* botanical.
—*n.m.* botanist. —**botanista,** *n.m.
& f.* botanist.

botar (bo'tar) *v.t.* 1, to cast; hurl. 2,
to throw away. 3, to launch; christen (a ship). 4, *Amer.* to squander. 5,
Amer. to dismiss. —*v.i.* to bounce;
jump.

botarate (bo·ta'ra·te) *n.m., colloq.*
1, madcap. 2, *Amer.* spendthrift.

botarel (bo·ta'rel) *n.m.* buttress;
brace.

botavara (bo·ta'βa·ra) *n.f., naut.*
boom; gaff.

bote ('bo·te) *n.m.* 1, boat. 2, thrust
with a weapon. 3, bounce; jump;
prance. 4, jar; can; pot.

botella (bo'te·ʎa; -ja) *n.f.* bottle;
flask.

botellero (bo·te'ʎe·ro; -'je·ro) *n.m.*
1, bottlemaker. 2, bottle rack.

botellón (bo·te'ʎon; -'jon) *n.m.* 1,
large bottle. 2, *Mex.* demijohn.

botica (bo'ti·ka) *n.f.* 1, drugstore.
2, medicine. —**boticario** (-'ka·rjo)
n.m. druggist; apothecary.

botija (bo'ti·xa) *n.f.* 1, earthen jug.
2, *Amer., colloq.* belly. 3, *Amer.,
colloq.* fat person.

botijo (bo'ti·xo) *n.m.* 1, earthen
jar with a spout and handle. 2,
colloq. fat person.

botín (bo'tin) *n.m.* 1, boot. 2, buskin; high shoe. 3, booty; plunder.
—**botinero,** *n.m.* shoemaker; bootmaker.

botiquín (bo·ti'kin) *n.m.* 1, medicine chest. 2, first-aid kit.

boto ('bo·to) *adj.* 1, blunt. 2, dullwitted.

botón (bo'ton) *n.m.* 1, button. 2,
bud. 3, knob. 4, push button.
—**botonadura** (-na'ðu·ra) *n.f.* set
of buttons. —**botón de oro,** buttercup.

botones (bo'to·nes) *n.m. sing & pl.*
bellboy; bellhop.

botulismo (bo·tu'lis·mo) *n.m.* botulism.

bóveda ('bo·βe·ða) *n.f.* 1, arch;
vault; arched roof. 2, cavern; crypt.

bovino (bo'βi·no) *adj. & n.m.* bovine.

boxear (bok·se'ar) *v.i.* to box.
—**boxeador** (-'ðor) *n.m.* boxer.
—**boxeo** (-'se·o) *n.m.* boxing.
bóxer ('bok·ser) *n.m.* boxer *(dog).*
boya ('bo·ja) *n.f.* **1,** buoy. **2,** net
float. —**boyante.** *adj.* buoyant.
—**boyar,** *v.i.* to float.
boyada (bo'ja·ða) *n.f.* drove of
oxen. —**boyera** ('je·ra) *n.f.* cattle
shed. —**boyero** (-ro) *n.m.* cowherd;
ox driver.
bozal (bo'θal; -'sal) *adj.* **1,** *colloq.*
inexperienced; green. **2,** stupid. **3,**
wild; untamed. —*n.m.* **1,** muzzle. **2,**
Amer. boor; coarse person.
bozo ('bo·θo; -so) *n.m.* **1,** fuzz or
down on the cheeks or upper lip. **2,**
part of the mouth around the lips.
braceaje (bra·θe'a·xe; bra·se-)
n.m. **1,** coinage. **2,** brewing.
bracear (bra·θe'ar; -se'ar) *v.i.* **1,** to
swing the arms. **2,** to swim the
crawl. **3,** to struggle. **4,** to brace.
—*v.t.* to brew.
bracero (bra'θe·ro; -'se·ro) *adj. (of
a weapon)* thrown with the hand.
—*n.m.* **1,** day laborer. **2,** one who
offers his arm, esp. to a lady. —**de
bracero,** arm in arm.
bracete (bra'θe·te; -'se·te) *n.m., in*
de bracete, arm in arm.
braco ('bra·ko) *adj.* pug-nosed.
—*n.m.* pointer *(dog).*
braga ('bra·ɣa) *n.f.* diaper.
—**bragas,** *n.f.pl.* **1,** breeches. **2,**
panties. —**bragadura** (-ɣa'ðu·ra)
n.f. crotch. —**braguero** (-'ɣe·ro)
n.m., med. truss; brace. —**bragueta**
(-'ɣe·ta) *n.f.* fly *(of trousers).*
brahmán (bra'man) *also,* **brahmín**
(-'min) *n.m.* Brahman. —**brahmanismo,** *n.m.* Brahmanism.
Braille (breil) *n.m.* Braille.
brama ('bra·ma) *n.f.* rut; mating
season.
bramar (bra'mar) *v.i.* to roar; bellow; to blare. —**bramador** (-'ðor)
adj. bellowing. —*n.m.* bellower;
roarer. —**bramante,** *adj.* bellowing.
—**bramido** (-'mi·ðo) *n.m.* bellow.
brancada (bran'ka·ða) *n.f.* dragnet.
branquia ('bran·kja) *n.f., ichthy.*
gill. —**branquial** (-'kjal) *adj.* branchial.
braquial (bra'kjal) *adj.* brachial.
brasa ('bra·sa) *n.f.* red-hot coal.
—**asar a la brasa,** to braise.
brasero (bra'se·ro) *n.m.* **1,** brazier.
2, *Mex.* hearth.

bravamente (bra·βa'men·te) *adv.*
1, bravely. **2,** cruelly. **3,** very well.
bravata (bra'βa·ta) *n.f.* brag;
boast; bravado.
bravear (bra·βe'ar) *v.i.* to bluster;
boast.
bravío (bra'βi·o) *adj.* wild; savage.
—*n.m.* ferocity.
bravo ('bra·βo) *adj.* **1,** brave; fearless. **2,** wild; fierce. **3,** excellent; elegant. **4,** ill-tempered; angry.
—*interj.* bravo!; well done!
bravucón (bra·βu'kon) *adj.* boastful. —*n.m.* [*fem.* **-ona**] braggart.
—**bravuconear,** *v.i.* to brag; boast.
—**bravuconería** (-ne'ri·a) *n.f.* bravado.
bravura (bra'βu·ra) *n.f.* **1,** courage; boldness; bravery. **2,** fierceness. **3,** bravado.
braza ('bra·θa; -sa) *n.f.* fathom.
brazada (bra'θa·ða; -'sa·ða) *n.f.* **1,**
armful. **2,** stroke or pull with the
arms.
brazado (bra'θa·ðo; -'sa·ðo) *n.m.*
armful.
brazal (bra'θal; -'sal) *n.m.* **1,** armband. **2,** irrigation ditch.
brazalete (bra·θa'le·te; bra·sa-)
n.m. bracelet.
brazo ('bra·θo; -so) *n.m.* **1,** arm. **2,**
foreleg of an animal. **3,** branch; division. **4,** *fig.* strength; power.
—**brazos,** *n.m.pl.* manual laborers;
hands. —**de** *or* **del brazo,** arm in
arm. —**no dar su brazo a torcer,**
to persevere; stick to one's guns.
brea ('bre·a) *n.f.* **1,** pitch; tar. **2,**
sackcloth; canvas.
brear (bre'ar) *v.t., colloq.* to annoy;
molest.
brebaje (bre'βa·xe) *n.m.* **1,** bad-
tasting potion. **2,** *naut.* grog.
brécol ('bre·kol) *n.m.* broccoli.
brecha ('bre·tʃa) *n.f.* breach; gap.
brega ('bre·ɣa) *n.f.* **1,** strife; struggle. **2,** trick; practical joke.
bregar (bre'ɣar) *v.i.* [*infl.:* **pagar,**
8] **1,** to fight; struggle. **2,** to work
hard; contend; strive.
brema ('bre·ma) *n.f., ichthy.* bream.
bren (bren) *n.m.* bran.
breña ('bre·ɲa) *also,* **breñal,
breñar,** *n.m.* craggy ground covered
with brambles. —**breñoso,** *adj.*
craggy; brambly.
bresca ('bres·ka) *n.f.* honeycomb.
Bretaña (bre'ta·ɲa) *n.f.* Britain;
Britannia.
brete ('bre·te) *n.m.* **1,** fetters;
shackles. **2,** perplexity; quandary.

bretón (bre'ton) *adj. & n.m.* Breton.

bretones (bre'to·nes) *n.m.pl.* Brussels sprouts.

breve ('bre·βe) *adj.* brief; short. —*n.f. mus.* breve. —**en breve, 1,** in short. **2,** soon; shortly.

brevedad (bre·βe'ðað) *n.f.* brevity; shortness.

brevete (bre'βe·te) *n.m.* memorandum.

breviario (bre'βja·rjo) *n.m.* breviary.

brezal (bre'θal; -'sal) *n.m.* heath. —**brezo** ('bre·θo; -so) *n.m.* heather; heath (*shrub*); brier.

bribón (bri'βon) *adj.* rascally. —*n.m.* rascal. —**bribonada,** *also,* **bribonería,** *n.f.* knavery; rascality. —**bribonear,** *v.i.* **1,** to loaf. **2,** to scheme.

bric-a-brac (brik·a'βrak) *n.m.* bric-a-brac.

bricho ('bri·tʃo) *n.m.* spangle.

brida ('bri·ða) *n.f.* **1,** bridle; rein. **2,** curb; check. —**a toda brida,** posthaste.

bridge (bridʒ; britʃ) *n.m.* bridge (*card game*).

brigada (bri'ɣa·ða) *n.f.* brigade. —*n.m.* staff sergeant. —**general de brigada,** brigadier general; brigadier.

brigadier (bri·ɣa'ðjer) *n.m.* **1,** brigadier; brigadier general. **2,** rear admiral.

brillante (bri'ʎan·te; bri'jan-) *adj.* brilliant; shining; sparkling. —*n.m.* diamond. —**brillantez** (-'teθ; -'tes) *n.f.* brilliance; splendor. —**brillar** (bri'ʎar; -'jar) *v.i.* to shine; gleam. —**brillo** ('bri·ʎo; -jo) *n.m.* sparkle; glitter; shine.

brincar (brin'kar) *v.i. & t.* [*infl.:* **tocar, 7**] to jump; hop; bounce. —**brinco** ('brin·ko) *n.m.* jump; leap; hop; bounce.

brindar (brin'dar) *v.i.* to drink a toast. —*v.t.* to offer; invite. —**brindis** ('brin·dis) *n.m.* toast (*to a person's health*).

brío ('bri·o) *n.m.* vigor; liveliness. —**brioso** (bri'o·so) *adj.* vigorous; lively.

brioche ('brjo·tʃe) *n.m.* brioche.

briqueta (bri'ke·ta) *n.f.* briquette.

brisa ('bri·sa) *n.f.* breeze.

británico (bri'ta·ni·ko) *adj.* British; Britannic. —**britano** (-'ta·no) *adj.* British. —*n.m.* Briton.

brizna ('briθ·na; 'bris-) *n.f.* **1,** fragment; chip. **2,** string; filament.

broca ('bro·ka) *n.f.* **1,** reel; bobbin. **2,** drill bit. **3,** shoemaker's tack.

brocado (bro'ka·ðo) *adj.* brocaded. —*n.m.* brocade.

brocal (bro'kal) *n.m.* **1,** edge of a well. **2,** metal rim.

bróculi ('bro·ku·li) *n.m.* broccoli.

brocha ('bro·tʃa) *n.f.* **1,** paint brush. **2,** shaving brush. —**de brocha gorda,** crude; amateurish. —**pintor de brocha gorda,** housepainter.

brochada (bro'tʃa·ða) *n.f.* brush stroke.

brochadura (bro·tʃa'ðu·ra) *n.f.* set of hook-and-eye fasteners.

brochazo (bro'tʃa·θo; -so) *n.m.* brush stroke.

broche ('bro·tʃe) *n.m.* **1,** brooch. **2,** clasp; fastener.

brocheta (bro'tʃe·ta) *n.f.* skewer.

broma ('bro·ma) *n.f.* **1,** joke; jest; gaiety. **2,** *Amer.* disappointment; contretemps. —**broma pesada,** crude practical joke.

bromear (bro·me'ar) *v.i.,* *also,* **bromearse,** *v.r.* to joke; have fun. —**bromista,** *n.m. & f.* joker.

bromo ('bro·mo) *n.m.* bromine. —**bromuro** ('mu·ro) *n.m.* bromide.

bronca ('bron·ka) *n.m.* quarrel; heated dispute.

bronce ('bron·θe; -se) *n.m.* bronze.

broncear (bron·θe'ar; -se'ar) *v.t.* to bronze; braze. —**broncearse,** *v.r.* to become tanned. —**bronceado,** *adj.* bronzed; tanned; sunburned.

broncíneo (bron'θi·ne·o; -'si·ne·o) *adj.* of bronze; bronzelike.

bronco ('bron·ko) *adj.* **1,** coarse; rough. **2,** brittle. **3,** hoarse; harsh. **4,** wild; untamed.

broncoscopio (bron·kos'ko·pjo) *n.m.* bronchoscope.

bronquedad (bron·ke'ðað) *n.f.* roughness; harshness; hoarseness.

bronquio ('bron·kjo) *n.m.* bronchus. —**bronquial** (-'kjal) *adj.* bronchial. —**bronquitis** (-'ki·tis) *n.f.* bronchitis.

brontosauro (bron·to'sau·ro) *n.m.* brontosaurus.

broquel (bro'kel) *n.m.* shield; buckler.

broqueta (bro'ke·ta) *n.f.* = **brocheta.**

brotar (bro'tar) *v.i.* **1,** to bud. **2,** to come out; gush; flow. —*v.t.* to grow; produce. —**brotadura** (-'ðu·ra) *n.f.* budding. —**brotador**

(-'ðor) *adj.* budding. **—brote** ('bro·te) *n.m.* bud; budding; sprouting.

broza ('bro·θa; -sa) *n.f.* **1,** brushwood. **2,** trash; rubbish. **3,** *fig.* nonsense.

bruces ('bru·θes; -ses) *n.m.pl.* lips. **—a** *or* **de bruces,** face downward.

bruja ('bru·xa) *n.f.* witch; sorceress; hag. **—brujería** (-xe'ri·a) *n.f.* witchcraft. **—brujo,** *n.m.* wizard; sorcerer. **—estar brujo,** *Amer.* to be penniless.

brujear (bru·xe'ar) *v.i.* to practice witchcraft.

brújula ('bru·xu·la) *n.f.* **1,** compass; magnetic needle. **2,** gunsight. **—brújula giroscópica,** gyrocompass.

bruma ('bru·ma) *n.f.* mist; fog; haze. **—brumal,** *adj.* foggy; hazy. **—brumoso,** *adj.* foggy; misty.

bruno ('bru·no) *adj.* dark brown.

bruñir (bru'ɲir) *v.t.* [*infl.:* **gruñir, 21**] to burnish; polish. **—bruñido** (-'ɲi·ðo) *adj.* burnished. **—bruñidor** (-'ðor) *adj.* burnishing; polishing. **—***n.m.* polisher.

brusco ('brus·ko) *adj.* brusque; rough; blunt. **—bruscamente,** *adv.* brusquely; abruptly. **—brusquedad** (-ke'ðað) *n.f.* brusqueness.

brutal (bru'tal) *adj.* brutal; savage. **—brutalidad,** *n.f.* brutality; savageness. **—brutalizar,** *v.t.* [*infl.:* **rezar, 10**] to brutalize.

bruteza (bru'te·θa; -sa) *n.f.* brutality; stupidity.

bruto ('bru·to) *adj.* **1,** brutish; gross; stupid. **2,** raw; unfinished. **—***n.m.* brute. **—datos en bruto,** raw data. **—diamante en bruto,** uncut diamond. **—peso bruto,** gross weight.

bruza ('bru·θa; -sa) *n.f.* hard scrubbing brush.

bu (bu) *interj.* boo! **—***n.m., colloq.* bogy; bugaboo.

buba ('bu·βa) *n.f.* pustule; swollen gland.

bubia ('bu·βja) *n.f.* gannet.

bubón (bu'βon) *n.m.* tumor; bubo. **—bubónico** (-'βo·ni·ko) *adj.* bubonic. **—peste bubónica,** bubonic plague.

bucal (bu'kal) *adj.* of or pert. to the mouth; oral.

bucanero (bu·ka'ne·ro) *n.m.* buccaneer.

bucarán (bu·ka'ran) *n.m.* buckram.

búcaro ('bu·ka·ro) *n.m.* vase.

buccino (buk'θi·no; -'si·no) *n.m., zoöl.* whelk.

buce ('bu·θe; -se) *v., pres.subjve.* of **buzar.**

bucear (bu·θe'ar; bu·se-) *v.i.* to dive. **—buceo** (-'θe·o; -'se·o) *n.m.* diving.

bucle ('bu·kle) *n.m.* curl; lock of hair.

bucólico (bu'ko·li·ko) *adj.* bucolic. **—bucólica,** *n.f.* bucolic.

buche ('bu·tʃe) *n.m.* **1,** crop *(of a bird)*. **2,** stomach. **3,** mouthful *(of fluid)*. **—buchada** (-'tʃa·ða) *n.f.* mouthful. **—buchón** (-'tʃon) *adj.* bulging; bellied.

Buda ('bu·ða) *n.m.* Buddha. **—budismo,** *n.m.* Buddhism. **—budista,** *adj. & n.m. & f.* Buddhist.

budín (bu'ðin) *n.m.* pudding. **—budinera** (-'ne·ra) *n.f.* pudding mold.

buen (bwen) *adj.* = **bueno** *before a masc. noun.*

buenaventura (bwe·na·βen'tu·ra) *n.f.* **1,** good luck. **2,** fortunate; fortunetelling.

bueno ('bwe·no) *adj.* **1,** good; kind; virtuous. **2,** useful; fit. **3,** great; strong. **4,** healthy. **5,** tasty. **—***adv.* **1,** very well. **2,** enough. **—de buenas a primeras,** suddenly. **—por las buenas,** willingly.

buey (bwei) *n.m.* ox; steer; bull; bullock.

bufa ('bu·fa) *n.f.* buffoonery. **—bufo,** *adj.* comic. **—ópera bufa,** comic opera.

búfalo ('bu·fa·lo) *n.m.* buffalo.

bufanda (bu'fan·da) *n.f.* muffler; scarf.

bufar (bu'far) *v.i.* to snort; puff angrily.

bufete (bu'fe·te) *n.m.* **1,** desk. **2,** lawyer's office.

buffet *also,* **bufet** (bu'fe) *n.m.* buffet; informal meal.

bufido (bu'fi·ðo) *n.m.* snort; bellow.

bufón (bu'fon) *adj.* comical. **—***n.m.* jester; buffoon. **—bufonada** (-'na·ða) *also,* **bufonería** (-ne'ri·a) *n.f.* buffoonery.

bufonearse (bu·fo·ne'ar·se) *v.r.* to jest; clown.

bugalla (bu'ɣa·ʎa; -ja) *n.f.* gallnut.

buganvilla (bu·ɣan'βi·ʎa; -ja) *n.f.* bougainvillaea.

buhardilla (bu·ar'ði·ʎa; -ja) *n.f.* **1,** garret. **2,** dormer; dormer window. **3**, skylight. *Also,* **buharda** (-ða).

búho (ˈbu·o) *n.m.* owl.

buhonero (bu·oˈne·ro) *n.m.* peddler. —**buhonería** (-neˈri·a) *n.f.* peddling.

buitre (ˈbwi·tre) *n.m.* vulture.

buitrero (bwiˈtre·ro) *adj.* vulturine; vulturous.

buje (ˈbu·xe) *n.m.* axle box; shaft pillow; bushing.

bujería (bu·xeˈri·a) *n.f.* trinket.

bujía (buˈxi·a) *n.f.* **1**, candle. **2**, candle power. **3**, spark plug.

bula (ˈbu·la) *n.f., eccles.* bull; edict.

bulbo (ˈbul·βo) *n.m.* bulb. —**bulbar**, *adj., pathol.* bulbous. —**bulboso**, *adj.* bulbous.

bulevar (bu·leˈβar) *n.m.* boulevard.

bulto (ˈbul·to) *n.m.* **1**, bulk; lump. **2**, bundle; package. **3**, shadowy object. —**escurrir** *or* **pasar el bulto**, to pass the buck.

bulla (ˈbu·ʎa; -ja) *n.f.* noise; clatter; bustle.

bullanguero (bu·ʎanˈge·ro; bu·jan-) *adj.* loud; vulgar.

bullicio (buˈʎi·θjo; -ˈji·sjo) *n.m.* noise; tumult. —**bullicioso**, *adj.* noisy.

bullir (buˈʎir; -ˈjir) *v.i.* [*infl.:* **19**] **1**, to boil; bubble. **2**, to budge; move; stir. **3**, to bustle; fidget. **4**, to swarm; teem. —*v.t.* to stir; budge.

bumerang (bu·meˈrang) *n.m.* [*pl.* **-rangs**] boomerang.

buniato (buˈnja·to) *n.m.* sweet potato.

buñuelo (buˈɲwe·lo) *n.m.* cruller; fritter. —**buñolero** (buˈɲoˈle·ro) *n.m.* one who makes or sells fritters.

buque (ˈbu·ke) *n.m.* ship; steamer. —**buque cisterna; buque tanque,** tanker. —**buque mercante,** merchant vessel. —**buque velero,** sailing vessel.

buqué (buˈke) *n.m.* bouquet (*of wine or flowers*).

burato (buˈra·to) *n.m.* crêpe; crêpe de Chine.

burbuja (burˈβu·xa) *n.f.* bubble; blob. —**burbujear** (-xeˈar) *v.i.* to bubble; burble. —**burbujeo** (-ˈxe·o) *n.m.* bubbling; burbling.

burdel (burˈðel) *n.m.* brothel.

burdo (ˈbur·ðo) *adj.* coarse; vulgar.

bureo (buˈre·o) *n.m.* amusement; diversion.

burgués (burˈɣes) *adj.* bourgeois; middle-class. —*n.m.* bourgeois;

middle-class person. —**burguesía** (-ɣeˈsi·a) *n.f.* bourgeoisie.

buriel (buˈrjel) *adj.* dark red.

buril (buˈril) *n.m.* **1**, burin. **2**, *dent.* explorer; burr. —**burilar**, *v.t.* to engrave.

burla (ˈbur·la) *n.f.* **1**, mockery; scoff. **2**, trick; joke.

burladero (bur·laˈðe·ro) *n.m.* **1**, safety door or screen in a bull ring. **2**, safety island.

burlador (bur·laˈðor) *adj.* joking; jesting. —*n.m.* **1**, practical joker; jester. **2**, seducer.

burlar (burˈlar) *v.t., fol. by* **de, 1**, to mock; scoff at. **2**, to deceive. —**burlarse**, *v.r.* to jest; jibe; ridicule.

burlería (bur·leˈri·a) *n.f.* **1**, trick; deception. **2**, tall tale; yarn. **3**, banter; ridicule.

burlesco (burˈles·ko) *adj.* comical; burlesque.

burlete (burˈle·te) *n.m.* weather strip.

burlón (burˈlon) *adj.* mocking. —*n.m.* mocker; scoffer.

buró (buˈro) *n.m.* desk; writing desk.

burocracia (bu·roˈkra·θja; -sja) *n.f.* bureaucracy. —**burócrata** (buˈro·kra·ta) *n.m.* & *f.* bureaucrat. —**burocrático** (-ˈkra·ti·ko) *adj.* bureaucratic.

burra (ˈbu·rra) *n.f.* **1**, she-ass. **2**, ignorant woman.

burrada (buˈrra·ða) *n.f.* **1**, drove of asses. **2**, stupid word or deed.

burro (ˈbu·rro) *n.m.* **1**, ass; donkey; burro. **2**, sawhorse. **3**, ignorant man. —**burrero**, *n.m.* donkey driver.

bursátil (burˈsa·til) *adj.* of or pert. to the stock exchange or stock market.

bursitis (burˈsi·tis) *n.f.* bursitis.

busardo (buˈsar·ðo) *n.m.* buzzard.

busca (ˈbus·ka) *n.f.* search; hunt. —**buscas**, *n.f.pl., Amer.* perquisites.

buscador (bus·kaˈðor) *adj.* searching. —*n.m.* **1**, searcher. **2**, divining rod.

buscapié (bus·kaˈpje) *n.m.* [*pl.* **-piés**] hint; clue; lead.

buscapleitos (bus·kaˈplei·tos) *n.m.* & *f. sing.* & *pl., Amer.* **1**, quarrelsome person; troublemaker. **2**, *colloq.* ambulance chaser.

buscar (busˈkar) *v.t.* [*infl.:* **tocar, 7**] to search; seek; hunt.

buscarruidos (bus·kaˈrrwi·ðos)

n.m. & f. sing. & pl. quarrelsome person; troublemaker.

buscavidas (bus·ka'βi·ðas) *n.m. & f. sing. & pl., colloq.* 1, busybody. 2, hustler; go-getter.

buscón (bus'kon) *n.m.* 1, searcher. 2, swindler; pilferer. —**buscona,** *n.f.* prostitute.

búsqueda ('bus·ke·ða) *n.f.* search; hunt.

busto ('bus·to) *n.m.* bust.

butaca (bu'ta·ka) *n.f.* 1, armchair. 2, orchestra seat. —**butacón** (-'kon) *n.m.* large armchair.

butano (bu'ta·no) *n.m.* butane.

butifarra (bu·ti'fa·rra) *n.f.* sausage. —**butifarrero,** *adj.* maker or seller of sausages.

butilo (bu'ti·lo) *n.m.* butyl. —**butileno** (-'le·no) *n.m.* butylene.

buz (buθ; bus) *n.m.* ceremonial kiss.

buzar (bu'θar; -'sar) *v.i.* [*infl.: rezar,* 10] *geol., mining* to dip. —**buzamiento,** *n.m.* dip.

buzo ('bu·θo; -so) *n.m.* diver.

buzón (bu'θon; -'son) *n.m.* 1, mailbox. 2, canal; sluice. 3, plug; stopper.

C

C, c (θe; se) *n.f.* 3rd letter of the Spanish alphabet.

cabal (ka'βal) *adj.* exact; perfect; faultless. —**estar en sus cabales,** to be in one's right mind. —**por sus cabales,** exactly; perfectly.

cábala ('ka·βa·la) *n.f.* 1, intrigue; scheme. 2, cabal. —**cabalista,** *n.m.* cabalist. —**cabalístico,** *adj.* cabalistic.

cabalgadura (ka·βal·ɣa'ðu·ra) *n.f.* 1, riding animal; mount. 2, beast of burden.

cabalgar (ka·βal'ɣar) *v.i.* [*infl.: pagar,* 8] 1, to ride horseback. 2, to parade on horseback. —*v.t.* to cover (a mare). —**cabalgador,** *n.m.* rider; horseman.

cabalgata (ka·βal'ɣa·ta) *n.f.* cavalcade.

caballa (ka'βa·ʎa; -ja) *n.f.* horse mackerel.

caballada (ka·βa'ʎa·ða; -'ja·ða) *n.f.* 1, herd of horses. 2, *Amer.* stupidity.

caballar (ka·βa'ʎar; -jar) *adj.* equine.

caballear (ka·βa·ʎe'ar; -je'ar) *v.i., colloq.* to ride horseback often; to be fond of riding.

caballejo (ka·βa'ʎe·xo; -'je·xo) *n.m.* poor horse; nag.

caballeresco (ka·βa·ʎe'res·ko; ka·βa·je-) *adj.* chivalrous.

caballerete (ka·βa·ʎe're·te; -je're·te) *n.m., colloq.* dude; dandy.

caballería (ka·βa·ʎe'ri·a; -je·'ri·a) *n.f.* 1, horse; mule; mount. 2, cavalry. 3, knighthood; chivalry. 4, chivalrous deed. 5, knightly privilege. 6, order of knights. 7, *Amer.* a

land measure of about 33 acres. —**caballería andante,** knighterrantry.

caballeriza (ka·βa·ʎe'ri·θa; -je·'ri·sa) *n.f.* 1, stable. 2, staff of grooms.

caballerizo (ka·βa·ʎe'ri·θo; -je'ri·so) *n.m.* chief groom.

caballero (ka·βa'ʎe·ro; -'je·ro) *n.m.* 1, gentleman. 2, nobleman. 3, knight. —*adj.* riding; on horseback. —**caballero andante,** knight-errant.

caballeroso (ka·βa·ʎe'ro·so; -je'ro·so) *adj.* gentlemanly; genteel. —**caballerosidad,** *n.f.* gentlemanliness.

caballerote (ka·βa·ʎe'ro·te; -je·'ro·te) *n.m., colloq.* gross, unpolished man.

caballete (ka·βa'ʎe·te; -'je·te) *n.m.* 1, *archit.* ridge of a roof. 2, sawhorse; trestle. 3, *paint.* easel. 4, *anat.* bridge of the nose. 5, *print.* gallows of a press.

caballista (ka·βa'ʎis·ta; -'jis·ta) *n.m.* riding performer; circus rider.

caballito (ka·βa'ʎi·to; -'ji·to) *n.m.* 1, *dim. of* **caballo.** 2, *Mex.* diaper. 3, *pl.* merry-go-round. 4, hobbyhorse. —**caballito del diablo,** dragonfly. —**caballito de mar,** sea horse.

caballo (ka'βa·ʎo; -jo) *n.m.* 1, horse. 2, *chess* knight. —**a caballo,** on horseback. —**caballo de fuerza,** horsepower. —**caballo marino,** sea horse.

caballón (ka·βa'ʎon; -'jon) *n.m.* 1, ridge (*in plowed soil*). 2, dike.

cabaña (ka'βa·ɲa) *n.f.* 1, cabin; hut. 2, drove of mules.

cabaret (ka·βa'ret; -'re) *n.m.* cabaret; nightclub.

cabecear (ka·βe·θe'ar; -se'ar) *v.i.* 1, to nod the head; nod in assent; bob the head. 2, *naut.* to pitch; lurch.

cabeceo (ka·βe'θe·o; -'se·o) *n.m.* 1, nodding of the head. 2, *naut.* pitching; lurching.

cabecera (ka·βe'θe·ra; -'se·ra) *n.f.* 1, beginning; head; heading. 2, headboard. 3, bolster. 4, capital of a province or district. 5, *print.* headpiece; vignette. 6, *journalism* headline. 7, foot *(of a bridge).* —**cabecera de puente,** bridgehead.

cabecero (ka·βe'θe·ro; -'se·ro) *n.m.* foreman of a mining crew.

cabecilla (ka·βe'θi·ʎa; -'si·ja) *n.f., dim. of* cabeza.

cabellera (ka·βe'ʎe·ra; -'je·ra) *n.f.* 1, long hair; head of hair. 2, *astron.* comet's tail.

cabello (ka'βe·ʎo; -jo) *n.m.* hair of the head. —**cabello de ángel,** 1, fine noodles; 2, cotton candy. 3, corn silk. —**en cabellos,** bareheaded.

cabelludo (ka·βe'ʎu·ðo; -'ju·ðo) *adj.* 1, hairy. 2, *bot.* fibrous.

caber (ka'βer) [*infl.:* 38] *v.i.* 1, to be admissible. 2, to fit; be contained. 3, *impers.* to befall *(as luck).* —*v.t.* to contain; include. —**no cabe duda,** there is no doubt. —**no cabe más,** that's the end. —**no caber en el pellejo; no caber en sí,** to be beside oneself.

cabestrillo (ka·βes'tri·ʎo; -jo) *n.m.* 1, sling; support for the arm. 2, *carp.* strap; diagonal tie. 3, *naut.* rope; cord.

cabestro (ka'βes·tro) *n.m.* 1, halter. 2, leading ox. —**traer del cabestro,** to lead by the nose.

cabeza (ka'βe·θa; -sa) *n.f.* 1, head. 2, chief; leader. 3, mind; brains. 4, origin; source. —**cabezas,** *n.f.pl.* bow and stern of a ship. —**cabeza de puente,** bridgehead.

cabezada (ka·βe'θa·ða; -'sa·ða) *n.f.* 1, a nod of the head, as in dozing. 2, *naut.* pitching of a ship. 3, = cabezazo. 4, headgear *(for a horse).*

cabezal (ka·βe'θal; -'sal) *n.m.* 1, pillow. 2, *med.* compress.

cabezalero (ka·βe·θa'le·ro; ka·βe·sa-) *n.m.* executor. —**cabezalera,** *n.f.* executrix.

cabezazo (ka·βe'θa·θo; -'sa·so) *n.m.* a blow with the head.

cabezón (ka·βe'θon -'son) *adj.* 1, big-headed. 2, stubborn.

cabezota (ka·βe'θo·ta; -'so·ta) *n.f., colloq.* stubborn person.

cabezudo (ka·βe'θu·ðo; -'su·ðo) *adj.* obstinate; stubborn. —*n.m.* mullet.

cabida (ka'βi·ða) *n.f.* space; room.

cabildear (ka·βil·de'ar) *v.i.* to lobby. —**cabildeo** (-'de·o) *n.m.* lobbying. —**cabildero** (-'de·ro) *n.m.* lobbyist.

cabildo (ka'βil·do) *n.m.* 1, cathedral chapter. 2, chapter meeting. 3, town council. 4, town hall.

cabilla (ka'βi·ʎa; -ja) *n.f., naut.* dowel.

cabillo (ka'βi·ʎo; -jo) *n.m.* 1, *bot.* stem; stalk. 2, end of a cord.

cabina (ka'βi·na) *n.f.* 1, cabin. 2, cab; driver's compartment. —**cabina telefónica,** telephone booth; call booth.

cabio ('ka·βjo) *n.m.* 1, joist. 2, lintel.

cabizbajo (ka·βiθ'βa·xo; ka·βis-) *adj.* sad; melancholy.

cable ('ka·βle) *n.m.* cable.

cablegrafiar (ka·βle·ɣra'fjar) *v.t. & i.* [*infl.:* enviar, 22] to cable. —**cablegráfico** (-'ɣra·fi·ko) *adj.* of or by cable.

cablegrama (ka·βle'ɣra·ma) *n.m.* cablegram.

cabo ('ka·βo) *n.m.* 1, end; extremity; tip. 2, *geog.* cape. 3, *naut.* chief; commander. 4, *naut.* rope; line. 5, *mil.* corporal. —**cabos,** *n.m.pl.* 1, mane of a horse. 2, accessories of apparel. —**al cabo,** at last. —**dar cabo a,** to finish. —**de cabo a cabo,** *also,* **de cabo a rabo,** from head to tail.

cabotaje (ka·βo'ta·xe) *n.m.* coastwise trade.

cabra ('ka·βra) *n.f.* goat. —**cabras,** *n.f.pl.* small white clouds. —**cabrero** (-'βre·ro), **cabrerizo** (-'ri·θo; -'ri·so) *n.m.* goatherd.

cabré (ka'βre) *v., fut. of* caber.

cabrería (ka·βre'ri·a) *n.f.* 1, herd of goats. 2, goat stable.

cabrestante (ka·βres'tan·te) *n.m.* capstan.

cabria ('ka·βrja) *n.f.* crane; windlass; hoist.

cabrilla (ka'βri·ʎa; -ja) *n.f.* 1, sawhorse. 2, *ichthy.* grouper. —**cabrillas,** *n.f.pl.* 1, whitecaps. 2, *cap., astron.* Pleiades.

cabrio ('ka·βrjo) *n.m.* joist; rafter.

cabrío (ka'βri·o) *adj.* of or pert. to goats; goatlike.

cabriola (ka'βrjo·la) *n.f.* caper; leap; somersault. —**cabriolar** (-'lar), **carbriolear** (-le'ar) *v.i.* to cut capers; prance.

cabriolé (ka·βrjo'le) *n.m.* 1, cabriolet. 2, sleeveless cloak.

cabrita (ka'βri·ta) *n.f.* she-kid.

cabritilla (ka·βri'ti·ʎa; -ja) *n.f.* kidskin; goatskin.

cabritillo (ka·βri'ti·ʎo; -jo) *n.m.* 1, kid; young goat. 2, kidskin.

cabrito (ka'βri·to) *n.m.* kid.

cabrón (ka'βron) *n.m.* 1, buck; he-goat 2, *colloq.* cuckold.

cabronada (ka·βro'na·ða) *n.f., vulg.* affront; indignity.

caca (''ka·ka) *n.f., vulg.* 1, feces; dung. 2, dirt; filth.

cacahual (ka·ka'wal) *n.m.* cacao plantation.

cacahuete (ka·ka'we·te) *n.m.* peanut. *Also* **cacahuate** (-'wa·te); **cacahué** (-'we); **cacahuey** (-'wei).

cacalote (ka·ka'lo·te) *n.m., Mex.* raven.

cacao (ka'ka·o) *n.m.* 1, cacao. 2, cocoa; chocolate. —**manteca de cacao,** cocoa butter.

cacaotal (ka·ka·o'tal) *n.m.* = **cacahual.**

cacareador (ka·ka·re·a'ðor) *adj.* 1, cackling; crowing. 2, *colloq.* bragging; boasting.

cacarear (ka·ka·re'ar) *v.i.* 1, to cackle *(as a hen);* crow *(as a cock).* 2, *colloq.* to brag; boast.

cacareo (ka·ka're·o) *n.m.* 1, crowing; cackling. 2, brag; boast.

cacatúa (ka·ka'tu·a) *n.f.* cockatoo.

cace (''ka·θe; -se) *v., pres.subjve.* of **cazar.**

cacé (ka'θe; -'se) *v., 1st pers. sing. pret.* of **cazar.**

cacera (ka'θe·ra; -'se·ra) *n.f.* canal; conduit.

cacería (ka·θe'ri·a; ka·se-) *n.f.* 1, hunt. 2, hunting party. 3, bag.

cacerina (ka·θe'ri·na; ka·se-) *n.f.* cartridge pouch.

cacerola (ka·θe'ro·la; ka·se-) *n.f.* casserole; saucepan.

cacique (ka'θi·ke; -'si·ke) *n.m.* 1, chief. 2, political boss. —**caciquear,** *v.i., colloq.* to act bossy. —**caciquismo** (-'kis·mo) *n.m.* political bossism.

caco (''ka·ko) *n.m.* 1, pickpocket; thief. 2, *colloq.* coward.

cacofonía (ka·ko·fo'ni·a) *n.f.* ca-cophony. —**cacofónico** (-'fo·ni·ko) *adj.* cacophonous.

cacto (''kak·to) *n.m.* cactus.

cacumen (ka'ku·men) *n.m.* 1, top; height. 2, acumen; insight.

cachalote (ka·tʃa'lo·te) *n.m.* sperm whale; cachalot.

cachano (ka'tʃa·no) *n.m., colloq.* the devil.

cachar (ka'tʃar) *v.t.* 1, to break in pieces. 2, to split lengthwise.

cacharro (ka'tʃa·rro) *n.m.* 1, coarse earthen pot. 2, worthless thing. 3, *pl.* crockery. —**tener cuatro cacharros,** to have nothing.

cachaza (ka'tʃa·θa; -sa) *n.f.* slowness; tardiness. —**cachazudo,** *adj.* slow.

cachear (ka·tʃe'ar) *v.t.* to frisk (a person) for hidden weapons. —**cacheo** (-'tʃe·o) *n.m.* frisking.

cachemir (ka·tʃe'mir) *n.m., also,* **cachemira** (-'mi·ra) *n.f.* = **casimir.**

cachete (ka'tʃe·te) *n.m.* 1, slap; cuff. 2, chubby cheek. —**cache-tudo,** *adj.* chubby-cheeked.

cachiporra (ka·tʃi'po·rra) *n.f.* club; cudgel. —**cachiporrazo,** *n.m.* blow with a club.

cachivache (ka·tʃi'βa·tʃe) *n.m.* 1, *derog.* junk; trash. 2, *colloq.* good-for-nothing. 3, *pl.* odds and ends; truck. 4, *pl.* pots and pans.

cacho (''ka·tʃo) *n.m.* 1, slice; piece. 2, *Amer.* horn.

cachondo (ka'tʃon·do) *adj.* 1, in heat; in rut. 2, *colloq.* passionate; sexy. —**cachondez** (-'deθ; -'des) *n.f.* heat, rut; lust.

cachorro (ka'tʃo·rro) *n.m.* 1, puppy; cub. 2, pocket pistol.

cachucha (ka'tʃu·tʃa) *n.f.* 1, rowboat. 2, a kind of cap. 3, an Andalusian dance.

cachuela (ka'tʃwe·la) *n.f.* 1, pork fricassee. 2, fricassee of rabbit's innards.

cada (''ka·ða) *adj.* each; every. —**cada cual,** everyone. —**cada uno,** each one. —**cada vez,** every time. —**cada vez más,** *(fol. by comp.)* more and more.

cadalso (ka'ðal·so) *n.m.* 1, platform; stage; stand. 2, scaffold; gallows.

cadáver (ka'ða·βer) *n.f.* cadaver; corpse. —**cadavérico** (-'βe·ri·ko) *adj.* cadaverous.

cadena (ka'ðe·na) *n.f.* 1, chain; bond. 2, *archit.* buttress. 3, [*also,*

cadena perpetua] life imprisonment. **4,** *radio; TV* hookup.

cadencia (ka'ðen·θja; -sja) *n.f.* **1,** cadence; rhythm. **2,** *mus.* cadenza. —**cadencioso,** *adj.* rhythmical.

cadente (ka'ðen·te) *adj.* decaying; declining.

cadera (ka'ðe·ra) *n.f.* hip.

caderillas (ka·ðe'ri·ʎas; -jas) *n.f.pl.* bustle.

cadete (ka'ðe·te) *n.m.,* mil. cadet.

cadmio ('kað·mjo) *n.m.* cadmium.

caducar (ka·ðu'kar) *v.t.* [*infl.:* **tocar,** 7] **1,** to be decrepit, senile or superannuated. **2,** to be out of date. **3,** *comm.; law* to lapse; expire.

caduceo (ka·ðu'θe·o; -'se·o) *n.m.* caduceus.

caducidad (ka·ðu·θi'ðað; -si· 'ðað) *n.f.* **1,** transitoriness. **2,** *comm.; law* expiration.

caduco (ka'ðu·ko) *adj.* **1,** senile; decrepit. **2,** transitory. **3,** *law* canceled.

caduquez (ka·ðu'keθ; -'kes) *n.f.* **1,** senility; decrepitude. **2,** *comm.; law* state of lapse or expiration.

caer (ka'er) *v.i.* [*infl.:* 39] to fall; drop; tumble down. —**caer bien, 1,** to fit. **2,** to be suitable; be becoming. **3,** to please; impress favorably. —**caer enfermo,** to fall sick. —**caer en gracia a,** to please; impress favorably. —**caer en la cuenta,** to catch on. —**dejar caer,** to drop.

café (ka'fe) *n.m.* **1,** coffee. **2,** coffee tree. **3,** coffeehouse; café. —*adj. & n.indecl.* brown.

cafeína (ka·fe'i·na) *n.f.* caffeine.

cafetal (ka·fe'tal) *n.m.* coffee plantation.

cafetera (ka·fe'te·ra) *n.f.* coffee pot.

cafetería (ka·fe·te'ri·a) *n.f.,* Amer. **1,** coffee seller's shop. **2,** cafeteria.

cafetero (ka·fe'te·ro) *n.m.* **1,** coffee grower. **2,** coffee seller. —*adj.* of or pert. to coffee.

cafeto (ka·fe'to) *n.m.* coffee tree.

cagar (ka'ɣar) *v.* [*infl.:* **pagar,** 8] —*v.i.* to defecate. —*v.t.* to soil. —**cagada** (-ɣa·ða) *n.f.* excrement. —**cagadero** (-ɣa·ðe·ro) *n.m.* latrine.

caí (ka'i) *v., 1st pers.sing. pret. of* **caer.**

caída (ka'i·ða) *n.f.* **1,** fall; tumble; downfall. **2,** *geol.* dip. —**caídas,** *n.f.pl.* coarse wool. —**a la caída de la tarde,** at dusk. —**a la caída del sol,** at sunset.

caído (ka'i·ðo) *v., p.p. of* **caer.** —*adj.* languid; downfallen. —**caídos,** *n.m.pl.* arrears of taxes.

caiga ('kai·ɣa) *v., pres.subjve. of* **caer.**

caigo ('kai·ɣo) *v., 1st pers.sing. pres.ind. of* **caer.**

caimán (kai'man) *n.m.* alligator.

caimiento (ka·i'mjen·to) *n.m.* **1,** fall; drop; decline. **2,** languor; torpor.

caja ('ka·xa) *n.f.* **1,** box; case; chest. **2,** safe; strongbox. **3,** coffin. **4,** cashier's office, desk or window. **5,** cabinet *(of a radio, TV set, etc.).* **6,** *print.* case. **7,** body *(of a car, carriage or wagon).* **8,** denture; set of false teeth; plate. **9,** hollow; socket. **10,** *bot.* capsule. **11,** stairwell; shaftway. —**caja de ahorros,** savings bank. —**caja de caudales,** safe; vault. —**caja de menores,** petty cash. —**caja de seguridad,** safe-deposit box. —**caja de sorpresa,** jack-in-the-box. —**caja registradora,** cash register. —**en caja, 1,** on hand. **2,** in good health; in good spirits. —**libro de caja,** cash book.

cajero (ka'xe·ro) *n.m.* **1,** boxmaker. **2,** cashier. **3,** treasurer.

cajeta (ka'xe·ta) *n.f.* little box.

cajetilla (ka·xe'ti·ʎa; -ja) *n.f.* **1,** little box. **2,** pack *(of cigarettes or snuff).*

cajista (ka'xis·ta) *n.m.,* print. compositor.

cajón (ka'xon) *n.m.* **1,** box; case; chest. **2,** Amer. coffin. **3,** locker. **4,** caisson. —**ser de cajón,** to go without saying.

cajonería (ka·xo·ne'ri·a) *n.f.* set of drawers.

cal (kal) *n.f.* lime. —**cal hidráulica,** cement; hydraulic lime. —**cal muerta** *or* **apagada,** slaked lime. —**cal viva,** quicklime.

cala ('ka·la) *n.f.* **1,** inlet. **2,** *naut.* bilge. **3,** calla lily. **4,** suppository. **5,** *surg.* probe.

calabaza (ka·la'βa·θa; -sa) *n.f.* pumpkin; gourd; calabash. —**dar calabazas,** *colloq.* **1,** to jilt. **2,** [*also,* **calabacear** (-θe'ar; -se'ar) *v.t.*] to flunk; fail.

calabozo (ka·la'βo·θo; -so) *n.m.* **1,** dungeon. **2,** jail; calaboose. **3,** jail cell.

calada (ka'la·ða) *n.f.* **1,** soak; soaking. **2,** dive; plunge; swoop.

calado (ka'la·ðo) *n.m.* **1,** openwork; fretwork. **2,** *naut.* draft.

—*adj.* soaked; wet. —**calados,** *n.m. pl.* lace.

calafatear (ka·la·fa·te'ar) *v.t.* to calk.

calamar (ka·la'mar) *n.m.* squid.

calambre (ka'lam·bre) *n.m.* cramp; crick.

calamidad (ka·la·mi'ðað) *n.f.* misfortune; calamity. —**calamitoso** (-'to·so) *adj.* calamitous.

calamina (ka·la'mi·na) *n.f.* calamine.

calandria (ka'lan·drja) *n.f.* 1, *ornith.* lark. 2, rolling press. —*n.m. & f.* malingerer.

calar (ka'lar) *v.t.* 1, to soak through; permeate. 2, to make open-work or fretwork in. 3, to wedge. 4, *naut.* to submerge (tackle). 5, *naut.* to draw (a specified depth of water). 6, to lower (a draw bridge). 7, to fix (a bayonet). 8, *colloq.* to size up. —**calarse,** *v.r.* to be soaked. — **calarse el sombrero,** to pull one's hat down on one's head.

calavera (ka·la'βe·ra) *n.f.* skull. —*n.m. & f., colloq.* madcap. —**calaverear,** *v.i.* to act foolishly. —**calaverada,** *n.f.* tomfoolery.

calcañal (kal·ka'ɲal) *n.m.* heel; heelbone. *Also,* **calcañar** (-'ɲar).

calcar (kal'kar) *v.t.* [*infl.:* tocar, 7] 1, to trace; copy. 2, to imitate; ape.

calcáreo (kal'ka·re·o) *adj.* calcareous.

calce ('kal·θe; -se) *n.m.* 1, wedge. 2, tire of a wheel. 3, wheel shoe.

calce ('kal·θe; -se) *v., pres.subjve. of* calzar.

calcé (kal'θe; -'se) *v., 1st pers.sing. pret. of* calzar.

calceta (kal'θe·ta; -'se·ta) *n.f.* hose; stocking. —**calcetería** (-te·ri·a) *n.f.* hosiery. —**calcetero** (-'te·ro) *n.m.* hosier. —**calcetín** (-'tin) *n.m.* half hose; sock. —**hacer calceta,** to knit.

calcificar (kal·θi·fi'kar; kal·si-) *v.t.* [*infl.:* tocar, 7] to calcify. —**calcificación,** *n.f.* calcification.

calcinar (kal·θi'nar; -si'nar) *v.t. & i.* to calcine. —**calcina** (-'θi·na; -'si·na) *n.f.* mortar.

calcio ('kal·θjo; -sjo) *n.m.* calcium.

calco ('kal·ko) *n.m.* tracing; drawing.

calcomanía (kal·ko·ma'ni·a) *n.f.* decalcomania; sticker.

calculador (kal·ku·la'ðor) *adj.* calculating. —**calculadora,** *n.f.* computer; calculator.

calcular (kal·ku'lar) *v.t. & i.* to calculate; compute; estimate. —**calculable,** *adj.* calculable. —**calculista,** *n.m. & f.* schemer.

cálculo ('kal·ku·lo) *n.m.* 1, calculation; computation. 2, *math.; med.* calculus.

caldear (kal·de'ar) *v.t.* 1, to warm; heat. 2, to weld (iron). —**calda** ('kal·da) *n.f.* warming; heating. —**caldas,** *n.f.pl.* hot mineral baths.

caldera (kal'de·ra) *n.f.* 1, caldron; boiler. 2, *mining* well sump. —**caldera de vapor,** steam boiler.

calderero (kal·de're·ro) *n.m.* brazier; coppersmith; boilermaker.

caldero (kal'de·ro) *n.m.* kettle.

calderón (kal·de'ron) *n.m.* 1, large kettle. 2, *print.* paragraph sign (¶). 3, *mus.* hold; fermata (⌒).

caldo ('kal·do) *n.m.* 1, broth; bouillon; sauce. 2, *Mex.* juice of sugar cane. 3, *Mex.* salad dressing. —**caldos,** *n.m.pl.* juices or liquids extracted from fruits. —**caldo de cultivo,** *biol.* culture.

calefacción (ka·le·fak'θjon; -'sjon) *n.f.* heating; heat.

calefactor (ka·le·fak'tor) *adj.* heating. —*n.m.* 1, heater. 2, heating element.

calendario (ka·len'da·rjo) *n.m.* almanac; calendar.

caléndula (ka'len·du·la) *n.f.* calendula.

calentar (ka·len'tar) [*infl.:* pensar, 27] *v.t.* to warm; heat. —**calentarse,** *v.r.* 1, to become warm. 2, to become angry. 3, to be in heat. —**calentador,** *n.m.* heater; warmer. —*adj.* heating; warming. —**calentamiento,** *n.m.* warming; heating. —**calentar a uno las orejas,** to scold someone. —**calentarse la cabeza** *or* **los sesos,** to rack one's brains.

calentura (ka·len'tu·ra) *n.f.* fever. —**calenturiento,** *adj.* feverish.

calera (ka'le·ra) *n.f.* lime kiln; lime pit.

calesa (ka'le·sa) *n.f.* chaise. —**calesín** (-'sin) *n.m.* light chaise.

caleta (ka'le·ta) *n.f.* inlet; cove.

caletre (ka'le·tre) *n.m., colloq.* judgment; good sense.

calibrar (ka·li'βrar) *v.t.* to calibrate; gauge; graduate. —**calibración,** *n.f.* calibration. —**calibrador,** *n.m.* caliper; micrometer.

calibre (ka·li·βre) *n.m.* **1,** caliber.
2, capacity.

calicanto (ka·li'kan·to) *n.m.* stone
masonry.

calicó (ka·li'ko) *n.m.* [*pl.* **calicós**
(-'kos)] calico.

calidad (ka·li'ðað) *n.f.* quality;
condition; character; rank. —**cali-
dades,** *n.f.pl.* **1,** conditions. **2,** personal qualifications. **3,** *cards* rules.
—**en calidad de,** in the capacity of.

cálido ('ka·li·ðo) *adj.* **1,** warm; hot.
2, piquant; spicy.

calidoscopio (ka·li·ðos'ko·pjo)
n.m. kaleidoscope. —**calidoscópico**
(-'ko·pi·ko) *adj.* kaleidoscopic.

calientapiés (ka·ljen·ta'pjes)
n.m.sing. & pl. foot warmer.

caliente (ka'ljen·te) *adj.* **1,** warm;
hot; scalding. **2,** *Amer., colloq.* ardent; hot. —**en caliente,** piping hot.

caliente *v.,pres.subjve.* of **calentar.**

caliento (ka'ljen·to) *v., 1st pers.
sing. pres.ind.* of **calentar.**

califa (ka'li·fa) *n.m.* caliph.
—**califato,** *n.m.* caliphate.

calificar (ka·li·fi'kar) *v.t. & i.*
[*infl.:* **tocar,** 7] to qualify. —**califi-
cable,** *adj.* qualifiable. —**calificación,** *n.f.* qualification; judgment;
educ. grade. —**calificado,** *adj.* qualified; competent. —**calificador,**
n.m. [*fem.* -**dora**] qualifier; censor.
—**calificativo,** *adj., gram.* qualifying. —*n.m.* appellation.

californio (ka·li'for·njo) *n.m.* californium.

caligrafía (ka·li·γra'fi·a) *n.f.* calligraphy. —**caligráfico** (-'γra·fi·ko)
adj. calligraphic. —**calígrafo** (-'li-
γra·fo) *n.m.* calligrapher.

calina (ka'li·na) *n.f.* haze; mist.

calistenia (ka·lis'te·nja) *n.f.* calisthenics. —**calisténico** (-'te·ni·ko)
adj. calisthenic.

cáliz ('ka·liθ; -lis) *n.m.* **1,** chalice.
2, *bot.* calyx. **3,** *poet.* cup; vase.

calizo (ka'li·θo; -so) *adj.* limy; of
lime or limestone. —**piedra caliza,**
limestone.

calma ('kal·ma) *n.f.* **1,** *naut.* calm;
calm weather. **2,** calmness; composure. **3,** cessation (*of pain*).

calmar (kal'mar) *v.t.* to calm;
quiet; compose; pacify. —*v.i.* to fall
calm. —**calmado,** *adj.* quiet; calm;
pacified. —**calmante,** *adj.* soothing; sedative. —*n.m.* narcotic; sedative. —**calmoso,** *adj.* calm.

calmo ('kal·mo) *adj.* **1,** empty of
vegetation; treeless, barren. **2,** uncultivated; unfilled. **3,** calm; quiet.

caló (ka'lo) *n.m.* cant; gypsy slang.

calofriarse (ka·lo·fri'ar·se) *also,*
calosfriarse (ka·los-) *v.r.* [*infl.:*
enviar, 22] to shiver with cold;
have a chill. —**calofriado, calos-
friado,** *adj.* = **escalofriado.**
—**calofrío, calosfrío,** *n.m.* = **escalofrío.**

calor (ka'lor) *n.m.* **1,** heat; glow;
warmth. **2,** excitement; animation;
vivacity. —**coger calor; entrar en
calor,** to warm oneself. —**hacer
calor,** to be warm or hot (*of the
weather*). —**tener calor,** to be (feel)
warm or hot.

caloría (ka·lo'ri·a) *n.f.* calorie. —**calórico** (-'lo·ri·ko) *adj.* caloric.

calorífero (ka·lo'ri·fe·ro) *n.m.*
stove; heater; furnace; radiator.
—*adj.* heating; producing heat.

caloso (ka'lo·so) *adj.* porous (*of
paper*).

calque ('kal·ke) *v., pres.subjve.* of
calcar.

calqué (kal'ke) *v., 1st pers.sing.
pret.* of **calcar.**

calumnia (ka'lum·nja) *n.f.* calumny; slander. —**calumnioso,** *adj.*
calumnious; slanderous.

calumniar (ka·lum'njar) *v.t.* to calumniate; slander. —**calumniador,**
n.m. calumniator; slanderer.

caluroso (ka·lu'ro·so) *adj.* warm;
hot.

calva ('kal·βa) *n.f.* **1,** bald spot. **2,**
clearing.

calvario (kal'βa·rjo) *n.m.* **1,** calvary. **2,** *colloq.* debt; tally; score.

calvez (kal'βeθ; -'βes) *n.f.* baldness. *Also,* **calvicie** (-'βi·θje;
-'βi·sje) *n.f.*

calvo ('kal·βo) *adj.* **1,** bald. **2,** barren; treeless.

calza ('kal·θa; -sa) *n.f.* **1,** wedge. **2,**
Amer. gold inlay or filling. **3,** *pl.*
breeches; trousers. **4,** *pl., colloq.*
hose; stockings. —**calza de arena,**
sandbag. —**en calzas prietas,** in
difficulties.

calzada (kal'θa·ða; -'sa·ða) *n.f.*
causeway; paved highway.

calzado (kal'θa·ðo, -'sa·ðo) *adj.* **1,**
shod (*usu. said of certain friars*). **2,**
(*of animals*) having feet of a different color. **3,** (*of birds*) having feathers down to the feet. —*n.m.* footwear.

calzador (kal·θa'ðor; -sa'ðor) *n.m.* shoehorn.

calzar (kal'θar; -'sar) *v.t.* [*infl.:* rezar, 10] 1, to put on (shoes, spurs, gloves, etc.). 2, to provide shoes for. 3, to wear or take (a certain size). 4, to wedge; put a wedge under. 5, *Amer.* to fill (a tooth).

calzo ('kal·θo; -so) *n.m.* 1, wedge. 2, wheel shoe. 3, wooden skid.

calzón (kal'θon; -'son) *n.m.* 1, *usu.pl.* breeches; trousers. 2, safety rope used by roofers and housepainters. 3, ombre (*card game*).

calzoncillos (kal·θon'θi·ʎos; -son'si·jos) *n.m.pl.* drawers; underdrawers.

callado (ka'ʎa·ðo; -'ja·ðo) *adj.* 1, quiet; silent. 2, secret; stealthy. —**callada**, *n.f., naut.* lull. —**de callada; a las calladas**, privately; on the quiet.

callar (ka'ʎar; -'jar) *v.t.* to silence. —*v.i.* 1, to be silent. 2, *poet.* to abate; fall into a lull. **callarse**, *v.r.* to shut up. —¡**calla!; ¡calle!**, you don't say! —**callarse el pico**, *colloq.* to hold one's tongue; to shut up.

calle ('ka·ʎe; -je) *n.f.* 1, street. 2, *colloq.* liberty. —*interj.* make way! —**calle abajo**, down the street. —**calle arriba**, up the street. —**hacer** *or* **abrir calle**, to make way. —**dejar en la calle**, leave penniless.

calleja (ka'ʎe·xa; -'je·xa) *n.f.* alley; lane.

callejear (ka·ʎe·xe'ar; ka·je-) *v.i.* to walk the streets; gad about. —**callejero** (-'xe·ro) *n.m.* loiterer; gadabout.

callejón (ka·ʎe'xon; ka·je-) *n.m.* lane; alley. —**callejón sin salida**, blind alley; cul-de-sac.

callejuela (ka·ʎe'xwe·la; ka·je-) *n.f.* 1, alley; lane. 2, *colloq.* subterfuge; shift.

callista (ka'ʎis·ta; -'jis·ta) *n.m. & f.* chiropodist.

callo ('ka·ʎo; -jo) *n.m.* corn; callus. —**callos**, *n.m.pl.* tripe.

calloso (ka'ʎo·so; ka'jo-) *adj.* callous. —**callosidad**, *n.f.* callosity.

cama ('ka·ma) *n.f.* 1, bed; couch; bedstead. 2, straw bedding (*for animals*). 3, *geol.* layer; stratum. —**cama doble**, double bed. —**cama sencilla**, single bed. —**hacer cama**, to be confined to bed. —**hacer la**

cama a uno, to work against someone behind his back.

camada (ka'ma·ða) *n.f.* 1, litter of animals. 2, bed; layer. 3, *colloq.* band of thieves.

camafeo (ka·ma'fe·o) *n.m.* cameo.

camaleón (ka·ma·le'on) *n.m.* 1, *zoöl.* chameleon. 2, *colloq.* self-serving person; one who changes his mind to suit his interests.

cámara ('ka·ma·ra) *n.f.* 1, hall; parlor. 2, chamber. 3, either house of a bicameral legislature. 4, chamber of a firearm. 5, inner tube. 6, camera. 7, *naut.* cabin. —**cámara de compensación**, *comm.* clearing house. —**cámara de oxígeno**, oxygen tent. —**cámara frigorífica**, cold storage room. —**cámaras**, *n.f.pl.* diarrhea. —**moza de cámara**, chambermaid.

camarada (ka·ma'ra·ða) *n.m.* 1, comrade; partner. 2, *colloq.* chum; buddy. —*n.f.* company or reunion of friends. —**camaradería**, *n.f.* camaradería.

camaranchón (ka·ma·ran'tʃon) *n.m.* garret; attic.

camarera (ka·ma're·ra) *n.f.* 1, chambermaid; housekeeper. 2, waitress. 3, lady in waiting. 4, stewardess.

camarero (ka·ma're·ro) *n.m.* 1, waiter. 2, steward. 3, chamberlain.

camarilla (ka·ma'ri·ʎa; -ja) *n.f.* 1, inner circle; clique. 2, political machine.

camarín (ka·ma'rin) *n.m.* 1, small room. 2, dressing room; boudoir. 3, *eccles.* niche behind an altar where images are kept.

camarlengo (ka·mar'len·go) *n.m.* chamberlain.

camarón (ka·ma'ron) *n.m.* shrimp. *Also,* **cámaro** ('ka·ma·ro).

camarote (ka·ma'ro·te) *n.m.* stateroom; cabin; berth.

cambalachear (kam·ba·la·tʃe·'ar) *v.t. & i.* to barter. —**cambalache** (-'la·tʃe) *n.m.* barter. —**cambalachero**, (-la'tʃe·ro) *adj.* bartering; of or by barter. —*n.m.* barterer.

cambiadiscos (kam·bja'ðis·kos) *n.m.sing. & pl.* record changer.

cambiador (kam·bja'ðor) *adj.* exchanging; bartering. —*n.m.* 1, changer; exchanger. 2, *Amer.* switch; switchman.

cambiante (kam'bjan·te) *adj.* changing; altering. —*n.m. usu.pl.* iridescence. —*n.m.* & *f.* money changer.

cambiar (kam'bjar) *v.t.* & *i.* to change; exchange; barter. —**cambiable,** changeable; exchangeable. —**cambiadizo,** *adj.* changeable; variable.

cambiavía (kam·bja'βi·a) *n.m.*, *Amer., R.R.* **1,** switch. **2,** switchman.

cambio ('kam·bjo) *n.m.* **1,** barter; exchange. **2,** *comm.* premium; rate. **3,** exchange value of currency. **4,** public or private bank. **5,** change *(coins or small bills).* **6,** gearshift. **7,** transmission. **8,** *bot.* [*also,* **cámbium**] cambium. —**casa de cambio,** foreign exchange office. —**en cambio,** on the other hand. —**letra de cambio,** bill of exchange. —**libre cambio,** free trade.

cambista (kam'bis·ta) *n.m.* banker; money broker; *Amer.* switchman.

cámbium ('kam·bi·um) *n.m.* cambium.

cambray (kam'brai) *n.m.* cambric.

camelia (ka'me·lja) *n.f.* camellia.

camello (ka'me·ʎo; -jo) *n.m.* **1,** camel. **2,** *naut.* caisson. —**camellero** (-'ʎe·ro; -'je·ro) *n.m.* camel driver.

camerino (ka·me'ri·no) *n.m.* dressing room.

camilla (ka'mi·ʎa; -ja) *n.f.* **1,** small bed; cot. **2,** stretcher. —**camillero** (-'ʎe·ro; -'je·ro) *n.m.* stretcher-bearer.

caminar (ka·mi'nar) *v.i.* & *t.* to go; travel; walk; march. —**caminata** (-'na·ta) *n.f.,* *colloq.* long walk; jaunt; promenade.

camino (ka'mi·no) *n.m.* **1,** way; course. **2,** road; highway. **3,** passage; trip; journey. —**camino real,** highroad; highway. —**camino vecinal,** country road. —**de camino,** on the way. —**ponerse en camino,** to set out.

camión (ka'mjon) *n.m.* **1,** truck; wagon; lorry. **2,** *Amer.* bus. —**camionaje** (-mjo'na·xe) *n.m.* truck transport; truckage. —**camionero,** *n.m.* truck driver.

camioneta (ka·mjo'ne·ta) *n.f.* **1,** small truck. **2,** *Amer.* station wagon. **3,** *Amer.* small bus.

camisa (ka'mi·sa) *n.f.* shirt; chemise. —**camisa de fuerza,** straitjacket. —**en mangas de camisa,** in shirt sleeves. —**meterse en camisa de once varas,** to bite off more

than one can chew. —**no tener camisa,** to be destitute.

camisería (ka·mi·se'ri·a) *n.f.* haberdashery. —**camisero** (-'se·ro) *n.m.* shirtmaker; haberdasher.

camiseta (ka·mi'se·ta) *n.f.* **1,** undershirt. **2,** T-shirt.

camisilla (ka·mi'si·ʎa; -ja) *n.f.* **1,** small shirt. **2,** *Amer.* undershirt.

camisola (ka·mi'so·la) *n.f.* ruffled shirt.

camisolín (ka·mi·so'lin) *n.m.* shirtfront; dickey.

camisón (ka·mi'son) *n.m.* **1,** long shirt, **2,** nightshirt. **3,** nightgown; nightdress.

camita (ka'mi·ta) *n.f.* small bed; cot; couch.

camita (ka'mi·ta) *adj.* & *n.m.* & *f.* Hamite. —**camítico** (-'mi·ti·ko) *adj.* Hamitic.

camomila (ka·mo'mi·la) *n.f.* camomile.

camón (ka'mon) *n.m.* large bed.

camorra (ka'mo·rra) *n.f.* **1,** quarrel; row. **2,** *cap.* Camorra. —**armar camorra,** to quarrel; raise a row. —**buscar camorra,** to look for trouble.

camorrista (ka·mo'rris·ta) *n.m.* & *f.* **1,** noisy, quarrelsome person. **2,** member of the Camorra.

campamento (kam·pa'men·to) *n.m.* encampment; camp.

campana (kam'pa·na) *n.f.* **1,** bell; any bell-shaped object. **2,** *fig.* parish; church. —**campana de buzo,** diving bell. —**campana de rebato,** alarm bell. —**picar la campana,** *naut.* to sound the bell.

campanada (kam·pa'na·ða) *n.f.* **1,** peal of a bell. **2,** *fig.* scandal; sensation. —**dar una campanada,** to cause scandal.

campanario (kam·pa'na·rjo) *n.m.* belfry; bell tower; campanile.

campanear (kam·pa·ne'ar) *v.t.* to ring; ring repeatedly. —*v.i.* to reverberate; chime. —**campaneo** (-'ne·o) *n.m.* bell ringing; chime.

campanero (kam·pa'ne·ro) *n.m.* **1,** bell ringer. **2,** bell founder.

campanilla (kam·pa'ni·ʎa; -ja) *n.f., dim.* **1,** small bell; hand bell. **2,** *anat.* uvula. **3,** *bot.* bellflower. —**campanillazo,** *n.m.* loud ringing.

campanudo (kam·pa'nu·ðo) *adj.* bell-shaped.

campaña (kam'pa·ɲa) *n.f.* **1,** campaign. **2,** *naut.* cruise.

campañol (kam·pa'ɲol) *n.m.* field mouse; vole.

campar (kam'par) *v.i.* **1,** to camp; encamp. **2,** to excel in ability or talent.

campear (kam·pe'ar) *v.i.* **1,** to be in the field; pasture. **2,** to grow green *(of fields)*. **3,** to excel; be eminent.

campechano (kam·pe'tʃa·no) *adj., colloq.* jovial; hearty.

campeón (kam·pe'on) *n.m.* champion; defender. **—campeonato,** *n.m.* championship.

campero (kam'pe·ro) *adj.* exposed to the outdoors; unsheltered. **—n.m.** field guard.

campesino (kam·pe'si·no) *n.m.* **1,** rustic; country dweller. **2,** farmer; peasant — *adj.* [*also,* **campestre** (-'pes·tre)] rural; pastoral.

campiña (kam'pi·ɲa) *n.f.* open country; fields *(pl.)*.

campo ('kam·po) *n.m.* **1,** country; field. **2,** camp. **3,** athletic field. **—a campo raso,** outdoors. **—campo de veraneo,** summer camp. **—dar campo a,** to give ground to.

camposanto (kam·po'san·to) *n.m.* cemetery.

camuflar (ka·mu'flar) *v.t.* to camouflage **—camuflaje** (-'fla·xe) *n.m.* camouflage.

can (kan) *n.m.* **1,** dog. **2,** trigger. **3,** *cap., astron.* Dog Star.

cana ('ka·na) *n.f.* gray hair. **—echar una cana al aire,** *colloq.* to go on a spree. **—peinar canas,** to be old; be grayhaired.

canadiense (ka·na'ðjen·se) *adj. & n.m. & f.* Canadian.

canal (ka'nal) *n.m.* **1,** channel; canal; duct. **2,** inlet; strait. **3,** *TV* channel. **—n.f.** **1,** natural underground waterway. **2,** long, narrow valley. **3,** *anat.* duct. **4,** roof gutter; gutter tile. **5,** pipe; conduit. **6,** dressed animal carcass. **—canalón,** *n.m.* large gutter; spout.

canalizar (ka·na·li'θar; -'sar) *v.t.* [*infl.:* **rezar, 10**] to canalize; channel; pipe **—canalización,** *n.f.* canalization; piping.

canalla (ka'na·ʎa; -ja) *n.f.* mob; rabble. **—n.m.** scoundrel. **—canallada,** *n.f.* low trick.

canallesco (ka·na'ʎes·ko; -'jes·ko) *adj.* **1,** of the rabble; low; vulgar. **2,** mean; scoundrelly.

canana (ka'na·na) *n.f.* cartridge belt. **—cananas,** *n.f.pl., Amer.* handcuffs.

canapé (ka·na'pe) *n.m.* **1,** couch; sofa. **2,** canapé.

canario (ka'na·rjo) *n.m.* canary. **—interj.** great Scott!

canasta (ka'nas·ta) *n.f.* **1,** basket. **2,** crate. **3,** canasta *(card game).*

canastero (ka·nas'te·ro) *n.m.* **1,** basketmaker. **2,** canasta player.

canasto (ka'nas·to) *also,* **canastro,** *n.m.* large basket; hamper. **—¡canastos!,** confound it!

cancán (kan'kan) *n.m.* cancan.

cancela (kan'θe·la; -'se·la) *n.f.* grating; grille.

cancelar (kan·θe'lar; kan·se-) *v.t.* to cancel. **—cancelación,** *n.f.* cancellation; obliteration.

cáncer ('kan·θer; -ser) *n.m.* **1,** cancer. **2,** *cap., astron.* Cancer. **—canceroso,** *adj.* cancerous.

cancerarse (kan·θe'rar·se; kan·se-) *v.r.* to become cancerous.

cancerígeno (kan·θe'ri·xe·no; kan·se-) *adj.* carcinogenic. **—agente cancerígeno,** carcinogen.

canciller (kan·θi'ʎer; -si'jer) *n.m.* chancellor.

cancillería (kan·θi·ʎe'ri·a; kan·si·je-) *n.f.* **1,** chancellery. **2,** chancellorship. **3,** chancery.

canción (kan'θjon; -'sjon) *n.f.* song; lyric poem; ballad. **—cancionero,** *n.m.* song book. **—cancionista,** *n.m. & f.* singer or composer.

cancha ('kan·tʃa) *n.f.* **1,** *sports* field; court; ground; (golf) links. **2,** cockpit. **3,** *Amer.* racetrack. **—interj.** make way!

candar (kan'dar) *v.t.* to lock; shut. **—candado** (-'da·ðo) *n.m.* padlock.

candela (kan'de·la) *n.f.* **1,** candle. **2,** *colloq.* light; flame; fire. **—estar con la candela en la mano,** *colloq.* to be dying. **—arrimar candela,** *colloq.* to spank; beat.

candelabro (kan·de'la·βro) *n.m.* candelabrum.

candelaria (kan·de'la·rja) *n.f.* **1,** mullein. **2,** *cap.* Candlemas.

candelero (kan·de'le·ro) *n.m.* candlestick. **—candeleros,** *n.m.pl., naut.* stanchions. **—estar en el candelero,** *colloq.* to be in the limelight.

candelilla (kan·de'li·ʎa; -ja) *n.f.* **1,** *surg.* catheter. **2,** *bot.* catkin. **3,** *Amer.* will-o'-the-wisp.

candente (kan'den·te) *adj.* incan-

descent; white hot. —**candencia,**
n.f. incandescence.

candidato (kan·di'ða·to) *n.m.* candidate. —**candidatura** (-'tu·ra) *n.f.*
candidacy.

candidez (kan·di'ðeθ; -'ðes) *n.f.* 1,
candor; simplicity; frankness. 2,
whiteness.

cándido ('kan·di·ðo) *adj.* 1, candid; simple; frank. 2, white.

candileja (kan·di'le·xa) *n.f.* small
oil lamp. —**candilejas,** *n.f.pl.,*
theat. footlights.

candor (kan'dor) *n.m.* 1, candor;
frankness. 2, innocence.

candoroso (kan·do'ro·so) *adj.* 1,
candid; frank. 2, innocent.

canela (ka'ne·la) *n.f.* 1, cinnamon.
2, *colloq.* an exquisite thing.
—**canelo,** *n.m.* cinnamon tree.

canelón (ka·ne'lon) *n.m.* 1, gargoyle. 2, roof gutter. —**canelones,**
n.m.pl. ends of a cat-o'-nine-tails.

cangreja (kan'gre·xa) *n.f.* foreand-aft sail. —**cangreja de popa,**
spanker.

cangrejo (kan'gre·xo) *n.m.* 1, crab;
crawfish. 2, *cap., astron.* Cancer.
—**cangrejo bayoneta** *or* **de las
Molucas,** horseshoe crab.

cangrena (kan'gre·na) *n.f.* =
gangrena. —**cangrenarse,** *v.r.* =
gangrenarse. —**cangrenoso,** *adj.* =
gangrenoso.

canguro (kan'gu·ro) *n.m.* kangaroo.

caníbal (ka'ni·βal) *n.m.* cannibal.
—*adj.* cannibalistic. —**canibalismo,** *n.m.* cannibalism.

canica (ka'ni·ka) *n.f.* 1, *pl.* game of
marbles. 2, marble.

canicie (ka'ni·θje; -sje) *n.f.* whiteness of the hair.

canícula (ka'ni·ku·la) *n.f.* 1, dog
days. 2, *cap., astron.* Dog Star.

canilla (ka'ni·ʎa; -ja) *n.f.* 1, long
bone. 2, petcock. 3, faucet. 4, spool;
reel. 5, rib or stripe *(in cloth).*
6, *slang* slender leg.

canillita (ka·ni'ʎi·ta; -'ji·ta) *n.m.,*
Amer. newsboy.

canino (ka'ni·no) *adj.* canine.
—*n.m.* canine tooth.

canjear (kan·xe'ar) *v.t.* to exchange. —**canje** ('kan·xe) *n.m.*
exchange. —**canjeable,** *adj.* exchangeable.

cano ('ka·no) *adj.* gray; grayhaired.

canoa (ka'no·a) *n.f.* 1, canoe. 2,
launch. 3, *Amer.* trough. 4, *Amer.*

water ditch or trench. —**canoero,**
n.m. canoeist.

canódromo (ka'no·ðro·mo) *n.m.*
dog track.

canon ('ka·non) *n.m.* canon.
—**canones,** *n.m.pl.* canon law.
—**canónico** (-'no·ni·ko) *adj.* canonical.

canonicato (ka·no·ni'ka·to) *n.m.*
= **canonjía.**

canonicidad (ka·no·ni·θi'ðað;
-si'ðað) *n.f.* canonicity.

canónigo (ka'no·ni·ɣo) *n.m.* canon
(churchman).

canonista (ka·no'nis·ta) *n.m.* canonist.

canonizar (ka·no·ni'θar; -'sar) *v.t.*
[infl.: rezar, 10] to canonize.
—**canonización,** *n.f.* canonization.

canonjía (ka·non'xi·a) *n.m.* 1, canonry. 2, *colloq.* sinecure.

canoro (ka'no·ro) *adj.* melodious;
musical. —**ave canora,** songbird.

canoso (ka'no·so) *adj.* gray; grayhaired.

canotié (ka·no'tje) *n.m.* straw hat
with a flat crown; sailor.

cansado (kan'sa·ðo) *adj.* 1, tired.
2, boring; tedious; tiresome. —*n.m.*
colloq. bore; tiresome person.

cansancio (kan'san·θjo; -sjo) *n.m.*
fatigue; weariness.

cansar (kan'sar) *v.t.* 1, to tire; fatigue. 2, to exhaust (land). —**cansarse,** *v.r.* to tire; become weary.

cantable (kan'ta·βle) *adj.* singable.

cantalupo (kan·ta'lu·po) *n.m.* cantaloupe.

cantante (kan'tan·te) *n.m. & f.*
singer. —*adj.* singing.

cantar (kan'tar) *v.t. & i.* 1, to sing.
2, *colloq.* to squeal; confess. 3,
poet. to compose; recite. —*n.m.*
song; singing.

cántara (kan·ta·ra) *n.f.* 1, liquid
measure equal to 16.13 liters, or
about 15 quarts. 2, = **cántaro.**

cantarín (kan·ta'rin) *n.m., colloq.*
songster; singer.

cántaro ('kan·ta·ro) *n.m.* pitcher;
jug. —**llover a cántaros,** to rain
cats and dogs.

cantata (kan'ta·ta) *n.f.* cantata.

cantatriz (kan·ta'triθ; -'tris) *n.f.*
singer.

cantazo (kan·ta·θo; -so) *n.m.* 1,
blow; cuff. 2, bump; knock.

cantera (kan'te·ra) *n.f.* 1, quarry.
2, *Amer.* block of stone. 3, *fig.* talents; genius. —**cantería** (-'te'ri·a)

n.f. stonecutting. —**cantero** (-'te·ro) *n.m.* stonecutter.

cántico ('kan·ti·ko) *n.m.* canticle; song.

cantidad (kan·ti'ðað) *n.f.* quantity.

cantilena (kan·ti'le·na) *n.f.* song; ballad. —**la misma cantilena,** the same old song or story.

cantimplora (kan·tim'plo·ra) *n.f.* 1, canteen. 2, siphon. 3, water cooler. 4, flask; decanter. 5, *Amer.* powder flask. 6, *Amer.* mumps.

cantina (kan'ti·na) *n.f.* 1, mess hall. 2, wine shop. 3, canteen. 4, *Amer.* barroom; tavern; saloon.

cantinela (kan·ti'ne·la) *n.f.* = **cantilena.**

cantinero (kan·ti'ne·ro) *n.m.* bartender; tavernkeeper.

canto ('kan·to) *n.m.* 1, song; singing. 2, epic poem. 3, canto. 4, *Amer.* small piece; bit. 5, edge; end. —**al canto de,** by the side of. —**al canto del gallo,** *colloq.* at daybreak.

cantón (kan'ton) *n.m.* 1, canton; region. 2, corner; edge.

cantonar (kan·to'nar) *v.t.* = **acantonar.**

cantonera (kan·to'ne·ra) *n.f.* 1, corner plate; angle iron. 2, *vulg.* streetwalker.

cantonero (kan·to'ne·ro) *n.m.* loafer; idler. —*adj.* loafing; idle.

cantor (kan'tor) *n.m.* [*fem.*-**tora**] 1, singer. 2, *colloq.* minstrel.

canturía (kan·tu'ri·a) *n.f.* 1, vocal music. 2, vocal exercise. 3, singsong. 4, singability; ease of singing or playing.

canturrear (kan·tu·rre'ar) *also,* **canturriar** (-tu'rrjar) *v.t. & i.* to hum; sing softly. —**canturreo** (-'rre·o) *n.m.* hum; humming.

cánula (ka·nu·la) *n.f., med.* 1, cannula. 2, hypodermic needle.

caña ('ka·ɲa) *n.f.* 1, cane; reed. 2, *Amer., colloq.* walking stick. 3, *naut.* helm. 4, *Amer., colloq.* bluff; boast. —**caña de pescar,** fishing rod.

cañada (ka'ɲa·ða) *n.f.* glen; dell.

cañal (ka'ɲal) *n.m.* 1, = **cañaveral.** 2, fishing channel. 3, weir (*for fishing*).

cañamazo (ka·ɲa·ma·θo; -so) *n.m.* canvas for embroidery.

cañamelar (ka·ɲa·me'lar) *n.m.* sugar cane plantation.

cañamiel (ka·ɲa'mjel) *n.f.* sugar cane.

cáñamo ('ka·ɲa·mo) *n.m.* hemp.

cañaveral (ka·ɲa·βe'ral) *n.m.* canebrake; cane field.

cañería (ka·ɲe'ri·a) *n.f.* 1, conduit; pipeline. 2, sewer pipe. 3, water or gas main. 4, *mus.* organ pipes.

caño ('ka·ɲo) *n.m.* 1, spout; faucet. 2, pipe; tube. 3, common sewer. 4, *mus.* organ pipe. 5, *naut.* channel. 6, *Amer.* gully; ravine.

cañón (ka'ɲon) *n.m.* 1, cannon. 2, pipe; tube. 3, barrel of a gun. 4, *mech.* socket. 5, canyon. —**cañón de chimenea,** chimney flue.

cañonear (ka·ɲo·ne'ar) *v.t.* to bombard; cannonade. —**cañonazo,** *n.m.* cannon shot. —**cañoneo,** *n.m.* bombardment.

cañonería (ka·ɲo·ne'ri·a) *n.f.* 1, cannonry; cannons collectively. 2, organ pipes collectively.

cañonero (ka·ɲo'ne·ro) *n.m.* [*also,* **lancha cañonera**] gunboat.

cañuto (ka'ɲu·to) *n.m.* small tube; small pipe.

caoba (ka'o·βa) *n.f.* mahogany tree; mahogany wood.

caobo (ka'o·βo) *n.m.* mahogany tree.

caos ('ka·os) *n.m.* chaos. —**caótico** (-'o·ti·ko) *adj.* chaotic.

capa ('ka·pa) *n.f.* 1, cape; cloak; mantle. 2, covering; coating. 3, layer; stratum.

capacidad (ka·pa·θi'ðað; -si'ðað) *n.f.* 1, capacity. 2, ability; talent. —**capacidad adquisitiva,** purchasing power. —**capacidad de ganancia,** earning power.

capacitar (ka·pa·θi'tar; -si'tar) *v.t.* 1, to enable; prepare. 2, to empower; authorize. 3, to train (*an employee*) —**capacitación,** training.

capacho (ka'pa·tʃo) *n.m.* 1, large basket; hamper. 2, *ornith.* barn owl.

capar (ka'par) *v.t.* 1, to castrate. 2, *vulg.* to curtail.

caparazón (ka·pa·ra'θon; -'son) *n.m.* 1, caparison. 2, horse blanket. 3, feedbag. 4, shell of insects or crustaceans.

capataz (ka·pa'taθ; -'tas) *n.m.* overseer; superintendent; foreman.

capaz (ka'paθ; -'pas) *adj.* 1, capable; competent. 2, spacious; roomy.

capcioso (kap'θjo·so; -'sjo·so) *adj.* captious; insidious. —**capciosidad,** *n.f.* captiousness.

capear (ka·pe'ar) *v.t.* 1, to challenge (a bull) with a cape. 2, to dodge; wait out. 3, to fool. —*v.i.* 1, *naut.* to lay to. 2, *colloq.* to lie low.

—**capeador,** *n.m.* [*fem.* **-dora**] bull-fighter who challenges a bull with a cape. —**capeo** (-'pe·o) *n.m.* challenging of a bull with a cape.
capellán (ka·pe'ʎan; -'jan) *n.m.* chaplain.
caperuza (ka·pe'ru·θa; -sa) *n.f.* **1,** hood; cowl. **2,** cap or covering, esp. cone-shaped.
capilar (ka·pi'lar) *adj. & n.m.* capillary. —**capilaridad,** *n.f.* capillarity.
capilla (ka'pi·ʎa; -ja) *n.f.* **1,** chapel. **2,** hood; cowl. **3,** *print.* proof sheet. **4,** death house. —**capilla ardiente,** funeral chapel. —**estar en capilla,** to await execution; *fig.* to be on pins and needles.
capillo (ka'pi·ʎo; -jo) *n.m.* **1,** child's cap. **2,** baptismal cap. **3,** christening fee.
capirotazo (ka·pi·ro'ta·θo; -so) *n.m.* fillip.
capirote (ka·pi'ro·te) *n.m.* **1,** hood. **2,** cone-shaped cap. **3,** fillip. —**tonto de capirote,** nincompoop.
capirucho (ka·pi'ru·tʃo) *n.m., colloq.* hood; cap.
capitación (ka·pi·ta'θjon; -'sjon) *n.f.* poll tax.
capital (ka·pi'tal) *adj.* capital. —*n.m.* **1,** capital; assets. **2,** asset. —*n.f.* capital *(city).* —**capital especulativo,** venture capital. —**capital líquido,** net worth. —**capital neto,** net worth. —**capital social,** capital stock.
capitalismo (ka·pi·ta'lis·mo) *n.m.* capitalism. —**capitalista,** *n.m. & f.* capitalist. —*adj.* capitalistic.
capitalizar (ka·pi·ta·li'θar; -'sar) *v.t.* [*infl.*: **rezar,** 10] **1,** *comm.* to capitalize. **2,** to compound (interest). —**capitalización,** *n.f.* capitalization.
capitán (ka·pi'tan) *n.m.* captain.
capitana (ka·pi'ta·na) *n.f.* **1,** flagship. **2,** captain's wife.
capitanear (ka·pi·ta·ne'ar) *v.t.* to command; head; lead.
capitanía (ka·pi·ta'ni·a) *n.f.* captainship; captaincy. —**Capitanía General,** Captaincy General; *l.c.* captain-generalcy.
capitel (ka·pi'tel) *n.m., archit.* capital.
capitolio (ka·pi'to·ljo) *n.m.* capitol.
capitulado (ka·pi·tu'la·ðo) *n.m.* capitulation; contract.

capitular (ka·pi·tu'lar) *v.i.* **1,** to conclude an agreement. **2,** to draw articles of a contract. **3,** *mil.* to capitulate. —*v.t.* to impeach. —*adj., eccles.* capitular; capitulary. —**capitulación,** *n.f.* capitulation; agreement. —**capitulaciones,** *n.f.pl.* marriage contract.
capítulo (ka'pi·tu·lo) *n.m.* **1,** chapter; division. **2,** *law* charge; count. —**capítulos matrimoniales,** articles of marriage. —**llamar a capítulo,** to call to account; bring to book.
capó (ka'po) *n.m.* = **capot.**
capolar (ka·po'lar) *v.t.* to mince; chop. —**capolado,** *n.m.* hash; minced meat.
capón (ka'pon) *n.m.* capon. —*adj.* castrated; gelded.
caporal (ka·po'ral) *n.m.* **1,** boss; chief. **2,** cattle boss.
capot (ka'pot) *n.m.* hood *(of an engine).*
capota (ka'po·ta) *n.f.* **1,** automobile top; convertible top. **2,** *aero.* cowling. **3,** = **capot.**
capotar (ka·po'tar) *v.i.* to turn or flip over.
capote (ka'po·te) *n.m.* **1,** bullfighter's cape. **2,** *mil.* close-fitting cloak with sleeves. **3,** *Amer.* beating; thrashing. —**capote de monte,** poncho. —**dar capote,** to win all the tricks, in certain card games. —**para mi capote,** (I said) to myself.
capotear (ka·po·te'ar) *v.t.* **1,** = **capear. 2,** to evade; shirk. **3,** to bamboozle.
capotera (ka·po'te·ra) *n.f., Amer.* clothes rack; clothes tree.
Capricornio (ka·pri'kor·njo) *n.m.* Capricorn.
capricho (ka'pri·tʃo) *n.m.* **1,** caprice; whim. **2,** desire; yen. **3,** *mus.* capriccio; caprice. —**caprichoso,** *adj.* capricious; whimsical; willful. —**caprichudo,** *adj.* obstinate; stubborn.
caprino (ka'pri·no) *adj.* = **cabrío.**
cápsula ('kap·su·la) *n.f.* **1,** bottle cap. **2,** cartridge. **3,** capsule. —**capsular,** *adj.* capsule; capsular. —*v.t.* to cap (a bottle).
captar (kap'tar) *v.t.* **1,** to catch; grasp. **2,** to capture; attract; win. **3,** to impound.
capturar (kap·tu'rar) *v.t.* to capture. —**captura** (-'tu·ra) *n.f.* capture.

capucha (ka'pu·tʃa) *n.f.* **1,** cowl; hood (*of a cloak*). **2,** *print.* circumflex accent.

capuchina (ka·pu'tʃi·na) *n.f.* nasturtium.

capuchino (ka·pu'tʃi·no) *adj.* & *n.m., eccles.* Capuchin. —*n.m., zoöl.* capuchin monkey.

capuchón (ka·pu'tʃon) *n.m.* **1,** hooded cloak. **2,** short domino.

capullo (ka'pu·ʎo; -jo) *n.m.* **1,** cocoon. **2,** flower bud.

capuz (ka'puθ; -'pus) *n.m.* **1,** cowl. **2,** hooded cloak.

caqui ('ka·ki) *adj.* & *n.m.* khaki. —*n.m., bot.* persimmon.

cara ('ka·ra) *n.f.* **1,** face; countenance. **2,** expression. **3,** façade; front. **4,** surface. **5,** heads (*of a coin*). **6,** side (*of a phonograph record*). —**cara a cara,** face to face. —**de cara,** opposite; facing. —**echar en cara; dar en cara,** to reproach (with). —**hacer cara a,** to face; confront. —**tener mala cara, 1,** to look ill. **2,** to make a bad appearance.

carabao (ka·ra'βa·o) *n.m.* water buffalo; carabao.

carabela (ka·ra'βe·la) *n.f.* caravel.

carabina (ka·ra'βi·na) *n.f.* carbine. —**carabinazo,** *n.m.* carbine shot.

carabinero (ka·ra·βi'ne·ro) *n.m.* **1,** carabineer. **2,** customs guard.

caracol (ka·ra'kol) *n.m.* **1,** snail; snail shell. **2,** seashell. **3,** *anat.* cochlea. **4,** *archit.* spiral. —¡**caracoles!,** *interj.* good heavens! —**escalera de caracol,** winding stairway.

caracolear (ka·ra·ko·le'ar) *v.i.* to caper; prance. —**caracoleo** (-'le·o) *n.m.* caper; prancing.

carácter (ka'rak·ter) *n.m.* [*pl.* caracteres (-'te·res)] **1,** character. **2,** mark; letter. **3,** *pl., print.* type; type faces.

característica (ka·rak·te'ris·ti·ka) *n.f.* **1,** characteristic; trait. **2,** character actress.

característico (ka·rak·te'ris·ti·ko) *adj.* characteristic; typical. —*n.m.* character actor.

caracterizado (ka·rak·te·ri'θa·ðo; -'sa·ðo) *adj.* characterized; distinguished.

caracterizar (ka·rak·te·ri'θar; -'sar) *v.t.* [*infl.:* rezar, 10] **1,** to characterize. **2,** *theat.* to play (a role). —**caracterización,** *n.f.* characterization.

caracul (ka·ra'kul) *n.m.* caracul.

carado (ka'ra·ðo) *adj., used only in:* **bien carado; biencarado,** kindfaced; pleasant; **mal carado; malcarado,** grim-faced; frowning.

caramba (ka'ram·ba) *interj. of surprise or annoyance* gracious!; darn it!

carámbano (ka'ram·ba·no) *n.m.* icicle.

carambola (ka·ram'bo·la) *n.f.* **1,** carom. **2,** *colloq.* trick; indirection. —**por carambola,** by chance.

carambolear (ka·ram·bo·le'ar) *v.t.* to carom.

caramelo (ka·ra'me·lo) *n.m.* **1,** caramel. **2,** candy; sugar drop. —**caramelizar** (-li'θar: -li'sar) *v.t.* [*infl.:* rezar, 10] = acaramelar.

caramente (ka·ra'men·te) *adv.* **1,** dearly. **2,** expensively.

caramillo (ka·ra'mi·ʎo; -jo) *n.m.* **1,** small flute. **2,** *colloq.* deceit; trick. —**armar un caramillo,** *colloq.* to raise a rumpus.

carapacho (ka·ra·pa·tʃo) *n.m.* shell; carapace.

carátula (ka·ra·tu·la) *n.f.* **1,** mask. **2,** *Amer.* title page.

caravana (ka·ra·βa·na) *n.f.* caravan.

caray (ka'rai) *n.m.* tortoise; tortoiseshell. —*interj.* = caramba.

carbohidrato (kar·βo·i'ðra·to) *n.m.* carbohydrate.

carbólico (kar'βo·li·ko) *n.m.* carbolic.

carbón (kar'βon) *n.m.* **1,** coal. **2,** carbon filament, electrode, etc. —**carbón de leña; carbón vegetal,** charcoal. —**carbón de piedra; carbón mineral,** coal. —**echar carbón,** *colloq.* to stir things up; inflame someone.

carbonado (kar·βo'na·ðo) *n.m.* black diamond.

carbonar (kar·βo'nar) *v.t.* to make into charcoal.

carbonatar (kar·βo·na'tar) *v.t.* to carbonate.

carbonato (kar·βo'na·to) *n.m.* **1,** carbonate. **2,** [*also,* carbonato de soda] washing soda. **3,** *erroneous* = bicarbonato. —*adj.* carbonated.

carboncillo (kar·βon'θi·ʎo; -'si·jo) *n.m.* **1,** small coal. **2,** charcoal pencil.

carbonear (kar·βo·ne'ar) *v.t.* to char; make into charcoal. —**carboneo** (-'ne·o) *n.m.* carbonization; charcoal burning.

carbonera (kar·βo'ne·ra) *n.f.* **1,** wood used for burning into charcoal. **2,** coal cellar; coal bin. **3,** a woman who sells coal; charcoal dealer; charcoal maker.

carbonería (kar·βo·ne'ri·a) *n.f.* coal yard; coal shed.

carbonero (kar·βo'ne·ro) *n.m.* charcoal dealer; charcoal maker; coal man. —*adj.* pert to coal or charcoal.

carbónico (kar'βo·ni·ko) *adj.* carbonic.

carbonífero (kar·βo'ni·fe·ro) *adj.* carboniferous.

carbonizar (kar·βo·ni'θar; -'sar) *v.t.* [*infl.:* rezar, 10] to carbonize; char. —**carbonización,** *n.f.* carbonization.

carbono (kar'βo·no) *n.m., chem.* carbon. —**carbonoso,** *adj.* carbonaceous.

carborundo (kar·βo'run·do) *n.m.* carborundum.

carbunclo (kar'βun·klo) *n.m.* **1,** = **carbunco. 2,** = **carbúnculo.**

carbunco (kar'βun·ko) *n.m., pathol.* carbuncle.

carbúnculo (kar'βun·ku·lo) *n.m., jewelry* carbuncle.

carburador (kar·βu·ra'ðor) *n.m.* carburetor.

carburante (kar·βu'ran·te) *n.m.* gas or liquid fuel.

carburo (kar'βu·ro) *n.m.* carbide.

carca ('kar·ka) *n.f., Amer.* grime.

carcaj (kar'kax) *also,* **carcax** (-'kaks) *n.m.* **carcaza** (-'ka·θa; -sa) *n.f.* quiver.

carcajada (kar·ka'xa·ða) *n.f.* loud laughter; guffaw.

cárcava ('kar·ka·βa) *n.f.* **1,** gully; ditch. **2,** grave.

cárcel ('kar·θel; -sel) *n.f.* **1,** jail. **2,** groove of a sluice gate. —**carcelario,** *adj.* of or pert. to a jail or prison. —**carcelero,** *n.m.* jailer; warden.

carcinoma (kar·θi'no·ma; kar·si-) *n.f.* carcinoma.

carcoma (kar'ko·ma) *n.f.* **1,** *entom.* wood borer. **2,** dry rot. **3,** anxiety. **4,** wasting; waste. **5,** wastrel.

carcomer (kar·ko'mer) *v.t.* to gnaw; rot; erode. —**carcomerse,** *v.r.* to become worm-eaten; decay.

carda ('kar·ða) *n.f.* **1,** carding. **2,** card (*for carding*).

cardar (kar'ðar) *v.t.* to card (fibers); tease (hair). —**cardador,** *n.m.*

[*fem.* -dora] carder. —**cardadora,** *n.f.* carding machine.

cardelina (kar·ðe'li·na) *n.f.* goldfinch; linnet.

cardenal (kar·ðe'nal) *n.m., eccles.; ornith.* cardinal. —**cardenalato,** *n.m.* cardinalate.

cardencha (kar'ðen·tʃa) *n.f.* **1,** *bot.* teasel. **2,** card (*for carding*).

cárdeno ('kar·ðe·no) *adj.* livid; purple.

cardíaco (kar'ði·a·ko) *adj. & n.m.* cardiac. —**ataque cardíaco,** heart attack.

cardialgia (kar·ði'al·xja) *n.f.* cardialgia; heartburn.

cardinal (kar·ði'nal) *adj.* cardinal; principal; fundamental.

cardiología (kar·ði·o·lo'xi·a) *n.f.* cardiology. —**cardiológico** (-'lo·xi·ko) *adj.* cardiological. —**cardiólogo** (-'o·lo·γo) *n.m.* cardiologist.

cardiopulmonar (kar·ðjo·pul·mo'nar) *adj.* cardiopulmonary.

carditis (kar'ði·tis) *n.f.* carditis.

cardo ('kar·ðo) *n.m.* thistle.

cardumen (kar'ðu·men) *also,* **cardume** (-me) *n.m.* school of fish.

carear (ka·re'ar) *v.t.* **1,** to confront. **2,** to bring face to face. **3,** to compare. —**carearse,** *v.r.* to assemble; meet face to face.

carecer (ka·re'θer; -'ser) *v.i.* [*infl.:* conocer, 13] to be in need. —**carecer de,** to lack; be in need of.

carena (ka're·na) *n.f., naut.* **1,** ship's bottom. **2,** cleaning and calking. —**dique de carena,** dry dock.

carencia (ka'ren·θja; -sja) *n.f.* lack; want; need.

careo (ka're·o) *n.m.* **1,** meeting; confrontation. **2,** comparison.

carero (ka're·ro) *adj., colloq.* expensive; overpriced.

carestía (ka·res'ti·a) *n.f.* **1,** scarcity; lack. **2,** high prices.

careta (ka're·ta) *n.f.* **1,** mask. **2,** wire mask (*esp. as used in fencing and beekeeping*).

carey (ka'rei) *n.m.* **1,** a kind of marine turtle. **2,** tortoise shell.

carga ('kar·γa) *n.f.* **1,** load; burden; charge. **2,** freight; cargo. **3,** charge (*of gunpowder*).

cargadero (kar·γa'ðe·ro) *n.m.* loading station or platform.

cargado (kar'γa·ðo) *adj.* **1,** loaded. **2,** thick; strong (*of drinks*). **3,** cloudy; overcast. **4,** sultry.

—**cargado de espaldas,** stoop-shouldered.

cargador (kar·ɣa'ðor) *n.m.* **1,** loader; stevedore. **2,** porter. **3,** battery charger.

cargamento (kar·ɣa'men·to) *n.m.* cargo.

cargar (kar'ɣar) *v.t. & i.* [*infl.:* **pagar,** 8] **1,** to load; charge. **2,** to burden. **3,** to entrust. **4,** *colloq.* to weary; annoy. **5,** *Amer.* to carry; lug. —**cargarse,** *v.r.* to lean; sway. —**cargar con,** to assume; take on oneself. —**cargar con el muerto,** to get the blame *(unjustly).* —**cargarse de,** to have in plenty.

cargazón (kar·ɣa'θon; -'son) *n.f.* **1,** cargo. **2,** feeling of heaviness *(in the head, stomach, etc.).* **3,** sultriness. **4,** *Amer., colloq.* bother; nuisance.

cargo ('kar·ɣo) *n.m.* **1,** act of loading; weight; burden. **2,** charge. **3,** position; job. —**cargo de conciencia,** remorse. —**hacerse cargo de, 1,** to realize. **2,** to take over; take charge of.

carguero (kar'ɣe·ro) *adj.* of burden; load-carrying; freight-carrying. —*n.m., Amer.* beast of burden.

cari ('ka·ri) *n.m.* curry.

cariarse (ka'rjar·se) *v.r.* [*infl.:* **enviar,** 22] to become carious; decay. —**cariado,** *adj.* carious; decayed.

caribe (ka'ri·βe) *adj.* Caribbean. —*adj. & n.m.* Carib. —*n.m.* savage.

caricatura (ka·ri·ka'tu·ra) *n.f.* caricature; cartoon. —**caricaturesco,** *adj.* in caricature.

caricaturista (ka·ri·ka·tu'ris·ta) *n.m. & f.* caricaturist; cartoonist.

caricaturizar (ka·ri·ka·tu·ri'θar; -'sar) *v.t.* [*infl.:* **rezar,** 10] to caricature. *Also,* **caricaturar.**

caricia (ka'ri·θja; -sja) *n.f.* caress; petting.

caridad (ka·ri'ðað) *n.f.* **1,** charity. **2,** alms.

caries ('ka·rjes) *n.f.pl.* caries.

carillón (ka·ri'ʎon; -'jon) *n.m.* carillon.

cariño (ka'ri·ɲo) *n.m.* **1,** affection; love. **2,** *colloq.* gift. —**cariños,** *n.m.pl.* affectionate regards. —**cariñoso,** *adj.* affectionate; loving; endearing.

carisma (ka'ris·ma) *n.m.* charisma. —**carismático** (-'ma·ti·ko) *adj.* charismatic.

caritativo (ka·ri·ta'ti·βo) *adj.* charitable.

cariz (ka'riθ; -'ris) *n.m.* appearance; look; aspect.

carlinga (kar'lin·ga) *n.f.* cockpit.

carmen ('kar·men) *n.m., in Granada,* a country house; a garden.

carmenar (kar·me'nar) *v.t.* **1,** to disentangle; unravel. **2,** *colloq.* to pull (someone's) hair). **3,** *fig.* to swindle.

carmesí (kar·me'si) *adj.* crimson. —*n.m.* cochineal powder.

carmín (kar'min) *adj. & n.m.* carmine.

carminativo (kar·mi·na'ti·βo) *adj. & n.m.* carminative.

carnal (kar'nal) *adj.* **1,** carnal. **2,** fleshy; sensual. —**carnalidad,** *n.f.* carnality; lustfulness.

carnaval (kar·na'βal) *n.m.* carnival; Mardi Gras. —**carnavalesco,** *adj.* like a carnival; of or pert. to a carnival.

carne ('kar·ne) *n.f.* meat; flesh. —**carne de gallina,** goose pimples. —**en carnes,** nude. —**ser de carne y hueso,** to be human.

carnero (kar'ne·ro) *n.m.* **1,** sheep; ram. **2,** mutton. **3,** *Amer.* namby-pamby; milquetoast.

carnicería (kar·ni·θe'ri·a; -se'ri·a) *n.f.* **1,** butcher store; meat market. **2,** *S.A.* slaughterhouse. **3,** slaughter.

carnicero (kar·ni'θe·ro; -'se·ro) *n.m.* butcher. —*adj.* **1,** carnivorous. **2,** *fig.* bloodthirsty.

carnívoro (kar'ni·βo·ro) *adj.* carnivorous. —*n.m.* carnivore.

carnoso (kar'no·so) *adj.* fleshy; meaty. *Also,* **carnudo.** —**carnosidad,** *n.f.* fleshiness.

caro ('ka·ro) *adj.* **1,** dear. **2,** expensive; costly. —*adv.* at a high price; expensively. —**cara mitad,** better half.

carona (ka'ro·na) *n.f.* saddle pad.

carótida (ka'ro·ti·ða) *n.f. & adj.* carotid.

carotina (ka·ro'ti·na) *n.f.* carotene.

carozo (ka'ro·θo; -so) *n.m.* **1,** corncob. **2,** core *(of a fruit).*

carpa ('kar·pa) *n.f.* **1,** *ichthy.* carp. **2,** *Amer.* tent.

carpelo (kar'pe·lo) *n.m.* carpel.

carpeta (kar'pe·ta) *n.f.* **1,** table cover. **2,** portfolio. **3,** letter file. **4,** *Amer.* school desk. **5,** writing pad.

carpintería (kar·pin·te'ri·a) *n.f.* **1,** carpentry. **2,** carpenter's shop.

carpintero (kar·pin'te·ro) *n.m.*

carpenter. —**pájaro carpintero,** woodpecker.

carraspear (ka·rras·pe'ar) *v.i.* to hawk; clear the throat. —**carraspeo** (-'pe·o) *n.m.* hawking; clearing the throat. —**carraspera,** *n.f., colloq.* hoarseness; sore throat.

carrera (ka'rre·ra) *n.f.* **1,** race. **2,** run; dash. **3,** route; course; run. **4,** career; profession. **5,** *mech.* stroke; travel. **6,** row; line. **7,** run *(as in a stocking).* **8,** *baseball* run; score. —**de carrera;** **a la carrera,** hastily.

carreta (ka'rre·ta) *n.f.* narrow cart; wagon.

carretada (ka·rre'ta·ða) *n.f.* cartload. —**a carretadas,** in great quantity; in heaps.

carretaje (ka·rre'ta·xe) *n.m.* cartage.

carrete (ka'rre·te) *n.m.* spool; reel.

carretear (ka·rre·te'ar) *v.t.* to cart; convey. —*v.i.* **1,** to drive a cart. **2,** *aero.* to taxi.

carretera (ka·rre'te·ra) *n.f.* highway.

carretero (ka·rre'te·ro) *n.m.* **1,** wagoner; carter. **2,** wheelwright.

carretilla (ka·rre'ti·ʎa; -ja) *n.f.* wheelbarrow; hand cart.

carretón (ka·rre'ton) *n.m.* **1,** cart. **2,** go-cart.

carril (ka'rril) *n.m.* **1,** cartway; narrow road. **2,** *R.R.* rail. **3,** lane *(of a road).*

carrillo (ka'rri·ʎo; -jo) *n.m.* cheek; jowl.

carriola (ka'rrjo·la) *n.f.* **1,** cariole. **2,** carryall. **3,** trundle bed; truckle bed.

carro ('ka·rro) *n.m.* **1,** car; railway car; streetcar. **2,** cart; wagon. **3,** *Amer.* automobile. **4,** chariot. **5,** carriage *(of a typewriter, printing press, etc.).* **6,** *cap., astron.* Dipper.

carrocería (ka·rro·θe'ri·a; -se·'ri·a) *n.f.* **1,** carriage shop, **2,** body *(of a vehicle).*

carromato (ka·rro'ma·to) *n.m.* a long, narrow covered cart with two wheels.

carroña (ka'rro·ɲa) *n.f.* **1,** carrion. **2,** carcass. **3,** trash. —**carroño,** *adj.* rotten.

carroza (ka'rro·θa; -sa) *n.f.* **1,** carriage of state. **2,** *Amer.* hearse; funeral car. **3,** [*also,* **carroza alegórica**] parade float.

carruaje (ka'rrwa·xe) *n.m.* carriage; coach; vehicle.

carrusel (ka·rru'sel) *n.m., Amer.* merry-go-round.

carta ('kar·ta) *n.f.* **1,** letter. **2,** playing card. **3,** charter. **4,** chart; map. **5,** bill of fare; menu. —**carta blanca,** carte blanche.

cartabón (kar·ta'βon) *n.m.* **1,** *carp.* square. **2,** *drafting* triangle. **3,** size stick.

Carta Magna ('kar·ta'mag·na) *n.f.* Magna Charta.

cártamo ('kar·ta·mo) *n.m.* safflower. *Also,* **cártama** (-ma) *n.f.*

cartapacio (kar·ta'pa·θjo; -sjo) *n.m.* **1,** notebook. **2,** portfolio; briefcase.

cartearse (kar·te'ar·se) *v.r.* to correspond.

cartel (kar'tel) *n.m.* **1,** poster; placard. **2,** *theat.* show bill. **3,** *comm.* cartel. —**prohibido fijar carteles,** post no bills.

cartela (kar'te·la) *n.f.* **1,** tag; slip; small card. **2,** part of a wall tablet bearing the inscription. **3,** bracket; support. **4,** *archit.* console.

cartelera (kar'te'le·ra) *n.f.* billboard. —**cartelero,** *n.m.* billposter.

cartelón (kar·te'lon) *n.m.* large poster.

cárter ('kar·ter) *n.m., mech.* housing; case.

cartera (kar'te·ra) *n.f.* **1,** portfolio. **2,** desk pad. **3,** wallet. **4,** letter file. **5,** *Amer.* handbag; purse.

carterista (kar·te'ris·ta) *n.m. & f.* pickpocket.

cartero (kar'te·ro) *n.m.* postman; mailman.

cartílago (kar'ti·la·ɣo) *n.m.* cartilage. —**cartilaginoso** (-xi'no·so) *adj.* [*also, zoöl.,* **cartilagíneo** (-'xi·ne·o)] cartilaginous.

cartilla (kar'ti·ʎa; -ja) *n.f.* **1,** primer. **2,** passbook. **3,** short treatise. —**cartilla de racionamiento,** ration book. —**no saber la cartilla,** to be ignorant. —**leer la cartilla a,** to reprimand; call down.

cartografía (kar·to·ɣra'fi·a) *n.f.* cartography. —**cartógrafo** (-'to·ɣra·fo) *n.m.* cartographer. —**cartográfico** (-'ɣra·fi·ko) *adj.* cartographic.

cartón (kar'ton) *n.m.* **1,** pasteboard; cardboard. **2,** carton; cardboard box. —**cartón piedra,** papier-maché. —**cartón yeso,** plasterboard.

cartonero (kar·to'ne·ro) *n.m.* vendor of pasteboard or cardboard.

cartucho (kar'tu·tʃo) *n.m.* cartridge. —**cartuchera** (-'tʃe·ra) *n.f.* cartridge belt.

cartulina (kar·tu'li·na) *n.f.* fine, stiff pasteboard or cardboard.

casa ('ka·sa) *n.f.* **1,** house; dwelling. **2,** home; household. **3,** *chess* square. **4,** *comm.* firm. —**casa de caridad,** poorhouse. —**casa de empeños,** pawnshop. —**casa editorial,** publishing house. —**casa rodante,** motor home. —**echar la casa por la ventana,** *colloq.* to blow the works. —**poner casa,** to set up house.

casaca (ka'sa·ka) *n.f.* coat; dress coat. —**cambiar de casaca,** *colloq.* to become a turncoat.

casadero (ka·sa'ðe·ro) *adj.* marriageable.

casado (ka'sa·ðo) *adj.* wed; married. —**recién casado,** *adj. & n.m.* [*fem.* **casada**] newlywed.

casamentero (ka·sa·men'te·ro) *n.m.* matchmaker. —*adj.* matchmaking.

casamiento (ka·sa'mjen·to) *n.m.* marriage; wedding. —**casamiento a la fuerza,** shotgun wedding.

casar (ka'sar) *v.i.* to marry; wed. —**casarse,** *v.r.* to marry; be or get married. —*v.t.* **1,** to marry; mate; unite in marriage. **2,** *fig.* to match; harmonize (colors). **3,** to blend (paint). —**casarse con,** to marry; get married to. —**no casarse con nadie,** *colloq.* to get tied up with nobody.

cascabel (kas·ka'βel) *n.f.* jingle bell; tinkle. —**cascabelear,** *v.i.* to jingle. —**serplente de cascabel** [*also, Amer.,* **cascabela** (-'βe·la) *n.f.*] rattlesnake.

cascabillo (kas·ka'βi·ʎo; -jo) *n.m.* chaff; husk; hull.

cascada (kas'ka·ða) *n.f.* cascade; waterfall.

cascado (kas'ka·ðo) *adj.* broken; burst.

cascajo (kas'ka·xo) *n.m.* **1,** gravel. **2,** *colloq.* rubbish. —**estar hecho un cascajo,** *colloq.* to be a wreck.

cascanueces (kas·ka'nwe·θes; -ses) *n.m.sing. & pl.* nutcracker.

cascar (kas'kar) *v.t.* [*infl.:* **tocar,** 7] **1,** to crack; break; burst. **2,** *Amer., colloq.* to beat; wallop. —**cascarse, cascárselas,** *Amer., colloq.* to beat it.

cáscara ('kas·ka·ra) *n.f.* shell; husk; rind. —**ser de la cáscara**

amarga, *colloq.* to be wild; *derog.* be extremist.

cascarón (kas·ka'ron) *n.m.* shell; eggshell.

cascarrabias (kas·ka'rra·βjas) *n.m. & f. sing. & pl., colloq.* grouch; crab.

cascarudo (kas·ka'ru·ðo) *adj.* thick-shelled; hard-shelled.

casco ('kas·ko) *n.m.* **1,** skull; cranium. **2,** helmet. **3,** cask. **4,** hoof (*of a horse, mule, etc.*). **5,** *naut.* hull. **6,** *colloq.* talent. —**caliente de cascos,** hot-headed. —**ligero** *or* **alegre de cascos,** frivolous. —**romperse los cascos,** to rack one's brains.

caseína (ka·se'i·na) *n.f.* casein.

casera (ka'se·ra) *n.f.* **1,** landlady. **2,** *Amer.* = **parroquiana.**

caserío (ka·se'ri·o) *n.m.* **1,** country house. **2,** hamlet; village.

casero (ka'se·ro) *n.m.* **1,** landlord; caretaker. **2,** *Amer.* = **parroquiano.** —*adj.* **1,** of the home; domestic. **2,** homely; homespun. **3,** *colloq.* home-loving, retiring.

caserón (ka·se'ron) *n.m.* large house.

caseta (ka'se·ta) *n.f.* small house; cottage. —**caseta de baños,** locker; bathhouse.

casete (ka'se·te) *n.m. or f.* cassette; tape cartridge.

casi ('ka·si) *adv.* almost; nearly.

casia ('ka·sja) *n.f.* cassia.

casilla (ka'si·ʎa; -ja) *n.f.* **1,** hut; booth. **2,** square (*on a sheet of paper; in checkers*). **3,** *Amer.* mail box (*at a residence*). **4,** ticket office. **5,** pigeonhole; cubbyhole. —**sacar de sus casillas,** *colloq.* to drive crazy. —**salirse de sus casillas,** *colloq.* to go crazy; forget oneself.

casillero (ka·si'ʎe·ro; -'je·ro) *n.m.* **1,** filing cabinet. **2,** desk with pigeonholes.

casimir (ka·si'mir) *n.m.* cashmere.

casino (ka'si·no) *n.m.* **1,** casino. **2,** club; clubhouse.

caso ('ka·so) *n.m.* **1,** case. **2,** event; chance; occurrence. —**caso fortuito,** mischance. —**dado caso que,** supposing that. —**en caso (de) que,** in case that; if. —**en todo caso,** in any case; in any event. —**en tal caso,** in such an event. —**hablar al caso; ir al caso,** to get to the point. —**hacer caso a** *or* **de,** to pay attention to. —**hacer caso omiso de; no hacer caso de,** to pass over.

casón (ka'son) *n.m.* large house.

casorio (ka'so·rjo) *n.m., colloq.* ill-considered marriage; mismatch.

caspa ('kas·pa) *n.f.* dandruff. —**casposo,** *adj.* full of dandruff.

caspera (kas'pe·ra) *n.f.* comb for removing dandruff; fine-toothed comb.

¡cáspita! ('kas·pi·ta) *interj.* **1,** great! **2,** confound it!

casque ('kas·ke) *v., pres.subjve. of* **cascar.**

casqué (kas'ke) *v., 1st pers.sing, pret. of* **cascar.**

casquete (kas'ke·te) *n.m.* **1,** helmet. **2,** skullcap.

casquivano (kas·ki'βa·no) *adj.* frivolous.

casta ('kas·ta) *n.f.* **1,** caste; race. **2,** generation. **3,** pedigree; kind; breed.

castaña (kas'ta·ɲa) *n.f.* chestnut. —**dar a uno para castaña,** to play a trick on someone.

castañal (kas·ta'ɲal) *n.m.* chestnut grove. Also, **castañar** (-'ɲar).

castañeo (kas·ta'ɲe·o) *n.m.* the sound of castanets. Also, **castañeteado** (-te'a·ðo).

castañero (kas·ta'ɲe·ro) *n.m.* chestnut vendor.

castañeta (kas·ta'ɲe·ta) *n.f.* **1,** castanet. **2,** snapping of the fingers.

castañetear (kas·ta·ɲe·te'ar) *v.i.* **1,** to rattle castanets. **2,** to chatter *(of the teeth).* **3,** to shudder; shiver. **4,** to crackle.

castañeteo (kas·ta·ɲe'te·o) *n.m.* **1,** the sound of castanets. **2,** chattering *(of the teeth).* **3,** snapping of the fingers.

castaño (kas'ta·ɲo) *n.m.* chestnut tree, wood or color. —*adj.* chestnut. —**pasar de castaño oscuro,** *colloq.* to be unbearable or too much.

castañuela (kas·ta'ɲwe·la) *n.f.* castanet.

castellano (kas·te'ʎa·no; -'ja·no) *adj. & n.m.* Castilian; Spanish. —*n.m.* lord of the castle.

castidad (kas·ti'ðað) *n.f.* chastity; virginity.

castigar (kas·ti'ɣar) *v.t.* [*infl.:* **pagar, 8**] to chastise; castigate; punish.

castigo (kas'ti·ɣo) *n.m.* punishment; chastisement; castigation.

castillo (kas'ti·ʎo; -jo) *n.m.* castle; fortress. —**castillo de proa,** fore-castle. —**hacer castillos en el aire,** to build castles in the air.

castizo (kas'ti·θo; -so) *adj.* **1,** of noble descent. **2,** pure *(of language).*

casto ('kas·to) *adj.* pure; chaste.

castor (kas'tor) *n.m.* **1,** beaver. **2,** *cap., astron.* Castor. **3,** [*also,* **aceite de castor**] castor oil. **4,** beaver hat.

castrado (kas'tra·ðo) *adj.* castrated. —*n.m.* **1,** eunuch. **2,** gelding.

castrar (kas'trar) *v.t.* to castrate; geld. —**castración,** *n.f.* castration; gelding.

casual (ka'swal) *adj.* casual; fortuitous.

casualidad (ka·swa·li'ðað) *n.f.* **1,** chance; hazard. **2,** coincidence. —**por casualidad,** by chance.

casucha (ka'su·tʃa) *n.f.* hut; shack; hovel. *Also,* **casuca** (-ka).

casuísta (ka·su'is·ta) *n.m. & f.* casuist. —*adj.* [*also,* **casuístico** (-'is·ti·ko)] casuistic. —**casuística** (-'is·ti·ka) *n.f.* casuistry.

casulla (ka'su·ʎa; -ja) *n.f.* chasuble.

cata ('ka·ta) *n.f.* **1,** tasting; sampling. **2,** taste; sample.

catabolismo (ka·ta·βo'lis·mo) *n.m.* catabolism. —**catabólico** (-'βo·li·ko) *adj.* catabolic.

cataclismo (ka·ta'klis·mo) *n.m.* cataclysm; deluge.

catacumbas (ka·ta'kum·bas) *n.f. pl.* catacombs.

catadura (ka.ta'ðu·ra) *n.f.* **1,** tasting; sampling. **2,** *colloq.* countenance.

catafalco (ka·ta'fal·ko) *n.m.* catafalque.

catalán (ka·ta'lan) *adj. & n.m.* [*fem.* **-lana**] Catalan; Catalonian.

catalejo (ka·ta'le·xo) *n.m.* spyglass.

catalepsia (ka·ta'lep·sja) *n.f.* catalepsy. —**cataléptico** (-'lep·ti·ko) *adj. & n.m.* cataleptic.

catálisis (ka'ta·li·sis) *n.m.* catalysis. —**catalítico** (-'li·ti·ko) *adj.* catalytic. —**catalizador** (-li·θa'ðor; -sa'ðor) *n.m.* catalyst.

catalogar (ka·ta·lo'ɣar) *v.t.* [*infl.:* **pagar, 8**] to catalogue; list.

catálogo (ka'ta·lo·ɣo) *n.m.* catalogue; table; list.

catalpa (ka'tal·pa) *n.f.* catalpa.

cataplasma (ka·ta'plas·ma) *n.f.* **1,** poultice; mustard plaster. **2,** *fig., colloq.* nuisance; bore.

catapulta (ka·ta'pul·ta) *n.f.* catapult. —**catapultar,** *v.t.* to catapult.

catar (ka'tar) *v.t.* to taste; sample.

catarata (ka·ta'ra·ta) *n.f.* **1,** cataract; cascade. **2,** *med.* cataract.

catarro (ka·ta·rro) *n.m.* **1,** catarrh. **2,** cold, esp. a head cold. —**catarral,** *adj.* catarrhal. —**catarroso,** *adj.* suffering from or subject to colds.

catarsis (ka'tar·sis) *n.f.* catharsis. —**catártico** (-ti·ko) *adj.* & *n.m.* cathartic.

catastro (ka'tas·tro) *n.m.* **1,** official land register. **2,** land office.

catástrofe (ka'tas·tro·fe) *n.f.* catastrophe. —**catastrófico** (-'tro·fi·ko) *adj.* catastrophic.

catavinos (ka·ta'βi·nos) *n.m.* & *f. sing.* & *pl.* **1,** winetaster. **2,** *colloq.* drunkard; tippler.

catear (ka·te'ar) *v.t.* **1,** *colloq.* to flunk. **2,** *S.A.* to prospect. **3,** *Mex.* to break into; search (a house).

catecismo (ka·te'θis·mo; -'sis·mo) *n.m.* catechism.

catecúmeno (ka·te'ku·me·no) *n.m.* catechumen.

cátedra ('ka·te·ðra) *n.f.* **1,** professorship. **2,** lecture room. **3,** *eccles.* cathedra. —**Cátedra del Espíritu Santo,** *n.f.* pulpit.

catedral (ka·te'ðral) *n.f.* & *adj.* cathedral.

catedrático (ka·te'ðra·ti·ko) *n.m.* [*fem.* -**ca**] professor.

categoría (ka·te·yo'ri·a) *n.f.* category; rank; class. —**categórico** (-'yo·ri·ko) *adj.* categorical. —**de categoría,** prominent; excellent.

catequismo (ka·te'kis·mo) *n.m.* catechism. *Also,* **catequesis** (ka·te'ke·sis) *n.f.*

catequista (ka·te'kis·ta) *n.m.* & *f.* catechist. —**catequístico,** *adj.* catechetical.

catequizador (ka·te·ki·θa'ðor; -sa 'ðor) *n.m.* [*fem.* -**dora**] persuader.

catequizante (ka·te·ki'θan·te; -'san·te) *adj.* catechizing. —*n.m.* & *f.* catechist.

catequizar (ka·te·ki'θar; -'sar) *v.t.* [*infl.:* rezar, 10] **1,** to catechize. **2,** *fig.* to induce; persuade. —**catequización,** *n.f.* catechizing.

catéter (ka'te·ter) *n.m.* catheter.

cateto (ka'te·to) *n.m., geom.* leg. —*adj.* & *n.m.* rustic.

catión (ka'tjon) *n.m.* cation.

cátodo ('ka·to·ðo) *n.m.* cathode.

catolicismo (ka·to·li'θis·mo; -'sis·mo) *n.m.* Catholicism.

católico (ka'to·li·ko) *adj.* **1,** Catholic. **2,** universal. —*n.m.* Catholic.

—**catolicidad** (-θi'ðað; -si'ðað) *n.f.* catholicity.

catorce (ka'tor·θe; -se) *adj.* fourteen; fourteenth (*in dates*).

catorzavo (ka·tor'θa·βo; -'sa·βo) *adj.* & *n.m.* fourteenth.

catre ('ka·tre) *n.m.* cot. —**catre de tijera,** field cot.

catrecillo (ka·tre'θi·ʎo; -'si·jo) *n.m.* canvas stool.

catrín (ka'trin) *n.m.* fop; dandy. —*adj.* foppish; dandified.

caucásico (kau'ka·si·ko) *adj.* & *n.m.* Caucasian.

cauce ('kau·θe; -se) *n.m.* riverbed.

caución (kau'θjon; -'sjon) *n.f.* **1,** security; pledge; bond. **2,** warning; foresight.

caucho (kau'tʃo) *n.m.* rubber.

caudal (kau'ðal) *n.m.* **1,** volume (*of fluids*). **2,** wealth; property; fortune. —*adj.* **1,** [*also,* **caudaloso**] containing water. **2,** *zoöl.* caudal.

caudillaje (kau·ði'ʎa·xe; -'ja·xe) *n.m.* **1,** military leadership. **2,** *Amer.* political bossism.

caudillo (kau'ði·ʎo; -jo) *n.m.* **1,** leader; commander. **2,** *Amer.* political boss.

causa ('kau·sa) *n.f.* **1,** cause. **2,** lawsuit. —**a causa de,** on account of.

causador (kau·sa'ðor) *adj.* causing. —*n.m.* [*fem.* -**dora**] one who causes; agent.

causal (kau'sal) *adj., gram.* causal. —*n.f.* ground; reason; motive.

causalidad (kau·sa·li'ðað) *n.f.* causality.

causar (kau'sar) *v.t.* to cause; produce.

cáustico ('kaus·ti·ko) *adj.* & *n.m.* caustic.

cautela (kau'te·la) *n.f.* **1,** caution; prudence. **2,** craftiness. —**cauteloso,** *adj.* cautious; wary.

cautelar (kau·te'lar) *v.t.* to prevent. —*v.i.* to proceed prudently; take necessary precautions.

cauterizar (kau·te·ri'θar; -'sar) *v.t.* [*infl.:* rezar, 10] to cauterize. —**cauterización,** *n.f.* cauterization. —**cauterizador,** *n.m.* cauterizer. —**cauterizante,** *adj.* cauterizing.

cautivar (kau·ti'βar) *v.t.* to captivate; charm.

cautiverio (kau·ti'βe·rjo) *n.m.* captivity; confinement. *Also,* **cautividad** (-βi'ðað) *n.f.*

cautivo (kau'ti·βo) *adj.* & *n.m.* captive.

cauto ('kau·to) *adj.* cautious.

cavado (ka'βa·ðo) *adj.* hollowed; excavated.

cavador (ka·βa'ðor) *n.m.* digger; sandhog.

cavadura (ka·βa'ðu·ra) *n.f.* digging.

cavar (ka'βar) *v.t.* to dig; excavate. —*v.i.* to penetrate far; dig.

caverna (ka'βer·na) *n.f.* cavern; cave. —**cavernoso,** *adj.* cavernous.

cavernícola (ka·βer'ni·ko·la) *adj.* cave-dwelling. —*n.m. & f.* cave man; cave woman.

caviar (ka'βjar) *also,* **cavial** (-'βjal) *n.m.* caviar.

cavidad (ka·βi'ðað) *n.f.* cavity.

cavilar (ka·βi'lar) *v.i.* to muse; ruminate. —**cavilación,** *n.f.* musing; rumination. —**caviloso,** *adj.* hesitant; reluctant.

cayado (ka'ja·ðo) *n.m. also,* **cayada** (-ða) *n.f.* **1,** shepherd's crook. **2,** walking stick. **3,** *eccles.* crozier.

cayo ('ka·jo) *n.m.* island reef; key.

cayó (ka'jo) *v., 3rd pers.sing. pret. of* **caer.**

caz (kaθ; kas) *n.m.* **1,** canal; ditch. **2,** channel of a stream. **3,** millrace.

caza ('ka·θa; -sa) *n.f.* **1,** chase; hunt; hunting. **2,** pursuit. —*n.m., aero.* pursuit plane. —**dar caza (a un empleo),** to pursue (a job).

cazabe (ka'θa·βe; -'sa·βe) *n.m.* cassava.

cazador (ka·θa'ðor; ka·sa-) *n.m.* hunter. —*adj.* hunting. —**cazadores,** *n.m.pl.* light infantry.

cazaperros (ka·θa·pe'rros; ka·sa-) *n.m. & f. sing. & pl.* dogcatcher.

cazar (ka'θar; -'sar) *v.t.* [*infl.:* **rezar,** 10] to chase; hunt. —**cazar moscas,** *colloq.* to dawdle.

cazatorpedero (ka·θa·tor·pe'ðe·ro; ka·sa-) *n.m.* destroyer.

cazo ('ka·θo; -so) *n.m.* dipper; ladle.

cazón (ka'θon; -'son) *n.m.* dogfish.

cazuela (ka'θwe·la; ka'swe-) *n.f.* **1,** stew. **2,** stewpan. **3,** theater gallery.

cea ('θe·a; 'se·a) *n.f.* = **cía.**

ceba ('θe·βa; 'se-) *n.f.* fattening *(of animals).*

cebada (θe'βa·ða; se-) *n.f.* barley.

cebadero (θe·βa'ðe·ro; se-) *n.m.* **1,** feeding place *(for animals).* **2,** breeder of hawks. **3,** barley dealer.

cebado (θe'βa·ðo; se-) *adj.* fattened; fed.

cebar (θe'βar; se-) *v.t.* **1,** to feed;

fatten (animals). **2,** to encourage (a passion). **3,** to bait (a fishhook). **4,** to prime (arms). **5,** *fig.* to penetrate. —**cebarse** *v.r.* to rage.

cebellina (θe·βe'ʎi·na; se·βe'ji-) *n.f.* sable.

cebo ('θe·βo; 'se-) *n.m.* **1,** fodder. **2,** primer; priming *(of firearms).* **3,** incentive; lure.

cebolla (θe'βo·ʎa; se'βo·ja) *n.f.* onion. —**cebollar,** *n.m.* onion patch.

cebollina (θe·βo'ʎi·na; se·βo'ji-) *n.f.* chive. *Also,* **cebollino,** *n.m.*

cebón (θe'βon; se-) *n.m.* fattened hog. —*adj.* fattened *(of animals).*

cebra ('θe·βra; 'se-) *n.f.* zebra —**cebrado,** *adj.* having zebralike stripes.

cebú (θe'βu; se-) *n.m.* zebu.

ceca ('θe·ka; 'se-) *n.f., archaic* royal mint. —**de ceca en meca; de la ceca a la meca,** to and fro.

cecear (θe·θe'ar; se-) *v.i.* **1,** to lisp. **2,** to pronounce *z* and *c* before *e* or *i* as θ.

ceceo (θe'θe·o) *n.m.* **1,** lisping. **2,** pronunciation as (θ) of *z* and of *c* before *e* or *i.* —**ceceoso,** *n.m.* lisper. —*adj.* lisping.

cecina (θe'θi·na; se'si-) *n.f.* dried beef; jerked beef. —**cecinar,** *v.t.* to cure (meat).

cecografía (θe·ko·ɣra'fi·a; se-) *n.f.* Braille. —**cecográfico** (-'ɣra·fi·ko) *adj.* of or in Braille. —**cecógrafo** (-'ko·ɣra·fo) *n.m.* Braille writer.

cedazo (θe'ða·θo; se'ða·so) *n.m.* sieve.

cedente (θe'ðen·te; se-) *adj.* granting; transferring. —*n.m.* grantor; transferrer.

ceder (θe'ðer; se-) *v.t.* **1,** to yield; cede; grant. **2,** to convey; transfer. —*v.i.* **1,** to yield; give in; give way. **2,** to diminish; abate. —**ceder el paso,** to make way; step aside.

cedilla (θe'ði·ʎa; se'ði·ja) *n.f.* cedilla.

cedro ('θe·ðro; 'se-) *n.m.* cedar.

cédula ('θe·ðu·la; 'se-) *n.f.* **1,** certificate; permit. **2,** government order; decree. —**cédula de vecindad; cédula personal,** identification papers.

cefálico (θe'fa·li·ko; se-) *adj.* cephalic.

cefalópodo (θe·fa'lo·po·ðo; se-) *adj. & n.m.* cephalopod.

céfiro ('θe·fi·ro; 'se-) *n.m.* zephyr.

cegajoso (θe·γa'xo·so; se-) *adj.* bleary-eyed.

cegar (θe'γar; se-) *v.i.* [*infl.*: pagar, 8; pensar, 27] to grow blind; become blind. —*v.t.* 1, to blind; 2, to block; close up (an opening).

cegato (θe'γa·to; se-) *adj.* dim-sighted; shortsighted. *Also,* cegatón.

ceguedad (θe·γe'ðað; se-) *n.f.* 1, blindness. 2, *fig.* ignorance.

ceguera (θe'γe·ra; se-) *n.f.* total blindness.

ceiba ('θei·βa; 'sei-) *n.f.* a tropical tree. —algodón de ceiba, kapok.

ceja ('θe·xa; 'se-) *n.f.* 1, eyebrow. 2, edge *(of clothes, books, etc.).* —fruncir las cejas, to frown. —hasta las cejas, to the utmost. —quemarse las cejas, to burn the midnight oil. —tener entre ceja y ceja, 1, *fol. by inf.* to have a yearning for (doing something). 2, to have a strong dislike for (a person).

cejar (θe'xar; se-) *v.i.* 1, to go back; step back. 2, to desist; give in; yield.

celada (θe'la·ða; se-) *n.f.* 1, helmet. 2, ambush. 3, artful trick.

celador (θe·la'ðor; se-) *n.m.* [*fem.* -dora] watcher; caretaker. —*adj.* vigilant.

celaje (θe'la·xe; se-) *n.m.* 1, skylight. 2, *usu.pl.* sky with many-hued clouds.

celar (θe'lar; se-) *v.t.* 1, to watch over; keep an eye on. 2, to conceal; cover; hide.

celda ('θel·da; 'sel-) *n.f.* cell.

celdilla (θel'di·ʎa; sel'di·ja) *n.f.* cell.

celebérrimo (θe·le'βe·rri·mo; se-) *adj., superl. of* célebre.

celebración (θe·le·βra'θjon; se·le·βra'sjon) *n.f.* celebration.

celebrante (θe·le'βran·te; se-) *n.m.* celebrant. —*adj.* celebrating.

celebrar (θe·le'βrar; se-) *v.t.* 1, to celebrate. 2, to praise; honor. 3, to hold (a conference, meeting, etc.). —*v.i.* to rejoice.

célebre ('θe·le·βre; 'se) *adj.* 1, celebrated; famous; known. 2, *colloq.* gay; funny.

celebridad (θe·le·βri'ðað; se-) *n.f.* 1, celebrity; fame. 2, celebration; pageant.

celeridad (θe·le·ri'ðað; se-) *n.f.* celerity; speed.

celerímetro (θe·le'ri·me·tro; se-) *n.m.* speedometer.

celeste (θe'les·te; se-) *adj.* 1, sky-blue. 2, celestial.

celestial (θe·les'tjal; se-) *adj.* celestial.

celestina (θe·les'ti·na; se-) *n.m.* 1, *mineral.* celestine;-celestite. 2, procuress.

célibe ('θe·li·βe; 'se-) *adj. & n.m.* celibate; bachelor. —celibato (-'βa·to) *n.m.* celibacy; bachelorhood.

celo ('θe·lo; 'se-) *n.m.* 1, zeal; ardor. 2, envy. 3, heat; rut *(of animals).* —celos, *n.m.pl.* 1, jealousy. 2, suspicions. —dar celos a, to make jealous. —tener celos, to be jealous.

celofana (θe·lo'fa·na; se-) *n.f.* cellophane. *Also,* celofán (-'fan) *n.m.*

celosía (θe·lo'si·a; se-) *n.f.* 1, lattice. 2, Venetian blind. 3, jalousie.

celoso (θe'lo·so; se-) *adj.* 1, zealous. 2, jealous. 3, suspicious.

celta ('θel·ta; 'sel-) *n.m. & f.* Celt. —*adj.* Celtic. —*n.m.* Celtic *(language).*

céltico ('θel·ti·ko; 'scl·) *adj.* Celtic.

célula ('θe·lu·la; 'se-) *n.f., bot.; zoöl.* cell. —celular, *adj.* cellular.

celuloide (θe·lu'loi·ðe; se-) *n.m.* celluloid.

celulosa (θe·lu'lo·sa; se-) *n.f.* cellulose.

celuloso (θe·lu'lo·so; se-) *adj.* cellulous.

cellisca (θe'ʎis·ka; se'jis-) *n.f.* sleet. —cellisquear (-ke'ar) *v.i.* to sleet.

cementar (θe·men'tar; se-) *v.t.* 1, to cement. 2, *mining* to precipitate.

cementerio (θe·men'te·rjo; se-) *n.m.* cemetery; graveyard.

cemento (θe'men·to; se-) *n.m.* cement.

cena ('θe·na; 'se-) *n.f.* supper; evening meal.

cenadero (θe·na'ðe·ro; se-) *n.m.* 1, supper room. 2, summerhouse.

cenador (θe·na'ðor; se-) *n.m.* arbor; summerhouse.

cenagal (θe·na'γal; se-) *n.m.* bog.

cenagoso (θe·na'γo·so; se-) *adj.* marshy.

cenar (θe'nar; se-) *v.t.* to eat (something) for supper; sup on. —*v.i.* to sup; have supper.

cenceño (θen'θe·ɲo; sen'se-) *adj.* lean; thin.

cencerrada (θen·θe'rra·ða; sen-se-) *n.f.* tin-pan serenade.

cencerrear (θen·θe·rre'ar;

sen·se-) *v.i.* **1,** to tinkle, as a cowbell. **2,** to jangle; clank.

cencerro (θen'θe·rro; sen'se-) *n.m.* cowbell.

cendal (θen'dal; sen-) *n.m.* gauze.

cenefa (θe'ne·fa; se-) *n.f.* border; edging; trim.

cenicero (θe·ni'θe·ro; se·ni'se-) *n.m.* **1,** ashtray. **2,** ash pit; ash bin.

Cenicienta (θe·ni'θjen·ta; se·ni·'sjen-) *n.f.* Cinderella.

ceniciento (θe·ni'θjen·to; se·ni·'sjen-) *adj.* ashen; ash-colored.

cenit (θe'nit; se-) *n.m.* zenith.

ceniza (θe'ni·θa; se'ni·sa) *n.f.* ash; ashes. —**cenizas,** *n.f.pl.* remains (*of a dead person*). —**huir de la ceniza, caer en las brasas,** to go from the frying pan into the fire.

cenizo (θe'ni·θo; se'ni·so) *adj.* ashen; ash-colored. —*n.m., colloq.* jinx.

cenotafio (θe·no'ta·fjo; se-) *n.m.* cenotaph.

censo ('θen·so; 'sen-) *n.m.* **1,** census. **2,** *law* rent. **3,** *fig.* burden; charge. —**censor** (-'sor) *n.m.* censor. —**censorio** (-'so·rjo) *adj.* censorial.

censura (θen'su·ra; sen-) *n.f.* **1,** censorship. **2,** office of censor. **3,** censure; critical review.

censurable (θen·su·ra'βle; sen-) *adj.* censurable.

censurador (θen·su·ra'ðor; sen-) *adj.* censorious. —*n.m.* censurer.

censurar (θen·su'rar; sen-) *v.t.* **1,** to censure. **2,** to review; judge.

centauro (θen'tau·ro; sen-) *n.m.* centaur.

centavo (θen'ta·βo; sen-) *adj.* hundredth. —*n.m.* **1,** hundredth part. **2,** cent.

centella (θen'te·ʎa; sen'te·ja) *n.f.* flash; spark.

centellar (θen·te'ʎar; sen·te'jar) *also,* **centellear** (-ʎe'ar; -je'ar) *v.i.* to flash; sparkle. —**centelleo** (-'ʎe·o; -'je·o) *n.m.* flash; sparkle.

centena (θen'te·na; sen-) *n.f.* hundred; quantity of a hundred.

centenada (θen·te'na·ða; sen-) *n.f.* quantity of about a hundred. —**a centenadas,** by hundreds.

centenar (θen·te'nar; sen-) *n.m.* hundred; quantity of a hundred. —**a centenares,** by hundreds.

centenario (θen·te'na·rjo; sen-) *n.m. & adj.* centenary; centenarian; centennial.

centeno (θen'te·no; sen-) *adj.* hundredth. —*n.m.* rye.

centésimo (θen'te·si·mo; sen-) *adj. & n.m.* hundredth; centesimal.

centiárea (θen·ti'a·re·a; sen-) *n.f.* centiare.

centígrado (θen'ti·γra·ðo; sen-) *adj.* centigrade.

centigramo (θen·ti'γra·mo; sen-) *n.m.* centigram.

centilitro (θen·ti'li·tro; sen-) *n.m.* centiliter.

centímetro (θen'ti·me·tro; sen-) *n.m.* centimeter.

céntimo ('θen·ti·mo; 'sen-) *adj. & n.m.* hundredth. —*n.m.* cent; centime; hundredth part of various monetary units.

centinela (θen·ti'ne·la; sen-) *n.m. & f.* sentry; guard. —**estar de centinela; hacer de centinela,** to be on guard duty; keep watch.

centón (θen'ton; sen-) *n.m.* crazy quilt.

central (θen'tral; sen-) *adj.* central. —*n.f.* **1,** main office; headquarters. **2,** powerhouse. —**central telefónica,** telephone exchange.

centralizar (θen·tra·li'θar; sen·tra·li'sar) *v.t.* [*infl.:* rezar, 10] to centralize. —**centralización,** *n.f.* centralization.

centrar (θen'trar; sen-) *v.t.* to center. —**centrarse,** *v.r.* to center; be centered.

céntrico ('θen·tri·ko; 'sen-) *adj.* central.

centrífugo (θen'tri·fu·o; sen-) *adj.* centrifugal. —**centrífuga,** *n.f.* centrifuge.

centrípeto (θen'tri·pe·to; sen-) *adj.* centripetal.

centro ('θen·tro; 'sen-) *n.m.* **1,** center; middle. **2,** hub; nucleus. **3,** headquarters; club. **4,** downtown.

centroamericano *adj. & n.m.* Central American.

centuplicar (θen·tu·pli'kar; sen-) *v.t. & v.i.* [*infl.:* tocar, 7] to centuple.

céntuplo ('θen·tu·plo; 'sen-) *n.m.* hundredfold. —*adj.* centuple.

centuria (θen'tu·rja; sen-) *n.f.* century.

centurio (θen'tu·rjo; sen-) *n.m.* centurium.

centurión (θen·tu'rjon; sen-) *n.m.* centurion.

ceñido (θe·'ɲi·ðo; se-) *adj.* **1,** moderate. **2,** tight; close-fitting.

ceñidor (θe·ɲi'ðor; se-) *n.m.* **1,** belt; sash. **2,** girdle.

ceñidura (θe·ɲi'ðu·ra; se-) *n.f.* **1,** act of girding. **2,** *fig.* contraction; reduction.

ceñir (θe'ɲir; se-) *v.t.* [*infl.:* reñir, 59] **1,** to gird; girdle. **2,** to surround. **3,** *fig.* to reduce; contract. —**ceñirse,** *v.r.* to limit oneself.

ceño ('θe·ɲo; 'se-) *n.m.* **1,** frown; scowl. **2,** countenance. **3,** brow. —**ceñudo,** *adj.* frowning.

cepa ('θe·pa; 'se-) *n.f.* **1,** stump; stub *(of a tree).* **2,** origin; stock *(of a family).*

cepilladura (θe·pi·ʎa'ðu·ra; se-pi·ja-) *n.f.* planing. —**cepilladuras,** *n.f.pl.* shavings.

cepillar (θe·pi'ʎar; se·pi'jar) *v.t.* **1,** to brush. **2,** to plane.

cepillo (θe'pi·ʎo; se'pi·jo) *n.m.* **1,** brush. **2,** plane. **3,** alms box.

cepo ('θe·po; 'se-) *n.m.* **1,** branch *(of a tree).* **2,** trap; snare *(for animals).* **3,** stocks *(instrument of punishment).* —**¡cepos quedos!,** *colloq.* cut it out!; enough!

cera ('θe·ra; 'se-) *n.f.* wax.

cerámico (θe'ra·mi·ko; se-) *adj.* ceramic; of or pert. to ceramics. —**cerámica,** *n.f.* ceramics.

cerbatana (θer·βa'ta·na; ser-) *n.f.* blowgun; popgun; peashooter.

cerca ('θer·ka; 'ser-) *n.f.* enclosure; fence. —**cercas,** *n.m.pl.* foreground *(of paintings).* —*adv.* near; close. —**cerca de,** near; about. —**de cerca,** close by. —**en cerca,** roundabout.

cercado (θer'ka·ðo; ser-) *adj.* enclosed; fenced in. —*n.m.* enclosure; fence.

cercador (θer·ka'ðor; ser-) *n.m.* **1,** enclosure. **2,** repoussé chisel. —*adj.* enclosing.

cercanía (θer·ka'ni·a; ser-) *n.f.* proximity. —**cercanías,** *n.f.pl.* surroundings; vicinity.

cercano (θer'ka·no; ser-) *adj.* near; neighboring.

cercar (θer'kar; ser-) *v.t.* [*infl.:* tocar, 7] **1,** to fence; enclose; encircle. **2,** *mil.* to besiege.

cercenadura (θer·θe·na'ðu·ra; ser-se-) *n.f.* clippings. —**cercenaduras,** *n.f.pl.* cuttings.

cercenar (θer·θe'nar; ser-se-) *v.t.* **1,** to pare; clip off. **2,** to curtail; reduce.

cerceta (θer'θe·ta; ser'se-) *n.f.* widgeon.

cerciorar (θer·θjo'rar; ser-sjo-) *v.t.* to assure; affirm. —**cerciorarse,** *v.r.* to ascertain; make sure.

cerco ('θer·ko; 'ser-) *n.m.* **1,** hoop; ring; rim. **2,** border; edge. **3,** siege. **4,** frame *(of a door).*

cerda ('θer·ða; 'ser-) *n.f.* **1,** bristle; horsehair. **2,** sow.

cerdear (θer·ðe'ar; ser-) *v.i.* **1,** to totter; stumble in the forelegs. **2,** to rasp; scrape roughly.

cerdo ('θer·ðo; 'ser-) *n.m.* hog; pig.

cerdoso (θer'ðo·so; ser-) *adj.* bristly.

cerdudo (θer'ðu·ðo; ser-) *adj.* **1,** bristly. **2,** hairy; hirsute.

cereal (θe·re'al; se-) *adj. & n.m.* cereal.

cerebelo (θe·re'βe·lo; se-) *n.m.* cerebellum.

cerebro (θe're·βro; se-) *n.m.* **1,** cerebrum. **2,** brain. **3,** *fig.* brains; talent; skill. —**cerebral** (-'βral) *adj.* cerebral.

ceremonia (θe·re'mo·nja; se-) *n.f.* ceremony.

ceremonial (θe·re·mo'njal; se-) *adj.* ceremonial. —*n.m.* book of ceremonies. —**ceremonioso** (-'njo·so) *adj.* ceremonious.

cerero (θe're·ro; se-) *n.m.* candlemaker.

cereza (θe're·θa; se're·sa) *n.f.* cherry. —**cerezo,** *n.m.* cherry tree. —**cerezal,** *n.m.* cherry orchard.

cerguillo (θer'yi·ʎo; ser'yi·jo) *n.m.* **1,** small circle; small hoop. **2,** seam; welt *(of a shoe).*

cerilla (θe'ri·ʎa; se'ri·ja) *n.f.* **1,** wax match; *colloq.* match. **2,** cerumen; earwax. **3,** taper.

cerillo (θe'ri·ʎo; se'ri·jo) *n.m., Amer.* wax match; match.

cerio ('θe·rjo; 'se-) *n.m.* cerium.

cernada (θer'na·ða; ser-) *n.f.* **1,** cinder. **2,** glue size; priming.

cernedor (θer·ne'ðor; ser-) *n.m.* sifter.

cerner (θer'ner; ser-) *v.t.* [*infl.:* perder, 29] **1,** to sift; bolt. **2,** *fig.* to refine. —*v.i.* **1,** to blossom; bud. **2,** *fig.* to drizzle. —**cernerse,** *v.r.* **1,** to hover. **2,** to be imminent; impend; threaten.

cernido (θer'ni·ðo; ser-) *adj.* sifted. —*n.m.* sifting.

cernir (θer'nir; ser-) *v.t. & i.* = **cerner.**

cero ('θe·ro; 'se-) *n.m.* zero; naught. —**ser un cero a la izquierda,** to be of no account.

ceroso (θe'ro·so; se-) *adj.* waxen; waxy.

cerque ('θer·ke; 'ser-) *v., pres. subjve. of* **cercar.**

cerqué (θer'ke; ser-) *v., 1st pers. sing. pret. of* **cercar.**

cerquita (θer'ki·ta; ser-) *n.f.* enclosure; fence. —*adv.* at a small distance. —**aquí cerquita,** just by.

cerradera (θe·rra'ðe·ra; se-) *n.f.* lock; clasp. —**echar la cerradera,** to turn a deaf ear.

cerradero (θe·rra'ðe·ro; se-) *adj.* of or pert. to a lock, or a thing or place that is locked. —*n.m.* **1,** lock; bolt; clasp. **2,** catch (*of a lock*). **3,** purse strings.

cerradizo (θe·rra'ði·θo; se·rra·'ði·so) *adj.* that may be locked.

cerrado (θe'rra·ðo; se-) *adj.* **1,** closed. **2,** secretive; concealed. **3,** reserved. **4,** *anat.* ductless. —*n.m.* fence; enclosure.

cerrador (θe·rra'ðor; se-) *n.m.* **1,** locker; lock. **2,** shutter.

cerradura (θe·rra'ðu·ra; se-) *n.f.* **1,** closure. **2,** lock. —**cerradura de golpe** *or* **muelle,** spring lock.

cerraja (θe'rra·xa; se-) *n.f.* lock.

cerrajería (θe·rra·xe'ri·a; se-) *n.f.* **1,** locksmith's trade; locksmith's store. **2,** light ironwork.

cerrajero (θe·rra'xe·ro; se-) *n.m.* locksmith.

cerrar (θe'rrar; se-) *v.t.* [*infl.:* **pensar,** 27] **1,** to lock; close; fasten. **2,** to clench (the fist). **3,** to fence in; enclose. **4,** to be stubborn in; persist in. —**cerrarse,** *v.r.* **1,** to remain firm in an opinion. **2,** to grow cloudy. **3,** to be shut up. **4,** to heal.

cerrazón (θe·rra'θon; se·rra'son) *n.m.* gathering storm clouds; blackening of the sky.

cerrero (θe'rre·ro; se-) *adj.* untamed (*of animals*); rude; rough (*of persons*).

cerril (θe'rril; se-) *adj.* **1,** wild; untamed. **2,** rude; boorish.

cerrillar (θe·rri'ʎar; se·rri'jar) *v.t.* to knurl.

cerrión (θe'rrjon; se-) *n.m.* icicle.

cerro ('θe·rro; 'se-) *n.m.* **1,** hill. **2,** neck (*of animals*); backbone. —**por los cerros de Ubeda,** *colloq.* off the track.

cerrojo (θe'rro·xo; se-) *n.m.* bolt; latch.

certamen (θer'ta·men; ser-) *n.m.* contest.

certero (θer'te·ro; ser-) *adj.* well-aimed; sharp.

certeza (θer'te·θa; ser'te·sa) *n.f.* certainty; assurance.

certidumbre (θer·ti'ðum·bre; ser-) *n.f.* = **certeza.**

certificación (θer·ti·fi·ka'θjon; ser·ti·fi·ka'sjon) *n.f.* **1,** certificate. **2,** certification.

certificado (θer·ti·fi·ka·ðo; ser-) *n.m.* **1,** certification. **2,** certificate; affidavit. —*adj.* **1,** certified. **2,** registered (*mail*). —**certificado de acciones,** stock certificate. —**certificado de defunción,** death certificate.

certificar (θer·ti·fi'kar; ser-) *v.t.* [*infl.:* **tocar,** 7] **1,** to certify. **2,** to register (*mail*).

certísimo (θer'ti·si·mo; ser-) *adj., superl. of* **cierto.**

certitud (θer·ti'tuð; ser-) *n.f.* = **certeza.**

cerúleo (θe'ru·le·o; se-) *adj.* cerulean.

cerumen (θe'ru·men; se-) *n.m.* cerumen; earwax.

cerval (θer'βal; ser-) *adj.* = **cervino.**

cervato (θer'βa·to; ser-) *n.m.* fawn.

cervecería (θer·βe·θe'ri·a; ser·βe·se-) *n.f.* **1,** brewery. **2,** *colloq.* saloon; tavern.

cervecero (θer·βe'θe·ro; ser·βe'se-) *n.m.* **1,** brewer. **2,** beer dealer. —*adj.* pert. to beer.

cerveza (θer'βe·θa; ser'βe·sa) *n.f.* beer. —**cerveza de barril,** draft beer.

cervical (θer·βi'kal; ser-) *adj.* cervical.

cervino (θer'βi·no; ser-) *adj.* deerlike; cervine.

cerviz (θer'βiθ; ser'βis) *n.f.* **1,** cervix. **2,** nape.

cesación (θe·sa'θjon; se·sa'sjon) *n.f.* cessation; suspension. *Also,* **cesamiento** (-'mjen·to) *n.m.*

cesante (θe'san·te; se-) *n.m.* **1,** dismissed employee. **2,** unemployed person.

cesantía (θe·san'ti·a; se-) *n.f.* **1,** unemployment. **2,** unemployment compensation. **3,** dismissal.

cesar (θe'sar; se-) *v.i.* to cease; stop; discontinue.

cesáreo (θe'sa·re·o; se-) *adj.* imperial; caesarean. —**operación cesárea,** caesarean operation.

cese ('θe·se; 'se·se) *n.m.* cessation;

stoppage, esp. of wages or pension.
—**cese de fuego,** cease-fire.
cesio (θe'·sjo· 'se-) *n.m.* cesium.
cesión (θe'sjon, se-) *n.f.* **1,** cession.
2, transfer, conveyance. —**cesionario,** *n.m.* grantee. —**cesionista,** *n.m.*
& *f.* grantor.
césped ('θes·peð; 'ses-) *n.m.* lawn;
turf; grass.
cesta ('θes·ta; 'ses-) *n.f.* basket.
cestería (θes·te'ri·a; ses-) *n.f.* basketwork; basketry; wickerwork.
cesto ('θes·to; 'ses-) *n.m.* **1,** basket.
2, hamper.
cesura (θe'su·ra; se-) *n.f.* caesura.
cetáceo (θe'ta·θe·o; se'ta·se·o) *adj.*
cetaceous. —*n.m.* cetacean.
cetona (θe'to·na; se-) *n.f.* ketone.
cetrería (θe·tre'ri·a; se-) *n.f.* falconry; hawking.
cetrino (θe'tri·no; se-) *adj.* **1,**
lemon-colored. **2,** *fig.* melancholic;
gloomy.
cetro ('θe·tro; 'se-) *n.m.* **1,** scepter.
2, *fig.* reign; throne (*of a king*). **3,**
perch; roost.
cía ('θi·a; 'si-) *n.f.* **1,** hipbone. **2,**
naut. sternway.
cianógeno (θja'no·xe·no; sja-)
n.m. cyanogen.
cianosis (θja'no·sis; sja-) *n.f.* cyanosis.
cianuro (θja'nu·ro; sja-) *n.m.* cyanide.
ciática ('θja·ti·ka; 'sja-) *n.f.* sciatica.
cibernética (θi·βer'ne·ti·ka; si-)
n.f. cybernetics. —**cibernético,** *adj.*
cybernetic.
cicatero (θi·ka'te·ro; si-) *adj.* miserly; stingy. —*n.m.* miser.
cicatriz (θi·ka'triθ; si·ka'tris) *n.f.*
scar.
cicatrizar (θi·ka·tri'θar; si·ka·tri'sar) *v.t.* [*infl.: rezar,* **10**] to heal.
cícero ('θi·θe·ro; 'si·se-) *n.m.,*
typog. pica.
cicerone (θi·θe'ro·ne; si·se-) *n.m.*
guide; cicerone.
ciclamino (θi·kla'mi·no; si-) *n.m.,*
bot. cyclamen.
cíclico ('θi·kli·ko; 'si-) *adj.* cyclical.
ciclismo (θi'klis·mo; si-) *n.m.* cycling.
ciclista (θi'klis·ta; si-) *n.m.* & *f.*
cyclist.
ciclo ('θi·klo; 'si-) *n.m.* cycle.
cicloide (θi'kloi·ðe; si-) *n.f.* cycloid. —**cicloidal,** *also,* **cicloideo**
(-'ðe·o) *adj.* cycloid; cycloidal.

ciclomotor (θi·klo·mo'tor; si-)
n.m. motorbike.
ciclón (θi'klon; si-) *n.m.* hurricane;
cyclone.
ciclonal (θi·klo'nal; si-) *adj.* cyclonic. *Also,* **ciclónico** (-'klo·ni·ko).
Cíclope ('θi·klo·pe; 'si-) *also,*
Ciclope (-'klo·pe) *n.m.* Cyclops.
—**ciclópeo** (-'klo·pe·o) *adj.* Cyclopean.
ciclorama (θi·klo'ra·ma; si-) *n.m.*
cyclorama.
ciclotrón (θi·klo'tron; si-) *n.m.* cyclotron.
cicuta (θi'ku·ta; si-) *n.f.* hemlock (*herb; poison*).
cid (θið; sið) *n.m.* hero; chief. —**el
Cid Campeador,** Rodrigo Díaz de
Vivar, Spain's national hero.
cidra ('θi·ðra; 'si-) *n.f.* citron.
cidro ('θi·ðro; 'si-) *n.m.* **1,** citron
tree. **2,** citrus.
cidronela (θi·ðro'ne·la; si-) *n.f.*
balm.
ciego ('θje·γo; 'sje-) *adj.* **1,** blind.
2, closed; blocked. **3,** without exit.
ciego ('θje·γo; 'sje-) *v., pres.ind. of*
cegar.
ciegue ('θje·γe; 'sje-) *v., pres.*
subjve. of **cegar.**
cielito (θje'li·to; sje-) *n.m.* **1,** a
S.A. dance. **2,** sweetheart.
cielo ('θje·lo; 'sje-) *n.m.* **1,** sky; firmament; heaven. **2,** *cap.* God; the
supreme power. **3,** glory; Paradise;
felicity. **4,** roof (*of the mouth*). **5,**
canopy. —**cielo raso,** ceiling; flat
ceiling. —**cielo de mi vida,** my
dear; my darling. —**¡cielo santo!,**
¡cielos santos! good heavens!
—**dormir a cielo raso,** to sleep
outdoors.
ciempiés (θjem'pjes; sjem-) *n.m.*
sing. & *pl.* centipede.
cien (θjen; sjen) *adj.* hundred (*used
when a larger number, or no
number, follows*). —**cien mil,** a
hundred thousand. —**cien millones,**
a hundred million.
ciénaga ('θje·na·γa; 'sje-) *n.f.*
marsh.
ciencia ('θjen·θja; 'sjen·sja) *n.f.* **1,**
science. **2,** knowledge. —**a ciencia
cierta,** knowingly.
cienmilésimo *adj.* & *n.m.*
hundred-thousandth.
cienmillonésimo *adj.* & *n.m.*
hundred-millionth.
cieno ('θje·no; 'sje-) *n.m.* mud;
slime.

científico (θjen'ti·fi·ko; sjen-) *adj.*
scientific. —*n.m.* scientist.
ciento ('θjen·to; 'sjen-) *adj. & n.m.*
hundred. —**por ciento,** percent.
cierna ('θjer·na; 'sjer-) *v., pres.
subjve. of* **cerner.**
cierne ('θjer·ne; 'sjer-) *n.m.* blossoming; flowering. —**en cierne, 1,**
in an early stage. **2,** in the offing. **3,**
hanging; pending.
cierno ('θjer·no; 'sjer-) *v., pres. ind.
of* **cerner.**
cierre ('θje·rre; 'sje-) *n.m.* **1,** closing; locking. **2,** snap; clasp. **3,** plug
(of a valve); lock. —**cierre de
seguridad,** safety lock. —**cierre de
corredera; cierre de cremallera;
cierre (de) relámpago,** zipper.
cierre *v., pres.subjve. of* **cerrar.**
cierro ('θje·rro; 'sje-) *n.m., S.A.* enclosure.
cierro ('θje·rro; 'sje-) *v., 1st pers.
sing. pres.ind. of* **cerrar.**
cierto ('θjer·to; 'sjer-) *adj.* certain;
sure; doubtless. —*adv.* surely.
cierva ('θjer·βa; 'sjer-) *n.f.* doe.
—**ciervo,** *n.m.* deer.
cifra ('θi·fra, 'si-) *n.f.* **1,** cipher;
number. **2,** cipher; code. **3,** sum;
figure. —**en cifra,** briefly; in short.
cifrar (θi'frar; si-) *v.t.* **1,** to cipher.
2, *fig.* to abridge. —**cifrador,** *n.m.*
cipherer. —*adj.* ciphering. —**cifrar
la esperanza en,** pin one's hopes
on.
cigarra (θi'ɣa·rra; si-) *n.f.* cicada;
locust.
cigarrera (θi·ɣa'rre·ra; si-) *n.f.* **1,**
cigarette maker. **2,** cigar box. **3,** cigar case.
cigarrería (θi·ɣa·rre'ri·a; si-) *ñ.f.*
Amer. cigar store.
cigarrero (θi·ɣa'rre·ro; si-) *n.m.*
cigar maker; cigar seller.
cigarrillo (θi·ɣa'rri·ʎo; si·ɣa'rri-
jo) *n.m.* cigarette.
cigarro (θi'ɣa·rro; si-) *n.m.* **1,** cigarette. **2,** cigar.
cigoñal (θi·ɣo'ɲal; si-) *n.m.* =
cigüeñal.
cigoto (θi'ɣo·to; si-) *n.m.* zygote.
cigüeña (θi'ɣwe·ɲa; si-) *n.f.* **1,**
stork. **2,** *mech.* crank.
cigüeñal (θi·ɣwe'ɲal; si-) **1,** *n.m.*
crankshaft. **2,** winch.
cilantro (θi'lan·tro; si-) *n.m.* coriander; cilantro.
ciliado (θi'lja·ðo; si-) *adj.* ciliate;
ciliated.
ciliar (θi'ljar; si-) *adj.* ciliary.

cilindrar (θi·lin'drar; si-) *v.t.* to
roll. —**cilindro** (-'lin·dro) *n.m.* cylinder; roller. —**cilindrado,** *adj.*
rolled. —**cilíndrico** (-'lin·dri·ko)
adj. cylindrical.
cilio ('θi·ljo; 'si-) *n.m.* cilium.
—**cilios,** *n.m.pl.* cilia.
cima ('θi·ma; 'si-) *n.f.* summit;
peak; apex.
cimarrón (θi·ma'rron; si-) *adj.,
Amer.* wild; untamed.
címbalo ('θim·ba·lo; 'sim-) *n.m.*
cymbal. —**cimbalero,** *n.m., also,*
cimbalista, *n.m. & f.* cymbalist.
cimbrar (θim'brar; sim-) *also,*
cimbrear (-bre'ar) *v.t.* to brandish
(a rod). —*v.t. & i.* to vibrate.
—**cimbrarse,** *v.r.* to bend; sway.
cimbreo (θim'bre·o; sim-) *n.m.*
bending; swaying.
cimentación (θi·men·ta'θjon;
si·men·ta'sjon) *n.f.* foundation.
cimentar (θi·men'tar; si-) *v.t.*
[*infl.:* **pensar, 27**] **1,** to lay the
foundation of. **2,** to refine (metals).
3, *fig.* to establish (principles);
found. —**cimentación,** *n.f.* foundation; laying of a foundation.
cimiento (θi'mjen·to; si-) *n.m.*
foundation; basis. —**abrir los
cimientos,** to break ground.
cimitarra (θi·mi'ta·rra; si-) *n.f.*
scimitar.
cimurgia (θi'mur·xja; si-) *n.f.*
zymurgy.
cinabrio (θi'na·βrjo; si-) *n.m* cinnabar.
cinc (θinƙ; sinƙ) *n.m.* zinc.
cincel (θin'θel; sin'sel) *n.m.* chisel.
cincelar (θin·θe'lar; sin·se-) *v.t.* to
chisel; engrave; carve. —**cince-
lador,** *n.m.* engraver; stonecutter.
—**cinceladura,** *n.f.* carving; chasing. —**cincelado,** *adj.* chiselled;
carved. —*n.m.* carving; engraving.
cinco ('θin·ko; 'sin-) *adj. & n.m.*
five.
cincuenta (θin'kwen·ta; sin-) *adj.
& n.m.* fifty.
cincuentavo (θin·kwen'ta·βo;
sin-) *adj. & n.m.* fiftieth.
cincuentena (θin·kwen'te·na;
sin-) *n.f.* a quantity of fifty.
cincuentón (θin·kwen'ton; sin-)
adj. & n.m. quinquagenarian.
cincha ('θin·tʃa; 'sin-) *n.f.* **1,** cinch.
2, girth.
cinchar (θin'tʃar; sin-) *v.t.* **1,** to
cinch. **2,** to bind, as with bands or
hoops.

cincho ('θin·tʃo; 'sin-) *n.m.* **1,** belt; girdle. **2,** iron hoop on a barrel.

cineasta (θi·ne'as·ta; si-) *n.m. & f.* film director or producer.

cinema (θi'ne·ma; si-) *also, colloq.* **cine** ('θi·ne; 'si-) *n.m.* **1,** motion pictures; movies. **2,** motion-picture theater.

cinematografía (θi·ne·ma·to·ɣra'fi·a; si-) *n.f.* cinematography; film production. —**cinematografiar** (-'fjar) *v.t.* [*infl.:* enviar, 22] to film. —**cinematográfico** (-'ɣra·fi·ko) *adj.* cinematographic; cinematic. —**cinematógrafo** (-'to·ɣrafo) *n.m.* **1,** motion-picture camera. **2,** film projector. **3,** movie theater.

cinético (θi'ne·ti·ko; si-) *adj.* kinetic. —**cinética,** *n.f.* kinetics.

cingalés (θin·ga'les; sin-) *adj. & n.m.* [*fem.* -**lesa**] Sri Lankan; formerly Singhalese; Ceylonese.

cíngaro ('θin·ga·ro; 'sin-) *adj. & n.m.* gypsy.

cíngulo ('θin·gu·lo; 'sin-) *n.m.* cingulum.

cínico ('θi·ni·ko; 'si-) *adj.* cynical. —*n.m.* cynic.

cinismo (θi'nis·mo; si-) *n.m.* cynicism.

cinosura (θi·no'su·ra; si-) *n.f.* cynosure.

cinta ('θin·ta; 'sin-) *n.f.* **1,** ribbon; band; tape. **2,** film. **3,** *naut.* wale. —**cinta adhesiva,** friction tape. —**cinta métrica,** tape measure. —**cinta magnetofónica,** recording tape. —**cinta transportadora,** conveyor belt.

cintillo (θin'ti·ʎo; sin'ti·jo) *n.m.* **1,** hatband. **2,** headband; snood.

cinto ('θin·to; 'sin-) *n.m.* belt; girdle.

cintura (θin'tu·ra; sin-) *n.f.* waist; waistline. —**cinturilla,** *n.f., Amer.* small girdle. —**meter en cintura,** to bring to heel.

cinturón (θin·tu'ron; sin-) *n.m.* belt. —**cinturón de seguridad,** safety belt; seat belt.

ciña ('θi·ɲa; 'si-) *v., pres.subjve. of* ceñir.

ciño ('θi·ɲo; 'si-) *v., 1st pers. sing. pres. ind. of* ceñir.

ciñó (θi'ɲo; si-) *v., 3rd pers.sing. pret. of* ceñir.

cipayo (θi'pa·jo; si-) *n.m.* sepoy.

ciprés (θi'pres; si-) *n.m.* cypress tree. —**cipresal,** *n.m.* cypress grove.

circo ('θir·ko; 'sir-) *n.m.* circus.

circón (θir'kon; sir-) *n.m.* zircon.

circonio (θir'ko·njo; sir-) *n.m.* zirconium.

circuir (θir·ku'ir; sir-) *v.t.* [*infl.:* huir, 26] to surround; encircle.

circuito (θir'kwi·to; sir-) *n.m.* circuit.

circulación (θir·ku·la'θjon; sir·ku·la'sjon) *n.f.* **1,** circulation. **2,** traffic.

circular (θir·ku'lar; sir-) *v.t. & i.* to circulate. —*adj.* circular. —*n.f.* circular; circular letter.

circulatorio (θir·ku·la'to·rjo; sir-) *adj.* circulatory.

círculo ('θir·ku·lo; 'sir-) *n.m.* **1,** circle. **2,** club.

circuncidar (θir·kun·θi'ðar; sir·kun·si-) *v.t.* to circumcise. —**circuncisión** (-'sjon) *n.f.* circumcision. —**circunciso** (-'θi·so; -'si·so) *adj.* circumcised.

circundar (θir·kun'dar; sir-) *v.t.* to circle; surround.

circunferencia (θir·kun·fe'ren·θja; sir·kun·fe'ren·sja) *n.f.* circumference.

circunflejo (θir·kun'fle·xo; sir-) *adj. & n.m.* circumflex.

circunlocución (θir·kun·lo·ku'θjon; sir·kun·lo·ku'sjon) *n.f.* circumlocution. Also, **circunloquio** (-'lo·kjo) *n.m.*

circunnavegar (θir·kun·na·βe'ɣar; sir-) *v.t* [*infl.:* pagar, 8] to circumnavigate. —**circunnavegación,** *n.f.* circumnavigation.

circunscribir (θir·kuns·kri'βir; sir-) *v.t.* **1,** to circumscribe. **2,** to limit; restrict. —**circunscripción** (-krip'θjon; -'sjon) *n.f.* circumscription.

circunspección (θir·kuns·pek'θjon; sir·kuns·pek'sjon) *n.f.* circumspection. —**circunspecto** (-'pek·to) *adj.* circumspect.

circunstancia (θir·kuns'tan·θja; sir·kuns'tan·sja) *n.f.* circumstance.

circunstanciado (θir·kuns·tan·'θja·ðo; sir·kuns·tan'sja·ðo) *adj.* detailed; minute.

circunstancial (θir·kuns·tan·'θjal; sir·kuns·tan'sjal) *adj.* circumstantial.

circunstante (θir·kuns'tan·te; sir-) *adj.* **1,** surrounding. **2,** present. —**circunstantes,** *n.m.pl.* bystanders.

circunvalar (θir·kun·βa'lar; sir-) *v.t.* to circle; surround. —**circunvalación,** *n.f.* **1,** surrounding rampart. **2,** traffic loop.

circunvecino (θir·kun·βe'θi·no; sir·kun·βe'si·no) *adj.* adjacent; surrounding.

cirila (θi'ri·la; si-) *n.f., bot.* titi.

cirílico (θi'ri·li·ko; si-) *adj. & n.m.* Cyrillic.

cirio ('θi·rjo; 'si-) *n.m., eccles.* wax candle.

cirro ('θi·rro; 'si-) *n.m.* cirrus.

cirrosis (θi'rro·sis; si-) *n.f.* cirrhosis.

ciruela (θi'rwe·la; si-) *n.f.* **1,** plum. **2,** [*also,* **ciruela pasa**] prune. —**ciruelo,** *n.m.* plum tree.

cirugía (θi·ru'xi·a; si-) *n.f.* surgery.

cirujano (θi·ru·xa·no; si-) *n.m.* surgeon.

cisma ('θis·ma; 'sis-) *n.m.* schism. —**cismático** (-'ma·ti·ko) *adj.* schismatic.

cisne ('θis·ne; 'sis-) *n.m.* swan.

cisterna (θis'ter·na; sis-) *n.f.* cistern.

cístico ('θis·ti·ko; 'sis-) *adj.* cystic.

cistitis (θis'ti·tis; sis-) *n.f.* cystitis.

cistología (θis·to·lo'xi·a; sis-) *n.f.* cystology.

cistoscopio (θis·tos'ko·pjo; sis-) *n.m.* cystoscope.

cita ('θi·ta; 'si-) *n.f.* **1,** appointment; engagement. **2,** quotation. **3,** assignation.

citable (θi'ta·βle; si-) *adj.* quotable.

citación (θi·ta'θjon; si·ta'sjon) *n.f.* **1,** citation. **2,** *law* summons.

citado (θi'ta·ðo; si-) *adj.* abovementioned.

citar (θi'tar; si-) *v.t.* **1,** to make an appointment with. **2,** to cite; quote. **3,** *law* to summon. **4,** *bullfighting* to incite.

cítara ('θi·ta·ra; 'si-) *n.f.* cithara; zither.

citología (θi·to·lo'xi·a; si-) *n.f.* cytology. —**citológico** (-'lo·xi·ko) *adj.* cytological. —**citólogo** (-'to·lo·ɣo) *n.m.* cytologist.

citoplasma (θi·to'plas·ma; si-) *n.m.* cytoplasm.

citrato (θi'tra·to; si-) *n.m.* citrate.

cítrico ('θi·tri·ko; 'si-) *adj.* citric; citrous.

ciudad (θju'ðað; sju-) *n.f.* city.

ciudadano (θju·ða·ða·no; sju-) *adj.* pert. to a city; civic. —*n.m.* citizen. —**ciudadanía** (-'ni·a) *n.f.* **1,** citizenship. **2,** citizenry.

ciudadela (θju·ða·ðe·la; sju-) *n.f.* citadel.

civeta (θi'βe·ta; si-) *n.f.* civet cat. —**civeto,** *n.m.* civet.

cívico ('θi·βi·ko; 'si-) *adj.* civic. —**civismo,** *n.m.* civic-mindedness.

civil (θi'βil; si-) *adj.* civil. —**civilidad,** *n.f.* civility.

civilizar (θi·βi·li'θar; si·βi·li'sar) *v.t.* [*infl.:* **rezar,** 10] to civilize. —**civilización,** *n.f.* civilization.

cizaña (θi'θa·ɲa; si'sa-) *n.f.* **1,** *bot.* darnel. **2,** *fig.* discord. **3,** *Bib.* tare.

clamar (kla'mar) *v.i.* to clamor. —*v.t.* to clamor for; cry out for.

clamor (kla'mor) *n.m.* clamor; uproar. —**clamoroso,** *adj.* clamorous; uproarious.

clamorear (kla·mo·re'ar) *v.t. & i.* to clamor. —*v.i.* to toll; knell.

clamoreo (kla·mo·re·o) *n.m.* **1,** clamor. **2,** toll; tolling.

clan (klan) *n.m.* clan.

clandestino (klan·des'ti·no) *adj.* clandestine; underhanded. —**clandestinidad,** *n.f.* clandestineness; underhandedness.

claque ('kla·ke) *n.f.* claque.

clara ('kla·ra) *n.f.* white (*of an* egg).

claraboya (kla·ra'βo·ja) *n.f.* skylight; transom.

clarear (kla·re'ar) *v.t.* to give light to. —*v.i.* to dawn; grow light. —**clarearse,** *v.r.* **1,** to be transparent. **2,** *colloq.* to give oneself away.

clarecer (kla·re'θer; -'ser) *v.i.* [*infl.:* **conocer,** 13] to dawn.

clarete (kla're·te) *n.m.* claret.

claridad (kla·ri'ðað) *n.f.* **1,** clarity; clearness. **2,** brightness. —**claridades,** *n.f.pl.* plain truth.

claridoso (kla·ri'ðo·so) *adj., Amer.* outspoken; blunt.

clarificar (kla·ri·fi'kar) *v.t.* [*infl.:* **tocar,** 7]. **1,** to brighten. **2,** to clarify. —**clarificación,** *n.f.* clarification.

clarín (kla'rin) *n.m.* bugle; clarion. —**clarinero,** *n.m.* bugler.

clarinete (kla·ri·ne·te) *n.m.* **1,** clarinet. **2,** [*also,* **clarinetista**] clarinet player.

clarión (kla'rjon) *n.m.* chalk; chalk crayon.

clarividencia (kla·ri·βi'ðen·θja; -sja) *n.f.* clairvoyance. —**clarividente,** *adj. & n.m. & f.* clairvoyant.

claro ('kla·ro) *adj.* **1,** clear; transparent. **2,** bright; serene (*of weather*). **3,** light (*of colors*). **4,** thin (*of liquids, hair, etc.*). **5,** weak (*of* *tea).* **6,** evident; indisputable. **7,** *fig.* shrewd; smart. —*n.m.* **1,** skylight. **2,** interval; pause. **3,** break; gap. —*adv.* clearly; of course; indeed. —**claro de luna,** moonlight. —**poner en claro,** to clarify. —**sacar en claro (de),** to understand; get the full meaning (of). —**a las claras,** openly. —**de claro en claro,** evidently.

claroscuro (kla·ros'ku·ro) *n.m.* chiaroscuro.

clase ('kla·se) *n.f.* **1,** class; category; rank. **2,** class of students; classroom. **3,** kind; sort.

clásico ('kla·si·ko) *adj.* **1,** classic; classical. **2,** *colloq.* customary. —*n.m.* classic. —**clasicismo** (-θis·mo; -'sis·mo) *n.m.* classicism. —**clasicista,** *n.m. & f.* classicist.

clasificar (kla·si·fi'kar) *v.t.* [*infl.:* tocar, 7] to classify; arrange. —**clasificación,** *n.f.* classification.

claustro ('klaus·tro) *n.m.* **1,** cloister. **2,** *educ.* faculty.

claustrofobia (klaus·tro'fo·βja) *n.f.* claustrophobia.

cláusula ('klau·su·la) *n.f.* **1,** *gram.* clause; sentence. **2,** *law* clause; stipulation.

clausura (klau'su·ra) *n.f.* **1,** confinement. **2,** adjournment. **3,** closure. **4,** restricted area in a convent or monastery.

clausurar (klau·su'rar) *v.t.* **1,** to close, as by official order. **2,** to seal off.

clava ('kla·βa) *n.f.* bat; club; cudgel.

clavado (kla'βa·ðo) *adj.* **1,** studded with nails. **2,** exact; just right.

clavar (kla'βar) *v.t.* **1,** to nail; stick *(as a bayonet).* **2,** to prick *(in horseshoeing).* **3,** *colloq.* to swindle.

clave ('kla·βe) *n.f.* **1,** key; code. **2,** *mus.* clef. —**clave de do,** tenor or C clef. —**clave de fa,** bass or F clef. —**clave de sol,** treble or G clef.

clavel (kla'βel) *n.m.* carnation.

clavetear (kla·βe·te'ar) *v.t.* **1,** to stud; trim with nails, tacks, etc. **2,** to tip with metal.

clavicémbalo (kla·βi'θem·ba·lo; -'sem·ba·lo) *n.m.* harpsichord.

clavicordio (kla·βi'kor·ðjo) *n.m.* clavichord.

clavícula (kla'βi·ku·la) *n.f.* clavicle.

clavija (kla'βi·xa) *n.f.* **1,** pin; peg. **2,** *mus.* peg *(of a stringed instrument).* **3,** *elect.* plug; jack. —**apretar las clavijas a,** *colloq.* to put the screws on.

clavijero (kla·βi'xe·ro) *n.m.* **1,** *mus.* pegbox *(of a stringed instrument).* **2,** hat and coat rack.

clavillo (kla'βi·ʎo; -jo) *n.m.* **1,** clove *(spice).* **2,** [*also,* **clavito**] brad; tack.

clavo ('kla·βo) *n.m.* **1,** nail; spike. **2,** clove *(spice).* **3,** corn *(on the foot).* **4,** *slang* disappointment; failure. —**dar en el clavo,** to hit the mark. —**agarrarse de un clavo ardiendo,** *colloq.* to grasp at a straw.

clemátide (kle'ma·ti·ðe) *n.f.* clematis.

clemencia (kle'men·θja; -sja) *n.f.* clemency. —**clemente,** *adj.* clement.

clepsidra (klep'si·ðra) *n.f.* hourglass.

cleptomanía (klep·to·ma'ni·a) *n.f.* kleptomania. —**cleptomaníaco** (-a·ko) *n.m. & adj.* kleptomaniac. *Also,* **cleptómano** (-'to·ma·no).

clerecía (kle·re'θi·a; -'si·a) *n.f.* clergy.

clerical (kle·ri'kal) *adj.* **1,** of or pert. to the clergy; clerical. **2,** favoring or supporting the interests of the clergy.

clericato (kle·ri'ka·to) *n.m.* office or dignity of a clergyman.

clericatura (kle·ri·ka'tu·ra) *n.f.*

clérigo ('kle·ri·ɣo) *n.m.* clergyman; cleric.

clero ('kle·ro) *n.m.* clergy.

cliente ('kljen·te) *n.m. & f.* client; customer.

clientela (kljen·te·la) *n.f.* clientele; customers.

clima ('kli·ma) *n.m.* **1,** climate. **2,** climatic zone. **3,** region; clime. **4,** *Amer., colloq.* weather.

climatérico (kli·ma'te·ri·ko) *adj.* climacteric.

climático (kli'ma·ti·ko) *adj.* climatic.

climatizar (kli·ma·ti'θar; -'sar) *v.t.* [*infl.:* rezar, 10] to air-condition. —**climatización,** *n.f.* air conditioning.

clímax ('kli·maks) *n.m.* climax.

clínico ('kli·ni·ko) *adj.* clinical. —*n.m.* clinician. —**clínica,** *n.f.* clinic.

clíper ('kli·per) *n.m.* clipper; clipper ship.

clisar (kli'sar) *v.t.* to stereotype.
—**clisé** (-'se) *n.m.* stereotype.
clítoris ('kli·to·ris) *n.m.* clitoris.
cloaca (klo'a·ka) *n.f.* **1**, sewer. **2**,
zoöl. large intestine; cloaca.
clocar (klo'kar) *v.i.* [*infl.: tocar, 7*;
mover, 30] to cluck.
clon (klon) *n.m.* clone.
cloque ('klo·ke) *n.m.* harpoon.
cloquear (klo·ke'ar) *v.i.* to cluck;
cackle. —**cloqueo** (-'ke·o) *n.m.*
cluck; cackle.
clorato (klo'ra·to) *n.m.* chlorate.
cloro ('klo·ro) *n.m.* chlorine.
clorofila (klo·ro'fi·la) *n.f.* chlorophyll. —**clorofílico** (-'fi·li·ko) *adj.*
of or pert. to chlorophyll.
cloroformizar (klo·ro·for·mi'θar;
-'sar) *v.t.* [*infl.: rezar, 10*] to chloroform.
cloroformo (klo·ro'for·mo) *n.m.*
chloroform.
cloruro (klo'ru·ro) *n.m.* chloride.
club (kluβ) *n.m.* [*pl. clubs*] club.
clueco ('klwe·ko) *adj.* **1**, broody. **2**,
feeble. —*v., pres.ind. of* **clocar**.
clueque ('klwe·ke) *v., pres.subjve.
of* **clocar**.

coacción (ko·ak'θjon; -'sjon)
n.f. compulsion; coercion. —**coaccionar** *v.t.* to coerce; bully.
coacusado (ko·a·ku'sa·ðo) *n.m.*
codefendant.
coadyuvar (ko·að·ju'βar) *v.i.* to
contribute. —*v.t.* to help; aid.
coagular (ko·a·ɣu'lar) *v.i.* to coagulate; curdle. —**coagulación,** *n.f.*
coagulation; curdling.
coágulo (ko'a·ɣu·lo) *n.m.* **1**, clot.
2, curd.
coalición (ko·a·li'θjon; -'sjon) *n.f.*
coalition.
coartada (ko·ar'ta·ða) *n.f.* alibi.
coartar (ko·ar'tar) *v.t.* to limit; restrict.
coaxial (ko·ak'sjal) *adj.* coaxial.
coba ('ko·βa) *n.f.* flattery; cajolery.
cobalto (ko'βal·to) *n.m.* cobalt.
cobarde (ko'βar·ðe) *n.m. & f.* coward. —*adj.* cowardly. —**cobardía,**
n.f. cowardice.
cobertera (ko·βer'te·ra) *n.f.* **1**, pot
lid; cover. **2**, procuress.
cobertizo (ko·βer'ti·θo; -so) *n.m.*
shed.
cobertor (ko·βer'tor) *n.m.* bedspread.
cobertura (ko·βer'tu·ra) *n.f.* cover; covering.
cobija (ko'βi·xa) *n.f.* **1**, overlapping

roof tile. **2**, *Amer.* blanket. **3**, *Amer.*
poncho. **4**, *pl., Amer.* bedclothes.
cobijar (ko·βi'xar) *v.t.* to cover;
protect; shelter. —**cobijadura,** *also,*
cobijo (-'βi·xo) *n.f.* covering.
—**cobijamiento,** *n.m.* lodging.
cobra ('ko·βra) *n.f.* cobra.
cobrable (ko'βra·βle) *adj.* collectible. *Also,* **cobradero** (-'ðe·ro).
cobrador (ko·βra'ðor) *n.m.* [*fem.*
-dora] **1**, collector. **2**, *R.R.* conductor. **3**, retriever.
cobranza (ko'βran·θa; -sa) *n.f.* **1**,
collection. **2**, retrieving (*of game*).
3, retrieval. **4**, payment. **5**, cashing
(*of a check*).
cobrar (ko'βrar) *v.t.* **1**, to collect. **2**,
to acquire; win (fame, etc.). **3**, to
retrieve (game). **4**, to pull in (a
rope). **5**, to charge (a certain price).
6, to cash (a check). —*v.i.* to get
hit; get a beating; be punished.
—**cobrarse,** *v.r.* to recover; come
to. —**cobrar ánimo,** to take courage. —**cobrar afición,** to take a liking. —**cobrar odio,** to take a dislike.
cobre ('ko·βre) *n.m.* **1**, copper. **2**,
brass cooking utensils. —**co-
bres,** *n.m.pl., mus.* brass instruments. —**batir el cobre,** *colloq.* to
bustle.
cobrizo (ko'βri·θo; -so) *adj.* **1**, of
or containing copper. **2**, copper-
colored.
cobro ('ko·βro) *n.m.* collection.
coca ('ko·ka) *n.f.* **1**, *bot.* coca. **2**,
colloq. [*also,* coco] head; brains. **3**,
Amer. eggshell. **4**, *Amer.* rind. —**de
coca,** *Amer.* **1**, free; gratis. **2**, in
vain.
cocaína (ko·ka'i·na) *n.f.* cocaine.
cocción (kok'θjon; -'sjon) *n.f.* cooking; boiling; baking; firing (*of ceramics*).
cóccix ('kok·θiks; -siks) *n.m.sing.
& pl.* coccyx.
cocear (ko·θe'ar; ko·se-) *v.i.* to
kick. —**coceadura,** *n.f., also,*
coceamiento, *n.m.* kicking.
cocedor (ko·θe'ðor; ko·se-) *n.m.*
baking oven.
cocer (ko'θer; -'ser) *v.t. & i.* [*infl.:
torcer, 66*] to boil; cook; bake; fire
(ceramics). —**cocerse,** *v.r.* to suffer
intense pain.
coces ('ko·θes; -ses) *n.f., pl. of* **coz.**
cocido (ko'θi·ðo; ko'si-) *n.m.* Spanish stew. —*adj.* boiled; cooked;
baked.

cociente (ko'θjen·te; ko'sjen-) *n.m.* = cuociente.

cocimiento (ko·θi'mjen·to; ko·si-) *n.m.* 1, cooking; boiling; baking. 2, brew of medicinal herbs.

cocina (ko'θi·na; ko'si-) *n.f.* 1, kitchen. 2, stove. 3, cookery; cuisine.

cocinar (ko·θi'nar; ko·si-) *v.i. & t.* 1, to cook. 2, *Amer.* to bake.

cocinero (ko·θi'ne·ro; ko·si-) *n.m.* cook; chef.

coco ('ko·ko) *n.m.* 1, coconut. 2, [*also*, **cocotero** (-'te·ro)] coconut tree. 3, coccus. 4, bugbear; bugaboo. 5, *colloq.* head; brains. 6, *Amer.* derby hat. 7, *Amer.* blow on the head. 8, *colloq.* face; grimace. —**hacer cocos a**, *colloq.* to make eyes at; flirt with.

cocodrilo (ko·ko'ðri·lo) *n.m.* crocodile.

cocotal (ko·ko'tal) *n.m.* coconut grove; coconut plantation.

coctel (kok'tel) *n.m.* cocktail. —**coctelera** (-'le·ra) *n.f.* cocktail shaker.

cocuyo (ko'ku·jo) *n.m.*, *Amer.* firefly.

coche ('ko·tʃe) *n.m.* 1, coach; carriage. 2, railway car. 3, car; automobile. —**coche de San Francisco**, Shank's mare.

cochecillo (ko·tʃe'θi·ʎo; -'si·jo) *n.m.* baby carriage; perambulator.

cochera (ko'tʃe·ra) *n.f.* 1, garage; carriage house. 2, *R.R.* depot.

cochería (ko·tʃe'ri·a) *n.f.*, *S.A.* car rental agency; livery.

cochero (ko'tʃe·ro) *n.m.* 1, coachman. 2, cab driver. —*adj.* easily cooked.

cochevira (ko·tʃe'βi·ra) *n.f.* lard.

cochina (ko'tʃi·na) *n.f.* sow.

cochinería (ko·tʃi·ne'ri·a) *n.f.*, *colloq.* dirtiness; filthiness. *Also*, **cochinada**.

cochinilla (ko·tʃi'ni·ʎa; -ja) *n.f.* 1, wood louse. 2, cochineal (*insect & dye*).

cochino (ko'tʃi·no) *n.m.* pig. —*adj.*, *colloq.* sloppy; filthy. —**cochinillo**, *n.m.* piglet; shoat.

cochitril (ko·tʃi'tril) *n.m.* pigsty.

coda ('ko·ða) *n.f.* 1, *mus.* coda. 2, *carp.* wedge.

codal (ko'ðal) *n.m.* 1, vineshoot. 2, *archit.* buttress. 3, frame (*of a saw*). 4, shore; prop. —*adj.* bent; elbowed.

codazo (ko'ða·θo; -so) *n.m.* nudge with the elbow.

codear (ko·ðe'ar) *v.i.* to elbow; jostle. —**codearse**, *v.r.* to mingle; hobnob.

codeína (ko·ðe'i·na) *n.f.* codeine.

codelincuente (ko·ðe·lin'kwen·te) *n.m. & f.* accomplice. —*adj.* jointly responsible; in complicity. —**codelincuencia**, *n.f.* complicity.

codemandado (ko·ðe·man'da·ðo) *n.m.* person sued jointly with another; co-respondent.

códice ('ko·ði·θe; -se) *n.m.* codex.

codicia (ko'ði·θja; -sja) *n.f.* covetousness; greed.

codiciar (ko·ði'θjar; -'sjar) *v.t.* to covet.

codicilo (ko·ði'θi·lo; -'si·lo) *n.m.* codicil.

codicioso (ko·ði'θjo·so; -'sjo·so) *adj.* greedy; covetous.

codificar (ko·ði·fi'kar) *v.t.* [*infl.* tocar, 7] 1, to codify. 2, to encode. —**codificación**, *n.f.* 1, codification. 2, encoding.

código ('ko·ði·ɣo) *n.m.* code. —**código penal**, criminal law; penal code.

codillo (ko'ði·ʎo; -jo) *n.m.* 1, bend; angle. 2, elbow. 3, stirrup.

codo ('ko·ðo) *n.m.* 1, *anat.* elbow. 2, *mech.* angle; elbow; —**hablar por los codos**, *colloq.* to chatter. —**empinar el codo**, *colloq.* to drink too much.

codorniz (ko·ðor'niθ; -'nis) *n.f.* quail.

coeducación (ko·e·ðu·ka'θjon; -'sjon) *n.f.* coeducation. —**coeducativo** (-'ti·βo) *adj.* coeducational.

coeficiente (ko·e·fi'θjen·te; -'sjen·te) *n.m. & adj.* coefficient.

coercer (ko·er'θer; -'ser) *v.t.* [*infl.*: vencer, 11] to coerce. —**coerción**, *n.f.* coercion.

coercible (ko·er'θi·βle; -'si·βle) *adj.* 1, coercible. 2, compressible.

coetáneo (ko·e'ta·ne·o) *adj. & n.m.* contemporary.

coevo (ko'e·βo) *adj.* coeval.

coexistir (ko·ek·sis'tir) *v.i.* to coexist. —**coexistencia**, *n.f.* coexistence.

cofia ('ko·fja) *n.f.* 1, coif. 2, hairnet.

cofín (ko'fin) *n.m.* small basket.

cofrade (ko'fra·ðe) *n.m. & f.* brother or sister (*of a confraternity*).

cofradía (ko·fra'ði·a) *n.f.* confraternity; brotherhood.

cofre ('ko·fre) *n.m.* trunk; coffer.

cogedero (ko·xe'ðe·ro) *adj.* ready for gathering. —*n.m.* handle.

coger (ko'xer) *v.t.* [*infl.:* 15] **1,** to pick; get; collect. **2,** to catch; seize; arrest. **3,** to occupy; take up (space). —*v.i.* to fit; have room.

cogida (ko'xi·ða) *n.f.* **1,** fruit harvest. **2,** catch (*in fishing*).

cogido (ko'xi·ðo) *n.m.* fold; pleat.

cognado (koɣ'na·ðo) *adj. & n.m.* cognate.

cognición (koɣ·ni'θjon; -'sjon) *n.f.* cognition. —**cognoscitivo** (koɣ·nos·θi'ti·βo; -no·si'ti·βo) *adj.* cognitive.

cognomen (koɣ'no·men) *n.m.* cognomen (*Roman family name*).

cognomento (koɣ·no'men·to) *n.m.* cognomen; appellation.

cogollo (ko'ɣo·ʎo; -jo) *n.m.* **1,** heart (*of vegetables*). **2,** shoot (*of plants*).

cogote (ko'ɣo·te) *n.m.* nape.

cogulla (ko'yu·ʎa; -ja) *n.f.* cowl.

cohabitar (ko·a·βi'tar) *v.i.* to cohabit. —**cohabitación**, *n.f.* cohabitation.

cohechar (ko·e't∫ar) *v.t.* to bribe.

cohecho (ko·e't∫o) *n.m.* **1,** bribe. **2,** bribery.

coheredero (ko·e·re'ðe·ro) *n.m.* coheir.

coherencia (ko·e'ren·θja; -sja) *n.f.* **1,** coherence. **2,** *physics* cohesion.

coherente (ko·e'ren·te) *adj.* **1,** coherent. **2,** *physics* cohesive.

cohesión (ko·e'sjon) *n.f.* cohesion.

cohesivo (ko·e'si·βo) *adj.* cohesive.

cohete (ko·e'te) *n.m.* **1,** rocket. **2,** *Amer.* firecracker.

cohibir (ko·i'βir) *v.t.* to restrain. —**cohibición**. *n.f.* restraint.

cohombro (ko'om·bro) *n.m.* cucumber.

cohorte (ko'or·te) *n.f.* cohort.

coima ('koi·ma) *n.f.*, *Amer.* graft; bribe; bribery. —**coimear**, *v.i. & t.*, *Amer.* to graft.

coincidencia (ko·in·θi'ðen·θja; -si'ðen·sja) *n.f.* coincidence. —**coincidente**, *adj.* coincident; coincidental.

coincidir (ko·in·θi'ðir; -si'ðir) *v.i.* **1,** to coincide. **2,** to agree. '

coito ('koi·to) *n.m.* coitus; coition.

coja ('ko·xa) *v.*, *pres.subjve.* of **coger.**

cojear (ko·xe'ar) *v.i.* **1,** to limp. **2,** to wobble (*as a table, chair, etc.*).

cojera (ko'xe·ra) *n.f.* limp; lameness.

cojín (ko'xin) *n.m.* **1,** cushion. **2,** saddle pad.

cojinete (ko·xi'ne·te) *n.m.* ball bearing.

cojo ('ko·xo) *adj.* **1,** (*of persons*) lame; crippled. **2,** (*of a table*) wobbly. —*n.m.* cripple. —**no ser cojo ni manco,** to be clever.

cojo ('ko·xo) *v.*, *1st pers.sing.pres. ind.* of **coger.**

cok (kok) *n.m.* coke.

col (kol) *n.f.* cabbage; cole; kale. —**col de Bruselas,** Brussels sprouts.

cola ('ko·la) *n.f.* **1,** tail. **2,** train (*of a gown*). **3,** hind part. **4,** line; queue. **5,** tail end; last place. **6,** glue. —**hacer cola,** to stand in line; queue up. —**tener** *or* **traer cola,** to have serious consequences.

colaborar (ko·la·βo'rar) *v.i.* to collaborate. —**colaboración**, *n.f.* collaboration. —**colaboracionista**, *n.* collaborationist. —**colaborador,** *n.m.* collaborator.

colación (ko·la'θjon; -'sjon) *n.f.* **1,** collation. **2,** *educ.* conferring (*of a degree, honor, etc.*). —**sacar** *or* **traer a colación,** to bring up; adduce.

colada (ko'la·ða) *n.f.* **1,** laundry; drenching; soaking (*of clothes*). **2,** tap (*of a furnace*).

coladera (ko·la'ðe·ra) *n.f.* **1,** strainer; colander. **2,** *Mex.* drain; sewer.

colado (ko'la·ðo) *adj.* cast (*of iron*).

colador (ko·la'ðor) *n.m.* strainer. Also, **coladero** (-'ðe·ro).

coladura (ko·la'ðu·ra) *n.f.* filtration.

colapso (ko'lap·so) *n.m.* collapse.

colar (ko'lar) *v.t. & i.* [*infl.:* **acostar, 28**] **1,** to strain; filter. **2,** to sneak in; slip in. **3,** to foist. —**colarse,** *v.r.* to sneak in or out; slip by. —**estar colado por,** *colloq.* to be madly in love with.

colateral (ko·la·te'ral) *adj.* collateral.

colerén (kol'kren) *n.m.* cold cream.

colcha ('kol·t∫a) *n.f.* quilt; bedspread; counterpane. —**colchadura,** *n.f.* quilting. —**colchar,** *v.t.* to quilt.

colchón (kol't∫on) *n.m.* mattress. —**colchón de muelles,** spring mattress. —**colchón neumático,** air mattress.

colchoneta (kol·tʃo'ne·ta) *n.f.* **1,** light mattress. **2,** mat *(for gymnastics).*

colear (ko·le'ar) *v.i.* **1,** to wag the tail. **2,** *Amer., colloq.* to move ridiculously *(in walking).* —**todavía colea,** *colloq.* it is not finished yet.

colección (ko·lek'θjon; -'sjon) *n.f.* collection. —**coleccionar,** *v.t.* to collect. —**coleccionista,** *n.m.* & *f.* collector; one who collects as a hobby.

colecta (ko'lek·ta) *n.f.* **1,** *liturgy* collect. **2,** money collected, esp. for charity.

colectar (ko·lek'tar) *v.t.* to collect.

colectividad (ko·lek·ti·βi'ðað) *n.f.* collectivity; community.

colectivo (ko·lek'ti·βo) *adj.* collective. —*n.m., Mex., Arg.* bus; public conveyance. —**colectivismo,** *n.m.* collectivism.

colector (ko·lek'tor) *n.m.* collector.

colega (ko'le·ɣa) *n.m.* & *f.* colleague.

colegiado (ko·le'xja·ðo) *adj.* collegiate.

colegial (ko·le'xjal) *adj.* collegiate. —*n.m.* & *f.* collegian.

colegiatura (ko·le·xja'tu·ra) *n.f.* fellowship; scholarship.

colegio (ko'le·xjo) *n.m.* **1,** college; school. **2,** professional association.

colegir (ko·le'xir) *v.t.* [*infl.:* **regir,** 57] **1,** to gather. **2,** to infer.

cólera ('ko·le·ra) *n.f.* anger; wrath. —*n.m.* [*also,* **cólera morbo**] cholera. —**montar en cólera,** to blow up; hit the ceiling.

colérico (ko'le·ri·ko) *adj.* **1,** irritable; choleric. **2,** of, pert. to or suffering from cholera.

colesterol (ko·les·te'rol) *n.m.* cholesterol. *Also,* **colesterina** (ko·les·te'ri·na) *n.f.*

coleta (ko'le·ta) *n.f.* ponytail; queue. —**cortarse la coleta,** to quit, esp. bullfighting.

coleto (ko'le·to) *n.m.* **1,** jacket. **2,** *colloq.* oneself; one's body. —**decir para su coleto,** to say to oneself. —**echarse (algo) al coleto,** to gulp down; polish off; toss off.

colgadero (kol·ɣa'ðe·ro) *n.m.* hanger. —*adj.* made to be hung up.

colgadizo (kol·ɣa'ði·θo; -so) *n.m.* lean-to.

colgadura (kol·ɣa'ðu·ra) *n.f.* hangings; tapestry; drapery.

colgante (kol'ɣan·te) *adj.* hanging. —*n.m.* earring. —**puente colgante,** suspension bridge.

colgar (kol'ɣar) *v.t.* [*infl.:* **pagar,** 8; **mover,** 30] **1,** to hang; suspend. **2,** to adorn *(with hangings).* **3,** *colloq.* to flunk. **4,** *colloq.* to hang; kill by hanging. **5,** to impute; attribute. —*v.i.* to hang.

colibrí (ko·li'βri) *n.m.* hummingbird.

cólico ('ko·li·ko) *adj.* & *n.m.* colic.

coliflor (ko·li'flor) *n.f.* cauliflower.

coligarse (ko·li'ɣar·se) *v.r.* [*infl.:* **pagar,** 8] to band together; join forces.

coligió (ko·li'xjo) *v., 3rd pers.sing. pret. of* **colegir.**

colija (ko'li·xa) *v., pres.subjve. of* **colegir.**

colijo (ko'li·xo) *v., 1st pers.sing. pres.ind. of* **colegir.**

colilla (ko'li·ʎa; -ja) *n.f.* stub; butt.

colina (ko'li·na) *n.f.* hill.

colinabo (ko·li'na·βo) *n.m.* kohlrabi.

colindar (ko·lin'dar) *v.i.* to abut; border. —**colindante,** *adj.* contiguous; adjacent.

coliseo (ko·li'se·o) *n.m.* **1,** theater; playhouse. **2,** coliseum.

colisión (ko·li'sjon) *n.f.* collision; clash.

colitis (ko'li·tis) *n.f.* colitis.

colmado (kol'ma·ðo) *adj.* full; chock-full; overflowing. —*n.m.* **1,** specialty restaurant, usu. a sea food house. **2,** food store.

colmar (kol'mar) *v.t.* **1,** to fill to the brim; heap up. **2,** to fulfill. **3,** to overwhelm.

colmena (kol'me·na) *n.f.* beehive.

colmenar (kol·me'nar) *n.m.* apiary.

colmenilla (kol·me'ni·ʎa; -ja) *n.f.* **1,** *dim. of* **colmena. 2,** morel.

colmillo (kol'mi·ʎo; -jo) *n.m.* **1,** *anat.* eyetooth; canine tooth, **2,** *zoöl.* fang; tusk.

colmo ('kol·mo) *n.m.* **1,** heap; mound. **2,** overflow. **3,** summit; top. —*adj.* heaping full; overflowing. —**a colmo,** abundantly. —**para colmo de,** *colloq.* to top off. —**esto es el colmo,** *colloq.* this is the limit.

colocación (ko·lo·ka'θjon; -'sjon) *n.f.* **1,** place; position. **2,** employment; job. **3,** placement.

colocar (ko·lo'kar) *v.* [*infl.:* **tocar,** 7] —*v.t.* **1,** to arrange; set. **2,** to place; put in place. **3,** *comm.* to invest. —*v.i.* to be placed; find employment.

colodión (ko·lo'ðjon) *n.m.* collodion.

colofón (ko·lo'fon) *n.m.* colophon.

colofonia (ko·lo·fo·nja) *n.f.* rosin.

coloide (ko'loi·ðe) *n.m.* colloid. —**coloideo** (-'ðe·o) *adj.* colloidal.

colon ('ko·lon) *n.m.* **1,** *anat.* colon. **2,** *gram.* clause, esp. main clause.

colón (ko'lon) *n.m.* monetary unit of El Salvador, Costa Rica; colón.

colonia (ko'lo·nja) *n.f.* **1,** colony. **2,** cologne; eau de cologne. —**colonial,** *adj.* colonial. —**colonialismo,** *n.m.* colonialism.

colonizar (ko·lo·ni'θar; -'sar) *v.t.* [*infl.:* **rezar,** 10] to colonize. —**colonización,** *n.f.* colonization.

colono (ko'lo·no) *n.m.* **1,** colonist; settler; colonial. **2,** tenant farmer.

coloque (ko'lo·ke) *v., pres.subjve. of* **colocar.**

coloqué (ko·lo'ke) *v., 1st pers. sing.pret. of* **colocar.**

coloquio (ko'lo·kjo) *n.m.* colloquy; conversation.

color (ko'lor) *n.m.* **1,** color. **2,** rouge. **3,** *fig.* character. —**dar color a,** *colloq.* to exaggerate. —**ponerse de mil colores,** *colloq.* to blush; turn a dozen colors. —**perder el color,** *colloq.* to become pale; pale. —**so color de,** under pretext of.

colorado (ko·lo'ra·ðo) *adj.* **1,** red; reddish. **2,** *fig.* embarrassed. **3,** off-color; risqué. —**ponerse colorado,** to blush.

colorante (ko·lo'ran·te) *adj. & n.m.* coloring.

colorar (ko·lo·rar) *v.t.* to dye; color; stain. —*v.i.* to blush. —**coloración,** *n.f.* coloration.

colorear (ko·lo·re'ar) *v.t.* to make plausible; palliate. —*v.i.* to redden.

colorete (ko·lo're·te) *n.m.* rouge.

colorido (ko·lo'ri·ðo) *n.m.* **1,** coloring. **2,** style.

colosal (ko·lo'sal) *adj.* colossal; huge.

coloso (ko·lo·so) *n.m.* colossus.

columbio (ko'lum·bjo) *n.m.* columbium.

columbrar (ko·lum'brar) *v.t.* **1,** to espy; perceive. **2,** to infer; guess.

columna (ko'lum·na) *n.f.* column. —**columnario,** *adj.* columnar.

columnata (ko·lum'na·ta) *n.f.* colonnade.

columnista (ko·lum'nis·ta) *n.m. & f.* columnist.

columpiar (ko·lum'pjar) *v.t.* to swing; sway.

columpio (ko'lum·pjo) *n.m.* **1,** swing. **2,** [*also,* **columpio de tabla**] seesaw.

colusión (ko·lu'sjon) *n.f.* collusion.

colusorio (ko·lu'so·rjo) *adj.* collusive.

colza ('kol·θa; -sa) *n.f., bot.* rape.

collado (ko'ʎa·ðo; ko'ja-) *n.m.* hill.

collar (ko'ʎar; -'jar) *n.m.* **1,** collar. **2,** necklace.

collera (ko'ʎe·ra; -'je·ra) *n.f.* collar.

coma ('ko·ma) *n.f.* comma. —*n.m.* coma. —**punto y coma,** semicolon.

comadre (ko'ma·ðre) *n.f.* **1,** midwife. **2,** gossip. **3,** *colloq.* go-between. **4,** the relationship between, and name used by a child's mother and godmother.

comadrear (ko·ma·ðre'ar) *v.i.* to gossip; tattle.

comadreja (ko·ma'ðre·xa) *n.f.* weasel.

comadrona (ko·ma'ðro·na) *n.f.* midwife.

comandar (ko·man'dar) *v.t.* to command. —**comandante,** *n.m.* commandant; commander; major.

comandita (ko·man'di·ta) *n.f.* silent partnership. —**comanditario,** *n.m.* silent partner.

comando (ko'man·do) *n.m.* **1,** command. **2,** control.

comarca (ko'mar·ka) *n.f.* county; district. —**comarcano,** *adj.* neighboring; bordering.

comatoso (ko·ma'to·so) *adj.* comatose.

comba ('kom·ba) *n.f.* **1,** bend; bulge; warp. **2,** jump rope. —**hacer combas,** *colloq.* to sway.

combar (kom'bar) *v.t.* to bend; warp.

combate (kom'ba·te) *n.m.* combat; battle.

combatiente (kom·ba'tjen·te) *adj. & n.m. & f.* combatant.

combatir (kom·ba'tir) *v.i.* to combat; fight. —*v.t.* to attack; beat. —**combativo,** *adj.* combative.

combinación (kom·bi·na'θjon; -'sjon) *n.f.* **1,** combination. **2,** *chem.* compound. **3,** lady's slip.

combinar (kom·bi'nar) *v.t.* to combine; blend; compound.

combo ('kom·bo) *adj.* bent; crooked; warped.

combustible (kom·bus'ti·βle) *adj.* combustible. —*n.m.* fuel.

combustión (kom·bus'tjon) *n.f.* combustion.

comedero (ko·me'ðe·ro) *n.m.*
feeding place *(for animals)*.

comedia (ko'me·ðja) *n.f.* comedy;
play; farce. **—hacer la comedia
(de)**, to pretend; make believe.

comedianta (ko·me'ðjan·ta) *n.f.*
actress; comedienne.

comediante (ko·me'ðjan·te) *n.m.*
comedian; player.

comedido (ko·me'ði·ðo) *adj.* **1**,
moderate. **2**, civil; polite.

comedirse (ko·me'ðir·se) *v.r.*
[*infl.:* **pedir, 33**] **1**, to refrain; to be
moderate. **2**, *Amer.* to volunteer.

comedón (ko·me'ðon) *n.m.* blackhead.

comedor (ko·me'ðor) *adj.* eating
much. **—n.m. 1**, dining room. **2**,
heavy eater.

comelón (ko·me'lon) *adj. & n.m.,
Amer.* = **comilón**.

comendador (ko·men·da'ðor)
n.m. **1**, knight commander. **2**, prefect of certain religious orders.

comensal (ko·men'sal) *n.m. &
f.* **1**, retainer; dependent. **2**, guest.

comentador (ko·men·ta'ðor) *n.m.*
commentator.

comentar (ko·men'tar) *v.t.* to comment on. *—v.i.* to comment.

comentario (ko·men'ta·rjo) *n.m.*
commentary; comment.

comentarista (ko·men·ta'ris·ta)
n.m. & f. commentator.

comento (ko'men·to) *n.m.* comment; commentary.

comenzar (ko·men'θar; -'sar) *v.t.*
& *v.i.* [*infl.:* **pensar, 27; rezar, 10**]
to commence; begin.

comer (ko'mer) *v.t.* **1**, to eat. **2**, to
consume; corrode. **3**, *chess, checkers* to take. **4**, to fade. **5**, to expend;
waste. *—v.i.* to eat; dine.
—comerse con los ojos, *colloq.* to
gaze at. **—comerse los codos**,
colloq. **1**, to be starved. **2**, to retract.
—dar de comer, *colloq.* to feed.
—tener qué comer, to have an income.

comerciable (ko·mer'θja·βle;
-'sja·βle) *adj.* **1**, salable; marketable. **2**, sociable.

comercial (ko·mer'θjal; -'sjal) *adj.*
commercial. **—comercializar**,
v.t. [*infl.:* **rezar, 10**] to commercialize.

comerciante (ko·mer'θjan·te;
-'sjan·te) *n.m. & f.* merchant; trader;
dealer.

comerciar (ko·mer'θjar; -'sjar) *v.i.*
to trade; deal.

comercio (ko·mer·θjo; -sjo) *n.m.*
commerce; trade; business. **—comercio exterior**, foreign trade.
—comercio interior, domestic
trade.

comestible (ko·mes'ti·βle) *adj.*
eatable; edible. **—comestibles**, *n.m.
pl.* provisions; groceries.

cometa (ko'me·ta) *n.m.* comet.
—n.f. kite.

cometer (ko·me'ter) *v.t.* **1**, to commit. **2**, to perpetrate.

cometido (ko·me'ti·ðo) *n.m.* **1**,
commitment; duty; task. **2**, purpose.

comezón (ko·me'θon; -'son) *n.f.* **1**,
itching. **2**, *fig.* desire.

cómico ('ko·mi·ko) *adj.* comic;
comical. **—n.m. 1**, comedian. **2**,
player; actor.

comida (ko'mi·ða) *n.f.* **1**, food; eating. **2**, dinner.

comience (ko'mjen·θe; -se) *v.,
pres.subjve.* of **comenzar**.

comienzo (ko'mjen·θo; -so) *v.,
pres.ind.* of **comenzar**. *—n.m.* origin; beginning.

comilitona (ko·mi·li'to·na) *n.f.,
colloq.* hearty meal; feast. *Also,*
comilona (-'lo·na).

comilón (ko·mi'lon) *n.m.* glutton.
—adj. gluttonous.

comillas (ko'mi·ʎas; -jas) *n.f.pl.*
quotation marks.

comino (ko'mi·no) *n.m., bot.*
cumin. **—no valer un comino**, to
be worthless.

comisaría (ko·mi·sa'ri·a) *n.f.* **1**,
police station. **2**, commissioner's
office. **3**, commissary.

comisario (ko·mi'sa·rjo) *n.m.* **1**,
commissioner. **2**, trustee. **3**, chief
of police; police official. **—comisariado**, *n.m.* commissariat.

comisión (ko·mi'sjon) *n.f.* **1**, commission. **2**, committee. **3**, assignment. **4**, errand.

comisionado (ko·mi·sjo'na·ðo)
adj. commissioned. **—n.m. 1**, commissioner. **2**, agent. **3**, trustee.

comisionar (ko·mi·sjo'nar) *v.t.* to
commission; appoint.

comisorio (ko·mi'so·rjo) *adj., law*
binding; compulsory.

comistrajo (ko·mis'tra·xo) *n.m.*
strange concoction of food; mess;
slop.

comité (ko·mi'te) *n.m.* committee.

comitiva (ko·mi'ti·βa) *n.f.* retinue.

como ('ko·mo) *adv. & conj.* **1**, how.
2, as *(in comparisons)*. **3**, why. **4**,
like; as. **5**, if. **—¿cómo?** what is it?

—¿**cómo no?** why not? —**como quiera que sea,** however.

cómoda ('ko·mo·ða) *n.f.* chest of drawers; bureau.

comodidad (ko·mo·ði'ðað) *n.f.* comfort; convenience.

comodín (ko·mo'ðin) *n.m., cards* joker.

cómodo ('ko·mo·ðo) *adj.* **1,** comfortable. **2,** convenient. **3,** comfort-loving; self-indulgent.

comodoro (ko·mo'ðo·ro) *n.m.* commodore.

compacto (kom'pak·to) *adj.* compact.

compadecer (kom·pa·ðe'θer; -'ser) *v.t. also, v.r.,* **compadecerse** [*infl.:* **conocer, 13**] *fol. by* **de,** to pity; feel compassion for.

compadrar (kom·pa'ðrar) *v.i.* to get along; be on good terms.

compadrazgo (kom·pa'ðraθ·ɣo; -'ðras·ɣo) *n.m.* **1,** relationship between a godfather and the parents of a child. **2,** *derog.* tight circle; clique.

compadre (kom'pa·ðre) *n.m.* **1,** godfather. **2,** *colloq.* crony.

compañerismo (kom·pa·ɲe'ris·mo) *n.m.* fellowship; companionship.

compañero (kom·pa'ɲe·ro) *n.m.* [*fem.* **-ra**] companion; friend; mate. —**compañero** *or* **compañera de habitación** *or* **cuarto,** roommate.

compañía (kom·pa'ɲi·a) *n.f.* **1,** company; society. **2,** companionship.

comparar (kom·pa'rar) *v.t.* to compare. —**comparable,** *adj.* comparable. —**comparación,** *n.f.* comparison. —**comparado,** *adj.* —**comparativo,** *adj.* comparative. —*n.m., gram.* comparative.

comparecencia (kom·pa·re'θen·θja; -'sen·sja) *n.f., law* appearance.

comparecer (kom·pa·re'θer; -'ser) *v.i.* [*infl.:* **conocer, 13**] **1,** to appear; turn up. **2,** *law* to appear (in court).

comparendo (kom·pa'ren·do) *n.m., law* **1,** summons. **2,** *Amer.* = **comparecencia.**

comparsa (kom'par·sa) *n.m. & f., theat.* extra; supernumerary. —*n.f.* extras collectively; chorus.

compartimiento (kom·par·ti·'mjen·to) *n.m.* division; compartment; department.

compartir (kom·par'tir) *v.t.* to divide; share.

compás (kom'pas) *n.m.* **1,** compass. **2,** calipers. **3,** *mus.* measure; time; beat. —**llevar el compás,** to beat or keep time. —**fuera de compás,** offbeat.

compasar (kom·pa'sar) *v.t.* to measure (*with a rule and compass*).

compasible (kom·pa'si·βle) *adj.* compassionate; lamentable.

compasión (kom·pa'sjon) *n.f.* compassion; pity.

compasivo (kom·pa'si·βo) *adj.* compassionate; humane.

compatible (kom·pa'ti·βle) *adj.* compatible. —**compatibilidad,** *n.f.* compatibility.

compatriota (kom·pa'trjo·ta) *n.m & f.* compatriot; fellow citizen.

compeler (kom·pe'ler) *v.t.* [*p.p.* **compulso**] to compel; force.

compendiar (kom·pen'djar) *v.t.* to abridge; condense.

compendio (kom'pen·djo) *n.m.* compendium; summary. —**compendioso,** *adj.* compendious.

compensación (kom·pen·sa'θjon; -'sjon) *n.f.* **1,** compensation. **2,** *comm.* clearing.

compensar (kom·pen'sar) *v.t.* **1,** to compensate. **2,** to compensate for; offset. —**compensatorio** (-'to·rjo) *also,* **compensativo** (-'ti·βo) *adj.* compensatory.

competencia (kom·pe'ten·θja; -sja) *n.f.* **1,** competition; rivalry. **2,** competence.

competente (kom·pe'ten·te) *adj.* competent; able; apt.

competer (kom·pe'ter) *v.i.* to be one's interest or concern; be incumbent on one.

competición (kom·pe·ti'θjon; -'sjon) *n.f.* contest; competition.

competidor (kom·pe·ti'ðor) *adj.* **1,** competing. **2,** competitive. —*n.m.* competitor; rival.

competir (kom·pe'tir) *v.i.* [*infl.:* **pedir, 33**] to compete; contend; vie. —**competitivo,** *adj.* competitive.

compilar (kom·pi'lar) *v.t.* to compile. —**compilación,** *n.f.* compilation.

compinche (kom'pin·tʃe) *n.m. & f., colloq.* chum; buddy.

complacencia (kom·pla'θen·θja; -'sen·sja) *n.f.* **1,** complacency; indulgence. **2,** pleasure; satisfaction.

complacer (kom·pla'θer; -'ser) *v.t.* [*infl.:* **placer, 52**] to please; accommodate. —**complacerse,** *v.r.* **1,** *fol.*

by **de** *or* **con,** to be pleased. **2,** *fol. by* **en,** to take pleasure in.

complaciente (kom·pla'θjen·te; -'sjen·te) *adj.* **1,** complacent. **2,** accommodating; obliging.

complejo (kom'ple·xo) *adj. & n.m.* complex. —**complejidad,** *n.f.* complexity.

complementar (kom·ple·men·'tar) *v.t.* to complement.

complementario (kom·ple·men·ta·rjo) *adj.* complementary.

complemento (kom·ple'men·to) *n.m.* **1,** complement. **2,** *gram.* object; complement.

completar (kom·ple'tar) *v.t.* to complete; finish. —**completamiento,** *n.m.* completion.

completo (kom'ple·to) *adj.* **1,** complete; finished. **2,** full; full to capacity.

complexión (kom·plek'sjon) *n.f.* **1,** complexion. **2,** constitution; nature.

complicar (kom·pli'kar) *v.t.* [*infl.:* tocar, 7] to complicate; entangle. —**complicación,** *n.f.* complication.

cómplice ('kom·pli·θe; -se) *n.m. & f.* accomplice; accessory.

complicidad (kom·pli·θi'ðað; -si'ðað) *n.f.* complicity.

complot (kom'plot) *n.m.* [*pl.* **complots**] plot; scheme.

componenda (kom·po'nen·da) *n.f.* **1,** arbitrary or unjust agreement or settlement. **2,** *colloq.* bribe; fix. **3,** *colloq.* excuse; blandishment.

componente (kom·po'nen·te) *adj. & n.m. & f.* component.

componer (kom·po'ner) *v.t.* [*infl.:* poner, 54] **1,** to compound. **2,** to repair; fix. **3,** to put in order; arrange. **4,** to settle (differences); reconcile. **5,** to write (poetry). **6,** to compose (music). **7,** *print.* to compose. **8,** to mix (drinks). **9,** to amount to; come to. —**componérselas,** to manage; get through (a task).

comportar (kom·por'tar) *v.t.* **1,** to endure; bear. **2,** *Amer.* to entail. —**comportarse,** *v.r.* to behave. —**comportamiento,** *n.m.* comportment; deportment.

composición (kom·po·si'θjon; -'sjon) *n.f.* **1,** composition. **2,** settlement; deal.

compositor (kom·po·si'tor) *adj.* composing. —*n.m.* [*fem.* -**tora**] **1,** composer. **2,** compositor.

compostura (kom·pos'tu·ra) *n.f.*

1, behavior; manners. **2,** repair; repairing. **3,** composure.

compota (kom'po·ta) *n.f.* compote. —**compotera** (-'te·ra) *n.f.* compote dish.

compra ('kom·pra) *n.f.* **1,** purchase. **2,** shopping; marketing. —**hacer compras; ir** *or* **salir de compras,** to go shopping.

comprador (kom·pra'ðor) *n.m.* buyer; shopper.

comprar (kom'prar) *v.t.* to buy. —*v.i.* to shop.

comprender (kom·pren'der) *v.t.* **1,** to comprehend; understand. **2,** to comprise; include.

comprensible (kom·pren'si·βle) *adj.* comprehensible. —**comprensibilidad,** *n.f.* comprehensibility.

comprensión (kom·pren'sjon) *n.f.* **1,** comprehension. **2,** comprehensiveness.

comprensivo (kom·pren'si·βo) *adj.* **1,** comprehensive. **2,** understanding.

compresa (kom'pre·sa) *n.f.* compress.

compresión (kom·pre'sjon) *n.f.* compression. —**compresible,** *adj.* compressible.

compresor (kom·pre'sor) *adj.* compressing. —*n.m.* compressor.

compresora (kom·pre'so·ra) *n.f.* compressor.

comprimido (kom·pri'mi·ðo) *adj.* compressed. —*n.m.* tablet; pill.

comprimir (kom·pri'mir) *v.t.* **1,** to compress. **2,** to constrain.

comprobación (kom·pro·βa·'θjon; -'sjon) *n.f.* verification; check; checking.

comprobante (kom·pro'βan·te) *n.m.* receipt; voucher; check.

comprobar (kom·pro'βar) *v.t.* [*infl.:* acostar, 28] to verify; check. —**comprobatorio,** *adj.* confirming.

comprometer (kom·pro·me'ter) *v.t.* **1,** to compromise. **2,** to involve; implicate. **3,** to endanger. —**comprometerse,** *v.r.* **1,** to commit oneself. **2,** to be or become engaged. —**comprometedor,** *adj.* compromising.

comprometido (kom·pro·me'ti·ðo) *adj.* **1,** engaged, **2,** committed. **3,** embarrassing.

compromisario (kom·pro·mi·'sa·rjo) *n.m.* arbitrator; umpire.

compromiso (kom·pro'mi·so) *n.m.* **1,** compromise; settlement; deal. **2,** appointment; engagement.

3, commitment. 4, embarrassment. 5, engagement; betrothal.

compuerta (kom'pwer·ta) *n.f.* 1, sluice; floodgate. 2, canal lock. 3, half door.

compuesto (kom'pwes·to) *v., p.p. of* **componer.** —*adj.* 1, composed; constituted. 2, repaired; fixed. 3, compound; composite; 4, calm; collected. —*n.m.* compound; composite.

compulsión (kom·pul'sjon) *n.f., law* compulsion.

compulsivo (kom·pul'si·βo) *adj.* compulsive.

compulso (kom'pul·so) *v., p.p. of* **compeler.**

compunción (kom·pun'θjon; -'sjon) *n.f.* compunction.

compungido (kom·pun'xi·ðo) *adj.* sorrowful; remorseful.

compungirse (kom·pun'xir·se) *v.r.* [*infl.:* **coger, 15**] to feel compunction.

computar (kom·pu'tar) *v.t.* to compute; calculate. —**computación,** *n.f.* 1, computation. 2, computer science. —**computadora,** *n.f.* computer. —**computarizar,** *v.t.* [*infl.:* **rezar, 10**] to computerize.

cómputo ('kom·pu·to) *n.m.* computation; calculation.

comulgante (ko·mul'ɣan·te) *n.m. & f., eccles.* communicant.

comulgar (ko·mul'ɣar) *v.* [*infl.:* **pagar, 8**] *v.t.* to be in agreement with; believe in. —*v.i.* to receive Communion. —**comulgar ruedas de molino,** to take everything for granted; believe everything.

común (ko'mun) *adj.* common; usual; general. —*n.m.* 1, community; public. 2, lavatory. —**por lo común,** in general.

comuna (ko'mu·na) *n.f.* commune; *Amer.* municipality.

comunal (ko·mu'nal) *adj.* common; communal. —*n.m.* community.

comunero (ko·mu'ne·ro) *n.m.* 1, shareholder; co-owner. 2, *hist.* a member of the old Castilian communities.

comunicación (ko·mu·ni·ka'θjon; -'sjon) *n.f.* communication.

comunicado (ko·mu·ni·ka·ðo) *n.m.* communiqué.

comunicar (ko·mu·ni'kar) *v.t.* [*infl.:* **tocar, 7**] 1, to communicate; transmit. 2, to connect; put in com-

munication. —**comunicable,** *adj.* communicable.

comunicativo (ko·mu·ni·ka·'ti·βo) *adj.* communicative.

comunidad (ko·mu·ni'ðað) *n.f.* 1, community. 2, commonwealth. —**de comunidad,** jointly.

comunión (ko·mu'njon) *n.f.* 1, communion. 2, political party. 3, *eccles.* congregation.

comunismo (ko·mu'nis·mo) *n.m.* communism. —**comunista,** *n.m. & f.* communist. —*adj.* communistic.

comunizar (ko·mu·ni'θar; -'sar) *v.t.* [*infl.:* **rezar, 10**] to communize.

comunmente (ko·mun'men·te) *adv.* commonly; generally; usually.

con (kon) *prep.* 1, with: *salí con él,* I left with him. 2, in spite of: *con todo esto,* in spite of all this. 3, *fol. by inf.* by: *con pedirlo lo tendrás,* by asking for it, you will get it. —**con tal (de) que,** provided that. —**con que,** so that; whereupon. —**con todo,** nevertheless.

conato (ko'na·to) *n.m.* endeavor; effort; attempt.

concatenar (kon·ka·te'nar) *v.t.* to concatenate; link. —**concatenación** (-te·na'θjon; -'sjon) *n.f.* concatenation; linking.

cóncavo ('kon·ka·βo) *adj.* concave; hollow. —**concavidad,** *n.f.* concavity; hollowness.

concebir (kon·θe'βir; -se'βir) *v.i. & v.t.* [*infl.:* **pedir, 33**] to conceive. —**concebible,** *adj.* conceivable.

conceder (kon·θe'ðer; kon·se-) *v.t.* to concede; grant.

concejal (kon·θe'xal; kon·se-) *n.m.* councilman; alderman.

concejo (kon'θe·xo; kon·se-) *n.m.* 1, city council. 2, town hall.

concentrar (kon·θen'trar; kon·sen-) *v.t.* to concentrate; center. —**concentración,** *n.f.* concentration.

concéntrico (kon'θen·tri·ko; kon·'sen-) *adj.* concentric. —**concentricidad** (-θi'ðað; -si'ðað) *n.f.* concentricity.

concepción (kon·θep'θjon; -sep·'sjon) *n.f.* conception.

concepto (kon'θep·to; -'sep·to) *n.m.* 1, concept; idea; 2, opinion; judgment. —**conceptual** (-'twal) *adj.* conceptual. —**conceptuar** (-'twar) *v.t.* [*infl.:* **continuar, 23**] to deem; judge.

concernir (kon·θer'nir; kon·ser-) *v.i., used only in 3rd pers.,* to concern; appertain. —**concernirse**, v.r., colloq. to concern oneself; to be concerned. —**concerniente** a, with (or in) regard to.

concertar (kon·θer'tar; -ser'tar) v.t. [infl.: **pensar, 27**] to concert; arrange. —**concertarse**, v.r. **1**, to agree. **2**, Amer., colloq. to hire out.

concertina (kon·θer'ti·na; kon·ser-) n.m. concertina.

concertino (kon·θer'ti·no; kon·ser-) n.f. first violin.

concesión (kon·θe'sjon; kon·se-) n.f. **1**, concession. **2**, grant.

concesionario (kon·θe·sjo'na·rjo; kon·se-) n.m. **1**, concessionaire. **2**, law grantee.

conceiba (kon'θi·βa; kon'si-) v., pres.subjve. of **concebir**.

concibió (kon·θi'·βjo; -si'βjo) v., 3rd pers.sing. pret. of **concebir**.

concibo (kon'θi·βo; -'si·βo) v., pres.ind. of **concebir**.

conciencia (kon'θjen·θja; -'sjen·sja) n.f. **1**, conscience. **2** consciousness. —**a conciencia, 1**, conscientiously. **2**, on purpose.

concienzudo (kon·θjen'θu·ðo; -sjen'su·ðo) adj. conscientious; businesslike.

concierna (kon'θjer·na; -'sjer·na) v., pres.subjve. of **concernir**.

concierne (kon'θjer·ne; -'sjer·ne) v., 3rd pers.sing.pres.ind. of **concernir**.

concierte (kon'θjer·te; kon'sjer-) v., pres.subjve. of **concertar**.

concierto (kon'θjer·to; -'sjer·to) v., pres.ind. of **concertar**.

concierto n.m. **1**, mus. concert; concerto. **2**, order; harmony. **3**, agreement; bargain.

conciliación (kon·θi·lja'θjon; -si·lja'sjon) n.f. **1**, conciliation. **2**, likeness; affinity. **3**, favor; protection.

conciliar (kon·θi'ljar; kon·si-) v.t. to conciliate; reconcile. —**conciliarse**, v.r. to gain; win.

conciliar adj. of or pert. to a council. —n.m. & f. council member.

conciliatorio (kon·θi·lja'to·rjo; kon·si-) adj. conciliatory.

concilio (kon'θi·ljo; kon'si-) n.m. council.

concisión (kon·θi'sjon; kon·si-) n.f. brevity; conciseness.

conciso (kon'θi·so; kon'si-) adj. concise; short.

conciudadano (kon·θju·ða'ða·no; kon·sju-) n.m. fellow citizen.

cónclave ('kon·kla·βe) also, **conclave** (kon'kla-) n.m. conclave.

concluir (kon·klu'ir) v.t. [infl.: **huir, 26**] **1**, to conclude; end; finish. **2**, to infer. —**concluirse**, v.r. to come to an end; conclude.

conclusión (kon·klu'sjon) n.f. **1**, conclusion; end. **2**, inference. —**conclusivo** (-'si·βo) adj. concluding; final; conclusive.

concluyente (kon·klu'jen·te) adj. conclusive; convincing.

concomerse (kon·ko'mer·se) v.r., colloq. **1**, to shrug the shoulders. **2**, to itch; twitch with an itch.

concomitancia (kon·ko·mi'tan·θja; -sja) n.f. concomitance. —**concomitante**, adj. concomitant.

concordancia (kon·kor'ðan·θja; -sja) n.f. **1**, concordance. **2**, gram. agreement; concord. **3**, mus. concord. **4**, pl. concordance; index of words and phrases. —**concordante**, adj. concordant.

concordar (kon·kor'ðar) v.i. [infl.: **mover, 30**] to accord; agree. —v.t. to harmonize; make agree.

concordia (kon'kor·ðja) n.f. **1**, concord; harmony. **2**, law agreement.

concreción (kon·kre'θjon; -'sjon) n.f. concretion.

concretar (kon·kre'tar) v.t. to define; make concrete. —**concretarse** a, to limit oneself to.

concreto (kon'kre·to) adj. concrete; real. —n.m. **1**, concrete. **2**, concretion. —**en concreto**, in sum; in conclusion.

concubina (kon·ku'βi·na) n.f. concubine. —**concubinato**, n.m. concubinage.

concuerde (kon'kwer·ðe) v., pres. subjve. of **concordar**.

concuerdo (kon'kwer·ðo) v., pres. ind. of **concordar**.

concupiscencia (kon·ku·pis·'θen·θja; -pi'sen·sja) n.f. concupiscence. —**concupiscente**, adj. concupiscent.

concurrencia (kon·ku'rren·θja; -sja) n.f. **1**, concurrence. **2**, attendance; gathering.

concurrente (kon·ku'rren·te) n.m. & f., usu.pl one present at a gathering, spectacle, etc. —adj. concurrent.

concurrir (kon·ku'rrir) v.i. **1**, to concur; agree. **2**, to attend; to be present. **3**, to compete. **4**, to frequent.

concurso (kon'kur·só) *n.m.* **1**, gathering; attendance; crowd. **2**, contest; competition. —**concursante**, *n.m. & f.* contestant; competitor.

concusión (kon·ku'sjon) *n.f.* **1**, concussion. **2**, *law* extortion.

concusionario (kon·ku·sjo'narjo) *adj.* extortionate. —*n.m.* extortioner.

concha ('kon·tʃa) *n.f.* **1**, shell; seashell. **2**, oyster. **3**, *theat.* prompter's shell. **4**, *Amer., colloq.* impudence.

conchabarse (kon·tʃa'βar·se) *v.r.*, *colloq.* to conspire; plot.

conchudo (kon'tʃu·ðo) *adj.* **1**, shell-like. **2**, *colloq.* crafty; sly. **3**, *Amer., colloq.* impudent.

conde ('kon·de) *n.m.* earl; count. —**condado** (-'da·ðo) *n.m.* earldom; county.

condecorar (kon·de·ko'rar) *v.t.* to decorate; confer a decoration upon. —**condecoración**, *n.f.* decoration; honor; medal.

condena (kon'de·na) *n.f.* term of imprisonment; sentence.

condenación (kon·de·na'θjon; -'sjon) *n.f.* **1**, condemnation. **2**, *theol.* damnation.

condenar (kon·de'nar) *v.t.* **1**, to condemn. **2**, to damn. **3**, to convict. **4**, to sentence.

condensar (kon·den'sar) *v.t.* to condense. —**condensación**, *n.f.* condensation. —**condensador**, *n.m.* condenser.

condesa (kon'de·sa) *n.f.* countess.

condescendencia (kon·des·θen·'den·θja; -de·sen'den·sja) *n.f.* **1**, condescension. **2**, indulgence; leniency.

condescender (kon·des·θén'der; -de·sen'der) *v.i.* [*infl.:* perder, 29] to condescend; to be complacent.

condescendiente (kon·des·θen·'djen·te; kon·de·sen-) *adj.* **1**, condescending. **2**, indulgent; lenient.

condición (kon·di'θjon; -'sjon) *n.f.* **1**, condition; quality. **2**, quality; rank. **3**, stipulation. —**a condición de que**, on condition that.

condicional (kon·di·θjo'nal; -sjo'nal) *adj.* conditional.

condicionar (kon·di·θjo'nar; -sjo'nar) *v.t.* = **acondicionar**. —*v.i.* to impose conditions.

condigno (kon'diɣ·no) *adj.* condign.

condimentar (kon·di·men'tar) *v.t.* to dress; season.

condimento (kon·di'men·to) *n.m.* seasoning; condiment.

condiscípulo (kon·dis'θi·pu·lo; -di'si·pu·lo) *n.m.* fellow student.

condolencia (kon·do'len·θja; -sja) *n.f.* condolence; sympathy.

condolerse (kon·do'ler·se) *v.r.* [*infl.:* mover, 30] to condole; feel sorry. —**condolerse de**, to feel sorry for; sympathize with.

condominio (kon·do'mi·njo) *n.m.* condominium.

condón (kon'don) *n.m.* condom.

condonar (kon·do'nar) *v.t.* to pardon; condone. —**condonación**, *n.f.* pardon; condonement.

cóndor ('kon·dor) *n.m.* condor.

conducción (kon·duk'θjon; -'sjon) *n.f.* **1**, conduction. **2**, conveyance. **3**, transportation. **4**, driving; drive. **5**, wage or price agreement.

conducente (kon·du'θen·te; -'sen·te) *adj.* conducive.

conducir (kon·du'θir; -'sir) *v.* [*infl.:* 40] —*v.t.* **1**, to convey; transport. **2**, to conduct; direct; lead. **3**, to drive (a vehicle). —*v.i.* to conduce; to be conducive. —**conducirse**, *v.r.* to conduct oneself; behave.

conducta (kon'duk·ta) *n.f.* behavior.

conductible (kon·duk'ti·βle) *adj.* conductible. —**conductibilidad**, *n.f.* conductibility.

conductivo (kon·duk'ti·βo) *adj.* conductive. —**conductividad**, *n.f.* conductivity.

conducto (kon'duk·to) *n.m.* **1**, conduit; tube; pipe. **2**, drain; sewer. **3**, channel; route. **4**, intermediary; go-between. **5**, *anat.* duct; canal. —**por conducto de**, through.

conductor (kon·duk'tor) *adj.* conducting. —*n.m.* conductor; driver.

conduela (kon·dwe·la) *v., pres. subjve. of* **condoler**.

conduelo (kon'dwe·lo) *v., 1st pers. sing. pres.ind. of* **condoler**.

conduje (kon'du·xe) *v., 1st pers. sing. pret. of* **conducir**.

conduzca (kon'duθ·ka; -'dus·ka) *v., pres.subjve. of* **conducir**.

conduzco (kon'duθ·ko; -'dus·ko) *v., 1st pers.sing.pres.ind. of* **conducir**.

conectar (ko·nek'tar) *v.t. & i.* to connect.

conectivo (ko·nek'ti·βo) *adj.* connective.

coneja (ko'ne·xa) *n.f.* female rabbit.

conejera (ko·ne'xe·ra) *n.f.* rabbit hutch; burrow; warren.

conejillo (ko·ne'xi·ʎo; -jo) *n.m.*, *dim.* of **conejo**. —**conejillo de Indias**, guinea pig.

conejo (ko'ne·xo) *n.m.* rabbit. —**conejo de Noruega**, lemming.

conexión (ko·nek'sjon) *n.f.* connection.

confabular (kon·fa·βu'lar) *v.t.* to discuss. —**confabularse**, *v.r.* to plot; scheme; connive. —**confabulación**, *n.f.* plotting; scheming; connivance. —**confabulador**, *n.m.* [*fem.* -**dora**] plotter; schemer; conniver. *Also*, **confabulista**.

confección (kon·fek'θjon; -'sjon) *n.f.*, **1**, confection. **2**, manufacture. **3**, ready-made clothing.

confeccionar (kon·fek·θjo'nar; -sjo'nar) *v.t.* to prepare; make.

confederar (kon·fe·ðe'rar) *v.t.* to confederate. —**confederación**, *n.f.* confederation; confederacy. —**confederado**, *adj.* & *n.m.* confederate.

conferencia (kon·fe'ren·θja; -sja) *n.f.* **1**, conference; meeting. **2**, lecture. —**conferenciante**, *n.m.* & *f.* lecturer. *Also*, **conferencista**.

conferenciar (kon·fe·ren'θjar; -'sjar) *v.i.* to confer; hold a conference.

conferir (kon·fe'rir) *v.t.* [*infl.:* **sentir**, 31] to confer; bestow.

confesar (kon·fe'sar) *v.t.* [*infl.:* **pensar**, 27] to confess; avow. —**confesarse**, *v.r.* to confess; make confession.

confesión (kon·fe'sjon) *n.f.* confession.

confesionario (kon·fe·sjo'na·rjo) *n.m.* **1**, confessional; book of confession. **2**, confessional box.

confeso (kon'fe·so) *adj.*, *law* confessed. —*n.m.* lay brother.

confesonario (kon·fe·so'na·rjo) *n.m.* confessional box.

confesor (kon·fe'sor) *n.m.* confessor.

confeti (kon'fe·ti) *n.m.* confetti.

confiado (kon'fja·ðo) *adj.* **1**, confident; self-confident. **2**, trusting; credulous.

confianza (kon'fjan·θa; -sa) *n.f.* **1**, confidence; trust; reliance. **2**, familiarity; camaraderie. —**de confianza**, trusted; reliable. —**en confianza**, **1**, confidentially. **2**, without formality.

confianzudo (kon·fjan'θu·ðo; -'su·ðo) *adj.*, *colloq.* **1**, overfamiliar; presumptuous. **2**, *Amer.* meddlesome.

confiar (kon'fjar) *v.i.* [*infl.:* **enviar**, 22] **1**, to hope. **2**, to have trust (in). —*v.t.* to confide; entrust.

confidencia (kon·fi'ðen·θja; -sja) *n.f.* confidence; secret. —**confidencial**, *adj.* confidential.

confidente (kon·fi'ðen·te) *n.m.* **1**, confidant. **2**, love seat. —*n.f.* confidante.

confiera (kon'fje·ra) *v.*, *pres. subjve.* of **conferir**.

confiero (kon'fje·ro) *v.*, *pres.ind.* of **conferir**.

confiese (kon'fje·se) *v.*, *pres. subjve.* of **confesar**.

confieso (kon'fje·so) *v.*, *pres.ind.* of **confesar**.

configurar (kon·fi·ɣu'rar) *v.t.* to outline; shape; give configuration to. —**configuración**, *n.f.* configuration.

confín (kon'fin) *n.m.* limit; boundary. —*adj.* bordering.

confinamiento (kon·fi·na'mjen·to) *n.m.* **1**, confinement. **2**, exile. **3**, restriction under surveillance.

confinar (kon·fi'nar) *v.t.* **1**, to confine. **2**, to exile; banish. —*v.i.* to border. —**confinar con**, to border on.

confines (kon'fi·nes) *n.m.pl.* confines; limits.

confiriendo (kon·fi'rjen·do) *v.*, *ger.* of **conferir**.

confirió (kon·fi'rjo) *v.*, *3rd pers. sing.pret.* of **conferir**.

confirmar (kon·fir'mar) *v.t.* to confirm. —**confirmación**, *n.f.* confirmation. —**confirmatorio**, *adj.* confirmatory.

confiscar (kon·fis'kar) *v.t.* [*infl.:* **tocar**, 7] to confiscate. —**confiscación**, *n.f.* confiscation.

confitar (kon·fi'tar) *v.t.* to candy; glaze.

confite (kon'fi·te) *n.m.* candy; sweetmeat.

confitería (kon·fi·te'ri·a) *n.f.* candy shop; confectionery. —**confitero** (-'te·ro) *n.m.* confectioner.

confitura (kon·fi'tu·ra) *n.f.* confection; preserve.

conflagración (kon·fla·ɣra·'θjon; -'sjon) *n.f.* conflagration.

conflicto (kon'flik·to) *n.m.* conflict.

confluencia (kon·flu'en·θja; -sja) *n.f.* confluence.

confluente (kon·flu'en·te) *adj.* confluent. —*n.m.* confluence.

confluir (kon·flu'ir) *v.i.* [*infl.:* **huir,** 26] **1,** to join; converge (*of roads or rivers*). **2,** to gather (*of crowds*).

conformar (kon·for'mar) *v.t.* & *i* to conform; adjust; fit. —**conformarse,** *v.r.* **1,** to conform; comply. **2,** *Amer.* to resign oneself; acquiesce. —**conformación,** *n.f.* conformation.

conforme (kon'for·me) *adj.* **1,** conformable; suited; in accordance. **2,** compliant; conforming. **3,** resigned. —**conforme a** *or* **con,** according to; in accordance with.

conformidad (kon·for·mi'ðað) *n.f.* **1,** agreement. **2,** conformity. —**de conformidad con,** in accordance with; according to.

conformista (kon·for'mis·ta) *n.m.* & *f.* conformist.

confort (kon'fort) *n.m.* comfort.

confortable (kon·for'ta·βle) *adj.* **1,** comforting. **2,** comfortable.

confortación (kon·for·ta'θjon; -'sjon) *n.f.* consolation; comfort.

confortante (kon·for'tan·te) *adj.* comforting. —*n.m.* & *f.* comforter.

confortar (kon·for'tar) *v.t.* & *i.* to comfort.

conforte (kon'for·te) *n.m.* = **confortación.**

confraternidad (kon·fra·ter·ni'ðað) *n.f.* fellowship; confraternity.

confrontación (kon·fron·ta'θjon; -'sjon) *n.f.* confrontation.

confrontar (kon·fron'tar) *v.t.* **1,** to confront; bring face to face. **2,** to compare. —*v.i.* to border. —**confrontarse con,** to face; confront.

confundir (kon·fun'dir) *v.t.* to confuse; confound. —**confundirse,** *v.r.* to be bewildered; to be abashed.

confusión (kon·fu'sjon) *n.f.* confusion.

confuso (kon'fu·so) *adj.* confused; perplexed.

confutar (kon·fu'tar) *v.t.* to confute. —**confutación,** *n.f.* confutation.

congelar (kon·xe'lar) *v.t.* to congeal; freeze. —**congelación,** *n.f.* freezing; freeze. —**congelador,** *n.m.* freezer.

congenial (kon·xe'njal) *adj.*

congenial. —**congeniar,** *v.i.* to get along; be congenial.

congénito (kon'xe·ni·to) *adj.* congenital.

congestión (kon·xes'tjon) *n.f.* congestion. —**congestionar** (-'nar) *v.t.* to congest, as with blood; cause congestion in.

conglomerar (kon·glo·me'rar) *v.t.* to conglomerate. —**conglomeración,** *n.f.* conglomeration. —**conglomerado,** *adj.* & *n.m.* conglomerate.

congoja (kon'go·xa) *n.f.* anguish; grief. —**congojar,** *v.t.* to distress; bring anguish upon.

congoleño (kon·go'le·ɲo) *adj.* & *n.m.* Congolese. *Also,* **congolés** [*fem.* **-esa**].

congraciar (kon·gra'θjar; -'sjar) *v.t.* to ingratiate. —**congraciador,** *adj.* ingratiating. —**congraciamiento,** *n.m.* ingratiation.

congratular (kon·gra·tu'lar) *v.t.* to congratulate. —**congratulación,** *n.f.* congratulation. —**congratulatorio,** *adj.* congratulatory.

congregación (kon·gre·ɣa'θjon; -'sjon) *n.f.* congregation. —**congregacionalista,** *adj.* congregational.

congregar (kon·gre'ɣar) *v.t.* [*infl.:* **pagar,** 8] to assemble; bring together. —**congregarse,** *v.r.* to congregate; assemble; meet.

congresista (kon·gre'sis·ta) *n.m.* & *f.* member of Congress.

congreso (kon'gre·so) *n.m.* **1,** congress; assembly. **2,** convention.

congrio ('kon·grjo) *n.m.* eel.

congruencia (kon'grwen·θja; -sja) *n.f.* **1,** congruence. **2,** congruity. **3,** congruousness.

congruente (kon'grwen·te) *adj.* **1,** congruent. **2,** congruous.

congruo ('kon·grwo) *adj.* congruous. —**congruidad,** *n.f.* congruousness; congruity.

cónico ('ko·ni·ko) *adj.* conical; conic.

conífero (ko'ni·fe·ro) *adj.* coniferous. —**conífera,** *n.f.* conifer.

conjetura (kon·xe'tu·ra) *n.f.* conjecture. —**conjetural,** *adj.* conjectural. —**conjeturar,** *v.t.* & *i.* to conjecture.

conjugar (kon·xu'ɣar) *v.t.* [*infl.:* **pagar,** 8] to conjugate. —**conjugación,** *n.f.* conjugation.

conjunción (kon·xun'θjon; -'sjon) *n.f.* conjunction.

conjuntivitis (kon·xun·ti'βi·tis) *n.f.* conjunctivitis.

conjuntivo (kon·xun'ti·βo) *adj.* conjunctive. —**conjuntiva,** *n.f.* conjunctiva.

conjunto (kon'xun·to) *n.m.* **1,** mass; whole; entirety. **2,** *mus.* ensemble. —*adj.* joined; related.

conjuración (kon·xu·ra'θjon; -'sjon) *n.f.* conspiracy; plot. *Also,* **conjura** (kon'xu·ra).

conjurado (kon·xu'ra·ðo) *n.m.* conspirator.

conjurar (kon·xu'rar) *v.t.* **1,** to entreat. **2,** to exorcise. **3,** to plot; scheme. —*v.i.* to conspire.

conjuro (kon'xu·ro) *n.m.* **1,** spell; incantation. **2,** entreaty; plea.

conmemorar (kon·me·mo'rar; ko·me-) *v.t.* to commemorate. —**conmemoración,** *n.f.* commemoration.

conmemorativo (kon·me·mo·ra 'ti·βo) *adj.* commemorative.

conmensurable (kon·men·su· 'ra·βlc) *adj.* commensurable. —**conmensurado** (-'ra·ðo) *adj.* commensurate.

conmigo (kon'mi·ɣo) with me; with myself.

conminar (kon·mi'nar) *v.t.* to threaten, esp. with punishment; denounce. —**conminación,** *n.f.* threat, esp. of punishment; denunciation. —**conminatorio,** *adj.* threatening; denunciatory.

conmiseración (kon·mi·se· ra'θjon; ko·mi·se·ra'sjon) *n.f.* commiseration; pity. —**conmiserarse,** *v.r.* to commiserate.

conmoción (kon·mo'θjon; -'sjon) *n.f.* commotion; excitement.

conmover (kon·mo'βer; ko·mo-) *v.t.* [*infl.:* mover, 30] **1,** to disturb; stir up; rouse. **2,** to move; affect emotionally. —**conmovedor** (-βe'ðor) *adj.* moving; touching.

conmutación (kon·mu·ta'θjon; ko·mu·ta'sjon) *n.f.* commutation.

conmutador (kon·mu·ta'ðor; ko·mu-) *adj.* commutating. —*n.m.* electric switch. —**cuadro conmutador,** switchboard.

conmutar (kon·mu'tar; ko·mu-) *v.t.* **1,** to commute; change. **2,** to barter; exchange.

connatural (kon·na·tu'ral) *adj.* inborn; inherent. —**connaturalización,** *n.f.* acclimation. —**connaturalizarse,** *v.r.* [*infl.:* rezar, 10] to become acclimated or accustomed.

connivencia (kon·ni'βen·θja; -sja) *n.f.* connivance.

connotar (kon·no'tar) *v.t.* to connote. —**connotación,** *n.f.* ćonnotation. —**connotado,** *adj., Amer.* outstanding.

cono ('ko·no) *n.m.* cone.

conocedor (ko·no·θe'ðor; -se'ðor) *adj.* expert; skilled. —*n.m.* connoisseur; critic.

conocer (ko·no'θer; -'ser) *v.t.* [*infl.:* 13] **1,** to know; be or become acquainted with. **2,** to perceive; distinguish. **3,** *law* to try (a case). —**conocible,** *adj.* knowable. —**dar a conocer,** to make known.

conocido (ko·no'θi·ðo; -'si·ðo) *adj.* well-known. —*n.m.* acquaintance.

conocimiento (ko·no·θi'mjen·to; ko·no·si-) *n.m.* **1,** knowledge; skill. **2,** understanding. **3,** consciousness. **4,** *Amer.* baggage check. —**conocimiento de embarque,** bill of lading.

conopeo (ko·no'pe·o) *n.m., eccles.* canopy.

conque ('kon·ke) *adv. & conj.* so then; now then. —*n.m., colloq.* condition; stipulation.

conquista (kon'kis·ta) *n.f.* conquest.

conquistar (kon·kis'tar) *v.t.* to conquer; vanquish. —**conquistador,** *n.m.* [*fem.* -dora] conqueror.

consabido (kon·sa'βi·ðo) *adj.* aforementioned.

consagrar (kon·sa'ɣrar) *v.t.* **1,** to consecrate. **2,** to dedicate; devote. **3,** to sanction. —**consagración,** *n.f.* consecration.

consanguíneo (kon·san'gi·ne·o) *adj.* consanguineous; kindred. —**consanguinidad** (-ni'ðað) *n.f.* consanguinity.

consciente (kons'θjen·te; kon· 'sjen·te) *adj. & n.m.* conscious. —**consciencia,** *n.f.* consciousness.

conscripción (kons·krip'θjon; -'sjon) *n.f.* conscription.

conscripto (kons'krip·to) *n.m.* conscript.

consecución (kon·se·ku'θjon; -'sjon) *n.f.* attainment; acquisition.

consecuencia (kon·se'kwen·θja; -sja) *n.f.* **1,** consequence; outcome. **2,** consistency; accordance. —**en consecuencia,** accordingly. —**por consecuencia,** therefore; consequently.

consecuente (kon·se'kwen·te) *adj.* consequent.

consecutivo (kon·se·ku'ti·βo) *adj.* consecutive.

conseguir (kon·se'ɣir) *v.t.* [*infl.:* seguir, 64] 1, to attain; achieve. 2, to get; obtain. 3, *colloq.* to find; locate.

conseja (kon'se·xa) *n.f.* saga; fairy tale.

consejero (kon·se'xe·ro) *n.m.* 1, counselor; adviser. 2, councilor; board member.

consejo (kon'se·xo) *n.m.* 1, counsel; advice. 2, council; board. —**consejo de guerra,** 1, council of war. 2, court-martial. —**consejo de ministros,** cabinet.

consenso (kon'sen·so) *n.m.* consensus.

consentido (kon·sen'ti·ðo) *adj.* 1, pampered; spoiled. 2, complaisant; indulgent.

consentimiento (kon·sen·ti·'mjen·to) *n.m.* consent.

consentir (kon·sen'tir) *v.* [*infl.:* sentir, 31] —*v.t.* 1, to permit; allow. 2, to consent to; agree to. 3, to spoil; pamper. —*v.i.* to weaken; become loose. —**consentirse,** *v.r.* to crack; give way.

conserje (kon'ser·xe) *n.m.* janitor; concierge; porter. —**conserjería,** *n.f.* porter's desk.

conserva (kon'ser·βa) *n.f.* conserve; preserve. —**conservas alimenticias,** canned goods. —**en conserva,** canned.

conservación (kon·ser·βa'θjon; -'sjon) *n.f.* 1, conservation. 2, preservation.

conservador (kon·ser·βa'ðor) *adj.* & *n.m.* 1, conservative. 2, preservative. —*n.m.* preserver; keeper; guardian.

conservar (kon·ser'βar) *v.t.* to conserve; keep. —**conservarse,** *v.r.* to take care of oneself; keep fit.

conservatorio (kon·ser·βa'to·rjo) *n.m.* conservatory; —*adj.* conservatory; preservative.

considerable (kon·si·ðe'ra·βle) *adj.* considerable.

consideración (kon·si·ðe·ra·'θjon; -'sjon) *n.f.* consideration.

considerado (kon·si·ðe'ra·ðo) *adj.* 1, considered. 2, considerate.

considerar (kon·si·de'rar) *v.t.* to consider.

consigna (kon'siɣ·na) *n.f.* 1, *mil.* password. 2, *R.R.* checkroom.

consignar (kon·siɣ'nar) *v.t.* 1, to assign. 2, to consign. 3, to point out; indicate. —**consignación,** *n.f.* consignment. —**consignador,** *n.m.* consignor. —**consignatario,** *n.m.* consignee.

consigo (kon'si·ɣo) with you; with him; with her; with them; with himself; with herself; with oneself; with yourself; with yourselves; with themselves.

consiguiente (kon·si'ɣjen·te) *adj.* consequent; consequential. —**por consiguiente,** therefore; consequently.

consistente (kon·sis'ten·te) *adj.* consistent. —**consistencia,** *n.f.* consistency.

consistir (kon·sis'tir) *v.i.* to consist. —**consistir en,** to consist of or in.

consistorio (kon·sis·to'rjo) *n.m.* consistory.

consocio (kon·so'θjo; -sjo) *n.m.* partner; associate.

consola (kon'so·la) *n.f.* console; console table.

consolar (kon·so'lar) *v.t.* [*infl.:* acostar, 28] to console; comfort. —**consolación,** *n.f.* consolation; comfort.

consolidar (kon·so·li'ðar) *v.t.* to consolidate. —**consolidación,** *n.f.* consolidation.

consomé *also,* **consommé** (kon·so'me) *n.m.* consommé.

consonancia (kon·so'nan·θja; -sja) *n.f.* 1, consonance. 2, harmony; accord. 3, rhyme.

consonante (kon·so'nan·te) *adj.* consonant; rhyming. —*n.m.* rhyme. —*n.f.* consonant.

consonar (kon·so'nar) *v.i.* [*infl.:* acostar, 28] to harmonize; rhyme.

consorcio (kon·sor·θjo; -sjo) *n.m.* 1, consortium. 2, partnership.

consorte (kon'sor·te) *n.m.* & *f.* consort. —**consortes,** *n.m.* & *f., pl., law* colitigants.

conspicuo (kons'pi·kwo) *adj.* conspicuous.

conspirar (kons·pi'rar) *v.i.* to conspire; plot. —**conspiración,** *n.f.* conspiracy. —**conspirador,** *n.m.* conspirator.

constancia (kons'tan·θja; -sja) *n.f.* 1, constancy. 2, certainty; proof.

constante (kons'tan·te) *adj.* constant; firm. —*n.f.* constant.

constar (kons'tar) *v.i.* 1, to be

clear; to be evident. **2,** to consist (in or of). —**hacer constar,** to state.

constatar (kons·ta'tar) *v.t.* to prove; establish. —**constatación,** *n.f.* proof.

constelación (kons·te·la'θjon; -'sjon) *n.f.* constellation.

consternar (kons·ter'nar) *v.t.* to consternate; upset. —**consternación,** *n.f.* consternation.

constipación (kons·ti·pa'θjon; -'sjon) *n.f.* **1,** cold. **2,** constipation.

constipado (kons·ti'pa·ðo) *adj.* **1,** suffering from a cold. **2,** constipated. —*n.m.* cold.

constipar (kons·ti'par) *v.t.* **1,** to constrict; stop up. **2,** to constipate. —**constiparse,** *v.r.* to catch cold.

constitución (kons·ti·tu'θjon; -'sjon) *n.f.* constitution. —**constitucional,** *adj.* constitutional. —*n.m. & f.* constitutionalist.

constituir (kons·ti·tu'ir) *v.t.* [*infl.:* **huir, 26**] to constitute.

constituyente (kons·ti·tu'jen·te) *adj. & n.m.* constituent; component. *Also,* **constitutivo** (-'ti·βo).

constreñimiento (kons·tre·ɲi·'mjen·to) *n.m.* constraint; compulsion.

constreñir (kons·tre'ɲir) *v.t.* [*infl.:* **reñir, 59**] **1,** to constrain; compel. **2,** to constipate.

constricción (kons·trik'θjon; -'sjon) *n.f.* constriction.

constrictor (kons·trik'tor) *adj.* constricting; constrictive. —*n.m., anat.* constrictor.

construcción (kons·truk'θjon; -'sjon) *n.f.* **1,** construction; fabrication. **2,** edifice; structure. **3,** *gram.* construction.

constructivo (kons·truk'ti·βo) *adj.* constructive.

constructor (kons·truk'tor) *adj.* building; constructing. —*n.m.* builder; constructor.

construir (kons·tru'ir) *v.t.* [*infl.:* **41**] **1,** to form; build; construct. **2,** to construe.

consubstanciación (kon·suß·stan·θja'θjon; -sja'sjon) *n.f.* consubstantiation.

consuegro (kon'swe·ɣro) *n.m.* father-in-law of one's son or daughter. —**consuegra** *n.f.* mother-in-law of one's son or daughter.

consuele (kon'swe·le) *v., pres. subjve. of* **consolar.**

consuelo (kon'swe·lo) *v., 1st pers. sing. pres.ind. of* **consolar.**

consuelo *n.m.* consolation; relief; comfort.

consuetudinario (kon·swe·tu·ði'na·rjo) *adj.* habitual; customary.

cónsul ('kon·sul) *n.m.* consul.

consulado (kon·su'la·ðo) *n.m.* consulate; consulship.

consulta (kon'sul·ta) *n.f.* **1,** consultation; conference. **2,** (professional) opinion.

consultación (kon·sul·ta'θjon; -'sjon) *n.f.* consultation; conference.

consultante (kon·sul'tan·te) *adj. & n.m. & f. =* **consultor.**

consultar (kon·sul'tar) *v.t.* **1,** to consult. **2,** to ask advice on; discuss. —*v.i.* to consult; confer. —**consultar con la almohada,** *colloq.* to sleep on a problem.

consultivo (kon·sul'ti·βo) *adj.* consultative; advisory.

consultor (kon·sul'tor) *adj.* consulting. —*n.m.* **1,** consultant. **2,** counsel; counselor.

consultorio (kon·sul'to·rjo) *n.m.* doctor's office.

consumado (kon·su'ma·ðo) *adj.* finished; accomplished; consummate. —*n.m.* consommé.

consumar (kon·su'mar) *v.t.* to consummate; finish. —**consumación,** *n.f.* consummation.

consumición (kon·su·mi'θjon; -'sjon) *n.f.* **1,** consumption. **2,** amount of food or drink consumed. —**consumición mínima,** minimum charge.

consumido (kon·su'mi·ðo) *adj.* emaciated; spent.

consumidor (kon·su·mi'ðor) *adj.* consuming. —*n.m.* **1,** consumer. **2,** restaurant customer; diner; drinker.

consumir (kon·su'mir) *v.t.* **1,** to consume. **2,** to eat; corrode. —**consumirse,** *v.r.* to waste away; languish.

consumo (kon'su·mo) *n.m.* consumption *(of food, goods, etc.).* —**bienes de consumo,** consumer goods.

consunción (kon·sun'θjon; -'sjon) *n.f., med.* consumption.

contabilidad (kon·ta·βi·li'ðað) *n.f.* bookkeeping; accounting.

contable (kon'ta·βle) *n.m.* accountant; bookkeeper. —*adj.* countable.

contacto (kon'tak·to) *n.m.* contact; touch.

contado (kon'ta·ðo) *adj.* rare;

scarce. —**contados,** *adj., pl.* few; à
few.—**al contado,** cash. —**de contado,** at once.
contador (kon·ta'ðor) *n.m.* **1,** accountant. **2,** *law* auditor. **3,** controller; accountant. **4,** meter; counter. **5,**
cash register. **6,** *naut.* purser.
contaduría (kon·ta·ðu'ri·a) *n.f.* **1,**
accountancy. **2,** cashier's or accountant's office. **3,** *theat.* box office.
contagiar (kon·ta'xjar) *v.t.* **1,** to
infect. **2,** to communicate (disease,
ideas, etc.).
contagio (kon'ta·xjo) *n.m.* contagion. —**contagioso** (-'xjo·so) *adj.*
contagious.
contaminar (kon·ta·mi'nar) *v.t.* to
contaminate; pollute. —**contaminación,** *n.f.* contamination; pollution.
—**contaminante,** *n.m.* contaminant;
pollutant.
contante (kon'tan·te) *adj. (of
money)* ready. —**dinero contante y
sonante,** ready cash.
contar (kon'tar) *v.t. & i.* [*infl.:*
acostar, 28] to count. —*v.t.* to tell;
relate. —**a contar desde,** starting
from or with. —**contar con, 1,** to
count on. **2,** to reckon with.
—**contar hacer (una cosa)** to count
on doing; expect to do.
contemplar (kon·tem'plar) *v.t. &
i.* to contemplate. —**contemplación,** *n.f.* contemplation. —**contemplativo,** *adj.* contemplative.
contemporáneo (kon·tem·po·
'ra·ne·o) *adj.* contemporaneous;
contemporary.
contemporizar (kon·tem·po·
ri'θar; -'sar) *v.i.* [*infl.:* **rezar, 10**] to
temporize.
contención (kon·ten'θjon; -'sjon)
n.f. **1,** contention. **2,** *law* litigation;
suit.
contencioso (kon·ten'θjo·so;
-'sjo·so) *adj.* **1,** quarrelsome. **2,** *law*
litigious; contentious.
contender (kon·ten'der) *v.i.* [*infl.:*
perder, 29] to contend; dispute.
—**contendiente,** *n.m. & f.* contender; contestant.
contener (kon·te'ner) *v.t.* [*infl.:*
tener, 65] to contain. —**contenerse,**
v.r. to keep one's temper; refrain.
contenido (kon·te'ni·ðo) *n.m.* contents; content.
contenta (kon'ten·ta) *n.f.* **1,** present; gift. **2,** *comm.* endorsement.
contentadizo (kon·ten·ta'ði·θo;
-so) *adj.* [*also,* **bien contentadizo**]

easy to please. —**mal contentadizo,** hard to please.
contentamiento (kon·ten·ta·
'mjen·to) *n.m.* contentment.
contentar (kon·ten'tar) *v.t.* **1,** to
please; content. **2,** *comm.* to endorse. **3,** *Amer.* = **reconciliar.**
—**contentarse,** *v.r.* to be satisfied.
contento (kon'ten·to) *adj.* glad;
happy; pleased. —*n.m.* joy; mirth.
conteo (kon'te·o) *n.m.* countdown.
contera (kon'te·ra) *n.f.* **1,** tip *(of a
cane, umbrella, etc.).* **2,** refrain *(of
a song or poem).*
contérmino (kon'ter·mi·no) *adj.*
contiguous.
contertulio (kon·ter'tu·ljo) *n.m.* **1,**
party guest. **2,** fellow member. *Also,*
contertuliano (-'lja·no).
contesta (kon'tes·ta) *n.f., Amer.* **1,**
answer. **2,** chat.
contestar (kon·tes'tar) *v.t. & i.* to
answer; reply. —**contestación,** *n.f.*
answer; reply.
contexto (kon'teks·to) *n.m.* context.
contextura (kon·teks'tu·ra) *n.f.*
texture; composition.
contienda (kon'tjen·da) *n.f.* contest; dispute.
contigo (kon'ti·ɣo) with you; with
thee; with yourself; with thyself.
contigüidad (kon·ti·ɣwi'ðað) *n.f.*
contiguity; proximity.
contiguo (kon'ti·ɣwo) *adj.* contiguous.
continencia (kon·ti'nen·θja; -sja)
n.f. continence.
continente (kon·ti'nen·te) *adj.*
continent; moderate. —*n.m.* **1,** container. **2,** *geog.* continent. **3,** countenance; mien. —**continental,** *adj.*
continental.
contingencia (kon·tin'xen·θja;
-sja) *n.f.* contingency.
contingente (kon·tin'xen·te) *adj.
& n.m.* contingent.
continuación (kon·ti·nwa'θjon;
-'sjon) *n.f.* **1,** continuation. **2,** continuance. —**a continuación,** following; next.
continuamente (kon·ti·nwa·
'men·te) *adv.* continuously. *Also,*
continuadamente (-nwa·ða'mente).
continuar (kon·ti'nwar) *v.t.* [*infl.:*
23] to continue; pursue. —*v.i.* **1,**
[*also,* **continuarse,** *v.r.*] to continue;
last; go on; keep on; keep up. **2,** to
stay; remain. —**continuar con,** to

adjoin. —**continuarse con**, to join; connect with.

continuidad (kon·ti·nwi'ðað) *n.f.* continuity. —**solución de continuidad**, break in continuity.

continuo (kon'ti·nwo) *adj.* **1,** continuous; continual. **2,** persistent. —*n.m.* continuum. —*adv.* [*also*, **de continuo**] continuously.

contonearse (kon·to·ne'ar·se) *v.r.* **1,** to strut; swagger. **2,** to waddle. —**contoneo** (-'ne·o) *n.m.* strut; swagger; waddle.

contorcerse (kon·tor'θer·se; -'ser·se) *v.r.* [*infl.:* **torcer, 66**] to be contorted; twist.

contornar (kon·tor'nar) *v.t.* **1,** to go around. **2,** to trace; outline. *Also*, **contornear** (-ne'ar).

contorno (kon'tor·no) *n.m.* **1,** contour; outline. **2,** *usu.pl.* environs; vicinity. —**en contorno**, around.

contorsión (kon·tor'sjon) *n.f.* contortion.

contorsionista (kon·tor·sjo'nis·ta) *n.m. & f.* contortionist.

contra ('kon·tra) *prep.* **1,** against; opposite; in opposition to. **2,** facing. —*n.m.* opposite opinion; con. —*n.f.* difficulty; obstacle. —**el pro y el contra**, the pros and cons. —**llevar la contra a**, *colloq.* to disagree with.

contraalmirante (kon·tra·al·mi'ran·te; -tral·mi'ran·te) *n.m.* rear admiral.

contraatacar (kon·tra·a·ta'kar; -tra·ta'kar) *v.t. & i.* [*infl.:* **tocar, 7**] to counterattack.

contraataque (kon·tra·a'ta·ke; -tra'ta·ke) *n.m.* counterattack.

contrabalancear (kon·tra·βa·lan·θe'ar; -se'ar) *v.t.* to counterbalance.

contrabandear (kon·tra·βan·de'ar) *v.t.* to smuggle. —**contrabandista**, *adj.* smuggling. —*n.m. & f.* smuggler.

contrabando (kon·tra'βan·do) *n.m.* **1,** contraband. **2,** smuggling.

contrabajo (kon·tra'βa·xo) *n.m.* bass; double bass.

contracarril (kon·tra·ka'rril) *n.m.* guard rail.

contracción (kon·trak'θjon; -'sjon) *n.f.* contraction.

contractual (kon·trak'twal) *adj.* contractual.

contracultura *n.f.* counterculture.

contradanza (kon·tra'ðan·θa; -sa) *n.f.* country dance; square dance.

contradecir (kon·tra·ðe'θir; -'sir) *v.t.* [*infl.:* **decir, 44**] to contradict.

contradicción (kon·tra·ðik'θjon; -'sjon) *n.f.* contradiction.

contradictorio (kon·tra·ðik'to·rjo) *adj.* contradictory.

contraer (kon·tra'er) *v.t. & i.* [*infl.:* **traer, 67**] **1,** to contract. **2,** to shrink.

contraespía (kon·tra·es'pi·a) *n.m. or f.* counterspy. —**contraespionaje** (-pjo'na·xe) *n.m.* counterespionage.

contrafuerte (kon·tra'fwer·te) *n.m.* **1,** stiffener (*for a shoe*). **2,** girth; strap (*for a saddle*). **3,** *archit.* buttress.

contragolpe (kon·tra'ɣol·pe) *n.m.* **1,** backlash. **2,** *mech.* back or reverse stroke.

contrahacer (kon·tra·a'θer; -tra'ser) *v.t.* [*infl.:* **hacer, 48**] **1,** to counterfeit; falsify. **2,** to mimic; ape.

contrahecho (kon·tra'e·tʃo) *v.*, *p.p. of* **contrahacer**. —*adj.* **1,** counterfeit. **2,** humpbacked. **3,** malformed. —*n.m.* humpback; hunchback.

contrahuella (kon·tra'we·ʎa; -ja) *n.f.* riser (*of a stair*).

contraindicar *v.t.* [*infl.:* **tocar, 7**] to contraindicate. —**contraindicación** *n.f.* contraindication.

contralor (kon·tra'lor) *n.m.*, *Amer.* comptroller; auditor.

contralto (kon'tral·to) *n.m. & f.* contralto.

contramaestre (kon·tra·ma'es·tre) *n.m.* **1,** foreman. **2,** *naut.* boatswain; petty officer.

contramandar (kon·tra·man'dar) *v.t.* to countermand. —**contramandato** (-'da·to) *n.m.* countermand.

contramano (kon·tra'ma·no) *adv.*, *in* **a contramano**, the wrong way; in the wrong direction.

contramarca (kon·tra'mar·ka) *n.f.* countermark. —**contramarcar**, *v.t.* [*infl.:* **tocar, 7**] to countermark.

contranatural (kon·tra·na·tu'ral) *adj.* unnatural; abnormal.

contraofensiva (kon·tra·o·fen'si·βa) *n.f.* counteroffensive.

contraorden (kon·tra·or·ðen) *n.f.* countermand.

contraparte (kon·tra'par·te) *n.f.* counterpart; complement.

contrapartida (kon·tra·par'ti·ða) *n.f., comm.* corrective entry.

contrapelo (kon·tra'pe·lo) *n.m., in* **a contrapelo,** against the grain.

contrapesar (kon·tra·pe'sar) *v.t.* to counterbalance. —**contrapeso** (-'pe·so) *n.m.* counterpoise; counterbalance.

contraponer (kon·tra·po'ner) *v.t.* [*infl.:* poner, 54] **1,** to oppose. **2,** to compare; contrast. —**contraposición,** *n.f.* **1,** opposition. **2,** comparison; contrast.

contraproducente (kon·tra·pro·ðu'θen·te; -'sen·te) *adj.* self-defeating; counterproductive.

contrapunto (kon·tra'pun·to) *n.m.* counterpoint.

contrariar (kon·tra'rjar) *v.t.* [*infl.:* enviar, 22] **1,** to contradict; oppose. **2,** to vex; annoy.

contrariedad (kon·tra·rje'ðað) *n.f.* **1,** contrariness; contradiction; opposition. **2,** vexation; annoyance.

contrario (kon'tra·rjo) *adj.* contrary; opposite. —*n.m.* **1,** opponent; competitor. **2,** obstacle. —**al contrario; por el contrario; por lo contrario,** on the contrary. —**llevar la contraria a,** *colloq.* to be against; disagree with.

contrarreferencia (kon·tra·rre·fe'ren·θja; -sja) *n.f.* cross reference.

contrarrestar (kon·tra·rres'tar) *v.t.* **1,** to resist. **2,** to offset; counteract. **3,** to hit back; return (a ball).

contrarrevolución (kon·tra·rre·βo·lu'θjon; -'sjon) *n.f.* counterrevolution. —**contrarrevolucionario,** *adj. & n.m.* counterrevolutionary.

contrasentido (kon·tra·sen'ti·ðo) *n.m.* **1,** contradiction. **2,** misinterpretation. **3,** absurdity.

contraseña (kon·tra'se·ɲa) *n.f.* **1,** countersign. **2,** baggage check. **3,** check; ticket stub. **4,** *mil.* countersign. —**contraseña de salida,** door pass; theater check.

contrastar (kon·tras'tar) *v.t.* **1,** to contrast; compare. **2,** to check (weights and measures). **3,** to assay. —*v.i.* to contrast.

contraste (kon'tras·te) *n.m.* **1,** contrast. **2,** assay. —*adj.* contrasting.

contrata (kon'tra·ta) *n.f.* contract; agreement.

contratar (kon·tra'tar) *v.t.* **1,** to contract for. **2,** to engage; hire.

contratiempo (kon·tra'tjem·po) *n.m.* mishap; accident; contretemps.

contratista (kon·tra'tis·ta) *n.m. & f.* contractor.

contrato (kon'tra·to) *n.m.* contract; covenant; agreement.

contravención (kon·tra·βen'θjon; -'sjon) *n.f.* contravention; infraction; violation.

contraveneno (kon·tra·βe'ne·no) *n.m.* antidote.

contravenir (kon·tra·βe'nir) *v.t.* [*infl.:* venir, 69] to contravene; infringe; violate.

contraventana (kon·tra·βen'ta·na) *n.f.* window shutter.

contravidriera (kon·tra·βi'ðrje·ra) *n.f.* storm window.

contribución (kon·tri·βu'θjon; -'sjon) *n.f.* **1,** contribution. **2,** tax.

contribuidor (kon·tri·βu·i'ðor) *adj.* **1,** contributing; contributory. **2,** taxpaying. —*n.m.* **1,** contributor. **2,** taxpayer.

contribuir (kon·tri·βu'ir) *v.t.* [*infl.:* huir, 26] **1,** to contribute. **2,** to pay (taxes).

contribuyente (kon·tri·βu'jen·te) *adj. & n.m. & f.* = **contribuidor.**

contrición (kon·tri'θjon; -'sjon) *n.f.* contrition.

contrincante (kon·trin'kan·te) *n.m. & f.* **1,** contestant; competitor. **2,** opponent; rival.

contrito (kon'tri·to) *adj.* contrite.

control (kon'trol) *n.m.* **1,** control. **2,** checkpoint. **3,** audit. —**control de la natalidad,** birth control.

controlador (kon·tro·la'ðor) *n.m., Amer.* = **contralor.**

controlar (kon·tro'lar) *v.t.* **1,** to control; check. **2,** to monitor. **3,** *Amer.* to audit.

controversia (kon·tro'βer·sja) *n.f.* controversy. —**controversial,** *adj.* controversial.

controvertir (kon·tro·βer'tir) *v.t.* [*infl.:* sentir, 31] to controvert. —**controvertible,** *adj.* controvertible.

contumacia (kon·tu'ma·θja; -sja) *n.f.* **1,** contumacy. **2,** *law* contempt.

contumaz (kon·tu'maθ; -'mas) *adj.* **1,** contumacious. **2,** *law* guilty of contempt.

contumelia (kon·tu'me·lja) *n.f.* contumely. —**contumelioso,** *adj.* contumelious.

contusión (kon·tu'sjon) *n.f.* contusion.

convalecer (kon·βa·le'θer; -'ser)

v.i. [*infl.:* **conocer,** 13] to convalesce. —**convalecencia,** *n.f.* convalescence. —**convaleciente,** *adj.* & *n.m.* & *f.* convalescent.

convalidar (kon·βa·li'ðar) *v.t.* to confirm.

convección (kon·βek'θjon; -'sjon) *n.f.* convection.

convecino (kon·βe'θi·no; -'si·no) *adj.* near; neighboring. —*n.m.* neighbor.

convencer (kon·βen'θer; -'ser) *v.t.* [*infl.:* **vencer,** 11] to convince. —**convencimiento** (-θi'mjen·to; -si'mjen·to) *n.m.* conviction; convincing.

convención (kon·βen'θjon; -'sjon) *n.f.* **1,** convention; assembly. **2,** agreement. —**convencional,** *adj.* conventional. —**convencionalismo,** *n.m.* conventionality.

conveniencia (kon·βe'njen·θja; -sja) *n.f.* **1,** conformity; congruity; propriety. **2,** advantage; comfort; convenience. **3,** agreement.

conveniente (kon·βe'njen·te) *adj.* **1,** convenient; advantageous. **2,** fit; suitable; proper.

convenio (kon'βe·njo) *n.m.* covenant; compact.

convenir (kon·βe'nir) *v.i.,* *also,* *refl.,* **convenirse** [*infl.:* **venir,** 69] **1,** to agree; come to an agreement. **2,** to gather; assemble; convene. **3,** to fit; to be suitable.

convento (kon·βen·to) *n.m.* convent.

converger (kon·βer'xer) *v.i.* [*infl.:* **coger,** 15] to converge. —**convergencia,** *n.f.* convergence. —**convergente,** *adj.* convergent.

conversar (kon·βer'sar) *v.i.* to converse. —**conversación,** *n.f.* conversation.

conversión (kon·βer'sjon) *n.f.* conversion.

converso (kon'βer·so) *n.m.* convert.

convertir (kon·βer'tir) *v.t.* [*infl.:* **sentir,** 31] to convert. —**convertible,** *adj.* convertible.

convexo (kon'βek·so) *adj.* convex. —**convexidad,** *n.f.* convexity.

convicción (kon·βik'θjon; -'sjon) *n.f.* conviction.

convicto (kon'βik·to) *adj.* convicted. —*n.m.* convict.

convidado (kon·βi'ða·ðo) *n.m.* guest.

convidar (kon·βi'ðar) *v.t.* **1,** to invite. **2,** to treat. —**convidarse,** *v.r.* to offer one's services.

convincente (kon·βin'θen·te; -'sen·te) *adj.* convincing.

convite (kon'βi·te) *n.m.* **1,** invitation. **2,** dinner party; banquet. —**convite a escote,** Dutch treat.

convival (kon·βi'βal) *adj.* convivial.

convivir (kon·βi'βir) *v.i.* to live together; cohabit.

convocar (kon·βo'kar) *v.t.* [*infl.:* **tocar,** 7] to convoke; call (a meeting). —**convocación,** *n.f.* convocation.

convocatoria (kon·βo·ka'to·rja) *n.f.* letter of convocation; summons.

convoy (kon'βoi) *n.m.* **1,** convoy. **2,** *Amer.* train. **3,** *colloq.* retinue.

convoyar (kon·βo'jar) *v.t.* to convoy; escort.

convulsión (kon·βul'sjon) *n.f.* convulsion. —**convulsivo** (-'si·βo) *adj.* convulsive. —**tos convulsiva,** whooping cough.

convulsionar (kon·βul·sjo'nar) *v.t.* to convulse.

conyugal (kon·ju'ɣal) *adj.* conjugal.

cónyuge ('kon·ju·xe) *n.m.* & *f.* spouse. —**cónyuges,** *n.m.pl.* married couple.

coñac (ko'ɲak) *n.m.* cognac.

cooperar (ko·o·pe'rar) *v.i.* to cooperate. —**cooperación,** *n.f.* cooperation. —**cooperativa,** *n.f.* cooperative. —**cooperativo,** *adj.* cooperative.

coordenado (ko·or·ðe'na·ðo) *adj.,* *math.* coordinate. —**coordenada,** *n.f., math.* coordinate.

coordinar (ko·or·ði'nar) *v.t.* to coordinate. —**coordinación,** *n.f.* coordination. —**coordinado,** *adj.* coordinated; coordinate. —**coordinador,** *n.m.* [*fem.* -**dora**] coordinator.

copa ('ko·pa) *n.f.* **1,** goblet; cup. **2,** treetop. **3,** crown (*of a hat*). **4,** *cards* heart (*in the French deck*); goblet (*in the Spanish deck*).

copar (ko'par) *v.t.* **1,** *mil.* to capture by surprise. **2,** to sweep (a game, election, etc.). **3,** to cover (a bet) completely.

coparticipación (ko·par·ti·θi·pa·'θjon; -si·pa'sjon) *n.f.* joint partnership. —**copartícipe** (-'ti·θi·pe; -si·pe) *n.m.* & *f.* joint partner.

copec *also,* **copeck** (ko'pek) *n.m.* [*pl.* **copecs,** *also,* **copecks** (ko'peks)] kopeck.

copete (ko'pe·te) *n.m.* **1**, tuft. **2**, crest. —**de alto copete**, of noble lineage; high-class.

copiar (ko'pjar) *v.t.* to copy. —**copia** ('ko·pja) *n.f.* copy. —**copiador,** *n.m.* [*fem.* **-dora**] copyist. —**copiadora,** *n.f.* copier; copying machine.

copiloto (ko·pi'lo·to) *n.m.* copilot.

copioso (ko'pjo·so) *adj.* copious; abundant. —**copiosidad,** *n.f.* copiousness; abundance.

copista (ko'pis·ta) *n.m. & f.* copyist.

copla ('ko·pla) *n.f.* **1**, couplet. **2**, popular song; ballad. —**coplas de ciego,** doggerel.

copo ('ko·po) *n.m.* **1**, tuft. **2**, ball (*of cotton, wool, etc.*). **3**, snowflake. **4**, coup; sweep.

copra ('ko·pra) *n.f.* copra.

copto ('kop·to) *adj.* Coptic. —*n.m.* **1**, Copt. **2**, Coptic (*language*). —**cóptico** ('kop·ti·ko) *adj.* Coptic.

cópula ('ko·pu·la) *n.f.* **1**, bond; tie. **2**, copula. **3**, copulation. **4**, = **cúpula.**

copular (ko·pu'lar) *v.i.* [*also, refl.,* **copularse**] to copulate. —**copulación,** *n.f.* copulation. —**copulativo,** *adj.* copulative.

coque ('ko·ke) *n.m.* coke.

coqueta (ko'ke·ta) *n.f.* **1**, coquette; flirt. **2**, dressing table. —*adj.* coquettish.

coquetear (ko·ke·te'ar) *v.i.* to flirt; act coquettishly. —**coquetería,** *n.f., also* **coqueteo** (-'te·o) *n.m.* flirtation; coquetry.

coquetón (ko·ke'ton) *adj.* [*fem.* **-ona**] flirtatious; coquettish.

coquina (ko'ki·na) *n.f., zoöl.* cockle; cockleshell.

coraje (ko'ra·xe) *n.m.* **1**, courage; spirit. **2**, anger.

coral (ko'ral) *adj., mus.* choral. —*n.m.* **1**, coral. **2**, *mus.* chorale. **3**, glee club; chorus. —*n.f., zoöl.* coral snake. —**corales,** *n.m.pl.* coral beads. —**ser más fino que el coral,** to be very shrewd.

coralino (ko·ra'li·no) *adj.* coral; of or resembling coral.

Corán (ko'ran) *n.m.* Koran.

coraza (ko'ra·θa; ·sa) *n.f.* **1**, armor; armor plate. **2**, *sports* guard; protector. **3**, shell (*of a crustacean*).

corazón (ko·ra'θon; -'son) *n.m.* **1**, heart. **2**, *fig.* love; affection. **3**, *fig.* courage. —**de corazón,** heartily.

—**hacer de tripas corazón,** to pluck up; take heart.

corazonada (ko·ra·θo'na·ða; -so'na·ða) *n.f.* hunch; presentiment.

corbata (kor'βa·ta) *n.f.* tie; cravat. —**corbata de lazo,** bow tie.

corbeta (kor'βe·ta) *n.f.* corvette.

corcel (kor'θel; -'sel) *n.m.* battle mount; charger.

corcova (kor'ko·βa) *n.f.* hump; hunch. —**corcovado,** *adj.* hunchbacked. —*n.m.* hunchback.

corcovo (kor'ko·βo) *n.m.* **1**, buck; leap, as of a horse. **2**, *colloq.* bend; curve. —**corcovear,** *v.i.* to buck; leap.

corchea (kor'tʃe·a) *n.f., mus.* eighth note; quaver.

corchete (kor'tʃe·te) *n.m.* **1**, hook and eye; hook (*of a hook and eye*). **2**, *typog.* bracket. —**corcheta,** *n.f.* eye (*of a hook and eye*).

corcho ('kor·tʃo) *n.m.* **1**, cork. **2**, stopper; cork. —**corchoso,** *adj.* corklike; corky.

cordaje (kor'ða·xe) *n.m.* **1**, cordage. **2**, *naut.* rigging.

cordal (kor'ðal) *n.m.* wisdom tooth.

cordel (kor'ðel) *n.m.* cord; string.

cordelería (kor·ðe·le'ri·a) *n.f.* = **cordaje.**

cordero (kor'ðe·ro) *n.m.* lamb.

cordial (kor'ðjal) *adj. & n.m.* cordial. —**cordialidad,** *n.f.* cordiality.

cordillera (kor·ði'ʎe·ra; -'je·ra) *n.f.* mountain range; cordillera.

cordobán (kor·ðo'βan) *n.m.* cordovan (*leather*).

cordón (kor'ðon) *n.m.* **1**, cord; braid. **2**, *mil.* line; cordon. **3**, shoelace.

cordoncillo (kor·ðon'θi·ʎo; -'si·jo) *n.m.* **1**, knurl; milling (*on coins*). **2**, piping; braid.

cordura (kor'ðu·ra) *n.f.* prudence.

corear (ko·re'ar) *v.t.* to chorus; sing or recite in chorus.

corégono (ko're·ɣo·no) *n.m.* whitefish.

coreografía (ko·re·o·ɣra'fi·a) *n.f.* choreography. —**coreógrafo** (-'o·ɣra·fo) *n.m.* choreographer. —**coreográfico** (-'ɣra·fi·ko) *adj.* choreographic.

corista (ko'ris·ta) *n.m. & f.* chorus singer; chorister. —*n.f.* chorus girl.

cormorán (kor·mo'ran) *n.m.* cormorant.

cornada (kor'na·ða) *n.f.* goring; thrust with a horn.

córnea ('kor·ne·a) *n.f.* cornea.

cornear (kor·ne'ar) *v.t.* = **acornear**.
corneja (kor'ne·xa) *n.f.* crow.
cornejo (kor'ne·xo) *n.m.* dogwood.
corneta (kor'ne·ta) *n.f.* **1**, cornet. **2**, bugle. —*n.m. or f.* **1**, cornetist. **2**, bugler. —**corneta acústica,** ear trumpet. —**corneta de monte,** hunting horn.
cornezuelo (kor·ne'θwe·lo; -'swe-lo) *n.m., bot.; pharm.* ergot.
cornisa (kor'ni·sa) *n.f.* cornice.
cornuda (kor'nu·ða) *n.f., ichthy.* hammerhead. *Also,* **cornudilla** (-'ði·ʎa; -ja).
cornudo (kor'nu·ðo) *adj.* **1**, horned; antlered. **2**, cuckold; cuckolded. —*n.m.* cuckold.
coro ('ko·ro) *n.m.* choir; chorus.
corola (ko'ro·la) *n.f., bot.* corolla.
corolario (ko·ro'la·rjo) *n.m.* corollary.
corona (ko'ro·na) *n.f.* **1**, crown. **2**, wreath. **3**, name of various coins. **4**, *astron.* corona. **5**, halo.
coronal (ko·ro'nal) *adj.* coronal.
coronar (ko·ro'nar) *v.t.* to crown. —**coronación,** *n.f.* coronation.
coronel (ko·ro'nel) *n.m.* colonel. —**coronelía,** *n.f.* colonelcy.
coronilla (ko·ro'ni·ʎa; -ja) *n.f.* **1**, small crown. **2**, crown of the head. —**estar hasta la coronilla (de),** *colloq.* to be fed up (with).
corpachón (kor·pa'tʃon) *n.m., colloq.* large body; carcass. *Also,* **corpanchón** (-pan'tʃon).
corpiño (kor'pi·ɲo) *n.m.* bodice.
corporación (kor·po·ra'θjon; -'sjon) *n.f.* corporation; association; society.
corporal (kor·po'ral) *adj.* corporal.
corpóreo (kor'po·re·o) *adj.* corporeal.
corpulento (kor·pu'len·to) *adj.* corpulent. —**corpulencia,** *n.f.* corpulence.
corpúsculo (kor'pus·ku·lo) *n.m.* corpuscle.
corral (ko'rral) *n.m.* **1**, corral. **2**, barnyard.
corralón (ko·rra'lon) *n.m., Amer.* vacant lot; sandlot.
correa (ko'rre·a) *n.f.* strap; belt. —**tener correa,** to be good-natured.
correcaminos (ko·rre·ka'mi·nos) *n.m. sing & pl.* roadrunner.
corrección (ko·rrek'θjon; -'sjon) *n.f.* **1**, correction. **2**, correctness. **3**, proofreading. —**correccional,** *adj.* corrective; correctional. —*n.m.* house of correction.

correctivo (ko·rrek'ti·βo) *adj. & n.m.* corrective.
correcto (ko'rrek·to) *adj.* correct; exact.
corrector (ko·rrek'tor) *adj.* corrective. —*n.m.* **1**, corrector. **2**, proofreader.
corredera (ko·rre'ðe·ra) *n.f.* **1**, *mech.* track; rail; tongue. **2**, race course. —**de corredera,** sliding.
corredizo (ko·rre'ði·θo; -so) *adj.* sliding; slipping. —**nudo corredizo,** slip knot; hangman's knot.
corredor (ko·rre'ðor) *n.m.* **1**, runner; racer. **2**, corridor. **3**, *comm.* broker. **4**, *mil.* scout. —*adj.* running; speeding.
corregidor (ko·rre·xi'ðor) *n.m.* former Spanish magistrate; corregidor.
corregir (ko·rre'xir) *v.t.* [*infl.: regir, 57*] **1**, to correct. **2**, to reprove. **3**, to proofread.
correlación (ko·rre·la'θjon; -'sjon) *n.f.* correlation. —**correlacionar** (-'nar) *v.t.* to correlate. —**correlativo** (-'ti·βo) *adj. & n.m.* correlative.
correligionario (ko'·rre·li·xjo·'na·rjo) *adj.* of the same religious or political beliefs. —*n.m.* coreligionist; fellow believer.
correo (ko'rre·o) *n.m.* **1**, mail; mail service. **2**, postman. **3**, post office. —**a vuelta de correo,** by return mail. —**echar al correo,** to mail.
correón (ko·rre'on) *n.m.* large strap.
correoso (ko·rre'o·so) *adj.* gristly; sinewy.
correr (ko'rrer) *v.t.* **1**, to run. **2**, to race (a car, horse, etc.). **3**, to draw (a curtain). **4**, to embarrass. —*v.i.* **1**, to run. **2**, to flow. —**a todo correr,** at full speed. —**correr de cuenta de uno,** to be on one's account. —**correr el albur,** to take the chance. —**correr el cerrojo,** to lock; turn the key. —**correrla,** *colloq.* to carouse.
correría (ko·rre'ri·a) *n.f.* **1**, raid; foray. **2**, tour; trip; circuit; *pl.* travels.
correspondencia (ko·rres·pon'den·θja; -sja) *n.f.* **1**, correspondence. **2**, mail. **3**, communication; contact. —**correspondencia urgente,** special delivery.
corresponder (ko·rres·pon'der) *v.t.* **1**, to return; reciprocate. **2**, to belong to; concern. —*v.i.* to corre-

spond; communicate. —**corresponderse,** *v.r.* **1,** to correspond. **2,** to agree.

correspondiente (ko·rres·pon·'djen·te) *adj.* correspondent; corresponding. —*n.m. & f.* correspondent.

corresponsal (ko·rres·pon'sal) *n.m. & f.* correspondent.

corretaje (ko·rre'ta·xe) *n.m.* commission; brokerage.

corretear (ko·rre·te'ar) *v.i.* **1,** to romp; run about. **2,** to roam; roam the streets.

correvedile (ko·rre·βe'ði·le) *n.m. & f.* **1,** gossipmonger. **2,** procurer; go-between. *Also,* **correveidile** (-βei'ði·le).

corrida (ko'rri·ða) *n.f.* **1,** race. **2,** course; travel. **3,** bullfight. —**de corrida,** fast; without stopping.

corrido (ko'rri·ðo) *adj.* **1,** over the weight or measure. **2,** experienced; worldly-wise. **3,** ashamed; abashed. **4,** elapsed; past *(of time).* **5,** flowing; fluent. **6,** uninterrupted; unbroken. —**de corrido = de corrida.**

corriente (ko'rrjen·te) *adj.* **1,** current; present. **2,** running; flowing. **3,** standard; common. —*n.f.* **1,** current; flow; stream. **2,** *elect.* current. —*adv.* all right. —**estar al corriente,** to be up-to-date; to be well-informed. —**seguir la corriente,** to follow the crowd.

corrigió (ko·rri'xjo) *v.,* 3rd *pers. sing. pret.* of **corregir.**

corrija (ko'rri·xa) *v., pres.subjve.* of **corregir.**

corrijo (ko'rri·xo) *v., pres.ind.* of **corregir.**

corrillo (ko'rri·ʎo; -jo) *n.m.* a group chatting intimately, apart from the main body; huddle.

corro ('ko·rro) *n.m.* group of people; circle.

corroborar (ko·rro·βo'rar) *v.t.* to corroborate. —**corroboración,** *n.f.* corroboration. —**corroborativo,** *adj.* corroborative.

corroer (ko·rro'er) *v.t.* [*infl.:* roer, 61] to corrode. —**corrosión** (-'sjon) *n.f.* corrosion. —**corrosivo** (-'si·βo) *adj.* corrosive.

corromper (ko·rrom'per) *v.t.* **1,** to corrupt; bribe. **2,** to rot; spoil. —**corromperse,** *v.r.* **1,** to rot; spoil. **2,** to become corrupted.

corrupción (ko·rrup'θjon; -'sjon) *n.f.* **1,** corruption; corruptness. **2,** stench; stink.

corrupto (ko'rrup·to) *v.,* —*adj.* corrupt; corrupted. —**corruptible** (-rrup'ti·βle) *adj.* corruptible.

corsario (kor'sa·rjo) *n.m.* **1,** privateer; corsair. **2,** pirate ship. **3,** pirate. —*adj.* privateering.

corsé (kor'se) *n.m.* corset.

corsear (kor·se'ar) *v.i.* to privateer.

corso ('kor·so) *n.m.* **1,** *hist.* privateering; cruise of a privateer. **2,** *S.A.* festive parade. —**ir** *or* **salir a corso,** to privateer; go privateering.

cortabolsas (kor·ta'βol·sas) *n.m. & f. sing. & pl., colloq.* pickpocket.

cortacircuito (kor·ta·θir'kwi·to; -sir'kwi·to) *n.m., Amer.* shortcircuit. —**cortacircuitos,** *n.m. sing. & pl.* circuit breaker; fuse.

cortacorriente (kor·ta·ko'rrjen·te) *n.m.* switch.

cortada (kor'ta·ða) *n.f., Amer.* cut; slash.

cortador (kor·ta'ðor) *adj.* cutting. —*n.m.* **1,** cutter. **2,** butcher. **3,** slicing machine.

cortadura (kor·ta'ðu·ra) *n.f.* cut; slash.

cortafuego (kor·ta'fwe·ɣo) *n.m.* firebreak.

cortalápiz (kor·ta'la·piθ; -pis) *n.m.* pencil sharpener. *Also,* **cortalápices** (-'la·pi·θes; -ses) *n.m. sing. & pl.*

cortante (kor'tan·te) *adj.* cutting; sharp. —*n.m.* butcher; meat cutter.

cortapapel (kor·ta·pa'pel) *n.m.* paper cutter; paper knife; letter opener. *Also,* **cortapapeles,** *n.m. sing. & pl.*

cortaplumas (kor·ta'plu·mas) *n.m.sing. & pl.* penknife.

cortar (kor'tar) *v.t.* **1,** to cut; cut out; cut off; disjoin. **2,** to intersect. —**cortarse,** *v.r.* **1,** to become confused; to be embarrassed. **2,** to be speechless. **3,** to sour; curdle. **4,** to chap *(of the skin).* **5,** to run *(of paint, varnish, etc.).*

corte ('kor·te) *n.m.* **1,** cut; cutting. **2,** cutting edge. **3,** material *(for a garment).* **4,** fit; cut *(of a garment).* —*n.f.* **1,** court; yard. **2,** *Amer.* court of justice. —**hacer la corte a,** to court; woo. —**darse corte,** *Amer.* to put on airs.

cortedad (kor·te'ðað) *n.f.* **1,** shortness. **2,** bashfulness; shyness.

cortejar (kor·te'xar) *v.t.* to court; woo.

cortejo (kor·te·xo) *n.m.* **1,** courtship. **2,** cortege. **3,** entourage.

cortés (kor·tes) *adj.* courteous; gracious.

Cortes ('kor·tes) *n.f.pl.* the Spanish Parliament.

cortesano (kor·te'sa·no) *adj.* courtly; courteous. —*n.m.* courtier. —**cortesana,** *n.f.* courtesan.

cortesía (kor·te'si·a) *n.f.* **1,** courtesy. **2,** gift. **3,** expression of respect. **4,** bow; curtsy.

corteza (kor·te·θa; -sa) *n.f.* **1,** bark; crust; skin; rind; peel. **2,** rusticity. **3,** *anat.; bot.* cortex.

cortical (kor·ti'kal) *adj.* cortical.

cortijo (kor'ti·xo) *n.m.* farmhouse; farm.

cortina (kor'ti·na) *n.f.* curtain; drape; screen.

cortisona (kor·ti'so·na) *n.f.* cortisone.

corto ('kor·to) *adj.* **1,** short. **2,** bashful. —**a la corta o a la larga,** sooner or later. —**corto de vista,** shortsighted.

cortocircuito (kor·to·θir'kwi·to; -sir-) *n.m.* short circuit.

corva ('kor·βa) *n.f.* back of the knee; ham.

corvadura (kor·βa'ðu·ra) *n.f.* bend; curvature.

corveta (kor'βe·ta) *n.* prance; rearing, as of a horse. —**corvetear,** *v.i.* to prance; rear.

corvo ('kor·βo) *adj.* hooked; arched; curved.

corzo ('kor·θo; -so) *n.m.* roe deer.

cosa ('ko·sa) *n.f.* thing; matter. —**a cosa hecha,** on purpose. —**como si tal cosa,** *colloq.* as if nothing had happened. —**cosa de, 1,** a matter of. **2,** about; approximately. —**cosa de otro jueves,** *colloq.* something unusual. —**cosas de,** doings of; pranks of. —**poquita cosa,** *colloq.* puny; feeble person.

cosaco (ko'sa·ko) *adj. & n.m.* Cossack.

cosecante (ko·se'kan·te) *n.f.* cosecant.

cosecha (ko·se'tʃa) *n.f.* crop; \ harvest. —**de su propia cosecha,** out of one's own imagination.

cosechar (ko·se'tʃar) *v.t. & i.* to reap; harvest. —**cosechadora,** *n.f., agric.* combine.

coseno (ko·se·no) *n.m.* cosine.

coser (ko'ser) *v.t.* to sew. —**coser a puñaladas,** to stab to death. —**co-**

ser y cantar, *colloq.* in a jiffy. —**ser coser y cantar,** to be a cinch.

cosmético (kos·me·ti·ko) *n.m. & adj.* cosmetic.

cósmico ('kos·mi·ko) *adj.* cosmic.

cosmogonía (kos·mo·ɣo'ni·a) *n.f.* cosmogony.

cosmografía (kos·mo·ɣra'fi·a) *n.f.* cosmography.

cosmología (kos·mo·lo'xi·a) *n.f.* cosmology.

cosmonauta (kos·mo'nau·ta) *n.m. or f.* cosmonaut; astronaut.

cosmopolita (kos·mo·po'li·ta) *adj.* cosmopolitan. —*n.m. & f.* cosmopolitan; cosmopolite.

cosmos ('kos·mos) *n.m.* cosmos.

cosquillas (kos·ki·ʎas; -jas) *n.f. pl.* **1,** tickles; tickling. **2,** ticklishness. —**hacer cosquillas a,** to tickle. —**tener cosquillas,** to be ticklish.

cosquillear (kos·ki·ʎe'ar; -je'ar) *v.t. (of things)* to tickle. *Also,* **cosquillar** (-'ʎar; -'jar).

cosquilleo (kos·ki'ʎe·o; -'je·o) *n.m.* tickle; tickling.

cosquilloso (kos·ki'ʎo·so; -'jo·so) *adj.* ticklish.

costa ('kos·ta) *n.f.* **1,** coast; shore. **2,** cost; expense. —**a costa de,** at the expense of. —**a toda costa,** at all costs; at any price.

costado (kos'ta·ðo) *n.m.* **1,** side. **2,** *mil.* flank. —**costados,** *n.m.pl.* lineage; ancestors. —**brazada de costado,** sidestroke.

costal (kos'tal) *n.m.* sack; bag.

costanera (kos·ta'ne·ra) *n.f.* slope. —**costaneras,** *n.f.pl.* rafters.

costanero (kos·ta'ne·ro) *adj.* **1,** coastal. **2,** sloping.

costar (kos'tar) *v.t. & i.* [*infl.:* acostar, 28] to cost. —**cueste lo que cueste,** cost what it may.

coste ('kos·te) *also,* **costo** (-to) *n.m.* cost; expense.

costear (kos·te'ar) *v.t.* to defray. —*v.i.* to navigate along the coast.

costero (kos·te'ro) *adj.* coastal.

costilla (kos'ti·ʎa; -ja) *n.f.* **1,** rib. **2,** *colloq.* wife; better half. **3,** cutlet, chop. **4,** rung *(of a chair).* **5,** stave *(of a barrel).* —**a las costillas de,** at the expense of.

costo ('kos·to) *n.m.* cost. —**costo de la vida,** cost of living.

costoso (kos'to·so) *adj.* expensive; dear; costly.

costra ('kos·tra) *n.f.* crust; scale;

scab. —**costroso,** *adj.* crusty; scaly; scabby.

costumbre (kos'tum·bre) *n.f.* custom; habit. —**de costumbre,** usual; usually. —**tener por costumbre,** to be used to; to be in the habit of.

costura (kos'tu·ra) *n.f.* **1,** sewing. **2,** seam. —**alta costura,** high fashion. —**sentar las costuras (a uno),** to call (someone) up on the carpet.

costurera (kos·tu're·ra) *n.f.* seamstress; dressmaker.

costurero (kos·tu're·ro) *n.m.* **1,** sewing table. **2,** sewing box. **3,** sewing room.

costurón (kos·tu'ron) *n.m.* **1,** large stitch or stitching. **2,** patch. **3,** prominent scar.

cota ('ko·ta) *n.f.* **1,** [*also,* **cota de malla**] coat of mail. **2,** *topog.* elevation; number on a map indicating elevation. **3,** coat of arms.

cotangente (ko·tan'xen·te) *n.f.* cotangent.

cotarro (ko'ta·rro) *n.m.* lodging for beggars. —**armar un cotarro,** *colloq.* to stir up a row.

cotejar (ko·te'xar) *v.t.* to compare; collate. —**cotejo** (-'te·xo) *n.m.* comparison; collation.

cotidiano (ko·ti'ðja·no) *adj.* **1,** daily. **2,** everyday.

cotiledón (ko·ti·le'ðon) *n.m.* cotyledon.

cotillón (ko·ti'ʎon; -'jon) *n.m.* cotillion.

cotización (ko·ti·θa'θjon; -sa·'sjon) *n.f.* **1,** price quotation. **2,** current price. **3,** dues; quota; assessment.

cotizar (ko·ti'θar; -'sar) *v.t.* [*infl.:* **rezar, 10**] **1,** to quote (prices). **2,** to prorate. —*v.i.* to pay or collect dues.

coto ('ko·to) *n.m.* **1,** enclosure of a pasture. **2,** preserve. **3,** limit; boundary.

cotorra (ko'to·rra) *n.f.* **1,** parrot. **2,** magpie. **3,** *colloq.* chatterbox. —**cotorrear** (-rre'ar) *v.i.,* *colloq.* to chatter. —**cotorreo** (-'rre·o) *n.m.,* *colloq.* chatter; chattering.

covacha (ko'βa·tʃa) *n.f.* **1,** small cave. **2,** *Amer.* cubbyhole. **3,** *Amer.* hut; shanty.

coyote (ko'jo·te) *n.m.* coyote.

coyuntura (ko·jun'tu·ra) *n.f.* **1,** juncture. **2,** *anat.* joint; articulation. **3,** opportunity.

coz (koθ; kos) *n.f.* **1,** kick. **2,** recoil (*of a gun*).

craal (kra'al) *n.m.* kraal.

cráneo ('kra·ne·o) *n.m.* cranium; skull. —**craneal,** *adj.* cranial.

crápula ('kra·pu·la) *n.f.* **1,** drunkenness. **2,** lewdness.

crapuloso (kra·pu'lo·so) *adj.* **1,** drunk. **2,** lewd.

crasitud (kra·si'tuð) *n.f.* **1,** obesity; corpulence. **2,** fattiness; greasiness. **3,** crassness; grossness.

craso ('kra·so) *adj.* **1,** fat; thick; coarse. **2,** fatty; greasy. **3,** crass; gross.

cráter ('kra·ter) *n.m.* crater.

crear (kre'ar) *v.t.* to create. —**creación,** *n.f.* creation. —**creador,** *adj.* creative. —*n.m.* creator.

crecer (kre'θer; -'ser) *v.i.* [*infl.:* **conocer, 13**] to grow; increase. —**crecerse,** *v.r.* to swell with pride.

crecida (kre'θi·ða; -'si·ða) *n.f.* freshet.

crecido (kre'θi·ðo; -'si·ðo) *adj.* **1,** large; grown. **2,** swollen.

creciente (kre'θjen·te; kre'sjen-) *adj.* **1,** growing; increasing. **2,** crescent. —*n.m.,* *her.* crescent; half moon. —*n.f.* **1,** high tide; flood tide. **2,** freshet. **3,** crescent (*of the moon*). **4,** sourdough.

crecimiento (kre·θi'mjen·to; kre·si-) *n.m.* growth; increase.

credenciales (kre·ðen'θja·les; -'sja·les) *n.f.pl.* credentials.

credibilidad (kre·ði·βi·li'ðað) *n.f.* credibility.

crédito ('kre·ði·to) *n.m.* credit.

credo ('kre·ðo) *n.m.* creed; credo. —**más viejo que el credo,** very ancient. —**no saber el credo,** to be very ignorant.

crédulo ('kre·ðu·lo) *adj.* credulous. —**credulidad** (-li'ðað) *n.f.* credulity.

creencia (kre'en·θja; -sja) *n.f.* belief.

creer (kre'er) *v.t. & i.* [*infl.:* **42**] to believe; think. —**creer que no,** to think not. —**creer que sí,** to think so. —**¡ya lo creo!,** *colloq.* I should say so!

creíble (kre'i·βle) *adj.* credible.

creído (kre'i·ðo) *v.,* *p.p. of* **creer.** —*adj.* **1,** credulous. **2,** conceited.

crema ('kre·ma) *n.f.* **1,** cream. **2,** *gram.* dieresis. —**cremoso,** *adj.* creamy.

cremación (kre·ma'θjon; -'sjon) *n.f.* cremation.

cremallera (kre·ma'ʎe·ra; -'je·ra)

n.f. **1,** *mech.* rack; toothed bar. **2,** zipper.

crematorio (kre·ma'to·rjo) *n.m.* crematory.

cremera (kre'me·ra) *n.f.* creamer.

crémor ('kre·mor) *n.m.* cream of tartar. *Also,* **crémor tártaro.**

creosota (kre·o'so·ta) *n.f.* creosote.

crepé (kre'pe) *n.m.* crêpe.

crepitación (kre·pi·ta'θjon; -'sjon) *n.f.* **1,** crackling; snapping. **2,** rattle *(of the breath).*

crepitar (kre·pi'tar) *v.i.* to crackle; snap.

crepúsculo (kre'pus·ku·lo) *n.m.* twilight. —**crepuscular,** *adj.* of or at twilight.

cresa ('kre·sa) *n.f.* maggot.

crescendo (kres'θen·do; kre'sen-) *adj., adv.* & *n.m.* crescendo.

crespo ('kres·po) *adj.* curly; curled. —*n.m.,* Amer. curl.

crespón (kres'pon) *n.m.* crêpe.

cresta ('kres·ta) *n.f.* **1,** crest. **2,** comb *(of birds).* —**cresta de gallo,** cockscomb.

creta ('kre·ta) *n.f.* limestone; chalk.

cretino (kre'ti·no) *n.m.* cretin. —**cretinismo,** *n.m.* cretinism.

cretona (kre'to·na) *n.f.* cretonne.

creyendo (kre'jen·do) *v., ger.* of **creer.**

creyente (kre'jen·te) *adj.* believing. —*n.m.* & *f.* believer.

creyó (kre'jo) *v., 3rd pers.sing. pret.* of **creer.**

creyón (kre'jon) *n.m.* **1,** crayon. **2,** charcoal pencil.

crezca ('kreθ·ka; 'kres-) *v., pres. subjve.* of **crecer.**

crezco ('kreθ·ko; 'kres-) *v., 1st. pers.sing. pres.ind.* of **crecer.**

cría ('kri·a) *n.f.* **1,** breeding; raising. **2,** brood; offspring. **3,** litter.

criadero (kri·a'ðe·ro) *n.m.* **1,** breeding place. **2,** nursery. **3,** fish hatchery. —*adj.* fruitful; prolific.

criado (kri'a·ðo) *n.m.* [*fem.* **criada**] servant. —*adj.* bred; raised.

criador (kri·a'ðor) *adj.* **1,** creative. **2,** fruitful. **3,** nurturing. —*n.m.* raiser; breeder. —**criadora,** *n.f.* wet nurse.

criandera (kri·an'de·ra) *n.f., Amer.* wet nurse.

crianza (kri'an·θa; -sa) *n.f.* breeding; raising. —**hermano de crianza,** foster brother.

criar (kri'ar) *v.t.* [*infl.:* **enviar, 22**] **1,** to raise; rear. **2,** to breed.

—**criarse,** *v.r.* **1,** to grow. **2,** to grow up; be raised.

criatura (kri·a'tu·ra) *n.f.* **1,** creature. **2,** baby.

criba ('kri·βa) *n.f.* sieve.

cribar (kri'βar) *v.t.* to sift.

crimen ('kri·men) *n.m.* crime.

criminal (kri·mi'nal) *adj.* & *n.m.* & *f.* criminal. —**criminalidad,** *n.f.* criminality.

criminalista (kri·mi·na'lis·ta) *n.m.* & *f.* criminologist. *Also,* **criminólogo,** *n.m.*

criminología (kri·mi·no·lo'xi·a) *n.f.* criminology.

crin (krin) *n.f.* **1,** mane, esp. of horses. **2,** horsehair.

crinolina (kri·no'li·na) *n.f.* crinoline.

criollo ('krjo·ʎo; -jo) *adj.* & *n.m.* **1,** native. **2,** creole.

cripta ('krip·ta) *n.f.* crypt.

criptografía (krip·to·ɣra'fi·a) *n.f.* cryptography. —**criptográfico** (-'ɣra·fi·ko) *adj.* cryptographic.

criptógrafo (krip'to·ɣra·fo) *n.m.* **1,** cryptographer. **2,** cryptograph *(device).*

criptograma (krip·to'ɣra·ma) *n.m.* cryptograph *(message);* cryptogram.

criptón (krip'ton) *n.m.* krypton.

crisálida (kri'sa·li·ða) *n.f.* chrysalis.

crisantemo (kri·san'te·mo) *n.m.* chrysanthemum. *Also,* **crisantema,** *n.f.*

crisis ('kri·sis) *n.f.* crisis.

crisol (kri'sol) *n.m.* crucible; melting pot.

crispar (kris'par) *v.t.* to contract; cause to twitch, as the muscles. —**crisparse,** *v.r.* to contract; twitch. —**crispamiento,** *n.m.* twitching; contraction.

cristal (kris'tal) *n.m.* **1,** crystal. **2,** glass. **3,** pane of glass.

cristalera (kris·ta'le·ra) *n.f.* **1,** sideboard; china closet. **2,** glass door.

cristalería (kris·ta·le'ri·a) *n.f.* glassware.

cristalino (kris·ta'li·no) *adj.* crystalline; transparent. —*n.m., anat.* crystalline lens.

cristalizar (kris·ta·li'θar; -'sar) *v.t.* [*infl.:* **rezar, 10**] to crystallize. —**cristalización.** *n.f.* crystallization.

cristianar (kris·tja'nar) *v.t., colloq.* to christen.

cristiandad (kris·tjan'dað) *n.f.* Christendom.

cristianismo (kris·tja'nis·mo) *n.m.* 1, Christianity; Christendom. 2, christening.

cristiano (kris'tja·no) *adj. & n.m.* 1, Christian. 2, person; human being. 3, Christian (i.e., Spanish) language. —**cristianizar,** *v.t.* [*infl.:* rezar, 10] to Christianize.

Cristo ('kris·to) *n.m.* Christ.

criterio (kri·te·rjo) *n.m.* 1, criterion. 2, judgment.

crítica ('kri·ti·ka) *n.f.* 1, criticism. 2, censure.

criticar (kri·ti'kar) *v.t.* [*infl.:* tocar, 7] 1, to criticize; judge. 2, to censure.

crítico ('kri·ti·ko) *adj.* critical. —*n.m.* critic. —*adj. & n.m., Amer.* = **criticón.**

criticón (kri·ti'kon) *adj., colloq.* critical; carping; faultfinding. —*n.m., colloq.* [*fem.* -**ona**] critic; faultfinder.

croar (kro'ar) *v.i.* to croak.

croata (kro'a·ta) *n.m. & f.* Croat; Croatian. —*adj.* Croatian.

croché (kro'tʃe) *n.m.* crochet.

cromado (kro'ma·ðo) *adj. & n.m.* chrome.

cromático (kro'ma·ti·ko) *adj.* chromatic.

cromo ('kro·mo) *n.m.* chromium.

cromosoma (kro·mo'so·ma) *n.m.* chromosome.

crónica ('kro·ni·ka) *n.f.* chronicle.

crónico ('kro·ni·ko) *adj.* chronic; long-standing.

cronista (kro'nis·ta) *n.m. & f.* 1, chronicler. 2, feature writer. —**cronista de radio,** newscaster.

cronología (kro·no·lo'xi·a) *n.f.* chronology. —**cronológico** (-'lo·xi·ko) *adj.* chronological.

cronómetro (kro'no·met·ro) *n.m.* 1, chronometer. 2, stopwatch. 3, *S.A.* watch.

croqueta (kro'ke·ta) *n.f.* croquette.

croquis ('kro·kis) *n.m. sing. & pl.* rough sketch; hand-drawn map.

cruce ('kru·θe; -se) *n.m.* 1, cross; crossing. 2, crossroads; intersection.

crucero (kru'θe·ro; -'se·ro) *n.m.* 1, cross-bearer. 2, crossing; intersection. 3, cruise. 4, cruiser. 5, crossbeam. 6, *archit.* transept.

crucial (kru'θjal; -'sjal) *adj.* crucial.

crucificar (kru·θi·fi'kar; kru·si-) *v.t.* [*infl.:* tocar, 7] to crucify.

crucifijo (kru·θi'fi·xo; kru·si-) *n.m.* crucifix.

crucifixión (kru·θi·fik'sjon; kru·si-) *n.f.* crucifixion.

crucigrama (kru·θi'ɣra·ma; kru·si-) *n.m.* crossword puzzle.

crudelísimo (kru·ðe'li·si·mó) *adj., superl. of* **cruel.**

crudeza (kru'ðe·θa; -sa) *n.f.* 1, rawness. 2, crudeness; crudity. 3, roughness; harshness.

crudo (kru·ðo) *adj.* 1, raw. 2, crude. 3, rough; harsh. —**agua cruda,** hard water. —**estar crudo,** *Amer.* to have a hangover.

cruel (krwel) *adj.* cruel. —**crueldad,** *n.f.* cruelty.

cruento (kru'en·to) *adj.* bloody.

crujido (kru'xi·ðo) *n.m.* 1, creak; crack; crackle. 2, gnashing *(of the teeth).*

crujir (kru'xir) *v.i.* 1, to creak; crack; crackle. 2, to make a gnashing sound, as the teeth.

crupié (kru'pje) *n.m.* croupier.

crustáceo (krus'ta·θe·o; -se·o) *adj. & n.m.* crustacean.

cruz (kruθ; krus) *n.f.* 1, cross. 2, reverse side of a coin; tails. 3, withers. 4, *math.* plus sign. —**cruz gamada** (ga'ma·ða) swastika. —**cruz y raya,** *colloq.* that's enough. —**en cruz,** crosswise. —**hacer la cruz a,** to be through with; wash one's hands of.

cruzada (kru'θa·ða; -'sa·ða) *n.f.* crusade.

cruzado (kru'θa·ðo; -'sa·ðo) *adj.* 1, crossed. 2, double-breasted. —*n.m.* crusader.

cruzamiento (kru·θa'mjen·to; kru·sa-) *n.m.* crossing.

cruzar (kru'θar; -'sar) *v.t.* [*infl.:* rezar, 10] 1, to cross. 2, *naut.* to cruise.

cuaderno (kwa'ðer·no) *n.m.* notebook.

cuadra ('kwa·ðra) *n.f.* 1, stable. 2, hospital ward. 3, quarter *(of a mile).* 4, *naut.* quarter. 5, *Amer.* city block.

cuadrado (kwa'ðra·ðo) *adj. & n.m.* 1, square. 2, quadrate. —*adj.* perfect; complete. —*n.m.* 1, ruler *(for drawing lines).* 2, clock; design in hose. 3, *print.* quad; quadrat.

cuadragésimo (kwa·ðra'xe·si·mo) *adj.* fortieth. —**Cuadragésima,** *n.f.* Lent; Quadragesima.

cuadrangular (kwa·ðran·gu'lar) *adj.* quadrangular. —*n.m., baseball* home run.

cuadrángulo (kwa'ðran·gu·lo) *adj.* quadrangular. —*n.m.* quadrangle.

cuadrante (kwa'ðran·te) *n.m.* 1, dial. 2, *math.* quadrant.

cuadrar (kwa'ðrar) *v.t.* 1, to square. 2, to arrange in squares. 3, *Amer.* to set aright. —*v.i.* to fit; suit. —**cuadrarse,** *v.r.* to stand at attention.

cuadrático (kwa'ðra·ti·ko) *adj.* quadratic. —**cuadrática,** *n.f.* quadratic equation.

cuadratín (kwa·ðra'tin) *n.m., print.* = **cuadrado.**

cuadricular (kwa·ðri·ku'lar) *v.t.* to divide into squares; rule squares in or on. —*adj.* squared. —**papel cuadriculado,** graph paper.

cuadrienio (kwa·ðri'e·njo) *n.m.* quadrennium. —**cuadrienal** (-'nal) *adj.* quadrennial.

cuadrilátero (kwa·ðri'la·te·ro) *adj.* & *n.m.* quadrilateral.

cuadrilla (kwa'ðri·ʎa; -ja) *n.f.* 1, group; gang. 2, quadrille. 3, *bullfighting* team.

cuadringentésimo (kwa·ðrin·xen'te·si·mo) *adj.* & *n.m.* fourhundredth.

cuadro ('kwa·ðro) *n.m.* 1, square. 2, picture; painting. 3, *mil.* cadre. 4, frame; support. 5, chart; table; schedule. 6, *theat.* scene; tableau. —*adj.* square. —**cuadro de distribución,** switchboard; control panel.

cuadrúmano (kwa'ðru·ma·no) *adj.* quadrumanous. —*n.m.* quadrumane.

cuadrúpedo (kwa'ðru·pe·ðo) *adj.* & *n.m.* quadruped.

cuádruple ('kwa·ðru·ple) *adj.* quadruple. —**cuádruplo,** *adj.* & *n.m.* quadruple.

cuadrúpleto (kwa'ðru·ple·to) *n.m.* quadruplet.

cuadruplicar (kwa·ðru·pli'kar) *v.t.* [*infl.:* tocar, 7] 1, to quadruple. 2, to quadruplicate. —**cuadruplicarse,** *v.r.* to quadruple. —**cuadruplicado,** *adj.* & *n.m.* quadruplicate.

cuajada (kwa'xa·ða) *n.f.* curd.

cuajado (kwa'xa·ðo) *n.m.* 1, curd. 2, mincemeat.

cuajar (kwa'xar) *v.t.* 1, to coagulate; curdle. 2, to adorn to excess. —*v.i.* 1, to take shape; jell. 2, to be pleasing. —**cuajarse,** *v.r.* 1, to coagulate; curdle. 2, to fill up; to be covered all over.

cuajo ('kwa·jo) *n.m.* 1, curd. 2, rennet. 3, clot. —**de cuajo,** by the roots.

cuákero ('kwa·ke·ro) *also, Amer.* **cuakero** (-'ke·ro) *adj.* & *n.m.* = **cuáquero, cuaquero.** —**cuakerismo,** *n.m.* = **cuaquerismo.**

cual (kwal) *rel.* & *indef. adj.* & *pron.* which. —*adv.* as; like. —**¿cuál?** *interr. adj.* & *pron.* which? what? —**cada cual,** each one. —**por lo cual,** for which reason. —**tal cual,** as is. —**tal ... cual,** like.... like. —**un tal por cual,** *colloq.* a good-for-nothing.

cualesquiera (kwa·les'kje·ra), **cualesquier** (-'kjer), *indef. adj.* & *pron., pl.* of **cualquiera, cualquier.**

cualidad (kwa·li'ðað) *n.f.* quality; property; characteristic.

cualificar (kwa·li·fi'kar) *v.t.* [*infl.:* tocar, 7] to qualify.

cualitativo (kwa·li·ta'ti·βo) *adj.* qualitative.

cualquier (kwal'kjer) *indef. adj.* & *pron.* = **cualquiera** *before a noun.*

cualquiera (kwal'kje·ra) *indef. adj.* & *pron.* anyone; whichever; any.

cuan (kwan) *adv., contr.* of **cuanto,** how; as. *Used only before adjs.* & *advs.*

cuando ('kwan·do) *adv.* & *conj.* when. —*prep.* during. —**aún cuando,** even though; although. —**cuando más,** at the most. —**cuando menos,** at least. —**cuando no,** if not; otherwise. —**¿de cuándo acá?** since when? —**de cuando en cuando; de vez en cuando,** from time to time; once in a while.

cuantía (kwan'ti·a) *n.f.* 1, quantity. 2, personal worth; esteem. 3, *law* degree (*specifying a criminal charge*).

cuántico ('kwan·ti·ko) *adj.* quantum. —**unidad cuántica,** quantum.

cuantioso (kwan'tjo·so) *adj.* 1, plentiful. 2, large; substantial.

cuantitativo (kwan·ti·ta'ti·βo) *adj.* quantitative.

cuanto ('kwan·to) *rel.adj.* & *pron.* as much as; as many as; all that. —*n.m.* [*pl.* **cuanta** (-ta)] quantum. —**¿cuánto?** *interr.adj.* & *pron.* how much? *pl.* how many? —**cuanto antes,** as soon as possible. —**en cuanto,** as soon as. —**en cuanto a,** as for. —**unos cuantos,** a few.

cuáquero ('kwa·ke·ro) *also, Amer.* **cuaquero** (-'ke·ro) *adj.* & *n.m.* Quaker. —**cuaquerismo**, *n.m.* Quakerism.

cuarenta (kwa'ren·ta) *n.m.* & *adj.* forty.

cuarentavo (kwa·ren'ta·βo) *adj.* & *n.m.* fortieth.

cuarentena (kwa·ren'te·na) *n.f.* 1, quarantine. 2, a quantity of forty.

cuarentón (kwa·ren'ton) *n.m.* a man in his forties.

cuaresma (kwa'res·ma) *n.f.* Lent.

cuarta ('kwar·ta) *n.f.* 1, quarter; one fourth. 2, *Amer.* span *(of the hand)*. 3, *Amer.* additional horses, etc., needed to perform a task. 4, *Amer.* horsewhip. 5, *mus.* fourth.

cuartear (kwar·te'ar) *v.t.* 1, to quarter. 2, to raise (a bid, price, etc.) by a quarter. 3, to zigzag along or over. 4, *Amer.* to whip. 5, to make a fourth in, as a card game. —*v.i.*, *Amer.* to back down; compromise. —**cuartearse**, *v.r.* to crack; split, as a wall or ceiling.

cuartel (kwar'tel) *n.m.* 1, quarter. 2, *mil.* barracks. —**cuartelada**, *n.f.* military uprising. —**cuartel general**, *mil.* headquarters.

cuarterón (kwar·te'ron) *n.m.* 1, quarter. 2, quarter of a pound. 3, door or window panel. 4, [*fem.* -ona] quarter-breed; quadroon.

cuarteto (kwar'te·to) *n.m.* 1, quartet. 2, quatrain.

cuartilla (kwar'ti·ʎa; -ja) *n.f.* 1, quarter sheet *(of paper)*. 2, a dry measure equal to about 1½ pecks. 3, a liquid measure equal to about 4 quarts. 4, quarter of an arroba.

cuartillo (kwar'ti·ʎo; -jo) *n.m.* 1, a dry measure equal to about ¼ peck. 2, a liquid measure equal to about a pint. 3, quarter of a real.

cuarto ('kwar·to) *n.m.* 1, room; bedroom. 2, quarter; fourth. —*adj.* fourth. —**cuarto doble**, double room. —**cuarto sencillo**, single room. —**de tres al cuarto**, insignificant; of little or no importance. —**echar su cuarto a espadas**, *colloq.* to butt into conversation. —**estar sin un cuarto; no tener un cuarto**, *colloq.* to be penniless; to be broke.

cuarzo ('kwar·θo; -so) *n.m.* quartz.

cuasar (kwa'sar) *n.m.* quasar.

cuasi ('kwa·si) *adv.* almost.

cuaternario (kwa·ter'na·rjo) *adj.* & *n.m.* quaternary.

cuaterno (kwa'ter·no) *adj.* quaternary.

cuatrero (kwa'tre·ro) *n.m.* horse thief; cattle thief.

cuatrillizo (kwa·tri'ʎi·θo; -'ji·so) *n.m.* quadruplet.

cuatrillón (kwa·tri'ʎon; -'jon) *n.m.* a billion quadrillion; *U.S.* septillion; *Brit.* quadrillion.

cuatro ('kwa·tro) *adj.* & *n.m.* four.

cuatrocientos (kwa·tro'θjen·tos; -'sjen·tos) *adj.* & *n.m. pl.* [*fem.* -tas] four hundred.

cuba ('ku·βa) *n.f.* 1, cask; vat. 2, *colloq.* tubby; fat person. 3, *colloq.* tippler; drunkard.

cubeta (ku'βe·ta) *n.f.* shallow pan or tray. *Mex.*, bucket.

cubicar (ku·βi'kar) *v.t.* [*infl.*: **tocar**, 7] 1, to determine the volume of. 2, *math.* to cube; raise to the third power.

cúbico ('ku·βi·ko) *adj.* cubic.

cubículo (ku'βi·ku·lo) *n.m.* cubicle; cubbyhole.

cubierta (ku'βjer·ta) *n.f.* 1, cover; bedspread. 2, *naut.* deck. 3, *auto.*; *aero.* cowling.

cubierto (ku'βjer·to) *v.*, *p.p.* of **cubrir**. —*n.m.* 1, tableware; silver. 2, place setting. 3, course; meal.

cubil (ku'βil) *n.m.* den, lair.

cubismo (ku'βis·mo) *n.m.* cubism. —**cubista**, *adj.* & *n.m.* & *f.* cubist.

cúbito ('ku·βi·to) *n.m.* ulna.

cubo ('ku·βo) *n.m.* 1, cube. 2, bucket. 3, hub.

cubrecama (ku·βre'ka·ma) *n.f.* bedspread; counterpane.

cubretablero (ku·βre·ta'βle·ro) *n.m.*, *auto.* cowl.

cubrir (ku'βrir) *v.t.* [*p.p.* **cubierto**] 1, to cover. 2, to hide; cloak. 3, to protect. —**cubrirse**, *v.r.* 1, to put on one's hat. 2, to insure oneself.

cucaracha (ku·ka'ra·tʃa) *n.f.* cockroach.

cuclillas (ku'kli·ʎas; -jas) *n.f.pl.*, *in* en cuclillas, squatting.

cuclillo (ku'kli·ʎo; -jo) *n.m.* cuckoo.

cuco ('ku·ko) *adj.* 1, shrewd; crafty. 2, *colloq.* dainty; neat. —*n.m.* 1, cuckoo. 2, a kind of caterpillar. 3, a card game. 4, *colloq.* cardsharp; gambler.

cucú (ku'ku) *n.m.* cry of the cuckoo.

cucurucho (ku·ku'ru·tʃo) *n.m.* 1, paper cone. 2, *Amer.* mountain cap; peak 3, *Amer.* = **capirote**.

cuchara (ku'tʃa·ra) *n.f.* spoon; tablespoon. —**cucharada**, *n.f.* spoon-

ful. —**cucharadita,** *n.f.* teaspoonful. —**cucharita,** *n.f.* teaspoon.
cucharear (ku·tʃa·re'ar) *v.t.* to
spoon; ladle.
cucharón (ku·tʃa'ron) *n.m.* large
spoon; ladle.
cuchichear (ku·tʃi·tʃe'ar) *v.t. & i.*
to whisper. —**cuchicheo** (-'tʃe·o)
n.m. whisper; whispering.
cuchilla (ku'tʃi·ʎa; -ja) *n.f.* **1,** large
knife; cleaver. **2,** *Amer.* jackknife. **3,**
blade; runner. —**cuchillada,** *n.f.*
slash; cut; knife wound.
cuchillería (ku·tʃi·ʎe'ri·a; -je·
'ri·a) *n.f.* **1,** cutlery. **2,** cutlery shop.
cuchillero (ku·tʃi'ʎe·ro; -'je·ro)
n.m. **1,** cutler. **2,** clamp; cleat.
cuchillo (ku'tʃi·ʎo; -jo) *n.m.* knife.
cuchitril (ku·tʃi'tril) *n.m.* **1,** hovel.
2, pigsty.
cuele ('kwe·le) *v., pres.subjve. of*
colar.
cuelgo ('kwel·ɣo) *v., 1st pers. sing.
pres.ind. of* **colgar.**
cuelgue ('kwel·ɣe) *v., pres.subjve.
of* **colgar.**
cuelo ('kwe·lo) *v., 1st pers. sing.
pres.ind. of* **colar.**
cuello ('kwe·ʎo; -jo) *n.m.* **1,** neck.
2, collar *(of a shirt, dress, etc.).*
cuenca ('kwen·ka) *n.f.* **1,** wooden
bowl. **2,** socket of the eye. **3,** river
basin; valley.
cuenco ('kwen·ko) *n.m.* **1,** earthen
bowl. **2,** cavity; hollow; depression.
cuenta ('kwen·ta) *n.f.* **1,** count; calculation. **2,** bill. **3,** account. **4,** bead.
—**caer en la cuenta,** to get the
point. —**dar cuenta,** to report.
—**darse cuenta de,** to realize.
—**tener en cuenta,** to take into account.
cuentagotas (kwen·ta'ɣo·tas)
n.m. sing. & pl. dropper.
cuentakilómetros (kwen·ta·
ki'lo·me·tros) *n.m.* odometer.
cuentapasos (kwen·ta'pa·sos)
n.m.sing. & pl. pedometer.
cuente ('kwen·te) *v., pres.subjve. of*
contar.
cuentista (kwen'tis·ta) *n.m. & f.*
1, storyteller. **2,** writer of stories or
tales. **3,** *colloq.* fibber; liar.
cuento ('kwen·to) *n.m.* story; tale.
—**sin cuento,** countless.
cuento ('kwen·to) *v., 1st pers. sing.
pres.ind. of* **contar.**
cuentón (kwen'ton) *n.m., colloq.*
[*fem.* **-ona**] **1,** gossip. **2,** fibber;
storyteller.
cuerda ('kwer·ða) *n.f.* **1,** cord;

rope; string. **2,** winding *(of a spring
mechanism).* **3,** watch spring. **4,**
anat. cord; tendon. **5,** *geom.* chord.
6, cord *(cubic measure).* —**aflojar
la cuerda,** to ease up. —**apretar
la cuerda,** to tighten up. —**bajo
cuerda,** underhandedly. —**dar
cuerda a, 1,** to wind. **2,** *fig.* to encourage.
cuerdo ('kwer·ðo) *adj.* **1,** wise;
prudent. **2,** rational; sane.
cuerear (kwe·re'ar) *v.t., Amer.* to
whip; flog. —**cuereada,** *n.f., Amer.*
whipping; flogging.
cuerno ('kwer·no) *n.m.* horn.
—*interj.* [*also,* **cuernos**] nuts!; hell!
cuero ('kwe·ro) *n.m.* hide; skin;
leather. —**en cueros,** nude.
cuerpear (kwer·pe'ar) *v.i., Amer.*
to dodge; evade one's responsibility. —**cuerpeada,** *n.f., Amer.* evasion; dodge.
cuerpo ('kwer·po) *n.m.* **1,** body. **2,**
build; figure. **3,** substance. **4,** *mil.*
corps. —**a cuerpo descubierto,** unprotected. —**cuerpo a cuerpo,** hand
to hand. —**hacer** *or* **irse del
cuerpo,** to move the bowels.
—**sacar el cuerpo,** to dodge.
cuervo ('kwer·ßo) *n.m.* crow;
raven.
cuesta ('kwes·ta) *n.f.* hill; slope.
—**cuesta abajo,** downhill. —**cuesta
arriba,** uphill.
cueste ('kwes·te) *v., pres.subjve. of*
costar.
cuestión (kwes'tjon) *n.f.* **1,** question; dispute. **2,** affair; matter.
cuestionar (kwes·tjo'nar) *v.t.* to
dispute; debate. —**cuestionable,**
adj. debatable; doubtful.
cuestionario (kwes·tjo'na·rjo)
n.m. questionnaire.
cuesto ('kwes·to) *v., 1st pers. sing.
pres.ind. of* **costar.**
cueva ('kwe·ßa) *n.f.* **1,** cave. **2,** cellar.
cueza ('kwe·θa; -sa) *v., pres.subjve.
of* **cocer.**
cuezo ('kwe·θo; -so) *v., 1st pers.
sing.pres.ind. of* **cocer.**
cuguar (ku'ɣwar) *n.m.* cougar.
cuico ('kwi·ko) *n.m., Amer.* **1,** outlander; foreigner. **2,** policeman; cop.
3, halfbreed. **4,** tubby; dumpy person.
cuidado (kwi'ða·ðo) *n.m.* care; attention. —*interj.* look out! —**al
cuidado de,** in care of. —**cuidado
con,** beware of. —**tener cuidado,**
to be careful; to take care.

cuidadoso (kwi·ða'ðo·so) *adj.* **1,** careful; attentive. **2,** concerned; anxious.

cuidaniños (kwi·ða'ni·ɲos) *n.m.* & *f., sing.* & *pl.* baby-sitter.

cuidar (kwi'ðar) *v.t.* to look after; take care of. —**cuidar de,** to take care of.

cuita ('kwi·ta) *n.f.* grief; misfortune.

cuitado (kwi'ta·ðo) *adj.* **1,** grieved; afflicted. **2,** timid; shy.

cuja ('ku·xa) *n.f.* bedstead.

culata (ku'la·ta) *n.f.* **1,** butt *(of a gun).* **2,** breech *(of a cannon).*

culatazo (ku·la'ta·θo; -so) *n.m.* **1,** recoil. **2,** a blow with the butt of a gun.

culebra (ku'le·βra) *n.f.* **1,** snake. **2,** *colloq.* cunning woman. —**culebra de cascabel,** rattlesnake.

culebrear (ku·le·βre'ar) *v.i.* to wriggle; zigzag; snake. —**culebreo** (-'βre·o) *n.m.* wriggling.

culinario (ku·li'na·rjo) *adj.* culinary.

culminar (kul·mi'nar) *v.i.* to culminate. —**culminación,** *n.f.* culmination; climax.

culo ('ku·lo) *n.m., slang* buttocks.

culombio (ku'lom·bjo) *n.m.* coulomb.

culpa ('kul·pa) *n.f.* guilt; blame; fault. —**echar la culpa a,** to blame.

culpable (kul'pa·βle) *adj.* culpable; guilty. —*n.m.* & *f.* culprit. —**culpabilidad,** *n.f.* culpability.

culpar (kul'par) *v.t.* to blame; accuse.

cultivador (kul·ti·βa'ðor) *adj.* cultivating; growing; farming. —*n.m.* cultivator; grower; farmer. —**cultivadora,** *n.f.* cultivator *(machine).*

cultivar (kul·ti'βar) *v.t.* **1,** to cultivate. **2,** *bacteriology* to culture. —**cultivación,** *n.f.* cultivation.

cultivo (kul'ti·βo) *n.m.* **1,** cultivation; farming. **2,** *bacteriology* culture.

culto ('kul·to) *n.m.* **1,** worship. **2,** cult. —*adj.* cultured; learned.

cultura (kul'tu·ra) *n.f.* culture. —**cultural,** *adj.* cultural.

cumbre ('kum·bre) *n.f.* summit. —*adj.* top; greatest.

cúmplase ('kum·pla·se) *n.m.* **1,** approval. **2,** decree. **3,** *Amer.* countersign *(of a decree).*

cumpleaños (kum·ple'a·ɲos) *n.m. sing* & *pl.* birthday.

cumplido (kum'pli·ðo) *adj.* **1,** complete; perfect. **2,** fulfilled. **3,** due. **4,** dutiful; correct. —*n.m.* courtesy; compliment.

cumplimentar (kum·pli·men'tar) *v.t.* **1,** to compliment. **2,** to fulfill; carry out.

cumplimiento (kum·pli'mjen·to) *n.m.* **1,** fulfillment. **2,** compliance. **3,** courtesy; compliment.

cumplir (kum'plir) *v.t.* to fulfill; accomplish. —*v.i.* to be quits. —**cumplir . . . . años,** to be. . . . years old. —**cumplir con,** to fulfill.

cúmulo ('ku·mu·lo) *n.m.* **1,** heap; pile; accumulation. **2,** cumulus.

cuna ('ku·na) *n.f.* **1,** cradle; crib. **2,** origin; ancestry.

cuneiforme (ku·ne·i'for·me) *adj.* & *n.m.* cuneiform.

cuneta (ku'ne·ta) *n.f.* gutter *(of a road).*

cuña ('ku·ɲa) *n.f.* **1,** wedge. **2,** *Amer., colloq.* influence; pull.

cuñado (ku'ɲa·ðo) *n.m.* brother-in-law. —**cuñada,** *n.f.* sister-in-law.

cuociente (kwo'θjen·te; -'sjen·te) *n.m.* quotient.

cuota ('kwo·ta) *n.f.* **1,** quota. **2,** fees; dues.

cuotidiano (kwo·ti'ðja·no) *adj.* = **cotidiano.**

cupe ('ku·pe) *v., pret.* of **caber.**

cupé (ku'pe) *n.m.* coupé.

cupido (ku'pi·ðo) *n.m.* cupid. —*cap., myth.* Cupid.

cupón (ku'pon) *n.m.* coupon.

cúpula ('ku·pu·la) *n.f.* dome; cupola.

cura ('ku·ra) *n.f.* cure; treatment. —*n.m.* priest; curate. —**no tener cura,** *colloq.* to be hopeless. —**ponerse en cura,** to undergo treatment.

curable (ku'ra·βle) *adj.* curable.

curación (ku·ra'θjon; -'sjon) *n.f.* healing; cure.

curador (ku·ra'ðor) *n.m.* **1,** caretaker; curator. **2,** *law* guardian. **3,** healer. —*adj.* curing; healing.

cúralotodo (ku·ra·lo'to·ðo) *n.m.* **1,** cure-all. **2,** quack.

curandero (ku·ran'de·ro) *n.m.* **1,** healer. **2,** witch doctor. **3,** quack. —**curanderismo** (-'ris·mo) *n.m., also,* **curandería** (-'ri·a) *n.f.* quackery.

curar (ku'rar) *v.t.* to treat; cure. —**curarse,** *v.r.* **1,** to undergo treatment. **2,** to recover. **3,** *Amer. colloq.*

to get drunk. —**curarse de,** to get over; recover from.

curativo (ku·ra'ti·βo) *adj.* curative. —**curativa,** *n.f.* curative; remedy; treatment.

curato (ku'ra·to) *n.m.* **1,** curacy. **2,** parish.

cúrcuma ('kur·ku·ma) *n.f.* turmeric.

curia ('ku·rja) *n.f., law* court.

curie (ku'ri) *n.m., physics* curie.

curio ('ku·rjo) *n.m.* curium.

curiosear (ku·rjo·se'ar) *v.i.* to snoop; pry. —**curioseo** (-'se·o) *n.m.* snooping; prying.

curioso (ku'rjo·so) *adj.* curious. —**curiosidad,** *n.f.* curiosity.

curro ('ku·rro) *adj., colloq.* gaudy; flashy. —*n.m., colloq.* fop; dandy.

curruca (ku'rru·ka) *n.f.* warbler.

currutaco (ku·rru·ta'ko) *adj., colloq.* affected or garish in dress. —*n.m., colloq.* loud dresser; sport.

cursi ('kur·si) *adj.* showy; gaudy; pretentious. —**cursilería** (-le'ri·a) *n.f.* pretentiousness; gaudiness.

cursivo (kur'si·βo) *adj.* **1,** cursive. **2,** *typog.* italic. —**cursiva,** *n.f.* **1,** cursive script. **2,** *typog.* italics.

curso ('kur·so) *n.m.* **1,** course; direction. **2,** school year. **3,** course of study.

cursor (kur'sor) *n.m.* cursor.

curtido (kur'ti·ðo) *n.m.* **1,** tanning. **2,** tanbark.

curtidor (kur·ti'ðor) *n.m.* tanner.

curtiduría (kur·ti·ðu'ri·a) *n.f.* tannery.

curtiembre (kur'tjem·bre) *n.f., Amer.* **1,** = **curtiduría. 2,** tanning.

curtir (kur'tir) *v.t.* **1,** to tan. **2,** to harden; inure. —**estar curtido en,** to be skilled in.

curva ('kur·βa) *n.f.* curve; bend.

curvar (kur'βar) *v.t.* **1,** to curve. **2,** to bend; warp.

curvatura (kur·βa'tu·ra) *n.f.* curvature.

curvo ('kur·βo) *adj.* curved; bent.

cuscurro (kus'ku·rro) *n.m.* crouton.

cúspide ('kus·pi·ðe) *n.f.* **1,** summit; peak. **2,** cusp. **3,** cuspid.

custodia (kus'to·ðja) *n.f.* **1,** custody. **2,** guard; escort.

custodiar (kus·to'ðjar) *v.t.* to guard; keep; have custody of.

custodio (kus'to·ðjo) *n.m.* guard; custodian.

cutáneo (ku'ta·ne·o) *adj.* cutaneous.

cúter ('ku·ter) *n.m., naut.* cutter.

cutí (ku'ti) *n.m.* **1,** ticking. **2,** crash (*cloth*).

cutícula (ku'ti·ku·la) *n.f.* cuticle.

cutis ('ku·tis) *n.m.* skin; complexion.

cuy (kwi) *n.m., S.A.* guinea pig.

cuyo ('ku·jo) *poss.adj.* whose; of whom; of which. —*n.m., colloq.* lover; beau.

czar (θar; sar) *n.m.* = **zar.**

czarevitz (θa·re'βits; sa-) *n.m.* = **zarevitz.**

czarina (θa'ri·na; sa-) *n.f.* = **zarina.**

CH

Ch, ch (tʃe) *n.f.* 4th letter of the Spanish alphabet.

cha (tʃa) *n.m.* shah.

chabacano (tʃa·βa'ka·no) *adj.* awkward; crude; tasteless; vulgar. —**chabacanería,** *n.f.* vulgarity; inane act or expression.

chabeta (tʃa'βe·ta) *n.f.* = **chaveta.**

chacal (tʃa'kal) *n.m.* jackal.

chacarero (tʃa·ka're·ro) *n.m. & adj., Amer.* farmhand.

chacó (tʃa'ko) *n.m.* shako.

chacota (tʃa'ko·ta) *n.f.* **1,** frolic. **2,** derision.

chacotear (tʃa·ko·te'ar) *v.i.* to banter; jest. —**chacotero** (-'te·ro) *adj.* waggish. —*n.m.* wag.

chacra ('tʃa·kra) *n.f., Amer.* small ranch or farm.

cháchara ('tʃa·tʃa·ra) *n.f.* chatter; prattle. —**chacharear,** *v.i.* to chatter.

chafar (tʃa'far) *v.t.* **1,** to flatten; level. **2,** to muss; rumple (clothing). —**chafadura,** *n.f.* leveling; flattening.

chafarrinar (tʃa·fa·rri'nar) *v.t.* to blot; taint.

chaflán (tʃa'flan) *n.m.* bevel; chamfer. —**chaflanar** (-'nar) *v.t.* = **achaflanar.**

chagra ('tʃa·ɣra) *n.f., Amer.* = **chacra.** —*adj. & n.m. & f., Amer.* peasant; rustic.

chal (tʃal) *n.m.* shawl.

chalado (tʃa'la·ðo) *adj. colloq.* **1,** eccentric; odd. **2,** madly in love; smitten.

chalán (tʃa'lan) *n.m.* **1,** huckster. **2,** horse dealer. **3,** *Amer.* broncobuster.

chalana (tʃa'la·na) *n.f.* barge; lighter.

chalanear (tʃa·la·ne'ar) *v.t.* **1,** to trade astutely. **2,** to deal in horses.

chalar (tʃa'lar) *v.t.* to drive (someone) mad. —**chalarse,** *v.r.* to be infatuated; to be smitten.

chaleco (tʃa'le·ko) *n.m.* vest.

chalet (tʃa'let) *n.m.* chalet.

chalina (tʃa'li·na) *n.f.* scarf; *Amer.* necktie.

chalote (tʃa'lo·te) *n.m.* shallot.

chalupa (tʃa'lu·pa) *n.f.* **1,** sloop. **2,** *Amer.* canoe. **3,** *Amer.* corncake.

chamaco (tʃa'ma·ko) *n.m., Mex.* boy. —**chamaca** (-ka) *n.f., Mex.* girl.

chamán (tʃa'man) *n.m.* shaman. —**chamanismo,** *n.m.* shamanism.

chamarasca (tʃa·ma'ras·ka) *n.f.* **1,** brushwood. **2,** brushwood fire.

chamarra (tʃa'ma·rra) *n.f.* a coarsely woven jacket; *Mex.* outdoor jacket.

chamarreta (tʃa·ma'rre·ta) *n.f.* **1,** loose jacket. **2,** *Amer.* poncho.

chambelán (tʃam·be'lan) *n.m.* chamberlain.

chambón (tʃam'bon) *adj.* clumsy; bungling. —*n.m.* [*fem.* **-bona**] blunderer; bungler. —**chambonada,** *n.f.* blunder; botch. —**chambonear,** *v.i.* to bungle; fumble.

chambra (tʃam·bra) *n.f.* woman's jacket.

chamicera (tʃa·mi'θe·ra; -'se·ra) *n.f.* burned-out woodland.

chamorro (tʃa'mo·rro) *adj.* shorn. —**chamorra,** *n.f.* shorn head.

champaña (tʃam'pa·ɲa) *n.m.* champagne.

champú (tʃam'pu) *n.m.* shampoo.

champurrar (tʃam·pu'rrar) *v.t.* to mix (drinks).

chamuscar (tʃa·mus'kar) *v.t.* [*infl.:* **tocar,** 7] to singe; scorch; sear.

chamusquina (tʃa·mus'ki·na) *n.f.* **1,** scorching; singeing. **2,** quarreling; wrangling. —**oler a chamusquina,** *colloq.* to smell fishy.

chancear (tʃan·θe'ar; -se'ar) *v.i.* to jest; fool. —**chancearse con,** to tease; banter.

chancero (tʃan'θe·ro; -'se·ro) *adj.* playful; jesting.

chancla (tʃan·kla) *n.f.* **1,** slipper. **2,** worn-out shoe. —**chancleta,** *n.f.* slipper. —**chanclo,** *n.m.* overshoe.

chancro (tʃan·kro) *n.m.* chancre.

chancho (tʃan·tʃo) *adj., colloq.* dirty. —*n.m., colloq.* hog; pig.

chanchullo (tʃan'tʃu·ʎo; -jo) *n.m., colloq.* trickery; collusion.

chanfaina (tʃan'fai·na) *n.f.* **1,** kind of stew; olio. **2,** hodgepodge; mixup.

changador (tʃan·ga'ðor) *n.m., Amer.* porter; handyman.

chango (tʃan·go) *n.m., Amer., colloq.* **1,** pest. **2,** whimsical person; wag. —*adj., Amer., colloq.* **1,** cumbersome; tiresome. **2,** whimsical; waggish.

chantaje (tʃan'ta·xe) *n.m.* blackmail. —**chantajear,** *v.t.* to blackmail. —**chantajista,** *n.m. & f.* blackmailer.

chantar (tʃan'tar) *v.t.* **1,** to put on; stick on; jam on. **2,** to tell (something) straight to someone's face. —**chantarse,** *v.r., cards* to stand pat.

chanza (tʃan·θa; -sa) *n.f.* joke; jest.

chapa (tʃa·pa) *n.f.* **1,** metal plate; foil. **2,** veneer. **3,** = **chapeta.** **4,** *colloq.* good sense; prudence. **5,** *Amer.* lock. **6,** *Amer.* auto license plate. —**chapas,** *n.f.pl.* a cointossing game.

chapalear (tʃa·pa·le'ar) *v.i.* to splash in the water; paddle.

chapaleteo (tʃa·pa·le'te·o) *n.m.* lapping or splashing of water.

chapapote (tʃa·pa'po·te) *n.m., Amer.* asphalt.

chapar (tʃa'par) *v.t.* to plate; coat. —**chapado a la antigua,** old-fashioned.

chaparral (tʃa·pa'rral) *n.m.* thicket; chaparral.

chaparrear (tʃa·pa·rre'ar) *v.i.* to rain heavily. —**chaparrón,** *n.m.* downpour.

chaparreras (tʃa·pa'rre·ras) *n.f. pl., Amer.* cowboy chaps; riding chaps.

chaparro (tʃa'pa·rro) *n.m.* **1,** evergreen oak. **2,** *Amer.* chubby, short person. —*adj.* short and thick.

chapear (tʃa·pe'ar) *v.t.* **1,** to inlay with metal. **2,** *Cuba* to clear (brush) with a machete.

chapeo (tʃaˈpe·o) *n.m.*, *colloq.* hat.

chapeta (tʃaˈpe·ta) *n.f.* rosy cheek.

chapitel (tʃa·piˈtel) *n.m.* **1**, *archit.* capital. **2**, spire.

chapotear (tʃa·po·teˈar) *v.t.* to moisten *(with a sponge or cloth)*. —*v.i.* = **chapalear.**

chapoteo (tʃa·poˈte·o) *n.m.* **1**, moistening; sponging. **2**, splashing.

chapucear (tʃa·pu·θeˈar; -seˈar) *v.t.* to bungle; work clumsily.

chapucería (tʃa·pu·θeˈri·a; -seˈri·a) *n.f.* bungle; botch.

chapucero (tʃa·puˈθe·ro; -seˈro) *adj.* clumsy; sloppy. —*n.m.* bungler.

chapulín (tʃa·puˈlin) *n.m.*, *Amer.* grasshopper; locust.

chapurrear (tʃa·pu·rreˈar) *v.t. & i.* to jabber. *Also,* **chapurrar.**

chapuz (tʃaˈpuθ; -ˈpus) *n.m.* **1**, ducking. **2**, bungle; botch.

chapuza (tʃaˈpu·θa; -sa) *n.f.* bungle; botch.

chapuzar (tʃa·puˈθar; -ˈsar) *v.t.* [*infl.:* rezar, 10] to duck; immerse. —*v.i.* to duck; dive.

chapuzón (tʃa·puˈθon; -ˈson) *n.m.* dip; ducking.

chaqué (tʃaˈke) *n.m.* cutaway; morning coat.

chaqueta (tʃaˈke·ta) *n.f.* jacket. —**chaquetón,** *n.m.* coat.

chaquete (tʃaˈke·te) *n.m.* backgammon.

charada (tʃaˈra·ða) *n.f.* charade.

charamusca (tʃa·raˈmus·ka) *n.f.*, *Mex.* candy twist. —**charamuscas,** *n.f.pl.*, *Amer.* firewood.

charanga (tʃaˈran·ga) *n.f.* **1**, fanfare. **2**, brass band.

charca (ˈtʃar·ka) *n.f.* pond. —**charco** (-ko) *n.m.* puddle.

charla (ˈtʃar·la) *n.f.* conversation; chat.

charlar (tʃarˈlar) *v.i.* **1**, to chatter; prate. **2**, to converse; chat.

charlatán (tʃar·la·ˈtan) *n.m.* **1**, charlatan. **2**, prattler. —*adj.* talkative; garrulous.

charlatanería (tʃar·la·ta·neˈri·a) *n.f.* **1**, charlatanism. **2**, garrulity.

charnela (tʃarˈne·la) *n.f.* hinge; joint; *mech.* knuckle.

charol (tʃaˈrol) *n.m.* **1**, patent leather. **2**, varnish. —**charolar** (-ˈlar) *v.t.* to varnish; polish.

charola (tʃaˈro·la) *n.f.*, *Mex.* tray.

charpa (ˈtʃar·pa) *n.f.* **1**, holster. **2**, *surg.* sling.

charqui (ˈtʃar·ki) *n.m.*, *Amer.* jerked beef. —**charquear,** *v.t.* to dry; cure.

charrada (tʃaˈrra·ða) *n.f.* **1**, rustic speech or action. **2**, gaudiness.

charrán (tʃaˈrran) *adj.* roguish. —*n.m.* rogue; knave.

charrería (tʃa·rreˈri·a) *n.f.* gaudiness; tawdriness.

charretera (tʃa·rreˈte·ra) *n.f.* epaulet.

charro (ˈtʃa·rro) *adj.* **1**, rustic. **2**, gaudy. —*n.m.*, *Mex.* horseman.

chascar (tʃasˈkar) *v.t.* [*infl.:* tocar, 7] **1**, to click (the tongue). **2**, to chew noisily; munch. —*v.i.* to crack; snap.

chascarrillo (tʃas·ka·ˈri·ʎo; -jo) *n.m.* joke; anecdote.

chasco (ˈtʃas·ko) *n.m.* **1**, joke; prank. **2**, disappointment. —**llevarse un chasco,** to be disappointed.

chasis (ˈtʃa·sis) *n.m. sing & pl.* chassis.

chasquear (tʃas·keˈar) *v.t.* **1**, to trick; dupe. **2**, to disappoint; disillusion. **3**, to crack (a whip).

chasqui (ˈtʃas·ki) *n.m.*, *Amer.* messenger.

chasquido (tʃasˈki·ðo) *n.m.* crack *(of a whip);* cracking sound; snap *(of the fingers).*

chata (ˈtʃa·ta) *n.f.* **1**, bedpan. **2**, *Amer.* barge; scow. **3**, *Amer.* flatcar.

chatarra (tʃaˈta·rra) *n.f.* scrap iron. —**chatarrería** (-rreˈri·a) *n.f.* junkyard.

chato (ˈtʃa·to) *adj.* **1**, flat; flattened; blunt. **2**, flat-nosed. —*n.m.* **1**, *colloq.* wine glass. **2**, [*fem.* **chata**] darling.

chauvinismo (tʃau·βiˈnis·mo) *n.m.* chauvinism. —**chauvinista,** *n.m. & f.* chauvinist. —*adj.* chauvinistic.

chaval (tʃaˈβal) *n.m.*, *colloq.* boy; kid. —**chavala** (-la) *n.f. colloq.* girl.

chaveta *also,* **chabeta** (tʃaˈβe·ta) *n.f.* **1**, forelock. **2**, pin; cotter pin. **3**, wedge. —**perder la chaveta,** to go out of one's mind.

chavo *n.m.*, *Mex.* kid; guy. —**chava,** *n.f.* kid; girl.

che (tʃe) *interj.*, *Amer.* hey!; ho! —*n.m.*, *colloq.* fellow; guy.

checo (ˈtʃe·ko) *adj. & n.m.* Czech.

checoslovaco *also,* **checoeslovaco** (-es·loˈβa·ko) *adj. & n.m.* Czechoslovak; Czechoslovakian.

chelín (tʃeˈlin) *n.m.* shilling.

chepa (ˈtʃe·pa) *n.f.* hump; hunch.

cheque ('tʃe·ke) *n.m.* check; bank draft. —**talonario de cheques,** checkbook.

cherna ('tʃer·na) *n.f.* sea bass.

cheslón (tʃes'lon) *n.m.* chaise longue.

cheviot (tʃe'βjot) *n.m.* [*pl.* **cheviots** (-'βjots)] cheviot.

chica ('tʃi·ka) *n.f.* 1, little girl. 2, girl servant.

chicano (tʃi'ka·no) *adj.* & *n.m.* Mexican-American; Chicano.

chicle ('tʃi·kle) *n.m.* chicle; chewing gum.

chico ('tʃi·ko) *adj.* 1, small. 2, young. —*n.m.* little boy.

chicoria (tʃi'ko·rja) *n.f.* = **achicoria.**

chicote (tʃi'ko·te) *n.m.* 1, sturdy youngster. 2, *naut.* end of a rope or cable. 3, *colloq.* cigar; cigar butt. 4, *Amer.* whip. 5, *Amer.* whiplash.

chicotear (tʃi·ko·te'ar) *v.t. Amer.* 1, to whip; flog. 2, to kill. —*v.i., Amer.* to quarrel.

chicoteo (tʃi·ko'te·o) *n.m., Amer.* 1, whipping; flogging. 2, killing. 3, quarreling.

chicuelo (tʃi'kwe·lo) *adj., n.m.* child; boy.

chicha ('tʃi·tʃa) *n.f., Amer.* 1, corn liquor. 2, *slang* breast.

chícharo ('tʃi·tʃa·ro) *n.m.* 1, pea. 2, *Amer.* poor cigar. 3, *Amer.* apprentice.

chicharra (tʃi'tʃa·rra) *n.f.* 1, cicada. 2, rattler. 3, *colloq.* chatterbox.

chicharrón (tʃi·tʃa'rron) *n.m.* 1, crisply fried pork rind. 2, burnt piece of meat.

chichear (tʃi·tʃe'ar) *v.t.* & *i.* to hiss. —**chicheo** (-'tʃe·o) *n.m.* hissing.

chichón (tʃi'tʃon) *n.m.* bump or lump on the head. —*adj., Amer.* joking; jesting. —**chichona,** *adj. fem., Amer.* bosomy.

chifla ('tʃi·fla) *n.f.* whistle; hoot.

chiflado (tʃi'fla·ðo) *adj., colloq.* 1, daffy; nutty. 2, enamored; smitten.

chifladura (tʃi·fla'ðu·ra) *n.f.* 1, whistling. 2, hissing. 3, mania; fad.

chiflar (tʃi'flar) *v.t.* to hiss; ridicule. —*v.i.* to whistle. —**chiflarse,** *v.r.* 1, to go crazy. 2, to fall in love.

chifle ('tʃi·fle) *n.m.* whistle.

chiflido (tʃi'fli·ðo) *n.m.* sound of a whistle.

chiflón (tʃi'flon) *n.m., Amer.* draft (*of air*).

chile ('tʃi·le) *n.m.* 1, chili. 2, red pepper.

chilindrina (tʃi·lin'dri·na) *n.f., colloq.* bagatelle.

chilla ('tʃi·ʎa; -ja) *n.f.* clapboard.

chillar (tʃi'ʎar; -'jar) *v.i.* 1, to shriek; scream; screech. 2, to creak; squeak. 3, *Amer.* to balk; protest. —**chillido** (-'ʎi·ðo; -'ji·ðo) *n.m.* shriek; scream.

chillón (tʃi'ʎon; -'jon) *adj.* 1, shrieking. 2, shrill. 3, gaudy. 4, *Amer.* whining. —*n.m.* screamer; shrieker.

chimenea (tʃi·me'ne·a) *n.f.* 1, chimney; smokestack. 2, fireplace.

chimpancé (tʃim·pan'θe; -'se) *n.m.* chimpanzee.

china ('tʃi·na) *n.f.* 1, pebble. 2, porcelain; chinaware. 3, *Amer.* maid; servant. 4, *W.I.* orange.

chinapo (tʃi'na·po) *n.m., Mex.* obsidian.

chinche ('tʃin·tʃe) *n.f.* 1, bedbug. 2, thumbtack. —*n.m.* & *f.* boring person. —**chincharrero** (-tʃa'rre·ro) *n.m.* place infested with bugs.

chinchilla (tʃin'tʃi·ʎa; -ja) *n.f.* chinchilla.

chinchorrería (tʃin·tʃo·rre'ri·a) *n.f.* malicious gossip; false report.

chinchorro (tʃin'tʃo·rro) *n.m.* small rowboat.

chinela (tʃi'ne·la) *n.f.* slipper.

chinero (tʃi'ne·ro) *n.m.* 1, china closet. 2, cupboard.

chinesco (tʃi'nes·ko) *adj.* Chinese.

chinito (tʃi'ni·to) *n.m., Amer.* [*fem.* -**ta**] darling; dear.

chino ('tʃi·no) *adj.* & *n.m.* Chinese.

chiquear (tʃi·ke'ar) *v.t., Cuba; Mex.* to fondle.

chiquero (tʃi'ke·ro) *n.m.* 1, pigsty. 2, *colloq.* messy place.

chiquitico (tʃi·ki'ti·ko) *adj.* tiny; wee. *Also,* **chiquirritico** (-rri'ti·ko).

chiquitín (tʃi·ki'tin) *adj.* [*fem.* -**tina**] tiny. —*n.m.* [*fem.* -**tina**] little child.

chiquito (tʃi'ki·to) *adj.* small; tiny. —*n.m.* little boy; tot. —**chiquita,** *n.f.* little girl.

chirigota (tʃi·ri'yo·ta) *n.f.* joke; jest.

chirimbolo (tʃi·rim'bo·lo) *n.m.* utensil; *pl.* pots and pans; trappings.

chirimía (tʃi·ri'mi·a) *n.f.* hornpipe.

chiripa (tʃi'ri·pa) *n.f.* 1, *billiards* fluke. 2, stroke of good luck.

chirivía (tʃi·ri'βi·a) *n.f.* parsnip.

chirona (tʃi'ro·na) *n.f., colloq.* jail.

chirriar (tʃiˈrrjar) *v.i.* **1,** to hiss; sizzle. **2,** to squeak; chirp. **3,** *colloq.* to sing off key.

chirrido (tʃiˈrri·ðo) *n.m.* **1,** chirping. **2,** shrill sound.

chisguete (tʃisˈɣe·te) *n.m., colloq.* spurt; squirt.

chisme (ˈtʃis·me) *n.m.* gossip; mischievous tattle. —**chismear** (-ˈar) *v.i.* to gossip; tattle. —**chismero,** also, **chismoso,** *adj.* gossiping. —*n.m.* gossip.

chismografía (tʃis·mo·ɣraˈfi·a) *n.f., colloq.* gossip.

chispa (ˈtʃis·pa) *n.f.* **1,** spark. **2,** sparkle. **3,** small particle; bit. **4,** small amount; drop. **5,** wit; acumen. **6,** *colloq.* tipsiness. **7,** *Amer.* false rumor. —**chisparse,** *v.r., Amer., colloq.* to get tipsy.

chispazo (tʃisˈpa·θo; -so) *n.m.* **1,** spark. **2,** burn caused by a spark.

chispeante (tʃis·peˈan·te) *adj.* witty; brilliant.

chispear (tʃis·peˈar) *v.i.* to sparkle; scintillate.

chispo (ˈtʃis·po) *adj., colloq.* tipsy. —*n.m., colloq.* nip; small drink.

chisporrotear (tʃis·po·rro·teˈar) *v.i.* **1,** to sizzle; sputter. **2,** to throw off sparks.

chisporroteo (tʃis·po·rro·teˈo) *n.m.* **1,** sizzling. **2,** sparkling.

chistar (tʃisˈtar) *v.i.* to mumble; mutter.

chiste (ˈtʃis·te) *n.m.* joke; witty sally. —**chistoso,** *adj.* humorous; witty.

chistera (tʃisˈte·ra) *n.f.* **1,** top hat. **2,** fish basket; creel.

¡chito! (ˈtʃi·to) *interj., colloq.* silence!; hist! *Also,* **chitón** (-ˈton).

chiva (ˈtʃi·βa) *n.f.* **1,** female goat. **2,** *Amer.* goatee. —**chivo,** *n.m.* male goat.

chocante (tʃoˈkan·te) *adj.* **1,** surprising; shocking. **2,** funny; amusing. **3,** *Amer.* impertinent; annoying.

chocar (tʃoˈkar) *v.* [*infl.:* **tocar,** 7] —*v.i.* **1,** to collide; clash. **2,** to be surprising; be shocking.

chocarrear (tʃo·ka·rreˈar) *v.i.* to joke; clown. —**chocarrería,** *n.f.* buffoonery; vulgarity. —**chocarrero,** *adj.* clownish; buffoonish. —*n.m.* buffoon; wiseacre.

choclo (ˈtʃo·klo) *n.m.* **1,** clog; sabot. **2,** *Amer.* ear of corn.

chocolate (tʃo·koˈla·te) *n.m.* chocolate. —**chocolatería,** *n.f.* **1,** chocolate shop. **2,** chocolate factory.

—**chocolatero,** *n.m.* **1,** chocolate maker. **2,** chocolate seller. —*adj.* fond of chocolate.

chocha (ˈtʃo·tʃa) *n.f.* woodcock.

chochear (tʃo·tʃeˈar) *v.i.* to dote; act senilely.

chochera (tʃoˈtʃe·ra) *n.f.* dotage; senility. *Also,* **chochez** (-ˈtʃeθ; -ˈtʃes) *n.f.*

chocho (ˈtʃo·tʃo) *adj.* **1,** doting. **2,** senile.

chofer (tʃoˈfer) *also,* **chófer** (ˈtʃo·fer) *n.m.* chauffeur.

chofeta (tʃoˈfe·ta) *n.f.* chafing dish.

cholo (ˈtʃo·lo) *n.m., Amer.* **1,** halfbreed. **2,** Indian.

cholla (ˈtʃo·ʎa; -ja) *n.f., colloq.* **1,** skull; head. **2,** brains; talent. **3,** *bot.* cholla.

chopo (ˈtʃo·po) *n.m.* black poplar.

choque (ˈtʃo·ke) *n.m.* **1,** shock; clash; collision. **2,** skirmish; conflict. **3,** dispute.

choque (ˈtʃo·ke) *v., pres.subjve.* of **chocar.**

choqué (tʃoˈke) *v., 1st. pers. sing.pret.* of **chocar.**

choquezuela (tʃo·keˈθwe·la; -ˈswe·la) *n.f.* kneecap.

chorizo (tʃoˈri·θo; -so) *n.m.* sausage.

chorlito (tʃorˈli·to) *n.m.* curlew; gray plover. —**cabeza de chorlito,** addle-brained person.

chorrear (tʃo·rreˈar) *v.i.* to drip; spout; gush. —**chorreo** (-ˈrre·o) *n.m.* dripping; spouting.

chorrera (tʃoˈrre·ra) *n.f.* **1,** spout. **2,** *colloq.* gush; spate. **3,** rapids. **4,** trace left by trickling.

chorro (ˈtʃo·rro) *n.m.* **1,** gush; spurt. **2,** stream.

chotacabras (tʃo·taˈka·βras) *n.m. sing. & pl.* **1,** nighthawk. **2,** goatsucker.

chotear (tʃo·teˈar) *v.i., Amer.* to mock; jeer; banter. —**chotearse de,** *colloq.* to tease; pull the leg of.

choza (ˈtʃo·θa; -sa) *n.f.* hut; hovel; shanty.

chubasco (tʃuˈβas·ko) *n.m.* squall.

chúcaro (ˈtʃu·ka·ro) *adj., Amer.* **1,** untamed. **2,** *fig.* diffident.

chucruta (tʃuˈkru·ta) *n.f.* sauerkraut.

chuchería (tʃu·tʃeˈri·a) *n.f.* trifle; trinket.

chucho (ˈtʃu·tʃo) *n.m., colloq.* dog.

chueco (ˈtʃwe·ko) *adj., Amer.* **1,** crooked; lopsided. **2,** bowlegged; knockkneed.

chufar (tʃu'far) *v.i.* to mock; scorn.
chufeta (tʃu'fe·ta) *n.f.* **1,** jest; joke. **2,** chafing dish.
chufleta (tʃu'fle·ta) *n.f.* **1,** taunt; jeer. **2,** jest; joke.
chuleta (tʃu'le·ta) *n.f.* cutlet; chop.
chulo ('tʃu·lo) *adj.* **1,** roguish. **2,** *Amer.* handsome; graceful. —*n.m.* **1,** dandy. **2,** clownish person. **3,** pimp. **4,** bullfighter's assistant.
chumacera (tʃu·ma'θe·ra; -'se·ra) *n.f.* **1,** *naut.* rowlock. **2,** *mech.* bearing; journal bearing.
chumbera (tʃum'be·ra) *n.f.* prickly pear cactus. —**higo chumbo** ('tʃum·bo) prickly pear.
chunga ('tʃun·ga) *n.f.* banter; jest.
chupada (tʃu'pa·ða) *n.f.* **1,** suck; sucking. **2,** sip; nip. **3,** *Amer.* puff; draw *(on a cigar or cigarette)*.
chupado (tʃu'pa·ðo) *adj. colloq.* gaunt; emaciated; shriveled.
chupador (tʃu·pa'ðor) *adj.* sucking; absorbent. —*n.m.* **1,** sucker. **2,** teething ring. **3,** [*fem.* -**dora**] heavy drinker; tippler.
chupaflor (tʃu·pa'flor) *n.m. Amer.* hummingbird. *Also,* **chuparrosa** (-'rro·sa).
chupar (tʃu'par) *v.t. & i.* to suck; draw; sip; absorb. —**chuparse,** *v.r.* to shrivel up.
chupete (tʃu'pe·te) *n.m.* **1,** nipple of a feeding bottle. **2,** teething ring.

3, *Amer.* pacifier. **4,** *Amer.* lollipop. —**de chupete,** *colloq.* splendid; great.
chupón (tʃu'pon) *n.m.* **1,** *bot.* sucker. **2,** *mech.* plunger. **3,** *colloq.* swindler.
churrasco (tʃu'rras·ko) *n.m., Amer.* roasted meat; barbecue. —**churrasquear** (-ke'ar) *v.t.* to roast; barbecue.
churre ('tʃu·rre) *n.m.* oozing grease; sweaty, greasy thing. —**churriento** (-'rrjen·to) *adj.* greasy.
churrigueresco (tʃu·rri·ye·'res·ko) *adj.* **1,** tawdry. **2,** rococo; in the style of Churriguera, 18th-century Spanish architect. —**churriguerismo,** *n.m., archit.* the style of Churriguera.
churro ('tʃu·rro) *n.m.* a fritter or cruller of oblong shape.
churruscar (tʃu·rrus'kar) [*infl.:* **tocar, 7**] *v.t.* to frizzle; make crisp, as by frying.
chuscada (tʃus'ka·ða) *n.f.* drollery; jest.
chusco ('tʃus·ko) *adj.* droll; amusing. —**perro chusco,** *Amer.* mongrel dog.
chusma ('tʃus·ma) *n.f.* rabble; mob.
chuzo ('tʃu·θo; -so) *n.m.* **1,** pike; lance. **2,** *Amer.* horsewhip.

D

D, d (de) *n.f.* 5th letter of the Spanish alphabet.
dable ('da·βle) *adj.* feasible; easy.
daca ('da·ka) *contr. of* **da acá,** give (it) here. —**andar al daca y toma,** *colloq.* to be at cross purposes.
dáctilo ('dak·ti·lo) *n.m.* **1,** *pros.* dactyl. **2,** *zoöl.* finger; toe. —**dactilado,** *adj.* finger-shaped. —**dactílico** (-'ti·li·ko) *adj.* dactylic.
dactilografía (dak·ti·lo·yra'fi·a) *n.f.* typewriting. —**dactilógrafo** (-'lo·yra·fo) *n.m.* [*fem.* –**grafa**] typist.
dádiva ('da·ði·βa) *n.f.* gift; grant. —**dadivoso,** *adj.* generous; munificent.
dado ('da·ðo) *n.m.* **1,** die; (*pl.*) dice. **2,** bushing; pivot collar. —*v., p.p. of* **dar.**

dador (da'ðor) *adj.* giving. —*n.m.* donor.
daga ('da·ya) *n.f.* dagger.
daguerrotipo (da·ye·rro'ti·po) *n.m.* daguerreotype.
dalia ('da·lja) *n.f.* dahlia.
daltonismo (dal·to'nis·mo) *n.m.* color blindness; Daltonism. —**daltoniano** (-to'nja·no) *n.m.* colorblind person. —*adj.* color-blind.
dallar (da'ʎar; -'jar) *v.t.* to mow.
dalle ('da·ʎe; -je) *n.m.* scythe; sickle.
dálmata ('dal·ma·ta) *adj. & n.m. & f.* Dalmatian.
dama ('da·ma) *n.f.* **1,** lady. **2,** checkers king. **3,** *chess; cards* queen. —**juego de damas,** checkers.
damajuana (da·ma'xwa·na) *n.f.* demijohn.

damasco (da·'mas·ko) *n.m.* **1,** damask *(fabric)* **2,** damson plum *(fruit);* apricot.

damisela (da·mi·'se·la) *n.f.* damsel.

damnificar (dam·ni·fi·'kar) *v.t.* [*infl.: tocar,* **7**] to injure; damage. —**damnificador,** *adj.* damaging. —*n.m.* injurer.

dance ('dan·θe; -se) *v., pres.subjve. of* **danzar.**

dancé (dan'θe; -'se) *v., 1st pers. sing. pret. of* **danzar.**

danés (da·'nes) *adj.* Danish. —*n.m.* **1,** Dane. **2,** Danish language.

danesa (da·'ne·sa) *n.f.* Danish woman.

danta ('dan·ta) *n.f.* tapir.

danza ('dan·θa; -sa) *n.f.* dance; ball. —**danza de figuras,** square dance.

danzante (dan'θan·te; -'san·te) *n.m.* **1,** dancer. **2,** *slang* hustler.

danzar (dan'θar; -'sar) *v.t.* [*infl.: rezar,* **10**] to dance.

danzarín (dan·θa'rin; sa'rin) *n.m.* **1,** dancer. **2,** *slang* meddler.

danzón (dan'θon; -'son) *n.m.* a Cuban dance.

dañado (da'ɲa·ðo) *adj.* **1,** spoiled; injured. **2,** wicked; damned.

dañar (da'ɲar) *v.t.* to damage; hurt; spoil.

dañino (da'ɲi·no) *adj.* harmful; noxious.

daño ('da·ɲo) *n.m.* **1,** damage. **2,** prejudice. **3,** loss. **4,** nuisance.

dañoso (da'ɲo·so) *adj.* = **dañino.**

dar (dar) *v.t.* [*infl.: 43*] **1,** to give, **2,** to supply; deliver. **3,** to grant; concede; yield. **4,** to emit. **5,** to cause. **6,** *theat.* to present. **7,** to deal (cards). **8,** to strike (the hour). —*v.i.* **1,** to forecast. **2,** to look out (on). **3,** to strike blows (on); give a beating (to). —**darse,** *v.r.* **1,** to surrender. **2,** to happen. —**dar con,** to find. —**dar de sí,** to stretch; give. —**dar en,** to hit upon; succeed in striking (a mark). —**dar por sentado,** to assume. —**dárselas de,** to boast of. —**darse por, 1,** to think oneself (to be something). **2,** *fol. by inf.* to take a notion to.

dardo ('dar·ðo) *n.m.* **1,** dart. **2,** *fig.* sarcasm.

dares y tomares ('da·res·i·to'ma·res) *colloq.* **1,** give and take. **2,** quarrel; dispute.

dársena ('dar·se·na) *n.f.* harbor; dockyard.

data ('da·ta) *n.f.* **1,** date. **2,** *comm.* item of a bill.

datar (da'tar) *v.t.* **1,** to date. **2,** *comm.* to credit. —*v.i.* to date; date back (to).

dátil ('da·til) *n.m.* date *(fruit).*

dativo (da'ti·βo) *adj.* & *n.m. gram.* dative. —**datos,** *n.m.pl.* data.

dato ('da·to) *n.m.* datum; fact.

de (de) *prep., denoting* **1,** (derivation) of; from; by. **2,** (possession) of; belonging to. **3,** (cause) from; because of. **4,** (character; material) of; made of; with. **5,** (time; measurement) of. **6,** (agency) by. **7,** (subject) about; concerning. **8,** (comparison) than: *mas de diez metros,* more than ten meters. **9,** (origin) from; of. **10,** *in adverbial phrases of manner* in; on; with: *caer de rodillas,* to fall on one's knees. **11,** *fol. by inf.,* equivalent to a conditional clause: *de correr yo ...,* if I were to run ....

dé (de) *v., pres.subjve. of* **dar.**

deán (de'an) *n.m., eccles.* dean.

debajo (de'βa·xo) *adv.* under; underneath; below.

debate (de'βa·te) *n.m.* debate; discussion; contest; quarrel.

debatir (de·βa'tir) *v.t.* **1,** to argue; debate. **2,** to battle; fight. —**debatirse,** *v.r.* to struggle helplessly; founder. —**debatible,** *adj.* arguable.

debe ('de·βe) *n., bookkeeping* debit; debit side of a ledger.

debelar (de·βe'lar) *v.t.* to subdue; conquer. —**debelación,** *n.f.* conquest.

deber (de'βer) *n.m.* duty; obligation; debt. —*v.t.* to owe; —*aux.v.* to be obliged (to); to have the duty (to); ought (to); must.

debido (de'βi·ðo) *adj.* due; just; exact; proper. —**debidamente,** *adv.* justly; duly; properly.

débil ('de·βil) *adj.* weak; feeble; debilitated. —**debilidad,** *n.f.* debility; weakness.

debilitar (de·βi·li'tar) *v.t.* to debilitate; weaken. —**debilitación,** *n.f.* debilitation.

débito ('de·βi·to) *n.m.* **1,** debt. **2,** *comm.* debit.

debutar (de·βu'tar) *v.t.* to begin. —*v.i.* to make one's debut. —**debutante,** *adj.* beginning. —*n.m. & f.* beginner; novice; debutante.

década ('de·ka·ða) *n.f.* decade.

decadente (de·ka'ðen·te) *adj.* &

n.m. & *f.* decadent. —**decadencia,** *n.f.* decadence.

decaedro (de·ka'e·ðro) *n.m.* decahedron.

decaer (de·ka'er) *v.i.* [*infl.:* **caer,** 39] to decay; decline; fade.

decágono (de'ka·yo·no) *n.m.* decagon.

decagramo (de·ka'yra·mo) *n.m.* decagram.

decaimiento (de·kai'mjen·to) *n.m.* **1,** decay; decline. **2,** weakness.

decalcomanía (de·kal·ko·ma'ni·a) *n.f.* decalcomania.

decalitro (de·ka'li·tro) *n.m.* decaliter.

decálogo (de'ka·lo·yo) *n.m.* decalogue.

decámetro (de'ka·me·tro) *n.m.* decameter.

decampar (de·kam'par) *v.i.* to decamp.

decano (de'ka·no) *n.m.* dean; senior member. —**decanato,** *n.m.* deanship.

decantar (de·kan'tar) *v.t.* **1,** to decant; pour. **2,** to exaggerate; exalt.

decapitar (de·ka·pi'tar) *v.t.* to decapitate. —**decapitación,** *n.f.* decapitation.

decárea (de'ka·re·a) *n.f.* decare.

decasílabo (de·ka'si·la·βo) *adj.* decasyllabic. —*n.m.* decasyllable.

decastéreo (de·ka'ste·re·o) *n.m.* decastere.

decatlon (de'ka·tlon) *n.m.* decathlon.

decena (de'θe·na; -'se·na) *n.f.* a quantity of ten.

decenal (de·θe'nal; -se'nal) *adj.* decennial.

decencia (de'θen·θja; -'sen·sja) *n.f.* decency; propriety. —**decente,** *adj.* decent; decorous.

decenio (de'θe·njo; -'se·njo) *n.m.* **1,** decade. **2,** decennial.

deceno (de'θe·no; -'se·no) *adj.* & *n.m.* tenth.

decentar (de·θen'tar; de·sen-) *v.t.* [*infl.:* **pensar,** 27] **1,** to use for the first time. **2,** to begin eroding, consuming, damaging (something). **3,** to injure.

decepción (de·θep'θjon; -sep'sjon) *n.f.* deception; illusion. —**decepcionar** (-'nar) *v.t.* to disappoint; disillusion.

deceso (de'θe·so; -'se·so) *n.m.* decease; death.

decibel (de·θi'βel; de·si-) *n.m.* decibel. *Also,* **decibelio** (-'βe·ljo).

decidir (de·θi'ðir; de·si-) *v.t.* to decide; resolve. —**decidirse,** *v.r.* to resolve; determine. —**decidido,** *adj.* decided; determined.

deciduo (de'θi·ðwo; -'si·ðwo) *adj.* deciduous.

decigramo (de·θi'yra·mo; de·si-) *n.m.* decigram.

decilitro (de·θi'li·tro; de·si-) *n.m.* deciliter.

decillón (de·θi'ʎon; de·si'jon) *n.m.* an octillion decillion; *Brit.* decillion.

décima ('de·θi·ma; 'de·si-) *n.f.* **1,** tenth; tenth part. **2,** = **diezmo.**

decimal (de·θi'mal; de·si-) *adj.* decimal.

decímetro (de'θi·me·tro; 'de·si-) *n.m.* decimeter.

décimo ('de·θi·mo; 'de·si-) *adj.* & *n.m.* tenth.

décimoctavo (de·θi·mok'ta·βo; de·si-) *adj.* & *n.m.* eighteenth.

décimocuarto (de·θi·mo'kwar·to; de·si-) *adj.* & *n.m.* fourteenth.

décimonono (de·θi·mo'no·no; de·si) *adj.* & *n.m.* nineteenth.

décimoquinto (de·θi·mo'kin·to; de·si-) *adj.* & *n.m.* fifteenth.

décimoséptimo (de·θi·mo'sep·ti·mo; de·si-) *adj.* & *n.m.* seventeenth.

décimosexto (de·θi·mo'seks·to; de·si-) *adj.* & *n.m.* sixteenth.

décimotercero (de·θi·mo·ter'θe·ro; de·si·mo·ter'se·ro) *adj.* & *n.m.* thirteenth.

décimotercio (de·θi·mo'ter·θjo; de·si·mo'ter·sjo) *adj.* & *n.m.* thirteenth.

decir (de'θir; -'sir) *v.t.* [*infl.:* **44**] **1,** to say; speak. **2,** to call; name. **3,** to assert; declare. **4,** to denote. —*n.m.* saying. —**decir de repente,** to improvise. —**es decir,** that is to say. —**querer decir,** to mean.

decisión (de·θi'sjon; de·si-) *n.f.* **1,** decision. **2,** judgment; verdict. —**decisivo,** *adj.* decisive.

declamar (de·kla'mar) *v.t.* to declaim; harangue. —**declamación,** *n.f.* declamation. —**declamador,** *n.m.* orator; declaimer. —*adj.* declaiming. —**declamatorio,** *adj.* declamatory.

declarar (de·kla'rar) *v.t.* **1,** to declare; state. **2,** to decide. —*v.i.* to testify. —**declaración,** *n.f.* declaration; testimony. —**declarante,** *adj.* declaring. —*n.m.* & *f., law* witness.

declinación (de·kli·na'θjon; -'sjon) *n.f.* **1,** *gram.* declension. **2,** slope. **3,** decay.

declinar (de·kli'nar) *v.i.* **1,** to decline; decay. **2,** to bend down. **3,** to diminish; abate. —*v.t.* **1,** to decline; reject. **2,** *gram.* to decline.

declive (de'kli·βe) *n.m.* declivity; descent. —**declividad,** *n.f.* declivity.

decocción (de·kok'θjon; -'sjon) *n.f.* decoction.

decoloración (de·ko·lo·ra'θjon; -'sjon) *n.f.* discoloration.

decolorar (de·ko·lo'rar) *v.t.* = **descolorar.**

decomisar (de·ko·mi'sar) *v.t.* to confiscate; seize. —**decomiso** (-'mi·so) *n.m.* confiscation; seizure.

decoración (de·ko·ra'θjon; -'sjon) *n.f.* **1,** decoration. **2,** stage scenery. **3,** commitment to memory.

decorado (de·ko'ra·ðo) *n.m.* **1,** decoration. **2,** something memorized.

decorar (de·ko'rar) *v.t.* **1,** to decorate; adorn. **2,** to memorize. **3,** to recite. —**decorador,** *n.m.* decorator. —**decorativo,** *adj.* decorative.

decoro (de'ko·ro) *n.m.* decorum; honor; respect; honesty. —**decoroso,** *adj.* decorous; decent.

decrecer (de·kre'θer; -'ser) *v.i.* [*infl.:* **conocer, 13**] to decrease. —**decreciente,** *adj.* decreasing. —**decremento,** *n.m.* decrement; decrease.

decrepitar (de·kre·pi'tar) *v.i.* to pop with the heat; crackle.

decrépito (de'kre·pi·to) *adj.* decrepit; broken down. —**decrepitud,** *n.f.* old age.

decretar (de·kre'tar) *v.t.* to decree; resolve. —**decreto** (-'kre·to) *n.m.* decree; decision.

decuplicar (de·ku·pli'kar) *v.t.* [*infl.:* **tocar, 7**] to multiply by ten; increase tenfold. *Also,* **decuplar.**

décuplo ('de·ku·plo) *adj.* tenfold.

dechado (de'tʃa·ðo) *n.m.* model; pattern; sample.

dedal (de'ðal) *n.m.* thimble.

dedicar (de·ði'kar) *v.t.* [*infl.:* **tocar, 7**] to dedicate; devote; consecrate. —**dedicación,** *n.f.* dedication; inscription. —**dedicatoria** (-'to·rja) *n.f.* dedication. —**dedicatorio,** *adj.* dedicatory.

dedillo (de'di·ʎo; -jo) *n.m.* little finger. —**saber al dedillo,** to have at one's fingertips.

dedo ('de·do) *n.m.* **1,** finger. **2,** toe. —**a dos dedos de,** *colloq.* within an ace of. —**dedo anular** *or* **médico,** ring finger. —**dedo auricular** *or* **meñique,** little finger. —**dedo cordial** *or* **del corazón,** *also,* **dedo mayor** *or* **de en medio,** middle finger. —**dedo índice** *or* **mostrador** *or* **saludador,** index finger; forefinger. —**dedo pulgar,** *also,* **dedo gordo, 1,** thumb. **2,** big toe.

deducción (de·ðuk'θjon; -'sjon) *n.f.* **1,** deduction. **2,** inference.

deducible (de·ðu'θi·βle; -'si·βle) *adj.* **1,** deducible. **2,** deductible.

deducir (de·ðu'θir; -'sir) *v.t.* [*infl.:* **conducir, 40**] **1,** to deduce; infer. **2,** to deduct.

deductivo (de·ðuk'ti·βo) *adj.* deductive.

defalcar (de·fal'kar) *v.t.* = **desfalcar.**

defecación (de·fe·ka'θjon; -'sjon) *n.f.* **1,** defecation. **2,** excrement.

defecar (de·fe'kar) *v.t.* [*infl.:* **tocar, 7**] **1,** to purify. **2,** to defecate.

defección (de·fek'θjon; -'sjon) *n.f.* defection.

defecto (de'fek·to) *n.m.* defect; fault; imperfection. —**defectible** *also,* **defectivo, defectuoso** (-'two·so) *adj.* defective; lacking; faulty.

defender (de·fen'der) *v.t.* [*infl.:* **perder, 29**] **1,** to defend; protect. **2,** to justify; to maintain. **4,** to resist. —**defendible,** *adj.* defensible.

defensa (de'fen·sa) *n.f.* **1,** defense; protection. **2,** justification. **3,** *Amer.* automobile bumper. —**defensiva,** *n.f.* defensive. —**defensivo,** *adj.* defensive. —*n.m.* defense; safeguard. —**defensor,** *adj.* defending. —*n.m.* defender; defense attorney.

defeque (de'fe·ke) *v., pres.subjve.* of **defecar.**

defequé (de·fe'ke) *v., pret.* of **defecar.**

deferir (de·fe'rir) *v.i.* [*infl.:* **sentir, 31**] to defer; submit; yield. —**deferencia,** *n.f.* deference. —**deferente,** *adj.* deferential.

deficiencia (de·fi'θjen·θja; -'sjen·sja) *n.f.* deficiency. —**deficiente,** *adj.* deficient; defective.

déficit ('de·fi·θit; -sit) *n.m.* deficit.

defienda (de'fjen·da) *v., pres. subjve.* of **defender.**

defiendo (de'fjen·do) *v., pres.ind.* of **defender.**

definible (de·fi'ni·βle) *adj.* definable.

definido (de·fi'ni·ðo) *adj.* definite; defined.

definir (de·fi'nir) *v.t.* **1,** to define. **2,** to determine. —**definición,** *n.f.* definition. —**definidor,** *adj.* defining. —*n.m.* definer.

definitivo (de·fi·ni'ti·βo) *adj.* **1,** definitive. **2,** conclusive.

deflagrar (de·fla'ɣrar) *v.i.* to burn rapidly. —**deflagración,** *n.f.* conflagration.

deflector (de·flek'tor) *n.m.* deflector.

deflexión (de·flek'θjon; -'sjon) *n.f.* deflection.

defoliación (de·fo·lja'θjon; -'sjon) *n.f.* defoliation. —**defoliante,** *adj.* & *n.f.* defoliant.

deformar (de·for'mar) *v.t.* to deform. —**deformación,** *n.f.* deformation.

deforme (de'for·me) *adj.* deformed; misshapen.

deformidad (de·for·mi'ðað) *n.f.* **1,** deformity. **2,** unsightliness. **3,** *fig.* crime; depravity.

defraudar (de·frau'ðar) *v.t.* **1,** to defraud. **2,** to frustrate. **3,** to disappoint. —**defraudación,** *n.f.* defrauding; cheating. —**defraudador,** *adj.* defrauding. —*n.m.* defrauder.

defuera (de'fwe·ra) *adv.* externally; on the outside.

defunción (de·fun'θjon; -'sjon) *n.f.* death; demise.

degenerar (de·xe·ne'rar) *v.i.* to degenerate. —**degeneración,** *n.f.* degeneration. —**degenerado,** *adj.* degenerate.

deglutir (de·ɣlu'tir) *v.t.* & *i.* to swallow. —**deglución,** *n.f.* swallowing.

degolladero (de·ɣo·ʎa'ðe·ro; -ja'ðe·ro) *n.m.* **1,** throat; windpipe. **2,** slaughterhouse. **3,** scaffold.

degollar (de·ɣo'ʎar; -'jar) *v.t.* [*infl.:* **acostar, 28**] **1,** to behead. **2,** to cut (a dress) low in the neck. —**degollación,** *n.f.* decapitation. —**degollado,** *n.m.* décolletage.

degradación (de·ɣra·ða'θjon; -'sjon) *n.f.* **1,** degradation; debasement. **2,** *paint.* blending; gradation.

degradar (de·ɣra'ðar) *v.t.* to degrade; debase.

degüelle (de'ɣwe·ʎe; -je) *v.,* pres. subjve. of **degollar.**

degüello (de'ɣwe·ʎo; -jo) *v.,* pres. ind. of **degollar.** —*n.m.* slaughter; massacre.

degustación (de·ɣus·ta'θjon; -'sjon) *n.f.* tasting.

dehesa (de'e·sa) *n.f.* pasture; meadow.

deidad (de·i'ðað) *n.f.* deity.

deificar (de·i·fi'kar) *v.t.* [*infl.:* **tocar, 7**] to deify. —**deificación,** *n.f.* deification.

deísmo (de'is·mo) *n.m.* deism. —**deísta,** *adj.* deistic. —*n.m.* & *f.* deist.

dejación (de·xa'θjon; -'sjon) *n.f.* **1,** abandonment. **2,** negligence. **3,** *law* assignment.

dejado (de'xa·ðo) *adj.* **1,** negligent; slovenly. **2,** *fig.* dejected. —**dejadez,** *n.f.* negligence; slovenliness.

dejar (de'xar) *v.t.* **1,** to leave; relinquish. **2,** to cease. **3,** to omit. **4,** to entrust. **5,** to permit. **6,** to fail; forsake. **7,** to bequeath. —*v.i.* to stop; cease. —**dejar mal,** to let down; disappoint. —**dejar plantado,** *slang* to leave in the lurch. —**dejarse de cuentos,** to ignore trivialities. —**no dejar de,** to be sure to; not fail to.

dejo ('de·xo) *n.m.* **1,** end. **2,** aftereffect. **3,** carelessness. **4,** aftertaste.

del (del) *contr.* of **de** + **el.**

delación (de·la'θjon; -'sjon) *n.f.* denunciation; accusation.

delantal (de·lan'tal) *n.m.* apron.

delante (de'lan·te) *adv.* in front; before; ahead; in the presence (of).

delantera (de·lan'te·ra) *n.f.* **1,** front; forefront. **2,** advantage; lead. —**delantero,** *adj.* foremost; first.

delatar (de·la'tar) *v.t.* **1,** to inform against; denounce. **2,** to betray; give away.

delator (de·la'tor) *adj.* denouncing; —*n.m.* informer; denouncer.

deleble (de'le·βle) *adj.* erasable.

delectación (de·lek·ta'θjon; -'sjon) *n.f.* delight; pleasure.

delegación (de·le·ɣa'θjon; -'sjon) *n.f.* **1,** delegation. **2,** group of delegates.

delegar (de·le'ɣar) *v.t.* [*infl.:* **pagar, 8**] to delegate. —**delegado,** *adj.* delegated. —*n.m.* delegate.

deleitar (de·lei'tar) *v.t.* to delight; please. —**deleitación,** *n.f.* enjoyment. —**deleitante,** *adj.* pleasing.

deleite (de'lei·te) *n.m.* delight; gratification. —**deleitoso,** *also,* **deleitable,** *adj.* delightful; delectable.

deletéreo (de·le'te·re·o) *adj.* deleterious.

deletrear (de·le·tre'ar) *v.i.* to

spell. —*v.t.* to decipher; interpret.
—**deletreo** (-'tre·o) *n.m.* spelling.
deleznable (de·le θ'na·βle; de·
les-) *adj.* **1,** slippery. **2,** brittle; fragile. **3,** perishable.
delfín (del'fin) *n.m.* **1,** dolphin. **2,**
dauphin.
delgadez (del·γa'δe θ; -'δes) *n.f.* **1,**
thinness; fineness; slenderness. **2,**
acuteness.
delgado (del'γa·δo) *adj.* **1,** thin;
delicate; gaunt. **2,** acute; ingenious.
deliberar (de·li·βe'rar) *v.t. & i.* to
deliberate; consider carefully.
—**deliberación,** *n.f.* deliberation.
—**deliberadamente,** *adv.* deliberately; resolutely. —**deliberativo,**
adj. deliberating; deliberative.
delicadez (de·li·ka'δe θ; -'δes) *n.f.*
1, delicacy; frailty. **2,** sensitiveness.
delicadeza (de·li·ka'δe·θa; -sa)
n.f. **1,** considerateness. **2,** daintiness; refinement; delicacy.
delicado (de·li'ka·δo) *adj.* **1,** delicate; frail. **2,** exquisite. **3,** considerate; tactful. **4,** palatable; tasty. **5,**
sensitive.
delicia (de'li·θja; -sja) *n.f.* delight.
—**delicioso,** *adj.* delicious; delightful.
delictuoso (de·lik'two·so) *adj.* unlawful; criminal. *Also,* **delictivo**
(-'ti·βo).
delicuescente (de·li·kwes' θen·te;
-kwe'sen·te) *adj.* deliquescent.
—**delicuescencia,** *n.f.* deliquescence.
delimitar (de·li·mi'tar) *v.t.* to delimit.
delincuente (de·lin'kwen·te) *adj.*
& *n.m. & f.* delinquent. —**delincuencia,** *n.f.* delinquency.
delinear (de·li·ne'ar) *v.t.* to delineate; sketch; describe; draft.
—**delineación,** *n.f.* delineation.
—**delineante,** *n.m.* draftsman.
delinquir (de·lin'kir) *v.i.* [*infl.:* 16]
to transgress. —**delinquimiento,**
n.m. transgression.
delirar (de·li'rar) *v.i.* to be delirious; rave. —**delirante,** *adj.* delirious.
delirio (de'li·rjo) *n.m.* **1,** delirium.
2, *fig.* nonsense.
delito (de'li·to) *n.m.* crime; transgression. —**delito menor,** misdemeanor. —**delito mayor,** felony.
delta ('del·ta) *n.f.* delta.
deludir (de·lu'δir) *v.t.* to delude;
deceive.

delusorio (de·lu'so·rjo) *also,*
delusivo (-'si·βo) *adj.* delusive.
demacrar (de·ma'krar) *v.t.* to emaciate. —**demacración,** *n.f.* emaciation. —**demacrado,** *adj.* emaciated.
demagogia (de·ma'γo·xja) *n.f.*
demagoguery. —**demagógico** (-'γo-
xi·ko) *adj.* demagogic. —**demagogo** (-'γo·γo) *adj.* demagogic.
—*n.m.* demagogue.
demanda (de'man·da) *n.f.* **1,** demand; petition. **2,** question; inquiry.
3, endeavor; quest. **4,** *law* claim;
lawsuit. **5,** *comm.* order.
demandar (de·man'dar) *v.t.* **1,**
to demand; ask; claim. **2,** *law* to
sue; file a suit against. —**demandado,** *n.m.* defendant; accused.
—**demandador,** *adj.* demanding.
—*n.m., law* claimant; plaintiff.
—**demandante,** *adj.* demanding.
—*n.m. & f.* plaintiff.
demarcar (de·mar'kar) *v.t.* [*infl.:*
tocar, 7] to survey; fix the bounda-
ries of. —**demarcación,** *n.f.* demarcation.
demás (de'mas) *adj.* other. —*adv.*
besides; moreover. —**lo demás,** the
rest. —**los** *or* **las demás,** the others.
—**por demás, 1,** too much; to excess. **2,** in vain. —**por lo demás,** as
for the rest.
demasía (de·ma'si·a) *n.f.* **1,** excess; surplus. **2,** insolence; boldness.
demasiado (de·ma'sja·δo) *adj.*
too much; excessive; *(pl.)* too
many. —*adv.* excessively; too.
demencia (de'men·θja; -sja) *n.f.*
dementia; insanity; —**dementar**
(-'tar) *v.t.* to drive mad. —**demente**
(-'men·te) *adj.* demented. —*n.m.*
& *f.* insane person.
demérito (de'me·ri·to) *n.m.* demerit.
democracia (de·mo'kra·θja; -sja)
n.f. democracy. —**demócrata**
(-'mo·kra·ta) *adj.* democratic.
—*n.m. & f.* democrat. —**democrático** (-'kra·ti·ko) *adj.* democratic.
democratizar (de·mo·kra·ti'θar;
-'sar) *v.t.* [*infl.:* **rezar,** 10] to democratize. —**democratización,** *n.f.* democratization.
demografía (de·mo·γra'fi·a)
n.f. demography. —**demográfico**
(-'γra·fi·ko) *adj.* demographic.
—**demógrafo** (-'mo·γra·fo) *n.m.*
demographer.
demoler (de·mo'ler) *v.t.* [*infl.:*

mover, 30] to demolish. —**demolición,** *n.f.* demolition.

demonio (de'mo·njo) *n.m.* demon; devil. —**demoníaco** (-'ni·a·ko) *adj.* demoniacal.

demontre (de'mon·tre) *n.m., colloq.* devil. —*interj.* damn!; the devil!

demora (de'mo·ra) *n.f.* delay.

demorar (de·mo'rar) *v.t.* to delay; hinder; detain. —**demorarse,** *v.r.* to linger; tarry.

demostrar (de·mos'trar) *v.t.* [*infl.:* acostar, 28] to demonstrate; show; prove. —**demostrable,** *adj.* demonstrable. —**demostración,** *n.f.* demonstration. —**demostrativo,** *adj.* demonstrative.

demudar (de·mu'ðar) *v.t.* **1,** to alter; change. **2,** to disguise. —**demudarse,** *v.r.* **1,** to become disturbed. **2,** (of the face) to change color suddenly. —**demudación,** *n.f.* alteration; change.

dendrita (den'dri·ta) *n.f.* dendrite.

denegar (de·ne'yar) *v.t.* [*infl.:* pagar, 8; pensar, 27] to deny; refuse. —**denegación,** *n.f.* denial; refusal.

dengue ('den·ge) *n.m.* **1,** coyness; affectation. **2,** *med.* dengue. —**dengoso** (-'go·so) *adj.* fastidious.

denigrar (de·ni'yrar) *v.t.* to defame; insult; revile. —**denigración,** *n.f.* defamation.

denodado (de·no'ða·ðo) *adj.* intrepid; bold.

denominar (de·no·mi'nar) *v.t.* to denominate; name. —**denominación,** *n.f.* denomination. —**denominador,** *adj.* denominating. —*n.m.* denominator. —**denominativo,** *adj.* denominative.

denostar (de·nos'tar) *v.t.* [*infl.:* acostar, 28] to affront; outrage; abuse.

denotar (de·no'tar) *v.t.* to denote; indicate; express. —**denotación,** *n.f.* denotation; indication.

densidad (den·si'ðað) *n.f.* **1,** density; thickness. **2,** *physics* specific gravity.

denso ('den·so) *adj.* dense; thick; compact.

dentado (den'ta·ðo) *adj.* toothed; serrated; cogged.

dentadura (den·ta'ðu·ra) *n.f.* **1,** teeth collectively. **2,** set of teeth; denture.

dental (den'tal) *also,* **dentario** (-'ta·rjo) *adj.* dental.

dentar (den'tar) *v.t.* [*infl.:* pensar, 27] - **1,** to provide with teeth or prongs. **2,** to indent. —*v.i.* to teethe.

dentellada (den·te'ʎa·ða; -'ja·ða) *n.f.* **1,** biting; bite. **2,** tooth mark.

dentellado (den·te'ʎa·ðo; -'ja·ðo) *adj.* **1,** toothed; serrated. **2,** bitten.

dentellar (den·te'ʎar; -'jar) *v.i.* (of the teeth) to chatter.

dentellear (den·te·ʎe'ar; -je'ar) *v.t.* to nibble.

dentición (den·ti'θjon; -'sjon) *n.f.* dentition.

dentífrico (den'ti·fri·ko) *n.m.* dentifrice. —**pasta dentífrica,** toothpaste.

dentina (den'ti·na) *n.f.* dentin.

dentista (den'tis·ta) *n.m. & f.* dentist.

dentro ('den·tro) *adv.* inside; within. —**hacia dentro,** toward the center or interior. —**dentro de poco,** soon.

denudar (de·nu'ðar) *v.t.* to denude. —**denudación,** *n.f.* denudation.

denuedo (de'nwe·ðo) *n.m.* intrepidity; bravery.

denueste (de'nwes·te) *v., pres. subjve. of* denostar.

denuesto (de'nwes·to) *v., pres.ind. of* denostar. —*n.m.* affront; outrage; abuse.

denuncia (de'nun·θja; -sja) *n.f.* **1,** denunciation; accusation. **2,** announcement. **3,** miner's claim.

denunciar (de·nun'θjar; -'sjar) *v.t.* **1,** to denounce; accuse. **2,** to advise; give notice. **3,** to predict. **4,** to register (a mining claim). —**denunciante,** *n.m. & f.* denouncer; informer. —**denuncio** (-'nun·θjo; -sjo) *n.m.* establishment of a mining claim.

denutrición (de·nu·tri'θjon; -'sjon) *n.f.* malnutrition.

deparar (de·pa'rar) *v.t.* to offer; present; furnish.

departamento (de·par·ta'men·to) *n.m.* **1,** department. **2,** *R.R.* compartment. **3,** *Mex., Arg.* apartment; room. —**departamental,** *adj.* departmental.

departir (de·par'tir) *v.i.* to talk; chat.

depauperación (de·pau·pe·ra·'θjon; -'sjon) *n.f.* **1,** impoverishment. **2,** weakening; debilitation. **3,** exhaustion; depletion.

depauperar (de·pau·pe'rar) *v.t.* **1,** to impoverish; pauperize. **2,** to weaken; debilitate. **3,** to exhaust; deplete.

dependencia (de·pen'den·θja; -sja) *n.f.* **1,** dependency. **2,** branch office. **3,** staff of employees.

depender (de·pen'der) *v.i.* to depend. —**depender de,** to depend on or upon; be dependent on or upon; rely on or upon.

dependiente (de·pen'djen·te) *adj.* dependent. —*n.m. & f.* **1,** dependent. **2,** salesclerk.

depilar (de·pi'lar) *v.t.* to depilate. —**depilación,** *n.f.* depilation. —**depilatorio,** *adj.* depilatory.

deplorar (de·plo'rar) *v.t.* to deplore; regret. —**deplorable,** *adj.* deplorable.

deponente (de·po'nen·te) *n.m. & f.* **1,** deposer. **2,** *law* deponent.

deponer (de·po'ner) *v.t.* [*infl.:* **poner, 54**] **1,** to depose; remove. **2,** *law* to testify. —*v.i.* to defecate.

deportar (de·por'tar) *v.t.* to deport. —**deportación,** *n.f.* deportation.

deporte (de·por·te) *n.m.* sport; recreation. —**deportista,** *n.m.* sportsman. —*n.f.* sportswoman. —**deportivo,** *adj.* sporting; sport *(attrib.).*

deposición (de·po·si'θjon; -'sjon) *n.f.* **1,** deposition; written testimony. **2,** dismissal or removal from office. **3,** bowel movement.

depositar (de·po·si'tar) *v.t.* **1,** to deposit. **2,** to entrust. **3,** to enclose. —**depositarse,** *v.r.* to settle *(of sediment).* —**depositario,** *adj.* depository. —*n.m.* receiver; trustee.

depositaría (de·po·si·ta'ri·a) *n.f.* **1,** depository. **2,** public treasury. **3,** receivership; trust.

depósito (de'po·si·to) *n.m.* **1,** deposit. **2,** depository. **3,** storehouse; warehouse. **4,** sediment.

depravar (de·pra'βar) *v.t.* to deprave; pervert. —**depravación,** *n.f.* depravity. —**depravado,** *adj.* depraved; perverted.

deprecar (de·pre'kar) *v.t.* [*infl.:* **tocar, 7**] to entreat; implore. —**deprecación,** *n.f.* entreaty; prayer. —**deprecatorio** (-ka'to·rjo) *adj.* entreating, imploring.

depreciar (de·pre'θjar; -'sjar) *v.t.* to depreciate; devaluate. —**depreciación,** *n.f.* depreciation.

depredar (de·pre'ðar) *v.t.* to rob; pillage; plunder. —**depredación,** *n.f.* depredation; embezzlement. —**depredador,** *n.m.* [*fem.* -**dora**] predatory person; predator.

depresión (de·pre'sjon) *n.f.* **1,** depression; dip. **2,** *econ.* depression;

decline. **3,** dejection. **4,** *meteorol.* low. —**depresivo** (-'si·βo) *adj.* depressive. —**depresor** (-'sor) *n.m.* depressor.

deprimir (de·pri'mir) *v.t.* to depress. —**deprimente,** *adj.* depressing; depressive.

depurar (de·pu'rar) *v.t.* to purify. —**depuración,** *n.f.* purification. —**depurativo,** *adj.* purifying. —*n.m.* purifier.

derecha (de're·tʃa) *n.f.* **1,** right; right side; right hand. **2,** *polit.* right; right wing.

derechista (de·re'tʃis·ta) *adj. & n.m. & f.* rightist.

derecho (de're·tʃo) *adj.* **1,** right. **2,** straight; direct. **3,** upright; vertical. **4,** just; lawful. —*adv.* straight; directly. —*n.m.* **1,** right. **2,** justice; law. **3,** tax; duty.

deriva (de'ri·βa) *n.f.* drift; drifting. —**ir a la deriva,** to drift.

derivar (de·ri'βar) *v.t.* **1,** to derive; trace. **2,** to lead; turn (one's attention). —*v.i.* **1,** to derive; be derived. **2,** to come (from); emanate (from). —**derivación,** *n.f.* derivation. —**derivado,** *adj. & n.m.* derivative. —**derivativo,** *adj.* derivative.

dermatitis (der·ma'ti·tis) *n.f.* dermatitis. *Also,* **dermitis,** *n.f.*

dermatología (der·ma·to·lo'xi·a) *n.f.* dermatology. —**dermatológico** (-'lo·xi·ko) *adj.* dermatological. —**dermatólogo** (-'to·lo·ɣo) *n.m.* dermatologist.

dermis (der'mis) *n.f.* dermis.

derogación (de·ro·ɣa'θjon; -'sjon) *n.f.* **1,** derogation. **2,** annulment; repeal.

derogar (de·ro'ɣar) *v.t.* [*infl.:* **pagar, 8**] **1,** to derogate. **2,** to annul; repeal.

derrabar (de·rra'βar) *v.t.* to cut or clip the tail of; dock.

derrama (de'rra·ma) *n.f.* tax assessment.

derramar (de·rra'mar) *v.t.* to spill; scatter. —**derramarse,** *v.r.* to overflow; leak. —**derramamiento,** *n.m.* spilling.

derrame (de'rra·me) *n.m.* **1,** leakage; spillage; overflow. **2,** declivity. **3,** discharge; hemorrhage.

derredor (de·rre'ðor) *n.m.* circumference; contour; circuit. —**al** *or* **en derredor,** around; about.

derrelición (de·rre·lik'θjon; -'sjon) *n.f.* dereliction; abandonment.

derrelicto (de·rre'lik·to) v., p.p. of **derrelinquir.** —adj. abandoned; derelict. —n.m., naut. derelict.

derrelinquir (de·rre·lin'kir) v.t. [infl.: **delinquir, 16**] to forsake; abandon.

derrengar (de·rren'gar) v.t. [infl.: **pagar, 8**] 1, to sprain the hip or spine of; cripple. 2, fig. to overburden; overwhelm.

derretimiento (de·rre·ti'mjen·to) n.m. 1, melting. 2, fig. consuming love.

derretir (de·rre'tir) v.t. [infl.: **pedir, 33**] 1, to melt; smelt. 2, fig. to waste; exhaust. —**derretirse,** v.r. to be infatuated; be smitten.

derribar (de·rri'βar) v.t. 1, to demolish; tear down; fell. 2, to overthrow; depose. —**derribo** (-'rri·βo) n.m. demolition; ruin.

derrocar (de·rro'kar) v.t. [infl.: **tocar, 7**] throw down; overthrow. —**derrocadero,** n.m. precipice. —**derrocamiento,** n.m. headlong fall; overthrow.

derrochar (de·rro'tʃar) v.t. to waste; dissipate. —**derrochador,** adj. wasteful. —n.m. spendthrift. —**derroche** (-'rro·tʃe) n.m. squandering; waste.

derrota (de'rro·ta) n.f. 1, defeat. 2, road; path. 3, naut. ship's course.

derrotar (de·rro'tar) v.t. 1, to defeat; rout. 2, to squander; destroy.

derrotero (de·rro'te·ro) n.m. 1, road; path. 2, naut. ship's course; route.

derrotismo (de·rro'tis·mo) n.m. defeatism. —**derrotista,** adj. & n.m. & f. defeatist.

derrubiar (de·rru'βjar) v.t. to erode; waste away. —**derrubio** (-'rru·βjo) n.m. erosion.

derruir (de·rru'ir) v.t. [infl.: **huir, 26**] to raze; destroy.

derrumbadero (de·rrum·ba'ðe·ro) n.m. precipice.

derrumbar (de·rrum'bar) v.t. to throw down. —**derrumbarse,** v.r. to crumble. —**derrumbamiento,** n.m. 1, collapse. 2, overthrow.

derrumbe (de'rrum·be) n.m. 1, landslide; collapse. 2, precipice.

derviche (der'βi·tʃe) n.m. dervish.

desabarrancar (des·a·βa·rran'kar) v.t. [infl.: **tocar, 7**] to pull out of a ditch; extricate.

desabastecer (des·a·βas·te'θer; -'ser) v.t. [infl.: **conocer, 13**] to cut off supplies from.

desabollar (des·a·βo'ʎar; -'jar) v.t. to remove the dents from.

desabono (des·a'βo·no) n.m. 1, injury; prejudice. 2, cancellation of a subscription. —**desabonarse** v.r. to cancel one's subscription.

desabotonar (des·a·βo·to'nar) v.t. to unbutton. —v.i., fig. to blossom.

desabrido (de·sa'βri·ðo) adj. 1, tasteless. 2, sour. 3, peevish. 4, unseasonable, as weather.

desabrigar (des·a·βri'yar) v.t. [infl.: **pagar, 8**] 1, to deprive of shelter. 2, to strip of warm or protective clothing.

desabrigo (des·a'βri·yo) n.m. 1, unsheltered state or condition; exposure. 2, lack of warm or protective clothing.

desabrir (de·sa'βrir) v.t. 1, to taint, as food. 2, to vex.

desabrochar (des·a·βro'tʃar) v.t. 1, to unbutton. 2, to burst open. —**desabrocharse,** v.r., fig. to confide; unburden oneself.

desacalorarse (des·a·ka·lo'rar·se) v.r. to cool off.

desacatar (des·a·ka'tar) v.t. to treat disrespectfully.

desacato (des·a'ka·to) n.m. 1, disrespect; irreverence. 2, law contempt of court.

desacerbar (des·a·θer'βar; -ser 'βar) v.t. to mitigate; temper.

desacertar (des·a·θer'tar; -ser'tar) v.i. [infl.: **pensar, 27**] to err; miss one's aim. —**desacierto** (-'θjer·to; -'sjer·to) n.m. blunder; error.

desacomodado (des·a·ko·mo·'ða·ðo) adj. 1, uncomfortable. 2, unemployed.

desacomodar (des·a·ko·mo'ðar) v.t. 1, to inconvenience. 2, to dismiss. 3, to disarrange.

desacomodo (des·a·ko'mo·ðo) n.m. 1, inconvenience. 2, dismissal.

desacompasado (des·a·kom·pa'sa·ðo) adj., Amer. = **descompasado,** def. 1.

desacoplar (des·a·ko'plar) v.t. to uncouple; disconnect.

desacordar (des·a·kor'ðar) v.t. [infl.: **acostar, 28**] to put out of tune. —**desacordarse,** v.r. to be forgetful.

desacorde (des·a'kor·ðe) adj. discordant.

desacostumbrado (des·a·kos·tum'bra·ðo) adj. unusual; unaccustomed.

desacostumbrar (des·a·kos·tum'brar) *v.t.* to break of a habit.

desacotar (des·a·ko'tar) *v.t.* 1, to lay open (a grazing ground). 2, to remove (a restriction). —**desacoto**, *n.m.* removal of a restriction.

desacreditado (des·a·kre·ði'ta·ðo) *adj.* 1, discredited. 2, disreputable; in disrepute.

desacreditar (des·a·kre·ði'tar) *v.t.* to discredit; disparage.

desactivar (des·ak·ti'βar) *v.t.* to deactivate.

desacuerdo (des·a'kwer·ðo) *n.m.* 1, discordance; disagreement. 2, inaccuracy. 3, forgetfulness.

desadvertido (des·að·βer'ti·ðo) *adj.* 1, inadvertent. 2, unnoticed.

desadvertir (des·að·βer'tir) *v.t.* [*infl.*: **sentir, 31**] to overlook; pay no heed (to).

desafección (des·a·fek'θjon; -'sjon) *n.f.* disaffection.

desafecto (des·a'fek·to) *adj.* opposed; alienated. —*n.m.* ill will; lack of affection. —**desafectado**, *adj.* disaffected.

desaferrar (des·a·fe'rrar) *v.t.* 1, to loosen; detach. 2, to persuade.

desafiar (des·a·fi'ar) *v.t.* [*infl.*: **enviar, 22**] to defy; dare; challenge. —**desafiador**, *adj.* challenging. —*n.m.* challenger; duelist.

desaficionar (des·a·fi·θjo'nar; -sjo'nar) *v.t.* to disaffect; disincline.

desafinar (des·a·fi'nar) *v.i.* 1, *mus.* to be discordant. 2, *fig.* to speak irrelevantly. —**desafinado**, *adj.* dissonant; out of tune.

desafío (des·a'fio) *n.m.* challenge; duel.

desaforar (des·a·fo'rar) *v.t.* [*infl.*: **acostar, 28**] to encroach on the rights of. —**desaforarse**, *v.r.* to be disorderly. —**desaforado**, *adj.* disorderly; impudent.

desafortunado (des·a·for·tu·'na·ðo) *adj.* unfortunate.

desafuero (-'fwe·ro) *n.m.* violation; outrage; abuse.

desagradar (des·a·γra'ðar) *v.t.* to displease. —**desagrado** (-'γra·ðo) *n.m.* displeasure. —**desagradable**, *adj.* disagreeable.

desagradecer (des·a·γra·ðe'θer; -'ser) *v.t.* [*infl.*: **conocer, 13**] to be ungrateful. —**desagradecido**, *adj.* ungrateful. —*n.m.* ingrate. —**desagradecimiento**, *n.m.* ingratitude.

desagraviar (des·a·γra'βjar) *v.t.* to make amends to; atone to.

—**desagravio** (-'γra·βjo) *n.m.* vindication; amends.

desagregar (des·a·γre'γar) *v.t.* [*infl.*: **pagar, 8**] to separate; disjoin. —**desagregación**, *n.f.* separation.

desaguar (des·a'γwar) *v.t.* [*infl.*: **averiguar, 9**] to drain; empty. —*v.i.* to flow into the sea. —**desaguadero**, *n.m.* drain. —**desagüe** (-'a·γwe) *n.m.* drainage; sluice.

desaguisado (des·a·γi'sa·ðo) *adj.* unjust; unfair. —*n.m.* outrage; wrong.

desahogado (des·a·o'γa·ðo) *adj.* 1, well-to-do; comfortable. 2, unencumbered. 3, petulant; impudent.

desahogar (des·a·o'γar) *v.t.* [*infl.*: **pagar, 8**] to relieve; alleviate. —**desahogarse**, *v.r.* 1, to recover from distress, fatigue or grief. 2, to vent one's feelings.

desahogo (des·a'o·γo) *n.m.* relief. —**vivir con desahogo**, to live comfortably.

desahuciar (des·au'θjar; -'sjar) *v.t.* 1, to give up (a patient) as hopeless. 2, to evict; dispossess. —**desahucio** (-'au·θjo; -sjo) *n.m.* eviction.

desahumar (des·a·u'mar) *v.t.* to clear of smoke. —**desahumado**, *adj.* vapid; flat, as champagne.

desairar (des·ai'rar) *v.t.* 1, to slight; snub (a person). 2, to disdain (a thing). —**desaire** (-'ai·re) *n.m.* slight; rebuff.

desajustar (des·a·xus'tar) *v.t.* to disarrange; put out of adjustment. —**desajustarse**, *v.r.* 1, to be or become out of adjustment. 2, to break an agreement. 3, to disagree; be incompatible.

desalar (de·sa'lar) *v.t.* to desalt; desalinate. —**desalazón** (-la'θon; -'son) *n.f.* desalination.

desalarse (des·a'lar·se) *v.r.* 1, to hasten. 2, *fig.* to be eager. —**desalado**, *adj.* eager; anxious.

desalentar (des·a·len'tar) *v.t.* [*infl.*: **pensar, 27**] to discourage. —**desalentador**, *adj.* discouraging. —**desaliento** (-'ljen·to) *n.m.* dismay; discouragement.

desalinear (des·a·li·ne'ar) *v.t.* to put out of alignment. —**desalineado**, *adj.* out of alignment.

desaliñar (des·a·li'ɲar) *v.t.* to ruffle; disarrange. —**desaliño** (-'li·ɲo) *n.m.* slovenliness; disarray; neglect.

desalivar (de·sa·li'βar) *v.i.* to salivate.

desalmar (des·al'mar) *v.t.* to weaken; deplete. —**desalmarse**, *v.r.* **1,** to be eager. **2,** to lose strength or spirit. —**desalmado**, *adj.* heartless; cruel; inhuman.

desalojar (des·a·lo'xar) *v.t.* to dislodge; dispossess; evict. —*v.i.* to move out. —**desalojamiento**, *n.m.* dislodgment.

desalquilar (des·al·ki'lar) *v.t.* to discontinue the lease or rental of. —**desalquilado**, *adj.* vacant; untenanted.

desalumbramiento (des·a·lum·bra'mjen·to) *n.m.* **1,** blindness. **2,** lack of knowledge or judgment.

desamarrar (des·a·ma'rrar) *v.t.* **1,** to untie; unfasten. **2,** *naut.* to cast off; unmoor.

desamistarse (des·a·mis'tar·se) *v.r.* to quarrel; have a falling out.

desamor (des·a'mor) *n.m.* **1,** coldness; indifference. **2,** dislike; enmity. —**desamorar**, *v.t.* to alienate. —**desamorado**, *adj.* coldhearted.

desamparar (des·am·pa'rar) *v.t.* to abandon; forsake. —**desamparo** (-'pa·ro) *n.m.* abandonment; helplessness; dereliction.

desamueblar (des·a·mwe'βlar) *v.t.* to strip of furniture; dismantle. —**desamueblado** also, **desamoblado** (-mo'βla·ðo) *adj.* unfurnished.

desandar (des·an'dar) *v.t.* [*infl.:* **andar, 35**] to retrace one's steps. —**desandadura**, *n.f.* turning back.

desangrar (de·san'grar) *v.t.* **1,** to bleed copiously. **2,** to drain. **3,** to impoverish. —**desangrarse**, *v.r.* to lose blood.

desanimar (des·a·ni'mar) *v.t.* to dishearten; discourage. —**desánimo** (-'a·ni·mo) *n.m.* discouragement.

desanudar (des·a·nu'ðar) also, **desañudar** (-ɲu'ðar) *v.t.* to untie; disentangle.

desaparecer (des·a·pa·re'θer; -'ser) *v.i.* [*infl.:* **conocer, 13**] to disappear. —**desaparición**, *n.f.* disappearance.

desaparejar (des·a·pa·re'xar) *v.t.* to unhitch; unrig.

desapasionarse (des·a·pa·sjo·'nar·se) *v.r.* to be or become indifferent. —**desapasionado**, *adj.* dispassionate; disinterested. —**desapasionamiento**, *n.m.* dispassion; disinterest.

desapegarse (des·a·pe'γar·se) *v.r.* [*infl.:* **pagar, 8**] to detach or dissociate oneself. —**desapego** (-'pe·γo) *n.m.* disinterest.

desapercibido (des·a·per·θi'βi·ðo; -si'βi·ðo) *adj.* **1,** unprepared; unprovided. **2,** unnoticed. —**desapercibimiento**, *n.m.* unpreparedness.

desaplicado (des·a·pli'ka·ðo) *adj.* indolent; negligent. —**desaplicación**, *n.f.* indolence; negligence.

desapoderar (des·a·po·ðe'rar) *v.t.* **1,** to dispossess. **2,** *law* to invalidate.

desapreciar (des·a·pre'θjar; -'sjar) *v.t.* to disparage; underestimate. —**desaprecio** (-'pre·θjo; -sjo) *n.m.* underestimation; disparagement.

desaprender (des·a·pren'der) *v.t.* to unlearn.

desaprobar (des·a·pro'βar) *v.t.* [*infl.:* **acostar, 28**] to disapprove; censure; reprove; *educ.* to fail (a student). —**desaprobación**, *n.f.* disapproval; censure; reproof; *educ.* failure.

desaprovechado (des·a·pro·βe·'tʃa·ðo) *adj.* **1,** unused; unexploited. **2,** unproductive. **3,** indolent.

desaprovechar (des·a·pro·βe·'tʃar) *v.t.* to waste; misspend; misuse.

desapuntalar (des·a·pun·ta'lar) *v.t.* to remove the props or supports of.

desarmar (des·ar'mar) *v.t.* **1,** to disarm. **2,** to dismount; dismantle. **3,** *fig.* to calm; pacify. —**desarmado**, *adj.* unarmed; defenseless. —**desarme** (-'ar·me) *n.m.* disarmament.

desarraigar (des·a·rrai'γar) *v.t.* [*infl.:* **pagar, 8**] **1,** to uproot; eradicate. **2,** to expel; banish.

desarraigo (des·a'rrai·γo) *n.m.* **1,** eradication. **2,** expulsion; banishment.

desarrapado *adj.* = **desharrapado**.

desarreglar (des·a·rre'γlar) *v.t.* to disarrange; discompose; upset. —**desarreglado**, *adj.* immoderate; extravagant. —**desarreglo** (-'rre·γlo) *n.m.* disorder; confusion.

desarrollar (des·a·rro'ʎar; -'jar) *v.t.* **1,** to develop; expand; improve. **2,** to explain; propound. —**desarrollarse**, *v.r.* **1,** to grow; become. **2,** to happen; befall. —**desarrollo** (-'rro·ʎo; -jo) *n.m.* development; course.

desarropar (des·a·rro'par) *v.t.* to uncover; remove a garment from.

desarrugar (des·a·rru'ɣar) *v.t.* [*infl.:* **pagar, 8**] to unwrinkle.

desarticular (des·ar·ti·ku'lar) *v.t.* 1, to disjoint; dislocate. 2, to break up; break apart.

desasear (des·a·se'ar) *v.t.* 1, to dirty. 2, to make a mess of; disorder. —**desaseado** (-'a·ðo) *adj.* unclean; slovenly. —**desaseo** (-'se·o) *n.m.* uncleanliness; slovenliness.

desasir (des·a'sir) *v.t.* [*infl.:* **asir, 36**] to loosen. —**desasirse,** *v.r.* 1, to disengage oneself. 2, to rid oneself (of).

desasociar (des·a·so'θjar; -'sjar) *v.t.* to disassociate; separate.

desasosegar (des·a·so·se'ɣar) *v.t.* [*infl.:* **pagar, 8; pensar, 27**] to disturb; make uneasy. —**desasosiego** (-'sje·ɣo) *n.m.* uneasiness.

desastrado (des·as'tra·ðo) *adj.* 1, unfortunate; unlucky. 2, shabby; seedy.

desastre (des·as·tre) *n.m.* disaster. —**desastroso,** *adj.* disastrous.

desatar (des·a'tar) *v.t.* to untie; loose. —**desatarse,** *v.r.* 1, to talk volubly; burst out talking. 2, to lose all restraint. 3, to loosen up. 4, to break loose; break out.

desatascar (des·a·tas'kar) *v.t.* [*infl.:* **tocar, 7**] 1, to unclog. 2, to extricate.

desataviar (des·a·ta'βjar) *v.t.* [*infl.:* **enviar, 22**] 1, to strip of ornaments. 2, to disarray. —**desatavío** (-'βi·o) *n.m.* slovenliness; disarray.

desatención (des·a·ten'θjon; -'sjon) *n.f.* 1, inattention. 2, discourtesy.

desatender (des·a·ten'der) *v.t.* [*infl.:* **perder, 29**] to neglect; disregard.

desatento (des·a'ten·to) *adj.* 1, inattentive. 2, discourteous.

desatinar (des·a·ti'nar) *v.i.* 1, to act or talk foolishly. 2, to blunder. —*v.t.* to confuse; bewilder. —**desatinarse,** *v.r.* to rave; lose one's bearings. —**desatinado,** *adj.* foolish; extravagant. —**desatino** (-'ti·no) *n.m.* blunder; error; extravagance.

desatracar (des·a·tra'kar) *v.t.* [*infl.:* **tocar, 7**] *naut.* to cast off.

desatrancar (des·a·tran'kar) *v.t.* [*infl.:* **tocar, 7**] 1, to unbar; unbolt. 2, to unclog.

desautorizar (des·au·to·ri'θar; -'sar) *v.t.* [*infl.:* **rezar, 10**] 1, to deprive of authority. 2, to disallow; deny approval of.

desavenencia (des·a·βe'nen·θja; -sja) *n.f.* disagreement; discord.

desavenirse (des·a·βe'nir·se) *v.r.* [*infl.:* **venir, 69**] to disagree; quarrel.

desayunar (des·a·ju'nar) *v.i.* [*also, refl.* **desayunarse**] to eat breakfast. —*v.t.* to have (something) for breakfast; breakfast on (something).

desayuno (des·a'ju·no) *n.m.* breakfast.

desazón (de·sa'θon; -'son) *n.m.* 1, uneasiness. 2, displeasure. 3, insipidity.

desazonar (de·sa·θo'nar; -so'nar) *v.t.* 1, to render insipid. 2, to annoy; disgust. —**desazonarse,** *v.r.* 1, to become restless. 2, to become indisposed.

desbancar (des·βan'kar) *v.t.* [*infl.:* **tocar, 7**] 1, *in gambling,* to break the bank. 2, to supplant (in affection).

desbandarse (des·βan'dar·se) *v.r.* 1, to disband; disperse. 2, *mil.* to desert. —**desbandada,** *n.f.* disbandment. —**a la desbandada,** in disorder; helter-skelter.

desbarajustar (des·βa·ra·xus'tar) *v.t.* to disarrange. —**desbarajuste** (-'xus·te) *n.m.* disorder; confusion.

desbaratar (des·βa·ra'tar) *v.t.* 1, to destroy; ruin. 2, to upset; disturb. 3, to disperse. —**desbarata-miento,** *n.m.* breakage; destruction. *Also,* **desbarate** (-'ra·te).

desbastar (des·βas'tar) *v.t.* 1, to plane; smooth. 2, to give social polish.

desbocado (des·βo·ka·ðo) *adj.* 1, runaway, as a horse. 2, unrestrained; uninhibited. 3, foulmouthed.

desbocarse (des·βo'kar·se) *v.r.* [*infl.:* **tocar, 7**] 1, (of horses) to run away. 2, to burst forth (in feeling, speech, etc.).

desbordar (des·βor'ðar) *v.i.* to overflow. —**desbordarse,** *v.r.* 1, to overflow. 2, to lose one's restraint; be carried away. —**desbordamiento,** *n.m.* overflow.

desbrozar (des·βro'θar; -'sar) *v.t.* [*infl.:* **rezar, 10**] to clear of brush. —**desbroce** (-'βro·θe; -se) *n.m.* clearing of brush. *Also,* **desbrozo** (-θo; -so).

descabal (des·ka'βal) *adj.* imperfect; incomplete. —**descabalar,** *v.t.* to break up; impair the unity or completeness of.

descabellar (des·ka·βe'ʎar; -'jar) *v.t.* to kill (an animal). —**descabellado,** *adj.* absurd; harebrained.

descabezar (des·ka·βe'θar; -'sar) *v.t.* [*infl.:* **rezar,** 10] to behead; lop off the head or top of. —**descabezarse,** *v.r.* to rack one's brain. —**descabezado,** *adj.* reckless; harebrained.

descaecer (des·ka·e'θer; -'ser) *v.i.* [*infl.:* **conocer,** 13] to decline; decay; decrease.

descaecimiento (des·ka·e·θi·'mjen·to; -si'mjen·to) *n.m.* 1, weakness; debility. 2, despondency; dejection.

descafeinar (des·ka·fei'nar) *v.t.* to decaffeinate.

descalabrar (des·ka·la'βrar) *v.t.* 1, to wound on the head. 2, *fig.* to hurt; offend. —**descalabrarse,** *v.r.* to suffer a head wound. —**descalabradura,** *n.f.* head wound or scar. —**descalabro** (-'la·βro) *n.m.* misfortune; loss.

descalificar (des·ka·li·fi'kar) *v.t.* [*infl.:* **tocar,** 7] to disqualify. —**descalificación,** *n.f.* disqualification.

descalzar (des·kal'θar; -'sar) *v.t.* [*infl.:* **rezar,** 10] 1, to bare the feet of. 2, *mech.* to remove a brake or impediment from. —**descalzarse,** *v.r.* to remove one's shoes. —**descalzarse los guantes,** to remove one's gloves.

descalzo (des'kal·θo; -so) *adj.* barefooted.

descaminar (des·ka·mi'nar) *v.t.* to mislead; lead astray.

descamisado (des·ka·mi'sa·ðo) *adj.* 1, shirtless. 2, destitute. —*n.m., colloq.* ragamuffin.

descampar (des·kam'par) *v.t.* to clear (land; forest). —*v.i.* (of the weather) to clear; clear up. —**descampado,** *adj.* clear; open.

descansar (des·kan'sar) *v.i.* to rest; relax. —*v.t.* 1, to rest; lean. 2, to relieve. —**descansadero,** *n.m.* resting place.

descanso (des'kan·so) *n.m.* 1, rest; relief. 2, stair landing.

descantear (des·kan·te'ar) *v.t.* to smooth the edges of.

descantillar (des·kan·ti'ʎar; -'jar)

v.t. to chip off. *Also,* **descantonar** (-to'nar).

descapotable (des·ka·po'ta·βle) *adj.* & *n.m.* convertible.

descararse (des·ka'rar·se) *v.r.* to behave impudently. —**descarado,** *adj.* impudent; brazen; shameless.

descarga (des'kar·ɣa) *n.f.* discharge; unloading.

descargador (des·kar·ɣa'ðor) *n.m.* unloader; longshoreman.

descargar (des·kar'ɣar) *v.t.* [*infl.:* **pagar,** 8] 1, to discharge; unload. 2, to empty. 3, to fire (a weapon). 4, to acquit; exonerate. 5, *elect.* to discharge. 6, *comm.* to discharge (a debt). 7, to deal; strike (a blow). 8, *fig.* to ease; unburden. —*v.i.* to burst, as clouds.

descargo (des'kar·ɣo) *n.m.* 1, [*also,* **descargue** (-ɣe)] unloading; discharge. 2, exoneration; acquittal. 3, *comm.* discharge (*of a debt*).

descarnar (des·kar'nar) *v.t.* 1, to remove the flesh from. 2, to corrode; eat away. —**descarnarse,** *v.r.* to lose flesh; become emaciated. —**descarnado,** *adj.* emaciated; fleshless.

descaro (des'ka·ro) *n.m.* effrontery; impudence.

descarriar (des·ka'rrjar) *v.t.* to mislead; lead astray. —**descarriarse,** *v.r.* to go astray.

descarrilar (des·ka·rri'lar) *v.i.* to derail; run off the rails; be derailed. —**descarrilamiento,** *n.m.* derailment.

descarrío (des·ka'rri·o) *n.m.* straying; going astray; waywardness.

descartar (des·kar'tar) *v.t.* to discard; put aside; dismiss.

descarte (des'kar·te) *n.m.* 1, discarding; discard. 2, subterfuge; evasion.

descasar (des·ka'sar) *v.t.* 1, to separate (a married couple). 2, to annul the marriage of. 3, to disturb or change the arrangement of. —**descasamiento,** *n.m.* divorce; annulment.

descascarar (des·kas·ka'rar) *v.t.* to shell; peel.

descastar (des·kas'tar) *v.t.* to exterminate.

descender (des·θen'der; de·sen'der) *v.i.* [*infl.:* **perder,** 29] 1, to descend; go down. 2, to come (from); be derived (from). —*v.t.* to let down; lower. —**descendencia,** *n.f.* descent; lineage. —**descendiente,**

adj. [*also,* **descendente**] descending. —*n.m.* descendant. —**descenso** (des·'θen·so; de'sen-) *n.m.* descent; lowering; degradation.

descentralizar (des·θen·tra·li·'θar; de·sen·tra·li'sar) *v.t.* [*infl.:* **rezar, 10**] to decentralize. —**descentralización** *n.f.* decentralization.

descentrar (des·θen'trar; de·sen-) *v.t.* to make eccentric; put off center.

desceñir (des·θe'ɲir; de·se-) *v.t.* [*infl.:* **reñir, 59**] to ungird; take off (a belt, girdle, etc.).

descifrar (des·θi'frar; de·si'frar) *v.t.* **1,** to decipher; decode. **2,** to interpret. **3,** *fig.* to unravel. —**descifrable,** *adj.* decipherable.

descifre (des'θi·fre; de'si·fre) *n.m.* decoding; deciphering; decipherment.

descoagular (des·ko·a·ɣu'lar) *v.t.* to dissolve (a clot).

descobijar (des·ko·βi'xar) *v.t.* to uncover; unwrap.

descocarse (des·ko'kar·se) *v.r., colloq.* [*infl.:* **tocar, 7**] to be impudent. —**descoco** (-'ko·ko) *n.m.* impudence; impertinence.

descocer (des·ko'θer; -'ser) *v.t.* [*infl.:* **torcer, 66**] to digest.

descogollar (des·ko·ɣo'ʎar; -'jar) *v.t.* **1,** to prune (a tree) of shoots. **2,** to remove the heart (of vegetables).

descolgar (des·kol'ɣar) *v.t.* [*infl.:* **pagar, 8; acostar, 28**] **1,** to take down; unhook. **2,** to remove the draperies, hangings, etc., from. —**descolgarse,** *v.r.* **1,** to descend gently; slip down. **2,** to appear unexpectedly. —**descolgar con,** to come out with; blurt out.

descolorar (des·ko·lo'rar) *v.t., also,* **descolorir** [*defective, used only in forms whose endings begin with* **i**] to fade; discolor. —**descoloramiento; descolorimiento,** *n.m.* discoloration.

descollar (des·ko'ʎar; -'jar) *v.i.* [*infl.:* **acostar, 28**] to stand out; excel.

descombrar (des·kom'brar) *v.t.* to disencumber. —**descombro** (-'kom·bro) *n.m.* disencumbrance.

descomedido (des·ko·me'ði·ðo) *adj.* **1,** immoderate; excessive. **2,** rude; insolent. —**descomedimiento,** *n.m.* rudeness.

descomodidad (des·ko·mo·ði'ðað) *n.f.* = **incomodidad.**

descompaginar (des·kom·pa·xi'nar) *v.t.* **1,** to disorganize; mix up. **2,** to confuse; fluster.

descompasado (des·kom·pa'sa·ðo) *adj.* **1,** [*also, Amer.,* **descompasado**] irregular; offbeat. **2,** extravagant; immoderate.

descompletar (des·kom·ple'tar) *v.t.* to make incomplete; break up (a set).

descomponer (des·kom·po'ner) *v.t.* [*infl.:* **poner, 54**] **1,** to upset; disturb. **2,** to put out of order. **3,** to decompose. **4,** *opt.* to disperse.

descomposición (des·kom·po·si·'θjon; -'sjon) *n.f.* **1,** discomposure. **2,** disarrangement. **3,** decomposition.

descompostura (des·kom·pos·'tu·ra) *n.f.* **1,** disorder; disarrangement. **2,** impudence; disrespect. **3,** untidiness; uncleanliness.

descomprimir (des·kom·pri'mir) *v.t.* to decompress. —**descompresión,** *n.f.* decompression.

descompuesto (des·kom'pwes·to) *adj.* **1,** out of order. **2,** insolent; brazen; indecent. —*v., p.p.* of **descomponer.**

descomulgado (des·ko·mul'ɣa·ðo) *adj.* **1,** excommunicated. **2,** wicked; perverse.

descomulgar (des·ko·mul'ɣar) *v.t.* [*infl.:* **pagar, 8**] to excommunicate.

descomunal (des·ko·mu'nal) *adj.* **1,** enormous. **2,** monstrous.

desconcertar (des·kon·θer'tar; -ser'tar) *v.t.* [*infl.:* **pensar, 27**] to disconcert; disturb; confound. —**desconcierto** (-'θjer·to; -'sjer·to) *n.m.* disagreement; disorder.

desconchar (des·kon'tʃar) *v.t.* to scrape off; peel off; chip off. —**desconchadura,** *n.f.* peeling; scaling.

desconectar (des·ko·nek'tar) *v.t.* to disconnect.

desconfiar (des·kon'fjar) *v.i.* [*infl.:* **enviar, 22**] to distrust. —**desconfiado,** *adj.* distrustful. —**desconfianza,** *n.f.* distrust.

desconformar (des·kon·for'mar) *v.i.* to disagree; dissent. —**desconforme** (-'for·me) *adj.* disagreeing; discordant. —**desconformidad,** *n.f.* disagreement; nonconformity.

descongelar (des·kon·xe'lar) *v.t.* to melt; thaw; defrost. —**descongelador,** *n.m.* defroster.

descongestionante (des·kon·xes·tjo'nan·te) *n.m.* decongestant.

descongestionar (des·kon·xes·tjo'nar) *v.t.* to relieve congestion in.

descongojar (des·kon·go'xar) *v.t.* to comfort; solace.

desconocer (des·ko·no'θer; -'ser) *v.t.* [*infl.:* conocer, 13] 1, to fail to recognize. 2, to disown; disavow. 3, to be ignorant of. 4, to pretend not to know. 5, to ignore; to overlook.

desconocido (des·ko·no'θi·ðo; -'si·ðo) *adj.* 1, unknown. 2, unrecognizable. —*n.m.* stranger.

desconocimiento (des·ko·no·θi'mjen·to; -si'mjen·to) *n.m.* 1, disregard. 2, ignorance. 3, oversight; failure to notice.

desconsiderado (des·kon·si·ðe'ra·ðo) *adj.* 1, inconsiderate. 2, thoughtless; rash; ill-considered. —**desconsideración,** *n.f.* thanklessness.

desconsolar (des·kon·so'lar) *v.t.* [*infl.:* acostar, 28] to grieve; sadden; afflict. —**desconsolarse,** *v.r.* to lose heart. —**desconsolado,** *adj.* disconsolate; sad. —**desconsuelo** (-'swe·lo) *n.m.* sadness; affliction; distress.

descontar (des·kon'tar) *v.t.* [*infl.:* acostar, 28] to discount; deduct.

descontentadizo (des·kon·ten·ta'ði·θo; -so) *adj.* 1, hard to please. 2, easily displeased.

descontentar (des·kon·ten'tar) *v.t.* to displease; dissatisfy. —**descontento** (-'ten·to) *adj.* discontented; displeased. —*n.m.* discontent; dissatisfaction.

descontinuar (des·kon·ti'nwar) *v.t.* [*infl.:* continuar, 23] to discontinue. —**descontinuación,** *n.f.* discontinuation; discontinuance. —**descontinuo** (-'ti·nwo) *adj.* discontinuous.

descontrol (des·kon'trol) *n.m.* decontrol. —**descontrolar,** *v.t.* to decontrol.

desconveniencia (des·kon·βe'njen·θja; -sja) *n.f.* 1, inconvenience. 2, disadvantage.

desconveniente (des·kon·βe·'njen·te) *adj.* 1, inconvenient. 2, unsuitable.

desconvenir (des·kon·βe'nir) *v.i.* [*infl.:* venir, 69] 1, to disagree. 2, to be mismatched or unsuited.

descoque (des'ko·ke) *v.,* *pres. subjve. of* descocar.

descoqué (des'ko·ke) *v.,* *1st pers. sing. pret. of* descocar.

descorazonar (des·ko·ra·θo'nar;

-so'nar) *v.t.* 1, to tear out the heart of. 2, to dishearten; discourage. —**descorazonamiento,** *n.f.* dejection; discouragement.

descorchar (des·kor'tʃar) *v.t.* 1, to uncork. 2, to strip of bark. 3, to break into.

descortés (des·kor'tes) *adj.* discourteous; ill-bred. —**descortesía,** *n.f.* discourtesy.

descortezar (des·kor·te'θar; -'sar) *v.t.* [*infl.:* rezar, 10] 1, to remove the bark, crust, shell, etc., of. 2, *colloq.* to refine; give social polish to.

descoser (des·ko'ser) *v.t.* to rip out (sewing); unstitch. —**descoserse,** *v.r.* to blab; let out a secret.

descosido (des·ko'si·ðo) *n.m.* rip; tear. —*adj.* 1, indiscreet. 2, wild; disorderly.

descostrar (des·kos'trar) *v.t.* to remove the crust or scale from.

descotar (des·ko'tar) *v.t.* to cut (a dress) low in the neck. —**descotado,** *adj.* décolleté. —**descote** (-'ko·te) *n.m.* décolletage.

descoyuntamiento (des·ko·jun·ta'mjen·to) *n.m.* 1, dislocation. 2, fatigue.

descoyuntar (des·ko·jun'tar) *v.t.* 1, to dislocate; disjoint. 2, *fig.* to annoy.

descrédito (des'kre·ði·to) *n.m.* discredit.

descreer (des·kre'er) *v.t.* [*infl.:* creer, 42] 1, to disbelieve. 2, to discredit; deny credit to.

descreído (des·kre'i·ðo) *adj.* unbelieving. —*n.m.* unbeliever. —**descreimiento,** *n.m.* unbelief.

describir (des·kri'βir) *v.t.* [*p.p.* descrito (-'kri·to), descripto (-'krip·to)] to describe; delineate. —**descripción,** *n.f.* description; design; delineation. —**descriptivo,** *adj.* descriptive.

descuajar (des·kwa'xar) *v.t.* 1, to liquefy; dissolve. 2, to root out. 3, *fig.* to dishearten.

descuajaringarse (des·kwa·xa·rin'gar·se) *v.r., colloq.* [*infl.:* pagar, 8] to collapse, as with fatigue; fall apart.

descuartizar (des·kwar·ti'θar; -'sar) *v.t.* [*infl.:* rezar, 10] 1, to carve. 2, to quarter. 3, to tear or cut into pieces.

descubrir (des·ku'βrir) *v.t.* [*p.p.* descubierto (-'βjer·to)] to discover; reveal; uncover. —**descubierto,**

adj. discovered; uncovered; exposed. —**descubridor,** *n.m.* discoverer; *mil.* scout. —**descubrimiento,** *n.m.* discovery.

descuelgo (des'kwel·ɣo) *v., 1st pers. sing. pres. ind. of* **descolgar.**

descuelgue (des'kwel·ɣe) *v., pres. subjve. of* **descolgar.**

descuelle (des'kwe·ʎe; -je) *v., pres.subjve. of* **descollar.**

descuello (des'kwe·ʎo; -jo) *v., 1st pers. sing. pres.ind. of* **descollar.**

descuente (des'kwen·te) *v., pres.subjve. of* **descontar.**

descuento (des'kwen·to) *v., 1st pers.sing. pres.ind. of* **descontar.**

descuidar (des·kui'ðar) *v.t.* 1, to neglect; overlook. 2, to distract. —*v.i.* to lack diligence; be careless. —**descuidarse,** *v.r.* 1, to be careless. 2, to be unwary. —**descuidado,** *adj.* negligent; careless; slovenly. —**descuido** (-'kwi·ðo) *n.m.* carelessness; neglect.

descuidero (des·kwi'ðe·ro) *n.m.* pickpocket.

desde ('des·ðe) *prep.* from; since; after. —**desde luego,** 1, of course. 2, at once. —**desde que,** ever since; since. —**desde ya,** *colloq.* right now; forthwith.

desdecir (des·ðe'θir; -'sir) *v.i.* [*infl.:* **decir, 44**] *fol. by* **de** 1, to degenerate; decline *(from an earlier condition).* 2, to detract (from). 3, to be out of harmony (with). —**desdecirse,** *v.r.* to retract.

desdén (des'ðen) *n.m.* disdain; scorn; contempt. —**al desdén,** contemptuously; with affected neglect.

desdentado (des·ðen'ta·ðo) *adj.* toothless.

desdeñar (des·ðe'ɲar) *v.t.* to disdain; scorn. —**desdeñable,** *adj.* contemptible.

desdeñoso (des·ðe'ɲo·so) *adj.* disdainful.

desdicha (des'ði·tʃa) *n.f.* misfortune; misery. —**desdichado,** *adj.* unfortunate; wretched. —*n.m.* wretch.

desdoblar (des·ðo'βlar) *v.t.* 1, to spread open; unfold. 2, to split; to break down. —**desdoblamiento,** *n.m.* 1, an unfolding; a spreading out. 2, split; breakdown.

desdorar (des·ðo'rar) *v.t.* 1, to tarnish. 2, to dishonor; sully.

desdoro (des'ðo·ro) *n.m.* 1, tarnish; blemish. 2, dishonor.

desear (de·se'ar) *v.t.* to desire;

want; wish; crave. —**deseable,** *adj.* desirable.

desecar (de·se'kar) *v.t.* [*infl.:* **tocar, 7**] 1, to desiccate; dry. 2, to drain. —**desecación,** *n.f.* desiccation. —**desecante,** *adj. & n.m.* desiccant.

desechar (des·e'tʃar) *v.t.* to reject; exclude; cast aside.

desecho (des'e·tʃo) *n.m.* 1, remainder; residue. 2, rubbish; debris. 3, reject. 4, *fig.* contempt.

desedificar (des·e·ði·fi'kar) *v.t.* [*infl.:* **tocar, 7**] to set a bad example for; demoralize.

desellar (de·se'ʎar; -'jar) *v.t.* to unseal.

desembalar (des·em·ba'lar) *v.t.* to unpack. —**desembalaje,** *n.m.* unpacking.

desembarazar (des·em·ba·ra'θar; -'sar) *v.t.* [*infl.:* **rezar, 10**] to disembarrass; disencumber; clear. —**desembarazo** (-'ra·θo; -so) *n.m.* ease; freedom.

desembarcadero (des·em·bar·ka'ðe·ro) *n.m.* wharf; dock; pier.

desembarcar (des·em·bar'kar) *v.t.* [*infl.:* **tocar, 7**] to unload. —*v.i.* to disembark; debark.

desembarco (des·em'bar·ko) *n.m.* unloading; debarkation *(of passengers).*

desembargar (des·em·bar'ɣar) *v.t.* [*infl.:* **pagar, 8**] 1, to lift the embargo on. 2, to free from a hindrance or encumbrance —**desembargo** (-'bar·ɣo) *n.m.* lifting of an embargo or encumbrance.

desembarque (des·em'bar·ke) *n.m.* unloading; debarkation *(of cargo).*

desembarrancar (des·em·ba·rran'kar) *v.t. & i.* [*infl.:* **tocar, 7**] to float, as a grounded ship.

desembocar (des·em·bo'kar) *v.i.* [*infl.:* **tocar, 7**] 1, to flow out; empty, as a stream. 2, to end, as a street. —**desembocadero** (-ka'ðe·ro) *n.m., also,* **desembocadura** (-ka'ðu·ra) *n.f.* mouth *(of a river or canal);* outlet; exit.

desembolsar (des·em·bol'sar) *v.t.* to disburse; pay out. —**desembolso** (-'bol·so) *n.m.* disbursement; expenditure.

desembotar (des·em·bo'tar) *v.t.* to sharpen (wits).

desembragar (des·em·bra'ɣar) *v.t.* [*infl.:* **pagar, 8**] *mech.* to disengage (gears); disconnect (a shaft).

desembriagar (des·em·brja'ɣar) *v.t.* [*infl.:* **pagar,** 8] to sober up.

desembrollar (des·em·bro'ʎar; -'jar) *v.t.* to unravel; untangle.

desemejar (de·se·me'xar) *v.i.* to be dissimilar. —*v.t.* to deform; disguise. —**desemejante,** *adj.* dissimilar. —**desemejanza,** *n.f.* dissimilarity.

desempacar (des·em·pa'kar) *v.t.* [*infl.:* **tocar,** 7] to unpack. —**desempacarse,** *v.r.* to become calm; calm down.

desempachar (des·em·pa'tʃar) *v.t.* to relieve of indigestion *(by disgorging)*. —**desempacharse,** *v.r.* to cast off one's timidity or inhibition.

desempacho (des·em'pa·tʃo) *n.m.* 1, ease; nonchalance. 2, boldness.

desempañar (des·em·pa'ɲar) *v.t.* 1, to clean (glass). 2, to remove tarnish from. 3, to defog.

desempaquetar (des·em·pa·ke'tar) *v.t.* to unpack, unwrap. —**desempaque** (-em'pa·ke) *n.m.* unpacking; unwrapping.

desempatar (des·em·pa'tar) *v.t.* 1, to make unequal. 2, to break a tie in (a score, a vote, etc.).

desempeñar (des·em·pe'ɲar) *v.t.* 1, to recover; redeem. 2, to free from obligation. 3, to perform (a duty or job); to act (a role).

desempeño (des·em'pe·ɲo) *n.m.* 1, recovery; redemption. 2, discharge; freedom from obligation. 3, fulfillment; performance.

desempleado (des·em·ple'a·ðo) *adj.* unemployed.

desempleo (des·em'ple·o) *n.m.* unemployment.

desempolvar (des·em·pol'βar) *also,* **desempolvorar** (-βo'rar) *v.t.* 1, to dust; remove the dust from. 2, *fig.* to dust off; resurrect.

desencadenar (des·en·ka·ðe'nar) *v.t.* 1, to unchain; free. 2, *fig.* to unleash; let forth. —**desencadenarse,** *v.r.* 1, to break loose. 2, to lose one's self-control. —**desencadenamiento,** *n.m.* unchaining; unleashing.

desencajar (des·en·ka'xar) *v.t.* to disjoint; disconnect. —**desencajarse,** *v.r.* 1, to get out of gear. 2, to be contorted *(with emotion or pain, as the face).*

desencallar (des·en·ka'ʎar; -'jar) *v.t.* to refloat (a grounded ship).

desencantar (des·en·kan'tar) *v.t.* to disenchant; disillusion. —**desen-**

canto (-'kan·to) *also,* **desencantamiento,** *n.m.* disenchantment.

desencarcelar (des·en·kar·θe·'lar; -se'lar) *v.t.* to set free; release from prison.

desencarnar (des·en·kar'nar) *v.t.* to disembody. —**desencarnarse,** *v.r.* to die.

desencoger (des·en·ko'xer) *v.t.* [*infl.:* **coger,** 15] to unfold; straighten out. —**desencogerse,** *v.r.* to grow bold.

desenconar (des·en·ko'nar) *v.t.* 1, to relieve (an inflammation or irritation). 2, to appease (anger, passion, etc.). —**desencono** (-'ko·no) *n.m.* mitigation; appeasement.

desencordar (des·en·kor'ðar) *v.t.* [*infl.:* **acostar,** 28] to unstring, esp. a musical instrument.

desencordelar (des·en·kor·ðe·'lar) *v.t.* to unstring; untie.

desenchufar (des·en·tʃu'far) *v.t.* to disconnect.

desenfadar (des·en·fa'ðar) *v.t.* to appease; calm. —**desenfadarse,** *v.r.* to calm down. —**desenfadaderas** (-ða'ðe·ras) *n.f.pl., colloq.* means of escaping difficulties; resourcefulness.

desenfado (des·en'fa·ðo) *n.m.* 1, ease; calmness. 2, presumptuousness; boldness.

desenfrenar (des·en·fre'nar) *v.t.* to unbridle. —**desenfrenarse,** *v.r.* to give vent to one's feelings. —**desenfrenado,** *adj.* unbridled; reckless; licentious. —**desenfreno** (-'fre·no) *n.m.* unruliness; wantonness; licentiousness.

desenganchar (des·en·gan'tʃar) *v.t.* 1, to unhook; unfasten. 2, to unhitch; unharness. 3, *R.R.* to uncouple.

desengañar (des·en·ga'ɲar) *v.t.* 1, to undeceive. 2, to disillusion; disappoint. —**desengaño** (-'ga·ɲo) *n.m.* disillusionment; disapointment.

desengranar (des·en·gra'nar) *v.t.* to put out of gear; disengage. —**desengrane** (-'gra·ne) *n.m.* disengagement *(of gears).*

desenlazar (des·en·la'θar; -'sar) *v.t.* [*infl.:* **rezar,** 10] 1, to unlace; untie. 2, to unravel, as the plot of a play, novel, etc. —**desenlace** (-'la·θe; -se) *n.m.* outcome; dénouement.

desenmarañar (des·en·ma·ra'ɲar) *v.t.* to disentangle; unravel.

desenmascarar (des·en·mas·ka'rar) *v.t.* to unmask; expose.

desenredar (des·en·re'ðar) *v.t.* **1,** to disentangle; unravel. **2,** to set in order. **3,** to clear up; resolve. —**desenredarse,** *v.r.* to extricate oneself; get clear.

desenredo (des·en·re·ðo) *n.m.* **1,** disentanglement. **2,** dénouement.

desenrollar (des·en·ro'ʎar; -'jar) *v.t.* to unroll; unwind.

desenroscar (des·en·ros'kar) *v.t.* [*infl.:* **tocar, 7**] to untwist; unscrew.

desensartar (des·en·sar'tar) *v.t.* to unstring; unthread.

desensibilizar (de·sen·si·βi·li'θar; -'sar) *v.t.* [*infl.:* **rezar, 10**] to desensitize.

desensillar (des·en·si'ʎar; -'jar) *v.t.* to unsaddle.

desentenderse (des·en·ten'der·se) *v.r.* [*infl.:* **perder, 29**] *fol. by* **de, 1,** to pretend not to understand. **2,** to ignore. **3,** to wash one's hands of. —**desentendido,** *adj.* unmindful; heedless.

desenterrar (des·en·te'rrar) *v.t.* [*infl.:* **pensar, 27**] **1,** to disinter; exhume. **2,** to dig up; unearth. **3,** *fig.* to recall to memory. —**desenterramiento,** *n.m.* disinterment.

desentonar (des·en·to'nar) *v.t.* to belittle; humble. —*v.i.* **1,** to be incongruous. **2,** *mus.* to be out of tune. —**desentonarse,** *v.r.* to speak or behave with impropriety.

desentono (des·en'to·no) *n.m.* **1,** discord; harsh tone. **2,** impropriety of speech or behavior.

desentrañar (des·en·tra'ɲar) *v.t.* **1,** to eviscerate. **2,** *fig.* to delve into. —**desentrañarse,** *v.r.* **1,** to give one's all, esp. to a loved one. **2,** *fol. by* **de** to give up; forsake.

desenvainar (des·en·βai'nar) *v.t.* to draw; draw out; unsheathe.

desenvoltura (des·en·βol'tu·ra) *n.f.* **1,** ease; poise. **2,** boldness; impudence.

desenvolver (des·en·βol'βer) *v.t.* [*infl.:* **mover, 30**] **1,** to unwrap; unfold. **2,** *fig.* to develop; evolve.

desenvuelto (des·en'βwel·to) *adj.* **1,** free; easy. **2,** forward; impudent.

deseo (de'se·o) *n.m.* desire; wish; longing. —**deseoso,** *adj.* desirous.

desequilibrar (des·e·ki·li'βrar) *v.t.* to unbalance. —**desequilibrado,** *adj.* unbalanced; foolish. —*n.m.* mental imbalance.

desequilibrio (des·e·ki'li·βrjo) *n.m.* imbalance.

deserción (de·ser'θjon; -'sjon) *n.f.* desertion.

desertar (de·ser'tar) *v.t.* to desert; abandon. —**desertor,** *n.m.* deserter.

deservir (de·ser'βir) *v.t.* [*infl.:* **pedir, 33**] to do a disservice to; fail. —**deservicio** (-'βi·θjo; -sjo) *n.m.* disservice.

deseslabonar (des·es·la·βo'nar) *v.t.* to unlink. —**deseslabonarse,** *v.r.* to withdraw; stand aloof.

desesperación (des·es·pe·ra·'θjon; -'sjon) *n.f.* despair; desperation; hopelessness.

desesperado (des·es·pe'ra·ðo) *adj.* **1,** desperate; hopeless. **2,** impatient. —*n.m.* bandit; desperado.

desesperanza (des·es·pe'ran·θa; -sa) *n.f.* despair. —**desesperanzado,** *adj.* despairing. —**desesperanzar,** *v.t.* [*infl.:* **rezar, 10**] to discourage; deprive of hope.

desesperar (des·es·pe'rar) *v.i.* to despair. —*v.t.* to exasperate; annoy. —**desesperarse,** *v.r.* to be or become impatient; to be annoyed.

desestimación (des·es·ti·ma·'θjon; -'sjon) *n.f.* **1,** low regard; contempt. **2,** rejection; denial, esp. of a plea or application. *Also,* **desestima** (-'ti·ma).

desestimar (des·es·ti'mar) *v.t.* **1,** to hold in low esteem; undervalue. **2,** to reject; deny; refuse, esp. a plea or application.

desfachatez (des·fa·tʃa'teθ; -'tes) *n.f.* impudence; shamelessness. —**desfachatado** (-'ta·ðo) *adj.* impudent; shameless.

desfalcar (des·fal'kar) *v.t.* [*infl.:* **tocar, 7**] to embezzle. —**desfalco** (-'fal·ko) *n.m.* embezzlement; defalcation. —**desfalcador,** *n.m.* [*fem.* -**dora**] embezzler.

desfallecer (des·fa·ʎe'θer; -je·'ser) *v.i.* [*infl.:* **conocer, 13**] to faint; languish. —*v.t.* to debilitate. —**desfallecimiento,** *n.m.* faintness; weakness; languor.

desfavorable (des·fa·βo'ra·βle) *adj.* unfavorable.

desfavorecer (des·fa·βo·re'θer; -'ser) *v.t.* [*infl.:* **conocer, 13**] **1,** to disfavor. **2,** to oppose; contradict.

desfigurar (des·fi·ɣu'rar) *v.t.* **1,** to disfigure. **2,** to misrepresent; distort. —**desfiguración,** *n.f.* disfigurement. *Also,* **desfiguramiento,** *n.m.*

desfiladero (des·fi·la'ðe·ro) *n.m.* defile.

desfilar (des·fi'lar) *v.i.* **1,** to file;

march in file. 2, to parade.
—**desfile** (-'fi·le) *n.m.* parade.

desflorar (des·flo'rar) *v.t.* to deflower. —**desfloración**, *n.f.* defloration. *Also*, **desfloramiento**, *n.m.*

desfogar (des·fo'yar) *v.t.* [*infl.:*
pagar, 8] 1, to give vent to. 2, to
slake (lime). —**desfogarse**, *v.r.*
to vent one's feelings.

desfondar (des·fon'dar) *v.t.* 1, to
break or remove the bottom of. 2,
naut. to pierce or sheer off the hull
of (a ship).

desgaire (des'yai·re) *n.m.* graceless manner; untidiness.

desgajar (des·ya'xar) *v.t.* to tear;
rend. —**desgajarse**, *v.r.* to fall off;
break off.

desgana (des'ya·na) *n.f.* 1, lack of
appetite. 2, indifference; boredom.

desganar (des·ya'nar) *v.t.* to dissuade. —**desganarse**, *v.r.* 1, to lose
one's appetite. 2, to be bored.

desgarbo (des'yar·βo) *n.m.* clumsiness. —**desgarbado** (-'βa·ðo) *adj.*
clumsy; ungainly.

desgarrado (des·ya'rra·ðo) *adj.* 1,
torn. 2, dissolute; wicked.

desgarradura (des·ya·rra'ðu·ra)
n.f. rip; rent; tear.

desgarrar (des·ya'rrar) *v.t.* to
rend; tear. —*v.i.*, *Amer.* to hawk;
clear the throat. —**desgarrador**,
adj. 1, heartrending. 2, bloodcur-
dling.

desgarro (des'ya·rro) *n.m.* 1, laceration; tear. 2, *fig.* boldness; impudence. —**desgarrón**, *n.m.* large tear.

desgastar (des·yas'tar) *v.t.* to
wear away; consume. —**desgaste**
(-'yas·te) *n.m.* wear and tear.

desglosar (des·ylo'sar) *v.t.* to separate the parts or divisions of; arrange under respective headings.

desgracia (des'yra·θja; -sja) *n.f.* 1,
misfortune; mishap; affliction. 2,
disgrace; dishonor. —**desgraciado**, *adj.* unfortunate; unhappy.
—*n.m.* wretch. —**desgraciadamente**, *adv.* unfortunately. *Also*,
por desgracia.

desgraciar (des·yra'θjar; -'sjar)
v.t. 1, to displease. 2, to spoil.
—**desgraciarse**, *v.r.* 1, to degenerate; to be spoiled. 2, to fall out of
favor. 3, to fail.

desgranar (des·yra'nar) *v.t.* to
thresh (grain); to shell (peas).

desgreñar (des·yre'ɲar) *v.t.* to dishevel.

desguarnecer (des·ywar·ne'θer)

-'ser) *v.t.* [*infl.:* **conocer,** 13] 1, to
strip of ornaments or trimmings. 2,
to unharness. 3, to dismantle; strip
down. 4, to unman (a garrison). 5,
to remove fortifications from.

desguazar (des·ywa'θar; -'sar) *v.t.*
[*infl.:* **rezar,** 10] 1, to hew. 2, *naut.*
to dismantle (a ship).

deshabitar (des·a·βi'tar) *v.t.* 1, to
vacate; move out of. 2, to depopulate. —**deshabitado**, *adj* uninhabited; vacant.

deshabituar (des·a·βi'twar) *v.t.*
[*infl.:* **continuar,** 23] to break
(someone) of a habit. —**deshabi-
tuarse**, *v.r.* to break (oneself) of a
habit.

deshacer (des·a'θer; -'ser) *v.t.*
[*infl.:* **hacer,** 48] 1, to undo; destroy. 2, to take apart; dissolve.
—**deshacerse**, *v.r.* 1, to melt; vanish. 2, to waste away. —**deshacerse
de**, to get rid of.

desharrapado *also*, **desarrapado**
(des·a·rra'pa·ðo) *adj.* ragged;
shabby; grubby.

deshebillar (des·e·βi'ʎar; -'jar)
v.t. to unbuckle.

deshecha (des'e·tʃa) *n.f.* feint;
sham.

deshecho (des'e·tʃo) *adj.* 1, undone; destroyed. 2, melted. 3, shattered.

deshelar (des·e'lar) *v.t.* [*infl.:*
pensar, 27] to thaw; melt.

desherbar (des·er'βar) *v.t.* [*infl.:*
pensar, 27] 1, to weed. 2, to pull
out (weeds).

desheredar (des·e·re'ðar) *v.t.* to
disinherit. —**desheredación**, *n.f.*,
also, **desheredamiento**, *n.m.* disinheritance.

deshidratar (des·i·ðra'tar) *v.t.* to
dehydrate. —**deshidratación**, *n.f.*
dehydration.

deshielo (des'je·lo) *n.m.* thaw.

deshierba (des'jer·βa) *n.f.* weeding.

deshilachar (des·i·la'tʃar) *v.t.* to
ravel; fray.

deshilar (des·i'lar) *v.t.* 1, to ravel.
2, *sewing* to draw threads from.

deshilvanar (des·il·βa'nar) *v.t.*,
sewing to unbaste; untack. —**deshilvanado**, *adj.* disconnected; incoherent.

deshojar (des·o'xar) *v.t.* to defoliate.

deshollejar (des·o·ʎe'xar; -je'xar)
v.t. to pare; peel; husk.

deshollinar (des·o·ʎi'nar; -ji'nar)

v.t. **1,** to sweep (a chimney) **2,** to remove soot from. **3,** to scrutinize. —**deshollinador,** *n.m.* [*fem.* -**dora**] **1,** chimney sweep. **2,** [*Also,* **deshollinadera,** *n.f.*] chimney brush or broom.

deshonestidad (des·o·nes·ti'ðað) *n.f.* **1,** dishonesty. **2,** immodesty.

deshonesto (des·o'nes·to) *adj.* **1,** dishonest. **2,** immodest.

deshonor (des·o'nor) *n.m.* dishonor.

deshonrar (des·on'rar) *v.t.* **1,** to dishonor. **2,** to defame. **3,** to seduce. —**deshonra** (-'on·ra) *n.f.* dishonor. —**deshonroso,** *adj.* dishonorable.

deshora (des'o·ra) *n.f.* inopportune time. —**a deshora,** untimely.

deshuesar (des·we'sar) *v.t.* = **desosar.**

deshuese (des'we·se) *v., pres. subjve.* of **desosar.**

deshueso (des'we·so) *v., pres.ind.* of **desosar.**

deshumanizar (des·u·ma·ni'θar; -'sar) *v.t.* [*infl.:* **rezar,** 10] to dehumanize. —**deshumanización,** *n.f.* dehumanization.

desidia (de'si·ðja) *n.f.* **1**laziness; idleness. —**desidioso,** *adj.* lazy; idle; listless.

desierto (de'sjer·to) *adj.* deserted. —*n.m.* desert; wilderness.

designar (de·siy'nar) *v.t.* to designate. —**designación,** *n.f.* designation; appointment.

designio (de'siy·njo) *n.m.* design; purpose.

desigualar (des·i·ywa'lar) *v.t.* to make dissimilar, unequal or uneven. —**desigual,** *adj.* dissimilar; unequal; uneven. —**desigualdad,** *n.f.* dissimilarity; inequality; unevenness.

desilusionar (des·i·lu·sjo'nar) *v.t.* **1,** to disillusion. **2,** to disappoint. —**desilusión** (-'sjon) **1,** disillusionment. **2,** disappointment.

desimantar (des·i·man'tar) *v.t.* to demagnetize.

desinclinar (des·in·kli'nar) *v.t.* to disincline. —**desinclinarse,** *v.r.* to disincline; be disinclined; be unwilling.

desincorporar (des·in·kor·po'rar) *v.t.* to dissolve; break up.

desinencia (de·si'nen·θja; -sja) *n.f., gram.* word ending.

desinfección (des·in·fek'θjon; -'sjon) *n.f.* disinfection.

desinfectar (des·in·fek'tar) *v.t.* to

disinfect. —**desinfectante,** *adj.* & *n.m.* disinfectant.

desinflar (des·in'flar) *v.t.* to deflate. —**desinflación,** *n.f.* deflation.

desintegrar (des·in·te'yrar) *v.t.* to disintegrate. —**desintegración,** *n.f.* disintegration.

desinterés (des·in·te'res) *n.m.* disinterestedness. —**desinteresado,** *adj.* disinterested; impartial.

desinteresarse (des·in·te·re'sar·se) *v.r., fol. by* **de,** to lose interest (in).

desintoxicar (des·in·tok·si'kar) *v.t.* [*infl.:* **tocar,** 7] to detoxify. —**desintoxicación,** *n.f.* detoxification.

desistimiento (de·sis·ti'mjen·to) *n.m.* **1,** desistance. **2,** *law* waiving; waiver. *Also,* **desistencia** (-'ten·θja; -sja) *n.f.*

desistir (de·sis'tir) *v.i.* **1,** to desist. **2,** *law* to waive.

desjarretar (des·xa·rre'tar) *v.t.* to hamstring.

desjuntar (des·xun'tar) *v.t.* to disjoin; separate. —**desjuntarse,** *v.r.* to separate; break away.

deslabonar (des·la·βo'nar) *v.t.* = **deseslabonar.**

deslavar (des·la'βar) *v.t.* **1,** to wash superficially. **2,** to weaken; fade. —**deslavado,** *adj.* impudent; barefaced.

deslazar (des·la'θar; -'sar) *v.t.* = **desenlazar.**

desleal (des·le'al) *adj.* disloyal. —**deslealtad,** *n.f.* disloyalty.

desleimiento (des·lei'mjen·to) *n.m.* **1,** dissolving. **2,** dilution. *Also,* **desleidura,** *n.f.*

desleír (des·le'ir) *v.t.* [*infl.:* **reír,** 58] **1,** to dissolve. **2,** to dilute. **3,** *fig.* to expatiate on; be prolix about.

deslenguado (des·len'gwa·ðo) *adj.* talkative; foul-mouthed.

desliar (des·li'ar) *v.t.* [*infl.:* **enviar,** 22] to untie; unwrap.

deslice (des'li·θe; -se) *v., pres. subjve.* of **deslizar.**

deslicé (des·li'θe; -'se) *v., 1st pers. sing. pret.* of **deslizar.**

desligar (des·li'yar) *v.t.* [*infl.:* **pagar,** 8] **1,** to untie; loosen. **2,** to disentangle. **3,** to release from an obligation.

deslindar (des·lin'dar) *v.t.* **1,** to demarcate. **2,** to define. —**deslinde** (-'lin·de) *n.m.* demarcation.

desliz (des'liθ; -'lis) *n.m.* **1,** slip; slide. **2,** error; false step.

deslizamiento (des·li·θa'mjen·to; -sa'mjen·to) n.m. 1, = **desliz**. 2, landslide.

deslizar (des·li'θar; -'sar) v.t. [infl.: **rezar**, 10] to let slide; let slip. —**deslizarse**, v.r. to slip away; shirk. —**deslizadero**, n.m. slippery place. —**deslizadizo**, adj. slippery. —**deslizador**, n.m. scooter; glider.

deslucir (des·lu'θir; -'sir) v.t. [infl.: **lucir**, 14] to mar; tarnish; discredit. —**deslucido**, adj. tarnished; dull. —**quedar** or **salir deslucido**, to be disappointing.

deslumbrar (des·lum'brar) v.t. to dazzle; daze. —**deslumbrante**, also, **deslumbrador**, adj. dazzling.

deslustrar (des·lus'trar) v.t. 1, to tarnish. 2, to sully (a reputation). —**deslustre** (-'lus·tre) n.m. stain; tarnish.

desmadejar (des·ma·ðe'xar) v.t. to weaken; enervate.

desmalezar (des·ma·le'θar; -'sar) v.t., Amer. [infl.: **rezar**, 10] to weed; grub; clear (the earth).

desmán (des'man) n.m. 1, misconduct; abuse. 2, disaster; misfortune.

desmandar (des·man'dar) v.t. countermand; rescind. —**desmandarse**, v.r. to get out of hand; go too far. —**desmandado**, adj. disobedient; impudent.

desmantelar (des·man·te'lar) v.t. to dismantle. —**desmantelamiento**, n.m. dismantling; dismantlement.

desmaña (des'ma·ɲa) n.f. clumsiness; awkwardness. —**desmañado**, adj. clumsy; awkward. —n.m. dub; duffer.

desmarañar (des·ma·ra'ɲar) v.t. = **desenmarañar**.

desmayar (des·ma'jar) v.t. to dismay; discourage. —v.i. to be dispirited or discouraged. —**desmayarse**, v.r. to faint.

desmayo (des'ma·jo) n.m. 1, faint; loss of strength. 2, discouragement; dismay.

desmedirse (des·me'ðir·se) v.r. [infl.: **pedir**, 33] to lose self-control; exceed the bounds of propriety. —**desmedido**, adj. immoderate; extravagant.

desmedrar (des·me'ðrar) v.t. to impair. —v.i. to deteriorate. —**desmedro** (-'me·ðro) n.m. detriment.

desmejorar (des·me·xo'rar) v.t. to impair; make worse.

desmelenar (des·me·le'nar) v.t. to dishevel.

desmembrar (des·mem'brar) v.t. [infl.: **pensar**, 27] 1, to dismember. 2, to separate. —**desmembrarse**, v.r. to disintegrate. —**desmembramiento**, n.m. dismemberment.

desmentir (des·men'tir) v.t. [infl.: **sentir**, 31] 1, to belie. 2, to disprove. 3, to dissemble. —**desmentida**, n.f. denial; contradiction.

desmenuzar (des·me·nu'θar; -'sar) v.t. [infl.: **rezar**, 10] 1, to chip; crumble; mince; shred. 2, to examine minutely.

desmerecer (des·me·re'θer; -'ser) v.t. [infl.: **conocer**, 13] to be or become unworthy of. —v.i. 1, to deteriorate. 2, to compare unfavorably (with something else). —**desmerecedor**, adj. unworthy; undeserving. —**desmerecimiento**, n.m. unworthiness.

desmesurar (des·me·su'rar) v.t. to exaggerate; overstate. —**desmesurarse**, v.r. to speak or act unbecomingly. —**desmesurado**, adj. immoderate.

desmigajar (des·mi·ɣa'xar) v.t. to crumble.

desmigar (des·mi'ɣar) v.t. [infl.: **pagar**, 8] to crumble (bread).

desmilitarizar (des·mi·li·ta·ri·'ɣar; -'sar) v.t. [infl.: **rezar**, 10] to demilitarize. —**desmilitarización**, n.f. demilitarization.

desmochar (des·mo'tʃar) v.t. 1, to cut off; lop. 2, to mutilate.

desmolado (des·mo'la·ðo) adj. toothless; without molars.

desmontar (des·mon'tar) v.t. 1, to dismount. 2, to dismantle. 3, to cut down (a forest); to clear or level (ground). —v.i. to dismount; alight. —**desmontable**, adj. dismountable.

desmoralizar (des·mo·ra·li'θar; -'sar) v.t. [infl.: **rezar**, 10] to demoralize; corrupt. —**desmoralización**, n.f. demoralization; depravity. —**desmoralizador**, adj. demoralizing.

desmoronar (des·mo·ro'nar) v.t. to crumble; abrade. —**desmoronamiento**, n.m. crumbling; wearing away.

desmotar (des·mo'tar) v.t. to gin (cotton). —**desmotadora**, n.f. cotton gin.

desmovilizar (des·mo·βi·li'θar; -'sar) v.t. [infl.: **rezar**, 10] to demobilize. —**desmovilización**, n.f. demobilization.

desnatar (des·na'tar) v.t. 1, to

skim (milk). **2,** *fig.* to remove the best part of. —**desnatadora,** *n.f.* skimmer; cream separator.

desnaturalizar (des·na·tu·ra·li'θar; -'sar) *v.t.* [*infl.:* rezar, 10] **1,** to denaturalize; deprive of citizenship. **2,** to denature. **3,** *fig.* to pervert.

desnivel (des·ni'βel) *n.m.* **1,** unevenness. **2,** gradient.

desnivelar (des·ni·βe'lar) *v.t.* **1,** to make uneven. **2,** to make unlevel.

desnucar (des·nu'kar) *v.t.* [*infl.:* tocar, 7] to break the neck of.

desnudar (des·nu'ðar) *v.t.* **1,** to undress. **2,** to denude. —**desnudez** (-'ðeθ; -'ðes) *n.f.* nudity; nakedness.

desnudo (des'nu·ðo) *adj.* **1,** naked; nude. **2,** *fig.* patent; evident. —**desnudista,** *adj.* & *n.m.* & *f.* nudist.

desnutrición (des·nu·tri'θjon; -'sjon) *n.f.* malnutrition.

desobedecer (des·o·βe·ðe'θer; -'ser) *v.t.* [*infl.:* conocer, 13] to disobey. —**desobediencia,** *n.f.* disobedience. —**desobediente,** *adj.* disobedient.

desobligar (des·o·βli'ɣar) *v.t.* [*infl.:* pagar, 8] **1,** to disoblige; offend. **2,** to free of an obligation.

desocupado (des·o·ku'pa·ðo) *adj.* **1,** empty; vacant. **2,** idle; unemployed. —**desocupación,** *n.f.* unemployment; idleness.

desocupar (des·o·ku'par) *v.t.* to vacate; empty.

desodorante (des·o·ðo'ran·te) *n.m.* & *adj.* deodorant.

desodorizar (des·o·ðo·ri'θar; -'sar) *v.t.* [*infl.:* rezar, 10] to deodorize. —**desodorización,** *n.f.* deodorization.

desoír (des·o'ir) *v.t.* [*infl.:* oír, 25] to be deaf to; not to hear or heed.

desolación (de·so·la'θjon; -'sjon) *n.f.* **1,** desolation; ruin. **2,** affliction; anguish.

desolar (de·so'lar) *v.t.* [*infl.:* acostar, 28] to desolate. —**desolarse,** *v.r.* to be forlorn. —**desolado,** *adj.* desolate.

desollar (des·o'ʎar; -'jar) *v.t.* [*infl.:* acostar, 28] **1,** to flay; skin. **2,** to fleece; swindle. —**desolladura,** *n.f.* flaying.

desorbitado (des·or·βi'ta·ðo) *adj.* **1,** out of orbit. **2,** *Amer.* pop-eyed; wide-eyed. **3,** *Amer.* unhinged; crazy.

desorden (des'or·ðen) *n.m.* disorder; confusion.

desordenar (des·or·ðe'nar) *v.t.* to disorder; disarrange; upset; confuse. —**desordenado,** *adj.* disordered; disorderly.

desorganizar (des·or·ɣa·ni'θar; -'sar) *v.t.* [*infl.:* rezar, 10] to disorganize. —**desorganización,** *n.f.* disorganization.

desorientar (des·o·rjen'tar) *v.t.* to disorient; confuse. —**desorientación,** disorientation.

desosar (des·o'sar) *v.t.* [*infl.:* 45] to bone; remove the bone from.

desovar (des·o'βar) *v.t.* to spawn. —**desove** (-'o·βe) *n.m.* spawning.

despabilado (des·pa·βi'la·ðo) *adj.* alert; lively. *Also,* **espabilado.**

despabilar (des·pa·βi'lar) *v.t.* **1,** to snuff (a candle). **2,** to trim (a wick). **3,** *fig.* to perk; rouse.

despacio (des'pa·θjo; -sjo) *adv.* slowly. —**despacioso,** *adj.* slow; deliberate.

despachar (des·pa't∫ar) *v.t.* **1,** to dispatch. **2,** to wait on (a customer) —**despachador,** *n.m.* dispatcher.

despacho (des'pa·t∫o) *n.m.* **1,** dispatch; shipment. **2,** office; study. **3,** official communication.

despachurrar (des·pa·t∫u'rrar) *v.t., colloq.* to squash; crush; mangle.

despampanarse (des·pam·pa·'nar·se) *v.r.* to be convulsed (*as with laughter, weeping, etc.*)

desparejar (des·pa·re'xar) *v.t.* **1,** to make uneven. **2,** to break up (a pair). —**desparejo** (-pa're·xo) *adj.* odd; uneven; unmatched.

desparpajar (des·par·pa'xar) *v.t.* **1,** to disarrange; upset. **2,** *Amer.* to scatter; disperse. —*v.i.* [*also,* **desparpajarse,** *v.r.*] *colloq.* to rant; rave.

desparpajo (des·par'pa·xo) *n.m., colloq.* **1,** poise; ease. **2,** boldness; presumptuousness. **3,** witticism.

desparramar (des·pa·rra'mar) *v.t.* **1,** to spread; scatter; spill. **2,** to squander. —**desparramo** (-'rra·mo) *n.m., Amer.* scattering; spreading.

despatillar (des·pa·ti'ʎar; -'jar) *v.t.* **1,** to groove (wood). **2,** *colloq.* to shave off (whiskers).

despavorido (des·pa·βo'ri·ðo) *adj.* terrified.

despearse (des·pe'ar·se) *v.r.* to weary one's feet by walking or standing. —**despeado,** *adj.* footsore.

despectivo (des·pek'ti·βo) *adj.*
derogatory; disparaging.

despechar (des·pe'tʃar) *v.t.* **1,** to
anger; vex. **2,** to displease. **3,** to
drive to despair. **4,** *colloq.* to wean.
—**despecharse,** *v.r.* **1,** to become
angry. **2,** to be displeased. **3,** to despair.

despecho (des'pe·tʃo) *n.m.* spite;
rancor. —**a despecho de,** in spite
of; despite.

despedazar (des·pe·ða'θar; -'sar)
v.t. [*infl.:* **rezar,** 10] to tear to
pieces.

despedida (des·pe'ði·ða) *n.f.* **1,**
farewell; parting. **2,** discharge; dismissal.

despedir (des·pe'ðir) *v.t.* [*infl.:*
pedir, 33] **1,** to dismiss; discharge.
2, to emit. **3,** to bid farewell.
—**despedirse,** *v.r.* to take one's
leave; say good-bye.

despegar (des·pe'γar) *v.t.* [*infl.:*
pagar, 8] **1,** to detach. **2,** to unglue;
unstick. —*v.i.,* *aero.* to take off.
—**despegable,** *adj.* detachable.
—**despegado,** *adj.* curt. —**despego**
(-'pe·γo) *n.m.* = **desapego.**

despeinar (des·pei'nar) *v.t.* to dishevel.

despegue (des'pe·γe) *n.m.,* *aero.*
take-off; lift-off.

despejado (des·pe'xa·ðo) *adj.* **1,**
bright; clear. **2,** unobstructed. **3,**
clever.

despejar (des·pe'xar) *v.t.* to clear;
remove obstacles from. —**despejarse,** *v.r.* to clear up *(as weather)*;
become bright.

despejo (des'pe·xo) *n.m.* **1,** clearing; removal of obstacles. **2,** cleverness.

despeluzar (des·pe·lu'θar; -'sar)
v.t. [*infl.:* **rezar,** 10] **1,** to muss; dishevel. **2,** to make (the hair) stand
on end. **3,** *Amer.* to clear out; clean
out; strip bare. *Also,* **despeluznar**
(-luθ'nar; -lus'nar).

despeluznante (des·pe·luθ'nan·
te; -lus'nan·te) *adj.* = **espeluznante.**

despellejar (des·pe·ʎe'xar;
-je'xar) *v.t.* to skin; flay.

despensa (des'pen·sa) *n.f.* pantry;
larder. —**despensero,** *n.m.* steward.

despeñar (des·pe'ɲar) *v.t.* to precipitate; cast down. —**despeñadero,** *n.m.* precipice.

despepitar (des·pe·pi'tar) *v.t.* to
remove the seeds from. —**despepi-
tarse por,** to yearn for.

desperdiciar (des·per·ði'θjar;

-'sjar) *v.t.* to waste; misuse.
—**desperdicio** (-'ði·θjo; -sjo) *n.m.*
waste. —**desperdicios,** *n.m.pl.* garbage; offal.

desperezarse (des·pe·re'θar·se;
-'sar·se) *v.r.* [*infl.:* **rezar,** 10] to
stretch; stretch one's legs. *Also,*
esperezarse.

desperfecto (des·per'fek·to) *n.m.*
damage; defect; flaw.

despertar (des·per'tar) *v.t.* [*infl.:*
pensar, 27] **1,** to awake; rouse. **2,** to
arouse; stimulate. —**despertador,**
adj. awakening; arousing. —*n.m.*
alarm clock.

despiadado (des·pja'ða·ðo) *adj.*
merciless; cruel.

despicar (des·pi'kar) *v.t.* [*infl.:*
tocar, 7] to satisfy; appease.

despida (des'pi·ða) *v.,* *pres.subjve.*
of **despedir.**

despido (des'pi·ðo) *n.m.* dismissal;
dispatch. —*v.,* *pres.ind.* of **despedir.**

despierto (des'pjer·to) *adj.* `**1,**
awake. **2,** alert.

despilfarrar (des·pil·fa'rrar) *v.t.*
to squander; waste. —**despilfarro**
(-'fa·rro) *n.m.* waste; prodigality.

despintarse (des·pin'tar·se) *v.r.* to
fade. —**no despintársele a uno,**
to remember (someone or something) well.

despique (des'pi·ke) *n.m.* revenge.

despistar (des·pis'tar) *v.t.* to
throw off the scent; mislead.

desplacer (des·pla'θer; -'ser) *v.t.*
[*infl.:* **placer,** 52] to displease.
—*n.m.* displeasure.

desplantar (des·plan'tar) *v.t.* **1,** to
uproot. **2,** to move or sway from an
upright position; throw off balance.
—**desplantador,** *n.m.* garden
trowel.

desplante (des'plan·te) *n.m.* barefaced act or attitude.

desplazar (des·pla'θar; -'sar) *v.t.*
[*infl.:* **rezar,** 10] to displace.
—**desplazamiento,** *n.m.,* *naut.* displacement.

desplegar (des·ple'γar) *v.t.* [*infl.:*
pagar, 8; **pensar,** 27] **1,** to unfold;
unfurl. **2,** *mil.* to deploy. **3,** to explain; show.

despliegue (des'plje·γe) *n.m.* **1,**
unfolding; unfurling. **2,** *mil.* deployment.

desplomar (des·plo'mar) *v.t.* to
put out of plumb. —**desplomarse,**
v.r. to slump; collapse; tumble
down. —**desplome** (-'plo·me) *n.m.*
collapse.

desplumar (des·plu'mar) *v.t.* **1,** to pluck (fowl). **2,** *colloq.* to fleece; rob.

despoblar (des·po'βlar) *v.t.* [*infl.:* **acostar, 28**] to depopulate. —**despoblado,** *n.m.* desert; uninhabited place.

despojar (des·po'xar) *v.t.* to despoil; divest; denude.

despojo (des'po·xo) *n.m.* **1,** spoils; booty; plunder. **2,** scrap; offal. **3,** despoilment; divestment. —**despojos,** *n.m.pl.* **1,** debris; rubble. **2,** leavings; leftovers. **3,** mortal remains. **4,** flotsam.

desportillar (des·por·ti'ʎar; -'jar) *v.t.* to chip; nick. —**desportilladura,** *n.f.* chip; fragment.

desposar (des·po'sar) *v.t.* to marry; wed. —**desposado,** *adj.* & *n.m.* newlywed.

desposeer (des·po·se'er) *v.t.* [*infl.:* **creer, 24**] **1,** to deprive. **2,** to dispossess. —**desposeimiento** (-sei'mjen·to) *n.m.* dispossession.

desposorio (des·po'so·rjo) *n.m.* **1,** betrothal; engagement. **2,** wedding.

déspota ('des·po·ta) *n.m.* despot. —**despótico** (-'po·ti·ko) *adj.* despotic. —**despotismo,** *n.m.* despotism.

despotricar (des·po·tri'kar) *v.i.* [*infl.:* **tocar, 7**] to rant; rave.

despreciar (des·pre'θjar; -'sjar) *v.t.* to disdain; scorn; despise. —**despreciable,** *adj.* despicable; contemptible. —**despreciativo** (-pre·θja'ti·βo; -sja'ti·βo) *adj.* scornful; contemptuous. —**desprecio** (-'pre·θjo; -sjo) *n.m.* disdain; contempt.

desprender (des·pren'der) *v.t.* to loosen; unfasten; detach. —**desprenderse,** *v.r.* to be inferred or inferable. —**desprenderse de,** to give up; dispose of.

desprendido (des·pren'di·ðo) *adj.* **1,** loose; detached. **2,** *fig.* generous.

desprendimiento (des·pren·di'mjen·to) *n.m.* **1,** separation; detaching. **2,** detachment; indifference. **3,** generosity.

despreocuparse (des·pre·o·ku'par·se) *v.r., fol. by* **de,** to ignore. —**despreocupación,** *n.f.* carelessness; indifference. —**despreocupado,** *adj.* careless; indifferent.

desprestigiar (des·pres·ti'xjar) *v.t.* **1,** to discredit. **2,** to sully (a reputation). —**desprestigio** (-'ti·xjo) *n.m.* discredit.

desprevenido (des·pre·βe'ni·ðo) *adj.* unprepared.

desproporción (des·pro·por'θjon; -'sjon) *n.f.* disproportion. —**desproporcionado,** *adj.* disproportionate. —**desproporcionar,** *v.t.* to make disproportionate.

desproveer (des·pro·βe'er) *v.t.* [*infl.:* **creer, 24**; *p.p.* **desproveído** (-βe'i·ðo), **desprovisto** (-'βis·to)] to deprive of provisions. —**desprovisto,** *adj.* deprived; lacking; devoid.

después (des'pwes) *adv.* after; afterwards; then; later. —**después de,** after (*prep.*). —**después (de) que,** after (*conj.*).

despuntar (des·pun'tar) *v.t.* **1,** to blunt. **2,** to crop. —*v.i.* **1,** to sprout. **2,** to excel. —**despuntar el alba,** to dawn.

desquiciar (des·ki'θjar; -'sjar) *v.t.* **1,** to unhinge. **2,** *fig.* to madden; enrage.

desquitarse (des·ki'tar·se) *v.r.* **1,** to recoup; recover. **2,** to retaliate; get even.

desquite (des'ki·te) *n.m.* **1,** retaliation; compensation. **2,** (in sports) return match.

desrazonable (des·ra·θo'na·βle; des·ra·so-) *adj.* unreasonable.

desrizar (des·ri'θar; -'sar) *v.t.* [*infl.:* **rezar, 10**] to uncurl.

destacar (des·ta'kar) *v.t.* [*infl.:* **tocar, 7**] **1,** to detach. **2,** to emphasize. —**destacarse,** *v.r.* to excel; stand out. —**destacamento,** *n.m., mil.* detachment; outpost.

destajar (des·ta'xar) *v.t.* **1,** to do (work) by the piece. **2,** to contract for (work) by the piece.

destajero (des·ta'xe·ro) *n.m.* pieceworker. *Also,* **destajista,** *n.m.* & *f.*

destajo (des'ta·xo) *n.m.* **1,** job; contract. **2,** piecework. —**a destajo, 1,** on contract. **2,** by the piece; on piecework. **3,** *fig.* eagerly; tirelessly.

destapar (des·ta'par) *v.t.* to uncover; remove the lid from.

destaponar (des·ta·po'nar) *v.t.* to uncork.

destartalado (des·tar·ta'la·ðo) *adj.* ramshackle; falling apart.

destejer (des·te'xer) *v.t.* **1,** to unweave; unknit. **2,** to upset; disturb.

destellar (des·te'ʎar; -'jar) *v.t.* to sparkle; flash. —**destello** (-'te·ʎo; -jo) *n.m.* sparkle; gleam.

destemplanza (des·tem'plan·θa;

-sa) *n.f.* 1, intemperance. 2, indisposition; distemper. 3, irregularity of the pulse.

destemplar (des·tem'plar) *v.t.* 1, to distemper. 2, to make discordant. 3, to jar; jangle. —**destemplarse,** *v.r.* 1, to become indisposed. 2, to behave intemperately. —**destemplado,** *adj.* 1, immoderate; intemperate. 2, *mus.* out of tune. 3, *med.* irregular.

destemple (des'tem·ple) *n.m.* 1, dissonance. 2, disorder. 3, indisposition.

desteñir (des·te'ɲir) *v.t.* [*infl.:* reñir, 59] to discolor; fade.

desternillarse (des·ter·ni'ʎar·se; -'jar·se) *v.r.* to split one's sides, as with laughter.

desterrar (des·te'rrar) *v.t.* [*infl.* pensar, 27] 1, to exile; banish. 2, to remove earth from, as roots.

destetar (des·te'tar) *v.t.* to wean. —**destete** (-'te·te) *n.m.* weaning.

destiempo (des'tjem·po) *in* a destiempo, untimely; inopportunely.

destierro (des'tje·rro) *n.m.* exile; banishment.

destilar (des·ti'lar) *v.t.* 1, to distil. 2, to filter. —*v.i.* to trickle. —**destilación,** *n.f.* distillation. —**destiladera,** *n.f.* still. —**destilería,** *n.f.* distillery. *Also,* **destilatorio,** *n.m.*

destinar (des·ti'nar) *v.t.* 1, to destine. 2, to designate; assign. —**destinación,** *n.f.* destination.

destinatario (des·ti·na'ta·rjo) *n.m.* addressee; consignee.

destino (des'ti·no) *n.m.* 1, destiny. 2, destination. 3, purpose. 4, assignment; post; job.

destitución (des·ti·tu'θjon; -'sjon) *n.f.* 1, destitution. 2, dismissal (*from a job*).

destituir (des·ti·tu'ir) *v.t.* [*infl.:* huir, 26] 1, to deprive. 2, to dismiss (*from a job*). —**destituído,** *adj.* destitute.

destocar (des·to'kar) *v.t.* [*infl.:* tocar, 7] 1, to remove the headgear of. 2, to undo the hair of.

destorcer (des·tor'θer; -'ser) *v.t.* [*infl.:* torcer, 66] to untwist.

destornillar (des·tor·ni'ʎar; -'jar) *v.t.* to unscrew. —**destornillarse,** *v.r.* to act foolishly; become unhinged. —**destornillador,** *n.m.* screwdriver.

destrabar (des·tra'βar) *v.t.* 1, to untie; unfetter. 2, to detach; separate.

destral (des'tral) *n.m.* small ax; hatchet.

destrenzar (des·tren'θar; -'sar) *v.t.* [*infl.:* rezar, 10] to unbraid.

destreza (des'tre·θa; -sa) *n.f.* dexterity.

destripar (des·tri'par) *v.t.* 1, to disembowel. 2, to crush; mash.

destrísimo (des'tri·si·mo) *adj., superl.* of diestro.

destrizar (des·tri'θar; -'sar) *v.t.* [*infl.:* rezar, 10] to break to bits; shatter. —**destrizarse,** *v.r.* to go to pieces.

destronar (des·tro'nar) *v.t.* to dethrone. —**destronamiento,** *n.m.* dethronement.

destroncar (des·tron'kar) *v.t.* [*infl.:* tocar, 7] 1, to truncate; lop. 2, to interrupt; cut short. 3, to behead; decapitate. —**destroncarse,** *v.r.* to come apart.

destrozar (des·tro'θar; -'sar) *v.t.* [*infl.:* rezar, 10] to destroy; shatter. —**destrozo** (-'tro·θo; -so) *n.m.* destruction; havoc.

destrucción (des·truk'θjon; -'sjon) *n.f.* destruction. —**destructivo** (-'ti·βo) *adj.* destructive.

destructible (des·truk'ti·βle) *adj.* destructible.

destructor (des·truk'tor) *adj.* destructive. —*n.m.* 1, destroyer. 2, naval destroyer.

destruíble (des·tru'i·βle) *adj.* destructible.

destruidor (des·tru·i'ðor) *adj.* destructive. —*n.m.* destroyer.

destruir (des·tru'ir) *v.t.* [*infl.:* construir, 41] to destroy.

destusar (des·tu'sar) *v.t., Amer.* to husk (corn).

desuele (de'swe·le) *v., pres.subjve.* of desolar.

desuelo (de'swe·lo) *v., pres.ind.* of desolar.

desuelle (des'we·ʎe; -je) *v., pres.subjve.* of desollar.

desuello (des'we·ʎo; -jo) *v., pres.ind.* of desollar.

desuncir (des·un'θir; -'sir) *v.t.* [*infl.:* esparcir, 12] to unyoke.

desunión (des·u'njon) *n.f.* disunion; disunity.

desunir (des·u'nir) *v.t.* 1, to disunite; divide; separate. 2, to set against one another. 3, to detach; disengage. —**desunirse,** *v.r.* to disintegrate; fall apart.

desusar (des·u'sar) *v.t.* to stop using; disuse. —**desusado**, *adj.* out of use; obsolete. —**desuso** (-'u·so) *n.m.* disuse.

desvaído (des·βa'i·ðo) *adj.* 1, lanky; gangling. 2, dull; faded.

desvainar (des·βai'nar) *v.t.* to shell (peas, beans, etc.).

desvalido (des·βa'li·ðo) *adj.* helpless; destitute.

desvalijar (des·βa·li'xar) *adj.* 1, to rifle (a bag). 2, to rob; fleece. —**desvalijamiento**, *n.m.* robbery; fleecing.

desvalorizar (des·βa·lo·ri'θar; -'sar) *v.t.* [*infl.:* rezar, 10] to devaluate; devalue. *Also,* **desvalorar** (-'rar). —**desvalorización**, *n.f.* devaluation.

desvaluación (des·βa·lwa'θjon; -'sjon) *n.f.* = **devaluación**.

desván (des'βan) *n.m.* attic; loft.

desvanecer (des·βa·ne'θer; -'ser) *v.t.* [*infl.:* conocer, 13] to banish; dispel. —**desvanecerse**, *v.r.* 1, to vanish; disappear. 2, to evaporate; dissipate. 3, to faint.

desvanecimiento (des·βa·ne·θi'mjen·to; -si'mjen·to) *n.m.* 1, disappearance. 2, evaporation; dissipation. 3, faint; swoon.

desvarar (des·βa'rar) *v.t.* 1, to slip; slide. 2, *naut.* to set afloat (a grounded ship).

desvariado (des·βa'rja·ðo) *adj.* 1, delirious; raving. 2, dreamy; vague. 3, nonsensical; incoherent.

desvariar (des·βa'rjar) *v.i.* [*infl.:* enviar, 22] to rave; rant.

desvarío (des·βa'ri·o) *n.m.* 1, raving; delirium. 2, madness; absurdity. 3, monstrosity.

desvedar (des·βe'ðar) *v.t.* to remove a prohibition or restriction from.

desvelar (des·βe'lar) *v.t.* to keep awake. —**desvelarse**, *v.r.* 1, to lose sleep; stay up all night. 2, to concern oneself.

desvelo (des'βe·lo) *n.m.* 1, wakefulness. 2, care; concern.

desvencijar (des·βen·θi'xar; -si'xar) *v.t.* to pull apart; loosen; wear out. —**desvencijarse**, *v.r.* to fall apart; wear out.

desventaja (des·βen'ta·xa) *n.f.* disadvantage. —**desventajoso**, *adj.* disadvantageous.

desventura (des·βen'tu·ra) *n.f.* misfortune. —**desventurado**, *adj.* unfortunate; wretched.

desvergonzarse (des·βer·ɣon'θar·se; -'sar·se) *v.r.* [*infl.:* rezar, 10; acostar, 28] to speak or act shamelessly. —**desvergonzado**, *adj.* shameless.

desvergüenza (des·βer'ɣwen·θa; -sa) *n.f.* shamelessness; impudence.

desvestir (des·βes'tir) *v.t.* [*infl.:* pedir, 33] to undress; denude.

desviar (des·βi'ar) *v.t.* [*infl.:* enviar, 22] to deviate; deflect; divert. —**desviarse**, *v.r.* 1, to turn aside; swerve. 2, to stray. 3, *aero.* to yaw. —**desviación**, *n.f.* deviation; deflection.

desvío (des'βi·o) *n.m.* 1, = **desviación**. 2, detour. 3, indifference. 4, aversion; dislike. 5, *aero.* yaw.

desvirgar (des·βir'ɣar) *v.t.*, *colloq.* [*infl.:* pagar, 8] to deflower.

desvirtuar (des·βir'twar) *v.t.* [*infl.:* continuar, 23] to detract from; diminish or destroy the value of. —**desvirtuarse**, *v.r.* to spoil; lose strength, flavor, etc.

desvivirse (des·βi'βir·se) *v.r.* 1, to long; yearn. 2, to be eager; strive.

desvolvedor (des·βol·βe'ðor) *n.m.* wrench.

desvolver (des·βol'βer) *v.t.* [*infl.:* mover, 30; *pp.* **desvuelto** (-'βwel·to)] 1, to change the shape of. 2, to turn up (the soil). 3, to unscrew; unbolt.

desyerbar (des·jer'βar) *v.t.* = **desherbar**. —**desyerba** (-'jer·βa) *n.f.* = **deshierba**.

detallar (de·ta'ʎar; -'jar) *v.t.* 1, to detail; enumerate. 2, to retail. —**detallista**, *n.m. & f.* retailer.

detalle (de'ta·ʎe; -je) *n.m.* 1, detail. 2, retail.

detective (de·tek'ti·βe) *n.m.* detective. *Also* **detectivo** (-βo).

detector (de·tek'tor) *n.m.* detector.

detención (de·ten'θjon; -'sjon) *n.f.* 1, detention; arrest. 2, stop; halt. 3, delay. 4, thoroughness; meticulousness. *Also,* **detenimiento** (de·te·ni'mjen·to) *n.m.*

detener (de·te'ner) *v.t.* [*infl.:* tener, 65] 1, to detain. 2, to stop; arrest. —**detenerse**, *v.r.* 1, to linger. 2, to pause.

detenido (de·te'ni·ðo) *adj.* 1, niggardly. 2, thorough; meticulous. 3, timid; backward. 4, detained; arrested.

detentar (de·ten'tar) *v.t.*, *law* to retain unlawfully. —**detentación**, *n.f., law* unlawful retention of property.

detergente (de·ter'xen·te) *adj. & n.m.* detergent.

deteriorar (de·te·rjo'rar) *v.t.* to deteriorate. —**deterioro** (de·te'rjo·ro) *n.m.* deterioration. *Also,* **deterioración**, *n.f.*

determinado (de·ter·mi'na·ðo) *adj.* **1,** determined; resolved. **2,** specified. **3,** definite; specific.

determinar (de·ter·mi'nar) *v.t.* **1,** to determine; decide. **2,** to specify; define. —**determinación**, *n.f.* determination.

detestar (de·tes'tar) *v.t.* to detest. —**detestable**, *adj.* detestable. —**detestación**, *n.f.* detestation.

detonar (de·to'nar) *v.t.* to detonate. —**detonación**, *n.f.* detonation. —**detonador**, *n.m.* detonator. —**detonante**, *adj. & n.m.* explosive.

detracción (de·trak'θjon; -'sjon) *n.f.* detraction.

detractar (de·trak'tar) *v.t.* to detract; defame. —**detractor**, *n.m.* detractor; defamer.

detraer (de·tra'er) *v.t.* [*infl.:* **traer, 67**] **1,** to detract; remove. **2,** = **detractar.**

detrás (de'tras) *adv.* behind; after. —**detrás de,** behind; in back of (*prep.*).

detrimento (de·tri'men·to) *n.m.* detriment.

detritus (de'tri·tus) *n.m.* detritus.

deuda ('deu·ða) *n.f.* debt; indebtedness.

deudo ('deu·ðo) *n.m.* kinsman.

deudor (deu'ðor) *adj.* indebted. —*n.m.* debtor.

deuterio (deu'te·rjo) *n.m.* deuterium.

deuterión (deu·te'rjon) *n.m.* deuteron.

devaluación (de·βa·lwa'θjon; -'sjon) *n.f.* devaluation.

devanar (de·βa'nar) *v.t.* to reel; wind, as yarn. —**devanadera**, *n.f.* reel; spool; bobbin. —**devanarse de risa,** *Amer.* to be convulsed with laughter. —**devanarse los sesos,** to cudgel one's brains.

devanear (de·βa·ne'ar) *v.i.* **1,** to rave; be delirious. **2,** to daydream. **3,** to flirt.

devaneo (de·βa'ne·o) *n.m.* **1,** frenzy; derangement. **2,** idle pursuit. **3,** flirtation.

devastar (de·βas'tar) *v.t.* to devastate. —**devastación**, *n.f.* devasta-

tion. —**devastador**, *adj.* devastating.

devengar (de·βen'gar) *v.t.* [*infl.:* **pagar, 8**] to earn.

devenir (de·βe'nir) *v.i.* [*infl.:* **venir, 69**] **1,** to happen. **2,** *philos.* to become.

devoción (de·βo'θjon; -'sjon) *n.f.* devotion. —**devocionario**, *n.m.* prayer book.

devolución (de·βo·lu'θjon; -'sjon) *n.f.* return; restitution.

devolutivo (de·βo·lu'ti·βo) *adj.* **1,** returnable. **2,** *law* restorable.

devolver (de·βol'βer) *v.t.* [*infl.:* **mover, 30**] to return; restore; repay.

devorar (de·βo'rar) *v.t.* to devour. —**devorador**, *adj.* voracious.

devoto (de'βo·to) *adj.* **1,** devout; pious. **2,** devoted; strongly attached. **3,** devotional. —*n.m.* **1,** devotee. **2,** object of devotion.

devuelto (de'βwel·to) *v., p.p. of* **devolver.**

dexteridad (deks·te·ri'ðað) *n.f.* dexterity.

dextrosa (deks'tro·sa) *n.f.* dextrose.

deyección (de·jek'θjon; -'sjon) *n.f.* **1,** volcanic debris. **2,** defecation; feces.

di (di) *v., impve.sing. of* **decir.**

dí (di) *v., 1st pers.sing.pret. of* **dar.**

día ('di·a) *n.m. day;* daylight. —**al día,** per day. —**al otro día,** the next day. —**buenos días,** good morning. —**dar los días, 1,** to greet someone. **2,** to give birthday greetings. —**de día,** by day; during the day. —**de hoy en ocho días,** a week from today. —**día diado,** appointed day. —**día natural,** from sunup to sundown. —**día quebrado,** halfholiday. —**en el mejor día,** some fine day. —**es de día,** it is daylight or daytime. —**estar al día,** to be up to date. —**hoy día,** nowadays. —**ser del día,** to be in style. —**tener días, 1,** to be old. **2,** to be moody. —**vivir al día,** to spend all one earns.

diabetes (dja'βe·tes) *n.f.* diabetes. —**diabético** (-'βe·ti·ko) *adj.* diabetic.

diablo ('dja·βlo) *n.m.* devil. —**diablura**, *n.f.* deviltry; mischievousness. —**diabólico** (-'βo·li·ko) *adj.* diabolical; devilish.

diáconisa (dja·ko'ni·sa) *n.f.* deaconess.

diácono ('dja·ko·no) *n.m.* deacon.

diacrítico (dja'kri·ti·ko) *adj.* **1**, *gram.* diacritical. **2**, *med.* diagnostic.

diadema (dja'ðe·ma) *n.f.* diadem.

diáfano ('dja·fa·no) *adj.* diaphanous. —**diafanidad**, *n.f.* transparency.

diafragma (dja'fraɣ·ma) *n.m.* diaphragm.

diagnosis (djaɣ'no·sis) *n.m. sing.* & *pl.* diagnosis. —**diagnóstico** (-'nos·ti·ko) *adj.* diagnostic. —*n.m.* diagnosis.

diagnosticar (djaɣ·nos·ti'kar) *v.t.* [*infl.*: **tocar, 7**] to diagnose.

diagonal (dja·ɣo'nal) *adj.* & *n.m.* diagonal.

diagrama (dja'ɣra·ma) *n.m.* diagram. —**diagramático** (-'ma·ti·ko) *adj.* diagrammatic.

dial (di'al) *n.m.* **1**, *radio* selector; dial. **2**, telephone dial.

dialéctica (dja'lek·ti·ka) *n.f.* logic; dialectics. —**dialéctico**, *adj.* logical; dialectical. —*n.m.* dialectician.

dialecto (dja'lek·to) *n.m.* dialect. —**dialectal**, *adj.* dialectal.

diálogo ('dja·lo·ɣo) *n.m.* dialogue.

diamante (dja'man·te) *n.m.* diamond.

diámetro (di'a·me·tro) *n.m.* diameter. —**diametral** (dja·me'tral) *adj.* diametrical.

diana ('dja·na) *n.f.* **1**, *mil.* reveille. **2**, target; bull's eye.

diantre ('djan·tre) *n.m.*, *slang* deuce; devil. *Also,* **dianche** (-tʃe).

diapasón (dja·pa'son) *n.m.* **1**, diapason. **2**, tuning fork.

diario ('dja·rjo) *adj.* daily. —*n.m.* **1**, diary; journal. **2**, daily newspaper. —**diariamente**, *adv.* daily. —**a diario**, daily. —**diario de navegación**, log book.

diarrea (dja'rre·a) *n.f.* diarrhea. —**diarreico** (-'rrei·ko) *adj.* diarrhetic.

Diáspora ('djas·po·ra) *n.f.* Diaspora.

diástole ('djas·to·le) *n.m.* diastole. —**diastólico** (-'to·li·ko) *adj.* diastolic.

diatermia (dja'ter·mja) *n.f.* diathermy. —**diatérmico**, *also,* **diatérmano**, *adj.* diathermic.

diatomea (dja·to'me·a) *n.f.*, *bot.* diatom.

diatónico (dja'to·ni·ko) *adj.*, *mus.* diatonic.

diatriba (dja'tri·βa) *n.f.* diatribe.

dibujar (di·βu'xar) *v.t.* to draw;

sketch; depict. —**dibujarse**, *v.r.* to appear; stand out. —**dibujante**, *n.m.* draftsman; designer.

dibujo (di'βu·xo) *n.m.* **1**, drawing. **2**, pattern; design.

dicción (dik'θjon; -'sjon) *n.f.* diction; phraseology.

diccionario (dik·θjo'na·rjo; dik·sjo-) *n.m.* dictionary. —**diccionarista**, *n.m.* & *f.* lexicographer.

diciembre (di'θjem·bre; di'sjem-) *n.m.* December.

diciendo (di'θjen·do; -'sjen·do) *v., ger. of* **decir.**

dicotomía (di·ko·to'mi·a) *n.f.* dichotomy.

dictado (dik'ta·ðo) *n.m.* **1**, dictation. **2**, rank; title. —**dictados**, *n.m.pl.* dictates; maxims.

dictador (dik·ta'ðor) *n.m.* dictator. —**dictadura**, *n.f.* dictatorship. —**dictatorial**, *also* **dictatorio**, *adj.* dictatorial.

dictáfono (dik·ta·fo·no) *n.m.* Dictaphone (T.N.).

dictamen (dik'ta·men) *n.m.* dictum; pronouncement. —**dictaminar** (-mi'nar) *v.i.* to pass judgment.

dictar (dik'tar) *v.t.* to dictate.

dicha ('di·tʃa) *n.f.* joy; good fortune. —**dichoso**, *adj.* fortunate; joyous.

dicharacho (di·tʃa'ra·tʃo) *n.m.*, *colloq.* **1**, wisecrack. **2**, vulgar expression.

dicho ('di·tʃo) *v., p.p. of* **decir.** —*adj.* said; aforesaid. —*n.m.* **1**, saying; proverb. **2**, witticism. —**dicho y hecho**, no sooner said than done.

didáctica (di'ðak·ti·ka) *n.f.* didactics. —**didáctico**, *adj.* didactic.

didimio (di'ði·mjo) *n.m.* didymium.

diecinueve (dje·θi'nwe·βe; dje·si-) *adj.* & *n.m.* nineteen. —**diecinueveavo**, *adj.* & *n.m.* nineteenth.

dieciocho (dje'θjo·tʃo; dje·sjo-) *adj.* & *n.m.* eighteen. —**dieciochavo**, *adj.* & *n.m.* eighteenth. *Also,* **dieciocheno.**

dieciséis (dje·θi'seis; dje·si-) *adj.* & *n.m.* sixteen. —**dieciseisavo**, *adj.* & *n.m.* sixteenth. *Also,* **dieciseiseno.**

diecisiete (dje·θi'sje·te; dje·si-) *adj.* & *n.m.* seventeen. —**diecisieteavo**, *adj.* & *n.m.* seventeenth.

diedro (di'e·ðro) *adj.* dihedral.

dieléctrico (di·e'lek·tri·ko) *adj.* & *n.m.* dielectric.

diente ('djen·te) *n.m.* **1,** tooth. **2,** cog. **3,** tine; prong. **4,** clove, as of garlic. —**diente de león,** dandelion. —**diente de leche; diente mamón,** baby tooth; milk tooth. —**diente de perro, 1,** sculptor's two-pointed chisel. **2,** *archit.* dogtooth. **3,** *bot.* dogtooth violet. —**pelar el diente,** *colloq.* to smile affectedly. —**tener buen diente,** *colloq.* to be a hearty eater.

diente ('djen·te) *v., pres.subjve.* of **dentar.**

diento ('djen·to) *v., pres.ind.* of **dentar.**

diéresis ('dje·re·sis) *n.f.* dieresis.

diestra ('djes·tra) *n.f.* right hand. —**a diestra y siniestra,** every which way.

diestro ('djes·tro) *adj.* **1,** skillful; dexterous. **2,** propitious; favorable. —*n.m., sports* expert; deft hand.

dieta ('dje·ta) *n.f.* **1,** diet *(regimen).* **2,** diet *(legislative body).* **3,** = honorarios.

dietética (dje'te·ti·ka) *n.f.* dietetics. —**dietético,** *adj.* dietetic; dietary.

diez (djeθ; djes) *adj. & n.m.* ten.

diezmar (djeθ'mar; djes-) *v.t.* **1,** to decimate. **2,** to pay a tithe of.

diezmilésimo (djeθ·mi'le·si·mo; djes-) *adj. & n.m.* ten-thousandth.

diezmo ('djeθ·mo; 'djes-) *n.m.* tithe; tenth part.

difamar (di·fa'mar) *v.t.* to defame. —**difamación,** *n.f.* defamation. —**difamatorio,** *adj.* defamatory.

diferencia (di·fe'ren·θja; -sja) *n.f.* difference.

diferencial (di·fe·ren'θjal; -'sjal) *adj. & n.m.* differential.

diferenciar (di·fe·ren'θjar; -'sjar) *v.t.* to differentiate. —**diferenciarse,** *v.r.* to differ; be distinguished. —**diferenciación,** *n.f.* differentiation.

diferente (di·fe'ren·te) *adj.* different.

diferir (di·fe'rir) *v.t.* [*infl.:* sentir, 31] to defer; delay. —*v.i.* to differ; have a different opinion.

difícil (di'fi·θil; -sil) *adj.* difficult.

dificultad (di·fi·kul'tað) *n.f.* difficulty. —**dificultar,** *v.t.* to make difficult; impede. —**dificultoso,** *adj.* difficult; laborious.

difidencia (di·fi'ðen·θja; -sja) *n.f.* distrust. —**difidente,** *adj.* distrustful.

difiera (di'fje·ra) *v., pres.subjve.* of **diferir.**

difiero (di'fje·ro) *v., pres.ind.* of **diferir.**

difracción (di·frak'θjon; -'sjon) *n.f.* diffraction. —**difractar** (-'tar) *v.t.* to diffract.

difteria (dif'te·rja) *n.f.* diphtheria.

difundir (di·fun'dir) *v.t.* to diffuse; spread; broadcast.

difunto (di'fun·to) *n.m.* corpse. —*adj.* defunct; dead.

difusión (di·fu'sjon) *n.f.* diffusion; broadcasting. —**difusor** (-'sor) *adj.* diffusive; broadcasting.

difuso (di'fu·so) *adj.* **1,** diffuse. **2,** verbose.

diga ('di·ɣa) *v., pres.subjve.* of **decir;** hello *(on telephone).*

digerir (di·xe'rir) *v.t.* [*infl.:* sentir, 31] to digest. —**digerible,** *adj.* digestible.

digestión (di·xes'tjon) *n.f.* digestion. —**digestible,** *adj.* digestible. —**digestivo,** *adj.* digestive.

digesto (di'xes·to) *n.m., law* digest.

digital (di·xi'tal) *adj.* digital. —*n.m.* digitalis.

dígito ('di·xi·to) *n.m.* digit. —*adj.* [*also,* **digital**] digital.

dignarse (diɣ'nar·se) *v.r.* to deign; condescend.

dignatario (diɣ·na'ta·rjo) *n.m.* dignitary.

dignidad (diɣ·ni'ðað) *n.f.* dignity; rank.

dignificar (diɣ·ni·fi'kar) *v.t.* [*infl.:* tocar, 7] to dignify.

digno ('diɣ·no) *adj.* **1,** worthy; deserving. **2,** fitting; appropriate.

digo ('di·ɣo) *v., 1st pers.sing. pres. ind.* of **decir.**

digresión (di·ɣre'sjon) *n.f.* digression. —**digresivo,** *adj.* digressive.

dije ('di·xe) *n.m.* **1,** bauble; charm. **2,** *colloq.* jewel *(person).*

dije ('di·xe) *v., 1st pers. sing. pret.* of **decir.**

dilación (di·la'θjon; -'sjon) *n.f.* delay.

dilapidación (di·la·pi·ða'θjon; -'sjon) *n.f.* **1,** dilapidation. **2,** squandering.

dilapidar (di·la·pi'ðar) *v.t.* **1,** to dilapidate. **2,** to squander.

dilatar (di·la'tar) *v.t.* **1,** to dilate. **2,** to retard; defer. —**dilatarse,** *v.r.* **1,** to expatiate. **2,** *Amer.* to be late. —**dilatación,** *n.f.* dilation; dilatation. —**dilatoria** (-'to·rja) *n.f.* delay. —**dilatorio** (-'to·rjo) *adj.* dilatory.

dilección (di·lek'θjon; -'sjon) *n.f.* love; affection. —**dilecto** (-'lek·to) *adj.* beloved.

dilema (di'le·ma) *n.m.* dilemma.

diletante (di·le'tan·te) *n.m.* dilettante.

diligencia (di·li'xen·θja; -sja) *n.f.* 1, diligence; industry. 2, stagecoach. 3, errand. —**diligente**, *adj.* diligent; active.

diligenciar (di·li·xen'θjar; -'sjar) *v.t.* to set about (something); apply oneself to (something).

dilucidar (di·lu·θi'ðar; -si'ðar) *v.t.* to elucidate. —**dilucidación**, *n.f.* elucidation.

diluir (di·lu'ir) *v.t.* [*infl.:* huir, 26] to dilute. —**dilución**, *n.f.* dilution. —**diluente**, *adj.* diluting; dissolving.

diluvio (di'lu·βjo) *n.m.* deluge; flood. —**diluvial**, *also,* **diluviano**, *adj.* diluvial.

dimanar (di·ma'nar) *v.i.* to emanate; proceed; stem. —**dimanación**, *n.f.* emanation; origin.

dimensión (di·men'sjon) *n.f.* dimension. —**dimensional**, *adj.* mensional.

dimes y diretes ('di·mes·i·ði· 're·tes) *colloq.* quibbling; bickering. —**andar en dimes y diretes**, to quibble; argue.

diminución (di·mi·nu'θjon; -'sjon) *n.f.* diminution; contraction. —**diminutivo**, *adj. & n.m.* diminutive.

diminuendo (di·mi'nwen·do) *adj., adv. & n.m., mus.* diminuendo.

diminuir (di·mi·nu'ir) *v.t.* [*infl.:* huir, 26] = **disminuir**. —**diminución**, *n.f.* = **disminución**.

diminuto (di·mi'nu·to) *adj.* diminutive; minute.

dimitir (di·mi'tir) *v.t.* to resign; relinquish. —**dimisión**, *n.f.* resignation.

dina ('di·na) *n.f.* dyne.

dinamarqués (di·na·mar'kes) *adj.* Danish. —*n.m.* 1, Dane. 2, Danish language.

dinámica (di'na·mi·ka) *n.f.* dynamics. —**dinámico**, *adj.* dynamic. —**dinamismo**, *n.m.* dynamism.

dinamita (di·na'mi·ta) *n.f.* dynamite. —**dinamitar**, *v.t.* to dynamite.

dínamo ('di·na·mo) *n.f.* [*also, Amer., n.m.*] dynamo.

dinamómetro (di·na'mo·me·tro) *n.m.* dynamometer.

dinastía (di·nas'ti·a) *n.f.* dynasty. —**dinasta** (-'nas·ta) *n.m.* dynast. —**dinástico** (-'nas·ti·ko) *adj.* dynastic.

din-dán (din'dan) *n.m.* ding-dong.

dinero (di'ne·ro) *n.m.* money; coin; currency. —**dineral**, *n.m.* a large sum of money.

dinosauro (di·no'sau·ro) *n.m.* dinosaur.

dintel (din'tel) *n.m.* 1, lintel. 2, doorway.

diócesis ('djo·θe·sis; -se·sis) *n.f.* diocese. —**diocesano** (-θe'sa·no; -se'sa·no) *adj.* diocesan.

díodo ('di·o·ðo) *n.m.* diode.

diorama (djo'ra·ma) *n.m.* diorama. —**diorámico**, *adj.* dioramic.

dios (djos) *n.m.* god; *cap.* God. —**a la buena de Dios**, *colloq.* 1, without malice; guilelessly. 2, at random; haphazardly. —**Dios mediante**, God willing.

diosa ('djo·sa) *n.f.* goddess.

dióspiro ('djos·pi·ro) *n.m.* persimmon.

dióxido (di'ok·si·ðo) *n.m.* dioxide.

diploma (di'plo·ma) *n.m.* diploma.

diplomático (di·plo'ma·ti·ko) *adj.* diplomatic. —*n.m.* diplomat. —**diplomacia** (-'ma·θja; -sja) *n.f.* diplomacy.

dipsomanía (dip·so·ma'ni·a) *n.f.* dipsomania. —**dipsómano** (-'so·ma·no) *also,* **dipsomaníaco** (-ma· 'ni·a·ko) *adj. & n.m.* dipsomaniac.

díptico ('dip·ti·ko) *n.m.* diptych.

diptongo (dip'ton·go) *n.m.* diphthong.

diputar (di·pu'tar) *v.t.* to depute; commission; delegate. —**diputación**, *n.f.* deputation. —**diputado**, *n.m.* deputy; representative; delegate.

dique ('di·ke) *n.m.* 1, dike; dam. 2, [*also,* **dique seco** *or* **de carena**] dry dock. —**dique flotante**, floating dry dock.

diré (di're) *v., fut. of* **decir**.

dirección (di·rek'θjon; -'sjon) *n.f.* 1, direction; course; aim. 2, management. 3, command; advice. 4, address. 5, director's office. —**direccional**, *adj.* directional.

directiva (di·rek'ti·βa) *n.f.* 1, directive. 2, [*also,* **junta directiva**] board of governors; board of directors.

directivo (di·rek'ti·βo) *adj.* directive; directing. —*adj.* & *n.m.* executive.

directo (di'rek·to) *adj.* direct; straight.

director (di·rek'tor) *adj.* directing. —*n.m.* **1,** director; manager. **2,** editor. **3,** *mus.* conductor.

directorio (di·rek'to·rjo) *n.m.* **1,** directorate. **2,** *cap., hist.* Directory.

dirigible (di·ri'xi·βle) *adj.* & *n.m.* dirigible.

dirigir (di·ri'xir) *v.t.* [*infl.:* coger, 15] **1,** to direct; guide; steer. **2,** to govern; manage; lead. **3,** *mus.* to conduct. —**dirigirse a, 1,** to address (someone). **2,** to betake oneself to. —**dirigente,** *n.m.* leader (*usu. one of a group of leaders*).

dirimir (di·ri'mir) *v.t.* to settle; adjust.

discante (dis'kan·te) *n.m.* descant. —**discantar** (-kan'tar) *v.t.* to descant.

discernir (dis-θer'nir; di·ser-) *v.t.* [*infl.:* perder, 29] to discern. —**discernimiento,** *n.m.* discernment.

disciplina (dis·θi'pli·na; di·si-) *n.f.* **1,** discipline. **2,** whip; scourge.

disciplinado (dis-θi·pli'na·ðo; di·si-) *adj.* **1,** disciplined. **2,** variegated (*of flowers*).

disciplinar (dis-θi·pli'nar; di·si-) *v.t.* **1,** to discipline. **2,** to scourge.

disciplinario (dis-θi·pli'na·rjo; di·si-) *adj.* disciplinary.

discípulo (dis'θi·pu·lo; di'si-) *n.m.* disciple; pupil.

disco ('dis·ko) *n.m.* **1,** disk. **2,** phonograph record. **3,** telephone dial. **4,** *sports* discus. **5,** *comput.* diskette.

díscolo ('dis·ko·lo) *adj.* unruly; disobedient.

disconforme (dis·kon'for·me) *adj.* = desconforme. —**disconformidad** (-mi'ðað) *n.f.* = desconformidad.

discontinuar (dis·kon·ti'nwar) *v.t.* [*infl.:* continuar, 23] to discontinue. —**discontinuación,** *n.f.* discontinuation; discontinuance.

discontinuo (dis·kon'ti·nwo) *adj.* discontinuous. —**discontinuidad,** *n.f.* discontinuity.

disconvenir (dis·kon·βe'nir) *v.i.* = desconvenir.

discordancia (dis·kor'ðan·θja; -sja) *n.f.* discord; disagreement. —**discordante,** *adj.* discordant.

discordar (dis·kor'ðar) *v.i.* [*infl.:* acostar, 28] **1,** to disagree. **2,** to be

out of tune. —**discorde** (-'kor·ðe) *adj.* discordant. —**discordia** (-'kor·ðja) *n.f.* discord.

discoteca (dis·ko'te·ka) *n.f.* **1,** record library. **2,** record cabinet. **3,** discotheque.

discreción (dis·kre'θjon; -'sjon) *n.f.* discretion. —**discrecional,** *adj.* discretionary; optional.

discrepancia (dis·kre'pan·θja; -sja) *n.f.* discrepancy. —**discrepante,** *adj.* disagreeing. —**discrepar,** *v.i.* to differ; disagree.

discreto (dis'kre·to) *adj.* **1,** discreet. **2,** discrete.

discriminar (dis·kri·mi'nar) *v.t.* to discriminate. —**discriminación,** *n.f.* discrimination.

disculpar (dis·kul'par) *v.t.* to exculpate; excuse; forgive. —**disculpa** (-'kul·pa) *n.f.* excuse; apology. —**disculpable,** *adj.* excusable.

discurrir (dis·ku'rrir) *v.i.* **1,** to ramble. **2,** to flow, as a river. **3,** to reason; reflect. **4,** to discourse. —*v.t.* **1,** to invent; scheme. **2,** to deduce; infer.

discurso (dis'kur·so) *n.m.* **1,** speech; discourse. **2,** course (*of time*).

discusión (dis·ku'sjon) *n.f.* discussion.

discutir (dis·ku'tir) *v.t.* & *i.* to discuss; argue. —**discutible,** *adj.* disputable.

disecar (di·se'kar) *v.t.* [*infl.:* tocar, 7] to dissect. —**disección,** *n.f.* dissection. —**disector,** *n.m.* dissector.

diseminar (di·se·mi'nar) *v.t.* to disseminate. —**diseminación,** *n.f.* dissemination.

disentería (di·sen·te'ri·a) *n.f.* dysentery.

disentir (di·sen'tir) *v.i.* [*infl.:* sentir, 31] to dissent. —**disención,** *n.f.* dissension. —**disentimiento,** *n.m.* dissent; dissension.

diseñar (di·se'ɲar) *v.t.* to design; draw. —**diseñador,** *n.m.* designer.

diseño (di·se·ɲo) *n.m.* **1,** drawing. **2,** design; pattern.

disertar (di·ser'tar) *v.i.* to discourse. —**disertación,** *n.f.* dissertation. —**disertante,** *n.m.* speaker; lecturer.

disfavor (dis·fa'βor) *n.m.* disfavor.

disformar (dis·for'mar) *v.t.* = deformar. —**disforme** (-'for·me) *adj.* = deforme. —**disformidad,** *n.f.* = deformidad.

disfraz (dis'fraθ; -'fras) *n.m.* disguise. —**baile de disfraces,** costume ball.

disfrazar (dis·fra'θar; -'sar) *v.t.* [*infl.:* rezar, 8] to disguise; conceal.

disfrutar (dis·fru'tar) *v.t.* [*also v.i., fol. by* de] to enjoy; have the benefit of; make use of. —**disfrute** (-'fru·te) *n.m.* enjoyment; benefit; use.

disfunción (dis·fun'θjon; -'sjon) *n.f.* dysfunction.

disgustar (dis·γus'tar) *v.t.* to displease; annoy. —**disgustarse,** *v.r.* to disagree; quarrel. —**disgusto** (-'γus·to) *n.m.* displeasure; annoyance.

disidir (di·si'ðir) *v.i.* to dissent. —**disidencia,** *n.f.* dissidence. —**disidente,** *adj.* dissident.

disimetría (di·si·me'tri·a) *n.f.* dissymmetry. —**disimétrico** (-'me·tri·ko) *adj.* dissymmetrical.

disímil (di'si·mil) *adj.* dissimilar. —**disimilitud,** *n.f.* dissimilarity.

disimilar (di·si·mi'lar) *adj.* dissimilar. —*v.t.* to dissimilate. —**disimilación,** *n.f.* dissimilation.

disimular (di·si·mu'lar) *v.t.* 1, to dissimulate; dissemble. 2, to overlook; tolerate. —**disimulación,** *n.f.* dissimulation; hypocrisy. —**disimulado,** *adj.* sly; underhanded.

disimulo (di·si'mu·lo) *n.m.* 1, dissimulation; deceit. 2, tolerance.

disipar (di·si'par) *v.t.* to dissipate; scatter. —**disipación,** *n.f.* dissipation. —**disipado,** *adj.* dissipated; dissolute.

dislate (dis'la·te) *n.m.* nonsense.

dislexia (dis'lek·sja) *n.f.* dyslexia. —**disléxico,** *adj.* dyslexic.

dislocar (dis·lo'kar) *v.t.* [*infl.:* tocar, 7] to dislocate. —**dislocación,** *n.f.* dislocation.

disminuir (dis·mi·nu'ir) *v.t.* [*infl.:* huir, 26] to diminish. —**disminución,** *n.f.* diminution.

disociar (di·so'θjar; -'sjar) *v.t.* to dissociate. —**disociación,** *n.f.* dissociation.

disolución (di·so·lu'θjon; -'sjon) *n.f.* 1, dissolution. 2, dissoluteness; licentiousness.

disoluto (di·so'lu·to) *adj.* dissolute.

disolver (di·sol'βer) *v.t.* [*infl.:* mover, 30; *p.p.* disuelto (-'swel·to)] to dissolve. —**disolvente,** *adj. & n.m.* dissolvent; solvent.

disonar (di·so'nar) *v.i.* [*infl.:* acostar, 28] to be dissonant. —**disonancia,** *n.f.* dissonance. —**disonante,** *also,* **dísono** ('di·so·no) *adj.* dissonant.

dispar (dis'par) *adj.* unlike; unequal.

disparar (dis·pa'rar) *v.t.* to shoot; fire; discharge. —**disparada,** *n.f., Amer.* flight; hurried start. —**disparador,** *n.m.* trigger.

disparate (dis·pa'ra·te) *n.m.* 1, absurdity; nonsense. 2, blunder. —**disparatado,** *adj.* absurd; foolish. —**disparatar,** *v.i.* to talk nonsense.

disparejo (dis·pa're·xo) *adj.* 1, unlike. 2, uneven.

disparidad (dis·pa·ri'ðað) *n.f.* disparity.

disparo (dis'pa·ro) *n.m.* shooting; discharge; shot.

dispendio (dis'pen·djo) *n.m.* expense, esp. an unusual or excessive one. —**dispendioso,** *adj.* expensive.

dispensar (dis·pen'sar) *v.t.* 1, to dispense. 2, to excuse; absolve. —**dispensa** (-'pen·sa) *also,* **dispensación,** *n.f.* dispensation. —**dispensable,** *adj.* dispensable.

dispensario (dis·pen'sa·rjo) *n.m.* dispensary.

dispepsia (dis'pep·sja) *n.f.* dyspepsia. —**dispéptico,** (-'pep·ti·ko) *adj.* dyspeptic.

dispersar (dis·per'sar) *v.t.* to disperse; rout. —**dispersión,** *n.f.* dispersion. —**disperso** (-'per·so) *adj.* dispersed.

displicente (dis·pli'θen·te; -'sen·te) *adj.* 1, unpleasant. 2, indifferent; aloof. —**displicencia,** *n.f.* indifference; aloofness.

disponer (dis·po'ner) *v.t. & i.* [*infl.:* poner, 54] to dispose; arrange. —**disponerse,** *v.r.* 1, to prepare oneself; dispose oneself. 2, to line up; align oneself. —**disponer de,** 1, to have available; have at one's disposal. 2, to make use of; put to use.

disponible (dis·po'ni·βle) *adj.* 1, disposable. 2, available. —**disponibilidad,** *n.f.* availability.

disposición (dis·po·si'θjon; -'sjon) *n.f.* 1, disposition; arrangement. 2, disposal. 3, aptitude; predisposition. 4, state of health. 5, decree; order.

dispositivo (dis·po·si'ti·βo) *n.m.* device; apparatus.

disprosio (dis'pro·sjo) *n.m.* dysprosium.

dispuesto (dis'pwes·to) v., p.p. of disponer. —adj. 1, disposed; ready. 2, apt.

disputa (dis'pu·ta) n.f. 1, dispute. 2, disputation; debate. —sin disputa, indisputably; beyond dispute.

disputar (dis·pu'tar) v.t. & i. to dispute. —disputable, adj. disputable. —disputador, n.m. disputant. —adj. disputatious.

disquete (dis'ke·te) n.m. diskette.

disquisición (dis·ki·si'θjon; -'sjon) n.f. disquisition.

disruptivo (dis·rup'ti·βo) adj., elect. disruptive.

distancia (dis'tan·θja; -sja) n.f. distance. —distanciar, v.t. to place at a distance; separate. —distanciarse, v.r. to be aloof; be distant.

distante (dis'tan·te) adj. distant.

distar (dis'tar) v.i. to be distant (from).

distender (dis·ten'der) v.t. [infl.: perder, 29] to distend. —distensión, n.f. distention.

distinguir (dis·tin'gir) v.t. [infl.: 17] to distinguish. —distinguirse, v.r. 1, to excel. 2, to differ; be different. —distinción, n.f. distinction. —distinguible, adj. distinguishable. —distinguido, adj. distinguished.

distinto (dis'tin·to) adj. distinct; different. —distintivo, adj. distinctive. —n.m. distinguishing mark or feature.

distorsión (dis·tor'sjon) n.f. distortion. —distorsionar, v.t. to distort.

distracción (dis·trak'θjon; -'sjon) n.f. 1, distraction. 2, amusement; pastime.

distraer (dis·tra'er) v.t. [infl.: traer, 67] 1, to distract; divert. 2, to amuse; beguile. —distraído, adj. distracted; absent-minded.

distribuir (dis·tri·βu'ir) v.t. [infl.: huir, 26] to distribute; allot. —distribución, n.f. distribution. —distribuidor, adj. distributing. —n.m. distributor.

distributivo (dis·tri·βu'ti·βo) adj. & n.m. distributive. —distributor (-'tor) n.m. distributor.

distrito (dis'tri·to) n.m. district.

distrofia (dis·tro'fi·a) n.f. dystrophy. —distrofia muscular, muscular dystrophy.

disturbar (dis·tur'βar) v.t. to disturb. —disturbio (-'tur·βjo) n.m. disturbance.

disuadir (di·swa'ðir) v.t. to dissuade. —disuasión, n.f. dissuasion. —disuasivo, adj. dissuasive.

disuelto (di'swel·to) adj. dissolved. —v., p.p. of disolver.

disyunción (dis·jun'θjon; -'sjon) n.f. disjunction. —disyuntivo (-'ti·βo) adj. disjunctive.

dita ('di·ta) n.f. surety; bond.

diuresis (di·u're·sis) n.f. diuresis. —diurético (-'re·ti·ko) adj. & n.m. diuretic.

diurno ('djur·no) adj. diurnal.

diva ('di·βa) n.f. 1, diva. 2, poet. goddess.

divagar (di·βa'γar) v.i. [infl.: pagar, 8] to digress; roam. —divagación, n.f. digression.

divalente (di·βa'len·te) adj. = bivalente.

diván (di'βan) n.m. divan.

divergir (di·βer'xir) v.i. [infl.: coger, 15] to diverge. —divergencia, n.f. divergence. —divergente, adj. divergent.

diversificar (di·βer·si·fi'kar) v.t. [infl.: tocar, 7] to diversify. —diversificación, n.f. diversification.

diversión (di·βer'sjon) n.f. 1, diversion. 2, amusement.

diverso (di'βer·so) adj. diverse. —diversidad, n.f. diversity.

divertir (di·βer'tir) v.t. [infl.: sentir, 31] 1, to turn aside, divert. 2, to amuse. —divertirse, v.r. to enjoy oneself; have a good time. —divertido, adj. diverting; amusing; fun.

dividendo (di·βi'ðen·do) n.m. dividend.

dividir (di·βi'ðir) v.t. 1, to divide. 2, to separate.

divieso (di'βje·so) n.m. boil (sore).

divinidad (di·βi·ni'ðað) n.f. 1, divinity; deity. 2, cap. God. 3, colloq. a beautiful woman; an exquisite object; a charming expression.

divinizar (di·βi·ni'θar; -'sar) v.t. [infl.: rezar, 10] to deify.

divino (di'βi·no) adj. divine.

divisa (di'βi·sa) n.f. 1, badge; emblem; motto. 2, currency (esp. foreign).

divisar (di·βi'sar) v.t. to glimpse; espy.

divisible (di·βi'si·βle) adj. divisible. —divisibilidad, n.f. divisibility.

división (di·βi'sjon) n.f. division. —divisional, adj. divisional.

divisivo (di·βi'si·βo) adj. divisive.

divisor (di·βi'sor) *adj.* dividing. —*n.m.* divisor.

divisorio (di·βi'so·rjo) *adj.* dividing. —**línea divisoria,** divide.

divorciar (di·βor'θjar; -'sjar) *v.t.* to divorce. —**divorciarse,** *v.r.* to be divorced; get a divorce. —**divorciado,** *n.m.* divorcé. —**divorciada,** *n.f.* divorcée.

divorcio (di'βor·θjo; -sjo) *n.m.* divorce.

divulgar (di·βul'γar) *v.t.* [*infl.*: **pagar, 8**] to divulge; spread abroad. —**divulgación,** *n.f.* divulgence.

do (do) *n.m., mus.* do; C.

dobladillo (do·βla'ði·ʎo; -jo) *n.m.* hem.

doblado (do'βla·ðo) *adj.* **1,** stocky; hefty. **2,** double-dealing; two-faced. **3,** uneven, as ground. **4,** folded.

doblar (do'βlar) *v.t.* **1,** to bend; fold. **2,** to double. **3,** to toll (a bell). **4,** to turn, as a corner. **5,** *motion pictures* to dub. —**doblarse,** *v.r.* to bend; stoop. —**dobladura,** *n.f.* fold; crease.

doble ('do·βle) *adj.* **1,** double; twofold. **2,** two-faced. —*adv.* double; doubly. —*n.m.* **1,** double. **2,** fold. **3,** hem. **4,** toll (*of a bell*).

doblegar (do·βle'γar) *v.t.* [*infl.*: **pagar, 8**] **1,** to bend; fold. **2,** to cause to yield; sway. —**doblegarse,** *v.r.* to bend; yield. —**doblegable,** *adj.* pliable; flexible.

doblez (do'βleθ; -'βles) *n.m.* **1,** fold. **2,** hem. **3,** trouser cuff. **4,** [*also fem.*] duplicity.

doce ('do·θe; -se) *adj. & n.m.* twelve.

docena (do'θe·na; -'se·na) *n.f.* dozen. —**docena del fraile,** baker's dozen.

doceno (do'θe·no; -'se·no) *adj.* twelfth.

docente (do'θen·te; do'sen-) *adj.* **1,** educational. **2,** teaching.

dócil ('do·θil; -sil) *adj.* docile; obedient. —**docilidad,** *n.f.* docility.

docto ('dok·to) *adj.* learned. —*n.m.* learned person.

doctor (dok'tor) *n.m.* doctor. —**doctorado,** *n.m.* doctorate. —**doctorar,** *v.t.* to confer a doctor's degree on.

doctrina (dok'tri·na) *n.f.* doctrine. —**doctrinal,** *adj.* doctrinal. —**doctrinario,** *adj. & n.m.* doctrinaire.

documentar (do·ku·men'tar) *v.t.* **1,** to document. **2,** to inform; brief.

—**documentación,** *n.f.* documentation.

documento (do·ku'men·to) *n.m.* document. —**documental,** *adj. & n.m.* documentary; documental.

dodo ('do·ðo) *also,* **dodó** (do'ðo) *n.m.* dodo.

dogal (do'γal) *n.m.* **1,** halter. **2,** dog collar. **3,** hangman's noose.

dogma ('doγ·ma) *n.m.* dogma. —**dogmático** (-'ma·ti·ko) *adj.* dogmatic. —**dogmatismo** (-'tis·mo) *n.m.* dogmatism.

dogo ('do·γo) *n.m.* [*fem.* **doga**] bulldog.

dólar ('do·lar) *n.m.* dollar.

dolencia (do'len·θja; -sja) *n.f.* ailment; disease.

doler (do'ler) *v.i.* [*infl.*: **mover, 30**] to pain; hurt. —**dolerse,** *v.r.,* *usu. fol. by* **de, 1,** to regret. **2,** to sympathize (with). **3,** to complain (of).

doliente (do'ljen·te) *adj.* **1,** suffering; sick. **2,** sorrowful. —*n.m. & f.* **1,** sufferer. **2,** mourner.

dolo ('do·lo) *n.m.* fraud; deceit. —**doloso,** *adj.* fraudulent; deceitful.

dolor (do'lor) *n.m.* **1,** pain. **2,** affliction. **3,** grief; sorrow.

dolorido (do·lo'ri·ðo) *adj.* pained; in pain.

doloroso (do·lo'ro·so) *adj.* painful.

doma ('do·ma) *n.f.* breaking; taming (*as of animals*).

domar (do'mar) *v.t.* to tame; subdue. —**domador,** *n.m.* tamer.

domeñar (do·me'ɲar) *v.t.* to tame; subdue; dominate.

domesticar (do·mes·ti'kar) *v.t.* [*infl.*: **tocar, 7**] to domesticate.

doméstico (do'mes·ti·ko) *adj. & n.m.* domestic. —**domesticidad** (-θi·'ðað; -si'ðað) *n.f.* domesticity.

domiciliar (do·mi·θi'ljar; -si'ljar) *v.t.* to house; lodge. —**domiciliarse,** *v.r.* **1,** to take up residence. **2,** to reside.

domicilio (do·mi'θi·ljo; -'si·ljo) *n.m.* domicile; residence.

dominante (do·mi'nan·te) *adj.* **1,** dominant. **2,** domineering.

dominar (do·mi'nar) *v.t.* to dominate; master; control. —*v.i.* to stand out; be conspicuous. —**dominación,** *n.f.* domination; dominance.

dómine ('do·mi·ne) *n.m.* schoolmaster; pedant.

domingo (do'min·go) *n.m.* Sunday. —**dominical** (-mi·ni'kal) *adj.* dominical; Sunday (*attrib.*).

dominicano (do·mi·ni'ka·no) *adj.* & *n.m.* Dominican.

dominico (do·mi'ni·ko) *adj.* & *n.m.* Dominican *(of the order of St. Dominic).*

dominio (do'mi·njo) *n.m.* 1, dominion. 2, domination. 3, domain. 4, *law* fee; ownership.

dominó (do·mi'no) *also,* **dómino** ('do·mi·no) *n.m.* 1, domino. 2, dominoes.

domo ('do·mo) *n.m.* dome; cupola.

don (don) *n.m.* 1, gift; talent. 2, *cap.,* title of respect; Don.

dona ('do·na) *n.f., Amer.* doughnut.

donador (do·na'ðor) *n.m.* donor; giver.

donaire (do'nai·re) *n.m.* 1, grace; elegance. 2, wit; witticism.

donairoso (do·nai'ro·so) *adj.* 1, graceful; elegant. 2, witty; clever.

donar (do'nar) *v.t.* to donate; give; bestow. —**donación,** *n.f., also,* **donativo,** *n.m.* donation. —**donante,** *adj.* donating. —*n.m.* & *f.* donor.

donatario (do·na'ta·rjo) *n.m.* grantee; donee.

doncel (don'θel; -'sel) *n.m.* young nobleman. —*adj.* gentle, mild.

doncella (don'θe·ʎa; -'se·ja) *n.f.* maiden; maid. —**doncellez,** *n.f.* maidenhood.

donde ('don·de) *rel.adv.* where. —*prep., colloq.* at, in or to the house or place of business of. —**a donde,** where; whither. —**de donde,** from where; whence. —**por donde,** whereby. —**dónde,** *interrog.* & *exclamatory adv.* where?; where!

dondequiera (don·de'kje·ra) *indef.* & *rel. adv.* anywhere; everywhere; wherever.

dondiego (don'dje·ɣo) *n.m.* morning-glory. *Also,* **dondiego de día.**

donoso (do'no·so) *adj.* graceful; charming. —**donosura,** *n.f.* grace; charm.

doña ('do·ɲa) *n.f.* 1, duenna. 2, *cap.* title of respect; Doña.

doquier (do'kjer) *also,* **doquiera** (-'kje·ra) *adv.* = **dondequiera.**

dorado (do'ra·ðo) *adj.* gilded; golden. —*n.m.* 1, gilt; gilding. 2, *ichthy.* dory.

dorar (do'rar) *v.t.* 1, to gild. 2, to palliate. 3, *cookery* to brown. —**dorador,** *n.m.* [*fem.* **-dora**] gilder.

dórico ('do·ri·ko) *adj.* Doric.

dormilón (dor·mi'lon) *n.m.* sleepyhead.

dormir (dor'mir) *v.i.* [*infl.:* **morir,** 32] to sleep. —**dormirse,** *v.r.* to fall asleep. —**dormir a pierna suelta,** *colloq.* to sleep soundly. —**dormir una siesta,** to take a nap.

dormitar (dor·mi'tar) *v.i.* to nap; doze.

dormitorio (dor·mi'to·rjo) *n.m.* 1, dormitory. 2, bedroom.

dorso ('dor·so) *n.m.* back. —**dorsal,** *adj.* dorsal.

dos (dos) *adj.* & *n.m.* two.

doscientos (dos'θjen·tos; do·'sjen·tos) *adj.* & *n.m.pl.* [*fem.* **-tas**] two hundred. —*adj.* two hundredth.

dosel (do'sel) *n.m.* canopy *(usu. over an altar, throne, statue, etc.).*

dosificar (do·si·fi'kar) *v.t.* [*infl.:* **tocar,** 7] *v.t.* to dose; measure out (medicine) in doses. —**dosificación,** *n.f.* dosage.

dosis ('do·sis) *n.f.* dose; dosage.

dotación (do·ta'θjon; -'sjon) *n.f.* 1, endowment. 2, equipment. 3, staff; crew.

dotal (do'tal) *adj.* of or pert. to endowment: **póliza dotal,** endowment policy.

dotar (do'tar) *v.t.* 1, to endow. 2, to equip; provide. —**dote** ('do·te) *n.m.* & *f.* dower; dowry. —**dotes,** *n.f.pl.* talents; natural gifts.

doxología (dok·so·lo'xi·a) *n.f.* doxology.

doy (doi) *v., 1st pers.sing. pres.ind.* of **dar.**

dozavo (do'θa·βo; -'sa·βo) *adj.* & *n.m.* twelfth.

dracma ('drak·ma) *n.f.* 1, drachma. 2, dram.

draga ('dra·ɣa) *n.f.* dredge.

dragado (dra'ɣa·ðo) *n.m.* 1, dredging. 2, dragging; drag.

dragaminas (dra·ɣa'mi·nas) *n.m.sing.* & *pl.* mine sweeper.

dragar (dra'ɣar) *v.t.* [*infl.:* **pagar,** 8] to dredge; drag.

dragón (dra'ɣon) *n.m.* 1, dragon. 2, dragoon.

drama ('dra·ma) *n.m.* drama. —**dramática** (-'ma·ti·ka) *n.f.* dramatics. —**dramático,** *adj.* dramatic. —**dramaturgo** (-'tur·ɣo) *n.m.* dramatist; playwright.

dramatizar (dra·ma·ti'θar; -'sar) *v.t.* [*infl.:* **rezar,** 10] to dramatize. —**dramatización,** *n.f.* dramatization.

drástico ('dras·ti·ko) *adj.* drastic.

drenar (dre'nar) *v.t.* to drain. —**drenaje,** *n.m.* drainage.

dríada ('dri·a·ða) *also,* **dríade** (-ðe) *n.f.* dryad.

driblar (dri'βlar) *v.t. & i., sports* to dribble. —**dribling** ('dri·βlin) *n.m.* dribble; dribbling.

dril (dril) *n.m.* **1,** drill *(cloth).* **2,** *zoöl.* mandrill.

driza ('dri·θa; -sa) *n.f.* halyard.

droga ('dro·ɣa) *n.f.* drug.

drogar (dro'ɣar) *v.t.* [*infl.:* **pagar, 8**] to drug. —**drogadicción** (-ɣa·dik'θjon; -'sjon) *n.f.* drug addiction. —**drogadicto** (-ɣa'ðik·to) *n.m.* drug addict. —**drogado,** *adj.* drugged; doped. —*n.m.* drug addict.

droguería (dro·ɣe'ri·a) *n.f.* **1,** drugstore. **2,** drug trade. **3,** hardware store.

droguista (dro'ɣis·ta) *n.m.* **1,** [*also,* **droguero** (-'ɣe·ro)] druggist. **2,** *Amer.,* impostor; cheat.

dromedario (dro·me'ða·rjo) *n.m.* dromedary.

druida ('drui·ða) *n.m.* druid.

drupa ('dru·pa) *n.f.* drupe.

dual (du'al) *adj.* dual. —**dualidad,** *n.f.* duality. —**dualismo,** *n.m.* dualism. —**dualístico,** *adj.* dualistic.

dubitable (du·βi'ta·βle) *adj.* doubtful; dubious. —**dubitación** (-ta'θjon; -'sjon) *n.f.* doubt; dubiety. —**dubitativo** (-ta'ti·βo) *adj.* doubtful.

ducado (du'ka·ðo) *n.m.* **1,** duchy; dukedom. **2,** ducat.

ducal (du'kal) *adj.* ducal.

ducentésimo (du·θen'te·si·mo; du·sen-) *adj. & n.m.* two-hundredth.

dúctil ('duk·til) *adj.* ductile. —**ductilidad,** *n.f.* ductility.

ducha ('du·tʃa) *n.f.* **1,** shower bath. **2,** douche.

duchar (du'tʃar) *v.t.* **1,** to douche. **2,** to give a shower bath to.

ducho ('du·tʃo) *adj.* skillful.

duda ('du·ða) *n.f.* doubt.

dudar (du'ðar) *v.t. & i.* to doubt. —**dudar de,** to distrust.

dudoso (du'ðo·so) *adj.* doubtful; dubious.

duela ('dwe·la) *v., pres.subjve. of* **doler.** —*n.f.* barrel stave.

duelo ('dwe·lo) *v., 1st pers. sing. pres.ind. of* **doler.**

duelo ('dwe·lo) *n.m.* **1,** duel. **2,** sorrow; affliction; bereavement. **3,** mourning. **4,** group of mourners. —**duelista,** *n.m.* duelist.

duende ('dwen·de) *n.m.* goblin; fairy; elf.

dueña ('dwe·ɲa) *n.f.* **1,** owner; mistress. **2,** duenna.

dueño ('due·ɲo) *n.m.* owner; master; landlord.

duerma ('dwer·ma) *v., pres.subjve. of* **dormir.**

duermo ('dwer·mo) *v., pres.ind. of* **dormir.**

dueto (du'e·to) *n.m.* duo; duet.

dulce ('dul·θe; -se) *adj.* **1,** sweet. **2,** gentle; mild. **3,** fresh, as water. —*n.m.* **1,** candy; sweetmeat. **2,** preserves. —**dulcería,** *n.f.* candy shop.

dulcero (dul'θe·ro; -'se·ro) *adj., colloq.* fond of sweets; having a sweet tooth. —*n.m.* **1,** confectioner. **2,** candy dish.

dulcificar (dul·θi·fi'kar; dul·si-) *v.t.* [*infl.:* **tocar, 7**] to sweeten. —**dulcificante,** *adj.* sweetening. —*n.m.* sweetener.

dulzura (dul'θu·ra; -'su·ra) *n.m.* **1,** sweetness. **2,** gentleness; mildness. **3,** pleasantness. *Also,* **dulzor** (-'θor; -'sor) *n.m.*

duna ('du·na) *n.f.* dune.

dúo ('du·o) *n.m.* duet; duo.

duodecimal (du·o·ðe·θi'mal; si·'mal) *adj.* duodecimal.

duodécimo (du·o'de·θi·mo; -si·mo) *adj. & n.m.* twelfth.

duodeno (dwo'ðe·no) *adj.* twelfth. —*n.m., anat.* duodenum. —**duodenal,** *adj.* duodenal.

duplicar (du·pli'kar) *v.t.* [*infl.:* **tocar, 7**] **1,** to duplicate. **2,** to repeat. **3,** to double. —**duplicación,** *n.f.* duplication; doubling. —**duplicado,** *n.m. & adj.* duplicate. —**duplicador,** *adj.* duplicating. —*n.m.* duplicator.

duplicidad (du·pli·θi'ðað; -si·'ðað) *n.f.* duplicity.

duplo ('du·plo) *adj. & n.m.* double; duplex.

duque ('du·ke) *n.m.* duke. —**duquesa** (-'ke·sa) *n.f.* duchess.

dura ('du·ra) *n.f., colloq.* durability.

durable (du'ra·βle) *adj.* durable. —**durabilidad,** *n.f.* durability.

duración (du·ra'θjon; -'sjon) *n.f.* duration.

duradero (du·ra'ðe·ro) *adj.* durable.

duramadre (du·ra'ma·ðre) *n.f.* dura mater. *Also,* **duramáter** (-'ma·ter).

durante (du'ran·te) *prep.* during.

durar (du'rar) *v.i.* to last; endure.

durazno (du'raθ·no; du'ras-) *n.m.*
1, peach. **2**, [*also*, **duraznero**]
peach tree.

dureza (du're·θa; -sa) *n.f.* **1**, hardness. **2**, harshness; cruelty. **3**, obstinacy.

durmiendo (dur'mjen·do) *v., ger. of* **dormir**. —*adj.* sleeping; dormant.

durmiente (dur'mjen·te) *v., pr.p. of* **dormir**. —*adj.* sleeping; dormant. —*n.m.* **1**, *archit.* girder; crossbeam. **2**, *Amer.* railroad tie; sleeper.

durmió (dur'mjo) *v., 3rd pers. sing.pret. of* **dormir**.

duro ('du·ro) *adj.* **1**, hard; solid. **2**, harsh; oppressive; cruel. **3**, stingy. **4**, obstinate. **5**, hard-boiled (*of eggs; also fig. sense*). —*adv.* hard. —*n.m.* a Spanish coin worth 5 pesetas; duro. —**a duras penas**, **1**, with great difficulty. **2**, hardly; scarcely. —**duro de corazón**, *also*, **de corazón duro**, hardhearted. —**duro de oído**, **1**, hard of hearing. **2**, tone deaf. —**duro de oreja**, hard of hearing. —**ser duro para (con)**, to be hard on. —**tomar las duras con las maduras**, *colloq.* to take the good with the bad.

E

E, e (e) *n.f.* 6th letter of the Spanish alphabet.

e (e) *conj.* and. *Used in place of y before words beginning with* i *or with* hi *when not followed by* e.

¡ea! ('e·a) *interj.* heigh!; heigh-ho!; ho!; now!; well!; there now! *Also, Amer.*, **¡epa!**

ebanista (e·βa'nis·ta) *n.m.* cabinetmaker.

ebanistería (e·βa·nis·te'ri·a) *n.f.* **1**, cabinetwork. **2**, cabinetmaker's shop. **3**, cabinetmaking.

ébano ('e·βa·no) *n.m.* ebony.

ebrio ('e·βrjo) *adj.* inebriated; intoxicated; drunk. —**ebriedad**, *n.f.* inebriety; intoxication; drunkenness.

ebullición (e·βu·ʎi'θjon; e·βu·ji'sjon) *also*, **ebulición** (e·βu·li-) *n.f.* ebullition; boiling.

ecléctico (e'klek·ti·ko) *adj. & n.m.* eclectic. —**eclecticismo** (-'θis·mo; -'sis·mo) *n.m.* eclecticism.

eclesiástico (e·kle'sjas·ti·ko) *adj.* ecclesiastical. —*n.m.* priest; clergyman; ecclesiastic.

eclipse (e'klip·se) *n.m.* eclipse. —**eclipsar**, *v.t.* to eclipse. —**eclipsarse**, *v.r.* to vanish; disappear.

eclíptico (e'klip·ti·ko) *adj.* ecliptic. —**eclíptica**, *n.f.* ecliptic.

écloga ('ek·lo·γa) *n.f.* eclogue.

eco ('e·ko) *n.m.* **1**, echo. **2**, news. **3**, response.

ecología (e·ko·lo'xi·a) *n.f.* ecology. —**ecológico** (-'lo·xi·ko) *adj.* ecological. —**ecólogo** (e'ko·lo·γo) *n.m.* ecologist.

economía (e·ko·no'mi·a) *n.f.* **1**, economy. **2**, economics. —**economías**, *n.f.pl.* savings. —**economista**, *n.m. & f.* economist. —**economía doméstica**, home economics.

económico (e·ko'no·mi·ko) *adj.* **1**, economic. **2**, economical; thrifty.

economizar (e·ko·no·mi'θar; -'sar) *v.t. & i.* [*infl.:* **rezar**, 10] to economize; save.

ecónomo (e'ko·no·mo) *n.m.* **1**, curator. **2**, trustee. **3**, *Amer.* economist.

ecosistema (e·ko·sis'te·ma) *n.m.* ecosystem.

ectoplasma (ek·to'plas·ma) *n.m.* ectoplasm.

ecuable (e'kwa·βle) *adj.* equable.

ecuación (e·kwa'θjon; -'sjon) *n.f.* equation.

ecuador (e·kwa'ðor) *n.m.* equator.

ecuánime (e'kwa·ni·me) *adj.* **1**, even-tempered; calm. **2**, fair; impartial. —**ecuanimidad**, *n.f.* equanimity.

ecuatorial (e·kwa·to'rjal) *adj.* equatorial.

ecuatoriano (e·kwa·to'rja·no) *adj. & n.m.* Ecuadoran; Ecuadorian.

ecuestre (e'kwes·tre) *adj.* equestrian.

ecuménico (e·ku'me·ni·ko) *adj.* ecumenical. —**ecumenismo**, *n.m.* ecumenism.

eczema (ek'θe·ma; ek'se-) *n.f.* eczema.

echadillo (e·tʃa'ði·ʎo; -jo) *n.m.* foundling.

echar (e'tʃar) *v.t.* **1**, to cast; throw; hurl. **2**, to pour; pour out. **3**, to turn or cast away. **4,** to eject; throw out. **5,** to put or throw in or on. **6,** to lay or set down. **7,** to deal out; distribute. **8,** to turn. **9,** to impute; ascribe. **10,** to move. **11,** to tell (fortunes). **12,** to discharge; dismiss. **13,** to sprout; put forth; grow. **14,** to emit; exude. **15,** to infer; gather; guess. **16,** to utter; pronounce. —*v.i.* **1,** to lean; tend; pull; turn *(in a certain direction).* **2,** to sprout. —**echarse,** *v.r.* **1,** to lie down. **2,** to throw or hurl oneself; plunge. **3,** to sit, as a hen. **4,** to devote oneself. —**echar a,** *fol. by inf.* to start. —**echar a perder,** to spoil. —**echar a pique,** to sink (a ship). —**echar de menos,** to miss. —**echar de ver,** to notice. —**echar el guante a,** to grab; arrest. —**echar en saco roto,** to disregard. —**echar mano a,** to grab. —**echarse a (reír, llorar,** *etc.***),** to burst out (laughing, crying, etc.). —**echársela** *or* **echárselas de,** to boast of; boast of being.

echazón (e·tʃaˈθon; -ˈson) *n.f.* jetti son; jetsam.

edad (eˈðað) *n.f.* age. —**edad media,** Middle Ages. —**edad mediana,** middle age; midlife. —**mayor de edad,** of age. —**menor de edad,** underage.

edecán (e·ðeˈkan) *n.m.* aide-decamp; aide.

edema (eˈðe·ma) *n.f.* edema.

Edén (eˈðen) *n.m.* Eden; paradise.

edición (e·ðiˈθjon; -ˈsjon) *n.f.* **1,** edition; issue. **2,** publication.

edicto (eˈðik·to) *n.m.* edict.

edificación (e·ði·fi·kaˈθjon; -ˈsjon) *n.f.* **1,** edification. **2,** building; erection.

edificar (e·ði·fiˈkar) *v.t. & i.* [*infl.:* **tocar,** 7] **1,** to edify. **2,** to build; erect. —**edificador,** *adj.* edifying. —*n.m.* builder.

edificio (e·ðiˈfi·θjo; -sjo) *n.m.* edifice; building.

editar (e·ðiˈtar) *v.t.* to publish; edit.

editor (e·ðiˈtor) *n.m.* **1,** publisher; editor. **2,** *colloq.* plagiarist. —*adj.* publishing; editing.

editorial (e·ði·toˈrjal) *adj. & n.m.* editorial. —*n.f.* publishing house. —*adj.* publishing *(attrib.).*

edredón (e·ðreˈðon) *n.m.* **1,** eider down. **2,** comforter.

educación (e·ðu·kaˈθjon; -ˈsjon) *n.f.* education; training; breeding.

educar (e·ðuˈkar) *v.t.* [*infl.:* **tocar,**

7] to educate; train. —**educador,** *n.* educator. —*adj.* educating. —**educativo,** *adj.* educational.

efectivamente (e·fek·ti·βaˈmen·te) *adv.* **1,** effectively. **2,** really.

efectivo (e·fekˈti·βo) *adj.* **1,** effective. **2,** true; certain; actual. —*n.m.* cash.

efecto (eˈfek·to) *n.m.* **1,** effect. **2,** impression. —**efectos,** *n.m.pl.* **1,** assets. **2,** merchandise; chattels; goods. **3,** drafts. —**efectos a pagar,** bills receivable. —**efectos de consumo,** consumer goods. —**efectos de resultado,** *comput.* output.

efectuar (e·fekˈtwar) *v.t.* [*infl.:* **continuar,** 23] to effect; effectuate; carry out; accomplish. —**efectuarse,** *v.r.* to occur; take place; take effect. —**efectuación,** *n.f.* accomplishment.

efemérides (e·fe·me·ri·ðes) *n.f. pl.* diary.

efervescencia (e·fer·βesˈθen·θja; -βcˈsen·sja) *n.f.* **1,** effervescence. **2,** ardor; ebullience. —**efervescente,** *adj.* effervescent.

eficaz (e·fiˈkaθ; -ˈkas) *adj.* effective. —**eficacia,** *n.f.* efficacy.

eficiente (e·fiˈθjen·te; -ˈsjen·te) *adj.* efficient. —**eficiencia,** *n.f.* efficiency.

efigie (eˈfi·xie) *n.f.* effigy.

efímero (eˈfi·me·ro) *adj.* ephemeral.

eflorescencia (e·flo·resˈθen·θja; -reˈsen·sja) *n.f.* efflorescence. —**eflorescente,** *adj.* efflorescent.

efluvio (eˈflu·βjo) *n.m.* effluvium.

efusión (e·fuˈsjon) *n.f.* effusion. —**efusivo,** *adj.* effusive.

égida (ˈe·xi·ða) *also,* **egida** (eˈxi-) *n.f.* aegis; egis; protection.

egipcio (eˈxip·θjo; -sjo) *adj. & n.m.* Egyptian.

eglantina (e·ɣlanˈti·na) *n.f.* sweetbrier; eglantine.

égloga (ˈe·ɣlo·ɣa) *also* **écloga** (ˈe·klo-) *n.f.* eclogue.

ego (ˈe·ɣo) *n.m.* ego.

egocéntrico (e·ɣoˈθen·tri·ko; -ˈsen·tri·ko) *adj.* egocentric.

egoísmo (e·ɣoˈis·mo) *n.m.* selfishness; egoism. —**egoísta,** *adj.* selfish; egoistic. —*n.m. & f.* egoist.

egolatría (e·ɣo·laˈtri·a) *n.f.* self-worship.

egotismo (e·ɣoˈtis·mo) *n.m.* egotism. —**egotista,** *n.m. & f.* egotist. —*adj.* egotistic; egotistical.

egregio (e'γre·xjo) *adj.* illustrious; excellent.

egresar (e·γre'sar) *v.i., Amer.* to leave; go away; graduate *(from school)*.

egreso (e'γre·so) *n.m.* 1, expense; debit. 2, *Amer.* graduation.

¡eh! (e) *interj.* eh!; here!; hey!

eíder (e'i·ðer) *n.m.* eider; eider duck.

einsteinio (ains'tai·njo) *n.m.* einsteinium.

eje ('e·xe) *n.m.* 1, axis. 2, axle. 3, shaft; spindle; arbor. 4, *fig.* crucial point; crux.

ejecutar (e·xe·ku'tar) *v.t.* 1, to execute; perform; carry out. 2, *law* to attach; seize. 3, to put to death. —**ejecución,** *n.f.* execution.

ejecutivo (e·xe·ku'ti·βo) *adj. & n.m.* executive.

ejecutor (e·xe·ku'tor) *adj.* executive. —*n.m.* 1, executor. 2, executive. —**ejecutor de la justicia,** executioner.

ejecutora (e·xe·ku'to·ra) *n.f.* 1, executrix. 2, executive.

ejecutorio (e·xe·ku'to·rjo) *adj., law* executory; effective; in force.

¡ejem! (e'xem) *interj.* hem!; ahem!

ejemplar (e·xem'plar) *adj.* exemplary. —*n.m.* 1, pattern; model. 2, example. 3, prototype; sample. 4, copy *(of a book or periodical).* —**sin ejemplar,** exceptional.

ejemplificar (e·xem·pli·fi'kar) *v.i.* [*infl.:* **tocar,** 7] to exemplify. —**ejemplificación,** *n.f.* exemplification.

ejemplo (e'xem·plo) *n.m.* 1, example. 2, pattern; exemplar. —**por ejemplo,** for example.

ejercer (e·xer'θer; -'ser) *v.t.* [*infl.:* **vencer,** 11] 1, to practice; exercise; perform. 2, to exert.

ejercicio (e·xer'θi·θjo; -'si·sjo) *n.m.* 1, exercise. 2, practice. 3, profession; task. 4, military drill. 5, fiscal year. 6, examination.

ejercitar (e·xer·θi'tar; -si'tar) *v.t.* 1, to exercise. 2, to train; drill.

ejército (e'xer·θi·to; -si·to) *n.m.* army.

ejido (e'xi·ðo) *n.m.* public land; common.

el (el) *def.art. masc.sing.* the. —*dem.pron. masc.sing.* that; the one (that).

él *pers.pron. masc.sing.* 1, *subj. of a verb* he; it. 2, *obj. of a prep.* him; it.

elaboración (e·la·βo·ra'θjon;

-'sjon) *n.f.* 1, elaboration. 2, manufacture.

elaborado (e·la·βo'ra·ðo) *adj.* 1, elaborate. 2, manufactured.

elaborar (e·la·βo'rar) *v.t.* 1, to elaborate. 2, to manufacture.

elación (e·la'θjon; -'sjon) *n.f.* 1, haughtiness; pride. 2, elevation; grandeur. 3, magnanimity. 4, ornateness of style.

elástico (e'las·ti·ko) *adj. & n.m.* elastic. —**elásticos,** *n.m.pl.* suspenders. —**elasticidad** (-θi'ðað; -si'ðað) *n.f.* elasticity; resiliency.

elección (e·lek'θjon; -'sjon) *n.f.* 1, election. 2, choice; selection.

electo (e'lek·to) *adj. & n.m.* elect; chosen. —**electivo,** *adj.* elective.

elector (e·lek'tor) *adj.* electing. —*n.m.* elector. —**electorado,** *n.m.* electorate. —**electoral,** *adj.* electoral.

electricidad (e·lek·tri·θi'ðað; -si'ðað) *n.f.* electricity.

electricista (e·lek·tri'θis·ta; -'sis·ta) *n.m. & f.* electrician.

eléctrico (e'lek·tri·ko) *adj.* electric; electrical.

electrificar (e·lek·tri·fi'kar) *v.t.* [*infl.:* **tocar,** 7] to electrify; provide with electricity. —**electrificación,** *n.f.* electrification.

electrizar (e·lek·tri'θar; -'sar) *v.t.* [*infl.:* **rezar,** 10] to electrify; stimulate. —**electrización,** *n.f.* electrification; stimulation.

electro (e'lek·tro) *n.m.* amber.

electrocardiograma (e·lek· tro·kar·ðjo'γra·ma) *n.m.* electrocardiogram.

electrocutar (e·lek·tro·ku'tar) *v.t.* to electrocute. —**electrocución,** *n.f.* electrocution. —**electrocutor,** *n.m.* electrocutionist.

electrodo (e·lek'tro·ðo) *n.m.* electrode.

electroencefalograma (e·lek· tro·en·θe·fa·lo'γra·ma; -en·se·fa· lo-) *n.m.* electroencephalogram.

electroimán (e·lek·tro·i'man) *n.m.* electromagnet.

electrolizar (e·lek·tro·li'θar; -'sar) *v.t.* [*infl.:* **rezar,** 10] to electrolyze. —**electrólisis** (-'tro·li·sis) *n.f.* electrolysis. —**electrolítico** (-'li·ti·ko) *adj.* electrolytic. —**electrólito** (-'tro·li·to) *n.m.* electrolyte.

electromagnético (e·lek·tro· maγ'ne·ti·ko) *adj.* electromagnetic.

—**electromagnetismo** (-'tis·mo) *n.m.* electromagnetism.
electromotor (e·lek·tro·mo'tor) *adj.* [*fem.* **-tora**] electromotive. —*n.m.* electromotor.
electromotriz (e·lek·tro·mo'triθ; -'tris) *adj.* electromotive.
electrón (e·lek'tron) *n.m.* electron. —**electrónico,** *adj.* electronic. —**electrónica,** *n.f.* electronics.
electrostática (e·lek·tros'ta·ti·ka) *n.f.* electrostatics. —**electrostático,** *adj.* electrostatic.
electrotecnia (e·lek·tro'tek·nja) *n.f.* electrical engineering.
electrotipo (e·lek·tro'ti·po) *n.m.* electrotype.
elefancía (e·le·fan'θi·a; -'si·a) *n.f.* elephantiasis.
elefante (e·le'fan·te) *n.m. & f.* elephant. —**elefantino,** *adj.* elephantine.
elefantiasis (e·le·fan'tja·sis) *n.f.* elephantiasis.
elegante (e·le'yan·te) *adj.* elegant. —**elegancia,** *n.f.* elegance.
elegía (e·le'xi·a) *n.f.* elegy. —**elegíaco,** *adj.* elegiac.
elegible (e·le'xi·βle) *adj.* eligible. —**elegibilidad,** *n.f.* eligibility.
elegir (e·le'xir) *v.t.* [*infl.:* **regir, 57**] **1,** to elect; choose. **2,** to name; nominate. —**elegido,** *adj.* elect.
elemental (e·le·men'tal) *adj.* **1,** elementary. **2,** elemental.
elemento (e·le'men·to) *n.m.* element.
elenco (e'len·ko) *n.m.* **1,** catalogue; list; index. **2,** *theat.* cast.
elevación (e·le·βa'θjon; -'sjon) *n.f.* elevation.
elevado (e·le'βa·ðo) *adj.* elevated.
elevador (e·le·βa'ðor) *n.m.* elevator; hoist; lift.
elevar (e·le'βar) *v.t.* **1,** to raise; elevate. **2,** to exalt. —**elevarse,** *v.r.* to rise; soar; ascend.
elfo (el'fo) *n.m.* elf.
elidir (e·li'ðir) *v.t.* to elide.
eligió (e·li'xjo) *v., 3rd pers.sing. pret.* of **elegir.**
elija (e'li·xa) *v., pres.subjve.* of **elegir.**
elijo (e'li·xo) *v., pres.ind.* of **elegir.**
eliminar (e·li·mi'nar) *v.t.* to eliminate. —**eliminación,** *n.f.* elimination.
elipse (e'lip·se) *n.f.* ellipse.
elipsis (e'lip·sis) *n.f.sing. & pl.* ellipsis.
elíptico (e'lip·ti·ko) *adj.* elliptical.

elisión (e·li'sjon) *n.f.* elision.
elitista (e·li'tis·ta) *adj.* elitist.
elíxir (e'lik·sir) *also,* **elixir** (-'sir) *n.m.* elixir.
elocución (e·lo·ku'θjon; -'sjon) *n.f.* elocution.
elocuente (e·lo'kwen·te) *adj.* eloquent. —**elocuencia,** *n.f.* eloquence.
elogiar (e·lo'xjar) *v.t.* to praise; eulogize. —**elogio** (e'lo·xjo) *n.m.* eulogy; praise.
elote (e'lo·te) *n.m., Amer.* ear of corn.
elucidar (e·lu·θi'ðar; -si'ðar) *v.t.* to elucidate. —**elucidación,** *n.f.* elucidation.
eludir (e·lu'ðir) *v.t.* to elude. —**eludible,** *adj.* avoidable. —**elusivo,** *adj.* elusive.
ella ('e·ʎa; 'e·ja) *pers.pron.fem. sing.* **1,** *subj. of a verb* she; it. **2,** *obj. of a prep.* her; it.
ellas ('e·ʎas; 'e·jas) *pers.pron., pl.* of **ella.**
ello ('e·ʎo; -jo) *pers. & dem.pron. neut.sing.* it; that.
ellos ('e·ʎos; 'e·jos) *pers.pron., pl.* of **él.**
emaciación (e·ma·θja'θjon; -sja'sjon) *n.f.* emaciation.
emanar (e·ma'nar) *v.i.* to emanate. —**emanación,** *n.f.* emanation.
emancipar (e·man·θi'par; -si'par) *v.t.* to emancipate. —**emancipación,** *n.f.* emancipation. —**emancipador,** *adj.* emancipating. —*n.m.* emancipator.
emasculación (e·mas·ku·la'θjon; -'sjon) *n.f.* emasculation.
emascular (e·mas·ku'lar) *v.t.* to emasculate; castrate. —**emasculación,** *n.f.* emasculation; castration.
embadurnar (em·ba·ður'nar) *v.t.* to smear; daub.
embajada (em·ba'xa·ða) *n.f.* **1,** embassy. **2,** errand. —**embajador,** *n.m.* ambassador.
embalar (em·ba'lar) *v.t.* to pack; bale. —*v.i.* to exert full force or speed. —**embalador,** *n.m.* packer. —**embalaje,** *n.m.* packing.
embaldosar (em·bal·do'sar) *v.t.* to tile; pave with tile. —**embaldosado,** *n.m.* tiling; tile floor or flooring.
embalsamar (em·bal·sa'mar) *v.t.* **1,** to embalm. **2,** to perfume. —**embalsamador,** *n.m.* embalmer. —**embalsamamiento,** *n.m.* embalming; embalmment.
embarazada (em·ba·ra'θa·ða; -'sa·ða) *adj., fem.* pregnant.

embarazar (em·ba·ra'θar; -'sar) v.t. [infl.: rezar, 10] 1, to embarrass. 2, colloq. to make pregnant. 3, to encumber.

embarazo (em·ba'ra·θo; -so) n.m. 1, encumbrance. 2, embarrassment. 3, pregnancy.

embarazoso (em·ba·ra'θo·so; -'so·so) adj. 1, cumbersome. 2, embarrassing.

embarcación (em·bar·ka'θjon; -'sjon) n.f. 1, vessel; boat; ship. 2, embarkation (of passengers).

embarcadero (em·bar·ka'ðe·ro) n.m. 1, pier; wharf. 2, R.R. platform.

embarcar (em·bar'kar) v.t. [infl.: tocar, 7] to ship. —**embarcarse**, v.r. to embark. —**embarcador**, n.m. shipper.

embarco (em'bar·ko) n.m. embarkation (of passengers).

embargar (em·bar'ɣar) v.t. [infl.: pagar, 8] 1, to embargo. 2, law to attach; seize. 3, to impede; restrain. 4, to seize; clutch.

embargo (em'bar·ɣo) n.m. 1, embargo. 2, law seizure; attachment. —**sin embargo**, nevertheless; however.

embarnizar (em·bar·ni'θar; -'sar) v.t. [infl.: rezar, 10] to varnish.

embarque (em'bar·ke) n.m. 1, embarkation (of cargo). 2, shipment.

embarradura (em·ba·rra'ðu·ra) n.f. smear; smearing.

embarrancar (em·ba·rran'kar) v.i. [infl.: tocar, 7] 1, to run aground. 2, to run into a ditch.

embarrar (em·ba'rrar) v.t. 1, to bemire; make muddy; soil. 2, Amer. to botch up; mess up. —**embarrarlas**, Amer., colloq. to foul things up.

embarullar (em·ba·ru'ʎar; -'jar) v.t., colloq. to botch; mess up.

embastar (em·bas'tar) v.t. to baste; tack. —**embaste** (-'bas·te) n.m. basting.

embate (em'ba·te) n.m. 1, pounding; banging. 2, sudden attack.

embaucar (em·bau'kar) v.t. [infl.: tocar, 7] to swindle; dupe. —**embaucador**, n.m. [fem. -**dora**] swindler; deceiver. —adj. tricky. —**embaucamiento**, n.m. deception; cock-and-bull story.

embebecer (em·be·βe'θer; -'ser) v.t. [infl.: conocer, 13] 1, to amuse; entertain. 2, to charm; fascinate. —**embebecido**, adj. amazed; rapt.

—**embebecimiento**, n.m. fascination; rapture.

embeber (em·be'βer) v.t. 1, to drink; absorb. 2, to soak; saturate. 3, to insert. 4, to shrink; shorten; compress. —v.i. to shrink. —**embeberse**, v.r. 1, to be delighted. 2, to be absorbed or engrossed. 3, fig. to immerse oneself; delve.

embelecar (em·be·le'kar) v.t. [infl.: tocar, 7] 1, to deceive; trick. 2, Amer., colloq. to give (someone) a line; string (someone) along.

embeleco (em·be'le·ko) n.m. 1, deceit; trickery. 2, Amer., colloq. humbug; bunk.

embelesar (em·be·le'sar) v.t. to charm; fascinate. —**embeleso** (-'le·so) n.m. charm; fascination.

embellecer (em·be·ʎe'θer; -je'ser) v.t. [infl.: conocer, 13] to adorn; embellish. —**embellecimiento**, n.m. embellishment.

embestida (em·bes'ti·ða) n.f. assault; onset.

embestir (em·bes'tir) v.t. [infl.: pedir, 33] to assail; attack.

emblandecer (em·blan·de'θer; -'ser) v.t. [infl.: conocer, 13] to soften; mollify.

emblanquecer (em·blan·ke'θer; -'ser) v.t. = **blanquecer**.

emblema (em'ble·ma) n.m. emblem; badge. —**emblemático** (-'ma·ti·ko) adj. emblematic.

embobar (em·bo'βar) v.t. 1, to amuse. 2, to fascinate.

embocadura (em·bo·ka'ðu·ra) n.f. 1, entrance; opening. 2, river mouth. 3, mus. mouthpiece. 4, taste, as of wine.

embolada (em·bo'la·ða) n.f. piston stroke.

embolado (em·bo'la·ðo) n.m. 1, a bull with tipped horns. 2, fig. ineffectual person. 3, theat. bit part. 4, colloq. trick; deception.

embolar (em·bo'lar) v.t. 1, to tip (a bull's horns) with wooden balls. 2, to black (shoes).

embolia (em'bo·lja) n.f. embolism. Also, **embolismo** (-'lis·mo).

émbolo ('em·bo·lo) n.m. 1, piston; plunger. 2, pathol. embolus.

embolsar (em·bol'sar) v.t. to pocket; put in one's pocket or purse.

embonar (em·bo'nar) v.t. to improve; make satisfactory.

emborrachar (em·bo·rra'tʃar) v.t. to intoxicate; make drunk. —**em-**

borracharse, *v.r.* to become intoxicated; get drunk.

emborrascar (em·bo·rras'kar) *v.t., colloq.* [*infl.:* tocar, 7] to anger. —**emborrascarse,** *v.r.* to become stormy, as weather.

emborronar (em·bo·rro'nar) *v.t.* **1,** to blur; blot. **2,** to scribble.

emboscar (em·bos'kar) *v.t.* [*infl.:* tocar, 7] to place in ambush. —**emboscarse,** *v.r.* **1,** to lie in ambush. **2,** *colloq.* to shirk. —**emboscada,** *n.f.* ambuscade; ambush.

embotar (em·bo'tar) *v.t.* to blunt; make dull.

embotellar (em·bo·te'ʎar; -'jar) *v.t.* to bottle; bottle up. —**embotellamiento,** *n.m.* bottleneck; traffic jam; gridlock.

embozar (em·bo'θar; -'sar) *v.t.* [*infl.:* rezar, 10] **1,** to muffle (the face). **2,** to cloak; conceal. **3,** to muzzle. —**embozarse,** *v.r.* to muffle one's face.

embragar (em·bra'ɣar) *v.t.* [*infl.:* pagar, 8] to engage (a clutch, driveshaft, etc.).

embrague (em'bra·ɣe) *n.m.* **1,** clutch; coupling. **2,** engaging (of a clutch, driveshaft, etc.).

embravecer (em·bra·βe'θer; -'ser) *v.t.* [*infl.:* conocer, 13] to enrage; irritate. —*v.i., bot.* to become strong. —**embravecerse,** *v.r.* **1,** to become enraged. **2,** to swell, as waves.

embrear (em·bre'ar) *v.t.* to coat with pitch.

embriagar (em·brja'ɣar) *v.t.* [*infl.:* pagar, 8] to intoxicate; inebriate. —**embriagado,** *adj.* intoxicated; drunk. —**embriaguez** (-'ɣeθ; -'ɣes) *n.f.* intoxication; drunkenness.

embridar (em·bri'ðar) *v.t.* to bridle; check; restrain.

embriología (em·brjo·lo'xi·a) *n.f.* embryology. —**embriólogo** (em'brjo·lo·ɣo) *n.m.* embryologist.

embrión (em·bri'on) *n.m.* embryo. —**embrionario,** *adj.* embryonic.

embrollador (em·bro·ʎa'ðor; -ja'ðor) *adj.* **1,** embroiling. **2,** troublesome. —*n.m.* **1,** muddler. **2,** troublemaker.

embrollar (em·bro'ʎar; -'jar) *v.t.* to entangle; embroil.

embrollo (em'bro·ʎo; -jo) *n.m.* tangle; muddle. *Also,* **embrolla,** *n.f., colloq.*

embromar (em·bro'mar) *v.t.* **1,** to tease; joke with. **2,** *Amer.* to bore; annoy. **3,** *Amer.* to detain; delay.

embrujar (em·bru'xar) *v.t.* to bewitch; charm. —**embrujo** (-'bru·xo) *n.m.* charm; bewitchment.

embrutecer (em·bru·te'θer; -'ser) *v.t.* [*infl.:* conocer, 13] to stupefy; make brutish or dull.

embudo (em'bu·ðo) *n.m.* **1,** funnel. **2,** *fig.* trick. —**ley del embudo,** *colloq.* unfairly applied law.

embuste (em'bus·te) *n.m.* **1,** fib; lie. **2,** trick; fraud. —**embustes,** *n.m.pl.* baubles; trinkets. —**embustero,** *n.m.* fibber; liar. —*adj.* lying; deceitful.

embutido (em·bu'ti·ðo) *adj.* inlaid. —*n.m.* **1,** inlaid work. **2,** salami; sausage. **3,** *Amer.* lace.

embutir (em·bu'tir) *v.t.* **1,** to inlay; insert. **2,** to stuff; cram. **3,** *colloq.* to gobble; gulp down.

emergencia (e·mer'xen·θja; -sja) *n.f.* **1,** emergence. **2,** emergency. —**emergente,** *adj.* emergent.

emerger (e·mer'xer) *v.i.* [*infl.:* coger, 15] to emerge.

emérito (e'me·ri·to) *adj.* emeritus.

emético (e'me·ti·ko) *n.m.* & *adj.* emetic.

emigración (e·mi·ɣra'θjon; -'sjon) *n.f.* **1,** emigration. **2,** migration.

emigrar (e·mi'ɣrar) *v.i.* **1,** to emigrate. **2,** to migrate. —**emigrado,** *n.m.* emigrant; emigré. —**emigrante,** *adj.* & *n.m.* & *f.* emigrant.

eminencia (e·mi'nen·θja; -sja) *n.f.* **1,** height; hill. **2,** eminence.

eminente (e·mi'nen·te) *adj.* **1,** eminent. **2,** lofty; high.

emir (e'mir) *n.m.* emir.

emisario (e·mi'sa·rjo) *n.m.* emissary.

emisión (e·mi'sjon) *n.f.* **1,** emission. **2,** *radio; TV* broadcast. **3,** *fin.* issue (of paper money, bonds, etc.).

emisor (e·mi'sor) *adj.* **1,** emitting. **2,** *radio; TV* broadcasting. —*n.m.* transmitter. —**emisora,** *n.f.* broadcasting station.

emitir (e·mi'tir) *v.t.* **1,** to emit. **2,** to issue, as bonds. **3,** to utter. **4,** *radio; TV* to broadcast.

emoción (e·mo'θjon; -'sjon) *n.f.* emotion. —**emocional,** *adj.* emotional.

emocionar (e·mo·θjo'nar; e·mo·sjo-) *v.t.* to move; touch; thrill. —**emocionante,** *adj.* moving; touching; thrilling.

emoliente (e·mo'ljen·te) *n.m.* & *adj.* emollient.

emolumento (e·mo·lu'men·to) *n.m.* emolument.

emotivo (e·mo'ti·βo) *adj.* emotive; emotional.

empacar (em·pa'kar) *v.t. & i.* [*infl.*: **tocar,** 7] to pack; package. —**empacado,** *n.m.* packing; packaging. —**empacador,** *n.m.* packer.

empachar (em·pa'tʃar) *v.t.* 1, to cause indigestion. 2, to gorge; glut. —**empacharse,** 1, to get indigestion. 2, to become embarrassed.

empacho (em·pa'tʃo) *n.m.* 1, scruple; restraint. 2, gorge; bellyful. 3, indigestion.

empadronar (em·pa·ðro'nar) *v.t.* to take a census of; register. —**empadronamiento,** *n.m.* census.

empalagar (em·pa·la'yar) *v.t.* [*infl.*: **pagar,** 8] 1, to cloy. 2, to weary; bore.

empalago (em·pa'la·yo) *n.m.* 1, surfeit. 2, bore.

empalagoso (em·pa·la'yo·so) *adj.* 1, cloying. 2, oversweet. 3, overrich; overornate. 4, boring.

empalar (em·pa'lar) *v.t.* to impale.

empalizar (em·pa·li'θar; -'sar) *v.t.* [*infl.*: **rezar,** 10] to fence; palisade. —**empalizada,** *n.f.* palisade; fence.

empalmar (em·pal'mar) *v.t.* to join; splice; couple. —*v.i. (of trains, conveyances, etc.)* to make connection.

empalme (em'pal·me) *n.m.* 1, joint; splice. 2, *R.R.* junction.

empanada (em·pa'na·ða) *n.f.* meat pie.

empanar (em·pa'nar) *v.t.* to bread. —**empanado,** *adj.* breaded. —*n.m.* turnover.

empañar (em·pa'ɲar) *v.t.* 1, to swaddle. 2, to darken; tarnish.

empañetar (em·pa·ɲe'tar) *v.t.* to plaster.

empapar (em·pa'par) *v.t.* to soak; saturate. —**empaparse,** *v.r.* to steep oneself; delve; get soaked.

empapelado (em·pa·pe'la·ðo) *n.m.* 1, wallpaper. 2, paperhanging.

empapelador (em·pa·pe·la'ðor) *n.m.* paperhanger.

empapelar (em·pa·pe'lar) *v.t.* to paper.

empaque (em'pa·ke) *n.m.* 1, packing. 2, *fig.* presence; bearing.

empaquetadura (em·pa·ke·ta·'ðu·ra) *n.f.* 1, packing. 2, gasket.

empaquetar (em·pa·ke'tar) *v.t.* to pack.

emparedado (em·pa·re'ða·ðo) *n.m.* 1, recluse. 2, sandwich. 3, prisoner. —*adj.* imprisoned; in confinement.

emparedar (em·pa·re'ðar) *v.t.* to confine; wall in.

emparejar (em·pa·re'xar) *v.t.* 1, to pair; match. 2, to level; make even. 3, to close (a door, window, etc.) without locking. —**emparejar con,** 1, to come abreast of; catch up with. 2, to be even with; be on a level with.

emparentar (em·pa·ren'tar) *v.i.* to be or become related by marriage.

emparrado (em·pa'rra·ðo) *n.m.* arbor; bower.

empastar (em·pas'tar) *v.t.* 1, *dent.* to fill (a tooth). 2, to paste. 3, to bind (a book) in a stiff cover. 4, *paint.* to impaste.

empaste (em'pas·te) *n.m.* 1, *dent.* filling. 2, stiff binding. 3, *paint.* impasto.

empatar (em·pa'tar) *v.t.* 1, to tie (a vote, score, etc.). 2, *Amer.* to couple; splice.

empate (em'pa·te) *n.m.* 1, tie; tie score. 2, *Amer.* joint; splice. 3, gridlock.

empatía (em·pa'ti·a) *n.f.* empathy.

empecé (em·pe'θe; -'se) *v., 1st pers.sing. pret. of* **empezar.**

empecinarse (em·pe·θi'nar·se; em·pe·si-) *v.r., Amer.* to be stubborn; persist. —**empecinado,** *adj., Amer.* stubborn; persistent.

empedernir (em·pe·ðer'nir) *v.t.* [*defective: used only in tenses with terminations beginning with* i] to harden. —**empedernido,** *adj.* hardhearted; hardcore.

empedrar (em·pe'ðrar) *v.t.* to pave with stones. —**empedrado,** *n.m.* stone pavement. —*adj.* dotted with clouds, as the sky.

empegado (em·pe'ya·ðo) *n.m.* tarpaulin.

empeine (em'pei·ne) *n.m.* 1, *anat.* groin. 2, *anat.* instep. 3, *pathol.* ringworm. 4, cotton blossom.

empellar (em·pe'ʎar; -'jar) *v.t.* [*infl.*: **pensar,** 27] to push; shove; jostle.

empeller (em·pe'ʎer; -'jer) *v.t.* [*infl.*: 18] = **empellar.**

empellón (em·pe'ʎon; -'jon) *n.m.* push; shove. —**a empellones,** rudely.

empeñar (em·pe'ɲar) *v.t.* 1, to pawn; pledge. 2, to compel; oblige.

—**empeñarse,** *v.r.* **1,** to bind oneself. **2,** to persist. **3,** to intercede.

empeño (em·pe·ɲo) *n.m.* **1,** pledge; pawn. **2,** longing; desire. **3,** determination. **4,** boldness. —**casa de empeños,** pawnshop. —**con empeño,** eagerly; persistently.

empeorar (em·pe·o'rar) *v.t. & i.* to worsen.

empequeñecer (em·pe·ke·ɲe'θer; -'ser) *v.t.* [*infl.:* **conocer, 13**] **1,** to diminish; make smaller. **2,** to belittle.

emperador (em·pe·ra'ðor) *n.m.* emperor.

emperatriz (em·pe·ra'triθ; -'tris) *n.f.* empress.

emperifollar (em·pe·ri·fo'ʎar; -'jar) *v.t.* to adorn; dress up.

empero (em'pe·ro) *conj.* yet; however; notwithstanding.

emperrarse (em·pe'rrar·se) *v.r.* to be or become stubborn.

empezar (em·pe'θar; -'sar) *v.t.* [*infl.:* **pensar, 27; rezar, 10**] to begin; commence.

empicotar (em·pi·ko'tar) *v.t.* to pillory; punish in a pillory.

empinado (em·pi'na·ðo) *adj.* **1,** high. **2,** steep. **3,** *fig.* conceited.

empinar (em·pi'nar) *v.t.* to raise. —**empinarse,** *v.r.* **1,** to rear up, as a horse. **2,** to stand on tiptoe. **3,** to tower. **4,** *aero.* to zoom. —**empinar el codo,** *colloq.* to drink heavily; bend the elbow.

empiojado (em·pjo'xa·ðo) *adj.* lousy.

empírico (em'pi·ri·ko) *adj.* empirical. —*n.m.* quack; charlatan.

empirismo (em·pi'ris·mo) *n.m.* **1,** empiricism. **2,** quackery.

empizarrar (em·pi·θa'rrar; -sa·'rrar) *v.t.* to slate; cover with slate.

emplastar (em·plas'tar) *v.t.* **1,** to plaster. **2,** to daub; smear.

emplasto (em'plas·to) *n.m.* **1,** plaster; poultice. **2,** unsatisfactory settlement; poor bargain. **3,** *colloq.* weakling; sickly or puny person.

emplazamiento *n.m.* **1,** summoning; summons. **2,** emplacement; location.

emplazar (em·pla'θar; -'sar) *v.t.* [*infl.:* **rezar, 10**] **1,** to summon. **2,** to place; locate.

empleado (em·ple'a·ðo) *adj.* employed. —*n.m.* [*fem.* **empleada**] employee.

emplear (em·ple'ar) *v.t.* **1,** to em-

ploy; engage. **2,** to spend; invest. **3,** to use.

empleo (em'ple·o) *n.m.* **1,** employ; employment. **2,** business; profession. **3,** investment. **4,** use.

emplomar (em·plo'mar) *v.t.* **1,** to lead; fill or line with lead. **2,** *Amer.* to fill (a tooth).

emplumar (em·plu'mar) *v.t.* to feather.

empobrecer (em·po·βre'θer; -'ser) *v.t.* [*infl.:* **conocer, 13**] to impoverish. —**empobrecerse,** *v.r.* **1,** to become poor. **2,** to languish; fade away. —**empobrecimiento,** *n.m.* impoverishment.

empolvar (em·pol'βar) *v.t.* **1,** to powder. **2,** to cover with dust or powder.

empollar (em·po'ʎar; -'jar) *v.t. & i.* to hatch. —*v.i., colloq.* to bone (up).

empollón (em·po'ʎon; -'jon) *n.m., colloq.* bookworm; grind.

emponzoñar (em·pon·θo'ɲar; -so'ɲar) *v.t.* **1,** to poison. **2,** to taint; corrupt. —**emponzoñador,** *n.m.* poisoner. —*adj.* poisoning; poisonous. —**emponzoñamiento,** *n.m.* poisoning.

emporio (em'po·rjo) *n.m.* emporium.

empotrar (em·po'trar) *v.t.* **1,** to imbed, as in a wall. **2,** *carp.* to mortise. **3,** *naut.* to fasten (cannon).

emprendedor (em·pren·de'ðor) *adj.* enterprising.

emprender (em·pren'der) *v.t.* **1,** to undertake. **2,** to begin. —**emprenderla con,** to squabble with.

empreñar (em·pre'ɲar) *v.t.* to impregnate; make pregnant.

empresa (em'pre·sa) *n.f.* **1,** enterprise; undertaking; company; business. **2,** design; purpose. **3,** *theat.* management.

empresario (em·pre'sa·rjo) *n.m.* **1,** entrepreneur. **2,** *theat.* impresario.

empréstito (em'pres·ti·to) *n.m.* corporation or government loan.

empujar (em·pu'xar) *v.t.* to push; propel.

empuje (em'pu·xe) *n.m.* **1,** push; impulse. **2,** *fig.* energy; enterprise. **3,** *mech.* thrust.

empujón (em·pu'xon) *n.m.* push; shove. —**a empujones, 1,** violently; rudely. **2,** by fits and starts.

empulgueras (em·pul'ye·ras) *n.f.pl.* thumbscrew (*instrument of torture*).

empuñadura (em·pu·ɲa'ðu·ra) *n.f.* **1,** hilt *(of a sword)* **2,** beginning *(of a story).* **3,** *Amer.* handle *(of an umbrella or cane).*

empuñar (em·pu'ɲar) *v.t.* to clutch; grasp.

emular (e·mu'lar) *v.t.* to emulate. —**emulación,** *n.f.* emulation.

émulo ('e·mu·lo) *adj.* emulous. —*n.m.* competitor; rival.

emulsión (e·mul'sjon) *n.f.* emulsion. —**emulsionar,** *v.t.* to emulsify. —**emulsionamiento,** *n.m.* emulsification. —**emulsor** (-'sor) *n.m.* emulsifier.

en (en) *prep.* **1,** in; into. **2,** at. **3,** on; upon. **4,** *fol. by ger., colloq.* on; upon.

enagua (e'na·ɣwa) *n.f., usu. pl.* petticoat.

enajenación (en·a·xe·na'θjon; -'sjon) *n.f.* **1,** alienation. **2,** absent-mindedness. **3,** rapture. —**enajenación mental,** mental derangement. *Also,* enajenamiento, *n.m.*

enajenar (en·a·xe'nar) *v.t.* **1,** to alienate. **2,** to transport; enrapture. —**enajenarse,** *v.r.* **1,** to become estranged. **2,** to be carried away.

enaltecer (en·al·te'θer; -'ser) *v.t.* [*infl.:* **conocer, 13**] to praise; extol; exalt. —**enaltecimiento,** *n.m.* praise; exaltation.

enamorado (en·a·mo'ra·ðo) *adj.* in love; enamored; smitten. —*n.m.* [*fem.* -**ada**] lover; sweetheart.

enamorar (en·a·mo'rar) *v.t.* **1,** to enamor. **2,** to court; woo. —**enamorarse,** *v.r., fol. by* **de,** to fall in love (with). —**enamoramiento,** *n.m.* love; being in love.

enano (e'na·no) *adj.* dwarfish; dwarf *(attrib.)* —*n.m.* [*fem.* **enana**] dwarf.

enarbolar (en·ar·βo'lar) *v.t.* to hoist; hang (a flag). —**enarbolarse,** *v.r.* = **encabritarse.**

enarcar (en·ar'kar) *v.t.* [*infl.:* **tocar, 7**] **1,** to arch. **2,** to hoop (a barrel).

enardecer (en·ar·ðe'θer; -'ser) *v.t.* [*infl.:* **conocer, 13**] to fire with passion; arouse; excite. —**enardecerse,** *v.r.* to be aroused or inflamed.

enarenar (en·a·re'nar) *v.t.* to sand; cover with sand or gravel.

encabestrar (en·ka·βes'trar) *v.t.* **1,** to put a halter on. **2,** to attract; seduce.

encabezamiento (en·ka·βe·θa·'mjen·to; -sa'mjen·to) *n.m.* **1,** =

empadronamiento. 2, tax; tax rate. **3,** heading *(of a document).* **4,** salutation *(of a letter).*

encabezar (en·ka·βe'θar; -'sar) *v.t.* [*infl.:* **rezar, 10**] **1,** = **empadronar. 2,** to give a heading or title to. **3,** to head; lead. **4,** *carp.* to join. *Also,* encabezonar (-θo'nar; -so·'nar).

encabritarse (en·ka·βri'tar·se) *v.r.* **1,** to rise on the hind legs; rear. **2,** to pitch with an upward motion. **3,** *fig.* to become aroused or excited.

encadenamiento (en·ka·ðe·na·'mjen·to) *n.m.* **1,** connection; linkage. **2,** concatenation. *Also,* encadenación (-'θjon; -'sjon) *n.f.*

encadenar (en·ka·ðe'nar) *v.t.* **1,** to chain; shackle. **2,** to subjugate; enslave. **3,** to connect; link together. **4,** to captivate.

encajar (en·ka'xar) *v.t.* **1,** to encase; insert. **2,** to fit closely, as a lid. **3,** *carp.* to join. **4,** *fig.* to toss in, as a remark. **5,** to deal or land (a blow). **6,** to palm off; foist. —*v.i.* to fit; be fitting. —**encajarse,** *v.r.* **1,** to intrude. **2,** to squeeze oneself in. **3,** to jam; become stuck.

encaje (en'ka·xe) *n.m.* **1,** fitting; fit. **2,** socket; groove. **3,** *carp.* join. **4,** lace. **5,** inlaid work; mosaic.

encajonar (en·ka·xo'nar) *v.t.* to pack; box; crate. —**encajonarse,** *v.r.* to narrow; become narrow. —**encajonado,** *adj.* narrow; boxed-in.

encallar (en·ka'ʎar; -'jar) *v.i., naut. & fig.* to run aground. —**encalladero,** *n.m.* sandbank; shoal.

encamarse (en·ka'mar·se) *v.r., colloq.* to take to one's bed. —**encamado,** *adj., colloq.* bedridden.

encaminar (en·ka·mi'nar) *v.t.* **1,** to guide; direct; show the way. **2,** to send (something) on its way. —**encaminarse,** *v.r.* **1,** to betake oneself. **2,** to start out.

encamotarse (en·ka·mo'tar·se) *v.r., Amer.* to become infatuated.

encandilar (en·kan·di'lar) *v.t.* to blind; dazzle. —**encandilarse,** *v.r.* to light up; be set aglow.

encanecer (en·ka·ne'θer; -'ser) *v.i.* [*infl.:* **conocer, 13**] to become gray-haired.

encanijarse (en·ka·ni'xar·se) *v.r.* to become sickly; become thin or emaciated.

encantador (en·kan·ta'ðor) *adj.*

delightful; charming; enchanting.
—*n.m.* [*fem.* **-dora**] enchanter;
charmer; sorcerer.

encantamiento (en·kan·ta·
'mjen·to) *n.m.* **1,** enchantment. **2,**
incantation. *Also,* **encantación.**

encantar (en·kan'tar) *v.t.* to enchant; charm.

encanto (en'kan·to) *n.m.* **1,** enchantment; spell. **2,** delight.

encapotado (en·ka·po'ta·ðo) **1,**
overcast. **2,** frowning; grim.

encapotadura (en·ka·po·ta'ðu·
ra) *n.f.* **1,** overcast. **2,** frown; grim
expression. *Also,* **encapotamiento**
(-'mjen·to) *n.m.*

encapotar (en·ka·po'tar) *v.t.* to
cloak; muffle. —**encapotarse,** *v.r.*
1, to become cloudy; darken; become overcast. **2,** to frown; lower.

encapricharse (en·ka·pri'tʃar·se)
v.r. **1,** to become stubborn. **2,**
colloq. to become infatuated.

encapuchar (en·ka·pu'tʃar) *v.t.* to
cover with a hood.

encaramar (en·ka·ra'mar) *v.t.* **1,**
to lift; raise; elevate. **2,** *fig.* to extol.
—**encaramarse,** *v.r.* to scramble
up; climb.

encarar (en·ka'rar) *v.t.* to aim;
point. —**encararse a** *or* **con,** to
confront; come face to face with.

encarcelar (en·kar·θe'lar; -se'lar)
v.t. **1,** to incarcerate; imprison. **2,**
archit. to imbed in mortar. **3,** *carp.*
to clamp. —**encarcelación,** *n.f.,*
also, **encarcelamiento,** *n.m.* incarceration; imprisonment.

encarecer (en·ka·re'θer; -'ser) *v.t.*
[*infl.:* **conocer, 13**] **1,** to increase
the price of. **2,** to praise; extol.
—*v.i.* to increase in price.

encarecidamente (en·ka·re·θi·
ða'men·te; -si·ða'men·te) *adv.* **1,**
exceedingly; highly. **2,** ardently;
earnestly.

encarecimiento (en·ka·re·θi·
'mjen·to; -si'mjen·to) *n.m.* **1,** increase; rise (*in price*). **2,** enhancement; exaggeration. —**con encarecimiento,** ardently; earnestly.

encargado (en·kar'ɣa·ðo) *n.m.* **1,**
agent. **2,** person in charge; foreman;
supervisor, etc. —**encargado de
negocios,** chargé d'affaires.

encargar (en·kar'ɣar) *v.t.* [*infl.:*
pagar, 8] **1,** to commend; entrust. **2,**
to recommend; counsel. **3,** to order;
commission; assign.

encargo (en'kar·ɣo) *n.m.* **1,**
charge; trust. **2,** recommendation;

counsel. **3,** order; commission; assignment. **4,** errand.

encariñarse (en·ka·ri'ɲar·se) *v.r.,*
fol. by **con,** to grow fond (of); become attached (to). —**encariñado,**
adj. fond; attached. —**encariñamiento,** *n.m.* fondness; attachment.

encarnar (en·kar'nar) *v.t.* **1,** to incarnate; embody. **2,** to bury in the
flesh, as a weapon; imbed. —*v.i.* to
become incarnate. —**encarnarse,**
v.r. **1,** to become incarnate. **2,** to
blend; fuse. **3,** to become ingrown,
as a nail. —**encarnación,** *n.f.* incarnation; embodiment.

encarnizado (en·kar·ni'θa·ðo;
-'sa·ðo) *adj.* **1,** irate; furious. **2,**
bloody.

encarnizar (en·kar·ni'θar; -'sar)
v.t. [*infl.:* **rezar, 10**] to provoke;
move to fury. —**encarnizarse,** *v.r.*
1, to be glutted with flesh. **2,** =
ensañarse. 3, to fight a bloody battle.

encaro (en'ka·ro) *n.m.* **1,** stare. **2,**
blunderbuss. **3,** stock (*of a rifle*).

encarrilar (en·ka·rri'lar) *v.t.* **1,** to
put on the right track; set aright. **2,**
to put (a train) back on the track.

encasillar (en·ka·si'ʎar; -'jar) *v.t.*
1, to pigeonhole. **2,** to sort; catalog.
—**encasillado,** *n.m.* set of pigeonholes.

encauchar (en·kau'tʃar) *v.t.* to
treat with rubber; rubberize.

encauzar (en·kau'θar; -'sar) *v.t.*
[*infl.:* **rezar, 10**] to channel; direct.

encefalitis (en·θe·fa'li·tis; en·se-)
n.f. encephalitis.

encefalograma (en·θe·fa·
lo'ɣra·ma; en·se·fa·lo-) *n.m.*
encephalogram.

encelar (en·θe'lar; en·se-) *v.t.* to
make jealous. —**encelarse,** *v.r.* to
become jealous.

encender (en·θen'der; en·sen-) *v.t.*
[*infl.:* **perder, 29**] **1,** to kindle;
light. **2,** *fig.* to inflame. —**encenderse,** *v.r.* to blush. —**encendedor,**
n.m. cigarette lighter.

encendido (en·θen'di·ðo; en·sen-)
adj. **1,** inflamed. **2,** blushing.
—*n.m., mech.* ignition.

encerado (en·θe'ra·ðo; en·se-) *adj.*
waxed. —*n.m.* **1,** coat of wax; polish. **2,** oilcloth. **3,** blackboard.

encerar (en·θe'rar; en·se-) *v.t.* to
wax; polish.

encerrar (en·θe'rrar; en·se-) *v.t.*
[*infl.:* **pensar, 27**] **1,** to lock up;
confine. **2,** to include; embrace;

comprise. —**encerrarse,** v.r. to live in seclusion.

encía (en'θi·a; -'si·a) n.f., anat. gum.

encíclico (en'θi·kli·ko; en'si-) adj. encyclical. —**encíclica,** n.f. encyclical.

enciclopedia (en·θi·klo'pe·ðja; en·si-) n.f. encyclopedia. —**enciclopédico** (-'pe·ði·ko) adj. encyclopedic. —**enciclopedista,** n.m. & f. encyclopedist.

encienda (en'θjen·da; -'sjen·da) v., pres.subjve. of **encender.**

enciendo (en'θjen·do; en'sjen-) v., pres.ind. of **encender.**

encierre (en'θje·rre; en'sje-) v., pres.subjve. of **encerrar.**

encierro (en'θje·rro; en'sje-) n.m. **1,** locking up; confinement. **2,** lockup. **3,** enclosure. —v., pres.ind. of **encerrar.**

encima (en'θi·ma; en'si-) adv. **1,** over; above. **2,** besides; over and above. —**encima de,** on; upon. —**por encima,** superficially. —**por encima de,** in spite of.

encina (en'θi·na; -'si·na) n.f. evergreen oak.

encinta (en'θin·ta; en'sin-) adj. fem. pregnant.

encintado (en·θin'ta·ðo; en·sin-) n.m. curb (of a sidewalk).

encintar (en·θin'tar; en·sin-) v.t. **1,** trim with ribbon. **2,** to put a curb on (a sidewalk).

enclaustrar (en·klaus'trar) v.t. to cloister; seclude.

enclavado (en·kla'βa·ðo) adj. hemmed in. —n.m. enclave.

enclavar (en·kla'βar) v.t. **1,** to nail down. **2,** to pierce through. **3,** colloq. to deceive.

enclave (en'kla·βe) n.m. enclave.

enclavijar (en·kla·βi'xar) v.t. **1,** to join; pin. **2,** to peg; put pegs on.

enclenque (en'klen·ke) adj. weak; feeble; sickly. —n.m. & f. weak or sickly person.

encocorar (en·ko·ko'rar) v.t., colloq. to annoy.

encoger (en·ko'xer) v.t. [infl.: **coger, 15**] **1,** to contract; shorten; shrink. **2,** fig. to abash; humble. —**encogerse,** v.r. **1,** to shrink; contract. **2,** to be abashed; humble oneself. —**encogerse de hombros,** to shrug one's shoulders.

encogido (en·ko'xi·ðo) adj. timid; shy.

encogimiento (en·ko·xi'mjen·to)

n.m. 1, contraction; shrinkage. **2,** pusillanimity. **3,** bashfulness; awkwardness.

encolar (en·ko'lar) v.t. to glue.

encolerizar (en·ko·le·ri'θar; -'sar) v.t. [infl.: **rezar, 10**] to anger; irritate. —**encolerizarse,** v.r. to become angry.

encomendable (en·ko·men'da·βle) adj. commendable.

encomendar (en·ko·men'dar) v.t. [infl.: **pensar, 27**] to commend; entrust. —**encomendarse,** v.r. to send one's compliments. —**encomendamiento,** n.m. commission; charge.

encomiar (en·ko'mjar) v.t. to eulogize; praise; extol.

encomienda (en·ko'mjen·da) n.f. **1,** commission; charge. **2,** complimentary message. **3,** hist. estate granted by the Spanish kings. **4,** colloq. errand. —**encomiendas,** n.f. pl. compliments; respects. —**encomienda postal,** Amer. parcel-post package.

encomio (en·ko·mjo) n.m. praise; eulogy; encomium.

enconamiento (en·ko·na'mjento) n.m. **1,** inflammation; festering. **2,** = **encono.**

enconar (en·ko'nar) v.t. **1,** to infect. **2,** to inflame; provoke. —**enconarse,** v.r. **1,** to fester. **2,** fig. to rankle.

encono (en·ko·no) n.m. malevolence; rancor.

enconoso (en·ko'no·so) adj. **1,** hurtful; prejudicial; malevolent. **2,** resentful; rancorous.

encontrado (en·kon'tra·ðo) adj. **1,** opposite; in front; facing. **2,** hostile; opposed; contrary.

encontrar (en·kon'trar) v.t. & i. [infl.: **acostar, 28**] **1,** to meet; encounter. **2,** to find; come upon. —**encontrarse,** v.r. **1,** to meet; come together. **2,** to be; find oneself. **3,** to feel; feel oneself to be. **4,** fig. to clash; conflict.

encontrón (en·kon'tron) n.m. bump; collision; jolt. Also, **encontronazo** (-'na·θo; -so).

encopetado (en·ko·pe'ta·ðo) adj. presumptuous; haughty; high-hat.

encopetar (en·ko·pe'tar) v.t. to dress (the hair) high on the head. —**encopetarse,** v.r. to become conceited.

encordar (en·kor'ðar) v.t. [infl.: **acostar, 28**] **1,** to provide with

encordelar 185 enderezar

strings. **2,** to string; tie or bind with string.

encordelar (en·kor·ðe'lar) *v.t.* to string; tie or bind with string. *Also,* **encordonar.**

encorralar (en·ko·rra'lar) *v.t.* to corral.

encorvada (en·kor'βa·ða) *n.f.* **1,** stoop; stooping. **2,** buck; bucking (*of an animal*).

encorvadura (en·kor·βa'ðu·ra) *n.f.* **1,** bending. **2,** crookedness; curvature. *Also,* **encorvamiento,** *n.m.*

encorvar (en·kor'βar) *v.t.* to bend; curve. —**encorvarse,** *v.r.* **1,** to bend; stoop. **2,** to be biased.

encrespar (en·kres'par) *v.t.* **1,** to curl; frizzle. **2,** to make (the hair) stand on end. **3,** to ruffle (feathers). —**encresparse,** *v.r.* **1,** to become rough, as the sea. **2,** *fig.* to bristle. **3,** to curl; become curly.

encristalar (en·kris·ta'lar) *v.t.* to glass; glaze; furnish with glass.

encrucijada (en·kru·θi'xa·ða; en·kru·si) *n.f.* **1,** intersection; crossroads. **2,** ambush. **3,** opportunity to harm someone.

encuadernador (en·kwa·ðer·na'ðor) *n.m.* **1,** binder (*for papers*). **2,** bookbinder.

encuadernar (en·kwa·ðer'nar) *v.t.* to bind (books). —**encuadernación,** *n.f.* binding.

encuadrar (en·kwa'ðrar) *v.t.* **1,** to frame. **2,** to fit in; insert. **3,** to encompass; comprise. **4,** *Amer.* to summarize.

encubridor (en·ku·βri'ðor) *n.m.* [*fem.* -**dora**] **1,** concealer. **2,** procurer; bawd. **3,** accessory after the fact. —*adj.* concealing.

encubrimiento (en·ku·βri'mjen·to) *n.m.* **1,** concealment. **2,** *law* being an accessory after the fact.

encubrir (en·ku'βrir) *v.t.* [*p.p.* **encubierto**] to hide; conceal.

encuentre (en'kwen·tre) *v.,* *pres.subjve.* of **encontrar.**

encuentro (en'kwen·tro) *v., pres. ind.* of **encontrar.** —*n.m.* **1,** encounter; sudden meeting. **2,** clash; collision. **3,** bout; match. **4,** find; finding. —**salirle al encuentro a** *or* **de, 1,** to go to meet. **2,** to oppose. **3,** to anticipate.

encuerar (en·kwe'rar) *v.t.* to strip (of clothes or money). —**encuerado,** *adj., Amer.* naked; ragged.

encuesta (en'kwes·ta) *n.f.* **1,** inquiry; inquest. **2,** poll; survey.

encuestador, *n.m.* [*fem.* -**dora**] pollster.

encumbrar (en·kum'brar) *v.t.* to raise; elevate. —**encumbrarse,** *v.r.* **1,** to rise; be raised. **2,** to become pretentious; put on airs. —**encumbrado,** *adj.* high; lofty. —**encumbramiento,** *n.m.* elevation; height.

encurtir (en·kur'tir) *v.t.* to pickle. —**encurtidos,** *n.m.pl.* pickled vegetables.

enchapado (en·tʃa'pa·ðo) *n.m.* **1,** veneer. **2,** overlay; plating.

enchapar (en·tʃa'par) *v.t.* **1,** to veneer. **2,** to overlay; cover with sheets or plates.

encharcar (en·tʃar'kar) *v.t.* [*infl.:* **tocar, 7**] to inundate; flood.

enchilada (en·tʃi'la·ða) *n.f., Amer.* enchilada.

enchufar (en·tʃu'far) *v.t.* **1,** to connect; plug in. **2,** to place in office through political favor.

enchufe (en'tʃu·fe) *n.m.* **1,** *elect.* plug; socket. **2,** pipe joint. **3,** *fig.* office obtained through political favor.

ende ('en·de) *in* **por ende,** consequently; therefore.

endeble (en'de·βle) *adj.* **1,** feeble; frail. **2,** flimsy.

endeblez (en·de'βleθ; -'βles) *n.f.* **1,** feebleness. **2,** flimsiness.

endecha (en'de·tʃa) *n.f.* dirge; lament.

endémico (en'de·mi·ko) *adj.* endemic.

endemoniado (en·de·mo'nja·ðo) *adj.* **1,** devilish; perverse. **2,** possessed.

endemoniar (en·de·mo'njar) *v.t., colloq.* to irritate; enrage.

endentar (en·den'tar) *v.t.* [*infl.:* **pensar, 27**] **1,** to mesh; engage. **2,** to put or form teeth in, as a saw, gearwheel, etc. —**endentadura,** *n.f.* serration.

enderezador (en·de·re·θa'ðor; -sa'ðor) *adj.* managing well. —*n.m.* **1,** good manager. **2,** [*also,* **enderezador de entuertos**] troubleshooter.

enderezamiento (en·de·re·θa'mjen·to; -sa'mjen·to) *n.m.* **1,** straightening. **2,** guiding; directing. **3,** setting right.

enderezar (en·de·re'θar; -'sar) *v.t.* [*infl.:* **rezar, 10**] **1,** to straighten; unbend. **2,** to rectify; set right. **3,** to manage well. **4,** to address. **5,** to guide; direct.

endeudarse (en·deu'ðar·se) *v.r.* to go into debt.

endiablado (en·dja'βla·ðo) *adj.* devilish; perverse.

endiablar (en·dja'βlar) *v.t.* **1,** to enrage. **2,** *fig.* to corrupt; pervert. —**endiablarse,** *v.r.* to become furious.

endibia (en'di·βja) *n.f.* endive; chicory.

endiosar (en·djo'sar) *v.t.* to deify. —**endiosarse,** *v.r.* to put on airs; be haughty. —**endiosamiento,** *n.m.* deification.

endocrino (en·do'kri·no) *adj.* & *n.m.* endocrine.

endomingarse (en·do·min'gar·se) *v.r.* [*infl.:* **pagar, 8**] to dress up in one's Sunday best.

endorsar (en·dor'sar) *v.t.* = endosar. —**endorso** (-'dor·so) *n.m.* = endoso.

endosar (en·do'sar) *v.t.* **1,** to endorse. **2,** to foist; palm off. **3,** to give; deal (a blow, insult, etc.). —**endosante,** *n.m.* endorser. —**endosatario,** *n.m.* endorsee. —**endoso** (-'do·so) *n.m.* endorsement.

endrino (en'dri·no) *n.m.,* **1,** sloe tree. **2,** sloe. —*adj.* sloe-colored; blue-black. —**endrina,** *n.f.* sloe.

endulzar (en·dul'θar; -'sar) *v.t.* [*infl.:* **rezar, 10**] **1,** to sweeten. **2,** to soothe; soften. —**endulzadura,** *n.f.* sweetening.

endurar (en·du'rar) *v.t.* **1,** to endure; bear. **2,** to put off; delay. **3,** to save; economize.

endurecer (en·du·re'θer; -'ser) *v.t.* [*infl.:* **conocer, 13**] to harden; stiffen. —**endurecido,** *adj.* hardened; hardcore. —**endurecimiento,** *n.m.* hardening; stiffening.

enea (e'ne·a) *n.f.* = **anea.**

enebro (e'ne·βro) *n.m.* juniper tree. —**enebrina,** *n.f.* juniper berry.

eneldo (e'nel·do) *n.m.* dill.

enema (e'ne·ma) *n.f.* enema.

enemigo (e·ne'mi·γo) *n.m.* enemy; foe. —*adj.* **1,** inimical; hostile. **2,** averse.

enésimo (e'ne·si·mo) *adj. n*th.

enemistad (e·ne·mis'taθ) *n.f.* enmity; hostility.

enemistar (e·ne·mis'tar) *v.t.* to alienate; estrange. —**enemistarse con,** to fall out with.

energía (en·er'xi·a) *n.f.* energy; power.

enérgico (e'ner·xi·ko) *adj.* energetic; vigorous.

energúmeno (e·ner'yu·me·no) *n.m.* **1,** violent person. **2,** madcap.

enero (e'ne·ro) *n.m.* January.

enervar (e·ner'βar) *v.t.* to enervate. —**enervarse,** *v.r.* to weaken. —**enervación,** *n.f.* enervation.

enfadar (en·fa'ðar) *v.t.* to vex; annoy. —**enfadarse,** *v.r.* **1,** to become annoyed. **2,** to fret. —**enfadadizo,** *adj.* irritable; peevish.

enfado (en'fa·ðo) *n.m.* annoyance; vexation. —**enfadoso,** *adj.* annoying; vexatious.

enfangar (en·fan'gar) *v.t.* [*infl.:* **pagar, 8**] to muddy. —**enfangarse,** *v.r.* **1,** to sink in the mud. **2,** to become muddy.

enfardar (en·far'ðar) *v.t.* to bale; pack; bundle. *Also,* **enfardelar** (-ðe'lar).

énfasis ('en·fa·sis) *n.m. or f.* emphasis. —**enfático** (en'fa·ti·ko) *adj.* emphatic.

enfermar (en·fer'mar) *v.i.* [*also, v.r.* **enfermarse**] to fall ill. —*v.t.* **1,** to make sick. **2,** *fig.* to weaken; enervate.

enfermedad (en·fer·me'ðaθ) *n.f.* sickness; illness.

enfermizo (en·fer'mi·θo; -so) *adj.* **1,** sickly; infirm. **2,** unwholesome; unhealthful.

enfermo (en'fer·mo) *adj.* sick; ill. —*n.m.* patient. —**enfermería,** *n.f.* infirmary. —**enfermero,** *n.m.* [*fem.* **-era**] nurse.

enfilar (en·fi'lar) *v.t.* **1,** to align; line up. **2,** to thread; string. **3,** *mil.* to enfilade. **4,** to bear or head toward. —**enfilada,** *n.f., mil.* enfilade.

enfisema (en·fi'se·ma) *n.m.* emphysema.

enflaquecer (en·fla·ke'θer; -'ser) *v.t. & i.* [*infl.:* **conocer, 13**] to weaken. —**enflaquecerse,** *v.r.* to weaken; be discouraged.

enfocar (en·fo'kar) *v.t.* [*infl.:* **tocar, 7**] to focus; focus on; bring into focus.

enfoque (en'fo·ke) *n.m.* **1,** focus; focusing. **2,** approach *(to a matter).*

enfrascamiento (en·fras·ka·'mjen·to) *n.m.* **1,** involvement. **2,** distraction; absent-mindedness.

enfrascar (en·fras'kar) *v.t.* [*infl.:* **tocar, 7**] to bottle; put in a flask or jar. —**enfrascarse,** *v.r.* to be absorbed or engrossed.

enfrenar (en·fre'nar) *v.t.* **1,** to restrain; bridle. **2,** to brake; put the brake on.

enfrentar (en·fren'tar) *v.t.* **1,** to confront; put face to face. **2,** to face; be situated opposite. —**enfrentarse a** *or* **con, 1,** to face. **2,** to oppose.

enfrente (en'fren·te) *adv.* opposite; facing. —**enfrente de,** opposite; in front of.

enfriamiento (en·fri·a'mjen·to) *n.m.* **1,** cooling; refrigeration. **2,** cold; chill.

enfriar (en·fri'ar) *v.t.* [*infl.:* **enviar,** 22] to cool; chill. —**enfriarse,** *v.r.* **1,** to cool. **2,** to grow cold. **3,** to catch cold.

enfundar (en·fun'dar) *v.t.* to sheathe; put in a case, sack, etc.

enfurecer (en·fu·re'θer; -'ser) *v.t.* [*infl.:* **conocer, 13**] to enrage; infuriate. —**enfurecerse,** *v.r.* to rage; become infuriated. —**enfurecimiento,** *n.m.* fury.

enfurruñarse (en·fu·rru'ɲar·se) *v.r., colloq.* to show annoyance; scowl.

enfurtir (en·fur'tir) *v.t.* **1,** to full (cloth). **2,** to tighten; frizzle (the hair).

engalanar (en·ga·la'nar) *v.t.* **1,** to deck out; adorn. **2,** *naut.* to dress (a ship).

enganchar (en·gan'tʃar) *v.t.* **1,** to hook; hang on a hook. **2,** to hitch. **3,** to connect; link; couple. **4,** *colloq.* to ensnare. **5,** *colloq.* to decoy into military service. —**engancharse,** *v.r.* **1,** to enlist. **2,** to engage; become hooked. **3,** to get caught on a hook.

enganche (en'gan·tʃe) *n.m.* **1,** enlistment. **2,** hooking. **3,** *R.R.* coupling; coupler. *Also,* **enganchamiento.**

engañar (en·ga'ɲar) *v.t.* **1,** to deceive; beguile; fool. **2,** to wile away (time). —**engañarse,** *v.r.* **1,** to be deceived. **2,** to be mistaken. —**engañadizo** (-'ði·θo; -so) *adj.* gullible. —**engañador,** *adj.* deceiving. —*n.m.* deceiver; cheat.

engañifa (en·ga'ɲi·fa) *n.f., colloq.* deception; inveiglement.

engaño (en·ga·ɲo) *n.m.* **1,** fraud; deceit. **2,** misunderstanding; mistake. **3,** lure; hoax. —**engañoso,** *adj.* false; deceitful; misleading.

engarzar (en·gar'θar; -'sar) *v.t.* [*infl.:* **rezar, 10**] **1,** to string, esp. jewels. **2,** = **engastar. 3,** *Amer.* to link; connect; couple. —**engarce** (-'gar·θe; -se) *n.m.* = **engaste.**

engastar (en·gas'tar) *v.t.* to chase; set; mount, esp. jewels. —**engaste** (-'gas·te) *n.m.* setting; mounting, esp. of jewels.

engatusar (en·ga·tu'sar) *v.t., colloq.* to inveigle; coax. —**engatusador,** *adj., colloq.* coaxing. —*n.m.* coaxer.

engendrar (en·xen'drar) *v.t.* **1,** to engender; beget. **2,** to create; produce.

engendro (en'xen·dro) *n.m.* **1,** fetus. **2,** shapeless offspring; monster. **3,** abortive scheme; botch.

englobar (en·glo'βar) *v.t.* to include; comprise.

engolfarse (en·gol'far·se) *v.r.* **1,** to go deeply (into); delve. **2,** to become absorbed or engrossed.

engolosinar (en·go·lo·si'nar) *v.t.* to lure; entice.

engomar (en·go'mar) *v.t.* to gum.

engordar (en·gor'ðar) *v.t. & i.* to fatten. —**engorde** (en'gor·ðe) *n.m.* fattening.

engoznar (en·goθ'nar; en·gos-) *v.t.* to hinge.

engranaje (en·gra'na·xe) *n.m.* gearing; gear; gears.

engranar (en·gra'nar) *v.t.* to gear; interlock. —*v.i.* to engage, as gears.

engrandecer (en·gran·de'θer; -'ser) *v.t.* [*infl.:* **conocer, 13**] **1,** to augment; aggrandize. **2,** to exalt; magnify.

engrandecimiento (en·gran·de·θi'mjen·to; -si'mjen·to) *n.m.* **1,** increase; aggrandizement. **2,** magnification.

engrane (en'gra·ne) *n.m.* **1,** mesh; meshing (of gears). **2,** = **engranaje.**

engrapador (en·gra·pa'ðor) *n.m.* stapler.

engrapar (en·gra'par) *v.t.* **1,** to cramp with irons. **2,** to staple.

engrasar (en·gra'sar) *v.t.* **1,** to oil; grease; lubricate. **2,** to stain with grease. —**engrasador,** *n.m.* oiler; lubricator. —**engrase** (-'gra·se); **engrasado** *n.m.* greasing; lubrication.

engreído (en·gre·i·ðo) *adj.* **1,** vain; conceited; spoiled. **2,** infatuated.

engreír (en·gre'ir) *v.t.* [*infl.:* **reír, 58**] **1,** to make vain or conceited; spoil, esp. a child. **2,** to infatuate. —**engreírse,** *v.r.* to become vain or conceited. —**engreimiento,** *n.m.* vanity; conceit; presumption.

enguantar (en·gwan'tar) *v.t.* to glove.

engrudo (en'gru·ðo) *n.m.* paste.

enguirnaldar (en·gir·nal'dar) *v.t.* **1,** to wreathe; garland. **2,** to trim; adorn.

engullir (en·gu'ʎir; -'jir) *v.t.* [*infl.:* **bullir, 19**] to gulp; devour.

enharinar (en·a·ri'nar) *v.t.* to flour; dredge.

enhebrar (en·e'βrar) *v.t.* to string; thread.

enhiesto (en'jes·to) *adj.* erect; upright.

enhilar (en·i'lar) *v.t.* **1,** to thread; string. **2,** to order; arrange. **3,** to direct; guide.

enhorabuena (en·o·ra'βwe·na) *n.f.* congratulations. —*adv.* well and good. —**estar de enhorabuena,** to be glad; be content.

enhuerar (en·we'rar) *v.t.* to addle.

enigma (e'niɣ·ma) *n.m.* enigma. —**enigmático** (-'ma·ti·ko) *adj.* enigmatic.

enjabonar (en·xa·βo'nar) *v.t.* **1,** to soap; lather. **2,** *colloq.* to softsoap. **3,** *colloq.* to reprimand.

enjaezar (en·xa·e'θar; -'sar) *v.t.* [*infl.:* **rezar, 10**] to harness.

enjalbegar (en·xal·βe'ɣar) *v.t.* [*infl.:* **pagar, 8**] **1,** to whitewash. **2,** to daub; smear (the face).

enjambre (en'xam·bre) *n.m.* **1,** swarm of bees. **2,** crowd; multitude. —**enjambrar,** *v.i.* to swarm.

enjaular (en·xau'lar) *v.t.* **1,** to cage. **2,** *colloq.* to jail.

enjoyar (en·xo'jar) *v.t.* to gem; bejewel.

enjuagadientes (en·xwa·ɣa·'ðjen·tes) *n.m. sing. & pl.* mouthwash.

enjuagar (en·xwa'ɣar) *v.t.* [*infl.:* **pagar, 8**] to rinse.

enjuague (en·xwa·ɣe) *n.m.* rinse.

enjugamanos (en·xu·ɣa'ma·nos) *n.m. sing. & pl.,* *Amer.* towel.

enjugar (en·xu'ɣar) *v.t.* [*infl.:* **pagar, 8**] **1,** to dry; wipe. **2,** to cancel; wipe out (a debt or deficit). —**enjugarse,** *v.r.* to become thin; take off weight.

enjuiciar (en·xwi'θjar; -'sjar) *v.t.* to judge; pass judgment on.

enjundia (en'xun·dja) *n.f.* **1,** nub; gist. **2,** vigor; vim.

enjuto (en'xu·to) *adj.* lean; gaunt.

enlace (en'la·θe; -se) *n.m.* **1,** con-nection. **2,** liaison; link. **3,** inter-locking. **4,** marriage.

enladrillado (en·la·ðri'ʎa·ðo; -'ja·ðo) *n.m.* **1,** brick pavement. **2,** brickwork.

enladrillar (en·la·ðri'ʎar; -'jar) *v.t.* to pave with brick. —**enladri-llador,** *n.m.* bricklayer.

enlatar (en·la'tar) *v.t.* to can.

enlazar (en·la'θar; -'sar) *v.t.* [*infl.:* **rezar, 10**] **1,** to tie; bind. **2,** to link; connect. **3,** to lasso. —**enla-zarse,** *v.r.* **1,** to be joined. **2,** to in-terlock. **3,** to be joined in marriage. **4,** to become related by marriage.

enlistonado (en·lis·to'na·ðo) *n.m.* furring; lathing.

enlodar (en·lo'ðar) *v.t.* **1,** to muddy; bemire. **2,** to sully; be-smirch.

enloquecer (en·lo·ke'θer; -'ser) *v.t.* [*infl.:* **conocer, 13**] to make in-sane; drive crazy. —*v.i.* [*also, v.r.,* **enloquecerse**] **1,** to become insane; be driven crazy. **2,** *(of trees)* to be-come barren. —**enloquecedor,** *adj.* maddening. —**enloquecimiento,** *n.m.* madness; insanity.

enlosar (en·lo'sar) *v.t.* to tile. —**enlosado,** *n.m.* tilework; tile floor.

enlutar (en·lu'tar) *v.t.* **1,** to put in mourning. **2,** to dress or drape with mourning. **3,** *fig.* to sadden.

enllantar (en·ʎan'tar; en·jan-) *v.t.* to shoe (a wheel).

enmaderar (en·ma·ðe'rar) *v.t.* to timber; construct or cover with tim-ber. —**enmaderamiento,** *n.m.* tim-berwork; woodwork.

enmarañar (en·ma·ra'ɲar) *v.t.* to tangle; entangle; confuse; mix up. —**enmarañamiento,** *n.m.* tangle; entanglement.

enmarcar (en·mar'kar) *v.t.* [*infl.:* **tocar, 7**] to frame.

enmascarar (en·mas·ka'rar) *v.t.* to mask. —**enmascararse,** *v.r.* to masquerade; disguise oneself.

enmelar (en·me'lar) *v.t.* [*infl.:* **pensar, 27**] **1,** to cover or smear with or as with honey. **2,** *fig.* to sweeten; sugar-coat.

enmendar (en·men'dar) *v.t.* [*infl.:* **pensar, 27**] **1,** to amend; emend. **2,** to make amends for. —**enmen-darse,** *v.r.* to mend one's ways. —**enmendación,** *n.f.* correction; amendment.

enmienda (en'mjen·da) *n.f.* **1,** correction; emendation. 2, amendment. 3, amends.

enmohecer (en·mo·e'θer; -'ser) v.t. [infl.: conocer, 13] 1, to mildew; mold. 2, to rust.

enmohecido (en·mo·e'θi·ðo; -'si·ðo) adj. 1, mildewed; moldy; musty. 2, rusty; rusted.

enmohecimiento (en·mo·e·θi·'mjen·to; -'si·mjen·to) n.m. 1, mustiness; moldiness. 2, rustiness; rust.

enmollecer (en·mo·ʎe'θer; -je'ser) v.t. [infl.: conocer, 13] to soften; mollify.

enmordazar (en·mor·ða'θar; -'sar) v.t. [infl.: rezar, 10] to gag; muzzle.

enmudecer (en·mu·ðe'θer; -'ser) v.t. [infl.: conocer, 13] to silence. —v.i. to be or become silent.

enmugrecer (en·mu·ɣre'θer; -'ser) v.t. [infl.: conocer, 13] to soil; dirty.

ennegrecer (en·ne·ɣre'θer; -'ser) v.t. [infl.: conocer, 13] to obscure; darken; blacken. —**ennegrecimiento**, n.m. blackening; darkening.

ennoblecer (en·no·βle'θer; -'ser) v.t. [infl.: conocer, 13] 1, to ennoble. 2, to adorn; embellish. —**ennoblecedor**, adj. ennobling. —**ennoblecimiento**, n.m. ennoblement.

enojadizo (e·no·xa'ði·θo; -so) adj. cross; irritable.

enojar (e·no'xar) v.t. to annoy; irritate. —**enojado**, adj. annoyed; peevish.

enojo (e·no·xo) n.m. annoyance; bother; trouble. —**enojoso**, adj. annoying; bothersome; troublesome.

enorgullecer (e·nor·ɣu·ʎe'θer; -je'ser) v.t. [infl.: conocer, 13] to make proud. —**enorgullecerse**, v.r. to be proud. —**enorgullecido**, adj. haughty; arrogant; extremely proud.

enorme (e'nor·me) adj. 1, huge; enormous. 2, horrible; wicked.

enormidad (e·nor·mi'ðað) n.f. 1, enormousness. 2, enormity.

enrabiar (en·ra'βjar) v.t. to enrage; anger.

enramada (en·ra'ma·ða) n.f. bower; arbor.

enramar (en·ra'mar) v.t. to decorate with branches. —v.i. to branch (of trees).

enranciar (en·ran'θjar; -'sjar) v.t. to make rancid; spoil. —**enranciarse**, v.r. to become rancid; spoil.

enrarecer (en·ra·re'θer; -'ser) v.t. [infl.: conocer, 13] to thin; rarefy. —**enrarecerse**, v.r. 1, to become rare or scarce. 2, to become stuffy, as the air in a room. —**enrarecimiento** (-θi'mjen·to; -si-) n.m. 1, thinning; rarefying. 2, rarity; scarcity.

enredadera (en·re·ða'ðe·ra) n.f. 1, climbing plant; vine. 2, bindweed. —adj.fem. climbing (of plants).

enredador (en·re·ða'ðor) adj. 1, mischievous. 2, gossipy. —n.m. 1, mischief-maker. 2, busybody; gossip.

enredar (en·re'ðar) v.t. 1, to entangle; confuse. 2, to intertwine. 3, to embroil. —v.i. 1, to fiddle; trifle. 2, to be frisky; romp.

enredo (en're·ðo) n.m. 1, tangle; entanglement. 2, mischief. 3, fib; mischievous lie. 4, plot (of a play). —**enredos**, n.m.pl. belongings.

enredoso (en·re'ðo·so) adj. tangled; complex; intricate.

enrejado (en·re'xa·ðo) n.m. 1, trellis; lattice. 2, grillwork; grating.

enrejar (en·re'xar) v.t. to provide with grillwork or latticework.

enrevesado (en·re·βe'sa·ðo) adj. = revesado.

enrielar (en·rje'lar) v.t., Amer. = encarrilar.

enriquecer (en·ri·ke'θer; -'ser) v.t. [infl.: conocer, 13] to enrich. —**enriquecerse**, v.r. to become rich. —**enriquecimiento**, n.m. enrichment.

enristrar (en·ris'trar) v.t. to string (onions, garlic, sausage, etc.).

enrocar (en·ro'kar) v.t. & i. [infl.: tocar, 7] chess to castle.

enrojecer (en·ro·xe'θer; -'ser) v.t. [infl.: conocer, 13] 1, to redden; 2, to make red-hot. 3, to cause to blush. —**enrojecerse**, v.r. 1, to blush. 2, to turn red. —**enrojecimiento** (-θi'mjen·to; -si-) n.m. reddening; blushing.

enrojecido (en·ro·xe'θi·ðo; -'si·ðo) adj. 1, reddened. 2, red-hot. 3, blushing.

enrolar (en·ro'lar) v.t. to enlist. —**enrolamiento**, n.m. enlistment.

enrollar (en·ro'ʎar; -'jar) v.t. to wind; coil; roll up.

enronquecer (en·ron·ke'θer; -'ser) v.t. [infl.: conocer, 13] to make hoarse. —**enronquecerse**, v.r.

to become hoarse. —**enronqueci-miento**, *n.m.* hoarseness.

enroscar (en·ros'kar) *v.t.* [*infl.:* **tocar,** 7] **1,** to twist; twine. **2,** to screw in. —**enroscadura**, *n.f.* coil; twist.

ensacar (en·sa'kar) *v.t.* [*infl.:* **tocar,** 7] to bag; put in a bag or sack.

ensalada (en·sa'la·ða) *n.f.* **1,** salad. **2,** *fig.* medley; hodgepodge. —**ensaladera,** *n.f.* salad bowl.

ensalmo (en'sal·mo) *n.m.* spell; incantation. —**ensalmista**, *n.m.* & *f.* quack; fake. —**por ensalmo**, miraculously.

ensalzar (en·sal'θar; -'sar) *v.t.* [*infl.:* **rezar,** 10] to exalt; extol. —**ensalzarse**, *v.r.* to vaunt oneself. —**ensalzamiento**, *n.m.* exaltation.

ensamblar (en·sam'blar) *v.t.* to join; assemble; dovetail; *carp.* to mortise. —**ensamblador**, *n.m.* joiner. —**ensambladura**, *n.f.* mortise; joint; dovetail.

ensanchar (en·san'tʃar) *v.t.* to stretch; extend; expand; enlarge; widen. —**ensanchador**, *n.m.* stretcher; expander. —**ensanchamiento**, *n.m.* extension; enlargement.

ensanche (en'san·tʃe) *n.m.* **1,** extension; enlargement; widening. **2,** *sewing* turn-in of a seam. **3,** undeveloped land on the outskirts of a city.

ensangrentar (en·san·gren'tar) *v.t.* [*infl.:* **pensar,** 27] to bloody; stain with blood.

ensartar (en·sar'tar) *v.t.* **1,** to string (beads). **2,** to thread (a needle). **3,** to link. —*v.i.* to talk rigmarole.

ensayar (en·sa'jar) *v.t.* **1,** to try; essay. **2,** to rehearse; practice. **3,** to test; assay. —**ensayarse**, *v.r.* to practice.

ensayo (en'sa·jo) *n.m.* **1,** test; assay. **2,** experiment; trial. **3,** practice; rehearsal. **4,** essay. —**ensayista**, *n.m.* & *f.* essayist.

enseguida (en·se'ɣi·ða) *adv.* at once; immediately. *Also,* **en seguida.**

ensenada (en·se'na·ða) *n.f.* inlet; cove.

enseña (en'se·ɲa) *n.f.* ensign; colors.

enseñanza (en·se'ɲan·θa; -sa) *n.f.* **1,** doctrine. **2,** teaching; instruction. **3,** education.

enseñar (en·se'ɲar) *v.t.* **1,** to train; teach. **2,** to show; point out.

enseñorarse (en·se·ɲo'rar·se) *v.r.* (*with* **de**) to take possession of; take over.

enseres (en'se·res) *n.m.pl.* furnishings; tools; equipment.

ensilaje (en·si'la·xe) *n.m.* ensilage. —**ensilar**, *v.t.* to ensile.

ensillar (eɲ·si'ʎar; -'jar) *v.t.* to saddle.

ensimismarse (en·si·mis'mar·se) *v.r.* to be engrossed; be abstracted. —**ensimismado**, *adj.* absorbed in thought; *Amer.* conceited. —**ensimismamiento**, *n.m.* absorption; engrossment.

ensoberbecer (en·so·βer·βe'θer; -'ser) *v.t.* [*infl.:* **conocer,** 13] to excite pride in; make proud or haughty. —**ensoberbecerse**, *v.r.* **1,** to become proud or haughty. **2,** to become rough or choppy, as the sea. —**ensoberbecimiento**, *n.m.* pride; haughtiness.

ensombrecer (en·som·bre'θer; -'ser) *v.t.* [*infl.:* **conocer,** 13] **1,** to darken; cloud. **2,** *fig.* to overshadow.

ensopar (en·so'par) *v.t.* to soak; steep.

ensordecer (en·sor·ðe'θer; -'ser) *v.t.* [*infl.:* **conocer,** 13] to deafen. —*v.i.* to become deaf. —**ensordecedor**, *adj.* deafening. —**ensordecimiento**, *n.m.* deafness.

ensortijar (en·sor·ti'xar) *v.t.* to curl; kink. —**ensortijado**, *adj.*, *colloq.* bejeweled.

ensuciar (en·su'θjar; -'sjar) *v.t.* to soil; dirty. —**ensuciarse**, *v.r.* **1,** to soil oneself. **2,** *colloq.* to be dishonest or corrupt.

ensueño (en'swe·ɲo) *n.m.* **1,** illusion; fantasy. **2,** dream.

entablar (en·ta'βlar) *v.t.* **1,** to cover with boards; board up. **2,** to start (a negotiation). **3,** *law* to bring (an action). —**entablarse**, *v.r.* to settle, as the wind.

entablillar (en·ta·βli'ʎar; -'jar) *v.t., surg.* to splint.

entallar (en·ta'ʎar; -'jar) *v.t.* **1,** to notch. **2,** to carve; engrave. **3,** to tailor; cut close to the figure. —*v.t. & i.* to fit, as a garment.

entapizar (en·ta·pi'θar; -'sar) *v.t.* [*infl.:* **rezar,** 10] to hang or adorn with tapestry.

entarimar (en·ta·ri'mar) *v.t.* to floor; provide with flooring.

—**entarimado,** *n.m.* hardwood floor.

ente ('en·te) *n.m.* **1,** being; entity. **2,** *comm.* firm; company.

enteco (en'te·ko) *adj.* sickly; emaciated. *Also,* **entecado** (-'ka·ðo).

entendedor (en·ten·de'ðor) *n.m.* perceptive or understanding person; expert.

entender (en·ten'der) *v.t. & i.* [*infl.:* **perder,** 29] **1,** to understand; comprehend. **2,** to suppose; guess. **3,** to conclude; infer. **4,** *fol. by* **de** *or* **en,** to be familiar with; be good at. **5,** *fol. by* **en** *or* **de,** to be in charge of; have authority or responsibility in. —**entenderse,** *v.r.* **1,** to be understood. **2,** to be meant. **3,** to know what one is about. **4,** to agree. **5,** to understand each other. **6,** to have an understanding. **7,** *fol. by* **con,** to deal with; have dealings with. —*n.m.* understanding; opinion.

entendido (en·ten'di·ðo) *adj.* **1,** experienced; able. **2,** well-informed. —**darse por entendido,** to take a hint; take notice.

entendimiento (en·ten·di'mjen·to) *n.m.* **1,** understanding. **2,** mind; intellect.

enterado (en·te'ra·ðo) *adj.* **1,** informed; aware. **2,** *Amer.* conceited; arrogant. —*n.m.* acknowledgment (by signing) that one has read and understood a document.

enteramente (en·te·ra'men·te) *adv.* completely; fully.

enterar (en·te'rar) *v.t.* to inform. —**enterarse de,** to find out; become aware of.

entereza (en·te're·θa; -sa) *n.f.* **1,** integrity. **2,** entirety. **3,** firmness; fortitude.

entérico (en·te'ri·ko) *adj.* enteric. —**enteritis** (en·te'ri·tis) *n.f.* enteritis.

enterizo (en·te'ri·θo; -so) *adj.* of one piece.

enternecer (en·ter·ne'θer; -'ser) *v.t.* [*infl.:* **conocer,** 13] **1,** to soften; make tender. **2,** to move to compassion. —**enternecedor,** *adj.* touching.

entero (en'te·ro) *adj.* **1,** entire; whole. **2,** sound; perfect. **3,** upright; honest. **4,** constant; firm. —*n.m.* **1,** *math.* integer. **2,** *Amer.* payment.

enterrador (en·te·rra'ðor) *n.m.* gravedigger.

enterramiento (en·te·rra'mjen-

to) *n.m.* **1,** burial; interment. **2,** grave; tomb.

enterrar (en·te'rrar) *v.t.* [*infl.:* **pensar,** 27] to bury; inter.

entibar (en·ti'βar) *v.i.* = **estribar.** —*v.t.* to prop; shore up. —**entibo** (-'ti·βo) *n.m.* prop; shoring.

entibiar (en·ti'βjar) *v.t.* **1,** to make lukewarm. **2,** to cool down (temper, passions, etc.).

entidad (en·ti'ðað) *n.f.* **1,** entity. **2,** value; importance. **3,** business establishment. **4,** group; body.

entierro (en'tje·rro) *n.m.* **1,** burial; interment. **2,** funeral. **3,** grave; tomb. **4,** buried treasure.

entintar (en·tin'tar) *v.t.* to ink; spread ink on; stain with ink.

entoldar (en·tol'dar) *v.t.* **1,** to cover with a hood or awning. **2,** to cover (walls) with tapestries, cloth, etc. —**entoldarse,** *v.r.* to become overcast.

entomología (en·to·mo·lo'xi·a) *n.f.* entomology. —**entomológico** (-'lo·xi·ko) *adj.* entomological. —**entomólogo** (-'mo·lo·ɣo) *n.m.* entomologist.

entonación (en·to·na'θjon; -'sjon) *n.f.* **1,** intonation. **2,** modulation *(of the voice).* **3,** *fig.* pride; presumption.

entonado (en·to·na·ðo) *adj.* arrogant; haughty.

entonar (en·to'nar) *v.t.* **1,** to modulate (the voice). **2,** to intone. **3,** *paint.* to harmonize (colors). **4,** *med.* to tone up. **5,** to make flexible; limber. —**entonarse,** *v.r.* to be conceited; put on airs.

entonces (en'ton·θes; -ses) *adv.* **1,** then; at that time. **2,** well then; now then; so then. —**en aquel entonces,** at that time.

entono (en'to·no) *n.m.* **1,** intonation. **2,** arrogance; haughtiness.

entontecer (en·ton·te'θer; -'ser) *v.t.* [*infl.:* **conocer,** 13] to stupefy; make foolish.

entornar (en·tor'nar) *v.t.* **1,** to half-open; set ajar. **2,** to half-close (the eyes).

entorpecer (en·tor·pe'θer; -'ser) *v.t.* [*infl.:* **conocer,** 13] to obstruct; hamper.

entorpecimiento (en·tor·pe·θi-'mjen·to; -si'mjen·to) *n.m.* **1,** delay; obstruction. **2,** stupidity.

entrada (en'tra·ða) *n.f.* **1,** entrance; door; gate. **2,** entry; admission; admittance. **3,** ticket of admission. **4,** total of admissions or receipts; gate. **5,** beginning. **6,** *cards* trump hand. **7,** main dish; entrée. **8,** earnings; income. **9,** *comm.* receipts; gross. **10,** ledger entry.

entrambos (en'tram·bos) *adj.* & *pron.masc.pl.* [*fem.* **entrambas**] both.

entrampar (en·tram'par) *v.t.* **1,** to trap; entrap. **2,** to trick. **3,** *colloq.* to entangle. **4,** *colloq.* to burden with debt. —**entrampamiento,** *n.m.* entrapment; ensnarement.

entramparse (en·tram'par·se) *v.r., colloq.* to fall into debt; become encumbered with debts.

entrante (en'tran·te) *adj.* **1,** entering. **2,** coming; next. —*n.m.* recessed part.

entraña (en'tra·ɲa) *n.f., usu.pl.* **1,** *anat.* entrail. **2,** core; center. **3,** *fig.* heart; soul.

entrañable (en·tra'ɲa·βle) *adj.* **1,** most affectionate. **2,** deep; profound.

entrañar (en·tra'ɲar) *v.t.* to contain; carry within; involve. —**entrañarse,** *v.r.* to become closely attached.

entrar (en'trar) *v.i.* **1,** to enter; go in; come in. **2,** to flow in. **3,** to join; become a member or part. **4,** to begin; enter (upon). —*v.t.* **1,** to introduce; put in. **2,** to invade; enter in force. **3,** to exercise influence in or on. **4,** *comm.* to enter *(in a ledger).* —**entrarse,** *v.r.* to enter; gain entry.

entre ('en·tre) *prep.* among; between. —**entre manos,** in hand. —**entre tanto,** in the meantime.

entreabrir (en·tre·a'βrir) *v.t.* [*p.p.* **entreabierto** (-'βjer·to)] to halfopen; set ajar. —**entreabierto,** *adj.* ajar.

entreacto (en·tre'ak·to) *n.m.* intermission; entr'acte.

entrecano (en·tre'ka·no) *adj.* grayish; graying *(of the hair).*

entrecara (en·tre'ka·ra) *n.f., physics; chem.* interface.

entrecasa (en·tre'ka·sa) *n.f., in de* or **para entrecasa,** to be worn in the house.

entrecejo (en·tre'θe·xo; -'se·xo) *n.m.* **1,** space between the eyebrows. **2,** *fig.* frown.

entrecerrar (en·tre·θe'rrar; -se'rrar) *v.t.* [*infl.:* **pensar, 27**] to half-close; leave ajar.

entrecoro (en·tre'ko·ro) *n.m.* chancel.

entrecortado (en·tre·kor'ta·ðo) *adj.* broken; interrupted; halting.

entrecruzar (en·tre·kru'θar; -'sar) *v.t.* [*infl.:* **rezar, 10**] to intercross; crisscross; interweave. —**entrecruzarse,** *v.r.* to cross each other; crisscross.

entredicho (en·tre'ði·tʃo) *n.m.* **1,** injunction; prohibition. **2,** interdict.

entrega (en'tre·ɣa) *n.f.* **1,** delivery; conveyance. **2,** surrender; submission. **3,** installment, as of a novel.

entregar (en·tre'ɣar) *v.t.* [*infl.:* **pagar, 8**] to give up; deliver. —**entregarse,** *v.r.* to surrender; submit.

entrelazar (en·tre·la'θar; -'sar) *v.t.* [*infl.:* **rezar, 10**] to interlace; interweave.

entremedias (en·tre'me·ðjas) *adv.* **1,** in the meantime. **2,** in between; amidst.

entremés (en·tre'mes) *n.m., theat.* interlude; farce. —**entremeses,** *n.m. pl.* hors d'oeuvres; appetizers.

entremeter (en·tre·me'ter) *v.t.* to insert; place between. —**entremeterse,** *v.r.* to intrude; meddle.

entremetido (en·tre·me'ti·ðo) *adj.* meddlesome; intrusive; officious. —*n.m.* **1,** meddler; intruder. **2,** go-between. **3,** busybody.

entremetimiento (en·tre·me·ti'mjen·to) *n.m.* intrusion; meddling.

entremezclar (en·tre·meθ'klar; -mes'klar) *v.t.* to intermingle.

entrenar (en·tre'nar) *v.t.* to train. —**entrenador,** *adj.* training. —*n.m.* trainer; coach. —**entrenamiento,** *n.m.* training.

entrepierna (en·tre'pjer·na) *n.f., usu.pl.* **1,** inner surface of the thigh. **2,** crotch *(of trousers).*

entreponer (en·tre·po'ner) *v.t.* [*infl.:* **poner, 54**] to interpose.

entresacar (en·tre·sa'kar) *v.t.* [*infl.:* **tocar, 7**] **1,** to pick out; cull. **2,** to thin out; trim.

entresuelo (en·tre'swe·lo) *n.m.* mezzanine.

entretanto (en·tre'tan·to) *adv.* & *n.m.* meanwhile; meantime.

entretejer (en·tre·te'xer) *v.t.* to interweave; intertwine.

entretela (en·tre'te·la) *n.f.* **1,** interlining. **2,** buckram. —**entretelas,** *n.f.pl., colloq.* innermost being; bowels.

entretener (en·tre·te'ner) *v.t.* [*infl.:* **tener, 65**] **1,** to amuse; entertain. **2,** to trifle with. **3,** to delay;

postpone. **4,** to detain. **—entrete-nido,** *adj.* entertaining; pleasant.

entretenimiento (en·tre·ten·i·'mjen·to) *n.m.* **1,** sport; amusement; entertainment. **2,** delay.

entretiempo (en·tre'tjem·po) *n.m.* middle season; spring or fall.

entrever (en·tre'βer) *v.t.* [*infl.:* ver, 70] **1,** to glimpse. **2,** to guess; divine.

entreverar (en·tre·βe'rar) *v.t.* to intermix; intermingle. **—entrevero,** *n.m.* intermingling; jumble.

entrevista (en·tre'βis·ta) *n.f.* interview. **—entrevistar** (-'tar) *v.t.* to interview. **—entrevistarse,** *v.r.* to be interviewed.

entristecer (en·tris·te'θer; -'ser) *v.t.* [*infl.:* conocer, 13] to grieve; sadden. **—entristecerse,** *v.r.* to grieve; grow sad. **—entristecimiento,** *n.m.* sadness.

entrometer (en·tro·me'ter) *v.t.* = **entremeter.** **—entrometido,** *adj.* & *n.m.* = entremetido. **—entrometimiento,** *n.m.* = entremetimiento.

entronar (en·tro'nar) *v.t.* = entronizar.

entronizar (en·tro·ni'θar; -'sar) *v.t.* [*infl.:* rezar, 10] to enthrone. **—entronización,** *n.f.* enthronement.

entropia (en'tro·pja) *n.f.* entropy.

entruchar (en·tru'tʃar) *v.t.* to lure; decoy. **—entruchón** (-'tʃon) *n.m.* decoy.

entuerto (en'twer·to) *n.m.* injustice; wrong. **—entuertos,** *n.m.pl.* afterpains.

entumecer (en·tu·me'θer; -'ser.) *v.t.* [*infl.:* conocer, 13] to benumb. **—entumecerse,** *v.r.* **1,** to become numb. **2,** to swell. **—entumecimiento,** *n.m.* **1,** numbness. **2,** swelling.

enturbiar (en·tur'βjar) *v.t.* **1,** to muddy. **2,** *fig.* to confuse; obscure. **3,** to upset; disarrange.

entusiasmar (en·tu·sjas'mar) *v.t.* to enrapture; transport. **—entusiasmarse,** *v.r.* to become enthusiastic; be enraptured. **—entusiasmado,** *adj.* enthusiastic.

entusiasmo (en·tu'sjas·mo) *n.m.* enthusiasm.

entusiasta (en·tu'sjas·ta) *n.m.* & *f.* enthusiast; fan. **—***adj.* enthusiastic.

entusiástico (en·tu'sjas·ti·ko) *adj.* enthusiastic.

enumerar (e·nu·me'rar) *v.t.* to

enumerate. **—enumeración,** *n.f.* enumeration.

enunciar (e·nun'θjar; -'sjar) *v.t.* to enunciate. **—enunciación,** *n.f.* [*also,* **enunciado,** *n.m.*] enunciation.

envainar (en·βai'nar) *v.t.* to sheathe (a sword).

envalentonar (en·βa·len·to'nar) *v.t.* to encourage; make bold. **—envalentonarse,** *v.r.* **1,** to become bold or courageous. **2,** to brag.

envanecer (en·βa·ne'θer; -'ser) *v.t.* [*infl.:* conocer, 13] to make vain. **—envanecerse,** *v.r.* to become vain. **—envanecimiento,** *n.m.* conceit.

envasar (en·βa'sar) *v.t.* **1,** to bottle; put into a barrel, cask, sack, or other container. **2,** *fig.* to drink to excess. **3,** *fig.* to thrust into the body, as a sword.

envase (en'βa·se) *n.m.* **1,** bottling. **2,** cask, barrel, or other container for liquids. **3,** packing.

envejecer (en·βe·xe'θer; -'ser) *v.t.* [*infl.:* conocer, 13] **1,** to make old. **2,** to make look old. **—v.i.** **1,** to grow old. **2,** to become inveterate. **—envejecerse,** *v.r.* **1,** to become old. **2,** to go out of use. **—envejecimiento,** *n.m.* aging; age.

envejecido (en·βe·xe'θi·ðo; -'si·ðo) *adj.* **1,** grown old. **2,** old-looking. **3,** inveterate. **4,** old-fashioned.

envenenar (en·βe·ne'nar) *v.t.* to poison; envenom. **—envenenador,** *adj.* poisonous. **—n.m.** poisoner.

envergadura (en·βer·ɣa'ðu·ra) *n.f.* **1,** wing span. **2,** *naut.* breadth (*of sails*). **3,** *fig.* compass; scope.

enviar (en·βi'ar) *v.t.* [*infl.:* 22] **1,** to send. **2,** to transmit; forward; convey. **—enviado,** *n.m.* envoy.

enviciar (en·βi'θjar; -'sjar) *v.t.* to corrupt; vitiate. **—enviciarse,** *v.r.* to acquire bad habits.

envidia (en'βi·ðja) *n.f.* envy; jealousy.

envidiable (en·βi'ðja·βle) *adj.* enviable; desirable.

envidiar (en·βi'ðjar) *v.t.* to envy; be jealous of.

envidioso (en·βi'ðjo·so) *adj.* **1,** envious; jealous. **2,** invidious.

envilecer (en·βi·le'θer; -'ser) *v.t.* [*infl.:* conocer, 13] to vilify; debase; degrade. **—envilecimiento,** *n.m.* vilification; debasement; degradation.

envío (en'βi·o) *n.m.* **1,** remittance. **2,** consignment; shipment.

envite (en'βi·te) *n.m., cards* bet; stake.

enviudar (en·βju'ðar) *v.i.* to become a widower or widow.

envoltorio (en·βol'to·rjo) *n.m.* **1,** bundle; package. **2,** covering; wrapping.

envoltura (en·βol'tu·ra) *n.f.* **1,** swaddling clothes. **2,** covering; wrapper; envelope.

envolvedor (en·βol·βe'ðor) *n.m.* **1,** cover; wrapping. **2,** wrapping clerk.

envolver (en·βol'βer) *v.t.* [*infl.:* **mover, 30;** *p.p.* envuelto] **1,** to wrap up. **2,** to diaper (a baby). **3,** to encircle; surround. **4,** to imply; involve. —**envolverse,** *v.r.* **1,** to be involved or implicated. **2,** to be mixed with a crowd. **3,** to bundle up.

envolvimiento (en·βol·βi'mjen·to) *n.m.* **1,** envelopment. **2,** involvement. **3,** encirclement.

envuelto (en'βwel·to) *v., p.p.* of **envolver.**

enyesar (en·je'sar) *v.t.* **1,** to plaster. **2,** to chalk. **3,** to whitewash. —**enyesado,** *n.m., also,* **enyesadura,** *n.f.* plaster; plastering; plasterwork.

enyugar (en·ju'ɣar) *v.t.* [*infl.:* **pagar, 8**] to yoke.

enzima (en'θi·ma; -'si·ma) *n.f.* enzyme.

enzunchar (en·θun'tʃar; en·sun-) *v.t.* to hoop; bind with hoops or bands.

eolítico (e·o'li·ti·ko) *adj.* eolithic.

¡epa! ('e·pa) *interj., Amer.* = **¡ea!**

eperlano (e·per'la·no) *n.m., ichthy.* smelt.

épica ('e·pi·ka) *n.f.* epic poetry. —**épico,** *adj.* epic.

epicentro (e·pi'θen·tro; -'sen·tro) *n.m.* epicenter.

epicúreo (e·pi'ku·re·o) *n.m.* epicure. —*adj.* epicurean.

epidemia (e·pi'ðe·mja) *n.f.* epidemic. —**epidémico** (-'ðe·mi·ko) *adj.* epidemic.

epidermis (e·pi'ðer·mis) *n.f.* epidermis.

Epifanía (e·pi·fa'ni·a) *n.f.* Epiphany.

epiglotis (e·pi'ɣlo·tis) *n.f.* epiglotis.

epigrama (e·pi'ɣra·ma) *n.m.* **1,** epigram. **2,** inscription. —**epigramático** (-'ma·ti·ko) *adj.* epigram-matic. —**epigramista** (-'mis·ta) *also,* **epigramatista** (-ma'tis·ta) *n.m. & f.* epigrammatist.

epigramatario (e·pi·ɣra·ma'ta·rjo) *adj.* epigrammatic. —*n.m.* **1,** collection of epigrams. **2,** = **epigramista.**

epígrafe (e'pi·ɣra·fe) *n.m.* epigraph. —**epigrafía** (-ɣra'fi·a) *n.f.* epigraphy.

epilepsia (e·pi'lep·sja) *n.f.* epilepsy. —**epiléptico** (-'lep·ti·ko) *adj. & n.m.* epileptic.

epilogar (e·pi·lo'ɣar) *v.t.* [*infl.:* **pagar, 8**] to sum up; recapitulate.

epílogo (e'pi·lo·ɣo) *n.m.* **1,** epilogue. **2,** recapitulation.

episcopado (e·pis·ko'pa·ðo) *n.m.* **1,** episcopacy; bishopric. **2,** episcopate.

episcopal (e·pis·ko'pal) *adj.* episcopal; *cap.* Episcopal. —**episcopalista,** *also,* **episcopaliano** (-pa'lja·no) *adj.* Episcopal. —*n.m.* Episcopalian.

episodio (e·pi'so·ðjo) *n.m.* episode. —**episódico** (-'so·ði·ko) *adj.* episodic.

epistemología (e·pis·te·mo·lo'xi·a) *n.f.* epistemology.

epístola (e'pis·to·la) *n.f.* epistle.

epistolar (e·pis·to'lar) *adj.* epistolary.

epistolario (e·pis·to'la·rjo) *n.m.* **1,** book or collection of letters. **2,** *eccles.* epistolary.

epitafio (e·pi'ta·fjo) *n.m.* epitaph.

epitelio (e·pi'te·ljo) *n.m.* epithelium.

epíteto (e'pi·te·to) *n.m.* epithet.

epítome (e'pi·to·me) *n.m.* epitome. —**epitomar** (-'mar) *v.t.* to epitomize.

época ('e·po·ka) *n.f.* **1,** epoch; age; era. **2,** time.

epopeya (e·po'pe·ja) *n.f.* epic.

equidad (e·ki'ðað) *n.f.* equity; fairness; justice.

equidistante (e·ki·ðis'tan·te) *adj.* equidistant.

equilátero (e·ki'la·te·ro) *adj.* equilateral.

equilibrar (e·ki·li'βrar) *v.t.* **1,** to equilibrate; balance. **2,** to counterbalance. —**equilibrado,** *adj.* **1,** balanced. **2,** sensible; prudent.

equilibrio (e·ki'li·βrjo) *n.m.* equilibrium; counterbalance. —**equilibrista** *n.m. & f.* (-'βris·ta) equilibrist; aerialist.

equino (e'ki·no) *adj.* equine.

equinoccio (e·ki'nok·θjo; -sjo) *n.m.* equinox. —**equinoccial** (-'θjal; -'sjal) *adj.* equinoctial.

equipaje (e·ki'pa·xe) *n.m.* **1,** luggage; baggage. **2,** equipment. **3,** crew.

equipar (e·ki'par) *v.t.* to equip; furnish.

equipo (e'ki·po) *n.m.* **1,** equipping; fitting out. **2,** equipment. **3,** team; crew.

equitación (e·ki·ta'θjon; -'sjon) *n.f.* horsemanship; equitation.

equitativo (e·ki·ta'ti·βo) *adj.* equitable; fair; just.

equivalente (e·ki·βa'len·te) *adj.* equal; tantamount; equivalent. —*n.m.* equivalent. —**equivalencia,** *n.f.* equivalence.

equivaler (e·ki·βa'ler) *v.i.* [*infl.:* **valer, 68**] to be equal; be equivalent.

equivocar (e·ki·βo'kar) *v.t.* [*infl.:* **tocar, 7**] to mistake; confuse. —**equivocarse,** *v.r.* **1,** to be mistaken. **2,** to make a mistake. —**equivocación,** *n.f.* error; mistake; blunder. —**equivocado,** *adj.* mistaken; wrong.

equívoco (e'ki·βo·ko) *adj.* equivocal. —*n.m.* **1,** equivocation. **2,** misinterpretation.

era ('e·ra) *n.f.* **1,** age; era; time. **2,** threshing floor.

era ('e·ra) *v., impf. of* **ser.**

erario (e'ra·rjo) *n.m.* public treasury.

erbio ('er·βjo) *n.m.* erbium.

erección (e·rek'θjon; -'sjon) *n.f.* erection. —**erectil,** *adj.* erectile.

eremita (e·re'mi·ta) *n.m.* hermit.

eres ('e·res) *v., 2nd pers.sing. pres. ind. of* **ser.**

erg ('erɣ) *n.m.* erg; unit of energy. *Also,* **ergio** ('er·xjo).

ergotina (er·ɣo'ti·na) *n.f.* ergotin.

ergotismo (er·ɣo'tis·mo) *n.m.* **1,** *plant pathol.* ergot. **2,** *pathol.* ergotism.

erguir (er'ɣir) *v.t.* [*infl.:* **46**] to put up straight; erect. —**erguirse,** *v.r.* **1,** to straighten; take an erect pose. **2,** to stiffen; take a proud stand.

erial (e'rjal) *n.m.* wasteland.

eriazo (e'rja·θo; -so) *adj.* uncultivated; untilled.

erigir (e·ri'xir) *v.t.* [*infl.:* **coger, 15**] **1,** to establish; found; erect. **2,** to raise; elevate (*to a position or situation*).

erisipela (e·ri·si'pe·la) *n.f.* erysipelas.

erizado (e·ri'θa·ðo; -'sa·ðo) *adj.* **1,** covered with bristles; bristly. **2,** bristling.

erizar (e·ri'θar; -'sar) *v.t.* [*infl.:* **rezar, 10**] **1,** to set on end, as the hair. **2,** to surround with difficulties; make bristle with difficulties. —**erizarse,** *v.r.* **1,** to bristle; stand on end. **2,** to become upset; become rattled.

erizo (e'ri·θo; -so) *n.m.* **1,** hedgehog; porcupine. **2,** *fig.* irascible person. **3,** *bot.* bur. —**erizo de mar,** sea urchin.

ermita (er'mi·ta) *n.f.* hermitage. —**ermitaño,** *n.m.* hermit.

erogar (e·ro'ɣar) *v.t.* [*infl.:* **pagar, 8**] **1,** to divide; apportion (an estate, money, etc.). **2,** *Amer.* to bring about; cause. —**erogación,** *n.f.* division; apportionment.

erógeno (e'ro·xe·no) *adj.* erogenous.

erosión (e·ro'sjon) *n.f.* erosion. —**erosivo** (-'si·βo) *adj.* erosive.

erótico (e'ro·ti·ko) *adj.* erotic. —**erótica,** *n.f.* erotica. —**erotismo** (-'θis·mo; -'sis·mo) *n.m.* eroticism. —**erotismo** (-'tis·mo) *n.m.* erotism.

errabundo (e·rra'βun·do) *adj.* wandering.

erradicar (e·rra·ði'kar) *v.t.* [*infl.:* **tocar, 7**] to eradicate. —**erradicación,** *n.f.* eradication. —**erradicador,** *n.m.* eradicator.

errado (e'rra·ðo) *adj.* mistaken; erroneous.

errante (e'rran·te) *adj.* errant; wandering; roving.

errar (e'rrar) *v.* [*infl.:* **47**] —*v.t.* **1,** to miss (a target). **2,** to mistake; choose erroneously. —*v.i.* **1,** to err. **2,** to roam; wander. —**errarse,** *v.r.* to be mistaken.

errata (e'rra·ta) *n.f.* erratum; misprint. —**fe de erratas,** list of errata.

errático (e'rra·ti·ko) *adj.* wandering; vagrant.

erróneo (e'rro·ne·o) *adj.* erroneous.

error (e'rror) *n.m.* error; mistake.

erso ('er·so) *adj. & n.m.* Erse.

eructación (e·ruk·ta'θjon; -'sjon) *n.f.* = **eructo.**

eructar (e·ruk'tar) *also,* **erutar** (e·ru'tar) *v.i.* to belch; eruct. —**eructo** (e'ruk·to) *also,* **eruto**

(e'ru·to) *n.m.* belch; belching; eructation.

erudito (e·ru'ði·to) *adj.* erudite. —*n.m.* scholar; pundit. —**erudición**, *n.f.* erudition.

erumpir (e·rum'pir) *v.i.* to erupt.

erupción (e·rup'θjon; -'sjon) *n.f.* eruption. —**eruptivo**, *adj.* eruptive.

es (es) *v., 3rd pers.sing. pres.ind. of* ser.

esa ('e·sa) *dem.adj.* [*pl.* **esas**] *fem. of* ese.

ésa ('e·sa) *dem.pron.* [*pl.* **ésas**] *fem. of* ése.

esbelto (es'βel·to) *adj.* svelte; lithe. —**esbeltez**, *n.f.* elegance of figure; litheness.

esbirro (es'βi·rro) *n.m.* **1,** bailiff. **2,** *colloq.* hired ruffian.

esbozar (es·βo'θar; -'sar) *v.t.* [*infl.:* **rezar, 10**] to sketch. —**esbozo** (-'βo·θo; -so) *n.m.* sketch; rough draft.

escabechar (es·ka·βe'tʃar) *v.t.* **1,** to pickle. **2,** *fig.* to dye (gray hair). **3,** *colloq.* to stab to death; cut to ribbons. **4,** *colloq.* to flunk.

escabeche (es·ka'βe·tʃe) *n.m.* **1,** pickled fish; pickled food of any kind. **2,** pickling solution.

escabel (es·ka'βel) *n.m.* stool; footstool.

escabiosis (es·ka'βjo·sis) *n.f.* scabies.

escabrosidad (es·ka·βro·si'ðað) *n.f.* **1,** cragginess; ruggedness. **2,** asperity; severity.

escabroso (es·ka'βro·so) *adj.* **1,** craggy; rugged (*of terrain*). **2,** difficult; touchy. **3,** risqué.

escabullirse (es·ka·βu'ʎir·se; -'jir·se) *v.r.* [*infl.:* bullir, 19] to slip away; escape. —**escabullimiento**, *n.m.* evasion.

escafandra (es·ka'fan·dra) *n.m.* diving suit.

escala (es'ka·la) *n.f.* **1,** ladder. **2,** *mus.* scale. **3,** proportion; scale. **4,** measuring scale. **5,** scale (*of values*). **6,** port of call. **7,** stop (*in an itinerary*).

escalador (es·ka·la'ðor) *n.m.* **1,** climber. **2,** burglar; housebreaker.

escalafón (es·ka·la'fon) *n.m.* **1,** roll; roster. **2,** rank; echelon.

escalar (es·ka'lar) *v.t.* **1,** to climb; scale. **2,** to enter surreptitiously. **3,** to measure according to a scale. —*v.i.* **1,** to climb up. **2,** to make one's way up. **3,** *naut.* to call (at a port).

escaldar (es·kal'dar) *v.t.* **1,** to scald; burn. **2,** to make red-hot. —**escaldarse**, *v.r.* to be vexed; become annoyed. —**escaldadura**, *n.f.* scald; scalding.

escaleno (es·ka'le·no) *adj.* scalene.

escalera (es·ka'le·ra) *n.f.* **1,** staircase; stairs. **2,** ladder. **3,** *poker* straight. —**escalera automática**, escalator. —**en escalera**, in sequence.

escalfar (es·kal'far) *v.t.* to poach (eggs). —**escalfador**, *n.m.* chafing dish.

escalinata (es·ka·li'na·ta) *n.f.* front step; front stoop.

escalo (es'ka·lo) *n.m.* **1,** housebreaking. **2,** climbing; scaling.

escalofrío (es·ka·lo'fri·o) *n.m.* chill; shiver. —**escalofriado** (-'frja·ðo) *adj.* chilled.

escalón (es·ka'lon) *n.m.* **1,** step (*of a stair*). **2,** stepping stone. **3,** echelon.

escalonar (es·ka·lo'nar) *v.t.* **1,** to arrange in steps or echelons. **2,** to terrace.

escaloña (es·ka·lo·ɲa) *n.f.* = ascalonia.

escalpar (es·kal'par) *v.t.* to scalp.

escalpelo (es·kal'pe·lo) *n.m.* scalpel.

escama (es'ka·ma) *n.f.* **1,** scale (*of fish, reptiles, etc.*); flake. **2,** *fig.* distrust; suspicion.

escamar (es·ka'mar) *v.t.* **1,** to scale (a fish). **2,** to ornament with a scaly design. **3,** *colloq.* to arouse suspicion in. —**escamarse**, *v.r.* to become cagy. —**escamoso**, *adj.* scaly; flaky.

escamotear (es·ka·mo·te'ar) *also*, **escamotar** (-'tar) *v.t.* **1,** to palm. **2,** to filch. **3,** to make disappear.

escamoteo (es·ka·mo'te·o) *n.m.* **1,** sleight-of-hand. **2,** filching; theft.

escampar (es·kam'par) *v.t.* to clear; unclutter. —*v.i.* **1,** to stop raining; clear up. **2,** *Amer.* to seek shelter from the rain.

escandalizar (es·kan·da·li'θar; -'sar) *v.t.* [*infl.:* **rezar, 10**] to scandalize.

escándalo (es'kan·da·lo) *n.m.* **1,** scandal. **2,** licentiousness. **3,** commotion.

escandaloso (es·kan·da'lo·so) *adj.* **1,** scandalous; scandalizing. **2,** noisy; boisterous.

escandinavo (es·kan·di'na·βo) *adj.* & *n.m.* Scandinavian.

escandio (es'kan·djo) *n.m.* scandium.

escandir (es·kan'dir) *v.t.* to scan (verse). —**escansión** (-'sjon) *n.f.* scansion.

escantillón (es·kan·ti'ʎon; -'jon) *n.m.* templet; pattern. —**escantillar** (-'ʎar; -'jar) *v.t.* to gauge; measure off.

escapada (es·ka·pa·ða) *n.f.* **1,** escape; fleeing. **2,** escapade.

escapar (es·ka'par) *v.i.* [*also, v.r.,* **escaparse**] to escape; flee.

escaparate (es·ka·pa'ra·te) *n.m.* **1,** glass cabinet. **2,** show window.

escapatoria (es·ka·pa'to·rja) *n.f.* **1,** escape; flight. **2,** way out (*of trouble, difficulties, etc.*); loophole. **3,** *colloq.* evasion; subterfuge.

escape (es'ka·pe) *n.m.* **1,** escape; flight. **2,** escapement. **3,** *mech.* exhaust. —**a escape,** at full speed.

escapismo (es·ka'pis·mo) *n m* escapism. —**escapista,** *adj.* & *n.m.* & *f.* escapist.

escápula (es'ka·pu·la) *n.f.* scapula. —**escapular,** *adj.* scapular. —**escapulario,** *n.m.* scapular.

escaque (es'ka·ke) *n.m.* check; square.

escara (es'ka·ra) *n.f., med.* slough.

escarabajo (es·ka·ra'βa·xo) *n.m.* **1,** scarab. **2,** stumpy person. —**escarabajos,** *n.m.pl.* scribble.

escaramuza (es·ka·ra'mu·θa; -sa) *n.f.* skirmish.

escaramuzar (es·ka·ra·mu'θar; -'sar) *v.i.* [*infl.:* **rezar,** 10] to skirmish. *Also,* **escaramucear** (-θe'ar; -se'ar).

escarbadientes (es·kar·βa'ðjentes) *n.m.* = **mondadientes.**

escarbar (es·kar'βar) *v.t.* **1,** to scrape; scratch (*as fowls*). **2,** to stir; poke. **3,** to dig into; delve into. **4,** to pick (the teeth).

escarcha (es'kar·tʃa) *n.f.* frost; hoarfrost.

escarchado (es·kar'tʃa·ðo) *adj.* frosted. —*n.m.* **1,** gold or silver embroidery. **2,** cake icing; frosting.

escarchar (es·kar'tʃar) *v.t.* & *i.* to freeze; frost. —*v.t.* to frost (a cake).

escarcho (es·kar'tʃo) *n.m., ichthy.* roach.

escarda (es'kar·ða) *n.* **1,** weeding; weeding time. **2,** weeding hoe; spud.

escardar (es·kar'ðar) *v.t.* & *i.* **1,** to weed. **2,** to cull; weed out.

escariar (es·ka'rjar) *v.t.* to ream. —**escariador,** *n.m.* reamer.

escarlata (es·kar'la·ta) *adj.* & *n.f.* scarlet. —*n.f.* = **escarlatina.**

escarlatina (es·kar·la'ti·na) *n.f.* scarlet fever.

escarmentar (es·kar·men'tar) *v.t.* [*infl.:* **pensar,** 27] to punish severely; teach a lesson. —*v.i.* to profit from experience; learn one's lesson.

escarmiento (es·kar'mjen·to) *n.m.* **1,** warning; lesson. **2,** chastisement.

escarnecer (es·kar·ne'θer; -'ser) *v.t.* [*infl.:* **conocer,** 13] **1,** to mock; jeer at. **2,** to besmirch. —**escarnio** (es'kar·njo) *n.f.* contempt; scoff.

escarola (es·ka'ro·la) *n.f.* escarole.

escarpa (es'kar·pa) *n.f.* scarp; escarpment. *Also,* **escarpadura; escarpe.**

escarpado (es·kar'pa·ðo) *adj.* steep; craggy.

escarpar (es·kar'par) *v.t.* to rasp; scrape.

escarpelo (es·kar'pe·lo) *n.m.* **1,** rasp. **2,** = **escalpelo.**

escarpia (es'kar·pja) *n.f.* **1,** hook; meat hook. **2,** spike.

escasamente (es·ka·sa'men·te) *adv.* **1,** sparingly; scantily. **2,** scarcely; barely; just.

escasear (es·ka·se'ar) *v.t.* to skimp; be sparing with. —*v.i.* to be scarce; be in short supply.

escasez (es·ka'seθ; -'ses) *n.f.* **1,** scarcity; lack; want. **2,** poverty; indigence. **3,** stinginess.

escaso (es'ka·so) *adj.* **1,** small; limited. **2,** sparing; niggardly. **3,** scarce; scanty. **4,** scant.

escatimar (es·ka·ti'mar) *v.t.* to scrimp; give sparingly of.

escatología (es·ka·to·lo'xi·a) *n.f.* **1,** eschatology. **2,** scatology. —**escatológico** (-'lo·xi·ko) *adj.* **1,** eschatological. **2,** scatological.

escena (es'θe·na; e'se·na) *n.f.* **1,** scene. **2,** *theat.* stage. —**poner en escena,** to stage (a play).

escenario (es·θe'na·rjo; e·se-) *n.m.* **1,** *theat.* stage. **2,** setting; background; scenery. **3,** site; scene.

escénico (es'θe·ni·ko; e'se-) *adj.* of or pert. to the stage.

escenificar (es·θe·ni·fi'kar; e·se-) *v.t.* [*infl.:* **tocar,** 7] **1,** to stage; portray. **2,** to dramatize; adapt for the stage.

escéptico (es'θep·ti·ko; e'sep-) *adj.* skeptical. —*n.m.* skeptic. —**escepticismo** (-'θis·mo; -'sis·mo) *n.m.* skepticism.

esclarecer (es·kla·re'θer; -'ser) *v.* [*infl.*: **conocer, 13**] —*v.t.* **1,** to illuminate; lighten. **2,** to give renown; make known. **3,** to elucidate. **4,** to enlighten (the mind). —*v.i.* to dawn.

esclarecido (es·kla·re'θi·ðo; -'si·ðo) *adj.* illustrious; prominent.

esclarecimiento (es·kla·re· θi'mjen·to; -si'mjen·to) *n.m.* **1,** elucidation; clarification. **2,** dawning. **3,** enlightenment.

esclavitud (es·kla·βi'tuð) *n.f.* slavery; enslavement.

esclavizar (es·kla·βi'θar; -'sar) *v.t.* [*infl.*: **rezar, 10**] **1,** to enslave. **2,** to hold in submission; make dependent. —**esclavización,** *n.f.* enslavement; enthrallment.

esclavo (es'kla·βo) *adj.* enslaved. —*n.m.* [*fem.* **esclava**] slave.

esclavón (es·kla'βon) *also,* **esclavonio** (-'βo·njo) *adj.* & *n.m.* = **eslavo.**

esclerosis (es·kle'ro·sis) *n.f.* sclerosis.

esclerótico (es·kle'ro·ti·ko) *adj.* sclerotic.

esclusa (es'klu·sa) *n.f.* **1,** canal lock. **2,** sluice; floodgate.

escoba (es'ko·βa) *n.f.* broom. —**escobar,** *v.t.* to sweep.

escobilla (es·ko'βi·ʎa; -ja) *n.f.* brush *(implement).* —**escobillar,** *v.t.* to brush.

escocer (es·ko'θer; -'ser) *v.i.* [*infl.*: **torcer, 66**] *also,* **escocerse,** *v.r.* to smart. —**escocedura,** *n.f., also,* **escocimiento,** *n.m.* = **escozor.**

escocés (es·ko'θes; -'ses) *adj.* Scotch; Scottish. —*n.m.* Scot; Scotsman. —**escocesa** (-'θe·sa; -'se·sa) *n.f.* Scotswoman.

escofina (es·ko'fi·na) *n.f.* rasp; file. —**escofinar,** *v.t.* to rasp; file.

escoger (es·ko'xer) *v.t.* [*infl.*: **coger, 15**] to select; choose. —**escogido,** *adj.* choice; select.

escogidamente (es·ko·xi·ða· 'men·te) *adv.* **1,** selectively; carefully. **2,** with excellence; completely.

escolar (es·ko'lar) *adj.* scholastic; school *(attrib.)* —*n.m.* student. —**escolástico** (-'las·ti·ko) *adj.* & *n.m.* scholastic.

escoltar (es·kol'tar) *v.t.* to escort. —**escolta** (-'kol·ta) *n.f.* escort.

escollera (es·ko'ʎe·ra; -'je·ra) *n.f.* jetty; breakwater.

escollo (es'ko·ʎo; -jo) *n.m.* **1,** hidden rock or reef. **2,** *fig.* difficulty; obstacle. **3,** *fig.* danger; risk. —**escollar,** *v.i.* to run aground.

escombro (es'kom·bro) *n.m.* **1,** rubble; debris. **2,** mackerel. —**escombrar,** *v.t.* to clear; sweep out.

esconder (es·kon'der) *v.t.* to conceal; hide. —**a escondidas,** covertly.

escondite (es·kon'di·te) *n.m.* hiding place; hide-out; cache. *Also,* **escondrijo** (-'dri·xo). —**jugar al escondite,** to play hide-and-seek.

escopeta (es·ko'pe·ta) *n.f.* shotgun.

escopetazo (es·ko·pe'ta·θo; -so) *n.m.* **1,** gunshot. **2,** gunshot wound. **3,** *fig.* sudden shock; surprise.

escoplo (es'ko·plo) *n.m.* chisel; gouge. —**escopladura,** *n.f.* notch; groove. —**escoplear** (-ple'ar) *v.t.* to chisel.

escopolamina (es·ko·po·la'mi·na) *n.f.* scopolamine.

escora (es'ko·ra) *n.f.* **1,** prop; shore. **2,** *naut.* list; heel.

escorar (es·ko'rar) *v.t.* to prop; shore. —*v.i., naut.* to list; heel.

escorbuto (es·kor'βu·to) *n.m.* scurvy. —**escorbútico,** *adj.* scorbutic.

escorchar (es·kor'tʃar) *v.t.* to flay; skin.

escoria (es'ko·rja) *n.f.* **1,** dross; slag. **2,** refuse; trash. —**escorial,** *n.m.* slag heap.

escorpión (es·kor'pjon) *n.m.* **1,** scorpion. **2,** *cap., astron.* Scorpio.

escota (es'ko·ta) *n.f., naut.* sheet; rope fastened to a sail.

escotado (es·ko'ta·ðo) *adj.* décolleté. —*n.m.* [*also,* **escotadura,** *n.f.*] décolletage.

escotar (es·ko'tar) *v.t.* **1,** to cut or trim to measurement. **2,** to cut (a bodice) low in the neck. **3,** to pay one's share of.

escote (es'ko·te) *n.m.* **1,** décolletage. **2,** share *(of a joint expense).*

escotilla (es·ko'ti·ʎa; -ja) *n.f.,* **1,** *naut.* hatchway. **2,** slide; chute. —**escotillón,** *n.m.* trapdoor.

escozor (es·ko'θor; -'sor) *n.m.* smart; smarting.

escriba (es·kri·βa) *n.m.*, *Bib.* scribe.

escribano (es·kri'βa·no) *n.m.* notary; scrivener. —**escribanía**, *n.f.* office or employment of a notary or scrivener. —**escribano del agua**, whirligig beetle.

escribiente (es·kri'βjen·te) *n.m.* & *f.* clerk; scribe.

escribir (es·kri'βir) *v.t.* [*p.p.* escrito] to write. —**escribirse**, *v.r.* to carry on correspondence; correspond. —**escribir a máquina**, to type. —**máquina de escribir**, typewriter.

escrito (es'kri·to) —*n.m.* 1, writing; manuscript. 2, literary composition. 3, report; paper. 4, *law* writ; brief. —**por escrito**, in writing.

escritor (es·kri'tor) *n.m.* [*fem.* escritora (-'to·ra)] writer; author.

escritorio (es·kri'to·rjo) *n.m.* 1, desk. 2, study. 3, business office.

escritura (es·kri'tu·ra) *n.f.* 1, penmanship; handwriting. 2, writing. 3, *law* instrument. 4, *cap.* Scripture.

escrófula (es'kro·fu·la) *n.f.* scrofula. —**escrofuloso**, *adj.* scrofulous.

escroto (es'kro·to) *n.m.* scrotum.

escrupulizar (es·kru·pu·li'θar; -'sar) *v.i.* [*infl.*: rezar, 10] to scruple; have or feel scruples; stickle.

escrúpulo (es'kru·pu·lo) *n.m.* 1, scruple. 2, [*also*, **escrupulosidad**, *n.f.*] scrupulousness; conscientiousness. 3, *pharm.* scruple. —**escrupuloso**, *adj.* scrupulous.

escrutar (es·kru'tar) *v.t.* 1, to scrutinize. 2, to count (votes) officially. —**escrutador**, *adj.* searching; scrutinizing. —*n.m.* examiner; inspector; teller (*of votes*).

escrutinio (es·kru'ti·njo) *n.m.* 1, scrutiny. 2, official count (*of election returns*).

escuadra (es'kwa·ðra) *n.f.* 1, L-shaped or T-shaped square. 2, *mil.* squad. 3, fleet. —**escuadrilla**, *n.f.* squadron. —**escuadrón**, *n.m.* squadron (*of cavalry*).

escuálido (es'kwa·li·ðo) *adj.* 1, squalid. 2, thin; emaciated. —**escualidez** (-li'ðeθ; -'ðes) (squalor; wretchedness.

escucha (es'ku·tʃa) *n.f.* 1, [*also*, *Amer.*, *n.m.*] advanced sentry; scout. 2, listening post. 3, listening. 4, monitor; listener. 5, monitoring; monitoring post. —**estar a la escucha**, to monitor; listen.

escuchar (es·ku'tʃar) *v.i.* to listen.

—*v.t.* to listen to. —**escucharse**, *v.r.* to be fond of one's own voice; speak with affectation.

escudar (es·ku'ðar) *v.t.* to shield.

escudero (es·ku'ðe·ro) *n.m.* 1, squire; shield-bearer. 2, henchman. 3, = hidalgo. 4, shieldmaker.

escudete (es·ku'ðe·te) *n.m.*, *sewing* gusset.

escudilla (es·ku'ði·ʎa; -ja) *n.f.* bowl; soup bowl.

escudo (es'ku·ðo) *n.m.* 1, shield. 2, coat of arms. 3, escudo (*coin*).

escudriñar (es·ku·ðri'ɲar) *v.t.* to scrutinize. —**escudriñador**, *adj.* searching; scrutinizing. —**escudriñamiento**, *n.m.* scrutiny.

escuela (es'kwe·la) *n.f.* 1, school. 2, schooling.

escuelante (es·kwe'lan·te) *n.m.*, *Amer.* schoolboy. —*n.f.*, *Amer.* schoolgirl.

escueto (es'kwe·to) *adj.* 1, free; unencumbered. 2, bare; raw (*of facts*).

esculcar (es·kul'kar) *v.t.* [*infl.*: tocar, 7] 1, to delve into; search. 2, *Amer.* to frisk; search (a person).

esculpir (es·kul'pir) *v.t.* 1, to sculpture. 2, to engrave; carve. —**esculpidor**, *n.m.* engraver.

escultura (es·kul'tu·ra) *n.f.* sculpture. —**escultural**, *adj.* sculptural. —**escultor**, *n.m.* sculptor; sculptress.

escullirse (es·ku'ʎir·se; -'jir·se) *v.r.* [*infl.*: bullir, 19] = escabullirse.

escuna (es'ku·na) *n.f.*, *naut.* schooner.

escupidera (es·ku·pi'ðe·ra) *n.f.* 1, spittoon; cuspidor. 2, *Amer.* chamber pot. 3, *Amer.* bedpan.

escupidero (es·ku·pi'ðe·ro) *n.m.* disgraceful situation or position.

escupir (es·ku'pir) *v.t.* & *i.* 1, to spit; expectorate. 2, to spew.

escupo (es'ku·po) *n.m.* spittle; expectoration.

escurridizo (es·ku·rri'ði·θo; -so) *adj.* 1, slippery. 2, *fig.* elusive.

escurrido (es·ku'rri·ðo) *adj.* narrow-hipped.

escurrimiento (es·ku·rri'mjen·to) *n.m.* 1, dripping. 2, *fig.* sneaking away.

escurrir (es·ku'rrir) *v.t.* & *i.* to drain. —**escurrirse**, *v.r.* to escape; slip away. —**escurridero**, *n.m.* drainboard; dishrack. —**escurridor**, *n.m.* colander.

esdrújulo (es'ðru·xu·lo) *adj.* accented on the antepenultimate syllable. **—n.m.** a word so accented.

ese ('e·se) *dem.adj.m.sing.* that.

ése ('e·se) *dem.pron.m.sing.* that; that one.

esencia (e'sen·θja; -sja) *n.f.* essence. **—esencial,** *adj.* essential. **—quinta esencia,** quintessence.

esfera (es'fe·ra) *n.f.* 1, sphere. 2, dial *(of a watch or clock).* **—esférico,** *adj.* spherical.

esferoide (es·fe'roi·ðe) *n.m.* spheroid. **—esferoidal,** *adj.* spheroidal.

esfinge (es'fin·xe) *n.f.,* also sometimes *masc.* sphinx.

esfínter (es'fin·ter) *n.m.* sphincter.

esforzado (es·for'θa·ðo; -'sa·ðo) *adj.* spirited; enterprising; daring.

esforzar (es·for'θar; -'sar) *v.t.* [*infl.:* rezar, 10; acostar, 28] 1, to invigorate; strengthen. 2, to encourage; give confidence. **—v.i.** to take courage. **—esforzarse,** *v.r.* to exert oneself.

esfuerzo (es'fwer·θo; -so) *n.m.* 1, effort. 2, spirit; daring. 3, *engin.* stress.

esfumar (es·fu'mar) *v.t., paint.* to tone down. **—esfumarse,** *v.r.* to vanish; dissipate.

esgrima (es'γri·ma) *n.f.* fencing; swordplay.

esgrimir (es·γri'mir) *v.t.* to wield; brandish. **—v.i.** to fence. **—esgrimidor,** *n.m.* fencer; swordsman. **—esgrimista,** *n.m. & f.* swordsman; swordswoman.

esguince (es'γin·θe; -se) *n.m.* 1, dodge; evasion. 2, frown; grimace. 3, sprain; wrenching *(of a joint).*

eslabón (es·la'βon) *n.m.* 1, link *(of a chain).* 2, steel for striking fire with a flint. 3, *fig.* tie; bond. **—eslabonar,** *v.t.* to link.

eslavo (es'la·βo) *adj. & n.m.* Slav; Slavic.

eslovaco (es·lo'βa·ko) *adj. & n.m.* Slovak.

esloveno (es·lo'βe·no) *adj. & n.m.* Slovene.

esmaltar (es·mal'tar) *v.t.* 1, to enamel. 2, *fig.* to adorn; embellish.

esmalte (es'mal·te) *n.m.* 1, enamel. 2, *fig.* polish; shine. *(Mex.)* nail polish.

esmaque (es'ma·ke) *n.m.* fishing smack.

esmerado (es·me'ra·ðo) *adj.* 1, carefully done. 2, careful; exacting.

esmeralda (es·me'ral·da) *n.f.* em-

erald. **—esmeraldino,** *adj.* emerald *(of color).*

esmerar (es·me'rar) *v.t.* to brighten; polish. **—esmerarse,** *v.r.* 1, to do one's best; take pains. 2, to strive for excellence.

esmerejón (es·me·re'xon) *n.m., ornith.* merlin.

esmeril (es·me'ril) *n.m.* emery. **—esmerilar,** *v.t.* to burnish.

esmero (es'me·ro) *n.m.* meticulousness.

esmoladera (es·mo·la'ðe·ra) *n.f.* whetstone.

esmoquin (es'mo·kin) *n.m.* [*pl.* esmoquins] tuxedo.

esnob (es'nob) *n.m. & f.* [*pl.* esnobs (es'nobs)] snob. **—esnobismo,** *n.m.* snobbism.

esnórquel (es'nor·kel) *n.m.* snorkel.

eso ('e·so) *dem.pron.neut.* that. **—eso de,** that matter of. **—eso es,** that's right. **—eso mismo,** the very thing; exactly. **—por eso,** for that reason; on that account.

esófago (e'so·fa·γo) *n.m.* esophagus.

esos ('e·sos) *dem.adj., pl. of* ese.

ésos ('e·sos) *dem.pron., pl. of* ése.

esotérico (e·so'te·ri·ko) *adj.* esoteric.

espabilar (es·pa·βi'lar) *v.t.* = despabilar.

espacial (es·pa'θjal; -'sjal) *adj.* 1, spatial. 2, space *(attrib.).*

espaciar (es·pa'θjar; -'sjar) *v.t.* 1, to space. 2, to disperse; diffuse. **—espaciarse,** *v.r.* 1, to expatiate. 2, to enjoy oneself; relax. **—espaciador,** *n.m.* space bar.

espacio (es'pa·θjo; -sjo) *n.m.* 1, space. 2, aerospace.

espacioso (es·pa'θjo·so; -'sjo·so) *adj.* 1, spacious. 2, slow; deliberate. **—espaciosidad,** *n.f.* spaciousness.

espada (es'pa·ða) *n.f.* 1, sword. 2, *often masc.* swordsman. 3, *cards* spade. **—pez espada,** swordfish.

espadachín (es·pa·ða'tʃin) *n.m.* 1, skillful swordsman. 2, bully.

espadilla (es·pa'ði·ʎa; -ja) *n.f.* 1, scull *(oar).* 2, *cards* ace of spades. 3, large hairpin.

espahí (es·pa'i) *n.m.* spahi.

espalda (es'pal·da) *n.f., also pl.,* espaldas, 1, *anat.* back. 2, rear; back. **—a espaldas,** treacherously; behind one's back. **—de espaldas,** on one's back. **—irse de espaldas,** to fall backwards.

espaldar (es·pal'dar) *n.m.* **1**, back. **2**, back (*of a chair*). **3**, dorsal section, as of armor, a turtle shell, etc. **4**, trellis. **5**, *pl.* hangings; tapestry.

espaldarazo (es·pal·da'ra·θo; -so) *n.m.* **1**, slap or pat on the back. **2**, dubbing (*of a knight*).

espaldera (es·pal'de·ra) *n.f.* trellis.

espaldudo (es·pal'du·ðo) *adj.* broad-shouldered.

espantada (es·pan'ta·ða) *n.f.* **1**, bolting (*of an animal*); stampede. **2**, *colloq.* sudden fright; cold feet.

espantadizo (es·pan·ta'ði·θo; -so) *adj.* scary; timid.

espantajo (es·pan'ta·xo) *n.m.* **1**, scary thing. **2**, scarecrow.

espantapájaros (es·pan·ta'pa·xa·ros) *n.m. sing. & pl.* scarecrow.

espantar (es·pan'tar) *v.t.* **1**, to frighten; terrify. **2**, to drive; chase away (*usu. animals*). —**espantarse,** *v.r.* to be astonished; be astounded.

espanto (es'pan·to) *n.m.* **1**, dread; terror. **2**, shock; astonishment. **3**, *pathol.* shock. **4**, *Amer.* ghost; apparition. **5**, *colloq.* horror.

espantoso (es·pan'to·so) *adj.* **1**, dreadful; terrifying. **2**, shocking; astonishing.

español (es·pa'ɲol) *adj.* Spanish, —*n.m.* **1**, Spanish language. **2**, Spaniard. —**española** (-'ɲo·la) *n.f.* Spanish woman.

esparadrapo (es·pa·ra'ðra·po) *n.m.* adhesive tape.

esparcir (es·par'θir; -'sir) *v.t.* [*infl.:* **12**] **1**, to scatter. **2**, to amuse; divert.

espárrago (es'pa·rra·ɣo) *n.m.* asparagus.

espartano (es·par'ta·no) *adj. & n.m.* Spartan.

esparto (es'par·to) *n.m.* esparto; esparto grass.

espasmo (es'pas·mo) *n.m.* spasm. —**espasmódico** (-'mo·ði·ko) *adj.* spasmodic.

espástico (es'pas·ti·ko) *adj. & n.m.* spastic.

espato (es'pa·to) *n.m., mineral.* spar.

espátula (es'pa·tu·la) *n.f.* **1**, spatula. **2**, *paint.* palette knife. **3**, *ornith.* spoonbill.

espavorido (es·pa·βo'ri·ðo) *adj.* = **despavorido.**

especia (es'pe·θja; -sja) *n.f.* spice.

especial (es·pe'θjal; -'sjal) *adj.*

special. —**en especial,** specially; in particular.

especialidad (es·pe·θja·li'ðað; -sja·li'ðað) *n.f.* specialty.

especialista (es·pe·θja'lis·ta; -sja'lis·ta) *n.m. & f.* specialist.

especializar (es·pe·θja·li'θar; -sja·li'sar) *v.t. & i.* [*infl.:* **rezar, 10**] to specialize. —**especialización,** *n.f.* specialization; *educ.* major.

especiar (es·pe'θjar; -'sjar) *v.t.* spice; season.

especie (es'pe·θje; -sje) *n.f.* **1**, species; kind. **2**, image; mental picture. —**en especie,** in kind.

especificar (es·pe·θi·fi'kar; es·pe·si-) *v.t.* [*infl.:* **tocar, 7**] to specify. —**especificación,** *n.f.* specification.

específico (es·pe'θi·fi·ko; es·pe'si-) *adj. & n.m.* specific. —*n.m.* proprietary medicine.

espécimen (es'pe·θi·men; -si·men) *n.m.* [*pl.* **especímenes** (-'θi·me·nes; -'si·me·nes)] specimen.

especiosidad (es·pe·θjʊ·si'ðað; -sjo·si'ðað). *n.f.* **1**, attractiveness; neatness. **2**, speciousness.

especioso (es·pe'θjo·so; -'sjo·so) *adj.* **1**, attractive; neat. **2**, specious.

espectáculo (es·pek'ta·ku·lo) *n.m.* spectacle; show. —**espectacular,** *adj.* spectacular.

espectador (es·pek·ta'ðor) *n.m.* spectator.

espectro (es'pek·tro) *n.m.* **1**, specter. **2**, spectrum. —**espectral,** *adj.* spectral.

espectrograma (es·pek·tro'ɣra·ma) *n.m.* spectrogram. —**espectrógrafo** (-'tro·ɣra·fo) *n.m.* spectrograph.

espectroscopio (es·pek·tros'ko·pjo) *n.m.* spectroscope. —**espectroscopia,** *n.f.* spectroscopy. —**espectroscópico** (-'ko·pi·ko) *adj.* spectroscopic.

especular (es·pe·ku'lar) *v.t.* **1**, to inspect; view. **2**, to speculate on; ponder. —*v.i.* to speculate. —**especulación,** *n.f.* speculation. —**especulador,** *n.m.* speculator. —**especulativo,** *adj.* speculative.

espejismo (es·pe'xis·mo) *n.m.* mirage.

espejo (es'pe·xo) *n.m.* mirror.

espejuelos (es·pe'xwe·los) *n.m.pl.* **1**, spectacles; eyeglasses. **2**, eyeglass lenses.

espelta (es'pel·ta) *n.f., bot.* spelt.

espeluznar (es·pe·luθ'nar; -lus-

'nar) *v.t.* to horrify; frighten; raise the hair of. —**espeluznante,** *adj.* frightful; hairraising.

espera (es'pe·ra) *n.f.* **1,** wait; waiting. **2,** respite. **3,** expectation. —**en espera,** waiting; expecting. —**en espera de,** waiting for. —**sala de espera,** waiting room.

esperanza (es·pe'ran·θa; -sa) *n.f.* hope; hopefulness. —**esperanzado,** *adj.* hopeful. —**esperanzar,** *v.t.* [*infl.:* **rezar, 10**] to encourage.

esperar (es·pe'rar) *v.t.* **1,** to hope for. **2,** to expect. **3,** to wait for; await. —*v.i.* **1,** to hope. **2,** to wait. —**esperarse,** *v.r.* to wait.

esperezarse (es·pe·re'θar·se; -'sar·se) *v.r.* = **desperezarse.**

esperma (es'per·ma) *n.f.* **1,** sperm. **2,** *also masc.* semen.

esperpento (es·per'pen·to) *n.m.* **1,** *colloq.* eyesore. **2,** absurdity; nonsense.

espesar (es·pe'sar) *v.t.* **1,** to thicken; make dense. **2,** to weave tighter.

espeso (es'pe·so) *adj.* **1,** thick; dense. **2,** *fig.* dirty; slovenly. **3,** *Amer., colloq.* boorish; loutish.

espesor (es·pe'sor) *n.m.* **1,** thickness. **2,** denseness; density.

espesura (es·pe'su·ra) *n.f.* **1,** denseness; thickness. **2,** thicket. **3,** filth; dirt.

espetar (es·pe'tar) *v.t.* **1,** to spit; skewer. **2,** *colloq.* to surprise (someone) with, as a blow, piece of news, etc.

espetera (es·pe'te·ra) *n.f.* scullery.

espetón (es·pe'ton) *n.m.* **1,** poker. **2,** skewer. **3,** large pin. **4,** poke; jab.

espía (es'pi·a) *n.m. & f.* spy. —*n.f., naut.* warp.

espiar (es·pi'ar) *v.t. & i.* [*infl.:* **enviar, 22**] to spy. —*v.i., naut.* to warp a ship.

espicanardo (es·pi·ka'nar·ðo) *n.m.* spikenard; nard.

espiga (es'pi·ɣa) *n.f.* **1,** spike or ear of grain. **2,** *carp.* tenon; dowel; pin; peg. **3,** *mech.* tongue; shank. **4,** brad. **5,** *naut.* masthead.

espigado (es·pi'ɣa·ðo) *adj.* **1,** ripe; eared. **2,** *fig.* tall; grown. **3,** spiky.

espigadora (es·pi·ɣa'ðo·ra) *n.f.* gleaner. *Also,* **espigadera** (-'ðe·ra).

espigar (es·pi'ɣar) *v.t.* [*infl.:* **pagar, 8**] **1,** to glean. **2,** *carp.* to tenon. —*v.i.* to ear, as grain. —**espigarse,** *v.r.* to grow tall.

espina (es'pi·na) *n.f.* **1,** thorn. **2,** spine; backbone. **3,** fishbone. **4,** splinter. —**dar mala espina,** *colloq.* to cause suspicion. —**sacarse la espina,** *colloq.* to get even.

espinaca (es·pi'na·ka) *n.f.* spinach.

espinal (es·pi'nal) *adj.* spinal; dorsal.

espinazo (es·pi'na·θo; -so) *n.m.* spine; backbone.

espineta (es·pi'ne·ta) *n.f.* spinet.

espinilla (es·pi'ni·ʎa; -ja) *n.f.* **1,** shinbone. **2,** blackhead.

espino (es'pi·no) *n.m.* hawthorn.

espinoso (es·pi'no·so) *adj.* **1,** spiny; thorny. **2,** *fig.* difficult; thorny; prickly.

espión (es·pi'on) *n.m.* spy.

espionaje (es·pj·o'na·xe) *n.m.* espionage.

espira (es'pi·ra) *n.f.* **1,** coil; spiral; spire. **2,** turn *(of a spiral).*

espiral (es·pi'ral) *adj.* spiral. —*n.f.* spiral. —*n.m.* hairspring of a watch.

espirar (es·pi'rar) *v.t. & i.* to exhale; expire. —**espiración,** *n.f.* exhalation; expiration.

espiritismo (es·pi·ri'tis·mo) *n.m.* spiritualism. —**espiritista,** *n.m. & f.* spiritualist. —*adj.* spiritualistic.

espíritu (es'pi·ri·tu) *n.m.* spirit. —**espiritual** (-'twal) *adj.* spiritual. —**espirituoso** (-'two·so) *adj.* spirituous.

espita (es'pi·ta) *n.f.* **1,** tap; spigot. **2,** *colloq.* tippler; drunkard.

esplendidez (es·plen·di'ðeθ; -'ðes) *n.f.* **1,** splendor; magnificence. **2,** liberality; largess.

espléndido (es·plen·di·ðo) *adj.* **1,** splendid; magnificent. **2,** liberal; munificent.

esplendor (es·plen'dor) *n.m.* splendor. —**esplendoroso,** *adj.* splendorous.

espliego (es·plje·ɣo) *n.m., bot.* lavender.

esplín (es'plin) *n.m.* **1,** *anat.* spleen. **2,** melancholy; depression.

espolear (es·po·le'ar) *v.t.* to spur.

espoleta (es·po'le·ta) *n.f.* **1,** fuse *(of a bomb or grenade).* **2,** wishbone.

espolón (es·po'lon) *n.m.* **1,** cock's spur. **2,** fetlock. **3,** beak; ram *(of a warship).* **4,** cutwater. **5,** mountain ridge or spur. **6,** breakwater; jetty. **7,** *archit.* buttress.

espolvorear (es·pol·βo·re'ar) *v.t.*

to dust; sprinkle with or as with dust.

espondeo (es·pon'de·o) *n.m.* spondee.

esponja (es'pon·xa) *n.f.* 1, sponge. 2, *colloq.* sponger. —**esponjoso,** *adj.* spongy.

esponjar (es·pon'xar) *v.t.* 1, to make spongy. 2, *Amer., colloq.* to sponge on. —**esponjarse,** *v.r.* 1, to swell; puff up (with pride). 2, to glow (with health).

esponsales (es·pon'sa·les) *n.m.pl.* betrothal; engagement.

espontáneo (es·pon'ta·ne·o) *adj.* spontaneous. —**espontaneidad** (-nei'ðað) *n.f.* spontaneity.

espora (es'po·ra) *n.f.* spore.

esporádico (es·po'ra·ði·ko) *adj.* sporadic.

esposa (es'po·sa) *n.f.* wife; spouse. —**esposas,** *n.f.pl.* handcuffs; fetters. —**esposar,** *v.t.* to shackle.

esposo (es'po·so) *n.m.* husband; spouse.

espuela (es'pwe·la) *n.f.* 1, spur. 2, *fig.* incitement; stimulus. —**espuela de caballero,** larkspur.

espuerta (es'pwer·ta) *n.f.* basket.

espulgar (es·pul'ɣar) *v.t.* [*infl.:* **pagar,** 8] 1, to delouse. 2, *fig.* to examine closely.

espuma (es'pu·ma) *n.f.* foam; scum; lather. —**espuma de caucho,** foam rubber. —**espuma de mar,** meerschaum.

espumar (es·pu'mar) *v.t.* to skim. —*v.i.* 1, to froth; foam. 2, to sparkle, as wine. 3, *fig.* to grow up. —**espumadera,** *n.f.* skimmer. —**espumante,** *adj.* = **espumoso.**

espumarajo (es·pu·ma'ra·xo) *n.m.* drivel; foam (*from the mouth*).

espumilla (es·pu'mi·ʎa; -ja) *n.f.* voile.

espumoso (es·pu'mo·so) *adj.* 1, frothy; foamy. 2, sparkling (*of wine*).

espurio (es'pu·rjo) *also,* **espúreo** (-'pu·re·o) *adj.* 1, bastard; illegitimate. 2, spurious; false.

esputar (es·pu'tar) *v.t.* to spit; expectorate.

esputo (es'pu·to) *n.m.* 1, spit; saliva. 2, sputum.

esquela (es'ke·la) *n.m.* 1, note. 2, announcement card, esp. an obituary notice.

esqueleto (es·ke'le·to) *n.m.* 1, skeleton. 2, framework. —**esquelético** (-'le·ti·ko) *adj.* thin; skinny.

esquema (es'ke·ma) *n.m.* 1, outline; sketch. 2, plan; scheme. —**esquemático** (-'ma·ti·ko) *adj.* schematic.

esquí (es'ki) *n.m.* 1, [*pl.* **esquís** *or* **esquíes**] ski. 2, skiing.

esquiar (es·ki'ar) *v.i.* [*infl.:* **enviar,** 22] to ski. —**esquiador,** *n.m.* skier.

esquiciar (es·ki'θjar; -'sjar) *v.t.* to sketch. —**esquicio** (-'ki·θjo; -sjo) *n.m.* sketch.

esquife (es'ki·fe) *n.m.* 1, skiff. 2, *archit.* barrel vault.

esquiísmo (es·ki'is·mo) *n.m.* skiing.

esquila (es'ki·la) *n.f.* 1, hand bell. 2, cowbell. 3, shearing.

esquilar (es·ki'lar) *v.t.* 1, to shear; crop; clip. 2, *fig.* to fleece; swindle.

esquileo (es·ki'le·o) *n.m.* 1, shearing. 2, shearing season.

esquimal (es·ki'mal) *adj. & n.m. & f.* Eskimo.

esquina (es'ki·na) *n.f.* corner.

esquinazo (es·ki'na·θo; -so) *n.m., colloq.* corner. —**dar esquinazo a uno,** *colloq.* to shake off someone.

esquirol (es·ki'rol) *n.m.* strikebreaker; scab.

esquisto (es'kis·to) *n.m.* schist; slate.

esquivar (es·ki'βar) *v.t.* to avoid; elude; shun. —**esquivarse,** *v.r.* to withdraw; be reserved; be coy. —**esquivez** (-'βeθ; -'βes) *n.f.* evasiveness; aloofness.

esquivo (es'ki·βo) *adj.* 1, elusive; evasive. 2, reserved; coy.

esquizofrenia (es·ki·θo'fre·nja; es·ki·so-) *n.f.* schizophrenia. —**esquizofrénico** (-'fre·ni·ko) *adj. & n.m.* schizophrenic; schizoid.

esta ('es·ta) *dem.adj., fem of* **este.**

ésta ('es·ta) *dem.pron., fem. of* **éste.**

estabilizar (es·ta·βi·li'θar; -'sar) *v.t.* [*infl.:* **rezar,** 10] to stabilize. —**estabilización,** *n.f.* stabilization. —**estabilizador,** *n.m.* stabilizer. —*adj.* stabilizing.

estable (es'ta·βle) *adj.* stable. —**estabilidad,** *n.f.* stability.

establecer (es·ta·βle'θer; -'ser) *v.t.* [*infl.:* **conocer,** 13] 1, to establish. 2, to fix; settle. 3, to decree.

establecimiento (es·ta·βle·θi'mjen·to; -si'mjen·to) *n.m.* 1, establishment. 2, settlement. 3, law; statute.

establo (es'ta·βlo) *n.m.* stable; barn.

estaca (es'ta·ka) *n.f.* 1, stake; pale.

2, cudgel; stick. —**estacada,** *n.f.* paling; fence. —**estacazo,** *n.m.* blow with a stick.

estacar (es·ta'kar) *v.t.* [*infl.:* **tocar,** 7] 1, to stake (an animal); tie to a stake. 2, to stake out; mark with stakes. —**estacarse,** *v.r.* to stand straight; stand stiff.

estación (es·ta'θjon; -'sjon) *n.f.* 1, station. 2, season. 3, stop; stay. 4, *eccles.* devotional church visit. —**estacional,** *adj.* seasonal.

estacionamiento (es·ta·θjo·na'mjen·to; -sjo·na'mjen·to) *n.m.* 1, placement; stationing. 2, parking.

estacionar (es·ta·θjo'nar; -sjo'nar) *v.t.* 1, to place; station. 2, to park. —**estacionarse,** *v.r.* 1, to stand; be or remain stationary. 2, to park; be parked.

estacionario (es·ta·θjo'na·rjo; -sjo'na·rjo) *adj.* stationary.

estada (es'ta·ða) *n.f.* stay; sojourn.

estadía (es·ta'ði·a) *n.f.* 1, *comm.; naut.* demurrage. 2, *Amer.* stay; sojourn.

estadio (es'ta·ðjo) *n.m.* stadium.

estadista (es·ta'ðis·ta) *n.m.* statesman.

estadística (es·ta'ðis·ti·ka) *n.f.* statistics. —**estadístico,** *adj.* statistical. —*n.m.* statistician.

estado (es'ta·ðo) *n.m.* 1, state. 2, condition. 3, estate; class; rank. 4, status. 5, account; statement. —**estado civil,** marital status. —**estado mayor,** general staff.

estadounidense (es·ta·ðo·u·ni·'ðen·se) *adj.* American; of or pert. to the United States. —*n.m. & f.* American (*of the United States*).

estafa (es'ta·fa) *n.f.* swindle; fraud.

estafar (es·ta'far) *v.t.* to swindle; defraud. —**estafador,** *n.m.* swindler.

estafeta (es·ta'fe·ta) *n.f.* 1, mail. 2, diplomatic courier. 3, [*also,* **estafeta de correos**] post office.

estafilococo (es·ta·fi·lo'ko·ko) *n.m.* staphylococcus.

estala (es'ta·la) *n.m., naut.* port of call.

estalactita (es·ta·lak'ti·ta) *n.f.* stalactite.

estalagmita (es·ta·laɣ'mi·ta) *n.f.* stalagmite.

estallar (es·ta'ʎar; -'jar) *v.i.* to explode; burst.

estallido (es·ta'ʎi·ðo; -'ji·ðo) *n.m.* 1, burst; explosion; report (*of a firearm*). 2, crack; snap.

estambre (es'tam·bre) *n.m.* 1, worsted; woolen yarn. 2, *bot.* stamen.

estameña (es·ta'me·ɲa) *n.f.* serge.

estampa (es'tam·pa) *n.f.* 1, print. 2, engraving. 3, *fig.* stamp; kind; sort. 4, image; portrait. 5, printing; press.

estampado (es·tam'pa·ðo) *n.m.* 1, cotton print. 2, stamping. 3, cloth printing.

estampar (es·tam'par) *v.t.* 1, to stamp; print. 2, to plant (a kiss); to impress (on the mind).

estampía (es·tam'pi·a) *in de estampía,* in a rush; precipitously.

estampida (es·tam'pi·ða) *n.f.* 1, stampede. 2, = **estampido.**

estampido (es·tam'pi·ðo) *n.m.* crash; explosion; report (*of a firearm*).

estampilla (es·tam'pi·ʎa; -ja) *n.f.* 1, signet; seal. 2, rubber stamp. 3, *Amer.* postage or tax stamp.

estancación (es·tan·ka'θjon; -'sjon) *n.f.* stagnation. *Also,* **estancamiento,** *n.m.*

estancar (es·tan'kar) *v.t.* [*infl.:* **tocar,** 7] 1, to stanch; stop; check. 2, to suspend. 3, *comm.* to monopolize. 4, to restrict the sale of. —**estancarse,** *v.r.* to be or become stagnant.

estancia (es'tan·θja; -sja) *n.f.* 1, sojourn; stay. 2, *Amer.* ranch. 3, sitting room; any large room. 4, stanza. —**estanciero,** *n.m., Amer.* rancher; ranchman.

estanco (es'tan·ko) *adj.* watertight. —*n.m.* 1, government monopoly. 2, monopoly store, esp. tobacco store. 3, file; archive. 4, *Amer.* liquor store.

estándar (es'tan·dar) *n.m., Amer.* standard; norm.

estandardizar (es·tan·dar·ði·'θar; -'sar) *v.t., Amer.* [*infl.:* **rezar,** 10] to standardize. *Also,* **estandarizar** (-ri'θar; -'sar). —**estandardización,** *n.f., Amer.* standardization.

estandarte (es·tan'dar·te) *n.m.* standard; banner.

estanque (es'tan·ke) *n.m.* reservoir; basin; pond.

estanquillo (es·tan'ki·ʎo; -jo) *n.m.* 1, tobacco store. 2, *Amer.* small store. 3, *Amer.* liquor store; tavern.

estante (es'tan·te) *adj.* 1, fixed; permanent. 2, extant. —*n.m.* 1, shelf. 2, book rack; bookcase. 3, support; post. —**estantería**, *n.f.* set of shelves; shelving.

estantío (es·tan'ti·o) *adj.* **1,** still; stagnant. **2,** slow; torpid.

estañar (es·ta'ɲar) *v.t.* **1,** to tin. **2,** to solder.

estaño (es·ta·ɲo) *n.m.* tin.

estaquilla (es·ta'ki·ʎa; -ja) *n.f.* **1,** peg; pin. **2,** brad. **3,** long nail; spike.

estar (es'tar) *v.i.* [*infl.:* 6] **1,** to be *(in a certain place or condition).* **2,** to remain; stay. —*aux.v.,* used with the gerund to form the progressive tenses: estoy escribiendo, I am writing. —**estarse,** *v.r.* **1,** to remain; stay. **2,** to be stopped or delayed. —**está bien,** fine; (it's) all right. —**¿a cuántos** *or* **a cómo estamos?,** what is today's date? —**estamos a diez,** today is the tenth. —**estar a (cierto precio),** to cost (a certain amount). —**estar a dos velas,** *colloq.* **1,** to know nothing. **2,** to be broke. —**estar al caer,** *colloq.* **1,** to be about to happen. **2,** to be about to strike *(of the hour).* —**estar a la que salta,** *colloq.* to be ready to make the most of something. —**estar a matar,** to be bitter enemies. —**estar a oscuras,** *colloq.* to know nothing. —**estar bien,** to be well. —**estar bien con,** *colloq.* to be on good terms with. —**estar con,** *colloq.* to be with; be on the side of; favor. —**estar con** *or* **en ánimo de,** to be in the mood for; like; feel like. —**estar** *or* **estarse de más,** *colloq.* **1,** to be idle. **2,** to be unnecessary. —**estar en,** *colloq.* **1,** to understand. **2,** to cost. —**estar en lo cierto,** to be sure. —**estar en todo,** *colloq.* **1,** to have a finger in everything. **2,** to take good care. —**estar mal, 1,** to be bad. **2,** to be ill. —**estar mal con,** to be on bad terms with. —**estar** *or* **estarse mano sobre mano,** *colloq.* **1,** to do nothing; be idle. **2,** to stand by idly. —**estar para,** to be ready or about to. —**estar por,** *colloq.* **1,** to favor; be in favor of; be for or with. **2,** *fol. by inf.* to remain to be; have yet to be. —**estar que bota; estar que estalla; estar que echa chispas,** to be in a rage. —**¿está Vd.?,** *colloq.* do you understand? do you follow me? —**estar sobre sí,** to control oneself. —**estar sobre uno** *or* **algo,** to watch cautiously.

estarcir (es·tar'θir; -'sir) *v.t.* [*infl.:*

esparcir, 12] to stencil. —**estarcido,** *n.m.* stencil.

estas ('es·tas) *dem.adj., fem.pl.* of **este.**

éstas ('es·tas) *dem.pron., fem.pl.* of **éste.**

estatal (es·ta'tal) *adj.* state *(attrib.).*

estático (es·ta·ti·ko) *adj.* static. —**estática,** *n.f.* **1,** statics. **2,** static.

estatidad (es·ta·ti'ðað) *n.f.* statehood.

estator (es·ta'tor) *n.m.* stator.

estatua (es·ta·twa) *n.f.* statue. —**estatuaria,** *n.f.* statuary. —**estatuilla,** *also,* **estatuita,** *n.f.* statuette.

estatuir (es·ta·tu'ir) *v.t.* [*infl.:* **huir, 26**] **1,** to enact; ordain. **2,** to demonstrate; prove.

estatura (es·ta'tu·ra) *n.f.* stature; height.

estatuto (es·ta·tu·to) *n.m.* statute; law; ordinance. —**estatutario,** *adj.* statutory.

estay (es'tai) *n.m.* [*pl.* **estayes**] *naut.* stay.

este ('es·te) *n.m.* **1,** east. **2,** east wind.

este ('es·te) *dem.adj.masc.* [*fem.* **esta;** *pl.* **estos, estas**] **1,** this; *pl.* these. **2,** latter.

éste ('es·te) *dem.pron.masc.* [*fem.* **ésta;** *pl.* **éstos, éstas**] **1,** this; this one; *pl.* these. **2,** the latter.

esté (es·te) *v., pres.subjve.* of **estar.**

esteatita (es·te·a'ti·ta) *n.f.* soapstone.

estela (es·te·la) *n.f.* trail; wake.

estelar (es·te'lar) *adj.* stellar.

estenografía (es·te·no·ɣra'fi·a) *n.f.* stenography. —**estenográfico** (-'ɣra·fi·ko) *adj.* stenographic. —**estenógrafo** (-'no·ɣra·fo) *n.m.* [*fem.* **-grafa**] stenographer.

estentóreo (es·ten'to·re·o) *adj.* stentorian.

estepa (es·te·pa) *n.f.* steppe.

éster ('es·ter) *n.m.* ester.

estera (es·te·ra) *n.f.* **1,** door mat. **2,** rug made of hemp, rope or fiber. —**esterado,** *adj.* matted; covered with a mat. —*n.m.* matting.

estercolar (es·ter·ko'lar) *v.t.* [*infl.:* **acostar, 28**] to manure; fertilize. —*n.m.* dunghill. —**estercoladura,** *n.f., also* **estercolamiento,** *n.m.* manuring; fertilizing.

estercolero (es·ter·ko'le·ro) *n.m.* **1,** manure collector. **2,** dunghill; manure pile.

estéreo (es·te·re·o) *n.m.* **1**, stere. **2**, stereo. —*adj.* stereo.

estereofónico (es·te·re·o'fo·ni·ko) *adj.* stereophonic.

estereoscopio (es·te·re·os'ko·pjo) *n.m.* stereoscope. —**estereoscópico** (-'ko·pi·ko) *adj.* stereoscopic. —**estereoscopia** (-'ko·pja) *n.f.* stereoscopy.

estereotipo (es·te·re·o'ti·po) *n.m.* stereotype. —**estereotipar,** *v.t.* to stereotype. —**estereotipia** (-'ti·pja) *n.f.* stereotypy. —**estereotípico** (-'ti·pi·ko) *adj.* stereotype *(attrib.)*.

estéril (es'te·ril) *adj.* sterile; barren; unproductive. —**esterilidad,** *n.f.* sterility; barrenness.

esterilizar (es·te·ri·li'θar; -'sar) *v.t.* [*infl.:* rezar, 10] to sterilize. —**esterilización,** *n.f.* sterilization. —**esterilizador,** *adj.* sterilizing. —*n.m.* sterilizer.

esterilla (es·te'ri·ʎa; -ja) *n.f.* small mat.

esterlina (es·ter'li·na) *adj.fem.* sterling. —**libra esterlina,** pound sterling.

esternón (es·ter'non) *n.m.* sternum.

estero (es'te·ro) *n.m.* **1**, inlet; creek. **2**, tideland. **3**, salt marsh.

estertor (es·ter'tor) *n.m.* **1**, death rattle. **2**, rattle in the throat. **3**, noisy breathing; panting. —**estertoroso,** *adj.* stertorous.

esteta (es'te·ta) *n.m. & f.* esthete.

estética (es'te·ti·ka) *n.f.* esthetics. —**estético,** *adj.* esthetic.

estetoscopio (es·te·tos'ko·pjo) *n.m.* stethoscope.

estiaje (es'tja·xe) *n.m.* low water.

estibar (es·ti'βar) *v.t.* **1**, to compress; bale. **2**, *naut.* to stow. —**estibador,** *n.m.* longshoreman.

estibio (es'ti·βjo) *n.m.* antimony.

estiércol (es'tjer·kol) *n.m.* **1**, dung; manure. **2**, *fig.* filth.

estigio (es'ti·xjo) *adj.* Stygian.

estigma (es'tiɣ·ma) *n.m.* stigma.

estigmatizar (es·tiɣ·ma·ti'θar; -'sar) *v.t.* [*infl.:* rezar, 10] to stigmatize; brand.

estilete (es·ti'le·te) *n.m.* **1**, stiletto. **2**, *surg.* probe.

estilista (es·ti'lis·ta) *n.m. & f.* stylist.

estilístico (es·ti'lis·ti·ko) *adj.* stylistic. —**estilística,** *n.f.* stylistics.

estilizar (es·ti·li'θar; -'sar) *v.t.* [*infl.:* rezar, 10] to stylize.

estilo (es'ti·lo) *n.m.* **1**, stylus. **2**, style. **3**, fashion; use; custom. **4**, kind; class; sort.

estilográfica (es·ti·lo'ɣra·fi·ka) *n.f.* fountain pen.

estima (es'ti·ma) *n.f.* **1**, esteem; respect. **2**, *naut.* dead reckoning.

estimable (es·ti'ma·βle) *adj.* **1**, estimable; worthy. **2**, computable.

estimación (es·ti·ma'θjon; -'sjon) *n.f.* **1**, esteem; regard. **2**, appraisal.

estimar (es·ti'mar) *v.t.* **1**, to esteem; regard. **2**, to estimate; appraise.

estimulante (es·ti·mu'lan·te) *adj.* stimulating. —*n.m.* stimulant.

estimular (es·ti·mu'lar) *v.t.* **1**, to stimulate. **2**, to encourage.

estímulo (es·ti·mu·lo) *n.m.* **1**, stimulus. **2**, stimulation.

estío (es'ti·o) *n.m.* summer.

estipendio (es·ti'pen·djo) *n.m.* stipend.

estíptico (es'tip·ti·ko) *adj. & n.m.* styptic. —*adj.* **1**, constipated. **2**, stingy; miserly.

estipular (es·ti·pu'lar) *v.t.* to stipulate. —**estipulación,** *n.f.* stipulation.

estirado (es·ti'ra·ðo) *adj.* **1**, stretched; expanded. **2**, *fig.* haughty; stiff. **3**, drawn *(of metals)*. —*n.m.* **1**, stretching. **2**, drawing.

estirar (es·ti'rar) *v.t.* **1**, to draw; pull. **2**, to stretch; extend. **3**, to draw (metals). —**estirarse,** *v.r.* **1**, to stretch. **2**, to grow haughty.

estirena (es·ti're·na) *n.f.* styrene.

estirón (es·ti'ron) *n.m.* **1**, strong pull; stretch. **2**, haul; hauling. **3**, *colloq.* rapid growth.

estirpe (es'tir·pe) *n.f.* ancestry; stock; pedigree.

estival (es·ti'βal) *adj.* summer *(attrib.)*.

esto ('es·to) *dem.pron.neut.* this. —**en esto,** at this moment. —**por esto,** hereby.

estocada (es·to'ka·ða) *n.f.* **1**, stab; thrust; lunge. **2**, stab wound.

estofa (es'to·fa) *n.f.* **1**, quilted cloth, usu. of silk. **2**, *fig.* quality.

estofado (es·to'fa·ðo) *adj.* **1**, quilted. **2**, stewed. —*n.m.* stew.

estofar (es·to'far) *v.t.* **1**, to quilt. **2**, to stew.

estoico (es'toi·ko) *adj.* stoic; stoical. —*n.m.* stoic. —**estoicismo** (-'θis·mo; -'sis·mo) *n.m.* stoicism.

estola (es'to·la) *n.f.* stole.

estólido (es'to·li·ðo) *adj.* stupid; foolish. —**estolidez,** *n.f.* stupidity.

estolón (es·to'lon) *n.m.; bot.; zoöl.* runner.

estomacal (es·to·ma'kal) *adj.* stomachic.

estomagar (es·to·ma'γar) *v.t.* [*infl.:* **pagar,** 8] to upset the stomach of. **—estomagársele a uno,** to annoy; upset; disgust (someone). **—estomagado,** *adj.* annoying; upsetting; disgusting.

estómago (es'to·ma·γo) *n.m.* 1, stomach. 2, *slang, fig.* nerve; insouciance.

estopa (es'to·pa) *n.f.* 1, tow. 2, oakum. 3, burlap.

estoque (cs'to·ke) *n.m.* 1, rapier. 2, sword cane. 3, *bot.* gladiolus. **—estoquear,** *v.t.* to pierce with a rapier.

estorbar (es·tor'βar) *v.t.* to hinder; obstruct. **—estorbo** (es'tor·βo) *n.m.* hindrance; obstacle.

estornino (es·tor'ni·no) *n.m.* starling.

estornudar (es·tor·nu'ðar) *v.i.* to sneeze. **—estornudo** (-'nu·ðo) *n.m.* sneeze.

estos ('es·tos) *dem.adj., pl. of* **este.**

éstos ('es·tos) *dem.pron., pl. of* **éste.**

estotro (es'to·tro) *dem.adj. & pron.* [*fem.* **estotra**] *archaic, contr. of* **este otro** (*or* **esta otra**), this other.

estoy (es'toi) *v., 1st pers.sing. pres.ind. of* **estar.**

estrabismo (es·tra'βis·mo) *n.m.* strabismus.

estrada (es'tra·ða) *n.f.* lane; road. **—batir la estrada,** *mil.* to reconnoiter.

estrado (es'tra·ðo) *n.m.* 1, dais. 2, drawing room.

estrafalario (es·tra·fa'la·rjo) *adj., colloq.* 1, extravagant; fantastic. 2, slovenly; slatternly. **—n.m.,** *colloq.* eccentric.

estragar (es·tra'γar) *v.t.* [*infl.:* **pagar,** 8] 1, to deprave; corrupt. 2, to ravage; ruin.

estrago (es'tra·γo) *n.m.* 1, ravage; ruin; havoc. 2, wickedness; depravity.

estragón (es·tra'γon) *n.m.* tarragon.

estrambótico (es·tram'bo·ti·ko) *adj.* eccentric; extravagant.

estrangular (es·tran·gu'lar) *v.t.* 1, to strangle; choke. 2, *med.* to strangulate. 3, *mech.* to throttle; choke. **—estrangulación,** *n.f.* strangulation; choking.

estraperlo (es·tra'per·lo) *n.m.* black market. **—estraperlista,** *n.m. & f.* black marketeer.

estratagema (es·tra·ta'xe·ma) *n.f.* 1, stratagem. 2, deception; trick. 3, craftiness.

estrategia (es·tra·te·xja) *n.f.* 1, strategy. 2, *fig.* craftiness. **—estratega** (-'te·γa) *also,* **estratego** (-'te·γo) *n.m.* strategist. **—estratégico** (-'te·xi·ko) *adj.* strategic. **—n.m.** strategist.

estratificar (es·tra·ti·fi'kar) *v.t.* [*infl.:* **tocar,** 7] to stratify. **—estratificación,** *n.f.* stratification.

estrato (es'tra·to) *n.m.* 1, stratum; layer; bed. 2, *meteorol.* stratus.

estratosfera (es·tra·tos'fe·ra) *n.f.* stratosphere.

estrechar (es·tre'tʃar) *v.t.* 1, to narrow. 2, to tighten. 3, to constrain; compel. **—estrecharse,** *v.r.* 1, to narrow; become narrow. 2, to tighten; become tight. 3, to restrict one's expenses. 4, to become more intimate; become friendlier. **—estrechar la mano,** to shake hands.

estrechez (es·tre'tʃeθ; -'tʃes) *n.f.* 1, narrowness. 2, tightness; snugness. 3, intimacy; closeness. 4, stinginess. 5, trouble; tight spot. 6, want; poverty.

estrecho (es'tre·tʃo) *adj.* 1, narrow. 2, tight; snug. 3, close; intimate. 4, strict; rigorous. 5, stingy. **—n.m.** strait.

estrechura (es·tre'tʃu·ra) *n.f.* 1, narrowness. 2, want; poverty.

estregar (es·tre'γar) *v.t.* [*infl.:* **pagar,** 8; **pensar,** 27] to rub; scrub; scour. **—estregamiento,** *n.m.* rubbing; scrubbing; scouring.

estrella (es'tre·ʎa; -ja) *n.f.* star. **—estrella fugaz,** shooting star. **—poner por las estrellas,** to praise to the skies.

estrellado (es·tre'ʎa·ðo; -'ja·ðo) *adj.* 1, starry. 2, *colloq.* smashed; cracked up. 3, (*of eggs*) sunny side up.

estrellamar (es·tre·ʎa'mar; -ja·'mar) *n.f.* [*also,* **estrella de mar**] starfish.

estrellar (es·tre'ʎar; -'jar) *v.t.* 1, to star; mark or sprinkle with stars. 2, *colloq.* to smash; dash to pieces. 3, to fry (eggs) sunny side up. **—estrellarse,** *v.r.* 1, to become starry. 2, to smash up; crash. 3, to fail; come to naught.

estrellón (es·tre'ʎon; -'jon) *n.m.* 1,

big star. **2,** *Amer.* smashup; crack-up. **—pegarse un estrellón,** *Amer., colloq.* to smash up; crash.

estremecer (es·tre·me'θer; -'ser) *v.t.* [*infl.:* conocer, 13] **1,** to shake; make tremble. **2,** to frighten; upset. **—estremecerse,** *v.r.* to tremble; shudder. **—estremecedor,** *adj.* frightening. **—estremecimiento,** *n.m.* shudder; tremor.

estrenar (es·tre'nar) *v.t.* **1,** to use for the first time. **2,** to open (a play, movie, etc.). **—estrenarse,** *v.r.* to make one's debut.

estreno (es'tre·no) *n.m.* **1,** opening; premiere. **2,** debut.

estrenuo (es'tre·nwo) *adj.* strenuous; vigorous. **—estrenuidad,** *n.f.* strenuousness; vigor.

estreñir (es·tre'ɲir) *v.t.* [*infl.:* reñir, 59] to constipate. **—estreñido,** *adj.* constipated. **—estreñimiento,** *n.m.* constipation.

estrépito (es'tre·pi·to) *n.m.* din; noise. **—estrepitoso,** *adj.* noisy; loud.

estreptococo (es·trep·to'ko·ko) *n.m.* streptococcus.

estreptomicina (es·trep·to·mi'θi·na; -'si·na) *n.f.* streptomycin.

estría (es'tri·a) *n.f.* groove; flute. **—estriado,** *adj.* striate; fluted. **—estriar,** *v.t.* [*infl.:* enviar, 22] to striate; flute.

estribación (es·tri·βa'θjon; -'sjon) *n.f.* foothill.

estribar (es·tri'βar) *v.i.* **1,** to rest; be supported. **2,** to be based.

estribillo (es·tri'βi·ʎo; -jo) *n.m.* refrain.

estribo (es'tri·βo) *n.m.* **1,** stirrup. **2,** abutment; buttress. **3,** running board; footboard. **4,** spur (*of a mountain range*). **—perder los estribos,** to lose one's head.

estribor (es·tri'βor) *n.m.* starboard.

estricnina (es·trik'ni·na) *n.f.* strychnine.

estricto (es'trik·to) *adj.* strict. **—estrictez,** *n.f., Amer.* strictness.

estridente (es·tri'ðen·te) *adj.* strident. **—estridencia,** *n.f.* stridency.

estriego (es'trje·ɣo) *v., pres.ind.* of estregar.

estriegue (es'trje·ɣe) *v., pres. subjve.* of estregar.

estro ('es·tro) *n.m.* estrus; rut.

estrobo (es'tro·βo) *n.m., naut.* grommet.

estroboscopio (es·tro·βos'ko·pjo) *n.m.* stroboscope.

estrofa (es'tro·fa) *n.f.* stanza; strophe.

estrógeno (es'tro·xe·no) *n.m.* estrogen.

estroncio (es'tron·θjo; -sjo) *n.m.* strontium.

estropajo (es·tro'pa·xo) *n.m.* **1,** scrubbing pad; scrub cloth. **2,** rag.

estropear (es·tro·pe'ar) *v.t.* **1,** to cripple; damage. **2,** to spoil.

estropeo (es·tro'pe·o) *n.m.* **1,** wear and tear. **2,** damage.

estructura (es·truk'tu·ra) *n.f.* structure. **—estructural,** *adj.* structural.

estruendo (es'trwen·do) *n.m.* **1,** thunderous noise. **2,** commotion; fracas. **3,** fanfare. **—estruendoso,** *adj.* thunderous.

estrujar (es·tru'xar) *v.t.* to squeeze. **—estrujadura,** *n.f., also,* **estrujamiento,** *n.m.* squeezing; squeeze.

estrujón (es·tru'xon) *n.m.* crush; squeeze.

estuario (es'twa·rjo) *n.m.* estuary.

estuco (es'tu·ko) *n.m.* stucco. **—estucado,** *n.m.* stuccowork. **—estucar** (-'kar) *v.t.* [*infl.:* tocar, 7] to stucco.

estuche (es'tu·tʃe) *n.m.* **1,** case; box; jewel box. **2,** *colloq.* man of many skills.

estudiante (es·tu'ðjan·te) *n.m. & f.* student. **—estudiantado** (-'ta·ðo) *n.m.* student body; students collectively. **—estudiantil** (-'til) *adj.* student (*attrib.*).

estudiar (es·tu'ðjar) *v.t.* to study.

estudio (es'tu·ðjo) *n.m.* **1,** study. **2,** studio.

estudioso (es·tu'ðjo·so) *adj.* studious.

estufa (es'tu·fa) *n.f.* **1,** stove; heater. **2,** hothouse; greenhouse. **3,** steam room; sauna.

estupefacto (es·tu·pe'fak·to) *adj.* stupefied. **—estupefacción,** *n.f.* stupefaction.

estupendo (es·tu'pen·do) *adj.* stupendous.

estúpido (es'tu·pi·ðo) *adj.* stupid. **—estupidez,** *n.f.* stupidity.

estupor (es·tu'por) *n.m.* **1,** stupor. **2,** stupefaction; amazement.

estuprar (es·tu'prar) *v.t.* to rape; violate. **—estuprador,** *n.m.* rapist. **—estupro** (-'tu·pro) *n.m.* rape, esp. statutory rape.

esturión (es·tu'rjon) *n.m.* sturgeon.

estuve (es·tu·βe) *v., 1st pers. sing. pret. of* **estar.**

esvástica (es·βas·ti·ka) *n.f.* swastika.

etano (e·ta·no) *n.m.* ethane.

etanol (e·ta·nol) *n.m.* ethanol.

etapa (e·ta·pa) *n.f.* **1,** *mil.* field ration. **2,** stage; step; phase.

etcétera (et·θe·te·ra; et·se-) *n.f.* et cetera.

éter ('e·ter) *n.m.* ether.

etéreo (e·te·re·o) *adj.* ethereal.

eternal (e·ter'nal) *adj.* = **eterno.**

eternamente (e·ter·na'men·te) *adv.* **1,** eternally; forever. **2,** evermore.

eterno (e·ter·no) *adj.* eternal. —**eternidad,** *n.f.* eternity. —**eternizar** (-ni'θar; -ni'sar) *v.t.* [*infl.;* **rezar, 10**] to perpetuate; prolong.

ética ('e·ti·ka) *n.f.* ethics. —**ético,** *adj.* ethical; ethic.

etileno (e·ti'le·no) *n.m.* ethylene.

etilo (e'ti·lo) *n.m.* ethyl.

etimología (e·ti·mo·lo'xi·a) *n.f.* etymology. —**etimológico** (-'lo·xi·ko) *adj.* etymological. —**etimologista,** *n.m.* & *f.* [*also,* **etimólogo** (-'mo·lo·ɣo) *n.m.*] etymologist.

etiología (e·tjo·lo'xi·a) *n.f.* etiology.

etíope (e'ti·o·pe) *also,* **etiope** (e'tjo·pe) *adj.* & *n.m.* & *f.* Ethiopian. —**etiópico** (e'tjo·pi·ko) *adj.* Ethiopian.

etiqueta (e·ti'ke·ta) *n.f.* **1,** etiquette. **2,** formality. **3,** label; tag. —**de etiqueta, 1,** formal. **2,** formally.

étnico ('et·ni·ko) *adj.* ethnic.

etnología (et·no·lo'xi·a) *n.f.* ethnology. —**etnológico** (-'lo·xi·ko) *adj.* ethnological. —**etnólogo** (-'no·lo·ɣo) *n.m.* ethnologist.

eucalipto (eu·ka'lip·to) *n.m.* eucalyptus.

Eucaristía (eu·ka·ris'ti·a) *n.f.* Eucharist. —**eucarístico** (-'ris·ti·ko) *adj.* Eucharistic.

eufemismo (eu·fe'mis·mo) *n.m.* euphemism. —**eufemístico,** *adj.* euphemistic.

eufonía (eu·fo'ni·a) *n.f.* euphony. —**eufónico** (-'fo·ni·ko) *adj.* euphonic; euphonious.

euforia (eu'fo·rja) *n.f.* euphoria. —**eufórico** (-'fo·ri·ko) *adj.* euphoric.

eugenesia (eu·xe'ne·sja) *n.f.* eugenics. —**eugenésico** (-'ne·si·ko) *adj.* eugenic.

eunuco (eu'nu·ko) *n.m.* eunuch.

eurásico (eu'ra·si·ko) *adj.* & *n.m.* Eurasian.

europeo (eu·ro'pe·o) *adj.* & *n.m.* European.

europio (eu'ro·pjo) *n.m.* europium.

eutanasia (eu·ta'na·sja) *n.f.* euthanasia.

evacuar (e·βa'kwar) *v.t.* & *i.* [*infl.:* **continuar, 23**] to evacuate —*v.t.* to discharge; fulfill. —**evacuación,** *n.f.* evacuation. —**evacuativo** (-kwa'ti·βo) *adj.* & *n.m* purgative.

evadir (e·βa'ðir) *v.t.* to escape; evade. —**evadirse,** *v.r.* to escape; get away; flee.

evaluar (e·βa'lwar) *v.t.* [*infl.:* **continuar, 23**] to evaluate. —**evaluación,** *n.f.* evaluation.

evanescente (e·βa·nes'θen·te; -ne'sen·te) *adj.* evanescent. —**evanescencia,** *n.f.* evanescence.

evangélico (e·βan'xe·li·ko) *adj.* **1,** evangelical. **2,** *also n.m.* Protestant.

evangelio (e·βan'xe·ljo) *n.m.* gospel; evangel. —**evangelismo** (-'lis·mo) *n.m.* evangelism. —**evangelista,** *n.m.* & *f.* evangelist.

evangelizar (e·βan·xe·li'θar; -'sar) *v.t.* [*infl.:* **rezar, 10**] to evangelize.

evaporar (e·βa·po'rar) *v.t.* to evaporate. —**evaporarse,** *v.r.* to vanish; evaporate. —**evaporación,** *n.f.* evaporation.

evaporizar (e·βa·po·ri'θar; -'sar) *v.t.* & *i.* = **vaporizar.** —**evaporización,** *n.f.* = **vaporización.**

evasión (e·βa'sjon) *n.f.* **1,** escape; flight. **2,** = **evasiva.**

evasiva (e·βa'si·βa) *n.f.* evasion; quibble. —**evasivo,** *adj.* evasive.

evasor (e·βa'sor) *adj.* evading; evasive. —*n.m.* evader; dodger.

evento (e'βen·to) *n.m.* event. —**eventual** (-'twal) *adj.* eventual. —**eventualidad,** *n.f.* eventuality.

evicción (e·βik'θjon; -'sjon) *n.f.* eviction.

evidencia (e·βi'ðen·θja; -sja) *n.f.* **1,** manifestness; obviousness. **2,** *Amer.* evidence; proof. —**evidenciar,** *v.t.* to evince; evidence. —**evidente,** *adj.* evident.

eviscerar (e·βis·θe'rar; e·βi·se-) *v.t.* to eviscerate. —**evisceración,** *n.f.* evisceration.

evitar (e·βi'tar) *v.t.* **1,** to prevent. **2,** to avoid.

evocar (e·βo'kar) *v.t.* [*infl.:* **tocar,**

7] to evoke. —**evocación,** *n.f.* evocation. —**evocador,** *adj.* evocative.

evolución (e·βo·lu'θjon; -'sjon) *n.f.* **1,** evolution; development. **2,** maneuver *(of troops or ships).*

evolucionar (e·βo·lu·θjo'nar; -sjo'nar) *v.i.* **1,** to evolve; develop. **2,** to engage in maneuvers; maneuver *(of ships or troops).* **3,** to become different; change *(in attitude or conduct).*

evolucionismo (e·βo·lu·θjo·'nis·mo; -sjo'nis·mo) *n.m.* evolutionism. —**evolucionista,** *adj.* evolutionary. —*n.m. & f.* evolutionist.

evolutivo (e·βo·lu'ti·βo) *adj.* evolutionary.

exacción (ek·sak'θjon; -'sjon) *n.f.* **1,** exaction. **2,** impost; tax.

exacerbar (ek·sa·θer'βar; -ser'βar) *v.t.* to exacerbate. —**exacerbación,** *n.f.* exacerbation.

exactitud (ek·sak·ti'tuð) *n.f.* **1,** precision; accuracy. **2,** exactitude. **3,** punctuality.

exacto (ek'sak·to) *adj.* **1,** exact; precise; accurate. **2,** punctual.

exagerar (ek·sa·xe'rar) *v.t.* to exaggerate. —**exageración,** *n.f.* exaggeration.

exaltado (ek·sal'ta·ðo) *adj.* **1,** excitable; hotheaded. **2,** exaggerated; extreme.

exaltar (ek·sal'tar) *v.t.* to exalt. —**exaltarse,** *v.r.* to be gripped by emotion; become elated. —**exaltación,** *n.f.* exaltation.

examen (ek'sa·men) *n.m.* examination.

examinar (ek·sa·mi'nar) *v.t.* to examine. —**examinarse,** *v.r.* to take an examination. —**examinador,** *n.m.* examiner.

exangüe (ek'san·gwe) *adj.* **1,** deprived of blood; bloodless. **2,** exhausted; spent. **3,** lifeless; dead.

exánime (ek'sa·ni·me) *adj.* **1,** unconscious. **2,** dead; lifeless. **3,** spiritless; dismayed.

exasperar (ek·sas·pe'rar) *v.t.* to exasperate. —**exasperación,** *n.f.* exasperation.

excarcelar (eks·kar·θe'lar; -se'lar) *v.t.* to release from prison.

excavar (eks·ka'βar) *v.t.* to excavate. —**excavación,** *n.f.* excavation. —**excavador,** *adj.* excavating. —*n.m.* excavator *(person).* —**excavadora,** *n.f.* excavator *(machine).*

excedente (eks·θe'ðen·te; eks·se-)

adj. excessive. —*adj. & n.m.* surplus; excess.

exceder (eks·θe'ðer; ek·se'ðer) *v.t.* to exceed; surpass. —*v.i.* [*also, v.r.,* **excederse**] to overstep oneself.

excelencia (eks·θe'len·θja; ek·se'len·sja) *n.f.* **1,** excellence; superiority. **2,** *cap.* Excellency. —**por excelencia,** par excellence.

excelente (eks·θe'len·te; ek·se-) *adj.* excellent. —**excelentísimo,** *adj.* most excellent.

excéntrico (eks'θen·tri·ko; ek'sen-) *adj.* eccentric. —**excéntrica,** *n.f.* [*also,* **excéntrico,** *n.m.*] *mech.* eccentric. —**excentricidad** (-θi'ðað; -si'ðað) *n.f.* eccentricity.

excepción (eks·θep'θjon; ek·sep'sjon) *n.f.* exception. —**excepcional,** *adj.* exceptional.

excepto (eks'θep·to; ek'sep·to) *adv.* except; excepting.

exceptuar (eks·θep'twar; ek·sep-) *v.t.* [*infl.:* **continuar, 23**] **1,** to except. **2,** to exempt.

excerpta (eks'θerp·ta; ek'serp-) *n.f.* excerpt; extract. *Also,* **exerta** (-ta).

exceso (eks'θe·so; ek'se-) *n.m.* excess. —**excesivo** (-'si·βo) *adj.* excessive.

excisión (eks·θi'sjon; ek·si-) *n.f.* excision.

excitable (eks·θi'ta·βle; ek·si-) *adj.* excitable. —**excitabilidad,** *n.f.* excitability.

excitación (eks·θi·ta'θjon; ek·si·ta'sjon) *n.f.* **1,** excitation. **2,** excitement.

excitado (eks·θi'ta·ðo; ek·si-) *adj.* excited; agitated.

excitante (eks·θi'tan·te; ek·si-) *adj.* exciting. —*n.m.* **1,** *elect.* exciter. **2,** stimulant.

excitar (eks·θi'tar; ek·si-) *v.t.* **1,** to excite. **2,** *elect.* to energize. —**excitarse,** *v.r.* to become excited.

exclamar (eks·kla'mar) *v.i.* to exclaim. —**exclamación,** *n.f.* exclamation. —**exclamatorio,** *also,* **exclamativo,** *adj.* exclamatory.

excluir (eks·klu'ir) *v.t.* [*infl.:* **huir, 26**] to exclude.

exclusión (eks·klu'sjon) *n.f.* exclusion.

exclusiva (eks·klu'si·βa) *n.f.* **1,** exclusion; denial of access. **2,** special privilege.

exclusive (eks·klu'si·βe) *adv.* exclusively. —*prep.* [*also,* **exclusive de**] not including; exclusive of.

exclusivo (eks·klu'si·βo) *adj.* exclusive. —**exclusivamente,** adv. exclusively. —**exclusividad,** n.f. exclusiveness. —**exclusivista,** adj. clannish; cliquish.

excluso (eks'klu·so) v., alt. p.p. of **excluir.**

excomulgado (eks·ko·mul'ɣa·ðo) adj. excommunicated. —n.m., colloq. miscreant.

excomulgar (eks·ko·mul'ɣar) v.t. [infl.: pagar, 8] **1,** to excommunicate. **2,** colloq. to ostracize.

excomunión (eks·ko·mu'njon) n.f. excommunication.

excoriar (eks·ko'rjar) v.t. **1,** to scrape off (the skin). **2,** fig. to excoriate; flay. —**excoriación,** n.f. excoriation.

excrecencia (eks·kre'θen·θja; -'sen·sja) n.f. excrescence. —**excrecente,** adj. excrescent.

excreción (eks·kre'θjon; -'sjon) n.f. excretion.

excremento (eks·kre'men·to) n.m. excrement.

excrescencia (eks·kres'θen·θja; -kre'sen·sja) n.f. = **excrecencia.**

excretar (eks·kre'tar) v.i. to excrete wastes.

exculpar (eks·kul'par) v.t. to exculpate. —**exculpación,** n.f. exculpation.

excursión (eks·kur'sjon) n.f. excursion; tour. —**excursionista,** n.m. & f. excursionist.

excusa (eks'ku·sa) n.f. **1,** excuse. **2,** law demurrer. —**a excusas,** cunningly; by subterfuge.

excusable (eks·ku·sa·βle) adj. excusable.

excusado (eks·ku·sa·ðo) adj. **1,** exempted; privileged. **2,** needless; unnecessary. **3,** reserved; private. —n.m. toilet; water closet.

excusar (eks·ku·sar) v.t. **1,** to excuse. **2,** to exempt. **3,** to eschew; avoid. **4,** fol. by inf. to excuse oneself from; refrain from. —**excusarse de,** to decline to.

execrar (ek·se'krar) v.t. to execrate. —**execrable,** adj. execrable. —**execración,** n.f. execration.

exégesis (ek'se·xe·sis) n.f.sing. & pl. exegesis. —**exégeta** (-ta) n.m. & f. exegete. —**exegético** (-'xe·ti·ko) adj. exegetic; exegetical.

exención (ek·sen'θjon; -'sjon) n.f. exemption.

exentar (ek·sen'tar) v.t. = **eximir.**

exento (ek'sen·to) adj. exempt; free; clear.

exequias (ek'se·kjas) n.f.pl. funeral rites.

exhalación (ek·sa·la'ðjon; -'sjon) n.f. **1,** exhalation. **2,** shooting star. **3,** flash; lightning.

exhalar (ek·sa'lar) v.t. to exhale. —**exhalarse,** v.r. = **desalarse.**

exhausto (ek'saus·to) adj. exhausted.

exhibición (ek·si·βi'θjon; -'sjon) n.f. exhibition. —**exhibicionismo,** n.m. exhibitionism. —**exhibicionista,** n.m. & f. exhibitionist.

exhibir (ek·si'βir) v.t. to exhibit; display.

exhortar (ek·sor'tar) v.t. to exhort. —**exhortación,** n.f. exhortation. —**exhortatorio,** adj. hortatory; exhortatory.

exhumar (ek·su'mar) v.t. to exhume. —**exhumación,** n.f. exhumation.

exigir (ek·si'xir) v.t. [infl.: coger, 15] to demand; require; exact. —**exigencia,** n.f. exigency; demand. —**exigente,** adj. exigent; demanding; exacting.

exiguo (ek'si·ɣwo) adj. exiguous; sparse; meager. —**exigüidad** (-ɣwi·'dad) n.f. exiguousness; meagerness.

exilio (ek'si·ljo) n.m. exile; banishment. —**exiliar** [also, Amer., **exilar** (-'lar)] v.t. to exile.

eximio (ek'si·mjo) adj. most excellent.

eximir (ek·si'mir) v.t. to exempt.

existencia (ek·sis'ten·θja; -sja) n.f. existence. —**existencias,** n.f.pl., comm. supply; stock.

existencial (ek·sis·ten'θjal; -'sjal) adj. existential. —**existencialismo,** n.m. existentialism. —**existencialista,** adj. & n.m. & f. existentialist.

existente (ek·sis'ten·te) adj. **1,** existent; extant. **2,** comm. on hand.

existir (ek·sis'tir) v.i. to exist.

éxito ('ek·si·to) n.m. **1,** end; termination. **2,** success. **3,** result; outcome. —**tener éxito,** to be successful.

exitoso (ek·si'to·so) adj., Amer. successful.

éxodo ('ek·so·ðo) n.m. exodus.

exonerar (ek·so·ne'rar) v.t. to exonerate. —**exonerar el vientre,** to move the bowels. —**exoneración,** n.f. exoneration.

exorbitante (ek·sor·βi'tan·te) adj. exorbitant. —**exorbitancia,** n.f. exorbitance.

exorcizar (ek·sor·θi'θar; -si'sar)

v.t. [*infl.:* **rezar, 10**] to exorcize.
—**exorcismo** (-'θis·mo; -'sis·mo)
n.m. exorcism. —**exorcista,** *n.m. &
f.* exorcist.

exotérico (ek·so·te·ri·ko) *adj.* exoteric.

exótico (ek'so·ti·ko) *adj.* exotic.
—**exotismo,** *n.m.* exoticism.

expandir (eks·pan'dir) *v.t., Amer.*
to expand.

expansible (eks·pan·si·βle) *adj.*
expansible.

expansión (eks·pan·sjon) *n.f.* **1,**
expansion. **2,** expansiveness. **3,** recreation; amusement.

expansionarse (eks·pan·
sjo'nar·se) *v.r.* **1,** to be or become
expansive. **2,** to rest or relax, esp.
by a change of activity.

expansivo (eks·pan'si·βo) *adj.* **1,**
expansive. **2,** expansile.

expatriar (eks·pa'trjar) *v.t.* [*infl.:*
enviar, 22] to exile; expatriate.
—**expatriarse,** *v.r.* to expatriate
oneself; leave one's country.
—**expatriación,** *n.f.* expatriation.
—**expatriado,** *adj. & n.m.* expatriate.

expectación (eks·pek·ta'θjon;
-'sjon) *n.f.* expectation; expectancy.
—**expectante,** *adj.* expectant.
—**expectativa,** *n.f.* expectation; expectancy. —**expectación de vida,**
life expectancy.

expectorar (eks·pek·to'rar) *v.t.* to
expectorate. —**expectoración,** *n.f.*
expectoration. —**expectorante,** *adj.
& n.m.* expectorant.

expedición (eks·pe·ði'θjon;
-'sjon) *n.f.* **1,** expedition. **2,** forwarding; sending; dispatch. —**expedicionario,** *adj.* expeditionary.
—*n.m.* **1,** member of an expedition.
2, sender; shipper.

expediente (eks·pe'ðjen·te) *n.m.*
1, expedient. **2,** dossier; record. **3,**
comm. procedure. **4,** *law* proceedings. **5,** expeditiousness; dispatch.

expedienteo (eks·pe·ðjen'te·o)
n.m. red tape.

expedir (eks·pe'ðir) *v.t.* [*infl.:*
pedir, 33] **1,** to expedite. **2,** to dispatch; send; forward. **3,** to issue
(a decree, order, etc.). —**expedidor,** *n.m.* [*fem.* -**dora**] sender; shipper.

expeditar (eks·pe·ði'tar) *v.t.,
Amer.* to expedite.

expeditivo (eks·pe·ði'ti·βo) *adj.*
expeditious.

expedito (eks·pe'ði·to) *adj.* **1,**
clear; unobstructed. **2,** ready.

expeler (eks·pe'ler) *v.t.* to expel;
eject. —**expelente,** *adj. & n.m. & f.*
expellant.

expender (eks·pen'der) *v.t.* **1,** to
expend; spend. **2,** to sell at retail.

expendio (eks'pen·djo) *n.m.* expenditure; expense.

expensas (eks'pen·sas) *n.f.pl.* expenses. —**a expensas de,** at the expense of.

experiencia (eks·pe'rjen·θja; -sja)
n.f. **1,** experience. **2,** experiment;
trial.

experimentar (eks·pe·ri·men'tar)
v.t. **1,** to experiment with; test. **2,** to
experience. —**experimentación,**
n.f. experimentation. —**experimentado,** *adj.* experienced.

experimento (eks·pe·ri'men·to)
n.m. experiment. —**experimental,**
adj. experimental.

experto (eks'per·to) *adj. & n.m.*
expert.

expiar (eks·pi'ar) *v.t.* [*infl.:* **enviar,
22**] to expiate; atone for.
—**expiación,** *n.f.* expiation; atonement.

expirar (eks·pi'rar) *v.i.* to expire.
—**expiración,** *n.f.* expiration.

explanada (eks·pla'na·ða) *n.f.* esplanade.

explayarse (eks·pla'jar·se) *v.r.* **1,**
to expatiate. **2,** to find solace; unburden oneself.

expletivo (eks·ple'ti·βo) *adj.* expletive.

explicable (eks·pli'ka·βle) *adj.*
explicable.

explicación (eks·pli·ka'θjon;
-'sjon) *n.f.* explanation.

explicar (eks·pli'kar) *v.t.* [*infl.:*
tocar, 7] to explain. —**explicarse,**
v.r. to make oneself understood.
—**explicarse una cosa,** to understand something.

explicativo (eks·pli·ka'ti·βo) *adj.*
explanatory; expository.

explícito (eks'pli·θi·to; -si·to) *adj.*
explicit.

explorador (eks·plo·ra'ðor) *adj.*
exploring. —*n.m.* **1,** explorer. **2,**
cap. Boy Scout. **3,** *elect.; comput.*
scanner.

explorar (eks·plo'rar) *v.t.* **1,** to explore. **2,** to scout; reconnoiter.
—**exploración,** *n.f.* exploration.
—**exploratorio,** *adj.* exploratory.

explosión (eks·plo'sjon) *n.f.* explosion. —**explosivo** (-'si·βo) adj. & n.m. explosive.

explotación (eks·plo·ta'θjon; -'sjon) n.f. 1, exploitation; development. 2, plant; works. 3, working; operation.

explotar (eks·plo'tar) v.t. 1, to exploit; develop. 2, to work; run; operate. —v.i. to explode.

exponente (eks·po'nen·te) adj. indicating; typifying. —n.m. exponent. —**exponencial** (-'θjal; -'sjal) adj. & n.f. exponential.

exponer (eks·po'ner) v.t. [infl.: poner, 54] 1, to expose; exhibit. 2, to endanger; risk. 3, to reveal; disclose. 4, to expound. —**exponerse**, v.r. to hazard; venture; risk.

exportar (eks·por'tar) v.t. to export. —**exportación**, n.f. exportation; export. —**exportador**, adj. exporting. —n.m. exporter.

exposición (eks·po·si'θjon; -'sjon) n.f. 1, exposition. 2, exposure. 3, exhibit; exhibition; fair.

expositivo (eks·po·si'ti·βo) adj. expository.

expósito (eks'po·si·to) adj. abandoned. —n.m. [fem. expósita] foundling.

expositor (eks·po·si'tor) n.m. 1, exponent; expositor. 2, commentator. 3, exhibitor. —adj. expository.

expresamente (eks·pre·sa'men·te) adv. 1, expressly. 2, clearly; decisively.

expresar (eks·pre'sar) v.t. to express; manifest. —**expresado**, adj. aforesaid; aforementioned.

expresión (eks·pre'sjon) n.f. expression.

expresivo (eks·pre'si·βo) adj. 1, expressive. 2, affectionate.

expreso (eks'pre·so) v., irreg. p.p. of **expresar**. —adj. 1, expressed; evident. 2, express; special. 3, clear; decisive. —adv. = **expresamente**. —n.m. 1, Amer. special delivery. 2, express agency. 3, express train.

exprimir (eks·pri'mir) v.t. 1, to squeeze; extract. 2, to wring. —**exprimidor**, n.m., also, **exprimidera**, n.f. juice extractor; wringer.

expropiar (eks·pro'pjar) v.t. to expropriate. —**expropiación**, n.f. expropriation.

expuesto (eks'pwes·to) v., p.p. of **exponer**. —adj. 1, exposed. 2, displayed. 3, liable. 4, at risk; in danger.

expugnar (eks·puɣ'nar) v.t. to

storm; take by storm. —**expugnación**, n.f. storming; taking by storm.

expulsar (eks·pul'sar) v.t. to expel; eject. —**expulsión** (-'sjon) n.f. expulsion; ejection. —**expulsivo** (-'si·βo) adj. & n.m. expellant. —**expulsor**, n.m. ejector (of a firearm).

expurgar (eks·pur'ɣar) v.t. [infl.: pagar, 8] 1, to expurgate. 2, to purge; purify. —**expurgo** (-'pur·ɣo) n.m., also, **expurgación**, n.f. expurgation.

exquisito (eks·ki'si·to) adj. exquisite. —**exquisitez**, n.f. exquisiteness.

extasiar (eks·ta'sjar) v.t. to delight. —**extasiarse**, v.r. to be delighted; be enraptured.

éxtasis ('eks·ta·sis) n.m. ecstasy. —**extático** (-'ta·ti·ko) adj. ecstatic.

extemporáneo (eks·tem·po'ra·ne·o) adj. 1, untimely; inopportune. 2, curt; abrupt.

extender (eks·ten'der) v.t. [infl.: perder, 29] 1, to extend; spread; stretch. 2, to draw up (a document). —**extenderse**, v.r. 1, to extend; spread; stretch out. 2, to expatiate.

extendido (eks·ten'di·ðo) adj. 1, extended; stretched out. 2, spacious; roomy. 3, general; widespread.

extensible (eks·ten'si·βle) adj. extensible.

extensión (eks·ten'sjon) n.f. 1, extension. 2, extent. 3, expanse. 4, geom. space; dimension.

extensivo (eks·ten'si·βo) adj. extensive; ample.

extenso (eks'ten·so) adj. 1, extended. 2, extensive.

extenuación (eks·te·nwa'θjon; -'sjon) n.f. 1, extenuation. 2, emaciation; exhaustion; enervation.

extenuado (eks·te'nwa·ðo) adj. 1, extenuated. 2, emaciated; exhausted; enervated.

extenuar (eks·te'nwar) v.t. [infl.: continuar, 23] to weaken; enervate.

exterior (eks·te'rjor) adj. & n.m. exterior; outside. —adj. foreign; external. —n.m. outward appearance.

exterioridad (eks·te·rjo·ri'ðað) n.f. 1, exterior thing. 2, demeanor; outward appearance.

exteriorizar (eks·te·rjo·ri'θar; -'sar) v.t. [infl.: rezar, 10] to make manifest; reveal.

exterminar (eks·ter·mi'nar) v.t. to

exterminate. —**exterminador,** *adj.*
exterminating. —*n.m.* exterminator.
exterminio (eks·ter'mi·njo) *n.m.*
extermination.
externo (eks'ter·no) *adj.* **1,** external. **2,** outward. —*n.m.* [*fem.* **externa**] day pupil.
extinción (eks·tin'θjon; -'sjon) *n.f.*
extinction; extinguishment.
extinguir (eks·tin'gir) *v.t.* [*infl.:*
distinguir, 17] to extinguish.
extinto (eks'tin·to) *adj.* **1,** extinguished. **2,** extinct.
extintor (eks·tin'tor) *n.m.* fire
extinguisher.
extirpar (eks·tir'par) *v.t.* to extirpate. —**extirpación,** *n.f.* extirpation.
extorsión (eks·tor'sjon) *n.f.* extortion. —**extorsionar,** *v.t.* to extort.
—**extorsionador,** *n.m.* [*fem.* **-dora**]
extortionist.
extra ('eks·tra) *prep.* without; besides; outside of. —*adj., colloq.*
extra; extraordinary; remarkable. —*n.m. or f.* extra.
extracción (eks·trak'θjon; -'sjon)
n.f. extraction.
extractar (eks·trak'tar) *v.t.* to abstract; abridge.
extracto (eks'trak·to) *n.m.* **1,** extract. **2,** summary; abstract. **3,**
number drawn in a lottery.
extractor (eks·trak'tor) *adj.* ex-
tracting. —*n.m.* extractor.
extracurricular (eks·tra·ku-
rri·ku'lar) *adj.* extracurricular.
extradición (eks·tra·ði'θjon;
-'sjon) *n.f.* extradition.
extraer (eks·tra'er) *v.t.* [*infl.:*
traer, 67] to extract.
extranjero (eks·tran'xe·ro) *adj.*
foreign; alien. —*n.m.* alien; foreigner. —**en el extranjero; al extranjero,** abroad.
extrañar (eks·tra'ɲar) *v.t.* **1,** to
banish; exile. **2,** to wonder at; be
amazed at. **3,** *Amer.* to miss; feel the
lack of.
extrañeza (eks·tra'ɲe·θa; -sa) *n.f.*
1, oddity; strangeness. **2,** wonderment; amazement.
extraño (eks·tra'ɲo) *adj.* **1,**
strange. **2,** extraneous; foreign.
extraordinario (eks·tra·or·ði-
'na·rjo) *adj.* extraordinary.
extrapolar (eks·tra·po'lar) *v.t.* to
extrapolate. —**extrapolación,** *n.f.*
extrapolation.
extraterrestre (eks·tra·te'rres-

tre) *adj.* extraterrestrial. —**extrate-
rreno** (-te'rre·no) *adj. & n.m.* extraterrestrial.
extraterritorial (eks·tra·te-
rri·to'rjal) *adj.* extraterritorial.
extravagante (eks·tra·βa'ɣan·te)
adj. extravagant. —**extravagancia,**
n.f. extravagance.
extravelocidad (eks·tra·βe-
lo·θi'ðað; -si'ðað) *n.f.* excessive
speed; speeding.
extraversión (eks·tra·βer'sjon)
n.f., psychol. extroversion.
extravertido (eks·tra·βer'ti·ðo)
adj. extroverted. —*n.m.* extrovert.
extraviado (eks·tra'βja·ðo) *adj.*
1, stray; wandering. **2,** strayed; mislaid. **3,** of unsound mind.
extraviar (eks·tra'βjar) *v.t.* [*infl.:*
enviar, 22] **1,** to lead astray. **2,** to
mislay; misplace. —**extraviarse,**
v.r. **1,** to go astray; lose one's way.
2, to err; deviate.
extravío (eks·tra'βi·o) *n.m.* **1,** deviation. **2,** going astray; straying. **3,**
misplacement. **4,** aberration; irregularity.
extremado (eks·tre'ma·ðo) *adj.*
extreme; excessive.
extremar (eks·tre'mar) *v.t.* to
carry to extreme. —**extremarse,** *v.r.*
to take special pains.
extremaunción (eks·tre·ma-
un'θjon; -'sjon) *n.f.* extreme unction.
extremidad (eks·tre·mi'ðað) *n.f.*
1, end; extremity. **2,** brink; border.
extremista (eks·tre'mis·ta) *n.m.*
& *f.* extremist.
extremo (eks'tre·mo) *adj.* extreme.
—*n.m.* **1,** end; extremity. **2,** extreme; utmost. —**en** *or* **por
extremo,** extremely.
extremoso (eks·tre'mo·so) *adj.*
extreme; vehement. —**extremosidad,** *n.f.* extremeness; vehemence.
extrínseco (eks'trin·se·ko) *adj.*
extrinsic.
extroversión (eks·tro·βer'sjon)
n.f. = **extraversión.** —**extrovertido**
adj. & n.m. = **extravertido.**
extrusión (eks·tru'sjon) *n.f.* extrusion (*of plastics, metals, etc.*).
exuberancia (ek·su·βe'ran·θja;
-sja) *n.f.* exuberance. —**exuberante,** *adj.* exuberant.
exudar (ek·su'ðar) *v.i.* to exude.
—**exudación,** *n.f.* exudation.
exultar (ek·sul'tar) *v.i.* to exult.
—**exultación,** *n.f.* exultation.
eyacular (e·ja·ku'lar) *v.t.* to ejacu-

late. —**eyaculación**, *n.f.* ejaculation.

eyector (e·jek'tor) *n.m.* ejector *(of a firearm)*.

F

F, f ('e·fe) *n.f.* 7th letter of the Spanish alphabet.

fa (fa) *n.m., mus.* fa; F.

fábrica ('fa·βri·ka) *n.f.* 1, factory; plant; mill. 2, fabric.

fabricar (fa·βri'kar) *v.t.* [*infl.:* **tocar, 7**] to manufacture; build; fabricate. —**fabricación**, *n.f.* manufacture; fabrication. —**fabricante**, *n.m.* manufacturer; builder. —**fabril** (fa'βril) *adj.* manufacturing.

fábula ('fa·βu·la) *n.f.* fable. —**fabulista**, *n.m.* & *f.* fabulist. —**fabuloso**, *adj.* fabulous.

facción (fak'θjon; -'sjon) *n.f.* faction; opposing group.

facciones (fak'θjo·nes; -'sjo·nes) *n.f.pl.* facial features.

faccioso (fak'θjo·so; -'sjo·so) *adj.* 1, partisan. 2, rebellious; factious. —*n.m.* rebel. —**faccionalismo**, *n.m.* factionalism.

faces ('fa·θes; -ses) *n.f., pl.* of **faz**.

faceta (fa'θe·ta; -'se·ta) *n.f.* facet.

facial (fa'θjal; -'sjal) *adj.* facial.

fácil ('fa·θil; -sil) *adj.* easy; facile. —**facilidad**, *n.f.* ease; facility.

facilitación (fa·θi·li·ta'θjon; fa·si·li·ta'sjon) *n.f.* 1, facilitation. 2, supplying; supply.

facilitar (fa·θi·li'tar; fa·si-) *v.t.* 1, to facilitate. 2, to supply; furnish.

facineroso (fa·θi·ne'ro·so; fa·si-) *adj.* wicked; rascally. —*n.m.* rascal; criminal.

facsímile (fak'si·mi·le) *n.m.* facsimile; *comput.* fax. *Also,* **facsímil** (-mil).

factible (fak'ti·βle) *adj.* feasible. —**factibilidad**, *n.f.* feasibility.

facticio (fak'ti·θjo; -sjo) *adj.* factitious.

factor (fak'tor) *n.m.* 1, factor; element. 2, *R.R.* baggagemaster. 3, *comm.* commission merchant; factor. —**factoraje**, *n.m., comm.* factoring. —**factorial**, *adj.* factorial.

factoría (fak·to'ri·a) *n.f.* 1, trading post. 2, *W.I.* factory. 3, *comm.* factoring. 4, *comm.* office of a factor.

factorizar (fak·to·ri'θar; -'sar) *v.t., Amer., math.* [*infl.:* **rezar, 10**] to factor.

factura (fak'tu·ra) *n.f.* invoice.

facturar (fak·tu'rar) *v.t.* 1, to invoice; bill. 2, *R.R.* to check (baggage). —**facturación**, *n.f.* invoicing; billing.

facultad (fa·kul'taδ) *n.f.* 1, faculty; capacity. 2, authority; authorization. 3, *educ.* faculty; department.

facultar (fa·kul'tar) *v.t.* to authorize; empower.

facultativo (fa·kul·ta'ti·βo) *n.m.* physician; surgeon. —*adj.* 1, facultative. 2, optional.

facundia (fa'kun·dja) *n.f.* eloquence. —**facundo** (-do) *adj.* eloquent.

facha ('fa·tʃa) *n f , colloq.* 1, appearance. 2, ludicrous person.

fachada (fa'tʃa·δa) *n.f.* 1, façade. 2, title page. 3, appearance; build. —**hacer fachada a**, to front on.

fachenda (fa'tʃen·da) *n.f.* airs; pretentiousness. —**fachendoso**, *adj.* pretentious.

faena (fa'e·na) *n.f.* task.

faetón (fa·e'ton) *n.m.* phaeton.

fagocito (fa·yo'θi·to; -'si·to) *n.m.* phagocyte.

fagot (fa'got) *n.m.* 1, bassoon. 2, bassoonist. —**fagotista**, *n.m.* & *f.* bassoonist.

Fahrenheit (fa·ren'xait; -'xeit) *n.m.* Fahrenheit.

faisán (fai'san) *n.m.* pheasant.

faja ('fa·xa) *n.f.* 1, girdle. 2, band; strip.

fajar (fa'xar) *v.t.* 1, to girdle. 2, to swaddle. 3, to bandage. 4, *Amer., colloq.* to beat; maul. —**fajarse**, *v.r.* 1, *Amer., colloq.* to fight; brawl. 2, to put on a girdle.

falacia (fa'la·θja; -sja) *n.f.* 1, deceit. 2, fallacy.

falange (fa'lan·xe) *n.f.* 1, phalanx. 2, *cap.* Falange. —**Falangista**, *n.m.* & *f.* Falangist.

falaz (fa'laθ; -'las) *adj.* 1, deceitful. 2, fallacious.

falda ('fal·da) *n.f.* 1, skirt. 2, flap; fold. 3, foothill. 4, *chiefly W.I.* lap. —**faldas**, *n.f.pl., colloq.* women; females.

faldear (fal·de'ar) *v.t.* to skirt (a hill).

faldero (fal'de·ro) *adj.* skirt (*attrib.*); lap (*attrib.*).

faldilla (fal'di·ʎa; -ja) *n.f.* flap (*of a garment*).

faldón (fal'don) *n.m.* **1,** flowing skirt. **2,** coattail; shirttail. **3,** gable.

falible (fa'li·βle) *adj.* fallible. —**falibilidad,** *n.f.* fallibility.

falo ('fa·lo) *n.m.* phallus. —**fálico,** *adj.* phallic.

falsario (fal'sa·rjo) *n.m.* faker; deceiver.

falsear (fal·se'ar) *v.t.* to falsify; misrepresent. —*v.i.* to weaken.

falsedad (fal·se'ðað) *n.f.* falsity; falsehood.

falsete (fal'se·te) *n.m.* **1,** falsetto. **2,** plug; bung.

falsía (fal'si·a) *n.f.* falsity; duplicity.

falsificar (fal·si·fi'kar) *v.t.* [*infl.:* **tocar, 7**] to counterfeit; forge; falsify. —**falsificación,** *n.f.* forgery; falsification. —**falsificador,** *n.m.* forger; counterfeiter.

falso ('fal·so) *adj.* **1,** false. **2,** forged; counterfeit. —*n.m., sewing* facing; padding. —**en falso, 1,** false(ly). **2,** mistaken(ly). **3,** improper(ly).

falta ('fal·ta) *n.f.* **1,** lack; want. **2,** fault; mistake. **3,** *colloq.* defect; flaw. **4,** misbehavior; misdemeanor. —**hacer falta,** to be wanting; be lacking; be needed. —**sin falta,** without fail.

faltar (fal'tar) *v.i.* **1,** to be lacking; be wanting; be needed. **2,** to fail; be derelict. **3,** to be absent. **4,** to offend. —**faltar a su palabra,** to break one's word. —**¡no faltaba más!,** the idea! what nonsense!

falto ('fal·to) *adj.* **1,** *fol. by* de, lacking; wanting. **2,** mean; base; low. **3,** *Amer.* stupid; cloddish.

faltriquera (fal·tri'ke·ra) *n.f.* **1,** purse. **2,** pocket.

falúa (fa'lu·a) *n.f., naut.* tender.

falla ('fa·ʎa; -ja) *n.f.* **1,** defect; flaw. **2,** *Amer.* fault; mistake. **3,** *geol.* fault.

fallada (fa'ʎa·ða; -'ja·ða) *n.f. cards* act of trumping; ruff.

fallar (fa'ʎar; -'jar) *v.i.* **1,** to fail. **2,** to miss. —*v.t. & i., law* to render judgment (on); pass sentence (on). —*v.t., cards* to trump.

fallecer (fa·ʎe'θer; -je'ser) *v.i.* [*infl.:* **conocer, 13**] to die; die out.

—**fallecido,** *adj.* late; dead. —**fallecimiento,** *n.m.* death.

fallido (fa'ʎi·ðo; -'ji·ðo) *adj.* **1,** frustrated; unsuccessful. **2,** bankrupt.

fallo ('fa·ʎo; -jo) *n.m.* **1,** decision; judgment. **2,** *law* verdict; sentence. —**estar fallo,** *cards* to be unable to follow suit.

fama ('fa·ma) *n.f.* fame; reputation. —**correr fama,** to be rumored.

famélico (fa'me·li·ko) *adj.* famished.

familia (fa'mi·lja) *n.f.* family.

familiar (fa·mi'ljar) *adj.* **1,** familial; domestic. **2,** familiar. —*n.m.* **1,** relative. **2,** house servant. **3,** familiar. —**familiaridad,** *n.f.* familiarity.

familiarizar (fa·mi·lja·ri'θar; -'sar) *v.t.* [*infl.:* **rezar, 10**] to familiarize.

famoso (fa'mo·so) *adj.* famous.

fanático (fa'na·ti·ko) *adj.* fanatic; fanatical. —*n.m.* fanatic. —**fanatismo,** *n.m.* fanaticism.

fandango (fan'dan·go) *n.m.* **1,** fandango. **2,** *colloq.* hullabaloo.

fanega (fa'ne·ɣa) *n.f.* Spanish grain measure (*about 1.5 bushels.*) —**fanega de tierra,** Spanish land measure (*about 1.6 acres*).

fanfarria (fan'fa·rrja) *n.f.* ostentation; fanfare.

fanfarrón (fan·fa'rron) *n.m.* braggart. —*adj.* boastful. —**fanfarronada** (fan·fa·rro'na·da) *n.f.* boast. —**fanfarronear** (-ne'ar) *v.i.* to boast; brag. —**fanfarronería,** *n.f.* boasting.

fango ('fan·go) *n.m.* mud; mire. —**fangal,** *n.m.* bog. —**fangoso,** *adj.* muddy.

fantasía (fan·ta'si·a) *n.f.* fantasy. —**de fantasía,** imitation (*of jewelry*).

fantasma (fan'tas·ma) *n.m.* phantom; ghost.

fantasmagoria (fan·tas·ma·'ɣo·rja) *n.f.* phantasmagoria. —**fantasmagórico** (-'ɣo·ri·ko) *adj.* phantasmagoric.

fantástico (fan'tas·ti·ko) *adj.* **1,** fantastic. **2,** *colloq.* swell; great.

fantoche (fan'to·tʃe) *n.m.* puppet.

fañoso (fa'ɲo·so) *adj., Amer.* nasal; twangy.

faquir (fa'kir) *n.m.* fakir.

faradio (fa'ra·ðjo) *n.m.* farad. *Also,* **farad** (fa'rað).

faralá (fa·ra'la) *n.m.* frill.

farallón (fa·ra'ʎon; -'jon) *n.m.* cliff; palisade.

faramalla (fa·ra'ma·ʎa; -ja) *n.f.*, *colloq.* show; affectation; frill.

farándula (fa'ran·du·la) *n.f.* **1**, theatrical troupe. **2**, bohemian life.

Faraón (fa·ra'on) *n.m.* **1**, Pharaoh. **2**, *l.c.* faro.

fardo ('far·ðo) *n.m.* bale; bundle. —**pasar el fardo,** *Amer., colloq.* to pass the buck.

farfolla (far'fo·ʎa; -ja) *n.f.* claptrap; nonsense.

farfulla (far'fu·ʎa; -ja) *n.f., colloq.* **1**, sputtering; stumbling. **2**, mumbling. **3**, [*also,* **farfolla**] idle talk; nonsense.

farfullar (far·fu'ʎar; -'jar) *v.t. & i., colloq.* **1**, to sputter; stumble (over). **2**, to mumble.

farináceo (fa·ri'na·θe·o; -se·o) *adj.* farinaceous.

faringe (fa'rin·xe) *n.f.* pharynx. —**faríngeo** (-xe·o), pharyngeal. —**faringitis,** *n.f.* pharyngitis.

fariseo (fa·ri'se·o) *n.m.* pharisee. —**farisaico** (-'sai·ko) *adj.* pharisaic.

farmacéutico (far·ma'θeu·ti·ko; -'seu·ti·ko) *n.m.* pharmacist; druggist. —*adj.* pharmaceutical.

farmacia (far'ma·θja; -sja) *n.f.* pharmacy.

farmacología (far·ma·ko·lo'xi·a) *n.f.* pharmacology. —**farmacológico** (-'lo·xi·ko) *adj.* pharmacological. —**farmacólogo** (-'ko·lo·go) *n.m.* [*fem.* **-ga**] pharmacologist.

farmacopea (far·ma·ko'pe·a) *n.f.* pharmacopeia.

faro ('fa·ro) *n.m.* **1**, lighthouse. **2**, beacon. **3**, floodlight. **4**, headlight. **5**, faro.

farol (fa'rol) *n.m.* **1**, lantern; headlight; street lamp. **2**, *fig.* bluff (*esp. in games*). **3**, *colloq.* = **fanfarrón.** —**farolear** (-le'ar) *v.i., colloq.* to boast; swagger.

farola (fa'ro·la) *n.f.* **1**, large street lamp. **2**, lighthouse.

farolero (fa·ro'le·ro) *n.m.* **1**, lamplighter. **2**, *colloq.* braggart. —*adj.* boastful.

farra ('fa·rra) *n.f., Amer.* spree.

farruco (fa'rru·ko) *adj.* **1**, bold; daring. **2**, *colloq.* impudent; saucy. —*n.m., Amer., colloq.* Galician or Asturian immigrant.

farsa ('far·sa) *n.f.* farce. —**farsante,** *adj. & n.m. & f.* fake.

fascículo (fas'θi·ku·lo; fa'si-) *n.m.* fascicle.

fascinar (fas·θi'nar; fa·si-) *v.t.* fascinate. —**fascinación,** *n.f.* fascination.

fascismo (fas'θis·mo; fa'sis-) *n.m.* fascism. —**fascista,** *n.m. & f.* fascist. —*adj.* fascistic.

fase ('fa·se) *n.f.* phase.

fastidiar (fas·ti'ðjar) *v.t.* **1**, to bother; bore. **2**, to disrupt; upset. —**fastidio** (-'ti·ðjo) *n.m.* boredom; nuisance. —**fastidioso,** *adj.* boring.

fasto ('fas·to) *adj.* auspicious; fortunate. —*n.m.* pomp, spectacle.

fastuoso (fas'two·so) *adj.* ostentatious.

fatal (fa'tal) *adj.* **1**, fatal. **2**, fateful. —**fatalidad** (fa·ta·li'ðað) *n.f.* **1**, fate; destiny. **2**, calamity; misfortune. **3**, fatality.

fatalismo (fa·ta'lis·mo) *n.m.* fatalism. —**fatalista,** *n.m. & f.* fatalist. —*adj.* fatalistic.

fatídico (fa'ti·ði·ko) *adj.* fateful.

fatiga (fa'ti·ya) *n.f.* **1**, fatigue. **2**, hardship; bother. —**fatigoso,** *adj.* tiring; tiresome.

fatigar (fa·ti'yar) *v.t.* [*infl.:* **pagar, 8**] to tire; fatigue.

fatuo ('fa·two) *adj.* fatuous. —**fatuidad,** *n.f.* fatuity.

fauna ('fau·na) *n.f.* fauna.

fauno ('fau·no) *n.m.* faun.

fausto ('faus·to) *n.m.* pomp; splendor. —*adj.* fortunate.

favor (fa'βor) *n.m.* favor. —**a favor de, 1**, in behalf of. **2**, in favor of. —**favor de,** *fol. by inf., Amer.* please. —**por favor,** please; if you please.

favorable (fa·βo'ra·βle) *adj.* favorable.

favorecer (fa·βo·re'θer; -'ser) *v.t.* [*infl.:* **conocer, 13**] to favor. —**favorecedor,** *adj.* favoring; becoming.

favorito (fa·βo'ri·to) *n.m. & adj.* favorite. —**favoritismo,** *n.m.* favoritism.

faz (faθ; fas) *n.f.* [*pl.* **faces**] face.

fe (fe) *n.f.* **1**, faith. **2**, testimony. —**dar fe, 1**, *fol. by* **de,** to attest. **2**, *fol. by* **a,** to believe; credit.

fealdad (fe·al'dað) *n.f.* ugliness.

febrero (fe'βre·ro) *n.m.* February.

febrífugo (fe'βri·fu·ɣo) *n.m.* febrifuge.

febril (fe'βril) *adj.* feverish.

fecal (fe'kal) *adj.* fecal.

fécula ('fe·ku·la) *n.f.* starch.

fecundo (fe'kun·do) *adj.* fecund. —**fecundar,** *v.t.* to fecundate.

—**fecundación,** *n.f.* fecundation.
—**fecundidad,** *n.f.* fecundity.
fecha ('fe·tʃa) *n.f.* date; day.
—**fechar,** *v.t.* to date. —**para estas
fechas,** by this time *(in the future).*
—**por estas fechas,** at this time *(in
the past).*
fechoría (fe·tʃo'ri·a) *n.f.* misdeed;
atrocity.
federal (fe·ðe'ral) *adj.* federal.
—**federalismo,** *n.m.* federalism.
—**federalista,** *n.m. & f.* federalist.
federar (fe·ðe'rar) *v.t.* to federate.
—**federación,** *n.f.* federation.
fehaciente (fe·a'θjen·te; -'sjen·te)
adj. authentic; genuine.
feldespato (fel·des'pa·to) *n.m.*
feldspar.
felicidad (fe·li·θi'ðað; -si'ðað) *n.f.*
happiness; good fortune. —**¡felicidades!,** congratulations!
felicitar (fe·li·θi'tar; -si'tar) *v.t.* to
congratulate. —**felicitación,** *n.f.*
congratulation.
feligrés (fe·li'ɣres) *n.m.* [*fem.*
-**gresa**] parishioner.
feligresía (fe·li·ɣre'si·a) *n.f.* **1,**
parish. **2,** parishioners collectively.
felino (fe'li·no) *adj. & n.m.* feline.
feliz (fe'liθ; -'lis) *adj.* happy.
—**Felices Pascuas** *or* **Navidades,**
Merry Christmas.
felón (fe'lon) *n.m.* felon; criminal.
—*adj.* criminal. —**felonía,** *n.f.* misdeed.
felpa ('fel·pa) *n.f.* plush.
felpilla (fel'pi·ʎa; -ja) *n.f.* chenille.
felpudo (fel'pu·ðo) *adj.* plushy.
—*n.m.* mat; plush mat.
femenil (fe·me'nil) *adj.* womanly;
womanish.
femenino (fe·me'ni·no) *adj.* feminine.
fementido (fe·men'ti·ðo) *adj.*
false; unfaithful.
femineidad (fe·mi·nei'ðað)
also, **feminidad** (-ni'ðað) *n.f.* femininity.
feminismo (fe·mi'nis·mo) *n.m.*
feminism. —**feminista,** *n.m & f.*
feminist.
fémur ('fe·mur) *n.m.* femur.
—**femoral** (-mo'ral) *adj.* femoral.
fenecer (fe·ne'θer; -'ser) *v.t.* [*infl.:*
conocer, 13] to finish; settle. —*v.i.*
to die; end. —**fenecido** (-'θi·ðo;
-'si-) *adj.* dead, deceased.
fenicio (fe'ni·θjo; -sjo) *adj. & n.m.*
Phoenician.
fénico ('fe·ni·ko) *adj.* carbolic.
fénix ('fe·niks) *n.m.* phoenix.

fenobárbito (fe·no'βar·βi·to) *n.m.*
phenobarbital.
fenol (fe'nol) *n.m.* phenol.
fenómeno (fe'no·me·no) *n.m.* phenomenon. —**fenomenal,** *adj.* phenomenal.
feo ('fe·o) *adj.* ugly; unbecoming.
—*n.m.* snub; slight. —**dar feo a,** to
insult. —**sexo feo,** the male sex.
feracidad (fe·ra·θi'ðað; -si'ðað)
n.f. fertility.
feral (fe'ral) *adj.* wild; feral.
feraz (fe'raθ; -'ras) *adj.* fruitful; fertile.
féretro ('fe·re·tro) *n.m.* coffin.
feria ('fe·rja) *n.f.* fair; market.
—**día feriado,** holiday.
feriante (fe'rjan·te) *n.m. & f.* peddler; hawker, esp. at fairs.
fermentar (fer·men'tar) *v.t. & i.* to
ferment. —**fermentación,** *n.f.* fermentation. —**fermento** (-'men·to)
n.m. ferment.
fermio ('fer·mjo) *n.m.* fermium.
feroz (fe'roθ;-'ros) *adj.* ferocious.
—**ferocidad** (-θi'ðað; -si'ðað) *n.f.*
ferocity.
férreo ('fe·rre·o) *adj.* **1,** ferrous;·
iron *(attrib.).* **2,** *fig.* stern; inflexible. —**via férrea,** railroad.
ferretería (fe·rre·te'ri·a) *n.f.* **1,**
hardware store. **2,** hardware.
—**ferretero** (-'te·ro) *n.m.* hardware
merchant.
ferrocarril (fe·rro·ka'rril) *n.m.*
railroad. —**ferrocarrilero,** *n.m.,*
Amer. = **ferroviario.**
ferroso (fe'rro·so) *adj.* ferrous.
ferrotipo (fe·rro'ti·po) *n.m.* tintype; ferrotype.
ferroviario (fe·rro'βja·rjo) *adj.*
railroad *(attrib.)* —*n.m.* railroad
employee.
ferruginoso (fe·rru·xi'no·so) *adj.*
containing iron; ferruginous.
fértil ('fer·til) *adj.* fertile. —**fertilidad,** *n.f.* fertility.
fertilizar (fer·ti·li'θar; -'sar) *v.t.*
[*infl.:* **rezar, 10**] to fertilize.
—**fertilización,** *n.f.* fertilization. —**fertilizante,** *n.m.* fertilizer.
—*adj.* [*also,* **fertilizador**] fertilizing.
férula ('fe·ru·la) *n.f.* **1,** ferule. **2,**
fig. rule; authority. **3,** *surg.* splint.
férvido ('fer·βi·ðo) *adj.* fervid.
ferviente (fer'βjen·te) *adj.* fervent.
Also, **fervoroso** (-βo'ro·so).
fervor (fer'βor) *n.m.* fervor.
festear (fes·te'ar) *v.i., colloq.* to

pay court; keep company. —**festeo** (-'te·o) *n.m., colloq.* courtship.

festejar (fes·te'xar) *v.t.* **1,** to entertain; fête. **2,** to celebrate; honor. **3,** to woo.

festejo (fes'te·xo) *n.m.* **1,** *usu.pl.* celebration; festivities. **2,** courtship.

festín (fes'tin) *n.m.* banquet; feast.

festinar (fes·ti'nar) *v.t., Amer.* to hasten; rush. —**festinado,** *adj.* precipitous; premature.

festival (fes·ti'βal) *n.m.* festival.

festivo (fes'ti·βo) *adj.* **1,** festive. **2,** humorous. —**festividad,** *n.f.* festivity.

festón (fes'ton) *n.m.* **1,** wreath; garland. **2,** edging.

festonear (fes·to·ne'ar) *v.t.* to wreathe; festoon. *Also,* **festonar.**

fetal (fe'tal) *adj.* fetal.

fetiche (fe'ti·tʃe) *n.m.* fetish; idol. —**fetichismo,** *n.m.* fetishism. —**fetichista,** *n.m. & f.* fetishist. —*adj.* fetishistic.

fétido ('fe·ti·ðo) *adj.* fetid. —**fetidez,** *n.f.* fetidness.

feto ('fe·to) *n.m.* fetus.

feudal (feu'ðal) *adj.* feudal. —**feudalismo,** *n.m.* feudalism.

feudo ('feu·ðo) *n.m.* fief. —**feudo franco,** freehold.

fez (feθ; fes) *n.m.* fez.

fiado (fi'a·ðo) *adj.* on credit. —**al fiado,** on credit. —**dar fiado,** to give credit.

fiador (fi·a'ðor) *n.m.* **1,** guarantor. **2,** bondsman. **3,** fastener; clasp. **4,** safety catch. **5,** tumbler *(of a lock).*

fiambre ('fjam·bre) *n.m.* **1,** cold cuts. **2,** *fig.* stale news. **3,** *slang* corpse. —*adj.* served cold, as food. —**fiambrera,** *n.f.* lunch basket.

fianza ('fjan·θa; -sa) *n.f.* **1,** bail. **2,** surety; guarantee.

fiar (fi'ar) *v.t.* [*infl.: enviar,* 22] **1,** to guarantee. **2,** to sell on credit. —**fiarse,** *v.r. fol. by* **de,** to trust. —**de fiar,** trustworthy.

fiasco ('fjas·ko) *n.m.* fiasco.

fibra ('fi·βra) *n.f.* **1,** fiber. **2,** *fig.* energy; firmness. —**fibra de vidrio,** fiberglass. —**fibroso,** *adj.* fibrous.

fibrosis (fi'βro·sis) *n.f.* fibrosis.

ficción (fik'θjon; -'sjon) *n.f.* fiction.

ficticio (fik'ti·θjo; -sjo) *adj.* fictitious.

ficha ('fi·tʃa) *n.f.* **1,** chip; token; counter. **2,** domino piece. **3,** card file; record. **4,** index card. **5,** *colloq.* character. **6,** dossier. —**fichar,** *v.t.*

to tag; peg (a person). —*v.t. & i.* to move in *(in dominoes).*

fichero (fi'tʃe·ro) *n.m.* **1,** file. **2,** filing cabinet.

fidedigno (fi·ðe'ðiɣ·no) *adj.* reliable.

fidelidad (fi·ðe·li'ðað) *n.f.* loyalty; fidelity.

fideo (fi'ðe·o) *n.m.* **1,** *usu.pl.* vermicelli; spaghetti. **2,** *colloq.* very thin person.

fiduciario (fi·ðu'θja·rjo; -'sja·rjo) *adj. & n.m.* fiduciary.

fiebre ('fje·βre) *n.f.* fever. —**limpiarse de fiebre,** to rid oneself of fever.

fiel (fjel) *adj.* faithful; true. —*n.m.* **1,** needle of a balance. **2,** inspector *(of weights and measures).*

fieltro ('fjel·tro) *n.m.* felt.

fiera ('fje·ra) *n.f.* **1,** wild beast. **2,** fiend.

fiero ('fje·ro) *adj.* **1,** wild; fierce. **2,** rude; rough. **3,** cruel. **4,** huge. —**fieros,** *n.m.pl.* boasts; threats. —**fiereza,** *n.f.* ferocity; cruelty.

fierro ('fje·rro) *n.m., Amer.* = **hierro.**

fiesta ('fjes·ta) *n.f.* **1,** festival; fiesta. **2,** party; entertainment. **3,** holy day; holiday. —**estar de fiesta,** to revel. —**hacer fiestas a,** to fawn on.

fiestero (fjes'te·ro) *adj.* fond of merrymaking. —*n.m.* merrymaker; reveler.

figón (fi'ɣon) *n.m.* cheap or unpretentious restaurant; joint.

figura (fi'ɣu·ra) *n.f.* **1,** figure; shape. **2,** mien; countenance. **3,** character; personage. **4,** design; pattern. **5,** figure of speech. **6,** face card.

figuración (fi·ɣu·ra'θjon; -'sjon) *n.f.* **1,** figuration. **2,** *Amer.* role; participation.

figurado (fi·ɣu'ra·ðo) *adj.* figurative.

figurar (fi·ɣu'rar) *v.t.* **1,** to shape; form. **2,** to portray; represent. **3,** to feign. —*v.i.* to figure; take part. —**figurarse,** *v.r.* to imagine; picture. —**figurante,** *n.m. & f., theat.* extra; walk-on.

figurativo (fi·ɣu·ra'ti·βo) *adj.* figurative.

figurín (fi·ɣu'rin) *n.m.* **1,** fashion plate. **2,** pattern book. **3,** *colloq.* dandy.

figurón (fi·ɣu'ron) *n.m.* figurehead.

fijación (fi·xa'θjon; -'sjon) *n.f.* **1**, fixation. **2**, setting; fixing.

fijado (fi'xa·ðo) *n.m., photog.* fixing; fixation.

fijar (fi'xar) *v.t.* to fix; set. —**fijarse**, *v.r.* to notice; pay attention. —**fijador**, *n.m.* **1**, hair spray. **2**, *photog.* fixative.

fijeza (fi'xe·θa; -sa) *n.f.* **1**, fixity. **2**, firmness.

fijo ('fi·xo) *adj.* **1**, fixed; set; agreed upon. **2**, firm; secure. **3**, stationary. **4**, fast *(of colors).* —**de fijo**, surely; undoubtedly.

fila ('fi·la) *n.f.* **1**, file; row; line. **2**, *mil.* rank.

filacteria (fi·lak'te·rja) *n.f.* phylactery.

filamento (fi·la'men·to) *n.m.* filament.

filantropía (fi·lan·tro'pi·a) *n.f.* philanthropy. —**filantrópico** (-'tro·pi·ko) *adj.* philanthropic. —**filántropo** (-'lan·tro·po) *n.m.* philanthropist.

filarmónico (fi·lar'mo·ni·ko) *adj.* philharmonic. —*n.m.* music lover.

filatelia (fi·la'te·lja) *n.f.* philately. —**filatélico** (-'te·li·ko) *adj.* philatelic. —**filatelista**, *n.m. & f.* philatelist.

filete (fi'le·te) *n.m.* **1**, fillet; filet. **2**, hem. **3**, screw thread. —**filetear**, *v.t.* to fillet. —**filete de solomillo**, filet mignon.

filiación (fi·lja'θjon; -'sjon) *n.f.* **1**, affiliation. **2**, personal description. **3**, filial relationship; descent.

filial (fi'ljal) *adj.* filial. —*n.f., comm.* branch; subsidiary.

filibustero (fi·li·βus'te·ro) *n.m.* freebooter.

filigrana (fi·li'ɣra·na) *n.f.* **1**, filigree. **2**, watermark. **3**, finely wrought object; jewel.

filipino (fi·li'pi·no) *adj. & n.m.* Philippine.

filisteo (fi·lis'te·o) *adj. & n.m.* Philistine. —*n.m.* tall, burly man.

film (film) *also,* **filme** ('fil·me) *n.m.* film.

filmar (fil'mar) *v.t.* to film; photograph. —**filmación**, *n.f.* filming.

filo ('fi·lo) *n.m.* **1**, edge; sharp edge. **2**, dividing line. **3**, *biol.* phylum. —**de filo**, *Amer.* directly; resolutely. —**por filo**, precisely.

filogenia (fi·lo'xe·nja) *n.f.* phylogeny.

filología (fi·lo·lo'xi·a) *n.f.* philology. —**filológico** (-'lo·xi·ko) *adj.*

philological. —**filólogo** (-'lo·lo·ɣo) *n.m.* philologist.

filón (fi'lon) *n.m.* **1**, lode. **2**, *fig.* gold mine.

filoso (fi'lo·so) *adj. Amer.* sharp.

filosofar (fi·lo·so'far) *v.i.* to philosophize.

filosofía (fi·lo·so'fi·a) *n.f.* philosophy. —**filosófico** (-'so·fi·ko) *adj.* philosophical. —**filósofo** (-'lo·so·fo) *n.m.* philosopher.

filtrar (fil'trar) *v.t. & i.* to filter; filtrate. —**filtrarse**, *v.r.* **1**, to filter or seep through. **2**, to be wasted away, as a fortune, money, etc. —**filtración**, *n.f.* filtration; seepage. —**filtrado**, *n.m.* filtrate.

filtro ('fil·tro) *n.m.* **1**, filter. **2**, love potion; philter.

filum ('fi·lum) *n.m., biol.* phylum.

fin (fin) *n.m.* end. —**a fin de**, in order to. —**a fin de que**, in order that. —**al fin; al fin y al cabo**, in the end; after all. —**en fin; por fin**, finally; at last.

finado (fi'na·ðo) *n.m.* deceased.

final (fi'nal) *adj.* final. —*n.m.* end; finish. —**finalista**, *n.m. & f.* finalist.

finalidad (fi·na·li'ðað) *n.f.* purpose; end.

finalizar (fi·na·li'θar; -'sar) *v.t. & i.* [*infl.:* **rezar**, 10] to finish; end. —**finalización**, *n.f.* conclusion; end.

financiar (fi·nan'θjar; -'sjar) *v.t.* to finance.

financiero (fi·nan'θje·ro; -'sje·ro) *adj.* financial. —*n.m.* financier.

finanzas (fi'nan·θas; -sas) *n.f.pl.* **1**, finances. **2**, finance.

finca ('fin·ka) *n.f.* **1**, estate; property. **2**, *Amer.* farm; ranch.

finés (fi'nes) *adj. & n.m.* [*fem.* **finesa** (-'ne·sa)] = **finlandés**.

fineza (fi'ne·θa; -sa) *n.f.* **1**, delicacy; graciousness. **2**, fineness. **3**, kind word or gesture. **4**, small gift; favor. **5**, *cards, Amer.* finesse.

fingir (fin'xir) *v.t.* [*infl.:* **coger**, 15] to feign; pretend. —**fingido**, *adj.* feigned; false. —**fingimiento**, *n.m.* feigning, deceit.

finiquitar (fi·ni·ki'tar) *v.t.* **1**, to close out (an account). **2**, to bring to an end; conclude. —**finiquito** (-'ki·to) *n.m.* closing out; settlement *(of an account).*

finito (fi'ni·to) *adj.* finite.

finlandés (fin·lan'des) *adj.* Finnish. —*n.m.* **1**, Finn. **2**, Finnish language.

fino ('fi·no) *adj.* **1,** fine. **2,** courteous; urbane. **3,** subtle.

finta ('fin·ta) *n.f.* feint.

finura (fi'nu·ra) *n.f.* **1,** daintiness. **2,** courtesy; urbanity. **3,** finesse; subtlety.

fiordo ('fjor·ðo) [*pl.* **fiordos**] *also,* **fiord** (fjorð) [*pl.* **fiores** ('fjo·res)] *n.m.* fiord.

firma ('fir·ma) *n.f.* **1,** signature. **2,** firm; company.

firmamento (fir·ma'men·to) *n.m.* firmament.

firmar (fir'mar) *v.t.* to sign; affix one's signature to. **—firmante,** *adj.* & *n.m.* & *f.* signatory.

firme ('fir·me) *adj.* firm. **—***adv.* firmly. **—***n.m., engin.* **1,** firm soil (*for foundations*). **2,** roadbed. **—de firme,** firmly; steadily. **—en firme,** *comm.* firm, as an offer. **—¡firmes!,** *mil.* attention!

firmeza (fir'me·θa; -sa) *n.f.* firmness.

firulete (fi·ru'le·te) *n.m., Amer., colloq.* frill; fanciness.

fiscal (fis'kal) *adj.* **1,** fiscal. **2,** governmental; of the public treasury. **—***n.m.* **1,** auditor of public moneys. **2,** public prosecutor; district attorney.

fiscalizar (fis·ka·li'θar; -'sar) *v.t.* [*infl.:* **rezar, 10**] **1,** to control; audit. **2,** *fig.* to criticize.

fisco ('fis·ko) *n.m.* public treasury.

fisgón (fis'ɣon) *adj.* prying; snoopy. **—***n.m.* prier; snoop.

fisgonear (fis·ɣo·ne'ar) *v.i.* to pry; snoop. **—fisgoneo** (-'ne·o) *n.m.* prying; snooping.

física ('fi·si·ka) *n.f.* physics.

físico ('fi·si·ko) *adj.* physical. **—***n.m.* **1,** physicist. **2,** physique. **3,** appearance. **4,** *archaic* physician.

fisiología (fi·sjo·lo'xi·a) *n.f.* physiology. **—fisiológico** (-'lo·xi·ko) *adj.* physiological. **—fisiólogo** (-'sjo·lo·ɣo) *n.m.* physiologist.

fisión (fi'sjon) *n.f.* fission. **—fisionable,** *adj.* fissionable. **—fisionar,** *v.t.* to split.

fisioterapia (fi·sjo·te'ra·pja) *n.f.* physiotherapy. **—fisioterapeuta** (-'peu·ta) *n.m.* & *f.* physiotherapist.

fisonomía (fi·so·no'mi·a) *n.f.* physiognomy. **—fisonómico** (-'no·mi·ko) *adj.* physiognomic.

fístula ('fis·tu·la) *n.f.* fistula.

fisura (fi'su·ra) *n.f.* fissure.

fizgar (fiθ'ɣar; fis-) *v.t.* [*infl.:* **pagar, 8**] **1,** to spear; harpoon. **2,** to pry into. **—fizgarse de,** to make fun of.

fláccido ('flak·θiðo; 'flak·si-) *adj.* flaccid. **—flaccidez,** *n.f.* flaccidity.

flaco ('fla·ko) *adj.* **1,** thin; lean; skinny. **2,** weak. **—***n.m.* weakness; weak point. **—flacura,** *n.f.* thinness; leanness; scrawniness.

flagelar (fla·xe'lar) *v.t.* to flagellate; whip. **—flagelación,** *n.f.* flagellation. **—flagelante,** *n.m.* & *f.* flagellant.

flagelo (fla'xe·lo) *n.m.* **1,** whip; lash. **2,** scourge.

flagrante (fla'ɣran·te) *adj.* flagrant. **—flagrancia,** *n.f.* flagrancy. **—en flagrante delito,** (caught) red-handed.

flama ('fla·ma) *n.f.* **1,** flame. **2,** firelight.

flamante (fla'man·te) *adj.* **1,** resplendent. **2,** brand new.

flamear (fla·me'ar) *v.i.* to flame; shine.

flamenco (fla'men·ko) *adj.* **1,** Flemish. **2,** gypsylike. **3,** roguish; bold. **—***n.m.* **1,** flamingo. **2,** Fleming. **3,** Flemish (*language*). **4,** Andalusian gypsy dance or song.

flan (flan) *n.m.* custard.

flanco ('flan·ko) *n.m.* flank; side. **—flanquear** (-ke'ar) *v.t.* to flank.

flaquear (fla·ke'ar) *v.i.* to weaken.

flaqueza (fla'ke·θa; -sa) *n.f.* **1,** = **flacura. 2,** weakness. **3,** *fig.* misstep.

flato ('fla·to) *n.m.* **1,** a breaking wind. **2,** *Amer., colloq.* hangover.

flatulento (fla·tu'len·to) *adj.* flatulent. **—flatulencia,** *n.f.* flatulence.

flauta ('flau·ta) *n.f.* flute. **—flautista,** *n.m.* & *f.* flutist.

flautín (flau'tin) *n.m.* piccolo.

flebitis (fle'βi·tis) *n.f.* phlebitis.

flebotomía (fle·βo·to'mi·a) *n.f.* phlebotomy.

fleco ('fle·ko) *n.m.* **1,** fringe; flounce. **2,** jagged or threadbare edge.

flecha ('fle·tʃa) *n.f.* arrow.

flechar (fle'tʃar) *v.t.* **1,** to fit an arrow to (a bow). **2,** to pierce with an arrow. **3,** *fig.* to inspire love in.

flechazo (fle'tʃa·θo; -so) *n.m.* **1,** stroke of an arrow. **2,** bowshot. **3,** arrow wound. **4,** *fig.* sudden love.

flechero (fle'tʃe·ro) *n.m.* **1,** bowman. **2,** arrowmaker.

fleje ('fle·xe) *n.m.* iron hoop; steel strap.

flema ('fle·ma) *n.f.* phlegm. —**flemático** (-'ma·ti·ko) *adj.* phlegmatic.

fleo ('fle·o) *n.m.* timothy; timothy grass.

flequillo (fle'ki·ʎo; -jo) *n.m.* bang (or bangs) of hair.

fletamento (fle·ta'men·to) *n.m.* **1,** charter or chartering of a vessel. **2,** charter party.

fletar (fle'tar) *v.t.* **1,** to charter (a vessel). **2,** *Amer.* to hire (a conveyance). **3,** *Amer., colloq.* to give (a blow, slap, etc.). —**fletarse,** *v.r., Amer. colloq.* to clear out; get out.

flete ('fle·te) *n.m.* **1,** freight charges. **2,** freight. **3,** *Amer.* hire; rental *(of a conveyance).*

flexible (flek'si·βle) *adj.* flexible. —**flexibilidad,** *n.f.* flexibility.

flexión (flek'sjon) *n.f.* **1,** bending; bend. **2,** *gram.* flexion; inflection. —**flexionar** (-'nar) *v.t.* to bend; flex.

flirtear (flir·te'ar) *v.i.* to flirt. —**flirteador,** *adj.* flirtatious. —*n.m.* [*fem.* **-dora**] flirt. —**flirteo** (-'te·o) *n.m.* flirtation.

flojear (flo·xe'ar) *v.i.* **1,** to idle; be lazy. **2,** to flag; weaken.

flojedad (flo·xe'ðað) *n.f.* **1,** looseness; slack. **2,** [*also, colloq.* **flojera** (-'xe·ra)] laziness; indolence.

flojel (flo'xel) *n.m.* **1,** nap *(of cloth).* **2,** soft feathers; down. —**pato de flojel,** eider duck.

flojo ('flo·xo) *adj.* **1,** loose; slack. **2,** feeble; lacking force. **3,** lazy; indolent. **4,** incompetent; poor.

flor (flor) *n.f.* **1,** flower. **2,** *fig.* compliment; flattery. —**a flor de agua,** afloat; at water level. —**a flor de labios,** on the tip of one's tongue. —**echar flores a,** *colloq.* to flatter; butter up. —**flor de lis, 1,** amaryllis. **2,** fleur-de-lis. —**flor de muerto,** marigold. —**flor de un día,** *colloq.* flash in the pan. —**flor y nata,** elite; cream. —**juegos florales,** poetry contest.

flora ('flo·ra) *n.f.* flora.

floración (flo·ra'θjon; -'sjon) *n.f.* flowering.

floral (flo'ral) *adj.* floral.

florear (flo·re'ar) *v.t.* to adorn with flowers. —*v.i.* **1,** to flit; gad about. **2,** *colloq.* to compliment; flatter. **3,** *Amer.* = **florecer.**

florecer (flo·re'θer; -'ser) *v.i.* [*infl.:* **conocer,** 13] **1,** to flower; blossom. **2,** to flourish; prosper. —**florecerse,** *v.r.* to become moldy.

—**floreciente,** *adj.* flourishing; prospering.

florecimiento (flo·re·θi'mjen·to; -si'mjen·to) *n.m.* **1,** flowering; blossoming. **2,** flourishing.

floreo (flo're·o) *n.m.* **1,** flourish; brandishing *(of a sword).* **2,** *colloq.* idle talk; nonsense. **3,** floweriness *(in speech or writing).*

florero (flo're·ro) *adj., fig.* flowery. —*n.m.* flower vase. —**florería,** *n.f., Amer.* flower shop.

florescencia (flo·res'θen·θja; -re'sen·sja) *n.f.* florescence.

floresta (flo'res·ta) *n.f.* forest; wood.

florete (flo're·te) *n.m.* fencing foil. —**floretista,** *n.m.* swordsman. —*n.f.* swordswoman.

floricultura (flo·ri·kul'tu·ra) *n.f.* floriculture. —**floricultor** (-'tor) *n.m.* [*fem.* **-tora**] floriculturist.

florido (flo'ri·ðo) *adj.* flowery. —**floridez** (-'ðeθ; -'ðes) floweriness.

florín (flo'rin) *n.m.* florin.

florista (flo'ris·ta) *n.m. & f.* florist. —**floristería,** *n.f.* flower shop.

flota ('flo·ta) *n.f.* fleet.

flotación (flo·ta'θjon; -'sjon) *n.f.* flotation; floating. —**línea de flotación,** waterline *(of a ship).*

flotar (flo'tar) *v.i.* to float. —**flotador,** *n.m.* float.

flote ('flo·te) *n.m.* = **flotación.** —**a flote,** afloat.

flotilla (flo'ti·ʎa; -ja) *n.f.* flotilla.

flox (floks) *n.m.* phlox.

fluctuar (fluk'twar) *v.i.* [*infl.:* **continuar,** 23] to fluctuate. —**fluctuación,** *n.f.* fluctuation.

fluidez (flu·i'ðeθ; -'ðes) *n.f.* **1,** fluidity. **2,** fluency.

flúido ('flu·i·ðo) *adj.* **1,** fluid. **2,** fluent. —*n.m.* **1,** fluid. **2,** electric current.

fluir (flu'ir) *v.i.* [*infl.:* **huir,** 26] to flow.

flujo ('flu·xo) *n.m.* **1,** flow; flux. **2,** rising tide. **3,** *med.* discharge; secretion. **4,** menstruation.

flúor ('flu·or) *n.m.* fluorine.

fluorescencia (flu·o·res'θen·θja; -re'sen·sja) *n.f.* fluorescence. —**fluorescente,** *adj.* fluorescent.

fluorización (flu·o·ri·θa'θjon; -sa'sjon) *n.f.* fluoridation.

fluoroscopio (flu·o·ros'ko·pjo) *n.m.* fluoroscope. —**fluoroscopia** (-pja) *n.f.* fluoroscopy. —**fluoroscópico** (-'ko·pi·ko) *adj.* fluoroscopic.

fluoruro (flu·o'ru·ro) *n.m.* fluoride.

fluvial (flu'βjal) *adj.* fluvial.

flux (fluks) *n.m.* 1, *cards* flush. 2, *Amer.* suit of clothes. —**hacer flux,** *colloq.* to go broke. —**tener flux,** *Amer., colloq.* to be lucky.

¡fo! (fo) *interj.* ¡pew!; ¡phew!

fobia ('fo·βja) *n.f.* phobia.

foca ('fo·ka) *n.f., zoöl.* seal.

foco ('fo·ko) *n.m.* 1, focus; center. 2, street lamp. 3, *Amer.* light bulb. 4, lamp globe. —**focal,** *adj.* focal.

fofo ('fo·fo) *adj.* flabby; spongy.

fogata (fo'γa·ta) *n.f.* bonfire; campfire.

fogón (fo'γon) *n.m.* hearth; stove.

fogonazo (fo·γo'na·θo; -so) *n.m.* flash.

fogonero (fo·γo'ne·ro) *n.m.* stoker; fireman.

fogoso (fo'γo·so) *adj.* 1, impetuous; fiery; spirited. 2, ardent; lustful. —**fogosidad,** *n.f.* impetuosity; fieriness; spirit.

folclor (fol'klor); **folklore** (fol·'klo·re) *n.m.* folklore. —**folclórico;** **folklórico** (-'klo·ri·ko) *adj.* folkloristic.

fólico ('fo·li·ko) *adj.* folic.

folículo (fo'li·ku·lo) *n.m.* follicle.

folio ('fo·ljo) *n.m.* folio.

follaje (fo'ʎa·xe; -'ja·xe) *n.m.* foliage.

folletín (fo·ʎe'tin; -je'tin) *n.m.* newspaper serial; regular newspaper feature; column. —**folletinista,** *n.m. & f.* columnist.

folleto (fo'ʎe·to; -'je·to) *n.m.* pamphlet; booklet.

fomentar (fo·men'tar) *v.t.* to foment; foster; promote.

fomento (fo'men·to) *n.m.* 1, fostering; promotion. 2, fomentation. 3, poultice.

fonda ('fon·da) *n.f.* 1, inn. 2, modest restaurant.

fondear (fon·de'ar) *v.t., naut.* to sound. —*v.i.* to cast anchor. —**fondeadero,** *n.m.* anchorage.

fondillos (fon'di·ʎos; -jos) *n.m. pl.* 1, seat of the pants. 2, buttocks.

fondista (fon'dis·ta) *n.m. & f.* innkeeper.

fondo ('fon·do) *n.m.* 1, bottom. 2, depth. 3, background. 4, fund. 5, essence; pith. 6, end *(of a street).* 7, back; rear *(of a house, room, etc.).* —**a fondo,** thoroughly. —**al fondo,** at the end; in the back. —**en el fondo,** 1, at heart. 2, in essence.

—**tener buen fondo,** to be good-natured.

fonducho (fon'du·tʃo) *n.m.* cheap restaurant; joint.

fonema (fo'ne·ma) *n.m.* phoneme.

fonética (fo'ne·ti·ka) *n.f.* phonetics. —**fonético,** *adj.* phonetic. —**fonetista,** *n.m. & f.* phonetician.

fónico ('fo·ni·ko) *adj.* phonic. —**fónica,** *n.f.* phonics.

fonocaptor (fo·no·kap'tor) *n.m.* pickup *(as of a phonograph).*

fonógrafo (fo'no·γra·fo) *n.m.* phonograph. —**fonográfico** (-'γra·fi·ko) *adj.* phonographic.

fontanería (fon·ta·ne'ri·a) *n.f.* plumbing. —**fontanero** (-'ne·ro) *n.m.* plumber.

foque ('fo·ke) *n.m., naut.* jib.

forajido (fo·ra'xi·ðo) *adj. & n.m.* outlaw; bandit.

foráneo (fo'ra·ne·o) *adj.* foreign.

forastero (fo·ras'te·ro) *n.m.* stranger; foreigner. —*adj.* strange; foreign.

forcé (for'θe; -'se) *v., 1st pers. sing.pret. of* **forzar.**

forcejear (for·θe·xe'ar; for·se-) *also,* **forcejar** (-'xar) *v.i.* to struggle; strive.

fórceps ('for·θeps; -seps) *n.m.* forceps.

forense (fo'ren·se) *adj.* forensic. —**médico forense,** coroner.

forestación (fo·res·ta'θjon; -'sjon) *n.f.* forestation; reforestation.

forestal (fo·res'tal) *adj.* forest *(attrib.).*

forja ('for·xa) *n.f.* 1, forge; smithy. 2, forging.

forjador (for·xa'ðor) *n.m.* 1, forger of metals; smith. 2, storyteller; fibber.

forjar (for'xar) *v.t.* 1, to forge. 2, *fig.* to fabricate; concoct. —**forjado,** *adj.* forged; wrought. —**forjadura,** *n.f.* forging.

forma ('for·ma) *n.f.* 1, form; shape. 2, manner; method. 3, pattern; mold. 4, format. —**formas,** *n.f.pl.* curves *(of a female figure).*

formación (for·ma'θjon; -'sjon) *n.f.* 1, formation; shape. 2, upbringing; training.

formal (for'mal) *adj.* 1, formal. 2, serious-minded; reliable.

formaldehído (for·mal·de'i·ðo) *n.m.* formaldehyde.

formalidad (for·ma·li'ðað) *n.f.* 1, formality. 2, seriousness; reliability.

formalismo (for·ma'lis·mo) *n.m.*

1, formalism. 2, formality; red tape.
—**formalista,** *adj.* formalistic.
—*n.m. & f.* formalist.

formalizar (for·ma·li'θar; -'sar)
v.t. [*infl.:* **rezar, 10**] to formalize.
—**formalizarse,** *v.r., colloq.* to become earnest.

formar (for'mar) *v.t.* **1,** to form;
constitute. **2,** to shape.

formativo (for·ma'ti·βo) *adj.*
formative.

formato (for'ma·to) *n.m.* format.

formidable (for·mi'ða·βle) *adj.* **1,**
formidable. **2,** *colloq.* tremendous.

formol (for'mol) *n.m.* formaldehyde.

formón (for'mon) *n.m.* chisel.

fórmula ('for·mu·la) *n.f.* **1,** formula. **2,** prescription. —**por
fórmula,** as a matter of form.

formular (for·mu'lar) *v.t.* to formulate. —**formulación,** *n.f.* formulation.

formulario (for·mu'la·rjo) *adj.*
formal; purely formal. —*n.m.*
blank; blank form.

formulismo (for·mu'lis·mo) *n.m.*
formality; red tape.

fornicar (for·ni'kar) *v.i.* [*infl.:*
tocar, 7] to fornicate. —**fornicación,** *n.f.* fornication.

fornido (for'ni·ðo) *adj.* husky; robust.

foro ('fo·ro) *n.m.* **1,** forum. **2,** bar;
legal profession. **3,** *theat.* back (of
the stage scenery).

forraje (fo'rra·xe) *n.m.* forage; fodder. —**forrajear,** *v.t. & i.* to forage.

forrar (fo'rrar) *v.t.* **1,** to line; put a
lining in. **2,** to put a cover on.

forro ('fo·rro) *n.m.* **1,** lining. **2,**
cover. **3,** bushing.

fortalecer (for·ta·le'θer; -'ser) *v.t.*
[*infl.:* **conocer, 13**] to strengthen;
fortify. —**fortalecimiento,** *n.m.*
strengthening; fortification.

fortaleza (for·ta'le·θa; -sa) *n.f.* **1,**
strength; vigor. **2,** fortitude. **3,** fortress.

fortificar (for·ti·fi'kar) *v.t.* [*infl.:*
tocar, 7] to fortify, —**fortificación,**
n.f. fortification.

fortín (for'tin) *n.m.* small fort.

fortísimo (for'ti·si·mo) *adj. &
adv.* **1,** *superl.* of **fuerte. 2,** *mus.*
fortissimo.

fortuito (for'twi·to) *adj.* fortuitous.

fortuna (for'tu·na) *n.f.* **1,** fortune;
chance. **2,** fate; luck. **3,** success;
good fortune. **4,** wealth.

forzado (for'θa·ðo;   -'sa·ðo)

adj. forced. —*n.m.* convict at hard
labor.

forzar (for'θar; -'sar) *v.t.* [*infl.:*
rezar, 10; acostar, 28] **1,** to force.
2, to ravish; rape.

forzosamente (for·θo·sa'men·te;
for·so-) *adv.* **1,** by force; forcibly. **2,**
forcefully. **3,** necessarily; perforce.

forzoso (for'θo·so; -'so·so) *adj.* inevitable; necessary; compulsory.
—**hacer la forzosa a,** *colloq.* to put
pressure on; coerce.

forzudo (for'θu·ðo; -'su·ðo) *adj.*
strong; robust.

fosa ('fo·sa) *n.f.* **1,** grave. **2,** pit;
cavity. —**fosas nasales,** nostrils.

fosca ('fos·ka) *n.f.* haze; mist.

fosco ('fos·ko) *adj.* **1,** dark. **2,** irritable; cross.

fosfato (fos'fa·to) *n.m.* phosphate.

fosforecer (fos·fo·re'θer; -'ser) *v.i.*
[*infl.:* **conocer, 13**] **1,** to be phos-
phorescent. **2,** to shine in the dark.
Also, **fosforescer** (-res'θer; -re'ser).

fosforescencia (fos·fo·res'θen·
θja; -re'sen·sja) *n.f.* phosphorescence. —**fosforescente,** *adj.* phos-
phorescent.

fósforo ('fos·fo·ro) *n.m.* **1,** phosphorus. **2,** match.

fósil ('fo·sil) *adj. & n.m.* fossil.

fosilizar (fo·si·li'θar; -'sar) *v.t.*
[*infl.:* **rezar, 10**] to fossilize.

foso ('fo·so) *n.m.* **1,** pit. **2,** moat.

foto ('fo·to) *n.f.* photo.

fotocopia (fo·to'ko·pja) *n.f.* photocopy. —**fotocopiar,** *v.t.* to photocopy.

fotoeléctrico (fo·to·e'lek·tri·ko)
adj. photoelectric.

fotogénico (fo·to'xe·ni·ko) *adj.*
photogenic.

fotograbado (fo·to·ɣra'βa·ðo)
n.m. **1,** photoengraving. **2,** photogravure.

fotograbar (fo·to·ɣra'βar) *v.t.* to
photoengrave.

fotografía (fo·to·ɣra'fi·a) *n.f.* **1,**
photography. **2,** photograph. **3,** photographic studio. —**fotográfico**
(-'ɣra·fi·ko) *adj.* photographic.
—**fotógrafo** (fo'to·ɣra·fo) *n.m.*
[*fem.* **-grafa**] photographer.

fotografiar (fo·to·ɣra'fjar) *v.t. &
i.* [*infl.:* **enviar, 22**] to photograph.

fotómetro (fo'to·me·tro) *n.m.* photometer.

fotón (fo'ton) *n.m.* photon.

fotosensible (fo·to·sen'si·βle)
adj. photosensitive.

fotosfera (fo·tos'fe·ra) *n.f.* photosphere.

fotosíntesis (fo·to'sin·te·sis) *n.f.* photosynthesis.

fotóstato (fo'tos·ta·to) *also,* **fotostato** (-'ta·to) *n.m.* photostat. —**fotostatar** (-'tar) *v.t. & i.* to photostat. —**fotostático** (-'ta·ti·ko) *adj.* photostatic.

frac (frak) *n.m.* [*pl.* **fracs** (fraks) *also,* **fraques** ('fra·kes)] full dress; tails.

fracaso (fra'ka·so) *n.m.* failure. —**fracasar,** *v.i.* to fail; come to naught.

fracción (frak'θjon; -'sjon) *n.f.* fraction. —**fraccionario,** *adj.* fractional.

fraccionar (frak·θjo'nar; -sjo'nar) *v.t.* to split; divide into parts or fractions. —**fraccionamiento,** *n.m.* division; *chem.* fractionation; cracking. —**destilación fraccionada,** fractional distillation.

fractura (frak'tu·ra) *n.f.* fracture. —**fracturar,** *v.t.* to fracture.

fragante (fra'ɣan·te) *adj.* 1, fragrant. 2, = **flagrante.** —**fragancia,** *n.f.* fragrance.

fragata (fra'ɣa·ta) *n.f.* frigate.

frágil ('fra·xil) *adj.* fragile. —**fragilidad,** *n.f.* fragility.

fragmentar (fraɣ·men'tar) *v.t.* to fragment. —**fragmentación,** *n.f.* fragmentation.

fragmento (fraɣ'men·to) *n.m.* fragment. —**fragmentario,** *adj.* fragmentary.

fragor (fra'ɣor) *n.m.* din; clamor. —**fragoroso,** *adj.* deafening; thunderous.

fragoso (fra'ɣo·so) *adj.* 1, rough; bumpy. 2, = **fragoroso.** —**fragosidad,** *n.f.* roughness; bumpiness.

fragua ('fra·ɣwa) *n.f.* forge.

fraguar (fra'ɣwar) *v.t.* [*infl.:* **averiguar,** 9] 1, to forge (metals). 2, to concoct; contrive; devise. —*v.i.* to set, as plaster, cement, etc.

fraile ('frai·le) *n.m.* friar.

frambesia (fram'be·sja) *n.f.* yaws.

frambuesa (fram'bwe·sa) *n.f.* raspberry. —**frambueso,** *n.m.* raspberry bush.

francachela (fran·ka'tʃe·la) *n.f., colloq.* 1, banquet. 2, revel.

francés (fran'θes; -'ses) *adj.* French. —*n.m.* 1, Frenchman. 2, French language. —**francesa** (-'θe·sa; -'se·sa) *n.f.* Frenchwoman.

francio ('fran·θjo; -sjo) *n.m.* francium.

francmasón (frank·ma'son) *n.m.* Freemason. —**francmasonería,** *ħ.f.* Freemasonry. —**francmasónico** (-'so·ni·ko) *adj.* Freemasonic.

franco ('fran·ko) *adj.* 1, frank. 2, free; open; clear. 3, generous; liberal. 4, exempt; privileged. —*n.m.* franc. —**franco a bordo,** *also,* **franco bordo,** free on board. —**franco de porte,** postpaid.

francote (fran'ko·te) *adj., colloq.* candid; frank.

francotirador (fran·ko·ti·ra'ðor) *n.m.* sniper.

franela (fra'ne·la) *n.f.* flannel.

franja ('fran·xa) *n.f.* 1, fringe; border. 2, stripe; band; strip.

franquear (fran·ke'ar) *v.t.* 1, to free; exempt. 2, to get over or across. 3, to clear; open. 4, to expedite; open the way to. 5, to pay postage on. —**franquearse,** *v.r.* to unbosom oneself.

franqueo (fran'ke·o) *n.m.* postage.

franqueza (fran'ke·θa; -sa) *n.f.* 1, frankness. 2, freedom; exemption. 3, generosity.

franquicia (fran'ki·θja; -sja) *n.f.* franchise; exemption. —**franquicia postal,** franking privilege.

frasco ('fras·ko) *n.m.* flask; vial.

frase ('fra·se) *n.f.* 1, phrase. 2, sentence. 3, phrasing. —**frasear** (fra·se'ar) *v.t.* to phrase.

fraseología (fra·se·o·lo'xi·a) *n.f.* 1, phraseology. 2, verbosity.

fraternal (fra·ter'nal) *adj.* fraternal; brotherly. —**fraternidad,** *n.f.* fraternity; brotherhood.

fraternizar (fra·ter·ni'θar; -'sar) *v.i.* [*infl.:* **rezar,** 10] to fraternize. —**fraternización,** *n.f.* fraternization.

fraterno (fra'ter·no) *adj.* = **fraternal.**

fratricida (fra·tri'θi·ða; -'si·ða) *adj.* fratricidal. —*n.m. & f.* fratricide (*agent*). —**fratricidio** (-'θi·ðjo; -'si·ðjo) *n.m.* fratricide (*act*).

fraude ('frau·ðe) *n.m.* fraud.

fraudulento (frau·ðu'len·to) *adj.* fraudulent. —**fraudulencia,** *n.f.* fraudulence.

fray (frai) *n.m., contr. of* **fraile** *used before a name*; Fra.

frazada (fra'θa·ða; -'sa·ða) *n.f.* blanket.

frecuencia (fre'kwen·θja; -sja) *n.f.*

frequency. —**frecuente,** *adj.* frequent.

frecuentar (fre·kwen'tar) *v.t.* to frequent. —**frecuentación,** *n.f.* frequentation. —**frecuentativo** (-ta'ti·βo) *adj.* frequentative.

fregar (fre'ɣar) *v.t.* [*infl.:* pagar, 8; pensar, 27] 1, to scrub; scour. 2, to wash (dishes). 3, *Amer., colloq.* to pester; annoy. —**fregadero,** *n.m.* sink. —**fregón,** *n.m., Amer.* [*fem.* -gona] pest; annoying person.

freír (fre'ir) *v.t.* [*infl.:* reír, 58; *p.p.* frito, *also,* freído] 1, to fry. 2, to pester; annoy.

fréjol ('fre·xol) *n.m.* = **frijol.**

frenar (fre'nar) *v.t.* 1, to brake. 2, to bridle; restrain.

frenesí (fre·ne'si) *n.m.* frenzy. —**frenético** (-'ne·ti·ko) *adj.* frantic; mad; furious.

frenillo (fre'ni·ʎo; -jo) *n.m., anat.* frenum.

freno ('fre·no) *n.m.* 1, brake. 2, bridle; bit. 3, restraint.

frenología (fre·no·lo'xi·a) *n.f.* phrenology. —**frenológico** (-'lo·xi·ko) *adj.* phrenological. —**frenólogo** (-'no·lo·ɣo) *n.m.* phrenologist.

frente ('fren·te) *n.m.* front. —*n.f.* forehead. —*adv.* = **enfrente.** —**al frente,** in front; out front. —**de frente,** 1, facing forward; abreast. 2, resolutely; directly. —**en frente,** opposite; across. —**frente a,** in front of. —**frente a frente,** face to face. —**hacer frente a,** to face; confront.

freón (fre'on) *n.m.* Freon *(T.N.).*

fresa ('fre·sa) *n.f.* 1, strawberry. 2, drill; bit. 3, milling cutter. 4, *dent.* burr.

fresar (fre'sar) *v.t.* 1, to mill (metals). 2, to ream. —**fresadora,** *n.f.* milling machine.

fresca ('fres·ka) *n.f.* 1, fresh air; cool *(of the morning or evening).* 2, *colloq.* wisecrack.

fresco ('fres·ko) *adj.* 1, fresh. 2, cool. 3, impudent. —*n.m.* 1, coolness; freshness. 2, fresco. 3, *colloq.* impudent person. 4, *Amer.* = **refresco.**

frescor (fres'kor) *n.m.* 1, freshness; coolness. 2, *paint.* vivid tone; glowing quality.

frescura (fres'ku·ra) *n.f.* 1, freshness; coolness. 2, impudence; boldness.

fresno ('fres·no) *n.m.* ash *(tree and wood).*

freza ('fre·θa; -sa) *n.f.* 1, spawn. 2, spawning. 3, spawning season. —**frezar,** *v.i.* [*infl.:* rezar, 10] to spawn.

fría ('fri·a) *v., pres.subjve.* of **freír.**

friable (fri'a·βle) *adj.* friable.

frialdad (fri·al'dað) *n.f.* 1, coldness; coolness. 2, frigidity.

fricasé (fri·ka'se) *n.m.* fricassee.

fricativo (fri·ka'ti·βo) *adj.* fricative. —**fricativa,** *n.f.* fricative (consonant).

fricción (frik'θjon; -'sjon) *n.f.* 1, friction. 2, rubbing. —**friccional,** *adj.* frictional. —**friccionar,** *v.t.* to rub.

friega ('frje·ɣa) *n.f.* 1, *colloq.* rubdown. 2, *slang* nuisance; bother.

friego ('frje·ɣo) *v., pres.ind.* of **fregar.**

friegue ('frje·ɣe) *v., pres.subjve.* of **fregar.**

friendo (fri'en·do) *v., ger.* of **freír.**

frígido ('fri·xi·ðo) *adj.* frigid. —**frigidez,** *n.f.* frigidity.

frigorífico (fri·ɣo'ri·fi·ko) *adj.* refrigerating. —*n.m.* cold storage plant.

frijol (fri'xol) *also,* **fríjol** ('fri·xol) *n.m.* bean; kidney bean.

frío ('fri·o) *adj.* cold; cool. —*n.m.* cold; chill. —**friolento** (frjo'len·to) *adj.* sensitive to cold. —**tener frío,** to be (feel) cold.

frío ('fri·o) *v., pres.ind.* of **freír.**

frió (fri'o) *v., 3rd pers.sing. pret.* of **freír.**

friolera (fri·o'le·ra) *n.f.* trifle; something trivial.

frisa ('fri·sa) *n.f.* 1, frieze *(cloth).* 2, *P.R.* blanket.

frisar (fri'sar) *v.t.* to rub. —*v.i.* *(with* con *or* en) to get along (with).

friso ('fri·so) *n.m.* 1, frieze. 2, baseboard. 3, dado.

fritada (fri'ta·ða) *n.f.* 1, fry. 2, fritter.

frito ('fri·to) *v., p.p.* of **freír.** —*n.m.* 1, fry. 2, fritter.

fritura (fri'tu·ra) *n.f.* = **fritada.**

frivolité (fri·βo·li'te) *n.m.* tatting.

frívolo ('fri·βo·lo) *adj.* frivolous. —**frivolidad,** *n.f.* frivolousness.

fronda ('fron·da) *n.f.* frond.

frondoso (fron'do·so) *adj.* luxuriant. —**frondosidad,** *n.f.* luxuriant growth.

frontal (fron'tal) *adj.* frontal.

frontera (fron'te·ra) *n.f.* 1, fron-

tier; border. **2,** = **frontispicio.**
—**fronterizo,** *adj.* frontier *(attrib.).*
frontispicio (fron·tis'pi·θjo; -sjo)
n.m. **1,** frontispiece. **2,** façade. *Also,*
frontis ('fron·tis) *n.m.sing. & pl.*
frontón (fron'ton) *n.m.* **1,** jai alai
wall or court. **2,** escarpment; scarp.
3, *archit.* frontispiece. **4,** [*also,*
juego de frontón] handball.
frotar (fro'tar) *v.t.* to rub. —**frote**
('fro·te) *n.m.* rub; rubbing.
frotis ('fro·tis) *n.m., med.* smear.
fructífero (fruk'ti·fe·ro) *adj.* =
fructuoso.
fructificar (fruk·ti·fi'kar) *v.i.*
[*infl.:* **tocar,** 7] to bear fruit; fructify. —**fructificación,** *n.f.* fructifica-
tion.
fructosa (fruk'to·sa) *n.f.* fructose.
fructuoso (fruk'two·so) *adj.* bearing fruit; fruitful.
frugal (fru'γal) *adj.* frugal. —**frugalidad,** *n.f.* frugality.
fruición (fru·i'θjon; -'sjon) *n.f.* enjoyment; gratification.
frunce ('frun·θe; -se) *n.m.* pleat;
shirr.
fruncir (frun'θir; -'sir) *v.t.* [*infl.:*
esparcir, 12] **1,** to wrinkle (the
brow, nose, etc.). **2,** to pucker. **3,**
sewing to gather; shirr. —**fruncirse,**
v.r. to frown.
fruslería (frus·le'ri·a) *n.f.* bauble.
frustrar (frus'trar) *v.t.* to frustrate.
—**frustración,** *n.f.* frustration.
fruta ('fru·ta) *n.f.* fruit —**frutal**
(fru'tal) *adj.* fruit-bearing. —*n.m.*
fruit tree. —**frutar,** *v.i.* to yield
fruit.
fruta bomba, *Cuba* papaya.
frutero (fru'te·ro) *adj.* fruit
(attrib.). —*n.m.* **1,** fruit bowl. **2,**
fruit seller; fruiterer. —**frutería,** *n.f.*
fruit shop.
fruto ('fru·to) *n.m.* **1,** fruit *(yield of
a plant).* **2,** *fig.* result; consequence.
3, *fig.* benefit; profit.
fucsia ('fuk·sja) *n.f.* fuchsia.
¡fuche! ('fu·t∫e; *Amer.* ugh!;
pew!; phew! *Also,* **¡fucha!** (-t∫a),
¡fuchi! (-t∫i).
fue (fwe) *v., 3rd pers.sing. pret. of*
ir *and* **ser.**
fuego ('fwe·γo) *n.m.* **1,** fire. **2,** light
(for a fire). **3,** itchy rash; skin eruption. —**fuego de Santelmo,** Saint
Elmo's fire. —**fuego fatuo,** will-o'-
the-wisp. —**fuegos artificiales,**
fireworks. —**hacer fuego,** to fire;
shoot. —**pegar fuego,** to set fire.
—**romper el fuego,** to open fire.

fuelle ('fwe·ʎe; -je) *n.m.* **1,** bellows. **2,** pucker; pleat; fold. **3,**
colloq. telltale, gossip.
fuente ('fwen·te) *n.f.* **1,** fountain. **2,**
spring; fountainhead. **3,** platter. **4,**
fig. source.
fuer (fwer) *n.m., contr. of* **fuero,** *in*
a fuer de, by reason of; by way of.
fuera ('fwe·ra) *adv.* out; outside;
without. —*interj.* out!; get out!
—**fuera de,** outside of. —**fuera de
sí,** beside oneself. —**por fuera,** on
the outside.
fuera ('fwe·ra) *v., impf.subjve. of* **ir**
and **ser.**
fuerce ('fwer·θe; -se) *v., pres.
subjve. of* **forzar.**
fuere ('fwe·re) *v., fut.subjve. of* **ir**
and **ser.**
fuero ('fwe·ro) *n.m.* **1,** jurisdiction;
authority. **2,** statute. **3,** exemption;
privilege. **4,** code of laws. **5,** *fig.* arrogance. —**fuero interno,** con-
science.
fueron ('fwe·ron) *v., 3rd pers.pl.
pret. of* **ir** *and* **ser.**
fuerte ('fwer·te) *adj.* **1,** strong. **2,**
loud. —*adv.* **1,** hard; vigorously. **2,**
loud. —*n.m.* **1,** fort. **2,** forte.
fuerza ('fwer·θa; -sa) *n.f.* **1,**
strength. **2,** force; power. —**fuerzas,** *n.f.pl., mil.* forces. —**a fuerza
de,** by dint of. —**con toda fuerza,**
all-out; full blast. —**fuerza mayor,**
act of God. —**por fuerza,** necessarily.
fuerzo ('fwer·θo; -so) *v., 1st
pers.sing. pres.ind. of* **forzar.**
fuese ('fwe·se) *v., impf.subjve. of* **ir**
and **ser.**
fuete ('fwe·te) *n.m., Amer.* = **látigo.**
—**fuetazo,** *n.m., Amer.* = **latigazo.**
fuga ('fu·γa) *n.f.* **1,** flight; escape.
2, *mus.* fugue.
fugarse (fu'γar·se) *v.r.* [*infl.:*
pagar, 8] to flee; escape.
fugaz (fu'γaθ; -'γas) *adj.* fleeting.
—**fugacidad** (-θi'ðað; -si'ðað) *n.f.*
brevity; fleeting quality.
fugitivo (fu·γi'ti·βo) *adj. & n.m.*
fugitive.
fui (fwi) *v., 1st pers.sing. pret. of* **ir**
and **ser.**
fulano (fu'la·no) *n.m.* so-and-so.
—**fulano de tal,** John Doe. —**fulano, zutano y mengano,** Tom, Dick
and Harry.
fular (fu'lar) *n.m.* foulard.
fulcro ('ful·kro) *n.m.* fulcrum.
fulgente (ful'xen·te) *adj.* fulgent.
—**fulgencia,** *n.f.* effulgence.

fulgor (ful'yor) *n.m.* brilliance; effulgence.

fulgurar (ful·yu'rar) *v.i.* to shine; gleam. —**fulguroso,** *adj.* bright; shining.

fúlica ('fu·li·ka) *n.f., ornith.* coot.

fulján (ful'xan) *n.m., poker* full house.

fulminante (ful·mi'nan·te) *adj.* 1, sudden; violent. 2, instantly fatal. —*n.m.* 1, percussion cap. 2, fulminate.

fulminar (ful·mi'nar) *v.t.* 1, to strike, as with lightning. 2, to hurl, as insults, threats, etc. 3, to fulminate against. —**fulminación,** *n.f.* fulmination.

fullería (fu·ʎe'ri·a; fu·je-) *n.f.* 1, cheating at games. 2, trickery.

fullero (fu'ʎe·ro; -'je·ro) *adj.* 1, cheating. 2, tricky. 3, mischievous. —*n.m.* [*fem.* **-ra**] 1, cheat. 2, trickster.

fumada (fu'ma·ða) *n.f.* 1, puff or draw (*in smoking*). 2, *Amer.* act of smoking; smoke.

fumadero (fu·ma'ðe·ro) *n.m.* smoking room.

fumador (fu·ma'ðor) *n.m.* [*fem.* **-dora**] smoker.

fumar (fu'mar) *v.t.* to smoke. —*v.i.* to smoke; fume. —**fumarse (algo),** to squander (something). —**fumarse (una persona)** *Amer., colloq.* to fix; take care of (someone). —**fumarse la clase,** to cut class.

fumarada (fu·ma'ra·ða) *n.f.* 1, puff (*of smoke*). 2, pipeful.

fumigar (fu·mi'yar) *v.t.* [*infl.:* **pagar,** 8] to fumigate. —**fumigación,** *n.f.* fumigation. —**fumigante,** *n.m.* fumigant. —**fumigador,** *n.m.* fumigator.

función (fun'θjon; -'sjon) *n.f.* 1, function. 2, *theat.* performance. —**funcional,** *adj.* functional.

funcionar (fun·θjo'nar; -sjo'nar) *v.i.* to function; perform. —**funcionamiento,** *n.m.* performance.

funcionario (fun·θjo'na·rjo; fun·sjo-) *n.m.* functionary; public official; civil servant.

funda ('fun·da) *n.f.* 1, covering; wrapper. 2, pillow slip.

fundamento (fun·da'men·to) *n.m.* 1, basis. 2, = **cimiento.** —**fundamental,** *adj.* fundamental. —**fundamentar,** *v.t.* lay the foundation of.

fundar (fun'dar) *v.t.* 1, to found. 2,

to base; rest. —**fundación,** *n.f.* foundation. —**fundadamente,** *adv.* with good reason. —**fundador,** *n.m.* [*fem.* **-dora**] founder.

fundente (fun'den·te) *n.m., chem.; metall.* flux.

fundible (fun'di·βle) *adj.* fusible.

fundición (fun·di'θjon; -'sjon) *n.f.* 1, foundry. 2, founding; casting. 3, fusion; melting. 4, *print.* font.

fundidor (fun·di'ðor) *n.m.* founder; foundryman.

fundillos (fun'di·ʎos; -jos) *n.m.pl.* = **fondillos.**

fundir (fun'dir) *v.t.* 1, to fuse; melt. 2, to cast; found. —**fundirse,** *v.r.* 1, to fuse; merge. 2, *Amer., colloq.* to fail; flop.

fúnebre ('fu·ne·βre) *adj.* funereal; gloomy. —**honras** *or* **pompas fúnebres,** funeral services.

funeral (fu·ne'ral) *n.m., often pl.* funeral. —*adj.* funeral.

funeraria (fu·ne'ra·rja) *n.f.* funeral parlor.

funerario (fu·ne'ra·rjo) *adj.* funeral (*attrib.*). —*n.m.* funeral director.

funesto (fu'nes·to) *adj.* 1, baneful; fatal. 2, regrettable; unfortunate.

fungicida (fun·xi'θi·ða; -'si·ða) *n.m.* fungicide. —*adj.* fungicidal.

fungo ('fun·go) *n.m.,* fungus. —**fungoso,** *adj.* fungous; spongy.

funicular (fu·ni·ku'lar) *adj.* & *n.m.* funicular.

furgón (fur'yon) *n.m.* 1, freight car. 2, caboose. 3, covered wagon.

furia ('fu·rja) *n.f.* fury.

furibundo (fu·ri'βun·do) *adj.* furious; maddened.

furioso (fu'rjo·so) *adj.* furious.

furor (fu'ror) *n.m.* rage; furor. —**hacer furor,** *colloq.* to be the rage.

furtivo (fur'ti·βo) *adj.* furtive.

furúnculo (fu'run·ku·lo) *n.m.* furuncle; boil.

fuselaje (fu·se'la·xe) *n.m.* fuselage.

fusible (fu'si·βle) *adj.* fusible. —*n.m., elect.* fuse. —**fusibilidad,** *n.f.* fusibility.

fusil (fu'sil) *n.m.* gun; rifle. —**fusilar,** *v.t.* to shoot; kill by shooting. —**fusilamiento,** *n.m.* shooting; execution by shooting.

fusilería (fu·si·le'ri·a) *n.f.* 1, rifles collectively. 2, body of fusiliers or riflemen.

fusilero (fu·si'le·ro) *n.m.* fusilier; rifleman.
fusión (fu'sjon) *n.f.* 1, fusion. 2, merger. —**fusionar,** *v.t.* to fuse; merge.
fusta ('fus·ta) *n.f.* 1, horsewhip. 2, switch; rod.
fustán (fus'tan) *n.m.* 1, fustian. 2, *Amer.* woman's slip.
fuste ('fus·te) *n.m.* 1, shaft. 2, *fig.* substance; sinew.
fustigar (fus·ti'gar) *v.t.* [*infl.:*

pagar, 8] to lash. —**fustigación,** *n.f.* lashing.
fútbol ('fut·βol) *n.m.* soccer; football. —**futbolista,** *n.m. & f.* football player; soccer player.
fútil ('fu·til) *adj.* futile. —**futilidad,** *n.f.* futility.
futuro (fu'tu·ro) *adj. & n.m.* future. —*n.m.* fiancé. —**futura,** *n.f.* fiancée. —**futurismo,** *n.m.* futurism. —**futurista,** *adj.* futuristic.

G

G, g (xe) *n.f.* 8th letter of the Spanish alphabet.
gabacho (ga'βa·tʃo) *adj. & n.m.* Pyrenean. —*adj., derog.* French. —*n.m.* 1, *derog.* Frenchman. 2, Gallicized Spanish.
gabán (ga'βan) *n.m.* 1, overcoat. 2, *W.I.* jacket.
gabardina (ga·βar'ði·na) *n.f.* 1, gabardine. 2, raincoat.
gabarra (ga'βa·rra) *n.f.* lighter; barge.
gabinete (ga·βi'ne·te) *n.m.* 1, cabinet. 2, study; office.
gablete (ga'βle·te) *n.m.* gable.
gacela (ga'θe·la; ga'se-) *n.f.* gazelle.
gaceta (ga'θe·ta; ga'se-) *n.f.* gazette.
gacetilla (ga·θe'ti·ʎa; ga·se'ti·ja) *n.f.* 1, short news item. 2, gossip column. 3, *colloq.* newsmonger; gossip. —**gacetillero,** *n.m.* newsmonger; gossip columnist.
gacha ('ga·tʃa) *n.f., often pl.* mush; pap; gruel.
gacho ('ga·tʃo) *adj.* turned downward; drooping. —**a gachas,** bending low; stooping; on all fours.
gadolinio (ga·ðo'li·njo) *n.m.* gadolinium.
gaélico (ga·e'li·ko) *adj. & n.m.* Gaelic.
gafa ('ga·fa) *n.f.* = **grapa.** —**gafas,** *n.f.pl.* spectacles.
gafe ('ga·fe) *n.m. & f., colloq.* jinx.
gago ('ga·ɣo) *adj. & n.m., Amer., colloq.* = **tartamudo.** —**gaguear** (ga·ɣe'ar) *v.i.* = **tartamudear.** —**gagueo** (ga'ɣe·o) *n.m.* = **tartamudez.**
gaita ('gai·ta) *n.f.* 1, bagpipe. 2,

colloq. bother; nuisance. —**gaitero,** *n.m.* piper.
gajes ('ga·xes) *n.m.pl.* wages. —**gajes del oficio,** occupational hazards or drawbacks.
gajo ('ga·xo) *n.m.* 1, torn or fallen branch. 2, segment (*of an orange, tangerine, etc.*).
gala ('ga·la) *n.f.* 1, finery; gala. 2, grace; pleasing manner. 3, pride and joy. —**de gala,** gala; festal. —**hacer gala de,** to make a display of; boast of.
galáctico (ga'lak·ti·ko) *adj.* galactic.
galán (ga'lan) *adj.* [*also,* **galano** (ga'la·no)] 1, spruce; dapper. 2, elegant; handsome. —*n.m.* 1, leading man. 2, suitor. 3, handsome man; gallant.
galante (ga'lan·te) *adj.* gallant; courtly; attentive.
galantear (ga·lan·te'ar) *v.t.* 1, to flatter; compliment (a woman). 2, to court; woo.
galanteo (ga·lan'te·o) *n.m.* 1, flattery; gallantry. 2, courtship; wooing.
galantería (ga·lan·te'ri·a) *n.f.* 1, compliment; flattery; gallantry. 2, courtesy; attention.
galanura (ga·la'nu·ra) *n.f.* 1, elegance. 2, grace; poise.
galápago (ga'la·pa·ɣo) *n.m.* turtle; terrapin.
garlardón (ga·lar'ðon) *n.m.* reward; prize; award. —**galardonar,** *v.t.* to reward.
galaxia (ga'lak·sja) *n.f.* galaxy.
galena (ga'le·na) *n.f.* galena.
galeno (ga'le·no) *n.m., colloq.* physician.

galeón (ga·le'on) *n.m.* galleon.
galeote (ga·le'o·te) *n.m.* galley slave.
galera (ga'le·ra) *n.f.* **1,** galley (*ship*). **2,** van; wagon. **3,** *print.* galley. **4,** *Amer.* top hat; silk hat.
galerada (ga·le'ra·ða) *n.f.* **1,** *print.* galley. **2,** *print.* galley proof. **3,** wagonload.
galería (ga·le'ri·a) *n.f.* **1,** gallery. **2,** *theat.* balcony. **3,** shopping mall.
galés (ga'les) *adj.* Welsh. —*n.m.* **1,** Welshman. **2,** Welsh language. —**galesa** (-'le·sa) *n.f.* Welsh woman.
galga ('gal·ɣa) *n.f.* **1,** female greyhound. **2,** wheel brake; skid. **3,** rash; mange.
galgo ('gal·ɣo) *n.m.* greyhound.
galicismo (ga·li'θis·mo; -'sis·mo) *n.m.* Gallicism.
galillo (ga'li·ʎo; -jo) *n.m.* uvula.
galio ('ga·ljo) *n.m.* gallium.
galo ('ga·lo) *adj.* Gallic. —*n.m.*, *cap.* Gaul; Gaulish (*language*).
galocha (ga'lo·tʃa) *n.f.* galosh; overshoe.
galón (ga'lon) *n.m.* **1,** gallon. **2,** chevron; stripe. **3,** braid; trimming. —**galonear,** *v.t.* to trim with braid.
galope (ga'lo·pe) *n.m.* gallop. —**galopar** (-'par) *also,* **galopear** (-pe'ar) *v.t.* to gallop. —**galopante,** *adj.* galloping. —**a galope tendido,** at full speed.
galvánico (gal'βa·ni·ko) *adj.* galvanic. —**galvanismo,** *n.m.* galvanism.
galvanizar (gal·βa·ni'θar; -'sar) *v.t.* [*infl.:* **rezar,** 10] to galvanize. —**galvanización,** *n.f.* galvanization.
galvanómetro (gal·βa'no·me·tro) *n.m.* galvanometer.
gallardete (ga·ʎar'ðe·te; ga·jar-) *n.m.* pennant.
gallardo (ga'ʎar·ðo; ga'jar-) *adj.* gallant. —**gallardear,** *v.i.* to behave with gallantry. —**gallardía,** *n.f.* gallantry.
gallear (ga·ʎe'ar; ga·je-) *v.i.*, *colloq.* to bluster.
gallego (ga'ʎe·ɣo; ga'je-) *adj. & n.m.* Galician.
galleta (ga'ʎe·ta; ga'je-) *n.f.* **1,** cracker; biscuit. **2,** *colloq.* slap in the face.
gallina (ga'ʎi·na; ga'ji-) *n.f.* hen; chicken. —*n.m. or f.*, *colloq.* coward; chickenhearted person. —**gallináceo** (-'na·θe·o; -'na·se·o) *adj.* gallinaceous.

gallinazo (ga·ʎi'na·θo; -ji'na·so) *n.m.* turkey buzzard.
gallinero (ga·ʎi'ne·ro; ga·ji-) *n.m.* **1,** poultry yard; chicken coop. **2,** poulterer. **3,** *colloq.* peanut gallery. —**gallinería,** *n.f.* **1,** poultry market. **2,** flock of hens.
gallo ('ga·ʎo; -jo) *n.m.* **1,** rooster; cock. **2,** *colloq.* bully. **3,** *colloq.* cracking of the voice. **4,** *ichthy.* dory. —*adj.*, *Amer.* cocky; brave. —**gallo de pelea,** gamecock. —**misa del gallo,** midnight Mass at Christmas. —**patas de gallo,** crow's-feet.
gama ('ga·ma) *n.f.* **1,** gamut. **2,** doe. **3,** = **gamma.**
gamba ('gam·ba) *n.f.* prawn.
gambito (gam'bi·to) *n.m.* gambit.
gamma ('ga·ma) *n.f.* gamma. —**rayos gamma,** gamma rays.
gamarra (ga'ma·rra) *n.f.* martingale (*piece of harness*).
gameto (ga'me·to) *n.m.* gamete.
gamo ('ga·mo) *n.m.* male fallow deer.
gamón (ga'mon) *n.m.* asphodel.
gamuza (ga'mu·θa; -sa) *n.f.* chamois.
gana ('ga·na) *n.f.* desire; inclination. —**de buena gana,** with pleasure; willingly. —**de mala gana,** unwillingly. —**no me da la gana,** *colloq.* I don't feel like it. —**tener gana(s) de,** to feel like; to be inclined to.
ganado (ga'na·ðo) *n.m.* livestock, esp. cattle. —**ganadería,** *n.f.* animal husbandry; cattle raising. —**ganadero,** *n.m.* rancher.
ganancia (ga'nan·θja; -sja) *n.f.* gain; profit; advantage. —**ganancia de capital,** capital gain. —**ganancial,** *adj.* profit (*attrib.*). —**ganancia líquida,** net profit.
ganar (ga'nar) *v.t.* **1,** to gain. **2,** to win. **3,** to earn. —**ganador,** *adj.* winning. —*n.m.* winner.
gancho ('gan·tʃo) *n.m.* **1,** hook. **2,** *Amer.* hairpin. **3,** *Amer.* coat hanger. **4,** *colloq.* charm; allure. —**echar el gancho a,** to trap; hook (someone).
gandul (gan'dul) *n.m.* loafer; ne'er-do-well. —**gandulear,** *v.i.* to loaf; idle. —**gandulería** (-le'ri·a) *n.f.* idleness; laziness.
ganga ('gan·ga) *n.f.* **1,** gangue. **2,** *colloq.* bargain; good buy. **3,** *colloq.* cinch; snap.
ganglio ('gan·gljo) *n.m.* ganglion.
gangoso (gan'go·so) *adj.* twangy;

nasal. —**gangosidad,** *n.f.* twanginess; twang.

gangrena (gan'gre·na) *n.f.* gangrene. —**gangrenarse,** *v. r.* to become gangrenous. —**gangrenoso,** *adj.* gangrenous.

gangster ('gang·ster) *n.m.* gangster.

ganguear (gan·ge'ar) *v.i.* to snuffle; talk through the nose. —**gangueo** (-'ge·o) *n.m.* snuffle; snuffling.

ganoso (ga'no·so) *adj.* 1, desirous. 2, *Amer.* spirited (*of a horse*).

ganso ('gan·so) *n.m.* 1, goose; gander. 2, *colloq.* oaf; lout.

ganzúa (gan'θu·a; -'su·a) *n.f.* picklock.

gañido (ga'ɲi·ðo) *n.m.* 1, yelp; yelping. 2, croak; croaking.

gañir (ga'ɲir) *v.i.* [*infl.:* gruñir, 21] 1, to yelp. 2, to croak (*of birds*). 3, to gasp; pant; wheeze.

garabato (ga·ra'βa·to) *n.m.* 1, scrawl; doodle. 2, grapnel; hook. —**garabatear,** *v.i.* to scrawl; doodle.

garaje *also* **garage** (ga'ra·xe) *n.m.* garage.

garante (ga'ran·te) *n.m.* guarantor.

garantía (ga·ran'ti·a) *n.f.* guarantee.

garantir (ga·ran'tir) *v.t.* [*defective: used only in forms whose endings begin with* i] to guarantee.

garantizar (ga·ran·ti'θar; -'sar) *v.t.* [*infl.:* rezar, 10] to guarantee.

garañón (ga·ra'ɲon) *n.m.* 1, stud jackass or camel. 2, *Amer.* stud horse; stallion.

garapiña (ga·ra'pi·ɲa) *n.f.* sugar coating; glaze. —**garapiñado,** *adj.* sugar-coated; glacé. —*n.m.* = garapiña. —**garapiñar,** *v.t.* to coat with sugar; glaze.

garbanzo (gar'βan·θo; -so) *n.m.* chick pea.

garbo ('gar·βo) *n.m.* grace; gallantry. —**garboso,** *adj.* graceful; gallant.

gardenia (gar'ðe·nja) *n.f.* gardenia.

garduño (gar'ðu·ɲo) *n.m.* pickpocket; thief.

garete (ga're·te) *n.m., in* al garete, adrift.

garfa ('gar·fa) *n.f.* claw.

garfio ('gar·fjo) *n.m.* gaff; hook.

gargajo (gar'ɣa·xo) *n.m.* phlegm.

garganta (gar'ɣan·ta) *n.f.* 1, throat. 2, ravine. 3, singing voice.

gárgara ('gar·ɣa·ra) *n.f.* gargle. —**hacer gárgaras,** to gargle.

gargarismo (gar·ɣa'ris·mo) *n.m.* gargle; gargling.

gargarizar (gar·ɣa·ri'θar; -'sar) *v.i.* [*infl.:* rezar, 10] to gargle.

gárgola ('gar·ɣo·la) *n.f.* gargoyle.

garita (ga'ri·ta) *n.f.* sentry box; gatekeeper's box.

garito (ga'ri·to) *n.m.* gambling den.

garlito (gar'li·to) *n.m.* trap; snare.

garra ('ga·rra) *n.f.* claw.

garrafa (ga'rra·fa) *n.f.* carafe; decanter. —**garrafón,** *n.m.* demijohn.

garrafal (ga·rra'fal) *adj.* outrageous; monstrous.

garranchuelo (ga·rran'tʃwe·lo) *n.m.* crabgrass.

garrapata (ga·rra'pa·ta) *n.f.* tick.

garrapato (ga·rra'pa·to) *n.m.* scribble; scrawl. —**garrapatear** (-te'ar) *v.i.* to scribble; scrawl.

garrocha (ga'rro·tʃa) *n.f.* 1, goad. 2, pole for vaulting. —**salto de garrocha,** pole vault.

garrote (ga'rro·te) *n.m.* 1, cudgel. 2, garrote. —**garrotazo,** *n.m.* blow with a cudgel.

garrotero (ga·rro'te·ro) *adj.,* *Amer.* stingy. —*n.m., Amer.* 1, brakeman. 2, loan shark.

garrucha (ga'rru·tʃa) *n.f.* pulley.

gárrulo ('ga·rru·lo) *adj.* garrulous. —**garrular,** *v.i.* to chatter. —**garrulería,** *n.f.* chatter. —**garrulidad,** *n.f.* garrulity.

garúa (ga'ru·a) *n.f., naut. & Amer.* drizzle.

garza ('gar·θa; -sa) *n.f.* heron.

garzo ('gar·θo; -so) *adj.* blue; bluish.

garzón (gar'θon; -'son) *n.m.* boy; lad.

gas (gas) *n.m.* gas. —**gas hilarante,** laughing gas. —**gas lacrimógeno,** tear gas.

gasa ('ga·sa) *n.f.* 1, gauze. 2, chiffon.

gaseoso (ga·se'o·so) *adj.* 1, gaseous. 2, gassy. —**gaseosa,** *n.f.* soda water; soda.

gasfitero (gas·fi'te·ro) *n.m., Amer.* plumber; gas fitter.

gasista (ga'sis·ta) *n.m.* gas fitter.

gasolina (ga·so'li·na) *n.f.* gasoline.

gasolinera (ga·so·li'ne·ra) *n.f.* 1, motorboat. 2, filling station.

gasómetro (ga'so·me·tro) *n.m.* 1, gas meter. 2, gas tank.

gastable (gas'ta·βle) *adj.* expendable.

gastar (gas'tar) *v.t.* **1,** to spend. **2,** to wear out. **3,** to use up; exhaust. **4,** to use or wear habitually. —**gastarse,** *v.r.* **1,** to burn oneself out. **2,** to wear out. —**gastador,** *n.m.* spendthrift. —**gastar una broma,** to play a joke. —**gastarlas,** to carry on.

gasto ('gas·to) *n.m.* **1,** expenditure; expense. **2,** use; consumption.

gástrico ('gas·tri·ko) *adj.* gastric.

gastritis (gas'tri·tis) *n.f.* gastritis.

gastronomía (gas·tro·no'mi·a) *n.f.* gastronomy. —**gastronómico** (-'no·mi·ko) *adj.* gastronomic. —**gastrónomo** (-'tro·no·mo) *n.m.* gourmet; gastronome.

gata ('ga·ta) *n.f.* female cat. —**a gatas,** on all fours.

gatear (ga·te'ar) *v.i.* **1,** to climb; clamber. **2,** to go on all fours. —*v.t.,* *colloq.* to claw.

gatillo (ga'ti·ʎo; -jo) *n.m.* **1,** trigger. **2,** hammer (*of a firearm*). **3,** *dent.* extractor. **4,** kitten. **5,** *colloq.* petty thief.

gato ('ga·to) *n.m.* **1,** cat. **2,** *mech.* jack. —**gatuno,** *adj.* feline; catlike. —**cuatro gatos,** a handful of people. —**dar gato por liebre,** to foist something off. —**gato montés,** wildcat. —**hay gato encerrado,** I smell a rat.

gatuperio (ga·tu'pe·rjo) *n.m.* **1,** hodgepodge. **2,** *colloq.* intrigue; hanky-panky.

gaucho ('gau·tʃo) *n.m.* gaucho. —**gauchesco,** *adj.* gaucho (*attrib.*).

gaulteria (gaul'te·rja) *n.f.* wintergreen.

gaveta (ga'βe·ta) *n.f.* drawer.

gavetero (ga·βe'te·ro) *n.m., Amer.* dresser; chest of drawers.

gavia ('ga·βja) *n.f.* topsail.

gavilán (ga·βi'lan) *n.m.* **1,** sparrow hawk. **2,** *Amer.* ingrown toenail.

gavilla (ga'βi·ʎa; -ja) *n.f.* **1,** sheaf (*of grain, hay, etc.*). **2,** gang; mob.

gaviota (ga'βjo·ta) *n.f.* sea gull.

gavota (ga'βo·ta) *n.f.* gavotte.

gaza ('ga·θa; -sa) *n.f.* loop; noose.

gazmoño (gaθ'mo·ɲo; gas-) *adj.* prudish. —*n.m.* prude. —**gazmoñería,** *n.f.* prudishness.

gaznate (gaθ'na·te; gas-) *n.m.* **1,** gullet. **2,** a kind of fritter. —**gaznatada,** *n.f.* a blow to the throat.

gazpacho (gaθ'pa·tʃo; gas-) *n.m.* a cold soup of various vegetables.

geiser ('xei·ser; 'gei-) *n.m.* geyser.

geisha ('xei·ʃa; 'gei-) *n.f.* geisha.

gelatina (xe·la'ti·na) *n.f.* gelatin. —**gelatinoso,** *adj.* gelatinous.

gélido ('xe·li·ðo) *adj., poet.* gelid.

gema ('xe·ma) *n.f.* gem.

gemelo (xe'me·lo) *adj.* twin. —*n.m.* **1,** twin. **2,** cuff link. —**gemelos,** *n.m.pl.* binoculars.

gemido (xe'mi·ðo) *n.m.* moan; howl.

geminar (xe·mi'nar) *v.t.* to geminate. —**geminación,** *n.f.* gemination. —**geminado,** *adj. & n.m.* geminate.

Géminis ('xe·mi·nis) *n.m.* Gemini.

gemir (xe'mir) *v.i.* [*infl.:* **pedir,** 33] to moan; howl.

gen (xen) *n.m.* gene. *Also,* **gene.**

genciana (xen'θja·na; xen'sja-) *n.f.* gentian.

gendarme (xen'dar·me) *n.m.* gendarme.

gene ('xe·ne) *n.m.* = **gen.**

genealogía (xe·ne·a·lo'xi·a) *n.f.* genealogy. —**genealógico** (-'lo·xi·ko) *adj.* genealogical. —**genealogista,** *n.m. & f.* genealogist.

generación (xe·ne·ra'θjon; -'sjon) *n.f.* generation.

generador (xe·ne·ra'ðor) *adj.* generating. —*n.m.* generator.

general (xe·ne'ral) *adj. & n.m.* general. —**general de brigada,** brigadier general. —**general de división,** major general. —**general en jefe,** commander in chief. —**generales,** *n.f.pl.* personal data. —**en** *or* **por lo general,** generally; usually.

generalato (xe·ne·ra'la·to) *n.m.* generalship.

generalidad (xe·ne·ra·li'ðað) *n.f.* **1,** majority; greater part. **2,** generality.

generalísimo (xe·ne·ra'li·si·mo) *n.m.* generalissimo.

generalizar (xe·ne·ra·li'θar; -'sar) *v.t.* [*infl.:* **rezar,** 10] to generalize. —**generalizarse,** *v.r.* to become general; spread. —**generalización,** *n.f.* generalization.

generar (xe·ne'rar) *v.t.* to generate.

generativo (xe·ne·ra'ti·βo) *adj.* generative.

genérico (xe'ne·ri·ko) *adj.* generic.

género ('xe·ne·ro) *n.m.* **1,** genus. **2,** manner. **3,** genre. **4,** textile. **5,** gender. —**género chico,** one-act play. —**género humano,** mankind.

generoso (xe·ne'ro·so) *adj.* generous. —**generosidad,** *n.f.* generosity.

genésico (xe'ne·si·ko) *adj.* genetic.

génesis ('xe·ne·sis) *n.f.* origin; genesis. —*n.m., cap.* Genesis.

genética (xe'ne·ti·ka) *n.f.* genetics. —**genético,** *adj.* genetic.

genial ('xe·njal) *adj.* endowed with genius; brilliant.

genialidad (xe·nja·li'ðað) *n.f.* **1,** genius. **2,** *colloq.* whim; fancy.

genio ('xe·njo) *n.m.* **1,** genius; brilliance. **2,** temperament; temper. **3,** genie.

genital (xe·ni'tal) *adj.* genital. —**genitales,** *n.m.pl.* genitals.

genitivo (xe·ni'ti·βo) *adj. & n.m.* genitive.

genocidio (xe·no'θi·ðjo; -'si·ðjo) *n.m.* genocide. —**genocida** (-'θi·ða; -'si·ða) *adj.* genocidal.

gente ('xen·te) *n.f.* **1,** people; folk. **2,** *colloq.* family. —**don de gentes,** social graces. —**gente baja,** rabble. —**gente bien,** the well-to-do. —**gente de bien,** honest folk. —**gente de mar,** seafaring folk. —**gente de medio pelo,** *derog.* lower classes. —**gente gorda** *or* **de peso,** *colloq.* big shots; brass. —**gente menuda,** children.

gentil (xen'til) *adj.* gentle; kind; gracious. —*adj. & n.m. & f.* gentile; pagan.

gentileza (xen·ti'le·θa; -sa) *n.f.* **1,** politeness. **2,** gracious gesture. **3,** gentility.

gentilhombre (xen·ti'lom·bre) *n.m.* nobleman; gentleman.

gentilicio (xen·ti'li·θjo; -sjo) *adj. & n.m., gram.* gentile.

gentío (xen'ti·o) *n.m.* throng.

gentuza (xen'tu·θa; -sa) *n.f.* rubble.

genuflexión (xe·nu·flek'sjon) *n.f.* genuflection.

genuino (xe'nwi·no) *adj.* genuine.

geocéntrico (xe·o'θen·tri·ko; -'sen·tri·ko) *adj.* geocentric.

geoda (xe'o·ða) *n.f.* geode.

geodesia (xe·o'ðe·sja) *n.f.* geodesy. —**geodésico** (-'ðe·si·ko) *adj.* **1,** geodesic. **2,** geodetic.

geofísica (xe·o'fi·si·ka) *n.f.* geophysics. —**geofísico,** *adj.* geophysical. —*n.m.* geophysicist.

geografía (xe·o·ɣra'fi·a) *n.f.* geography. —**geográfico** (-'ɣra·fi·ko)

adj. geographic. —**geógrafo** (xe'o·ɣra·fo) *n.m.* geographer.

geología (xe·o·lo'xi·a) *n.f.* geology. —**geológico** (-'lo·xi·ko) *adj.* geological. —**geólogo** (xe'o·lo·ɣo) *n.m.* geologist.

geometría (xe·o·me'tri·a) *n.f.* geometry. —**geómetra** (xe'o·me·tra) *n.m. & f.* geometrician. —**geométrico** (-'me·tri·ko) *adj.* geometric. —**geometría del espacio,** solid geometry.

geopolítica (xe·o·po'li·ti·ka) *n.f.* geopolitics. —**geopolítico,** *adj.* geopolitical.

geranio (xe'ra·njo) *n.m.* geranium.

gerencia (xe'ren·θja; -sja) *n.f.* **1,** management, **2,** manager's office.

gerente (xe'ren·te) *n.m. & f.* manager.

geriatría (xe·rja'tri·a) *n.f.* geriatrics. —**geriátrico** (-'rja·tri·ko) *adj.* geriatric.

germanía (xer·ma'ni·a) *n.f.* thieves' slang; cant; argot. —**germanesco,** *adj.* slang *(attrib.).*

germánico (xer'ma·ni·ko) *adj.* Germanic.

germanio (xer'ma·njo) *n.m.* germanium.

germano (xer'ma·no) *adj.* = **alemán.**

germen ('xer·men) *n.m.* **1,** germ. **2,** origin; source.

germicida (xer·mi'θi·ða; -'si·ða) *n.m.* germicide. —*adj.* germicidal.

germinal (xer·mi'nal) *adj.* germinal.

germinar (xer·mi'nar) *v.i.* to germinate. —**germinación,** *n.f.* germination.

gerontología (xe·ron·to·lo'xi·a) *n.f.* gerontology. —**gerontólogo** (-'to·lo·ɣo) *n.m.* gerontologist.

gerundio (xe'run·djo) *n.m.* gerund.

gesta ('xes·ta) *n.f.* feat.

gestar (xes'tar) *v.t.* to gestate. —**gestación,** *n.f.* gestation.

gesticular (xes·ti·ku'lar) *v.i.* to gesticulate. —**gesticulación,** *n.f.* gesticulation.

gestión (xes'tjon) *n.f.* **1,** effort. **2,** step; measure. **3,** démarche. **4,** management. —**gestionar,** *v.t.* to take steps or measures to attain (something).

gesto ('xes·to) *n.m.* **1,** gesture; expression. **2,** appearance. —**estar de buen gesto,** to be agreeable. —**hacer gestos, 1,** to gesture. **2,** to signal. —**poner gesto,** *colloq.* to show anger.

gestor (xes'tor) *adj.* contriving; endeavoring. —*n.m.* agent.

géyser ('xei·ser) *n.m.* = **géiser.**

ghetto ('ge·to) *n.m.* ghetto.

giba ('xi·βa) *n.f.* hump; hunch. —**gibar,** *v.t.* **1,** to bend; curve. **2,** *colloq.* to bother; annoy. —**giboso,** *adj.* **1,** hunchbacked. **2,** gibbous.

gibón (xi'βon) *n.m.* gibbon.

giga ('xi·γa) *n.f.* gigue.

gigante (xi'γan·te) *n.m.* giant. —*adj.* gigantic. —**giganta,** *n.f.* giantess. —**gigantesco,** *adj.* gigantic. —**gigantez,** *n.f.* [*also,* **gigantismo,** *n.m.*] gigantic size; giantism.

gígolo ('xi·γo·lo) *n.m.* gigolo.

gigote (xi'γo·te) *n.m.* minced-meat stew.

gima ('xi·ma) *v., pres.subjve.* of **gemir.**

gimiendo (xi'mjen·do) *v., ger.* of **gemir.**

gimió (xi'mjo) *v., 3rd pers.sing. pret.* of **gemir.**

gimnasia (xim'na·sja) *also,* **gimnástica** (-'nas·ti·ka) *n.f.* gymnastics —**gimnasta** (-'nas·ta) *n.m. & f.* gymnast. —**gimnástico,** *adj.* gymnastic.

gimnasio (xim'na·sjo) *n.m.* gymnasium.

gimo ('xi·mo) *v., pres.ind.* of **gemir.**

gimotear (xi·mo·te'ar) *v.i., colloq.* to whine. —**gimoteo** (-'te·o) *n.m., colloq.* whining.

ginebra (xi'ne·βra) *n.f.* **1,** gin. **2,** confusion; bedlam.

ginecología (xi·ne·ko·lo'xi·a) *n.f.* gynecology. —**ginecológico** (-'lo·xi·ko) *adj.* gynecological. —**ginecólogo** (-'ko·lo·γo) *n.m.* gynecologist.

gingivitis (xin·xi'βi·tis) *n.f.* gingivitis.

gira ('xi·ra) *n.f.* outing; picnic.

giradiscos (xi·ra'ðis·kos) *n.m. sing. & pl.* **1,** record player. **2,** turntable.

giralda (xi'ral·da) *n.f.* weather vane.

girar (xi'rar) *v.i.* **1,** to turn; gyrate. **2,** *comm.* to draw (a check, draft, etc.). **3,** *mech.* to spin. —**girar contra** *or* **a cargo de,** *comm.* to draw on.

girasol (xi·ra'sol) *n.m.* sunflower.

giratorio (xi·ra'to·rjo) *adj.* gyrating; revolving.

giro ('xi·ro) *n.m.* **1,** gyration; rota-

tion. **2,** trend. **3,** *comm.* draft; note; money order. **4,** *comm.* gross; turnover *(of business).* **5,** turn of phrase; figure of speech.

giroscopio (xi·ros'ko·pjo) *also,* **giróscopo** (xi'ros·ko·po) *n.m.* gyroscope.

gitanería (xi·ta·ne'ri·a) *n.f.* **1,** flattery; cajolery. **2,** gypsies collectively. **3,** *slang* dirty trick.

gitano (xi'ta·no) *adj. & n.m.* gypsy. —*n.m.* Gypsy *(language).* —**gitana,** *n.f.* gypsy woman. —**gitanesco,** *adj.* gypsy.

glacial (gla'θjal; -'sjal) *adj.* glacial.

glaciar (gla'θjar; -'sjar) *n.m.* glacier.

gladiador (gla·ðja'ðor) *n.m.* gladiator.

gladiolo (gla'ðjo·lo) *n.m.* gladiolus. *Also, Amer.,* **gladiola,** *n.f.*

glande ('glan·de) *n.m.* glans; penis.

glándula ('glan·du·la) *n.f.* gland. —**glandular,** *adj.* glandular.

glaseado (gla·se'a·ðo) *adj.* glossy.

glasto ('glas·to) *n.m.* woad.

glaucoma (glau'ko·ma) *n.m.* glaucoma.

glicerina (gli·θe'ri·na; gli·se-) *n.f.* glycerin.

glicógeno (gli'ko·xe·no) *n.m.* glycogen.

glicol (gli'kol) *n.m.* glycol.

glifo ('gli·fo) *n.m.* **1,** *archit.; sculp.* groove or channel, usu. vertical. **2,** symbol; glyph.

globo ('glo·βo) *n.m.* **1,** globe. **2,** balloon. —**global,** *adj.* **1,** global. **2,** whole; total.

globulina (glo·βu'li·na) *n.m.* globulin. —**globulina gama,** gamma globulin.

glóbulo ('glo·βu·lo) *n.m.* globule; corpuscle. —**globular,** *adj.* globular.

gloria ('glo·rja) *n.f.* **1,** glory. **2,** heaven; paradise. **3,** blessing. —**estar en sus glorias,** *colloq.* to be in seventh heaven. —**saber a gloria,** *colloq.* to taste heavenly.

gloriar (glo'rjar) *v.t.* [*infl.:* **enviar,** 22] to glorify. —**gloriarse,** *v.r.* (*with* **de** *or* **en**) to glory (in); to boast (of).

glorieta (glo'rje·ta) *n.f.* **1,** summerhouse; bower. **2,** small city park. **3,** traffic circle.

glorificar (glo·ri·fi'kar) *v.t.* [*infl.:* **tocar,** 7] to glorify. —**glorificación,** *n.f.* glorification.

glorioso (glo'rjo·so) *adj.* **1,** glorious. **2,** blessed.

glosa ('glo·sa) *n.f.* gloss; comment. —**glosar,** *v.t.* to gloss; comment on.

glosario (glo'sa·rjo) *n.m.* glossary.

glotis ('glo·tis) *n.f.* glottis. —**glotal,** *adj.* glottal.

glotón (glo'ton) *n.m.* **1,** glutton. **2,** *zoöl.* glutton; wolverine. —*adj.* gluttonous. —**glotonear,** *v.i.* to gorge (on food or drink). —**glotonería,** *n.f.* gluttony.

glucemia (glu'θe·mja; -'se·mja) *n.f.* glycemia.

glucinio (glu'θi·njo; -'si·njo) *n.m.* glucinium.

glucosa (glu'ko·sa) *n.f.* glucose.

gluglú (glu'ɣlu) *n.m.* **1,** gurgle; gurgling. **2,** gobble *(of a turkey).*

gluglutear (glu·ɣlu·te'ar) *v.i.* **1,** to gurgle. **2,** to gobble, as a turkey.

gluten ('glu·ten) *n.m.* gluten. —**glutinoso** (-ti'no·so) *adj.* glutinous.

gnomo ('gno·mo; 'no·mo) *n.m.* gnome.

gnóstico ('gnos·ti·ko; 'nos-) *adj.* & *n.m.* gnostic. —**gnosticismo** (-'θis·mo; -'sis·mo) *n.m.* gnosticism.

gobernación (go·βer·na'θjon; -'sjon) *n.f.* government. —**Ministerio de la Gobernación,** Department of the Interior.

gobernador (go·βer·na'ðor) *n.m.* governor.

gobernadora (go·βer·na'ðo·ra) *n.f.* **1,** lady governor. **2,** governor's wife.

gobernar (go·βer'nar) *v.t.* [*infl.:* **pensar,** 27] **1,** to govern; rule. **2,** to control; steer. —**gobernante,** *adj.* governing; ruling. —*n.m. or f.* ruler.

gobierno (go'βjer·no) *n.m.* **1,** government; administration. **2,** governorship. **3,** governor's offices; the building housing them. **4,** control; steering. **5,** helm; rudder. —**para su gobierno,** for your information and guidance. —**servir de gobierno,** to serve as guide. —**sin gobierno,** adrift.

gobio ('go·βjo) *n.m., ichthy.* gudgeon.

goce ('go·θe; -se) *n.m.* enjoyment.

goce ('go·θe; -se) *v., pres.subjve. of* **gozar.**

gocé (go'θe; -'se) *v., 1st pers.sing. pret. of* **gozar.**

godo ('go·ðo) *n.m.* Goth. —*adj.* Gothic.

gofio ('go·fjo) *n.m.* roasted corn meal.

gol (gol) *n.m., sports* goal.

gola ('go·la) *n.f.* throat; gullet.

goleta (go'le·ta) *n.f.* schooner.

golf (golf) *n.m.* golf.

golfa ('gol·fa) *n.f.* moll; tramp.

golfo ('gol·fo) *n.m.* **1,** gulf; bay. **2,** ragamuffin. **3,** faro.

golilla (go'li·ʎa; -ja) *n.f.* ruff; lace collar.

golondrina (go·lon'dri·na) *n.f.* swallow. —**golondrino,** *n.m.* **1,** male swallow. **2,** vagabond. **3,** *mil.* deserter. **4,** swelling in the armpit.

golosina (go·lo'si·na) *n.f.* **1,** delicacy; tidbit. **2,** sweet tooth. —**golosinar,** *v.i.* to nibble on sweets.

goloso (go'lo·so) *adj.* sweet-toothed.

golpe ('gol·pe) *n.m.* **1,** blow; stroke. **2,** bump; bruise. **3,** knock *(at a door).* **4,** attack; fit. **5,** disappointment; blow. —**caer** *or* **caerse de golpe,** *colloq.* to collapse. —**de golpe,** suddenly. —**de golpe y porrazo,** *colloq.* **1,** in a rush. **2,** unexpectedly. —**de un golpe,** all at once. —**golpe de gente,** crowd; throng. —**golpe de mar,** tidal wave. —**golpe seco,** sharp blow. —**golpe de vista,** glance. —**no dar golpe,** *colloq.* not to hit a lick.

golpear (gol·pe'ar) *v.t.* **1,** to beat; strike. **2,** to knock. **3,** to bruise; bump.

golpetear (gol·pe·te'ar) *v.t. & i.* to knock; pound; rattle. —**golpeteo** (-'te·o) *n.m.* knocking; pounding; rattling.

gollería (go·ʎe'ri·a; go·je-) *n.f.* **1,** delicacy; dainty. **2,** extra; superfluity.

goma ('go·ma) *n.f.* **1,** gum. **2,** rubber. **3,** mucilage. **4,** rubber band. **5,** tire. **6,** eraser. —**gomas,** *n.f.pl., Amer.* galoshes; overshoes. —**goma de mascar,** chewing gum. —**goma hinchable,** bubble gum.

gomoso (go'mo·so) *adj.* gummy. —*n.m.* dandy; fop.

gonado (go'na·ðo) *n.m.* gonad. *Also,* **gónada** ('go·na·ða) *n.f.*

góndola ('gon·do·la) *n.f.* gondola. —**gondolero,** *n.m.* gondolier.

gong (gong) *n.m.* [*pl.* **gongs**] gong.

gonococo (go·no'ko·ko) *n.m.* gonococcus.

gonorrea (go·no'rre·a) *n.f.* gonorrhea.

gordiflón (gor·ði'flon) *also,*
gordinflón (gor·ðin-) *adj., colloq.*
fat; obese; chubby. —*n.m., colloq.*
[*fem.* **-flona**] chubby person.

gordo ('gor·ðo) *adj.* **1,** fat; stout;
plump. **2,** fatty; greasy. —*n.m.* **1,**
fat; grease. **2,** fat person. —**gordu-**
ra, *n.f.* stoutness. —**algo gordo,**
something important. —**armar la**
gorda, *colloq.* **1,** to have a fight. **2,**
to create a furor. —**hacer la vista**
gorda, to close one's eyes; pretend
not to notice.

gordolobo (gor·ðo'lo·βo) *n.m.*
mullein.

gorgojo (gor'γo·xo) *n.m.* weevil;
grub.

gorgorito (gor·γo'ri·to) *n.m.* **1,**
warble; trill. **2,** inarticulate sound;
gurgle.

gorgoteo (gor·γo'te·o) *n.m.* gurgle; gurgling. —**gorgotear,** *v.i.* to
gurgle.

gorila (go'ri·la) *n.m.* gorilla.

gorjear (gor·xe'ar) *v.i.* **1,** to warble; trill. **2,** to gurgle. —**gorjeador,**
adj. warbling. —*n.m.* warbler.

gorjeo (gor'xe·o) *n.m.* **1,** warble;
warbling. **2,** gurgle; gurgling.

gorra ('go·rra) *n.f.* cap —*n.m.,*
colloq. sponger. —**pegar la gorra;**
ir *or* **andar de gorra,** *colloq.* to
sponge.

gorrear (go·rre'ar) *v.t. & i., colloq.*
to sponge; grub; beg.

gorrino (go'rri·no) *n.m.* hog; pig.
—*adj.* hoggish; piggish.

gorrión (go'rrjon) *n.m.* sparrow.

gorro ('go·rro) *n.m.* cap; bonnet.

gorrón (go'rron) *n.m.* **1,** sponger. **2,**
pebble. **3,** *mech.* spindle.

gota ('go·ta) *n.f.* **1,** drop. **2,** *pathol.*
gout. —**gota a gota,** drop by drop.
—**gotas amargas,** bitters. —**sudar**
la gota gorda, *colloq.* to sweat
blood.

gotear (go·te'ar) *v.i.* to drip; leak.
—**goteo** (-'te·o) *n.m.* dripping; leak-
ing.

gotera (go'te·ra) *n.f.* leak; drip;
dripping. —**goteras,** *n.f.pl.* aches;
pains.

gotero (go'te·ro) *n.m., Amer.* =
cuentagotas.

gótico ('go·ti·ko) *adj. & n.m.*
Gothic. —**niño gótico,** coxcomb.

gourmet (gur'me) *n.m. & f.* [*pl.*
gourmets (-'mes)] gourmet.

gozar (go'θar; -'sar) *v.t.* [*infl.:*
rezar, 10] *often fol. by* **de,** **1,** to enjoy; have the benefit of. **2,** to enjoy;

derive pleasure from. —*v.i.* to have
enjoyment or pleasure. —**gozarse,**
v.r., often fol. by **de, en** *or* **con, 1,** to
rejoice. **2,** to enjoy oneself. —**gozar**
mucho, *Amer., colloq.* to have a
good time.

gozne ('goθ·ne; 'gos-) *n.m.* hinge.

gozo ('go·θo; -so) *n.m.* joy.
—**gozoso,** *adj.* joyful; gleeful. —**el**
gozo en el pozo, all hope is gone.
—**no caber de gozo,** to be beside
oneself with joy.

gozque ('goθ·ke; 'gos-) *n.m.* small
barking dog. *Also,* **gozquejo** (-'ke·
xo).

grabación (gra·βa'θjon; -'sjon)
n.f. **1,** engraving. **2,** recording.

grabado (gra'βa·ðo) *n.m.* **1,** engraving; print. **2,** illustration. —*adj.*
1, engraved. **2,** drawn; pictured. **3,**
graven.

grabador (gra·βa'ðor) *n.m.* engraver. —*adj.* recording.

grabadora (gra·βa'ðo·ra) *n.f.,*
also, **grabadora de cinta,** tape recorder; answering machine.

grabar (gra'βar) *v.t.* **1,** to engrave.
2, to record (on a disc, tape, etc.).

gracejo (gra'θe·xo; -'se·xo) *n.m.* **1,**
wit; grace. **2,** *Amer.* buffoon.
—**gracejar** (-'xar) *v.i.* to be witty.
—**gracejada** (-'xa·ða) *n.f., Amer.*
buffoonery.

gracia ('gra·θja; -sja) *n.f.* **1,** grace.
2, charm. **3,** favor. **4,** (*as a polite*
formula) name of a person. **5,** joke.
—**gracias,** *n.f.pl.* thanks. —**caer en**
gracia, to find favor; be favorably
received. —**hacer gracia,** to be
funny or amusing. —**no estar para**
gracias, to be in no mood for jokes.
—**¡tiene gracia!,** isn't it funny!

gracioso (gra'θjo·so; -'sjo·so) *adj.*
1, funny; witty. **2,** gracious; charming. —*n.m.* clown; fool.

grada ('gra·ða) *n.f.* **1,** step (*in front*
of a building or an altar). **2,** *often*
pl. bleachers. **3,** harrow. —**gradar,**
v.t. to harrow.

gradación (gra·ða'θjon; -'sjon)
n.f. gradation.

gradería (gra·ðe'ri·a) *n.f.* **1,** series
of steps. **2,** stands (*in an arena*). **3,**
bleachers. —**gradería cubierta,**
grandstand.

grado ('gra·ðo) *n.m.* **1,** degree. **2,**
grade. **3,** rank. —**de buen grado,**
with pleasure. —**de mal grado,** unwillingly.

graduación (gra·ðwa'θjon; -'sjon)
n.f. **1,** graduation; measurement. **2,**

mil. rank. **3**, proof *(of alcohol)*. **4**, *Amer.* school or college graduation.

graduado (gra'ðwa·ðo) *adj.* **1**, graduated. **2**, graded. **3**, *mil.* brevet. —*adj. & n.m.* graduate. —**probeta graduada**, *chem.* graduate.

gradual (gra'ðwal) *adj.* gradual.

graduar (gra'ðwar) *v.t.* [*infl.*: **continuar, 23**] **1**, to grade. **2**, to graduate. **3**, to adjust. —**graduarse**, *v.r.* to graduate.

gráfico ('gra·fi·ko) *adj.* graphic —*n.m.* diagram. —**gráfica**, *n.f.* graph.

grafito (gra'fi·to) *n.m.* graphite.

gragea (gra'xe·a) *n.f.* **1**, sugar plum. **2**, sugar-coated pill.

grajo ('gra·xo) *n.m., ornith.* rook.

grama ('gra·ma) *n.f.* grass.

gramática (gra'ma·ti·ka) *n.f.* grammar. —**gramatical**, *adj.* grammatical. —**gramático**, *adj.* grammatical. —*n.m.* grammarian. —**gramática parda**, shrewdness.

gramo ('gra·mo) *n.m.* gram.

gramófono (gra'mo·fo·no) *n.m.* phonograph; gramophone.

grampa ('gram·pa) *n.f.* = **grapa**.

gran (gran) *adj.*, *contr.* of **grande** *before a sing. noun.*

grana ('gra·na) *n.f.* **1**, ripening season. **2**, cochineal. **3**, scarlet dye or color. **4**, scarlet cloth.

granada (gra'na·ða) *n.f.* **1**, grenade. **2**, pomegranate. —**granadero**, *n.m.* grenadier.

granadina (gra·na'ði·na) *n.f.* grenadine.

granado (gra'na·ðo) *n.m.* pomegranate tree. —*adj.* **1**, mature; expert. **2**, choice; select.

granar (gra'nar) *v.i.* **1**, to ripen. **2**, *fig.* to become real.

granate (gra'na·te) *n.m.* garnet.

grande ('gran·de) *adj.* **1**, large. **2**, great; grand. —*n.m.* grandee. —**a lo grande**, in high style.

grandeza (gran'de·θa; -sa) *n.f.* **1**, greatness; grandeur. **2**, rank of a grandee. **3**, grandees collectively.

grandilocuente (gran·di·lo·'kwen·te) *adj.* grandiloquent. —**grandilocuencia**, *n.f.* grandiloquence.

grandioso (gran'djo·so) *adj.* grandiose. —**grandiosidad**, *n.f.* grandeur; grandiosity.

granel (gra'nel) *n.m., in* **a granel, 1**, *comm.* in bulk; in odd lots. **2**, in abundance. **3**, at random.

granero (gra'ne·ro) *n.m.* **1**, gran-

ary; barn. **2**, grain-producing district.

granito (gra'ni·to) *n.m.* **1**, granite. **2**, small grain. **3**, pimple.

granizar (gra·ni'θar; -'sar) *v. impers.* [*infl.*: **rezar, 10**] to hail.

granizo (gra'ni·θo; -so) *n.m.* hail; hailstones *(pl).* —**granizada**, *n.f.* hailstorm. —**granizado**, *n.m.* snow cone.

granja ('gran·xa) *n.f.* farm; grange. —**granjero**, *n.m.* farmer.

granjear (gran·xe'ar) *v.t.* to win (friendship, favor, etc.).

grano ('gra·no) *n.m.* **1**, grain. **2**, boil; pimple. —**granoso** (-'no·so), *adj.* grainy. —**al grano**, to the point.

granuja (gra'nu·xa) *n.m.* rogue; rascal. —**granujada**, *n.f.* roguery; rascality.

granujoso (gra·nu'xo·so) *adj.* pimpled; pimply.

granular (gra·nu'lar) *v.t.* to granulate. —*adj.* granular. —**granulación**, *n.f.* granulation.

gránulo ('gra·nu·lo) *n.m.* granule.

grapa ('gra·pa) *n.f.* clamp; staple.

grasa ('gra·sa) *n.f.* grease; fat. —**grasiento**, *also*, **grasoso**, *adj.* greasy. —**graso**, *adj.* fatty.

grata ('gra·ta) *n.f., Amer.* = **atenta**.

gratificación (gra·ti·fi·ka'θjon; -'sjon) *n.f.* **1**, gratification. **2**, bonus; perquisite. **3**, expense allowance.

gratificar (gra·ti·fi'kar) *v.t.* [*infl.*: **tocar, 7**] **1**, to gratify. **2**, to reward; tip.

gratis ('gra·tis) *adv.* gratis; free.

gratitud (gra·ti'tuð) *n.f.* gratitude.

grato ('gra·to) *adj.* pleasant; pleasing.

gratuito (gra'twi·to) *adj.* **1**, free; free of charge. **2**, gratuitous.

grava ('gra·βa) *n.f.* gravel.

gravamen (gra'βa·men) *n.m.* **1**, burden; obligation. **2**, *law* lien; mortgage.

gravar (gra'βar) *v.t.* **1**, to burden. **2**, *law* to encumber. **3**, to tax (a property).

grave ('gra·βe) *adj.* **1**, grave. **2**, *mus.* bass. **3**, accented on the penultimate syllable. —**gravedad**, *n.f.* gravity.

grávida ('gra·βi·ða) *adj.fem.* pregnant.

gravidez (gra·βi'ðeθ; -'ðes) *n.f.* pregnancy.

gravitar (gra·βi'tar) *v.i.* to gravitate. —**gravitación**, *n.f.* gravitation.

gravoso (gra'βo·so) *adj.* burdensome.

graznar (graθ'nar; gras-) *v.i.* to croak; caw.

graznido (graθ'ni·ðo; gras-) *n.m.* croak; caw.

greca ('gre·ka) *n.f.* **1**, fret; fretwork. **2**, *Amer.* coffee maker; coffee pot.

grecorromano (gre·ko·rro'ma·no) *adj.* Greco-Roman.

greda ('gre·ða) *n.f.* fuller's earth.

gregario (gre'ɣa·rjo) *adj.* gregarious. —**gregarismo** (-'ris·mo) *n.m.* gregariousness.

gremio ('gre·mjo) *n.m.* **1**, guild; trade union. **2**, social or occupational group. —**gremial,** *adj.* of or pert. to a guild or trade union.

greña ('gre·ɲa) *n.f.* matted lock of hair. —**greñudo,** *adj.* matted.

grey (grei) *n.f.* congregation; flock.

grial (grjal) *n.m.* grail.

griego ('grje·ɣo) *adj. & n.m.* Greek; Grecian.

grieta ('grje·ta) *n.f.* **1**, crevice. **2**, cleft; crack.

grifo ('gri·fo) *n.m.* **1**, griffin. **2**, faucet; spigot. —*adj.* kinky; tangled.

grilla ('gri·ʎa; -ja) *n.f.* **1**, grid. **2**, female cricket.

grillete (gri'ʎe·te; -'je·te) *n.m.* shackle.

grillo ('gri·ʎo; -jo) *n.m., entom.* cricket. —**grillos,** *n.m.pl.* shackles.

grima ('gri·ma) *n.f.* disgust.

gringo ('grin·go) *n.m., slang* gringo; foreigner, esp. of the U.S.

gripe ('gri·pe) *n.f.* grippe. —**gripal,** *adj.* of or like the grippe.

gris (gris) *adj. & n.m.* gray. —**grisáceo,** *adj.* grayish.

gritar (gri'tar) *v.i.* to shout; cry.

griterío (gri·te'ri·o) *n.m.* shouting; outcry; howl. *Also,* **gritería,** *n.f.*

grito ('gri·to) *n.m.* shout; cry. —**a grito pelado,** at the top of one's lungs.

gritón (gri'ton) *adj.* vociferous.

gro (gro) *n.m.* grosgrain.

grosella (gro'se·ʎa; -ja) *n.f.* red currant. —**grosella blanca** *or* **silvestre,** gooseberry.

grosero (gro'se·ro) *adj.* coarse; uncouth. —**grosería,** *n.f.* coarseness; vulgarity; a vulgar word.

grosor (gro'sor) *n.m.* thickness.

grotesco (gro'tes·ko) *adj.* grotesque.

grúa ('gru·a) *n.f., mech.* crane; tow truck.

gruesa ('grwe·sa) *n.f.* gross.

grueso ('grwe·so) *adj.* **1**, thick. **2**, stout. —*n.m.* **1**, thickness. **2**, greater part; bulk.

grulla ('gru·ʎa; -ja) *n.f., ornith.* crane.

grumete (gru'me·te) *n.m.* cabin boy.

grumo ('gru·mo) *n.m.* clot. —**grumo de la leche,** curd.

gruñido (gru'ɲi·ðo) *n.m.* grunt; growl.

gruñir (gru'ɲir) *v.i.* [*infl.:* 21] to grunt; growl; grumble. —**gruñón,** *adj., colloq.* grumpy; grouchy. —*n.m., colloq.* [*fem.* -**ñona**] grouch; griper.

grupa ('gru·pa) *n.f.* croup; rump. —**grupera,** *n.f.* pillion. —**volver grupas,** to turn tail.

grupo ('gru·po) *n.m.* group.

gruta ('gru·ta) *n.f.* grotto.

guaca ('gwa·ka) *n.f., Amer.* Indian burial ground.

guacal (gwa'kal) *n.m., Amer.* wooden crate.

guacamayo (gwa·ka'ma·jo) *n.m.* macaw.

guacamole (gwa·ka'mo·le) *n.m.,* **1**, *Amer.* avocado salad. **2**, *Mex.* avocado.

guacho ('gua·tʃo) *n.m.* **1**, young bird; chick. **2**, young animal. —*adj. & n.m., Amer.* orphan; foundling. —*adj., Amer.* odd; unmatched; without pair.

guadaña (gwa'ða·ɲa) *n.f.* scythe. —**guadañada,** *n.f.* swath. —**guadañar,** *v.t.* to mow.

guagua ('gwa·gwa) *n.f.* **1**, *W.I.* omnibus; bus. **2**, *S.A.* baby. —**de guagua,** free.

guaje ('gwa·xe) *n.m., Amer.* **1**, a kind of gourd or calabash. **2**, trinket; bauble. **3**, fool; simpleton. **4**, knave; rogue. —*adj., Amer.* **1**, foolish; simple. **2**, knavish; roguish.

guajiro (gwa'xi·ro) *n.m. & adj., Amer.* rustic.

guajolote (gwa·xo'lo·te) *n.m., Mex.* turkey.

guanaco (gwa'na·ko) *n.m.* guanaco.

guanajo (gwa'na·xo) *n.m., Amer.* turkey.

guano ('gwa·no) *n.m.* guano.

guante ('gwan·te) *n.m.* glove. —**arrojar el guante,** to challenge. —**echar el guante a,** to seize; nab. —**guantero,** *n.m.* glover. —**guantera,** *n.f.* glove compartment.

guantelete (gwan·te'le·te) *n.m.* gauntlet.

guapo ('gwa·po) *adj.* 1, handsome. 2, *Amer., colloq.* brave. —*n.m.* 1, dandy. 2, bully. —**guapear**, *v.i., Amer.* to bluster. —**guapería**, *n.f., Amer.* bluster.

guarache (gwa'ra·tʃe) *n.m., Mex.* 1, leather sandal. 2, tire patch.

guarapo (gwa'ra·po) *n.m.* sugarcane juice, esp. fermented.

guarda ('gwar·ða) *n.m. & f.* guard; custodian. —*n.f.* 1, custody. 2, ward (*of a lock*). 3, flyleaf. 4, *mech.* guard; shield.

guardabarreras (gwar·ða·βa·'rre·ras) *n.m. & f.sing. & pl.* gatekeeper.

guardabarro (gwar·ða'βa·rro) *n.m., usu.pl.* fender; mudguard.

guardabosque (gwar·ða'βos·ke) *n.m.* game warden.

guardabrisa (gwar·ða'βri·sa) *n.m.* = parabrisa.

guardacostas (gwar·ða'kos·tas) *n.m.sing. & pl.* coast guard cutter.

guardaespaldas (gwar·ða·es'pal·das) *n.m. & f.sing. & pl.* bodyguard.

guardafango (gwar·ða'fan·go) *n.m.* fender (*of an automobile*).

guardafrenos (gwar·ða'fre·nos) *n.m.sing. & pl.* brakeman.

guardafuegos (gwar·ða'fwe·yos) *n.m.sing. & pl.* fender (*of a fireplace*).

guardagujas (gwar·ða'yu·xas) *n.m.sing. & pl., R.R.* switchman.

guardalmacén (gwar·ðal·ma'θen; -'sen) *n.m.* 1, keeper of supplies or stores; storekeeper. 2, warehouseman. *Also,* **guardaalmacén** (gwar·ða·al-).

guardameta (gwar·ða'me·ta) *n.m.* goalkeeper; goalie.

guardapelo (gwar·ða'pe·lo) *n.m.* locket.

guardapolvo (gwar·ða'pol·βo) *n.m.* 1, dust cover. 2, duster; light coat.

guardar (gwar'ðar) *v.t.* 1, to hold; keep. 2, to save; store. 3, to watch over; protect. —**guardarse**, *v.r.* to take care; be wary. —**guardarse de**, to guard against; avoid. —**guardar cama**, to stay in bed; to be confined to bed.

guardarropa (gwar·ða'rro·pa) *n.m.* 1, cloakroom. 2, wardrobe; clothes closet. —*n.m. & f.* cloakroom attendant; *theat.* property

man. —**guardarropía**, *n.f., theat.* property room.

guardavía (gwar·ða'vi·a) *n.m., R.R.* lineman; section hand.

guardería (gwar·ðe'ri·a) *n.f.* 1, occupation of a guard or keeper. 2, [*also,* **guardería infantil**] nursery; day nursery; nursery school.

guardia ('gwar·ðja) *n.f.* 1, guard. 2, *naut.* watch. 3, protection; guarding. —*n.m.* policeman. —**guardia civil**, rural police or policeman. —**guardia marina**, *n.m.* midshipman.

guardián (gwar'ðjan) *n.m.* 1, guardian; custodian. 2, keeper.

guarecer (gwa·re'θer; -'ser) *v.t.* [*infl.:* **conocer**, 13] to shelter.

guarida (gwa'ri·ða) *n.f.* den; lair.

guarismo (gwa'ris·mo) *n.m.* digit; figure; number.

guarnecer (gwar·ne'θer; -'ser) *v.t.* [*infl.:* **conocer**, 13] 1, to adorn; bedeck. 2, to provide; equip. 3, to garrison.

guarnición (gwar·ni'θjon; -'sjon) *n.f.* 1, adornment; trim. 2, guard (*of a sword*). 3, garrison. 4, setting or mounting for a jewel. 5, *pl.* harness; trappings; gear. 6, *pl.* fittings; fixtures.

guasa ('gwa·sa) *n.f.* 1, jest. 2, insipidity.

guasca ('gwas·ka) *n.f., Amer.* 1, leather thong. 2, rope. 3, whip.

guaso ('gwa·so) *adj. & n.m., Amer.* rustic; yokel. —*n.m.* gaucho.

guasón (gwa'son) *adj., colloq.* waggish; humorous. —*n.m., colloq.* [*fem.* **-sona**] joker; wag.

guata ('gwa·ta) *n.f.* 1, padding; quilt. 2, *Amer.* belly.

guau (gwau) *interj. & n.m.* bowwow.

guayaba (gwa'ja·βa) *n.f.* guava. —**guayabo**, *n.m.* guava tree.

guayabera (gwa·ja'βe·ra) *n.f.* lightweight shirt, usu. worn outside the waist.

gubernamental (gu·βer·na·men'tal) *adj.* governmental.

gubernativo (gu·βer·na'ti·βo) *adj.* governmental.

gubia ('gu·βja) *n.f.* gouge (*tool*).

guedeja (ge'ðe·xa) *n.f.* long lock of hair. —**guedejas**, *n.f.pl.* mane.

güero ('gwe·ro) *adj., Amer.* blond. *Also,* **huero**.

guerra ('ge·rra) *n.m.* war. —**guerrera**, *n.f.* soldier's jacket. —**gue-**

rrero, *adj.* martial; warlike. —*n.m.* warrior. —**dar guerra,** *colloq.* to be a nuisance. —**hacer guerra,** to wage war.

guerrear (ge·rre'ar) *v.i.* to wage war.

guerrilla (ge'rri·ʎa; -ja) *n.f.* **1,** guerrilla band. **2,** *mil.* open formation. —**guerrillear,** *v.i.* to wage guerrilla warfare. —**guerrillero,** *n.m.* guerrilla fighter; guerrilla.

guía ('gi·a) *n.m. & f.* guide. —*n.f.* **1,** guidebook. **2,** sign; signpost. **3,** *mech.* rule; guide. **4,** *bot.* young shoot. **5,** directory. **6,** norm; guiding principle.

guiar (gi'ar) *v.t. & i.* [*infl.:* **enviar,** 22] **1,** to guide; lead. **2,** to steer.

guija ('gi·xa) *n.f.* pebble.

guijarro (gi'xa·rro) *n.m.* large pebble; cobblestone.

guijo ('gi·xo) *n.m.* gravel.

guillotina (gi·ʎo'ti·na; gi·jo-) *n.f.* guillotine. —**guillotinar,** *v.t.* to guillotine. —**ventana de guillotina,** sash window.

guinda ('gin·da) *n.f.* **1,** wild cherry. **2,** *colloq.* easy job; cinch.

guindar (gin'dar) *v.t.* **1,** to hoist. **2,** *colloq.* to hang; hang up. **3,** *colloq.* to win; gain *(esp. by beating out someone else).* **4,** *slang* to steal; filch.

guindo ('gin·do) *n.m.* wild cherry tree.

guinea (gi'ne·a) *n.f.* **1,** guinea. **2,** guinea hen.

guineo (gi'ne·o) *n.m., Amer.* banana.

guinga ('gin·ga) *n.f.* gingham.

guiñada (gi'ɲa·ða) *n.f.* **1,** wink. **2,** *naut.* yaw.

guiñapo (gi'ɲa·po) *n.m.* **1,** rag. **2,** ragged person; ragpicker. **3,** *colloq.* a nobody. —**dejar hecho un guiñapo; poner como un guiñapo, 1,** to beat to a pulp. **2,** *fig.* to dress down; crush.

guiñar (gi'ɲar) *v.t.* to wink. —*v.i., naut.* to yaw. —**guiño** ('gi·ɲo) *n.m.* wink.

guión (gi'on) *n.m.* **1,** standard; pennant. **2,** leader. **3,** outline; guide. **4,** hyphen; dash. **5,** *theat.* script.

güira ('gwi·ra) *n.f.* **1,** calabash tree. **2,** gourd used as a container.

—**güiro,** *n.m.* bottle gourd *(musical instrument).*

guirnalda (gir'nal·da) *n.f.* garland.

guisa ('gi·sa) *n.f.* manner. —**a guisa de,** in the manner of; like; as.

guisado (gi'sa·ðo) *n.m.* stew.

guisante (gi'san·te) *n.m.* pea. —**guisante de olor,** sweet pea.

guisar (gi'sar) *v.t.* to cook; stew.

guiso ('gi·so) *n.m.* **1,** stew. **2,** *fig., colloq.* mess; disorder. —**guisote** (-'so·te) *n.m.* slop.

guitarra (gi'ta·rra) *n.f.* guitar. —**guitarrista,** *n.m. & f.* guitarist.

gula ('gu·la) *n.f.* gluttony.

gurrumino (gu·rru'mi·no) *adj.* **1,** mean; despicable. **2,** uxorious; henpecked. —*n.m.* henpecked husband. —**gurrumina,** *n.f., colloq.* uxoriousness.

gusaniento (gu·sa'njen·to) *adj.* wormy.

gusanillo (gu·sa'ni·ʎo; -jo) *n.m.* **1,** small worm. **2,** *mech.* gimlet; auger bit. **3,** *mech.* small spring.

gusano (gu'sa·no) *n.m.* **1,** worm. **2,** any wormlike creature, as a maggot, caterpillar, etc. —**gusanear,** *v.i.* to crawl with or as with worms. —**gusanoso,** *adj.* wormy.

gusarapo (gu·sa'ra·po) *n.m.* water-breeding larva.

gustar (gus'tar) *v.t.* **1,** to taste. **2,** to try; test —*v.i.* to please; be pleasing; be liked; *Me gustan los dulces,* I like candy; *Me gusta ir al teatro,* I like to go to the theater. —**gustar de,** to like (to); take pleasure in.

gustativo (gus·ta'ti·βo) *adj.* gustatory.

gustazo (gus'ta·θo; -so) *n.m.* **1,** great pleasure. **2,** fiendish delight.

gusto ('gus·to) *n.m.* **1,** taste. **2,** liking. **3,** pleasure. **4,** caprice; whim. —**a gusto, 1,** at will. **2,** to one's taste or liking. **3,** at ease; in comfort. —**con (mucho) gusto,** with (great) pleasure. —**tener gusto en,** to be pleased to. —**tomar gusto a,** to take a liking to.

gustoso (gus'to·so) *adj.* **1,** tasty. **2,** willing; content. **3,** enjoyable.

gutapercha (gu·ta'per·tʃa) *n.f.* gutta-percha.

gutural (gu·tu'ral) *adj.* guttural.

H

H, h ('a·tʃe) *n.f.* 9th letter of the Spanish alphabet.

ha (a) **1**, *v.*, *3rd pers.sing. pres.ind. of* **haber**. **2**, *contr. of* **hace** *in expressions of time elapsed: dos años ha,* two years ago.

¡ha! (a) *interj.* ha!

haba ('a·βa) *n.f.* **1**, broad bean; horse bean. **2**, *Amer.* Lima bean.

habanera (a·βa'ne·ra) *n.f.* a Cuban dance; the music and rhythm of this dance.

habano (a'βa·no) *n.m.* havana cigar.

haber (a'βer) *v.t.* [*infl.:* 4] **1**, *archaic* to have; own; possess. **2**, *archaic* to catch; lay hold of: *la maestra lee cuantos libros puede haber,* the teacher reads all the books she can lay hold of. —*v.i.,* used only in 3rd pers. to be; exist; *no había piano en la casa,* there was no piano in the house. —*aux.v.,* used with p.p. to form compound tenses: *el año ha terminado,* the year has ended; *he dado el sombrero a mi hermano,* I have given the hat to my brother. —*n.m.* **1**, bookkeeping credit; credit side of a ledger. **2**, wage; wages. —**haberes**, *n.m.pl.* assets. —**haber de, 1**, to have to: *he de salir temprano,* I have to leave early. **2**, to be to: *hemos de comer a las seis,* we are to dine at six o'clock. —**haber que**, to be necessary: *hubo que matarlo,* it was necessary to kill him. —**habérselas con**, to face; deal with.

habichuela (a·βi'tʃwe·la) *n.f.* kidney bean. —**habichuela verde**, string bean.

hábil ('a·βil) *adj.* skillful; clever; capable. —**dia hábil** *or* **laborable**, work day.

habilidad (a·βi·li'ðað) *n.f.* talent; skill; ability.

habilidoso (a·βi·li'ðo·so) *adj.* skillful; able.

habilitar (a·βi·li'tar) *v.t.* **1**, to habilitate. **2**, to qualify; enable.

habitable (a·βi·ta'βle) *adj.* habitable.

habitación (a·βi·ta'θjon; -'sjon) *n.f.* **1**, room. **2**, habitation; dwelling. **3**, habitat.

habitante (a·βi'tan·te) *n.m. & ɟ.* inhabitant.

habitar (a·βi'tar) *v.t.* to inhabits live in; dwell in.

hábito ('a·βi·to) *n.m.* habit.

hábitat ('a·βi·tat) *n.m.* habitat.

habitual (a·βi'twal) *adj.* customary; habitual.

habituar (a·βi'twar) *v.t.* [*infl.: continuar,* 23] to accustom; habituate. —**habituarse**, *v.r.* to become accustomed; accustom oneself.

habitué (a·βi·tu'e) *n.m.* habitué.

habla ('a·βla) *n.f.* speech; tongue language. —**al habla**, in verbal contact; *(in answering the telephone)* speaking. —**de habla española**, Spanish-speaking.

hablador (a·βla'ðor) *adj.* talkative —*n.m.* [*fem.* **-dora**] chatterbox.

habladuría (a·βla·ðu'ri·a) *n.f* gossip; rumor.

hablanchín (a·βlan'tʃin) *adj.* talkative. —*n.m.* [*fem.* **-china**] chatterbox; gossip.

hablar (a'βlar) *v.t.* **1**, to speak. **2** to utter. —*v.i.* **1**, to speak. **2**, to talk —**hablarse**, *v.r.* **1**, to be on speaking terms. **2**, *colloq.* to go steady —**bien hablado**, well-spoken —**hablar a chorros**, to speak fast —**hablar a gritos**, to shout —**hablar por hablar**, to talk idly —**hablar por los codos**, to talk too much. —**mal hablado**, ill-tongued —**¡ni hablar!**, don't think of it!

hablilla (a'βli·ʎa; -ja) *n.f.* = **habladuría**.

habré (a'βre) *v., 1st pers.sing. fut of* **haber**.

hacedero (a·θe'ðe·ro; a·se-) *adj* feasible.

hacedor (a·θe'ðor; a·se-) *n.m* [*fem.* **-dora**] maker.

hacendado (a·θen'da·ðo; a·sen-) *adj.* landed; owning land. —*n.m.* **1** landholder. **2**, *Amer.* cattle rancher.

hacendoso (a·θen'do·so; a·sen-) *adj.* industrious; diligent.

hacer (a'θer; a'ser) *v.t.* [*infl.:* 48] **1** to do. **2**, to make. **3**, to prepare. **4** to produce. **5**, to cause; bring about —*v.i.* **1**, to matter. **2**, to be pertinent —*v. impers.* **1**, *in expressions of weather: hace buen tiempo,* it is good weather; *hace calor,* it is

241

warm; *hace frío,* it is cold; *hace mal tiempo,* it is bad weather; *hace viento,* it is windy. **2,** *in expressions of time:* ¿*Cuánto hace?* How long ago? *Hace poco,* A short time ago. ¿*Cuánto hace que Vd. me espera?* How long have you been waiting for me? ¿*Cuánto tiempo hace que salieron?* How long ago did they leave? How long has it been since they left? *Hace tiempo que salieron,* They left a long time ago. *Hace tiempo me gustaba bailar,* A long time ago I was fond of dancing. —**hacerse,** *v.r.* **1,** to become. **2,** to pretend to be. **3,** to move; move over. **4,** to accustom oneself. —**hacer alarde,** to boast. —**hacer caso,** to mind; pay attention. —**hacer daño,** to hurt; harm. —**hacer falta,** to be lacking; be missing. —**hacer hacer una cosa,** to have something done: *Hicimos construir una casa,* We had a house built. —**hacerle a uno hacer algo,** to have someone do something: *Le hicimos venir ayer,* We had him come yesterday. —**hacer la maleta,** to pack one's suitcase. —**hacer un viaje,** to take a trip. —**hacer vida de artista,** to lead an artist's life. —**hacerse rogar,** to want to be coaxed. —**no le hace,** *colloq.* never mind; it makes no difference.

haces ('a·θes; 'a·ses) *n.m.* or *f., pl.* of *haz.*

hacia ('a·θja; 'a·sja) *prep.* **1,** toward. **2,** near; about: *hacia las ocho,* about eight o'clock. —**hacia acá,** this way. —**hacia adelante,** forward. —**hacia atrás,** backwards.

hacienda (a'θjen·da; a'sjen·) *n.f.* **1,** estate. **2,** large ranch. **3,** *Amer.* cattle. —**Ministerio de Hacienda,** Ministry of Finance or Economics; U.S. Department of the Treasury.

hacinar (a·θi'nar; a·si·) *v.t.* **1,** to stack; heap. **2,** to overcrowd.

hacha ('a·tʃa) *n.f.* ax; hatchet. —**hachazo,** *n.m.* blow of an ax or hatchet.

hachear (a·tʃe'ar) *v.t.* to chop; hew.

hachís (a'tʃis) *n.m.* = **haxix.**

hada ('a·ða) *n.f.* fairy.

hado ('a·ðo) *n.m.* destiny; fate.

hafnio ('af·njo) *n.m.* hafnium.

haga ('a·ɣa) *v., pres.subjve.* of *hacer.*

hago ('a·ɣo) *v., 1st pers.sing. pres. ind.* of *hacer.*

¡**hala!** ('a·la) *also,* ¡**hale!** ('a·le) *interj.* get going!; pull!

halagar (a·la'ɣar) *v.t.* [*infl.:* **pagar,** 8**]** **1,** to flatter. **2,** to please; delight.

halago (a'la·ɣo) *n.m.* flattery.

halagüeño (a·la'ɣwe·ɲo) *adj.* **1,** attractive; delightful. **2,** flattering.

halar (a'lar) *v.t.* to pull; tug; haul.

halcón (al'kon) *n.m.* falcon. —**halconería,** *n.f.* falconry. —**halconero,** *n.m.* falconer.

halibut (a·li'ßut) *n.m.* halibut.

hálito ('a·li·to) *n.m.* **1,** breath. **2,** *poet.* breeze.

halitosis (a·li'to·sis) *n.f.* halitosis.

halo ('a·lo) *n.m.* halo.

halógeno (a'lo·xe·no) *adj. & n.m.* halogen.

hallar (a'ʎar; -'jar) *v.t.* to find; come upon. —**hallarse,** *v.r.* **1,** to be (in a certain place or condition). **2,** to feel (well or ill).

hallazgo (a'ʎaθ·ɣo; -'jas·ɣo) *n.m.* discovery; find; findings.

hamaca (a'ma·ka) *n.f.* hammock. —**hamacar,** *v.t., Amer.* [*infl.:* **tocar,** 7**]** to swing; rock.

hamamelis (a·ma'me·lis) *n.m.* witch hazel.

hambre ('am·bre) *n.f.* hunger. —**tener hambre,** to be hungry.

hambrear (am·bre'ar) *v.t. & i.* to starve.

hambriento (am'brjen·to) *adj.* hungry; starved.

hambruna (am'bru·na) *n.f., Amer.* famine.

hamburguesa (am·bur'ɣe·sa) *n.f., Amer.* hamburger.

hampa ('am·pa) *n.f.* underworld. —**hampón,** *n.m.* thug; goon.

hámster ('ams·ter) *n.m. & f.* [*pl.* **hámsters**] hamster.

han (an) *v., 3rd. pers.pl. pres.ind.* of *haber.*

handicap ('an·di·kap) *n.m.* handicap.

hangar (an'gar) *n.m.* hangar.

haragán (a·ra'ɣan) *n.m.* loafer; lazy person. —*adj.* lazy; indolent.

haraganear (a·ra·ɣa·ne'ar) *v.i.* **1,** to be lazy. **2,** to idle; loaf.

harakiri (a·ra'ki·ri) *n.m.* harakiri.

harapo (a'ra·po) *n.m.* rag. —**harapiento,** *also,* **haraposo,** *adj.* tattered; ragged.

haré (a're) *v., 1st pers.sing. fut.* of *hacer.*

harén (a'ren) *also,* **harem** (a'rem) *n.m.* harem.

harina (a'ri·na) *n.f.* **1,** flour. **2,**

meal; grounds; *Amer.* coffee grounds. —**harina de otro costal,** *colloq.* a horse of a different color.
harinoso (a·ri'no·so) *adj.* mealy.
harmonía (ar·mo'ni·a) *n.f.* = **armonía.**
harnero (ar'ne·ro) *n.m.* sifter; sieve.
harpa ('ar·pa) *n.f.* = **arpa.**
harpía (ar'pi·a) *n.f.* = **arpía.**
harpillera (ar·pi'ʎe·ra; -'je·ra) *n.f.* burlap.
hartar (ar'tar) *v.t.* **1,** to satiate. **2,** to glut. **3,** *fig.* to bother. —**hartarse,** *v.r.* **1,** to overeat. **2,** *colloq.* to be fed up. —**hartazgo** (-'taθ·ɣo; -'tas·ɣo) *n.m.* fill; bellyful.
harto ('ar·to) *adj.* **1,** satiated; full. **2,** *colloq.* fed up. —*adv.* enough.
has (as) *v.,* *2nd pers.sing. pres.ind. of* **haber.**
hasta ('as·ta) *prep.* until; as far as; up to. —*conj.* also; even. —**hasta ahora, 1,** heretofore. **2,** *colloq.* = **hasta luego.** —**hasta luego,** see you later; so long.
hastiar (as'tjar) *v.t.* [*infl.:* **enviar, 22**] **1,** to surfeit. **2,** to bore. **3,** to disgust; sicken.
hastío (as'ti·o) *n.m.* **1,** excess; surfeit. **2,** boredom. **3,** disgust.
hato ('a·to) *n.m.* **1,** herd; flock. **2,** heap; lot. **3,** gang; band. —**liar el hato** *or* **el petate,** to get ready to go; pack.
haxix ('a·ʃiʃ) *n.m.* hashish.
hay (ai) *adverbial expression* (*formed from* **ha** + *archaic* **y,** there) there is; there are: *hay mucho que ver en esta ciudad,* there is much to see in this city. —**hay para,** *fol. by a noun* **1,** there is enough: *hay comida para todos,* there is enough food for everybody. **2,** there is something: *hay para todos los gustos,* there is something for every taste. **3,** *Fol. by inf.* it makes you want to: *Hay para reírse,* It makes you want to laugh. *Hay para matarlo,* It makes you want to kill him. —**hay que,** it is necessary. —**no hay de qué,** you're welcome; don't mention it. —**no hay remedio,** it can't be helped. —**¿qué hay?,** what's the matter? —**¿qué hay de nuevo?,** what's new?
haya ('a·ja) *n.f.* beech tree. —**hayuco** (a'ju·ko) *n.m.* beechnut.
haya ('a·ja) *v.,* *pres.subjve. of* **haber.**
haz (aθ; as) *n.m.* [*pl.* **haces**] **1,** bun-

dle; fagot; sheaf. **2,** beam, as of light. —*n.m. or f.* face; surface.
haz (aθ; as) *v.,* *impve.sing. of* **hacer.**
hazaña (a'θa·ɲa; a'sa-) *n.f.* deed; feat.
hazmerreír (aθ·me·rre'ir; as-) *n.m.* laughingstock.
he (e) *interj.* behold; *usu.fol. by* **aquí** *or* **allí** *or by a pronoun: he aquí,* here you have; here is; here are. *Heme aquí,* Here I am. *Helos allí,* There they are. *He aquí que llegó,* Lo and behold, he has arrived.
he (e) *v.,* *1st pers.sing. pres.ind. of* **haber.**
hebilla (e'βi·ʎa; -ja) *n.f.* buckle; clasp.
hebra ('e·βra) *n.f.* **1,** thread. **2,** fiber. **3,** *mining* vein. **4,** grain (*of wood*). —**de una hebra,** *Amer.* all at once.
hebreo (e'βre·o) *adj.* & *n.m.* Hebrew.
hebraico (e'βrai·ko) *adj.* Hebrew; Hebraic.
hebroso (e'βro·so) *adj.* fibrous; stringy.
hecatombe (e·ka'tom·be) *n.f.* hecatomb.
heces ('e·θes; 'e·ses) *n.f.pl.* **1,** feces. **2,** dregs. **3,** *fig.* scum; riffraff.
hectárea (ek'ta·re·a) *n.f.* hectare.
hectogramo (ek·to'ɣra·mo) *n.m.* hectogram.
hectolitro (ek·to'li·tro) *n.m.* hectoliter.
hectómetro (ek'to·me·tro) *n.m.* hectometer.
hechicero (e·tʃi'θe·ro; -'se·ro) *adj.* bewitching. —*n.m.* sorcerer. —**hechicera,** *n.f.* witch. —**hechicería,** *n.f.* witchcraft; sorcery.
hechizar (e·tʃi'θar; -'sar) *v.t.* [*infl.:* **rezar, 10**] to bewitch.
hechizo (e'tʃi·θo; -so) *n.m.* enchantment; spell.
hecho ('e·tʃo) *v.,* *p.p. of* **hacer.** —*adj.* **1,** made. **2,** ready-made. **3,** done. **4,** ripe. —*n.m.* **1,** fact. **2,** act; deed. **3,** event. —**bien hecho, 1,** well done. **2,** right. —**hecho y derecho,** perfect. —**mal hecho, 1,** badly done. **2,** wrong.
hechura (e'tʃu·ra) *n.f.* **1,** creation; handiwork. **2,** form; cut; shape. **3,** image; likeness. **4,** workmanship. —**hechuras,** *n.f.pl.* cost of making.
heder (e'ðer) *v.i.* [*infl.:* **perder, 29**] to stink.
hediondo (e'ðjon·do) *adj.* stink-

ing; fetid. —**hediondez,** *n.f.* fetidness.

hedonismo (e·ðo'nis·mo) *n.m.* hedonism. —**hedonista,** *n.m.* & *f.* hedonist. —*adj.* hedonistic.

hedor (e'ðor) *n.m.* stench; stink.

hegemonía (e·xe·mo'ni·a) *n.f.* hegemony.

helada (e'la·ða) *n.f.* frost.

heladera (e·la'ðe·ra) *n.f.* **1,** [*also,* **heladora**] ice cream freezer. **2,** *Amer.* refrigerator.

heladería (e·la·ðe'ri·a) *n.f., Amer.* ice cream parlor.

helado (e'la·ðo) *adj.* frozen. —*n.m.* ice cream.

helar (e'lar) *v.t.* [*infl.:* **pensar, 27**] **1,** to freeze; congeal. **2,** *fig.* to shock; stupefy.

helecho (e'le·tʃo) *n.m.* fern.

helénico (e'le·ni·ko) *adj.* Hellenic; Greek.

heleno (e'le·no) *adj.* Hellenic; Greek. —*n.m.* Hellene; Greek.

hélice ('e·li·θe; -se) *n.f.* **1,** helix. **2,** propeller.

helicóptero (e·li'kop·te·ro) *n.m.* helicopter.

helio ('e·ljo) *n.m.* helium.

heliocéntrico (e·ljo'θen·tri·ko; -'sen·tri·ko) *adj.* heliocentric.

heliógrafo (e'ljo·ɣra·fo) *n.m.* heliograph.

heliotropo (e·ljo'tro·po) *n.m.* heliotrope.

helipuerto (e·li'pwer·to) *n.m.* heliport.

hembra ('em·bra) *n.f.* **1,** female. **2,** *sewing* eye of a hook. **3,** *mech.* nut of a screw.

hembrilla (em'bri·ʎa; -ja) *n.f.* grommet; eyelet.

hemiplejía (e·mi·ple'xi·a) *n.f.* hemiplegia. —**hemipléjico** (-'ple·xi·ko) *adj.* & *n.m.* hemiplegic.

hemisferio (e·mis'fe·rjo) *n.m.* hemisphere. —**hemisférico** (-'fe·ri·ko) *adj.* hemispheric; hemispherical.

hemofilia (e·mo'fi·lja) *n.f.* hemophilia. —**hemofílico** (-'fi·li·ko) *adj.* hemophilic. —*n.m.* hemophiliac.

hemoglobina (e·mo·ɣlo'βi·na) *n.f.* hemoglobin.

hemorragia (e·mo'rra·xja) *n.f.* hemorrhage.

hemorroides (e·mo'rroi·ðes) *n.f. pl.* hemorrhoids.

hemos ('e·mos) *v. 1st pers.pl. pres. ind. of* **haber**.

henal (e'nal) *n.m.* = **henil.**

henar (e'nar) *n.m.* hayfield.

henchir (en'tʃir) *v.t.* [*infl.:* **pedir, 33**] to fill up; stuff; heap.

hender (en'der) *v.t.* [*infl.:* **perder, 29**] to crack; split.

hendidura (en·di'ðu·ra) *also,* **hendedura** (en·de-) *n.f.* crack; fissure.

henequén (e·ne'ken) *n.m.* **1,** sisal plant. **2,** sisal fiber.

henil (e'nil) *n.m.* hayloft.

heno ('e·no) *n.m.* hay.

heñir (e'ɲir) *v.t.* [*infl.:* **reñir, 59**] to knead.

hepática (e'pa·ti·ka) *n.f.* hepatica.

hepático (e'pa·ti·ko) *adj.* hepatic.

hepatitis (e·pa'ti·tis) *n.f.* hepatitis.

heptágono (ep'ta·ɣo·no) *n.m.* heptagon. —**heptagonal,** *adj.* heptagonal.

heraldo (e'ral·do) *n.m.* herald. —**heráldico,** *adj.* heraldic. —**heráldica,** *n.f.* heraldry.

herbáceo (er'βa·θe·o; -se·o) *adj.* herbaceous.

herbaje (er'βa·xe) *n.m.* herbage; grass.

herbario (er'βa·rjo) *adj.* herbal. —*n.m.* **1,** herbarium. **2,** herbal.

herbazal (er·βa'θal; -'sal) *n.m.* field of grass.

herbicida (er·βi'θi·ða; -'si·ða) *n.m.* herbicide.

herbívoro (er'βi·βo·ro) *adj.* herbivorous. —*n.m.* herbivore.

herboso (er'βo·so) *adj.* grassy.

hercúleo (er'ku·le·o) *adj.* Herculean.

heredad (e·re'ðað) *n.f.* country estate.

heredar (e·re'ðar) *v.t.* to inherit. —**heredable,** *adj.* heritable.

heredera (e·re'ðe·ra) *n.f.* heiress.

heredero (e·re'ðe·ro) *n.m.* heir; inheritor. —**heredero forzoso,** heir apparent. —**presunto heredero,** heir presumptive.

hereditario (e·re·ði'ta·rjo) *adj.* hereditary.

hereje (e're·xe) *n.m.* & *f.* heretic. —**herejía,** *n.f.* heresy.

herencia (e'ren·θja; -sja) *n.f.* **1,** estate. **2,** heritage. **3,** heredity.

herético (e're·ti·ko) *adj.* heretical.

herida (e'ri·ða) *n.f.* wound.

herir (e'rir) *v.t.* [*infl.:* **sentir, 31**] to wound; hurt.

hermafrodita (er·ma·fro'ði·ta) *n.m.* & *f.* hermaphrodite. —*adj.* hermaphroditic.

hermana (er'ma·na) *n.f.* sister.

hermanar (er·ma'nar) *v.t. & i.* to match; harmonize; conform.

hermanastro (er·ma'nas·tro) *n.m.* stepbrother. **—hermanastra,** *n.f.* stepsister.

hermandad (er·man'dað) *n.f.* 1, brotherhood; fraternity. 2, sisterhood; sorority.

hermano (er'ma·no) *n.m.* brother. **—hermanos,** *n.m.pl.* brothers; brothers and sisters. **—hermano de leche** *or* **de crianza,** foster brother. **—hermano político,** brother-in-law.

hermético (er'me·ti·ko) *adj.* hermetic; airtight.

hermosear (er·mo·se'ar) *v.t.* to beautify.

hermoso (er'mo·so) *adj.* beautiful; handsome; lovely. **—hermosura,** *n.f.* beauty; handsomeness.

hernia (er'nja) *n.f.* hernia.

héroe ('e·ro·e) *n.m.* hero.

heroico (e'roi·ko) *adj.* heroic.

heroína (e·ro'i·na) *n.f.* 1, heroine. 2, heroin.

heroísmo (e·ro'is·mo) *n.m.* heroism.

herpes ('er·pes) *n.m. or f.pl.* herpes.

herpetologia (er·pe·to·lo'xi·a) *n.f.* herpetology. **—herpetólogo** (-'to·lo·ɣo) *n.m.* herpetologist.

herrador (e·rra'ðor) *n.m.* blacksmith.

herradura (e·rra'ðu·ra) *n.f.* horseshoe.

herraje (e'rra·xe) *n.m.* 1, ironwork; iron fittings. 2, horseshoe and nails.

herramienta (e·rra'mjen·ta) *n.f.* tool; implement.

herrar (e'rrar) *v.t.* [*infl.:* **pensar,** 27] 1, to shoe (a horse). 2, to brand (cattle).

herrería (e·rre'ri·a) *n.f.* 1, blacksmithing. 2, blacksmith's shop.

herrero (e'rre·ro) *n.m.* blacksmith.

herrumbre (e'rrum·bre) *n.f.* 1, rust. 2, iron taste.

hervidero (er·βi'ðe·ro) *n.m.* 1, bubbling (*of boiling liquids*). 2, bubbling spring. 3, swarm; mass; throng.

hervir (er'βir) *v.t. & i.* [*infl.:* **sentir,** 31] to boil.

hervor (er'βor) *n.m.* 1, boiling. 2, boiling point. 3, *fig.* restlessness; fervor.

hesitar (e·si'tar) *v.i., rare* to hesitate. **—hesitación,** *n.f., rare* hesitation.

heterodoxo (e·te·ro'ðok·so) *adj.* heterodox. **—heterodoxia** (-'ðok·sja) *n.f.* heterodoxy.

heterogéneo (e·te·ro'xe·ne·o) *adj.* heterogeneous.

heterosexual (e·te·ro·sek'swal) *adj. & n.m. & f.* heterosexual.

heurístico (eu'ris·ti·ko) *adj.* heuristic. **—heurística,** *n.f.* heuristic; heuristics.

hexágono (ek'sa·ɣo·no) *n.m.* hexagon. **—hexagonal,** *adj.* hexagonal.

hexagrama ('eks·a'ɣra·ma) *n.m.* hexagram.

hez (eθ; es) *n.f.* [*pl.* **heces**] scum.

hiato (i'a·to) *n.m.* hiatus.

hibernal (i·βer'nal) *adj.* hibernal.

hibernar (i·βer'nar) *v.t.* to hibernate. **—hibernación,** *n.f.* hibernation.

hibisco (i'βis·ko) *n.m.* hibiscus.

híbrido ('i·βri·ðo) *adj. & n.m.* hybrid; mongrel. **—hibridismo,** *n.m.* hybridism.

hice ('i·θe; 'i·se) *v., 1st pers.sing. pret. of* **hacer.**

hidalgo (i'ðal·ɣo) *n.m.* [*fem.* **hidalga**] Spanish nobleman. **—***adj.* noble.

hidalguía (i·ðal'ɣi·a) *n.f.* nobility.

hidratar (i·ðra'tar) *v.t.* to hydrate. **—hidratación,** *n.m.* hydration.

hidrato (i'ðra·to) *n.m.* hydrate.

hidráulico (i'ðrau·li·ko) *adj.* hydraulic. **—hidráulica,** *n.f.* hydraulics.

hidroavión (i·ðro·a'βjon) *n.m.* hydroplane; seaplane.

hidrocarburo (i·ðro·kar'βu·ro) *n.m.* hydrocarbon.

hidrocefalia (i·dro·θe'fa·lja; -se·'fa·lja) *n.f.* hydrocephaly. **—hidrocéfalo** (-'θe·fa·lo; -'se·fa·lo) *adj.* hydrocephalic.

hidrodinámico (i·ðro·ði'na·mi·ko) *adj.* hydrodynamic. **—hidrodinámica,** *n.f.* hydrodynamics.

hidroeléctrico (i·ðro·e'lek·tri·ko) *adj.* hydroelectric. **—hidroeléctrica,** *n.f.* hydroelectrics.

hidrófilo (i'ðro·fi·lo) *adj.* absorbent.

hidrofobia (i·ðro'fo·βja) *n.f.* hydrophobia. **—hidrófobo** (i'ðro·fo·βo) *adj.* hydrophobic. **—***n.m.* hydrophobe.

hidrogenar (i·ðro·ɣe'nar) *v.t.* to hydrogenate. **—hidrogenación,** *n.f.* hydrogenation.

hidrógeno (i'ðro·xe·no) *n.m.* hydrogen.

hidrólisis (i'ðro·li·sis) *n.f.* hydrolysis.

hidrómetro (i'ðro·me·tro) *n.m.* hydrometer.

hidromiel (i·ðro'mjel) *n.m.* mead. *Also,* **hidromel** (-'mel).

hidropesía (i·ðro·pe'si·a) *n.f.* dropsy.

hidrópico (i'ðro·pi·ko) *adj.* 1, dropsical. 2, extremely thirsty. 3, insatiable.

hidroplano (i·ðro'pla·no) *n.m.* = **hidroavión**.

hidroponía (i·ðro·po'ni·a) *n.f.* hydroponics. *Also,* **hidropónica** (-'po·ni·ka) *n.f.* —**hidropónico** *adj.* hydroponic.

hidróxido (i'ðrok·si·ðo) *n.m.* hydroxide.

hieda ('je·ða) *v., pres.subjve.* of **heder**.

hiedo ('je·ðo) *v., 1st pers.sing. pres.ind.* of **heder**.

hiedra ('je·ðra) *n.f.* ivy.

hiel (jel) *n.f.* 1, gall; bile. 2, *fig.* bitterness.

hiele ('je·le) *v., pres.subjve. of* **helar**.

hielo ('je·lo) *n.m.* ice.

hielo ('je·lo) *v., 1st pers.sing. pres.ind.* of **helar**.

hiena ('je·na) *n.f.* hyena.

hienda ('jen·da) *v., pres.subjve.* of **hender**.

hiendo ('jen·do) *v., 1st pers.sing. pres.ind.* of **hender**.

hiera ('je·ra) *v.t, pres.subjve.* of **herir**.

hierba ('jer·ßa) *n.f.* 1, grass; weed. 2, herb. —**mala hierba,** *colloq.* 1, wayward person. 2, ill-bred person.

hierbabuena (jer·ßa'ßwe·na) *n.f.* mint.

hierba mora ('mo·ra) nightshade.

hiero ('je·ro) *v., 1st pers.sing. pres.ind.* of **herir**.

hierre ('je·rre) *v., pres.subjve.* of **herrar**.

hierro ('je·rro) *n.m.* iron. —**hierro colado** *or* **fundido,** cast iron. —**hierro dulce,** wrought iron.

hierro ('je·rro) *v., 1st pers.sing. pres.ind.* of **herrar**.

hierva ('jer·ßa) *v., pres.subjve.* of **hervir**.

hiervo ('jer·ßo) *v., 1st pers.sing. pres.ind.* of **hervir**.

higa ('i·ɣa) *n.f.* contemptuous gesture. —**darle una higa a uno,** to thumb one's nose at someone.

hígado ('i·ɣa·ðo) *n.m.* liver. —**echar los hígados,** *colloq.* to work hard; slave. —**hasta los hígados,** *colloq.* wholeheartedly.

higiene (i'xje·ne) *n.f.* hygiene. —**higiene pública,** public health.

higiénico (i'xje·ni·ko) *adj.* hygienic; sanitary.

higienista (i·xje'nis·ta) *n.m. & f.* hygienist.

higo ('i·ɣo) *n.m.* fig. —**higo chumbo; higo de tuna,** prickly pear. —**no doy un higo por,** I don't give a rap for. —**no se me da un higo,** I don't care a rap.

higrómetro (i'ɣro·me·tro) *n.m.* hygrometer. —**higrométrico** (-'me·tri·ko) *adj.* hygrometric.

higuera (i'ɣe·ra) *n.f.* fig tree. —**higuera chumba; higuera de tuna,** prickly pear cactus. —**higuera india,** banyan.

hija ('i·xa) *n.f.* daughter.

hijastro (i'xas·tro) *n.m.* stepchild; stepson. —**hijastra,** *n.m.* stepdaughter.

hijo ('i·xo) *n.m.* 1, son; child. 2, junior; Jr. —**hijo de leche** *or* **de crianza,** foster child. —**hijo político,** son-in-law.

hila ('i·la) *n.f.* 1, row; line. 2, *usu. pl.* dressing for a wound.

hilacha (i'la·tʃa) *n.f.* shred. —**hilachas,** *n.f.pl.* lint. —**hilachos,** *n.m.pl., Amer.* tatters. —**hilachoso,** *adj.* tattered; ragged.

hilada (i'la·ða) *n.f.* 1, course (of masonry). 2, = **hilera**.

hilado (i'la·ðo) *n.m.* 1, spinning. 2, yarn.

hilandera (i·lan'de·ra) *n.f.* spinner.

hilandería (i·lan·de'ri·a) *n.f.* 1, spinning. 2, spinning mill.

hilar (i'lar) *v.t. & i.* to spin.

hilarante (i·la'ran·te) *adj.* hilarious.

hilaridad (i·la·ri'ðað) *n.f.* hilarity.

hilaza (i'la·θa; -sa) *n.f.* coarse thread.

hilera (i'le·ra) *n.f.* row; line.

hilo ('i·lo) *n.m.* 1, thread; fine yarn. 2, string. 3, wire. 4, linen. —**a hilo,** without interruption. —**al hilo, 1,** along the weave. 2, = **al filo**. —**hilo bramante,** twine. —**hilo de Escocia,** lisle. —**hilo de medianoche** (*or* **mediodía**), midnight (*or* noon) sharp.

hilván (il'βan) *n.m.*, *sewing* basting; tacking.

hilvanar (il·βa'nar) *v.t.* 1, *sewing* to baste; tack. 2, *fig.* to do hastily; patch.

himen ('i·men) *n.m.* hymen.

himeneo (i·me'ne·o) *n.m.* marriage; hymen.

himno ('im·no) *n.m.* hymn. —**himnario,** *n.m.* hymnal.

hincapié (in·ka'pje) *n.m.*, in **hacer hincapié en,** to emphasize.

hincar (in'kar) *v.t.* [*infl.:* **tocar, 7**] to thrust in; drive in. —**hincarse,** *v.r.* to kneel. —**hincar el diente,** to bite.

hincha ('in·tʃa) *n.m.* & *f.*, *colloq.* 1, grudge; ill will. 2, *sports* fan; rooter.

hincha ('in·tʃa) *v.*, *pres.subjve.* of henchir.

hinchar (in'tʃar) *v.t.* to swell; inflate. —**hincharse,** *v.t.* 1, to swell. 2, to become conceited; put on airs.

hinchazón (in·tʃa'θon; -'son) *n.m.* 1, swelling. 2, *fig.* conceit; vanity. 3, *fig.*, *colloq.* bellyful.

hinchió (in'tʃjo) *v.*, *3rd pers.sing. pret.* of henchir.

hincho ('in·tʃo) *v.*, *1st pers.sing. pres.ind.* of henchir.

hindú (in'du) *adj.* & *n.m.* & *f.* Hindu. —**hinduísmo,** *n.m.* Hinduism.

hinojo (i'no·xo) *n.m.* 1, fennel. 2, knee; *only in* **de hinojos,** kneeling.

hinque ('in·ke) *v.*, *pres.subjve.* of hincar.

hinqué (in'ke) *v.*, *1st.pers.sing. pret.* of hincar.

hiña ('i·ɲa) *v.*, *pres.subjve.* of heñir.

hiñendo (i'ɲen·do) *v.*, *ger.* of heñir.

hiño ('i·ɲo) *v.*, *1st pers.sing. pres.ind.* of heñir.

hiñó (i'ɲo) *v.*, *3rd pers.sing. pret.* of heñir.

hipar (i'par) *v.i.* 1, to hiccup. 2, to pant. —**hipar por,** to yearn for; crave.

hipérbola (i'per·βo·la) *n.f.* hyperbola. —**hiperbólico** (-'βo·li·ko) *adj.* hyperbolic.

hipérbole (i'per·βo·le) *n.f.* hyperbole.

hipercrítico (i·per'kri·ti·ko) *adj.* excessively critical; severe in judgment.

hipersensible (i·per·sen'si·βle) *adj.* hypersensitive.

hipertensión (i·per·ten'sjon) *n.f.*

hypertension; high blood pressure. —**hipertenso** (-'ten·so) *adj.* hypertensive.

hipertrofia (i·per'tro·fja) *n.f.* hypertrophy. —**hipertrofiarse** (-'fjar·se) *v.r.* to hypertrophy.

hípico ('i·pi·ko) *adj.* horse (*attrib.*); equestrian.

hípido (i'pi·ðo) *n.m.* hiccups.

hipnosis (ip'no·sis) *n.f.* hypnosis. —**hipnótico** (-'no·ti·ko) *adj.* hypnotic. —**hipnotismo** (-'tis·mo) *n.m.* hypnotism.

hipnotizar (ip·no·ti'θar; -'sar) *v.t.* [*infl.:* **rezar, 10**] to hypnotize. —**hipnotizador,** *n.m.* [*fem.* **-dora**] hypnotist.

hipo ('i·po) *n.m.* 1, hiccup. 2, panting. —**tener hipo de** *or* **por,** to yearn for; crave.

hipocondría (i·po·kon'dri·a) *n.f.* hypochondria. —**hipocondríaco,** *adj.* & *n.m.* hypochondriac.

hipocresía (i·po·kre'si·a) *n.f.* hypocrisy; insincerity.

hipócrita (i'po·kri·ta) *n.m.* & *f.* hypocrite. —*adj.* hypocritical.

hipodérmico (i·po'ðer·mi·ko) *adj.* & *n.m.* hypodermic.

hipódromo (i'po·ðro·mo) *n.m.* hippodrome; race track.

hipoglucemia (i·po·ɣlu'θe·mja; -'se·mja) *n.f.* hypoglycemia.

hipopótamo (i·po'po·ta·mo) *n.m.* hippopotamus.

hiposo (i'po·so) *adj.* suffering from hiccups.

hipoteca (i·po'te·ka) *n.f.* mortgage. —**hipotecario,** *adj.* mortgage (*attrib.*).

hipotecar (i·po·te'kar) *v.t.* [*infl.:* **tocar, 7**] to mortgage.

hipotenusa (i·po·te'nu·sa) *n.f.* hypotenuse.

hipótesis (i'po·te·sis) *n.f.* hypothesis. —**hipotético** (-'te·ti·ko) *adj.* hypothetical.

hiriendo (i'rjen·do) *v.*, *ger.* of herir.

hiriente (i'rjen·te) *v.*, *pr.p.* of herir. —*adj.* cutting; hurtful.

hirió (i'rjo) *v.*, *3rd pers.sing. pret.* of herir.

hirsuto (ir'su·to) *adj.* hirsute.

hirviendo (ir'βjen·do) *v.*, *ger.* of hervir.

hirviente (ir'βjen·te) *adj.* boiling.

hirvió (ir'βjo) *v.*, *3rd pers.sing. pret.* of hervir.

hisopo (i'so·po) *n.m.* hyssop.

ıispánico (is·pa·ni·ko) *adj.* Hispanic.

ıispano (is·pa·no) *adj.* **1,** Hispanic; Spanish. **2,** Spanish-American. —*n.m.* **1,** Spaniard. **2,** Spanish-American.

hispanoamericano (is·pa·no·a·me·ri·ka·no) *adj. & n.m.* Spanish-American.

hispanohablante (is·pa·no·a·'βlan·te) *adj.* Spanish-speaking. —*n.m. & f.* Spanish speaker.

histamina (is·ta·'mi·na) *n.f.* histamine.

histerectomía (is·te·rek·to'mi·a) *n.f.* hysterectomy.

histeria (is'te·rja) *n.f.* **1,** hysteria. **2,** hysterics. *Also,* **histerismo,** *n.m.*

histérico (is'te·ri·ko) *adj.* hysterical. —*n.m.* hysteric.

histología (is·to·lo'xi·a) *n.f.* histology. —**histológico** (-'lo·xi·ko) *adj.* histological. —**histólogo** (-'to·lo·ɣo) *n.m.* histologist.

historia (is'to·rja) *n.f.* **1,** history. **2,** story. **3,** fable; tale. —**historias,** *n.f.pl.* idle talk; palaver.

historiado (is·to'rja·ðo) *adj.* **1,** ornate; elaborate. **2,** *colloq.* storytelling; full of stories.

historiador (is·to·rja'ðor) *n.m.* historian.

historial (is·to'rjal) *n.* case history; record.

historiar (is·to'rjar) *v.t.* to write the history or story of.

histórico (is'to·ri·ko) *adj.* historical; historic. —**historicidad** (-θi·'ðað; -si'ðað) *n.f.* historicity.

historieta (is·to'rje·ta) *n.f.* **1,** short story. **2,** *pl.* comics; comic strips.

histriónico (is'trjo·ni·ko) *adj.* histrionic. —**histrionismo,** *n.m.* histrionics.

hito ('i·to) *adj.* **1,** fixed; firm. **2,** adjacent; adjoining. —*n.m.* landmark; guidepost; milestone. —**dar en el hito,** to hit the mark. —**mirar de hito en hito,** to fix with one's gaze.

hizo ('i·θo; -so) *v. 3rd pers.sing. pret.* of **hacer.**

hoce ('o·θe; 'o·se) *v., pres.subjve.* of **hozar.**

hocé (o'θe; o'se) *v., 1st pers.sing. pret.* of **hozar.**

hoces ('o·θes; 'o·ses) *n.f., pl.* of **hoz.**

hocicar (o·θi'kar; o·si-) *v.t. [infl.: tocar, 7]* **1,** to root. **2,** to nuzzle.

—*v.i., colloq.* to run smack up against a difficulty.

hocico (o'θi·ko; o'si-) *n.m.* **1,** snout. **2,** *slang* mug; kisser. **3,** *colloq.* pout; sulk. —**darse de hocicos, 1,** to fall flat on one's face. **2,** = **hocicar,** *v.i.*

hockey ('xo·ki) *n.m.* hockey.

hogaño (o'ɣa·ɲo) *adv.* nowadays.

hogar (o'ɣar) *n.m.* **1,** hearth; fireplace. **2,** home.

hogareño (o·ɣa're·ɲo) *adj.* **1,** homeloving. **2,** homey; cozy. **3,** of the home or family.

hoguera (o'ɣe·ra) *n.f.* blaze; bonfire.

hoja ('o·xa) *n.f.* **1,** leaf. **2,** sheet *(of paper or metal)*. **3,** veneer. **4,** blade. **5,** pane; panel. —**hoja de lata,** tin plate. —**hoja electrónica,** *comput.* spreadsheet. —**hoja suelta,** leaflet.

hojalata (o·xa'la·ta) *n.f.* tin plate.

hojalatería (o·xa·la·te'ri·a) *n.f.* **1,** tinware. **2,** tin shop. —**hojalatero** (-'te·ro) *n.m.* tinsmith.

hojaldre (o'xal·dre) *n.m. or f.* puff paste.

hojarasca (o·xa'ras·ka) *n.f.* **1,** dead leaves. **2,** excessive foliage. **3,** *fig.* rubbish.

hojear (o·xe'ar) *v.t.* to leaf through (a book). —*v.i.* to flake; scale off.

hojuela (o'xwe·la) *n.f.* **1,** pancake. **2,** gold or silver foil, used esp. in embroidery. **3,** tin foil or other metal foil.

¡hola! ('o·la) *interj.* hello! hi!

holanda (o'lan·da) *n.f.* Dutch linen.

holandés (o·lan'des) *adj.* Dutch. —*n.m.* **1,** Dutchman. **2,** Dutch language. —**holandesa** (-'de·sa) *n.f.* Dutch woman.

holgado (ol'ɣa·ðo) *adj.* **1,** loose; wide; roomy. **2,** comfortable; well-off. **3,** idle; at one's ease.

holganza (ol'ɣan·θa; -sa) *n.f.* **1,** leisure. **2,** idleness. **3,** recreation.

holgar (ol'ɣar) *v.i. [infl.: pagar, 8; mover, 30]* **1,** to rest. **2,** to be idle. —**holgarse,** *v.r.* **1,** to be glad. **2,** to amuse oneself.

holgazán (ol·ɣa'θan; -'san) *n.m. [fem.* **holgazana**] loafer; idler. —*adj.* lazy; insolent. —**holgazanear,** *v.i.* to idle; loiter. —**holgazanería,** *n.f.* idleness.

holgorio (ol'ɣo·rjo; xol-) *n.m., colloq.* revel; frolic. *Also,* **jolgorio.**

holgué (ol'ɣe) *v., 1st pers.sing.pret. of* **holgar.**

holgura (ol'ɣu·ra) *n.f.* **1**, comfort; ease. **2**, roominess; looseness.

holismo (o'lis·mo) *n.m.* holistics. —**holístico,** *adj.* holistic.

holmio ('ol·mjo) *n.m.* holmium.

holocausto (o·lo'kaus·to) *n.m.* holocaust.

hológrafo (o'lo·ɣra·fo) *adj.* & *n.m.* = **ológrafo.** —**holografía** = **olografía.**

holograma (o·lo'ɣra·ma) *n.m.* hologram.

hollar (o'ʎar; -'jar) *v.t.* [*infl.:* **acostar, 28**] to tread upon; step on.

hollejo (o'ʎe·xo; o'je-) *n.m.* thin skin or peel of certain fruits and vegetables.

hollín (o·ʎin; o'jin) *n.m.* soot. —**holliniento,** *adj.* sooty.

hombrada (om'bra·ða) *n.f.* manly deed; act of valor.

hombre ('om·bre) *n.m.* **1**, man. **2**, mankind. **3**, *colloq.* husband. —**hombre al agua,** man overboard. —**hombre de bien,** man of honor or integrity.

hombría (om'bri·a) *n.f.* manliness; courage. —**hombría de bien,** honesty; integrity.

hombro ('om·bro) *n.m.* shoulder. —**arrimar el hombro,** to lend a hand. —**echarse al hombro,** to shoulder; take responsibility for. —**encogerse de hombros,** to shrug one's shoulders. —**mirar por encima del hombro,** to shrug off; ignore.

hombruno (om'bru·no) *adj., colloq., derog.* mannish.

homenaje (o·me'na·xe) *n.m.* homage. —**homenajear,** *v.t.* to pay homage to.

homeopatía (o·me·o·pa'ti·a) *n.f.* homeopathy. —**homeópata** (-'o·pa·ta) *n.m.* homeopath. —**homeopático** (-'pa·ti·ko) *adj.* homeopathic.

homicida (o·mi'θi·ða; -'si·ða) *n.m.* murderer. —*n.f.* murderess. —*adj.* murderous; homicidal.

homicidio (o·mi'θi·ðjo; -'si·ðjo) *n.m.* homicide; murder.

homilético (o·mi'le·ti·ko) *adj.* homiletic. —**homilética,** *n.f.* homiletics.

homilía (o·mi'li·a) *n.f.* homily.

homófono (o'mo·fo·no) *adj.* homophonous; homophonic. —*n.m.* homophone. —**homofonía** (-'ni·a) *n.f.* homophony.

homógamo (o'mo·ɣa·mo) *adj.* homogamous.

homogéneo (o·mo'xe·ne·o) *adj.* homogenous. —**homogeneidad,** (-ne·i'ðað) *n.f.* homogeneity.

homogenizar (o·mo·xe·ni'θar; -'sar) *v.t.* [*infl.:* **rezar, 10**] to homogenize. —**homogenización,** *n.f.* homogenization.

homólogo (o'mo·lo·ɣo) *adj.* homologous. —**homología** (-'xi·a) *n.f.* homology.

homónimo (o'mo·ni·mo) *adj.* homonymous. —*n.m.* **1**, homonym. **2**, namesake. —**homonimia** (-'ni·mja) *n.f.* homonymy.

homosexual (o·mo·sek'swal) *adj.* & *n.m.* & *f.* homosexual. —**homosexualidad,** *n.f.* homosexuality.

homúnculo (o'mun·ku·lo) *n.m.* **1**, homunculus. **2**, *colloq.* little man; dwarf.

honda ('on·da) *n.f.* sling; slingshot.

hondo ('on·do) *adj.* deep. —*n.m.* bottom; depth.

hondonada (on·do'na·ða) *n.f.* hollow; dale.

hondura (on'du·ra) *n.f.* depth. —**meterse en honduras,** *colloq.* to get in over one's depth.

honesto (o'nes·to) *adj.* honest; upright; decent. —**honestidad,** *n.f.* honesty; uprightness.

hongo ('on·go) *n.m.* **1**, mushroom. **2**, fungus. **3**, derby hat.

honor (o'nor) *n.m.* honor. —**de honor,** honorary.

honorable (o·no'ra·βle) *adj.* honorable.

honorario (o·no'ra·rjo) *adj.* honorary. —**honorarios,** *n.m.pl.* fee; honorarium.

honorífico (o·no'ri·fi·ko) *adj.* **1**, honorary. **2**, honorific. —**mención honorífica,** honorable mention.

honra ('on·ra) *n.f.* **1**, honor. **2**, reputation. **3**, reverence. —**tener a mucha honra,** to be proud of.

honradez (on·ra'ðeθ; -'ðes) *n.f.* honesty.

honrado (on'ra·ðo) *adj.* **1**, honest. **2**, honored.

honrar (on'rar) *v.t.* to honor. —**honrarse,** *v.r.* **1**, to be honored. **2**, to take pleasure.

honroso (on'ro·so) *adj.* **1**, honorable. **2**, honoring; conferring honor.

hopo ('o·po; 'xo·po) *n.m.* **1**, bushy tail. **2**, tuft of hair.

hora ('o·ra) *n.f.* **1**, hour. **2**, time. —*adv., colloq.* = **ahora.** —**a buena**

hora, 1, on time; punctually. **2,** in time; opportunely. **3,** *ironic* in good time. —**a estas horas,** at this time. —**a última hora,** at the last moment. —**dar hora,** to set the time. —**dar la hora,** to strike the hour. —**de última hora,** latest; up to date. —**no ver la hora de,** to be eager to. —**¿qué hora es?,** what time is it? —**hora civil,** standard time. —**hora de verano,** daylight saving time.

horadar (o·ra'ðar) *v.t.* to perforate; pierce; drill.

horario (o'ra·rjo) *n.m.* **1,** timetable; schedule. **2,** hour hand. —*adj.* hourly.

horca ('or·ka) *n.f.* **1,** gallows. **2,** pitchfork. **3,** forked prop. **4,** string *(of garlic or onions).* **5,** yoke *(for animals).*

horcajadas (or·ka'xa·ðas) *n.f.pl.,* in **a horcajadas,** astride; astraddle.

horcón (or'kon) *n.m.* **1,** pitchfork. **2,** forked prop. **3,** *Amer.* roof support.

horda ('or·ða) *n.f.* horde.

horizontal (o·ri·θon'tal; -son'tal) *adj. & n.m.* horizontal.

horizonte (o·ri'θon·te; -'son·te) *n.m.* horizon.

horma ('or·ma) *n.f.* **1,** mold. **2,** hatter's block. **3,** shoemaker's last. —**hallar la horma de su zapato,** *colloq.* **1,** to find just what one has been looking for. **2,** to meet one's match.

hormiga (or'mi·ɣa) *n.f.* ant. —**hormiga blanca,** termite.

hormigón (or·mi'ɣon) *n.m.* concrete. —**hormigón armado,** reinforced concrete.

hormiguear (or·mi·ɣe'ar) *v.i.* **1,** to crawl like ants. **2,** to itch. —**hormigueo** (-'ɣe·o) *n.m.* itching.

hormiguero (or·mi'ɣe·ro) *n.m.* anthill; ant nest. —**oso hormiguero,** anteater.

hormona (or'mo·na) *n.f.* hormone.

hornada (or'na·ða) *n.f.* quantity baked at one time; batch.

hornear (or·ne'ar) *v.i.* to bake.

hornero (or'ne·ro) *n.m.* baker.

hornilla (or'ni·ʎa; -ja) *n.f.* **1,** kitchen grate or stove. **2,** pigeonhole.

hornillo (or'ni·ʎo; -jo) *n.m.* **1,** portable stove; small stove. **2,** kitchen stove.

horno ('or·no) *n.m.* **1,** oven. **2,** kiln. **3,** furnace.

horología (o·ro·lo'xi·a) *n.f.* horology. —**horólogo** (o'ro·lo·ɣo) *n.m.* horologist.

horóscopo (o'ros·ko·po) *n.m.* horoscope.

horqueta (or'ke·ta) *n.f.* **1,** fork *(of a tree).* **2,** forked stick. **3,** anything forked or bifurcated.

horquilla (or'ki·ʎa; -ja) *n.f.* **1,** forked stick. **2,** fork *(of a tree).* **3,** pitchfork. **4,** hairpin.

horrendo (o'rren·do) *adj.* horrible; horrendous.

horrible (o'rri·βle) *adj.* horrible.

horrificar (o·rri·fi'kar) *v.t.* [*infl.:* **tocar, 1**] to horrify. —**horrífico** (o'rri·fi·ko) *adj.* horrific.

horripilar (o·rri·pi'lar) *v.t.* to horrify; cause revulsion in.

horror (o'rror) *n.m.* horror. —**horroroso,** *adj.* horrid; horrible.

horrorizar (o·rro·ri'θar; -'sar) *v.t.* [*infl.* **rezar, 10**] to horrify; shock.

hortaliza (or·ta'li·θa; -sa) *n.f.* garden vegetable.

hortelano (or·te'la·no) *n.m.* **1,** gardener who tends a vegetable garden. **2,** *ornith.* ortolan.

hortensia (or'ten·sja) *n.f.* hydrangea.

hortícola (or'ti·ko·la) *adj.* horticultural.

horticultura (or·ti·kul'tu·ra) *n.f.* horticulture. —**horticultor,** *n.m.* [*fem.* **-tora**] horticulturist.

hosanna (o'sa·na) *interj. & n.m.* hosanna.

hosco ('os·ko) *adj.* **1,** dark-colored. **2,** sullen; glum.

hospedaje (os·pe'ða·xe) *n.m.* lodging.

hospedar (os·pe'ðar) *v.t.* to lodge; provide lodging for. —**hospedarse,** *v.r.* to lodge; stay.

hospedería (os·pe·ðe'ri·a) *n.f.* hostel; inn.

hospedero (os·pe'ðe·ro) *n.m.* innkeeper; host.

hospicio (os'pi·θjo; -sjo) *n.m.* **1,** poorhouse. **2,** orphanage. **3,** asylum.

hospital (os·pi'tal) *n.m.* hospital.

hospitalario (os·pi·ta'la·rjo) *adj.* hospitable.

hospitalidad (os·pi·ta·li'ðað) *n.f.* hospitality.

hospitalizar (os·pi·ta·li'θar; -'sar) [*infl.:* **rezar, 10**] to hospitalize. —**hospitalización,** *n.f.* hospitalization.

hosquedad (os·ke'ðað) *n.f.* glumness; sullenness.

hostelero (os·te'le·ro) *n.m.* innkeeper; host. —**hostelería,** *n.f.* 1, hotel business. 2, hotel management.

hostería (os·te'ri·a) *n.f.* inn; hostel.

hostia ('os·tja) *n.f., eccles.* Host.

hostigar (os·ti'ɣar) *v.t.* [*infl.:* pagar, 8] 1, to harass. 2, *Amer.* to sicken; cloy.

hostil (os'til) *adj.* hostile. —**hostilidad,** *n.f.* hostility.

hostilizar (os·ti·li'θar; -'sar) *v.t.* [*infl.:* rezar, 10] to harry; harass.

hotel (o'tel) *n.m.* hotel. —**hotelero,** *n.m.* hotel manager. —*adj.* hotel (*attrib.*).

hoy (oi) *adv.* 1, today. 2, at the present time. —**de hoy en adelante,** from now on. —**hoy día,** *also,* **hoy en día,** nowadays. —**hoy por hoy,** at the present time.

hoya ('o·ja) *n.f.* 1, dale; hollow. 2, grave. 3, *Amer.* river basin. 4, hole or dip in a river bed or sea bottom.

hoyo ('o·jo) *n.m.* 1, hole; pit. 2, grave.

hoyuelo (o'jwe·lo) *n.m.* 1, dimple. 2, small hole.

hoz (oθ; os) *n.f.* [*pl.* **hoces**] 1, sickle. 2, ravine.

hozar (o'θar; -'sar) *v.t.* [*infl.:* rezar, 10] to root; root up.

huaca ('wa·ka) *n.f.* = **guaca.**

huacal (wa'kal) *n.m.* = **guacal.**

huarache (wa'ra·tʃe) *n.m., Mex.* = **guarache.**

huasca ('was·ka) *n.f., Amer.* = **guasca.**

huaso (wa·so) *adj. & n.m., Amer.* = **guaso.**

hube ('u·βe) *v., pret. of* **haber.**

hucha ('u·tʃa) *n.f.* 1, = **alcancía.** 2, nest egg.

hueco ('we·ko) *adj.* 1, hollow. 2, *fig.* shallow. —*n.m.* 1, hole. 2, gap. 3, *colloq.* place; opening.

huela ('we·la) *v., pres.subjve. of* **oler.**

huelga ('wel·ɣa) *n.f.* labor strike. —**huelguista** (-'ɣis·ta) *n.m. & f.* striker.

huelgue ('wel·ɣe) *v., pres.subjve. of* **holgar.**

huelgo ('wel·ɣo) *v., pres.ind. of* **holgar.**

huelo ('we·lo) *v., pres.ind. of* **oler.**

huella ('we·ʎa; -ja) *n.f.* 1, footprint. 2, track; trail. 3, trace; sign. —**huellas digitales** *or* **dactilares,** fingerprints.

huelle ('we·ʎe; -je) *v., pres.subjve. of* **hollar.**

huello ('we·ʎo; -jo) *v., pres.ind. of* **hollar.**

huérfano ('wer·fa·no) *adj. & n.m.* orphan.

huero ('we·ro) *adj.* 1, empty; vain. 2, *Amer.* = **güero.** 3, rotten (*of an egg*).

huerta ('wer·ta) *n.f.* large vegetable patch.

huerto ('wer·to) *n.m.* 1, orchard. 2, vegetable garden; garden patch.

hueso ('we·so) *n.m.* 1, bone. 2, stone; pit (*of fruits*). 3, *fig.* drudgery. 4, *Amer.* dross. —**la sin hueso,** *colloq.* the tongue. —**estar en los huesos,** *colloq.* to be nothing but skin and bones.

huésped ('wes·peð) *n.m.* 1, [*fem.* **huéspeda**] guest. 2, *biol.* host; host organism. —**casa de huéspedes,** boarding house.

hueste ('wes·te) *n.f.* 1, host; army. 2, body of followers or partisans.

huesudo (we'su·ðo) *adj.* bony.

hueva ('we·βa) *n.f.* roe.

huevera (we'βe·ra) *n.f.* 1, ovary of birds. 2, egg cup.

huevero (we'βe·ro) *n.m.* 1, egg dealer. 2, egg server.

huevo ('we·βo) *n.m.* egg.

huída (u'i·ða) *n.f.* escape; flight.

huir (u'ir) *v.i.* [*infl.:* 26] to flee; escape. —*v.t.* to avoid; shun. —**huirse,** *v.r.* to escape.

hule ('u·le) *n.m.* 1, oilcloth. 2, rubber.

hulla ('u·ʎa; -ja) *n.f.* soft coal. —**hulla blanca,** water power.

humanar (u·ma'nar) *v.t.* = **humanizar.**

humanidad (u·ma·ni'ðað) *n.f.* 1, humanity. 2, humaneness. 3, *colloq.* corpulence.

humanismo (u·ma'nis·mo) *n.m.* humanism. —**humanista,** *n.m. & f.* humanist. —*adj.* humanistic.

humanitario (u·ma·ni'ta·rjo) *adj.* humanitarian.

humanizar (u·ma·ni'θar; -'sar) *v.t.* [*infl.:* rezar, 10] to humanize. —**humanizarse,** *v.r.* to become more humane; soften.

humano (u'ma·no) *adj.* 1, human. 2, humane. —*n.m.* [*fem.* **humana**] human.

humanoide (u·ma'noi·ðe) *adj. & n.m. & f.* humanoid.

humareda (u·ma're·ða) *n.f.* cloud of smoke.

humear (u·me'ar) *v.i.* to smoke; fume.

humedad (u·me'ðað) *n.f.* humidity; dampness; moisture.

humedecer (u·me·ðe'θer; -'ser) *v.t.* [*infl.:* **conocer, 13**] to moisten; dampen.

húmedo ('u·me·ðo) *adj.* humid; moist; damp.

húmero ('u·me·ro) *n.m.* humerus.

humidificar (u·mi·ði·fi'kar) *v.t.* [*infl.:* **tocar, 7**] to humidify. —**humidificación**, *n.f.* humidification.

humildad (u·mil'dað) *n.f.* **1,** humility. **2,** humbleness. **3,** meekness.

humilde (u'mil·de) *adj.* **1,** humble. **2,** meek.

humillar (u·mi'ʎar; -'jar) *v.t.* **1,** to humiliate. **2,** to humble. —**humillarse**, *v.r.* to humble oneself. —**humillación**, *n.f.* humiliation.

humillos (u'mi·ʎos; -jos) *n.m.pl.* airs; conceit.

humita (u'mi·ta) *n.f., S.A.* a kind of tamale.

humo ('u·mo) *n.m.* **1,** smoke. **2,** vapor; fume. —**humos**, *n.m.pl.* airs; conceit.

humor (u'mor) *n.m.* **1,** humor. **2,** disposition; mood.

humorada (u·mo·ra·ða) *n.f.* drollery; humorous sally.

humorado (u·mo·ra·ðo) *adj.* in **bien humorado**, good-humored; **mal humorado**, ill-humored.

humorismo (u·mo·ris·mo) *n.m.* humor; humorous style; humorous literature. —**humorista**, *n.m. & f.* humorist. —**humorístico**, *adj.* humorous; humoristic.

humoso (u'mo·so) *adj.* smoky.

humus ('u·mus) *n.m.* humus.

hundir (un'dir) *v.t.* **1,** to sink. **2,** to plunge. **3,** to crush; overwhelm. **4,** to destroy; ruin.

hundirse (un'dir·se) *v.r.* **1,** to sink.

2, to cave in; collapse. **3,** *colloq.* to melt away; vanish.

huracán (u·ra'kan) *n.m.* hurricane.

huraño (u'ra·ɲo) *adj.* shy; retiring. —**huranía** (-'ɲi·a) *also,* **hurañez** (-'ɲeθ; -'ɲes) *n.f.* shyness; diffidence.

hurgar (ur'ɣar) *v.t.* [*infl.:* **pagar, 8**] **1,** to stir; poke. **2,** to search; rummage through.

hurgón (ur'ɣon) *n.m.* poker (*for a fire*).

hurgonear (ur·ɣo·ne'ar) *v.t.* to stir; poke. —*v.i., colloq.* to meddle; stir up trouble.

hurón (u'ron) *n.m.* **1,** *zoöl.* ferret. **2,** *colloq.* busybody; snoop. —**huronear**, *v.i., colloq.* to pry; snoop.

¡hurra! ('u·rra) *interj.* hurrah!

hurraca (u'rra·ka) *n.f.* = **urraca.**

hurtadillas (ur·ta'ði·ʎas; -jas) *n.f.pl.,* in **a hurtadillas,** furtively.

hurtar (ur'tar) *v.t.* **1,** to steal; filch. **2,** to shortweight; shortchange, etc. —**hurtarse**, *v.r.* to withdraw; hide; steal away.

hurto ('ur·to) *n.m.* **1,** theft; filching. **2,** stolen article. —**a hurto**, furtively.

húsar ('u·sar) *n.m.* hussar. —**sombrero de húsar**, busby.

husmear (us·me'ar) *v.t.* **1,** to sniff; smell. **2,** *colloq.* to pry into; snoop into. —*v.i.* to smell; reek.

husmeo (us'me·o) *n.m.* **1,** sniffing; smelling. **2,** *colloq.* prying; snooping.

huso ('u·so) *n.m.* **1,** spindle. **2,** bobbin.

¡huy! (ui) *interj.* wow!; ouch!

huya ('u·ja) *v., pres.subjve.* of **huir.**

huyendo (u'jen·do) *v., ger.* of **huir.**

huyo ('u·jo) *v., 1st pers.sing. pres.ind.* of **huir.**

huyó (u'jo) *v., 3rd pers.sing. pret.* of **huir.**

I

I, i (i) *n.f.* 10th letter of the Spanish alphabet.

iba ('i·βa) *v., impf.* of **ir.**

ibérico (i'βe·ri·ko) *adj.* Iberian.

ibero (i'βe·ro) *n.m. & adj.* Iberian. —**iberoamericano**, *n.m. & adj.* Latin American.

íbice ('i·βi·θe; -se) *n.m.* ibex.

ibis ('i·βis) *n.m.* ibis.

ice ('i·θe; -se) *v., pres.subjve.* of **izar.**

icé (i'θe; -'se) *v., 1st pers.sing. pret.* of **izar.**

iceberg ('ais·βerɣ) *n.m.* iceberg.

icono (i'ko·no) *n.m.* icon. *Also,* **icón** (i'kon).

iconoclasta (i·ko·no'klas·ta) *n.m.* & *f.* iconoclast. —*adj.* iconoclastic. —**iconoclasia** (-'kla·sja) *n.f.* iconoclasm.

iconografía (i·ko·no·ɣra'fi·a) *n.f.* iconography.

ictericia (ik·te'ri·θja; -sja) *n.f.* jaundice. —**ictérico** (-'te·ri·ko) *adj.* jaundiced.

ictiología (ik·tjo·lo'xi·a) *n.f.* ichthyology. —**ictiológico** (-'lo·xi·ko) *adj.* ichthyological. —**ictiólogo** (ik·'tjo·lo·ɣo) *n.m.* ichthyologist.

id (ið) *v.*, 2nd pers.pl. impve. of **ir**.

id (ið) *n.m.*, *psych.* id:

ida ('i·ða) *n.f.* departure; going. —**ida y vuelta**, round trip. —**idas y venidas**, comings and goings.

idea (i'ðe·a) *n.f.* idea.

ideación (i·ðe·a'θjon; -'sjon) *n.f.* ideation.

ideal (i·ðe'al) *adj.* & *n.m.* ideal. —**idealismo**, *n.m.* idealism. —**idealista**, *n.m.* & *f.* idealist. —*adj.* idealistic.

idealizar (i·ðe·a·li'θar; -'sar) *v.t.* [*infl.:* rezar, 10] to idealize. —**idealización**, *n.f.* idealization.

idear (i·ðe'ar) *v.t.* 1, to form an idea of; ideate. 2, to devise; plan.

ideático (i·ðe'a·ti·ko) *adj.*, *Amer.* crazy; touched.

ídem ('i·ðem) *pron.* idem; the same; ditto.

idéntico (i'ðen·ti·ko) *adj.* identical.

identidad (i·ðen·ti'ðað) *n.f.* identity.

identificar (i·ðen·ti·fi'kar) *v.t.* [*infl.:* tocar, 7] to identify. —**identificable**, *adj.* identifiable. —**identificación**, *n.f.* identification.

ideograma (i·ðe·o'ɣra·ma) *n.m.* ideogram; ideograph.

ideología (i·ðe·o·lo'xi·a) *n.f.* ideology. —**ideológico** (-'lo·xi·ko) *adj.* ideological.

idilio (i'ði·ljo) *n.m.* idyl. —**idílico** (i'ði·li·ko) *adj.* idyllic.

idioma (i'ðjo·ma) *n.m.* language; idiom.

idiomático (i·ðjo'ma·ti·ko) *adj.* idiomatic.

idiosincrasia (i·ðjo·sin'kra·sja) *n.f.* idiosyncrasy. —**idiosincrásico** (-'kra·si·ko) *adj.* idiosyncratic.

idiota (i'ðjo·ta) *n.m.* & *f.* idiot. —*adj.* idiotic. —**idiotez**, *n.f.* idiocy.

idiotismo (i·ðjo'tis·mo) *n.* 1, ignorance; lack of learning. 2, idiocy. 3, = **modismo**.

idiotizar (i·ðjo·ti'θar; -'sar) *v.t.* [*infl.:* rezar, 10] to stultify; stupefy.

ido ('i·ðo) *adj.*, *colloq.* 1, absent-minded. 2, *Amer.* drunk.

ido ('i·ðo) *v.*, *p.p.* of **ir**.

idólatra (i'ðo·la·tra) *adj.* idolatrous. —*n.m.* & *f.* idolater.

idolatrar (i·ðo·la'trar) *v.t.* to idolize; worship.

idolatría (i·ðo·la'tri·a) *n.f.* idolatry.

ídolo ('i·ðo·lo) *n.m.* idol.

idóneo (i'ðo·ne·o) *adj.* competent; qualified. —**idoneidad** (-nei'ðað) *n.f.* competence; capacity.

idus ('i·ðus) *n.m.pl.* ides.

iglesia (i'ɣle·sja) *n.f.* church.

iglú (i'ɣlu) *n.m.* igloo.

ígneo ('iɣ·ne·o) *adj.* igneous.

ignición (iɣ·ni'θjon; -'sjon) *n.f.* ignition. —**ignito** (-'ni·to) *adj.* ignited.

ignoble (iɣ'no·βle) *adj.*, *Amer.* = **innoble**.

ignominia (iɣ·no'mi·nja) *n.f.* ignominy. —**ignominioso**, *adj.* ignominious.

ignorado (iɣ·no'ra·ðo) *adj.* unknown.

ignorante (iɣ·no'ran·te) *adj.* ignorant. —*n.m.* & *f.* ignoramus. —**ignorancia**, *n.f.* ignorance.

ignorar (iɣ·no'rar) *v.t.* 1, to be ignorant of. 2, to ignore.

ignoto (iɣ'no·to) *adj.* unknown.

igual (i'ɣwal) *adj.* 1, equal. 2, even; level. 3, equable. —*n.m.* equal. —*adv.* in like manner. —**al igual**, equally. —**al igual que**, as well as; the same as. —**es igual**, *colloq.* it's all the same.

igualación (i·ɣwa·la'θjon; -'sjon) *n.f.* 1, equalization. 2, agreement; stipulation.

igualar (i·ɣwa'lar) *v.t.* 1, to make equal; equalize. 2, to equal. 3, to even; level. 4, to equate. —*v.i.* to be equal. —**igualarse**, *v.t.* to compare oneself; put oneself on a par. —**igualador**, *adj.* equalizing. —*n.m.* [*fem.* -**dora**] equalizer.

igualdad (i·ɣwal'dað) *n.f.* 1, equality. 2, evenness; uniformity.

igualmente (i·ɣwal'men·te) *adv.* 1, equally. 2, likewise.

iguana (i'ɣwa·na) *n.f.* iguana.

ijada (i'xa·ða) *n.f.* flank; side. *Also*, **ijar** (i'xar) *n.m.*

ilación (i·la'θjon; -'sjon) *n.f.* 1, inference. 2, logical sequence; connection.

ilegal (i·le'ɣal) *adj.* illegal; unlawful. —**ilegalidad,** *n.f.* illegality.

ilegible (i·le'xi·βle) *adj.* illegible.

ilegítimo (i·le'xi·ti·mo) *adj.* illegitimate. —**ilegitimidad,** *n.f.* illegitimacy.

íleon ('i·le·on) *n.m., anat.* ileum.

ileso (i'le·so) *adj.* unhurt; uninjured.

iletrado (i·le'tra·ðo) *adj.* = **iliterato.**

ilíaco (i'li·a·ko) *also,* **ilíaco** (i'lja·ko) *adj.* iliac.

iliberal (i·li·βe'ral) *adj.* illiberal. —**iliberalidad,** *n.f.* illiberality.

ilícito (i'li·θi·to; -si·to) *adj.* illicit; unlawful.

ilimitable (i·li·mi'ta·βle) *adj.* illimitable.

ilimitado (i·li·mi'ta·ðo) *adj.* unlimited; boundless.

iliterato (i·li·te'ra·to) *adj. & n.m.* illiterate.

ilógico (i'lo·xi·ko) *adj.* illogical.

iluminar (i·lu·mi'nar) *v.t.* **1,** to illuminate; light. **2,** to enlighten. —**iluminación,** *n.f.* illumination; lighting.

ilusión (i·lu'sjon) *n.f.* **1,** illusion. **2,** false hope. —**ilusionista,** *n.m. & f.* illusionist; magician.

ilusionar (i·lu·sjo'nar) *v.t., Amer.* **1,** to give false hopes to. **2,** to delude (by sleight). —**ilusionarse,** *v.r.* **1,** to become hopeful. **2,** to build up high hopes; be overconfident.

ilusivo (i·lu'si·βo) *adj.* illusive.

iluso (i'lu·so) *adj.* deluded; deceived. —*n.m.* dreamer.

ilusorio (i·lu'so·rjo) *adj.* illusory.

ilustración (i·lus·tra'θjon; -'sjon) *n.f.* **1,** illustration. **2,** culture; learning.

ilustrado (i·lus'tra·ðo) *adj.* **1,** illustrated. **2,** learned; cultured.

ilustrador (i·lus·tra'ðor) *n.m.* illustrator.

ilustrar (i·lus'trar) *v.t.* **1,** to illustrate. **2,** to enlighten. —**ilustrativo,** *adj.* illustrative.

ilustre (i'lus·tre) *adj.* illustrious; distinguished.

imagen (i'ma·xen) *n.f.* **1,** image. **2,** statue.

imaginar (i·ma·xi'nar) *v.t.* to imagine. —**imaginable,** *adj.* imaginable. —**imaginación,** *n.f.* imagination. —**imaginario,** *adj.* imaginary. —**imaginativo,** *adj.* imaginative.

imán (i'man) *n.m.* **1,** magnet. **2,** attraction.

imantación (i·man·ta'θjon; -'sjon) *also* **imanación** (i·ma·na'θjon; -'sjon) *n.f.* magnetization.

imantar (i·man'tar) *also,* **imanar** (i·ma'nar) *v.t.* to magnetize.

imbécil (im'be·θil; -sil) *n.m. & f.* imbecile. —*adj.* imbecilic. —**imbecilidad,** *n.f.* imbecility.

imberbe (im'ber·βe) *adj.* beardless.

imborrable (im·bo'rra·βle) *adj.* indelible.

imbuir (im·bu'ir) *v.t.* [*infl.: huir,* 26] to imbue. —**imbuimiento,** *n.m.* imbuement.

imitar (i·mi'tar) *v.t.* to imitate. —**imitable,** *adj.* imitable. —**imitación,** *n.f.* imitation. —**imitado,** *adj.* [*also,* **de imitación**] imitation. —**imitador,** *n.m.* imitator. —**imitativo,** *adj.* imitative.

impacientar (im·pa·θjen'tar; -sjen'tar) *v.t.* **1,** to make impatient. **2,** to vex; irritate. —**impacientarse,** *v.r.* to lose patience.

impaciente (im·pa'θjen·te; -'sjen·te) *adj.* impatient. —**impaciencia,** *n.f.* impatience.

impactado (im·pak'ta·ðo) *adj., dent.* impacted.

impacto (im'pak·to) *n.m.* impact.

impagable (im·pa'ɣa·βle) *adj.* **1,** unpayable. **2,** *Amer., colloq.* invaluable; priceless.

impago (im'pa·ɣo) *adj., Amer., colloq.* unpaid.

impalpable (im·pal'pa·βle) *adj.* impalpable. —**impalpabilidad,** *n.f.* impalpability.

impar (im'par) *adj.* **1,** unequal. **2,** unmatched. **3,** matchless; without equal. —**número impar,** odd number.

imparcial (im·par'θjal; -'sjal) *adj.* impartial. —**imparcialidad,** *n.f.* impartiality.

impartir (im·par'tir) *v.t.,* **1,** to impart. **2,** to grant; concede.

impasable (im·pa'sa·βle) *adj.* **1,** impassable. **2,** *Amer., colloq.* unbearable; that cannot be swallowed.

impasible (im·pa'si·βle) *adj.* impassive. —**impasibilidad,** *n.f.* impassiveness.

impávido (im'pa·βi·ðo) *adj.* dauntless. —**impavidez,** *n.f.* dauntlessness.

impecable (im·pe'ka·βle) *adj.* impeccable. —**impecabilidad,** *n.f.* impeccability.

impediencia (im·pe·'ðjen·θja; -sja) *also,* **impedancia** (-'ðan·θja; -sja) *n.f., elect.* impedance.

impedimenta (im·pe·ði'men·ta) *n.f.* impedimenta.

impedimento (im·pe·ði'men·to) *n.m.* impediment.

impedir (im·pe·'ðir) *v.t.* [*infl.:* **pedir, 33**] to prevent; impede. —**impedido,** *adj.* disabled; crippled.

impeditivo (im·pe·ði'ti·βo) *adj.* preventive; deterrent.

impeler (im·pe·'ler) *v.t.* to impel.

impenetrable (im·pe·ne'tra·βle) *adj.* impenetrable. —**impenetrabilidad,** *n.f.* impenetrability.

impenitente (im·pe·ni'ten·te) *adj.* impenitent. —**impenitencia,** *n.f.* impenitence.

impensable (im·pen'sa·βle) *adj.* unthinkable.

impensado (im·pen'sa·ðo) *adj.* unexpected; unforeseen. —**impensadamente,** *adv.* inadvertently; thoughtlessly.

imperar (im·pe'rar) *v.i.* to rule; reign; hold sway.

imperativo (im·pe·ra'ti·βo) *adj.* & *n.m.* imperative.

imperceptible (im·per·θep'ti·βle; im·per·sep-) *adj.* imperceptible. —**imperceptibilidad,** *n.f.* imperceptibility.

imperdible (im·per'ði·βle) *n.m.* safety pin.

imperdonable (im·per·ðo'na·βle) *adj.* unpardonable; unforgivable.

imperecedero (im·pe·re·θe'ðe·ro; -se'ðe·ro) *adj.* everlasting; imperishable.

imperfección (im·per·fek'θjon; -'sjon) *n.f.* imperfection.

imperfecto (im·per'fek·to) *adj.* & *n.m.* imperfect.

imperial (im·pe'rjal) *adj.* imperial. —*n.f.* top (*of a bus, carriage, etc.*).

imperialismo (im·pe·rja'lis·mo) *n.m.* imperialism. —**imperialista,** *n.m.* & *f.* imperialist. —*adj.* imperialistic.

impericia (im·pe'ri·θja; -sja) *n.f.* **1,** unskillfulness. **2,** inexperience.

imperio (im·pe·rjo) *n.m.* **1,** empire. **2,** rule; command. **3,** *fig.* haughtiness; pride. **4,** *fig.* imperiousness.

imperioso (im·pe'rjo·so) *adj.* **1,** imperious; domineering. **2,** urgent. —**imperiosidad,** *n.f.* imperiousness.

imperito (im·pe'ri·to) *adj.* unskilled; inexperienced.

impermeabilizar (im·per·me·a·βi·li'θar; -'sar) *v.t.* [*infl.:* **rezar, 10**] to waterproof. —**impermeabilización,** *n.f.* waterproofing.

impermeable (im·per·me'a·βle) *adj.* waterproof; impermeable; impervious. —*n.m.* raincoat. —**impermeabilidad,** *n.f.* impermeability; imperviousness.

impermutable (im·per·mu'ta·βle) *adj.* **1,** unchangeable. **2,** unexchangeable.

impersonal (im·per·so'nal) *adj.* impersonal.

impersuasible (im·per·swa'si·βle) *adj.* unpersuadable.

impertérrito (im·per'te·rri·to) *adj.* unruffled; undaunted.

impertinente (im·per·ti'nen·te) *adj.* **1,** impertinent; saucy. **2,** irrelevant. —**impertinentes,** *n.m.pl.* lorgnette. —**impertinencia,** *n.f.* impertinence; sauciness.

imperturbable (im·per·tur·'βa·βle) *adj.* imperturbable. —**imperturbabilidad,** *n.f.* imperturbability. —**imperturbado,** *adj.* unperturbed; undisturbed.

impétigo (im'pe·ti·yo) *n.m.* impetigo.

impetrar (im·pe'trar) *v.t.* to entreat; beseech. —**impetración,** *n.f.* plea; entreaty.

ímpetu ('im·pe·tu) *n.m.* **1,** impetus. **2,** impulse. **3,** attack; fit.

impetuoso (im·pe'two·so) *adj.* **1,** impetuous. **2,** violent. —**impetuosidad,** *n.f.* impetuosity.

impida (im'pi·ða) *v., pres.subjve. of* **impedir**.

impidió (im·pi'ðjo) *v., 3rd pers. sing. pret. of* **impedir.**

impido (im'pi·ðo) *v., 1st pers.sing. pres.ind. of* **impedir.**

impiedad (im·pje'ðað) *n.f.* impiety; impiousness.

impío (im'pi·o) *adj.* impious; irreligious.

implacable (im·pla·ka·βle) *adj.* implacable; relentless. —**implacabilidad,** *n.f.* implacability.

implantar (im·plan'tar) *v.t.* **1,** to implant; instill; inculcate. **2,** to introduce; establish.

implicación (im·pli·ka'θjon; -'sjon) *n.f.* **1,** implication. **2,** contradiction.

implicar (im·pli'kar) *v.t.* [*infl.:* **tocar, 7**] **1,** to implicate; involve. **2,**

to imply. —*v.i.* to imply contradiction (*usu. with adverbs of negation*).

implícito (im'pli·θi·to; -si·to) *adj.* implicit; implied —*n.m., elect.; comput.* default.

implorar (im·plo'rar) *v.t.* to implore; entreat. —**imploración,** *n.f.* entreaty.

implosión (im·plo'sjon) *n.f.* implosion. —**implosionar,** *v.t.* to implode.

implume (im'plu·me) *adj.* unfledged; without feathers.

impolítico (im·po'li·ti·ko) *adj.* 1, impolite. 2, impolitic. —**impolítica,** *n.f.* discourtesy; impoliteness.

impoluto (im·po'lu·to) *adj.* unpolluted; pure.

imponderable (im·pon·de'ra·βle) *adj.* 1, imponderable. 2, beyond praise.

imponente (im·po'nen·te) *adj.* imposing.

imponer (im·po'ner) *v.t.* [*infl.:* **poner,** 54] 1, to impose. 2, to acquaint; inform. —**imponerse,** *v.t.* to dominate; prevail.

imponible (im·po'ni·βle) *adj.* taxable; dutiable.

impopular (im·po·pu'lar) *adj.* unpopular. —**impopularidad,** *n.f.* unpopularity.

importante (im·por'tan·te) *adj.* important. —**importancia,** *n.f.* importance.

importar (im·por'tar) *v.t.* 1, to import. 2, to cost; cause expenditure of. —*v.i.* to matter. —**importación,** *n.f.* importation; import. —**importador,** *adj.* importing. —*n.m.* importer. —**no importa,** no matter; never mind. —**¿qué importa?,** what does it matter?

importe (im'por·te) *n.m.* 1, *comm.* amount. 2, cost; price; value.

importunar (im·por·tu'nar) *v.t.* to importune. —**importunación,** *n.f.* annoying insistence.

importuno (im·por'tu·no) *adj.* 1, inopportune. 2, importunate; annoying. —**importunidad,** *n.f.* importunity.

imposibilitar (im·po·si·βi·li·'tar) *v.t.* 1, to make impossible. 2, to disable; incapacitate.

imposible (im·po'si·βle) *adj.* impossible. —**imposibilidad,** *n.f.* impossibility.

imposición (im·po·si'θjon; -'sjon) *n.f.* imposition.

impostergable (im·pos·ter'ɣa·βle) *adj.* that cannot be postponed.

impostor (im·pos'tor) *n.m.* impostor.

impostura (im·pos'tu·ra) *n.f.* 1, imputation. 2, imposture.

impotente (im·po'ten·te) *adj.* impotent. —**impotencia,** *n.f.* impotence.

impracticable (im·prak·ti'ka·βle) *adj.* impracticable. —**impracticabilidad,** *n.f.* impracticability.

impráctico (im'prak·ti·ko) *adj.* impractical.

imprecar (im·pre'kar) *v.t.* [*infl.:* **tocar,** 7] to imprecate; curse. —**precación,** *n.f.* imprecation; curse.

impreciso (im·pre'θi·so; -'si·so) *adj.* not precise; vague; indefinite. —**imprecisión,** *n.f.* absence of precision; indefiniteness.

impregnar (im·preɣ'nar) *v.t.* to impregnate; saturate. —**impregnable,** *adj.* impregnable; saturable. —**impregnación,** *n.f.* impregnation; saturation.

impremeditado (im·pre·me·ði·'ta·ðo) *adj.* unpremeditated.

imprenta (im'pren·ta) *n.f.* 1, printing. 2, printing shop or office. 3, print; character. 4, publication. —**pie de imprenta,** publisher's mark; imprint.

imprescindible (im·pres·θin'di·βle; -pre·sin'di·βle) *adj.* essential; indispensable.

imprescriptible (im·pres·krip'ti·βle) *adj.* inadvisable; not recommendable.

impresentable (im·pre·sen'ta·βle) *adj.* unpresentable.

impresión (im·pre'sjon) *n.f.* 1, impression. 2, impress; stamp. 3, edition. 4, print. 5, printing. —**impresión digital,** fingerprint.

impresionante (im·pre·sjo'nan·te) *adj.* impressive.

impresionar (im·pre·sjo'nar) *v.t.* to impress. —**impresionable,** *adj.* impressionable.

impresionismo (im·pre·sjo'nis·mo) *n.m.* impressionism. —**impresionista,** *n.m. & f.* impressionist. —*adj.* impressionistic.

impreso (im'pre·so) *v., p.p. of* **imprimir.** —*adj.* 1, printed. 2, stamped. —*n.m.* 1, print; copy. 2, booklet; pamphlet; handbill. —**impresos,** *n.m.pl.* printed matter.

impresor (im·pre'sor) *n.m.* printer.

—**impresora** (–'so·ra) *n.f.* printer; printing machine.
imprevisible (im·pre·βi'si·βle) *adj.* unforeseeable.
imprevisión (im·pre·βi'sjon) *n.f.* improvidence; lack of foresight.
imprevisto (im·pre'βis·to) *adj.* unforeseen. —*n.m.* unforeseen thing or event. —**imprevistos,** *n.m. pl.* incidental or unforeseen expenses.
imprimir (im·pri'mir) *v.t.* [*p.p.* **impreso**] **1,** to print. **2,** to impress; imprint.
improbable (im·pro'βa·βle) *adj.* improbable. —**improbabilidad,** *n.f.* improbability.
ímprobo ('im·pro·βo) *adj.* **1,** dishonest. **2,** laborious; backbreaking. —**improbidad,** *n.f.* dishonesty; improbity.
improcedencia (im·pro·θe'ðen·θja; -se'ðen·sja) *n.* **1,** lack of legal sanction. **2,** untimeliness. **3,** inappropriateness.
improcedente (im·pro·θe'ðen·te; -se'ðen·te) *adj.* **1,** unlawful; unsanctioned. **2,** untimely; inopportune. **3,** inappropriate.
improductivo (im·pro·ðuk'ti·βo) *adj.* unproductive.
impronunciable (im·pro·nun'θja·βle; -'sja·βle) *adj.* unpronounceable.
improperio (im·pro'pe·rjo) *n.m.* insult; abuse.
impropio (im'pro·pjo) *adj.* improper. —**impropiedad,** *n.f.* impropriety.
improrrogable (im·pro·rro'ya·βle) *adj.* that cannot be extended or postponed.
impróspero (im'pros·pe·ro) *adj.* unprosperous.
impróvido (im'pro·βi·ðo) *adj.* improvident. —**improvidencia,** *n.f.* improvidence.
improvisación (im·pro·βi·sa·'θjon; -'sjon) *n.f.* **1,** improvisation. **2,** sudden rise to fame or success. **3,** *mus.* impromptu.
improvisar (im·pro·βi'sar) *v.t.* to improvise. —**improvisado,** *adj.* improvised; impromptu.
improviso (im·pro'βi·so) *also,* **improvisto** (-'βis·to) *adj.* unforeseen. —**de improviso; a la improvista,** suddenly; unexpectedly.
imprudente (im·pru'ðen·te) *adj.* imprudent. —**imprudencia,** *n.f.* imprudence.
impúber (im'pu·βer) *also,*

impúbero (-βe·ro) *adj.* below the age of puberty; immature.
impudente (im·pu'ðen·te) *adj.* impudent. —**impudencia,** *n.f.* impudence.
impúdico (im'pu·ði·ko) *adj.* immodest; brash. —**impudicia** (-'ði·θja; -sja) *n.f., also,* **impudor** (-'ðor) *n.m.* immodesty; brashness.
impuesto (im'pwes·to) *v., p.p. of* **imponer.** —*n.m.* tax; duty.
impugnar (im·puy'nar) *v.t.* to impugn. —**impugnable,** *adj.* impugnable. —**impugnación,** *n.f.* impugnment.
impulsar (im·pul'sar) *v.t.* **1,** to impel; urge. **2,** *mech.* to drive.
impulsión (im·pul'sjon) *n.f.* = **impulso.**
impulsivo (im·pul'si·βo) *adj.* impulsive. —**impulsividad,** *n.f.* impulsiveness.
impulso (im'pul·so) *n.m.* **1,** impulse. **2,** impetus.
impulsor (im·pul'sor) *n.m.* impeller. —*adj* impelling.
impune (im'pu·ne) *adj.* unpunished. —**impunemente,** *adv.* with impunity.
impunidad (im·pu·ni'ðað) *n.f.* impunity.
impuro (im'pu·ro) *adj.* impure. —**impureza,** *n.f.* impurity.
impuse (im'pu·se) *v., 1st pers.sing. pret. of* **imponer.**
imputar (im·pu'tar) *v.t.* to impute. —**imputable,** *adj.* imputable. —**imputación,** *n.f.* imputation.
inabarcable (in·a·βar'ka·βle) *adj.* unencompassable.
inabordable (in·a·βor'ða·βle) *adj.* **1,** unapproachable. **2,** incapable of being boarded, as a ship, train, etc.
inabrogable (in·a·βro'ya·βle) *adj.* irrevocable.
inacabado (in·a·ka'βa·ðo) *adj.* unfinished.
inacabable (in·a·ka'βa·βle) *adj.* endless; interminable.
inaccesible (in·ak·θe'si·βle; in·ak·se-) *adj.* inaccessible. —**inaccesibilidad,** *n.f.* inaccessibility.
inacción (in·ak'θjon; -'sjon) *n.f.* inaction.
inacentuado (in·a·θen'twa·ðo; in·a·sen-) *adj.* unaccented.
inaceptable (in·a·θep'ta·βle; in·a·sep-) *adj.* unacceptable.
inacostumbrado (in·a·kos·tum·'bra·ðo) *adj.* unaccustomed.

inactivo (in·ak'ti·βo) *adj.* inactive.
—**inactividad**, *n.f.* inactivity.

inadaptable (in·a·ðap'ta·βle) *adj.*
unadaptable.

inadecuado (in·a·ðe'kwa·ðo)
adj. 1, inadequate. 2, inappropriate.

inadmisible (in·að·mi'si·βle) *adj.*
inadmissible. —**inadmisibilidad**,
n.f. inadmissibility.

inadoptable (in·a·ðop'ta·βle)
adj. unadoptable; impracticable.

inadulterado (in·a·ðul·te'ra·ðo);
adj. unadulterated.

inadvertido (in·að·βer'ti·ðo) *adj.*
1, inadvertent. 2, unnoticed; unseen.
—**inadvertencia**, *n.f.* inadvertency;
oversight.

inafectado (in·a·fek'ta·ðo) *adj.*
unaffected.

inagotable (in·a·ɣo'ta·βle) *adj.*
inexhaustible.

inaguantable (in·a·ɣwan'ta·βle)
adj. unbearable; unendurable.

inalámbrico (in·a'lam·bri·ko)
adj. wireless.

inalcanzable (in·al·kan'θa·βle;
-'sa·βle) *adj.* unattainable.

inalienable (in·a·lje'na·βle) *also,*
inajenable (-xe'na·βle) *adj.* inalienable.

inalterable (in·al·te'ra·βle) *adj.*
unalterable; unchangeable. —**inalterado** (-'ra·ðo) *adj.* unaltered; unchanged.

inamovible (in·a·mo'βi·βle) *adj.*
immovable.

inane (i'na·ne) *adj.* inane.
—**inanidad**, *n.f.* inanity.

inanición (i·na·ni'θjon; -'sjon) *n.f.*
inanition; starvation.

inanimado (in·a·ni'ma·ðo) *adj.*
inanimate.

inánime (i'na·ni·me) *adj.* 1, =
exánime. 2, inanimate.

inanunciado (in·a·nun'θja·ðo;
-'sja·ðo) *adj.* unannounced.

inapagable (in·a·pa'ɣa·βle) *adj.*
inextinguishable; unquenchable.

inapelable (in·a·pe'la·βle) *adj.* 1,
unappealable. 2, irremediable.

inapercibido (in·a·per·θi'βi·ðo;
-si'βi·ðo) *adj.* unnoticed; unseen.

inapetente (in·a·pe'ten·te) *adj.*
without appetite. —**inapetencia**,
n.f. lack of appetite.

inaplazable (in·a·pla'θa·βle;
-'sa·βle) *adj.* that cannot be postponed.

inaplicable (in·a·pli'ka·βle) *adj.*
inapplicable. —**inaplicabilidad**, *n.f.*
inapplicability.

inaplicado (in·a·pli'ka·ðo) *adj.* =
desaplicado. —**inaplicación**, *n.f.* =
desaplicación.

inapreciable (in·a·pre'θja·βle;
-'sja·βle) *adj.* 1, invaluable. 2, inappreciable.

inapropiado *adj.* inappropriate.

inaprovechable (in·a·pro·βe'tʃa·
βle) *adj.* unusable.

inapto (in'ap·to) *adj.* = **inepto**.
—**inaptitud**, *n.f.* = **ineptitud**.

inarmónico (in·ar'mo·ni·ko) *adj.*
inharmonious.

inarticulado (in·ar·ti·ku'la·ðo)
adj. inarticulate.

inartístico (in·ar'tis·ti·ko) *adj.* inartistic.

inasequible (in·a·se'ki·βle) *adj.*
1, unattainable. 2, unapproachable.

inasimilable (in·a·si·mi'la·βle)
adj. unassimilable.

inasistencia (in·a·sis'ten·θja;
-sja) *n.f.* absence; unattendance.

inasociable (in·a·so'θja·βle;
-'sja·βle) *adj.* that cannot be associated; unrelatable.

inastillable (in·as·ti'ʎa·βle;
-'ja·βle) *adj.* splinterproof; shatterproof.

inatacable (in·a·ta'ka·βle) *adj.*
unassailable.

inatento *adj.* unattentive. —**ina-
tención**, *n.f.* inattention.

inaudible (in·au'ði·βle) *adj.* inaudible.

inaudito (in·au'ði·to) *adj.* unheard-of.

inaugurar (in·au·ɣu'rar) *v.t.* to
inaugurate. —**inauguración**, *n.f.*
inauguration. —**inaugural**, *adj.* inaugural.

inaveriguable (in·a·βe·ri'ɣwa·
βle) *adj.* unascertainable.

inca ('in·ka) *n.m. & adj.* Inca.
—**incaico** (in'kai·ko) *adj.* Incan.

incalculable (in·kal·ku'la·βle)
adj. incalculable.

incalificable (in·ka·li·fi'ka·βle)
adj. 1, unqualifiable. 2, unspeakable.

incambiable (in·kam'bja·βle)
adj. 1, unchangeable. 2, unexchangeable.

incandescente (in·kan·des'θen·
te; -des'sen·te) *adj.* incandescent.
—**incandescencia**, *n.f.* incandescence.

incansable (in·kan'sa·βle) *adj.*
untiring; tireless.

incapaz (in·ka'paθ; -'pas) *adj.* incapable; unable. —*adj. & n.m. & f.*

incompetent. —**incapacidad** (-θi·'ðað; -si'ðað) *n.f.* incapacity. —**incapacitar**, *v.t.* to incapacitate.

incasto (in'kas·to) *adj.* unchaste.

incautarse (in·kau'tar·se) *v.r., fol. by* **de**, to attach (money, property, etc.). —**incautación**, *n.f.* attachment of property.

incauto (in'kau·to) *adj.* incautious; unwary.

incendiar (in·θen'djar; in·sen-) *v.t.* to set on fire. —**incendiarse**, *v.r.* to catch fire.

incendiario (in·θen'dja·rjo; in·sen-) *adj. &* incendiary.

incendio (in'θen·djo; in'sen-) *n.m.* conflagration; fire.

incensar (in·θen'sar; in·sen-) *v.t.* [*infl.:* pensar, 27] to flatter.

incensurable (in·θen·su'ra·βle; in·sen-) *adj.* uncensurable; unimpeachable.

incentivo (in·θen'ti·βo; in·sen-) *n.m.* incentive.

incertidumbre (in·θer·ti'ðum·bre; in·ser-) *n.f.* uncertainty.

incesante (in·θe'san·te; in·se-) *adj.* incessant; unceasing.

incesto (in'θes·to; in'ses-) *n.m.* incest. —**incestuoso** (-'two·so) *adj.* incestuous.

incidencia (in·θi'ðen·θja, -si·'ðen·sja) *n.f.* incidence.

incidental (in·θi·ðen'tal; in·si-) *adj.* incidental.

incidente (in·θi'ðen·te; in·si-) *adj. & n.m.* **1**, incidental. **2**, incident.

incidir (in·θi'ðir; in·si-) *v.i., usu. fol. by* **en**, to fall into; fall upon.

incienso (in'θjen·se; in'sjen-) *v., pres.subjve. of* **incensar**.

incienso (in'θjen·so; -'sjen·so) *n.m.* **1**, incense. **2**, *fig.* flattery.

inciensò (in'θjen·so; -'sjen·so) *v., 1st pers.sing. pres.ind. of* **incensar**.

incierto (in'θjer·to; in'sjer-) *adj.* **1**, uncertain. **2**, untrue.

incinerar (in·θi·ne'rar; in·si-) *v.t.* to incinerate. —**incineración**, *n.f.* incineration. —**incinerador**, *adj.* incinerating. —*n.m.* incinerator.

incipiente (in·θi'pjen·te; in·si-) *adj.* incipient.

incircunciso (in·θir·kun'θi·so; -sir·kun'si·so) *adj.* uncircumcised.

incircunscrito (in·θir·kuns'kri·to; in·sir-) *adj.* uncircumscribed.

incisión (in·θi'sjon; in·si-) *n.f.* incision.

incisivo (in·θi'si·βo; in·si-) *adj.*

incisive. —**incisivos**, *n.m.pl.* incisors.

inciso (in'θi·so; -'si·so) *adj.* concise; terse *(of style).* —*n.m.* **1**, clause; paragraph. **2**, comma.

incitar (in·θi'tar; in·si-) *v.t.* to incite. —**incitación**, *n.f.* incitement. —**incitante**, *adj.* inciting; appealing.

incivil (in·θi'βil; in·si-) *adj.* uncivil. —**incivilidad**, *n.f.* incivility.

incivilizado (in·θi·βi·li'θa·ðo; -si·βi·li'sa·ðo) *adj.* uncivilized.

inclasificable (in·kla·si·fi'ka·βle) *adj.* unclassifiable; nondescript.

inclasificado (in·kla·si·fi'ka·ðo) *adj.* unclassified.

inclemente (in·kle'men·te) *adj.* inclement. —**inclemencia**, *n.f.* clemency.

inclinación (in·kli·na'θjon; -'sjon) *n.f.* **1**, inclination; bent. **2**, bow; curtsy. **3**, slant; tilt.

inclinado (in·kli'na·ðo) *adj.* inclined.

inclinar (in·kli'nar) *v.t. & i.* to incline. —*v.t.* **1**, to nod. **2**, to bend; bow; lean. —**inclinarse**, *v.r.* **1**, to be inclined; tend. **2**, to bow; curtsy. **3**, to slant; tilt.

ínclito ('in·kli·to) *adj.* illustrious; famed.

incluir (in·klu'ir) *v.t.* [*infl.:* huir, 26] **1**, to include. **2**, to enclose.

inclusa (in'klu·sa) *n.f.* foundling home.

inclusión (in·klu'sjon) *n.f.* **1**, inclusion. **2**, access; intimacy.

inclusive (in·klu'si·βe) *adv.* inclusively.

inclusivo (in·klu'si·βo) *adj.* inclusive. —**inclusivamente**, *adv.* inclusively.

incluso (in'klu·so) *adj.* enclosed; included. —*adv.* inclusively. —*prep.* including; inclusive of.

incoativo (in·ko·a'ti·βo) *adj., gram.* inceptive; inchoative.

incobrable (in·ko'βra·βle) *adj.* **1**, uncollectible. **2**, irrecoverable.

incógnito (in'koγ·ni·to) *adj.* unknown; incognito. —**incógnita**, *n.f., math.* unknown; unknown quantity. —**de incógnito**, incognito.

incognoscible (in·koγ·nos'θi·βle; -no'si·βle) *adj.* unknowable.

incoherente (in·ko·e'ren·te) *adj.* incoherent. —**incoherencia**, *n.f.* incoherence.

incoloro (in·ko·lo·ro) *adj.* colorless.

incólume (in'ko·lu·me) *adj.* unharmed; safe and sound.

incombustible (in·kom·bus'ti·βle) *adj.* incombustible.

incomible (in·ko'mi·βle) *adj.* inedible. *Also,* **incomestible.**

incomodar (in·ko·mo'ðar) *v.t.* to inconvenience; incommode.

incomodidad (in·ko·mo·ði'ðað) *n.f.* 1, inconvenience. 2, discomfort.

incómodo (in'ko·mo·ðo) *adj.* 1, inconvenient. 2, uncomfortable.

incomparable (in·kom·pa'ra·βle) *adj.* incomparable.

incompasivo (in·kom·pa'si·βo) *adj.* unmerciful; lacking compassion.

incompatible (in·kom·pa'ti·βle) *adj.* incompatible. **—incompatibilidad,** *n.f.* incompatibility.

incompetente (in·kom·pe'ten·te) *adj.* incompetent. **—incompetencia,** *n.f.* incompetence.

incompleto (in·kom'ple·to) *adj.* incomplete.

incomplexo (in·kom'plek·so) *also,* **incomplejo** (-'ple·xo) *adj.* 1, unencumbered; free. 2, uncomplicated; simple.

incomprensible (in·kom·pren·'si·βle) *adj.* incomprehensible.

incomprensión (in·kom·pren·'sjon) *n.f.* lack of understanding. **—incomprensivo,** *adj.* lacking understanding.

incompresible (in·kom·pre'si·βle) *adj.* incompressible.

incomunicable (in·ko·mu·ni·'ka·βle) *adj.* incommunicable.

incomunicado (in·ko·mu·ni'ka·ðo) *adj.* incommunicado; isolated.

incomunicar (in·ko·mu·ni'kar) *v.t.* [*infl.:* **tocar, 7**] to isolate; place incommunicado.

inconcebible (in·kon·θe'βi·βle; -se'βi·βle) *adj.* inconceivable.

inconciliable (in·kon·θi'lja·βle; -si'lja·βle) *adj.* irreconcilable.

inconcluso (in·kon'klu·so) *adj.* 1, unfinished. 2, inconclusive.

incondicional (in·kon·di·θjo·'nal; -sjo'nal) *adj.* unconditional.

inconducente (in·kon·du'θen·te; -'sen·te) *adj.* nonconducive.

inconexo (in·ko'nek·so) *adj.* 1, unconnected. 2, incoherent; disconnected.

inconfesable (in·kon·fe'sa·βle) *adj.* that cannot be confessed; too shameful for mention.

inconfeso (in·kon'fe·so) *adj.* 1, unconfessed. 2, unshriven.

inconfundible (in·kon·fun'di·βle) *adj.* unmistakable.

incongruente (in·kon'grwen·te) *adj.* incongruent; incongruous. **—incongruencia,** *n.f.* incongruence; incongruousness.

incongruo (in'kon·grwo) *adj.* incongruous. **—incongruidad** (-grwi'ðað) *n.f.* incongruity; incongruousness.

inconmensurable (in·kon·men·su'ra·βle) *adj.* incommensurable. **—inconmensurabilidad,** *n.f.* incommensurability.

inconmovible (in·kon·mo'βi·βle; in·ko·mo-) *adj.* unyielding; unpitying.

inconquistable (in·kon·kis'ta·βle) *adj.* unconquerable.

inconsciencia (in·kons'θjen·θja; -kon'sjen·sja) *n.f.* 1, unconsciousness. 2, unawareness.

inconsciente (in·kons'θjen·te; -kon'sjen·te) *adj.* 1, unconscious. 2, unaware. 3, unconscionable. 4, *colloq.* irresponsible.

inconsecuente (in·kon·se'kwen·te) *adj.* inconsequent; inconsistent. **—inconsecuencia** (-θja; -sja) *n.f.* inconsequence.

inconsiderado (in·kon·si·ðe'ra·ðo) *adj.* inconsiderate. **—inconsideración,** *n.f.* inconsiderateness.

inconsiguiente (in·kon·si'ɣjen·te) *adj.* inconsequent.

inconsistente (in·kon·sis'ten·te) *adj.* 1, lacking consistency; loose; thin. 2, inconsistent. **—inconsistencia,** *n.f.* inconsistency.

inconsolable (in·kon·so'la·βle) *adj.* inconsolable.

inconstante (in·kons'tan·te) *adj.* inconstant. **—inconstancia,** *n.f.* inconstancy.

inconstitucional (in·kons·ti·tu·θjo'nal; -sjo'nal) *adj.* unconstitutional.

incontable (in·kon'ta·βle) *adj.* countless; innumerable.

incontaminado (in·kon·ta·mi'na·ðo) *adj.* uncontaminated.

incontenible (in·kon·te'ni·βle) *adj.* irrepressible.

incontestable (in·kon·tes'ta·βle) *adj.* unquestionable.

incontestado (in·kon·tes'ta·ðo) *adj.* uncontested.

incontinente (in·kon·ti'nen·te)

adj. incontinent. —**incontinencia,** *n.f.* incontinence.

incontinenti (in·kon·ti'nen·ti) *adv.* at once; immediately.

incontrolable (in·kon·tro'la·βle) *adj.* uncontrollable.

incontrovertible (in·kon·tro· βer'ti·βle) *adj.* incontrovertible. —**incontrovertibilidad,** *n.f.* incontrovertibility.

inconvencible (in·kon·βen'θi· βle; -'si·βle) *adj.* unpersuadable.

inconveniencia (in·kon·βe· 'njen·θja; -sja) *n.f.* 1, inconvenience; hardship. 2, untimeliness. 3, indelicacy; impertinence.

inconveniente (in·kon· βe'njen·te) *adj.* 1, inconvenient; difficult. 2, unsuitable; unseemly. —*n.m.* 1, difficulty; hardship. 2, objection; impediment.

inconversable (in·kon·βer'sa· βle) *adj.* unsociable; uncommunicative.

inconvertible (in·kon·βer'ti·βle) *adj., fin.* inconvertible; irredeemable.

incorporal (in·kor·po'ral) *adj.* 1, incorporeal. 2, insubstantial; unreal.

incorporar (in·kor·po'rar) *v.t.* 1, to incorporate. 2, to embody; include. —**incorporarse,** *v.r.* 1, to incorporate; form a group, society, etc. 2, to sit up; stand up; straighten up. —**incorporación,** *n.f.* incorporation.

incorpóreo (in·kor'po·re·o) *adj.* incorporeal.

incorrección (in·ko·rrek'θjon; '-sjon) *n.f.* 1, incorrectness. 2, impropriety.

incorrecto (in·ko'rrek·to) *adj.* incorrect.

incorregible (in·ko·rre'xi·βle) *adj.* incorrigible. —**incorregibilidad,** *n.f.* incorrigibility.

incorrupto (in·ko'rrup·to) *adj.* 1, incorrupt; uncorrupted. 2, chaste; pure. —**incorruptible,** *adj.* incorruptible. —**incorruptibilidad,** *n.f.* incorruptibility.

incredibilidad (in·kre·ði·βi·li· 'ðað) *n.f.* incredibility.

incrédulo (in'kre·ðu·lo) *adj.* incredulous; unbelieving. —*n.m.* unbeliever. —**incredulidad,** *n.f.* incredulity.

increíble (in·kre'i·βle) *adj.* incredible.

incrementar (in·kre·men'tar) *v.t.* to increase.

incremento (in·kre'men·to) *n.m.* increment.

increpar (in·kre'par) *v.t.* to scold; reprimand. —**increpación,** *n.f.* rebuke; reprimand.

incriminar (in·kri·mi'nar) *v.t.* to incriminate. —**incriminación,** *n.f.* incrimination.

incrustación (in·krus·ta'θjon; -'sjon) *n.f.* 1, incrustation. 2, scale; flaky deposit. 3, inlay; inlaying.

incrustar (in·krus'tar) *v.t.* 1, to inlay. 2, to incrust. 3, to imbed.

incubadora (in·ku·βa'ðo·ra) *n.f.* incubator.

incubar (in·ku'βar) *v.t. & i.* to incubate; hatch. —**incubación,** *n.f.* incubation; hatching.

íncubo ('in·ku·βo) *n.m.* incubus.

incuestionable (in·kwes·tjo'na· βle) *adj.* unquestionable.

inculcar (in·kul'kar) *v.t.* [*infl.:* tocar, 7] to inculcate. —**inculcación,** *n.f.* inculcation.

inculpar (in·kul'par) *v.t.* to inculpate. —**inculpación,** *n.f.* inculpation.

incultivable (in·kul·ti'βa·βle) *adj.* untillable; not arable.

inculto (in'kul·to) *adj.* 1, uncultured; unrefined. 2, uncultivated; untilled.

incultura (in·kul'tu·ra) *n.f.* lack of education; ignorance.

incumbencia (in·kum'ben·θja; -sja) *n.f.* 1, charge; care; concern. 2, incumbency.

incumbir (in·kum'bir) *v.i.* [*defective; used only in forms whose endings begin with* **i**] 1, to pertain; apply. 2, to be incumbent (upon one).

incumplible (in·kum'pli·βle) *adj.* unenforceable.

incumplido (in·kum'pli·ðo) *adj.* 1, unfulfilled. 2, *colloq.* unreliable; untrustworthy.

incurable (in·ku'ra·βle) *adj.* incurable.

incuria (in'ku·rja) *n.f.* carelessness.

incurrir (in·ku'rrir) *v.i., fol. by* **en,** to fall or run (into sin, error, debt, etc.).

incursión (in·kur'sjon) *n.f.* incursion; inroad.

indagador (in·da·ɣa'ðor) *n.m.* [*fem.* -**dora**] investigator; inquirer. —*adj.* investigating; inquiring. *Also,* **indagatorio.**

indagar (in·da'ɣar) *v.t.* [*infl.:* pagar, 8] to investigate; inquire into. —**indagación,** *n.f.* investigation; inquiry; inquest. —**indagatoria** (-'to·rja) *n.f., law* unsworn statement taken from a suspect.

indebidamente (in·de·βi·ða·'men·te) *adv.* unduly; improperly.

indebido (in·de'βi·ðo) *adj.* undue; unwarranted; improper.

indecente (in·de'θen·te; -'sen·te) *adj.* indecent. —**indecencia,** *n.f.* indecency.

indecible (in·de'θi·βle; -'si·βle) *adj.* inexpressible; unutterable.

indecisión (in·de·θi'sjon; -si·'sjon) *n.f.* 1, indecision. 2, indecisiveness.

indeciso (in·de'θi·so; -'si·so) *adj.* 1, undecided. 2, indecisive.

indecoro (in·de'ko·ro) *n.m.* indecorum; indecorousness. —**indecoroso,** *adj.* indecorous; unbecoming.

indefectible (in·de·fek'ti·βle) *adj.* unfailing.

indefendible (in·de·fen'di·βle) *adj.* indefensible.

indefenso (in·de'fen·so) *adj.* defenseless.

indefinible (in·de·fi'ni·βle) *adj.* indefinable.

indefinido (in·de·fi'ni·ðo) *adj.* 1, undefined. 2, indefinite.

indeleble (in·de'le·βle) *adj.* indelible.

indeliberado (in·de·li·βe'ra·ðo) *adj.* unpremeditated; unconsidered.

indemne (in'dem·ne) *adj.* undamaged; unhurt; intact.

indemnidad (in·dem·ni'ðað) *n.f.* exemption from loss or liability; indemnity.

indemnización (in·dem·ni·θa·'θjon; -sa'sjon) *n.f.* 1, indemnification. 2, indemnity.

indemnizar (in·dem·ni'θar; -'sar) *v.t.* [*infl.:* rezar, 10] to indemnify.

independencia (in·de·pen'den·θja; -sja) *n.f.* independence.

independiente (in·de·pen'djen·te) *adj.* independent.

independizar (in·de·pen·di'θar; -'sar) *v.t.* [*infl.:* rezar, 10] *Amer.* to grant independence to. —**independizarse,** *v.r.* to become independent.

indescifrable (in·des·θi'fra·βle; in·de·si-) *adj.* undecipherable.

indescriptible (in·des·krip'ti·βle) *adj.* indescribable.

indeseable (in·de·se'a·βle) *adj.* undesirable.

indestructible (in·des·truk'ti·βle) *adj.* indestructible.

indeterminado (in·de·ter·mi·'na·ðo) *adj.* 1, indeterminate. 2, irresolute. 3, *gram.* indefinite. —**indeterminable,** *adj.* indeterminable.

indiada (in'dja·ða) *n.f., Amer.* 1, group or multitude of Indians. 2, Indian-like act or remark.

indiano (in'dja·no) *adj.* native of or resident in America. —*n.m.* nabob; one who returns rich from America.

indicación (in·di·ka'θjon; -'sjon) *n.f.* 1, indication. 2, suggestion.

indicado (in·di'ka·ðo) *adj.* 1, indicated. 2, appropriate.

indicador (in·di·ka'ðor) *n.m.* indicator; pointer; gauge. —*adj.* indicating.

indicar (in·di'kar) *v.t.* [*infl.:* tocar, 7] 1, to indicate; point out. 2, to suggest.

indicativo (in·di·ka'ti·βo) *adj. & n.m.* indicative.

índice ('in·di·θe; -se) *n.m.* 1, index. 2, table of contents. 3, forefinger. 4, hand; pointer *(of a clock, gauge, etc.)*. 5, rate *(of births, deaths, growth, etc.)*.

indicio (in'di·θjo; -sjo) *n.m.* sign; clue; hint.

índico ('in·di·ko) *adj.* Indian *(of India)*. —**Océano Indico,** Indian Ocean.

indiferente (in·di·fe'ren·te) *adj.* indifferent. —**indiferencia,** *n.f.* indifference.

indígena (in'di·xe·na) *adj.* indigenous; native. —*m. & f.* native.

indigente (in·di'xen·te) *adj.* indigent. —**indigencia,** *n.f.* indigence.

indigestarse (in·di·xes'tar·se) *v.r.* 1, to cause indigestion. 2, to have indigestion. 3, *colloq.* (*usu. of persons*) to be unbearable; be hard to take.

indigestible (in·di·xes'ti·βle) *adj.* indigestible.

indigestión (in·di·xes'tjon) *n.f.* indigestion.

indigesto (in·di'xes·to) *adj.* 1, = **indigestible.** 2, undigested. 3, stodgy; crude.

indignar (in·diɣ'nar) *v.t.* to anger; make indignant. —**indignación,** *n.f.* indignation. —**indignado,** *adj.* indignant.

indigno (in'diɣ·no) *adj.* 1, unworthy. 2, despicable; low. —**indignidad,** *n.f.* indignity.

índigo ('in·di·ɣo) *n.m.* indigo.

indio ('in·djo) *adj.* & *n.m.* Indian. —*n.m., chem.* indium.

indique (in'di·ke) *v., pres.subjve. of* **indicar**.

indiqué (in·di'ke) *v., 1st pers. sing. pret. of* **indicar**.

indirecta (in·di'rek·ta) *n.f.* 1, innuendo; hint. 2, *colloq.* dig; sarcasm.

indirecto (in·di'rek·to) *adj.* indirect.

indiscernible (in·dis·θer'ni·βle; in·di·ser-) *adj.* undiscernible.

indisciplina (in·dis·θi'pli·na; in·di·si-) *n.f.* lack of discipline.

indisciplinado (in·dis·θi·pli'na·ðo; in·di·si-) *adj.* undisciplined.

indisciplinarse (in·dis·θi·pli·'nar·se; in·di·si-) *v.r.* to rebel; defy discipline.

indiscreción (in·dis·kre'θjon; -'sjon) *n.f.* 1, indiscreetness. 2, indiscretion.

indiscreto (in·dis'kre·to) *adj.* indiscreet.

indiscutible (in·dis·ku'ti·βle) *adj.* indisputable; unquestionable.

indisoluble (in·di·so'lu·βle) *adj.* indissoluble. —**indisolubilidad**, *n.f.* indissolubility.

indispensable (in·dis·pen'sa·βle) *adj.* indispensable.

indisponer (in·dis·po'ner) *v.t.* [*infl.:* **poner**, 54] 1, to indispose; upset. 2, to prejudice; turn (someone) against. —**indisponerse**, *v.r.* 1, to become ill. 2, to quarrel; fall out.

indisponible (in·dis·po'ni·βle) *adj.* unavailable.

indisposición (in·dis·po·si'θjon; -'sjon) *n.f.* indisposition.

indispuesto (in·dis'pwes·to) *v., p.p. of* **indisponer**. —*adj.* indisposed.

indisputable (in·dis·pu'ta·βle) *adj.* indisputable.

indistinguible (in·dis·tin'gi·βle) *adj.* indistinguishable.

indistinto (in·dis'tin·to) *adj.* 1, indistinct. 2, indiscriminate.

individual (in·di·βi'ðwal) *adj.* individual. —**individualidad**, *n.f.* individuality. —**individualismo**, *n.m.* individualism. —**individualista**, *adj.* individualistic. —*n.m.* & *f.* individualist. —**individualizar**, *v.t.* [*infl.:* **rezar**, 10] to individualize.

individuo (in·di'βi·dwo) *n.m.* individual; person.

indivisible (in·di·βi'si·βle) *adj.*

indivisible. —**indivisibilidad**, *n.f.* indivisibility.

indiviso (in·di·'βi·so) *adj.* undivided.

indócil (in'do·θil; -sil) *adj.* unruly; unmanageable. —**indocilidad**, *n.f.* unruliness.

indocto (in'dok·to) *adj.* uneducated; untutored.

indocumentado *adj.* undocumented; lacking identification.

indoeuropeo (in·do·eu·ro'pe·o) *adj.* & *n.m.* Indo-European.

índole ('in·do·le) *n.f.* 1, disposition; nature. 2, kind; class.

indolente (in·do'len·te) *adj.* indolent. —**indolencia**, *n.f.* indolence.

indomable (in·do'ma·βle) *adj.* 1, untamable. 2, indomitable.

indomado (in·do'ma·ðo) *adj.* untamed; unsubdued.

indómito (in'do·mi·to) *adj.* 1, untamed. 2, indomitable.

indubitable (in·du·βi'ta·βle) *adj.* = **indudable**.

inducción (in·duk'θjon, -'sjon) *n.f.* 1, inducement. 2, *physics; logic* induction.

inducir (in·du'θir; -'sir) *v.t.* [*infl.:* **conducir**, 40] to induce. —**inducimiento**, *n.m.* inducement.

inductivo (in·duk'ti·βo) *adj.* inductive.

indudable (in·du'ða·βle) *adj.* undoubted; indubitable.

indulgente (in·dul'xen·te) *adj.* indulgent. —**indulgencia**, *n.f.* indulgence.

indultar (in·dul'tar) *v.t.* to pardon; remit.

indulto (in'dul·to) *n.m.* pardon; remission.

indumentaria (in·du·men'ta·rja) *n.f.* apparel; dress.

indumento (in·du'men·to) *n.m.* garment.

induración (in·du·ra'θjon; -'sjon) *n.f.* hardening; induration; callosity.

industria (in'dus·trja) *n.f.* industry. —**industrial**, *adj.* industrial. —*n.m.* & *f.* industrialist. —**de industria**, intentionally; on purpose.

industrialismo (in·dus·trja'lis·mo) *n.m.* industrialism. —**industrialista**, *n.m.* & *f., Amer.* industrialist.

industrializar (in·dus·trja·li'θar; -'sar) *v.t.* [*infl.:* **rezar**, 10] to industrialize. —**industrialización**, *n.f.* industrialization.

industrioso (in·dus'trjo·so) *adj.* industrious.

induzca (in'duθ·ka; in'dus-) *v., pres.subjve. of* **inducir**.

induzco (in'duθ·ko; in'dus-) *v., 1st pers.sing.pres.ind. of* **inducir**.

inédito (in'e·ði·to) *adj.* unpublished.

ineducable (in·e·ðu'ka·βle) *adj.* uneducable. —**ineducación,** *n.f.* lack of education. —**ineducado,** *adj.* uneducated.

inefable (in·e'fa·βle) *adj.* ineffable. —**inefabilidad,** *n.f.* ineffability.

ineficaz (in·e·fi'kaθ; -'kas) *adj.* inefficacious; ineffective; ineffectual. —**ineficacia,** *n.f.* inefficacy; inefficiency.

ineficiente (in·e·fi'θjen·te; -'sjen·te) *adj.* inefficient. —**ineficiencia,** *n.f.* inefficiency.

inelegante (in·e·le'ɣan·te) *adj.* inelegant. —**inelegancia,** *n.f.* inelegance; inelegancy.

inelegible (in·e·le'xi·βle) *adj.* ineligible. —**inelegibilidad,** *n.f.* ineligibility.

ineluctable (in·e·luk'ta·βle) *adj.* ineluctable.

ineludible (in·e·lu'ði·βle) *adj.* unavoidable; inescapable.

inepto (in'ep·to) *adj.* inept. —**ineptitud,** *also* **inepcia** (in'ep·θja; -sja) *n.f.* ineptness; ineptitude.

inequívoco (in·e'ki·βo·ko) *adj.* unmistakable; unequivocal.

inercia (i'ner·θja; -sja) *n.f.* **1,** inertness. **2,** inertia.

inerme (in'er·me) *adj.* unarmed.

inerte (i'ner·te) *adj.* inert.

inescrupuloso (in·es·kru·pu'lo·so) *adj.* unscrupulous. —**inescrupulosidad,** *n.f.* unscrupulousness.

inescrutable (in·es·kru'ta·βle) *adj.* inscrutable. —**inescrutabilidad,** *n.f.* inscrutability.

inesperado (in·es·pe'ra·ðo) *adj.* unexpected.

inestable (in·es'ta·βle) *adj.* unstable. —**inestabilidad,** *n.f.* instability.

inestimable (in·es·ti'ma·βle) *adj.* inestimable.

inevitable (in·e·βi'ta·βle) *adj.* inevitable. —**inevitabilidad,** *n.f.* inevitability.

inexacto (in·ek'sak·to) *adj.* inexact; inaccurate. —**inexactitud,** *n.f.* inaccuracy; inexactness.

inexcusable (in·eks·ku'sa·βle) *adj.* inexcusable.

inexistente (in·ek·sis'ten·te) *adj.* nonexistent. —**inexistencia,** *n.f.* nonexistence.

inexorable (in·ek·so'ra·βle) *adj.* inexorable. —**inexorabilidad,** *n.f.* inexorableness; inexorability.

inexperiencia (in·eks·pe'rjen·θja; -sja) *n.f.* inexperience.

inexperto (in·eks'per·to) *adj.* inexperienced; unskillful.

inexpiable (in·eks·pi'a·βle) *adj.* inexpiable.

inexplicable (in·eks·pli'ka·βle) *adj.* inexplicable. —**inexplicado** (-'ka·ðo) *adj.* unexplained.

inexplorado (in·eks·plo'ra·ðo) *adj.* unexplored.

inexpresable (in·eks·pre'sa·βle) *adj.* inexpressible. —**inexpresado** (-'sa·ðo) *adj.* unexpressed.

inexpresivo (in·eks·pre'si·βo) *adj.* inexpressive.

inexpugnable (in·eks·puɣ'na·βle) *adj.* impregnable.

inextinguible (in·eks·tin'gi·βle) *adj.* inextinguishable.

inextirpable (in·eks·tir'pa·βle) *adj.* ineradicable.

inextricable (in·eks·tri'ka·βle) *adj.* inextricable.

infalible (in·fa'li·βle) *adj.* infallible. —**infalibilidad,** *n.f.* infallibility.

infamar (in·fa'mar) *v.t.* to defame.

infame (in'fa·me) *adj.* infamous. —*n.m. & f.* scoundrel; infamous person.

infamia (in'fa·mja) *n.f.* infamy.

infancia (in'fan·θja; -sja) *n.f.* infancy; childhood.

infando (in'fan·do) *adj.* unmentionable.

infanta (in'fan·ta) *n.f.* infanta.

infante (in'fan·te) *n.m.* **1,** infant. **2,** infante. **3,** infantryman.

infantería (in·fan·te'ri·a) *n.f.* infantry.

infanticida (in·fan·ti'θi·ða; -'si·ða) *n.m. & f.* infanticide *(agent).* —**infanticidio** (-'θi·ðjo; -'si·ðjo) *n.m.* infanticide *(act).*

infantil (in·fan'til) *adj.* infantile; childish.

infatigable (in·fa·ti'ɣa·βle) *adj.* indefatigable.

infatuación (in·fa·twa'θjon; -'sjon) *n.f.* **1,** vanity; conceit. **2,** infatuation.

infatuar (in·fa'twar) *v.t.* [*infl.*: **continuar,** 23] **1,** to make vain or conceited. **2,** to infatuate. —**infa-**

tuarse, *v.r.* **1**, to become vain or conceited. **2**, to become infatuated.

infausto (in'faus·to) *adj.* unfortunate; unlucky.

infección (in·fek'θjon; -'sjon) *n.f.* infection. —**infeccioso**, *adj.* infectious.

infectar (in·fek'tar) *v.t.* to infect. —**infectarse**, *v.r.* to become infected.

infecto (in'fek·to) *adj.* polluted; infected; corrupt.

infecundo (in·fe'kun·do) *adj.* infecund. —**infecundidad**, *n.f.* infecundity.

infelicidad (in·fe·li·θi'ðað; -si'ðað) *n.f.* misfortune.

infeliz (in·fe'liθ; -'lis) *adj.* unhappy; unfortunate. —*n.m.* & *f.* wretch.

inferior (in·fe'rjor) *adj.* **1**, inferior; subordinate. **2**, lower. —*n.m.* inferior. —**inferioridad**, *n.f.* inferiority.

inferir (in·fe'rir) *v.t.* [*infl.:* sentir, 31] **1**, to infer. **2**, to imply. **3**, to inflict. —**inferencia**, *n.f.* inference.

infernal (in·fer'nal) *adj.* infernal.

infestar (in·fes'tar) *v.t.* to infest. —**infestación**, *n.f.* infestation.

inficionar (in·fi·θjo'nar; -sjo'nar) *v.t.* **1**, to infect; contaminate. **2**, to corrupt.

infidelidad (in·fi·ðe·li'ðað) *n.f.* infidelity.

infiel (in'fjel) *adj.* unfaithful. —*adj.* & *n.m.* & *f.* infidel.

infierno (in'fjer·no) *n.m.* hell; inferno. —**en el quinto infierno**, *colloq.* far away.

infiltrar (in·fil'trar) *v.t.* to infiltrate. —**infiltración**, *n.f.* infiltration.

ínfimo ('in·fi·mo) *adj.* **1**, lowest. **2**, least.

infinidad (in·fi·ni'ðað) *n.f.* **1**, infinity. **2**, crowd; multitude.

infinitesimal (in·fi·ni·te·si'mal) *adj.* infinitesimal.

infinitivo (in·fi·ni·ti·βo) *adj.* & *n.m.* infinitive.

infinito (in·fi'ni·to) *adj.* infinite. —*n.m.* infinity. —*adv.*, *colloq.* a great deal; much.

inflación (in·fla'θjon; -'sjon) *n.f.* inflation. —**inflacionista**, *adj.* inflationary.

inflamable (in·fla'ma·βle) *adj.* inflammable.

inflamación (in·fla·ma'θjon; -'sjon) *n.f.* inflammation.

inflamar (in·fla'mar) *v.t.* to inflame. —**inflamarse**, *v.r.* to become inflamed; become swollen.

inflamatorio (in·fla·ma'to·rjo) *adj.* inflammatory.

inflar (in'flar) *v.t.* to inflate. —**inflarse**, *v.r.* to puff up with pride; become elated.

inflexible (in·flek'si·βle) *adj.* inflexible. —**inflexibilidad**, *n.f.* inflexibility.

inflexión (in·flek'sjon) *n.f.* inflection.

infligir (in·fli'xir) *v.t.* [*infl.:* coger, 15] to inflict.

influencia (in·flu'en·θja; -sja) *n.f.* influence.

influenza (in·flu'en·θa; -sa) *n.f.* influenza.

influir (in·flu'ir) *v.i.* [*infl.:* huir, 26] to have or exert influence. —**influir en**, to influence.

influjo (in'flu·xo) *n.m.* **1**, influence. **2**, influx.

influyente (in·flu'jen·te) *adj.* influential.

información (in·for·ma'θjon; -'sjon) *n.f.* **1**, information. **2**, *law* inquiry.

informal (in·for'mal) *adj.* **1**, informal. **2**, *colloq.* unreliable; untrustworthy. —**informalidad**, *n.f.* informality.

informante (in·for'man·te) *n.m.* & *f.* **1**, informant. **2**, informer.

informar (in·for'mar) *v.t.* **1**, to inform. **2**, *philos.* to give form to. —*v.i.* **1**, *law* to plead. **2**, to submit a report; report.

informática (in·for'ma·ti·ka) *n.f.*, *comput.* **1**, data processing. **2**, computer science. —**informático**, *n.m.* computer expert or technician.

informativo (in·for·ma'ti·βo) *adj.* informative.

informe (in'for·me) *n.m.* **1**, report; account. **2**, *law* plea. —*adj.* shapeless; formless.

infortunio (in·for'tu·njo) *n.m.* misfortune. —**infortunado**, *adj.* & *n.m.* unfortunate.

infracción (in·frak'θjon; -'sjon) *n.f.* infraction; transgression. —**infractor** (-'tor) *n.m.* transgressor.

infraestructura (in·fra·es·truk·'tu·ra) *n.f.* infrastructure.

infrangible (in·fran'xi·βle) *adj.* infrangible.

infranqueable (in·fran·ke·a·βle) *adj.* insurmountable.

infrarrojo (in·fra'rro·xo) *adj.* infrared.

infrascrito (in·fras'kri·to) *n.m.* undersigned.

infrecuente (in·fre'kwen·te) *adj.* infrequent. —**infrecuencia,** *n.f.* infrequency.

infringir (in·frin'xir) *v.t.* [*infl.:* coger, 15] to infringe; violate.

infructuoso (in·fruk'two·so) *adj.* fruitless; futile.

ínfulas ('in·fu·las) *n.f.pl.* conceit; airs.

infundado (in·fun'da·ðo) *adj.* groundless.

infundir (in·fun'dir) *v.t.* **1,** to infuse. **2,** to inspire; instill.

infusión (in·fu'sjon) *n.f.* infusion.

ingeniar (in·xe'njar) *v.t.* to contrive; invent. —**ingeniárselas,** to manage.

ingeniería (in·xe·nje'ri·a) *n.f.* engineering.

ingeniero (in·xe'nje·ro) *n.m.* [*fem.* **-ra**] engineer.

ingenio (in'xe·njo) *n.m.* **1,** ingenuity. **2,** talent. **3,** genius; talented person. **4,** engine; mechanical device. —**ingenio de azúcar, 1,** sugar refinery. **2,** sugar plantation.

ingenioso (in·xe'njo·so) *adj.* ingenious. —**ingeniosidad,** *n.f.* ingenuity.

ingénito (in'xe·ni·to) *adj.* inborn; innate.

ingenuo (in'xe·nwo) *adj.* ingenuous. —**ingenuidad,** *n.f.* ingenuousness.

ingerir (in·xe'rir) *v.t.* [*infl.:* sentir, 31] to ingest. —**ingestión** (in·xes'tjon) *n.f.* ingestion.

ingle ('in·gle) *n.f.* groin.

inglés (in'gles) *adj.* English. —*n.m.* **1,** Englishman. **2,** English (*language*) —**inglesa,** *n.f.* Englishwoman. —**a la inglesa,** in English fashion. —**ir a la inglesa,** *Amer.* to go Dutch.

inglesar (in·gle'sar) *v.t.* to Anglicize.

inglete (in'gle·te) *n.m.* miter; miter joint.

ingobernable (in·go·βer'na·βle) *adj.* ungovernable; uncontrollable.

ingramatical (in·gra·ma·ti'kal) *adj.* ungrammatical.

ingrato (in'gra·to) *adj.* **1,** ungrateful. **2,** thankless. **3,** disagreeable; unpleasant. —*n.m.* [*fem.* **-ta**] ingrate. —**ingratitud,** *n.f.* ingratitude.

ingrediente (in·gre'ðjen·te) *n.m.* ingredient.

ingresar (in·gre'sar) *v.t.* **1,** to enter; go in. **2,** to join; become a member.

ingreso (in'gre·so) *n.m.* **1,** entrance. **2,** *usu.pl.* income; revenue.

inhábil (in·a'βil) *adj.* inept; unskillful. —**día inhábil,** holiday. —**hora inhábil,** hour when an office is closed for business.

inhabilidad (in·a·βi·li'ðað) *n.f.* **1,** ineptitude. **2,** disability; impediment.

inhabilitar (in·a·βi·li'tar) *v.t.* **1,** to incapacitate. **2,** to disqualify. —**inhabilitación,** *n.f.* incapacitation.

inhabitable (in·a·βi'ta·βle) *adj.* uninhabitable. —**inhabitado** (-'ta·ðo) *adj.* uninhabited.

inhalador (in·a·la'ðor) *n.m.* **1,** inhalant. **2,** inhaler; inhalator.

inhalar (in·a'lar) *v.t. & i.* to inhale. —**inhalación,** *n.f.* inhalation.

inherente (in·e'ren·te) *adj.* inherent. —**inherencia,** *n.f.* inherence.

inhibir (in·i'βir) *v.t.* to inhibit. —**inhibirse,** *v.r. fol. by* de *or* en, to eschew; abstain from. —**inhibición,** *n.f.* inhibition.

inhospitalario (in·os·pi·ta'la·rjo) *adj.* inhospitable. *Also,* **inhóspito** (in'os·pi·to).

inhospitalidad (in·os·pi·ta·li·'ðað) *n.f.* inhospitability.

inhumano (in·u'ma·no) *adj.* **1,** inhuman. **2,** inhumane. —**inhumanidad,** *n.f.* inhumanity.

inhumar (in·u'mar) *v.t.* to bury; inter. —**inhumación,** *n.f.* burial; interment.

inicial (i·ni'θjal; -'sjal) *adj. & n.f.* initial.

iniciar (i·ni'θjar; -'sjar) *v.t.* to initiate. —**iniciarse,** *v.r.* to be initiated. —**iniciación,** *n.f.* initiation. —**iniciador,** *adj.* initiating. —*n.m.* [*fem.* **-dora**] initiator.

iniciativa (i·ni·θja'ti·βa; i·ni·sja·) *n.f.* initiative. —**iniciativo,** *adj.* initiating.

inicio (i'ni·θjo; -sjo) *n.m.* beginning; start.

inicuo (i'ni·kwo) *adj.* iniquitous.

inigualado (in·i·ɣwa'la·ðo) *adj.* unequaled.

inimaginable (in·i·ma·xi'na·βle) *adj.* unimaginable.

inimitable (in·i·mi'ta·βle) *adj.* inimitable.

ininteligible (in·in·te·li'xi·βle) *adj.* unintelligible.

ininterrumpido (in·in·te·rrum-
'pi·ðo) *adj.* uninterrupted.
iniquidad (in·i·ki'ðað) *n.f.* iniquity.
injerir (in·xe'rir) *v.t.* [*infl.:* **sentir,**
31] to insert. —**injerirse,** *v.r.* to become involved.
injertar (in·xer'tar) *v.t.* to graft;
implant.
injerto (in'xer·to) *n.m.* graft; implant.
injuria (in'xu·rja) *n.f.* **1,** affront;
insult. **2,** injury; wrong.
injuriar (in·xu'rjar) *v.t.* **1,** to
affront; insult. **2,** to wrong; injure.
injurioso (in·xu'rjo·so) *adj.* **1,** insulting; offensive. **2,** injurious; hurtful.
injusticia (in·xus'ti·θja; -sja) *n.f.*
injustice.
injustificable (in·xus·ti·fi'ka-
βle) *adj.* unjustifiable.
injustificado (in·xus·ti·fi'ka·ðo)
adj. unjustified.
injusto (in'xus·to) *adj.* unjust; unfair.
inmaculado (in·ma·ku'la·ðo;
i·ma-) *adj.* immaculate.
inmaduro (in·ma'ðu·ro; *also,*
i·ma-) *adj.* **1,** unripe. **2,** immature.
—**inmadurez** (-'reθ; -'res) *adj.* immaturity.
inmanejable (in·ma·ne'xa·βle;
i·ma-) *adj.* unmanageable.
inmanente (in·ma'nen·te; i·ma-)
adj. immanent. —**inmanencia,** *n.f.*
immanence.
inmarchitable (in·mar·tji'ta·βle)
adj. unfading.
inmaterial (in·ma·te'rjal; i·ma-)
adj. inmaterial. —**inmaterialidad,**
n.f. immateriality.
inmaturo (in·ma'tu·ro; i·ma-) *adj.*
immature; unripe.
inmediación (in·me·ðja'θjon;
-'sjon; *also,* i·me-) *n.f.* immediate
vicinity; proximity. —**inmediaciones,** *n.f.pl.* environs.
inmediatamente (in·me·ðja-
ta'men·te; i·me-) *adv.* immediately;
at once.
inmediato (in·me'ðja·to; i·me-)
adj. immediate. —**de inmediato,**
immediately.
inmejorable (in·me·xo'ra·βle;
i·me-) *adj.* most excellent; unsurpassable.
inmemorial (in·me·mo'rjal;
i·me-) *adj.* immemorial.
inmenso (in'men·so; i'men-) *adj.*

immense. —**inmensidad,** *n.f.* immensity.
inmensurable (in·men·su'ra·βle;
i·men-) *adj.* immeasurable.
inmerecido (in·me·re'θi·ðo;
-'si·ðo; *also,* i·me-) *adj.* undeserved; unmerited.
inmersión (in·mer'sjon; i·mer-)
n.f. immersion.
inmigrar (in·mi'γrar; i·mi-) *v.i.* to
immigrate. —**inmigración,** *n.f.* immigration. —**inmigrante,** *n.m. & f.
& adj.* immigrant.
inminente (in·mi'nen·te; i·mi-)
adj. imminent. —**inminencia,** *n.f.*
imminence.
inmiscuir (in·mis·ku'ir; i·mis-)
v.t. [*infl.:* **huir,** 26] to mix; blend.
—**inmiscuirse,** *v.r.* to meddle.
inmoderado (in·mo·ðe'ra·ðo;
i·mo-) *adj.* immoderate. —**inmoderación,** *n.f.* immoderation.
inmodesto (in·mo'ðes·to; i·mo-)
adj. immodest. —**inmodestia,** *n.f.*
immodesty.
inmolar (in·mo'lar; i·mo-) *v.t.* to
immolate. —**inmolación,** *n.f.* immolation.
inmoral (in·mo'ral; i·mo-) *adj.*
immoral. —**inmoralidad,** *n.f.* immorality.
inmortal (in·mor'tal; i·mor-) *adj.
& n.m. & f.* immortal. —**inmortalidad,** *n.f.* immortality.
inmortalizar (in·mor·ta·li'θar;
-'sar; *also, i·mor-) v.t.* [*infl.:* **rezar,**
10] to immortalize. —**inmortaliza-
ción,** *n.f.* immortalization.
inmoto (in'mo·to; i'mo-) *adj.* unmoved.
inmovible (in·mo'βi·βle; i·mo-)
adj. immovable.
inmóvil (in'mo·βil; i'mo-) *adj.* immobile; motionless. —**inmovilidad,**
n.f. immobility.
inmovilizar (in·mo·βi·li'θar;
-'sar; *also,* i·mo-) *v.t.* [*infl.:* **rezar,**
10] to immobilize. —**inmoviliza-
ción,** *n.f.* immobilization.
inmueble (in'mwe·βle; i'mwe-)
adj., law real *(of property).* —*n.m.*
1, real property. **2,** building.
inmundicia (in·mun'di·θja; -sja;
also, i·mun-) *n.f.* filth. —**inmundo**
(in'mun·do; i'mun-) *adj.* filthy.
inmune (in'mu·ne; i'mu-) *adj.* immune. —**inmunidad,** *n.f.* immunity.
inmunizar (in·mu·ni'θar; -'sar;
also, i·mu-) *v.t.* [*infl.:* **rezar,** 10] to
immunize. —**inmunización,** *n.f.*
immunization.

inmunología (in·mu·no·lo'xi·a; i·mu-) *n.f.* immunology.

inmutable (in·mu'ta·βle; i·mu-) *adj.* immutable. —**inmutabilidad,** *n.f.* immutability.

inmutar (in·mu'tar; i·mu-) *v.t.* to alter; change. —**inmutarse,** *v.r.* to become ruffled; change countenance.

innato (in'na·to; i'na-) *adj.* innate; inborn.

innatural (in·na·tu'ral; i·na-) *adj.* unnatural.

innecesario (in·ne·θe'sa·rjo; -se'sa·rjo; *also,* i·ne-) *adj.* unnecessary.

innegable (in·ne'ɣa·βle; .i·ne-) *adj.* undeniable.

innoble (in'no·βle; i'no-) *adj.* ignoble.

innocuo (in'no·kwo; i'no-) *adj.* innocuous; harmless.

innominado (in·no·mi'na·ðo; i·no-) *adj.* **1,** unnamed; nameless. **2,** *anat.* innominate.

innovar (in·no'βar; i·no-) *v.t.* to innovate. —**innovación,** *n.f.* innovation. —**innovador,** *adj.* innovating. —*n.m.* [*fem.* **-dora**] innovator.

innumerable (in·nu·me'ra·βle; i·nu-) *adj.* innumerable.

inobservable (in·oβ·ser'βa·βle) *adj.* unobservable.

inobservancia (in·oβ·ser'βan·θja; -sja) *n.f.* noncompliance; nonobservance.

inocente (i·no'θen·te; -'sen·te) *adj.* & *n.m.* & *f.* innocent. —**inocencia,** *n.f.* innocence. —**Día de Inocentes,** April Fool's Day (in the Spanish-speaking world, December 28).

inocentón (i·no·θen'ton; -sen'ton) *n.m.* [*fem.* **-tona**] dupe; gull; simpleton.

inocuidad (i·no·kwi'ðað) *n.f.* innocuousness; harmlessness. —**inocuo** (i'no·kwo) *adj.* = innocuo.

inocular (i·no·ku'lar) *v.t.* to inoculate. —**inoculación,** *n.f.* inoculation.

inodoro (in·o'ðo·ro) *adj.* odorless. —*n.m.* **1,** deodorizer. **2,** *Amer.* water closet; toilet.

inofensivo (in·o·fen'si·βo) *adj.* inoffensive.

inolvidable (in·ol·βi'ða·βle) *adj.* unforgettable. —**inolvidado** (-'ða·ðo) *adj.* unforgotten.

inoperable (in·o·pe'ra·βle) *adj.* inoperable.

inoperante (in·o·pe'ran·te) *adj.* inoperative.

inopia (i'no·pja) *n.f.* **1,** poverty; indigence. **2,** *colloq.* blissful ignorance.

inopinado (in·o·pi'na·ðo) *adj.* unexpected.

inoportuno (in·o·por'tu·no) *adj.* inopportune. —**inoportunidad,** *n.f.* inopportuneness.

inorgánico (in·or'ɣa·ni·ko) *adj.* inorganic.

inorganizado (in·or·ɣa·ni'θa·ðo; -'sa·ðo) *adj.* unorganized.

inoxidable (in·ok·si'ða·βle) *adj.* stainless; rustproof.

inquebrantable (in·ke·βran'ta·βle) *adj.* unbreakable.

inquietar (in·kje'tar) *v.t.* to disquiet; disturb; worry.

inquieto (in'kje·to) *adj.* **1,** uneasy; worried. **2,** restless.

inquietud (in·kje'tuð) *n.f.* **1,** restlessness. **2,** uneasiness; worry.

inquilino (in·ki'li·no) *n.m.* [*fem.* **-na**] tenant. —**inquilinato,** *n.m.* **1,** lease; leasing. **2,** tenancy; occupancy.

inquina (in'ki·na) *n.f.* aversion; hatred.

inquirir (in·ki'rir) *v.t.* [*infl.:* adquirir, 34] to inquire into; investigate.

inquisición (in·ki·si'θjon; -'sjon) *n.f.* inquisition. —**inquisidor,** *n.m.* [*fem.* **-dora**] inquisitor.

inquisitivo (in·ki·si'ti·βo) *adj.* inquisitive.

insabible (in·sa'βi·βle) *adj.* unknowable; unascertainable.

insaciable (in·sa'θja·βle; -'sja·βle) *adj.* insatiable. —**insaciabilidad,** *n.f.* insatiability.

insalubre (in·sa'lu·βre) *adj.* insalubrious; unhealthful; unsanitary.

insano (in'sa·no) *adj.* insane.

insatisfecho (in·sa·tis'fe·tʃo) *adj.* unsatisfied. —**insatisfacción,** *n.f.* dissatisfaction. —**insatisfactorio,** *adj.* unsatisfactory.

inscribir (ins·kri'βir) *v.t.* [*p.p.* inscrito (-'kri·to)] **1,** to inscribe. **2,** to register; enroll.

inscripción (ins·krip'θjon; -'sjon) *n.f.* **1,** inscription. **2,** registration; enrollment.

insecticida (in·sek·ti'θi·ða; -'si·ða) *adj.* insecticidal. —*n.m.* insecticide.

insectívoro (in·sek'ti·βo·ro) *adj.* insectivorous. —*n.m.* insectivore.

insecto (in'sek·to) *n.m.* insect.
inseguro (in·se'yu·ro) *adj.* 1, insecure. 2, uncertain. —**inseguridad,** *n.f.* insecurity.
inseminar (in·se·mi'nar) *v.t.* to inseminate. —**inseminación,** *n.f.* insemination.
insensato (in·sen'sa·to) *adj.* senseless; mad. —*n.m.* fool; madman. —**insensata,** *n.f.* madwoman. —**insensatez,** *n.f.* senselessness; madness.
insensible (in·sen'si·βle) *adj.* 1, insensible. 2, insensitive; unfeeling. —**insensibilidad,** *n.f.* insensibility.
inseparable (in·se·pa'ra·βle) *adj.* inseparable.
insepulto (in·se'pul·to) *adj.* unburied.
inserción (in·ser'θjon; -'sjon) *n.f.* 1, insertion. 2, insert.
insertar (in·ser'tar) *v.t.* [*p.p.* **insertado,** *also,* **inserto** (in'ser·to)] to insert.
inservible (in·ser'βi·βle) *adj.* useless
insidia (in'si·δja) *n.f.* 1, snare; ambush. 2, insidiousness. —**insidioso,** *adj.* insidious.
insigne (in'siɣ·ne) *adj.* renowned; famous.
insignia (in'siɣ·nja) *n.f.* 1, insignia; badge; emblem. 2, flag; pennant.
insignificante (in·siɣ·ni·fi'kan·te) *adj.* insignificant. —**insignificancia,** *n.f.* insignificance.
insincero (in·sin'θe·ro; -'se·ro) *adj.* insincere. —**insinceridad,** *n.f.* insincerity.
insinuar (in·si'nwar) *v.t.* [*infl.:* **continuar, 23**] to insinuate; hint. —**insinuación,** *n.f.* insinuation; hint.
insípido (in'si·pi·δo) *adj.* insipid. —**insipidez,** *n.f.* insipidity.
insistir (in·sis'tir) *v.i.* to insist. —**insistencia,** *n.f.* insistence. —**insistente,** *adj.* insistent.
insobornable (in·so·βor'na·βle) *adj.* incorruptible.
insociable (in·so'θja·βle; -'sja·βle) *adj.* unsociable.
insolación (in·so·la'θjon; -'sjon) *n.f.* sunstroke.
insolar (in·so'lar) *v.t.* to expose to the sun. —**insolarse,** *v.r.* to suffer sunstroke.
insolentar (in·so·len'tar) *v.t.* to make insolent. —**insolentarse,** *v.r.* to be or become insolent.

insolente (in·so'len·te) *adj.* insolent. —**insolencia,** *n.f.* insolence.
insolicitado (in·so·li·θi'ta·δo; -si'ta·δo) *adj.* unasked; unsolicited.
insólito (in'so·li·to) *adj.* 1, uncommon; unusual. 2, unaccustomed.
insoluble (in·so'lu·βle) *adj.* insoluble. —**insolubilidad,** *n.f.* insolubility.
insolvente (in·sol'βen·te) *adj.* insolvent. —**insolvencia,** *n.f.* insolvency.
insomnio (in'som·njo) *n.m.* insomnia. —**insomne** (in'som·ne) *adj.* sleepless.
insondable (in·son'da·βle) *adj.* unfathomable.
insonoro (in·so'no·ro) *adj.* 1, soundless. 2, dull-sounding. 3, *phonet.* voiceless; unvoiced.
insoportable (in·so·por'ta·βle) *adj.* insupportable; unbearable.
insospechado (in·sos·pe'tʃa·δo) *adj.* unsuspected.
insostenible (in·sos·te'ni·βle) *adj.* untenable.
inspección (ins·pek'θjon; -'sjon) *n.f.* inspection. —**inspeccionar,** *v.t.* to inspect. —**inspector** (-'tor) *n.m.* [*fem.* **-tora**] inspector.
inspirar (ins·pi'rar) *v.t.* 1, to inhale. 2, to inspire. —**inspirarse,** *v.r.* to become inspired. —**inspiración,** *n.f.* inspiration.
instabilidad (ins·ta·βi·li'δað) *n.f.* = **inestabilidad.**
instalar (ins·ta'lar) *v.t.* to install; set up. —**instalación,** *n.f.* installation.
instancia (ins'tan·θja; -sja) *n.f.* 1, instance; urging. 2, petition.
instantáneo (ins·tan'ta·ne·o) *adj.* 1, instantaneous. 2, instant *(attrib.).* —**instantánea,** *n.f.* snapshot.
instante (ins'tan·te) *n.m.* instant. —**al instante, 1,** at once. **2,** instant *(attrib.).*
instar (ins'tar) *v.t.* to urge; beseech. —*v.i.* **1,** to insist. **2,** to be urgent.
instaurar (ins·tau'rar) *v.t.* to restore; renovate. —**instauración,** *n.f.* restoration; renovation.
instigar (ins·ti'ɣar) *v.t.* [*infl.:* **pagar, 8**] to instigate. —**instigación,** *n.f.* instigation. —**instigador,** *n.m.* [*fem.* **-dora**] instigator.
instilar (ins·ti'lar) *v.t.* to instill. —**instilación,** *n.f.* instillation.
instinto (ins'tin·to) *n.m.* instinct. —**instintivo,** *adj.* instinctive.

institución (ins·ti·tu'θjon; -'sjon) *n.f.* institution. —**institucional**, *adj.* institutional.

instituir (ins·ti·tu'ir) *v.t.* [*infl.*: **huir**, 26] to institute.

instituto (ins·ti'tu·to) *n.m.* 1, institute. 2, constitution; statutes.

institutriz (ins·ti·tu'triθ; -'tris) *n.f.* governess.

instrucción (ins·truk'θjon; -'sjon) *n.f.* 1, instruction. 2, education; knowledge.

instructivo (ins·truk'ti·βo) *adj.* instructive.

instructor (ins·truk'tor) *n.m.* [*fem.* **-tora**] instructor.

instruir (ins·tru'ir) *v.t.* [*infl.*: **huir**, 26] 1, to instruct; train; educate. 2, to apprise; inform. —**instruido**, *adj.* well-read; learned.

instrumento (ins·tru'men·to) *n.m.* instrument. —**instrumentación**, *n.f.* instrumentation. —**instrumental**, *adj.* instrumental. —**instrumentar**, *v.t.* to provide instrumentation for.

insubordinar (in·su·βor·ði'nar) *v.t.* to incite to insubordination. —**insubordinarse**, *v.r.* to rebel; commit insubordination. —**insubordinación**, *n.f.* insubordination. —**insubordinado**, *adj.* & *n.m.* insubordinate.

insubsanable (in·suβ·sa'na·βle) *adj.* irremediable; irreparable.

insubstancial (in·suβs·tan'θjal; -'sjal) *adj.* insubstantial.

insuficiente (in·su·fi'θjen·te; -'sjen·te) *adj.* insufficient. —**insuficiencia**, *n.f.* insufficiency.

insufrible (in·su'fri·βle) *adj.* insufferable; unbearable.

ínsula ('in·su·la) *n.f.* 1, = **isla**. 2, *fig.* unimportant place, town, etc.

insular (in·su'lar) *adj.* insular. —**insularidad**, *n.f.* insularity.

insulina (in·su'li·na) *n.f.* insulin.

insulso (in'sul·so) *adj.* 1, insipid; tasteless. 2, dull; vapid.

insultada (in·sul'ta·ða) *n.f.*, *Amer.* 1, insult. 2, act of insulting.

insultar (in·sul'tar) *v.t.* to insult. —**insulto** (-'sul·to) *n.m.* insult.

insumergible (in·su·mer'xi·βle) *adj.* unsinkable.

insuperable (in·su·pe'ra·βle) *adj.* 1, insuperable. 2, matchless; unsurpassable. —**insuperado** (-'ra·ðo) *adj.* unmatched; unsurpassed.

insurgente (in·sur'xen·te) *adj.* &

n.m. & *f.* insurgent. —**insurgencia**, *n.f.* insurgence.

insurrección (in·su·rrek'θjon; -'sjon) *n.f.* insurrection. —**insurreccionarse**, *v.r.* to revolt.

insurrecto (in·su'rrek·to) *adj.* & *n.m.* insurgent. —*n.m.* insurrectionist.

insustancial (in·sus·tan'θjal; -'sjal) *adj.* = **insubstancial**.

intacto (in'tak·to) *adj.* intact.

intachable (in·ta'tʃa·βle) *adj.* irreproachable; faultless.

intangible (in·tan'xi·βle) *adj.* intangible. —**intangibilidad**, *n.f.* intangibility.

integral (in·te'γral) *adj.* & *n.f.* integral.

integrar (in·te'γrar) *v.t.* to integrate. —**integración**, *n.f.* integration.

integridad (in·te·γri'ðað) *n.f.* 1, integrity. 2, maidenhood; virginity. 3, whole; entirety.

íntegro ('in·te·γro) *adj.* 1, entire; whole; complete. 2, honest; just; upright.

integumento (in·te·γu'men·to) *n.m.* integument.

intelecto (in·te'lek·to) *n.m.* intellect.

intelectual (in·te·lek'twal) *adj.* & *n.m.* & *f.* intellectual. —**intelectualidad**, *n.f.* intelligentsia. —**intelectualizar**, *v.t.* [*infl.*: **rezar**, 10] to intellectualize.

inteligencia (in·te·li'xen·θja; -sja) *n.f.* intelligence. —**inteligente**, *adj.* intelligent.

inteligible (in·te·li'xi·βle) *adj.* intelligible. —**inteligibilidad**, *n.f.* intelligibility.

intemperante (in·tem·pe'ran·te) *adj.* intemperate. —**intemperancia**, *n.f.* intemperance.

intemperie (in·tem'pe·rje) *n.f.* raw weather. —**a la intemperie**, outdoors; exposed to the weather.

intempestivo (in·tem·pes'ti·βo) *adj.* 1, untimely; ill-timed. 2, unseasonable.

intención (in·ten'θjon; -'sjon) *n.f.* intention. —**intencional**, *adj.* intentional.

intencionado (in·ten·θjo'na·ðo; -sjo'na·ðo) *adj.*, *usu.preceded by* **bien, mal, mejor** *or* **peor**, intended; meant.

intendencia (in·ten'den·θja; -sja) *n.f.* 1, administration. 2, mayor's or governor's office.

intendente (in·ten'den·te) *n.m.* **1,** administrator. **2,** *Amer.* governor of a province. **3,** *Amer.* = **alcalde.**

intensificar (in·ten·si·fi'kar) *v.t.* [*infl.:* **tocar, 7**] to intensify. —**intensificación,** *n.f.* intensification.

intenso (in'ten·so) *adj.* intense. —**intensidad,** *n.f.* intensity. —**intensivo,** *adj.* intensive.

intentar (in·ten'tar) *v.t.* **1,** to try; attempt. **2,** to intend.

intento (in·ten'to) *n.m.* **1,** intent; purpose. **2,** attempt.

intentona (in·ten'to·na) *n.f., colloq.* try; attempt.

interacción (in·ter·ak'θjon; -'sjon) *n.f.* interaction.

intercalar (in·ter·ka'lar) *v.t.* to intercalate. —**intercalación,** *n.f.* intercalation.

intercambio (in·ter'kam·bjo) *n.m.* interchange. —**intercambiable,** *adj.* interchangeable. —**intercambiar,** *v.t.* to interchange.

interceder (in·ter·θe'ðer; -se'ðer) *v.i.* to intercede.

interceptar (in·ter·θep'tar; -sep'tar) *v.t.* to intercept. —**interceptación,** *also,* **intercepción** (-'θjon; -'sjon) *n.f.* interception. —**interceptor** (-'tor) *n.m.* interceptor.

intercesión (in·ter·θe'sjon; -se'sjon) *n.f.* intercession. —**intercesor,** *n.m.* [*fem.* **-sora**] intercessor. —*adj.* interceding.

intercomunicarse (in·ter·ko·mu·ni'kar·se) *v.r.* [*infl.:* **tocar, 7**] to intercommunicate. —**intercomunicación,** *n.f.* intercommunication.

interdecir (in·ter·ðe'θir; -'sir) *v.t.* [*infl.:* **decir, 44**] to interdict. —**interdicción** (-ðik'θjon; -'sjon) *n.f.* interdiction. —**interdicto** (-'ðik·to) *n.m.* interdict.

interdependiente (in·ter·ðe·pen'djen·te) *adj.* interdependent. —**interdependencia,** *n.f.* interdependence.

interés (in·te'res) *n.m.* interest. —**intereses creados,** vested interests.

interesado (in·te·re·sa'ðo) *adj.* **1,** interested. **2,** selfish; mercenary. —*n.m.* **1,** interested party. **2,** self-seeker.

interesante (in·te·re·san'te) *adj.* interesting.

interesar (in·te·re·sar) *v.i.* to be interesting. —*v.t.* **1,** to interest. **2,** to

give an interest to. **3,** to involve. **4,** *med.* to affect (an organ) —**interesarse,** *v.r.* to be interested; take an interest.

interestelar (in·ter·es·te'lar) *adj.* interstellar.

interferir (in·ter·fe'rir) *v.i.* [*infl.:* **sentir, 31**] to interfere. —**interferencia,** *n.f.* interference.

interferona (in·ter·fe'ro·na) *n.f.* interferon.

ínterin ('in·te·rin) *n.m.* interim; meantime. —**interino** (-'ri·no) *adj.* temporary; provisional.

interior (in·te'rjor) *adj.* interior; inner; internal. —*n.m.* interior; inside. —**interioridades,** *n.f.pl.* private matters.

interiorizar (in·te·rjo·ri'θar; -'sar) *v.t., Amer., colloq.* [*infl.:* **rezar, 10**] to inform in detail; familiarize.

interjección (in·ter·xek'θjon; -'sjon) *n.f.* interjection.

interlinear (in·ter·li·ne'ar) *v.t.* to interline (a writing). —**interlineal,** *adj.* interlinear.

interlocución (in·ter·lo·ku'θjon; -'sjon) *n.f.* interlocution. —**interlocutor,** *n.m.* [*fem.* **-tora**] interlocutor. —**interlocutorio,** *adj., law* interlocutory.

interludio (in·ter'lu·ðjo) *n.m.* interlude.

intermediar (in·ter·me'ðjar) *v.t.* = **mediar.**

intermediario (in·ter·me'ðja·rjo) *adj. & n.m.* intermediary.

intermedio (in·ter'me·ðjo) *adj.* intermediate. —*n.m.* **1,** interim. **2,** interlude. **3,** intermission. —**por intermedio de,** *Amer.* through the intervention of.

interminable (in·ter·mi·na'βle) *adj.* interminable; endless.

intermisión (in·ter·mi'sjon) *n.f.* intermission.

intermitente (in·ter·mi'ten·te) *adj.* intermittent. —**intermitencia,** *n.f.* intermittence.

internacional (in·ter·na·θjo'nal; -sjo'nal) *adj.* international. —**internacionalismo,** *n.m.* internationalism. —**internacionalista,** *n.m. & f.* internationalist. —*adj.* internationalistic.

internado (in·ter'na·ðo) *n.m.* **1,** boarding school. **2,** boarding students collectively. **3,** boarding status. **4,** internship. **5,** internee.

internar (in·ter'nar) *v.t.* to intern.

—*v.i.* [*also, refl.,* **internarse**] 1, to penetrate; go in or through. 2, to delve. —**internación,** *n.f.* 1, hospitalization. 2, confinement. —**internamiento,** *n.m.* internment.

internista (in·ter'nis·ta) *n.m. & f., med.* internist.

interno (in'ter·no) *adj.* internal. —*n.m.* 1, boarding school student. 2, intern.

interpelar (in·ter·pe'lar) *v.t.* to question; interrogate. —**interpelación** *n.f.* appeal; plea.

interplanetario (in·ter·pla·ne'ta·rjo) *adj.* interplanetary.

interpolar (in·ter·po'lar) *v.t.* to interpolate. —**interpolación,** *n.f.* interpolation.

interponer (in·ter·po'ner) *v.t.* [*infl.:* **poner, 54**] to interpose. —**interponerse,** *v.r.* 1, to intercede; intervene. 2, to come between. —**interposición** (-po·si'θjon; -'sjon) *n.f.* interposition.

interpretar (in·ter·pre'tar) *v.t.* to interpret. —**interpretación,** *n.f.* interpretation. —**interpretativo,** *adj.* interpretative.

intérprete (in'ter·pre·te) *n.m. & f.* interpreter.

interracial (in·te·rra'θjal; -'sjal) *adj.* interracial.

interrogación (in·te·rro·ɣa'θjon; -'sjon) *n.f.* 1, interrogation; inquiry. 2, question mark.

interrogar (in·te·rro'ɣar) *v.t.* [*infl.:* **pagar, 8**] to interrogate; question. —**interrogador,** *n.m.* interrogator. —**interrogativo,** *adj.* interrogative.

interrogatorio (in·te·rro·ɣa'to·rjo) *n.m.* 1, interrogatory. 2, interrogation; questioning.

interrumpir (in·te·rrum'pir) *v.t.* to interrupt. —**interrupción** (-rrup'θjon; -'sjon) *n.f.* interruption.

interruptor (in·te·rrup'tor) *adj.* interrupting; interruptive. —*n.m.* 1, circuit breaker. 2, light switch; electric switch.

intersecarse (in·ter·se'kar·se) *v.r.* [*infl.:* **tocar, 7**] to intersect.

interdenominational (in·ter·sek'ta·rjo) *adj.* interdenominational.

intersección (in·ter·sek'θjon; -'sjon) *n.f.* intersection.

intersticio (in·ter'sti·θjo; -sjo) *n.m.* interstice.

interurbano (in·ter·ur'βa·no) *adj. & n.m.* interurban.

intervalo (in·ter'βa·lo) *n.m.* interval.

intervención (in·ter·βen'θjon; -'sjon) *n.f.* 1, intervention. 2, auditing of accounts. 3, *surg.* operation.

intervenir (in·ter·βe'nir) *v.i.* [*infl.:* **venir, 69**] to intervene. —*v.t.* 1, to intervene in. 2, to audit. 3, to place under official control or regulation.

interventor (in·ter·βen'tor) *n.m.* [*fem.* **-tora**] 1, mediator; intervener. 2, comptroller; auditor.

interviú (in·ter'βju) *n.f.* interview.

intestado (in·tes·ta·ðo) *adj. & n.m.* intestate.

intestino (in·tes'ti·no) *adj.* internal. —*n.m.* intestine. —**intestinal,** *adj.* intestinal. —**intestino ciego,** caecum. —**intestino delgado,** small intestine. —**intestino grueso,** large intestine.

intimar (in·ti'mar) *v.t.* to intimate; make known; announce. —*v.i.* [*also, refl.,* **intimarse**] 1, to become intimate. 2, to permeate; soak in. —**intimación,** *n.f.* intimation; announcement.

intimidar (in·ti·mi'ðar) *v.t.* to intimidate. —**intimidación,** *n.f.* intimidation.

íntimo ('in·ti·mo) *adj.* 1, intimate. 2, inner; inmost. —**intimidad,** *n.f.* intimacy.

intitular (in·ti·tu'lar) *v.t.* 1, to entitle. 2, to confer (*on someone or something*) the title of.

intocable (in·to'ka·βle) *adj. & n.m. & f.* untouchable.

intolerable (in·to·le'ra·βle) *adj.* intolerable. —**intolerabilidad,** *n.f.* intolerability.

intolerante (in·to·le'ràn·te) *adj.* intolerant. —**intolerancia,** *n.f.* intolerance.

intoxicar (in·tok·si'kar) *v.t.* [*infl.:* **tocar, 7**] to poison; intoxicate. —**intoxicación,** *n.f.* poisoning; intoxication.

intraducible (in·tra·ðu'θi·βle; -'si·βle) *adj.* untranslatable.

intranquilidad (in·tran·ki·li·'ðað) *n.f.* 1, restlessness. 2, uneasiness.

intranquilo (in·tran'ki·lo) *adj.* 1, restless. 2, uneasy.

intransigente (in·tran·si'xen·te) *adj.* intransigent; uncompromising. —**intransigencia,** *n.f.* intransigence.

intransitable (in·tran·si'ta·βle)
adj. impassable.

intransitivo (in·tran·si'ti·βo) *adj.*
intransitive.

intratable (in·tra'ta·βle) *adj.* 1,
intractable. 2, unsociable; uncommunicative. —**intratabilidad,** *n.f.*
intractability.

intrauterino (in·tra·u·te'ri·no)
adj. intrauterine. —**dispositivo
intrauterino,** intrauterine device.

intravenoso (in·tra·βe'no·so) *adj.*
intravenous.

intrépido (in'tre·pi·ðo) *adj.* intrepid; daring. —**intrepidez,** *n.f.* intrepidity; daring.

intriga (in'tri·γa) *n.f.* intrigue.

intrigante (in·tri'γan·te) *adj.* 1,
intriguing. 2, plotting; scheming.
—*n.m. & f.* intriguer; plotter;
schemer.

intrigar (in·tri'γar) *v.t.* [*infl.:*
pagar, 8] to intrigue. —*v.i.* to plot;
scheme.

intrincado (in·trin'ka·ðo) *adj.* intricate, involved. —**intrincación,**
n.f. intricacy.

intrínseco (in'trin·se·ko) *adj.* intrinsic.

introducción (in·tro·ðuk'θjon;
-'sjon) *n.f.* introduction.

introducir (in·tro·ðu'θir; -'sir) *v.t.*
[*infl.:* **conducir, 40**] to introduce.
—**introducirse,** *v.r.* to interfere;
meddle. —**introductivo,** *adj.* introductory.

intromisión (in·tro·mi'sjon) *n.f.*
1, interposition. 2, interference;
meddling.

introspección (in·tros·pek'θjon;
-'sjon) *n.f.* introspection. —**introspectivo** (-'ti·βo) *adj.* introspective.

introvertido (in·tro·βer'ti·ðo)
adj. introverted. —*n.m.* introvert.
—**introversión** (-'sjon) *n.f.* introversion.

intrusear (in·tru·se'ar) *v.i., Amer.,
colloq.* to intrude; poke in.

intrusión (in·tru'sjon) *n.f.* intrusion.

intruso (in'tru·so) *adj.* intrusive.
—*n.m.* intruder.

intuición (in·twi'θjon; -'sjon) *n.f.*
intuition.

intuir (in·tu'ir) *v.t.* [*infl.:* **huir, 26**]
to grasp intuitively; perceive by intuition.

intuitivo (in·twi'ti·βo) *adj.* intuitive.

inundar (i·nun'dar) *v.t.* to flood;

inundate. —**inundación,** *n.f.* flooding; inundation.

inusitado (i·nu·si'ta·ðo) *adj.* 1,
unusual. 2, unused; out of use.

inútil (in'u·til) *adj.* 1, useless. 2,
incapacitated; noneffective. —*n.m.
& f.* 1, useless person; good-for-
nothing. 2, incapacitated person;
noneffective.

inutilidad (in·u·ti·li'ðað) *n.f.* 1,
uselessness. 2, incapacity.

inutilizar (in·u·ti·li'θar; -'sar) *v.t.*
[*infl.:* **rezar, 10**] to render useless;
disable.

invadir (in·βa'ðir) *v.t.* to invade.

invalidar (in·βa·li'ðar) *v.t.* invalidate. —**invalidación,** *n.f.* invalidation.

invalidez (in·βa·li'ðeθ; -'ðes) *n.f.*
1, invalidity. 2, state of being an invalid.

inválido (in'βa·li·ðo) *adj.* 1, invalid. 2, null; void. —*n.m.* invalid.

invariable (in·βa'rja·βle) *adj.* invariable. —**invariabilidad,** *n.f.* invariability.

invasión (in·βa'sjon) *n.f.* invasion.
—**invasor,** *adj.* invading. —*n.m.*
[*fem.* **-sora**] invader.

invectiva (in·βek'ti·βa) *n.f.* invective.

invencible (in·βen'θi·βle; -'si·βle)
adj. invincible. —**invencibilidad,**
n.f. invincibility.

invención (in·βen'θjon; -'sjon) *n.f.*
invention.

invendible (in·βen'di·βle) *adj.*
unsaleable.

inventar (in·βen'tar) *v.t.* to invent.

inventario (in·βen'ta·rjo) *n.m.* inventory. —**inventariar,** *v.t.* [*infl.:*
enviar, 22] to inventory.

inventivo (in·βen'ti·βo) *adj.* inventive. —**inventiva,** *n.f.* inventiveness; ingenuity.

invento (in'βen·to) *n.m.* invention.

inventor (in·βen'tor) *n.m.* [*fem.*
-tora] inventor.

invernáculo (in·βer'na·ku·lo)
n.m. greenhouse; hothouse.

invernadero (in·βer·na'ðe·ro)
n.m. 1, winter quarters. 2, winter
pasture. 3, greenhouse; hothouse.

invernal (in·βer'nal) *adj.* winter
(*attrib.*); wintry. —*n.m.* winter stable.

invernar (in·βer'nar) *v.i.* [*infl.:*
pensar, 27] to winter; hibernate.

inverosímil (in·βe·ro'si·mil)
also, **inverisímil** (in·βe·ri-) *adj.* unbelievable; improbable.

inversión (in·βer'sjon) *n.f.* 1, inversion. 2, investment. 3, input. —**inversionista,** *n.m. & f.* investor.

inverso (in'βer·so) *adj.* inverse. —**a** *or* **por la inversa,** 1, on the contrary. 2, in reverse order; upsidedown.

invertebrado (in·βer·te'βra·ðo) *adj. & n.m.* invertebrate.

invertir (in·βer'tir) *v.t.* [*infl.:* **sentir, 31**] 1, to invert; reverse. 2, to invest.

investidura (in·βes·ti'ðu·ra) *n.f.* 1, investiture. 2, installation (*in office*).

investigación (in·βes·ti·ɣa·'θjon; -'sjon) *n.f.* 1, investigation; inquiry. 2, research.

investigador (in·βes·ti·ɣa'ðor) *n.m.* [*fem.* **-dora**] 1, investigator. 2, researcher. —*adj.* investigating; investigative.

investigar (in·βes·ti'ɣar) *v.t. & i.* [*infl.:* **pagar, 8**] to investigate.

investir (in·βes'tir) *v.t.* [*infl.:* **pedir, 33**] to invest; vest.

inveterado (in·βe·te'ra·ðo) *adj.* inveterate.

invicto (in'βik·to) *adj.* undefeated; unvanquished.

invierne (in'βjer·ne) *v.,* pres. subjve. *of* **invernar.**

invierno (in'βjer·no) *n.m.* winter.

invierno (in'βjer·no) *v., 1st pers.sing. pres.ind. of* **invernar.**

invierta (in'βjer·ta) *v.,* pres.subjve. *of* **invertir.**

invierto (in'βjer·to) *v., 1st pers.sing. pres.ind. of* **invertir.**

inviolable (in·βjo'la·βle) *adj.* inviolable. —**inviolabilidad,** *n.f.* inviolability.

inviolado (in·βjo'la·ðo) *adj.* inviolate.

invirtiendo (in·βir'tjen·do) *v.,* ger. *of* **invertir.**

invirtió (in·βir'tjo) *v., 3rd pers. sing. pret. of* **invertir.**

invisible (in·βi'si·βle) *adj.* invisible. —**invisibilidad,** *n.f.* invisibility.

invitación (in·βi·ta'θjon; -'sjon) *n.f.* 1, invitation. 2, *colloq.* treat.

invitado (in·βi'ta·ðo) *n.m.* invited guest; company.

invitar (in·βi'tar) *v.t.* 1, to invite. 2, to treat.

invocar (in·βo'kar) *v.t.* [*infl.:* **tocar, 7**] to invoke. —**invocación,** *n.f.* invocation.

involución (in·βo·lu'θjon; -'sjon) *n.f.* involution.

involucrar (in·βo·lu'krar) *v.t.* to involve; entail.

involuntario (in·βo·lun'ta·rjo) *adj.* involuntary.

invulnerable (in·βul·ne'ra·βle) *adj.* invulnerable. —**invulnerabilidad,** *n.f.* invulnerability.

inyección (in·jek'θjon; -'sjon) *n.f.* injection.

inyectado (in·jek'ta·ðo) *adj.* bloodshot.

inyectar (in·jek'tar) *v.t.* to inject. —**inyector** (-'tor) *n.m.* injector.

ión (i'on) *n.m.* ion.

ionio (i'o·njo) *n.m.* ionium.

ionosfera (i·o·nos'fe·ra) *n.f.* ionosphere.

ipecacuana (i·pe·ka'kwa·na) *n.f.* ipecac.

ir (ir) *v.i.* [*infl.:* **49**] 1, to go. 2, to fit; suit; be becoming. 3, to concern; affect. 4, *expressing condition or progress* to be; do; get along: *El enfermo va bien,* the patient is doing well. *¿Cómo van los negocios?* How is business? 5, *in expressions of time* to be; elapse: *Van tres años que no lo veo,* It has been three years since I saw him. —aux.v. 1, *used with the gerund to form the progressive tenses: Va amaneciendo,* It is getting light. 2, *used with the past participle to express the passive: Va vendido,* it is sold. 3, *fol. by* **a** + *inf., expressing the immediate future: Voy a hablarle,* I am going to speak to him. *Van a cerrar,* they are about to close. —**irse,** *v.r.* 1, to go; go away; leave. 2, to fail; give way; collapse. 3, to die; succumb. 4, to fade; fade away. —**ir a caballo,** to go on horseback. —**ir a pie,** to go on foot. —**ir en automóvil, tren, barco,** etc., to go by car, train, boat, etc. —**ir por,** 1, to be for; follow. 2, to go after; pursue. 3, to be at (a certain state or stage): *Voy por la mitad del libro,* I am at the middle of the book. —**irse a pique,** to sink. —**No me va ni me viene,** It makes no difference to me. —**¡qué va!,** nonsense!; you don't say! —**¿Quién va?,** Who's there?

ira ('i·ra) *n.f.* ire; wrath.

iracundo (i·ra'kun·do) *adj.* ireful; wrathful.

irascible (i·ras'θi·βle; i·ra'si·βle) *adj.* irascible. —**irascibilidad,** *n.f.* irascibility.

irga ('ir·ɣa) v., pres.subjve. of erguir.

irguiendo (ir'ɣjen·do) v., ger. of erguir.

irguió (ir'ɣjo) v., 3rd pers.sing. pret. of erguir.

iridio (i'ri·ðjo) n.m. iridium.

iridiscente (i·ri·ðis'θen·te; -ði·'sen·te) adj. iridescent. —**iridiscencia**, n.f. iridescence.

iris ('i·ris) n.m. 1, iris. 2, [also, arco iris] rainbow.

irisado (i·ri'sa·ðo) adj. iridescent.

irlandés (ir·lan'des) adj. Irish. —n.m. 1, Irishman. 2, Irish language. —**irlandesa**, n.f. Irish woman.

ironía (i·ro'ni·a) n.f. irony. —**irónico** (i'ro·ni·ko) adj. ironic; ironical.

irracional (i·rra·θjo'nal; -sjo'nal) adj. irrational. —**irracionalidad**, n.f. irrationality.

irradiar (i·rra'ðjar) v.t. to irradiate. —**irradiación**, n.f. irradiation.

irrazonable (i·rra·θo'na·βle; -so'na·βle) adj. unreasonable.

irreal (i·rre'al) adj. unreal.

irrealidad (i·rre·a·li'ðað) n.f. unreality.

irrealizable (i·rre·a·li'θa·βle; -'sa·βle) adj. unrealizable.

irrebatible (i·rre·βa'ti·βle) adj. irrefutable.

irreconciliable (i'rre·kon·θi'lja·βle; -si'lja·βle) adj. irreconcilable.

irreconocible (i·rre·ko·no'θi·βle; -'si·βle) adj. unrecognizable. —**irreconocido** (-'θi·ðo; -'si·ðo) adj. unrecognized.

irrecuperable (i·rre·ku·pe'ra·βle) adj. irrecoverable.

irrecusable (i·rre·ku'sa·βle) adj. unexceptionable; unimpeachable.

irredimible (i·rre·ði'mi·βle) adj., comm. irredeemable.

irreducible (i·rre·ðu'θi·βle) -'si·βle) also, **irreductible** (-ðuk'ti·βle) adj. irreducible.

irreemplazable (i·rre·em·pla·'θa·βle; -'sa·βle) adj. irreplaceable.

irreflexión (i·rre·flek'sjon) n.f. thoughtlessness. —**irreflexivo** (-'si·βo) adj. thoughtless.

irrefrenable (i·rre·fre'na·βle) adj. uncontrollable; unbridled.

irrefutable (i·rre·fu'ta·βle) adj. irrefutable.

irregular (i·rre·ɣu'lar) adj. irregular. —**irregularidad**, n.f. irregularity.

irreligioso (i·rre·li'xjo·so) adj. irreligious. —**irreligiosidad**, n.f. irreligiousness.

irremediable (i·rre·me'ðja·βle) adj. irremediable.

irremovible (i·rre·mo'βi·βle) adj. irremovable.

irreparable (i·rre·pa'ra·βle) adj. irreparable.

irreprensible (i·rre·pren'si·βle) adj. irreproachable; unimpeachable.

irreprimible (i·rre·pri'mi·βle) adj. irrepressible.

irreprochable (i·rre·pro'tʃa·βle) adj. irreproachable.

irresistible (i·rre·sis'ti·βle) adj. irresistible.

irresoluto (i·rre·so'lu·to) adj. irresolute. —**irresolución**, n.f. irresoluteness.

irrespetuoso (i·rres·pe'two·so) adj. disrespectful.

irresponsable (i·rres·pon'sa·βle) adj. irresponsible. —**irresponsabilidad**, n.f. irresponsibility.

irresponsive (i·rres·pon'si·βc) adj. irresponsive.

irreverente (i·rre·βe'ren·te) adj. irreverent. —**irreverencia**, n.f. irreverence.

irreversible (i·rre·ver'si·βle) adj. irreversible.

irrevocable (i·rre·βo'ka·βle) n.f. irrevocable. —**irrevocabilidad**, n.f. irrevocability.

irrigar (i·rri'ɣar) v.t. [infl.: pagar, 8] to irrigate. —**irrigación**, n.f. irrigation.

irrisión (i·rri'sjon) n.f. 1, derision; ridicule. 2, laughable person or thing; object of ridicule.

irrisorio (i·rri'so·rjo) adj. 1, laughable. 2, piddling; inconsequential.

irritable (i·rri'ta·βle) adj. irritable. —**irritabilidad**, n.f. irritability.

irritado (i·rri'ta·ðo) adj. 1, irate. 2, irritated.

irritar (i·rri'tar) v.t. to irritate. —**irritación**, n.f. irritation. —**irritante**, adj. irritating. —n.m. irritant.

irrompible (i·rrom'pi·βle) adj. unbreakable.

irrumpir (i·rrum'pir) v.i. to burst in.

irrupción (i·rrup'θjon; -'sjon) n.f. irruption.

isla ('is·la) n.f. island.

Islam (is'lam) n.m. Islam.

—**islámico** (-'la·mi·ko) *adj.* Islamic. —**islamismo,** *n.m.* Mohammedanism. —**islamita,** *adj. & n.m. & f.* Mohammedan.

isleño (is'le·ɲo) *adj.* island (*attrib.*). —*n.m.* islander.

islote (is'lo·te) *n.m.* isle; islet.

ismo ('is·mo) *n.m.* ism.

isométrico (i·so'me·tri·ko) *adj.* isometric.

isósceles (i'sos·θe·les; i'so·se·les) *adj.* isosceles.

isótopo (i'so·to·po) *n.m.* isotope.

israelí (is·ra·e'li) *adj. & n.m. & f.* Israeli. —**israelita** (-'li·ta) *adj. & n.m. & f.* Israelite.

istmo ('ist·mo; 'is·mo) *n.m.* isthmus.

italiano (i·ta'lja·no) *adj. & n.m.* Italian.

itálico (i'ta·li·ko) *adj.* Italic. —**letra itálica,** italics.

ítem ('i·tem) *adv.* moreover; also. —*n.m.* item.

iterar (i·te'rar) *v.t.* to iterate. —**iteración,** *n.f.* iteration.

iterbio (i'ter·βjo) *n.m.* ytterbium.

itrio ('i·trjo) *n.m.* yttrium.

izar (i'θar; i'sar) *v.t.* [*infl.:* rezar, 10] to raise; hoist; haul up.

izquierda (iθ'kjer·ða; is-) *n.f.* left; left hand; left side.

izquierdista (iθ·kjer'ðis·ta; is-) *adj. & n.m. & f.* leftist.

izquierdo (iθ'kjer·ðo; is-) *adj.* **1,** left. **2,** = zurdo. —**levantarse por el lado izquierdo,** to get up on the wrong side of the bed.

J

J, j ('xo·ta) *n.f.* 11th letter of the Spanish alphabet.

¡ja! (xa) *interj.* ha!

jabalí (xa·βa'li) *n.m.* wild boar.

jabalina (xa·βa'li·na) *n.f.* **1,** javelin. **2,** *fem. of* jabalí.

jábega ('xa·βe·ɣa) *n.f.* seine.

jabón (xa'βon) *n.m.* **1,** soap. **2,** *Amer.* fear; scare. —**dar jabón,** *colloq.* to softsoap. —**dar un jabón,** *colloq.* to scold.

jabonadura (xa·βo·na'ðu·ra) *n.f., also, Amer.* **jabonada** (-'na·ða) soaping; washing; lathering. —**jabonaduras,** *n.f.pl.* suds.

jabonar (xa·βo'nar) *v.t.* to soap; lather.

jabonera (xa·βo'ne·ra) *n.f.* **1,** soap dish. **2,** soapwort.

jabonoso (xa·βo'no·so) *adj.* soapy.

jaca ('xa·ka) *n.f.* small horse; cob.

jacal (xa'kal) *n.m., Mex.* shack; Indian hut.

jácara ('xa·ka·ra) *n.f.* **1,** lilt; merry ballad. **2,** group of merrymakers. **3,** merrymaking. **4,** *colloq.* bother; nuisance. **5,** *colloq.* fib; lie.

jacinto (xa'θin·to; -'sin·to) *n.m.* hyacinth.

jaco ('xa·ko) *n.m.* inferior horse; nag.

jactancia (xak'tan·θja; -sja) *n.f.* swagger; boasting. —**jactancioso,** *adj.* boastful.

jactarse (xak'tar·se) *v.r.* to boast; brag.

jaculatoria (xa·ku·la'to·rja) *n.f.* short prayer.

jade ('xa·ðe) *n.m., mineral.* jade.

jadear (xa·ðe'ar) *v.i.* to pant; gasp for breath. —**jadeante,** *adj.* panting; out of breath. —**jadeo** (-'ðe·o) *n.m.* pant; panting.

jaez (xa'eθ; -'es) *n.m.* **1,** harness; trappings. **2,** sort; nature.

jaguar (xa'ɣwar) *n.m.* jaguar.

jai alai (xai·a'lai) *n.m.* jai alai.

jaiba ('xai·βa) *n.f., Amer.* crab.

jalar (xa'lar) *v.t., colloq.* **1,** = halar. **2,** *W.I.* to woo. —**jalarse,** *v.r., Amer., colloq.* **1,** to get drunk. **2,** to get out; scram.

jalea (xa'le·a) *n.f.* jelly.

jalear (xa·le'ar) *v.t.* **1,** to urge; spur on; encourage loudly. **2,** *Amer., colloq.* to poke fun at.

jaleo (xa'le·o) *n.m.* **1,** boisterous encouragement; rooting. **2,** Andalusian dance. **3,** *colloq.* merrymaking. **4,** *colloq.* brawl; rumpus.

jaletina (xa·le'ti·na) *n.f.* fine, clear gelatine.

jalón (xa'lon) *n.m.* **1,** surveyor's pole. **2,** landmark. **3,** *Amer., colloq.* swig; drink, esp. of liquor. **4,** *Amer.* jerk; pull; tug. **5,** *Amer.* distance; stretch.

jamás (xa'mas) *adv.* **1,** never. **2,** ever. —**nunca jamás,** nevermore.

—**por siempre jamás,** for evermore.

jamba ('xam·ba) *n.f.* jamb.

jamelgo (xa'mel·go) *n.m.* nag; hack; jade.

jamón (xa'mon) *n.m.* ham.

jamona (xa'mo·na) *n.f.* fat middleaged woman.

japonés (xa·po'nes) *adj.* & *n.m.* [*fem.* **japonesa**] Japanese *(language)*.

jaque ('xa·ke) *n.m.* 1, *chess* check. 2, swashbuckler. —**jaquear,** *v.t., chess* to check. —**en jaque,** in check; at bay. —**jaque mate,** checkmate.

jaqueca (xa'ke·ka) *n.f.* migraine; headache.

jarabe (xa'ra·βe) *n.m.* 1, syrup. 2, sweet drink or infusion. 3, *colloq.* sweet talk. 4, a Mexican dance.

jarana (xa'ra·na) *n.f.* 1, carousal; revel; romp. 2, *colloq.* brawl; quarrel. 3, *colloq.* trick; joke. —**jaranear,** *v.i.* to carouse; revel. —**jaranero,** *adj.* fun-loving. —*n.m.* reveler.

jardín (xar'ðin) *n.m.* garden. —**jardinera,** *n.f.* jardinière. —**jardinería,** *n.f.* gardening. —**jardinero,** *n.m.* gardener. —**jardín de infancia; jardín infantil,** kindergarten.

jarra ('xa·rra) *n.f.* pitcher; jug. —**de** *or* **en jarras,** akimbo.

jarretera (xa·rre'te·ra) *n.f.* garter; *(cap.)* Order of the Garter.

jarro ('xa·rro) *n.m.* jug; mug.

jarrón (xa'rron) *n.m.* ornamental pot; vase; urn.

jaspe ('xas·pe) *n.m.* jasper. —**jaspeado,** *adj.* marbled; veined; mottled. —*n.m.* veins; streaks; mottle; streaking. —**jaspear,** *v.t.* to vein; streak; mottle.

jaula ('xau·la) *n.f.* 1, cage. 2, *colloq.* jail.

jauría (xau'ri·a) *n.f.* pack, as of hounds.

jazmín (xaθ'min; xas-) *n.m.* jasmine.

jazz (dʒas, *also,* xas) *n.m.* jazz.

jebe ('xe·βe) *n.m.* 1, = **alumbre.** 2, *Amer.* rubber; raw rubber. 3, *Amer.* elastic; rubber band.

jedive (xe'ði·βe) *n.m.* khedive.

jeep (dʒip) *n.m.* jeep.

jefatura (xe·fa'tu·ra) *n.f.* 1, position of chief; chieftaincy; leadership. 2, headquarters.

jefe ('xe·fe) *n.m.* [*fem.* **jefa**] chief;

leader; head; boss. —**en jefe,** chief; principal; highest; head.

Jehová (xe·o'βa) *n.m.* Jehovah.

jején (xe'xen) *n.m., Amer.* gnat.

jengibre (xen'xi·βre) *n.m.* ginger.

jeque ('xe·ke) *n.m.* sheik.

jerarca (xe'rar·ka) *n.m.* hierarch. —**jerarquía** (-'ki·a) *n.f.* hierarchy. —**jerárquico** (xe'rar·ki·ko) *adj.* hierarchical.

jeremiada (xe·re'mja·ða) *n.f.* jeremiad.

jerez (xe'reθ; -'res) *n.m.* sherry.

jerga ('xer·γa) *n.f.* 1, frieze; coarse cloth. 2, jargon; cant; argot. 3, = **jerigonza.** 4, = **jergón.**

jergón (xer'γon) *n.m.* 1, pallet; straw mat. 2, *colloq.* rags; shabby dress. 3, *colloq.* lazy lummox.

jerigonza (xe·ri'γon·θa; -sa) *n.f., colloq.* 1, lingo. 2, gibberish; jabber; balderdash. 3, rigmarole.

jeringa (xe'rin·ga) *n.f.* 1, syringe. 2, *colloq.* bother; nuisance.

jeringar (xe·rin'gar) *v.t.* [*infl.:* **pagar,** 8] 1, to squirt or inject with a syringe. 2, *colloq.* to vex; annoy; bother.

jeroglífico (xe·roγ'li·fi·ko) *adj.* & *n.m.* hieroglyphic.

jersey (xer'sei) *n.m.* jersey.

Jesucristo (xe·su'kris·to) *n.m.* Jesus Christ.

jesuita (xe'swi·ta) *adj.* & *n.m.* Jesuit. —**jesuítico,** *adj.* jesuitic; jesuitical.

Jesús (xe'sus) *n.m.* Jesus.

jeta ('xe·ta) *n.f.* 1, protruding lips. 2, snout. 3, *colloq.* mug; face. —**poner jeta,** to pout.

jíbaro ('xi·βa·ro) *adj., Amer.* rustic; uncivilized. —*n.m.* rustic; hick.

jibia ('xi·βja) *n.f.* cuttlefish.

jícara ('xi·ka·ra) *n.f.* mug; chocolate cup.

jifa ('xi·fa) *n.f.* offal.

¡ji, ji! ('xi'xi) *interj.* te-hee!

jilguero (xil'γe·ro) *n.m.* linnet. —**jilguero de América,** yellowbird.

jineta (xi'ne·ta) *n.f.* horsewoman. —**a la jineta,** (to ride) with very short stirrups.

jinete (xi'ne·te) *n.m.* 1, horseman. 2, thoroughbred horse.

jinetear (xi·ne·te'ar) *v.i.* to ride horseback for show; prance. —*v.t. Amer.* to break in; tame (a horse).

jingo ('xin·go) *n.m.* jingo. —**jingoísmo,** *n.m.* jingoism. —**jingoísta,** *adj.* & *n.m.* & *f.* jingoist.

jinrikisha (xin·ri'ki·ʃa) *n.m.* jin-rikisha.

jipijapa (xi·pi'xa·pa) *n.m.* straw hat; Panama hat.

jira ('xi·ra) *n.f.* **1**, excursion; tour. **2**, outing; picnic.

jirafa (xi'ra·fa) *n.f.* giraffe.

jirón (xi'ron) *n.m.* **1**, strip of cloth. **2**, rag; tatter. **3**, *fig.* shred; bit.

jitomate (xi·to'ma·te) *n.m., Amer.* a kind of tomato.

jiu-jitsu (xju'xit·su) *n.m.* jujitsu.

jockey ('dʒo·ki) *n.m.* jockey.

jocoso (xo'ko·so) *adj.* jocose; jocular. —**jocosidad,** *n.f.* jocosity; jocularity.

jocundo (xo'kun·do) *adj.* jocund. —**jocundidad,** *n.f.* jocundity.

jofaina (xo'fai·na) *n.f.* washbasin.

jolgorio (xol'ɣo·rjo) *n.m.* = **holgorio.**

jónico ('xo·ni·ko) *adj.* Ionic.

jonrón (xon'ron) *n.m., baseball* home run.

jornada (xor'na·ða) *n.f.* **1**, journey. **2**, day's journey. **3**, day's work.

jornal (xor'nal) *n.m.* **1**, day's wages. **2**, day's work. —**jornal mínimo,** minimum wage.

jornalero (xor·na'le·ro) *n.m.* laborer; day laborer.

joroba (xo'ro·βa) *n.f.* **1**, hump; humpback. **2**, *colloq.* bother; nuisance; importunity.

jorobado (xo·ro'βa·ðo) *adj.* **1**, humpbacked. **2**, *colloq.* in a fix. —*n.m.* hunchback; humpback.

jorobar (xo·ro'βar) *v.t., colloq.* to importune; bother; annoy.

jota ('xo·ta) *n.f.* **1**, the letter *j*. **2**, iota; jot. **3**, a Spanish dance.

joule (dʒul) *n.m., physics* joule.

joven ('xo·βen) *adj.* young. —*n.m. & f.* youth; young person.

jovial (xo'βjal) *adj.* jovial. —**jovialidad,** *n.f.* joviality.

joya ('xo·ja) *n.f.* gem; jewel. —**joyas de fantasía,** costume jewelry.

joyel (xo'jel) *n.m.* small jewel.

joyería (xo·je'ri·a) *n.f.* **1**, jewelry trade. **2**, jewelry shop. —**joyero** (-'je·ro) *n.m.* jeweler.

juanete (xwa'ne·te) *n.m.* **1**, bunion. **2**, *naut.* topgallant sail.

jubilación (xu·βi·la'θjon; -'sjon) *n.f.* **1**, retirement. **2**, pension.

jubilado (xu·βi'la·ðo) *adj.* retired. —*n.m.* pensioner.

jubilar (xu·βi'lar) *v.t.* to retire; pension.

jubileo (xu·βi'le·o) *n.m.* jubilee.

júbilo ('xu·βi·lo) *n.m.* jubilation; joy. —**jubiloso,** *adj.* jubilant.

jubón (xu'βon) *n.m.* **1**, doublet; jerkin. **2**, tight blouse; basque.

judaico (xu'ðai·ko) *adj.* Judaic. —**judaísmo** (xu·ða'is·mo) *n.m.* Judaism.

judería (xu·ðe'ri·a) *n.f.* ghetto.

judía (xu'ði·a) *n.f.* **1**, Jewess. **2**, kidney bean.

judicatura (xu·ði·ka'tu·ra) *n.f.* **1**, judicature. **2**, judiciary.

judicial (xu·ði'θjal; -'sjal) *adj.* judicial; judiciary.

judío (xu'ði·o) *adj.* Jewish. —*n.m.* Jew.

judo ('xu·ðo) *n.m.* judo.

juego ('xwe·ɣo) *n.m.* **1**, game. **2**, gambling. **3**, play; move. **4**, matching set; set. **5**, works; movement; mechanism. **6**, *mech.* play. —*v.*, *1st pers.sing.pres.ind.* of **jugar.** —**hacer juego [con],** to match; go (with). —**juego de palabras,** play on words; pun. —**juego limpio,** fair play. —**juego sucio,** foul play. —**juegos malabares,** juggling; jugglery.

juegue ('xwe·ɣe) *v.*, *pres.subjve.* of **jugar.**

juerga ('xwer·ɣa) *n.f.* spree; revelry; carousal. —**juerguista** (-'ɣis·ta) *n.m. & f.* merrymaker; reveler.

jueves ('xwe·βes) *n.m.sing. & pl.* Thursday.

juez (xweθ; xwes) *n.m.* judge.

jugada (xu'ɣa·ða) *n.f.* **1**, play; move; stroke. **2**, *fig.* trick; prank.

jugador (xu·ɣa'ðor) *adj.* gambling. —*n.m.* **1**, player. **2**, gambler.

jugar (xu'ɣar) *v.i.* [*infl.:* pagar, 8; acostar, 28] **1**, to play; engage in playing. **2**, to toy; trifle. **3**, to match; fit; suit. **4**, to gamble. **5**, *mech.* to have play. —*v.t.* **1**, to play; play at. **2**, to gamble; gamble away. **3**, to move; wield.

jugarreta (xu·ɣa'rre·ta) *n.f. colloq.* **1**, bad play; wrong move. **2**, mischief; misdeed.

juglar (xu'ɣlar) *n.m.* minstrel. —**juglaría,** *n.f.* minstrelsy.

jugo ('xu·ɣo) *n.m.* **1**, juice. **2**, *fig.* substance; meat; marrow. —**jugoso,** *adj.* juicy.

jugué (xu'ɣe) *v.*, *1st pers.sing. pret.* of **jugar.**

juguete (xu'ɣe·te) *n.m.* toy; plaything.

juguetear (xu·ɣe·te'ar) *v.i.* **1,** to toy; trifle. **2,** to frolic; romp.
juguetería (xu·ɣe·te·ri·a) *n.f.* toy-shop.
juguetón (xu·ɣe'ton) *adj.* playful; frolicsome.
juicio ('xwi·θjo; -sjo) *n.m.* **1,** judgment. **2,** sense; wisdom. **3,** sanity. **4,** trial; lawsuit. —**juicioso,** *adj.* judicious; wise; sensible.
julepe (xu'le·pe) *n.m.* **1,** julep. **2,** *colloq.* scolding; reprimand. **3,** *Amer., colloq.* fear; fright. **4,** *Amer., colloq.* fuss; to-do.
julio ('xu·ljo) *n.m.* **1,** July. **2,** joule.
jumento (xu'men·to) *n.m.* ass; donkey.
juncia ('xun·θja; -sja) *n.f.* sedge.
junco ('xun·ko) *n.m.* **1,** *bot.* rush. **2,** junk *(ship)*.
jungla ('xun·gla) *n.f.* jungle.
junio ('xu·njo) *n.m.* June.
junípero (xu'ni·pe·ro) *n.m.* juniper.
junquillo (xun'ki·ʎo; -jo) *n.m.* **1,** *bot.* jonquil. **2,** rattan.
junta ('xun·ta) *n.f.* **1,** junta; assembly; board. **2,** meeting; gathering. **3,** joint; seam. **4,** junction. —**junta directiva,** board of directors.
juntar (xun'tar) *v.t.* **1,** to join; unite; place together. **2,** to collect; gather; amass. **3,** to close (a door or window) incompletely. **4,** to assemble; congregate. **5,** to pool. —**juntarse,** *v.r.* **1,** to meet; assemble. **2,** *fol. by* **a,** to get close to; hug. **3,** *fol. by* **con** *or* **a,** to associate with.
junto ('xun·to) *adj.* joined; united; placed together. —**juntos,** *adv.* together; jointly. —**junto a,** next to; beside. —**junto con,** together with.
juntura (xun'tu·ra) *n.f.* joint; juncture.
Júpiter ('xu·pi·ter) *n.m.* Jupiter; Jove.
jura ('xu·ra) *n.f.* oath; pledge.

jurado (xu'ra·ðo) *adj.* sworn. —*n.m.* **1,** jury. **2,** juror.
juramentar (xu·ra·men'tar) *v.t.* to swear in. —**juramentarse,** *v.r.* to take an oath.
juramento (xu·ra'men·to) *n.m.* oath. —**juramento falso,** perjury.
jurar (xu'rar) *v.t.* **1,** to swear; vow. **2,** to be sworn into; take the oath of (a public office). —*v.i.* to curse; swear. —**jurársela a uno,** *colloq.* to have it in for someone. —**jurar en falso,** to commit perjury.
jurel (xu'rel) *n.m., ichthy.* yellow jack.
jurídico (xu'ri·ði·ko) *adj.* juridical.
jurisconsulto (xu·ris·kon'sul·to) *n.m.* **1,** jurist. **2,** lawyer.
jurisdicción (xu·ris·ðik'θjon; -'sjon) *n.f.* jurisdiction. —**jurisdiccional,** *adj.* jurisdictional.
jurisperito (xu·ris·pe'ri·to) *n.m.* legal expert.
jurisprudencia (xu·ris·pru'ðen·θja; -sja) *n.f.* jurisprudence.
jurista (xu'ris·ta) *n.m.* jurist.
justa ('xus·ta) *n.f.* **1,** joust. **2,** contest.
justicia (xus'ti·θja; -sja) *n.f.* **1,** justice. **2,** police; law enforcement authority. —**justiciar,** *v.t.* **1,** to condemn. **2,** to execute.
justiciero (xus·ti'θje·ro; -'sje·ro) *adj.* strictly fair; stern.
justificar (xus·ti·fi'kar) *v.t.* [*infl.:* **tocar, 7**] to justify. —**justificable,** *adj.* justifiable. —**justificación,** *n.f.* justification.
justo ('xus·to) *adj.* **1,** just; fair. **2,** correct; exact. **3,** tight. —*adv.* **1,** just; exactly. **2,** just right. **3,** tight.
juvenil (xu·βe'nil) *adj.* juvenile; youthful.
juventud (xu·βen'tuð) *n.f.* youth.
juzgado (xuθ'ɣa·ðo; jus-) *n.m.* tribunal; court of justice.
juzgar (xuθ'ɣar; xus-) *v.t. & i.* [*infl.:* **pagar, 8**] to judge.

K

K, k (ka) *n.f.* 12th letter of the Spanish alphabet.
káiser ('kai·ser) *n.m.* Kaiser.
kajak (ka'xak) *n.m.* kayak.
kaki ('ka·ki) *adj. & n.m.* = **caqui.**
kaleidoscopio (ka·lei·ðos'ko·pjo) *n.m.* = **calidoscopio.**

kan (kan) *n.m.* khan. —**kanato** (-'na·to) *n.m.* khanate.
kanguro (kan'gu·ro) *n.m.* = **canguro.**
kapok (ka'pok) *n.m.* kapok.
kayak (ka'jak) *n.m.* = **kajak.**
kepis ('ke·pis) *n.m.sing. & pl.* kepi.

kerosina (ke·ro'si·na) *n.f., also,*
Amer., **kerosén** (-'sen), **kerosene**
(-'se·ne) *n.m.* kerosene.
kilo ('ki·lo) *n.m.* = **kilogramo.**
kilociclo (ki·lo'θi·klo; -'si·klo)
n.m. kilocycle.
kilogramo (ki·lo'γra·mo) *n.m.*
kilogram.
kilolitro (ki·lo'li·tro) *n.m.* kiloliter.
kilometraje (ki·lo·me'tra·xe)
n.m. distance in kilometers.
kilométrico (ki·lo'me·tri·ko) *adj.*
1, kilometric. **2,** *colloq.* lengthy.
kilómetro (ki'lo·me·tro) *n.m.* kilometer.
kilovatio (ki·lo'βa·tjo) *n.m.* kilowatt.
kimono (ki'mo·no) *n.m.* = **quimono.**

kindergarten (kin·der'γar·ten)
n.m. kindergarten.
kinescopio (ki·nes'ko·pjo) *n.m.*
kinescope.
kiosco *also,* **kiosko** ('kjos·ko)
n.m. = **quiosco.**
kiwi ('ki·wi) *n.m.* kiwi.
klaxson ('klak·son) *n.m., Amer.*
automobile horn.
knockout (no'kaut) *n.m.* knockout.
knut *also,* **knout** (nut) *n.m.*
knout.
koala (ko'a·la) *n.m.* koala.
kopek (ko'pek) *n.m.* kopeck.
Kremlin ('krem·lin) *n.m.* Kremlin.
kriptón (krip'ton) *n.m.* = **criptón.**
kulak (ku'lak) *n.m.* kulak.

L

L, l ('e·le) *n.f.* 13th letter of the
Spanish alphabet.
la (la) *def.art. fem.sing.* the. *—pers.*
pron. fem.sing., used as dir. obj. of
a verb her; it; you. *—dem. pron.*
fem.sing. that; the one (that).
la (la) *n.m., mus.* la; A.
laberinto (la·βe'rin·to) *n.m.* labyrinth. **—laberíntico,** *adj.* labyrinthine.
labia ('la·βja) *n.f., colloq.* glibness.
labial (la'βjal) *adj.* labial.
labihendido (la·βi·en'di·ðo) *adj.*
harelipped.
labio ('la·βjo) *n.m.* lip. **—labio
leporino,** harelip.
labor (la'βor) *n.f.* **1,** labor; work. **2,**
embroidery; needlework. **3,** tillage;
tilling.
laborar (la·βo'rar) *v.t.* = **labrar.**
—v.i. to work; labor; strive.
—laborable, *adj.* arable. **—día
laborable,** workday; working
day.
laboratorio (la·βo·ra'to·rjo) *n.m.*
laboratory.
laborioso (la·βo'rjo·so) *adj.* **1,** laborious. **2,** industriousness. **—laboriosidad,** *n.f.* industriousness; industry.
laborista (la·βo'ris·ta) *n.m. & f.*
Laborite. **—partido laborista,** Labor Party.
labrado (la'βra·ðo) *adj.* **1,** tilled;
cultivated. **2,** wrought; worked.
—n.m. **1,** working; carving; forg-

ing. **2,** tillage. **3,** *usu.pl.* cultivated
land.
labrador (la·βra'ðor) *n.m.* **1,** farmer; peasant. **2,** farmhand.
labrantío (la·βran'ti·o) *n.m.* tillable land. *—adj.* tillable.
labranza (la'βran·θa; -sa) *n.f.* tillage; farming.
labrar (la'βrar) *v.t. & i.* **1,** to till. **2,**
to work; carve; forge. **3,** to build.
labriego (la'βrje·γo) *n.m.* farmhand; peasant.
laca ('la·ka) *n.f.* lac; lacquer; shellac.
lacayo (la'ka·jo) *n.m.* lackey.
lace ('la·θe; -se) *v., pres.subjve.* of
lazar.
lacé (la'θe; -'se) *v., 1st pers.sing.*
pret. of **lazar.**
lacear (la·θe'ar; la·se-) *v.t.* **1,** to
adorn or tie with bows. **2,** *Amer.* to
lasso.
lacerar (la·θe'rar; la·se-) *v.t.* to lacerate. **—laceración,** *n.f.* laceration.
lacio ('la·θjo; -sjo) *adj.* **1,** withered;
shriveled. **2,** flaccid; limp; weak. **3,**
straight; lank *(of hair).*
lacónico (la'ko·ni·ko) *adj.* laconic.
—laconismo (-'nis·mo) *n.m.* brevity.
lacra ('la·kra) *n.f.* **1,** scar. **2,** blemish; defect. **3,** *Amer.* scab. **4,** *fig.*
scum.
lacrar (la'krar) *v.t.* **1,** to impair the
health of. **2,** to seal *(with sealing
wax).*

lacre ('la·kre) *n.m.* sealing wax.

lacrimal (la·kri'mal) *adj.* lachrymal. —**lacrimoso** (-'mo·so) *adj.* lachrymose; tearful.

lacrimógeno (la·kri'mo·xe·no) *adj.* tear-producing. —**gas lacrimógeno,** tear gas.

lactar (lak'tar) *v.t. & i.* to suckle; nurse. —**lactación,** *also,* **lactancia,** *n.f.* lactation.

lácteo ('lak·te·o) *adj.* lacteal; milky. —**Vía Láctea,** Milky Way.

láctico ('lak·ti·ko) *adj.* lactic.

lactosa (lak'to·sa) *also,* **lactina** (-'ti·na) *n.f.* lactose.

ladeado (la·ðe'a·ðo) *adj.* **1,** tilted; lopsided. **2,** turned sideways.

ladear (la·ðe'ar) *v.t. & i.* to tilt; tip; lean. —*v.t.* to turn sideways. —*v.i.* to skirt around; go around the side.

ladeo (la'ðe·o) *n.m.* leaning; tilting; tilt.

ladera (la'ðe·ra) *n.f.* hillside; slope.

ladilla (la'ði·ʎa; -ja) *n.f.* crab louse.

ladino (la'ði·no) *adj.* sly; shifty.

lado ('la·ðo) *n.m.* **1,** side. **2,** direction. —**al lado,** alongside; next door. —**al lado de, 1,** next to; beside. **2,** on the side of. —**de lado,** sideways; tilted.

ladrar (la'ðrar) *v.i.* to bark. —**ladrido** (la'ðri·ðo) bark; barking.

ladrillo (la'ðri·ʎo; -jo) *n.m.* brick. —**ladrillado,** *n.m.* = **enladrillado.** —**ladrillar,** *n.m.* brickyard. —*v.t.* = **enladrillar.**

ladrón (la'ðron) *n.m.* thief. —*adj.* thieving; thievish.

ladronera (la·ðro'ne·ra) *n.f.* **1,** den of thieves. **2,** sluice gate.

lagaña (la'ya·ɲa) *n.f.* = **legaña.**

lagar (la'yar) *n.m.* **1,** wine press. **2,** winery.

lagartija (la·yar'ti·xa) *n.f.* a kind of small lizard.

lagarto (la'yar·to) *n.m.* **1,** lizard. **2,** *Mex.* alligator. **3,** *colloq.* sly person.

lago ('la·yo) *n.m.* lake.

lágrima ('la·yri·ma) *n.f.* tear; teardrop. —**lagrimal,** *adj.* lachrymal. —**lagrimar,** *v.i.* = **llorar.** —**lagrimoso,** *adj.* tearful; lachrymose.

lagrimear (la·yri·me'ar) *v.i.* **1,** to weep readily; be easily moved to tears. **2,** (of the eyes) to water; tear.

laguna (la'yu·na) *n.f.* **1,** lagoon; pond. **2,** lacuna.

laicismo (lai'θis·mo; -'sis·mo) *n.m.* secularism.

laico ('lai·ko) *adj.* lay; laic. *Also,* **laical.** —**laicado,** *n.m.* laity.

laja ('la·xa) *n.f.* slab; flagstone.

lama ('la·ma) *n.f.* **1,** slime; ooze. **2,** = **lamé.**

lama ('la·ma) *n.m.* lama. —**lamaísmo,** *n.m.* Lamaism. —**lamaísta,** *adj. & n.m. & f.* Lamaist. —**lamasería** (-se'ri·a) *n.f.* lamasery.

lamber (lam'ber) *v.t.* **1,** *Amer.* to lick. **2,** to fawn on; toady to.

lamé (la'me) *n.m., also,* **lama** ('la·ma) *n.f.* lamé.

lamedal (la·me'ðal) *n.m.* bog; quagmire.

lamedor (la·me'ðor) *adj.* **1,** licking. **2,** *fig. & colloq.* fawning; cajoling. —*n.m.* **1,** licker. **2,** syrup.

lamedura (la·me'ðu·ra) *n.f.* lick; licking.

lamentar (la·men'tar) *v.t. & i.* to lament. —**lamentable,** *adj.* lamentable. —**lamentación,** *n.f.* lamentation.

lamento (la'men·to) *n.m.* lament. —**lamentoso,** *adj.* plaintive; mournful.

lamer (la'mer) *v.t.* to lick; lap against.

lámina ('la·mi·na) *n.f.* **1,** plate; sheet. **2,** illustration; picture. **3,** stamp; die.

laminar (la·mi'nar) *v.t.* **1,** to laminate. **2,** to roll (metal) into sheets. —*adj.* laminate. —**laminado,** *adj.* laminated. —*n.m.* [*also,* **laminación,** *n.f.*] lamination.

lampa ('lam·pa) *n.f., Amer.* shovel. —**lampear** (-pe'ar) *v.t., Amer.* to shovel.

lampacear (lam·pa·θe'ar; -se'ar) *v.t., naut.* to mop; swab. —**lampazo,** *n.m., naut.* mop; swab.

lámpara ('lam·pa·ra) *n.f.* lamp.

lamparón (lam·pa'ron) *n.m.* **1,** grease spot. **2,** scrofula.

lampiño (lam'pi·ɲo) *adj.* beardless; hairless.

lamprea (lam'pre·a) *n.f.* lamprey. —**lamprea glutinosa,** hagfish.

lana ('la·na) *n.f.* wool. —**lanado,** *adj.* woolly; fleecy.

lanar (la'nar) *adj.* wool-producing; woolbearing. —**ganado lanar,** sheep.

lance ('lan·θe; -se) *n.m.* **1,** throw; cast. **2,** incident; episode; happening. **3,** situation; predicament. **4,** dispute; quarrel; fight. **5,** *Amer.*

chance; risk. —**de lance,** bargain
(*attrib.*); bought or sold at a bargain.

lance ('lan·θe; -se) *v., pres.subjve.
of* **lanzar.**

lancé (lan'θe; -'se) *v., 1st pers.
sing.pret. of* **lanzar.**

lancear (lan·θe'ar; lan·se-) *v.t.* to
pierce; wound, as with a lance.

lancero (lan'θe·ro; -'se·ro) *n.m.*
lancer.

lanceta (lan'θe·ta; -'se·ta) *n.f.* lancet; surgical knife. —**lancetada,** *n.f.
also,* **lancetazo,** *n.m.* cut; lancing;
incision.

lancha ('lan·tʃa) *n.f.* launch; boat.

lanchón (lan'tʃon) *n.m.* barge;
scow.

landa ('lan·da) *n.f.* moor; heath.

lanero (la'ne·ro) *adj.* woolen.
—*n.m.* **1,** wool dealer. **2,** wool
warehouse.

langaruto (lan·ga'ru·to) *adj.,
colloq.* = **larguirucho.**

langosta (lan'gos·ta) *n.f.* **1,** lobster. **2,** locust. —**langostín** (-'tin)
also, **langostino** (-'ti·no) *n.m.* crawfish.

languidecer (lan·gi·ðe'θer; -'ser)
v.i. [*infl.:* **conocer, 13**] to languish.
—**languidecimiento,** *n.m.* languishment.

lánguido ('lan·gi·ðo) *adj.* languid.
—**languidez,** *n.f.* languor; languidness.

lanilla (la'ni·ʎa; -ja) *n.f.* **1,** lightweight wool cloth. **2,** nap.

lanolina (la·no'li·na) *n.f.* lanolin.

lantano (lan'ta·no) *n.m.* lanthanum.

lanudo (la'nu·ðo) *adj.* woolly;
fleecy. *Also,* **lanoso** (-'no·so).

lanza ('lan·θa; -sa) *n.f.* lance; spear.

lanzada (lan'θa·ða; -'sa·ða) *n.f.* **1,**
thrust of a lance. **2,** wound from a
lance or spear. *Also,* **lanzazo**
(-'θa·θo; -'sa·so) *n.m.*

lanzadera (lan·θa'ðe·ra; lan·sa-)
n.f. shuttle of a loom or sewing machine.

lanzamiento (lan·θa'mjen·to;
lan·sa-) *n.m.* **1,** throwing; hurling.
2, ejection; ousting. **3,** launching.

lanzar (lan'θar; -'sar) *v.t.* [*infl.:*
rezar, 10] **1,** to hurl; throw. **2,** to
eject. **3,** to launch. —**lanzador,** *n.m.*
[*fem.* **-dora**] *baseball* pitcher.

lapa ('la·pa) *n.f.* **1,** *zoöl.* limpet. **2,**
Amer., colloq. hanger-on; leech.

lapicero (la·pi'θe·ro; -'se·ro) *n.m.,*

also, Amer. **lapicera,** *n.f.* mechanical pencil.

lápida ('la·pi·ða) *n.f.* **1,** tombstone.
2, stone tablet. **3,** stone slab.

lapidar (la·pi'ðar) *v.t.* **1,** to stone.
2, *Amer.* to cut (gems).

lapidario (la·pi'ða·rjo) *adj. &
n.m.* lapidary. —*adj.* concise; pithy.

lapislázuli (la·pis'la·θu·li; -su·li)
n.m. lapis lazuli.

lápiz ('la·piθ; -pis) *n.m.* pencil.
—**lápiz para los labios; lápiz de
labios,** lipstick.

lapón (la'pon) *adj. & n.m.* Lapp.

lapso ('lap·so) *n.m.* lapse.

laquear (la·ke'ar) *v.t.* to lacquer;
shellac.

lar (lar) *n.m.* **1,** hearth. **2,** *usu.pl.*
lares, home; family.

lardear (lar·ðe'ar) *also,* **lardar**
(-'ðar) *v.t.* **1,** to lard. **2,** to baste.

lardo ('lar·ðo) *n.m.* lard.

largar (lar'ɣar) *v.t.* [*infl.:* **pagar, 8**]
1, to let loose; let go. **2,** to unfurl.
—**largarse,** *v.r., colloq.* to get out;
leave.

largo ('lar·ɣo) *adj.* **1,** long. **2,** generous; liberal. **3,** abundant. —*n.m.*
1, length. **2,** *mus.* largo. —*adj. &
adv., mus.* largo. —*interj.* out!; get
out! —**a la larga, 1,** lengthwise. **2,**
at length. **3,** in the long run. —**a lo
largo, 1,** along; lengthwise. **2,** at
length. **3,** in the distance. —**de
largo,** in formal dress; full length.

largor (lar'ɣor) *n.m.* length.

largueza (lar'ɣe·θa; -sa) *n.f.* largess.

larguirucho (lar·ɣi'ru·tʃo) *adj.,
colloq.* lanky; gawky.

larguísimo (lar'ɣi·si·mo) *adj.*
very long.

largura (lar'ɣu·ra) *n.f.* extent;
length.

laringe (la'rin·xe) *n.f.* larynx.
—**laríngeo,** *adj.* laryngeal. —**laringitis** (-'xi·tis) *n.f.* laryngitis.

larva ('lar·βa) *n.f.* larva; grub.
—**larval,** *adj.* larval.

las (las) *def.art. fem.pl.* the. —*pers.
pron. fem.pl., used as dir.obj. of a
verb* them; you. —*dem.pron. fem.pl.*
those.

lascivo (las'θi·βo; la'si-) *adj.* lascivious. —**lascivia,** *n.f.* lasciviousness.

láser ('la·ser) *n.m.* laser. —**rayo
láser,** laser beam.

lasitud (la·si'tuð) *n.f.* lassitude.

lástima ('las·ti·ma) *n.f.* pity; compassion.

lastimadura (las·ti·ma'ðu·ra) *n.f.* hurt; injury.

lastimar (las·ti'mar) *v.t.* to hurt; injure.

lastimero (las·ti'me·ro) *adj.* mournful.

lastimoso (las·ti'mo·so) *adj.* pitiful.

lastra ('las·tra) *n.f.* slab; flagstone.

lastre ('las·tre) *n.m.* ballast; dead weight. —**lastrar,** *v.t.* to ballast.

lata ('la·ta) *n.f.* **1,** tin; tin plate; tin can. **2,** *colloq.* bore; nuisance.

latente (la'ten·te) *adj.* latent.

lateral (la·te'ral) *adj.* lateral.

látex ('la·teks) *n.m.* latex.

latido (la'ti·ðo) *n.m.* beat; throb.

latifundio (la·ti'fun·djo) *n.m.* landed estate. —**latifundista,** *n.m. & f.* large landowner.

látigo ('la·ti·ɣo) *n.m.* whip. —**latigazo,** *n.m.* lash; whiplash; crack of a whip.

latigudo (la·ti'ɣu·ðo) *adj., S.A.* = **correoso.**

latín (la'tin) *n.m.* Latin; Latin language. —**latinidad,** *n.f.* Latinity.

latinizar (la·ti·ni'θar; -'sar) *v.t. & i.* [*infl.:* **rezar,** 10] to Latinize. —**latinización,** *n.f.* Latinization.

latino (la'ti·no) *adj. & n.m.* Latin. —**vela latina,** lateen sail.

latinoamericano (la·ti·no·a·me·ri'ka·no) *adj. & n.m.* Latin American.

latir (la'tir) *v.i.* to beat; throb.

latitud (la·ti'tuð) *n.f.* latitude. —**latitudinal** (-ði'nal) *adj.* latitudinal.

lato ('la·to) *adj.* extended; broad.

latón (la'ton) *n.m.* brass. —**latonería,** *n.f.* brass shop; brass works. —**latonero,** *n.m.* brazier; brass dealer.

latoso (la'to·so) *adj., colloq.* annoying; boring.

latrina (la'tri·na) *n.f.* = **letrina.**

latrocinio (la·tro'θi·njo; -'si·njo) *n.m.* larceny; theft.

laucha ('lau·tʃa) *n.f., Amer.* mouse. —*adj., Amer., colloq.* shifty; shrewd.

laúd (la'uð) *n.m.* **1,** lute. **2,** catboat.

laudable (lau'ða·βle) *adj.* laudable.

láudano ('lau·ða·no) *n.m.* laudanum.

laudatorio (lau·ða'to·rjo) *adj.* laudatory.

laureado (lau·re·a'ðo) *adj. & n.m.* laureate.

laurear (lau·re'ar) *v.t.* to honor.

laurel (lau'rel) *n.m.* **1,** laurel. **2,** honor; distinction. —**lauredal** (lau·re'ðal) *n.m.* laurel grove.

laurencio (lau'ren·θjo; -sjo) *n.m.* lawrencium.

lauréola (lau're·o·la) *n.f.* laurel wreath.

lauro ('lau·ro) *n.m.* honor; glory; praise.

lava ('la·βa) *n.f.* lava.

lavable (la'βa·βle) *adj.* washable.

lavabo (la'βa·βo) *n.m.* **1,** washstand. **2,** lavatory.

lavadero (la·βa'ðe·ro) *n.m.* washing place; laundry shed.

lavado (la'βa·ðo) *n.m.* wash; washing. *Also,* **lavada,** *n.f.* —**lavado en seco,** dry cleaning.

lavadora (la·βa'ðo·ra) *n.f.* washer; washing machine.

lavadura (la·βa'ðu·ra) *n.f.* **1,** washing. **2,** dishwater; dirty water.

lavamanos (la·βa'ma·nos) *n.m. sing. & pl.* washstand; washbowl.

lavanda (la'βan·da) *n.f.* lavender.

lavandera (la·βan'de·ra) *n.f.* laundress. —**lavandería,** *n.f.* laundry. —**lavandero,** *n.m.* launderer.

lavaplatos (la·βa'pla·tos) *n.m. & f. sing. & pl.* dishwasher.

lavar (la'βar) *v.t.* **1,** to wash. **2,** *fig.* to wash away. —**lavar en seco,** to dry-clean.

lavarropas (la·βa'rro·pas) *n.m. sing. & pl.* washing machine.

lavativa (la·βa'ti·βa) *n.f.* **1,** enema. **2,** syringe. **3,** *colloq.* nuisance; annoyance.

lavatorio (la·βa'to·rjo) *n.m.* **1,** wash; washing. **2,** washbowl. **3,** *Amer.* washroom; lavatory.

lavazas (la'βa·θas; -sas) *n.f.pl.* wash water.

laxante (lak'san·te) *also,* **laxativo** (-'ti·βo) *adj.* loosening; slackening. —*adj. & n.m.* laxative.

laxar (lak'sar) *v.t.* to loosen; slacken.

laxo ('lak·so) *adj.* lax. —**laxitud,** *n.f.* laxity; laxness.

lay (lai) *n.m., hist.* lay; ballad.

laya ('la·ja) *n.f.* **1,** sort; kind. **2,** garden spade. —**layar,** *v.t.* to spade; dig with a spade.

lazada (la'θa·ða; -'sa·ða) *n.f.* bow; bowknot.

lazar (la'θar; -'sar) *v.t.* [*infl.:* **rezar,** 10] to lasso; rope.

lazarillo (la·θa'ri·ʎo; la·sa'ri·jo) *n.m.* blindman's guide.

lázaro ('la·θa·ro; 'la·sa-) *n.m.* **1,** beggar. **2,** leper.

lazo ('la·θo; -so) *n.m.* **1,** bow; loop. **2,** lasso. **3,** bond; tie. **4,** trap; snare.

le (le) *pers.pron.m. & f.sing.* **1,** used as dir.obj. of a verb him. **2,** used as indir.obj. of a verb to him; to her; to it; to you.

leal (le'al) *adj.* loyal. —**lealtad,** *n.f.* loyalty.

lebrato (le'βra·to) *n.m.* young hare.

lebrel (le'βrel) *n.m.* whippet.

lebrillo (le'βri·ʎo; -jo) *n.m.* earthenware tub.

lebrón (le'βron) *n.m.* **1,** large hare. **2,** *colloq.* coward.

lebruno (le'βru·no) *adj.* leporine.

lección (lek'θjon; -'sjon) *n.f.* lesson.

lecitina (le·θi'ti·na; le·si-) *n.f.* lecithin.

lector (lek'tor) *n.m.* **1,** reader. **2,** lecturer. —*adj.* fond of reading.

lectura (lek'tu·ra) *n.f.* reading.

lecha ('le·tʃa) *n.f.,ichthy.* **1,** milt. **2,** milt sac.

lechada (le'tʃa·ða) *n.f.* **1,** thin grout. **2,** paper pulp. **3,** whitewash.

leche ('le·tʃe) *n.f.* milk. —**tener leche,** *Amer., colloq.* to be lucky; have luck.

lechera (le'tʃe·ra) *n.f.* **1,** milkmaid. **2,** milk can; milk pitcher. —*adj. fem.* milch.

lechería (le·tʃe'ri·a) *n.f.* dairy.

lechero (le'tʃe·ro) *n.m.* milkman. —*adj.* **1,** of milk; milk *(attrib.).* **2,** milch. **3,** *Amer., colloq.* lucky.

lechigada (le·tʃi'ɣa·ða) *n.f.* litter *(of animals).*

lecho ('le·tʃo) *n.m.* **1,** bed. **2,** straw bedding.

lechón (le'tʃon) *n.m.* **1,** suckling pig. **2,** *colloq.* babe in the woods.

lechosa (le'tʃo·sa) *n.f.* papaya.

lechoso (le'tʃo·so) *adj.* milky.

lechuga (le'tʃu·ɣa) *n.f.* lettuce.

lechuguilla (le·tʃu'ɣi·ʎa; -ja) *n.f.* **1,** wild lettuce. **2,** frill; frilled collar; ruff.

lechuza (le'tʃu·θa; -sa) *n.f.* owl.

leer (le'er) *v.t.* [*infl.:* **creer,** 42] to read.

legacía (le·ɣa'θi·a; -'si·a) *n.f.* legateship.

legación (le·ɣa'θjon; -'sjon) *n.f.* legation.

legado (le'ɣa·ðo) *n.m.* **1,** legate. **2,** legacy.

legajo (le'ɣa·xo) *n.m.* sheaf *(of papers or documents).*

legal (le'ɣal) *adj.* legal. —**legalidad,** *n.f.* legality.

legalizar (le·ɣa·li'θar; -'sar) *v.t.* [*infl.:* **rezar,** 10] to legalize. —**legalización,** *n.f.* legalization.

légamo ('le·ɣa·mo) *n.m.* silt; mud. —**legamoso,** *adj.* silty; muddy.

legaña (le'ɣa·ɲa) *n.f.* eye secretion; rheum. —**legañoso,** *adj.* blear-eyed; bleary.

legar (le'ɣar) *v.t.* [*infl.:* **pagar,** 8] **1,** to bequeath. **2,** to send as envoy.

legatario (le·ɣa'ta·rjo) *n.m.* legatee.

legendario (le·xen'da·rjo) *adj.* legendary.

legible (le'xi·βle) *adj.* legible. —**legibilidad,** *n.f.* legibility.

legión (le'xjon) *n.f.* legion. —**legionario,** *adj.* legionary. —*n.m.* legionnaire.

legislar (le·xis'lar) *v.t. & i.* to legislate. —**legislación,** *n.f.* legislation. —**legislador,** *n.m.* legislator. —**legislativo,** *adj.* legislative. —**legislatura,** *n.f.* legislature.

legista (le'xis·ta) *n.m. & f.* legal expert; student of the law.

legitimar (le·xi·ti'mar) *v.t.* to legitimize. —**legitimación,** *n.f.* legitimation.

legítimo (le'xi·ti·mo) *adj.* **1,** legitimate. **2,** genuine. —**legitimidad,** *n.f.* legitimacy.

lego (le'ɣo) *adj.* **1,** laic; lay. **2,** uninformed; ignorant. —*n.m.* **1,** layman. **2,** lay brother.

legua ('le·ɣwa) *n.f.* league *(measure).*

legue ('le·ɣe) *v., pres.subjve.* of **legar.**

legué (le'ɣe) *v., 1st pers.sing. pret.* of **legar.**

leguleyo (le·ɣu'le·jo) *n.m.* dabbler at law; shyster.

legumbre (le'ɣum·bre) *n.f.* **1,** legume. **2,** vegetable *(edible).* —**leguminoso** (le·ɣu·mi'no·so) *adj.* leguminous.

leí (le'i) *v., 1st pers.sing. pret.* of **leer.**

leíble (le'i·βle) *adj.* **1,** legible. **2,** readable.

leída (le'i·ða) *n.f.* reading.

leído (le'i·ðo) *v., p.p.* of **leer.** —*adj.* well-read.

lejano (le'xa·no) *adj.* distant; remote. —**lejanía,** *n.f.* distance; remoteness.

lejía (le'xi·a) *n.f.* lye.
lejos ('le·xos) *adv.* far; afar; far off. —**a lo lejos**, in the distance; far away. —**de lejos; desde lejos**, from afar; from a distance.
lelo ('le·lo) *also, Amer.* **lele** ('le·le) *adj.* **1,** slow-witted; doltish. **2,** stupefied; aghast. —*n.m.* ninny; dolt.
lema ('le·ma) *n.m.* **1,** motto; slogan. **2,** theme. **3,** caption.
lémur ('le·mur) *n.m.* lemur.
lencería (len·θe'ri·a; len·se-) *n.f.* **1,** dry goods. **2,** dry goods store. **3,** lingerie.
lene ('le·ne) *adj.* soft; mild; gentle; light.
lengua ('len·gwa) *n.f.* **1,** tongue. **2,** language. —**lengua materna**, mother tongue.
lenguado (len'gwa·ðo) *n.m., ichthy.* sole; flounder.
lenguaje (len'gwa·xe) *n.m.* language; idiom; speech.
lenguaraz (len·gwa'raθ; -'ras) *adj.* foulmouthed; loose-tongued.
lengüeta (len'gwe·ta) *n.f.* **1,** tongue (*of a shoe*). **2,** pin (*of a buckle*). **3,** pointer (*of a scale*). **4,** *mus.* tongue; reed. **5,** epiglottis. **6,** *carp.* tongue.
lengüetada (len·gwe'ta·ða) *n.f.* lick; lap. *Also,* **lengüetazo,** *n.m.*
lenidad (le·ni'ðað) *n.f.* leniency.
lenitivo (le·ni'ti·βo) *adj. & n.m.* emollient. —*n.m., fig.* salve; balm; relief.
lentamente (len·ta'men·te) *adv.* slowly.
lente ('len·te) *n.m. or f.* lens. —**lentes,** *n.m.pl.* eyeglasses.
lenteja (len'te·xa) *n.f.* lentil.
lentejuela (len·te'xwe·la) *n.f.* spangle.
lenticular (len·ti·ku'lar) *adj.* lenticular.
lento ('len·to) *adj.* slow; sluggish; tardy. —*adj. & adv., mus.* lento. —**lentitud,** *n.f.* slowness; sluggishness; tardiness.
leña ('le·ɲa) *n.f.* **1,** firewood; kindling. **2,** *colloq.* drubbing. —**leñador,** *n.m.* woodcutter; woodman. —**leñera,** *n.f.* woodshed.
leño ('le·ɲo) *n.m.* timber; heavy piece of wood. —**leñoso,** *adj.* woody; ligneous.
Leo ('le·o) *n.m., astron.* Leo.
león (le'on) *n.m.* lion. —**leona** (le'o·na) *n.f.* lioness.
leonado (le·o'na·ðo) *adj.* tawny; yellowish brown.
leonera (le·o'ne·ra) *n.f.* **1,** lion's cage. **2,** *colloq.* untidy room. **3,** *colloq.* gambling den.
leonino (le·o'ni·no) *adj.* leonine.
leontina (le·on'ti·na) *n.f., Amer.* watch chain.
leopardo (le·o'par·ðo) *n.m.* leopard.
leotardo (le·o'tar·ðo) *n.m.* leotard.
lépero ('le·pe·ro) *adj., Amer.* **1,** vulgar; coarse. **2,** *W.I.* shrewd; sly.
leporino (le·po'ri·no) *adj.* leporine. —**labio leporino,** harelip.
lepra ('le·pra) *n.f.* leprosy. —**leproso,** *adj.* leprous. —*n.m.* leper.
lerdo ('ler·ðo) *adj.* **1,** slow; dull. **2,** clumsy.
les (les) *pers.pron.m. & f.pl.* **1,** *used as dir.obj. of a verb* them; you. **2,** *used as ind.obj. of a verb* to them; to you.
lesa ('le·sa) **majestad** lese majesty.
lesbiano (les'βja·no) *adj. & n.m.* lesbian. *Also,* **lesbio** ('les·βjo). —**lesbia,** *n.f.* lesbian; homosexual woman.
lesión (le'sjon) *n.f.* lesion. —**lesionar,** *v.t.* to injure; wound.
lesna ('les·na) *n.f.* = **lezna.**
leso ('le·so) *adj.* injured; wronged.
letal (le'tal) *adj.* lethal.
letanía (le·ta'ni·a) *n.f.* litany.
letargo (le'tar·yo) *n.m.* lethargy. —**letárgico** (-xi·ko) *adj.* lethargic.
letra ('le·tra) *n.f.* **1,** letter (*written character*). **2,** handwriting. **3,** words of a song; lyrics. —**al pie de la letra; a la letra,** to the letter; literally. —**letra de cambio,** bill of exchange. —**letra de imprenta,** type. —**letra de molde,** printed letter. —**letra magnética,** laser printing. —**letra negrilla,** boldface. —**letras humanas,** humanities.
letrado (le'tra·ðo) *adj.* learned; erudite. —*n.m.* lawyer.
letrero (le'tre·ro) *n.m.* poster; sign.
letrina (le'tri·na) *n.f.* latrine; privy.
leucemia (leu'θe·mja; -'se·mja) *n.f.* leukemia.
leucocito (leu·ko'θi·to; -'si·to) *n.m.* leucocyte.
leudar (leu'ðar) *v.t.* to leaven. —**leudarse,** *v.r.* to ferment, as a leaven. —**leudo** ('leu·ðo) *adj.* leavened.
leva ('le·βa) *n.f.* **1,** departure (*from port*); weighing of anchor. **2,** levy (*of troops*). **3,** cam.
levadizo (le·βa'ði·θo; -so) *adj.*

that can be raised. —**puente levadizo,** drawbridge; lift bridge.

levadura (le·βa'ðu·ra) *n.f.* yeast; leaven.

levantar (le·βan'tar) *v.t.* **1,** to raise; lift. **2,** to recruit. **3,** to erect. **4,** to clear (the table). —**levantarse,** *v.r.* to rise. —**levantado,** *adj.* elevated; high; sublime. —**levantamiento,** *n.m.* uprising.

levante (le'βan·te) *n.m.* East; Orient; Levant. —**levantino,** *adj.* & *n.m.* Levantine.

levar (le'βar) *v.t.* to weigh (anchor). —**levarse,** *v.r.* to set sail.

leve ('le·βe) *adj.* **1,** light; of little weight. **2,** slight; of little importance.

levedad (le·βe'ðað) *n.f.* **1,** levity. **2,** lightness; unimportance.

leviatán (le·βja'tan) *n.m.* leviathan.

levita (le'βi·ta) *n.m.* Levite. —*n.f.* frock coat. —**levítico,** *adj.* Levitical.

levitación (le·βi·ta'θjon; -'sjon) *n.f.* levitation.

léxico ('lek·si·ko) *n.m.* [*also,* **lexicón** (-'kon)] lexicon. —*adj.* lexical.

lexicografía (lek·si·ko·ɣra'fi·a) *n.f.* lexicography. —**lexicográfico** (-'ɣra·fi·ko) *adj.* lexicographic. —**lexicógrafo** (-'ko·ɣra·fo) *n.m.* lexicographer.

ley (lei) *n.f.* **1,** law. **2,** rule; norm. **3,** legal standard. **4,** loyalty; devotion. **5,** fineness (*of metals*). —**mala ley,** animosity; dislike.

leyenda (le'jen·da) *n.f.* legend.

leyendo (le'jen·do) *v., ger. of* **leer.**

leyó (le'jo) *v., 3rd pers.sing. pret. of* **leer.**

lezna ('leθ·na; 'les-) *n.f.* awl.

liar (li'ar) *v.t.* [*infl.:* **enviar, 22**] **1,** to bind; tie; bundle. **2,** to embroil. —**liarse,** *v.r.* to become involved.

libar (li'βar) *v.t.* to sip; taste; savor. —*v.i.* to make a libation. —**libación,** *n.f.* libation.

libelo (li'βe·lo) *n.m.* libel. —**libelista,** *n.m.* & *f.* libeler.

libélula (li'βe·lu·la) *n.f.* dragonfly.

liberación (li·βe·ra'θjon; -'sjon) *n.f.* **1,** liberation. **2,** *law* quittance.

liberal (li·βe'ral) *adj.* & *n.m.* & *f.* liberal. —**liberalismo,** *n.m.* liberalism.

liberalidad (li·βe·ra·li'ðað) *n.f.* liberality.

liberalizar (li·βe·ra·li'θar; -'sar)

v.t. [*infl.:* **rezar, 10**] to liberalize. —**liberalización,** *n.f.* liberalization.

liberar (li·βe'rar) *v.t.* to free; liberate; exempt.

libérrimo (li'βe·rri·mo) *adj., superl. of* **libre.**

libertad (li·βer'tað) *n.f.* liberty; freedom.

libertar (li·βer'tar) *v.t.* to liberate; free. —**libertador,** *n.m.* liberator. —*adj.* liberating.

libertario (li·βer'ta·rjo) *adj.* & *n.m.* libertarian.

libertino (li·βer'ti·no) *adj.* & *n.m.* libertine. —**libertinaje,** *n.m.* licentiousness.

liberto (li'βer·to) *n.m.* emancipated slave; freedman.

libídine (li'βi·ði·ne) *n.f.* lust; lewdness. —**libidinoso,** *adj.* libidinous.

libido (li'βi·ðo) *n.m.* libido.

libra ('li·βra) *n.f.* **1,** pound. **2,** *cap., astron.* Libra.

librado (li'βra·ðo) *n.m., comm.* drawee.

librador (li·βra'ðor) *n.m.* **1,** deliverer. **2,** *comm.* drawer (*of a draft or check*).

libramiento (li·βra'mjen·to) *n.m.* **1,** delivery; deliverance. **2,** *comm.* draft.

libranza (li'βran·θa; -sa) *n.f.* draft; bill of exchange. —**libranza postal,** money order.

librar (li'βrar) *v.t.* **1,** to free; deliver. **2,** to exempt. **3,** to issue; draw up. **4,** *comm.* to draw (a draft or check). **5,** to give (battle). —*v.i.* to deliver; give birth. —**librarse,** *v.r., fol. by* **de, 1,** to get out from; free oneself from. **2,** to avoid; keep away from. —**librarse de buena,** *colloq.* to have a close call. —**salir bien librado,** to get out (of something) well. —**salir mal librado,** to come out badly.

libre ('li·βre) *adj.* **1,** free. **2,** vacant; available. —*n.m., Mex.* taxi.

librea (li'βre·a) *n.f.* livery. —**de librea,** liveried.

librepensador (li·βre·pen·sa·'ðor) *n.m.* freethinker. —**libre pensamiento,** free thought.

librería (li·βre'ri·a) *n.f.* **1,** bookstore. **2,** bookshelf; bookcase.

librero (li'βre·ro) *n.m.* **1,** bookseller. **2,** *Amer.* bookcase.

libreta (li'βre·ta) *n.f.* notebook.

libreto (li'βre·to) *n.m.* libretto. —**libretista,** *n.m.* & *f.* librettist.

libro ('li·βro) *n.m.* book. —**libro borrador**, blotter. —**libro copiador**, *comm.* letter book. —**libro de actas**, minute book. —**libro de asiento** *or* **de cuentas**, account book. —**libro de caja**, cashbook. —**libro de memoria**, memorandum book. —**libro diario**, *comm.* journal. —**libro mayor**, ledger.

licántropo (li·kan·tro·po) *n.m.* werewolf.

licencia (li'θen·θja; li·sɛn·sja) *n.f.* 1, license. 2, leave of absence. 3, leave; furlough. 4, *mil.* discharge. 5, licentiousness.

licenciado (li·θen'θja·ðo; -sen'sja·ðo) *n.m.* 1, person licensed in a profession. 2, *Amer.* lawyer. 3, holder of a master's degree. 4, discharged soldier.

licenciar (li·θen'θjar; -sen'sjar) *v.t.* 1, to license. 2, *mil.* to discharge. —**licenciarse**, *v.r.* to graduate; earn a master's degree. —**licenciatura**, *n.f.* master's degree. *Mex.*, bachelor's degree.

licencioso (li·θen'θjo·so; li·sen'sjo-) *adj.* licentious.

liceo (li'θe·o; -'se·o) *n.m.* 1, lyceum. 2, high school.

licitar (li·θi'tar; li·si-) *v.t.* to bid for. —**licitación**, *n.f.* bid; bidding. —**licitador**, *also*, **licitante**, *n.m.* bidder.

lícito ('li·θi·to; 'li·si-) *adj.* lawful; licit; permitted.

licor (li'kor) *n.m.* 1, liquor. 2, liqueur.

licuar (li'kwar) *v.t.* [*infl.:* **continuar**, 23] to liquefy. —**licuable**, *adj.* liquefiable. —**licuación**, *also*, **licuefacción** (li·kwe·fak'θjon; -'sjon) *n.f.* liquefaction. —**licuado**, fruit drink/shake. —**licuadora**, *n.f.* blender; liquefier.

licuescente (li·kwes'θen·te; -kwe'sen·te) *adj.* liquescent. —**licuescencia**, *n.f.* liquescence.

lid (lið) *n.f.* struggle; fray.

líder ('li·ðer) *n.m.* leader.

lidia ('li·ðja) *n.f.* fight, esp. bull-fight.

lidiar (li'ðjar) *v.i.* to fight; contend; struggle. —*v.t.* to fight, esp. a bull. —**lidiador**, *n.m.* [*fem.* **-dora**] fighter; combatant.

líe ('li·e) *v. pres.subjve.* of **liar**.

lié (li'e) *v. 1st pers.sing. pret.* of **liar**.

liebre ('lje·βre) *n.f.* hare; *(fig.)* coward. —**dar gato por liebre**, to swindle.

lienzo ('ljen·θo; -so) *n.m.* 1, linen or cotton cloth. 2, canvas.

liga ('li·ɣa) *n.f.* 1, league; alliance. 2, garter. 3, alloy. 4, band; rubber band. —**hacer ligas con**, to get along with.

ligado (li'ɣa·ðo) *adj. & adv., mus.* legato. —*n.m.* ligature.

ligadura (li·ɣa'ðu·ra) *n.f.* 1, ligature. 2, bond; tie. 3, tourniquet

ligamento (li·ɣa'men·to) *n.m.* ligament.

ligar (li'ɣar) *v.t.* [*infl.:* **pagar**, 8] 1, to bind; tie. 2, to alloy. 3, *Amer., colloq.* to get (something) by chance. —*v.i., cards* to draw matching cards; fill in. —**ligarse**, *v.r.* to ally; associate.

ligazón (li·ɣa'θon;* -'son) *n.f.* union; bond.

ligereza (li·xe're·θa; -sa) *n.f.* 1, lightness. 2, swiftness. 3, frivolity; levity.

ligero (li'xe·ro) *adj.* 1, light; slight. 2, swift; nimble; fast. 3, fickle. —*adv., Amer.* fast. —**a la ligera**, recklessly. —**ligero de cascos**, lightheaded. —**ligero de lengua**, loose-tongued.

lignito (liɣ'ni·to) *n.m.* lignite.

ligue ('li·ɣe) *v., pres.subjve.* of **ligar**.

ligué (li'ɣe) *v., 1st pers.sing. pret.* of **ligar**.

lija ('li·xa) *n.f.* sandpaper. —**lijar**, *v.t.* to sandpaper.

lila ('li·la) *n.f.* lilac.

lima ('li·ma) *n.f.* 1, lime. 2, lime tree. 3, file (*tool*).

limar (li'mar) *v.t.* to file; smooth. —**limar asperezas**, to smooth over differences.

limaza (li'ma·θa; -sa) *n.f.* snail; slug.

limbo ('lim·bo) *n.m.* 1, limbo. 2, edge; hem.

limero (li'me·ro) *n.m.* lime tree.

limitar (li·mi'tar) *v.t.* to limit; to bound; to restrict. —*v.i.* to border; abut. —**limitación**, *n.f.* limitation.

límite ('li·mi·te) *n.m.* limit; boundary; border.

limítrofe (li'mi·tro·fe) *adj.* bordering; contiguous.

limo ('li·mo) *n.m.* mud; slime.

limón (li'mon) *n.m.* 1, lemon. 2, lemon tree. —**limonada**, *n.f.* lemonade. —**limonar**, *n.m.* lemon grove. **—limonero,** *n.m.* lemon tree.

limosna (li'mos·na) *n.f.* alms.

limosnero (li·mos'ne·ro) *adj.* charitable. **—***n.m.* **1,** almoner. **2,** beggar.

limousine (li·mu'sin) *n.m.* limousine.

limpiabotas (lim·pja'βo·tas) *n.m.sing.* & *pl.* bootblack.

limpiachimeneas (lim·pja·tʃi·me'ne·as) *n.m.* & *f. sing.* & *pl.* chimney sweep.

limpianieves (lim·pja'nje·βes) *n.m.sing.* & *pl.* snowplow.

limpiaparabrisas (lim·pja·pa·ra'βri·sas) *n.m.sing.* & *pl.* windshield wiper.

limpiar (lim'pjar) *v.t.* to clean; cleanse. **—limpiador,** *n.m.* cleaner; cleanser. **—limpiar en seco,** to dry-clean.

límpido ('lim·pi·ðo) *adj.* limpid. **—limpidez,** *n.f.* limpidity.

limpieza (lim'pje·θa; -sa) *n.f.* **1,** cleaning. **2,** cleanliness. **3,** *fig.* integrity; honesty. **—limpieza en seco,** dry cleaning.

limpio ('lim·pjo) *adj.* **1,** clean; neat. **2,** clear; pure. **3,** honest; upright. **—en limpio,** free and clear; net. **—quedar limpio,** *colloq.* to go broke; be cleaned out.

linaje (li'na·xe) *n.m.* **1,** lineage. **2,** family; line.

linaza (li'na·θa; -sa) *n.f.* linseed; flaxseed.

lince ('lin·θe; -se) *n.m.* **1,** lynx. **2,** *colloq.* sharp person. **—adj.** sharp-eyed; shrewd.

linchar (lin'tʃar) *v.t.* to lynch. **—linchamiento,** *n.f.* lynching.

lindar (lin'dar) *v.i.* to border; adjoin. **—lindante,** *adj.* contiguous; bordering.

linde ('lin·de) *n.m.* & *f.* boundary; limit. **—lindero,** *n.m.* limit; boundary. **—adj.** contiguous; bordering.

lindo ('lin·do) *adj.* pretty; comely; handsome. **—lindeza,** *also,* **lindura,** *n.f.* prettiness; comeliness.

línea ('li·ne·a) *n.f.* line. **—lineal,** *adj.* lineal; linear. **—lineamento,** *n.m.* lineament. **—guardar la línea,** to keep one's figure. **—línea aérea,** airline. **—línea política,** policy. **—línea de montaje,** assembly line. **—línea de tiro,** line of fire.

linear (li·ne'ar) *v.t.* to line; draw lines on. **—adj.** linear.

linfa ('lin·fa) *n.f.* lymph. **—linfático** (-'fa·ti·ko) *adj.* lymphatic.

lingote (lin'go·te) *n.f.* ingot.

lingual (lin'gwal) *adj.* lingual.

lingüista (lin'gwis·ta) *n.m.* & *f.* linguist. **—lingüística,** *n.f.* linguistics. **—lingüístico,** *adj.* linguistic.

linimento (li·ni'men·to) *n.m.* liniment.

lino ('li·no) *n.m.* **1,** flax. **2,** linen.

linóleo (li'no·le·o) *n.m.* linoleum.

linón (li'non) *n.m.* lawn (*fabric*).

linotipia (li·no'ti·pja) *n.f.* linotype (*machine*). **—linotipista** (-'ti'pis·ta) *n.m.* & *f.* linotypist. **—linotipo** (-'ti·po) *n.m.* linotype (*plate*).

linterna (lin'ter·na) *n.f.* lantern; flashlight.

liño ('li·ɲo) *n.m.* row of trees or plants.

lío ('li·o) *n.m.* **1,** bundle; pack. **2,** *colloq.* mess; muddle. **3,** *colloq.* trouble; row. **—v.,** *1st pers.sing. pres.ind. of* liar.

liquen (li'ken) *n.m.* lichen.

liquidación (li·ki·ða'θjon; -'sjon) *n.f.* **1,** liquidation. **2,** *comm.* clearance; clearance sale.

liquidar (li·ki'ðar) *v.t.* **1,** to liquidate. **2,** *comm.* to close out. **3,** *comm.* to settle; close (an account). **—liquidable,** *adj.,* *comm.* liquid; fluid (*of assets*).

líquido ('li·ki·ðo) *adj.* **1,** liquid; fluid. **2,** *comm.* net; clear. **—***n.m.* **1,** liquid. **2,** *comm.* net; balance. **—liquidez,** *n.f.* liquidity.

lira ('li·ra) *n.f.* **1,** lyre. **2,** lira.

lírico ('li·ri·ko) *adj.* lyric; lyrical. **—***n.m.* lyricist. **—lírica,** *n.f.* lyric poetry. **—lirismo,** *n.m.* lyricism.

lirio ('li·rjo) *n.m.* lily.

lirón (li'ron) *n.m.* dormouse.

lisiar (li'sjar) *v.t.* to maim; cripple. **—lisiado,** *adj.* crippled; maimed. **—***n.m.* cripple.

liso (li'so) *adj.* **1,** smooth; even. **2,** simple; plain. **3,** *Amer., colloq.* impudent; fresh.

lisonja (li'son·xa) *n.f.* flattery; fawning. **—lisonjear,** *v.t.* to flatter; fawn on. **—lisonjero,** *adj.* flattering. **—***n.m.* flatterer.

lista ('lis·ta) *n.f.* **1,** list; roll. **2,** strip; stripe. **3,** *law* docket. **—listado,** *adj.* striped. **—pasar lista,** to call roll.

listar (lis'tar) *v.t.* **1,** to list; enter in a list. **2,** *Amer.* to stripe; streak.

listo ('lis·to) *adj.* **1,** ready; prompt.

2, clever; cunning. —**listeza,** n.f. cleverness; cunning.

listón (lis'ton) n.m. lath.

listonado (lis·to'na·ðo) n.m. lathing; lathwork.

lisura (li'su·ra) n.f. **1,** smoothness; evenness. **2,** Amer. impudence.

litera (li'te·ra) n.f. **1,** litter (portable bed). **2,** berth.

literal (li·te'ral) adj. literal.

literario (li·te'ra·rjo) adj. literary.

literato (li·te'ra·to) adj. literate. —n.m. writer; pl. literati.

literatura (li·te·ra'tu·ra) n.f. literature.

litigar (li·ti'ɣar) v.t. & i, [infl.: **pagar,** 8] to litigate. —**litigación,** n.f. litigation. —**litigante,** adj. & n.m. & f. litigant. —**litigio** (li'ti·xjo) n.m. lawsuit; litigation. —**litigioso,** adj. litigious.

litio ('li·tjo) n.m. lithium.

litografía (li·to·ɣra'fi·a) n.f. **1,** lithography. **2,** lithograph. —**litográfico** (-'ɣra·fi·ko) adj. lithographic. —**litógrafo** (-'to·ɣra·fo) n.m. lithographer.

litografiar (li·to·ɣra'fjar) v.t. [infl.: **enviar,** 22] to lithograph.

litoral (li·to'ral) adj. & n.m. littoral.

litorina (li·to'ri·na) n.f., zoöl. periwinkle.

litosfera (li·tos'fe·ra) n.f. lithosphere.

litro ('li·tro) n.m. **1,** liter. **2,** W.I. quart.

liturgia (li'tur·xja) n.f. liturgy. —**litúrgico** (-xi·ko) adj. liturgical.

liviandad (li·βjan'daθ) adj. **1,** lightness. **2,** frivolity.

liviano (li'βja·no) adj. **1,** light; slight. **2,** frivolous.

lívido ('li·βi·ðo) adj. livid. —**lividez,** n.f. lividness.

liza ('li·θa; -sa) n.f. **1,** lists. **2,** = **lid.**

lo (lo) def.art. neut.sing., used with adjs. & advs. the: lo bueno, the good; a lo más temprano, at the earliest; that matter: lo que deseo, what I want; lo de Zuriaga, that matter of Zuriaga. —pers.pron. masc. & neut.sing., used as dir.obj. of a verb him; you; it. —adverbial qualifier, used with adjs. & advs. how: Se ve lo hermoso que es, One can see how beautiful it is. Tú no sabes lo fuerte que trabajo, You don't know how hard I'm working.

loa ('lo·a) n.f. praise; panegyric. —**loable,** adj. praiseworthy. —**loar** (lo'ar) v.t. to praise; extol.

loba ('lo·βa) n.f. she-wolf.

lobanillo (lo·βa'ni·ʎo; -jo) n.m. wen.

lobato (lo'βa·to) n.m. wolf cub.

lobero (lo'βe·ro) adj. wolfish. —n.m. wolf hunter.

lobo ('lo·βo) n.m. **1,** wolf. **2,** lobe.

lobotomía (lo·βo·to'mi·a) n.f. lobotomy.

lóbrego ('lo·βre·ɣo) adj. dark; tenebrous. —**lobreguez** (-'ɣeθ; 'ɣes) n.f. darkness; gloominess.

lóbulo ('lo·βu·lo) n.m. lobule; lobe.

locación (lo·ka'θjon; -'sjon) n.f. rental; leasing.

local (lo'kal) adj. local. —n.m. place; premises. —**localidad,** n.f. locality; location.

localización (lo·ka·li·θa'θjon -sa'sjon) n.f. **1,** localization. **2,** location.

localizar (lo·ka·li'θar; -'sar) v.t. [infl.: **rezar,** 10] **1,** to localize. **2,** to locate.

locatario (lo·ka'ta·rjo) n.m. tenant; lessee.

loción (lo'θjon; -'sjon) n.f. lotion.

loco ('lo·ko) adj. insane; mad. —n.m. madman. —**loca,** n.f. madwoman. —**a tontas y a locas,** colloq. any old way. —**hacerse el loco,** to play dumb. —**loco rematado,** colloq. stark, raving mad.

locomoción (lo·ko·mo'θjon; -'sjon) n.f. locomotion.

locomotor (lo·ko·mo'tor) also, **locomotriz** (-'triθ; -'tris) adj. locomotor; locomotive. —**locomotora,** n.f. locomotive.

locuaz (lo'kwaθ; -'kwas) adj. loquacious. —**locuacidad** (-θi'ðaθ; -si'ðað) n.f. loquacity.

locución (lo·ku'θjon; -'sjon) n.f. locution.

locura (lo'ku·ra) n.f. madness; insanity; folly.

locutor (lo·ku'tor) n.m., radio; TV [fem. **-tora**] announcer; speaker.

lodazal (lo·ða'θal; -'sal) n.m. muddy ground; mudhole.

lodo ('lo·ðo) n.m. mud; mire. —**lodoso,** adj. muddy; miry.

logaritmo (lo·ɣa'rit·mo) n.m. logarithm. —**logarítmico,** adj. logarithmic.

logia ('lo·xja) n.f. **1,** lodge (of a fraternal order). **2,** archit. loggia.

lógica ('lo·xi·ka) *n.f.* logic.
—**lógico,** *adj.* logical. —*n.m.* logician.

logicial (lo·xi'θjal; -'sjal) *n.f.,*
comput. software.

logotipo (lo·γo'ti·po) *n.m.* logotype.

logística (lo'xis·ti·ka) *n.f.* logistics. —**logístico,** *adj.* logistic; logistical.

lograr (lo'γrar) *v.t.* to gain; attain; achieve. —*v.i.* to succeed. —**logrero,** *n.m.* usurer; profiteer.

logro ('lo·γro) *n.m.* **1,** profit; lucre. **2,** attainment.

loma ('lo·ma) *n.f.* hillock; slope.

lombarda (lom'bar·ða) *n.f.* red cabbage.

lombriz (lom'briθ; -'bris) *n.f.* earthworm; intestinal worm. —**lombriz solitaria,** tapeworm.

lomo ('lo·mo) *n.m.* **1,** loin; back. **2,** spine; back (*of an animal, book, etc.*). **3,** ridge between furrows.

lona ('lo·na) *n.f.* canvas.

loncha ('lon·tʃa) *n.f.* **1,** slice. **2,** thin, flat stone.

lonche ('lon·tʃe) *n.m., Amer.* lunch. —**lonchería,** *n.f. Amer.* lunchroom.

longánimo (lon'ga·ni·mo) *adj.* **1,** forbearing. **2,** magnanimous. —**longanimidad,** *n.f.* forbearance.

longaniza (lon·ga'ni·θa; -sa) *n.f.* a kind of sausage.

longevo (lon'xe·βo) *adj.* long-lived. —**longevidad,** *n.f.* longevity.

longitud (lon·xi'tud) *n.f.* **1,** length. **2,** longitude.

longitudinal (lon·xi·tu·ði'nal) *adj.* **1,** lengthwise. **2,** longitudinal.

lonja ('lon·xa) *n.f.* **1,** exchange; stock exchange. **2,** slice; strip. **3,** thong.

lontananza (lon·ta'nan·θa; -sa) *n.f.* background; distance.

loor (lo'or) *n.m.* praise.

loquear (lo·ke'ar) *v.i.* to act foolishly.

lorán (lo'ran) *n.m.* loran.

loro ('lo·ro) *n.m.* parrot.

los (los) *def.art.masc.pl.* the. —*pers.pron. masc.pl., used as dir. obj. of a verb* them; you. —*dem. pron. masc.pl.* those.

losa ('lo·sa) *n.f.* **1,** slab. **2,** flagstone.

losange (lo'san·xe) *n.m.* lozenge; diamond-shaped figure.

losar (lo'sar) *v.t.* = **enlosar.** —**losado,** *n.m.* = **enlosado.**

loseta (lo'se·ta) *n.f.* small flagstone; tile.

lote ('lo·te) *n.m.* **1,** lot; share; portion. **2,** *Amer.* lot; plot of land.

lotear (lo·te'ar) *v.t., Amer.* to divide into lots.

lotería (lo·te'ri·a) *n.f.* lottery; raffle.

loto ('lo·to) *n.m.* lotus.

loza ('lo·θa; -sa) *n.f.* crockery; porcelain.

lozanear (lo·θa·ne'ar; lo·sa-) *v.i.* **1,** to luxuriate. **2,** to be vigorous; be full of life.

lozanía (lo·θa'ni·a; lo·sa-) *n.f.* **1,** luxuriance. **2,** vigor; vitality.

lozano (lo'θa·no; -'sa·no) *adj.* **1,** luxuriant. **2,** vigorous; healthy.

lubricar (lu·βri'kar) *v.t.* [*infl.: tocar,* 7] to lubricate. —**lubricación,** *n.f.* lubrication. —**lubricante,** *adj. & n.m.* lubricant.

lubricidad (lu·βri·θi'ðað; -si'ðað) *n.f.* **1,** slipperiness. **2,** lechery.

lúbrico ('lu·βri·ko) *adj.* **1,** slippery. **2,** lecherous.

lucerna (lu'θer·na; -'ser·na) *n.f.* **1,** chandelier. **2,** skylight.

lucero (lu'θe·ro; -'se·ro) *n.m.* **1,** bright star. **2,** brightness. **3,** *poet.* eye.

luces ('lu·θes; -ses) *n.f., pl. of* **luz,** **1,** culture; enlightenment. **2,** understanding.

lucido (lu'θi·ðo; -'si·ðo) *adj.* **1,** gracious; elegant. **2,** *colloq.* done for; fouled up.

lúcido ('lu·θi·ðo; 'lu·si-) *adj.* lucid. —**lucidez,** *n.f.* lucidity.

luciente (lu'θjen·te; -'sjen·te) *adj.* **1,** shining; lucid. **2,** outstanding.

luciérnaga (lu'θjer·na·γa; lu·'sjer-) *n.f.* firefly; glowworm.

Lucifer (lu·θi'fer; lu·si-) *n.m.* **1,** Lucifer. **2,** morning star.

lucífero (lu'θi·fe·ro; lu'si-) *adj.* shining. —*n.m., cap.* morning star.

lucimiento (lu·θi'mjen·to; lu·si-) *n.m.* **1,** brightness; brilliancy. **2,** dash; display.

lucir (lu'θir; -'sir) *v.i.* [*infl.:* 14] **1,** to shine; be bright. **2,** to befit. —*v.t.* to display; show to advantage. —**lucirse,** *v.r.* **1,** to appear to advantage. **2,** *colloq.* to appear ridiculous; make oneself a laughingstock.

lucita (lu'θi·ta; -'si·ta) *n.f.* lucite (*marc.reg.*).

lucro ('lu·kro) *n.m.* lucre; gain. —**lucrarse,** *v.r.* to profit (*in work or* *business).* —**lucrativo,** *adj.* lucrative.

luctuoso (luk'two·so) *adj.* mournful.

lucubrar (lu·ku'βrar) *v.i.* to lucubrate. —**lucubración,** *n.f.* lucubration.

lucha ('lu·tʃa) *n.f.* 1, strife; struggle; battle. 2, wrestling; wrestling match.

luchar (lu'tʃar) *v.t.* 1, to wrestle. 2, to struggle; contend. —**luchador,** *n.m.* wrestler.

ludibrio (lu'ði·βrjo) *n.m.* scorn; mockery.

lúe ('lu·e) *n.f.* 1, infection. 2, syphilis.

luego ('lwe·yo) *adv.* 1, immediately; directly. 2, soon. 3, then; thereupon. —*conj.* therefore. —**desde luego,** naturally; of course. —**hasta luego,** so long; good-bye. —**luego como; luego que,** as soon as.

luengo ('lwen·go) *adj.* long.

lugar (lu'yar) *n.m.* 1, place. 2, space; room. 3, occasion; opportunity. 4, small village. —**en lugar de,** in lieu of; instead of. —**lugar geométrico,** locus. —**tener lugar,** to take place. —**lugareño,** *adj.* village *(attrib.).* —*n.m.* villager.

lugarteniente (lu·yar·te'njen·te) *n.m. & f.* 1, deputy; substitute. 2, lieutenant. —**lugartenencia,** *n.f.* lieutenancy.

lúgubre ('lu·yu·βre) *adj.* lugubrious.

lujo ('lu·xo) *n.m.* luxury; extravagance. —**lujoso,** *adj.* luxurious. —**de lujo,** deluxe.

lujuria (lu'xu·rja) *n.f.* lust; lechery. —**lujurioso,** *adj.* lustful; lecherous.

lujuriante (lu·xu'rjan·te) *adj.* 1, luxuriant. 2, lustful.

lumbago (lum'ba·yo) *n.m.* lumbago.

lumbar (lum'bar) *adj.* lumbar.

lumbre ('lum·bre) *n.f.* 1, fire; light. 2, brightness. 3, lucidity. 4, space admitting light.

lumbrera (lum'bre·ra) *n.f.* 1, luminary. 2, louver.

luminaria (lu·mi'na·rja) *n.f.* luminary; light.

luminiscente (lu·mi·nis'θen·te)

-ni'sen·te) *adj.* luminescent. —**luminiscencia,** *n.f.* luminescence.

luminoso (lu·mi'no·so) *adj.* luminous. —**luminosidad,** *n.f.* luminosity.

luna ('lu·na) *n.f.* 1, moon. 2, glass; plate glass. —**luna creciente,** crescent moon. —**luna de miel,** honeymoon. —**luna llena,** full moon. —**luna menguante,** waning moon. —**luna nueva,** new moon. —**media luna,** half moon.

lunar (lu'nar) *adj.* lunar. —*n.m.* 1, mole; blemish. 2, polka dot.

lunático (lu'na·ti·ko) *adj. & n.m.* lunatic.

lunes ('lu·nes) *n.m.sing. & pl.* Monday.

luneta (lu'ne·ta) *n.f.* 1, eyeglass; lens. 2, *theat.* orchestra; orchestra seat.

lupa ('lu·pa) *n.f.* magnifying glass.

lupanar (lu·pa'nar) *n.m.* brothel.

lupino (lu'pi·no) *adj.* lupine.

lúpulo ('lu·pu·lo) *n.m., bot.* hops.

lusitano (lu·si'ta·no) *adj. & n.m.* Lusitanian; Portuguese.

lustrabotas (lus·tra'βo·tas) *n.m. sing. & pl., Amer.* bootblack.

lustrar (lus'trar) *v.t.* to polish; shine.

lustre ('lus·tre) *n.m.* 1, polish; gloss; luster. 2, glory; renown. —**lustroso,** *adj.* lustrous; shiny.

lutecio (lu'te·θjo; -sjo) *n.m.* lutecium.

luterano (lu·te'ra·no) *adj. & n.m.* Lutheran. —**luteranismo,** *n.m.* Lutheranism.

luto ('lu·to) *n.m.* mourning. —**de luto,** 1, in mourning. 2, mourning *(attrib.).*

luz (luθ; lus) *n.f.* [*pl.* **luces**] 1, light. 2, lamp; candle. 3, span *(of a bridge).* 4, opening; clearance. 5, headroom. —**a primera luz,** 1, at daybreak. 2, at first sight. —**a toda luz; a todas luces,** by all means. —**dar a luz,** to give birth. —**entre dos luces,** 1, at twilight. 2, half drunk; tipsy. 3, confused; bewildered.

luzca ('luθ·ka; 'lus-) *v., pres.subjve. of* **lucir.**

luzco ('luθ·ko; 'lus-) *v., 1st pers. sing.pres.ind. of* **lucir.**

LL

Ll, ll ('e·ʎe; 'e·je) *n.f.* 14th letter of the Spanish alphabet.

llaga ('ʎa·ɣa; 'ja-) *n.f.* sore; ulcer.

llagar (ʎa'ɣar; ja-) *v.t.* [*infl.:* **pagar, 8**] **1,** to ulcerate. **2,** to wound; injure.

llama ('ʎa·ma; 'ja-) *n.f.* **1,** flame. **2,** llama.

llamada (ʎa'ma·ða; ja-) *n.f.* **1,** call. **2,** sign; signal. **3,** knock. **4,** reference mark.

llamamiento (ʎa·ma'mjen·to; ja-) *n.m.* **1,** call; calling. **2,** convening; convocation.

llamar (ʎa'mar; ja-) *v.t.* **1,** to call. **2,** to cite; summon. —*v.i.* to knock. —**llamarse,** *v.r.* to be named; be called: *¿Cómo se llama Vd.?* What is your name? —**llamativo,** *adj.* showy; gaudy.

llamarada (ʎa·ma'ra·ða; ja-) *n.f.* **1,** blaze; flame. **2,** *fig.* flare-up; outburst (*of temper*).

llamear (ʎa·me'ar; ja-) *v.i.* to flame; blaze.

llana ('ʎa·na; 'ja-) *n.f.* trowel.

llanada (ʎa'na·ða; ja-) *n.f.* plain.

llanero (ʎa'ne·ro; ja-) *n.m., Amer.* plainsman.

llaneza (ʎa'ne·θa; ja'ne·sa) *n.f.* plainness; simplicity.

llano ('ʎa·no; 'ja-) *adj.* **1,** plain; level; even. **2,** straightforward; simple. **3,** accented on the penultimate syllable. —*n.m.* plain; flat ground.

llanta ('ʎan·ta; 'jan-) *n.f.* **1,** tire. **2,** wheel rim.

llantén (ʎan'ten; jan-) *n.m.* plantain (*weed*).

llanto ('ʎan·to; 'jan-) *n.m.* weeping; crying.

llanura (ʎa'nu·ra; ja'nu-) *n.f.* **1,** plain; prairie. **2,** evenness; flatness.

llares ('ʎa·res; 'ja-) *n.f.pl.* pothook.

llave ('ʎa·βe; 'ja-) *n.f.* **1,** key. **2,** wrench. **3,** faucet; tap; spigot. —**llave inglesa,** monkey wrench.

llavero (ʎa'βe·ro; ja-) *n.m.* **1,** key ring. **2,** keymaker. **3,** turnkey.

llavín (ʎa'βin; ja-) *n.m.* small key; latchkey.

llegar (ʎe'ɣar; je-) *v.i.* [*infl.:* **pagar, 8**] **1,** to arrive; come. **2,** to reach; attain. **3,** to succeed. **4,** to amount; come to. —**llegarse,** *v.r.* **1,** to approach. **2,** to go; betake oneself.

—**llegada,** *n.f.* arrival; coming. —**llegar a las manos,** *colloq.* to come to blows. —**llegar a saber,** to find out. —**llegar a ser,** to become.

llena ('ʎe·na; 'je-) *n.f.* flood; overflow.

llenar (ʎe'nar; je-) *v.t.* **1,** to fill. **2,** to satisfy. **3,** to fill out; complete.

lleno ('ʎe·no; 'je-) *adj.* full. —*n.m.* **1,** fullness. **2,** capacity audience; full house. **3,** full moon. —**de lleno,** fully; completely.

llenura (ʎe'nu·ra; je-) *n.f.* fullness; fill.

llevadero (ʎe·βa'ðe·ro; je-) *adj.* light; easy to bear.

llevar (ʎe'βar; je-) *v.t.* **1,** to carry; transport. **2,** to wear. **3,** to keep (books, accounts, etc.) **4,** to take; lead; guide. **5,** to take off or away; carry off. **6,** to bear; endure. **7,** to charge (someone) for (something). **8,** to run; manage (a business, organization, etc.). **9,** to be ahead (a certain time, distance, etc.) of someone or something: *Este alumno lleva al otro dos años,* This student is two years ahead of the other. *Este tren lleva al otro diez kilómetros,* This train is ten kilometers ahead of the other. **10,** to be older than (someone) by: *Mi hijo lleva al suyo tres años,* My son is three years older than yours. **11,** *colloq.* to take (a certain time): *Me llevó una hora ir a la oficina,* It took me an hour to get to the office. **12,** to have been or gone (a certain time): *Lleva cinco días enfermo,* He has been sick five days. *Llevo tres días sin comer,* I have gone three days without eating. —**llevarse,** *v.r.* **1,** *with* **bien** *or* **mal,** to get along (well or badly). **2,** to be apart (*a certain time*): *Mi hijo y el suyo se llevan dos años,* My son and yours are two years apart. —**llevar a cabo,** to succeed in; bring about; accomplish. —**llevar las de perder,** to be doomed; be bound to fail. —**llevar y traer,** *colloq.* to carry gossip.

llorar (ʎo'rar; jo-) *v.i.* to weep; cry. —*v.t.* to mourn; lament.

lloriquear (ʎo·ri·ke'ar; jo-) *v.i.* to whine; whimper. —**lloriqueo** (-'ke·o) *n.m.* whining; whimpering.

lloro ('ʎo·ro; 'jo-) *n.m.* weeping.

llorón (ʎo'ron; jo-) *n.m.* [*fem.* **llorona**] weeper; whiner. —*adj.* weeping; whining. —**sauce llorón,** weeping willow.

lloroso (ʎo'ro·so; jo-) *adj.* 1, weeping; tearful. 2, sad; heartrending.

llovedizo (ʎo·βe'ði·θo; jo-βe'ði·so) *adj.* leaky. —**agua llovediza,** rain water.

llover (ʎo'βer; jo-) *v.impers.* [*infl.:* **mover, 30**] to rain; pour. —**llover a cántaros,** to rain cats and dogs. —**llueva o no,** rain or shine.

llovizna (ʎo'βiθ·na; jo'βis-) *n.f.* drizzle. —**lloviznar,** *v.impers.* to drizzle.

llueca ('ʎwe·ka; 'jwe-) *n.f.* brooding hen.

llueva ('ʎwe·βa; -'jwe-) *v., pres.subjve.* of **llover.**

llueve ('ʎwe·βe; -'jwe-) *v. pres.ind.* of **llover.**

lluvia ('ʎu·βja; 'ju-) *n.f.* 1, rain; shower. 2, *fig.* flood; deluge. —**lluvioso,** *adj.* rainy; wet. —**lluvia atómica,** radioactive fallout.

M

M, m ('e·me) *n.f.* 15th letter of the Spanish alphabet.

maca ('ma·ka) *n.f.* 1, bruise (*in a fruit*). 2, *colloq.* fraud; deceit; trickery.

macabro (ma'ka·βro) *adj.* macabre.

macaco (ma'ka·ko) *n.m.* 1, macaque. 2, *Mex.* hobgoblin. —*adj. Amer., colloq.* ugly; ill-shaped.

macadán (ma·ka'ðan) *also,* **macádam** (-'ka·ðam) *n.m.* macadam. —**macadamizar** [*infl.:* **rezar, 10**] to macadamize.

macana (ma'ka·na) *n.f., Amer.* 1, a kind of flint ax. 2, cudgel; club. 3, *colloq.* nonsense.

macanudo (ma·ka'nu·ðo) *adj., Amer., colloq.* 1, tremendous; extraordinary. 2, superb.

macareo (ma·ka're·o) *n.m.* riptide.

macarrón (ma·ka'rron) *n.m.* 1, macaroon. 2, macaroni. —**macarrones,** *n.m.pl.* macaroni.

macarse (ma'kar·se) *v.r.* to begin to rot, as bruised fruit.

macerar (ma·θe'rar; ma·se-) *v.t.* to macerate. —**maceración,** *n.f., also,* **maceramiento,** *n.m.* maceration.

macero (ma'θe·ro; -'se·ro) *n.m.* mace-bearer.

maceta (ma'θe·ta; -'se·ta) *n.f.* 1, flowerpot. 2, small mallet.

macias ('ma·θjas; -sjas) *n.f.* mace (*spice*). *Also,* **macis** ('ma·θis; -sis).

macilento (ma·θi'len·to; ma·si-) *adj.* gaunt; thin.

macillo (ma'θi·ʎo; -'si·jo) *n.m.* hammer (*of a percussion instrument*).

macizar (ma·θi'θar; -si'sar) *v.t.* [*infl.:* **rezar, 10**] to fill in (a hole or gap).

macizo (ma'θi·θo; -'si·so) *adj.* massive; solid. —*n.m.* mass; cluster (*of mountains, buildings, trees, flowers, etc.*). —**macicez,** *n.f.* massiveness.

macrocosmo (ma·kro'kos·mo) *n.m.* macrocosm.

macroeconomía (ma·kro·e·ko·no'mi·a) *n.f.* macroeconomics.

macroscópico (ma·kros'ko·pi·ko) *adj.* macroscopic.

mácula ('ma·ku·la) *n.f.* stain; spot.

machaca (ma'tʃa·ka) *n.f.* crusher; pounder. —*n.m. & f.* importunate person; bore. —**machacar,** *v.t.* [*infl.:* **tocar, 7**] to crush; pound. —*v.i., colloq.* to harp (on); insist. —**machacón** (-'kon) *n.m.* [*fem.* **-cona**] importunate person; bore. —*adj.* importunate; boring.

machada (ma'tʃa·ða) *n.f.* 1, flock of male goats. 2, *colloq.* stupidity. 3, *Amer., colloq.* manly, virile action.

machar (ma'tʃar) *v.t.* = **machacar.** —**macharse,** *v.r., Amer.* to get drunk.

machete (ma'tʃe·te) *n.m.* machete. —**machetazo,** *n.m.* blow with a machete. —**machetear** (-te'ar) *v.t.* to strike or cut with a machete.

machihembrado (ma·tʃi·em'bra·ðo) *n.m.* tongue and groove.

machihembrar (ma·tʃi·em'brar) *v.t.* to dovetail; mortise.

machina (ma'tʃi·na) *n.f.* 1, crane; derrick. 2, pile-driver.

macho ('ma·tʃo) *adj.* 1, male. 2, *colloq.* masculine; manly. 3, *mech.*

male. —*n.m.* male. —**machismo** (-'tʃis·mo) *n.m.* male pride; virility.

machucar (ma·tʃu'kar) *v.t.* [*infl.*: **tocar**, 7] to crush; pound; bruise. —**machucamiento**, *n.m.* crushing; pounding; bruising.

machucho (ma'tʃu·tʃo) *adj.* **1**, staid; judicious. **2**, advancing in years.

madama (ma'ða·ma) *n.f.* madam.

madeja (ma'ðe·xa) *n.f.* **1**, hank; skein. **2**, *fig.* tangle; complication.

madera (ma'ðe·ra) *n.f.* **1**, wood. **2**, timber; lumber. —*n.m.* madeira wine. —**madera laminada**, plywood.

maderamen (ma·ðe'ra·men) *also*, **maderaje**, *n.m.* timberwork; timber.

maderero (ma·ðe're·ro) *adj.* lumbering; of the lumber industry. —*n.m.* lumberman. —**maderería**, *n.f.* lumberyard.

madero (ma'ðe·ro) *n.m.* **1**, beam; timber. **2**, *colloq.* blockhead.

madona (ma'ðo·na) *n.f.* Madonna.

madrastra (ma'ðras·tra) *n.f.* stepmother.

madre ('ma·ðre) *n.f.* **1**, mother. **2**, bed *(of a river)*. —**madre de familia**, housewife. —**madre de leche**, wet nurse. —**madre política**, mother-in-law. —**sacar de madre**, to make (someone) lose patience. —**salirse de madre**, *(of a stream)* to overflow its banks.

madreperla (ma·ðre'per·la) *n.f.* mother-of-pearl.

madreselva (ma·ðre'sel·βa) *n.f.* honeysuckle.

madrigado (ma·ðri'ɣa·ðo) *adj.* **1**, *(of an animal, esp. a bull)* that has sired. **2**, *(of a woman)* twice-wed. **3**, *colloq.* experienced; versed.

madrigal (ma·ðri'ɣal) *n.m.* madrigal.

madriguera (ma·ðri'ɣe·ra) *n.f.* **1**, burrow. **2**, den; lair.

madrileño (ma·ðri'le·ɲo) *adj.* & *n.m.* of Madrid; Madrilenian; Madrilene.

madrina (ma'ðri·na) *n.f.* **1**, godmother. **2**, maid or matron of honor. **3**, patroness.

madroño (ma'ðro·ɲo) *n.m.* arbutus.

madrugada (ma·ðru'ɣa·ða) *n.f.* **1**, daybreak; dawn. **2**, early rising. —**de madrugada**, at dawn.

madrugador (ma·ðru·ɣa'ðor) *adj.* early-rising. —*n.m.* early riser.

madrugar (ma·ðru'ɣar) *v.i.* [*infl.*:

pagar, 8] **1**, to rise early. **2**, to come or arrive early. —**madrugarse a**, *Amer., colloq.* to steal a march on.

madrugón (ma·ðru'yon) *adj.* early-rising.

madurar (ma·ðu'rar) *v.t.* & *i.* to ripen. —*v.i.* to mature; become mature. —**maduración**, *n.f.* ripening; aging.

madurez (ma·ðu'reθ; -'res) *n.f.* **1**, ripeness. **2**, maturity. **3**, wisdom; prudence.

maduro (ma'ðu·ro) *adj.* **1**, ripe. **2**, mature; middle-aged. **3**, wise; prudent.

maelstrom (ma·els'trom) *n.m.* maelstrom.

maestra (ma·es·tra) *n.f.* **1**, teacher. **2**, mistress.

maestría (ma·es'tri·a) *n.f.* **1**, mastery. **2**, mastership. **3**, master's degree.

maestro (ma·es·tro) *adj.* master. —*n.m.* **1**, teacher. **2**, master. —**maestro** [*fem.* **maestra**] **de ceremonias**, master [*fem.* mistress] of ceremonies. —**maestro de obras**, contractor; builder.

magaña (ma'ɣa·ɲa) *n.f.* **1**, cleverness. **2**, stratagem.

magenta (ma'xen·ta) *adj.* & *n.m.* magenta.

magia ('ma·xja) *n.f.* magic.

magiar (ma'xjar) *adj.* & *n.m.* & *f.* Magyar.

mágico ('ma·xi·ko) *adj.* magic; magical. —*n.m.* magician.

magín (ma'xin) *n.m., colloq.* imagination.

magisterial (ma·xis·te'rjal) *adj.* **1**, of or pert. to teachers or teaching. **2**, pompous; magisterial.

magisterio (ma·xis'te·rjo) *n.m.* **1**, mastery; control. **2**, professorship; professoriate. **3**, teachers collectively; teaching profession.

magistrado (ma·xis'tra·ðo) *n.m.* magistrate.

magistral (ma·xis'tral) *adj.* masterly; superb. —**obra magistral**, masterpiece; masterwork.

magistratura (ma·xis·tra'tu·ra) *n.f.* magistracy.

magma ('maɣ·ma) *n.m., geol.* magma.

magnánimo (maɣ'na·ni·mo) *adj.* magnanimous. —**magnanimidad**, *n.f.* magnanimity.

magnate (maɣ'na·te) *n.m.* magnate.

magnesia (maɣ'ne·sja) *n.f.* magnesia.

magnesio (maɣ'ne·sjo) *n.m.* magnesium.

magnetismo (maɣ·ne'tis·mo) *n.m.* magnetism. —**magnético** (-'ne·ti·ko) *adj.* magnetic.

magnetita (maɣ·ne'ti·ta) *n.f.* magnetite.

magnetizar (maɣ·ne·ti'θar; -'sar) *v.t.* [*infl.*: **rezar, 10**] **1**, to magnetize. **2**, to hypnotize.

magneto (maɣ'ne·to) *n.m.* magneto.

magnetófono (maɣ·ne·to'fo·no) *n.m.* wire or tape recorder.

magnificar (maɣ·ni·fi'kar) *v.t.* [*infl.*: **tocar, 7**] to magnify. —**magnificación**, *n.f.* magnification.

magnífico (maɣ'ni·fi·ko) *adj.* magnificent. —**magnificencia** (-'θen·θja; -'sen·sja) *n.f.* magnificence.

magnitud (maɣ·ni'tuð) *n.f.* magnitude.

magno ('maɣ·no) *adj.* great.

magnolia (maɣ'no·lja) *n.f.* magnolia.

mago ('ma·ɣo) *n.m.* magician; wizard. —**los reyes magos**, the Magi.

magro ('ma·ɣro) *adj.* lean; thin. —**magra**, *n.f.* slice of ham. —**magrez**, *n.f.* leanness.

magullar (ma·ɣu'ʎar; -'jar) *v.t.* to bruise. —**magulladura**, *n.f.* bruise.

maharajá (ma·a·ra'xa; ma·ra'xa) *n.m.* maharajah.

maharaní (ma·a·ra'ni; ma·ra'ni) *n.f.* maharanee.

mahometano (ma·o·me'ta·no) *adj. & n.m.* Mohammedan. —**mahometismo**, *n.m.* Mohammedanism.

maitines (mai'ti·nes) *n.m.pl.* matins.

maíz (ma'iθ; -'is) *n.m.* corn; maize. —**maizal**, *n.m.* cornfield.

majada (ma'xa·ða) *n.f.* **1**, sheepfold. **2**, dung; manure.

majadería (ma·xa·ðe'ri·a) *n.f.* **1**, absurdity; nonsense. **2**, importunity; bother. —**majadero**, *adj.* annoying; importunate.

majar (ma'xar) *v.t.* **1**, to pound; crush; mash. **2**, *colloq.* to annoy; importune.

majestad (ma·xes'tað) *n.f.* majesty.

majestuoso (ma·xes'two·so) *adj.* majestic. —**majestuosidad**, *n.f.* majesty; grandeur.

majo ('ma·xo) *adj.* **1**, gallant; bold. **2**, elegant; handsome. —*n.m.* gallant.

majuelo (ma'xwe·lo) *n.m.* white hawthorn.

mal (mal) *adj., var. of* **malo** *before a masc. noun.* —*n.m.* **1**, evil. **2**, harm; hurt; mischief. **3**, illness; disease. —*adv.* badly; bad; poorly. —**estar mal con**, to be on bad terms with. —**mal de ojo**, evil eye. —**mal que bien**, anyhow; at any rate. —**mal que le pese (a uno)**, in spite of (someone); however (someone) may dislike it. —**parar mal**, to end up badly. —**tomar a mal**, to misconstrue; take amiss.

malabarismo (ma·la·βa'ris·mo) *n.m.* [*also,* **juegos malabares**] jugglery; juggling. —**malabarista**, *n.m. & f.* juggler.

malaconsejado (mal·a·kon·se'xa·ðo) *adj.* ill-advised.

malacostumbrado (mal·a·kos·tum'bra·ðo) *adj.* pampered.

malacrianza (ma·la·kri'an·θa; -sa) *n.f.,. Amer.* **1**, poor manners. **2**, vulgarity; indelicacy.

malagradecido (mal·a·ɣra·ðe'θi·ðo; -'si·ðo) *adj.* ungrateful.

malagua (ma'la·ɣwa) *n.f., Amer.* = **medusa**.

malandanza (mal·an'dan·θa; -sa) *n.f.* misfortune; misery.

malandrín (ma·lan'drin) *n.m.* rascal; scoundrel. —*adj.* rascally; scoundrelly.

malaquita (ma·la'ki·ta) *n.f.* malachite.

malar (ma'lar) *adj.* malar.

malaria (ma'la·rja) *n.f.* malaria.

malavenido (mal·a·βe'ni·ðo) *adj.* unfriendly; unsociable.

malaventura (mal·a·βen'tu·ra) *also,* **malaventuranza** (-'ran·θa; -sa) *n.f.* misfortune; unhappiness. —**malaventurado**, *adj.* unfortunate.

malayo (ma'la·jo) *adj. & n.m.* Malay; Malayan.

malbaratar (mal·βa·ra'tar) *v.t.* to squander.

malcarado (mal·ka'ra·ðo) *adj.* **1**, surly; grim. **2**, ill-looking; ugly.

malcasado (mal·ka'sa·ðo) *adj.* **1**, unfaithful; adulterous. **2**, married beneath one's station.

malcontento (mal·kon'ten·to) *adj. & n.m.* malcontent.

malcriar (mal·kri'ar) *v.t.* [*infl.*: **enviar, 22**] to spoil; pamper.

—**malcriado,** *adj.* ill-bred; spoiled; pampered. —**malcriadez,** *n.f., Amer.* brattiness; poor breeding.

maldad (mal'daθ) *n.f.* wickedness; evil.

maldecir (mal·ðe'θir; -'sir) *v.t. & i.* [*infl.:* **bendecir,** 37] to damn; curse. —**maldecir de,** to speak evil of; backbite.

maldición (mal·di'θjon; -'sjon) *n.f.* 1, malediction; curse. 2, damnation.

maldispuesto (mal·dis'pwes·to) *adj.* ill-disposed; reluctant.

maldito (mal'di·to) *adj.* 1, perverse. 2, accursed; damned. 3, blasted; confounded.

maleable (ma·le·a'βle) *adj.* malleable. —**maleabilidad,** *n.f.* malleability.

malear (ma·le'ar) *v.t.* to spoil; corrupt. —**maleante,** *n.m.* hoodlum; bandit.

malecón (ma·le'kon) *n.m.* mole; dike; sea wall.

maledicencia (ma·le·ði'θen·θja; -'sen·sja) *n.f.* slander; evil talk.

maleducado (mal·e·ðu'ka·ðo) *adj.* ill-mannered.

maleficiar (ma·le·fi'θjar; -'sjar) *v.t.* 1, to injure; harm. 2, to cast evil spells on.

maleficio (ma·le'fi·θjo; -sjo) *n.m.* 1, evil spell. 2, harm; injury.

maléfico (ma'le·fi·ko) *adj.* maleficent. —**maleficencia** (-'θen·θja; -'sen·sja) *n.f.* maleficence.

malentendido (mal·en·ten'di·ðo) *n.m.* misunderstanding.

malestar (ma·les'tar) *n.m.* uneasiness; discomfort; malaise.

maleta (ma'le·ta) *n.f.* suitcase. —*n.m. & f., colloq.* incompetent.

maletín (ma·le'tin) *n.m.* valise.

malévolo (ma'le·βo·lo) *adj.* malevolent. —**malevolencia,** *n.f.* malevolence.

maleza (ma'le·θa; -sa) *n.f.* 1, thicket. 2, growth of weeds.

malformación (mal·for·ma'θjon; -'sjon) *n.f.* malformation.

malgastar (mal·ɣas'tar) *v.t.* to misspend; squander. —**malgastador,** *adj. & n.m.* [*fem.* **-dora**] spendthrift.

malhablado (mal·a'βla·ðo) *adj.* foul-mouthed.

malhadado (mal·a'ða·ðo) *adj.* unfortunate; ill-starred.

malhaya (ma'la·ja) *interj.* damn!

malhechor (mal·e'tʃor) *n.m.* [*fem.*

-**chora**] malefactor; criminal; bandit.

malhumor (mal·u'mor) *n.m.* bad mood. —**malhumorado,** *adj.* ill-humored.

malicia (ma'li·θja; -sja) *n.f.* 1, malice. 2, shrewdness. 3, suspicion; inkling.

maliciar (ma·li'θjar; -'sjar) *v.t.* to suspect; mistrust.

malicioso (ma·li'θjo·so; -'sjo·so) *adj.* 1, malicious. 2, suspicious; distrustful. 3, shrewd; knowing.

málico ('ma·li·ko) *adj.* malic. —**ácido málico,** malic acid.

maligno (ma'liɣ·no) *adj.* malign; malignant. —**malignidad,** *n.f.* malignancy; malignity.

malintencionado (mal·in·ten·θjo'na·ðo; -sjo'na·ðo) *adj.* ill-intentioned; malicious.

malmandado (mal·man'da·ðo) *adj.* disobedient; unruly.

malo ('ma·lo) *adj.* 1, bad; evil. 2, ill. 3, naughty. 4, defective; poor. —*n.m.* bad one; evil one. —**a las malas,** with evil intentions. —**estar de malas,** 1, to be out of luck. 2, to be out of sorts. —**por** *or* **a la mala,** by force; against one's will. —**por malas o por buenas,** 1, by hook or by crook. 2, willingly or unwillingly.

malograr (ma·lo'ɣrar) *v.t.* 1, to spoil; impair. 2, to break; put out of order. —**malograrse,** *v.r.* 1, to spoil. 2, to go wrong; miscarry; fail. —**malogrado,** *adj.* frustrated; disappointed.

malogro (ma'lo·ɣro) *n.m.* 1, spoiling. 2, miscarriage; a going wrong; failure.

maloliente (mal·o'ljen·te) *adj.* malodorous.

malón (ma'lon) *n.m.* 1, mean trick. 2, *Amer.* surprise attack. 3, *Amer.* surprise party.

malparado (mal·pa'ra·ðo) *adj.* 1, beaten; defeated. 2, shaken up; mauled.

malparir (mal·pa'rir) *v.i.* to miscarry; have a miscarriage.

malparto (mal'par·to) *n.m.* miscarriage.

malpensado (mal·pen'sa·ðo) *adj.* evil-minded.

malquerencia (mal·ke·ren'θja; -sja) *n.f.* 1, dislike. 2, ill will.

malquerer (mal·ke'rer) *v.t.* [*infl.:* **querer,** 55] 1, to dislike. 2, to wish (someone) ill.

malquistar (mal·kis'tar) *v.t.* to alienate.

malquisto (mal'kis·to) *adj.* 1, alienated. 2, disliked; unpopular.

malsano (mal'sa·no) *adj.* unwholesome.

malta ('mal·ta) *n.f.* malt.

maltés (mal'tes) *adj. & n.m.* [*fem.* maltesa] Maltese.

maltosa (mal'to·sa) *n.f.* maltose.

maltraer (mal·tra'er) *v.t.* [*infl.:* traer, 67] to mistreat.

maltratar (mal·tra'tar) *v.t.* to maltreat; mistreat. —**maltrato** (-'tra·to) *n.m.* mistreatment.

maltrecho (mal'tre·t∫o) *adj.* battered; in bad shape.

malva ('mal·βa) *n.f.* mallow. —*adj. & n.m.* mauve.

malvado (mal'βa·ðo) *adj.* perverse; bad; evil. —*n.m.* evildoer.

malvavisco (mal·βa'βis·ko) *n.m.* marshmallow.

malvender (mal·βen'der) *v.t.* to sell unprofitably.

malversar (mal·βer'sar) *v.t.* to misappropriate. —**malversación,** *n.f.* misappropriation.

malvís (mal'βis) *n.m.* mavis.

malla ('ma·ʎa; -ja) *n.f.* 1, mesh. 2, coat of mail. 3, sweater; jersey. 4, *S.A.* bathing suit.

mama ('ma·ma) *n.f.* 1, mamma; breast. 2, = **mamá.**

mamá (ma'ma) *n.f.* mother; mamma; mama.

mamada (ma'ma·ða) *n.f.* 1, breast feeding. 2, *colloq.* suck; sucking.

mamadera (ma·ma'ðe·ra) *n.f.* 1, breast pump. 2, *Amer.* nursing bottle.

mamar (ma'mar) *v.t.* 1, to suck. 2, *colloq.* to gobble; gobble up. —*v.i.* to suckle. —**mamarse,** *v.r., Amer., slang* to get drunk. —**dar de mamar,** to breast-feed. —**mamarla,** *colloq.* to be taken in. —**mamarse a uno,** *colloq.* 1, to get the best of someone. 2, to do away with someone.

mamario (ma'ma·rjo) *adj.* mammary.

mamarracho (ma·ma'rra·t∫o) *n.m., colloq.* 1, mess; sight. 2, good-for-nothing; ne'er-do-well.

mambo ('mam·bo) *n.m.* mambo.

mamífero (ma'mi·fe·ro) *n.m.* mammal. —*adj.* mammalian.

mamita (ma'mi·ta) *n.f.* mammy; mama.

mammón (ma'mon) *n.m.* Mammon.

mamografía (ma·mo·ɣra'fi·a) *n.f.* 1, mammography. 2, mammogram.

mamola (ma'mo·la) *n.f.* chuck (*under the chin*). —**hacer la mamola a,** to chuck (someone) under the chin.

mamón (ma'mon) *adj. & n.m.* suckling. —*n.m., bot.* shoot; sucker.

mampara (mam'pa·ra) *n.f.* screen; room divider.

mamparo (mam'pa·ro) *n.m., naut.* bulkhead.

mampostería (mam·pos·te'ri·a) *n.f.* masonry.

mampuesto (mam'pwes·to) *n.m.* 1, parapet. 2, roughhewn stone. 3, *Amer.* arm rest (*for firing a weapon*). —**mampuesta,** *n.f.* course (*of masonry*).

mamut (ma'mut) *n.m.* mammoth.

maná (ma'na) *n.m.* manna.

manada (ma'na·ða) *n.f.* herd; drove; pack.

manantial (ma·nan'tjal) *n.m.* spring; fountain. —*adj.* spring (*attrib.*).

manar (ma'nar) *v.i.* to flow; spring forth. —*v.i. & t.* to gush.

manatí (ma·na'ti) *n.m.* manatee.

manceba (man'θe·βa; -'se·βa) *n.f.* mistress; concubine.

mancebo (man'θe·βo; -'se·βo) *n.m.* 1, young man; young lad. 2, bachelor.

mancilla (man'θi·ʎa; -'si·ja) *n.f.* blemish; stain; dishonor. —**mancillar,** *v.t.* to stain; taint; dishonor.

manco ('man·ko) *adj.* 1, maimed; lacking one or both hands or arms. 2, crippled in one or both hands or arms.

mancomún (man·ko'mun) *n.m., in de mancomún,** jointly; in common.

mancomunidad (man·ko·mu·ni'ðað) *n.f.* 1, commonwealth. 2, joint authority or administration. —**mancomunar** (-'nar) *v.t.* to associate; unite.

mancha ('man·t∫a) *n.f.* spot; stain; blemish. —**manchado,** *adj.* spotted; stained; soiled. —**manchar,** *v.t.* to spot; stain; soil.

manchú (man't∫u) *adj. & n.m. & f.* [*pl.* manchús *or* manchúes] Manchu.

manda ('man·da) *n.f.* 1, offer; promise; pledge. 2, legacy; donation.

mandamiento (man·da'mjen·to) *n.m.* **1**, commandment. **2**, *law* writ.

mandar (man'dar) *v.t. & i.* **1**, to command; order. **2**, to govern. —*v.t.* to send. —**mandarse cambiar,** *colloq.* to get out; clear out. —**mandado,** *n.m.* **1**, order; command. **2**, errand; chore. —¿**mande?,** *Mex.* pardon me?; what did you say?

mandarín (man·da'rin) *n.m.* mandarin.

mandarina (man·da'ri·na) *n.f.* tangerine.

mandatario (man·da'ta·rjo) *n.m.* **1**, legal representative; mandatory. **2**, *Amer.* high official.

mandato (man'da·to) *n.m.* **1**, mandate. **2**, command; order.

mandíbula (man'di·βu·la) *n.f.***1**, jaw. **2**, mandible; jawbone. —**mandibular,** *adj.* mandibular.

mandil (man'dil) *n.m.* full-length apron.

mandioca (man'djo·ka) *n.f.* manioc.

mando ('man·do) *n.m.* **1**, command; authority. **2**, *mech.* control; drive; steering.

mandolina (man·do'li·na) *n.f.* mandolin.

mandón (man'don) *adj.* bossy; domineering. —*n.m.* [*fem.* -**dona**] domineering person.

mandrágora (man'dra·ɣo·ra) *n.f.* mandrake.

mandril (man'dril) *n.m.* **1**, *zoöl.* mandrill; baboon. **2**, *mech.* chuck.

manducar (man·du'kar) *v.t.* [*infl.:* **tocar, 7**] *colloq.* to eat up; gobble. —**manducatoria** (-ka'to·rja) *n.f.,* *colloq.* food.

manear (ma·ne'ar) *v.t.* **1**, to hobble (an animal). **2**, = **manejar.**

manecilla (ma·ne'θi·ʎa; -'si·ja) *n.f.* **1**, *dim. of* **mano. 2**, hand (*of a timepiece*). **3**, pointer; needle.

manejar (ma·ne'xar) *v.t.* **1**, to handle. **2**, *Amer.* to manage. **3**, *Amer.* to drive (a car); ride (a bicycle). **4**, to operate (an instrument, machine, etc.). —**manejable,** *adj.* manageable.

manejo (ma'ne·xo) *n.m.* **1**, handling. **2**, *Amer.* management. **3**, operation (*of a machine, device, etc.*). **4**, *Amer.* driving (*of a vehicle, conveyance, etc.*). **5**, intrigue; stratagem.

manera (ma'ne·ra) *n.f.* manner; way. —**de manera que,** so that.

—**de todas maneras, 1**, by all means. **2**, in any case; anyway. —**sobre manera,** extremely.

manés (ma'nes) *adj. & n.m.* [*fem.* **manesa**] Manx.

manga ('man·ga) *n.f.* **1**, sleeve. **2**, = **manguera. 3**, *Amer.* cloth strainer. **4**, *naut.* beam. —**manga de agua,** squall; shower. —**manga de viento,** whirlwind; tornado. —**tener manga ancha,** *colloq.* to be easygoing.

manganeso (man·ga'ne·so) *n.m.* manganese. —**mangánico** (-'ga·ni·ko) *adj.* manganic.

mangle ('man·gle) *n.m.* mangrove.

mango ('man·go) *n.m.* **1**, handle. **2**, mango.

mangonear (man·go·ne'ar) *v.i.,* *colloq.* to meddle; butt in. —*v.t.,* *colloq.* to boss; manage.

mangosta (man'gos·ta) *n.f.* mongoose.

manguera (man'ge·ra) *n.f.* hose; water hose.

manguito (man'gi·to) *n.m.* **1**, muff. **2**, gas mantle.

maní (ma'ni) *n.m.* [*pl.* **maníes** (-'ni·es) *or* **manises** (-'ni·ses)] peanut.

manía (ma'ni·a) *n.f.* **1**, mania. **2**, whim; caprice. **3**, habit. —**maníaco** (-'ni·a·ko) *adj.* maniacal; maniac. —*n.m.* maniac. —**maniacodepresivo,** *adj.* manic depressive.

maniabierto (ma·ni·a'βjer·to) *adj.* generous.

maniatar (ma·nja'tar) *v.t.* to manacle; tie the hands of.

maniático (ma'nja·ti·ko) *adj. & n.m.* **1**, eccentric. **2**, = **maníaco.**

manicomio (ma·ni'ko·mjo) *n.m.* **1**, mental hospital. **2**, madhouse.

manicura (ma·ni'ku·ra) *n.f.* **1**, manicure. **2**, manicurist.

manicuro (ma·ni'ku·ro) *n.m.* manicurist. *Also, Amer.,* **manicurista** (-'ris·ta) *n.m. & f.*

manido (ma'ni·ðo) *adj.* worn; threadbare.

manifestación (ma·ni·fes·ta·'θjon; -'sjon) *n.f.* **1**, manifestation. **2**, public demonstration.

manifestar (ma·ni·fes'tar) *v.t.* [*infl.:* **pensar, 27**] **1**, to manifest; evince; show. **2**, to state; declare.

manifiesto (ma·ni'fjes·to) *adj. & n.m.* mànifest. —*n.m.* manifesto.

manija (ma'ni·xa) *n.f.* **1**, handle (*of certain tools*). **2**, crank. **3**, clamp. **4**, hobble (*for an animal*).

manilla (ma'ni·ʎa; -ja) n.f. **1,** manacle. **2,** bracelet.

manillar (ma·ni'ʎar; -'jar) n.m. handlebar.

maniobra (ma'njo·βra) n.f. maneuver. —**maniobrabilidad,** n.f. maneuverability. —**maniobrable,** adj. maneuverable. —**maniobrar,** v.t. & i. to maneuver.

maniota (ma'njo·ta) n.f. hobble.

manipular (ma·ni·pu'lar) v.t. to handle; manipulate. —**manipulación,** n.f. handling; manipulation. —**manipulador,** n.m. manipulator. —**manipuleo** (-'le·o) n.m., colloq. manipulation; hanky-panky.

maniquí (ma·ni'ki) n.m. manikin; mannequin.

manirroto (ma·ni'rro·to) adj. lavish; prodigal. —n.m. spendthrift.

manivela (ma·ni'βe·la) n.f. handle; crank.

manjar (man'xar) n.m. **1,** delicacy, food; dish.

mano ('ma·no) n.f. **1,** hand. **2,** side (right or left). **3,** coat, as of paint. **4,** quire. **5,** Amer., slang pal. —**a la mano,** at hand; handy. —**a mano, 1,** by hand. **2,** at hand; handy. —**buenas manos,** skill; dexterity. —**echar mano de,** colloq. to have recourse to; resort to. —**llegar a las manos,** to come to blows. —**mano de obra,** labor. —**manos aguadas,** colloq. butterfingers. —**¡manos arriba!,** hands up! —**mano sobre mano,** idle; idly. —**ser mano,** to lead (in a game). —**tener mano con,** colloq. to have pull with.

manojo (ma'no·xo) n.m. handful; bunch.

manómetro (ma'no·me·tro) n.m. manometer. —**manométrico** (-'me·tri·ko) adj. manometric.

manopla (ma'no·pla) n.f. **1,** gauntlet; armored glove. **2,** Amer. brass knuckles.

manosear (ma·no·se'ar) v.t. to handle; finger; paw. —**manoseo** (-'se·o) n.m. handling; fingering; pawing.

manotada (ma·no'ta·ða) n.f., also **manotazo** (-θo; -so) n.m. blow with the hand.

manotear (ma·no·te'ar) v.t. **1,** to beat with the hands; cuff; buffet. **2,** Amer. to snatch; filch. —v.i. to move the hands; gesticulate.

manquear (man·ke'ar) v.i. **1,** to be crippled in the hand or arm. **2,** to pretend to be so crippled.

manquedad (man·ke'ðað) also, colloq., **manquera** (-'ke·ra) n.f. lack of, or impediment in, one or both arms or hands.

mansalva (man'sal·βa) n.f., in a **mansalva,** without risk; from a safe position.

mansarda (man'sar·ða) n.f. mansard.

mansedumbre (man·se'ðum·bre) n.f. meekness.

mansión (man'sjon) n.f. **1,** dwelling; abode. **2,** mansion.

manso ('man·so) adj. **1,** meek; gentle. **2,** tame; domesticated. **3,** Amer., colloq. gullible. —n.m. lead animal.

manta ('man·ta) n.f. **1,** blanket; coverlet. **2,** mantle; cloak. **3,** Amer. poncho. **4,** manta ray. **5,** colloq. = zurra.

mantear (man·te'ar) v.t. to toss in a blanket. —**manteamiento,** n.m. tossing in a blanket.

manteca (man'te·ka) n.f. **1,** lard; fat; grease. **2,** = mantequilla. —**mantecoso,** adj. greasy.

mantecado (man·te'ka·ðo) n.m. **1,** biscuit made with lard. **2,** ice cream.

mantel (man'tel) n.m. tablecloth. —**mantelería,** n.f. table linen.

mantener (man·te'ner) v.t. [infl.: tener, 65] to maintain; hold; keep. —**mantenerse,** v.r. to sustain oneself.

mantenimiento (man·te·ni·'mjen·to) n.m. **1,** maintenance. **2,** sustenance.

manteo (man'te·o) n.m. **1,** tossing in a blanket. **2,** priest's cloak.

mantequera (man·te'ke·ra) also, Amer., **mantequillera** (-ki'ʎe·ra; -'je·ra) n.f. **1,** churn. **2,** butter dish.

mantequilla (man·te'ki·ʎa; -ja) n.f. butter.

mantilla (man'ti·ʎa; -ja) n.f. **1,** mantilla. **2,** infant's frock. —**estar en mantillas,** to be in infancy.

mantillo (man'ti·ʎo; -jo) n.m. = humus.

mantis ('man·tis) n.m. mantis.

mantisa (man'ti·sa) n.f. mantissa.

manto ('man·to) n.m. **1,** mantle; cloak. **2,** mantel. **3,** stratum.

mantón (man'ton) n.m. a large shawl, usu. of wool. —**mantón de Manila,** embroidered silk shawl.

manuable (ma'nwa·βle) adj. easily handled.

manual (ma'nwal) adj. **1,** manual;

hand (*attrib.*). **2,** = **manuable.** —*n.m.* manual; handbook.

manubrio (ma'nu·βrjo) *n.m.* **1,** handle; crank. **2,** *Amer.* handlebar; handlebars. **3,** *Amer.* steering wheel.

manufactura (ma·nu·fak'tu·ra) *n.f.* manufacture. —**manufacturar,** *v.t.* to manufacture. —**manufacturero,** *adj.* manufacturing. —*n.m.* manufacturer.

manumitir (ma·nu·mi'tir) *v.t.* to manumit. —**manumisión** (-'sjon) *n.f.* manumission.

manuscrito (ma·nus'kri·to) *adj.* handwritten. —*n.m.* manuscript.

manutención (ma·nu·ten'θjon; -'sjon) *n.f.* **1,** maintenance; support. **2,** sustenance.

manzana (man'θa·na; -'sa·na) *n.f.* **1,** apple. **2,** city block. **3,** *Amer.* Adam's apple. —**manzanar,** *also,* **manzanal,** *n.m.* apple orchard. —**manzano,** *n.m.* apple tree.

manzanilla (man·θa'ni·ʎa; -sa'ni·ja) *n.f.* camomile.

maña ('ma·ɲa) *n.f.* **1,** skill; ingenuity; knack. **2,** craftiness; cunning. —**darse maña,** to contrive; manage.

mañana (ma'ɲa·na) *n.f.* morning. —*n.m.* morrow; future. —*adv.* tomorrow. —**muy de mañana,** early in the morning. —**pasado mañana,** the day after tomorrow.

mañanear (ma·ɲa·ne'ar) *v.i.* to rise early; be an early riser.

mañanero (ma·ɲa'ne·ro) *adj.* **1,** early-rising. **2,** *colloq.* morning (*attrib.*).

mañoso (ma'ɲo·so) *adj., colloq.* **1,** ingenious; facile; adroit. **2,** tricky.

mapa ('ma·pa) *n.m.* map. —**mapamundi** (-'mun·di) *n.m.* map of the world.

mapache (ma'pa·tʃe) *n.m.* raccoon.

maquiavélico (ma·kja'βe·li·ko) *adj.* Machiavellian. —**maquiavelismo,** *n.m.* Machiavellism. —**maquiavelista,** *adj. & n.m. & f.* Machiavellian.

maquillar (ma·ki'ʎar; -'jar) *v.t.* to make up; apply cosmetics to. —**maquillaje,** *n.m.* makeup.

máquina ('ma·ki·na) *n.f.* machine; machinery; contrivance. —**maquinal,** *adj.* mechanical. —**a toda máquina,** at full speed.

maquinar (ma·ki'nar) *v.t. & i.* to machinate; plot; scheme. —**maquinación,** *n.f.* machination; plot. —**maquinador,** *adj.* plotting;

scheming. —*n.m.* [*fem.* **-dora**] plotter; schemer.

maquinaria (ma·ki'na·rja) *n.f.* **1,** machinery. **2,** machine design; machine construction. **3,** *comput.* hardware.

maquinista (ma·ki'nis·ta) *n.m. & f.* **1,** engineer; machinist. **2,** machine designer; machine builder.

mar (mar) *n.m. or f.* sea. —**alta mar,** the high seas. —**a mares,** copiously. —**la mar de,** *colloq.* a lot of; no end of. —**mar de fondo,** **1,** ocean swell; ground swell. **2,** *fig.* turmoil.

marabú (ma·ra'βu) *n.m.* marabou.

maraña (ma'ra·ɲa) *n.f.* **1,** tangle. **2,** dense growth. **3,** plot; intrigue.

marasmo (ma'ras·mo) *n.m.* **1,** *pathol.* marasmus. **2,** *fig.* torpor.

maratón (ma·ra'ton) *n.f.* marathon.

maravedí (ma·ra·βe'ði) *n.m.* [*pl.* **maravedís, -díes** *or* **-dises**] a name given to various old Spanish coins.

maravilla (ma·ra'βi·ʎa; -ja) *n.f.* **1,** marvel; wonder. **2,** *bot.* marigold. —**maravilloso,** *adj.* marvelous; wonderful.

maravillar (ma·ra·βi'ʎar; -'jar) *v.t.* to strike with wonder; delight; amaze. —**maravillarse de** *or* **con,** to marvel at; wonder at.

marbete (mar'βe·te) *n.m.* **1,** label; tag; sticker. **2,** border; fillet.

marca ('mar·ka) *n.f.* **1,** mark. **2,** [*also,* **marca registrada**] brand; make; trademark. **3,** brand (*of animals*). **4,** *sports* record. —**de marca mayor,** outstanding; first rate. —**de marca,** of quality.

marcar (mar'kar) *v.t.* [*infl.:* **tocar,** 7] **1,** to brand; mark. **2,** to designate; point out. **3,** to monogram. **4,** to point to; show (the hour). **5,** to dial (a telephone number). **6,** *sports* to score.

marcasita (mar·ka'si·ta) *n.f.* marcasite.

marcial (mar'θjal; -'sjal) *adj.* martial.

marciano (mar'θja·no; -'sja·no) *adj. & n.m.* Martian.

marco ('mar·ko) *n.m.* **1,** frame. **2,** standard (*of weight*). **3,** mark (*monetary unit*).

marcha ('mar·tʃa) *n.f.* **1,** march. **2,** course; progress. **3,** watch movement. **4,** running; functioning. —**a toda marcha,** at full speed. —**en marcha,** in motion; in process. —**marcha atrás,** *mech.* reverse.

—**sobre la marcha, 1,** offhand; on the spot. **2,** in the course of events.

marchamo (mar'tʃa·mo) *n.m.* **1,** customhouse mark. **2,** *fig.* mark; label.

marchar (mar'tʃar) *v.i.* **1,** to march. **2,** to proceed; go. **3,** to run; function. —**marcharse,** *v.r.* to leave.

marchitar (mar·tʃi'tar) *v.t.* to wither; fade. —**marchitamiento,** *n.m., also,* **marchitez,** *n.f.* withering; fading. —**marchito** (-'tʃi·to) *adj.* withered; faded.

marea (ma're·a) *n.f.* tide.

marear (ma·re'ar) *v.t.* **1,** to make seasick; make dizzy. **2,** to bother; importune. —**marearse,** *v.r.* to be seasick; be dizzy. —**mareado,** *adj.* seasick; dizzy.

marejada (ma·re'xa·ða) *n.f.* **1,** ocean swell; ground swell. **2,** *fig.* commotion; turmoil.

mareo (ma're·o) *n.m.* **1,** [*also,* **mareamiento**] seasickness; dizziness. **2,** bother; annoyance.

marfil (mar'fil) *n.m.* ivory. —**marfileño,** *adj.* ivory (*attrib.*); ivory-like.

marga ('mar·ɣa) *n.f.* loam. —**margoso,** *adj.* loamy.

margarina (mar·ɣa'ri·na) *n.f.* margarine.

margarita (mar·ɣa'ri·ta) *n.f.* **1,** daisy; marguerite. **2,** pearl.

margen ('mar·xen) *n.m. & f.* **1,** margin. **2,** verge; fringe. **3,** *agric.* row. —**marginal** (-xi'nal) *adj.* marginal. —**dar margen,** to give cause or opportunity.

marginar (mar·xi'nar) *v.t.* **1,** to make marginal notes of or in. **2,** to leave a margin in.

mariachi (ma'rja·tʃi) *n.m.* **1,** a Mexican dance, similar to the fandango. **2,** music for this dance. **3,** ensemble that plays such music.

marica (ma'ri·ka) *n.m.* milksop; effeminate man.

maricón (ma·ri'kon) *n.m.* **1,** *colloq.* sissy. **2,** *vulg.* homosexual.

marido (ma'ri·ðo) *n.m.* husband.

marihuana (ma·ri'wa·na) *n.f.* marijuana. *Also,* **mariguana** (-'ɣwa·na).

marimacho (ma·ri'ma·tʃo) *n.m., colloq.* hoyden; tomboy.

marimba (ma'rim·ba) *n.f.* marimba.

marina (ma'ri·na) *n.f.* **1,** shore; coast. **2,** fleet; navy. **3,** seascape.

marinar (ma·ri'nar) *v.t.* to marinate.

marinera (ma·ri'ne·ra) *n.f.* sailor's blouse.

marinería (ma·ri·ne'ri·a) *n.f.* **1,** seamanship. **2,** ship's crew. **3,** seamen collectively.

marinero (ma·ri'ne·ro) *n.m.* sailor. —*adj.* **1,** = **marino. 2,** seaworthy.

marino (ma'ri·no) *n.m.* sailor; seaman. —*adj.* marine; nautical.

marioneta (ma·rjo'ne·ta) *n.f.* marionette.

mariposa (ma·ri'po·sa) *n.f.* **1,** butterfly. **2,** night light. **3,** wing nut. **4,** butterfly valve. —*n.m.* homosexual. —**mariposear,** *v.i.* to flit.

mariquita (ma·ri'ki·ta) *n.f.* ladybug; ladybird. —*n.m., colloq.* sissy.

mariscal (ma·ris'kal) *n.m., mil.* marshal. —**mariscalato,** *n.m., also,* **mariscalía,** *n.f.* marshalship.

marisco (ma'ris·ko) *n.m.* [*also pl.* **mariscos**] shellfish; seafood.

marisma (ma'ris·ma) *n.f.* marsh; swamp.

marisquero (ma·ris'ke·ro) *n.m.* fisher or seller of shellfish or any seafood. —**marisquería,** *n.f.* seafood shop or restaurant.

marital (ma·ri'tal) *adj.* marital.

marítimo (ma'ri·ti·mo) *adj.* maritime; marine.

marjal (mar'xal) *n.m.* bog; fen.

marlín (mar'lin) *n.m.* marlin.

marmita (mar'mi·ta) *n.f.* kettle.

mármol ('mar·mol) *n.m.* marble. —**marmolista,** *n.m.* marbleworker. —**marmóreo** (-'mo·re·o) *adj.* marble (*attrib.*); marmoreal.

marmolería (mar·mo·le'ri·a) *n.f.* **1,** marblework. **2,** marble works.

marmota (mar'mo·ta) *n.f.* **1,** marmot. **2,** sleepyhead.

maroma (ma'ro·ma) *n.f.* **1,** hemp rope; hawser. **2,** tightrope. **3,** *Amer.* acrobatic feat; stunt. —**maromero,** *n.m., Amer.* tightrope walker; acrobat.

marque ('mar·ke) *v., pres.subjve. of* **marcar.**

marqué (mar'ke) *v., 1st pers.sing. pret. of* **marcar.**

marqués (mar'kes) *n.m.* marquis. —**marquesa,** *n.f.* marchioness. —**marquesado,** *n.m.* marquisate.

marquesina (mar·ke'si·na) *n.f.* marquee; awning.

marquetería (mar·ke·te'ri·a) *n.f.* marquetry.

marra ('ma·rra) *n.f.* **1,** lack; deficiency. **2,** sledgehammer.

marranada (ma·rra'na·ða) *also,* **marranería,** *n.f., colloq.* **1,** filthiness. **2,** swinishness; dirty trick.

marrano (ma'rra·no) *n.m.* **1,** pig; hog. **2,** *colloq., derog.* swine.

marrar (ma'rrar) *v.i.* & *t.* to fail; miss.

marras ('ma·rras) *adv., colloq., usu. in* **de marras, 1,** aforementioned. **2,** previous.

marrasquino (ma·rras'ki·no) *n.m.* maraschino.

marro ('ma·rro) *n.m.* **1,** a game resembling prisoner's base. **2,** a game resembling quoits. **3,** *colloq.* evasion; dodge.

marrón (ma'rron) *adj.* chestnut; brown. —*n.m.* **1,** quoit. **2,** marron.

marroquín (ma·rro'kin) *n.m.* morocco *(leather).*

marrubio (ma'rru·βjo) *n.m.* horehound.

marrullería (ma·rru·ʎe'ri·a; -je'ri·a) *n.f.* cunning; cajolery. —**marrullero,** *adj.* crafty; cunning. —*n.m.* crafty person.

Marsellesa (mar·se'ʎe·sa; -'je·sa) *n.f.* Marseillaise.

marsopa (mar'so·pa) *n.f.* porpoise.

marsupial (mar·su'pjal) *adj.* & *n.m.* & *f.* marsupial.

marta ('mar·ta) *n.f.* marten. —**marta cebellina,** sable.

Marte ('mar·te) *n.m., astron.; myth.* Mars.

martes ('mar·tes) *n.m. sing.* & *pl.* Tuesday. —**martes de carnaval** *or* **carnestolendas,** Shrove Tuesday.

martillar (mar·ti'ʎar; -'jar) *v.t.* & *i.* to hammer. *Also,* **martillear.**

martillazo (mar·ti'ʎa·θo; -'ja·so) *n.m.* hammer blow.

martilleo (mar·ti'ʎe·o; -'je·o) *n.m.* hammering.

martillo (mar'ti·ʎo; -jo) *n.m.* **1,** hammer; claw hammer. **2,** persistent person. **3,** auction room. —**a macha** ('ma·tʃa) **martillo,** *also,* **a machamartillo, 1,** roughly made. **2,** insistently; firmly.

martín (mar'tin) **pescador,** *n.m., ornith.* kingfisher.

martinete (mar·ti'ne·te) *n.m.* **1,** a kind of heron. **2,** drop hammer. **3,** pile driver.

martingala (mar·tin'ga·la) *n.f., colloq.* **1,** trick; artifice. **2,** gambling system.

martini (mar'ti·ni) *n.m.* martini.

mártir ('mar·tir) *n.m.* & *f.* martyr. —**martirio** (mar'ti·rjo) *n.m.* martyrdom.

martirizar (mar·ti·ri'θar; -'sar) *v.t.* [*infl.:* **rezar, 10**] to martyrize; torment.

marxismo (mark'sis·mo) *n.m.* Marxism. —**marxista,** *n.m.* & *f.* Marxist. —*adj.* Marxian.

marzo ('mar·θo; -so) *n.m.* March.

mas (mas) *conj.* but; yet.

más (mas) *adv.* **1,** more. **2,** most. **3,** longer. **4,** rather. **5,** besides; in addition. **6,** plus. —**a lo más,** at most; at best. —**a más y mejor,** copiously; to one's heart's content. —**de más,** extra; superfluous. —**más bien,** rather. —**más de,** more than *(fol. by a number or expression of quantity).* —**más que,** more than *(fol. by the second term of a comparison).* —**más que nunca,** more than ever. —**por más que,** however much. —**sin más ni más,** *colloq.* **1,** without further ado. **2,** suddenly; unexpectedly.

masa ('ma·sa) *n.f.* **1,** mass. **2,** dough. **3,** mash. **4,** populace; rabble. —**en masa,** in a group; en masse. —**producción en masa,** mass production.

masacre (ma'sa·kre) *n.f.* massacre. —**masacrar,** *v.t.* to massacre.

masaje (ma'sa·xe) *n.m.* massage. —**masajista,** *n.m.* masseur. —*n.f.* masseuse.

masajear (ma·sa·xe'ar) *v.t., Amer.* to massage.

mascar (mas'kar) *v.t.* [*infl.:* **tocar, 7**] to chew.

máscara ('mas·ka·ra) *n.f.* **1,** mask. **2,** disguise. —*n.m.* & *f.* masquerader; mummer. —**máscaras,** *n.f.pl.* masquerade.

mascarada (mas·ka'ra·ða) *n.f.* masquerade; mummery; masque.

mascarilla (mas·ka'ri·ʎa; -ja) *n.f.* death mask.

mascarón (mas·ka'ron) *n.m.* stone mask. —**mascarón de proa,** figurehead.

mascota (mas'ko·ta) *n.f.* mascot.

masculino (mas·ku'li·no) *adj.* male; manly; masculine. —**masculinidad,** *n.f.* masculinity.

mascullar (mas·ku'ʎar; -'jar) *v.t.* & *i.* to mumble.

masía (ma'si·a) *n.f.* farm; farmhouse.

masilla (ma'si·ʎa; -ja) *n.f.* putty.

masivo (ma'si·βo) *adj.* **1,** massive. **2,** mass (*attrib.*).

masón (ma'son) *n.m.* Freemason; Mason. —**masonería,** *n.f.* Freemasonry; Masonry. —**masónico,** *adj.* Masonic; Freemasonic.

masonita (ma·so'ni·ta) *n.f.*, *T.N.* Masonite.

masoquismo (ma·so'kis·mo) *n.m.* masochism. —**masoquista,** *n.m. & f.* masochist. —*adj.* masochistic. —**masoquístico,** *adj.* masochistic.

masque ('mas·ke) *v.*, *pres.subjve. of* mascar.

masqué (mas'ke) *v.*, *1st pers.sing. pret. of* mascar.

mastelero (mas·te'le·ro) *n.m.* topmast.

masticar (mas·ti'kar) *v.t.* [*infl.:* **tocar,** 7] **1,** to masticate; chew. **2,** to mull; ponder; ruminate. —**masticación,** *n.f.* mastication.

mástil ('mas·til) *n.m.* **1,** mast. **2,** stanchion. **3,** neck (*of a violin, guitar, etc.*).

mastín (mas'tin) *n.m.* mastiff.

mástique ('mas·ti·ke) *n.m.* mastic.

mastitis (mas'ti·tis) *n.f.* mastitis.

mastodonte (mas·to'ðon·te) *n.m.* mastodon.

mastoides (mas'toi·ðes) *adj. & n.f. sing. & pl.* mastoid. —**mastoideo** (-'ðe·o) *adj.* mastoidal. —**mastoiditis,** *n.f.* mastoiditis.

mastuerzo (mas'twer·θo; -so) *n.m.* **1,** dolt; oaf. **2,** cress.

masturbarse (mas·tur'βar·se) *v.r.* to masturbate. —**masturbación,** *n.f.* masturbation.

mata ('ma·ta) *n.f.* **1,** bush. **2,** sprig. **3,** grove. **4,** clump of grass; hassock. —**mata de pelo,** mass of hair; head of hair.

matadero (ma·ta'ðe·ro) *n.m.* slaughterhouse.

matador (ma·ta'ðor) *adj.* killing. —*n.m.* [*fem.* **-dora**] **1,** matador. **2,** killer; murderer. **3,** *cards* trump.

matadura (ma·ta'ðu·ra) *n.f.* sore; gall.

matalobos (ma·ta'lo·βos) *n.m. sing.* wolfsbane.

matamoros (ma·ta'mo·ros) *n.m. sing. & pl.* blusterer; fire-eater.

matamoscas (ma·ta'mos·kas) *n.m. sing. & pl.* fly swatter.

matanza (ma'tan·θa; -sa) *n.f.* killing; slaughter.

mataperro (ma·ta'pe·rro) *n.m.*, *colloq.* urchin; ragamuffin; gamin.

mataperrear, *v.i.*, *Amer.*, *colloq.* to roam the streets doing mischief.

matar (ma'tar) *v.t.* **1,** to kill. **2,** to gall. **3,** to tone down; subdue; dull. **4,** *cards* to beat; outrank. —**matarse,** *v.r.* **1,** to kill oneself. **2,** to strive; strain.

matarife (ma·ta'ri·fe) *n.m.* butcher; slaughterer.

matasanos (ma·ta'sa·nos) *n.m. sing. & pl.* quack doctor.

matasellos (ma·ta'se·ʎos; -'se·jos) *n.m. sing. & pl.* postmark.

match (matʃ) *n.m.*, *sports* match.

mate ('ma·te) *n.m.* **1,** mate; checkmate. **2,** *bot.* maté. —*adj.* mat.

matemáticas (ma·te'ma·ti·kas) *n.f.pl.*, *also, sing.*, **matemática,** mathematics. —**matemático,** *adj.* mathematical. —*n.m.* mathematician.

materia (ma'te·rja) *n.f.* **1,** matter. **2,** material. **3,** *educ.* subject. —**materia prima,** raw material.

material (ma·te'rjal) *adj. & n.m.* material. —**materialidad,** *n.f.* materiality.

materialismo (ma·te·rja'lis·mo) *n.m.* materialism. —**materialista,** *n.m. & f.* materialist. —*adj.* materialistic.

materializar (ma·te·rja·li'θar; -'sar) *v.t.* [*infl.:* **rezar,** 10] to materialize. —**materialización,** *n.f.* materialization.

maternal (ma·ter'nal) *adj.* maternal. *Also,* **materno** (-'ter·no).

maternidad (ma·ter·ni'ðað) *n.f.* **1,** maternity. **2,** motherliness; motherly affection.

matinal (ma·ti'nal) *adj.* matinal; matutinal.

matiné (ma·ti'ne) *n.m. or f.* matinee.

matiz (ma'tiθ; -'tis) *n.m.* shade; tint; tone.

matizar (ma·ti'θar; -'sar) *v.t.* [*infl.:* **rezar,** 10] to shade; color.

matón (ma'ton) *n.m.*, *colloq.* bully. —**matonería,** *n.f.*, *colloq.* braggadocio; bravado.

matorral (ma·to'rral) *n.m.* bush; scrub.

matraca (ma'tra·ca) *n.f.* **1,** noisemaker; rattle. **2,** *colloq.* annoying insistence. **3,** *colloq.* rattle; rattling. **4,** *colloq.* monotony; humdrum.

matrero (ma'tre·ro) *adj.* **1,** shrewd; cunning. **2,** *Amer.* = **arisco.**

matriarca (ma'trjar·ka) *n.f.* matriarch. —**matriarcado,** *n.m.* matriarchy. —**matriarcal**, *adj.* matriarchal.

matricida (ma·tri'θi·ða; -'si·ða) *adj.* matricidal. —*n.m. & f.* matricide (*agent*). —**matricidio** (-θi·ðjo; -'si·ðjo) *n.m.* matricide (*act*).

matrícula (ma'tri·ku·la) *n.f.* 1, matriculation; enrollment. 2, registration. 3, list; register.

matricular (ma·tri·ku'lar) *v.t.* 1, to matriculate; enroll. 2, to register; record.

matrimonio (ma·tri'mo·njo) *n.m.* 1, matrimony; marriage. 2, married couple. —**matrimonial**, *adj.* matrimonial.

matriz (ma'triθ; -'tris) *n.f.* 1, uterus; womb. 2, matrix. 3, mold. —*adj.* 1, principal. 2, parent (*attrib.*).

matrona (ma'tro·na) *n.f.* 1, matron. 2, midwife. —**matronal**, *adj.* matronly.

matute (ma'tu·te) *n.m.* 1, smuggling. 2, smuggled goods. —**matutear** (-te'ar) *v.i.* to smuggle.

matutino (ma·tu'ti·no) *also*, **matutinal** (-'nal) *adj.* matutinal; morning (*attrib.*).

maula ('mau·la) *n.f.* 1, defective article; lemon. 2, remnant. 3, trick; ruse. —*n.m. & f.* deceitful person.

maullar (mau'ʎar; -'jar) *v.i.* [*infl.*: **reunir**, 60] to meow. —**maullador**, *adj.* meowing.

maullido (mau'ʎi·ðo; -'ji·ðo) *also*, **maúllo** (ma'u·ʎo; -jo) *n.m.* meow.

mausoleo (mau·so'le·o) *n.m.* mausoleum.

maxilar (mak·si'lar) *adj. & n.m.* maxillary.

máxima ('mak·si·ma) *n.f.* maxim.

máxime ('mak·si·me) *adv.* mainly; chiefly; especially.

máximo ('mak·si·mo) *n.m. & adj.* maximum. —*adj.* maximal.

máximum ('mak·si·mum) *n.m.* [*pl.* -**mums**] maximum.

maya ('ma·ja) *adj. & n.m. & f.* Mayan. —*n.m. & f.* Maya.

mayal (ma'jal) *n.m.* flail.

mayar (ma'jar) *v.i.* = **maullar**.

mayo ('ma·jo) *n.m.* 1, May. 2, Maypole.

mayonesa (ma·jo'ne·sa) *n.f.* mayonnaise. *Also*, **mahonesa** (ma·o-).

mayor (ma'jor) *adj.* A *comp. of* **grande**, 1, greater; larger. 2, more; further. 3, older; elder. 4, *mus.* major. B *superl. of* **grande**, 1, greatest; largest. 2, oldest; eldest. 3, principal; main. —*n.m., mil:* major. —*n.f., logic* major premise; major term. —**mayores**, *n.m. & f.pl.* ancestors. —**mayor de edad**, of age. —**por mayor**; **al por mayor**, wholesale.

mayoral (ma·jo'ral) *n.m.* foreman; boss.

mayorazgo (ma·jo'raθ·ɣo; -'ras·ɣo) *n.m.* 1, primogeniture. 2, estate inherited by primogeniture.

mayordomo (ma·jor'ðo·mo) *n.m.* 1, majordomo. 2, steward. 3, manservant.

mayoría (ma·jo'ri·a) *n.f.* majority.

mayoridad (ma·jo·ri'ðað) *n.f.* legal age; majority.

mayorista (ma·jo'ris·ta) *n.m. & f.* wholesaler.

mayormente (ma·jor'men·te) *adv.* greatly; especially.

mayúsculo (ma'jus·ku·lo) *adj.* 1, good-sized; great. 2, capital; uppercase. —**mayúscula**, *n.f.* capital letter.

maza ('ma·θa; -sa) *n.f.* 1, mace; club. 2, hammer of a pile driver; drop hammer.

mazacote (ma·θa'ko·te; ma·sa-) *n.m.* lump; lumpy mass; mess. —**mazacotudo**, *adj.* lumpy; gooey; messy.

mazamorra (ma·θa'mo·rra; ma·sa-) *n.f.* 1, *colloq.* hodgepodge. 2, *Amer.* dessert made with corn starch and fruits.

mazapán (ma·θa'pan; ma·sa-) *n.m.* marzipan.

mazazo (ma'θa·θo; -'sa·so) *n.m., also,* **mazada** (-ða) *n.f.* blow with a mace or mallet.

mazmorra (maθ'mo·rra; mas-) *n.f.* dungeon.

mazo ('ma·θo; -so) *n.m.* 1, large wooden hammer; mallet; maul. 2, bundle; bunch. 3, stack (*of cards*).

mazorca (ma'θor·ka; ma'sor-) *n.f.* ear of corn.

mazurca (ma'θur·ka; ma'sur-) *n.f.* mazurka.

me (me) *pers.pron.* 1st *pers.sing., used as obj. of a verb* me; to me; myself.

meandro (me'an·dro) *n.m.* meandering; loop.

mear (me'ar) *v.i., vulg.* to urinate. —**meada**, *n.f., vulg.* urination. —**meadero**, *n.m., vulg.* urinal.

mecánica (me'ka·ni·ka) *n.f.* mechanics. —**mecánico**, *adj.* mechanic; mechanical. —*n.m.* mechanic. —**mecanismo**, *n.m.* mechanism.

mecanizar (me·ka·ni'θar; -'sar) *v.t.* [*infl.*: **rezar, 10**] to mechanize. —**mecanización**, *n.f.* mechanization.

mecanografía (me·ka·no·γra·'fi·a) *n.f.* typewriting. —**mecanográfico** (-'γra·fi·ko) *adj.* typewriting *(attrib.)*. —**mecanógrafo** (-'no·γra·fo) *n.m.* [*fem.* -**grafa**] typist.

mecanografiar (me·ka·no·γra'fjar) *v.t. & i.* [*infl.*: **enviar, 22**] to typewrite; type.

mecedor (me·θe'ðor; -se'ðor) *adj.* rocking; swinging. —*n.m.* swing; porch glider. —**mecedora**, *n.f.* rocking chair.

mecer (me'θer; -'ser) *v.t.* [*infl.*: **vencer, 11**] to rock; swing.

mecha ('me·tʃa) *n.f.* **1**, wick. **2**, wick fuse; fuse. **3**, = **mechón. 4**, thin strip of bacon.

mechar (me'tʃar) *v.t.* to lard with bacon strips.

mechero (me'tʃe·ro) *n.m.* **1**, burner. **2**, oil or gas lamp. **3**, wick lighter.

mechón (me'tʃon) *n.m.* lock; tuft of hair.

medalla (me'ða·ʎa; -ja) *n.f.* medal. —**medallón** (-'ʎon; -'jon) *n.m.* medallion; locket.

médano ('me·ða·no) *n.m.* **1**, dune. **2**, sandbank. *Also,* **medaño** (me'ða·ɲo).

media ('me·ðja) *n.f.* **1**, stocking. **2**, *Amer.* sock. **3**, *math.* mean. —**a medias**, by halves; halfway; fifty-fifty.

mediación (me·ðja'θjon; -'sjon) *n.f.* mediation. —**mediador**, *adj.* mediating. —*n.m.* [*fem.* -**dora**] mediator.

mediado (me'ðja·ðo) *adj.* **1**, half full. **2**, halfway; in the middle. —**a mediados de**, towards the middle of *(the month, year, etc.)*.

mediana (me'ðja·na) *n.f., geom.* median.

medianamente (me·ðja·na·'men·te) *adv.* **1**, moderately; reasonably. **2**, halfway; incompletely.

medianero (me·ðja'ne·ro) *adj.* intervening; intermediate. —*n.m.* = **mediador**. —**medianera**, *n.f.* party wall.

medianía (me·ðja'ni·a) *n.f.* **1**, mediocrity. **2**, mediocre person. **3**, tenant farming on a fifty-fifty basis.

mediano (me'ðja·no) *adj.* **1**, me-

dium; average. **2**, moderate. **3**, mediocre.

medianoche (me·ðja'no·tʃe) *n.f.* midnight.

mediante (me'ðjan·te) *adj.* mediating; interceding. —*prep.* by means of; with the help of; through. —**Dios mediante**, God willing.

mediar (me'ðjar) *v.i.* **1**, to be in the middle; be at the midpoint. **2**, to intervene. **3**, to mediate.

medicar (me·ði'kar) *v.t.* [*infl.*: **tocar, 7**] to medicate. —**medicación**, *n.f.* medication. —**medicamento**, *n.m.* medicament.

medicastro (me·ði'kas·tro) *n.m.* quack doctor.

medicina (me·ði'θi·na; -'si·na) *n.f.* medicine. —**medicinal**, *adj.* medicinal.

medicinar (me·ði·θi'nar; -si'nar) *v.t.* to medicate.

medición (me·ði'θjon; -'sjon) *n.f.* measurement; measuring; mensuration.

médico ('me·ði·ko) *adj.* medical. —*n.m.* [*fem.* **médica**] physician. —**médico de cabecera**, family physician. —**médico forense**, medical examiner.

medida (me'ði·ða) *n.f.* **1**, measure. **2**, measurement. **3**, proportion; correspondence. —**a medida de**, according to. —**a medida que**, as; while. —**hecho a la medida**, made-to-order.

medidor (me·ði'ðor) *adj.* measuring. —*n.m., Amer.* meter.

medieval (me·ðje'βal) *adj.* medieval. *Also,* **medioeval** (me·ðjo·e-).

medievo (me'ðje·βo) *n.m.* Middle Ages. *Also,* **medioevo** (me·ðjo'e-).

medio ('me·ðjo) *adj. & adv.* half. —*adj.* **1**, middle. **2**, medium. —*n.m.* **1**, middle; center. **2**, agency; means. **3**, medium; surroundings; environment. **4**, = **médium. 5**, *math.* one half; a half. **6**, *math.* mean. —**medios**, *n.m.pl.* means. —**a medio**, *fol. by inf.* half done: *a medio vestir*, half dressed. —**de medio a medio**, **1**, right on center; on the button. **2**, from *a* to *z*; completely. —**de por medio**, in between; between. —**echar por medio**, *colloq.* to go at it firmly; ride roughshod. —**edad media**, Middle Ages. —**en medio de**, in the midst of; amidst. —**meterse de por medio** *or* **por en medio**, to intervene. —**poner los medios**, to take steps; take measures. **—quitar de en medio,** *colloq.* to put out of the way; do away with. **—quitarse de en medio,** to get out of the way.

mediocre (me'ðjo·kre) *adj.* mediocre. **—mediocridad,** *n.f.* mediocrity.

mediodía (me·ðjo'ði·a) *n.m.* **1,** noon. **2,** south.

medioevo (me·ðjo'e·βo) *n.m.* = medievo. **—medioeval,** *adj.* = medieval.

mediopensionista (me·ðjo·pen·sjo'nis·ta) *n.m.* & *f.* day student.

medir (me'ðir) *v.t.* [*infl.:* pedir, 33] **1,** to measure; size. **2,** to fit; try on. **—medirse,** *v.r.* to moderate one's behavior; restrain oneself. **—¿Cuánto mide Vd.?,** How tall are you?

meditabundo (me·ði·ta'βun·do) *also, Amer., colloq.* **meditativo** (-'ti·βo) *adj.* meditative.

meditar (me·ði'tar) *v.t.* & *i.* to meditate. **—meditación,** *n.f.* meditation.

mediterráneo (me·ði·te'rra·ne·o) *adj.* & *n.m.* Mediterranean.

médium ('me·ðjum) *n.m.* & *f.* [*pl.* **médium** *or* **médiums**] spiritualistic medium.

medra ('me·ðra) *n.f.* progress; improvement; thriving. *Also,* **medro,** *n.m.,* **medros,** *n.m.pl.*

medrar (me'ðrar) *v.i.* to thrive; prosper.

medroso (me'ðro·so) *adj.* **1,** timorous. **2,** frightful.

médula (me·ðu·la) *n.f.* **1,** medulla. **2,** marrow. **3,** pith. **4,** *fig.* core; essence.

medular (me·ðu'lar) *adj.* **1,** medullary. **2,** basic; essential.

meduloso (me·ðu'lo·so) *adj.* pulpy; pithy.

medusa (me'ðu·sa) *n.f.* jellyfish; medusa; *cap., myth.* Medusa.

mefítico (me'fi·ti·ko) *adj.* mephitic.

megaciclo (me·ɣa'θi·klo; -'si·klo) *n.m.* megacycle.

megáfono (me'ɣa·fo·no) *n.m.* megaphone.

megalomanía (me·ɣa·lo·ma'ni·a) *n.f.* megalomania. **—megalómano** (-'lo·ma·no) *adj.* & *n.m.* megalomaniac.

megaocteto (me·ɣa·ok'te·to) *n.m.* megabyte.

megatón (me·ɣa'ton) *n.m.* megaton.

meiosis (me'jo·sis) *n.f.* meiosis.

mejicano (me·xi'ka·no) *adj.* & *n.m.* Mexican. *Also,* **mexicano.**

mejilla (me'xi·ʎa; -ja) *n.f.* cheek.

mejillón (me·xi'ʎon; -'jon) *n.m.* mussel.

mejor (me'xor) *adj.* **1,** *comp. of* bueno; better. **2,** *superl. of* bueno; best. **—adv. 1,** *comp. of* bien; better. **2,** *superl.* of bien; best. **3,** rather; preferably. **—a lo mejor,** perhaps; maybe. **—mejor dicho,** rather; more exactly. **—mejor que mejor,** much better; much the better; very well. **—tanto mejor,** so much the better; all the better.

mejora (me'xo·ra) *n.f.* **1,** improvement; melioration. **2,** *law* special bequest.

mejoramiento (me·xo·ra'mjen·to) *n.m.* improvement; melioration.

mejorana (me·xo'ra·na) *n.f.* marjoram.

mejorar (me·xo'rar) *v.t.* **1,** to improve; meliorate. **2,** to outbid. **3,** *law* to give a special bequest to. **—v.i.** [*also, refl.,* **mejorarse**] to improve; recover.

mejoría (me·xo'ri·a) *n.f.* improvement.

mejunje (me'xun·xe) *n.m.* hodgepodge. *Also,* **menjunje.**

melado (me'la·ðo) *adj.* honeycolored.

melancolía (me·lan·ko'li·a) *n.f.* **1,** melancholy. **2,** melancholia. **—melancólico,** *adj.* melancholic; melancholy.

melanesio (me·la'ne·sjo) *adj.* & *n.m.* Melanesian.

melanoma (me·la'no·ma) *n.m.* melanoma.

melaza (me'la·θa; -sa) *n.f.* molasses.

melcocha (mel'ko·tʃa) *n.f.* taffy.

melena (me'le·na) *n.f.* **1,** loose hair; long hair. **2,** mane.

melifluo (me'li·flwo) *adj.* mellifluous. **—melifluidad,** *n.f.* mellifluousness.

melindre (me'lin·dre) *n.m.* **1,** ladyfinger. **2,** priggishness. **—melindroso,** *adj.* & *n.m.* namby-pamby.

melocotón (me·lo·ko'ton) *n.m.* peach. **—melocotonero,** *n.m.* peach tree.

melodía (me·lo'ði·a) *n.f.* melody. **—melódico** (-'lo·ði·ko) *adj.* melodic. **—melodioso** (-'ðjo·so) *adj.* melodious.

melodrama (me·lo'ðra·ma) *n.m.*

melodrama. **—melodramático**
(-'ma·ti·ko) *adj.* melodramatic.

melón (me'lon) *n.m.* melon; muskmelon. **—melonar,** *n.m.* melon
patch. **—melonero,** *n.m.* melon
vendor.

meloso (me'lo·so) *adj.* excessively
sweet; unctuous. **—melosidad,** *n.f.*
excessive sweetness; unctuousness.

mella ('me·ʎa; -ja) *n.f.* **1,** notch;
nick; dent. **2,** hollow; gap. **—hacer
mella a,** to impress; affect. **—hacer
mella en,** to impair.

mellado (me'ʎa·ðo; -'ja·ðo) *adj.* **1,**
jagged; notched. **2,** toothless.

mellar (me'ʎar; -'jar) *v.t.* to notch;
nick; dent.

mellizo (me'ʎi·θo; -'ji·so) *adj.* &
n.m. twin.

membrana (mem'bra·na) *n.f.*
membrane. **—membranoso,** *adj.*
membranous.

membresía (mem·bre'si·a) *n.f.*
membership.

membrete (mem'bre·te) *n.m.* **1,**
letterhead. **2,** inside address. **3,** caption; heading. **4,** *journalism* masthead.

membrillo (mem'bri·ʎo; -jo) *n.m.*
1, quince. **2,** [*also,* **membrillero**]
quince tree.

membrudo (mem'bru·ðo) *adj.*
muscular; brawny.

memento (me'men·to) *n.m.* memento.

memo ('me·mo) *adj.* silly; foolish.
—n.m. simpleton.

memorable (me·mo'ra·βle) *adj.*
memorable.

memorándum (me·mo'ran·dum)
n.m. [*pl.* **-mums**] memorandum.

memoria (me'mo·rja) *n.f.* **1,** memory. **2,** remembrance. **3,** account. **4,**
note; memorandum. **—memorias,**
n.f.pl. **1,** memoirs. **2,** regards. **—de
memoria,** by heart; from memory.
—flaco de memoria, forgetful.
—hacer memoria de, to recall.
—memoria de gallo, poor memory; short memory.

memorial (me·mo'rjal) *n.m.*
formal petition; memorial.

memorizar (me·mo·ri'θar; -'sar)
v.t. [*infl.:* **rezar,** 10] to memorize.

menaje (me'na·xe) *n.m.* household
furniture and furnishings.

mención (men'θjon; -'sjon) *n.f.*
mention; reference. **—mencionar,**
v.t. to mention; name.

mendaz (men'daθ; -'das) *adj.* men-

dacious. **—mendacidad,** *n.f.* mendacity.

mendicante (men·di'kan·te) *adj.*
& *n.m.* & *f.* mendicant.

mendicidad (men·di·θi'ðað;
-si'ðað) *n.f.* beggary; mendicancy.

mendigar (men·di'ɣar) *v.t.* [*infl.:*
pagar, 8] to beg. **—mendigo**
(-'di·ɣo) *n.m.* [*fem.* **-ga**] beggar.

mendrugo (men'dru·ɣo) *n.m.* crust
of bread; bit of stale bread.

menear (me·ne'ar) *v.t.* to shake;
wag. **—meneo** (-'ne·o) *n.m.* wag;
wagging

menester (me·nes'ter) *n.m.* **1,**
need. **2,** task; chore. **—menestero-
so,** *adj.* needy. **—es menester,** it is
necessary.

menestra (me'nes·tra) *n.f.* **1,** vegetable stew. **2,** *pl.* dried vegetables.

mengua ('men·gwa) *n.f.* **1,** diminution; decrease; wane. **2,** want;
lack. **3,** poverty; indigence. **4,** discredit.

menguante (men'ɣwan·te) *adj.*
waning; decreasing. **—n.f.** wane.

menguar (men'ɣwar) *v.t.* & *i.*
[*infl.:* **averiguar,** 9] to decrease;
wane. **—menguado,** *adj.* cowardly.
—n.m. coward.

menhir (men'ir) *n.m.* menhir.

meningitis (me·nin'xi·tis) *n.f.*
meningitis.

menjunje (men'xun·xe) *n.m.* =
mejunje.

menonita (me·no'ni·ta) *adj.* &
n.m. & *f.* Mennonite.

menopausia (me·no'pau·sja) *n.f.*
menopause.

menor (me'nor) *adj.* A *comp. of*
pequeño, 1, smaller. **2,** younger. **3,**
mus. minor. B *superl. of* **pequeño,
1,** smallest. **2,** youngest. **—n.m.** &
f. minor. **—n.f.,** *logic* minor premise; minor term. **—menor de edad,**
under age. **—por menor; al por
menor,** retail.

menoría (me·no'ri·a) *n.f.* **1,** inferiority. **2,** minority; condition of a
minor or underage person.

menorista (me·no'ris·ta) *n.m.* &
f., Amer. retailer.

menos ('me·nos) *adv.* **1,** less. **2,**
least. **3,** except. **4,** minus. **5,** *in expressions of time* to; before: *las dos
menos cuarto,* a quarter to or before
two. **—prep.** less; minus; except.
—conj. but; except. **—al menos; a
lo menos,** at least. **—a menos que,**
unless. **—de menos,** lacking; less.
—echar de menos, to miss.

—**menos de,** less than (*fol. by a number or expression of quantity*). —**menos que,** less than (*fol. by the second term of a comparison*). —**no poder menos de** *or* **que,** to be unable to do other than: *No pude menos que hacerlo,* I could not help doing it. —**por lo menos,** at least. —**por menos que,** however little. —**sin más ni menos** = **sin más ni más.** —**tener a** *or* **en menos,** to belittle; scorn. —**venir a menos,** to decline.

menoscabar (me·nos·ka'βar) *v.t.* **1,** to reduce; diminish. **2,** to impair. **3,** to discredit; disparage.

menoscabo (me·nos'ka·βo) *n.m.* **1,** diminution. **2,** impairment. **3,** disparagement.

menospreciar (me·nos·pre'θjar; -'sjar) *v.t.* **1,** to underrate; undervalue. **2,** to belittle; scorn. —**menospreciable,** *adj.* contemptible.

menosprecio (me·nos'pre·θjo; -sjo) *n.m.* **1,** undervaluation; underestimation. **2,** scorn.

mensaje (men'sa·xe) *n.m.* **1,** message. **2,** errand. —**mensajero,** *n.m.* messenger.

menstruar (mens'trwar) *v.t.* [*infl.:* continuar, 23] to menstruate. —**menstruación,** *n.f.* menstruation. —**menstrual,** *adj.* menstrual.

menstruo ('mens·trwo) *adj.* menstrual. —*n.m.* **1,** menstruation. **2,** menstrual fluid.

mensual (men'swal) *adj.* monthly. —**mensualidad,** *n.f.* monthly salary; monthly payment.

mensurar (men·su'rar) *v.t.* to measure. —**mensurable,** *adj.* measurable; mensurable.

menta ('men·ta) *n.f.* mint.

mentado (men'ta·ðo) *adj.* noted; famous.

mental (men'tal) *adj.* mental. —**mentalidad,** *n.f.* mentality.

mentar (men'tar) *v.t.* [*infl.:* pensar, 27] to mention; cite.

mente ('men·te) *n.f.* mind.

mentecato (men·te'ka·to) *adj.* silly; stupid. —*n.m.* fool.

mentir (men'tir) *v.i.* [*infl.:* sentir, 31] to lie; speak falsely.

mentira (men'ti·ra) *n.f.* lie; falsehood. —**de mentiras,** jokingly; in jest. —**mentira oficiosa,** white lie.

mentiroso (men·ti'ro·so) *adj.* lying; false. —*n.m.* [*fem.* -**rosa**] liar.

mentirijillas (men·ti·ri'xi·ʎas;

-jas) *n.f.pl.,* in **de mentirijillas,** make-believe.

mentís (men'tis) *n.m.* flat denial. —**dar el mentís a,** give the lie to.

mentol (men'tol) *n.m.* menthol. —**mentolado,** *adj.* mentholated.

mentón (men'ton) *n.m.* chin.

mentor (men'tor) *n.m.* mentor.

menú (me'nu) *n.m.* menu.

menudear (me·nu·de'ar) *v.i.* **1,** to be frequent; occur often. **2,** to enumerate details or trifles. **3,** to fall abundantly, as rain. —*v.t., colloq.* to repeat; do often.

menudencia (me·nu'ðen·θjá; -sja) *n.f.* **1,** smallness; minuteness. **2,** trifle; detail. —**menudencias,** *n.f.pl.* minutiae.

menudeo (me·nu'ðe·o) *n.m.* **1,** frequent occurrence. **2,** detailed account. **3,** retail. —**al menudeo,** at retail.

menudillos (me·nu'ði·ʎos; -jos) *n.m.pl.* giblets.

menudo (me'nu·ðo) *adj.* **1,** small; little; minute. **2,** petty; picayune. **3,** (*ironic*) fine!; great! —*n.m.* **1,** loose change. **2,** *Mex.* tripe and hominy stew. —**a menudo,** often. —¡**menudo triunfo!,** big deal! —**por menudo,** minutely.

meñique (me'ɲi·ke) *n.m.* little finger.

meollo (me'o·ʎo; -jo) *n.m.* **1,** brain. **2,** marrow. **3,** essence.

mequetrefe (me·ke'tre·fe) *n.* coxcomb; busybody.

meramente (me·ra'men·te) *adv.* merely; solely.

mercachifle (mer·ka'tʃi·fle) *n.m.* **1,** peddler; hawker. **2,** *colloq.,* petty dealer; huckster.

mercadeo (mer·ka'ðe·o) *n.m.* marketing. —**mercadear,** *v.i.* to deal; trade.

mercader (mer·ka'ðer) *n.m.* merchant. —**mercadería,** *n.f.* merchandise.

mercado (mer·ka·ðo) *n.m.* **1,** market. **2,** marketing; shopping.

mercancía (mer·kan'θi·a; -'si·a) *n.f., usu.pl.* goods; merchandise. —**tren mercancías** *or* **de mercancías,** freight train.

mercante (mer'kan·te) *adj.* & *n.m.,* merchant.

mercantil (mer·kan'til) *adj.* mercantile. —**mercantilismo,** *n.m.* mercantilism. —**derecho mercantil,** commercial law.

mercar (mer'kar) *v.t.* [*infl.:* **tocar, 7**] to buy.

merced (mer'θed; -'sed) *n.f.* grace; mercy; favor. **—a merced de,** in the hands of; subject to the will of. **—merced a,** thanks to. **—vuestra merced,** your grace; your honor.

mercenario (mer·θe'na·rjo; mer·se-) *adj.* & *n.m.* mercenary.

mercería (mer·θe'ri·a; mer·se-) *n.f.* **1,** notions. **2,** notions store. **3,** haberdashery. **—mercero** (-'θe·ro; -'se·ro) *n.m.* mercer.

mercerizar (mer·θe·ri'θar; -se·ri'sar) *v.t.* [*infl.:* **rezar, 10**] to mercerize.

mercurial (mer·ku'rjal) *adj.* **1,** pert. to mercury or the god Mercury. **2,** [*also,* **mercúrico** (-'ku·ri·ko)] mercuric; mercury (*attrib.*).

mercurio (mer'ku·rjo) *n.m.* **1,** mercury. **2,** *cap.* Mercury.

mercurocromo (mer·ku·ro'kro·mo) *n.m.* mercurochrome.

merecer (me·re'θer; -'ser) *v.t.* [*infl.:* **conocer, 13**] **1,** to merit; deserve. **2,** to be worth; be worthy of. **—v.i.** to be worthy or deserving. **—merecimiento,** *n.m.* merit. **—merecedor,** *adj.* deserving; worthy. **—merecido,** *n.m.* (just) deserts.

merendar (me·ren'dar) *v.i.* [*infl.:* **pensar, 27**] **1,** to have an afternoon snack or tea. **2,** to picnic. **—v.t.** to have as an afternoon snack.

merendero (me·ren'de·ro) *n.m.* **1,** patio restaurant. **2,** picnic stand.

merengue (me'ren·ge) *n.m.* **1,** meringue. **2,** merengue.

meretricio (me·re'tri·θjo; -sjo) *adj.* meretricious.

meretriz (me·re'triθ; -'tris) *n.f.* prostitute.

mergo ('mer·yo) *n.m.* merganser. *Also,* **mergánsar** (-'yan·sar).

meridiano (me·ri'ðja·no) *adj.* **1,** meridional. **2,** noon. **—n.m.** meridian. **—meridional,** *adj.* southern.

merienda (me'rjen·da) *n.f.* **1,** afternoon snack or tea. **2,** picnic.

merino (me'ri·no) *adj.* & *n.m.* merino.

mérito ('me·ri·to) *n.m.* **1,** merit; worth. **2,** excellence. **—meritorio,** *adj.* worthy; meritorious. **—n.m.** unpaid trainee.

merla ('mer·la) *n.f.* blackbird; merle. *Also,* **mirlo,** *n.m.*

merlín (mer'lin) *n.m.* marline.

merluza (mer'lu·θa; –sa) *n.f.* **1,** hake. **2,** haddock. **3,** *colloq.* drunkenness.

merma ('mer·ma) *n.f.* **1,** diminution; decrease. **2,** *comm.* leakage.

mermar (mer'mar) *v.i.* to diminish; decrease. **—v.t.** to reduce.

mermelada (mer·me'la·ða) *n.f.* marmalade; jam.

mero ('me·ro) *adj.* **1,** pure; simple; mere. **2,** *Mex.* very; self. **—n.m.** jewfish. **—lo mero mero,** *slang* the nitty-gritty.

merodeador (me·ro·ðe·a'ðor) *adj.* **1,** foraging. **2,** marauding. **—n.m.** **1,** forager. **2,** marauder.

merodear (me·ro·ðe'ar) *v.i.* **1,** to forage. **2,** to maraud.

merodeo (me·ro'ðe·o) *n.m.* **1,** foraging. **2,** marauding.

merque ('mer·ke) *v., pres.subjve. of* **mercar.**

merqué (mer'ke) *v., 1st pers.sing. pret. of* **mercar.**

mes (mes) *n.m.* **1,** month. **2,** monthly pay or payment. **3,** *colloq.* menstruation. **—mesada,** *n.f.* monthly pay. **—meses mayores,** last months of pregnancy.

mesa ('me·sa) *n.f.* **1,** table. **2,** desk; bureau. **3,** counter. **4,** executive board. **5,** = **meseta.** **—a mesa puesta,** *colloq.* without trouble or expense. **—hacer mesa limpia,** *colloq.* to make a clean sweep. **—levantar la mesa,** to clear the table. **—mesa revuelta,** *colloq.* topsy-turvy. **—poner la mesa,** to set the table.

mesana (me'sa·na) *n.f.* mizzen. **—palo de mesana,** mizzenmast.

mesar (me'sar) *v.t., usu.v.r.* **mesarse,** to tear out (one's hair).

mescolanza (mes·ko'lan·θa; -sa) *n.f.* mixture; medley.

mesero (me'se·ro) *n.m.* **1,** worker paid by the month. **2,** *Mex.* waiter. **—mesera,** *n.f.* waitress.

meseta (me'se·ta) *n.f.* **1,** tableland; plateau. **2,** stair landing.

Mesías (me'si·as) *n.m.* Messiah. **—mesiánico** (-'sja·ni·ko) *adj.* Messianic.

mesmerismo (mes·me'ris·mo) *n.m.* mesmerism. **—mesmeriano** (-'rja·no) *adj.* mesmeric.

mesnada (mes'na·ða) *n.f.* **1,** retinue. **2,** band; troupe. **—mesnadero,** *n.m.* retainer; follower.

mesolítico (me·so'li·ti·ko) *adj.* mesolithic.

mesón (me'son) *n.m.* **1,** inn; tavern.

2, meson. —**mesonero,** *n.m.* innkeeper; tavernkeeper.

mesotrón (me·so'tron) *n.m.* mesotron.

mesozoico (me·so'θoi·ko; -'soiko) *adj.* Mesozoic.

mestizo (mes'ti·θo; -so) *adj.* & *n.m.* mestizo.

mesurar (me·su'rar) *v.t.* to temper; moderate. —**mesurarse,** *v.r.* to control oneself.

meta ('me·ta) *n.f.* **1,** end; limit. **2,** goal. **3,** *sports* finish line.

metabolismo (me·ta·βo'lis·mo) *n.m.* metabolism. —**metabólico** (-'βo·li·ko) *adj.* metabolic.

metacarpo (me·ta'kar·po) *n.m.* metacarpus. —**metacarpiano** ('pjano) *adj.* metacarpal.

metadona (me·ta'ðo·na) *n.f.* methadone.

metafísica (me·ta'fi·si·ka) *n.f.* metaphysics. —**metafísico,** *adj.* metaphysical. —*n.m.* metaphysician.

metáfora (me'ta·fo·ra) *n.f.* metaphor. —**metafórico** (-'fo·ri·ko) *adj.* metaphoric.

metal (me'tal) *n.m.* **1,** metal. **2,** tone or timbre of the voice. —**metal blanco,** nickel silver.

metálico (me'ta·li·ko) *adj.* metallic. —*n.m.* coin; specie.

metalífero (me·ta'li·fe·ro) *adj.* metalliferous.

metalizarse (me·ta·li'θar·se; -'sar·se) *v.r.* [*infl.:* **rezar,** 10] to be dominated by love of money.

metaloide (me·ta'loi·ðe) *adj.* & *n.m.* metalloid.

metalurgia (me·ta'lur·xja) *n.f.* metallurgy. —**metalúrgico** (-'lurxi·ko) *adj.* metallurgic. —*n.m.* metallurgist.

metamorfosis (me·ta·mor'fo·sis) *also,* **metamórfosis** (-'mor·fo·sis) *n.f.sing.* & *pl.* metamorphosis. —**metamórfico** (-'mor·fi·ko) *adj.* metamorphic. —**metamorfosear** (-se'ar) *v.t.* to metamorphose.

metano (me'ta·no) *n.m.* methane.

metanol (me·ta'nol) *n.m.* methanol.

metaplasma (me·ta'plas·ma) *n.m.* metaplasm.

metástasis (me'tas·ta·sis) *n.f.* metastasis. —**metastático** (-'tati·ko) *adj.* metastatic.

metatarso (me·ta'tar·so) *n.m.* metatarsus. —**metatarsiano** (-'sja·no) *adj.* metatarsal.

metazoario (me·ta·θo'a·rjo; -so'arjo) *adj.* & *n.m.* Metazoan.

metazoo (me·ta'θo·o; -'so·o) *adj.* & *n.m.* Metazoan. —**metazoos,** *n.m.pl.* Metazoa.

metempsicosis (me·temp·si'ko·sis) *also,* **metempsícosis** (-'si·ko·sis) *n.f.sing.* & *pl.* metempsychosis.

meteorito (me·te·o'ri·to) *n.m.* meteorite.

meteoro (me·te'o·ro) *n.m.* meteor. —**meteórico,** *adj.* meteoric.

meteorología (me·te·o·ro·lo'xi·a) *n.f.* meteorology. —**meteorológico** (-'lo·xi·ko) *adj.* meteorological. —**meteorologista** (-'xis·ta) *n.m.* & *f., also,* **meteorólogo** (-'ro·lo·γo) *n.m.* meteorologist.

meter (me'ter) *v.t.* **1,** to put in; insert. **2,** to bring in; introduce. **3,** to raise; stir up; produce. **4,** to invest; stake. **5,** to put forth; utter. —**meterse,** *v.r.* **1,** to interfere; meddle. **2,** to become involved. —**meterse con,** *colloq.* to pick a quarrel with.

meticuloso (me·ti·ku'lo·so) *adj.* meticulous. —**meticulosidad,** *n.f.* meticulousness.

metido (me'ti·ðo) *adj.* **1,** *fol. by* **en,** profuse in; abounding in. **2,** *Amer.* meddlesome. —*n.m., Amer.* meddler.

metileno (me·ti'le·no) *n.m.* methylene.

metilo (me'ti·lo) *n.m.* methyl. —**metílico,** *adj.* methylic. —**alcohol metílico,** methyl alcohol.

metodista (me·to'ðis·ta) *adj.* & *n.m.* & *f.* Methodist. —**metodismo,** *n.m.* Methodism.

método ('me·to·ðo) *n.m.* method. —**metódico** (-'to·ði·ko) *adj.* methodical. —**metodología** (-ðo·lo 'xi·a) *n.f.* methodology.

metraje (me'tra·xe) *n.m., motion pictures* length; footage. —**(de) corto metraje,** short. —**(de) largo metraje,** full-length.

metralla (me'tra·ʎa; -ja) *n.f.* grapeshot.

métrica ('me·tri·ka) *n.f.* metrics.

métrico ('me·tri·ko) *adj.* **1,** metric. **2,** metrical.

metro ('me·tro) *n.m.* **1,** meter. **2,** = **metropolitano.**

metrónomo (me'tro·no·mo) *n.m.* metronome.

metrópoli (me'tro·po·li) *n.f.* metropolis. —**metropolitano** (-'ta·no) *adj.* & *n.m.* metropolitan. —*n.m.*

[*also,* **metro**] city transit system; subway.

mexicano (me·xi'ka·no) *adj.* & *n.m., Amer.* = **mejicano.**

meza ('me·θa; -sa) *v., pres.subjve. of* **mecer.**

mezcal (meθ'kal; mes-) *n.m.* mescal.

mezcla ('meθ·kla; 'mes-) *n.f.* mixture; mix; mixing.

mezcladora (meθ·kla'ðo·ra; mes-) *n.f.* mixing machine; mixer.

mezcladura (meθ·kla'ðu·ra; mes-) *n.f.* = **mezcla.**

mezclamiento (meθ·kla'mjen·to; mes-) *n.m.* = **mezcla.**

mezclar (meθ'klar; mes-) *v.t.* to mix. —**mezclarse,** *v.r.* to mingle.

mezcolanza (meθ·ko'lan·θa; mes·ko'lan·sa) *n.f.* mixture; hodgepodge; medley.

mezo ('me·θo; -so) *v., 1st pers. sing. pres.ind. of* **mecer.**

mezquindad (meθ·kin'daθ; mes-) *n.f.* **1,** miserliness. **2,** smallness; pettiness; meanness. **3,** meagerness. **4,** wretchedness; poverty.

mezquino (meθ'ki·no; mes-) *adj.* **1,** miserly. **2,** small; petty; mean. **3,** meager. **4,** wretched; poor.

mezquita (meθ'ki·ta; mes-) *n.f.* mosque.

mezquite (meθ'ki·te; mes-) *n.m.* mesquite.

mezzo-soprano (me·so·so·'pra·no) *n.f.* mezzo-soprano.

mi (mi) *poss.adj. masc.* & *fem.sing.* [*m.* & *f.pl.* **mis**], *agreeing in number with the thing possessed* my.

mi (mi) *n.m., mus.* mi; E.

mí (mi) *pers.pron. 1st pers.sing., used after a prep.* me; myself.

mía ('mi·a) *poss.pron. fem.sing.* mine. —*poss.adj.f.sing., used after a noun* my; mine; of mine.

mías ('mi·as) *poss.pron. fem.pl.* mine. —*poss.adj fem.pl. used after a noun* my; mine; of mine.

miasma ('mjas·ma) *n.m.* miasma. —**miasmático** (-'ma·ti·ko) *adj.* miasmal; miasmatic.

miastenia (mjas'te·nja) *n.f.* myasthenia.

miau (mjau) *n.m.* meow.

mica ('mi·ka) *n.f.* mica.

micado (mi'ka·ðo) *n.m.* mikado.

micción (mik'θjon; -'sjon) *n.f.* urination.

micra ('mi·kra) *n.f.* micron.

microbio (mi'kro·βjo) *n.m.* mi-crobe. —**micróbico** (-βi·ko) *adj.* microbic.

microcircuito (mi·kro·θir'kwi·to; -sir'kwi·to) *n.m.* microcircuit.

microcomputadora (mi·kro·kom·pu·ta'ðo·ra) *n.f.* microcomputer.

microcosmo (mi·kro'kos·mo) *n.m.* microcosm. —**microcósmico,** *adj.* microcosmic.

microeconomía (mi·kro·e·ko·no'mi·a) *n.f.* microeconomics.

microficha (mi·kro'fi·tʃa) *n.f.* microfiche.

microfilm (mi·kro'film) *n.m.* microfilm.

micrófono (mi'kro·fo·no) *n.m.* microphone.

microfotografía (mi·kro·fo·to·ɣra'fi·a) *n.f.* **1,** microphotography. **2,** microphotograph.

micrografía (mi·kro·ɣra'fi·a) *n.f.* **1,** micrograph. **2,** micrography.

micrómetro (mi'kro·me·tro) *n.m.* micrometer.

micrón (mi'kron) *n.m.* micron.

micronesio (mi·kro'ne·sjo) *adj.* & *n.m.* Micronesian.

microonda (mi·kro'on·da) *n.f.* microwave. —**horno de microondas,** microwave oven.

microordenador (mi·kro·or·ðe·na'ðor) *n.m.* microcomputer.

microorganismo (mi·kro·or·ɣa'nis·mo) *n.m.* microörganism.

microplaqueta (mi·kro·pla'ke·ta) *n.f.* microchip.

microscopio (mi·kros'ko·pjo) *n.m.* microscope. —**microscópico** (-'ko·pi·ko) *adj.* microscopic.

microteléfono (mi·kro·te'le·fo·no) *n.m.* handset.

micrótomo (mi'kro·to·mo) *n.m.* microtome.

mida ('mi·ða) *v., pres.subjve. of* **medir.**

midiendo (mi'ðjen·do) *v., ger. of* **medir.**

midió (mi'ðjo) *v., 3rd pers.sing. pret. of* **medir.**

mido ('mi·ðo) *v., 1st pers.sing. pres.ind. of* **medir.**

miedo ('mje·ðo) *n.m.* fear. —**miedoso,** *adj.* scary; fearful; afraid. —**dar miedo,** to frighten; be frightening. —**miedo cerval,** animal fear; dreadful fear. —**tener miedo,** to be afraid.

miel (mjel) *n.f.* honey. —**miel de caña,** molasses; sugar cane juice.

mielitis (mje'li·tis) *n.f.* myelitis.

miembro ('mjem·bro) *n.m.* **1**, member. **2**, limb.

mienta ('mjen·ta) *v.*, *pres.subjve.* of **mentir**.

miente ('mjen·te) *n.f.*, *usu.pl.* mind; thought. —**parar** *or* **poner mientes en**, to consider; pay attention to. —**traer a las mientes**, to recall; bring to mind.

miente ('mjen·te) *v.*, *pres.subjve.* of **mentar**.

miento ('mjen·to) *v.*, *1st pers.sing. pres.ind.* of **mentir** *and* **mentar**.

mientras ('mjen·tras) *conj.* while; as; whereas. —*prep.* during. —*adv.* meanwhile; in the meantime. —**mientras más**, the more. —**mientras menos**, the less. —**mientras que**, while; as; so long as. —**mientras tanto**, meanwhile; in the meantime.

miércoles ('mjer·ko·les) *n.m. sing. & pl.* Wednesday. —**miércoles de ceniza**, Ash Wednesday.

mierda ('mjer·ða) *n.f.*, *vulg.* excrement; filth.

mies (mjes) *n.f.* **1**, ripe grain. **2**, harvest season. —**mieses**, *n.f.pl.* grainfields.

miga ('mi·ɣa) *n.f.* **1**, crumb. **2**, soft part of bread. **3**, *colloq.* substance; gist. —**hacer buenas (malas) migas**, to be on good (bad) terms.

migaja (mi'ɣa·xa) *n.f.* crumb.

migración (mi·ɣra'θjon; -'sjon) *n.f.* migration. —**migratorio** (-'to·rjo) *adj.* migratory.

mijo ('mi·xo) *n.m.* millet.

mil (mil) *adj. & n.m.* **1**, thousand. **2**, thousandth; one-thousandth. —**a las mil y quinientas**, at an unearthly hour. —**armar las mil y quinientas**, to raise a row. —**cantar las mil y quinientas**, **1**, to give someone a dressing-down. **2**, to talk nonsense. —**mil millones**, billion (*U.S.*); milliard (*Brit.*).

milagro (mi'la·ɣro) *n.m.* miracle. —**milagroso**, *adj.* miraculous.

milano (mi'la·no) *n.m.*, *ornith.* kite.

milenario (mi·le'na·rjo) *adj.* **1**, millenary. **2**, millennial. —*n.m.* millennium.

milenio (mi'le·njo) *n.m.* millennium.

milenrama (mil·en'ra·ma) *n.f.* yarrow.

milésimo (mi'le·si·mo) *adj. & n.m.* thousandth. —**milésima**, *n.f.* thousandth part.

milhojas (mil'o·xas) *n.f.sing. & pl.* yarrow.

miliar (mi'ljar) *adj.*, *in* **erupción miliar**, miliaria. —**poste miliar**, milepost; milestone.

milicia (mi'li·θja; -sja) *n.f.* militia. —**miliciano**, *n.m.* militiaman; armed civilian. —*adj.* militia (*attrib.*).

milico (mi'li·ko) *n.m.*, *Amer., colloq.* **1**, rookie. **2**, cop; policeman. **3**, *derog.* soldier.

miligramo (mi·li'ɣra·mo) *n.m.* milligram.

mililitro (mi·li'li·tro) *n.m.* milliliter.

milímetro (mi'li·me·tro) *n.m.* millimeter.

militante (mi·li'tan·te) *adj.* militant. —*n.m.* active member.

militar (mi·li'tar) *adj.* military. —*n.m.* soldier; military man. —*v.i.* to be an active member; militate. —**militarismo**, *n.m.* militarism. —**militarista**, *n.m. & f.* militarist. —*adj.* militaristic.

militarizar (mi·li·ta·ri'θar; -'sar) *v.t.* [*infl.: rezar*, **10**] to militarize. —**militarización**, *n.f.* militarization.

milonga (mi'lon·ga) *n.f.*, *Amer.* **1**, a South American dance and air. **2**, street dancing.

milpiés (mil'pjes) *n.m.sing. & pl.* millipede.

milla ('mi·ʎa; -ja) *n.f.* mile. —**millaje**, *n.m.* mileage. —**milla marina**, nautical mile. —**milla terrestre**, statute mile.

millar (mi'ʎar; -'jar) *n.m.* a quantity of a thousand. —**millarada**, *n.f.* about a thousand.

millo ('mi·ʎo; -jo) *n.m.* = **mijo**.

millón (mi'ʎon; -'jon) *n.m.* million. —**millonada**, *n.f.* about a million.

millonario (mi·ʎo'na·rjo; mi·jo-) *n.m.* millionaire.

millonésimo (mi·ʎo'ne·si·mo; mi·jo-) *adj. & n.m.* millionth.

mimar (mi'mar) *v.t.* to pamper; pet.

mimbre ('mim·bre) *n.m.* osier. —**mimbrera** (-'bre·ra) *n.f.* osier (*plant*).

mimeógrafo (mi·me'o·ɣra·fo) *n.m.* mimeograph. —**mimeografía**, *n.f.* **1**, mimeographing. **2**, mimeograph. —**mimeografiar** (-'fjar) *v.t.* [*infl.: enviar*, **22**] to mimeograph.

mimetismo (mi·me'tis·mo) *n.m.*, *biol.* protective coloration; mimicry.

mímica ('mi·mi·ka) *n.f.* mimicry. —**mímico**, *adj.* mimic; imitative.

mimo ('mi·mo) *n.m.* **1,** mime. **2,** mimic. **3,** caress; pampering; petting. **4,** care; gentleness. —**mimoso,** *adj.* fastidious; delicate.

mimosa (mi'mo·sa) *n.f.* mimosa.

mina ('mi·na) *n.f.* **1,** mine. **2,** lead *(of a pencil).*

minador (mi·na'ðor) *n.m.* **1,** mine-layer. **2,** demolition expert.

minar (mi'nar) *v.t.* **1,** to mine *(as for demolition).* **2,** to undermine.

minarete (mi·na're·te) *n.m.* minaret.

mineral (mi·ne'ral) *adj. & n.m.* mineral.

mineralogía (mi·ne·ra·lo'xi·a) *n.f.* mineralogy. —**mineralógico** (-'lo·xi·ko) *adj.* mineralogical. —**mineralogista,** *n.m. & f.* mineralogist.

minería (mi·ne'ri·a) *n.f.* mining.

minero (mi'ne·ro) *adj.* mining. —*n.m.* miner.

mingitorio (min·xi'to·rjo) *n.m.* urinal.

miniatura (mi·nja'tu·ra) *n.f.* miniature.

minifalda (mi·ni'fal·da) *n.f.* miniskirt.

mínima ('mi·ni·ma) *n.f.* minim.

mínimo ('mi·ni·mo) *adj.* least; smallest. —*n.m.* minimum; least.

mínimum ('mi·ni·mum) *n.m.* minimum.

minino (mi'ni·no) *n.m., colloq.* pussy cat.

miniordenador (mi·ni·or·ðe·na'ðor) *n.m.* minicomputer.

ministerial (mi·nis·te'rjal) *adj.* **1,** ministerial. **2,** cabinet *(attrib.).*

ministerio (mi·nis'te·rjo) *n.m.* ministry.

ministrar (mi·nis'trar) *v.t. & i.* to minister. —*v.t.* **1,** to administer. **2,** to supply. —**ministrador,** *adj. & n.m.* ministrant. —**ministrante,** *adj. & n.m. & f.* ministrant. —*n.m. & f.* nurse; ward nurse.

ministril (mi·nis'tril) *n.m.* marshal *(law-enforcement officer).*

ministro (mi'nis·tro) *n.m.* minister.

minivestido (mi·ni·ßes'ti·ðo) *n.m.* minidress. *Also,* **minitraje.**

minorar (mi·no'rar) *v.t.* = **aminorar.** —**minorativo,** *adj. & n.m.* laxative, esp. mild.

minoría (mi·no'ri·a) *n.f.* minority. —**minoridad,** *n.f.* minority *(of age).*

minorista (mi·no'ris·ta) *adj.* retail. —*n.m.* retailer.

mintiendo (min'tjen·do) *v., ger. of* **mentir.**

mintió (min'tjo) *v., 3rd pers.sing. pret. of* **mentir.**

minucia (mi'nu·θja; -sja) *n.f.* trifle; detail; *pl.* minutiae.

minucioso (mi·nu'θjo·so; -'sjo·so) *adj.* minute; detailed; thorough. —**minuciosidad,** *n.f.* minuteness of detail.

minué (mi'nwe) *n.m.* minuet.

minuendo (mi·nu'en·do) *n.m.* minuend.

minúsculo (mi'nus·ku·lo) *adj.* **1,** minute; tiny. **2,** minuscule. **3,** lowercase. —**minúscula,** *n.f.* lower-case letter.

minuta (mi'nu·ta) *n.f.* **1,** note; memorandum. **2,** rough draft. **3,** menu; bill of fare.

minutero (mi·nu'te·ro) *n.m.* minute hand *(of a timepiece).*

minuto (mi'nu·to) *adj.* = **diminuto.** —*n.m.* minute.

mío ('mi·o) *poss.pron. masc.sing.* *[fem.* **mía;** *pl.* **míos, mías],** *agreeing in number and gender with the thing or things possessed* mine. —*poss.adj., used after a noun* my; mine; of mine: *hermanos míos,* my brothers; brothers mine (or of mine).

miopía (mi·o'pi·a) *n.f.* myopia; nearsightedness. —**miope** (mi'o·pe) *adj.* myopic; nearsighted. —*n.m. & f.* nearsighted person.

miosis (mi'o·sis) *n.f.* myosis. —**miótico** (-ti·ko) *adj.* myotic.

mira ('mi·ra) *n.f.* **1,** eyepiece; sight. **2,** aim; intent. **3,** leveling rod.

mirada (mi'ra·ða) *n.f.* glance; look.

mirado (mi'ra·ðo) *adj.* thoughtful; cautious. —**bien mirado,** well-thought-of. —**mal mirado,** ill-regarded.

mirador (mi·ra'ðor) *n.m.* **1,** lookout; watch tower. **2,** balcony; terrace. —*adj.* watching; looking.

miramiento (mi·ra'mjen·to) *n.m.* **1,** look; looking. **2,** consideration; regard. **3,** prudence; circumspection. **4,** misgiving; scruple.

mirar (mi'rar) *v.t.* **1,** to look at or upon; gaze at or upon; watch; observe. **2,** to regard; consider. —*v.i.* **1,** to look; gaze. **2,** to face; look *(in a certain direction).* —**mirarse en,** to look up to; follow the example of. —**mirar por,** to look after; look out for.

mirasol (mi·ra'sol) *n.m.* sunflower.

miríada (mi'ri·a·ða) *n.f.* myriad.

mirilla (mi'ri·ʎa; -ja) *n.f.* peep-hole.

miriñaque (mi·ri'ɲa·ke) *n.m.* hoopskirt.

mirlo ('mir·lo) *n.m.* blackbird; merle.

mirón (mi'ron) *n.m.* **1,** looker-on; bystander. **2,** kibitzer.

mirra ('mi·rra) *n.f.* myrrh.

mirto ('mir·to) *n.m.* myrtle.

mis (mis) *poss.adj., pl. of* **mi** *(agreeing in number with the things possessed)* my.

misa ('mi·sa) *n.f.* Mass. —**misal,** *n.m.* missal. —**misa del gallo,** midnight Mass. —**misa mayor,** High Mass; principal Mass. —**misa rezada,** Low Mass.

misantropía (mi·san·tro'pi·a) *n.f.* misanthropy. —**misantrópico** (-'tro·pi·ko) *adj.* misanthropic. —**misántropo** (-'san·tro·po) *n.m.* misanthrope.

miscelánea (mis·θe'la·ne·a; mi·se-) *n.f.* miscellany. —**misceláneo,** *adj.* miscellaneous.

miscible (mis'θi·βle; -'si·βle) *adj.* miscible. —**miscibilidad,** *n.f.* miscibility.

miserable (mi·se'ra·βle) *adj.* **1,** miserable; wretched. **2,** paltry. **3,** tightfisted; stingy. —*n.m.* **1,** wretch. **2,** tightwad; miser.

miseria (mi'se·rja) *n.f.* **1,** misery; wretchedness. **2,** stinginess; miserliness. **3,** paltry thing; paltry sum.

misericordia (mi·se·ri'kor·ðja) *n.f.* mercy; pity. —**misericordioso,** *adj.* compassionate; merciful.

mísero ('mi·se·ro) *adj.* = **miserable.**

misérrimo (mi'se·rri·mo) *adj., superl. of* **mísero.**

misil (mi'sil) *n.m.* missile.

misión (mi'sjon) *n.f.* mission. —**misional,** *adj.* missionary.

misionario (mi·sjo'na·rjo) *n.m.* **1,** = **misionero. 2,** delegate; envoy.

misionero (mi·sjo'ne·ro) *n.m.* missionary.

misiva (mi'si·βa) *n.f.* missive; note.

mismísimo (mis'mi·si·mo) *adj. & pron., colloq., superl. of* **mismo,** very same.

mismo ('mis·mo) *adj.* same; self;

very; selfsame. —*pron.* same; very same.

misogamia (mi·so'ɣa·mja) *n.f.* misogamy. —**misógamo** (-'so·ɣa·mo) *adj.* misogamous. —*n.m.* misogamist.

misoginia (mi·so'xi·nja) *n.f.* misogyny. —**misógino** (-'so·xi·no) *adj.* misogynous. —*n.m.* misogynist.

misterio (mis'te·rjo) *n.m.* mystery. —**misterioso,** *adj.* mysterious.

mística ('mis·ti·ka) *n.f.* **1,** mysticism. **2,** mystique.

místico ('mis·ti·ko) *adj. & n.m.* mystic. —*adj.* mystical. —**misticismo** (-'θis·mo; -'sis·mo) *n.m.* mysticism.

mistificar (mis·ti·fi'kar) *v.t.* = **mixtificar.** —**mistificación,** *n.f.* = **mixtificación.** —**mistificador,** *adj.* = **mixtificador.**

mitad (mi'tað) *n.f.* **1,** half. **2,** middle. —**mi cara mitad,** *colloq.* my better half.

mítico ('mi·ti·ko) *adj.* mythical.

mitigar (mi·ti'ɣar) *v.t.* [*infl.:* **pagar, 8**] to mitigate. —**mitigación,** *n.f.* mitigation.

mitin ('mi·tin) *n.m.* [*pl.* **mítines**] meeting; public assembly.

mito ('mi·to) *n.m.* myth.

mitología (mi·to·lo'xi·a) *n.f.* thology. —**mitológico** (-'lo·xi·ko) *adj.* mythological.

mitón (mi'ton) *n.m.* mitt; mitten.

mitosis (mi'to·sis) *n.f., biol.* mitosis.

mitra ('mi·tra) *n.f.* **1,** miter *(bishop's headdress).* **2,** bishopric.

mixtificar (miks·ti·fi'kar) *v.t.* [*infl.:* **tocar, 7**] to mystify. —**mixtificación,** *n.f.* mystification. —**mixtificador,** *adj.* mystifying.

mixto ('miks·to) *adj.* **1,** mixed; mingled. **2,** composite. —*n.m.* **1,** sulfur match. **2,** explosive.

mixtura (miks'tu·ra) *n.f.* mixture. —**mixturar,** *v.t.* to mix.

mnemotecnia (ne·mo'tek·nja) *n.f.* mnemonics. —**mnemotécnico** (-ni·ko) *adj.* mnemonic.

moaré (mo·a're) *n.f.* moire. Also, **muaré.**

mobiliario (mo·βi'lja·rjo) *adj., comm.* negotiable. —*n.m.* furniture; household goods.

moblaje (mo'βla·xe) *n.m.* furniture.

moca *also,* **moka** ('mo·ka) *n.f.* mocha.

mocasín (mo·ka'sin) *n.m.* mocca-sin.

mocear (mo·θe'ar; mo·se-) *v.i.* to sow wild oats.

mocedad (mo·θe'ðað; mo·se-) *n.f.* 1, youth; boyhood. 2, carefree living.

mocetón (mo·θe'ton; mo·se-) *n.m.* strapping youngster.

moción (mo'θjon; -'sjon) *n.f.* motion.

moco ('mo·ko) *n.m.* 1, mucus. 2, viscous substance. 3, snuff *(of a candle).* 4, candle drippings. —**moco del bauprés,** *naut.* martin-gale. —**moco de pavo,** 1, cockscomb. 2, *colloq.* trifle.

mocoso (mo'ko·so) *adj.* 1, snivelly. 2, full of mucus. 3, impudent; saucy. —*n.m.* brat; upstart youth.

mochar (mo'tʃar) *v.t.* 1, to butt; strike with the head or horns. 2, = **desmochar.** —**mochada,** *n.f.* butt; blow with the head or horns.

mochila (mo'tʃi·la) *n.f.* knapsack.

mocho ('mo·tʃo) *adj.* 1, blunt; stub-pointed. 2, cut short; cropped; lopped. 3, stub-horned, as a bull. —*n.m.* butt; butt end; stub.

mochuelo (mo'tʃwe·lo) *n.m.* red owl. —**cargar con el mochuelo,** to get (or give) the worst part.

moda ('mo·ða) *n.f.* fashion; mode.

modal (mo'ðal) *adj.* modal. —**modales,** *n.m.pl.* manners.

modalidad (mo·ða·li'ðað) *n.f.* 1, modality. 2, *colloq.* manner; sort.

modelar (mo·ðe'lar) *v.t. & i.* to model. —**modelado,** *n.m.* modeling.

modelo (mo'ðe·lo) *n.m.* model; pattern; norm. —*n.m. & f.* artist's model; fashion model. —*adj. indecl.* model: *casa modelo,* model house. —**desfile de modelos,** fashion show. —**modelo a escala,** scale model.

modem ('mo·ðem) *n.m., comput.; radio* modem.

moderar (mo·ðe'rar) *v.t.* to moderate; restrain. —**moderación,** *n.f.* moderation; temperance. —**moderado,** *adj.* moderate; restrained. —**moderador,** *n.m.* moderator.

modernizar (mo·ðer·ni'θar; -'sar) *v.t.* [*infl.: rezar,* 10] to modernize. —**modernización,** *n.f.* modernization.

moderno (mo'ðer·no) *adj. & n.m.* modern. —**modernismo,** *n.m.* mod-

ernism. —**modernista,** *n.m. & f.* modernist. —*adj.* modernistic.

modesto (mo'ðes·to) *adj.* modest. —**modestia,** *n.f.* modesty.

módico ('mo·ði·ko) *adj.* 1, frugal; sparing. 2, moderate *(of prices).*

modificar (mo·ði·fi'kar) *v.t.* [*infl.: tocar,* 7] to modify. —**modifica-ción,** *n.f.* modification. —**modifica-dor,** *n.m.* modifier. —*adj.* modi-fying.

modismo (mo'ðis·mo) *n.m.* idiom; idiomatic expression.

modista (mo'ðis·ta) *n.m. & f.* dressmaker; modiste. —**modistería,** *n.f.* dress shop.

modo ('mo·ðo) *n.m.* 1, mode; manner. 2, *gram.* mood. 3, *mus.* mode. —**modoso,** *adj.* well-mannered; well-behaved. —**de modo que,** so; and so. —**de ningún modo,** by no means. —**de todos modos,** anyhow; at any rate. —**de un modo u otro,** somehow; in one way or another. —**en cierto modo,** to some extent. —**ni modo,** *Mex.,* oh, well; too bad.

modorra (mo'ðo·rra) *n.f.* drowsiness.

modular (mo·ðu'lar) *v.t. & i.* to modulate. —**modulación,** *n.f.* modulation. —**modulador,** *n.m.* modulator.

módulo ('mo·ðu·lo) *n.m.* 1, module. 2, *mus.* modulation. 3, modulus. —**modular,** *adj.* modular.

mofa ('mo·fa) *n.f.* mockery; jeer. —**mofar,** *v.i.* [*also, refl.,* **mofarse**] to deride; mock.

moflete (mo'fle·te) *n.m.* chub-cheek. —**mofletudo,** *adj.* chubcheeked.

mogol (mo'ɣol) *n.m.* 1, mogul. 2, Mongol. —*adj.* [*also,* **mogólico**] Mongolian.

mogote (mo'ɣo·te) *n.m.* hummock.

mohín (mo'in) *n.m.* face; pout; grimace.

mohina (mo'i·na) *n.f.* displeasure.

mohino (mo'i·no) *adj.* crestfallen.

moho ('mo·o) *n.m.* 1, rust. 2, mildew; mold; must.

mohoso (mo'o·so) *adj.* 1, rusty. 2, mildewed; moldy; musty.

mojar (mo'xar) *v.t.* to wet; moisten. —*v.i., fig.* to be involved.

mojicón (mo·xi'kon) *n.m.* 1, biscuit; bun. 2, *colloq.* punch, esp. in the face.

mojiganga (mo·xi'ɣan·ga) *n.f.* 1, grimace. 2, horseplay; clowning.

mojigato (mo·xi'ɣa·to) *adj.* prud-

ish. —*n.m.* prude. —**mojigatería,**
n.f. prudery; prudishness.

mojón (mo'xon) *n.m.* **1,** landmark.
2, heap. **3,** turd.

moka ('mo·ka) *n.f.* = **moca.**

molar (mo'lar) *adj. & n.m.* molar.

molde ('mol·de) *n.m.* **1,** mold; cast.
2, model; example. **3,** *print.* form.
—**de molde,** printed. —**venir de
molde,** to come as a godsend.

moldear (mol·de'ar) *v.t.* to mold;
cast. —**moldeado,** *n.m.* molding.
—**moldeador,** *n.m.* molder.

moldura (mol'du·ra) *n.f.* molding.

mole ('mo·le) *adj.* soft. —*n.f.* mass;
bulk. —*n.m., Mex.* fricassee of meat
and chili.

molécula (mo'le·ku·la) *n.f.* molecule. —**molecular,** *adj.* molecular.

moler (mo'ler) *v.t.* [*infl.:* **mover,**
30] **1,** to grind; mill. **2,** to weary;
wear out. —**moledor,** *n.m.* grinder.
—**moler a palos,** to beat up.

molestar (mo·les'tar) *v.t.* to
molest; bother; disturb.

molestia (mo'les·tja) *n.f.* **1,** molestation. **2,** bother; trouble. **3,**
discomfort. **4,** hardship.

molesto (mo'les·to) *adj.* **1,** annoying; bothersome. **2,** uncomfortable.

molibdeno (mo·liβ'ðe·no) *n.m.*
molybdenum. —**molíbdico** (mo·
'liβ·ði·ko) *adj.* molybdic.

molicie (mo'li·θje; -sje) *n.f.* **1,** softness. **2,** soft living.

molienda (mo'ljen·da) *n.f.* **1,**
grinding; milling. **2,** grist. **3,** *fig.*
weariness; fatigue.

molificar (mo·li·fi'kar) *v.t.* [*infl.:*
tocar, 7] to mollify; soften. —**molificación,** *n.f.* mollification. —**moli-
ficativo,** *adj.* mollifying.

molinete (mo·li'ne·te) *n.m.* **1,**
windlass. **2,** pinwheel; windmill
(*toy*). **3,** turnstile. **4,** exhaust fan. **5,**
flourish (*with a sword, stick, etc.*).

molinillo (mo·li'ni·ʎo; -jo) *n.m.* **1,**
hand mill. **2,** coffee grinder. **3,** pinwheel; windmill (*toy*).

molino (mo'li·no) *n.m.* mill.
—**molinero,** *n.m.* miller. —*adj.*
milling (*attrib.*).

molusco (mo'lus·ko) *n.m.* mollusk.

molla ('mo·ʎa; -ja) *n.f.* **1,** lean
meat. **2,** soft part of bread. **3,** bulge
of flesh.

molleja (mo'ʎe·xa; -'je·xa) *n.f.* **1,**
gizzard. **2,** sweetbread.

mollera (mo'ʎe·ra; -'je·ra) *n.f.* **1,**
crown of the head. **2,** *fig.* brains; in-

tellect. —**cerrado de mollera,** *also,*
duro de mollera, stubborn; dense.

mollete (mo'ʎe·te; -'je·te) *n.m.*
muffin.

momento (mo'men·to) *n.m.* **1,** moment. **2,** momentum. —**momentáneo** (-'ta·ne·o) *adj.* momentary.

momia ('mo·mja) *n.f.* mummy.

momificar (mo·mi·fi'kar) *v.t.*
[*infl.:* **tocar,** 7] to mummify. —**momificación,** *n.f.* mummification.

mona ('mo·na) *n.f.* **1,** female
monkey. **2,** *colloq.* drunkenness;
hangover. —*adj., fem. of* **mono.**

monacal (mo·na'kal) *adj.* monastic.

monacato (mo·na'ka·to) *n.m.* monasticism.

monacillo (mo·na'θi·ʎo; -'si·jo)
n.m., colloq. = **monaguillo.**

monada (mo'na·ða) *n.f.* **1,** grimace. **2,** *colloq.* monkeyshine. **3,**
colloq. pretty child; charming girl.

mónada ('mo·na·ða) *n.f.* monad.

monaguillo (mo·na'yi·ʎo; -jo)
n.m. acolyte; altar boy.

monarca (mo'nar·ka) *n.m.* monarch. —**monarquía** (-'ki·a) *n.f.*
monarchy. —**monárquico** (-ki·ko)
adj. monarchal. —*n.m.* monarchist.
—**monarquismo** (-'kis·mo) *n.m.*
monarchism.

monasterio (mo·nas'te·rjo) *n.m.*
monastery.

monástico (mo'nas·ti·ko) *adj.* monastic.

monda ('mon·da) *n.f.* **1,** pruning. **2,**
pruning season.

mondadientes (mon·da'ðjen·tes)
n.m.sing. & pl. toothpick.

mondar (mon'dar) *v.t.* **1,** to prune.
2, to hull; peel.

mondo ('mon·do) *adj.* clean; pure.

mondongo (mon'don·go) *n.m.* **1,**
tripe. **2,** *colloq.* guts.

moneda (mo'ne·ða) *n.f.* **1,** money.
2, coin. —**moneda de curso legal,**
legal tender.

monedero (mo·ne'ðe·ro) *n.m.* **1,**
coiner. **2,** change purse.

monería (mo·ne'ri·a) *n.f.* **1,** grimace. **2,** monkeyshine.

monetario (mo·ne'ta·rjo) *adj.*
monetary.

monetizar (mo·ne·ti'θar; -'sar) *v.t.*
[*infl.:* **rezar,** 10] **1,** to monetize. **2,**
to mint; coin.

mongol (mon'gol) *adj. & n.m.* =
mogol. —**mongólico,** *adj.* =
mogólico. —**mongolismo,** *n.m.*
mongolism; Down's syndrome.

monigote (mo·ni'γo·te) *n.m.* **1,**
colloq. bumpkin. **2,** puppet.

monismo (mo'nis·mo) *n.m.* monism. **—monista,** *adj.* monistic.
—*n.m.* & *f.* monist.

monitor (mo·ni'tor) *n.m.* [*fem.*
-tora] monitor; adviser; *comput.*
monitor.

monja ('mon·xa) *n.f.* nun.

monje ('mon·xe) *n.m.* monk.

monjil (mon'xil) *n.m.* widow's
weeds. **—***adj.* nunnish; of or pert. to
a nun.

mono ('mo·no) *adj., colloq.* pretty;
cute. **—***n.m.* **1,** monkey. **2,** cover-
alls; jeans.

monocarril (mo·no·ka'rril) *n.m.*
monorail.

monociclo (mo·no'θi·klo; -'si·klo)
n.m. unicycle.

monocromo (mo·no'kro·mo) *adj.*
& *n.m.* monochrome. **—monocromático** (-'ma·ti·ko) *adj.* monochromatic.

monóculo (mo'no·ku·lo) *n.m.*
monocle. **—monocular,** *adj.* monocular.

monogamia (mo·no'γa·mja) *n.f.*
monogamy. **—monógamo** (mo'no·
γa·mo) *adj.* monogamous. **—***n.m.*
monogamist.

monografía (mo·no·γra'fi·a) *n.f.*
monograph. **—monográfico** (-'γra-
fi·ko) *adj.* monographic.

monograma (mo·no'γra·ma) *n.m.*
monogram.

monolito (mo·no'li·to) *n.m.* monolith. **—monolítico,** *adj.* monolithic.

monologar (mo·no·lo'γar) *v.i.*
[*infl.:* **pagar, 8**] to soliloquize.

monólogo (mo'no·lo·γo) *n.m.*
monologue.

monomanía (mo·no·ma'ni·a) *n.f.*
monomania. **—monomaníaco,** *adj.*
& *n.m.* monomaniac.

monometalismo (mo·no·me·
ta'lis·mo) *n.m.* monometallism.

monomio (mo'no·mjo) *n.m.* monomial.

mononucleosis (mo·no·nu·
kle'o·sis) *n.f.* mononucleosis.

monoplano (mo·no'pla·no) *n.m.*
monoplane.

monopolio (mo·no'po·ljo) *n.m.*
monopoly. **—monopolista** (-'lis·ta)
n.m. & *f.* monopolist. **—monopolizar** (-li'θar; -li'sar) *v.t.* [*infl.:* **rezar,
10**] to monopolize.

monosílabo (mo·no'si·la·βo) *n.m.*
monosyllable. **—monosilábico**
(-'la·βi·ko) *adj.* monosyllabic.

monoteísmo (mo·no·te'is·mo)
n.m. monotheism. **—monoteísta,**
n.m. & *f.* monotheist. **—***adj.* monotheistic.

monotipia (mo·no'ti·pja) *n.f.*
monotype (*process*). **—monotipo**
(-po) *n.m.* monotype (*machine*).

monotonía (mo·no·to'ni·a) *n.f.* **1,**
monotone. **2,** monotony.

monótono (mo'no·to·no) *adj.* monotonous.

monovalente (mo·no·βa'len·te)
adj. monovalent.

monóxido (mo'nok·si·ðo) *n.m.*
monoxide.

monseñor (mon·se'ɲor) *n.m.*
Monsignor.

monserga (mon'ser·γa) *n.f.* gibberish.

monstruo ('mons·trwo) *n.m.* monster. **—***adj., colloq.* monstrous; extraordinary.

monstruoso (mons'trwo·so) *adj.*
monstrous; extraordinary. **—monstruosidad,** *n.f.* monstrosity.

monta ('mon·ta) *n.f.* **1,** act of
mounting. **2,** *mil.* signal or call to
mount. **3,** sum; total; amount. **4,**
value; worth. **—de poca monta,** of
little account; insignificant.

montacargas (mon·ta'kar·γas)
n.m. **1,** hoist; lift; cargo elevator. **2,**
dumbwaiter.

montadura (mon·ta'ðu·ra) *n.f.* **1,**
mounting. **2,** *jewelry* setting.

montaje (mon'ta·xe) *n.m.* **1,**
mounting; assembly. **2,** *photog.*
montage. **3,** *motion pictures* editing.
4, *mech.* mount. **—montaje musical,** musical setting.

montante (mon'tan·te) *n.m.* **1,**
broadsword. **2,** upright; post; strut.
3, transom. **4,** sum; total; amount.
—*n.f.* high or flood tide.

montaña (mon'ta·ɲa) *n.f.* **1,**
mountain. **2,** highlands. **—montaña
rusa,** roller coaster.

montañero (mon·ta'ɲe·ro) *n.m.*
mountain climber. **—***adj.* mountaineering (*attrib.*).

montañés (mon·ta'ɲes) *n.m.*
mountain dweller; highlander.
—*adj.* highland (*attrib.*).

montañismo (mon·ta'ɲis·mo)
n.m. mountaineering.

montañoso (mon·ta'ɲo·so) *adj.*
mountainous.

montar (mon'tar) *v.i.* **1,** to mount;
to get on or in. **2,** to ride. **—***v.t.* **1,**
to mount; set. **2,** to ride (a horse). **3,**
to cock (a firearm). **4,** to carry (*in a*

vehicle). **5,** to cover *(of animals).*
—**montar en cólera,** to fly into a rage.

montaraz (mon·ta'raθ; -'ras) *adj.* **1,** mountain bred. **2,** wild; untamed. —*n.m.* forester; ranger.

monte ('mon·te) *n.m.* **1,** mountain; mount. **2,** monte *(card game).* **3,** *fig.* obstruction. **4,** forest; woodland. —**monte de piedad,** a pawnshop operated by a bank or the state.

montecillo (mon·te'θi·ʎo; -'si·jo) *n.m.* hillock; mound; knoll.

montepío (mon·te'pi·o) *n.m.* **1,** pension fund. **2,** emergency fund.

montera (mon'te·ra) *n.f.* bullfighter's cap.

montería (mon·te'ri·a) *n.f.* hunting; hunt. —**montero,** *n.m.* hunter; beater.

montés (mon'tes) *adj.* wild; feral.

montículo (mon'ti·ku·lo) *n.m.* mound.

monto ('mon·to) *n.m.* sum; total.

montón (mon'ton) *n.m.* heap; pile; mass.

montonera (mon·to'ne·ra) *n.f.* guerrilla band. —**montonero,** *n.m.* guerrilla fighter.

montuoso (mon'two·so) *adj.* hilly.

montura (mon'tu·ra) *n.f.* **1,** mount *(animal).* **2,** harness; saddle. **3,** mounting. **4,** *jewelry* setting.

monumento (mo·nu'men·to) *n.m.* monument. —**monumental,** *adj.* monumental.

monzón (mon'θon; -'son) *n.m.* monsoon.

moño ('mo·ɲo) *n.m.* chignon; topknot.

moquear (mo·ke'ar) *v.i.* to snivel; have a runny nose.

moquillo (mo'ki·ʎo; -jo) *n.m., vet.* distemper.

mora ('mo·ra) *n.f.* **1,** blackberry. **2,** mulberry.

morada (mo'ra·ða) *n.f.* abode.

morado (mo'ra·ðo) *adj. & n.m.* purple.

morador (mo·ra'ðor) *adj.* dwelling; residing. —*n.m.* [*fem.* **-dora**] dweller; resident.

moral (mo'ral) *adj.* moral. —*n.m.* black mulberry tree. —*n.f.* **1,** ethics; morals. **2,** morale.

moraleja (mo·ra'le·xa) *n.f.* moral *(of a story).*

moralidad (mo·ra·li'ðað) *n.f.* morality.

moralista (mo·ra'lis·ta) *n.m. & f.* moralist.

moralizar (mo·ra·li'θar; -'sar) *v.t. & i.* [*infl.:* **rezar,** 10] to moralize.

morar (mo'rar) *v.i.* to dwell.

moratoria (mo·ra'to·rja) *n.f.* moratorium. —**moratorio,** *adj.* moratory.

morbidez (mor·βi'ðeθ; -'ðes) *n.f.* **1,** morbidity. **2,** *fig.* lusciousness.

mórbido ('mor·βi·ðo) *adj.* **1,** morbid; diseased. **2,** *fig.* luscious; inviting.

morbo ('mor·βo) *n.m.* disease. —**morboso,** *adj.* morbid. —**morbosidad,** *n.f.* morbidity.

morcilla (mor'θi·ʎa; -'si·ja) *n.f.* **1,** blood pudding. **2,** *theat.* ad lib. **3,** *colloq.* long-winded speech.

mordaz (mor'ðaθ; -'ðas) *adj.* **1,** corrosive. **2,** sarcastic; pungent. —**mordacidad,** *n.f.* sarcasm; pungency.

mordaza (mor'ða·θa; -sa) *n.f.* gag; muzzle.

mordedor (mor·ðe'ðor) *adj.* **1,** biting; snapping. **2,** sarcastic. —*n.m.* **1,** biter; snapper. **2,** carper; harsh critic.

mordelón (mor·ðe'lon) *adj., Amer.* biting; given to biting. —*n.m., Amer.* **1,** biter; snapper. **2,** grafter.

morder (mor'ðer) *v.t.* [*infl.:* **mover,** 30] **1,** to bite. **2,** to gnaw. **3,** to corrode. —**mordedura,** *n.f.* bite.

mordida (mor'ði·ða) *n.f., Amer.* **1,** bite; snap. **2,** graft; bribe.

mordiente (mor'ðjen·te) *also,* **mordente** (-'ðen·te) *adj. & n.m.* mordant.

mordiscar (mor·ðis'kar) *v.t.* [*infl.:* **tocar,** 7] to nibble.

mordisco (mor'ðis·ko) *n.m.* bite.

morena (mo're·na) *n.f.* **1,** moraine. **2,** moray. **3,** brunette.

moreno (mo're·no) *adj.* **1,** brown; swarthy. **2,** brunette. **3,** *Amer., colloq.* negro.

morera (mo're·ra) *n.f.* white mulberry tree.

moretón (mo·re'ton) *n.m.* livid bruise.

morfina (mor'fi·na) *n.f.* morphine. —**morfinómano** (-'no·ma·no) *n.m.* morphine addict; drug addict.

morfología (mor·fo·lo'xi·a) *n.f.* morphology. —**morfológico** (-'lo·xi·ko) *adj.* morphological.

morfosis (mor'fo·sis) *n.f.* morphosis.

morganático (mor·ɣa'na·ti·ko) *adj.* morganatic.

morgue ('mor·ɣe) *n.f.* morgue.

moribundo (mo·ri'βun·do) *adj.* dying; moribund.

morillo (mo'ri·ʎo; -jo) *n.m.* andiron.

morir (mo'rir) *v.i.* [*infl.:* 32] 1, to die. 2, to end; come to an end. —*v.t., colloq., in compound tenses only* to kill. —**morirse,** *v.r.* to die. —**morirse por,** to yearn for.

morisco (mo'ris·ko) *adj.* Moorish. —*n.m.* Christianized Moor.

mormón (mor'mon) *adj. & n.m.* Mormon. —**mormonismo,** *n.m.* Mormonism.

moro ('mo·ro) *adj.* Moorish. —*n.m.* Moor.

moroso (mo'ro·so) *adj.* slow; tardy. —**morosidad,** *n.f.* slowness; tardiness.

morral (mo'rral) *n.m.* 1, game bag. 2, rustic.

morriña (mo'rri·ɲa) *n.f.* 1, sadness; blues; homesickness. 2, a parasitic disease of animals; rot.

morro ('mo·rro) *n.m.* 1, snout. 2, round hill or cliff. 3, nose cone. —**estar de morro** *or* **morros,** *colloq.* to be on the outs. —**poner morro,** *colloq.* to pout; grimace.

morsa ('mor·sa) *n.f.* walrus.

mortaja (mor'ta·xa) *n.f.* shroud.

mortal (mor'tal) *adj.* 1, mortal. 2, fatal; deadly. 3, dying. —*n.m.* mortal; man.

mortalidad (mor·ta·li'ðað) *n.f.* 1, mortality. 2, death rate.

mortandad (mor·tan'dað) *n.f.* 1, mortality. 2, massacre.

mortecino (mor·te'θi·no; -'si·no) *adj.* 1, dying. 2, pale; wan. —**hacer la mortecina,** *colloq.* to play dead.

mortero (mor'te·ro) *n.m.* 1, mortar *(mixing vessel).* 2, mortar *(cement).* 3, mortar *(artillery weapon).* 4, howitzer. —**mano de mortero,** pestle.

mortífero (mor'ti·fe·ro) *adj.* death-dealing; fatal.

mortificar (mor·ti·fi'kar) *v.i.* [*infl.:* tocar, 7] 1, to mortify. 2, *Amer., colloq.* to bother; annoy. —**mortificación,** *n.f.* mortification.

mortuorio (mor'two·rjo) *adj.* mortuary; obituary. —*n.m.* funeral.

moruno (mo'ru·no) *adj.* Moorish.

mosaico (mo'sai·ko) *adj. & n.m.* mosaic.

mosca ('mos·ka) *n.f.* fly. —**aflojar** *or* **soltar la mosca,** *colloq.* to fork out; shell out. —**mosca muerta,** *colloq.* 1, milquetoast. 2, hypocrite. —**papar moscas,** *colloq.* to gape. —**peso mosca,** flyweight.

moscardón (mos·kar'ðon) *n.m.* 1, bumblebee. 2, horsefly. 3, = **moscón.**

moscatel (mos·ka'tel) *adj. & n.m. & f.* muscat. —*n.m.* muscatel.

mosco ('mos·ko) *n.m.* 1, gnat. 2, any small fly.

moscón (mos'kon) *n.m., colloq.* hanger-on. *Also,* **moscardón.**

moscovita (mos·ko'βi·ta) *adj. & n.m. & f.* Muscovite.

mosqueado (mos·ke'a·ðo) *adj.* speckled; mottled.

mosquear (mos·ke'ar) *v.t., colloq.* 1, to elude; give the slip to. 2, to deceive; dupe. —*v.i., colloq.* to smell fishy; look suspicious. —**mosquearse,** *v.r., colloq.* to be suspicious or distrustful.

mosquete (mos'ke·te) *n.m.* musket. —**mosquetazo,** *n.m.* musket shot.

mosquetero (mos·ke'te·ro) *n.m.* musketeer. —**mosquetería,** *n.f.* musketry.

mosquito (mos'ki·to) *n.m.* 1, mosquito. 2, gnat. —**mosquitero,** *n.m.* mosquito net.

mostacho (mos'ta·tʃo) *n.m.* mustache.

mostaza (mos'ta·θa; -sa) *n.f.* mustard.

mosto ('mos·to) *n.m.* wine, esp. new wine.

mostrar (mos'trar) *v.t.* [*infl.:* acostar, 28] to show; point out; demonstrate. —**mostrarse,** *v.r.* to appear. —**mostrador,** *n.m.* showcase; counter.

mostrenco (mos'tren·ko) *adj.* 1, homeless; vagrant. 2, dull; stupid. —**bienes mostrencos,** ownerless goods.

mota ('mo·ta) *n.f.* 1, mote; speck. 2, slight defect. 3, knoll. 4, *Amer.* powder puff.

mote ('mo·te) *n.m.* 1, motto. 2, nickname. 3, riddle.

motear (mo·te'ar) *v.t.* to speckle; mottle.

motejar (mo·te'xar) *v.t., usu.fol. by* **de,** to call; brand (as).

motel (mo'tel) *n.m.* motel.

motilidad (mo·ti·li'ðað) *n.f.* motility.

motín (mo'tin) *n.m.* mutiny; uprising.

motivar (mo·ti'βar) *v.t.* **1**, to motivate; cause. **2**, to justify; explain the reason for. —**motivación**, *n.f.* motivation.

motivo (mo'ti·βo) *adj.* motive; moving. —*n.m.* **1**, cause; reason; motive. **2**, motif.

motocicleta (mo·to·θi'kle·ta; -si'kle·ta) *n.f.* motorcycle.

motón (mo'ton) *n.m.*, *naut.* block; pulley.

motoneta (mo·to'ne·ta) *n.f.* motor scooter.

motor (mo'tor) *n.m.* **1**, motor. **2**, mover. —*adj.* motor; motive; moving.

motora (mo'to·ra) *n.f.*, *also*, **lancha motora**, motorboat.

motorista (mo·to'ris·ta) *n.m.* & *f.* **1**, motorist. **2**, *Amer.* motorman.

motorizar (mo·to·ri'θar; -'sar) *v.t.* [*infl.*: **rezar**, **10**] to motorize.

motriz (mo'triθ; -'tris) *adj.* motor; motive; moving.

movedizo (mo·βe'ði·θo; -so) *adj.* **1**, moving; movable. **2**, easily moved; shaky; unsteady.

mover (mo'βer) *v.t.* [*infl.*: **30**] **1**, to move. **2**, to persuade; induce.

movible (mo'βi·βle) *adj.* movable; mobile; motile.

móvil (mo·βil) *adj.* movable; mobile; motile. —*n.m.* **1**, motive. **2**, moving body.

movilidad (mo·βi·li'ðað) *n.f.* **1**, mobility; motility. **2**, unsteadiness.

movilizar (mo·βi·li'θar; -'sar) *v.t.* [*infl.*: **rezar**, **10**] to mobilize. —**movilización**, *n.f.* mobilization.

movimiento (mo·βi'mjen·to) *n.m.* **1**, movement; motion. **2**, agitation; activity. **3**, *comm.* lively trade.

moza (mo'θa; -sa) *n.f.* **1**, girl; young woman. **2**, maid. **3**, mistress. —**moza de cámara**, chambermaid.

mozalbete (mo·θal'βe·te; mo·sal-) *n.m.* lad; boy.

mozárabe (mo'θa·ra·βe; mo'sa-) *adj.* Mozarabic. —*n.m.* & *f.* Mozarab.

mozo (mo'θo; -so) *n.m.* **1**, young man. **2**, bachelor. **3**, waiter; porter. —*adj.* **1**, young. **2**, unmarried.

mozuelo (mo'θwe·lo; -'swe·lo) *n.m.* boy; lad. —**mozuela**, *n.f.* girl; lass.

muaré (mwa're) *n.f.* = **moaré**.

mucílago (mu'θi·la·γo; mu'si-)

n.m. mucilage. —**mucilaginoso**, *adj.* mucilaginous.

mucoso (mu'ko·so) *adj.* mucous. —**mucosa**, *n.f.* mucous membrane. —**mucosidad**, *n.f.* mucosity; mucus.

muchacha (mu'tʃa·tʃa) *n.f.* **1**, girl; lass; young woman. **2**, maid; servant. —*adj.* girlish.

muchachada (mu·tʃa'tʃa·ða) *n.f.* **1**, boyishness; boyish behavior. **2**, group of boys; boys collectively.

muchachez (mu·tʃa'tʃeθ; -'tʃes) *n.f.* childhood.

muchacho (mu'tʃa·tʃo) *n.m.* boy. —*adj.* boyish.

muchedumbre (mu·tʃe'ðum·bre) *n.f.* crowd; multitude; swarm.

muchísimo (mu'tʃi·si·mo) *adj.* & *adv.*, *superl. of* **mucho**.

mucho ('mu·tʃo) *adj.*, *adv.* & *pron.* **1**, much; very much; a great deal (of); a lot (of). **2**, *colloq.* too much; overmuch. —**muchos**, *adj.* & *pron.pl.* **1**, many. **2**, *colloq.* too many. —**con mucho**, by far. —**ni con mucho**, *also*, **ni mucho menos**, not by any means. —**por mucho que**, however much. —**tener a** *or* **en mucho**, to hold in high esteem.

muda ('mu·ða) *n.f.* **1**, change. **2**, molting; molting time.

mudable (mu'ða·βle) *adj.* changeable; mutable.

mudadizo (mu·ða'ði·θo; -so) *adj.* fickle; changeable.

mudanza (mu'ðan·θa; -sa) *n.f.* **1**, change; changing. **2**, moving; change of residence. **3**, inconstancy; fickleness.

mudar (mu'ðar) *v.t.* **1**, to change. **2**, to move; change the position or location of. **3**, to molt. —**mudarse**, *v.r.* **1**, to change. **2**, to move; change residence or location.

mudez (mu'ðeθ; -'ðes) *n.f.* **1**, dumbness; muteness. **2**, silence.

mudo ('mu·ðo) *adj.* **1**, dumb; mute. **2**, silent.

mueblaje (mwe'βla·xe) *n.m.* furniture.

mueble ('mwe·βle) *adj.* movable; mobile. —*n.m.* piece of furniture. —**bienes muebles**, liquid assets; chattels.

mueblería (mwe·βle'ri·a) *n.f.* furniture store. —**mueblista**, *n.m.* & *f.* furniture dealer.

mueca ('mwe·ka) *n.f.* grimace.

muecín (mu·e'θin; -'sin) *n.m.* muezzin.

muela ('mwe·la) *n.f.* **1,** grindstone. **2,** millstone. **3,** molar. —**dolor de muelas,** toothache. —**muela del juicio,** wisdom tooth.

muela ('mwe·la) *v., pres.subjve. of* **moler.**

muelo ('mwe·lo) *v., 1st pers.sing. pres.ind. of* **moler.**

muellaje (mwe'ʎa·xe; -'ja·xe) *n.m.* dockage; wharfage.

muelle ('mwe·ʎe; -je) *adj.* soft; comfortable. —*n.m.* **1,** *mech.* spring. **2,** pier; dock. —**muelle real,** mainspring.

muera ('mwe·ra) *v., pres.subjve. of* **morir.**

muerda ('mwer·ða) *v., pres.subjve. of* **morder.**

muérdago ('mwer·ða·ɣo) *n.m.* mistletoe.

muerdo ('mwer·ðo) *v., 1st pers.sing. pres.ind. of* **morder.**

muero ('mwe·ro) *v., 1st pers.sing. pres.ind. of* **morir.**

muerte ('mwer·te) *n.f.* **1,** death. **2,** ruin; destruction. —**de mala muerte,** poor; wretched.

muerto ('mwer·to) *v., p.p. of* **morir.** —*adj.* dead. —*n.m.* **1,** dead person; dead body. **2,** *cards* dummy. —**echarle a uno el muerto,** to put the onus on someone.

muesca ('mwes·ka) *n.f.* **1,** notch. **2,** mortise.

muestra ('mwes·tra) *n.f.* **1,** sample. **2,** sign; token. **3,** sign *(of a shop, inn, etc.).* **4,** face *(of a watch or clock).* —**muestrario,** *n.m.* sample book; collection of samples.

muestre ('mwes·tre) *v., pres. subjve. of* **mostrar.**

muestro ('mwes·tro) *v., 1st pers.sing. pres.ind. of* **mostrar.**

mueva ('mwe·βa) *v., pres.subjve. of* **mover.**

muevo ('mwe·βo) *v., 1st pers.sing. pres.ind. of* **mover.**

muftí (muf'ti) *n.m.* mufti *(Muslim religious officer).*

mugir (mu'xir) *v.i.* [*infl.:* **coger,** 15] to moo; low. —**mugido,** *n.m.* moo; low.

mugre ('mu·ɣre) *n.f.* dirt; grime. —**mugriento** (-'ɣrjen·to) *adj.* dirty; grimy. *Also,* **mugroso.**

muja ('mu·xa) *v., pres.subjve. of* **mugir.**

mujer (mu'xer) *n.f.* **1,** woman. **2,** wife.

mujercilla (mu·xer'θi·ʎa; -'si·ja) *n.f.* floozy.

mujeriego (mu·xe'rje·ɣo) *adj.* skirt-chasing. —*n.m.* womanizer. —**a mujeriegas,** (riding) sidesaddle.

mujeril (mu·xe'ril) *adj.* feminine; womanly.

mujerzuela (mu·xer'θwe·la; -'swe·la) *n.f.* floozy.

mujo ('mu·xo) *v., 1st pers.sing. pres.ind. of* **mugir.**

mújol ('mu·xol) *n.m.* mullet.

mula ('mu·la) *n.f.* mule; she-mule.

muladar (mu·la'ðar) *n.m.* trash heap; garbage dump.

mulato (mu'la·to) *adj. & n.m.* mulatto.

mulero (mu'le·ro) *n.m.* mule driver; muleteer.

muleta (mu'le·ta) *n.f.* **1,** crutch. **2,** red flag used by bullfighters.

muletilla (mu·le'ti·ʎa; -ja) *n.f.* **1,** refrain; cliché. **2,** = **muleta.**

mulo ('mu·lo) *n.m.* mule. —*adj.* stubborn; mulish.

multa ('mul·ta) *n.f.* fine; penalty. —**multar,** *v.t.* to fine.

multicolor (mul·ti·ko'lor) *adj.* multicolored; motley.

multicopista (mul·ti·ko'pis·ta) *n.m.* duplicator; duplicating machine.

multiforme (mul·ti'for·me) *adj.* multiform.

multilátero (mul·ti'la·te·ro) *adj., geom.* multilateral. *Also, fig.,* **multilateral** (-'ral).

multimillonario (mul·ti·mi·ʎo'na·rjo; -jo'na·rjo) *n.m. & adj.* multimillionaire.

multipartito (mul·ti·par'ti·to) *adj.* multipartite.

múltiple ('mul·ti·ple) *adj.* multiple.

multiplicar (mul·ti·pli'kar) *v.t.* [*infl.:* **tocar,** 7] to multiply. —**multiplicación,** *n.f.* multiplication. —**multiplicador,** *adj.* multiplying. —*n.m.* multiplier. —**multiplicando** (-'kan·do) *n.m.* multiplicand.

multiplicidad (mul·ti·pli·θi·'ðað; -si'ðað) *n.f.* multiplicity.

múltiplo ('mul·ti·plo) *n.m. & adj.* multiple.

multiprocesador (mul·ti·pro·θe·sa'ðor; -se·sa'ðor) *n.m., comput.* multiprocessor.

multitud (mul·ti'tuð) *n.f.* multitude. —**multitudinario** (-ði'na·rjo) *adj.* multitudinous.

mullido (mu'ʎi·ðo; -'ji·ðo) *adj.*

soft; fluffy. —*n.m.* **1,** fluff. **2,** straw bedding.

mullir (mu'ʎir; -'jir) *v.t.* [*infl.: bullir,* 19] to fluff.

mundanalidad (mun·da·na·li'ðað) *n.f.* worldliness; mundaneness. *Also,* **mundanería** (-ne'ri·a).

mundano (mun'da·no) *adj.* worldly; mundane. *Also,* **mundanal.**

mundial (mun'djal) *adj.* worldwide; world (*attrib.*).

mundo ('mun·do) *n.m.* world; earth. —**todo el mundo,** everyone.

munición (mu·ni'θjon; -'sjon) *n.f.* **1,** *often pl.* munitions; provisions; rations. **2,** charge; load (*of a firearm*). **3,** birdshot. —**municionar,** *v.t.* to munition; supply; provide.

municipal (mu·ni·θi'pal; -si'pal) *adj.* municipal. —*n.m.* city policeman. —**municipalidad,** *n.f.* = **municipio.**

municipio (mu·ni'θi·pjo; -'si·pjo) *n.m.* **1,** municipality; city; township. **2,** town hall; city hall. **3,** town council.

munificencia (mu·ni·fi'θen·θja; -'sen·sja) *n.f.* munificence. —**munificente,** *adj.* = **munífico.**

munífico (mu'ni·fi·ko) *adj.* munificent.

muñeca (mu'ɲe·ka) *n.f.* **1,** wrist. **2,** doll. **3,** *colloq.* dressmaker's form; manikin.

muñeco (mu'ɲe·ko) *n.m.* puppet; doll; manikin; dummy.

muñón (mu'ɲon) *n.m.* stump (*esp. of an amputated limb*).

murajes (mu'ra·xes) *n.m.pl.* pimpernel.

mural (mu'ral) *adj.* mural. —**muralista,** *n.m.* & *f.* muralist.

muralla (mu'ra·ʎa; -ja) *n.f.* rampart; wall.

murciélago (mur'θje·la·ɣo; mur'sje-) *n.m.,* *zoöl.* bat.

murga ('mur·ɣa) *n.f.,* *colloq.* band of street musicians. —**dar murga a,** *colloq.* to bother; annoy.

muriendo (mu'rjen·do) *v., ger. of* **morir.**

murió (mu'rjo) *v., 3rd pers.sing. pret. of* **morir.**

murmullo (mur'mu·ʎo; -jo) *n.m.* murmur.

murmurar (mur·mu'rar) *v.i.* **1,** to murmur. **2,** to grumble. **3,** to gossip. —**murmuración,** *n.f.* backbiting;

gossip. —**murmurador,** *n.m.* detractor; backbiter. —**murmurio** (-'mu·rjo) *n.m.* murmur.

muro ('mu·ro) *n.m.* wall, esp. a thick or supporting wall.

murria ('mu·rrja) *n.f.,* *colloq.* melancholy; blues.

musa ('mu·sa) *n.f.* Muse.

musaraña (mu·sa'ra·ɲa) *n.f.* shrew; shrewmouse. —**pensar en las musarañas,** *colloq.* to be absentminded.

músculo ('mus·ku·lo) *n.m.* muscle. —**muscular,** *adj.* muscular. —**musculatura,** *n.f.* musculature. —**musculoso,** *adj.* muscular. —**musculosidad,** *n.f.* muscularity.

muselina (mu·se'li·na) *n.f.* muslin.

museo (mu'se·o) *n.m.* museum.

musgo ('mus·ɣo) *n.m.* moss. —**musgoso,** *adj.* mossy.

música ('mu·si·ka) *n.f.* music. —**musical,** *adj.* musical.

músico ('mu·si·ko) *adj.* musical. —*n.m.* musician. —**musicología** (-ko·lo'xi·a) *n.f.* musicology. —**musicólogo** (-'ko·lo·ɣo) *n.m.* musicologist.

musitar (mu·si'tar) *v.i.* & *t.* to mumble; whisper; muse.

muslime (mus'li·me) *adj.* & *n.m.* Moslem. —**muslímico,** *adj.* Moslem.

muslo ('mus·lo) *n.m.* thigh.

mustango (mus'tan·go) *n.m., Amer.* mustang.

mustio (mus·tjo) *adj.* **1,** withered; wilted. **2,** sad; melancholy. **3,** *Mex.* hypocritical; two-faced. —**mustiarse,** *v.r.* to fade; wither.

musulmán (mu·sul'man) *adj.* & *n.m.* [*fem.* -**mana**] Moslem.

mutabilidad (mu·ta·βi·li'ðað) *n.f.* mutability.

mutación (mu·ta'θjon; -'sjon) *n.f.* change; mutation.

mutante (mu'tan·te) *adj.* & *n.m.* & *f.* mutant.

mutilar (mu·ti'lar) *v.t.* to mutilate; maim. —**mutilación,** *n.f.* mutilation.

mutis ('mu·tis) *n.m., esp. theat.* exit. —**hacer mutis,** *esp. theat.* to exit.

mutismo (mu'tis·mo) *n.m.* muteness; silence.

mutual (mu'twal) *adj.* = **mutuo.**

mutualidad (mu·twa·li'ðað) *n.f.* **1,** mutuality. **2,** credit union.

mutuo ('mu·two) *adj.* mutual; reciprocal.

muy (mui) *adv.* very; greatly; most. —**muy señor mío,** Dear Sir.

N

N, n ('e·ne) *n.f.* 16th letter of the Spanish alphabet.

nabab (na'βaβ) *n.m.* nabob.

nabo ('na·βo) *n.m.* 1, turnip. 2, newel.

nácar ('na·kar) *n.m.* mother-of-pearl; nacre. —**nacarino,** *also,* **nacarado,** *adj.* nacreous.

nacencia (na'θen·θja; -'sen·sja) *n.f.* tumor; growth.

nacer (na'θer; -'ser) *v.i.* [*infl.:* conocer, 13] 1, to be born; come to life. 2, to rise; emerge; appear. —**nacer de pie,** *also, Amer.* **nacer parado,** to be born under a lucky star.

nacida (na'θi·ða; -'si·ða) *adj. fem.* born; née.

nacido (na'θi·ðo, -'si·ðo) *adj.* 1, born. 2, inborn; innate. 3, natural; proper. —*n.m.* 1, human being. 2, = nacencia. —**bien nacido,** well-born. —**mal nacido,** lowborn; low.

naciente (na'θjen·te; -'sjen·te) *adj.* 1, nascent. 2, rising (*of the sun*). —*n.m.* east.

nacimiento (na·θi'mjen·to; na·si-) *n.m.* 1, birth. 2, Nativity scene; crèche. 3, source (*of a river*).

nación (na'θjon; -'sjon) *n.f.* nation. —**nacional,** *adj.* & *n.m.* national. —**nacionalidad,** *n.f.* nationality.

nacionalismo (na·θjo·na'lis·mo; na·sjo-) *n.m.* nationalism. —**nacionalista,** *adj.* nationalistic. —*n.m.* & *f.* nationalist.

nacionalización (na·θjo·na·li·θa'θjon; na·sjo·na·li·sa'sjon) *n.f.* 1, nationalization. 2, naturalization.

nacionalizar (na·θjo·na·li'θar; -sjo·na·li'sar) *v.t.* [*infl.:* rezar, 10] 1, to nationalize. 2, to naturalize. —**nacionalizarse,** *v.r.* to become naturalized; become a citizen.

nacre ('na·kre) *n.m.* = nácar.

nada ('na·ða) *indef.pron.* nothing; not anything; naught. —*n.f.* 1, nothing; nothingness. 2, nonentity. —*adv.* not at all. —**de nada,** think nothing of it; don't mention it; not at all; you're welcome. —**nada de eso,** nothing of the sort. —**nada entre dos platos,** nothing of substance. —**por nada,** 1, for nothing. 2, under no circumstances; in no way.

nadada (na'ða·ða) *n.f., Amer.* swim.

nadadera (na·ða'ðe·ra) *n.f.* 1, swim bladder. 2, *pl.* water wings.

nadadero (na·ða'ðe·ro) *n.m.* swimming hole.

nadar (na'ðar) *v.i.* 1, to swim. 2, to fit loosely (in). —**nadador,** *n.m.* [*fem.* -dora] swimmer. —*adj.* swimming.

nadería (na·ðe'ri·a) *n.f.* trifle; nothing.

nadie ('na·ðje) *indef.pron.* nobody; no one. —*n.m.* & *f.* nobody; nonentity.

nadir (na'ðir) *n.m.* nadir.

nafta ('naf·ta) *n.f.* 1, naphtha. 2, *Amer.* gasoline.

naftalina (naf·ta'li·na) *n.f.* naphthalene.

naipe ('nai·pe) *n.m.* 1, playing card. 2, *pl.* cards; card games.

nalga ('nal·ɣa) *n.f.* buttock; rump. —**nalgada,** *n.f.* a blow on or with the buttocks; spanking.

nana ('na·na) *n.f., colloq.* 1, grandmother. 2, nanny; nurse. 3, lullaby.

nao ('na·o) *n.f., archaic* = nave.

napoleón (na·po·le'on) *n.m.* napoleon (*coin*).

naranja (na'ran·xa) *n.f.* orange. —**naranjada,** *n.f.* orangeade. —**naranjal,** *n.m.* orange grove. —**naranjo,** *n.m.* orange tree. —**mi media naranja,** my better half. —**naranja de ombligo,** navel orange. —**¡naranjas!,** *interj.* You don't say!; no!; no way!

narcisismo (nar·θi'sis·mo; nar·si-) *n.m.* narcissism. —**narcisista,** *n.m.* & *f.* narcissist. —*adj.* narcissistic.

narciso (nar'θi·so; nar'si-) *n.m.* narcissus; daffodil.

narcómano (nar'ko·ma·no) *n.m.* drug addict. —**narcomanía,** *n.f.* drug addiction.

narcosis (nar'ko·sis) *n.f.* narcosis.

narcótico (nar'ko·ti·to) *adj.* &

n.m. narcotic. —**narcotismo,** *n.m.* narcotism.

narcotizar (nar·ko·ti'θar; -'sar) *v.t.* [*infl.:* **rezar, 10**] to drug; administer a narcotic to.

narcotraficante (nar·ko·tra·fi'kan·te) *n.m. & f.* drug dealer.

nardo ('nar·ðo) *n.m.* nard; spikenard; tuberose.

narigón (na·ri'ɣon) *n.m.* large nose. —*adj.* = **narigudo.**

narigudo (nari'ɣu·ðo) *adj.* large-nosed.

nariz (na'riθ; -'ris) *n.f.* **1,** nose. **2,** *usu.pl.* nostrils. —**nariz respingona** *or* **respingada,** turned-up nose. —**sonarse las narices,** *colloq.* to blow one's nose.

narrar (na'rrar) *v.t. & i.* to narrate. —**narración,** *n.f.* narration. —**narrador,** *n.m.* [*fem.* **-dora**] narrator. —**narrativa,** *n.f.* narrative. —**narrativo,** *adj.* narrative.

narria ('na·rrja) *n.f.* **1,** sled; sledge. **2,** heavy carriage; drag. **3,** *colloq.* corpulent woman.

narval (nar'βal) *n.m.* narwhal.

nasal (na'sal) *adj.* nasal. —**nasalidad,** *n.f.* nasality. —**nasalizar,** *v.t.* [*infl.:* **rezar, 10**] to nasalize.

nata ('na·ta) *n.f.* **1,** cream. **2,** skin that forms on milk. **3,** *fig.* [*also,* **flor y nata**] cream; pick; elite.

natación (na·ta'θjon; -'sjon) *n.f.* swimming.

natal (na'tal) *adj.* natal; native. —**natalidad,** *n.f.* birth rate.

natalicio (na·ta'li·θjo; -sjo) *adj. & n.m.* birthday.

natátil (na'ta·til) *adj.* natant.

natatorio (na·ta'to·rjo) *adj.* swimming (*attrib.*). —*n.m.,* *Amer.* natatorium.

natillas (na'ti·ʎas; -jas) *n.f.pl.* custard.

natividad (na·ti·βi'ðað) *n.f.* nativity.

nativo (na'ti·βo) *adj. & n.m.* native. —*adj.* natural; occurring naturally.

nato ('na·to) *adj.* by nature or birth; born.

natrón (na'tron) *n.m.* natron.

natura (na'tu·ra) *n.f.* = **naturaleza.**

natural (na·tu'ral) *adj.* natural; native. —*n.m. & f.* native. —*n.m.* natural inclination; nature. —**al natural,** in the raw; in the natural state. —**del natural,** from nature; from life.

naturaleza (na·tu·ra'le·θa; -sa)

n.f. nature. —**naturaleza muerta,** still life.

naturalidad (na·tu·ra·li'ðað) *n.f.* ease; spontaneity; naturalness.

naturalismo (na·tu·ra'lis·mo) *n.m.* naturalism. —**naturalista,** *adj.* naturalistic. —*n.m. & f.* naturalist.

naturalizar (na·tu·ra·li'θar; -'sar) *v.t.* [*infl.:* **rezar, 10**] to naturalize. —**naturalizarse,** *v.r.* to become naturalized. —**naturalización,** *n.f.* naturalization.

naufragar (nau·fra'ɣar) *v.i.* [*infl.:* **pagar, 8**] to be shipwrecked.

naufragio (nau'fra·xjo) *n.m.* shipwreck.

náufrago ('nau·fra·ɣo) *adj.* shipwrecked. —*n.m.* castaway.

náusea ('nau·se·a) *n.f.* nausea. —**nauseabundo** (-'βun·do) *adj.* nauseous; nauseating. —**nausear,** *v.i.* to feel nauseated. —**nauseado** (-'a·ðo) *adj.* nauseated.

nauta ('nau·ta) *n.m.* seaman.

náutica ('nau·ti·ka) *n.f.* navigation (*as an art or discipline*). —**náutico,** *adj.* nautical.

nautilo (nau'ti·lo) *n.m.* nautilus.

navaja (na'βa·xa) *n.f.* razor; jackknife; folding blade. —**navajazo,** *n.m.* razor slash; knife slash. —**navaja de resorte,** switchblade.

naval (na'βal) *adj.* naval.

nave ('na·βe) *n.f.* **1,** ship; vessel; craft. **2,** nave. —**nave espacial,** spaceship.

navegar (na·βe'ɣar) *v.t. & i.* [*infl.:* **pagar, 8**] to navigate. —**navegable,** *adj.* navigable. —**navegación,** *n.f.* navigation. —**navegador,** *n.m.* [*fem.* **-dora**] navigator. —*adj.* navigating. —**navegante,** *n.m. & f.* navigator. —*adj.* navigating.

Navidad (na·βi'ðað) *n.f.* Christmas; Nativity. —**Navidades,** *n.f.pl.* Christmas season; Yuletide.

naviero (na'βje·ro) *adj.* of ships or shipping. —*n.m.* shipowner.

navío (na'βi·o) *n.m.* ship.

náyade ('na·ja·ðe) *n.f.* naiad.

nazca ('naθ·ka; 'nas-) *v., pres. subjve. of* **nacer.**

nazco ('naθ·ko; 'nas-) *v., 1st pers. sing.pres. ind. of* **nacer.**

nazi ('na·θi; -si) *adj. & n.m.* Nazi. —**nazismo,** *n.m.* Nazism.

neandertal (ne·an·der'tal) *adj. & n.m. & f.* Neanderthal.

nébeda ('ne·βe·ða) *n.f.* catnip.

neblina (ne'βli·na) *n.f.* fog. —**neblinoso,** *adj.* foggy.

nebulosa (ne·βu'lo·sa) *n.f.* nebula.
—**nebulosidad,** *n.f.* nebulosity.
—**nebuloso,** *adj.* nebulous; nebular.

necear (ne·θe'ar; ne·se-) *v.i.* **1,** to
utter nonsense. **2,** to behave foolishly.

necedad (ne·θe'ðað; ne·se-) *n.f.* **1,**
foolishness; inanity. **2,** impertinence; nonsense. **3,** tomfoolery.

necesario (ne·θe'sa·rjo; ne·se-)
adj. necessary.

neceser (ne·θe'ser; ne·se-) *n.m.* **1,**
toilet case; vanity case. **2,** sewing
kit; sewing basket.

necesidad (ne·θe·si'ðað; ne·se-)
n.f. **1,** necessity; need. **2,** *usu.pl.*
bodily needs.

necesitado (ne·θe·si'ta·ðo; ne·
se-) *adj.* in need; needy. —*n.m.*
needy person.

necesitar (ne·θe·si'tar; ne·se-) *v.t.*
1, to necessitate. **2,** to need. —*v.i.* to
need; be in need. —**necesitarse,** *v.r.*
to be necessary.

necio ('ne·θjo; -sjo) *adj.* **1,** foolish;
inane. **2,** impertinent. —*n.m.* **1,**
fool. **2,** importunate person; pest.

necrofilia (ne·kro'fi·lja) *n.f.* necrophilia.

necrología (ne·kro·lo'xi·a) *n.f.*
obituary. —**necrológico** (-'lo·xi·ko)
adj. obituary.

necromancia (ne·kro'man·θja;
-sja) *n.f.* necromancy.

necrópolis (ne'kro·po·lis) *n.f.* necropolis.

necrosis (ne'kro·sis) *n.f.* necrosis.
—**necrótico** (-'kro·ti·ko) *adj.* necrotic.

néctar ('nek·tar) *n.m.* nectar.

neerlandés (ne·er·lan'des) *adj.*
Dutch. —*n.m.* **1,** Dutchman. **2,**
Dutch language. —**neerlandesa,**
n.f. Dutch woman.

nefando (ne'fan·do) *adj.* unspeakable; infamous.

nefario (ne'fa·rjo) *adj.* nefarious.

nefasto (ne'fas·to) *adj.* ominous;
fateful.

nefrita (ne'fri·ta) *n.f.* nephrite.

nefritis (ne'fri·tis) *n.f.* nephritis.
—**nefrítico,** *adj.* nephritic.

negación (ne·ya'θjon; -'sjon) *n.f.*
1, negation. **2,** denial. **3,** *gram.* negative.

negar (ne'yar) *v.t.* [*infl.:* **pagar, 8;**
pensar, 27] **1,** to negate; deny. **2,** to
refuse. **3,** to prohibit. **4,** to disown;
disclaim. —**negarse,** *v.r.* to deny
oneself; sacrifice one's own interests. —**negarse a, 1,** to refuse; turn

away from. **2,** *fol. by inf.* to refuse
to.

negativa (ne·ya'ti·βa) *n.f.* negative; denial; refusal.

negativo (ne·ya'ti·βo) *adj.* negative. —*n.m.,* *photog.; elect.* negative. —**negatividad,** *n.f.* negativity.

negligente (ne·yli'xen·te) *adj.*
negligent. —**negligencia** (-θja; -sja)
n.f. negligence.

negociado (ne·yo'θja·ðo; -'sja·ðo)
n.m. **1,** deal; business. **2,** *Amer.*
shady business; shady deal.

negociador (ne·yo·θja'ðor;
-sja'ðor) *adj.* negotiating. —*n.m.*
[*fem.* -**dora**] negotiator.

negociar (ne·yo'θjar; -'sjar) *v.t. &*
i. to negotiate. —*v.i.* to deal; trade.
—**negociable,** *adj.* negotiable.
—**negociación,** *n.f.* negotiation.
—**negociante,** *n.m. & f.* dealer;
businessman (or -woman); tradesman (or -woman).

negocio (ne'yo·θjo; -sjo) *n.m.* **1,**
business; concern. **2,** transaction; dealing. **3,** profit; benefit;
gain. **4,** *Amer.* place of business; office; store. —**negocios,** *n.m.pl.*
business affairs. —**encargado de**
negocios, chargé d'affaires.
—**negocio redondo,** *colloq.* clearly
profitable deal; sound business.

negrear (ne·yre'ar) *v.i.* to look
black; be blackish.

negrero (ne'yre·ro) *adj.* of or pert.
to the slave trade.—*n.m.* slaver.

negrilla (ne'yri·ʎa; -ja) *n.f., print.*
boldface.

negro ('ne·yro) *adj. & n.m.* **1,**
black. **2,** negro. —**negra,** *n.f.* negress; *Amer.* darling. —**negro de**
humo, lampblack. —**pasarlas**
negras, *colloq.* to have a hard time
of it.

negroide (ne'yroi·ðe) *adj.* negroid.

negrura (ne'yru·ra) *n.f.* blackness.
Also, **negror** (-'yror) *n.m.*

negruzco (ne'yruθ·ko; -'yrus·ko)
adj. blackish.

negué (ne'ye) *v., 1st pers.sing. pret.*
of **negar.**

nematoda (ne·ma'to·ða) *n.f.* nematode.

némesis ('ne·me·sis) *n.m.* nemesis.

nene ('ne·ne) *n.m., colloq.* [*fem.*
nena] baby; child.

nenúfar (ne'nu·far) *n.m.* white water lily.

neoceno (ne·o'θe·no; -'se·no) *adj.*
Neocene.

neodimio (ne·o'ði·mjo) *n.m.* neodymium.

neófito (ne'o·fi·to) *n.m.* neophyte; novice.

neolítico (ne·o'li·ti·ko) *adj.* neolithic.

neologismo (ne·o·lo'xis·mo) *n.m.* neologism.

neón (ne'on) *n.m.* neon.

neonato (ne·o'na·to) *adj. & n.m.* newborn; neonate.

neoplasma (ne·o'plas·ma) *n.m.* neoplasm.

neoyorquino (ne·o·jor'ki·no) *adj.* of New York; New York *(attrib.).* —*n.m.* New Yorker.

nepotismo (ne·po'tis·mo) *n.m.* nepotism.

neptunio (nep'tu·njo) *n.m.* neptunium.

Neptuno (nep'tu·no) *n.m.* Neptune.

nereida (ne'rei·ða) *n.f.* nereid.

nervadura (ner·βa'ðu·ra) *n.f.* 1, nervure. 2, nervation.

nérveo ('ner·βe·o) *adj.* neural.

nervio ('ner·βjo) *n.m.* 1, nerve. 2, vein *(of a leaf).*

nerviosidad (ner·βjo·si'ðað) *n.f.* 1, nervousness. 2, = **nervosidad.**

nervioso (ner'βjo·so) *adj.* 1, nervous. 2, sinewy.

nervosidad (ner·βo·si'ðað) *n.f.* 1, force; vigor. 2, cogency *(of an argument).* 3, flexibility.

nervoso (ner'βo·so) *adj.* = **nervioso.**

nervudo (ner'βu·ðo) *adj.* 1, vigorous. 2, sinewy.

nesciencia (nes'θjen·θja; ne'sjen·sja) *n.f.* nescience. —**nesciente,** *adj.* nescient; ignorant.

nesga ('nes·ɣa) *n.f., sewing* gore.

neto ('ne·to) *adj.* 1, clear; pure; clean. 2, net.

neumático (neu'ma·ti·ko) *adj.* pneumatic. —*n.m.* tire.

neumonía (neu·mo'ni·a) *n.f.* pneumonia.

neuralgia (neu'ral·xja) *n.f.* neuralgia. —**neurálgico** (-xi·ko) *adj.* neuralgic.

neurastenia (neu·ras'te·nja) *n.f.* neurasthenia. —**neurasténico** (-ni·ko) *adj. & n.m.* neurasthenic.

neuritis (neu'ri·tis) *n.f.* neuritis.

neurología (neu·ro·lo'xi·a) *n.f.* neurology. —**neurológico** (-'lo·xi·ko) *adj.* neurological. —**neurólogo** (-'ro·lo·ɣo) *n.m.* neurologist.

neurona (neu'ro·na) *n.f.* neuron.

neurosis (neu'ro·sis) *n.f.* neurosis.

neurótico (-'ro·ti·ko) *adj. & n.m.* neurotic.

neutral (neu'tral) *adj. & n.m. & f.* neutral. —**neutralidad,** *n.f.* neutrality.

neutralizar (neu·tra·li'θar; -'sar) *v.t.* [*infl.:* **rezar, 10**] to neutralize. —**neutralización,** *n.f.* neutralization.

neutrino (neu'tri·no) *n.m.* neutrino.

neutro ('neu·tro) *adj.* 1, neuter. 2, neutral. 3, *gram.* intransitive.

neutrón (neu'tron) *n.m.* neutron.

nevar (ne'βar) *v.impers.* [*infl.:* **pensar, 27**] to snow. —**nevada,** *n.f.* snowfall. —**nevado,** *adj.* snow-covered. —*n.m.* snow-capped mountain.

nevasca (ne'βas·ka) *n.f.* snowfall; snowstorm.

nevera (ne'βe·ra) *n.f.* icebox; refrigerator.

nevisca (ne'βis·ka) *n.f.* snow flurry; light snow.

neviscar (ne·βis'kar) *v.impers.* [*infl.:* **tocar, 7**] to snow lightly.

nevoso (ne'βo·so) *adj.* snowy.

nexo ('nek·so) *n.m.* bond; connection; nexus.

ni (ni) *conj.* neither; nor. —**ni . . . ni,** neither . . . nor. —**ni que, 1,** as if. **2,** would that. —**ni siquiera,** not even.

nicotina (ni·ko'ti·na) *n.f.* nicotine. —**nicotínico,** *adj.* nicotinic.

nicho ('ni·tʃo) *n.m.* niche.

nidada (ni'ða·ða) *n.f.* brood; covey.

nidal (ni'ðal) *n.m.* 1, nest. 2, nest egg.

nido ('ni·ðo) *n.m.* nest.

niebla ('nje·βla) *n.f.* fog; mist.

niego ('nje·ɣo) *v., 1st pers.sing. pres.ind.* of **negar.**

niegue ('nje·ɣe) *v., pres.subjve.* of **negar.**

nieta ('nje·ta) *n.f.* granddaughter.

nieto ('nje·to) *n.m.* grandson.

nieva ('nje·βa) *v., pres.ind.* of **nevar.**

nieve ('nje·βe) *n.f.* 1, snow. 2, *Amer.* sherbet. —**nieve carbónica,** dry ice.

nieve ('nje·βe) *v., pres.subjve.* of **nevar.**

nigromancia (ni·ɣro'man·θja; -sja) *n.f.* necromancy. —**nigromante,** *n.m. & f.* necromancer.

nihilismo (ni·i'lis·mo) *n.m.*

nihilism.—**nihilista,** *n.m. & f.* nihilist. —*adj.* nihilistic.

nilón (ni'lon) *n.m.* nylon.

nimbo ('nim·bo) *n.m.* nimbus.

nimiedad (ni·mje'ðað) *n.f.* 1, trifle. 2, meticulousness; minuteness. 3, fastidiousness.

nimio ('ni·mjo) *adj.* 1, trivial; trifling. 2, meticulous; minute. 3, fastidious.

ninfa ('nin·fa) *n.f.* nymph.

ninfomanía (nin·fo·ma'ni·a) *n.f.* nymphomania. —**ninfomaníaca,** *n.f.* nymphomaniac.

ningún (nin'gun) *adj.* = **ninguno** *before a masc. noun.* —**de ningún modo,** by no means; not at all; nowise.

ninguno (nin'gu·no) *adj.* not any; no. —*pron.* none; no one; nobody.

niña ('ni·ɲa) *n.f.* 1, girl. 2, pupil *(of the eye).*

niñada (ni'ɲa·ða) *n.f.* childishness; childish behavior.

niñera (ni'ɲe·ra) *n.f.* nursemaid.

niñería (ni·ɲe'ri·a) *n.f.* 1, = **niñada.** 2, trifle.

niño ('ni·ɲo) *adj.* childish. —*n.m.* boy; child. —**niñez,** *n.f.* childhood.

niobio ('njo·βjo) *n.m.* niobium; columbium.

nipón (ni'pon) *adj.* & *n.m.* [*fem.* **-pona**] Nipponese.

níquel ('ni·kel) *n.m.* nickel. —**niquelar,** *v.t.* to nickel-plate. —**niquelado,** *adj.* nickel-plated. —*n.m.* nickelplating.

nirvana (nir'βa·na) *n.m.* nirvana.

níspero ('nis·pe·ro) *n.m.* medlar.

nítido ('ni·ti·ðo) *adj.* clear; clean; well defined. —**nitidez,** *n.f.* clarity.

nitón (ni'ton) *n.m.* = **radón.**

nitos ('ni·tos) *adv. & interj., slang* nix; no.

nitrato (ni'tra·to) *n.m.* nitrate.

nítrico (ni'tri·ko) *adj.* nitric.

nitro ('ni·tro) *n.m.* niter; saltpeter.

nitrocelulosa (ni·tro·θe·lu'lo·sa; -se·lu'lo·sa) *n.f.* nitrocellulose.

nitrógeno (ni'tro·xe·no) *n.m.* nitrogen. —**nitrogenado,** *adj.* nitrogenous.

nitroglicerina (ni·tro·γli·θe'ri·na; -se'ri·na) *n.f.* nitroglycerine.

nitroso (ni'tro·so) *adj.* nitrous.

nivel (ni'βel) *n.m.* level. — **a nivel,** on a level line; level. —**a nivel con,** on a level with. —**nivel de vida,** standard of living; lifestyle.

nivelado (niβe'la·ðo) *adj.* 1, level; even. 2, horizontal.

nivelar (ni·βe'lar) *v.t.* to level; make even. —**nivelación,** *n.f.* leveling.

níveo ('ni·βe·o) *adj.* snowy; like snow.

no (no) *adv.* no; not. *Preceding nouns and adjectives, equivalent to Eng. prefix* **non-:** *no beligerante,* nonbelligerent; *no intervención,* nonintervention. —*n.m.* refusal; denial; nay; no. —**a no ser que,** unless. —**no bien,** no sooner. —**no más,** only. —**no obstante,** notwithstanding; nevertheless. —**no sea que,** lest. —**por sí o por no,** just in case. —**ya no,** no longer.

nobelio (no'βe·ljo) *n.m.* nobelium.

noble ('no·βle) *adj.* noble. —*n.m.* nobleman. —**nobleza,** *n.f.* nobility. —**mujer noble,** noblewoman.

noción (no'θjon; -'sjon) *n.f.* notion; idea. —**nociones,** *n.f.pl.* rudiments; elements.

nocivo (no'θi·βo; -'si·βo) *adj.* noxious. —**nocividad,** *n.f.* noxiousness.

nocturno (nok'tur·no) *adj.* nocturnal. —*n.m.* nocturne.

noche ('no·tʃe) *n.f.* 1, night. 2, evening. 3, dark; darkness. —**buenas noches,** good evening; good night. —**de la noche a la mañana,** suddenly; unexpectedly. —**de noche,** at night; by night. —**es de noche,** it is night. —**hacer noche,** to stop for the night. —**pasar la noche en claro,** not to sleep a wink.

nochebuena (no·tʃe'βwe·na) *n.f.* Christmas Eve.

nodo ('no·ðo) *n.m.* node. —**nodal,** *adj.* nodal.

nodriza (no'ðri·θa; -sa) *n.f.* wet nurse.

nódulo ('no·ðu·lo) *n.m.* nodule. —**nodular,** *adj.* nodular.

nogal (no'γal) *n.m.* 1, walnut tree. 2, walnut *(wood and color).*

nómada ('no·ma·ða) *adj.* [*also,* **nómade** (-ðe)] nomadic. —*n.m. & f.* nomad.

nomás (no'mas) *adv., Mex.* just; only.

nombradía (nom·bra'ði·a) *n.f.* fame; renown.

nombrado (nom'bra·ðo) *adj.* celebrated; renowned.

nombrar (nom'brar) *v.t.* 1, to name. 2, to appoint; nominate. —**nonbramiento,** *n.m.* appointment; commission.

nombre ('nom·bre) *n.m.* 1, name. 2, noun. —**de nombre,** renowned.

—**nombre de pila**, given name.
—**no tiene nombre**, there's no word for it; unbelievable; impossible.

nomenclatura (no·men·kla'tu·ra) *n.f.* nomenclature.

nomeolvides (no·me·ol'βi·ðes) *n.m.sing. & pl.* forget-me-not.

nómina ('no·mi·na) *n.f.* list; roll, esp. payroll.

nominal (no·mi'nal) *adj.* nominal.

nominar (no·mi'nar) *v.t.* to nominate; appoint. —**nominación,** *n.f.* nomination; appointment.

nominativo (no·mi·na'ti·βo) *adj. & n.m.* nominative.

non (non) *adj.* odd; uneven. —*n.m.* odd number. —**nones,** *n.m.pl. & interj.* emphatic no; nix.

nona ('no·na) *n.f.* nones *(canonical hour).* —**nonas,** *n.f.pl.* nones *(in the ancient calendar).*

nonada (no'na·ða) *n.f.* trifle; nothing.

nonagenario (no·na·xe'na·rjo) *adj. & n.m.* nonagenarian.

nonagésimo (no·na'xe·si·mo) *adj. & n.m.* ninetieth.

nonágono (no'na·γo·no) *n.m.* nonagon.

nonato (no'na·to) *adj.* **1,** born by cesarean section. **2,** unborn; still to come.

nonillón (no·ni'ʎon; -'jon) *n.m. U.S.* a septillion nonillion; *Brit.* nonillion.

noningentésimo (no·nin·xen'te·si·mo) *adj. & n.m.* ninehundredth.

nono ('no·no) *adj.* ninth.

nopal (no'pal) *n.m.* nopal.

noquear (no·ke'ar) *v.t., slang* to knock out; kayo.

nordestal (nor·ðes'tal) *adj.* northeastern; northeasterly.

nordeste (nor'ðes·te) *n.m.* northeast. *Also,* **noreste** (no'res·te).

nórdico ('nor·ði·ko) *adj. & n.m.* Nordic; Norse.

noria ('no·rja) *n.f.* noria; waterwheel.

norma ('nor·ma) *n.f.* **1,** norm; rule. **2,** carpenter's or mason's square.

normal (nor'mal) *adj.* normal. —*adj. & n.m. or f., geom.* perpendicular. —**normalidad,** *n.f.* normalcy; normality.

normalizar (nor·ma·li'θar; -'sar) *v.t.* [*infl.:* **rezar, 10**] to normalize; standardize.

normando (nor'man·do) *adj.* **1,**

Norman. **2,** Norse. —*n.m.* **1,** Norman. **2,** Norseman; Northman; *pl.* the Norse.

normativo (nor·ma'ti·βo) *n.m.* normative.

noroeste (nor·o'es·te) *n.m.* northwest.

norte ('nor·te) *adj. & n.m.* north. —*n.m., fig.* guiding light; aim.

norteamericano (nor·te·a·me·ri'ka·no) *adj. & n.m.* **1,** North American. **2,** American *(of the U.S.A.).*

norteño (nor'te·ɲo) *adj.* **1,** northern. **2,** northerly. —*n.m.* northerner.

nos (nos) *pers.pron. 1st pers.pl., used as obj. of a verb* us; to us; ourselves.

nosotros (no'so·tros) *pers.pron. 1st pers.m.pl.* [*fem.* **nosotras**] *used as subject of a verb or object of a preposition* we; us.

nostalgia (nos'tal·xja) *n.f.* nostalgia. —**nostálgico** (-xi·ko) *adj.* nostalgic.

nota ('no·ta) *n.f.* **1,** note. **2,** grade; mark *(in school).*

notable (no'ta·βle) *adj.* notable; noteworthy. —*n.m. & f.* notable. —**notabilidad,** *n.f.* notability.

notación (no·ta'θjon; -'sjon) *n.f.* notation.

notar (no'tar) *v.t.* **1,** to note. **2,** to notice; perceive.

notaría (no·ta'ri·a) *n.f.* **1,** notary public's office. **2,** profession of notary public.

notario (no'ta·rjo) *n.m.* notary public; notary. —**notarial,** *adj.* notarial.

notarizar (no·ta·ri'θar; -'sar) *v.t., Amer.* [*infl.:* **rezar, 10**] to notarize.

noticia (no'ti·θja; -sja) *n.f.* news; information. —**noticias,** *n.f.pl.* news. —**noticiar,** *v.t., colloq.* to give news of.

noticiario (no·ti'θja·rjo; -'sja·rjo) *n.m.* **1,** newsreel. **2,** newscast.

noticiero (no·ti'θje·ro; -'sje·ro) *n.m.* **1,** news writer. **2,** newscaster. **3,** newsreel. —*adj.* **1,** news *(attrib.).* **2,** *colloq.* newsy.

noticioso (no·ti'θjo·so; -'sjo·so) *adj.* newsy; informative.

notificar (no·ti·fi'kar) *v.t.* [*infl.:* **tocar, 7**] to notify. —**notificación,** *n.f.* notification; notice.

notorio (no'to·rjo) *adj.* notorious. —**notoriedad,** *n.f.* notoriety.

nova ('no·βa) *n.f., astron.* nova.

novatada (no·βa'ta·ða) *n.f.* **1,** hazing. **2,** beginner's blunder.

novato (no'βa·to) *n.m.* tyro; tenderfoot; greenhorn.

novecientos (no·βe'θjen·tos; -sjen·tos) *adj. & n.m.pl.* [*fem.* **-tas**] nine hundred. —*adj.* ninehundredth.

novedad (no·βe'ðað) *n.f.* **1,** novelty. **2,** bit of news; latest news. —**sin novedad, 1,** all is quiet; no news to report. **2,** safely; without mishap.

novedoso (no·βe'ðo·so) *adj.* novel; original; newfangled.

novel (no'βel) *adj.* new; beginning; inexperienced.

novela (no'βe·la) *n.f.* **1,** novel. **2,** tale; fiction; falsehood. **3,** soap opera. —**novela policíaca**, detective story. —**novelizar**, *v.t.* [*infl.: rezar, 10*] to novelize. —**novelización,** *n.f.* novelization.

novelería (no·βe·le'ri·a) *n.f.* **1,** bit of news; gossip. **2,** fad. **3,** faddishness.

novelero (no·βe'le·ro) *adj.* **1,** fond of gossip; gossiping. **2,** faddish. —*n.m.* **1,** gossipmonger; talebearer. **2,** faddist.

novelesco (no·βe'les·ko) *adj.* **1,** fictional. **2,** romantic.

novelista (no·βe'lis·ta) *n.m. & f.* novelist.

novena (no'βe·na) *n.f.* **1,** *eccles.* novena. **2,** *mus.* ninth.

noveno (no'βe·no) *adj. & n.m.* ninth.

noventa (no'βen·ta) *adj. & n.m.* ninety. —**noventavo,** *adj. & n.m.* ninetieth.

noventón (no·βen'ton) *adj. & n.m.* [*fem.* **-tona**] nonagenarian.

novia (no'·βja) *n.f.* **1,** bride. **2,** fiancée. **3,** sweetheart; girlfriend.

noviazgo (no'βjaθ·γo; -'βjas·γo) *n.m.* betrothal; engagement.

novicio (no'βi·θjo; -sjo) *n.m.* novice. —*adj.* inexperienced. —**noviciado,** *n.m.* novitiate.

noviembre (no'βjem·bre) *n.m.* November.

novilunio (no·βi'lu·njo) *n.m.* new moon.

novillero (no·βi'ʎe·ro; -'je·ro) *n.m.* **1,** herdsman, esp. for young cattle. **2,** fighter of young bulls; novice bullfighter. **3,** truant.

novillo (no'βi·ʎo; -jo) *n.m.* young bull. —**novilla,** *n.f.* heifer. —**novillada,** *n.f.* mock bullfight with young bulls. —**hacer novillos,** to play hooky.

novio (no'·βjo) *n.m.* **1,** bridegroom. **2,** fiancé. **3,** sweetheart; boyfriend.

novísimo (no'βi·si·mo) *adj., superl. of* **nuevo.**

novocaína (no·βo·ka'i·na) *n.f.* novocaine.

nube ('nu·βe) *n.f.* **1,** cloud. **2,** swarm. **3,** cataract (*in the eye*). —**nubarrón** (-βa'rron) storm cloud.

núbil ('nu·βil) *adj.* nubile; marriageable. —**nubilidad,** *n.f.* nubility; marriageability.

nubio ('nu·βjo) *adj. & n.m.* Nubian.

nublado (nu'βla·ðo) *adj.* cloudy. —*n.m..* cloud formation; storm clouds.

nublar (nu'βlar) *v.t.* to cloud; becloud. —**nublarse,** *v.r.* to cloud over; become cloudy.

nubloso (nu'βlo·so) *adj.* **1,** cloudy; overcast. **2,** unfortunate. *Also,* **nuboso** (-'βo·so). —**nublosidad,** *n.f.* cloudiness.

nuca ('nu·ka) *n.f.* nape.

nuclear (nu·kle'ar) *adj.* nuclear.

núcleo ('nu·kle·o) *n.m.* nucleus.

nucléolo (nu'kle·o·lo) *n.m.* nucleolus.

nucleón (nu·kle'on) *n.m.* nucleon.

nudillo (nu'ði·ʎo; -jo) *n.m.* knuckle.

nudismo (nu'ðis·mo) *n.m.* nudism. —**nudista,** *adj. & n.m. & f.* nudist.

nudo ('nu·ðo) *n.m.* **1,** knot. **2,** tangle. **3,** cluster, esp. of mountains. **4,** *naut.* knot. **5,** bump. **6,** crux; crucial point. —**nudo corredizo,** slipknot. —**nudoso,** *adj.* knotty.

nuégado ('nwe·γa·ðo) *n.m.* nougat.

nuera ('nwe·ra) *n.f.* daughter-in-law.

nuestro ('nwes·tro) *poss.adj. & pron.m.sing.* [*fem.* **nuestra**; *pl.* **nuestros, nuestras**], *agreeing in number and gender with the thing or things possessed* our; ours. —**los nuestros,** our side.

nueva ('nwe·βa) *n.f.* = **noticia.**

nueve ('nwe·βe) *adj. & n.m.* nine.

nuevo ('nwe·βo) *adj.* new. —**de nuevo,** again. —¿**Qué hay de nuevo?,** What's new?

Nuevo Testamento New Testament.

nuez (nweθ; nwes) *n.f.* **1,** *bot.* nut. **2,** walnut. **3,** Adam's apple. —**nuez moscada,** nutmeg.

nulidad (nu·li'ðað) *n.f.* **1,** nullity. **2,** incompetent; good-for-nothing.

nulo ('nu·lo) *adj.* **1,** null. **2,** incompetent; good-for-nothing.

numeración (nu·me·ra'θjon; -'sjon) *n.f.* **1,** numbering. **2,** numeration.

numerador (nu·me·ra'ðor) *n.m.* numerator.

numeral (nu·me'ral) *adj.* numeral.

numerar (nu·me'rar) *v.t.* **1,** to number; count. **2,** to express in numbers. **3,** to assign a number to. —**asiento numerado,** reserved seat. —**sesión numerada,** reserved-seat performance.

numerario (nu·me'ra·rjo) *n.m.* cash; specie.

numérico (nu·me·ri·ko) *adj.* numerical.

número ('nu·me·ro) *n.m.* **1,** number. **2,** numeral. —**numerosidad,** *n.f.* numerousness. —**numeroso,** *adj.* numerous.

numerología (nu·me·ro·lo'xi·a) *n.f.* numerology. —**numerólogo** (-'ro·lo·ɣo) *n.m.* numerologist.

numismática (nu·mis'ma·ti·ka) *n.f.* numismatics. —**numismático,** *adj.* numismatic. —*n.m.* numismatist.

nunca ('nun·ka) *adv.* never. —**nunca jamás,** nevermore.

nuncio ('nun·θjo; -sjo) *n.m.* **1,** nuncio. **2,** harbinger.

nupcial (nup'θjal; -'sjal) *adj.* nuptial.

nupcias ('nup·θjas; -sjas) *n.f.pl.* nuptials; wedding.

nutria ('nu·trja) *n.f.* **1,** otter. **2,** nutria.

nutrición (nu·tri'θjon; -'sjon) *n.f.* nutrition.

nutrido (nu'tri·ðo) *adj.* **1,** *fig.* abounding; abundant. **2,** *mil.* uninterrupted; thick *(of fire or firing).* —**bien nutrido,** well-fed. —**mal nutrido,** ill-fed.

nutrimento (nu·tri'men·to) *also,* **nutrimiento** (-'mjen·to) *n.m.* nutriment.

nutrir (nu'trir) *v.t.* to nourish; nurture.

nutritivo (nu·tri'ti·βo) *adj.* nutrient; nutritive; nutritious.

Ñ

Ñ, ñ ('e·ɲe) *n.f.* 17th letter of the Spanish alphabet.

ña (ɲa) *n.f., Amer. colloq.* = **doña.**

ñame ('ɲa·me) *n.m.* yam.

ñandú (ɲan'du) *n.m.* American ostrich.

ñáñigo ('ɲa·ɲi·ɣo) *adj. & n.m., Cuba* voodoo.

ñapa ('ɲa·pa) *n.f., Amer.* bonus; extra. —**de ñapa,** to boot; in the bargain.

ñaque ('ɲa·ke) *n.m.* assortment of junk; odds and ends.

ñato ('ɲa·to) *adj., Amer.* pug-nosed; flat-nosed.

ñeque ('ɲe·ke) *n.m., Amer.* vigor; enterprise.

ño (ɲo) *n.m., Amer., colloq.* = **don.**

ñongo ('ɲon·go) *adj., Amer. derog.* lazy; ignorant.

ñoño ('ɲo·ɲo) *adj., colloq.* mawkish. —**ñoñería,** *n.f.* drivel; mawkishness. —**ñoñez,** *n.f.* mawkishness.

ñu (ɲu) *n.m.* gnu.

ñudo ('ɲu·ðo) *n.m.* = **nudo.** —**ñudoso** = nudoso.

O

O, o (o) *n.f.* 18th letter of the Spanish alphabet.

o (o) *conj.* or; either. —**o . . . o,** either . . . or. —**o sea,** that is.

oasis (o'a·sis) *n.m.sing. & pl.* oasis.

obcecar (oβ·θe'kar; -se'kar) *v.t.* [*infl.:* **tocar, 7**] to blind; obsess. —**obcecarse,** *v.r.* to be obsessed.

—**obcecación,** *n.f.* obsession; blind stubbornness.

obedecer (o·βe·ðe'θer; -'ser) *v.t. & i.* [*infl.:* **conocer, 13**] to obey. —**obedecer a, 1,** to yield to. **2,** to be due to; arise from.

obediente (o·βe'ðjen·te) *adj.* obedient. —**obediencia,** *n.f.* obedience.

obelisco (o·βe'lis·ko) *n.m.* obelisk.

obenques (o'βen·kes) *n.m.pl.*, *naut.* shrouds.

obertura (o·βer'tu·ra) *n.f.*, *mus.* overture.

obeso (o'βe·so) *adj.* obese. —**obesidad**, *n.f.* obesity.

óbice ('o·βi·θe; -se) *n.m.* impediment; obstacle.

obispalía (o·βis·pa'li·a) *n.f.* 1, bishop's palace. 2, diocese.

obispo (o'βis·po) *n.m.* bishop. —**obispado**, *n.m.* bishopric; diocese. —**obispal**, *adj.* episcopal.

óbito ('o·βi·to) *n.m.* decease; demise.

obituario (o·βi'twa·rjo) *n.m.* obituary.

objeción (oβ·xe'θjon; -'sjon) *n.f.* objection.

objetar (oβ·xe'tar) *v.t.* to object.

objeto (oβ'xe·to) *n.m.* object. —**objetivo**, *adj.* & *n.m.* objective. —**objetividad**, *n.f.* objectivity.

oblación (o·βla'θjon; -'sjon) *n.f.* oblation.

oblato (o'βla·to) *n.m.* oblate.

oblea (o'βle·a) *n.f.* 1, adhesive wafer. 2, *pharm.* capsule.

oblicuo (o'βli·kwo) *adj.* oblique. —**oblicuidad**, *n.f.* obliquity.

obligación (o·βli·ɣa'θjon; -'sjon) *n.f.* 1, obligation. 2, *comm.* bond. —**obligacionista**, *n.m.* & *f.* bondholder.

obligar (o·βli'ɣar) *v.t.* [*infl.*: **pagar**, 8] to obligate; compel.

obligatorio (o·βli·ɣa'to·rjo) *adj.* obligatory; compulsory.

oblongo (oβ'lon·go) *adj.* oblong.

oboe (o'βo·e) *n.m.* 1, oboe. 2, oboist.

óbolo ('o·βo·lo) *n.m.* mite; small contribution.

obra ('o·βra) *n.f.* 1, work. 2, construction. 3, *theat.* play. 4, *mus.* composition. —**obra maestra**, masterpiece. —**¡manos a la obra!**, to work!

obrar (o'βrar) *v.t.* & *i.* 1, to work. 2, to build. —**obrador**, *n.m.* workshop.

obrerismo (o·βre'ris·mo) *n.m.* 1, labor movement. 2, working class.

obrero (o'βre·ro) *adj.* working. —*n.m.* worker.

obsceno (oβs'θe·no; oβ'se·no) *adj.* obscene. —**obscenidad**, *n.f.* obscenity.

obscurecer (oβs·ku·re'θer; -'ser) *v.t.* [*infl.*: **conocer**, 13] to darken;

becloud; obscure. —*v.impers.* to grow dark.

obscuridad (oβs·ku·ri'ðað) *n.f.* 1, darkness. 2, obscurity.

obscuro (oβs'ku·ro) *adj.* 1, dark. 2, obscure. —**a obscuras**, in the dark.

obsequiar (oβ·se'kjar) *v.t.* 1, to give; present. 2, to treat; regale.

obsequio (oβ'se·kjo) *n.m.* gift; compliment. —**en obsequio de**, in deference to.

obsequioso (oβ·se'kjo·so) *adj.* obsequious. —**obsequiosidad**, *n.f.* obsequiousness.

observable (oβ·ser'βa·βle) *adj.* observable.

observar (oβ·ser'βar) *v.t.* to observe. —**observación**, *n.f.* observation. —**observador**, *n.m.* [*fem.* -**dora**] observer. —*adj.* observant. —**observancia**, *n.f.* observance. —**observatorio**, *n.m.* observatory.

obsesión (oβ·se'sjon) *n.f.* obsession. —**obsesionar**, *v.t.* to obsess. —**obsesivo** (-'si·βo) *adj.* obsessive.

obsidiana (oβ·si'ðja·na) *n.f.* obsidian.

obstáculo (oβs'ta·ku·lo) *n.m.* obstacle.

obstante (oβs'tan·te) *adv.*, *in* **no obstante**, nevertheless; notwithstanding.

obstar (oβs'tar) *v.i.* (*with* **a** *or* **para**) to stand in the way (of); to be opposed (to).

obstetricia (oβs·te'tri·θja; -sja) *n.f.* obstetrics. —**obstétrico** (-'te·tri·ko) *adj.* obstetrical.

obstinarse (oβs·ti'nar·se) *v.r.* to persist; be obstinate. —**obstinación**, *n.f.* obstinacy. —**obstinado**, *adj.* obstinate.

obstruccionismo (oβs·truk·θjo'nis·mo; -sjo'nis·mo) *n.m.* obstructionism. —**obstruccionista**, *adj.* & *n.m.* & *f.* obstructionist.

obstruir (oβs·tru'ir) *v.t.* [*infl.*: **construir**, 41] to obstruct. —**obstrucción** (-truk'θjon; -'sjon) *n.f.* obstruction. —**obstructor** (-'tor) *adj.* [*also*, **obstructivo** (-'ti·βo)] obstructive. —*n.m.* obstructionist.

obtener (oβ·te'ner) *v.t.* [*infl.*: **tener**, 65] to get; obtain. —**obtención**, *n.f.* obtaining; attainment. —**obtenible**, *adj.* obtainable.

obturador (oβ·tu·ra'ðor) *adj.* stopping; plugging. —*n.m.* 1, plug; stopper. 2, *mech.* choke. 3, *photog.* shutter.

obturar (oβ·tu'rar) *v.t.* **1,** to stop up; plug. **2,** *mech.* to choke.

obtuso (oβ'tu·so) *adj.* obtuse.

obtuve (oβ'tu·βe) *v., 1st pers.sing. pret.* of **obtener.**

obús (o'βus) *n.m.* **1,** artillery shell. **2,** howitzer.

obviar (oβ'βjar) *v.t.* to obviate.

obvio ('oβ·βjo) *adj.* obvious.

oca ('o·ka) *n.f.* goose.

ocasión (o·ka'sjon) *n.f.* occasion; opportunity. **—ocasional,** *adj.* occasional; casual. **—ocasionar,** *v.t.* to occasion; provoke. **—de ocasión,** bargain *(attrib.).*

ocaso (o'ka·so) *n.m.* **1,** setting *(of a star)*; sunset. **2,** *fig.* decline; fall; twilight.

occidente (ok·θi'ðen·te; ok·si-) *n.m.* west; occident. **—occidental,** *adj.* occidental; western; west *(attrib.).* **—n.m. & f.** westerner; occidental. **—occidentalizar** (-li'θar; -'sar) *v.t.* [*infl.:* **rezar, 10**] to westernize.

occipucio (ok·θi'pu·θjo; ok·si·'pu·sjo) *n.m.* occiput. **—occipital** (-pi'tal) *adj.* occipital.

océano (o'θe·a·no; o'se-) *n.m.* ocean. **—oceánico** (-'a·ni·ko) *adj.* oceanic.

oceanografía (o·θe·a·no·ɣra·'fi·a; o·se-) *n.f.* oceanography. **—oceanográfico** (-'ɣra·fi·ko) *adj.* oceanographic. **—oceanógrafo** (-'no·ɣra·fo) *n.m.* oceanographer.

ocelote (o·θe'lo·te; o·se-) *n.m.* ocelot.

ocio ('o·θjo; 'o·sjo) *n.m.* idleness; leisure. **—ociosidad,** *n.f.* idleness; laziness. **—ocioso,** *adj.* idle; lazy; useless.

ocluir (o·klu'ir) *v.t.* [*infl.:* **huir, 26**] to occlude. **—oclusión** (-'sjon) *n.f.* occlusion. **—oclusivo** (-'si·βo) *adj.* occlusive.

ocre ('o·kre) *n.m.* ocher.

octaedro (ok·ta'e·ðro) *n.m.* octahedron. **—octaédrico,** *adj.* octahedral.

octágono (ok'ta·yo·no) *n.m.* octagon. **—octagonal,** *adj.* octagonal.

octano (ok'ta·no) *n.m.* octane.

octante (ok'tan·te) *n.m.* octant.

octava (ok'ta·βa) *n.f.* octave.

octavilla (ok·ta'βi·ʎa; -ja) *n.f.* handbill.

octavo (ok'ta·βo) *adj. & n.m.* eighth. **—en octavo,** octavo.

octeto (ok'te·to) *n.m.* octet; *comput.* byte.

octillón (ok·ti'ʎon; -'jon) *n.m. U.S.* a sextillion octillion; *Brit.* octillion.

octingentésimo (ok·tin·xen'te·si·mo) *adj. & n.m.* eight-hundredth.

octogenario (ok·to·xe'na·rjo) *adj. & n.m.* octogenarian.

octogésimo (ok·to'xe·si·mo) *adj. & n.m.* eightieth.

octubre (ok'tu·βre) *n.m.* October.

óctuple ('ok·tu·ple) *adj. & n.m. & f.* octuple. *Also,* **óctuplo** (-plo) *adj. & n.m.* **—octuplicar** (-pli'kar) *v.t.* [*infl.:* **tocar, 7**] to octuple.

ocular (o·ku'lar) *adj.* ocular. **—n.m.** eyepiece.

oculista (o·ku'lis·ta) *n.m. & f.* oculist.

ocultación (o·kul·ta'θjon; -'sjon) *n.f.* **1,** concealment. **2,** *astron.* occultation.

ocultar (o·kul'tar) *v.t.* to hide; conceal.

oculto (o'kul·to) *adj.* hidden; concealed; occult. **—ocultismo,** *n.m.* occultism. **—ocultista,** *adj. & n.m. & f.* occultist.

ocupación (o·ku·pa'θjon; -'sjon) *n.f.* **1,** occupation. **2,** occupancy.

ocupante (o·ku'pan·te) *n.m. & f.* occupant. **—adj.** occupying.

ocupar (o·ku'par) *v.t.* to occupy. **—ocuparse,** *v.r.* **1,** to occupy oneself; be busy. **2,** *fol. by* **de,** to take charge of; concern oneself with; take care of. **—ocupado,** *adj.* busy; engaged; occupied.

ocurrencia (o·ku'rren·θja; -sja) *n.f.* **1,** occurrence. **2,** *fig.* bright idea. **—ocurrente,** *adj.* witty.

ocurrir (o·ku'rrir) *v.i.* to occur.

ochavo (o'tʃa·βo) *n.m.* **1,** an ancient brass coin. **2,** *Amer., colloq.* small coin; *pl.* money.

ochavón (o·tʃa'βon) *adj. & n.m.* octoroon.

ochenta (o'tʃen·ta) *adj. & n.m.* eighty. **—ochentavo,** *adj. & n.m.* eightieth.

ocho ('o·tʃo) *adj. & n.m.* eight.

ochocientos (o·tʃo'θjen·tos; -'sjen·tos) *adj. & n.m.pl.* [*fem.* **-tas**] eight hundred. **—adj.** eight-hundredth.

oda ('o·ða) *n.f.* ode.

odalisca (o·ða'lis·ka) *n.f.* odalisque.

odiar (o'ðjar) *v.t.* to hate.

odio ('o·ðjo) *n.m.* **1,** hate; hatred. **2,** odium.

odioso (o'ðjo·so) *adj.* hateful; odious. —**odiosidad,** *n.f.* hatefulness; odiousness.

odisea (o·ði'se·a) *n.f.* odyssey.

odómetro (o'ðo·me·tro) *n.m.* odometer.

odontología (o·ðon·to·lo'xi·a) *n.f.* odontology; dentistry. —**odontológico** (-'lo·xi·ko) *adj.* odontological. —**odontólogo** (-'to·lo·ɣo) *n.m.* odontologist; dentist.

odorífero (o·ðo'ri·fe·ro) *adj.* odoriferous.

odre ('o·ðre) *n.m.* **1,** wineskin. **2,** *colloq.* drunkard; tippler.

oeste (o'es·te) *n.m.* west.

ofender (o·fen'der) *v.t.* to offend. —**ofenderse,** *v.r.* to take offense.

ofensa (o'fen·sa) *n.f.* offense.

ofensiva (o·fen'si· βa) *n.f.* offensive.

ofensivo (o·fen'si·βo) *adj.* offensive.

ofensor (o·fen'sor) *adj.* offending. —*n.m.* offender.

oferta (o'fer·ta) *n.f.* offer; bid. —**oferta en competencia,** competitive bid. —**oferta y demanda,** supply and demand.

ofertorio (o·fer'to·rjo) *n.m.* offertory.

oficial (o·fi'θjal; -'sjal) *adj.* official. —*n.m.* **1,** official. **2,** officer.

oficialidad (o·fi·θja·li'ðað; -sja·li'ðað) *n.f.* **1,** officers collectively. **2,** official nature.

oficiar (o·fi'θjar; -'sjar) *v.i.* to officiate. —**oficiante,** *n.m., eccles.* celebrant.

oficina (o·fi'θi·na; -'si·na) *n.f.* office. —**oficinista,** *n.m. & f.* office clerk.

oficio (o'fi·θjo; -sjo) *n.m.* **1,** craft; trade. **2,** function; office. **3,** official communication. —**oficios,** *n.m.pl., eccles.* office; services. —**gajes del oficio,** occupational hazards.

oficioso (o·fi'θjo·so; -'sjo·so) *adj.* **1,** officious. **2,** helpful. —**oficiosidad,** *n.f.* officiousness.

ofrecer (o·fre'θer; -'ser) *v.t.* [*infl.:* conocer, 13] **1,** to offer. **2,** to present; show. —**ofrecerse,** *v.r.* to offer oneself; volunteer. —**ofrecimiento,** *n.m.* offer; offering. —**¿Qué se le ofrece?,** What do you wish?

ofrenda (o'fren·da) *n.f.* offering; gift. —**ofrendar,** *v.t.* to present.

oftálmico (of'tal·mi·ko) *adj.* ophthalmic.

oftalmología (of·tal·mo·lo'xi·a) *n.f.* ophthalmology. —**oftalmólogo**

(-'mo·lo·ɣo) *n.m.* ophthalmologist; oculist.

ofuscar (o·fus'kar) *v.t.* [*infl.:* tocar, 7] to obfuscate; bewilder. —**ofuscación,** *n.f., also,* **ofuscamiento,** *n.m.* bewilderment.

ogro ('o·ɣro) *n.m.* ogre.

¡Oh! (o) *interj.* Oh!

ohmio ('o·mjo) *n.m.* ohm. *Also,* **ohm** (om).

oíble (o'i·βle) *adj.* audible.

oído (o'i·ðo) *n.m.* **1,** ear. **2,** hearing. —**oídas,** *n.f.pl., in* de *or* por oídas, by hearsay.

oigo ('oi·ɣo) *v., 1st pers. sing. pres.ind. of* **oír.**

oír (o'ir) *v.t. & i.* [*infl.:* 25] to hear; listen. —**oír decir (que),** to hear (that). —**oír hablar (de),** to hear (about).

ojal (o'xal) *n.m.* **1,** buttonhole. **2,** eyelet. **3,** grommet.

¡ojalá! (o·xa'la) *interj., usu. followed by subjve.* God grant . . . !; Would that . . . !

ojeada (o·xe'a·ða) *n.f.* glance.

ojear (o·xe'ar) *v.t.* to eye; ogle.

ojera (o'xe·ra) *n.f.* eyecup. —**ojeras,** *n.f.pl.* rings under the eyes.

ojeriza (o·xe'ri·θa; -sa) *n.f.* ill will; grudge.

ojeroso (o·xe'ro·so) *adj.* having rings under the eyes; haggard.

ojete (o'xe·te) *n.m.* eyelet.

ojiva (o'xi·βa) *n.f.* ogive.

ojo ('o·xo) *n.m.* **1,** eye. **2,** look; regard. **3,** opening between bridge supports. —**a ojo de buen cubero,** *colloq.* roughly; approximately. —**a ojos vistas,** clearly; openly. —**costar un ojo de la cara,** *colloq.* to cost an arm and a leg. —**dar en los ojos,** *also,* **saltar a los ojos,** to be obvious. —**¡Dichosos los ojos!,** You're a sight for sore eyes! —**echar el ojo a,** to set one's eye on. —**echar un ojo a,** to keep an eye on. —**globo del ojo,** eyeball. —**mal de ojo,** evil eye. —**mirar con buenos** (*or* **malos**) **ojos,** to look favorably (*or* unfavorably) upon. —**¡mucho ojo!** *also,* **¡ojo!,** beware! —**no pegar los ojos,** *colloq.* not to sleep a wink. —**ojo amoratado,** black eye. —**ojo avizor,** sharp eye. —**ojo de buey, 1,** *bot.* oxeye. **2,** *naut.* porthole. —**ojo de la cerradura,** keyhole. —**ojos saltones,** popeyes.

ola ('o·la) *n.f.* wave. —**correr las olas,** to surf.

olaje (o'la·xe) *n.m.* = oleaje.

¡olé! (o'le) *also,* **¡ole!** ('o·le) *interj.* bravo!; ole!

oleada (o·le'a·ða) *n.f.* **1,** big wave. **2,** pounding of waves. **3,** press; crush *(of a crowd).*

oleaginoso (o·le·a·xi'no·so) *adj.* oily; oleaginous.

oleaje (o·le'a·xe) *n.m.* **1,** surf. **2,** heavy sea. **3,** waves.

óleo ('o·le·o) *n.m.* oil.

oleoducto (o·le·o'ðuk·to) *n.m.* oil pipeline.

oleomargarina (o·le·o·mar·ya'ri·na) *n.f.* oleomargarine.

oleoso (o·le'o·so) *adj.* oily.

oler (o'ler) *v.t.* [*infl.:* 51] to smell; sniff. —*v.i.* to smell; stink. —**oler a,** to smell of.

olfatear (ol·fa·te'ar) *v.t.* & *i.* to smell; sniff; scent. —**olfateo** (-'te·o) *n.m.* sniffing.

olfato (ol'fa·to) *n.m.* **1,** sense of smell. **2,** *fig.* perspicacity. —**olfatorio,** *adj.* olfactory.

oligarquía (o·li·yar'ki·a) *n.f.* oligarchy. —**oligarca** (-'yar·ka) *n.m.* oligarch. —**oligárquico** (-'yar·ki·ko) *adj.* oligarchical.

Olimpo (o'lim·po) *n.m.* Olympus. —**olímpico,** *adj.* Olympic. —**olimpíada** (-'pi·a·ða) *n.f.* Olympic Games; Olympiad.

oliva (o'li·βa) *n.f.* olive. —**olivar,** *n.m.* olive grove. —**olivo,** *n.m., also* **olivera** (-'βe·ra) *n.f.* olive tree.

olmo ('ol·mo) *n.m.* elm. —**olmeda,** *n.f.* grove of elms.

ológrafo (o'lo·yra·fo) *adj.* & *n.m.* holograph. —*adj.* holographic. —**olografía** (o·lo·yra'fi·a) *n.f.* holography.

olor (o'lor) *n.m.* odor. —**oloroso,** *adj.* odorous; fragrant.

olvidar (ol·βi'ðar) *v.i.* to forget. —**olvidarse,** *v.r.* **1,** to be forgotten; slip one's mind. **2,** *fol. by* de, to forget. —**olvidadizo,** *adj.* forgetful.

olvido (ol'βi·ðo) *n.m.* **1,** forgetfulness. **2,** oversight. **3,** oblivion. —**echar al** *or* **en olvido,** to forget.

olla ('o·ʎa; 'o·ja) *n.f.* **1,** pot. **2,** stew. —**olla de grillos,** bedlam. —**olla podrida,** a Spanish stew.

ollar (o'ʎar; -'jar) *n.m.* nostril.

ombligo (om'bli·yo) *n.m.* navel.

omega (o'me·ya) *n.f.* omega.

ominoso (o·mi'no·so) *adj.* ominous. —**ominosidad,** *n.f.* ominousness.

omiso (o'mi·so) *adj.* careless; remiss. —**hacer caso omiso de,** to omit; overlook; ignore.

omitir (o·mi'tir) *v.t.* to omit. —**omisión** (-'sjon) omission.

ómnibus ('om·ni·βus) *n.m.sing.* & *pl.* omnibus; bus.

omnipotente (om·ni·po'ten·te) *adj.* omnipotent. —**omnipotencia,** *n.f.* omnipotence.

omnipresente (om·ni·pre'sen·te) *adj.* omnipresent. —**omnipresencia,** *n.f.* omnipresence.

omnisciente (om·nis'θjen·te; -ni'sjen·te) *adj.* omniscient. —**omnisciencia,** *n.f.* omniscience.

omnívoro (om'ni·βo·ro) *adj.* omnivorous.

omóplato (o'mo·pla·to) *n.m.* shoulder blade; scapula.

once ('on·θe; -se) *adj.* & *n.m.* eleven. —**onceavo,** *adj.* & *n.m.* = onzavo.

onceno (on'θe·no; -'se·no) *adj.* & *n.m.* eleventh.

onda ('on·da) *n.f.* wave; ripple. —**ondear,** *v.i.* to wave; ripple; flutter. —**ondeado,** *adj.* wavy.

ondular (on·du'lar) *v.t.* to wave, esp. the hair. —*v.i.* to undulate; wave; wriggle. —**ondulación,** *n.f.* undulation; wave. —**ondulado,** *adj.* wavy. —**ondulante,** *adj.* waving; undulant.

oneroso (o·ne'ro·so) *adj.* onerous. —**onerosidad,** *n.f.* onerousness.

ónice ('o·ni·θe; -se) *n.m. or f.* onyx. *Also,* **ónix.**

ónix ('o·niks) *n.m. or f. sing.* & *pl.* onyx.

onomástico (o·no'mas·ti·ko) *n.m., also,* **onomástica,** *n.f.* name day.

onomatopeya (o·no·ma·to'pe·ja) *n.f.* onomatopoeia. —**onomatopéyico** (-'pe·ji·ko) *adj.* onomatopoetic.

ontología (on·to·lo'xi·a) *n.f.* ontology. —**ontológico** (-'lo·xi·ko) *adj.* ontological. —**ontólogo** (-'to·lo·yo) *n.m.* ontologist.

onza ('on·θa; -sa) *n.f.* **1,** ounce. **2,** snow leopard; ounce.

onzavo (on'θa·βo; -'sa·βo) *adj.* & *n.m.* eleventh.

opaco (o'pa·ko) *adj.* opaque. —**opacidad** (-θi'ðað; -si'ðað) *n.f.* opacity.

opalescente (o·pa·les'θen·te;

-le'sen·te) *adj.* opalescent. —**opalescencia,** *n.f.* opalescence.
opalino (o·pa'li·no) *adj.* opaline.
ópalo ('o·pa·lo) *n.m.* opal.
opción (op'θjon; -'sjon) *n.f.* option.
—**opcional,** *adj.* optional.
ópera ('o·pe·ra) *n.f.* opera.
operable (o·pe·ra·βle) *adj.* operable.
operación (o·pe·ra'θjon; -'sjon)
n.f. operation.
operador (o·pe·ra'ðor) *adj.* operating; operative. —*n.m.* [*fem.* **-dora**]
operator. —**operador cinematográfico,** 1, cameraman. 2, projectionist.
operante (o·pe'ran·te) *adj.* 1, operating; operative. 2, effective. *Also,*
operativo.
operar (o·pe'rar) *v.t. & i., surg.* to
operate. —*v.i.* 1, to operate; work.
2, *comm.* to speculate.
operático (o·pe'ra·ti·ko) *adj.* operatic.
operatorio (o·pe·ra·to·rjo) *adj.,
surg.* operative.
opereta (o·pe're·ta) *n.f.* operetta.
opiado (o'pja·ðo) *adj.* opiate.
opiata (o'pja·ta) *n.f.* opiate. *Also,*
opiato (-to) *n.m.*
opinar (o·pi'nar) *v.i.* to think;
opine.
opinión (o·pi'njon) *n.f.* opinion.
opio ('o·pjo) *n.m.* opium.
—**opiómano** (o'pjo·ma·no) *n.m.*
opium addict.
opíparo (o'pi·pa·ro) *adj.* lavish;
sumptuous.
oponer (o·po'ner) *v.t.* [*infl.:* **poner,**
54] to oppose; place against.
—**oponerse,** *v.r.* to object; be opposed.
oporto (o'por·to) *n.m.* port *(wine).*
oportunidad (o·por·tu·ni'ðað)
n.f. 1, opportunity. 2, opportuneness.
oportuno (o·por'tu·no) *adj.* 1, opportune. 2, quick-witted. —**oportunismo,** *n.m.* opportunism.
—**oportunista,** *n.m. & f.* opportunist. —*adj.* opportunistic.
oposición (o·po·si'θjon; -'sjon) *n.f.*
1, opposition. 2, *usu.pl.* competitive
examinations. —**oposicionista,**
n.m. & f. oppositionist; member of
the opposition. —*adj.* opposition
(attrib.).
opositor (o·po·si'tor) *n.m.* [*fem.*
-tora] 1, competitor, esp. in a competitive examination. 2, opponent.
opresión (o·pre'sjon) *n.f.* oppres-

sion. —**opresivo** (-'si·βo) *adj.* oppressive. —**opreso,** *adj.* oppressed.
—**opresor** (-'sor) *n.m.* [*fem.* **-sora**]
oppressor. —*adj.* oppressive.
oprimir (o·pri'mir) *v.t.* [*p.p.*
oprimido *or* **opreso**] 1, to press. 2,
to oppress.
oprobio (o'pro·βjo) *n.m.* opprobrium. —**oprobioso,** *adj.* opprobrious.
optar (op'tar) *v.i.* to choose; decide.
—**optativo,** *adj.* optional. —*adj. &
n.m., gram.* optative.
óptica ('op·ti·ka) *n.f.* 1, optics. 2,
optical shop. —**óptico,** *n.m.* optician. —*adj.* optic; optical.
optimismo (op·ti'mis·mo) *n.m.*
optimism. —**optimista,** *adj.* optimistic. —*n.m. & f.* optimist.
óptimo ('op·ti·mo) *adj., superl.* of
bueno. —*adj. & n.m.* optimum.
optometría (op·to·me'tri·a) *n.f.*
optometry. —**optómetra** (-'to·me-
tra) *also,* **optometrista** (-'tris·ta)
n.m. & f. optometrist. —**optómetro**
(-'to·me·tro) *n.m.* optometer.
opuesto (o'pwes·to) *v., p.p.* of
oponer. —*adj. & n.m.* opposite;
contrary.
opulento (o·pu'len·to) *adj.* opulent. —**opulencia,** *n.f.* opulence.
opúsculo (o'pus·ku·lo) *n.m.* tract;
booklet.
opuse (o'pu·se) *v., 1st pers.sing.
pret.* of **oponer.**
oquedad (o·ke'ðað) *n.f.* 1, cavity;
hollow. 2, *fig.* hollowness; emptiness.
ora ('o·ra) *conj. (in correlative constructions)* now: *ora rico, ora
pobre,* now rich, now poor.
oración (o·ra'θjon; -'sjon) *n.f.* 1,
speech; oration. 2, prayer. 3, *gram.*
sentence. —**partes de la oración,**
parts of speech.
oráculo (o'ra·ku·lo) *n.m.* oracle.
—**oracular,** *adj.* oracular.
orador (o·ra'ðor) *n.m.* [*fem.* **-dora**]
orator; speaker.
oral (o'ral) *adj.* oral.
orangután (o·ran·gu'tan) *n.m.*
orangutan.
orar (o'rar) *v.i.* 1, to pray. 2, to
speak; orate.
orate (o'ra·te) *n.m. & f.* lunatic.
oratoria (o·ra·to·rja) *n.f.* oratory;
eloquence.
oratorio (o·ra·to·rjo) *n.m.* 1, small
chapel; oratory. 2, oratorio. —*adj.*
oratorical.
orbe ('or·βe) *n.m.* 1, orb. 2, world.

órbita ('or·βi·ta) *n.f.* orbit. —**orbital,** *adj.* orbital.

orca ('or·ka) *n.f., also,* **orco** (-ko) *n.m.* killer whale.

ordalías (or·ða'li·as) *n.f.pl., hist.* ordeal.

orden ('or·ðen) *n.m.* order; arrangement. —*n.f.* **1,** order; command. **2,** *comm.* order. **3,** religious order; order of knighthood; honor society. —**órdenes,** *n.f.pl.* holy orders. —**a sus órdenes,** at your service. —**orden del día,** agenda.

ordenación (or·ðe·na'θjon; -'sjon) *n.f.* **1,** *eccles.* ordination. **2,** arrangement; disposition.

ordenado (or·ðe'na·ðo) *adj.* ordered; orderly. —**ordenada,** *n.f., geom.* ordinate.

ordenador (or·ðe·na'ðor) *n.m.* computer; data processor.

ordenancista (or·ðe·nan'θis·ta; -'sis·ta) *n.* disciplinarian; martinet.

ordenanza (or·ðe'nan·θa; -sa) *n.f.* ordinance; bylaw. —*n.m.* **1,** *mil.* orderly. **2,** office boy.

ordenar (or·ðe'nar) *v.t.* **1,** to order; command. **2,** to arrange. **3,** to direct. **4,** *eccles.* to ordain.

ordeñar (or·ðe'ɲar) *v.t. & i.* **1,** to milk. **2,** to strip, as olives from the branch.

ordeño (or'ðe·ɲo) *n.m.* **1,** milking. **2,** stripping, as from a branch.

ordinal (or·ði'nal) *adj. & n.m.* ordinal.

ordinario (or·ði'na·rjo) *adj.* **1,** ordinary; common; usual. **2,** coarse; vulgar. —*n.m.* **1,** *eccles.* bishop. **2,** delivery man; expressman. —**ordinariez,** *n.f.* vulgarity. —**de ordinario,** usually.

orégano (o're·ɣa·no) *n.m.* oregano.

oreja (o're·xa) *n.f.* **1,** ear; outer ear. **2,** *mech.* lug. —**orejera,** *n.f.* earflap; earmuff. —**calentar las orejas a,** to scold sharply; dress down. —**con las orejas caídas** *or* **gachas,** crestfallen. —**enseñar la oreja,** to show one's true colors.

orfanato (or·fa'na·to) *n.m.* orphanage.

orfandad (or·fan'daθ) *n.f.* orphanhood; orphanage.

orfebre (or'fe·βre) *n.m.* goldsmith; silversmith. —**orfebrería,** *n.f.* goldsmith's or silversmith's trade.

orfelinato (or·fe·li'na·to) *n.m.* orphanage.

orfeón (or·fe'on) *n.m.* glee club;

choral society. —**orfeonista,** *n.m. & f.* chorister.

organdí (or·ɣan'di) *n.m.* organdy.

orgánico (or'ɣa·ni·ko) *adj.* organic.

organillo (or·ɣa'ni·ʎo; -jo) *n.m.* hand organ; barrel organ; hurdygurdy. —**organillero,** *n.m.* organ grinder.

organismo (or·ɣa'nis·mo) *n.m.* **1,** organism. **2,** organization.

organista (or·ɣa'nis·ta) *n.m. & f.* organist.

organizar (or·ɣa·ni'θar; -'sar) *v.t.* [*infl.:* **rezar, 10**] to organize. —**organización,** *n.f.* organization. —**organizador,** *n.m.* [*fem.* -**dora**] organizer. —*adj.* organizing.

órgano ('or·ɣa·no) *n.m.* **1,** organ. **2,** pipe organ. **3,** *fig.* medium; instrument.

orgasmo (or'ɣas·mo) *n.m.* orgasm.

orgía (or'xi·a) *n.f.* orgy. —**orgiástico** (or'xjas·ti·ko) *adj.* orgiastic.

orgullo (or'ɣu·ʎo; -jo) *n.m.* pride; haughtiness. —**orgulloso,** *adj.* proud; haughty.

oriental (o·rjen'tal) *adj.* **1,** eastern. **2,** Oriental. —*n.m. & f.* **1,** easterner. **2,** Oriental.

orientar (o·rjen'tar) *v.t.* **1,** to orient. **2,** to brief; inform. —**orientación,** *n.f.* orientation.

oriente (o'rjen·te) *n.m.* **1,** east. **2,** *cap.* Orient.

orificar (o·ri·fi'kar) *v.t.* [*infl.:* **tocar, 7**] to fill (a tooth) with gold. —**orificación,** *n.f.* gold filling.

orificio (o·ri'fi·θjo; -sjo) *n.m.* orifice.

origen (o'ri·xen) *n.m.* origin.

original (o·ri·xi'nal) *adj. & n.m. & f.* original. —**originalidad,** *n.f.* originality.

originar (o·ri·xi'nar) *v.t.* to originate; start; give rise to. —**originarse,** *v.r.* to originate; arise. —**originador,** *n.m.* [*fem.* -**dora**] originator. —*adj.* originating; causing.

originario (o·ri·xi'na·rjo) *adj.* **1,** originating. **2,** native.

orilla (o'ri·ʎa; -ja) *n.f.* **1,** edge. **2,** shore; bank. **3,** shoulder (*of a road*). —**orillar,** *v.t.* **1,** to trim; edge. **2,** to conclude; wind up (an affair). —**orillarse,** *v.r.* to come to shore.

orillo (o'ri·ʎo; -jo) *n.m.* selvage.

orín (o'rin) *n.m.* **1,** rust. **2,** *usu.pl.* urine.

orina (o'ri·na) *n.f.* urine. —**orinar,** *v.i.* to urinate. —**orinal,** *n.m.* chamber pot; urinal.

oriol (o'rjol) *n.m.* oriole.

Orión (o'rjon) *n.m.* Orion.

oriundo (o'rjun·do) *adj.* native.

orla (or'la) *n.f.* **1,** fringe; trimming. **2,** fillet; molding. **3,** ornamental border. **4,** mat; border for a picture.

orlar (or'lar) *v.t.* to border; edge; trim.

orlón (or'lon) *n.m.* orlon.

ornado (or'na·ðo) *adj.* ornate; adorned.

ornamento (or·na'men·to) *n.m.* **1,** ornament. **2,** *pl., eccles.* vestments. —**ornamentación,** *n.f.* ornamentation. —**ornamental,** *adj.* ornamental. —**ornamentar,** *v.t.* = **adornar.**

ornar (or'nar) *v.t.* = **adornar.**

ornato (or'ña·to) *n.m.* adornment; decoration.

ornitología (or·ni·to·lo'xi·a) *n.f.* ornithology. —**ornitológico** (-'lo·xi·ko) *adj.* ornithological. —**ornitólogo** (-'to·lo·ɣo) *n.m.* ornithologist.

ornitorrinco (or·ni·to'rrin·ko) *n.m.* platypus.

oro ('o·ro) *n.m.* **1,** gold. **2,** gold coin. **3,** *pl., cards* in the Spanish deck, the suit corresponding to diamonds. —**pan de oro; oro batido** gold leaf.

orondo (o'ron·do) *adj.* **1,** puffed out; puffy. **2,** *colloq.* puffed up; vain; conceited.

oropel (o·ro'pel) *n.m.* tinsel.

oropéndola (o·ro'pen·do·la) *n.f.* yellowbird.

orquesta (or'kes·ta) *n.m.* orchestra. —**orquestal,** *adj.* orchestral.

orquestar (or·kes'tar) *v.t. & i.* to orchestrate. —**orquestación,** *n.f.* orchestration.

orquídea (or'ki·ðe·a) *n.f.* orchid.

ortiga (or'ti·ɣa) *n.f.* nettle.

ortodoncia (or·to'ðon·θja; -sja) *n.f.* orthodontia. —**ortodontista,** *adj.* orthodontic. —*n.m. & f.* orthodontist.

ortodoxo (or·to'ðok·so) *adj.* orthodox. —**ortodoxia** (-'ðok·sja) *n.f.* orthodoxy.

ortogonal (or·to·ɣo'nal) *adj.* orthogonal.

ortografía (or·to·ɣra'fi·a) *n.f.* spelling; orthography. —**ortográfico** (-'ɣra·fi·ko) *adj.* orthographic.

ortopedia (or·to'pe·ðja) *n.f.* orthopedics. —**ortopédico** (-ði·ko) *adj.* orthopedic. —*n.m.* [*also,* **ortopedista,** *n.m. & f.*] orthopedist.

oruga (o'ru·ɣa) *n.f.* caterpillar.

orzuelo (or'θwe·lo; -'swe·lo) *n.m.* **1,** *pathol.* sty. **2,** snare.

os (os) *pers.pron. 2nd pers.pl., used as obj. of a verb* you; to you; yourselves.

osa ('o·sa) *n.f.* she-bear. —**Osa Mayor,** Ursa Major; Big Dipper. —**Osa Menor,** Ursa Minor; Little Dipper.

osado (o'sa·ðo) *adj.* daring; bold. —**osadía,** *n.f.* daring; boldness.

osar (o'sar) *v.i.* to dare; venture.

osario (o'sa·rjo) *n.m.* ossuary.

oscilar (os·θi'lar; o·si-) *v.i.* to oscillate. —**oscilación,** *n.f.* oscillation. —**oscilador,** *n.m.* oscillator. —**oscilante,** *adj.* oscillating. —**oscilatorio,** *adj.* oscillating.

oscilógrafo (os·θi'lo·ɣra·fo; o·si-) *n.m.* oscillograph.

osciloscopio (os·θi·los'ko·pjo; o·si-) *n.m.* oscilloscope.

ósculo ('os·ku·lo) *n.m.* kiss.

oscurecer (os·ku·re'θer; -'ser) *v.* = **obscurecer.** —**oscuridad,** *n.f.* = **obscuridad.** —**oscuro,** *adj.* = **obscuro.**

óseo ('o·se·o) *adj.* osseous.

osezno (o'seθ·no; -'ses·no) *n.m.* bear cub.

osificarse (o·si·fi'kar·se) *v.r.* [*infl.:* **tocar,** 7] to ossify. —**osificación,** *n.f.* ossification.

osmio ('os·mjo) *n.m.* osmium.

ósmosis ('os·mo·sis) *also,* **osmosis** (-'mo·sis) *n.f.* osmosis. —**osmótico** (-'mo·ti·ko) *adj.* osmotic.

oso ('o·so) *n.m.* bear. —**oso blanco,** polar bear. —**oso gris,** grizzly bear. —**oso hormiguero,** anteater. —**oso marino,** fur seal. —**oso pardo,** brown bear.

ostensible (os·ten'si·βle) *adj.* ostensible; apparent.

ostentar (os·ten'tar) *v.t.* to exhibit; display. —**ostentación,** *n.f.* ostentation; display. —**ostentoso,** *adj.* ostentatious.

osteología (os·te·o·lo'xi·a) *n.f.* osteology. —**osteólogo** (-'o·lo·ɣo) *n.m.* osteologist.

osteopatía (os·te·o·pa'ti·a) *n.f.* osteopathy. —**osteópata** (-'o·pa·ta) *n.m. & f.* osteopath.

ostra ('os·tra) *n.f.* oyster.

ostracismo (os·tra'θis·mo; -'sis·mo) *n.m.* ostracism.

ostrón (os'tron) *n.m.* a kind of large oyster. *Also,* **ostión** (-'tjon).

osuno (o'su·no) *adj.* bearlike.

otero (o'te·ro) *n.m.* hill; hillock.

otitis (o'ti·tis) *n.f.* otitis.

otología (o·to·lo'xi·a) *n.f.* otology. —**otólogo** (o'to·lo·ɣo) otologist.

otomano (o·to'ma·no) *adj. & n.m.* Ottoman. —**otomana,** *n.f.* ottoman; divan.

otoño (o'to·ɲo) *n.m.* autumn; fall. —**otoñal,** *adj.* autumnal; fall (*attrib.*).

otorgar (o·tor'ɣar) *v.t.* [*infl.:* **pagar,** 8] 1, to grant. 2, to consent to. 3, *law* to execute (a document). —**otorgante,** *n.m. & f.* grantor.

otramente (o·tra'men·te) *adv.* otherwise.

otro (o'·tro) *adj. & pron.* other; another. —**al otro día,** on the next day. —**al otro día de,** on the day after. —**la otra vida,** the hereafter. —**otro que tal,** another such. —**otros tantos,** as many more.

otrora (o'tro·ra) *adv.* formerly.

otrosí (o·tro'si) *adv.* furthermore.

ovación (o·βa'θjon; -'sjon) *n.f.* ovation.

ovado (o'βa·ðo) *adj.* ovate.

óvalo ('o·βa·lo) *n.m.* oval. —**ovalado,** *also,* **oval** (o'βal) *adj.* oval.

ovario (o'βa·rjo) *n.m.* ovary. —**ovárico** (o'βa·ri·ko) *adj.* ovarian.

oveja (o'βe·xa) *n.f.* ewe. —**ovejero,** *n.m.* shepherd; sheep raiser. —**ovejuno,** *adj.* of sheep; sheep (*attrib.*).

overol (o·βe'rol) *n.m., Amer.* overalls. *Also,* **overoles,** *n.m.pl.*

ovillo (o'βi·ʎo; -jo) *n.m.* skein; clew. —**ovillar,** *v.t.* to roll up; wind.

ovino (o'βi·no) *adj.* ovine.

ovíparo (o'βi·pa·ro) *adj.* oviparous.

ovni ('oβ·ni) *n.m., abbr. of* **objeto volante no identificado,** unidentified flying object.

ovoide (o'βoi·ðe) *adj. & n.m.* ovoid.

óvulo ('o·βu·lo) *n.m.* 1, ovule. 2, ovum. —**ovular,** to ovulate. —**ovulación,** *n.f.* ovulation.

oxálico (ok'sa·li·ko) *adj.* oxalic.

oxiacetilénico (ok·si·a·θe·ti'le·ni·ko; ok·si·a·'se-) *adj.* oxyacetylene.

óxido ('ok·si·ðo) *n.m.* oxide. —**oxidar,** *v.t.* to oxidize. —**oxidación,** *n.f.* oxidation.

oxigenar (ok·si·xe'nar) *v.t.* to oxygenate. —**oxigenación,** *n.f.* oxygenation.

oxígeno (ok'si·xe·no) *n.m.* oxygen. —**agua oxigenada,** hydrogen peroxide.

oxímoron (ok'si·mo·ron) *n.m.* oxymoron.

oye (o'·je) *v.* [see **oír,** 25]

oyen (o'·jen) *v.* [see **oír,** 25]

oyendo (o'jen·do) *v., ger. of* **oír.**

oyente (o'jen·te) *v., pr.p. of* **oír.** —*n.m. & f.* listener; hearer.

oyes (o'·jes) *v.* [see **oír,** 25]

oyó (o'jo) *v.* [see **oír,** 25]

ozono (o'θo·no; o'so-) *n.m.* ozone. —**ozonosfera** (-nos'fe·ra) *n.f., also,* **capa de ozono,** ozone layer.

P

P, p (pe) *n.f.* 19th letter of the Spanish alphabet.

pa (pa) *prep., colloq.* = **para.**

pabellón (pa·βe'ʎon; -'jon) *n.m.* 1, pavilion. 2, flag; colors. 3, canopy.

pabilo (pa'βi·lo) *n.m.* 1, candlewick. 2, snuff of a candle.

pábulo ('pa·βu·lo) *n.m.* nourishment; food. —**dar pábulo a,** to encourage; abet.

pacana (pa'ka·na) *n.f.* pecan. —**pacano,** *n.m.* pecan tree.

pacato (pa'ka·to) *adj.* timorous; pacific; quiet.

pacedura (pa·θe'ðu·ra; pa·se-) *n.f.* pasturage.

pacer (pa'θer; -'ser) *v.i. & t.* [*infl.:* **conocer,** 13] to pasture; graze.

paces ('pa·θes; -ses) *n.f., pl. of* **paz.** —**hacer las paces,** to make peace; make one's peace.

paciente (pa'θjen·te; pa'sjen-) *adj. & n.m. & f.* patient. —**paciencia,** *n.f.* patience.

pacienzudo (pa·θjen'θu·ðo; pa·sjen'su-) *adj.* patient; forbearing.

pacificar (pa·θi·fi'kar; pa·si-) *v.t.* [*infl.:* **tocar,** 7] to pacify; appease. —**pacificarse,** *v.r.* to calm

down; quiet down. —**pacificación,**
n.f. pacification. —**pacificador,** *adj.*
appeasing; peacemaking. —*n.m.*
[*fem.* -**dora**] peacemaker.
pacífico (pa'θi·fi·ko; pa'si-) *adj.*
pacific; peaceful. —*n.m., cap.* Pacific.
pacifismo (pa·θi'fis·mo; pa·si-)
n.m. pacifism. —**pacifista,** *adj.* pacifistic. —*n.m.* & *f.* pacifist.
paco ('pa·ko) *n.m., Amer.* **1,** alpaca. **2,** *slang* cop; policeman.
pacotilla (pa·ko'ti·ʎa; -ja) *n.f.*
bauble; bagatelle; knickknack. —**de
pacotilla,** cheap; shoddy.
pactar (pak'tar) *v.t.* to agree to or
upon.
pacto ('pak·to) *n.m.* pact; agreement; covenant.
pachá (pa'tʃa) *n.m.* pasha.
pachamanca (pa·tʃa'man·ka) *n.f.*
Amer. **1,** barbecue. **2,** *slang* petting;
necking.
pachorra (pa'tʃo·rra) *n.f.* sluggishness; slowness. *Also,* **pachocha**
(-'tʃa).
padecer (pa·ðe'θer; -'ser) *v.t.* [*infl.:*
conocer, 13] to suffer. —*v.i., fol. by*
de, to suffer from or with. —**padecimiento,** *n.m.* suffering.
padilla (pa'ði·ʎa; -ja) *n.f.* **1,** small
frying pan. **2,** bread oven.
padrastro (pa'ðras·tro) *n.m.* **1,**
stepfather. **2,** hangnail.
padre ('pa·ðre) *n.m.* **1,** father. **2,**
priest; padre. —**padres,** *n.m.pl.* parents. —**armar el lío padre,** *colloq.*
to raise a row. —**de padre y señor
mío,** *colloq.* terrific. —**padre
adoptivo,** foster father. —**padre
político,** father-in-law.
padrenuestro (pa·ðre'nwes·tro)
n.m. the Lord's Prayer.
padrinazgo (pa·ðri'naθ·ɣo;
-'nas·ɣo) *n.m.* **1,** godfathership. **2,**
patronage; sponsorship.
padrino (pa'ðri·no) *n.m.* **1,** godfather. **2,** second (*in a duel*). **3,** best
man. **4,** patron; protector.
padrón (pa'ðron) *n.m.* **1,** pattern;
model. **2,** census; registration. **3,**
mark of infamy. **4,** *Mex.* boss.
paella (pa'e·ʎa; -ja) *n.f.* a dish of
rice with meats and seafood; paella.
¡paf! (paf) *interj.* imitating the
sound of a blow, slap, fall, etc.;
pow!
paga ('pa·ɣa) *n.f.* **1,** pay; payment.
2, wages; salary. **3,** requital of love
or friendship.

pagadero (pa·ɣa'ðe·ro) *adj.* **1,**
payable. **2,** due. **3,** easily paid.
pagado (pa'ɣa·ðo) *adj., Amer.* self-
satisfied; conceited.
pagador (pa·ɣa'ðor) *n.m.* **1,** payer.
2, paymaster. **3,** paying teller.
pagaduría (pa·ɣa·ðu'ri·a) *n.f.*
paymaster's office; disbursement
office.
pagamento (pa·ɣa'men·to) *n.m.*
pay; payment.
pagano (pa'ɣa·no) *adj.* & *n.m.* pagan. —*n.m., colloq.* [*also,* **pagote**
(-'ɣo·te)] fall guy; scapegoat.
—**paganismo,** *n.m.* paganism.
pagar (pa'ɣar) *v.t.* [*infl.:* 8] **1,** to
pay. **2,** to return; reciprocate.
—**pagarse,** *v.r.* **1,** *fol. by* **de,** to become infatuated with; become fond
of. **2,** to be self-satisfied; be conceited.
pagaré (pa·ɣa're) *n.m.* promissory
note.
página ('pa·xi·na) *n.f.* page.
paginar (pa·xi'nar) *v.t.* to paginate.
—**paginación,** *n.m.* pagination;
paging.
pago ('pa·ɣo) *n.m.* **1,** payment. **2,**
country district, esp. of vineyards or
olive groves. **3,** hamlet. **4,** *S.A.*
home; home town or region. —*adj.,
colloq.* paid.
pagoda (pa'ɣo·ða) *n.f.* pagoda.
pagro ('pa·ɣro) *n.m.* porgy.
pague ('pa·ɣe) *v., pres.subjve.* of
pagar.
pagué (pa'ɣe) *v., 1st pers.sing. pret.*
of **pagar.**
paila ('pai·la) *n.f.* **1,** washbowl;
washbasin. **2,** shallow pot.
pairar (pai'rar) *v.i., naut.* to lie to
with all sails set. —**pairo** ('pai·ro)
n.m., in **al pairo,** lying to.
país (pa'is) *n.m.* country. —**del
país,** domestic; national.
paisaje (pai'sa·xe) *n.m.* landscape.
—**paisajista,** *n.m.* & *f.* landscape
painter.
paisana (pai'sa·na) *n.f.* a country
dance.
paisanaje (pai·sa·na·xe) *n.m.* **1,**
peasantry; countryfolk. **2,** nationality or citizenship in common.
paisano (pai'sa·no) *adj.* **1,** of or
from the same country or locality.
2, civilian. —*n.m.* **1,** fellow countryman; compatriot. **2,** civilian.
paja ('pa·xa) *n.f.* **1,** straw; chaff. **2,**
trash; refuse. —**dormirse en las
pajas,** *Amer.* to let the grass grow
under one's feet. —**echar paja,**

Amer., colloq. **1,** to talk nonsense. **2,** to fib; tell tall tales. —**echar pajas,** to draw lots. —**en un quítame allá esas pajas,** *colloq.* in a jiffy. —**paja de madera,** excelsior. —**por quítame allá esas pajas,** *colloq.* for a straw; (to quarrel) over a trifle.

pajar (pa'xar) *n.m.* barn.

pájara ('pa·xa·ra) *n.f.* **1,** female bird. **2,** = **pajarita. 3,** paper kite. **4,** crafty woman.

pajarear (pa·xa·re'ar) *v.i.* **1,** to hunt birds. **2,** to wander about; loaf. **3,** *Amer.* to be absentminded; be bemused.

pajarera (pa·xa're·ra) *n.f.* **1,** aviary. **2,** bird cage.

pajarete (pa·xa're·te) *n.m.* fine sherry wine.

pajarita (pa·xa'ri·ta) *n.f.* folded paper figure, esp. in the form of a bird.

pájaro ('pa·xa·ro) *n.m.* **1,** bird. **2,** *colloq.* character; guy. —**pájaro mosca,** humming bird. —**pájaro bobo,** *also* **pájaro niño,** penguin. —**pájaro de cuenta,** sharper; cunning fellow.

paje ('pa·xe) *n.m.* page; groom.

pajizo (pa'xi·θo; ·so) *adj.* **1,** of, resembling or filled with straw. **2,** straw-colored.

pajonal (pa·xo'nal) *n.m., Amer.* place abounding in tall grass.

pala ('pa·la) *n.f.* **1,** shovel; spade. **2,** blade *(of an oar, spade, etc.).* **3,** paddle. **4,** *colloq.* craft; cleverness. **5,** upper *(of a shoe).* —**hacer la pala,** *colloq.* to stall; speak or act evasively.

palabra (pa'la·βra) *n.f.* word. —**palabreo** (-'βre·o) *n.m.* chatter. —**palabrota** (-'βro·ta) *n.f.* swearword. —**empeñar la palabra,** to pledge one's word. —**palabras mayores, 1,** serious matter. **2,** angry words; quarrel. —**pedir la palabra,** to ask for the floor. —**tener la palabra,** to have the floor. —**tratar mal de palabra,** to scold; berate.

palabrero (pa·la'βre·ro) *adj.* talkative; wordy. —*n.m.* chatterbox. —**palabrería,** *n.f.* wordiness; palaver.

palabrita (pa·la'βri·ta) *n.f.* a bit of good sense; a word of advice.

palacete (pa·la'θe·te; -'se·te) *n.m.* small palace.

palacio (pa'la·θjo; -sjo) *n.m.* **1,** palace. **2,** public building; hall.

—**palaciego** (-'θje·ɣo; -'sje·ɣo) *adj.* palace *(attrib.);* court *(attrib.).* —*n.m.* courtier.

palada (pa'la·ða) *n.f.* **1,** shovelful. **2,** stroke of an oar.

paladar (pa·la'ðar) *n.m.* **1,** palate. **2,** taste.

paladear (pa·la·ðe'ar) *v.t.* **1,** to taste; savor. **2,** to relish; enjoy. —**paladeo** (-'ðe·o) *n.m.* relishing; savoring; tasting.

paladín (pa·la'ðin) *n.m.* paladin.

paladio (pa'la·ðjo) *n.m.* palladium.

palafrén (pa·la'fren) *n.m.* palfrey.

palafrenero (pa·la·fre'ne·ro) *n.m.* **1,** groom. **2,** attendant on horseback; outrider.

palanca (pa'lan·ka) *n.f.* **1,** lever. **2,** push rod; handle. **3,** *Amer., colloq.* influence; pull.

palangana (pa·lan'ga·na) *n.f.* washbowl. —*n.m., Amer., colloq.* braggart. —**palanganearse,** *v.r., Amer., colloq.* to brag.

palangre (pa'lan·gre) *n.m.* trotline.

palanqueta (pa·lan'ke·ta) *n.f.* **1,** small lever or handle. **2,** jimmy.

palanquín (pa·lan'kin) *n.m.* **1,** public porter. **2,** palanquin.

palastro (pa'las·tro) *n.m.* sheet iron; sheet steel.

palatal (pa·la'tal) *adj. & n.f.* palatal.

palatino (pa·la'ti·no) *adj.* palatal. —*adj. & n.m.* palatine. —**palatinado,** *n.m.* palatinate.

palazo (pa'la·θo; -so) *n.m.* blow with a shovel.

palco ('pal·ko) *n.m.* **1,** theater box. **2,** grandstand. —**palco escénico,** stage.

palear (pa·le'ar) *v.t. & i.* to shovel; stoke (coal). —**paleador,** *n.m.* shoveler; stoker.

palenque (pa'len·ke) *n.m.* **1,** barrier; palisade. **2,** lists; arena. **3,** *theat.* passage from pit to stage. **4,** hitching post.

paleografía (pa·le·o·ɣra'fi·a) *n.f.* paleography. —**paleográfico** (-'ɣra·fi·ko) *adj.* paleographic. —**paleógrafo** (-'o·ɣra·fo) *n.m.* paleographer.

paleolítico (pa·le·o'li·ti·ko) *adj.* paleolithic.

paleontología (pa·le·on·to·lo'xi·a) *n.f.* paleontology. —**paleontológico** (-'lo·xi·ko) *adj.* paleontological. —**paleontólogo** (-'to·lo·ɣo) *n.m.* paleontologist.

paleozoico (pa·le·o'θoi·ko; -'soi·ko) *adj.* Paleozoic.

palero (pa'le·ro) *n.m.* **1**, maker or seller of shovels. **2**, *Amer., colloq.* weaver of tall tales; fibber.

palestino (pa·les'ti·no) *adj.* & *n.m.* Palestinian.

palestra (pa'les·tra) *n.f.* **1**, lists; arena. **2**, contest; struggle.

paleta (pa'le·ta) *n.f.* **1**, palette. **2**, paddle. **3**, trowel. **4**, small shovel.

paletear (pa·le·te'ar) *v.t.* to row or paddle ineffectively.

paletilla (pa·le'ti·ʎa; -ja) *n.f.* shoulderblade.

paleto (pa'le·to) *adj.* & *n.m.* rustic; yokel.

paletó (pa·le'to) *n.m.* overcoat; greatcoat.

paliar (pa'ljar) *v.t.* **1**, to palliate. **2**, to cloak; dissimulate. —**paliación**, *n.f.* palliation. —**paliativo**, *adj.* & *n.m.* palliative.

palidecer (pa·li·ðe'θer; -'ser) *v.i.* [*infl.:* conocer, 13] to pale.

pálido ('pa·li·ðo) *adj.* pale; pallid. —**palidez**, *n.f.* paleness; pallor.

palillo (pa'li·ʎo; -jo) *n.m.* **1**, small stick. **2**, toothpick. **3**, *mus.* drumstick. **4**, knitting needle. **5**, *pl.* castanets. **6**, *pl.* chopsticks.

palíndromo (pa'lin·dro·mo) *n.m.* palindrome.

palio ('pa·ljo) *n.m.* **1**, pallium. **2**, canopy used in religious processions.

paliza (pa'li·θa; -sa) *n.f.* beating; drubbing.

palizada (pa·li'θa·ða; -'sa·ða) *n.f.* paling.

palma ('pal·ma) *n.f.* **1**, palm tree. **2**, palm leaf. **3**, palm of the hand. **4**, pad *(of an animal's foot)*. —**batir palmas**, to clap.

palmacristi (pal·ma'kris·ti) *n.f.* = ricino.

palmada (pal'ma·ða) *n.f.* **1**, slap. **2**, handclap.

palmar (pal'mar) *adj.* palmar. —*n.m.* palm grove. —*v.i., colloq.* to die.

palmario (pal'ma·rjo) *adj.* plain; evident.

palmatoria (pal·ma'to·rja) *n.f.* candlestick.

palmeado (pal·me'a·ðo) *also,* **palmado** (-'ma·ðo) *adj.* webbed.

palmear (pal·me'ar) *v.t.* to pat. —*v.i.* to clap the hands.

palmera (pal'me·ra) *n.f.* palm tree. —**palmeral**, *n.m.* palm grove.

palmeta (pal'me·ta) *n.f.* **1**, ferule. **2**, [*also,* **palmetazo**, *n.m.*] slap with a ferule.

palmípedo (pal'mi·pe·ðo) *n.m.* web-footed.

palmito (pal'mi·to) *n.m.* **1**, dwarf fan palm; palmetto. **2**, heart of palm. **3**, *colloq.* woman's face.

palmo ('pal·mo) *n.m.* **1**, span of the hand. **2**, unit of length of approximately 8 inches. —**dejar con un palmo de narices**, to disappoint; leave in the cold. —**palmo a palmo**, inch by inch.

palmotear (pal·mo·te'ar) *v.i.* to clap the hands. —*v.t.* to pat; give pats on.

palmoteo (pal·mo'te·o) *n.m.* **1**, clapping. **2**, patting.

palo ('pa·lo) *n.m.* **1**, stick; piece of wood. **2**, club; cudgel. **3**, blow with a stick or club. **4**, *cards* clubs *(in the Spanish deck).* **5**, suit *(at cards).* **6**, *naut.* mast. **7**, hook of a letter. **8**, *Amer.* drink, esp. of liquor. **9**, *W.I.* tree. —**dar de palos**, to drub; beat. —**moler a palos**, to beat to a pulp. —**palo dulce**, licorice. —**palo mayor**, mainmast.

paloduz (pa·lo'ðuθ; -'ðus) *n.m., also,* **palo dulce**, licorice.

paloma (pa'lo·ma) *n.f.* **1**, pigeon; dove. **2**, meek person. **3**, *pl.* whitecaps. —**paloma buchona**, pouter. —**paloma emigrante**, passenger pigeon. —**paloma mensajera**, carrier pigeon; homing pigeon. —**paloma moñuda**, ruff. —**paloma torcaz**, ringdove; wood pigeon; wild pigeon. —**paloma triste**, mourning dove.

palomar (pa·lo'mar) *n.m.* pigeon house; dovecot.

palomilla (pa·lo'mi·ʎa; -ja) *n.f.* **1**, nocturnal butterfly. **2**, grain moth. **3**, any small moth or butterfly. **4**, *mech.* wing nut. **5**, *Amer., colloq.* urchin; ragamuffin. **6**, palomino. —**palomillas**, *n.f.pl.* whitecaps.

palomitas (pa·lo'mi·tas) *n.f.pl., Amer.* popcorn.

palomo (pa'lo·mo) *n.m.* male pigeon.

palote (pa'lo·te) *n.m.* **1**, stick. **2**, scribble; scrawl. **3**, drumstick. **4**, pothook; curlicue.

pallar (pa'ʎar; -'jar) *v.i.* = payar.

palpable (pal'pa·βle) *adj.* palpable.

palpación (pal·pa'θjon; -'sjon) *n.f.*

1, [*also,* **palpadura,** *n.f.,* **palpamiento,** *n.m.*] feeling; touching; groping. **2,** *med.* palpation.
palpar (pal'par) *v.t. & i.* **1,** to feel; touch. **2,** to grope. **3,** to know positively. **4,** *med.* to palpate.
palpitante (pal·pi'tan·te) *adj.* **1,** palpitating; throbbing. **2,** *fig.* burning; highly controversial.
palpitar (pal·pi'tar) *v.i.* to palpitate; throb. —**palpitación,** *n.f.* palpitation; throbbing.
pálpito ('pal·pi·to) *n.m., Amer.* hunch; premonition.
palpo ('pal·po) *n.m., zoöl.* feeler.
palta ('pal·ta) *n.f., S.A.* avocado. —**palto,** *n.m., S.A.* avocado tree.
palúdico (pa'lu·ði·ko) *adj.* **1,** swampy; marshy. **2,** malarial. —**paludismo,** *n.m.* malaria.
palurdo (pa'lur·ðo) *adj.* rustic; rude. —*n.m.* rustic; boor.
palustre (pa'lus·tre) *n.m.* trowel.
palla (pa'ja) *n.f., S.A.* = **paya.**
pallador (pa·ja'ðor) *n.m., S.A.* = **payador.** —**pallar** (pa·jar) *v.i.* = **payar.**
pampa ('pam·pa) *n.f.* pampa.
pámpana ('pam·pa·na) *n.f.* vine leaf. —**zurrar la pámpana a,** *colloq.* to thrash.
pámpano ('pam·pa·no) *n.m.* **1,** vine leaf. **2,** vine shoot; tendril. **3,** *ichthy.* gilthead; *Amer.* pompano.
pampeano (pam·pe'a·no) *adj., S.A.* of or pert. to the pampas.
pampear (pam·pe'ar) *v.i., S.A.* to travel through the pampas.
pampero (pam'pe·ro) *n.m.* **1,** dweller of the pampas. **2,** *Amer.* violent wind blowing from the pampas. —*adj.* pampas (*attrib.*).
pampirolada (pam·pi·ro'la·ða) *n.f.* **1,** garlic sauce. **2,** *colloq.* nonsense.
pamplemusa (pam·ple'mu·sa) *n.f.* shaddock.
pamplina (pam'pli·na) *also,* **pamplinada,** *n.f., colloq.* nonsense.
pamporcino (pam·por'θi·no; -'si·no) *n.m.* cyclamen.
pan (pan) *n.m.* **1,** bread. **2,** cake; loaf; patty. **3,** pastry crust. —**pan bendito,** manna. —**pan de oro,** gold leaf.
pana ('pa·na) *n.f.* **1,** velveteen; corduroy. **2,** *Amer.* liver. **3,** *Amer., colloq.* nerve; gall.
panacea (pa·na'θe·a; -'se·a) *n.f.* panacea.

panadero (pa·na'ðe·ro) *n.m.* baker. —**panadería,** *n.f.* bakery.
panadizo (pa·na'ði·θo; -so) *n.m., pathol.* felon.
panal (pa'nal) *n.m.* **1,** honeycomb. **2,** hornet's nest.
panamá (pa·na'ma) *n.m.* panama hat.
panamericano (pan·a·me·ri'ka·no) *adj.* Pan-American. —**panamericanismo,** *n.m.* Pan-Americanism.
panatela (pa·na'te·la) *n.f.* sponge cake.
pancista (pan'θis·ta; -'sis·ta) *adj.* noncommittal; politic; straddling. —*n.m. & f.* straddler; one who is on the fence; politician.
páncreas ('pan·kre·as) *n.m.* pancreas. —**pancreático** (-kre'a·ti·ko) *also,* **pancrático** (-'kra·ti·ko) *adj.* pancreatic.
pancromático (pan·kro'ma·ti·ko) *adj.* panchromatic.
panda ('pan·da) *n.m.* panda.
pandear (pan·de'ar) *v.i.* [*also, v.r.,* **pandearse**] to bend; warp; bulge out.
pandémico (pan'de·mi·ko) *adj.* pandemic. —**pandémica,** *n.f.* pandemic.
pandemónium (pan·de'mo·njum) *n.m.* pandemonium.
pandereta (pan·de're·ta) *n.f., also,* **pandera** (-'de·ra) *n.f.,* **pandero** (-'de·ro) *n.m.* tambourine.
panderetear (pan·de·re·te'ar) *v.i.* to play on the tambourine.
pandereteo (pan·de·re'te·o) *n.m.* **1,** playing on the tambourine. **2,** merriment.
pandilla (pan'di·ʎa; -ja) *n.f.* **1,** gang; clique. **2,** group of merrymakers.
pandorga (pan'dor·ɣa) *n.f.* **1,** kite. **2,** *colloq.* fat, hulking woman.
panecillo (pa·ne'θi·ʎo; -'si·jo) *n.m.* bread roll.
panegírico (pa·ne'xi·ri·ko) *n.m.* panegyric. —*adj.* panegyrical.
panel (pa'nel) *n.m.* **1,** panel. **2,** pane.
panela (pa'ne·la) *n.f.* **1,** a kind of biscuit. **2,** *Amer.* unrefined sugar.
panera (pa'ne·ra) *n.f.* **1,** breadbox. **2,** breadbasket.
pánfilo ('pan·fi·lo) *n.m.* dullard; sad sack.
panfleto (pan'fle·to) *n.m.* pamphlet. —**panfletista,** *n.m. & f.* pamphleteer.

pánico ('pa·ni·ko) *n.m.* & *adj.* panic.

panizo (pa'ni·θo; -so) *n.m.* millet.

panoja (pa'no·xa) *n.f.* panicle; ear of grain. *Also,* **panocha** (-·tʃa).

panoplia (pa'no·plja) *n.f.* panoply.

panóptico (pa'nop·ti·ko) *n.m., Amer.* penitentiary.

panorama (pa·no'ra·ma) *n.m.* panorama. —**panorámico,** *adj.* panoramic.

panoso (pa'no·so) *adj.* mealy.

panqueque (pan'ke·ke) *n.m., Amer.* pancake.

pantalón (pan·ta'lon) *n.m., also pl.,* **pantalones,** trousers; pantaloons; pants. —**pantalones vaquero,** jeans.

pantaloncito (pan·ta·lon'θi·to; -'si·to) *n.m.* panties.

pantalla (pan'ta·ʎa; -ja) *n.f.* 1, lamp shade. 2, screen.

pantano (pan'ta·no) *n.m.* 1, swamp; marsh; bog. 2, hindrance; obstacle. —**pantanal,** *n.m.* marshy terrain. —**pantanoso,** *adj.* marshy; swampy.

panteísmo (pan·te'is·mo) *n.m.* pantheism. —**panteísta,** *n.m.* & *f.* pantheist. —*adj.* [*also,* **panteístico**] pantheistic.

panteón (pan·te'on) *n.m.* pantheon.

pantera (pan'te·ra) *n.f.* panther.

pantógrafo (pan'to·ɣra·fo) *n.m.* pantograph.

pantomima (pan·to'mi·ma) *n.f.* pantomime. —**pantomímico,** *adj.* pantomimic. —**pantomimo,** *n.m.* mimic; pantomimist.

pantoque (pan'to·ke) *n.m., naut.* bilge.

pantorrilla (pan·to'rri·ʎa; -ja) *n.f.* calf of the leg. —**pantorrillera,** *n.f.* padded stocking. —**pantorrilludo,** *adj.* having thick calves.

pantufla (pan'tu·fla) *n.f., also,* **pantuflo,** *n.m.* slipper.

panza ('pan·θa; -sa) *n.f.* belly; paunch. —**panzudo,** *also,* **panzón,** *adj.* paunchy.

panzada (pan'θa·ða; -'sa·ða) *n.f.* 1, push with the paunch. 2, *colloq.* bellyful.

pañal (pa'ɲal) *n.m.* 1, diaper. 2, tail (*of a shirt*). —**pañales,** *n.m.pl.* swaddling clothes.

pañero (pa'ɲe·ro) *n.m.* dealer in cloth or dry goods.

paño ('pa·ɲo) *n.m.* 1, cloth. 2, film; opacity. —**paños calientes,** half measures. —**paños menores,** 1, underclothes. 2, state of undress.

pañol (pa'ɲol) *n.m., naut.* storeroom. —**pañolero,** *n.m.* storekeeper; yeoman.

pañoleta (pa·ɲo'le·ta) *n.f.* triangular shawl.

pañolón (pa·ɲo'lon) *n.m.* large square shawl.

pañuelo (pa'ɲwe·lo) *n.m.* 1, handkerchief. 2, shawl.

papa ('pa·pa) *n.f.* 1, Pope. 2, *Amer.* potato. 3, pap. 4, = **paparrucha.** 5, = **papá.**

papá (pa'pa) *n.m.* [*pl.* **papás**] papa; dad.

papada (pa'pa·ða) *n.f.* double chin.

papado (pa'pa·ðo) *n.m.* papacy.

papagayo (pa·pa'ɣa·jo) *n.m.* parrot; macaw.

papahuevos (pa·pa'we·βos) *n.m.* & *f. sing.* & *pl.* = **papanatas.**

papal (pa'pal) *adj.* papal.

papalote (pa·pa'lo·te) *n.m., Mex.* paper kite.

papamoscas (pa·pa'mos·kas) *n.m.* & *f. sing.* & *pl.,* *ornith.* flycatcher. 2, *colloq.* = **papanatas.**

papanatas (pa·pa'na·tas) *n.m.* & *f. sing.* & *pl., colloq.* simpleton; dolt.

papar (pa'par) *v.t.* 1, to eat without chewing (*as pap, gruel, etc.*). 2, *colloq.* to eat. —**papar moscas,** *colloq.* to gape.

paparrucha (pa·pa'rru·tʃa) *n.f., colloq.* humbug; nonsense.

papaya (pa'pa·ja) *n.f.* papaya; papaw. —**papayo,** *n.m.* papaya tree; papaw tree.

papazgo (pa'paθ·ɣo; pa'pas-) *n.m.* papacy.

papel (pa'pel) *n.m.* 1, paper. 2, part; role. —**hacer buen papel,** to show to advantage; make a fine show. —**papel cebolla,** onionskin. —**papel cuadriculado,** graph paper. —**papel de calcar,** tracing paper. —**papel de estraza,** brown wrapping paper. —**papel encerado,** waxed paper. —**papel de lija,** sandpaper. —**papel de oficio,** foolscap. —**papel higiénico** *or* **sanitario,** toilet paper. —**papel majado** *or* **maché** (ma'tʃe) papier-maché. —**papel rayado,** lined paper. —**papel secante,** blotting paper.

papelear (pa·pe·le'ar) *v.i.* 1, to rummage through papers. 2, *colloq.* to do paperwork.

papeleo (pa·pe'le·o) *n.m.* 1, rummaging through papers. **2,** *colloq.* papers; paperwork.

papelera (pa·pe'le·ra) *n.f.* **1,** file; filing cabinet. **2,** wastebasket.

papelería (pa·pe·le'ri·a) *n.f.* **1,** heap of papers. **2,** stationery store.

papelero (pa·pe'le·ro) *adj.* paper *(attrib.).* —*n.m.* stationer.

papeleta (pa·pe'le·ta) *n.f.* **1,** card; ticket. **2,** blank form. **3,** *Amer.* traffic ticket.

papelillo (pa·pe'li·ʎo; -jo) *n.m.* **1,** packet *(for medicinal powders).* **2,** hand-rolled cigarette.

papelón (pa·pe'lon) *n.m.* **1,** pasteboard. **2,** *Amer., colloq.* ludicrous performance; howler.

papelucho (pa·pe'lu·tʃo) *n.m.* scrap of paper. *Also,* **papelote** (-'lo·te).

papera (pa'pe·ra) *n.f.* goiter. —**paperas,** *n.f.pl.* mumps.

papi ('pa·pi) *n.m., colloq.* = **papá.**

papila (pa'pi·la) *n.f.* papilla. —**papilar,** *adj.* papillary.

papilla (pa'pi·ʎa; -ja) *n.f.* **1,** pap. **2,** *colloq.* deceitful talk; cajolery.

papiro (pa'pi·ro) *n.m.* papyrus.

papirote (pa·pi'ro·te) *also,* **papirotazo,** *n.m.,* **papirotada,** *n.f.* fillip.

papismo (pa'pis·mo) *n.m.* popery. —**papista,** *n.m. & f.* papist. —*adj.* papist; popish.

papito (pa'pi·to) *n.m., colloq.* = **papá.**

papo ('pa·po) *n.m.* **1,** double chin. **2,** gizzard *(of fowl).* **3,** thistledown. **4,** wattle *(of animals).*

papudo (pa'pu·ðo) *adj.* double-chinned.

pápula ('pa·pu·la) *n.f.* papule.

paquebote (pa·ke'βo·te) *n.m.* packet boat; steamer.

paquete (pa'ke·te) *n.m.* package; pack; packet. —*adj., Amer.* **1,** dapper; spruce. **2,** insincere.

paquetería (pa·ke·te'ri·a) *n.f.* retail store.

paquidermo (pa·ki'ðer·mo) *n.m.* pachyderm.

par (par) *adj.* **1,** equal; on a par. **2,** alike; matching. **3,** even *(of numbers).* —*n.m.* **1,** pair; couple. **2,** mate; match. **3,** peer. **4,** *mech.* couple. —**a la par, 1,** jointly. **2,** equally. **3,** par; at par. —**a pares,** two by two; by pairs. —**de par en par,** unobstructedly; wide open *(as a door, window, etc.).* —**ir a la par,** to go halves. —**pares y nones,** the game of odds and evens. —**sin par,** peerless; matchless.

para ('pa·ra) *prep.* **1,** for. **2,** toward. **3,** to. **4,** in order to. —**para con,** toward; with. —**para eso,** for that; for that matter. —**para mí,** for my part; as far as I am concerned. —**para nunca,** *colloq.* **1,** poorly; badly. **2,** endlessly. —**para que,** so that; in order that. —**¿para qué?,** what for? what is the use? —**para siempre,** forever.

parabién (pa·ra'βjen) *n.m.* congratulation; felicitation.

parábola (pa'ra·βo·la) *n.f.* **1,** parable. **2,** parabola. —**parabólico** (-'βo·li·ko) *adj.* parabolic.

parabrisas (pa·ra'βri·sas) *n.f. sing. & pl.* windshield.

paracaídas (pa·ra·ka'i·ðas) *n.m. sing. & pl.* parachute. —**paracaidista** (-kai'ðis·ta) *n.m. & f.* parachutist.

parachoques (pa·ra'tʃo·kes) *n.m.sing. & pl.* bumper.

parada (pa'ra·ða) *n.f.* **1,** stop *(of a vehicle).* **2,** halt. **3,** parade; review. **4,** *fencing* parry. —**parada en seco,** dead stop.

paradero (pa·ra'ðe·ro) *n.m.* **1,** whereabouts. **2,** stopping place; stop. **3,** end; final stop.

paradigma (pa·ra'ðiɣ·ma) *n.m.* paradigm.

paradisíaco (pa·ra·ði'si·a·ko) *adj.* paradisiacal; heavenly.

parado (pa'ra·ðo) *adj.* **1,** stopped; standing still; at a standstill. **2,** slow; slack; sluggish. **3,** unemployed. **4,** *Amer.* standing. **5,** *Amer.* arrogant; standoffish. —**salir bien parado,** to come out well. —**salir mal parado,** to come out poorly; get the worst of it.

paradoja (pa·ra'ðo·xa) *n.f.* paradox. —**paradójico,** *adj.* paradoxical.

parador (pa·ra'ðor) *n.m.* inn; road stop; motor court.

parafina (pa·ra'fi·na) *n.f.* paraffin.

parafrasear (pa·ra·fra·se'ar) *v.t. & i.* to paraphrase.

paráfrasis (pa'ra·fra·sis) *n.f. sing. & pl.* paraphrase. —**parafrástico** (-'fras·ti·ko) *adj.* paraphrastic.

paragolpes (pa·ra'ɣol·pes) *n.m. sing. & pl.* bumper.

parágrafo (pa'ra·ɣra·fo) *n.m.* = **párrafo.**

paraguas (pa·ra'ɣwas) *n.m.sing. & pl.* umbrella.

paragüero (pa·ra·'ɣwe·ro) *n.m.* **1,** umbrella man. **2,** umbrella stand. —**paragüería,** *n.f.* umbrella shop.

paraíso (pá·ra·'i·so) *n.m.* **1,** paradise. **2,** *theat., colloq.* upper gallery.

paraje (pa'ra·xe) *n.m.* place; spot.

paralaje (pa·ra'la·xe) *n.m.* parallax.

paralelar (pa·ra·le'lar) *v.t.* to parallel.

paralelepípedo (pa·ra·le·le'pi·pe·ðo) *n.m.* parallelepiped.

paralelo (pa·ra'le·lo) *adj. & n.m.* parallel. —**paralelas,** *n.f.pl.* parallel bars. —**paralelismo,** *n.m.* parallelism.

paralelogramo (pa·ra·le·lo·'ɣra·mo) *n.m.* parallelogram.

Paralipómenos (pa·ra·li'po·me·nos) *n.m.pl., Bib.* Chronicles.

parálisis (pa'ra·li·sis) *n.f.* paralysis. —**paralítico** (-'li·ti·ko) *adj. & n.m.* paralytic.

paralización (pa·ra·li·θa'θjon; -sa'sjon) *n.f.* **1,** paralyzation. **2,** stoppage.

paralizar (pa·ra·li'θar; -'sar) *v.t.* [*infl.:* rezar, 10] to paralyze.

paralogizar (pa·ra·lo·xi'θar; -'sar) *v.t.* [*infl.:* rezar, 10] to confuse; befuddle.

paramecio (pa·ra·me·θjo; -sjo) *n.m.* paramecium.

paramédico (pa·ra·me·ði·ko) *adj.* paramedical.

paramento (pa·ra'men·to) *n.m.* ornament; trappings. —**paramentar,** *v.t.* to adorn; bedeck.

parámetro (pa'ra·me·tro) *n.m.* parameter.

páramo ('pa·ra·mo) *n.m.* **1,** flat, barren land; paramo. **2,** *Amer.* cold drizzle.

parangón (pa·ran'gon) *n.m.* **1,** comparison. **2,** model; paragon. —**parangonar,** *v.t.* to compare.

paraninfo (pa·ra'nin·fo) *n.m.* auditorium, esp. in an academic institution.

paranoia (pa·ra'no·ja) *n.f.* paranoia. —**paranoico** (-'noi·ko) *adj. & n.m.* paranoiac.

parapetarse (pa·ra·pe'tar·se) *v.r.* to take cover, as behind a parapet.

parapeto (pa·ra'pe·to) *n.m.* parapet.

paraplejía (pa·ra·ple'xi·a) *n.f.* paraplegia. —**parapléjico** (-'ple·xi·ko) *adj. & n.m.* paraplegic.

parapsicología (pa·ra·si·ko·lo'xi·a) *n.f.* parapsychology.

parar (pa'rar) *v.t. & i.* to stop; check. —*v.t.* **1,** to parry. **2,** *Amer.* to stand; stand up; place upright. —*v.i.* **1,** to end up (as or in). **2,** to put up; lodge. —**pararse,** *v.r.* **1,** to stop. **2,** *Amer.* to stand up. —**parar en seco,** to stop dead. —**parar las orejas,** *Amer.* to prick up one's ears. —**pararse en,** to notice; pay attention to. —**sin parar,** at once.

pararrayos (pa·ra'rra·jos) *n.m. sing. & pl.* lightning rod.

parásito (pa'ra·si·to) *n.m.* parasite. —*adj.* parasitic. —**parasitario,** *also,* **parasítico,** *adj.* parasitic.

parasol (pa·ra'sol) *n.m.* parasol.

paratifoide (pa·ra·ti'foi·ðe) *adj.* paratyphoid. *Also,* **paratífico** (-'ti·fi·ko). —**paratifoidea** (-'ðe·a) *n.f.* paratyphoid fever.

parca ('par·ka) *n.f., often cap.* Death.

parcamente (par·ka'men·te) *adv.* sparingly.

parcela (par'θe·la; -'se·la) *n.f.* parcel of land.

parcelar (par·θe'lar; -se'lar) *v.t.* to divide into lots; parcel. —**parcelación,** *n.f.* division into lots; parceling.

parcial (par'θjal; -'sjal) *adj.* partial. —**parcialidad,** *n.f.* partiality.

parco ('par·ko) *adj.* moderate; sparing; spare.

parchar (par'tʃar) *v.t., Amer.* to patch; mend.

parche ('par·tʃe) *n.m.* **1,** plaster; poultice. **2,** patch; added piece. **3,** daub; blotch. **4,** drumhead. **5,** drum. —**pegar un parche a,** *colloq.* to swindle.

pardal (par'ðal) *adj.* rustic. —*n.m.* **1,** sparrow. **2,** = pardillo. **3,** = leopardo. **4,** *colloq.* crafty fellow.

pardear (par·ðe'ar) *v.i.* to be or become grayish brown.

¡pardiez! (par'ðjeθ; -'ðjes) *interj., colloq.* by heavens!; by Jove!

pardillo (par'ði·ʎo; -jo) *n.m.* linnet.

pardo ('par·ðo) *adj. & n.m.* grayish brown; dun. —*n.m.* = leopardo. —**pardusco** (-'ðus·ko) *adj.* brownish.

parear (pa·re'ar) *v.t.* **1,** to pair. **2,** to match. —**parearse,** *v.r.* to pair off.

parecer (pa·re'θer; -'ser) *v.i.* [*infl.:* conocer, 13] **1,** to appear; seem. **2,** to look like; appear to be. —*n.m.* **1,** opinion; view. **2,** countenance;

mien. —**parecerse,** *v.r.* **1,** to look alike; resemble each other. **2,** *fol. by* **a,** to look like; resemble. —**al parecer,** *also,* **a lo que parece,** seemingly; apparently.

parecido (pa·re'θi·ðo; -'si·ðo) *adj.* like; alike; similar. —*n.m.* likeness; resemblance. —**bien parecido,** good-looking. —**mal parecido,** ill-favored; ugly.

pared (pa'reð) *n.f.* wall. —**hasta la pared de enfrente,** *colloq.* to the limit. —**pared maestra,** main wall. —**pared medianera,** party wall.

paredaño (pa·re'ða·ɲo) *adj.* having a common wall; adjoining.

paredón (pa·re'ðon) *n.m.* thick wall.

paregórico (pa·re'ɣo·ri·ko) *n.m.* paregoric.

pareja (pa're·xa) *n.f.* **1,** pair. **2,** couple. **3,** mate; partner. —**correr parejas con,** to go hand in hand with.

parejo (pa're·xo) *adj.* **1,** level; flush; even. **2,** equal; like. —*n.m.,* W.I. mate; partner.

parentela (pa·ren'te·la) *n.f.* kin; relations.

parentesco (pa·ren'tes·ko) *n.m.* relationship; kinship.

paréntesis (pa'ren·te·sis) *n.m. sing. & pl.* parenthesis.

paresa (pa're·sa) *n.f.* peeress.

paresia (pa're·sja) *n.f.* paresis. *Also,* **paresis** (-sis). —**parético** (-ti·ko) *adj. & n.m.* paretic.

parezca (pa'reθ·ka; -'res·ka) *v., pres.subjve.* of **parecer.**

parezco (pa'reθ·ko; -'res·ko) *v., 1st pers.sing.pres.ind.* of **parecer.**

parfait (par'fe) *n.m.* [*pl.* **parfaits** (-'fes)] parfait.

pargo ('par·ɣo) *n.m.* = **pagro.**

paria (pa·rja) *n.m. & f.* pariah.

parida (pa'ri·ða) *adj.fem.* recently delivered.

paridad (pa·ri'ðað) *n.f.* parity.

pariente (pa'rjen·te) *n.m.* [*fem.* **parienta**] relation; relative.

parihuela (pa·ri'we·la) *n.f., usu. pl.* litter; stretcher.

parir (pa'rir) *v.t.* to give birth to. —*v.i.* to give birth; be delivered.

parla ('par·la) *n.f.* **1,** loquacity. **2,** talk; chatter.

parlamentar (par·la·men'tar) *v.i.* to parley; negotiate.

parlamentario (par·la·men'ta·rjo) *adj.* parliamentary. —*n.m.* **1,** parliamentarian. **2,** envoy; emissary (*to parley*).

parlamentarismo (par·la·men·ta'ris·mo) *n.m.* parliamentarism.

parlamento (par·la'men·to) *n.m.* **1,** parliament. **2,** parley.

parlanchín (par·lan'tʃin) *adj.* chattering. —*n.m.* [*fem.* **-china**] chatterer; chatterbox.

parlante (par'lan·te) *adj., Amer.* talking; speaking. —*n.m., Amer.* loudspeaker.

parlar (par'lar) *v.t. & i.* **1,** to talk; chatter. **2,** to speak glibly.

parlero (par'le·ro) *adj.* **1,** talkative. **2,** gossipy.

parlotear (par·lo·te'ar) *v.i.* to prattle. —**parloteo** (-'te·o) *n.m.* prattle.

parnaso (par'na·so) *n.m.* **1,** (literary anthology; literary coterie) Parnassus. **2,** *cap.* Mount Parnassus.

parné (par'ne) *n.m., colloq.* money.

paro ('pa·ro) *n.m.* **1,** titmouse. **2,** work stoppage. **3,** lockout. **4,** *Amer.* throw of the dice. —**paro y pinta,** *Amer.* game of dice; craps.

parodia (pa'ro·ðja) *n.f.* parody. —**parodiar** (-'ðjar) *v.t.* to parody. —**parodista** (-'ðis·ta) *n.m. & f.* writer of parodies.

parótida (pa'ro·ti·ða) *n.f.* **1,** parotid. **2,** mumps. —**parotídeo** (-'ti·ðe·o) *adj.* parotid. —**parotiditis,** *n.f.* parotiditis; mumps.

paroxismo (pa·rok'sis·mo) *n.m.* paroxysm.

parpadear (par·pa·ðe'ar) *v.i.* to blink. —**parpadeo** (-'ðe·o) *n.m.* blinking; blink.

párpado ('par·pa·ðo) *n.m.* eyelid.

parpar (par'par) *v.i.* to quack.

parque ('par·ke) *n.m.* **1,** park. **2,** parking field. **3,** *mil.* depot; dump. **4,** equipment, esp. for a public service. —**parque de atracciones,** amusement park.

parquear (par·ke'ar) *v.t. & i., Amer.* to park. —**parqueadero,** *n.m., Amer.* parking lot. —**parqueo** (-'ke·o) *n.m., Amer.* parking; parking lot.

parquedad (par·ke'ðað) *n.f.* paucity.

parra ('pa·rra) *n.f.* grapevine.

parrafada (pa·rra'fa·ða) *n.f., colloq.* private talk; chat.

párrafo (pa·rra·fo) *n.m.* paragraph. —**echar un párrafo,** to chat amicably.

parral (pa'rral) *n.m.* vine arbor; grape arbor.

parranda (pa'rran·da) *n.f.* revel; carousal. —**parrandero,** *adj.* fond of carousing. —*n.m.* [*also,* **parrandista**] *n.m. & f.* carouser; reveler.

parrandear (pa·rran·de'ar) *v.i.* to revel; carouse.

parricida (pa·rri'θi·ða; -'si·ða) *n.m. & f.* parricide; patricide (*agent*). —*adj.* parricidal; patricidal. —**parricidio** (-'θi·ðjo; -'si·ðjo) *n.m.* parricide; patricide (*act*).

parrilla (pa'rri·ʎa; -ja) *n.f.* **1,** gridiron; grill. **2,** barbecue; grillroom.

párroco ('pa·rro·ko) *n.m.* parson.

parroquia (pa'rro·kja) *n.f.* **1,** parish. **2,** parish church. —**parroquial,** *adj.* parochial.

parroquiano (pa·rro'kja·no) *n.m.* **1,** customer; patron; habitué. **2,** parishioner. —*adj.* = **parroquial.**

parsimonia (par·si'mo·nja) *n.f.* parsimony. —**parsimonioso,** *adj.* parsimonious.

parte ('par·te) *n.f.* **1,** part. **2,** side; place; hand. **3,** *law* party. —*n.m.* **1,** dispatch; message. **2,** official communication; writ. —**en parte,** in part; partly. —**dar parte,** to inform; notify. —**de algún tiempo a esta parte,** for some time past. —**de mi parte,** for my part; on my behalf. —**de parte a parte,** from side to side; through. —**de parte de,** **1,** from; by courtesy or command of. **2,** on the side of; favoring. —**¿de parte de quién?,** who's calling? —**echar a mala parte,** **1,** to take amiss. **2,** to misuse or misconstrue (a word or expression). —**en ninguna parte,** nowhere. —**por todas partes,** everywhere.

partenogénesis (par·te·no'xe·ne·sis) *n.f.* parthenogenesis.

partera (par'te·ra) *n.f.* midwife. —**partería,** *n.f.* midwifery. —**partero,** *n.m.* male midwife.

parterre (par'te·rre) *n.m.* parterre.

partición (par·ti'θjon; -'sjon) *n.f.* partition; division.

participación (par·ti·θi·pa'θjon; -si·pa'sjon) *n.f.* **1,** participation. **2,** notification.

participante (par·ti·θi'pan·te; -si'pan·te) *n.m. & f.* **1,** participant. **2,** informant. —*adj.* sharing.

participar (par·ti·θi'par; -si'par) *v.t.* to notify; communicate. —*v.i.* **1,** *fol. by* **de,** to share in. **2,** *fol. by* **en,** to participate in.

partícipe (par'ti·θi·pe; -si·pe) *n.m. & f. & adj.* participant.

participio (par·ti'θi·pjo; -'si·pjo) *n.m.* participle. —**participial,** *adj.* participial.

partícula (par'ti·ku·la) *n.f.* particle.

particular (par·ti·ku'lar) *adj.* **1,** particular. **2,** private. **3,** special; peculiar. —*n.m.* **1,** *also fem.* individual; private person. **2,** particular. —**particularizar** (-la·ri'θar; -'sar) *v.t.* [*infl.:* **rezar, 10**] **1,** to specify. **2,** to detail.

particularidad (par·ti·ku·la·ri·'ðað) *n.f.* **1,** peculiarity. **2,** detail; particular.

partida (par'ti·ða) *n.f.* **1,** departure. **2,** item in an account; entry. **3,** lot. **4,** game; match. **5,** certificate (*of birth, marriage, etc.*). **6,** band; gang; party. **7,** start. **8,** consignment. —**partida de campo,** picnic. —**partida doble,** *comm.* double entry. —**partida simple,** *comm.* single entry.

partidario (par·ti'ða·rjo) *adj. & n.m.* partisan. —*n.m.* follower; supporter. —**partidario de,** supporting; in favor of.

partidismo (par·ti'ðis·mo) *n.m.* partisanship. —**partidista,** *adj.* partisan.

partido (par'ti·ðo) *adj.* split; broken. —*n.m.* **1,** *polit.* party. **2,** match; contest; game. **3,** advantage. **4,** expedient; measure. **5,** players; team. **6,** odds; handicap. —**buen partido,** desirable suitor; good catch. —**mal partido,** undesirable suitor; bad catch. —**tomar partido,** to take sides; choose.

partidura (par·ti'ðu·ra) *n.f.* part (*in the hair*).

partir (par'tir) *v.t.* **1,** to divide; split. **2,** to crack; rend; shatter. **3,** *math.* to divide. —*v.i.* **1,** to depart; leave. **2,** to start; set out. —**partirse,** *v.r., fig.* to be torn apart. —**a partir de,** starting from; as of.

partitivo (par·ti'ti·βo) *adj.* partitive.

partitura (par·ti'tu·ra) *n.f., mus.* score.

parto ('par·to) *n.m.* **1,** parturition. **2,** birth; delivery. **3,** being or thing that is born. —**estar de parto,** to labor; be in difficulties.

parturienta (par·tu'rjen·ta) *also,* **parturiente** (-te) *adj.fem.* parturient. —*n.f.* woman in childbirth.

parva ('par·βa) *n.f.* **1,** stack; rick

(of straw, hay, etc.). **2,** heap; multitude.

parvada (par'βa·ða) *n.f.* **1,** row of haystacks. **2,** brood; covey.

parvedad (par·βe'ðað) *n.f.* **1,** smallness; sparseness. **2,** light snack, esp. one taken on the morning of a fast day.

párvulo ('par·βu·lo) *n.m.* small child; tot. —*adj.* **1,** very small. **2,** innocent.

pasa ('pa·sa) *n.f.* **1,** raisin. **2,** tight curl; kink *(of hair).* —**pasa de Corinto,** currant.

pasable (pa'sa·βle) *adj.* **1,** passable. **2,** tolerable.

pasada (pa'sa·ða) *n.f.* **1,** passing; pass; passage. **2,** trick; trickery; chicanery. —**de pasada, 1,** in passing. **2,** hastily; cursorily.

pasadera (pa·sa'ðe·ra) *n.f.* stepping stone.

pasadero (pa·sa'ðe·ro) *adj.* = **pasable.**

pasadizo (pa·sa'ði·θo; -so) *n.m.* passageway.

pasado (pa'sa·ðo) *adj.* **1,** past. **2,** last; just past. **3,** stale. **4,** spoiled *(of fruit).* **5,** out of date; antiquated. —*n.m.* past. —**pasado mañana,** the day after tomorrow.

pasador (pa·sa'ðor) *n.m.* **1,** door bolt. **2,** cotter pin. **3,** hairpin. **4,** hatpin. **5,** marlinespike.

pasagonzalo (pa·sa·γon'θa·lo; -'sa·lo) *n.m., colloq.* flip; flick; light rap.

pasaje (pa'sa·xe) *n.m.* **1,** passage. **2,** fare; ticket. **3,** ship's passengers; passenger list.

pasajero (pa·sa'xe·ro) *adj.* passing; transitory. —*n.m.* passenger.

pasamano (pa·sa'ma·no) *n.m.* **1,** handrail; banister. **2,** trimming.

pasante (pa'san·te) *n.m.* **1,** assistant *(to a teacher, lawyer, physician, etc.).* **2,** tutor.

pasaporte (pa·sa'por·te) *n.m.* passport.

pasar (pa'sar) *v.t. & i.* to pass. —*v.t.* **1,** to pass on; convey; transmit. **2,** to run through; pierce. **3,** to swallow. **4,** to cross; pass through. —*v.i.* **1,** to last; endure. **2,** to manage; get along; make do. —*v.impers.* to come to pass; happen. —**pasarse,** *v.r.* **1,** to pass. **2,** to go over (to); change allegiance (to). **3,** to spoil *(of food).* **4,** to become permeated; be soaked through. —**pasar a cuchillo,** to put to the sword. —**pasar de largo,** to go through; go by. —**pasar en blanco** *or* **claro,** to pass over; disregard. —**pasar lista,** to call the roll. —**pasar por alto,** to overlook. —**pase lo que pase,** come what may; no matter what.

pasarela (pa·sa're·la) *n.f.* **1,** gangplank; gangway. **2,** footbridge. **3,** catwalk.

pasatiempo (pa·sa'tjem·po) *n.m.* pastime.

pascua ('pas·kwa) *n.f.* **1,** *usu.pl.* Christmas; Yuletide. **2,** Easter. **3,** Passover.

pascual (pas'kwal) *adj.* paschal.

pase ('pa·se) *n.m.* **1,** pass; permit. **2,** *fencing* thrust. **3,** pass *(in certain games and sports).* **4,** movement; motion; pass.

paseante (pa·se'an·te) *n.m. & f.* promenader; stroller.

pasear (pa·se'ar) *v.i.* [*also, v.r.,* **pasearse**] **1,** to promenade; stroll; take a walk. **2,** to take a ride. **3,** *Amer., colloq.* to take a trip; travel. —*v.t.* to take out for a walk or a ride.

paseo (pa'se·o) *n.m.* **1,** walk; stroll. **2,** drive; ride. **3,** promenade; boulevard. —**dar un paseo,** to take a walk or ride. —**mandar a paseo,** *colloq.* to send flying; send off; send packing.

pasillo (pa'si·ʎo; -jo) *n.m.* **1,** corridor. **2,** aisle. **3,** *theat.* sketch; farce.

pasión (pa'sjon) *n.f.* passion.

pasional (pa·sjo'nal) *adj.* **1,** of or pert. to passion. **2,** passionate.

pasionaria (pa·sjo'na·rja) *n.f.* passionflower.

pasito (pa'si·to) *n.m.* short step. —*adv., colloq.* gently; softly.

pasivo (pa'si·βo) *adj.* passive. —*n.m.* liabilities. —**pasividad,** *n.f.* passivity.

pasmado (pas'ma·ðo) *adj.* stunned; amazed.

pasmar (pas'mar) *v.t.* **1,** to stun; benumb. **2,** to astound. **3,** to stunt. **4,** to freeze *(as a plant).* —**pasmarse,** *v.r.* **1,** to freeze; become rigid. **2,** to suffer from lockjaw. **3,** to marvel; be astounded.

pasmo ('pas·mo) *n.m.* **1,** astonishment. **2,** wonder; marvel. **3,** lockjaw; cold; chill. —**pasmoso,** *adj.* astounding; marvelous.

paso ('pa·so) *n.m.* **1,** step; pace. **2,** way; path; pass. **3,** predicament; tight spot. **4,** an event of the life of

Christ; sculptured figure or group representing such event. —*adj.* dried *(of fruit).* —**a cada paso,** frequently. —**al paso que,** while; as. —**paso a nivel,** grade crossing. —**de paso, 1,** on the way. **2,** passing or traveling through. —**llevar el paso, 1,** to lead *(in dancing).* **2,** to keep step. —**marcar el paso,** to mark time. —**prohibido el paso,** no trespassing.

pasquín (pas'kin) *n.m.* lampoon; pasquinade. —**pasquinar,** *v.t.* to lampoon.

pasquinada (pas·ki'na·ða) *n.f.* pasquinade; skit.

pasta ('pas·ta) *n.f.* **1,** paste. **2,** batter; dough. **3,** metal bullion. **4,** *colloq.* money. —**pastas,** *n.f.pl.* pasta; noodles; macaroni.

pastadero (pas·ta'ðe·ro) *n.m.* grazing field; pasture. *Also,* **pastal** (-'tal).

pastar (pas'tar) *v.i.* to pasture; graze. —*v.t.* to lead (cattle) to graze.

pastel (pas'tel) *n.m.* **1,** pie; pastry; tart. **2,** *print.* pie. **3,** *colloq.* jumble. —*adj. & n.m.* pastel.

pastelería (pas·te·le'ri·a) *n.f.* **1,** pastry shop. **2,** pastry.

pastelero (pas·te'le·ro) *n.m.* **1,** pastry baker. **2,** pastry seller.

pastellillo (pas·te'li·ʎo; -jo) *n.m.* patty; pasty.

pasteurizar (pas·teu·ri'θar; -'sar) *also,* **pasterizar** (pas·te·ri-) *v.t.* [*infl.:* **rezar,** 10] to pasteurize. —**pasteurización,** *also,* **pasterización,** *n.f.* pasteurization.

pastiche (pas'ti·tʃe) *n.m.* pastiche.

pastilla (pas'ti·ʎa; -ja) *n.f.* **1,** lozenge; pastille. **2,** cake; tablet; block *(as of soap, chocolate, etc.).*

pastinaca (pas·ti'na·ka) *n.f.* **1,** *ichthy.* stingray. **2,** *bot.* parsnip.

pastizal (pas·ti'θal; -'sal) *n.m.* rich pasture, esp. for horses.

pasto ('pas·to) *n.m.* **1,** pasture. **2,** grass; herbage. **3,** *fig.* food; fuel.

pastor (pas'tor) *n.m.* **1,** shepherd. **2,** pastor; clergyman. —**pastora,** *n.f.* **1,** shepherdess. **2,** (woman) pastor; clergywoman.

pastoral (pas·to'ral) *adj.* pastoral. —*n.f.* pastorale.

pastorear (pas·to·re'ar) *v.t. & i.* to pasture.

pastoreo (pas·to're·o) *n.m.* **1,** pasturing. **2,** tending of flocks.

pastoril (pas·to'ril) *adj.* shepherd *(attrib.).*

pastoso (pas'to·so) *adj.* **1,** pasty; doughy. **2,** mellow. —**pastosidad,** *n.f.* pastiness; doughiness.

pastura (pas'tu·ra) *n.f.* pasture; pasturage.

pata ('pa·ta) *n.f.* **1,** leg or paw of an animal. **2,** *colloq.* human leg or foot. **3,** leg of a chair, table, etc. **4,** female of the drake; duck. **5,** pocket flap. —**a pata,** *colloq.* on foot. —**enseñar la pata,** *colloq.* to show one's ignorance. —**estirar la pata,** *colloq.* to die; to kick the bucket. —**meter la pata,** *colloq.* to botch; bungle. —**pata de palo,** peg leg. —**tener mala pata,** *colloq.* **1,** to be jinxed. **2,** to be churlish. —**salir, quedar** *or* **estar patas,** *colloq.* to end in a draw or tie.

patada (pa'ta·ða) *n.f.* kick. —**a patadas,** *colloq.* plentifully.

patalear (pa·ta·le'ar) *v.i.* **1,** to kick about violently. **2,** to stamp the feet. **3,** *colloq.* to raise a ruckus.

pataleo (pa·ta'le·o) *n.m.* **1,** kicking. **2,** stamping of the feet. —**derecho a pataleo,** *colloq.* the right to complain.

pataleta (pa·ta'le·ta) *n.f.,* *colloq.* **1,** convulsion; fit. **2,** tantrum.

patán (pa'tan) *adj.* **1,** rustic; churlish. **2,** unmannerly. —*n.m.* churl; boor. —**patanería,** *n.f.* churlishness; boorishness.

patata (pa'ta·ta) *n.f.* potato. —**patatal,** *also,* **patatar,** *n.m.* potato patch. —**patatero,** *adj.,* *colloq.,* *often derog.* potato-eating.

patatús (pa·ta'tus) *n.m.,* *colloq.* swoon; fainting fit.

pateadura (pa·te·a'ðu·ra) *n.f.* **1,** kicking. **2,** drubbing. **3,** *colloq.* dressing down.

patear (pa·te'ar) *v.t.* **1,** to kick; trample. **2,** to boo; hoot off. —*v.i.,* *colloq.* to rage; stamp.

patentar (pa·ten'tar) *v.t.* to patent.

patente (pa'ten·te) *adj. & n.f.* patent.

paternal (pa·ter'nal) *adj.* fatherly; paternal. —**paternalismo,** *n.m.* paternalism. —**paternalista,** *adj.* paternalistic.

paternidad (pa·ter·ni'ðað) *n.f.* **1,** paternity. **2,** title of respect used with clergymen; Reverence.

paterno (pa'ter·no) *adj.* paternal; of or inherited from the father.

paternóster (pa·ter'nos·ter) *n.m.*
sing. & *pl.* paternoster.
patético (pa'te·ti·ko) *adj.* pathetic.
—**patetismo** (-'tis·mo) *n.m.* pathos.
patiabierto (pa·tja'βjer·to) *adj.*
bowlegged.
patibulario (pa·ti·βu'la·rjo) *adj.*
repulsive; villainous.
patíbulo (pa'ti·βu·lo) *n.m.* gallows; scaffold.
patilla (pa'ti·ʎa; -ja) *n.f.* **1,**
sideburn. **2,** *Amer., colloq.* thingum-
bob. —**patillas,** *n.m.pl.* Old Nick.
patín (pa'tin) *n.m.* **1,** ice skate;
roller skate. **2,** child's scooter. **3,**
skiff. **4,** *ornith.* petrel. **5,** runner *(of
a sled).*
pátina ('pa·ti·na) *n.f.* patina.
patinadero (pa·ti·na'ðe·ro) *n.m.*
skating rink; skating pond.
patinador (pa·ti·na'ðor) *n.m.*
[*fem.* **-dora**] skater.
patinaje (pa·ti'na·xe) *n.m.* skating.
patinar (pa·ti'nar) *v.i.* **1,** to skate.
2, to skid. —**patinamiento; pati-
nazo** *n.m., also, Amer.,* **patinada,**
n.f. skidding; skid.
patio ('pa·tjo) *n.m.* **1,** patio; courtyard. **2,** *theat.* pit; orchestra.
patitieso (pa·ti'tje·so) *adj., colloq.*
1, unconscious; knocked out. **2,**
stunned; overwhelmed.
patituerto (pa·ti'twer·to) *adj.* **1,**
crook-legged; bowlegged or knock-
kneed. **2,** crooked; lopsided.
patizambo (pa·ti'θam·bo;
-'sam·bo) *adj.* knockkneed.
pato ('pa·to) *n.m.* duck; drake.
—**pagar el pato,** *colloq.* to be the
scapegoat. —**pato de flojel,** eider
duck. —**pato negro,** mallard.
—**pato silvestre,** wild duck.
patochada (pa·to'tʃa·ða) *n.f.* tomfoolery.
patógeno (pa'to·xe·no) *adj.* pathogenic.
patología (pa·to·lo'xi·a) *n.f.* pathology. —**patológico** (-'lo·xi·ko)
adj. pathological. —**patólogo** (-'to-
lo·ɣo) *n.m.* pathologist.
patraña (pa'tra·ɲa) *n.f.* humbug;
fib.
patria ('pa·trja) *n.f.* fatherland; native land.
patriarca (pa'trjar·ka) *n.m.* patriarch. —**patriarcado,** *n.m.* patriarchate; patriarchy. —**patriarcal,**
adj. patriarchal.
patricio (pa'tri·θjo; -sjo) *n.m.* &
adj. patrician.
patrimonio (pa·tri'mo·njo) *n.m.*

patrimony. —**patrimonial,** *adj.* patrimonial.
patrio ('pa·trjo) *adj.* **1,** of the fatherland. **2,** = **paterno.**
patriota (pa'trjo·ta) *n.m.* & *f.* patriot. —**patriótico,** *adj.* patriotic.
—**patriotismo,** *n.m.* patriotism.
patriotero (pa·trjo'te·ro) *adj.* &
n.m. chauvinist; jingoist. —**patriotería,** *n.f.* chauvinism; jingoism.
patrocinar (pa·tro·θi'nar; -si'nar)
v.t. to sponsor; patronize. —**patrocinador,** *adj.* sponsoring; patronizing. —*n.m.* [*fem.* **-dora**] sponsor;
patron. —**patrocinio** (-'θi·njo;
-'si·njo) *n.m.* sponsorship; patronage.
patrón (pa'tron) *h.m.* **1,** employer;
boss. **2,** patron; sponsor. **3,** patron
saint. **4,** pattern; model; standard. **5,**
skipper.
patrona (pa'tro·na) *n.f.* **1,** mistress;
boss. **2,** landlady; housekeeper. **3,**
patroness.
patronal (pa·tro'nal) *adj.* **1,** patronal. **2,** of or pert. to an employer
or employers.
patronato (pa·tro'na·to) *n.m.* **1,**
employers' association. **2,** welfare
organization. **3,** [*also,* **patronazgo**]
patronage.
patronímico (pa·tro'ni·mi·ko)
adj. & *n.m.* patronymic.
patrono (pa'tro·no) *n.m.* **1,** patron.
2, employer; boss.
patrulla (pa'tru·ʎa; -ja) *n.f.* **1,** patrol. **2,** band; gang. —**patrullaje,**
n.m. patrolling; patrol. —**patrullar,** *v.t.* & *i.* to patrol. —**patrullero,** *adj.* patrol *(attrib.).* —*n.m.*
patrol car; patrol plane; patrol boat.
patuá (pa'twa) *n.m.* patois.
paulatino (pau·la'ti·no) *adj.* gradual; slow.
pauperismo (pau·pe'ris·mo) *n.m.*
pauperism.
paupérrimo (pau·pe·rri·mo) *adj.*
very poor; destitute; penniless.
pausa ('pau·sa) *n.f.* **1,** pause.
2, *mus.* rest. **3,** slowness. —**pausado,** *adj.* slow; deliberate. —*adv.*
slow; slowly. —**pausar,** *v.i.* to
pause. —**con pausa,** slowly.
pauta ('pau·ta) *n.f.* **1,** ruler. **2,** ruled
lines. **3,** norm; standard; model.
pava ('pa·βa) *n.f.* **1,** turkey hen. **2,**
large furnace bellows. **3,** *Amer.* kettle. **4,** *W.I.* farmer's straw hat. **5,**
colloq. graceless woman. —**pelar
la pava,** *colloq.* to engage in amorous chat.

pavada (pa'βa·ða) n.f. **1,** flock of turkeys. **2,** Amer. foolishness; silliness; nonsense.

pavesa (pa'βe·sa) n.f. ember.

pavía (pa'βi·a) n.f. cling peach.

pavimento (pa·βi'men·to) n.m. pavement. —**pavimentar,** v.t. to pave. —**pavimentación,** n.f. paving. —**pavimentado,** adj. paved.

pavo ('pa·βo) n.m. **1,** turkey. **2,** colloq. oaf; sad sack; fool. —adj., colloq. oafish; foolish. —**pavo real,** peacock. —**ponerse hecho un pavo,** to blush. —**subírsele a uno el pavo,** to put on airs.

pavón (pa'βon) n.m. peacock.

pavonear (pa·βo·ne'ar) v.i. [also, refl., **pavonearse**] to strut; show off.

pavor (pa'βor) n.m. dread. —**pavoroso,** adj. dreadful; awful. —**pavura,** n.f. dread; terror.

paya ('pa·ja) n.f., S.A. song improvised to the tune of the guitar. —**payar,** v.i., to sing a paya. —**payador,** n.m., singer; improviser.

payaso (pa'ja·so) n.m. clown. —**payasada,** n.f. clownery; tomfoolery. —**payasear,** v.i., Amer. to clown.

payo ('pa·jo) adj. & n.m. rustic. —n.m., slang fellow; guy.

payuelas (pa'jwe·las) n.f.pl. chicken pox.

paz (paθ; pas) n.f. peace.

pazca ('paθ·ka; 'pas-) v., pres. subjve. of **pacer.**

pazco ('paθ·ko; 'pas-) v., 1st pers. sing.pres.ind. of **pacer.**

pazguato (paθ'ɣwa·to; pas-) n.m. dolt; simpleton. —**pazguatería,** n.f. foolishness.

pe (pe) n.f., in **de pe a pa,** from beginning to end; from A to Z.

peaje (pe'a·xe) n.m. toll. —**peajero,** n.m. toll collector.

peatón (pe·a'ton) n.m. **1,** pedestrian. **2,** rural postman.

pebete (pe'βe·te) n.m. **1,** incense. **2,** Amér., colloq. kid; small boy. **3,** colloq. malodorous thing.

pebre ('pe·βre) n.m. or f. sauce of pepper, garlic and spice. —**hacer pebre,** colloq. to maul; beat.

peca ('pe·ka) n.f. freckle.

pecadillo (pe·ka'ði·ʎo; -jo) n.m. peccadillo.

pecado (pe'ka·ðo) n.m. sin. —**de mis pecados,** of mine; my own.

—**los siete pecados capitales,** the seven deadly sins.

pecador (pe·ka'ðor) n.m. sinner. —adj. sinning.

pecaminoso (pe·ka·mi'no·so) adj. sinful.

pecar (pe'kar) v.i. [infl.: **tocar, 7**] to sin. —**pecar de** (fol. by adj.), to be too . . .

pecarí (pe·ka'ri) n.m. peccary.

pecblenda (pek'βlen·da) n.f. pitchblende.

pecera (pe'θe·ra; -'se·ra) n.f. fish bowl; fish tank.

pecíolo (pe'θi·o·lo; pe'si-) n.m. petiole.

pécora ('pe·ko·ra) n.f. **1,** head of sheep; sheep. **2,** colloq. hussy; minx.

pecoso (pe'ko·so) adj. freckly; freckled.

pectina (pek'ti·na) n.f. pectin.

pectoral (pek·to'ral) adj. pectoral; chest (attrib.). —n.m., eccles. pectoral.

pecuario (pe'kwa·rjo) adj. of or pert. to livestock.

peculado (pe·ku'la·ðo) n.m. embezzlement; peculation.

peculiar (pe·ku'ljar) adj. peculiar. —**peculiaridad,** n.f. peculiarity.

peculio (pe'ku·ljo) n.m. personal wealth; belongings; possessions.

pecunia (pe'ku·nja) n.f., colloq. hard cash; money.

pecuniario (pe·ku'nja·rjo) adj. pecuniary.

pechar (pe'tʃar) v.t. & i. to shoulder (a burden or responsibility). —v.i., Amer. to contend; struggle. —v.t. to breast; confront.

pechblenda (petʃ'βlen·da) n.f. = **pecblenda.**

pechera (pe'tʃe·ra) n.f. **1,** shirt front. **2,** chest protector. **3,** colloq. chest; bosom. —**pechero,** n.m. bib.

pechicolorado (pe·tʃi·ko·lo'ra·ðo) n.m. linnet.

pecho ('pe·tʃo) n.m. **1,** chest; thorax. **2,** breast. **3,** bosom. **4,** fig. courage; fortitude. **5,** mus. strength of the voice. —**abrir el pecho,** to open one's heart; confide. —**dar el pecho, 1,** to suckle; nurse. **2,** to face; confront. —**entre pecho y espalda,** colloq. deep down inside. —**tomar a pecho,** to take to heart.

pechuga (pe'tʃu·ɣa) n.f. **1,** breast (of fowl). **2,** colloq. bosom; breasts. **3,** Amer., colloq. nerve); gall.

pechugón (pe·tʃu'ɣon) adj., Amer.,

colloq. brazenly demanding. —*n.m., Amer., colloq.* [*fem.* **-gona**] sponger; demanding person.

pedagogía (pe·ða·γo'xi·a) *n.f.* pedagogy. —**pedagógico** (-'γo·xi·ko) *adj.* pedagogical. —**pedagogo** (-'γo·γo) pedagogue; educator.

pedal (pe'ðal) *n.m.* pedal; treadle. —**pedalear,** *v.t. & i.* to pedal.

pedáneo (pe'ða·ne·o) *n.m., also,* **alcalde pedáneo,** reeve; bailiff.

pedante (pe'ðan·te) *n.m. & f.* pedant. —*adj.* pedantic. —**pedantear,** *v.i.* to act the pedant. —**pedantería,** *n.f.* pedantry. —**pedantesco,** *adj.* pedantic (*of style*).

pedazo (pe'ða·θo; -so) *n.m.* piece; fragment; slice.

pederasta (pe·ðe'ras·ta) *n.m.* pederast. —**pederastia** (-tja) *n.f.* pederasty.

pedernal (pe·ðer'nal) *n.m.* flint.

pedestal (pe·ðes'tal) *n.m.* pedestal.

pedestre (pe'ðes·tre) *adj.* pedestrian.

pediatría (pe·ðja'tri·a) *n.f.* pediatrics. —**pediatra** (pe'ðja·tra) *n.m. & f.* pediatrician. —**pediátrico** (pe·'ðja·tri·ko) *adj.* pediatric.

pedicura (pe·ði'ku·ra) *n.f.* pedicure.

pedicuro (pe·ði'ku·ro) *n.m.* chiropodist; pedicure.

pedida (pe'ði·ða) *adj.fem.* spoken for. —*n.f.* request for the hand of a woman in marriage.

pedido (pe'ði·ðo) *n.m.* **1,** demand; request; call. **2,** *comm.* order.

pedidor (pe·ði'ðor) *adj.* demanding. —*n.m.* [*fem.* **-dora**] demanding person.

pedigüeño (pe·ði'γwe·ɲo) *adj., colloq.* importunate. *Also,* **pedigón** (-'γon)

pedir (pe'dir) *v.t.* [*infl.:* **33**] **1,** to request; ask; beg. **2,** to order. —**a pedir de boca,** at just the right moment; just as hoped for. —**pedir prestado,** to borrow; ask for the loan of.

pedo ('pe·ðo) *n.m.* fart; breaking wind.

pedorrero (pe·ðo'rre·ro) *adj.* farting; farty. —**pedorrera,** *n.f.* farting; flatulence.

pedorreta (pe·ðo'rre·ta) *n.f., colloq.* Bronx cheer.

pedrada (pe'ðra·ða) *n.f.* **1,** stone's throw. **2,** blow with a stone. **3,** *colloq.* taunt; insinuation.

pedregal (pe·ðre'γal) *n.m.* stony

terrain. —**pedregoso,** *adj.* stony; rocky.

pedrería (pe·ðre'ri·a) *n.f.* jewelry.

pedrusco (pe'ðrus·ko) *n.m.* boulder; rough stone.

pedúnculo (pe'ðun·ku·lo) *n.m.* stem; stalk.

pega ('pe·γa) *n.f.* **1,** = **pegadura. 2,** *Amer., colloq.* paste; glue. **3,** *Amer., colloq.* soft job; racket.

pegadizo (pe·γa'ði·θo; -so) *adj.* **1,** sticky; adhesive. **2,** catching; contagious. **3,** catchy (*of a tune*).

pegadura (pe·γa'ðu·ra) *n.f.* **1,** pasting; sticking. **2,** adhesion.

pegajoso (pe·γa'xo·so) *adj.* **1,** sticky. **2,** catching; contagious. **3,** catchy (*of a tune*). **4,** clammy. —**pegajosidad,** *n.f.* stickiness.

pegar (pe'γar) *v.t.* [*infl.:* **pagar, 8**] **1,** to stick; glue. **2,** to attach; fasten. **3,** to sew on. **4,** to give (a vice or disease). **5,** to strike (a blow). —*v.i.* **1,** to take hold. **2,** to take; catch on. —**pegarse,** *v.r.* **1,** to stick; scorch (*of food*). **2,** to become ingrained; become fixed. —**pegársela a uno,** to dupe someone.

pegote (pe'γo·te) *n.* **1,** sticky mass; goo. **2,** hanger-on; leech.

peinado (pei'na·ðo) *n.m.* coiffure; hairdo. —*adj.* overnice (*of style*).

peinador (pei·na'ðor) *n.m.* peignoir.

peinar (pei'nar) *v.t.* to comb. —**peinarse,** *v.r.* to comb one's hair.

peine ('pei·ne) *n.m.* comb.

peineta (pei'ne·ta) *n.f.* ornamental comb.

peje ('pe·xe) *n.m.* **1,** fish. **2,** *colloq.* crafty fellow.

pejerrey (pe·xe'rrei) *n.m.* a variety of smelt.

pejesapo (pe·xe'sa·po) *n.m., ichthy.* angler.

peladilla (pe·la'ði·ʎa; -ja) *n.f.* **1,** candied almond. **2,** small pebble.

pelado (pe'la·ðo) *adj.* **1,** plucked. **2,** bald; hairless. **3,** bare. **4,** *colloq.* penniless; broke. —*n.m.* **1,** *colloq.* penniless person. **2,** *Mex.* peasant. **3,** *Amer.* infant; child.

pelafustán (pe·la·fus'tan) *n.m., colloq.* ne'er-do-well; loafer.

pelágico (pe'la·xi·ko) *adj.* pelagic.

pelagatos (pe·la'γa·tos) *n.m.sing. & pl., colloq.* tramp.

pelagra (pe'la·γra) *n.f.* pellagra.

pelaje (pe'la·xe) *n.m.* **1,** coat; hair; fur. **2,** aspect; complexion.

pelambre (pe'lam·bre) *n.f.* **1,** hair;

hairiness. **2,** [*also,* **pelambrera**] shed hair or fur. **3,** [*also,* **pelambrera**] bare or bald spot.

pelar (pe'lar) *v.t.* **1,** to cut or pull off (the hair). **2,** to pluck (feathers). **3,** to peel; skin. **4,** *colloq.* to clean out; make bankrupt. —**pelarse,** *v.r.* **1,** to lose the hair. **2,** to peel off; flake. **3,** [*also,* **pelárselas**] *usu. fol. by* **por,** to be eager to; be raring to; be excited about. **4,** [*also,* **pelárselas**] *usu.fol. by* **de,** to be intensely affected by.

peldaño (pel'da·ɲo) *n.m.* **1,** step (*of a staircase*). **2,** rung (*of a ladder*).

pelea (pe'le·a) *n.f.* fight; quarrel.

pelear (pe·le'ar) *v.i.* to fight; quarrel. —**pelearse,** *v.r.* **1,** to have a fight; scuffle. **2,** to be on bad terms.

pelechar (pe·le'tʃar) *v.i.* to molt; shed.

pelele (pe'le·le) *n.m.* **1,** stuffed figure; dummy. **2,** *fig.* straw man.

peletero (pe·le'te·ro) *n.m.* furrier. —**peletería,** *n.f.* furrier's shop or trade.

peliagudo (pe·li·a'ɣu·ðo; pe·lja-) *adj.* **1,** having long, thin hair. **2,** *colloq.* difficult; tough; crucial.

pelícano (pe'li·ka·no) *n.m.* pelican.

película (pe'li·ku·la) *n.f.* film.

peligrar (pe·li'ɣrar) *v.i.* to be in danger.

peligro (pe'li·ɣro) *n.m.* danger; peril. —**peligroso,** *adj.* dangerous; perilous.

pelillo (pe'li·ʎo; -jo) *n.m.* **1,** hair; trifle. **2,** *usu.pl.* bone of contention; gripe. —**echar pelillos a la mar,** *colloq.* to bury the hatchet. —**pararse en pelillos,** *colloq.* to quibble; haggle.

pelirrojo (pe·li'rro·xo) *adj.* redheaded. —*n.m.* redheaded person; redhead.

pelmazo (pel'ma·θo; -so) *n.m., also,* **pelma** ('pel·ma) *n.m. & f.* **1,** thick lump. **2,** *colloq.* slow, sluggish person. **3,** *colloq.* nuisance; bore.

pelo ('pe·lo) *n.m.* hair. —**al pelo; a pelo,** just right; to a T. —**a pelo,** with the grain. —**agarrarse a un pelo,** to grasp at a straw. —**contra pelo,** against the grain. —**de pelo en pecho,** *colloq.* manly; virile. —**en pelo,** bareback. —**estar hasta los pelos,** to be fed up. —**pelos y señales,** *colloq.* minute details; characteristics. —**tomar el pelo,** *colloq.* to pull one's leg; josh.

pelón (pe'lon) *adj.* hairless; bald. —*n.m.* bald person; baldhead.

pelota (pe'lo·ta) *n.f.* **1,** ball. **2,** jai alai, soccer, or any of several games of ball. —**en pelota,** naked; stripped.

pelotear (pe·lo·te'ar) *v.i.* to bandy a ball; play catch.

pelotera (pe·lo'te·ra) *n.f., colloq.* brawl; riot; tumult.

pelotón (pe·lo'ton) *n.m.* **1,** bunch; crowd. **2,** hank; knot. **3,** platoon.

peltre ('pel·tre) *n.m.* pewter.

peluca (pe'lu·ka) *n.f.* wig.

peluche (pe'lu·tʃe) *n.m.* plush. —**oso de peluche,** teddy bear.

peludo (pe'lu·ðo) *adj.* hairy. —*n.m.* fiber mat.

peluquería (pe·lu·ke'ri·a) *n.f.* **1,** hairdresser's shop. **2,** barber shop.

peluquero (pe·lu'ke·ro) *n.m.* **1,** barber. **2,** [*fem.* **peluquera**] hairdresser.

pelusa (pe'lu·sa) *n.f.* fuzz; down.

pelvis ('pel·βis) *n.f.* pelvis. —**pelviano** ('βja·no) *adj.* pelvic.

pellejo (pe'ʎe·xo; -'je·xo) *n.m.* **1,** skin; pelt. **2,** wineskin.

pelliza (pe'ʎi·θa; -'ji·sa) *n.f.* pelisse.

pellizcar (pe;ʎiθ'kar; pe·jis'kar) *v.t.* [*infl.:* **tocar, 7**] to pinch; nip. —**pellizcarse,** *v.r.* to long; pine.

pellizco (pe'ʎiθ·ko; pe'jis-) *n.m.* pinch; nip.

pena ('pe·na) *n.f.* **1,** penalty; punishment. **2,** sorrow. **3,** suffering; pain. **4,** toil; hardship. **5,** mortification; embarrassment. **6,** *Amer.* spirit; ghost. —**a duras penas,** barely; just barely. —**dar pena,** to evoke sorrow; cause to be sorry. —**merecer** *or* **valer la pena,** to be worthwhile. —**tener pena,** to be sorry.

penacho (pe'na·tʃo) *n.m.* **1,** tuft of feathers. **2,** plume; crest.

penado (pe'na·ðo) *n.m.* convict. —*adj.* = **penoso.**

penal (pe'nal) *adj.* penal. —*n.m.* prison.

penalidad (pe·na·li'ðað) *n.f.* **1,** hardship. **2,** *law* penalty.

penalista (pe·na'lis·ta) *n.m. & f.* penologist.

penalizar (pe·na·li'θar; -'sar) *v.t.* [*infl.:* **rezar, 10**] to penalize.

penar (pe'nar) *v.i.* **1,** to suffer; experience sorrow. **2,** to be in torment (*in the afterlife*). **3,** to long; pine. —*v.t.* to impose a penalty on.

—**penarse,** *v.r.* to grieve; mourn; lament.

penca ('pen·ka) *n.f.* **1,** rawhide; whip. **2,** pulpy leaf of some plants, as cactus. —**coger una penca,** *Amer., colloq.* to get drunk.

penco ('pen·ko) *n.m., colloq.* nag; plug.

pendejo (pen'de·xo) *n.m.* **1,** pubic hair. **2,** *Amer., vulg.* fool; jerk. **3,** coward. —*adj.* cowardly.

pendencia (pen'den·θja; -sja) *n.f.* quarrel; wrangle; brawl. —**pendenciar,** *v.i.* to quarrel; wrangle. —**pendenciero,** *adj.* quarrelsome; wrangling; brawling. —*n.m.* wrangler; brawler.

pender (pen'der) *v.i.* **1,** to hang; dangle. **2,** to pend. **3,** to depend.

pendiente (pen'djen·te) *adj.* **1,** pendent; hanging. **2,** pending. —*n.f.* slope; gradient. —*n.m.* pendant; earring.

péndola ('pen·do·la) *n.f.* **1,** pendulum. **2,** pendulum clock.

pendolista (pen·do'lis·ta) *n.m.* penman.

pendón (pen'don) *n.m.* **1,** standard; banner; pennant. **2,** tiller; shoot. **3,** *colloq.* so-and-so; hussy *(if applied to a woman).*

péndulo ('pen·du·lo) *n.m.* pendulum. —*adj.* pendulous. —**pendular,** *adj.* of or like a pendulum.

pene ('pe·ne) *n.m.* penis.

penetrar (pene'trar) *v.t.* to penetrate. —**penetrable,** *adj.* penetrable. —**penetración,** *n.f.* penetration.

penicilina (pe·ni·θi'li·na; pe·ni·si-) *n.f.* penicillin.

península (pe'nin·su·la) *n.f.* peninsula. —**peninsular,** *adj.* peninsular.

penique (pe'ni·ke) *n.m.* British penny.

penitencia (pe·ni'ten·θja; -sja) *n.f.* penitence; penance. —**penitencial,** *adj.* penitential.

penitenciaría (pe·ni·ten·θja'ri·a; -sja'ri·a) *n.f.* penitentiary. —**penitenciario** (-'θja·rjo; -'sja·rjo) *adj.* penitentiary *(attrib.).*

penitente (pe·ni'ten·te) *adj.* & *n.m.* & *f.* penitent.

penol (pe'nol) *n.m.* yardarm.

penología (pe·no·lo'xi·a) *n.f.* penology.

penoso (pe'no·so) *adj.* **1,** painful. **2,** grieving. **3,** embarrassing.

pensado (pen'sa·ðo) *adj.* deliberate; reasoned. —**bien pen-**sado, **1,** well-considered. **2,** well-intentioned. —**de pensado,** deliberately. —**mal pensado, 1,** badly thought out. **2,** evil-minded.

pensador (pen·sa'ðor) *n.m.* thinker. —*adj.* thinking.

pensamiento (pen·sa'mjen·to) *n.m.* **1,** thought. **2,** mind. **3,** *bot.* pansy.

pensar (pen'sar) *v.t.* & *i.* [*infl.:* 27] to think. —**pensar en,** to think of; think about.

pensativo (pen·sa'ti·βo) *adj.* pensive.

pensión (pen'sjon) *n.f.* **1,** pension. **2,** boarding house. **3,** board; meals. —**pensionar,** *v.t.* to pension.

pensionado (pen·sjo'na·ðo) *adj.* pensioned. —*n.m.* **1,** pensioner. **2,** boarding school.

pensionista (pen·sjo'nis·ta) *n.m.* & *f.* **1,** boarder. **2,** pensioner.

pentaedro (pen·ta'e·ðro) *n.m.* pentahedron.

pentágono (pen'ta·γo·no) *n.m.* pentagon. —**pentagonal,** *adj.* pentagonal.

pentagrama (pen·ta'γra·ma) *n.m., mus.* staff.

pentámetro (pen'ta·me·tro) *n.m.* pentameter.

Pentateuco (pen·ta'teu·ko) *n.m.* Pentateuch.

péntatlo ('pen·ta·tlo) *n.m.* pentathlon.

Pentecostés (pen·te·kos'tes) *n.m.* Pentecost. —**pentecostal,** *adj.* & *n.m.* & *f.* Pentecostal.

pentotal (pen·to'tal) *n.m.* pentothal.

penúltimo (pe'nul·ti·mo) *adj.* penultimate; next to last. —**penúltima,** *n.f.* penult; next-to-last syllable.

penumbra (pe'num·bra) *n.f.* penumbra; twilight. —**penumbroso,** *adj.* penumbral.

penuria (pe'nu·rja) *n.f.* penury.

peña ('pe·ɲa) *n.f.* rock.

peñasco (pe'ɲas·ko) *n.m.* large rock. —**peñascal,** *n.m.* rocky terrain. —**peñascoso,** *adj.* rocky.

peñón (pe'ɲon) *n.m.* rocky prominence.

peón (pe'on) *n.m.* **1,** laborer; peon. **2,** spinning top. **3,** *chess* pawn. **4,** *checkers* man. **5,** foot soldier. **6,** pedestrian.

peonada (pe·o'na·ða) *n.f.* **1,** day's work *(of a peon).* **2,** gang of peons. **3,** = **peonaje.**

peonaje (pe·o'na·xe) *n.m.* **1,** peonage. **2,** peons collectively. **3,** foot soldiers collectively.

peonía (pe·o'ni·a) *n.f.* peony.

peonza (pe'on·θa; -sa) *n.f.* spinning top.

peor (pe'or) *adj. & adv.* **1,** *comp. of* **malo;** worse. **2,** *superl. of* **malo;** worst. **—cada vez peor,** worse and worse. **—peor que peor,** from bad to worse. **—tanto peor,** so much the worse.

pepa ('pe·pa) *n.f., Amer.* **1,** seed; pit. **2,** playing marble.

pepinillos (pe·pi'ni·ʎos; -jos) *n.m.pl.* **1,** gherkins. **2,** pickled cucumbers.

pepino (pe'pi·no) *n.m.* cucumber. **—no importar un pepino** *or* **tres pepinos,** *colloq.* not to matter a bit.

pepita (pe'pi·ta) *n.f.* **1,** pip; seed. **2,** pip *(disease of fowls).* **3,** nugget.

pepitoria (pe·pi'to·rja) *n.f.* **1,** giblet fricassee. **2,** hodgepodge.

pepón (pe'pon) *n.m.* watermelon.

pepsina (pep'si·na) *n.f.* pepsin.

péptico ('pep·ti·ko) *adj.* peptic.

péptido ('pep·ti·ðo) *n.m.* peptide.

peptona (pep'to·na) *n.f.* peptone.

peque ('pe·ke) *v., pres.subjve. of* **pecar.**

pequé (pe'ke) *v., 1st pers.sing. pret. of* **pecar.**

pequeñez (pe·ke'ɲeθ; -'ɲes) *n.f.* **1,** smallness. **2,** meanness; pettiness. **3,** trifle. **4,** infancy; childhood.

pequeño (pe'ke·ɲo) *adj.* **1,** small; little. **2,** petty; trifling. **—n.m.** child; tot; little one.

pequeñuelo (pe·ke'ɲwe·lo) *n.m.* baby; infant; tot. **—adj.** very small.

pera ('pe·ra) *n.f.* **1,** pear. **2,** goatee; imperial. **3,** rubber bulb. **4,** *colloq.* light bulb. **—pedir peras al olmo,** to expect the impossible. **—ponerle a uno las peras a cuarto,** to çall down; reprimand.

peral (pe'ral) *n.m.* pear tree.

peralte (pe'ral·te) *n.m.* **1,** superelevation; banking *(of curves).* **2,** *archit.* rise of an arch.

perca ('per·ka) *n.f., ichthy.* perch.

percal (per'kal) *n.m.* percale; muslin.

percance (per'kan·θe; -se) *n.m.* mishap.

percatar (per·ka'tar) *v.i.* [*usu. v.r.,* **percatarse**] to perceive; apprehend; realize.

percebe (per'θe·βe; -'se·βe) *n.m.* barnacle.

percentil (per·θen'til; -sen'til) *n.m.* percentile.

percepción (per·θep'θjon; -sep'sjon) *n.f.* perception.

perceptibilidad (per·θep·ti·βi·li·'ðað; per·sep-) *n.f.* **1,** perceptibility. **2,** perceptivity.

perceptible (per·θep'ti·βle; per·sep-) *adj.* **1,** perceptible; perceivable. **2,** *comm.* receivable.

perceptivo (per·θep'ti·βo; per·sep-) *adj.* perceptive.

percibir (per·θi'βir; per·si-) *v.t.* **1,** to perceive. **2,** to receive (salary, monies, etc.).

percudir (per·ku'ðir) *v.t.* **1,** to tarnish. **2,** to soil; begrime.

percusión (per·ku'sjon) *n.f.* percussion.

percusor (per·ku'sor) *n.m.* hammer *(of a firearm).*

percha ('per·tʃa) *n.f.* **1,** perch; roost. **2,** hat or clothes rack. **3,** = **perca.**

perchero (per'tʃe·ro) *n.m.* hat or clothes rack.

perdedor (per·ðe'ðor) *n.m.* [*fem* **-dora**] loser. **—adj.** losing.

perder (per'ðer) *v.t.* [*infl.:* **29**] **1,** to lose. **2,** to waste; throw away. **3,** to miss (a train, opportunity, etc.). **4,** to corrupt. **—v.i.** to lose. **—perderse,** *v.r.* **1,** to be lost. **2,** to lose one's way. **3,** to go wrong; go astray. **4,** to disappear. **5,** to be smitten. **—perder los estribos,** to lose one's self-control. **—¡pierda Vd. cuidado!,** don't worry!; forget it!

perdición (per·ði'θjon; -'sjon) *n.f.* perdition.

pérdida ('per·ði·ða) *n.f.* **1,** loss. **2,** *comm.* leakage.

perdido (per'ði·ðo) *adj.* **1,** lost. **2,** mislaid. **—adj. & n.m.** profligate.

perdigón (per·ði'ɣon) *n.m.* **1,** young partridge. **2,** bird shot. **—perdigonada,** *n.f.* volley of bird shot.

perdiguero (per·ði'ɣe·ro) *n.m.* setter; retriever.

perdiz (per'ðiθ; -'ðis) *n.f.* partridge.

perdón (per'ðon) *n.m.* **1,** pardon; forgiveness. **2,** reprieve. **3,** remission *(of a debt).* **—interj.** I beg your pardon; excuse me. **—con perdón,** by your leave; begging your pardon.

perdonable (per·ðo'na·βle) *adj.* pardonable; forgivable.

perdonar (per·ðo'nar) *v.t.* **1,** to pardon; forgive. **2,** to remit (a debt).

3, to excuse. 4, to overlook (a fault or mistake).

perdonavidas (per·ðo·na'βi·ðas) *n.m. & f. sing. & pl., colloq.* bully.

perdulario (per·ðu'la·rjo) *adj.* **1,** careless; slovenly. **2,** dissolute; unregenerate. —*n.m.* **1,** slovenly person. **2,** profligate.

perdurar (per·ðu'rar) *v.i.* to last; endure. —**perdurable,** *adj.* lasting; everlasting. —**perdurabilidad,** *n.f.* permanence.

perecedero (pe·re·θe'ðe·ro; pe·re·se·) *adj.* perishable; not lasting.

perecer (pe·re'θer; -'ser) *v.i.* [*infl.:* conocer, 13] to perish; die. —**perecerse,** *v.r.* to crave; pine.

peregrinación (pe·re·ɣri·na'θjon; -'sjon) *n.f.,* also, **peregrinaje** (-'na·xe) *n.m.* **1,** peregrination. **2,** pilgrimage.

peregrinar (pe·re·ɣri'nar) *v.i.* **1,** to roam. **2,** to go on a pilgrimage.

peregrino (pe·re·ɣri'no) *adj.* **1,** migratory. **2,** singular; extraordinary. —*n.m.* pilgrim.

perejil (pe·re'xil) *n.m.* **1,** parsley. **2,** *colloq.* dressiness; garishness.

perenne (pe'ren·ne; pe're·ne) *adj.* **1,** perennial. **2,** evergreen.

perentorio (pe·ren'to·rjo) *adj.* peremptory.

pereza (pe're·θa; -sa) *n.f.* laziness; sloth.

perezca (pe're θ·ka; -'res·ka) *v., pres.subjve.* of **perecer**.

perezco (pe're θ·ko; -'res·ko) *v., 1st pers.sing. pres.ind.* of **perecer**.

perezoso (pe·re'θo·so; -'so·so) *adj.* lazy; slothful. —*n.m.* **1,** idler; lazybones. **2,** zoöl. sloth.

perfección (per·fek'θjon; -'sjon) *n.f.* **1,** perfection. **2,** perfect thing.

perfeccionar (per·fek·θjo'nar; -sjo'nar) *v.t.* to perfect. —**perfeccionamiento,** *n.m.* perfecting; perfection. —**perfeccionista,** *adj. & n.m. & f.* perfectionist.

perfecto (per'fek·to) *adj.* perfect.

perfidia (per'fi·ðja) *n.f.* perfidy. —**pérfido** ('per·fi·ðo) *adj.* perfidious. —*n.m.* traitor.

perfil (per'fil) *n.m.* **1,** profile; outline. **2,** cross section. —**perfiles,** *n.m.pl.* final touches.

perfilado (per·fi'la·ðo) *adj.* **1,** elongated (*of the face*). **2,** cleancut; well-shaped.

perfilar (per·fi'lar) *v.t.* **1,** to draw in profile; outline. **2,** to finish; pol-

ish. —**perfilarse,** *v.r.* **1,** to place oneself in profile. **2,** to emerge; begin to stand out. **3,** *colloq.* to preen oneself; primp.

perforación (per·fo·ra'θjon; -'sjon) *n.f.* perforation.

perforador (per·fo·ra'ðor) *adj.* perforating; boring; drilling. —*n.m.* [also, **perforadora,** *n.f.*] borer; perforator; driller.

perforar (per·fo'rar) *v.t.* to perforate; bore; drill.

perfume (per'fu·me) *n.m.* perfume. —**perfumador,** *n.m.* atomizer. —**perfumar,** *v.t.* to perfume.

perfumista (per·fu'mis·ta) *n.m. & f.,* also, **perfumero,** *n.m.* perfumer. —**perfumería,** *n.f.* perfumery.

perfunctorio (per·funk'to·rjo) *adj.* perfunctory.

pergamino (per·ɣa'mi·no) *n.m.* parchment.

pergeñar (per·xe'ɲar) *v.t.* to sketch; outline; frame. —**pergeño** (-'xe·ɲo) *n.m.* sketch.

pericardio (pe·ri'kar·ðjo) *n.m.* pericardium.

pericarpio (pe·ri'kar·pjo) *n.m.* pericarp.

pericia (pe'ri·θja; -sja) *n.f.* skill; expertness.

perico (pe'ri·ko) *n.m.* parakeet. —**Perico de los palotes,** John Doe.

periferia (pe·ri'fe·rja) *n.f.* periphery. —**periférico** (-'fe·ri·ko) *adj.* peripheral.

perifollos (pe·ri'fo·ʎos; -jos) *n.m.pl.* frippery.

perífrasis (pe'ri·fra·sis) *n.f.* periphrasis. —**perifrástico** (-'fras·ti·ko) *adj.* periphrastic.

perigeo (pe·ri'xe·o) *n.m.* perigee.

perihelio (pe·ri'e·ljo) *n.m.* perihelion.

perilla (pe'ri·ʎa; -ja) *n.f.* **1,** pear-shaped ornament. **2,** goatee. **3,** lobe of the ear. **4,** *Amer.* doorknob. —**de perilla** *or* **perillas,** most opportune or opportunely.

perillán (pe·ri'ʎan; -'jan) *n.m.* rascal; crafty person.

perímetro (pe'ri·me·tro) *n.m.* perimeter.

periódico (pe'rjo·ði·ko) *n.m.* **1,** newspaper. **2,** periodical. —*adj.* **1,** periodic. **2,** periodical.

periodismo (pe·rjo'ðis·mo) *n.m.* journalism. —**periodista,** *n.m. & f.* journalist. —**periodístico,** *adj.* journalistic.

período (pe'ri·o·ðo) *n.m.* **1,** period,

(of time). **2,** *rhet.; music; physics* period. **3,** *elect.* cycle. **4,** *colloq.* menses; menstrual period.

peripatético (pe·ri·pa'te·ti·ko) *adj. & n.m.* peripatetic. —*adj. colloq.* highfalutin; high-sounding; ridiculous.

peripecia (pe·ri'pe·θja; -sja) *n.f.* **1,** vicissitude. **2,** mischance; misadventure.

peripuesto (pe·ri'pwes·to) *adj., colloq.* dandified; foppish.

periquito (pe·ri'ki·to) *n.m.* parakeet.

periscopio (pe·ris'ko·pjo) *n.m.* periscope.

peristalsis (pe·ris'tal·sis) **perístole** ('ris·to·le) *n.f.sing. & pl.* peristalsis. —**peristáltico** (-ti·ko) *adj.* peristaltic.

peristilo (pe·ris'ti·lo) *n.m.* peristyle.

perito (pe'ri·to) *n.m. & adj.* expert.

peritoneo (pe·ri·to'ne·o) *n.m.* peritoneum. —**peritonitis,** *n.f.* peritonitis.

perjudicar (per·xu·ði'kar) *v.t.* [*infl.:* **tocar, 7**] to harm; impair; jeopardize.

perjudicial (per·xu·ði'θjal; -'sjal) *adj.* harmful; prejudicial.

perjuicio (per'xwi·θjo; -sjo) *n.m.* injury; damage. —**sin perjuicio de,** without affecting.

perjurar (per·xu'rar) *v.i.* **1,** to commit perjury. **2,** to swear; be profane. —**perjurarse,** *v.r.* to perjure oneself. —**jurar y perjurar,** to swear over and over.

perjurio (per'xu·rjo) *n.m.* perjury. —**perjuro** (-'xu·ro) *adj.* perjured. —*n.m.* perjurer.

perla ('per·la) *n.f.* pearl. —**de perlas,** *colloq.* just right; to a T.

perlado (per'la·ðo) *adj.* pearly; pearled.

perlesía (per·le'si·a) *n.f.* palsy.

permanecer (per·ma·ne'θer; -'ser) *v.i.* [*infl.:* **conocer, 13**] to stay; remain. —**permanencia** (-'nen·θja; -sja) *n.f.* **1,** stay; sojourn. **2,** permanence. —**permanente,** *adj. & n.f.* permanent.

permeable (per·me'a·βle) *adj.* permeable. —**permeabilidad,** *n.f.* permeability.

permisible (per·mi'si·βle) *adj.* permissible. —**permisión** (-'sjon) *n.f.* permission. —**permisivo** (-'si·βo) *adj.* permissive.

permiso (per'mi·so) *n.m.* **1,** permission. **2,** license; permit. —**con permiso,** excuse me. —**¿permiso?,** may I come in? —**permiso de conducir,** driver's license.

permitir (per·mi'tir) *v.t.* to allow; permit.

permuta (per'mu·ta) *n.f.* barter; exchange.

permutación (per·mu·ta'θjon; -'sjon) *n.f.* **1,** barter; exchange. **2,** permutation.

permutar (per·mu'tar) *v.t.* **1,** to barter; exchange. **2,** to permute. —**permutable,** *adj.* exchangeable.

pernada (per'na·ða) *n.f.* **1,** kick; blow with the leg. **2,** shake of the leg.

pernaza (per'na·θa; -sa) *n.f.* large or thick leg.

pernetas (per'ne·tas) *n.f.pl., in* **en pernetas,** barelegged.

pernicioso (per·ni'θjo·so; -'sjo·so) *adj.* pernicious. —**perniciosidad,** *n.f.* perniciousness.

pernil (per'nil) *n.m.* **1,** hock; ham *(of animals).* **2,** [*also,* **pernera** (-'ne·ra)] *n.f.* trouser leg.

perno ('per·no) *n.m.* **1,** bolt. **2,** pin; spike. **3,** hook of a door hinge. **4,** *mech.* joint pin; crank pin.

pernoctar (per·nok'tar) *v.i.* to spend the night.

pero ('pe·ro) *conj.* but; except that; yet. —*n.m., colloq.* fault; objection. —**no hay pero que valga,** *colloq.* no buts about it. —**poner peros,** *colloq.* to find fault; object.

perogrullada (pe·ro·yru'ʎa·ða; -'ja·ða) *n.f.* **1,** truism; platitude. **2,** nonsense; tomfoolery.

perol (pe'rol) *n.m.* kettle.

peroné (pe·ro'ne) *n.m., anat.* fibula.

perorar (pe·ro'rar) *v.i.* **1,** to orate. **2,** to discourse; hold forth. —**peroración,** *n.f.* peroration. —**perorata** (-'ra·ta) *n.f., colloq.* harangue; spiel.

peróxido (pe'rok·si·ðo) *n.m.* peroxide.

perpendicular (per·pen·di·ku'lar) *adj. & n.f.* perpendicular.

perpetrar (per·pe'trar) *v.t.* to perpetrate. —**perpetración,** *n.f.* perpetration. —**perpetrador,** *n.m.* [*fem.* -**dora**] perpetrator.

perpetua (per'pe·twa) *n.f., bot.* immortelle; everlasting.

perpetuar (per·pe'twar) *v.t.* [*infl.:* **continuar, 23**] to perpetuate. —**perpetuación,** *n.f.* perpetuation. —**perpetuidad,** *n.f.* perpetuity.

perpetuo (per'pe·two) *adj.* perpetual.

perplejo (per'ple·xo) *adj.* perplexed; puzzled. —**perplejidad**, *n.f.* perplexity; puzzlement.

perra ('pe·rra) *n.f.* 1, female dog; bitch. 2, *colloq.* tantrum. 3, *colloq.* drunken fit. —**perra chica**, Spanish coin of 5 céntimos. —**perra gorda**, *also,* **perro gordo**, Spanish coin of 10 céntimos.

perrada (pe'rra·ða) *n.f.* 1, pack of dogs. 2, *colloq.* dastardly deed.

perrera (pe'rre·ra) *n.f.* 1, kennel; doghouse. 2, dog catcher's wagon. 3, *colloq.* tantrum. 4, drudgery; thankless job.

perrero (pe'rre·ro) *n.m.* 1, kennel; doghouse. 2, dog catcher's wagon. 3, *colloq.* tantrum.

perrería (pe·rre'ri·a) *n.f.* 1, = **perrada**. 2, churlishness.

perrito (pe'rri·to) *also,* **perrillo**, *n.m.* 1, small dog. 2, puppy.

perro ('pe·rro) *n.m.* dog. —*adj.,* *colloq.* dastardly. —**perro braco**, pointer. —**perro de aguas**, spaniel. —**perro cobrador**, retriever. —**perro de lanas**, poodle. —**perro de presa**, bulldog. —**perro de Terranova**, Newfoundland dog. —**perro dogo**, bulldog. —**perro faldero**, lap dog. —**perro lobo**, wolfhound. —**perro ovejero**, sheepdog. —**perro sabueso**, bloodhound.

perruno (pe'rru·no) *adj.* 1, canine. 2, churlish.

persa ('per·sa) *adj. & n.m. & f.* Persian.

persecución (per·se·ku'θjon; -'sjon) *n.f.* 1, persecution. 2, pursuit. *Also,* **perseguimiento** (-ɣi'mjen·to) *n.m.*

perseguidor (per·se·ɣi'ðor) *n.m.* [*fem.* -**dora**] 1, pursuer. 2, persecutor. —**perseguidora**, *n.f., Amer., colloq.* hangover.

perseguir (per·se'ɣir) *v.t.* [*infl.:* **seguir**, 64] 1, to persecute. 2, to pursue.

perseverancia (per·se·βe'ran·θja; -sja) *n.f.* 1, perseverance. 2, persistence; continuance. —**perseverante**, *adj.* persevering.

perseverar (per·se·βe'rar) *v.i.* 1, to persevere. 2, to persist; continue.

persiana (per'sja·na) *n.f.* 1, shutter. 2, louver. 3, Venetian blind.

pérsico ('per·si·ko) *adj.* Persian. —*n.m.* 1, peach. 2, peach tree.

persiga (per'si·ɣa) *v., pres.subjve.* of **perseguir**.

persignarse (per·siɣ'nar·se) *v.r.* to cross oneself.

persigo (per'si·ɣo) *v., 1st pers.sing pres.ind.* of **perseguir**.

persiguiendo (per·si'ɣjen·do) *v., ger.* of **perseguir**.

persiguió (per·si'ɣjo) *v., 3rd pers.sing. pret.* of **perseguir**.

persistir (per·sis'tir) *v.i.* to persist. —**persistencia**, *n.f.* persistence. —**persistente**, *adj.* persistent.

persona (per'so·na) *n.f.* person.

personaje (per·so·na'xe) *n.m.* 1, personage. 2, character (*in a story, play, etc.*).

personal (per·so'nal) *adj.* personal. —*n.m.* personnel; staff.

personalidad (per·so·na·li'ðað) *n.f.* 1, personality. 2, *law* person. 3, legal capacity.

personalizar (per·so·na·li'θar; -'sar) *v.t. & i.* [*infl.:* **rezar**, 10] to personalize.

personería (per·so·ne'ri·a) *n.f.* 1, solicitorship. 2, legal capacity.

personero (per·so'ne·ro) *n.m.* solicitor; agent.

personificar (per·so·ni·fi'kar) *v.t.* [*infl.:* **tocar**, 7] to personify. —**personificación**, *n.f.* personification.

personilla (per·so'ni·ʎa; -ja) *n.f.* person of no importance; nonentity.

perspectiva (pers·pek'ti·βa) *n.f.* perspective.

perspicaz (pers·pi'kaθ; -'kas) *adj.* perspicacious. —**perspicacia** (-'ka·θja; -sja) *n.f.* perspicacity.

perspicuo (pers'pi·kwo) *adj.* perspicuous. —**perspicuidad**, *n.f.* perspicuity.

persuadir (per·swa'ðir) *v.t.* to persuade. —**persuadidor**, *adj.* persuading. —*n.m.* [*fem.* -**dora**] persuader.

persuasible (per·swa'si·βle) *adj.* persuasible; persuadable.

persuasión (per·swa'sjon) *n.f.* persuasion.

persuasivo (per·swa'si·βo) *adj.* persuasive. —**persuasiva**, *n.f.* persuasiveness.

pertenecer (per·te·ne'θer; -'ser) *v.i.* [*infl.:* **conocer**, 13] 1, to belong; appertain. 2, to pertain.

pertenencia (per·te'nen·θja; -sja) *n.f.* 1, ownership. 2, tenure; holding. 3, personal belonging; property.

4, appurtenance; accessory. **5,** *fig.* province; domain.

pértica ('per·ti·ka) *n.f.* perch *(land measure).* .

pértiga ('per·ti·ɣa) *n.f.* staff; pole; rod.

pertinaz (per·ti'naθ; -'nas) *adj.* pertinacious. —**pertinacia** (-'na·θja; -sja) *n.f.* pertinacity.

pertinente (per·ti'nen·te) *adj.* pertinent. —**pertinencia,** *n.f.* pertinence.

pertrechar (per·tre'tʃar) *v.t., mil.* to stock; equip; supply.

pertrechos (per'tre·tʃos) *n.m.pl., mil.* supplies; stores.

perturbar (per·tur'βar) *v.t.* to upset; perturb. —**perturbable,** *adj.* readily perturbed. —**perturbación,** *n.f.* upset; perturbation. —**perturbador,** *adj.* perturbing; disturbing.

peruano (pe'rwa·no) *adj. & n.m.* Peruvian. *Also,* **peruviano** (pe·ru·'βja·no).

perulero (pe·ru'le·ro) *adj. & n.m., hist.* **1,** Peruvian. **2,** one returning rich from Peru.

perversión (per·βer'sjon) *n.f.* perversion.

perverso (per'βer·so) *adj.* perverse. —**perversidad,** *n.f.* perversity.

pervertir (per·βer'tir) *v.t.* [*infl.:* **sentir,** 31] to pervert. —**pervertirse,** *v.r.* to become depraved.

pervinca (per'βin·ka) *n.f.* periwinkle *(plant).*

pesa ('pe·sa) *n.f.* **1,** weight *(used on scales).* **2,** clock weight. **3,** counterweight. **4,** dumbbell.

pesacartas (pe·sa'kar·tas) *n.m. sing. & pl.* letter scale.

pesada (pe'sa·ða) *n.f.* **1,** weighing. **2,** quantity weighed.

pesadez (pe·sa'ðeθ; -'ðes) *n.f.* **1,** heaviness; weight. **2,** impertinence; importunity. **3,** bother; unpleasantness.

pesadilla (pe·sa'ði·ʎa; -ja) *n.f.* nightmare.

pesado (pe'sa·ðo) *adj.* **1,** heavy. **2,** tedious; tiresome. **3,** annoying; importunate. —*n.m.* **1,** bore. **2,** tease.

pesadumbre (pe·sa'ðum·bre) *n.f.* sorrow; grief; affliction.

pésame ('pe·sa·me) *n.m.* condolence.

pesantez (pe·san'teθ; -'tes) *n.f.* heaviness; weight.

pesar (pe'sar) *v.t. & i.* to weigh. —*n.m.* sorrow; regret. —**a pesar**

de, in spite of; notwithstanding. —**pese a quien pese,** no matter who gets hurt; whether anybody likes it or not.

pesario (pe'sa·rjo) *n.m.* pessary.

pesaroso (pe·sa'ro·so) *adj.* sorrowful; regretful.

pesca ('pes·ka) *n.f.* **1,** fishing. **2,** catch *(of fish).*

pescada (pes'ka·ða) *n.f.* hake.

pescadería (pes·ka·ðe'ri·a) *n.f.* fish market. —**pescadero** (-'ðe·ro) *n.m.* fishmonger.

pescadilla (pes·ka'ði·ʎa; -ja) *n.f., ichthy.* whiting.

pescado (pes'ka·ðo) *n.m.* edible fish taken from the water.

pescador (pes·ka'ðor) *n.m.* **1,** fisherman. **2,** = **pejesapo.** —*adj.* fishing *(attrib.).*

pescante (pes'kan·te) *n.m.* **1,** davit. **2,** boom; jib; hoist. **3,** driver's seat.

pescar (pes'kar) *v.t. & i.* [*infl.:* **tocar,** 7] to fish. —*v.t., colloq.* **1,** to grab. **2,** to catch in the act.

pescozón (pes·ko'θon; -'son) *n.m.* slap on the head or neck. *Also,* **pescozada,** *n.f.*

pescozudo (pes·ko'θu·ðo; -'su·ðo) *adj.* thick-necked; bullnecked.

pescuezo (pes'kwe·θo; -so) *n.m.* **1,** neck *(of an animal).* **2,** *fig.* haughtiness.

pesebre (pe'se·βre) *n.m.* manger. —**pesebrera,** *n.f.* stable.

peseta (pe'se·ta) *n.f.* **1,** peseta; monetary unit of Spain. **2,** *Amer.* quarter; any coin of comparable size.

pesimismo (pe·si'mis·mo) *n.m.* pessimism. —**pesimista,** *n.m. & f.* pessimist. —*adj.* pessimistic.

pésimo ('pe·si·mo) *adj., superl.* of **mal,** extremely bad.

peso ('pe·so) *n.m.* **1,** weight. **2,** peso; monetary unit of several Spanish-American countries. **3,** *Amer., colloq.* dollar. —**caerse de su propio peso,** to be self-evident; go without saying. —**de peso,** of due weight; of importance. —**en peso, 1,** bodily. **2,** wholly; in toto. **3,** in the balance. —**peso bruto,** gross weight. —**peso duro,** *also,* **peso fuerte,** a silver coin weighing one ounce. —**peso liviano,** lightweight. —**peso medio,** middleweight. —**peso mosca,** flyweight. —**peso pesado,** heavyweight. —**peso semimedio,** welterweight.

pesque ('pes·ke) v., pres.subjve. of pescar.

pesqué (pes'ke) v., 1st pers.sing. pret. of pescar.

pesquera (pes'ke·ra) n.f. fishing grounds.

pesquería (pes·ke'ri·a) n.f. 1, fishing. 2, fishery. 3, = pesquera.

pesquero (pes'ke·ro) adj. fishing (attrib.).

pesquis ('pes·kis) n.m. acumen; cleverness.

pesquisa (pes'ki·sa) n.f. inquiry; investigation; search. —n.m., Amer. police investigator; plainclothesman.

pesquisar (pes·ki'sar) v.t. to investigate; inquire into. —pesquisidor (-si'ðor) n.m. [fem. -dora] inquirer; investigator. —adj. inquiring; investigating.

pestaña (pes'ta·ɲa) n.f. 1, eyelash. 2, sewing fag end; fringe; edging. 3, cilium. 4, flange.

pestañear (pes·ta·ɲe'ar) v.i. to blink. —pestañeo (-'ɲe·o) n.m. blinking.

peste ('pes·te) n.f. 1, pest; nuisance. 2, plague. 3, stench; foul smell. 4, colloq. swarm; lot; lots. 5, usu.pl. profanities; swearwords.

pesticida (pes·ti'θi·ða; -'si·ða) n.m. pesticide.

pestífero (pes'ti·fe·ro) adj. 1, pestiferous. 2, malodorous; stinking.

pestilencia (pes·ti'len·θja; -sja) n.f. 1, pestilence. 2, stench; foulness. —pestilencial, adj. = pestilente.

pestilente (pes·ti'len·te) adj. 1, pestilent. 2, malodorous.

pestillo (pes'ti·ʎo; -jo) n.m. door bolt; latch; bolt of a lock.

pesuña (pe'su·ɲa) n.f. = pezuña.

pesuño (pe'su·ɲo) n.m. each half of a cloven hoof.

petaca (pe'ta·ka) n.f. 1, cigar or cigarette case. 2, tobacco pouch. 3, Amer., colloq. piece of luggage; bag.

pétalo ('pe·ta·lo) n.m. petal.

petardo (pe'tar·ðo) n.m. 1, petard. 2, large firecracker. 3, fraud; swindle.

petate (pe'ta·te) n.m., Amer. 1, sleeping mat. 2, colloq. luggage; baggage. 3, colloq. worthless fellow. —liar el petate, colloq. 1, to pack up and go. 2, to die.

petición (pe·ti'θjon; -'sjon) n.f. petition. —peticionario, n.m. petitioner.

petimetre (pe·ti'me·tre) n.m. fop; beau; dude. —petimetra, n.f. clotheshorse.

petirrojo (pe·ti'rro·xo) n.m. redbreast.

petitorio (pe·ti'to·rjo) adj. petitionary. —n.m., colloq. impertinent petitioning. —petitoria, n.f., colloq. petition; petitioning.

peto ('pe·to) n.m. 1, breastplate. 2, dickey.

petrel (pe'trel) n.m. petrel.

pétreo ('pe·tre·o) adj. petrous.

petrificar (pe·tri·fi'kar) v.t. [infl.: tocar, 7] to petrify. —petrificación, n.f. petrification.

petrografía (pe·tro·yra'fi·a) n.f. petrography. —petrográfico (-'yra·fi·ko) adj. petrographic.

petróleo (pe'tro·le·o) n.m. petroleum; oil. —petróleo bruto or crudo, crude oil. —petróleo combustible, fuel oil.

petrolero (pe·tro'le·ro) adj. of or pertaining to petroleum; oil (attrib.). —n.m. 1, tanker. 2, Amer. oil man. 3, incendiary; saboteur (esp. one using kerosene, gasoline, etc.).

petrolífero (pe·tro'li·fe·ro) adj. oil-bearing; oil (attrib.).

petroquímica (pe·tro'ki·mi·ka) n.f. petrochemistry. —petroquímico, adj. petrochemical.

petroso (pe'tro·so) adj. 1, rocky; stony. 2, anat. petrous.

petulante (pe·tu'lan·te) adj. petulant. —petulancia, n.f. petulance.

petunia (pe'tu·nja) n.f. petunia.

peyorativo (pe·jo·ra'ti·βo) adj. pejorative.

pez (peθ; pes) n.m. fish. —n.f. pitch; tar. —pez blanca; pez griega, rosin.

pezón (pe'θon; -'son) n.m. 1, stem (of fruits). 2, stalk (of a leaf or flower). 3, nipple; teat.

pezuña (pe'θu·ɲa; pe'su-) n.f. 1, hoof; toe of animals. 2, Amer., colloq. foot odor.

pi (pi) n.f. pi (Greek letter; math.).

piache ('pja·tʃe) in tarde piache, colloq. too late.

piada (pi'a·ða) n.f. chirp; chirping. —piador, adj. chirping.

piadoso (pja'ðo·so) adj. 1, pious. 2, compassionate.

piafar (pja'far) v.i. to stamp (of horses).

pial (pjal) *n.m., S.A.* lasso.
—**pialar,** *v.t., S.A.* to lasso.
píamente (pi·a'men·te) *adv.* piously.
pianísimo (pja'ni·si·mo) *adj. & adv.* pianissimo.
pianista (pi·a'nis·ta) *n.m. & f.* pianist.
piano ('pja·no) *n.m.* piano. —*adv.* slowly; step by step. —*adj. & adv., mus.* piano. —**piano de cola,** grand piano. —**piano de media cola,** baby grand. —**piano vertical** *or* **recto,** upright piano.
pianoforte (pja·no'for·te) *n.m.* pianoforte.
pianola (pja'no·la) *n.f.* pianola.
piar (pi'ar) *v.i.* [*infl.:* **enviar, 22**] 1, to chirp; peep. 2, *colloq.* to plead; whine.
piara ('pja·ra) *n.f.* herd, esp. of swine.
piastra ('pjas·tra) *n.f.* piaster.
pibe ('pi·βe) *n.m., Arg.* kid; child.
pica ('pi·ka) *n.f.* 1, pike; lance. 2, bullfighter's goad. 3, stonecutter's hammer. 4, *colloq.* pique. —**poner una pica en Flandes,** to put a feather in one's cap.
picacho (pi'ka·tʃo) *n.m.* peak; mountaintop.
picada (pi'ka·ða) *n.f.* 1, sting; stinging; bite. 2, = **picotazo.** 3, *Amer.* trail; narrow pass. 4, dive; swoop. 5, *Amer.* jackrabbit start.
picadero (pi·ka'ðe·ro) *n.m.* 1, riding school. 2, boat skid; boat block.
picadillo (pi·ka'ði·ʎo; -jo) *n.m.* 1, minced meat. 2, hash.
picado (pi'ka·ðo) *adj.* 1, perforated; stippled. 2, minced; ground; diced. 3, *colloq.* piqued; irritated. 4, *colloq.* tipsy. 5, *mus.* staccato. —*n.m.* 1, minced meat; hash. 2, *aero.* dive; diving.
picador (pi·ka'ðor) *n.m.* 1, horsebreaker. 2, bullfighter armed with a goad; picador. 3, chopping block.
picadura (pi·ka'ðu·ra) *n.f.* 1, prick; pricking. 2, sting; bite. 3, cut tobacco. 4, cavity; decay in a tooth. 5, pinking.
picaflor (pi·ka'flor) *n.m.* 1, hummingbird. 2, *Amer., colloq.* fickle person; butterfly.
picamaderos (pi·ka·ma'ðe·ros) *n.m.sing. & pl.* woodpecker.
picana (pi'ka·na) *n.f., Amer.* goad.
—**picanear,** *v.t., Amer.* to goad.
picante (pi'kan·te) *adj.* 1, hot; piquant; highly seasoned. 2, risqué.

—*n.m.* 1, piquancy. 2, hot, spicy seasoning.
picapedrero (pi·ka·pe'ðre·ro) *n.m.* stonemason.
picapica (pi·ka'pi·ka) *n.f.* 1, itching powder. 2, *Amer.* any plant that causes itching.
picapleitos (pi·ka'plei·tos) *n.m. sing. & pl., colloq.* 1, = **pleitista.** 2, *Amer.* shyster; pettifogger. 3, ambulance chaser.
picaporte (pi·ka'por·te) *n.m.* 1, latch; spring lock. 2, *Amer.* slide bolt; door bolt.
picaposte (pi·ka'pos·te) *n.m.* woodpecker.
picar (pi'kar) *v.t.* [*infl.:* **tocar, 7**] 1, to prick; puncture. 2, to sting. 3, to bite (*said only of serpents, birds or insects*). 4, to bite (the bait). 5, to stipple. 6, to mince; chop. 7, to spur; goad. 8, to peck. 9, to strike, as with a pick. 10, *colloq.* to pique; vex. 11, to ring clearly. 12, *billiards* to strike (the ball) with english. —*v.i.* 1, to smart. 2, to itch. 3, to be hot or sharp to the taste; burn. 4, to strike; take the bait. 5, to dive; swoop. 6, *fig., fol. by* **en,** to border on; verge on. —**picarse,** *v.r.* 1, to become choppy (*as the sea*). 2, to become vexed; become annoyed. 3, to be motheaten. 4, to sour; spoil. 5, to boast. 6, *Amer.* to make a jackrabbit start. 7, *Amer.* to get tipsy. —**picar (muy) alto,** to aim (too) high.
picardía (pi·kar'ði·a) *n.f.* 1, mischievousness; impishness. 2, roguery.
picaresco (pi·ka'res·ko) *adj.* 1, picaresque. 2, mischievous; roguish.
pícaro ('pi·ka·ro) *adj.* 1, knavish; roguish. 2, mischievous. —*n.m.* rascal; knave; rogue.
picarón (pi·ka'ron) *n.m.* 1, rascal. 2, *Amer.* doughnut-shaped fritter; cruller.
picazo (pi'ka·θo; -so) *n.m.* 1, blow with a pickax or mattock. 2, insect bite.
picazón (pi·ka'θon; -'son) *n.f.* itch; itching.
picea (pi'θe·a; -'se·a) *also,* **pícea** ('pi-) *n.f.* spruce.
pico ('pi·ko) *n.m.* 1, beak. 2, pick; pickax; mattock. 3, pouring spout. 4, peak (*of a cap, mountain, etc.*). 5, *colloq.* mouth. 6, = **picamaderos.** —**andar de picos pardos,** *colloq.* to loaf; goof off. —**pico de**

oro, *colloq.* 1, gift of gab. 2, great talker. —**sobras y picos,** odds and ends. —**y pico,** and some; and some odd; and change; a little after *(in expressions of time).*

picofeo (pi·ko'fe·o) *n.m., Amer.* toucan.

picota (pi'ko·ta) *n.f.* 1, gallows. 2, pillory.

picotazo (pi·ko'ta·θo; -so) *n.m.* peck; blow with the beak. *Also,* **picotada,** *n.f.*

picotear (pi·ko·te'ar) *v.t.* to peck; nibble. —*v.i.* 1, to bob the head up and down *(as a horse).* 2, to chatter; prattle. —**picotearse,** *v.r.* to squabble *(said of women).*

pícrico ('pi·kri·ko) *adj.* picric.

pictografía (pik·to·γra'fi·a) *n.f.* pictograph.

pictórico (pik'to·ri·ko) *adj.* of or pert. to painting; pictorial.

picudo (pi'ku·ðo) *adj.* 1, beaked; having a long beak. 2, pointed. 3, *colloq.* garrulous. —*n.m.* spit; skewer.

pichel (pi'tʃel) *n.m.* tankard.

pichincha (pi'tʃin·tʃa) *n.f., Amer., colloq.* very good buy; bargain.

pichón (pi'tʃon) *n.m.* 1, squab; young pigeon. 2, *colloq.* darling; dove. 3, *colloq.* babe in the woods; novice. 4, *Amer.* nestling.

pida ('pi·ða) *v., pres.subjve.* of **pedir.**

pidiendo (pi'ðjen·do) *v., ger.* of **pedir.**

pidió (pi'ðjo) *v., 3rd pers.sing.pret.* of **pedir.**

pido ('pi·ðo) *v., 1st pers. sing. pres.ind.* of **pedir.**

pidón (pi'ðon) *adj., colloq.* = **pedigüeño.**

pie (pje) *n.m.* 1, foot. 2, footing; basis. 3, leg *(of a piece of furniture).* 4, stem *(of a glass).* —**al pie de la letra,** to the letter; literally. —**a pie,** on foot. —**a pie juntillas,** closely; rigidly. —**buscar tres pies al gato,** *colloq.* to go poking for trouble. —**de pie; de pies,** 1, up; out of bed. 2, standing. —**echar pie a tierra,** to dismount; alight. —**en pie = de pie.** —**no dar pie con bola,** *colloq.* to have everything go wrong with one. —**pie de grabado,** caption. —**poner pies en polvorosa,** *colloq.* to light out; take to one's heels.

piedad (pje'ðað) *n.f.* 1, piety. 2, mercy; pity.

piedra ('pje·ðra) *n.f.* stone. —**a piedra y lodo,** sealed; sealed up. —**piedra angular,** cornerstone. —**piedra de amolar,** whetstone. —**piedra de toque,** touchstone. —**piedra imán,** lodestone. —**piedra pómez,** pumice.

piel (pjel) *n.f.* 1, skin. 2, hide; pelt. 3, fur.

piélago ('pje·la·γo) *n.m., poet.* sea.

piense ('pjen·se) *v., pres.subjve.* of **pensar.**

pienso ('pjen·so) *v., 1st pers.sing. pres.ind.* of **pensar.** —*n.m.* feed; fodder. —**ni por pienso,** *colloq.* 1, not even in dreams. 2, not for anything.

pierda ('pjer·ða) *v., pres.subjve.* of **perder.**

pierdo ('pjer·ðo) *v., 1st pers.sing. pres.ind.* of **perder.**

pierna ('pjer·na) *n.f.* 1, *anat.* leg. 2, leg *(of a compass).* —**a pierna suelta,** in a carefree manner. —**dormir a pierna suelta,** to sleep soundly.

pieza ('pje·θa; -sa) *n.f.* 1, piece; part. 2, room *(of a house).* 3, bag; catch *(in hunting or fishing).* 4, bolt *(of cloth).* —**quedarse de una pieza,** to be stunned; be astonished.

pífano ('pi·fa·no) *n.m.* fife.

pifia ('pi·fja) *n.f.* 1, *billiards* miscue. 2, *Amer.* jeer; hiss; hoot.

pifiar (pi'fjar) *v.i.* 1, *billiards* to miscue. 2, *Amer.* to jeer; hiss; hoot.

pigmento (piγ'men·to) *n.m.* pigment. —**pigmentación,** *n.f.* pigmentation.

pigmeo (piγ'me·o) *adj. & n.m.* pygmy.

pijama (pi'xa·ma) *n.m.* pajama; pajamas.

pila ('pi·la) *n.f.* 1, basin; trough. 2, font, esp. baptismal font. 3, pile; heap. 4, pilaster; pile; pier. 5, dry cell battery.

pilar (pi'lar) *n.m.* 1, pillar. 2, pallbearer.

pilastra (pi'las·tra) *n.f.* pilaster.

pilcha ('pil·tʃa) *n.f., Amer., usu. pl.* 1, various typical country garments. 2, *colloq., derog.* clothes; clothing.

píldora ('pil·do·ra) *n.f.* pill.

pileta (pi'le·ta) *n.f.* 1, small font; bowl. 2, *S.A.* swimming pool.

pilón (pi'lon) *n.m.* 1, basin *(of a fountain).* 2, trough; water trough. 3, mortar *(bowl).* 4, pylon. 5, drop hammer. **6,** counterweight. **7,** sugar loaf.

píloro ('pi·lo·ro) *n.m.* pylorus. —**pilórico** (-'lo·ri·ko) *adj.* pyloric.

piloso (pi'lo·so) *adj.* pilose; downy; hairy.

pilotaje (pi·lo'ta·xe) *n.m.* **1,** pilotage. **2,** piles; piling.

pilotar (pi·lo'tar) *also,* **pilotear,** *v.t.* **1,** to pilot. **2,** *Amer.* to drive, esp. in racing.

pilote (pi'lo·te) *n.m.* pile *(support).*

piloto (pi'lo·to) *n.m.* **1,** pilot. **2,** *naut.* mate. **3,** *Amer.* driver, esp. racing driver.

piltrafa (pil'tra·fa) *n.f.* **1,** scum; riffraff. **2,** *Amer.* rag; tatter. **3,** *pl.* scraps; castoffs.

pillada (pi'ʎa·ða; -'ja·ða) *n.f.* **1,** rascality. **2,** *Amer., colloq.* a catching by surprise.

pillaje (pi'ʎa·xe; pi'ja-) *n.m.* pillage; plunder.

pillar (pi'ʎar; -'jar) *v.t.* **1,** to pillage; plunder. **2,** to catch; get. **3,** to grab. **4,** *colloq.* to surprise; catch by surprise.

pillastre (pi'ʎas·tre; -'jas·tre) *n.m.* = **pillo.**

pillería (pi·ʎe'ri·a; pi·je-) *n.f.* **1,** rascality. **2,** shrewdness. **3,** band of rogues.

pillo ('pi·ʎo; -jo) *adj.* **1,** roguish; rascally. **2,** shrewd. —*n.m.* rogue; rascal.

pilluelo (pi'ʎwe·lo; -'jwe·lo) *n.m.* gamin; street Arab.

pimentero (pi·men'te·ro) *n.m.* **1,** pepper bush. **2,** pepper shaker.

pimentón (pi·men'ton) *n.m.* **1,** pimento. **2,** ground red pepper. **3,** paprika.

pimienta (pi'mjen·ta) *n.f.* pepper. —**tener pimienta,** to be racy or risqué.

pimiento (pi'mjen·to) *n.m.* **1,** pimento. **2,** red pepper.

pimpollo (pim'po·ʎo; -jo) *n.m.* **1,** sapling. **2,** shoot; sprout; bud. **3,** rosebud. **4,** *fig.* pretty girl.

pinacoteca (pi·na·ko'te·ka) *n.f.* museum of paintings.

pináculo (pi'na·ku·lo) *n.m.* pinnacle.

pinado (pi'na·ðo) *adj.* = **pinnado.**

pinar (pi'nar) *n.m.* pine grove.

pincel (pin'θel; -'sel) *n.m.* **1,** brush; paintbrush. **2,** brushwork. —**pincelada,** *n.f.* brush stroke.

pincelar (pin·θe'lar; -se'lar) *v.t.* **1,** to paint. **2,** to portray.

pincha ('pin·tʃa) *n.f.* **1,** kitchen maid. **2,** = **pincho.**

pinchadura (pin·tʃa'ðu·ra) *n.f.* **1,** prick; pricking. **2,** puncture.

pinchar (pin'tʃar) *v.t.* **1,** to prick. **2,** to puncture. —**ni pinchar ni cortar,** *colloq.* to have nothing to do (with a matter).

pinchazo (pin'tʃa·θo; -so) *n.m.* **1,** prick; puncture. **2,** *fig.* goading; prodding.

pinche ('pin·tʃe) *n.m. & f.* kitchen helper; scullion.

pincho ('pin·tʃo) *n.m.* **1,** prickle; thorn. **2,** skewer.

pindonguear (pin·don·ge'ar) *v.i., colloq.* = **callejear.**

pineal (pi·ne'al) *adj.* pineal.

pingajo (pin'ga·xo) *n.m., colloq.* rag; tatter.

pingar (pin'gar) *v.i.* [*infl.:* **pagar,** 8] **1,** to drip. **2,** to jump; skip. —*v.t., colloq.* to incline.

pingo ('pin·go) *n.m., colloq.* = **pingajo.**

pingorotudo (pin·go·ro'tu·ðo) *adj., colloq.* highfalutin.

ping-pong *also,* **pinpón** (pin'pon) *n.m.* ping-pong.

pingüe ('pin·gwe) *adj.* substantial; fat; juicy.

pingüino (pin'gwi·no) *n.m.* penguin.

pinitos (pi'ni·tos) *n.m.pl.* child's first steps.

pinnado (pin'na·ðo; pi'na·ðo) *adj., bot.* pinnate.

pino ('pi·no) *n.m.* pine. —*adj.* steep.

pinocle (pi'no·kle) *n.m.* pinochle.

pinocha (pi'no·tʃa) *n.f.* pine needle.

pinoso (pi'no·so) *adj.* piny; abounding in pines.

pinta ('pin·ta) *n.f.* **1,** spot; mark. **2,** distinctive mark. **3,** *colloq.* appearance; looks. **4,** pint.

pintado (pin'ta·ðo) *adj.* **1,** colored; colorful. **2,** *Amer.* like; alike. —*adv.* fitly; just right. —**el más pintado,** *colloq.* the best; the bravest.

pintar (pin'tar) *v.t.* **1,** to paint. **2,** to portray; depict. —*v.i.* to color with ripening *(said of fruit).* —**pintarse,** *v.r.* to put on makeup. —**pintarla,** to play a part; cut a figure. —**pintarse para,** to be skilled in. —**¿Qué pintas tú aquí?,** *colloq.* What are you doing here?

pintarrajear (pin·ta·rra·xe'ar)

also, **pintarrajar** (-'xar) *v.t., colloq.* = **pintorrear.**

pintear (pin·te'ar) *v.i.* = **lloviznar.**

pintiparado (pin·ti·pa'ra·ðo) *adj.* **1,** just right; most suitable. **2,** exactly like; closely resembling.

pinto ('pin·to) *adj. & n.m.* pinto; piebald.

pintonear (pin·to·ne'ar) *v.i., Amer.* to begin to ripen; color with ripening.

pintor (pin'tor) *n.m.* painter *(artist and tradesman).* **—pintor de brocha gorda, 1,** painter *(tradesman).* **2,** dauber.

pintoresco (pin·to'res·ko) *adj.* picturesque; colorful.

pintorrear (pin·to·rre'ar) *v.t.* to daub; daub paint on. **—pintorrearse,** *v.r.* to daub makeup on.

pintura (pin'tu·ra) *n.f.* **1,** paint. **2,** painting. **3,** portrayal.

pinza ('pin·θa; -sa) *n.f.* **1,** clothespin. **2,** *sewing* dart. **3,** *pl.* pincers; pliers. **4,** *pl.* tweezers.

pinzón (pin'θon; -'son) *n.m.* finch.

piña ('pi·ɲa) *n.f.* **1,** pine cone. **2,** pineapple. **3,** *colloq.* crowd. **4,** *Amer., colloq.* = **puñetazo.**

piñata (pi'ɲa·ta) *n.f.* **1,** pot. **2,** pot filled with party goodies; piñata.

piñón (pi'ɲon) *n.m.* **1,** pine seed. **2,** pinion.

pío ('pi·o) *adj.* pious. **—n.m. 1,** peep; chirp. **2,** *colloq.* yen; craving.

piojo ('pjo·xo) *n.m.* louse. **—piojento,** *adj.* lousy. **—piojería,** *n.f.* lousiness.

piojoso (pjo'xo·so) *adj.* **1,** lousy. **2,** *colloq.* mean; stingy.

pión (pi'on) *adj.* **1,** chirping; tweeting. **2,** *colloq.* demanding; exigent.

pionero (pi·o'ne·ro) *n.m.* pioneer.

piorrea (pjo'rre·a) *n.f.* pyorrhea.

pipa ('pi·pa) *n.f.* **1,** cask; butt. **2,** smoking pipe. **3,** reed pipe. **4,** *Amer., colloq.* belly; paunch. **5,** seed; pip.

pipeta (pi'pe·ta) *n.f.* pipette.

pipí (pi'pi) *n.m., colloq.* urine. **—hacer pipí,** *colloq.* to urinate.

pipiar (pi'pjar) *v.i.* [*infl.:* enviar, 22] to chirp; peep.

pipiolo (pi'pjo·lo) *n.m., colloq.* **1,** beginner; greenhorn. **2,** pipsqueak.

pique ('pi·ke) *n.m.* **1,** pique. **2,** chigger. **3,** *Amer., colloq.* pickup; acceleration. **—a pique de,** close to; on the verge of. **—echar a pique,** to sink; send to the bottom.

—irse a pique, to sink; go to the bottom.

pique ('pi·ke) *v., pres.subjve. of* **picar.**

piqué (pi'ke) *v., 1st pers.sing. pret. of* **picar.** **—n.m.** piqué.

piqueta (pi'ke·ta) *n.f.* pickax; mattock.

piquete (pi'ke·te) *n.m.* **1,** jab; prick. **2,** picket.

pira ('pi·ra) *n.f.* pyre.

piragua (pi'ra·ɣwa) *n.f.* pirogue.

piramidal (pi·ra·mi'ðal) *adj.* **1,** pyramidal. **2,** colossal.

pirámide (pi'ra·mi·ðe) *n.f.* pyramid.

piraña (pi'ra·ɲa) *n.f.* piranha.

pirata (pi'ra·ta) *adj.* **1,** pirate *(attrib.).* **2,** pirated. **—n.m. & f.** pirate. **—piratear** (-te'ar) *v.i.* to practice piracy. **—piratería** (-te'ri·a) *n.f.* piracy. **—pirático** (-'ra·ti·ko) *adj.* piratical.

pirita (pi'ri·ta) *n.f.* **1,** pyrite. **2,** pyrites.

piromanía (pi·ro·ma'ni·a) *n.f.* pyromania. **—pirómano** (-'ro·ma·no) *also,* **piromaníaco** (-ma'ni·a·ko) *n.m.* pyromaniac.

piropo (pi'ro·po) *n.m., colloq.* compliment; gallantry. **—piropear,** *v.t.* to flatter; compliment.

pirotecnia (pi·ro'tek·nja) *n.f.* pyrotechnics. **—pirotécnico** (-'tek·ni·ko) *adj.* pyrotechnic. **—n.m.** maker or seller of fireworks.

pirrarse (pi'rrar·se) *v.r., colloq., fol. by* **por,** to die for; pine for.

pírrico ('pi·rri·ko) *adj.* pyrrhic.

pirueta (pi'rwe·ta) *n.f.* **1,** pirouette. **2,** prank; caper. **—piruetear** (-te'ar) *v.i.* to pirouette.

pirulí (pi·ru'li) *n.m.* sucker; lollipop.

pisa ('pi·sa) *n.f.* **1,** pressing *(of grapes, olives, etc.).* **2,** *colloq.* beating; kicking.

pisada (pi'sa·ða) *n.f.* **1,** step; footstep. **2,** footprint. **3,** stepping on the foot.

pisadura (pi·sa'ðu·ra) *n.f.* = **pisada.**

pisapapeles (pi·sa·pa'pe·les) *n.m. sing. & pl.* paperweight.

pisar (pi'sar) *v.t.* **1,** to step on; tread on. **2,** to crush; stamp. **3,** to overlap. **4,** to cover *(said of birds).* **5,** *colloq.* to steal (an idea, plan, etc.). **—pisarse,** *v.r., Amer., colloq.* to be fooled; be deceived.

pisaverde (pi·sa'βer·ðe) *n.m.,*

colloq. fop; beau. —*n.f., colloq.* clotheshorse.

piscatorio (pis·ka'to·rjo) *adj.* piscatorial.

piscicultura (pis·θi·kul'tu·ra; pi·si-) *n.f.* pisciculture.

piscina (pis'θi·na; pi'si-) *n.f.* pool; swimming pool.

Piscis ('pis·θis; 'pi·sis) *n.m.* Pisces.

piscolabis (pis·ko'la·βis) *n.m. sing. & pl., colloq.* light snack; tidbit.

piso ('pi·so) *n.m.* **1**, floor. **2**, ground. **3**, pavement. **4**, story *(of a building).* **5**, apartment; flat.

pisón (pi'son) *n.m.* tamper; rammer.

pisonear (pi·so·ne'ar) *v.t.* = apisonar.

pisotear (pi·so·te'ar) *v.t.* to step on; stamp on; trample. —**pisoteo** (-'te·o) *n.m.* trampling.

pisotón (pi·so'ton) *n.m.* stepping on the foot.

pista ('pis·ta) *n.f.* **1**, track; course. **2**, trace; trail. **3**, clue; hint.

pistacho (pis'ta·tʃo) *n.m.* pistachio.

pistilo (pis'ti·lo) *n.m.* pistil.

pisto ('pis·to) *n.m.* **1**, meat juice; broth. **2**, *Amer., colloq.* money; dough. **3**, a diced vegetable dish. —**darse pisto**, to put on airs.

pistola (pis'to·la) *n.f.* **1**, pistol. **2**, spray gun; sprayer.

pistolera (pis·to'le·ra) *n.f.* gun holster.

pistolero (pis·to'le·ro) *n.m.* gunman; armed bandit.

pistoletazo (pis·to·le'ta·θo; -so) *n.f.* gunshot; gun wound.

pistón (pis'ton) *n.m.* **1**, piston. **2**, primer *(of a shell).*

pita ('pi·ta) *n.f.* **1**, American agave; pita. **2**, *Amer.* string; cord. **3**, *colloq.* chicken. —**enredar la pita**, *Amer., colloq.* to foul up the works.

pitada (pi'ta·ða) *n.f.* whistle; whistling.

pitagórico (pi·ta'ɣo·ri·ko) *adj.* Pythagorean.

pitanza (pi'tan·θa; -sa) *n.f.* **1**, quota; ration; allowance. **2**, food allowance; ration. **3**, *colloq.* daily food consumption.

pitar (pi'tar) *v.i.* **1**, to whistle; blow a whistle. **2**, *Amer., colloq.* to smoke a cigarette. —*v.t., colloq.* to whistle or hoot (a performer) off the stage.

pitecántropo (pi·te'kan·tro·po) *n.m.* pithecanthropus.

pitido (pi'ti·ðo) *n.m.* whistle; hoot.

pitillo (pi'ti·ʎo; -jo) *n.m.* cigarette. —**pitillera**, *n.f.* cigarette case.

pito ('pi·to) *n.m.* **1**, whistle *(instrument).* **2**, *Amer., colloq.* fag; cigarette. —**no dársele** *or* **importársele a uno un pito**, *colloq.* not to give a hoot. —**no tocar pito**, *colloq.* to be out of place; not belong. —**pitos y flautas**, *colloq.* nonsense.

pitón (pi'ton) *n.m.* **1**, beginnings of a horn *(in an animal).* **2**, small hornlike protuberance. **3**, nozzle; spout. **4**, python.

pituitario (pi·twi'ta·rjo) *adj.* pituitary.

pituso (pi'tu·so) *adj.* cute; darling *(usu. said of children).*

pivote (pi'βo·te) *n.m.* pivot.

piyama (pi'ja·ma) *n.m.* = pijama.

pizarra (pi'θa·rra; pi'sa-) *n.f.* **1**, shale. **2**, slate. **3**, blackboard. —**pizarroso**, *adj.* slaty.

pizarrón (pi·θa'rron; pi·sa-) *n.m., Amer.* blackboard.

pizca ('piθ·ka; 'pis-) *n.f. colloq.* **1**, bit. **2**, dash; pinch *(of seasonings).* **3**, jot; iota.

pizpireta (piθ·pi're·ta; pis-) *adj. fem., colloq.* vivacious.

placa ('pla·ka) *n.f.* **1**, badge. **2**, plaque; plate. **3**, *photog.* plate. **4**, film; coating. **5**, shingle *(of a professional person).* **6**, *elect.; comput.* chip; board.

placaminero (pla·ka·mi'ne·ro) *n.m.* persimmon.

placativo (pla·ka'ti·βo) *adj.* placatory.

pláceme ('pla·θe·me; 'pla·se-) *n.m., usu.pl.* congratulation.

placenta (pla'θen·ta; pla'sen-) *n.f.* placenta. —**placentario**, *adj. & n.m.* placental.

placentero (pla·θen'te·ro; pla·sen-) *adj.* pleasant.

placer (pla'θer; -'ser) *v.t.* [*infl.:* 52] to please; gratify; content. —*n.m.* pleasure. —**a placer**, at one's convenience. —**que me place**, it gives me pleasure.

placero (pla'θe·ro; -'se·ro) *n.m.* **1**, dealer or seller in the marketplace. **2**, gadabout; idle fellow.

plácido ('pla·θi·ðo; 'pla·si-) *adj.* placid. —**placidez**, *n.f.* placidity.

plaga ('pla·ɣa) *n.f.* **1**, plague. **2**, *fig.* swarm; crowd.

plagar (pla'ɣar) *v.t.* [*infl.:* pagar, 8] to plague; infest. —**plagarse**, *v.r.*

usu.fol. by **de,** to be infested with; be full of; swarm with.

plagiar (pla'xjar) *v.t.* **1,** to plagiarize. **2,** *Amer.* to kidnap.

plagiario (pla'xja·rjo) *n.m.* **1,** plagiarist. **2,** *Amer.* kidnapper.

plagio ('pla·xjo) *n.m.* **1,** plagiarism. **2,** *Amer.* kidnapping.

plan (plan) *n.m.* plan. —**plan de estudios,** curriculum.

plana ('pla·na) *n.f.* **1,** page; side *(of a sheet).* **2,** flat; flatland. **3,** record; docket. —**enmendar la plana a uno,** *colloq.* **1,** to show someone up. **2,** to patch things up with someone. —**plana mayor,** *mil.* staff.

plancton *also,* **plankton** ('plankton) *n.m.* plankton.

plancha ('plan·tʃa) *n.f.* **1,** plate; metal plate. **2,** plank; gangplank. **3,** iron; flatiron. **4,** *print.* plate. **5,** *colloq.* ridiculous mistake; boner; howler.

planchada (plan'tʃa·ða) *n.f.* gangplank.

planchado (plan'tʃa·ðo) *n.m.* **1,** ironing; pressing. **2,** items ironed or ready for pressing. —*adj.* **1,** *Amer., colloq.* penniless; broke. **2,** *Mex.* courageous; forthright.

planchadora (plan·tʃa'ðo·ra) *n.f.* **1,** pressing machine; mangle. **2,** ironer; presser; ironing woman.

planchar (plan'tʃar) *v.t.* to iron; press. —**planchador,** *n.m.* presser.

planchear (plan·tʃe'ar) *v.t.* to plate; cover with metal sheets.

planeador (pla·ne·a'ðor) *n.m., aero.* glider.

planear (pla·ne'ar) *v.t. & i.* to plan. —*v.i.* to glide. —**planeación,** *n.f.;* **planeamiento,** *n.m.* planning. —**planeo** (-'ne·o) *n.m.* gliding; glide.

planeta (pla'ne·ta) *n.m.* planet.

planetario (pla·ne'ta·rjo) *adj.* planetary. —*n.m.* planetarium.

planetoide (pla·ne'toi·ðe) *n.m.* planetoid.

planicie (pla'ni·θje; -sje) *n.f.* plain; flat terrain.

planificar (pla·ni·fi'kar) *v.t.* [*infl.:* **tocar, 7**] to plan. —**planificación,** *n.f.* planning.

planilla (pla'ni·ʎa; -ja) *n.f., Amer.* **1,** roll; list. **2,** blank form.

plano ('pla·no) *adj.* **1,** plane; flat. **2,** level; smooth; even. —*n.m.* **1,** plan; blueprint. **2,** map. **3,** *geom.* plane. **4,** flat; flat part. —**de plano,** flatly; plainly. —**primer plano, 1,**

foreground. **2,** forefront. **3,** *photog.* close-up.

planta ('plan·ta) *n.f.* **1,** plant. **2,** sole *(of the foot).* **3,** *engin.* plan; top view. **4,** *archit.* floor plan. **5,** position; stance; attitude. **6,** disposition. —**buena planta,** good looks; handsome appearance. —**planta baja,** ground floor.

plantación (plan·ta'θjon; -'sjon) *n.f.* **1,** plantation. **2,** planting.

plantador (plan·ta'ðor) *n.m.* [*fem.* -**dora**] planter.

plantaina (plan'tai·na) *n.f.* plantain *(weed).*

plantar (plan'tar) *v.t.* **1,** to plant. **2,** to strike; land (a blow). **3,** to leave in the lurch; stand up. —**plantarse,** *v.r.* **1,** to stand pat. **2,** to balk; refuse to move. **3,** *colloq.* to dash; get to a place quickly. **4,** *colloq.* to post oneself; set oneself. —**dejar plantado,** to leave in the lurch; stand up.

planteamiento (plan·te·a'mjen·to) *n.m.* **1,** a stating; setting forth. **2,** framing; outline. **3,** setting up; establishment. **4,** posing *(of a question or problem). Also,* **planteo** (-'te·o).

plantear (plan·te'ar) *v.t.* **1,** to state; set forth. **2,** to frame; outline. **3,** to set up; establish. **4,** to pose (a question or problem).

plantel (plan'tel) *n.m.* center *(of education or training).*

plantificar (plan·ti·fi'kar) *v.t.* [*infl.:* **tocar, 7**] **1,** to set up; establish. **2,** *colloq.* to strike; land (a blow). **3,** *colloq.* to put; place; plant. —**plantificarse,** *v.r.* **1,** *colloq.* to dash; get to a place quickly. **2,** *W.I., colloq.* to spruce up.

plantilla (plan'ti·ʎa; -ja) *n.f.* **1,** insole. **2,** templet. **3,** table of organization.

plantillar (plan·ti'ʎar; -'jar) *v.t.* to sole (shoes).

plantío (plan'ti·o) *n.m.* **1,** plantation. **2,** vegetable field. **3,** planting.

plantón (plan'ton) *n.m.* **1,** seedling; slip. **2,** *colloq.* long wait.

planudo (pla'nu·ðo) *adj.* flatbottomed.

plañir (pla'ɲir) *v.i.* [*infl.:* **gruñir, 21**] to make a plaintive sound; wail; moan. —**plañido,** *n.m.* plaint; wail; moan. —**plañidero,** *adj.* plaintive.

plaqué (pla'ke) *n.m.* **1,** plate; plating. **2,** plated ware.

plaqueta (pla'ke·ta) *n.f.* **1,** small

plaque; brooch. **2**, platelet. **3**, *elect.; comput.* chip.

plasma ('plas·ma) *n.m.* plasma.

plasmar (plas'mar) *v.t.* to mold; shape; give shape to.

plasta ('plas·ta) *n.f.* **1**, mush; soft mass. **2**, something flat, as a pancake. **3**, *colloq.* mess; poor job.

plástica ('plas·ti·ka) *n.f.* plastic arts.

plástico ('plas·ti·ko) *adj. & n.m.* plastic. —**plasticidad** (-θi'ðað; -si'ðað) *n.f.* plasticity.

plata ('pla·ta) *n.f.* **1**, silver. **2**, money. **3**, silver coin. —**en plata**, briefly; in substance.

plataforma (pla·ta'for·ma) *n.f.* platform.

platal (pla'tal) *n.m.* great wealth; great quantity of money.

platanal (pla·ta'nal) *n.m.* banana plantation. *Also,* **platanar** (-'nar).

platanero (pla·ta'ne·ro) *n.m.* banana tree. —*adj., W.I.* of hurricane strength.

plátano ('pla·ta·no) *n.m.* **1**, banana; plantain. **2**, banana tree; plantain tree. **3**, plane tree.

platazo (pla'ta·θo; -so) *n.m.* **1**, large dish. **2**, dishful; plateful. **3**, blow with a dish or plate.

platea (pla'te·a) *n.f., theat.* orchestra circle; parterre.

platear (pla·te'ar) *v.t.* to silver. —**plateado**, *adj.* silver *(attrib.)*; silvered; silverplated. —**plateadura**, *n.f.* silvering; silver plating.

platero (pla'te·ro) *n.m.* silversmith. —**platería**, *n.f.* silversmith's shop or trade.

plática ('pla·ti·ka) *n.f.* **1**, talk; chat; conversation. **2**, brief or informal lecture or sermon.

platicar (pla·ti'kar) *v.i.* [*infl.:* **tocar, 7**] to chat; converse; talk informally.

platija (pla'ti·xa) *n.f.* plaice.

platillo (pla'ti·ʎo; -jo) *n.m.* **1**, small dish; saucer. **2**, pan *(of a balance)*. **3**, cymbal. —**platillo volador**, flying saucer.

platina (pla'ti·na) *n.f.* **1**, table of a microscope. **2**, = **platino**. **3**, platen.

platinado (pla·ti'na·ðo) *adj.* **1**, platinum plated. **2**, platinum *(attrib.)*. —*n.m.* platinum plating.

platinar (pla·ti'nar) *v.t.* **1**, to plate with platinum. **2**, to give a platinum sheen to.

platino (pla'ti·no) *n.m.* platinum.

platique (pla'ti·ke) *v., pres.subjve. of* **platicar**.

platiqué (-'ke) *v., 1st pers.sing. pret. of* **platicar**.

plato ('pla·to) *n.m.* **1**, dish; plate. **2**, plateful. **3**, pan *(of a balance)*. **4**, turntable *(of a phonograph)*. —**plato volador**, flying saucer. —**ser un plato**, *Amer., colloq.* to be a riot; be funny; be a card.

platónico (pla'to·ni·ko) *adj.* platonic.

platudo (pla'tu·ðo) *adj., Amer., colloq.* rich; loaded with money.

plausible (plau'si·βle) *adj.* plausible. —**plausibilidad**, *n.f.* plausibility.

playa ('pla·ja) *n.f.* beach; shore.

plaza ('pla·θa; -sa) *n.f.* **1**, plaza; square. **2**, local market; marketplace. **3**, position; opening; place. **4**, *mil.* fortified place. —**plaza de toros**, bullring. —**plaza fuerte**, stronghold; fortress. —**¡plaza, plaza!**, clear the way!; make room! —**sacar a plaza**, to publish; make public. —**sentar plaza**, *mil.* to enlist.

plazca ('plaθ·ka; 'plas-) *v., pres. subjve. of* **placer**. *Also,* **plazga** (-ɣa).

plazco ('plaθ·ko; 'plas-) *v., 1st pers.sing.pres.ind. of* **placer**. *Also,* **plazgo** (-ɣo).

plazo ('pla·θo; -so) *n.m.* **1**, term; period of time. **2**, installment. —**a corto plazo**, **1**, soon. **2**, short-term. —**a largo plazo**, long-term; long-range.

plazoleta (pla·θo'le·ta; pla·so-) *n.f.* small plaza or square. *Also,* **plazuela** (-'θwe·la; -'swe·la).

pleamar (ple·a'mar) *n.f.* high water; high tide.

plebe ('ple·βe) *n.f.* common people; populace. —**plebeyo** (-'βe·jo) *adj. & n.m.* plebeian.

plebiscito (ple·βis'θi·to; -βi'si·to) *n.m.* plebiscite.

plectro ('plek·tro) *n.m.* **1**, plectrum. **2**, *fig.* poetic inspiration; muse.

plega ('ple·ɣa) *v., 3rd pers.sing. pres.subjve. of* **placer**.

plegable (ple'ɣa·βle) *also,* **plegadizo** (-'ði·θo; -'ði·so) *adj.* folding; that can fold or be folded.

plegado (ple'ɣa·ðo) *n.m.* **1**, plait; plaiting. **2**, fold; folding. **3**, pleated.

plegadura (ple·ɣa'ðu·ra) *n.f.* **1**, plait; pleat. **2**, fold; crease.

plegar (ple'ɣar) *v.t.* [*infl.:* **pagar, 8**;

pensar, 27] 1, to fold. **2,** to pleat; plait. —**plegarse,** *v.r.* **1,** to fold up; give in; submit. **2,** to adhere; give one's support.

plegaria (ple'ɣa·rja) *n.f.* prayer; supplication.

plegue ('ple·ɣe) *v., pres.subjve. of* **placer.**

plegué (ple'ɣe) *v., 1st pers.sing. pret. of* **plegar.**

pleistoceno (pleis·to'θe·no; -'se·no) *n.m. & adj.* Pleistocene.

pleiteador (plei·te·a'ðor) *n.m.* [*fem.* **-dora**] **1,** [*also,* **pleiteante**] litigant; pleader. **2,** squabbler.

pleitear (plei·te'ar) *v.t.* to take to court; fight in court.

pleitesía (plei·te'si·a) *n.f.* homage; tribute.

pleitista (plei'tis·ta) *adj.* squabbling; quarrelsome. —*n.m. & f.* wrangler; squabbler.

pleito ('plei·to) *n.m.* **1,** lawsuit; litigation. **2,** dispute; wrangle; quarrel. —**conocer de un pleito,** to pass judgment on a lawsuit. —**contestar el pleito,** to fight the case. —**salir con el pleito,** to win the case. —**pleito homenaje,** due homage.

plenamar (ple·na'mar) *n.f.* = **pleamar.**

plenario (ple'na·rjo) *adj.* plenary.

plenilunio (ple·ni'lu·njo) *n.m.* full moon.

plenipotenciario (ple·ni·po·ten'θja·rjo; -'sja·rjo) *adj. & n.m.* plenipotentiary.

plenitud (ple·ni'tuð) *n.f.* plenitude.

pleno ('ple·no) *adj.* full; complete. —*n.m.* plenary session. —**en pleno,** in the middle of; smack on center. —**a** *or* **en pleno día,** in broad daylight.

pleonasmo (ple·o'nas·mo) *n.m.* pleonasm; redundancy. —**pleonástico** (-'nas·ti·ko) *adj.* pleonastic; redundant.

plétora ('ple·to·ra) *n.f.* plethora. —**pletórico** (-'to·ri·ko) *adj.* plethoric.

pleura ('pleu·ra) *n.f.* pleura. —**pleural,** *adj.* pleural.

pleuresía (pleu·re'si·a) *n.f.* pleurisy. —**pleurítico** (-'ri·ti·ko) *adj.* pleuritic.

plexo ('plek·so) *n.m.* plexus.

Pléyades ('ple·ja·ðes) *n.f.pl.* Pleiades. *Also,* **Pléyadas** (-ðas).

plica ('pli·ka) *n.f.* escrow.

pliego ('plje·ɣo) *n.m.* **1,** sheet of paper. **2,** dossier. **3,** legal sheet. —**pliego de cargos,** bill of particulars. *v., 1st pers.sing. pres.ind. of* **plegar.**

pliegue ('plje·ɣe) *n.m.* **1,** fold; crease. **2,** pleat; plait.

pliegue ('plje·ɣe) *v., pres.subjve. of* **plegar.**

plioceno (pli·o'θe·no; -'se·no) *adj. & n.m.* Pliocene.

plisar (pli'sar) *v.t.* to pleat; plait. —**plisado,** *adj.* plaited. —*n.m.* plait; pleat.

plomada (plo'ma·ða) *n.f.* **1,** plumb; plumb bob. **2,** *naut.* lead; sounding lead. **3,** *fishing* sinker.

plomazo (plo'ma·θo; -so) *n.m.* **1,** gunshot. **2,** gunshot wound.

plomería (plo·me'ri·a) *n.f.* **1,** lead sheeting. **2,** *Amer.* plumbing.

plomero (plo'me·ro) *n.m.* **1,** worker in lead. **2,** *Amer.* plumber.

plomizo (plo'mi·θo; -so) *adj.* leaden; gray.

plomo ('plo·mo) *n.m.* **1,** lead (*metal*). **2,** plumb bob. **3,** *colloq.* bullet. **4,** *colloq.* bore; dullard. —**andar con pies de plomo,** to proceed with great caution. —**a plomo,** true; plumb. —**caer a plomo,** to fall down; fall flat. —**caer como plomo,** *colloq.* to be a pain in the neck.

plugo ('plu·ɣo) *v., 3rd pers.sing. pret. of* **placer.**

pluguiera (plu'ɣje·ra) *v., impf. subjve. of* **placer.**

pluma ('plu·ma) *n.f.* **1,** feather; plume. **2,** writing pen. **3,** nib; pen point. —**pluma estilográfica; pluma fuente,** fountain pen.

plumada (plu'ma·ða) *n.f.* **1,** pen stroke. **2,** *fig.* flourish. **3,** brief writing.

plumado (plu'ma·ðo) *adj.* feathered; feathery.

plumaje (plu'ma·xe) *n.m.* plumage.

plumero (plu'me·ro) *n.m.* **1,** feather duster. **2,** *Amer.* penholder.

plumista (plu'mis·ta) *n.m. & f.* scrivener.

plumón (plu'mon) *n.m.* **1,** down. **2,** down quilt. **3,** plume.

plumoso (plu'mo·so) *adj.* feathery.

plural (plu'ral) *adj. & n.m.* plural.

pluralidad (plu·ra·li'ðað) *n.f.* plurality.

pluralizar (plu·ra·li'θar; -'sar) *v.t.*

[*infl.:* **rezar, 10**] to make plural; pluralize.

plus (plus) *n.m.* plus; extra.

pluscuamperfecto (plus·kwam·per'fek·to) *adj. & n.m.* pluperfect.

plusvalía (plus·βa'li·a) *n.f.* increased value or valuation.

plutocracia (plu·to'kra·θja; -sja) *n.f.* plutocracy. —**plutócrata** (-'to·kra·ta) *n.m. & f.* plutocrat. —**plutocrático** (-'kra·ti·ko) *adj.* plutocratic.

Plutón (plu'ton) *n.m., myth.; astron.* Pluto.

plutonio (plu'to·njo) *n.m.* plutonium.

pluvial (plu'βjal) *adj.* pluvial; rain (*attrib.*).

pobeda (po'βe·ða) *n.f.* poplar grove.

población (po·βla'θjon; -'sjon) *n.f.* 1, population. 2, city; town; village.

poblacho (po'βla·tʃo) *n.m.* poor village or hamlet.

poblado (po'βla·ðo) *adj.* populated; inhabited. —*n.m.* town; settlement.

poblador (po·βla'ðor) *n.m.* [*fem.* -**dora**] settler.

poblar (po'βlar) *v.t.* [*infl.:* **acostar, 28**] 1, to populate; people. 2, to settle; colonize. 3, to plant; stock. —*v.i.* to increase; multiply. —**poblarse**, *v.r.* 1, to bud; leaf. 2, to be covered (with); be overrun (with); teem (with).

pobre ('po·βre) *adj.* poor. —*n.m. & f.* pauper; poor person.

pobrete (po'βre·te) *adj.* poor; wretched. —*n.m.* poor fellow; poor wretch.

pobreza (po'βre·θa; -sa) *n.f.* 1, poverty. 2, paucity; dearth. 3, meanness; pettiness.

pocilga (po'θil·ɣa; po'sil-) *n.f.* pigsty; pigpen.

pocillo (po'θi·ʎo; -'si·jo) *n.m.* 1, well; container. 2, bowl; mug.

pócima ('po·θi·ma; 'po·si-) *n.f.* potion; draught.

poción (po'θjon; -'sjon) *n.f.* potion.

poco ('po·ko) *adj.* 1, little; not much. 2, *pl.* few; not many —*adv. & n.m.* little. —**pocos**, *n.m. & pron.pl.* few. —**a poco**, shortly; soon; *Mex.* really? you're kidding. —**a poco de**, shortly after. —**poco a poco**, 1, little by little. 2, slow; easy. —**por poco**, 1, by a hair. 2, almost. —**tener en poco**, to think little of; hold in low esteem.

poda ('po·ða) *n.f.* 1, pruning. 2,

pruning season. —**podar**, *v.t.* to prune.

podadera (po·ða'ðe·ra) *n.f.* pruning hook; pruning knife.

podenco (po'ðen·ko) *n.m.* hound.

poder (po'ðer) *n.m.* 1, power; strength. 2, power of attorney. 3, possession. —**poderes**, *n.m.pl.* authority. —**a poder de**, by dint of. —**por poderes**, by proxy.

poder (po'ðer) *v.i.* [*infl.:* **53**] to be able to; can; may. —*v.t.* to be capable of; be able to do. —*v.impers.* to be possible; may. —**a más no poder**, with all possible strength or effort. —**no poder con**, not to be able to handle. —**no poder más**, to be at the end of one's strength or patience. —**no poder menos de . . .**, not to be able to help. . . . —**no poder ver**, not to be able to stand the sight of; loathe.

poderío (po·ðe'ri·o) *n.m.* power; might.

poderoso (po·ðe'ro·so) *adj.* 1, powerful; mighty. 2, influential.

podiatría (po·ðja'tri·a) *n.f.* podiatry. —**podiatra** (po'ðja·tra) *n.m. & f.* podiatrist.

podio ('po·ðjo) *n.m.* podium.

podómetro (po'ðo·me·tro) *n.m.* pedometer.

podré (po'ðre) *v., 1st pers.sing. fut.* of **poder**.

podredumbre (po·ðre'ðum·bre) *n.f.* decay; putrescence.

podredura (po·ðre'ðu·ra) *n.f.* putrescence; corruption.

podrir (po'ðrir) *v.t. & i.* [*also, refl.,* **podrirse**] to rot; putrefy. *Defective, inf. & p.p. only; all other forms are taken from* **pudrir**.

poema (po'e·ma) *n.m.* poem.

poesía (po·e'si·a) *n.f.* 1, poetry. 2, poem.

poeta (po'e·ta) *n.m.* poet.

poetastro (po·e'tas·tro) *n.m.* poetaster.

poético (po'e·ti·ko) *adj.* poetic. —**poética**, *n.f.* poetics.

poetisa (po·e'ti·sa) *n.f.* poetess.

poetizar (po·e·ti'θar; -'sar) *v.i.* [*infl.:* **rezar, 10**] 1, to compose poetry. 2, to wax poetic. —*v.t.* to make poetic; lyricize.

poinsetia (poin'se·tja) *n.f.* poinsettia.

póker ('po·ker) *n.m.* poker (*card game*).

polaco (po'la·ko) *adj. & n.m.* Polish. —*n.m.* Pole.

polaina (po'lai·na) *n.f.* legging.
polar (po'lar) *adj.* polar. —**Estrella polar,** Polaris; polestar; North Star.
polaridad (po·la·ri'ðað) *n.f.* polarity.
polarizar (po·la·ri'θar; -'sar) *v.t.* [*infl.:* **rezar, 10**] to polarize. —**polarización,** *n.f.* polarization.
polca ('pol·ka) *n.f.* polka. —**polcar,** *v.i.* [*infl.:* **tocar, 7**] to dance the polka.
polea (po'le·a) *n.f.* **1,** pulley. **2,** tackle block; block pulley. —**poleame** (-'a·me) *n.m.* set of pulleys; tackle.
polémica (po'le·mi·ka) *n.f.* **1,** polemic. **2,** polemics. —**polémico,** *adj.* polemical. —**polemista** (-'mis·ta) *n.m. & f.* polemist; polemicist. —**polemizar** (-mi'θar; -mi'sar) *v.i.* [*infl.:* **rezar, 10**] to argue; engage in polemic.
polen ('po·len) *n.m.* pollen.
poliandria (po·li'an·drja) *n.f.* polyandry. —**poliándrico** (-'an·dri·ko) *adj.* [*also, bot.,* **poliandro** (-'an·dro)] polyandrous.
policía (po·li'θi·a; -'si·a) *n.f.* police. —*n.m.* policeman; policewoman.
policíaco (po·li'θi·a·ko; -'si·a·ko) *adj.* police (*attrib.*). —**novela policíaca,** detective story.
policial (po·li'θjal; -'sjal) *adj., Amer.* = **policíaco.**
policlínico (po·li'kli·ni·ko) *adj.* polyclinic. —**policlínica,** *n.f.* polyclinic.
policromía (po·li·kro'mi·a) *n.f.* **1,** polychrome. **2,** polychromy.
policromo (po'li·kro·mo) *also,* **policromo** (-'kro·mo) *adj.* polychrome.
polichinela (po·li·tʃi'ne·la) *n.m.* Punch; punchinello.
poliedro (po·li'e·ðro) *n.m.* polyhedron. —**poliédrico,** *adj.* polyhedral.
poliéster (po·li'es·ter) *n.m.* polyester.
polígala (po'li·ɣa·la) *n.f.* milkwort.
poligamia (po·li'ɣa·mja) *n.f.* polygamy.
polígamo (po'li·ɣa·mo) *adj.* polygamous. —*n.m.* polygamist.
políglota (po'li·ɣlo·ta) *adj. & n.m. & f.* polyglot. *Also,* **poligloto** (-'ɣlo·to) *adj. & n.m.*
poligonal (po·li·ɣo'nal) *adj.* polygonal.
polígono (po'li·ɣo·no) *adj.* polyg-

onal. —*n.m.* **1,** polygon. **2,** target range.
polilla (po'li·ʎa; -ja) *n.f.* **1,** moth. **2,** rot; something causing rot. **3,** *colloq.* pest; nuisance.
polimerizar (po·li·me·ri'θar; -'sar) *v.t.* [*infl.:* **rezar, 10**] to polymerize. —**polimerización,** *n.f.* polymerization.
polímero (po'li·me·ro) *adj.* polymeric. —*n.m.* polymer.
polinesio (po·li'ne·sjo) *adj. & n.m.* Polynesian.
polinizar (po·li·ni'θar; -'sar) *v.t.* [*infl.:* **rezar, 10**] to pollinate. —**polinización,** *n.f.* pollination.
polinomio (po·li'no·mjo) *n.m.* polynomial.
poliomielitis (po·ljo·mje'li·tis) *n.f.* poliomyelitis; polio.
pólipo (po'li·po) *n.m.* polyp.
polisílabo (po·li'si·la·βo) *adj.* polysyllabic. —*n.m.* polysyllable.
polisón (po·li'son) *n.m.* bustle (*woman's dress*).
polista (po'lis·ta) *n.m.* polo player.
Politburó (po·lit·βu'ro) *n.m.* Politburo.
politécnico (po·li'tek·ni·ko) *adj.* polytechnic.
politeísmo (po·li·te'is·mo) *n.m.* polytheism. —**politeísta,** *n.m. & f.* polytheist. —*adj.* polytheistic.
política (po'li·ti·ka) *n.f.* **1,** policy. **2,** politics. **3,** polity. **4,** tact. **5,** female politician. —**política exterior,** foreign policy. —**por política,** out of courtesy.
políticamente (po·li·ti·ka'men·te) *adv.* **1,** politically. **2,** civilly.
politicastro (po·li·ti'kas·tro) *n.m.* petty politician; ward heeler.
político (po'li·ti·ko) *adj.* **1,** political. **2,** politic. **3,** tactful. **4,** in-law: *padre político,* father-in-law. —*n.m.* politician.
politiquear (po·li·ti·ke'ar) *v.i., colloq.* **1,** to politick. **2,** to talk politics. —**politiqueo** (-'ke·o) *n.m., colloq.* politicking.
politiquería (po·li·ti·ke'ri·a) *n.f., Amer., colloq.* political chicanery. —**politiquero,** *n.m., Amer., colloq.* petty politician.
politizar (po·li·ti'θar; -'sar) *v.t.* [*infl.:* **rezar, 10**] to politicize.
poliuretano (po·li·u·re'ta·no) *n.m.* polyurethane.
polivalente (po·li·βa'len·te) *adj.* polyvalent.

póliza ('po·li·θa; -sa) *n.f.* **1,** [*also,* **póliza de seguro**] insurance policy. **2,** tax stamp. **3,** [*also,* **póliza de crédito**] letter of credit. **4,** scrip.

polizón (po·li'θon; -'son) *n.m.* **1,** vagrant. **2,** stowaway.

polizonte (po·li'θon·te; -'son·te) *n.m., colloq., derog.* cop; flatfoot.

polo ('po·lo) *n.m.* **1,** *geog.; physics* pole. **2,** polo.

polonés (po·lo'nes) *adj.* Polish. —*n.m.* Pole.

polonesa (po·lo'ne·sa) *adj., fem. of* **polonés.** —*n.f.* **1,** Polish woman. **2,** polonaise.

polonio (po'lo·njo) *n.m.* polonium.

poltrón (pol'tron) *adj.* lazy; slothful. —**poltrona,** *n.f.* easy chair. —**poltronería,** *n.f.* laziness; indolence.

polución (po·lu'θjon; -'sjon) *n.f.* pollution.

poluto (po'lu·to) *adj.* polluted; unclean.

polvareda (pol·βa're·ða) *n.f.* **1,** cloud of dust. **2,** tiff; free-for-all.

polvera (pol'βe·ra) *n.f.* **1,** powder box. **2,** compact.

polvillo (pol'βi·ʎo; -jo) *n.m.* fine dust.

polvo ('pol·βo) *n.m.* **1,** dust. **2,** powder; face powder. **3,** *pl.* toilet powder. —**hacer polvo,** *colloq.* to beat to a pulp. —**limpio de polvo y paja,** *colloq.* free of all charges; net.

pólvora ('pol·βo·ra) *n.f.* **1,** powder; gunpowder. **2,** *colloq.* fireball; spitfire.

polvorear (pol·βo·re'ar) *v.t.* = espolvorear.

polvoriento (pol·βo'rjen·to) *adj.* dusty; dust-covered.

polvorín (pol·βo'rin) *n.m.* **1,** powder magazine. **2,** powder flask; powder horn. **3,** *colloq.* touchy or irascible person.

polvoroso (pol·βo'ro·so) *adj.* = polvoriento. —**poner pies en polvorosa,** *colloq.* to take flight; take to one's heels.

polla ('po·ʎa; -ja) *n.f.* **1,** spring chicken; pullet. **2,** *S.A.* first prize (*in a lottery*).

pollada (po'ʎa·ða; po'ja-) *n.f.* hatch; brood; covey.

pollera (po'ʎe·ra; po'je-) *n.f.* **1,** child's walker. **2,** chicken coop. **3,** *S.A.* skirt.

pollino (po'ʎi·no; po'ji-) *n.m.* ass; donkey.

pollita (po'ʎi·ta; po'ji-) *n.f.* **1,** pullet. **2,** *colloq.* girl; lass.

pollito (po'ʎi·to; po'ji-) *n.m.* **1,** chick. **2,** *colloq.* boy; lad.

pollo ('po·ʎo; -jo) *n.m.* **1,** chicken. **2,** boy; lad.

polluelo (po'ʎwe·lo; -'jwe·lo) *n.m.* chick.

poma ('po·ma) *n.f.* pome; apple.

pomada (po'ma·ða) *n.f.* pomade; salve.

pomar (po'mar) *n.m.* orchard, esp. apple orchard.

pomelo (po'me·lo) *n.m.* grapefruit.

pómez ('po·meθ; -mes) *n.f.* pumice.

pomo ('po·mo) *n.m.* **1,** flask; phial. **2,** pommel; knob. **3,** bunch; cluster. **4,** *bot.* pome.

pompa ('pom·pa) *n.f.* **1,** pomp. **2,** bubble. **3,** *naut.* pump.

pompón (pom'pon) *n.m.* **1,** pompon. **2,** *Amer.* chrysanthemum.

pomposo (pom'po·so) *adj.* pompous. —**pomposidad,** *n.f.* pomposity.

pómulo ('po·mu·lo) *n.m.* cheekbone.

pon (pon) *v., impv.sing. of* **poner.** —*n.m., W.I.* lift; free ride.

ponche ('pon·tʃe) *n.m.* punch (*drink*). —**ponchera,** *n.f.* punch bowl.

poncho ('pon·tʃo) *n.m.* poncho. —*adj.* lax; lazy.

ponderable (pon·de'ra·βle) *adj.* **1,** ponderable. **2,** admirable.

ponderación (pon·de·ra'θjon; -'sjon) *n.f.* **1,** tact; prudence. **2,** praise.

ponderado (pon·de·ra·ðo) *adj.* tactful; prudent.

ponderar (pon·de'rar) *v.t.* **1,** to ponder; weigh. **2,** to praise.

ponderoso (pon·de'ro·so) *adj.* **1,** heavy; ponderous. **2,** serious; circumspect.

ponedero (po·ne'ðe·ro) *adj.* egg-laying. —*n.m.* hen's nest.

ponedor (po·ne'ðor) *adj.* egg-laying.

poner (po'ner) *v.t.* [*infl.:* 54] **1,** to put; place; set. **2,** to set (the table). **3,** [*also, refl.,* **ponerse**] to put on (a garment). **4,** to put up; wager; stake. **5,** to lay (eggs). **6,** to suppose; assume. **7,** to give (a name). **8,** to take (a period of time). **9,** *fol. by* **de, por** *or* **como,** to show (someone) up as. **10,** *fol. by adj.* to turn; make; cause to be or become. **11,** *fol. by* **en,** to get (someone) into. —**ponerse,** *v.r.*

1, to become. **2,** to set, as the sun. **3,** *fol. by* **en,** to make it to; get to (a place or position). **4,** *fol. by* **de** *or* **como,** to set oneself up as. —**poner bien,** to commend; put in a favorable light. —**poner mal,** to discredit; put in a bad light.

poniente (po'njen·te) *n.m.* west. —**sol poniente,** setting sun.

pontear (pon·te'ar) *v.t.* to bridge. —*v.i.* to build a bridge.

pontificado (pon·ti·fi'ka·ðo) *n.m.* pontificate.

pontifical (pon·ti·fi'kal) *adj.* pontifical.

pontificar (pon·ti·fi'kar) *v.i.* [*infl.:* **tocar,** 7] to pontificate. —**pontificación,** *n.f.* pontification.

pontífice (pon'ti·fi·θe; -se) *n.m.* pontiff.

pontificio (pon·ti'fi·θjo; -sjo) *adj.* papal; pontifical.

pontón (pon'ton) *n.m.* pontoon.

ponzoña (pon'θo·ɲa; -'so·ɲa) *n.f.* venom; poison. —**ponzoñoso,** *adj.* venomous; poisonous.

popa ('po·pa) *n.f.* poop; stern.

popelina (po·pe'li·na) *n.f.* poplin.

populachería (po·pu·la·tʃe'ri·a) *n.f.* **1,** vulgar manners; vulgar behavior. **2,** crowd response. **3,** = **populacho.** **4,** popular appeal; rabble rousing.

populachero (po·pu·la'tʃe·ro) *adj.* **1,** vulgar; uncouth. **2,** of or characteristic of the rabble. **3,** catering to the populace; rabble-rousing.

populacho (po·pu·la'tʃo) *n.m.* populace; rabble.

popular (po·pu'lar) *adj.* popular. —**popularidad,** *n.f.* popularity.

popularizar (po·pu·la·ri'θar;-'sar) *v.t.* [*infl.:* **rezar,** 10] to popularize.—**popularización,** *n.f.* popularization.

populismo (po·pu'lis·mo) *n.m.* populism. —**populista,** *adj. & n.m. & f.* populist.

populoso (po·pu'lo·so) *adj.* populous.

popurrí (po·pu'rri) *n.m.* potpourri.

poquedad (po·ke'ðað) *n.f.* **1,** shortness; paucity. **2,** timidity; pusillanimity. **3,** trifle.

póquer ('po·ker) *n.m.* = **póker.**

poquito (po'ki·to) *adj.* very little. —**a poquitos,** bit by bit. —**poquito a poco,** *also,* **a poquito,** little by little.

por (por) *prep.* **1,** by; by way of; through: *por las calles,* through the

streets. **2,** throughout the extent of; over: *Los perros andan sueltos por el prado,* The dogs are running loose over the meadow. **3,** by; by means or agency of: *Fue aplastado por el auto,* He was run over by the car. **4,** *in expressions of time* in: *por la mañana,* in the morning. **5,** for; because of: *por haber hecho esto,* for having done this. **6,** for the sake of; on behalf of: *Lo hizo por mí,* He did it for my sake. **7,** to; in order to: *No llevo corbata por ir más cómodo.* I am not wearing a tie in order to be more comfortable. **8,** for; in quest of: *Fue por el médico,* He went for the doctor. **9,** by; multiplied by; times: *siete por seis,* seven times six; seven by six. **10,** *denoting price or cost* for: *Pagué cinco dólares por la camisa,* I paid five dollars for the shirt. **11,** per; a; each: *cinco por ciento,* five percent; *Pagué treinta centavos por docena,* I paid thirty cents a dozen. **12,** for; as: *La tomó por esposa,* He took her as his wife. **13,** for; instead of; in place of: *El vicepresidente firmó por el presidente,* The vice-president signed for the president. —**estar por,** *fol. by inf.* **1,** to be ready to or disposed to: *Estamos por salir,* We are ready to leave. **2,** to be; be still to be: *La casa está por barrer,* The house is still to be swept.—**por cuanto,** whereas; inasmuch as. —**por donde, 1,** where; whereabout. **2,** whereby; wherefore. —**por que = porque.** —**por qué,** why. —**por si acaso,** in case.

porcachón (por·ka'tʃon) *adj.* piggish; hoggish. *Also, colloq.,* **porcacho** ('ka·tʃo).

porcelana (por·θe'la·na; por·se-) *n.f.* porcelain.

porcentaje (por·θen'ta·xe; por·sen-) *n.m.* percentage. —**porcentual** (-'twal) *adj.* on a percentage basis.

porcino (por'θi·no; -'si·no) *adj.* porcine.

porción (por'θjon; -'sjon) *n.f.* portion.

porche ('por·tʃe) *n.m.* porch.

pordiosear (por·ðjo·se'ar) *v.t. & i.* to beg.

pordiosero (por·ðjo'se·ro) *n.m.* beggar. —*adj.* mendicant; begging. —**pordiosería,** *n.f.* begging; beggary.

porfía (por'fi·a) *n.f.* **1,** stubbornness. **2,** altercation; quarrel. **—a porfía,** in competition.

porfiado (por'fja·ðo) *adj.* stubborn. *—n.m.* stubborn man.

porfiar (por'fjar) *v.i.* [*infl.:* enviar, 22] **1,** to fight; dispute stubbornly. **2,** to be stubborn; be obstinate.

pórfido ('por·fi·ðo) *n.m.* porphyry.

pormenor (por·me'nor) *n.m.* detail; particular.

pormenorizar (por·me·no·ri'θar; -'sar) *v.t.* [*infl.:* rezar, 10] **1,** to detail; relate in detail. **2,** to itemize.

pornografía (por·no·ɣra'fi·a) *n.f.* pornography. **—pornográfico** (-'ɣra·fi·ko) *adj.* pornographic.

poro ('po·ro) *n.m.* pore. **—poroso,** *adj.* porous. **—porosidad,** *n.f.* porosity.

poroto (po'ro·to) *n.m., S.A.* bean. **—apuntarse un poroto,** *S.A., colloq.* to make a point; hit the mark.

porque ('por·ke) *conj.* **1,** because. **2,** so that; in order that.

porqué (por'ke) *n.m.* reason; motive; cause; the why; the wherefore. **—los porqués y los cómos,** the whys and wherefores.

porquería (por·ke'ri·a) *n.f.* **1,** filth. **2,** *colloq.* mess; botch. **3,** *colloq.* trifle; junk. **4,** *colloq.* dirty trick.

porqueriza (por·ke'ri·θa; -sa) *n.f.* pigsty; sty. **—porquerizo,** *n.m.* swineherd.

porra ('po·rra) *n.f.* **1,** mace; truncheon. **2,** stick; club; bludgeon. **3,** *colloq.* gall; brazenness. *—interj.* confound it! **—irse a la porra,** to go to the dickens.

porrada (po'rra·ða) *n.f.* **1,** = **porrazo. 2,** *colloq.* nonsense; inanity. **3,** *colloq.* heap; slew.

porrazo (po'rra·θo; -so) *n.m.* **1,** blow; clubbing. **2,** fall; bump.

porro ('po·rro) *adj., colloq.* dull; stupid. *—n.m., colloq.* dullard.

porrón (po'rron) *n.m.* **1,** glass jug with a spout for drinking wine. **2,** earthen jar.

portaaviones (por·ta·a'βjo·nes; por·ta'βjo-) *n.m.sing. & pl.* aircraft carrier.

portacartas (por·ta'kar·tas) *n.m. sing. & pl.* mail pouch; mailbag.

portada (por'ta·ða) *n.f.* **1,** façade; front. **2,** cover (*of a book, magazine, etc.*).

portado (por'ta·ðo) *adj., in* **bien** *or*

mal portado, well or poorly attired or behaved.

portador (por·ta'ðor) *adj.* bearing; carrying. *—n.m.* [*fem.* **-dora**] bearer; carrier.

portaequipajes (por·ta·e·ki'pa·xes) *n.m. sing. & pl.* **1,** baggage trunk. **2,** luggage rack.

portafolio (por·ta'fo·ljo) *n.m.* portfolio.

portafusil (por·ta·fu'sil) *n.m.* rifle sling.

portal (por'tal) *n.m.* **1,** portal: entrance. **2,** doorstep. **3,** portico.

portalón (por·ta'lon) *n.m.* **1,** large door; portal. **2,** *naut.* side hatchway.

portamantas (por·ta'man·tas) *n.m. sing. & pl.* carrying straps.

portamonedas (por·ta·mo'ne·ðas) *n.m.sing. & pl.* pocketbook; purse.

portaobjetos (por·ta·oβ'xe·tos) *n.m.sing. & pl.* microscope slide.

portapapeles (por·ta·pa'pe·les) *n.m.sing. & pl.* **1,** briefcase. **2,** paper rack; paper holder.

portapliegos (por·ta'plje·ɣos) *n.m.sing. & pl.* briefcase.

portaplumas (por·ta'plu·mas) *n.m.sing. & pl.* penholder.

portar (por'tar) *v.t.* to carry; bear (*esp. arms*). *—v.i., naut.* to bear well before the wind. **—portarse,** *v.r.* to behave; comport oneself.

portátil (por'ta·til) *adj.* portable.

portaviandas (por·ta'βjan·das) *n.m.sing. & pl.* = **fiambrera.**

portavoz (por·ta'βoθ; -'βos) *n.m.* **1,** megaphone. **2,** spokesman. **3,** organ (*publication*).

portazgo (por'taθ·ɣo; -'tas·ɣo) *n.m.* toll; road toll.

portazo (por'ta·θo; -so) *n.m.* slam or slamming of a door.

porte ('por·te) *n.m.* **1,** transport; transportation. **2,** portage. **3,** shipping costs; postage. **4,** carriage; demeanor. **5,** deportment. **6,** import; importance.

portear (por·te'ar) *v.t.* to carry; transport. *—v.i.* to slam, as a door. **—portearse,** *v.r.* to migrate, esp. as birds.

portento (por'ten·to) *n.m.* portent. **—portentoso,** *adj.* portentous.

porteño (por'te·ɲo) *adj.* inhabiting or coming from a seaport, esp. Buenos Aires, Cadiz, and other principal ports. *—n.m.* inhabitant or native of a seaport.

portería (por·te'ri·a) *n.f.* **1,** porter's desk, office or quarters. **2,** gatehouse. **3,** *sports* goal.

portero (por'te·ro) *n.m.* **1,** porter; gatekeeper; doorman. **2,** goalkeeper.

portezuela (por·te'θwe·la; -'swe-la) *n.f.* small door, usu. of a vehicle.

pórtico ('por·ti·ko) *n.m.* portico.

portier (por'tjer) *n.m.* portiere.

portilla (por'ti·ʎa; -ja) *n.f.* port-hole.

portillo (por'ti·ʎo; -jo) *n.m.* **1,** aperture; opening; gap. **2,** wicket; barnyard gate. **3,** *colloq.* break; crack.

portón (por'ton) *n.m.* large door; gate.

portorriqueño (por·to·rri'ke·ɲo) *adj. & n.m.* = **puertorriqueño.**

portuario (por'twa·rjo) *adj.* **1,** port *(attrib.).* **2,** dock *(attrib.);* docking *(attrib.).*

portugués (por·tu'ɣes) *adj. & n.m. [fem.* **-guesa]** Portuguese.

porvenir (por·βe'nir) *n.m.* future.

pos (pos) *in* **en pos** *or* **en pos de,** after; following; in pursuit of.

posada (po'sa·ða) *n.f.* **1,** inn; lodge. **2,** lodging; lodgings.

posaderas (po·sa'ðe·ras) *n.f.pl.* buttocks.

posadero (po·sa'ðe·ro) *n.m.* inn-keeper.

posar (po'sar) *v.i.* **1,** to rest; repose. **2,** to lodge; room. **3,** *art; photog.* to pose. —*v.t.* **1,** to put; place. **2,** to lay down (a burden). —**posarse,** *v.r.* to light; alight; come to rest; settle.

posas ('po·sas) *n.f.pl., colloq.* = **posaderas.**

posdata (pos'ða·ta) *n.f.* postscript.

pose ('po·se) *n.f.* **1,** pose. **2,** *photog.* exposure; take.

poseedor (po·se·e'ðor) *n.m. [fem.* **-dora]** possessor; holder. —*adj.* possessing.

poseer (po·se'er) *v.t. [infl.:* **creer,** **24] 1,** to possess. **2,** to master; have knowledge or command of. **3,** to seize; take possession of. —**poseerse,** *v.r.* to be self-possessed.

poseído (po·se'i·ðo) *adj.* possessed. *Also,* **poseso.**

posesión (po·se'sjon) *n.f.* possession.

posesionar (po·se·sjo'nar) *v.t.* to give possession (of something) to. —**posesionarse,** *v.r.* to take possession; seize control.

posesivo (po·se'si·βo) *adj. & n.m.* possessive.

poseso (po'se·so) *adj. & n.m.* possessed.

poseyendo (po·se'jen·do) *v., ger. of* **poseer.**

poseyó (po·se'jo) *v., 3rd pers.sing. pret. of* **poseer.**

posfecha (pos'fe·tʃa) *n.f.* postdate. —**posfechar,** *v.t.* to postdate.

posguerra (pos'ɣe·rra) *n.f.* = **postguerra.**

posible (po'si·βle) *adj.* possible. —**posibilidad,** *n.f.* possibility. —**posibilitar,** *v.t.* to make possible.

posición (po·si'θjon; -'sjon) *n.f.* position.

positivismo (po·si·ti'βis·mo) *n.m.* positivism. —**positivista,** *n.m. & f.* positivist. —*adj.* positivistic.

positivo (po·si'ti·βo) *adj. & n.m.* positive. —**positiva,** *n.f., photog.* positive. —**positividad,** *n.f.* positivity.

positrón (po·si'tron) *n.m.* positron.

posma ('pos·ma) *n.m. & f., colloq.* sluggard; slowpoke. —*n.f., colloq.* sluggishness; phlegm.

posmeridiano (pos·me·ri'ðja·no) *adj.* = **postmeridiano.**

poso ('po·so) *n.m.* **1,** sediment; dregs. **2,** quiet; repose.

posología (po·so·lo'xi·a) *n.f.* dosage.

posponer (pos·po'ner) *v.t. [infl.:* **poner, 54]** to postpone.

posta ('pos·ta) *n.f.* **1,** relay of horses; express post. **2,** stagecoach run; distance between posts. **3,** meat repast. **4,** *gambling* pool; pot. —**a posta,** *also,* **aposta,** *adv.* on purpose.

postal (pos'tal) *adj.* postal; post *(attrib.);* postage *(attrib.).* —*n.f.* postcard.

postdata (post'ða·ta) *n.f.* = **posdata.**

postdiluviano (post·ði·lu'βja·no) *adj.* postdiluvian.

poste ('pos·te) *n.m.* post; pole. —**poste miliar,** milepost, milestone. —**ser un poste, 1,** to be deaf; be impassive. **2,** to be clumsy.

postergar (pos·ter'ɣar) *v.t. [infl.:* **pagar, 8] 1,** to postpone; put off. **2,** to hold back; check. —**postergación,** *n.f.* postponement; deferment.

posteridad (pos·te·ri'ðað) *n.f.* posterity.

posterior (pos·te'rjor) *adj. & n.m.* posterior. —*adj.* subsequent. —**posterioridad,** *n.f.* posteriority. —**con posterioridad,** after; subsequently.

posteriormente (pos·te·rjor·'men·te) *adv.* **1,** after. **2,** later.

postgraduado (post·γra'ðwa·ðo) *adj. & n.m.* postgraduate.

postguerra (post'γe·rra) *n.f.* postwar period.

postigo (pos'ti·γo) *n.m.* **1,** wicket. **2,** shutter. **3,** postern. **4,** peephole.

postilla (pos'ti·ʎa; -ja) *n.f.* scab.

postillón (pos·ti'ʎon; -'jon) *n.m.* postillion.

postín (pos'tin) *n.m., colloq.* dash; cockiness.

postizo (pos'ti·θo; -so) *adj.* false; artificial.

postludio (post'lu·ðjo) *n.m.* postlude.

postmeridiano (post·me·ri'ðja·no) *adj.* postmeridian.

post mortem (post'mor·tem) postmortem.

postor (pos'tor) *n.m.* [*fem.* **-tora**] bidder. —**mejor postor,** highest bidder.

postrar (pos'trar) *v.t.* to prostrate. —**postrarse,** *v.r.* to kneel down; lie prone. —**postración,** *n.f.* prostration. —**postrador,** *adj.* prostrating.

postre ('pos·tre) *adj.* = **postrero.** —*n.m.* dessert. —**a la postre,** at last; finally

postrer (pos'trer) *adj.* = **postrero** *before a masc. noun.*

postrero (pos'tre·ro) *adj. & n.m.* **1,** last; last remaining. **2,** hindmost.

postrimería (pos·tri·mc'ri·a) *n.f., usu.pl.* end; final or late stages, esp. of life.

postulado (pos·tu'la·ðo) *n.m.* postulate.

postulante (pos·tu'lan·te) *adj.* requesting admission, esp. in a religious community. —*n.m.* [*fem.* **postulanta**] candidate for admission; postulant.

postular (pos·tu'lar) *v.t.* **1,** to postulate. **2,** to request; petition for.

póstumo ('pos·tu·mo) *adj.* posthumous.

postura (pos'tu·ra) *n.f.* **1,** posture. **2,** bid. **3,** = **puesta. 4,** *Amer.* a trying on; fitting.

potable (po'ta·βle) *adj.* potable.

potaje (po'ta·xe) *n.m.* pottage; stew.

potasa (po'ta·sa) *n.f.* potash.

potasio (po'ta·sjo) *n.m.* potassium. —**potásico** (-'ta·si·ko) *adj.* potassic.

pote ('po·te) *n.m.* **1,** pot. **2,** jug; jar.

potencia (po'ten·θja; -sja) *n.f.* **1,** power. **2,** potency. —**en potencia,** potentially.

potencial (po·ten'θjal; -'sjal) *adj. & n.m.* **1,** potential. **2,** *gram.* conditional. —**potencialidad,** *n.f.* potentiality.

potenciar (po·ten'θjar; -'sjar) *v.t.* to utilize; exploit.

potentado (po·ten'ta·ðo) *n.m.* potentate.

potente (po'ten·te) *adj.* potent; powerful.

potestad (po·tes'tað) *n.f.* jurisdiction; power. —**patria potestad,** parental jurisdiction.

potestativo (po·tes·ta'ti·βo) *adj., law* facultative.

potra ('po·tra) *n.f.* **1,** young mare. **2,** *colloq.* hernia. —**tener potra,** *colloq.* to have it made; be happy.

potranca (po'tran·ka) *n.f.* filly; young mare. —**potranco,** *n.m., Amer.* colt.

potrero (po'tre·ro) *n.m.* **1,** grazing field for horses. **2,** colt tender.

potro ('po·tro) *n.m.* **1,** colt. **2,** torture rack. **3,** *gymnastics* horse.

poza ('po·θa; -sa) *n.f.* puddle.

pozo ('po·θo; -so) *n.m.* **1,** well. **2,** shaft; pit. **3,** hole or dip in the bed of a river or the sea. **4,** *cards* jackpot; kitty. —**pozo negro,** cesspool.

práctica ('prak·ti·ka) *n.f.* practice.

practicable (prak·ti'ka·βle) *adj.* practicable; feasible.

practicanta (prak·ti'kan·ta) *n.f.* **1,** female nurse. **2,** *pharm.* female clerk.

practicante (prak·ti'kan·te) *adj.* practicing. *n.m.* **1,** practitioner. **2,** intern. **3,** male nurse. **4,** *pharm.* clerk.

practicar (prak·ti'kar) *v.t.* [*infl.:* **tocar,** 7] to practice.

práctico ('prak·ti·ko) *adj.* **1,** practical. **2,** skillful; experienced. —*n.m.* harbor pilot.

pradera (pra'ðe·ra) *n.f.* prairie; meadow.

prado ('pra·ðo) *n.m.* **1,** field; meadow. **2,** grassy spot; park.

pragmático (praγ'ma·ti·ko) *adj.* pragmatic. —*n.m.* interpreter of the law; jurist.

pragmatismo (praγ·ma'tis·mo) *n.m.* pragmatism. —**pragmatista,** *n.m. & f.* pragmatist.

praseodimio (pra·se·o'ði·mjo) *n.m.* praseodymium.

preámbulo (pre·am·bu·lo) *n.m.* **1,**

preamble. **2,** *colloq.* evasion; circumlocution.

prebenda (pre'βen·da) *n.f.* **1,** prebend. **2,** *colloq.* soft job.

preboste (pre'βos·te) *n.m.* provost.

precario (pre'ka·rjo) *adj.* precarious.

precaución (pre·kau'θjon; -'sjon) *n.f.* precaution; caution. **—precaucionarse,** *v.r.* to take precautions; be on guard.

precautela (pre·kau'te·la) *n.f., Amer.* caution; precaution.

precautorio (pre·kau'to·rjo) *adj.* precautionary.

precaver (pre·ka'βer) *v.t.* to forestall. **—precaverse,** *v.r., fol. by* **de** *or* **contra,** to guard against; take precautions against.

precavido (pre·ka'βi·ðo) *adj.* **1,** careful; cautious. **2,** forewarned.

precedencia (pre·θe'ðen·θja; -se'ðen·sja) *n.f.* precedence. **—precedente,** *adj.* preceding; foregoing. **—***n.m.* precedent.

preceder (pre·θe'ðer; pre·se-) *v.t. & i.* to precede.

precepto (pre'θep·to; pre'sep-) *n.m.* precept. **—preceptivo,** *adj.* preceptive. **—preceptor,** *n.m.* [*fem.* **-tora**] preceptor.

preceptuar (pre·θep'twar; pre·sep-) *v.t.* [*infl.:* **continuar, 23**] **1,** to rule on; advise on. **2,** to prescribe.

preces ('pre·θes; -ses) *n.f.pl.* **1,** prayers; devotions. **2,** supplications.

preciado (pre'θja·ðo; -'sja·ðo) *adj.* **1,** valuable; precious. **2,** valued; esteemed. **3,** presumptuous; vain.

preciador (pre·θja'ðor; -sja'ðor) *n.m.* [*fem.* **-dora**] appraiser.

preciar (pre'θjar; -'sjar) *v.t.* **1,** to appraise; price. **2,** to value; appreciate. **—preciarse,** *v.r.* to take pride; boast.

precinto (pre'θin·to; -'sin·to) *n.m.* strap; strapping. **—precintar,** *v.t.* to strap; bind.

precio ('pre·θjo; -sjo) *n.m.* **1,** price. **2,** value; esteem. **—precio al contado,** cash price. **—precio de cierre,** closing price. **—precio de lista,** list price. **—precio de venta,** selling price. **—tener en precio,** to esteem; value highly.

preciosidad (pre·θjo·si'ðað; pre·sjo-) *n.f.* **1,** preciousness. **2,** precious thing. **3,** *colloq.* beauty; pretty thing; precious one.

precioso (pre'θjo·so; pre'sjo-) *adj.*

1, precious. **2,** *colloq.* beautiful. **—preciosismo,** *n.m.* preciosity.

preciosura (pre·θjo'su·ra; pre·sjo-) *n.f., Amer.* = **preciosidad.**

precipicio (pre·θi'pi·θjo; -si'pi·sjo) *n.m.* precipice.

precipitación (pre·θi·pi·ta'θjon; -si·pi·ta'sjon) *n.f.* **1,** haste; precipitancy. **2,** precipitation.

precipitadero (pre·θi·pi·ta'ðe·ro; pre·si-) *n.m.* precipice; steep cliff.

precipitado (pre·θi·pi'ta·ðo; pre·si-) *n.m. & adj.* precipitate.

precipitar (pre·θi·pi'tar; pre·si-) *v.t. & i.* to precipitate. **—precipitarse,** *v.r.* to rush headlong; hasten.

precisamente (pre·θi·sa'men·te; pre·si-) *adv.* **1,** precisely; exactly. **2,** necessarily; unavoidably.

precisar (pre·θi'sar; -si'sar) *v.t.* **1,** to fix; set; determine exactly. **2,** *Amer.* to need; have need of. **—***v.i.* **1,** to be precise. **2,** *Amer.* to be necessary.

precisión (pre·θi'sjon; pre·si-) *n.f.* **1,** necessity. **2,** precision; accuracy.

preciso (pre'θi·so; -'si·so) *adj.* **1,** necessary; indispensable. **2,** precise; exact. **3,** concise. **—tiempo preciso,** just time enough.

precitado (pre·θi'ta·ðo; pre·si-) *adj.* aforesaid; aforementioned.

preclaro (pre'kla·ro) *adj.* famous; illustrious; prominent.

precocidad (pre·ko·θi'ðað; -si·'ðað) *n.f.* precocity.

precognición (pre·koɣ·ni'θjon; -'sjon) *n.f.* precognition.

precolombino (pre·ko·lom'bi·no) *adj.* pre-Columbian.

preconcebir (pre·kon·θe'βir; -se·'βir) *v.t.* [*infl.:* **pedir, 33**] to preconceive.

preconizar (pre·ko·ni'θar; -'sar) *v.t.* [*infl.:* **rezar, 10**] to herald; proclaim.

preconocer (pre·ko·no'θer; -'ser) *v.t.* [*infl.:* **conocer, 13**] to foreknow.

precoz (pre'koθ; -'kos) *adj.* precocious.

precursor (pre·kur'sor) *adj.* preceding. **—***n.m.* [*fem.* **-sora**] precursor; harbinger.

predecesor (pre·ðe·θe'sor; -se'sor) *n.m.* [*fem.* **-sora**] predecessor.

predecir (pre·ðe'θir; -'sir) *v.t.* [*infl.:* **decir, 44**] to predict; foretell; forecast.

predestinar (pre·ðes·ti'nar) *v.t.* to

predestine. —**predestinación**, *n.f.* predestination.

predeterminar (pre·ðe·ter·mi'nar) *v.t.* to predetermine. —**predeterminación**, *n.f.* predetermination.

prédica ('pre·ði·ka) *n.f.* preachment; sermon.

predicación (pre·ði·ka'θjon; -'sjon) *n.f.* 1, preaching. 2, predication.

predicado (pre·ði·ka·ðo) *n.m.* predicate.

predicador (pre·ði·ka·ðor) *n.m.* [*fem.* **-dora**] preacher. —*adj.* preaching.

predicamento (pre·ði·ka·men·to) *n.m.* 1, position; status. 2, *logic* predicament; category.

predicar (pre·ði'kar) *v.t. & i.* [*infl.*: **tocar, 7**] to preach. —*v.t.* 1, to make public; make known. 2, *colloq.* to lecture; reprimand. 3, to predicate.

predicativo (pre·ði·ka·ti·βo) *adj.* predicative.

predicción (pre·ðik'θjon; -'sjon) *n.f.* prediction.

predicho (prc'ði·tʃo) *adj.* aforesaid.

predilecto (pre·ði'lek·to) *adj.* favorite; preferred. —**predilección**, *n.f.* predilection.

predio ('pre·ðjo) *n.m.* 1, landed property; real property. 2, *usu.pl.*, *Amer.* taxes on real property.

predisponer (pre·ðis·po'ner) *v.t.* [*infl.*: **poner, 54**] to predispose. —**predisposición** (-si'θjon; -'sjon) *n.f.* predisposition.

predominar (pre·ðo·mi'nar) *v.t. & i.* to predominate. —**predominancia**, *also*, **predominación**, *n.f.* predominance. —**predominante**, *adj.* predominant.

predominio (pre·ðo'mi·njo) *n.m.* predominance.

preeminente (pre·e·mi'nen·te) *adj.* preëminent. —**preeminencia**, *n.f.* preëminence.

preescolar (pre·es·ko'lar) *adj.* preschool (*attrib*).

preexistir (pre·ek·sis'tir) *v.i.* to preexist. —**preexistencia**, *n.f.* preexistence. —**preexistente**, *adj.* preexisting.

prefabricar (pre·fa·βri'kar) *v.t.* [*infl.*: **tocar, 7**] to prefabricate. —**prefabricación**, *n.f.* prefabrication.

prefacio (pre'fa·θjo; -sjo) *n.m.* preface.

prefecto (pre'fek·to) *n.m.* prefect. —**prefectura**, *n.f.* prefecture.

preferencia (pre·fe'ren·θja; -sja) *n.f.* preference. —**preferente**, *adj.* preferential. —**preferible**, *adj.* preferable.

preferir (pre·fe'rir) *v.t.* [*infl.*: **sentir, 31**] to prefer.

prefijar (pre·fi'xar) *v.t.* 1, to fix beforehand; predetermine. 2, to prefix.

prefijo (pre'fi·xo) *n.m.* prefix.

pregón (pre'yon) *n.m.* announcement; proclamation. —**pregonero**, *adj.* proclaiming; divulging. —*n.m.* town crier.

pregonar (pre·yo'nar) *v.t.* 1, to announce; proclaim. 2, to hawk (wares). 3, to divulge. 4, to praise publicly.

preguerra (pre'ye·rra) *n.f.* prewar period.

pregunta (pre'yun·ta) *n.f.* question; query. —**hacer una pregunta**, to ask a question.

preguntar (pre·yun'tar) *v.t.* to ask; question. —*v·i.* to ask; inquire. —**preguntarse**, *v.r.* to wonder; ask oneself.

preguntón (pre·yun'ton) *adj.*, *colloq.* nosy; inquisitive; prying. —*n.m.* [*fem.* **-tona**] nosy person.

prehistoria (pre·is'to·rja) *n.f.* prehistory. —**prehistórico** (-'to·ri·ko) *adj.* prehistoric.

prejuicio (pre·'xwi·θjo; -sjo) *n.m.* prejudice; bias. —**prejuiciado**, *adj.* prejudiced; biased. —**prejuiciar** *v.t.* to prejudice.

prejuzgar (pre·xuθ'yar; -xus'yar) *v.t.* [*infl.*: **pagar, 8**] to prejudge.

prelacía (pre·la'θi·a; -'si·a) *n.f.* prelacy.

prelación (pre·la'θjon; -'sjon) *n.f.* preference.

prelada (pre'la·ða) *n.f.* abbess.

prelado (pre'la·ðo) *n.m.* prelate —**prelado doméstico**, monsignor.

preliminar (pre·li·mi'nar) *adj. & n.m.* preliminary.

preludio (pre'lu·ðjo) *n.m.* prelude —**preludiar**, *v.t. & i.* to prelude.

prematuro (pre·ma'tu·ro) *adj* premature.

premédico (pre'me·ði·ko) *adj* premedical. —**premédica**, *n.f.* pre medical training.

premeditar (pre·me·ði'tar) *v.t.* to

premeditate. —**premeditación,** *n.f.* premeditation.

premiar (pre'mjar) *v.t.* **1,** to reward. **2,** to give an award to.

premio ('pre·mjo) *n.m.* **1,** reward. **2,** prize. **3,** premium.

premioso (pre'mjo·so) *adj.* **1,** pressing; urging. **2,** exacting. **3,** clumsy; heavy.

premisa (pre'mi·sa) *n.f.* premise.

premonitorio (pre·mo·ni'to·rjo) *adj.* premonitory.

premura (pre'mu·ra) *n.f.* urgency; haste.

prenatal (pre·na'tal) *adj.* prenatal.

prenda ('pren·da) *n.f.* **1,** pledge; security; pawn. **2,** household or personal effect. **3,** pledge; token. **4,** *pl.* talents; natural gifts. **5,** loved one. **6,** *W.I.* jewel. —**juego de prendas,** game of forfeits.

prendar (pren'dar) *v.t.* **1,** to pledge; pawn. **2,** to charm; please. —**prendarse,** *v.r.* to become enamored; be smitten.

prendedor (pren·de'ðor) *n.m.* brooch; pin; clasp.

prender (pren'der) *v.t.* **1,** to seize; apprehend. **2,** to pin; fasten. **3,** *Amer.* to turn on (a light, gas jet, etc.); to light (a fire, match, etc.). —*v.t. & i.* to catch; entangle. —*v.i.* **1,** to take; take root. **2,** *Amer.* to light up; be lit; be set afire. **3,** to take; take effect.

prendero (pren'de·ro) *n.m.* secondhand dealer.

prensa ('pren·sa) *n.f.* **1,** press; vise. **2,** printing press. **3,** press; publishing.

prensar (pren'sar) *v.t.* to press; squeeze. —**prensado,** *n.m.* press; pressing; compressing. —**prensador,** *n.m.* [*fem.* **-dora**] presser.

prensil (pren'sil) *adj.* prehensile.

prensista (pren'sis·ta) *n.m.* pressman.

prenupcial (pre·nup'θjal; -'sjal) *adj.* prenuptial.

preñado (pre'ɲa·ðo) *adj.* **1,** pregnant. **2,** full; loaded. —*n.m.* pregnancy.

preñar (pre'ɲar) *v.t.* to make pregnant.

preñez (pre'ɲeθ; -'ɲes) *n.f.* pregnancy.

preocupación (pre·o·ku·pa'θjon; -'sjon) *n.f.* **1,** preoccupation. **2,** worry; concern.

preocupar (pre·o·ku'par) *v.t.* **1,** to preoccupy. **2,** to worry; concern.

cause anxiety to. —**preocuparse,** *v.r.* to worry; to be concerned.

preordinar (pre·or·ði'nar) *v.t.* to preordain. —**preordinación,** *n.f.* preordination.

preparación (pre·pa·ra'θjon; -'sjon) *n.f.* **1,** preparation. **2,** *Amer.* education; learning.

preparado (pre·pa'ra·ðo) *adj.* **1,** prepared; concocted. **2,** ready. **3,** *Amer.* capable; learned. —*n.m.* preparation; concoction.

preparar (pre·pa'rar) *v.t.* to prepare; ready. —**preparativo,** *adj.* preparatory. —*n.m.* preparation. —**preparatorio,** *adj.* preparatory.

preponderar (pre·pon·de'rar) *v.t.* to preponderate. —**preponderancia,** *n.f.* preponderance. —**preponderante,** *adj.* preponderant.

preposición (pre·po·si'θjon; -'sjon) *n.f.* preposition. —**preposicional,** *also,* **prepositivo** (-'ti·βo) *adj.* prepositional.

prepósito (pre'po·si·to) *n.m.* chairman; president; chief officer or official.

preposterar (pre·pos·te'rar) *v.t.* to reverse; transpose; disarrange.

prepóstero (pre'pos·te·ro) *adj.* **1,** reversed; transposed; out of order. **2,** inopportune.

prepotente (pre·po'ten·te) *adj.* overpowering; dominant. —**prepotencia,** *n.f.* dominance.

prepucio (pre'pu·θjo; -sjo) *n.m.* prepuce.

prerrogativa (pre·rro·ɣa'ti·βa) *n.f.* prerogative.

presa ('pre·sa) *n.f.* **1,** prey. **2,** morsel; portion. **3,** dam. **4,** millpond. **5,** ditch; trench. **6,** booty; prize. **7,** *fem. of* **preso.** —**hacer presa de,** to grab; seize.

presagiar (pre·sa'xjar) *v.t.* to presage; forebode. —**presagio** (-'sa·xjo) *n.m.* presage; foreboding.

presbicia (pres'βi·θja; -sja) *n.f.* farsightedness.

présbita ('pres·βi·ta) *also,* **présbite,** *adj.* farsighted.

presbiterado (pres·βi·te'ra·ðo) *n.m.* **1,** priesthood. **2,** presbytery.

presbiteriano (pres·βi·te'rja·no) *adj. & n.* Presbyterian.

presbiterio (pres·βi'te·rjo) *n.m.* **1,** presbytery. **2,** chancel.

presbítero (pres'βi·te·ro) *n.m.* **1,** presbyter. **2,** priest.

presciencia (pres'θjen·θja; pre·'sjen·sja) *n.f.* prescience.

prescindir (pres·θin'dir; pre·sin-) *v.i., fol. by* de, to do without; dispense with. —**prescindible,** *adj.* nonessential; expendable.

prescribir (pres·kri'βir) *v.t. & i.* [*p.p.* **prescrito**] to prescribe.

prescripción (pres·krip'θjon; -'sjon) *n.f.* prescription.

prescripto (pres'krip·to) *adj. & n.m.* prescript.

presencia (pre'sen·θja; -sja) *n.f.* 1, presence. 2, appearance; bearing. —**presencia de ánimo,** presence of mind.

presencial (pre·sen'θjal; -'sjal) *adj.* present. —**testigo presencial,** eyewitness.

presenciar (pre·sen'θjar; -'sjar) *v.t.* to witness; be present at.

presentable (pre·sen·ta·βle) *adj.* presentable.

presentación (pre·sen·ta'θjon; -'sjon) *n.f.* 1, presentation. 2, personal introduction. —**a presentación,** *comm.* at sight; on demand.

presentar (pre·sen'tar) *v.t.* 1, to present. 2, to introduce. —**presentarse,** *v.r.* 1, to appear; present oneself. 2, to introduce oneself.

presente (pre'sen·te) *adj. & n.m.* present. —**hacer presente,** to call attention to; point out. —**por la presente,** by these presents. —**tener presente,** to bear in mind.

presentir (pre·sen'tir) *v.t.* [*infl.:* **sentir,** 31] to have a presentiment or premonition of. —**presentimiento,** *n.m.* presentiment; premonition.

preservar (pre·ser'βar) *v.t.* to preserve; keep. —**preservación,** *n.f.* preservation. —**preservador,** *adj.* preserving. —*n.m.* [*fem.* -**dora**] preserver.

preservativo (pre·ser·βa'ti·βo) *adj. & n.m.* preservative. —*n.m.* prophylactic; contraceptive.

presidencia (pre·si'ðen·θja; -sja) *n.f.* 1, presidency. 2, chairmanship; chair. —**presidencial,** *adj.* presidential.

presidente (pre·si'ðen·te) *n.m.* [*fem.* **presidenta**] 1, president. 2, chairman or chairwoman; presiding officer. —*adj.* presiding.

presidiario (pre·si'ðja·rjo) *also,* **presidario** (-'ða·rjo) *n.m.* convict.

presidio (pre'si·ðjo) *n.m.* 1, penitentiary. 2, imprisonment.

presidir (pre·si'ðir) *v.t.* to preside over. —*v.i.* to preside.

presilla (pre'si·ʎa; -ja) *n.f.* 1, loop; eye; bight. 2, buttonhole stitching. 3, paper clip.

presión (pre'sjon) *n.f.* pressure.

presionar (pre·sjo'nar) *v.t., Amer.* to press; exert pressure on.

preso ('pre·so) *adj.* imprisoned; in jail; held captive. —*n.m.* [*fem.* **presa**] prisoner; person apprehended.

prestación (pres·ta'θjon; -'sjon) *n.f.,* 1, lending; loan. 2, services. —**prestación de juramento,** swearing-in.

prestador (pres·ta'ðor) *n.m.* [*fem.* -**dora**] lender.

prestamista (pres·ta'mis·ta) *n.m. & f.* moneylender; pawnbroker.

préstamo ('pres·ta·mo) *n.m.* loan.

prestancia (pres'tan·θja; -sja) *n.f.* 1, excellence. 2, handsomeness.

prestar (pres'tar) *v.t.* 1, to lend; loan. 2, to give (help, attention, etc.). 3, to keep (silence, patience, etc.). —**prestarse,** *v.r.* to lend oneself or itself. —**dar prestado,** to lend; loan. —**pedir prestado,** to borrow; ask for loan of. —**tomar prestado,** to borrow; take as a loan.

presteza (pres'te·θa; -sa) *n.f.* promptness; speed; haste.

prestidigitación (pres·ti·ði·xi·ta'θjon; -'sjon) *n.f.* prestidigitation. —**prestidigitador,** *n.m.* [*fem.* -**dora**] prestidigitator.

prestigio (pres'ti·xjo) *n.m.* prestige. —**prestigioso,** *adj.* renowned; reputable.

presto ('pres·to) *adj.* 1, quick; swift; prompt. 2, ready; prepared. —*adv.* soon; quickly. —**de presto,** promptly; swiftly.

presumible (pre·su'mi·βle) *adj.* presumable.

presumido (pre·su'mi·ðo) *adj.* conceited; presumptuous.

presumir (pre·su'mir) *v.t.* to presume; surmise; conjecture. —*v.i.* to presume; boast; be conceited.

presunción (pre·sun'θjon; -'sjon) *n.f.* 1, presumption. 2, presumptuousness; conceit.

presuntamente (pre·sun·ta·'men·te) *adv.* 1, presumptively. 2, seemingly.

presuntivo (pre·sun'ti·βo) *adj.* presumptive; supposed.

presunto (pre'sun·to) *adj.* 1, presumed; assumed. 2, presumptive.

presuntuoso (pre·sun'two·so) *adj.* presumptuous. —**presuntuosidad,** *n.f.* presumptuousness.

presuponer (pre·su·po'ner) *v.t.*
[*infl.:* poner, 54] **1,** to presuppose.
2, to estimate; draw up a budget of.
presuposición (pre·su·po·si'θjon;
-'sjon) *n.f.* presupposition.
presupuesto (pre·su'pwes·to)
n.m. budget. —**presupuestar,** *v.t. &*
i. to budget. —**presupuestario,** *adj.*
budgetary.
presura (pre'su·ra) *n.f.* **1,** anxiety.
2, promptness; haste. **3,** obstinacy;
persistence.
presuroso (pre·su'ro·so) *adj.*
prompt; hasty.
pretencioso (pre·ten'θjo·so;
-'sjo·so) *adj.* pretentious.
pretender (pre·ten'der) *v.t.* **1,** to
pretend. **2,** to aspire to. **3,** to seek
to; attempt to. **4,** *Amer.* to court;
woo.
pretendiente (pre·ten'djen·te)
n.m. **1,** pretender. **2,** *Amer.* suitor.
pretensión (pre·ten'sjon) *n.f.* **1,**
pretension. **2,** pretentiousness.
—**pretensioso,** *adj.* pretentious.
preterir (pre·te'rir) *v.t.* [*defective,*
used only in inf. & p.p.] to ignore;
omit.
pretérito (pre'te·ri·to) *adj. & n.m.*
preterit.
preternatural (pre·ter·na·tu'ral)
adj. preternatural.
pretexto (pre'teks·to) *n.m.* pretext.
—**pretextar,** *v.t.* to give as pretext.
pretil (pre'til) *n.m.* railing; parapet.
pretina (pre'ti·na) *n.f.* **1,** waistband. **2,** belt; girdle; sash.
pretor (pre'tor) *n.m.* praetor.
—**pretorial,** *adj.* praetorial. —**pretoriano,** *adj.* praetorian.
prevalecer (pre·βa·le'θer; -'ser)
v.i. [*infl.:* conocer, 13] to prevail.
prevaler (pre·βa'ler) *v.i.* [*infl.:*
valer, 68] = **prevalecer.** —**pre-
valerse,** *v.r.* to avail oneself.
prevaricación (pre·βa·ri·ka·
'θjon; -'sjon) *n.f.* **1,** prevarication. **2,**
dereliction; remissness.
prevaricador (pre·βa·ri·ka'ðor)
adj. **1,** prevaricating. **2,** remiss; inobservant. —*n.m.* prevaricator.
prevaricar (pre·βa·ri'kar) *v.i.*
[*infl.:* tocar, 7] **1,** to prevaricate. **2,**
to be remiss or derelict. **3,** to transgress. **4,** *colloq.* to talk nonsense;
ramble.
prevención (pre·βen'θjon; -'sjon)
n.f. **1,** prevention. **2,** preparation;
preparedness. **3,** supply; store (*as of*
provisions). **4,** bias; prejudice. **5,**
police station. **6,** guardhouse;

guardroom. —**a prevención,** just in
case.
prevenido (pre·βe'ni·ðo) *adj.* **1,**
ready; prepared. **2,** forewarned. **3,**
alert; watchful; vigilant. **4,** well
stocked; well supplied.
prevenir (pre·βe'nir) *v.t.* [*infl.:*
venir, 69] **1,** to prepare; make
ready. **2,** to forewarn. **3,** to warn;
admonish. **4,** to forestall. —**prevenirse,** *v.r.* to prepare oneself; make
ready.
preventivo (pre·βen'ti·βo) *adj.*
preventive. —*adj. & n.m.* preventative.
prever (pre'βer) *v.t.* [*infl.:* ver, 70]
to foresee; anticipate.
previo ('pre·βjo) *adj.* previous;
prior.
previsible (pre·βi'si·βle) *adj.*
foreseeable.
previsión (pre·βi'sjon) *n.f.* foresight; providence. —**previsión social,** social security.
previsor (pre·βi'sor) *adj.* foresighted; provident.
previsto (pre'βis·to) *v., p.p. of*
prever. —*adj.* **1,** foreseen. **2,** provided.
prez (preθ; pres) *n.m. or f.* praise;
honor.
priesa ('prje·sa) *n.f.* = **prisa.**
prieto ('prje·to) *adj.* **1,** dark; black.
2, closely packed; firm. **3,** miserly;
tight. —*adj. & n.m., Amer.* negro.
prima ('pri·ma) *n.f.* **1,** female
cousin. **2,** *comm.* premium. **3,**
bounty; allowance. **4,** government
grant; subsidy.
primacía (pri·ma'θi·a; -'si·a) *n.f.*
primacy.
primada (pri'ma·ða) *n.f., colloq.* **1,**
hoax; prank. **2,** naïveté; naïve act.
primado (pri'ma·ðo) *n.m.* primate;
bishop.
prima donna ('pri·ma 'ðon·na;
-'ðo·na) *n.f.* [*pl.* **prima donnas**]
prima donna.
primar (pri'mar) *v.i.* to excel.
primario (pri'ma·rjo) *adj.* primary.
primate (pri'ma·te) *n.m., zoöl.* primate.
primavera (pri·ma'βe·ra) *n.f.* **1,**
spring; springtime; prime. **2,** primrose. **3,** gaiety; liveliness; color.
primaveral (pri·ma·βe'ral) *adj.* **1,**
spring (*attrib.*); springlike. **2,** gay;
lively; colorful.
primazgo (pri'maθ·γo; -'mas·γo)
n.m. cousinship.
primer (pri'mer) *adj.* = **primero**

before a *masc.* noun. —**Primer Ministro,** Prime Minister.

primera (pri'me·ra) *n.f.* **1,** *mech.* first gear. **2,** *fencing* first position.

primerizo (pri·me'ri·θo; -so) *adj.* **1,** earliest; beginning; maiden. **2,** firstborn. —*n.m.* **1,** firstborn; firstling. **2,** novice; beginner.

primero (pri'me·ro) *adj., adv. & n.m.* first. —*adj.* **1,** foremost. **2,** former; original. —*adv.* firstly. —**de buenas a primeras,** all at once; suddenly. —**de primera,** of superior quality; firstrate. —**primera dama,** *theat.* leading lady. —**primeros auxilios,** first aid.

primicia (pri'mi·θja; -sja) *n.f.* **1,** first fruits; first pickings. **2,** *journalism, Amer.* scoop.

primitivo (pri·mi'ti·βo) *adj. & n.m.* primitive.

primo (pri'mo) *adj.* **1,** prime; first. **2,** excellent; choice. —*n.m.* **1,** cousin. **2,** *colloq.* naïve person. —**primo hermano; primo carnal,** first cousin.

primogénito (pri·mo'xe·ni·to) *adj. & n.m.* firstborn. —**primogenitura,** *n.f.* primogeniture.

primor (pri'mor) *n.m.* **1,** artistry; delicacy. **2,** exquisite beauty. **3,** artistic gem.

primordial (pri·mor'ðjal) *adj.* primordial.

primoroso (pri·mo'ro·so) *adj.* artistic; delicate; exquisite.

princesa (prin'θe·sa; -'se·sa) *n.f.* princess.

principado (prin·θi'pa·ðo; prin·si-) *n.m.* principality.

principal (prin·θi'pal; -si'pal) *adj. & n.m. & f.* principal; main; chief.

príncipe ('prin·θi·pe; -si·pe) *n.m.* prince. —*adj.* first; foremost. —**príncipe consorte,** prince consort. —**príncipe heredero,** crown prince. —**principesco** (-'pes·ko) *adj.* princely.

principiante (prin·θi'pjan·te; prin·si-) *n.m.* [*fem.* **-ta**] beginner; apprentice.

principiar (prin·θi'pjar; prin·si-) *v.t.* to begin.

principio (prin'θi·pjo; -'si·pjo) *n.m.* **1,** principle. **2,** beginning. **3,** origin.

pringar (prin'gar) *v.t.* [*infl.:* **pagar, 8**] **1,** to dip in grease. **2,** to smear. —**pringarse,** *v.r., colloq.* to profiteer; make shady profits.

pringón (prin'gon) *adj., colloq.* greasy; dirty. —*n.m., colloq.* grease stain.

pringoso (prin'go·so) *adj.* greasy; fat.

pringue ('prin·ge) *n.m.* **1,** fat; dripping. **2,** dirt; filth.

prior (pri'or) *n.m.* prior. —**priora,** *n.f.* prioress.

prioridad (pri·o·ri'ðað; prjo-) *n.f.* priority.

prisa ('pri·sa) *n.f.* haste; promptness. —**a prisa,** quickly; swiftly. —**dar prisa a,** to hurry (someone). —**darse prisa,** to hurry; make haste. —**estar de prisa; tener prisa,** to be in a hurry.

prisco ('pris·ko) *n.m.* a variety of peach.

prisión (pri'sjon) *n.f.* **1,** prison. **2,** imprisonment. **3,** shackle; fetter; bond.

prisionero (pri·sjo'ne·ro) *n.m.* prisoner.

prisma ('pris·ma) *n.m.* prism. —**prismático** (-'ma·ti·ko) *adj.* prismatic. —**prismáticos,** *n.m.pl.* binoculars.

prístino ('pris·ti·no) *adj.* pristine; primeval.

privación (pri·βa'θjon; -'sjon) *n.f.* privation.

privada (pri'βa·ða) *n.f.* privy.

privado (pri'βa·ðo) *adj.* **1,** private. **2,** unconscious; senseless; stunned. —*n.m.* confidant; favorite.

privanza (pri'βan·θa; -sa) *n.f.* favor; special regard; favoritism.

privar (pri'βar) *v.t.* **1,** to deprive. **2,** to make unconscious; render senseless. —*v.i.* to have favor; enjoy favor. —**privarse,** *v.r.* **1,** to deprive oneself. **2,** to become unconscious. —**privarse de,** to forgo; give up.

privativo (pri·βa'ti·βo) *adj.* **1,** personal; peculiar. **2,** privative.

privilegio (pri·βi'le·xjo) *n.m.* privilege. —**privilegiado,** *adj.* privileged. —**privilegiar,** *v.t.* to favor; grant privilege to.

pro (pro) *prep., adv. & n.m. or f.* pro. —**¡buena pro!,** hearty appetite! —**de pro,** worthy. —**el pro y el contra,** the pros and cons. —**en pro,** for; in favor.

proa ('pro·a) *n.f.* **1,** prow; bow. **2,** *aero.* nose.

probable (pro'βa·βle) *adj.* probable. —**probabilidad,** *n.f.* probability.

probación (pro·βa'θjon; -'sjon) *n.f.* 1, probation. 2, = **prueba.**

probado (pro'βa·ðo) *adj.* tried; proven.

probador (pro·βa'ðor) *n.m.* 1, [*fem* **-dora**] sampler; taster; tester; fitter. 2, fitting room. —*adj.* sampling; tasting.

probadura (pro·βa'ðu·ra) *n.f.* sampling; tasting.

probar (pro'βar) *v.t.* [*infl.:* **acostar,** 28] 1, to prove. 2, to sample; try; taste. 3, to try on. —*v.i.* 1, *fol. by* **a,** to try to; attempt to. 2, to suit; be suitable.

probatorio (pro·βa'to·rjo) *adj.* probationary.

probeta (pro'βe·ta) *n.f.* 1, test tube. 2, mercury manometer. 3, *photog.* developing pan.

probidad (pro·βi'ðað) *n.f.* probity.

problema (pro'βle·ma) *n.m.* problem. —**problemático** (-'ma·ti·ko) *adj.* problematic.

probo ('pro·βo) *adj.* upright; honest.

probóscide (pro'βos·θi·ðe; -'βo·si·ðe) *n.f.* .proboscis.

procaz (pro'kaθ; -'kas) *adj.* impudent; pert. —**procacidad** (-θi'ðað; -si'ðað) *n.f.* impudence; pertness.

procedencia (pro·θe'ðen·θja; -se'ðen·sja) *n.f.* 1, source. 2, place of origin.

procedente (pro·θe'ðen·te; pro·se-) *adj.* 1, originating. 2, fitting; apt. 3, rightful; lawful.

proceder (pro·θe'ðer; -se'ðer) *v.i.* 1, to proceed; go on. 2, to act; behave. 3, to arise; stem; originate. 4, to be fitting; be rightful. 5, *fol. by* **contra,** to bring suit against; proceed against. —*n.m.* conduct; behavior; action.

procedimiento (pro·θe·ði·'mjen·to; pro·se-) *n.m.* 1, procedure. 2, *law* proceedings.

prócer ('pro·θer; -ser) *adj.* exalted; lofty. —*n.m.* exalted personage; great patriot.

procesado (pro·θe'sa·ðo; pro·se-) *adj.* 1, legal; of or pert. to legal proceedings. 2, accused; indicted. —*n.m.* defendant.

procesal (pro·θe'sal; -se'sal) *adj.* of or pert. to legal proceedings; legal.

procesamiento (pro·θe·sa'mjen·to; pro·se-) *n.m.* 1, prosecution. 2, indictment. 3, *comput.* processing.

—**procesamiento de datos,** data processing.

procesar (pro·θe'sar; -se'sar) *v.t.* 1, to process. 2, to indict; prosecute.

procesión (pro·θe'sjon; -se'sjon) *n.f.* procession. —**procesional,** *adj.* processional.

proceso (pro'θe·so; -'se·so) *n.m.* 1, process. 2, *law* trial; proceedings.

proclama (pro'kla·ma) *n.f.* 1, announcement; public notice. 2, manifesto. 3, *usu.pl.* marriage banns.

proclamar (pro·kla'mar) *v.t.* to proclaim. —**proclamación,** *n.f.* proclamation.

proclive (pro'kli·βe) *adj.* inclined; disposed. —**proclividad,** *n.f.* proclivity.

procomún (pro·ko'mun) *n.m.* public welfare. *Also,* **procumunal.**

procónsul (pro'kon·sul) *n.m.* proconsul. —**proconsulado,** *n.m.* proconsulate. —**proconsular,** *adj.* proconsular.

procrear (pro·kre'ar) *n.f.* to procreate. —**procreación** *n.f.* procreation. —**procreador,** *adj.* procreating. —*n.m.* [*fem.* **-dora**] procreator.

procura (pro'ku·ra) *n.f.* 1, power of attorney; commission. 2, = **procuraduría.** 3, diligence. —**en procura de,** *Amer.* 1, in search of. 2, in an attempt to.

procuración (pro·ku·ra'θjon; -'sjon) *n.f.* 1, enterprise; diligence. 2, power of attorney; commission. 3, = **procuraduría.** 4, procurement.

procurador (pro·ku·ra'ðor) *n.m.* 1, procurator. 2, solicitor; attorney. 3, agent; proctor; representative. 4, *polit.* deputy.

procuraduría (pro·ku·ra·ðu'ri·a) *n.f.* office of a legal representative, proctor, attorney, solicitor, etc.

procurar (pro·ku'rar) *v.t.* 1, to procure; secure. 2, to attempt; endeavor. 3, to manage; look after. 4, *Amer.* to cause; bring about.

prodigalidad (pro·ði·ya·li'ðað) *n.f.* prodigality.

prodigar (pro·ði'yar) *v.t.* [*infl.:* **pagar, 8**] to lavish; squander.

prodigio (pro'ði·xjo) *n.m.* prodigy. —**prodigioso,** *adj.* prodigious.

pródigo ('pro·ði·yo) *adj. & n.m.* prodigal.

producción (pro·ðuk'θjon; -'sjon) *n.f.* production. —**producción en serie,** mass production.

producir (pro·ðu'θir; -'sir) v.t. [infl.: conducir, 40] 1, to produce. 2, to yield; bear. 3, to cause; bring about. —**producirse**, v.r. to happen; come about.

productivo (pro·ðuk'ti·βo) adj. productive; fruitful. —**productividad**, n.f. productivity.

producto (pro'ðuk·to) n.m. 1, product. 2, often pl. produce.

productor (pro·ðuk'tor) adj. 1, producing. 2, productive. —n.m. [fem. -tora] 1, producer. 2, worker.

proemio (pro'e·mjo) n.m. preface; introduction. —**proemial**, adj. prefatory; introductory.

proeza (pro'e·θa; -sa) n.f. prowess; heroic deed.

profanar (pro·fa'nar) v.t. to profane; defile. —**profanación**, n.f., also, **profanamiento**, n.m. profanation. —**profanador**, adj. profaning; defiling. —n.m. [fem. -dora] profaner; defiler.

profanidad (pro·fa·ni'ðað) n.f. 1, profanity. 2, immodesty; excess.

profano (pro'fa·no) adj. 1, profane. 2, secular. 3, lay; uninformed.

profecía (pro·fe'θi·a; -'si·a) n.f. prophecy.

proferir (pro·fe'rir) v.t. [infl.: sentir, 31] to utter.

profesar (pro·fe'sar) v.t. 1, to profess. 2, to exercise; practice (an art or science). 3, to teach. —v.i. to take the vows of a religious order.

profesión (pro·fe'sjon) n.f. profession. —**profesional**, adj. & n.m. & f. professional.

profeso (pro'fe·so) adj. professed; avowed.

profesor (pro·fe'sor) n.m. [fem. -sora] professor; teacher.

profesorado (pro·fe·so'ra·ðo) n.m. 1, professorate. 2, professoriate. 3, professorship.

profesoral (pro·fe·so'ral) adj. professorial.

profeta (pro'fe·ta) n.m. prophet. —**profético**, adj. prophetic. —**profetisa**, n.f. prophetess.

profetizar (pro·fe·ti'θar; -'sar) v.t. & i. [infl.: rezar, 10] to prophesy.

proficiente (pro·fi'θjen·te; -'sjen·te) adj. proficient. —**proficiencia**, n.f. proficiency.

profiláctico (pro·fi'lak·ti·ko) adj. & n.m. prophylactic. —n.m. condom. —**profiláctica**, n.f. hygiene.

profilaxis (pro·fi'lak·sis) n.f. prophylaxis.

prófugo ('pro·fu·ɣo) adj. escaping; escaped; fugitive. —n.m. 1, fugitive from justice; escapee. 2, mil. deserter.

profundizar (pro·fun·di'θar; -'sar) v.t. [infl.: rezar, 10] 1, to deepen. 2, to fathom; delve into.

profundo (pro'fun·do) adj. deep; profound. —**profundidad**, n.f. depth; profundity.

profuso (pro'fu·so) adj. profuse. —**profusión**, n.f. profusion; profuseness.

progenie (pro'xe·nje) n.f. 1, ancestry; lineage. 2, progeny.

progenitor (pro·xe·ni'tor) n.m. parent; progenitor. —**progenitura**, n.f. primogeniture.

progesterona (pro·xes·te'ro·na) n.f. progesterone.

prognosis (proɣ'no·sis) n.f. prognosis.

programa (pro'ɣra·ma) n.m. program.

programar (pro·ɣra'mar) v.t., elect.; comput. to program. —**programación**, n.f., programming. —**programador** n.m. [fem. -dora] programmer.

progresar (pro·ɣre'sar) v.i. to progress.

progresión (pro·ɣre'sjon) n.f. progression.

progresista (pro·ɣre'sis·ta) adj. & n.m. & f. progressive.

progresivo (pro·ɣre'si·βo) adj. progressive.

progreso (pro'ɣre·so) n.m. progress.

prohibición (pro·i·βi'θjon; -'sjon) n.f. prohibition. —**prohibicionista**, n.m. & f. prohibitionist.

prohibir (pro·i'βir) v.t. to prohibit; forbid.

prohibitivo (pro·i·βi'ti·βo) adj. prohibitive.

prohibitorio (pro·i·βi'to·rjo) adj. prohibitory.

prohijar (pro·i'xar) v.t. to adopt. —**prohijamiento**, n.m., also, **prohijación**, n.f. adoption.

prohombre (pro'om·bre) n.m. great man; respected man.

prójima ('pro·xi·ma) n.f., colloq. woman of questionable reputation.

prójimo ('pro·xi·mo) n.m. fellow being; Bib. neighbor.

prole ('pro·le) n.f. offspring; progeny.

proletario (pro·le'ta·rjo) adj. &

n.m. proletarian. —**proletariado,** *n.m.* proletariat.

proliferar (pro,li·fe'rar) *v.i.* to proliferate. —**proliferación,** *n.f.* proliferation.

prolífico (pro'li·fi·ko) *adj.* prolific.

prolijidad (pro·li·xi'ðað) *n.f.* 1, neatness; fastidiousness. 2, prolixity.

prolijo (pro'li·xo) *adj.* 1, excessively tidy or neat; fastidious. 2, prolix; tedious.

prologar (pro·lo'ɣar) *v.t.* [*infl.:* **pagar,** 8] to write a prologue or preface to.

prólogo ('pro·lo·ɣo) *n.m.* prologue; preface.

prolongación (pro·lon·ga'θjon; -'sjon) *n.f., also,* **prolongamiento,** *n.m.* prolongation; extension.

prolongado (pro·lon'ga·ðo) *adj.* 1, elongated. 2, prolonged; extended.

prolongar (pro·lon'gar) *v.t.* [*infl.:* **pagar,** 8] to prolong; extend. —**prolongarse,** *v.r.* to last; extend.

promediar (pro·me'ðjar) *v.t.* to average. —*v.i.* 1, to mediate. 2, to reach the middle; be half over: *antes de promediar el mes de agosto,* before the middle of August.

promedio (pro'me·ðjo) *n.m.* 1, average. 2, *math.* mean.

promesa (pro'me·sa) *n.f.* promise. —**cumplir una promesa,** to keep one's promise. —**faltar a su promesa,** to break one's promise.

prometedor (pro·me·te'ðor) *adj.* promising.

Prometeo (pro·me'te·o) *n.m.* Prometheus.

prometer (pro·me'ter) *v.t.* to promise. —*v.i.* to give promising indications. —**prometerse,** *v.r.* to become betrothed; become engaged.

prometido (pro·me'ti·ðo) *n.m.* 1, betrothed; fiancé. 2, promise. —**prometida,** *n.f.* betrothed; fiancée.

prometio (pro·me'tjo) *n.m.* promethium.

prominente (pro·mi'nen·te) *adj.* prominent. —**prominencia,** *n.f.* prominence.

promiscuo (pro'mis·kwo) *adj.* promiscuous. —**promiscuidad,** *n.f.* promiscuity.

promisión (pro·mi'sjon) *n.f.* promise.

promisorio (pro·mi'so·rjo) *adj.* promissory.

promoción (pro·mo'θjon; -'sjon) *n.f.* 1, promotion. 2, group of individuals promoted or graduated together; class.

promontorio (pro·mon'to·rjo) *n.m.* promontory.

promotor (pro·mo'tor) *adj.* promoting. —*n.m.* [*fem.* **-tora**] promoter. *Also,* **promovedor** (-βe'ðor) [*fem.* **-dora**].

promover (pro·mo'βer) *v.t.* [*infl.:* **mover,** 30] to promote.

promulgar (pro·mul'ɣar) *v.t.* [*infl.:* **pagar,** 8] to promulgate. —**promulgación,** *n.f.* promulgation. —**promulgador,** *n.m.* [*fem.* **-dora**] promulgator.

prono ('pro·no) *adj.* prone.

pronombre (pro'nom·bre) *n.m.* pronoun. —**pronominal** (-mi'nal) *adj.* pronominal.

pronosticar (pro·nos·ti'kar) *v.t.* [*infl.:* **tocar,** 7] to prognosticate; forecast. —**pronosticación,** *n.f.* prognostication. —**pronosticador,** *adj.* prognostic; forecasting.

pronóstico (pro'nos·ti·ko) *n.m.* 1, forecast; prediction. 2, prognosis. —**pronóstico de vida,** life expectancy.

prontamente (pron·ta'men·te) *adv.* promptly.

prontitud (pron·ti'tuð) *n.f.* 1, promptness. 2, quick wit. 3, quick temper.

pronto ('pron·to) *adj.* 1, prompt; quick. 2, ready; prepared. —*n.m., colloq.* sudden impulse. —*adv.* 1, soon. 2, promptly; quickly. —**al pronto,** at first. —**de pronto,** 1, suddenly. 2, *comm., Mex.* down; as down payment. —**por lo pronto,** in the meantime; for the time being; provisionally. —**tan pronto como,** as soon as.

prontuario (pron'twa·rjo) *n.m.* 1, compendium; handbook. 2, dossier; record.

pronunciación (pro·nun·θja'θjon; -sja'sjon) *n.f.* pronunciation.

pronunciamiento (pro·nun·θja'mjen·to; -sja'mjen·to) *n.m.* 1, military uprising; insurrection. 2, *law* pronouncement of a sentence.

pronunciar (pro·nun'θjar; -'sjar) *v.t.* 1, to pronounce; utter. 2, to deliver (a speech). —**pronunciarse,** *v.r.* 1, to rebel; rise in mutiny. 2, to declare oneself; decide.

propagación (pro·pa·ɣa'θjon; -'sjon) *n.f.* **1**, propagation. **2**, dissemination; spreading.

propagador (pro·pa·ɣa'ðor) *adj.* propagating. —*n.m.* [*fem.* **-dora**] propagator.

propaganda (pro·pa'ɣan·da) *n.f.* propaganda. —**propagandista**, *n.m. & f.* propagandist.

propagar (pro·pa'ɣar) *v.t.* [*infl.:* **pagar, 8**] to propagate.

propalar (pro·pa'lar) *v.t.* to divulge.

propano (pro'pa·no) *n.m.* propane.

propasarse (pro·pa'sar·se) *v.r.* to overstep one's bounds; forget oneself.

propender (pro·pen'der) *v.i.* to tend; be prone; be inclined.

propensión (pro·pen'sjon) *n.f.* propensity; tendency.

propenso (pro'pen·so) *adj.* inclined; susceptible.

propiciar (pro·pi'θjar; -'sjar) *v.t.* to propitiate. —**propiciación**, *n.f.* propitiation. —**propiciatorio**, *adj.* propitiatory.

propicio (pro'pi·θjo; -sjo) *adj.* propitious; favorable.

propiedad (pro·pje'ðað) *n.f.* **1**, property. **2**, ownership. **3**, propriety. **4**, quality; peculiarity. —**propiedad literaria** *or* **artística**, copyright.

propietario (pro·pje'ta·rjo) *n.m.* proprietor; owner; landlord. —*adj.* proprietary.

propina (pro'pi·na) *n.f.* **1**, gratuity; tip. **2**, *Amer.* child's allowance.

propinar (pro·pi'nar) *v.t.* **1**, to give a drink to; treat to a drink. **2**, to administer (a medicine). **3**, to deliver (a blow, beating, etc.).

propincuo (pro'pin·kwo) *adj.* close; near. —**propincuidad**, *n.f.* propinquity.

propio ('pro·pjo) *adj.* **1**, one's own; peculiar. **2**, suitable; proper. **3**, characteristic; typical. **4**, natural. **5**, very same; identical. —*n.m.* **1**, municipal land or resources. **2**, messenger.

proponer (pro·po'ner) *v.t.* [*infl.:* **poner, 54**] **1**, to propose. **2**, to propound. —**proponerse**, *v.r.* to resolve; determine. —**proponente**, *n.m. & f.* proponent.

proporción (pro·por'θjon; -'sjon) *n.f.* **1**, proportion. **2**, extent; scope. **3**, chance; opportunity. —**a proporción de**, in accordance with; commensurate with.

proporcionado (pro·por·θjo'na-

ðo; -sjo'na·ðo) *adj.* **1**, proportionate. **2**, proportioned. **3**, convenient; suitable.

proporcional (pro·por·θjo'nal; -sjo'nal) *adj.* proportional.

proporcionar (pro·por·θjo'nar; -sjo'nar) *v.t.* **1**, to proportion. **2**, to provide; furnish. **3**, to adjust; adapt.

proposición (pro·po·si'θjon; -'sjon) *n.f.* **1**, proposition. **2**, proposal. **3**, *gram.* sentence; clause.

propósito (pro'po·si·to) *n.m.* purpose. —**a propósito, 1**, by the way. **2**, apropos. **3**, [*also,* **de propósito**] on purpose. —**fuera de propósito**, irrelevant; beside the point.

propuesta (pro'pwes·ta) *n.f.* proposal.

propuesto (pro'pwes·to) *v., p.p. of* **proponer**.

propugnar (pro·puɣ'nar) *v.t.* to champion; support.

propulsa (pro'pul·sa) *n.f.* rejection.

propulsar (pro·pul'sar) *v.t.* to propel.

propulsión (pro·pul'sjon) *n.f.* propulsion.

propulsor (pro·pul'sor) *n.m.* propellant. —*adj.* propellent; propulsive.

prorrata (pro'rra·ta) *n.f.* quota; assessment. —**a prorrata**, in proportion.

prorratear (pro·rra·te'ar) *v.t.* to prorate. —**prorrateo** (-'te·o) *n.m.* proportioning; proration.

prórroga ('pro·rro·ɣa) *also,* **prorrogación**, *n.f.* extension of time; deferment.

prorrogar (pro·rro'ɣar) `v.t.` [*infl.:* **pagar, 8**] to extend; defer.

prorrumpir (pro·rrum'pir) *v.i., usu.fol. by* **en**, to burst into (tears, laughter, etc.).

prosa ('pro·sa) *n.f.* **1**, prose. **2**, *colloq.* verbosity; wordiness.

prosaico (pro'sai·ko) *adj.* prosaic.

prosapia (pro'sa·pja) *n.f.* ancestry; lineage.

proscenio (pros'θe·njo; pro'se-) *n.m.* proscenium.

proscribir (pros·kri'βir) *v.t.* [*p.p.* **proscrito**] **1**, to proscribe. **2**, to banish; exile.

proscripción (pros·krip'θjon; -'sjon) *n.f.* proscription; exile.

proscrito (pros'kri·to) *v., p.p. of* **proscribir**. —*n.m.* outlaw; exile.

prosecución (pro·se·ku'θjon;

-'sjon) *n.f.* **1,** prosecution; continuance. **2,** pursuit.

proseguir (pro·se'γir) *v.t. & i.* [*infl.:* seguir, 64] to continue. —*v.i.* to proceed.

prosélito (pro'se·li·to) *n.m.* proselyte. —**proselitista,** *adj.* proselyting.

prosista (pro'sis·ta) *n.m. & f.* prose writer.

prosodia (pro'so·ðja) *n.f.* prosody. —**prosódico** (-'so·ði·ko) *adj.* prosodic.

prospecto (pros'pek·to) *n.m.* **1,** prospectus. **2,** *Amer.* prospect.

prosperar (pros·pe'rar) *v.t. & i.* to prosper.

próspero ('pros·pe·ro) *adj.* **1,** prosperous; thriving. **2,** propitious. —**prosperidad,** *n.f.* prosperity.

próstata ('pros·ta·ta) *n.f.* prostate gland. —**prostático** (-'ta·ti·ko) *adj.* prostatic.

prosternarse (pros·ter'nar·se) *v.r.* to prostrate oneself.

prostíbulo (pros'ti·βu·lo) *n.m.* house of prostitution.

prostituir (pros·ti·tu'ir) *v.t.* [*infl.:* huir, 26] to prostitute. —**prostitución,** *n.f.* prostitution.

prostituta (pros·ti'tu·ta) *n.f.* prostitute.

protactinio (pro·tak'ti·njo) *n.m.* = protoactinio.

protagonista (pro·ta·γo'nis·ta) *n.m. & f.* protagonist; star. —**protagonizar,** *v.t.* [*infl.:* rezar, 10] to star in (a play, film, etc.).

protección (pro·tek'θjon; -'sjon) *n.f.* protection. —**proteccionismo,** *n.m.* protectionism. —**proteccionista,** *adj. & n.m. & f.* protectionist.

protector (pro·tek'tor) *adj.* protecting; protective. —*n.m.* protector; patron. —**protectora,** *n.f.* protectress; patroness.

protectorado (pro·tek·to'ra·ðo) *n.m.* protectorate.

protectriz (pro·tek'triθ; -'tris) *adj.fem.* protecting; protective. —*n.f.* protectress.

proteger (pro·te'xer) *v.t.* [*infl.:* coger, 15] to protect.

protegido (pro·te'xi·ðo) *n.m.* protégé. —**protegida,** *n.f.* protégée.

proteico (pro'tei·ko) *adj.* protean.

proteína (pro·te'i·na) *n.f.* protein.

prótesis ('pro·te·sis) *n.f.* prosthesis. —**protético** (pro'te·ti·ko) *adj.* prosthetic.

protesta (pro'tes·ta) *n.f.* **1,** protest. **2,** protestation. *Also,* **protestación.**

protestante (pro·tes'tan·te) *adj. & n.m. & f.* Protestant; (*l.c.*) (one) protesting; remonstrant. —**protestantismo,** *n.m.* Protestantism.

protestar (pro·tes'tar) *v.t. & i.* to protest.

protesto (pro'tes·to) *n.m., comm.* protest.

protoactinio (pro·to·ak'ti·njo) *n.m.* protactinium.

protocolizar (pro·to·ko·li'θar; -'sar) *v.t.* [*infl.:* rezar, 10] **1,** to incorporate in a protocol. **2,** *colloq.* to make official; put official sanction on.

protocolo (pro·to'ko·lo) *n.m.* protocol. —**protocolar,** *adj.* of or pert. to protocol. —**protocolario,** *adj.* in accordance with protocol.

protón (pro'ton) *n.m.* proton.

protoplasma (pro·to'plas·ma) *n.m.* protoplasm. —**protoplasmático** (-'ma·ti·ko) *adj.* protoplasmic.

prototipo (pro·to'ti·po) *n.m.* prototype.

protozoario (pro·to·θo'a·rjo; -so'a·rjo) *adj. & n.m.* protozoan. *Also,* **protozoo** (-'θo·o; -'so·o).

protuberancia (pro·tu·βe'ran·θja; -sja) *n.f.* protuberance. —**protuberante,** *adj.* protuberant.

provecho (pro'βe·tʃo) *n.m.* benefit; advantage; good. —**¡buen provecho!,** *colloq.* good appetite! —**de provecho,** useful; of use.

provechoso (pro·βe'tʃo·so) *adj.* **1,** profitable. **2,** beneficial; good. **3,** useful; advantageous.

proveedor (pro·βe·e'ðor) *n.m.* **1,** purveyor; supplier. **2,** caterer. **3,** provider.

proveeduría (pro·βe·e·ðu'ri·a) *n.f.* **1,** storehouse. **2,** purveyor's shop.

proveer (pro·βe'er) *v.t.* [*infl.:* creer, 24; *p.p.* proveído, provisto (-'βis·to)] **1,** to provide. **2,** to stock; provision. **3,** to confer (a title, honor, etc.). **4,** *law* to decide.

proveído (pro·βe'i·ðo) *n.m., law* judgment; decision.

proveimiento (pro·βei'mjen·to) *n.m.* supply; provisioning.

provenir (pro·βe'nir) *v.i.* [*infl.:* venir, 69] **1,** to arise; originate. **2,** to result.

proverbio (pro'βer·βjo) *n.m.* proverb. —**proverbial,** *adj.* proverbial.

providencia (pro·βi'ðen·θja; -sja)

n.f. **1,** provision; preparation; measure. **2,** foresight. **3,** providence. —**providencial,** *adj.* providential.
providente (pro·βi'ðen·te) *adj.* provident.
próvido ('pro·βi·ðo) *adj.* **1,** provident. **2,** propitious; benevolent.
provincia (pro'βin·θja; -sja) *n.f.* province. —**provincial,** *adj.* provincial. —**provincialismo,** *n.m.* provincialism.
provinciano (pro·βin'θja·no; -'sja·no) *adj.* & *n.m.* provincial.
provisión (pro·βi'sjon) *n.f* provision. —**provisional,** *adj.* provisional.
provisorio (pro·βi'so·rjo) *adj.* provisional; temporary.
provisto (pro'βis·to) *v., p.p. of* **proveer.**
provocador (pro·βo·ka'ðor) *adj.* **1,** provoking; provocative. **2,** inviting; tempting.
provocar (pro·βo'kar) *v.t.* [infl.: **tocar,** 7] **1,** to provoke. **2,** to move; incite. **3,** to invite; tempt. —**provocación,** *n.f.* provocation. —**provocativo,** *adj.* provocative.
proxeneta (prok·se'ne·ta) *n.m.* procurer; go-between. —*n.f.* procuress.
próximamente (prok·si·ma·'men·te) *adv.* **1,** immediately; closely. **2,** soon. **3,** approximately.
proximidad (prok·si·mi'ðað) *n.f.* proximity. —**proximidades,** *n.f.pl.* environs; vicinity.
próximo ('prok·si·mo) *adj.* **1,** next. **2,** close; near. —**el próximo pasado,** last month.
proyección (pro·jek'θjon; -'sjon) *n.f.* projection.
proyectar (pro·jek'tar) *v.t.* **1,** to project. **2,** to plan.
proyectil (pro·jek'til) *n.m.* projectile; missile.
proyectista (pro·jek'tis·ta) *n.m.* & *f.* designer; planner.
proyecto (pro'jek·to) *n.m.* project; plan. —**proyecto de ley,** bill.
proyector (pro·jek'tor) *n.m.* projector. —**proyector cinematográfico,** movie projector.
prudencia (pru'ðen·θja; -sja) *n.f.* prudence. —**prudencial,** *adj.* prudential.
prudente (pru'ðen·te) *adj.* prudent.
prueba ('prwe·βa) *n.f.* **1,** proof. **2,** trial; test. **3,** ordeal. **4,** fitting; trying on. **5,** sample; sampling. **6,** *Amer.*

sporting event. **7,** tryout. —**a prueba,** *comm.* **1,** on trial; on approval. **2,** warranted; perfect. —**a prueba de,** proof against; -proof: *a prueba de agua,* waterproof. —**de prueba,** firm; solid; durable.
pruebe ('prwe·βe) *v., pres.subjve. of* **probar.**
pruebo ('prwe·βo) *v., 1st pers.sing. pres.ind. of* **probar.**
prurito (pru'ri·to) *n.m.* **1,** itch. **2,** *fig.* yen; craving.
prusiano (pru'sja·no) *adj.* & *n.m.* Prussian.
pseudo ('seu·ðo) *adj.* pseudo.
pseudónimo (seu'ðo·ni·mo) *adj.* & *n.m.* = **seudónimo.**
psicoanálisis (si·ko·a'na·li·sis) *n.m.* psychoanalysis. —**psicoanalista** (-'lis·ta) *n.m.* & *f.* psychoanalyst. —**psicoanalítico** (-'li·ti·ko) *adj.* psychoanalytic. —**psicoanalizar** *v.t.* [infl.: **rezar,** 10] to psychoanalyze.
psicodélico (si·ko'ðe·li·ko) *adj.* psychedelic.
psicología (si·ko·lo'xi·a) *n.f.* psychology. —**psicológico** (-'lo·xi·ko) *adj.* psychological. —**psicólogo** (-'ko·lo·γo) *n.m.* psychologist.
psiconeurosis (si·ko·neu'ro·sis) *n.f.* psychoneurosis.
psicópata (si'ko·pa·ta) *n.m.* & *f.* psychopath. —**psicopatía** (-'ti·a) *n.f.* psychopathy. —**psicopático** (-'pa·ti·ko) *adj.* psychopathic.
psicopatología (si·ko·pa·to·lo'xi·a) *n.f.* psychopathology.
psicosis (si'ko·sis) *n.f.* psychosis.
psicosomático (si·ko·so'ma·ti·ko) *adj.* psychosomatic.
psicoterapia (si·ko·te'ra·pja) *n.f.* psychotherapy. —**psicoterapeuta** (-'peu·ta) *n.m.* & *f.* psychotherapist.
psicótico (si'ko·ti·ko) *adj.* & *n.m.* psychotic.
psique ('si·ke) *n.m. or f.* psyche. —*cap., myth.* Psyche.
psiquiatría (si·kja'tri·a) *n.f.* psychiatry. —**psiquiatra** (-'kja·tra) *n.m.* & *f.* psychiatrist. —**psiquiátrico** (-'kja·tri·ko) *adj.* psychiatric.
psíquico ('si·ki·ko) *adj.* psychic.
psiquis ('si·kis) *n.m. or f.* psyche.
psitacosis (si·ta'ko·sis) *n.f.* psittacosis; parrot fever.
psoriasis (so'ri·a·sis) *also,* **psoriasis** (so'rja·sis) *n.f.* psoriasis.
pterodáctilo (te·ro'ðak·ti·lo) *n.m.* pterodactyl.

ptomaína (to·ma'i·na) *n.f.* pto-maine. *Also,* **tomaína.**

¡pu! (pu) *interj.* ugh!

púa ('pu·a) *n.f.* **1,** spine; quill; barb; prickle. **2,** tooth *(of a comb).* **3,** phonograph needle. **4,** plectrum. **5,** *colloq.* wily person; sharp person.

púber ('pu·βer) *also,* **púbero** ('pu·βe·ro) *adj.* pubescent.

pubertad (pu·βer'tað) *n.f.* puberty.

pubescencia (pu·βes'θen·θja; -βe'sen·sja) *n.f.* pubescence. —**pubescente,** *adj.* pubescent.

pubis ('pu·βis) *n.m.sing.* & *pl.* **1,** pubis. **2,** pubes. —**púbico** ('pu·βi·ko) *adj.* pubic.

publicación (pu·βli·ka'θjon; -'sjon) *n.f.* publication.

publicano (pu·βli'ka·no) *n.m.* publican.

publicar (pu·βli'kar) *v.t.* [*infl.:* **tocar,** 7] **1,** to publish. **2,** to publicize; make public.

publicidad (pu·βli·θi'ðað; -si'ðað) *n.f.* **1,** publicity. **2,** advertising. —**en publicidad,** publicly.

publicista (pu·βli'θis·ta; -'sis·ta) *n.m.* & *f.* publicist.

publicitario (pu·βli·θi'ta·rjo; -si'ta·rjo) *adj.* **1,** publicity *(attrib.).* **2,** advertising *(attrib.).*

público ('pu·βli·ko) *adj.* public. —*n.m.* **1,** public. **2,** audience.

puchero (pu'tʃe·ro) *n.m.* **1,** pot. **2,** = **puches.** **3,** pout; grimace.

puches ('pu·tʃes) *n.m.* or *f.pl.* pap; porridge; gruel. —**ganarse el puche,** *colloq.* to earn one's daily bread.

pucho ('pu·tʃo) *n.m., Amer.* **1,** cigar or cigarette stub; butt. **2,** butt end. **3,** leftover; trash; rubbish.

pude ('pu·ðe) *v., 1st pers.sing. pret.* of **poder.**

pudelar (pu·ðe'lar) *v.t.* to puddle (iron). —**pudelación,** *n.f.* puddling. —**pudelador,** *n.m.* puddler.

pudendo (pu'ðen·do) *adj., in partes pudendas,* private parts; pudenda.

pudibundez (pu·ði·βun'deθ; -'des) *n.f.* prudery; priggery.

pudibundo (pu·ði'βun·do) *adj.* = **pudoroso.**

pudicicia (pu·ði'θi·θja; -'si·sja) *n.f.* modesty; chastity; decorum.

púdico ('pu·ði·ko) *adj.* modest; chaste.

pudiendo (pu'ðjen·do) *v., ger.* of **poder.**

pudiente (pu'ðjen·te) *adj.* rich; well-to-do.

pudín (pu'ðin) *n.m.* = **budín.**

pudor (pu'ðor) *n.m.* modesty; decency. —**pudoroso,** *adj.* modest; decent.

pudrición (pu·ðri'θjon; -'sjon) *n.f.* = **putrefacción.**

pudrimiento (pu·ðri'mjen·to) *n.m.* putrefaction; rotting.

pudrir (pu'ðrir) *v.t.* [*p.p.* **podrido**] **1,** to putrefy; rot. **2,** to pester; annoy. —*v.i.* [*also, refl.,* **pudrirse**] to rot; rot away.

pueble ('pwe·βle) *v., pres.subjve.* of **poblar.**

pueblerino (pue·βle'ri·no) *adj.* small-town.

pueblo ('pwe·βlo) *n.m.* **1,** small town; village. **2,** people; populace. **3,** people; nation. **4,** pueblo.

pueblo ('pwe·βlo) *v., 1st pers.sing. pres.ind.* of **poblar.**

pueda ('pwe·ða) *v., pres.subjve.* of **poder.**

puedo ('pwe·ðo) *v., 1st pers.sing. pres.ind.* of **poder.**

puente ('pwen·te) *n.m.* **1,** bridge. **2,** *naut.* deck. —**puente colgante,** suspension bridge. —**puente levadizo,** drawbridge.

puerca ('pwer·ka) *n.f.* **1,** sow; pig. **2,** slut.

puerco ('pwer·ko) *n.m.* **1,** pig; hog. **2,** pork. —*adj.* piggish. —**puerco espín** (es'pin) porcupine.

pueril (pwe'ril) *adj.* puerile. —**puerilidad,** *n.f.* puerility.

puerperal (pwer·pe'ral) *adj.* puerperal.

puerro ('pwe·rro) *n.m.* leek.

puerta ('pwer·ta) *n.f.* door; gate. —**puerta corrediza,** sliding door. —**puerta falsa; puerta excusada,** private door; back door. —**puerta giratoria,** revolving door. —**puerta trasera,** back door; back gate.

puerto ('pwer·to) *n.m.* **1,** port. **2,** mountain pass; defile. **3,** harbor; haven. —**puerto seco,** inland port of entry.

puertorriqueño (pwer·to·rri'ke·ɲo) *adj.* & *n.m.* Puerto Rican.

pues (pwes) *conj.* **1,** for; since; because; inasmuch as. **2,** then; therefore. —*interj.* well; why; well; yes. —**pues bien,** now then; well. —**pues que,** since; inasmuch as. —**¿pues qué?,** so what?

puesta ('pwes·ta) *n.f.* **1,** setting *(as of the sun).* **2,** stake *(at cards).* **3,**

bet; amount bet. **4**, clutch of eggs.
5, *colloq.* a putting on or wearing of
a garment.

puestero (pwes'te·ro) *n.m.* vendor;
seller *(at a stand or booth).*

puesto ('pwes·to) *v., p.p.* of **poner.**
—*adj., usu. with* **bien** *or* **mal,**
dressed; attired. —*n.m.* **1,** post; station. **2,** position; place. **3,** stand;
booth. —**puesto que, 1,** though. **2,**
for; since.

¡puf! (puf) *interj.* ugh!

púgil ('pu·xil) *n.m.* pugilist; boxer.

pugilato (pu·xi'la·to) *n.m.* **1,** pugilism; boxing. **2,** fight; boxing
match. **3,** contention; rivalry.

pugilismo (pu·xi'lis·mo) *n.m.* pugilism; boxing. —**pugilista,** *n.m. &*
f., Amer. pugilist; boxer.

pugna ('puɣ·na) *n.f.* struggle;
strife.

pugnacidad (puɣ·na·θi'ðað; -si-
'ðað) *n.f.* pugnacity.

pugnar (puɣ'nar) *v.i.* to struggle;
strive

pugnaz (puɣ'naθ; -'nas) *adj.* pugnacious.

puja ('pu·xa) *n.f.* **1,** bid; bidding. **2,**
struggle.

pujador (pu·xa'ðor) *n.m.* [*fem.*
-dora] bidder.

pujanza (pu'xan·θa; -sa) *n.f.* vigor;
energy; might. —**pujante,** *adj.* vigorous; energetic.

pujar (pu'xar) *v.t.* **1,** to push; further; advance. **2,** to bid up. —*v.i.* **1,**
to struggle; push. **2,** to bid *(as in an
auction).* **3,** *colloq.* to snivel; pout.

pujo ('pu·xo) *n.m.* **1,** straining at
stool or in urinating. **2,** irresistible
impulse. **3,** craving; desire; eagerness. **4,** attempt, esp. an unsuccessful one.

pulcro ('pul·kro) *adj.* neat; tidy.
—**pulcritud** (-kri'tuð) *n.f.* pulchritude.

pulchinela (pul·tʃi'ne·la) *n.m.* =
polichinela.

pulga ('pul·ɣa) *n.f.* flea. —**juego
de ·la pulga,** tiddlywinks. —**no
aguantar pulgas,** *colloq.* to brook
no nonsense. —**tener malas
pulgas,** *colloq.* to have a nasty disposition; be irascible.

pulgada (pul'ɣa·ða) *n.f.* inch.

pulgar (pul'ɣar) *n.m.* thumb.

pulgoso (pul'ɣo·so) *adj.* fleabitten; flea-ridden. *Also, Amer.,*
pulguiento (-'yjen·to).

pulido (pu·li·ðo) *adj.* polished; re-

fined. —**pulidez** (-'ðeθ; -'ðes) *n.f.*
polish; refinement.

pulidor (pu·li'ðor) *n.m.* polisher.
—*adj.* polishing.

pulimentar (pu·li·men'tar) *v.t.* to
polish; buff.

pulimento (pu·li'men·to) *n.m.*
polish; gloss.

pulir (pu'lir) *v.t.* to polish.

pulmón (pul'mon) *n.m.* lung.
—**pulmonado,** *adj.* pulmonate.
—**pulmonar,** *adj.* pulmonary.

pulmonía (pul·mo'ni·a) *n.f.* pneumonia.

pulmotor (pul·mo'tor) *n.m.* pulmotor.

pulóver (pu'lo·βer) *n.m.* pullover.

pulpa ('pul·pa) *n.f.* pulp.

pulpería (pul·pe'ri·a) *n.f., Amer.*
general store. —**pulpero,** *n.m.,*
Amer. storekeeper.

púlpito ('pul·pi·to) *n.m.* pulpit.

pulpo ('pul·po) *n.m.* cuttlefish; octopus.

pulposo (pul'po·so) *adj.* pulpy.

pulque ('pul·ke) *n.m.* fermented
juice of the maguey; pulque.

pulsación (pul·sa·θjon; -'sjon) *n.f.*
pulsation.

pulsada (pul'sa·ða) *n.f.* pulse beat.

pulsador (pul·sa'ðor) *n.m.* push
button.

pulsar (pul'sar) *v.t.* **1,** to pluck;
strum. **2,** to take the pulse of. —*v.i.*
to pulse; pulsate; throb.

pulsear (pul·se'ar) *v.i.* to hand-
wrestle.

pulsera (pul'se·ra) *n.f.* bracelet;
wristlet.

pulso ('pul·so) *n.m.* **1,** pulse. **2,**
wrist. —**a pulso, 1,** by sheer exertion. **2,** freehand, as in drawing.

pulular (pu·lu'lar) *v.i.* to swarm;
teem.

pulverización (pul·βe·ri·
θa'θjon; -sa'sjon) *n.f.* **1,** pulverization. **2,** spraying.

pulverizar (pul·βe·ri'θar; -'sar)
v.t. [*infl.: rezar,* 10] **1,** to pulverize.
2, to spray; spray with an atomizer.
—**pulverizador,** *n.m.* **1,** pulverizer.
2, paint sprayer. **3,** atomizer.

pulla ('pu·ʎa; -ja) *n.f.* satirical remark; barb; gibe.

¡pum! (pum) *interj.* bang!; wham!;
pop!

puma ('pu·ma) *n.m.* puma; cougar.

puna ('pu·na) *n.f., S.A.* **1,** highland;
mountain heights. **2,** mountain sickness.

punce ('pun·θe; -se) *v., pres.subjve. of* **punzar.**

puncé (pun·'θe; -'se) *v., 1st pers. sing.pret. of* **punzar.**

punción (pun'θjon; -'sjon) *n.f., med.* puncture; puncturing; lancing.

pundonor (pun·do'nor) *n.m.* honor; pride; integrity.

pundonoroso (pun·do·no'ro·so) *adj.* **1,** delicate; touchy *(in matters of honor).* **2,** upright; honorable.

punible (pu'ni·βle) *adj.* punishable.

punición (pu·ni'θjon; -'sjon) *n.f.* punishment.

punitivo (pu·ni'ti·βo) *adj.* punitive.

punta ('pun·ta) *n.f.* **1,** point; tip; end. **2,** touch; trace; tinge. **3,** grain; speck; bit. **4,** *Amer.* bunch; lot. **5,** = **colilla.** —**puntas,** *n.f.pl.* needlepoint lace. —**a punta de,** *Amer.* by dint of. —**de punta en blanco,** *colloq.* all dressed up. —**de puntas** = **de puntillas.** —**estar de punta,** to be on bad terms.

puntada (pun'ta·ða) *n.f.* **1,** stitch. **2,** hint. **3,** *Amer.* = **punzada.**

puntaje (pun'ta·xe) *n.m.* score; points.

puntal (pun'tal) *n.m.* **1,** prop; support. **2,** *Amer., colloq.* snack. **3,** *naut.* depth of hold.

puntapié (pun·ta'pje) *n.m.* kick.

puntazo (pun'ta·θo; -so) *n.m., Amer.* stab; jab.

punteado (pun·te'a·ðo) *n.m.* pattern of dots or stipples; stippling.

puntear (pun·te'ar) *v.t.* **1,** to dot. **2,** to stitch. **3,** to pluck; strum. —*v.i., naut.* to tack.

punteo (pun'te·o) *n.m.* strumming; plucking.

puntera (pun'te·ra) *n.f.* **1,** toecap. **2,** darn; patch *(on socks or stockings).* **3,** *colloq.* = **puntapié.**

puntería (pun·te'ri·a) *n.f.* **1,** aim. **2,** marksmanship.

puntero (pun'te·ro) *n.m.* **1,** pointer. **2,** hole punch. **3,** stonecutter's chisel. **4,** *Amer.* hand *(of a timepiece).*

puntiagudo (pun·tja'ɣu·ðo) *adj.* pointed; sharp.

puntilla (pun'ti·ʎa; -ja) *n.f.* **1,** lace; lace edging. **2,** brad. **3,** sharp, slender pick. —**dar la puntilla,** *colloq.* to finish off. —**de puntillas,** on tiptoe.

puntillazo (pun·ti'ʎa·θo; -'ja·so) *n.m., colloq.* kick.

puntillo (pun'ti·ʎo; -jo) *n.m.* puntilio. —**puntilloso,** *adj.* punctilious.

punto ('pun·to) *n.m.* **1,** point. **2,** dot; speck. **3,** period *(punctuation).* **4,** stitch. **5,** notch *(of a belt, strap, etc.).* **6,** catch *(in a stocking).* **7,** aim. **8,** ideal state or condition; peak. **9,** point of honor. **10,** taxi stand. **11,** *colloq.* shrewd one. —**al punto, 1,** right away; immediately. **2,** = **a punto.** —**a punto, 1,** ready. **2,** just right; at the right point. **3,** to the point; pertinent. —**a punto de,** at or on the point of; just about to. —**a punto fijo,** exactly; with certainty. —**bajar de punto,** to cool off; calm down. —**de punto,** knit; knitted. —**de todo punto,** entirely; completely. —**dos puntos,** colon. —**en punto,** sharp; on the dot. —**poner los puntos sobre las íes,** *colloq.* to get down to brass tacks. —**por punto general,** as a rule; generally. —**por puntos, 1,** from one moment to the next. **2,** point by point; in detail. **3,** scarcely; barely. —**punto en boca,** silence; mum. —**punto final,** end; finish. —**punto menos (que),** almost; well nigh; practically. —**puntos seguidos,** *print.* leaders. —**puntos suspensivos,** suspension points. —**punto y aparte,** period *(at the end of a paragraph).* —**punto y coma,** semicolon. —**punto y seguido,** period *(at the end of a sentence, within a paragraph).* —**subir de punto,** to come up to a peak state or condition.

puntuación (pun·twa'θjon; -'sjon) *n.f.* punctuation.

puntual (pun'twal) *adj.* punctual. —**puntualidad,** *n.f.* punctuality.

puntualizar (pun·twa·li'θar; -'sar) *v.t. [infl.:* **rezar, 10]** **1,** to define; set forth in detail. **2,** to give the finishing touches to. **3,** to fix in one's memory.

puntuar (pun'twar) *v.t. [infl.:* **continuar, 23]** to punctuate.

puntura (pun'tu·ra) *n.f.* puncture.

punzada (pun'θa·ða; -'sa·ða) *n.f.,* **1,** [*also,* **punzadura**] prick; pricking. **2,** sharp pain; pang.

punzar (pun'θar; -'sar) *v.t. [infl.:* **rezar, 10]** **1,** to prick; pierce. **2,** to cause a sharp pain in; hurt. —**punzante,** *adj.* sharp.

punzó (pun'θo; -'so) *n.m.* poppy red.

punzón (pun'θon; -'son) *n.m.* **1,** punch; puncheon. **2,** awl. **3,** die punch. —**punzón de trazar,** scriber.

puñada (pu'ɲa·ða) *n.f.* = **puñetazo.**

puñado (pu'ɲa·ðo) *n.m.* handful. —**a puñados, 1,** by fistfuls; abundantly. **2,** by handfuls; sparsely.

puñal (pu'ɲal) *n.m.* dagger. —**puñalada,** *n.f.* stab.

puñetazo (pu·ɲe'ta·θo; -so) *n.m.* blow with the fist; punch. *Also,* **puñete** (-'ɲe·te).

puño ('pu·ɲo) *n.m.* **1,** fist. **2,** cuff; wristband. **3,** handle *(of an umbrella, cane, etc.).* **4,** hilt *(of a sword, dagger, etc.).* **5,** fistful. **6,** *colloq.* hand. **7,** *colloq.* courage; strength. **8,** *Amer.* = **puñetazo.**

pupa ('pu·pa) *n.f.* **1,** cold sore; chap *(of the lips).* **2,** = **postilla. 3,** childish expression of pain.

pupila (pu'pi·la) *n.f.* **1,** pupil; student. **2,** ward. **3,** *anat.* pupil.

pupilaje (pu·pi'la·xe) *n.m.* ward ship.

pupilo (pu'pi·lo) *n.m.* **1,** pupil; student. **2,** ward.

pupitre (pu'pi·tre) *n.m.* school desk.

puré (pu're) *n.m.* purée.

pureza (pu're·θa; -sa) *n.f.* purity.

purga (pur'ɣa) *n.f.* purge.

purgación (pur·ɣa'θjon; -'sjon) *n.f.* **1,** purge; purgation. **2,** *usu.pl.* gonorrhea.

purgador (pur·ɣa'ðor) *adj.* purging. —*n.m.* steam valve.

purgante (pur'ɣan·te) *adj.* & *n.m.* & *f.* purgative.

purgar (pur'ɣar) *v.t.* [*infl.:* **pagar, 8**] to purge; cleanse.

purgativo (pur·ɣa'ti·βo) *adj.* & *n.m.* purgative.

purgatorio (pur·ɣa'to·rjo) *n.m.* purgatory.

purificar (pu·ri·fi'kar) *v.t.* [*infl.:* **tocar, 7**] to purify. —**purifica-**

ción, *n.f.* purification. —**purificador,** *adj.* purifying. —*n.m.* [*fem.* -**dora**] purifier.

purismo (pu'ris·mo) *n.m.* purism. —**purista,** *adj.* puristic. —*n.m.* & *f.* purist.

puritano (pu·ri'ta·no) *adj.* puritanical. —*n.m.* puritan. —**puritanismo,** *n.m.* puritanism.

puro ('pu·ro) *adj.* **1,** pure. **2,** sheer; mere. —*n.m.*, cigar. —**oro puro,** solid gold.

púrpura ('pur·pu·ra) *adj.* & *n.f.* purple.

purpúreo (pur'pu·re·o) *adj.* purple; purplish. *Also,* **purpurino** (-'ri·no).

purulento (pu·ru'len·to) *adj.* purulent. —**purulencia,** *n.f.* purulence.

pus (pus) *n.f.* pus.

puse ('pu·se) *v., pret. of* **poner.**

pusilánime (pu·si'la·ni·me) *adj.* pusillanimous. —**pusilanimidad,** *n.f.* pusillanimity.

pústula ('pus·tu·la) *n.f.* pustule. —**pustuloso,** *adj.* pustular.

puta ('pu·ta) *n.f.* whore.

putaísmo (pu·ta'is·mo) *n.m.* **1,** harlotry; whoring. **2,** brothel.

putativo (pu·ta'ti·βo) *adj.* putative.

putear (pu·te'ar) *v.i., colloq.* to whore.

putería (pu·te'ri·a) *n.f.* **1,** = **putaísmo. 2,** [*also,* **putada** (-'ta·ða)] *colloq.* dirty trick.

putero (pu'te·ro) *adj., colloq.* lewd; lecherous. —*n.m.* lecher.

putesco (pu'tes·ko) *adj.* whorish.

putrefacción (pu·tre·fak'θjon; -'sjon) *n.f.* putrefaction.

putrefacto (pu·tre'fak·to) *adj.* putrefied; putrid.

pútrido ('pu·tri·ðo) *adj.* putrid. —**putridez** (-'ðeθ; -'ðes) *n.f.* rottenness.

puya ('pu·ja) *n.f.* **1,** goad. **2,** snide remark; dig.

Q

Q, q (ku) *n.f.* 20th letter of the Spanish alphabet.

quantum ('kwan·tum) *n.m.* [*pl.* -**ta**] quantum.

que (ke) *rel.pron.* who; whom; that; which. —*conj.* **1,** *in subordinate* *clauses* that: *Él dice que lo hará,* He says that he will do it. *In subjunctive constructions denoting command or request, the clause introduced by* **que** *is usually rendered in Eng. by* to + *inf.: Quiero que* *vengas,* I want you to come. **2,** *in correlative constructions* whether . . . or: *que quiera que no quiera,* whether he wants to or not. **3,** *in coordinate clauses, indicating repetition or continuance of an action:* habla que habla, talk, talk; talking and talking. **4,** *colloq.* since; for; as: *Léalo, que es interesante,* Read it, for it is interesting. **5,** *in comparisons* than: *Más vale tarde que nunca,* Better late than never. **6,** *in independent clauses expressing indirect command or request,* que *is rendered in Eng. by* let: *Que lo haga,* Let him do it. **7,** *colloq.* = para que: *Dame el dinero que te compre el libro,* Give me the money so I may buy you the book. —**por . . . que,** no matter how . . .; however . . . : *por enfermo que esté, tiene que venir,* However sick he is, he has to come.

qué (ke) *interrog. adj. & pron.* which; what. —*adj., in exclamations* what a: *¡qué lástima!,* what a pity! —*adv., in exclamations* how: *¡qué bonita!,* how pretty! —**a qué,** why; what for. —**no hay de qué,** you're welcome; don't mention it. —**¿para qué?,** what for? —**¿por qué?,** why? —**¿pues y qué?,** why not?; so what? —**¡qué de . . . !,** how much . . . !; how many . . . !—**¿qué hay?,** what's up?; what's the matter? —**¿Qué más da?,** What's the difference?; What does it matter? —**¿qué tal?,** how goes it? —**¡qué va!,** You don't say!; Come on! —**un no sé qué,** an indefinable something —**¿y qué?,** so what?

quebracho (ke'βra·tʃo) *n.m.* a tropical tree with very hard wood. *Also,* **quiebrahacha** (kje'βra·tʃa).

quebrada (ke'βra·ða) *n.f.* **1,** ravine; gorge. **2,** bankruptcy; failure. **3,** *Amer.* brook.

quebrado (ke'βra·ðo) *adj.* **1,** broken. **2,** bankrupt. —*n.m., math.* fraction. —**quebradizo,** *adj.* breakable; fragile; frail.

quebradura (ke·βra'ðu·ra) *n.f.* **1,** break; fracture; rupture. **2,** hernia.

quebrantador (ke·βran·ta'ðor) *adj.* **1,** harrowing; distressing. **2,** debilitating. —*n.m.* breaker.

quebrantahuesos (ke·βran·ta·'we·sos) *n.m.* osprey.

quebrantamiento (ke·βran·ta·'mjen·to) *n.m.* **1,** breakdown; collapse. **2,** breaking; breach. **3,** violation.

quebrantar (ke·βran'tar) *v.t.* **1,** to break; breach. **2,** to crush; break down. **3,** to harrow; distress. **4,** to cool (something hot); take the chill off (something cold). —**quebrantarse,** *v.r.* **1,** to break; become broken. **2,** to break down.

quebranto (ke'βran·to) *n.m.* **1,** breakdown. **2,** despair. **3,** affliction. **4,** damage; loss. **5,** commiseration; pity.

quebrar (ke'βrar) *v.t. & i.* [*infl.:* **pensar,** 27] to break. —*v.t.* to break; bend. —*v.i.* **1,** to break down; give; fail. **2,** to fail; become bankrupt. —**quebrarse,** *v.r.* **1,** to break; become broken. **2,** to break off; end. **3,** *colloq.* to put forth great effort.

quebrazón (ke·βra'θon; -'son) *n.m.* breaking; breakage.

queche ('ke·tʃe) *n.m.* ketch.

queda ('ke·ða) *n.f.* curfew.

quedar (ke'ðar) *v.i.* **1,** to rest; remain. **2,** to stay; tarry. **3,** to be left; be or become; find oneself or itself. **4,** *fol. by* en, to agree. **5,** *fol. by* en, to come to; result in. **6,** *fol. by* por or como, to be taken for; come to be regarded as; seem. **7,** to fit, as clothes. **8,** to come out; turn out. **9,** *Amer.* to be; to be located. —*aux.v., fol. by p.p.* to be or become. —**quedarse,** *v.r.* **1,** to remain. **2,** *fol. by* con, to keep; hold on to.

quedo ('ke·ðo) *adj.* quiet; silent. —*adv.* softly; quietly.

quehacer (ke·a'θer; -'ser) *n.m.* occupation; chore; odd job.

queja ('ke·xa) *n.f.* **1,** plaint; plaintive cry. **2,** complaint.

quejarse (ke'xar·se) *v.r.* **1,** to cry; lament. **2,** to complain; *fol. by* con to complain to; *(with* de) to complain of or about.

quejido (ke'xi·ðo) *n.m.* plaintive sound; groan; moan.

quejón (ke'xon) *adj.* whining; complaining. —*n.m.* [*fem.* **quejona**] whiner; complainer.

quejoso (ke'xo·so) *adj.* complaining; grumbling; disgruntled.

quejumbre (ke'xum·bre) *n.f.* constant complaining; querulousness.

quejumbroso (ke·xum'bro·so) *adj.* plaintive; querulous.

quema ('ke·ma) *n.f.* **1,** burning. **2,** fire. —**a quema ropa; a quema-rropa** (a·ke·ma'rro·pa) point-blank.

quemadero (ke·ma'ðe·ro) *n.m.* incinerator.

quemado (ke'ma·ðo) *n.m.* 1, something burning or burnt. 2, *colloq.* burnt portion, esp. of rice.

quemador (ke·ma'ðor) *adj.* burning; scorching. —*n.m.* burner.

quemadura (ke·ma'ðu·ra) *n.f.* 1, burn. 2, frostbite.

quemar (ke'mar) *v.t. & i.* to burn. —**quemarse,** *v.r.* to burn; be burning.

quemazón (ke·ma'θon; -'son) *n.f.* 1, burn; burning. 2, burning sensation. 3, itch; irritation.

quepa ('ke·pa) *v., pres.subjve.* of **caber.**

quepis ('ke·pis) *n.m.sing. & pl.* = **kepis.**

quepo ('ke·po) *v., 1st pers.sing. pres.ind.* of **caber.**

queratina (ke·ra'ti·na) *n.f., biol.* keratin.

querella (ke're·ʎa; -ja) *n.f.* 1, plaint; complaint. 2, quarrel; dispute; disagreement. 3, *law* complaint.

querellado (ke·re'ʎa·ðo; -'ja·ðo) *n.m.* defendant.

querellante (ke·re'ʎan·te; -'jan·te) *n.m. & f.* complainant; plaintiff.

querellarse (ke·re'ʎar·se; -'jar·se) *v.r.* to complain.

querelloso (ke·re'ʎo·so; -'jo·so) *adj.* querulous.

querencia (ke'ren·θja; -sja) *n.f.* 1, love; fondness; affection. 2, yearning; longing. 3, haunt; nest; lair.

querendón (ke·ren'don) *adj.* affectionate.

querer (ke'rer) *v.t. & i.* [*infl.:* 55] 1, to want; wish; will. 2, to love; like; be fond (of). —*v.impers.* to threaten; be about to. —*n.m.* love; affection. —**como quiera que,** however; no matter how. —**como quiera que sea,** in any case; no matter what. —**cuando quiera,** at any time; whenever. —**donde quiera,** anywhere; wherever. —**querer decir,** to mean. —**sin querer,** involuntarily; unwittingly.

querida (ke'ri·ða) *n.f.* 1, darling; dear. 2, mistress.

querido (ke'ri·ðo) *adj.* dear. —*n.m.* 1, beloved; darling. 2, lover.

querúbico (ke'ru·βi·ko) *adj.* cherubic.

querubín (ke·ru'βin) *n.m.* cherub. Also, **querube** (-'ru·βe).

quesadilla (ke·sa'ði·ʎa; -ja) *n.f.*

1, cheese cake. 2, a kind of tart. 3, *Mex.* tortilla with melted cheese inside.

quesera (ke'se·ra) *n.f.* 1, cheese vat. 2, cheese container. 3, cheese dish.

quesería (ke·se'ri·a) *n.f.* 1, cheese store. 2, cheese dairy.

quesero (ke'se·ro) *adj.* cheese (*attrib.*). —*n.m.* maker or seller of cheese.

queso ('ke·so) *n.m.* cheese. —**queso de nata,** cream cheese.

quevedos (ke'βe·ðos) *n.m.pl.* pince-nez.

¡quia! (kja) *interj.* come now!; you don't say!

quicio ('ki·θjo; -sjo) *n.m.* 1, hinge post (*of a door or window*). 2, eye of a hinge. —**fuera de quicio,** unhinged; put out. —**sacar de quicio,** to unhinge; exasperate.

quid (kið) *n.m.* gist; substance; point.

quiebra ('kje·βra) *n.f.* 1, break; fissure. 2, bankruptcy.

quiebre ('kje·βre) *v., pres.subjve.* of **quebrar.**

quiebro ('kje·βro) *n.m.* 1, dodge; shift; twist. 2, trill. 3, break or catch in the voice. —*v., 1st pers.sing. pres.ind.* of **quebrar.**

quien (kjen) *rel.pron.* [*pl.* **quienes** ('kje·nes)] who; whom; whoever; whomever; which; whichever. —**quien . . . quien . . . ,** one . . . another . . . : *Quien iba a pie, quien a caballo,* One (some) went on foot, another (others) on horseback. —**de quien o de quienes,** whose.

quién (kjen) *interrog.pron.* [*pl.* **quiénes** ('kje·nes)] who; whom; which.

quienquiera (kjen'kje·ra) *indef. pron.* [*pl.* **quienesquiera** (kje·nes-)] whoever; whosoever; whomever; whomsoever; whichever.

quiera ('kje·ra) *v., pres.subjve.* of **querer.**

quiero ('kje·ro) *v., 1st pers.sing. pres.ind.* of **querer.**

quieto ('kje·to) *adj.* still; quiet; calm. —**quietud,** *n.f.* quietude; quiet; stillness.

quijada (ki'xa·ða) *n.f.* jaw; jawbone.

quijote (ki'xo·te) *n.m.* quixotic person. —**quijotada,** *n.f.* quixotic deed or undertaking. —**quijotesco,** *adj.* quixotic. —**quijotismo,** *n.m.* quixotism.

quilate (ki'la·te) *n.m.* carat.

quilo ('ki·lo) *n.m.* = **kilo**.

quilla ('ki·ʎa; -ja) *n.f.* keel.

quimera (ki'me·ra) *n.f.* chimera. —**quimérico** (-'me·ri·ko) *adj.* chimerical.

química ('ki·mi·ka) *n.f.* chemistry.

químico ('ki·mi·ko) *adj.* chemical. —*n.m.* [*fem.* -**ca**] chemist.

quimioterapia (ki·mjo·te'ra·pja) *n.f.* chemotherapy.

quimono (ki'mo·no) *n.m.* kimono.

quina ('ki·na) *n.f.* **1,** cinchona bark. **2,** quint (*in games of chance*).

quincalla (kin'ka·ʎa; -ja) *n.f.* **1,** metalware; hardware. **2,** small wares; novelties. **3,** costume jewelry. —**quincallería,** *n.f.* shop dealing in metalware, novelties, etc. —**quincallero,** *n.m.* dealer in metalware, novelties, etc.

quince ('kin·θe; -se) *adj.* & *n.m.* fifteen. —**quince días,** fortnight.

quinceañera (kin·θe·a'ɲe·ra; kin·se-) *n.f.* fifteen-year-old girl; debutante.

quincena (kin'θe·na; -'se·na) *n.f.* **1,** fortnight. **2,** biweekly allowance or pay. —**quincenal,** *adj.* fortnightly; biweekly.

quinceno (kin'θe·no; -'se·no) *adj.* fifteenth.

quincuagenario (kin·kwa·xe'na·rjo) *adj.* & *n.m.* = **cincuentón.**

quincuagésimo (kin·kwa'xe·si·mo) *adj.* & *n.m.* fiftieth. —**Quincuagésima,** *n.f.* Quinquagesima.

quindécimo (kin'de·θi·mo; -si·mo) *adj.* & *n.m.* fifteenth.

quinestesia (ki·nes'te·sja) *n.f., physiol.* kinesthesia.

quingentésimo (kin·xen'te·si·mo) *adj.* & *n.m.* five-hundredth.

quingombó (kin·gom'bo) *n.m.* **1,** okra. **2,** gumbo.

quinientos (ki'njen·tos) *adj.* & *n.m.pl.* [*fem.* -**tas**] five hundred. —*adj.* five-hundredth.

quinina (ki'ni·na) *n.f.* quinine.

quino ('ki·no) *n.m.* cinchona tree.

quinqué (kin'ke) *n.m.* **1,** kerosene lamp; hurricane lamp. **2,** globe lamp.

quinquenio (kin'ke·njo) *n.m.* five-year period; quinquennium. —**quinquenal** (-'nal) *adj.* five-year; quinquennial.

quinta ('kin·ta) *n.f.* **1,** country house; villa. **2,** draft; levy. **3,** *mus.* fifth; quint. **4,** *cards* five of a kind.

quintaesencia (kin·ta·e'sen·θja; -sja) *n.f.* quintessence.

quintal (kin'tal) *n.m.* quintal. —**quintal métrico,** 100 kilograms.

quinteto (kin'te·to) *n.m.* quintet.

quintillizo (kin·ti'ʎi·θo; -'ji·so) *adj.* & *n.m.* quintuplet.

quintillón (kin·ti'ʎon; -'jon) *n.m.* a trillion quintillion; *U.S.* nonillion; *Brit.* quintillion.

quinto ('kin·to) *adj.* & *n.m.* fifth. —*n.m.* draftee; conscript.

quíntuple (kin·tu·ple) *n.m.* & *f., Amer.* quintuplet.

quintuplicar (kin·tu·pli'kar) *v.t.* [*infl.:* **tocar, 7**] to quintuple; multiply by five.

quíntuplo ('kin·tu·plo) *adj.* & *n.m.* quintuple.

quinzavo (kin'θa·βo; -'sa·βo) *adj.* & *n.m.* fifteenth.

quiosco *also,* **kiosco** ('kjos·ko) *n.m.* kiosk; stand; booth.

quiquiriquí (ki·ki·ri'ki) *interj.* & *n.m.* cock-a-doodle-doo.

quirófano (ki'ro·fa·no) *n.m.* **1,** operating room. **2,** surgical amphitheater.

quiromancia (ki·ro'man·θja; -sja) *n.f.* chiromancy; palmistry. —**quiromántico** (-ti·ko) *adj.* of or pert. to chiromancy or palmistry. —*n.m.* chiromancer; palmist.

quiropráctica (ki·ro'prak·ti·ka) *n.f.* chiropractic. —**quiropráctico,** *adj.* chiropractic. —*n.m.* chiropractor.

quirúrgico (ki'rur·xi·ko) *adj.* surgical.

quise ('ki·se) *v., pret. of* **querer.**

quisling ('kwis·lin; 'kis-) *n.m.* traitor; quisling.

quisquilla (kis'ki·ʎa; -ja) *n.f.* **1,** petty nuisance. **2,** = **camarón.**

quisquilloso (kis·ki'ʎo·so; -'jo·so) *adj.* **1,** fastidious. **2,** touchy; skittish.

quiste ('kis·te) *n.m.* cyst.

quisto ('kis·to) *adj., in* **bien quisto,** well-liked; **mal quisto,** disliked.

quita ('ki·ta) *n.f.* acquittance; release (*from debt*).

¡quita! ('ki·ta) *inter., colloq.* get out!; get off it!; come on!

quitamanchas (ki·ta'man·tʃas) *n.m.sing.* & *pl.* **1,** spot remover; cleaning fluid. **2,** dry cleaner.

quitanieves (ki·ta'nje·βes) *n.m. sing.* & *pl.* snow plow; snow remover.

quitanza (ki'tan·θa; -sa) *n.f.* quittance.

quitar (ki'tar) *v.t.* **1,** to remove; take away; take off. **2,** to prevent; preclude. —**quitarse,** *v.r.* **1,** to remove; take off, as clothing. **2,** *fol. by* **de,** to quit; abstain from. —**(de) quita y pon, 1,** removable; detachable. **2,** *(of clothing)* casual; slip-on. **3,** *also,* **juego de quita y pon,** the game of put and take.ʼ —**quitar del medio** *or* **de en medio,** to get out of the way; to get rid of. —**quitarse de encima,** to get rid of; get off one's shoulders.

quitasol (ki·ta'sol) *n.m.* parasol; sunshade.

quite ('ki·te) *n.m.* **1,** side-stepping; dodge. **2,** parry.

quizás (ki'θas; -'sas) *adv.* maybe; perhaps. *Also,* **quizá.**

quórum ('kwo·rum) *n.m.sing. & pl.* quorum.

R

R, r ('e·rre; 'e·re) *n.f.* 21st letter of the Spanish alphabet.

rabada (ra'βa·ða) *n.f.* rump.

rabadán (ra·βa'ðan) *n.m.* head shepherd.

rabadilla (ra·βa'ði·ʎa; -ja) *n.f.* **1,** coccyx; small of the back. **2,** tail end of a bird.

rábano ('ra·βa·no) *n.m.* radish. —**tomar el rábano por las hojas,** *colloq.* to be off the track; get one's wires crossed.

rabí (ra'βi) *n.m.* rabbi.

rabia ('ra·βja) *n.f.* **1,** rage; fury. **2,** rabies.

rabiar (ra'βjar) *v.i.* **1,** to rage; be mad. **2,** to be rabid; have rabies. —**a rabiar,** *colloq.* madly; exceedingly. —**rabiar por,** *colloq.* to crave; be eager for.

rabicorto (ra·βi'kor·to) *adj.* stubtailed; short-tailed.

rábido ('ra·βi·ðo) *adj.* rabid.

rabieta (ra'βje·ta) *n.f., colloq.* tantrum; fit.

rabillo (ra'βi·ʎo; -jo) *n.m., dim. of* **rabo.** —**rabillo del ojo,** corner of the eye.

rabínico (ra'βi·ni·ko) *adj.* rabbinical.

rabino (ra'βi·no) *n.m.* rabbi.

rabioso (ra'βjo·so) *adj.* **1,** mad; rabid. **2,** furious; raging.

rabo ('ra·βo) *n.m.* **1,** tail. **2,** tail end. **3,** corner of the eye.

rabona (ra'βo·na) *n.f., in* **hacer rabona,** *also* **hacerse la rabona,** to play hooky.

rabotada (ra·βo'ta·ða) *n.f.* insolent remark; grossness.

racial (ra'θjal; -'sjal) *adj.* racial.

racimo (ra'θi·mo; -'si·mo) *n.m.* **1,** bunch; cluster. **2,** *bot.* raceme.

raciocinar (ra·θjo·θi'nar; ra·sjo·si-) *v.i.* to reason; ratiocinate. —**raciocinación,** *n.f.* ratiocination.

raciocinio (ra·θjo'θi·njo; ra·sjo'si-) *n.m.* reasoning; ratiocination.

ración (ra'θjon; -'sjon) *n.f.* ration.

racional (ra·θjo'nal; -sjo'nal) *adj.* rational. —*n.m. or f.* rationale. —**racionalidad,** *n.f.* rationality. —**racionalizar,** *v.t.* [*infl.:* **rezar,** 10] to rationalize.

racionalismo (ra·θjo·na'lis·mo; ra·sjo-) *n.m.* rationalism. —**racionalista,** *adj.* rationalistic. —*n.m. & f.* rationalist.

racionar (ra·θjo'nar; ra·sjo-) *v.t.* to ration. —**racionamiento,** *n.m.* rationing.

racismo (ra'θis·mo; -'sis·mo-) *n.m.* racism. —**racista,** *adj. & n.m. & f.* racist.

racha ('ra·tʃa) *n.f.* **1,** gust of wind. **2,** *colloq.* gush; spate. **3,** *colloq.* streak (of luck).

rada ('ra·ða) *n.f.* small bay; inlet; roadstead.

radar (ra'ðar) *n.m.* radar.

radiación (ra·ðja'θjon; -'sjon) *n.f.* radiation.

radiactivo (ra·ði·ak'ti·βo) *adj.* radioactive. —**radiactividad,** *n.f.* radioactivity.

radiado (ra'ðja·ðo) *adj.* radiate.

radiador (ra·ðja'ðor) *n.m.* radiator.

radial (ra'ðjal) *adj.* radial.

radián (ra'ðjan) *n.m.* radian.

radiante (ra'ðjan·te) *adj.* radiant.

radiar (ra'ðjar) *v.t. & i.* **1,** to radiate. **2,** to broadcast.

radical (ra·ði'kal) *adj. & n.m. & f.* radical. —*n.m., math.; chem.; gram.* radical.

radicalismo (ra·ði·ka'lis·mo) *n.m.* radicalism.

radicar (ra·ði'kar) *v.i.* [*infl.:* **tocar,** 7] **1,** to settle; be or become rooted. **2,** to reside; have roots. —**radicarse,** *v.r.* to settle; establish residence.

radio ('ra·ðjo) *n.m.* **1,** radius. **2,** [*also,* **rádium**] radium. **3,** *also fem.* radio set; radio. **4,** spoke; ray. —*n.f.* = **radiodifusión.**

radioactivo (ra·ðjo·ak'ti·βo) *adj.* radioactive. —**radioactividad,** *n.f.* radioactivity.

radioaficionado *n.m.* ham radio operator.

radiocomunicación (ra·ðjo·ko·mu·ni·ka'θjon; -'sjon) *n.f.* radio communication.

radiodifundir (ra·ðjo·ði·fun'dir) *v.i.* to broadcast.

radiodifusión (ra·ðjo·ði·fu'sjon) *n.f.* radio broadcasting.

radiodifusora (ra·ðjo·ði·fu'so·ra) *n.f.* [*also,* **estación radiodifusora**] broadcasting station.

radiodirigido (ra·ðjo·ði·ri'xi·ðo) *adj.* radio-controlled.

radioemisor (ra·ðjo·e·mi'sor) *adj.* transmitting. —*n.m.* radio transmitter. —**radioemisora,** *n.f.* = **radiodifusora.**

radioescucha (ra·ðjo·es'ku·tʃa) *n.m. & f.* **1,** radio listener. **2,** radio monitor. **3,** short-wave listener.

radiofonía (ra·ðjo·fo'ni·a) *n.f.* = **radiotelefonía.**

radiofrecuencia (ra·ðjo·fre·'kwen·θja; -sja) *n.f.* radio frequency.

radiografía (ra·ðjo·ɣra'fi·a) *n.f.* **1,** X-ray photograph; radiograph. **2,** radiography. —**radiografiar,** *v.t.* [*infl.:* **enviar,** 22] to X-ray. —**radiográfico** (-'ɣra·fi·ko) *adj.* of or for X rays; X-ray (*attrib.*).

radiograma (ra·ðjo'ɣra·ma) *n.m.* radiogram.

radiolocutor (ra·ðjo·lo·ku'tor) *n.m.* [*fem.* **-tora**] radio announcer.

radiología (ra·ðjo·lo'xi·a) *n.f.* radiology. —**radiológico** (-'lo·xi·ko) *adj.* radiological. —**radiólogo** (ra·'ðjo·lo·ɣo) *n.m.* radiologist.

radiorreceptor (ra·ðjo·rre·θep'tor; -sep'tor) *adj.* receiving. —*n.m.* radio receiver.

radioscopia (ra·ðjos'ko·pja) *n.f.* radioscopy.

radiosonda (ra·ðjo'son·da) *n.f.* radiosonde.

radiotécnico (ra·ðjo'tek·ni·ko)

n.m. radio technician. —**radiotecnia** (-'tɛk·nja) *n.f.* radio technology; radio repair.

radiotelefonía (ra·ðjo·te·le·fo·'ni·a) *n.f.* **1,** radiotelephony. **2,** radio; radio communication. —**radioteléfono** (-'le·fo·no) *n.m.* radiotelephone.

radiotelefotografía (ra·ðjo·te·le·fo·to·ɣra'fi·a) *n.f.* **1,** telephotography. **2,** telephotograph.

radiotelegrafía (ra·ðjo·te·le·ɣra'fi·a) *n.f.* wireless telegraphy. —**radiotelegrafiar** (-te·le·ɣra'fjar) *v.t.* [*infl.:* **enviar,** 22] to radiotelegraph. —**radiotelegrafista,** *n.m. & f.* wireless operator. —**radiotelégrafo** (-te'le·ɣra·fo) *n.m.* radiotelegraph.

radioterapia (ra·ðjo·te'ra·pja) *n.f.* radiotherapy.

radiotransmisor (ra·ðjo·trans·mi'sor) *n.m.* radio transmitter.

radioyente (ra·ðjo'jen·te) *n.m. & f.* radio listener.

radique (ra'ði·ke) *v., pres.subjve. of* **radicar.**

radiqué (ra·ði'ke) *v., 1st pers. sing.pret. of* **radicar.**

rádium ('ra·ðjum) *n.m.* radium.

radón (ra'ðon) *n.m.* radon.

raer (ra'er) *v.t.* [*infl.:* 56] to abrade; wear away; fray.

ráfaga ('ra·fa·ɣa) *n.f.* **1,** gust of wind. **2,** flash. **3,** burst; volley.

rafia ('ra·fja) *n.f.* raffia.

raglán (ra'ɣlan) *n.m.* raglan.

raído (ra'i·ðo) *adj.* **1,** abraded; worn out. **2,** frayed; threadbare. **3,** disreputable; seedy.

raiga ('rai·ɣa) *v., pres.subjve. of* **raer.**

raigambre (rai'ɣam·bre) *n.f.* **1,** *lit. & fig.* root; roots. **2,** intertwining of roots.

raigo ('rai·ɣo) *v., 1st pers.sing. pres.ind. of* **raer.**

raigón (rai'ɣon) *n.m.* root (*of a tooth*).

rail (rail) *n.m., R.R.* rail; track.

raíz (ra'iθ; -'is) *n.f.* root. —**a raíz de,** following upon. —**de raíz,** by the roots; entirely. —**echar raíces,** to take root; grow roots. —**raíz cuadrada,** square root.

raja ('ra·xa) *n.f.* **1,** crack; split. **2,** slice. **3,** splinter; split piece of wood.

rajá (ra'xa) *n.m.* rajah.

rajadura (ra·xa'ðu·ra) *n.f.* crack; split; fissure.

rajar (ra'xar) *v.t.* to split; crack.

—*v.i.*, *colloq.* to boast; brag. —**rajarse**, *v.r.*, *colloq.* 1, to quit; give up. 2, *Amer.* to get out; scram. 3, to jabber; prattle.

ralea (ra'le·a) *n.f.* sort; breed.

ralear (ra·le'ar) *v.i.* 1, to thin out; become sparse. 2, to show one's true colors.

ralo ('ra·lo) *adj.* 1, sparse. 2, *Amer.* thin; weak; watery. —**raleza**, *n.f.* sparseness; thinning out.

rallador (ra·ʎa'ðor; ra·ja-) *n.m.* grater.

ralladura (ra·ʎa'ðu·ra; ra·ja-) *n.f.* 1, shavings; gratings. 2, scrape; scratch.

rallar (ra'ʎar; -'jar) *v.t.* to grate; shred.

rallo ('ra·ʎo, -jo) *n.m.* = **rallador.**

rama ('ra·ma) *n.f.* 1, branch. 2, *print.* chase. —**andarse por las ramas**, to beat around the bush. —**de rama en rama**, shifting; changing. —**en rama**, in unfinished state; unprocessed.

ramada (ra'ma·ða) *n.f.* 1, = **ramaje.** 2, = **enramada.**

ramaje (ra'ma·xe) *n.m.* branches; boughs; mass of branches.

ramal (ra'mal) *n.m.* 1, branch; spur. 2, ramification; offshoot. 3, strand *(of a rope).*

ramalazo (ra·ma'la·θo; -so) *n.m.* lash; blow.

rambla ('ram·bla) *n.f.* boulevard.

ramera (ra'me·ra) *n.f.* whore; harlot.

ramificarse (ra·mi·fi'kar·se) *v.r.* [*infl.:* tocar, 7] to ramify; branch off. —**ramificación**, *n.f.* ramification; branching off.

ramillete (ra·mi'ʎe·te; -'je·te) *n.m.* 1, bouquet *(of flowers).* 2, centerpiece. 3, bevy of young girls.

ramilletero (ra·mi·ʎe'te·ro; ra·mi·je-) *n.m.* 1, maker or seller of bouquets. 2, flower vase. —**ramilletera**, *n.f.* flower girl.

ramo ('ra·mo) *n.m.* 1, small branch. 2, bunch; cluster. 3, sprig; spray. 4, bouquet. 5, branch *(of knowledge, study, etc.).* 6, line *(of trade, business, etc.).* —**Domingo de Ramos**, Palm Sunday.

ramojo (ra'mo·xo) *n.m.* brushwood.

rampa ('ram·pa) *n.f.* ramp.

rampante (ram'pan·te) *adj.* rampant.

ramplón (ram'plon) *adj.* rude; gross; vulgar. —*n.m.* calk *(of a horseshoe).* —**ramplonería**, *n.f.* vulgarity; grossness.

rana ('ra·na) *n.f.* frog. —**no ser rana**, *colloq.* to be no slouch.

rancio ('ran·θjo; -sjo) *adj.* 1, rancid. 2, age-old; ancient. 3, aged. —**ranciarse** (-'θjar·se; -'sjar·se) *v.r.* to become rancid. —**rancidez** (-θi'ðeθ; -si'ðes) *also,* **ranciedad** (-θje'ðað; -sje'ðað) *n.f.* rancidity.

ranchería (ran·tʃe'ri·a) *n.f.* group of huts or cabins; small settlement.

ranchero (ran'tʃe·ro) *n.m.*, *Amer.* rancher; ranchman.

rancho ('ran·tʃo) *n.m.* 1, mess. 2, large hut or cabin. 3, *Amer.* ranch. —**hacer rancho**, *colloq.* to make room; move aside. —**hacer rancho aparte**, *colloq.* to go one's own way.

rango ('ran·go) *n.m.* 1, rank; position. 2, *Amer.* high social rank. 3, *Amer.* airs; stateliness; pomposity. —**de rango**, *Amer.* high-class.

raní (ra'ni) *n.f.* ranee.

ranúnculo (ra'nun·ku·lo) *n.m.*, *bot.* buttercup.

ranura (ra'nu·ra) *n.f.* 1, groove. 2, slot; slit.

rapacería (ra·pa·θe'ri·a; -se'ri·a) *n.f.* 1, = **rapacidad.** 2, mischievous prank.

rapacidad (ra·pa·θi'ðað; -si'ðað) *n.f.* rapacity.

rapador (ra·pa'ðor) *adj.* shaving. —*n.m.*, *colloq.* barber.

rapadura (ra·pa'ðu·ra) *n.f.* shaving; shave; cropping.

rapapolvo (ra·pa'pol·βo) *n.m.*, *colloq.* sharp reproof; dressing down.

rapar (ra'par) *v.t.* 1, to shave. 2, to crop (the hair). 3, *colloq.* to clean out; rob.

rapaz (ra'paθ; -'pas) *adj.* 1, rapacious. 2, predatory. —*n.m.* young boy; lad. —**ave rapaz**, bird of prey.

rape ('ra·pe) *n.m.*, *colloq.* shave; cropping; trimming. —**al rape**, clean; bald.

rapé (ra'pe) *n.m.* snuff.

rápido ('ra·pi·ðo) *adj.* quick; swift; rapid. —*adv.* [*also,* **rapidamente**] quickly. —*n.m.* 1, *usu.pl.* rapids. 2, express train. —**rapidez**, *n.f.* rapidity; swiftness.

rapiña (ra'pi·ɲa) *n.f.* pillage; rapine. —**de rapiña**, of prey.

raposa (ra'po·sa) *n.f.* = **zorra.**

raposear (ra·po·se'ar) *v.i.* to be foxy.

raposera (ra·po'se·ra) n.f. foxhole.
raposo (ra'po·so) n.m. = zorro.
rapsoda (rap'so·ða) n.m. bard; reciter of poetry.
rapsodia (rap'so·ðja) n.f. rhapsody. —**rapsódico** (-'so·ði·ko) rhapsodic.
raptar (rap'tar) v.t. to abduct; kidnap. —**raptor**, n.m. abductor; kidnapper.
rapto ('rap·to) n.m. 1, abduction; kidnapping. 2, rapture. 3, seizure; spell.
raqueta (ra'ke·ta) n.f. 1, racket (used in games). 2, snowshoe. 3, croupier's rake.
raquis ('ra·kis) n.m.sing. & pl. backbone; spine. —**raquídeo** (ra·'ki·ðe·o) adj. spinal.
raquítico (ra'ki·ti·ko) adj. 1, rachitic. 2, rickety; weak. —**raquitismo**, n.m. rickets.
raramente (ra·ra'men·te) adv. 1, rarely. 2, oddly.
rarefacción (ra·re·fak'θjon; -'sjon) n.f. rarefaction.
rareza (ra're·θa; -sa) n.f. 1, rarity. 2, oddity.
raro ('ra·ro) adj. 1, rare; uncommon. 2, strange; odd. —**rara vez,** also, **raras veces,** seldom.
ras (ras) n.m. level. —**a ras de,** level with; even with.
rasar (ra'sar) v.t. 1, to skim; graze. 2, to level off; make even. —**rasante,** adj. grazing; barely touching. —n.f. slope. —**vuelo rasante,** low-level flight.
rascacielos (ras·ka'θje·los; -'sje·los) n.m.sing. & pl. skyscraper.
rascar (ras'kar) v.t. [infl.: tocar, 7] to scratch; scrape. —**rascador,** n.m. scratcher; scraper. —**rascadura,** n.f. scratching; scraping. —**rascazón** (-ka'θon; -ka'son) n.f. itch; itching.
rascatripas (ras·ka'tri·pas) n.m. & f.sing. & pl. poor violinist; fiddler.
rascón (ras'kon) adj. tart; sour. —n.m., ornith. rail.
rasero (ra'se·ro) n.m. 1, leveling stick; skimmer. 2, [also, **rasera,** n.f.] egg turner; spatula. —**medir con el mismo rasero,** to treat impartially.
rasgado (ras'ɣa·ðo) adj. 1, torn; rent. 2, almond-shaped (of the eyes). 3, wide (of the mouth). —n.m. = rasgón.
rasgar (ras'ɣar) v.t. [infl.: pagar, 8] to tear; rend; rip.

rasgo ('ras·ɣo) n.m. 1, pen stroke; flourish. 2, trait; feature. 3, gesture; act. —**a grandes rasgos,** broadly; in outline.
rasgón (ras'ɣon) n.m. rent; tear; rip.
rasguear (ras·ɣe'ar) v.i. to strum; pluck; stroke. —**rasgueo** (ras'ɣe·o) n.m. stroking; strumming.
rasguñar (ras·ɣu'ɲar) v.t. 1, to scratch. 2, to sketch. —**rasguño** (-'ɣu·ɲo) n.m. scratch.
raso ('ra·so) adj. 1, clear; open. 2, plain. 3, flat. —n.m. satin. —**al raso,** in the open; outdoors. —**cielo raso,** 1, flat ceiling. 2, clear sky. —**soldado raso,** private soldier.
raspa ('ras·pa) n.f. 1, rasp. 2, fishbone; spine of a fish. 3, Amer., colloq. dressing down; scolding.
raspador (ras·pa'ðor) n.m. scraper.
raspadura (ras·pa'ðu·ra) n.f. 1, scraping. 2, scrape; scratch. 3, erasure. 4, usu.pl. shavings.
raspar (ras'par) v.t. 1, to rasp; scrape. 2, to graze.
rasque ('ras·ke) v., pres.subjve. of rascar.
rasqué (ras'ke) v., 1st pers.sing. pret. of rascar.
rasqueta (ras'ke·ta) n.f. scraper.
rasquetear (ras·ke·te'ar) v.t., Amer. to scrape; scratch.
rastra ('ras·tra) n.f. 1, rake. 2, agric. harrow; drag. 3, naut. drag; grapnel. 4, string (as of dried fruit). 5, trace; sign. 6, dredge. —**a la rastra; a rastra; a rastras,** 1, dragging. 2, crawling. 3, fig. unwillingly.
rastreador (ras·tre·a'ðor) n.m. 1, drag; dredge. 2, tracker; scout.
rastrear (ras·tre'ar) v.t. to track; trail. —v.t. & i. 1, to rake; harrow. 2, to drag; dredge. —v.i. to skim or hug the ground.
rastreo (ras'tre·o) n.m. dragging; dredging.
rastrero (ras'tre·ro) adj. 1, creeping; crawling. 2, abject; groveling.
rastrillar (ras·tri'ʎar; -'jar) v.t. & i. 1, to hackle; comb (flax). 2, to rake. —**rastrillador,** n.m. flax dresser.
rastrillo (ras'tri·ʎo; -jo) n.m. 1, hackle; flax rake. 2, rake. 3, portcullis.
rastro ('ras·tro) n.m. 1, track; trail. 2, rake. 3, slaughterhouse. 4, vestige; trace. 5, [also, Amer. **rastri-**

llo] open-air bargain market, esp. that of Madrid. **6,** harrow.

rastrojo (ras'tro·xo) *n.m.* stubble. —**rastrojera,** *n.f.* stubble field.

rasurar (ra·su'rar) *v.t.* to shave. —**rasuración,** *also,* **rasura** (ra'su·ra) *n.f.* shaving.

rata ('ra·ta) *n.f.* rat. —*n.m., colloq.* = **ratero.**

rataplán (ra·ta'plan) *n.m.* sound of a drum; rub-a-dub.

ratear (ra·te'ar) *v.i.* to pick pockets; filch.

ratería (ra·te'ri·a) *n.f.* **1,** petty theft. **2,** pettiness; skulduggery.

ratero (ra'te·ro) *adj.* **1,** low; mean; contemptible. **2,** thieving. —*n.m.* pickpocket; petty thief.

ratificar (ra·ti·fi'kar) *v.t.* [*infl.: **tocar,** 7*] to ratify; confirm. —**ratificación,** *n.f.* ratification; confirmation.

rato ('ra·to) *n.m.* period of time; moment; while. —**a ratos perdidos,** in spare time. —**de rato en rato,** *also,* **a ratos,** occasionally

ratón (ra'ton) *n.m.* mouse.

ratonar (ra·to'nar) *v.t.* to gnaw.

ratonera (ra·to'ne·ra) *n.f.* **1,** mouse-trap. **2,** mousehole. **3,** *fig., colloq.* rathole; hole in the wall.

ratonil (ra·to'nil) *adj.* of or pert. to mice; mousy. *Also,* **ratonesco** (-'nes·ko).

raudal (rau'ðal) *n.m.* stream; torrent; flood.

raudo ('rau·ðo) *adj.* rapid; impetuous.

ravioles (ra'vjo·les) *n.m.pl.* ravioli.

raya ('ra·ja) *n.f.* **1,** stroke; dash; streak; stripe. **2,** boundary; limit. **3,** part (*of the hair*). **4,** *ichthy.* ray; skate. —**a raya,** within bounds. —**pasar de la raya, 1,** [*also, refl.,* **pasarse** . . .] to overstep oneself. **2,** to top it; be the last straw. —**(juego de las) tres en raya,** ticktacktoe.

raya ('ra·ja) *v., pres.subjve. of* **raer.**

rayadillo (ra·ja'ði·ʎo; -jo) *n.m.* striped cotton duck.

rayado (ra'ja·ðo) *adj.* lined; ruled; striped. —*n.m.* ruling; lines.

rayar (ra'jar) *v.t.* **1,** to draw lines in or on; rule. **2,** to scratch; score. **3,** to underline. —*v.i.* **1,** to stand out; excel. **2,** to break, as the dawn. **3,** to border; verge.

rayendo (ra'jen·do) *v., ger. of* **raer.**

rayo ('ra·jo) *n.m.* **1,** beam; ray. **2,** spoke. **3,** thunderbolt. **4,** *fig.* wit;

live wire. —**echar rayos,** *colloq.* to blow up; make the sparks fly.

rayó (ra'jo) *v., 3rd pers.sing.pret. of* **raer.**

rayón (ra'jon) *n.m.* rayon.

raza ('ra·θa; -sa) *n.f.* **1,** race. **2,** lineage. **3,** breed; sort. —**de raza,** thoroughbred.

razón (ra'θon; -'son) *n.f.* **1,** reason. **2,** reasoning; argument. **3,** cause; motive. **4,** right; justification. **5,** *math.* ratio. —**a razón de,** at the rate of. —**dar razón de, 1,** to inform of. **2,** to give account of. —**en razón de** *or* **a,** concerning; regarding. —**meter (a uno) en razón,** to enjoin reason (upon someone). —**no tener razón,** to be wrong. —**razón comercial,** business concern; trade name. —**razón social,** company; firm; company name. —**tener razón,** to be right. —**tomar razón de, 1,** to note down; make a note of. **2,** to record; register.

razonable (ra·θo'na·βle; ra·so-) *adj.* **1,** reasonable. **2,** moderate.

razonamiento (ra·θo·na'mjen·to; ra·so-) *n.m.* reasoning; argument.

razonar (ra·θo'nar; ra·so-) *v.i.* to reason; argue. —*v.t.* **1,** to reason out; explain. **2,** to corroborate; support with evidence.

re (re) *n.m., mus.* re; D.

reabrir (rc·a'βrir) *v.t.* [*p.p.* **reabierto** (-'βjer·to)] to reopen.

reacción (re·ak'θjon; -'sjon) *n.f.* reaction. —**reaccionar,** *v.i.* to react.

reaccionario (re·ak·θjo'na·rjo; re·ak·sjo-) *adj. & n.m.* reactionary.

reacio (re'a·θjo; -sjo) *adj.* obstinate; stubborn.

reactivar (re·ak·ti'βar) *v.t.* to reactivate. —**reactivación,** *n.f.* reactivation; *econ.* recovery.

reactivo (re·ak'ti·βo) *adj.* reactive. —*n.m.* reagent.

reactor (re·ak'tor) *n.m.* reactor.

reafirmar (re·a·fir'mar) *v.t.* to reaffirm.

reagrupar (re·a·ɣru'par) *v.t.* to regroup. —**reagruparse,** *v.r.* to regroup.

reajustar (re·a·xus'tar) *v.t.* to readjust. —**reajuste** (-'xus·te) *n.m.* readjustment.

real (re'al) *adj.* **1,** real. **2,** royal; kingly. **3,** fine; splendid. —*n.m.* **1,** *mil.* camp. **2,** fair grounds. **3,** a Spanish coin; real. —**sentar los re-**

ales, to encamp. **—levantar los reales,** to break camp.

realce (re'al·θe; -se) *n.m.* **1,** embossment. **2,** splendor; magnificence. **3,** highlight. **4,** emphasis. **5,** enhancement.

realengo (re·a'len·go) *adj.* **1,** royal. **2,** unappropriated, as land. *—n.m.* royal patrimony.

realeza (re·a'le·θa; -sa) *n.f.* royalty.

realidad (re·a·li'ðað) *n.f.* **1,** reality; fact. **2,** truth; sincerity.

realismo (re·a'lis·mo) *n.m.* **1,** royalism. **2,** realism.

realista (re·a'lis·ta) *adj. & n.m. & f.* **1,** royalist. **2,** realist. *—adj.* realistic.

realizable (re·a·li'θa·βle; -'sa·βle) *adj.* **1,** realizable. **2,** *comm.* liquid.

realización (re·a·li·θa'θjon; -sa'sjon) *n.f.* **1,** realization; fulfillment. **2,** *comm.* sale; liquidation.

realizar (re·a·li'θar; -'sar) *v.t.* [*infl.:* **rezar, 10**] **1,** to realize; fulfill. **2,** *comm.* to sell; liquidate. **3,** *cinema* to produce; film. **—realización,** *n.f.* **1,** fulfillment. **2,** *comm.* sale; liquidation. **3,** *cinema* production; filming.

realzar (re·al'θar; -'sar) *v.t.* [*infl.:* **rezar, 10**] **1,** to emboss. **2,** to highlight. **3,** to enhance; heighten.

reanimar (re·a·ni'mar) *v.t.* **1,** to cheer; comfort. **2,** to reanimate; resuscitate. **—reanimarse,** *v.r.* to recover.

reanudar (re·a·nu'ðar) *v.t.* to resume; continue. **—reanudación,** *n.f.* resumption; continuation.

reaparecer (re·a·pa·re'θer; -'ser) *v.i.* [*infl.:* **conocer, 13**] to reappear.

reaparición (re·a·pa·ri'θjon; -'sjon) *n.f.* reappearance.

rearmar (re·ar'mar) *v.t.* to rearm. **—rearme** (-'ar·me) *n.m.* rearmament.

reasumir (re·a·su'mir) *v.t.* to resume. **—reasunción** (-sun'θjon; -'sjon) *n.f.* resumption.

reata (re'a·ta) *n.f.* **1,** rope; tether. **2,** string of mules or asses.

reavivar (re·a·βi'βar) *v.t.* to revive.

rebaba (re'βa·βa) *n.f.* **1,** burr; mold mark; rough seam. **2,** flange; rim.

rebaja (re'βa·xa) *n.f.* **1,** abatement; diminution. **2,** *comm.* discount; rebate.

rebajar (re·βa'xar) *v.t.* **1,** to lessen; diminish; abate. **2,** to reduce. **3,** to

lower. **4,** to deduct; discount. **5,** *mil.* to relieve or excuse *(from a detail)*. **6,** to abase; demean. **7,** to make paler; lighten (a color).

rebanar (re·βa'nar) *v.t.* to slice; cut. **—rebanada,** *n.f.* slice. **—rebanador,** *adj.* slicing. *—n.m.* [*also,* **rebanadora,** *n.f.*] slicer.

rebañar (re·βa'ñar) *v.t.* to sop up.

rebaño (re'βa·ño) *n.m.* flock.

rebasar (re·βa'sar) *v.t.* **1,** to exceed; go beyond. **2,** *naut.* to skirt; sail past. *—v.i.,* *Amer.* to escape; dodge.

rebate (re'βa·te) *n.m.* fight; encounter.

rebatir (re·βa'tir) *v.t.* **1,** to repel; resist. **2,** to refute. **—rebatible,** *adj.* refutable; vulnerable.

rebato (re'βa·to) *n.m.* **1,** alarm; tocsin. **2,** commotion. **3,** *mil.* surprise attack.

rebelarse (re·βe'lar·se) *v.r.* **1,** to revolt; rebel. **2,** to resist.

rebelde (re'βel·de) *adj.* **1,** rebellious. **2,** stubborn. *—n.m. & f.* rebel.

rebeldía (re·βel'di·a) *n.f.* **1,** rebelliousness. **2,** stubbornness. **3,** *law* default; contempt.

rebelión (re·βe'ljon) *n.f.* rebellion; revolt; insurrection.

rebenque (re'βen·ke) *n.m.* whip; lash. **—rebencazo** (-'ka·θo; -so) *n.m.* blow with a lash.

rebisabuelo (re·βis·a'βwe·lo) *n.m.* great-great-grandfather. **—rebisabuela,** *n.f.* great-great-grandmother.

rebisnieto (re·βis'nje·to) *n.m.* great-great-grandson. **—rebisnieta,** *n.f.* great-great-granddaughter.

reblandecer (re·βlan·de'θer; -'ser) *v.t.* [*infl.:* **conocer, 13**] to soften. **—reblandecimiento,** *n.m.* softening.

reborde (re'βor·ðe) *n.m.* rim; edge; flange.

rebosar (re·βo'sar) *v.i.* **1,** to run over; overflow. **2,** to abound; teem. **—rebosamiento,** *n.m.* overflow; overflowing.

rebotar (re·βo'tar) *v.i.* to rebound; ricochet. *—v.t.* **1,** to cause to rebound. **2,** to clinch (a spike or nail). **3,** to repel. **4,** to raise the nap of. **5,** *colloq.* to annoy.

rebote (re'βo·te) *n.m.* rebound. **—de rebote, 1,** indirectly; incidentally. **2,** on the rebound.

rebozar (re·βo'θar; -'sar) *v.t.* [*infl.:*

rezar, 10] **1,** to muffle up. **2,** *cooking* to coat with batter.

rebozo (re'βo·θo; -so) *n.m.* **1,** shawl; muffler. **2,** muffling up. **3,** pretext. **—de rebozo,** secretly. **—sin rebozo,** frankly; candidly.

rebujo (re'βu·xo) *n.m.* **1,** muffler; wrapper. **2,** clumsy bundle.

rebullir (re·βu'ʎir; -'jir) *v.t.* [*infl.:* **bullir, 19**] to stir; boil up. *Also, v.r.,* **rebullirse.**

rebusca (re'βus·ka) *n.f.* **1,** gleaning. **2,** gleanings. **3,** *colloq.* rummaging; searching.

rebuscado (re·βus'ka·ðo) *adj.* **1,** affected; precious. **2,** recherché. **—rebuscamiento,** *n.m.* affectation.

rebuscar (re·βus'kar) *v.t.* [*infl.:* **tocar, 7**] **1,** to rummage; search through. **2,** to glean. **—rebuscárselas,** *colloq.* to contrive; manage.

rebuznar (re·βuθ'nar; re·βus-) *v.i.* to bray. **—rebuzno** (-'βuθ·no; -'βus·no) *n.m.* bray; braying.

recabar (re·ka'βar) *v.t.* to request; obtain by request.

recado (re'ka·ðo) *n.m.* **1,** message. **2,** errand. **3,** gift; compliment. **4,** daily shopping or marketing. **5,** advice; warning. **6,** *pl.* compliments; regards. **7,** implements; tools. **—recado de escribir,** writing materials.

recaer (re·ka'er) *v.i.* [*infl.:* **caer, 39**] **1,** to relapse. **2,** to fall upon; befall. **—recaída** (-ka'i·ða) *n.f.* relapse.

recalar (re·ka'lar) *v.i., naut.* to reach land. **—v.t.** to soak; drench. **—recalada,** *n.f.* landfall.

recalcar (re·kal'kar) *v.t.* [*infl.:* **tocar, 7**] **1,** to emphasize. **2,** to bear down on. **—v.i., naut.** to heel; list. **—recalcarse,** *v.r.* to speak emphatically.

recalcitrar (re·kal·θi'trar; -si'trar) *v.i.* to resist; be recalcitrant. **—recalcitrante,** *adj.* recalcitrant.

recalentamiento (re·ka·len·ta'mjen·to) *n.m.* **1,** reheating. **2,** overheating.

recalentar (re·ka·len'tar) *v.t.* [*infl.:* **pensar, 27**] **1,** to reheat. **2,** to overheat. **—recalentarse,** *v.r.* **1,** to become overheated. **2,** to be spoiled by heat.

recamar (re·ka'mar) *v.t.* to embroider with raised work. **—recamado,** *n.m.* raised embroidery.

recámara (re'ka·ma·ra) *n.f.* **1,** antechamber. **2,** dressing room. **3,**

breech *(of a gun)*. **4,** chamber *(of a firearm).* **5,** *Mex.* bedroom.

recambiar (re·kam'bjar) *v.t.* **1,** to exchange anew. **2,** *comm.* to redraw.

recambio (re'kam·bjo) *n.m.* **1,** *comm.* reexchange. **2,** *mech.* [*also,* **pieza de recambio**] replacement part.

recamo (re'ka·mo) *n.m.* **1,** = **recamado. 2,** frog *(ornamental fastening).*

recapacitar (re·ka·pa·θi'tar; -si'tar) *v.t.* **1,** to think over; consider. **2,** *Amer.* to rehabilitate.

recapitular (re·ka·pi·tu'lar) *v.t.* to recapitulate. **—recapitulación,** *n.f.* recapitulation.

recargar (re·kar'γar) *v.t.* [*infl.:* **pagar, 8**] **1,** to overload. **2,** to overburden. **3,** to reload; recharge. **4,** to surcharge. **5,** to bear down on. **6,** *law* to increase (the sentence of a convict). **7,** to overadorn. **—recargarse,** *v.r., med.* to suffer an increase in temperature.

recargo (re'kar·γo) *n.m.* **1,** extra load; extra burden. **2,** overload; overloading. **3,** surcharge. **4,** *med.* rise in temperature. **5,** *law* new or additional charge.

recatado (re·ka'ta·ðo) *adj.* **1,** circumspect; cautious. **2,** modest; decorous.

recatar (re·ka'tar) *v.t.* **1,** to cloak; conceal. **2,** to sample or taste again. **—recatarse,** *v.r.* to be circumspect; be cautious.

recato (re'ka·to) *n.m.* **1,** circumspection; caution. **2,** modesty; decorousness.

recauchar (re·kau'tʃar) *v.t.* to retread (a tire). *Also,* **recauchutar** (-tʃu'tar). **—recauchaje,** *n.m.* retread; retreading.

recaudación (re·kau·ða'θjon; -'sjon) *n.f.* **1,** collection, esp. of taxes. **2,** collector's office.

recaudar (re·kau'ðar) *v.t.* **1,** to collect, esp. rents or taxes. **2,** to set aside; put in reserve. **—recaudador,** *n.m.* tax collector. **—recaudamiento,** *n.m.* tax collection.

recaudo (re'kau·ðo) *n.m.* **1,** collection, esp. of taxes. **2,** precaution. **3,** reserve; store. **4,** *law* bail; security. **—a buen recaudo, 1,** in safekeeping. **2,** present in one's mind; well in mind.

rece ('re·θe; -se) *v., pres.subjve.* of **rezar.**

recé (re'θe; -'se) v., *1st pers.sing. pret. of* rezar.

recelar (re·θe'lar; re·se-) v.t. to fear; suspect; distrust. —**recelarse**, v.r. to be afraid; be suspicious. —**recelo** (-'θe·lo; -'se·lo) n.m. fear; suspicion; distrust. —**receloso**, adj. suspicious; distrustful.

recental (re·θen'tal; re·sen-) adj. milk-fed; suckling.

recentísimo (re·θen'ti·si·mo; re·sen-) adj., superl. of reciente.

recepción (re·θep'θjon; -sep'sjon) n.f. 1, reception. 2, admission; acceptance. 3, receiving; receipt. —**recepcionista**, n.m. & f. receptionist.

receptáculo (re·θep'ta·ku·lo; re·sep-) n.m. receptacle.

receptar (re·θep'tar; re·sep-) v.t. 1, to receive; welcome. 2, to harbor (a fugitive). 3, to receive (stolen goods).

receptivo (re·θep'ti·βo; re·sep-) adj. receptive. —**receptividad**, n.f. receptivity; receptiveness.

receptor (re·θep'tor; re·sep-) adj. receiving. —n.m. receiver.

recesión (re·θe'sjon; re·se-) n.f. recession.

receso (re'θe·so; re'se-) n.m. adjournment; recess.

receta (re'θe·ta; re'se-) n.f. 1, prescription. 2, recipe.

recetar (re·θe'tar; re·se-) v.t. to prescribe.

recetario (re·θe'ta·rjo; re·se-) n.m. 1, prescription book. 2, recipe book.

recibí (re·θi'βi; re·si-) n.m., comm. receipt; payment received.

recibidero (re·θi·βi'ðe·ro; re·si-) adj. receivable.

recibidor (re·θi·βi'ðor; re·si-) n.m. 1, parlor; drawing room. 2, reception room; waiting room. 3, receiver; recipient. —adj. receiving.

recibimiento (re·θi·βi'mjen·to; re·si-) n.m. 1, reception. 2, hall; salon. 3, anteroom; reception room.

recibir (re·θi'βir; re·si-) v.t. 1, to receive; admit; accept. 2, to meet; greet; welcome. 3, to suffer; sustain. —**recibirse**, v.r. 1, to graduate. 2, to be admitted or received.

recibo (re'θi·βo; re'si-) n.m. 1, reception. 2, receiving; receipt. —**acusar recibo**, comm. to acknowledge receipt. —**estar de recibo**, to be at home to callers.

reciclar (re·θi'klar; re·si-) v.t. to recycle. —**reciclarse**, v.r. to be re-

trained. —**reciclaje** (-'kla·xe) n.m. 1, recycling. 2, retraining.

recidiva (re·θi'ði·βa; re·si-) n.f., med. relapse.

reciedumbre (re·θje'ðum·bre; re·sje-) n.f. strength; vigor.

recién (re'θjen; -'sjen) adv. = **recientemente** before a p.p.

reciente (re'θjen·te; re'sjen-) adj. recent; new; fresh. —**recientemente**, adv. recently; newly; lately.

recinto (re'θin·to; re'sin-) n.m. enclosure; precinct; confines.

recio ('re·θjo; -sjo) adj. 1, strong; robust. 2, thick; stout; sturdy. 3, rude; coarse. 4, hard; severe; rigorous. 5, loud. 6, sudden; violent. —adv. 1, strongly. 2, suddenly; violently. 3, loud; loudly.

recipiente (re·θi'pjen·te; re·si-) adj. receiving. —n.m. 1, recipient. 2, container; receptacle.

recíproca (re'θi·pro·ka; re'si-) n.f., math. reciprocal.

reciprocar (re·θi·pro'kar; re·si-) v.t. [infl.: tocar, 7] to reciprocate; match. —**reciprocación**, n.f. reciprocation.

recíproco (re'θi·pro·ko; re'si-) adj. reciprocal. —**reciprocidad** (-θi·'ðað; -si'ðað) n.f. reciprocity.

recital (re·θi'tal; re·si-) n.m. recital.

recitar (re·θi'tar; re·si-) v.t. & i. to recite. —**recitación**, n.f. recitation. —**recitado**, n.m. recitative.

reclamación (re·kla·ma'θjon; -'sjon) n.f. 1, demand; claim; complaint. 2, reclamation.

reclamar (re·kla'mar) v.t. 1, to claim; reclaim; demand. 2, to decoy (birds). 3, to call; attract. —v.i. to protest; complain. —**reclamante**, n.m. & f. claimant.

reclamo (re'kla·mo) n.m. 1, decoy bird. 2, bird call. 3, allurement; attraction. 4, advertisement. 5, catchword. 6, demand; claim; complaint.

reclinar (re·kli'nar) v.t. to rest; lean; recline. —**reclinación**, n.f. reclining; recumbency. —**reclinado**, adj. reclining; recumbent. —**reclinable**, adj. reclining (seat).

reclinatorio (re·kli·na'to·rjo) n.m. prie-dieu.

recluir (re·klu'ir) v.t. [infl.: huir, 26] to seclude; shut in; confine.

reclusión (re·klu'sjon) n.f seclusion; confinement.

recluso (re'klu·so) n.m. inmate; prisoner.

recluta (re'klu·ta) *n.m.* & *f.* recruit. —*n.f.* [*also,* **reclutamiento,** *n.m.*] recruiting; recruitment. —**reclutar,** *v.t.* to recruit.

recobrar (re·ko'βrar) *v.t.* to recover; regain; recoup. —**recobrarse,** *v.r.* to recover; recuperate. —**recobro** (-'ko·βro) *n.m.* recovery; recuperation.

recocer (re·ko'θer; -'ser) *v.t.* [*infl.:* **torcer,** 66] 1, to recook. 2, to overcook. 3, to anneal. —**recocerse,** *v.r.* to be consumed with passion.

recocido (re·ko'θi·ðo; -'si·ðo) *adj.* veteran; experienced. —*n.m.* 1, overcooking. 2, reheating. 3, annealing.

recodo (re'ko·ðo) *n.m.* turn; bend; twist.

recoger (re·ko'xer) *v.t.* [*infl.:* **coger,** 15] 1, to get back; receive in return. 2, to gather; pick up. 3, to harvest; reap. 4, to shrink; contract. 5, to lock up. 6, to shelter. 7, to call back; withdraw from distribution. —**recogerse,** *v.r.* 1, to take shelter. 2, to go to bed; retire. 3, to shut oneself off; withdraw.

recogida (re·ko'xi·ða) *n.f.* 1, withdrawal. 2, harvest; reaping. 3, gathering; collection. 4, a picking up; pickup.

recogido (re·ko'xi·ðo) *adj.* shy; withdrawn. —*n.m.* inmate.

recogimiento (re·ko·xi'mjen·to) *n.m.* 1, withdrawal; seclusion. 2, absorption; raptness. 3, house of correction for women.

recolección (re·ko·lek'θjon; -'sjon) *n.f.* 1, reaping; harvest. 2, collection; gathering.

recolectar (re·ko·lek'tar) *v.t.* to collect; gather.

recoleto (re·ko'le·to) *adj.* retired; secluded.

recomendable (re·ko·men'da·βle) *adj.* 1, advisable. 2, commendable.

recomendación (re·ko·men·da'θjon; -'sjon) *n.f.* 1, recommendation; advice. 2, commendation; praise.

recomendar (re·ko·men'dar) *v.t.* [*infl.:* **pensar,** 27] 1, to recommend; advise. 2, to commend. —**recomendado,** *n.m.* protégé. —**recomendada,** *n.f.* protégée.

recompensa (re·kom'pen·sa) *n.f.* recompense; reward. —**recompensar,** *v.t.* to recompense; reward.

recomponer (re·kom·po'ner) *v.t.* [*infl.:* **poner,** 54] to mend; repair.

reconcentrar (re·kon·θen'trar; -sen'trar) *v.t.* 1, to concentrate. 2, *fig.* to store up, as feelings. —**reconcentrarse,** *v.r.* to be absorbed or engrossed.

reconciliar (re·kon·θi'ljar; -si'ljar) *v.t.* to reconcile. —**reconciliable,** *adj.* reconcilable. —**reconciliación,** *n.f.* reconciliation.

reconcomio (re·kon'ko·mjo) *n.m.* 1, urge; itch. 2, *colloq.* gnawing suspicion; misgiving.

recóndito (re'kon·di·to) *adj.* recondite; hidden. —**reconditez,** *n.f.,* *colloq.* reconditeness; obscurity.

reconocer (re·ko·no'θer; -'ser) *v.t.* [*infl.:* **conocer,** 13] 1, to recognize. 2, to acknowledge. 3, to appreciate; be thankful for. 4, to confess; admit; avow. 5, to reconnoiter. —**reconocible,** *adj.* recognizable.

reconocido (re·ko·no'θi·ðo; -'si·ðo) *adj.* 1, acknowledged. 2, grateful.

reconocimiento (re·ko·no·θi'mjen·to; -si'mjen·to) *n.m.* 1, recognition. 2, acknowledgment. 3, gratitude. 4, reconnaissance.

reconquistar (re·kon·kis'tar) *v.t.* to reconquer. —**reconquista** (-'kis·ta) *n.f.* reconquest.

reconsiderar (re·kon·si·ðe'rar) *v.t.* to reconsider.

reconstituir (re·kons·ti·tu'ir) *v.t.* [*infl.:* **huir,** 26] to reconstitute. —**reconstitución,** *n.f.* reconstitution. —**reconstituyente,** *adj.* & *n.m.* reconstituent.

reconstruir (re·kons·tru'ir) *v.t.* [*infl.:* **construir,** 41] to reconstruct. —**reconstrucción,** *n.f.* reconstruction.

recontar (re·kon'tar) *v.t.* [*infl.:* **acostar,** 28] 1, to tell; retell. 2, to recount; count again.

reconvención (re·kon·βen'θjon; -'sjon) *n.f.* 1, reproof; reproach. 2, remonstrance.

reconvenir (re·kon·βe'nir) *v.t.* [*infl.:* **venir,** 69] 1, to reproach; reprove. 2, to remonstrate.

recopilación (re·ko·pi·la'θjon; -'sjon) *n.f.* 1, compendium; abridgment; summary. 2, compilation; digest.

recopilar (re·ko·pi'lar) *v.t.* 1, to abridge; summarize. 2, to compile. —**recopilador,** *n.m.* [*fem.* **-dora**] compiler.

récord ('re·korð) *n.m. & adj.* record.

recordación (re·kor·ða'θjon; -'sjon) *n.f.* remembering; remembrance.

recordar (re·kor'ðar) *v.t.* [*infl.:* acostar, 28] **1**, to remember; recall. **2**, to remind; call to mind. —**recordativo**, *adj.* reminding. —**recordatorio**, *n.m.* reminder; memento.

recorrer (re·ko'rrer) *v.t.* **1**, to traverse; pass over or through. **2**, to travel; go over. **3**, to examine. **4**, to glance through; scan.

recorrido (re·ko'rri·ðo) *n.m.* **1**, route; course. **2**, a going over. **3**, *print.* overrun. *Also,* **recorrida** (-ða) *n.f.*

recortar (re·kor'tar) *v.t.* **1**, to cut away; clip; trim. **2**, to outline; mark out. —**recortado**, *n.m.* paper cutout. —*adj.* jagged; irregular in outline.

recorte (re·kor·te) *n.m.* **1**, cutting; clipping; trimming. **2**, item (*in a newspaper*).

recoser (re·ko'ser) *v.t.* to resew; mend.

recostado (re·kos'ta·ðo) *adj.* reclining; recumbent.

recostar (re·kos'tar) *v.t.* [*infl.:* acostar, 28] to rest; recline. —**recostarse**, *v.r.* **1**, to lie down; rest. **2**, to lean back.

recoveco (re·ko'βe·ko) *n.m.* **1**, turning; winding. **2**, nook; cranny. **3**, ruse; artifice.

recrear (re·kre'ar) *v.t.* **1**, to amuse; delight. **2**, to re-create; create anew. —**recreación**, *n.f.* recreation. —**recreativo**, *adj.* recreative.

recrecer (re·kre'θer; -'ser) *v.t. & i.* [*infl.:* conocer, 13] to increase; grow.

recreo (re·'kre·o) *n.m.* recreation; leisure.

recriminar (re·kri·mi'nar) *v.t.* to recriminate. —**recriminación**, *n.f.* recrimination.

recrudecer (re·kru·ðe'θer; -'ser) *v.i.* [*infl.:* conocer, 13] to recrudesce. —**recrudecimiento**, *n.m.* recrudescence.

recrudescente (re·kru·ðes·'θen·te; -ðe'sen·te) *adj.* recrudescent. —**recrudescencia**, *n.f.* recrudescence.

recrujir (re·kru'xir) *v.i.* to creak loudly.

recta ('rek·ta) *n.f.* **1**, straightaway. **2**, straight line.

rectal (rek'tal) *adj.* rectal.

rectángulo (rek'tan·gu·lo) *adj.* right; right-angled. —*n.m.* rectangle. —**rectangular**, *adj.* rectangular.

rectificar (rek·ti·fi'kar) *v.t.* [*infl.:* tocar, 7] to rectify. —**rectificación**, *n.f.* rectification; rectifying. —**rectificador**, *adj.* rectifying. —*n.m.* rectifier. —**rectificativo**, *adj. & n.m.* corrective.

rectitud (rek·ti'tuð) *n.f.* **1**, rectitude. **2**, straightness; directness.

recto ('rek·to) *adj.* **1**, straight. **2**, upright; honest. **3**, *geom.* right. —*n.m.* rectum.

rector (rek'tor) *n.m.* rector. —**rectorado**, *n.m.* rectorate.

rectoría (rek·to'ri·a) *n.f.* **1**, rectorate. **2**, rectory.

recua ('re·kwa) *n.f.* **1**, string of pack animals. **2**, *fig.* string; pack; slew.

recuadro (re'kwa·ðro) *n.m.* square section; panel.

recubrir (re·ku'βrir) *v.t.* [*p.p.* recubierto] **1**, to cover; coat. **2**, to recover. —**recubrimiento**, *n.m.* cover; covering; coating.

recuento (re'kwen·to) *n.m.* **1**, recount. **2**, inventory.

recuerde (re'kwer·ðe) *v., pres. subjve. of* **recordar**.

recuerdo (re'kwer·ðo) *v., 1st. pers.sing. pres.ind. of* **recordar**.

recuerdo (re'kwer·ðo) *n.m.* **1**, remembrance; memory. **2**, memento; keepsake; souvenir. —**recuerdos**, *n.m.pl.* regards; best wishes.

recuestar (re·kwes'tar) *v.t.* to request. —**recuesta** (-'kwes·ta) *n.f.* request.

recueza (re'kwe·θa; -sa) *v., pres. subjve. of* **recocer**.

recuezo (re'kwe·θo; -so) *v., 1st pers.sing. pres.ind. of* **recocer**.

reculada (re·ku'la·ða) *n.f.* **1**, rearing back; recoil. **2**, *colloq.* backing down; backing out.

recular (re·ku'lar) *v.i.* **1**, to rear back; recoil. **2**, *colloq.* to back down; back out.

reculones (re·ku'lo·nes) *n.m.pl. in* **a reculones**, *colloq.* rearing back; recoiling.

recuperar (re·ku·pe'rar) *v.t.* to recover; regain; recoup. —**recuperarse**, *v.r.* to recover; recuperate. —**recuperación**, *n.f.* recovery; recuperation. —**recuperativo**, *adj.* recuperative; restorative.

recurrir (re·ku'rrir) *v.i.* **1**, to resort; have recourse. **2,** to recur. **3,** to return; repair; revert. —**recurrente,** *adj.* recurrent. —*n.m.* & *f.* petitioner.

recurso (re'kur·so) *n.m.* **1,** recourse; resort. **2,** resource; *pl.* means. **3,** petition; appeal.

recusar (re·ku'sar) *v.t.* to disallow; refuse; deny. —**recusación,** *n.f.* refusal; denial; recusancy. —**recusante,** *adj.* & *n.m.* & *f.* recusant.

rechazar (re·tʃa'θar; -'sar) *v.t.* [*infl.:* **rezar, 10**] **1,** to reject. **2,** to repel; repulse.

rechazo (re'tʃa·θo; -so) *n.m.* **1,** rebound. **2,** rejection; rebuff. —**de rechazo,** incidentally; accidentally.

rechifla (re'tʃi·fla) *n.f.* catcall; hoot; razz. —**rechiflar,** *v.t.* & *i.* to catcall; hoot; razz.

rechinamiento (re·tʃi·na'mjen·to) *n.m.* **1,** grating; grinding; grating or grinding sound. **2,** gnashing of the teeth. *Also,* **rechinido** (-'ni·ðo), **rechino** (re'tʃi·no).

rechinar (re·tʃi'nar) *v.i.* to grate; grind. —*v.t.* & *i.* to gnash (the teeth)

rechistar (re·tʃis'tar) *v.i., usu. with* **sin** *or* **no,** to protest; grumble.

rechoncho (re'tʃon·tʃo) *adj., colloq.* chubby.

rechupete (re·tʃu'pe·te) *n.m., in* **de rechupete,** *colloq.* wonderful; fine; exquisite.

red (reð) *n.f.* **1,** net. **2,** netting. **3,** network. **4,** snare; trap.

redacción (re·ðak'θjon; -'sjon) *n.f.* **1,** writing; editing; redaction. **2,** editorial staff. **3,** newsroom. **4,** editorial office.

redactar (re·ðak'tar) *v.t.* to write; edit; redact.

redactor (re·ðak'tor) *n.m.* [*fem.* **-tora**] writer; editor.

redada (re'ða·ða) *n.f.* **1,** cast or casting of a net. **2,** catch; haul. **3,** dragnet.

redar (re'ðar) *v.t.* to net; catch.

redecilla (re·ðe'θi·ʎa; -'si·ja) *n.f.* **1,** small net. **2,** hairnet. **3,** netting; mesh.

rededor (re·ðe'ðor) *n.m.* **1,** contour; outline. **2,** immediate vicinity or surroundings. —**al** *or* **en rededor = alrededor.**

redención (re·ðen'θjon; -'sjon) *n.f.* redemption.

redentor (re·ðen'tor) *n.m.* [*fem.* **-tora**] redeemer. —*adj.* redeeming.

redicho (re'ði·tʃo) *adj.* affected or over-precise in speech.

redil (re'ðil) *n.m.* fold; sheepfold.

redimir (re·ði'mir) *v.t.* to redeem. —**redimible,** *adj.* redeemable.

redingote (re·ðin'go·te) *n.m.* **1,** riding coat. **2,** overcoat; greatcoat.

rédito ('re·ði·to) *n.m.* interest; return; income. —**reditual** (-'twal) *adj.* interest-bearing; income-producing.

redituar (re·ði'twar) *v.t.* [*infl.:* **continuar, 23**] to yield (interest or income).

redivivo (re·ði'βi·βo) *adj.* risen; resurrected.

redoblado (re·ðo'βla·ðo) *adj.* **1,** redoubled. **2,** double-folded. **3,** double-quick. **4,** thickset. —*n.m.* double fold.

redoblar (re·ðo'βlar) *v.t.* **1,** to redouble. **2,** to double-fold. **3,** to clinch (*as a nail or with nails*). —*v.t.* & *i.* to roll (*as a drum*).

redoble (re'ðo·βle) *n.m.* **1,** redoubling; redouble. **2,** drum roll.

redoblona (re·ðo'βlo·na) *n.f., S.A.* combination bet; parlay.

redolente (re·ðo'len·te) *adj.* aching; suffering a dull pain.

redolor (re·ðo'lor) *n.m.* dull ache or pain; afterpain.

redoma (re'ðo·ma) *n.f.* flask; phial.

redomado (re·ðo'ma·ðo) *adj.* artful; crafty; cunning.

redomón (re·ðo'mon) *adj., S.A.* half-tamed.

redonda (re'ðon·da) *n.f.* **1,** surrounding neighborhood. **2,** *mus.* semibreve. —**a la redonda,** around; in a circle; about.

redondear (re·ðon·de'ar) *v.t* **1,** to round; round off. **2,** to settle; pay off; discharge; clear. —**redondearse,** *v.r., colloq.* to be or become well-off.

redondel (re·ðon'del) *n.m., colloq.* **1,** circle; ring. **2,** arena.

redondez (re·ðon'deθ; -'des) *n.f.* **1,** roundness. **2,** curvature. **3,** round or curved surface.

redondilla (re·ðon'di·ʎa; -ja) *n.f.* quatrain.

redondo (re'ðon·do) *adj.* **1,** round. **2,** *typog.* roman. —*n.m.* **1,** roundness; round shape. **2,** *colloq.* coin; cash. —**en redondo,** around; round; full circle.

redopelo (re·ðo'pe·lo) *n.m.* hassle; squabble. —**a** *or* **al redopelo,** the wrong way; against the grain.

reducir (re·ðu'θir; -'sir) *v.t.* [*infl.*: **conducir, 40**] to reduce. —**redu-cirse,** *v.r.* **1,** to be or become reduced; confine oneself. **2,** *fol.* by **en,** to cut down on. —**reducción,** *n.f.* reduction. —**reducible,** *also* **reductible,** *adj.* reducible. —**redu-cido,** *adj.* reduced; small; confined.

reducto (re'ðuk·to) *n.m.* redoubt.

redundante (re·ðun'dan·te) *adj.* redundant. —**redundancia,** *n.f.* redundancy.

redundar (re·ðun'dar) *v.i.* **1,** to redound. **2,** to be redundant. **3,** to overflow; run over.

reduplicar (re·ðu·pli'kar) *v.t.* [*infl.*: **tocar, 7**] **1,** to reduplicate. **2,** to redouble. —**reduplicación,** *n.f.* reduplication.

reelegir (re·e·le'xir) *v.t.* [*infl.*: **coger, 15**] to reelect. —**reelección,** *n.f.* reelection. —**reelegible,** *adj.* eligible for reelection.

reembarcar (re·em·bar'kar) *v.t.* [*infl.*: **tocar, 7**] to reship. —**reem-barcarse,** *v.r.* to reembark.

reembarque (re·em'bar·ke) *n.m.* **1,** reshipment. **2,** [*also,* **reembarco** (-ko)] reembarkation.

reembolsar (re·em·bol'sar) *v.t.* to reimburse. —**reembolsable,** *adj.* reimbursable. —**reembolso** (-'bol·so) *n.m.* reimbursement. —**a** *or* **contra reembolso,** cash on delivery.

reemplazar (re·em·pla'θar; -'sar) *v.t.* [*infl.*: **rezar, 10**] to replace; substitute. —**reemplazante,** *adj.* replacing. —*n.m. & f.* replacement. —**reemplazo** (-'pla·θo; -so) *n.m.* replacement; substitution.

reencarnar (re·en·kar'nar) *v.i.* to be reincarnated. —**reencarnación,** *n.f.* reincarnation.

reentrar (re·en'trar) *v.i.* to reenter.

reenviar (re·en·βi'ar) *v.t.* [*infl.*: **enviar, 22**] to forward; send on.

reenvío (re·en'βi·o) *n.m.* forwarding; reshipment.

reexpedir (re·eks·pe'ðir) *v.t.* to forward; reship. —**reexpedición,** *n.f.* forwarding; reshipment.

refacción (re·fak'θjon; -'sjon) *n.f.* **1,** refection; repast. **2,** repair; repairing. —**refaccionar,** *v.t., Amer.* to repair; remake; do over.

refajo (re'fa·xo) *n.m.* underskirt.

refección (re·fek'θjon; -'sjon) *n.f.* = **refacción.**

refectorio (re·fek'to·rjo) *n.m.* refectory.

referencia (re·fe'ren·θja; -sja) *n.f.* **1,** reference. **2,** account; report.

referendum (re·fe'ren·dum) *n.m.* referendum.

referente (re·fe'ren·te) *adj.* referring; relating.

referir (re·fe'rir) *v.t.* [*infl.*: **sentir, 31**] **1,** to refer. **2,** to tell; relate. —**referirse,** *v.r.* to refer; relate; have reference.

refilón (re·fi'lon) *n.m., colloq.* glancing blow. —**de refilón,** obliquely; aslant; glancing.

refinar (re·fi'nar) *v.t.* to refine. —**refinación,** *n.f.* refining. —**refinado,** *adj.* refined. —**refinamiento,** *n.m.* refinement. —**refinería,** *n.f.* refinery.

reflectar (re·flek'tar) *v.t.* to reflect (light, sound, etc.).

reflector (re·flek'tor) *adj.* reflecting. —*n.m.* **1,** reflector. **2,** searchlight. **3,** headlight.

reflejar (re·fle'xar) *v.t.* **1,** to reflect. **2,** to mirror.

reflejo (re·fle'xo) *adj.* **1,** reflected. **2,** reflex. **3,** *gram.* reflexive. —*n.m.* **1,** reflection; reflected light. **2,** reflex.

reflexión (re·flek'sjon) *n.f.* reflection.

reflexionar (re·flek·sjo'nar) *v.t. & i.* to reflect (on); to ponder.

reflexivo (re·flek'si·βo) *adj.* **1,** thoughtful; considerate. **2,** *gram.* reflexive.

refluir (re·flu'ir) *v.i.* [*infl.*: **huir, 26**] **1,** to flow back. **2,** to redound; come back; react.

reflujo (re'flu·xo) *n.m.* **1,** reflux; ebbing. **2,** ebb tide.

refocilar (re·fo·θi'lar; -si'lar) *v.t.* to please; bring enjoyment to. —**refocilarse,** *v.r.* to enjoy oneself. —**refocilación,** *n.f.* enjoyment; pleasure.

reforestación (re·fo·res·ta'θjon; -'sjon) *n.f., Amer.* reforestation.

reforma (re'for·ma) *n.f.* **1,** reform. **2,** reformation; *cap.* Reformation.

reformación (re·for·ma'θjon; -'sjon) *n.f.* reformation; reforming; reform.

reformar (re·for'mar) *v.t.* **1,** to reform. **2,** to reshape; remake; alter. —**reformarse,** *v.r.* to reform; be reformed. —**reformador,** *adj.* reforming. —*n.m.* [*fem.* **-dora**] reformer.

reformatorio (re·for·ma'to·rjo) *n.m.* reformatory.

reformista (re·for'mis·ta) *adj.* reform; reformist. —*n.m. & f.* advocate of reform; reformist.

reforzar (re·for'θar; -'sar) *v.t.* [*infl.*: rezar, 10; acostar, 28] to reinforce; strengthen; fortify.

refracción (re·frak'θjon; -'sjon) *n.f.* refraction.

refractar (re·frak'tar) *v.t.* to refract.

refractario (re·frak'ta·rjo) *adj.* refractory; unyielding.

refractor (re·frak'tor) *n.m.* refractor.

refrán (re'fran) *n.m.* 1, proverb; saying. 2, refrain. —**refranero**, *n.m.* collection of sayings.

refregadura (re·fre·ɣa'ðu·ra) *n.f.* 1, rub; rubbing. 2, scratch; bruise; abrasion.

refregar (re·fre'ɣar) *v.t.* [*infl.*; pagar, 8; pensar, 27] to rub; rub in. —**refregamiento**, *n.m.* rub; rubbing.

refregón (re·fre'ɣon) *n.m.* = **refregadura**.

refreír (re·fre'ir) *v.t.* [*infl.*: reír, 58] 1, to refry. 2, to overfry.

refrenar (re·fre'nar) *v.t.* to restrain; curb; rein. —**refrenamiento**, *n.m.* restraining; restraint.

refrendar (re·fren'dar) *v.t.* 1, to countersign. 2, to visé. 3, to approve; sanction. 4, to support; corroborate. —**refrendario**, *n.m.* countersigner. —**refrendata** (-'da·ta) *n.f.* countersignature.

refrescar (re·fres'kar) *v.t. & i.* [*infl.*: tocar, 7] to refresh. —*v.i.* 1, to become cool, as weather. 2, to cool off; take refreshment. —**refrescarse**, *v.r.* 1, to cool off; take refreshment. 2, to become brisk (*said of the wind*). —**refrescante**, *adj.* refreshing.

refresco (re'fres·ko) *n.m.* 1, refreshment. 2, soft drink. —**de refresco**, 1, relief; fresh. 2, refreshed; renewed.

refresquería (re·fres·ke'ri·a) *n.f.*, *Amer.* refreshment stand.

refriega (re'frje·ɣa) *n.f.* fray; affray; battle.

refrigerador (re·fri·xe·ra'ðor) *adj.* refrigerating; cooling. —*n.m.* [*also*, refrigeradora, *n.f.*] refrigerator; ice box; cooler.

refrigerar (re·fri·xe'rar) *v.t.* to refrigerate. —**refrigeración**, *n.f.* refrigeration. —**refrigerante**, *adj. & n.m.* refrigerant.

refrigerio (re·fri'xe·rjo) *n.m.* 1, refreshment; snack. 2, relief; solace.

refringir (re·frin'xir) *v.t.* [*infl.*: coger, 15] to refract. —**refringente**, *adj.* refracting; refractive.

refrito (re'fri·to) *v.*, *p.p. of* refreír. —*adj.*, *Amer.*, *colloq.* done; fouled up; done for. —*n.m.*, *colloq.* rehash.

refuerzo (re'fuer·θo; -so) *n.m.* reinforcement.

refugiar (re·fu'xjar) *v.t.* to shelter; harbor; give refuge to. —**refugiarse**, *v.r.* to take refuge; take shelter. —**refugiado**, *n.m.* refugee.

refugio (re'fu·xjo) *n.m.* 1, refuge. 2, shelter.

refulgencia (re·ful'xen·θja; -sja) *n.f.* refulgence. —**refulgente**, *adj.* refulgent.

refulgir (re·ful'xir) *v.i.* [*infl.*: coger, 15] to shine; glow.

refundición (re·fun·di'θjon; -'sjon) *n.f.* recasting; revision; abridgment.

refundir (re·fun'dir) *v.t.* 1, to remelt. 2, to recast; revise; abridge. 3, to contain; include. 4, *Amer.*, *colloq.* to lose; misplace; bury among assorted things.

refunfuñar (re·fun·fu'ɲar) *v.i.* to grumble. —**refunfuño** (-'fu·ɲo) *n.m.* grumble; grumbling. —**refunfuñón** (-'ɲon) *adj.* grumbling; grumbly. —*n.m.* [*fem.* -ñona] grumbler.

refutar (re·fu'tar) *v.t.* to refute. —**refutación**, *n.f.* refutation.

regadera (re·ɣa'ðe·ra) *n.f.* 1, watering pot. 2, sprinkler. 3, shower.

regadío (re·ɣa'ði·o) *adj.* irrigable. —*n.m.* [*also*, tierras de regadío] irrigated land.

regalado (re·ɣa'la·ðo) *adj.* 1, delicate; exquisite. 2, pleasing; delightful. 3, easy; pleasant. 4, *colloq.* fond of being waited upon; fond of easy living. 5, free; gratis. 6, cheap; bargain-priced.

regalar (re·ɣa'lar) *v.t.* 1, to give; present. 2, to regale; entertain. —**regalarse**, *v.r.* to regale oneself.

regalía (re·ɣa'li·a) *n.f.* 1, royal prerogative. 2, exemption; privilege. 3, bonus; *pl.* perquisites. 4, *Amer.* muff. 5, royalties.

regaliz (re·ɣa'liθ; -'lis) *n.m.* licorice. *Also*, **regaliza** (-'li·θa; -sa) *n.f.*

regalo (re'ɣa·lo) *n.m.* 1, present; gift. 2, pleasure; comfort. 3, regalement.

regalón (re·γa'lon) *adj.*, *Amer.*, *colloq.* pampered; spoiled.

regañar (re·γa'ɲar) *v.i.* **1**, to grumble; gripe. **2**, *colloq.* to bicker; squabble. —*v.t.*, *colloq.* to scold. —(a) **regañadientes** (re·γa·ɲa·'ðjen·tes) reluctantly; grumblingly.

regaño (re'γa·ɲo) *n.m.* **1**, grumble; gripe. **2**, *colloq.* scolding.

regañón (re·γa'ɲon) *adj.*, *colloq.* **1**, grumbly; griping. **2**, scolding. —*n.m.*, *colloq.* grouch. —**regañona**, *n.f.* scold; nag.

regar (re'γar) *v.t.* [*infl.:* pagar, 8; pensar, 27] **1**, to water. **2**, to spread; strew.

regata (re'γa·ta) *n.f.* regatta.

regate (re'γa·te) *n.m.* dodge; evasion.

regatear (re·γa·te'ar) *v.t.* **1**, to dicker or haggle over (price). **2**, to sell (bargain goods); sell at retail. **3**, *colloq.* to shirk. **4**, to begrudge. —*v.i.* **1**, to bargain. **2**, to dodge. **3**, to engage in a boat race.

regateo (re·γa'te·o) *n.m.* haggling; dickering; bargaining.

regatero (re·γa'te·ro) *n.m.* **1**, hawker. **2**, *colloq.* haggler; bargain hunter.

regato (re'γa·to) *n.m.* **1**, rill; rivulet. **2**, pool; puddle. *Also,* **regajo** (-xo).

regazo (re'γa·θo; -so) *n.m.* lap.

regencia (re'xen·θja; -sja) *n.f.* regency.

regenerar (re·xe·ne'rar) *v.t.* to regenerate. —**regeneración**, *n.f.* regeneration. —**regenerativo**, *adj.* regenerative.

regentar (re·xen'tar) *v.t.* to rule, esp. as regent.

regente (re'xen·te) *adj.* ruling; regent. —*n.m.* & *f.* **1**, regent. **2**, [*fem.* **regenta**] manager of a small establishment.

regentear (re·xen·te'ar) *v.t.* **1**, to rule sternly or arbitrarily; boss. **2**, to manage (a small establishment, store, etc.).

regicida (re·xi'θi·ða; -'si·ða) *n.m.* & *f.* regicide (*agent*). —**regicidio** (-'θi·ðjo; -'si·ðjo) *n.m.* regicide (*act*).

regidor (re·xi'ðor) *adj.* ruling; governing. —*n.m.* alderman; councilman. —**regiduría** (-ðu'ri·a) *n.f.* office or dignity of an alderman or councilman.

régimen ('re·xi·men) *n.m.* [*pl.* **regímenes** (re'xi·me·nes)] **1**, regime. **2**, regimen; order; plan. **3**, diet. **4**, *gram.* government.

regimental (re·xi·men'tal) *adj.* regimental.

regimentar (re·xi·men'tar) *v.t.* [*infl.:* **pensar, 27**] to regiment. —**regimentación**, *n.f.* regimentation.

regimiento (re·xi'mjen·to) *n.m.* **1**, regiment. **2**, ruling; rule. **3**, council; board of aldermen.

regio ('re·xjo) *adj.* regal.

región (re'xjon) *n.f.* region. —**regional**, *adj.* regional.

regionalismo (re·xjo·na'lis·mo) *n.m.* regionalism. —**regionalista**, *adj.* regionalistic. —*n.m.* & *f.* regionalist.

regir (re'xir) *v.t.* [*infl.:* 57] **1**, to rule; govern. **2**, *gram.* to govern. —*v.i.* **1**, to be in force or effect. **2**, to govern; prevail.

registrador (re·xis·tra'ðor) *adj.* registering. —*n.m.* **1**, register; cash register. **2**, registering device; meter. **3**, [*fem.* **-dora**] registrar; recorder.

registrar (re·xis'trar) *v.t.* **1**, to register. **2**, to search; inspect. **3**, to rummage; rummage through. —**registrarse**, *v.r.* to register.

registro (re'xis·tro) *n.m.* **1**, register. **2**, registry. **3**, registration. **4**, record; entry. **5**, search; inspection. **6**, *mech.* regulator. **7**, bookmark.

regla ('re·γla) *n.f.* **1**, rule. **2**, ruler; straightedge. **3**, period; menses. —**en regla**, in order; properly.

reglamentación (re·γla·men·ta'θjon; -'sjon) *n.f.* **1**, rule; regulation. **2**, set of rules or regulations.

reglamentar (re·γla·men'tar) *v.t.* to set rules or regulations for.

reglamentario (re·γla·men'ta·rjo) *adj.* **1**, regulation (*attrib.*); prescribed by regulation. **2**, ruling; regulatory. **3**, mandatory; necessary.

reglamento (re·γla'men·to) *n.m.* **1**, collection of rules, regulations or bylaws. **2**, regulation; rule; bylaw. —**de reglamento = reglamentario**.

reglar (re'γlar) *v.t.* **1**, to rule; draw lines on. **2**, to regulate; order. —*v.i.*, *Arg.* to menstruate. —*adj.*, *eccles.* regular. —**reglarse**, *v.r.* to restrict oneself; limit oneself.

regleta (re'γle·ta) *n.f.*, *print.* lead. —**regletear**, *v.t.* to lead.

regocijar (re·γo·θi'xar; -si'xar) *v.t.* to gladden; rejoice. —**regocijarse**, *v.r.* to rejoice; be gladdened.

regocijo (re·ɣo'θi·xo; -'si·xo) *n.m.*
1, joy. 2, rejoicing.

regodearse (re·ɣo·ðe'ar·se) *v.r.* 1,
to enjoy oneself; delight. 2, *colloq.*
to frolic. 3, *colloq.* to coddle oneself.

regodeo (re·ɣo'ðe·o) *n.m., colloq.*
1, coddling; pampering; indulgence.
2, frolic.

regojo (re'ɣo·xo) *n.m.* 1, bread
crumb. 2, *colloq.* small boy; shaver.

regoldar (re·ɣol'dar) *v.i., colloq.*
[*infl.:* **acostar, 28; averiguar, 9**] to
belch.

regordete (re·ɣor'ðe·te) *adj.,
colloq.* pudgy; chubby.

regresar (re·ɣre'sar) *v.i.* 1, to return; go or come back. 2, to regress.

regresión (re·ɣre'sjon) *n.f.* regression. —**regresivo** (-'si·βo) *adj.* regressive.

regreso (re'ɣre·so) *n.m.* 1, return;
going or coming back. 2, regress.

regué (re'ɣe) *v., 1st pers.sing. pret.
of* **regar.**

regüelde (re'ɣwel·de) *v., pres.
subjve. of* **regoldar.**

regüeldo (re'ɣwel·do) *v., pres.ind.
of* **regoldar.** —*n.m., colloq.* belch.

reguera (re'ɣe·ra) *n.f.* ditch; irrigation ditch.

reguero (re'ɣe·ro) *n.m.* 1, trail *(of
something spilled or scattered).* 2,
trickle; thin stream. 3, irrigation
ditch.

regulación (re·ɣu·la'θjon; -'sjon)
n.f. regulation.

regulador (re·ɣu·la'ðor) *adj.* regulating. —*n.m.* 1, regulator. 2, throttle.

regular (re·ɣu'lar) *adj.* 1, regular.
2, medium; average. —*adj. & adv.,
colloq.* so-so. —*n.m. & f.* regular.
—*v.t.* to regulate; adjust. —**por lo
regular,** usually; ordinarily.

regularidad (re·ɣu·la·ri'ðað) *n.f.*
regularity.

regularizar (re·ɣu·la·ri'θar; -'sar)
v.t. [*infl.:* **rezar, 10**] to regularize.
—**regularización,** *n.f.* regularization.

regulativo (re·ɣu·la'ti·βo) *adj.*
regulating.

régulo ('re·ɣu·lo) *n.m.* 1, petty
king; kinglet. 2, *ornith.* kinglet. 3, =
basilisco.

regurgitar (re·ɣur·xi'tar) *v.i.* to
regurgitate. —**regurgitación,** *n.f.*
regurgitation.

rehabilitar (re·a·βi·li'tar) *v.t.* to

rehabilitate. —**rehabilitación,** *n.f.*
rehabilitation.

rehacer (re·a'θer; -'ser) *v.t.* [*infl.:*
hacer, 48] 1, to redo; do over. 2, to
remake; make over. 3, to rebuild. 4,
to revive; restore. —**rehacerse,** *v.r.*
1, to recover; get back on one's
feet. 2, to reorganize; reassemble.

rehacimiento (re·a·θi'mjen·to;
re·a·si-) *n.m.* 1, recovery; recover-
ing. 2, remaking; rebuilding.

rehecho (re'e·tʃo) *v., p.p. of*
rehacer. —*adj.* heavy-set.

rehén (re'en) *n.m.* hostage. —**en
rehenes,** 1, in or as hostage. 2, in or
as pledge.

rehervir (re·er'βir) *v.t.* [*infl.:*
sentir, 31] to reboil. —*v.i.* to burn
with love. —**rehervirse,** *v.r.* to ferment.

rehogar (re·o'ɣar) *v.t.* [*infl.:*
pagar, 8] to cook slowly in a covered pan.

rehuir (re·u'ir) *v.t.* [*infl.:* **huir, 26**]
1, to shirk; avoid; shrink from. 2, to
refuse; decline. —**rehuída** ('i·ða)
n.f. shirking; avoidance.

rehusar (re·u'sar) *v.t.* to refuse.

reidor (re·i'ðor) *adj.* laughing;
jolly.

reimprimir (re·im·pri'mir) *v.t.*
[*p.p.* **reimpreso** (-'pre·so)] to reprint. —**reimpresión** (-pre'sjon) *n.f.*
reprint.

reina ('rei·na) *n.f.* queen.

reinado (rei'na·ðo) *n.m.* reign.

reinar (rei'nar) *v.i.* to reign.
—**reinante,** *adj.* 1, ruling; reigning.
2, prevailing.

reincidir (re·in·θi'ðir; -si'ðir) *v.i.*
to relapse; repeat an error or offense. —**reincidencia,** *n.f.* relapse;
recidivism. —**reincidente,** *adj.* re-
lapsing; recidivous. —*n.m. & f.* recidivist.

reingresar (re·in·gre'sar) *v.i.* to
reenter; rejoin —**reingreso** (-'gre·
so) *n.m.* reentry; rejoining.

reino ('rei·no) *n.m.* 1, kingdom. 2,
reign.

reinstalar (re·ins·ta'lar) *v.t.* to reinstate; reinstall. —**reinstalación,**
n.f. reinstatement; reinstallation.

reintegración (re·in·te·ɣra'θjon;
-'sjon) *n.f.* 1, return; restitution. 2,
reimbursement.

reintegrar (re·in·te'ɣrar) *v.t.* 1, to
restore; return. 2, to refund; reimburse. —**reintegrarse,** *v.r.* 1, to return; rejoin. 2, to reimburse oneself.

reintegro (re·in'te·ɣro) *n.m.* 1, =

reintegración. 2, *comm.* withdrawal.

reír (re'ir) *v.i.* [*also, v.r.,* **reírse**] [*infl.:* 58] 1, to laugh. 2, to sneer; scoff. —*v.t.* to laugh at; laugh about.

reiterar (re·i·te'rar; rei-) *v.t.* to reiterate. —**reiteración**, *n.f.* reiteration.

reivindicación (re·i·βin·di·ka·'θjon; -'sjon) *n.f.* 1, vindication. 2, assertion (*of a legal right*). 3, repossession.

reivindicar (re·i·βin·di'kar) *v.t.* [*infl.:* tocar, 7] 1, to vindicate. 2, to assert (a legal right). 3, to regain possession of.

reja ('re·xa) *n.f.* 1, grille; grating, esp. in a window. 2, plowshare. —**entre rejas**, behind bars; in prison.

rejado (re'xa·ðo) *n.m.* = **verja**.

rejilla (re'xi·ʎa; -ja) *n.f.* 1, lattice; grating. 2, grate. 3, luggage rack. 4, rattan or cane for chair backs, seats, etc.

rejo ('re·xo) *n.m.* 1, spike; goad. 2, sting; barb. 3, *Amer.* lash; whip.

rejón (re'xon) *n.m.* 1, spear; lance. 2, dagger.

rejonear (re·xo·ne'ar) *v.t.* to spear or lance (a bull). —**rejoneo** (-'ne·o) *n.m.* lancing; spearing.

rejuvenecer (re·xu·βe·ne'θer; -'ser) *v.t.* [*infl.:* conocer, 13] to rejuvenate. —*v.i.* [*also, v.r.,* **rejuvenecerse**] to be or become rejuvenated. —**rejuvenecedor**, *adj.* rejuvenating. —**rejuvenecimiento**, *n.m.* rejuvenation.

relación (re·la'θjon; -'sjon) *n.f.* 1, relation. 2, account; report. —**tener relaciones con,** to be engaged to.

relacionar (re·la·θjo'nar; -sjo'nar) *v.t.* to relate. —**relacionarse**, *v.r.* 1, to be or become related. 2, to become involved; become acquainted.

relajación (re·la·xa'θjon; -'sjon) *n.f.* 1, relaxation. 2, laxity. 3, hernia.

relajado (re·la'xa·ðo) *adj.* morally lax; dissolute; licentious.

relajamiento (re·la·xa'mjen·to) *n.m.* = **relajación**.

relajar (re·la'xar) *v.t.* 1, to relax. 2, to weaken morally. 3, *law* to release. —**relajarse**, *v.r.* 1, to be or become lax or relaxed. 2, to become morally lax; become dissolute.

relamer (re·la'mer) *v.t.* to lick over; lick again. —**relamerse**, *v.r.* 1, to smack the lips. 2, to gloat.

relamido (re·la'mi·ðo) *adj.* 1, prim; overnice; affected. 2, *Amer.* blasé.

relámpago (re'lam·pa·ɣo) *n.m.* lightning; lightning flash. —**relampaguear** (-ɣe'ar) *v.i.* to flash as with lightning. —**relampagueo** (-'ɣe·o) *n.m.* flashing; flash of lightning.

relapso (re'lap·so) *adj.* relapsed into error. —*n.m.* 1, relapse. 2, backslider.

relatar (re·la'tar) *v.t.* to tell; relate; report.

relativo (re·la'ti·βo) *adj.* relative. —**relatividad**, *n.f.* relativity. —**relativismo**, *n.m.* relativism.

relato (re'la·to) *n.m.* 1, statement; report. 2, story; narrative.

relator (re·la'tor) *n.m.* [*fem.* -tora] narrator.

releer (re·le'er) *v.t.* [*infl.:* creer, 42] to reread.

relegar (re·le'ɣar) *v.t.* [*infl.:* pagar, 8] to relegate. —**relegación**, *n.f.* relegation.

relente (re'len·te) *n.m.* night dew.

relevación (re·le·βa'θjon; -'sjon) *n.f.* 1, relief; release. 2, enhancement; enhancing.

relevante (re·le'βan·te) *adj.* prominent; excellent.

relevar (re·le'βar) *v.t.* 1, to relieve (*as from duty or a duty*). 2, to put or bring into relief. 3, to overrate; overpraise. 4, to give relief to; succor. 5, to release; absolve. —*v.i.* to be in relief; stand out.

relevo (re'le·βo) *n.m.* 1, relief; replacement. 2, change of watch, guard, shift, etc. 3, *pl.* [*also,* **carrera de relevos**] relay race.

relicario (re·li'ka·rjo) *n.m.* 1, shrine. 2, reliquary. 3, locket.

relieve (re'lje·βe) *n.m.* 1, relief. 2, prominence; importance. —**de** or **en relieve,** in relief.

religa (re'li·ɣa) *n.f.* alloy; metal added to an alloy.

religión (re·li'xjon) *n.f.* religion.

religiosidad (re·li·xjo·si'ðað) *n.f.* 1, religiousness. 2, religiosity. 3, scrupulousness.

religioso (re·li'xjo·so) *adj.* religious. —*n.m.* member of a religious order.

relimpio (re'lim·pjo) *adj., colloq.* very clean.

relinchar (re·lin'tʃar) *v.i.* to neigh;

whinny. —**relincho** (-'lin·tʃo) *n.m.* neigh; whinny.

relindo (re'lin·do) *adj.* very pretty.

reliquia (re'li·kja) *n.f.* 1, relic. 2, vestige; trace.

reloj (re'lox; re'lo) *n.m.* 1, clock. 2, watch. —**reloj despertador,** alarm clock. —**reloj de pulsera,** wristwatch.

relojera (re·lo'xe·ra) *n.f.* 1, watchcase. 2, watch pocket.

relojería (re·lo·xe'ri·a) *n.f.* 1, clockmaking; watchmaking. 2, watchmaker's shop.

relojero (re·lo'xe·ro) *n.m.* watchmaker; clockmaker.

relucir (re·lu'θir; -'sir) *v.i.* [*infl.:* **lucir, 14**] 1, to shine; glow. 2, to stand out; excel. —**sacar a relucir,** to bring out; bring to view. —**salir a relucir,** to come out; come to view.

reluctancia (re·luk'tan·θja; -sja) *n.f., elect.* reluctance.

reluctante (re·luk'tan·te) *adj.* recalcitrant; intractable.

relumbrar (re·lum'brar) *v.i.* to sparkle; shine; glare. —**relumbre** (-'lum·bre) *n.m.* glare; brilliance.

relumbro (re'lum·bro) *n.m.* 1, flash. 2, tinsel.

relumbrón (re·lum'bron) *n.m.* = relumbro. —**de relumbrón,** tinsel; showy; gaudy.

rellenar (re·ʎe'nar; re·je-) *v.t.* 1, to refill. 2, to fill completely; cram. 3, to stuff. —**rellenarse,** *v.r., colloq.* to be stuffed; be satiated.

relleno (re'ʎe·no; re'je-) *adj.* 1, stuffed. 2, *colloq.* satiated; full. —*n.m.* 1, stuffing. 2, padding. 3, meatball; dumpling.

remachado (re·ma'tʃa·ðo) *n.m.* riveting; clinching.

remachar (re·ma'tʃar) *v.t.* to clinch; rivet; nail down.

remache (re'ma·tʃe) *n.m.* 1, clinching; riveting. 2, rivet. 3, *colloq.* clincher.

remada (re'ma·ða) *n.f.* 1, stroke of the oar. 2, *colloq.* rowing; row.

remador (re·ma'ðor) *n.m.* = remero.

remanente (re·ma'nen·te) *adj.* residual; remaining. —*n.m.* residue; remnant.

remangar (re·man'gar) *v.t.* [*infl.:* **pagar, 8**] to roll up, esp. the sleeves.

remanso (re'man·so) *n.m.* 1, river pond; backwater. 2, *fig.* haven; oa-

sis. —*adj., S.A. colloq.* timorous; timid.

remar (re'mar) *v.i.* to row; paddle.

rematado (re·ma'ta·ðo) *adj.* 1, finished; ended; lost. 2, hopeless; irremediable. —**loco rematado,** stark mad.

rematar (re·ma'tar) *v.t.* 1, to end; finish; close; terminate. 2, to finish off; give the final stroke to. 3, to auction; knock down.

remate (re'ma·te) *n.m.* 1, end. 2, auction. 3, crown; top piece; topping. 4, *cards* bidding.

remecer (re·me'θer; -'ser) *v.t.* [*infl.:* **vencer, 11**] to rock; swing back and forth.

remedar (re·me'ðar) *v.t.* to imitate; mimic; ape. —**remedable,** *adj.* imitable. —**remedador,** *n.m.* [*fem.* **-dora**] imitator; mimic.

remediar (re·me'ðjar) *v.t.* to remedy; help. —**remediable,** *adj.* remediable.

remedio (re'me·ðjo) *n.m.* remedy; help. —**No hay remedio,** It can't be helped.

remedo (re'me·ðo) *n.m.* imitation; parody.

remembranza (re·mem'bran·θa; -sa) *n.f.* remembrance.

rememorar (re·me·mo'rar) *v.t.* to remember; recall. —**rememorativo,** *adj.* reminding; recalling.

remendar (re·men'dar) *v.t.* [*infl.:* **pensar, 27**] to patch; mend; darn.

remendón (re·men'don) *n.m.* 1, patcher; mender. 2, cobbler.

remero (re'me·ro) *n.m.* rower; oarsman.

remesa (re'me·sa) *n.f.* 1, shipment. 2, remittance.

remesar (re·me'sar) *v.t.* 1, to pull (the hair). 2, *comm.* to send; remit.

remeter (re·me'ter) *v.t.* to take in (a garment); to take up (a hem).

remiendo (re'mjen·do) *n.m.* 1, patch; mend; darn. 2, patching; mending; darning.

remilgarse (re·mil'γar·se) *v.r.* [*infl.:* **pagar, 8**] to fuss; be fussy. —**remilgado,** *adj.* fussy; overfastidious.

remilgo (re'mil·γo) *n.m.* 1, primness; priggishness. 2, fastidiousness.

reminiscencia (re·mi·nis'θen·θja; -ni'sen·sja) *n.f.* reminiscence.

remirar (re·mi'rar) *v.t.* to recheck; look at again; review. —**remirarse,**

v.r. **1,** to take great pains. **2,** to primp.

remisión (re·mi'sjon) *n.f.* **1,** remission. **2,** remittance. **3,** delivery.

remiso (re'mi·so) *adj.* remiss.

remitente (re·mi'ten·te) *n.m. & f.* sender.

remitido (re·mi'ti·ðo) *n.m.* personal notice.

remitir (re·mi'tir) *v.t.* **1,** to remit; send. **2,** to forgive. **3,** to defer; postpone. **4,** to refer. —*v.i.* [*also, v.r.,* **remitirse**] to abate, as the wind. —**remitirse,** *v.r.* **1,** to submit. **2,** to abide; hold fast.

remo ('re·mo) *n.m.* **1,** oar; paddle. **2,** rowing. **3,** *usu.pl., zoöl.* leg; *ornith.* wing; *colloq.* limb.

remoce (re'mo·θe; -se) *v., pres. subjve. of* **remozar.**

remocé (re·mo'θe; -'se) *v., 1st pers.sing. pret. of* **remozar.**

remoción (re·mo'θjon; -'sjon) *n.f.* removal.

remojar (re·mo'xar) *v.t.* **1,** to steep; soak. **2,** to wet; wet down. —**remojo** (-'mo·xo) *n.m.* steeping; soaking.

remolacha (re·mo'la·tʃa) *n.f.* beet.

remolcador (re·mol·ka'ðor) *adj.* towing. —*n.m.* **1,** tug; towboat. **2,** tow truck.

remolcar (re·mol'kar) *v.t.* [*infl.:* **tocar, 7**] to tow; haul.

remolino (re·mo'li·no) *n.m.* **1,** whirl; swirl. **2,** whirlwind. **3,** whirlpool. **4,** cowlick. **5,** crowd; throng. **6,** disturbance; commotion.

remolón (re·mo'lon) *adj.* indolent; lazy. —*n.m.* [*fem.* **-lona**] loiterer; idler; sluggard. —**remolonear,** *v.i.* to lag; loiter; shirk.

remolque (re'mol·ke) **1,** towing; tow. **2,** trailer. —**a remolque,** in tow.

remontar (re·mon'tar) *v.t.* **1,** to raise; lift; bear aloft. **2,** to mount (a stream); go upstream. **3,** to surmount; overcome. **4,** to repair (a saddle). **5,** to resole (a shoe). —**remontarse,** *v.r.* **1,** to soar. **2,** to go back to (in time); date from.

remonte (re'mon·te) *n.m.* **1,** repairing. **2,** remounting. **3,** soaring.

remoque (re'mo·ke) *n.m., colloq.* jibe; scoff.

remoquete (re·mo'ke·te) *n.m.* **1,** nickname; epithet. **2,** witticism; sally.

rémora ('re·mo·ra) *n.f.* **1,** *ichthy.* remora. **2,** hindrance; obstacle.

remorder (re·mor'ðer) *v.t.* [*infl.:* **mover, 30**] **1,** to gnaw; corrode. **2,** to prick; pierce; sting. —**remorderse,** *v.r.* to show worry, remorse, etc. —**remordimiento,** *n.m.* remorse.

remoto (re'mo·to) *adj.* remote.

remover (re·mo'βer) *v.t.* [*infl.:* **mover, 30**] **1,** to remove. **2,** to stir. —**removimiento,** *n.m.* removal.

remozar (re·mo'θar; -'sar) *v.t.* [*infl.:* **rezar, 10**] to give a fresh look to; renovate. —**remozarse,** *v.r.* to look young or new. —**remozamiento,** *n.m.* new appearance; renovation.

rempujar (rem·pu'xar) *v.t.* to push; shove. —**rempujo** (-'pu·xo) *also,* **rempujón** (-'xon) *n.m.* push; shove.

remudar (re·mu'ðar) *v.t.* to change; replace. —**remuda** (-'mu·ða) *n.f.* change; replacement.

remunerar (re·mu·ne'rar) *v.t.* to remunerate. —**remuneración,** *n.f.* remuneration. —**remuneratorio,** *adj.* remunerative.

renacer (re·na'θer; -'ser) *v.i.* [*infl.:* **conocer, 13**] to be born again; spring up anew. —**renaciente,** *adj.* renascent.

renacimiento (re·na·θi'mjen·to; re·na·si-) *n.m.* renascence; renaissance.

renacuajo (re·na'kwa·xo) *n.m.* **1,** tadpole. **2,** *colloq.* runt.

renal (re'nal) *adj.* renal.

rencilla (ren'θi·ʎa; -'si·ja) *n.f.* quarrel; falling out. —**rencilloso,** *adj.* peevish; quarrelsome.

renco ('ren·ko) *adj.* lame in the hip.

rencor (ren'kor) *n.m.* rancor. —**rencoroso,** *adj.* rancorous.

rendición (ren·di'θjon; -'sjon) *n.f.* **1,** surrender; submission. **2,** yield.

rendido (ren'di·ðo) *adj.* **1,** obsequious; devoted. **2,** exhausted; worn out.

rendija (ren'di·xa) *n.f.* crack; fissure; split.

rendimiento (ren·di'mjen·to) *n.m.* **1,** exhaustion; fatigue. **2,** submission. **3,** tribute. **4,** yield. **5,** *mech.* efficiency.

rendir (ren'dir) *v.t.* [*infl.:* **pedir, 33**] **1,** to overcome; subdue. **2,** to yield. **3,** to exhaust; fatigue. **4,** to render; pay; obey. **5,** to give back; return. —**rendirse,** *v.r.* **1,** to surrender; submit; yield. **2,** to collapse; give way.

renegado (re·ne'ɣa·ðo) *n.m.* **1,** renegade. **2,** ombre *(card game).* —*adj.* renegade.

renegar (re·ne'ɣar) *v.t.* [*infl.:* **pagar, 8; pensar, 27**] **1,** to deny vehemently. **2,** *often fol. by* **de,** to disown; renounce, **3,** to execrate. —*v.i.* **1,** to apostatize. **2,** to blaspheme. **3,** to swear. **4,** *colloq.* to rant; rave.

renegón (re·ne'ɣon) *adj., colloq.* **1,** profane; swearing. **2,** ranting; raving.

renegrido (re·ne'ɣri·ðo) *adj.* livid; black and blue.

renglón (ren'glon) **1,** line *(of writing or printing).* **2,** *comm.* line *(of merchandise).* **3,** *bookkeeping* item. **4,** *colloq.* affair; matter. —**renglonadura,** *n.f.* ruling *(of paper).* —**a renglón seguido,** immediately following; below.

rengo ('ren·go) *adj.* **1,** lame in the hip. **2,** *Amer.* lame. —**renguear** (-ge'ar) *v.i., Amer.* to limp.

reniego (re'nje·ɣo) *n.m.* **1,** blasphemy. **2,** *colloq.* swearing; curse; cursing.

renio ('re·njo) *n.m.* rhenium.

reno ('re·no) *n.m.* reindeer.

renombre (re'nom·bre) *n.m.* renown. —**renombrado** (-'bra·ðo) *adj.* renowned.

renovación (re·no·βa'θjon; -'sjon) *n.f.* **1,** renewal. **2,** renovation.

renovar (re·no'βar) *v.t.* [*infl.:* **acostar, 28**] **1,** to renew; restore. **2,** to renovate.

renquear (ren·ke'ar) *v.i.* to limp.

renta ('ren·ta) *n.f.* **1,** rent. **2,** rental. **3,** income; return. **4,** revenue. **5,** annuity. —**rentado,** *adj.* living on an income.

rentar (ren'tar) *v.t.* to yield; return (income).

rentista (ren'tis·ta) *n.m.* **1,** financier. **2,** bondholder. **3,** one living on an income.

renuente (re·nu'en·te) *adj.* reluctant; unwilling. —**renuencia,** *n.f.* reluctance; unwillingness.

renuevo (re'nwe·βo) *n.m.* **1,** sprout; shoot. **2,** renewal. **3,** renovation.

renuncia (re'nun·θja; -sja) *n.f.* **1,** resignation *(of a right or an office).* **2,** abdication.

renunciar (re·nun'θjar; -'sjar) *v.t.* **1,** to renounce. **2,** to resign. **3,** to abdicate. —*v.i., cards* to revoke. —**renunciación,** *n.f.* renunciation.

renuncio (re'nun·θjo; -sjo) *n.m., cards* revoke.

reñido (re'ɲi·ðo) *adj.* **1,** on bad terms; on the outs. **2,** hard-fought; bitter.

reñidor (re·ɲi'ðor) *adj.* **1,** quarrelsome. **2,** scolding; nagging.

reñir (re'ɲir) *v.t. & i.* [*infl.:* **59**] to fight. —*v.i.* to quarrel. —*v.t.* to scold.

reo ('re·o) *n.m. & f.* **1,** offender; culprit. **2,** defendant. —*adj.* culpable; guilty.

reojo (re'o·xo) *n.m., in* **de reojo,** sideways; out of the corner of one's eye.

reorganizar (re·or·ɣa·ni'θar; -'sar) *v.t.* [*infl.:* **rezar, 10**] to reorganize. —**reorganización,** *n.f.* reorganization.

reóstato (re'os·ta·to) *n.m.* rheostat.

repagar (re·pa'ɣar) *v.t.* [*infl.:* **pagar, 8**] **1,** to repay. **2,** to overpay.

repantigarse (re·pan·ti'ɣar·se) *v.r.* [*infl.:* **pagar, 8**] to stretch out; slump down.

reparable (re·pa'ra·βle) *adj.* **1,** reparable. **2,** noticeable; noteworthy.

reparación (re·pa·ra'θjon; -'sjon) *n.f.* **1,** reparation. **2,** reparations. **3,** repair.

reparador (re·pa·ra'ðor) *adj.* **1,** repairing; restorative. **2,** faultfinding. —*n.m.* repairer; repairman.

reparar (re·pa'rar) *v.t.* **1,** to repair. **2,** to restore. **3,** to make amends for. **4,** to observe; note; mark. —*v.i.* **1,** *fol. by* **en,** to notice; take note of. **2,** to stop. —**repararse,** *v.r.* to refrain; forbear.

reparo (re'pa·ro) *n.m.* **1,** repair; restoration. **2,** remark; advice; warning. **3,** objection; difficulty. **4,** defense; protection.

repartimiento (re·par·ti'mjen·to) *n.m.* partition; apportionment; distribution.

repartir (re·par'tir) *v.t.* **1,** to divide; distribute; apportion. **2,** to deal (cards). —**repartición,** *n.f.* division; distribution. —**repartidor,** *n.m.* [*fem.* **-dora**] **1,** distributor. **2,** deliverer.

reparto (re'par·to) *n.m.* **1,** = **repartimiento. 2,** *theat.* cast. **3,** delivery; delivery route.

repasar (re·pa'sar) *v.t.* **1,** *also v.i.* to repass; pass again. **2,** to review. **3,** to go over; look over. **4,** to mend (clothes).

repaso (re'pa·so) *n.m.* **1,** review. **2,** *colloq.* reprimand.

repatriar (re·pa'trjar) *v.t.* to repatriate. —*v.i.* [*also,* *v.r.,* **repatriarse**] to return to one's own country. —**repatriación,** *n.f.* repatriation.

repechar (re·pe'tʃar) *v.i.* to go uphill.

repecho (re'pe·tʃo) *n.m.* **1,** short, steep slope. **2,** window sill. **3,** *colloq.* mantelpiece. —**a repecho,** uphill.

repelar (re·pe'lar) *v.t.* **1,** to pull the hair of. **2,** to trim; crop. **3,** to gnaw down; gnaw clean.

repeler (re·pe'ler) *v.t.* to repel; repulse. —**repelente,** *adj.* repellent; repelling; repulsive.

repelo (re'pe·lo) *n.m.* **1,** anything that goes against the grain. **2,** cross grain. **3,** *colloq.* slap; set-to.

repelón (re·pe'lon) *n.m.* **1,** pulling of the hair. **2,** torn piece; tatter. —**a repelones,** *colloq.* **1,** by degrees; little by little. **2,** by fistfuls. —**de repelón,** *colloq.* **1,** in passing. **2,** quick as a flash.

repeloso (re·pe'lo·so) *adj.* **1,** rough-grained. **2,** *colloq.* touchy; peevish.

repensar (re·pen'sar) *v.t.* [*infl.:* **pensar, 27**] to reconsider.

repente (re'pen·te) *n.m., colloq.* sudden movement; outburst. —**de repente,** suddenly.

repentino (re·pen'ti·no) *adj.* sudden; abrupt.

repercutir (re·per·ku'tir) *v.i.* **1,** to rebound. **2,** to resound; echo. **3,** to have repercussions. —**repercusión** (-'sjon) *n.f.* repercussion.

repertorio (re·per'to·rjo) *n.m.* repertory; repertoire.

repetidor (re·pe·ti'ðor) *adj.* **1,** repeating. **2,** repetitious. —*n.m.* repeater.

repetir (re·pe'tir) *v.t.* [*infl.:* **pedir, 33**] to repeat. —*v.i.* to repeat; have an aftertaste. —**repetición** (-'θjon; -'sjon) *n.f.* repetition. —**repetitivo,** *adj.* repetitive.

repicar (re·pi'kar) *v.t.* [*infl.:* **tocar, 7**] **1,** to chop; mince. **2,** to peal, as a bell. —**repicarse,** *v.r.* to boast.

repique (re'pi·ke) *n.m.* **1,** chopping, mincing. **2,** peal of a bell. **3,** spat; set-to.

repiquetear (re·pi·ke·te'ar) *v.t.* to ring or sound rapidly. —**repiquete-arse,** *v.r.* to quarrel. —**repiqueteo** (-'te·o) *n.m.* ringing; sounding.

repisa (re'pi·sa) *n.f.* **1,** shelf; ledge. **2,** mantelpiece. **3,** bracket. **4,** sill.

repita (re'pi·ta) *v., pres.subjve.* of **repetir.**

repitiendo (re·pi'tjen·do) *v., ger.* of **repetir.**

repitió (re·pi'tjo) *v., 3rd pers.sing. pret.* of **repetir.**

repito (re'pi·to) *v., 1st pers.sing. pres.ind.* of **repetir.**

repizcar (re·piθ'kar; re·pis-) *v.t.* [*infl.:* **tocar, 7**] to pinch. —**repizco** (-'piθ·ko; -'pis·ko) *n.m.* pinch.

repleción (re·ple'θjon; -'sjon) *n.f.* repletion.

replegar (re·ple'ɣar) *v.t.* [*infl.:* **pagar, 8; pensar, 27**] to refold; fold over and over. —**replegarse,** *v.r.,* *mil.* to retire in good order.

repleto (re'ple·to) *adj.* replete; full.

réplica ('re·pli·ka) *n.f.* **1,** reply; answer. **2,** retort; repartee. **3,** objection. **4,** replica.

replicar (re·pli'kar) *v.i.* [*infl.:* **tocar, 7**] **1,** to reply; answer. **2,** to retort. **3,** to object.

repliegue (re'plje·ɣe) *n.m.* **1,** folding. **2,** *mil.* withdrawal.

repoblación (re·po·βla'θjon; -'sjon) *n.f.* **1,** repopulation. **2,** reforestation. **3,** restocking (with fish or game).

repoblar (re·po'βlar) *v.t.* [*infl.:* **acostar, 28**] **1,** to repopulate. **2,** to reforest. **3,** to restock (with fish or game).

repollo (re'po·ʎo; -jo) *n.m.* **1,** cabbage. **2,** head (*of cabbage, lettuce, etc.*).

reponer (re·po'ner) *v.t.* [*infl.:* **poner, 54**] **1,** to replace; restore. **2,** *theat.* to revive. —**reponerse,** *v.r.* to recover; regain one's health or composure.

reportaje (re·por'ta·xe) *n.m.* **1,** reportage. **2,** report.

reportar (re·por'tar) *v.t.* **1,** to repress; restrain. **2,** to attain; obtain. **3,** to bring; carry. —**reportarse,** *v.r.* to restrain oneself.

reporte (re'por·te) *n.m.* **1,** report; news. **2,** gossip; rumor.

reportero (re·por'te·ro) *n.m.* reporter. *Also,* **repórter** (re'por·ter).

reposapiés (re·po·sa'pjes) *n.m. sing. & pl.* footrest.

reposar (re·po'sar) *v.i.* to rest; repose. —**reposarse,** *v.r.* to settle, as liquids. —**reposado,** *adj.* quiet; peaceful; calm.

reposición (re·po·si'θjon; -'sjon) *n.f.* **1,** replacement. **2,** *theat.* revival.

repositorio (re·po·si'to·rjo) *n.m.* repository.

reposo (re'po·so) *n.m.* rest; repose.

repostada (re·pos'ta·ða) *n.f.,* *Amer.* sharp answer; retort.

repostar (re·pos'tar) *v.t.* to refuel; reprovision.

repostería (re·pos·te'ri·a) *n.f.* **1,** pastry; confectionery. **2,** pastry shop. —**repostero** (-'te·ro) *n.m.* pastry baker; confectioner.

reprender (re·pren'der) *v.t.* to reprehend; reprimand; scold. —**reprensible** (-'si·βle) *adj.* reprehensible. —**reprensión** (-'sjon) *n.f.* reprehension. —**reprensor** (-'sor) *adj.* reprehensive.

represa (re'pre·sa) *n.f.* dam.

represalia (re·pre'sa·lja) *n.f.* reprisal.

represar (re·pre'sar) *v.t.* **1,** to bank; dam. **2,** to repress.

representación (re·pre·sen·ta·'θjon; -'sjon) *n.f.* **1,** representation. **2,** *theat.* performance. **3,** authority; dignity.

representante (re·pre·sen'tan·te) *n.m.* **1,** representative. **2,** *comm.* agent; salesman.

representar (re·pre·sen'tar) *v.t.* **1,** to represent. **2,** *theat.* to perform. —**representarse,** *v.r.* to imagine. —**representativo,** *adj.* representative.

represión (re·pre'sjon) *n.f.* repression. —**represivo** (-'si·βo) *also,* **represor** (-'sor) *adj.* repressive.

reprimenda (re·pri'men·da) *n.f.* reprimand.

reprimir (re·pri'mir) *v.t.* to repress; restrain.

reprobar (re·pro'βar) *v.t.* [*infl.:* **acostar, 28**] to reprove.

réprobo ('re·pro·βo) *adj. & n.m.* reprobate; damned.

reprochar (re·pro'tʃar) *v.t.* to reproach (someone) with. —**reproche** (-'pro·tʃe) *n.m.* reproach.

reproducir (re·pro·ðu'θir; -'sir) *v.t.* [*infl.:* **conducir, 40**] to reproduce. —**reproducción** (-ðuk'θjon; -'sjon) *n.f.* reproduction. —**reproductivo** (-'ti·βo) *adj.* reproductive. —**reproductor** (-'tor) *adj.* reproducing. —*n.m.* [*fem.* **-tora**] reproducer.

repropiarse (re·pro'pjar·se) *v.r.* to balk; be restive, as a horse. —**repropio** (-'pro·pjo) *adj.* balky; restive.

reptar (rep'tar) *v.i.* to crawl.

reptil (rep'til) *n.m.* reptile. —*adj.* reptilian.

república (re'pu·βli·ka) *n.f.* republic. —**republicano,** *adj. & n.m.* republican. —**republicanismo,** *n.m.* republicanism.

repudiar (re·pu'ðjar) *v.t.* to repudiate. —**repudio** (-'pu·ðjo) *n.m.,* *also,* **repudiación,** *n.f.* repudiation.

repudrirse (re·pu'ðrir·se) *v.r.,* *colloq.* [*p.p.* **repodrido**] to pine away.

repuesto (re'pwes·to) *v., pp. of* **reponer.** —*n.m.* replacement part; spare part. —**de repuesto,** extra; spare.

repugnar (re·puɣ'nar) *v.t.* **1,** to disgust; revolt. **2,** to abhor; view with disgust. —*v.i.* to be repugnant. —**repugnancia,** *n.f.* repugnance. —**repugnante,** *adj.* **1,** repugnant; causing disgust. **2,** feeling repugnance; disgusted.

repujar (re·pu'xar) *v.t.* to work (metal) in repoussé; emboss (leather). —**repujado,** *adj. & n.m.* repoussé; embossing.

repulgado (re·pul'ɣa·ðo) *adj.,* *colloq.* affected.

repulgar (re·pul'ɣar) *v.t.* [*infl.:* **pagar, 8**] to hem; border.

repulgo (re'pul·ɣo) *n.m.* **1,** hem. **2,** edging (*of pie or pastry*).

repulir (re·pu'lir) *v.t.* **1,** to re-polish; refurbish. **2,** to dress up. —**repulido,** *adj.* slick; shiny.

repulsar (re·pul'sar) *v.t.* to repulse. —**repulsa** (-'pul·sa) *n.f.* repulse. —**repulsión** (-'sjon) *n.f.* repulsion; repugnance. —**repulsivo** (-'si·βo) *adj.* repulsive.

repullo (re'pu·ʎo; -jo) *n.m.* start; jump.

reputar (re·pu'tar) *v.t.* to esteem; repute. —**reputación,** *n.f.* reputation.

requebrar (re·ke'βrar) *v.t.* [*infl.:* **pensar, 27**] to flatter; address gallantries to.

requemar (re·ke'mar) *v.t.* **1,** to burn again. **2,** to overcook; scorch. **3,** to parch. —**requemarse,** *v.r.* to smolder.

requerir (re·ke'rir) *v.t.* [*infl.:* **adquirir, 34**] **1,** to require; need; call for. **2,** to demand; request. **3,** to court; woo. —**requerimiento,** *n.m.* demand; request.

requesón (re·ke'son) *n.m.* cottage cheese.

requetebién (re·ke·te'βjen) *adv., colloq.* wonderfully.

requiebro (re'kje·βro) *n.m.* flattery; gallantry.

réquiem ('re·kjem) [*pl.* **réquiems**] *n.m.* requiem.

requiera (re'kje·ra) *v., pres.subjve. of* **requerir.**

requiero (re'kje·ro) *v., 1st pers. sing. pres.ind. of* **requerir.**

requilorios (re·ki'lo·rjos) *n.m.pl., colloq.* hemming and hawing; beating about the bush.

requiriendo (re·ki'rjen·do) *v., ger. of* **requerir.**

requirió (re·ki'rjo) *v., 3rd pers. sing.pret. of* **requerir.**

requisa (re'ki·sa) *n.f.* **1,** tour of inspection. **2,** requisition. **3,** confiscation; expropriation.

requisar (re·ki'sar) *v.t.* **1,** to requisition. **2,** to confiscate; expropriate.

requisición (re·ki·si'θjon; -'sjon) *n.f.* requisition.

requisito (re·ki'si·to) *n.m.* requisite.

res (res) *n.f.* **1,** head, esp. of cattle. **2,** bovine animal.

resabiar (re·sa'βjar) *v.t.* to incline to bad habits; give bad habits to. —**resabiarse,** *v.r.* **1,** to spoil; acquire bad taste. **2,** to be miffed; be piqued. **3,** to fester.

resabido (re·sa'βi·ðo) *adj.* wellknown.

resabio (re'sa·βjo) *n.m.* **1,** unpleasant aftertaste. **2,** touch; tinge. **3,** bad habit or tendency.

resaca (re'sa·ka) *n.f.* **1,** undertow; backflow. **2,** hangover. **3,** *comm.* redraft.

resalado (re·sa'la·ðo) *adj., colloq.* **1,** very graceful; charming. **2,** amusing; spicy.

resalir (re·sa'lir) *v.i.* [*infl.:* **salir,** 63] to jut out; project.

resaltar (re·sal'tar) *v.i.* **1,** to stand out; show up clearly. **2,** to be evident; be clear. **3,** to jut out; project.

resalto (re'sal·to) *n.m., also,* **resalte** (-te) **1,** jutting part; projection. **2,** prominence; conspicuousness.

resarcir (re·sar'θir; -'sir) *v.t.* [*infl.:* **esparcir,** 12] to compensate; repay; indemnify. —**resarcirse,** *v.r., fol. by* **de,** to recover; recoup. —**resarci-**

miento, *n.m.* compensation; indemnification.

resbalar (res·βa'lar) *v.i.* **1,** to slip; slide. **2,** to err; fall into error. —**resbaladizo,** *also,* **resbaloso,** *adj.* slippery. —**resbalón** (-'lon) *n.m.* slip.

rescatar (res·ka'tar) *v.t.* **1,** to rescue; free; save. **2,** to extricate; disentangle. **3,** to ransom. **4,** to redeem; recover.

rescate (res'ka·te) *n.m.* **1,** rescue. **2,** ransom. **3,** redemption.

rescindir (res·θin'dir; re·sin-) *v.t.* to rescind. —**rescisión** (res·θi'sjon; re·si-) *n.f.* rescission.

rescoldo (res'kol·do) *n.m.* **1,** ember; embers. **2,** grudge; sore spot; rankling. **3,** scruple; qualm; misgiving.

rescripto (res'krip·to) *n.m.* rescript; edict.

resecar (re·se'kar) *v.t.* [*infl.:* **tocar,** 7] **1,** to dry up. **2,** to wither; shrivel. —**resecación,** *n.f.* a drying up.

reseco (re'se·ko) *adj.* dried up. —*n.m.* dried-up part.

reseda (re'se·ða) *n.f.* mignonette.

resentido (re·sen'ti·ðo) *adj.* **1,** sore; tender. **2,** angry; annoyed; resentful.

resentirse (re·sen'tir·se) *v.r.* [*infl.:* **sentir,** 31] **1,** to be or become sore or tender. **2,** to be resentful; be annoyed or angry. —**resentir,** *v.t., colloq.* to resent. —**resentimiento,** *n.m.* resentment.

reseña (re'se·ɲa) *n.f.* **1,** brief description; note; sketch. **2,** review.

reseñar (re·se'ɲar) *v.t.* **1,** to make a review of; review. **2,** to outline; sketch.

resero (re'se·ro) *n.m., Amer.* **1,** cowboy; cattle herder. **2,** livestock dealer.

reserva (re'ser·βa) *n.f.* **1,** reserve. **2,** *mil.* reserve; reserves. **3,** reservation; qualification.

reservación (re·ser·βa'θjon; -'sjon) *n.f.* reservation.

reservado (re·ser'βa·ðo) *adj.* **1,** reserved. **2,** private; confidential. —*n.m.* compartment or room reserved for special use or occasion.

reservar (re·ser'βar) *v.t.* **1,** to reserve. **2,** to keep; hold back, retain. —**reservarse,** *v.r.* **1,** to become reserved. **2,** to hold back; hold off.

reservista (re·ser'βis·ta) *n.m. & f.* reservist.

resfriado (res·fri'a·ðo) *n.m.* cold; catarrh. *Also,* **resfrío** (-'fri·o).

resfriarse (res·fri'ar·se) *v.r.* [*infl.:* enviar, 22] to catch cold.

resguardar (res·γwar'ðar) *v.t.* to guard; shield; protect. —**resguardarse**, *v.r.* 1, to shield oneself. 2, to take shelter.

resguardo (res'γwar·ðo) *n.m.* 1, guard; shield; protection. 2, *comm.* guaranty; security.

residencia (re·si'ðen·θja; -sja) *n.f.* residence. —**residencial**, *adj.* residential. —**residente**, *adj.* & *n.m.* & *f.* resident.

residir (re·si'ðir) *v.i.* to reside.

residuo (re'si·ðwo) *n.m.* 1, residue. 2, *math.* remainder. —**residual**, *adj.* residual.

resignar (re·siγ'nar) *v.t.* & *i.* to resign. —**resignarse**, *v.r.* to resign oneself; be resigned. —**resignación**, *n.f.* resignation.

resina (re'si·na) *n.f.* 1, resin. 2, rosin. —**resinoso**, *adj.* resinous.

resistencia (re·sis'ten·θja; -sja) *n.f.* resistance. —**resistente**, *adj.* resistant.

resistible (re·sis'ti·βle) *adj.* resistible.

resistir (re·sis'tir) *v.t.* & *i.* 1, to resist; withstand. 2, to endure; bear. —**resistirse**, *v.r.* 1, to resist. 2, *fol. by* **a**, to refuse.

resistor (re·sis'tor) *n.m.* resistor.

resma ('res·ma) *n.f.* ream.

resobrino (re·so'βri·no) *n.m.* grandnephew; great-nephew. —**resobrina**, *n.f.* grandniece; great-niece.

resol (re'sol) *n.m.* sun glare.

resolución (re·so·lu'θjon; -'sjon) *n.f.* 1, resolution. 2, resolve. —**en resolución**, in short; by way of concluding.

resoluto (re·so'lu·to) *adj.* resolute.

resolver (re·sol'βer) *v.t.* [*infl.:* mover, 30; *p.p.* **resuelto**] 1, to resolve. 2, to solve. —**resolverse**, *v.r.* to resolve; make up one's mind.

resollar (re·so'ʎar; -'jar) *v.i.* [*infl.:* acostar, 28] 1, to breathe noisily or heavily. 2, *colloq.* to breathe. 3, *colloq.* to talk; make a peep.

resonador (re·so·na'ðor) *adj.* resonating. —*n.m.* resonator.

resonante (re·so'nan·te) *adj.* 1, resonant. 2, resounding. —**resonancia**, *n.f.* resonance.

resonar (re·so'nar) *v.i.* [*infl.:* acostar, 28] to resound.

resoplar (re·so'plar) *v.i.* to breathe noisily; snort; puff. —**resoplido** *also,* **resoplo** (-'so·plo) *n.m.* snort; puff.

resorte (re'sor·te) *n.m.* 1, *mech.* spring. 2, springiness. 3, recourse; resort. 4, elastic.

respaldar (res·pal'dar) *v.t.* to back; support. —*n.m.* back (*of a seat*). —**respaldarse**, *v.r.* 1, to find support; be backed. 2, to sit back.

respaldo (res'pal·do) *n.m.* 1, back (*of a seat*). 2, backing; support. 3, back of a sheet of paper.

respectar (res·pek'tar) *v.t.* to concern; relate to.

respectivo (res·pek'ti·βo) *adj.* respective.

respecto (res'pek·to) *n.m.* concern; relation; bearing; respect. —**al respecto,** in that respect; in that regard. —**con respecto a; respecto a,** as concerns; respecting; with respect to.

résped ('res·peð) *n.f.* 1, serpent's tongue. 2, barb; sting.

respetable (res·pe'ta·βle) *adj.* respectable. —**respetabilidad,** *n.f.* respectability.

respetar (res·pe'tar) *v.t.* to respect.

respeto (res'pe·to) *n.m.* respect. —**respetuoso** (-'two·so) *adj.* respectful.

respingado (res·pin·ga·ðo) *adj.* turned up, as the nose. *Also,* **respingón** (-'gon).

respingar (res·pin'gar) *v.i.* [*infl.:* pagar, 8] 1, to buck; rear. 2, *colloq.* to wince.

respingo (res'pin·go) *n.m.* 1, buck; bucking. 2, *colloq.* wince.

respiración (res·pi·ra'θjon; -'sjon) *n.f.* respiration; breathing. —**sin respiración,** breathless; panting.

respiradero (res·pi·ra'ðe·ro) *n.m.* 1, vent; air hole. 2, small window or skylight. 3, *colloq.* breather; respite. 4, *colloq.* respiratory system.

respirador (res·pi·ra'ðor) *adj.* 1, breathing. 2, respiratory. —*n.m.* respirator.

respirar (res·pi'rar) *v.i.* & *t.* to breathe. —*v.i.* to breathe freely; rest; relax.

respiratorio (res·pi·ra'to·rjo) *adj.* respiratory.

respiro (res'pi·ro) *n.m.* 1, breath. 2, pause; respite.

resplandecer (res·plan·de'θer; -'ser) *v.i.* [*infl.:* conocer, 13] to shine; glow; glitter. —**resplande-ciente,** *adj.* resplendent.

resplandor (res·plan'dor) *n.m.* shine; glitter; glow; resplendence.

respondedor (res·pon·de'ðor) *adj.* 1, respondent. 2, responsive. —*n.m.* [*fem.* **-dora**] respondent.

responder (res·pon'der) *v.t. & i.* to answer. —*v.i.* to respond.

respondón (res·pon'don) *adj., colloq.* cheeky; impertinent; saucy.

responsabilizar (res·pon·sa·βi·li'θar; -'sar) *v.t.* [*infl.:* **rezar, 10**] to make responsible. —**responsa-bilizarse,** *v.r.* to be responsible; take responsibility. —**responsabilizarse de,** to take responsibility for.

responsable (res·pon'sa·βle) *adj.* responsible. —**responsabilidad,** *n.f.* responsibility.

responsar (res·pon'sar) *v.i.* to recite prayers for the dead. —*v.t.* 1, to say prayers for (a dead person). 2, *colloq.* to scold; lecture. *Also, colloq.,* **responsear** (-se'ar).

responsivo (res·pon'si·βo) *adj.* responsive.

responso (res·pon·so) *n.m.* 1, prayer for the dead. 2, *colloq.* scolding; lecture.

respuesta (res'pwes·ta) *n.f.* answer; reply; response.

resquebradura (res·ke·βra·'ðu·ra) *n.f.* crack; cracking. *Also,* **resquebrajadura** (-xa'ðu·ra) *n.f.,* **resquebrajo** (-'βra·xo) *n.m.*

resquebrajar (res·ke·βra'xar) *v.t.* to crack; damage; break. —**resque-brajarse,** *v.r.* to crack; break. —**resquebrajadizo,** *adj.* brittle; fragile.

resquebrar (res·ke'βrar) *v.t.* [*infl.:* **pensar, 27**] to cause to give way; crack; split.

resquemar (res·ke'mar) *v.t. & i.* 1, to sting; bite (the tongue). 2, to itch.

resquemor (res·ke'mor) *n.m.* 1, burn; bite; smarting. 2, *fig.* itch; restlessness.

resquicio (res·ki·θjo; -sjo) *n.m.* 1, chink; crack; slit. 2, chance; opening.

resta ('res·ta) *n.f., math.* 1, subtraction. 2, difference; remainder.

restablecer (res·ta·βle'θer; -'ser) *v.t.* [*infl.:* **conocer, 13**] to reestablish; restore. —**restablecerse,** *v.r.* to recuperate; recover.

restablecimiento (res·ta·βle·θi'mjen·to; -si'mjen·to) *n.m.* 1, rees-

tablishment; restoration. 2, recovery; recuperation.

restallar (res·ta'ʎar; -'jar) *v.i.* to crack, as a whip; snap. —**restalli-do,** *n.m.* snap; crack.

restante (res'tan·te) *n.m.* rest; remainder. —*adj.* remaining.

restañar (res·ta'ɲar) *v.t.* to stanch.

restar (res'tar) *v.t. & i.* to subtract. —*v.i.* to be left; be left over; remain.

restaurante (res·tau'ran·te) *n.m.* restaurant.

restaurar (res·tau'rar) *v.t.* to restore. —**restauración,** *n.f.* restoration. —**restaurativo,** *adj. & n.m.* restorative.

restituir (res·ti·tu'ir) *v.t.* [*infl.:* **huir, 26**] to return; restore. —**restituirse,** *v.r.* to go back; return. —**restitución,** *n.f.* restitution.

resto ('res·to) *n.m.* rest; remainder. —**restos,** *n.m.pl.* 1, remains. 2, leftovers. —**echar el resto,** to do one's best.

restorán (res·to'ran) *n.m., Amer.* restaurant.

restregar (res·tre'ɣar) *v.t.* [*infl.:* **pagar, 8; pensar, 27**] to scrub; rub. —**restregadura,** *n.f. also,* **restre-gón** (-'ɣon) *n.m.* scrubbing; rubbing.

restringir (res·trin'xir) *v.t* [*infl.:* **coger, 15**] to restrict. —**restricción** (-trik'θjon; -'sjon) *n.f.* restriction. —**restrictivo** (-'ti·βo) *adj.* restrictive.

resucitar (re·su·θi'tar; -si'tar) *v.t. & i.* to resuscitate; revive. —*v.t.* to resurrect. —*v.i.* to rise from the dead. —**resucitación,** *n.f.* resuscitation.

resudar (re·su'ðar) *v.i.* to perspire lightly. —**resudor** (-'ðor) *n.m.* light sweat.

resuelto (re'swel·to) *v., pp. of* **re-solver.** —*adj.* resolute.

resuelva (re'swel·βa) *v., pres. subjve. of* **resolver.**

resuelvo (re'swel·βo) *v., 1st pers.-sing. pres.ind. of* **resolver.**

resuelle (re'swe·ʎe; -je) *v., pres. subjve. of* **resollar.**

resuello (re'swe·ʎo; -jo) *v., 1st pers.sing. pres.ind. of* **resollar.** —*n.m.* 1, breath; breathing. 2, pant; panting.

resuene (re'swe·ne) *v., pres. subjve. of* **resonar.**

resueno (re'swe·no) *v., 1st pers.sing. pres.ind. of* **resonar.**

resulta (re'sul·ta) *n.f.* result; consequence. —**de resultas,** as a result.

resultado (re·sul'ta·ðo) *n.m.* result.

resultante (re·sul'tan·te) *adj.* & *n.f.* resultant. —*adj.* resulting.

resultar (re·sul'tar) *v.i.* 1, to result. 2, to come out; turn out.

resumen (re'su·men) *n.m.* summary; abridgment; résumé. —**en resumen,** in short.

resumidero (re·su·mi'ðe·ro) *n.m., Amer.* = **sumidero.**

resumir (re·su'mir) *v.t.* 1, to summarize; abridge.

resurgir (re·sur'xir) *v.i.* [*infl.:* **coger,** 15] 1, to resurge. 2, to revive; be revived or resurrected. —**resurgimiento,** *n.m.* resurgence.

resurrección (re·su·rrek'θjon; -'sjon) *n.f.* resurrection.

retablo (re'ta·βlo) *n.m.* 1, altarpiece; retable. 2, tableau.

retaco (re'ta·ko) *adj., colloq.* stubby. —*n.m.* 1, short, stubby shotgun. 2, stubby person.

retador (re·ta'ðor) *n.m.* [*fem.* -**dora**] challenger.

retaguardia (re·ta'ɣwar·ðja) *n.f.* 1, rear guard. 2, rearward sector; rear.

retahíla (re·ta'i·la) *n.f.* slew; string.

retal (re'tal) *n.m.* remnant.

retama (re'ta·ma) *n.f., bot.* broom; furze.

retar (re'tar) *v.t.* 1, to challenge. 2, *colloq.* to scold; reprimand.

retardar (re·tar'ðar) *v.t.* to retard; delay. —**retardarse,** *v.r.* to be delayed; be late. —**retardo** (-'tar·ðo) *n.m., also,* **retardación,** *n.f.* retardation; delay.

retazo (re'ta·θa; -so) *n.m.* 1, remnant; strip. 2, part; fragment.

retemblar (re·tem'blar) *v.i.* [*infl.:* **pensar,** 27] to tremble or shake violently and repeatedly.

retén (re'ten) *n.m.* 1, provision; reserve. 2, reserve troops. 3, house of detention; city jail.

retener (re·te'ner) *v.t.* [*infl.:* **tener,** 65] 1, to retain. 2, to detain; confine. 3, to contain; hold back. —**retención,** *n.f.* retention.

reténgase (re'ten·ga·se) *v., print.* stet.

retentivo (re·ten'ti·βo) *adj.* retentive. —**retentiva,** *n.f.* retentiveness; memory.

reticencia (re·ti'θen·θja; -'sen·sja)

n.f. reticence. —**reticente,** *adj.* reticent.

retina (re'ti·na) *n.f.* retina.

retintín (re·tin'tin) *n.m.* 1, tinkling. 2, *colloq.* ironic tone. 3, ringing in the ears.

retinto (re'tin·to) *adj.* dark brown.

retiñir (re·ti'ɲir) *v.i.* [*infl.:* **gruñir,** 21] 1, to tinkle; jingle. 2, to ring, as the ears.

retirada (re·ti'ra·ða) *n.f.* retreat; withdrawal.

retirado (re·ti'ra·ðo) *adj.* 1, retired. 2, distant; removed; remote. —*n.m., mil.* retired officer.

retirar (re·ti'rar) *v.t.* 1, to retire. 2, to take back; withdraw; remove. —**retirarse,** *v.r.* 1, to withdraw. 2, to retire.

retiro (re'ti·ro) *n.m.* 1, retirement. 2, retreat.

reto ('re·to) *n.m.* challenge.

retocar (re·to'kar) *v.t.* [*infl.:* **tocar,** 7] to retouch.

retoño (re'to·ɲo) *n.m.* 1, sprout; shoot. 2, *colloq.* child; offspring. —**retoñar,** *v.i.* to sprout; shoot.

retoque (re'to·ke) *n.m.* 1, beat; beating; pounding. 2, retouching. 3, finishing touch. 4, touch; mild attack, as of a disease.

retorcer (re·tor'θer; -'ser) *v.t.* [*infl.:* **torcer,** 66] 1, to twist. 2, to wring (the hands). —**retorcerse,** *v.r.* to twist; writhe. —**retorcimiento,** *n.m.* twisting; twisting.

retórica (re'to·ri·ka) *n.f.* 1, rhetoric. 2, *usu.pl., colloq.* sophistries; roundabout talk. —**retórico,** *adj.* rhetorical. —*n.m.* rhetorician.

retornar (re·tor'nar) *v.i.* 1, to return. 2, to recede. —*v.t.* to give back; return; restore. —**retorno** (-'tor·no) *n.m.* return.

retorta (re'tor·ta) *n.f., chem.* retort.

retortero (re·tor'te·ro) *n.m.* twirl; whirl; twist. —**andar al retortero,** to bustle around; hover about.

retortijar (re·tor·ti'xar) *v.t.* to twist; curl. —**retortijón** (-'xon) *n.m.* twisting. —**retortijón de tripas,** *colloq.* bellyache.

retozar (re·to'θar; -'sar) *v.i.* [*infl.:* **rezar,** 10] to romp; frolic. —**retozo** (-'to·θo; -so) *n.m.* romping; frolicking. —**retozo de la risa,** titter; snicker.

retozón (re·to'θon; -'son) *adj.* playful; frolicsome.

retractar (re·trak'tar) *v.t.* to retract. —**retractarse,** *v.r.* to retract;

recant. —**retracción,** *n.f.* retraction.
—**retractación,** *n.f.* recantation.
—**retráctil** (-'trak·til) *adj.* retractable.

retractor (re·trak'tor) *n.m.* retractor.

retraer (re·tra'er) *v.t.* [*infl.:* traer, 67] to dissuade. —**retraerse,** *v.r.* to retire; withdraw. —**retraído,** *adj.* shy; retiring.

retraimiento (re·tra·i'mjen·to) *n.m.* 1, shyness; reserve. 2, retreat; withdrawal.

retransmitir *v.t.* 1, to retransmit. 2, to relay. 3, to rebroadcast.

retraqueo (re·tra'ke·o) *n.m.,* *archit.* setback.

retrasar (re·tra'sar) *v.t.* 1, to defer; delay. 2, to set back, as a clock. —*v.i.* to go back; retrogress. —**retrasarse,** *v.r.* 1, to be backward. 2, to be late.

retraso (re'tra·so) *n.m.* 1, delay. 2, slowness. 3, backwardness.

retratar (re·tra'tar) *v.t.* 1, to portray; describe. 2, to photograph. —**retratista,** *n.m. & f.* portrait painter.

retrato (re'tra·to) *n.m.* 1, portrait; description. 2, resemblance; likeness.

retrechar (re·tre'tʃar) *v.i.* to move backward.

retrechero (re·tre'tʃe·ro) *adj.,* *colloq.* 1, sly; cunning; evasive. 2, bewitching; attractive.

retreta (re'tre·ta) *n.f.,* *mil.* retreat.

retrete (re'tre·te) *n.m.* toilet; rest room.

retribuir (re·tri·βu'ir) *v.t.* [*infl.:* huir, 26] to recompense. —**retribución,** *n.f.* retribution. —**retributivo** (-'ti·βo) *adj.* retributive.

retroactivo (re·tro·ak'ti·βo) *adj.* retroactive. —**retroactividad,** *n.f.* retroactivity.

retroalimentación (re·tro·a·li·men·ta'θjon; -'sjon) *n.f.* feedback.

retroceder (re·tro·θe'ðer; -se'ðer) *v.i.* to turn back; recede.

retroceso (re·tro'θe·so; -'se·so) *n.m.* 1, setback. 2, backward movement; recession. 3, *med.* relapse.

retrogradar (re·tro·ɣra'ðar) *v.i.* 1, to retrogress. 2, *astron.* to retrograde. —**retrogradación,** *n.f.,* *astron.* retrogradation.

retrógrado (re'tro·ɣra·ðo) *adj.* 1, retrograde. 2, retrogressive. —*adj. & n.m., polit.* reactionary.

retrogresión (re·tro·ɣre'sjon) *n.f.* retrogression.

retronar (re·tro'nar) *v.i.* [*infl.:* acostar, 28] to thunder; rumble.

retropropulsión (re·tro·pro·pul'θjon; -'sjon) *n.f.* jet propulsion.

retrospección (re·tros·pek'θjon; -'sjon) *n.f.* 1, retrospect. 2, retrospection. —**retrospectivo** (-'ti·βo) *adj.* retrospective.

retrotraer (re·tro·tra'er) *v.t.* [*infl.:* traer, 67] to antedate.

retrovisor (re·tro·βi'sor) *n.m.* rearview mirror.

retruécano (re'trwe·ka·no) *n.m.* pun; play on words.

retuerza (re'twer·θa; -sa) *v., pres. subjve. of* retorcer.

retuerzo (re'twer·θo; -so) *v., 1st pers.sing. pres.ind. of* retorcer.

retumbar (re·tum'bar) *v.i.* to resound; reverberate; rumble. —**retumbo** (-'tum·bo) *n.m.* reverberation; rumble.

reuma ('reu·ma) *n.m. or f.* = **reumatismo.**

reumatismo (reu·ma'tis·mo) *n.m.* rheumatism. —**reumático** (-'ma·ti·ko) *adj. & n.m.* rheumatic.

reunión (re·u'njon) *n.f.* 1, reunion. 2, gathering; assembly.

reunir (re·u'nir) *v.t.* [*infl.:* 60] 1, to reunite. 2, to unite; join. 3, to gather. —**reunirse,** *v.r.* to meet; gather.

revalidar (re·βa·li'ðar) *v.t.* to confirm; validate. —**revalidación,** *n.f.* confirmation; validation. —**reválida** (-'βa·li·ða) *n.f.* final examination for an academic degree.

revancha (re'βan·tʃa) *n.f.* 1, revenge; retaliation. 2, return game or match.

revelar (re·βe'lar) *v.t.* 1, to reveal. 2, *photog.* to develop. —**revelación,** *n.f.* revelation. —**revelado,** *n.m., photog.* developing. —**revelador,** *adj.* revealing. —*n.m.* 1, revealer. 2, *photog.* developer.

revendedor (re·βen·de'ðor) *n.m.* [*fem.* -**dora**] 1, retailer. 2, *colloq.* ticket scalper.

revender (re·βen'der) *v.t.* to resell; retail. —**revendedor,** *n.m.* [*fem.* -**dora**] 1, retailer. 2, *colloq.* ticket scalper.

revenirse (re·βe'nir·se) *v.r.* [*infl.:* venir, 69] to become shriveled; spoil; turn.

reventa (re'βen·ta) *n.f.* 1, resale. 2, retail.

reventar (re·βen'tar) *v.i.* [*infl.:* **pensar, 27**] **1,** to burst; blow up; blow out. **2,** to break, as waves. **3,** to blossom; burst into bloom. **4,** *colloq. fol. by* **por,** to crave; long. **5,** *slang* to die; croak. —*v.t.* **1,** to burst; crack open. **2,** to break down (a horse). **3,** *colloq.* to ruin; destroy; smash. **4,** *colloq.* to overburden; crush. **5,** *colloq.* to tire; exhaust.

reventón (re·βen'ton) *adj.* bursting. —*n.m.* **1,** burst; explosion. **2,** blowout; flat tire. **3,** *colloq.* back-breaking job.

reverberar (re·βer·βe'rar) *v.i.* to reverberate. —**reverbero** (-'βe·ro) *n.m., also,* **reverberación,** *n.f.* reverberation.

reverdecer (re·βer·ðe'θer; -'ser) *v.i.* [*infl.:* **conocer, 13**] to grow green again; regain freshness.

reverencia (re·βe'ren·θja; -sja) *n.f.* **1,** reverence. **2,** curtsy; bow. —**reverencial,** *adj.* reverential; awesome.

reverenciar (re·βe·ren'θjar; -'sjar) *v.t.* to revere. —**reverenciable,** *adj.* venerable.

reverendo (re·βe'ren·ðo) *adj. & n.m.* reverend.

reverente (re·βe'ren·te) *adj.* reverent.

reversible (re·βer'si·βle) *adj.* reversible. —**reversibilidad,** *n.f.* reversibility.

reversión (re·βer'sjon) *n.f.* reversion.

reverso (re'βer·so) *n.m.* reverse. —**el reverso de la medalla,** the exact opposite.

reverter (re·βer'ter) *v.i.* [*infl.:* **perder, 29**] to overflow.

revertir (re·βer'tir) *v.i.* [*infl.:* **sentir, 31**] to revert.

revés (re'βes) *n.m.* **1,** other side; reverse. **2,** backhanded slap or blow. **3,** setback; reverse. —**al revés,** backwards; inside out; wrong side out (or up); the opposite way.

revesado (re·βe'sa·ðo) *adj.* **1,** complex; intricate. **2,** wild; unruly.

revestir (re·βes'tir) *v.t.* [*infl.:* **pedir, 33**] **1,** to dress; clothe. **2,** to invest; endow. **3,** to cover; coat; face. —**revestirse,** *v.r.* to gird oneself. —**revestimiento,** *also,* **revestido,** *n.m.* facing; coating.

revezar (re·βe'θar; -'sar) *v.t.* [*infl.:* **rezar, 10**] to replace temporarily; spell; relieve.

reviente (re'βjen·te) *v., pres.subjve. of* **reventar.**

reviento (re'βjen·to) *v., 1st pers. sing. pres.ind. of* **reventar.**

revisar (re·βi'sar) *v.t.* **1,** to review. **2,** to inspect; examine; check. **3,** to revise. **4,** to audit.

revisión (re·βi'sjon) *n.f.* **1,** review. **2,** inspection; examination; check. **3,** revision. **4,** audit.

revisor (re·βi'sor) *n.m.* [*fem.* **-sora**] **1,** inspector; examiner. **2,** reviser. **3,** auditor.

revista (re'βis·ta) *n.f.* **1,** review. **2,** magazine; journal; review. **3,** *theat.* revue. —**pasar revista,** *also,* **revistar,** *v.t.* to review; inspect. —**revistero,** *n.m.* magazine rack.

revivir (re·βi'βir) *v.i.* to revive.

revocable (re·βo'ka·βle) *adj.* revocable.

revocador (re·βo·ka'ðor) *n.m.* **1,** revoker. **2,** plasterer; whitewasher; painter.

revocar (re·βo'kar) *v.t.* [*infl.:* **tocar, 7**] **1,** to revoke. **2,** to repaint or refinish, esp. the walls of a building. —**revocable,** *adj.* revocable. —**revocación,** *n.f.* revocation. —**revocadura,** *n.f.* refinishing; repainting.

revolcar (re·βol'kar) *v.t.* [*infl.:* **tocar, 7; acostar, 28**] to knock down; trample; drag in the dust. —**revolcarse,** *v.r.* **1,** to wallow, as in mud. **2,** to roll over and over on the ground. —**revolcadero,** *n.m.* wallow.

revolcón (re·βol'kon) *n.m., colloq.* **1,** a rolling over; writhing in the dust. **2,** trampling; mauling. **3,** wallowing; tumbling. **4,** *colloq.* rebuff; rebuke. **5,** *colloq.* bawling-out; dressing-down.

revolotear (re·βo·lo·te'ar) *v.i.* **1,** to flutter; flit. **2,** to tumble through the air.

revoloteo (re·βo·lo'te·o) *n.m.* **1,** fluttering; flitting. **2,** tumbling through the air.

revolqué (re·βol'ke) *v., 1st pers. sing. pret. of* **revolcar.**

revoltijo (re·βol'ti·xo) *also,* **revoltillo,** (-'ti·ʎo; -'ti·jo) *n.m.* **1,** jumble; mess; scramble. **2,** hodgepodge. —**revoltijo** [*also,* **revoltillo**] **de huevos,** scrambled eggs.

revoltoso (re·βol'to·so) *adj.* **1,** mischievous; unruly. **2,** turbulent; riotous.

revolución (re·βo·lu'θjon; -'sjon)

n.f. revolution. —**revolucionar,** *v.t.* to revolutionize. —**revolucionario,** *adj.* & *n.m.* revolutionary. —*n.m.* revolutionist.

revólver (re'βol·βer) *n.m.* revolver.

revolver (re·βol'βer) *v.t.* [*infl.:* **mover,** 30; *p.p.* **revuelto**] **1,** to mix; stir. **2,** to turn over; rummage through. **3,** to mix up; confuse. **4,** to arouse; stir up. **5,** to turn; turn over; revolve. —**revolverse,** *v.r.* **1,** to turn; turn around; wheel. **2,** to toss and turn. **3,** to squirm; wriggle.

revoque (re'βo·ke) *n.m.* **1,** = **revocadura. 2,** whitewash; plaster; finishing materials. —*v.,* *pres.subjve.* of **revocar.**

revoqué (re·βo'ke) *v.,* *1st pers. sing. pret.* of **revocar.**

revuelco (re'βwel·ko) *n.m.* **1,** upset; tumble. **2,** wallow; wallowing. —*v.,* *1st pers.sing. pres.ind.* of **revolcar.**

revuelo (re'βwe·lo) *n.m.* **1,** circling in flight. **2,** uproar; commotion. —**de revuelo,** in passing.

revuelque (re'βwel·ke) *v.,* *pres. subjve.* of **revolcar.**

revuelta (re'βwel·ta) *n.f.* **1,** turn; return. **2,** revolt. **3,** turn; turning. **4,** quarrel.

revuelto (re'βwel·to) *v.,* *p.p.* of **revolver.** —*adj.* **1,** disordered; upset. **2,** jumbled; scrambled. **3,** churned up; rough. **4,** mischievous; unruly.

revuelva (re'βwel·βa) *v.,* *pres. subjve.* of **revolver.**

revuelvo (re'βwel·βo) *v.,* *1st pers.sing. pres.ind.* of **revolver.**

revulsión (re·βul'sjon) *n.f.* revulsion.

rey ('rei) *n.m.* king.

reyerta (re'jer·ta) *n.f.* quarrel; dispute.

reyezuelo (re·je'θwe·lo; -'swe·lo) *n.m.* kinglet; wren.

rezagar (re·θa'yar; re·sa-) *v.t.* [*infl.:* **pagar,** 8] **1,** to leave behind; outstrip. **2,** to put off. —**rezagarse,** *v.r.* to fall behind; lag. —**rezagado,** *adj.* & *n.m.* laggard. —**rezago** (-'θa·yo; -'sa·yo) *n.m.* residue; remainder. —**venta de rezagos,** rummage sale.

rezar (re'θar; -'sar) *v.t.* [*infl.:* 10] **1,** to say or recite (prayers, mass, etc.). **2,** *colloq.* to say; state. —*v.i.* **1,** to pray; recite prayers. **2,** *colloq.* to say; read. **3,** *colloq.* to grumble;

whine. —**rezar con,** to concern; pertain to.

rezo ('re·θo; -so) *n.m.* **1,** prayer. **2,** prayers; devotions.

rezongar (re·θon'gar; re·son-) *v.i.* [*infl.:* **pagar,** 8] to grumble. —**rezongador,** *adj.* grumbling. —*n.m.* [*fem.* **-dora**] grumbler. *Also, colloq.* **rezongón** (-'gon) [*fem.* **-gona**].

rezumar (re·θu'mar; re·su-) *v.t.* & *i.* **1,** to ooze; exude. **2,** to percolate. —**rezumarse,** *v.r.* **1,** to seep; leak. **2,** *fig.* to leak out; be divulged.

ría ('ri·a) *n.f.* mouth of a river.

ría ('ri·a) *v.,* *pres.subjve.* of **reír.**

¡riá! (ri'a) *interj.* haw!

riachuelo (ri·a'tʃwe·lo) *n.m.* stream; rivulet. *Also,* **riacho** (ri'a·tʃo).

riada (ri'a·ða) *n.f.* freshet; flood.

ribazo (ri'βa·θo; -so) *n.m.* embankment.

ribera (ri'βe·ra) *n.f.* shore; bank.

ribereño (ri'βe·re·ɲo) *adj.* of or by the riverside; riparian. —*n.m.* riverside dweller.

ribero (ri'βe·ro) *n.m.* dike; levee.

ribete (ri'βe·te) *n.m.* **1,** edge; binding; border. **2,** trimming. **3,** embellishment. —**ribetes,** *n.m.pl.,* signs; indications.

ribetear (ri·βe·te'ar) *v.t.* **1,** to edge; bind; border. **2,** to trim; adorn.

riboflavina (ri·βo·fla'βi·na) *n.f.* riboflavin.

ricacho (ri'ka·tʃo) *adj.* & *n.m., colloq., derog.* nouveau riche; filthy rich. *Also,* **ricachón** [*fem.* **-chona**].

rice ('ri·θe; -se) *v.,* *pres.subjve.* of **rizar.**

ricé (ri'θe; -'se) *v.,* *1st pers.sing. pret.* of **rizar.**

ricino (ri'θi·no; ri'si-) *n.m.* castor oil plant. —**aceite de ricino,** castor oil.

rico ('ri·ko) *adj.* **1,** rich; wealthy. **2,** delicious; exquisite. —*n.m., colloq., as a term of endearment* cutie; precious.

ridiculez (ri·ði·ku'leθ; -'les) *n.f.* **1,** ridiculousness. **2,** extravagance; oddity. **3,** excessive nicety; squeamishness.

ridiculizar (ri·ði·ku·li'θar; -'sar) *v.t.* [*infl.:* **rezar,** 10] to ridicule.

ridículo (ri'ði·ku·lo) *adj.* **1,** ridiculous. **2,** extravagant; odd. **3,** excessively nice; squeamish. —*n.m.* **1,** ridiculousness. **2,** ridicule.

riego ('rje·yo) *v.,* *1st pers.sing.*

pres.ind. of **regar.** —*n.m.* irrigation. —**boca de riego,** hydrant.

riegue ('rje·ɣe) *v., pres.subjve.* of **regar.**

riel (rjel) *n.m.* rail.

rielar (rje'lar) *v.i., poet.* to gleam; glitter.

rienda ('rjen·da) *n.f.* rein. —**rienda suelta,** free rein.

riendo ('rjen·do) *v., ger.* of **reír.**

riente ('rjen·te) *adj.* laughing; cheerful.

riesgo ('rjes·ɣo) *n.m.* danger; risk.

rifa ('ri·fa) *n.f.* raffle. —**rifar,** *v.t.* to raffle.

rifle ('ri·fle) *n.m.* rifle.

riflero (ri'fle·ro) *n.m.* rifleman.

rígido ('ri·xi·ðo) *adj.* rigid; inflexible. —**rigidez,** *n.f.* rigidity; inflexibility.

rigiendo (ri'xjen·do) *v., ger.* of **regir.**

rigió (ri'xjo) *v., 3rd pers.sing.pret.* of **regir.**

rigor (ri'ɣor) *n.m.* rigor; strictness. —**de rigor,** strictly required. —**en rigor,** *also,* **en rigor de verdad,** strictly speaking; as a matter of fact.

rigoroso (ri·ɣo'ro·so) *adj.* = **riguroso.** —**rigorosidad,** *n.f.* = **rigurosidad.**

riguroso (ri·ɣu'ro·so) *adj.* rigorous; strict; severe. —**rigurosidad,** *n.f.* rigorousness; severity.

rija ('ri·xa) *v., pres.subjve.* of **regir.** —*n.f.* lachrymal fistula.

rijo ('ri·xo) *v., 1st pers.sing.pres. ind.* of **regir.**

rima ('ri·ma) *n.f.* rhyme; *pl.* poems. —**rimar,** *v.t. & i.* to rhyme.

rimbombante (rim·bom'ban·te) *adj.* resounding; bombastic.

rimero (ri'me·ro) *n.m.* heap; pile.

rincón (rin'kon) *n.m.* corner; nook.

rinconada (rin·ko'na·ða) *n.f.* corner; angle.

rinconera (rin·ko'ne·ra) *n.f.* corner cupboard; corner table.

rinda ('rin·da) *v., pres.subjve.* of **rendir.**

rindiendo (rin'djen·do) *v., ger.* of **rendir.**

rindió (rin'djo) *v., 3rd pers.sing. pret.* of **rendir.**

rindo ('rin·do) *v., 1st pers.sing. pres.ind.* of **rendir.**

ringlera (rin'gle·ra) *n.f.* row; file; line.

ringorrango (rin·go'rran·go) *n.m., colloq.* frill; fanciness.

rinoceronte (ri·no·θe'ron·te; ri·no·se-) *n.m.* rhinoceros.

riña ('ri·ɲa) *n.f.* quarrel; squabble. —*v., pres.subjve.* of **reñir.**

riñendo (ri'ɲen·do) *v., ger.* of **reñir.**

riño ('ri·ɲo) *v., 1st pers.sing. pres.ind.* of **reñir.**

riñó (ri'ɲo) *v., 3rd pers.sing.pret.* of **reñir.**

riñón (ri'ɲon) *n.m.* **1,** kidney. **2,** *fig.* heart; core. —**tener el riñón cubierto,** *colloq.* to be well-off.

río ('ri·o) *n.m.* river. —**a río revuelto,** in confusion.

río ('ri·o) *v., 1st pers.sing. pres.ind.* of **reír.**

rió (rjo) *v., 3rd pers.sing.pret.* of **reír.**

riostra ('rjos·tra) *n.f., archit.* brace; stay.

ripio ('ri·pjo) *n.m.* **1,** refuse; debris; rubble. **2,** superfluous word or words; padding.

riqueza (ri'ke·θa; -sa) *n.f.* **1,** riches; wealth. **2,** richness. **3,** abundance.

risa ('ri·sa) *n.f.* laugh; laughter.

risada (ri'sa·ða) *n.f.* = **risotada.**

risco ('ris·ko) *n.m.* crag; cliff. —**riscoso,** *adj.* steep; craggy.

risible (ri'si·βle) *adj.* risible; laughable. —**risibilidad,** *n.f.* risibility.

risita (ri'si·ta) *also,* **risica,** *n.f.* giggle; titter.

risotada (ri·so'ta·ða) *n.f.* guffaw; loud laugh.

ristra ('ris·tra) *n.f.* **1,** string (*of onions, garlic, sausage, etc.*) **2,** row; file.

risueño (ri'swe·ɲo) *adj.* **1,** smiling; cheerful. **2,** favorable; promising. **3,** optimistic.

ritmo ('rit·mo) *n.m.* rhythm. —**rítmico,** *adj.* rhythmical.

rito ('ri·to) *n.m.* rite; ceremony. —**ritual** (-'twal) *adj. & n.m.* ritual. —**ritualista,** *adj.* ritualistic.

rival (ri'βal) *n.m. & f.* rival. —**rivalidad,** *n.f.* rivalry. —**rivalizar,** *v.i.* [*infl.:* **rezar,** 10] to compete. —**rivalizar con,** to rival; compete against.

rizar (ri'θar; -'sar) *v.t.* [*infl.:* **rezar,** 10] **1,** to curl. **2,** to crinkle; frizzle. **3,** to ripple, as water. —**rizador,** *n.m.* curler; curling iron.

rizo ('ri·θo; -so) *adj.* curly. —*n.m.* **1,** curl; ringlet. **2,** *aero.* loop. **3,** *naut.* reef. **4,** ripple.

rizoma (ri'θo·ma; -'so·ma) *n.f.* rhizome.

roano (ro'a·no) *adj.* = **ruano.**

róbalo ('ro·βa·lo) *also,* **robalo** (ro-'βa·lo) *n.m., ichthy.* bass; sea bass.

robar (ro'βar) *v.t.* **1,** to rob; steal. **2,** to abduct. **3,** to erode. **4,** *cards* to draw.

roble ('ro·βle) *n.m.* **1,** oak. **2,** *fig.* very strong person. —**roblizo,** *adj.* hard; strong.

robledal (ro·βle'ðal) *n.m.* oak woods. *Also,* **robleda,** *n.f.,* **robledo,** *n.m.*

robo ('ro·βo) *n.m.* robbery; theft.

robot (ro'βot) *n.m.* [*pl.* **robots**] robot.

robustecer (ro·βus·te'θer; -'ser) *v.t.* [*infl.:* **conocer, 13**] to strengthen; fortify.

robusto (ro'βus·to) *adj.* robust. —**robustez,** *n.f.* robustness.

roca ('ro·ka) *n.f.* rock. —**rocalla** (-'ka·ʎa; -ja) *n.f.* pebbles.

roce ('ro·θe; -se) *n.m.* **1,** friction. **2,** contact; intimacy. —*v., pres. subjve. of* **rozar.**

rocé (ro'θe; -'se) *v., 1st pers.sing. pret. of* **rozar.**

rociada (ro'θja·ða; -'sja·ða) *n.f.* **1,** sprinkle; spray; splash. **2,** *colloq.* scolding; dressing down.

rociar (ro'θjar; -'sjar) *v.i.* [*infl.:* **enviar, 22**] to fall as dew. —*v.t.* to spray; sprinkle; spatter. —**rociadera,** *n.f., also* **rociador,** *n.m.* watering can; sprinkler; sprayer.

rocín (ro'θin; -'sin) *n.m.* nag; jade.

rocío (ro'θi·o; -'si·o) *n.m.* dew.

rococó (ro·ko'ko) *adj. & n.m.* rococo.

rocoso (ro'ko·so) *adj.* rocky.

roda (ro·ða) *n.f.* stem (of a ship).

rodaballo (ro·ða'βa·ʎo; -jo) *n.m.* a fish resembling the turbot or the brill.

rodada (ro'ða·ða) *n.f.* **1,** rut; wheel track. **2,** *Amer.* fall; tumble.

rodadura (ro·ða'ðu·ra) *n.f.* rolling; wheeling.

rodado (ro'ða·ðo) *adj.* **1,** dappled. **2,** well-beaten; well-traveled; easy.

rodaja (ro'ða·xa) *n.f.* **1,** small wheel or disk. **2,** caster. **3,** round slice. **4,** rowel.

rodaje (ro'ða·xe) *n.m.* **1,** wheels; set of wheels; wheelwork. **2,** filming; shooting (of a film).

rodar (ro'ðar) *v.i.* [*infl.:* **acostar, 28**] **1,** to roll; run on wheels. **2,** to spin; turn. **3,** to fall; tumble. **4,** to

wander; drift. **5,** to follow in quick succession. —*v.t.* to film; shoot (a film).

rodear (ro·ðe'ar) *v.i.* **1,** to go around. **2,** to take the long way around. —*v.t.* **1,** to surround; encircle. **2,** to circle; go around. **3,** *Amer.* to round up (cattle).

rodeo (ro'ðe·o) *n.m.* **1,** turn. **2,** roundabout way. **3,** *Amer.* rodeo. **4,** corral. **5,** circumlocution; beating about the bush.

rodilla (ro'ði·ʎa; -ja) *n.f.* knee. —**rodillazo,** *n.m.* thrust with the knee. —**de rodillas,** on one's knees; kneeling.

rodillera (ro·ði'ʎe·ra; -'je·ra) *n.f.* **1,** kneecap. **2,** knee guard. **3,** bagging of trousers at the knees.

rodillo (ro'ði·ʎo; -jo) *n.m.* **1,** roller. **2,** rolling pin.

rodio ('ro·ðjo) *n.m.* rhodium.

rododendro (ro·ðo'ðen·dro) *n.m.* rhododendron.

rodrigar (ro·ðri'ɣar) *v.t.* [*infl.:* **pagar, 8**] to prop up (vines). —**rodrigazón,** *n.m.* propping season.

rodrigón (ro·ðri'ɣon) *n.m.* **1,** vine prop. **2,** *hist.* a male retainer who accompanied ladies.

roedor (ro·e'ðor) *adj.* gnawing. —*n.m.* rodent.

roedura (ro·e'ðu·ra) *n.f.* **1,** gnawing; gnawed part. **2,** corrosion; corroded part.

roer (ro'er) *v.t.* [*infl.:* **61**] **1,** to gnaw. **2,** to corrode.

rogación (ro·ɣa'θjon; -'sjon) *n.f.* request; petition. —**rogaciones,** *n.f. pl.* = **rogativa.**

rogar (ro'ɣar) *v.t.* [*infl.:* **pagar, 8; acostar, 28**] **1,** to pray; ask. **2,** to beg; plead.

rogativa (ro·ɣa'ti·βa) *n.f., eccles.* rogation; Rogation Days.

rojo ('ro·xo) *adj.* **1,** red. **2,** ruddy; reddish. —**rojez,** *n.f.* redness. —**rojizo,** *adj.* reddish. —**rojura,** *n.f.* redness.

roldana (rol'da·na) *n.f.* pulley wheel.

rollizo (ro'ʎi·θo; -'ji·so) *adj.* plump; robust. —*n.m.* log.

rollo ('ro·ʎo; -jo) *n.m.* **1,** roll. **2,** roller. **3,** log.

romadizo (ro·ma'ði·θo; -so) *n.m.* head cold.

romana (ro'ma·na) *n.f.* **1,** steelyard. **2,** scale; balance.

romance (ro'man·θe; -se) *adj.* Romance. —*n.m.* **1,** Romance language, esp. Spanish. **2,** romance; tale. **3,** historical ballad. **4,** *pl., colloq.* excuses; evasions. —**hablar en romance,** to speak plainly.

romancero (ro·man'θe·ro; -'se·ro) *n.m.* **1,** romancer. **2,** collection of ballads, esp. Spanish. **3,** *colloq.* fibber. —*adj., colloq.* evasive; fibbing.

románico (ro'ma·ni·ko) *adj.* **1,** Romanesque. **2,** Romanic; Romance.

romanista (ro·ma'nis·ta) *n.m.* Romanist.

romano (ro'ma·no) *adj. & n.m.* Roman.

romántico (ro'man·ti·ko) *adj.* romantic. —*n.m.* romanticist. —**romanticismo** (-'θis·mo; -'sis·mo) *n.m.* romanticism.

romanza (ro'man·θa; -sa) *n.f., mus.* romance; song.

romaza (ro'ma·θa; -sa) *n.f., bot.* dock.

rombo ('rom·bo) *n.m.* rhombus.

romboide (rom'boi·ðe) *n.m.* rhomboid. —**romboidal,** *also,* **romboideo** (-'boi·ðe·o) *adj.* rhomboidal.

romero (ro'me·ro) *n.m.* **1,** pilgrim. **2,** *bot.* rosemary. —**romería,** *n.f.* pilgrimage; religious excursion.

romo ('ro·mo) *adj.* **1,** blunt; stubby. **2,** flat-nosed. **3,** obtuse.

rompecabezas (rom·pe·ka'βe·θas; -sas) *n.m.sing. & pl.* **1,** puzzle; riddle; brain teaser. **2,** jigsaw puzzle.

rompehielos (rom·pe'je·los) *n.m. sing. & pl.* icebreaker.

rompehuelgas (rom·pe'wel·ɣas) *n.m. sing. & pl.* strikebreaker; scab.

rompeolas (rom·pe'o·las) *n.m. sing. & pl.* breakwater; mole; jetty.

romper (rom'per) *v.t.* [*p.p.* **roto**] **1,** to break. **2,** to rend; rip; tear. —*v.i.* **1,** to break; come apart; burst. **2,** to break; break forth (into action, utterance, etc.). **3,** to start; begin; open. **4,** *fol. by* **con,** to break with. **5,** to break, as the day. —**romperse,** *v.r., colloq.* to give one's all. —**de rompe y rasga,** confidently; resolutely.

rompiente (rom'pjen·te) *n.m.* reef; rocky shore; shoal; surf.

rompimiento (rom·pi'mjen·to) *n.m.* **1,** break; breaking; breakage. **2,** a breaking off; estrangement. **3,** break; opening.

ron (ron) *n.m.* rum.

roncador (ron·ka'ðor) *adj.* **1,** snor-

ing. **2,** growling; roaring; bellowing. —*n.m.* **1,** [*fem.* **-dora**] snorer. **2,** *ichthy.* small bass.

roncar (ron'kar) *v.i.* [*infl.:* **tocar,** 7] **1,** to snore. **2,** to growl; roar; bellow. **3,** *colloq.* to be or act important; cut a figure.

roncear (ron·θe'ar; -se'ar) *v.i.* **1,** to shilly-shally; drag one's heels. **2,** to flatter; cajole. **3,** *naut.* to move slowly; make slow headway.

roncería (ron·θe'ri·a; -se'ri·a) *n.f.* **1,** shilly-shallying; heel-dragging. **2,** *colloq.* flattery; blandishment.

roncero (ron'θe·ro; -'se·ro) *adj.* **1,** slow; lazy; reluctant. **2,** uncooperative; malingering.

ronco ('ron·ko) *adj.* hoarse; raucous.

roncha ('ron·tʃa) *n.f.* **1,** welt; wale. **2,** *colloq.* brazen swindle. **3,** round slice. —**levantar** *or* **sacar ronchas,** *colloq.* to annoy; rankle.

ronda ('ron·da) *n.f.* **1,** round; circuit; regular course. **2,** watch; patrol. **3,** *colloq.* round, as of drinks. **4,** group of revelers. **5,** round of reveling; carousing. —**coger la ronda a,** to catch in the act. —**hacer la ronda a,** to court.

rondalla (ron'da·ʎa; -ja) *n.f.* **1,** tale; fib. **2,** making the rounds; carousing.

rondar (ron'dar) *v.t. & i.* **1,** to prowl. **2,** to circle; move around. **3,** to roam, as the streets. **4,** to make the rounds (of); go the rounds (of).

rondín (ron'din) *n.m.* **1,** round of inspection. **2,** *S.A.* night watchman.

rondó (ron'do) *n.m.* rondo.

ronque ('ron·ke) *v., pres.subjve. of* **roncar.**

ronqué (ron'ke) *v., 1st pers.sing. pret. of* **roncar.**

ronquear (ron·ke'ar) *v.i.* to speak hoarsely.

ronquedad (ron·ke'ðað) *n.f.* raucousness.

ronquera (ron'ke·ra) *n.f.* hoarseness.

ronquido (ron'ki·ðo) *n.m.* **1,** snore. **2,** hoarse sound.

ronronear (ron·ro·ne'ar) *v.i.* to purr. —**ronroneo** (-'ne·o) *n.m.* purr; purring.

ronzal (ron'θal; -'sal) *n.m.* halter.

roña ('ro·ɲa) *n.f.* **1,** rust. **2,** scabies; mange. **3,** grime. **4,** rot; rottenness; decay. **5,** *colloq.* stinginess; miserliness.

roñería (ro·ɲe'ri·a) *n.f., colloq.* miserliness; stinginess.

roñoso (ro'ɲo·so) *adj.* 1, rusty. 2, moldy. 3, scabby; mangy. 4, grimy. 5, *colloq.* miserly; stingy.

ropa ('ro·pa) *n.f.* clothes; clothing. —**a quema ropa,** point-blank; at close range. —**ropa blanca,** 1, underwear; underclothes. 2, linen. —**ropa de quita y pon,** knockabout clothes; casual wear. —**ropa hecha,** ready-made clothes.

ropaje (ro'pa·xe) *n.m.* 1, dress; garb. 2, wardrobe.

ropavejero (ro·pa·βe'xe·ro) *n.m.* old-clothes dealer. —**ropavejería,** *n.f.* secondhand clothing shop.

ropería (ro·pe'ri·a) *n.f.* 1, clothier's trade. 2, clothing shop. 3, wardrobe; clothes room.

ropero (ro'pe·ro) *n.m.* 1, clothier; clothes dealer. 2, clothes cabinet; wardrobe; clothes closet.

roque ('ro·ke) *n.m., chess* rook.

roqueño (ro'ke·ɲo) *adj.* = **rocoso.**

rorcual (ror'kwal) *n.m.* rorqual.

rorro ('ro·rro) *n.m., colloq.* babe in arms.

rosa ('ro·sa) *n.f. & adj.* rose. —**rosa de los vientos; rosa náutica,** mariner's compass.

rosáceo (ro'sa·θe·o; -se·o) *adj.* 1, rose-colored. 2, rosaceous.

rosada (ro'sa·ða) *n.f.* rime.

rosado (ro'sa·ðo) *adj.* 1, rosy; rose-colored; pink. 2, frosted, as a drink. 3, *(of wine)* rosé.

rosal (ro'sal) *n.m.* rosebush.

rosaleda (ro·sa'le·ða) *n.f.* rose patch; rose thicket. *Also,* **rosalera.**

rosario (ro'sa·rjo) *n.m.* 1, rosary. 2, *fig.* series; train; chain.

rosbif (ros'bif) *n.m.* roast beef.

rosca ('ros·ka) *n.f.* 1, bolt and nut. 2, loop; twist; coil. 3, thread *(of a screw, bolt, nut, etc.).* 4, pastry ring; ring-shaped bread or roll. 5, roll of fat, esp. of children. 6, *S.A. colloq.* hassle; commotion.

roscado (ros'ka·ðo) *adj.* 1, threaded; having threads. 2, looped; coiled.

róseo ('ro·se·o) *adj.* rosy; roseate; rose-colored.

roseta (ro'se·ta) *n.f.* 1, rosette. 2, small rose. 3, *pl.* [*also,* **rositas**] popcorn.

rosetón (ro·se'ton) *n.m.* rose window.

rosillo (ro'si·ʎo; -jo) *adj.* 1, light red. 2, roan.

rosquilla (ros'ki·ʎa; -ja) *n.f.* ring-shaped pastry or roll.

rostro ('ros·tro) *n.m.* face; visage; countenance. —**hacer rostro a,** to face; face up to.

rostropálido, *adj., derog.* paleface.

rota ('ro·ta) *n.f.* 1, rout; utter defeat. 2, rattan; rattan palm.

rotación (ro·ta'θjon; -'sjon) *n.f.* rotation.

rotativo (ro·ta'ti·βo) *adj.* rotary. —*n.m., S.A.* continuous show.

rotatorio (ro·ta'to·rjo) *adj.* rotatory.

rotén (ro'ten) *also* **roten** ('ro·ten) *n.m.* 1, rattan; rattan palm. 2, rattan cane or stick.

roto ('ro·to) *v., p.p. of* **romper.** —*adj.* 1, broken; broken down. 2, ragged; raggedy.

rotonda (ro'ton·da) *n.f.* rotunda.

rotor (ro'tor) *n.m.* rotor.

rotoso (ro'to·so) *adj., S.A.* ragged; raggedy.

rótula ('ro·tu·la) *n.f.* kneepan; kneecap.

rotular (ro·tu'lar) *v.t.* 1, to label. 2, to put a heading on; place an inscription on. —**rotulación,** *n.f.* labeling.

rótulo ('ro·tu·lo) *n.m.* 1, identifying label. 2, poster; sign. 3, title; heading.

rotundo (ro'tun·do) *adj.* 1, rotund. 2, round; complete. —**rotundidad,** *n.f.* rotundity.

rotura (ro'tu·ra) *n.f.* 1, break; breaking; crack. 2, tear; rip. 3, rupture.

roturar (ro·tu'rar) *v.t.* to break up (ground) for cultivation. —**roturación,** *n.f.* breaking of ground.

royendo (ro'jen·do) *v., ger. of* **roer.**

royó (ro'jo) *v., 3rd pers.sing.pret. of* **roer.**

rozadura (ro·θa'ðu·ra; ro·sa-) *n.f.* 1, light touch in passing; brush. 2, scrape; abrasion; graze.

rozamiento (ro·θa'mjen·to; ro·sa-) *n.m.* friction.

rozar (ro'θar; -'sar) *v.t.* [*infl.:* **rezar,** 10] 1, to touch or brush lightly. 2, to scrape; scuff; graze. —**rozarse,** *v.r.* 1, to be scuffed. 2, to have contact; come into contact; meet. 3, to come close; be similar.

roznar (roθ'nar; ros-) *v.i.* to bray. —**roznido,** *n.m.* braying.

rúa ('ru·a) *n.f.* road; lane.

ruana ('rwa·na) *n.f., S.A.* = **poncho.**

ruano (ru'a·no; 'rwa·no) *adj.* roan.

rúbeo ('ru·βe·o) *adj.* ruddy; reddish.

rubéola (ru'βe·o·la) *n.f.* rubella; German measles.

rubí (ru'βi) *n.m.* & *adj.* ruby.

rubia ('ru·βja) *adj.* & *n.f.* blond. —*n.f.,* bot. madder.

rubicundo (ru·βi'kun·do) *adj.* rubicund; ruddy. —**rubicundez,** *n.f.* rubicundity; ruddiness.

rubidio (ru'βi·ðjo) *n.m.* rubidium.

rubio ('ru·βjo) *adj.* blond; fair. —*n.m.* 1, blond. 2, *ichthy.* roach.

rublo ('ru·βlo) *n.m.* ruble.

rubor (ru'βor) *n.m.* blush. —**ruboroso,** *adj.* blushing.

ruborizar (ru·βo·ri'θar; -'sar) *v.t.* [*infl.:* **rezar,** 10] to cause to blush. —**ruborizarse,** *v.r.* to blush.

rúbrica ('ru·βri·ka) *n.f.* 1, fancy or distinctive signature marked by a flourish. 2, rubric. —**de rúbrica,** *colloq.* by the letter of the word; in accordance with standard procedure.

rubricar (ru·βri'kar) *v.t.* [*infl.:* **tocar,** 7] 1, to sign with a flourish. 2, to put one's mark of approval on; subscribe to.

rucio ('ru·θjo; -sjo) *adj.* 1, *(of animals)* grayish; whitish. 2, *(of persons)* gray-haired; graying.

ruda ('ru·ða) *n.f.,* bot. rue.

rudeza (ru'ðe·θa; -sa) *n.f.* rudeness; roughness.

rudimento (ru·ði'men·to) *n.m.* rudiment. —**rudimentario,** *also,* **rudimental,** *adj.* rudimentary.

rudo ('ru·ðo) *adj.* rude; rough.

rueca ('rwe·ka) *n.f.* distaff.

rueda ('rwe·ða) *n.f.* 1, wheel. 2, roller; caster. 3, circular arrangement; circle. 4, turn; sequence. 5, round slice. 6, group; circle; ring. 7, *ichthy.* sunfish. —**hacer la rueda a,** *colloq.* 1, to flatter; wheedle. 2, to pursue; run after. —**rueda de presos** *or* **sospechosos,** police lineup.

ruede ('rwe·ðe) *v., pres.subjve.* of **rodar.**

ruedo ('rwe·ðo) *v., 1st pers.sing. pres.ind.* of **rodar.**

ruedo ('rwe·ðo) *n.m.* 1, hem; border; edge. 2, perimeter; circumference. 3, ring; arena.

ruego ('rwe·ɣo) *n.m.* plea; entreaty; supplication. —*v., 1st pers.sing. pres.ind.* of **rogar.**

ruegue ('rwe·ɣe) *v., pres.subjve.* of **rogar.**

ruejo ('rwe·xo) *n.m.* mill-wheel.

rufián (ru'fjan) *n.m.* 1, ruffian. 2, pimp. —**rufianería,** *n.f.* ruffianism. —**rufianesco,** *adj.* ruffianly.

rugir (ru'xir) *v.i.* [*infl.:* **coger,** 15] to roar; rumble; growl. —**rugido,** *n.m.* roar; rumble; growl.

rugoso (ru'ɣo·so) *adj.* wrinkled; corrugated. —**rugosidad,** *n.f.* wrinkle; corrugation.

ruibarbo (ru·i'βar·βo) *n.m.* rhubarb.

ruido ('rwi·ðo) *n.m.* 1, noise. 2, fuss; clamor.

ruidoso (rwi'ðo·so) *adj.* 1, noisy. 2, sensational.

ruin (ru'in; rwin) *adj.* 1, base; vile. 2, mean; wretched. 3, stingy; miserly; paltry.

ruina ('rwi·na) *n.f.* ruin. —**ruinar,** *v.t.* = **arruinar.**

ruindad (rwin'dað) *n.f.* 1, baseness; vileness. 2, meanness; wretchedness. 3, stinginess; miserliness.

ruinoso (rwi'no·so) *adj.* ruinous.

ruiseñor (rwi·se'ɲor) *n.m.* nightingale.

ruja ('ru·xa) *v., pres.subjve.* of **rugir.**

rujo ('ru·xo) *v., 1st pers.sing.pres. ind.* of **rugir.**

ruleta (ru'le·ta) *n.f.* roulette.

rulo ('ru·lo) *n.m.* 1, round object; ball. 2, roller. 3, *Amer.* lock; curl.

ruma ('ru·ma) *n.f., S.A. colloq.* heap; bunch.

rumano (ru'ma·no) *n.m.* & *adj.* Romanian.

rumba ('rum·ba) *n.f.* 1, rumba. 2, *Amer.* spree.

rumbear (rum·be'ar) *v.i.* 1, *Amer.* to dance the rumba. 2, *W.I., colloq.* to go on a spree. 3, *S.A., colloq.* to take a course; choose a direction.

rumbo ('rum·bo) *n.m.* 1, direction; course; bearing. 2, *colloq.* lavishness; pomp; show. —**rumboso,** *adj., colloq.* lavish; openhanded.

rumia ('ru·mja) *n.f.* rumination. *Also,* **rumiadura.**

rumiar (ru'mjar) *v.t.* & *i.* to ruminate. —**rumiante,** *adj.* & *n.m.* ruminant.

rumor (ru'mor) *n.m.* 1, rumor. 2, murmur. —**rumoroso,** *adj.* murmuring; murmurous.

rumorear (ru·mo·re'ar) *v.t.* [*also,*

Amer., **rumorar** (-'rar)] to rumor. **—rumorearse,** *also, Amer.,* **rumorarse,** *v.r.* to be rumored.

runfla ('run·fla) *n.f.* **1,** *cards* sequence. **2,** *colloq.* series; row.

runrún (run'run) *n.m., colloq.* murmur: purr. **—runrunearse,** *v.r., colloq.* = **rumorearse.**

rupia ('ru·pja) *n.f.* rupee.

rupicabra (ru·pi'ka·βra) *n.f.* chamois. *Also,* **rupicapra** (-pra).

ruptura (rup'tu·ra) *n.f.* rupture.

rural (ru'ral) *adj.* rural.

ruso ('ru·so) *adj. & n.m.* Russian.

rústico ('rus·ti·ko) *adj. & n.m.* rustic. **—rusticidad** (-θi'ðað; -si'ðað) *n.f.* rusticity. **—en rústica; a la rústica,** paperbound; paperback.

ruta ('ru·ta) *n.f.* route.

rutenio (ru'te·njo) *n.m.* ruthenium.

rutilar (ru·ti'lar) *v.i., poet* to twinkle; sparkle; shine.

rutina (ru'ti·na) *n.f.* routine. **—rutinario,** *adj.* routine.

S

S, s ('e·se) *n.f.* 22nd letter of the Spanish alphabet.

sábado ('sa·βa·ðo) *n.m.* Saturday.

sábalo ('sa·βa·lo) *n.m.* shad.

sabana (sa'βa·na) *n.f.* savanna.

sábana ('sa'βa·na) *n.f.* sheet; bedsheet.

sabandija (sa·βan'di·xa) *n.f.* vermin; small noxious animal.

sabañón (sa·βa'ɲon) *n.m.* chilblain.

sabático (sa'βa·ti·ko) *adj.* **1,** Sabbath *(attrib.).* **2,** sabbatical.

sabatino (sa·βa'ti·no) *adj.* Saturday *(attrib.).* **—sabatina,** *n.f.* Saturday devotions to the Virgin Mary.

sabedor (sa·βe'ðor) *adj.* informed; aware.

sábelotodo (sa·βe·lo'to·ðo) *n.m. & f. sing. & pl., colloq.* know-it-all.

saber (sa'βer) *v.t. & i.* [*infl.:* 62] **1,** to know; have knowledge (of). **2,** *fol. by inf.* to know how to; can. **—***v.i., fol. by* **a,** to taste of; have the flavor of. **—***n.m.* knowledge; wisdom; learning. **—a saber,** that is; to wit.

sabido (sa'βi·ðo) *adj.* **1,** learned; well-informed. **2,** *colloq.* shrewd; cunning. **—de** *or* **por sabido,** surely; of course.

sabiduría (sa·βi·ðu'ri·a) *n.f.* wisdom; learning.

sabiendas (sa'βjen·das) *in* **a sabiendas,** knowingly; consciously.

sabiente (sa'βjen·te) *adj.* informed; knowing.

sabihondo (sa·βi'on·do) *also,* **sabiondo** (sa'βjon·do) *adj. & n.m., colloq.* know-it-all.

sabio ('sa·βjo) *adj.* sage; wise. **—***n.m.* sage.

sablazo (sa'βla·θo; -so) *n.m.* **1,** blow or wound with a saber. **2,** *colloq.* a cadging of money; touch.

sable ('sa·βle) *n.m.* saber; cutlass. **—***adj. & n.m., her.* sable; black.

sablista (sa'βlis·ta) *n.m. & f., colloq.* sponger; cadger. *Also,* **sableador** (sa·βle·a'ðor) *n.m.* [*fem.* **-dora**].

sabor (sa'βor) *n.m.* taste; savor; flavor. **—saborear,** *v.t.* to savor; enjoy the flavor of.

sabotaje (sa·βo'ta·xe) *n.m.* sabotage. **—saboteador,** *n.m.* [*fem.* **-dora**] saboteur. **—sabotear,** *v.t.* to sabotage.

sabré (sa'βre) *v., fut. of* **saber.**

sabroso (sa'βro·so) *adj.* savory; flavorful; tasty.

sabueso (sa'βwe·so) *n.m.* **1,** hound; bloodhound; beagle. **2,** *colloq.* investigator; sleuth.

sábulo ('sa·βu·lo) *n.m.* coarse sand.

saburra (sa'βu·rra) *n.f.* coating or fur on the tongue. **—saburroso,** *adj.* furred or coated, as the tongue.

saca ('sa·ka) *n.f.* **1,** extraction; taking out. **2,** sack; bag.

sacabocados (sa·ka·βo'ka·ðos) *n.m. sing. & pl., mech.* punch.

sacacorchos (sa·ka'kor·tʃos) *n.m. sing. & pl.* corkscrew.

sacamanchas (sa·ka'man·tʃas) *n.m. & f. sing. & pl.* dry cleaner.

sacamiento (sa·ka'mjen·to) *n.m.* removal.

sacamuelas (sa·ka'mwe·las) *n.m. & f. sing. & pl., colloq.* **1,** dentist. **2,** charlatan; quack.

sacapuntas (sa·ka'pun·tas) *n.m. sing. & pl.* pencil sharpener.

sacar (sa'kar) *v.t.* [*infl.:* tocar, 7] **1,** to take out; withdraw. **2,** to bring out; get out. **3,** to take off; remove. **4,** to get; gain; acquire. **5,** to show; bring to notice. **6,** to make (a copy). **7,** to take (photographs). **8,** to take; take down (notes, information, etc.). **9,** to figure out; find out; get at. **10,** to give or apply (a name or nickname). —*v.t. & i., sports* to serve. —**sacar adelante, 1,** to further; advance. **2,** to rear; bring up. —**sacar a luz,** to publish. —**sacar el cuerpo,** to dodge; duck. —**sacar a uno de sí,** to drive one out of one's mind; drive one mad. —**sacar en limpio** *or* **claro, 1,** to understand; deduce. **2,** to gain; benefit.

sacarina (sa·ka·ri'na) *n.f.* saccharin. —**sacarino,** *adj.* saccharine.

sacerdote (sa·θer'ðo·te; sa·ser-) *n.m.* priest. —**sacerdocio** (-'ðo·θjo; -sjo) *n.m.* priesthood. —**sacerdotal,** *adj.* sacerdotal. —**sacerdotisa,** *n.f.* priestess.

saciar (sa'θjar; -'sjar) *v.t.* to satiate; sate. —**saciable,** *adj.* satiable. —**saciedad,** *n.f.* satiety; satiation. —**sacio** ('sa·θjo; -sjo) *adj.* satiated; sated.

saco ('sa·ko) *n.m.* **1,** sack; bag. **2,** *anat.; bot.; zoöl.* sac. **3,** plunder; loot; sack. **4,** *Amer.* jacket. **5,** *colloq.* pack; bunch. —**saco de noche,** overnight bag.

sacramento (sa·kra'men·to) *n.m.* sacrament. —**sacramental,** *adj.* sacramental. —**sacramentar,** *v.t.* to administer the last rites to.

sacratísimo (sa·kra'ti·si·mo) *adj.* most sacred.

sacrificar (sa·kri·fi'kar) *v.t.* [*infl.:* tocar, 7] **1,** to sacrifice. **2,** to slaughter (animals) for use.

sacrificatorio (sa·kri·fi·ka'to·rjo) *adj.* sacrificial.

sacrificio (sa·kri'fi·θjo; -sjo) *n.m.* sacrifice.

sacrilegio (sa·kri'le·xjo) *n.m.* sacrilege. —**sacrílego** (sa'kri·le·ɣo) *adj.* sacrilegious.

sacroilíaco (sa·kro·i'li·a·ko) *adj.* sacroiliac. —**región sacroilíaca,** sacroiliac region.

sacristán (sa·kris'tan) *n.m.* sexton; sacristan. —**sacristía,** *n.f.* sacristy; vestry.

sacro ('sa·kro) *n.m., also,* **hueso sacro,** sacrum. —*adj.* **1,** sacred. **2,** sacral.

sacrosanto (sa·kro'san·to) *adj.* sacrosanct.

sacudir (sa·ku'ðir) *v.t.* **1,** to shake; jerk back and forth. **2,** to jolt. **3,** to shake off; dust off. **4,** to beat; strike repeatedly; pound. —**sacudirse,** *v.r., colloq.* get out; get off. —**sacudida,** *n.f.* shake; jerk; jolt. —**sacudidura,** *n.f.* a shaking off; dusting. —**sacudimiento,** *n.m.* jolt; jolting; shaking. —**sacudón,** *n.m.* jerk; jolt; shock.

sachar (sa'tʃar) *v.t.* to weed. —**sacho** ('sa·tʃo) *n.m.* hoe; weeder.

sadismo (sa'ðis·mo) *n.m.* sadism. —**sádico** ('sa·ði·ko) *n.m. also,* **sadista,** *n.m. & f.* sadist. —*adj.* sadistic.

sadomasoquismo (sa·ðo·ma·so'kis·mo) *n.m.* sadomasochism. —**sadomasoquista** (-'kis·ta) *n.m. & f.* sadomasochist. —*adj.* sadomasochistic.

saeta (sa'e·ta) *n.f.* **1,** arrow; dart. **2,** hand of a clock. **3,** poignant religious song of Holy Week; saeta. —**saetazo,** *n.m.* stroke or wound of a dart or arrow.

safari (sa'fa·ri) *n.m.* safari.

saga ('sa·ɣa) *n.f.* saga.

sagaz (sa'ɣaθ; -'ɣas) *adj.* sagacious. —**sagacidad** (-θi'ðað; -si'ðað) *n.f.* sagacity.

Sagitario (sa·xi'ta·rjo) *n.m.* Sagittarius.

sagrado (sa'ɣra·ðo) *adj.* sacred.

sagrario (sa'ɣra·rjo) *n.m.* **1,** sanctuary. **2,** *eccles.* tabernacle.

sahína (sa'i·na) *n.f.* = zahína.

sahumar (sa·u'mar) *v.t.* to perfume (a room) by burning aromatic substances. —**sahumador,** *n.m.* incense burner.

sahumerio (sa·u'me·rjo) *n.m.* **1,** perfuming by burning of aromatic substances. **2,** a substance so used.

sainete (sa·i'ne·te) *n.m.* **1,** one-act farce. **2,** morsel; tidbit. **3,** tang; flavor.

saíno (sa'i·no) *n.m.* peccary.

sajar (sa'xar) *v.t.* to slit; cut. —**saja** ('sa·xa) *also,* **sajadura,** *n.f.* slit; cut; incision.

sajón (sa'xon) *adj. & n.m.* [*fem.* -jona] Saxon.

sal (sal) *n.f.* **1,** salt. **2,** wit; grace; charm. **3,** *colloq.* color; spice; zest. —*v., impv. sing. of* salir. —**sal de la Higuera,** Epsom salts.

sala ('sa·la) *n.f.* **1,** living room; parlor. **2,** hall; room; gallery. **3,** auditorium; theater. **—sala de espectácu-los,** theater; hall. **—sala de espera,** waiting room. **—sala de estar,** living room. **—sala de fiestas,** cabaret.

saladar (sa·la'ðar) *n.m.* **1,** salt marsh. **2,** barren, saline soil. **3,** salt lick.

salado (sa'la·ðo) *adj.* **1,** salt; salty. **2,** witty; graceful; charming. **3,** colorful; spicy; zestful. **4,** *Amer., colloq.* unlucky.

salamandra (sa·la'man·dra) *n.f.* **1,** salamander. **2,** coal stove.

salar (sa'lar) *v.t.* **1,** to salt; cure by salting. **2,** to make salty. **3,** *Amer., colloq.* to give bad luck to; make unlucky. **4,** *Amer., colloq.* to spoil; ruin.

salario (sa'la·rjo) *n.m.* salary; pay.

salaz (sa'laθ; -'las) *adj.* salacious. **—salacidad** (-θi'ðað; -si'ðað) *n.f.* salaciousness.

salazón (sa·la'θon; -'son) *n.m.* **1,** salt meat or fish. **2,** salt meat and fish trade.

salcochar (sal·ko'tʃar) *v.t.* to boil (meat, fish, etc.).

salchicha (sal'tʃi·tʃa) *n.f.* small sausage. **—salchichón,** *n.m.* salami.

saldar (sal'dar) *v.t.* **1,** to pay in full; close; settle (an account). **2,** to liquidate; close out. **3,** to settle (a question or dispute).

saldo ('sal·do) *n.m.* **1,** *comm.* balance; difference. **2,** closeout; bargain.

saldré (sal'dre) *v., fut. of* **salir.**

saledizo (sa·le'ði·θo; -so) *adj.* projecting; jutting. **—n.m.** = **salidizo.**

salero (sa'le·ro) *n.m.* **1,** salt shaker; salt cellar. **2,** wit; piquancy; charm. **—saleroso,** *adj.* witty; charming; piquant.

salga ('sal·ɣa) *v., pres.subjve. of* **salir.**

salgo ('sal·ɣo) *v., 1st pers.sing. pres.ind. of* **salir.**

salicilato (sa·li·θi'la·to; -si'la·to) *n.m.* salicylate. **—salicílico** (-'θi·li·ko; -'si·li·ko) *adj.* salicylic.

salida (sa'li·ða) *n.f.* **1,** exit; way out. **2,** a going or coming out. **3,** leaving; departure. **4,** outset; start. **5,** expenditure. **6,** sally. **7,** outlet. **8,** = **saliente. 9,** *colloq.* remark; crack. **—salida de baño,** bathrobe. **—salida de teatro,** *Amer.* evening wrap. **—tener salida,** to sell well.

salidizo (sa·li'ði·θo; -so) *n.m.* projection; ledge.

saliente (sa'ljen·te) *adj.* salient; jutting. **—n.f.** projection; protuberance; salient.

salina (sa'li·na) *n.f., usu.pl.* salt pit; salt mine.

salino (sa'li·no) *adj.* saline; salt. **—salinidad,** *n.f.* (-ni'ðað) salinity.

salir (sa'lir) *v.i.* [*infl.:* 63] **1,** to go out; get out. **2,** to come out. **3,** to emerge; arise. **4,** to open; give access; lead. **5,** to leave; depart. **6,** to project; protrude. **7,** to flow out. **8,** *games* to open; lead; begin. **—salirse,** *v.r.* to overflow; leak out. **—salir a,** to resemble **—salir de, 1,** to escape; get out of. **2,** to get rid of; dispose of. **—salirse con la suya,** to have one's way.

salitre (sa'li·tre) *n.m.* saltpeter. **—salitral,** *adj.* nitrous. **—n.m.** [*also,* **salitrera,** *n.f.*] nitrate bed. **—salitrero,** *also,* **salitroso,** *adj.* nitrous.

saliva (sa'li·βa) *n.f.* saliva. **—salival,** *adj.* salivary.

salivar (sa·li'βar) *v.i.* to salivate. **—salivación,** *n.f.* salivation. **—salivazo,** *n.m.* spit; spitting.

salmo ('sal·mo) *n.m.* psalm. **—salmista,** *n.m.* psalmist. **—salmodia** (-'mo·ðja) *n.f.* psalmody.

salmodiar (sal·mo'ðjar) *v.t. & i.* to chant; sing or speak monotonously.

salmón (sal'mon) *n.m.* salmon.

salmonete (sal·mo'ne·te) *n.m.* red mullet.

salmuera (sal'mwe·ra) *n.f.* brine; pickle.

salobral (sa·lo'βral) *n.m.* **1,** barren, saline soil. **2,** salt lick. **—adj.** = **salobre.**

salobre (sa'lo·βre) *adj.* salty; briny; brackish. **—salobridad,** *n.f.* saltiness; brackishness.

salón (sa'lon) *n.m.* **1,** salon; parlor. **2,** drawing room. **3,** hall; room; saloon. **4,** gallery; art exhibit.

salpicar (sal·pi'kar) *v.t.* [*infl.:* **tocar,** 7] to spatter; sprinkle; splash. **—salpicadura,** *n.f.* spattering; sprinkling; splashing.

salpicón (sal·pi'kon) *n.m.* **1,** splash; spatter. **2,** salmagundi. **3,** hash; mincemeat. **4,** *colloq.* hodgepodge; jumble. **5,** *S.A.* cold fruit drink.

salpullido (sal·pu'ʎi·ðo; -'ji·ðo) *n.m.* rash; skin rash.

salsa ('sal·sa) *n.f.* sauce; gravy;

dressing. —**salsera,** *n.f.* gravy boat; sauce dish or tray.

saltador (sal·ta'ðor) *adj.* jumping; leaping. —*n.m.* **1,** [*fem.* **-dora**] jumper; dancer. **2,** jump rope; skipping rope.

saltamontes (sal·ta'mon·tes) *n.m. sing. & pl.* grasshopper.

saltar (sal'tar) *v.t. & i.* **1,** to jump; leap; spring; bounce. **2,** to skip. **3,** to break; snap; crack. —*v.i.* **1,** to stand out; be evident. **2,** to shift or change suddenly; start. —**saltar a la vista; saltar a los ojos,** to be obvious.

saltarín (sal·ta'rin) *adj.* gamboling; frolicking. —*n.m.* **1,** restless boy; jumping jack. **2,** [*fem.* **-rina**] jumper; dancer.

saltear (sal·te'ar) *v.t.* **1,** to assault; rob; hold up. **2,** to sauté. —**salteador,** *n.m.* [*fem.* **-dora**] bandit; robber. —**salteo** (-'te·o) *n.m.* = **asalto.**

saltimbanqui (sal·tim'ban·ki) *also,* **saltimbanco** (-ko) *n.m.* **1,** mountebank; charlatan; quack. **2,** tumbler; acrobat. **3,** *colloq.* ne'er-do-well.

salto ('sal·to) *n.m.* **1,** leap; jump; spring. **2,** gap; hiatus. **3,** cliff; precipice. —**salto de agua,** waterfall. —**salto mortal,** somersault.

saltón (sal'ton) *adj.* jumping; hopping. —*n.m.* **1,** grasshopper. **2,** maggot.

salubre (sa'lu·βre) *adj.* salubrious; healthful.

salubridad (sa·lu·βri'ðað) *n.f.* **1,** salubriousness; salubrity. **2,** public health.

salud (sa'luð) *n.f.* health. —**vender salud,** *colloq.* to be the picture of health.

saludable (sa·lu'ða·βle) *adj.* **1,** salutary; healthful. **2,** healthy.

saludar (sa·lu'ðar) *v.t.* to greet; salute. —**saludador,** *adj.* salutatory. —*n.m.* [*fem.* **-dora**] salutatorian.

saludo (sa'lu·ðo) *n.m.* **1,** greeting; salutation. **2,** salute.

salutación (sa·lu·ta'θjon; -'sjon) *n.f.* **1,** salutation. **2,** salutatory.

salva ('sal·βa) *n.f.* salvo; burst.

salvación (sal·βa'θjon; -'sjon) *n.f.* salvation.

salvado (sal'βa·ðo) *n.m.* bran.

salvador (sal·βa'ðor) *n.m.* savior. —*adj.* saving.

salvadoreño (sal·βa·ðo're·ɲo) *adj. & n.m.* Salvadoran.

salvaguardar (sal·βa·ɣwar·'ðar) *v.t.* to safeguard; protect.

salvaguardia (sal·βa'ɣwar·ðja) *n.m.* **1,** guard; watchman. **2,** safeguard; protection. —*n.f.* **1,** token of immunity or privilege. **2,** = **salvo-conducto.**

salvaje (sal'βa·xe) *adj.* savage; wild. —*n.m. & f.* savage. —**salvajada,** *n.f.* wild action; vandalism. —**salvajismo,** *n.m.* savagery; atrocity.

salvamanteles (sal·βa·man·'te·les) *n.m. sing. & pl.* place mat.

salvamento (sal·βa'men·to) *n.m.* **1,** salvage. **2,** salvation; rescue. **3,** refuge; retreat.

salvar (sal'βar) *v.t.* **1,** to save; rescue. **2,** to salvage. **3,** to pass; leap over; clear. **4,** to except; exclude. **5,** to skip; omit.

salvavidas (sal·βa'βi·ðas) *n.m. sing. & pl.* life preserver. —**lancha salvavidas,** lifeboat.

salve ('sal·βe) *interj.* hail! —*n.f., eccles.* Salve Regina.

salvedad (sal·βe'ðað) *n.f.* condition; exception; reservation.

salvia ('sal·βja) *n.f., bot.* sage.

salvo ('sal·βo) *adj.* **1,** safe; saved. **2,** left out; omitted; excepted. —*prep.* save; except. —**a salvo,** safe; safely; in safety. —**dejar a salvo,** to except; make an exception of. —**en salvo, 1,** at liberty. **2,** safe; out of danger. —**salvo que,** save that; unless.

salvoconducto (sal·βo·kon'duk·to) *n.m.* safe-conduct; pass.

sallar (sa'ʎar; -'jar) *v.t.* to weed.

samario (sa'ma·rjo) *n.m.* samarium.

samaritano (sa·ma·ri'ta·no) *adj. & n.m.* Samaritan.

samba ('sam·ba) *n.f.* samba.

samovar (sa·mo'βar) *n.m.* samovar.

sampán (sam'pan) *n.m.* sampan.

samurai (sa·mu'rai) *n.m.* samurai.

san (san) *adj., contr. of* **santo,** *used before masculine names of saints, except* Tomás, Tomé, Toribio *and* Domingo.

sánalotodo (sa·na·lo'to·ðo) *n.m. sing. & pl.* cure-all.

sanamente (sa·na'men·te) *adv.* sincerely; candidly.

sanar (sa'nar) *v.t.* to heal; cure; make whole. —*v.i.* to heal; be cured; recover.

sanatorio (sa·na'to·rjo) *n.m.* sanatorium; sanitarium; *Amer.* hospital.
sanción (san'θjon; -'sjon) *n.f.* 1, sanction. 2, *sports* penalty. —**sancionar,** *v.t.* to sanction.
sancochar (san·ko'tʃar) *v.t.* to parboil. —**sancocho** (-'ko·tʃo) *n.m., Amer.* stew.
sandalia (san'da·lja) *n.f.* sandal.
sándalo ('san·da·lo) *n.m.* sandalwood.
sandez (san'deθ; -'des) *n.f.* silliness; foolishness.
sandía (san'di·a) *n.f.* watermelon.
sandio ('san·djo) *adj.* foolish; silly. —*n.m.* fool; simpleton.
sandunga (san'dun·ga) *n.f.* 1, *colloq.* grace; charm. 2, *Amer.* spree. —**sandunguero** (-'ge·ro) *adj., colloq.* charming.
sandwich ('san·dwitʃ) *n.m.* sandwich.
saneamiento (sa·ne·a'mjen·to) *n.m.* 1, sanitation; cleansing. 2, improvement, as of land. 3, *law* reparation; indemnification.
sanear (sa·ne'ar) *v.t.* 1, to make sanitary; cleanse. 2, to improve (land, swampy terrain, etc.). 3, *law* to pay damages or reparations to.
sangre ('san·gre) *n.f.* blood. —**sangrar,** *v.t. & i.* 1, to bleed. 2, *print.* to indent. —**estar sangrando,** to be recent; to be still painfully present in memory.
sangría (san'gri·a) *n.f.* 1, bleeding; bloodletting. 2, *print.* indentation. 3, *colloq.* cold drink of wine and fruits; wine cooler.
sangriento (san'grjen·to) *adj.* bloody.
sangüesa (san'gwe·sa) *n.f.* raspberry.
sanguijuela (san·gi'xwe·la) *n.f.* leech.
sanguinario (san·gi'na·rjo) *adj.* sanguinary; bloodthirsty.
sanguíneo (san'gi·ne·o) *adj.* sanguine; blood (*attrib.*). —**grupo sanguíneo,** blood group.
sanguinolento (san·gi·no'len·to) *adj.* bloody; sanguinolent.
sanidad (sa·ni'ðað) *n.f.* public health; sanitation.
sanitario (sa·ni'ta·rjo) *adj.* sanitary.
sano ('sa·no) *adj.* healthy; sound; whole. —**sano y salvo,** safe and sound.
sánscrito ('sans·kri·to) *adj. & n.m.* Sanskrit.

sanseacabó (san·se·a·ka'βo) *also,* **sansacabó** (san·sa-) *interj., colloq.* that's the end!; that does it!
santa ('san·ta) *n.f.* saint.
santabárbara (san·ta'βar·βa·ra) *n.f.* powder magazine.
santiamén (san·tja'men) *n.m., colloq.* instant; jiffy.
santidad (san·ti'ðað) *n.f.* 1, sanctity; holiness; saintliness. 2, sainthood.
santificar (san·ti·fi'kar) *v.t.* [*infl.*: tocar, 7] to sanctify. —**santificación,** *n.f.* sanctification.
santiguarse (san·ti·ɣwar·se) *v.r.* [*infl.*: averiguar, 9] to cross oneself.
santísimo (san'ti·si·mo) *adj.* most holy. —*n.m.* the Holy Sacrament. —**todo el santísimo día,** the livelong day.
santo ('san·to) *adj.* saintly; holy. —*n.m.* 1, [*fem.* **santa**] saint. 2, saint's day; name day. 3, *colloq.* holy card or stamp. —**santa voluntad,** one's own will. —**¿a santo de qué?,** *colloq.* why on earth? —**santo y seña,** watchword; password. —**todo el santo día,** the livelong day.
santón (san'ton) *n.m.* 1, dervish. 2, = santurrón.
santoral (san·to'ral) *n.m.* calendar of saints.
santuario (san'twa·rjo) *n.m.* 1, shrine. 2, sanctuary.
santurrón (san·tu'rron) *adj.* sanctimonious. —*n.m.* [*fem.* **-rrona**] *colloq.* hypocrite. —**santurronería,** *n.f.* sanctimony.
saña ('sa·ɲa) *n.f.* 1, rage; fury. 2, vindictive cruelty; malice. —**sañoso,** *also,* **sañudo,** *adj.* vindictive; cruel.
sápido ('sa·pi·ðo) *adj.* sapid. —**sapidez,** *n.f.* sapidity.
sapiencia (sa'pjen·θja; -sja) *n.f.* sapience. —**sapiente,** *adj.* sapient.
sapo ('sa·po) *n.m.* toad. —**echar sapos y culebras,** *colloq.* to pour forth abuse. —**sapo marino,** *ichthy.* angler.
saponaria (sa·po'na·rja) *n.f.* soapwort.
saque ('sa·ke) *v., pres.subjve.* of sacar. —*n.m., sports* 1, serve; service. 2, taking away (of a ball).
saqué (sa'ke) *v., 1st pers.sing.pret.* of sacar.
saquear (sa·ke'ar) *v.t.* to sack;

plunder. —**saqueo** (-'ke·o) *n.m.* sacking; plunder.

saquillo (sa'ki·ʎo; -jo) *n.m.* handbag; satchel.

sarampión (sa·ram'pjon) *n.m.* measles.

sarao (sa'ra·o) *n.m.* soirée; informal dance.

sarape (sa'ra·pe) *n.m.*, *Amer.* serape; shawl.

sarcasmo (sar'kas·mo) *n.m.* sarcasm. —**sarcástico** (-ti·ko) *adj.* sarcastic.

sarcófago (sar'ko·fa·ɣo) *n.m.* sarcophagus.

sarcoma (sar'ko·ma) *n.f.* sarcoma.

sardina (sar'di·na) *n.f.* sardine.

sardineta (sar·ði'ne·ta) *n.f.* 1, small sardine. 2, chevron.

sardónico (sar'ðo·ni·ko) *adj.* sardonic.

sarga ('sar·ɣa) *n.f.* 1, serge. 2, willow.

sargazo (sar'ɣa·θo; -so) *n.m.* sargasso.

sargento (sar'xen·to) *n.m.* sergeant.

sarmiento (sar'mjen·to) *n.m.* 1, shoot or branch of a grapevine. 2, *fig.* offshoot.

sarna ('sar·na) *n.f.* mange; scabies. —**sarnoso,** *adj.* mangy.

sarong (sa'ron) *n.m.* sarong.

sarpullido (sar·pu'ʎi·ðo; -'ji·ðo) *n.m.* = **salpullido.**

sarraceno (sa·rra'θe·no; -'se·no) *adj. & n.m.* Saracen.

sarro ('sa·rro) *n.m.* 1, crust; sediment. 2, tartar *(on teeth)*. 3, coating or fur on the tongue. —**sarroso,** *adj.* furred or coated, as the tongue.

sarta ('sar·ta) *n.f.* string; row; series.

sartén (sar'ten) *n.f.* frying pan.

sasafrás (sa·sa'fras) *n.m.* sassafras.

sastre ('sas·tre) *n.m.* tailor. —**traje sastre,** woman's tailored suit.

sastrería (sas·tre'ri·a) *n.f.* 1, tailor shop. 2, tailoring.

Satán (sa'tan) *also,* **Satanás** (-'nas) *n.m.* Satan. —**satánico,** *adj.* satanic.

satélite (sa'te·li·te) *n.m.* satellite.

satén (sa'ten) *also,* **satín** (-'tin) *n.m.* sateen. —**satinar,** *v.t.* to glaze; make glossy.

satín (sa'tin) *n.m.* 1, satinwood. 2, = satén.

sátira ('sa·ti·ra) *n.f.* satire. —**satírico** (-'ti·ri·ko) *adj.* satirical,

—*n.m. & f.* satirist. —**satirizar,** *v.t* [*infl.:* **rezar, 10**] to satirize.

sátiro ('sa·ti·ro) *n.m.* satyr.

satisfacer (sa·tis·fa'θer; -'ser) *v.t* [*infl.:* **hacer, 48**] to satisfy —**satisfacción** (-fak'θjon; -'sjon *n.f.* satisfaction. —**satisfactoriᴏ** (-fak'to·rjo) *adj.* satisfactory.

satisfecho (sa·tis'fe·tʃo) *v., p.p. ᴏ* **satisfacer.** —*adj.* satisfied.

sátrapa ('sa·tra·pa) *n.m.* satrap —**satrapía** (-'pi·a) *n.f.* satrapy.

saturar (sa·tu'rar) *v.t.* to saturate —**saturación,** *n.f.* saturation —**saturable,** *adj.* saturable.

Saturno (sa'tur·no) *n.m.* Saturn —**saturnino,** *adj.* saturnine.

sauce ('sau·θe; -se) *n.m.* willow —**sauce llorón,** weeping willow —**sauzal** (-'θal; -'sal) willow grove

saúco (sa'u·ko) *n.m.*, *bot.* elder.

savia ('sa·βja) *n.f.* sap.

saxofonista (sak·so·fo'nis·ta *n.m. & f.* saxophonist.

saxófono (sak'so·fo·no) *n.m* saxophone. *Also,* **saxofón** (-'fon)

saya ('sa·ja) *n.f.* 1, skirt. 2, half slip; petticoat.

sayo ('sa·jo) *n.m.* 1, cassock 2, tunic.

sazón (sa'θon; -'son) *n.f.* 1, maturity; ripeness. 2, seasoning; flavoring. 3, ripe moment; right time. —**ᴀ la sazón;** at the time; at the moment; then. —**en sazón, 1,** in season; ripe. 2, opportunely; in due season.

sazonar (sa·θo'nar; sa·so-) *v.t.* 1 to season. 2, to ripen. —**sazonado** *adj.* witty; pithy.

se (se) *pers. pron. 3rd pers.m. & f sing. & pl. refl.,* used as obj. of ᴄ *verb* oneself; yourself; himself; her self; itself; yourselves; themselves each other; one another. —*pers pron., used to replace a 3rᴅ pers.ind. obj.pron. when fol. by ᴄ 3rd pers.dir.obj.pron.: se lo doy,* give it to him (to her, to it, to them to you).

sé (se) *v.* 1, *1st pers.sing.pres.ind. ᴏ* **saber.** 2, *impv.sing. of* **ser.**

sea ('se·a) *v., pres.subjve. of* **ser.**

sebáceo (se'βa·θe·o; -se·o) *adj.* se baceous.

sebo ('se·βo) *n.m.* tallow; suet; fat sebum. —**seborrea** (se·βo'rre·a *n.f.* seborrhea. —**seboso** (se'βo·sᴏ *adj.* greasy; fatty.

seca ('se·ka) *n.f.* drought; dry pe

riod or season. **—a secas, 1,** simply; baldly. **2,** drily; curtly; coldly.

secano (se'ka·no) *n.m.* dry or unwatered land.

secante (se'kan·te) *adj.* blotting; drying. **—***n.m.* blotter; dryer. **—***n.f.* secant.

secar (se'kar) *v.t.* [*infl.:* tocar, 7] to dry. **—secarse,** *v.r.* to dry; dry up. **—secador,** *n.m.* hair dryer. **—secadora,** *n.f.* clothes dryer. **—secamiento,** *n.m.* drying up; withering.

sección (sek'θjon; -'sjon) *n.f.* section. **—seccional,** *adj.* sectional. **—seccionar,** *v.t.* to section.

secesión (se·θe'sjon; se·se-) *n.f.* secession. **—secesionismo,** *n.m.* secessionism. **—secesionista,** *adj.* & *n.m.* & *f.* secessionist.

seco ('se·ko) *adj.* **1,** dry. **2,** withered; parched. **3,** *fig.* curt; aloof. **—en seco,** suddenly; abruptly.

secoya (se'ko·ja) *n.f.* sequoia.

secreción (se·kre'θjon; -'sjon) *n.f.* secretion.

secretar (se·kre'tar) *v.t., biol.* to secrete.

secretaría (se·kre·ta'ri·a) *n.f.* **1,** secretary's office. **2,** secretaryship. **3,** secretariat.

secretario (se·kre'ta·rjo) *n.m.* [*fem.* **-ria**] secretary. **—secretariado,** *n.m.* **1,** secretariat. **2,** secretaryship.

secretear (se·kre·te'ar) *v.i.* to whisper; talk in secret.

secreto (se'kre·to) *adj.* secret. **—***n.m.* **1,** secret. **2,** secrecy. **—secreto a voces,** open secret.

secretor (se·kre'tor) *adj.* secretory. *Also,* **secretorio** (-to'rjo).

secta ('sek·ta) *n.f.* sect. **—sectario,** *adj.* & *n.m.* sectarian. **—sectarismo,** *n.m.* sectarianism.

sector (sek'tor) *n.m.* sector.

secuaz (se'kwaθ; -'kwas) *n.m.* & *f.* **1,** adherent; follower. **2,** henchman.

secuela (se'kwe·la) *n.f.* sequel; continuation.

secuencia (se'kwen·θja; -sja) *n.f.* sequence.

secuestrar (se·kwes'trar) *v.t.* **1,** to sequester. **2,** to kidnap. **3,** to hijack.

secuestro (se'kwes·tro) *n.m.* **1,** sequestration. **2,** kidnapping. **3,** hijacking.

secular (se·ku'lar) *adj.* & *n.m.* secular. **—secularismo,** *n.m.* secularism. **—secularista,** *adj.* secularistic. **—***n.m.* & *f.* secularist.

secularizar (se·ku·la·ri'θar; -'sar) *v.t.* [*infl.:* rezar, 10] to secularize. **—secularización,** *n.f.* secularization.

secundar (se·kun'dar) *v.t.* to second; support.

secundario (se·kun'da·rjo) *adj.* secondary.

sed (seð) *n.f.* thirst. **—tener sed,** to be thirsty.

seda ('se·ða) *n.f.* silk.

sedal (se'ðal) *n.m.* fishline.

sedán (se'ðan) *n.m.* sedan.

sedar (se'ðar) *v.t.* **1,** to calm; pacify. **2,** to allay; soothe. **—sedación,** *n.f.* sedation. **—sedante,** *also,* **sedativo,** *adj.* & *n.m.* sedative.

sede ('se·ðe) *n.f.* **1,** see. **2,** seat (*of government or authority*). **3,** *fig.* seat; center; heart.

sedentario (se·ðen'ta·rjo) *adj.* sedentary.

sedición (se·ði'θjon; -'sjon) *n.f.* sedition. **—sedicioso,** *adj.* seditious.

sediento (se'ðjen·to) *adj.* **1,** thirsty. **2,** eager; craving.

sedimento (se·ði'men·to) *n.m.* sediment. **—sedimentar,** *v.t.* to deposit as sediment. **—sedimentarse,** *v.r.* to be deposited as sediment. **—sedimentación,** *n.f.* sedimentation. **—sedimentario,** *adj.* sedimentary.

sedoso (se'ðo·so) *adj.* silky.

seducir (se·ðu'θir; -'sir) *v.t.* [*infl.:* conducir, 40] to seduce. **—seducción** (se·ðuk'θjon; -'sjon) *n.f.* seduction.

seductor (se·ðuk'tor) *adj.* seductive; charming. **—***n.m.* [*fem.* **-tora**] seducer; tempter; charmer. **—seductivo,** *adj.* seductive.

segada (se'ya·ða) *n.f.* = **siega.**

segadera (se·ya'ðe·ra) *n.f.* sickle.

segar (se'yar) *v.t.* [*infl.:* pagar, 8; pensar, 27] to reap; harvest; mow. **—segador,** *n.m.* reaper; harvester. **—segadora,** *n.f.* reaper; harvester (*machine*).

seglar (se'ylar) *adj.* secular; worldly. **—***n.m.* layman. **—***n.f.* laywoman.

segmento (sey'men·to) *n.m.* segment. **—segmentación,** *n.f.* segmentation. **—segmental,** *adj.* segmental.

segregación (se·yre·ya'θjon; -'sjon) *n.f.* **1,** segregation. **2,** *biol.* secretion. **—segregacionista,** *adj.* & *n.m.* & *f.* segregationist.

segregar (se·yre'yar) *v.t.* [*infl.:*

pagar, 8] **1,** to segregate; separate. **2,** *biol.* to secrete.

segué (se'ɣe) *v., 1st pers.sing.pret. of* **segar.**

segueta (se'ɣe·ta) *n.f.* **1,** hacksaw. **2,** jigsaw.

seguida (se'ɣi·ða) *n.f.* **1,** pursuit. **2,** continuance; continuation; succession. *Obs. except in the following phrases:* **de seguida, 1,** one after another; in succession. **2,** at once; immediately. —**en seguida,** at once; immediately.

seguido (se'ɣi·ðo) *adj.* **1,** continued; successive. **2,** straight; direct. —*adv.* **1,** at once; immediately. **2,** straight; directly. **3,** in quick succession; thick and fast.

seguidor (se·ɣi'ðor) *n.m.* [*fem.* **-dora**] follower.

seguimiento (se·ɣi'mjen·to) *n.m.* pursuit; chase; quest.

seguir (se'ɣir) *v.t. & i.* [*infl.:* 64] **1,** to follow. **2,** to continue. —**seguirse,** *v.r.* to follow as a consequence; arise; spring.

según (se'ɣun) *prep.* according to; in accordance with. —*adv.* accordingly; correspondingly; depending. —*conj.* [*also,* **según que; según lo que**] **1,** according to how or what; depending upon how or what. **2,** as; in the same way as. **3,** to the degree that. —**según y como; según y conforme, 1,** in the same way or manner. **2,** it depends.

segunda (se'ɣun·da) *n.f., mus.* second.

segundar (se·ɣun'dar) *v.t.* **1,** to do again; repeat. **2,** to second; be second to.

segundario (se·ɣun'da·rjo) *adj.* secondary. —*n.m., S.A.* second hand *(of a timepiece).*

segundero (se·ɣun'de·ro) *n.m.* second hand *(of a timepiece). Also, S.A.* **segundario.**

segundo (se'ɣun·do) *adj. & n.m.* second. —**de segunda mano,** secondhand. —**segunda intención,** double meaning; ulterior motive; malice. —**sin segundo,** without equal; without peer.

segur (se'ɣur) *n.m.* **1,** ax. **2,** sickle.

seguridad (se·ɣu·ri'ðað) *n.f.* **1,** security; safety. **2,** certainty.

seguro (se'ɣu·ro) *adj.* **1,** safe; secure. **2,** sure; certain. —*adv., colloq.* sure; for sure. —*n.m.* **1,** insurance. **2,** lock; safety lock. —**de**

seguro, surely; assuredly. —**sobre seguro,** with full assurance.

seis (seis) *adj. & n.m.* six.

seisavo (sei'sa·βo) *adj. & n.m.* sixth.

seiscientos (seis'θjen·tos; sei·'sjen-) *adj. & n.m.* [*fem.* **-tas**] six hundred.

seiseno (sei'se·no) *adj.* sixth.

seísmo (se'is·mo) *n.m.* = **sismo.**

selección (se·lek'θjon; -'sjon) *n.f.* selection. —**seleccionar,** *v.t.* to select.

selecto (se'lek·to) *adj.* select. —**selectividad,** *n.f.* selectivity. —**selectivo,** *adj.* selective.

selenio (se'le·njo) *n.m.* selenium.

seltz (selts) *n.f., also,* **agua de seltz,** seltzer.

selva ('sel·βa) *n.f.* forest; jungle. —**selvático** (-'βa·ti·ko) *adj.* forest *(attrib.);* sylvan.

sellar (se'ʎar; -'jar) *v.t.* **1,** to seal. **2,** to stamp.

sello ('se·ʎo; -jo) *n.m.* **1,** seal; stamp. **2,** postage stamp. **3,** *pharm.* wafer.

semáforo (se'ma·fo·ro) *n.m.* **1,** semaphore. **2,** traffic signal.

semana (se'ma·na) *n.f.* week.

semanal (se·ma'nal) *adj.* weekly. —**semanalmente,** *adv.* weekly.

semanario (se·ma'na·rjo) *adj. & n.m.* weekly.

semántica (se'man·ti·ka) *n.f.* semantics. —**semántico,** *adj.* semantic.

semblante (sem'blan·te) *n.m.* **1,** semblance; countenance; aspect. **2,** face.

semblanza (sem'blan·θa; -sa) *n.f.* **1,** likeness. **2,** biographical sketch.

sembrado (sem'bra·ðo) *n.m.* cultivated field. *Also, S.A.,* **sembrío** (-'bri·o).

sembrar (sem'brar) *v.t.* [*infl.:* **pensar,** 27] to sow; seed; plant. —**sembradora** (-bra'ðo·ra) *n.f.* planter *(machine).*

semejante (se·me'xan·te) *adj.* **1,** similar; like. **2,** such; such a. —*n.m.* fellow man; like.

semejanza (se·me'xan·θa; -sa) *n.f.* similarity; resemblance. —**semejar** (-'xar) *v.i.* [*also, v.r.,* **semejarse**] to resemble; be similar.

semen ('se·men) *n.m.* semen.

semental (se·men'tal) *adj.* breeding. —*n.m.* breeding male animal.

semestre (se'mes·tre) *n.m.* semester. —**semestral,** *adj.* semiannual.

semibreve (se·mi'βre·βe) *n.f.* semibreve; whole note.

semicírculo (se·mi'θir·ku·lo; se·mi'sir-) *n.m.* semicircle. —**semicircular,** *adj.* semicircular.

semicorchea (se·mi·kor'tʃe·a) *n.f., mus.* semiquaver.

semidiós (se·mi'ðjos) *n.m.* demigod.

semifinal (se·mi·fi'nal) *adj.* & *n.m.* semifinal. —**semifinalista,** *adj.* & *n.m.* & *f.* semifinalist.

semilunio (se·mi'lu·njo) *n.m.* half moon.

semilla (se'mi·ʎa; -ja) *n.f.* seed.

semillero (se·mi'ʎe·ro; -'je·ro) *n.m.* **1,** seed bed. **2,** plant nursery. **3,** *fig.* hotbed.

seminal (se·mi'nal) *adj.* seminal.

seminario (se·mi'na·rjo) *n.m.* **1,** seminary. **2,** seminar. —**seminarista,** *n.m.* & *f.* theological student.

semipesado (se·mi·pe'sa·ðo) *adj.* & *n.m.* light heavyweight.

semiprecioso (se·mi·pre'θjo·so; -'sjo·so) *adj.* semiprecious.

semirremolque (se·mi·rre'mol·ke) *n.m.* semitrailer.

semita (se'mi·ta) *n.m.* & *f.* Semite. —**semítico,** *adj.* Semitic.

semitono (se·mi'to·no) *n.m.* half tone.

sémola ('se·mo·la) *n.f.* semolina.

sempiterno (sem·pi'ter·no) *adj.* perpetual; eternal.

sena ('se·na) *n.f.* a six at dice.

senado (se'na·ðo) *n.m.* senate. —**senador,** *n.m.* senator. —**senaduría** (-ðu'ri·a) *n.f.* senatorship. —**senatorial** (-to'rjal) *also,* **senatorio** (-'to·rjo) *adj.* senatorial.

sencillo (sen'θi·ʎo; -'si·jo) *adj.* **1,** simple. **2,** plain; unadorned. —*n.m., Amer.* change; silver. —**sencillez,** *n.f.* simplicity.

senda ('sen·da) *n.f.* path; trail; way. *Also,* **sendero** (-'de·ro) *n.m.*

sendos ('sen·dos) *adj.m.pl.* [*fem.* **-das**] one each; one for each.

senectud (se·nek'tuð) *n.f.* old age; senescence.

senescal (se·nes'kal) *n.m.* seneschal.

senil (se'nil) *adj.* senile. —**senilidad,** *n.f.* senility.

seno ('se·no) *n.m.* **1,** bosom; breast. **2,** *fig.* womb. **3,** sinus. **4,** *geom.* sine. **5,** inlet.

sensación (sen·sa'θjon; -'sjon) *n.f.* sensation. —**sensacional,** *adj.* sensational. —**sensacionalismo,** *n.m.* sensationlism.

sensato (sen'sa·to) *adj.* sensible; reasonable; wise. —**sensatez,** *n.f.* good sense; wisdom.

sensibilizar (sen·si·βi·li'θar; -'sar) *v.t.* [*infl.:* **rezar, 10**] to sensitize.

sensible (sen'si·βle) *adj.* **1,** sensible; perceptible. **2,** sensitive; readily affected. **3,** regrettable; grievous. —**sensibilidad,** *n.f.* sensitivity; sensibility.

sensiblería (sen·si·βle'ri·a) *n.f.* sentimentality; mawkishness. —**sensiblero,** *adj.* maudlin; mawkish; sentimental.

sensitivo (sen·si'ti·βo) *adj.* sensitive. —**sensitiva,** *n.f.* mimosa.

sensor (sen'sor) *n.m.* sensor.

sensorio (sen'so·rjo) *adj.* sensory. *Also,* **sensorial.**

sensual (sen'swal) *adj.* sensual; sensuous. —**sensualidad,** *n.f.* sensuality; sensuousness. —**sensualismo,** *n.m.* sensualism. —**sensualista,** *adj.* sensualistic. —*n.m.* & *f.* sensualist.

sentado (sen'ta·ðo) *adj.* **1,** steady; quiet; sedate. **2,** settled. **3,** seated; sitting. —**dar por sentado,** to assume; take for granted. —**dejar por sentado,** to establish; fix; set.

sentar (sen'tar) *v.t.* [*infl.:* **pensar, 27**] to seat; sit. —*v.i.* to agree (with); go well (with). —**sentarse,** *v.r.* to sit; sit down.

sentencia (sen'ten·θja; -sja) *n.f.* **1,** *law* sentence. **2,** maxim. —**sentenciar,** *v.t.* to sentence. —**sentencioso,** *adj.* sententious.

sentido (sen'ti·ðo) *adj.* **1,** heartfelt. **2,** sensitive; touchy. **3,** offended; hurt. —*n.m.* **1,** sense. **2,** direction. **3,** consciousness.

sentimental (sen·ti·men'tal) *adj.* sentimental. —**sentimentalismo,** *n.m.* sentimentalism; sentimentality.

sentimiento (sen·ti'mjen·to) *n.m.* **1,** sentiment; feeling. **2,** regret.

sentina (sen'ti·na) *n.f.* **1,** bilge. **2,** *fig.* cesspool; sink.

sentir (sen'tir) *v.t.* [*infl.:* **31**] **1,** to feel; experience. **2,** to sense; perceive. **3,** to hear; be aware of (a sound). **4,** to regret; be sorry for. —*n.m.* feeling. —**sentirse,** *v.r.* **1,** to feel. **2,** to be sensitive to the touch;

pain; hurt. **3,** to take offense; feel hurt.

seña ('se·ɲa) *n.f.* **1,** sign; mark. **2,** password. **—señas,** *n.f.pl.* address. **—señas personales,** personal description. **—por (más) señas,** *colloq.* to put it more plainly.

señal (se'ɲal) *n.f.* **1,** signal. **2,** sign; mark. **3,** indication; token.

señalado (se·ɲa'la·ðo) *adj.* signal; eminent.

señalar (se·ɲa'lar) *v.t.* **1,** to mark; put a mark on. **2,** to signal; indicate; point out. **3,** to signalize. **4,** to single out; point to. —*v.t. & i.* to point. **—señalarse,** *v.r.* to distinguish oneself.

señero (se'ɲe·ro) *adj.* **1,** singular; rare. **2,** solitary; alone.

señor (se'ɲor) *n.m.* **1,** mister; sir. **2,** lord; master. **3,** gentleman.

señora (se'ɲo·ra) *n.f.* **1,** mistress; madam. **2,** lady.

señorear (se·ɲo·re'ar) *v.t.* to command; be master of. **—señorearse,** *v.r.* **1,** to take command, become master. **2,** to look imposing; put on grandiose manners.

señoría (se·ɲo'ri·a) *n.f.* lordship. **—señorial** (-'rjal) *adj.* lordly. **—señoril** (-'ril) *adj.* lordly; noble.

señorío (se·ɲo'ri·o) *n.m.* **1,** noble rank; nobility. **2,** dominion; domain. **3,** lordliness.

señorita (se·ɲo'ri·ta) *n.f.* miss; young lady.

señorito (se·ɲo'ri·to) *n.m.* **1,** young master. **2,** young gentleman. **3,** *colloq.* fop; dandy.

señuelo (se'ɲwe·lo) *n.m.* lure; bait; decoy.

seó (se'o) *n.m.,* *colloq.,* *contr.* of señor. *Also,* **seor** (se'or).

seora (se'o·ra) *n.f.,* *colloq.,* *contr.* of señora.

sepa ('se·pa) *v.,* *pres.subjve.* of saber.

sépalo ('se·pa·lo) *n.m.* sepal.

separar (se·pa'rar) *v.t.* **1,** to separate. **2,** to set aside; set apart; remove. **—separarse,** *v.r.* **1,** to separate; come apart. **2,** to part company; sever connections. **—separable,** *adj.* separable. **—separación,** *n.f.* separation. **—separado,** *adj.* separate; apart.

separatismo (se·pa·ra'tis·mo) *n.m.* separatism. **—separatista,** *adj. & n.m. & f.* separatist.

sepelio (se'pe·ljo) *n.m.* burial.

sepia ('se·pja) *n.f.* **1,** sepia. **2,** cuttlefish.

sepsis ('sep·sis) *n.f.* sepsis.

septeno (sep'te·no) *adj. & n.m.* seventh.

septentrional (sep·ten·trjo'nal) *adj.* north; northern; northerly. **—septentrión** (-'trjon) *n.m.* north.

septeto (sep'te·to) *n.m.* septet.

séptico ('sep·ti·ko) *adj.* septic.

septiembre (sep'tjem·bre) *n.m.* September. *Also,* **setiembre.**

septillón (sep·ti'ʎon; -'jon) *n.m.* a quintillion septillion; *Brit.* septillion.

séptimo ('sep·ti·mo) *adj. & n.m.* seventh. **—séptima,** *n.f., mus.* seventh.

septingentésimo (sep·tin·xen'te·si·mo) *adj. & n.m.* sevenhundredth.

septo ('sep·to) *n.m.* septum.

septuagenario (sep·twa·xe'na·rjo) *adj. & n.m.* septuagenarian.

septuagésimo (sep·twa'xe·si·mo) *adj. & n.m.* seventieth. **—Septuagésima,** *n.f.* Septuagesima.

séptuplo ('sep·tu·plo) *adj.* septuple. **—septuplicar** (-pli'kar) *v.t.* [*infl.:* **tocar, 7**] to septuple.

sepulcro (se'pul·kro) *n.m.* sepulcher. **—sepulcral,** *adj.* sepulchral.

sepultar (se·pul'tar) *v.t.* to bury. **—sepultador,** *n.m.* gravedigger. **—sepulto** (se'pul·to) *adj.* buried.

sepultura (se·pul'tu·ra) *n.f.* **1,** grave. **2,** burial. **—sepulturero,** *n.m.* gravedigger.

seque ('se·ke) *v.,* *pres.subjve.* of secar.

sequé (se'ke) *v.,* *1st pers. sing. pret.* of secar.

sequedad (se·ke'ðað) *n.f.* **1,** dryness. **2,** asperity; brusqueness.

sequía (se'ki·a) *n.f.* drought.

séquito ('se·ki·to) *n.m.* retinue; following.

ser (ser) *v.i.* [*infl.:* **5**] **1,** *copulative* to be; have the intrinsic quality, property, nature or status of. **2,** to happen; come about. **3,** *expressing identity or equality* to be; make; be the same as; be equal to: *Dos y dos son cuatro,* Two and two are (or make) four; *Amar es sufrir,* To love is to suffer. **4,** *expressing existence; fact; reality* to be; exist: *Esto no puede ser,* This cannot be. **5,** *fol. by* **de,** *denoting origin* to be from; come from: *¿De dónde eres?,*

Where are you from?; *denoting material* to be of; be made of: *La mesa es de madera*, The table is (made) of wood. **6,** *fol. by de and a noun or poss. adj. or pronoun* to belong to; pertain to: *La pluma es de Pedro*, The pen is Peter's; *La pluma es mía*, The pen is mine. **7,** *fol. by de and inf.*, expressing tendency or expectation: *Es de esperar*, It is to be expected. —*aux.v.*, used with p.p. to form the passive voice: *Es temido por todos*, He is feared by all. —*n.m.* **1,** being. **2,** nature. —**a no ser por,** were it not for. —**a no ser que,** unless. —¡**cómo es eso!**, *colloq.*, how's that!; what's the idea! —¡**Cómo ha de ser!, 1,** How can it be? **2,** That's the way it is. —**de ser Vd.**, if I were you; in your place. —**érase que se era,** once upon a time there was. —**no sea que,** lest. —**no ser para menos,** to have good cause; be justified: *Ella lloró y no era para menos*, She cried, and with good cause. —**sea lo que sea; sea lo que fuere; sea como sea, 1,** come what may. **2,** be that as it may; anyhow. —**sea o no sea,** be that as it may —**ser de lo que no hay,** *colloq.* to be unbelievable; be unheard of. —**ser para,** *fol. by inf.* **1,** *colloq.* to make one want to . . . : *Es para matarlo*, It makes you want to kill him. **2,** to be . . . ; be meant to be . . . : *Estos papeles son para tirar* or *tirarlos*, These papers are to be thrown away. —**si yo fuera Vd.**, if I were you; if I were in your place. —**soy con Vd.**, *colloq.* I'll be right with you.

sera ('se·ra) *n.f.* basket, usu. without handles.
serafín (se·ra'fin) *n.m.* seraph. —**seráfico** (-'ra·fi·ko) *adj.* seraphic.
serenar (se·re'nar) *v.t.* to make serene; calm. —*v.i.* [*also, v.r.,* **serenarse**] to become serene; calm.
serenata (se·re'na·ta) *n.f.* serenade.
sereno (se're·no) *adj.* serene; unruffled. —*n.m.* **1,** night watchman. **2,** night cold; night air; night dew. —**serenidad,** *n.f.* screnity.
serial (se'rjal) *n.f.* serial.
sérico ('se·ri·ko) *adj.* silken.
serie ('se·rje) *n.f.* series; sequence.
serio ('se·rjo) *adj.* **1,** serious. **2,** serious-minded; sober. —**seriedad,**

n.f. seriousness. —**en serio,** seriously.
sermón (ser'mon) *n.m.* sermon. —**sermoneador,** *adj.* [*fem.* -**dora**] sermonizing; preaching. —**sermonear,** *v.i. & t.* to sermonize; lecture.
seroja (se'ro·xa) *n.f., also,* **serojo,** *n.m.* **1,** dry leaf. **2,** brushwood.
serón (se'ron) *n.m.* large basket, usu. without handles.
seroso (se'ro·so) *adj.* serous. —**serosidad,** *n.f.* serosity.
serpentear (ser·pen·te'ar) *v.i.* to wind; meander; twist.
serpentín (ser·pen'tin) *n.m.* cooling coil; coil of a still.
serpentina (ser·pen'ti·na) *n.f.* **1,** paper streamer; festoon. **2,** = **serpentín. 3,** *mineral.* serpentine.
serpentino (ser·pen'ti·no) *adj.* serpentine.
serpiente (ser'pjen·te) *n.f.* serpent.
serpollo (ser'po·ʎo; -jo) *n.m.* shoot; tiller.
serrado (se'rra·ðo) *adj.* serrate.
serrador (se·rra'ðor) *n.m.* sawyer.
serrallo (se'rra·ʎo; -jo) *n.f.* seraglio.
serrano (se'rra·no) *adj.* highland; mountain (*attrib.*). —*n.m.* highlander. —**serranía,** *n.f.* mountain region; highlands.
serrar (se'rrar) *v.t.* [*infl.:* **pensar, 27**] to saw. —**serrería** (se·rre'ri·a) *n.f.* sawmill.
serrín (se'rrin) *n.m.* sawdust.
serrucho (se'rru·tʃo) *n.m.* handsaw; carpenter's saw.
servible (ser'βi·βle) *adj.* serviceable; useful.
servicio (ser'βi·θjo; -sjo) *n.m.* **1,** service. **2,** help; servants. **3,** tableware. **4,** *Amer.* toilet; water closet. —**servicial,** *adj.* helpful; obliging.
servidor (ser·βi'ðor) *n.m.* [*fem.* -**dora**] servant. —**servidor de Vd.**, your servant; at your service.
servidumbre (ser·βi'ðum·bre) *n.f.* **1,** servants collectively; help. **2,** serfdom; servitude. —**servidumbre de paso** or **de vía**, right of way.
servil (ser'βil) *adj.* servile. —**servilismo,** *n.m.* servility.
servilleta (ser·βi'ʎe·ta; -'je·ta) *n.f.* serviette; napkin. —**servilletero,** napkin ring; napkin holder.
servio ('ser·βjo) *adj. & n.m.* Serbian; Serb.
servir (ser'βir) *v.t. & i.* [*infl.:* **pedir, 33**] **1,** to serve. **2,** to be of

use (to); avail. **—servirse,** *v.r.* **1,** to be willing; be pleased. **2,** to help oneself; take. **3,** *fol. by* **de,** to make use of. **—sírvase** ('sir·βa·se) *fol. by inf.* please. **—ir servido; ir bien servido,** to get one's due; get one's just deserts.

servocroata (ser·βo·kro'a·ta) *adj. & n.m. & f.* Serbo-Croatian.

sésamo ('se·sa·mo) *n.m.* sesame.

sesear (se·se'ar) *v.i.* to pronounce (s) for *z* and for *c* before *e* or *i.* **—seseo** (-'se·o) pronunciation as (s) of *z* and *c* before *e* or *i.*

sesenta (se'sen·ta) *adj. & n.m.* sixty. **—sesentavo,** *adj. & n.m.* sixtieth.

sesentón (se·sen'ton) *adj. & n.m.* [*fem.* **-tona**], *colloq., usu. derog.* = **sexagenario.**

sesgar (ses'γar) *v.t.* [*infl.:* **pagar, 8**] **1,** to cut on a bias; cut or tear obliquely. **2,** to bevel. **3,** to pass or cross at a slant or at an angle. **4,** to skew; slant. **—sesgado,** *adj.* aslant; askew; oblique; beveled. **—sesgadura,** *n.f.* slanting or oblique cut.

sesgo ('ses·γo) *n.m.* **1,** slant; skew; bevel; bias. **2,** *fig.* grimace; bad face. **3,** *fig.* course; direction; way. **—al sesgo, 1,** obliquely; slantingly. **2,** through; across.

sesión (se'sjon) *n.f.* **1,** session. **2,** conference; consultation.

seso ('se·so) *n.f.* brain; brains. **—devanarse los sesos,** to rack one's brain.

sestear (ses·te'ar) *v.i.* to nap; take a siesta.

sesudo (se'su·ðo) *adj.* **1,** intelligent; wise; brainy. **2,** *Amer.* stubborn.

seta ('se·ta) *n.f.* **1,** mushroom. **2,** bristle.

setecientos (se·te'θjen·tos; -'sjen·tos) *adj. & n.m.* [*fem.* **-tas**] seven hundred.

setenta (se'ten·ta) *adj. & n.m.* seventy. **—setentavo,** *adj. & n.m.* seventieth.

setentón (se·ten'ton) *adj. & n.m.* [*fem.* **-tona**] *colloq.* = **septuagenario.**

setiembre (se'tjem·bre) *n.m.* = **septiembre.**

sétimo ('se·ti·mo) *adj. & n.m.* = **séptimo.**

seto ('se·to) *n.m.* fence; garden fence; hedge.

seudo ('seu·ðo) *adj.* pseudo.

seudónimo (seu'ðo·ni·mo) *n.m.* pseudonym.

severo (se'βe·ro) *adj.* severe. **—severidad,** *n.f.* severity.

sevicia (se'βi·θja; -sja) *n.f.* excessive cruelty.

sexagenario (sek·sa·xe'na·rjo) *adj. & n.m.* sexagenarian.

sexagésimo (sek·sa'xe·si·mo) *adj. & n.m.* sixtieth. **—Sexagésima,** *n.f.* Sexagesima.

sexagonal (sek·sa·γo'nal) *adj.* = **hexagonal.**

sexcentésimo (seks·θen'te·si·mo; sek·sen-) *adj. & n.m.* six-hundredth.

sexo ('sek·só) *n.m.* **1,** sex. **2,** genitals. **—sexista,** *adj. & n.m. & f.* sexist.

sexta ('seks·ta) *n.f., mus.* sixth.

sextante (seks'tan·te) *n.m.* sextant.

sexteto (seks'te·to) *n.m.* sextet.

sextillón (seks·ti'ʎon; -'jon) *n.m.* a quadrillion sextillion; *Brit.* sextillion.

sexto ('seks·to) *adj. & n.m.* sixth.

séxtuplo ('seks·tu·plo) *adj.* sextuple. **—sextuplicar** (-pli'kar) *v.t.* [*infl.:* **tocar, 7**] to sextuple.

sexual (sek'swal) *adj.* sexual. **—sexualidad,** *n.f.* sexuality.

si (si) *conj.* **1,** if. **2,** whether. **3,** *archaic* although. **—por si,** in case; in the event that. **—si bien,** while; though. **—si no, 1,** otherwise. **2,** unless.

si (si) *n.m., mus.* si; B.

sí (si) *adv.* yes; indeed. **—n.m.** assent; consent; yea; aye; yes. **—por sí o por no,** in any case. **—sí que,** certainly. **—sí tal,** yes indeed.

sí (si) *refl.pron. 3rd pers. m. & f. sing. & pl.,* used after a prep. oneself; yourself; yourselves; himself; herself; itself; themselves. **—de por sí,** by itself. **—sobre sí,** on guard.

siamés (si·a'mes) *adj & n.m.* [*fem.* **siamesa**] Siamese.

sibarita (si·βa'ri·ta) *n.m.* sybarite. **—adj.** sybaritic. **—sibarítico,** *adj.* sybaritic.

sibila (si'βi·la) *n.f.* sibyl.

sibilante (si·βi'lan·te) *adj. & n.f.* sibilant.

sicario (si'ka·rjo) *n.m.* **1,** hired assassin. **2,** henchman.

siclo ('si·klo) *n.m.* shekel.

sicoanálisis *n.m.* = **psicoanálisis.** **—sicoanalista,** *n.m. & f.* = **psicoanalista. —sicoanalítico,** *adj.* =

psicoanalítico. —sicoanalizar, v.t.
= psicoanalizar.
sicofante (si·ko'fan·te) also,
sicofanta (-ta) n.m. sycophant.
sicología n.f. = **psicología.**
—sicológico, adj. = **psicológico.**
—sicólogo, n.m. = **psicólogo.**
sicómoro (si'ko·mo·ro) n.m. sycamore.
sicópata n.m. = **psicópata.**
—sicopatía, n.f. = **psicopatía.**
—sicopático, adj. = psicopático.
sicopatología n.f. = psicopatología.
sicosis n.f. = psicosis.
sicosomático adj. = psicosomático.
sicoterapia n.f. = psicoterapia.
SIDA, abbr. of **síndrome de
inmunodeficiencia adquirida,** acquired immune deficiency syndrome (abbr. AIDS).
sideral (si·ðe'ral) adj. sidereal.
Also, **sidéreo** (-'ðe·re·o).
siderurgia (si·ðe'rur·xja) n.f. iron
or steel metallurgy. —**siderúrgico**
(-xi·ko) adj. of or pert. to the iron
or steel industry; steel (attrib.).
sido ('si·ðo) v., p.p. of **ser.**
sidra ('si·ðra) n.f. cider.
siega ('sje·ɣa) n.f. harvest; harvesting; reaping.
siego ('sje·ɣo) v., 1st pers.sing.
pres. ind. of **segar.**
siegue ('sje·ɣe) v., pres.subjve. of
segar.
siembra ('sjem·bra) n.f. **1,** sowing.
2, sowing season. **3,** = **sembrado.**
siembre ('sjem·bre) v., pres.subjve.
of **sembrar.**
siembro (-'bro) v., 1st pers.sing.
pres.ind. of **sembrar.**
siempre ('sjem·pre) adv. **1,** always; ever; forever. **2,** Amer. anyway; in any case. —**de siempre,** accustomed; usual. —**por siempre
jamás,** forever and ever. —**siempre que, 1,** whenever. **2,** [also,
siempre y cuando que] provided.
siempreviva (sjem·pre'βi·βa)
n.f., bot. everlasting; immortelle.
sien (sjen) n.f., anat. temple.
siena ('sje·na) n.f. sienna.
siendo ('sjen·do) v., ger. of **ser.**
sienta ('sjen·ta) v. **1,** pres.subjve.
of **sentir. 2,** 3rd pers.sing.pres.ind.
of **sentar.**
siente ('sjen·te) v. **1,** pres.subjve.
of **sentar. 2,** 3rd pers.sing.pres.ind.
of **sentir.**
siento ('sjen·to) v., 1st

pers.sing.pres.ind. of **sentar** and
sentir.
sierpe ('sjer·pe) n.f. serpent.
sierra ('sje·rra) n.f. **1,** saw. **2,**
mountain range. **3,** sawfish.
sierre ('sje·rre) v., pres.subjve. of
serrar.
sierro ('sje·rro) v., 1st pers.sing.
pres.ind. of **serrar.**
siervo ('sjer·βo) n.m. **1,** serf; slave.
2, servant.
siesta ('sjes·ta) n.f. siesta.
siete ('sje·te) adj. & n.m. seven.
—n.m. a V-shaped rent or tear.
sífilis ('si·fi·lis) n.f. syphilis.
—**sifilítico** (-'li·ti·ko) adj. & n.m.
syphilitic.
sifón (si'fon) n.m. siphon.
siga ('si·ɣa) v., pres.subjve. of
seguir.
sigilar (si·xi'lar) v.t. **1,** to conceal;
secrete. **2,** archaic to seal.
sigilo (si'xi·lo) n.m. **1,** secrecy. **2,**
stealth. **3,** caution; reserve. **4,** archaic seal.
sigiloso (si·xi'lo·so) adj. **1,** secretive. **2,** stealthy. **3,** reticent; reserved.
sigla ('si·ɣla) n.f. acronym.
siglo ('si·ɣlo) n.m. **1,** century. **2,**
age; epoch. **3,** fig. world; worldly
affairs.
signar (siɣ'nar) v.t. **1,** to stamp;
mark. **2,** archaic to sign. —**signar-
se,** v.r. to cross oneself three times
(on the brow, on the mouth, and on
the breast) invoking divine deliverance from enemies.
signatario (siɣ·na'ta·rjo) adj. &
n.m. signatory.
signatura (siɣ·na'tu·ra) n.f. **1,**
sign; mark. **2,** signing; signature. **3,**
print. signature.
significado (siɣ·ni·fi'ka·ðo)
adj. important; significant; eminent.
—n.m. **1,** meaning; significance. **2,**
[also, **significación,** n.f.] signification.
significar (siɣ·ni·fi'kar) v.t. [infl.:
tocar, 7] to signify; mean. —v.i. to
have importance; be significant.
—**significativo; significante,** adj.
significant.
signo ('siɣ·no) n.m. sign; mark;
character; symbol.
sigo ('si·ɣo) v., 1st pers.sing.
pres.ind. of **seguir.**
siguiendo (si'ɣjen·do) v., ger. of
seguir.
siguiente (si'ɣjen·te) adj. following; next.

siguió (si'yjo) *v., 3rd pers.sing. pret. of* seguir.

sílaba ('si·la·βa) *n.f.* syllable. —**silabario** (-'βa·rjo) *n.m.* spelling book. —**silábico** (si'la·βi·ko) *adj.* syllabic.

silabear (si·la·βe'ar) *v.t.* to syllabicate. —*v.i.* to speak in syllables. —**silabeo** (-'βe·o) *n.m.* syllabication.

sílabo ('si·la·βo) *n.m.* syllabus.

silbar (sil'βar) *v.t. & i.* to whistle. —*v.i.* to hiss (a performance). —**silbato** (-'βa·to) *n.m.* whistle (*device*). —**silbido** (-'βi·ðo) *n.m.* whistling; whistle; hiss.

silenciar (si·len'θjar; -'sjar) *v.t.* to silence. —**silenciador**, *n.m.* silencer; muffler.

silencio (si'len·θjo; -sjo) *n.m.* silence. —**silencioso**, *adj.* silent.

sílfide ('sil·fi·ðe) *n.f.* sylph.

silfo ('sil·fo) *n.m.* sylph.

silicato (si·li'ka·to) *n.m.* silicate.

sílice ('si·li·θe; -se) *n.m.* silica.

silíceo (sɪ'li·θe·o; -se·o) *adj.* siliceous.

silicio (si'li·θjo; -sjo) *n.m.* silicon.

silicón (si·li'kon) *n.m.* silicone.

silicosis (si·li'ko·sis) *n.f.* silicosis.

silo ('si·lo) *also,* **silero** (si'le·ro) *n.m.* silo.

silogismo (si·lo'xis·mo) *n.m.* syllogism.

silueta (si'lwe·ta) *n.f.* silhouette.

silvestre (sil'βes·tre) *adj.* wild; uncultivated.

silla ('si·ʎa; -ja) *n.f.* 1, chair. 2, saddle. 3, *eccles.* see. —**silleta**, *n.f.* folding chair. —**sillón**, *n.m.* armchair.

sillín (si'ʎin; -'jin) *n.m.* 1, light riding saddle. 2, bicycle or motorcycle seat.

sima ('si·ma) *n.f.* abyss; chasm.

simbiosis (sim'bjo·sis) *n.f.* symbiosis. —**simbiótico** (-'bjo·ti·ko) *adj.* symbiotic.

símbolo ('sim·bo·lo) *n.m.* symbol; token. —**simbólico** (-'bo·li·ko) *adj.* symbolic. —**simbolismo**, *n.m.* symbolism. —**simbolizar** (-li'θar; -'sar) *v.t.* [*infl.:* rezar, 10] to symbolize.

simetría (si·me'tri·a) *n.f.* symmetry. —**simétrico** (-'me·tri·ko) *adj.* symmetrical.

símico ('si·mi·ko) *adj.* simian.

simiente (si'mjen·te) *n.f.* seed.

simiesco (si'mjes·ko) *adj.* simian.

símil ('si·mil) *adj.* similar; like —*n.m.* 1, similarity. 2, simile.

—**similar**, *adj.* similar. —**similitud**, *n.f.* similitude.

similor (si·mi'lor) *n.m.* imitation gold; ormolu.

simio ('si·mjo) *n.m.* male ape or monkey; simian.

simonía (si·mo'ni·a) *n.f.* simony.

simpatía (sim·pa'ti·a) *n.f.* 1, sympathy. 2, congeniality.

simpático (sim'pa·ti·ko) *adj.* 1, sympathetic. 2, congenial; likable. 3, pleasant; agreeable.

simpatizar (sim·pa·ti'θar; -'sar) *v.i.* [*infl.:* rezar, 10] 1, to sympathize. 2, to be congenial; get along.

simple ('sim·ple) *adj.* 1, simple; plain. 2, single. 3, silly; foolish.

simpleza (sim'ple·θa; -sa) *n.f.* 1, simpleness; plainness. 2, silliness; foolishness. 3, trifle.

simplicidad (sim·pli·θi'ðað; -si'ðað) *n.f.* 1, simplicity. 2, candor; ingenuousness.

simplificar (sim·pli·fi'kar) *v.t.* [*infl.:* tocar, 7] to simplify. —**simplificación**, *n.f.* simplification.

simplón (sim'plon) *n.m.* [*fem.* -plona] simpleton.

simulacro (si·mu'la·kro) *n.m.* 1, image. 2, sham; parody. 3, *mil.* training exercise; combat drill.

simular (si·mu'lar) *v.t.* to simulate. —**simulación**, *n.f.* simulation.

simultáneo (si·mul'ta·ne·o) *adj.* simultaneous. —**simultaneidad**, *n.f.* simultaneousness.

simún (si'mun) *n.m.* simoom.

sin (sin) *prep.* without. —**sin que**, without: *Salió sin que lo viéramos,* He left without our seeing him.

sinagoga (si·na'yo·ya) *n.f.* synagogue.

sinapismo (si·na'pis·mo) *n.m.* 1, mustard plaster. 2, = cataplasma.

sinapsis (si'nap·sis) *n.f.* synapse.

sincerarse (sin·θe'rar·se; sin·se-) *v.r.* to speak candidly; unbosom oneself.

sincero (sin'θe·ro; -'se·ro) *adj.* sincere. —**sinceridad**, *n.f.* sincerity.

síncopa ('sin·ko·pa) *n.f.* 1, *gram.* syncope. 2, *mus.* syncopation. —**sincopar**, *v.t.* to syncopate.

síncope ('sin·ko·pe) *n.m.* 1, *gram.* = síncopa. 2, *med.* syncope; fainting spell.

sincrónico (sin'kro·ni·ko) *adj.* synchronous.

sincronizar (sin·kro·ni'θar; -'sar) *v.t.* [*infl.:* rezar, 10] to synchronize.

—**sincronización,** *n.f.* synchronization.

sindicalismo (sin·di·ka'lis·mo) *n.m.* unionism. —**sindicalista,** *n.m. & f.* unionist.

sindicar (sin·di'kar) *v.t.* [*infl.:* **tocar,** 7] to syndicate; unionize. —**sindicación,** *n.f.* syndication; unionization. —**sindicato** (-'ka·to) *n.m.* syndicate; union.

síndico ('sin·di·ko) *n.m.* **1,** *law* receiver. **2,** trustee; board member.

sindiós (sin'djos) *adj. & n.m. & f. sing. & pl.* godless.

síndrome ('sin·dro·me) *n.m.* syndrome.

sinecura (si·ne'ku·ra) *n.f.* sinecure.

sinfín (sin'fin) *n.m.* endless number or quantity.

sinfonía (sin·fo'ni·a) *n.f.* symphony. —**sinfónico** (-'fo·ni·ko) *adj.* symphonic.

singlón (sin'glon) *n.m.* yardarm.

singular (sin·gu'lar) *adj.* singular; unique. —**singularidad,** *n.f.* singularity; uniqueness. —**singularizarse** (-ri'θar·se; -'sar·se) *v.r.* [*infl.:* **rezar,** 10] to distinguish oneself.

sinhueso (sin'we·so) *n.f., colloq.* tongue.

siniestro (si'njes·tro) *adj.* **1,** sinister. **2,** left. —*n.m.* disaster. —**siniestra,** *n.f.* left hand; left side.

sinnúmero (sin'nu·me·ro) *n.m.* countless number. —**un sinnúmero de ... ,** countless ...

sino ('si·no) *conj.* but; except; only. —*n.m.* fate.

sínodo ('si·no·ðo) *n.m.* synod. —**sinodal,** *adj.* synodal.

sinónimo (si'no·ni·mo) *adj.* synonymous. —*n.m.* synonym.

sinopsis (si'nop·sis) *n.f. sing. & pl.* synopsis. —**sinóptico** (-'nop·ti·ko) *adj.* synoptic.

sinrazón (sin·ra'θon; -'son) *n.f.* **1,** unreason. **2,** injustice; wrong.

sinsabor (sin·sa'βor) *n.m.* **1,** insipidity. **2,** *fig.* trouble; worry.

sinsonte (sin'son·te) *n.m.* mockingbird.

sintaxis (sin'tak·sis) *n.f.* syntax. —**sintáctico** (-'tak·ti·ko) *adj.* syntactical.

síntesis ('sin·te·sis) *n.f. sing. & pl.* synthesis. —**sintético** (-'te·ti·ko) *adj.* synthetic. —**sintetizar** (-ti'θar; -'sar) *v.t.* [*infl.:* **rezar,** 10] to synthesize. —**sintetizador** (sin·te·ti·θa'ðor; -sa'ðor) *n.m.* synthesizer.

sintiendo (sin'tjen·do) *v., ger. of* **sentir.**

sintió (sin'tjo) *v., 3rd pers.sing. pret. of* **sentir.**

sintoísmo (sin·to'is·mo) *n.m.* Shinto; Shintoism. —**sintoísta,** *adj.* Shinto; Shintoist. —*n.m. & f.* Shintoist.

síntoma ('sin·to·ma) *n.m.* symptom; sign. —**sintomático** (-'ma·ti·ko) *adj.* symptomatic.

sintonizar (sin·to·ni'θar; -'sar) *v.t.* [*infl.:* **rezar,** 10] to tune in. —**sintonización,** *n.f.* tuning. —**sintonizador,** *n.m.* tuner.

sinuoso (si'nwo·so) *adj.* sinuous. —**sinuosidad,** *n.f.* sinuosity.

sinusitis (si·nu'si·tis) *n.f.* sinusitis.

sinvergonzonería (sin·βer·γon·θo·ne'ri·a; -so·ne'ri·a) *n.f., colloq.* **1,** shamelessness; brazenness. **2,** low trick; dastardly act. —**sinvergonzón** (-'θon; -'son) *n.m.* [*fem.* **-zona**] *colloq.* scamp; so-and-so.

sinvergüenza (sin·βer'γwen·θa; -sa) *adj.* shameless; brazen. —*n.m.* rascal; scoundrel. —*n.f.* wanton; hussy. —**sinvergüenzada,** *n.f., colloq.* low trick; dastardly act. —**sinvergüencería** (-θe'ri·a; -se'ri·a) *n.f., colloq.* = **sinvergonzonería.** —**sinvergüenzón** (-'θon; -'son) *n.m.* = **sinvergonzón.**

Sión (si'on) *n.f.* Zion. —**sionismo,** *n.m.* Zionism. —**sionista,** *adj. & n.m. & f.* Zionist.

sique *n.f.* = **psique.**

siquiatría *n.f.* = **psiquiatría.** —**siquiatra,** *n.m. & f.* = **psiquiatra.** —**siquiátrico,** *adj.* = **psiquiátrico.**

síquico *adj.* = **psíquico.**

siquiera (si'kje·ra) *adv.* at least. —*conj.* though; although. —**ni siquiera,** not even.

siquis *n.f.* = **psiquis.**

sirena (si're·na) *n.f.* siren.

sirga ('sir·γa) *n.f.* tow rope; tow line.

Sirio ('si·rjo) *n.m.* Dog Star; Sirius.

siroco (si'ro·ko) *n.m.* sirocco.

sirsaca (sir'sa·ka) *n.f.* seersucker.

sirva ('sir·βa) *v., pres.subjve. of* **servir.**

sirviendo (sir'βjen·do) *v., ger. of* **servir.**

sirviente (sir'βjen·te) *n.m.* [*fem.* **sirvienta**] servant; domestic.

sirvió (sir'βjo) *v., 3rd pers.sing. pret. of* **servir.**

sirvo ('sir·βo) v., 1st pers.sing. pres.ind.of **servir**.

sisa ('si·sa) n.f. **1**, pilferage; cheating, esp. in domestic accounts. **2**, dart in a garment.

sisal (si'sal) n.m., Amer. sisal; sisal hemp.

sisar (si'sar) v.t. **1**, to cheat; pilfer. **2**, to take in (a garment).

sisear (si·se'ar) v.t. & i. to hiss. —**siseo** (-'se·o) n.m. hissing.

sísmico ('sis·mi·ko) adj. seismic.

sismo ('sis·mo) n.m. earthquake.

sismógrafo (sis'mo·yra·fo) n.m. seismograph. —**sismográfico** (-'yra·fi·ko) adj. seismographic. —**sismograma** (-'yra·ma) n.m. seismogram.

sismología (sis·mo·lo'xi·a) n.f. seismology. —**sismológico** (-'lo·xi·ko) adj. seismological. —**sismólogo** (-'mo·lo·yo) n.m., also, **sismologista** (-'xis·ta) n.m. & f. seismologist. —**sismómetro** (sis'mo·me·tro) n.m. seismometer.

sistema (sis'te·ma) n.m. system. —**sistemático** (-'ma·ti·ko) adj. systematic. —**sistematizar** (-ti'θar; -'sar) v.t. [infl.: rezar, 10] to systematize.

sístole ('sis·to·le) n.m. systole. —**sistólico** (-'to·li·ko) adj. systolic.

sitial (si'tjal) n.m. seat of honor.

sitiar (si'tjar) v.t. to besiege; surround.

sitio ('si·tjo) n.m. **1**, place; site; location. **2**, siege.

sito ('si·to) adj. situated; located.

situación (si·twa'θjon; -'sjon) n.f. **1**, situation; position; location. **2**, condition; circumstances.

situar (si'twar) v.t. [infl.: continuar, 23] to situate; locate; place.

smoking ('smo·kin) n.m. [pl. smokings (-kins)] dinner jacket; tuxedo.

snob (snob) n.m. & f. = **esnob**. —**snobismo**, n.m. = **esnobismo**.

so (so) prep. under; below. —interj. whoa!

soasar (so·a'sar) v.t. to roast lightly; broil.

soba ('so·βa) n.f. **1**, squeezing; pressing; kneading. **2**, rub; rubbing; massage. **3**, colloq. pawing; fondling. **4**, colloq. fawning; servile flattery. **5**, colloq. drubbing. **6**, colloq. bother; annoyance.

sobaco (so'βa·ko) n.m. armpit.

sobado (so'βa·ðo) adj. trite; hackneyed; stale. —n.m. = **sobadura**.

sobadura (so·βa'ðu·ra) n.f. **1**, rub; rubbing; massage. **2**, squeezing; pressing; kneading.

sobajar (so·βa'xar) v.t. **1**, to handle; paw. **2**, Amer. to degrade; humiliate.

sobajear (so·βa·xe'ar) v.t., Amer. to handle; paw. —**sobajeo** (-'xe·o) n.m. handling; pawing.

sobaquera (so·βa'ke·ra) n.f. **1**, armhole. **2**, shield for the armpit. **3**, Amer. = **sobaquina**.

sobaquina (so·βa'ki·na) n.f. underarm perspiration.

sobar (so'βar) v.t. **1**, to squeeze; press; knead. **2**, to rub; massage. **3**, colloq. to paw; fondle. **4**, colloq. to fawn on; toady to. **5**, colloq. to beat; give a drubbing to. **6**, colloq. to displease; molest.

soberano (so·βe'ra·no) n.m. & adj. sovereign. —**soberanía**, n.f. sovereignty.

soberbia (so'βer·βja) n.f. **1**, arrogance; haughtiness. **2**, magnificence.

soberbio (so'βer·βjo) adj. **1**, arrogant; haughty; overbearing. **2**, magnificent; superb.

sobina (so'βi·na) n.f. wooden pin; peg.

sobón (so'βon) adj., colloq. fawning; obsequious. —n.m., colloq. toady.

sobornal (so·βor'nal) n.m. surcharge.

sobornar (so·βor'nar) v.t. to suborn; bribe. —**sobornación**, n.f. bribing; subornation. —**soborno** (so'βor·no) n.m. bribe; bribing; subornation.

sobra ('so·βra) n.f. excess; remainder. —**sobras**, n.f.pl. leftovers. —**de sobra**, **1**, ample; amply; more than enough. **2**, redundant; unnecessary; superfluous.

sobrado (so'βra·ðo) adj. **1**, redundant; superfluous; excessive. **2**, well-provided; well-off. **3**, intemperate; immoderate. —adv. **1**, amply; well. **2**, too; too much. —n.m. **1**, attic; garret. **2**, usu.pl., Amer. leftovers.

sobrante (so'βran·te) adj. excess; extra; leftover. —n.m. excess; remainder.

sobrar (so'βrar) v.t. **1**, to exceed. **2**, to excel. —v.i. **1**, to be ample; be more than sufficient. **2**, to be unnecessary; be superfluous. **3**, to be left over; remain.

sobre ('so·βre) *prep & adv.* over; above. —*prep.* **1**, on; upon; on top of. **2**, about; concerning. **3**, after; following. **4**, beyond; besides. —*n.m.* **1**, envelope. **2**, = **sobrescrito.**

sobreabundante (so·βre·a·βun'dan·te) *adj.* superabundant. —**sobreabundancia,** *n.f.* superabundance.

sobreagudo (so·βre·a'ɣu·ðo) *adj. & n.m., mus.* treble.

sobrealiento (so·βre·a'ljen·to) *n.m.* labored breathing.

sobrealzar (so·βre·al'θar; -'sar) *v.t.* [*infl.:* **rezar, 10**] to extol; laud.

sobrecama (so·βre'ka·ma) *n.f.* bedspread.

sobrecarga (so·βre'kar·ɣa) *n.f.* overload; surcharge. —**sobrecargar,** *v.t.* [*infl.:* **pagar, 8**] to overload; surcharge.

sobrecargo (so·βre'kar·ɣo) *n.m.* supercargo.

sobreceja (so·βre'θe·xa; -'se·xa) *n.f.* ridge of the brow.

sobreceño (so·βre'θe·ɲo; -'se·ɲo) *n.m.* frown.

sobrecincha (so·βre'θin·tʃa; -'sin·tʃa) *n.f.* surcingle. *Also,* **sobrecincho,** *n.m.*

sobrecoger (so·βre·ko'xer) *v.t.* [*infl.:* **coger, 15**] to catch up with; overtake. —**sobrecogerse,** *v.r.* **1**, to be overcome; be overwhelmed. **2**, to be seized with fear or apprehension. —**sobrecogimiento,** *n.m.* fear.

sobrecubierta (so·βre·ku'βjer·ta) *n.f.* **1**, double wrapper. **2**, dust jacket. **3**, *naut.* upper deck.

sobredicho (so·βre'ði·tʃo) *adj.* aforesaid.

sobreentender (so·βre·en·ten·'der) *v.t.* = **sobrentender.**

sobreestimar (so·βre·es·ti'mar) *v.t.* to overestimate. —**sobreestimación,** *n.f.* overestimation.

sobreexceder (so·βre·eks·θe'ðer; -ek·se'ðer) *v.t.* = **sobrexceder.**

sobreexcitar (so·βre·eks·θi'tar; -ek·si'tar) *v.t.* to overexcite. —**sobreexcitación,** *n.f.* overexcitement.

sobreexponer (so·βre·eks·po·'ner) *v.t.* [*infl.:* **poner, 54**] to overexpose. —**sobreexposición** (-po·si·'θjon; -'sjon) *n.f.* overexposure.

sobrefalda (so·βre'fal·da) *n.f.* overskirt.

sobregirar (so·βre·xi'rar) *v.t. & i.,* comm. to overdraw. —**sobregiro** (-'xi·ro) *n.m.* overdraft.

sobrehilar (so·βre·i'lar) *v.t., sewing* to overcast. —**sobrehilado,** *adj. & n.m.* overcast.

sobrehumano (so·βre·u'ma·no) *adj.* superhuman.

sobrellenar (so·βre·ʎe'nar; -je·'nar) *v.t.* to overfill; overflow.

sobrellevar (so·βre·ʎe'βar; -je·'βar) *v.t.* to endure; put up with.

sobremanera (so·βre·ma'ne·ra) *adv.* exceedingly.

sobremarcha (so·βre'mar·tʃa) *n.f., mech.* overdrive.

sobremesa (so·βre'me·sa) *n.f.* **1**, tablecloth; table cover. **2**, after-dinner amenities. —**de sobremesa,** after-dinner.

sobrenadar (so·βre·na'ðar) *v.i.* to float; swim on the surface.

sobrenatural (so·βre·na·tu'ral) *adj.* supernatural.

sobrenombre (so·βre'nom·bre) *n.m.* nickname; cognomen.

sobrentender (so·βren·ten'der) *v.t.* [*infl.:* **perder, 29**] to understand; assume; take for granted.

sobrepasar (so·βre·pa'sar) *v.t.* to surpass. —**sobrepasarse,** *v.r.* to overstep one's bounds.

sobrepelliz (so·βre·pe'ʎiθ; -'jis) *n.f.* surplice.

sobrepeso (so·βre'pe·so) *n.m.* overweight; excess weight.

sobreponer (so·βre·po'ner) *v.t.* [*infl.:* **poner, 54**] to superimpose. —**sobreponerse,** *v.r., fol. by* **a,** to overcome; master.

sobreprecio (so·βre'pre·θjo; -sjo) *n.m.* surcharge.

sobrepuesto (so·βre'pwes·to) *v.,* *p.p.* of **sobreponer.** —*adj. & n.m.* appliqué. —*n.m., Amer.* patch; mend.

sobrepujar (so·βre·pu'xar) *v.t.* to outdo; outstrip.

sobresaliente (so·βre·sa'ljen·te) *adj.* **1**, outstanding; excellent. **2**, projecting; protruding. —*n.m.* [*fem.* **sobresalienta**] substitute; understudy.

sobresalir (so·βre·sa'lir) *v.i.* [*infl.:* **salir, 63**] **1**, to stand out; excel. **2**, to project; protrude.

sobresaltar (so·βre·sal'tar) *v.t.* to startle; frighten. —*v.i.* to stand out; show up clearly. —**sobresaltarse,** *v.r.* to take fright; be startled. —**sobresalto** (-'sal·to) *n.m.* start; fright. —**de sobresalto,** suddenly.

sobrescribir (so·βres·kri'βir) v.t. [p.p. **sobrescrito** (-'kri·to)] **1,** to superscribe. **2,** to address (a letter or package). —**sobrescrito,** n.m. address (on a letter or package).

sobrestante (so·βres'tan·te) n.m. foreman; supervisor.

sobrestimar (so·βres·ti'mar) v.t. = **sobreestimar.**

sobresueldo (so·βre'swel·do) n.m. extra pay; bonus.

sobretodo (so·βre'to·ðo) n.m. overcoat.

sobrevenir (so·βre·βe'nir) v.i. [infl.: venir, 69] to befall; happen; supervene.

sobrevivir (so·βre·βi'βir) v.t. & i. to survive. —**sobreviviente,** adj. & n.m. & f. survivor.

sobrexceder (so·βreks·θe'ðer; so·βrek·se'ðer) v.t. to exceed; outdo; excel; surpass.

sobriedad (so·βrje'ðað) n.f. **1,** sobriety. **2,** frugality.

sobrina (so'βri·na) n.f. niece. —**sobrino,** n.m. nephew.

sobrio (so'βrjo) adj. **1,** sober. **2,** sparing; frugal.

socaire (so'kai·re) n.m. lee; shelter. —**estar** or **ponerse al socaire,** colloq. to shirk.

socapa (so'ka·pa) n.f. pretense; pretext; cloak. —**a socapa,** surreptitiously.

socarrar (so·ka'rrar) v.t. to singe. —**socarra** (-'ka·rra) n.f. singe; singeing.

socarrón (so·ka'rron) adj. **1,** ironic; jesting; mocking. **2,** cunning; roguish; rascally.

socarronería (so·ka·rro·ne'ri·a) n.f. **1,** irony; mockery; jest. **2,** roguishness; cunning.

socavar (so·ka'βar) v.t. to undermine; dig under. —**socavación,** also, **socava** (-'ka·βa) n.f. undermining; digging under. —**socavón** (-'βon) n.m. tunnel; dugout.

sociable (so'θja·βle; -'sja·βle) adj. sociable. —**sociabilidad,** n.f. sociability.

social (so'θjal; -'sjal) adj. **1,** social. **2,** of or pert. to a company or association. **3,** colloq. sociable.

socialismo (so·θja'lis·mo; so·sja-) n.m. socialism. —**socialista,** adj. & n.m. & f. socialist. —adj. socialistic.

socializar (so·θja·li'θar; -sja·li'sar) v.t. [infl.: rezar, 10] to social-

ize. —**socialización,** n.f. socialization.

sociedad (so·θje'ðað; so·sje-) n.f. **1,** society. **2,** high society; the fashionable world. **3,** partnership. **4,** corporation; company; organization. —**sociedad anónima,** stock company; corporation.

socio ('so·θjo; -sjo) n.m. partner; member; associate. —**socio fundador,** charter member.

sociología (so·θjo·lo'xi·a; so·sjo-) n.f. sociology. —**sociológico** (-'lo·xi·ko) adj. sociological. —**sociólogo** (so'θjo·lo·ɣo; -'sjo·lo·ɣo) n.m. sociologist.

socolor (so·ko'lor) n.m. guise; pretense.

socorrer (so·ko'rrer) v.t. **1,** to succor; give help or relief to. **2,** to favor.

socorrido (so·ko'rri·ðo) adj. **1,** well-stocked; well-supplied. **2,** hackneyed; worn; trite.

socorro (so'ko·rro) n.m. succor; help; aid.

soda ('so·ða) n.f. soda.

sodio ('so·ðjo) n.m. sodium.

sodomía (so·ðo'mi·a) n.f. sodomy. —**sodomita,** n.m. & f. sodomite.

soez (so'eθ; -'es) adj. low; vulgar.

sofá (so'fa) n.m. sofa.

sófbol ('sof·βol) n.m. softball.

sofisma (so'fis·ma) n.m. sophism. —**sofista,** adj. sophistic. —n.m. & f. sophist. —**sofistería,** n.f. sophistry.

sofisticar (so·fis·ti'kar) v.t. [infl.: tocar, 7] to sophisticate. —**sofisticación,** n.f. sophistication.

soflama (so'fla·ma) n.f. **1,** flicker; glow. **2,** blush. **3,** derog. bombastic speech.

sofocar (so·fo'kar) v.t. [infl.: tocar, 7] to suffocate; smother. —**sofocarse,** v.r. **1,** to suffocate. **2,** to be discomfited or embarrassed. —**sofocación,** n.f. suffocation. —**sofocante,** adj. suffocating; oppressive.

sofoco (so'fo·ko) n.m. **1,** suffocation. **2,** shame; embarrassment. **3,** shock; jolt; upset.

sofreír (so·fre'ir) v.t. [infl.: reír, 58] to fry lightly.

sofrenar (so·fre'nar) v.t. to curb; check; restrain.

sofrito (so'fri·to) v., p.p. of **sofreír.** —n.m. fry.

soga ('so·ɣa) n.f. rope.

sois (sois) v., 2nd pers.pl.pres.ind. of **ser.**

soja ('so·xa) *n.f.* = **soya.**

sojuzgar (so·xuθ'yar; so·xus-) *v.t.* [*infl.*: **pagar,** 8] to subjugate; subdue.

sol (sol) *n.m.* 1, sun. 2, sunshine; sunlight. 3, *mus.* sol; G. 4, monetary unit of Peru; sol. —**hacer sol,** to be sunny.

solacear (so·la·θe'ar; -se'ar) *v.t.* = **solazar.**

solamente (so·la'men·te) *adv.* only; merely; just; solely. —**solamente que,** only that; unless.

solana (so'la·na) *n.f.* 1, sun porch. 2, sunny spot.

solano (so'la·no) *n.m.* 1, nightshade. 2, east wind.

solapa (so'la·pa) *n.f.* 1, lapel. 2, *fig.* pretext; cloak. —**solapado,** *adj.* deceitful; underhanded. —**de solapa,** underhandedly; deceitfully.

solar (so'lar) *n.m.* 1, lot; plot of ground. 2, ancestry; lineage; house. 3, heritage. —*adj.* solar.

solar (so'lar) *v.t.* [*infl.*: **acostar,** 28] 1, to sole (shoes). 2, to pave; floor.

solariego (so·la'rje·yo) *adj.* ancestral. —**casa solariega,** family home; homestead; manor.

solario (so'la·rjo) *n.m.* solarium.

solaz (so'laθ; -'las) *n.m.* 1, solace. 2, enjoyment; recreation.

solazar (so·la'θar; -'sar) *v.t.* [*infl.*: **rezar,** 10] to solace.

soldado (sol'da·ðo) *n.m.* soldier. —**soldadesca,** *n.f.* soldiery. —**soldadesco,** *adj.* soldierly. —**soldado raso,** private.

soldador (sol·da'ðor) *n.m.* 1, [*fem.* -**dora**] welder; solderer. 2, soldering iron; soldering gun.

soldadura (sol·da'ðu·ra) *n.f.* 1, solder. 2, soldering. 3, weld.

soldar (sol'dar) *v.t.* [*infl.*: **acostar,** 28] to solder; weld.

solear (so·le'ar) *v.t.* to sun.

solecismo (so·le'θis·mo; -'sis·mo) *n.m.* solecism.

soledad (so·le'ðað) *n.f.* solitude; loneliness.

solemne (so'lem·ne) *adj.* solemn. —**solemnidad,** *n.f.* solemnity. —**solemnizar** (-ni'θar, -'sar) *v.t.* [*infl.*: **rezar,** 10] to solemnize.

solenoide (so·le'noi·ðe) *n.m.* solenoid.

soler (so'ler) *v.i.* [*infl.*: **mover,** 30] *defective, used only in pres.ind., pres.subjve. and impf.* to be used (to); be accustomed (to); be customary (to); do often.

solera (so'le·ra) *n.f.* crossbeam.

solevantar (so·le·βan'tar) *v.t.* 1, to agitate; stir; stir up. 2, = **solevar.** —**solevantado,** *adj.* restless; excited. —**solevantamiento,** *n.m.* upheaval; uprising.

solevar (so·le'βar) *v.t.* to raise; lift.

solfa ('sol·fa) *n.f.* 1, solmization. 2, *fig.* music. 3, *colloq.* beating; drubbing. 4, *colloq.* reprimand; scolding. 5, *colloq.* harping; ranting. —**poner en solfa,** to set to music.

solfear (sol·fe'ar) *v.t. & i.* 1, to sing or play in solmization. 2, *colloq.* to harp (on); rant. —**solfeo** (-'fe·o) *n.m.* solmization.

solferino (sol·fe'ri·no) *adj.* reddish-purple.

solicitar (so·li·θi'tar; -si'tar) *v.t.* 1, to solicit; entreat. 2, to request; demand. 3, to further; promote. —**solicitación,** *n.f.* solicitation. —**solicitado,** *adj.* in demand; sought after. —**solicitador,** *n.m.* [*fem.* -**dora**] solicitor. —**solicitante,** *n.m. & f.* applicant; petitioner.

solícito (so'li·θi·to; -si·to) *adj.* solicitous.

solicitud (so·li·θi'tuð; -si'tuð) *n.f.* 1, solicitude. 2, application; request; appeal; demand.

solidar (so·li'ðar) *v.t.* 1, = **consolidar.** 2, to affirm; establish.

solidario (so·li'ða·rjo) *adj.* 1, solidary. 2, united; unanimous; at one. —**solidaridad,** *n.f.* solidarity.

solidarizar (so·li·ða·ri'θar; -'sar) *v.i.* [*infl.*: **rezar,** 10] *fol. by* **con,** to make common cause with; stand together with.

solidificar (so·li·ði·fi'kar) *v.t.* [*infl.*: **tocar,** 7] to solidify. —**solidificación,** *n.f.* solidification.

sólido ('so·li·ðo) *adj. & n.m.* solid. —**solidez,** *n.f.* solidity.

soliloquio (so·li'lo·kjo) *n.m.* soliloquy. —**soliloquiar,** *v.i., colloq.* to soliloquize.

solista (so'lis·ta) *n.m. & f.* soloist.

solitaria (so·li'ta·rja) *n.f.* tapeworm.

solitario (so·li'ta·rjo) *adj. & n.m.* solitary. —*n.m.* solitaire.

sólito ('so·li·to) *adj.* accustomed; usual.

solitud (so·li'tuð) *n.f.* solitude.

soliviantar (so·li·βjan'tar) *v.t.* to arouse; incite. —**soliviantado,** *adj.* restless; excited; aroused.

soliviar (so·li'βjar) *v.t.* to raise; prop; lift.

solo ('so·lo) *adj.* **1,** alone. **2,** single; only; sole. **3,** lonely. —*n.m.* solo. —**sólo,** *adv.* = **solamente.**

solomillo (so·lo'mi·ʎo; -jo) *also,* **solomo** (so'lo·mo) *n.m.* loin; sirloin.

solsticio (sols'ti·θjo; -sjo) *n.m.* solstice.

soltar (sol'tar) *v.t.* [*infl.:* **acostar,** 28] **1,** to untie. **2,** to loosen; let out. **3,** to let go; loose; release. —**soltarse,** *v.r.* **1,** to loosen; become loose. **2,** to come off. **3,** to lose restraint. —**soltar a,** *fol. by inf.* to begin; set out.

soltería (sol·te'ri·a) *n.f.* **1,** bachelorhood. **2,** spinsterhood.

soltero (sol'te·ro) *adj.* unmarried. —*n.m.* bachelor; unmarried man. —**soltera,** *n.f.* spinster. —**solterón,** *n.m.* confirmed bachelor. —**solterona,** *n.f.* old maid.

soltura (sol'tu·ra) *n.f.* **1,** loosing. **2,** ease; freedom. **3,** fluency.

soluble (so'lu·βle) *adj.* soluble. —**solubilidad,** *n.f.* solubility.

solución (so·lu'θjon; -'sjon) *n.f.* solution. —**solucionar,** *v.t.* to solve.

solventar (sol·βen'tar) *v.t.* **1,** to pay; settle (an account). **2,** to resolve; solve.

solvente (sol'βen·te) *adj. & n.m.* solvent. —**solvencia,** *n.f.* solvency.

sollastre (so'ʎas·tre; so'jas-) *n.m.* kitchen helper; scullion. —**sollastría,** *n.f.* scullery.

sollo ('so·ʎo; -jo) *n.m.* sturgeon.

sollozar (so·ʎo'θar; -jo'sar) *v.i.* [*infl.:* **rezar,** 10] to sob. —**sollozo** (-'ʎo·θo; -'jo·so) *n.m.* sob.

soma ('so·ma) *n.m.* soma. —**somático** (-'ma·ti·ko) *adj.* somatic.

somanta (so'man·ta) *n.f., colloq.* beating; drubbing.

sombra ('som·bra) *n.f.* **1,** shade; shadow. **2,** protection; shelter. **3,** image. **4,** umbra. —**a la sombra,** *colloq.* in jail. —**tener mala sombra,** *colloq.* **1,** (of persons) [*also,* **ser una mala sombra**] to be baneful; be detestable. **2,** (of things) to be a jinx. —**tierra de sombra,** umber.

sombraje (som'bra·xe) *n.m.* shade; awning.

sombrar (som'brar) *v.t.* to shade; provide shade for.

sombrear (som·bre'ar) *v.t.* to shade (a drawing or painting). —**sombreado,** *n.m.* shading.

sombrero (som'bre·ro) *n.m.* hat.

—**sombrerera,** *n.f.* hatbox. —**sombrerería,** *n.f.* hat shop. —**sombrero,** *n.m.* hatter. —**sombrero de copa,** high hat; top hat. —**sombrero de jipijapa; sombrero panamá,** Panama hat. —**sombrero de muelles,** opera hat. —**sombrero de pelo,** *Amer.* high hat. —**sombrero hongo,** derby.

sombrilla (som'bri·ʎa; -ja) *n.f.* **1,** parasol; sunshade. **2,** umbrella.

sombrío (som'bri·o) *adj.* somber; gloomy.

somero (so'me·ro) *adj.* superficial; summary.

someter (so·me'ter) *v.t.* **1,** to subject. **2,** to submit; propose. **3,** to entrust; commit. —**someterse,** *v.r.* to submit; yield.

sometimiento (so·me·ti'mjen·to) *n.m.* **1,** subjection; subjugation. **2,** submission.

sommier (so'mjer) *n.m.* bedspring.

somnambulismo (som·nam·bu'lis·mo) *n.m.* = **sonambulismo.** —**somnámbulo** (som'nam·bu·lo) *n.m.* = **sonámbulo.**

somnífero (som'ni·fe·ro) *adj.* somniferous. —*n.m.* sleeping pill or potion.

somnolencia (som·no'len·θja; -sja) *n.f.* somnolence.

somorgujar (so·mor·ɣu'xar) *v.t. & i.* to dip; dunk. —*v.i.* to dive; duck. —**somorgujo** (-'ɣu·xo) *n.m.* merganser; loon.

somos ('so·mos) *v., 1st pers.pl. pres.ind. of* **ser.**

son (son) *n.m.* **1,** sound. **2,** tune. **3,** fame; report. **4,** *fig.* manner; guise; tenor. —*¿a son de qué?, also, ¿a qué son?,* why?; for what reason? —*sin son, also, sin ton ni son, colloq.* without rhyme or reason.

son (son) *v., 3rd pers.pl.pres.ind. of* **ser.**

sonado (so'na·ðo) *adj.* **1,** noted; famous. **2,** notorious.

sonaja (so'na·xa) *n.f.* **1,** tambourine. **2,** noisemaker. **3,** [*also,* **sonajero,** *n.m.*] baby rattle.

sonambulismo (so·nam·bu'lis·mo) *n.m.* somnambulism. —**sonámbulo** (so'nam·bu·lo) *n.m.* sleepwalker; somnambulist.

sonante (so'nan·te) *adj.* sounding; ringing. —**dinero sonante,** *also,* **dinero contante y sonante,** hard cash.

sonar (so'nar) *v.t.* [*infl.:* **acostar,** 28] **1,** to sound; ring. **2,** to blow (the nose). —*v.i.* **1,** to sound; ring. **2,** to sound familiar. **3,** to strike *(of the clock or the hour).* **4,** *colloq.* to be finished; be done for. —**sonarse,** *v.r.* **1,** to blow one's nose. **2,** to be rumored. —**sonar a,** to sound like.

sonar (so'nar) *n.m.* sonar.

sonata (so'na·ta) *n.f.* sonata.

sonda ('son·da) *n.f.* **1,** sounding. **2,** sounding line. **3,** borer; drill. **4,** *med.* catheter. **5,** *surg.* probe.

sondear (son·de'ar) *also,* **sondar** (-'dar) *v.t.* to sound; probe.

sondeo (son'de·o) *n.m.* **1,** sounding. **2,** boring; drilling.

sonetista (so·ne'tis·ta) *n.m. & f.* sonneteer.

soneto (so'ne·to) *n.m.* sonnet. —**sonetillo,** *n.m.* light sonnet.

sónico ('so·ni·ko) *adj.* sonic.

sonido (so'ni·ðo) *n.m.* sound.

soniquete (so·ni'ke·te) *n.m.* click; clack; rattle.

sonorizar (so·no·ri'θar; -'sar) *v.t.* [*infl.:* **rezar, 10**] *phonet.* to voice. —**sonorización,** *n.f.* voicing.

sonoro (so'no·ro) *adj.* **1,** sonorous. **2,** *phonet.* voiced. —**sonoridad,** *n.f.* sonority.

sonreír (son·re'ir) *v.i.* [*infl.:* **reír, 58**] to smile; grin. —**sonrisa** (-'ri·sa) *n.f.* smile; grin.

sonrojar (son·ro'xar) *v.t.* to cause to blush. —**sonrojarse,** *v.r.* to blush. —**sonrojo** (-'ro·xo) *n.m.* blush; blushing.

sonrosado (son·ro'sa·ðo) *adj.* pink; rosy.

sonsacar (son·sa'kar) *v.t.* [*infl.:* **tocar, 7**] to cajole; get by cajolery; wheedle. —**sonsaca** (-'sa·ka) *n.f., also,* **sonsaque** (-'sa·ke) *n.m.* cajolery; wheedling.

sonsonete (son·so'ne·te) *n.m.* **1,** clicking; clacking; rattle. **2,** ironic tone of the voice. **3,** singsong.

soñar (so'ɲar) *v.t. & i* [*infl.:* **acostar, 28**] to dream. —**soñador,** *adj.* dreaming. —*n.m.* [*fem.* **-dora**] dreamer. —**soñar con,** to dream of or about.

soñoliento (so·ɲo'ljen·to) *adj.* sleepy; somnolent. —**soñolencia,** *n.f.* sleepiness; somnolence.

sopa ('so·pa) *n.f.* soup. —**sopas,** *n.f.pl.* sops; pieces of bread soaked in soup or milk. —**a la sopa boba,** sponging; without effort or exertion. —**estar hecho una sopa,** to be soaking wet.

sopaipa (so'pai·pa) *n.f.* **1,** *also,*

sopaipilla (-'pi·ʎa; -ja) honey fritter. **2,** *colloq.* gooey mass.

sopanda (so'pan·da) *n.f.* brace; joist.

sopapo (so'pa·po) *n.m. colloq.* slap; box; blow. —**sopapear,** *v.t.* to slap. —**sopapina,** *n.f., Amer., colloq.* drubbing.

sopera (so'pe·ra) *n.f.* tureen. —**sopero,** *n.m., also,* **plato sopero,** soup plate.

sopetear (so·pe·te'ar) *v.t., colloq.* to sop; dip; dunk. —*v.i., colloq.* to snoop around. —**sopeteo** (-'te·o) *n.m., colloq.* sopping; dipping; dunking.

sopetón (so·pe'ton) *n.m.* slap; box; blow. —**de sopetón,** suddenly.

soplado (so'pla·ðo) *adj., colloq.* **1,** dapper; neat. **2,** conceited; vain. —*n.m.* deep crevice.

soplar (so'plar) *v.t. & i.* to blow; puff. —*v.t.* **1,** to inflate; blow up. **2,** to blow out (a flame). **3,** to blow away. **4,** *colloq.* to disclose; inform of or about. **5,** *colloq.* to whisper (information, answers to examination questions, etc.). **6,** *checkers* to take (a piece) for failing to jump. **7,** *slang* to filch. —**soplarse,** *v.r.* to be puffed up; swell with pride. —**¡sopla!,** wow! —**soplador,** *adj.* blowing. —*n.m.* blower; fire bellows.

soplete (so'ple·te) *n.m.* **1,** blowtorch. **2,** blowpipe.

soplido (so'pli·ðo) *n.m.* blowing; puffing; puff.

soplillo (so'pli·ʎo; -jo) *n.m.* **1,** ventilator; blower. **2,** chiffon; gauze. **3,** chiffon cake.

soplo (so'plo) *n.m.* **1,** blow; blowing; puff. **2,** *colloq.* instant; moment. **3,** *colloq.* informing; squealing. —**en un soplo,** in the twinkling of an eye.

soplón (so'plon) *adj., colloq.* **1,** tattling; gossiping. **2,** informing; squealing. —*n.m.* [*fem.* **-plona**] *colloq.* **1,** tattletale. **2,** informer.

soplonería (so·plo·ne'ri·a) *n.f., colloq.* **1,** tattling; gossip. **2,** informing; squealing.

soponcio (so'pon·θjo; -sjo) *n.m., colloq.* faint; swoon.

sopor (so'por) *n.m.* **1,** stupor. **2,** drowsiness.

soporífico (so·po'ri·fi·ko) *adj. & n.m.* soporific. *Also,* **soporífero** (-'fe·ro).

soportal (so·por'tal) *n.m.* **1,** porch. **2,** portico. **3,** arcade.

soportar (so·por'tar) *v.t.* **1,** to support. **2,** to tolerate; bear; endure. —**soportable,** *adj.* tolerable; bearable. —**soporte** (-'por·te) *n.m.* prop; support.

soprano (so'pra·no) *n.m. & f.* soprano.

sopuntar (so·pun'tar) *v.t.* to underscore with dots.

sor (sor) *n.f.*, *eccles.*, *used before a name* sister.

sorber (sor'ßer) *v.t.* **1,** to sip; suck. **2,** to sniff; sniffle. **3,** to soak up; absorb. —**sorber los vientos por,** *colloq.* to be crazy about.

sorbete (sor'ße·te) *n.m.* sherbet.

sorbo ('sor·ßo) *n.m.* **1,** sip; gulp. **2,** sniff; sniffle.

sordera (sor'ðe·ra) *n.f.* deafness; hardness of hearing. *Also, colloq.*, **sordez.**

sordez (sor'ðeθ; -'ðes) *n.f.* **1,** *phonet.* voicelessness. **2,** = **sordera.**

sórdido ('sor·ði·ðo) *adj.* sordid. —**sordidez,** *n.f.* sordidness.

sordina (sor'ði·na) *n.f.*, *mus.* mute.

sordo ('sor·ðo) *adj.* **1,** deaf; hard of hearing. **2,** silent; muffled. **3,** *phonet.* voiceless. —**a sordas; a la sorda,** silently.

sordomudo (sor·ðo'mu·ðo) *n.m.* deafmute.

sorgo ('sor·ɣo) *n.m.* sorghum.

soriasis (so'ri·a·sis) *also,* **soriasis** (so'rja·sis) *n.f.* = **psoriasis.**

sorna ('sor·na) *n.f.* **1,** irony; sarcasm; scorn. **2,** malingering; heel-dragging.

soroche (so'ro·tʃe) *n.m.*, *S.A.* **1,** mountain sickness. **2,** *colloq.* blush.

sorprender (sor·pren'der) *v.t.* **1,** to surprise. **2,** to amaze; astound. —**sorprendente** (-'den·te) *adj.* surprising; amazing. —**sorpresa** (-'pre·sa) *n.f.* surprise. —**sorpresivo** (-'si·ßo) *adj.* sudden; surprise *(attrib.)*.

sortear (sor·te'ar) *v.i.* **1,** to raffle; choose or assign by lot. **2,** to dodge; elude. —**sorteo** (-'te·o) *n.m.* raffle; drawing or casting of lots.

sortija (sor'ti·xa) *n.f.* ring.

sortilegio (sor·ti'le·xjo) *n.m.* **1,** sorcery. **2,** magic spell. —**sortílego** (-'ti·le·ɣo) *n.m.* sorcerer.

sosa ('so·sa) *n.f.*, *chem.* soda.

sosegar (so·se'ɣar) *v.t.* [*infl.:* **pagar, 8; pensar, 27**] to assuage; calm. —*v.i.* to rest.

—**sosegarse,** *v.r.* to calm down; become calm. —**sosiego** (-'sje·ɣo) *n.m.* peace; stillness; calm.

sosería (so·se'ri·a) *n.f.* insipidity. *Also, colloq.*, **sosera** (so'se·ra).

soslayar (sos·la'jar) *v.t.* **1,** to avoid; sidestep. **2,** to put or place obliquely.

soslayo (sos'la·jo) *adj.* oblique. —**al soslayo,** obliquely; on the bias. —**de soslayo,** obliquely; sideways; askance.

soso ('so·so) *adj.* insipid.

sospecha (sos'pe·tʃa) *n.f.* suspicion. —**sospechar,** *v.t.* to suspect. —*v.i.* to be suspicious. —**sospechoso,** *adj.* suspicious; suspect. —*n.m.* suspect.

sosquín (sos'kin) *n.m.* treacherous blow.

sostén (sos'ten) *n.m.* **1,** support. **2,** brassiere.

sostener (sos·te'ner) *v.t.* [*infl.:* **tener, 65**] **1,** to support; sustain; maintain. **2,** to endure; suffer. —**sostenido,** *adj. & n.m.*, *mus.* sharp. —**sostenimiento,** *n.m.* support; sustenance; maintenance.

sota ('so·ta) *n.f.*, *cards* jack.

sotabanco (so·ta'ßan·ko) *n.m.* garret; attic.

sotana (so'ta·na) *n.f.* cassock.

sótano ('so·ta·no) *n.m.* cellar; basement.

sotavento (so·ta'ßen·to) *n.m.* leeward; lee.

sotechado (so·te'tʃa·ðo) *n.m.* shed.

soterrar (so·te'rrar) *v.t.* [*infl.:* **pensar, 27**] to bury.

soto ('so·to) *n.m.* thicket; grove.

sotrozo (so'tro·θo; -so) *n.f.* cotter pin; axle pin.

soviet (so'ßjet) *n.m.* [*pl.* **soviets**] soviet. —**soviético,** *adj. & n.m.* soviet.

soy (soi) *v.*, *1st pers.sing.pres.ind. of* **ser.**

soya ('so·ja) *n.f.* soy; soybean.

staccato (sta'ka·to) *adj.*, *mus.* staccato.

su (su) *poss.adj. m. & f. sing.* [*m. & f.pl.* **sus**], *agreeing in number with the thing possessed* his; her; its; one's; your; their.

suave ('swa·ße) *adj.* **1,** soft; smooth. **2,** mild; gentle.

suavidad (swa·ßi'ðað) *n.f.* **1,** softness; smoothness. **2,** gentleness.

suavizar (swa·ßi'θar; -'sar) *v.t.* [*infl.:* **rezar, 10**] **1,** to soften;

smooth. **2,** to mitigate; temper. —**suavizador,** *adj.* softening; smoothing. —*n.m.* **1,** softener. **2,** razor strop.

subalterno (suβ·al'ter·no) *adj.* & *n.m.* subaltern; subordinate.

subarrendar (suβ·a·rren'dar) *v.t.* [*infl.:* **pensar, 27**] to sublease. —**subarriendo** (-'rrjen·do) *n.m.* sublease.

subastar (su·βas'tar) *v.t.* to auction. —**subasta** (su'βas·ta) *n.f.* auction.

subatómico (suβ·a'to·mi·ko) *adj.* subatomic.

subcomisión (suβ·ko·mi'sjon) *n.f.* subcommittee. *Also,* **subcomité** (-'te) *n.m.*

subconsciente (suβ·kons'θjen·te; -kon'sjen·te) *adj.* & *n.m.* subconscious. —**subconsciencia,** *n.f.* subconscious; subconsciousness.

subcontinente (suβ·kon·ti·'nen·te) *n.m.* subcontinent.

subcontratar (suβ·kon·tra'tar) *v.t.* & *i.* to subcontract. —**subcontrato** (-'tra·to) *n.m.* subcontract. —**subcontratista** (-'tis·sta) *n.m.* & *f.* subcontractor.

subcutáneo (suβ·ku'ta·ne·o) *adj.* subcutaneous.

subdesarrollado (suβ·ðes·a·rro'ʎa·ðo; -'ja·ðo) *adj.* underdeveloped.

subdirector (suβ·ði·rek'tor) *n.m.* [*fem.* **-tora**] assistant director; manager; editor, etc.

súbdito ('suβ·ði·to) *adj.* subject. —*n.m.* subject; citizen; national.

subdividir (suβ·ði·βi'ðir) *v.t.* to subdivide. —**subdivisión** (-'sjon) *n.f.* subdivision.

subestimar (suβ·es·ti'mar) *v.t.* to underestimate. —**subestimación,** *n.f.* underestimation.

subgobernador (suβ·γo·βer·na'ðor) *n.m.* [*fem.* **-dora**] lieutenant governor.

subida (su'βi·ða) *n.f.* **1,** rise; rising. **2,** raise; raising. **3,** upgrade; rising slope. **4,** climbing; mounting; ascent. **5,** increase.

subido (su'βi·ðo) *adj.* **1,** raised; high. **2,** bright; deep; loud (*of color*).

subilla (su'βi·ʎa; -ja) *n.f.* awl.

subir (su'βir) *v.t.* to raise; lift. —*v.i.* **1,** to rise. **2,** *comm.* to amount to; come to. —*v.t.* & *i.* **1,** to climb; mount; ascend. **2,** to increase. —**su-**

birse, *v.r., usu.fol.by* **a,** to get on; go up on or into.

súbitamente (su·βi·ta'men·te) *adv.* suddenly.

súbito ('su·βi·to) *adj.* sudden. —*adv.* = **súbitamente.** —**de súbito,** suddenly.

subjefe (suβ'xe·fe) *n.m.* assistant chief; assistant manager.

subjetivo (suβ·xe'ti·βo) *adj.* subjective. —**subjetividad,** *n.f.* subjectivity.

subjuntivo (suβ·xun'ti·βo) *adj.* subjunctive.

sublevar (suβ·le'βar) *v.t.* **1,** to incite to rebellion. **2,** to arouse; excite. —**sublevarse,** *v.r.* to rise up; rebel. —**sublevación,** *n.f.,* *also,* **sublevamiento,** *n.m.* revolt; insurrection.

sublimar (su·βli'mar) *v.t.* to sublimate. —**sublimación,** *n.f.* sublimation. —**sublimado,** *n.m.* sublimate.

sublime (su'βli·me) *adj.* sublime. —**sublimidad,** *n.f.* sublimity.

submarino (suβ·ma'ri·no) *adj.* & *n.m.* submarine.

subnormal *adj.* subnormal.

suboficial (suβ·o·fi'θjal; -'sjal) *n.m.* **1,** noncommissioned officer. **2,** warrant officer.

suborbital (suβ·or·βi'tal) *adj.* suborbital.

subordinar (suβ·or·ði'nar) *v.t.* to subordinate. —**subordinación,** *n.f.* subordination. —**subordinado,** *adj.* & *n.m.* subordinate.

subproducto (suβ·pro'ðuk·to) *n.m.* by-product.

subrayar (suβ·ra'jar) *v.t.* to underline; underscore. —**subrayado,** *n.m.* underlining; underscoring.

subrepticio (suβ·rep'ti·θjo; -sjo) *adj.* surreptitious. —**subrepción** (-'θjon; -'sjon) *n.f.* underhandedness.

subrogar (suβ·ro'γar) *v.t.* [*infl.:* **pagar, 8**] to subrogate. —**subrogación,** *n.f.* subrogation.

subsanar (suβ·sa'nar) *v.t.* to remedy; put right; set aright.

subscribir (suβs·kri'βir) *v.t.* = suscribir. —**subscripción,** *n.f.* = suscripción. —**subscriptor, subscritor,** *n.m.* = **suscriptor, suscritor.**

subsecretario (suβ·se·kre'ta·rjo) *n.m.* undersecretary.

subsecuente (suβ·se'kwen·te) *adj.* subsequent.

subsidiario (suβ·si'ðja·rjo) *adj.* & *n.m.* subsidiary.

subsidio (suβ'si·ðjo) *n.m.* subsidy. —**subsidiar,** *v.t.* to subsidize.

subsiguiente (suβ·si'γjen·te) *adj.* subsequent; following.

subsistir (suβ·sis'tir) *v.i.* to subsist. —**subsistencia,** *n.f.* subsistence. —**subsistente,** *adj.* subsisting.

subsónico (suβ'so·ni·ko) *adj.* subsonic.

substancia (suβs'tan·θja; —sja) *n.f.* = **sustancia.** —**substancial,** *adj.* = **sustancial.** —**substanciación,** *n.f.* = **sustanciación.** —**substanciar,** *v.t.* = **sustanciar.** —**substancioso,** *adj.* = **sustancioso.**

substantivo (suβs·tan'ti·βo) *adj.* & *n.m.* = **sustantivo.**

substituir (suβs·ti·tu'ir) *v.t.* = **sustituir.** —**substitución,** *n.f.* = **sustitución.** —**substituto,** *adj.* & *n.m.* = **sustituto.**

substraer (suβs·tra'er) *v.t.* = **sustraer.** —**substracción,** *n.f.* = **sustracción.** —**substraendo,** *n.m.* = **sustraendo.**

substrato (suβs'tra·to) *n.m.* substratum.

subsuelo (suβ'swe·lo) *n.m.* **1,** subsoil. **2,** basement.

subsumir (suβ·su'mir) *v.t.* to subsume.

subtender (suβ·ten'der) *v.t.* to subtend.

subteniente (suβ·te'njen·te) *n.m.* second lieutenant.

subterfugio (suβ·ter'fu·xjo) *n.m.* subterfuge.

subterráneo (suβ·te'rra·ne·o) *adj.* subterranean. —*n.m.* underground passage; subway.

subtítulo (suβ'ti·tu·lo) *n.m.* subtitle.

subtropical (suβ·tro·pi'kal) *adj.* subtropical.

suburbio (su'βur·βjo) *n.m.* suburb. —**suburbano** (-'βa·no) *adj.* suburban. —*n.m.* suburbanite.

subvención (suβ·βen'θjon; -'sjon) *n.f.* subsidy. —**subvencionar,** *v.t.* to subsidize.

subvenir (suβ·βe'nir) *v.t.* [*infl.*: **venir,** 69] to aid; assist; provide for.

subvertir (suβ·βer'tir) *v.t.* [*infl.*: **sentir,** 31] to subvert. —**subversión** (-'sjon) *n.f.* subversion. —**subversivo** (-'si·βo) *adj.* subversive. —**subversor** (-'sor) *n.m.* subversive; subverter.

subyacente (suβ·ja'θen·te; -'sen·te) *adj.* underlying.

subyugar (suβ·ju'γar) *v.t.* [*infl.*: **pagar,** 8] to subjugate. —**subyugación,** *n.f.* subjugation.

succión (suk'θjon; -'sjon) *n.f.* suction. —**succionar,** *v.t.* to suck.

sucedáneo (su·θe'ða·ne·o; su·se-) *adj.* & *n.m.* substitute.

suceder (su·θe'ðer; su·se-) *v.i.* to follow; succeed. —*v.impers.* to happen; occur. —**sucedido,** *n.m.* event; happening.

sucesión (su·θe'sjon; su·se-) *n.f.* **1,** succession. **2,** issue; offspring. **3,** *law* estate. —**sucesivamente,** *adj.* successively. —**sucesivo** (-'si·βo) *adj.* successive; next. —**en lo sucesivo,** from now on; hereafter. —**y así sucesivamente,** and so on.

suceso (su'θe·so; su'se-) *n.m.* **1,** event; occurrence. **2,** outcome; issue.

sucesor (su·θe'sor; su·se-) *n.m.* successor.

sucinto (su'θin·to; su'sin-) *adj.* succinct.

sucio ('su·θjo; -sjo) *adj.* **1,** dirty; soiled; filthy. **2,** obscene. —**suciedad,** *n.f.* dirt; filth.

sucre ('su·kre) *n.m.* monetary unit of Ecuador; sucre.

sucrosa (su'kro·sa) *n.f.* sucrose.

súcula ('su·ku·la) *n.f.* windlass.

suculento (su·ku'len·to) *adj.* succulent. —**suculencia,** *n.f.* succulence.

sucumbir (su·kum'bir) *v.i.* to succumb.

sucursal (su·kur'sal) *adj.* subsidiary; branch (*attrib.*). —*n.f.* branch office.

sud (suð) *n.m.* = **sur.**

sudamericano (suð·a·me·ri'ka·no) *adj.* & *n.m.* South American.

sudar (su'ðar) *v.t.* & *i.* to sweat.

sudario (su'ða·rjo) *n.m.* shroud.

sudeste (suð'es·te) *adj.* & *n.m.* southeast; southeastern; southeasterly.

sudoeste (suð·o'es·te) *adj.* & *n.m.* southwest; southwestern; southwesterly.

sudor (su'ðor) *n.m.* sweat. —**sudoroso,** *adj.* sweating; sweaty. —**sudoso** (-'ðo·so) *adj.* sweaty.

sudsudeste (suð·suð'es·te) *adj.* & *n.m.* south southeast.

sudsudoeste (suð·suð·o'es·te) *adj.* & *n.m.* south southwest.

sueco ('swe·ko) *adj.* Swedish. —*n.m.* **1,** Swede. **2,** Swedish *(language).* —**hacerse el sueco,** *colloq.* to play dumb; pretend not to understand.

suegra ('swe·ɣra) *n.f.* mother-in-law. —**suegro,** *n.m.* father-in-law.

suela ('swe·la) *n.f.* sole of a shoe.

suela ('swe·la) *v., pres.subjve. of* **soler.**

suelde ('swel·de) *v., pres.subjve. of* **soldar.**

sueldo ('swel·do) *n.m.* salary.

sueldo ('swel·do) *v., 1st pers.sing. pres.ind. of* **soldar.**

suele ('swe·le) *v., pres.subjve. of* **solar.**

suelo ('swe·lo) *n.m.* **1,** floor. **2,** ground.

suelo ('swe·lo) *v., 1st pers.sing. pres.ind. of* **solar** *and* **soler.**

suelta ('swel·ta) *n.f.* release.

suelte ('swel·te) *v., pres.subjve. of* **soltar.**

suelto ('swel·to) *adj.* **1,** loose. **2,** nimble. **3,** easy; flowing. —*n.m.* **1,** change; small change; silver. **2,** bit of news; item.

suelto ('swel·to) *v., 1st pers.sing. pres.ind. of* **soltar.**

suene ('swe·ne) *v., pres.subjve. of* **sonar.**

sueno ('swe·no) *v., 1st pers.sing. pres.ind. of* **sonar.**

sueñe ('swe·ɲe) *v., pres.subjve. of* **soñar.**

sueño ('swe·ɲo) *n.m.* **1,** sleep; sleeping. **2,** desire to sleep; sleepiness. **3,** dream. —*v., 1st pers.sing. pres.ind. of* **soñar. —en** *or* **entre sueños,** in one's sleep; dreaming. —**ni por sueños,** by no means. —**tener sueño,** to be sleepy.

suero ('swe·ro) *n.m.* **1,** serum. **2,** whey.

suerte ('swer·te) *n.f.* **1,** luck. **2,** fate; lot. **3,** chance; share of luck. **4,** kind; sort. **5,** manner; way. **6,** trick; maneuver. —**de suerte que,** so that; in such a way that. —**echar suertes,** to cast or draw lots.

suertudo (swer'tu·ðo) *adj., colloq.* lucky. —*n.m., colloq.* lucky fellow.

suéter ('swe·ter) *n.m. or f.* sweater.

suficiente (su·fi'θjen·te; -'sjen·te) *adj.* sufficient. —**suficiencia,** *n.f.* sufficiency.

sufijo (su'fi·xo) *adj.* suffixed; affixed. —*n.m.* suffix.

sufragar (su·fra'ɣar) *v.t.* [*infl.:* **pagar,** 8] to defray; pay; bear the costs of. —*v.i., S.A., fol. by* **por,** to vote (for).

sufragio (su'fra·xjo) *n.m.* **1,** suffrage. **2,** aid; help; support. **3,** mass or prayers for the dead.

sufragista (su·fra'xis·ta) *adj.* & *n.m.* & *f.* suffragist. —*n.f.* suffragette.

sufrimiento (su·fri'mjen·to) *n.m.* **1,** suffering. **2,** sufferance; forbearance.

sufrir (su'frir) *v.t.* & *i.* to suffer. —*v.t.* **1,** to bear; endure. **2,** to undergo. —**sufrido,** *adj.* patient; forbearing.

sufusión (su·fu'sjon) *n.f.* suffusion.

sugerir (su·xe'rir) *v.t.* [*infl.:* **sentir,** 31] to suggest. —**sugerencia,** *n.f.* suggestion. —**sugerente,** *adj.* suggesting; suggestive.

sugestión (su·xes'tjon) *n.f.* suggestion. —**sugestionar,** *v.t.* to influence or impress by suggestion. —**sugestionable,** *adj.* suggestible; impressionable.

sugestivo (su·xes'ti·βo) *adj.* suggestive.

suicida (sui'θi·ða; -'si·ða) *adj.* suicidal. —*n.m.* & *f.* suicide *(agent).* —**suicidarse** (-'ðar·se) *v.r.* to commit suicide. —**suicidio** (-'θi·ðjo; -'si·ðjo) *n.m.* suicide *(act).*

suizo ('swi·θo; -so) *adj.* & *n.m.* Swiss.

sujeción (su·xe'θjon; -'sjon) *n.f.* subjection; restraint.

sujetalibros (su·xe·ta'li·βros) *n.m. sing.* & *pl.* bookend.

sujetapapeles (su·xe·ta·pa'pe·les) *n.m.sing.* & *pl.* paper clip.

sujetar (su·xe'tar) *v.t.* **1,** to hold; grasp. **2,** to fasten; secure. **3,** to subject; subdue. —**sujetarse,** *v.r.* **1,** to subject oneself; submit. **2,** *fol. by* **a,** to abide by; hold to.

sujeto (su'xe·to) *adj.* subject; liable. —*n.m.* **1,** subject; theme. **2,** *philos.; logic; gram.* subject. **3,** individual; person. **4,** *derog.* character; guy.

sulfa ('sul·fa) *n.f.* & *adj.* sulfa.

sulfato (sul'fa·to) *n.m.* sulfate.

sulfurar (sul·fu'rar) *v.t.* **1,** to sulfurate. **2,** to anger; annoy. —**sulfurarse,** *v.r.* to be angry; be annoyed.

sulfuro (sul'fu·ro) *n.m.* sulfide. —**sulfúrico,** *adj.* sulfuric. —**sulfuroso,** *adj.* sulfurous.

sultán (sul'tan) *n.m.* sultan. —**sultana,** *n.f.* sultana. —**sultanía,** *n.f., also,* **sultanato,** *n.m.* sultanate.

suma ('su·ma) *n.f.* 1, sum. 2, *math.* addition. —**en suma,** in short; summing up; in sum.

sumadora (su·ma'ðo·ra) *n.f., also,* **máquina de sumar,** adding machine.

sumamente (su·ma'men·te) *adv.* extremely; exceedingly.

sumando (su'man·do) *n.m.* addend.

sumar (su'mar) *v.t. & i., math.* to add. —*v.t.* 1, to add up to; reach a total of. 2, to summarize; sum up. —**sumarse,** *v.r., usu. fol. by* **a,** to join; become part of.

sumario (su'ma·rjo) *adj.* summary. —*n.m.* 1, summary. 2, *law* indictment.

sumergir (su·mer'xir) *v.t.* [*infl.:* **coger, 15**] to submerge. —**sumergible,** *adj.* submersible. —*n.m.* submarine. —**sumersión** (su·mer'sjon) *n.f.* submersion.

sumidero (su·mi'ðe·ro) *n.m.* sewer; drain.

suministrar (su·mi·nis'trar) *v.t.* 1, to supply; furnish; provide. 2, to give; administer. —**suministro** (-'nis·tro) *n.m.* supply.

sumir (su'mir) *v.t.* to sink; plunge. —**sumirse,** *v.r.* 1, to sink. 2, *Amer.* to shrink; shrivel. 3, *Amer.* to cringe; cower.

sumiso (su'mi·so) *adj.* submissive; meek; humble. —**sumisión** (-'sjon) *n.f.* submission.

sumo ('su·mo) *adj.* highest; supreme. —**a lo sumo,** at most. —**de sumo,** thoroughly; perfectly.

suntuoso (sun'two·so) *adj.* sumptuous. —**suntuosidad,** *n.f.* sumptuousness.

supe ('su·pe) *v., pret. of* **saber.**

supeditar (su·pe·ði'tar) *v.t.* 1, to make subservient or subordinate. 2, to subject; subdue.

superable (su·pe'ra·βle) *adj.* 1, surmountable. 2, improvable. 3, surpassable.

superabundante (su·per·a·βun'dan·te) *adj.* superabundant. —**superabundancia,** *n.f.* superabundance.

superalimentador (su·per·a·li·men·ta'ðor) *n.m.* supercharger.

superar (su·pe'rar) *v.t.* 1, to surpass; exceed; excel. 2, to overcome;

surmount; prevail over. 3, to improve; improve upon.

superávit (su·pe'ra·βit) *n.m.* surplus.

superchería (su·per·tʃe'ri·a) *n.f.* 1, deceit; fraud. 2, superstition; mumbo jumbo. —**superchero** (-'tʃe·ro) *adj.* deceitful; fraudulent.

super ego ('su·per'e·ɣo) super-ego.

superentender (su·per·en·ten'der) *v.t.* [*infl.:* **perder, 29**] to supervise; manage.

superestructura (su·per·es·truk'tu·ra) *n.f.* superstructure.

superficie (su·per'fi·θje; -sje) *n.f.* 1, surface. 2, area. —**superficial,** *adj.* superficial. —**superficialidad,** *n.f.* superficiality.

superfino (su·per'fi·no) *adj.* superfine.

superfluo (su'per·flwo) *adj.* superfluous. —**superfluidad,** *n.f.* superfluity.

superfortaleza (su·per·for·ta'le·θa; -sa) *n.f.* superfortress.

superheterodino (su·per·e·te·ro'ði·no) *adj.* superheterodyne.

superhombre (su·per'om·bre) *n.m.* superman.

superintendente (su·per·in·ten'den·te) *n.m. & f.* superintendent. —**superintendencia,** *n.f.* superintendency.

superior (su·pe'rjor) *adj. & n.m.* superior. —*adj.* higher; highest; upper; uppermost. —**superioridad,** *n.f.* superiority.

superiora (su·pe'rjo·ra) *n.f.* superior, esp. mother superior.

superlativo (su·per·la'ti·βo) *adj. & n.m.* superlative.

supermercado (su·per·mer'ka·do) *n.m.* supermarket.

superno (su'per·no) *adj.* supreme; supernal.

supernumerario (su·per·nu·me'ra·rjo) *adj. & n.m.* supernumerary.

superponer (su·per·po'ner) *v.t.* [*infl.:* **poner, 54**] to superpose; superimpose.

superposición (su·per·po·si'θjon; -'sjon) *n.f.* superposition; superimposition.

superpotencia (su·per·po'ten·θja; -sja) *n.f.* superpower.

supersónico (su·per'so·ni·ko) *ajd.* supersonic.

superstición (su·pers·ti'θjon;

-'sjon) *n.f.* superstition. —**supersti-cioso,** *adj.* superstitious.

superveniencia (su·per·βe'njen·θja; -sja) *n.f.* supervention. —**supervenir** (-βe'nir) *v.i.* = sobrevenir.

supervisar (su·per'βi·sar) *v.t. & i.* to supervise. —**supervisión,** *n.f.* supervision.

supervisor (su·per·βi'sor) *n.m.* [*fem.* **-sora**] **1,** overseer. **2,** controller; examiner.

superviviente (su·per·βi'βjen·te) *adj. & n.m. & f.* = sobreviviente. —**supervivencia** (-'βen·θja; -sja) *n.f.* survival.

supino (su'pi·no) *adj.* **1,** supine. **2,** crass; gross.

suplantar (su·plan'tar) *v.t.* to supplant.

suplemento (su·ple'men·to) *n.m.* supplement. —**suplementar,** *v.t.* to supplement. —**suplementario,** *adj.* supplementary; supplemental.

suplente (su'plen·te) *adj. & n.m. & f.* substitute.

suplicar (su·pli'kar) *v.t.* [*infl.:* **tocar, 7**] to supplicate; beseech; entreat. —**súplica** ('su·pli·ka) *n.f.* supplication. —**suplicante,** *adj. & n.m. & f.* supplicant; suppliant.

suplicio (su'pli·θjo; -sjo) *n.m.* **1,** torture; torment. **2,** execution.

suplir (su'plir) *v.t.* **1,** to supply. **2,** to take the place of; substitute for. **3,** to supplement. —**suplidor,** *adj. & n.m.* [*fem.* **-dora**] = suplente.

suponer (su·po'ner) *v.t.* [*infl.:* **poner, 54**] to suppose. —**suposición** (-si'θjon; -'sjon) *n.f.* supposition.

supositorio (su·po·si'to·rjo) *n.m.* suppository.

supremo (su'pre·mo) *adj.* supreme —**supremacía** (-ma'θi·a; -'si·a) *n.f.* supremacy.

supresión (su·pre'sjon) *n.f.* suppression. —**supresor,** *adj. & n.m.* suppressant.

suprimir (su·pri'mir) *v.t.* **1,** to suppress; abolish; cancel. **2,** to omit; leave out.

supuesto (su'pwes·to) *v., p.p. of* suponer. —*adj.* supposed; assumed. —*n.m.* supposition; assumption. —**por supuesto,** certainly.

supurar (su·pu'rar) *v.i.* to suppurate. —**supuración,** *n.f.* suppuration. —**supurante,** *adj.* suppurating.

sur (sur) *n.m.* south. *Also,* sud.

surcar (sur'kar) *v.t.* [*infl.:* **tocar, 7**] **1,** to furrow. **2,** to cleave through; plow through.

surco ('sur·ko) *n.m.* furrow; groove; wrinkle.

sureño (su're·ɲo) *adj., Amer.* southern; of or from the South.

surgir (sur'xir) *v.i.* [*infl.:* **coger, 15**] **1,** to surge; rise; spurt out; squirt out. **2,** to emerge; appear. —**surgimiento,** *n.m.* emergence.

surrealismo (su·rre·a'lis·mo) *n.m.* surrealism. —**surrealista,** *adj. & n.m. & f.* surrealist. —*adj.* surrealistic.

surtidor (sur·ti'ðor) *n.m.* **1,** waterspout; jet; fountain. **2,** supplier.

surtir (sur'tir) *v.t.* **1,** to supply; provide. **2,** to gush; spurt. —**surtido,** *adj.* assorted. —*n.m.* assortment.

sus (sus) *poss.adj., pl. of* su (*agreeing in number with the things possessed*).

¡sus! (sus) *interj.* forward!; get on!; *hunting* halloo!

susceptible (sus·θep'ti·βle; su·sep-) *adj.* susceptible. —**susceptibilidad,** *n.f.* susceptibility.

suscitar (sus·θi'tar; su·si-) *v.t.* to stir up; arouse.

suscribir (sus·kri'βir) *v.t.* [*p.p.* suscrito (-'kri·to)] **1,** to subscribe. **2,** to subscribe to; endorse; adhere to. —**suscribirse,** *v.r.* to subscribe.

suscripción (sus·krip'θjon; -'sjon) *n.f.* subscription. —**suscriptor** (-krip'tor) *also,* **suscritor** (-kri'tor) *n.m.* [*fem.* **-tora**] subscriber.

susodicho (su·so'ði·tʃo) *adj.* aforesaid.

suspender (sus·pen'der) *v.t.* **1,** to suspend. **2,** to fail; flunk.

suspensión (sus·pen'sjon) *n.f.* suspension. —**suspensivo** (-'si·βo) *adj.* suspensive; suspension (*attrib.*). —**puntos suspensivos,** suspension points.

suspenso (sus'pen·so) *adj.* **1,** suspended. **2,** astonished; enthralled. —*n.m.* **1,** suspense. **2,** *educ.* failing grade; failure.

suspensores (sus·pen'so·res) *n.m.pl., Amer.* suspenders.

suspensorio (sus·pen'so·rjo) *adj. & n.m.* suspensory.

suspicaz (sus·pi'kaθ; -'kas) *adj.* suspicious. —**suspicacia** (-'ka·θja; -sja) *n.f.* suspiciousness.

suspirar (sus·pi'rar) *v.i.* **1,** to sigh. **2,** to pine; long.

suspiro (sus'pi·ro) *n.m.* **1,** sigh. **2,**

mus. quarter rest. **3,** a kind of meringue.

sustancia (sus·tan·θja; -sja) *n.f.* substance. —**sustancial,** *adj.* substantial. —**sustanciar,** *v.t.* to substantiate.

sustancioso (sus·tan'θjo·so; -'sjo·so) *adj.* **1,** substantial. **2,** nourishing.

sustantivo (sus·tan'ti·vo) *adj.* substantive. —*n.m.,* *gram.* substantive.

sustentar (sus·ten'tar) *v.t.* to sustain; support; maintain. —**sustento** (-'ten·to) *n.m.* sustenance; support.

sustituir (sus·ti·tu'ir) *v.t.* [*infl.:* **huir, 26**] to substitute; replace. —**sustitución,** *n.f.* substitution; replacement. —**sustituto** (-'tu·to) *adj.* & *n.m.* substitute; replacement.

susto ('sus·to) *n.m.* fright; scare.

sustracción (sus·trak'θjon; -'sjon) *n.f.* subtraction.

sustraendo (sus·tra'en·do) *n.m.* subtrahend.

sustraer (sus·tra'er) *v.t.* [*infl.:* **traer, 67**] **1,** to subtract; deduct. **2,** to remove; withdraw. —**sustraerse,** *v.r.* to withdraw. —**sustraerse a** or **de,** to evade; avoid; dodge.

susurrar (su·su'rrar) *v.i.* **1,** to whisper. **2,** to rustle. —**susurrarse,** *v.r.* to be rumored.

susurro (su'su·rro) *n.m.* **1,** whisper. **2,** rustle.

sutura (su'tu·ra) *n.f.* suture.

sutil (su'til) *adj.* **1,** subtle. **2,** thin; slender. **3,** fine; sheer; delicate. —**sutileza,** *n.f.* subtlety; subtleness.

sutilizar (su·ti·li'θar; -'sar) *v.i.* [*infl.:* **rezar, 10**] to cavil; quibble. —*v.t.* **1,** to make thin; taper. **2,** to file; smooth; rub smooth. **3,** to cavil at or about; find fault with.

suyo ('su·jo) *poss.pron.m.sing.* [*fem.* **suya;** *pl.* **suyos, suyas**], *agreeing in number and gender with the thing or things possessed* his; hers; its own; one's own; yours; theirs. —**de suyo,** by itself. —**hacer de las suyas,** to be up to one's tricks. —**una de las suyas,** one of his tricks.

svástica ('sβas·ti·ka) *n.f.* swastika.

T

T, t (te) *n.f.* 23rd letter of the Spanish alphabet.

¡ta! (ta) *interj.* **1,** tut, tut! **2,** rat-tat-tat.

tabaola (ta·βa'o·la) *n.f., colloq.* = **batahola.**

tabaco (ta'βa·ko) *n.m.* **1,** tobacco. **2,** cigar. **3,** snuff. —**tabacal,** *n.m.* tobacco plantation. —**tabacalero,** *adj.* tobacco (*attrib.*). —*n.m.* tobacco grower.

tabalear (ta·βa·le'ar) *v.t.* to shake; rock. —*v.i.* to drum; beat; tap, as with the fingers.

tabanco (ta'βan·ko) *n.m.* market stand.

tábano ('ta·βa·no) *n.m.* gadfly; horsefly.

tabaquera (ta·βa'ke·ra) *n.f.* **1,** cigar case. **2,** tobacco pouch. **3,** pipe bowl. **4,** snuff box. —**tabaquería,** *n.f.* cigar store. —**tabaquero,** *n.m.* tobacconist; cigar maker or dealer.

tabardillo (ta·βar'ði·ʎo; -jo) *n.m.* **1,** malignant fever. **2,** *colloq.* sunstroke. **3,** *colloq.* pest; nuisance.

tabasco (ta'βas·ko) *n.m.* tabasco.

taberna (ta'βer·na) *n.f.* **1,** tavern. **2,** bar; pub.

tabernáculo (ta·βer'na·ku·lo) *n.m.* tabernacle.

tabernero (ta·βer'ne·ro) *n.m.* **1,** tavern keeper. **2,** bartender.

tabes ('ta·βes) *n.m.* tabes.

tabicar (ta·βi'kar) *v.t.* [*infl.:* **tocar, 7**] **1,** to wall up; seal. **2,** to partition; divide with partitions.

tabique (ta'βi·ke) *n.m.* **1,** thin wall; partition. **2,** septum.

tabla ('ta·βla) *n.f.* **1,** board. **2,** table (*list, tabular arrangement, etc.*). **3,** slab; tablet. **4,** flat, broad part of anything. —**a raja tabla,** *colloq.* at any cost; all out. —**hacer tabla rasa de, 1,** to omit; ignore. **2,** *Amer.* to clear the way for. —**tabla de salvación,** salvation; lifesaver.

tablado (ta'βla·ðo) *n.m.* **1,** flooring. **2,** wooden platform; scaffold. **3,** stage; stage floor. **4,** boarding; boards. —**tablaje** (-'βla·xe) *n.m.* boarding; boards.

tablas ('ta·βlas) *n.f.pl.* **1,** draw; tie.

2, *theat.* stage. **—estar** *or* **quedar tablas,** *colloq.* **1,** to be tied. **2,** to be even; be quits.

tablazón (ta·βla'θon; -'son) *n.f.* **1,** boards; planks; planking. **2,** *naut.* deck; decking.

tablero (ta'βle·ro) *n.m.* **1,** instrument or control panel; dashboard. **2,** playing board, esp. for chess or checkers. **3,** thin board. **4,** board of a table. **5,** writing slate. **—poner** *or* **traer al tablero,** to risk; hazard.

tableta (ta'βle·ta) *n.f.* tablet; lozenge.

tablilla (ta'βli·ʎa; -ja) *n.f.* **1,** splint; slat. **2,** wooden tablet. **3,** bulletin board.

tablón (ta'βlon) *n.m.* **1,** plank; board. **2,** *colloq.* drunkenness; intoxication. **—coger un tablón,** *colloq.* to get drunk.

tabú (ta'βu) *adj.* & *n.m.* taboo.

tabular (ta·βu'lar) *adj.* tabular. **—***v.t.* to tabulate. **—tabulación,** *n.f.* tabulation. **—tabulador,** *n.m.* tabulator.

taburete (ta·βu're·te) *n.m.* stool; taboret.

tac (tak) *interj.* & *n.m.* tick; ticktock.

taca ('ta·ka) *n.f.* small cupboard.

tacaño (ta'ka·ɲo) *adj.* stingy. **—tacañería,** *n.f.* stinginess.

tacita (ta'θi·ta; -'si·ta) *n.f.* small cup; demitasse.

tácito ('ta·θi·to; -si·to) *adj.* tacit.

taciturno (ta·θi'tur·no; ta·si-) *adj.* taciturn. **—taciturnidad,** *n.f.* taciturnity.

taco ('ta·ko) *n.m.* **1,** plug; slug. **2,** wedge; stopper. **3,** wad; wadding. **4,** billiard cue. **5,** ramrod; rammer. **6,** drink, esp. of wine. **7,** pea shooter. **8,** *colloq.* snack. **9,** *Mex.* taco. **10,** *colloq.* tangle; jam; **11,** *S.A.* heel of a shoe. **12,** *Amer., colloq.* stumpy person or thing. **13,** *colloq.* swear word; profanity. **—darse taco,** *Amer., colloq.* to put on airs. **—soltar tacos,** *colloq.* to swear; use profanity.

tacómetro (ta'ko·me·tro) *n.m.* tachometer.

tacón (ta'kon) *n.m.* heel of a shoe. **—taconazo,** *n.m.* thump or kick with the heel.

taconear (ta·ko·ne'ar) *v.i.* **1,** to tap the heels. **2,** to strut. **—taconeo** (-'ne·o) *n.m.* tapping of the heels, esp. in dancing.

táctica ('tak·ti·ka) *n.f.* **1,** tactic. **2,** tactics.

táctico ('tak·ti·ko) *adj.* tactical. **—***n.m.* **1,** tactic. **2,** tactician.

táctil ('tak·til) *adj.* tactile.

tacto ('tak·to) *n.m.* **1,** touch; sense of touch. **2,** tact.

tacha ('ta·tʃa) *n.f.* **1,** flaw; fault. **2,** stain; smirch.

tachable (ta'tʃa·βle) *adj.* exceptionable; censurable.

tachadura (ta·tʃa'ðu·ra) *n.f.* erasure; deletion.

tachar (ta'tʃar) *v.t.* **1,** to find fault; censure. **2,** to label; depict. **3,** to cross off or out; delete.

tacho ('ta·tʃo) *n.m., Amer.* large, cylindrical can, esp. a garbage can.

tachón (ta'tʃon) *n.m.* **1,** erasure; scratch; blot. **2,** braid; trimming. **3,** stud; boss. **—tachonar,** *v.t.* to stud.

tachuela (ta'tʃwe·la) *n.f.* **1,** tack. **2,** hobnail. **3,** thumbtack.

tafetán (ta·fe'tan) *n.m.* taffeta.

tafilete (ta·fi'le·te) *n.m.* morocco; morocco leather.

tagalo (ta'ɣa·lo) *adj.* & *n.m.* Tagalog.

tagarote (ta·ɣa'ro·te) *n.m.* **1,** sparrow hawk. **2,** lanky, gawky person.

tahalí (ta·a'li) *n.m.* baldric; shoulder belt.

tahona (ta'o·na) *n.f.* **1,** bakery. **2,** grist mill.

tahonero (ta·o'ne·ro) *n.m.* **1,** baker. **2,** miller.

tahúr (ta'ur) *n.m.* [*fem.* **tahura**] gambler; cardsharp.

taimado (tai'ma·ðo) *adj.* sly; crafty. **—taimarse,** *v.r., Amer.* to sulk; become stubborn.

taita ('tai·ta) *n.m., Amer., colloq.* dad; daddy.

taja ('ta·xa) *n.f.* **1,** incision; cut. **2,** = **tajada.**

tajada (ta'xa·ða) *n.f.* slice; cut.

tajado (ta'xa·ðo) *adj.* **1,** sliced; cut. **2,** steep; sheer.

tajador (ta·xa'ðor) *n.m.* **1,** cutter; chopper; slicer. **2,** *Amer.* = **tajalápiz.**

tajalápiz (ta·xa'la·piθ; -pis) *n.m., also,* **tajalápices,** *n.m.sing.* & *pl.* pencil sharpener.

tajamar (ta·xa'mar) *n.m.* cutwater.

tajar (ta'xar) *v.t.* **1,** to cut; chop; cleave; slash. **2,** to sharpen (a pencil). **—tajadura,** *n.f.* cut; slash. **—tajante,** *adj.* cutting; incisive.

tajo ('ta·xo) *n.m.* **1,** cut. **2,** gash;

slash. **3,** sheer cliff. **4,** cutting edge. **5,** chopping block.

tal (tal) *adj.* such; such a. —*indef. pron.* such; such a one; so-and-so. —*adv.* thus; so. —**con tal que,** provided that. —**el tal,** that person; the so-called. —¿**qué tal?,** how are you? —**tal cual, 1,** such as; just as. **2,** just so; so-so. —**tal para cual,** exactly alike; exactly suited. —**un tal por cual,** a no-account person.

tala ('ta·la) *n.f.* felling; cutting down.

talabarte (ta·la'βar·te) *n.m.* sword belt.

talabartero (ta·la·βar'te·ro) *n.m.* saddler; harness maker. —**talabartería** (-te'ri·a) *n.f.* saddlery; harness shop.

taladrar (ta·la'ðrar) *v.t.* to drill; bore; pierce.

taladro (ta'la·ðro) *n.m.* **1,** drill; borer; auger. **2,** drill hole.

tálamo ('ta·la·mo) *n.m.* **1,** bridal bed. **2,** thalamus. —**talámico** (ta'la·mi·ko) *adj.* thalamic.

talán (ta'lan) *interj. & n.m.* ding-dong.

talanquera (ta·lan'ke·ra) *n.f.* breastwork; parapet; fence.

talante (ta'lan·te) *n.m.* **1,** disposition; will; mood. **2,** looks; appearance.

talar (ta'lar) *v.t.* **1,** to fell (trees). **2,** to desolate; destroy; ravage. —*adj.* full length; reaching to the ankles: *traje talar,* cassock.

talco ('tal·ko) *n.m.* talc; talcum.

talega (ta'le·γa) *n.f.* bag; sack; moneybag.

talego (ta'le·γo) *n.m.* **1,** bag; sack; duffel bag. **2,** *colloq.* dumpy person; rolypoly.

talento (ta'len·to) *n.m.* talent. —**talentoso,** *adj.* talented.

talio ('ta·ljo) *n.m.* thallium.

talión (ta'ljon) *n.m.* talion; retribution. —**la ley del talión,** an eye for an eye.

talismán (ta·lis'man) *n.m.* talisman; charm.

Talmud (tal'muð) *n.m.* Talmud. —**talmúdico** (-'mu·ði·ko) *adj.* Talmudic. —**talmudista** (-'ðis·ta) *n.m. & f.* Talmudist.

talón (ta'lon) *n.m.* **1,** heel. **2,** stub; coupon. **3,** talon.

talonario (ta·lo'na·rjo) *n.m.* **1,** book of stubs; coupon book. **2,** checkbook.

taltuza (tal'tu·θa; -sa) *n.f., Amer.* gopher.

talud (ta'luð) *n.m.* talus; slope; embankment.

talla ('ta·ʎa; -ja) *n.f.* **1,** height; stature. **2,** size *(of a garment).* **3,** carving; cutting. **4,** ransom. **5,** reward for the capture of a criminal or a fugitive.

tallar (ta'ʎar; -'jar) *v.t.* **1,** to cut; carve. **2,** to engrave. **3,** *cards* to have (the deck) as dealer. **4,** to evaluate; appraise. —*v.i., Amer., colloq.* to figure; have a say. —**tallado,** *adj.* carved; cut. —*n.m.* carving; cutting. —**talladura,** *n.f.* carving; cutting.

tallarín (ta·ʎa'rin; ta·ja-) *n.m.* noodle.

talle ('ta·ʎe; -je) *n.m.* **1,** waist, esp. a slender waist. **2,** form; figure; shape. **3,** fit *(of a garment).* **4,** *Amer.* bodice.

taller (ta'ʎer; -'jer) *n.m.* **1,** workshop; factory; mill. **2,** studio.

tallo ('ta·ʎo; -jo) *n.m.* **1,** stem; stalk. **2,** sprout; shoot.

tamal (ta'mal) *n.m.* tamale.

tamaño (ta'ma·ɲo) *n.m.* size. —*adj.* **1,** great; large; big. **2,** *colloq.* such a big . . . : *tamaño error,* such a big mistake.

tamarindo (ta·ma'rin·do) *n.m.* tamarind.

tambalear (tam·ba·le'ar) *v.i.* to stagger; totter. —**tambaleo** (-'le·o) *n.m.* staggering; tottering.

también (tam'bjen) *adv.* also; too; as well; besides.

tambo ('tam·bo) *n.m., S.A.* trading post.

tambor (tam'bor) *n.m.* **1,** drum. **2,** drummer. **3,** eardrum. —**tambor mayor,** drum major.

tambora (tam'bo·ra) *n.f.* bass drum.

tamborilear (tam·bo·ri·le'ar) *v.i.* **1,** to play the tambourine or tabor. **2,** to drum, beat or tap as with the fingers. —**tamborileo** (-'le·o) *n.m.* drumbeat. —**tamborilero** (-'le·ro) *n.m.* drummer.

tamborín (tam·bo'rin) *n.m.* tambourine; tabor. *Also,* **tamboril** (-'ril).

tamiz (ta'miθ; -'mis) *n.f.* sifter; fine sieve. —**tamizar** (-'θar; -'sar) *v.t.* [*infl.: rezar,* 10] to sift; strain.

tamo ('ta·mo) *n.m.* fuzz; fluff; lint.

tampoco (tam'po·ko) *adv.,* neither; not either; nor.

tampón (tam'pon) *n.m.* **1,** stamp pad. **2,** tampon.

tam-tam (tam'tam) *n.m.* tom-tom.

tan (tan) *adv.* as; so; so much. —**tan ... como,** as ... as; so ... as. —**tan siquiera,** at least. —**tan sólo,** only.

tanda ('tan·da) *n.f.* **1,** turn; round. **2,** shift; relay. **3,** series; string. **4,** *colloq.* great deal; lot. **5,** *Amer.* performance; showing *(of a play or movie)*. **6,** *colloq.* drubbing; beating.

tándem ('tan·dem) *n.m.* tandem.

tángara ('tan·ga·ra) *n.f.* tanager.

tangente (tan'xen·te) *adj. & n.m.* tangent. —**tangencia,** *n.f.* tangency. —**tangencial,** *adj.* tangential.

tangible (tan'xi·βle) *adj.* tangible.

tango ('tan·go) *n.m.* tango.

tanino (ta'ni·no) *n.m.* tannin. —**tánico** ('ta·ni·ko) *adj.* tannic.

tanque ('tan·ke) *n.m.* **1,** tank. **2,** *Amer.* pool; reservoir. **3,** *mil.* tank.

tantalio (tan'ta·ljo) *n.m.* tantalum.

tantán (tan'tan) *n.m.* **1,** gong. **2,** clang; clanging.

tantarantán (tan·ta·ran'tan) *n.m.* sound of a drum; rub-a-dub.

tantear (tan·te'ar) *v.t.* **1,** to feel; probe. **2,** to feel out; sound out. **3,** to try out; test. **4,** to sketch; outline. **5,** *Amer., colloq.* to estimate; calculate. —*v.i.* to feel one's way.

tanteo (tan'te·o) *n.m.* **1,** test; trial. **2,** estimate; calculation. **3,** score *(of a game)*. **4,** *Amer., colloq.* groping; feeling. —**al tanteo,** by guess; by feel; by eye.

tanto ('tan·to) *adj. & pron.* so much; as much; *pl.* so many; as many. —*adv.* so; so much; so long; in such a manner. —*n.m.* **1,** a certain amount; so much; *pl.* a certain number; so many. **2,** point *(in a game)*. **3,** counter *(in games)*. **4,** copy; duplicate. —**a tantos de mayo,** on such-and-such day in May. —**en su tanto,** within proper bounds; within rights. —**en tanto; entre tanto,** meanwhile. —**estar al tanto, 1,** to be or keep informed; be aware; be in the know. **2,** to look out; be on the lookout. —**las tantas,** a late hour. —**mientras tanto,** meanwhile. —**otro tanto, 1,** the same; equally. **2,** as much more. —**poner al tanto,** to inform; brief. —**por tanto; por lo tanto,** therefore. —**por tanto que,** inasmuch as; since. —**tanto por ciento,** per-

centage. —**un tanto,** *fol. by adj. or adv.* somewhat. —**y tantos,** and some; and some odd.

tañer (ta'ɲer) *v.t.* [*infl.:* 20] to pluck (a stringed instrument). —*v.t. & i.* **1,** to twang; sound, as strings. **2,** to peal; toll, as a bell.

tañido (ta'ɲi·ðo) *n.m.* **1,** pluck; plucking; twang. **2,** peal; toll *(of a bell)*.

tapa ('ta·pa) *n.f.* **1,** lid; cover; cap; top. **2,** pocket flap. **3,** *usu.pl.* tidbits; hors d'oeuvres.

tapabarro (ta·pa'βa·rro) *n.m., Amer.* mudguard.

tapada (ta'pa·ða) *n.f.* veiled woman.

tapadera (ta·pa'ðe·ra) *n.f.* cover; lid.

tapado (ta'pa·ðo) *n.m., Amer.* **1,** cloak; cape. **2,** buried treasure.

tapar (ta'par) *v.t.* **1,** to cover; cover up. **2,** to plug; stop up. **3,** to cap; put a lid on. **4,** *Amer.* to fill (a tooth).

taparrabo (ta·pa'rra·βo) *n.m.* loincloth. *Also,* **taparrabos,** *n.m. sing. & pl.*

tapete (ta'pe·te) *n.m.* **1,** small carpet; runner. **2,** table cover; table mat. —**sobre el tapete,** on the carpet.

tapia ('ta·pja) *n.f.* adobe wall. —**tapiar,** *v.t.* to wall up; wall in.

tapicería (ta·pi·θe'ri·a; -se'ri·a) *n.f.* **1,** tapestries. **2,** upholstery. **3,** tapestry shop and trade. **4,** upholstery shop.

tapicero (ta·pi'θe·ro; -'se·ro) *n.m.* **1,** carpet maker. **2,** tapestry maker. **3,** upholsterer.

tapioca (ta'pjo·ka) *n.f.* tapioca.

tapir (ta'pir) *n.m.* tapir.

tapiz (ta'piθ; -'pis) *n.m.* tapestry.

tapizar (ta·pi'θar; -'sar) *v.t.* [*infl.:* rezar, 10] **1,** to cover with tapestry. **2,** to carpet; cover over. **3,** to upholster.

tapón (ta'pon) *n.m.* **1,** plug; stopper; cap. **2,** tampon. **3,** fuse. **4,** *W.I.* traffic jam. —**taponazo,** *n.m.* pop *(of a cap or cork)*.

taponamiento (ta·po·na'mjen·to) *n.m.* **1,** act of corking or stopping up. **2,** bottleneck.

taponar (ta·po'nar) *v.t.* to plug; stopper; cap.

tapujo (ta'pu·xo) *n.m.* **1,** muffler; scarf; face wrap. **2,** *colloq.* concealment; subterfuge.

taquigrafía (ta·ki·ɣra'fi·a) *n.f.* stenography; shorthand. —**taquigrafiar**, *v.t.* [*infl.:* enviar, 22] to take down in shorthand. —**taquigráfico** (-'ɣra·fi·ko) *adj.* stenographic. —**taquígrafo** (-'ki·ɣra·fo) *n.m.* stenographer.

taquilla (ta'ki·ʎa; -ja) *n.f.* **1**, ticket office. **2**, box office. **3**, ticket rack. **4**, letter file. **5**, *Amer.* barroom; tavern. —**taquillero**, *n.m.* ticket agent. —*adj.*, in **éxito taquillero**, box-office hit.

tara ('ta·ra) *n.f.* **1**, *comm.* tare. **2**, defect; handicap.

tarabilla (ta·ra'βi·ʎa; -ja) *n.f.* fastener; catch.

taracear (ta·ra·θe'ar; -se'ar) *v.t.* to inlay; set with marquetry. —**taracea** (-'θe·a; -'se·a) *n.f.* inlaid work; marquetry.

tarambana (ta·ram'ba·na) *n.m. & f.*, *colloq.* madcap; flighty person.

tarantela (ta·ran'te·la) *n.f.* tarantella.

tarántula (ta'ran·tu·la) *n.f.* tarantula.

tararear (ta·ra·re'ar) *v.t. & i.* to hum (a tune). —**tarareo** (-'re·o) *n.m.* hum; humming.

tarasca (ta'ras·ka) *n.f.*, *colloq.* **1**, gluttony. **2**, *Amer.* mouth; big mouth.

tarascar (ta·ras'kar) *v.t.* [*infl.:* tocar, 7] to bite; snap.

tardanza (tar'ðan·θa; -sa) *n.f.* delay; tardiness.

tardar (tar'ðar) *v.i.* to delay; be late; take time; be long. —*v.t.* to take (a certain time). —**a más tardar**, at the latest.

tarde ('tar·ðe) *n.f.* afternooon. —*adv.* late; too late. —**de tarde en tarde**, from time to time. —**más tarde**, later. —**tarde o temprano**, sooner or later.

tardecer (tar·ðe'θer; -'ser) *v.i.* [*infl.:* conocer, 13] to grow late; approach nightfall.

tardío (tar'ði·o) *adj.* tardy.

tardo ('tar·ðo) *adj.* **1**, tardy; slow; sluggish. **2**, retarded.

tarea (ta're·a) *n.f.* task; job; assignment.

tarifa (ta'ri·fa) *n.f.* **1**, tariff. **2**, rate. **3**, fare.

tarima (ta'ri·ma) *n.f.* **1**, platform; stand. **2**, low bench or stool.

tarjeta (tar'xe·ta) *n.f.* **1**, card. **2**, label. —**tarjetero**, *n.m.* card file; card case. —**tarjeta postal**, postcard.

taro ('ta·ro) *n.m.* taro.

tarpón (tar'pon) *n.m.* tarpon.

tarquín (tar'kin) *n.m.* mud; silt.

tarraya (ta'rra·ja) *n.f.* casting net.

tarro ('ta·rro) *n.m.* **1**, can; jar. **2**, pail. **3**, *Amer.* high hat; top hat.

tarso ('tar·so) *n.m.* tarsus.

tarta ('tar·ta) *n.f.* tart.

tartajear (tar·ta·xe'ar) *v.i.* to stammer; stutter. —**tartajeo** (-'xe·o) *n.m.* stammering; stuttering.

tartalear (tar·ta·le'ar) *v.i.*, *colloq.* **1**, to fumble; dawdle; dodder. **2**, to be dumfounded.

tartamudear (tar·ta·mu·ðe'ar) *v.i.* to stammer; stutter. —**tartamudeo** (-'ðe·o) *n.m.* stammering; stuttering.

tartamudo (tar·ta'mu·ðo) *adj.* stuttering, stammering. —*n.m.* stutterer; stammerer. —**tartamudez**, *n.f.* affliction with stuttering or stammering.

tartán (tar'tan) *n.m.* tartan.

tártaro ('tar·ta·ro) *adj. & n.m.* Tartar. —*n.m.* **1**, hell. **2**, tartar. —**tártrico** ('tar·tri·ko) *also*, **tartárico** (-'ta·ri·ko) *adj.* tartaric.

tartera (tar'te·ra) *n.f.* **1**, baking pan; pie pan. **2**, lunch basket.

tarugo (ta'ru·ɣo) *n.m.* **1**, peg; pin. **2**, plug; bung. **3**, *Amer.*, *colloq.* cheat.

tasa ('ta·sa) *n.f.* **1**, assessment; appraisal; estimate. **2**, rate. **3**, price, esp. fixed price. **4**, measure; moderation.

tasación (ta·sa'θjon; -'sjon) *n.f.* appraisal; assessment.

tasador (ta·sa'ðor) *n.m.* [*fem.* -dora] appraiser; assessor.

tasajo (ta'sa·xo) *n.m.* **1**, jerked beef. **2**, piece of meat.

tasar (ta'sar) *v.t.* **1**, to appraise; assess; evaluate. **2**, to fix (a price, quota, etc.).

tasca ('tas·ka) *n.f.* gambling den; dive.

tascar (tas'kar) *v.t.* [*infl.:* tocar, 7] **1**, to crunch; chew noisily. **2**, to champ.

tata ('ta·ta) *n.m. Amer.*, *colloq.* dad.

tatarabuelo (ta·ta·ra'βwe·lo) *n.m.* great-great-grandfather. —**tatarabuela**, *n.f.* great-great-grandmother.

tataranieto (ta·ta·ra'nje·to) *n.m.* great-great-grandson. —**tataranieta**, *n.f.* great-great-granddaughter.

¡tate! ('ta·te) *interj.* **1**, easy!; careful! **2**, that's it!; I have it!

tato ('ta·to) *n.m.* stutterer with a lisp.

tatuar (ta'twar) *v.t.* [*infl.*: **continuar, 23**] to tattoo. —**tatuaje,** *n.m.* tattoo.

taumaturgo (tau·ma'tur·ɣo) *n.m.* miracle worker.

taurino (tau'ri·no) *adj.* taurine.

Tauro ('tau·ro) *n.m.* Taurus.

tauromaquia (tau·ro'ma·kja) *n.f.* the art of bullfighting. —**taurómaco** (-'ro·ma·ko) *adj.* bullfighting (*attrib.*). —*n.m.* expert in bullfighting.

taurófilo (tau'ro·fi·lo) *n.m.* bullfight fan.

tautología (tau·to·lo'xi·a) *n.f.* tautology. —**tautológico** (-'lo·xi·ko) *adj.* tautological.

taxativo (tak·sa'ti·βo) *adj.* limiting; restrictive.

taxear (tak·se'ar) *v.i.*, *aero.* to taxi.

taxi ('tak·si) *n.m.* taxi; taxicab.

taxidermia (tak·si'ðer·mja) *n.f.* taxidermy. —**taxidermista** (-'mis·ta) *n.m. & f.* taxidermist.

taxímetro (tak'si·me·tro) *n.m.* **1,** taximeter. **2,** taxicab.

taxista (tak'sis·ta) *n.m. & f.* taxi driver.

taxonomía (tak·so·no'mi·a) *n.f.* taxonomy. —**taxonómico** (-'no·mi·ko) *adj.* taxonomic. —**taxonomista** (-'mis·ta) *n.m. & f.* taxonomist.

taza ('ta·θa; -sa) *n.f.* **1,** cup. **2,** toilet bowl.

tazón (ta'θon; -'son) *n.m.* large cup; bowl.

te (te) *pers.pron. 2nd per.sing.*, used as *obj.* of a verb you; to you; yourself; thee; to thee; thyself.

té (te) *n.m.* tea.

tea ('te·a) *n.f.* torch; firebrand.

teatro (te'a·tro) *n.m.* **1,** theater. **2,** theatrics. —**teatral** (-'tral) *adj.* theatrical.

teca ('te·ka) *n.f.* teak.

tecla ('te·kla) *n.f.* key (*of a keyboard*). —**teclado,** *n.m.* keyboard. —**dar en (la) tecla,** to hit the mark; hit the nail on the head.

teclear (te·kle'ar) *v.i.* **1,** to operate a keyboard. **2,** *colloq.* to thrum; drum the fingers. **3,** to click; clack. —*v.t.*, *colloq.* to try out; feel out.

tecleo (te'kle·o) *n.m.* **1,** fingering (*of a keyboard*). **2,** *colloq.* thrumming; drumming the fingers. **3,** clicking; clacking.

tecnecio (tek'ne·θjo; -sjo) *n.m.* technetium.

técnica ('tek·ni·ka) *n.f.* **1,** technique. **2,** technics. —**técnico,** *adj.* technical. —*n.m.* technician.

tecnicismo (tek·ni'θis·mo; -'sis·mo) *n.m.* technicality.

tecnicolor (tek·ni·ko'lor) *n.m.* technicolor.

tecnocracia (tek·no'kra·θja; -sja) *n.f.* technocracy. —**tecnócrata** (-'no·kra·ta) *n.m. & f.* technocrat. —**tecnocrático** (-'kra·ti·ko) *adj.* technocratic.

tecnología (tek·no·lo'xi·a) *n.f.* technology. —**tecnológico** (-'lo·xi·ko) *adj.* technological. —**tecnólogo** (-'no·lo·ɣo) *n.m.* technologist.

tectónica (tek'to·ni·ka) *n.f.* tectonics. —**tectónico,** *adj.* tectonic.

techado (te'tʃa·ðo) *n.m.* roof; roofing. *Also,* **techumbre** (te'tʃum·bre) *n.f.* —**techador,** *n.m.* roofer. —**techar,** *v.t.* to roof; provide with a roof.

techo ('te·tʃo) *n.m.* **1,** roof. **2,** ceiling. —**techar,** *v.t.* to roof.

tedio ('te·ðjo) *n.m.* tedium; boredom. —**tedioso,** *adj.* tedious.

tee (ti) *n.m.*, golf tee.

tegumento (te·ɣu'men·to) *n.m.* tegument.

teísmo (te'is·mo) *n.m.* theism. —**teísta,** *n.m. & f.* theist. —*adj.* theistic.

teja ('te·xa) *n.f.* roof tile. —**tejado,** *n.m.* roof. esp. tiled roof. —**tejar,** *v.t.* to tile; roof with tiles. —*n.m.* tile works.

tejamaní (te·xa·ma'ni) *n.m.*, *Amer.* roof shingle. *Also,* **tejamanil** (-'nil).

tejeduría (te·xe·ðu'ri·a) *n.f.* **1,** weaving art or trade. **2,** weaving mill.

tejemaneje (te·xe·ma'ne·xe) *n.m.*, *colloq.* **1,** knack; cleverness. **2,** scheming; maneuvering.

tejer (te'xer) *v.t. & i.* **1,** to weave. **2,** to spin (a web, cocoon, etc.). **3,** *colloq.* to knit; crochet. —**tejedor,** *adj.* weaving; spinning. —*n.m.* [*fem.* **-dora**] weaver; spinner. —**tejedura,** *n.f.* weave; weaving.

tejido (te'xi·ðo) *n.m.* **1,** fabric; textile. **2,** weave. **3,** tissue.

tejo ('te·xo) *n.m.* **1,** quoit; disk. **2,** metal disk. **3,** yew; yew tree.

tejón (te'xon) *n.m.* **1,** badger. **2,** disk; round slug.

tela ('te·la) *n.f.* **1,** cloth; fabric. **2,**

skin; membrane. **3,** *paint.* canvas. **4,** insect web; cobweb. **5,** subject matter; material. —**en tela de juicio,** in doubt; in question. —**tela metálica,** wire mesh; wire netting.

telar (te'lar) *n.m.* **1,** loom; weaving machine. **2,** frame, as for weaving. **3,** *theat.* flies.

telaraña (te·la·ra'ɲa) *n.f., also,* **tela de araña,** cobweb; spider web.

teledifundir (te·le·ði·fun'dir) *v.t.* to telecast. —**teledifusión** (-fu'sjon) *n.f.* telecast.

teledirigir (te·le·ði·ri'xir) *v.t.* [*infl.:* coger, 15] to guide by remote control. —**teledirigido,** *adj.* remote-controlled.

teléfono (te'le·fo·no) *n.m.* telephone. —**telefonazo** (-'na·θo; -so) *n.m., colloq.* telephone call. —**telefonear** (-ne'ar) *v.t. & i.* to telephone. —**telefonía,** *n.f.* telephony. —**telefónico** (-'fo·ni·ko) *adj.* telephonic. —**telefonista,** *n.m. & f.* telephone operator.

telefoto (te·lc'fo·to) *n.m.* telephoto. —**telefotografía** (-ɣra'fi·a) *n.f.* telephotography. —**telefotográfico** (-'ɣra·fi·ko) *adj.* telephotographic.

telégrafo (te'le·ɣra·fo) *n.m.* telegraph. —**telegrafía** (-'fi·a) *n.f.* telegraphy. —**telegrafiar** (-'fjar) *v.t.* [*infl.:* enviar, 22] to telegraph. —**telegráfico** (-'ɣra·fi·ko) *adj.* telegraphic. —**telegrafista,** *n.m. & f.* telegraph operator; telegrapher.

telegrama (te·le'ɣra·ma) *n.m.* telegram.

telemando (te·le'man·do) *n.m.* remote control.

telémetro (te'le·me·tro) *n.m.* telemeter; range finder. —**telemetría,** *n.f.* telemetry.

telenovela (te·le·no'βe·la) *n.f.* TV soap opera.

teleología (te·le·o·lo'xi·a) *n.f.* teleology. —**teleológico** (-'lo·xi·ko) *adj.* teleological.

telepatía (te·le·pa'ti·a) *n.f.* telepathy. —**telepático** (-'pa·ti·ko) *adj.* telepathic.

telequinesis (te·le·ki'ne·sis) *n.f.* telekinesis.

telescopio (te·les'ko·pjo) *n.m.* telescope. —**telescópico** (-'ko·pi·ko) *adj.* telescopic.

teletipo (te·le'ti·po) *n.m.* teletype.

televidente (te·le·βi'ðen·te) *n.m. & f.* television viewer; televiewer.

televisión (te·le·βi'sjon) *n.f.* television. —**televisar** (-'sar) *v.t.* to televise. —**televisor** (-'sor) *n.m.* television set. —*adj.* television (*attrib.*).

telilla (te'li·ʎa; -ja) *n.f.* **1,** thin, light fabric. **2,** thin membrane; film.

telón (te'lon) *n.m.* theater curtain; drop curtain. —**telón de boca,** front curtain. —**telón de foro** *or* **fondo,** backdrop.

telurio (te'lu·rjo) *n.m.* tellurium.

tema (te'ma) *n.m.* **1,** theme; subject. **2,** *gram.* stem; base. —*n.f.* mania; obsession. —**temático** (te'ma·ti·ko) *adj.* thematic.

temblar (tem'blar) *v.i.* [*infl.:* pensar, 27] **1,** to tremble; shake; quake. **2,** to shiver; shudder. —**tembladera,** *n.f., Amer., colloq.* fit of shakes. —**tembladero,** *n.m.* = **tremedal.**

tembleque (tem'ble·ke) *adj.* **1,** shaky. **2,** trembling; quaking. —**temblequear,** *v.i., colloq.* to shiver; quiver; have the shakes.

temblón (tem'blon) *adj., colloq.,* **1,** shaky. **2,** quaking; trembling.

temblor (tem'blor) *n.m.* **1,** tremor; trembling. **2,** quake; earth tremor.

tembloroso (tem·blo'ro·so) *adj.* quaking; trembling; tremulous.

temer (te'mer) *v.t.* [*infl.:* 2] to fear. —*v.i.* to be afraid; fear.

temerario (te·me'ra·rjo) *adj.* temerarious; rash. —**temeridad** (-ri'ðað) *n.f.* temerity.

temeroso (te·me'ro·so) *adj.* **1,** fearful; afraid. **2,** timorous.

temible (te'mi·βle) *adj.* fearful; fearsome.

temor (te'mor) *n.m.* fear; dread.

témpano (tem'pa·no) *n.m.* **1,** kettledrum; tympanum. **2,** drumskin. **3,** block of ice; ice floe. **4,** [*also,* **témpano de hielo**] iceberg. **5,** barrelhead. **6,** thick slice, as of bacon.

temperado (tem·pe'ra·ðo) *adj.* = **templado.**

temperamento (tem·pe·ra'men·to) *n.m.* temperament. —**temperamental,** *adj.* temperamental.

temperancia (tem·pe'ran·θja; -sja) *n.f.* temperance.

temperante (tem·pe'ran·te) *adj.* **1,** temperate; moderate. **2,** tempering; moderating.

temperar (tem·pe'rar) *v.t.* to temper; moderate; calm.

temperatura (tem·pe·ra'tu·ra) *n.f.* temperature.

temperie (tem'pe·rje) *n.f.* weather; state of the weather.

tempestad (tem·pes'taθ) *n.f.* tempest; storm. —**tempestuoso** (-'two·so) *adj.* tempestuous; stormy.

templa ('tem·pla) *n.f.* tempera.

templado (tem'pla·ðo) *adj.* 1, temperate; moderate. 2, tempered. 3, tepid; lukewarm. 4, *Amer., colloq.* drunk.

templanza (tem'plan·θa; -sa) *n.f.* 1, temperance. 2, mildness. 3, moderation.

templar (tem'plar) *v.t.* 1, to temper. 2, to take the chill out of; warm; make lukewarm. 3, to stretch; make taut. 4, to tune; put in tune. 5, *naut.* to trim or adjust (the sails) to the wind. —*v.i.* to warm up; become warmer. —**templarse**, *v.r.* 1, to become temperate; exercise temperance. 2, *Amer., colloq.* to become tipsy; get drunk.

temple ('tem·ple) *n.m.* 1, temperature. 2, temper, as of metals. 3, disposition; mood; temperament. 4, courage. 5, *mus.* tuning; tempering. —**al temple**, *paint.* in tempera.

templete (tem'ple·te) *n.m.* canopy; pavilion.

templo ('tem·plo) *n.m.* temple; sanctuary.

temporada (tem·po'ra·ða) *n.f.* time; period of time; season.

temporal (tem·po'ral) *adj.* 1, temporal; secular. 2, temporary; transitory. 2, *anat.* temporal. —*n.m.* 1, tempest; storm. 2, temporal bone.

temporario (tem·po'ra·rjo) *adj.* temporary. *Also,* **temporáneo** (-'ra·ne·o).

temporero (tem·po're·ro) *adj.* provisional; temporary.

temporizar (tem·po·ri'θar; -'sar) *v.i.* [*infl.:* **rezar,** 10] to temporize.

tempranero (tem·pra'ne·ro) *adj.* early.

tempranito (tem·pra'ni·to) *adv., colloq.* early; very early.

temprano (tem'pra·no) *adj. & adv.* early.

tenacidad (te·na·θi'ðað; -si'ðað) *n.f.* tenacity.

tenacillas (te·na'θi·ʎas; -'si·jas) *n.f.pl.* 1, tweezers; pincers, small tongs. 2, sugar tongs. 3, curling irons.

tenada (te'na·ða) *n.f.* shed.

tenaz (te'naθ; -'nas) *adj.* tenacious.

tenaza (te'na·θa; -sa) *n.f., also pl.* **tenazas,** 1, pincers; claws. 2, tongs.

3, pliers. 4, pincer-like hold. —**tenazuelas,** *n.f.pl.* tweezers.

tenca ('ten·ka) *n.f.* tench.

tendal (ten'dal) *n.m.* 1, awning. 2, clothes spread out for drying. 3, cloth spread out to catch fruit. 4, *S.A.* apron.

tendalera (ten·da'le·ra) *n.f., colloq.* slew; scattered lot; litter. *Also, Amer.,* **tendalada** (-'la·ða).

tendencia (ten'den·θja; -sja) *n.f.* 1, tendency. 2, tendentiousness. —**tendencioso,** *adj.* tendentious.

ténder ('ten·der) *n.m., R.R.* tender.

tender (ten'der) *v.t.* [*infl.:* **perder,** 29] 1, to stretch; lay out. 2, to hang out (laundry) for drying. 3, to lay down. 4, to extend; tender; offer. —*v.i.* to tend.

tenderete (ten·de're·te) *n.m.* 1, = **tendalera.** 2, market stall.

tendero (ten'de·ro) *n.m.* storekeeper.

tendido (ten'di·ðo) *adj.* accelerated; at full speed. —*n.m.* 1, laying out; laying down. 2, bleachers.

tendón (ten'don) *n.m.* tendon.

tendré (ten'dre) *v., fut. of* **tener.**

tenebroso (te·ne'βro·so) *adj.* dark; gloomy. —**tenebrosidad,** *n.f.* darkness; gloom.

tenedor (te·ne'ðor) *n.m.* 1, fork; table fork. 2, holder; keeper. —**tenedor de libros,** bookkeeper.

teneduría (te·ne·ðu'ri·a) *n.f., also,* **teneduría de libros,** bookkeeping.

tenencia (te'nen·θja; -sja) *n.f.* 1, tenure; holding. 2, lieutenancy.

tener (te'ner) *v.t.* [*infl.:* 65] 1, to have. 2, to hold; take or have hold of. 3, to contain. 4, to have or experience the feeling of, as cold, hunger, etc.: *tener sed, calor, etc.,* to be thirsty, warm, etc. 5, to be (a certain age): *tiene cinco años,* he is five years old. —*aux.v.,* sometimes used in place of **haber:** *tengo dicho,* I have said. *When the p.p. is construed as a participial adjective, it agrees in gender and number with the object:* Tengo escritos dos libros, I have written two books (i.e., I have two books written). *The combination of aux.v. and p.p. is sometimes equivalent to the simple form of the verb:* Tengo entendido que irás, I understand you will go; Tengo pensado comprar una casa, I intend to buy a house. —**tenerse,** *v.r.* to hold (oneself or itself); keep (oneself or itself). **—no tener en qué** (or **donde**) **caerse muerto,** to be penniless; be destitute. **—no tenerlas todas consigo,** to be scared; be worried. **—tener lugar,** to take place; occur; happen. **—tener que,** *fol. by inf.* to have to; must: *Tengo que salir,* I have to go out. **—tener (algo) que ...** to have (something) to ... : *Tengo mucho que decir,* I have much to say. **—tener que ver,** to be pertinent. **—tener que ver con,** to have to do with; be concerned with.

tenería (te·ne'ri·a) *n.f.* tannery.

tenia ('te·nja) *n.f.* tapeworm.

teniente (te'njen·te) *n.m.* lieutenant. **—adj. 1,** having; holding. **2,** *colloq.* hard of hearing. **—teniente de alcalde,** deputy mayor.

tenis ('te·nis) *n.m.* tennis. **—tenista,** *n.m. & f.* tennis player.

tenor (te'nor) *n.m.* **1,** tenor; purport. **2,** *mus.* tenor. **3,** kind; nature; sort.

tenorio (te'no·rjo) *n.m.* Don Juan; rake.

tensar (ten'sar) *v.t.* to tauten; tighten.

tensión (ten'sjon) *n.m.* **1,** tension. **2,** tensity. **—tensión arterial,** blood pressure.

tenso ('ten·so) *adj.* tense.

tensor (ten'sor) *n.m.* tensor. **—adj. 1,** tensile. **2,** producing tension.

tentación (ten·ta'θjon; -'sjon) *n.f.* temptation.

tentáculo (ten·ta·ku·lo) *n.m.* tentacle.

tentador (ten·ta'ðor) *adj.* tempting. **—n.m.** tempter. **—tentadora,** *n.f.* temptress.

tentalear (ten·ta·le'ar) *v.t.* to feel; grope about for.

tentar (ten'tar) *v.t.* [*infl.:* **pensar,** 27] **1,** to tempt. **2,** to try; attempt. **3,** to touch; feel. **4,** to grope for. **5,** to probe.

tentativa (ten·ta·ti·βa) *n.f.* attempt; trial. **—tentativo,** *adj.* tentative.

tenue ('te·nwe) *adj.* **1,** thin; light; slender. **2,** tenuous. **—tenuidad** (te·nwi'ðað) *n.f.* tenuousness.

teñir (te'ɲir) *v.t.* [*infl.:* **reñir,** 59] to dye; stain. **—teñido,** *n.m.* dyeing.

teocracia (te·o'kra·θja; -sja) *n.f.* theocracy. **—teocrático** (-'kra·ti·ko) *adj.* theocratic.

teologal (te·o·lo'ɣal) *adj.* theologi-

cal. **—virtudes teologales,** theological virtues.

teología (te·o·lo'xi·a) *n.f.* theology. **—teológico** (-'lo·xi·ko) *adj.* theological. **—teólogo** (te'o·lo·ɣo) *n.m.* theologian.

teorema (te·o're·ma) *n.m.* theorem.

teoría (te·o'ri·a) *n.f.* theory. **—teórica** (te'o·ri·ka) *n.f.* theoretics. **—teórico,** *adj.* theoretical. **—n.m.** theorist.

teorizar (te·o·ri'θar; -'sar) *v.i.* [*infl.:* **rezar,** 10] to theorize. **—v.t.** to treat theoretically.

teosofía (te·o·so'fi·a) *n.f.* theosophy. **—teosófico** (-'so·fi·ko) *adj.* theosophical. **—teósofo** (te'o·so·fo) *n.m.* theosophist.

tepe ('te·pe) *n.m.* block of turf or sod.

tequila (te'ki·la) *n.f.* tequila.

terapéutica (te·ra'peu·ti·ka) *n.f.* **1,** therapeutics. **2,** therapy. **—terapeuta** (-'peu·ta) *n.m. & f.* therapist. **—terapéutico** (-'peu·ti·ko) *adj.* therapeutic. **—terapia** (-'ra·pja) *n.f.* therapy.

terbio ('ter·βjo) *n.m.* terbium.

tercer (ter'θer; -'ser) *adj.* = **tercero** *before a masc. noun.*

tercera (ter'θe·ra; -'se·ra) *n.f.* **1,** *mus.* third. **2,** procuress.

tercería (ter·θe'ri·a; -se'ri·a) *n.f.* **1,** mediation. **2,** *law* right of third party. **3,** one-third interest or partnership.

tercero (ter'θe·ro; -'se·ro) *adj. & n.m.* third. **—n.m. 1,** third party. **2,** mediator; go-between.

terciana (ter'θja·na; -'sja·na) *n.f., usu.pl.* tertian fever.

terciar (ter'θjar; -'sjar) *v.t.* **1,** to divide into thirds. **2,** to slant; place aslant. **3,** *mil.* to port (a rifle). **—v.i. 1,** to mediate; intercede. **2,** to take part; participate. **3,** to come up; happen; intervene. **—terciarse,** *v.r.* **1,** to be fitting; be propitious. **2,** *colloq.* to accede; come around; agree. **—terciado,** *adj.* crosswise.

terciario (ter'θja·rjo; -'sja·rjo) *adj. & n.m.* tertiary. **—n.m.** member of a tertiary order.

tercio ('ter·θjo; -sjo) *adj. & n.m.* third. **—hacer tercio,** to take equal share; join in as an equal.

terciopelo (ter·θjo'pe·lo; ter·sjo-) *n.m.* velvet. **—terciopelado,** *adj.* = **aterciopelado. —n.m.** velours.

terco ('ter·ko) *adj.* obstinate; stubborn.

tergiversar (ter·xi·βer'sar) *v.t., fig.* to distort; twist. —**tergiversación,** *n.f., fig.* distortion.

termal (ter'mal) *adj.* thermal.

termas ('ter·mas) *n.f.pl.* **1,** thermal waters; hot springs. **2,** Roman baths.

termes ('ter·mes) *n.m.* termite.

térmico ('ter·mi·ko) *adj.* thermal; thermic.

terminable (ter·mi·na·βle) *adj.* terminable.

terminal (ter·mi'nal) *adj. & n.m.* terminal. —*n.f.* terminal station.

terminante (ter·mi'nan·te) *adj.* **1,** definite; unequivocal. **2,** definitive; final.

terminar (ter·mi'nar) *v.t. & i.* to finish; terminate; end. —**terminación,** *n.f.* termination. —**terminado,** *adj.* finished. —*n.m.* finish; polish.

término ('ter·mi·no) *n.m.* **1,** term. **2,** end. **3,** boundary; limit; terminus. **4,** place; position. **5,** terminal. —**primer término,** foreground. —**término medio, 1,** average. **2,** middle ground. —**término municipal,** township.

terminología (ter·mi·no·lo'xi·a) *n.f.* terminology.

termita (ter'mi·ta) *n.m.* termite. —*n.f.* thermit.

termodinámica (ter·mo·ði'na·mi·ka) *n.f.* thermodynamics. —**termodinámico,** *adj.* thermodynamic.

termoeléctrico (ter·mo·e'lek·tri·ko) *adj.* thermoelectric.

termómetro (ter'mo·met·ro) *n.m.* thermometer. —**termométrico** (-'me·tri·ko) *adj.* thermometric.

termonuclear (ter·mo·nu·kle'ar) *adj.* thermonuclear.

termos ('ter·mos) *n.m.sing. & pl.* thermos bottle. *Also,* **termo,** *n.m.sing.*

termosifón (ter·mo·si'fon) *n.m.* water heater.

termostático (ter·mos'ta·ti·ko) *adj.* thermostatic.

termóstato (ter'mos·ta·to) *n.m.* thermostat.

terna ('ter·na) *n.f.* **1,** group or set of three. **2,** slate of three candidates.

ternario (ter'na·rjo) *adj. & n.m.* ternary.

ternera (ter'ne·ra) *n.f.* **1,** female calf. **2,** veal. —**ternero,** *n.m.* calf; male calf.

terneza (ter'ne·θa; -sa) *n.f.* **1,** = **ternura. 2,** *usu.pl.* sweet nothings.

ternilla (ter'ni·ʎa; -ja) *n.f.* cartilage.

terno ('ter·no) *n.m.* **1,** suit of clothes, usu. including a vest. **2,** swear word; profanity. **3,** group or set of three.

ternura (ter'nu·ra) *n.f.* tenderness.

terquear (ter·ke'ar) *v.i.* to be stubborn.

terquedad (ter·ke'ðað) *n.f.* obstinacy; stubbornness.

terracota (te·rra'ko·ta) *n.f.* terra cotta.

terrado (te'rra·ðo) *n.m.* flat roof; terrace.

terramicina (te·rra·mi'θi·na; -'si·na) *n.f.* terramycin.

terraplén (te·rra'plen) *n.m.* embankment; terrace.

terraplenar (te·rra·ple'nar) *v.t.* **1,** to level (land). **2,** to terrace by cut or fill. **2,** to embank.

terráqueo (te'rra·ke·o) *adj.* **1,** terraqueous. **2,** terrestrial.

terrario (te'rra·rjo) *n.m.* terrarium.

terrateniente (te·rra·te'njen·te) *n.m.* landholder; landowner.

terraza (te'rra·θa; -sa) *n.f.* terrace.

terregoso (te·rre'yo·so) *adj.* **1,** lumpy; full of clods. **2,** paved with dirt.

terremoto (te·rre'mo·to) *n.m.* earthquake.

terrenal (te·rre'nal) *adj.* worldly; earthly; mundane.

terreno (te'rre·no) *n.m.* **1,** terrain; ground. **2,** grounds. **3,** plot of land. —*adj.* **1,** terrestrial. **2,** = **terrenal.**

terrestre (te'rres·tre) *adj.* **1,** terrestrial. **2,** land *(attrib.)*.

terrible (te'rri·βle) *adj.* terrible. —**terribilidad,** *n.f.* terribleness.

terrier (te'rrjer) *n.m.* terrier.

terrífico (te'rri·fi·ko) *adj.* terrific; terrifying.

territorio (te·rri'to·rjo) *n.m.* territory. —**territorial,** *adj.* territorial.

terrón (te'rron) *n.m.* lump; clod.

terror (te'rror) *n.m.* terror. —**terrorífico** (-rro'ri·fi·ko) *adj.* = **terrífico.**

terrorismo (te·rro'ris·mo) *n.m.* terrorism. —**terrorista,** *n.m. & f.* terrorist. —*adj.* terroristic.

terruño (te'rru·ɲo) *n.m.* soil; land, esp. native land.

terso ('ter·so) *adj.* **1,** smooth. **2,** terse.

tersura (ter'su·ra) *n.f.* **1,** smoothness. **2,** terseness.

tertulia (ter'tu·lja) *n.f.* **1,** social gathering; tea party; salon. **2,** conversation; talk. **3,** *S.A.* orchestra; parquet *(of a theater).* —**salón de tertulia,** lounge.

tesar (te'sar) *v.t.,* naut. to make taut.

tesauro (te'sau·ro) *n.m.* thesaurus.

tesis ('te·sis) *n.f.sing. & pl.* thesis.

teso ('te·so) *adj.* = **tieso.**

tesón (te'son) *n.m.* tenacity; firmness. —**tesonería,** *n.f.* stubbornness; pertinacity. —**tesonero,** *adj.* pertinacious; tenacious.

tesoro (te'so·ro) *n.m.* **1,** treasure. **2,** treasury. —**tesorería,** *n.f.* treasury. —**tesorero,** *n.m.* treasurer.

test (test) *n.m.* test.

testa ('tes·ta) *n.f.* head.

testaferro (tes·ta'fe·rro) *n.m.* figurehead; dummy. *Also,* **testaférrea** (-rre·a).

testamentaría (tes·ta·men·ta'ri·a) *n.f.* **1,** testamentary execution. **2,** inheritance; estate.

testamento (tes·ta'men·to) *n.m.* **1,** testament. **2,** will. —**testamentaria,** *n.f.* executrix. —**testamentario,** *adj.* testamentary. —*n.m.* executor.

testar (tes'tar) *v.i.* to make a will. —**testación,** *n.f.* making of a will. —**testado,** *adj.* testate. —**testador,** *n.m.* testator. —**testadora,** *n.f.* testatrix.

testarudo (tes·ta'ru·ðo) *adj.* stubborn. —**testarudez,** *n.f.* stubbornness.

teste ('tes·te) *n.m.* testicle. —**testes,** *n.m.pl.* testes.

testículo (tes'ti·ku·lo) *n.m.* testicle.

testificar (tes·ti·fi'kar) *v.t. & i.* [*infl.:* **tocar,** 7] to testify. —**testificación,** *n.f.* testifying; attestation.

testigo (tes'ti·ɣo) *n.m. & f.* witness. —*n.m.* proof; evidence. —**testigo de cargo,** witness for the prosecution. —**testigo de descargo,** witness for the defense. —**testigo de vista; testigo ocular,** eyewitness.

testimonio (tes·ti'mo·njo) *n.m.* testimony. —**testimonial,** *adj.* confirmatory; attesting; testifying.

—*n.f.* testimonial. —**testimoniar,** *v.t. & i.* to testify; attest.

testosterona (tes·tos·te'ro·na) *n.f.* testosterone.

testuz (tes'tuθ; -'tus) *n.m.* **1,** nape. **2,** forehead *(of animals).*

teta ('te·ta) *n.f.* teat. —**tetar,** *v.t.* to suckle; nurse.

tétano ('te·ta·no) *n.m.* tetanus. *Also,* **tétanos.**

tetera (te'te·ra) *n.f.* teapot; teakettle.

tetero (te'te·ro) *n.m., S.A.* nursing bottle.

tetilla (te'ti·ʎa; -ja) *n.f.* nipple.

tetraedro (te·tra'e·ðro) *n.m.* tetrahedron. —**tetraédrico,** *adj.* tetrahedral.

tetrágono (te'tra·ɣo·no) *n.m.* tetragon. —**tetragonal,** *adj.* tetragonal.

tetrarca (te'trar·ka) *n.m.* tetrarch. —**tetrarquía** (-'ki·a) *n.f.* tetrarchy.

tétrico ('te·tri·ko) *adj.* sad; gloomy; dark.

teutón (tcu'ton) *n.m.* Teuton. —**teutónico** (-'to·ni·ko) *adj. & n.m.* Teutonic.

textil (teks'til) *adj. & n.m.* textile.

texto ('teks·to) *n.m.* **1,** text. **2,** textbook. —**textual** (-'twal) *adj.* textual.

textura (teks'tu·ra) *n.f.* **1,** texture. **2,** weave.

tez (teθ; tes) *n.f.* complexion.

tezado (te'θa·ðo; -'sa·ðo) *adj.* = **atezado.**

ti (ti) *pers.pron. 2nd pers.sing., used after a prep.* you; yourself; thee; thyself.

tía ('ti·a) *n.f.* **1,** aunt. **2,** *derog.* woman; female. —**no hay tu tía,** *colloq.* there's nothing to be done about it. —**quedarse para tía,** to remain an old maid. —**tía abuela,** great-aunt.

tiamina (ti·a'mi·na) *n.f.* thiamine.

tiara ('tja·ra) *n.f.* tiara.

tibia ('ti·βja) *n.f.* tibia.

tibio ('ti·βjo) *adj.* tepid; lukewarm. —**tibieza,** *n.f.* tepidity; tepidness; lukewarmness.

tiburón (ti·βu'ron) *n.m.* shark.

tic (tik) *n.m.* **1,** [*pl.* **tiques** ('ti·kes)] tic. **2,** [*also,* **tictac** (tik'tak)] tick; ticking.

ticket ('ti·ket) *n.m.* [*pl.* **tickets**] ticket.

tiemble ('tjem·ble) *v., pres.subjve. of* **temblar.**

tiemblo ('tjem·blo) v., 1st pers. sing. pres.ind. of **temblar.**

tiempo ('tjem·po) n.m. 1, time. 2, epoch; age; times. 3, period; season. 4, weather. 5, gram. tense. 6, mus. tempo. 7, phase; measure. —a tiempo, in time; at the right time. —a su tiempo, in good time. —a un tiempo, in unison; at once. —cargarse or cerrarse el tiempo, to cloud over; become cloudy. —con tiempo, 1, in time; eventually. 2, ahead of time; with foresight. —cuanto tiempo, how long. —de un tiempo a esta parte, for some time; for some time now. —fuera de tiempo, untimely. —¿Qué tiempo hace?, How is the weather?

tienda ('tjen·da) n.f. 1, store; shop. 2, tent. —tienda de campaña, army tent.

tienda ('tjen·da) v., pres.subjve. of **tender.**

tiendo ('tjen·do) v., 1st pers.sing. pres.ind. of **tender.**

tienes ('tje·nes) v., 2nd pers.sing.pres.ind. of **tener.**

tienta ('tjen·ta) n.f. 1, probe. 2, shrewdness. —a tientas, gropingly; groping one's way.

tiente ('tjen·te) v., pres.subjve. of **tentar.**

tiento ('tjen·to) n.m. 1, touch; feel. 2, tact. 3, care; caution. 4, steady hand. 5, feeler. 6, try; test. 7, blind man's stick. 8, colloq. slap; blow; poke. 9, colloq. swig; swallow. —dar un tiento a, colloq. to have a try at; take a crack at.

tiento ('tjen·to) v., 1st pers.sing. pres.ind. of **tentar.**

tierno ('tjer·no) adj. tender.

tierra ('tje·rra) n.f. 1, earth. 2, land; soil. 3, ground. —tierra adentro, inland. —tierra firme, 1, mainland. 2, terra firma.

tieso ('tje·so) adj. stiff. —adv. stiffly. —tiesura, n.f. stiffness.

tiesto ('tjes·to) n.m. pot; flowerpot.

tifo ('ti·fo) adj., colloq. full; satiated. —n.m. typhus. —tifo asiático, cholera. —tifo de América, yellow fever. —tifo de Oriente, bubonic plague.

tifoideo (ti·foi'ðe·o) adj. typhoid. —tifoidea, n.f. typhoid fever.

tifón (ti'fon) n.m. typhoon.

tifus ('ti·fus) n.m.sing. & pl. typhus.

tigre ('ti·yre) n.m. 1, tiger. 2, Amer.

jaguar. —tigra, n.f., Amer. female jaguar. —tigresa, n.f. tigress.

tijeras (ti'xe·ras) n.f.pl., also sing. tijera, scissors; shears. —tijerada, n.f. = tijeretazo. —(de) tijera, folding; scissor (attrib.).

tijeretear (ti·xe·re·te'ar) v.t. to snip; cut with scissors. —tijeretazo (-'ta·θo; -so) n.m. snip or cut with scissors. —tijereteo (-'te·o) n.m. snipping; cutting.

tila ('ti·la) n.f. 1, linden flower. 2, tea made of linden flowers.

tildar (til'dar) v.t. 1, to put a tilde on. 2, usu.fol. by de, to brand as; label as. 3, strike out; erase.

tilde ('til·de) n.m. or f. 1, tilde. 2, flaw; blemish. 3, brand; stigma. —n.f. jot; speck.

tilín (ti'lin) n.m. tinkle. —hacer tilín, to be likable; be well-liked.

tilo ('ti·lo) n.m. 1, linden tree. 2, tea made of linden flowers.

tilla ('ti·ʎa; -ja) n.f. deck board, esp. of a small boat. —tillado, n.m. wood floor. —tillar, v.t. to floor.

timar (ti'mar) v.t. to cheat; swindle. —timarse, v.r., colloq. to make eyes at each other. —timador, n.m., colloq. [fem. -dora] cheat; swindler.

timbal (tim'bal) n.f. 1, kettledrum. 2, tabor; drum. 3, meat pie. —timbalero, n.m. tympanist.

timbrado (tim'bra·ðo) adj. 1, stamped. 2, sonorous.

timbrar (tim'brar) v.t. to stamp; affix a stamp to. —v.t. & i., Amer., colloq. to ring.

timbre ('tim·bre) n.m. 1, stamp; seal. 2, official stamp; tax stamp. 3, Amer. postage stamp. 4, timbre. 5, electric bell; buzzer; call bell; doorbell. —timbre de gloria, 1, milestone of glory; outstanding achievement. 2, pride; object of pride.

tímido ('ti·mi·ðo) adj. timid; bashful; shy. —timidez, n.f. timidity; bashfulness; shyness.

timo ('ti·mo) n.m. 1, thymus. 2, colloq. cheat; swindle.

timón (ti'mon) n.m. 1, helm; rudder. 2, steering wheel. 3, beam of a plow. —timonear, v.t. & i. to steer (a vessel). —timonel, also, timonero, n.m. helmsman; boatsman; yachtsman. —timón de profundidad, aero. elevator.

timorato (ti·mo'ra·to) adj. timorous.

tímpano ('tim·pa·no) *n.m.* **1,** *anat.* tympanum; eardrum. **2,** *archit.* tympanum; pediment. **3,** drum; kettledrum.

tina ('ti·na) *n.f.* **1,** = **tinaja. 2,** bathtub.

tinaja (ti'na·xa) *n.f.* large earthen jar.

tinajero (ti·na'xe·ro) *n.m.* **1,** maker or seller of water jars. **2,** stand for water jars.

tinglado (tin'gla·ðo) *n.m.* **1,** shed; tent. **2,** wooden stand or platform. **3,** trick; scheme. **4,** *colloq.* brawl; scramble.

tiniebla (ti'nje·βla) *n.f., usu.pl.* **1,** darkness. **2,** abysmal ignorance.

tino ('ti·no) *n.m.* **1,** good sense; good judgment. **2,** accuracy; precision; good aim. **3,** tact. —**sacar de tino,** *colloq.* to drive (someone) mad.

tinta ('tin·ta) *n.f.* **1,** ink. **2,** dye; color. —**de buena tinta,** on good authority. —**media tinta,** halftone. —**tinta china,** India ink. —**tinta simpática,** invisible ink.

tintar (tin'tar) *v.t.* to dye; tint; stain.

tinte ('tin·te) *n.m.* **1,** hue; tint; tinge. **2,** dye; stain; color. **3,** dyeing; coloring; staining.

tinterillo (tin·te'ri·ʎo; -jo) *n.m., Amer.* shyster; pettifogger.

tintero (tin'te·ro) *n.m.* inkwell; inkstand. —**dejar en el tintero,** *colloq.* to forget.

tintinar (tin·ti'nar) *v.i.* = **tintinear.**

tintinear (tin·ti·ne'ar) *v.i.* to tinkle; jingle. —**tintineo** (-'ne·o) *n.m.* tinkling; jingling; tintinnabulation.

tinto ('tin·to) *adj.* **1,** dyed; tinted. **2,** deep-colored. —**vino tinto,** red wine. —**café tinto,** *Amer.* black coffee.

tintorería (tin·to·re'ri·a) *n.f.* **1,** dyer's shop or trade. **2,** dry cleaning store. —**tintorero** (-'re·ro) *n.m.* **1,** dyer. **2,** dry cleaner.

tintura (tin'tu·ra) *n.f.* **1,** tincture. **2,** dye; tint; stain. **3,** dyeing; staining. **4,** smattering. —**tinturar,** *v.t.* to tincture; tinge.

tiña ('ti·ɲa) *n.f.* **1,** mange. **2,** scalp ringworm. **3,** *colloq.* stinginess.

tiña ('ti·ɲa) *v., pres.subjve.* of **teñir.**

tiñendo (ti'ɲen·do) *v., ger* of **teñir.**

tiño ('ti·ɲo) *v., 1st pers.sing. pres.ind.* of **teñir.**

tiñó (ti'ɲo) *v., 3rd pers.sing.pret.* of **teñir.**

tiñoso (ti'ɲo·so) *adj.* **1,** mangy; scabby. **2,** stingy.

tío ('ti·o) *n.m.* **1,** uncle. **2,** *colloq.* guy; fellow; bloke. —**tío abuelo,** great-uncle.

tiovivo (ti·o'βi·βo) *n.m.* merry-go-round.

tipejo (ti'pe·xo) *n.m., derog.* insignificant person; jerk.

tipiador (ti·pja'ðor) *n.m.* = **mecanógrafo.** —**tipiadora,** *n.f.* typewriter. —**tipiar** (ti'pjar) *v.t.* & *i., Amer.* to type; typewrite.

típico ('ti·pi·ko) *adj.* typical.

tipificar (ti·pi·fi'kar) *v.t.* [*infl.:* **tocar,** 7] to typify.

tiple ('tip·le) *n.m.* treble; soprano. —*n.m.* & *f.* soprano singer.

tipo ('ti·po) *n.m.* **1,** type. **2,** presence; bearing; appearance. **3,** *colloq.* guy; fellow. **4,** *Amer.* rate (*of interest, discount, exchange, etc.*).

tipografía (ti·po·ɣra'fi·a) *n.f.* typography. —**tipográfico** (-'ɣra·fi·ko) *adj.* typographical. —**tipógrafo** (-'po·ɣra·fo) *n.m.* typographer.

tipómetro (ti'po·me·tro) *n.m.* type gauge.

tiquete (ti'ke·te) *n.m., Amer., colloq.* ticket.

tiquismiquis (ti·kis'mi·kis) *n.m.pl., colloq.* **1,** squeamishness; fastidiousness. **2,** priggishness; affectation.

tira ('ti·ra) *n.f.* strip. —**tiras,** *n.f. pl., Amer.* tatters; shreds.

tirabuzón (ti·ra·βu'θon; -'son) *n.m.* **1,** curl; corkscrew curl. **2,** corkscrew. **3,** *aero.* spin.

tirada (ti'ra·ða) *n.f.* **1,** throw. **2,** distance; stretch. **3,** space or lapse of time. **4,** issue; printing; edition. **5,** outpouring; tirade. **6,** string; series. —**de** *or* **en una tirada,** at one stroke; all at once.

tirado (ti'ra·ðo) *adj.* **1,** thrown away; discarded. **2,** *colloq.* cheap; dirt-cheap. **3,** *colloq.* plentiful; abundant.

tirador (ti·ra'ðor) *n.m.* **1,** thrower. **2,** shooter. **3,** marksman. **4,** pull cord; pull chain. **5,** slingshot **6,** pea shooter. **7,** = **tiralíneas.**

tiralíneas (ti·ra'li·ne·as) *n.m. sing.* & *pl.* ruling pen.

tiranía (ti·ra'ni·a) *n.f.* tyranny. —**tiránico** (ti'ra·ni·ko) *adj.* tyrannical.

tiranizar (ti·ra·ni'θar; -'sar) *v.t.* & *i.* [*infl.:* **rezar,** 10] to tyrannize.

tirano (ti'ra·no) *adj.* tyrannical. —*n.m.* tyrant.

tiranosauro (ti·ra·no'sau·ro) *n.m.* tyrannosaurus.

tirante (ti'ran·te) *adj.* 1, taut; tight; pulling. 2, tense; strained. —*n.m.* 1, harness trace. 2, brace; joist; truss. 3, guy rope. —**tirantes**, *n.m.pl.* suspenders.

tirantez (ti·ran'teθ; -'tes) *n.f.* 1, tautness; tightness. 2, tension; strain.

tirar (ti'rar) *v.i.* 1, to pull; draw; exert a pull or attraction. 2, to tend; bear (*in a given direction*). 3, to bear up; hold out. 4, to fire; shoot. —*v.t.* 1, to throw; cast; fling. 2, to throw away; cast off. 3, to shoot; shoot off; fire. 4, to squander. 5, to stretch; draw. 6, to draw (a line). 7, to give (a blow, pinch, kick, etc.). 8, to knock down; throw down. 9, to print; draw from the presses. —**tirarse**, *v.r.* to throw oneself; lunge; plunge; jump. —**tirarse a**, *Amer., colloq.* to finish off; polish off. —**a todo tirar**, at the most; at the outmost. —**tirar a**, 1, to shade toward. 2, to resemble; look like. 3, to aim at or toward. —**tirar de**, 1, to pull out; draw (a weapon). 2, to pull on; tug at. —**tirarla de**, *also*, **tirárselas de**, to boast of; boast of being. —**tira y afloja**, give and take; blowing hot and cold.

tiritar (ti·ri'tar) *v.i.* to shiver. —**tiritón**, *n.m.* shiver.

tiro ('ti·ro) *n.m.* 1, shot. 2, throw; cast. 3, trajectory. 4, shooting range. 5, team (*of draft animals*). 6, draft; chimney draft. 7, length (*of a piece of cloth*). 8, *Amer., colloq.* run; sweep. —**a tiro**, within range. —**de tiros largos**, *colloq.* all dressed up. —**ni a tiros**, *colloq.* not by wild horses. —**salir el tiro por la culata**, *colloq.* to backfire; boomerang. —**tiro al blanco**, target shooting. —**tiro de pichón**, trapshooting.

tiroides (ti'roi·ðes) *n.m. sing & pl.* thyroid gland. —**tiroideo** (-'ðe·o) *adj.* thyroid.

tirón (ti'ron) *n.m.* 1, pull; tug. 2, stretch. —**de un tirón**, all at once; at one blow.

tirotear (ti·ro·te'ar) *v.t.* to shoot; shoot at. —**tirotearse**, *v.r.* to exchange shots. —**tiroteo** (-'te·o) *n.m.* shooting.

tirria ('ti·rrja) *n.f., colloq.* antipathy; aversion.

tisana (ti'sa·na) *n.f.* herb tea.

tisis ('ti·sis) *n.f.* tuberculosis; consumption. —**tísico** ('ti·si·ko) *adj. & n.m.* consumptive.

tisú (ti'su) *n.m.* gold or silver lamé.

titán (ti'tan) *n.m.* titan. —**titánico**, *adj.* titanic.

titanio (ti'ta·njo) *n.m.* titanium. —*adj.* = **titánico**.

titano (ti'ta·no) *n.m.* = **titanio**.

títere ('ti·te·re) *n.m.* 1, puppet. 2, *colloq.* clown; buffoon. —**títeres**, *n.m.pl.* jugglers' show. —**titerotada** (-'ta·ða) *n.f., colloq.* clowning; buffoonery.

tití (ti'ti) *n.m., S.A.* monkey; titi.

titilar (ti·ti'lar) *v.i.* 1, to quiver. 2, to twinkle. —**titilación**, *n.f.* = **titileo**.

titileo (ti·ti'le·o) *n.m.* 1, quiver; quivering; titillation. 2, twinkle; twinkling.

titiritar (ti·ti·ri'tar) *v.t.* = **tiritar**.

titiritero (ti·ti·ri'te·ro) *n.m.* 1, puppeteer. 2, ropewalker. 3, juggler.

titubear (ti·tu·βe'ar) *v.i.* 1, to vacillate; hesitate. 2, to toddle. *Also*, **titubar** (-'βar).

titubeo (ti·tu'βe·o) *n.m.* 1, vacillation; hesitation. 2, toddling; toddle.

titular (ti·tu'lar) *adj.* titular. —*n.m. & f.* 1, holder; bearer. 2, incumbent. —*n.f.* large type capital letter. —*n.m.* headline. —*v.t.* to title. —**titularse**, *v.r.* to be called; call oneself.

título ('ti·tu·lo) *n.m.* 1, title. 2, diploma. 3, academic degree. 4, bond; certificate. 5, qualification; requisite. —**a título de**, 1, by way of; as. 2, by right of being; as.

tiza ('ti·θa; -sa) *n.f.* chalk.

tizne ('tiθ·ne; 'tis-) *n.m. or f.* 1, soot. 2, black smudge; smut. —*n.m.* charred stick used for blacking. —**tiznar**, *v.t.* to soot; cover with or as with soot.

tizón (ti'θon; -'son) *n.m.* 1, smudge; smut. 2, charred stick used for blacking. 3, flaming stick; brand. 4, *fig.* stigma; dishonor.

tizona (ti'θo·na; -'so·na) *n.f., colloq.* sword.

toalla (to'a·ʎa) *n.f.* towel. —**toallero**, *n. m.* towel rack.

tobillo (to'βi·ʎo; -jo) *n.m.* ankle. —**tobillera**, *n.f.* 1, ankle support; ankle guard. 2, bobbysoxer.

tobogán (to·βo'ɣan) *n.m.* toboggan.

toca ('to·ka) *n.f.* **1,** toque. **2,** coif.

tocadiscos (to·ka'ðis·kos) *n.m. sing. & pl.* pickup; record player.

tocado (to'ka·ðo) *n.m.* coiffure; headdress. —*adj.* **1,** touched; slightly unbalanced. **2,** spoiled; bruised, esp. of fruits.

tocador (to·ka'ðor) *n.m.* **1,** player (*of a musical instrument*). **2,** dressing room; boudoir. **3,** dresser; vanity. **4,** vanity case.

tocar (to'kar) *v.t. & i.* [*infl.:* 7] **1,** to touch. **2,** to play (music, an instrument, etc.); perform. **3,** to knock; rap. **4,** to ring; toll; peal; sound (*a bell, buzzer, etc.*); strike (*the hour*); blow (*a whistle, horn, etc.*). —*v.t.* **1,** to knock on; rap on. **2,** to touch up. **3,** to do (the hair). **4,** to concern. —*v.i.* **1,** to fall; befall. **2,** to be one's turn. **3,** to be due; be one's share or portion. **4,** to fall to one's lot (*as something inherited, won, etc.*). **5,** *usu.fol. by* **a,** to behoove; be incumbent (upon); be fitting. **6,** to be related; be kin: ¿*Qué le toca Juan? Es mi primo,* What is John to you? He is my cousin. —**tocarse,** *v.r.* **1,** to touch (oneself or each other). **2,** to cover one's head; put on a hat. **3,** *fol. by* **de,** to become touched (with); have a touch (of).

tocayo (to'ka·yo) *n.m.* namesake.

tocino (to'θi·no; -'si·no) *n.m.* bacon; salt pork. *Also, W.I. & C.A.,* **tocineta,** *n.f.*

tocología (to·ko·lo'xi·a) *n.f.* obstetrics. —**tocólogo** (-'ko·lo·ɣo) *n.m.* obstetrician.

tocón (to'kon) *n.m.* tree stump. —*adj., colloq.* fond of touching.

tocuyo (to'ku·jo) *n.m., Amer.* a coarse cotton cloth.

tocho ('to·tʃo) *adj.* rustic; homespun.

todavía (to·ða'βi·a) *adv.* still; yet; even. —**todavía no,** not yet.

todo ('to·ðo) *adj.* **1,** all. **2,** every; each and every. **3,** all of; the whole (of). **4,** full: *a todo correr,* at full speed. —*pron.* everything; all. —*n.m.* all; whole —**todos,** *pron. m.pl.* all; everybody; everyone. —**ante todo,** first of all. —**con todo,** still; however; all in all. —**del todo,** entirely; completely. —**por todo,** throughout. —**todo el que,** everybody who. —**todos cuantos,** all those that.

todopoderoso (to·ðo·po·ðe'ro·so) *adj.* almighty.

toga ('to·ɣa) *n.f.* **1,** toga. **2,** magistrate's robe.

tojino (to'xi·no) *n.m.* cleat.

tojo ('to·xo) *n.m.* furze.

toldilla (tol'di·ʎa; -ja) *n.f., naut.* **1,** poop deck. **2,** roundhouse.

toldo ('tol·do) *n.m.* **1,** awning; canopy; tilt. **2,** *Amer.* hut; shelter.

tolemaico (to·le'mai·ko) *adj.* Ptolemaic.

tolerante (to·le'ran·te) *adj.* tolerant. —**tolerancia,** *n.f.* tolerance; toleration.

tolerar (to·le'rar) *v.t.* to tolerate. —**tolerable,** *adj.* tolerable.

tolete (to'le·te) *n.m., Amer.* **1,** club; cudgel. **2,** *colloq.* blow; rap.

tolmo ('tol·mo) *n.m.* boulder; outcropping of rock.

tolondro (to'lon·dro) *also,* **tolondrón** (-'dron) *adj.* giddy; scatterbrained; reckless. —*n.m.* **1,** scatterbrain. **2,** = **chichón.**

tolteca (tol'te·ka) *adj. & n.m. & f.* Toltec.

tolueno (to'lwe·no) *n.m.* toluene.

tolva ('tol·βa) *n.f.* **1,** mill hopper. **2,** slot; box with a slot.

tolvanera (tol·βa'ne·ra) *n.f.* **1,** whirling dust; dust storm. **2,** *fig.* whirlwind; tempest.

tollo ('to·ʎo; -jo) *n.m.* **1,** dogfish. **2,** hunting blind.

toma ('to·ma) *n.f.* **1,** take; taking. **2,** seizure; capture. **4,** dose. **5,** tap. **6,** intake. **7,** outlet; source. —*interj., colloq.* **1,** Well, how about that!; You don't say! **2,** There!

tomaína (to·ma'i·na) *n.f.* = **ptomaína.**

tomar (to'mar) *v.t.* **1,** to take; get. **2,** to take hold of; grasp. **3,** to seize; capture. **4,** to take in; receive. **5,** to take on; hire. **6,** to drink. **7,** to have; partake of, as food or drink. —*v.i.* **1,** to proceed; go; head (*in a given direction*). **2,** to drink; have a drink or drinks; *Amer.* to tipple. **3,** *Amer.* to take; catch (*as a fire, flame, etc.*); take effect (*as a vaccine*). —**tomarse,** *v.r.* **1,** to become rusty; rust. **2,** to be scorched, as food, clothing, etc. —**tomador,** *n.m., Amer.* [*fem.* **-dora**] drinker; tippler. —**tomar a bien, a mal,** *etc.,* to take (something) well, ill, etc. —**tomar el pelo a,** *colloq.* to poke fun at; tease; pull the leg of. —**tomarla con (uno),** to pick on; take it out on. —**tomarla con (algo),** *colloq.* to get into the habit of. —**toma y daca,** *colloq.* give and take.

tomate (to'ma·te) *n.m.* tomato. —**tomatera** (-'te·ra) *n.f.* tomato plant.

tómbola ('tom·bo·la) *n.f.* **1,** raffle. **2,** charity bazaar.

tomillo (to'mi·ʎo; -jo) *n.m.* thyme.

tomo ('to·mo) *n.m.* **1,** tome; volume. **2,** importance; consequence; weight. —**de tomo y lomo, 1,** of great importance or moment. **2,** *colloq.* tremendous.

ton (ton) *n.m., contr. of* **tono.** —**sin ton ni son,** without rhyme or reason.

tonada (to'na·ða) *n.f.* air; tune; song. —**tonadilla,** *n.f.* light tune.

tonal (to'nal) *adj.* tonal. —**tonalidad,** *n.f.* tonality.

tonante (to'nan·te) *adj.* thundering; thunderous.

tonel (to'nel) *n.m.* barrel; cask. —**tonelero,** *n.m.* cooper. —**tonelería,** *n.f.* cooperage.

tonelada (to·ne'la·ða) *n.f.* ton. —**tonelaje,** *n.m.* tonnage.

tongo ('ton·go) *n.m.* **1,** fix; rigging *(of a contest)*; throwing *(of a race, game, etc.)*; dive *(in boxing).* **2,** *S.A.* derby hat.

tónica ('to·ni·ka) *n.f.* **1,** *mus.* tonic. **2,** *fig.* keynote.

tónico ('to·ni·ko) *adj. & n.m.* tonic. —**tonicidad** (-θi'ðað; -si'ðað) *n.f.* tonicity.

tonificar (to·ni·fi'kar) *v.t.* [*infl.:* **tocar,** 7] to give tone or tonicity to; invigorate. —**tonificación,** *n.f.* strengthening; invigoration. —**tonificador,** *adj.* strengthening; invigorating.

tonina (to'ni·na) *n.f.* tunny.

tono ('to·no) *n.m.* **1,** tone. **2,** *mus.* pitch. **3,** *mus.* key. **4,** tune; accord; agreement. —**darse tono,** *colloq.* to put on airs. —**de buen (mal) tono,** in or of good (bad) taste. —**subirse de tono,** to assume a lofty attitude; be supercilious.

tonsila (ton'si·la) *n.f.* = **amígdala.** —**tonsilectomía,** *n.f.* tonsillectomy. —**tonsilitis,** *n.f.* tonsillitis.

tonsura (ton'su·ra) *n.f.* tonsure. —**tonsurar,** *v.t.* to tonsure.

tontería (ton·te'ri·a) *n.f.* foolishness; nonsense. *Also,* **tontera.**

tonto ('ton·to) *adj.* foolish. —*n.m.* fool. —**tontear,** *v.i.* to act foolishly. —**a tontas y a locas,** recklessly.

topacio (to'pa·θjo; -sjo) *n.m.* topaz.

topar (to'par) *v.t. & i.* **1,** to butt; ram with the head. **2,** to bump (into); run (into). **3,** to hit upon; come upon.

tope ('to·pe) *n.m.* **1,** top; summit. **2,** butt; collision; bump.

topetar (to·pe'tar) *v.t. & i.* to butt; bump. *Also,* **topetear** (-te'ar).

topetazo (to·pe'ta·θo; -so) *n.m.* butt; bump; collision. *Also,* **topetada,** *n.f.,* **topetón,** *n.m.*

tópico ('to·pi·ko) *adj.* topical; local. —*n.m.* topic; subject.

topo ('to·po) *n.m.* mole. —**topinera** (-pi'ne·ra) *n.f.* molehill; mole hole.

topografía (to·po·ɣra'fi·a) *n.f.* topography. —**topográfico** (-'ɣra·fi·ko) *adj.* topographical. —**topógrafo** (-'po·ɣra·fo) *n.m.* topographer.

toque ('to·ke) *n.m.* **1,** touch. **2,** knock. **3,** beat, as of a drum. **4,** ring; peal. **5,** test; crucial point. **6,** *mil.* call. **7,** *Amer.* painting *(of the throat).* —**piedra de toque,** touchstone. —**toque de diana,** reveille. —**toque de queda,** curfew.

toque ('to·ke) *v., pres.subjve. of* **tocar.**

toqué (to'ke) *v., 1st pers.sing. pret. of* **tocar.**

toquilla (to'ki·ʎa; -ja) *n.f.* **1,** hatband. **2,** bandanna.

Tora *also,* **Torah** ('to·ra) *n.f.* Torah.

tórax ('to·raks) *n.m. sing. & pl.* thorax. —**torácico** (-'ra·θi·ko; 'ra·si·ko) *adj.* thoracic.

torbellino (tor·βe'ʎi·no; -'ji·no) *n.m.* whirlwind; vortex.

torcaz (tor'kaθ; -'kas) *adj.* ring-necked *(esp. of birds).* See **paloma torcaz.**

torcedura (tor·θe'ðu·ra; tor·se-) *n.f.* twisting; sprain.

torcer (tor'θer; -'ser) *v.t.* [*infl.:* 66] **1,** to twist. **2,** to bend; put a bend in; make crooked. **3,** to turn; change the course or direction of. **4,** to sprain. **5,** to distort; pervert. —*v.i.* to twist; bend; turn; swerve. —**torcerse,** *v.r.* **1,** to twist; turn; writhe. **2,** to turn sour, esp. milk or wine. **3,** to go astray; fall into evil ways. **4,** to go awry; come to naught; fail.

torcido (tor'θi·ðo; -'si·ðo) *adj.* twisted; crooked; bent. —*n.m.* twist, as of yarn or pastry. —**torcida,** *n.f.* wick.

torcijón (tor·θi'xon; tor·si-) *n.m.* colic; stomach cramp; cramps.

tordillo (tor'ði·ʎo; -jo) *adj.* gray; dapple-gray. —*n.m.* dapple-gray horse.

tordo ('tor·ðo) *n.m.* **1**, thrush. **2**, dapple-gray horse. —*adj.* dapple-gray.

torear (to·re'ar) *v.t. & i.* **1**, to fight (bulls). **2**, to tease. —**toreador,** *n.m.* toreador.

toreo (to're·o) *n.m.* bullfighting.

torero (to're·ro) *n.m.* bullfighter. —*adj.* bullfighting; bullfighter (*attrib.*).

toril (to'ril) *n.m.* bull pen.

torio ('to·rjo) *n.m.* thorium.

tormenta (tor'men·ta) *n.f.* **1**, storm; tempest. **2**, misfortune; trouble. —**tormentoso,** *adj.* stormy.

tormento (tor'men·to) *n.m.* torment; torture.

torna ('tor·na) *n.f.* **1**, return. **2**, small dam placed in an irrigation ditch for diverting the flow of water. —**volver las tornas,** to turn tables; return tit for tat: *Se volvieron las tornas,* The worm turned.

tornadizo (tor·na'ði·θo; -so) *adj.* changeable; fickle.

tornado (tor'na·ðo) *n.m.* tornado.

tornapunta (tor·na'pun·ta) *n.f.* brace; strut.

tornar (tor'nar) *v.t. & i.* to return. —*v.t.* to turn; make; cause to become. —**tornarse,** *v.r.* to turn; become. —**tornar a,** *fol. by inf.* to go back to (doing something); do again.

tornasol (tor·na'sol) *n.m.* **1**, sunflower. **2**, litmus. **3**, iridescence. —**tornasolado,** *adj.* changing colors; iridescent. —**tornasolar,** *v.t.* to make iridescent.

tornavía (tor·na'βi·a) *n.f.*, *R.R.* turntable.

tornavoz (tor·na'βoθ; -'βos) *n.m.* sounding board.

tornear (tor·ne'ar) *v.t.* to shape in a lathe. —*v.i.* to compete in a tourney or tournament. —**torneado,** *adj.* turned; shaped. —*n.m.* turning; shaping; shape. —**tornero** (-'ne·ro) *n.m.* turner; lathe operator.

torneo (tor'ne·o) *n.m.* **1**, tourney; tournament. **2**, turning (*on a lathe*).

tornillo (tor'ni·ʎo; -jo) *n.m.* **1**, screw. **2**, bolt. **3**, clamp; vise. —**faltarle a uno un tornillo; tener flojos los tornillos,** *colloq.* to have

a screw loose. —**tornillo de mariposa,** wing bolt.

torniquete (tor·ni'ke·te) *n.m.* **1**, tourniquet. **2**, turnbuckle.

torno ('tor·no) *n.m.* **1**, lathe. **2**, winch. **3**, turnstile. **4**, wheel (*for spinning, potterymaking, etc.*). **5**, turn; gyration. —**en torno,** around.

toro ('to·ro) *n.m.* bull. —**toros,** *n.m.pl.* bullfight. —**plaza de toros,** bullring; arena.

toronja (to'ron·xa) *n.f.* grapefruit. —**toronjo,** *n.m.* grapefruit tree.

toronjil (to·ron'xil) *n.m.*, *bot.* a kind of balm.

torpe ('tor·pe) *adj.* **1**, dull; stupid; torpid. **2**, clumsy. **3**, lewd; obscene.

torpedo (tor'pe·ðo) *n.m.* torpedo. —**torpedear** (-ðe'ar) *v.t.* to torpedo. —**torpedero,** *n.m.* torpedo boat.

torpeza (tor'pe·θa; -sa) *n.f.* **1**, dullness; stupidity. **2**, clumsiness. **3**, lewdness; turpitude.

torpor (tor'por) *n.m.* torpor. —**tórpido** ('tor·pi·ðo) *adj.* torpid.

torrar (to'rrar) *v.t.* **1**, to toast. **2**, to parch; burn. —**torrado,** *n.m.* toasted chick pea.

torre ('to·rre) *n.f.* **1**, tower. **2**, turret. **3**, *chess* rook. **4**, steeple. **5**, villa. —**torre del homenaje,** keep. —**torre de perforación,** oil derrick.

torrecilla (to·rre'θi·ʎa; -'si·ja) *n.f.* turret.

torrefacción (to·rre·fak'θjon; -'sjon) *n.f.* roasting; toasting. —**torrefacto** (-'fak·to) *adj.* roasted; toasted.

torrentada (to·rren'ta·ða) *n.f.* flash flood; cloudburst.

torrente (to'rren·te) *n.m.* torrent. —**torrencial** (-'θjal; -'sjal) *adj.* torrential.

torrentera (to·rren'te·ra) *n.f.* bed of a torrent; gully.

torrentoso (to·rren'to·so) *adj.*, *Amer.* torrential (*of streams and rivers*).

torreón (to·rre'on) *n.m.* fortified tower; watchtower.

torrero (to'rre·ro) *n.m.* lighthouse keeper.

tórrido ('to·rri·ðo) *adj.* torrid.

torrija (to'rri·xa) *n.f.* a kind of French toast. *Also,* **torrijo.**

torsión (tor'sjon) *n.f.* torsion. —**torsional,** *adj.* torsional.

torso ('tor·so) *n.m.* torso.

torta ('tor·ta) *n.f.* **1**, cake. **2**, tart;

patty. **3,** *Mex.* type of sandwich. **4,** *print.* font. **5,** *colloq.* slap; buffet.

tortera (tor'te·ra) *n.f.* baking pan; pie pan.

tortícolis (tor'ti·ko·lis) *n.f.* stiff neck.

tortilla (tor'ti·ʎa; -ja) *n.f.* **1,** omelet. **2,** *Mex.* tortilla.

tórtola ('tor·to·la) *n.f.* turtledove. —**tórtolos** (-los) *n.m.pl.*, *colloq.* lovebirds.

tortuga (tor'tu·ɣa) *n.f.* tortoise; turtle.

tortuoso (tor'two·so) *adj.* tortuous. —**tortuosidad,** *n.f.* tortuousness.

tortura (tor'tu·ra) *n.f.* torture. —**torturar,** *v.t.* to torture.

torvo ('tor·βo) *n.m.* grim; fierce.

tory ('to·ri) *adj. indecl. & n.m. & f.* conservative; tory.

torzal (tor'θal; -'sal) *n.m.* cord; silk twist.

tos (tos) *n.f.* cough. —**tos ferina,** whooping cough.

tosco ('tos·ko) *adj.* coarse; rough.

toser (to'ser) *v.i.* to cough. —*v.t.*, *colloq.* to match; outdo *(esp. in courage).* —**toser fuerte,** to boast.

tósigo ('to·si·ɣo) *n.m.* poison.

tosquedad (tos·ke'ðað) *n.f.* coarseness; roughness.

tostada (tos'ta·ða) *n.f.* toast. —**dar** *or* **pegar la tostada a,** *colloq.* to cheat; dupe.

tostado (tos'ta·ðo) *adj.* **1,** toasted. **2,** roasted. **3,** tanned; sunburnt. **4,** tan; brown. —*n.m.* **1,** toasting. **2,** roasting. **3,** toasted or roasted part.

tostador (tos·ta'ðor) *adj.* toasting. —*n.m.* [*also,* **tostadora,** *n.f.*] toaster.

tostar (tos'tar) *v.t.* [*infl.:* **acostar,** 28] **1,** to toast. **2,** to roast. **3,** to tan. —**tostarse,** *v.r.* **1,** to tan; become tanned. **2,** to roast.

tostón (tos'ton) *n.m.* **1,** toasted corn. **2,** roast suckling. **3,** *colloq.* nuisance; bore. **4,** *Amer.* fried plantain.

total (to'tal) *adj. & n.m.* total. —**totalidad,** *n.f.* totality; entirety. —**totalizar,** *v.t.* [*infl.:* **rezar,** 10] to total.

totalitario (to·ta·li'ta·rjo) *adj.* totalitarian. —**totalitarismo,** *n.m.* totalitarianism.

tótem ('to·tem) *n.m.* [*pl.* **tótems**] totem. —**totémico** (-'te·mi·ko) *adj.* totem *(attrib.).* —**totemismo,** *n.m.* totemism.

totuma (to'tu·ma) *n.f.*, *Amer.* = **güira.**

toxemia (tok'se·mja) *n.f.* toxemia.

tóxico ('tok·si·ko) *adj.* toxic. —*n.m.* toxicant; poison. —**toxicidad** (-θi'ðað; -si'ðað) *n.f.* toxicity.

toxicología (tok·si·ko·lo'xi·a) *n.f.* toxicology. —**toxicológico** (-'lo·xi·ko) *adj.* toxicological. —**toxicólogo** (-'ko·lo·ɣo) *n.m.* toxicologist.

toxicómano (tok·si'ko·ma·no) *adj.* addicted to drugs. —*n.m.* drug addict. —**toxicomanía,** *n.f.* drug addiction.

toxina (tok'si·na) *n.f.* toxin.

toza ('to·θa; -sa) *n.f.* **1,** log; stump; wooden block. **2,** piece of bark.

tozo ('to·θo; -so) *adj.* dwarfish; stumpy.

tozudo (to'θu·ðo; to'su-) *adj.* stubborn. —**tozudez,** *n.f.* stubbornness.

traba ('tra·βa) *n.f.* **1,** bond; tie. **2,** lock; trammel; shackle. **3,** impediment; obstacle.

trabado (tra'βa·ðo) *adj.* **1,** connected; joined. **2,** blocked; trammeled; inhibited. **3,** strong; sinewy. **4,** *Amer.* tongue-tied; slurred; slurring. **5,** *phonet.* closed *(syllable).*

trabajar (tra·βa'xar) *v.t. & i.* to work. —*v.t.* to mold; shape; form. —**trabajador,** *adj.* industrious; hardworking. —*n.m.* [*fem.* **-dora**] worker; laborer.

trabajo (tra'βa·xo) *n.m.* **1,** work. **2,** occupation; employment. **3,** task; undertaking; duty. **4,** work; product of work. **5,** workmanship. **6,** labor. **7,** *mech.* work. —**trabajos,** *n.m.pl.* **1,** hardships; tribulations. **2,** works; construction. —**Día del Trabajo,** Labor Day.

trabajoso (tra·βa'xo·so) *adj.* difficult; laborious.

trabalenguas (tra·βa'len·gwas) *n.m.sing. & pl.* tongue twister.

trabar (tra'βar) *v.t. & i.* **1,** to join; bind; fasten. **2,** to engage; lock. **3,** to grab; grasp; seize. **4,** to tie in (with); mesh. —*v.t.* **1,** to entangle. **2,** to shackle; fetter. **3,** to enter upon; engage in. —**trabarse,** *v.r.* **1,** to become entangled; catch; lock. **2,** to tangle (with). —**trabarse la lengua,** to stammer; stutter.

trabazón (tra·βa'θon; -'son) *n.f.* **1,** bond; connection; union. **2,** thickness; consistency.

trabilla (tra'βi·ʎa; -ja) *n.f.* **1,** strap. **2,** loose stitch; end stitch.

trabucar (tra·βu'kar) *v.t.* [*infl.:*
tocar, 7] to jumble; garble; confuse.
trabuco (tra'βu·ko) *n.m.* blunderbuss.
tracalada (tra·ka'la·ða) *n.f., Amer.
colloq.* slew; scads.
tracción (trak'θjon; -'sjon) *n.f.*
traction. —**tracción delantera,**
front-wheel drive.
trace ('tra·θe; -se) *v., pres.subjve.
of* **trazar.**
tracé (tra'θe; -'se) *v., 1st pers.
sing.pret. of* **trazar.**
tracería (tra·θe'ri·a; -se'ri·a) *n.f.*
tracery.
tracoma (tra'ko·ma) *n.f.* trachoma.
tracto ('trak·to) *n.m.* stretch; extent; tract.
tractor (trak'tor) *n.m.* tractor.
tradición (tra·ði'θjon; -'sjon) *n.f.*
tradition. —**tradicional,** *adj.* traditional. —**tradicionalismo,** *n.m.* traditionalism. —**tradicionalista,** *adj.
& n.m. & f.* traditionalist.
traducir (tra·ðu'θir; -'sir) *v.t.*
[*infl.;* **conducir,** 40] to translate;
render. —**traducción** (-ðuk'θjon;
-'sjon) *n.f.* translation; render-
ing. —**traductor** (-ðuk'tor) *n.m.*
[*fem.* -**tora**] translator.
traer (tra'er) *v.t.* [*infl.:* 67] **1,** to
bring. **2,** to fetch; carry. **3,** to bring
on; bring about; cause. **4,** to have;
hold; bear. **5,** to have on; wear. **6,** to
bring up; introduce; bring forward.
7, *fol. by adj.* denoting state or con-
dition, to have (one) . . . ; cause
(one) to be . . . : *Esto me trae aburrido,* This has me bored. —**tra-
erse,** *v.r. (fol. by adv. of manner)* **1,**
to dress. **2,** to comport oneself. **3,** to
be up to; be doing. —**traérselas, 1,**
to be up to something. **2,** to have
more than meets the eye. —**traer a
mal traer,** to put (someone) in a
bad way. —**traer y llevar,** *colloq.*
to carry gossip.
traeres (tra'e·res) *n.m.pl.* finery.
trafagar (tra·fa'γar) *v.i.* [*infl.:*
pagar, 8] **1,** to trade; traffic. **2,** to
travel; rove.
tráfago ('tra·fa·γo) *n.m.* **1,** traffic;
trade. **2,** hustle and bustle. **3,** drudgery.
traficar (tra·fi'kar) *v.i.* [*infl.:* **tocar,**
7] **1,** to traffic; trade. **2,** to travel;
roam; rove. —**traficante,** *n.m. & f.*
trafficker; trader.
tráfico ('tra·fi·ko) *n.m.* **1,** traffic. **2,**
trade.
tragaderas (tra·γa'ðe·ras) *n.f.pl.*

gullet. —**tener (buenas) tragade-
ras,** *colloq.* **1,** to be gullible. **2,** to
be lax; be indulgent.
tragadero (tra·γa'ðe·ro) *n.m.* **1,**
gullet. **2,** drain.
tragaldabas (tra·γal'da·βas) *n.m.
& f.sing. & pl., colloq.* **1,** big eater;
glutton. **2,** gullible person; gull.
tragaluz (tra·γa'luθ; -'lus) *n.f.*
skylight.
tragamonedas (tra·γa·mo'ne·
ðas) *n.m.sing. & pl., colloq.* slot
machine. *Also,* **traganíqueles**
(-'ni·ke·les).
tragar (tra'γar) *v.t.* [*infl.:* **pagar,** 8]
1, to swallow; gulp. **2,** *fig., colloq.*
to stomach; be able to bear; be able
to put up with.
tragedia (tra'xe·ðja) *n.f.* tragedy.
trágico ('tra·xi·ko) *adj.* tragic.
—*n.m.* tragedian. —**trágica,** *n.f.*
tragedienne.
tragicomedia (tra·xi·ko'me·ðja)
n.f. tragicomedy. —**tragicómico**
(-'ko·mi·ko) *adj.* tragicomic.
trago ('tra·γo) *n.m.* **1,** drink. **2,**
swallow; gulp. **3,** *fig.* calamity; misfortune. —**a tragos,** little by little.
tragón (tra'γon) *adj., colloq.* gluttonous; voracious. —*n.m., colloq.*
glutton.
traición (trai'θjon; -'sjon) *n.f.* treason; treachery. —**traicionar,** *v.t.* to
betray. —**traicionero,** *adj.* treacherous. —*n.m.* treacherous person;
double-dealer.
traída (tra'i·ða) *n.f.* bringing in;
carrying in. —**traída de aguas,** water supply.
traído (tra'i·ðo) *adj.* threadbare;
worn out.
traidor (trai'ðor) *n.m.* [*fem.* -**dora**]
traitor. —*adj.* traitorous; treacherous.
traiga ('trai·γa) *v., pres.subjve. of*
traer.
traigo ('trai·γo) *v., 1st pers.
sing.pres.ind. of* **traer.**
trailla (tra'i·ʎa; -ja) *n.f.* **1,** leash. **2,**
road scraper. **3,** lash. —**traillar,** *v.t.*
to level.
traje ('tra·xe) *n.m.* **1,** dress. **2,** suit.
3, gown; costume. —*v., pret. of*
traer. —**traje de baño,** swimsuit.
—**traje de etiqueta** *or* **ceremonia,**
formal wear. —**traje de luces,** bullfighter's costume. —**traje de
montar,** riding habit. —**traje
sastre,** lady's tailored suit.
trajear (tra·xe'ar) *v.t.* to dress;
clothe.

trajín (tra'xin) *n.m.* bustle; activity.

trajinar (tra·xi'nar) *v.t.* **1,** to carry; cart (merchandise). **2,** *colloq.* to push; peddle. —*v.i.* to run or travel back and forth; bustle.

tralla ('tra·ʎa; -ja) *n.f.* lash; whip. —**trallazo,** *n.m.* lash; crack of a whip.

trama ('tra·ma) *n.f.* **1,** weave; woof; texture. **2,** plot; scheme.

tramar (tra'mar) *v.t.* **1,** to weave. **2,** to plot; scheme.

tramilla (tra'mi·ʎa; -ja) *n.f.* twine.

tramitar (tra·mi'tar) *v.t.* to negotiate; arrange; expedite. —**tramitación,** *n.f.* procedure; arrangement; expediting.

trámite ('tra·mi·te) *n.m.* procedure; formality; step.

tramo ('tra·mo) *n.m.* **1,** stretch; lap; span. **2,** flight *(of stairs).* **3,** *fig.* literary passage.

tramoya (tra'mo·ja) *n.f.* **1,** stage machinery. **2,** sham; artifice; contrivance. **3,** plot *(of a play, novel, etc.).*

tramoyista (tra·mo'jis·ta) *n.m.* **1,** stage machinist. **2,** scene shifter; stagehand. —*n.m. & f.* schemer; swindler; humbug. —*adj.* scheming; swindling.

trampa ('tram·pa) *n.f.* **1,** trap; snare. **2,** trapdoor. **3,** trick; fraud. —**hacer trampa,** to cheat.

trampear (tram·pe'ar) *v.t. & i.,* *colloq.* to cheat.

trampería (tram·pe'ri·a) *n.f.* cheating; trickery.

trampero (tram'pe·ro) *n.m.* trapper.

trampista (tram'pis·ta) *adj. & n.m. & f.* = **tramposo.**

trampolín (tram·po'lin) *n.m.* **1,** springboard. **2,** diving board. **3,** trampoline.

tramposo (tram'po·so) *adj.* cheating; swindling. —*n.m.* cheat; swindler.

tranca ('tran·ka) *n.f.* **1,** bar; crossbar; bolt. **2,** club; stick. **3,** *Amer.* drunk; spree.

trancada (tran'ka·ða) *n.f.* stride; step. —**en dos trancadas,** *colloq.* in a jiffy.

trancar ('tran·kar) *v.t.* [*infl.:* **tocar, 7**] **1,** to bolt; bar. **2,** to block; obstruct. —**trancarse,** *v.r., colloq.* **1,** to seclude oneself. **2,** *Amer.* to stuff oneself; gorge.

trancazo (tran'ka·θo; -so) *n.m.* blow with a stick or club.

trance ('tran·θe; -se) *n.m.* **1,** strait; predicament. **2,** *law* seizure. —**a todo trance,** at any cost. —**en trance de,** at the point of; in the act of. —**trance de armas,** feat of arms. —**último trance,** last moment; death throes.

trance ('tran·θe; -se) *v., pres.subjve.* of **tranzar.**

trancé (tran'θe; -'se) *v., 1st pers.sing.pret.* of **tranzar.**

tranco ('tran·ko) *n.m.* **1,** stride; long step. **2,** threshold. —**a trancos,** at a stride; hurriedly. —**a un tranco,** one step away; on the threshold.

tranque ('tran·ke) *v., pres.subjve.* of **trancar.**

tranqué (tran'ke) *v., 1st pers.sing.pret.* of **trancar.**

tranquear (tran·ke'ar) *v.i., colloq.* to walk with long strides.

tranquera (tran'ke·ra) *n.f.* **1,** stockade; palisade. **2,** *Amer.* fence gate; corral gate.

tranquilo (tran'ki·lo) *adj.* **1,** tranquil; calm. **2,** easygoing. —**tranquilidad,** *n.f.* tranquillity; calm. —**tranquilizar** (-li'θar; -'sar) *v.t.* [*infl.:* **rezar, 10**] to tranquilize; calm. —**tranquilizarse,** *v.r.* to calm down. —**tranquilizante,** *n.m.* tranquilizer.

transacción (tran·sak'θjon; -'sjon) *n.f.* **1,** transaction. **2,** compromise; accommodation.

transar (tran'sar) *v.t., Amer.* to compromise; settle; adjust.

transatlántico (trans·a'tlan·ti·ko) *adj.* transatlantic. —*n.m.* ocean liner.

transbordador (trans·βor·ða'ðor) *n.m.* **1,** ferry. **2,** funicular; cable car; aerial car. —**transbordador espacial,** space shuttle.

transbordar (trans·βor'ðar) *v.t.* to transship; transfer. —*v.i.* to transfer; change vehicles. —**transbordo** (-'βor·ðo) *n.m.* transshipment; transfer.

transcender (trans·θen'der; tran·sen-) *v.t.* = **trascender.** —**transcendencia,** *n.f.* = trascendencia. —**transcendental,** *adj.* = trascendental. —**transcendente,** *adj.* = trascendente.

transceptor (trans·θep'tor; -sep'tor) *n.m.* transceiver.

transcontinental (trans·kon·ti·nen'tal) *adj.* transcontinental.

transcribir (trans·kri'βir) *v.t.* to

transcribe. —**transcrito** (-'kri·to) *also,* **transcripto** (-'krip·to) *adj.* transcribed. —**transcripción** (-krip·'θjon; -'sjon) *n.f.* transcription; transcript. —**transcriptor** (-krip'tor) —*n.m.,* Amer. *n.m.* [*fem.* **-tora**] transcriber.

transcurrir (trans·ku'rrir) *v.i.* to elapse; pass. —**transcurso** (-'kur·so) *n.m.* course *(as of time).*

transeúnte (tran·se'un·te) *adj.* transient; transitory. —*n.m. & f.* **1,** passerby. **2,** transient.

transferencia (trans·fe'ren·θja; -sja) *n.f.* **1,** transference. **2,** transfer.

transferir (trans·fe'rir) *v.t.* [*infl.:* **sentir,** 31] to transfer. —**transferible,** *adj.* transferable.

transfigurar (trans·fi·ɣu'rar) *v.t.* to transfigure. —**transfigurarse,** *v.r.* to be transfigured. —**transfiguración,** *n.f.* transfiguration; transfigurement.

transfixión (trans·fik'sjon) *n.f.* transfixion. —**transfijo** (-'fi·xo) *adj.* transfixed.

transflorar (trans·flo'rar) *v.i.* to show through. —*v.t.* **1,** to trace against the light. **2,** to paint (metal).

transformar (trans·for'mar) *v.t.* to transform. —**transformación** *n.f.* transformation. —**transformador,** *n.m.* transformer. —*adj.* transforming.

transformista (trans·for'mis·ta) *n.m. & f.* **1,** quick-change artist. **2,** transformist. —**transformismo,** *n.m.* transformism.

tránsfuga ('trans·fu·ɣa) *n.m. & f.* fugitive; deserter; turncoat.

transfundir (trans·fun'dir) *v.t.* to transfuse. —**transfusión** (-fu'sjon) *n.f.* transfusion.

transgredir (trans·ɣre'ðir) *v.t.* [*defective: used only in tenses with terminations beginning with* i] to transgress. —**transgresión** (-'sjon) *n.f.* transgression. —**transgresor** (-'sor) *n.m.* transgressor.

transición (tran·si·'θjon; -'sjon) *n.f.* transition.

transido (tran'si·ðo) *adj.* overcome; overwhelmed *(with fear, emotion, etc.);* pierced *(with pain, suffering, etc.).*

transigir (tran·si'xir) *v.i & t.* [*infl.:* **coger,** 15] to compromise; concede; yield. —**transigencia,** *n.f.* tolerance. —**transigente,** *adj.* tolerant; accommodating.

transistor (tran·sis'tor) *n.m.* transistor.

transitar (tran·si'tar) *v.i.* to travel; pass. —**transitable,** *adj.* passable; capable of bearing traffic. —**transitado,** *adj.* bearing traffic; traveled.

transitivo (tran·si'ti·βo) *adj. & n.m.* transitive.

tránsito ('tran·si·to) *n.m.* **1,** transit. **2,** traffic.

transitorio (tran·si'to·rjo) *adj.* **1,** transitory; transient; passing. **2,** transitional. —**transitoriedad** (-rje·'ðað) *n.f.* transitoriness; transience.

translación (trans·la'θjon; -'sjon) *n.f.* = **traslación.**

translimitar (trans·li·mi'tar) *v.t.* to go beyond; cross over; overstep.

transliteración (trans·li·te·ra·'θjon; -'sjon) *n.f.* transliteration.

translúcido (trans'lu·θi·ðo; -si·ðo) *adj.* translucent. —**translucidez,** *n.f.* translucence.

transmigrar (trans·mi'ɣrar) *v.i.* to transmigrate. —**transmigración,** *n.f.* transmigration.

transmisión (trans·mi'sjon) *n.f.* **1,** transmission. **2,** transmittal. **3,** broadcast.

transmisor (trans·mi'sor) *n.m.* transmitter. —*adj.* transmitting.

transmitir (trans·mi'tir) *v.t.* to transmit. —**transmisible** (-'si·βle) *adj.* transmissible. —**transmisibilidad,** *n.f.* transmissibility.

transmutar (trans·mu'tar) *v.t.* to transmute. —**transmutación,** *n.f.* transmutation.

transoceánico (trans·o·θe'a·ni·ko; -o·se-) *adj.* transoceanic.

transónico (tran'so·ni·ko) *adj.* transsonic.

transparentarse (trans·pa·ren'tar·se) *v.r.* **1,** to become transparent. **2,** to be visible; show through.

transparente (trans·pa'ren·te) *adj.* transparent. —**transparencia,** *n.f.* transparency.

transpiración (trans·pi·ra'θjon; -'sjon) *n.f.* **1,** perspiration. **2,** transpiration.

transpirar (trans·pi'rar) *v.i.* **1,** to perspire. **2,** to transpire.

transplantar (trans·plan'tar) *v.t.* = **trasplantar.** —**transplante,** *n.m.* = **trasplante.**

transponer (trans·po'ner) *v.t.* [*infl.:* **poner,** 54] to transpose.

transportación (trans·por·ta·

'θjon; -'sjon) *n.f.* **1,** transportation. **2,** *mus.* transposition.

transportador (trans·por·ta'ðor) *adj.* transporting. —*n.m.* **1,** transporter. **2,** protractor.

transportar (trans·por'tar) *v.t.* **1,** to transport. **2,** *mus.* to transpose. —**transportarse,** *v.r.* to be transported; be rapt.

transporte (trans·por·te) *n.m.* **1,** transport. **2,** transportation.

transposición (trans·po·si'θjon; -'sjon) *n.f.* transposition.

transpuesto (trans'pwes·to) *v., p.p.* of transponer.

transubstanciar (tran·suβs· tan'θjar; -'sjar) *v.t.* to transubstantiate. —**transubstanciación,** *n.f.* transubstantiation.

transversal (trans·βer'sal) *adj.* **1,** transverse. **2,** intersecting. —*n.f.* **1,** transversal. **2,** cross street. —**corte** *or* **sección transversal,** cross section.

transverso (trans'βer·so) *adj.* transverse.

transvertir (trans·βer'tir) *v.t.* [*infl.:* sentir, 31] to change; change over; transform.

transvestismo (trans·βes'tis·mo) *also,* **transvestitismo** (-ti'tis·mo) *n.m.* transvestism. —**transvestista,** *adj.* transvestic. —*n.m.* & *f.* transvestite.

tranvía (tran'βi·a) *n.f.* **1,** streetcar. **2,** tramway; trolley system. —**tranviario** (-'βja·rjo) *adj.* streetcar (*attrib.*).

tranzar (tran'θar; -'sar) *v.t.* [*infl.:* rezar, 10] = **tronchar.**

trapacear (tra·pa·θe'ar; -se'ar) *v.t.* to deceive; swindle; cheat. —**trapacería,** *n.f.* fraud; swindle. —**trapacero,** *also,* **trapacista,** *adj.* cheating; swindling. —*n.m.* cheater; swindler.

trapajo (tra'pa·xo) *n.m.* rag; tatter. —**trapajoso,** *adj.* ragged; tattered.

trapalear (tra·pa·le'ar) *v.i., colloq.* **1,** to clatter; patter. **2,** to jabber; babble. **3,** to cheat.

trapear (tra·pe'ar) *v.t., Amer.* to mop; swab. —**trapeador,** *n.m., Amer.* mop; swab.

trapecio (tra'pe·θjo; -sjo) *n.m.* **1,** trapeze. **2,** *anat.* trapezium. **3,** *geom.* trapezoid. —**trapecista,** *n.m.* & *f.* trapeze artist.

trapense (tra'pen·se) *adj.* & *n.m.* Trappist.

trapero (tra'pe·ro) *n.m.* ragpicker.

—**trapería** (-pe'ri·a) *n.f.* **1,** rags. **2,** secondhand clothing store.

trapezoide (tra·pe'θoi·ðe; -'soi·ðe) *n.m.* **1,** *geom.* trapezium. **2,** *anat.* trapezoid. —**trapezoidal,** *adj.* trapezoidal.

trapiche (tra'pi·tʃe) *n.m.* **1,** sugar mill. **2,** *S.A.* ore crusher. **3,** press; juice extractor. **4,** *colloq.* wringer.

trapichear (tra·pi·tʃe'ar) *v.i., colloq.* **1,** to deal at retail. **2,** to scheme; wangle.

trapisonda (tra·pi'son·da) *n.f., colloq.* **1,** brawl; uproar. **2,** prank.

trapo ('tra·po) *n.m.* **1,** rag. **2,** sails. —**trapos,** *n.m.pl.* duds. —**a todo trapo,** *colloq.* at full speed; full sail. —**soltar el trapo,** *colloq.* to burst out (laughing or crying).

traposo (tra'po·so) *adj., Amer.* ragged; tattered.

traque ('tra·ke) *n.m.* clack; crack; crackle.

tráquea ('tra·ke·a) *n.f.* trachea. —**traqueal** (tra·ke'al) *adj.* tracheal.

traquear (tra·ke'ar) *v.i.* = **traquetear.**

traquearteria (tra·ke·ar'te·rja) *n.f.* = **tráquea.**

traqueotomía (tra·ke·o·to'mi·a) *n.f.* tracheotomy.

traquetear (tra·ke·te'ar) *v.t.* & *i.* **1,** to shake; rattle. **2,** to clack; crack; crackle.

traqueteo (tra·ke'te·o) *n.m.* **1,** shaking; rattling. **2,** clacking; cracking; crackling. **3,** *Amer.* uproar; racket; din.

traquido (tra'ki·ðo) *n.m.* **1,** report (*of a firearm*). **2,** crack; snap.

tras (tras) *prep.* **1,** after; behind. **2,** beyond. —**tras de, 1,** after; behind. **2,** besides; in additon to.

¡tras! (tras) *interj.* knock!—¡**tras, tras!,** knock, knock!

trasbordador (tras·βor·ða'ðor) *n.m.* = **transbordador.** —**trasbordar,** *v.t.* & *i.* = **transbordar.** —**trasbordo,** *n.m.* = **transbordo.**

trasca ('tras·ka) *n.f.* leather thong.

trascendencia (tras·θen'den·θja; tra·sen'den·sja) *n.f.* **1,** importance; consequence. **2,** transcendence; transcendency.

trascendental (tras·θen·den·'tal; tra·sen-) *adj.* **1,** important; momentous. **2,** transcendental. —**trascendentalismo,** *n.m.* transcendentalism. —**trascendente** (-'den·te) *adj.* transcendent.

trascender (tras·θen'der; tra·sen-)

v.i. [*infl.*: **perder, 29**] **1,** to come to be known; become known. **2,** to spread. **3,** to be transcendent. —*v.t.* **1,** to transcend. **2,** to penetrate; fathom.

trascocina (tras·ko'θi·na; -'si·na) *n.f.* scullery.

trascolar (tras·ko'lar) *v.t.* [*infl.*: **acostar, 28**] to percolate; strain.

trascurrir (tras·ku'rrir) *v.i.* = **transcurrir.** —**trascurso** (-'kur·so) *n.m.* = **transcurso.**

trasechar (tras·e'tʃar) *v.t.* to waylay.

trasegar (tra·se'ɣar) *v.t.* [*infl.*: **pagar, 8; pensar, 27**] **1,** to pour; decant. **2,** to upset; turn topsy-turvy. **3,** *colloq.* to guzzle.

trasero (tra·se·ro) *adj.* rear; hind; back. —*n.m.* rump; posterior. —**trasera,** *n.f.* back.

trasgo ('tras·ɣo) *n.m.* sprite; goblin.

trasgredir (tras·ɣre'ðir) *v.t.* = **transgredir.** —**trasgresión,** *n.f.* = **transgresión.** —**trasgresor,** *n.m.* = **transgresor.**

trashojar (tras·o'xar) *v.t.* to leaf through; skim.

traslación (tras·la'θjon; -'sjon) *n.f.* **1,** conveying; moving; transfer. **2,** *mech.* translation.

trasladar (tras·la'ðar) *v.t.* **1,** to move; convey. **2,** to transfer; relocate. **3,** to postpone; reschedule *(for an earlier or later date).* —**trasladarse,** *v.r.* to move; change residence or location.

traslado (tras'la·ðo) *n.m.* **1,** moving; conveying. **2,** transfer; relocation. **3,** *law* notification.

traslucir (tras·lu'θir; -'sir) *v.t.* [*infl.*: **lucir, 14**] to show up; bring to light; evince. —**traslucirse,** *v.r.* **1,** to show up; be seen; show through. **2,** to be translucent.

trasluz (tras'luθ; -'lus) *n.m.* diffuse light. —**al trasluz,** against the light.

trasmallo (tras'ma·ʎo; -jo) *n.m.* trammel net.

trasnochada (tras·no'tʃa·ða) *n.f.* **1,** long night; sleepless night. **2,** last night. —**darse la trasnochada,** *colloq.* to make a night of it.

trasnochado (tras·no'tʃa·ðo) *adj.* **1,** weary; haggard *(from lack of sleep).* **2,** stale; old. **3,** passé.

trasnochar (tras·no'tʃar) *v.i.* **1,** to stay up all night; go without sleep. **2,** to spend the night. **3,** to keep late

hours. —**trasnochador,** *adj. & n.m.* [*fem.* -**dora**] night owl.

trasnoche (tras'no·tʃe) *n.m.* [*also,* **trasnocho** (-tʃo)] long night; sleepless night. —*n.f., Amer., colloq.* night before last.

traspapelar (tras·pa·pe'lar) *v.t.* to misplace (a letter or papers) among other papers.

traspasar (tras·pa'sar) *v.t.* **1,** to cross; cross over; pass over. **2,** to pierce; run through; transfix. **3,** to transfer; turn over. **4,** to trespass; transgress. —**traspasarse,** *v.r.* to overstep one's bounds.

traspaso (tras'pa·so) *n.m.* **1,** transfer. **2,** trespass; transgression. **3,** grief; pain. **4,** sale; transfer (of property).

traspié (tras'pie) *n.m.* trip; stumble; slip. —**dar traspiés,** *also,* **dar un traspié,** to trip; stumble; slip.

trasplantar (tras·plan'tar) *v.t.* to transplant.

trasplante (tras'plan·te) *n.m.* **1,** transplanting; transplantation. **2,** transplant.

trasponer (tras·po'ner) *v.t.* = **transponer.**

trasportación (tras·por·ta'θjon; -'sjon) *n.f.* = **transportación.** —**trasportador,** *adj. & n.m.* = **transportador.** —**trasportar,** *v.t.* = **transportar.** —**trasporte,** *n.m.* = **transporte.**

trasposición (tras·po·si'θjon; -'sjon) *n.f.* = **transposición.** —**traspuesto,** *p.p.* = **transpuesto.**

traspunte (tras'pun·te) *n.m.* **1,** prompter. **2,** prompting.

trasquilar (tras'ki·lar) *v.t.* to shear; crop; cut; clip. —**trasquila** (-'ki·la) *also,* **trasquilada,** **trasquiladura,** *n.f., colloq.* cropping; trim; clipping.

trasquilón (tras·ki'lon) *n.m., colloq.* **1,** scissor slash. **2,** swindle; something swindled. **3,** = **trasquila.**

trastabillar (tras·ta·βi'ʎar; -'jar) *v.i.* **1,** to stumble. **2,** to stagger; reel. —**trastabillón,** *n.m., Amer.* = **traspié.**

trastada (tras'ta·ða) *n.f., colloq.,* low trick; bad turn.

trastazo (tras'ta·θo; -so) *n.m., colloq.* **1,** blow; whack. **2,** bump; thump.

traste ('tras·te) *n.m.* **1,** fret *(of a stringed instrument).* **2,** *chiefly Amer.* = **trasto. 3,** *Amer., colloq.* =

trasero. **—dar al traste con,** to ruin; undo; spoil.

trastear (tras'te·ar) *v.i.* to move or change things around. —*v.t.* **1,** to strum. **2,** to make passes at (a bull) with the *muleta.* **3,** *colloq.* to handle; manage. **—trastearse,** *v.r.,* *colloq.* to move; move one's belongings.

trastera (tras'te·ra) *n.f.* [*also,* **cuarto trastero** *or* **de los trastos**] attic; storeroom; junk room.

trastienda (tras'tjen·da) *n.f.* back or back room of a store.

trasto ('tras·to) *n.m.* **1,** piece; thing. **2,** piece of junk. **3,** *colloq.* good-for-nothing. **—trastos,** *n.m. pl.* **1,** things; personal belongings. **2,** odds and ends; junk; rummage.

trastornar (tras·tor'nar) *v.t.* **1,** to upset; disturb. **2,** to unbalance; derange.

trastorno (tras'tor·no) *n.m.* **1,** upset; disturbance. **2,** derangement.

trastrabillar (tras·tra·βi'ʎar; -'jar) *v.i.* = **trastabillar.**

trastrocar (tras·tro'kar) *v.t.* [*infl.:* **tocar, 7; acostar, 28**] to reverse; invert; change the order of.

trasudar (tra·su'ðar) *v.i.* to perspire lightly. **—trasudor** (-'ðor) *n.m.* light perspiration.

trasunto (tra'sun·to) *n.m.* likeness; image; copy. **—trasuntar,** *v.t.* **1,** to copy. **2,** to summarize.

trasversal (tras·βer'sal) *adj.* & *n.f.* = **tansversal. —trasverso,** *adj.* = **transverso.**

trasverter (tras·βer'ter) *v.i.* [*infl.:* **perder, 29**] to overflow; run over.

trata ('tra·ta) *n.f.* trade; traffic. **—trata de blancas,** white slavery. **—trata de esclavos,** slave trade.

tratable (tra'ta·βle) *adj.* **1,** tractable. **2,** approachable; accessible.

tratado (tra'ta·ðo) *n.m.* **1,** treaty; agreement. **2,** treatise.

tratamiento (tra·ta'mjen·to) *n.m.* **1,** treatment. **2,** form of address; title. **3,** process; processing.

tratante (tra'tan·te) *n.m. & f.* trader; dealer; merchant.

tratar (tra'tar) *v.t.* **1,** to treat. **2,** to handle; manage. **3,** to discuss. **4,** *also v.i., fol. by* **de** *or* **sobre,** to deal with; have to do with; be about. **5,** *fol. by* **de,** to call; address (someone) as. —*v.i.* **1,** *fol. by* **de,** to try to; attempt to. **2,** *fol. by* **en,** to deal (in); trade (in). **—tratarse,** *v.r.* **1,**

fol. by **de,** to deal with; have to do with; be about. **2,** *fol. by* **con,** to have dealings with; have to do with.

trato ('tra·to) *n.m.* **1,** treatment. **2,** trade; dealings. **3,** manner; behavior. **4,** *colloq.* agreement; deal. **5,** form of address; title. **6,** [*also,* **trato de gentes**] social intercourse; social graces. **—trato hecho,** *colloq.* it's a deal; agreed.

trauma ('trau·ma) *n.f.* trauma. **—traumático** (-'ma·ti·ko) *adj.* traumatic. **—traumatismo** (-'tis·mo) *n.m.* traumatism. **—traumatizar** (-ti'θar; -ti'sar) *v.t.* [*infl.:* **rezar, 10**] to traumatize.

través (tra'βes) *n.m.* **1,** bias; slant; diagonal. **2,** reverse; misfortune. **—al través; a través,** through; across. **—al través; de través, 1,** transversely; diagonally. **2,** askance; sideways.

travesaño (tra·βe'sa·ɲo) *n.m.* **1,** crossbeam; crossbar. **2,** bolster.

travesear (tra·βe·se'ar) *v.i.* **1,** to misbehave; be naughty or mischievous. **2,** to frolic; romp.

travesía (tra·βe'si·a) *n.f.* **1,** crossing; traversing. **2,** cross street; crossroad.

travesura (tra·βe'su·ra) *n.f.* mischief; prank.

traviesa (tra'βje·sa) *n.f.* railroad tie.

travieso (tra'βje·so) *adj.* **1,** mischievous; naughty. **2,** frolicsome. **—a campo travieso,** cross-country.

trayecto (tra'jek·to) *n.m.* **1,** course; route. **2,** journey; passage. **3,** distance; stretch.

trayectoria (tra·jek'to·rja) *n.f.* trajectory.

trayendo (tra'jen·do) *v., ger. of* **traer.**

traza ('tra·θa; -sa) *n.f.* **1,** plan; sketch; drawing. **2,** aspect; appearance. **3,** indication; sign. **4,** way; means. **—darse trazas (de),** to manage (to); find a way (to). **—tener trazas de,** to look like.

trazado (tra'θa·ðo; -'sa·ðo) *n.m.* **1,** trace; outline; contour. **2,** tracing; outlining. **—bien trazado,** handsome; good-looking. **—mal trazado,** homely; ill-looking.

trazar (tra'θar; -'sar) *v.t.* [*infl.:* **rezar, 10**] to trace; outline. **—trazante,** *adj.* tracer *(attrib.);* tracing.

trazo ('tra·θo; -so) *n.m.* **1,** line; trace. **2,** outline; contour.

trazumar (tra·θu'mar; -su'mar) *v.i.* to ooze; seep.

trébedes ('tre·βe·ðes) *n.f.pl.* trivet.

trebejo (tre'βe·xo) *n.m.* 1, thing; piece. 2, utensil; implement. —**trebejos,** *n.m.pl.* 1, things; personal belongings. 2, pots and pans. 3, odds and ends; rummage. 4, stuff; nonsense.

trébol ('tre·βol) *n.m.* 1, trefoil; clover. 2, *cards* club.

trece ('tre·θe; -se) *adj. & n.m.* thirteen. —**estar** *or* **seguir en sus trece,** to stick to one's guns.

treceno (tre'θe·no; -'se·no) *adj. & n.m.* thirteenth.

trecientos (tre'θjen·tos; tre'sjen-) *adj. & n.m.* = **trescientos.**

trecho ('tre·tʃo) *n.m.* distance; space; stretch. —**a trechos,** at intervals. —**de trecho en trecho,** from time to time; here and there.

tregua ('tre·ɣwa) *n.f.* 1, truce. 2, rest; respite.

treinta ('trein·ta) *adj. & n.m.* thirty.

treintavo (trein'ta·βo) *adj. & n.m.* thirtieth.

treintena (trein'te·na) *n.f.* 1, a quantity of thirty. 2, a thirtieth part.

treinteno ((trein'te·no) *adj.* thirtieth.

tremebundo (tre·me'βun·do) *adj.* dreadful; fearful.

tremedal (tre·me'ðal) *n.m.* marsh; bog; quagmire.

tremendo (tre'men·do) *adj.* 1, tremendous. 2, terrible; awful.

trementina (tre·men'ti·na) *n.f.* turpentine.

tremolar (tre·mo'lar) *v.t.* to wave; fly, as a flag.

trémolo ('tre·mo·lo) *n.m.* tremolo.

tremor (tre'mor) *n.m.* tremor; trembling.

trémulo ('tre·mu·lo) *adj.* tremulous; trembling.

tren (tren) *n.m.* 1, train. 2, retinue. 3, gear; equipment; outfit. 4, pace; speed. 5, show; pomp. 6, convoy. —**en tren de,** in the garb of; ready for. —**tren de aterrizaje,** landing gear. —**tren de vida,** mode of living.

trencilla (tren'θi·ʎa; -'si·ja) *n.f.* braid.

trenza ('tren·θa; -sa) *n.f.* 1, braid; tress. 2, pastry twist.

trenzar (tren'θar; -'sar) *v.t.* [*infl.:* **rezar,** 10] to braid; plait.

—**trenzarse,** *v.r., Amer., colloq.* to tangle; get into a fight.

trepa ('tre·pa) *n.f.* 1, climb; climbing. 2, *colloq.* somersault; turn. 3, *colloq.* beating; drubbing.

trepador (tre·pa'ðor) *adj.* climbing. —*n.m.* [*fem.* **-dora**] climber.

trepanar (tre·pa'nar) *v.t.* to trepan. —**trepanación,** *n.f.* trepanning.

trépano ('tre·pa·no) *n.m.* trepan.

trepar (tre'par) *v.t. & i.* 1, to climb. 2, to creep up.

trepidar (tre·pi'ðar) *v.i.* 1, to tremble; shake; vibrate. 2, *Amer.* to fear; be fearful. —**trepidación,** *n.f.* trepidation.

tres (tres) *adj. & n.m.* three.

trescientos (tres'θjen·tos; tre'sjen-) *adj. & n.m.pl.* [*fem.* **-tas**] three hundred. —*adj.* three-hundredth.

tresillo (tre'si·ʎo; -jo) *n.m.* 1, ombre *(card game).* 2, *mus.* triplet. 3, trio; ensemble of three.

treta ('tre·ta) *n.f.* trick; wile; ruse.

trezavo (tre'θa·βo; -'sa·βo) *adj. & n.m.* thirteenth.

tríada ('tri·a·ða) *n.f.* triad.

triángulo ('trjan·gu·lo) *n.m.* triangle. —*adj.* triangular. —**triangulación,** *n.f.* triangulation. —**triangular,** *adj.* triangular. —*v.t.* to triangulate.

tribu ('tri·βu) *n.f.* tribe. —**tribual** (tri'βwal) *also,* **tribal** (-'βal) *adj.* tribal.

tribulación (tri·βu·la'θjon; -'sjon) *n.f.* tribulation.

tribuna (tri'βu·na) *n.f.* 1, tribune; dais; rostrum. 2, stand; grandstand. —**tribuna de la prensa,** press box. —**tribuna de los acusados,** dock.

tribunal (tri·βu'nal) *n.m.* tribunal; court.

tribuno (tri'βu·no) *n.m.* tribune.

tributario (tri·βu'ta·rjo) *adj. & n.m.* tributary.

tributo (tri'βu·to) *n.m.* tribute. —**tributable,** *adj.* taxable. —**tributar,** *v.t.* to pay; render (homage, admiration, etc.).

trice ('tri·θe; -se) *v., pres.subjve. of* **trizar.**

tricé (tri'θe; -'se) *v., 1st pers.sing. pret. of* **trizar.**

tricentenario (tri·θen·te'na·rjo; tri·sen-) *n.m.* tercentenary.

tricentésimo (tri·θen'te·si·mo; tri·sen-) *adj. & n.m.* three-hundredth.

tríceps ('tri·θeps; -seps) *n.m.* triceps.

triciclo (tri'θi·klo; -'si·klo) *n.m.* tricycle.

tricolor (tri·ko'lor) *adj.* & *n.m.* tricolor.

tricornio (tri'kor·njo) *adj.* tricorn; three-cornered. —*n.m.* three-cornered hat.

tricot (tri'ko) *n.m.* tricot.

tricota (tri'ko·ta) *n.f.* turtleneck sweater.

tricúspide (tri'kus·pi·ðe) *adj.* & *n.f.* tricuspid.

tridente (tri'ðen·te) *adj.* & *n.m.* trident.

tridimensional (tri·ði·men·sjo'nal) *adj.* three-dimensional.

triedro (tri'e·ðro) *adj.* trihedral. —*n.m.* trihedron.

trienio (tri'e·njo) *n.m.* triennium. —**trienal** (-e'nal) *adj.* triennial.

trifásico (tri'fa·si·ko) *adj.* three-phase.

trifocal (tri·fo'kal) *adj.* trifocal. —**lentes trifocales,** trifocal lenses.

trifoliado (tri·fo'lja·ðo) *adj.* trifoliate.

trifulca (tri'ful·ka) *n.f., colloq.* free-for-all; brawl; row.

trifurcar (tri·fur'kar) *v.t.* [*infl.:* **tocar,** 7] to trifurcate. —**trifurcación,** *n.f.* trifurcation. —**trifurcado,** *adj.* trifurcate.

trigésimo (tri'xe·si·mo) *adj.* & *n.m.* thirtieth.

trigo ('tri·ɣo) *n.m.* wheat. —**trigal** (-'ɣal) *n.m.* wheat field.

trigonometría (tri·ɣo·no·me·'tri·a) *n.f.* trigonometry. —**trigonométrico** (-'me·tri·ko) *adj.* trigonometric.

trigueño (tri'ɣe·ɲo) *adj.* brunet; olive-skinned; swarthy.

trilátero (tri·la·te·ro) *adj.* trilateral; three-sided.

trilogía (tri·lo'xi·a) *n.f.* trilogy.

trilla ('tri·ʎa; -ja) *n.f.* **1,** threshing. **2,** threshing time.

trillado (tri'ʎa·ðo; -'ja·ðo) *adj.* **1,** threshed; beaten. **2,** hackneyed.

trillar (tri'ʎar; -'jar) *v.t.* **1,** to thresh. **2,** *colloq.* to mistreat. —**trillador,** *adj.* threshing. —*n.m.* thresher. —**trilladora,** *n.f.* threshing machine. —**trilladura,** *n.f.* threshing.

trillizo (tri'ʎi·θo; -'ji·so) *n.m.* triplet.

trillo ('tri·ʎo; -jo) *n.m.* **1,** thresher;

threshing machine. **2,** *Amer.* trail; footpath.

trillón (tri'ʎon; -'jon) *n.m.* a million trillion; *U.S.* quintillion; *Brit.* trillion. —**trillonésimo,** *adj.* & *n.m., U.S.* quintillionth; *Brit.* trillionth.

trimensual (tri·men'swal) *adj.* thrice monthly.

trimestre (tri'mes·tre) *n.m.* trimester; quarter. —**trimestral,** *adj.* quarterly.

trimotor (tri·mo'tor) *adj.* three-engined. —*n.m.* three-engined airplane.

trinar (tri'nar) *v.i.* **1,** to trill; warble. **2,** *colloq.* to be angry; rage; rave.

trinca ('trin·ka) *n.f.* **1,** triad. **2,** *naut.* rope; cable; lanyard. **3,** binding; fastening. **4,** *colloq.* pinioning. **5,** *Amer., colloq.* drunk; drunkenness; spree.

trincar (trin'kar) *v.t.* [*infl.:* **tocar,** 7] **1,** to cut into pieces. **2,** to fasten; bind. **3,** to pinion. —*v.t.* & *i., colloq.* to drink; tipple.

trinchar (trin'tʃar) *v.t.* & *i.* **1,** to carve; slice **2,** *colloq.* to decide; dispose; settle. —**trinchante,** *n.m.* carving fork. —*adj.* carving. —**trinche,** *n.m., Amer., colloq.* fork.

trinchera (trin'tʃe·ra) *n.f.* **1,** trench. **2,** trench coat.

trineo (tri'ne·o) *n.m.* sled; sleigh.

trinidad (tri·ni'ðað) *n.f.* trinity.

trinitrotolueno (tri·ni·tro·to·'lwe·no) *n.m.* trinitrotoluene; TNT.

trino ('tri·no) *n.m.* **1,** trill; warble. **2,** *mus.* trill.

trinomio (tri'no·mjo) *n.m.* trinomial.

trinque ('trin·ke) *v., pres.subjve. of* **trincar.**

trinqué (trin'ke) *v., 1st pers.sing. pret. of* **trincar.**

trinquete (trin'ke·te) *n.m.* **1,** foremast. **2,** foreyard. **3,** foresail. **4,** ratchet; pawl. **5,** rackets *(game).* —**a cada trinquete,** *colloq.* at every turn.

trinquis ('trin·kis) *n.m.sing.* & *pl., colloq.* swig; drink.

trío ('tri·o) *n.m.* trio.

tríodo (tri·o·ðo) *n.m.* triode.

tripa ('tri·pa) *n.f.* **1,** intestine; gut. **2,** *often pl.* tripe. **3,** *pl.* entrails. —**hacer de tripas corazón,** *colloq.* to pluck up courage; make the best of it. —**tener malas tripas,** *colloq.* to be cruel.

tripartito (tri·par'ti·to) *adj.* tripartite. —**tripartir,** *v.t.* to divide into three parts. —**tripartición,** *n.f.* division into three parts.

tripe ('tri·pe) *n.m.* shag (*fabric*).

triplano (tri'pla·no) *n.m.* triplane.

triple ('tri·ple) *adj. & n.m.* triple; triplex.

triplicación (tri·pli·ka'θjon; -'sjon) *n.f.* **1,** tripling; trebling. **2,** triplication.

triplicado (tri·pli'ka·ðo) *adj. & n.m.* triplicate. —**por** *or* **en triplicado,** in triplicate.

triplicar (tri·pli'kar) *v.t.* [*infl.:* tocar, 7] **1,** to triple; treble. **2,** to triplicate.

tríplice ('tri·pli·θe; -se) *adj.* = **triple.**

trípode ('tri·po·ðe) *n.m.* tripod.

tríptico ('trip·ti·ko) *n.m.* triptych.

triptongo (trip'ton·go) *n.m.* triphthong.

tripulación (tri·pu·la'θjon; -'sjon) *n.f.* crew (*of a ship or aircraft*). —**tripulante,** *n.m.* crew member. —**tripular,** *v.t.* to man (a ship or aircraft).

trique ('tri·ke) *n.m.* **1,** click; crack; clack. **2,** *Amer.* trinket. —**a cada trique,** at every turn.

triquina (tri'ki·na) *n.f.* trichina. —**triquinosis,** *n.f.* trichinosis.

triquiñuela (tri·ki'ɲwe·la) *n.f., colloq.* chicanery; subterfuge; trick.

triquitraque (tri·ki'tra·ke) *n.m.* **1,** click; clack; clacking. **2,** *colloq.* noisemaker. **3,** firecracker.

trirreme (tri'rre·me) *n.m.* trireme.

tris (tris) *n.m.* **1,** crack; crackle. **2,** *colloq.* trice; instant. **3,** *colloq.* trifle; bit. —**en un tris,** within an ace; within an inch.

trisar (tri'sar) *v.t., S.A.* to crack; chip (glass, porcelain, etc.).

trisca ('tris·ka) *n.f.* **1,** crunch; crunching; crackle. **2,** ruckus; uproar. **3,** *Amer., colloq.* bit; speck.

triscar (tris'kar) *v.i.* [*infl.:* tocar, 7] **1,** to crunch; crackle. **2,** to romp; frolic. —*v.t.* **1,** to set (the teeth of a saw). **2,** *colloq.* to ball up; foul.

trisecar (tri·se'kar) *v.t.* [*infl.:* tocar, 7] to trisect. —**trisección** (-sek'θjon; -'sjon) *n.f.* trisection.

trisílabo (tri'si·la·βo) *adj.* trisyllabic. —*n.m.* trisyllable.

triste ('tris·te) *adj.* sad; gloomy. —**tristeza,** *n.f.* sadness; gloom.

tristón (tris'ton) *adj.* somewhat sad; somewhat gloomy.

tritio ('tri·tjo) *n.m.* tritium.

tritón (tri'ton) *n.m.* **1,** triton; merman. **2,** newt.

triturar (tri·tu'rar) *v.t.* to triturate; crush; grind. —**trituración,** *n.f.* trituration. —**triturador,** *adj.* triturating; crushing. —*n.m.* crusher. —**trituradora,** *n.f.* crushing machine.

triunfar (trjun'far) *v.i.* **1,** to triumph. **2,** *cards* to trump. —**triunfal,** *adj.* triumphal. —**triunfador,** *n.m.* [*fem.* **-dora**] victor; winner. —**triunfante,** *adj.* triumphant.

triunfo ('trjun·fo) *n.m.* **1,** triumph. **2,** *cards* trump. —**costar un triunfo,** to cost a great effort. —**sin triunfo,** no trump.

triunvirato (trjun·βi'ra·to) *n.m.* triumvirate. —**triunviro** (-'βi·ro) *n.m.* triumvir.

trivalente (tri·βa'len·te) *adj.* trivalent.

trivial (tri'βjal) *adj.* trivial. —**trivialidad,** *n.f.* triviality.

triza ('tri·θa; -sa) *n.f.* shred; fragment; bit. —**hacer trizas,** to shatter; break to bits.

trizar (tri'θar; -'sar) *v.t.* [*infl.:* rezar, 10] to shatter.

trocaico (tro'kai·ko) *adj. & n.m.* trochaic.

trocar (tro'kar) *v.t.* [*infl.:* tocar, 7; acostar, 28] **1,** to change; exchange. **2,** to barter. **3,** to transform; convert. —**trocable,** *adj.* changeable; exchangeable.

trocatinta (tro·ka'tin·ta) *n.f., colloq.* mixup.

troce ('tro·θe; -se) *v., pres.subjve.* of **trozar.**

trocé (tro'θe; -'se) *v., 1st pers.sing. pret.* of **trozar.**

trocla ('tro·kla) *n.f.* pulley.

trocha ('tro·tʃa) *n.f.* **1,** trail; path. **2,** *Amer., R.R.* gauge. **3,** *Amer.* wheelbase.

trochemoche (tro·tʃe'mo·tʃe) *n.m., in* a **trochemoche,** *also,* a **troche y moche,** helter-skelter; pell-mell.

trofeo (tro'fe·o) *n.m.* trophy.

trófico ('tro·fi·ko) *adj.* trophic.

troglodita (tro·ɣlo'ði·ta) *n.m.* **1,** troglodyte. **2,** *colloq.* glutton. —*adj.* [*also,* **troglodítico** (-'ði·ti·ko)] troglodytic.

troica ('troi·ka) *n.f.* troika.

troj (trox) *n.f.* **1,** granary; barn. **2,** bin. *Also,* **troje** ('tro·xe).

trole ('tro·le) *n.m.* trolley.

trolebús (tro·le'βus) *n.m.* trolley bus.

tromba ('trom·ba) *n.f.* **1,** [*also,* **tromba marina**] waterspout. **2,** [*also,* **tromba de viento**] whirlwind; tornado.

trombón (trom'bon) *n.m.* **1,** trombone. **2,** trombonist.

trombosis (trom'bo·sis) *n.f.* thrombosis.

trompa ('trom·pa) *n.f.* **1,** horn; French horn. **2,** elephant's trunk. **3,** proboscis. **4,** snout. **5,** *colloq.* mouth; puss. **6,** *med.* tube; canal; duct: *trompa de Eustaquio,* Eustachian tube; *trompa de Falopio,* Fallopian tube.

trompada (trom'pa·ða) *n.f., colloq.* blow with the fist; punch. *Also,* **trompazo** (-'pa·θo; -so) *n.m.*

trompear (trom·pe'ar) *v.t., Amer.* to punch. **—trompearse,** *v.r., Amer., colloq.* to have a fist fight.

trompeta (trom'pe·ta) *n.f.* **1,** trumpet; bugle. **2,** *also masc.* trumpeter; bugler. **3,** *colloq.* good-for-nothing; scamp. **—trompetazo,** *n.m., also,* **trompetada,** *n.f., colloq.* trumpet blast. **—trompetero,** *n.m.* trumpeter.

trompetear (trom·pe·te'ar) *v.i., colloq.* to trumpet. **—trompeteo** (-'te·o) *n.m.* trumpeting. .

trompetilla (trom·pe'ti·ʎa; -ja) *n.f.* **1,** ear trumpet. **2,** *Amer., colloq.* Bronx cheer.

trompicar (trom·pi'kar) *v.t.* [*infl.:* **tocar,** 7] to trip; cause to stumble. **—trompicón** (-'kon) *n.m.* stumble.

trompis ('trom·pis) *n.m., colloq.* = **trompada.**

trompo ('trom·po) *n.m.* top; spinning top.

tronada (tro'na·ða) *n.f.* thunderstorm.

tronar (tro'nar) *v.i.* [*infl.:* **acostar,** 28] **1,** to thunder. **2,** *colloq.* to collapse; be finished; be ruined. **—***v.t., Amer., colloq.* to finish off; kill. **—por lo que pueda tronar,** *colloq.* just in case. **—tronar** *or* **tronarse con,** *colloq.* to fall out with; quarrel with. **—tronar los dedos,** to snap the fingers.

troncal (tron'kal) *adj.* **1,** of or pert. to a trunk. **2,** growing out of a trunk.

troncar (tron'kar) *v.t.* [*infl.:* **tocar,**

7] to truncate; lob. **—tronca** ('tron·ka) *n.f.* = **truncamiento.**

tronce ('tron·θe; -se) *v., pres. subjve. of* **tronzar.**

troncé (tron'θe; -'se) *v., 1st pers. sing.pret. of* **tronzar.**

tronco ('tron·ko) *n.m.* **1,** trunk *(of a tree, body, etc.).* **2,** main trunk or stem. **3,** log. **4,** team *(of animals).* **5,** frustum. **—estar hecho un tronco,** *colloq.* **1,** to be dead to the world; be out cold. **2,** to be fast asleep; be sleeping like a log.

troncha ('tron·tʃa) *n.f., Amer., colloq.* **1,** slice; cut; hunk. **2,** sinecure.

tronchar (tron'tʃar) *v.t.* **1,** to snap; break. **2,** to twist; wrench. **3,** to mutilate; damage.

tronera (tro'ne·ra) *n.f.* **1,** porthole. **2,** small opening or window. **3,** *billiards* pocket. **4,** *also masc., colloq.* fly-by-night; scatterbrain.

tronido (tro'ni·ðo) *n.m.* thunder; thunderous sound.

trono ('tro·no) *n.m.* throne.

tronque ('tron·ke) *v., pres.subjve. of* **troncar.**

tronqué (tron'ke) *v., 1st pers. sing.pret. of* **troncar.**

tronzar (tron'θar; -'sar) *v.t.* [*infl.:* **rezar,** 10] **1,** = **tronchar. 2,** to pleat (a skirt). **3,** to exhaust; fatigue.

tropa ('tro·pa) *n.f.* **1,** troop; troops. **2,** *Amer.* herd; drove; troop.

tropel (tro'pel) *n.m.* **1,** rush; rushing; bustle. **2,** gang; crowd; pack.

tropelía (tro·pe'li·a) *n.f.* **1,** abuse; outrage. **2,** confusion.

tropezar (tro·pe'θar; -'sar) *v.i.* [*infl.:* **rezar,** 10; **pensar,** 27] to stumble; trip. **—tropezar con,** *colloq.* to chance upon; stumble upon; meet.

tropezón (tro·pe'θon; -'son) *n.m.* **1,** stumble. **2,** slip; error.

trópico ('tro·pi·ko) *n.m.* tropic. **—tropical,** *adj.* tropical.

tropiece (tro'pje·θe; -se) *v., pres.subjve. of* **tropezar.**

tropiezo (tro'pje·θo; -so) *n.m.* **1,** stumble. **2,** trouble; difficulty. **3,** obstacle; stumbling block. **4,** slip; error. **5,** mishap. **—***v., 1st pers.sing. pres.ind. of* **tropezar.**

tropismo (tro'pis·mo) *n.m.* tropism.

tropo ('tro·po) *n.m.* figure of speech; trope.

troposfera (tro·pos'fe·ra) *n.f.* troposphere.

troqué (tro'ke) *v.*, *1st pers. sing.pret. of* **trocar.**

troquel (tro'kel) *n.m.* die; stamp. —**troquelar,** *v.t.* to die-stamp.

troqueo (tro'ke·o) *n.m.* trochee.

trotacalles (tro·ta'ka·ʎes; -jes) *n.m. & f., sing. & pl.* gadabout.

trotamundos (tro·ta'mun·dos) *n.m. & f.sing. & pl.* globetrotter.

trotar (tro'tar) *v.i.* **1,** to trot; jog. **2,** *colloq.* to be on the run; hustle. —**trotón,** *adj.* trotting. —*n.m.* horse, esp. a trotter.

trote ('tro·te) *n.m.* **1,** trot; jog. **2,** *colloq.* chore; hard task. —**al trote, 1,** on the double; fast. **2,** at a trot.

troupe ('tru·pe) *n.f.* troupe.

trousseau (tru'so) *n.m. or f.* trousseau.

trova ('tro·βa) *n.f.* song; ballad; lyric; love song. —**trovador,** *n.m.* troubadour. —**trovar,** *v.i. & t.* to versify; lyricize.

Troya ('tro·ja) *n.f.* Troy, *in* **ahí, allí** *or* **aquí fué Troya,** *colloq.* that's when (or where) the fireworks started. —**ardió Troya,** *colloq.* the fireworks started; all hell broke loose.

troza ('tro·θa; -sa) *n.f.* log; timber.

trozar (tro'θar; -'sar) *v.t.* [*infl.:* **rezar, 10**] to cut off; lop.

trozo ('tro·θo; -so) *n.m.* **1,** piece; chunk; bit. **2,** passage; excerpt.

truco ('tru·ko) *n.m.* **1,** trick; legerdemain. **2,** card game. —**trucos,** *n.m.pl.* pool *(game)*.

truculento (tru·ku'len·to) *adj.* truculent. —**truculencia,** *n.f.* truculence.

trucha ('tru·tʃa) *n.f.* **1,** trout. **2,** derrick.

trueco ('trwe·ko) *v.*, *1st pers.sing. pres.ind. of* **trocar.** —*n.m.* = **trueque.**

truene ('trwe·ne) *v.*, *pres.subjve. of* **tronar.**

trueno ('trwe·no) *n.m.* **1,** thunder. **2,** thunderclap. —*v.*, *1st pers.sing. pres.ind. of* **tronar.**

trueque ('trwe·ke) *n.m.* **1,** exchange. **2,** barter; bartering. **3,** change; transformation. —*v., pres.subjve. of* **trocar.** —**a trueque de,** instead of. —**a** *or* **en trueque,** in exchange.

trufa ('tru·fa) *n.f.* **1,** truffle. **2,** lie; fib. —**trufar,** *v.t.* to stuff with truffles. —*v.i.* to lie.

truhán (tru'an) *adj.* scoundrelly; rascally. —*n.m.* scoundrel; rascal.

—**truhanear,** *v.i.* to cheat. —**truhanesco,** *adj.* rascally; knavish.

truhanada (tru·a'na·ða) *n.f.* **1,** rascally act. **2,** gang of crooks.

truhanería (tru·a·ne'ri·a) *n.f.* **1,** knavery; rascality. **2,** mischievousness; buffoonery. **3,** gang of rascals.

trujamán (tru·xa'man) *also,* **trujimán** (tru·xi-) *n.m.* wizard; whiz; expert.

trullo ('tru·ʎo; -jo) *n.m.* teal.

truncar (trun'kar) *v.t.* [*infl.:* **tocar, 7**] **1,** to truncate; lop. **2,** to make or leave incomplete. **3,** to block; hinder; disrupt. —**truncamiento,** *n.m.* truncation. —**trunco,** *adj.* truncated.

trusa ('tru·sa) *n.f., Amer.* bathing suit; trunks.

tsetsé (tse'tse) *n.f.* tsetse.

tu (tu) *poss.adj.m. & f.sing.* [*m. & f.pl.* **tus**], *agreeing in number with the thing possessed* your; thy; thine.

tú (tu) *pers.pron.2ndpers.sing.* you; thou. —**de tú por tú,** on intimate terms.

tualet (twa'let) *n.m.* [*pl.* **tualets**] toilet; lavatory.

tuba ('tu·βa) *n.f.* tuba.

tuberculina (tu·βer·ku'li·na) *n.f.* tuberculin.

tubérculo (tu'βer·ku·lo) *n.m.* **1,** tubercle. **2,** tuber.

tuberculosis (tu·βer·ku'lo·sis) *n.f.* tuberculosis. —**tuberculoso,** *adj.* tuberculous; tubercular. —*n.m.* tubercular.

tubería (tu·βe'ri·a) *n.f.* **1,** pipes; tubing. **2,** plumbing. **3,** pipeline.

tuberosa (tu·βe'ro·sa) *n.f.* tuberose.

tuberoso (tu·βe'ro·so) *adj.* tuberous.

tubo ('tu·βo) *n.m.* **1,** tube. **2,** pipe. —**tubular** (-βu'lar) *adj.* tubular.

tucán (tu'kan) *n.m.* toucan.

tudesco (tu'ðes·ko) *adj.* Teutonic; German. —*n.m.* Teuton; German.

tuerca ('twer·ka) *n.f., mech.* nut. —**tuerca de mariposa,** wing nut.

tuerto ('twer·to) *adj.* **1,** one-eyed. **2,** crosseyed. —*n.m.* **1,** one-eyed person. **2,** crosseyed person. **3,** *obs.* wrong; injustice. —**a tuertas,** wrongly; contrariwise. —**a tuertas o a derechas,** *also,* **a tuerto o a derecho,** rightly or wrongly.

tuerza ('twer·θa; -sa) *v.*, *pres. subjve. of* **torcer.**

tuerzo ('twer·θo; -so) *v., 1st pers.sing.pres.ind. of* **torcer.**

tueste ('twes·te) *v., pres.subjve. of* **tostar.**

tuesto ('twes·to) *v., 1st pers.sing. pres.ind. of* **tostar.**

tuétano ('twe·ta·no) *n.m.* marrow.

tufo ('tu·fo) *n.f.* **1,** fume; vapor. **2,** *colloq.* unpleasant odor; reek. **3,** *often pl., colloq.* haughtiness; airs. **4,** lock of hair; tuft; bang.

tugurio (tu'ɣu·rjo) *n.m.* **1,** shepherd's hut. **2,** *colloq.* hovel; dump.

tul (tul) *n.m.* **1,** tulle. **2,** = **tule.**

tule ('tu·le) *n.m., Amer.* a kind of reed used in making cane chairs, straw hats, etc. *Also,* **tul.**

tulio ('tu·ljo) *n.m.* thulium.

tulipa (tu'li·pa) *n.f.* light globe.

tulipán (tu·li'pan) *n.m.* tulip.

tullido (tu'ʎi·ðo; -'ji·ðo) *adj.* crippled; lame. —*n.m.* cripple.

tullir (tu'ʎir; -'jir) *v.t.* [*infl.:* **bullir, 19**] to cripple; lame. —**tullirse,** *v.r.* to become crippled.

tumba ('tum·ba) *n.f.* **1,** tomb. **2,** *Amer.* felling, as of trees. **3,** *Amer.* forest clearing.

tumbar (tum'bar) *v.t.* to fell; knock down; tumble. —**tumbarse,** *v.r., colloq.* to lie down.

tumbo ('tum·bo) *n.m.* tumble; tumbling.

tumefacción (tu·me·fak'θjon; -'sjon) *n.f.* tumefaction; tumidity. —**tumefacto** (-'fak·to) *adj.* tumid.

tumescente (tu·mes'θen·te; -me'sen·te) *adj.* tumescent. —**tumescencia,** *n.f.* tumescence.

túmido ('tu·mi·ðo) *adj.* tumid; swollen.

tumor (tu'mor) *n.m.* tumor.

túmulo ('tu·mu·lo) *n.m.* **1,** burial mound; tomb. **2,** catafalque. **3,** mound.

tumulto (tu'mul·to) *n.m.* tumult. —**tumultuoso** (-'two·so) *adj.* tumultuous.

tumultuar (tu·mul'twar) *v.t.* [*infl.:* **continuar, 23**] to incite to riot. —**tumultuarse,** *v.r.* to riot.

tuna ('tu·na) *n.f.* **1,** prickly pear. **2,** *colloq.* dissolute life. —**tunal,** *n.m.* prickly pear cactus.

tunanta (tu'nan·ta) *n.f.* hussy; wench.

tunante (tu'nan·te) *n.m.* **1,** rogue; scoundrel. **2,** bum; loafer.

tunar (tu'nar) *v.i.* to bum around; be a hobo.

tunda ('tun·da) *n.f., colloq.* beating; whipping.

tundir (tun'dir) *v.t.* **1,** to beat; whip; drub. **2,** to shear.

tundra ('tun·dra) *n.f.* tundra.

tunear (tu·ne'ar) *v.i.* to live or behave as a scoundrel.

túnel ('tu·nel) *n.m.* tunnel.

tungsteno (tuŋs'te·no) *n.m.* tungsten.

túnica ('tu·ni·ka) *n.f.* tunic; robe.

tuno ('tu·no) *adj.* scoundrelly; rascally. —*n.m.* scoundrel; rascal.

tuntún (tun'tun) *n.m., in* **al (buen) tuntún,** *colloq.* **1,** gropingly; by trial and error. **2,** blindly; helterskelter.

tupé (tu'pe) *n.m.* **1,** toupee. **2,** nerve; audacity.

tupido (tu'pi·ðo) *adj.* **1,** thick; dense. **2,** obstructed; blocked; stopped up. **3,** filled; crammed.

tupir (tu'pir) *v.t.* **1,** to fill; cram. **2,** to obstruct; block; stop up. —**tupirse,** *v.r.* **1,** to become full; be gorged. **2,** to become obstructed. **3,** *Amer.* to become morose; become stultified. **4,** *Amer.* to be astonished.

turba ('tur·βa) *n.f.* **1,** mob; crowd. **2,** peat; turf.

turbante (tur'βan·te) *n.m.* turban.

turbar (tur'βar) *v.t.* to disturb; trouble; upset; discomfit. —**turbación,** *n.f.* perturbation; discomfiture.

túrbido ('tur·βi·ðo) *adj.* muddy; turbid. —**turbidez** (-'ðeθ; -'ðes) *n.f.* muddiness; turbidity.

turbina (tur'βi·na) *n.f.* turbine.

turbio ('tur·βjo) *adj.* **1,** turbid; murky. **2,** muddled; confused. —**turbiedad** (-βje'ðað) *n.f.* muddiness. —**turbios,** *n.m.pl.* dregs, esp. oil dregs.

turbión (tur'βjon) *n.m.* **1,** squall; thunderstorm. **2,** maelstrom. **3,** *fig.* hail; avalanche.

turbonada (tur·βo'na·ða) *n.f.* squall; pelting shower.

turbopropulsor (tur·βo·pro·pul'sor) *adj. & n.m.* turboprop.

turborreactor (tur·βo·rre·ak'tor) *adj. & n.m.* turbojet.

turbulento (tur·βu'len·to) *adj.* turbulent. —**turbulencia,** *n.f.* turbulence.

turco ('tur·ko) *adj. & n.m.* Turkish. —*n.m.* Turk.

turf (turf) *n.m., sports* turf.

turgente (tur'xen·te) *adj.* turgid. —**turgencia,** *n.f.* turgidity.

turista (tu'ris·ta) *n.m. & f.* tourist.

—**turismo,** *n.m.* touring; tourism.

—**turístico,** *adj.* tourist *(attrib.)*.

turmalina (tur·ma'li·na) *n.f.* tourmaline.

turnar (tur'nar) *v.i.* **1,** to alternate; take turns. **2,** to work shifts.

turno ('tur·no) *n.m.* **1,** turn. **2,** shift. —**de turno,** on duty; open *(said of a drugstore)*.

turquesa (tur'ke·sa) *n.f.* turquoise.

turquí (tur'ki) *adj.* & *n.m.* deep blue; indigo.

turrón (tu'rron) *n.m.* **1,** nougat. **2,** *fig.* toothsome morsel. —**romper el turrón,** *Amer.* to switch from polite to informal address.

turulato (tu·ru'la·to) *adj., colloq.* stunned; agape; dumfounded.

tus (tus) *poss.adj., pl. of* **tu** *(agreeing in number with the things possessed)* your; thy; thine.

tusa ('tu·sa) *n.f., Amer.* **1,** corncob. **2,** corn husk. **3,** *fig.* rubbish.

tusar (tu'sar) *v.t., Amer.* to cut; crop; shear.

tutear (tu·te'ar) *v.t.* & *i.* to use the familiar pronouns **tú** and **te** in addressing someone. —**tuteo** (-'te·o) *n.m.* use of **tú** and **te.**

tutela (tu'te·la) *n.f.* **1,** tutelage; guardianship. **2,** tutorage. —**tutelar,** *adj.* tutelary.

tutiplén (tu·ti'plen) *n.m., in a tutiplén,* in abundance.

tutor (tu'tor) *n.m.* tutor. —**tutora,** *n.f.* female tutor. —**tutoría,** *n.f.* tutelage.

tutti-frutti ('tu·ti'fru·ti) *n.m.* tutti-frutti.

tuturuto (tu·tu'ru·to) *adj., Amer., colloq.* = **turulato.**

tuturutú (tu·tu·ru'tu) *n.m.* trumpet or bugle call.

tuve ('tu·βe) *v., .1st pers.sing. pret. of* **tener.**

tuyo ('tu·jo) *poss.pron.m.sing.* [*fem.* **tuya;** *pl.* **tuyos, tuyas**] yours; thine. —*poss.adj.m.sing., used after a noun* your; of yours; thy; of thine.

tuza ('tu·θa; -sa) *n.f., Amer.* gopher.

U

U, u (u) *n.f.* 24th letter of the Spanish alphabet.

U. *abbr. of* **usted.**

u (u) *conj.* or. *Used in place of* **o** *before words beginning with* o *or* ho.

ubérrimo (u'βe·rri·mo) *adj.* extremely fruitful, fertile or abundant.

ubicación (u·bi·ka'θjon; -'sjon) *n.f.* **1,** location; situation. **2,** *Amer.* placing; placement.

ubicar (u·βi'kar) *v.i.* [*infl.: tocar,* 7] to lie; be situated. —*v.t., Amer.* to locate; situate; place. —**ubicarse,** *v.r.* **1,** to lie; be situated. **2,** *Amer.* to orient oneself; take one's bearings. **3,** to be hired; land a job.

ubicuo (u'βi·kwo) *adj.* ubiquitous. —**ubicuidad** (-kwi'ðað) *n.f.* ubiquity.

ubre ('u·βre) *n.f.* udder; teat.

ubrera (u'βre·ra) *n.f.* thrush *(disease)*.

ucase (u'ka·se) *n.m.* = **ukase.**

ucranio (u'kra·njo) *adj.* & *n.m.* Ukrainian.

Ud. *abbr. of* **usted.**

Uds. *abbr. of* **ustedes.**

¡uf! (uf) *interj.* ugh! *(denoting weariness or annoyance)*.

ufanarse (u·fa'nar·se) *v.r.* to boast; brag.

ufanía (u·fa'ni·a) *n.f.* **1,** conceit; airs. **2,** airiness; jauntiness. **3,** contentment; satisfaction.

ufano (u'fa·no) *adj.* **1,** conceited; haughty. **2,** airy; jaunty. **3,** content; satisfied.

ujier (u'xjer) *n.m.* usher; doorman.

ukase *also,* **ucase** (u'ka·se) *n.m.* ukase.

ukulele (u·ku'le·le) *n.m.* ukulele.

úlcera ('ul·θe·ra; 'ul·se-) *n.f.* ulcer. —**ulceroso,** *adj.* ulcerous.

ulcerar (ul·θe'rar; ul·se-) *v.t.* to ulcerate. —**ulcerarse,** *v.r.* to ulcerate; become ulcerated. —**ulceración,** *n.f.* ulceration.

ulterior (ul·te'rjor) *adj.* **1,** ulterior. **2,** subsequent.

últimamente (ul·ti·ma'men·te) *adv.* **1,** finally; lastly. **2,** lately.

ultimar (ul·ti'mar) *v.t.* to finish; end; finish off.

ultimátum (ul·ti'ma·tum) *n.m. sing.* & *pl.* **1,** ultimatum. **2,** *colloq.* last say; final say.

último ('ul·ti·mo) *adj.* last; final; ultimate. —**a la última (moda),** in the latest (fashion). —**a la última**

hora, at the last moment; at the eleventh hour. **—a últimos de,** at the end of (a month). **—estar en las últimas,** to be at one's (or its) end; be on one's (or its) last legs. **—por último,** in the end; at last; finally.

ultra ('ul·tra) *adj.* ultra; extreme. **—***n.m.* & *f.* ultra; extremist.

ultraje (ul'tra·xe) *n.m.* outrage. **—ultrajar,** *v.t.* to outrage. **—ultrajante,** *adj.* outrageous.

ultramar (ul·tra'mar) *n.m.* land beyond the sea. **—de ultramar,** overseas.

ultramarino (ul·tra·ma'ri·no) *adj.* & *n.m.* ultramarine. **—tienda de ultramarinos,** delicatessen.

ultranza (ul'tran·θa; -sa) *in* **a ultranza,** to the end; to the utmost.

ultrasónico (ul·tra'so·ni·ko) *adj.* ultrasonic.

ultrasonido (ul·tra·so'ni·ðo) *n.m.* ultrasound.

ultratumba (ul·tra'tum·ba) *adv.* beyond the grave.

ultravioleta (ul·tra·βjo'le·ta) *adj.* ultraviolet.

ulular (u·lu'lar) *v.i.* to ululate; howl. **—ululación,** *n.f.,* also, **ululato,** *n.m.* ululation; howl; howling.

umbilical (um·bi·li'kal) *adj.* umbilical.

umbral (um'bral) *n.m.* **1,** threshold; doorsill. **2,** lintel.

umbría (um'bri·a) *n.f.* shade; shadow.

umbrío (um'bri·o) *adj.* shady; dark.

umbroso (um'bro·so) *adj.* shady; umbrageous.

un (un) *indef.article m.sing.* a; an. **—***adj.m.sing.* one.

una ('u·na) *indef.article,* *adj.* & *pron., fem.* of **un** *or* **uno. —a una, 1,** jointly; together. **2,** at one; of one accord. **—la una,** one o'clock.

unánime (u'na·ni·me) *adj.* unanimous. **—unanimidad,** *n.f.* unanimity. **—por unanimidad,** unanimously.

unas ('u·nas) *indef.pron. pl.* & *adj. pl., fem.* of **unos.**

unción (un'θjon; -'sjon) *n.m.* unction.

uncir (un'θir; -'sir) *v.t.* [*infl.:* **esparcir,** 12] to yoke.

undécimo (un'de·θi·mo; -si·mo) *adj.* & *n.m.* eleventh.

undular (un·du'lar) *v.i.* = **ondular. —undulación,** *n.f.* = **ondulación.**

ungir (un'xir) *v.t.* [*infl.:* **coger,** 15]

to anoint. **—ungimiento,** *n.m.* anointment.

ungüento (un'gwen·to) *n.m.* ointment.

ungulado (un·gu'la·ðo) *adj.* & *n.m.* ungulate.

unicameral (u·ni·ka·me'ral) *adj.* unicameral.

unicelular (u·ni·θe·lu'lar; u·ni·se-) *adj.* unicellular.

unicidad (u·ni·θi'ðað; -si'ðað) *n.f.* **1,** singularity. **2,** uniqueness.

único ('u·ni·ko) *adj.* **1,** only; sole; single. **2,** unique. **—únicamente,** *adv.* only; solely.

unicornio (u·ni'kor·njo) *n.m.* unicorn.

unidad (u·ni'ðað) *n.f.* **1,** unity. **2,** unit.

unidamente (u·ni·ða'men·te) *adv.* jointly; together; unitedly.

unido (u'ni·ðo) *adj.* **1,** united; joined. **2,** close.

unificar (u·ni·fi'kar) *v.t.* [*infl.:* **tocar,** 7] to unify. **—unificación,** *n.f.* unification.

uniformar (u·ni·for'mar) *v.t.* **1,** to make uniform. **2,** to uniform; furnish with a uniform. **—uniforme** (-'for·me) *adj.* & *n.m.* uniform. **—uniformidad,** *n.f.* uniformity.

unigénito (u·ni'xe·ni·to) *adj.* only-begotten.

unilateral (u·ni·la·te'ral) *adj.* unilateral.

unión (u'njon) *n.f.* **1,** union. **2,** joining; uniting. **3,** unity; concord. **4,** combination; fusion. **5,** junction; juncture. **6,** joint; seam. **7,** merging; merger.

unionismo (u·njo'nis·mo) *n.m.* unionism. **—unionista,** *n.m.* & *f.* unionist.

unipersonal (u·ni·per·so'nal) *adj., gram.* impersonal.

unir (u'nir) *v.t.* **1,** to unite. **2,** to join; connect; merge. **—unirse,** *v.r.* **1,** to unite; join; merge. **2,** *fol. by* **a,** to join; become a member of. **3,** to wed; be married.

unisexo (u·ni'sek·so) *adj.* unisex.

unisexual (u·ni·sek'swal) *adj.* unisexual.

unisón (u·ni'son) *adj.* = **unísono. —***n.m.* unison.

unísono (u'ni·so·no) *adj.* **1,** sounding alike; of like sound. **2,** sounding together; in unison. **—al unísono,** in unison.

unitario (u·ni'ta·rjo) *adj.* **1,** unitary; unit *(attrib.)*. **2,** unitarian. **3,** *polit.* centralized; advocating centralization. —*n.m.* **1,** unitarian. **2,** *polit.* advocate of centralization.

univalente (u·ni·βa'len·te) *adj.* univalent.

univalvo (u·ni'βal·βo) *adj. & n.m.* univalve.

universal (u·ni·βer'sal) *adj.* **1,** universal. **2,** world *(attrib.)*. —**universalidad,** *n.f.* universality.

universalismo (u·ni·βer·sa'lis·mo) *n.m.* universalism. —**universalista,** *adj. & n.m. & f.* universalist.

universalizar (u·ni·βer·sa·li·'θar; -'sar) *v.t.* [*infl.:* rezar, 10] to universalize.

universidad (u·ni·βer·si'ðað) *n.f.* **1,** university. **2,** = **universalidad.** —**universitario,** *adj.* university *(attrib.)*. —*n.m.* university student.

universo (u·ni'βer·so) *n.m.* universe. —*adj.* universal.

unja ('un·xa) *v., pres.subjve.* of **ungir.**

unjo ('un·xo) *v., 1st per.sing. pres.ind.* of **ungir.**

uno ('u·no) *indef.pron.* **1,** one. **2,** oneself **3,** someone; somebody. —*adj. & n.m.* one. —**de uno en uno; uno a uno,** one by one. —**uno a otro,** each other; one another. —**uno de tantos,** one of many; one of the lot. —**uno que otro,** one here and there; some; a few. —**uno y otro,** both.

unos ('u·nos) *indef.pron.pl.* some: *Unos cantan, otros lloran,* Some sing, some weep. —*indef.adj.pl.* **1,** some; several; a few: *Compré unos libros,* I bought some books. **2,** *fol. by a numeral* some; approximately; about; more or less: *unos veinte libros,* about twenty books. —**unos cuantos,** a few; some; several.

untar (un'tar) *v.t.* **1,** to spread; smear; daub. **2,** *colloq.* to tip; bribe; grease: *untar las manos,* to grease the palm. —**untarse,** *v.r.* **1,** to spread or daub oneself with ointment, grease, etc. **2,** to line one's pockets; engage in pilferage. —**untadura,** *n.f.* = **untura.** —**untamiento,** *n.m.* daubing; smearing.

unto ('un·to) *n.m.* **1,** ointment; pomade. **2,** grease. **3,** animal fat.

untuoso (un'two·so) *also,* **untoso** (-'to·so) *adj.* unctuous; greasy. —**untuosidad,** *n.f.* unctuousness.

untura (un'tu·ra) *n.f.* **1,** ointment; pomade. **2,** daubing; smearing.

unza ('un·θa; -sa) *v., pres.subjve.* of **uncir.**

unzo ('un·θo; -so) *v., 1st pers. sing.pres.ind.* of **uncir.**

uña ('u·ɲa) *n.f.* **1,** nail; fingernail; toenail. **2,** hoof. **3,** claw; hook. **4,** plectrum. **5,** *colloq.* greed; itchy fingers. —**a uña de caballo,** at full gallop. —**enseñar** *or* **mostrar las uñas,** to show one's claws. —**ser uña y carne,** to be very close friends; be hand in glove. —**tener uñas largas,** to have itchy fingers.

uñada (u'ɲa·ða) *n.f.* scratch.

uñero (u'ɲe·ro) *n.m.* ingrown toenail.

uñir (u'ɲir) *v.t., dial.* [*infl.:* gruñir, 21] = **uncir.**

¡upa! ('u·pa) *interj.* up, up!; hoopla!

uranálisis (u·ra'na·li·sis) *n.m. or f.sing. & pl* urinalysis.

uranio (u'ra·njo) *n.m.* uranium.

Urano (u'ra·no) *n.m.* Uranus.

urbanidad (ur·βa·ni'ðað) *n.f.* urbanity; civility; manners.

urbanismo (ur·βa'nis·mo) *n.m.* city planning.

urbanización (ur·βa·ni·θa'θjon; -sa'sjon) *n.f.* **1,** urbanization. **2,** *chiefly Amer.* housing development.

urbanizar (ur·βa·ni'θar; -'sar) *v.t.* [*infl.:* rezar, 10] **1,** to urbanize. **2,** to develop (land).

urbano (ur'βa·no) *adj.* **1,** urban. **2,** urbane; polite.

urbe ('ur·βe) *n.f.* city; metropolis.

urdimbre (ur'ðim·bre) *also,* **urdiembre** (-'ðjem·bre) *n.f.* **1,** weaving warp. **2,** *lit. & fig.* weave.

urdir (ur'ðir) *v.t.* **1,** to twine; warp; weave. **2,** *fig.* to weave; concoct; plot.

urea (u're·a) *n.f.* urea.

uremia (u're·mja) *n.f.* uremia. —**urémico** (u're·mi·ko) *adj.* uremic.

uréter (u're·ter) *n.m.* ureter.

uretra (u're·tra) *n.f.* urethra.

urgente (ur'xen·te) *adj.* urgent. —**urgencia,** *n.f.* urgency. —**de urgencia, 1,** urgent. **2,** urgently.

urgir (ur'xir) *v.i.* [*infl.:* coger, 15] **1,** to be urgent. **2,** to urge; insist. —*v.t., Amer.* to urge.

úrico ('u·ri·ko) *adj.* uric.

urinación (u·ri·na'θjon; -'sjon) *n.f.* urination.

urinal (u·ri'nal) *adj.* urinary. —*n.m.* urinal.

urinálisis (u·ri'na·li·sis) *n.m. or f.sing. & pl.* urinalysis.

urinario (u·ri'na·rjo) *adj.* urinary. —*n.m.* urinal.

urna ('ur·na) *n.f.* 1, urn. 2, showcase. 3, ballot box; *pl.* polls.

urología (u·ro·lo'xi·a) *n.f.* urology. —**urológico** (-'lo·xi·ko) *adj.* urological. —**urólogo** (u'ro·lo·ɣo) *n.m.* urologist.

urraca (u'rra·ka) *n.f.* magpie.

úrsido ('ur·si·ðo) *adj.* ursine; bear *(attrib.).* —*n.m.* member of the bear family.

ursino (ur'si·no) *adj.* ursine.

urticaria (ur·ti'ka·rja) *n.f., pathol.* hives.

usado (u'sa·ðo) *adj.* 1, used; worn. 2, customary. 3, second-hand. 4, experienced; skilled.

usanza (u'san·θa; -sa) *n.f.* usage; custom; fashion.

usar (u'sar) *v.t.* 1, to use. 2, *fol. by* de, to make use of; take advantage of. 3, to wear. 4, to exercise; practice; follow. —*v.i., fol. by inf.* to be accustomed to; be used to; be wont to. —**usarse**, *v.r.* 1, to be used; be employed. 2, to be usual; be in fashion or usage; be customary.

usía (u'si·a) *pers.pron., contr. of* **vuestra señoría,** your lordship.

usina (u'si·na) *n.f., Amer.* 1, powerhouse. 2, gas works. 3, industrial plant.

uso ('u·so) *n.m.* 1, use. 2, usage; custom; fashion. 3, habit; practice. 4, wearing; wear. 5, wear and tear. —**en buen uso,** *colloq.* in good condition. —**uso de razón,** discernment; understanding.

usted (us'teð) *pers.pron.* [*pl.* **ustedes**] you; yourself (*or* yourselves). *Used as subject of a verb or object of a preposition in polite or formal address. Construed with the verb in the third person.*

usual (u'swal) *adj.* usual. —**usualmente,** *adv.* usually.

usuario (u'swa·rjo) *n.m.* user.

usufructo (u·su'fruk·to) *n.m.* 1,

usufruct. 2, benefits; advantage; profit.

usufructuar (u·su·fruk'twar) [*infl.:* **continuar, 23**] *v.t.* 1, to have the usufruct of. 2, to make use of; turn to account; enjoy the benefits of.

usura (u'su·ra) *n.f.* usury. —**usurario,** *adj.* usurious. —**usurero,** *n.m.* usurer.

usurpar (u·sur'par) *v.t.* to usurp. —**usurpación,** *n.f.* usurpation. —**usurpador,** *adj.* usurping. —*n.m.* [*fem.* **-dora**] usurper.

utensilio (u·ten'si·ljo) *n.m.* utensil.

útero ('u·te·ro) *n.m.* uterus. —**uterino** (-'ri·no) *adj.* uterine.

útil ('u·til) *adj.* 1, useful; usable. 2, *law* allowable (time). —*n.m.* 1, *usu. pl.* utensils; tools. 2, usefulness.

utilidad (u·ti·li'ðað) *n.f.* 1, utility. 2, profit. 3, usefulness.

utilitario (u·ti·li'ta·rjo) *adj.* utilitarian. —**utilitarismo** (-'ris·mo) *n.m.* utilitarianism. —**utilitarista** (-'ris·ta) *adj. & h.m. & f.* utilitarian.

utilizar (u·ti·li'θar; -'sar) *v.t.* [*infl.:* **rezar, 10**] to utilize. —**utilizable,** *adj.* utilizable. —**utilización,** *n.f.* utilization.

utopía (u·to'pi·a) *also,* **utopia** (u'to·pja) *n.f.* Utopia. —**utópico** (u'to·pi·ko) *adj.* Utopian. —**utopismo,** *n.m.* utopianism. —**utopista,** *adj. & n.m. & f.* Utopian.

utrero (u'tre·ro) *n.m.* calf between two and three years old.

UU. *abbr. of* **ustedes.**

uva ('u·βa) *n.f.* 1, grape. 2, bunch of grapes. 3, grapes collectively. —**uvero,** *adj.* grape *(attrib.).* —*n.m.* grape vendor. —**uva pasa,** raisin.

úvula ('u·βu·la) *n.f.* uvula. —**uvular,** *adj.* uvular.

uxoricidio (uk·so·ri'θi·ðjo; -'si·ðjo) *n.m.* uxoricide *(act).* —**uxoricida** (-'θi·ða; -'si·ða) *n.m. or f.* uxoricide *(agent).*

¡uy! (uj) *interj.* oh!; ouch!

V

V, v (be) *n.f.* 25th letter of the Spanish alphabet.
V. *abbr. of* **usted.**

va (ba) *v.,* *3rd pers.sing.pres.ind. of* **ir.**

vaca ('ba·ka) *n.f.* 1, cow. 2, beef. 3,

cowhide. —**hacerse la vaca; hacer vacas,** *Amer., colloq.* to play hooky. —**vaca marina,** sea cow.

vacación (ba·ka'θjon; -'sjon) *n.f., usu.pl.* vacation.

vacada (ba'ka·ða) *n.f.* drove of cattle.

vacancia (ba'kan·θja; -sja) *n.f.* vacancy; unfilled position; opening.

vacante (ba'kan·te) *adj.* vacant; unoccupied. —*n.f.* 1, vacancy; unfilled position; opening. 2, vacation.

vacar (ba'kar) *v.i.* [*infl.: tocar,* 7] 1, to be idle; be not working. 2, to be vacant, as a position. —*v.t.* to vacate.

vaciado (ba'θja·ðo; -'sja·ðo) *n.m.* cast; casting; molding.

vaciar (ba'θjar; -'sjar) *v.t.* [*infl.: enviar,* 22] 1, to empty. 2, to vacate. 3, to hollow. 4, to cast; mold. 5, to grind; put a cutting edge on. —*v.i.* to discharge; empty; flow out or away. —**vaciarse,** *v.r.* 1, to become empty or vacant. 2, *colloq.* to unbosom oneself. 3, *colloq.* to let the cat out of the bag. 4, *Amer., colloq.* to come to naught; be foiled.

vaciedad (ba·θje'ðað; -sje'ðað) *n.f.* empty statement; tomfoolery.

vacilación (ba·θi·la'θjon; -si·la'sjon) *n.f.* 1, swaying; tottering. 2, hesitation; vacillation.

vacilar (ba·θi'lar; -si'lar) *v.i.* 1, to vacillate; waver; hesitate. 2, to sway; totter.

vacío (ba'θi·o; -'si·o) *adj.* 1, empty; void. 2, vacuous. 3, unoccupied; untenanted. 4, idle. 5, concave; hollow. 6, vain; presumptuous. —*n.m.* 1, void; emptiness. 2, vacuum. 3, vacancy. 4, concavity; hollowness. 5, blank; gap. —**hacer el vacío a,** 1, to ignore; shun. 2, to isolate.

vacuidad (ba·kwi'ðað) *n.f.* emptiness; vacuity.

vacuna (ba'ku·na) *n.f.* 1, cowpox. 2, vaccine.

vacunar (ba·ku'nar) *v.t.* to vaccinate. —**vacunación,** *n.f.* vaccination.

vacuno (ba'ku·no) *adj.* bovine. —**ganado vacuno,** cattle.

vacuo ('ba·kwo) *adj.* empty; vacuous.

vacuola (ba'kwo·la) *n.f.* vacuole.

vadear (ba·ðe'ar) *v.t.* 1, to wade; ford. 2, to get around; circumvent. 3, to get through; get over.

—**vadearse,** *v.r.* to behave; conduct oneself.

vado ('ba·ðo) *n.m.* ford.

vagabundear (ba·ɣa·βun·de'ar) *v.i.* to wander; rove. 2, to loaf; idle. —**vagabundeo** (-'de·o) *n.m.* vagabondage; vagrancy.

vagabundo (ba·ɣa'βun·do) *adj.* & *n.m.* & *f.* vagabond; vagrant. *Also,* **vagamundo** (-'mun·do).

vagamente (ba·ɣa'men·te) *adv.* vaguely.

vagancia (ba'ɣan·θja; -sja) *n.f.* vagrancy. —**vagante,** *adj.* & *n.m.* & *f.* vagrant.

vagar (ba'ɣar) *v.i.* [*infl.: pagar,* 8] 1, to roam; wander. 2, to idle; loiter. —*n.m.* 1, wandering; roaming. 2, idleness.

vagaroso (ba·ɣa'ro·so) *adj.* flitting.

vagido (ba'xi·ðo) *n.m.* wail, esp. of a newborn child.

vagina (ba'xi·na) *n.f.* vagina. —**vaginal,** *adj.* vaginal.

vago ('ba·ɣo) *adj.* 1, roaming; wandering. 2, vague, indistinct. 3, lax; loose. 4, lazy; slothful. 5, *paint.* misty; hazy. —*n.m.* loafer; vagrant.

vagón (ba'ɣon) *n.m.* 1, railroad car. 2, wagon; van. —**vagón de cola,** caboose. —**vagón de mercancías,** freight car.

vagonada (ba·ɣo'na·ða) *n.f.* wagonload; carload.

vagoneta (ba·ɣo'ne·ta) *n.f.* 1, *R.R.* gondola. 2, dump car. 3, station wagon. 4, *Amer.* delivery truck; pickup.

vague ('ba·ɣe) *v., pres.subjve.* of **vagar.**

vagué (ba'ɣe) *v., 1st pers.sing. pret. of* **vagar.**

vaguear (ba·ɣe'ar) *v.i.* = **vagar.**

vaguedad (ba·ɣe'ðað) *n.f.* vagueness; ambiguity.

vaharada (ba·a'ra·ða) *n.f.* breath; puff.

vahido (ba'i·ðo) *n.m.* dizziness; fainting spell.

vaho ('ba·o) *n.m.* 1, breath; exhalation. 2, vapor; condensation. 3, reek; stench.

vaina ('bai·na) *n.f.* 1, scabbard; sheath. 2, pod. 3, *colloq.* bother; nuisance. 4, *colloq.* tripe; humbug. 5, *Amer., colloq.* luck. —**salirse de la vaina,** *Amer., colloq.* to fly off the handle.

vainica (bai'ni·ka) *n.f.* hemstitch.

vainilla (bai'ni·ʎa; -ja) *n.f.* 1, vanilla. 2, = **vainica**.

vais (bais) *v.*, *2nd pers.pl.pres.ind. of* **ir**.

vaivén (bai'βen) *n.m.* 1, swinging; swaying. 2, coming and going. 3, *usu.pl.* ups and downs.

vajilla (ba'xi·ʎa; -ja) *n.f.* table service; set of dishes. —**vajilla de plata**, silverware. —**vajilla de porcelana**, chinaware.

val (bal) *n.m.*, *contr. of* **valle**. *Used chiefly in place names.*

valdré (bal'dre) *v.*, *fut. of* **valer**.

vale ('ba·le) *n.m.* 1, bond; promissory note. 2, voucher; coupon. 3, farewell. —*n.m. & f.*, *Amer.* pal; chum.

valedero (ba·le'ðe·ro) *adj.* worthy; valuable.

valedor (ba·le'ðor) *n.m.* [*fem.* -**dora**] 1, defender; protector. 2, *Amer.* comrade.

valencia (ba'len·θja; -sja) *n.f.*, *chem.* valence.

valentía (ba·len'ti·a) *n.f.* valor; courage; bravery.

valentón (ba·len'ton) *adj.* blustering; swaggering. —*n.m.* [*fem.* -**tona**] swaggerer; blusterer; braggart. —**valentonada**, *n.f.* boast; boasting; bluster. —**valentonería**, *n.f.* bravado; bluster.

valer (ba'ler) *v.i.* [*infl.*: **68**] 1, to be worth. 2, to be worthy; have value. 3, to cost. 4, to avail; be effective; be useful or helpful. 5, to have power or authority. 6, to be valid; count. 7, to be good; be acceptable. —*v.t.* to produce; yield; bring about. —*n.m.* 1, worth; value. 2, power; influence. —**hacer valer**, 1, to assert. 2, to make good; make effective. —**no poder valerse**, to be helpless. —**valer la pena**, to be worthwhile; be worth the trouble. —**valer más**, to be better; be preferable. —**valer por**, 1, to be good for; be sufficient for. 2, to be worth; be equal to; be as good as. —**valerse de**, to take advantage of; avail oneself of. —**¡Válgame Dios!**, Bless my soul!

valeriana (ba·le'rja·na) *n.f.* valerian.

valeroso (ba·le'ro·so) *adj.* brave; courageous; valorous. —**valerosidad**, *n.f.* courage.

valga ('bal·ɣa) *v.*, *pres.subjve. of* **valer**.

valgo ('bal·ɣo) *v.*, *1st pers.sing. pres.ind. of* **valer**.

valía (ba'li·a) *n.f.* 1, value; worth. 2, favor; influence. 3, political sympathy.

validar (ba·li'ðar) *v.t.* to validate. —**validación**, *n.f.* validation.

valido (ba'li·ðo) *adj.* accepted; credited. —*n.m.* favorite; protégé.

válido ('ba·li·ðo) *adj.* valid. —**validez** (-'ðeθ; -'ðes) *n.f.* validity.

valiente (ba'ljen·te) *adj.* 1, valiant; brave; courageous. 2, *usu. ironic* great; big. —*n.m.* 1, brave man. 2, = **valentón**.

valija (ba'li·xa) *n.f.* 1, valise; suitcase. 2, mail bag; pouch. 3, *Amer.* brief case; leather case.

valimiento (ba·li'mjen·to) *n.m.* 1, benefit; advantage. 2, favor; influence.

valioso (ba'ljo·so) *adj.* 1, valuable. 2, influential; powerful.

valor (ba'lor) *n.m.* 1, value. 2, worth. 3, valor; courage. 4, staunchness. 5, effrontery; audacity. 6, *pl.* securities; stocks; bonds.

valoración (ba·lo·ra'θjon; -'sjon) *n.f.* 1, valuation; appraisal. 2, increase in value.

valorar (ba·lo'rar) *v.t.* 1, to appraise; evaluate. 2, to value; prize. 3, to increase the value of.

valorización (ba·lo·ri·θa'θjon; -sa'sjon) *n.f.* 1, valuation; appraisal. 2, increase in value or price.

valorizar (ba·lo·ri'θar; -'sar) *v.t.* [*infl.*: **rezar**, **10**] 1, to appraise; evaluate. 2, to increase the value or price of. —**valorizarse**, *v.r.* to increase in value or price.

vals (bals) *n.m.* waltz. —**valsar**, *v.i.* to waltz.

valuar (ba'lwar) *v.t.* [*infl.*: **continuar**, **23**] to appraise; evaluate; value. —**valuación**, *n.f.* valuation.

valva ('bal·βa) *n.f.*, *bot.*; *zoöl.* valve.

válvula ('bal·βu·la) *n.f.* 1, valve. 2, *elect.* tube. —**valvular**, *adj.* valvular.

valla ('ba·ʎa; -ja) *n.f.* 1, paling; fence; stockade. 2, barrier; barricade. 3, obstacle; impediment. 4, *sports* hurdle.

valle ('ba·ʎe; -je) *n.m.* valley; vale.

vamos ('ba·mos) *v.*, *1st pers. pl.pres.ind. & impv. of* **ir**. —*interj.* well!; come, now!; why!; go on!;

let's go!; stop! **—vámonos** ('ba·mo·nos) *v.r.* let's go; let's leave.

vampiresa (bam·pi're·sa) *n.f.* vamp.

vampiro (bam'pi·ro) *n.m.* **1,** vampire. **2,** vampire bat.

van (ban) *v., 3rd pers.pl.pres.ind.* of **ir.**

vanadio (ba'na·ðjo) *n.m.* vanadium.

vanagloria (ba·na'ɣlo·rja) *n.f.* vainglory. **—vanagloriarse** (-'rjar·se) *v.r.* to boast. **—vanaglorioso,** *adj.* vainglorious.

vanamente (ba·na'men·te) *adv.* vainly.

vándalo ('ban·da·lo) *adj. & n.m.* vandal. **—vandálico** (-'da·li·ko) *adj.* vandal *(attrib.).* **—vandalismo,** *n.m.* vandalism.

vanguardia (ban'gwar·ðja) *n.f.* vanguard; van.

vanidad (ba·ni'ðað) *n.f.* vanity; conceit. **—vanidoso** (-'ðo·so) *adj.* vain; conceited.

vano ('ba·no) *adj.* vain. *—n.m.* bay; recess; door or window opening. **—en vano,** in vain.

vapor (ba'por) *n.m.* **1,** vapor; steam. **2,** exhalation; fume. **3,** steamboat; steamer. **4,** *usu.pl.* vertigo; faintness.

vaporizar (ba·po·ri'θar; -'sar) *v.t. & i.* [*infl.:* **rezar,** 10] to vaporize. **—vaporización,** *n.f.* vaporization. **—vaporizador,** *n.m.* vaporizer. *—adj.* vaporizing.

vaporoso (ba·po'ro·so) *adj.* vaporous. **—vaporosidad,** *n.f.* vaporousness.

vapulear (ba·pu·le'ar) *v.t.* to thrash; beat. **—vapuleo** (-'le·o) *n.m.* thrashing; beating.

vaque ('ba·ke) *v., pres.subjve.* of **vacar.**

vaqué (ba'ke) *v., 1st pers.sing. pret. of* **vacar.**

vaquería (ba·ke'ri·a) *n.f.* **1,** = **vacada. 2,** dairy.

vaquerizo (ba·ke'ri·θo; -so) *adj.* cattle *(attrib.). — n.m.* cattle tender; herdsman. **—vaqueriza,** *n.f.* winter stable for cattle.

vaquero (ba'ke·ro) *adj.* cattle *(attrib.). —n.m.* cowboy; cowhand.

vaqueta (ba'ke·ta) *n.f.* cowhide; calfskin.

vara ('ba·ra) *n.f.* **1,** rod; stick; shaft. **2,** wand; staff. **3,** a measure of length of about 33 inches; vara. **4,** influence; power; authority.

varada (ba'ra·ða) *n.f.* **1,** a running aground; grounding; stranding. **2,** *colloq.* frustrating experience.

varadero (ba·ra'ðe·ro) *n.m.* boatyard; graving beach. **—varadera,** *naut.* skid *(supporting a ship in drydock).*

varadura (ba·ra'ðu·ra) *n.f.* grounding; stranding.

varar (ba'rar) *v.i.* **1,** to run aground. **2,** to halt; come to a standstill. *—v.t.* **1,** to strand. **2,** to beach.

varear (ba·re'ar) *v.t.* **1,** to beat; club. **2,** to goad (a bull). **3,** to measure or sell by the vara. **—varearse,** *v.r.* to weaken; flag.

variable (ba'rja·βle) *adj. & n.f.* variable. **—**adj. changeable; fickle. **—variabilidad,** *n.f.* variability.

variación (ba·rja'θjon; -'sjon) *n.f.* **1,** variation. **2,** variance; divergence.

variado (ba'rja·ðo) *adj.* **1,** varied. **2,** variegated.

variante (ba'rjan·te) *adj.* variant; variable; changeable. **—**n.f. variant; variation.

variar (ba'rjar) *v.t. & i.* [*infl.:* **enviar,** 22] to vary; change.

várice ('ba·ri·θe; -se) *n.f.* varicosity; varicose vein.

varicela (ba·ri'θe·la; -'se·la) *n.f.* varicella; chicken pox.

varicosis (ba·ri'ko·sis) *n.f.* varicose veins. **—varicoso,** *adj.* varicose. **—varicosidad,** *n.f.* varicosity.

variedad (ba·rje'ðað) *n.f.* variety. **—variedades,** *n.f.pl.* variety show.

varilla (ba'ri·ʎa; -ja) *n.f.* **1,** thin rod or stick. **2,** wand. **3,** rib, as of a fan, umbrella, etc. **—varillaje,** *n.m.* ribs; ribbing.

vario ('ba·rjo) *adj.* **1,** varied; various. **2,** variegated. **3,** fickle; variable. **—varios,** *adj.pl.* several; various.

variola (ba'rjo·la) *n.f.* variola.

varón (ba'ron) *n.m.* **1,** male person; male. **2,** man; adult man. **—varonil** (ba·ro'nil) *adj.* manly.

vas (bas) *v., 2nd pers.sing.pres.ind. of* **ir.**

vasallo (ba'sa·ʎo; -jo) *adj. & n.m. & f.* vassal. **—vasallaje,** *n.m.* vassalage.

vascular (bas·ku'lar) *adj.* vascular.

vasectomía (ba·sek·to'mi·a) *n.f.* vasectomy.

vaselina (ba·se'li·na) *n.f.* Vaseline *(T.N.);* petroleum jelly.

vasija (ba'si·xa) *n.f.* **1,** vessel; receptacle. **2,** pottery; vessels collectively.

vaso ('ba·so) *n.m.* **1,** glass; drinking glass. **2,** glassful. **3,** vase. **4,** *anat.; bot.* vessel. **5,** vessel; container. **6,** washbowl; toilet bowl; urinal bowl.

vasomotor (ba·so·mo'tor) *adj.* vasomotor.

vástago ('bas·ta·ɣo) *n.m.* **1,** shoot; sprout. **2,** offspring; descendant; scion. **3,** *mech.* driving rod, esp. piston rod.

vasto ('bas·to) *adj.* vast. —**vastedad,** *n.f.* vastness.

vate ('ba·te) *n.m.* **1,** prophet. **2,** poet.

vatiaje (ba'tja·xe) *n.m.* wattage.

Vaticano (ba·ti'ka·no) *n.m.* Vatican. —**vaticano,** *adj.* Vatican *(attrib.)*.

vaticinio (ba·ti'θi·njo; -'si·njo) *n.m.* prophecy; prediction. —**vaticinar** (-θi'nar; -si'nar) *v.t.* to prophesy; predict. —**vaticinador,** *adj.* prophetic. —*n.m.* [*fem.* **-dora**] seer.

vatímetro (ba'ti·me·tro) *n.m.* watt meter. *Also,* **vatiómetro** (ba'tjo–).

vatio ('ba·tjo) *n.m.* watt.

vaya ('ba·ja) *v., pres.subjve. of* **ir.** —*interj.* well now!; look here!; you don't say! —**¡vaya una idea!,** what an idea! —*n.f.* scoff; jest.

Vd. *abbr. of* **usted.**

Vds. *abbr. of* **ustedes.**

ve (be) *v.* **1,** *2nd pers.sing.impv. of* **ir. 2,** *3rd pers.sing.pres.ind. of* **ver.**

vea ('be·a) *v., pres.subjve. of* **ver.** —**véase,** see *(used in references).*

vecinal (be·θi'nal; -si'nal) *adj.* neighborhood *(attrib.);* local.

vecindad (be·θin'dað; -sin'dað) *n.f.* **1,** vicinity. **2,** neighborhood.

vecindario (be·θin'da·rjo; be·sin·) *n.m.* neighborhood; community.

vecino (be'θi·no; -'si·no) *adj.* **1,** neighboring; near. **2,** like. —*n.m.* **1,** neighbor. **2,** local resident. —**vecino a,** close to; bordering on or upon.

vector (bek'tor) *adj. & n.m.* vector. —**vectorial,** *adj.* vector *(attrib.).*

veda ('be·ða) *n.f.* **1,** prohibition. **2,** closed season.

vedado (be'ða·ðo) *n.m.* game park; game preserve.

vedar (be'ðar) *v.t.* to prohibit; forbid.

vedeja (be'ðe·xa) *n.f.* = **guedeja.**

vedette (be'ðet) *n.f.* [*pl.* **vedettes** (be'ðets)] principal actress in musical shows.

vedija (be'ði·xa) *n.f.* **1,** mat or tangle of hair. **2,** curl of smoke.

veedor (be·e'ðor) *adj.* peering; prying; observant. —*n.m.* [*fem.* **-dora**] **1,** inquisitive, observant person. **2,** overseer; inspector.

vega ('be·ɣa) *n.f.* **1,** fertile plain. **2,** *Amer.* tobacco plantation.

vegetación (be·xe·ta'θjon; -sjon) *n.f.* vegetation.

vegetal (be·xe'tal) *adj.* vegetal; vegetable. —*n.m.* plant; vegetable.

vegetar (be·xe'tar) *v.i.* to vegetate.

vegetariano (be·xe·ta'rja·no) *adj. & n.m.* vegetarian. —**vegetarianismo,** *n.m.* vegetarianism.

vegetativo (be·xe·ta'ti·βo) *adj.* vegetative.

vehemente (be·e'men·te) *adj.* vehement. —**vehemencia,** *n.f.* vehemence.

vehículo (be'i·ku·lo) *n.m.* vehicle. —**vehicular,** *adj.* vehicular.

veintavo (bein'ta·βo) *adj. & n.m.* twentieth.

veinte ('bein·te) *adj. & n.m.* twenty; twentieth.

veintena (bein'te·na) *n.f.* score; quantity of twenty.

veinteno (bein'te·no) *adj. & n.m.* twentieth.

veintésimo (bein'te·si·mo) *adj. & n.m.* = **vigésimo.**

vejación (be·xa'θjon; -'sjon) *n.f.* **1,** vexation. **2,** abuse; ill-treatment.

vejamen (be'xa·men) *n.m.* **1,** ill-treatment; abuse. **2,** taunt; sarcasm.

vejancón (be·xan'kon) *adj., colloq.* old; oldish. —*n.m., colloq.* oldster; old fellow.

vejar (be'xar) *v.t.* **1,** to vex; annoy. **2,** to criticize; censure.

vejatorio (be·xa'to·rjo) *adj.* vexatious; annoying.

vejestorio (be·xes'to·rjo) *n.m., derog.* old man; relic.

vejete (be'xe·te) *n.m., colloq.* old codger.

vejez (be'xeθ; -'xes) *n.f.* **1,** old age. **2,** oldness; age. **3,** trite story; old story. **4,** senile act or behavior.

vejiga (be'xi·ɣa) *n.f.* **1,** bladder. **2,** blister.

vela ('be·la) *n.f.* **1,** wakefulness. **2,** vigil; watch. **3,** candle. **4,** sail. —**dar vela (a uno) en un entierro,** *colloq.* to let (someone) in on a matter; let (someone) have a say. —**en vela,** awake; wakeful —**estar a dos velas,** *colloq.* **1,** to be broke. **2,** to be blissfully ignorant.

—**hacerse a la vela,** to sail; set sail.
—**no tener vela en un entierro,** to have no say in a matter.

velaciones (be·la'θjo·nes; -'sjo·nes) *n.f.pl., also,* **misa de velaciones,** nuptial Mass.

velada (be'la·ða) *n.f.* **1,** evening. **2,** soirée. —**velada musical,** musicale.

velado (be'la·ðo) *adj.* **1,** veiled. **2,** fogged; blurred.

velador (be·la'ðor) *adj.* **1,** wakeful. **2.** watching; watchful. —*n.m.* **1,** watcher; watchman; guard. **2,** pedestal table; café table. **3,** *Amer.* night table.

velamen (be'la·men) *n.m.* sail; sails; rigging. *Also,* **velaje** (-xe).

velar (be'lar) *v.t.* **1,** to veil. **2,** to fog; blur (the eyes, a photograph, etc.). **3,** to hold a wake over. **4,** to watch; watch over; take care of. **5,** to keep vigil over. —*v.i.* **1,** to be awake; stay awake. **2,** to keep watch; keep vigil. —**velar por que** . . . , to take care that . . . ; be on the watch that. . . .

velar (be'lar) *adj.* velar.

velatorio (be·la'to·rjo) *n.m.* wake; vigil over the deceased.

veleidad (be·lei'ðað) *n.f.* **1,** whim; whimsy. **2,** fickleness; inconstancy. —**veleidoso,** *adj.* fickle; inconstant.

velero (be'le·ro) *adj.* **1,** sail (*attrib.*); sailing. **2,** swift; swift-sailing. —*n.m.* **1,** sailboat. **2,** sailmaker. **3,** candlemaker.

veleta (be'le·ta) *n.f.* **1,** vane; weather vane; weathercock. **2,** bob; float. —*n.m. & f.* fickle person; weathercock.

velís (be'lis) *n.m., Amer.* valise.

velo ('be·lo) *n.m.* **1,** veil. **2,** veiling; curtain. **3,** [*also,* **velo del paladar**] velum.

velocidad (be·lo·θi'ðað; -si'ðað) *n.f.* velocity; speed.

velocímetro (be·lo'θi·me·tro; -'si·me·tro) *n.m.* speedometer.

velocípedo (be·lo'θi·pe·ðo; -'si·pe·ðo) *n.m.* velocipede.

velódromo (be'lo·ðro·mo) *n.m.* velodrome.

velorio (be'lo·rjo) *n.m.* = **velatorio.**

veloz (be'loθ; -'los) *adj.* swift; speedy; fleet.

vello ('be·ʎo; -jo) *n.m.* **1,** body hair. **2,** fuzz; down.

vellón (be'ʎon; -'jon) *n.m.* **1,** fleece. **2,** tuft of wool. **3,** an ancient Spanish coin. **4,** *W.I.* dime.

vellonera (be·ʎo'ne·ra; be·jo-) *n.f., W.I.* **1,** juke box. **2,** vending machine.

velloso (be'ʎo·so; -'jo·so) *adj.* **1,** fuzzy; downy. **2,** hairy.

velludillo (be·ʎu'ði·ʎo; be·ju'ði·jo) *n.m.* velveteen.

velludo (be'ʎu·ðo; be'ju-) *adj.* hairy. —*n.m.* velvet; plush.

vena ('be·na) *n.f.* vein. —**estar en** *or* **de vena,** to be in the mood.

venablo (be'na·βlo) *n.m.* a short javelin or spear.

venado (be'na·ðo) *n.m.* **1,** deer; stag. **2,** venison. —**pintar venado,** *Amer.* to play hooky.

venal (be'nal) *adj.* **1,** venal. **2,** venous. —**venalidad,** *n.f.* venality.

venático (be'na·ti·ko) *adj. colloq.* eccentric; erratic.

vencedor (ben·θe'ðor; -se'ðor) *adj.* winning; victorious. —*n.m.* [*fem.* **-dora**] winner; victor.

vencedero (ben·θe'ðe·ro; ben·se-) *adj.* payable; due.

vencejo (ben'θe·xo; -'se·xo) *n.m., ornith.* martin; swift.

vencer (ben'θer; -'ser) *v.t.* [*infl.:* 11] **1,** to vanquish; defeat. **2,** to conquer; overcome; surmount. **3,** to best. **4,** to force; strain (a mechanism). **5,** to impair through use or misuse. —*v.i.* **1,** to win; be victorious; **2,** to fall due; mature. **3,** to expire; terminate. **4,** to sag; twist or bend out of shape. —**vencerse,** *v.r,* **1,** to control oneself. **2,** to bend. **3,** to collapse.

vencida (ben'θi·ða; -'si·ða) *n.f., en a la tercera va la vencida,* the third time does it. —**ir de vencida, 1,** to be losing; be getting the worst of it. **2,** to be nearly over.

vencido (ben'θi·ðo; -'si·ðo) *adj.* **1,** defeated; frustrated. **2,** broken; worn; sagging. **3,** due; overdue. **4,** expired.

vencimiento (ben·θi'mjen·to; ben·si-) *n.m.* **1,** expiration. **2,** majority. **3,** due date. **4,** defeat.

venda ('ben·da) *n.f.* **1,** bandage. **2,** blindfold.

vendaje (ben'da·xe) *n.m.* bandage; dressing. —**vendaje de yeso,** *surg.* plaster cast.

vendar (ben'dar) *v.t.* **1,** to bandage. **2,** to blindfold.

vendaval (ben·da'βal) *n.m.* strong, blustery wind.

vendedor (ben·de'ðor) *adj.* vending; selling. —*n.m.* [*fem.* **-dora**] **1,**

seller; vendor. **2,** salesman; sales-person.

vender (ben'der) *v.t. & i.* to sell; vend. —*v.t.* to sell out; betray. —**venderse,** *v.r.* **1,** to sell; be sold; be for sale. **2,** to sell oneself; sell out. **3,** *usu.fol. by* **por,** to offer one's all for; give all for. **4,** *usu.fol. by* **por,** to pose as; pass oneself off as.

vendetta (ben'de·ta) *n.f.* vendetta.

vendible (ben'di·βle) *adj.* salable; marketable.

vendimia (ben'di·mja) *n.f.* grape harvest; vintage.

vendré (ben'dre) *v., fut. of* **venir.**

venduta (ben'du·ta) *n.f., Amer.* **1,** auction. **2,** vegetable shop.

veneciano (be·ne'θja·no; -'sja·no) *adj. & n.m.* Venetian. —**veneciana,** *n.f.* Venetian blind.

veneno (be'ne·no) *n.m.* poison; venom. —**venenoso,** *adj.* poison-ous.

venerable (be·ne'ra·βle) *adj.* ven-erable. —**venerabilidad,** *n.f.* vener-ability; venerableness.

venerar (be·ne'rar) *v.t.* to venerate; honor. —**veneración,** *n.f.* venera-tion. —**venerando,** *adj.* venerable.

venéreo (be'ne·re·o) *adj.* venereal.

venero (be'ne·ro) *n.m.* **1,** water spring. **2,** origin; source. **3,** *mining* lode.

venga ('ben·ga) *v., pres.ṣubjve. of* **venir.**

venganza (ben'gan·θa; -sa) *n.f.* vengeance; revenge.

vengar (ben'gar) *v.t.* [*infl.:* **pagar,** 8] to avenge; revenge. —**vengarse,** *v.r.* to take vengeance; avenge one-self. —**vengador,** *adj.* avenging. —*n.m.* [*fem.* **-dora**] avenger.

vengativo (ben·ga'ti·βo) *adj.* vengeful; vindictive.

vengo ('ben·go) *v., 1st pers. sing.pres.ind. of* **venir.**

venia ('be·nja) *n.f.* **1,** pardon; for-giveness. **2,** leave; permission. **3,** bow of the head; nod.

venial (be'njal) *adj.* venial. —**venialidad,** *n.f.* veniality.

venida (be'ni·ða) *n.f.* **1,** coming. **2,** coming back.

venidero (be·ni'ðe·ro) *adj.* future; coming.

venido (be'ni·ðo) *adj.* come; ar-rived. —**bien venido,** welcome.

venir (be'nir) *v.i.* [*infl.:* **69**] **1,** to come. **2,** to suit; fit; befit. **3,** to con-cern; be of interest: *Eso no me va ni me viene,* That doesn't concern me

one way or the other. —*aux. v., used with the gerund to form the progressive tenses: Vengo dicién-dolo desde hace un año,* I have been saying it for a year. —*¿A qué viene esto?,* To what purpose is this? —**lo por venir,** the future. —**que viene,** coming; next: *el mes que viene,* next month. —**venir al caso; venir a cuento,** to be to the point; be appropriate. —**venirse abajo; venirse al suelo,** to fall; col-lapse.

venoso (be'no·so) *adj.* **1,** venous. **2,** veiny; veined.

venta ('ben·ta) *n.f.* **1,** sale. **2,** sell-ing. **3,** roadside inn.

ventada (ben'ta·ða) *n.f.* gust of wind.

ventaja (ben'ta·xa) *n.f.* **1,** advan-tage. **2,** lead *(in a race or contest): Llevaba dos cuerpos de ventaja,* He had a two-length lead. **3,** odds given at play: *Te doy seis puntos de ventaja,* I spot you six points.

ventajista (ben·ta'xis·ta) *n.m. & f.* opportunist.

ventajoso (ben·ta'xo·so) *adj.* ad-vantageous.

ventana (ben'ta·na) *n.f.* **1,** win-dow. **2,** [*also,* **ventana de la nariz**] nostril. **3,** *anat.* fenestra.

ventanal (ben·ta'nal) *n.m.* large window; multiple window; bay window; church window.

ventanilla (ben·ta'ni·ʎa; -ja) *n.f.* **1,** small window; opening. **2,** win-dow *(of a conveyance).* **3,** window offering information, service, etc. to the public.

ventarrón (ben·ta'rron) *n.m.* stiff wind; windstorm.

ventear (ben·te'ar) *also,* **ventar** (-'tar) *v.impers.* to blow, as wind. —*v.t.* **1,** to sniff; scent. **2,** to air. —*v.i.* = **ventosear.**

ventero (ben'te·ro) *n.m.* innkeeper.

ventilador (ben·ti·la'ðor) *n.m.* **1,** ventilator. **2,** fan; blower.

ventilar (ben·ti'lar) *v.t.* **1,** to venti-late; air. **2,** *fig.* to thrash out. —**ventilación,** *n.f.* ventilation.

ventisca (ben'tis·ka) *n.f.* **1,** snow-storm; blizzard. **2,** wind-driven snow.

ventiscar (ben·tis'kar) *v.impers.* [*infl.:* **tocar,** 7] **1,** to blow, as a bliz-zard. **2,** to be driven by the wind, as snow. *Also,* **ventisquear** (-ke'ar).

ventisquero (ben·tis'ke·ro) *n.m.* **1,** mountain glacier. **2,** = **ventisca.**

ventolera (ben·to'le·ra) *n.f.* **1,** gust of wind. **2,** *colloq.* draft; breeze. **3.** *colloq.* airs. **4,** *colloq.* caprice; whim.

ventosa (ben'to·sa) *n.f.* **1,** *zoöl.* sucker. **2,** cupping glass.

ventosear (ben·to·se'ar) *v.i.* to break wind.

ventoso (ben'to·so) *adj.* **1,** windy. **2,** flatulent. —**ventosidad,** *n.f.* flatulence.

ventral (ben'tral) *adj.* ventral.

ventrera (ben'tre·ra) *n.f.* **1,** sash; waistband. **2,** cinch (of a harness).

ventrículo (ben'tri·ku·lo) *n.m.* *anat.* ventricle. —**ventricular,** *adj.* ventricular.

ventrílocuo (ben'tri·lo·kwo) *n.m.* ventriloquist. —**ventriloquia** (-'lo·kja) *n.f.* ventriloquism.

ventura (ben'tu·ra) *n.f.* **1,** felicity; bliss. **2,** chance; luck; fortune. **3,** hazard; risk. —**venturoso,** *adj.* lucky; fortunate. —**a la ventura,** aimlessly; at random. —**buena ventura,** fortune; fortunetelling. —**por ventura,** by chance; perchance. —**probar ventura,** to try one's luck; venture.

Venus ('be·nus) *n.f.* Venus; beautiful woman. —*n.m., astron.* Venus.

venza ('ben·θa; -sa) *v., pres. subjve. of* vencer.

venzo ('ben·θo; -so) *v., 1st pers. sing. pres.ind. of* vencer.

ver (ber) *v.t. & i.* [*infl.:* **70**] to see. —*v.t.* **1,** to look into; examine. **2,** *fol. by* de + *inf.* to see about; try to: *Veré de hacerlo,* I will see about doing it; I will try to do it. —*n.m.* **1,** sight. **2,** appearance; looks. **3,** view; opinion. —**verse,** *v.r.* **1,** to appear; seem; look. **2,** to be visible. **3,** to be obvious; be evident. **4,** to find oneself; happen to be. —**a** *or* **hasta más ver,** *colloq.* so long. —**allá veremos,** we shall see. —**a ver,** let's see. —**estar por ver,** to remain to be seen. —**no poder ver a (uno),** not to be able to stand (someone); hate the sight of. —**no tener nada que ver con,** to have nothing to do with; be irrelevant to. —**ser de ver,** to be worth seeing. —**tener que ver con,** to have to do with; deal with. —**vérselas con,** to come face to face with; confront. —**ver y creer,** seeing is believing. —**ya se ve,** of course; it is obvious.

vera ('be·ra) *n.f.* edge; border; side.

—**a la vera de,** by the side of; near; beside.

veracidad (be·ra·θi'ðað; -si'ðað) *n.f.* veracity.

veranda (be'ran·da) *n.f.* veranda.

veranear (be·ra·ne'ar) *v.i.* to summer; spend the summer. —**veraneo** (-'ne·o) *n.m.* summering; summer vacation.

veraniego (be·ra'nje·ɣo) *adj.* summer (*attrib.*).

veranillo (be·ra'ni·ʎo; -jo) *n.m.* Indian summer. *Also,* **veranillo de San Martín.**

verano (be'ra·no) *n.m.* **1,** summer. **2,** *Amer.* dry season.

veras ('be·ras) *n.f.pl.* fact; truth. —**de veras,** truly; really.

veraz (be'raθ; -'ras) *adj.* veracious; truthful.

verba ('ber·βa) *n.f.* eloquence; fluency.

verbal (ber'βal) *adj.* verbal.

verbatim (ber'βa·tim) *adj. & adv.* verbatim.

verbena (ber'βe·na) *n.f.* **1,** evening festival. **2,** *bot.* verbena.

verbigracia (ber·βi'ɣra·θja; -sja) for example; that is.

verbo ('ber·βo) *n.m.* **1,** verb. **2,** *cap., theol.* Word.

verborrea (ber·βo'rre·a) *n.f., colloq.* verbosity; verbiage.

verboso (ber'βo·so) *adj.* verbose. —**verbosidad,** *n.f.* verbosity.

verdad (ber'ðað) *n.f.* truth —**a decir verdad; a la verdad,** to be truthful; truthfully. —**de verdad, 1,** true; real. **2,** in fact; truly; really. —**¿es verdad?,** is it (or that) so? —**¿no es verdad?,** *also,* **¿verdad?,** isn't it (or that) so?

verdadero (ber·ða'ðe·ro) *adj.* **1,** true; real; genuine. **3,** truthful. —**verdaderamente,** *adv.* truly; verily.

verde ('ber·ðe) *adj.* **1,** green. **2,** verdant. **3,** unripe. **4,** off-color; risqué. **5,** *colloq.* unpromising; improbable. —*n.m.* **1,** green. **2,** greenery. —**estar verde,** *colloq.* to be annoyed. —**poner verde,** *colloq.* **1,** to scold. **2,** *Amer.* to annoy. —**viejo verde,** *colloq.* old fop; old goat; old rake.

verdear (ber·ðe'ar) *v.i.* **1,** to tend to green; look greenish. **2,** to sprout; begin to grow; turn green. —**verdeante,** *adj.* verdant.

verdete (ber'ðe·te) *n.m.* verdigris.

verdolaga (ber·ðo'la·ɣa) *n.f.* purslane.

verdor (ber'ðor) *n.m.* **1,** verdure; verdancy. **2,** greenness.

verdoso (ber'ðo·so) *adj.* greenish.

verdugo (ber'ðu·ɣo) *n.m.* **1,** executioner. **2,** = **verdugón. 3,** *hortic.* shoot; sucker; **4,** *fig.* torment. **5,** rapier.

verdugón (ber·ðu'ɣon) *n.m.* **1,** welt; wale. **2,** whip; lash.

verdulería (ber·ðu·le'ri·a) *n.f.* vegetable shop. —**verdulero** (-'le·ro) *n.m.* vegetable man; vegetable vendor. —**verdulera,** *n.f.,* *colloq.* hussy; fishwife.

verdura (ber'ðu·ra) *n.f.* **1,** verdure; verdancy. **2,** greenness. **3,** green; vegetable. **4,** greenery.

verdusco (ber'ðus·ko) *adj.* greenish; dark-green.

vereda (be·re'ða) *n.f.* **1,** path; trail. **2,** *Amer.* sidewalk. —**poner en vereda,** to set aright; put on the right path.

veredicto (be·re'ðik·to) *n.m.* verdict.

verga ('ber·ɣa) *n.f.* **1,** *naut.* yard; spar. **2,** penis (of animals; also, vulg., of the human male).

vergajo (ber'ɣa·xo) *n.m.* **1,** short whip, esp. one made from a bull's penis. **2.** *colloq.* wretch; scoundrel.

vergel (ber'xel) *n.f.* garden; garden spot.

vergonzante (ber·ɣon'θan·te; -'san·te) *adj.* shameful.

vergonzoso (ber·ɣon'θo·so; -'so·so) *adj.* **1,** shameful. **2,** bashful; modest.

vergüenza (ber'ɣwen·θa; -sa) *n.f.* **1,** shame. **2,** bashfulness; modesty. **3,** embarrassment. **4,** *pl.* pudenda. —**sin vergüenza,** shameless(ly). —**tener vergüenza,** to be ashamed.

vericueto (be·ri'kwe·to) *n.m.* **1,** rough, difficult ground. **2,** *often pl.* twists and turns; maze.

verídico (be'ri·ði·ko) *adj.* true; truthful.

verificar (be·ri·fi'kar) *v.t.* [*infl.:* **tocar,** 7] **1,** to verify. **2,** to fulfill; cause to take place; carry out. —**verificarse,** *v.r.* **1,** to be verified; prove true. **2,** to take place. —**verificable,** *adj.* verifiable. —**verificación,** *n.f.* verification.

verija (be'ri·xa) *n.f.* **1,** pubic parts; pubes. **2,** *Amer.* groin.

verja ('ber·xa) *n.f.* **1,** railing; fence. **2,** grating.

verme ('ber·me) *n.m.* intestinal worm.

vermicida (ber·mi'θi·ða; -'si·ða) *n.m.* vermicide. —*adj.* vermicidal.

vermicular (ber·mi·ku'lar) *adj.* vermiculate; vermicular.

vermiforme (ber·mi'for·me) *adj.* vermiform.

vermífugo (ber·mi·fu·ɣo) *adj.* & *n.m.* vermifuge.

verminoso (ber·mi'no·so) *adj.* verminous.

vermut (ber'mut) *n.m.* vermouth.

vernáculo (ber'na·ku·lo) *adj.* & *n.m.* vernacular.

vernal (ber'nal) *adj.* vernal; spring (attrib.).

vernier (ber'njer) *n.m.* vernier.

verónica (be·ro·ni·ka) *n.f.* **1,** *bot.* veronica. **2,** a pass in bullfighting; veronica.

verosímil (be·ro'si·mil) *adj.* **1,** probable; likely. **2,** credible. *Also,* **verisímil** (be·ri-).

verosimilitud (be·ro·si·mi·li'tuð) *n.f.* verisimilitude. *Also,* **verisimilitud** (be·ri-).

verraco (be'rra·ko) *n.m.* male hog; domestic boar.

verriondo (be'rrjon·do) *adj.* in rut; rutting; in heat.

verruga (be'rru·ɣa) *n.f.* wart. —**verrugoso,** *adj.* warty.

versado (ber'sa·ðo) *adj.* versed; informed.

versar (ber'sar) *v.i.,* fol. by **sobre** or **acerca de,** to be about; treat of; deal with. —**versarse,** *v.r.* to become versed; become informed.

versátil (ber'sa·til) *adj.* **1,** turning easily. **2,** fickle; inconstant. **3,** *bot.; zoöl.* versatile.

versatilidad (ber·sa·ti·li'ðað) *n.f.* **1,** ability to turn easily. **2,** fickleness; inconstancy. **3,** *bot.; zoöl.* versatility.

versículo (ber'si·ku·lo) *n.m.* verse, esp. of the Bible.

versificar (ber·si·fi'kar) *v.t.* & *i.* [*infl.:* **tocar,** 7] to versify. —**versificación,** *n.f.* versification.

versión (ber'sjon) *n.f.* version.

verso ('ber·so) *n.m.* **1,** verse. **2,** verso.

versus ('ber·sus) *prep.* versus.

vértebra ('ber·te·βra) *n.f.* vertebra. —**vertebrado,** *adj.* & *n.m.* vertebrate. —**vertebral,** *adj.* vertebral.

vertedero (ber·te'ðe·ro) *n.m.* **1,** dumping ground; dump. **2,** spillway.

verter (ber'ter) *v.t.* [*infl.:* **71**] **1,** to pour; spill; shed. **2,** to tip (a container). **3,** to translate. —*v.i.* to flow; empty; run.

vertical (ber·ti'kal) *adj. & n.f.* vertical.

vértice ('ber·ti·θe; -se) *n.m.* vertex.

vertiente (ber'tjen·te) *n.m. or f.* **1,** watershed. **2,** slope. —*n.f., Amer.* spring; fount.

vertiginoso (ber·ti·xi'no·so) *adj.* vertiginous.

vértigo ('ber·ti·γo) *n.m.* **1,** dizziness; vertigo. **2,** fit of insanity. **3,** *fig.* whirl; bustle.

vesícula (be·si·ku·la) *n.f.* vesicle. —**vesicular,** *adj.* vesicular. —**vesiculoso,** *adj.* vesiculate.

vespasiana (bes·pa'sja·na) *n.f., S.A.* public urinal.

vespertino (bes·per'ti·no) *adj.* evening (*attrib.*).

vestal (bes'tal) *adj. & n.f.* vestal.

vestíbulo (bes'ti·βu·lo) *n.m.* vestibule; hall; lobby.

vestido (bes'ti·ðo) *n.m.* **1,** dress; suit. **2,** clothing; clothes; attire.

vestidura (bes·ti'ðu·ra) *n.f.* dress; garment; vestment.

vestigio (bes'ti·xjo) *n.m.* vestige. —**vestigial,** *adj.* vestigial.

vestiglo (bes'ti·γlo) *n.m.* monster.

vestimenta (bes·ti'men·ta) *n.f.* **1,** clothing; clothes. **2,** garment. **3,** *usu.pl.* vestments.

vestir (bes'tir) *v.t.* [*infl:* pedir, **33**] **1,** to clothe; dress. **2,** to deck; adorn. **3,** to cover; cloak. **4,** to wear. —*v.i.* **1,** to dress. **2,** to be dressy; be decorative. —**vestirse,** *v.r.* **1,** to dress oneself. **2,** to be clothed. **3,** *fol. by* **de,** to put on; assume.

vestuario (bes'twa·rjo) *n.m.* **1,** wardrobe; supply of clothing. **2,** uniform. **3,** cloakroom. **4,** vestry. **5,** clothing allowance. **6,** *theat.* wardrobe; dressing room.

veta ('be·ta) *n.f.* **1,** *mining* vein; seam; lode. **2,** grain; streak; vein, as in wood or marble. —**vetado,** *adj.* veined; streaked.

vetar (be'tar) *v.t.* to veto.

vetear (be·te'ar) *v.t.* to grain; streak. —**veteado,** *adj.* veined; streaked. —*n.m.* veining; graining; streaks.

veterano (be·te'ra·no) *adj. & n.m.* veteran. —**veteranía,** *n.f.* **1,** seniority. **2,** long experience.

veterinario (be·te·ri'na·rjo) *adj.* veterinary. —*n.m.* veterinary; veterinarian. —**veterinaria,** *n.f.* veterinary medicine.

veto ('be·to) *n.m.* veto.

vetusto (be'tus·to) *adj.* ancient; hoary. —**vetustez,** *n.f.* great age; antiquity; hoariness.

vez (beθ; bes) *n.f.* [*pl.* **veces** ('be·θes; -ses)] **1,** time; occasion. **2,** turn. —**a la vez,** at once; at one time; at the same time. —**a la vez que,** while; at the same time as. —**algunas veces,** at times; sometimes; occasionally. —**alguna vez,** some time; at some time. —**alguna vez que otra** = **de vez en cuando.** —**a veces,** at times; sometimes. —**cada vez,** each time; every time. —**de una vez, 1,** all at once. **2,** [*also,* **de una vez para siempre**] once and for all. —**de vez en cuando,** from time to time; once in a while; occasionally. —**en vez de,** instead of; in place of; in lieu of. —**érase una vez,** once upon a time. —**hacer las veces de,** to substitute for; take the place of. —**las más veces,** most of the time; in most cases. —**muchas veces,** often. —**otra vez, 1,** again; once more. **2,** at another time. —**pocas veces,** seldom. —**rara vez; raras veces,** very seldom; once in a great while. —**tal vez,** perhaps; maybe. —**tomar la vez a,** to steal a march on. —**una que otra vez, 1,** a few times. **2,** once in a while. —**unas veces,** at times; sometimes. —**una vez, 1,** once; one time. **2,** at one time; at some time. **3,** once upon a time.

vi (bi) *v., 1st pers.sing. pret. of* ver

vía ('bi·a) *n.f.* **1,** way; road; street. **2,** path; route; way. **3,** *R.R.* track. **4,** *R.R.* gauge. **5,** method; procedure. **6,** *law* process. **7,** *anat.* canal; passage; tract. —*prep.* via; by way of. —**en vías de,** in the process of. —**vía crucis** ('kru·θis; -sis) **1,** Way of the Cross. **2,** [*also,* **víacrucis** *n.m.*] affliction; burden. —**vía férrea,** railroad; railway; track; rail.

viabilidad (bi·a·βi·li'ðað) *n.f.* **1,** feasibility; practicability. **2,** viability.

viable (bi'a·βle) *adj.* **1,** feasible; practicable. **2,** viable.

viaducto (bi·a'ðuk·to) *n.m.* viaduct.

viajante (bja'xan·te) *adj.* traveling. —*n.m.* & *f.* **1**, traveler. **2**, traveling salesman or saleswoman.

viajar (bja'xar) *v.t.* & *i.* to travel; journey.

viaje ('bja·xe) *n.m.* **1**, journey; voyage; trip. **2**, passage; fare. —**viaje de ida y vuelta**, round trip.

viajero (bja'xe·ro) *adj.* traveling. —*n.m.* [*fem.* **viajera**] **1**, traveler. **2**, passenger.

vianda ('bjan·da) *n.f.* **1**, food; viand; victuals. **2**, *W.I.* staple; starchy food, esp. tubers.

viandante (bjan'dan·te) *n.m.* & *f.* passerby.

viático ('bja·ti·ko) *n.m.* **1**, *eccles.* viaticum. **2**, travel allowance; viaticum.

víbora ('bi·βo·ra) *n.f.* viper.

vibración (bi·βra'θjon; -'sjon) *n.f.* **1**, vibration. **2**, vibrancy.

vibrante (bi'βran·te) *adj.* **1**, vibrating. **2**, vibrant.

vibráfono (bi'βra·fo·no) *n.m.* vibraphone; vibraharp.

vibrar (bi'βrar) *v.t.* & *i.* to vibrate. —*v.t.* **1**, to brandish. **2**, to throw; hurl. —**vibrador,** *adj.* vibrating; vibratory. —*n.m.* vibrator.

vibrátil (bi'βra·til) *adj.* vibratile. —**vibratorio** (-'to·rjo) *adj.* vibratory.

viburno (bi'βur·no) *n.m.* viburnum.

vicaría (bi·ka'ri·a) *n.f.* **1**, vicarage. **2**, vicarship; vicariate.

vicario (bi'ka·rjo) *adj.* **1**, vicarial. **2**, vicarious. —*n.m.* vicar. —**vicariato,** *n.m.* vicarship; vicariate.

vicealmirante (bi·θe·al·mi'ran·te; bi·se-) *n.m.* vice-admiral.

vicecónsul (bi·θe·kon'sul; bi·se-) *n.m. or f.* vice consul.

vicegerente *n.m. or f.* assistant manager.

vicegobernador *n.m.* [*fem.* **-dora**] lieutenant governor.

vicenio (bi'θe·njo; -'se·njo) *n.m.* vicennial. —**vicenal** (bi·θe'nal; -se'nal) *adj.* vicennial.

vicepresidente (bi·θe·pre·si·'ðen·te; bi·se-) *n.m. or f.* vice-president. —**vicepresidencia,** *n.f.* vice-presidency.

viceversa (bi·θe'βer·sa; bi·se-) *adv.* vice versa.

viciar (bi'θjar; -'sjar) *v.t.* **1**, to vitiate; spoil; corrupt. **2**, to foul; contaminate. **3**, to misconstrue; distort. —**viciación,** *n.f.* vitiation.

vicio ('bi·θjo; -sjo) *n.m.* **1**, vice. **2**, habit, esp. bad habit. **3**, defect.

vicioso (bi'θjo·so; -'sjo·so) *adj.* **1**, vicious. **2**, given to vice; depraved. **3**, defective. **4**, incorrect; wrong.

vicisitud (bi·θi·si'tuð; bi·si-) *n.f.* vicissitude.

víctima ('bik·ti·ma) *n.f.* **1**, victim. **2**, scapegoat. **3**, underdog.

victoria (bik'to·rja) *n.f.* **1**, victory. **2**, victoria (*carriage*). —**victorioso,** *adj.* victorious.

victoriano (bik·to'rja·no) *adj.* Victorian.

vicuña (bi'ku·ɲa) *n.f.* vicuña; vicuna.

vid (bið) *n.f.* vine; grapevine.

vida ('bi·ða) *n.f.* **1**, life. **2**, living. **3**, vitality. —**hacer vida,** to live together; cohabit. —**vida mía; mi vida,** dearest; darling.

vidente (bi'ðen·te) *adj.* seeing. —*n.m.* seer. —*n.f.* seeress.

video (bi'ðe·o) *n.m. or f.* video. —**videocasete,** *n.m. or f.* videocassette. —**videocinta,** *n.f.* videotape. —**videodisco,** *n.m.* videodisc.

videocámara *n.f.* video camera; camcorder.

videocasetera *n.f.* videocassette recorder or player. *Abbr.* **VCR.**

vidriado (bi'ðrja·ðo) *adj.* **1**, glassy. **2**, glazed. —*n.m.* **1**, glaze; glazing. **2**, glazed earthenware.

vidriar (bi'ðrjar) *v.t.* to glaze.

vidriera (bi'ðrje·ra) *n.f.* **1**, glass window or partition. **2**, *Amer.* glass case; showcase; show window. **3**, [*also,* **vidriera de colores**] stained-glass window.

vidriero (bi'ðrje·ro) *n.m.* **1**, glazier. **2**, glass blower. **3**, glass maker. **4**, glass dealer.

vidrio ('bi·ðrjo) *n.m.* **1**, glass. **2**, piece of glass; something made of glass. **3**, pane of glass. —**vidrioso,** *adj.* glassy. —**pagar los vidrios rotos,** to be the scapegoat.

viejo ('bje·xo) *adj.* **1**, old. **2**, aged. **3**, ancient. **4**, stale. —*n.m.* **1**, old man. **2**, *Amer.*, *colloq.* term of endearment applied to parents, spouses, etc. —**vieja,** *n.f.* old woman. —**viejos,** *n.m.pl.*, *Amer.*, *colloq.* parents; folks.

viendo ('bjen·do) *v.*, *ger.* of **ver.**

vienes ('bje·nes) *v.*, 2nd pers. sing.pres.ind. of **venir.**

viento ('bjen·to) *n.m.* **1**, wind. **2**, vanity; airs. **3**, brace; guy; bracing rope. **4**, *naut.* course. **5**, scent;

smell. —**beber los vientos por,** *colloq.* to be head over heels for. —**contra viento y marea,** come hell or high water; against all odds. —**viento en popa, 1,** before the wind. **2,** *fig.* very successfully.

vientre ('bjen·tre) *n.m.* **1,** abdomen; belly; bowels. **2,** womb.

viernes ('bjer·nes) *n.m.sing. & pl.* Friday. —**comer de viernes,** to fast. —**Viernes Santo,** Good Friday.

vierta ('bjer·ta) *v., pres.subjve. of* **verter.**

vierto ('bjer·to) *v., 1st pers.sing. pres.ind. of* **verter.**

viga ('bi·ɣa) *n.f.* beam; girder; joist; rafter.

vigente (bi'xen·te) *adj.* in force; in effect; standing. —**vigencia,** *n.f.* force; effect.

vigésimo (bi'xe·si·mo) *adj. & n.m.* twentieth. —**vigesimal,** *adj.* vigesimal.

vigía (bi'xi·a) *n.f.* **1,** watchtower. **2,** watch; watching. **3,** *naut.* jutting rock; reef. —*n.m. or f.* lookout.

vigilar (bi·xi'lar) *v.t. & i.* to watch; guard. —**vigilancia,** *n.f.* vigilance; watchfulness. —**vigilante,** *adj.* vigilant; watchful. —*n.m.* **1,** watchman; guard. **2,** vigilante.

vigilia (bi'xi·lja) *n.f.* **1,** vigil. **2,** *esp. eccles.* = **víspera. 3,** *eccles.* fast; fasting. **4,** *esp.mil. & naut.* period of duty; watch; division of the night.

vigor (bi'ɣor) *n.m.* vigor. —**vigoroso,** *adj.* vigorous. —**en vigor,** in force; in effect.

vigorizar (bi·ɣo·ri'θar; -'sar) *v.t.* [*infl.:* **rezar, 10**] to strengthen; invigorate. —**vigorización,** *n.f.* invigoration. —**vigorizador,** *adj.* invigorating. —*n.m.* invigorant; tonic.

vihuela (bi'we·la) *n.f.* a medieval type of guitar.

viking ('bi·kiŋ) *n.m.* [*pl.* **vikings**] viking.

vil (bil) *adj.* vile; mean.

vileza (bi'le·θa; -sa) *n.f.* vileness; meanness.

vilipendiar (bi·li·pen'djar) *v.t.* to vilify; revile. —**vilipendio** (-'pen·djo) *n.m.* vilification; revilement.

vilo ('bi·lo) *n.m., in* **en vilo, 1,** up in the air; hanging. **2,** in suspense.

villa ('bi·ʎa; -ja) *n.f.* **1,** country house; villa. **2,** village. **3,** *chiefly hist.* city; town.

villadiego (bi·ʎa'ðje·ɣo; bi·ja-)

n.m., in **coger** *or* **tomar las de villadiego,** to turn tail; sneak out.

villanada (bi·ʎa'na·ða; bi·ja-) *n.f.* villainous act; villainy.

villancico (bi·ʎan'θi·ko; bi·jan'si·ko) *n.m.* carol; Christmas carol.

villanía (bi·ʎa'ni·a; bi·ja-) *n.f.* villainy.

villano (bi'ʎa·no; -'ja·no) *adj.* **1,** villainous. **2,** *hist.* boorish; rustic. —*n.m.* **1,** villain. **2,** *hist.* rustic; peasant; villager.

villorrio (bi'ʎo·rrjo; bi'jo-) *n.m.* hamlet; one-horse town.

vinagre (bi'na·ɣre) *n.m.* vinegar. —**vinagreta,** *n.f.* vinegar sauce.

vinagrera (bi·na'ɣre·ra) *n.f.* **1,** cruet. **2,** *S.A.* acid stomach.

vinatero (bi·na'te·ro) *adj.* wine (*attrib.*). —*n.m.* vintner. —**vinatería,** *n.f.* wine shop.

vincular (bin·ku'lar) *v.t.* **1,** to bind; tie. **2,** to relate; associate; refer. **3,** *law* to entail. —**vinculación,** *n.f., law* entailment.

vínculo ('bin·ku·lo) *n.m.* **1,** tie; bond; relationship; **2,** *law* entailment.

vindicar (bin·di'kar) *v.t.* [*infl.:* **tocar, 7**] to vindicate. —**vindicación,** *n.f.* vindication. —**vindicativo,** *also,* **vindicatorio,** *adj.* vindicatory.

vine ('bi·ne) *v., 1st pers.sing. pret. of* **venir.**

vinícola (bi'ni·ko·la) *adj.* wine (*attrib.*).

vinicultor (bi·ni·kul'tor) *n.m.* winegrower. —**vinicultura** (-'tu·ra) *n.f.* winegrowing.

viniendo (bi'njen·do) *v., ger. of* **venir.**

vinilo (bi'ni·lo) *n.m.* vinyl.

vino ('bi·no) *n.m.* wine. —*v., 3rd pers.sing.pret. of* **venir.**

vinoso (bi'no·so) *adj.* of or like wine; winy.

viña ('bi·ɲa) *n.f.* vineyard. *Also,* **viñedo** (-'ɲe·ðo) *n.m.*

viñeta (bi'ɲe·ta) *n.f.* vignette.

vió (bjo) *v., 3rd pers.sing.pret. of* **ver.**

viola ('bjo·la) *n.f.* **1,** viol. **2,** viola. —*n.m. & f.* violist.

violáceo (bjo'la·θe·o; -se·o) *adj.* purplish; resembling violet. *Also,* **violado** (-ðo).

violar (bjo'lar) *v.t.* **1,** to violate. **2,** to ravish; rape. **3,** to profane; desecrate; defile. —**violación**, *n.f.* violation.

violencia (bjo'len·θja; -sja) *n.f.* violence.

violentar (bjo·len'tar) *v.t.* **1,** to do violence to. **2,** to break into; force. —**violentarse**, *v.r.* to force oneself; control one's unwillingness.

violento (bjo'len·to) *adj.* **1,** violent; furious. **2,** forced; distorted. **3,** shocking; repugnant.

violeta (bjo'le·ta) *adj. indecl.* violet. —*n.f.* violet (*flower*). —*n.m.* violet (*color*).

violín (bjo'lin) *n.m.* violin. —**violinista**, *n.m. & f.* violinist.

violón (bjo'lon) *n.m.* bass; double bass. —**tocar el violón**, *colloq.* to dawdle.

violoncelo (bjo·lon'θe·lo; -'se·lo) *n.m.* violoncello; cello. —**violoncelista**, *n.m. & f.* violoncellist; cellist.

viperino (bi·pe'ri·no) *adj.* **1,** viperine. **2,** viperous; viperish.

vira ('bi·ra) *n.f.* **1,** dart; arrow. **2,** welt of a shoe.

virada (bi'ra·ða) *n.f.* turn; sudden turn; veer.

virago (bi'ra·ɣo) *n.f.* virago.

viraje (bi'ra·xe) *n.m.* turn.

virar (bi'rar) *v.t. & i.* **1,** to turn; veer. **2,** *naut.* to tack.

virazón (bi·ra'θon; -'son) *n.f.* **1,** sea breeze. **2,** change of wind.

virgen ('bir·xen) *adj. & n.f.* virgin. —**virginidad**, *n.f.* virginity. —**virginal**, *adj.* virginal. —*n.m., mus.* virginal.

virgo ('bir·ɣo) *n.m.* **1,** maidenhead. **2,** *cap., astron.* Virgo.

vírgula ('bir·ɣu·la) *n.f., print.* virgule.

viril (bi'ril) *adj.* virile. —**virilidad**, *n.f.* virility.

virola (bi'ro·la) *n.f.* metal collar or clasp.

virolento (bi·ro'len·to) *adj.* **1,** of or pert. to smallpox. **2,** afflicted with smallpox. **3,** pockmarked.

virreina (bi'rrei·na) *n.f.* wife of a viceroy.

virreinal (bi·rrei'nal) *adj.* viceregal.

virrey (bi'rrei) *n.m.* viceroy. —**virreinato** (-'na·to) *also,* **virreino** (-'rrei·no) *n.m.* viceroyalty; viceroyship.

virtual (bir'twal) *adj.* virtual.

virtud (bir'tuð) *n.f.* **1,** virtue. **2,** quality; property. **3,** power; capacity.

virtuoso (bir'two·so) *adj.* virtuous. —*n.m.* virtuoso. —**virtuosidad**, *n.f.* virtuousness. —**virtuosismo**, *n.m.* virtuosity.

viruela (bi'rwe·la) *n.f.* **1,** pock; pockmark. **2,** *often pl.* smallpox. —**viruelas locas**, chicken pox.

virulento (bi·ru'len·to) *adj.* virulent. —**virulencia**, *n.f.* virulence.

virus ('bi·rus) *n.m.sing. & pl.* virus.

viruta (bi'ru·ta) *n.f.* shaving (*of wood or metal*).

vis (bis) *n.f., in* **vis cómica**, comic verve or dash.

visa ('bi·sa) *n.f., Amer.* visa.

visado (bi'sa·ðo) *n.m.* **1,** visa. **2,** endorsement of a visa.

visaje (bi'sa·xe) *n.m.* **1,** gesture; grimace. **2,** image.

visar (bi'sar) *v.t.* **1,** to visa; endorse a visa. **2,** to endorse; check.

víscera ('bis·θe·ra; 'bi·se-) *n.f., usu.pl.* viscera; vitals. —**visceral**, *adj.* visceral.

viscosa (bis'ko·sa) *n.f.* viscose.

viscoso (bis'ko·so) *adj.* viscous. —**viscosidad**, *n.f.* viscosity.

visera (bi'se·ra) *n.f.* visor.

visible (bi'si·βle) *adj.* **1,** visible. **2,** conspicuous; evident. —**visibilidad**, *n.f.* visibility.

visigodo (bi·si'ɣo·ðo) *n.m.* Visigoth. —*adj. & n.m.* Visigothic. —**visigótico**, *adj.* Visigothic.

visillo (bi'si·ʎo; -jo) *n.m.* a sheer window curtain.

visión (bi'sjon) *n.f.* **1,** vision. **2,** sight. **3,** grotesque figure. —**quedarse (uno) como quien ve visiones**, *colloq.* to be agape or aghast. —**ver visiones**, to see things.

visionario (bi·sjo'na·rjo) *adj. & n.m.* visionary.

visir (bi'sir) *n.m.* vizier.

visita (bi'si·ta) *n.f.* **1,** visit. **2,** visitor; caller; company. **3,** call; house call; social call.

visitar (bi·si'tar) *v.t.* to visit; call on or at. —**visitación**, *n.f.* visitation. —**visitador**, *n.m. [fem. -dora]* visiting inspector. —**visitante**, *adj.* visiting. —*n.m. & f.* visitor; visitant.

vislumbrar (bis·lum'brar) *v.t.* **1,** to glimpse. **2,** to foresee; envisage.

vislumbre (bis'lum·bre) *n.m.* **1,** glimmer; glimpse. **2,** hint; surmise.

viso ('bi·so) *n.m.* **1,** shimmer; sheen. **2,** gleam; glitter. **3,** indication; appearance. **4,** ladies' slip.

visón (bi'son) *n.m.* mink.

visor (bi'sor) *n.m.* **1,** sight; sighting device. **2,** *photog.* viewfinder.

visorio (bi'so·rjo) *adj.* visual. —*n.m.* expert examination.

víspera ('bis·pe·ra) *n.f.* eve. —**vísperas,** *n.f.pl.* vespers. —**en vísperas de,** near; close to.

vista ('bis·ta) *n.f.* **1,** sight. **2,** vision; eyesight. **3,** view. **4,** vista. **5,** looks; appearance. **6,** = **vistazo. 7,** *law* hearing. —*n.m.* customs inspector. —**a la vista, 1,** at or on sight. **2,** in plain view; evident. —**corto de vista,** shortsighted; nearsighted. —**de vista,** by sight. —**en vista de,** in view of; because of. —**hacer la vista gorda,** to close one's eyes; pretend not to see. —**hasta la vista,** until we meet again; good-bye; so long.

vista ('bis·ta) *v., pres.subjve. of* **vestir.**

vistaria (bis'ta·rja) *n.f.* wisteria.

vistazo (bis'ta·θo; -so) *n.m.* look; glance.

vistiendo (bɪs'tjen·do) *v., ger. of* **vestir.**

vistió (bis'tjo) *v., 3rd pers. sing.pret. of* **vestir.**

visto ('bis·to) *v.* **1,** *p.p. of* **ver. 2,** *1st pers.sing. pres.ind. of* **vestir.**

visto ('bis·to) *adj.* **1,** obvious; evident; clear. **2,** considered; thought out. —**bien** (or **mal**) **visto,** well (or poorly) regarded. —**visto bueno, 1,** approved; passed. **2,** approval; endorsement. —**visto que,** whereas; since; seeing that.

vistoso (bis'to·so) *adj.* attractive; showy. —**vistosidad,** *n.f.* attractiveness; showiness.

visual (bi'swal) *adj.* visual. —*n.f.* line of sight.

visualizar (bi·swa·li'θar; -'sar) *v.t.* [*infl.:* **rezar,** 10] to visualize. —**visualización,** *n.f.* visualization.

vital (bi'tal) *adj.* vital. —**vitalidad,** *n.f.* vitality.

vitalicio (bi·ta·li'θjo; -sjo) *adj.* lifelong; life (*attrib.*); for life.

vitalismo (bi·ta'lis·mo) *n.m.* vitalism. —**vitalista,** *adj.* vitalistic. —*n.m. & f.* vitalist.

vitalizar (bi·ta·li'θar; -'sar) *v.t.* [*infl.:* **rezar,** 10] to vitalize. —**vitalización,** *n.f.* vitalization.

vitamina (bi·ta'mi·na) *n.f.* vitamin. —**vitamínico** (-'mi·ni·ko) *adj.* vitamin (*attrib.*).

vitela (bi'te·la) *n.f.* vellum.

viticultura (bi·ti·kul'tu·ra) *n.f.* viticulture.

vitorear (bi·to·re'ar) *v.t.* to cheer; acclaim.

vítreo ('bi·tre·o) *adj.* vitreous.

vitrificar (bi·tri·fi'kar) *v.t.* [*infl.:* **tocar,** 7] to vitrify. —**vitrificación,** *n.f.* vitrification.

vitrina (bi'tri·na) *n.f.* **1,** showcase; show window. **2,** glass cabinet.

vitriolo (bi'trjo·lo) *n.m.* vitriol. —**vitriólico** (-'trjo·li·ko) *adj.* vitriolic.

vitualla (bi'twa·ʎa; -ja) *n.f., usu. pl.* victuals.

vituperar (bi·tu·pe'rar) *v.t.* to vituperate. —**vituperación,** *n.f.* vituperation.

vituperio (bi·tu'pe·rjo) *n.m.* insult; vituperation. —**vituperioso,** *adj.* vituperative.

viuda ('bju·ða) *n.f.* widow.

viudedad (bju·ðe'ðað) *n.f.* widow's inheritance; dower.

viudez (bju'ðeθ; -'ðes) *n.f.* **1,** widowhood. **2,** condition of a widower.

viudo ('bju·ðo) *adj.* widowed. —*n.m.* widower.

viva ('bi·βa) *n.m.* cheer; acclamation. —*interj.* long live!; hurrah!

vivac (bi'βak) *n.m.* [*pl.* **vivaques** (-kes)] = **vivaque.**

vivacidad (bi·βa·θi'ðað; -si'ðað) *n.f.* vivacity.

vivamente (bi·βa'men·te) *adv.* **1,** energetically. **2,** vividly; clearly. **3,** to the quick.

vivandero (bi·βan'de·ro) *n.m.* sutler.

vivaque (bi'βa·ke) *n.m.* bivouac. —**vivaquear,** *v.i.* to bivouac.

vivar (bi'βar) *n.m.* **1,** warren; burrow. **2,** fish hatchery. —*v.t., Amer.* to cheer; acclaim.

vivaracho (bi·βa'ra·tʃo) *adj., colloq.* gay; sprightly.

vivaz (bi'βaθ; -'βas) *adj.* **1,** vivacious; lively. **2,** *bot.* perennial.

víveres ('bi·βe·res) *n.m.pl.* provisions; food supplies.

vivero (bi'βe·ro) *n.m.* **1,** warren. **2,** hatchery. **3,** plant nursery. **4,** *fig.* hotbed.

viveza (bi'βe·θa; -sa) *n.f.* **1,** alacrity. **2,** alertness; sharpness. **3,** liveliness; animation; sparkle. **4,** vividness. **5,** clever ruse; sharp trick.

vívido ('bi·βi·ðo) *adj.* vivid.

vivido (bi'βi·ðo) *adj.* personally experienced; firsthand.

vividor (bi·βi'ðor) *adj.* **1,** fond of

good or high living. **2,** *colloq.* opportunistic; sponging. —*n.m.* [*fem.* **-dora**] **1,** one fond of good or high living. **2,** *colloq.* opportunist; sponger.

vivienda (bi'βjen·da) *n.f.* dwelling; house; abode.

viviente (bi'βjen·te) *adj.* living.

vivificar (bi·βi·fi'kar) *v.t.* [*infl.:* **tocar,** 7] **1,** to vivify. **2,** to refresh; revivify. —**vivificación,** *n.f.* vivification. —**vivificador,** *adj.* vivifying.

vivíparo (bi'βi·pa·ro) *adj.* viviparous.

vivir (bi'βir) *v.i. & t.* [*infl.:* 3] to live. —*n.m.* living; life. —¿**Quién vive?,** Who goes there? —¡**Vive Dios!,** By God! —**vivir para ver,** live and learn.

vivisección (bi·βi·sek'θjon; -'sjon) *n.f.* vivisection.

vivo ('bi·βo) *adj.* **1,** alive; living. **2,** vivid; intense. **3,** lively; brisk. **4,** sharp; quick. **5,** expressive; forceful. **6,** *colloq.* foxy; sly; cunning. —*n.m.* **1,** edge; sharp edge. **2,** edging; fringe; trimming. **3,** *colloq.* sly fox. —**carne viva,** raw flesh; quick. —**en lo vivo,** to the quick. —**en vivo,** *radio; TV* live.

vizcaíno (biθ·ka'i·no; bis-) *adj. & n.m.* Biscayan. —**vizcainada** (-kai'na·ða) *n.f.* ungrammatical speech.

vizconde (biθ'kon·de; bis-) *n.m.* viscount. —**vizcondado,** *n.m.* viscountship. —**vizcondesa** (-'de·θa; -sa) *n.f.* viscountess.

vocablo (bo'ka·βlo) *n.m.* word; term; vocable.

vocabulario (bo·ka·βu'la·rjo) *n.m.* vocabulary.

vocación (bo·ka'θjon; -'sjon) *n.f.* vocation. —**vocacional,** *adj.* vocational.

vocal (bo'kal) *adj.* vocal. —*n.f., gram.* vowel. —*n.m. & f.* board member; director. —**vocálico** (-'ka·li·ko) *adj.* vocalic; vowel (*attrib.*).

vocalista (bo·ka'lis·ta) *n.m. & f.* vocalist.

vocalizar (bo·ka·li'θar; -'sar) *v.t. & i.* [*infl.:* **rezar,** 10] **1,** to vocalize. **2,** to enunciate; articulate. —**vocalización,** *n.f.* vocalization.

vocativo (bo·ka'ti·βo) *adj. & n.m.* vocative.

vocear (bo·θe'ar; -se'ar) *v.t. & i.* to cry; shout. —*v.t.* **1,** to proclaim; an-

nounce. **2,** to hail. **3,** to boast of; brag about. —**voceador,** *n.m.* town crier. —**voceo** (-'θe·o; -'se·o) *n.m.* crying; shouting.

vocería (bo·θe'ri·a; bo·se-) *n.f.* **1,** = **vocerío. 2,** spokesmanship.

vocerío (bo·θe'ri·o; bo·se-) *n.m.* shouting; uproar.

vocero (bo'θe·ro; bo'se-) *n.m.* spokesman.

vociferar (bo·θi·fe'rar; bo·si-) *v.i.* to vociferate; be vociferous. —*v.t.* to boast loudly of. —**vociferación,** *n.f.* vociferation. —**vociferador,** *adj.* [*also,* **vociferante**] vociferous. —*n.m.* barker; hawker.

vocinglero (bo·θin'gle·ro; bo·sin-) *adj.* **1,** loud; loud-voiced. **2,** garrulous; verbose; windy. —**vocinglería,** *n.f. also,* **vocingleo** (-'gle·o) *n.m.* loud chatter; shouting.

vodevil (bo·ðe'βil) *n.m.* vaudeville.

vodka ('boð·ka) *n.f.* vodka.

vodú (bo'ðu) *n.m. & adj.* voodoo. —**voduismo** (bo·ðu'is·mo) *n.m.* voodooism. —**voduista,** *n.m. & f.* voodooist.

volada (bo'la·ða) *n.f.* flight; short flight. —**de una volada,** *Amer., colloq.* = **de un vuelo.**

voladero (bo·la'ðe·ro) *adj.* flying; fleeting. —*n.m.* precipice.

volado (bo'la·ðo) *adj.* **1,** *print.* superior. **2,** *Amer., colloq.* absentminded. —*n.m., S.A.* frill; ruffle.

volador (bo·la'ðor) *adj.* flying. —*n.m.* skyrocket.

voladura (bo·la'ðu·ra) *n.f.* blast; blasting.

volandas (bo'lan·das) *n.f.pl.,* **en volandas, 1,** through the air; suspended. **2,** *colloq.* speedily; flying.

volandero (bo·lan'de·ro) *adj.* **1,** poised, as for flight. **2,** flighty. **3,** occurring by chance; fortuitous.

volante (bo'lan·te) *adj.* hovering; fluttering; flying. —*n.m.* **1,** frill; ruffle. **2,** flier; leaflet. **3,** flywheel. **4,** balance wheel. **5,** steering wheel. **6,** shuttlecock. **7,** the game of battledore and shuttlecock; badminton. **8,** crack driver; auto racer.

volantín (bo·lan'tin) *n.m., Amer.* **1,** paper kite. **2,** = **volatín.**

volar (bo'lar) *v.i. & t.* [*infl.:* **acostar,** 28] to fly. —*v.i.* **1,** to flutter; hover. **2,** to vanish; disappear. **3,** to blow up; explode. —*v.t.* **1,** to blast; blow up. **2,** to make angry; enrage.

volátil (bo'la·til) *adj.* volatile. —**volatilidad,** *n.f.* volatility.

volatilizar (bo·la·ti·li'θar; -'sar) *v.t.* [*infl.:* **rezar,** 10] to volatilize; vaporize.

volatín (bo·la'tin) *n.m.* acrobatic feat; tumble.

volatinero (bo·la·ti'ne·ro) *n.m.* tumbler; acrobat; aerialist.

volcán (bol'kan) *n.m.* volcano. —**volcánico,** *adj.* volcanic. —**volcanismo,** *n.m.* volcanism.

volcar (bol'kar) *v.t.* & *i.* [*infl.:* **tocar,** 7; **acostar,** 28] 1, to tip over; upset; overturn. 2, to capsize. 3, to pour; spill.

volear (bo·le'ar) *v.t.* 1, *games* to volley. 2, to throw; let fly.

voleo (bo'le·o) *n.m.* 1, *games* volley. 2, blow; strike. —**al voleo,** overhand.

volframio (bol'fra·mjo) *n.m.* wolfram

volibol (bo·li'βol) *n.m.* volleyball.

volición (bo·li'θjon; -'sjon) *n.f.* volition. —**volitivo** (-'ti·βo) *adj.* volitional; volitive.

volqué (bol'ke) *v., 1st pers.sing. pret.* of **volcar.**

volt (bolt) *n.m.* [*pl.* **volts** (bolts)] volt.

voltaico (bol'tai·ko) *adj.* voltaic. —**voltaísmo** (-ta'is·mo) *n.m.* voltaism.

voltaje (bol'ta·xe) *n.m.* voltage.

voltear (bol·te'ar) *v.t.* & *i.* 1, to turn; turn over. 2, to turn around. 3, to overturn; upset. —*v.t.* 1, to swing; spin; whirl. 2, to arch; vault. 3, to peal (a bell). 4, *Amer., colloq.* to knock over; knock down.

volteo (bol'te·o) *n.m.* 1, whirling; revolving; turning. 2, overturning; upsetting. 3, tumbling. 4, peal (*of a bell*). 5, *Amer., colloq.* knocking down; felling.

voltereta (bol·te're·ta) *n.f.* tumble; somersault.

voltímetro (bol'ti·me·tro) *n.m.* voltmeter.

voltio ('bol·tjo) *n.m.* volt.

volubilidad (bol·lu·βi·li'ðað) *n.f.* 1, changeableness; fickleness; inconstancy. 2, volubility.

voluble (bo'lu·βle) *adj.* 1, changeable; fickle; inconstant. 2, voluble.

volumen (bo'lu·men) *n.m.* volume.

voluminoso (bo·lu·mi'no·so) *adj.* voluminous. —**voluminosidad,** *n.f.* voluminousness.

voluntad (bo·lun'tað) *n.f.* 1, will.

2, [*also,* **buena voluntad**] goodwill. 3, disposition; inclination. 4, [*also,* **fuerza de voluntad**] will power. 5, free will. —**mala voluntad,** ill will. —**última voluntad,** last will and testament.

voluntariedad (bo·lun·ta·rje·'ðað) *n.f.* 1, voluntariness. 2, willfulness; stubbornness.

voluntario (bo·lun'ta·rjo) *adj.* voluntary. —*n.m.* volunteer.

voluntarioso (bo·lun·ta'rjo·so) *adj.* 1, willful; self-willed; stubborn. 2, tenacious; determined.

voluptuoso (bo·lup'two·so) *adj.* voluptuous. —*n.m.* voluptuary. —**voluptuosidad,** *n.f.* voluptuousness.

voluta (bo'lu·ta) *n.f.* 1, volute. 2, wisp or curl of smoke.

volver (bol'βer) *v.t.* [*infl.:* **mover,** 30; *p.p.* **vuelto**] 1, to turn; turn over. 2, = **devolver.** 3, to put back; replace; restore. 4, to change; convert; turn: *Volvió el agua en vino,* He changed water into wine. 5, to make; cause to become. —*v.i.* 1, *fol. by* **a** + *inf.* to do again (the action expressed by the verb): *Volvió a salir,* He went out again. 2, to return; go or come back. 3, to turn; change direction. —**volverse,** *v.r.* 1, to turn; turn into; become. 2, to return. —**volver en sí,** to come to. —**volverse atrás,** 1, to turn back; go back. 2, to back out; withdraw. —**volverse contra,** to turn on; turn against.

vomitado (bo·mi'ta·ðo) *adj., colloq.* pale; sickly.

vomitar (bo·mi'tar) *v.t.* 1, to vomit. 2, to disgorge; belch forth.

vomitivo (bo·mi'ti·βo) *adj.* & *n.m.* emetic.

vómito ('bo·mi·to) *n.m.* vomit.

voracidad (bo·ra·θi'ðað; -si'ðað) *n.f.* voracity; voraciousness.

vorágine (bo'ra·xi·ne) *n.f.* vortex; maelstrom. —**voraginoso,** *adj.* turbulent.

voraz (bo'raθ; -'ras) *adj.* voracious.

vórtice ('bor·ti·θe; -se) *n.m.* vortex.

vos (bos) *pers.pron. 2nd pers.sing. & pl., used as subj. or obj. of a verb or obj. of a prep., in addressing God, a saint or an important personage; in Amer.colloq. usage often replacing* **tú, te, ti,** *you; to you; ye; yourself; thou; thee; to thee; thyself.*

vosear (bo·se'ar) *v.t. & i.* to use **vos** in addressing a person or persons. —**voseo** (-'se·o) *n.m.* use of **vos**.

vosotros (bo'so·tros) *pers.pron. 2nd pers.m.pl.* [*fem.* **vosotras**] you; ye; yourselves.

votación (bo·ta'θjon; -'sjon) *n.f.* **1**, voting; balloting. **2**, vote; number of votes cast.

votar (bo'tar) *v.i. & t.* **1**, to vote. **2**, to vow. —*v.i.* to swear; utter an oath. —**votante**, *n.m. & f.* voter. —*adj.* voting.

votivo (bo'ti·βo) *adj.* votive.

voto ('bo·to) *n.m.* **1**, vote. **2**, vow. **3**, oath; curse. —**hacer votos por**, to pray for; wish that. —¡**voto a tal!**, confound it!

voy (boi) *v., 1st pers.sing.pres.ind. of* **ir**.

voz (boθ; bos) *n.f.* **1**, voice. **2**, shout; cry. **3**, clamor; outcry. **4**, *gram.* voice. **5**, word; expression; vocable. —**a voces**, shouting; crying loudly. —**a voz en cuello; a voz en grito**, at the top of one's voice. —**correr la voz (que)**, to be rumored (that). —**dar voces**, to shout; cry out. —**en voz alta**, aloud. —**tener voz**, to have a (or one's) say.

vozarrón (bo·θa'rron; -sa'rron) *n.m.* strong, deep voice.

vudú (bu'ðu) *adj. & n.m.* = **vodú**.

vuecencia (bwe'θen·θja; -'sen·sja) *n.m. & f., contr. of* **vuestra excelencia**, your excellency. *Also,* **vuecelencia** (bwe-θe'len·θja; -se'len·sja).

vuelco ('bwel·ko) *n.m.* **1**, upset; overturn. **2**, a tumbling; tumble; somersault. —**darle a uno un vuelco el corazón**, *colloq.* **1**, to feel one's heart leap. **2**, to have a foreboding or premonition.

vuelco ('bwel·ko) *v., 1st pers.sing. pres.ind. of* **volcar**.

vuele ('bwe·le) *v., pres.subjve. of* **volar**.

vuelo ('bwe·lo) *n.m.* **1**, flight; flying. **2**, flare, as of a skirt. **3**, *fig.* scope; breadth; reach. **4**, *Amer.* take-off distance; running start. —**al vuelo**, **1**, at once; in a jiffy. **2**, on the wing; on the fly. —**alzar el vuelo**, to take flight. —**de un vuelo**, in one fell swoop. —**echar a vuelo las campanas**, to set the bells ringing; ring a full peal. —**levantar el vuelo**, to take off; take flight. —**tomar vuelo**, **1**, to grow; grow

wings; progress. **2**, *Amer.* to take a running start.

vuelo ('bwe·lo) *v., 1st pers.sing. pres.ind. of* **volar**.

vuelque ('bwel·ke) *v., pres.subjve. of* **volcar**.

vuelta ('bwel·ta) *n.f.* **1**, turn; turning; a turning around. **2**, bend; twist. **3**, walk; stroll. **4**, ride; trip. **5**, outing; excursion. **6**, tour. **7**, other side; reverse. **8**, return. **9**, return trip. **10**, change; money returned. —**a la vuelta**, **1**, on or upon returning. **2**, *colloq.* around the corner; close by. —**a la vuelta de**, **1**, at the end of; after. **2**, around; just off; just past. —**a vuelta de**, **1**, after; following upon. **2**, about to; on the point of. —**a vuelta de correo**, by return mail. —**dar una vuelta**, to take a stroll, walk, ride, etc. —**dar vuelta**, to turn. —**dar vueltas**, **1**, to circle. **2**, to go around and around. —**de vuelta**, on returning. —**estar de vuelta**, to be back. —**media vuelta**, about-face. —**no tiene vuelta**, that's that; no two ways about it. —**poner a uno de vuelta y media**, to give a tongue-lashing to. —**vuelta de campana**, tumble; somersault.

vuelto ('bwel·to) *n.m.* **1**, verso. **2**, *Amer.* change; money returned. —*v., p.p. of* **volver**.

vuelva ('bwel·βa) *v., pres.subjve. of* **volver**.

vuelvo ('bwel·βo) *v., 1st pers.sing. pres.ind. of* **volver**.

vuestro ('bwes·tro) *poss.adj & pron.m.sing.* [*fem.* **vuestra**; *pl.* **vuestros, vuestras**]. *agreeing in number and gender with the thing or things possessed* your; yours.

vulcanita (bul·ka'ni·ta) *n.f.* vulcanite.

vulcanizar (bul·ka·ni'θar; -'sar) *v.t.* [*infl.:* **rezar, 10**] to vulcanize. —**vulcanización**, *n.f.* vulcanization.

vulgacho (bul'γa·tʃo) *n.m.* rabble; riffraff.

vulgar (bul'γar) *adj.* **1**, vulgar. **2**, common; ordinary. —**vulgaridad**, *n.f.* vulgarity. —**vulgarismo**, *n.m.* vulgarism. —**idioma** *or* **lengua vulgar**, vernacular. —**vulgar y corriente**, run-of-the-mill.

vulgarizar (bul·γa·ri'θar; -'sar) *v.t.* [*infl.:* **rezar, 10**] **1**, to vulgarize. **2**, to popularize. —**vulgarización**, *n.f.* **1**, vulgarization. **2**, popularization.

Vulgata (bul'ɣa·ta) *n.f.* Vulgate.
vulgo ('bul·ɣo) *n.m.* **1,** common people; populace. **2,** laymen collectively; the uninitiated.
vulnerar (bul·ne'rar) *v.t.* to wound. —**vulnerable,** *adj.* vulnera-ble. —**vulnerabilidad,** *n.f.* vulnera-bility.
vulpino (bul'pi·no) *adj.* vulpine.
vultuoso (bul'two·so) *adj.* bloated, as the face.
vulva ('bul·βa) *n.f.* vulva.
V.V., VV *abbr. of* **ustedes.**

W

W, w (be'ðo·βle; 'u·βe'ðo·βle) *n̄.f.* w; *not properly a letter of the Spanish alphabet; found only in foreign words.*
wagogo (wa'ɣo·ɣo) *n.m.* African arrow poison.
wagón (va'gon) *n.m.* = **vagón.**
wat (wat) *n.m.* [*pl.* **wats** (wats)] = **vatio.**
water-closet ('va·ter 'klo·set) *n.m.* water closet; lavatory. *Abbr.* **W.C.**
watt (wat) *n.m.* = **wat.**
whig (wig) *adj. indecl. & n.m. or f.* liberal; Whig.
whisky ('wis·ki) *n.m.* whiskey.
whist (wist) *n.m.* whist.
wigwam ('wig·wam) *n.m.* wig-wam.
winche ('win·tʃe) *n.m., Amer.* winch.
wolfram ('vol·fram) *n.m.* = **volfra-mio.**

X

X, x ('e·kis) *n.f.* 26th letter of the Spanish alphabet.
xanteína (ksan·te'i·na) *n.f.* xan-thein.
xantina (ksan'ti·na) *n.f.* xanthin.
xenia ('kse·nja) *n.f.* xenia.
xeno ('kse·no) *n.m.* = **xenón.**
xenofobia (kse·no'fo·βja) *n.f.* xenophobia. —**xenófobo** (-'no·fo·βo) *adj.* xenophobic. —*n.m.* xeno-phobe.
xenón (kse'non) *n.m.* xenon.
xerografía (kse·ro·ɣra'fi·a) *n.f.* xerography. —**xerografiar** (-'fjar) *v.t.* [*infl.:* **enviar, 22**] to photocopy; xerox. —**xerográfico** (-'ɣra·fi·ko) *adj.* xerographic.
xilema (ksi'le·ma) *n.m.* xylem.
xilófago (ksi'lo·fa·ɣo) *adj.* xy-lophagous.
xilófono (ksi'lo·fo·no) *n.m.* xylo-phone.
xilografía (ksi·lo·ɣra'fi·a) *n.f.* **1,** xylography. **2,** xylograph. —**xilo-gráfico** (-'ɣra·fi·ko) *adj.* xylo-graphic.

Y

Y, y (i'ɣrje·ɣa; *also,* je) *n.f.* 27th let-ter of the Spanish alphabet.
y (i) *conj.* and.
ya (ja) *adv.* **1,** already: *Ya comí,* I have already eaten. **2,** now; at once: *Hazlo ya,* Do it now. **3,** *in questions* yet: *¿Está ya en casa tu padre?,* Is your father at home yet? **4,** pres-ently; in a while; eventually: *Ya saldrá,* He will come out presently; *Ya vendrá,* He will come eventually.
5, *intensifying the immediacy of an action: Ya voy,* I'm coming; *Ya lo veré,* I'll see to it. —*interj.* yes!; of course!; I see!; so! —**no ya . . . . sino,** not only . . . . but also: *no ya los vivos, sino los muertos,* not only the living but also the dead. —**si ya,** if only; so long as; provided: *Lo haré si ya no me molestas,* I will do it if only you will not bother me. —**ya . . . . ya, 1,** whether . . . . or; as

well ... as: *Ya en política ya en letras, es un maestro,* Whether in politics or in letters, he is an expert; As well in politics as in letters he is an expert. **2,** now ..... now: *ya rico, ya pobre,* now rich, now poor. —**¡ya lo creo!,** of course! —**ya no,** no longer. —**ya que,** as long as; since: *Lo haré ya que lo dije,* I will do it as long as I have said so.

yacer (ja'θer; -'ser) *v.i.* [*infl.:* 72] to lie; rest.

yacimiento (ja·θi'mjen·to; ja·si-) *n.m., geol.* deposit.

yaga ('ja·ɣa) *v., pres.subjve. of* **yacer.** —**yago** (-ɣo) *v., 1st pers. sing.pres.ind. of* **yacer.**

yagua ('ja·ɣwa) *n.f., W.I.* **1,** royal palm. **2,** palm leaf, used for thatching.

yaguar (ja'ɣwar) *n.m.* = **jaguar.**

yak (jak) *n.m.* yak.

yambo ('jam·bo) *n.m.* iamb; iambic. —**yámbico,** *adj.* iambic.

yanqui (jan·ki) *adj. & n.m. & f.* Yankee. ·

yantar (jan'tar) *v.t., rare* to eat; dine. —*n.m.* food.

yapa ('ja·pa) *n.f., Amer.* bonus; extra.

yarda ('jar·ða) *n.f.* **1,** yard (*measure*). **2,** yardstick.

yate ('ja·te) *n.m.* yacht.

yautía (jau'ti·a) *n.f., W.I.* a tropical tuber; yautia.

yaz (jaθ; jas) *v., impv. of* **yacer.** —**yazca** ('jaθ·ka; 'jas-) *also,* **yazga** (-ɣa) *v., pres.subjve. of* **yacer.** —**yazco** ('jaθ·ko; 'jas-) *also,* **yazgo** (-ɣo) *v., 1st pers.sing.pres.ind. of* **yacer.**

yedra ('je·ðra) *n.f.* = **hiedra.**

yegua ('je·ɣwa) *n.f.* mare. —**yeguada,** *n.f.* herd of mares or horses.

yeísmo (je'is·mo) *n.m.* pronunciation of Spanish ll as y (j).

yelmo ('jel·mo) *n.m.* helmet.

yema ('je·ma) *n.f.* **1,** yolk. **2,** bud. **3,** candied egg yolk. —**yema del dedo,** finger tip.

yen (jen) *n.m.* yen (*monetary unit*).

yendo ('jen·do) *v., ger. of* **ir.**

yerba ('jer·βa) *n.f.* = **hierba.** —**yerba mate,** maté.

yerbajo (jer'βa·ꭓo) *n.m.* useless plant; weed.

yerga ('jer·ɣa) *v., pres.subjve. of*

erguir. —**yergo** (-ɣo) *v., 1st pers.sing. pres.ind. of* **erguir.**

yermo ('jer·mo) *adj.* **1,** lifeless; desolate. **2,** barren; waste. —*n.m.* wasteland.

yerno ('jer·no) *n.m.* son-in-law.

yerre ('je·rre) *v., pres.subjve. of* **errar.**

yerro ('je·rro) *v., 1st pers.sing. pres.ind. of* **errar.** —*n.m.* mistake; error.

yerto ('jer·to) *adj.* inert; rigid.

yesal (je'sal) *n.m.* gypsum pit; gypsum quarry. *Also,* **yesar** (-'sar).

yesca ('jes·ka) *n.f.* **1,** tinder; kindling. **2,** *fig.* incentive to passion.

yeso ('je·so) *n.m.* **1,** gypsum. **2,** plaster. **3,** plaster cast. —**yeso blanco,** finishing plaster. —**yeso mate,** *also,* **yeso de París,** plaster of Paris. —**yeso negro,** coarse plaster.

yesoso (je'so·so) *adj.* of or like gypsum or plaster; chalky.

yiddish ('ji·ðiʃ) *adj. & n.m.* Yiddish.

yo (jo) *pers.pron.* I. —*n.m.* ego; self.

yodo ('jo·ðo) *n.m.* iodine. —**yodado,** *adj.* iodized.

yodoformo (jo·ðo'for·mo) *n.m.* iodoform.

yoduro (jo'ðu·ro) *n.m.* iodide. —**yodurar,** *v.t.* to iodize.

yoga ('jo·ɣa) *n.m.* yoga. —**yogi** (-ɣi) *n.m.* yogi.

yogurt (jo'ɣurt) *n.m.* yogurt.

yola ('jo·la) *n.f.* yawl.

yo-yo ('jo·jo) *n.m.* yoyo.

yuan (ju'an) *n.m.* yuan.

yuca ('ju·ka) *n.f.* **1,** cassava. **2,** yucca.

yudo ('ju·ðo) *n.m.* judo.

yugo ('ju·ɣo) *n.m.* yoke.

yugoslavo (ju·ɣos'la·βo) *also,* **yugoeslavo** (-es'la·βo) *adj. & n.m.* Yugoslav; Yugoslavian.

yugular (ju·ɣu'lar) *adj.* jugular.

yunque ('jun·ke) *n.m.* anvil.

yunta ('jun·ta) *n.f.* yoke of draft animals, esp. oxen. —**yuntero,** *n.m.* plowboy.

yute ('ju·te) *n.m.* jute.

yuxtaponer (juks·ta·po'ner) *v.t.* [*infl.:* **poner,** 54] to juxtapose. —**yuxtaposición** (-si'θjon; -'sjon) *n.f.* juxtaposition.

yuyo ('ju·jo) *n.m., S.A.* = **yerbajo.**

yuyuba (ju'ju·βa) *n.f.* jujube.

Z

Z, z ('θe·ta; 'se·ta, *also*, 'θe·ða; 'se·ða) *n.f.* 28th letter of the Spanish alphabet.

zacate (θa'ka·te; sa-) *n.m., Amer.* hay; fodder.

zafacoca (θa·fa'ko·ka; sa-) *n.f., Amer., colloq.* row; melée.

zafado (θa·fa'ðo; sa-) *adj., Amer.* **1,** braven; barefaced. **2,** alert; wide-awake. **3,** out of joint; dislocated. **4,** *colloq.* screwloose; daft.

zafar (θa'far; sa-) *v.t.* **1,** to free; release; disengage. **2,** *Amer.* to dislocate; put out of joint. **—zafarse,** *v.r., fol. by* **de, 1,** to get out of; avoid. **2,** to get rid of; shake off. **3,** to become loose. **4,** *Amer., colloq.* to go out of one's mind.

zafarrancho (θa·fa'rran·tʃo; sa-) *n.m.* **1,** a clearing for action. **2,** *colloq.* melée; row. **3,** *Amer., colloq.* mess; confusion.

zafio ('θa·fjo; 'sa-) *adj.* rustic; coarse; uncouth. **—n.m.** rustic; boor. **—zafiedad,** *n.f.* coarseness; uncouthness.

zafiro (θa'fi·ro; sa-) *n.m.* sapphire. **—zafirino** (-'ri·no) *also*, **zafireo** (-'fi·re·o) *adj.* sapphirine; sapphire-colored.

zafra ('θa·fra; sa-) *n.f.* **1,** sugar harvest. **2,** sugar making. **3,** *Sp.* olive harvest. **4,** oil jar or vat.

zaga ('θa·ya; 'sa-) *n.f.* end; rear; back. **—a la zaga,** *also*, **en zaga, a zaga,** *usu.fol. by* **de,** behind; after; following.

zagal (θa'yal; sa-) *n.m.* **1,** youth; lad. **2,** [*also*, **zagalejo** (-'le·xo)] shepherd boy.

zagala (θa'ya·la; sa-) *n.f.* **1,** girl; lass. **2,** [*also*, **zagaleja** (-'le·xa)] shepherd girl.

zagalejo (θa·ya'le·xo; sa-) *n.m.* **1,** shepherd boy. **2,** peasant skirt.

zaguán (θa'ywan; sa-) *n.m.* entrance; entrance hall; vestibule.

zaguero (θa'ye·ro; sa-) *adj.* rear; back; hind. **—n.m.,** *sports* back.

zaherir (θa·e'rir; sa-) *v.t.* [*infl.:* **sentir, 31**] **1,** to blame; censure; scold. **2,** to hurt; offend.

zahína (θa'i·na; sa-) *n.f.* a variety of sorghum.

zahones (θa'o·nes; sa-) *n.m.pl.* leather trousers; hunting breeches.

zahorí (θa·o'ri; sa-) *n.m.* **1,** diviner; clairvoyant. **2,** perspicacious person.

zaino ('θai·no; 'sai-) *adj.* **1,** untrustworthy; tricky. **2,** chestnut-colored (*of a horse*). **—n.m.** chestnut-colored horse.

zalagarda (θa·la'yar·ða; sa-) *n.f.* **1,** row; rumpus. **2,** trap; snare; ambush.

zalamero (θa·la'me·ro; sa-) *adj.* sugary; flattering; fawning. **—zalamería,** *n.f.* fawning; adulation.

zalea (θa'le·a; sa-) *n.f.* unsheared sheepskin; fur of sheep.

zalema (θa'le·ma; sa-) *n.f.* **1,** salaam. **2,** = **zalamería.**

zamarra (θa'ma·rra; sa-) *n.f.* **1,** sheepskin jacket. **2,** sheepskin.

zamarrear (θa·ma·rre'ar; sa-) *v.t.* **1,** to shake violently. **2,** to jolt; jar. **3,** to drub; trounce. *Also*, **zamarronear** (-rro·ne'ar).

zamarro (θa'ma·rro; sa-) *adj., Amer., colloq.* sly; shrewd. **—n.m. 1,** = **zamarra. 2,** *pl., S.A.* chaps.

zambo ('θam·bo; 'sam-) *adj.* knock-kneed. **—adj. & n.m.** *Amer.* person of Indian and Negro ancestry.

zambomba (θam'bom·ba; sam-) *n.f.* a kind of rustic drum. **—interj.** wow!

zambra ('θam·bra; 'sam-) *n.f.* a gypsy dance.

zambullir (θam·bu'ʎir; sam·bu'jir) *v.t.* [*infl.:* **bullir, 19**] to dip; plunge. **—zambullirse,** *v.r.* to dive; plunge. **—zambullida,** *n.f.* dive; plunge.

zampar (θam'par; sam-) *v.t.* **1,** to thrust in; jam. **2,** to gobble; devour. **3** *Amer., colloq.* to give (a blow). **—zamparse,** *v.r.* **1,** to rush in; barge in. **2,** *colloq.* to slip in; crash the gate.

zanahoria (θa·na'o·rja; sa-) *n.f.* carrot.

zanca ('θan·ka; 'san-) *n.f.* leg; long leg. **—zancada,** *n.f.* long step; stride. **—en dos zancadas,** *colloq.* in a jiffy.

zancadilla (θan·ka'ði·ʎa; san·ka'ði·ja) *n.f.* trip; a tripping up. **—echar una zancadilla a,** to trip; trip up.

zanco ('θan·ko; 'san-) *n.m.* stilt.

zancón (θan'kon; san-) *adj.* **1,** *colloq.* long-legged. **2,** *Amer.* too short, as a skirt or dress.

zancudo (θan'ku·ðo; san-) *adj.* **1,** long-legged. **2,** *ornith.* wading. —*n.m.,* *Amer.* mosquito. —**zancuda,** *n.f.,* also, **ave zancuda,** wading bird.

zángano ('θan·ga·no; 'san-) *n.m.* **1,** *entom.* drone. **2,** *colloq.* loafer; good-for-nothing. —**zanganada,** *n.f., colloq.* impertinence; nuisance. —**zanganear,** *v.i., colloq.* to loaf.

zangolotear (θan·go·lo·te'ar; san-) *v.t., colloq.* to shake; rattle. —*v.i., colloq.* to fuss about; fidget. —**zangolotearse,** *v.r., colloq.* to be loose; move about; rattle.

zanguango (θan'gwan·go; san-) *n.m., colloq.* lazybones. —**zanguanga,** *n.f., colloq.* malingering.

zanja ('θan·xa; 'san-) *n.f.* ditch.

zanjar (θan'xar; san-) *v.t.* **1,** to open ditches in. **2,** to settle; resolve.

zanquilargo (θan·ki'lar·ɣo; san-) *adj.* long-legged; lanky.

zapa ('θa·pa; 'sa-) *n.f., mil.* **1,** sapper's spade. **2,** sap; trench. —**zapador,** *n.m., mil.* sapper. —**labor de zapa,** undermining; subversion.

zapallo (θa'pa·ʎo; sa'pa·jo) *n.m., S.A.* **1,** pumpkin; squash; gourd. **2,** *colloq.* stroke of luck; chance.

zapapico (θa·pa'pi·ko; sa-) *n.m.* pick mattock.

zapata (θa'pa·ta; sa-) *n.f.* shoe *(curved part of a brake, anchor, etc.).*

zapateado (θa·pa·te'a·ðo; sa-) *n.m.* **1,** a typical Spanish clog dance. **2,** *Amer.* tap dance.

zapatear (θa·pa·te'ar; sa-) *v.t.* to tap or stamp with the feet. —**zapateo** (-'te·o) *n.m.* tapping or stamping with the feet.

zapatería (θa·pa·te'ri·a; sa-) *n.f.* **1,** shoe store; bootery. **2,** shoemaking; bootmaking. **3,** cobbler's shop; shoe repair shop.

zapatero (θa·pa'te·ro; sa-) *n.m.* **1,** shoemaker; cobbler. **2,** *games* player who fails to score a point, or take a trick. —**zapatero a tus zapatos,** mind your own business.

zapatilla (θa·pa'ti·ʎa; sa·pa'ti·ja) *n.f.* **1,** slipper; pump. **2,** leather or rubber washer.

zapato (θa'pa·to; sa-) *n.m.* shoe.

¡zape! ('θa·pe; 'sa·pe) *interj.* **1,** scat! **2,** gee!; gee whiz!

zaque ('θa·ke; 'sa-) *n.m.* **1,** wineskin. **2,** drunk; drunkard.

zaquizamí (θa·ki·θa'mi; sa·ki·sa-) *n.m.* **1,** attic; garret. **2,** hole in the wall; rathole. **3,** *fig., colloq.* scrape; tight spot.

zar (θar; sar) *n.m.* czar; tsar. —**zarevitz** (θa·re'βits; sa-) *n.m.* czarevitch. —**zarevna** (θa'reβ·na; sa-) *n.f.* czarevna.

zarabanda (θa·ra'βan·da; sa-) *n.f.* saraband.

zarandaja (θa·ran'da·xa; sa-) *n.f., usu.pl.* trivia.

zarandear (θa·ran·de'ar; sa-) *v.t.* **1,** to sift. **2,** to shake; move to and fro. —**zarandearse,** *v.r., Amer.* to strut; swagger; sway the hips.

zaraza (θa'ra·θa; sa'ra·sa) *n.f.* chintz; printed cotton.

zarcillo (θar'θi·ʎo; sar'si·jo) *n.m.* **1,** tendril. **2,** drop earring.

zarco ('θar·ko; 'sar-) *adj.* light blue.

zarigüeya (θa·ri'ɣwe·ja; sa-) *n.f.* opossum.

zarina (θa'ri·na; sa-) *n.f.* czarina.

zarpa ('θar·pa; 'sar-) *n.f.* paw; claw. —**echar la zarpa a,** *colloq.* to grab; nab.

zarpada (θar'pa·ða; sar-) *n.f.* **1,** blow with the paw. **2,** grabbing; grab. *Also,* **zarpazo** (-θo; -so) *n.m.*

zarpar (θar'par; sar-) *v.i.* to weigh anchor; sail.

zarrapastroso (θa·rra·pas'tro·so; sa-) *adj.* ragged; tattered. —*n.m.* ragamuffin.

zarria ('θarr·ja; 'sa-) *n.f.* **1,** dirt; grime. **2,** rag; tatter. **3,** leather thong.

zarza ('θar·θa; 'sar·sa) *n.f.* **1,** bramble; brier. **2,** blackberry; dewberry.

zarzal (θar'θal; sar'sal) *n.m.* **1** brier patch; brambles. **2,** blackberry patch; dewberry patch.

zarzamora (θar·θa'mo·ra; sar·sa-) *n.f.* brambleberry; blackberry.

zarzaparrilla (θar·θa·pa'rri·ʎa; sar·sa·pa'rri·ja) *n.f.* sarsaparilla.

zarzo (θar'θo; sar'so) *n.m.* wattle.

zarzoso (θar'θo·so; sar'so-) *adj.* brambly.

zarzuela (θar'θwe·la; sar'swe-) *n.f.* traditional Spanish musical drama; zarzuela.

¡zas! (θas; sas) *interj.* pow!; smack!

zeda ('θe·ða; 'se-) *n.f.* name of the letter *z;* zed.

zenit (θe'nit; se-) *n.m.* = **cenit.**

zeta ('θe·ta; 'se-) *n.f.* **1,** zeta. **2,** name of the letter *z;* zed.

zigzag (θiɣ'θaɣ; siɣ'saɣ) *n.m.* zigzag. **—zigzaguear** (-ɣe'ar) *v.i.* to zigzag. **—zigzagueo** (-'ɣe·o) *n.m.* zigzag; zigzagging.

zimurgia (θi'mur·xja; si-) *n.f.* = **cimurgia**.

zinc (θink; sink) *n.m.* zinc.

zinia ('θi·nja; 'si-) *n.f.* zinnia.

zipizape (θi·pi'θa·pe; si·pi'sa·pe) *n.m., colloq.* rumpus.

¡zis, zas! ('θis'θas; 'sis'sas) *interj.* 1, wham! bam! 2, swish! swish!

zócalo ('θo·ka·lo; 'so-) *n.m.* 1, base of a column, pedestal, etc. 2, dado. 3, baseboard. 4, *Amer.* public square.

zodíaco (θo'ði·a·ko; so-) *n.m.* zodiac. **—zodiacal** (-ðja'kal) *adj.* zodiacal.

zombi ('θom·bi; 'som-) *n.m. & f.* zombi.

zona ('θo·na; 'so-) *n.f.* 1, zone. 2, *pathol.* shingles.

zonzo ('θon·θo; 'son·so) *adj.* 1, insipid; inane. 2, slow-witted; dull. *—n.m.* boob; fool; ninny. **—zoncería** (-θe'ri·a; -se'ri·a) *also, Amer.*, **zoncera** (-'θe·ra; -'se·ra) *n.f.* inanity; foolishness.

zoología (θo·o·lo'xi·a; so-) *n.f.* zoölogy. **—zoológico** (-'lo·xi·ko) *adj.* zoölogical. **—zoólogo** (-'o·lo·ɣo) *n.m.* zoölogist.

zopenco (θo'pen·ko; so-) *n.m., colloq.* blockhead. **—adj., colloq.** stupid.

zopilote (θo·pi'lo·te; so-) *n.m., Amer.* turkey buzzard.

zopo ('θo·po; 'so-) *adj.* crippled; deformed. *—n.m.* cripple.

zoquete (θo'ke·te; so-) *n.m.* 1, stub; chunk; stump (*of wood, bread, etc.*). 2, *colloq.* stumpy or stubby fellow. 3, *colloq.* blockhead; dolt. *—adj.* doltish.

zoroástrico (θo·ro'as·tri·ko; so-) *adj.* Zoroastrian. **—zoroastrismo,** *n.m.* Zoroastrianism.

zorra ('θo·rra; 'so-) *n.f.* 1, fox. 2, she-fox; vixen. 3, *colloq.* drunkenness. 4, *colloq.* prostitute. 5, heavy truck; dray.

zorrero (θo'rre·ro; so-) *n.m., also,* **perro zorrero,** foxhound.

zorrillo (θo'rri·ʎo; so'rri·jo) *n.m., Amer.* skunk.

zorro ('θo·rro; 'so-) *n.m.* 1, fox; male fox. 2, *fig.* sly, crafty person. **—estar hecho un zorro,** to be drowsy. **—hacerse el zorro,** to play dumb; play deaf.

zorruno (θo'rru·no; so-) *adj.* fox (*attrib.*); foxlike.

zorzal (θor'θal; sor'sal) *n.m.* 1, thrush. 2, *colloq.* sharp fellow; fox. 3, *S.A., colloq.* booby; dupe.

zote ('θo·te; 'so-) *n.m. colloq.* blockhead.

zozobra (θo'θo·βra; so'so-) *n.f.* 1, shipwreck; danger of shipwreck. 2, anguish; anxiety. **—zozobrar,** *v.i.* to founder; sink.

zuavo ('θwa·βo; 'swa-) *n.m.* Zouave.

zucarino (θu·ka'ri·no; su-) *adj.* = **sacarino**.

zueco ('θwe·ko; 'swe-) *n.m.* sabot; clog.

zulú (θu'lu; su-) *adj. & n.m. & f.* Zulu.

zumaque (θu'ma·ke; su-) *n.m.* sumac.

zumba ('θum·ba; 'sum-) *n.f.* 1, banter; raillery. 2, *colloq.* jeer; hiss; hoot. 3, *Amer., colloq.* beating. 4, bullroarer.

zumbar (θum'bar; sum-) *v.i.* to buzz; hum. *—v.t.* 1, *colloq.* to throw (a punch, blow, missile, etc.). 2, *Amer., colloq.* to put out; throw out. **—zumbarse,** *v.r.* 1, *colloq.* to become sassy. 2, *Amer., colloq.* to scram; clear out.

zumbido (θum'bi·ðo; sum-) *n.m.* hum; buzz.

zumbón (θum'bon; sum-) *adj.* waggish; jesting. *—n.m.* [*fem.* **-bona**] wag; jester.

zumo ('θu·mo; 'su-) *n.m.* juice. **—zumoso,** *adj.* juicy.

zuncho ('θun·tʃo; 'sun-) *n.m.* 1, hoop; metal strap. 2, ferrule. **—zunchar,** *v.t.* to strap; bind with hoops or straps.

zunzún (θun'θun; sun'sun) *n.m., Amer.* a kind of hummingbird.

zurcir (θur'θir; sur'sir) *v.t.* [*infl.:* **esparcir,** 12] to darn. **—zurcido,** *n.m., also,* **zurcidura,** *n.f.* darn; patch.

zurdo ('θur·ðo; 'sur-) *adj.* 1, left-handed. 2, gauche. **—a zurdas,** 1, lefthandedly. 2, clumsily.

zuro ('θu·ro; 'su-) *n.m.* corncob. **—adj.** wild (*of doves or pigeons*).

zurra ('θu·rra; 'su-) *n.f.* 1, flogging; beating; trouncing. 2, *colloq.* continuous task; grind. 3, fight; brawl. 4, treating; curing (*of hides*).

zurrapa (θu'rra·pa; su-) *n.f.* dregs.

zurrar (θu'rrar; su-) *v.t.* 1, to flog;

beat; trounce. **2,** to berate; upbraid. **3,** to treat; cure (hides). —**zurrarse,** *v.r.* **1,** to befoul oneself. **2,** *colloq.* to be scared stiff.

zurrón (θu'rron; su-) *n.m.* **1,** game bag; shepherd's pouch; shoulder bag. **2,** membranous covering; sac.

zurullo (θu'ru·ʎo; su'ru·jo) *n.m.* round lump; gob.

zurza ('θur·θa; 'sur·sa) *v., pres. subjve. of* **zurcir.**

zurzo ('θur·θo; 'sur·so) *v., 1st pers.sing.pres.ind. of* **zurcir.**

zutano (θu'ta·no; su-) *n.m.* See **fulano.**

SUMMARY OF SPANISH

I. The Alphabet

The Spanish alphabet consists of the following 28 letters:

Letter	Name	Pronunciation
a	a	(a)
b	be	(be)
c	ce	(θe; se)
ch	che	(tʃe)
d	de	(de)
e	e	(e)
f	efe	('e·fe)
g	ge	(xe)
h	hache	('a·tʃe)
i	i	(i)
j	jota	('xo·ta)
l	ele	('e·le)
ll	elle	('e·ʎe; -je)
m	eme	('e·me)
n	ene	('e·ne)
ñ	eñe	('e·ɲc)
o	o	(o)
p	pe	(pe)
q	cu	(ku)
r	ere	('e·re)
rr	erre	('e·rre)
s	ese	('e·se)
t	te	(te)
u	u	(u)
v	ve, uve	(be; 'u·βe)
x	equis	('e·kis)
y	i griega	(i'ɣrje·ɣa)
z	zeda *or* zeta	('θe·ða; -ta; 'se·ða; -ta)

k (ka) and **w** (doble u) are found only in words of foreign origin. The letters **ch, ll, ñ,** and **rr** are counted as separate letters and (except for **rr**) are so treated in the alphabetization of Spanish words.

II. Key to Spanish Pronunciation

The center dot (·) is used to divide syllables. This is the *phonetic* division of syllables, which may often not agree with the orthographic rules for division of syllables. The stress mark (') is used instead of the center dot to mark the stresses. It is placed at the beginning of the stressed syllable. The symbol (,) denoting secondary stress, which appears in the pronunciation of many words in the English-Spanish section of this dictionary, is not used in the Spanish pronunciations, since the

Spanish speech level is quite even in all syllables except the syllable bearing primary stress.

If a pronunciation is broken at the end of a line, the center dot is placed after the syllable that ends the line. This is done even when the syllable beginning the next line is preceded by the stress mark, which would otherwise replace the center dot. ◂

VOWELS

Phonetic Symbol	Approximate English Sound	Examples
a	like *a* in *what, father*	**bala** ('ba·la) **acá** (a'ka)
e	when followed by a single consonant or any vowel, or standing at the end of a word, pronounced like *é* in *café*	**pelo** ('pe·lo) **peor** (pe'or) **ante** ('an·te)
	when followed by more than one consonant, or by a single consonant at the end of a word, pronounced like *e* in *let*	**vengo** ('ben·go) **perro** ('pe·rro) **hotel** (o'tel)
i	when not preceded or followed by a vowel, or when stressed even though preceded or followed by a vowel, pronounced like *i* in *machine*	**misa** ('mi·sa) **ibis** ('i·βis) **país** (pa'is) **río** ('ri·o)
	when preceded by a vowel (except **u**) in the same syllable, pronounced like *y* in *day, boy* (see the diphthongs **ai, ei, oi,** and the triphthongs **jai, jei, wai, wei**)	**reino** ('rei·no) **boina** ('boi·na) **fraile** ('frai·le)
o	when followed by a single consonant or any vowel, or standing at the end of a word, pronounced like *o* in *note, going, piano,* but only about half as long and without the *w* sound usually heard at the end of the English vowel	**moda** ('mo·ða) **coágulo** (ko'a·ɣu·lo) **paso** ('pa·so)
	when followed by more than one consonant, or by a single consonant at the end of a word, pronounced like *o* in *order*	**bolsa** ('bol·sa) **farol** (fa'rol)
u	when not preceded or followed by a vowel, or when stressed even though preceded or followed by a vowel, pronounced like *u* in *June*	**ruta** ('ru·ta) **unir** (u'nir) **ataúd** (a·ta'uð) **falúa** (fa'lu·a)

Phonetic Symbol	*Approximate English Sound*	*Examples*
	when preceded by another vowel (except **i**) in the same syllable, pronounced like *w* in *how* (see the diphthongs **au, eu**)	**pausa** ('pau·sa) **deuda** ('deu·ða)

DIPHTHONGS

ai	like *i* in *site*	**baile** ('bai·le) **hay** (ai)
au	like *ow* in *brow*	**fauna** ('fau·na)
ei	like *a* in *gate*	**reino** ('rei·no) **ley** (lei)
eu	like *ay* in *wayward*	**deuda** ('deu·ða)
oi	like *oi* in *boil*	**boina** ('boi·na) **estoy** (es'toi)
ja	like *ya* in *yacht*	**enviamos** (en'βja·mos) **guayaba** (gwa'ja·βa)
je	like *ye* in *yes*	**tiene** ('tje·ne) **huye** ('u·je)
jo	like *yo* in *yore*	**biombo** ('bjom·bo) **peyote** (pe'jo·te)
ju	like *u* in *use*	**viuda** ('bju·ða) **ayuda** (a'ju·ða)
wa	like *wa* in *watch*	**cuanto** ('kwan·to)
we	like *wa* in *wake*	**bueno** ('bwe·no)
wi	like *wee* in *weed*	**cuidado** (kwi'ða·ðo)
wo	like *uo* in *quorum*	**cuota** ('kwo·ta)

TRIPHTHONGS

jai	like *yi* in the exclamation *yikes!*	**cambiáis** (kam'bjais)
jei	like the English word *yea*	**cambiéis** (kam'bjeis)
wai	like *wi* in *wide*	**uai** between consonants: **insinuáis** (in·si'nwais) **uay** at the end of a word: **Paraguay** (pa·ra'ɣwai)
wei	like *wai* in *wait*	**uei** between consonants: **insinuéis** (in·si'nweis) **uey** at the end of a word: **buey** (bwei)

CONSONANTS

Phonetic Symbol	Approximate English Sound	Examples
b	like *b* in *cabin*	**b** or **v** at the beginning of a word: **bola** ('bo·la) **vaya** ('ba·ja) **b** following **m**: **rumbo** ('rum·bo)
β	like *v* in *ever,* but with both lips nearly touching (not, as in English *v,* with the lower lip between the upper and lower teeth)	**b** in all positions except at the beginning of a word or following **m**: **cabo** ('ka·βo) **sobre** ('so·βre) **alba** ('al·βa) **v** in all positions except at the beginning of a word: **envío** (en'βi·o) **vivir** (bi'βir) **tuve** ('tu·βe) **salvo** ('sal·βo)
p	like *p* in *tepid*	**pata** ('pa·ta) **supe** ('su·pe)
f	like *f* in *knife*	**fonda** ('fon·da) **gafa** ('ga·fa)
m	like *m* in *some*	**mana** ('ma·na) **lomo** ('lo·mo)
t	like *t* in *satin,* but with the tip of the tongue touching the upper teeth, not (as in English) the alveolar ridge	**toma** ('to·ma) **meta** ('me·ta)
θ	like *th* in *think*	**c** (in *ceceo* pronunciation) before **e** or **i**: **cena** ('θe·na) **cita** ('θi·ta) **acción** (ak'θjon) **z** in all positions (in *ceceo* pronunciation): **zumo** ('θu·mo) **moza** ('mo·θa) **caz** (kaθ)
d	like *d* in *day,* but with the tip of the tongue touching the upper teeth, not (as in English) the alveolar ridge	**d** at the beginning of a word, or following **l** or **n**: **damos** ('da·mos) **falda** ('fal·da) **hondo** ('on·do)

Phonetic Symbol	Approximate English Sound	Examples
ð	like *th* in *rather*	**d** between vowels, or following a consonant other than **l** or **n**, or preceded by a vowel and followed by **r**, or at the end of a word: **modelo** (mo'ðe·lo) **nardo** ('nar·ðo) **madre** ('ma·ðre) **pared** (pa'reð)
n	like *n* in *unity*	**nada** ('na·ða) **hongo** ('on·go)
s	like *s* in *see*	**s** in all positions: **seso** ('se·so) **estar** (es'tar) **lunes** ('lu·nes) **c** (in *seseo* pronunciation) before **e** or **i**: **cena** ('se·na) **cita** ('si·ta) **acción** (ak'sjon) **z** in all positions (in *seseo* pronunciation): **zumo** ('su·mo) **moza** ('mo·sa) **caz** (kas)
k	like *c* in *care* or *k* in *keen*	**c** before **a, o, u** or a consonant: **caber** (ka'ßer) **cosa** ('ko·sa) **cuna** ('ku·na) **activo** (ak'ti·ßo) **qu** (always followed by **e** or **i**): **queda** ('ke·ða) **quinta** ('kin·ta) **quiosco** ('kjos·ko) **x** (the first element): **exacto** (ek'sak·to) **sexo** ('sek·so) **k** in some words of foreign origin: **kilogramo** (ki·lo'ɣra·mo)

Phonetic Symbol	Approximate English Sound	Examples
g	like *g* in *go*	g at the beginning of a word and followed by **a, o,** or **u,** or in the middle of a word and preceded by **n:** **gato** ('ga·to) **gorra** ('go·rra) **gusano** (gu'sa·no) **mango** ('man·go)
ɣ	like *g* in *cigar,* but with greatly reduced tension and with vibration of the uvula	g in the middle of a word and followed by **a, o,** or **u** and not preceded by **n:** **paga** ('pa·ɣa) **digo** ('di·ɣo) **laguna** (la'ɣu·na) **cargo** ('kar·ɣo) **vulgar** (bul'ɣar)
x	like *ch* in Scottish *loch* or German *ach*	j in all positions, except sometimes at the end of a word: **justo** ('xus·to) **traje** ('tra·xe) **reloj** (re'lo) *but* **relojes** (re'lo·xes) g followed by **e** or **i:** **gemir** (xe'mir) **angina** (an'xi·na) x in a few words: **México** ('me·xi·ko) h in some words, as a variant pronunciation (**h** is usually silent): **holgorio** (ol'ɣo·rjo) *or* (xol'ɣo·rjo)
tʃ	like *ch* in *chat*	ch in all positions: **chino** ('tʃi·no) **mucho** ('mu·tʃo) **cancha** ('kan·tʃa)
ɲ	like *ny* in *canyon*	ñ in all positions: **caña** ('ka·ɲa) **ñame** ('ɲa·me)
ʎ	like *lli* in *million*	ll in all positions: **llamar** (ʎa'mar) **pollo** ('po·ʎo)

Phonetic Symbol	Approximate English Sound	Examples
j	like *y* in *yet*	**y** in all positions except at the end of a word: **ya** (ja) **huyo** ('u·jo) *but* **carey** (ka'rei)
		i as first element in a diphthong (see **ja, je, jo, ju**) or triphthong (see **jai, jei**)
		ll as a variant pronunciation in many regions: **llamar** (ja'mar) **pollo** ('po·jo)
l	like *l* in *love*	**l** in all positions: **lata** ('la·ta) **calma** ('kal·ma) **útil** ('u·til)
r	at the end of a word, or in the middle of a word and not preceded by **l, n,** or **s,** pronounced with a single flap of the tongue, somewhat like the British pronunciation of *r* in *very* or the relaxed pronunciation of *dd* in *ladder*	**deber** (de'βer) **pero** ('pe·ro) **otro** ('o·tro) **forma** ('for·ma)
	at the beginning of a word, or in the middle of a word and preceded by **l, n,** or **s,** strongly trilled, like *rr*	**roto** ('ro·to) **alrededor** (al·re·ðe'ðor) **enredo** (en're·ðo) **israelita** (is·ra·e'li·ta)
rr	strongly trilled, like the Scottish burr	**rr** (so written only between vowels): **perro** ('pe·rro) **corro** ('ko·rro)
w	like *w* in *wet*	**u** as first element in a diphthong (see **wa, we, wi, wo**) or triphthong (see **wai, wei**)
		w or **wh** in some foreign words: **wat** (wat) **whiskey** ('wis·ki)

FURTHER REMARKS ON SPANISH PRONUNCIATION

1. Regional and variant pronunciations. The following are regularly shown in our notation:

a. *Ceceo* and *seseo* alternates. *Ceceo* (θe'θe·o) and the related verb *cecear* (θe·θe'ar) are used to refer to speakers of Spanish who regularly use (θ) for z in all positions and for c before e or i; see (θ) in the pronunciation table. *Ceceo* speakers are concentrated largely in central and northern Spain, notably in Castile. Also, certain areas of the New World, particularly Peru, Colombia, and Ecuador, have a considerable number of *ceceo* speakers, especially among the more conservative or aristocratic classes. Furthermore, a number of educated speakers in all regions deliberately cultivate *ceceo,* in the belief that it is the truer and nobler form of Spanish.

Seseo (se'se·o) and the related verb *sesear* (se·se'ar) are used to refer to speakers of Spanish who regularly use (s) for z in all positions and for c before e or i; see (s) in the pronunciation table. *Seseo* is almost universal in the New World and in insular Spain (Canary Islands, etc.) as well as over most of southern Spain. The speakers of Judeo-Spanish, or Ladino, also regularly use *seseo.*

b. *Yeísmo* (je'is·mo) and the related noun *yeísta* (je'is·ta) are used to refer to speakers of Spanish who do not distinguish between ll and y, pronouncing both as (j); see (ʎ) and (j) in the pronunciation table. *Yeísmo* has gradually encroached upon the use of (ʎ) to the extent that today it may be said to be universal in all regions except among the more conservative or scholarly groups. In some regions not only have both sounds been merged but they have been further evolved to (ʒ) or (dʒ); see **2a,** below.

2. Regional and variant pronunciations not shown in our notation:

a. Variant pronunciation—chiefly in Argentina, Uruguay, Paraguay, and parts of Chile—of ll and also of y as (ʒ) or (dʒ):

calle ('ka·ʎe) *or* ('ka·je) *or* ('ka·ʒe)
yo (jo) *or* (ʒo) *or* (dʒo)

b. Common variant pronunciation of s as (z), especially before a voiced consonant:

mismo ('mis·mo) *or* ('miz·mo)
sesgo ('ses·ɣo) *or* ('sez·ɣo)

c. Common variant pronunciation of nv as (mb):
convenir (kon·βe'nir) *or* (kom·be'nir)

d. Common variant pronunciation of x as (s), especially before consonants:

extático (eks'ta·ti·ko) *or* (es'ta·ti·ko)

also sometimes between vowels:

exacto (ek'sak·to) *or* (e'sak·to)

another variant between vowels is (ɣz):

existe (ek'sis·te) *or* (eɣ'zis·te)

e. Common variant pronunciation of **j** and of **g** before **e** and **i** as (h):

justo ('xus·to) *or* ('hus·to)

traje ('tra·xe) *or* ('tra·he)

f. Syntactical phonetics: the treatment of groups of words in spoken utterance as a unit. In this dictionary, we naturally give the pronunciation of each word as if standing alone or at the beginning of an utterance. In normal speech, the initial sound of a word will often undergo certain modifications, as though it were in the middle of a word.

d at the beginning of a word may be pronounced as (ð) rather than (d) if it follows closely upon a word ending in a vowel or in a consonant other than **l** or **n**:

vamos a dormir ('ba·mo·sa·ðor'mir)

b at the beginning of a word may be pronounced as (β) rather than (b) if it follows closely upon a word ending in a vowel or in a consonant other than **m**:

agua bien fría ('a·ɣwa·βjen'fri·a)

s at the end of a word may be pronounced as (z) rather than (s) if the next word begins with a voiced consonant:

los dientes (loz'ðjen·tes)

g. Aspiration, or loss of **s**. In many regions, and especially in the West Indies, **s** at the end of a word or preceded by a vowel and followed by a consonant may be pronounced as a mere aspiration (h) or may be elided altogether; in the latter case, however, there is usually lengthening of the preceding vowel:

bonitos (bo'ni·tos) *or* (bo'ni·toh) *or* (bo'ni·to:)

postre ('pos·tre) *or* ('poh·tre) *or* ('po:·tre)

III. Stress and Accentuation

Spanish uses regularly only one written accent, the "acute" accent (´). The following simple rules govern its use:

1. Words ending in a vowel (not including **y**) or in **n** or **s** are stressed on the syllable before the last: hablado, vinieron, españoles.

2. Words ending in a consonant other than **n** or **s** (but including **y**) are stressed on the last syllable: entender, arrabal, codorniz, estoy.

3. Words not stressed according to one or the other of the above rules must have the written accent over the vowel of the stressed syllable: rubí, acá, cayó, nación, cortés, carácter, fácil, páramo.

4. The orthographic accent often serves to distinguish words that are spelled alike but differ in meaning:

se, reflexive pronoun
sé, I know

tu, possessive adjective
tú, personal pronoun

este, demonstrative adjective
éste, demonstrative pronoun

como, declarative
¿cómo?, interrogative; **¡cómo!,** exclamatory

In most cases, the written accent represents a genuine stress, or preserves a historic stress, on the words so marked. Its use is nevertheless
governed by orthographic rather than phonetic rule.

5. Adjectives that have a written accent retain the accent when adding
-mente to form adverbs, even though the stress shifts to the syllable before the last: fácilmente, últimamente, cortésmente.

Words that have a written accent often retain the accent when joined
to other words to form compounds: décimotercio or decimotercio;
décimoséptimo or decimoséptimo.

Verb forms that have a written accent retain the accent when an object
pronoun is added: déme, el acabóse.

6. The written accent over the vowel **i** or **u** serves to show that the
sound does not form a diphthong with an adjacent vowel or a triphthong
with two adjacent vowels: hacían, veíamos, evalúo. The vowels **i** and **u**
(commonly called "weak" vowels) would otherwise form a diphthong
with an adjacent **a, e,** or **o** ("strong" vowels)—averiguo, hacia—or a
triphthong with any two adjacent vowels—cambiáis, evaluáis. When the
vowels **i** and **u** come together and do not form a diphthong, one of them
must have a written accent: destruís, flúido.

The written accent is always placed over the strong vowel in a diphthong or triphthong whenever it is required to mark the stressed syllable,
in accordance with rules (1), (2), and (3) above: cantáis, habéis,
continuáis, evaluéis.

7. The pronouncements of the Spanish Royal Academy issued in 1952
permit departures from the rules hitherto in effect in the following
classes of words:

a. The combination **ui** is considered always to form a diphthong, and
neither vowel needs to be marked orthographically unless otherwise required by rules (1), (2), and (3) above. Thus, without accent: jesuita,
huido, juicio, construido, fluido; with accent: benjuí, casuístico.

b. The silent letter **h** between vowels does not prevent these vowels
from forming a diphthong: desahucio (de'sau·θjo). Consequently, when
such vowels do not form a diphthong, the stressed vowel of the pair
may be written with or without accent: vahído, búho, rehúso or vahido,
buho, rehuso.

c. Monosyllabic verb forms do not require a written accent: fue, fui,
vio, dio. This rule is even extended to include infinitives, which now
are often written without accent: oir, reir, huir.

IV. Punctuation and Capitalization

Spanish punctuation differs from English in the following respects:
1. The **question mark** and the **exclamation mark** are used at both the
beginning and the end of interrogative and exclamatory sentences, respectively, the first sign being inverted:

¿Dónde está Juan?
¡Qué bueno!

In longer sentences in which only a part of the sentence is a question or exclamation the signs are placed only at the beginning and the end of that part:

Dime: ¿que harás en mi lugar?

Cuando salí de la Habana ¡Válgame Dios!
Nadie me ha visto salir si no fui yo . . .

2. Quotation marks («   ») are used to indicate direct quotations or citations from a text:
«Veo que las leyes son contra los flacos, dice Luis Mejía, como las telarañas contra las moscas.»

Dialogue, however, is set off by the use of dashes. The dash precedes each change of speaker:

——¡Qué barbaridad! Se me olvidó la cartera.
——María, ¿necesitas dinero?
——Sí, tengo que comprarle un regalo a mi hermano.
——¿Cuánto piensas gastar?
——Como cinco dólares.
3. Capitalization is more restricted in Spanish than in English. Nouns and adjectives denoting nationality, religion, language, etc., names of the days of the week, the months of the year, and the pronoun *yo* are usually not capitalized; un francés, la nación rusa, el idioma inglés, un presbiteriano, martes, junio, yo.

V. Division of Syllables in Spanish

CONSONANTS

1. **ch, ll, rr** count as single letters and are never separated:
pe·cho   o·lla   pe·rro

2. Single consonants between vowels go with the second vowel:
ca·be·za   pa·re·cer

Note: y is treated as a consonant when it is followed by a vowel; in other cases it is treated as a vowel.

3. The groups **pr, pl, br, bl, fr, fl, tr, dr, cr, cl, gr, gl** go with the following vowel and are never separated:

re·pri·mir   co·pla   te·cla

4. In other groups of two consonants, whether identical or different, the consonants are divided between the preceding and the following vowel:

res·pi·ro   hon·ra   ac·ción   in·noble   at·las

5. In groups of three consonants, the first two go with the preceding vowel and the third with the following vowel:

ins·tin·to   obs·tá·cu·lo

Exception: The groups listed in (3), above, are not separated:

en·tre   com·pra   tem·plo   ins·tru·men·to

Note: A group of four consonants that does not contain one of the groups listed in (3), above, is rarely found, if at all.

VOWELS

6. In any combination of two of the letters **a, e, o,** the syllable is divided between the two vowels:

ca·o·ba   i·de·a·ción

7. In any combination of two vowels in which one is **a, e,** or **o** and the other is **i** or **u,** and there is no accent mark on the **i** or **u,** the vowels form a diphthong and are not separated:

jo·fai·na   vian·da   em·bau·car   men·guan·te
vi·rrei·na   con·tien·da   en·deu·dar·se   con·sue·lo
co·loi·dal   na·cio·nal   duo·de·no

If there is an accent mark on the **a, e,** or **o** of the group, the two vowels still form a diphthong and are not separated:

es·táis   es·co·géis   cuán·do

If the accent mark falls on the **i** or **u** of the group, the two vowels do not form a diphthong and are separated:

ca·í·da   pen·sa·rí·a·mos   a·ta·úd   re·ú·ne

8. In any combination of **i** and **u,** that is **ui** or **iu,** no division of syllables is made between these two vowels. This holds whether there is an accent mark or not:

ciu·dad   rui·do   ca·suís·ti·co

9. In any combination of three vowels (more than three do not occur), there is no division of syllables between any two vowels of the group. This holds whether there is an accent mark on any of the vowels or not:

a·pre·ciáis

VI. Nouns

1. *Gender*

Spanish nouns have grammatical rather than natural gender. Consequently, the gender of a noun may have nothing to do with the fact that it denotes a male or female being or something inanimate. Nouns have either masculine or feminine gender. The neuter gender in Spanish is limited to the neuter pronouns.

In this dictionary all nouns and pronouns are labeled to show gender. To determine the gender of nouns not included in this dictionary, some general rules (though there are exceptions) may be applied:

    a. Nouns denoting male human beings or animals are generally masculine: el señor, el caballo. *But:* la guardia, la centinela.

    Nouns ending in **-o** are generally masculine: el cuarto, el mexicano. *But:* la mano.

    Days of the week, months, rivers, lakes, seas, oceans, mountains are generally masculine: el lunes, el marzo, el Paraná, el Atlántico, los Pirineos.

Nouns of Greek origin ending in **-ma** are masculine: el tema, el drama.

b. Nouns denoting female human beings or animals are generally feminine: la señora, la vaca.

Nouns ending in **-a** are generally feminine. *But:* el mapa, el día.

Nouns ending in **-ez, -dad, -ion, -tad, -tud, -umbre** are generally feminine: la vejez, la humanidad, la nación, la dificultad, la juventud, la certidumbre.

Abstract nouns ending in **-ón** are generally feminine: la razón, la comezón. *But:* nouns with augmentative suffix **-ón** are masculine: el montón (the feminine augmentative suffix is **-ona**: la regañona).

Letters of the alphabet and phonetic sounds or symbols are feminine: la b, la g, la d.

c. Abstract nouns formed from adjectives are neuter and take the article lo: lo bueno, lo largo.

d. Some nouns are either masculine or feminine, with little or no difference in meaning: el *or* la azúcar, el *or* la mar.

e. Some nouns have different meanings in the masculine and in the feminine: el guía (the guide), la guía (guidebook, directory); el capital (money), la capital (seat of government).

f. Nouns denoting persons and ending in **-ista, -ante, -cida,** etc., have only one form for the masculine and the feminine, the gender being shown only in the article: el *or* la artista, el *or* la paciente, el *or* la estudiante, el *or* la homicida.

2. *Formation of the Plural*

a. Nouns ending in an unstressed vowel add **s:** el palo, los palos; la casa, las casas.

b. Nouns ending in a consonant or **y** add **es:** la mujer, las mujeres; el cristal, los cristales; el buey, los bueyes; la ley, las leyes.

c. Nouns ending in a stressed vowel (except **é**) usually add **es,** but sometimes **s:** el rubí, los rubíes; el cebú, los cebúes; el bajá, los bajaes; el paletó, los paletoes. *But:* el papá, los papás; la mamá, las mamás; el bongó, los bongós.

d. Nouns ending in stressed **e** add **s:** el bebé, los bebés; el café, los cafés.

e. Nouns of more than one syllable ending in **s** preceded by an unstressed vowel remain unchanged in the plural: la crisis, las crisis; el jueves, los jueves. *But:* el mes, los meses; el dios, los dioses.

f. Foreign nouns or recent borrowings ending in a consonant may form the plural by adding **s** or **es,** though usage tends more and more to favor **s:** el club, los clubs (*or* clubes); el complot, los complots (*or* complotes); el álbum, los álbums (*or* álbumes).

g. Spelling and accentuation of plural forms.

1) Nouns ending in **z** change the **z** to **c** when adding **es** to form the plural: el lápiz, los lápices; la raíz, las raíces.

2) With but few exceptions, the stressed vowel of the singular is stressed also in the plural. Consequently a written accent may have to be dropped or added, in accordance with the rules of Spanish accentuation:

written accent dropped { la nación, las naciones
                          el mohín, los mohines

written accent added { el crimen, los crímenes
                        el joven, los jóvenes

Exceptions: the stress ⎫ el carácter, los caracteres
shifts to a different sylla- ⎬ el régimen, los regímenes
ble in the plural ⎭

3. *Formation of the Feminine*

a. Nouns ending in **o** change the **o** to **a:** el muchacho, la muchacha; el tío, la tía.

b. Nouns ending in **-án, -ón, -or, -ol, -és, -ín,** add **a** to form the feminine:

el haragán, la haragana
el burlón, la burlona
el profesor, la profesora
el español, la española
el francés, la francesa
el bailarín, la bailarina

c. Nouns ending in **-ista, -ante, -ente, -cida,** etc., do not change in the feminine (see **1f,** above).

A few nouns ending in **-ante** or **-ente** change the **e** to **a** in the feminine: el asistente, la asistenta; el ayudante, la ayudanta; el practicante, la practicanta; el sirviente, la sirvienta.

d. Some nouns have a different suffix in the feminine: el poeta, la poetisa; el actor, la actriz; el diácono, la diaconisa; el emperador, la emperatriz; el duque, la duquesa; el abad, la abadesa.

VII. Adjectives

1. *Agreement of Adjectives*
a. Formation of the Feminine

1) Adjectives ending in **o** change the **o** to **a** in the feminine: bueno, buena; malo, mala.

2) Adjectives ending in a consonant or a vowel other than **o** have the same form for the masculine and the feminine: débil, familiar, común, verde, elegante, egoísta, etc.

3) Adjectives of nationality ending in a consonant add **a** to form the feminine: español, española; inglés, inglesa.

4) Adjectives ending in **-án, -ón,** and **-or** (except comparatives) add **a** to form the feminine: holgazán, holgazana; querendón, querendona.

5) Comparatives ending in **-or** do not change in the feminine: mejor, peor, mayor, menor, inferior, superior, etc.

b. Formation of the Plural

Adjectives follow in general the same rules for formation of the plural as nouns (see **VI 2,** above).

2. *Comparison of Adjectives*

a. The comparative of most adjectives (and adverbs) is formed by placing **más** (or **menos**) before the adjective or adverb. The superlative is the same as the comparative, except that it usually requires the definite article or a possessive adjective before it.

fácil, easy   *más fácil,* easier   *el (la) más fácil,* (the) easiest

tarde, late   *más tarde,* later   *(lo) más tarde,* (the) latest

b. Some adjectives (and adverbs) have special forms for the comparative and superlative. (Most of these permit also the regularly formed comparative and superlative.)

bueno, good   *mejor,* better   *el (la) mejor,* (the) best
malo, bad   *peor,* worse   *el (la) peor,* (the) worst

grande, large   *mayor,* larger, older   *el (la) mayor,* (the) largest, oldest

pequeño, small   *menor,* smaller, younger   *el (la) menor,* (the) smallest, youngest

alto, high   *superior,* higher, upper   *el (la) superior,* (the) highest, uppermost

bajo, low   *inferior,* lower, nether   *el (la) inferior,* (the) lowest, nethermost

bien, well   *mejor,* better   *mejor,* best
mal, badly   *peor,* worse   *peor,* worst

mucho, much ⎱
muchos, many ⎰ *más,* more   *más,* most

poco, little   *menos,* less   *menos,* least
pocos, few   *menos,* fewer   *menos,* fewest

3. *The Absolute Superlative*

The superlative described in **a** and **b,** above, is known as the **relative superlative.** It signifies a quality possessed by a person or thing in a higher degree than any of the other persons or things with which it is compared. The **absolute superlative,** on the other hand, signifies only a quality possessed by a person or thing in a very high degree, without direct comparison with any other persons or things.

The absolute superlative is formed by adding the suffix **-ísimo** to the stem of the adjective:

rapidísimo, most rapid, very rapid
facilísimo, most easy, very easy

Adverbs ending in **-mente** form the absolute superlative by inserting **-ísima** between the stem of the adjective and the suffix **-mente:** *bravísimamente,* most bravely, very bravely.

Other adverbs form the absolute superlative in the same way as adjectives:

muchísimo, most, very much
poquísimo, least, very little

4. *Irregular Superlatives*

bueno—óptimo, bonísimo (*or* buenísimo)
malo—pésimo, malísimo
grande—máximo, grandísimo
pequeño—mínimo, pequeñísimo
acre—acérrimo
antiguo—antiquísimo
pobre—paupérrimo
mísero—misérrimo
probable—probabilísimo (similarly all adjectives ending in **-ble**)

VIII. *Adverbs*

1. *Regular Adverbs*

These are formed in Spanish from nearly all adjectives by adding the
suffix **-mente** to the *feminine* form of the adjective:

> *solo,* solamente
> *feliz,* felizmente
> *rápido,* rápidamente

(Adjectives that have an orthographic accent retain the accent when
adding **-mente** even though the principal stress moves to the penultimate
syllable.)

2. *Special Forms*

Adjective	Adverb
bueno, good	*bien,* well
malo, bad	*mal,* badly, ill
mucho, much (adj. & adv.)	
poco, little (adj. & adv.)	
tardío, tardy	*tarde,* late
cercano, near, neighboring	*cerca,* near, close by
lejano, far, remote	*lejos,* far, far off

3. *Comparison of Adverbs*
See *Comparison of Adjectives,* **VII 2,** above.

IX. *Verbs*

(See also the Reference List of Model Spanish Verbs, p. 536.)

1. *Regular Conjugations*

Spanish has three regular classes of verbs, with infinitives ending in
-ar (1st conjugation), **-er** (2nd conjugation), and **-ir** (3rd conjugation).
The regular tenses are formed by dropping the ending **-ar, -er,** or **-ir**
of the infinitive and adding the endings shown below in boldface type.

	Infinitive	*Gerund*	*Past Participle*
1st conjugation	am**ar**	am**ando**	am**ado**
2nd conjugation	tem**er**	tem**iendo**	tem**ido**
3rd conjugation	viv**ir**	viv**iendo**	viv**ido**

PRESENT INDICATIVE

	1st Conjugation	2nd Conjugation	3rd Conjugation
yo	amo	temo	vivo
tú	amas	temes	vives
él, ella, Vd.	ama	teme	vive
nosotros	amamos	tememos	vivimos
vosotros	amáis	teméis	vivís
ellos, ellas, Vds.	aman	temen	viven

IMPERATIVE

The imperative is normally used only in the second person singular, second person plural, and first person plural. Of these, the first two are properly imperatives; the last is the subjunctive form used as an imperative. There are furthermore no negative forms in Spanish. The negative imperative is expressed by the appropriate subjunctive forms.

1st Conjugation	2nd Conjugation	3rd Conjugation
ama (tú)	teme (tú)	vive (tú)
no ames	no temas	no vivas
amad (vosotros)	temed (vosotros)	vivid (vosotros)
no améis	no temáis	no viváis
amemos (nosotros)	temamos (nosotros)	vivamos (nosotros)
no amemos	no temamos	no vivamos

IMPERFECT INDICATIVE

	1st Conjugation	2nd Conjugation	3rd Conjugation
yo	amaba	temía	vivía
tú	amabas	temías	vivías
él, ella, Vd.	amaba	temía	vivía
nosotros	amábamos	temíamos	vivíamos
vosotros	amabais	temíais	vivíais
ellos, ellas, Vds.	amaban	temían	vivían

FUTURE INDICATIVE

yo	amaré	temeré	viviré
tú	amarás	temerás	vivirás
él, ella, Vd.	amará	temerá	vivirá
nosotros	amaremos	temeremos	viviremos
vosotros	amaréis	temeréis	viviréis
ellos, ellas, Vds.	amarán	temerán	vivirán

CONDITIONAL

	1st Conjugation	2nd Conjugation	3rd Conjugation
yo	amaría	temería	viviría
tú	amarías	temerías	vivirías
él, ella, Vd.	amaría	temería	viviría
nosotros	amaríamos	temeríamos	viviríamos
vosotros	amaríais	temeríais	viviríais
ellos, ellas, Vds.	amarían	temerían	vivirían

PRETERIT INDICATIVE

yo	amé	temí	viví
tú	amaste	temiste	viviste
él, ella, Vd.	amó	temió	vivió
nosotros	amamos	temimos	vivimos
vosotros	amasteis	temisteis	vivisteis
ellos, ellas, Vds.	amaron	temieron	vivieron

PRESENT SUBJUNCTIVE

yo	ame	tema	viva
tú	ames	temas	vivas
él, ella, Vd.	ame	tema	viva
nosotros	amemos	temamos	vivamos
vosotros	améis	temáis	viváis
ellos, ellas, Vds.	amen	teman	vivan

IMPERFECT SUBJUNCTIVE

yo	amara / amase	temiera / temiese	viviera / viviese
tú	amaras / amases	temieras / temieses	vivieras / vivieses
él, ella, Vd.	amara / amase	temiera / temiese	viviera / viviese
nosotros	amáramos / amásemos	temiéramos / temiésemos	viviéramos / viviésemos
vosotros	amarais / amaseis	temierais / temieseis	vivierais / vivieseis
ellos, ellas, Vds.	amaran / amasen	temieran / temiesen	vivieran / viviesen

FUTURE SUBJUNCTIVE

	1st Conjugation	2nd Conjugation	3rd Conjugation
yo	amare	temiere	viviere
tú	amares	temieres	vivieres
él, ella, Vd.	amare	temiere	viviere
nosotros	amáremos	temiéremos	viviéremos
vosotros	amareis	temiereis	viviereis
ellos, ellas, Vds.	amaren	temieren	vivieren

2. *Auxiliary Verbs*

The principal auxiliary verbs of Spanish are **haber,** to have; **ser,** to be; and **estar,** to be. **Haber** has little use as an independent verb and functions largely as the auxiliary verb in forming (with the past participle) the **compound tenses** of all verbs. **Ser,** in addition to its other uses, functions as the auxiliary verb in forming (with the past participle) the **passive voice. Estar,** in addition to its other uses, functions as the auxiliary in forming (with the gerund) the **progressive tenses.** The conjugations of **haber, ser,** and **estar** are given below. A few other verbs, principally **tener** and **ir,** are used occasionally as auxiliaries. **Tener** is sometimes used in place of **haber** as a more emphatic auxiliary in forming the compound tenses:

> **tengo dicho . . . ,** I have said . . .
> (that is, authoritatively)

Ir is sometimes used in place of **estar** in forming the progressive tenses:

> **va creciendo,** it is growing
> (that is, keeps on growing)

CONJUGATIONS OF AUXILIARY VERBS

Infinitive	*Gerund*	*Past Participle*
haber	habiendo	habido
ser	siendo	sido
estar	estando	estado

PRESENT INDICATIVE

haber	**ser**	**estar**
he	soy	estoy
has	eres	estás
ha	es	está
hemos (*also,* habemos)	somos	estamos
habéis	sois	estáis
han	son	están

IMPERATIVE

haber	ser	estar
(impve. rarely used)		
hé (tú)	sé (tú)	está (tú)
no hayas	no seas	no estés
habed (vosotros)	sed (vosotros)	estad (vosotros)
no hayáis	no seáis	no estéis
hayamos	seamos	estemos
(nosotros)	(nosotros)	(nosotros)
no hayamos	no seamos	no estemos

IMPERFECT INDICATIVE

había	era	estaba
habías	eras	estabas
había	era	estaba
habíamos	éramos	estábamos
habíais	erais	estabais
habían	eran	estaban

FUTURE INDICATIVE

habré	seré	estaré
habrás	serás	estarás
habrá	será	estará
habremos	seremos	estaremos
habréis	seréis	estaréis
habrán	serán	estarán

CONDITIONAL

habría	sería	estaría
habrías	serías	estarías
habría	sería	estaría
habríamos	seríamos	estaríamos
habríais	seríais	estaríais
habrían	serían	estarían

PRETERIT INDICATIVE

hube	fui	estuve
hubiste	fuiste	estuviste
hubo	fue	estuvo
hubimos	fuimos	estuvimos
hubisteis	fuisteis	estuvisteis
hubieron	fueron	estuvieron

PRESENT SUBJUNCTIVE

haya	sea	esté
hayas	seas	estés
haya	sea	esté

hayamos	seamos	estemos
hayáis	seáis	estéis
hayan	sean	estén

IMPERFECT SUBJUNCTIVE

yo	{ hubiera / hubiese	{ fuera / fuese	{ estuviera / estuviese
tú	{ hubieras / hubieses	{ fueras / fueses	{ estuvieras / estuvieses
él, ella, Vd.	{ hubiera / hubiese	{ fuera / fueśe	{ estuviera / estuviese
nosotros	{ hubiéramos / hubiésemos	{ fuéramos / fuésémos	{ estuviéramos / estuviésemos
vosotros	{ hubierais / hubieseis	{ fuerais / fueseis	{ estuvierais / estuvieseis
ellos, ellas, Vds.	{ hubieran / hubiesen	{ fueran / fuesen	{ estuvieran / estuviesen

FUTURE SUBJUNCTIVE

hubiere	fuere	estuviere
hubieres	fueres	estuvieres
hubiere	fuere	estuviere
hubiéremos	fuéremos	estuviéremos
hubiereis	fuereis	estuviereis
hubieren	fueren	estuvieren

3. *Compound Tenses*

These are normally formed with the appropriate tense of **haber** followed by the past participle. Only the first person singular of each tense is given below.

	amar	**temer**	**vivir**
Perfect infinitive	haber amado	haber temido	haber vivido
Perfect gerund	habiendo amado	habiendo temido	habiendo vivido
Perfect indicative	he amado	he temido	he vivido
Pluperfect indicative }	había amado	había temido	había vivido
Future perfect indicative }	habré amado	habré temido	habré vivido
Conditional perfect }	habría amado	habría temido	habría vivido

Past anterior	hube amado	hube temido	hube vivido
Perfect subjunctive }	haya amado	haya temido	haya vivido
Pluperfect subjunctive }	hubiera amado hubiese amado	hubiera temido hubiese temido	hubiera vivido hubiese vivido
Future perfect subjunctive }	hubiere amado	hubiere temido	hubiere vivido

4. Irregular Verbs

a. Radical-Changing Verbs

These are the true irregular verbs. The orthographic-changing verbs described in the following section are on the whole phonetically regular, and the changes in their inflected forms affect only the spelling. Radical-changing verbs, on the other hand, exhibit irregularities in their stem vowels under the influence of the shifting pattern of stress. These inflectional changes date back to the earliest stages in the development of the Spanish language from the parent Latin. Consequently, many of the most basic and most common verbs will be found to have irregularities of one kind or another. It is entirely possible, furthermore, for a verb to be both radical-changing and orthographic-changing. The radical-changing verbs may conveniently be grouped into three classes, according to the kind of change that is undergone by the stem vowel (that is, the last vowel before the infinitive ending **-ar, -er,** or **-ir**).

Class I consists of verbs of the 1st and 2nd conjugations in which the stem vowels **e** and **o** change to the diphthongs **ie** and **ue**, respectively, whenever they are stressed. This change affects the 1st, 2nd, and 3rd persons singular and the 3rd person plural of the present indicative and present subjunctive, and the 2nd person singular affirmative imperative. These are shown in the table below in boldface type.

	pensar		**perder**	
Present indicative	**pienso**	pensamos	**pierdo**	perdemos
	piensas	pensáis	**pierdes**	perdéis
	piensa	**piensan**	**pierde**	**pierden**
Present subjunctive	**piense**	pensemos	**pierda**	perdamos
	pienses	penséis	**pierdas**	perdáis
	piense	**piensen**	**pierda**	**pierdan**
Imperative	**piensa**		**pierde**	

	acostar		**mover**	
Present indicative	**acuesto**	acostamos	**muevo**	movemos
	acuestas	acostáis	**mueves**	movéis
	acuesta	**acuestan**	**mueve**	**mueven**
Present subjunctive	**acueste**	acostemos	**mueva**	movamos
	acuestes	acostéis	**muevas**	mováis
	acueste	**acuesten**	**mueva**	**muevan**
Imperative	**acuesta**		**mueve**	

Class II consists of verbs of the 3rd conjugation in which the stem vowels **e** and **o** change to **ie** and **ue**, respectively, whenever they are stressed, just as in Class I. In addition, the stem vowels **e** and **o** change to **i** and **u**, respectively, whenever they are unstressed and followed by an ending containing **a, ió,** or **ie.** This second change affects the gerund, the 1st and 2nd persons plural of the present subjunctive, the 3rd person singular and plural of the preterit indicative, and the entire imperfect subjunctive and future subjunctive. The irregular forms showing either of these changes are in boldface type in the table below.

	sentir		**morir**	
Gerund	**sintiendo**		**muriendo**	
Present indicative	**siento**	sentimos	**muero**	morimos
	sientes	sentís	**mueres**	morís
	siente	**sienten**	**muere**	**mueren**
Present subjunctive	**sienta**	**sintamos**	**muera**	**muramos**
	sientas	**sintáis**	**mueras**	**muráis**
	sienta	**sientan**	**muera**	**mueran**
Preterit indicative	sentí	sentimos	morí	morimos
	sentiste	sentisteis	moriste	moristeis
	sintió	**sintieron**	**murió**	**murieron**
Imperfect subjunctive	**sintiera,** etc.		**muriera,** etc.	
	sintiese, etc.		**muriese,** etc.	
Future subjunctive	**sintiere,** etc.		**muriere,** etc.	

Class III consists of verbs of the 3rd conjugation in which the stem vowel **i** changes to **i** whenever it is stressed. This change affects the 1st, 2nd, and 3rd persons singular and the 3rd person plural of the present indicative and present subjunctive, and the 2nd person singular affirmative imperative. In addition, the stem vowel **e** changes to **i** whenever it is unstressed and followed by an ending containing **a, ió,** or **ie,** just as in Class II. The irregular forms showing either of these changes are in boldface type in the following table.

	pedir				
Gerund	**pidiendo**		*Preterit indicative*	pedí	pedimos
				pediste	pedisteis
Present indicative	**pido**	pedimos		**pidió**	**pidieron**
	pides	pedís			
	pide	**piden**	*Imperfect subjunctive*	**pidiera,** etc.	
Present subjunctive	**pida**	**pidamos**		**pidiese,** etc.	
	pidas	**pidáis**	*Future subjunctive*	**pidiere,** etc.	
	pida	**pidan**			

b. Orthographic-Changing Verbs

In the conjugation of some regular as well as irregular verbs, it is necessary to change the final letters of the stem before adding certain

personal endings. Such verbs are on the whole phonetically regular,
but require the indicated changes in order to preserve the same sound
of the final stem consonant throughout and still conform to the rules
of Spanish spelling.

RULES FOR ORTHOGRAPHIC-CHANGING VERBS

Infinitive Ending	Change Required	Tenses Affected	Examples
-car	c to qu	}	tocar: toqué; toque, toques, etc.
-gar	insert u	1st pers. sing. pret. ind.; entire pres. subjve.	pagar: pagué; pague, pagues, etc.
-guar	change u to ü	before e	averiguar: averigüé; averigüe, averigües, etc.
-zar	change z to c	}	rezar: recé; rece, reces, etc.

Infinitive Ending	Change Required	Tenses Affected	Examples
-cer preceded by a consonant	change c to z	before a or o	vencer: venzo; venza, venzas, etc.
-cir preceded by a consonant		1st pers. sing. pres. ind.; entire pres. subjve.	esparcir: esparzo; esparza, esparzas, etc.

Infinitive Ending	Change Required	Tenses Affected	Examples
-cer preceded by a vowel	insert z before c	before a or o	conocer: conozco; conozca, conozcas, etc.
-cir preceded by a vowel		1st pers. sing. pres. ind.; entire pres. subjve.	lucir: luzco; luzca, luzcas, etc.

(Exceptions: **mecer,** to rock; **cocer,** to cook; **escocer,** to smart, which follow the model of **vencer,** above, and **decir** and **hacer** and their compounds, which are irregular.)

Infinitive Ending	Change Required	Tenses Affected	Examples
-ger	change g to j	}	coger: cojo; coja, cojas, etc.
-gir		before a or o	dirigir: dirijo; dirija, dirijas, etc.
-quir	change qu to c	1st pers. sing. pres. ind.; entire pres. subjve.	delinquir: delinco; delinca, delincas, etc.
-guir	drop the u of gu	}	distinguir: distingo; distinga, distingas, etc.

-ller			empeller: empellendo; empelló, empelleron; empellera; empellese; empellere
-llir	drop the **i** from the ending **-ió** and from all endings beginning with **-ie**	gerund; 3rd pers. sing. and 3rd pers. pl. of pret. ind.; entire impf. subjve. and fut. subjve.	bullir: bullendo; bulló, bulleron; bullera; bullese; bullere
-ñer			tañer: tañendo; tañó, tañeron; tañera; tañese; tañere
-ñir			gruñir: gruñendo; gruñó, gruñeron; gruñera; gruñese; gruñere

(The preceding rule affects also certain verbs that have **j** in the stem of some tenses in which the **i** is dropped from endings beginning with **-ie-**: decir: 3rd pers. pl. pret. ind., **dijeron;** impf. subjve., **dijera, dijese;** fut. subjve., **dijere.**)

-iar	the **i** or **u** of the stem adds a written accent when stressed before one-syllable endings	1st, 2nd, 3rd pers. sing. and 3rd pers. pl. of the pres. ind. and pres. subjve; 2nd pers. sing. impve.	enviar: envío, envías, envía; envían; envíe, envíes, envíe; envíen; envía
-uar			continuar: continúo, continúas, continúa, continúan; continúe, continúes, continúe, continúen; continúa

The rules of Spanish spelling require that the vowel **i** when unstressed and standing at the beginning of a word and followed by a vowel, or in the middle of a word between two other vowels, become phonetically a consonant and be written **y** [see the vowel (i), the diphthongs (ja), (je), (jo), (ju), and the consonant (j) in the pronunciation section]. This rule affects verb forms in all tenses in which the stem ends in a vowel and the ending begins with an unstressed **i** followed by another vowel. In all such cases **i** must be changed in writing to **y.** This rule affects verbs of the following types:

creer *ger.,* creyendo; *3rd pers. sing. & pl. pret. ind.,* creyó, creyeron; *impf. subjve.,* creyera, etc., creyese, etc.; *fut. subjve.,* creyere, etc.

oír *ger.,* oyendo; *2nd pers. sing., 3rd pers. sing. & pl. pres. ind.,* oyes, oye, oyen (the 1st pers. sing. is irregular: oigo, not oyo); *3rd pers. sing. & pl. pret. ind.,* oyó, oyeron; *impf. subjve.,* oyera, etc., oyese, etc.; *fut. subjve.,* oyere, etc.

huir *ger.,* huyendo; *entire sing. and 3rd pl. pres. ind.,* huyo, huyes, huye, huyen (but huímos, huís); *entire pres. subjve.,* huya, huyas, etc.; *3rd pers. sing. & pl. pret. ind.,* huyó, huyeron; *impf. subjve.,* huyera, etc., huyese, etc.; *fut. subjve.,* huyere, etc.

ir *ger.,* yendo.

REFERENCE LIST OF MODEL SPANISH VERBS

Boldface is used to indicate forms that show a change in the stem of the verb.

REGULAR VERBS

1. amar (to love)

Gerund & P.P.	amando, amado
Pres.Ind.	amo, amas, ama, amamos, amáis, aman
Impve.	ama, amad
Impf.Ind.	amaba, amabas, amaba, amábamos, amabais, amaban
Fut.Ind.	amaré, amarás, amará, amaremos, amaréis, amarán
Conditional	amaría, amarías, amaría, amaríamos, amaríais, amarían
Preterit	amé, amaste, amó, amamos, amasteis, amaron
Pres.Subjve.	ame, ames, ame, amemos, améis, amen
Impf. Subjve.	
(-ra form)	amara, amaras, amara, amáramos, amarais, amaran
(-se form)	amase, amases, amase, amásemos, amaseis, amasen
Fut.Subjve.	amare, amares, amare, amáremos, amareis, amaren

2. temer (to fear)

Gerund & P.P.	temiendo, temido
Pres.Ind.	temo, temes, teme, tememos, teméis, temen
Impve.	teme, temed
Impf.Ind.	temía, temías, temía, temíamos, temíais, temían
Fut.Ind.	temeré, temerás, temerá, temeremos, temeréis, temerán
Conditional	temería, temerías, temería, temeríamos, temeríais, temerían
Preterit	temí, temiste, temió, temimos, temisteis, temieron
Pres.Subjve.	tema, temas, tema, temamos, temáis, teman
Impf.Subjve.	temiera, temieras, temiera, temiéramos, temierais,
(-ra form)	temieran
(-se form)	temiese, temieses, temiese, temiésemos, temieseis, temiesen
Fut.Subjve.	temiere, temieres, temiere, temiéremos, temiereis, temieren

3. vivir (to live)

Gerund & P.P.	viviendo, vivido
Pres.Ind.	vivo, vives, vive, vivimos, vivís, viven
Impve.	vive, vivid
Impf.Ind.	vivía, vivías, vivía, vivíamos, vivíais, vivían
Fut.Ind.	viviré, vivirás, vivirá, viviremos, viviréis, vivirán
Conditional	viviría, vivirías, viviría, viviríamos, viviríais, vivirían
Preterit	viví, viviste, vivió, vivimos, vivisteis, vivieron
Pres.Subjve.	viva, vivas, viva, vivamos, viváis, vivan
Impf.Subjve.	
(-ra form)	viviera, vivieras, viviera, viviéramos, vivierais, vivieran
(-se form)	viviese, vivieses, viviese, viviésemos, vivieseis, viviesen
Fut.Subjve.	viviere, vivieres, viviere, viviéremos, viviereis, vivieren

AUXILIARY VERBS

4. haber (to have)

Gerund & P.P.	habiendo, habido
Pres.Ind.	**he, has, ha, hemos,** habéis, **han**
Impve.	**hé,** habed
Fut.Ind.	**habré, habrás, habrá, habremos, habréis, habrán**
Conditional	**habría, habrías, habría, habríamos, habríais, habrían**
Preterit	**hube, hubiste, hubo, hubimos, hubisteis, hubieron**
Pres.Subjve.	**haya, hayas, haya, hayamos, hayáis, hayan**
Impf.Subvjve. (-ra form)	**hubiera, hubieras, hubiera, hubiéramos, hubierais, hubieran**
(-se form)	**hubiese, hubieses, hubiese, hubiésemos, hubieseis, hubiesen**
Fut.Subjve.	**hubiere, hubieres, hubiere, hubiéremos, hubiereis, hubieren**

5. ser (to be)

Gerund & P.P.	siendo, sido
Pres.Ind.	**soy, eres, es, somos, sois, son**
Impve.	**sé,** sed
Impf.Ind.	**era, eras, era, éramos, erais, eran**
Preterit	**fui, fuiste, fue, fuimos, fuisteis, fueron**
Pres.Subjve.	**sea, seas, sea, seamos, seáis, sean**
Impf.Subjve. (-ra form)	**fuera, fueras, fuera, fuéramos, fuerais, fueran**
(-se form)	**fuese, fueses, fuese, fuésemos, fueseis, fuesen**
Fut.Subjve.	**fuere, fueres, fuere, fuéremos, fuereis, fueren**

6. estar (to be)

Gerund & P.P.	estando, estado
Pres.Ind.	estoy, **estás, está,** estamos, estáis, **están**
Impve.	**está,** estad
Preterit	**estuve, estuviste, estuvo, estuvimos, estuvisteis, estuvieron**
Pres.Subjve.	**esté, estés, esté,** estemos, estéis, **estén**
Impf.Subjve. (-ra form)	**estuviera, estuvieras, estuviera, estuviéramos, estuvierais, estuvieran**
(-se form)	**estuviese, estuvieses, estuviese, estuviésemos, estuvieseis, estuviesen**
Fut.Subjve.	**estuviere, estuvieres, estuviere, estuviéremos, estuviereis, estuvieren**

ORTHOGRAPHIC-CHANGING VERBS

7. tocar (to touch; play)

Preterit	**toqué,** tocaste, tocó, tocamos, tocasteis, tocaron
Pres.Subjve.	**toque, toques, toque, toquemos, toquéis, toquen**

8. pagar (to pay)

Preterit	**pagué,** pagaste, pagó, pagamos, pagasteis, pagaron
Pres.Subjve.	**pague, pagues, pague, paguemos, paguéis, paguen**

9. averiguar (to ascertain)

Preterit	**averigüé,** averiguaste, averiguó, averiguamos, averiguasteis, averiguaron
Pres.Subjve.	**averigüe, averigües, averigüe, averigüemos, averigüéis, averigüen**

10. rezar (to pray)

Preterit	**recé,** rezaste, rezó, rezamos, rezasteis, rezaron
Pres.Subjve.	**rece, reces, rece, recemos, recéis, recen**

11. vencer (to conquer; win)

Pres.Ind.	**venzo,** vences, vence, vencemos, vencéis, vencen
Pres.Subjve.	**venza, venzas, venza, venzamos, venzáis, venzan**

12. esparcir (to scatter)

Pres.Ind.	**esparzo,** esparces, esparce, esparcimos, esparcís, esparcen
Pres.Subjve.	**esparza, esparzas, esparza, esparzamos, esparzáis, esparzan**

13. conocer (to know; to be acquainted with)

Pres.Ind.	**conozco,** conoces, conoce, conocemos, conocéis, conocen
Pres.Subjve.	**conozca, conozcas, conozca, conozcamos, conozcáis, conozcan**

14. lucir (to shine)

Pres.Ind.	**luzco,** luces, luce, lucimos, lucís, lucen
Pres.Subjve.	**luzca, luzcas, luzca, luzcamos, luzcáis, luzcan**

15. coger (to pick; seize)

Pres.Ind.	**cojo,** coges, coge, cogemos, cogéis, cogen
Pres.Subjve.	**coja, cojas, coja, cojamos, cojáis, cojan**

16. delinquir (to transgress)

Pres.Ind.	**delinco,** delinques, delinque, delinquimos, delinquís, delinquen
Pres.Subjve.	**delinca, delincas, delinca, delincamos, delincáis, delincan**

17. distinguir (to distinguish)

Pres.Ind.	**distingo,** distingues, distingue, distinguimos, distinguís, distinguen
Pres.Subjve.	**distinga, distingas, distinga, distingamos, distingáis, distingan**

18. empeller (to push; shove)

Gerund & P.P.	**empellendo,** empellido
Preterit	empellí, empelliste, **empelló,** empellimos, empellisteis, **empelleron**
Impf.Subjve. (-ra form)	**empellera, empelleras, empellera, empelléramos, empellerais, empelleran**
(-se form)	**empellese, empelleses, empellese, empellésemos, empelleseis, empellesen**

Fut.Subjve.	**empellere, empelleres, empellere, empelléremos, empellereis, empelleren**

19. bullir (to boil)

Gerund & P.P.	**bullendo,** bullido
Preterit	bullí, bulliste, **bulló,** bullimos, bullisteis, **bulleron**
Impf.Subjve. (-ra form)	**bullera, bulleras, bullera, bulléramos, bullerais, bulleran**
(-se form)	**bullese, bulleses, bullese, bullésemos, bulleseis, bullesen**
Fut.Subjve.	**bullere, bulleres, bullere, bulléremos, bullereis, bulleren**

20. tañer (to pluck; twang; peal)

Gerund & P.P.	**tañendo,** tañido
Preterit	tañí, tañiste, **tañó,** tañimos, tañisteis, **tañeron**
Impf.Subjve. (-ra form)	**tañera, tañeras, tañera, tañéramos, tañerais, tañeran**
(-se form)	**tañese, tañeses, tañese, tañésemos, tañeseis, tañesen**
Fut.Subjve.	**tañere, tañeres, tañere, tañéremos, tañereis, tañeren**

21. gruñir (to grunt)

Gerund & P.P.	**gruñendo,** gruñido
Preterit	gruñí, gruñiste, **gruñó,** gruñimos, gruñisteis, **gruñeron**
Impf.Subjve. (-ra form)	**gruñera, gruñeras, gruñera, gruñéramos, gruñerais, gruñeran**
(-se form)	**gruñese, gruñeses, gruñese, gruñésemos, gruñeseis, gruñesen**
Fut.Subjve.	**gruñere, gruñeres, gruñere, gruñéremos, gruñereis, gruñeren**

22. enviar (to send)

Pres.Ind.	**envío, envías, envía,** enviamos, enviáis, **envían**
Impve.	**envía,** enviad
Pres.Subjve.	**envíe, envíes, envíe,** enviemos, enviéis, **envíen**

23. continuar (to continue)

Pres.Ind.	**continúo, continúas, continúa,** continuamos, continuáis, **continúan**
Impve.	**continúa,** continuad
Pres.Subjve.	**continúe, continúes, continúe,** continuemos, continuéis, **continúen**

24. creer (to believe)

Gerund & P.P.	**creyendo,** creído
Preterit	creí, creíste, **creyó,** creímos, creísteis, **creyeron**
Impf. Subjve. (-ra form)	**creyera, creyeras, creyera, creyéramos, creyerais, creyeran**
(-se form)	**creyese, creyeses, creyese, creyésemos, creyeseis, creyesen**
Fut. Subjve.	**creyere, creyeres, creyere, creyéremos, creyereis, creyeren**

25. oír (to hear)

Gerund & P.P.	**oyendo,** oído
Pres.Ind.	**oigo, oyes, oye,** oímos, oís, **oyen**
Impve.	**oye,** oíd
Preterit	oí, oíste, **oyó,** oímos, oísteis, **oyeron**
Pres.Subjve.	**oiga, oigas, oiga, oigamos, oigáis, oigan**
Impf.Subvjve.	
(-ra form)	**oyera, oyeras, oyera, oyéramos, oyerais, oyeran**
(-se form)	**oyese, oyeses, oyese, oyésemos, oyeseis, oyesen**
Fut.Subjve.	**oyere, oyeres, oyere, oyéremos, oyereis, oyeren**

26. huir (to flee)

Gerund & P.P.	**huyendo,** huído
Pres.Ind.	**huyo, huyes, huye,** huímos, huís, **huyen**
Impve.	**huye,** huid
Preterit	huí, huiste, **huyó,** huimos, huisteis, **huyeron**
Pres.Subjve.	**huya, huyas, huya, huyamos, huyáis, huyan**
Impf.Subjve.	**huyera, huyeras, huyera, huyéramos, huyerais,**
(-ra form)	**huyeran**
(-se form)	**huyese, huyeses, huyese, huyésemos, huyeseis,**
	huyesen
Fut.Subjve.	**huyere, huyeres, huyere, huyéremos, huyereis,**
	huyeren

RADICAL-CHANGING VERBS

27. pensar (to think)

Pres.Ind.	**pienso, piensas, piensa,** pensamos, pensáis, **piensan**
Impve.	**piensa,** pensad
Pres.Subjve.	**piense, pienses, piense,** pensemos, penséis, **piensen**

28. acostar (to lay down; [refl. lie down]

Pres.Ind.	**acuesto, acuestas, acuesta,** acostamos, acostáis, **acuestan**
Impve.	**acuesta,** acostad
Pres.Subjve.	**acueste, acuestes, acueste,** acostemos, acostéis, **acuesten**

29. perder (to lose)

Pres.Ind.	**pierdo, pierdes, pierde,** perdemos, perdéis, **pierden**
Impve.	**pierde,** perded
Pres.Subjve.	**pierda, pierdas, pierda,** perdamos, perdáis, **pierdan**

30. mover (to move)

Pres.Ind.	**muevo, mueves, mueve,** movemos, movéis, **mueven**
Impve.	**mueve,** moved
Pres.Subjve.	**mueva, muevas, mueva,** movamos, mováis, **muevan**

31. sentir (to feel)

Gerund & P.P.	**sintiendo,** sentido
Pres.Ind.	**siento, sientes, siente,** sentimos, sentís, **sienten**
Impve.	**siente,** sentid
Preterit	sentí, sentiste, **sintió,** sentimos, sentisteis, **sintieron**

Pres.Subjve.	**sienta, sientas, sienta, sintamos, sintáis, sientan**
Impf.Subjve.	**sintiera, sintieras, sintiera, sintiéramos, sintierais,**
(-ra form)	**sintieran**
(-se form)	**sintiese, sintieses, sintiese, sintiésemos, sintieseis,**
	sintiesen
Fut.Subjve.	**sintiere, sintieres, sintiere, sintiéremos, sintiereis,**
	sintieren

32. morir (to die)

Gerund & P.P.	**muriendo, muerto**
Pres.Ind.	**muero, mueres, muere,** morimos, morís, **mueren**
Impve.	**muere,** morid
Preterit	morí, moriste, **murió,** morimos, moristeis, **murieron**
Pres.Subjve.	**muera, mueras, muera, muramos, muráis, mueran**
Impf. Subjve.	**muriera, murieras, muriera, muriéramos,**
(-ra form)	**murierais, murieran**
(-se form)	**muriese, murieses, muriese, muriésemos, murieseis,**
	muriesen
Fut.Subjve.	**muriere, murieres, muriere, muriéremos, muriereis,**
	murieren

33. pedir (to ask; request)

Gerund & P.P.	**pidiendo,** pedido
Pres.Ind.	**pido, pides, pide,** pedimos, pedís, **piden**
Impve.	**pide,** pedid
Preterit	pedí, pediste, **pidió,** pedimos, pedisteis, **pidieron**
Pres.Subjve.	**pida, pidas, pida, pidamos, pidáis, pidan**
Impf.Subjve.	**pidiera, pidieras, pidiera, pidiéramos, pidierais,**
(-ra form)	**pidieran**
(-se form)	**pidiese, pidieses, pidiese, pidiésemos, pidieseis,**
	pidiesen
Fut.Subjve.	**pidiere, pidieres, pidiere, pidiéremos, pidiereis,**
	pidieren

IRREGULAR VERBS

34. adquirir (to acquire)

Pres.Ind.	**adquiero, adquieres, adquiere,** adquirimos, adquirís,
	adquieren
Impve.	**adquiere,** adquirid
Pres.Subjve.	**adquiera, adquieras, adquiera,** adquiramos,
	adquiráis, **adquieran**

35. andar (to walk; go)

Preterit	**anduve, anduviste, anduvo, anduvimos, anduvisteis,**
	anduvieron
Impf.Subjve.	**anduviera, anduvieras, anduviera, anduviéramos,**
(-ra form)	**anduvierais, anduvieran**
(-se form)	**anduviese, anduvieses, anduviese, anduviésemos,**
	anduvieseis, anduviesen
Fut.Subjve.	**anduviere, anduvieres, anduviere, anduviéremos,**
	anduviereis, anduvieren

36. asir (to seize)
Pres.Ind.   **asgo,** ases, ase, asimos, asís, asen
Pres.Subjve.   **asga, asgas, asga, asgamos, asgáis, asgan**

37. bendecir (to bless)
Gerund & P.P.   **bendiciendo,** bendecido
Pres.Ind.   **bendigo, bendices, bendice,** bendecimos, bendecís,
                   bendicen
Impve.   **bendice,** bendecid
Preterit   **bendije, bendijiste, bendijo, bendijimos, bendijisteis,**
                   bendijeron
Pres.Subjve.   **bendiga, bendigas, bendiga, bendigamos, bendigáis,**
                   bendigan
Impf.Subjve.   **bendijera, bendijeras, bendijera, bendijéramos,**
(-ra form)   **bendijerais, bendijeran**
  (-se form)   **bendijese, bendijeses, bendijese, bendijésemos,**
                   bendijeseis, bendijesen
Fut.Subjve.   **bendijere, bendijeres, bendijere, bendijéremos,**
                   bendijereis, bendijeren

38. caber (to fit; to be contained)
Pres.Ind.   **quepo,** cabes, cabe, cabemos, cabéis, caben
Fut.Ind.   **cabré, cabrás, cabrá, cabremos, cabréis, cabrán**
Conditional   **cabría, cabrías, cabría, cabríamos, cabríais, cabrían**
Preterit   **cupe, cupiste, cupo, cupimos, cupisteis, cupieron**
Pres.Subjve.   **quepa, quepas, quepa, quepamos, quepáis, quepan**
Impf.Subjve.   **cupiera, cupieras, cupiera, cupiéramos, cupierais,**
(-ra form)   **cupieran**
  (-se form)   **cupiese, cupieses, cupiese, cupiésemos, cupieseis,**
                   cupiesen
Fut.Subjve.   **cupiere, cupieres, cupiere, cupiéremos, cupiereis,**
                   cupieren

39. caer (to fall)
Gerund & P.P.   **cayendo,** caído
Pres.Ind.   **caigo,** caes, cae, caemos, caéis, caen
Preterit   caí, caíste, **cayó,** caímos, caísteis, **cayeron**
Pres.Subjve.   **caiga, caigas, caiga, caigamos, caigáis, caigan**
Impf.Subjve.   **cayera, cayeras, cayera, cayéramos, cayerais,**
(-ra form)   **cayeran**
  (-se form)   **cayese, cayeses, cayese, cayésemos, cayeseis, cayesen**
Fut.Subjve.   **cayere, cayeres, cayere, cayéremos, cayereis, cayeren**

40. conducir (to lead; conduct)
Pres.Ind.   **conduzco,** conduces, conduce, conducimos, conducís,
                   conducen
Preterit   **conduje, condujiste, condujo, condujimos,**
                   condujisteis, condujeron
Pres.Subjve.   **conduzca, conduzcas, conduzca, conduzcamos,**
                   conduzcáis, conduzcan
Impf.Subjve.   **condujera, condujeras, condujera, condujéramos,**
(-ra form)   **condujerais, condujeran**
  (-se form)   **condujese, condujeses, condujese, condujésemos,**
                   condujeseis, condujesen

Fut.Subjve.	**condujere, condujeres, condujere, condujéremos, condujereis, condujeren**

41. construir (to construct)

Gerund & P.P.	**construyendo,** construído
Pres.Ind.	**construyo, construyes, construye,** construimos, construís, **construyen**
Impve.	**construye,** construid
Preterit	construí, construiste, **construyó,** construimos, construisteis, **construyeron**
Pres.Subjve.	**construya, construyas, construya, construyamos, construyáis, construyan**
Impf.Subjve. (-ra form)	**construyera, construyeras, construyera, construyéramos, construyerais, construyeran**
(-se form)	**construyese, construyeses, construyese, construyésemos, construyeseis construyesen**
Fut.Subjve.	**construyere, construyeres, construyere, construyéremos, construyereis, construyeren**

42. creer (to believe)

Gerund & P.P.	**creyendo,** creído
Preterit	creí, creíste, **creyó,** creímos, creísteis, **creyeron**
Impf.Subjve. (-ra form)	**creyera, creyeras, creyera, creyéramos, creyerais, creyeran**
(-se form)	**creyese, creyeses, creyese, creyésemos, creyeseis, creyesen**
Fut.Subjve.	**creyere, creyeres, creyere, creyéremos, creyereis, creyeren**

43. dar (to give)

Pres.Ind.	**doy,** das, da, damos, dais, dan
Preterit	**di, diste, dió, dimos, disteis, dieron**
Pres.Subjve.	**dé,** des, **dé,** demos, deis, den
Impf.Subjve. (-ra form)	**diera, dieras, diera, diéramos, dierais, dieran**
(-se form)	**diese, dieses, diese, diésemos, dieseis, diesen**
Fut.Subjve.	**diere, dieres, diere, diéremos, diereis, dieren**

44. decir (to say; tell)

Gerund & P.P.	**diciendo, dicho**
Pres.Ind.	**digo, dices, dice,** decimos, decís, **dicen**
Impve.	**di,** decid
Fut.Ind.	**diré, dirás, dirá, diremos, diréis, dirán**
Conditional	**diría, dirías, diría, diríamos, diríais, dirían**
Preterit	**dije, dijiste, dijo, dijimos, dijisteis, dijeron**
Pres.Subjve.	**diga, digas, diga, digamos, digáis, digan**
Impf.Subjve. (-ra form)	**dijera, dijeras, dijera, dijéramos, dijerais, dijeran**
(-se form)	**dijese, dijeses, dijese, dijésemos, dijeseis, dijesen**
Fut.Subjve.	**dijere, dijeres, dijere, dijéremos, dijereis, dijeren**

45. desosar (to bone)
Pres.Ind.	**deshueso, deshuesas, deshuesa,** desosamos, desosáis, **deshuesan**
Impve.	**deshuesa,** desosad
Pres.Subjve.	**deshuese, deshueses, deshuese,** desosemós, desoséis, **deshuesen**

46. erguir (to erect)
Gerund & P.P.	**irguiendo,** erguido
Pres.Ind.	**yergo [irgo], yergues [irgues], yergue [irgue],** erguimos, erguís, **yerguen [irguen]**
Impve.	**yergue [irgue],** erguid
Preterit	erguí, erguiste, **irguió,** erguimos, erguisteis, **irguieron**
Pres.Subjve.	**yerga [irga], yergas [irgas], yerga [irga], irgamos, irgáis, yergan [irgan]**
Impf.Subjve. (-ra form)	**irguiera, irguieras, irguiera, irguiéramos, irguierais, irguieran**
(-se form)	**irguiese, irguieses, irguiese, irguiésemos, irguieseis, irguiesen**
Fut.Subjve.	**irguiere, irguieres, irguiere, irguiéremos, irguiereis, irguieren**

47. errar (to mistake; err)
Pres.Ind.	**yerro, yerras, yerra,** erramos, erráis, **yerran**
Impve.	**yerra,** errad
Pres.Subjve.	**yerre, yerres, yerre,** erremos, erréis, **yerren**

48. hacer (to make; do)
Gerund & P.P.	haciendo, **hecho**
Pres.Ind.	**hago,** haces, hace, hacemos, hacéis, hacen
Impve.	**haz,** haced
Fut.Ind.	**haré, harás, hará, haremos, haréis, harán**
Conditional	**haría, harías, haría, haríamos, haríais, harían**
Preterit	**hice, hiciste, hizo,** hicimos, hicisteis, hicieron
Pres.Subjve.	**haga, hagas, haga, hagamos, hagáis, hagan**
Impf.Subjve. (-ra form)	**hiciera, hicieras, hiciera, hiciéramos, hicierais, hicieran**
(-se form)	**hiciese, hicieses, hiciese, hiciésemos, hicieseis, hiciesen**
Fut.Subjve.	**hiciere, hicieres, hiciere, hiciéremos, hiciereis, hicieren**

49. ir (to go)
Gerund & P.P.	**yendo,** ido
Pres.Ind.	**voy, vas, va, vamos, vais, van**
Impve.	**ve, vamos,** id
Impf.Ind.	**iba, ibas, iba, íbamos, ibais, iban**
Preterit	**fui, fuiste, fue, fuimos, fuisteis, fueron**
Pres.Subjve.	**vaya, vayas, vaya, vayamos, vayáis, vayan**
Impf.Subjve. (-ra form)	**fuera, fueras, fuera, fuéramos, fuerais, fueran**
(-se form)	**fuese, fueses, fuese, fuésemos, fueseis, fuesen**
Fut.Subjve.	**fuere, fueres, fuere, fuéremos, fuereis, fueren**

50. jugar (to play)

Pres.Ind.	**juego, juegas, juega,** jugamos, jugáis, **juegan**
Impve.	**juega,** jugad
Preterit	**jugué,** jugaste, jugó, jugamos, jugasteis, jugaron
Pres.Subjve.	**juegue, juegues, juegue, juguemos, juguéis, jueguen**

51. oler (to smell)

Pres.Ind.	**huelo, hueles, huele,** olemos, oléis, **huelen**
Impve.	**huele,** oled
Pres.Subjve.	**huela, huelas, huela,** olamos, oláis, **huelan**

52. placer (to please)

Pres.Ind.	**plazco [plazgo],** places, place, placemos, placéis, placen
Preterit	plací, placiste, plació **[plugo],** placimos, placisteis, placieron
Pres.Subjve.	**plazca [plazga], plazcas, plazca, plazcamos, plazcáis, plazcan**
Impf.Subjve.	
(-ra form)	(3rd pers.sing.) placiera **[pluguiera]**
(-se form)	(3rd pers.sing.) placiese **[pluguiese]**
Fut.Subjve.	(3rd pers.sing.) placiere **[piuguiere]**

53. poder (to be able; can; may)

Gerund & P.P.	**pudiendo,** podido
Pres.Ind.	**puedo, puedes, puede,** podemos, podéis, **pueden**
Fut.Ind.	**podré, podrás, podrá, podremos, podréis, podrán**
Conditional	**podría, podrías, podría, podríamos, podríais, podrían**
Preterit	**pude, pudiste, pudo, pudimos, pudisteis, pudieron**
Pres.Subjve.	**pueda, puedas, pueda,** podamos, podáis, **puedan**
Impf.Subjvc.	**pudiera, pudieras, pudiera, pudiéramos, pudierais,**
(-ra form)	**pudieran**
(-se form)	**pudiese, pudieses, pudiese, pudiésemos, pudieseis, pudiesen**
Fut.Subjve.	**pudiere, pudieres, pudiere, pudiéremos, pudiereis, pudieren**

54. poner (to put; place; set)

Gerund & P.P.	poniendo, **puesto**
Pres.Ind.	**pongo,** pones, pone, ponemos, ponéis, ponen
Impve.	**pon,** poned
Fut.Ind.	**pondré, pondrás, pondrá, pondremos, pondréis, pondrán**
Conditional	**pondría, pondrías, pondría, pondríamos, pondríais, pondrían**
Preterit	**puse, pusiste, puso, pusimos, pusisteis, pusieron**
Pres.Subjve.	**ponga, pongas, ponga, pongamos, pongáis, pongan**
Impf.Subjve.	**pusiera, pusieras, pusiera, pusiéramos, pusierais,**
(-ra form)	**pusieran**
(-se form)	**pusiese, pusieses, pusiese, pusiésemos, pusieseis, pusiesen**

| Fut.Subjve. | pusiere, pusieres, pusiere, pusiéremos, pusiereis, pusieren |

55. querer (to want; love)

Pres.Ind.	quiero, quieres, quiere, queremos, queréis, quieren
Impve.	quiere, quered
Fut.Ind.	querré, querrás, querrá, querremos, querréis, querrán
Conditional	querría, querrías, querría, querríamos, querríais, querrían
Preterit	quise, quisiste, quiso, quisimos, quisisteis, quisieron
Pres.Subjve.	quiera, quieras, quiera, queramos, queráis, quieran
Impf.Subjve. (-ra form)	quisiera, quisieras, quisiera, quisiéramos, quisierais, quisieran
(-se form)	quisiese, quisieses, quisiese, quisiésemos, quisieseis, quisiesen
Fut.Subjve.	quisiere, quisieres, quisiere, quisiéremos, quisiereis, quisieren

56. raer (to abrade; wear away; fray)

Gerund & P.P.	rayendo, raído
Pres.Ind.	raigo [rayo], raes, rae, raemos, raéis, raen
Preterit	raí, raíste, rayó, raímos, raísteis, rayeron
Pres.Subjve.	raiga [raya], raigas, raiga, raigamos, raigáis, raigan
Impf.Subjve. (-ra form)	rayera, rayeras, rayera, rayéramos, rayerais, rayeran
(-se form)	rayese, rayeses, rayese, rayésemos, rayeseis, rayesen
Fut.Subjve.	rayere, rayeres, rayere, rayéremos, rayereis, rayeren

57. regir (to rule)

Gerund & P.P.	rigiendo, regido
Pres.Ind.	rijo, riges, rige, regimos, regís, rigen
Impve.	rige, regid
Preterit	regí, registe, rigió, regimos, registeis, rigieron
Pres.Subjve.	rija, rijas, rija, rijamos, rijáis, rijan
Impf.Subjve. (-ra form)	rigiera, rigieras, rigiera, rigiéramos, rigierais, rigieran
(-se form)	rigiese, rigieses, rigiese, rigiésemos, rigieseis, rigiesen
Fut.Subjve.	rigiere, rigieres, rigiere, rigiéremos, rigiereis, rigieren

58. reir (to laugh)

Gerund & P.P.	riendo, reído
Pres.Ind.	río, ríes, ríe, reímos, reís, ríen
Impve.	ríe, reíd
Preterit	reí, reíste, rió, reímos, reísteis, rieron
Pres.Subjve.	ría, rías, ría, riamos, riáis, rían
Impf.Subjve.	
(-ra form)	riera, rieras, riera, riéramos, rierais, rieran
(-se form)	riese, rieses, riese, riésemos, rieseis, riesen
Fut.Subjve.	riere, rieres, riere, riéremos, riereis, rieren

59. reñir (to fight; quarrel)
Gerund & P.P.   **riñendo,** reñido
Pres.Ind.   **riño, riñes, riñe,** reñimos, reñís, **riñen**
Impve.   **riñe,** reñid
Preterit   reñí, reñiste, **riñó,** reñimos, reñisteis, **riñeron**
Pres.Subjve.   **riña, riñas, riña, riñamos, riñáis, riñan**
Impf.Subjve.
(-ra form)   **riñera, riñeras, riñera, riñéramos, riñerais, riñeran**
(-se form)   **riñese, riñeses, riñese, riñésemos, riñeseis, riñesen**
Fut.Subjve.   **riñere, riñeres, riñere, riñéremos, riñereis, riñeren**

60. reunir (to unite; reunite)
Pres.Ind.   **reúno, reúnes, reúne,** reunimos, reunís, **reúnen**
Impve.   **reúne,** reunid
Pres.Subjve.   **reúna, reúnas, reúna,** reunamos, reunáis, **reúnan**

61. roer (to gnaw; corrode)
Gerund & P.P.   **royendo,** roído
Pres.Ind.   roo **[roigo, royo],** roes, roe, roemos, roéis, roen
Preterit   roí, roíste, **royó,** roímos, roísteis, **royeron**
Pres.Subjve.   roa **[roiga, roya],** roas, roa, roamos, roáis, roan
Impf.Subjve.   **royera, royeras, royera, royéramos, royerais,**
(-ra form)   **royeran**
(-se form)   **royese, royeses, royese, royésemos, royeseis, royesen**
Fut.Subjve.   **royere, royeres, royere, royéremos, royereis, royeren**

62. saber (to know)
Pres.Ind.   **sé,** sabes, sabe, sabemos, sabéis, saben
Fut. Ind.   **sabré, sabrás, sabrá, sabremos, sabréis, sabrán**
Conditional   **sabría, sabrías, sabría, sabríamos, sabríais, sabrían**
Preterit   **supe, supiste, supo, supimos, supisteis, supieron**
Pres.Subjve.   **sepa, sepas, sepa, sepamos, sepáis, sepan**
Impf.Subjve.   **supiera, supieras, supiera, supiéramos, supierais,**
(-ra form)   **supieran**
(-se form)   **supiese, supieses, supiese, supiésemos, supieseis,**
  supiesen
Fut.Subjve.   **supiere, supieres, supiere, supiéremos, supiereis,**
  supieren

63. salir (to go out; leave)
Pres.Ind.   **salgo,** sales, sale, salimos, salís, salen
Impve.   **sal,** salid
Fut.Ind.   **saldré, saldrás, saldrá, saldremos, saldréis, saldrán**
Conditional   **saldría, saldrías, saldría, saldríamos, saldríais,**
  saldrían
Pres.Subjve.   **salga, salgas, salga, salgamos, salgáis, salgan**

64. seguir (to follow)
Gerund & P.P.   **siguiendo,** seguido
Pres.Ind.   **sigo, sigues, sigue,** seguimos, seguís, **siguen**
Impve.   **sigue,** seguid
Preterit   seguí, seguiste, **siguió,** seguimos, seguisteis, **siguieron**
Pres.Subjve.   **siga, sigas, siga, sigamos, sigáis, sigan**

Impf.Subjve.	**siguiera, siguieras, siguiera, siguiéramos, siguierais,**
(-ra form)	**siguieran**
(-se form)	**siguiese, siguieses, siguiese, siguiésemos, siguieseis,**
	siguiesen
Fut.Subjve.	**siguiere, siguieres, siguiere, siguiéremos, siguiereis,**
	siguieren

65. tener (to have; hold)

Pres.Ind.	**tengo, tienes, tiene,** tenemos, tenéis, **tienen**
Impve.	**ten,** tened
Fut.Ind.	**tendré, tendrás, tendrá, tendremos, tendréis,**
	tendrán
Conditional	**tendría, tendrías, tendría, tendríamos, tendríais,**
	tendrían
Preterit	**tuve, tuviste, tuvo, tuvimos, tuvisteis, tuvieron**
Pres.Subjve.	**tenga, tengas, tenga, tengamos, tengáis, tengan**
Impf.Subjve.	**tuviera, tuvieras, tuviera, tuviéramos, tuvierais,**
(-ra form)	**tuvieran**
(-se form)	**tuviese, tuvieses, tuviese, tuviésemos, tuvieseis,**
	tuviesen
Fut.Subjve.	**tuviere, tuvieres, tuviere, tuviéremos, tuviereis,**
	tuvieren

66. torcer (to twist)

Pres.Ind.	**tuerzo, tuerces, tuerce,** torcemos, torcéis, **tuercen**
Impve.	**tuerce,** torced
Pres.Subjve.	**tuerza, tuerzas, tuerza, torzamos, torzáis, tuerzan**

67. traer (to bring)

Gerund & P.P.	**trayendo,** traído
Pres.Ind.	**traigo,** traes, trae, traemos, traéis, traen
Preterit	**traje, trajiste, trajo, trajimos, trajisteis, trajeron**
Pres.Subjve.	**traiga, traigas, traiga, traigamos, traigáis, traigan**
Impf.Subjve.	**trajera, trajeras, trajera, trajéramos, trajerais,**
(-ra form)	**trajeran**
(-se form)	**trajese, trajeses, trajese, trajésemos, trajeseis,**
	trajesen
Fut.Subjve.	**trajere, trajeres, trajere, trajéremos, trajereis,**
	trajeren

68. valer (to be worth)

Pres.Ind.	**valgo,** vales, vale, valemos, valéis, valen
Fut.Ind.	**valdré, valdrás, valdrá, valdremos, valdréis, valdrán**
Conditional	**valdría, valdrías, valdría, valdríamos, valdríais,**
	valdrían
Pres.Subjve.	**valga, valgas, valga, valgamos, valgáis, valgan**

69. venir (to come)

Gerund & P.P.	**viniendo,** venido
Pres.Ind.	**vengo, vienes, viene,** venimos, venís, **vienen**
Impve.	**ven,** venid
Fut.Ind.	**vendré, vendrás, vendrá, vendremos, vendréis,**
	vendrán

Conditional	**vendría, vendrías, vendría, vendríamos, vendríais, vendrían**
Preterit	**vine, viniste, vino, vinimos, vinisteis, vinieron**
Pres.Subjve.	**venga, vengas, venga, vengamos, vengáis, vengan**
Impf.Subjve.	**viniera, vinieras, viniera, viniéramos, vinierais,**
(-ra form)	**vinieran**
(-se form)	**viniese, vinieses, viniese, viniésemos, vinieseis, viniesen**
Fut.Subjve.	**viniere, vinieres, viniere, viniéremos, viniereis, vinieren**

70. ver (to see)

Gerund & P.P.	viendo, **visto**
Pres.Ind.	**veo,** ves, ve, vemos, veis, ven
Impf.Ind.	**veía, veías, veía, veíamos, veíais, veían**
Preterit	**vi,** viste, **vió,** vimos, visteis, vieron
Pres.Subjve.	**vea, veas, vea, veamos, veáis, vean**
Impf.Subjve.	
(-ra form)	**viera, vieras, viera, viéramos, vierais, vieran**
(-se form)	**viese, vieses, viese, viésemos, vieseis, viesen**
Fut.Subjve.	**viere, vieres, viere, viéremos, viereis, vieren**

71. verter (to pour; flow)

Pres.Ind.	**vierto, viertes, vierte,** vertemos, vertéis, **vierten**
Impve.	**vierte,** verted
Pres.Subjve.	**vierta, viertas, vierta,** vertamos, vertáis, **viertan**

72. yacer (to lie; rest)

Pres.Ind.	**yazco [yazgo, yago],** yaces, yace, yacemos, yacéis, yacen
Impve.	**yaz [yace],** yaced
Pres.Subjve.	**yazca [yazga, yaga], yazcas, yazca, yazcamos, yazcáis, yazcan**

SPANISH PREFIXES

	English Equivalents, If Any	Meanings and Uses	Examples
a-	a-	**1,** *Var. of* **ab-** *before* m, p, v **2,** *Var. of* **ad-** **3,** not; without	*aversión,* aversion *aspirar,* aspire *asimetría,* assymetry *amoral,* amoral
ab-	ab-	**1,** off; away; from **2,** origin	*absolver,* absolve; *abjurar,* abjure *aborígenes,* aborigines
abs-	abs-	*Var. of* **ab-** *before* c, t	*abstracto,* abstract; *abscisa,* abscissa
ac-	ac-	*Var. of* **ad-** *before* c *In some words,* *reduced to* **a-**	*acceder,* accede *aceptar,* accept
acro-	acro-	top; tip; edge	*acrópolis,* acropolis; *acrobacia,* acrobatics
ad-	ad-	*Denoting* direction toward; tendency; addition	*adherirse,* adhere
aero-; aeri-	aero-; aeri-	air	*aerodinámica,* aerodynamics; *aeriforme,* aeriform
al-	—	*In words of Arabic* *origin, representing* *the Arabic definite* *article*	*Alcorán,* (the) Koran
alo-	allo-	divergency; alternative	*alopatía,* allopathy
alto-; alti-	alto-; alti-	high; height	*alto-cúmulo,* alto- cumulus; *altímetro,* altimeter
ambi-	ambi-	**1,** both; on both sides **2,** around; about	*ambidiestro,* ambidextrous *ambiente,* ambient

	English Equivalents, If Any	Meanings and Uses	Examples
an-	an-	1, not; without; *var. of* **a-** *before a vowel*	*anarquía,* anarchy
		2, *Var. of* **ana-** *before a vowel*	*ánodo,* anode
ana-	ana-	1, up	*anatema,* anathema
		2, back; against	*anagrama,* anagram; *anacronismo,* anachronism
		3, again	*anabaptista,* Anabaptist
		4, thorough; thoroughly	*análisis,* analysis
		5, in accordance	*analogía,* analogy
andro-	andro-	1, man; male	*andrógino,* androgynous
		2, *bot.* stamen	*androceo,* androecium
anfi-	amphi-	1, around	*anfiteatro,* amphitheater
		2, at both sides or ends	*anfipróstilo,* amphiprostyle
		3, of both kinds	*anfibología,* amphibology; *anfibio,* amphibious
anglo-	Anglo-	English; England	*angloamericano,* Anglo-American *anglófobo,* Anglophobe
ante-	ante-	1, before; prior to	*antecedente,* antecedent
		2, in front of	*antecámara,* antechamber
anti-	anti-	1, against; opposed	*anticlerical,* anticlerical
		2, false; rival	*antipapa,* antipope
		3, located opposite; against	*antípoda,* antipode
		4, *med.* preventive; curative	*antitoxina,* antitoxin; *antídoto,* antidote
		Before vowels sometimes **ant-**	*antártico,* Antarctic

	English Equivalents, If Any	Meanings and Uses	Examples
anto-	antho-	flower	*antología*, anthology
antropo-	anthropo-	man	*antropología*, anthropology
apo-	apo-	off; from; away	*apogeo*, apogee; *apotema*, apothem
archi-; arqui-; arz-	arch-; archi-	first; chief	*archiduque*, archduke; *arquitecto*, architect; *arzobispo*, archbishop
arque-	arche-	*Var. of* **archi-**	*arquetipo*, archetype
arqueo-	archeo-	ancient	*arqueología*, archaeology
astro-	astro-	star	*astrología*, astrology
audio-; audi-	audio-; audi-	hearing	*audiómetro*, audiometer; *audífono*, audiphone
auto-; aut-	auto-; aut-	self	*autobiografía*, autobiography; *autarquía*, autarchy
avi-	avi-	bird	*avicultura*, aviculture
bati-	bathy-	deep	*batiscafo*, bathyscaphe
bato-	batho-	depth	*batómetro*, bathometer
bene-; ben-	bene-	good; well	*benéfico*, beneficial; *bendición*, benediction
bi-	bi-	1, two 2, doubly 3, every other 4, twice	*biáxico*, biaxial *bilingüe*, bilingual *bienal*, biennial *bisemanal*, twice weekly

	English Equivalents, If Any	Meanings and Uses	Examples
biblio-	biblio-	1, book	*bibliografía,* bibliography
		2, Bible	*bibliolatría,* bibliolatry
bin-	bin-	*Var. of* **bi-**	*binocular,* binocular
bio-	bio-	life	*bioquímica,* biochemistry
bis-	—	*Var. of* **bi-** *before a vowel*	*bisabuelo,* great-grandfather
biz-	—	*Var. of* **bis-**	*biznieto,* great-grandson; *bizcocho,* biscuit
braqui-	brachy-	short	*braquicéfalo,* brachycephalic
brevi-	brevi-	brief; short	*brevipenne,* brevipennate
cardio-; **cardi-**	cardio-; cardi-	heart	*cardiograma,* cardiogram *cardialgia,* cardialgia
cata-	cata-	*Forming nouns and adjectives denoting*	
		1, against	*catapulta,* catapult
		2, down; downward	*catabolismo,* catabolism
		3, completely; away	*cataclismo,* cataclysm
ceno-	ceno-	1, common	*cenobita,* cenobite
		2, new; recent	*cenozoico,* Cenozoic
cent-	cent-	*Var. of* **centi-** *before a vowel*	*centenario,* centennial
centi-	centi-	1, hundred	*centígrado,* centigrade
		2, hundredth	*centímetro,* centimeter
centro-; **centri-**	centro-; centri-	center; central	*centrosoma,* centrosome; *centrífugo,* centrifugal

	English Equivalents, If Any	Meanings and Uses	Examples
cerebro-	cerebro-	brain; mind	*cerebroespinal,* cerebrospinal
ciclo-	cyclo-	circle; circular	*ciclorama,* cyclorama
circum-; **circun-**	circum-	around	*circumpolar,* circumpolar; *circunnavegar,* circumnavigate
cito-	cyto-	cell	*citología,* cytology
co-	co-	*Var. of* **com-** **1,** association **2,** joint action **3,** *math.* complement of	*coautor,* coauthor *cooperación,* cooperation *coseno,* cosine
com-	com-	with; jointly; entirely *The form* **com-** *is used before* b *and* p *The form* **co-** *is used before vowels and before* h, l, m, r *(with doubling of* r*) and* y *The form* **con-** *is used before* c, d, f, g, j, ll, n, q, s, t, v	*combinar,* combine; *componer,* compose *coalición,* coalition; *cohabitar,* cohabit; *colateral,* collateral; *comarca,* province; *corresponder,* correspond; *coyuntura,* joint
contra-	contra-	against; opposite	*contravenir,* contravene
cosmo-	cosmo-	cosmos	*cosmografía,* cosmography
cripto-	crypto-	hidden	*criptograma,* cryptogram
crom-	chrom-	*Var. of* **cromo-** *before a vowel or* h	*cromidrosis,* chromidrosis
cromato-	chromato-	**1,** color **2,** chromatin	*cromatología,* chromatology *cromatólisis,* chromatolysis

	English Equivalents, If Any	Meanings and Uses	Examples
cromi-	chromi-	*Var. of* **cromo-**	*cromífero,* chromiferous
cromo-	chromo-	**1,** color	*cromolitografía,* chromolithography
		2, *chem.* chromium	*cromo-arseniato,* chromo-arsenate
crono-	chrono-	time	*cronología,* chronology
cuadri-; **cuadr-**	quadri-; quadr-	four	*cuadrinomio,* quadrinomial; *cuadrángulo,* quadrangle
cuasi-	quasi-	almost	*cuasicontrato,* quasicontract
de-	de-	**1,** down	*degradar,* degrade
		2, negation	*demérito,* demerit
		3, privation	*defoliación,* defoliation
		4, intensification	*demostrar,* demonstrate, prove
deca-	deca-	ten	*decámetro,* decameter
deci-	deci-	**1,** ten	*decimal,* decimal
		2, one-tenth	*decímetro,* decimeter
dermo-; **derm-**	dermo-; derm-	skin	*dermoblasto,* dermoblast *dermalgia,* dermalgia
dermato-; **dermat-**	dermato-; dermat-	skin	*dermatología,* dermatology *dermatemia,* dermathemia
des-	dis-; di-	**1,** negation	*desconfiar,* distrust
		2, opposition	*descrédito,* discredit
		3, apart; asunder; in different directions	*desunir,* disjoin; *desechar,* reject; *desplazar,* displace
dextro-	dextro-	right; turning to the right	*dextrógiro,* dextrogyrate

	English Equivalents, If Any	Meanings and Uses	Examples
di-	dis- — dis- di- di-	**1,** opposition **2,** origin **3,** diffusion; extension **4,** two; twofold; double **5,** *Var. of* **dia-** *before vowels*	*disentir,* dissent *dimanar,* to spring *disolución,* dissolution *dígrafo,* digraph; *dicloruro,* dichloride *dieléctrico,* dielectric
dia-	dia-	**1,** separation **2,** opposition **3,** through; across	*diacrítico,* diacritical *diamagnético,* diamagnetic *diagonal,* diagonal
dina-	dyna-	force; power	*dinatrón,* dynatron
dinamo-	dynamo-	power	*dinamómetro,* dynamometer
dis-	dis- dis- dis- dys-	**1,** negation **2,** opposition; reversal **3,** apart; asunder; in different directions **4,** *med.* difficulty; illness	*dispar,* dissimilar *discordancia,* discordancy *disparar,* discharge, shoot *dispepsia,* dyspepsia
duo-	duo-	two	*duodecimal,* duodecimal
e-	e-	*Var. of* **ex-**	*emerger,* emerge; *evasión,* evasion
ecto-	ecto-	outer; external	*ectodermo,* ectoderm
electro-; electri-	electro-; electri-	electricity	*electrocardiograma,* electrocardiogram; *electrificar,* electrify
em-	em-	*Var. of* **en-** *before* b, p	*embalsamar,* embalm; *empobrecer,* impoverish
en-	en-	**1,** in; into **2,** *Forming verbs from nouns and adjectives*	*encerrar,* enclose; *encierro,* enclosure *endiosar,* deify; *engordar,* fatten

	English Equivalents, If Any	Meanings and Uses	Examples
		3, in (*esp. in words of Greek origin*)	*endémico,* endemic
endo-	endo-	internal; within	*endocrino,* endocrine
ento-	ento-	inside; within	*entofita,* entophyte
entomo-	entomo-	insect	*entomología,* entomology
entre-	inter-	**1,** between; among **2,** *Limiting the force of verbs and adjectives*	*entrelazar,* interlace *entreabrir,* to half-open; *entrecano,* graying (of hair)
eo-	eo-	early; primitive	*eolítico,* eolithic
ep-	ep-	*Var. of* **epi-** *before vowels*	*epónimo,* eponym
epi-	epi-	on; upon; over; among	*epicentro,* epicenter; *epidemia,* epidemic
equi-	equi-	equal	*equivalente,* equivalent
esclero-	sclero-	hard	*esclerodermia,* scleroderma
esfero-	sphero-	sphere	*esferómetro,* spherometer
eso-	eso-	into; internal; hidden	*esotérico,* esoteric
espiro-	spiro-	**1,** breath; respiration **2,** spiral	*espirómetro,* spirometer *espiroqueta,* spirochete
esporo-	sporo-	spore	*esporocarpio,* sporocarp
esquizo-	schizo-	split; division; cleavage	*esquizofrenia,* schizophrenia
estato-	stato-	stable; stability	*estatocisto,* statocyst

	English Equivalents, If Any	Meanings and Uses	Examples
estereo-	stereo-	solid; three-dimensional	*estereofónico,* stereophonic
estomato-	stomato-	mouth	*estomatología,* stomatology
estrati-; estrato-	strati-; strato-	stratum; layer	*estratificación,* stratification; *estratosfera,* stratosphere
etno-	ethno-	people; race	*etnografía,* ethnography
eu-	eu-	well; good	*eufónico,* euphonic
ex-	ex-	1, beyond; forth 2, out; out of; off 3, former; formerly	*extender,* extend *expulsar,* expel *expresidente,* ex-president
exo-	exo-	outside; out; external	*exógeno,* exogenous
extra-	extra-	beyond; outside	*extralegal,* extralegal
extro-	extro-	*Var. of* **extra-**	*extrovertido,* extrovert
fago-	phago-	eating	*fagocito,* phagocyte
ferro-; ferri-	ferro-; ferri-	iron	*ferrocromo,* ferrochromium; *ferríferro,* ferriferous
fil-	phil-	*Var. of* **filo-** *before vowels*	*filantropía,* philanthropy
filo-	philo- phyll(o)-	1, liking; loving 2, leaf	*filología,* philology *filoxera,* phylloxera; *filoma,* phyllome
fisio-	physio-	nature; natural	*fisiología,* physiology
fito-	phyto-	plant; vegetable	*fitogénesis,* phytogenesis
flebo-	phlebo-	vein	*flebotomía,* phlebotomy

	English Equivalents, If Any	Meanings and Uses	Examples
flori-	flori-	flower	*floricultura,* floriculture
fono-	phono-	sound; voice	*fonógrafo,* phonograph
foto-	photo-	light; photography	*fotoeléctrico,* photoelectric
franco-	Franco-	French	*francoamericano,* Franco-American
galo-	Gallo-	French; Gallic	*galófilo,* Gallophile
galvano-	galvano-	electricity	*galvanómetro,* galvanometer
gamo-	gamo-	joined; united	*gamopétalo,* gamopetalous
gastro-	gastro-	stomach	*gastrónomo,* gastronome
gene-	gene-	ancestry; generation	*genealogía,* genealogy
geno-	geno-	people; race	*genocidio,* genocide
geo-	geo-	earth	*geocéntrico,* geocentric
gine-; gin-	gyne-; gyn	woman; female	*gineolatría,* gyneolatry; *ginandro,* gynandrous
gineco-	gyneco-	woman	*ginecología,* gynecology
gino-	gyno-	*Var. of* **gine-**	*ginóforo,* gynophore
giro-	gyro-	ring; circle; spiral	*giróscopo,* gyroscope
gono-	gono-	related or pertaining to sex or the organs of reproduction	*gonorrea,* gonorrhea
grafo-	grapho-	writing; drawing	*grafología,* graphology

	English Equivalents, If Any	Meanings and Uses	Examples
greco-	Greco-	Greek	*grecorromano,* Greco-Roman
halo-	halo-	salt	*halógeno,* halogen
hecto-	hecto-	hundred	*hectogramo,* hectogram
helico-	helico-	spiral; helix	*helicóptero,* helicopter
helio-	helio-	sun	*heliógrafo,* heliograph
hema-; hemo-	hema-; hemo-	blood	*hemacroma,* hemachrome; *hemorragia,* hemorrhage
hemato-; hemat-	hemato-; hemat-	blood	*hematólisis,* hematolysis; *hematémesis,* hematemesis
hemi-	hemi-	half	*hemiciclo,* hemicycle
hepta-	hepta-	seven	*heptágono,* heptagon
hetero-	hetero-	other; different	*heterosexual,* heterosexual
hexa-	hexa-	six	*hexágono,* hexagon
hidro-	hydro-	**1,** water	*hidroeléctrico,* hydroelectric
		2, *chem.* hydrogen	*hidrocarbono,* hydrocarbon
hiper-	hyper-	over; above; beyond	*hipersensitivo,* hypersensitive
hipo-	hippo-	**1,** horse	*hipódromo,* hippodrome
	hypo-	**2,** beneath; below; under	*hipodérmico,* hypodermic; *hipotaxis,* hypotaxis; *hipoplasia,* hypoplasia
	hypo-	**3,** *chem.* least degree of oxidation	*hiposulfuro,* hyposulfite

	English Equivalents, If Any	Meanings and Uses	Examples
histero-	hystero-	1, womb; uterus	*histerotomía,* hysterotomy
		2, hysteria	*histerógeno,* hysterogenic
histo-	histo-	tissue	*histología,* histology
holo-	holo-	entire; whole	*holocausto,* holocaust
homeo-	homeo-	similar; like	*homeopatía,* homeopathy
homo-	homo-	same	*homogéneo,* homogeneous
i-	il-	*Var. of* in- *before* l	*ilegal,* illegal
ictio-	ichthyo-	fish	*ictiosauro,* ichthyosaur
ideo-	ideo-	idea	*ideología,* ideology
idio-	idio-	peculiar; personal	*idiosincrasia,* idiosyncrasy
im-	im-	*Var. of* in- *before* b *and* p	*imberbe,* beardless; *imposible,* impossible
in-	in-	1, not; without	*incauto,* incautious; *inarticulado,* inarticulate
		2, in; into; within; toward	*innato,* inborn; *interior,* inland
		3, *Forming verbs denoting* existence, motion or direction inward	*incluir,* inclose; *inducir,* induce
		4, *Sometimes used as a mere intensive*	*inculpar,* to blame
infra-	infra-	below; under	*infrarrojo,* infrared
inter-	inter-	between; during	*internacional,* international; *interregno,* interregnum

	English Equivalents, If Any	Meanings and Uses	Examples
intra-	intra-	within	*intravenoso,* intravenous
intro-	intro-	within; into; inward	*introducir,* introduce; *introvertido,* introvert
ir-	ir-	*Var. of* **in-** *before* r	*irradiar,* irradiate; *irracional,* irrational
iso-	iso-	equal	*isoterma,* isotherm
kilo-	kilo-	thousand	*kilogramo,* kilogram
lacto-; lacti-	lacto-; lacti-	milk	*lactómetro,* lactometer; *lactífero,* lactiferous
levo-	levo-	left	*levógiro,* levogyrate
lito-	litho-	stone	*litografía,* lithography
loco-	loco-	place	*locomoción,* locomotion
logo-	logo-	word; speech	*logotipo,* logotype
luni-	luni-	moon	*lunisolar,* lunisolar
macro-	macro-	long; large; great	*macroscópico,* macroscopic
magni-	magni-	large; great	*magnífico,* magnificent
mal-	mal-; mis-; ill-	bad; badly	*maltratar,* maltreat, mistreat; *malajustado,* maladjusted; *malgastar,* misspend; *malintencionado,* ill-intentioned
male-	male-	*Var. of* **mal-**	*maledicencia,* malediction
mani-; manu-	mani-; manu-	hand	*manicura,* manicure; *manufactura,* manufacture

	English Equivalents, If Any	Meanings and Uses	Examples
matri-	matri-	mother	*matriarcado,* matriarchy
medio-; medi-	mid-; medi-	middle	*mediocentro,* midcenter; *medieval,* also *medioeval,* medieval
mega-	mega-	1, large; great 2, million; millionfold	*megalito,* megalith *megaciclo,* megacycle
megalo-	megalo-	very large	*megalocéfalo,* megalocephalic
melano-	melano-	black	*melanosis,* melanosis
melo-	melo-	song; music	*melómano,* melomaniac
meso-	meso-	middle	*mesocarpio,* mesocarp
meta-	meta-	1, along with; after; over; in or of the middle 2, change; transformation	*metacentro,* metacenter; *metafísica,* metaphysics *metátesis,* metathesis
metro-	metro-	1, measure 2, womb; uterus 3, mother	*metrología,* metrology *metrorragia,* metrorrhagia *metrópolis,* metropolis
mico-	myco-	fungus	*micología,* mycology
mile-	mille-	thousand	*milépora,* millepore
mili-	milli-	thousandth part	*milímetro,* millimeter
mio-	myo-	muscle	*miocardio,* myocardium
miria-	myria-	1, many 2, ten thousand	*miriápodo,* myriapod *miriámetro,* myriameter

	English Equivalents, If Any	Meanings and Uses	Examples
miso-	miso-	hatred; dislike	*misoginia,* misogyny
mono-	mono-	one; alone; single	*monoteísta,* monotheist
morfo-	morpho-	form	*morfología,* morphology
muco-	muco-	mucous membrane; mucus	*mucoproteína,* mucoprotein
multi-	multi-	many	*multimillonario,* multimillionaire
naso-	naso-	nose	*nasofrontal,* nasofrontal
necro-	necro-	dead; death	*necrología,* necrology
nefro-; nefr-	nephro-; nephr-	kidney	*nefrotomía,* nephrotomy; *nefritis,* nephritis
nemato-	nemato-	thread; threadlike	*nematocisto,* nematocyst
neo-	neo-	new; recent	*neoclásico,* neoclassical
neumato-	pneumato-	1, air; vapor 2, breathing	*neumatólisis,* pneumatolysis *neumatómetro,* pneumatometer
neumo-	pneumo-	lung	*neumoconiosis,* pneumoconiosis
neumono-	pneumono-	lung	*neumonóforo,* pneumonophore
neuro-; neur-	neuro-; neur-	nerve	*neurología,* neurology; *neuralgia,* neuralgia
nitro-	nitro-	nitrogen; compound of nitrogen	*nitrobencina,* nitrobenzene; *nitrocelulosa,* nitrocellulose

	English Equivalents, If Any	Meanings and Uses	Examples
nocti-; **noct-**	nocti-; noct-	night	*noctíluco,* noctiluca *noctambulismo,* noctambulism
o-	o-; ob-	*Var. of* **ob-** *before* f, m, p	*ofuscar,* obfuscate; *omitir,* omit; *oponer,* oppose
ob-	ob-	1, toward; facing 2, against 3, upon; over 4, inversely	*oblicuo,* oblique *objetar,* object *observar,* observe *obovoide,* obovoid
octa-	octa-	*Var. of* **octo-**	*octágono,* octagon
octo-; oct-	octo-; oct-	eight	*octogenario,* octogenarian; *octeto,* octet
oculo-	oculo-	eye	*oculomotor,* oculomotor
oleo-	oleo-	oil	*oleomargarina,* oleomargarine
oligo-; **olig-**	oligo-; olig-	few; scanty	*oligopolio,* oligopoly; *oligarquía,* oligarchy
omni-	omni-	all	*omnipotente,* omnipotent
onoma-	onoma-	name	*onomatopeya,* onomatopoeia
oo-	oo-	egg	*oogénesis,* oogenesis
ornito-	ornitho-	bird	*ornitología,* ornithology
orto-	ortho-	upright; straight; correct	*ortostático,* orthostatic; *ortodoxo,* orthodox
osteo-	osteo-	bone	*osteología,* osteology
oto-; ot-	oto-; ot-	ear	*otología,* otology; *otalgia,* otalgia

	English Equivalents, If Any	Meanings and Uses	Examples
ovi-	ovi-	egg	*oviforme*, oviform
oxi-	oxy-	1, oxygen 2, acute; sharp	*oxisulfuro*, oxysulfide *oxicefálico*, oxycephalic
paleo-	paleo-	ancient; primitive	*paleología*, paleology
pan-	pan-	all; every; universal	*panamericano*, Pan-American; *pandemia*, pandemic
panto-	panto-	*Var. of* **pan-**	*pantógrafo*, pantograph
para-	para-	1, near; beside; beyond 2, *pathol.* abnormal 3, guard; protection	*paramilitar*, paramilitary; *paráfrasis*, paraphrase *paranoia*, paranoia *paracaídas*, parachute; *parabrisas*, windshield
pari-	pari-	equal	*paripinado*, paripinnate
pati-	—	leg; having a (specified) kind or defect of legs	*patizambo*, knockkneed; *patilargo*, longlegged
pato-	patho-	disease	*patología*, pathology
patri-	patri-	father	*patriarcado*, patriarchate
pedi-	pedi-	1, foot 2, child	*pedicura*, pedicure; *pediforme*, pediform *pediatría*, pediatrics
pedo-	pedo-	child	*pedodoncia*, pedodontia
peni-	penni-	feather	*peniforme*, penniform
penta-	penta-	five	*pentágono*, pentagon

	English Equivalents, If Any	Meanings and Uses	Examples
per-	per-	**1,** through	*perenne,* perennial
		2, thoroughly; very; completely	*persuadir,* persuade
		3, *chem.* maximum or high valence	*peróxido,* peroxide
peri-	peri-	around; about	*periferia,* periphery
petro-; petri-	petro-; petri-	stone; rock	*petrografía,* petrography; *petrificar,* petrify
piro-	pyro-	fire	*pirómetro,* pyrometer
pisci-	pisci-	fish	*piscicultura,* pisciculture
plasmo-	plasmo-	plasma; form; mold	*plasmólisis,* plasmolysis
plati-	platy-	broad	*platirrino,* platyrrhine
plexi-	plexi-	twining; interwoven	*plexiforme,* plexiform
pluri-	pluri-	many; several	*pluricelular,* pluricellular
podo-; pod-	pedo-; pod-	foot	*podómetro,* pedometer; *podiatra,* podiatrist
poli-	poly-	many	*poligamia,* polygamy
porta-	—	*Forming nouns denoting* carrying; holding	*portaaviones,* aircraft carrier; *portaplumas,* penholder
pos-; post-	post-	after; behind	*posponer,* postpone; *postguerra,* postwar
pre-	pre-	before *(in time, place, or rank)*	*precedencia,* precedence; *predecesor,* predecessor; *preeminente,* preeminent
preter-	preter-	beyond; more than	*preternatural,* preternatural

	English Equivalents, If Any	Meanings and Uses	Examples
pro-	pro-	1, in favor of	*profrancés,* pro-French
		2, on behalf of; in place of	*procónsul,* proconsul
		3, forward	*proseguir,* proceed
		4, outward	*proyectar,* project
		5, before *(in time or place)*	*prólogo,* prologue; *proscenio,* proscenium
proto-	proto-	1, first	*protomártir,* protomartyr
		2, *chem.* having a lower proportion than that of the other members in a series of compounds	*protocloruro,* protochloride
pseudo-; seudo-	pseudo-	false; deceptive	*pseudomorfo, seudomorfo,* pseudomorph
psico-; sico-	psycho-	mind; mental process	*psicología, sicología,* psychology
ptero-	ptero-	wing	*pterodáctilo,* pterodactyl
quilo-	kilo-	*Var. of* **kilo-**	*quilogramo,* kilogram
quinque-	quinque-	five	*quinquenal,* quinquennial
quiro-	chiro-	hand	*quiromancia,* chiromancy
radio-	radio-	1, radio	*radiotelegrafía,* radiotelegraphy
		2, radium; radioactive	*radioterapia,* radiotherapy
·re-	re-	1, back; reverse action	*reacción,* reaction
		2, again; anew	*reelegir,* reelect
		3, resistance; opposition	*rechazar,* reject
		4, emphasis; intensification	*refuerzo,* reinforcement

	English Equivalents, If Any	Meanings and Uses	Examples
recti-; rect-	recti-; rect-	straight	*rectilíneo*, rectilinear *rectángulo*, rectangle
reo-	rheo-	flow; current	*reómetro*, rheometer
requete-; rete-	—	*Used to intensify meaning of various parts of speech*	*requetebién*, very well, marvelous(ly); *reteviejo*, very old, doddering
retro-	retro-	1, back; backwards *(in space or time)* 2, anterior; prior	*retrospección*, retrospection; *retrogresión*, retrogression *retroactivo*, retroactive
rino-	rhino-	nose	*rinoplastia*, rhinoplasty
rizo-	rhizo-	root	*rizópodo*, rhizopod
sangui-	sangui-	blood	*sanguífero*, sanguiferous
sarco-	sarco-	flesh	*sarcófago*, sarcophagus
sauro-	sauro-	lizard	*saurópodo*, sauropod
semi-	semi-	1, half 2, partly	*semicírculo*, semicircle *semidormido*, half-asleep
sept-	sept-	*Var. of* **septi-**, seven	*septeto*, septet
septi-	septi-	1, seven 2, decomposition; rot 3, septum; partition	*septilateral*, septilateral *septicemia*, septicemia *septífraga*, septifragal
sero-	sero-	serum	*serología*, serology
sesqui-	sesqui-	one and a half	*sesquicentenario*, sesquicentennial

	English Equivalents, If Any	Meanings and Uses	Examples
seudo-	pseudo-	*Var. of* **pseudo-**	*seudónimo,* pseudonym
sex-	sex-	six	*sexenio,* sexennial
sico-	psycho-	*Var. of* **psico-**	*sicología,* psychology
sim-	sym-	*Var. of* **sin-** *before* b, p	*simbiosis,* symbiosis; *simposio,* symposium
sin-	syn-	**1,** with; together with	*sincrónico,* synchronic
	—	**2,** without	*sinrazón,* unreason, injustice
sinistro-	sinistro-	left	*sinistrorso,* sinistrorse
sino-	Sino-	Chinese; China	*sinología,* Sinology
sismo-	seismo-	earthquake; temblor	*sismómetro,* seismometer
so-	—	**1,** below; under **2,** expressing partial or incomplete performance of an action	*socavar,* undermine *soasar,* roast lightly
sobre-	over-; super-; sur-	over; beyond; extra	*sobrealimentación,* overfeeding; *sobreabundante,* superabundant; *sobrecarga,* surcharge; *sobrepasar,* surpass
soli-	soli-	single; alone	*soliloquio,* soliloquy
somato-	somato-	body	*somatología,* somatology
su-	sup-	*Var. of* **sub-** *before* p	*suponer,* suppose
sub-	sub-	**1,** under; below; beneath **2,** lesser in degree **3,** inferior; lower in rank or position **4,** forming a division; formed by division	*subsuelo,* subsoil *subtropical,* subtropical *subordinado,* subordinate *subgrupo,* subgroup; *subarrendar,* sublease

	English Equivalents, If Any	Meanings and Uses	Examples
subter-	subter-	below	*subterfugio,* subterfuge
super-	super-	over; above; beyond; superior	*supereminencia,* supereminence; *superhombre,* superman; *supervisar,* supervise; *supersónico,* supersonic
supra-	supra-	over; above	*suprarrenal,* suprarenal
sus-	sus-	*Var. of* **sub-** *before* c	*susceptible,* susceptible
taxi-; taxo-	taxi-; taxo-	arrangement; order	*taxidermia,* taxidermy; *taxonomía,* taxonomy
tele-	tele-	far off; distant	*telescopio,* telescope
teo-	theo-	god; divine	*teología,* theology
termo-	thermo-	heat	*termonuclear,* thermonuclear
tetra-	tetra-	four	*tetraedro,* tetrahedron
tipo-	typo-	type	*tipografía,* typography
topo-	topo-	place	*toponimia,* toponymy
toxico-	toxico-	toxic; poison	*toxicógeno,* toxicogenic
toxo-; tox-	toxo-; tox-	poison	*toxoplasmosis,* toxoplasmosis; *toxemia,* toxemia
tra-	trans-	*Var. of* **trans-**	*traducir,* translate; *tramitar,* arrange, expedite

	English Equivalents, If Any	Meanings and Uses	Examples
trans-	trans-	**1,** across; over; beyond	*transatlántico,* transatlantic
		2, through	*translúcido,* translucent
		3, change	*transformar,* transform
		Also, usually less correctly, **tras-**	*trasformador,* transformer
traqueo-; traque-	tracheo-; trache-	trachea	*traqueotomía,* tracheotomy; *traqueítis,* tracheitis
tras-	trans-	*Var. of* **trans-**	*trasladar,* transfer
tri-	tri-	**1,** three	*triciclo,* tricycle
		2, three times	*triplicar,* triplicate
		3, every third	*trienio,* triennial
trofo-	tropho-	nutrition	*trofoplasma,* trophoplasm
tropo-	tropo-	change; transformation	*troposfera,* troposphere
ultra-	ultra-	**1,** on the other side of; beyond	*ultravioleta,* ultraviolet; *ultramar,* land beyond the sea
		2, extreme; excessive	*ultranacionalismo,* ultranationalism
uni-	uni-	one; as one; single	*unísono,* unison; *unicornio,* unicorn
uro-	uro-	urine; urinary tract	*uroscopia,* uroscopy; *urología,* urology
vaso-	vaso-	vessel	*vasomotor,* vasomotor
vermi-	vermi-	worm	*vermicida,* vermicide
vice-	vice-	**1,** substitute	*vicepresidente,* vice-president
		2, subordinate	*vicecónsul,* vice-consul
viz-; vi-	vis-; —	*Var. of* **vice-**	*vizconde,* viscount *virrey,* viceroy

	English Equivalents, If Any	Meanings and Uses	Examples
xanto-	xantho-	yellow	*xantofilia,* xanthophilia
xeno-	xeno-	strange; foreign	*xenofobia,* xenophobia
xero-	xero-	dry	*xeroftalmia,* xerophthalmia
xilo-	xylo-	wood	*xilófono,* xylophone
yuxta-	juxta-	near; together; close	*yuxtaposición,* juxtaposition
zoo-	zoö-	animal	*zoología,* zoölogy

SPANISH SUFFIXES

	English Equivalents, If Any	Meanings and Uses	Examples
-able	-able	*Forming adjectives expressing* ability; capability	*favorable,* favorable
-áceas		*fem. pl. form of* **-áceo.** *See* **-áceo**	
-áceo	-aceous	*Forming adjectives and nouns expressing* quality; relationship	*cetáceo,* cetaceous
-áceos; fem. **-áceas**	-acea; -aceae	*bot.; zool., plural forms naming families, orders, and classes*	*crustáceos,* crustacea; *gramináceas,* graminaceae
-acia	-acy	*Forming nouns expressing* quality; condition	*aristocracia,* aristocracy
-acidad	-acity	*Forming nouns denoting* quality; tendency	*pugnacidad,* pugnacity
-ación	-ation	*Forming verbal nouns expressing* action; result of action	*abdicación,* abdication
-aco	-ac	*Forming adjectives expressing* 1, characteristic of 2, relating to; of 3, affected by; possessed by 4, nationality 5, derog. sense, in some nouns	*elegíaco,* elegiac *cardíaco,* cardiac *maníaco,* maniac *austríaco,* Austrian *libraco,* poor or cheap book
-acho	—	*Forming nouns and adjectives with* derog. sense	*hombracho,* husky big fellow; *ricacho,* vulgar rich person

	English Equivalents, If Any	Meanings and Uses	Examples
-ada		*Forming nouns expressing*	
	-ade	**1,** action; result of action	*emboscada,* ambuscade
	-ade	**2,** group; ensemble; structure	*empalizada,* palisade
	-ade	**3,** names of some drinks	*limonada,* lemonade
	-ade	**4,** period of time	*década,* decade
	—	**5,** amount held or contained	*brazada,* armful; *cucharada,* spoonful
-adero	—	*Var. of* **-dero**	*invernadero,* greenhouse; *pagadero,* payable
-adizo	—	*Var. of* **-izo**	*voladizo,* projecting
-ado	—	*Forming adjectives and nouns*	
		1, equivalent to a past participle	*aislado,* isolated
		2, likeness; shape	*almendrado,* almond-shaped
		3, office; dignity	*profesorado,* professorship
		4, place	*consulado,* consulate
		5, period of time	*reinado,* reign
-ador	—	*Var. of* **-dor**	*creador,* creator; *encantador,* enchanter
-adura	—	*Forming verbal nouns expressing* action; result of action; means	*quemadura,* burn; *añadidura,* addition; *desembocadura,* opening; outlet
-aje	-age; -ing	*Forming nouns expressing*	
		1, action	*pillaje,* pillage
		2, action and result	*embalaje,* wrapping, packing
		3, place	*hospedaje,* boarding house
		4, fee charged for a service	*almacenaje,* storage
		5, group; ensemble	*follaje,* foliage
		6, state; condition	*aprendizaje,* apprenticeship

	English Equivalents, If Any	Meanings and Uses	Examples
-ajo	—	*Forming nouns, usu. with derog. meaning*	*lagunajo,* puddle; *espantajo,* scarecrow
-al	-al	**1,** *Forming adjectives expressing* relation; connection	*arbitral,* arbitral; *esferoidal,* spheroidal
	——	**2,** *Forming nouns expressing place where something abounds*	*cerezal,* cherry orchard; *peñascal,* rocky ground
-alla	—	*Forming collective nouns*	*vitualla,* victuals; *canalla,* rabble
-amen	—	*Forming collective nouns*	*certamen,* contest; *velamen,* rigging
-án	—	*Forming nouns and adjectives [fem.* **-ana**] *expressing* characteristic; relation	*holgazán,* lazy; *patán,* peasant
-ancia	-ance; -ancy	*Forming nouns from adjectives ending in* **-ante**	*vigilancia,* vigilance
-andro	-androus	male	*monandro,* monandrous
-áneo	-an; -aneous	*Forming adjectives expressing* relation; connection	*mediterráneo,* Mediterranean; *instantáneo,* instantaneous
-ano	-an	**1,** *Forming adjectives and nouns expressing* relation; connection	*americano,* American
	-ane	**2,** *chem. denoting* saturated hydrocarbons	*metano,* methane

	English Equivalents, If Any	Meanings and Uses	Examples
-ante	-ant; -ing	1, *Forming adjectives equivalent to participles*	*desafiante,* defiant
		2, *Forming nouns denoting* activity; occupation	*ayudante,* adjutant
-anto	-anthous	flower	*monanto,* monanthous
-anza	-ance; -ancy	*Var. of* **-ancia**	*templanza,* temperance
-ar	—	1, *Forming verbs*	*pasear,* walk, ride
		2, *Forming adjectives and nouns indicating* manner; relation; connection	*regular,* regular; *tejar,* tile works; *yesar,* gypsum quarry
-arca	-arch	ruler; chief	*monarca,* monarch; *tetrarca,* tetrarch
-ardo	-ard	*Forming nouns and adjectives, usu. with derog. meaning*	*bastardo,* bastard
-aria	—	*Forming feminine nouns expressing* relation; connection	*funeraria,* funeral home
-ario	-ary; -arian; -arious; -arium	*Forming adjectives and nouns expressing* relation; connection	*voluntario,* voluntary; *autoritario,* authoritarian; *temerario,* temerarious; *acuario,* aquarium
-arquía	-archy	rule; dignity	*jerarquía,* hierarchy
-asa	-ase	*Forming nouns denoting* enzymes	*diastasa,* diastase
-asis	-asis	*Forming nouns denoting* disease	*elefantíasis,* elephantiasis
-asmo	-asm	*Forming nouns denoting* action; tendency; quality	*orgasmo,* orgasm; *entusiasmo,* enthusiasm; *pleonasmo,* pleonasm

	English Equivalents, If Any	Meanings and Uses	Examples
-asta	-ast	*Forming nouns of agency corresponding to nouns ending in* **-asmo**	*entusiasta,* enthusiast
-astro; -astra; -astre	-aster	*Forming nouns with dim. or derog. meaning*	*poetastro,* poetaster *hijastro,* stepson; *madrastra,* stepmother; *pillastre,* scoundrel
-atario	-atory; -atary	*Forming adjectives and nouns expressing agency; relation; connection*	*arrendatario,* renter; *mandatario,* mandatory; *signatario,* signatory
-ate	—	*Forming nouns expressing* 1, action; result 2, quality; condition	*disparate,* blunder *botarate,* madcap
-ático	-atic	*Forming adjectives expressing connection; relation*	*fanático,* fanatic; *acuático,* aquatic
-ativo	-ative	*Forming adjectives expressing* 1, tendency; disposition 2, relation; connection	*formativo,* formative *demostrativo,* demonstrative
-ato	-ate; -ship	1, *Forming nouns expressing* office; dignity 2, *Forming nouns denoting* the young of animals	*cardenalato,* cardinalate; *generalato,* generalship *ballenato,* young whale
-atorio	-atory	1, *Forming adjectives denoting* relation; connection 2, *Forming nouns denoting* place	*declaratorio,* declaratory *lavatorio,* lavatory
-avo	-th	*Forming ordinal numerals*	*dozavo,* twelfth

	English Equivalents, If Any	Meanings and Uses	Examples
-az	-acious	*Forming adjectives denoting* tendency; disposition	*locuaz,* loquacious
-azgo	-ty; -ship	*Forming nouns expressing*	
		1, office, dignity	*almirantazgo,* admiralship
		2, function	*padrinazgo,* godfathership, sponsorship
		3, state; condition	*noviazgo,* courtship
		4, action; result	*hallazgo,* discovery
-azo	—	1, *Forming augmentative nouns and adjectives, often derog.*	*animalazo,* big beast
		2, *Forming nouns denoting* blow; stroke	*latigazo,* stroke with a whip
-azón	—	*Forming nouns of augmentative and derog. meaning*	*ligazón,* ligament; *cargazón,* burden; heaviness
-biosis	-biosis	way of life	*simbiosis,* symbiosis
-ble	-ble	*Var. of* **-able** *or* **-ible**	*soluble,* soluble
-bundo	-bund	*Forming adjectives expressing* tendency; beginning of an action	*vagabundo,* wandering; *moribundo,* moribund
-ceno	-cene	recent; new	*mioceno,* Miocene
-cia	-cy	*Forming nouns denoting*	
		1, qualities; abstract entities	*conveniencia,* expediency; *democracia,* democracy
		2, arts; professions	*nigromancia,* necromancy

	English Equivalents, If Any	Meanings and Uses	Examples
-cico; -cica	—	*Var. of* **-ico**; *forming diminutives, often expressing endearment*	*corazoncico,* little heart, dear heart; *mujercica,* little woman, dear girl
-cida	-cide	**1,** *Forming nouns denoting* killer; substance that kills	*homicida,* killer; *insecticida,* insecticide
	-cidal	**2,** *Forming adjectives denoting* relation to killing	*homicida,* homicidal
-cidio	-cide	*Forming nouns denoting* act of killing	*homicidio,* homicide
-cillo; -cilla	—	*Var. of* **-illo** *forming diminutives*	*dolorcillo,* slight pain; *piedrecilla,* little stone
-ción	-tion	*Forming verbal nouns expressing* action; result of action	*concepción,* conception
-cioso	-tious	*Forming adjectives corresponding to nouns ending in* **-ción** *or* **-cia**	*tendencioso,* tendentious; *sedicioso,* seditious
-cito; -cita	—	**1,** *Var. of* **-ito,** *forming diminutives*	*cochecito,* small coach; *jovencita,* young girl
	-cyte	**2,** cell	*trombocito,* thrombocyte
-cracia	-cracy	*Forming nouns denoting* **1,** rule	*autocracia,* autocracy
		2, ruling class	*aristocracia,* aristocracy
		3, form of government	*democracia,* democracy
-crata	-crat	*Forming nouns denoting* persons, *corresponding to nouns ending in* **-cracia**	*autócrata,* autocrat; *aristócrata,* aristocrat; *demócrata,* democrat

	English Equivalents, If Any	Meanings and Uses	Examples
-crático	-cratic	*Forming adjectives from nouns ending in* **-crata** *or* **-cracia**	*autocrático,* autocratic; *aristocrático,* aristocratic; *democrático,* democratic
-cromo	-chrome	1, color	*polícromo,* polychrome
		2, *chem.* chromium	*mercuro-cromo,* mercurochrome
-culo; -cula	-cule	*Forming diminutives of nouns and adjectives*	*minúsculo,* minuscule; *molécula,* molecule
-dad	-ty; -ness	*Forming abstract and collective nouns*	*vecindad,* vicinity, neighborhood; *maldad,* wickedness
-dermo	-derm	skin	*paquidermo,* pachyderm
-dero; -dera	—	1, *Forming nouns (usu. masc.) denoting* place	*abrevadero,* watering place
		2, *Forming nouns (usu. fem.) denoting* instrument	*regadera,* watering pot
		3, *Forming adjectives expressing* ability; capability	*pagadero,* payable; *hacedero,* feasible
-dino	-dyne	power	*superheterodino,* superheterodyne
-dizo	—	*Var. of* **-izo**	*olvidadizo,* forgetful
-dor	-tor	1, *Forming nouns [fem.* **-dora**] *denoting* agent; instrument	*vendedor,* salesman; *vendedora,* saleswoman; *batidor,* beater
		2, *Forming adjectives expressing* tendency	*encantador,* enchanting

	English Equivalents, If Any	Meanings and Uses	Examples
-dura	—	*Forming nouns denoting* 1, action; result	*bordadura,* embroidery
		2, collectivity	*brochadura,* set of hooks and eyes
-ear	—	*Forming verbs from nouns or adjectives*	*telefonear,* telephone; *blanquear,* whiten
-ecer	-esce	*Forming verbs of inceptive or inchoative sense*	*convalecer,* convalesce
-ectomía	-ectomy	excision; surgical removal	*apendectomía,* appendectomy
-edad	—	*Var. of* **-dad** *in trisyllabic nouns*	*variedad,* variety; *suciedad,* dirt, filth
-edal	—	*Forming nouns expressing place where something abounds*	*bojedal,* growth of boxwood
-edero	—	*Var. of* **-dero** *[fem.* **-edera**]	*comedero,* feeding trough; *raedera,* scraper; *valedero,* valid
-edizo	—	*Var. of* **-izo** *[fem.* **-ediza**]	*acogedizo,* easy to gather; *advenedizo,* strange
-edo	—	*Forming collective nouns [fem.* **-eda**]	*robledo,* oak grove; *alameda,* poplar grove
-edor	—	*Var. of* **-dor** *[fem.* **-edora**]	*vendedor,* seller; *vendedora,* saleswoman; *tenedor,* holder, fork; *bebedor,* given to drink
-édrico	-hedral	*Forming adjectives corresponding to nouns ending in* **-edro**	*poliédrico,* polyhedral

	English Equivalents, If Any	Meanings and Uses	Examples
-edro	-hedron	*Forming nouns denoting geometrical solid figures having a specified number of faces*	*poliedro,* polyhedron
-ejo	—	*Forming nouns and adjectives, usu. with derog. meaning*	*caballejo,* nag; *medianejo,* fair to middling
-emia	-emia	*Forming nouns denoting* condition or disease of the blood	*anemia,* anemia
-ena	—	**1,** *Forming fem. collective numeral nouns* **2,** *fem. of* **-eno**	*docena,* dozen; *cuarentena,* quantity of forty
-encia	-ence; -ency	*Forming nouns corresponding to adjectives ending in* **-ente** *or* **-ento**	*urgencia,* urgency; *violencia,* violence
-eno	—	**1,** *Forming ordinal numerals* **2,** *Forming adjectives denoting* quality; relation; tendency	*noveno,* ninth *terreno,* terrestrial; *moreno,* dark brown
	-ene	**3,** *Forming names of certain hydrocarbons*	*etileno,* ethylene
-ente	-ent	**1,** *Forming adjectives equivalent to the present participle* Some are used as nouns **2,** *Forming nouns denoting* agent; actor	*diferente,* different *gerente,* manager *regente,* regent
-ento	-ent	*Forming adjectives denoting* manner; tendency	*violento,* violent, *amarillento,* yellowish

	English Equivalents, If Any	Meanings and Uses	Examples
-eo	—	1, *Forming adjectives denoting* quality; condition	*arbóreo,* arboreal; *acotiledóneo,* acotyledonous
		2, *Forming nouns of action from verbs ending in* **-ear**	*baileteo,* prancing
-ería	-ery	*Forming nouns denoting*	
		1, collectivity	*ferretería,* hardware
		2, quality; condition	*tontería,* foolishness
		3, place where something is made or sold	*cervecería,* brewery; *mercería,* haberdashery
-ero; -era	—	1, *Forming nouns denoting* agency; function	*aduanero,* customs officer; *carretero,* cartwright; *ramilletera,* flower girl
		2, *Forming names of trees*	*melocotonero,* peach tree
		3, *Forming nouns denoting* place	*abejera,* apiary
		4, *Forming adjectives denoting* relation; tendency; quality	*algodonero,* pert. to cotton; *parlero,* talkative; *verdadero,* true
-erón	—	*Forming augmentatives, usu. with derog. sense*	*caserón,* old ramshackle house
-es	—	1, *Forming the 2nd pers.sing. pres.ind. of verbs of the 2nd and 3rd conjugations*	*temes,* you are afraid; *vives,* you live
		2, *Forming the plural of nouns and adjectives ending in a consonant, or* y, *or an accented vowel other than* e	*árbol, árboles; ley, leyes; rubí, rubíes;* but *café, cafés*

	English Equivalents, If Any	Meanings and Uses	Examples
-és; -esa	-ese; -ish	1, *Forming nouns and adjectives denoting* origin; nationality; language	*francés*, French; Frenchman; *francesa*, Frenchwoman; *portugués*, Portuguese; *danés*, Danish
	—	2, *Forming adjectives denoting* relation; tendency; quality	*cortés*, courteous
-esa	-ess	1, *Forming feminine nouns of* dignity; profession	*abadesa*, abbess; *princesa*, princess
	—	2, *fem. of* -és	*portuguesa*, Portuguese woman
-escencia	-escence	*Forming nouns corresponding to adjectives ending in* -escente	*adolescencia*, adolescence
-escente	-escent	*Forming adjectives and nouns with inceptive or inchoative meaning*	*adolescente*, adolescent
-esco	-esque	having the form or manner of	*pintoresco*, picturesque
-ésimo	-th	*Forming ordinal numerals above the 20th*	*centésimo*, hundredth
-estre	—	*Forming adjectives denoting* relation; connection	*campestre*, of the country, rural
-eta	-et	1, *forming fem. diminutive nouns*	*trompeta*, trumpet; *isleta*, islet
		2, *fem. of* -ete	*silleta*, low chair, bedpan
-ete; -eta	-et; -ish	1, *Forming adjectives denoting* lesser or inferior quality or degree	*clarete*, claret; *agrete*, sourish
		2, *Forming masc. diminutive nouns and adjectives, often with derog. sense*	*mozalbete*, lad; *pobrete*, wretch, wretched

	English Equivalents, If Any	Meanings and Uses	Examples
-ez	—	*Forming abstract nouns from adjectives*	*vejez,* old age, senility; *niñez,* childhood; *avidez,* greediness
-eza	—	*Forming abstract nouns from adjectives*	*alteza,* Highness; *aspereza,* roughness
-faciente	-facient	making; tending to make	*estupefaciente,* stupefacient
-fagia	-phagy	eating; devouring	*antropofagia,* anthropophagy
-fago	-phagous	**1,** *forming adjectives denoting* eating; devouring	*antropófago,* anthropophagous
	-phage	**2,** *forming nouns denoting* eater; devourer	*xilófago,* xylophage
-fana	-phane	resembling	*cimofana,* cymophane
-fasia	-phasia	speech disorder	*afasia,* aphasia
-fero	-ferous	containing; yielding; producing	*conífero,* coniferous
-ficación	-fication	*Forming nouns from verbs ending in* **-ficar**	*glorificación,* glorification
-ficar	-fy	make	*purificar,* purify
-fico	-fic	causing; producing	*terrorífico,* terrific
-fila	-phyl	leaf	*clorofila,* chlorophyll
-filia	-philia; -philism	*Forming nouns from adjectives ending in* **-filo**	*cromatofilia,* chromatophilia; *bibliofilia,* bibliophilism
-filo	-phile -phyllous	**1,** liking; loving **2,** having a specified number or kind of leaves	*bibliófilo,* bibliophile *clorófilo,* chlorophyllous

	English Equivalents, If Any	Meanings and Uses	Examples
-fito	-phyte	*Forming nouns denoting* a plant of a specified habit or nature	*saprófito*, saprophyte
-floro	-florous	bearing a specified kind or number of flowers	*unífloro*, uniflorous
-fobia	-phobia	dread; fear; hatred	*claustrofobia*, claustrophobia
-fobo	-phobe	fearing; hating	*anglófobo*, Anglophobe
-fonía	-phony; -phonia	voice; sound	*telefonía*, telephony *afonía*, aphonia
-fono	-phone	producing or relating to sound, voice, etc.	*teléfono*, telephone
-foro	-phore	bearer	*electróforo*, electrophore
-fuga	-fuge	agent or instrument that expels	*centrífuga*, centrifuge
-fugo	-fugal	expelling	*centrífugo*, centrifugal
-gamia	-gamy	*Forming nouns denoting* marriage; union	*bigamia*, bigamy
-gamo	-gamous	*Forming adjectives denoting* marriage; union	*monógamo*, monogamous
-gena	-genous	*Forming adjectives denoting* born; produced	*indígena*, indigenous
-genia	-geny	*Forming nouns denoting* origin	*ontogenia*, ontogeny
-génico	-genic	*Forming adjectives corresponding to nouns ending in* **-geno** *or* **-genia**	*fotogénico*, photogenic

	English Equivalents, If Any	Meanings and Uses	Examples
-génito	—	begotten; born	*primogénito*, firstborn
-geno	-genous	1, *Forming adjectives denoting* born; produced	*nitrógeno*, nitrogenous
	-gen	2, **a.** *chem.*, *forming nouns denoting* something that produces	*halógeno*, halogen
		b. *biol.*, something produced	*exógeno*, exogen
-ginia	-gyny	*Forming nouns from adjectives ending in* **-gino**	*androginia*, androgyny
-gino	-gynous	female	*andrógino*, androgynous
-glota	-glot	tongue; language	*políglota*, polyglot
-gonía	-gony	genesis; origin	*cosmogonía*, cosmogony
-gono	-gon	*Forming nouns denoting geometrical plane figures with a specified number of sides or angles*	*polígono*, polygon
-grado	-grade	*Forming adjectives denoting* 1, walking; movement	*digitígrado*, digitigrade
		2, gradation	*centígrado*, centigrade
-grafía	-graphy	*Forming nouns denoting* 1, descriptive sciences and studies	*geografía*, geography; *biografía*, biography
		2, pictorial and representational arts	*fotografía*, photography; *coreografía*, choreography

	English Equivalents, If Any	Meanings and Uses	Examples
		3, the use of instruments for writing, drawing, recording, etc.	*telegrafía*, telegraphy
		4, writing; representation in writing	*ortografía*, orthography
	-graph	5, writing; drawing; recording; representation	*monografía*, monograph; *fotografía*, photograph
-grafo	-graph	1, an instrument for writing, drawing, recording, etc.	*telégrafo*, telegraph; *fonógrafo*, phonograph
	-grapher	2, [*fem.* **-grafa**] a person engaged in an art, science, study or craft of writing, drawing, recording, etc.	*biógrafo*, biographer; *coreógrafo*, choreographer; *calígrafo*, calligrapher
-grama	-gram	*Forming nouns denoting* something written, drawn or recorded	*telegrama*, telegram; *diagrama*, diagram
-gramo	-gram	metric units of weight	*kilogramo*, kilogram
-ia	-y; -ia	1, *Forming abstract and collective nouns*	*falacia*, fallacy; *milicia*, militia
		2, *Forming names of diseases*	*atrofia*, atrophy; *difteria*, diphtheria
		3, *Forming names of countries and regions*	*Francia*, France; *Galicia*, Galicia
		4, *Forming names of plants*	*gardenia*, gardenia
-ía	-y	*Forming nouns denoting*	
		1, sciences	*astronomía*, astronomy
		2, office; rank; dignity; jurisdiction	*alcaldía*, mayoralty; *abadía*, abbacy
		3, quality; condition	*alevosía*, treachery; *bastardía*, bastardy
		4, collectivity	*mayoría*, majority

	English Equivalents, If Any	Meanings and Uses	Examples
		5, place	*sacristía,* sacristy
		6, geographical names	*Turquía,* Turkey; *Lombardía,* Lombardy
-ial	-ial	*Forming adjectives expressing* relation; connection	*ministerial,* ministerial
-íasis	-iasis	disease	*elefantíasis,* elephantiasis
-iatra	-iatrist	medical practitioner	*psiquiatra,* psychiatrist
-iatría	-iatry; -iatrics	science or treatment of diseases	*psiquiatría,* psychiatry; *pediatría,* pediatrics
-iátrico	-iatric	*Forming adjectives from nouns ending in* **-iatra** *and* **-iatría**	*psiquiátrico,* psychiatric
-ible	-ible	*Forming adjectives expressing* ability; capability	*legible,* legible
-ica	-ics	*Forming nouns denoting* science; study; craft	*física,* physics; *gramática,* grammar; *gimnástica,* gymnastics
-icia	-ice	*Forming fem. abstract nouns denoting* quality; condition	*justicia,* justice; *avaricia,* avarice
-icio	-ice	1, *Forming masc. abstract nouns denoting* quality; condition	*servicio,* service
	-itious	2, *Forming adjectives denoting* tendency; relation	*alimenticio,* nutritious; *ficticio,* fictitious

	English Equivalents, If Any	Meanings and Uses	Examples
-ición	-ition	*Forming verbal nouns expressing* action; result of action	*aparición,* apparition
-icioso	-icious; -itious	*Forming adjectives denoting* quality; relation	*pernicioso,* pernicious; *supersticioso,* superstitious
-ico	-ic	**1,** *Forming adjectives denoting* quality; relation	*poético,* poetic
	-ic	**2,** *chem.,* indicating presence of an element in a compound at a higher valence	*nítrico,* nitric
	-ician	**3,** *Forming nouns denoting* practitioner	*matemático,* mathematician
	—	**4,** *colloq., forming diminutives*	*pajarico,* small bird
-idad	-ity	*Forming nouns denoting* condition; quality	*actividad,* activity; *benignidad,* benignity
-ido	—	**1,** *Forming adjectives equivalent to a past participle*	*cocido,* cooked
	—	**2,** *Forming nouns expressing* sound; outcry	*quejido.* whine; *aullido,* howl
	-id	**3,** *Forming adjectives denoting* quality; relation	*tórrido,* torrid; *flúido,* fluid
	-id	**4,** *zoöl.* member of a family or group	*arácnido,* arachnid
-iente	-ent	*Var. of* **-ente**	*paciente,* patient
-iento	—	*Var. of* **-ento**	*harapiento,* ragged
-iguar	—	*Forming verbs from nouns and adjectives*	*apaciguar,* pacify; *atestiguar,* testify
-ijo	—	**1,** *Forming diminutives*	*atadijo,* small bundle
		2, *Forming nouns expressing* action; result of action	*revoltijo,* mess

	English Equivalents, If Any	Meanings and Uses	Examples
-il	-il; -ile	*Forming adjectives expressing* relation; tendency	*civil*, civil; *frágil*, fragile
-illo	—	*Forming diminutives* [*fem.* **-illa**]	*chiquillo*, small boy, lad *pesadilla*, nightmare
-imo	-th	*Forming ordinal numerals*	*décimo*, tenth
-ín	—	*Forming diminutives* [*fem.* **-ina**]	*chiquitín*, very small (child); *gallina*, hen, chicken
-ina	-in; -ine	1, *Forming nouns denoting* chemical elements and compounds; minerals; pharmaceutical substances	*glicerina*, glycerine; *calamina*, calamine
	-ine	2, *Forming abstract nouns*	*disciplina*, discipline
	-ine	3, *Forming feminine nouns*	*heroína*, heroine
-íneo	—	*Forming adjectives expressing* condition; character; form	*sanguíneo*, sanguineous; *lacticíneo*, lacteal, milky
-ino	-ine	*Forming adjectives and nouns meaning* like; made of; pertaining to	*opalino*, opaline; *sanguino*, sanguine; *canino*, canine
-io	-ium	*Forming nouns used in scientific terms*	*geranio*, geranium; *actinio*, actinium
-ío	—	*Forming adjectives denoting*	
	-ish	1, intensity	*bravío*, fierce
		2, related or pert. to	*cabrío*, goatish; goat (*attrib.*)
		3, *Forming collective nouns*	*griterío*, uproar; *gentío*, crowd

	English Equivalents, If Any	Meanings and Uses	Examples
-ión	-ion	1, *Forming abstract nouns* 2, *Forming concrete nouns denoting* persons or things	*opinión*, opinion; *fusión*, fusion *centurión*, centurion; *legión*, legion
-ioso	-ious	*Forming adjectives often corresponding to nouns ending in* **-ión**	*religioso*, religious; *ansioso*, anxious
-isa	-ess	*Forming fem. nouns from masc. nouns ending in a vowel*	*poetisa*, poetess; *sacerdotisa*, priestess
-isco	—	*Forming adjectives meaning* having; pert. or related to	*arenisco*, sandy
-ismo	-ism	*Forming nouns denoting* doctrine; theory; practice; system; principle	*socialismo*, socialism
-ista	-ist	*Forming nouns, sometimes used as adjectives, denoting* one who practices, studies, believes, advocates	*pacifista*, pacifist; *socialista*, socialist
-ística	-istics	*Forming nouns from adjectives ending in* **-ista** *or* **-ístico** *denoting* practice or science of	*lingüística*, linguistics; *balística*, ballistics
-ístico	-istic	*Forming adjectives often corresponding to nouns ending in* **-ista**	*artístico*, artistic
-ita	-ite	*Forming nouns denoting* 1, origin; tribe 2, follower; disciple 3, rock; mineral 4, explosives 5, *Fem. of* **-ito**.	 *israelita*, Israelite *carmelita*, Carmelite *dolomita*, dolomite *dinamita*, dynamite; *cordita*, cordite *chiquita*, little girl

	English Equivalents, If Any	Meanings and Uses	Examples
-ítico	-itic; -itical	*Forming adjectives denoting*	
		1, origin	*levítico,* Levitical
		2, like; pertaining to	*granítico,* granitic; *político,* political
-itis	-itis	inflammation	*bronquitis,* bronchitis
-itivo	-itive	*Forming adjectives expressing relation; tendency*	*sensitivo,* sensitive
-ito	-ite	**1,** *Forming adjectives*	*contrito,* contrite; *erudito,* erudite
	-ite	**2,** *Forming names of minerals*	*grafito,* graphite
	-ite	**3,** *Forming names of chemical compounds, esp. salts of acids with names ending in* **-oso**	*sulfito,* sulfite
	—	**4,** [*fem.* **-ita**] *forming diminutives*	*pajarito,* little bird; *estatuita,* statuette
-ivo	-ive	*Forming adjectives of quality from verbs and nouns denoting function; tendency; disposition*	*nutritivo,* nutritive; *formativo,* formative
-iza	—	*Forming nouns denoting*	
		1, place	*porqueriza,* pigpen; *caballeriza,* stable
		2, action; result of action	*paliza,* beating
-izar	-ize	*Forming verbs from nouns and adjectives, expressing*	
		1, *in transitive verbs,* make, render, treat, act upon in a particular way	*civilizar,* civilize; *realizar,* realize
		2, *in intransitive verbs,* act, function, practice in a particular way	*economizar,* economize; *cristalizar,* crystallize

	English Equivalents, If Any	Meanings and Uses	Examples
-izo	—	*Forming adjectives expressing* 1, tendency; similarity 2, having; containing 3, tendency; capability	*enfermizo,* sickly; *pajizo,* straw-colored, pale *cobrizo,* copper-colored, cupric *arrojadizo,* easily thrown
-latra	-later; -lator	worshipper; worshipping	*idólatra,* idolater; *ególatra,* self-worshipping
-latría	-latry	worship	*idolatría,* idolatry
-lisis	-lysis	disintegration; destruction	*análisis,* analysis; *parálisis,* paralysis
-lita	-lite	*Forming names of minerals*	*criolita,* cryolite
-lítico	-lithic	1, *Forming adjectives from nouns ending in* -lito	*monolítico,* monolithic
	-lytic	2, *Forming adjectives from nouns ending in* -lisis	*analítico,* analytic; *paralítico,* paralytic
-lito	-lith -lyte	1, stone 2, *Forming nouns denoting result or product of disintegration or destruction*	*monolito,* monolith *electrolito,* electrolyte
-lizar	-lyze	*Forming verbs from nouns ending in* -lisis	*paralizar,* paralyze; *analizar,* analyze
-logía	-logy	1, science; doctrine; treatise 2, collection; group	*cosmología,* cosmology *antología,* anthology
-lógico	-logic; -logical	*Forming adjectives from nouns ending in* -logía	*cosmológico,* cosmologic(al)

	English Equivalents, If Any	Meanings and Uses	Examples
-logo	-logist	1, *Forming nouns corresponding to nouns ending in* **-logía,** *denoting* expert; practitioner	*geólogo,* geologist
	-logue; -log	2, *Forming nouns denoting* speech; writing; description	*diálogo,* dialogue; *catálogo,* catalog, catalogue
-mancia	-mancy	divination	*nigromancia,* necromancy
-mente	-ly	*Forming adverbs*	*lentamente,* slowly
-mento	-ment	*Forming nouns denoting* action; result of action	*armamento,* armament
-metría	-metry	measurement	*antropometría,* anthropometry
-metro	-meter	1, measure	*termómetro,* thermometer
		2, units in the metric system	*kilómetro,* kilometer
		3, *in versification,* having a specified number of feet	*hexámetro,* hexameter
-miento	-ment	*Forming nouns denoting* action; result of action	*lanzamiento,* launching; *rompimiento,* breaking
-monia; -monio	-mony	*Forming nouns denoting,* quality; condition	*acrimonia,* acrimony; *matrimonio,* matrimony
-mórfico	-morphic	*Forming adjectives denoting* likeness in form or appearance	*antropomórfico,* anthropomorphic
-morfismo	-morphism	*Forming nouns corresponding to adjectives ending in* **-mórfico**	*antropomorfismo,* anthropomorphism

	English Equivalents, If Any	Meanings and Uses	Examples
-morfo	-morph	1, *Forming nouns denoting* form; appearance	*isomorfo,* isomorph
	-morphous	2, *Forming adjectives expressing* likeness in form or appearance	*antropomorfo,* anthropomorphous
-motor	-motor; -motive	*Forming nouns and adjectives denoting* motion; propulsion	*vasomotor,* vasomotor; *locomotor,* locomotive
-motriz	-motive; -motor	*Forming adjectives denoting* motion; propulsion	*automotriz,* automotive; *locomotriz,* locomotor
-nomía	-nomy	*Forming nouns denoting* 1, science; study; body of knowledge 2, arrangement; management; government	*astronomía,* astronomy *taxonomía,* taxonomy; *autonomía,* autonomy
-nomo	—	*Forming nouns and adjectives corresponding to nouns ending in* **-nomía**	*astrónomo,* astronomer; *autónomo,* autonomous
-oda	-ode	*Forming nouns and adjectives denoting* like; in the form of	*geoda,* geode; *nematoda,* nematode
-odo	-ode	*Forming nouns denoting* path; way	*cátodo,* cathode
-oide; **-oideo**	-oid	*Forming adjectives and nouns expressing* similarity; resemblance	*celuloide,* celluloid; *mastoideo,* mastoid

	English Equivalents, If Any	Meanings and Uses	Examples
-ol	-ol	*Forming nouns denoting* alcohol or phenol derivative	*mentol,* menthol
-ole	-ole	*Forming* names of some organic compounds	*azole,* azole
-olento	—	*Forming adjectives denoting* quality; condition	*sanguinolento,* bloody
-oma	-oma	morbid growth	*fibroma,* fibroma
-ón, -ona	—	**1,** *Forming nouns and adjectives with augmentative, and often derogatory, force*	*hombrón,* big, burly man; *solterona,* spinster, old maid; *bravucón,* fourflusher, fourflushing
		2, *affixed to numbers, denotes* of a certain age	*cincuentón,* quinquagenarian
		3, *added to verbs, forms nouns and adjectives expressing* tendency or instinct to do the action contained in the verb	*acusón,* talebearing, tattletale
		4, *forming nouns from verbs denoting* rough, sudden action	*apretón,* squeeze
		5, *forming nouns from verbs denoting in physics,* subatomic particles: *in chemistry,* inert gases	*protón,* proton; *argón,* argon
-ona	-one	*chem., forming names of ketones*	*acetona,* acetone
-onimia	-onymy	*Forming nouns corresponding to nouns and adjectives ending in* **ónimo**	*toponimia,* toponymy

	English Equivalents, If Any	Meanings and Uses	Examples
-ónimo	-onym; -onymous	*Forming nouns and adjectives denoting* name; appellation	*sinónimo,* synonym, synonymous
-ope	-opic; -ope	*Forming nouns and adjectives denoting* having a (specified) kind or defect of eye	*miope,* myopic, myope
-opía	-opia;	*Forming nouns corresponding to nouns and adjectives ending in* **-ope**	*miopía,* myopia
-or	-or; -er	1, *Forming nouns* [*fem.* **-ora**] *denoting* agent	*pintor,* painter; *escritora,* (female) writer; *eyector,* ejector
	-or; -ness	2, *Forming abstract nouns denoting* quality; condition	*langor,* languor; *dulzor,* sweetness
-orama	-orama	*Forming nouns denoting* sight; view	*diorama,* diorama
-orio	-ory; -orious	1, *Forming adjectives denoting, in an active or passive sense,* aptitude; suitability	*meritorio,* meritorious; *transitorio,* transitory
	-ory; -orium	2, *Forming nouns denoting* place	*refectorio,* refectory; *sanatorio,* sanatorium
	-ory	3, *Forming nouns denoting* action; result of action	*interrogatorio,* interrogatory
-osa	-ose	*Forming names of carbohydrates*	*celulosa,* cellulose
-osidad	-osity	*Forming nouns corresponding to adjectives ending in* **-oso**	*belicosidad,* bellicosity
-osis	-osis	*Forming nouns denoting* 1, action; condition 2, diseased condition	*ósmosis,* osmosis *avitaminosis,* avitaminosis

	English Equivalents, If Any	Meanings and Uses	Examples
-oso	-ose; -ous	**1,** *Forming adjectives denoting* full of; having; characterized by	*belicoso*, bellicose; *vicioso*, vicious
	-ous	**2,** *chem., denoting* a lower valence in a compound than that denoted by **-ico**	*sulfuroso*, sulfurous
-paro	-parous	producing; giving birth to	*ovíparo*, oviparous
-pata	-path	*Forming nouns denoting* persons corresponding to nouns ending in **-patía**	*homeópata*, homeopath; *psicópata*, psychopath
-patía	-pathy; -pathia	**1,** feeling; suffering	*antipatía*, antipathy
		2, disease	*psicopatía*, psychopathy, psychopathia
		3, treatment of disease	*homeopatía*, homeopathy
-pático	-pathic	*Forming adjectives from nouns ending in* **-pata** *and* **-patía**	*psicopático*, psychopathic; *homeopático*, homeopathic
-pedia	-pedia; -pedics	education; conditioning	*enciclopedia*, encyclopedia; *ortopedia*, orthopedics
-pédico	-pedic	*Forming adjectives from nouns ending in* **-pedia**	*enciclopédico*, encyclopedic
-pedo	-ped; -pede	foot; having a (specified) kind or number of feet	*cuadrúpedo*, quadruped; *alípedo*, aliped; *velocípedo*, velocipede
-pepsia	-pepsia	digestion	*dispepsia*, dyspepsia
-péptico	-peptic	*Forming adjectives from nouns ending in* **-pepsia**	*dispéptico*, dyspeptic

	English Equivalents, If Any	Meanings and Uses	Examples
-plano	-plane	aircraft; plane	*hidroplano,* hydroplane
-plasia; -plasis	-plasia; -plasis	formation; development	*hipoplasia,* hypoplasia; *metaplasis,* metaplasis
-plasma	-plasm	formation; molding; a thing molded or formed	*protoplasma,* protoplasm
-plastia	-plasty	*Forming nouns denoting* 1, a manner of growth or development 2, an operation in plastic surgery	*dermatoplastia,* dermatoplasty *rinoplastia,* rhinoplasty
-plasto	-plast	*Forming nouns denoting* a structure of protoplasm	*cromoplasto,* chromoplast
-plejía	-plegia	stroke; paralysis	*hemiplejía,* hemiplegia
-ploide	-ploid	*Forming adjectives denoting* having a specified number of chromosomes	*diploide,* diploid
-podo	-ped; -pod	foot	*cirrópodo,* cirriped; *pseudópodo,* pseudopod
-polis	-polis	city	*cosmópolis,* cosmopolis
-ptero	-pterous; -pter	*Forming adjectives and nouns denoting* having a specified number or kind of wings	*himenóptero,* hymenopterous, hymenopter
-rragia	-rrhage	abnormal or excessive flow	*hemorragia,* hemorrhage
-rrea	-rrhea	flow; discharge	*diarrea,* diarrhea

	English Equivalents, If Any	Meanings and Uses	Examples
-rrino	-rrhine	nose	*platirrino,* platyrrhine
-sauro	-saur	lizard; lizardlike	*dinosauro,* dinosaur
-scopia	-scopy	viewing or observing through optical instruments	*fluoroscopia,* fluoroscopy
-scopio	-scope	instrument or means for viewing	*fluoroscopio,* fluoroscope
-sión	-sion	*Forming nouns denoting* action; result of action; quality; condition	*admisión,* admission; *confusión,* confusion
-sofía	-sophy	knowledge; thought	*filosofía,* philosophy
-sófico	-sophic; -sophical	*Forming adjectives from nouns ending in* **-sofía**	*filosófico,* philosophic, philosophical
-soma	-some	body	*cromosoma,* chromosome
-sperma	-sperm	seed; sperm	*gimnosperma,* gymnosperm
-spora	-spore	spore	*endospora,* endospore
-sporo	-sporous	having spores	*gimnosporo,* gymnosporous
-stática	-statics	*Forming names of sciences dealing with the equilibrium of physical forces*	*hidrostática,* hydrostatics
-stático	-static	*Forming adjectives corresponding to nouns ending in* **-stática** *or* **-stato**	*hidrostático,* hydrostatic; *fotostático,* photostatic

	English Equivalents, If Any	Meanings and Uses	Examples
-stato	-stat	*Forming nouns denoting* 1, equilibrium; stationary position or condition	*aeróstato,* aerostat
		2, instrument for maintaining a system in a fixed position or condition	*termóstato,* thermostat
-tad	-ty	*Forming abstract nouns denoting* quality; state; condition	*lealtad,* loyalty; *enemistad,* enmity
-tario	——	*Var. of* **-ario**	*arrendatario,* tenant, lessee; *autoritario,* authoritarian
-taxis	-taxis	order; arrangement	*termotaxis,* thermotaxis
-tecnia	-technics	*Forming nouns denoting* art; science; industry	*electrotecnia,* electrotechnics
-técnico	-technic; -technical	*Forming adjectives corresponding to nouns ending in* **-tecnia**	*electrotécnico,* electrotechnic(al)
-terma	-therm	heat	*isoterma,* isotherm
-termia	-thermy	*Forming abstract nouns from nouns ending in* **-terma**	*diatermia,* diathermy
-tipia	-typy; -type	printing; printing process	*linotipia,* linotype *electrotipia,* electrotypy
-tipo	-type	1, example; representative form	*prototipo,* prototype
		2, print; stamp	*daguerrotipo,* daguerrotype
-tomía	-tomy	1, a cutting; dividing	*dicotomía,* dichotomy
		2, surgical operation	*apendectomía,* appendectomy

	English Equivalents, If Any	Meanings and Uses	Examples
-tomo	-tome	*Forming nouns denoting* cutter; cutting instrument	*micrótomo,* microtome
-tor; -tora	-tor	*Forming nouns and adjectives denoting* agency	*director,* director, directing; *directora,* directress
-torio	——	*Var. of* **-orio**	*auditorio,* audience
-triz	-ess; -trix	*Forming fem. nouns of agency corresponding to some masc. nouns ending in* **-tor** *and* **-dor**	*actriz,* actress; *emperatriz,* empress; *bisectriz,* bisectrix
-trofia	-trophy	nutrition	*atrofia,* atrophy
-trófico	-trophic	*Forming adjectives corresponding to nouns ending in* **-trofia**	*hipertrófico,* hypertrophic
-tropía	-tropy	change; transformation	*entropía,* entropy
-trópico	-tropic	*Forming adjectives corresponding to nouns ending in* **-tropismo**	*heliotrópico,* heliotropic
-tropismo	-tropism	tendency to turn toward; turning	*heliotropismo,* heliotropism
-tud	-tude; -ness	*Forming abstract nouns denoting* quality; condition; state	*verosimilitud,* verisimilitude; *acritud,* acridness
-ucho; -ucha	—	*Forming diminutives, usu. derog.*	*cuartucho,* hut; *debilucho,* feeble; *casucha,* shack
-udo	—	*Forming adjectives denoting* strongly characterized by; having an abundance of	*cabezudo,* obstinate, thickheaded; *barbudo,* heavy-bearded

	English Equivalents, If Any	Meanings and Uses	Examples
-uelo; -uela	—	*Forming diminutives*	*mozuelo* youngster, lad; *chicuela,* little girl
-ula	-ule	*Forming diminutives*	*espórula,* sporule
-ulento	-ulent	*Forming adjectives expressing* full of	*virulento.* virulent
-ulo	-ulous	*Forming adjectives expressing* inclination; tendency	*trémulo,* tremulous; *crédulo,* credulous
-umbre	—	*Forming abstract nouns denoting* quality; condition	*muchedumbre,* crowd, multitude *pesadumbre,* sorrow
-undo	-und	*Forming adjectives denoting* quality; condition	*rubicundo,* rubicund; *rotundo,* rotund
-uno	—	*Forming adjectives denoting* having the characteristic of; like	*gatuno,* catlike, feline
-ura	-ure	*Forming nouns denoting* 1, quality; condition	*compostura,* composure; *bravura,* bravery
		2, action; result of action; process	*pintura,* picture, painting
		3, means; instrument	*embocadura,* mouthpiece, opening
		4, art	*escultura,* sculpture
		5, office; function	*prefectura,* prefecture
-uria	-uria	urine; diseased condition of the urine	*albuminuria,* albuminuria
-uro	-ide	*chem., forming names of binary compounds*	*cloruro,* chloride
-usco	—	*Var. of* **-uzco**	*verdusco,* greenish

	English Equivalents, If Any	Meanings and Uses	Examples
-uzco	—	*Forming adjectives, esp. relating to colors, denoting* likeness; tendency toward	*blancuzco,* whitish
-uzo; -uza	—	*Forming nouns and adjectives, often derog.*	*lechuzo,* suckling mule; *carnuza,* coarse, cheap meat
-valente	-valent	*chem., forming adjectives denoting* valence	*monovalente,* monovalent
-voro	-vorous; -vore	*Forming adjectives and nouns denoting* eating; eater	*carnívoro,* carnivorous, carnivore
-zoico	-zoic	*Forming adjectives denoting* 1, animal; animal life 2, *geol.* fossil era	*fanerozoico,* phanerozoic *mesozoico,* Mesozoic
-zoo	-zoon	animal	*espermatozoo,* spermatozoon
-zuelo	—	*Forming diminutives*	*bribonzuelo,* little rascal

GEOGRAPHICAL NAMES—
NOMBRES GEOGRÁFICOS

(L) = language (N) = native; inhabitant; citizen; resident

CONTINENTS	Derivatives	CONTINENTES	Derivados
Africa	African	África	africano
America	American	América	americano
Antarctica	Antarctic	Antártica	antártico
Asia	Asian; Asiatic	Asia	asiático
Central America	Central American	Centroamérica; América Central	centroamericano
Eurasia	Eurasian	Eurasia	eurasiático
Europe	European	Europa	europeo
North America	North American	Norteamérica; América del Norte	norteamericano
South America	South American	Sudamérica; América del Sur	sudamericano

COUNTRIES, REGIONS	Derivatives	PAISES, REGIONES	Derivados
Aden		Adén	
Afghanistan	Afghan	Afganistán	afgano
Albania	Albanian	Albania	albanés (-esa)
Algeria	Algerian	Argelia	argelino
Andalusia	Andalusian	Andalucía	andaluz
Andorra	Andorran	Andorra	andorrano
Angola	Angolan	Angola	angoleño; angolés (-esa)
Antigua		Antigua	
Arabia	Arabian	Arabia	árabe
Argentina	Argentinian; Argentine	Argentina	argentino
Armenia	Armenian	Armenia	armenio
Asia Minor		Asia Menor	
Australasia	Australasian	Austrolasia	
Australia	Australian	Australia	australiano
Austria	Austrian	Austria	austríaco
Azerbaijan	Azerbaijani	Azerbaiján	azerbaijaní; azerbeyaní
Bahamas	Bahamian	Bahamas	bahamés (-esa)
Bahrain; Bahrein		Bahrein	
Bangladesh	Bangladeshi	Bangladesh	
Barbados	Barbadian	Barbados	barbadense

COUNTRIES, REGIONS	Derivatives	PAISES, REGIONES	Derivados
Bavaria	Bavarian	Baviera	
Belarus	Belorussian	Bielorusia	bielorruso
Belgium	Belgian	Bélgica	belga
Belize	Belizan	Belice	
Benelux		Países Bajos	
Benin		Benín	
Bessarabia	Bessarabian	Besarabia	
Bhutan	Bhutanese	Bután	butanés (-esa)
Bohemia	Bohemian	Bohemia	boemio
Bolivia	Bolivian	Bolivia	boliviano
Bosnia	Bosnian	Bosnia	
Botswana		Botswana	
Brazil	Brazilian	Brasil	brasileño
Britain	British	Gran Bretaña	británico
British Isles	British	Islas Británicas	británico
Brittany	Breton	Bretaña	bretón (-ona)
Brunei		Brunei	
Bulgaria	Bulgarian	Bulgaria	búlgaro
Burgundy	Burgundian	Borgoña	borgoñón (-ñona)
Burkina Faso		Burkina Faso	
Burma (Myanmar)	Burman (N); Burmese (L)	Birmania	birmano
Burundi	Burundian	Burundi	burundés (-esa)
Cambodia; Kampuchea	Cambodian	Camboya; Kampuchea	camboyano
Cameroon	Cameroonian	Camerún	camerunés (-esa); camerunense
Canada	Canadian	Canadá	canadiense
Cape Verde, Republic of		República de Cabo Verde	
Castile	Castilian	Castilla	castellano
Catalonia	Catalonian	Cataluña	catalán (-ana)
Central African Republic		República Centroafricana	
Ceylon; Sri Lanka	Ceylonese; Sin(g)halese	Ceilán	cingalés (-esa)
Chad	Chadian	Chad	chadiano
Chile	Chilean	Chile	chileno
China	Chinese	China	chino
Colombia	Colombian	Colombia	colombiano
Comoros, Republic of the		República de los Comores	
Congo	Congolese	Congo	congolés (-esa); congoleño
Cornwall	Cornish	Cornualles	córnico
Corsica	Corsican	Córcega	corso
Costa Rica	Costa Rican	Costa Rica	costarriqueño; costarricense

COUNTRIES, REGIONS	Derivatives	PAISES, REGIONES	Derivados
Crimea	Crimean	Crimea	
Croatia	Croatian	Croacia	croata
Cuba	Cuban	Cuba	cubano
Cyprus	Cyprian; Cypriote	Chipre	chipriota
Czechoslovakia	Czechoslovakian	Checoslovaquia	checoslovaco
Dalmatia	Dalmatian	Dalmacia	dálmata
Denmark	Danish (L); Dane (N)	Dinamarca	danés (-esa)
Djibouti		Djibouti	
Dominica		Dominica	
Dominican Republic	Dominican	República Dominicana	dominicano
East Germany		Alemania Oriental	
Ecuador	Ecuadorian (-ean)	Ecuador	ecuatoriano
Egypt	Egyptian	Egipto	egipcio
El Salvador	Salvadorian (-ean)	El Salvador	salvadoreño
England	English	Inglaterra	inglés (-esa)
Equatorial Guinea		Guinea Ecuatorial	ecuatoguineano
Eritrea	Eritrean	Eritrea	
Est(h)onia	Est(h)onian	Estonia	estonio
Ethiopia	Ethiopian	Etiopía	etíope; etiope
Fiji	Fijian	Fidji	
Finland	Finn (N); Finnish (L)	Finlandia	finlandés (-esa)
Flanders	Fleming (N); Flemish (L)	Flandes	flamenco
France	French	Francia	francés (-esa)
Gabon	Gabonese	Gabón	gabonés (-esa)
Galicia	Galician	Galicia	gallego
Gambia	Gambian	Gambia	gambiano
Georgia	Georgian	Georgia	
Germany	German	Alemania	alemán (-ana)
Ghana	Ghanian; Ghanaian	Ghana	ganés (-esa)
Gibraltar		Gibraltar	
Great Britain	British	Gran Bretaña	británico
Greece	Greek; Grecian	Grecia	griego
Greenland	Greenlander (N)	Groenlandia	groenlandés (-esa)
Grenada		Grenada; Granada	
Guatemala	Guatemalan	Guatemala	guatemalteco
Guinea	Guinean	Guinea	guineo; guineano
Guinea-Bissau		Guinea-Bissau	

COUNTRIES, REGIONS	Derivatives	PAÍSES, REGIONES	Derivados
Guyana	Guyanian; Guyanese	Guyana	guyanés (-esa)
Haiti	Haitian	Haití	haitiano
Holland	Dutch	Holanda	holandés (-esa)
Honduras	Honduran	Honduras	hondureño
Hong Kong		Hong Kong	
Hungary	Hungarian	Hungría	húngaro
Iberia	Iberian	Iberia	ibérico
Iceland	Icelandic (L); Icelander (N)	Islandia	islandés (-esa)
India	Indian	India	indio; hindú
Indochina	Indochinese	Indochina	indochino (N)
Indonesia	Indonesian	Indonesia	indonesio; indonésico
Iran	Iranian	Irán	iraní (N); iranio (L)
Iraq; Irak	Iraqi; Iraki	Iraq; Irak	iraquí; irakí
Ireland	Irish	Irlanda	irlandés (-esa)
Israel	Israeli	Israel	israelí; israelita
Italy	Italian	Italia	italiano
Ivory Coast		la Costa de Marfil	
Jamaica	Jamaican	Jamaica	jamaiquino; jamaicano
Japan	Japanese	Japón	japonés (-esa)
Jordan	Jordanian	Jordania	jórdano
Kashmir		Cachemira	
Kenya	Kenyan	Kenya; Kenia	keniano
Kiribati		Kiribati	
Korea	Korean	Corea	coreano
Kuwait	Kuwaiti	Kuwait; Koweit	kuwaití; koweití
Labrador	Labradoran	Labrador	labradoresco
Laos	Laotian	Laos	laosiano
Latin America	Latin American	Latinoamérica; América Latina	latinoamericano
Latvia	Latvian; Lett (N); Lettish (L)	Latvia	latvio; letón
Lebanon	Lebanese	Líbano	libanés (-esa)
Lesotho		Lesotho	
Liberia	Liberian	Liberia	liberiano
Libya	Libyan	Libia	libio
Liechtenstein		Liechtenstein	
Lithuania	Lithuanian	Lituania	lituano
Luxemb(o)urg	Luxemb(o)urgian	Luxemburgo	luxemburgués (-esa)
Macao		Macao	
Macedonia	Macedonian	Macedonia	macedón (-ona); macedonio; macedónico
Malawi	Malawian	Malawi	malawiano

COUNTRIES, REGIONS	Derivatives	PAISES, REGIONES	Derivados
Malaysia	Malaysian	Malasia	malasio
Maldives	Maldive	Maldivas	maldivo
Malgasy Republic	Malgasy	República Malgache	malgache
Mali	Malian	Malí	maliense
Malta	Maltese	Malta	maltés (-esa)
Manchuria	Manchu; Manchurian	Manchuria	manchú; manchuriano
Mauritania	Mauritanian	Mauritania	mauritano
Mauritius	Mauritian	Mauricio	mauriciano
Mesopotamia	Mesopotamian	Mesopotamia	mesopotámico
Mexico	Mexican	México	mexicano
Micronesia	Micronesian	Micronesia	micronesio
Monaco	Monacan	Mónaco	monegasco
Mongolia	Mongol (N); Mongolian (L)	Mongolia	mongol
Morocco	Moroccan	Marruecos	marroquí
Mozambique	Mozambican	Mozambique	mozambiqueño
Myanmar (see Burma)			
Namibia	Namibian	Namibia	namibio
Nauru	Nauruan	Nauru	nauruano
Nepal	Nepalese	Nepal	nepalés (-esa); nepalí
Netherlands	Netherlander (N)	Países Bajos	neerlandés (-esa)
New Zealand	New Zealander (N)	Nueva Zelandia	neozelandés (-esa)
New England	New Englander (N)	Nueva Inglaterra	
New Guinea		Nueva Guinea	
Newfoundland		Terranova	
Nicaragua	Nicaraguan	Nicaragua	nicaragüense
Niger		Níger	nigerio; nigerino
Nigeria	Nigerian	Nigeria	nigeriano; nigerio
Normandy	Norman	Normandía	normando
North Korea	North Korean	Corea del Norte	norcoreano
Northern Ireland		Irlanda del Norte	
Norway	Norwegian	Noruega	noruego
Oceania	Oceanian	Oceanía	oceánico
Oman	Omani	Omán	omaní
Pakistan	Pakistani	Pakistán; Paquistán	pakistaní; paquistaní; pakistano; paquistano
Palestine	Palestinian	Palestina	palestino
Panama	Panamanian	Panamá	panameño

COUNTRIES, REGIONS	Derivatives	PAISES, REGIONES	Derivados
Papua New Guinea		Papua-Nueva Guinea	
Paraguay	Paraguayan	Paraguay	paraguayo
Patagonia	Patagonian	Patagonia	
Persia	Persian	Persia	persa (N,L); pérsico (L); persiano (N)
Peru	Peruvian	Perú	peruano
Philippines	Filipino; Filipine	Filipinas	filipino
Phoenicia	Phoenician	Fenicia	fenicio
Poland	Pole (N); Polish (L)	Polonia	polonés (-esa); polaco
Polynesia	Polynesian	Polinesia	polinesio
Portugal	Portuguese	Portugal	portugués (-esa)
Prussia	Prussian	Prusia	prusiano
Puerto Rico	Puerto Rican	Puerto Rico	puertorriqueño
Punjab	Punjabi	Pendjab	penjabo; penjabi
Qatar		Qatar; Katar	
Romania; Rumania	Romanian; Rumanian	Rumania	rumano
Russia	Russian	Rusia	ruso
Rwanda	Rwandan	Ruanda	ruandés (-esa)
Samoa	Samoan	Samoa	samoano
San Marino	San Marinese	San Marino	sanmarinense
Sardinia	Sardinian	Cerdeña	sardo
Saudi Arabia	Saudi; Saudi Arabian	Arabia Saudita	árabe saudita
Scandinavia	Scandinavian	Escandinavia	escandinavo
Scotland	Scot (N); Scotch; Scottish (L)	Escocia	escocés (-esa)
Senegal	Senegalese	Senegal	senegalés (-esa)
Seychelles		República de Seychelles	
Serbia	Serbian; Serbo-Croatian (L)	Serbia; Servia	servio; servocroata (L)
Siam	Siamese	Siam	siamés (-esa)
Siberia	Siberian	Siberia	siberiano
Sicily	Sicilian	Sicilia	siciliano
Sierra Leone		República de Sierra Leona	sierraleonés (-esa)
Singapore	Singaporean	Singapur	singapurense
Slovakia	Slovakian	Eslovaquia	eslovaco
Slovenia	Slovene; Slovenian	Eslovenia	esloveno
Somalia	Somali; Somalian	Somalia	somalí
South Africa	South African	África del Sur; República Sudafricana	sudafricano

COUNTRIES, REGIONS	Derivatives	PAISES, REGIONES	Derivados
South Korea	South Korean	Corea del Sur	surcoreano
Soviet Union	Soviet	Unión Soviética	soviético
Spain	Spaniard (N); Spanish (L)	España	español (-ola)
Sri Lanka	Sri Lankan	Sri Lanka	cingalés (-esa); ceilandés (-esa)
Sudan	Sudanese	Sudán	sudanés (-esa)
Surinam	Surinamese	Suriname	surinamés (-esa)
Swaziland	Swazi	Swazilandia	swazi; swazilandés (-esa)
Sweden	Swede (N); Swedish (L)	Suecia	sueco
Switzerland	Swiss	Suiza	suizo
Syria	Syrian	Siria	sirio
Taiwan	Taiwanese	Taiwán	taiwanés (-esa)
Tanzania	Tanzanian	Tanzanía	tanzaniano
Thailand	Thai	Tailandia	tailandés (-esa)
Tibet	Tibetan	Tíbet	tibetano
Togo	Togolese	Togo	togolés (-esa)
Tonga	Tongan	Tonga	tongano
Trinidad and Tobago		Trinidad y Tobago	
Tunisia	Tunisian	Túnez	tunecino
Turkey	Turk (N); Turkish (L)	Turquía	turco
Tuvalu	Tuvaluan	Tuvalu	tuvaluano
Tyrol	Tyrolean	Tirol	tirolés (-esa)
Uganda	Ugandan	Uganda	ugandés (-esa)
Ukraine	Ukrainian	Ucrania	ucranio; ucraniano
United Kingdom	British	Reino Unido	británico
United States of America	American	Estados Unidos de América	norteamericano; estadounidense
United Arab Emirates		Emiratos Árabes Unidos	
Upper Volta (Bourkina Fasso)	Upper Voltan	Alto Volta (Burkina Faso)	voltense
Uruguay	Uruguayan	Uruguay	uruguayo
Vanuatu		Vanuatu	
Vatican		Vaticano	
Venezuela	Venezuelan	Venezuela	venezolano
Vietnam	Vietnamese	Viet Nam	vietnamita; vietnamés (-esa)
Wales	Welsh	Gales	galés (-esa)
West Germany		Alemania Occidental	

COUNTRIES, REGIONS	Derivatives	PAISES, REGIONES	Derivados
Yemen	Yemeni; Yemenite	Yemen	yemení; yemenita
Yucatan		Yucatán	
Yukon		Yukón	
Yugoslavia	Yugoslav (N); Yugoslavian	Yugoslavia	yugoslavo
Zaire	Zairean; Zairian	Zaire	zairense
Zambia	Zambian	Zambia	zambiano; zambés (-esa)
Zimbabwe	Zimbabwean	Zimbabwe	simbabwense

CITIES	Derivatives	CIUDADES	Derivados
Addis Ababa, Ethiopia		Addis Ababa	
Ahmadabad, India		Ahmadabad	
Alexandria, Egypt		Alejandría	
Algiers	Algerian	Argel	argelino
Amsterdam, Holland		Amsterdam	
Ankara, Turkey		Ankara	
Athens, Greece	Athenian	Atenas	
Baghdad, Iraq		Bagdad	
Bangalore, India		Bangalore	
Bangkok, Thailand		Bangkok	
Barcelona, Spain		Barcelona	
Beijing (Peking), China		Beijing (Pekín)	
Beirut, Lebanon		Beirut	
Belgrade, Yugoslavia (Serbia)		Belgrado	
Belo Horizonte, Brazil		Belo Horizonte	
Berlin, Germany	Berliner (N)	Berlín	
Bethlehem, Israel		Belén	
Bogotá, Colombia		Bogotá	bogotano
Bombay, India		Bombay	
Boston, USA	Bostonian	Boston	
Brussels, Belgium		Bruselas	
Bucharest, Romania		Bucarest	
Budapest, Hungary		Budapest	

CITIES	Derivatives	CIUDADES	Derivados
Buenos Aires, Argentina		Buenos Aires	porteño
Cairo, Egypt		El Cairo	
Calcutta, India		Calcuta	
Canton (Guangzhou), China		Cantón	
Caracas, Venezuela		Caracas	
Casablanca, Morocco		Casablanca	
Chengdu, China		Chengdu	
Chicago, USA	Chicagoan	Chicago	
Chongqing; Chungking, China		Chongqing	
Copenhagen, Denmark		Copenhague	
Dallas, USA		Dallas	
Damascus, Syria		Damasco	
Delhi, India		Delhi	
Detroit, USA		Detroit	
Dhaka, Bangladesh		Dacca	
Edinburgh, Scotland		Edimburgo	
Essen, Germany		Essen	
Florence, Italy	Florentine	Florencia	florentino
Geneva, Switzerland		Ginebra	
Guadalajara, Spain; Mexico		Guadalajara	
Guangzhou (Canton), China		Guangzhou	
Hague (The), Holland		La Haya	
Hamburg, Germany		Hamburgo	hamburgués (-esa)
Harbin, China		Harbín; Jarbín	
Havana, Cuba	habanero	La Habana	habanero
Ho Chi Minh City (Saigon), Vietnam		Ho Chi Minh	
Hong Kong		Hongkong	
Houston, USA		Houston	
Hyderabad, India		Haiderabad	
Islamabad, Pakistan		Islamabad	
Istanbul, Turkey		Estambul	

CITIES	Derivatives	CIUDADES	Derivados
Jakarta, Indonesia		Yakarta	
Jerusalem, Israel		Jerusalén	
Karachi, Pakistan		Karachi	
Kiev, Ukraine		Kiev	
Kinshasa, Zaire		Kinshasa	
Kobe, Japan		Kobe	
Kyoto, Japan		Kyoto	
Lagos, Nigeria		Lagos	
Lahore, Pakistan		Lahore	
Leningrad, Russia		Leningrado	
Lima, Peru		Lima	
Lisbon, Portugal		Lisboa	
London, England	Londoner (N)	Londres	londinense
Los Angeles, USA	Angeleno (N)	Los Angeles	
Madras, India		Madrás	
Madrid, Spain	Madrilene	Madrid	madrileño
Manchester, England		Manchester	
Manila, Philippines		Manila	
Marseille(s), France		Marsella	
Mecca, Saudi Arabia		La Meca	
Melbourne, Australia		Melbourne	
Mexico City		México, D.F.	
Milan, Italy	Milanese	Milán	milanés
Monterrey, Mexico		Monterrey	
Montreal, Canada		Montreal	
Moscow, Russia	Muscovite	Moscú	moscovita
Munich, Germany		Munich	
Nagoya, Japan		Nagoya	
Nanking, China		Nankín	
Naples, Italy	Neapolitan	Nápoles	napolitano
New Delhi, India		Nueva Delhi	
New York, USA	New Yorker (N)	Nueva York	neoyorquino
Odessa, Ukraine		Odesa	
Osaka, Japan		Osaka	
Oslo, Norway		Oslo	
Ottawa, Canada		Ottawa	
Paris, France	Parisian	París	parisiense

CITIES	Derivatives	CIUDADES	Derivados
Peking (Beijing), China		Pequín, Pekín	
Philadelphia, USA		Filadelfia	
Poona, India		Poona	
Port-au-Prince, Haiti		Puerto Príncipe	
Porto Alegre, Brazil		Porto Alegre	
Prague, Czechoslovakia		Praga	
Pusan, South Korea		Pusan	
Rangoon (Yaugôn), Myanmar		Rangún	
Rio de Janeiro, Brazil		Río de Janeiro	
Riyadh, Saudi Arabia		Riyadh	
Rome, Italy	Roman	Roma	romano
Saigon (Ho Chi Minh City), Vietnam		Saigón	
Salvador, Brazil		Salvador	
San Francisco, USA		San Francisco	
Santiago, Chile		Santiago de Chile	
Santiago, Cuba		Santiago de Cuba	
São Paulo, Brazil		São Paulo	
Sarajevo, Bosnia		Sarajevo	
Seoul, South Korea		Seúl	
Seville, Spain		Sevilla	sevillano
Shanghai, China		Shangai	
Shenyang, China		Shenyang	
Singapore		Singapur	
Sofia, Bulgaria		Sofía	
Stockholm, Sweden		Estocolmo	
Surabaya, Indonesia		Surabaya	
Sydney, Australia		Sidney	
Taegu, South Korea		Taegu	
Taipei, Taiwan		Taipei	

CITIES	Derivatives	CIUDADES	Derivados
Tangiers, Morocco		Tanger	
Tashkent, Uzbekistan		Tashkent	
Tehran, Iran		Teherán	
Tianjin (Tientsin), China		Tianjin	
Tokyo, Japan		Tokio	
Toronto, Canada		Toronto	
Troy	Trojan	Troya	troyano
Tunis, Tunisia		Túnez	
Venice, Italy	Venetian	Venecia	veneciano
Vienna, Austria	Viennese	Viena	vienés (-esa)
Warsaw, Poland		Varsovia	
Washington, D.C., USA		Washington	
Wuhan, China		Wuhan	
Yaugôn, Myanmar		Yaugôn	
Yokohama, Japan		Yokohama	
Zagreb, Serbia		Zagreb	

ISLANDS		ISLAS	
Aleutian Is.		Is. Aleutianas	
Antigua		Antigua	
Antilles		Antillas	
Aruba		Aruba	
Azores		Azores	
Baffin I.		Tierra de Baffín	
Balearic Is.		Is. Baleares	
Bali		Bali	
Bermuda		Bermuda	
Borneo		Borneo	
Canary Is.		Is. Canarias	
Cape Verde Is.		Is. Cabo Verde	
Caroline Is.		Is. Carolinas	
Celebes		Célebes	
Channel Is.		Is. de la Mancha	
Comoros		Comores	
Corfu		Corfú	
Crete		Creta	
Curaçao		Curaçao	
East Indies		Indias Orientales	
Easter I.		I. De Pascua	
Falkland Is.		Is. Malvinas	
Faroe Is.		Is. Feroé	
Galapagos Is.		Is. Galápagos	
Greater Antilles		Antillas Mayores	

ISLANDS	ISLAS
Greenland	Groenlandia
Guadalcanal	Guadalcanal
Guadeloupe	Guadalupe
Guam	Guam
Hebrides	Is. Hébridas
Hispaniola	Hispaniola
Hokkaido	Hokkaido
Honshu	Hondo
Iceland	Islandia
Iwo Jima	Iwo Jima
Java	Java
Kyushu	Kiushiu
Leeward Is.	Is. de Sotavento
Lesser Antilles	Antillas Menores
Leyte	Leyte
Long I.	Long Island
Luzon	Luzón
Madagascar	Madagascar
Made(i)ra Is.	Maderas
Majorca	Mallorca
Maldive Is.	Is. Maldivas
Man, Isle of	Isla de Man
Mariana Is.	Is. Marianas
Marquesas Is.	Is. Marquesas
Marshall Is.	Is. Marshall
Martinique	Martinica
Mindanao	Mindanao
Minorca	Menorca
Newfoundland	Terranova
Okinawa	Okinawa-Jima
Orkney Is.	Is. Orcadas
Prince Edward I.	I. Príncipe Eduardo
Réunion	Réunion
Rhodes	Rodas
Ryukyu Is.	Is. Ryukyu
Sakhalin	Sajalín
Shetland Is.	Is. Shetland
Shikoku	Shikoku
Solomon Is.	Is. Salomón
Sumatra	Sumatra
Tahiti	Tahití
Tasmania	Tasmania
Tierra del Fuego	Tierra del Fuego
Timor	Timor
Vancouver I.	I. Vancouver
Victoria I.	I. de Victoria
Virgin Is.	Is. Vírgenes
West Indies (Antilles)	Indias Occidentales (Antillas)
Windward Is.	Is. de Barlovento
Zanzibar	I. Zanzíbar

OCEANS	OCEANOS
Antarctic Ocean	Océano Antártico
Arctic Ocean	Océano Artico
Atlantic Ocean	Océano Atlántico
Indian Ocean	Océano Indico
Pacific Ocean	Océano Pacífico

SEAS	MARES
Adriatic Sea	Mar Adriático
Aegean Sea	Mar Egeo
Arabian Sea	Mar Arábigo
Aral Sea	Lago Aral
Azov, Sea of	Mar de Azov
Baltic Sea	Mar Báltico
Bering Sea	Mar de Bering
Black Sea	Mar Negro
Caribbean Sea	Mar Caribe; Mar de las Antillas
Caspian Sea	Mar Caspio
Dead Sea	Mar Muerto
East China Sea	Mar Oriental de la China
Irish Sea	Mar de Irlanda
Japan, Sea of	Mar del Japón
Mediterranean Sea	Mar Mediterráneo
North Sea	Mar del Norte
Okhotsk, Sea of	Mar de Okhotsk
Red Sea	Mar Rojo
Sargasso Sea	Mar de los Sargazos
South China Sea	Mar Meridional de la China
Tasman Sea	Mar Tasmán; Mar de Tasmania
White Sea	Mar Blanco
Yellow Sea	Mar Amarillo

LAKES	LAGOS
Albert Nyanza	Alberto Nyanza
Baikal	Baikal
Chad	Chad
Erie	Erie
Geneva	Lago Léman; Lago de Ginebra
Great Bear	Gran Lago de los Osos
Great Lakes	Los Grandes Lagos
Great Salt	Gran Lago Salado
Great Slave	Gran Lago de los Esclavos
Huron	Hurón
Ladoga	Ladoga
Michigan	Michigan
Nyassa	Nyassa
Onega	Onega
Ontario	Ontario
Superior	Superior
Tanganyika	Tanganika
Titicaca	Titicaca
Victoria Nyanza	Victoria Nyanza

RIVERS	RIOS
Amazon	R. Amazonas
Amur	R. Amur
Columbia	R. Columbia
Congo	R. Congo
Danube	R. Danubio
Delaware	R. Delaware
Dnieper	R. Dniéper
Dniester	R. Dniéster
Don	R. Don
Elbe	R. Elba
Euphrates	R. Eufrates
Ganges	R. Ganges
Huang Ho	R. Huang Ho
Hudson	R. Hudson
Indus	R. Indus *o* Singh
Irawaddy	R. Irauadi
Irtysh	R. Irtish
Jordan	R. Jordán
Lena	R. Lena
Loire	R. Loira
Mackenzie	R. Mackenzie
Mekong	R. Mekong
Mississippi	R. Misisipí
Missouri	R. Misuri
Niger	R. Níger
Nile	R. Nilo
Ob	R. Ob *u* Obi
Oder	R. Oder
Ohio	R. Ohio
Orinoco	R. Orinoco
Paraná	R. Paraná
Po	R. Po
Potomac	R. Potomac
Rhine	R. Rin
Rhône	R. Ródano
Rio Grande	R. Grande
St. Lawrence	R. San Lorenzo
Seine	R. Sena
Susquehanna	R. Susquehanna
Thames	R. Támesis
Tigris	R. Tigris
Ural	R. Ural
Vistula	R. Vístula
Volga	R. Volga
Volta	R. Volta
Yangtze	R. Yan Tse Kiang *o* R. Azul
Yellow	R. Amarillo
Yenisei	R. Yenisei
Yukon	R. Yukón
Zambezi; Zambesi	R. Zameze

GULFS, BAYS, STRAITS, CHANNELS, CANALS	GOLFOS, BAHIAS, ESTRECHOS, CANALES
Aden, Gulf of	Golfo de Adén
Bengal, Bay of	Golfo de Bengala
Bering Strait	Estrecho de Bering
Biscay, Bay of	Golfo de Vizcaya
Bosporus	Bósforo
California, Gulf of	Golfo de California; Mar de Cortez
English Channel	Canal de la Mancha
Florida Strait	Canal de Florida
Gibraltar, Strait of	Estrecho de Gibraltar
Hudson Bay	Bahía *o* Mar de Hudson
Magellan, Strait of	Estrecho de Magallanes
Mexico, Gulf of	Golfo de México
Panama Canal	Canal de Panamá
Persian Gulf	Golfo Pérsico
St. Lawrence, Gulf of	Golfo de San Lorenzo
St. Lawrence Seaway	Vía Marítima San Lorenzo
Suez Canal	Canal de Suez

MOUNTAIN RANGES	SIERRAS, CORDILLERAS
Adirondack Mts., USA	Mtes. Adirondacks
Allegheny Mts., USA	Mtes. Allegheny
Alps Mts., Europe	Alpes
Andes Mts., South America	C. de los Andes
Appalachian Mts., USA	Mtes. Apalaches
Balkans, Europe	Balcanes
Carpathian Mts., Europe	Mtes. Cárpatos
Cascade Range, USA-Canada	C. de las Cascadas
Catskill Mts., USA	Mtes. Catskills
Caucasus Mts., Europe	Mtes. Caucaso
Himalaya Mts., Asia	C. de los Himalaya
Pyrenees Mts., Europe	Mtes. Pirineos
Rocky Mts., USA	Montañas Rocosas
Sierra Nevada, USA	Sierra Nevada
St. Elias Mts., Alaska-Yukon	Mtes. San Elías
Ural Mts., Russia-Siberia	Mtes. Urales

MOUNTAIN PEAKS	PICOS
Aconcagua, Argentina (Andes)	Aconcagua
Elbrus, Europe (Caucasus)	Elbrus
Etna, Sicily	Etna
Everest, Nepal-Tibet (Himalayas)	Everest
Fujiyama, Japan	Fujiyama
Kilimanjaro, Tanzania	Kilimanjaro
Logan, Canada (St. Elias Mts.)	Logan
Matterhorn, Switzerland (Alps)	Matterhorn; Cervino
Mauna Loa, Hawaii	Mauna Loa
McKinley, Alaska	McKinley
Mont Blanc, France-Italy (Alps)	Monte Blanco
Monte Rosa, Switzerland (Alps)	Monte Rosa

MOUNTAIN PEAKS	PICOS
Orizaba, Mexico	Orizaba
Pikes Peak, USA (Rockies)	Pikes Peak
Popocatepetl, Mexico	Popocatépetl
Rainier, USA (Cascades)	Rainier
Shasta, USA (Cascades)	Shasta
Sinai, Egypt	Sinaí
Vesuvius, Italy	Vesubio
Whitney, USA (Sierra Nevada)	Whitney

A

A, a (ei) **1,** primera letra del alfabeto inglés. **2,** *mus.* la. **3,** (*denota*) primera clase; mejor calidad; primer grado; excelencia.

a (ə; ei *bajo acento*) *adj., art. indef.* un; *fem.* una. También (*ante vocal o* h *muda*) **an.**

aback (ə'bæk) *adv.* atrás; detrás; al fondo. —**taken aback,** desconcertado; aturdido.

abacus ('æb·ə·kəs) *n.* ábaco.

abandon (ə'bæn·dən) *v.t.* abandonar; dejar; desechar; desistir de. —*n.* desenfado; indiferencia. —**abandoned,** *adj.* abandonado; indiferente; descuidado. —**abandonment,** *n.* abandono; desamparo.

abase (ə'beis) *v.t.* degradar; rebajar; humillar. —**abasement,** *n.* abatimiento; humillación.

abash (ə'bæʃ) *v.t.* avergonzar; desconcertar; aturdir.

abate (ə'beit) *v.t.* **1,** (reduce) reducir; disminuir; rebajar. **2,** *law* suprimir; condonar; suspender. —*v.i.* mermar; menguar. —**abatement,** *n.* rebaja; disminución.

abbé (æ'be) *n.* abate.

abbess ('æb·ɛs) *n.* abadesa; superiora; prelada.

abbey ('æb·i) *n.* abadía; monasterio.

abbot ('æb·ət) *n.* abad. —**abbacy** ('æb·ə·si) *n.* [*pl.* **-cies** (-siz)] abadía.

abbreviate (ə'bri·vi·eit) *v.t.* abreviar; acortar; compendiar. —**abbreviation,** *n.* abreviación; abreviatura.

abc's (ei·bi'siːz) *n.* abecé; rudimentos.

abdicate ('æb·də·keit) *v.t. & i.* abdicar; renunciar. —**abdication,** *n.* abdicación; renuncia.

abdomen ('æb·də·mən) *n.* abdomen; vientre. —**abdominal** (æb'dam·ɪ·nəl) *adj.* abdominal.

abduct (æb'dʌkt) *v.t.* secuestrar. —**abduction** (-'dʌk·ʃən) *n.* secuestro. —**abductor,** *n.* secuestrador.

abeam (ə'biːm) *adv., naut.* a través; por el lado; en dirección lateral.

abed (ə'bɛd) *adv.* en cama; acostado.

aberrant (æb'ɛr·ənt) *adj.* errado; irregular; anómalo. —**aberrance,**

aberrancy, *n.* error; equivocación; extravío.

aberration (æb·ə'rei·ʃən) *n.* **1,** (displacement; deviation) error; extravío; desviación. **2,** *astron.; opt.* aberración.

abet (ə'bet) *v.t.* [**abetted, -ting**] instigar; inducir; animar. —**abetter, abettor,** *n.* instigador; cómplice. —**abetment,** *n.* instigación.

abeyance (ə'bei·əns) *n.* suspensión; expectación; dilación.

abhor (æb'hɔːr) *v.t.* [**abhorred, abhorring**] aborrecer; detestar; odiar. —**abhorrence** (æb'har·əns) *n.* aborrecimiento; aversión; odio. —**abhorrent,** *adj.* aborrecible; detestable.

abide (ə'baid) *v.t.* soportar; aguantar. —*v.i.* [*pret. & p.p.* **abode**] **1,** (remain) permanecer. **2,** (continue) continuar; seguir. **3,** (dwell) morar. **4,** (stand firm) permanecer; sostenerse.

ability (ə'bɪl·ə·ti) *n.* **1,** (capacity) habilidad; capacidad. **2,** (skill) ingenio; competencia; aptitud.

abject ('æb·dʒekt) *adj.* abyecto; vil; despreciable. —**abjectness,** *n.* abyección.

abjure (æb'dʒʊr) *v.t.* abjurar; renunciar. —**abjuration** (ˌæb·dʒə'rei·ʃən) *n.* abjuración.

ablative ('æb·lə·tɪv) *adj. & n.* ablativo.

ablaze (ə'bleiz) *adv.* en llamas. —*adj.* **1,** (afire) encendido. **2,** (lit up) iluminado; alumbrado.

able ('ei·bəl) *adj.* **1,** (capable) apto; capaz. **2,** (talented) competente; hábil; talentoso. —**ably** ('ei·bli) *adv.* hábilmente.

able-bodied ('ei·bəl'ba·did) *adj.* robusto; fuerte; sano. —**able-bodied seaman,** marinero ordinario.

abnegate ('æb·nə·geit) *v.t.* renunciar a; privarse de; negar. —**abnegation,** *n.* abnegación; renunciación.

abnormal (æb'nor·məl) *adj.* **1,** (unusual) anormal; desusado; raro. **2,** (deviating) anormal; contranatural. —**abnormality** (ˌæb·nor·'mæl·ə·ti) *n.* anormalidad; anomalía.

aboard (ə'bord) *adv.* & *prep.* a bordo (de). —**all aboard!**, ¡pasajeros al tren!

abode (ə'boːd) *v., pret.* & *p.p. de* **abide**. —*n.* 1, (dwelling place) domicilio; morada. 2, (sojourn) estancia; permanencia.

abolish (ə'bal·ıʃ) *v.t.* abolir; derogar; suprimir. —**abolishment**, *n.* abolición; anulamiento; derogación.

abolition (,æb·ə'lıʃ·ən) *n.* abolición; supresión; derogación. —**abolitionism**, *n.* abolicionismo. —**abolitionist**, *n.* abolicionista.

A-bomb ('ei,bam) *n.* bomba atómica.

abominable (ə'bam·ı·nə·bəl) *adj.* abominable; odioso.

abominate (ə'bam·ı·neit) *v.t.* abominar; aborrecer; odiar. —**abomination**, *n.* abominación; repugnancia; odio.

aboriginal (,æb·ə'rıdʒ·ı·nəl) *adj.* aborigen; indígena. —**aborigines** (-niz) *n.pl.* [*sing.* **-ne** (-ni)] aborígenes; indígenas.

abort (ə'bort) *v.i.* abortar.—*v.t.* 1, (deliver prematurely) abortar. 2, (produce abortion in) hacer abortar. —**abortive**, *adj.* abortivo. —**abortion** (ə'bor·ʃən) *n.* aborto. —**abortionist**, *n.* abortista.

abound (ə'baund) *v.i.* abundar. —**abound in**, tener en cantidad; abundar en o de.

about (ə'baut) *adv.* alrededor; poco más o menos; aproximadamente. —*prep.* en o con referencia a; acerca de; por. —**about to**, a punto de.

about-face *n.* media vuelta.

above (ə'bʌv) *prep.* sobre; encima de; superior a. —*adv.* arriba; antes. —*adj.* antedicho; ya mencionado. —**above all**, sobre todo; principalmente.

aboveboard (ə'bʌv,bord) *adj.* franco; sincero. —*adv.* al descubierto; sin rodeos.

abracadabra (,æb·rə·kə'dæb·rə) *n.* abracadabra.

abrade (ə'breid) *v.t.* raer; raspar.

abrasion (ə'brei·ʒən) *n.* raedura; raspadura; abrasión. —**abrasive** (-sıv) *adj.* & *n.* abrasivo.

abreast (ə'brest) *adv.* 1, (side by side) de frente. 2, (in marching) en fondo.

abridge (ə'brıdʒ) *v.t.* 1, (shorten) condensar; resumir; compendiar. 2,

(curtail) cortar; privar. —**abridgment**, *n.* compendio; resumen.

abroad (ə'broːd) *adv.* 1, (in a foreign country) en el extranjero. 2, (in circulation) entre el público. 3, (outdoors) afuera.

abrogate ('æb·rə,geit) *v.t.* revocar por ley; abolir; abrogar. —**abrogation**, *n.* abrogación.

abrupt (ə'brʌpt) *adj.* 1, (suddenly changing) repentino; brusco; impensado. 2, (precipitous) abrupto; escarpado; áspero. —**abruptness**, *n.* aspereza.

abscess ('æb·sɛs) *n.* absceso.

abscissa (æb'sıs·ə) *n., geom.* abscisa.

abscond (æb'skand) *v.i.* evadirse; esconderse; desaparecer.

absence ('æb·səns) *n.* ausencia; falta.

absent ('æb·sənt) *adj.* ausente; no presente. —**absentee** (,æb·sən'tiː) *n.* ausente. —**absenteeism**, *n.* absentismo. —**absent** (æb'sent) **oneself**, ausentarse; irse; retirarse.

absentminded ('æb·sənt,main·dıd) *adj.* abstraído; distraído; olvidadizo. —**absentmindedness**, *n.* distracción; olvido.

absinthe ('æb·sınθ) *n.* absintio; ajenjo.

absolute (æb·sə'lut) *adj.* 1, (unqualified) absoluto; perfecto. 2, (complete) completo; total. —**absoluteness**, *n.* lo absoluto. —**absolutely**, *adv.* en absoluto; terminantemente.

absolution (æb·sə'lu·ʃən) *n.* absolución; perdón.

absolutism ('æb·sə·lu·tiz·əm) *n.* absolutismo.

absolve (æb'salv) *v.t.* absolver; perdonar; justificar.

absorb (æb'sorb) *v.t.* 1, (suck up or in) absorber. 2, (assimilate) asimilar. 3, (engulf completely) preocupar. —**absorbed**, *adj.* absorto; absorbido. —**absorbent**, *adj.* absorbente. —**absorbency**, *n.* absorbencia. —**absorbing**, *adj.* absorbente; interesante.

absorption (æb'sorp·ʃən) *n.* 1, (a sucking in) absorción. 2, (assimilation) asimilación. 3, (preoccupation) preocupación. —**absorptive** (-tıv) *adj.* absorbente.

abstain (æb'stein) *v.i.* abstenerse; retraerse; privarse. —**abstainer**, *n.* abstinente.

abstemious (æb'stiː·mi·əs) *adj.*

abstemio; sobrio; parco.
—**abstemiousness**, *n.* sobriedad.
abstention (æb'stɛn·ʃən) *n.*
abstención. —**abstentious**, *adj.*
abstinente.
abstinence ('æb·stɪ·nəns) *n.*
abstinencia. —**abstinent**, *adj.*
abstinente.
abstract (æb'strækt) *v.t.* 1, (consider) considerar; abstraer. 2, (take away) separar; alejar. 3, (epitomize) compendiar; resumir; extractar. —*n.* ('æb·strækt) 1, (summary) resumen; extracto. 2, (essential aspect) extracto; meollo. —*adj.* abstracto. —**abstracted**, *adj.* abstraído; desatento; preocupado.
abstraction (æb'stræk·ʃən) *n.* 1, abstracción. 2, (absentmindedness) descuido; desatención.
abstruse (æb'strus) *adj.* abstruso; oscuro. —**abstruseness**, *n.* oscuridad.
absurd (æb'sʌrd) *adj.* absurdo; ilógico; ridículo; disparatado. —**absurdity**, *n.* disparate; ilógica; absurdo.
abundance (ə'bʌn·dəns) *also,* **abundancy**, *n.* abundancia; plenitud; afluencia. —**abundant**, *adj.* abundante; lleno; copioso.
abuse (ə'bjuːz) *v.t.* 1, (misapply) usar mal. 2, (do wrong to) abusar de. 3, (injure) maltratar; ultrajar. 4, (revile) denostar; ofender. —*n.* (ə'bjus) abuso; maltrato; insulto. —**abusive** (-sɪv) *adj.* abusivo.
abut (ə'bʌt) *v.t.* [abutted, -ting] limitar con; colindar con; confinar.
abutment (ə'bʌt·mənt) *n.* 1, (juxtaposition) contigüidad; yuxtaposición. 2, *archit.* contrafuerte; estribo.
abysmal (ə'bɪz·məl) *adj.* abismal; insondable.
abyss (ə'bɪs) *n.* abismo; sima.
acacia (ə'kei·ʃə) *n.* acacia.
academe ('æk·ə‚dim) *n.* ámbito académico. —**academia** (‚æk·ə'diː·mi·ə) *n.* los académicos; los universitarios.
academy (ə'kæd·ə·mi) *n.* academia; centro de enseñanza. —**academic** (‚æk·ə'dɛm·ɪk) *adj. & n.* académico. —**academician** (ə‚kæd·ə·'mɪʃ·ən) *n.* académico.
acanthus (ə'kæn·θəs) *n.* acanto.
accede (æk'siːd) *v.i.* acceder; asentir; consentir.
accelerate (æk'sɛl·ə·reit) *v.t.* acelerar; precipitar. —*v.i.* acelerarse; precipitarse; apresurarse.

—**acceleration**, *n.* aceleración; precipitación. —**accelerator**, *n.* acelerador.
accent ('æk·sɛnt) *n.* acento; énfasis. —*v.t.* (*también,* æk'sɛnt) acentuar.
accentuate (æk'sən·tʃu·eit) *v.t.* acentuar; hacer énfasis en. —**accentuation**, *n.* acentuación.
accept (æk'sɛpt) *v.t.* 1, (take in a formal way) aceptar; acoger bien. 2, (agree to) aceptar; admitir.
acceptable (æk'sɛp·tə·bəl) *adj.* aceptable. —**acceptability**, *n.* aceptabilidad.
acceptance (æk'sɛp·təns) *n.* aceptación; admisión.
acceptation (‚æk·sɛp'tei·ʃən) *n.*, *gram.* acepción.
access ('æk·sɛs) *n.* acceso. —**accessible** (æk'sɛs·ə·bəl) *adj.* accesible. —**accessibility**, *n.* accesibilidad.
accession (æk'sɛʃ·ən) 1, (attainment) accesión; advenimiento. 2, (increase) incremento. 3, (consent) consentimiento; asentimiento.
accessory (æk'sɛs·ə·ri) *n.* 1, (subordinate part) accesorio; secundario. 2, *law* cómplice. —*adj.* 1, (belonging to) accesorio; adjunto. 2, (contributory) contribuyente. —**accessories**, *n.pl.* accesorios; extras; repuestos.
accident ('æk·sɪ·dənt) *n.* accidente; contratiempo; percance.
accidental (‚æk·sɪ'dɛn·təl) *adj.* 1, (occurring by chance) accidental; casual. 2, (subsidiary) secundario. —*n., mus.* acorde accidental.
acclaim (ə'kleim) *v.t.* aclamar; vitorear; aplaudir. —*n.* aplauso. —**acclamation** (æk·lə'mei·ʃən) *n.* aclamación.
acclimate (ə'klai·mət) *también,* **acclimatize** *v.t.* aclimatar; acostumbrar. —*v.i.* aclimatarse; acostumbrarse. —**acclimation** (‚æk·lə'mei·ʃən), **acclimatization** (ə‚klai·mə·tɪ'zei·ʃən) *n.* aclimatación.
accommodate (ə'kɑm·ə·deit) *v.t.* 1, (adapt) acomodar; arreglar; ordenar. 2, (lodge) acomodar; hospedar. 3, (serve) ayudar. 4, (please; satisfy) complacer. —**accommodating**, *adj.* complaciente.
accommodation (ə‚kɑm·ə'dei·ʃən) *n.* 1, (adaptation) arreglo; acomodo. 2, (readiness to serve) servicio; favor. 3, *pl.* (facilities) facilidades; conveniencias.

accompany (ə'kʌm·pə·ni) *v.t.* acompañar. —**accompanist,** *n.* acompañador. —**accompaniment,** *n.* acompañamiento.

accomplice (ə'kam·plɪs) *n.* cómplice.

accomplish (ə'kam·plɪʃ) *v.t.* **1,** (do) realizar; cumplir. **2,** (achieve) lograr; conseguir. **3,** (complete) concluir; culminar. —**accomplishment,** *n.* resultado; logro; éxito.

accomplished (ə'kam·plɪʃt) *adj.* **1,** (done) realizado; cumplido. **2,** (talented) perfecto; consumado; diestro.

accord (ə'kord) *v.t.* **1,** (agree) acordar; pactar; convenir. **2,** (concede) conceder; acceder. —*v.i.* avenirse. —*n.* acuerdo; pacto. —**of one's own accord,** espontáneamente. —**with one accord,** unánimemente.

accordance (ə'kord·əns) *n.* conformidad. —**accordant,** *adj.* acorde; conforme. —**in accordance with,** de acuerdo con; de conformidad a o con.

according (ə'kor·dɪŋ) *adv.* acorde; según. —**accordingly,** *adv.* por lo tanto; por consiguiente. —**according to,** de acuerdo con; conforme a.

accordion (ə'kor·di·ən) *n.* acordeón. —**accordionist,** *n.* acordeonista.

accost (ə'kost) *v.t.* abordar; acercarse a.

account (ə'kaunt) *n.* **1,** (business record) cuenta. **2,** (enumeration) enumeración; cuenta; relato. **3,** (explanation) explicación; razón. —*v.t.* estimar; calificar; imputar. —**account for,** explicar; responder de. —**on account,** *comm.* a cuenta. —**on account of, 1,** (because of) porque. **2,** (for the sake of) en favor de; por. —**no account,** de ninguna manera. —**take account of,** *también,* **take into account,** considerar; tener o tomar en cuenta.

accountable (ə'kaun·tə·bəl) *adj.* **1,** (explicable) explicable. **2,** (responsible) responsable.

accountant (ə'kaunt·ənt) *n.* contador; tenedor de libros. —**accountancy; accounting,** *n.* contabilidad; teneduría de libros.

account executive ejecutivo de cuentas.

accouterments (ə'ku·tər·mənts) *n.pl.* adornos; atavío(s).

accredit (ə'kred·ɪt) *v.t.* **1,** (believe) dar crédito a; creer. **2,** (attribute to) atribuir a. **3,** (bring into favor) acreditar; abonar. **4,** (confer authority upon) dar credenciales a; autorizar.

accretion (ə'kri·ʃən) *n.* acreción; acrecencia.

accrue (ə'kru) *v.i.* **1,** (come about) provenir; resultar. **2,** (increase) acrecentarse; aumentar; crecer. —**accrual,** *n.* acrecencia; acrecentamiento.

accumulate (ə'kju·mjə·leit) *v.t.* acumular; amasar. —*v.i.* acumularse; amontonarse. —**accumulation,** *n.* acumulación; acopio. —**accumulative** (-lə·tɪv) *adj.* acumulador.

accuracy ('æk·ju·rə·si) *n.* precisión; minuciosidad; exactitud.

accurate ('æk·ju·rət) *adj.* correcto; verdadero; exacto. —**accurateness,** *n.* precisión; esmero.

accursed (ə'kʌr·səd) *también,* **accurst** ('kʌrst) *adj.* maldito; maldecido; perverso; detestable. —**accursedness,** *n.* maldición; desventura; infamia.

accusative (ə'kju·zə·tɪv) *adj.* & *n., gram.* acusativo.

accuse (ə'kjuz) *v.t.* acusar; inculpar; denunciar. —**accusation** (,æk·ju'zei·ʃən) *n.* acusación; denuncia; cargo.

accustom (ə'kʌs·təm) *v.t.* acostumbrar; habituar. —**accustomed,** *adj* acostumbrado; usual.

ace (eis) *n.* as. —*adj.* experto; sobresaliente. —**within an ace of,** a dos dedos de.

acerbity (ə'sʌr·bə·ti) *n.* acerbidad; amargura.

acetanilide (,æs·ɪ'tæn·ə·lɪd) *n.* acetanilida.

acetate ('æs·ə·teit) *n.* acetato. —**cellulose acetate,** *n.* acetato de celulosa.

acetic (ə'si·tɪk) *adj.* acético. —**acetic acid,** ácido acético.

acetone ('æs·ə·ton) *n.* acetona.

acetylene (ə'sɛt·ə·lɪn; -liːn) *n.* acetileno. —**acetylene torch,** soplete oxiacetilénico.

ache (eik) *n.* dolor. —*v.i.* **1,** (cause pain) doler. **2,** (suffer pain) tener dolor. —**ache for,** *colloq.* desear; anhelar.

achieve (ə'tʃiv) *v.t.* conseguir; realizar; lograr. —**achievement,** *n.* resultado; logro.

acid ('æs·ɪd) *n.* ácido. —*adj.* ácido;

agrio. —**acidify,** *v.t.* acidificar.
—*v.i.* acidificarse. —**acidity** (æ'sɪd·ə·ti) *n.* acidez.

ack-ack ('æk'æk) *n.* fuego antiaéreo.

acknowledge (æk'nal·ɪdʒ) *v.t.* **1,** (admit) reconocer; admitir; aceptar. **2,** (certify receipt of) acusar recibo de. —**acknowledgment; acknowledgement,** *n.* reconocimiento; aceptación; admisión.

acme ('æk·mi) *n.* cima; cumbre; colmo.

acne ('æk·ni) *n.* acné.

acolyte ('æk·ə·ˌlait) *n.* acólito; monaguillo.

aconite ('æk·ə,nait) *n.* acónito.

acorn ('ei·kɔrn) *n.* bellota.

acoustic (ə'kus·tɪk) *adj.* acústico. —**acoustics,** *n.pl.* acústica.

acquaint (ə'kweint) *v.t.* **1,** (make familiar with) familiarizar. **2,** (inform) enterar; informar.

acquaintance (ə'kwein·təns) *n.* **1,** (knowledge) conocimiento; noción. **2,** (person) conocido. —**acquaintanceship,** *n.* conocimiento; relación.

acquiesce (ˌæk·wi'ɛs) *v.i.* consentir; acceder. —**acquiesce in,** aprobar; admitir.

acquiescent (ˌæk·wi'ɛs·ənt) *adj.* condescendiente; conforme; acorde. —**acquiescence,** *n.* aquiescencia; consentimiento; aprobación.

acquire (ə'kwair) *v.t.* adquirir; conseguir; alcanzar; obtener. —**acquirement,** *n.* obtención.

acquisition (æk·wə'zɪʃ·ən) *n.* adquisición.

acquisitive (ə'kwɪz·ə·tɪv) *adj.* avaricioso; codicioso. —**acquisitiveness,** *n.* avaricia; codicia.

acquit (ə'kwɪt) *v.t.* [**acquitted, -ting**] **1,** (absolve) exonerar; absolver. **2,** (settle, as debts) pagar; cancelar. —**acquit oneself,** conducirse; comportarse.

acquittal (ə'kwɪt·əl) *n.* **1,** (discharge of duty) descargo; licencia. **2,** *law* exoneración; absolución.

acre ('ei·kər) *n.* acre (40.469 áreas). —**acreage,** *n.* superficie medida en acres.

acrid ('æk·rɪd) *adj.* acre; amargo; agrio. —**acridity** (ə'krɪd·ə·ti); **acridness,** *n.* acritud; acidez; mordacidad.

acrimony ('æk·rə·mo·ni) *n.* acrimonia; aspereza. —**acrimo-**

nious (-'mo·ni·əs) *adj.* acrimonioso; áspero.

acrobat ('æk·rə·bæt) *n.* acróbata. —**acrobatic** (-'bæt·ɪk) *adj.* acrobático. —**acrobatics,** *n.* acrobacia; acrobatismo.

acronym ('æk·rə·nɪm) *n.* sigla.

acrophobia (ˌæk·rə'fo·bi·ə) *n.* acrofobia.

across (ə'krɔs) *adv.* a través; de través; al otro lado; transversalmente. —*prep.* al otro lado de; por; a través de. —**across-the-board,** *adj.* general; que incluye todos. —**come across, 1,** encontrarse con; dar en; hallar. **2,** (*con* **with**) entregar.

acrylic (ə'krɪl·ɪk) *adj.* & *n.* acrílico.

act (ækt) *v.i.* **1,** (do something) actuar; hacer; obrar. **2,** (behave) comportarse; conducirse. **3,** *theat.* representar; actuar. —*v.t.* **1,** (do) actuar; obrar. **2,** *theat.* actuar; representar *o* desempeñar el papel de. —*n.* **1,** (deed) acto; acción; hecho. **2,** *law* decreto. **3,** *theat.* acto. —**put on an act,** *colloq.* hacer escenas.

acting ('ækt·ɪŋ) *n.* **1,** *theat.* actuación; representación. **2,** (affected behavior) simulación; fingimiento. —*adj.* interino; provisional; suplente.

actinic (æk'tɪn·ɪk) *adj.* actínico.

actinium (æk'tɪn·i·əm) *n.* actinio.

actinon ('æk·tɪ·nən) *n.* actinón.

action ('æk·ʃən) *n.* **1,** (act) acción; hecho; obra. **2,** (behavior) acto; gesto. **3,** *mil.* acción; batalla. **4,** (of a play or narrative) acción; desarrollo; argumento. **5,** *law* demanda; proceso. —**actionable,** *adj.* litigable; procesable. —**bring action,** demandar; procesar. —**in action, 1,** (operating) obrando; actuando; activo. **2,** *mil.* en el combate; en campaña. —**take action, 1,** *law* procesar. **2,** (begin to act) comenzar a actuar; obrar.

activate ('æk·tə,veit) *v.t.* activar. —**activation,** *n.* activación. —**activator,** *n.* activador.

active ('æk·tɪv) *adj.* **1,** (brisk) activo; enérgico. **2,** *gram.* activo; transitivo. —**activeness; activity** (-'tɪv·ə·ti) *n.* actividad; viveza. —**activities,** *n.pl.* ocupaciones; actividades.

actor ('æk·tər) *n.* actor. —**actress** (-trɪs) *n.* actriz.

actual ('æk·tʃu·əl) *adj.* **1,** (real) real; verdadero. **2,** (present) actual; presente; existente. —**actuality** (-'æl·ə·ti) *n.* realidad. —**actualize,** *v.t.* realizar. —**actually,** *adv.* realmente; en realidad.

actuary ('æk·tʃu‚ɛr·i) *n.* actuario. —**actuarial** (-'ɛr·i·əl) *adj.* actuarial.

actuate ('æk·tʃu·eit) *v.t.* actuar; activar; impulsar; mover. —**actuation,** *n.* actuación; impulso.

acuity (ə'kju·ə·ti) *n.* agudeza.

acumen (ə'kju·mən) *n.* cacumen; acumen; perspicacia.

acupuncture ('æk·ju‚pʌŋk·tʃər) *n.* acupuntura.

acute (ə'kjut) *adj.* **1,** (sharp) agudo; penetrante. **2,** (perceptive) ingenioso; vivo; sutil. —**acuteness,** *n.* agudeza.

ad (æd) *n., colloq.* = **advertisement.**

adage ('æd·idʒ) *n.* adagio; proverbio.

adagio (ə'dɑ‚·ʒo) *n., mus.* adagio.

adamant ('æd·ə·mənt) *adj.* reacio; porfiado; duro; inflexible. —*n.* diamante.

Adam's apple ('æd·əmz) nuez.

adapt (ə'dæpt) *v.t.* adaptar; convertir; arreglar. —*v.i.* adaptarse. —**adaptable,** *adj.* adaptable; transformable; convertible. —**adaptation** (‚æd·əp'tei·ʃən) *n.* adaptación; arreglo.

add (æd) *v.t.* añadir; agregar; unir. —*v.i.* sumar.

adder ('æd·ər) *n.* serpiente; víbora.

addict ('æd·ikt) *n.* **1,** (enthusiast) adicto; adepto; partidario. **2,** (drug addict) vicioso de drogas; morfinómano. —**addicted** (ə'dik·tid) *adj.* adicto; aficionado.

addiction (ə'dik·ʃən) *n.* **1,** inclinación; tendencia; propensión. **2,** afición a las drogas; morfinomanía.

adding machine máquina de sumar; calculadora.

addition (ə'dif·ən) *n.* **1,** *aritm.* suma; adición. **2,** (something added) añadidura. —**in addition (to),** además (de).

additional (ə'dif·ən·əl) *adj.* adicional; aditicio.

additive ('æd·ə·tiv) *adj. & n.* aditivo.

addle ('æd·əl) *adj.* huero. —*v.t.* **1,** (make rotten) enhuerar. **2,** (confuse) ofuscar; enturbiar. —*v.i.* enhuerarse.

address (ə'drɛs) *v.t.* **1,** (speak or write to) hablar con o a; escribir a; dirigirse a. **2,** (pay court to) piropear; galantear. —*n.* **1,** (speech) alocución; discurso. **2,** (dwelling or mailing place) señas; domicilio; dirección. **3,** (formal utterance) petición. —**address oneself to,** volverse a; aplicarse a; dedicarse a. —**addressee,** *n.* destinatario. —**addresser; addressor,** *n.* remitente.

adduce (ə'djus) *v.t.* aducir; alegar.

adenoid ('æd·ə·noid) *n.* adenoide. —**adenoidal** (-'noid·əl) *adj.* adenoideo.

adept *n.* ('æd·ɛpt) & *adj.* (ə'dɛpt) adepto; eficiente. —**adeptness** (ə'dɛpt·nəs) *n.* eficiencia; pericia.

adequate ('æd·ɪ·kwət) *adj.* adecuado; apto; oportuno. —**adequacy,** *n.* oportunidad; pertinencia.

adhere (æd'hɪr) *v.i.* adherirse; pegarse; unirse. —**adherence,** *n.* adherencia. —**adherent,** *adj. & n.* adherente.

adhesion (æd'hiʒ·ʒən) *n.* adhesión.

adhesive (æd'hiʒ·siv) *adj.* adhesivo; pegajoso; pertinaz. —*n.* adhesivo. —**adhesive tape,** esparadrapo.

adieu (ə'dju) *interj.* adiós. —*n.* [*pl.* **adieus; adieux** (ə'djuːz)] despedida; adiós.

adipose ('æd·ɪ·pos) *adj.* adiposo.

adjacent (ə'dʒei·sənt) *adj.* adyacente; contiguo; colindante. —**adjacency,** *n.* contigüidad; colindancia.

adjective ('ædʒ·ək·tiv) *n. & adj.* adjetivo. —**adjectival** (-'tai·vəl) *adj.* adjetival.

adjoin (ə'dʒɔin) *v.t. & i.* yuxtaponer; lindar; colindar. —**adjoining,** *adj.* contiguo.

adjourn (ə'dʒʌrn) *v.t.* aplazar; diferir; dilatar. —**adjournment,** *n.* aplazamiento; dilación.

adjudge (ə'dʒʌdʒ) *v.t.* **1,** (decree) decretar; juzgar. **2,** (award) adjudicar; conferir.

adjudicate (ə'dʒu·di·ket) *v.t. & i.* juzgar. —**adjudication,** *n.* sentencia; fallo.

adjunct ('æ·dʒʌŋkt) *n. & adj.* anexo; adjunto; asociado.

adjuration (‚ædʒ·rei·ʃən) *n.* **1,** (command) orden imperiosa. **2,** (entreaty) conjuro; ruego.

adjure (ə'dʒur) *v.t.* **1,** (command) ordenar. **2,** (entreat) conjurar; rogar.

adjust (ə'dʒʌst) *v.t.* **1,** (adapt) ajustar; adaptar. **2,** (put in order) acomodar; arreglar; ordenar. **3,** (settle) asegurar; ajustar; asentar. —*v.i.* ajustarse. —**adjustment,** *n.* ajuste; arreglo.

adjutant ('ædʒ·ə·tənt) *n.* ayudante; asistente.

ad-lib (ˌæd'lɪb) *v.t.* & *i.* improvisar. —*adj.* improvisado. —*n.* improvisación.

administer (æd'mɪn·ɪs·tər) *v.t.* **1,** (manage) administrar; regentar; conducir. **2,** (supply) proveer; suplir; dispensar. —**administer to,** ayudar; socorrer.

administration (æd,mɪn·ɪ'streɪ·ʃən) *n.* administración.

administrative (æd'mɪn·ɪˌstreɪ·tɪv) *adj.* administrativo.

administrator (æd'mɪn·ɪˌstreɪ·tər) *n.* administrador.

administratrix (æd,mɪn·ɪs'treɪ·trɪks) *n.* [*pl.* **-trices** (-trəˌsiːz)] administradora.

admirable ('æd·mə·rə·bəl) *adj.* admirable; excelente; estupendo.

admiral ('æd·mə·rəl) *n.* almirante. —**admiralty,** *n.* almirantazgo.

admiration (æd·mə'reɪ·ʃən) *n.* admiración.

admire (æd'maɪr) *v.t.* admirar; apreciar; estimar.

admirer (æd'maɪr·ər) *n.* **1,** (one who admires) admirador. **2,** *colloq.* (suitor) pretendiente; enamorado.

admissible (æd'mɪs·ə·bəl) *adj.* admisible; aceptable; válido. —**admissibility,** *n.* validez; aceptabilidad.

admission (æd'mɪʃ·ən) *n.* **1,** (acknowledgment; act of admitting) admisión; confesión. **2,** (entrance fee) entrada; admisión.

admit (æd'mɪt) *v.t.* [**admitted, -ting**] **1,** (allow to enter) admitir; permitir entrar. **2,** (acknowledge) admitir; reconocer; confesar. —**admittance,** *n.* entrada.

admonish (æd'man·ɪʃ) *v.t.* **1,** (reprove mildly) amonestar; censurar. **2,** (exhort) exhortar; aconsejar. —**admonishment,** *n.* amonestación; reprensión; consejo.

admonition (æd·mə'nɪʃ·ən) *n.* **1,** (reproof) admonición; amonestación; reprensión. **2,** (warning) consejo; aviso.

ado (ə'duː) *n.* alharaca; trabajo; dificultad.

adobe (ə'doʊ·bi) *n.* adobe. —*adj.* de adobe.

adolescent (æd·ə'lɛs·ənt) *n.* &

adj. adolescente. —**adolescence,** *n.* adolescencia.

adopt (ə'dapt) *v.t.* **1,** (take as one's own) adoptar; prohijar. **2,** (vote to accept) aceptar; tomar; resolver. —**adoption** (ə'dap·ʃən) *n.* adopción; aceptación. —**adoptive,** *adj.* adoptivo.

adorable (ə'dor·ə·bəl) *adj.* adorable.

adore (ə'doːr) *v.t.* adorar; venerar. —**adoration** (æd·ə'reɪ·ʃən) *n.* adoración; veneración.

adorn (ə'dorn) *v.t.* adornar; embellecer. —**adornment,** *n.* adorno; gala; ornato.

adrenal (ə'driː·nəl) *adj.* suprarrenal.

adrenaline (ə'drɛn·ə·lɪn) *n.* adrenalina.

adrift (ə'drɪft) *adj.* flotante. —*adv.* a la deriva; al pairo.

adroit (ə'drɔɪt) *adj.* experto; hábil; diestro. —**adroitness,** *n.* habilidad; destreza.

adsorb (æd'sorb) *v.t.* adsorber. —**adsorption** (-'sorp·ʃən) *n.* adsorción. —**adsorptive** (-tɪv) *adj.* adsorptivo.

adulate ('æd·ju·let) *v.t.* adular. —**adulation,** *n.* adulación.

adult (ə'dʌlt) *n.* & *adj.* adulto; crecido; mayor. —**adulthood,** *n.* edad adulta.

adulterant (ə'dʌl·tə·rənt) *adj.* & *n.* adulterante.

adulterate (ə'dʌl·tə·reɪt) *v.t.* adulterar; falsear; viciar. —**adulteration,** *n.* adulteración; falseamiento; corrupción.

adulterer (ə'dʌl·tər·ər) *n.* adúltero. —**adulteress** (-tər·əs; -trɪs) *n.* adúltera.

adultery (ə'dʌl·tə·ri) *n.* adulterio. —**adulterous,** *adj.* adúltero.

ad valorem ('æd·və'lor·rəm) según el valor (*abbr.* **ad val.**).

advance (æd'væns) *v.t.* **1,** (bring forward) avanzar; adelantar. **2,** (suggest) sugerir; insinuar; ofrecer. **3,** *comm.* adelantar; anticipar. **4,** (promote) promover; mejorar. —*v.i.* **1,** (move forward) adelantarse; avanzar. **2,** (make progress) progresar; adelantar. **3,** (rise in price) subir. —*n.* **1,** (a move forward) avance; adelanto. **2,** (improvement) progreso; mejora. **3,** *comm.* anticipo; adelanto. —**in advance, 1,** *comm.* anticipado; por adelantado. **2,** (in front) al frente. **3,** (beforehand) antes; de antemano.

advancement (æd'væns·mənt) *n.* **1,** (forward movement) adelantamiento. **2,** (promotion) ascenso; promoción. **3,** (improvement) mejoría; prosperidad.

advantage (æd'væn·tɪdʒ) *n.* **1,** (favorable circumstance) ventaja; facilidad. **2,** (gain) beneficio; ganancia. **3,** (superiority) superioridad; preponderancia. **4,** *tennis* ventaja. —**advantageous** (ˌæd·vən'tei·dʒəs) *adj.* ventajoso. —**be of advantage to,** favorecer. —**have the advantage of,** llevar ventaja a. —**take advantage of, 1,** (for one's benefit) aprovecharse de; valerse de. **2,** (impose upon) imponerse a.

advent ('æd·vent) *n.* **1,** (arrival) llegada; venida; advenimiento. **2,** *cap., eccles.* Adviento.

adventure (æd'ven·tʃər) *n.* **1,** (remarkable event) aventura; incidente. **2,** (hazardous undertaking) aventura; riesgo; percance. —*v.t.* aventurar; arriesgar. —*v.i.* aventurarse; arriesgarse. —**adventurer,** *n.* aventurero; explorador. —**adventuress,** *n.* aventurera. —**adventurous,** *adj.* aventurado; arriesgado.

adverb ('æd·vʌrb) *n.* adverbio. —**adverbial** (æd'vʌrb·i·əl) *adj.* adverbial.

adversary ('æd·vər·ser·i) *n.* adversario; enemigo; contrincante.

adverse (æd'vʌrs) *adj.* adverso; hostil; desfavorable.

adversity (æd'vʌr·sə·ti) *n.* adversidad; infortunio; malaventura.

advertise *también,* **advertize** ('æd·vər·taiz) *v.t. & i.* anunciar; avisar. —**advertisement** (-'taiz·mənt) *n.* anuncio; aviso; noticia. —**advertising,** *n.* publicidad. —*adj.* publicitario.

advice (æd'vais) *n.* aviso; consejo; advertencia. —**take advice,** aconsejarse; orientarse.

advisable (æd'vai·zə·bəl) *adj.* aconsejable; recomendable; conveniente.

advise (æd'vaiz) *v.t.* **1,** (give counsel to) avisar; aconsejar. **2,** (give information to) advertir; orientar. **3,** (recommend) recomendar. —**advised,** *adj.* avisado; advertido; aconsejado. —**adviser; advisor** (-zər) *n.* aconsejador; consejero. —**advisement,** *n.* parecer; opinión;

consideración. —**advisory,** *adj.* consultor; consejero.

advocacy ('æd·vɔ·kə·si) *n.* defensa; vindicación.

advocate ('æd·vɔ,keit) *v.t.* abogar por; defender; interceder por. —*n.* (-kət) abogado; defensor.

adz *también,* **adze** (ædz) *n.* azuela.

aegis *también,* **egis** ('iː·dʒɪs) *n.* égida.

aerate ('e·ɔr,et; 'eɪr-) *v.t.* **1,** (expose to air) airear; ventilar. **2,** (charge with air) impregnar o saturar con aire. —**aeration,** *n.* aeración. —**aerator,** *n.* aparato para aeración; fumigadora.

aerial ('eɪr·i·əl; e'ɪr-) *adj.* **1,** *lit.* aéreo. **1,** *fig.* etéreo; sutil; leve. —*n.* ('eɪr·i·əl) antena. —**aerialist,** *n.* trapecista.

aerie ('eɪr·i; 'ɪr·i) *n.* = **eyrie.**

aerobe ('eɪr,rob) *n.* aerobio.

aerobic (e'ro·bɪk) *adj.* aeróbico. —**aerobics,** *n.sing.* o *pl.* ejercicios aeróbicos.

aerodynamics (ˌeɪr·o·dai'næm·ɪks) *n.pl.* aerodinámica. —**aerodynamic,** *adj.* aerodinámico.

aerosol ('eɪr·ə,sɔl) *n.* aerosol.

aerospace ('eɪr·o,speis) *adj.* aero(e)spacial. —*n.* (todo) el espacio.

aerostat ('eɪr·ə,stæt) *n.* aeróstato.

aerostatic (ˌeɪr·ə'stæt·ɪk) *adj.* aerostático. —**aerostatics,** *n.* aerostática.

aesthete ('es·θit) *n.* = **esthete.** —**aesthetic** (es'θɛt·ɪk) *adj.* = **esthetic.** —**aesthetics** *n.* = **esthetics.**

afar (ə'faɪr) *adv.* lejos; distante.

affable ('æf·ə·bəl) *adj.* afable; cariñoso; condescendiente. —**affability,** *n.* afabilidad; condescendencia.

affair (ə'feɪr) *n.* **1,** (event; matter) suceso; acontecimiento; hecho. **2,** *colloq.* (involvement of love) aventura. **3,** *pl.* (business) asuntos; cosas; negocios.

affect (ə'fɛkt) *v.t.* **1,** (change) afectar; cambiar; influenciar. **2,** (feign) simular; fingir. **3,** (make a show of) impresionar; conmover.

affectation (ˌæf·ɛk'tei·ʃən) *n.* afectación; amaneramiento; pretensión; presunción.

affected (ə'fɛk·tɪd) *adj.* **1,** (influenced) afectado; influenciado; influido. **2,** (artificial in manner) amanerado; afectado. **3,** (moved by emotion) conmovido. **4,** (afflicted) afectado; atacado; afligido.

affecting (ə'fɛk·tiŋ) *adj.* conmovedor; emocionante; tierno.

affection (ə'fɛk·ʃən) *n.* afección; afecto; cariño. —**affectionate,** *adj.* afecto; afectuoso; cariñoso.

affective (ə'fɛk·tiv) *adj.* afectivo.

affidavit (ˌæf·ɪ'dei·vɪt) *n.* aval; garantía; declaración jurada.

affiliate (ə'fɪl·i·eit) *v.i.* afiliarse; asociarse. —*v.t.* afiliar; asociar; incorporar. —*n.* (-ət) afiliado; asociado; socio. —**affiliation,** *n.* afiliación; asociación.

affinity (ə'fɪn·ə·ti) *n.* afinidad.

affirm (ə'fʌrm) *v.t.* **1,** (assert) afirmar; aseverar; sostener. **2,** (confirm) confirmar; ratificar. **3,** *law* jurar. —**affirmation** (ˌæf·ər'mei·ʃən) *n.* afirmación; ratificación. —**affirmative** (ə'fʌr·mə·tiv) *adj.* & *n.* afirmativo; aseverativo.

affix (ə'fɪks) *v.t.* **1,** (add; append) añadir; juntar. **2,** (fasten) fijar; pegar. —*n.* ('æf·ɪks) **1,** *gram.* afijo. **2,** (an addition) añadidura.

afflatus (ə'flei·təs) *n.* soplo; inspiración.

afflict (ə'flɪkt) *v.t.* afligir; acongojar; angustiar. —**afflicting,** *adj.* aflictivo. —**affliction** (ə'flɪk·ʃən) *n.* aflicción; congoja; pena.

affluence ('æf·lu·əns) *n.* afluencia. —**affluent,** *adj.* & *n.* afluente.

afford (ə'ford) *v.t.* **1,** (be able to) poder. **2,** (have the means for) proporcionar. **3,** (yield) dar; producir; deparar.

affront (ə'frʌnt) *n.* afrenta; agravio; ofensa. —*v.t.* afrentar; agraviar; ofender.

Afghan ('æf·gæn) *n.* **1,** (dog) perro afgano. **2,** [*también adj.*] (native of Afghanistan) afgano; afganistaní. **3,** *l.c.* (woolen blanket or shawl) cubrecama o manta de estambre.

afield (ə'fild) *adv.* lejos de casa; por el campo; en la campiña.

afire (ə'fair) *adv.* en llamas. —*adj.* ardiente; encendido.

aflame (ə'fleim) *adv.* en llamas; en ascuas. —*adj.* ardiente; inflamado.

afloat (ə'flot) *adv.* a flote; flotando. —*adj.* flotante.

aflutter (ə'flʌt·ər) *adj.* agitado. —*adv.* agitadamente.

afoot (ə'fut) *adv.* & *adj.* **1,** (walking) a pie; moviéndose; andando. **2,** (underway) en preparación.

aforementioned (ə'for,mɛn·ʃənd) *adj.* antepuesto; ya mencionado.

aforesaid (ə'for·sɛd) *adj.* antedicho; ya mencionado.

aforethought (ə'for,θɔt) *adj.* premeditado.

afoul (ə'faul) *adv.* en colisión. —*adj.* enredado. —**run afoul of,** enredarse con; tener una pelea o altercado con.

afraid (ə'freid) *adj.* atemorizado; amedrentado; temeroso. —**be afraid,** tener miedo.

African ('æf·rɪ·kən) *n.* & *adj.* africano.

Afro-American ('æf·ro·ə'mɛr·ɪ·kən) *adj.* & *n.* afroamericano.

aft (æft) *adv.* a popa.

after ('æf·tər) *prep.* después (de); tras (de); detrás. —*conj.* después que; después de que. —*adv.* después; detrás; atrás. —*adj.* siguiente; posterior.

afterbirth ('æf·tər,bʌrθ) *n.* placenta.

aftereffect ('æf·tər·ə,fɛkt) *n.* efecto subsiguiente.

afterlife ('æf·tər,laif) *n.* vida futura.

aftermath ('æf·tər·mæθ) *n.* consecuencias; resultados.

afternoon (æf·tər'nuːn) *n.* tarde.

afterpains ('æf·tər,peinz) *n.pl.* entuertos.

aftershave lotion ('æf·tər·ʃeiv) loción para después de afeitarse.

aftertaste ('æf·tər,teist) *n.* dejo; resabio.

afterthought ('æf·tər,θɔt) *n.* idea tardía; segundo *o* nuevo pensamiento.

afterward ('æf·tər·wərd) *también,* **afterwards** (-wərdz) *adv.* después; más tarde; posteriormente.

again (ə'gɛn) *adv.* además; otra vez; de nuevo; asimismo. —**again and again,** una y otra vez; muchas veces. —**now and again,** de cuando en cuando; a veces.

against (ə'gɛnst) *prep.* **1,** (in opposite direction to; hostile to) contra. **2,** (toward) frente; enfrente. **3,** (in provision for) por. **4,** (adjoining) junto a; contra.

agape (ə'geip) *adj.* & *adv.* boquiabierto.

agate ('æg·ət) *n.* ágata.

agave (ə'gei·vi; ə'ga·vi) *n.* agave.

age (eidʒ) *n.* **1,** (years since birth) edad; años. **2,** (stage of life) edad;

época; período. **3,** (lifetime) vida; existencia. **4,** *hist.; geol.* época; era; período. **5,** *colloq.* [*también,* **ages**] (a long time) mucho tiempo. —*v.i.* envejecer; envejecerse. —*v.t.* madurar; curar; envejecer. —**aged** ('ei·dʒd; eidʒd) *adj.* viejo; anciano; senil. —**ageless,** *adj.* inmutable; perenne. —**coming of age,** mayoría de edad. —**of age,** mayor de edad. —**underage,** menor de edad.

agency ('ei·dʒən·si) *n.* **1,** (means) acción; gestión. **2,** (office) agencia. **3,** (government bureau) organismo; departamento.

agenda (ə'dʒɛn·də) *n.* [*sing.* **agendum** (-dəm)] agenda; diario.

agent ('ei·dʒənt) *n.* agente.

agglomerate (ə'glam·ə·reit) *v.t.* aglomerar; amontonar; hacinar. —*v.i.* aglomerarse; amontonarse; hacinarse. —*adj.* (-rət) aglomerado; amontonado. —**agglomeration,** *n.* aglomeración; amontonamiento.

agglutinate (ə'glu·tə͵neit) *v.t.* aglutinar. —**agglutinant,** *adj.* & *n.* aglutinante. —**agglutination,** *n.* aglutinación.

aggrandize ('æg·rən͵daiz) *v.t.* **1,** (increase; extend) engrandecer; exaltar; agrandar; ensanchar. **2,** (exaggerate) exagerar; aumentar. —**aggrandizement** (ə'græn·dɪz·mənt) *n.* **1,** (increase) engrandecimiento; ensanche. **2,** (exaggeration) exageración.

aggravate ('æg·rə͵veit) *v.t.* **1,** (make worse) agravar; empeorar; deteriorar. **2,** *colloq.* (vex) irritar; provocar. —**aggravation,** *n.* agravación; agravamiento.

aggregate ('æg·rə·gət) *n.* agregado. —*adj.* en bruto; en total. —**aggregation,** *n.* agregación.

aggression (ə'grɛʃ·ən) *n.* agresión; ataque; provocación.

aggressive (ə'grɛs·ɪv) *adj.* **1,** (hostile) agresivo; provocador; hostil. **2,** (vigorous) agresivo; emprendedor; vigoroso. —**aggressiveness,** *n.* agresividad.

aggressor (ə'grɛs·ər) *n.* agresor; atacante; enemigo.

aggrieved (ə'griːvd) *adj.* agraviado; ofendido; oprimido.

aghast (ə'gæst) *adj.* espantado; aterrorizado; atónito.

agile ('æd͡ʒ·əl) *adj.* ágil; vivo; ligero; rápido. —**agility** (ə'dʒɪl·ə·ti) *n.* agilidad; ligereza.

agitate ('ædʒ·ɪ·teit) *v.t.* **1,** (shake briskly) agitar; mover; sacudir. **2,** (perturb) agitar; perturbar. —*v.i.* inquietar el ánimo; alborotar; perturbar al público. —**agitation,** *n.* agitación; alboroto.

agitator ('ædʒ·ɪ͵te·tər) *n.* **1,** (person) agitador; perturbador. **2,** (device) agitador.

aglow (ə'glo) *adj.* fulgurante.

agnostic (æg'nas·tɪk) *n.* & *adj.* agnóstico. —**agnosticism** (-tɪ·siz·əm) *n.* agnosticismo.

ago (ə'go) *adv.* & *adj.* hace (*often contracted to* ha): *a short time ago,* hace poco; *long ago,* hace mucho tiempo; *two years ago,* hace dos años *o* dos años ha.

agog (ə'gɔg) *adj.* ansioso; anhelante. —*adv.* ansiosamente; con ansia.

agonize ('æg·ə·naiz) *v.i.* agonizar; extinguirse; languidecer. —*v.t.* angustiar; causar gran pena.

agony ('æg·ə·ni) *n.* agonía; congoja; lucha.

agoraphobia (͵æg·ə·rə'fo·bi·ə) *n.* agorafobia.

agrarian (ə'grɛːr·i·ən) *adj.* agrario; rural; campesino.

agree (ə'griː) *v.i.* **1,** (give assent) asentir; consentir. **2,** (arrive at a settlement) entenderse; ponerse de acuerdo; convenir. **3,** (be similar) corresponder. **4,** (be in accord) estar de acuerdo. **5,** *gram.* concordar. —**agree on,** convenir en. —**agree that,** coincidir en que. —**agree to,** consentir en.

agreeable (ə'gri·ə·bəl) *adj.* **1,** (pleasing) agradable; satisfactorio. **2,** (conformable) conveniente; oportuno; lógico. **3,** (willing to consent) complaciente; condescendiente.

agreement (ə'gri·mənt) *n.* **1,** (concord) acuerdo; armonía. **2,** (arrangement) contrato; acuerdo. **3,** (among nations) pacto; convenio.

agriculture ('æg·rɪ͵kʌl·tʃər) *n.* agricultura. —**agricultural** (-'kʌl·tʃər·əl) *adj.* agrícola.

agriculturist (͵æg·rɪ'kʌl·tʃər·ɪst) *n.* **1,** (expert) perito agrícola. **2,** (farmer) agricultor.

agronomy (ə'gran·ə·mi) *n.* agronomía. —**agronomist,** *n.* agrónomo.

aground (ə'graund) *adv.* & *adj.* varado; encallado.

ah (ɑː) *interj.* ¡ah!

aha (a'haɹ) *interj.* ¡ajá!

ahead (ə'hɛd) *adv.* 1, (in front) adelante; al frente; delante. 2, (in advance) antes; delante.

ahem (ə'hɛm) *interj.* ¡ejem!

aid (eid) *v.t.* 1, (help) ayudar; asistir; socorrer. 2, (facilitate) facilitar; favorecer; promover. —*n.* 1, (assistance) ayuda; asistencia; auxilio. 2, (helper) ayudante; auxiliar; colaborador.

aide (eid) *n.* ayudante.

aide-de-camp ('eid·də'kæmp) *n.* ayuda de campo; edecán.

AIDS (eidz) *abr. de* **acquired immune deficiency syndrome** síndrome de inmunodeficiencia adquirida (*abbr.* SIDA).

ail (eil) *v.t.* afligir; padecer; molestar. —*v.i.* indisponerse; sentirse mal.

aileron ('ei·lə·ran) *n.* alerón.

ailment ('eil·mənt) *n.* dolencia; enfermedad; padecimiento.

aim (eim) *n.* 1, (direction) trayectoria; mira; dirección. 2, (act of aiming) apuntamiento. 3, (intention; purpose) objetivo; intención; mira. —*v.t.* apuntar; dirigir. —*v.i.* aspirar; pretender; luchar (por). —**aimless**, *adj.* desorientado; despistado; sin norte.

ain't (eint) *colloq., contr. of* **am not, is not, are not, has not** *and* **have not.**

air (eɹr) *n.* 1, (atmosphere) aire; atmósfera. 2, (light breeze) aire; brisa. 3, (outward appearance) aire; impresión; sensación. 4, (personal bearing) aire; semblante; talente. 5, *pl.* (affected manners) aires; ínfulas; presunción. 6, *mus.* aire; tonada; melodía. —*v.t.* 1, (ventilate) airear; ventilar. 2, (bring to public notice) airear; sacar a relucir; pregonar. —*adj.* 1, (by or in the air) aéreo; de aire. 2, (operated by air) neumático. —**put on airs,** darse aires; darse ínfulas. —**up in the air,** 1, (undecided) en la luna; indeciso. 2, *colloq.* (excited) enojado; enfadado.

air base base aérea.

airborne ('ɛr,born) *adj.* 1, (aloft) en vuelo. 2, (transported by air) aéreo; llevado por aire.

air brake freno neumático.

aircoach ('ɛr,kotʃ) *n.* clase turista.

air conditioner acondicionador de aire. —**air conditioned,** refrigerado; climatizado; aire acondi-

cionado. —**air conditioning,** acondicionamiento de aire; aire acondicionado.

aircraft ('ɛr,kræft) *n.* aeronave; avión; aeroplano. —**aircraft carrier,** portaaviones.

airfield ('ɛr,fiɹld) *n.* aeropuerto; campo de aviación.

air force fuerza aérea militar; fuerzas de aviación; aviación militar.

air hole respiradero.

airiness ('ɛr·i·nəs) *n.* 1, (ventilation) ventilación; aire. 2, *fig.* (jauntiness) ligereza; viveza.

airing ('ɛr·ɪŋ) *n.* 1, (exposure to air) aireo; ventilación. 2, (walk) paseo.

airlift ('ɛr,lɪft) *n.* ayuda aérea.

airline ('ɛr,lain) *n.* compañia *o* línea aérea; aerolínea. —**airliner,** *n.* aeronave.

air mail correo aéreo. —**by air mail,** por avión.

airman ('ɛr·mən) *n.* [*pl.* -**men**] aviador; aeronauta; soldado de la aviación militar.

airplane ('ɛr,plein) *n.* aeroplano; avión; *colloq.* aparato.

airport ('ɛr,port) *n.* aeropuerto.

air pressure presión atmosférica.

air raid bombardeo; ataque aéreo.

airsick ('ɛr,sɪk) *adj.* mareado. —**airsickness,** *n.* mal de altura.

airstrip ('ɛr,strɪp) *n.* pista de aterrizaje.

airtight ('ɛr,tait) *adj.* hermético.

airway ('ɛr·we) *n.* aerovía; vía aérea.

airy ('ɛr·i) *adj.* 1, (like air) ligero; sutil; etéreo. 2, (well-ventilated) aireado; ventilado. 3, (unreal) idealista; visionario. 4, (pretentious) vanidoso; pretencioso.

aisle (ail) *n.* pasillo; paso.

ajar (ə'dʒar) *adj.* entreabierto; entornado. —*adv.* a medio abrir.

akimbo (ə'kɪm·bo) *adj. & adv.* de *o* en jarras.

akin (ə'kɪn) *adj.* 1, (related) consanguíneo. 2, (similar) parecido; semejante.

alabaster ('æl·ə·bæs·tər) *n.* alabastro. —*adj.* alabastrino.

a la carte (a·lə'kart) a la carta.

alacrity (ə'læk·rə·ti) *n.* presteza; prontitud; alacridad.

a la mode (a·lə'mord) a la moda; de moda.

alarm (ə'larm) *v.t.* 1, (frighten) alarmar; atemorizar; inquietar. 2, (warn of danger) avisar; dar la alarma a. —*n.* **1,** (warning of danger) alarma; aviso. **2,** (device) alarma. **3,** (apprehension of danger) ansiedad; temor; inquietud. —**alarming,** *adj.* alarmante. —**alarmist,** *n.* alarmista. —**alarm clock,** despertador.

alas (ə'læs) *interj.* ¡ay!, ¡ay de mí!

albacore ('æl·bə,kor) *n.* albacora.

albatross ('æl·bə,trɒs) *n.* albatros.

albeit (ɔl'bi·ɪt) *conj.* a pesar de que; aunque.

albinism ('æl·bə·nɪz·əm) *n.* albinismo.

albino (æl'bai·no) *n.* & *adj.* albino.

album ('æl·bəm) *n.* álbum.

albumen (æl'bju·mən) *n.* **1,** (white of egg) clara. **2,** *chem.* albumen.

albumin (æl'bju·mɪn) *n.* albúmina.

alchemy ('æl·kə·mi) *n.* alquimia. —**alchemist,** *n.* alquimista.

alcohol ('æl·kə·hɒl; -hal) *n.* alcohol. —**alcoholic** (-'hal·ɪk) *adj.* & *n.* alcohólico. —**alcoholism,** *n.* alcoholismo; dipsomanía.

alcove ('æl·kouv) *n.* alcoba; recámara.

aldehyde ('æl·də,haid) *n.* aldehido.

alder ('ɔl·dər) *n.* aliso.

alderman ('ɔl·dər·mən) *n.* [*pl.* -**men**] concejal.

ale (eil) *n.* cerveza inglesa.

alert (ə'lʌrt) *n.* alerta; aviso. —*adj.* **1,** (watchful) vigilante. **2,** (nimble) vivo; despierto; inteligente. —*v.t.* alertar; avisar; prevenir. —**alertness,** *n.* vigilancia; atención. —**on the alert,** vigilante; alerta.

alfalfa (æl'fæl·fə) *n.* alfalfa.

alga ('æl·gə) [*pl.* **ulgae** (-dʒi)] *n.* alga.

algebra ('æl·dʒə·brə) *n.* álgebra. —**algebraic** (-'brei·ɪk) *adj.* algebraico.

alias ('ei·li·əs) *n.* alias. —*adv.* conocido como.

alibi ('æl·ə·bai) *n.* **1,** *law* coartada. **2,** *colloq.* excusa; pretexto.

alien ('eil·jən) *n.* & *adj.* extranjero; forastero. —*adj.* extraño; ajeno; diferente.

alienable ('eil·jə·nə·bəl) *adj.* alienable; enajenable; transferible.

alienate ('eil·jə·neit) *v.t.* **1,** (estrange) enajenar; alejar; malquistar. **2,** *law* enajenar.

alienation (eil·jə'nei·ʃən) *n.* **1,** (estrangement) enajenación; desunión; desapego; desvío. **2,** (mental aberration) enajenación; locura; desvarío.

alienist ('eil·jə·nɪst) *n.* alienista; psiquiatra.

alight (ə'lait) *v.i.* bajar; desmontar; descender; apearse. —*adj.* brillante; luminoso.

align *también,* **aline** (ə'lain) *v.t.* alinear. —**alignment,** *n.* alineamiento; alineación.

alike (ə'laik) *adv.* igualmente; a semejanza; de igual forma. —*adj.* igual; semejante; parecido.

alimentary (æl·ə'men·tə·ri) *adj.* alimenticio.

alimony ('æl·ɪ·mo·ni) *n.* alimentos; manutención.

alive (ə'laiv) *adj.* **1,** (living) vivo; existente. **2,** (active) animado; activo. **3,** (susceptible) impresionable; susceptible.

alkali ('æl·kə·lai) *n.,* *chem.* álcali. —**alkaline** (-lain) *adj.* alcalino. —**alkalinity** (-'lɪn·ə·ti) *n.* alcalinidad. —**alkalize** (-laiz) *v.t.* & *i.* alcalizar. —**alkalization** (-lɪ'zei·ʃən) *n.* alcalización.

alkaloid ('æl·kə·lɔid) *n.* alcaloide.

all (ɔːl) *n.,* *adj.* & *pron.* todo. —*adv.* completamente; por entero; totalmente. —**above all,** sobre todo; ante todo. —**after all,** después de todo. —**all in all,** en conjunto. —**all the better** o **worse,** tanto mejor o peor. —**all the more,** tanto más. —**all the same,** a pesar de todo. —**at all,** en absoluto; de ninguna forma. —**not at all,** de ninguna manera; por nada. —**once and for all,** por última vez.

Allah ('ɑː·la) *n.* Alá.

All-American ('ɔːl·ə'mer·ɪ·kən) *adj., sports* que representa al conjunto de los EE.UU. —*n.* equipo o miembro de equipo estadounidense selecto.

all-around *también,* **all-round,** *adj.* completo; cabal; versátil.

allay (æ'lei) *v.t.* **1,** (pacify) aquietar; pacificar. **2,** (mitigate) aliviar; mitigar; calmar.

allegation (,æl·ə'gei·ʃən) *n.* alegación; alegato.

allege (ə'ledʒ) *v.t.* alegar; sostener.

allegiance (ə'li·dʒəns) *n.* fidelidad; devoción; lealtad.

allegory ('æl·ə,gor·i) *n.* alegoría; figura; símbolo. —**allegorical** (-'gor·ɪ·kəl) *adj.* alegórico; simbólico.

allegro (ə'lɛg·ro) *adv. & n., mus.* alegro; allegro.

alleluia (æl·ə'luː·jə) *n. & interj.* aleluya.

allergen ('æl·ər·dʒən) *n.* alergeno. —**allergenic** (-'dʒɛn·ɪk) *adj.* que produce alergia.

allergy ('æl·ər·dʒi) *n.* alergia. —**allergic** (ə'lʌr·dʒɪk) *adj.* alérgico.

alleviate (ə'liː·vi·eit) *v.t.* aliviar; aligerar; mitigar. —**alleviation,** *n.* alivio; mitigación; desahogo.

alley ('æl·i) *n.* callejón; travesía; pasadizo. —**blind alley,** callejón sin salida.

alliance (ə'lai·əns) *n.* alianza; pacto; unión.

allied (ə'laid; 'æl·aid) *adj.* aliado; socio; unido.

alligator ('æl·ɪ͵gei·tər) *n.* caimán; *Mex.* lagarto. —**alligator pear,** aguacate.

alliteration (ə͵lɪt·ə'rei·ʃən) *n.* aliteración. —**alliterative** (ə'lɪt·ə·rə·tɪv) *adj.* aliterado.

allocate ('æl·ə·keit) *v.t.* colocar; distribuir. —**allocation,** *n.* colocación; distribución.

allopathy (ə'lap·ə·θi) *n.* alopatía. —**allopathic** (æl·ə'pæθ·ɪk) *adj.* alopático.

allot (ə'lat) *v.t.* [**allotted, -ting**] **1,** (parcel out) parcelar; distribuir; prorratear. **2,** (appoint for a purpose; assign) señalar; asignar.

allotment (ə'lat·mənt) *n.* **1,** (portion) parcela; trozo; prorrateo. **2,** (appointment) asignación.

allotrope ('æl·ə·trop) *n.* alótropo. —**allotropic** (-'trap·ɪk) *adj.* alotrópico. —**allotropy** (ə'lat·rə·pi), **allotropism,** *n.* alotropía.

all-out ('ɔl͵aut) *adj.* completo; vigoroso.

allow (ə'lau) *v.t.* **1,** (permit) autorizar; permitir. **2,** (yield) ceder; condescender. **3,** (admit) admitir; confesar. **4,** *comm.* descontar. —**allow for, 1,** (leave room for) dejar sitio o espacio para. **2,** (reckon with) tener en cuenta.

allowance (ə'lau·əns) *n.* **1,** (permission) autorización; permiso. **2,** (allotment, as of money) asignación; subvención. **3,** *comm.* descuento; deducción. **4,** (compensation, as for weight) margen.

alloy ('æl·ɔi) *n.* aleación; mezcla. —*v.t.* (ə'lɔi) alear; ligar; mezclar.

all right 1, (satisfactory) bueno;

satisfactorio. **2,** (unhurt) bien. **3,** (expression of assent) muy bien; por seguro; de acuerdo.

All Saints' Day Día de Todos los Santos.

All Souls' Day Día de los Difuntos.

allude (ə'luːd) *v.i.* aludir; mencionar; referirse.

allure (ə'lur) *v.t.* atraer; seducir; tentar. —*n.* [*también,* **allurement**] atracción; seducción. —**alluring,** *adj.* seductor; atrayente; fascinante.

allusion (ə'luː·ʒən) *n.* alusión; referencia. —**allusive** (-sɪv) *adj.* alusivo; referente.

alluvium (ə'lu·vi·əm) *n.* aluvión. —**alluvial,** *adj.* aluvial.

ally (ə'lai) *v.t.* unir; ligar; enlazar. —*v.i.* aliarse; unirse. —*n.* (*también,* 'æl·ai) aliado.

almanac ('ɔl·mə·næk) *n.* almanaque.

almighty (ɔl'mai·ti) *adj.* omnipotente; todopoderoso. —**the Almighty,** Dios; el Todopoderoso.

almond ('aː·mənd; 'ɔl·mənd) *n.* **1,** (tree) almendro. **2,** (fruit) almendra.

almoner ('æl·mən·ər) *n.* limosnero.

almost ('ɔl·most) *adv.* casi.

alms (aːmz) *n.* limosna; caridad.

almshouse ('aːmz͵haus) *n.* asilo; hospicio.

aloe ('æl·o) *n.* áloe. —**aloes,** *n. sing.* áloe.

aloft (ə'lɔft) *adj.* flotante; aéreo. —*adv.* en el aire; en alto.

alone (ə'loːn) *adj.* solo; único. —*adv.* tan solo; aparte; solitariamente.

along (ə'lɔŋ) *prep.* por; a lo largo de. —*adv.* a lo largo; junto; en compañía. —**all along,** desde el principio; todo el tiempo. —**along with,** junto con; en compañía de.

alongside (ə'lɔŋ·said) *adv. & prep.* a lo largo (de).

aloof (ə'luːf) *adv.* a distancia; desde lejos. —*adj.* retraído; apartado; huraño. —**aloofness,** *n.* reserva; retraimiento.

aloud (ə'laud) *adv.* fuerte; con fuerza; en voz alta.

alpaca (æl'pæk·ə) *n.* alpaca.

alpha ('æl·fə) *n.* alfa.

alphabet ('æl·fə·bet) *n.* alfabeto. —**alphabetical** (-'bet·ɪ·kəl), **alphabetic,** *adj.* alfabético. —**alphabetize** (-bə·taiz) *v.t.* alfabetizar.

alpine ('æl·pain) *adj.* alpino.

—**alpinism** ('æl·pə·nɪz·əm) n. alpinismo. —**alpinist** ('æl·pə·nɪst) n. alpinista.

already (ɔl'rɛd·ɪ) adv. ya; con anterioridad; anteriormente.

also ('ɔl·so) adv. además; también; asimismo.

altar ('ɔl·tər) n. altar. —**altar boy**, acólito; monaguillo.

altarpiece ('əl·tar,pis) n. retablo.

alter ('ɔl·tər) v.t. alterar; cambiar; variar. —v.i. alterarse; cambiarse; modificarse.

alteration (ɔl·tər'ei·ʃən) n. 1, (change) alteración; cambio. 2, (renovation) arreglo.

altercate ('ɔl·tər,keit) v.t. altercar. —**altercation**, n. altercación; altercado.

alternate ('ɔl·tər,neit) v.t. alternar; hacer turnos de. —v.i. alternarse; turnarse; elect. alternar. —n. (-nət) substituto; suplente. —adj. (-nət) alterno. —**alternation**, n. alternación; turno. —**alternating current**, corriente alterna.

alternative (ɔl'tʌr·nə·tɪv) n. alternativa; dilema. —adj. alternativo.

although (ɔl'ðoɪ) conj. aunque; si bien.

altimeter (æl'tɪm·ə·tər) n. altímetro.

altitude ('æl·tɪ·tud) n. altitud; altura.

alto ('æl·toɪ) adj. & n. [pl. -tos] 1, mus. alto. 2, (voice) contralto.

altogether (ɔl·tə'gɛð·ər) adv. completamente; del todo. —**in the altogether**, colloq. desnudo; en cueros.

altruism ('æl·tru·ɪz·əm) n. altruísmo. —**altruist**, n. altruísta. —**altruistic**, adj. altruísta.

alum ('æl·əm) n. alumbre.

alumina (ə'luɪ·mə·nə) n. alúmina.

aluminum (ə'luɪ·mɪn·əm) también, Brit., **aluminium** (,æl·ju'mɪn·i·əm) n. aluminio.

alumnus (ə'lʌm·nəs) n. [pl. -ni (-nai)] graduado. —**alumna** (-nə) n. [pl. -nae (-ni)] graduada.

alveolus (æl'vi·ə·ləs) n. [pl. -li (-lai)] alvéolo. —**alveolar**, adj. alveolar.

always ('ɔl·wiz; -weiz) adv. siempre; por siempre.

am (æm) v., primera persona del sing. del pres. de **be**.

amalgam (ə'mæl·gəm) n. amalgama; compuesto; mezcla.

amalgamate (ə'mæl·gə,meit) v.t. amalgamar; mezclar; combinar. —v.i. mezclarse; combinarse; amalgamarse. —**amalgamation**, n. amalgamación.

amanuensis (ə,mæn·ju'ɛn·sis) n. amanuense.

amaranth ('æm·ə·rænθ) n. amaranto.

amaryllis (æm·ə'rɪl·is) n. 1, bot. amarilis. 2, cap., poet. Amarilis.

amass (ə'mæs) v.t. amasar; amontonar; acumular.

amateur ('æm·ə·tʃur; -tʌr) n. & adj. aficionado; principiante. —**amateurish**, adj. de aficionado; inexperto. —**amateurism**, n. inexperiencia; impericia.

amatory ('æm·ə,tor·i) adj. amatorio.

amaze (ə'meiz) v.t. asombrar. —**amazement**, n. asombro. —**amazing**, adj. asombroso.

amazon ('æm·ə·zan) n. amazona.

ambassador (æm'bæs·ə·dər) n. embajador. —**ambassadorial** (-'dor·i·əl) adj. de la embajada; del embajador. —**ambassadress** (-drəs) n. embajadora.

amber ('æm·bər) n. ámbar. —adj. ambarino.

ambergris ('æm·bər,gris) n. ámbar gris.

ambidexterity (,æm·bɪ·dɛk·'stɛr·ə·ti) n. 1, (skill with both hands) habilidad o destreza con ambas manos. 2, fig. (duplicity) doblez.

ambidextrous (æm·bɪ'dɛks·trəs) adj. 1, (apt with both hands) ambidextro; ambidiestro. 2, fig. (deceitful) falso; engañoso.

ambience [también, **ambiance**] ('æm·bi·əns) n. ambiente; atmósfera.

ambiguity (,æm·bɪ'gju·ə·ti) n. ambigüedad; equívoco; oscuridad. —**ambiguous** (-'bɪg·ju·əs) adj. ambiguo; equívoco; confuso.

ambit ('æm·bit) n. ámbito; ambiente; contorno.

ambition (æm'bɪʃ·ən) n. ambición; aspiración; codicia. —**ambitious** (-əs) adj. ambicioso.

ambivalent (æm'bɪv·ə·lənt) adj. ambivalente. —**ambivalence**, n. ambivalencia.

amble ('æm·bəl) v.i. amblar.

ambrosia (æm'broɪ·ʒə) n. ambrosía. —**ambrosial** (-ʒəl) adj. superior; delicioso.

ambulance ('æm·bjə·ləns) *n.* ambulancia.

ambulatory ('æm·bjə·lə‚tor·i) *adj.* ambulante; ambulatorio.

ambush ('æm·bʊʃ) *v.t.* acechar; emboscar. —*n.* emboscada; celada.

ameba (ə'mi·bə) *n.* = **amoeba.**

ameliorate (ə'miːl·jə·reit) *v.t.* mejorar; perfeccionar. —*v.i.* mejorarse. —**ameliorable** (-rə·bəl) *adj.* mejorable; perfeccionable. —**amelioration,** *n.* mejoría; adelanto; progreso. —**ameliorative** (-rə·tɪv) *adj.* mejorador; perfeccionador.

amen ('ei'mɛn; 'a-) *adv., n.* & *interj.* amén.

amenable (ə'miː·nə·bəl; ə'mɛn-) *adj.* **1,** (tractable) sumiso; dócil. **2** (answerable) responsable.

amend (ə'mɛnd) *v.t.* **1,** (correct) enmendar; corregir; mejorar. **2,** (alter) enmendar; alterar; cambiar. —*v.i* enmendarse; corregirse; mejorarse. —**amends,** *n.pl.* compensación; reparación; enmienda. —**make amends (for),** compensar; enmendar.

amendment (ə'mɛnd·mənt) *n.* enmienda; cambio; corrección.

amenity (ə'mɛn·ə·ti) *n.* amenidad.

ament ('æm·ənt; 'ei·mənt) *n.* amento; candelilla.

American (ə'mɛr·ɪ·kən) *n.* & *adj.* americano. —**American plan,** pensión completa; plan americano.

Americana (ə‚mɛr·ɪ'ka·nə) *n.* colección de arte, artesanía, literatura, historia, etc. que representa los EE.UU.

Americanism (ə'mɛr·ɪ·kan‚ɪz·əm) *n.* americanismo.

Americanize (ə'mɛr·ɪ·kə‚naiz) *v.t.* americanizar. —**Americanization** (-nɪ'zei·ʃən) *n.* americanización.

americium (æm·ə'rɪs·i·əm; -'rɪʃ·jəm) *n.* americio; américo.

amethyst ('æm·ə·θɪst) *n.* & *adj.* amatista.

amiable ('ei·mi·ə·bəl) *adj.* amable; cordial; afable. —**amiability, amiableness,** *n.* cordialidad; amabilidad; afabilidad.

amicable ('æm·ɪ·kə·bəl) *adj.* amistoso; sociable; afectuoso. —**amicability,** *n.* cordialidad; sociabilidad.

amid (ə'mɪd) *también,* **amidst** (ə'mɪdst) *prep.* entre; en medio de.

amidships (ə'mɪd‚ʃɪps) *adv.* en medio del barco.

amino ('æm·ə·no; ə'mi·no) **acid** aminoácido.

amiss (ə'mɪs) *adv.* impropiamente; equivocadamente; fuera de sitio o de tono; demás. —*adj.* impropio; inoportuno. —**take amiss,** llevar o tomar a mal.

amity ('æm·ə·ti) *n.* amistad; cordialidad; concordia.

ammeter ('æm·mi·tər) *n.* amperímetro.

ammo ('æ·mo) *n., contr. de* **ammunition.**

ammonia (ə'moːn·jə) *n., chem.* amoníaco.

ammoniate (ə'mo·ni·eit) *v.t.* tratar con amoníaco. —*n.* (-ət) amoniuro.

ammonium (ə'mo·ni·əm) *n.* amonio.

ammunition (‚æm·ju'nɪʃ·ən) *n.* munición.

amnesia (æm'niː·ʒə) *n.* amnesia. —**amnesic** (-zɪk) *adj.* & *n.* amnésico.

amnesty ('æm·nəs·ti) *n.* amnistía; indulto; perdón.

amoeba, *también* **ameba** (ə'mi·bə) *n.* ameba; amiba.

amok (ə'mɔk) *adv.* = **amuck.**

among (ə'mʌŋ) *también* **amongst** (ə'mʌŋst) *prep.* entre; en medio de.

amoral (ei'mɔr·əl) *adj.* amoral. —**amorality** (‚ei·mə'ræl·ə·ti) *n.* amoralidad.

amorous ('æm·ə·rəs) *adj.* amoroso; apasionado. —**amorousness,** *n.* enamoramiento; apasionamiento.

amorphous (ə'mor·fəs) *adj.* amorfo.

amortize ('æm·ər‚taiz; ə'mor-) *v.t.* amortizar. —**amortization** (-tɪ'zei·ʃən) *n.* amortización.

amount (ə'maunt) *n.* cantidad; suma; importe. —*v.i.* sumar; ascender; importar.

ampere ('æm·pɪr) *n.* amperio. —**amperage,** *n.* amperaje.

amphetamine (æm'fɛt·ə·min) *n.* anfetamina.

amphibian (æm'fɪb·i·ən) *n.* anfibio. —**amphibious,** *adj.* anfibio.

amphitheater ('æm·fə‚θi·ə·tər) *n.* anfiteatro.

amphora ('æm·fə·rə) *n.* [*pl.* **-rae** (-ri) *o* **-ras** (-rəz)] ánfora.

ample ('æm·pəl) *adj.* **1,** (large) amplio; capaz; suficiente. **2,** (plentiful) abundante; copioso; bastante.

amplifier ('æm·plɪ‚fai·ər) *n.* amplificador.

amplify ('æm·plɪ·fai) *v.t.* amplificar; ampliar. —**amplification** (-fɪ'kei·ʃən) *n.* amplificación; ampliación.

amplitude ('æm·plɪ·tud) *n.* amplitud. —**amplitude modulation,** *también,* AM ('ei'ɛm) modulación dilatada o de extensión.

ampoule ('æm·pul) *n.* ampolla; ampolleta.

amputate ('æm·pjə·teit) *v.t.* amputar; cortar un miembro. —**amputation,** *n.* amputación. —**amputee** (-'tiː) *n.* amputado.

amuck (ə'mʌk) *adv.* con frenesí; con rabia. —**run amuck,** correr o ir a troche y moche.

amulet ('æm·ju·lɛt) *n.* amuleto.

amuse (ə'mjuːz) *v.t.* divertir; entretener; recrear. —**amusement,** *n.* diversión; distracción; entretenimiento. —**amusing,** *adj.* divertido. —**amusement park,** parque de atracciones o diversiones.

an (ən; æn) *indef.art.* = a *(ante vocal o h muda).*

anabolism (ə'næb·ə,lɪz·əm) *n.* anabolismo. —**anabolic** (,æn·ə'bal·ɪk) *adj.* anabólico.

anachronism (ə'næk·rə·nɪz·əm) *n.* anacronismo. —**anachronistic** (-'nɪs·tɪk) *adj.* anacrónico.

anaconda (æn·ə'kan·də) *n.* anaconda.

anaerobe ('æn·ə,rob) *n.* anaerobio. —**anaerobic** (-'ro·bɪk) *adj.* anaerobio.

anagram ('æn·ə,græm) *n.* anagrama.

anal ('ei·nəl) *adj.* anal.

analgesia (,æn·əl'dʒi·ʒə) *n.* analgesia. —**analgesic** (-'dʒi·zɪk) *adj.* analgésico.

analogous (ə'næl·ə·gəs) *adj.* análogo; similar; semejante.

analogue ('æn·ə,lɔg) *n.* término análogo.

analogy (ə'næl·ə·dʒi) *n.* analogía. —**analogical** (,æn·ə'ladʒ·ɪ·kəl) *adj.* analógico.

analysis (ə'næl·ə·sɪs) *n.* [*pl.* -ses (-siz)] análisis; estudio. —**analyst** ('æn·ə·lɪst) *n.* analista; analizador. —**analytical** (æn·ə'lɪt·ɪ·kəl) *n.*; ana-lytic, *adj.* analítico.

analyze ('æn·ə·laiz) *v.t.* analizar; estudiar.

anamorphosis (,æn·ə'mor·fə·sɪs) *n.* [*pl.* -ses (-siz)] anamorfosis.

anapest ('æn·ə·pɛst) *n.* anapesto.

—**anapestic** (-'pɛst·ɪk) *adj.* anapéstico.

anarchism ('æn·ər·kɪz·əm) *n.* anarquismo. —**anarchist** (-kɪst) *n.* anarquista. —**anarchistic** (-'kɪs·tɪk) *adj.* anarquista.

anarchy ('æn·ər·ki) *n.* anarquía. —**anarchic** (æn'ark·ɪk), **anarchical,** *adj.* anárquico.

anathema (ə'næθ·ə·mə) *n.* anatema. —**anathematize** (-taiz) *v.t. & i.* anatematizar.

anatomist (ə'næt·ə·mɪst) *n.* anatomista.

anatomize (ə'næt·ə,maiz) *v.t.* anatomizar.

anatomy (ə'næt·ə·mi) *n.* anatomía. —**anatomical** (,æn·ə'tam·ɪ·kəl) *adj.* anatómico.

ancestor ('æn·sɛs·tər) *n.* antepasado; ascendiente. —**ancestress** (-trəs) *n.* antepasada.

ancestral (æn'sɛs·trəl) *adj.* ancestral; atávico; antiguo.

ancestry ('æn·sɛs·tri) *n.* ascendencia; genealogía; linaje.

anchor ('æŋ·kər) *n.* ancla. —*v.t.* asegurar; sujetar; amarrar. —*v.i.* anclar; echar anclas; fondear. —**anchorage,** *n.* anclaje; ancladero; fondeadero.

anchorite ('æŋ·kə·rait) *n.* anacoreta.

anchorman *n.* [*pl.* -men (-mən)] locutor; anunciador. —**anchorwoman** *n.fem.* [*pl.* -women (-'wɪm·ən)] locutora; anunciadora.

anchovy ('æn·tʃo·vi) *n.* anchoa.

ancient ('ein·ʃənt) *adj.* antiguo; remoto.

and (ænd) *conj.* y; e (*before a word beginning with* i *or* hi).

andante (an'dan·ti) *n., mus.* andante.

Andean (æn'di·ən) *adj.* andino.

andiron ('ænd,ai·ərn) *n.* morillo.

android ('æn·drɔid) *n.* androide.

anecdote ('æn·ɛk·dot) *n.* anécdota.

anemia (ə'niː·mi·ə) *n.* anemia. —**anemic,** *adj. & n.* anémico.

anemometer (,æn·ə'mam·ə·tər) *n.* anemómetro.

anemone (ə'nɛm·ə·ni) *n.* anémona.

aneroid ('æn·ər·ɔid) *adj.* aneroide.

anesthesia (,æn·əs'θiː·ʒə) *n.* anestesia. —**anesthetic** (-'θɛt·ɪk) *n. & adj.* anestésico. —**anesthetist** (ə'nɛs·θə·tɪst), **anesthetician** (-'tɪʃ·ən) *n.* anestesista. —**anesthetize** (ə'nɛs·θə,taiz) *v.t.* anestesiar.

aneurysm *también,* **aneurism** ('æn·jə‚rɪz·əm) *n.* aneurisma.

anew (ə'nju‚) *adv.* de nuevo; nuevamente; otra vez.

angel ('ein·dʒəl) *n.* ángel. —**angelic** (æn'dʒel·ɪk), **angelical,** *adj.* angélico; angelical.

anger ('æŋ·gər) *n.* furia; cólera; enfado. —*v.t.* encolerizar; enfurecer; irritar.

angina (æn'dʒai·nə) *n.* angina. —**angina pectoris** ('pek·tə·rɪs) angina de pecho.

angle ('æŋ·gəl) *n.* **1,** *geom.* ángulo. **2,** (corner) ángulo; rincón. **3,** (point of view) aspecto; faceta. —*v.t. & i.* **1,** (form an angle) hacer o formar ángulo. **2,** *colloq.* (focus; direct) enfocar. —*v.i.* **1,** (fish) pescar con caña. **2,** (scheme) maquinar; intrigar. —**angler** (-glər) *n.* pescador de caña. —**angling** (-glɪŋ) *n.* pesca.

Angle ('æŋ·gəl) *n.* anglo. —**Anglian** ('æŋ·gli·ən) *adj.* anglo.

angleworm ('æŋ·gəl‚wʌrm) *n.* lombriz.

Anglican ('æŋ·gli·kən) *n. & adj.* anglicano. —**Anglicanism,** *n.* anglicanismo.

Anglicism ('æŋ·gli‚sɪz·əm) *n.* anglicismo.

Anglicize ('æŋ·gli‚saiz) *v.t.* inglesar; hacer inglés. —**Anglicization** (-sɪ'zei·ʃən) *n.* anglicización.

Anglo ('æŋ·glo) *adj. & n.* = Anglo-American.

Anglo-American *adj. & n.* angloamericano.

Anglophile ('æŋ·glo‚fail) *n. & adj.* anglófilo.

Anglophobe ('æŋ·glo‚fob) *n.* anglófobo.

Anglo-Saxon (‚æŋ·glo'sæk·sən) *adj. & n.* anglo-sajón.

angry ('æŋ·gri) *adj.* airado; colérico; violento; inflamado.

anguish ('æŋ·gwɪʃ) *n.* angustia; congoja; ansia. —*v.t.* angustiar; acongojar; aquejar. —*v.i.* angustiarse; acongojarse.

angular ('æŋ·gju·lər) *adj.* **1,** (forming angles) angular. **2,** (bony; gaunt) angular; anguloso; huesudo. —**angularity** (-'lær·ə·ti) *n.* angulosidad.

aniline ('æn·ə·lɪn) *n.* anilina.

animadversion (‚æn·ɪ·mæd·'vʌr·ʒən) *n.* **1,** (criticism) animadversión; censura. **2,** (bias) animadversión; animosidad; antipatía.

animal ('æn·ə·məl) *n. & adj.* animal; bestia; bruto. —**animality** (-'mæl·ə·ti) *n.* animalidad.

animate ('æn·ɪ·meit) *v.t.* **1,** (give life to) animar; dar vida a; vivificar. **2,** (incite to action) alentar; impulsar; dar ánimo a. —*adj.* (-mət) animado; viviente. —**animated,** *adj.* vivaz; vivo; animado. —**animated cartoon,** dibujos animados. —**animation,** *n.* animación; viveza.

animism ('æn·ə·mɪz·əm) *n.* animismo. —**animist,** *n.* animista. —**animistic** (-'mɪs·tɪk) *adj.* animista.

animosity (‚æn·ɪ'mas·ə·ti) *n.* animosidad; enemistad.

anion ('æn‚ai·ən) *n.* anión.

anise ('æn·ɪs) *n.* anís.

aniseed ('æn·ə‚sid) *n.* anís; grano de anís.

anisette (æn·ɪ'set) *n.* anisete; anisado.

ankle ('æŋ·kəl) *n.* tobillo. —**ankle bone,** hueso del tobillo.

anklet ('æŋ·klɪt) *n.* tobillera.

annals ('æn·əlz) *n. pl.* anales. —**annalist** (-əl·ɪst) *n.* analista.

anneal (ə'nil) *v.t.* **1,** (treat glass, metals, etc.) recocer. **2,** *fig.* (strengthen) fortalecer; vigorizar.

annex (ə'neks) *v.t.* anexar; añadir; agregar. —*n.* ('æn·eks) anexo; adjunto; apéndice. —**annexation** (‚æn·ek'sei·ʃən) *n.* anexión.

annihilate (ə'nai·ə·leit) *v.t.* aniquilar; destruir; arrasar. —**annihilation,** *n.* aniquilación; destrucción.

anniversary (‚æn·ə'vʌr·sə·ri) *n. & adj.* aniversario.

anno Domini (‚æ·no'dɔ·mi·ni) año de Cristo.

annotate ('æn·ə·teit) *v.t. & i.* anotar; explicar; comentar. —**annotation,** *n.* anotación; nota; apunte.

announce (ə'nauns) *v.t.* anunciar; proclamar; avisar.

announcement (ə'nauns·mənt) *n.* **1,** (information) anuncio; comunicación. **2,** (public notice) aviso; prospecto.

announcer (ə'naun·sər) *n.* anunciador; *radio; TV* locutor.

annoy (ə'nɔi) *v.t.* enojar; incomodar; irritar. —**annoyance** (-əns) *n.* enojo; disgusto.

annual ('æn·ju·əl) *adj.* anual. —*n.* anuario.

annuity (ə'nju·ə·ti) *n.* anualidad; prima anual.

annul (ə'nʌl) *v.t.* [**annulled, -nulling**] anular; revocar; suprimir. —**annulment,** *n.* anulación; cancelación; revocación.

annunciation (ə,nʌn·si'ei·ʃən) *n., usu.cap.* anunciación.

anode ('æn·od) *n.* ánodo.

anodyne ('æn·ə,dain) *adj. & n.* anodino.

anoint (ə'nɔint) *v.t.* ungir. —**anointment,** *n.* ungimiento.

anomaly (ə'nam·ə·li) *n.* anomalía; anormalidad; irregularidad. —**anomalous** (-ləs) *adj.* anómalo; anormal; irregular.

anon (ə'nan) *adv., arcaico* pronto; dentro de poco.

anonymity (,æn·ə'nɪm·ə·ti) *n.* anonimato. —**anonymous** ('nan·ə·məs) *adj.* anónimo; desconocido.

anopheles (ə'naf·ə,liz) *n.sing. & pl.* anofeles.

anorexia (,æn·ə'ɪɛk·si·ə) *n.* anorexia. —**anorexic,** *adj. & n.* que (o quien) padece de anorexia.

another (ə'nʌð·ər) *adj. & pron.* otro; diferente. —**one another,** uno a otro; entre sí.

answer ('æn·sər) *n.* **1,** (reply) respuesta; contestación. **2,** (solution) solución; resultado. **3,** *law* defensa; refutación. —*v.i.* **1,** *también,* *v.t.* (reply) contestar; replicar; responder. **2,** (be responsible) ser responsable; responder. **3,** (be in conformity) responder; concordar. —*v.t.* **1,** (comply with) servir; satisfacer. **2,** (refute) refutar. **3,** (suit) corresponder a; responder a.

answerable ('æn·sər·ə·bəl) *adj.* **1,** (that can be answered) explicable. **2,** (responsible) responsable.

answering machine contestador automático.

ant (ænt) *n.* hormiga.

antacid (ænt'æs·ɪd) *n. & adj.* antiácido.

antagonism (æn'tæg·ə,nɪz·əm) *n.* antagonismo; oposición; enemistad. —**antagonist** (-nɪst) *n.* antagonista; adversario; contrincante. —**antagonistic** (-'nɪs·tɪk) *adj.* antagónico; opuesto; hostil.

antagonize (æn'tæg·ə,naiz) *v.t.* antagonizar; contrariar.

antalkali (ænt'æl·kə·lai) *n.* antialcalino.

antarctic (ænt'ark·tɪk) *adj.* antártico. —*n., cap.* Antártica.

ante ('æn·ti) *n.* **1,** *cards* puesta. **2,** (share) cuota. —*v.t.* **1,** *cards* apostar. **2,** [*también,* **ante up**] (pay) pagar. —*v.i.* **1,** *cards* poner su apuesta. **2,** [*también* **ante up**] (pay one's share) pagar su cuota.

anteater ('ænt,i·tər) *n.* oso hormiguero.

antecedent (,æn·tə'si·dənt) *n.* antecedente. —*adj.* antecedente; anterior; precedente. —**antecedence,** *n.* precedencia; anterioridad.

antechamber ('æn·ti,tʃeim·bər) *n.* antecámara.

antedate ('æn·ti,deit) *v.t.* antedatar. —*n.* antedata.

antelope ('æn·tə·lop) *n.* antílope.

antenna (æn'tɛn·ə) *n.* **1,** *radio* antena. **2,** *zoöl.* [*pl.* **-nae** (-i)] antena.

anterior (æn'tɪr·i·ər) *adj.* **1,** (in space) delantero; del frente. **2,** (in time) anterior; precedente; previo.

anteroom ('æn·ti,rum) *n.* antesala; vestíbulo; recibimiento.

anthem ('æn·θəm) *n.* **1,** *eccles.* antífona. **2,** (national) himno nacional.

anther ('æn·θər) *n.* antera.

anthill ('ænt,hil) *n.* hormiguero.

anthology (æn'θal·ə·dʒi) *n.* antología.

anthracite ('æn·θrə·sait) *n.* antracita. —*adj.* color carbón.

anthrax ('æn·θræks) *n.* ántrax.

anthropoid ('æn·θrə·poid) *adj. & n.* antropoideo; antropoide.

anthropology (æn·θrə'pal·ə·dʒi) *n.* antropología. —**anthropological** (-pə'ladʒ·ɪ·kəl) *adj.* antropológico. —**anthropologist** (-'pal·ə·dʒɪst) *n.* antropólogo.

antiaircraft ('æn·ti'er,kræft) *adj.* antiaéreo.

antibiotic (,æn·tɪ·bai'at·ɪk) *n. & adj.* antibiótico.

antibody ('æn·tɪ,bad·i) *n.* anticuerpo.

antic ('æn·tɪk) *adj.* extraño; ridículo. —*n., usu.pl.* bufonadas. —*v.i.* bufonear; bufonearse.

Antichrist ('æn·ti,kraist) *n.* Anticristo.

anticipate (æn'tɪs·ɪ·peit) *v.t.* **1,** (expect) esperar. **2,** (foresee) anticipar; prever. **3,** (forestall) impedir; frustrar. **4,** (be ahead of) anticiparse a; adelantarse a. —**anticipation**, n. anticipación; antelación. —**anticipatory** (-pə,tor·i) adj. anticipante.

anticlerical (,æn·ti'klɛr·ɪ·kəl) adj. anticlerical.

anticlimax (,æn·tɪ'klai·mæks) n. anticlímax. —**anticlimactic** (-klai'mæk·tɪk) adj. desengañador; decepcionante.

antidote ('æn·tɪ·dot) n. antídoto; remedio.

antifreeze ('æn·ti,friːz) n. anticongelante.

antiknock ('æn·ti,nak) adj. & n. antidetonante.

antimony ('æn·tə,mo·ni) n. antimonio.

antipathy (æn'tɪp·ə·θi) n. antipatía; antagonismo. —**antipathetic** (,æn·tɪ·pə'θɛt·ɪk) adj. antipático.

antiphon ('æn·tə,fan) n. antífona.

antipode ('æn·tə,pod) n. antípoda. —**antipodal** (æn'tɪp·ə·dəl) adj. antípoda.

antipope ('æn·ti·pop) n. antipapa.

antiquary ('æn·tɪ,kwɛr·i) n. anticuario. —**antiquarian** (-'kwɛr·i·ən) n. & adj. anticuario.

antiquated ('æn·tɪ·kwei·tɪd) adj. anticuado; arcaico; desusado.

antique (æn'tik) adj. antiguo; pasado de moda. —n. antigualla; pl. antigüedades.

antiquity (æn'tɪk·wə·ti) n. antigüedad; vetustez.

anti-Semite (,æn·ti'sɛm·ait) n. antisemita. —**anti-Semitic** (-sə'mɪt·ɪk) adj. antisemítico; anti-judío. —**anti-Semitism** (-'sɛm·ə·tiz·əm) n. antisemitismo.

antiseptic (æn·tɪ'sɛp·tɪk) adj. & n. antiséptico; desinfectante. —**antisepsis** (-sɪs) n. antisepsia.

antisocial (,æn·ti'so·ʃəl) adj. antisocial.

anti-tank adj. antitanque.

antithesis (æn'tɪθ·ə·sɪs) n. [pl. -ses (-siz)] antítesis. —**antithetical** (æ·tɪ'θɛt·ɪ·kəl) adj. antitético.

antitoxin (,æn·tɪ'tak·sɪn) n. antitoxina. —**antitoxic,** adj. antitóxico.

antitrust (,æn·tɪ'trʌst) adj. antimonopolio.

antler ('ænt·lər) n. asta o cuerno de venado.

antonym ('æn·tə·nɪm) n. antónimo; vocablo opuesto.

antonymous (æn'tan·ə·məs) adj. antónimo.

anus ('ei·nəs) n. ano.

anvil ('æn·vəl) n. yunque.

anxiety (æŋ'zai·ə·ti) n. ansiedad; angustia; zozobra.

anxious ('æŋk·ʃəs) adj. 1, (worried) preocupado; intranquilo. 2, (eager) ansioso; deseoso.

anxiousness ('æŋk·ʃəs·nəs) n. 1, (yearning) ansiedad; anhelo. 2, (impatience) impaciencia; intranquilidad.

any ('ɛn·i) adj. & pron. algún; alguno; cualquiera. —adv. algo.

anybody ('ɛn·i,bad·i) pron. alguien; alguno; cualquiera.

anyhow ('ɛn·i,hau) adv. de cualquier forma; de todos modos; como sea.

anyone ('ɛn·i,wʌn) pron. alguien; alguno; cualquiera.

anything ('ɛn·i,θɪŋ) pron. algo; cualquier cosa; alguna cosa.

anyway ('ɛn·i,wei) adv. 1, = anyhow. 2, (carelessly) descuidadamente; no importa como.

anywhere ('ɛn·i,hwɛr) adv. en o por cualquier sitio; doquiera; dondequiera.

aorta (ei'or·tə) n. aorta.

Apache (ə'pætʃ·i) n. apache.

apart (ə'part) adv. aparte; separadamente.

apartment (ə'part·mənt) n. apartamiento; piso; Arg., Mex. departamento. —**apartment house,** casa de apartamientos.

apathy ('æp·ə·θi) n. apatía; insensibilidad; flema. —**apathetic** (-'θɛt·ɪk) adj. apático; indolente; indiferente.

ape (eip) n. 1, (animal) mono. 2, fig. (mimic) imitador; parodista. —v.t. imitar; remedar; parodiar.

aperitif (ə·pɛr·ə'tif) n. aperitivo.

aperture ('æp·ər·tʃur) n. 1, (opening) apertura; abertura. 2, (hole) agujero; vacío.

apex ('ei·pɛks) n. ápice; cima.

aphasia (ə'fei·ʒə) n. afasia. —**aphasic** (-zɪk) adj. & n. que o quien padece de afasia.

aphelion (ə'fi·li·ən) n. afelio.

aphid ('æf·ɪd) n. áfido.

aphorism ('æf·ə·rɪz·əm) n. aforismo. —**aphoristic** (-'rɪs·tɪk) adj. aforístico.

aphrodisiac (,æf·rə'diz·i·æk) adj. & n. afrodisíaco.

apiary ('ei·pi,ɛr·i) n. abejera.

apiece (ə'pis) *adv.* cada uno; por persona.

aplomb (ə'plorm) *n.* aplomo.

apocalypse (ə'pak·ə·lɪps) *n.* **1,** *cap., Bib.* Apocalipsis. **2,** (revelation) revelación; profecía. **—apocalyptic** (-'lɪp·tɪk) *adj.* apocalíptico.

Apocrypha (ə'pak·rə·fə) *n.pl., Bib.* libros apócrifos. **—apocryphal** (-fəl) *adj.* apócrifo; falso.

apogee ('æp·ə·dʒiɪ) *n.* apogeo.

apologetic (ə,pal·ə'dʒɛt·ɪk) *adj.* **1,** (regretful) pesaroso; compungido. **2,** (defending) apologético.

apologist (ə'pal·ə·dʒɪst) *n.* apologista.

apologize (ə'pal·ə·dʒaiz) *v.i.* **1,** (express regret) excusarse; disculparse. **2,** (make a formal defense) apologizar; defenderse; justificarse.

apology (ə'pal·ə·dʒi) *n.* **1,** (formal defense) apología; defensa; elogio. **2,** (expression of regret) excusa; disculpa. **3,** (makeshift) expediente.

apoplexy ('æp·ə·plɛk·si) *n.* apoplejía. **—apoplectic** (-'plɛk·tɪk) *adj.* apoplético.

apostasy (ə'pas·tə·si) *n.* apostasía; repudio. **—apostate** (-teit) *n. & adj.* apóstata; renegado. **—apostatize** (-tə·taiz) *v.i.* apostatar; repudiar; renegar.

apostle (ə'pas·əl) *n.* apóstol. **—apostolic** (,æp·ə'stal·ɪk) *adj.* apostólico.

apostolate (ə'pas·tə,leit; -lɪt) *n.* apostolado.

apostrophe (ə'pas·trə·fi) *n.* **1,** (direct address) apóstrofe. **2,** *gram.* apóstrofo. **—apostrophize** (-faiz) *v.t. & i.* apostrofar.

apothecary (ə'paθ·ə,kɛr·i) *n.* boticario. **—apothecary's shop,** botica.

apotheosis (ə,paθ·i'o·sɪs) *n.* [*pl.* **-ses** (-siz)] apoteosis.

appall *también,* **appal** (ə'pɔl) *v.t.* horrorizar; aterrar; espantar.

apparatus (,æp·ə'rei·təs) *n.* aparato; aparejo.

apparel (ə'pær·əl) *n.* **1,** (clothing) vestidos; trajes; ropa. **2,** (outward aspect) aspecto; apariencia. **—v.t.** vestir; ataviar.

apparent (ə'pær·ənt) *adj.* **1,** (obvious) patente; evidente; indubable. **2,** (seeming) aparente; presunto.

apparently (ə'pær·ənt·li) *adv.* **1,** (clearly) evidentemente; claramente; sin duda. **2,** (seemingly) aparentemente; presuntamente.

apparition (,æp·ə'rɪʃ·ən) *n.* aparición; espectro; fantasma.

appeal (ə'piːl) *v.i.* **1,** (seek help) acudir; pedir ayuda; implorar. **2,** (resort) volverse; recurrir. **3,** (be attractive) atraer; interesar. **—v.t. & i.,** *law* apelar; recurrir a un tribunal superior. **—n.** **1,** (call for aid) llamamiento; súplica. **2,** (attractiveness) atracción. **3,** *law* apelación; instancia. **—appealing,** *adj.* atractivo; atrayente.

appear (ə'pɪr) *v.i.* **1,** (become visible) aparecer; aparecerse. **2,** (seem to be) parecer; figurar; asemejar; asemejarse. **3,** (be known) manifestarse. **4,** (be published) aparecer. **5,** *law* comparecer.

appearance (ə'pɪr·əns) **1,** (act of appearing) aparición. **2,** (outward aspect) aspecto; porte; apariencia. **3,** (presence) comparecencia.

appease (ə'piz) *v.t.* **1,** (placate) apaciguar; aplacar. **2,** (satisfy) aplacar; calmar. **—appeasement,** *n.* apaciguamiento; pacificación.

appellate (ə'pɛl·ət) *adj.* de apelación.

appellation (,æp·ə'lei·ʃən) *n.* apelativo; nombre.

appellative (ə'pɛl·ə·tɪv) *n. & adj.* apelativo.

append (ə'pɛnd) *v.t.* añadir; agregar; fijar; acompañar. **—appendage** (-ɪdʒ) *n.* añadidura; adición; accesorio.

appendectomy (,æp·ən'dɛk·tə·mi) *n.* apendectomía.

appendicitis (ə'pɛn·dɪ'sai·tɪs) *n.* apendicitis.

appendix (ə'pɛn·dɪks) *n.* [*pl.* **-dixes, -dices** (-də,siz)] **1,** (of a document or book) apéndice; suplemento. **2,** *anat.* apéndice.

appertain (,æp·ər'tein) *v.i.* pertenecer; relacionarse.

appetite ('æp·ə·tait) *n.* **1,** (readiness to eat) apetito. **2,** (strong desire) apetencia; deseo; anhelo.

appetizing ('æp·ə·taiz·ɪŋ) *adj.* apetecible; sabroso; apetitoso; deleitable. **—appetizer** (-ər) *n.* aperitivo; apetito.

applaud (ə'plɔd) *v.t.* aplaudir; aclamar. **—v.i.** ovacionar; aprobar.

applause (ə'plɔz) *n.* aplauso; aclamación; ovación.

apple ('æp·əl) *n.* **1,** (fruit) manzana; poma. **2,** (tree) manzano.

—**apple butter,** manteca de manzana. —**apple of one's eye,** el niño (o la niña) de sus ojos. —**apple orchard,** manzanal; manzanar. —**apple pie,** pastel de manzana. —**apple polisher,** adulador.

applesauce ('æp·əl‚sɔs) n. 1, (food) compota de manzana. 2, slang (nonsense) tontería; disparate.

appliance (ə'plai·əns) n. 1, (tool; utensil) utensilio; instrumento. 2, (act of putting to use) aplicación; uso.

applicable ('æp·lɪ·kə·bəl) adj. aplicable; pertinente. —**applicability,** n. aplicabilidad.

applicant ('æp·lɪ·kənt) n. aspirante; candidato; solicitante.

application (‚æp·lɪ'kei·ʃən) n. 1, (act of applying; thing applied) aplicación. 2, (request) solicitud; instancia; petición. 3, (diligence) aplicación; diligencia; estudio.

applicator ('æp·lɪ‚kei·tər) n. instrumento que sirve para aplicar alguna cosa.

appliqué (‚æp·lə'kei) adj. & n. sobrepuesto.

apply (ə'plai) v.t. 1, (lay on) aplicar. 2, (put to use) usar; aplicar. 3, (concentrate on) applicarse a o en. —v.i. 1, (be applicable or pertinent) aplicarse; atribuirse. 2, (request) pedir; solicitar.

appoint (ə'pɔint) v.t. 1, (assign) nombrar; designar. 2, (prescribe) ordenar; decretar. 3, (rig) surtir; equipar. —**appointive,** adj. electivo; elegible.

appointment (ə'pɔint·mənt) n. 1, (act) nombramiento; elección. 2, (position) puesto; cargo; posición. 3, (scheduled meeting) cita. 4, pl. (furnishings) equipo.

apportion (ə'pɔr·ʃən) v.t. prorratear; dividir proporcionalmente. —**apportionment,** n. prorrateo; división.

apposite ('æp·ə·zɪt) adj. adecuado; apropiado; oportuno. —**apposition** (-'zɪʃ·ən) n. adición; añadidura; gram. aposición.

appraisal (ə'prei·zəl) n. valuación; tasación; cálculo.

appraise (ə'preiz) v.t. valorar; estimar; apreciar. —**appraiser** (-ər) n. tasador; estimador.

appreciable (ə'priː·ʃə·bəl) adj. apreciable; estimable; considerable.

appreciate (ə'priː·ʃi·eit) v.t. 1, (esteem) apreciar; estimar; valorar.

2, (be thankful for) agradecer. —v.i. subir (de precio o valor).

appreciation (ə‚priː·ʃi'ei·ʃən) n. 1, (esteem) apreciación. 2, (grateful recognition) reconocimiento; agradecimiento. 3, (sensitive awareness) percepción; apreciación. 4, (estimate) valuación. 5, (rise in value) alza.

appreciative (ə'priː·ʃə·tɪv) adj. agradecido.

apprehend (æp·rɪ'hɛnd) v.t. 1, (seize physically) prender; detener. 2, (understand) comprender; entender; percibir. 3, (fear) temer; recelar; sospechar.

apprehension (æp·rɪ'hɛn·ʃən) n. 1, (seizure) aprehensión; presa; captura. 2, (understanding) comprensión; percepción. 3, (fear) aprensión; temor; recelo.

apprehensive (æp·rɪ'hɛn·sɪv) adj. aprensivo; receloso. —**apprehensiveness,** n. aprensión; sospecha; recelo.

apprentice (ə'prɛn·tɪs) n. aprendiz; principiante. —v.t. poner de aprendiz. —**apprenticeship** (-ʃɪp) n. aprendizaje.

apprise también, **apprize** (ə'praiz) v.t. informar.

approach (ə'protʃ) v.t. 1, (draw near) acercar. 2, (resemble) parecerse a. 3, (make advances or proposals to) abordar. —v.i. acercarse; aproximarse. —n. 1, (act of approaching) acercamiento. 2, (avenue) acceso; vía. 3, (nearness) proximidad; cercanía.

approbation (æp·rə'bei·ʃən) n. aprobación; autorización; consentimiento.

appropriate (ə'proː·pri·eit) v.t. 1, (allot) asignar. 2, (take possession of) apropiarse de. 3, (steal) robar. —adj. (-ət) apropiado; adecuado. —**appropriateness,** n. propiedad; lo adecuado.

appropriation (ə‚proː·pri'ei·ʃən) n. 1, (allotment) asignación. 2, (act of appropriating) apropiación.

approve (ə'pruːv) v.t. 1, (pronounce good) sancionar; confirmar. 2, (ratify) aprobar; asentir. —v.i. aprobar; sancionar. —**approval** (-əl) n. aprobación; consentimiento. —**on approval,** a prueba.

approximate (ə'prak·sɪ·mət) adj. 1, (nearly correct) parecido; aproximado. 2, (close together) cercano; inmediato. —v.t. (-meit) 1, (approach) aproximarse a; acercarse a. **2,** (resemble) parecerse a. —**approximately,** *adv.* aproximadamente; más o menos. —**approximation,** *n.* aproximación.

appurtenance (ə'pʌr·tə·nəns) *n.* **1,** *law* adjunto. **2,** (accessory) accesorio. **3,** (appendage) añadidura; apéndice. **4,** (that which appertains) pertenencia. **5,** *pl.* (furnishings) accesorios; instrumentos. —**appurtenant,** *adj.* perteneciente.

apricot ('ei·pri·kat) *n.* **1,** (fruit) albaricoque. **2,** (tree) albaricoquero.

April ('ei·prəl) *n.* abril. —**April fool,** inocente; tonto; burlado. —**April Fool's Day,** Día de Inocentes (in the Spanish-speaking world, *usu.* December 28).

apron ('ei·prən) *n.* delantal; mandil.

apropos (æp·rə'poɹ) *adv.* a propósito. —*adj.* adecuado; oportuno. —**apropos of,** con referencia a.

apse (æps) *n.* ábside.

apt (æpt) *adj.* **1,** (suited) apto; adecuado. **2,** (quick to learn) vivo; listo. **3,** (inclined) propenso; inclinado. —**aptness,** *n.* aptitud; competencia.

aptitude ('æp·ti·tud) *n.* aptitud; habilidad; competencia.

aquamarine (,æk·wə·mə'riɹn) *n.* aguamarina. —*adj.* de color aguamarina.

aquarium (ə'kweɹ·i·əm) *n.* acuario.

Aquarius (ə'kweɹ·i·əs) *n., astron.* Acuario.

aquatic (ə'kwæt·ik) *adj.* acuático.

aquatint ('æk·wə·tint) *n.* acuatinta.

aqueduct ('æk·wi·dʌkt) *n.* acueducto; *Mex.* cañería.

aqueous ('ei·kwi·əs) *adj.* ácueo; acuoso. —**aqueous humor,** humor ácueo.

aquiline ('æk·wə·lin) *adj.* aguileño; *poet.* aquilino.

Arab ('ær·əb) *n. & adj.* árabe.

arabesque (ær·ə'bɛsk) *n.* arabesco.

Arabian (ə'rei·bi·ən) *n.* árabe. —*adj.* árabe; arábico; arábigo.

Arabic ('ær·ə·bik) *adj.* árabe; arábico; arábigo. —*n.* árabe; arábigo.

arable ('ær·ə·bəl) *adj.* arable; labrable; cultivable.

arachnid (ə'ræk·nid) *n.* arácnido.

Aramaic (ær·ə'mei·ik) *n. & adj.* arameo.

arbiter ('ar·bi·tər) *n.* árbitro; juez.

arbitrage ('ar·bi,traʒ) *n.* arbitraje.

arbitrary ('ar·bi,trɛr·i) *adj.* **1,** (not regulated by rule) arbitrario; voluble. **2,** (despotic) absoluto; despótico. **3,** (unreasonable) injusto; irrazonable. —**arbitrariness,** *n.* arbitrariedad.

arbitrate ('ar·bi·treit) *v.t. & i.* arbitrar; mediar; intervenir. —**arbitration,** *n.* arbitraje; mediación. —**arbitrator** (-tər) *n.* árbitro; mediador; intermediario.

arbor ('ar·bər) *n.* **1,** [*también,* **arbour**] (bower) emparrado; pérgola; enramada. **2,** *mech.* eje; árbol. —**arboreal** (ar'bor·i·əl) *adj.* arbóreo.

arboretum (ar·bə'ri·təm) *n.* jardín botánico, esp. de árboles raros y exóticos; arboreto.

arbutus (ar'bju·təs) *n.* arbusto; madroño.

arc (ark) *n.* arco. —**arc lamp; arc light,** lámpara de arco. —**arc welder,** soldador de arco. —**arc welding,** soldadura de arco.

arcade (ar'keid) *n.* arcada; galería o pasadizo abovedado.

arch (artʃ) *n.* arco. —*v.t.* arquear; enarcar. —*v.i.* hacer un arco o arcos. —*adj.* **1,** (preeminent) principal; prominente. **2,** (sly) travieso; pícaro.

archaeology (ar·ki'al·ə·dʒi) *n.* arqueología. —**archaeological** (-ə'ladʒ·i·kəl) *adj.* arqueológico. —**archaeologist** (-'al·ə·dʒist) *n.* arqueólogo.

archaic (ar'kei·ik) *adj.* arcaico; antiguo; vetusto. —**archaism** ('ar·ki·iz·əm) *n.* arcaísmo.

archangel (ark'ein·dʒəl) *n.* arcángel.

archbishop ('artʃ,biʃ·əp) *n.* arzobispo. —**archbishopric** (-rik) *n.* arzobispado.

archdeacon ('artʃ,di·kən) *n.* arcediano; archidiácono.

archdiocese (artʃ'dai·ə·sis) *n.* archidiócesis.

archduke ('artʃ,duk) *n.* archiduque. —**archducal** ('du·kəl) *adj.* archiducal. —**archduchess** (-,dʌtʃ·əs) *n.* archiduquesa. —**archduchy** (-,dʌtʃ·i) *n.* archiducado.

archer ('ar·tʃər) *n.* arquero. —**archery,** *n.* tiro al arco.

archetype ('ar·kɪ·taip) *n.* arquetipo; prototipo; modelo.

archfiend ('artʃ,find) *n.* archienemigo; *cap.* el diablo; Satanás.

archiepiscopal (,ar·ki·ɪ'pɪs·kə·pəl) *adj.* arzobispal.

archipelago (ar·kə'pɛl·ə·go) *n.* archipiélago.

architect ('ar·kə·tɛkt) *n.* arquitecto. —**architecture** (-,tɛk·tʃər) *n.* arquitectura. —**architectural** (-'tɛk·tʃər·əl) *adj.* arquitectónico.

archives ('ar·kaivz) *n.pl.* archivos. —**archivist** ('ar·kɪ·vɪst; 'ar,kai·vɪst) *n.* archivero.

archpriest ('artʃ,prist) *n.* arcipreste.

archway ('artʃ·wei) *n.* arcada; bóveda; pasaje abovedado.

arctic ('ark·tɪk) *adj.* ártico. —*n.*, *cap.* Ártica.

ardent ('ar·dənt) *adj.* 1, (burning) ardiente; en llamas. 2, (passionate) fogoso; apasionado. —**ardency,** *n.* ardor; incandescencia.

ardor *también,* **ardour** ('ar·dər) *n.* ardor; pasión.

arduous ('ar·dju·əs) *adj.* arduo; difícil; penoso. —**arduousness,** *n.* arduidad; dificultad.

are (ar) *v., segunda persona del sing. y todas las personas del pl. del pres. de* **be.**

are (ɛr) *n.* área.

area ('ɛːr·i·ə) *n.* 1, (surface) área; superficie. 2, (region) región. 3, (scope) área; extensión; alcance. —**area code,** código de área telefónica.

arena (ə'riː·nə) *n.* 1, (enclosure for sports) anfiteatro; arena; estadio. 2, (bull ring) plaza de toros; redondel.

aren't (arnt; 'a·rənt) *contr. de* **are not.**

argon ('ar·gan) *n.* argo; argón.

argot ('ar·go) *n.* argot; jerga.

argue ('ar·gju) *v.i.* argüir; disputar. —*v.t.* 1, (discuss) argüir; discutir; debatir. 2, (try to prove) razonar; probar.

argument ('ar·gju·mənt) *n.* 1, (debate) discusión; debate. 2, (reasoning) razonamiento. 3, (summary) argumento. —**argumentation** (-mən'tei·ʃən) *n.* argumentación; razonamiento; debate. —**argumentative** (-'mɛn·tə·tɪv) *adj.* argumentativo; disputador; contencioso.

argyrol ('ar·dʒɪ·rol) *n., T.N.* argirol.

aria ('ar·i·ə) *n.* aria.

arid ('ær·ɪd) *adj.* 1, (dry) árido; reseco; estéril. 2, *fig.* (dull) árido; aburrido. —**aridity** (ə'rɪd·ə·ti) *n.* aridez; sequedad.

Aries ('ɛr·iz) *n., astron.* Aries.

aright (ə'rait) *adv.* rectamente; justamente. —**set aright,** rectificar.

arise (ə'raiz) *v.i.* [**arose, arisen** (ə'riz·ən)] 1, (move upward) surgir; elevarse. 2, (get up; come into being or action) levantarse; sublevarse.

aristocracy (,ær·ɪs'tak·rə·si) *n.* aristocracia. —**aristocrat** (ə'rɪs·tə·kræt) *n.* aristócrata; noble. —**aristocratic** (-'kræt·ɪk) *adj.* aristocrático; distinguido.

arithmetic (ə'rɪθ·mə·tɪk) *n.* aritmética. —**arithmetical** (,ær·ɪθ'mɛt·ɪ·kəl), **arithmetic,** *adj.* aritmético. —**arithmetician,** (ə,rɪθ·mə'tɪʃ·ən) *n.* aritmético.

ark (ark) *n.* arca.

arm (arm) *n.* 1, *anat.* brazo. 2, (of a river) brazo. 3, (weapon) arma. 4, *fig.* (helpful person or thing) rama. —*v.t.* armar. —*v.i.* armarse. —**arm in arm,** de o del brazo; de bracero; de bracete. —**with open arms,** con los brazos abiertos.

armada (ar'ma·də) *n.* armada; flota.

armadillo (ar·mə'dɪl·o) *n.* [*pl.* -los] armadillo.

armament ('ar·mə·mənt) *n.* armamento.

armature ('ar·mə·tʃur) *n.* 1, (armor) armadura. 2, (for horses) arnés. 3, *elect.* (of a magnet) armadura; (of a dynamo) inducido.

armband ('arm,bænd) *n.* brazal.

armchair ('arm,tʃeir) *n.* sillón; butaca.

armed (armd) *adj.* armado. —**armed forces,** fuerzas armadas; ejército.

armful ('arm,ful) *n.* brazada.

armhole ('arm,hol) *n.* sobaquera.

armistice ('ar·mɪ·stɪs) *n.* armisticio.

armlet ('arm·lət) *n.* brazal; brazalete.

armor ('ar·mər) *n.* armadura; coraza; blindaje. —*v.t.* blindar; acorazar. —*v.i.* acorazarse; ponerse coraza. —**armored,** *adj.* blindado. —**armor plate,** plancha blindada; blindaje.

armory ('ar·mə·ri) *n.* 1, (arsenal)

armería; arsenal. **2,** (heraldry) heráldica; blasones; armas.

armpit ('arm,pɪt) n. axila; sobaco.

arms (armz) n.pl. **1,** (weapons) armas. **2,** her. armas; blasones. —**bear arms,** estar armado; cargar armas. —**be up in arms,** levantarse en armas. —**lay down one's arms,** rendir las armas; rendirse. —**take up arms,** tomar las armas. —**to arms!,** ¡a las armas!.

army ('ar·mi) n. **1,** mil. ejército. **2,** fig. multitud.

arnica ('ar·nɪk·ə) n. árnica.

aroma (ə'ro·mə) n. aroma; fragancia. —**aromatic** (ær·ə'mæt·ɪk) adj. aromático; fragante; oloroso.

arose (ə'roːz) v., pret. de **arise.**

around (ə'raund) adv. a la redonda; en derredor; alrededor; a la vuelta; por todos lados. —prep. cerca de; en; alrededor de.

arouse (ə'rauz) v.t. excitar; impulsar; despertar.

arraign (ə'rein) v.t. procesar; acusar. —**arraignment,** n. procesamiento; proceso; acusación.

arrange (ə'reɪndʒ) v.t. **1,** (put in order) ordenar; arreglar. **2,** (settle) ajustar; acordar. **3,** (plan) preparar; planear. **4,** mus. arreglar; adaptar.

arrangement (ə'reɪndʒ·mənt) n. **1,** (order) orden; arreglo; colocación. **2,** (settlement) acuerdo; arreglo. **3,** pl. (plans) medidas; preparativos. **4,** mus. adaptación; arreglo.

arrant ('ær·ənt) adj. **1,** (notorious) conocido; manifiesto. **2,** (downright) absoluto; categórico.

array (ə'rei) n. **1,** (arrangement) orden; colocación. **2,** mil. formación. **3,** (apparel) vestido; indumentaria. —v.t. **1,** (place in order) ordenar; organizar. **2,** (bedeck) vestir; adornar.

arrears (ə'rɪrz) n.pl. atrasos; deudas vencidas. —**in arrears,** atrasado.

arrest (ə'rest) v.t. **1,** (capture) arrestar; capturar. **2,** (stop forcibly) detener; impedir. —n. **1,** (detention) arresto; detención. **2,** (capture) captura. **3,** mech. interrupción. **4,** med. detención. —**arresting,** adj. impresionante. —**under arrest,** detenido; arrestado.

arrival (ə'rai·vəl) n. **1,** (act of arriving) arribo; llegada. **2,** (person or thing that arrives) llegado; arribado.

arrive (ə'raiv) v.i. **1,** (reach) llegar; arribar. **2,** (occur) suceder; ocurrir;

acontecer. **3,** (attain success) lograr; llegar.

arrogant ('ær·ə·gənt) adj. arrogante; altanero; despectivo. —**arrogance,** n. arrogancia; altanería.

arrogate ('ær·ə,geit) v.t. arrogarse; atribuirse; usurpar. —**arrogation,** n. arrogación.

arrow ('ær·o) n. flecha; saeta.

arrowhead ('ær·o,hɛd) n. punta de flecha.

arrowroot ('ær·o,rut) n. arrurruz.

arroyo (ə'rɔi·o) n. arroyo.

arse (ars) n., slang culo; nalgas.

arsenal ('ar·sə·nəl) n. arsenal.

arsenic ('ar·sə·nɪk) n. arsénico. —**arsenical** (-'sən·ɪ·kəl) adj. arsenical; de arsénico.

arson ('ar·sən) n. incendio premeditado.

art (art) n. arte. —**arts and crafts,** artes y artesanías.

art (art) v., arcaico, segunda persona del sing. del pres. de **be.**

arteriosclerosis (ar,tɪr·i·o·skle'ro·sɪs) n. arteriosclerosis.

artery ('ar·tə·ri) n. arteria. —**arterial** (-'tɪr·i·əl) adj. arterial.

artesian well (ar'tiː·ʒən) pozo artesiano.

artful ('art·fəl) adj. **1,** (wily) engañoso; artificial. **2,** (skillful) diestro; ingenioso.

artfulness ('art·fəl·nəs) n. **1,** (cunning) engaño; artificio. **2,** (skill) habilidad; destreza.

arthritis (ar'θrai·tɪs) n. artritis. —**arthritic** (-'θrɪt·ɪk) adj. artrítico.

arthropod ('ar·θro·pad) n., zoöl. artrópodo.

artichoke ('ar·tɪ,tʃok) n. alcachofa; Sp. alcacil.

article ('ar·tɪ·kəl) n. artículo.

articulate (ar'tɪk·ju·leit) v.t. & i. **1,** (enunciate) articular; enunciar. **2,** (join) enlazar; unir. —adj. (-lət) **1,** (expressive) claro. **2,** (having joints) articulado. —**articulation,** n. articulación.

artifact ('ar·tə,fækt) n. artefacto.

artifice ('ar·tɪ·fɪs) n. **1,** (crafty device) artificio. **2,** (trickery) treta; engaño; ardid.

artificer (ar'tɪf·ə·sər) n. artífice.

artificial (ar·tɪ'fɪʃ·əl) adj. **1,** (man-made) artificial. **2,** (pretended) falso; postizo. **3,** (fictitious) ficticio; fingido; artificioso. **4,** (affected) afectado; artificial. —**artificiality** (-,fɪʃ·i'æl·ə·ti) n. artificialidad. —**artificial respiration,** resucitación por medidas artificiales.

artillery (ar'tıl·ə·ri) *n.* artillería. —**artilleryman** (-mən) *n.* [*pl.* -men] artillero.

artisan ('ar·tı·zən) *n.* artesano.

artist ('ar·tıst) *n.* artista. —**artistic** (-tis'tık) *adj.* artístico. —**artistry** (-ri) *n.* arte; maña; habilidad artística.

artless ('art·ləs) *adj.* natural; simple; sincero. —**artlessness,** *n.* naturalidad; sencillez.

Aryan *también,* **Arian** ('eır·i·ən; 'ær-) *n.* & *adj.* ario.

as (æz) *adv.* **1,** (to the same degree) tan; como. **2,** (for example) como; por ejemplo. —*conj.* **1,** (to the same degree that) así como; como; a medida que. **2,** (in the same manner that) como; según. **3,** (while) cuando; mientras; a la vez que. **4,** (because) porque; puesto que; ya que. **5,** (though) aunque; aun. —*rel.pron.* que; lo que; como. —*prep.* como; por. —**as.... as,** tan.... como. —**as for,** en cuanto a. —**as if,** como si. —**as if to,** como para. —**as is,** tal cual; sin condición. —**as it were,** por decirlo así. —**as though,** como si. —**as to, 1,** (concerning) en cuanto a. **2,** = **as if to.** —**as well,** también. —**as well as,** así como. —**as yet,** todavía; aún. —**so.... as,** tan.... como. —**such as, 1,** (the same as) tal cual; como. **2,** (who) quien (o quienes); los (o las) que. —**the same as,** el mismo que.

asafetida (,æs·ə'fεt·ı·də) *n.* asafétida.

asbestos (æz'bεs·təs) *n.* asbesto; amianto.

ascend (ə'sεnd) *v.i.* ascender; elevarse. —*v.t.* escalar; subir.

ascendant (ə'sεn·dənt) *adj.* **1,** (rising) ascendente. **2,** (dominant) superior; predominante. —*n.* predominio; influjo. —**ascendancy,** *n.* ascendiente; poder.

ascension (ə'sεn·ʃən) *n.* **1,** (ascent) subida; ascensión. **2,** *cap., relig.* Ascensión.

ascent (ə'sεnt) *n.* **1,** (upward movement) ascenso; ascensión; subida. **2,** (upward slope) pendiente; cuesta.

ascertain (æs·ər'tein) *v.t.* indagar; inquirir; averiguar. —**ascertainment,** *n.* indagación; averiguación.

ascetic (ə'sεt·ık) *adj.* ascético. —*n.*

asceta; eremita. —**asceticism** (-ı,sız·əm) *n.* ascetismo.

ascorbic acid (ə'skor·bık 'æs·ıd) *n.* ácido ascórbico.

ascribe (ə'skraib) *v.t.* adscribir; atribuir; imputar. —**ascription** (ə'skrıp·ʃən) *n.* adscripción.

asepsis (ə'sεp·sıs) *n.* asepsia. —**aseptic** (-tık) *adj.* aséptico.

asexual (ei'sεk·ʃu·əl) *adj.* asexual; ambiguo; indeterminado.

ash (æʃ) *n.* **1,** (residue) ceniza. **2,** (tree) fresno. **3,** *pl.* (human remains) cenizas; despojos. —**ash tray,** cenicero. —**ash can, 1,** (for trash) cubo de basura; basurero. **2,** *slang* (depth charge) carga de profundidad.

ashamed (ə'ʃeimd) *adj.* avergonzado; abochornado; confundido.

ashen ('æʃ·ən) *adj.* ceniciento; pálido; exangüe.

ashore (ə'ʃor) *adv.* en o a tierra.

Ash Wednesday miércoles de Ceniza.

ashy ('æʃ·i) *adj.* ceniciento; gris. —**ashiness,** *n.* palidez; cualidad de ceniza.

Asian ('ei·ʒən) *también,* **Asiatic** (ei·ʒi'æt·ık) *adj.* & *n.* asiático. —**Asian** *or* **Asiatic flu,** gripe asiática.

aside (ə'said) *adv.* **1,** (on or to one side) al lado; aparte; a un lado. **2,** (regardless) sin consideración o atención. —*n., theat.* aparte. —**aside from,** aparte de; además de.

asinine ('æs·ə·nain) *adj.* asnal; estúpido; idiota. —**asininity** (-'nın·ə·ti) *n.* asnada; asnería; estupidez.

ask (æsk) *v.t.* **1,** (interrogate) preguntar; interrogar. **2,** (request) solicitar; rogar; pedir. **3,** (invite) invitar; convidar.

askance (ə'skæns) *adv.* desconfiadamente; con recelo.

askew (ə'skju:) *adv.* oblicuamente; de soslayo. —*adj.* oblicuo; sesgado.

aslant (ə'slænt) *adv.* oblicuamente. —*adj.* oblicuo; inclinado.

asleep (ə'sli:p) *adj.* **1,** (sleeping) dormido. **2,** (numb) insensible. —*adv.* dormidamente.

asp (æsp) *n.* áspid; serpiente venenosa.

asparagus (ə'spær·ə·gəs) *n.* **1,** (plant) espárrago. **2,** (shoots used as food) espárragos.

aspect ('æs·pεkt) *n.* **1,** (viewpoint)

aspecto. **2,** (appearance) semblante; aspecto; talante; cariz. **3,** (view) vista.

aspen ('æs·pən) *n.* álamo temblón.

asperity (æs'pɛr·ə·ti) *n.* aspereza; severidad.

asperse (ə'spʌrs) *v.t.* difamar; inculpar; calumniar.

aspersion (ə'spʌr·ʒən) *n.* **1,** (sprinkling) aspersión. **2,** (defamation) calumnia; difamación.

asphalt ('æs·fɔlt) *n.* asfalto.

asphodel ('æs·fə·dɛl) *n.* asfódelo; gamón.

asphyxia (æs'fɪk·si·ə) *n.* asfixia; sofocación; ahogo.

asphyxiate (æs'fɪk·si·eit) *v.t.* asfixiar; sofocar; ahogar. —*v.i.* asfixiarse; sofocarse; ahogarse. —**asphyxiation,** *n.* asfixia; sofocación.

aspic ('æs·pɪk) *n.* jalea de carne u hortalizas.

aspirant ('æs·pər·ənt) *n.* aspirante; candidato.

aspirate ('æs·pə·reit) *v.t.* aspirar. —*n. & adj.* (-rət) aspirado.

aspiration (,æs·pə'rei·ʃən) *n.* **1,** (desire) aspiración; deseo; anhelo. **2,** (breathing) aspiración.

aspire (ə'spair) *v.i.* aspirar; anhelar; desear.

aspirin ('æs·pə·rɪn) *n.* aspirina.

ass (æs; as) *n.* **1,** (donkey) asno; burro. **2,** *slang* (dunce) burro; idiota. **3,** *slang* culo; nalgas.

assail (ə'seil) *v.t.* asaltar; atacar; acometer. —**assailant** (-ənt) *n.* atacador; agresor.

assassin (ə'sæs·ɪn) *n.* asesino; homicida.

assassinate (ə'sæs·ə·neit) *v.t.* asesinar. —**assassination,** *n.* asesinato.

assault (ə'sɔlt) *v.t.* **1,** (attack physically) asaltar; atacar; agredir. **2,** (attack verbally) asaltar; abusar. —*n.* asalto; agresión; ataque. —**assault and battery,** asalto y agresión.

assay (ə'sei) *v.t.* examinar; probar; *metall.* ensayar; analizar; *chem.* analizar. —*n.* ('æs·ei) prueba; examen; *metall.* ensayo; análisis; *chem.* análisis.

assemblage (ə'sɛm·blɪdʒ) *n.* **1,** (gathering of persons) asamblea; reunión. **2,** (group of things) grupo; conjunto. **3,** *mech.* montaje.

assemble (ə'sɛm·bəl) *v.t.* **1,** (persons) convocar; reunir. **2,** (things)

montar; unir; ensamblar. —*v.i.* congregarse; reunirse; agruparse.

assembly (ə'sɛm·bli) *n.* **1,** (meeting) asamblea; reunión; junta. **2,** *mech.* juego de piezas. —**assembly line,** línea de montaje.

assent (ə'sɛnt) *v.i.* asentir; consentir; aprobar. —*n.* ('æs·ɛnt) asenso; consentimiento; aprobación.

assert (ə'sʌrt) *v.t.* **1,** (aver) aseverar; afirmar; ratificar; **2,** (claim and defend) defender; sostener; mantener. —**assert oneself,** hacer valer sus derechos.

assertion (ə'sʌr·ʃən) *n.* aserción; afirmación; aseveración.

assertive (ə'sʌr·tɪv) *adj.* aseverativo; afirmativo.

assess (ə'sɛs) *v.t.* **1,** (evaluate) tasar; evaluar; valorar. **2,** (tax) fijar o poner impuestos. **3,** (require a contribution of) imponer contribución a.

assessment (ə'sɛs·mənt) *n.* **1,** (evaluation) tasación; valoración. **2,** (amount of tax) impuesto; contribución.

assessor (ə'sɛs·ər) *n.* **1,** (tax appraiser) tasador. **2,** (adviser) asesor.

asset ('æs·ɛt) *n.* **1,** (anything advantageous) ventaja. **2,** *usu.pl., comm.* capital; activo.

assiduous (ə'sɪdʒ·u·əs) *adj.* asiduo; constante; diligente. —**assiduousness, assiduity** (,æs·ɪ'dju·ə·ti) *n.* asiduidad; diligencia; constancia.

assign (ə'sain) *v.t.* **1,** (allot) asignar; repartir; distribuir. **2,** (appoint) asignar; designar; nombrar. **3,** *law* consignar; ceder. —*v.i., law* hacer cesión. —*n., law* cesionario.

assignation (,æs·ɪg'nei·ʃən) *n.* **1,** *law* asignación; cesión. **2,** (tryst) cita amorosa ilícita.

assignee (,æs·ə'niː; ə,sai'niː) *n., law* cesionario.

assignment (ə'sain·mənt) *n.* **1,** (allotment) asignación. **2,** (appointment) designación. **3,** (task) tarea; misión. **4,** *law* documento de cesión o traspaso.

assimilate (ə'sɪm·ə·leit) *v.t.* **1,** (absorb) asimilar; absorber. **2,** (adapt) asimilar; adaptar; asemejar. —*v.i.* asemejarse; asimilarse. —**assimilation,** *n.* asimilación.

assist (ə'sɪst) *v.t.* asistir; ayudar; atender. —*v.i.* asistir; concurrir; atender.

assistance (ə'sɪs·təns) *n.*

asistencia; ayuda; auxilio. —**assistant,** *n.* asistente; ayudante.

associate (ə'so·ʃi·eit) *v.t.* unir; juntar; asociar. —*v.i.* asociarse; juntarse; unirse. —*n.* (-ət) asociado; socio; consocio. —*adj.* (-ət) asociado.

association (ə,so·si'ei·ʃən) *n.* **1,** (act of associating) unión; reunión. **2,** (a society) asociación; sociedad; compañía. **3,** (of ideas) asociación.

assonance ('æs·ə·nəns) *n.* asonancia. —**assonant,** *adj.* asonante.

assort (ə'sort) *v.t.* **1,** (classify) arreglar; clasificar; distribuir. **2,** (supply with various goods) surtir; proveer; suministrar. —**assort with,** asociarse con.

assortment (ə'sort·mənt) *n.* **1,** (classification) arreglo; clasificación. **2,** (variety) surtido; variedad.

assuage (ə'sweidʒ) *v.t.* **1,** (lessen) aminorar; mitigar. **2,** (calm) pacificar; sosegar; calmar. —**assuagement,** *n.* mitigación.

assume (ə'sum) *v.t.* **1,** (believe without proof) asumir; presumir. **2,** (take for oneself) usurpar; apropiarse de. **3,** (undertake) asumir; tomar. **4,** (pretend to have) presumir de. **5,** (take for granted) presumir; dar por sentado o descontado.

assumption (ə'sʌmp·ʃən) *n.* **1,** (belief without proof) asunción. **2,** (acceptance on faith) presunción; hipótesis. **3,** *cap., eccles.* Asunción de María.

assurance (ə'ʃur·əns) *n.* **1,** (confidence) seguridad; confianza. **2,** (certainty) certeza; convicción. **3,** (boldness) valor; arrojo. **4,** (impudence) descaro. **5,** (insurance) seguro.

assure (ə'ʃur) *v.t.* **1,** (make certain) asegurar; afirmar. **2,** (make confident) inspirar confianza en.

Assyrian (ə'sɪr·i·ən) *adj. & n.* asirio.

astatine ('æs·tə,tin) *n.* astacio.

aster ('æs·tər) *n.* áster.

asterisk ('æs·tər·ɪsk) *n.* asterisco.

astern (ə'stʌrn) *adv. & adj.* a popa.

asteroid ('æs·tər·ɔid) *n.* asteroide.

asthma ('æz·mə) *n.* asma. —**asthmatic** (-'mæt·ɪk) *adj. & n.* asmático.

astigmatism (ə'stig·mə·tiz·əm) *n.* astigmatismo. —**astigmatic** (,æs·tɪg'mæt·ɪk) *adj.* astigmático.

astir (ə'stʌr) *adv.* **1,** (actively) afanosamente; vivamente. **2,** (out of bed) fuera de la cama. —*adj.* activo; laborioso.

astonish (ə'stan·ɪʃ) *v.t.* asombrar; sorprender; pasmar. —**astonishment,** *n.* asombro; pasmo; sorpresa.

astound (ə'staund) *v.t.* aturdir; espantar; aterrar.

astraddle (ə'stræd·əl) *adv.* a horcajadas. —*prep.* a horcajadas en.

astral ('æs·trəl) *adj.* astral.

astray (ə'strei) *adv.* desviadamente; fuera del camino. —*adj.* extraviado; perdido; descarriado.

astride (ə'straid) *adv.* a horcajadas. —*prep.* a horcajadas en.

astringe (ə'strindʒ) *v.t.* astringir; constreñir; contraer.

astringent (ə'strin·dʒənt) *n.* astringente; constringente. —*adj.* **1,** (tending to constrict) astringente; constringente. **2,** (severe) severo; riguroso; áspero. —**astringency** (-dʒən·si) *n.* astringencia; contracción.

astrology (ə'stral·ə·dʒi) *n.* astrología. —**astrologer** (-dʒər) *n.* astrólogo. —**astrological** (,æs·trə'ladʒ·ɪ·kəl) *adj.* astrológico.

astronaut ('æs·trə·nɔt) *n.* astronauta. —**astronautics** (-'nɔː·tɪks) *n.* astronáutica.

astronomy (ə'stran·ə·mi) *n.* astronomía. —**astronomer** (-mər) *n.* astrónomo. —**astronomical** (,æs·trə'nam·ɪ·kəl) *adj.* astronómico.

astrophysics (,æs·tro'fɪz·ɪks) *n.* astrofísica. —**astrophysical** (-ɪ·kəl) *adj.* astrofísico.

astute (ə'stut) *adj.* astuto; sagaz; taimado. —**astuteness,** *n.* astucia; sagacidad.

asunder (ə'sʌn·dər) *adj.* separado; dividido; desunido. —*adv.* aparte; por separado; desunidamente.

asylum (ə'sai·ləm) *n.* asilo.

asymmetry (ei'sim·ə·tri) *n.* asimetría. —**asymmetrical** (,ei·sə'met·rɪk·əl) *adj.* asimétrico.

at (æt) *prep.* **1,** (expressing location) a. **2,** (expressing direction or goal) a. **3,** (in the state of) en. **4,** (by; near) por. **5,** (expressing price, speed, etc.) a.

atavism ('æt·ə·vɪz·əm) *n.* atavismo. —**atavistic** (-'vɪs·tɪk) *adj.* atávico.

ataxia (ə'tæk·si·ə) *n.* ataxia.

ate (eit) *v., pret. de* eat.

atheism ('ei·θi·ɪz·əm) *n.* ateísmo. —**atheist**, *n.* ateo; ateísta. —**atheistic** (-'ɪs·tɪk) *adj.* ateo; ateísta; ateístico.

athenium (æ'θiː·ni·əm) *n., chem.* atenio.

athlete ('æθ·lit) *n.* atleta. —**athlete's foot,** pie de atleta; infección entre los dedos de los pies.

athletic (æθ'let·ɪk) *adj.* atlético. —**athletics**, *n.pl.*. deportes; atletismo.

athwart (ə'θwort) *prep.* **1,** (across) a o de través de. **2,** (against) contra; en oposición a. —*adv.* **1** (crosswise) oblicuamente; contrariamente. **2,** (perversely) aviesamente; perversamente.

Atlantic (æt'læn·tɪk) *adj.* atlántico. —*n., cap.* Atlántico.

atlas ('æt·ləs) *n.* atlas.

atmosphere ('æt·məs,fɪr) *n.* **1,** (air) atmósfera. **2,** *fig.* (environment) ambiente; medio. —**atmospheric** (-'fɛr·ɪk) *adj.* atmosférico.

atoll ('æ·tal) *n.* atolón.

atom ('æt·əm) *n.* átomo. —**atomic** (ə'tam·ɪk) *adj.* atómico. —**atom bomb; atomic bomb,** bomba atómica. —**atomic pile,** reactor atómico.

atomize ('æt·ə·maiz) *v.t.* pulverizar; rociar; atomizar. —**atomizer,** *n.* pulverizador; atomizador.

atonal (ei'to·nəl) *adj.* atonal. —**atonality** (,ei·to'næl·ə·ti) *n.* atonalidad.

atone (ə'toːn) *v.i.* arrepentirse; enmendarse; expiar. —**atonement,** *n.* expiación; arrepentimiento; enmienda.

atop (ə'tap) *adj.* elevado; alto. —*adv.* encima; en la cima. —*prep.* sobre; encima de.

atrium ('ei·tri·əm) *n.* atrio.

atrocious (ə'tro·ʃəs) *adj.* atroz; cruel; perverso. —**atrociousness,** *n.* perversidad; crueldad.

atrocity (ə'tras·ə·ti) *n.* atrocidad; brutalidad.

atrophy ('æt·rə·fi) *n.* atrofia. —*v.i.* atrofiarse.

atropine ('æt·rə,pin) *n.* atropina.

attach (ə'tætʃ) *v.t.* **1,** (fasten) adherir; sujetar; fijar. **2,** *law* embargar. **3,** (appoint) designar; nombrar. **4,** (associate) unir; asociar; enlazar. —*v.i.* pegarse; unirse; adherirse.

attaché (æt·ə'ʃei) *n.* agregado diplomático. —**attaché case,** portafolio; cartera.

attachment (ə'tætʃ·mənt) *n.* **1,** (adhesion) adhesión; adherencia. **2,** (devotion) afición; afecto. **3,** *mech.* accesorio.

attack (ə'tæk) *v.t.* **1,** (assault) atacar; agredir; asaltar. **2,** (assail) acusar; acometer. —*n.* **1,** (assault) ataque; agresión. **2,** *mil.* ataque; combate. **3,** (illness) ataque; acometida.

attain (ə'tein) *v.t.* obtener; conseguir; lograr; realizar.

attainment (ə'tein·mənt) *n.* **1,** (acquisition) obtención; logro; realización. **2,** (acquired honor or ability) conocimiento; don.

attar ('æt·ər) *n.* aceite esencial.

attempt (ə'tɛmpt) *v.t.* intentar; procurar; probar. —*n.* intento; tentativa; esfuerzo.

attend (ə'tend) *v.t.* **1,** (be present at) asistir a; concurrir a. **2,** (take care of) cuidar; atender. **3,** (go with) acompañar. **4,** (heed) atender; escuchar.

attendance (ə'ten·dəns) *n.* **1,** (presence) concurrencia; asistencia. **2,** (help) asistencia; ayuda.

attendant (ə'ten·dənt) *n.* **1,** (one who serves) asistente; sirviente. **2,** (one who is present) asistente. **3,** (follower) acompañante; seguidor. —*adj.* **1,** (serving or being present) asistente. **2,** (accompanying) concomitante; acompañante.

attention (ə'ten·ʃən) *n.* **1,** (mindfulness; care) atención; cuidado. **2,** (act of civility) cortesía; fineza; atención. —*interj., mil.* ¡atención!; ¡firmes!

attentive (ə'ten·tɪv) *adj.* **1,** (intent) atento; aplicado. **2,** (polite) atento; educado; cortés. —**attentiveness,** *n.* atención; fijeza; finura.

attenuate (ə'ten·ju·eit) *v.t.* atenuar; disminuir; aminorar. —*v.i.* atenuarse; disminuirse; aminorarse. —**attenuation,** *n.* atenuación; disminución.

attest (ə'tɛst) *v.t.* **1,** (testify) atestiguar; declarar. **2,** (prove) probar; garantizar; confirmar. **3,** *law* deponer; declarar.

attestation (,æt·ɛs'tei·ʃən) *n.* atestación; deposición; declaración.

attic ('æt·ɪk) *n.* ático; desván.

Attic ('æt·ɪk) *adj.* ático.

attire (ə'tair) *n.* atavío; traje;

vestido. —*v.t.* vestir; adornar;
ataviar.

attitude ('æt·ɪ·tud) *n.* **1,** (feeling; opinion) actitud; gesto;
posición. **2,** (posture) actitud;
postura.

attorney (ə'tʌr·ni) *n.* abogado.
—**attorney at law,** procurador.
—**attorney general,** ministro de
justicia; fiscal de la nación.
—**power of attorney,** poder.

attract (ə'trækt) *v.t.* atraer.

attraction (ə'træk·ʃən) *n.* atracción.

attractive (ə'træk·tɪv) *n.*
atrayente; seductor.

attribute (ə'trɪb·jut) *v.t.* atribuir;
achacar; imputar. —*n.* ('æt·rɪ·bjut)
atributo; característica. —**attribution** (,æt·rɪ'bju·ʃən) *n.* atribución.
—**attributive** (ə'trɪb·ju·tɪv) *adj.* &
n. atributivo.

attrition (ə'trɪʃ·ən) *n.* desgaste;
rozadura; *fig.* agotamiento.

attune (ə'tun) *v.t.* **1,** (tune) afinar;
templar. **2,** (bring into accord)
armonizar; poner de acuerdo.

atypical (ei'tɪp·ɪ·kəl) *adj.*
desusado; anormal.

auburn ('ɔ·bərn) *adj.* castañorojizo.

auction ('ɔk·ʃən) *n.* subasta; remate. —*v.t.* subastar. —**auctioneer**
(-'ɪr) *n.* subastador; rematador.

audacious (ɔ'dei·ʃəs) *adj.* **1,** (daring) audaz; intrépido; valiente. **2,**
(unrestrained) atrevido; insolente;
descarado.

audacity (ɔ'dæs·ə·ti) *n.* **1,** (daring)
audacia; intrepidez. **2,** (impudence)
atrevimiento; insolencia.

audible ('ɔ·də·bəl) *adj.* audible;
oíble; perceptible. —**audibility,** *n.*
sonoridad; perceptibilidad.

audience ('ɔ·di·əns) *n.* **1,** (listeners) oyentes. **2,** (assembly) auditorio; concurso. **3,** (formal interview) audiencia.

audio ('ɔ·di·o) *n.* parte audible de
una emisión. —*adj.* audible.

audion ('ɔ·di·an) *n.* audión.

audiovisual (,ɔ·di·o'vɪʒ·u·əl) *adj.*
audiovisual.

audiphone ('ɔ·də,fon) *n.* audífono.

audit ('ɔ·dɪt) *n.* inspección. —*v.t.*
inspeccionar.

audition (ɔ'dɪʃ·ən) *n.* **1,** (act of
hearing) audición. **2,** (test performance) audición; *mus.* recital. —*v.t.*
dar audición a. —*v.i.* dar una
audición.

auditor ('ɔ·dɪ·tər) *n.* **1,** (listener)
oyente. **2,** *comm.* contador; revisor
o inspector de contabilidad.

auditorium (ɔ·də'tor·i·əm) *n.* **1,**
(for a small group) paraninfo. **2,**
(for the public) sala de espectáculos.

auditory ('ɔ·də·tor·i) *adj.* auditivo.

auger ('ɔ·gər) *n.* barrena; taladro.

aught (ɔt) *n.* algo; alguna cosa; *(en
proposiciones negativas)* nada.
—*adv.* de cualquier forma; en
absoluto.

augment (ɔg'mɛnt) *v.t.* aumentar;
incrementar. —*v.i.* crecer; hacerse
más grande. —*n.* ('ɔg·mɛnt) aumento. —**augmentation** (,ɔg·mɛn'tei·ʃən) *n.* aumentación; aumento;
incremento. —**augmentative**
(ɔg'mɛn·tə·tɪv) *adj.* aumentativo.

augur ('ɔ·gər) *v.t.* & *i.* predecir;
presagiar; augurar. —*n.* augur;
agorero; adivino.

augury ('ɔ·gju·ri) *n.* **1,** (omen)
augurio; presagio. **2,** (bad omen)
mal agüero.

august (ɔ'gʌst) *adj.* augusto;
solemne; impresionante.

August ('ɔ·gəst) *n.* agosto.

auk (ɔk) *n.* alca.

aunt (ant; ænt) *n.* tía.

aura ('ɔ·rə) *n.* aura.

aural ('ɔ·rəl) *adj.* auditivo.

aureole ('or·i·ol) *n.* aureola.

aureomycin (,or·i·o'mai·sɪn) *n.*
aureomicina.

auricle ('ɔ·rə·kəl) *n.* **1,** (outer ear)
oreja. **2,** (chamber of the heart)
aurícula. —**auricular** (ɔ'rɪk·jə·lər)
adj. auricular.

auriferous (ɔ'rɪf·ər·əs) *adj.*
aurífero.

aurora (ɔ'ror·ə) *n.* **1,** (dawn)
amanecer; alborada. **2,** (atmospheric
phenomenon) aurora. —**aurora borealis** (bor·i'æl·ɪs) aurora boreal.
—**aurora australis** (ɔ'strei·lɪs) aurora austral.

auscultate ('ɔs·kəl,teit) *v.t.*
auscultar. —**auscultation,** *n.* auscultación.

auspice ('ɔ·spɪs) *n., usu.pl.*
auspicios; protección. —**auspicious**
(ɔ'spɪʃ·əs) *adj.* favorable; propicio;
benigno. —**auspiciousness,** *n.*
benignidad; prosperidad.

austere (ɔ'stɪr) *adj.* **1,** (unadorned) austero; sobrio. **2,** (severe)
severo; estricto; riguroso.

—**austerity** (ɔ'stɛr·ə·ti) *n.* austeridad.

austral ('ɔ·strəl) *adj.* austral.

autarchy ('ɔ·tar·ki) *n.* autarquía. —**autarchic** (ɔ'tar·kɪk) *adj.* autárquico.

autarky ('ɔ·tar·ki) *n.* autarquía. —**autarkic** (ɔ'tar·kɪk); **autarkical,** *adj.* autárquico.

authentic (ɔ'θɛn·tɪk) *adj.* auténtico; genuino; verdadero. —**authenticity** (ˌɔ·θɛn'tɪs·ə·ti) *n.* autenticidad.

authenticate (ɔ'θɛn·tɪ·keit) *v.t.* autenticar; validar; autorizar. —**authentication,** *n.* autenticación.

author ('ɔ·θər) *n.* autor. —**authoress** (-əs) *n.* autora.

authoritative (ə'θar·ə·tei·tɪv) *adj.* **1,** (official) autoritario. **2,** (based on authority) autorizado.

authority (ə'θar·ə·ti) *n.* autoridad; poder; mando. —**authoritarian** (-'tɛr·i·ən) *n.* & *adj.* autoritario.

authorize ('ɔ·θə·raiz) *v.t.* autorizar; permitir; sancionar. —**authorization** (-rɪ'zei·ʃən) *n.* autorización; licencia; permiso.

autism ('ɔ·tɪz·əm) *n.* autismo. —**autistic,** *adj.* autista.

auto ('ɔ·to) *n., colloq.* auto; automóvil; coche; *Amer.* carro.

autobiography (ˌɔ·to·bai'ag·rə·fi) *n.* autobiografía. —**autobiographical** (-ə'græf·ɪ·kəl) *adj.* autobiográfico.

autocracy (ɔ'tak·rə·si) *n.* autocracia. —**autocrat** ('ɔ·tə·kræt) *n.* autócrata. —**autocratic** (-'kræt·ɪk) *adj.* autocrático.

autograph ('ɔ·tə·græf) *n.* autógrafo.

automate ('ɔ·tə·ˌmeit) *v.t.* automatizar.

automatic (ˌɔ·tə'mæt·ɪk) *adj.* **1,** *mech.* automático. **2,** *fig.* habitual; reflejo; automático. —*n.* (pistola) automática.

automation (ˌɔ·tə'mei·ʃən) *n.* automatización.

automaton (ɔ'tam·ə·tan) *n.* autómata.

automobile ('ɔ·tə·mə·bil) *n.* & *adj.* (-'moʊ·bəl) automóvil.

automotive (ˌɔ·tə'mo·tɪv) *adj.* automotor.

autonomic (ˌɔ·tə'nam·ɪk) *adj.* autonómico.

autonomy (ɔ'tan·ə·mi) *n.* autonomía. —**autonomous** (-məs) *adj.* autónomo.

autopsy ('ɔˌtap·si) *n.* autopsia.

autosuggestion ('ɔ·to·səgˌdzɛs·tʃən) *n.* autosugestión.

autumn ('ɔ·təm) *n.* otoño. —**autumnal** (ɔ'tʌm·nəl) *adj.* otoñal; autumnal.

auxiliary (ɔg'zɪl·jə·ri) *adj.* **1,** (assisting) auxiliar; ayudante. **2,** (subordinate) asistente; subordinado. **3,** (additional) adicional; suplementario. —*n.* ayudante; asistente; auxiliar.

avail (ə'veil) *v.t.* aprovechar; servir; ayudar. —*v.i.* ser ventajoso; ser de provecho. —*n.* provecho. —**avail oneself of,** aprovecharse de; valerse de. —**to no avail,** inútilmente.

available (ə'veil·ə·bəl) *adj.* disponible. —**availability,** *n.* disponibilidad.

avalanche ('æv·əˌlæntʃ) *n.* avalancha; alud.

avant-garde (æ·van'gard) *n.* vanguardia.

avarice ('æv·ə·rɪs) *n.* avaricia; codicia. —**avaricious** ('rɪʃ·əs) *adj.* avaricioso; codicioso.

Ave Maria ('a·və·ma'ri·ə; 'a·ve-) avemaría.

avenge (ə'vɛndʒ) *v.t.* vengar; vindicar.

avenue ('æ·və·nju) *n.* **1,** (wide street) avenida. **2,** *fig.* (approach) entrada; acceso; vía.

aver (ə'vʌr) *v.t.* [**averred, averring**] **1,** (assert) afirmar; aseverar. **2,** *law* (prove) confirmar; justificar.

average ('æv·ə·rɪdʒ) *n.* promedio. —*adj.* promedio; ordinario; normal. —*v.i.* calcular el promedio; ser o tener el promedio de. —*v.t.* hacer un promedio de; promediar; prorratear.

averse (ə'vʌrs) *adj.* contrario; opuesto.

aversion (ə'vʌr·ʒən) *n.* aversión; repulsión; antipatía.

avert (ə'vʌrt) *v.t.* **1,** (ward off) prevenir; evitar. **2,** (turn away) alejar; desviar.

aviary ('ei·vi·ɛr·i) *n.* pajarera; jaula.

aviation (ei·vi'ei·ʃən) *n.* aviación.

aviator ('ei·vi·e·tər) *n.* aviador. —**aviatrix** (-'e·trɪks) *n.* [*pl.* **-trices** (-trɪ·siz)] aviadora; aviatriz.

avid ('æv·ɪd) *adj.* ávido; ansioso; codicioso.

avidity (ə'vɪd·ə·ti) *n.* avidez; ansiedad; codicia.

avocado (æv·ə'ka·do) *n.* [*pl.*-dos] aguacate.

avocation (æv·ə'kei·ʃən) *n.* afición; entretenimiento; pasatiempo.

avoid (ə'vɔid) *v.t.* evitar; esquivar; eludir. —**avoidance** (-əns) *n.* evasión; escape.

avoirdupois (,æv·ər·də'pɔiz) *n.* 1, (measure) sistema de peso basado en la libra de 16 onzas. 2, *colloq.* (obesity) gordura.

avouch (ə'vautʃ) *v.t.* 1, (vouch for) justificar; garantizar. 2, (assert) afirmar; sostener.

avow (ə'vau) *v.t.* declarar abiertamente; admitir; confesar; reconocer. —**avowal** (-əl) *n.* reconocimiento; confesión; admisión.

await (ə'weit) *v.t.* aguardar; esperar.

awake (ə'weik) *v.t.* [*pret. & p.p.* **awoke** o **awaked**] —*v.t.* 1, (rouse) despertar. 2, (call into action) despabilar; animar. —*v.i.* despertarse. —*adj.* despierto; despabilado; alerta.

awaken (ə'wei·kən) *v.t. & i.* = **awake.** —**awakening,** *n.* el despertar; el abrir los ojos.

award (ə'wɔrd) *v.t.* premiar; conceder; *law* adjudicar. —*n.* 1, (prize) premio; galardón. 2, *law* adjudicación.

aware (ə'weːr) *adj.* enterado; consciente; informado.

awash (ə'waʃ) *adj.* anegado en agua; inundado. —*adv.* a flor de agua.

away (ə'wei) *adv.* 1, (off) lejos. 2, (aside) aparte. 3, (at once) en seguida. 4, (out of one's presence, etc.) afuera; fuera. —*adj.* 1, (absent) ausente. 2, (distant) lejano; distante.

awe (ɔ) *n.* pavor; temor reverencial. —*v.t.* impresionar.

aweigh (ə'wei) *adj., naut.* levado.

awesome ('ɔː·səm) *adj.* impresionante; pavoroso.

awestruck ('ɔː·strʌk) *adj.* despavorido; espantado; impresionado.

awful ('ɔː·fəl) *adj.* 1, (inspiring awe) tremendo; abrumador. 2, (terrifying) horripilante; terrible. 3, *colloq.* (very bad) detestable; muy malo; desagradable. 4, *colloq.* (great) grande; excesivo.

awfully ('ɔf·li) *adv.* 1, (horribly) horriblemente. 2, *colloq.* (very) muy.

awhile (ə'hwail) *adv.* (por) un rato; (por) un momento.

awkward ('ɔk·wərd) *adj.* 1, (unskilled) torpe; poco diestro. 2, (clumsy) desmañado; tosco. 3, (illadapted) indócil. 4, (difficult to handle) delicado; peligroso. —**awkwardness,** *n.* tosquedad; torpeza.

awl (ɔl) *n.* lezna; punzón.

awn (ɔn) *n.* arista.

awning ('ɔː·nɪŋ) *n.* toldo.

awoke (ə'woːk) *v., pret. de* **awake.**

awry (ə'rai) *adv.* oblicuamente; al través. —*adj.* desviado; perverso.

ax *también,* **axe** (æks) *n.* hacha. —*v.t.* 1, (cut with an ax) hachear. 2, *slang* (dismiss) despedir. —**have an ax to grind,** tener fines interesados.

axial ('æk·si·əl) *adj.* axial.

axiom ('æk·si·əm) *n.* axioma. —**axiomatic** (-ə'mæt·ɪk) *adj.* axiomático.

axis ('æk·sɪs) *n.* [*pl.* **-es** (-siz)] 1, (pivot) eje. 2, *anat.* axis.

axle ('æk·səl) *n.* 1, (of a wheel) eje. 2, (of a machine) árbol.

ay 1, [*también,* **aye**] (ei) *adv., poet.* siempre. 2, (ai) *adv. & n.* = **aye.**

aye 1, [*también,* **ay**] (ai) *adv. & n.* sí. 2, (ei) *adv., poet.* = **ay.**

azalea (ə'zeil·jə) *n.* azalea.

azimuth ('æz·e·məθ) *n.* azimut; acimut.

azoic (ə'zo·ɪk) *adj.* azoico.

Aztec ('æz·tek) *n. & adj.* azteca.

azure ('æʒ·ər) *n. & adj.* azur.

B

B, b (biː) 1, segunda letra del alfabeto inglés. 2, *mus.* si. 3, denota segunda clase; segundo grado; suficiencia.

baa (baː) *v.i.* [**baaed** (baːd), **baaing**] balar. —*n.* balido.

babble ('bæb·əl) *v.i.* 1, (chatter) charlar; parlotear. 2, (utter words imperfectly) balbucear; balbucir. **3.** (murmur) murmurar. —*v.t.* **1,** (utter incoherently) mascullar; barbotar. **2,** (murmur) murmurar. —*n.* **1,** (prattle) balbuceo; barboteo. **2,** (murmur) murmullo.

babe (beib) *n.* **1,** = baby. **2,** *slang* (girl) muchachita; chiquita; nena.

babel ('bei·bəl) *n.* babel; confusión; *cap.* Babel.

baboon (bæ'buːn) *n.* babuino.

baby ('bei·bi) *n.* **1,** (infant) bebé; niño; criatura; nene (*fem.* nena). **2,** (youngest child) menor. **3,** (young of an animal) pequeño. **4,** *slang* (pet) monada. —*adj.* **1,** (infantile) infantil; de o para niños. **2,** (small) pequeño. —*v.t.* mimar; tratar como niño. —**babyhood,** *n.* niñez; infancia. —**babyish,** *adj.* pueril; aniñado. —**baby carriage,** cochecillo de niño. —**baby talk,** habla infantil.

Babylon ('bæb·ə‚lan) *n.* Babilonia. —**Babylonian** (-'lo·ni·ən) *adj.* babilonio; babilónico.

babysit ('bei·bi·sɪt) *v.i.* cuidar niños. —**babysitter,** *n.* cuidaniños.

baccalaureate (bæk·ə'lɔr·i·ət) *n.* bachillerato. —*adj.* de bachiller; de bachillerato.

baccarat ('bæk·ə‚ra) *n.* bacará.

bacchanal ('bæk·ə·nəl; -nal) *n.* **1,** (orgy) bacanal. **2,** (reveler) calavera; borracho. —**bacchanalia** (-'nei·li·ə) *n.pl.* bacanales. —**bacchanalian,** *adj.* bacanal; ebrio.

bachelor ('bætʃ·ə·lər) *n.* **1,** (unmarried man) soltero. **2,** (college graduate) bachiller. —**bachelorhood,** *n.* soltería.

bacillus (bə'sɪl·əs) *n.* [*pl.* **-li** (-lai)] bacilo.

back (bæk) *n.* **1,** (of an animal) lomo; espinazo. **2,** (of a person) espalda. **3,** (rear or hind part) trasero; respaldo. **4,** (of a book) lomo. **5,** (support; stiffening) respaldo. **6,** (reverse side) reverso; revés. —*adj.* **1,** (behind) trasero; posterior. **2,** (distant) distante; lejano. **3,** (of past time) atrasado; retrasado. —*v.t.* [*también,* **back up**] **1,** (support) respaldar; apoyar; sostener. **2,** (cause to move backward) hacer retroceder; mover hacia atrás; dar marcha atrás a. —*v.i.* [*también,* **back up**] retroceder; retirarse; moverse hacia atrás; dar marcha atrás. —*adv.* **1,** (toward the rear) atrás; detrás. **2,** (again) otra vez; de nuevo. **3,** (returned or restored) de vuelta. **4,** (ago) hace: *three months back,* hace tres meses. —**back and fill,** vacilar; dudar. —**back and forth,** de una parte a otra; de aquí para allá. —**back down,** ceder; rendirse; acobardarse. —**back entrance,** puerta trasera. —**back order,** pedido pendiente. —**back out,** retractarse; volverse atrás. —**back water,** *naut.* recular. **2,** (withdraw) retirarse. —**be back,** estar de vuelta. —**come back,** volver. —**go back on,** *colloq.* desertar; abandonar; faltar a. —**slap** o **pat on the back,** espaldarazo.

backache ('bæk·eik) *n.* dolor de espalda.

backbite ('bæk·bait) *v.t.* & *i.* calumniar; desacreditar.

backbone ('bæk·bo‚rn) *n.* **1,** (spine) espina dorsal; columna vertebral; espinazo. **2,** (mainstay) nervio; fundamento. **3,** (firmness) firmeza; resolución.

backbreaking ('bæk·breik·ɪŋ) *adj.* abrumador; extenuante.

backdate ('bæk‚deit) *v.t.* atrasar la fecha de.

backfire ('bæk·fair) *n.* **1,** *mech.* explosión prematura de un motor o fusil. **2,** (fire to check another fire) cinturón de cenizas; claro abierto. **3,** (undesired outcome) resultado contrario u opuesto. —*v.i.* **1,** (explode) explotar prematuramente. **2,** (go awry) tener resultado contrario.

backgammon ('bæk‚gæm·ən) *n.* chaquete.

background ('bæk‚graund) *n.* **1,** (setting) fondo. **2,** (past history) antecedentes.

backhand ('bæk‚hænd) *n.* **1,** (writing) escritura inclinada a la izquierda. **2,** *tennis; jai alai* revés.

backing ('bæk·ɪŋ) *n.* **1,** (supporting material) respaldo. **2,** (endorsement; aid) sostén; apoyo; ayuda.

backlash ('bæk‚laʃ) *n.* contragolpe.

backlog ('bæk‚lɔg) *n.* acumulación. —*v.t.* & *i.* acumular(se).

backorder ('bæk‚or·dər) *v.t.* reservar (un pedido).

backtrack ('bæk‚træk) *v.i.* retroceder; volverse atrás.

backup ('bæk‚ʌp) *n.* reserva; repuesto. —*adj.* de reserva; de repuesto.

backward ('bæk·wərd) *también,* **backwards** (-wərdz) *adv.* 1, (toward the rear) para o hacia atrás. 2, (with back foremost) de espaldas. 3, (in reverse order) invertidamente. 4, (inside out) al revés. 5, (in past time) con atraso; retrasadamente. —*adj.* 1, (retarded) atrasado; retrasado. 2, (shy) retraído; esquivo.

backwater ('bæk,wat·ər; -,wɔ·tər) *n.* lugar remoto; lugar culturalmente atrasado.

backwoods ('bæk,wʊdz) *n.* bosque remoto.

bacon ('bei·kən) *n.* tocino; *W.I.; C.A.* tocineta.

bacteria (bæk'tɪr·i·ə) *n.* [*sing.* **-um** (əm)] bacterias [*sing.* **bacteria**]. —**bacterial,** *adj.* bacterial; bactérico. —**bacterial warfare,** guerra bacteriológica.

bactericide (bæk'tɪr·ə·said) *n.* bactericida.

bacteriology (bæk,tɪr·i'al·ə·dʒi) *n.* bacteriología. —**bacteriological** (-ə'ladʒ·ɪ·kəl) *adj.* bacteriológico. —**bacteriologist,** *n.* bacteriólogo.

bad (bæɪd) *adj.* [**worse, worst**] 1, (wicked) malo; perverso. 2, (defective) defectuoso; dañado. 3, (noxious) nocivo; dañino. 4, (unfavorable) desfavorable; desafortunado. 5, (sick) malo; enfermo; indispuesto. —*n.* el mal; lo malo. —**in a bad way,** de mala manera. —**in bad,** *colloq.* en desgracia. —**be to the bad** (financially or morally) resultar o salir perdiendo.

bade (bæɪd) *v., pret.* de **bid.**

badge (bæɪdʒ) *n.* divisa; distintivo; emblema.

badger ('bæ·dʒər) *n., zoöl.* tejón. —*v.t.* fastidiar; molestar; importunar.

badly ('bæð·li) *adv.* 1, (poorly) mal; malamente. 2, (seriously) gravemente. 3, *colloq.* (very much) muy; mucho; muchísimo.

badminton ('bæd·min·tən) *n.* juego del volante.

badness ('bæd·nəs) *n.* maldad.

baffle ('bæf·əl) *v.t.* 1, (impede) frustrar; impedir. 2, (bewilder) confundir; aturdir. —*n.* deflector. —**bafflement,** *n.* confusión; aturdimiento.

bag (bæɪg) *n.* 1, (portable receptacle) bolsa; saco. 2, (suitcase) maleta. 3, (purse) bolso; cartera. 4, (hunter's catch) morral. 5, *slang* (money collected) bolsa. 6, (udder) ubre; teta. —*v.t.* [**bagged, bagging**] capturar; cazar. —*v.i.* 1, (swell) inflamarse; hincharse. 2, (hang loosely) hacer bolsas; abolsarse. —**baggy,** *adj.* abolsado.

bagatelle (,bæg·ə'tel) *n.* bagatela.

baggage ('bæg·ɪdʒ) *n.* 1, (luggage) equipaje. 2, *mil.* bagaje. 3, (lewd woman) ramera; bagasa.

bagpipe ('bæg·paip) *n.* gaita.

bail (beil) *n., law* 1, (money or credit) fianza. 2, (person) fiador. —*v.t.* 1, (deliver in trust for) poner como fianza. 2, [*también,* **bail out**] libertar o poner en libertad bajo fianza. 3, (pay money for release of) poner fianza o salir fiador de o por. —**bailsman,** *n.* [*pl.* **-men**] fiador; fianza. —**bail out,** 1, *naut.* desaguar; achicar. 2, *aero.* tirarse o saltar con paracaídas.

bailiff ('bei·lɪf) *n.* alguacil.

bailiwick ('bei·lə·wɪk) *n.* bailía.

bait (beit) *n.* cebo; anzuelo. —*v.t.* 1, (provide with a lure) cebar; poner cebo a. 2, (tease) molestar; enojar.

baize (beiz) *n.* bayeta.

bake (beik) *v.t.* cocer al horno; hornear. —*v.i.* (be baked) hornearse; cocerse; endurecerse al horno.

bakelite ('bei·kə,lait) *n.* baquelita; bakelita.

baker ('bei·kər) *n.* panadero. —**bakery,** *n.* panadería. —**baker's dozen,** docena del fraile.

baking ('bei·kɪŋ) *n.* cocimiento; hornada. —**baking powder,** levadura en polvo. —**baking soda,** bicarbonato de soda.

balance ('bæl·əns) *n.* 1, (scale) balanza. 2, (equal distribution of weight) balance; equilibrio. 3, (mental stability) buen juicio. 4, *comm.* saldo; balance. 5, (remainder) resto. —*v.t.* 1, (equalize) equilibrar; igualar. 2, (weigh) pesar. 3, (estimate) ponderar; comparar. 4, *comm.* saldar. —*v.i.* equilibrarse; contrarrestarse; balancear. —**balance beam,** balancín. —**balance of payments,** balanza de pagos. —**balance of power,** equilibrio político. —**balance of trade,** balanza de comercio. —**balance sheet,** balance. —**balancing pole,** balancín.

balcony ('bæl·kə·ni) *n.* 1, *archit.* balcón. 2, *theat.* galería; paraíso.

bald (bɔːld) *adj.* 1, (hairless) calvo. 2, (without covering) descubierto. 3, (bare) soso; desnudo. 4, (unqualified) puro; mero; escueto. **—balding,** adj. volviéndose calvo. **—bald-faced,** adj. descarado.

balderdash ('bɔl·dər,dæʃ) n. jerigonza; jerga.

baldness ('bɔld·nəs) n. **1,** (lack of hair) calvicie. **2,** (bareness) desnudez; simplicidad.

baldric ('bɔl·drɪk) n. tahalí.

bale (beil) n. bala. —v.t. embalar; empacar.

baleen (bə'liːn) n. ballena.

baleful ('beil·fəl) adj. **1,** (menacing) amenazante; peligroso. **2,** (malign) nocivo; maligno. **—balefulness,** n. malignidad.

balk (bɔːk) n. **1,** (obstacle) obstáculo; impedimento. **2,** (blunder) derrota; fracaso. **3,** (piece of timber) viga. **4,** sports falta. —v.t. impedir; frustrar. —v.i. resistirse; rebelarse. **—balky,** adj. porfiado; obstinado.

Balkan ('bɔl·kən) adj. balcánico. **—the Balkans,** los Balcanes.

ball (bɔl) n. **1,** (round body) bola; esfera; globo. **2,** sports pelota; balón. **3,** (bullet) bala. **4,** (dance) baile. **5,** (of yarn) ovillo. **6,** (of the finger) yema del dedo. **—ball up,** slang desordenar; enredar.

ballad ('bæl·əd) n. balada.

ballast ('bæl·əst) n. **1,** (stabilizing material) lastre. **2,** R.R. balasto.

ball bearing cojinete.

ballerina (bæl·ə'riː·nə) n. bailarina de ballet.

ballet (bæl'eiː) n. baile; ballet.

ballistics (bə'lɪs·tɪks) n. sing. o pl. balística. **—ballistic,** adj. balístico.

balloon (bə'luːn) n. **1,** (inflated sphere) globo. **2,** aero. globo aerostático; aeróstato. —v.i. hincharse; inflarse. **—ballooning,** n. aerostación. **—balloonist,** n. aeronauta; ascensionista.

ballot ('bæl·ət) n. **1,** (voting ticket) balota; papeleta o cédula de votación; voto. **2,** (voting; total vote) voto; votación. —v.i. votar; balotar.

ballpoint pen ('bɔl·pɔint) bolígrafo.

ballroom ('bɔl·rum) n. salón de baile.

ballyhoo ('bæl·i,hu) n., slang alharaca; bombo —v.t. dar bombo a.

balm (bɑːm) n. bálsamo; ungüento.

balmy ('bɑ·mi) adj. **1,** (mild)

suave. **2,** (fragrant) fragante; balsámico. **3,** slang (mildly demented) alocado. **—balminess,** n. untuosidad; suavidad; fragancia.

baloney (bə'lo·ni) n. **1,** slang (nonsense) tontería; disparate. **2,** = **bologna.**

balsa ('bɔl·sə) n. balsa.

balsam ('bɔl·səm) n. bálsamo.

Baltic ('bɔl·tɪk) adj. báltico. —n. Báltico.

baluster ('bæl·əs·tər) n. balaustre. **—balustrade** (-treid) n. balaustrada; barandilla.

bamboo (bæm'buː) n. bambú.

ban (bæːn) v.t. [**banned, banning**] proscribir; prohibir; suprimir. —n. **1,** (prohibition) prohibición; supresión; proscripción. **2,** (medieval proclamation) bando; proclama; pregón. **3,** eccles. excommunión.

banal ('bei·nəl) adj. banal; trivial. **—banality** (bə'næl·ə·ti) n. banalidad; trivialidad.

banana (bə'næn·ə) n. banana; Sp. & Mex. plátano; W.I., C.A., northern S.A. guineo.

band (bæːnd) n. **1,** (strip) banda; faja; franja. **2,** (metal strip) fleje; abrazadera. **3,** (zone marked off) precinto; tira. **4,** (group of persons) cuadrilla; grupo; pandilla. **5,** (group of musicians) banda. **6,** radio banda. —v.t. **1,** (mark or fasten with a band) zunchar. **2,** (group together) unir; reunir; juntar. —v.i. [también, **band together**] unirse; reunirse; juntarse.

bandage ('bæn·dɪdʒ) n. vendaje; venda. —v.t. vendar.

bandanna (bæn'dæn·ə) n. pañuelo grande.

banderilla (,bæn·də'ri·jə) n. banderilla. **—banderillero** (-ri'je·ro) n. banderillero.

bandit ('bæn·dɪt) n. bandido; bandolero; ladrón. **—banditry,** n. bandolerismo; bandidaje.

bandoleer (,bæn·də'lir) n. bandolera.

bandstand ('bænd·stænd) n. quiosco o concha de música.

bandwagon ('bænd,wæg·ən) n. carro de banda. **—get on the bandwagon,** colloq. adherirse al partido que gana.

bandy ('bæn·di) v.t. cambiar; tirar o pasar de una parte a otra. —adj. zambo; combado. **—bandy a ball,** pelotear. **—bandy words,** trocar palabras.

bandylegged ('bæn·di,lɛgd) *adj.* patizambo; patituerto.

bane (bein) *n.* **1,** (poison) veneno. **2,** (destroyer) ruina; azote; calamidad. —**baneful,** *adj.* dañino; pernicioso.

bang (bæ:ŋ) *n.* **1,** (noise) ruido; golpe seco; porrazo. **2,** *slang* (energy) energía; vigor. **3,** *slang* (thrill) emoción; fascinación. **4,** (hair over the forehead) flequillo. —*v.t.* golpear ruidosamente; arrojar. —*v.i.* dar golpes; hacer estrépito. —*adv.* de repente; de golpe.

bangle ('bæŋ·gəl) *n.m.* ajorca.

banish ('bæn·ɪʃ) *v.t.* **1,** (exile) desterrar; proscribir. **2,** (dismiss) expulsar; expeler; desechar. —**banishment,** *n.* proscripción.

banister ('bæn·ɪs·tər) *n.* pasamano; barandal.

banjo ('bæn·dʒo) *n.* [*pl.* -**jos**] banjo. —**banjoist,** *n.* banjoísta.

bank (bæŋk) *n.* **1,** (mound; ridge) banco; loma; montón de tierra o nubes. **2,** (river edge) orilla; ribera; margen. **3,** (shoal) bajío. **4,** (financial establishment) banco. **5,** (row; tier) hilera; fila. **6,** *mus.* teclado. **7,** *aero.* inclinación lateral. **8,** *gambling* banca. **9,** (sloping curve, as of a road) peralte. —*v.t.* **1,** (pile up) amontonar; apilar. **2,** (dam; hold back, as water) represar. **3,** (cover, as a fire) cubrir; soterrar. **4,** (deposit in a bank) depositar o guardar en un banco. **5,** *aero.* ladear. —*v.i.* **1,** (engage in banking) ocuparse en banca; ser banquero. **2,** (maintain a bank account) tener su cuenta (en o con). —**bank on,** *colloq.* confiar en; contar con.

banker ('bæŋk·ər) *n.* banquero. —**banking,** *n.* banca.

banknote ('bæŋk·not) *n.* billete; billete de banco.

bankroll ('bæŋk,rol) *n.* fondos disponibles. —*v.t.* financiar; subvencionar.

bankrupt ('bæŋk·rʌpt) *n. & adj.* quebrado; fallido; insolvente. —*v.t.* quebrar. —**bankruptcy,** *n.* bancarrota.

banner ('bæn·ər) *n.* **1,** (flag) bandera; enseña. **2,** (symbol; standard) estandarte; enseña. **3,** (newspaper headline) titular. —*adj.* sobresaliente; primero.

banns (bæ:nz) *n.pl.* amonestaciones.

banquet ('bæŋ·kwɪt) *n.* banquete; festín. —*v.t. & i.* banquetear.

bantam ('bæn·təm) *n.* **1,** gallo Bantam; gallo de India. **2,** cualquier animal pequeño.

bantamweight ('bæn·təm,weit) *n.* peso gallo.

banter ('bæn·tər) *n.* chanza; zumba. —*v.t.* chancearse con; chotearse de. —*v.i.* hacer zumba; chancear; chotear.

banyan ('bæn·jən) *n.* higuera india; baniano.

baptism ('bæp·tɪz·əm) *n.* bautismo. —**baptismal** (-'tɪz·məl) *adj.* bautismal.

Baptist ('bæp·tɪst) *adj. & n.* bautista.

baptistery *también,* **baptistry** ('bæp·tɪst·ri) *n.* bautisterio; baptisterio.

baptize ('bæp·taiz) *v.t.* **1,** (consecrate) bautizar; cristianar. **2,** (name) poner nombre.

bar (ba:r) *n.* **1,** (rod) barra; palanca. **2,** (crossbar; bolt) tranca. **3,** (obstruction) impedimento; obstáculo. **4,** [*también,* **barroom**] (place serving liquor) bar; cantina. **5,** (counter) mostrador. **6,** (lawyers collectively) abogacía. **7,** (tribunal) tribunal; foro. **8,** *mus.* barra. —*v.t.* [**barred,** **barring**] **1,** (block) impedir; prohibir. **2,** (close; bolt) cerrar; trancar. **3,** (shut out) excluir. —*prep.* con excepción de; excepto. —**bar none,** sin excepción.

barb (ba:rb) *n.* **1,** (points bent backward, as on a fishhook) lengüeta; púa; punta. **2,** (beardlike growth) barba.

barbarian (bar'bɛr·i·ən) *adj. & n.* bárbaro. —**barbarism** ('bar·bə·rɪz·əm) *n.* barbarismo.

barbaric (bar'bær·ɪk) *adj.* barbárico; bárbaro.

barbarity (bar'bær·ə·ti) *n.* barbaridad.

barbarous ('bar·bə·rəs) *adj.* bárbaro. —**barbarousness,** *n.* barbaridad.

barbecue ('bar·bə·kju) *n.* barbacoa. —*v.t.* hacer barbacoa.

barbed (ba:rbd) *adj.* **1,** (having a sharp point) erizado; barbado. **2,** *fig.* (stinging) punzante; mordaz. —**barbed wire,** alambrada.

barber ('bar·bər) *n.* barbero. —*v.t.* afeitar; hacer la barba a; cortar el pelo a. —**barber shop** [*también,*

barbershop, *n.*] barbería; peluquería.

barbiturate (bar'bɪt·ju‚reit) *n.* barbiturato. —**barbituric** (‚bar·bɪ'tjur·ɪk) *adj.* barbitúrico.

barcarole ('bar·kə·rol) *n.* barcarola.

bard (bɑːrd) *n.* bardo; juglar; poeta.

bare (beir) *adj.* **1,** (naked) desnudo; en cueros. **2,** (empty; unequipped) pelado; desnudo. **3,** (unadorned) simple; sencillo. **4,** (open to view) descubierto; público. **5,** (just sufficient) escaso; solo. —*v.t.* **1,** (uncover) desnudar; desposeer. **2,** (open to view) descubrir. —**bareness,** *n.* desnudez.

bareback ('beir‚bæk) *adj. & adv.* en pelo; sin silla.

barefaced ('beir·feist) *adj.* descarado; insolente.

barefoot ('beir·fʊt) *adj.* descalzo.

bareheaded ('beir‚hɛd·ɪd) *adj.* descubierto; en cabellos.

barely ('beir·li) *adv.* **1,** (scarcely) apenas. **2,** (openly) abiertamente.

bargain ('bar·gən) *n.* **1,** (agreement) convenio; contrato. **2,** (advantageous purchase) ganga. —*v.i.* **1,** (discuss terms) negociar; tratar. **2,** (haggle) regatear. —*adj.* barato. —**bargain sale,** baratillo; barato; *Amer.* barata.

barge (bɑːrdʒ) *n.* gabarra; barcaza; lanchón. —*v.i.* moverse pesadamente. —**barge in,** entremeterse; irrumpir. —**barge into,** chocar con.

baritone ('bær·ə·ton) *n. & adj.* barítono.

barium ('bær·i·əm) *n.* bario.

bark (bɑːrk) *n.* **1,** (cry of a dog, animal or person) ladrido. **2,** (tree covering) corteza. **3,** (small ship) barca; barqueta. —*v.i.* ladrar. —*v.t.* descortezar; desollar.

barker ('bar·kər) *n.* vociferador.

barley ('bar·li) *n.* cebada.

barmaid ('bar·med) *n.* camarera.

barman ('bar·mən) *n.* [*pl.* **-men**] cantinero; tabernero.

barn (bɑːrn) *n.* **1,** (storage place for fodder) almiar; pajar. **2,** (granary) granero; troj; troje. **3,** (stable) cuadra; establo. **4,** (depot; garage) cochera.

barnacle ('bar·nə·kəl) *n.* percebe.

barnyard ('barn‚jard) *n.* corral.

barometer (bə'ram·ə·tər) *n.* barómetro. —**barometric** (‚bæ·rə·'mɛt·rɪk) *adj.* barométrico.

baron ('bær·ən) *n.* barón. —**baronage,** *n.* baronía. —**baroness,** *n.* baronesa. —**baronet,** *n.* baronet. —**baronial** (bə'ro·ni·əl) *adj.* del barón. —**barony,** *n.* baronía.

baroque (bə'roːk) *n. & adj.* barroco.

barrack ('bær·ək) *n., usu.pl.* cuartel; barraca.

barracuda (‚bær·ə·'ku·də) *n.* barracuda.

barrage (bə'raːʒ) *n.* **1,** *mil.* cortina de fuego. **2,** *engin.* presa o dique (de contención).

barratry ('bær·ə·tri) *n.* baratería.

barrel ('bær·əl) *n.* barril; barrica; tonel. —**barrel organ,** organillo.

barren ('bær·ən) *adj.* estéril; árido; improductivo. —**barrenness,** *n.* esterilidad; aridez; improductividad.

barricade ('bær·ə·keid) *n.* **1,** (barrier) empalizada; cerca. **2,** *mil.* barricada; trinchera. —*v.t.* obstruir; impedir.

barrier ('hær·i·ər) *n* barrera; impedimento.

barring ('bar·ɪŋ) *prep.* con excepción de; excepto; salvo.

barrister ('bær·ɪs·tər) *n., Brit.* abogado.

barroom ('bar‚rum) *n.* bar; cantina.

barrow ('bær·o) *n.* **1,** (hand barrow) angarillas. **2,** (wheelbarrow) carretón; carretilla. **3,** (burial mound) túmulo.

bartender ('baːr‚tɛn·dər) *n.* cantinero.

barter ('bar·tər) *v.t.* trocar; cambiar. —*v.i.* traficar. —*n.* trueque; cambio.

basal ('bei·səl) *adj.* basal. —**basal metabolism,** metabolismo basal.

basalt (bə'sɔlt) *n.* basalto.

bascule ('bæs·kjul) *n.* balanza oscilante; balancín. —**bascule bridge,** puente levadizo de contrapeso.

base (beis) *n.* **1,** (bottom) base; fondo. **2,** (fundamental) fundamento. **3,** *chem.; math.* base. **4,** (depot) base. **5,** *baseball* base. —*v.t.* **1,** (found) establecer; poner base a. **2,** (establish as fact) basar; apoyar; fundamentar. —*adj.* **1,** (mean) bajo; ruin; vil. **2,** (low in rank) inferior; secundario. **3,** (of little value, esp. of metals) bajo de ley. —**baseness,** *n.* bajeza; vileza; ruindad. —**baseless,** *adj.* infundado. —**basely,** *adv.*

bajamente. —**base metal,** metal común.

baseball ('beis,bɔl) n. 1, (game) béisbol. 2, (ball) pelota.

baseboard ('beis,bord) n. friso; zócalo.

baseborn ('beis,born) adj. de humilde linaje; ilegítimo.

basement ('beis·mənt) n. sótano.

bases ('bei·siz) n., pl. de basis.

bash (bæʃ) v.t., colloq. aporrear. —n., colloq. jarana; juerga.

bashful ('bæʃ·fəl) adj. vergonzoso; tímido. —**bashfulness,** n. timidez; cortedad.

basic ('bei·sik) adj. 1, (standard) básico; fundamental; corriente. 2, chem. básico.

basil ('bei·zəl) n. albahaca.

basilica (bə'sil·ə·kə) n. basílica.

basilisk ('bæs·ə·lisk) n. basilisco.

basin ('bei·sən) n. 1, (bowl for liquids) palangana; jofaina; W.I. ponchera. 2, (lowland) valle; cuenca; Amer. hoya. 3, (pond; pool) estanque; represa. 4, (hollow of a fountain) pilón.

basis ('bei·sis) n. [pl. -ses (-siz)] 1, (fundamental principle) base; fundamento; principio. 2, (chief ingredient) base; elemento principal.

bask (bæsk) v.i. calentarse. —**bask in the sun,** tomar el sol; asolearse.

basket ('bæs·kit) n. 1, (small container) cesto; cesta; canasta. 2, (large container) espuerta. 3, basketball cesta.

basketball ('bæs·kit,bɔl) n. baloncesto; básquetbol.

basketry ('bæs·kit·ri) n. cestería.

basketwork ('bæs·kit,wʌrk) n. cestería.

Basque (bæsk) adj. & n. vasco; vascuence. —n., l.c. (blouse) blusa ajustada; jubón.

bas-relief ('ba·rə,lif) n. bajorrelieve.

bass (beis) adj. & n., mus. bajo. —**bass clef,** clave de fa. —**bass drum,** bombo. —**bass viol** [también, **bass; double bass**] violón; contrabajo.

bass (bæs) n. 1, ichthy. róbalo. 2, = basswood.

basso ('bæs·o) n., mus. bajo.

bassoon (bæ'su:n) n. fagot; bajón. —**bassoonist,** n. fagotista; bajonista.

basswood ('bæs·wʊd) n. tilo.

bastard ('bæs·tərd) n. bastardo. —adj. 1, (of illegitimate birth)

bastardo; ilegítimo. 2, (impure) espurio; impuro; degenerado. —**bastardy,** n. bastardía.

bastardize ('bæs·tərd·aiz) v.t. 1, (make bastard of) probar la bastardía de; bastardear. 2, (debase) adulterar; degenerar; depravar.

baste (beist) v.t. 1, (sew) embastar; hilvanar. 2, (moisten meat) untar o pringar la carne; lardear. 3, (beat) golpear con un palo. —**basting,** n. baste; basta.

bastion ('bæs·tʃən) n. bastión; baluarte.

bat (bæt) n. 1, (heavy club) estaca; garrote. 2, sports bate. 3, zoöl. murciélago. —v.t. [**batted, batting**] 1, sports batear. 2, colloq. (blink) pestañear. —**go on a bat,** slang ir de parranda. —**go to bat for,** colloq. salir a la defensa de.

batch (bætʃ) n. 1, (quantity made at one time) cochura; hornada. 2, (mound of dough) masa. 3, slang (lot) montón; cantidad.

bath (bæθ) n. 1, (a washing) baño. 2, (bathroom) cuarto de baño. 3, fig. baño; inundación.

bathe (beið) v.t. bañar. —v.i. bañarse. —**bathing suit,** traje de baño.

bathhouse ('bæθ,haus) n. caseta de baños.

bathos ('bei·θɔs) n. exceso de sensiblería.

bathrobe ('bæθ·rob) n. albornoz; bata de baño.

bathroom ('bæθ·ru:m) n. cuarto de baño; baño.

bathtub ('bæθ·tʌb) n. bañera; Amer. bañadera.

bathyscaphe ('bæθ·ɪ,skeif) también, **bathyscaph** (-,skæf) n. batiscafo.

bathysphere ('bæθ·ɪ·sfir) n. batisfera.

batiste (bə'tist) n. batista.

baton (bæ'tan) n. 1, (symbol of authority) bastón de mando. 2, mus. batuta. 3, (weapon) porra.

battalion (bə'tæl·jən) n., mil. batallón.

batten ('bæt·ən) v.i. 1, (overeat) engordar; cebar. 2, (grow fat) engordar; engruesar; ponerse obeso. 3, (thrive) medrar; prosperar. —v.t. 1, (overfeed) cebar. 2, carp. construir con listones o latas. 3, naut. (fasten with battens) tapar (las escotillas) con listones. —n. listón.

batter ('bæt·ər) v.i. & t. batir;

golpear. —n. 1, (dough) masa; pasta; batido. 2, *baseball* bateador.

battery ('bæt·ə·ri) n. 1, (for cars) batería; acumulador. 2, (for flashlight) pila. 3, *mil.* batería. 4, *law* agresión.

batting ('bæt·ɪŋ) n. 1, (stuffing) relleno. 2, *baseball* bateo.

battle ('bæt·əl) n. batalla; lucha; pelea. —v.i. batallar; luchar; pelear. —v.t. luchar con.

battleax ('bæt·əl‚æks) n. 1, hacha de combate. 2, *colloq.* mujer regañona.

battledore ('bæt·əl‚dor) n. raqueta. —**battledore and shuttlecock,** volante; raqueta y volante.

battlefield ('bæt·əl‚fild) *también,* **battleground** (-‚graund) n. campo de batalla.

battlement ('bæt·əl·mənt) n. muralla almenada.

battleship ('bæt·əl‚ʃɪp) n. acorazado.

batty ('bæt·i) adj., *colloq.* loco; chiflado.

bauble ('bɔ·bəl) n. bagatela; chuchería; fruslería.

baud (bɔd) n., *comput.* baudio.

bauxite ('bɔks·aɪt) n. bauxita.

bawd (bɔd) n. alcahueta.

bawdy ('bɔ·di) adj. indecente; obsceno; sucio. —**bawdiness,** n. obscenidad; indecencia.

bawl (bɔl) n. 1, (howl) berrido; bramido. 2, *colloq.* (loud weeping) llanto. —v.i. gritar; vocear; chillar. —v.t. vocear. —**bawl out,** *colloq.* regañar; reprender.

bay (bei) n. 1, (inlet) bahía. 2, (protruding turret) mirador; ventana salediza; balcón. 3, (niche; alcove) receso. 4, *bot.* laurel. 5, (animal bark) ladrido; aullido. 6, (reddish-brown horse) caballo bayo. —v.i. ladrar; aullar. —**at bay,** acosado; acorralado. —**bay leaf,** hoja de laurel. —**bay rum,** ron con aceite esencial de laurel.

bayberry ('bei·bɛr·i) n. arrayán.

bayonet ('be·jə·nɛt) n. bayoneta. —v.t. cargar o herir a bayoneta.

bay window mirador; ventana salediza.

bazaar (bə'zɑr) n. bazar.

bazooka (bə'zu·kə) n., *mil.* cañón antitanques.

be (bi) v.i. & *copulativo* [p.pr. **being;** p.p. **been;** *pres. de ind.:* I **am,** thou **art** (*arcaico*), he, she, it **is,** we, you, they **are;** *pret.:* I, he, she, it **was,** we, you, they **were,** thou **wert** (*arcaico*), he, she, it **wast** (*arcaico*)] 1, (expressing permanent condition; ownership; source; material; time; impersonal state) ser. 2, (expressing temporary condition; location; result, etc.) estar.

beach (bitʃ) n. playa; ribera. —v.t. varar.

beachhead ('bitʃ‚hɛd) n. desembarco armado; cabeza de puente.

beacon ('bi·kən) n. faro; señal luminosa.

bead (bid) n. 1, (small ball) cuenta; abalorio. 2, pl. (rosary) rosario 3, (bubble) gota; burbuja. 4, (small globular body) glóbulo. —v.t. adornar con abalorios. —**beady,** adj. de o como abalorios. —**draw a bead on,** apuntar con arma de fuego.

beadle ('bi·dəl) n. bedel. —**beadleship,** n. bedelía.

beagle ('bi·gəl) n. sabueso.

beak (bik) n. 1, (of bird) pico. 2, (of animal) hocico. 3, *hist.* (prow of a warship) espolón.

beaker ('bi·kər) n. 1, (drinking vessel) vaso; copa. 2, *chem.* vaso picudo.

beam (bim) n. 1, (structural member) viga; vigueta. 2, (crossbar) astil; brazo de balanza. 3, *naut.* manga. 4, (light ray) rayo de luz. 5, (smile) sonrisa. —v.i. 1, (shine brightly) destellar; irradiar. 2, (smile warmly) rebosar (de alegría). —v.t. 1, (emit) emitir. 2, *aero.* (guide by radio) dirigir por radio. —**on the beam,** *colloq.,* en el buen camino.

bean (bin) n. habichuela; haba; judía; frijol. —v.t., *slang* pegar en la cabeza.

bear (bɛr) v.t. [**bore, borne**] 1, (hold up) sostener. 2, (support) soportar; llevar. 3, (endure) aceptar; tolerar. 4, (bring forward) producir; rendir. 5, (possess) tener; poseer. 6, (show) mostrar; enseñar. 7, (exercise) ejercitar; desempeñar. 8, (give birth to) dar a luz; alumbrar; parir. —v.i. 1, (remain firm) aguantar; soportar. 2, (press) apretar; oprimir. 3, (be productive) fructificar. 4, (go in a given direction) llevar rumbo o dirección. —n. 1, (animal) oso. 2, *fin.* bajista. —adj., *fin.* bajista. —**bear down,** apretar; ejercer presión; hacer esfuerzo. —**bear in**

mind, tener presente; recordar; tener en cuenta. **—bear off, 1,** (carry away) quitar; llevarse. **2,** *naut.* salvar; esquivar. **—bear on,** referirse a. **—bear out, 1,** (support) apoyar; sostener. **2,** (confirm) confirmar. **—bear up,** sostener; resistir. **—bear with,** tolerar; soportar; tener paciencia con.

bearable ('bɛr·ə·bəl) *adj.* soportable; tolerable.

beard (bɪrd) *n.* **1,** (hair on the face) barba. **2,** (tuft of hair) mechón. **3,** *bot.* arista.

bearer ('bɛr·ər) *n.* **1,** (carrier) portador; dador; mensajero. **2,** (pallbearer) pilar. **3,** (productive tree) árbol fructífero.

bearing ('bɛr·ɪŋ) *n.* **1,** (behavior) comportamiento; modales; actuación. **2,** (ability to produce) fertilidad; producción. **3,** (support) apoyo; sostén; soporte. **4,** (relation of parts) conexión; relación. **5,** (compass direction) orientación. **6,** *pl.* (position) rumbo; posición. **7,** *archit.* apoyo; apuntalamiento. **8,** *mech.* cojinete.

bearish ('bɛr·ɪʃ) *adj.* **1,** (of or like a bear) ursino. **2,** *fin.* bajista.

beast (bist) *n.* bestia; animal; bruto. **—beastly,** *adj.* bestial; brutal; animal. **—beast of burden,** animal de carga. **—beast of prey,** animal de presa.

beat (bit) *v.t. & i.* [**beat, beaten, beating**] **1,** (strike repeatedly) golpear; sacudir. **2,** *colloq.,* (defeat) superar; vencer. **—v.t. 1,** (overcome) sobrepasar; superar. **2,** (whip, as eggs or metal) batir. **3,** *mus.* marcar (el compás). **4,** *mil.* batir; abatir. **5,** (move the wings) aletear. **6,** (force) abrirse paso. **—v.i.** latir; palpitar. **—n. 1,** (blow) golpe; sonido repetido. **2,** (throb) latido; palpitación; pulsación. **3,** (stress) fuerza; énfasis. **4,** (habitual path) ronda; recorrido.

beatify (bi'æt·ə·fai) *v.t.* beatificar. **—beatific** (,bi·ə'tɪf·ɪk) *adj.* beatífico. **—beatification** (-fɪ'kei·ʃən) *n.* beatificación.

beatitude (bi'æt·ə·tud) *n.* **1,** (bliss) beatitud; bienaventuranza. **2,** *cap., usu.pl., Bib.* Bienaventuranzas. **3,** *cap., eccles.* (title of the Pope) Beatitud.

beatnik ('bit·nɪk) *n., slang* bohemio.

beat-up ('bit,ʌp) *adj., slang* arruinado; destartalado.

beau (boʊ) *n.* [*pl.* **beaus, beaux**] **1,** (male admirer) galán. **2,** (fop) petimetre.

beauteous ('bju·ti·əs) *adj.* hermoso; bello. **—beauteousness,** *n.* belleza; hermosura; donaire.

beautician (bju'tɪʃ·ən) *n.* peluquero de señoras.

beautiful ('bju·tɪ·fəl) *adj.* hermoso; bello. **—beautify** ('bju·tɪ·fai) *v.t.* hermosear; embellecer; adornar. **—v.i.** hermosearse; acicalarse. **—beautification** (-fɪ'kei·ʃən) *n.* embellecimiento.

beauty ('bju·ti) *n.* belleza. **—beauty shop,** salón de belleza.

beaux (boʊz) *n., pl. de* beau.

beaver ('bi·vər) *n.* **1,** *zoöl.* castor. **2,** (hat) castor. **3,** (high silk hat) sombrero de copa.

becalm (bi'kɑrm) *v.t.* calmar; tranquilizar; sosegar. **—becalmed,** *adj., naut.* encalmado; al pairo.

because (bi'kɔz) *conj.* porque; pues; puesto que. **—because of,** a causa de; por.

beck (bɛk) *n.* seña. **—at the beck and call of,** a disposición de; a las órdenes de.

beckon ('bɛk·ən) *v.t.* hacer señas a; llamar con señas. **—v.i.** hacer señas.

becloud (bi'klaʊd) *v.t.* obscurecer; anublar.

become (bi'kʌm) *v.i.* [**became, becoming**] convertirse en; hacerse. **—v.t.** quedar, sentar o caer bien. **—becoming,** *adj.* atractivo; apropiado; que cae bien.

bed (bɛd) *n.* **1,** (furniture) lecho; cama. **2,** (foundation) cimientos **3,** *geol.* capa; estrato. **4,** (bottom of a river, lake, etc.) madre; lecho. **5,** (plot for planting) tabla; cuadro. **—v.t.** [**bedded, -ding**] **1,** (put to bed) acostar; dar cama a. **2,** (place in a bed) asentar. **—v.i. 1,** (go to bed) acostarse; descansar. **2,** (have sexual intercourse) cohabitar; acostarse.

bedbug ('bɛd·bʌg) *n.* chinche.

bedchamber *n.* = **bedroom.**

bedclothes ('bɛd,kloʊz) *también,* **bedding** ('bɛd·ɪŋ) *n.* ropa de cama.

bedeck (bi'dɛk) *v.t.* decorar; adornar; engalanar.

bedevil (bi'dɛv·əl) *v.t.* **1,** (torment maliciously) enloquecer; maleficiar.

2, (bewitch) embrujar. 3, (harass) endiablar; atormentar.

bedfellow ('bɛd,fɛl·o) n. compañero de cama.

bedlam ('bɛd·ləm) n. 1, (lunatic asylum) manicomio. 2, fig. (uproar) confusión; desbarajuste; babel.

Bedouin ('bɛ·du·ɪn) n. & adj. beduíno.

bedpan ('bɛd,pæn) n. chata.

bedraggled (bɪ'dræg·əld) adj. desaliñado; desaseado.

bedridden ('bɛd·rɪd·ən) adj. imposibilitado; postrado en cama.

bedrock ('bɛd,rak) n. lecho de roca.

bedroom ('bɛd,rum) también, **bedchamber** (-,tʃeim·bər) n. alcoba; dormitorio; Mex. recámara.

bedside ('bɛd·said) n. lado de cama.

bedspread ('bɛd·sprɛd) n. cubrecama; colcha.

bedspring ('bɛd,sprɪŋ) n. colchón de muelles; sommier.

bedstead ('bɛd·stɛd) n. cuja; armazón de cama.

bedtime ('bɛd·taim) n. hora de dormir.

bee (biː) n. 1, (insect) abeja. 2, (social gathering) reunión; tertulia.

beech (bitʃ) n. haya. —**beechen** (-ən) adj. de haya.

beechnut ('bitʃ,nʌt) n. hayuco; nuez de haya.

beef (bif) n. 1, (meat) carne de res. 2, [pl. beeves] (steer) novillo. 3, colloq. (muscle) fuerza; músculo. 4, colloq. (complaint) queja. —v.i., colloq. quejarse; dar quejas. —**beefeater,** n. guardián del palacio real británico o de la Torre de Londres. —**beefy,** adj. carnoso; fornido. —**beef tea,** caldo de res. —**roast beef,** rosbif.

beefsteak ('bif,steik) n. bistec.

beekeeping ('bi,ki·pɪŋ) n. apicultura. —**beekeeper,** n. apicultor.

been (bɪn) v., p.p. de be.

beep (bip) n. señal de bocina o de diversos aparatos. —v.i. emitir un sonido agudo.

beer (bɪr) n. 1, (alcoholic) cerveza. 2, (non-alcoholic) gaseosa.

beet (bit) n. remolacha.

beetle ('bi·təl) n. 1, (insect) escarabajo. 2, (mallet) mazo. 3, slang (slow racehorse) jamelgo. —v.t. martillar con un mazo. —v.i. sobresalir.

beeves (biːvz) n., pl. de beef.

befall (bi'fɔl) v.i. suceder; ocurrir; acontecer. —v.t. suceder o pasar a.

befit (bi'fɪt) v.t. [**befitted, -ting**] cuadrar; convenir; acomodarse a.

before (bi'fɔr) prep. 1, (earlier than) antes de o que. 2, (in front of) delante de; enfrente de. 3, (in presence of) ante; frente a. 4, (in preference to) antes que. —conj. 1, (previous to) primero que. 2, (rather than) antes que. —adv. 1, (ahead) antes; delante. 2, (previously) previamente; anteriormente. —**beforehand,** adv. de antemano; con antelación.

befoul (bi'faul) v.t. 1, (make dirty) ensuciar. 2, (defame) calumniar.

befriend (bi'frɛnd) v.t. 1, (act as a friend) tener amistad con; brindar amistad a. 2, (favor) favorecer; patrocinar; proteger.

befuddle (bi'fʌd·əl) v.t. aturdir; confundir.

beg (bɛg) v.t. [**begged, begging**] rogar; suplicar; pedir. —v.i. 1, (ask for alms) pedir limosna. 2, (live by asking alms) mendigar.

began (bi'gæn) v., pret. de begin.

begat (bi'gæt) v., arcaico, pret. de beget.

beget (bi'gɛt) v.t. [**begot, begot o begotten, begetting**] 1, (procreate) engendrar; procrear. 2, (result in) causar; resultar en.

beggar ('bɛg·ər) n. limosnero; pordiosero. —v.t. empobrecer; arruinar. —**beggary,** n. mendicidad.

begin (bi'gɪn) v.t. & i. [**began, begun, beginning**] comenzar; empezar. —v.t. iniciar. —v.i. 1, (come into existence) nacer; tomar forma. 2, (arise) levantarse; surgir. —**beginner,** n. principiante; novicio.

beginning (bi'gɪn·ɪŋ) n. 1, (early stage) comienzo; fuente. 2, (origin) principio; origen.

begone (bi'gɔn) interj. fuera; afuera. —v.i., irse; marcharse.

begonia (bi'go·ni·ə) n. begonia.

begot (bi'gat) v., pret. & p.p. de beget.

begotten (bi'gat·ən) v., p.p. de beget.

begrime (bi'graim) v.t. embarrar; enlodar; encenagar.

begrudge (bi'grʌdʒ) v.t. 1, (be disinclined to) refunfuñar; rezongar. 2, (envy) envidiar; codiciar.

beguile (bi'gail) v.t. 1, (delude)

defraudar; engañar. **2,** (divert) divertir; entretener. —**beguilement,** *n.* engaño; entretenimiento.

begun (bi'gʌn) *v., p.p. de* begin.

behalf (bi'hæf) *n.* interés; favor. —**in, on** o **upon behalf of,** por; en o a nombre de; en o a favor de.

behave (bi'heiv) *v.i.* **1,** (conduct oneself) comportarse; conducirse. **2,** (act) proceder; actuar.

behavior (bi'heiv·jər) *n.* comportamiento; conducta; modales.

behaviorism (bi'heiv·jər·iz·əm) *n.* behaviorismo. —**behaviorist,** *n.* & *adj.* behaviorista. —**behavioristic,** *adj.* behaviorista.

behead (bi'hɛd) *v.t.* decapitar; degollar.

beheld (bi'hɛld) *v., pret. & p.p. de* **behold.**

behemoth ('bi·ə·məθ; bə'hi-) *n.* bestia colosal; cualquier cosa enorme. *Bib.* behemot.

behind (bi'haind) *prep.* **1,** (in the rear of) detrás de; tras. **2,** (inferior to) después de; tras. **3,** (later than) más tarde que o de. —*adv.* **1,** toward the back) detrás; atrás. **2,** (slow) con atraso; retrasadamente. —*adj.* atrasado; retrasado. —*n., colloq.* trasero; nalgas.

behindhand (bi'haind·hænd) *adv.* atrasadamente; con retraso.

behold (bi'hold) *v.t.* [**beheld, beholding**] observar; mirar; vigilar. —*interj.* ¡he aquí!; ¡aquí está! —**beholden** (bɪ'hol·dən) *adj.* obligado; agradecido.

behoove (bi'huːv) *v.i. impers.* **1,** (be fitting) corresponder a; cuadrar a. **2,** (be necessary) corresponder; necesitar; tocar.

beige (beiʒ) *adj.* & *n.* moreno amarillento.

being ('bi·ɪŋ) *n.* **1,** (existence) existencia; vida. **2,** (a human) ser; ente; criatura. —*v., p.pr. de* be.

bejewel (bi'ju·əl) *v.t.* enjoyar; alhajar.

belabor (bi'lei·bər) *v.t.* **1,** (thump) apalear; dar de puñadas. **2,** (scold) criticar; acusar.

belated (bi'lei·tɪd) *adj.* retrasado; demorado; tardío.

belay (bi'lei) *v.t.* amarrar; detener.

belch (bɛltʃ) *v.i.* **1,** (eructate) eructar; regoldar. **2,** (spurt) vomitar. —*v.t.* vomitar; despedir. —*n.* eructo; regüeldo.

beleaguer (bi'li·gər) *v.t.* sitiar; asediar; bloquear.

belfry ('bɛl·fri) *n.* campanario.

Belgian ('bɛl·dʒən) *adj.* & *n.* belga.

belie (bi'lai) *v.t.* **1,** (misrepresent) mentir; engañar. **2,** (disguise) disfrazar; falsear. **3,** (contradict) contradecir; desmentir.

belief (bi'lif) *n.* creencia; convicción.

believe (bi'liːv) *v.t.* & *i.* creer. —**believable,** *adj.* creíble. —**believer,** *n.* creyente.

belittle (bi'lɪt·əl) *v.t.* rebajar; disminuir; atenuar.

bell (bɛl) *n.* **1,** (device emitting sound) campana. **2,** *elect.* timbre. **3,** *naut.* campanada. —*v.i.* crecer o hincharse como campana. —*v.t.* poner campana a.

belladonna (bɛl·ə'dan·ə) *n.* belladona.

bell-bottom ('bɛl,bat·əm) *adj.* ensanchado. —**bell bottoms,** pantalones ensanchados.

bellboy ('bɛl,bɔi) *n.* botones. *Also,* bellhop.

belle (bɛl) *n.* belleza; mujer hermosa.

bellflower ('bɛl,flau·ər) *n.* campanilla.

bellicose ('bɛl·ə·kos) *adj.* belicoso; beligerante. —**bellicosity** (-'kas·ə·ti) *n.* belicosidad.

belligerent (bə'lɪdʒ·ə·rənt) *adj.* **1,** (pert. to war) beligerante. **2,** (bellicose) belicoso; peleante. **3,** (at war) beligerante; en guerra. —*n.* beligerante. —**belligerence,** *n.* beligerancia.

bellow ('bɛl·o) *v.i.* & *t.* rugir; bramar; mugir. —*n.* bramido; alarido.

bellows ('bɛl·oz) *n.* fuelle.

bellwether ('bɛl,wɛð·ər) *n.* guía *(de rebaño)*; precursor.

belly ('bɛl·i) *n.* **1,** (stomach) vientre; abdomen; estómago. **2,** (the inside of anything) entrañas. —*v.i.* hartarse; hincharse. —*v.t.* inflar; hinchar. —**belly laugh,** carcajada; risotada.

bellyache ('bɛl·i,eik) *n.* **1,** dolor de estómago. **2,** *slang* queja. —*v.i., slang* quejarse.

bellybutton ('bɛl·i,bʌt·ən) *n., colloq.* ombligo.

bellydance ('bɛl·i,dæns) *n.* danza del vientre. —**bellydancer,** *n.* bailadora de esta danza.

belong (bɪ'lɔːŋ) *v.i.* pertenecer. —**belong to**, pertenecer a; ser de. —**belong with** o **among**, pertenecer a.

belongings (bɪ'lɔŋ·ɪŋz) *n.pl.* posesiones; pertenencias; propiedad.

beloved (bɪ'lʌv·ɪd) *n. & adj.* amado; querido.

below (bɪ'loʊ) *adv.* 1, (in a lower place) abajo; debajo. 2, (coming later in a writing) más adelante; más abajo. —*prep.* 1, (under) bajo. 2, (beneath) bajo; debajo de.

belt (bɛlt) *n.* 1, (strap) correa; cinturón. 2, *geog.* zona. 3, *slang* (blow) porrazo; zurra. 4, *slang* (swig) trago. —*v.t.* 1, (gird) ceñir. 2, *slang* (beat) aporrear; zurrar.

bemire (bɪ'maɪr) *v.t.* enlodar; embarrar.

bemoan (bɪ'moʊn) *v.t.* deplorar; lamentar.

bemused (bɪ'mjuːzd) *adj.* confundido; aturdido.

bench (bɛntʃ) *n.* 1, (seat) banco; asiento. 2, *law* judicatura. 3, (shelf) estante; tabla. —**benchmark,** punto de referencia.

bend (bɛnd) *v.t.* [*pret. & p.p.* **bent**] 1, (curve) doblar; combar. 2, (turn) doblar. 3, (force into submission) doblegar; vencer; doblar. —*v.i.* 1, (become curved) doblarse; combarse. 2, (yield) someterse; doblegarse. —*n.* 1, (curve) curva; curvatura; codo. 2, *naut.* nudo. 3, *pl.* (sickness) calambres. —**bender,** *n., slang* juerga; parranda.

beneath (bɪ'niθ) *adv.* debajo; abajo. —*prep.* bajo; debajo de.

Benedictine (bɛn·ə'dɪk·tɪn; -tin) *adj. & n.* benedictino.

benediction (bɛn·ə'dɪk·ʃən) *n.* bendición.

benefaction (bɛn·ə'fæk·ʃən) *n.* 1, (good deed) beneficencia; bondad. 2, (benefit; charity) beneficio; merced; gracia. —**benefactor,** *n.* benefactor; bienhechor.

benefice ('bɛn·ə·fɪs) *n.* beneficio.

beneficient (bə'nɛf·ɪ·sənt) *adj.* benéfico; caritativo. —**beneficence,** *n.* beneficiencia; caridad.

beneficial (bɛn·ə'fɪʃ·əl) *adj.* beneficioso; benéfico; provechoso.

beneficiary (bɛn·ə'fɪʃ·i·ɛr·i) *n.* beneficiario.

benefit ('bɛn·ə·fɪt) *n.* 1, (profit) beneficio; utilidad. 2, (kind act) beneficio; ventaja. 3, *theat.* función de beneficio; beneficio. —*v.i.*

[-**fitted,** -**ting**] beneficiarse; aprovecharse. —*v.t.* beneficiar; aprovechar; mejorar.

benevolent (bə'nɛv·ə·lənt) *adj.* benévolo; bondadoso. —**benevolence** (-ləns) *n.* benevolencia.

benighted (bɪ'naɪ·tɪd) *adj.* ignorante.

benign (bɪ'naɪn) *adj.* 1, (gracious) gracioso; benigno. 2, (favorable) propicio; favorable. 3, *med.* ligero; leve; benigno. —**benignity** (bɪ'nɪg·nə·ti) *n.* benignidad; dulzura.

benignant (bɪ'nɪg·nənt) *adj.* bondadoso; afable. —**benignancy,** *n.* benignidad; bondad; afabilidad.

bent (bɛnt) *adj.* 1, (curved) doblado; curvado. 2, (determined) decidido; resuelto. —*n.* tendencia; inclinación. —*v., pret. & p.p. de* **bend.**

benumb (bɪ'nʌm) *v.t.* entumecer; paralizar.

benzedrine ('bɛn·zə,drɪn) *n.* bencedrina.

benzene ('bɛn·zin) *n.* benceno.

benzine ('bɛn·zin) *n.* bencina.

benzoate ('bɛn·zo·ət) *n.* benzoato.

benzoic (bɛn'zo·ɪk) *adj.* benzoico.

benzoin ('bɛn·zo·ɪn) *n.* benjuí.

benzol ('bɛn·zol) *n.* benzol.

bequeath (bɪ'kwiθ) *v.t.* legar; dejar (en testamento).

bequest (bɪ'kwɛst) *n.* legado; donación.

berate (bɪ'reɪt) *v.t.* regañar; reñir; reprender.

Berber ('bɑr·bər) *n. & adj.* bereber; berberí.

bereave (bɪ'riːv) *v.t.* [*pret. & p.p. a veces* **bereft**] despojar; desposeer; arrebatar.

bereavement *n.* 1, (deprivation) despojo; privación. 2, (loss through death) aflicción; duelo; luto.

bereft (bɪ'rɛft) *v., pret. & p.p. de* **bereave.** —*adj.* despojado; privado; desposeído.

beret (bə'reɪ) *n.* boina.

beriberi ('bɛr·i'bɛr·i) *n.* beriberi.

berkelium ('bɑrk·li·əm) *n.* berkelio.

berry ('bɛr·i) *n.* baya; grano. —*v.i.* echar bayas. —*v.t.* recoger o coger bayas.

berserk (bər'sʌrk) *adj.* frenético; colérico.

berth (bɑrθ) *n.* 1, (bed on a train or ship) camarote. 2, (bunk) litera. 3, (dock) amarradero. 4, (job) empleo;

trabajo. —*v.t.* **1,** dar litera o empleo. **2,** *naut.* atracar. —*v.i.* tener u ocupar una litera.

beryl ('bɛr-əl) *n.* berilo.

beryllium (bə'rɪ·li·əm) *n.* berilio.

beseech (bi'siʧ) *v.t.* [*pret. & p.p.* **besought**] suplicar; rogar; implorar.

beset (bi'sɛt) *v.t.* [**beset, besetting**] **1,** (attack) sitiar; acosar; rodear. **2,** (harass) importunar; fastidiar; fatigar.

beside (bi'said) *prep.* **1,** (at the side of) al lado de; junto a. **2,** (near) cerca de. **3,** [*también*, **besides**] (in addition to) además de. **4,** (unconnected with) aparte de. —*adv.* [*también*, **besides**] **1,** (moreover) además; también. **2,** (in addition) aparte; por otra parte. —**beside oneself,** loco; fuera de sí.

besiege (bi'siʤ) *v.t.* **1,** (lay siege to) asediar; sitiar. **2,** (harass) asediar; demandar; acosar.

besmirch (bi'smʌrʧ) *v.t.* manchar; escarnecer.

besotted (bi'sat·ɪd) *adj.* **1,** (foolish) embrutecido; entontecido. **2,** (intoxicated) embriagado; emborrachado. **3,** (infatuated) enamorado; chiflado.

besought (bi'sɔt) *v., pret. & p.p.* de **beseech.**

best (bɛst) *adj., superl. de* **good;** óptimo; mejor; superior. —*adv., superl. de* **well;** más; mejor. —*n.* lo sumo; lo más; lo mayor; lo mejor. —*v.t.* derrotar; vencer; ganar. —**at best,** a lo más; a lo mejor. —**get the best of, 1,** (outdo) vencer; ganar. **2,** (outwit) ser más listo que; sobrepasar a. —**make the best of,** aprovecharse de. —**best man,** padrino de boda. —**best seller,** el de más venta; éxito de librería.

bestial ('bɛs·ʧəl) *adj.* **1,** (beast-like) brutal; irracional. **2,** (pert. to beasts) bestial. —**bestiality,** *n.* bestialidad; brutalidad.

bestir (bi'stʌr) *v.t. & i.* mover(se).

bestow (bi'stoʊ) *v.t.* **1,** (give) dar; conferir; otorgar. **2,** (give in marriage) dar o entregar en matrimonio. —**bestowal,** *n.* dádiva; donación.

bestride (bi'straid) *v.t.* [**bestrode, bestridden**] **1,** (straddle) montar a horcajadas. **2,** (step over) cruzar de un salto; saltar a.

bet (bɛt) *v.t. & i.* [**bet, betting**] apostar. —*n.* apuesta; envite. —**better; bettor,** *n.* apostador.

beta ('be·tə) *n.* beta. —**beta parti-**

cle, partícula beta. —**beta ray,** rayo beta.

betake (bi'teik) *v.t., usu.v.r.* irse; marcharse; dirigirse.

betel ('bi·təl) *n.* betel. —**betel nut,** fruto del betel.

bethink (bɪ'θɪŋk) *v., usu.v.r.* ocurrírsele; recordarse.

betide (bi'taid) *v.i.* acontecer; suceder; pasar. —*v.t.* indicar; presagiar.

betoken (bi'to·kən) *v.t.* señalar; representar; denotar.

betray (bi'trei) *v.t.* traicionar; denunciar. —**betrayal** (-əl) *n.* traición; denuncia.

betroth (bi'trɔθ; bi'troʊð) *v.t.* desposar; contraer esponsales; prometer en matrimonio. —**betrothal,** *n.* desposorios; esponsales; compromiso. —**betrothed,** *n.* novio; prometido.

better ('bɛt·ər) *adj., comp. of* **good;** mejor. —*adv., comp. of* **well;** mejor; más bien. —*v.t.* **1,** (improve) mejorar. **2,** (surpass) aventajar. —*v.i.* mejorarse. —*n.* **1,** (superior thing) lo mejor. **2,** (superior person) el mejor. **3,** (advantage) ventaja; superioridad. —**get the better of, 1,** (outdo) sobrepasar a. **2,** (outwit) ser más listo que. —**think better of,** considerar; reconsiderar. —**better oneself,** mejorar; adelantar. —**betterment,** *n.* mejora; mejoría.

between (bi'twin) *prep.* entre. —*adv.* en medio; entremedias.

betwixt (bi'twikst) *prep.* entre.

bevel ('bɛv·əl) *n.* **1,** (instrument) cartabón. **2,** (angle) ángulo agudo u obtuso. **3,** (sloping part) bisel; chaflán. —*v.i. & t.* biselar; achaflanar. —*adj.* biselado; oblicuo.

beverage ('bɛv·ər·ɪʤ) *n.* bebida.

bevy ('bɛv·i) *n.* bandada.

bewail (bi'weil) *v.t. & i.* lamentar.

beware (bi'wɛr) *v.i.* precaverse; guardarse. —*v.i.* vigilar; tener cuidado con.

bewilder (bi'wɪl·dər) *v.t.* confundir; aturdir; aturullar. —**bewilderment,** *n.* aturdimiento; perplejidad.

bewitch (bi'wɪʧ) *v.t.* **1,** (charm) encantar; fascinar; hechizar. **2,** (cast a spell upon) embrujar; maleficiar. —**bewitching,** *adj.* encantador; hechicero.

beyond (bi'jand) *adv.* más lejos; más allá. —*prep.* tras; superior a; más allá de.

bias ('bai·əs) n. **1,** (oblique direction) oblicuidad; inclinación. **2,** (prejudice) prejuicio; propensión. —v.t. prejuzgar; predisponer; inclinar. —adj. inclinado; sesgado; diagonal.

bib (bɪb) n. babero.

Bible ('bai·bəl) n. Biblia. —**Biblical** ('bɪb·lɪ·kəl) adj. bíblico.

bibliography (,bɪb·li'ag·rə·fi) n. bibliografía. —**bibliographical** (-ə'græf·ɪ·kəl) adj. bibliográfico.

bibliomania (bɪb·li·o'mei·ni·ə) n. bibliomanía. —**bibliomaniac** (-æk) n. bibliómano.

bibliophile ('bɪb·li·o·fail) n. bibliófilo.

bibulous ('bɪb·jə·ləs) adj. **1,** (highly absorbent) poroso; absorbente. **2,** (addicted to liquor) borrachín; bebedor. —**bibulousness,** n. porosidad; absorbencia.

bicameral (bai'kæm·ər·əl) adj. bicameral; de dos cámaras legislativas.

bicarbonate of soda (bai'kar·bə·nət) bicarbonato de soda.

bicentennial (bai·sɛn'tɛn·i·əl) n. & adj. bicentenario.

biceps ('bai·sɛps) n. bíceps.

bichloride (bai'klo·raid) n. bicloruro.

bicker ('bɪk·ər) n. altercado; camorra. —v.i. argumentar; disputar.

bicolor ('bai,kʌl·ər) adj. bicolor. También, **bicolored.**

bicron ('bai·krɒn) n. bicrón.

bicuspid (bai'kʌs·pɪd) adj. bicúspide. —n. gran molar.

bicycle ('bai·sɪk·əl) n. bicicleta.

bid (bɪd) v.t. [**bade, bidden,** -**ding**] **1,** (command) mandar; ordenar. **2,** [pret. & p.p. **bid**] (invite) invitar; convidar. **3,** (offer a price of) proponer; ofrecer. —v.i. pujar. —n. **1,** (offer) oferta; postura; puja. **2,** (attempt) ensayo; prueba. **3,** (invitation) invitación; oferta. —**bidder,** n. postor; licitador; pujador.

bidding n. **1,** (command) orden; mandato. **2,** (request) ruego; favor. **3,** cards or auction apuesta; puja; (in bridge) remate.

bide (baid) v.t. [**bided** o **bode, biding**] aguantar; soportar. —v.i. **1,** (dwell) residir; vivir. **2,** (stay) continuar; permanecer. **3,** (wait) esperar; aguardar.

biennial (bai'ɛn·i·əl) adj. bienal. —**biennium** (-əm) n. bienio.

bier (bɪr) n. túmulo; estrado funeral.

bifocal (bai'fo·kəl) adj. bifocal. —**bifocals,** n.pl. bifocales.

bifurcate ('bai·fər,keit) adj. [también, **bifurcated**] bifurcado. —v.i. bifurcarse. —v.t. dividir en dos ramales. —**bifurcation,** n. bifurcación.

big (bɪg) adj. [**bigger,** -**gest**] **1,** (large) grande; enorme. **2,** (important) importante; principal; sobresaliente. **3,** (generous) generoso; magnánimo. **4,** (fullgrown) mayor. —**big game, 1,** (hunting) caza mayor. **2,** colloq. empresa peligrosa. —**big shot,** slang persona importante. —**big top,** circo; tienda de un circo.

bigamist ('bɪg·ə·mɪst) n. bígamo.

bigamy ('bɪg·ə·mi) n. bigamia. —**bigamous** (-məs) adj. bígamo.

bigfoot ('bɪg,fʊt) n. monstruo enorme legendario de las selvas.

big-hearted adj. de gran corazón; generoso.

bighorn ('bɪg,hɔrn) n. carnero salvaje de los montes del noroeste de EE.UU.

bigot ('bɪg·ət) n. intolerante; fanático; beatón. —**bigoted,** adj. fanático. —**bigotry,** n. fanatismo; intolerancia.

bigwig ('bɪg·wɪg) n., colloq. persona importante; pájaro de cuenta.

bike (baik) n., colloq. bicicleta; motocicleta. —v.i., colloq. montar en bicicleta o motocicleta.

bilateral (bai'læt·ər·əl) adj. bilateral.

bilberry ('bɪl·bɛr·i) n. arándano.

bile (bail) n. **1,** (secretion) bilis. **2,** (peevishness) cólera; mal humor; mal genio.

bilge (bɪldʒ) n. **1,** naut. pantoque. **2,** (bulge of a barrel) barriga. **3,** slang (nonsense) tontería. —**bilge water,** agua de pantoque.

bilingual (bai'lɪŋ·gwəl) adj. bilingüe. —**bilingualism,** n. bilingüismo.

bilious ('bɪl·jəs) adj. bilioso. —**biliousness,** n. biliosidad.

bilk (bɪlk) v.t. defraudar; estafar.

bill (bɪl) n. **1,** (account of money owed) factura; cuenta. **2,** comm. letra; giro; pagaré. **3,** (money) billete. **4,** (proposed law) proyecto de ley. **5,** (handbill) prospecto; aviso. **6,** theat. espectáculo; representación. **7,** (beak) pico. —v.t. **1,** (send a bill to) facturar. **2,** (enter on a bill) entrar; cargar; adeudar. **3,**

theat. anunciar. —**bill and coo,** arrullarse. —**bill of fare,** menú. —**bill of rights,** declaración de derechos; *cap.* las diez primeras enmiendas a la Constitución de los EE.UU. —**bill of sale,** escritura de venta. —**bill of lading,** conocimiento de embarque.

billboard ('bɪl·bord) *n.* cartelera.

billet ('bɪl·ɪt) *n.* **1,** *mil.* cuartel; alojamiento militar. **2,** (assignment) trabajo; tarea; empleo. **3,** (ticket) billete; boleto; entrada. **4,** (written note) billete; esquela. **5,** (stick) zoquete de leña. —*v.t.* **1,** *mil.* alojar; aposentar. **2,** (assign) designar; señalar.

billet-doux (,bɪl·i'duɹ) *n.* [*pl.* **billets-doux** ('bɪl·i'duɹz)] esquela amorosa.

billfold ('bɪl·fold) *n.* cartera; *Amer.* billetera.

billiards ('bɪl·jərdz) *n.* billar. —**billiard,** *n.* carambola.

billing ('bɪl·iŋ) *n.,* *theat.* elenco; reparto.

billion ('bɪl·jən) *n.* *(U.S.)* mil millones; *(Brit.)* un millón de millones; billón. —**billionaire** (-jə'neɹr) *n.* billonario. —**billionth,** *adj.* & *n.* *(U.S.)* mil millonésimo; *(Brit.)* billonésimo.

billow ('bɪl·o) *n.* ola; oleada. —*v.i.* crecer o hincharse como ola. —**billowy,** *adj.* hinchado como ola.

billy ('bɪl·i) *n.* [*también,* **billy club**] porra; bastón de policía.

billygoat ('bɪl·i,got) *n.* macho cabrío; cabrón.

bimetallism (bai'mɛt·əl·ɪz·əm) *n.* bimetalismo.

bimonthly (bai'mʌnθ·li) *adj.* bimestral; bimestre. —*adv.* bimestralmente.

bin (bɪn) *n.* depósito; hucha; arca.

binary ('bai·nə·ri) *adj.* binario.

binaural (bai'nor·əl) *adj.* binaural; binauricular.

bind (baind) *v.t.* [*pret.* & *p.p.* **bound**] **1,** (tie) atar; ligar; apretar. **2,** (wrap) envolver. **3,** (bandage) vendar. **4,** (hem) ribetear; galonear. **5,** (obligate) obligar; precisar; exigir. —*v.i.* **1,** (cohere) pegarse; endurecerse. **2,** (be necessary) ser obligatorio.

binder ('bain·dər) *n.* **1,** (wrapper) atador; encuadernador. **2,** (cord) atadura; lazo. **3,** (adhesive) adhesivo; pegante. —**bindery,** *n.* taller de encuadernación.

binding ('bain·diŋ) *n.* **1,** (fastening; wrapping) ligadura; faja; venda. **2,** (covering of a book) encuadernación.

bindweed ('baind,wiɹd) *n.* enredadera.

binge (bɪndʒ) *n.* parranda. —*v.i.* hartarse; saciarse.

binnacle ('bɪn·ə·kəl) *n.* bitácora.

binocular (bɪ'nak·jə·lər) *adj.* binocular. —**binoculars,** *n.pl.* anteojos; gemelos.

binomial (bai'no·mi·əl) *adj.* binómico. —*n.* binomio.

biochemistry (,bai·o'kɛm·ɪs·tri) *n.* bioquímica. —**biochemical,** *adj.* bioquímico. —**biochemist,** *n.* bioquímico.

biodegradable (,bai·o·di'grei·də·bəl) *adj.* biodegradable.

biography (bai'ag·rə·fi) *n.* biografía. —**biographer,** *n.* biógrafo. —**biographical** (,bai·ə'græf·ɪ·kəl) *adj.* biográfico.

biology (bai'al·ə·dʒi) *n.* biología. —**biological** (-ə'lɑdʒ·ɪ·kəl) *adj.* biológico. —**biologist** (-'al·ə·dʒɪst) *n.* biólogo.

bionic (bai'ɑn·ɪk) *adj.* biónico. —**bionics** *n. sing.* & *pl.* biónica.

biophysics (,bai·o'fɪz·ɪks) *n.* biofísica.

biopsy ('bai·ap·si) *n.* biopsia.

bipartisan (bai'par·tɪ·zən) *adj.* de dos (o ambos) partidos políticos.

bipartite (bai'par·tait) *adj.* bipartido; *polit.* bipartito.

biped ('bai·ped) *n.* bípedo. —*adj.* bípede; bípedo.

birch (bʌrtʃ) *n.* abedul. —*v.t.* varear.

bird (bʌrd) *n.* ave; pájaro. —**bird's-eye,** *adj.* general; global; superficial. —**bird shot,** perdigón.

biretta (bə'ret·ə) *n.* birreta.

birth (bʌrθ) *n.* **1,** (act of being born) nacimiento; alumbramiento. **2,** (descent) linaje; ascendencia; descendencia. **3,** (beginning) origen; principio.

birth control control de los nacimientos; control de la natalidad.

birthday ('bʌrθ·dei) *n.* cumpleaños.

birthmark ('bʌrθ·mark) *n.* marca de nacimiento.

birthplace ('bʌrθ·pleis) *n.* sitio o lugar de nacimiento.

birthright ('bʌrθ·rait) *n.* **1,** (rights conferred by birth) derechos de

---

nacimiento. **2,** (right of the first-born) primogenitura.

Biscayan (bɪs'kei·ən) *adj.* & *n.* vizcaíno.

biscuit ('bɪs·kɪt) *n.* galleta; bizcocho.

bisect (bai'sɛkt) *v.t.* bisecar. —**bisection** (-'sɛk·ʃən) *n.* bisección.

bisector (bai'sɛk·tər) *n.* bisectriz. *También,* **bisectrix** (-trɪks) [*pl.* -**trices** (-'trai·siz)].

bisexual (bai'sɛk·ʃʊ·əl) *adj.* & *n.* bisexual.

bishop ('bɪʃ·əp) *n.* **1,** *eccles.* obispo. **2,** *chess* alfil. —**bishopric** (-rɪk) *n.* obispado.

bismuth ('bɪz·məθ) *n.* bismuto.

bison ('bai·sən) *n.* bisonte.

bisque (bɪsk) *n.* **1,** (thick soup) sopa espesa. **2,** *ceramics* bizcocho. **3,** *games* (handicap) ventaja.

bissextile (bɪ'sɛks·tɪl) *adj.* bisiesto.

bit (bɪt) *v., pret. de* **bite.** —*n.* **1,** (small piece) pizca; trocito; ardite. **2,** (small coin) monedita. **3,** (mouthpiece) bocado del freno. **4,** (tool) taladro; hoja. **5,** *comput.* bitio.

bitch (bɪtʃ) *n.* **1,** (dog) perra. **2,** (malicious woman) ramera. **3,** *slang* (complaint) queja. —*v.i., slang* quejarse. —*v.t., slang* estropear; chapucear.

bite (bait) *v.t.* [**bit, bitten, biting**] **1,** (grip with the teeth) morder; mordiscar; picar. **2,** (grasp) apresar; agarrar. **3,** (corrode) comer; corroer. —*v.i.* **1,** (take a bait) picar. **2,** (be duped) ser engañado. **3,** (take hold) hacer presa. —*n.* **1,** (act or effect of biting) mordedura; picadura. **2,** (small piece) mordisco. **3,** *slang* (extortion) exacción; extorsión. **4,** *slang* (graft) concusión; *Amer.* mordida.

bitten ('bɪt·ən) *v., p.p. de* **bite.**

bitter ('bɪt·ər) *adj.* **1,** (harsh-tasting) amargo; áspero. **2,** *fig.* (grievous) doloroso; penoso; desagradable. **3,** *fig.* (piercing) mordaz. **4,** *fig.* (severe) encarnizado. —**bitters,** *n.pl.* licor amargo. —**to the bitter end,** hasta la muerte; hasta el extremo.

bittern ('bɪt·ərn) *n.* avetoro.

bitterness ('bɪt·ər·nəs) *n.* **1,** (harsh taste) amargura; amargor. **2,** (grief) dolor; pena. **3,** (severity) encarnizamiento.

bittersweet *adj.* & *n.* agridulce.

bitumen (bɪ'tu·mən) *n.* betún.

—**bituminous** (-mɪn·əs) *adj.* bituminoso.

bivalent (bai'vei·lənt) *adj.* bivalente. —**bivalence,** *n.* bivalencia.

bivalve ('bai·vælv) *n.* & *adj.* bivalvo.

bivouac ('bɪv·wæk) *n.* vivac; vivaque. —*v.i.* [**bivouacked, -acking**] vivaquear.

bizarre (bɪ'zɑːr) *adj.* raro; caprichoso; grotesco. —**bizarreness,** *n.* extravagancia.

blab (blæb) *v.t.* [**blabbed, blabbing**] revelar; divulgar. —*v.i.* chismear.

blabber ('blæb·ər) *v.i.* parlotear; cotorrear. —*n.* parloteo; cotorreo.

blabbermouth ('blæb·ər,mauθ) *n.* bocaza.

black (blæk) *n.* negro. —*adj.* **1,** (dark) negro; obscuro. **2,** *fig.* (wicked) atroz; horrible. **3,** *fig.* (sad) triste; calamitoso. —*v.t.* & *i.* = **blacken.** —**black and blue,** lívido; amoratado. —**black hole,** agujero negro. —**black sheep,** garbanzo negro; oveja descarriada.

blackball ('blæk·bɔl) *v.t.* rechazar; votar en contra.

blackberry ('blæk·bɛr·i) *n.* zarzamora.

blackbird ('blæk·bʌrd) *n.* mirlo.

blackboard ('blæk,bord) *n.* pizarra; encerado.

blacken ('blæk·ən) *v.t.* **1,** (make black) ennegrecer; obscurecer; betunar. **2,** (defame) difamar; denigrar; calumniar. —*v.i.* ennegrecerse; obscurecerse.

blackguard ('blæ·gərd) *n.* tunante; pillo; pelagatos.

blackhead ('blæk,hed) *n.* comedón; espinilla.

blackjack ('blæk·dʒæk) *n.* **1,** (heavy club) cachiporra; porra. **2,** (card game) veintiuna. —*v.t.* **1,** (strike) aporrear. **2,** (coerce) coaccionar; obligar; forzar.

blacklist ('blæk·lɪst) *n.* lista negra. —*v.t.* votar en contra; rechazar.

blackmail ('blæk·meil) *n.* chantaje. —*v.t.* chantajear. —**blackmailer,** *n.* chantajista.

Black Maria (mə'rai·ə) *colloq.* coche celular; camión de policía.

black market mercado negro; estraperlo. —**black marketeer,** estraperlista.

blackout ('blæk·aut) *n.* **1,** (extinction of lights) apagón. **2,** (fainting spell) inconsciencia; desvanecimiento. **3,** (loss of memory) amnesia.

blacksmith ('blæk·smiθ) *n.* herrador; herrero; forjador.

blacktop ('blæk·tap) *n.* asfalto. —*v.t.* asfaltar.

bladder ('blæd·ər) *n.* vejiga.

blade (bleid) *n.* **1,** (weapon) espada. **2,** (cutting edge) hoja; cuchilla. **3,** (plant leaf) hoja. **4,** *colloq.* (rakish man) calavera.

blah (bla) *adj., slang* aburrido; insípido. —**to have** o **get the blahs,** *slang* estar abatido; desanimarse.

blame (bleim) *v.t.* acusar; culpar; censurar. —*n.* censura; acusación; culpa; reproche. —**blameless,** *adj.* inculpable.

blameworthy ('bleim,wʌr·ði) *adj.* culpable.

blanch (blæntʃ) *v.t.* emblanquecer; blanquear. —*v.i.* palidecer.

bland (blænd) *adj.* suave; dulce; blando. —**blandness,** *n.* suavidad; blandura.

blandish ('blænd·ɪʃ) *v.t.* ablandar; halagar; lisonjear; engatusar. —**blandishment,** *n.* halago; lisonja; engatusamiento.

blank (blæŋk) *adj.* **1,** (bare) vacío; sin adorno. **2,** (without marks) sin llenar; en blanco. **3,** (utter) completo; total. **4,** (colorless) pálido; descolorido. —*n.* **1,** (vacant space) blanco; espacio en blanco; libre. **2,** (form) impreso en blanco. **3,** *mech.* madera o metal para ser trabajado. —*v.t.* **1,** [también, **blank out**] (cancel) anular; borrar. **2,** *colloq.* (prevent from scoring) confundir. —**blank check,** carta blanca.

blanket ('blæŋk·ət) *n.* manta; frazada; cobertor de lana; *fig.* manto. —*adj.* comprensivo; general. —*v.t.* **1,** (cover) cubrir con manta; mantear. **2,** (overwhelm) suprimir; cubrir; oscurecer.

blankness ('blæŋk·nəs) *n.* **1,** (empty space) hueco; espacio. **2,** (mental confusion) turbación; confusión.

blare (bleɪr) *v.t.* trompetear; publicar. —*v.i.* vociferar; bramar. —*n.* **1,** (trumpet sound) trompeteo. **2,** (blatant sound, color, etc.) trompetada; estridencia.

blarney ('blar·ni) *n.* adulación; lisonja. —*v.t. & i.* lisonjear.

blasé (bla'zei) *adj.* hastiado; cansado; aburrido.

blaspheme (blæs'firm) *v.i.* blasfemar. —*v.t.* maldecir; vilipendiar. —**blasphemer,** *n.* blasfemador; blasfemante; blasfemo.

blasphemy ('blæs·fə·mi) *n.* blasfemia. —**blasphemous,** *adj.* blasfemo; blasfemador.

blast (blæst) *n.* **1,** (gust of air) golpe de viento; ráfaga de aire. **2,** (blowing of a horn) resoplido; soplo. **3,** (explosion) explosión; estallido. —*v.t.* **1,** (explode) explotar; estallar. **2,** (destroy) arruinar; destruir. —**blast furnace,** alto horno.

blast-off *n.* despegue (*de un cohete*). —**blast off,** despegar un cohete.

blatancy ('blei·tən·si) *n.* **1,** (noise) vocinglería. **2,** (obtrusiveness) lo entremetido; lo intruso.

blatant ('blei·tənt) *adj.* **1,** (noisy) vocinglero; bramante; ruidoso. **2,** (obtrusive) entremetido; intruso.

blather ('blæð·ər) *n.* disparates; necedades —*v.i.* disparatar; decir necedades.

blaze (bleiz) *n.* **1,** (fire) llama; fuego. **2,** (brilliant light) luz brillante. **3,** (outburst) llamarada; hoguera. **4,** (mark on an animal's face) mancha; señal. —*v.i.* quemarse; encenderse; brillar. —*v.t.* **1,** (inflame) encender; inflamar. **2,** (proclaim) pregonar; proclamar.

blazer ('blei·zər) *n.* chaqueta deportiva.

blazon ('blei·zən) *n.* **1,** (heraldry) blasón; escudo de armas. **2,** (display) divulgación; proclamación. —*v.t.* **1,** *her.* blasonar. **2,** (embellish) adornar. **3,** (proclaim) divulgar; proclamar. —**blazonry,** *n.* heráldica; blasón.

bleach (blitʃ) *v.t.* blanquear; decolorar. —*v.i.* palidecer; decolorarse; empalidecer. —*n.* lejía.

bleachers ('blitʃ·ərz) *n.pl.* gradas descubiertas.

bleak (blik) *adj.* **1,** (desolate) desolado; desierto; yermo. **2,** (cold) frío; helado; desabrigado. **3,** (dreary) apático; indiferente; sin entusiasmo. —**bleakness,** *n.* desolación; frialdad.

blear (blɪr) *v.t.* nublar; ofuscar. —*adj.* [también, **bleary**] legañoso; ofuscado; nublado.

bleat (blit) *n.* (of a sheep or goat)

balido; (of a calf) mugido. —*v.i.* balar; mugir.

bleed (bli:d) *v.i.* [*pret. & p.p.* **bled**] **1,** (emit blood) sangrar; echar sangre. **2,** (flow from a plant) exudar. **3,** *fig.* (pity) apiadarse; compadecerse; angustiarse. —*v.t.* **1,** (draw blood from) sangrar a. **2,** *colloq.* (extort money from) dar un sablazo. **3,** *print.* sangrar. —**bleeder,** *n.* hemofílico.

bleep (blip) *n.* señal electrónico, esp. para suprimir ciertas palabras ofensivas.

blemish ('blɛm·ɪʃ) *v.t.* **1,** (mar) afear; manchar. **2,** (defame) denigrar; infamar. —*n.* tacha; mancha.

blend (blɛːnd) *v.t.* mezclar; combinar. —*v.i.* **1,** (harmonize) armonizar. **2,** (mix paints) casar colores. —*n.* mezcla; combinación.

bless (blɛs) *v.t.* **1,** (consecrate) bendecir; santificar. **2,** (make happy) hacer feliz. **3,** (extol) alabar; glorificar. —**blessed** ('blɛs·ɪd) *adj.* ·bendito; feliz. —**blessedness,** *n.* felicidad. —**blessed event,** nacimiento de un niño.

blessing ('blɛs·ɪŋ) *n.* **1,** (benediction) bendición; bien; gracia. **2,** (approval) bendición; aprobación; consentimiento.

blew (blu:) *v.,* *pret. de* **blow.**

blight (blait) *n.* plaga. —*v.t.* **1,** (cause to decay) plagar; marchitar; agostar. **2,** (ruin) arruinar; frustrar.

blimp (blɪmp) *n.* globo dirigible.

blind (blaind) *adj.* **1,** (sightless) ciego. **2,** (unaware) ignorante; insensato. **3,** (heedless) irrazonable; descuidado. **4,** (secret) oculto; secreto. —*v.t.* **1,** (deprive of sight) cegar; quitar la vista a. **2,** (conceal) oscurecer; esconder. —*n.* **1,** (obstruction) obstáculo. **2,** (ruse) evasiva; pretexto. **3,** (deceit) disfraz; engaño. **4,** (hunters' shelter) refugio para cazadores. **5,** (window shade) transparente. —**blind alley,** callejón sin salida. —**blind date,** *slang* cita a ciegas. —**Venetian blind,** celosía; persiana.

blindfold ('blaind·fold) *n.* venda ocular. —*adj.* que tiene vendados los ojos. —*v.t.* vendar los ojos a.

blink (blɪŋk) *v.i.* **1,** (wink rapidly) parpadear; pestañear. **2,** (flash) destellar; fulgurar. —*n.* **1,** (wink) guiño; parpadeo; pestañeo. **2,**

(flash) destello. **3,** (glimpse) mirada. —**blink at,** ignorar; disimular.

blinker ('blɪŋ·ər) *n.* **1,** (flashing light) parpadeo luminoso. **2,** *pl.* (shades for a horse's eyes) anteojeras.

blip (blɪp) *n.* centella que aparece en la pantalla del radar.

bliss (blɪs) *n.* **1,** (supreme joy) bienaventuranza; gloria. **2,** (delight) deleite; alegría; felicidad. —**blissful,** *adj.* dichoso; bienaventurado; contento.

blister ('blɪs·tər) *n.* ampolla; vejiga. —*v.t.* **1,** (cause to swell) ampollar. **2,** *fig.* (vituperate) mortificar; vituperar. —*v.i.* ampollarse.

blithe (blaið; blaiθ) *también,* **blithesome** (-səm) *adj.* contento; feliz; alegre; gozoso. —**blitheness,** *n.* gozo; alegría; júbilo.

blithering ('blið·ər·ɪŋ) *adj.* que dice necedades o disparates.

blitz (blɪts) *n.* **1,** *mil.* ataque blindado. **2,** (sudden onslaught) matanza; aniquilación. —*v.t.* atacar violentamente. *También,* **blitzkrieg** (-,kri:g).

blizzard ('blɪz·ərd) *n.* **1,** (snowstorm) nevada. **2,** (windstorm with sleet) ventisca.

bloat (blot) *v.t.* **1,** (cause to swell) hinchar; entumecer. **2,** (smoke, as fish) curar; ahumar. —*v.i.* hincharse; abotagarse. —*n.,* *vet.med.* inflamación del abdomen.

bloater ('blot·ər) *n.* pescado ahumado.

blob (blɑb) *n.* burbuja; pompa.

bloc (blɑk) *n.* grupo político; bloc; unión.

block (blɑk) *n.* **1,** (solid mass) bloque. **2,** (obstacle) obstáculo; impedimento. **3,** (city block) manzana; *Amer.* cuadra. **4,** (base for work) mesa; bloque. **5,** (auction platform) plataforma. **6,** *mech.* bloque de cilindros. **7,** *print.* bloque de grabado. **8,** *R.R.* tramo; sección. **9,** *naut.* motón; sistema de poleas. —*v.t.* **1,** (mount on a block) montar. **2,** [*usu.,* **block out**] (plan) delinear; esbozar. **3,** (obstruct) bloquear; obstruir. **4,** (shape, as a hat) conformar.

blockade (blɑ'keid) *n.* **1,** (barrier) bloqueo. **2,** (obstruction) obstrucción; impedimento. —*v.t.* bloquear.

blockbuster ('blɑk,bʌs·tər) *n.* bomba rompemanzanas.

blockhead ('blak·hɛd) *n.* necio; estúpido; bruto. —**blockheaded,** *adj.* estúpido; lerdo.

blond (blaːnd) *n.* & *adj.* [*fem.* **blonde**] blondo; rubio; *Amer.* güero (o huero).

blood (blʌd) *n.* 1, (body fluid) sangre. 2, (plant sap) savia. 3, (lineage) ascendencia; linaje; parentesco. —**blood bank,** banco de sangre. —**blood count,** suma de glóbulos rojos y blancos por unidad de volumen. —**blood relation,** parentesco directo. —**blood vessel,** vena; arteria.

bloodhound ('blʌd·haund) *n.* perro sabueso.

bloodless ('blʌd·ləs) *adj.* 1, (without blood) desangrado; exangüe; incruento. 2, (pale) pálido; lívido. 3, (cowardly) indeciso; apático; sin sangre.

bloodshed ('blʌd·ʃɛd) *n.* matanza; carnicería.

bloodshot ('blʌd·ʃat) *adj.* inyectado de sangre; sanguinolento.

bloodstream ('blʌd,strim) *n.* corriente sanguíneo.

bloodsucker ('blʌd·sʌk·ər) *n.* 1, (leech) sanguijuela. 2, *slang* (extortionist) usurero.

bloodthirsty ('blʌd·θʌrst·i) *adj.* sanguinario; cruel. —**bloodthirstiness,** *n.* encarnizamiento; sed de sangre.

bloody ('blʌ·di) *adj.* 1, (gory) sangriento; ensangrentado. 2, (marked by bloodshed) sanguinario; cruel. 3, *slang* (damned) maldito. —*v.t.* ensangrentar. —**bloodiness,** *n.* sanguinolencia; ensangrentamiento.

bloom (bluːm) *n.* 1, (flower) flor. 2, (foliage) floración; florecimiento. 3, (healthful glow) flor; frescura; juventud. 4, (fuzz on fruit) pelusilla. 5, *metall.* lingote. —*v.i.* 1, (flower) florecer. 2, (keep young) ser joven; disfrutar de salud. 3, (glow) brillar vivamente. —**bloomer,** *n.* desatino; disparate.

bloomers ('blum·ərz) *n.pl.* pantalones de mujer holgados.

blooming ('blu·mɪŋ) *adj.* floreciente; (*Brit.,* *slang*) desdichado; despreciable.

blooper ('bluː·pər) *n.* error ridículo; disparate.

blossom ('bla·səm) *n.* 1, (flower) flor. 2, (foliage) floración. —*v.i.* 1,

(bloom) florecer; echar flor. 2, (ripen) desarrollarse; madurar.

blot (blat) *n.* 1, (spot) borrón; mancha. 2, (moral stain) mancilla; mancha. —*v.t.* [**blotted, -ting**] 1, (stain) manchar; ensuciar. 2, (spot with ink; scribble) emborronar. 3, (dry; soak up) secar. —*v.i.* mancharse; emborronarse; empañarse; ensuciarse.

blotch (blatʃ) *n.* pintarrajo; mancha; borrón. —*v.t.* manchar; pintarrajear; empañar.

blotter (bla·tər) *n.* 1, (absorbent paper) papel secante. 2, (police journal) libro registro o borrador.

blow (bloː) *v.i.* [**blew, blown** (bloːn), **blowing**] 1, (send forth air) soplar; hacer viento. 2, (produce sound) sonar. 3, (breathe hard) respirar fuerte. 4, (pant) jadear. 5, (explode; burst) explotar; estallar; reventarse. 6, (be carried by the wind) llevarse por el viento. 7, *colloq.* (boast) jactarse. 8, (bloom) florecer. 9, *slang* (leave) irse; marcharse. 10, (burn out, as a fuse) quemarse. —*v.t.* 1, (drive by air) soplar. 2, (cause to sound) sonar; tocar. 3, (scatter) limpiar o diseminar a chorro. 4, (explode) hacer estallar. 5, (burn out, as a fuse) quemar. 6, *slang* (waste) disipar; malgastar. —*n.* 1, (blast) golpe de aire; vendaval; borrasca. 2, (stroke) golpe; manotazo; puñetazo. 3, (disaster) desastre; desdicha; calamidad. 4, (bloom) florescencia. 5, *slang* (boast) jactancia. —**blow down,** derribar. —**blow hot and cold,** vacilar; estar indeciso. —**blow in,** *slang* 1, (arrive) llegar. 2, (spend) gastar; disipar. —**blow off,** 1, (let out pressure) descargar; descargarse; escaparse. 2, *slang* (boast) jactarse. —**blow off steam,** *slang* desahogarse. —**blow out,** 1, (extinguish) apagar. 2, (burst) reventar; reventarse. 3, (escape suddenly) escaparse. 4, (burn out, as a fuse) quemar; quemarse. —**blow over,** pasar; disiparse; olvidarse. —**blow up,** 1, (inflate) inflar. 2, (swell) hinchar; hincharse. 3, (explode; burst) explotar; estallar; saltar; reventar. 4, (become stormy) emborrascarse. 5, (lose one's temper) reventar de ira; enfurecerse.

blowgun ('blo,gʌn) *n.* cerbatana.

blowout ('blo·aut) *n.* 1, (rupture)

escape; reventón; estallido. **2,** *colloq.* (spree) juerga.

blowpipe ('blo,paip) *n.* soplete.

blowtorch ('blo,tortʃ) *n.* soplete; antorcha a soplete.

blubber ('blʌb·ər) *n.* grasa *(de ballena u otro animal).* —*v.i.* gimotear. —*v.t.* hablar con lágrimas; llorar. —**blubber lip,** bezo.

bludgeon ('blʌdʒ·ən) *n.* cachiporra; garrote; porra. —*v.t.* **1,** (strike) aporrear. **2,** (bully) obligar; coaccionar.

blue (bluː) *n.* azul. —*adj.* **1,** (color) azul. **2,** (pallid in face) lívido; exangüe. **3,** (depressed) triste; melancólico; abatido. **4,** (morally strict) puritano; exigente; riguroso. —*v.t.* azular. —**blue law,** ley que limita o prohíbe ciertas actividades los domingos.

bluebell ('bluː·bel) *n.* campanilla.

blueberry ('bluː·ber·i) *n.* mora azul.

bluebird ('bluː·bʌrd) *n.* pájaro cantor; azulejo.

blueblood ('bluː·blʌd) *n., colloq.* aristócrata; sangre azul.

blue-collar *adj.* de obreros; de la clase social de obreros.

bluefish ('bluː·fiʃ) *n.* pez azul.

blueprint ('bluː·prɪnt) *n.* plano. —*v.t.* hacer un plano de; levantar un plano de.

blues (bluːz) *n.pl.* **1,** *mus.* variedad de música de jazz. **2,** (sadness) tristeza; melancolía.

bluff (blʌf) *v.t. & i.* alardear; baladronear. —*n.* **1,** (deception) fanfarronada; alarde; baladronada. **2,** (hill) colina o risco escarpado. —*adj.* **1,** (abrupt) rudo; áspero. **2,** (broad) abierto; ancho.

bluish ('bluː·ɪʃ) *adj.* azulado; azulino.

blunder ('blʌn·dər) *n.* disparate; dislate; estupidez. —*v.i.* **1,** (err grossly) disparatar. **2,** (move blindly) desatinar. —*v.t.* **1,** (confuse) confundir. **2,** (bungle) chapucear.

blunderbuss ('blʌn·dər·bʌs) *n.* trabuco.

blunt (blʌnt) *adj.* **1,** (not sharp) obtuso; romo. **2,** (abrupt) bronco; brusco; abrupto. —*v.t.* **1,** (dull) embotar; enervar. **2,** (lessen pain) calmar un dolor. —**bluntness,** *n.* embotadura; brusquedad.

blur (blʌr) *v.t.* [**blurred, blurring**] **1,** (obscure) empañar; hacer borro-

so. **2,** (stain) manchar; ensuciar. —*v.i.* empañarse. —*n.* mancha; borrón; trazo borroso. —**blurry,** *adj.* emborronado; confuso. —**blurriness,** *n.* emborronamiento; ensuciamiento.

blurt (blʌrt) *v.t.* decir o hablar abruptamente; hablar a tontas y a locas.

blush (blʌʃ) *v.i.* sonrojarse; ruborizarse; avergonzarse. —*n.* rubor; sonrojo.

bluster ('blʌs·tər) *v.i.* **1,** (swagger) fanfarronear; bravear. **2,** (bellow) bramar; rugir. —*n.* **1,** (bravado) fanfarronada; jactancia. **2,** (loud roar) rugido; bramido.

boa ('boː·ə) *n.* boa.

boar (borr) *n.* jabalí; verraco.

board (bord) *n.* **1,** (wooden strip) tabla; tablero. **2,** (table) mesa. **3,** (meals) pensión; alimentos. **4,** (group of officials) consejo; junta. **5,** *naut.* bordo; borde. **6,** *comput.* tarjeta; placa. —*v.t.* **1,** (cover with wood) entablar; enmaderar. **2,** (give meals) tomar a pupilaje. **3,** (embark) abordar. —*v.i.* estar de pupilo. —**boarding house,** pensión; casa de huéspedes. —**board of directors,** junta directiva.

boast (bost) *v.i.* **1,** (brag) jactarse; alardear. **2,** (be justly proud) alabarse. —*v.t.* **1,** (exult) exaltar. **2,** (show off) ostentar. —*n.* jactancia; alarde; ostentación. —**boastful,** *adj.* jactancioso; fanfarrón.

boat (bot) *n.* **1,** (vessel) bote; barca. **2,** (gravy dish) salsera. —*v.i.* navegar; embarcarse. —**boater,** *n.* **1,** barquero. **2,** sombrero de paja rígida. —**boating,** *n.* paseo en bote. —**be in the same boat,** correr la misma suerte.

boat hook bichero.

boatman ('bot·mən) *n.* [*pl.* **-men**] barquero.

boatswain ('boː·sən) *n.* contramaestre.

bob (bab) *n.* **1,** (jerk) sacudida; tirón; sacudimiento. **2,** (pendant) colgante. **3,** (plumb line) plomada. **4,** (fishing float) flotador de pesca. **5,** (haircut) pelo corto. **6,** *colloq.* (shilling) chelín. —*v.i.* [**bobbed, bobbing**] sacudirse; bambolear. —*v.t.* **1,** (cut short) cortar corto (el pelo). **2,** (rap) dar con el codo o la mano.

bobbin ('bab·ɪn) *n.* bobina; carrete.

bobby socks, *también,* **bobby sox,** medias cortas.

bobbysoxer ('bɔb·i,sɔk·sər) *n.* tobillera.

bobcat ('bɔb,kæt) *n.* gato montés.

bobsled ('bɔb,slɛd) *n.* trineo de balancín.

bode (boːd) *v.t. & i.* presagiar; pronosticar; vaticinar.

bode (boːd) *v., pret. & p.p. de* **bide.**

bodice ('bad·ɪs) *n.* corpiño; jubón.

bodily ('bad·ə·li) *adj.* corpóreo; corporal.

body ('ba·di) *n.* **1,** *anat.* cuerpo. **2,** (group) corporación; gremio; cuerpo. **3,** (collection) colección. **4,** (density) espesor; consistencia. **5,** (of a car) carrocería. **6,** (of a truck) caja.

bodyguard ('ba·di,gard) *n.* salvaguardia.

Boer (boːr) *n. & adj.* bóer.

bog (baːg) *n.* pantano; ciénaga; fangal. —*v.t. & i.* (**bogged, bogging**) empantanar(se); enfangar(se).

boggle ('bɔg·əl) *v.t. & i.* espantar(se); sobresaltar(se).

bogus ('bo·gəs) *adj.* engañoso; falso; fingido.

bogy ('bo·gi) *también,* **bogie** *n.* fantasma; espectro; coco; bu.

Bohemian (bo'hi·mi·ən) *n. & adj., también, l.c.* bohemio.

boil (bɔil) *v.i.* **1,** (become hot) hervir; bullir. **2,** *fig.* (be excited) agitarse; excitarse; airarse. —*v.t.* **1,** (cook) hervir; cocer. **2,** [*usu.,* **boil down**] (condense) condensar. —*n.* **1,** (boiling state) hervor; ebullición. **2,** (skin sore) furúnculo; divieso.

boiler ('bɔi·lər) *n.* **1,** (caldron) caldera. **2,** (water heater) termosifón.

boilermaker ('bɔi·lər,mei·kər) *n.* calderero.

boisterous ('bɔi·stə·rəs) *adj.* ruidoso; tempestuoso; vocinglero. —**boisterousness,** *n.* turbulencia; vociglería; impetuosidad.

bold (boːld) *adj.* **1,** (daring) valiente; bravo; audaz. **2,** (impudent) impudente; temerario; descarado. **3,** (conspicuous) prominente; sobresaliente. —**boldness,** *n.* valentía; audacia.

boldface ('bold·fes) *n., print.* negrilla.

bolero (bo'lɛr·o) *n.* [*pl.* -**ros**] bolero.

boll (boːl) *n.* cápsula. —**boll weevil,** gorgojo.

bologna (bə'lo·njə; -ni) *n.* boloña.

bolo knife ('bo·lo) bolo.

boloney (bə'lo·ni) *n., slang* = **baloney.**

Bolshevik ('bol·ʃə·vɪk) *n.* [*pl.* -**viki** (-vi·ki)] bolchevique. —**Bolshevism,** *n.* bolchevismo; bolcheviquismo. —**Bolshevist,** *n.* bolchevique.

bolster ('bols·stər) *n.* **1,** (long pillow) amohadón cilíndrico. **2,** (support) soporte; travesero. —*v.t.* soportar; reforzar.

bolt (bolt) *n.* **1,** (metal pin) perno. **2,** (bar in a lock) pestillo. **3,** (arrow) dardo; flecha. **4,** (roll of material) pieza o rollo de tela. **5,** (stroke of thunder or lightning) rayo. **6,** (flight) fuga; deserción. **7,** (lock) cerrojo; pestillo. —*v.t.* **1,** (lock) cerrar; asegurar. **2,** (swallow) engullir; tragar. **3,** (sift) cerner. —*v.i.* desertar; escapar. —*adv.* repentinamente; abruptamente.

bomb (bam) *n.* **1,** (missile) bomba. **2,** (lava mass) masa de lava. **3,** *slang* (failure) fracaso; fiasco. —*v.t. & i.* bombardear. —*v.i., slang* (fail) fracasar. —**bomber,** *n.* bombardero.

bombard (bam'baːrd) *v.t.* bombardear. —**bombardier** (-bər'dɪr) *n.* bombardero. —**bombardment,** *n.* bombardeo.

bombast ('bam·bæst) *n.* palabras altisonantes. —**bombastic** (bam'bæs·tɪk) *adj.* bombástico; altisonante; ampuloso.

bombshell ('bam,ʃɛl) *n.* **1,** (bomb) bomba. **2,** *slang, fig.* catástrofe; estallido.

bona fide ('bo·nə·faid) buena fe. —*adj.* sincero; franco; genuino.

bonanza (bo'næn·zə) *n.* bonanza.

bonbon ('ban·ban) *n.* bombón.

bond (baːnd) *n.* **1,** (binder) lazo; vínculo; unión. **2,** (duty) obligación. **3,** *comm.* bono; obligación. **4,** (binding substance) adhesivo. **5,** (type of paper) papel de tina o marca. —*v.t.* **1,** (give in trust) depositar. **2,** (pledge) empeñar. **3,** (form into a mass) ligar; trabar. —*v.i.* adherirse; juntarse.

bondman ('bɔnd·mən) *n.* [*pl.* -**men**] esclavo. —**bondwoman** [*pl.* -**women**] esclava. *También,* **bondmaid.**

bondage ('ban·dɪdʒ) *n.* esclavitud; servidumbre; cautiverio.

bondholder ('band,hol·dər) *n.* obligacionista.

bondsman ('bandz·mən) *n.* [*pl.* -men] fiador; fianza.

bone (boːn) *n.* 1, *anat.* hueso. 2, (of fish) espina. 3, (ivory) marfil. 4, (corset stiffening) ballena. —*v.t.* 1, (remove bones) desosar; deshuesar. 2, (stiffen) emballenar. —*v.i., colloq.* (study hard) empollar. —bone up on, empollar sobre.

bonehead ('bon‚hɛd) *n.* estúpido; ignorante.

bonfire ('ban·fair) *n.* fogata; hoguera.

boner ('bo·nər) *n. colloq.* plancha; error ridículo.

bong (bɔŋ) *n.* sonido de una campana o semejante. —*v.t. & i.* sonar como campana.

bongo drum ('baŋ·go) bongó.

bonito (bə'ni·to) *n., ichthy.* bonito.

bonnet ('ban·ɪt) *n.* cofia; sombrero de cofia.

bonny ('ban·i) *adj.* bonito [*fem.* bonita].

bonus ('bo·nəs) *n.* bono; gratificación económica.

bony ('bo·ni) *adj.* 1, (with or like bones) huesudo; anguloso. 2, (thin) delgado; flaco. —boniness, *n.* delgadez; flacura.

boo (buː) *interj.* 1, (to frighten) ¡bu! 2, (to express disapproval) ¡fuera! —*n.* chifla; rechifla. —*v.t. & i.* rechiflar.

boob (buːb) *n., slang* necio; tonto. —boob tube, *colloq.* televisión.

booby ('bu·bi) *n.* 1, (stupid person) estúpido. 2, (person with the worst score) bobo. 3, *ornith.* pato bobo. —booby trap, trampa explosiva.

boodle ('bu·dəl) *n.* 1, (bribe; graft) soborno. 2, (loot) botín.

book (bʊk) *n.* 1, (printed work) libro. 2, (notebook) libreta. 3, *theat.* libreto. —*v.t.* inscribir; registrar; reservar; planear.

bookbinder ('bʊk‚bain·dər) *n.* encuadernador. —bookbindery, *n.* taller de encuadernación. —bookbinding, *n.* encuadernación.

bookcase ('bʊk‚keis) *n.* armario para libros; biblioteca.

bookend ('bʊk‚ɛnd) *n.* sujetalibros.

bookie ('bʊk·i) *n., colloq.* = bookmaker.

bookish ('bʊk·ɪʃ) *adj.* pedante; estudioso.

bookkeeper ('bʊk·kip·ər) *n.* contador; tenedor de libros. —bookkeeping, *n.* contabilidad; teneduría de libros.

booklet ('bʊk·lət) *n.* folleto; opúsculo.

bookmaker ('bʊk‚mei·kər) *n.* corredor de apuestas.

bookworm ('bʊk·wʌrm) *n.* 1, (insect) polilla de libros. 2, (diligent reader) ratón de biblioteca; empollón.

boom (buːm) *n.* 1, (sound) estampido. 2, (increase) alza; auge. 3, *naut.* botalón; botavara. 4, (arm of a derrick) brazo de grúa o de taladro. 5, (underwater trap) barrera de puerto. —*v.t.* 1, (announce loudly) anunciar a bombo y platillo. 2, (promote) promover. —*v.i.* 1, (emit a sound) hacer estampido. 2, (flourish) estar en auge.

boomerang ('bu·mə‚ræŋ) *n.* bumerang. —*v.i.* tener resultado malo, opuesto al que se esperaba.

boon (buːn) *n.* 1, (welcome gift) dádiva; donación; regalo. 2, (favor) gracia; favor. —*adj.* convival; festivo.

boondocks ('buːn‚dɔks) *n.* selva; lugar remoto.

boondoggle ('buːn‚dɔg·əl) *n.* proyecto pródigo o derrochador. —*v.i.* montar tal proyecto.

boor (buːr) *n.* 1, (rude person) zafio; tosco. 2, (peasant) patán; aldeano. —boorish, *adj.* tosco; grosero.

boost (buːst) *v.t.* 1, (raise) empujar hacia arriba; alzar. 2, *colloq.* (promote) ayudar; favorecer; alentar. —*n.* 1, (lift) empujón hacia arriba; alza. 2, (help) asistencia; ayuda.

booster ('bust·ər) *n.* 1, *elect.* elevador de potencial. 2, (supporter) partidario; entusiasta.

boot (but) *n.* 1, (footwear) bota. 2, (kick) puntapié; patada. 3, *slang* (dismissal) patada. 4, *comput.* carga inicial. —*v.t.* 1, (kick) dar puntapiés; patear. 2, *slang* (expel) despedir; echar. 3, *colloq.* (botch) chapucear. 4, (put shoes on) calzar. 5, *comput.* poner en marcha (un sistema). —to boot, además.

bootblack ('but‚blæk) *n.* limpiabotas.

booth (buθ) *n.* casilla; cabina.

bootleg ('but‚lɛg) *n.* licor de contrabando. —*v.t & i.* [bootlegged, -legging] contrabandear en licores. —bootlegger, *n.* contrabandista de licores.

bootmaker ('but‚mei·kər) *n.* botinero.

booty ('bu·ti) *n*. botín.

booze (buːz) *n*., *colloq*. licor. —*v.i.* emborracharse; beber inmoderadamente. —**boozy,** *adj*. borrachín.

borate ('bor·et) *n*. borato. —**borated,** *adj*. boratado.

borax ('bor·æks) *n*. bórax.

bordello (bor'dɛl·o) *n*. burdel; prostíbulo.

border ('bor·dər) *n*. **1,** (edge) borde; orilla; margen. **2,** (boundary) frontera; límite. **3,** (ornament) franja; banda; ribete; orla. —*v.i.* **1,** (touch upon) aproximarse; acercarse. **2,** (confine) confinar; lindar. —*v.t.* ribetear; repulgar.

bore (bor) *n*. **1,** (drill) taladro; barrena. **2,** (hole) agujero. **3,** (of a firearm) calibre. **4,** *mech*. diámetro interno de cilindro. **5,** (tiresome person) pelma; cargante; jorobón. —*v.t.* **1,** (drill) taladrar; barrenar; perforar. **2,** (tire) aburrir; fastidiar. —*v.i.* **1,** (drill) hacer agujeros. **2,** (push ahead) avanzar; adelantarse.

bore (bor) *v.,* *pret. de* **bear.**

boreal ('bor·i·əl) *adj*. boreal; nórdico.

boredom ('bor·dəm) *n*. tedio; fastidio; aburrimiento.

borer ('bor·ər) *n*. **1,** *mech*. barrena; taladro. **2,** *entom*. barrenillo.

boric ('bor·ɪk) *adj*. bórico. —**boric acid,** ácido bórico.

born (born) *adj*. **1,** (innate) nato; congénito. **2,** (entered life) nacido. —**be born,** nacer.

borne (born) *v.,* *p.p. de* **bear.** —*adj*. **1,** (carried) llevado; sostenido. **2,** (endured) sobrellevado; resistido.

boron ('bor·an) *n*. boro.

borough ('bʌr·o) *n*. villa; municipio incorporado; división administrativa (*esp. de una ciudad*).

borrow ('ba·ro) *v.t.* **1,** (take temporarily) tomar prestado; tomar fiado. **2,** (plagiarize) apropiar. —*v.i.* conseguir un préstamo.

borsch (borʃ) *también*, **borsht** (borʃt) *n*. sopa de remolachas.

bosh (baʃ) *n.,* *slang* nadería; tontería.

bosom ('buˑzəm) *n*. **1,** *anat*. seno; pecho. **2,** *fig*. (heart) amor; cariño; corazón. **3,** (dress front) pechera. —*adj*. familiar; querido; íntimo. —*v.t.* **1,** (cherish) abrazar; estimar; acariciar. **2,** (hide) ocultar; esconder.

boss (bɔs) *n*. **1,** *colloq*. (supervisor) jefe; patrón; dueño. **2,** *colloq*. (political chief) jefe; cacique. **3,** (protuberance) nudo; protuberancia; joroba. —*v.t.,* *colloq*. mandar; ordenar; dirigir. —**bossy,** *adj*. dominante.

botany ('bat·ə·ni) *n*. botánica. —**botanical** (bə'tæn·ɪ·kəl) *adj*. botánico. —**botanist,** *n*. botánico; botanista.

botch (batʃ) *v.t.* chapucear; estropear por ineptitud. —*n*. chapucería.

both (boθ) *adj. & pron*. ambos; los dos; entrambos. —*adv. & conj*. tanto como; así como; a la vez; igualmente.

bother ('ba·ðər) *v.t.* molestar; fastidiar; incomodar. —*v.i.* molestarse; incomodarse. —*n*. fastidio; molestia; enojo. —*interj., colloq*. ¡joroba! —**bothersome,** *adj*. enojoso; fastidioso; importuno.

bottle ('bat·əl) *n*. botella; frasco. —*v.t.* embotellar; enfrascar; envasar. —**bottle up,** contener; refrenar.

bottleneck ('bat·əl·nɛk) *n*. taponamiento; congestión; obstáculo.

bottom ('bat·əm) *n*. **1,** (base) fondo; base; cimiento; asiento. **2,** (bed of a river) lecho fluvial. **3,** *naut*. quilla; buque; barco. **4,** (buttocks) asiento; asentaderas. —*adj.* **1,** (lowest) inferior; hondo. **2,** (basic) fundamental; básico. —*v.t.* **1,** (furnish with a bottom) cimentar; asentar; apoyar. **2,** (fathom) repasar; profundizar; escudriñar. —*v.i.* **1,** (be based; rest) apoyarse; reclinarse. **2,** (run aground) encallar.

botulism ('batʃ·ə·lɪz·əm) *n*. botulismo.

boudoir ('bu·dwar) *n*. tocador; gabinete de señora.

bougainvillea (ˌbu·gən'vɪl·jə) *n*. buganvilla.

bough (bau) *n*. rama.

bought (bɔt) *v.,* *pret. & p.p. de* **buy.**

bouillon ('bʊl·jan) *n*. caldo; consomé; consumado.

boulder *también*, **bowlder** ('bol·dər) *n*. peña; roca; canto rodado.

boulevard ('bʊl·ə·ˌvard) *n*. avenida; paseo; bulevar.

bounce (bauns) *v.i.* botar; rebotar; brincar; saltar. —*v.t.* **1,** (toss up and down) hacer saltar o botar. **2,** *slang* (dismiss) despedir; expulsar. —*n.* **1,** (motion) despido; salta; brinco. **2,** *slang* (discharge) expulsión; despido. **3,** (energy) energía; vigor; fuerza. —**bouncing,** *adj.* fuerte; gordiflón.

bound (baund) *pret. & p.p. de* **bind.** —*v.i.* saltar; dar saltos; rebotar. —*v.t.* **1,** (cause to bounce or leap) hacer saltar o botar. **2,** (limit) limitar; lindar. —*n.* **1,** (leap) salto; bote; brinco. **2,** (limit) límite; lindero. **3,** *pl.* (limited area) territorio fronterizo; limítrofe. —*adj.* **1,** (tied) atado; sujeto; ligado. **2,** (covered, as a book) encuadernado. **3,** (obliged) obligado; forzado. **4,** (determined) determinado; resuelto. **5,** (traveling to) destinado; con destino a.

boundary ('baun·də·ri) *n.* límite; frontera.

bounder ('baun·dər) *n., colloq.* bribón; pícaro; maleante.

bounteous ('baun·ti·əs) *adj.* generoso; dadivoso; munífico.

bountiful ('baun·ti·fəl) *adj.* dadivoso; generoso; munífico. —**bountifulness,** *n.* munificencia; liberalidad; generosidad.

bounty ('baun·ti) *n.* **1,** (generosity) generosidad; largueza. **2,** (favor) dádiva; gracia. **3,** (premium) prima; premio.

bouquet (bu'kei) *n.* **1,** (bunch of flowers) buqué; ramillete. **2,** (of wine) buqué; aroma.

bourbon ('bʌr·bən) *n.* **1,** *cap.* (French royal family) Borbón. **2,** (corn whiskey) whisky.

bourgeois (bur'ʒwa) *n. & adj.* burgués. —**bourgeoisie** (-'zi) *n.* burguesía.

bout (baut) *n.* **1,** (contest) combate; pelea; lucha. **2,** (period of struggle) ataque; crisis. **3,** (round; turn) turno; vez.

boutique (bu'tik) *n.* tienda pequeña, esp. de prendas de moda.

bovine ('bo·vain) *adj.* **1,** (oxlike) bovino; vacuno. **2,** (stolid) bruto; estúpido. —*n.* bovino; res.

bow (bau) *v.i.* **1,** (bend) doblarse; inclinarse; arquearse. **2,** (yield) ceder; someterse. **3,** (worship; salute) hacer reverencia; inclinarse. —*v.t.* **1,** (cause to bend) doblar; arquear; inclinar. **2,** (subdue) someter; forzar; obligar. —*n.* **1,** (bend) inclinación; reverencia; saludo. **2,** *naut.* proa.

bow (boː) *n.* **1,** (weapon) arco. **2,** *mus.* arco. **3,** (knot) lazo. **4,** (curve) curva. —*adj.* arqueado; curvado; doblado. —*v.i.* doblarse; arquearse. —*v.t.* doblar; arquear. —**bow compass,** bigotera. —**bow tie,** corbata de lazo.

bowel ('bau·əl) *n.* intestino; *pl.* tripas; entrañas. —**bowel movement,** **1,** (passing of waste) defecación. **2,** (feces) heces; excremento. —**move the bowels,** hacer o irse del cuerpo.

bower ('bau·ər) *n.* **1,** (shaded retreat) emparrado; glorieta. **2,** *poet.* (rustic cottage) enramada; cenador. **3,** *cards* sota.

bowl (boːl) *n.* **1,** (deep dish) cuenco; plato hondo; escudilla. **2,** (basin) palangana; jofaina. **3,** (large cup) tazón. **4,** (cup of a tobacco pipe) hornillo de pipa. **5,** (of a toilet) taza. **6,** (ball) bola. —*v.i.* **1,** (play at bowls) bolear; jugar a bolos. **2,** [*usu.,* **bowl along**] (glide) deslizarse. —*v.t.* **1,** rodar. **2,** [*usu.,* **bowl over** o **down**] (upset) desconcertar; (knock down) derribar.

bowleg ('boː·leg) *n.* pierna corva. —**bowlegged** (-əd) *adj.* patiabierto.

bowling ('boːl·ɪŋ) *n.* juego de bolos; bolos; boliche. —**bowling alley,** bolera; boliche.

bowman ('bo·mən) *n.* [*pl.* **-men**] arquero.

bowls (boːlz) *n.sing.* juego de bolos; bolos.

bowsprit ('bau·sprɪt; 'bo-) *n.* bauprés.

bowwow ('bau'wau) *n.* ladrido. —*v.i.* ladrar.

box (baks) *n.* **1,** (container) caja; (small box) estuche; (large box) cajón. **2,** *theat.* palco. **3,** (outdoor booth or privy) garita; casilla. **4,** (socket; pit) caja. **5,** (enclosed area) cuadro; cuadrado. **6,** (blow) bofetón; bofetada. **7,** *bot.* boj. —*v.t.* **1,** (put in a box) encajonar; guardar; almacenar. **2,** (strike) abofetear; dar puñetazos. —*v.i.* boxear. —**box office,** taquilla.

boxer ('bak·sər) *n.* **1,** (pugilist) boxeador; púgil. **2,** (dog) bóxer.

boxing ('baks·ɪŋ) *n.* **1,** (sport) boxeo; pugilismo. **2,** (packing) embalaje; empaque.

boxwood ('baks·wʊd) *n.* boj.

boy (bɔi) *n.* **1,** (male child) niño; chico; muchacho. **2,** (servant) mozo; sirviente; criado. —**boy-**

hood, *n.* niñez; infancia. —**boyish,** *adj.* aniñado. —**boyfriend, 1,** *colloq.* (escort) amigo; íntimo. **2,** *colloq.* (sweetheart) novio.

boycott ('bɔi·kat) *n.* boicot; boicoteo. —*v.t.* boicotear.

Boy Scout explorador.

bra (braː) *n.*, *colloq.* = **brassiere.**

brace (breis) *n.* **1,** (fastener) abrazadera; grapa; traba. **2,** (support, as for guy wire) tirante; refuerzo. **3,** *archit.* riostra. **4,** *dent.* mordaza. **5,** *carp.*, berbiquí. **6,** *pl.* (suspenders) tirantes. **7,** *mus.* corchete. **8,** (couple) par; pareja. —*v.t.* **1,** (join) juntar; ligar. **2,** (make tense) reforzar; fortalecer. —**brace up,** resolverse; decidirse.

bracelet ('breis·lət) *n.* **1,** (wrist band) brazalete; pulsera. **2,** (handcuff) esposas.

brachial ('brei·ki·əl) *adj.* braquial.

bracket ('bræk·ɪt) *n.* **1,** (shelf support) brazo; soporte. **2,** (small shelf) repisa. **3,** *print.* paréntesis angular. **4,** (category) categoría; clase. —*v.t.* **1,** (support) aguantar; sostener. **2,** *print.* poner paréntesis a. **3,** (classify) clasificar; agrupar.

brackish ('bræk·ɪʃ) *adj.* salado; salobre. —**brackishness,** *n.* salobridad.

brad (bræd) *n.* clavo corto y delgado.

brag (bræːg) *v.i.* [**bragged, bragging**] fanfarronear; jactarse; vanagloriarse. —*n.* **1,** (boast) fanfarronada; jactancia. **2,** (boaster) fanfarrón; jactancioso.

braggadocio (ˌbræg·ə'do·ʃi,o) *n.* [*pl.* -**os** (-,oːz)] **1,** (vain boasting) fanfarronada. **2,** (braggart) fanfarrón.

braggart ('bræg·ərt) *n.* fanfarrón; jactancioso.

Brahman ('braː·mən) *también,* **Brahmin** (-mɪn) *n.* brahmán. —**Brahmanism,** *n.* brahmanismo.

braid (breid) *v.t.* **1,** (plait) entrelazar; trenzar. **2,** (weave) entretejer. —*n.* **1,** (ornamental tape) galón; fleco; cordoncillo. **2,** (braided hair) trenza.

Braille (breil) *n.* Braille.

brain (brein) *n.* **1,** *anat.* cerebro. **2,** *usu.pl.*, (intelligence) inteligencia; conocimiento. —*v.t.* descalabrar. —**brainy,** *adj.* inteligente; entendido; listo.

brainstorm ('brein·storm) *n.*, *colloq.* ocurrencia; idea.

brain teaser ('tiː·zər) rompecabezas.

brain trust *slang* grupo de especialistas consejeros.

brainwashing ('brein,woʃ·ɪŋ) *n.* adoctrinamiento forzoso. —**brainwash,** *v.t.* adoctrinar por persuasión intensa.

braise (breiz) *v.t.* asar a la brasa.

brake (breik) *n.* **1,** (stopping device) freno. **2,** (thicket) matorral; maleza. —*v.t.* frenar; parar.

brakeman ('breik·mən) *n.* [*pl.* -**men**] guardafrenos.

bramble ('bræm·bəl) *n.* zarza; espino. —**brambly** (-bli) *adj.* zarzoso; espinoso.

bran (bræːn) *n.* salvado; afrecho; bren.

branch (bræntʃ) *n.* **1,** (limb of a tree) rama; (of a vine) sarmiento. **2,** (offshoot) rama; sección; división. **3,** (arm of a river) riachuelo; tributario; brazo. **4,** *comm.* sucursal. —*v.i.* **1,** (put forth branches) enramar. **2,** (extend) ramificarse; extenderse. —**branch off,** bifurcarse; apartarse. —**branch out,** extenderse; ramificarse.

branchial ('bræn·ki·əl) *adj.* branquial.

brand (bræːnd) *n.* **1,** (flaming stick) tizón. **2,** (identifying mark) marca a fuego. **3,** (marking iron) marcador. **4,** (label; make) marca; nombre. **5,** (quality) calidad; clase. **6,** (stigma) estigma; baldón. —*v.t.* **1,** (mark) marcar. **2,** (stigmatize) infamar; tildar; manchar. —**brand new,** sin usar; nuevo.

brandish ('bræn·dɪʃ) *v.t.* blandir; sacudir; mover.

brandy ('bræn·di) *n.* coñac. —*v.t.* aromatizar con o mojar en coñac. —**brandied,** adj. con o en coñac.

brash (bræʃ) *adj.* **1,** (reckless) impetuoso; temerario. **2,** (impudent) desvergonzado; impudente.

brashness ('bræʃ·nəs) *n.* **1,** (recklessness) impetuosidad. **2,** (impudence) impudicia.

brass (bræs) *n.* **1,** (alloy) latón. **2,** *mus.* metales; instrumentos metálicos de viento. **3,** *colloq.* (impudence) desvergüenza; impudicia. **4,** *slang* (persons in authority) peces gordos.

brassard ('bræs·ard) *n.* brazal.

brass band charanga.

brassiere (brə'ziːr) *n.* sostén; corpiño; *Amer.* ajustador.

brassiness ('bræs·ɪ·nəs) *n.* **1,** (brassy quality) calidad de latón. **2,** *colloq.* (impudence) desfachatez; desvergüenza; descaro.

brassy ('bræs·i) *adj.* **1,** (of brass) de latón. **2,** *colloq.* (impudent) desvergonzado; desfachatado.

brat (bræt) *n.* niño malcriado.

bravado (brə'va·do) *n.* bravata; bravuconería.

brave (breiv) *adj.* bravo; valiente; intrépido. —*n.* guerrero indio. —*v.t.* arrostrar; desafiar. —**braveness, bravery,** *n.* bravura; valor; coraje.

bravo ('bra·vo) *interj.* ¡bravo!

bravura (brə'vjʊ·rə) *n.* **1,** *mus.* ejecución virtuosa. **2,** valentía; intrepidez.

brawl (brɔːl) *n.* **1,** (quarrel) pendencia; disputa; camorra. **2,** *slang* (noisy party) juerga; alboroto; jaleo. —*v.i.* **1,** (quarrel noisily) pendenciar; disputar. **2,** *slang* (carouse) jaranear; alborotar.

brawn (brɔːn) *n.* **1,** (muscular strength) músculo; vigor. **2,** (meat) carne dura; carne de jabalí. —**brawny,** *adj.* muscular; membrudo; fuerte.

bray (brei) *n.* rebuzno. —*v.i.* rebuznar. —*v.t.* triturar; pulverizar; moler.

braze (breiz) *v.t.* **1,** (solder) soldar con latón. **2,** (cover with brass) broncear.

brazen ('brei·zən) *adj.* **1,** (of brass) de latón. **2,** (shameless) insolente; descarado. —*v.t.* [*usu.,* **brazen out**] sostener descaradamente; encarar con insolencia. —**brazenness,** *n.* desvergüenza; desfachatez.

brazier ('brei·ʒ·ər) *n.* **1,** (worker in brass) latonero; calderero. **2,** (iron vessel) brasero; calentador.

breach (britʃ) *n.* **1,** (break) brecha; abertura. **2,** *law* infracción; violación. **3,** (disagreement) interrupción; brecha; disensión. —*v.t.* romper; quebrar.

bread (brɛd) *n.* **1,** (food) pan. **2,** *fig.* (necessities of life) sustento; comida; alimentos. —*v.t.* empanar.

breadfruit ('brɛd·frut) *n.* **1,** (fruit) fruto del pan. **2,** (tree) árbol del pan.

breadstuff ('brɛd·stʌf) *n.* harina; cereal.

breadth (brɛdθ) *n.* **1,** (width) anchura; ancho. **2,** (liberality) amplitud; liberalidad. **3,** (broadness) holgura.

breadwinner ('brɛd·wɪn·ər) *n.* productor; trabajador; quien gana el pan.

break (breik) *v.t.* [**broke, broken, breaking**] **1,** (shatter) romper; quebrar; destrozar. **2,** (interrupt) interrumpir. **3,** (discontinue) suspender; discontinuar. **4,** (change) cambiar. **5,** (tame) adiestrar; entrenar; amansar. **6,** (violate) infringir; violar. **7,** (make known) descubrir. **8,** (demote) degradar; destituir. **9,** (soften; weaken) amortiguar; debilitar. **10,** (surpass) batir; exceder. **11,** (bankrupt) arruinar; quebrar. **12,** [*usu.,* **break down**] (analyze) dividir; separar; analizar. **13,** [*usu.,* **break off**] (discontinue) suspender; cesar. —*v.i.* **1,** (be shattered) romperse; quebrarse. **2,** (change) cambiar; variar. **3,** (burst) reventar. **4,** (come into being) rayar; apuntar. **5,** [*usu.,* **break in**] (force one's way) forzar; entrar violentamente. **6,** [*usu.,* **break down**] (fall ill) enfermarse; quebrantarse. **7,** (give way to emotions) desfallecer; desanimarse. **8,** [*usu.,* **break up** o **with**] (quarrel) disband) pelear; separarse; romper. —*n.* **1,** (breach) brecha; abertura; grieta. **2,** (interruption) pausa; descanso; suspensión; interrupción. **3,** (sudden change) desviación. —**breakable,** *n. & adj.* frágil.

breakage ('breik·ɪdʒ) *n.* **1,** (break) rotura; fractura. **2,** (indemnity) indemnización.

breakdown ('breik·daun) *n.* **1,** *med.* trastorno; agotamiento; colapso. **2,** *mech.* parada; derrumbamiento.

breaker ('breik·ər) *n.* **1,** (tool; worker) roturador; rompedor. **2,** (ocean wave) ola rompiente.

breakfast ('brɛk·fəst) *n.* desayuno. —*v.i.* desayunar.

breakneck ('breik·nɛk) *adj.* precipitado; peligroso; apresurado.

breakthrough ('breik·θru) *n.* brecha; abertura.

breakup ('breik·ʌp) *n.* ruptura.

breakwater ('breik·wat·ər) *n.* escollera; rompeolas.

bream (briːm) *n., ichthy.* brema.

breast (brɛst) *n.* **1,** (chest) pecho. **2,** (mammary gland) pezón. **3,** *fig.* (seat of emotions) corazón. —*v.t.* **1,** (move forward against) empujar con el pecho. **2,** (face) arrostrar; encarar; apechugar.

breastbone ('brɛst·bon) *n.* esternón.

breastwork ('brɛst·wʌrk) *n.* parapeto; barricada.

breath (brɛθ) *n.* **1,** (air inhaled or exhaled) aliento. **2,** (light breeze) hálito; soplo. **3,** (moment) instante; segundo. **4,** (faint scent) vaharada. **5,** (trifle) fruslería; friolera; trivialidad. —**catch one's breath, 1,** (pant) jadear; palpitar. **2,** (rest) recuperarse; recobrar el aliento. —**in one breath,** en seguida; de un tirón. —**under one's breath,** en voz baja; en un murmullo. —**with bated breath,** con aliento pasmado.

breathe (briːð) *v.i.* **1,** (respire) respirar; alentar. **2,** (live) vivir. **3,** (rest) descansar; reposar. —*v.t.* **1,** (inhale and exhale) respirar; inhalar; exhalar. **2,** (whisper) susurrar; murmurar. —**breather,** *n., colloq.* respiro; descanso.

breathless ('brɛθ·ləs) *adj.* **1,** (panting) jadeante; sofocado; sin aliento. **2,** (thrilled) emocionante; impresionante; tenso. —**breathlessness,** *n.* sofocación; desaliento.

breathtaking ('brɛθ·teik·ɪŋ) *adj.* impresionante; excitante; emocionante.

bred (brɛd) *v.,* pret. & p.p. de **breed.**

breech (britʃ) *n.* **1,** (of a gun) culata. **2,** (buttocks) trasero; nalgas; posaderas.

breechcloth ('britʃ·klɔθ) *n.* taparrabo.

breeches ('britʃ·əz) *n.* calzones.

breed (briːd) *v.t.* [*pret.* & *p.p.* **bred**] **1,** (beget) engendrar; procrear. **2,** (produce) producir; crear. **3,** (rear) criar; educar. —*v.i.* **1,** (be produced) producirse; criarse. **2,** (reproduce) reproducirse; desarrollarse —*n.* raza; casta.

breeder ('briː·dər) *n.* **1,** (reproducing plant or animal) generador; (person) criador. **2,** (source) causa; fuente; origen.

breeding ('bri·dɪŋ) *n.* **1,** (upbringing) crianza. **2,** (gentility) modales; educación.

breeze (briːz) *n.* **1,** (light wind) brisa; soplo. **2,** *colloq.* (disturbance) conmoción; barullo. —*v.i.* **1,** (blow lightly) soplar. **2,** *colloq.* (move briskly) volar.

breezy ('briz·i) *adj.* **1,** (mildly windy) refrescado con brisas. **2,**

(brisk) animado; vivo. **3,** *colloq.* (pert) descarado; atrevido.

brethren ('brɛð·rən) *n.pl.* **1,** (brothers) hermanos. **2,** (associates) compañeros; *relig.* correligionarios.

Breton ('brɛt·ən) *adj.* & *n.* bretón.

breve (briːv) *n.* **1,** *mus.* breve. **2,** *print.*; *gram.* marca de brevedad.

brevet (brə'vɛt) *adj.* graduado; honorario. —*n.* grado honorario; comisión honoraria. —*v.t.* dar un ascenso honorífico; dar una comisión honoraria.

breviary ('bri·vi·ɛr·i) *n.* breviario.

brevity ('brɛv·ə·ti) *n.* brevedad; concisión.

brew (bruː) *v.t.* **1,** (ferment) fermentar. **2,** (steep, as tea) hervir. —*v.i.* (gather) formarse; fraguarse. —*n.* mezcla; cocción; cerveza.

brewer ('bru·ər) *n.* cervecero. —**brewery,** *n.* cervecería; fábrica de cerveza.

briar ('brai·ər) *n.* = **brier.**

bribe (braib) *n.* soborno; cohecho. —*v.t.* sobornar; cohechar. —**bribery,** *n.* soborno; cohecho.

bric-a-brac ('brɪk·ə·bræk) *n.* bric-a-brac; chucherías; curiosidades.

brick (brɪk) *n.* **1,** (block) ladrillo; loseta; *Mex.* adobe. **2,** *colloq.* (good fellow) buen chico. —*adj.* de ladrillos. —*v.t.* [*usu.,* **brick up**] enladrillar.

brickbat ('brɪk·bæt) *n.* ladrillo; teja.

bricklayer ('brɪk,lei·ər) *n.* enladrillador.

brickwork ('brɪk·wʌrk) *n.* enladrillado.

bridal ('brai·dəl) *adj.* **1,** (of or pert. to a bride or bridal couple) de novia; de novios. **2,** (nuptial) nupcial. —*n.* boda.

bride (braid) *n.* **1,** (before marriage) novia. **2,** (after marriage) desposada; recién casada.

bridegroom ('braid·grum) *n.* novio.

bridesmaid ('braidz·meid) *n.* madrina de boda.

bridge (brɪdʒ) *n.* **1,** (structure) puente. **2,** (of the nose) caballete; puente. **3,** *naut.*; *mus.* puente. **4,** (card game) bridge. **5,** *elect.* paralelo. **6,** *dent.* puente. —*v.t.* **1,** (build a bridge across) tender un puente sobre. **2,** (span; get across) salvar; cruzar.

bridgehead ('brɪdʒ·hɛd) *n.* cabeza de puente.

bridle (brai·dəl) *n.* **1,** (of a horse) brida. **2,** (restraint) freno; sujeción. —*v.t.* embridar; refrenar; controlar. —*v.i.* erguirse; alterarse. —**bridle path,** camino de herradura.

brief (brif) *adj.* breve; corto; conciso. —*n.* sumario; resumen. —*v.t.* **1,** (epitomize) condensar; resumir. **2,** (inform) informar; dar cuenta a o de. —**briefing,** *n.* resumen; información breve. —**briefness,** *n.* brevedad.

briefcase ('brif·keis) *n.* cartera; portafolio.

brier también, **briar** ('brai·ər) *n.* **1,** (prickly shrub) zarza. **2,** (tree heath, used for making pipes) brezo. —**briar patch,** zarzal. —**brier pipe,** pipa hecha de madera de brezo.

brig (brɪg) *n.* **1,** (ship) bergantín. **2,** (ship's prison) calabozo (de un buque).

brigade (brɪ'geid) *n.* brigada.

brigadier (,brɪg·ə'dɪr) *n.* brigadier. —**brigadier general,** general de brigada; brigadier.

brigand ('brɪg·ənd) *n.* bandido; salteador; bandolero. —**brigandage,** *n.* bandidaje; bandolerismo.

brigantine ('brɪg·ən·tin; -tain) *n.* bergantín.

bright (brait) *adj.* **1,** (shining) claro; brillante; reluciente. **2,** (sunny) asoleado; luminoso. **3,** (clever) despejado; vivaz; despierto. **4,** (vivacious) alegre; feliz; vivaz. **5,** (illustrious) eminente; preclaro; ilustre.

brighten ('brait·ən) *v.t.* **1,** (make bright) abrillantar; aclarar. **2,** (cheer up) alegrar; animar. —*v.i.* **1,** (become bright) aclararse; despejarse. **2,** (gladden) alegrarse; animarse.

brightness ('brait·nəs) *n.* **1,** (quality) brillo; esplendor. **2,** (cleverness) agudeza; viveza.

brilliance ('brɪl·jəns) *n.* **1,** (luster) brillantez; lustre; magnificencia. **2,** (mental superiority) inteligencia; brillantez. **3,** (vivacity) agudeza; viveza. —**brilliant,** *adj.* brillante. —*n.* brillante; diamante.

brim (brɪm) *n.* **1,** (edge) borde; orilla. **2,** (rim of a hat) ala. —**brimful,** *adj.* rebosante; colmado.

brimstone ('brɪm·ston) *n.* azufre. —*adj.* azufroso; sulfuroso.

brine (brain) *n.* **1,** (salt solution) salmuera. **2,** (the sea) mar. —**briny**

(-ni) *adj.* salobre; salado. —*n.,* *slang* el mar.

bring (brɪŋ) *v.t.* [*pret. & p.p.* **brought**] **1,** (carry) traer; llevar. **2,** (yield) producir; dar. **3,** [*usu.,* **bring around**] (induce) inducir; persuadir. **4,** (command as a price) tener; alcanzar. **5,** [*usu.,* **bring about**] (cause) resultar; causar. **6,** *law* presentar. —**bring forth, 1,** (give birth to) parir; dar a luz. **2,** (produce) producir; dar. **3,** (disclose) descubrir; poner de manifiesto. —**bring in, 1,** (import) importar; traer. **2,** (produce as income) producir; entrar; obtener. **3,** (give a verdict) dar un fallo. **4,** (report) informar; presentar. —**bring off,** completar; realizar. —**bring on,** causar; comenzar. —**bring to, 1,** (revive) reanimar. **2,** *naut.* ponerse a la capa. —**bring up, 1,** (raise) educar; criar. **2,** (introduce) traer a colación; introducir.

brink (brɪŋk) *n.* borde; margen.

brioche (bri'ɔʃ) *n.* bollo; brioche.

briquette (brɪ'ket) *n.* briqueta.

brisk (brɪsk) *adj.* vivo; fuerte; enérgico. —**briskness,** *n.* animación; viveza; energía.

bristle ('brɪs·əl) *n.* **1,** (of hair) cerda. **2,** (of a brush) cerda; púa. —*v.i.* erizarse. —**bristly** (-li) *adj.* erizado.

bristling ('brɪs·lɪŋ) *adj.* **1,** (prickly) espinoso; erizado. **2,** (resentful) rencoroso; resentido.

Britain ('brɪt·ən) *n.* Bretaña; la gran Bretaña.

Britannia (brɪ'tæn·i·ə) *n.* = Britain. —**britannia metal,** metal británico.

Britannic (brɪ'tæn·ɪk) *adj.* británico.

British ('brɪt·ɪʃ) *adj.* británico; britano; inglés. —**the British,** los britanos; los ingleses.

Briton ('brɪt·ən) *n.* britano; inglés.

brittle ('brɪt·əl) *adj.* **1,** (fragile) frágil; quebradizo. **2,** (crisp) tieso; crespo. —*n.* dulce acaramelado duro. —**brittleness,** *n.* fragilidad.

broach (brotʃ) *n.* **1,** (tool) broca; lezna. **2,** (brooch) broche; prendedor. —*v.t.* **1,** (pierce) taladrar; agujerear. **2,** (bring up) introducir; presentar; abordar.

broad (brɔd) *adj.* **1,** (wide) ancho; amplio. **2,** (widespread) abierto; claro. **3,** (liberal) tolerante; liberal. **4,** (pronounced openly) abierto.

5, (extensive) general; amplio. 6, (indelicate) descomedido; rudo. —**broaden,** *v.t.* & *i.* ensanchar(se). —**broad jump,** salto de longitud.

broadcast ('brɔd·kæst) *adj.* conocido; público. —*n.* emisión; radiodifusión. —*v.t.* [*pret.* & *p.p.* **-cast** o **-casted**] 1, (scatter) diseminar; esparcir. 2, *radio; TV* emitir; radiar. —*v.i.* radiar; radiodifundir; dar emisiones. —*adv.* por todas partes. —**broadcasting,** *n.* emisión; radiodifusión.

broadcloth ('brɔd,klɔθ) *n.* paño fino.

broadminded ('brɔd,main·dɪd) *adj.* liberal; tolerante; comprensivo.

broad-shouldered ('brɔd,ʃol·dərd) *adj.* espaldudo; ancho de espaldas.

broadside ('brɔd·said) *n.* 1, *naut.* (side of a ship) costado. 2, *naut.* (discharge of guns) andanada. 3, *fig.* ataque; andanada. 4, *colloq.* (announcement) anuncio impreso.

broadsword ('brɔd,sord) *n.* montante.

brocade (bro'keid) *n.* brocado. —**brocaded,** *adj.* brocado.

broccoli ('brak·ə·li) *n.* bróculi; brécol.

brochure (bro'ʃur) *n.* folleto.

brogue (broɪg) *n.* 1, [*también,* **brogan** ('bro·gən)] (shoe) zapato fuerte y pesado, muchas veces con perforaciones decorativas. 2, (accent) acento regional, esp. irlandés.

broil (brɔil) *v.t.* asar en parrillas; soasar. —*v.i.* asarse; torrarse. —*n.* soasado; carne soasada.

broiler ('brɔil·ər) *n.* 1, (cooking appliance) parrilla. 2, (fowl) ave para asar.

broke (brok) *v., pret. de* **break.** —*adj., slang* pelado; sin dinero; arruinado.

broken (bro·kən) *v., p.p. de* **break.** —*adj.* 1, (rough; hilly) quebrado; áspero; irregular. 2, (shattered) roto; avenado. 3, (imperfectly spoken) chapurreado; imperfecto. 4, (sick) enfermo; débil; agotado. 5, (breached; violated) quebrantado; roto. 6, (tamed) amaestrado; domado. 7, (subdued) desanimado; desalentado.

broken-down *adj.* impotente; decrépito.

broken-hearted *adj.* angustiado; destrozado; desesperado.

broker ('bro·kər) *n., fin.* corredor

de comercio. —**brokerage** (-ɪdʒ) *n.* corretaje; comisión.

bromide ('bro·maid) *n.* 1, *chem.* bromuro. 2, *colloq.* (cliché) perogrullada; trivialidad. —**bromidic** (-'mɪd·ɪk) *adj., colloq.* trillado; trivial.

bromine ('bro·min) *n.* bromo.

bronchial ('braŋ·ki·əl) *adj.* bronquial.

bronchitis (braŋ'kai·tɪs) *n.* bronquitis.

broncho ('braŋ·ko) *n.* [*pl.* **-chos**] = **bronco.**

bronchoscope ('braŋ·ko·skop) *n.* broncoscopio.

bronchus ('braŋ·kəs) *n.* [*pl.* **-chi** (-kai)] bronquio.

bronco ('braŋ·ko) *n.* [*pl.* **-cos**] potro o caballo bronco.

broncobuster *n.* domador; *Amer.* chalán.

brontosaurus (,bran·tə'sor·əs) *n.* brontosauro.

Bronx cheer (braŋks) pedorreta; *Amer.* trompetilla.

bronze (branz) *n.* bronce. —*v.t.* broncear. —*adj.* broncíneo.

brooch (brotʃ; brutʃ) *n.* broche; prendedor. *También,* **broach.**

brood (brurd) *n.* 1, (litter of animals) cría; (of birds) nidada. 2, (breed; kind) tipo; clase. —*v.i.* 1, (hatch eggs) empollar. 2, (ponder) ponderar; cavilar. —*v.t.* 1, (sit on, as eggs) empollar. 2, (protect) cobijar; amparar. —**broody,** *adj.* preocupado; intranquilo.

brook (bruk) *n.* arroyo; arroyuelo; *Amer.* quebrada. —*v.t.* tolerar; sufrir; aguantar.

broom (brurm) *n.* 1, (brush) escoba. 2, *bot.* retama.

broomstick ('brum·stɪk) *n.* palo de escoba.

broth (brɔθ) *n.* caldo.

brothel ('braθ·əl; braθ-) *n.* burdel; prostíbulo.

brother ('brʌð·ər) *n.* hermano. —**brotherhood,** *n.* fraternidad; hermandad; cofradía. —**brotherly,** *adj.* fraternal. —**brotherliness,** *n.* fraternidad.

brother-in-law *n.* [*pl.* **brothers-in-law**] cuñado; hermano político.

brought (brɔt) *v., pret. & p.p. de* **bring.**

brow (brau) *n.* 1, (eyebrow) ceja. 2, (forehead) frente; sienes. 3, (edge of a cliff) cresta.

browbeat ('brau·bit) *v.t.* intimidar; atemorizar; mirar mal.

brown (braun) *n.* color castaño. —*adj.* pardo; castaño; moreno. —*v.t.* broncear; *cookery* dorar. —**in a brown study,** preocupado.

brownie ('brau·ni) *n.* **1,** (elf) duendecillo. **2,** (kind of cake) galleta de chocolate.

brownout ('braun·aut) *n.* apagón parcial.

brownstone ('braun·ston) *n.* piedra arenisca.

browse (brauz) *n.* pimpollos; renuevos. —*v.t.* ramonear; mordiscar. —*v.i.* **1,** (feed; graze) ramonear; mordiscar. **2,** (read cursorily) hojear. **3,** (look around idly) mirar; curiosear.

bruin ('bru·in) *n.* oso.

bruise (bru:z) *n.* contusión; golpe. —*v.t.* magullar; golpear.

bruiser ('bru·zər) *n.* **1,** (fight) pelea. **2,** (fighter) púgil. **3,** (bully) matón.

brunch (brʌntʃ) *n.*, *colloq.* almuerzo, esp. a hora temprana.

brunette (bru'nɛt) *n. & adj. fem.* trigueña; morena. —**brunet** (-'nɛt) *n. & adj. masc.* trigueño; moreno.

brunt (brʌnt) *n.* choque; esfuerzo.

brush (brʌʃ) *n.* **1,** (shrub) matorral; maleza. **2,** (bristled cleaning tool) escobilla; cepillo. **3,** (for painting) pincel; brocha. **4,** (for shaving) brocha. **5,** (light touch) roce; rozadura. **6,** *elect.* escobilla. **7,** (skirmish) pelea; discusión. —*v.t.* **1,** (sweep) barrer; limpiar. **2,** (rub) frotar; restregar. **3,** (touch lightly) rozar. —*v.i.* **1,** [*usu.,* **brush by**] (sweep past) pasar rápidamente. **2,** [*usu.,* **brush up**] (clean up) limpiar. **3,** [*usu.,* **brush up**] (refresh one's memory) acordarse; recordarse. —**brush stroke,** brochada; brochazo.

brushwood ('brʌʃ·wud) *n.* broza.

brusque (brʌsk) *adj.* brusco; rudo; abrupto. —**brusqueness,** *n.* brusquedad; rudeza.

Brussels sprouts ('brʌs·əlz'sprauts) *n.* bretones; col de Bruselas.

brutal ('bru·təl) *adj.* brutal; cruel; bárbaro. —**brutality** (bru'tæl·ə·ti) *n.* brutalidad; barbarie. —**brutalize,** *v.t.* tratar brutalmente; brutalizar.

brute (brut) *n. & adj.* bruto; bestia; animal. —**brutish,** *adj.* brutal; bes-

tial. —**brutishness,** *n.* brutalidad; salvajismo.

bubble ('bʌb·əl) *n.* **1,** (gas or air film) burbuja. **2,** (unsound idea) tontería; bagatela. —*v.i.* **1,** (effervesce) burbujear. **2,** (boil) bullir; hervir. —**bubble gum,** goma hinchable.

bubo ('bju·bo) *n.* bubón. —**bubonic** (-'ban·ɪk) *adj.* bubónico. —**bubonic plague,** peste bubónica.

buccaneer (,bʌk·ə'nɪr) *n.* bucanero.

buck (bʌk) *n.* **1,** (male of various animals) macho. **2,** *slang* (dollar) dólar; *Amer.* peso. **3,** (sawhorse) cabrilla; caballete de aserrar. **4,** *colloq.* (young man) petimetre. **5,** (leap, as of a horse) corcovo. —*v.i.* **1,** (make twisting leaps) corcovear. **2,** (suddenly demur) embestir. —*v.t.* **1,** (unseat by leaping) despedir por la cerviz. **2,** *colloq.* (go against) oponerse a. —**pass the buck,** *colloq.* pasar el bulto; no responsabilizarse. —**buck up,** *colloq.* animarse; reanimarse.

buckaroo (,bʌk·ə'ru:) *n.* vaquero.

bucket ('bʌk·ɪt) *n.* **1,** (pail) pozal; cubo; balde. **2,** (scoop of a dredge) cangilón. —**bucket shop,** oficina ilegal de transacciones ficticias. —**kick the bucket,** *slang* morirse.

buckle ('bʌk·əl) *n.* **1,** (belt clasp) hebilla. **2,** (clasp of a strap) presilla; grapa. **3,** (kink in metal) horquilla; hebilla. —*v.t.* **1,** (fasten) hebillar; engrapar. **2,** (crumple) doblar; arrugar. —*v.i.* **1,** [*usu.,* **buckle down**] (work hard) empeñarse; decidirse. **2,** (warp) combarse; doblarse.

buckram ('bʌk·rəm) *n.* bucarán.

buckshot ('bʌk·ʃat) *n.* balines.

buckskin ('bʌk·skɪn) *n.* piel de gamo; ante; *pl.* artículos de ante.

bucktooth ('bʌk·tuθ) *n.* diente saliente. —**bucktoothed** (-,tu:ðd) *adj.* con o de diente saliente.

buckwheat ('bʌk·hwit) *n.* **1,** (cereal) alforfón; trigo moro. **2,** (flour) harina de alforfón.

bucolic (bju'ka·lɪk) *adj.* bucólico. —*n.* bucólica.

bud (bʌd) *n.* **1,** (unopened leaf) botón; yema; (unopened flower) capullo. **2,** (undeveloped thing or person) brote; germen. **3,** *colloq.* (debutante) joven presentada en sociedad. —*v.i.* [**budded, -ding**] florecer; germinar; brotar.

Buddha ('bud·ə) *n.* Buda.
—**Buddhism,** *n.* budismo.
—**Buddhist,** *n. & adj.* budista.

buddy ('bʌd·i) *n., colloq.* camarada; compañero; amigo.

budge (bʌdʒ) *v.t.* mover; revolver. —*v.i.* moverse; revolverse.

budget ('bʌdʒ·ɪt) *n.* presupuesto. —*v.t. & i.* presuponer. —**budgetary,** *adj.* presupuestario.

buff (bʌf) *n.* 1, (kind of leather) piel de ante. 2, (tan color) color de ante. 3, *colloq.* (enthusiast) aficionado; seguidor; entusiasta. —*v.t.* 1, (polish) pulimentar; adelgazar. 2, (deaden) amortiguar. —**in the buff,** en cueros.

buffalo ('bʌf·ə·lo) *n.* búfalo.

buffer ('bʌf·ər) *n.* 1, (polisher) lustrador. 2, (mitigator) amortiguador. —**buffer state,** nación parachoques; estado neutral. —**buffer zone,** zona de neutralidad.

buffet ('bʌf·ɪt) *n.* golpe; bofetón. —*v.t.* 1, (beat) golpear. 2, (contend against) contender con; pelear contra.

buffet (bə'fei) *n.* 1, (sideboard) aparador; mostrador. 2, (food for self-service) bufet; refrigerio. —*adj.* informal; sin etiqueta.

buffoon (bə'fuːn) *n.* bufón. —**buffoonery,** *n.* bufonería; bufonada.

bug (bʌg) *n.* 1, (insect) chinche. 2, *colloq.* (germ) microbio. 3, *slang* (zealot) fanático; intransigente. 4, *slang* (difficulty) defecto; dificultad; tropiezo. 5, *slang* micrófono oculto. 6, *comput.* defecto o falla (en un sistema). —*v.t., slang* 1, molestar; importunar. 2, poner micrófono oculto en (un lugar).

bugaboo ('bʌg·ə·bu) *también,* **bugbear** ('bʌg,beːr) *n.* espantajo; fantoche; coco; bu.

buggy ('bʌg·i) *n.* cabriolé; birlocho.

bughouse ('bʌg,haus) *n., slang* manicomio. —*adj., slang* [*también,* **bugs**] loco.

bugle ('bju·gəl) *n.* corneta. —**bugler** (-glər) *n.* corneta.

build (bɪld) *v.t.* [*pret. & p.p.* **built**] 1, (erect) construir; edificar; fabricar. 2, (found) fundar; establecer. 3, (strengthen) reforzar; rigorizar. —*v.i.* edificar —*n.* estructura; (of a person) talle. —**builder,** *n.* constructor. —**building,** *n.* edificio.

buildup ('bɪld·ʌp) *n.* refuerzo; vigorización; *colloq.* propaganda.

built (bɪlt) *v., pret. & p.p. de* **build.**

built-in *adj.* incorporado; estructural.

bulb (bʌlb) *n.* 1, (plant root) bulbo. 2, (light bulb) bombilla; *Amer.* foco; bombillo; bombita. —**bulbous,** *adj.* bulboso.

bulge (bʌldʒ) *n.* comba; pandeo; panza. —*v.t.* combar. —*v.i.* pandearse; combarse.

bulk (bʌlk) *n.* 1, (mass) bulto; grueso; volumen. 2, (the major part) mayoría. —*v.i.* abultar; hincharse. —**bulky,** *adj.* abultado; voluminoso.

bulkhead ('bʌlk·hed) *n.* mamparo.

bull (bul) *n.* 1, (ox) buey; (fighting bull) toro. 2, *fin.* alcista. 3, *eccles.* (edict) bula. 4, (blunder) disparate; desatino. 5, *cap., astron.* Tauro.

bulldog ('bul·dɔg) *n.* buldog; dogo; perro de presa. —*adj.* testarudo; tenaz.

bulldoze ('bul·doz) *v.t.* intimidar; atemorizar. —**bulldozer,** *n.* niveladora o removedora a tracción.

bullet ('bul·ɪt) *n.* bala.

bulletin ('bul·ə·tən) *n.* boletín.

bullfight ('bul,fait) *n.* lidia; corrida de toros. —**bullfighter,** *n.* torero; toreador. —**bullfighting,** *n.* toreo; tauromaquia. —*adj.* torero; taurómaco.

bullfinch ('bul·fɪntʃ) *n.* pinzón real.

bullfrog ('bul,frɔg) *n.* rana macho.

bullheaded ('bul,hed·ɪd) *adj., colloq.* obstinado; testarudo.

bullion ('bul·jən) *n.* oro o plata en lingotes.

bullish ('bul·ɪʃ) *adj.* 1, (of or like a bull) taurino. 2, *fin.* alcista. 3, *colloq.* (foolish) disparatado.

bullnecked ('bul,nɛkt) *adj.* pescozudo.

bullock ('bul·ək) *n.* buey; ternero.

bull ring plaza de toros.

bullroarer ('bul,rɔr·ər) *n.* zumba.

bull's-eye ('bulz·ai) *n.* 1, (round window) claraboya; tragaluz. 2, (convex lens) linterna sorda. 3, (target) diana.

bully ('bul·i) *n.* camorrista; matón. —*v.t.* intimidar; amedrentar. —*adj. & interj., colloq.* excelente; estupendo.

bulrush ('bul·rʌʃ) *n.* anea; junco; *Bib.* planta del papiro.

bulwark ('bʊl·wərk) *n.* parapeto; defensa; baluarte.

bum (bʌm) *n. & adj., slang* holgazán; pordiosero. —*v.i. slang* [**bummed, bumming**] haraganear; holgazanear. —*v.t.* pordiosear; mendigar.

bumblebee ('bʌm·bəl·biː) *n.* abejarrón; moscardón.

bumbling ('bʌm·blɪŋ) *adj.* desmañado; chapuceado.

bump (bʌmp) *n.* 1, (shock) choque; colisión; topetón. 2, (protuberance) giba; joroba; protuberancia. 3, (swelling) chichón; *Amer.* bodoque. —*v.t.* topar; chocar. —*v.i.* chocar; estrellarse. —**bumpy**, *adj.* abollado; traqueteado.

bumper ('bʌm·pər) *n.* 1, (protective bar) parachoques. 2, (filled glass) vaso ɔ copa colmada. —*adj., colloq.* enorme.

bumpkin ('bʌmp·kɪn) *n.* zafio; patán; rústico.

bun (bʌn) *n.* 1, (biscuit) bollo. 2, (roll of hair) relleno.

bunch (bʌntʃ) *n.* (cluster of flowers) manojo; ramo; (of fruits) ramo; racimo. —*v.t.* arracimar; agrupar. —*v.i.* arracimarse; juntarse.

bundle ('bʌn·dəl) *n.* (loose package) atado; bulto; envoltorio; (neat package) paquete; bulto. —*v.t.* 1, (tie) atar; envolver; empaquetar. 2, [*usu.*, **bundle off**] *colloq.* (send away) deshacerse de. —*v.i.* 1, *colloq.* [*usu.*, **bundle off**] (depart) marcharse. 2, (lie in bed fully clothed) acostarse vestido.

bung (bʌŋ) *n.* bitoque.

bungalow ('bʌŋ·gə·lo) *n.* bungalow; casa de una planta.

bunghole *n.* boca de tonel.

bungle ('bʌŋ·gəl) *v.t.* estropear; chapucear. —*v.i.* hacer chapucerías. —**bungler** (-glər) *n.* chapucero.

bunion ('bʌn·jən) *n.* juanete.

bunk (bʌŋk) *n.* 1, (bed) litera. 2, *slang* (nonsense) tontería; banalidad. —*v.i., colloq.* acostarse.

bunker ('bʌŋk·ər) *n.* 1, (storage bin) depósito. 2, (coal bin) pañol del carbón; carbonera. 3, *mil.* fortín. 4, *golf* hoya de arena.

bunny ('bʌn·i) *n., colloq.* conejo.

Bunsen burner ('bʌn·sən) mechero Bunsen.

bunting ('bʌn·tɪŋ) *n.* 1, (fabric) estameña; lanilla. 2, *ornith.* calandria. 3, (infant's garment) capa cerrada con capucha.

buoy ('buː·i) *n.* boya; baliza. —*v.t.* [*usu.*, **buoy up**] 1, (keep afloat) mantener a flote. 2, *fig.* (encourage) apoyar; sostener; alentar.

buoyancy ('bɔɪ·ən·si) *n.* 1, (floating) flotación. 2, *fig.* (exuberance) animación; alegría.

buoyant ('bɔɪ·ənt) *adj.* 1, (floating) boyante; flotante. 2, (lighthearted) alegre; vivaz; animado.

bur *también,* **burr** (bʌr) *n.* erizo.

burble ('bʌr·bəl) *n.* burbujeo. —*v.i.* burbujear.

burden ('bʌr·dən) *también,* **burthen** (-ðən) *n.* 1, (load) carga; peso. 2, *comm.* porte. 3, (main theme) tema; estribillo. 4, (encumbrance) estorbo; embarazo; obstáculo. 5, *mus.* bordón. —*v.t.* cargar; agobiar; imponer. —**burdensome**, *adj.* gravoso; oneroso; pesado; molesto.

bureau ('bjʊr·o) *n.* 1, (dresser) tocador; cómoda. 2, (government agency) oficina; agencia; departamento.

bureaucracy (bjuˈrak·rə·si) *n.* burocracia. —**bureaucrat** ('bjʊ·rə·kræt) *n.* burócrata. —**bureaucratic** (-rəˈkræt·ɪk) *adj.* burocrático.

burgeon ('bʌr·dʒən) *v.i.* brotar; crecer.

burglar ('bʌrg·lər) *n.* escalador. —**burglarize**, *v.t.* escalar; robar. —**burglary**, *n.* escalo; robo.

Burgundy ('bʌr·gən·di) *n.* borgoña.

burial ('bɛr·i·əl) *n.* entierro; funeral.

burin ('bjʊr·ɪn) *n.* buril.

burlap ('bʌr·læp) *n.* harpillera.

burlesque (bərˈlɛsk) *n.* 1, *theat.* parodia. 2, (satire) sátira. —*v.t.* parodiar; remedar. —*adj.* burlesco; satírico.

burly ('bʌr·li) *adj.* musculoso; robusto; firme.

burn (bʌrn) *v.t.* [*pret. & p.p.* **burned** ɔ **burnt**] 1, (destroy by fire) quemar; incendiar. 2, (scorch) socarrar; chamuscar. 3, (consume as fuel) quemar; consumir. 4, (inflame) inflamar. —*v.i.* 1, (be on fire) quemarse; incendiarse. 2, (be charred) chamuscarse; socarrarse. 3, *fig.* (become inflamed) inflamarse; abrasarse; consumirse. —*n.* quemadura; *Amer.* quemada.

burner ('bʌr·nər) *n.* 1, (heating unit) mechero. 2, (apparatus for burning) quemador. 3, (worker) quemador.

burnish ('bʌr·nɪʃ) *v.t.* bruñir; pulir.

burnoose (bʌr'nuːs) *n.* albornoz.

burnt (bʌrnt) *v., pret. & p.p. de* **burn.**

burp (bʌrp) *n., slang* eructo; regüeldo. —*v.i., slang* eructar; regoldar.

burr (bʌːr) *n.* **1,** (roughness after cutting) viruta; rebaba. **2,** = **bur. 3,** *dent.* buril. **4,** *phonet.* pronunciación gutural de la *r.* —*v.t.* **1,** (make rough or jagged) poner serrado o dentado. **2,** (pronounce with a burr) pronunciar con sonido gutural (la *r*).

burro ('bʌr·o) *n.* [*pl.* **-ros**] burro.

burrow ('bʌr·o) *n.* madriguera. —*v.t.* minar; agujerear.

bursa ('bʌr·sə) *n., anat.* [*pl.* **-sas** (-səz) o **-sae** (-si)] bolsa.

bursitis (bʌr'saɪ·tɪs) *n.* bursitis.

burst (bʌrst) *v.i.* **1,** (break) estallar; explotar; reventar. **2,** [*usu.,* **burst into**] (display suddenly) deshacerse en; prorrumpir en; desatarse en. **3,** (appear suddenly) irrumpir. —*v.t.* reventar; quebrar; explotar. —*n.* **1,** (outburst) explosión; reventón. **2,** (rush) carrera; precipitación. **3,** (firearms) andanada.

burthen *n. & v.t., arcaico* = **burden.**

bury ('ber·i) *v.t.* **1,** (inter) sepultar; enterrar. **2,** (conceal) ocultar; esconder. —**bury oneself,** abstraerse; concentrarse.

bus (bʌs) *n.* autobús; ómnibus; *W.I.; C.A.* guagua; *Mex.* camión. —**bus driver,** conductor de autobús.

busboy ('bʌs·bɔɪ) *n.* ayudante de camarero.

busby ('bʌz·bi) *n.* sombrero de húsar; birretina.

bush (bʊʃ) *n.* **1,** (shrub) zarza; arbusto. **2,** (uncleared land) matorral; chaparral. —**bushed,** *adj. colloq.* cansado; exhausto.

bushing ('bʊʃ·ɪŋ) *n., mech.* forro; buje.

bushman ('bʊʃ·mən) *n.* hombre montaraz.

bushy ('bʊʃ·i) *adj.* **1,** (like a bush) espeso; tupido. **2,** (hairy) peludo. —**bushiness,** *n.* espesura.

business ('bɪz·nəs) *n.* **1,** (occupation) profesión; trabajo; oficio. **2,** (enterprise) empresa; compañía. **3,** *comm.* negocio. **4,** (aim) deber; obligación. **5,** (affair) asunto; cosa. **6,** *theat.* actuación.

businesslike ('bɪz·nəs·laik) *adj.* metódico; ordenado.

businessman ('bɪz·nəs·mæn) *n.* [*pl.* **-men**] hombre de negocios; comerciante. —**businesswoman** [*pl.* **-women** (-ˌwɪm·ən)] mujer de negocios; comerciante.

buskin ('bʌs·kɪn) *n.* borceguí.

busman ('bʌs·mən) *n.* [*pl.* **-men**] conductor de autobús. —**busman's holiday,** vacaciones que no se distinguen de las actividades del acostumbrado trabajo de uno.

buss (bʌs) *v.t.* besar. —*n.* beso.

bust (bʌst) *n.* **1,** *anat.* busto; pecho. **2,** *sculp.* busto. **3,** *slang* (failure) fallo; fracaso. **4,** *slang* (spree) juerga; parranda. —*v.i., slang.* **1,** (burst) reventar; estallar. **2,** (fail) fallar; fracasar. —**busted,** *adj., slang* sin dinero; tronado.

buster ('bʌs·tər) *n., slang* **1,** (something noteworthy) maravilla; sensación. **2,** (spree) francachela; juerga. **3,** *often cap., usu. derog.* (boy) chico; muchacho.

bustle ('bʌs·əl) *v.i.* pulular; bullir. —*n.* **1,** (stir) agitación; ruido; bulla. **2,** (pad on the back of a skirt) caderillas; almohadillas.

busy ('bɪz·i) *adj.* atareado; ocupado. —*v.t.* ocupar; atarear. —**busy oneself,** atarearse; ocuparse.

busybody ('bɪz·i·bad·i) *n.* chismoso; entremetido; enredador.

but (bʌt) *adv.* sólo; simplemente. —*conj.* mas; pero; no obstante; sin embargo. —*prep.* excepto; salvo. —**all but,** casi todo. —**but for,** a excepción de; salvo; si no es por o si no fuese por.

butane (bju'tein) *n.* butano.

butcher ('bʊtʃ·ər) *n.* **1,** (cutter or seller of meat) carnicero. **2,** *fig.* (assassin) asesino. —*v.t.* **1,** (slaughter) matar. **2,** *fig.* (murder) asesinar. —**butchery,** *n.* matanza; carnicería. —**butcher shop,** carnicería.

butler ('bʌt·lər) *n.* mayordomo.

butt (bʌt) *n.* **1,** (cask) tonel; barril; pipa. **2,** (thick end) extremo; mango. **3,** (target) blanco. **4,** (cigarette end) colilla. **5,** (blow with the head) topetazo. **6,** (of a gun) culata. —*v.t.* **1,** (strike with the head) topar; embestir; chocar con; arremeter contra. **2,** (abut on) confinar con; lindar con. —**butt in,** *slang* interferir; entremeterse.

butte (bjuːt) *n.* otero escarpado.

butter ('bʌt·ər) *n.* mantequilla; *Sp.*

manteca de vaca. —*v.t.* **1,** (put butter on) untar con mantequilla. **2,** *colloq.* [*también,* **butter up**] (flatter) adular; halagar. —**buttery,** *adj.* con o de mantequilla.

buttercup (′bʌt·ər·kʌp) *n.* ranúnculo; botón de oro.

butterfat (′bʌt·ər·fæt) *n.* grasa de la leche.

butterfingers (′bʌt·ər‚fɪŋ·gərz) *n.* desmañado; torpe.

butterfly (′bʌt·ər·flai) *n.* **1,** (insect) mariposa. **2,** *colloq.* (flirtatious girl) mujer alegre.

buttermilk (′bʌt·ər·mɪlk) *n.* nata agria o suero agrio de la leche.

butterscotch (′bʌt·ər‚skatʃ) *n.* dulce de azúcar acaramelado.

buttocks (′bʌt·əks) *n.pl.* (of a person) nalgas; asentaderas; trasero; asiento; (of an animal) ancas.

button (′bʌt·ən) *n.* botón. —*v.t.* abotonar; abrochar.

buttonhole (′bʌt·ən·hol) *n.* ojal. —*v.t.* **1,** (slit) hacer ojales; abrir ojales. **2,** *colloq.* (grasp by the lapel) coger por las solapas.

buttonwood (′bʌt·ən·wʊd) *n.* plátano.

buttress (′bʌt·rɪs) *n.* **1,** *archit.* contrafuerte. **2,** *fig.* (prop) refuerzo; apoyo. —*v.t.* reforzar; entibar.

butyl (′bju·tɪl) *n.* butilo. —**butylene** (-tə′liːn) *n.* butileno.

buxom (′bʌk·səm) *adj.* robusto; fuerte; desarrollado. —**buxomness,** *n.* robustez; desarrollo.

buy (bai) *v.t.* [**bought, buying**] **1,** (purchase) comprar. **2,** (win by striving) lograr; obtener; alcanzar. **3,** (bribe) comprar; sobornar. —*n.,* *colloq.* compra.

buyer (′bai·ər) *n.* **1,** *comm.* (purchasing agent) comprador. **2,** (purchaser) cliente; parroquiano.

buzz (bʌz) *n.* **1,** (hum) zumbido. **2,** *slang* (telephone call) telefonazo. —*v.i.* **1,** (hum) zumbar; sonar. **2,** (gossip) chismear; cuchichear. **3,** (bustle) atarearse; afanarse. —*v.t.,* *slang* **1,** *aero.* volar muy bajo por encima de. **2,** (telephone) telefonear. —**buzzer,** *n.* zumbador; vibrador.

buzzard (′bʌz·ərd) *n.* busardo.

buzzword (′bʌz‚wʌrd) *n.* término de jerga muy corriente.

by (bai) *prep.* **1,** (beside; near) a; en; cerca a o de; junto a. **2,** (along; over) por; hacia. **3,** (past; beyond) después de; tras. **4,** (through the action or agency of) por; con. **5,** (in or to amount or degree of) a; por. **6,** (before; no later than) a; en; de; por. **7,** (with permission of) por. **8,** (according to; in) de acuerdo a o con; según; por. **9,** (with respect to) por. —*adv.* **1,** (beside) cerca; al lado. **2,** (aside) aparte; a un lado. **3,** (past) ya. —**by oneself,** solo; por sí mismo; sin ayuda. —**by the way,** a propósito; entre paréntesis; de paso. —**by way of,** por medio de. —**by and large,** en general; en conjunto.

bygone (′bai·gan) *adj.* pasado; anterior. —*adv.* anteriormente. —**bygones,** *n.pl.* cosas pasadas; hechos pasados; sucesos.

bylaw (′bai·lɔ) *n.* estatuto; reglamento; ordenanza.

byline (′bai·lain) *n.* nombre de autor.

bypass (′bai·pæs) *n.* **1,** (detour) desviación; desvío; **2,** *mech.; elect.* derivación. —*v.t.* rodear.

bypath (′bai·pæθ) *n.* **1,** (side road) sendero. **2,** (detour) desviación; desvío.

byplay (′bai·plei) *n.* acción aparte.

by-product *n.* subproducto; residuo.

byroad (′bai‚rod) *n.* camino vecinal.

bystander (′bai‚stæn·dər) *n.* espectador; mirón.

byte (bait) *n., comput.* byte; octeto.

byway (′bai·wei) *n.* camino accesorio.

byword (′bai‚wʌrd) *n.* **1,** (axiom) proverbio; refrán. **2,** (slogan) mote. **3,** (nickname) apodo.

Byzantine (′bɪz·ən‚tin) *n. & adj.* bizantino.

C

C, c (siː) tercera letra del alfabeto inglés. —*n., mus.* do.

cab (kæːb) *n.* **1,** (hired vehicle) taxímetro; taxi; coche. **2,** (driver's compartment) cabina. —**cab driver; cabman,** *n.* taxista; cochero; chofer.

cabal (kə'bæl) *n.* cábala. —*v.i.* intrigar; maquinar. —**cabalist** ('kæb·ə,lɪst) *n.* cabalista. —**cabalistic,** *adj.* cabalístico; oculto.

cabaret (kæ'bə'rei) *n.* sala de fiestas; cabaret.

cabbage ('kæb·ɪdʒ) *n.* col; berza; repollo. —**cabbage patch,** berzal.

cabin ('kæ·bɪn) *n.* 1, (house) cabaña; choza; barraca; *W.I.* bohío. 2, (stateroom on a ship) camarote; cabina; cámara. 3, (airplane compartment) cabina.

cabinet ('kæb·ɪ·nət) *n.* 1, (cupboard) alacena. 2, (for medicines) botiquín. 3, (of a radio) caja; mueble. 4, (advisory body) gabinete; ministerio. 5, (showcase) escaparate; vitrina. 6, (study) gabinete.

cabinetmaker ('kæb·ɪ·nət-,mei·kər) *n.* ebanista.

cabinetwork ('kæb·ɪ·nət,wʌrk) *n.* ebanistería.

cable ('kei·bəl) *n.* 1, (rope) maroma; cuerda. 2, (wire) cable. 3, *naut.* (hawser) amarra. 4, = **cablegram.** 5, (measure of 120 fathoms) cable. —*v.t. & i.* cablegrafiar. —**cable address,** dirección cablegráfica.

cablegram ('kei·bəl,græm) *n.* cablegrama.

caboose (kə'bus) *n., R.R.* furgón de cola.

cabriolet (,kæb·ri·ə'lei) *n.* cabriolé.

cacao (kə'ka·o) *n.,* cacao.

cache (kæʃ) *n.* 1, (hiding place) escondrijo; escondite. 2, (hidden supply) depósito; repuesto. —*v.t.* esconder; ocultar.

cackle ('kæk·əl) *n.* 1, (sound of fowl) cacareo. 2, (chatter) charla; cháchara. 3, (laughter) risotada; carcajada. —*v.i.* 1, (of fowl) cacarear. 2, (chatter) charlar. 3, (laugh raucously) dar risotadas o carcajadas; reír estrepitosamente.

cacophony (kə'kaf·ə·ni) *n.* cacofonía. —**cacophonous,** *adj.* cacofónico.

cactus ('kæk·təs) *n.* [*pl.* **-ti** (-tai)] cacto.

cad (kæd) *n.* sinvergüenza; canalla. —**caddish** ('kæd·ɪʃ) *adj.* canallesco; inescrupuloso.

cadaver (kə'dæv·ər) *n.* cadáver. —**cadaverous,** *adj.* cadavérico.

caddie *también,* **caddy** ('kæd·i) *n.* muchacho de golf. —*v.i.* ser o servir de muchacho de golf.

cadence ('kei·dəns) *n.* cadencia; ritmo.

cadenza (kə'dɛn·zə) *n., mus.* cadencia.

cadet (kə'dɛt) *n.* 1, *mil.* (student) cadete. 2, (younger brother) hermano menor. 3, (younger son) hijo menor.

cadmium ('kæd·mi·əm) *n.* cadmio.

cadre ('ka·drei) *n.* 1, (nucleus) núcleo. 2, *mil.* (officer corps) cuadro de jefes.

caduceus (kə'du·si·əs) *n.* [*pl.* **-cei** (-si·ai)] caduceo.

caecum ('si·kəm) *n.* intestino ciego.

Caesarean (sɪ'zɛr·i·ən) *adj.* cesáreo; imperial. —**cesarean operation** o **section,** operación cesárea; cesárea.

caesura (sɪ'ʒur·ə) *n.* cesura.

café (kæ'fei) *n.* café.

cafeteria (,kæf·ə'tɪr·i·ə) *n.* restaurante de autoservicio; *Amer.* cafetería.

caffeine ('kæf·in) *n.* cafeína.

cage (keidʒ) *n.* jaula; alambrera. —*v.t.* enjaular.

caisson ('kei·sən) *n.* 1, *mil.* cajón. 2, *engin.* cajón hidráulico. 3, *naut.* camello; cajón de suspensión.

cajole (kə'dʒol) *v.t. & i.* halagar; lisonjear; adular. —**cajolery,** *n.* lisonja; adulación.

cake (keik) *n.* 1, (pastry) bizcocho; pastel; torta. 2, (loaflike mass) pastilla. —*v.t.* endurecer. —*v.i.* endurecerse.

calabash ('kæl·ə,bæʃ) *n.* calabaza.

calaboose ('kæl·ə·bus) *n., slang* calabozo.

calamine ('kæl·ə,main) *n.* calamina.

calamity (kə'læm·ə·ti) *n.* calamidad; desastre; desgracia. —**calamitous,** *adj.* calamitoso; desastroso.

calcareous (kæl'kɛr·i·əs) *adj.* calcáreo; calizo.

calcify ('kæl·sɪ,fai) *v.t.* calcificar. —*v.i.* calcificarse. —**calcification** (-fɪ'kei·ʃən) *n.* calcificación.

calcimine *también,* **kalsomine** ('kæl·sə,main) *n.* lechada. —*v.t.* dar lechada a.

calcine ('kæl·sain) *v.t. & i.* calcinar.

calcium ('kæl·si·əm) *n.* calcio.

calculate ('kæl·kju·leit) *v.t.* **1,** *math.* calcular; computar. **2,** (plan) proyectar; planear. **3,** *colloq.* (guess) pretender; creer; suponer. —*v.i.* hacer cálculos. —**calculable,** *ad.* calculable. —**calculation,** *n.* cálculo; calculación. —**calculator,** *n.* calculador.

calculus ('kæl·kju·ləs) *n.* **1,** *math.* cálculo. **2,** [*pl.* **-li** (-lai)] *pathol.* cálculo; piedra.

caldron *también,* **cauldron** ('kɔl·drən) *n.* caldera.

calendar ('kæl·ən·dər) *n.* **1,** (list or table of dates) calendario. **2,** *law* orden del día; lista de pleitos. —*v.t.* incluir en el calendario; poner en lista.

calendula (kə'lɛnd·jə·lə) *n.* caléndula.

calf (kæf) *n.* [*pl.* **calves**] **1,** (young animal) ternero; becerro. **2,** (calfskin) piel de becerro. **3,** *anat.* pantorrilla.

caliber *también,* **calibre** ('kæl·ə·bər) *n.* **1,** (diameter) calibre. **2,** (ability) calibre; aptitud; capacidad.

calibrate ('kæl·ə·breit) *v.t.* calibrar; graduar. —**calibration,** *n.* calibración; graduación.

calico ('kæl·ɪ,ko) *n.* calicó.

californium (,kæl·ə'for·ni·əm) *n.* californio.

caliper *también,* **calliper** ('kæl·ɪ·pər) *n.* calibrador. —*v.t. & i.* medir el calibre; calibrar.

caliph ('kei·lɪf) *n.* califa. —**caliphate** ('kæl·ɪ·feit) *n.* califato.

calisthenics (kæl·əs'θɛn·ɪks) *n.pl.* calistenia. —**calisthenic,** *adj.* calisténico.

calk (kɔk) *n.* ramplón. —*v.t.* [*también,* **caulk**] calafatear.

call (kɔl) *v.t.* **1,** (speak loudly) llamar; anunciar; proclamar. **2,** (demand the attention of) atraer. **3,** (summon) citar; llamar. **4,** (designate) nombrar; designar. **5,** (telephone) telefonear; llamar por teléfono. —*v.i.* **1,** (shout) gritar; dar voces. **2,** (visit) hacer una visita; visitar. —*n.* **1,** (cry; shout) llamada; grito. **2,** (call of an animal, bird, bugle, etc.) llamada; reclamo. **3,** (notice; summons; invitation) aviso; citación; invitación. **4,** (visit) visita.

5, *comm.* demanda. —**close call,** escape por un pelo.

calla ('kæl·ə) *n.* cala. *También,* **calla lily.**

caller ('kɔl·ər) *n.* **1,** (device) llamador. **2,** (visitor) visitante; visita.

call girl prostituta que uno solicita por teléfono.

calligraphy (kə'lɪg·rə·fi) *n.* caligrafía. —**calligrapher,** *n.* calígrafo. —**calligraphic** (,kæl·ə'græf·ɪk) *adj.* caligráfico.

calling (kɔl·ɪŋ) *n.* **1,** (vocation) profesión; oficio; vocación. **2,** (summons) invitación. —**calling card,** tarjeta de visita.

callous ('kæl·əs) *adj.* **1,** (hardened) calloso; endurecido. **2,** *fig.* (insensitive) insensible; duro; seco. —**callousness,** *n.* callosidad. —**callosity** (kə'las·ə·ti) *n.* callosidad; dureza.

callow ('kæl·o) *adj.* **1,** (immature) inexperto; joven; inmaturo. **2,** (unfledged) desplumado; pelado. —**callowness,** *n.* inexperiencia.

callus ('kæl·əs) *n.* callo; dureza.

calm (kɑm) *adj.* tranquilo; sereno; quieto. —*n.* calma; tranquilidad; serenidad. —*v.t.* aquietar; tranquilizar. —*v.i.* [*también,* **calm down**] calmarse; tranquilizarse. —**calmness,** *n.* quietud; serenidad.

calomel ('kæl·ə·məl) *n.* calomel.

calorie ('kæl·ə·ri) *n.* caloría. —**caloric** (kə'lor·ɪk) *adj.* calórico.

calumniate (kə'lʌm·ni·eit) *v.t.* calumniar. —**calumniation,** *n.* calumnia. —**calumnious,** *adj.* calumnioso.

calumny ('kæl·əm·ni) *n.* calumnia.

calvary ('kæl·və·ri) *n.* calvario.

calve (kæv) *v.i.* parir una vaca.

calves (kævz) *n., pl. de* **calf.**

calyx ('kei·lɪks) *n.* [*pl.* **calyxes** (-ɪz) o **calyces** ('kei·lə,siz)] cáliz.

cam (kæm) *n., mech.* leva.

camaraderie (,ka·mə'ra·də·ri) *n.* camaradería.

cambium ('kæm·bi·əm) *n.* [*pl.* **-ums**] cámbium; cambio.

cambric ('keim·brɪk) *n.* cambray; batista.

camcorder ('kæm,kɔr·dər) *n.* videocámara.

came (keim) *v., pret. de* **come.**

camel ('kæm·əl) *n.* camello.

camellia (kə'mil·jə) *n.* camelia.

cameo ('kæm·i·o) n. [pl. -os] camafeo.

camera ('kæm·ə·rə) n. cámara fotográfica. —**in camera,** en secreto.

cameraman n. [pl. -men] operador.

camisole ('kæm·ə·sol) n. camiseta de mujer.

camomile ('kæm·ə,mail) n. camomila; manzanilla.

Camorra (kə'mor·ə) n. Camorra.

camouflage ('kæm·ə·flaʒ) n. 1, (disguise) disfraz; mil. camuflaje. 2, (false pretense) engaño; fingimiento. —v.t. disfrazar; mil. camuflar.

camp (kæmp) n. 1, (shelter) campamento; campo; colonia. 2, fig. (group) partido; agrupación; cuerpo; clase. —v.i. acampar. —**camper,** n. acampado; quien va a acampar.

campaign (kæm'pein) n. campaña. —v.i. hacer campaña.

campanile (,kæm·pə'ni·li) n. campanario.

campfire ('kæmp,fair) n. fuego u hoguera de campamento.

camphor ('kæm·fər) n. alcanfor. —**camphorate** (-eit) v.t. alcanforar.

campus ('kæm·pəs) n. jardines o terrenos de un centro universitario.

can (kæ:n) v.aux. [pret. could] 1, (be able) poder. 2, colloq. (may) tener permiso para; poder. —n. lata; bote. —v.t. [canned, canning] 1, (preserve) enlatar. 2, slang (dismiss) despedir; dejar cesante. —**can opener,** abrelatas.

Canadian (kə'nei·di·ən) adj. & n. canadiense.

canal (kə'næ:l) n. canal.

canalize ('kæn·ə,laiz) v.t. canalizar. —**canalization** (-lɪ'zei·ʃən) n. canalización.

canapé ('kæn·ə·pi; -,pe) n. entremés; aperitivo; bocadito.

canard (kə'nɑːrd) n. decepción; engaño; burla.

canary (kə'nɛr·i) n. 1, (bird) canario. 2, (color) amarillo canario.

canasta (kə'næs·tə) n. canasta.

cancan ('kæn·kæn) n. cancán.

cancel ('kæn·səl) v.t. & i. 1, (strike out) cancelar; anular; invalidar. 2, math.; print. suprimir. —**cancellation,** n. cancelación; invalidación; (of stamps or currency) inutilización.

cancer ('kæn·sər) n., 1, pathol.

cáncer. 2, cap., astron. Cáncer. —**cancerous,** adj. canceroso.

candelabrum (kæn·də'la·brəm) n. [pl. -bra (-brə)] candelabro.

candid ('kæn·dɪd) adj. sincero; franco. —**candidness,** n. sinceridad; franqueza.

candidate ('kæn·də·det) n. candidato; aspirante. —**candidacy** (-də·si) n. candidatura.

candied ('kæn·did) adj. azucarado; almibarado; confitado.

candle ('kæn·dəl) n. candela; vela; bujía. —v.t. examinar; probar (huevos). —**candlepower,** n. fuerza de iluminación; bujía.

candlemaker ('kæn·dəl,mei·kər) n. velero; cerero.

Candlemas ('kæn·dəl·məs) n. Candelaria.

candlestick ('kæn·dəl·stɪk) n. candelero.

candor también, **candour** ('kæn·dər) n. candor; sinceridad; integridad.

candy ('kæn·di) n. dulce; bombón; caramelo. —v.t. 1, (cook) almibarar; garapiñar. 2, fig. (make agreeable) endulzar; suavizar. —**candy dish, candy box,** bombonera. —**candy store** o **shop,** dulcería.

cane (kein) n. 1, (stick) bastón; caña; palo. 2, bot. caña. 3, (woody fiber) mimbre; junco. —v.t. 1, (flog) apalear. 2, (weave) tejer con mimbre o junco.

canebrake ('kein,breik) n. cañaveral.

canine ('kei·nain) n. & adj. canino. —**canine tooth,** diente canino.

canister ('kæn·ɪs·tər) n. bote; lata; frasco.

canker ('kæŋ·kər) n. llaga ulcerosa o gangrenosa. —v.t. 1, (ulcerate) gangrenar; ulcerar; 2, fig. (corrupt) corromper; emponzoñar. —v.i. gangrenarse; ulcerarse. —**cankerous,** adj. gangrenoso.

cannabis ('kæn·ə·bɪs) n. cáñamo índico.

canner ('kæn·ər) n. enlatador; envasador. —**cannery,** n. fábrica de conservas.

cannibal ('kæn·ə·bəl) n. caníbal; antropófago. —**cannibalism,** n. canibalismo. —**cannibalistic,** adj. caníbal. —**cannibalize,** v.t. recuperar las piezas servibles de.

cannon ('kæn·ən) n. 1, (gun) cañón. 2, (carom) carambola. —**cannonade** (,kæn·ə'neid)

cañoneo. —*v.t.* & *i.* cañonear.
—**cannonry** (-ri) *n.* cañonería.
cannot ('kæn·at) = can not.
cannula ('kæn·jə·lə) *n.* [*pl.* -lae
(-li)] cánula.
canny ('kæn·i) *adj.* prudente;
sagaz; sensato. —**canniness,** *n.*
sagacidad; sensatez.
canoe (kə'nuɪ) *n.* canoa. —*v.i.*
navegar o ir en canoa. —**canoeist,**
n. canoero.
canon ('kæn·ən) *n.* **1,** (rule; law)
canon; regla; ley eclesiástica. **2,**
Bib. libros canónicos. **3,** (church official) canónigo. —**canon law,** *n.*
derecho canónico.
cañon ('kæn·jən) *n.* = **canyon.**
canonical (kə'nan·i·kəl) *adj.*
canónico. —**canonicals,** *n.pl.*
vestiduras.
canonicity (ˌkæ·nə'nɪs·ə·ti) *n.*
canonicidad.
canonist ('kæn·ən·ɪst) *n.* canonista.
canonize ('kæn·ə,naɪz) *v.t.* canonizar. —**canonization** (-nɪ'zeɪ·ʃən) *n.*
canonización.
canonry ('kæn·ən·ri) *n.* canonjía.
canopy ('kæn·ə·pi) *n.* dosel;
pabellón; *fig.* cielo.
cant (kæɪnt) *n.* **1,** (insincerity)
hipocresía. **2,** (jargon) jerga; jerigonza; argot. **3,** (slant) inclinación;
sesgo. **4,** (salient angle) esquina;
canto. —*v.i.* hablar en jerga. —*v.t.*
achaflanar; inclinar; poner al sesgo.
can't (kæɪnt; kant) *v.,* *contr. de* **cannot.**
cantaloupe ('kæn·tə,lop) *n.*
cantalupo.
cantankerous (kæn'tæŋ·kər·əs)
adj. pendenciero; camorrista; mal
inclinado. —**cantankerousness,** *n.*
camorra; pendencia.
cantata (kɔn'ta·tə) *n.* cantata.
canteen (kæn'tiɪn) *n.* **1,** (shop)
cantina. **2,** (container) cantimplora.
canter ('kæn·tər) *n.* medio galope.
—*v.i.* ir a medio galope.
cantilever ('kæn·tə,li·vər) *n.*
modillón; soporte. —*adj.* a
modillones.
canto ('kæn·to) *n.* canto.
canton ('kæn·tən) *n.* cantón. —*v.t.*
cantonar; acantonar. —**cantonment**
(-'tan·mənt) *n.* acantonamiento;
acuartelamiento.
cantor ('kæn·tər) *n.* cantor, esp. de
sinagoga.
canvas ('kæn·vəs) *n.* **1,** (cloth)
lona; cáñamazo; lienzo. **2,** (sail)

vela; lona. **3,** (painting) óleo;
cuadro.
canvass ('kæn·vəs) *v.t.* **1,** (solicit
votes) recorrer pidiendo votos. **2,**
(investigate) examinar; discutir;
averiguar. —*v.i.* pedir o solicitar
votos, opiniones, impresiones, etc.
—*n.* **1,** (campaign) campaña para
pedir votos. **2,** (survey) examen;
investigación; encuesta.
canyon ('kæn·jən) *n.* cañón.
cap (kæp) *n.* **1,** (hat) gorro; gorra. **2,**
(top) tapadera; tapa. **3,** (peak; summit) cima; cumbre; pináculo. **4,** (explosive device) fulminante. —*v.t.*
[**capped, capping**] **1,** (cover) tapar;
cubrir. **2,** (culminate) completar;
finalizar; coronar. **3,** (surpass)
mejorar; aventajar.
capable ('kei·pə·bəl) *adj.* capaz;
competente; eficiente. —**capability,**
n. capacidad; competencia; eficiencia.
capacious (kə'pei·ʃəs) *adj.* capaz;
amplio;   holgado;   espacioso.
—**capaciousness,** *n.* capacidad; espaciosidad.
capacity (kə'pæs·ə·ti) *n.* **1,** (volume) capacidad; cabida; volumen.
2, (ability) capacidad; aptitud;
idoneidad. **3,** (function) capacidad;
facultad; poder.
caparison (kə'pær·ɪ·sən) *n.* **1,**
(trappings) caparazón. **2,** (clothing)
equipo; vestido fastuoso. —*v.t.*
enjaezar.
cape (keip) *n.* **1,** (garment) capa. **2,**
(point of land) cabo.
caper ('kei·pər) *v.i.* cabriolear;
cabriolar. —*n.* **1,** (leap) cabriola;
voltereta. **2,** (bud) alcaparra. **3,**
(prank) travesura; broma. **4,** (crime)
estratagema; intriga.
capillary ('kæp·ə·lɛr·i) *adj.*
capilar. —*n.* capilar; vaso capilar.
—**capillarity** (-'lɛr·ə·ti) *n.*
capilaridad.
capital ('kæp·ɪ·təl) *n.* **1,** (city) capital. **2,** (letter) mayúscula. **3,** *archit.*
capitel; chapitel. **4,** *econ.* capital.
—*adj.* **1,** (chief) principal; capital;
excelente. **2,** *law* capital. —**capital gain,** ganancia de capital.
—**capital punishment,** pena capital; pena de muerte. —**capital ship,**
acorazado grande.
capitalism ('kæp·ɪ·təl,ɪz·əm) *n.*
capitalismo.   —**capitalist,**   *n.*
capitalista.   —**capitalistic,**   *adj.*
capitalista.
capitalization (ˌkæp·ɪ·tə·lɪ'zei·

ʃən) *n.* **1,** *fin.* capitalización. **2,** (profitable use) aprovechamiento. **3,** *ortho.* escritura o imprenta en mayúsculas.

capitalize ('kæp·ɪ·tə,laiz) *v.t.* **1,** *fin.* capitalizar. **2,** [*usu.,* **capitalize on**] (use to advantage) sacar provecho de. **3,** *ortho.* poner en mayúsculas.

capitol ('kæp·ɪ·təl) *n.* capitolio.

capitular (kə'pɪt·jə·lər) *adj.* capitular. También, **capitulary** (-,lɛr·ɪ).

capitulate (kə'pɪtʃ·ə·leit) *v.i.* capitular; rendirse. —**capitulation,** *n.* capitulación.

capon ('kei·pan) *n.* capón.

caprice (kə'pris) *n.* capricho; antojo; veleidad. —**capricious** (-'prɪʃ·əs) *adj.* caprichoso; veleidoso.

Capricorn ('kæp·rɪ,korn) *n.* Capricornio.

capsize (kæp'saiz) *v.t.* volcar; zozobrar. —*v.i.* volcarse.

capstan ('kæp·stən) *n.* cabrestante.

capsule ('kæp·səl) *n.* cápsula. —**capsular,** *adj.* capsular.

captain ('kæp·tən) *n.* capitán. —*v.i.* mandar; gobernar; dirigir. —**captaincy,** *n.* capitanía. —**captainship,** *n.* capitanía.

caption ('kæp·ʃən) *n.* titular; título; encabezamiento; pie de grabado; pie de foto. —*v.t.* poner un subtítulo a; titular.

captious ('kæp·ʃəs) *adj.* capcioso; quisquilloso. —**captiousness,** *n.* capciosidad.

captivate ('kæp·tɪ·veit) *v.t.* cautivar; fascinar. —**captivation,** *n.* fascinación.

captive ('kæp·tɪv) *n.* & *adj.* cautivo; prisionero.

captivity (kæp'tɪv·ə·ti) *n.* **1,** (physical) cautividad; esclavitud; cautiverio. **2,** (mental) sujeción; fascinación.

captor ('kæp·tər) *n.* aprehensor; apresador.

capture ('kæp·tʃər) *v.t.* capturar; apresar; detener. —*n.* **1,** (act) captura; aprehensión; detención. **2,** (prey) presa; botín.

Capuchin ('kæp·ju·ʃɪn) *adj.* & *n.,* *eccles.* capuchino. —*n.,* *zoöl.* [*también,* **capuchin monkey**] (mono) capuchino.

car (kar) *n.* **1,** (automobile) automóvil; coche; *Amer.* carro. **2,** (elevator) caja de ascensor. **3,** *R.R.* vagón. —**closed car,** sedán.

carabao (,kar·ə'ba·o) *n.* carabao.

caracul ('kær·ə·kəl) *n.* caracul.

carafe (kə'ræf) *n.* garrafa; botella de cristal.

caramel ('kær·ə·məl) *n.* caramelo.

caramelize ('kær·ə·mə,laiz) *v.t.* acaramelar. —*v.i.* acaramelarse.

carapace ('kær·ə,pes) *n.* carapacho.

carat *también,* **karat** ('kær·ət) *n.* quilate.

caravan ('kær·ə·væn) *n.* **1,** (group) caravana. **2,** (vehicle) camión de mudanzas.

caravel ('kær·ə,vel) *n.* carabela.

caraway ('kær·ə·wei) *n.* alcaravea.

carbide ('kar·baid) *n.* carburo.

carbine ('kar·bain) *n.* carabina.

carbohydrate (,kar·bo'hai·dret) *n.* hidrato de carbono; carbohidrato.

carbolic (kar'bal·ɪk) *adj.* carbólico.

carbon ('kar·bən) *n.* **1,** *chem.* carbono. **2,** *elect.* carbón (de filamento, de batería). **3,** (paper) papel carbón. **4,** (copy) copia al o de carbón.

carbonaceous (,kar·bə'nei·ʃəs) *adj.* carbonoso.

carbonate ('kar·bə·neit) *v.t.* carbonatar. —*n.* (-nət) carbonato. —**carbonated water,** agua de soda.

carbonic (kar'ban·ɪk) *adj.* carbónico.

carboniferous (,kar·bə'nɪf·ər·əs) *adj.* carbonífero.

carbonize ('kar·bə,naiz) *v.t.* carbonizar. —*v.i.* carbonizarse. —**carbonization** (-nɪ'zei·ʃən) *n.* carbonización.

carbon dioxide bióxido de carbono.

carbon monoxide (ma'nak·said) monóxido de carbono.

carbon tetrachloride (,tət·rə 'klor·aid) tetracloruro de carbón.

carborundum (,kar·bə'rʌn·dəm) *n.* carborundo.

carboy ('kar·boi) *n.* bombona.

carbuncle ('kar·bʌŋ·kəl) *n.* **1,** (gem) carbúnculo. **2,** *pathol.* carbunco.

carburetor ('kar·bə,re·tər) *n.* carburador.

carcass ('kar·kəs) *n.* animal muerto.

carcinoma (,kar·sə'no·mə) *n.* carcinoma.

carcinogen (kar'sɪn·ə·dʒɪn) *n.* agente cancerígeno. —**carcinogenic** (-'dʒɛn·ɪk) *adj.* cancerígeno.

card (kard) *n.* **1,** (social) tarjeta. **2,** (for games) carta; naipe. **3,** (program) anuncio; papeleta; aviso. **4,** (bill of fare) carta. **5,** (cardboard) tarjeta; cartulina. **6,** (tool) carda; cardencha. **7,** *colloq.* (amusing person) chistoso; bromista. —*v.t.* **1,** (comb) cardar. **2,** (schedule) señalar; designar; preparar. —**lay one's cards on the table,** descubrir el juego.

cardamom ('kar·də·məm) *n.* cardamomo. *También,* **cardamon.**

cardboard ('kard·bord) *n.* cartón.

cardiac ('kar·di·æk) *adj. & n.* cardíaco.

cardialgia (,kar·di·'æl·dʒi·ə) *n.* cardialgia.

cardinal ('kar·də·nəl) *adj.* **1,** (fundamental) cardinal; principal; fundamental. **2,** (color) púrpura; violeta; cardenal. —*n., eccles.; ornith.* cardenal. —**cardinalate,** *n.* cardenalato.

cardiogram ('kar·di·o,græm) *n.* cardiograma. —**cardiograph** (-,græf) *n.* cardiógrafo. —**cardiographic** (-'græf·ɪk) *adj.* cardiográfico. —**cardiography** (,kar·di'agrə·fi) *n.* cardiografía.

cardiology (,kar·di'al·ə·dʒi) *n.* cardiología. —**cardiological** (-ə'ladʒ·ɪ·kəl) *adj.* cardiológico. —**cardiologist,** *n.* cardiólogo.

cardiopulmonary (,kar·di·o'pʊl·mə·nɛr·i) *adj.* cardiopulmonar. —**cardiopulmonary resuscitation,** resucitación cardiopulmonar.

carditis (kar'dai·tɪs) *n.* carditis.

cardsharp ('kard,ʃarp) *también,* **cardsharper** *n.* tahur.

care (kɛr) *n.* **1,** (heed) cuidado; atención; solicitud. **2,** (anxiety) zozobra; ansiedad. **3,** (protection) custodia; cargo —*v.i.* preocuparse; cuidarse; hacer caso. —**care for, 1,** (tend) cuidar; cuidar de; proteger. **2,** (be fond of) querer; estimar; apreciar. **3,** (desire) desear; gustar. —**in care of,** al cuidado de; a cargo de. —**take care,** tener cuidado.

careen (kə'riːn) *v.t.* inclinar; volcar. —*v.i.* volcarse; echarse de costado.

career (kə'rɪr) *n.* **1,** (course of events) curso. **2,** (speed) carrera. **3,** (calling) carrera; profesión. —*v.i.* correr a carrera tendida o a toda marcha.

carefree ('kɛr·fri) *adj.* sin preocupaciones; libre de cuidados.

careful ('kɛr·fəl) *adj.* cuidadoso; cauteloso; prudente. —**carefulness,** *n.* prudencia; cautela; atención.

careless ('kɛr·ləs) *adj.* **1,** (reckless) descuidado; desatento; negligente. **2,** (unworried) despreocupado. —**carelessness,** *n.* descuido; negligencia; despreocupación.

caress (kə'rɛs) *v.t.* acariciar; mimar. —*n.* caricia; mimo; terneza.

caret ('kær·ət) *n.* signo de intercalación (^).

caretaker ('kɛr·tek·ər) *n.* guardián; celador; vigilante.

careworn (kɛr·worn) *adj.* agobiado; abatido; cansado.

cargo (kar·go) *n.* carga; cargamento.

Carib ('kær·ɪb) *adj. & n.* caribe.

Caribbean ('kær·ə'bi·ən; kə·'rɪb·i-) *adj.* caribe. —*n.* mar Caribe.

caricature ('kær·i·kə,tʃur) *n.* caricatura. —*v.t.* caricaturizar. —**caricaturist,** *n.* caricaturista.

caries ('kɛr·iz) *n.* caries.

carillon ('kær·ə,lan) *n.* carillón. —**carillonneur** (-lə'nʌr) *n.* campanero.

cariole ('kar·i,ol) *n.* carriola.

carious ('kɛr·i·əs) *adj.* cariado.

carload ('kar·lod) *n.* **1,** *R.R.* vagonada; carga de un vagón. **2,** *fig.* (load) cargamento.

carminative ('kar·mɪn·ə·tɪv; 'kar·mə,ne·tɪv) *adj. & n.* carminativa.

carmine ('kar·mɪn) *n. & adj.* carmín; color carmín.

carnage ('kar·nɪdʒ) *n.* carnicería; matanza.

carnal ('kar·nəl) *adj.* carnal; impúdico; lascivo. —**carnality** (-'næl·ə·ti) *n.* carnalidad; lascivia.

carnation (kar'nei·ʃən) *n.* clavel. —*adj.* encarnado; rosado.

carnival ('kar·nə·vəl) *n.* **1,** (festival) carnaval. **2,** (amusement park) feria. —*adj.* carnavalesco.

carnivore ('kar·nə·vor) *n.* carnívoro. —**carnivorous** (kar'nɪv·ə·rəs) *adj.* carnívoro.

carob ('kær·əb) *n.* **1,** (fruit) algarroba. **2,** (tree) algarrobo; algarrobera.

carol ('kær·əl) *n.* canción alegre; villancico. —*v.t. & i.* cantar (villancicos); cantar alegremente.

carom ('kær·əm) *n.* carambola. —*v.t.* & *i.* carambolear.

carotid (kə'rat·ɪd) *adj.* & *n.* carótida.

carouse (kə'rauz) *v.i.* parrandear; jaranear. —**carousal,** *n.* parranda; holgorio.

carp (karp) *n., ichthy.* carpa. —*v.i.* criticar; censurar.

carpel ('kar·pəl) *n.* carpelo.

carpenter ('kar·pən·tər) *n.* carpintero. —**carpentry** (-tri) *n.* carpintería.

carpet ('kar·pɪt) *n.* alfombra; tapiz. —*v.t.* alfombrar. —**carpeting,** *n.* tejido de alfombras; alfombrado. —**on the carpet,** *colloq.* 1, (under consideration) en consideración. 2, (being reprimanded) castigado; reprendido.

carriage ('kær·ɪdʒ) *n.* 1, (vehicle) carruaje; coche. 2, (posture) presencia; modales; porte. 3, *mech.* soporte; jinete. 4, (transport) acarreo; porte.

carrier ('kær·i·ər) *n.* 1, (person) portador; mensajero; ordinario. 2, *naval* portaaviones. 3, (transporter) acarreador.

carriole ('kær·i,ol) *n.* = **cariole.**

carrion ('kær·i·ən) *n.* carroña.

carrot ('kær·ət) *n.* zanahoria.

carrousel *también,* **carousel** (,kær·ə'sɛl) *n.* tiovivo; caballitos; *Amer.* carrusel.

carry ('kær·i) *v.t.* 1, (convey) transportar; acarrear; llevar. 2, (support) aguantar; sostener. 3, (pass as legislation) adoptar; aprobar; aceptar. 4, (win the votes of) ganar; conseguir; lograr. 5, *comm.* (stock) vender; tener surtido de. 6, (transfer) trasladar; pasar. —*v.i.* alcanzar; llegar. —*n.* 1, (distance) alcance. 2, (portage) porteo. —**carry away,** 1, (remove) quitar; llevarse. 2, *fig.* (delight) entusiasmar; encantar; llevar violentamente. —**carry forward,** *comm.* pasar a la cuenta; llevar. —**carried forward,** *comm.* suma y sigue. —**carry off,** 1, (win) ganar; lograr. 2, *colloq.* (kill) llevar; matar. —**carry on,** 1, (engage in) ocuparse en; practicar. 2, (persist) proseguir; continuar. 3, *colloq.* (act foolishly) tontear; hacer el oso. —**carry out,** 1, (put into practice) aplicar. 2, (accomplish) realizar; llevar a cabo. —**carry over,** aplazar; posponer. —**carry through,** 1, (accomplish) realizar;

ejecutar. 2, (sustain) ayudar; sostener hasta el final.

carryall ('kær·i,ɔl) *n.* carriola.

cart (kart) *n.* 1, (small) carretilla; carrito. 2, (medium) carretón. 3, (big) carro; carreta; carromato. —*v.t.* & *i.* acarrear.

cartage ('kart·ɪdʒ) *n.* carretaje; acarreo.

carte blanche (kart'blanʃ) carta blanca.

cartel (kar'tɛl) *n.* cartel; reglamento; sociedad para un monopolio.

carter ('kar·tər) *n.* carretero.

cartilage ('kar·tə·lɪdʒ) *n.* cartílago. —**cartilaginous** (,kar·tə·'lædʒ·ə·nəs) *adj.* cartilaginoso.

cartography (kar'tag·rə·fi) *n.* cartografía. —**cartographer,** *n.* cartógrafo. —**cartographic** (,kar·tə'græf·ɪk) *adj.* cartográfico.

carton ('kar·tən) *n.* caja de cartón.

cartoon (kar'tuːn) *n.* 1, (caricature) caricatura. 2, (sketch) boceto. 3, (comic strip) historieta. 4, (film) dibujos animados. —**cartoonist,** *n.* dibujante; caricaturista.

cartridge ('kar·trɪdʒ) *n.* 1, (of ammunition) cartucho; bala; munición. 2, (for a phonograph) cartucho. 3, (of film) rollo.

carve (karv) *v.t.* & *i.* 1, (sculpture) tallar; esculpir; cincelar. 2, (slice food) trinchar.

cascade (kæs'keid) *n.* cascada; catarata; salto de agua.

case (keis) *n.* 1, (event) caso. 2, (condition; problem) caso; problema. 3, *law* causa; pleito; caso. 4, *med.* (disease) caso; (person) paciente. 5, *gram.* caso. 6, (box) caja; estuche; (of a knife) vaina. 7, *print.* caja. 8, *mech.* forro; cubierta. —*v.t.* 1, (enclose) embalar; cubrir. 2, *slang* (investigate) inspeccionar; registrar; examinar. —**upper case,** letra mayúscula. —**lower case,** letra minúscula.

casein ('kei·si·ɪn) *n.* caseína.

casement ('keis·mənt) *n.* marco de ventana; puerta ventana.

cash (kæʃ) *n.* 1, (currency) dinero; efectivo. 2, (immediate payment) contado; dinero contante y sonante. —*v.t.* cobrar; hacer efectivo; cambiar. —**cash and carry,** compra al contado. —**cash flow,** flujo del efectivo. —**cash in,** 1, (convert to cash) cobrar; cambiar. 2, *slang* (die) morirse; terminar. —**cash on deliv-**

ery, contra reembolso. **—cash register,** registradora; caja.

cashew ('kæʃ·uɪ) n. anacardo.

cashier (kæˈʃɪr) n. cajero. —v.t. degradar; destituir.

cashmere ('kæʃ·mɪr) n. casimir.

casino (kəˈsiːno) n. [pl. -nos] casino.

cask (kæsk) n. barril; tonel; cuba.

casket ('kæs·kət) n. 1, (small box) joyero; estuche; cofrecito. 2, (coffin) ataúd; féretro.

cassava (kəˈsa·və) n. cazabe.

casserole ('kæs·ə·rol) n. cacerola.

cassia ('kæʃ·ə) n. casia.

cassock ('kæs·ək) n. 1, (clerical garment) sotana. 2, (coat) balandrán.

cast (kæst; kast) v.t. [pret. & p.p. **cast**] 1, (hurl) tirar; lanzar. 2, (shed) despedir; echar. 3, (arrange) calcular; planear; computar. 4, theat. (assign roles) elegir (actores); repartir (papeles de una obra). 5, (mold) vaciar; moldear. —v.i. 1, (throw) tirar. 2, (conjecture) idear; pronosticar; conjeturar. —n, 1, (throw) tiro; lanzamiento. 2, [también, **casting**] (thing made from a mold) molde. 3, theat. (the company) reparto. 4, (tendency) inclinación; tendencia. 5, (computation) recuento; computación. **—cast a ballot,** votar. **—cast away,** 1, (discard) abandonar; desechar. 2, naut. naufragar. **—cast down,** 1, (project downward) abatir; derribar. 2, (sadden) abatir; desanimar. **—cast off,** 1, abandon) desechar; abandonar. 2, (free) libertar; librar. 3, naut. desamarrar.

castanets (kæs·təˈnɛts) n. castañuelas; palillos.

castaway ('kæst·ə·wei) n. abandonado; náufrago.

caste (kæst; kast) n. casta; clase social.

caster ('kæs·tər) n. 1, (molder) fundidor; vaciador; moldeador. 2, fig. (guesser) adivino. 3, (small wheel) rodaja de mobiliario. 4, (cruet) vinagrera.

castigate ('kæs·tɪ·geit) v.t. castigar; reprender; corregir. **—castigation,** n. castigo; corrección.

Castilian (kæsˈtɪl·jən) adj. & n. castellano.

casting ('kæst·ɪŋ) n. 1, (molding) fundición; vaciado. 2, [también, **cast**] (thing molded) molde.

cast-iron adj. 1, lit. de hierro colado. 2, fig. (hardy) inflexible; duro; rígido. **—cast iron,** hierro fundido; hierro colado.

castle ('kæs·əl) n. 1, (fortress) castillo; fortaleza. 2, chess castillo. —v.i. & t., chess enrocar.

castoff ('kæst·af) adj. & n. abandonado; desechado.

castor oil ('kæs·tər,ɔil) n. aceite de ricino; aceite de castor.

castrate ('kæs·treit) v.t. capar; castrar. **—castration,** n. castración.

casual ('kæʒ·u·əl) adj. 1, (offhand) casual; eventual; fortuito. 2, (careless) negligente; sin cuidado. —n. trabajador temporero o provisional. **—casualness,** n. casualidad; contingencia.

casualty ('kæʒ·u·əl·ti) n. 1, (injury; death) accidente. 2, (person) accidentado. 3, mil. baja.

casuist ('kæʒ·u·ɪst) n. casuista. **—casuistic,** adj. casuista; casuístico. **—casuistry,** n. casuística.

cat (kæt) n. 1, (domesticated) gato. 2, (wild) felino. 3, colloq. (spiteful woman) mujer despreciable. **—cat nap,** siesta corta.

catabolism (kəˈtæb·ə,lɪz·əm) n. catabolismo. **—catabolic** (,kæt·əˈbal·ɪk) adj. catabólico.

cataclysm ('kæt·ə·klɪz·əm) n. cataclismo. **—cataclysmic** (-ˈklɪz·mɪk) adj. desastroso.

catacomb ('kæt·ə·kom) n. catacumba.

catafalque ('kæt·ə,fælk) n. catafalco.

catalepsy ('kæt·ə·lɛp·si) n. catalepsia. **—cataleptic** (-ˈlɛp·tɪk) adj. cataléptico.

catalog también, **catalogue** ('kæt·ə·lag) n. catálogo; lista; índice. —v.t. catalogar; registrar; inventariar; clasificar.

Catalan ('kæt·ə,læn) adj. & n. catalán.

Catalonian (,kæt·əˈlo·ni·ən) adj. & n. catalán.

catalpa (kəˈtæl·pə) n. catalpa.

catalysis (kəˈtæl·ə·sɪs) n. catálisis. **—catalyst** ('kæt·ə·lɪst) n. catalizador. **—catalytic** (-ˈlɪt·ɪk) adj. catalítico.

catamount ('kæt·ə·maunt) n. gato montés.

catapult ('kæt·ə,pʌlt) n. catapulta. —v.t. arrojar como catapulta. —v.i. saltar o brincar repentinamente.

cataract ('kæt·ə,rækt) n. 1, (water) catarata; cascada. **2,** *pathol.* catarata.

catarrh (kə'taːr) *n.* catarro. —**catarrhal,** *adj.* catarral.

catastrophe (kə'tæs·trə·fi) *n.* catástrofe; desastre. —**catastrophic** (ˌkæt·ə'straf·ɪk) *adj.* catastrófico; desastroso.

catcall ('kæt·kɔl) *n.* chifla; rechifla. —*v.t.* & *i.* chiflar; rechiflar.

catch (kætʃ) *v.t.* [*pret.* & *p.p.* **caught**] **1,** (seize) atrapar; agarrar; capturar. **2,** (overtake) atajar; interceptar. **3,** (halt) detener; controlar. **4,** (entrap) engañar. **5,** (get) coger; obtener. **6,** *colloq.* (understand) comprender; entender. —*v.i.* enredarse; pegarse; engancharse. —*n.* **1,** (act) captura; detención; prendimiento. **2,** (thing caught) presa; botín. **3,** *mech.* freno; tope; pestillo. **4,** *colloq.* (trick) trampa; engaño. **5,** *colloq.* (desirable thing) atractivo; ventaja. —**catching,** *adj.* **1,** (infectious) contagioso. **2,** (alluring) atrayente; fascinante. —**catch on, 1,** (become popular) prender; popularizarse. **2,** *colloq.* (understand) comprender; entender. —**catch 22,** paradoja. —**catch up,** ponerse al día.

catch-all *n.* **1,** (box) arca; cofre. **2,** (room) ático; desván.

catchup ('kætʃ·əp) *n.* salsa de setas o tomate. *También,* **catsup, ketchup.**

catchword *n.* **1,** (key word) reclamo. **2,** *theat.* (cue) pie.

catchy ('kætʃ·i) *adj., colloq.* atrayente; agradable.

catechetical (ˌkæt·ə'ket·ɪ·kəl) *adj.* catequístico.

catechism ('kæt·ə·kɪz·əm) *n.* catecismo. —**catechist,** *n.* catequista; catequizante. —**catechize,** *v.t.* catequizar; adoctrinar.

catechumen (ˌkæt·ə'kju·mən) *n.* catecúmeno.

category ('kæt·ə·gor·i) *n.* categoría; clase. —**categorical** (-'gor·ɪ·kəl) *adj.* categórico; absoluto.

cater ('kei·tər) *v.i.* proveer; abastecer. —**caterer,** *n.* abastecedor; proveedor; despensero.

cater-cornered ('kæt·ər͵kornərd) *adj.* diagonal. —*adv.* diagonalmente.

caterpillar ('kæt·ər·pɪl·ər) *n.* **1,** (larva) oruga; larva. **2,** (tractor) tractor oruga.

catgut ('kæt͵gʌt) *n.* cuerda de tripa.

catharsis (kə'θar·sɪs) *n., med.* catarsis; purga. —**cathartic** (-tɪk) *n.* & *adj.* catártico; purgante.

cathedra (kə'θi·drə) *n., eccles.* cátedra.

cathedral (kə'θiː·drəl) *n.* catedral.

catheter ('kæθ·ə·tər) *n.* catéter.

cathode ('kæθ·od) *n.* cátodo.

catholic ('kæθ·ə·lɪk) *adj.* **1,** (universal) católico; universal. **2,** *cap., relig.* católico. —**Catholicism** (kə'θal·ə·sɪz·əm) *n.* catolicismo. —**catholicity** (ˌkæθ·ə'lɪs·ə·ti) *n.* catolicidad.

cation ('kæt͵ai·ən) *n.* catión.

catkin ('kæt·kɪn) *n.* amento; candelilla.

catnip ('kæt·nɪp) *n.* nébeda.

cat-o'-nine-tails (ˌkæt·ə'nainteilz) *n.* disciplina con nueve azotes.

cat's-paw ('kæts͵pɔ) *n.* víctima engañada a que se arriesgue por otro.

catsup ('kæt·səp; 'kætʃ·əp) = **catchup.**

cattail ('kæt͵teil) *n.* anea.

cattle ('kæt·əl) *n.* ganado vacuno.

catty ('kæt·i) *también,* **cattish,** *adj.* malicioso; felino.

Caucasian (kə'kei·ʒən) *n.* & *adj.* caucásico.

caucus ('kɔ·kəs) *n.* junta política o electoral. —*v.i.* reunirse en camarilla·política.

caudal ('kɔ·dəl) *adj.* caudal.

caught (cɔt) *v., pret.* & *p.p.* de **catch.**

caul (kɔl) *n.* redaño.

cauldron ('kɔl·drən) *n.* = **caldron.**

cauliflower ('kɔ·lɪ͵flau·ər) *n.* coliflor.

caulk (kɔk) *v.t.* = **calk.**

causal ('kɔ·zəl) *adj.* causal. —**causality** (kɔ'zæl·ə·ti) *n.* causalidad.

causation (kɔ'zei·ʃən) *n.* causa; origen. —**causative** ('kɔ·zə·tɪv) *adj.* causante.

cause (kɔːz) *n.* **1,** (source of a result) causa; motivo. **2,** *law* causa; litigio; proceso. —*v.t.* causar; hacer.

causeway ('kɔːz͵wei) *n.* calzada; calzada elevada.

caustic ('kɔs·tɪk) *n.* & *adj.* cáustico.

cauterize ('kɔ·tər͵aiz) *v.t.* cauterizar. —**cauterization** (-ɪ'zei·ʃən) *n.* cauterización.

caution ('kɔ·ʃən) *n.* **1,** (prudence)

cautela; cuidado, precaución. **2,** (warning) advertencia; aviso. —*v.t.* avisar; aconsejar; advertir.

cautious ('kɔ·ʃəs) *adj.* precavido; cauto; cauteloso.

cavalcade ('kæv·əl·keid) *n.* cabalgata.

cavalier (,kæv·ə'lɪr) *n.* **1,** (knight) caballero. **2,** (escort) caballero; galán. **3,** *cap., hist.* partidario del rey Carlos I de Inglaterra. —*adj.* **1,** (gay) alegre; caballeroso. **2,** (haughty) arrogante; altivo.

cavalry ('kæv·əl·ri) *n., mil.* caballería. —**mechanized cavalry,** cuerpo motorizado.

cave (keiv) *n.* cueva; caverna. —*v.t.* cavar. —**cave in,** hundirse; *fig.* rendirse. —**cave man; cave woman,** cavernícola.

cavern ('kæv·ərn) *n.* caverna; cueva. —**cavernous,** *adj.* cavernoso.

caviar ('kæv·i,ar) *n.* caviar; cavial.

cavil ('kæv·əl) *v.i.* sutilizar; rodear. —*n.* sutileza; rodeo. —**cavil at** o **about,** sutilizar.

cavity ('kæv·ə·ti) *n.* **1,** (hole) cavidad; hueco. **2,** *dent.* caries.

cavort (kə'vort) *v.i.* cabriolear; corvetear.

caw (kɔ) *n.* graznido. —*v.i.* graznar.

cay (ki) *n.* cayo.

cease (sis) *v.i.* cesar; desistir; pararse. —*v.t.* suspender; parar. —**ceaseless,** *adj.* incesante; sin descanso.

cease-fire *n.* cese de fuego.

cedar ('si·dər) *n.* cedro.

cede (sid) *v.t.* ceder; transferir; traspasar.

cedilla (sɪ'dɪl·ə) *n.* cedilla.

ceiling ('si·lɪŋ) *n.* **1,** (in a room) techo. **2,** *aero.* máxima altitud. —**ceiling price,** tope legal de precios.

celebrate ('sɛl·ə·breit) *v.t.* **1,** (commemorate; perform) celebrar; solemnizar. **2,** (praise) encomiar; alabar; elogiar. —*v.i.* estar de fiesta. —**celebrant** (-brənt) *n.* celebrante; oficiante. —**celebrated,** *adj.* famoso; conocido; célebre. —**celebration,** *n.* celebración.

celebrity (sə'lɛb·rə·ti) *n.* **1,** (fame) celebridad; renombre; fama. **2,** (person) celebridad.

celerity (sə'lɛr·ə·ti) *n.* celeridad; rapidez; ligereza.

celery ('sɛl·ə·ri) *n.* apio.

celestial (sə'lɛs·tʃəl) *adj.* **1,** (sky) celeste. **2,** (divine) celestial; divino; angélico.

celestite ('sɛl·əs,tait) *n.* celestina. *También,* **celestine** (-tɪn).

celibacy ('sɛl·ə·bə·si) *n.* celibato. —**celibate** (-bət) *n.* & *adj.* célibe.

cell (sɛl) *n.* **1,** (prison) celda; calabozo. **2,** (small room) cuarto; celda. **3,** (mouth) alvéolo. **4,** (group; protoplasm) célula. **5,** *elect.* célula eléctrica. **6,** (honeycomb) celdilla. **7,** (hole) nicho; cavidad.

cellar ('sɛl·ər) *n.* sótano; bodega.

cello ('tʃɛl·o) *n.* [*pl.* -**los**] violoncelo. —**cellist,** *n.* violoncelista.

cellophane ('sɛl·ə·fein) *n.* celofán.

cellular ('sɛl·jə·lər) *adj.* celular.

celluloid ('sɛl·jə·lɔid) *n.* celuloide.

cellulose ('sɛl·jə·los) *n.* celulosa.

cellulous ('sɛl·jə·ləs) *adj.* celuloso.

Celt (sɛlt) *también,* **Kelt** (kɛlt) *n.* celta.

Celtic ('sɛl·tɪk) *también,* **Keltic** ('kɛl-) *adj.* celta; céltico. —*n.* celta.

cement (sɪ'mɛnt) *n.* **1,** (adhesive) aglutinante; adhesivo; pegamento. **2,** (powdered lime) cemento. —*v.t.* pegar; aglutinar; asegurar. —*v.i.* pegarse; aglutinarse.

cemetery ('sɛm·ə·tɛr·i) *n.* cementerio.

cenotaph ('sɛn·ə,taf; -,tæf) *n.* cenotafio.

censor ('sɛn·sər) *n.* **1,** (examiner) censor. **2,** (faultfinder) crítico; censurador. —*v.t.* censurar; criticar. —**censorship,** *n.* censura.

censorial (sɛn'sor·i·əl) *adj.* censorio.

censorious (sɛn'sor·i·əs) *adj.* crítico; severo. —**censoriousness,** *n.* predisposición a censurar.

censure ('sɛn·ʃər) *v.t.* censurar; reprobar; criticar. —*n.* censura; reprobación.

census ('sɛn·səs) *n.* censo; padrón; empadronamiento.

cent (sɛnt) *n.* centavo; *Sp.* céntimo.

centaur ('sɛn·tor) *n.* centauro.

centenarian (,sɛn·tə'nɛr·i·ən) *n.* centenario. —**centenary** ('sɛn·tə·nɛr·i) *n.* & *adj.* centenario.

centennial (sɛn'tɛn·i·əl) *n.* & *adj.* centenario.

center *también,* **centre** ('sɛn·tər) *n.* centro. —*v.t.* centrar. —*v.i.* centrarse; concentrarse.

centesimal (sɛn'tɛs·ə·məl) *adj.* centésimo.

centiare ('sɛn·ti,ɛɹɹ) *n.* centiárea.

centigrade ('sɛn·tə,greid) *adj.* centígrado.

centigram ('sɛn·tə,græm) *n.* centigramo.

centiliter ('sɛn·tə,li·tər) *n.* centilitro.

centime ('san·tim) *n.* céntimo.

centimeter ('sɛn·tə,mi·tər) *n.* centímetro.

centipede ('sɛn·tə·pid) *n.* ciempiés.

central ('sɛn·trəl) *n.* central. —*adj.* central; céntrico.

centralize ('sɛn·trə,laiz) *v.t.* centralizar. —*v.i.* centralizarse. —**centralization** (-lɪ'zei·ʃən) *n.* centralización.

centrifugal (sɛn'trɪf·jə·gəl) *adj.* centrífugo.

centrifuge ('sɛn·trɪ,fjudʒ) *n.* máquina centrífuga.

centripetal (sɛn'trɪp·ə·təl) *adj.* centrípeto.

centuple ('sɛn·tju·pəl) *adj.* céntuplo. —*v.t.* centuplicar.

centurion (sɛn'tjur·i·ən) *n.* centurión.

centurium (sɛn'tjur·i·əm) *n.* centurio.·

century ('sɛn·tʃə·ri) *n.* centuria; siglo.

cephalic (sə'fæl·ɪk) *adj.* cefálico.

cephalopod ('sɛf·ə·lə,pad) *n. & adj.* cefalópodo.

ceramics (sə'ræm·ɪks) *n.sing.* cerámica. —*n.pl.* objetos de cerámica. —**ceramic,** *adj.* cerámico.

cereal ('sɪr·i·əl) *n.* cereal; grano. —*adj.* cereal.

cerebellum (,sɛr·ə'bɛl·əm) *n.* cerebelo.

cerebral ('sɛr·ə·brəl) *adj.* cerebral. —**cerebral palsy,** parálisis cerebral.

cerebrum ('sɛr·ə·brəm) *n.* cerebro.

ceremonial (sɛr·ə'mo·ni·əl) *adj.* ceremonial. —*n.* ceremonial; rito externo.

ceremony ('sɛr·ə,mo·ni) *n.* **1,** (rite) ceremonia; rito. **2,** (politeness) etiqueta; formalidad. —**ceremonious** (-'mo·ni·əs) *adj.* ceremonioso. —**stand on ceremony,** estar de etiqueta; estar de ceremonia.

cerium ('sɪr·i·əm) *n.* cerio.

certain ('sɑr·tən) *adj.* **1,** (sure) cierto; seguro; inevitable. **2,** (unspecified) algún; cierto. —**certainly,**

adv. cierto; por supuesto. —**certainty** (-ti) *n.* certidumbre; certeza.

certificate (sər'tʊf·ɪ·kət) *n.* **1,** (legal document) certificado. **2,** (written testimonial) atestado; certificación. **3,** *comm.* obligación; título; bono. —*v.t.* (-,keit) certificar. —**certification,** *n.* certificación.

certify ('sɑr·tə,fai) *v.t.* certificar; atestiguar. —**certified public accountant,** contador público titulado.

certitude ('sɑr·tɪ·tjud) *n.* certitud; certeza; certidumbre.

cerulean (sə'ru·li·ən) *adj.* cerúleo.

cerumen (sə'ru·mən) *n.* cerilla; cerumen.

cervine ('sɑr·vain) *adj.* cervino.

cervix ('sɑr·vɪks) *n.* cerviz; nuca. —**cervical** (-vɪ·kəl) *adj.* cervical.

cesium ('si·zi·əm) *n.* cesio.

cessation (sɛ'sei·ʃən) *n.* cesación; cesamiento; cese.

cession ('sɛʃ·ən) *n.* **1,** (act of ceding) cesión; traspaso; transferencia. **2,** (surrender) rendición.

cesspool ('sɛs,pul) *n.* pozo negro.

cetacean (sə'tei·ʃən) *n.* cetáceo.

cetaceous (sə'tei·ʃəs) *adj.* cetáceo.

chafe (tʃeif) *v.t.* **1,** (rub) escoriar; raer; escaldar. **2,** *fig.* (annoy) irritar; enojar. —*v.i.* **1,** (be roughened) escoriarse; raerse; desgastarse. **2,** *fig.* (be annoyed) acalorarse; enojarse; irritarse.

chaff (tʃæf) *n.* **1,** (husk) hollejo; cascabillo. **2,** (fodder) broza; desperdicios; pienso. **3,** (raillery) burla; zumba. —*v.t.* molestar; burlarse de. —*v.i.* burlarse.

chafing dish chofeta.

chagrin (ʃə'grɪn) *n.* mortificación; desazón. —*v.t., usu. pasivo* mortificar; disgustar.

chain (tʃein) *n.* **1,** (connected links) cadena. **2,** *pl.* (fetters) cautiverio; esclavitud; servidumbre. **3,** (connected events, objects) encadenamiento; sucesión. **4,** (measuring device) cadena de medir. —*v.t.* encadenar; enlazar. —**chain gang,** cuadrilla de malhechores encadenados. —**chain reaction,** reacción en cadena. —**chain store,** tienda de cadena.

chair (tʃeɹɹ) *n.* **1,** (seat) silla; asiento. **2,** *fig.* (leadership) presidencia. **3,** (professorship) cátedra. **4,** (presiding officer) presidente [*fem.* -ta].

chairlift ('tʃeir,lɪft) *n.* ascensor funicular con sillas para esquiadores.

chairman ('tʃɛr·mən) *n.* [*pl.* -men] presidente. —**chairwoman**, *n.fem.* [*pl.* -women] presidenta.

chaise (ʃeiz) *n.* calesa; calesín.

chaise longue (ʃeiz'lɔŋ) *n.* cheslón.

chalet (ʃa'lei) *n.* chalet.

chalice ('tʃæl·ɪs) *n.* cáliz.

chalk (tʃɔk) *n.* **1,** (limestone) creta. **2,** (crayon) tiza; clarión. —*v.t.* enyesar. —**chalk up, 1,** (write; draw) escribir o dibujar con tiza. **2,** (score; record) llevar cuenta; apuntar.

challenge ('tʃæl·əndʒ) *n.* **1,** (defiance) desafío; reto. **2,** *mil.* contraseña; santo y seña. **3,** *law* recusación. **4,** (objection) oposición; objeción. —*v.t.* **1,** (invite to fight or debate) desafiar; retar. **2,** (demand explanation of) demandar; exigir. **3,** *law* recusar. **4,** (object to) contradecir; disputar; objetar. —**challenger,** *n.* retador.

chamber ('tʃeim·bər) *n.* **1,** (room) cámara. **2,** (bedroom) habitación; dormitorio. **3,** (legislature) cámara. **4,** *law* tribunal. **5,** (cavity) cámara. **6,** (of a firearm) recámara. —**chamber music,** música de cámara. —**chamber of commerce,** cámara de comercio. —**chamber pot,** orinal.

chamberlain ('tʃeim·bər·lɪn) *n.* chambelán; camarlengo.

chambermaid ('tʃeim·bər ˌmeid) *n.* doncella; camarera.

chameleon (kə'mi·li·ən) *n.* camaleón.

chamfer ('tʃæm·fər) *n.* chaflán. —*v.t.* achaflanar.

chamois ('ʃæm·i) *n.* **1,** (antelope) gamuza; ante. **2,** (skin) piel de gamuza o ante.

champ (tʃæmp) *v.t. & i.* mordiscar; morder; mascar. —*n., colloq.* = champion.

champagne (ʃæm'pein) *n.* champaña.

champion ('tʃæm·pi·ən) *n.* **1,** (winner) campeón. **2,** (defender) paladín; defensor. —*adj.* campeón. —*v.t.* defender; apoyar; propugnar.

championship ('tʃæm·pi·ən·ˌʃip) *n.* **1,** (supremacy) campeonato. **2,** (support) apoyo; defensa.

chance (tʃæns) *n.* **1,** (fortuity) casualidad; azar. **2,** (risk) peligro; riesgo. **3,** (opportunity) oportunidad. **4,** (unexpected event) contingencia. **5,** *usu. pl.* (probability) pro-

babilidad. —*v.t.* (hazard) arriesgar; probar. —*v.i.* (befall) acaecer; acontecer; suceder. —*adj.* casual; fortuito.

chancel ('tʃæn·səl) *n.* entrecoro; presbiterio.

chancellery ('tʃæn·sə·lə·ri) *n.* cancillería.

chancellor ('tʃæn·sə·lər) *n.* canciller. —**chancellorship,** *n.* cancillería.

chancery ('tʃæn·sə·ri) *n.* cancillería. —**in chancery,** en posición difícil o embarazosa.

chancre ('ʃæŋ·kər) *n.* chancro.

chandelier (ˌʃæn·də'lɪr) *n.* araña de luces.

chandler ('tʃænd·lər) *n.* **1,** (dealer) tendero; abacero. **2,** (candlemaker) velero; cerero.

change (tʃeindʒ) *v.t.* **1,** (alter) cambiar; mudar. **2,** (replace) substituir; reemplazar. **3,** (exchange) cambiar; convertir; intercambiar. —*v.i.* alterarse; cambiarse. —*n.* **1,** (modification) modificación; alteración; transformación. **2,** (substitution) cambio; substitución. **3,** (money) cambio; vuelta. —**changeless,** *adj.* inmutable; invariable. —**change of life,** menopausia.

changeable ('tʃeindʒ·ə·bəl) *adj.* **1,** (liable to change) cambiable; variable. **2,** (changing readily) cambiadizo; mudable.

changeling ('tʃeindʒ·lɪŋ) *n.* niño trocado por otro.

channel ('tʃæn·əl) *n.* **1,** (waterway) canal. **2,** (river bed) cauce; lecho. **3,** *fig.* (route) conducto; vía; canal; medio. **4,** (groove) surco; estría. **5,** *radio; TV* canal; estación. **6,** *pl., slang* (involved routing) conducto reglamentario. —*v.t.* **1,** (direct) conducir; encauzar. **2,** (groove) estriar; acanalar.

chant (tʃænt) *n.* canto; salmodia. —*v.t. & i.* cantar monótonamente; salmodiar.

chaos ('kei·as) *n.* caos. —**chaotic** (ke'at·ɪk) *adj.* caótico.

chap (tʃæp) *v.t.* [**chapped, chapping**] **1,** (harm the skin) agrietar; resquebrajar. **2,** (roughen) hender; rajar. —*v.i.* agrietarse; resquebrajarse; henderse. —*n., colloq.* chico; mozo; amigo.

chaparral ('tʃæp·ər·əl) *n.* chaparral.

chapel ('tʃæp·əl) *n.* capilla.

chaperon *también,* **chaperone**

('ʃæp·ə·rən) n. acompañante de señoritas; rodrigón. —v.t. & i. acompañar; vigilar.

chaplain ('tʃæp·lɪn) n. capellán.

chaps (tʃæps) n.pl. zahones; Amer. chaparreras.

chapter ('tʃæp·tər) n. 1, (part of a book; council; branch of an association) capítulo. 2, eccles. cabildo.

char (tʃar) v.t. [**charred, charring**] 1, (burn to charcoal) carbonizar; hacer carbón. 2, (scorch) socarrar; chamuscar. —v.i. 1, (become charcoal) carbonizarse; hacerse carbón. 2, (perform domestic work) trabajar a jornal.

character ('kær·ɪk·tər) n. 1, (personality) carácter; personalidad. 2, (trait) índole; genio. 3, (reputation) reputación; fama. 4, colloq. (an eccentric) persona; tipo. 5, theat. (role) personaje; parte; papel. 6, (symbol) tipo de letra; tipo.

characteristic (,kær·ɪk·tə'rɪs·tɪk) adj. característico; peculiar. —n. característica.

characterize ('kær·ɪk·tə,raiz) v.t. caracterizar; señalar. —**characterization** (-rɪ'zei·ʃən) n. caracterización.

charade (ʃə'reid) n. charada.

charcoal ('tʃar·kol) n. 1, (burnt wood) carbón. 2, (for drawing) carbón; carboncillo.

chard (tʃard) n. acelga.

charge (tʃardʒ) v.t. 1, (load) cargar. 2, (command) mandar; comisionar. 3, (accuse) censurar; acusar. 4, (ask as a price) poner precio; pedir. 5, (defer payment) cargar en cuenta. 6, (attack) acometer; atacar. 7, (prepare arms) apuntar; preparar. —v.i. (attack) embestir; atacar. —n. 1, (load) carga; peso. 2, (command) mandato; orden; encargo. 3, (duty) obligación; deber. 4, (accusation) cargo; acusación. 5, (price) coste; precio. 6, (professional fee) honorario. 7, (violent onslaught) embestida; ataque. —**in charge, 1**, (responsible) encargado. 2, (substitute) suplente; interino. 3, Brit. (under arrest) bajo arresto; arrestado. —**in charge of**, a cargo de.

chargé d'affaires (ʃar'ʒei da'feːr) n. [pl. **chargés d'affaires** (ʃar'ʒei)] encargado de negocios.

charger ('tʃar·dʒər) n. 1, (war horse) caballo de guerra; corcel. 2,

(tray) fuenta o plato grande. 3, elect. cargador.

chariot ('tʃær·ɪ·ət) n. carro de guerra o combate; carro. —**charioteer** (-ə'tɪr) n. auriga.

charisma (kə'rɪz·mə) n. carisma. —**charismatic** (,kær·ɪz'mæt·ɪk) adj. carismático.

charity ('tʃær·ə·ti) n. 1, (benevolence) caridad; tolerancia; amor. 2, (alms) caridad; limosna. —**charitable**, adj. caritativo; benéfico.

charlatan ('ʃar·lə·tən) n. charlatán. —**charlatanism**, n. charlatanería.

charm (tʃarm) n. 1, (attractiveness) atractivo; encanto. 2, (spell) hechizo. 3, (amulet) talismán; amuleto; dije. —v.t. encantar; hechizar; atraer. —v.i. embelesar; arrobar. —**charming**, adj. atrayente; atractivo; encantador.

chart (tʃart) n. 1, (map) mapa; naut. carta hidrográfica o de navegación. 2, (record) gráfico; cuadro. —v.t. poner en o hacer una carta hidrográfica o gráfico.

charter ('tʃar·tər) n. 1, (grant of rights) cédula; título. 2, (constitution) reglamento; estatutos; carta. 3, (lease) alquiler. —v.t. 1, (authorize) estatuir; incorporar o instituir legítimamente. 2, (hire) alquilar; fletar. —**charter member**, socio fundador.

charwoman n. [pl. **-women**] asalariada; criada a jornal.

chary ('tʃer·i) adj. precavido; cauteloso. —**chariness**, n. cautela; precaución; circunspección.

chase (tʃeis) v.t. 1, (hunt; pursue) cazar; perseguir; acosar. 2, (drive away) espantar; ahuyentar. 3, (of jewelry) cincelar; montar; engastar. —v.i. corretear. —n. 1, (chasing) caza; persecución. 2, (quarry) caza. 3, (sport) caza; montería. 4, print. rama.

chaser ('tʃei·sər) n. 1, (one who chases) cazador. 2, colloq. (drink) bebida que sigue a un trago fuerte. 3, colloq. (licentious person) libertino.

chasm ('kæz·əm) n. 1, (fissure) abismo; grieta; hendedura. 2, fig. (difference) divergencia; laguna; separación.

chassis ('ʃæs·i) n. [pl. **chassis**] 1, (framework) armazón; cuerpo; bastidor. 2, mech. chasis.

chaste (tʃeist) *adj.* **1,** (pure) casto; puro. **2,** (restrained in style) puro; castizo. —**chasteness,** *n.* = **chastity.**

chasten ('tʃei·sən) *v.t.* **1,** (punish) reprimir; castigar; corregir. **2,** (make chaste) purificar; limpiar.

chastise (tʃæs'taiz) *v.t.* castigar; disciplinar. —**chastisement,** *n.* castigo; corrección; disciplina.

chastity ('tʃæs·tə·ti) *n.* castidad; continencia; pureza.

chasuble ('tʃæz·ju·bəl) *n.* casulla.

chat (tʃæt) *v.i.* [**chatted, chatting**] charlar; conversar. —*n.* charla; conversación íntima. —**chatty,** *adj.,* *colloq.* locuaz; hablador; charlador.

chattel ('tʃæt·əl) *n.* bienes muebles.

chatter ('tʃæt·ər) *v.i.* **1,** (rattle; vibrate noisily) traquetear; golpetear. **2,** (click together, as the teeth) castañetear. **3,** (prattle) parlotear; chacharear; cotorrear. —*n.* **1,** (noisy vibration) traqueteo; golpeteo. **2,** (clicking, as of the teeth) castañeteo. **3,** (prattle) parloteo; cháchara; cotorreo.

chatterbox ('tʃæt·ər·baks) *n.* hablador; parlanchín.

chauffeur ('ʃo·fər) *n.* chofer; conductor.

chauvinism ('ʃo·və·nɪz·əm) *n.* chauvinismo; patriotería. —**chauvinist,** *n.* chauvinista; patriotero. —**chauvinistic,** *adj.* chauvinista; patriotero.

cheap (tʃip) *adj.* **1,** (low-priced) barato; asequible. **2,** *fig.* (vulgar) de poco precio; despreciable; mezquino. —**cheapness,** *n.* baratura; *fig.* mezquindad.

cheapen ('tʃi·pən) *v.t.* abaratar; rebajar. —*v.i.* rebajar de precio; regatear.

cheat (tʃit) *v.t.* **1,** (mislead) engañar; equivocar; defraudar. **2,** (swindle) timar; chasquear. —*v.i.* cometer fraude o engaño. —*n.* **1,** (swindler) timador; tramposo. **2,** (act of fraud) engaño; timo; trampa.

check (tʃek) *n.* **1,** (obstruction) obstáculo; impedimento. **2,** (brake) freno; tope. **3,** (rebuff) contratiempo; descalabro. **4,** [*usu.,* check-up] (test) verificación; comprobación. **5,** (mark) contraseña. **6,** [*también,* **cheque**] (money order) cheque; talón de cuenta corriente. **7,** (receipt; token) talón; billete de reclamo. **8,** (square)

escaque; cuadrito. **9,** (restaurant bill) cuenta; factura. **10,** *chess* jaque. **11,** (chip) ficha. —*v.t.* **1,** (impede) impedir; reprimir; parar. **2,** (test) investigar; comprobar; verificar. **3,** (mark) hacer una contraseña; marcar. **4,** (put in temporary custody) dar a guardar; dejar en consigna. **5,** (send baggage) facturar. **6,** *chess* dar jaque. —*v.i.* **1,** (prove to be accurate) concordar; estar de acuerdo. **2,** (stop) pararse; detenerse. —*interj., slang* ¡muy bien! —**check in,** registrarse; inscribirse. —**check out,** despedirse; *slang* (die) morir. —**check up,** comprobar. —**in check,** controlado; *chess* en jaque.

checkbook ('tʃek·bʊk) *n.* talonario de cheques.

checker ('tʃek·ər) *n.* **1,** (record-keeper) archivista. **2,** (store clerk) cajero. **3,** (tester; watcher) verificador; examinador; vigilante. **4,** (playing piece) pieza de damas. —**checkered,** *adj.* a o de cuadros; ajedrezado.

checkerboard ('tʃek·ər·bord) *n.* tablero de damas.

checkers ('tʃek·ərz) *n.* juego de damas.

checkmate ('tʃek·meit) *n.* **1,** *chess* jaque mate; mate. **2,** (defeat) derrota. —*v.t.* **1,** *chess* dar mate a. **2,** (overthrow) derrotar; deshacer; destruir.

checkroom ('tʃek·rum) *n.* guardarropía; guardarropa; *R.R.* consigna.

check-up *n.* **1,** = **check;** *n.* **4.** **2,** (medical) reconocimiento médico.

cheek (tʃik) *n.* **1,** *anat.* mejilla; carrillo. **2,** *colloq.* (impudence) descaro; atrevimiento. —**cheeky,** *adj., colloq.* atrevido; descarado.

cheekbone ('tʃik·bon) *n.* pómulo.

cheep (tʃip) *n.* pío; chirrido. —*v.t. & i.* piar; chirriar.

cheer (tʃɪr) *n.* **1,** (joyful feeling) alegría; regocijo; buen humor. **2,** (shout of joy) viva; aplauso; vítores —*v.t. & i.* animar; alentar; aplaudir. —**cheers!,** *interj.* ¡a la salud!; ¡salud!

cheerful ('tʃɪr·fəl) *adj.* jovial; alegre; animado. —**cheerfulness,** *n.* jovialidad; animación; alegría.

cheery ('tʃɪr·i) *adj.* alegre; jubiloso. —**cheeriness,** *n.* júbilo; animación.

cheese (tʃiz) *n.* queso.

cheesecloth ('tʃiz,klɔθ) *n.* estopilla de algodón.

cheetah ('tʃiːtə) *n.* leopardo cazador.

chef (ʃɛf) *n.* primer cocinero; jefe de cocina.

chemical ('kɛm·ɪ·kəl) *adj.* químico. —*n.* producto químico.

chemise (ʃə'miːz) *n.* camisa; camisola; camisón.

chemist ('kɛm·ɪst) *n.* químico.

chemistry ('kɛm·ɪs·trɪ) *n.* química.

chemotherapy (,kɛm·ə'θɛr·ə·pi; ,ki·mə-) *n.* quimoterapia.

chenille (ʃə'niːl) *n.* felpilla.

cheque (tʃɛk) *n.*, *Brit.* = check.

chequer ('tʃɛk·ər) *n.*, *Brit.* = checker. —**chequered**, *adj.*, *Brit.* = checkered.

cherish ('tʃɛr·ɪʃ) *v.t.* 1, (hold dear) estimar; apreciar. 2, *fig.* (take care of) acariciar; alimentar; abrigar.

cherry ('tʃɛr·i) *n.* 1, (tree and wood) cerezo. 2, (fruit; color) cereza.

cherub ('tʃɛr·əb) *n.* [*pl.* **cherubim** ('tʃɛr·ə·bɪm)] querube; querubín. —**cherubic** (tʃə'ru·bɪk) *adj.* querúbico.

chess (tʃɛs) *n.* ajedrez. —**chessboard**, *n.* tablero de ajedrez. —**chessman**, *n.* [*pl.* -**men**] pieza de ajedrez.

chest (tʃɛst) *n.* 1, (box) cofre; arca; baúl. 2, *anat.* pecho; tórax. —**get off one's chest**, *colloq.* descargarse (de).

chestnut ('tʃɛs·nʌt) *n.* 1, (tree and wood) castaño. 2, (nut) castaña. 3, (color) color castaño; marrón. 4, *slang* (cliché) broma o frase gastada. —*adj.* castaño.

chevalier (,ʃɛv·ə'lɪr) *n.* caballero.

cheviot ('ʃɛv·i·ət) *n.* lanilla; paño de lana; cheviot.

chevron ('ʃɛv·rən) *n.* galón; sardineta.

chew (tʃuː) *v.t.* 1, (grind) masticar; mascar. 2, *fig.* (consider) rumiar; considerar; meditar. —*n.* mascadura; *Chile & Arg.* mascada. —**chew the rag**, *slang* hablar mucho. —**chewing gum**, *slang* goma de mascar.

chiaroscuro (,kja·rə'skʊr·o) *n.* claroscuro.

chic (ʃik) *adj.* elegante; bien hecho; de moda.

chicanery (ʃɪ'kei·nə·ri) *n.* embrollo; trampa legal; sofistería.

chick (tʃɪk) *n.* 1, (fowl) polluelo;

pichón. 2, *slang* (girl) jovencita; *Amer.* gallina.

chicken ('tʃɪk·ən) *n.* 1, (fowl) pollo. 2, *slang* = chick. 3, *slang* cobarde. —*adj.*, *slang* tímido; encogido. —**chicken feed**, *slang* pitanza.

chickenhearted ('tʃɪk·ən,har·tɛd) *adj.* tímido; cobarde.

chicken pox *n.* varicela.

chickpea ('tʃɪk,pi) *n.* garbanzo.

chicle ('tʃɪk·əl) *n.* chicle; goma para o de mascar.

chicory ('tʃɪk·ə·ri) *n.* achicoria.

chide (tʃaid) *v.t.* [*pret. & p.p.* **chid** (tʃɪd), *p.p. también*, **chidden** ('tʃɪd·ən)] reprobar; echar en cara; culpar; increpar. —*v.i.* regañar; refunfuñar.

chief (tʃif) *n.* jefe; líder. —*adj.* principal; el más importante; primero. —**chiefly**, *adv.* principalmente; ante todo.

chieftain ('tʃif·tən) *n.* 1, (of a tribe) jefe. 2, (of a clan or band) jefe; capitán; caudillo.

chiffon (ʃɪ'fan) *n.* gasa; soplillo.

chigger ('tʃɪg·ər) *n.* garrapata; pique. *También*, **chigoe** (-o).

chignon (ʃin·jan) *n.* moño.

chilblain ('tʃɪl·blein) *n.* sabañón.

child (tʃaild) *n.* [*pl.* **children**] niño; infante; hijo. —**with child**, embarazada; preñada. —**child's play**, juego de niños.

childbirth ('tʃaild,bʌrθ) *n.* parto; alumbramiento.

childhood ('tʃaild·hʊd) *n.* niñez; infancia.

childish ('tʃaild·dɪʃ) *adj.* pueril; aniñado. —**childishness**, *n.* puerilidad; niñería.

childless ('tʃaild·ləs) *adj.* sin hijos.

childlike ('tʃaild·laik) *adj.* pueril; aniñado.

childproof ('tʃaild·pruf) *adj.* a prueba de niños.

children ('tʃɪl·drən) *n.*, *pl. de* **child**.

chili (tʃɪl·i) *n.* chile.

chill (tʃɪl) *n.* 1, (sensation) escalofrío; estremecimiento. 2, (degree of cold) frío. —*v.t.* 1, (make cold) enfriar; helar. 2, *fig.* (repulse) desanimar; desalentar; enfriar. —*v.i.* desanimarse; desalentarse. —**chilly**, *adj.* frío; helado.

chime (tʃaim) *n.* 1, (bell or set of bells) campana; juego de campanas. 2, (ringing sound) repique; campaneo. **3,** *fig.* (concord) armonía; conformidad. —*v.t.* **1,** (cause to ring) repicar; tañer; tocar. **2,** (say in chorus) decir al unísono. —*v.i.* **1,** (ring) tañer; sonar. **2,** *fig.* (harmonize) armonizar; concordar. —**chime in,** *colloq.* **1,** (agree) convenir; consentir; estar de acorde. **2,** (interrupt) interrumpir; entremeterse.

chimera (kɪ'mɪr·ə) *n.* quimera. —**chimerical** (kɪ'mɛr·ɪ·kəl) *adj.* quimérico.

chimney ('tʃɪm·ni) *n.* chimenea.

chimpanzee (tʃɪm'pæn·zi) *tambien,* **chimp,** *n.* chimpancé.

chin (tʃɪn) *n.* barbilla. —*v.i.* [**chinned, chinning**] *slang* charlar; hablar.

china ('tʃai·nə) *n.* porcelana; loza fina. —**china closet,** chinero; cristalera.

Chinaman ('tʃai·nə·mən) *n.* [*pl.* -**men**] chino.

chinaware *n.* vajilla de porcelana.

chinch (tʃɪntʃ) *n.* chinche.

chinchilla (tʃɪn'tʃɪl·ə) *n.* chinchilla.

Chinese (tʃai'niːz) *adj.* chino; chinesco. —*n.* **1,** (person) chino. **2,** (language) idioma chino.

chink (tʃɪŋk) *n.* grieta; raja; hendedura. —*v.i.* **1,** (crack) hender; rajar. **2,** (ring) sonar; resonar. —*v.t.* **1,** (split) hender; partir; rajar. **2,** (fill cracks) rellenar hendiduras; calafatear.

chintz (tʃɪnts) *n.* zaraza. —**chintzy,** *adj., colloq.* de relambrón.

chip ('tʃɪp) *n.* **1,** (fragment of wood) astilla. **2,** (counter; bus token) ficha. **3,** *elect.; comput.* placa; plaqueta. —*v.t.* [**chipped, chipping**] astillar. —*v.i.* astillarse. —**chip in,** contribuir; ayudar.

chipmunk ('tʃɪp·mʌŋk) *n.* ardilla norteamericana; ardilla listada.

chipper ('tʃɪp·ər) *v.i.* gorjear; piar. —*adj., colloq.* jovial; alegre.

chiropody (kai'rap·ə·di) *n.* pedicura. —**chiropodist** (-dɪst) *n.* pedicuro; callista.

chiropractic (ˌkai·ro'præk·tɪk) *n.* quiropráctica. —*adj.* quiropráctico. —**chiropractor,** *n.* quiropráctico.

chirp (tʃʌrp) *n.* **1,** (of birds) gorjeo. **2,** (of insects) chirrido. —*v.i.* **1,** gorjear. **2,** chirriar.

chisel ('tʃɪz·əl) *n.* cincel; formón; escoplo. —*v.t. & i.* **1,** (cut) cincelar;

esculpir. **2,** *slang* (cheat) engañar; defraudar; conseguir engañando.

chit (tʃɪt) *n.* **1,** (memo) comunicación; esquela. **2,** (girl) chiquilla. **3,** (animal) cachorro; cría.

chitchat ('tʃɪt·tʃæt) *n., colloq.* cháchara; charla; plática.

chivalry ('ʃɪv·əl·ri) *n.* **1,** (medieval knighthood) caballería. **2,** *fig.* (knightly manners) caballerosidad; hidalguía. —**chivalrous** (-rəs); **chivalric** (-rɪk) *adj.* caballeresco.

chive (tʃaiv) *n.* cebollina.

chlorate ('klor·et) *n.* clorato.

chloride ('klor·aid) *n.* cloruro.

chlorine ('klor·in) *n.* cloro. —**chloride** ('klor·aid) *n.* cloruro. —**chlorinate** ('klor·ɪ·neit) *v.t.* clorinar. —**chlorination,** *n.* tratamiento con cloro.

chloroform ('klor·ə·form) *n.* cloroformo. —*v.t.* cloroformizar.

chlorophyll ('klor·ə·fɪl) *n.* clorofila.

chock (tʃak) *n.* cuña; calzo. —**chock-full,** *adj.* lleno; colmado.

chocolate ('tʃak·lɪt; -ə·lɪt) *n. & adj.* chocolate.

choice (tʃois) *n.* **1,** (act of choosing) elección; preferencia. **2,** (option) oportunidad; opción. **3,** (thing chosen) lo elegido; lo escogido. **4,** (the best part) lo mejor; lo más escogido. —*adj.* selecto; superior; excelente. —**choiceness,** *n.* discernimiento; gusto; delicadeza.

choir (kwair) *n.* coro.

choke (tʃok) *v.t.* **1,** (strangle) ahogar; estrangular; sofocar. **2,** (obstruct) tapar; obstruir. **3,** *mech.* obturar. —*v.i.* **1,** (suffocate) sofocarse; ahogarse; atorarse. **2,** (be overcrowded) rebosar; estar de bote en bote. —*n.* **1,** (obstruction) opresión; sofocamiento; ahogo. **2,** *mech.* obturador. —**choke up,** emocionarse.

choker ('tʃo·kər) *n.* **1,** (necklace) gargantilla. **2,** (collar) cuello alto.

choler ('ka·lər) *n.* cólera; ira. —**choleric** (kə'lɛr·ɪk) *adj.* colérico, irascible.

cholera ('kal·ər·ə) *n.* cólera morbo.

cholesterol (kə'lɛs·tə·rɔl) *n.* colesterol.

cholla ('tʃɔi·jə) *n., bot.* cholla.

choose (tʃuːz) *v.t.* [**chose, chosen, choosing**] elegir; escoger; decidir. —*v.i.* preferir.

chop (tʃap) *v.t.* [**chopped, chopping**] **1,** (hew) tajar; hender; rajar.

2, (mince) picar; desmenuzar. —*v.i.*
1, (hew) hachear; dar tajos. 2, (turn;
shift) virar; cuartearse. —*n.* 1, (cut
of meat) chuleta. 2, *usu.pl.* (jaw)
quijada; labios. 3, (act of chopping)
tajo; corte. 4, (ocean wave) oleada.
—**chopper,** *n.*, 1, (tool) hacha;
cuchilla (de carnicería). 2, *colloq.*
helicóptero.

choppy ('tʃap·i) *adj.* adusto; violento.

chopsticks ('tʃap,stɪks) *n.pl.*
palillos.

choral ('kor·əl) *adj.* coral.

chorale (kə'ræl) *n.* coral.

chord (kord) *n.* 1, (cord) cordón;
cordel. 2, *mus.* acorde. 3, *geom.;*
anat.; aero. cuerda. 4, *engin.* viga
de celosía o reticulada.

chore (tʃor) *n.* tarea.

chorea (kə'ri·ə) *n.* baile de San
Vito.

choreography (kor·i'ag·rə·fi) *n.*
coreografía. —**choreographer**
(-fər) *n.* coreógrafo. —**choreo-**
graph ('kor·i·ə,græf) *v.t.* montar la
coreografía de. —**choreographic**
(-'græf·ɪk) *adj.* coreográfico.

chorine ('kor·in) *n., colloq.* corista.

chorister ('kor·ɪs·tər) *n.* corista.

chorus ('kor·əs) *n.* 1, (group of
singers) coro. 2, (refrain) estribillo;
coro. —*v.i.* cantar en o a coro. —*v.t.*
corear.

chorus girl (o boy) corista.

chose (tʃoz) *v.t., pret. de* **choose.**

chosen ('tʃo·zən) *v., p.p. de*
choose.

chow (tʃau) *n.*, 1, (dog) perro chino.
2, *slang* (food) comida; alimentos.

chowder ('tʃau·dər) *n.* sancocho o
sopa, esp. de pescado o almejas.

Christ (kraist) *n.* Cristo.

christen ('krɪs·ən) *v.t.* bautizar.
—**christening,** *n.* bautizo; bautismo.

Christendom ('krɪs·ən·dəm) *n.*
cristiandad; cristianismo.

Christian ('krɪs·tʃən) *n. & adj.*
cristiano. —**Christian name,**
nombre de pila; nombre.

Christianity (,krɪs·tʃi'æn·ə·ti) *n.*
cristianismo.

Christmas ('krɪs·məs) *n.* Navi-
dad. —**Christmas carol,** villancico.
—**Christmas Eve,** Nochebuena.
—**Christmas tree,** árbol de Navi-
dad. —**Merry Christmas,** felices
Pascuas; Feliz Navidad.

chromatic (kro'mæt·ɪk) *adj.*
cromático.

chrome (kroːm) *n. & adj.* cromado.

chromium ('kro·mi·əm) *n.* cromo.

chromosome ('kro·mə·som) *n.*
cromosoma.

chronic ('kran·ɪk) *adj.* crónico; habitual; inveterado; continuo.

chronicle ('kran·ɪ·kəl) *n.* 1, (history) crónica. 2, *pl., cap., Bib.*
Paralipómenos; Crónicas. —*v.t.*
escribir una crónica de. —**chroni-**
cler (-klər) *n.* cronista.

chronology (krə'nal·ə·dʒi) *n.*
cronología. —**chronological**
(,kran·ə'ladʒ·ɪ·kəl) *adj.* cronológico.

chronometer (krə'nam·ə·tər) *n.*
cronómetro.

chrysalis ('krɪs·ə·lɪs) *n.* crisálida.

chrysanthemum (krɪ'sæn·θə·
məm) *n.* crisantemo.

chubby ('tʃʌb·i) *adj.* gordezuelo;
gordiflón; rechoncho.

chuck (tʃʌk) *n.* 1, *mech.* mandril. 2,
(wedge) calzo; cuña. 3, (cut of beef)
carne del cuello del buey. 4, (tap,
esp. under the chin) mamola. —*v.t.*
1, (tap under the chin) hacer la
mamola a. 2, (toss) tirar. 3, [*usu.,*
chuck out] *colloq.* (throw away)
echar; arrinconar. —*v.i.* (cackle)
cloquear.

chuckle ('tʃʌk·əl) *v.i.* reír conte-
nidamente. —*n.* risita; risa aho-
gada.

chug (tʃʌg) *n.* ruido explosivo
corto. —*v.i.* [**chugged, chugging**]
hacer o moverse con ruidos
explosivos cortos.

chum (tʃʌm) *n., colloq.* compañero;
compinche. —*v.i.* [**chummed,**
chumming] ser compañero; ser
compinche.

chunk (tʃʌŋk) *n.* 1, (piece) trozo;
pedazo grande. 2, *colloq.* (large
piece) cantidad importante.
—**chunky,** *adj.* grueso; carnoso;
rechoncho.

church (tʃʌrtʃ) *n.* iglesia.

churchman ('tʃʌrtʃ·mən) *n.* [*pl.*
-**men**] 1, (clergyman) eclesiástico.
2, (church member) hombre de
iglesia; militante. —**churchwoman,**
n. [*pl.* -**women**] *n.* feligresa.

churchyard ('tʃʌrtʃ·jard) *n.* patio
o jardín de iglesia.

churl (tʃʌrl) *n.* 1, (boor) patán. 2,
(rustic) rústico. —**churlish,** *adj.*
patán; zafio.

churn (tʃʌrn) *n.* 1, (for making butter) mantequera. 2, (agitator)
batidora; agitadora. —*v.t.* (stir)

batir; agitar. —*v.i., fig.* (be stirred up) agitarse; alterarse.

chute (ʃut) *n.* **1,** (inclined duct) canal; conducto; escotilla. **2,** (mail duct) tubo del correo. **3,** (parachute) paracaídas.

cicada (sɪˈkeiˑdə) *n.* chicharra; cigarra.

cicerone (ˌsɪsˑəˈroˑni) *n.* cicerone.

cider (ˈsaiˑdər) *n.* sidra.

cigar (sɪˈgar) *n.* puro; habano; *Amer.* cigarro; tabaco.

cigarette *también,* **cigaret** (ˌsɪgˑəˈrɛt) *n.* cigarrillo; cigarro.

cigarillo (ˌsɪgˑəˈrɪlˑo) *n.* cigarrillo.

cilantro (sɪˈlænˑtro) *n.* cilantro.

cilia (ˈsɪlˑiˑə) *n.pl.* [*sing.* **cilium** (-əm)] cilios. —**ciliary,** *adj.* ciliar. —**ciliate,** *adj.* ciliado.

cinch (sɪntʃ) *n.* **1,** (girth; strap) cincha; cincho. **2,** *slang* (easy task) ganga. **3,** (sure thing) cosa asegurada. —*v.t.* **1,** (tighten) cinchar. **2,** (assure) asegurar; afianzar.

cinchona (sɪnˈkoˑnə) *n.* **1,** (tree) chinchona. **2,** (bark) quina.

cincture (ˈsɪŋkˑtʃər) *n.* cinto; ceñido. —*v.t.* ceñir.

cinder (ˈsɪnˑdər) *n.* **1,** (burnt particle) cernada; pavesa. **2,** *pl.* (ashes) cenizas. —**cinder block,** bloque de cenizas.

Cinderella (sɪnˑdəˈrɛlˑə) *n.* Cenicienta.

cinema (ˈsɪnˑəˑmə) *n.* cinema; cine. —**cinematic** (sɪnˑəˈmætˑɪk); **cinematographic** (ˌsɪnˑəˌmætˑəˈgræfˑɪk) *adj.* cinematográfico. —**cinematograph** (sɪnˑəˈmætˑəˑgræf) *n.* cinematógrafo; cine. —**cinematography** (ˌsɪnˑəˑməˈtagˑrəˑfi) *n.* cinematografía.

cingulum (ˈsɪŋˑgjəˑləm) *n.* cíngulo.

cinnabar (ˈsɪnˑəˌbar) *n.* cinabrio.

cinnamon (ˈsɪnˑəˑmən) *n.* **1,** (tree) canelo; árbol de la canela. **2,** (spice) canela.

cipher (ˈsaiˑfər) *n.* **1,** (zero) cero. **2,** (numeral) cifra. **3,** (code; its key) clave. —*v.t.* **1,** (calculate) calcular. **2,** (write in code) cifrar.

circle (ˈsɑrˑkəl) *n.* **1,** *geom.* círculo; circunferencia; **2,** (ring) anillo. **3,** (cycle) ciclo; círculo. **4,** (social group) círculo; grupo; clase. —*v.t.* circundar; rodear. —*v.i.* dar vueltas.

circuit (ˈsɑrˑkɪt) *n.* **1,** *elect.* circuito. **2,** (boundary) radio; contorno. **3,** (itinerary) itinerario. —**circuitry,** *n.* conjunto de circuitos.

circuit breaker cortacircuitos.

circuitous (sərˈkjuˑɪˑtəs) *adj.* tortuoso; indirecto. —**circuitousness,** *n.* tortuosidad; rodeo.

circular (ˈsɑrˑkjəˑlər) *adj.* **1,** (round) circular; redondo. **2,** (indirect) tortuoso; sinuoso. —*n.* circular; aviso.

circulate (ˈsɑrˑkjuˑleit) *v.i.* circular; moverse. —*v.t.* propalar; divulgar; esparcir. —**circulatory** (-ləˌtorˑi) *adj.* circulatorio.

circulation (ˌsɑrˑkjuˈleiˑʃən) *n.* circulación.

circumcision (ˈsɑrˑkəmˌsɪʒˑen) *n.* circuncisión. —**circumcise** (ˈsɑrˑkəmˌsaiz) *v.t.* circuncidar.

circumference (sərˈkʌmˑfərˑəns) *n.* circunferencia.

circumflex (ˈsɑrˑkəmˌflɛks) *n.* circunflejo; acento circunflejo (^).

circumlocution (ˌsɑrˑkəmˑloˈkjuˑʃən) *n.* circunlocución; circunloquio; rodeo.

circumnavigate (ˌsɑrˑkəmˈnævˑəˌgeit) *v.t.* circunnavegar. —**circumnavigation,** *n.* circunnavegación.

circumscribe (ˌsɑrˑkəmˈskraib) *v.t.* circunscribir; limitar. —**circumscription** (-ˈskrɪpˑʃən) *n.* circunscripción; limitación.

circumspect (ˈsɑrˑkəmˌspɛkt) *adj.* circunspecto; discreto. —**circumspection** (-ˈspɛkˑʃən) *n.* circunspección: recato; discreción.

circumstance (ˈsɑrˑkəmˌstæns) *n.* circunstancia. —**in easy circumstances,** en buena posición; acomodado. —**under no circumstances,** de ninguna manera.

circumstantial (ˌsɑrˑkəmˈstænˑʃəl) *adj.* circunstancial.

circumstantiate (ˌsɑrˑkəmˈstænˑʃiˌet) *v.t.* comprobar en todos los detalles.

circumvent (sɑrˑkəmˈvɛnt) *v.t.* **1,** (evade) esquivar. **2,** (outwit) engañar; embaucar. —**circumvention** (-ˈvɛnˑʃən) *n.* evasión; engaño.

circus (ˈsɑrˑkəs) *n.* circo.

cirrhosis (sɪˈroˑsɪs) *n.* cirrosis.

cirrus (ˈsɪrˑəs) *n.* [*pl.* **cirri** (-ai)] cirro.

cistern (ˈsɪsˑtərn) *n.* cisterna.

citadel (ˈsɪtˑəˑdəl) *n.* ciudadela; fortaleza.

citation (saiˈteiˑʃən) *n.* **1,** (quotation) cita. **2,** (commendation)

citación; mención. **3,** *law* emplazamiento.
cite (sait) *v.t.* **1,** (mention) citar; mencionar; referirse a. **2,** *law* emplazar.
cithara ('sıθ·ə·rə) *n.* cítara.
citified ('sıt·ı,faid) *adj.*, *colloq.* urbano; con costumbres de ciudad.
citizen ('sıt·ə·zən) *n.* ciudadano. —**citizenry** (-ri) *n.* nación; gente; población. —**citizenship,** *n.* ciudadanía; nacionalidad. —**fellow citizen,** conciudadano.
citrate ('sai·tret; 'sıt·ret) *n.* citrato.
citric ('sıt·rık) *adj.* cítrico.
citron ('sıt·rən) *n.* **1,** (tree) cidro. **2,** (fruit) cidra.
citrus ('sıt·rəs) *n.* cidro. —*adj.* [*también,* **citrous**] cítrico.
city ('sıt·i) *n.* ciudad. —**city council,** ayuntamiento; concejo municipal. —**city hall,** ayuntamiento; alcaldía; municipio.
civet ('sıv·ıt) *n.* civeto. —**civet cat,** civeta.
civic ('sıv·ık) *adj.* cívico. —**civics,** *n.* ciencia del gobierno civil.
civil ('sıv·əl) *adj.* **1,** (pert. to citizens) civil. **2,** (polite) civil; educado; cortés. —**civil defense,** defensa civil. —**civil engineering,** ingeniería civil; *Sp.* ingeniería de caminos, canales y puertos. —**civil law,** derecho civil. —**civil liberty,** libertad de ciudadanos. —**civil marriage,** matrimonio civil. —**civil rights,** derechos de ciudadanos. —**civil servant,** funcionario; empleado de administración pública. —**civil service,** servicio civil o de administración pública. —**civil war,** guerra civil.
civilian (sə'vıl·jən) *n.* ciudadano. —*adj.* civil.
civility (sə'vıl·ə·ti) *n.* civilidad; sociabilidad; urbanidad.
civilization (,sıv·ə·lı'zei·ʃən) *n.* civilización.
civilize ('sıv·ə,laiz) *v.t.* civilizar.
clack (klæk) *n.* chasquido; ruido seco. —*v.t.* chasquear. —*v.i.* chascar.
clad (klæd) *v.*, *pret.* & *p.p. de* **clothe.** —*adj.* vestido; cubierto.
claim (kleim) *v.t.* **1,** (demand) demandar; reclamar. **2,** *colloq.* (assert) pretender; debatir; contender. —*n.* demanda; reclamación. —**claimant,** *n.* demandante; peticionario.

clairvoyance (klɛr'vɔi·əns) *n.* clarividencia; lucidez. —**clairvoyant,** *n.* & *adj.* clarividente.
clam (klæm) *n.* **1,** (mollusk) almeja. **2,** *fig.* (reticent person) ostra. —**clam up,** *slang* callarse.
clamber ('klæm·bər) *v.i.* gatear; encaramarse; trepar.
clammy ('klæm·i) *adj.* pegajoso; pastoso; gelatinoso. —**clamminess,** *n.* viscosidad; pegajosidad.
clamor *también,* **clamour** ('klæm·ər) *n.* clamor; alboroto; vocería. —*v.i.* clamorear; gritar; vociferar. —**clamorous,** *adj.* clamoroso; vociferante; vinglero.
clamp (klæmp) *n.* grapa; abrazadera. —*v.t.* sujetar; afianzar; coser con grapas. —**clamp down (on),** *colloq.* ponerse serio (con); volverse riguroso (con).
clan (klæn) *n.* **1,** (tribe) clan; tribu. **2,** *fig.* (kin) familia. **3,** (clique) camarilla; pandilla. —**clannish** (-ısh) *adj.* gregario; exclusivista.
clandestine (klæn'dɛs·tın) *adj.* clandestino; furtivo. —**clandestineness,** *n.* clandestinidad.
clang (klæŋ) *n.* retintín. —*v.t.* hacer sonar; resonar. —*v.i.* sonar o vibrar metálicamente.
clank (klæŋk) *n.* chirrido o golpe metálico. —*v.i.* rechinar; chirriar.
clansman ('klænz·mən) *n.* [*pl.* **-men**] pariente; miembro de un clan.
clap (klæp) *v.t.* [**clapped, clapping**] **1,** (strike the hands) palmotear; aplaudir. **2,** *slang* (place or dispose of swiftly) empujar; tirar; arrojar. —*v.i.* batir; aplaudir. —*n.* **1,** (applause) aplauso; ovación. **2,** (a blow) palmada. **3,** *slang* gonorrea.
clapboard ('klæb·ərd) *n.* chilla.
clapper ('klæp·ər) *n.* badajo.
claptrap ('klæp,træp) *n.* engañifa; faramalla.
claque (klæk) *n.* claque.
claret ('klær·ət) *n.* vino clarete.
clarify ('klær·ə,fai) *v.t.* **1,** (make clear) clarificar; aclarar. **2,** *fig.* (explain) esclarecer. —*v.i.* aclararse; clarificarse. —**clarification** (-fı'kei·ʃən) *n.* clarificación; aclaración.
clarinet (klær·ə'nɛt) *n.* clarinete. —**clarinetist,** *n.* clarinete.
clarion ('klær·i·ən) *n.* clarín.
clarity ('klær·ə·ti) *n.* claridad.
clash (klæʃ) *v.i.* **1,** (collide) chocar; entrechocar. **2,** *fig.* (oppose) encontrarse; oponerse; antagonizar.

—*v.t.* golpear violentamente. —*n.* **1,** (collision) choque; colisión. **2,** *fig.* (conflict) encuentro; disputa.

clasp (klæsp) *n.* **1,** (latch) abrazadera; broche; hebilla. **2,** (embrace) abrazo; apretón. —*v.t.* **1,** (lock) abrochar; enganchar; asegurar. **2,** (embrace) apretar; abrazar.

class (klæs) *n.* **1,** (category) clase; categoría; rango; condición. **2,** (academic) clase. **3,** *colloq.* (refinement) elegancia; belleza; madera. —*v.t.* clasificar.

classic ('klæs·ɪk) *n.* clásico; obra clásica; autor clásico. —*adj.* [también, **classical**] clásico.

classicism ('klæs·ə·sɪz·əm) *n.* clasicismo. —**classicist,** *n.* clasicista.

classification (,klæs·ɪ·fɪ'kei·ʃən) *n.* clasificación.

classified ('klæs·ɪ,faid) *adj.* **1,** (grouped) clasificado. **2,** *mil.* secreto; confidencial.

classify ('klæs·ɪ,fai) *v.t.* clasificar.

classroom ('klæs·rum) *n.* sala o salón de clase; aula.

clatter ('klæt·ər) *n.* estruendo; ruido; martilleo. —*v.t.* hacer retumbar. —*v.i.* resonar; hacer ruido.

clause (klɔːz) *n.* **1,** *gram.* cláusula; período. **2,** (stipulation) cláusula; condición.

claustrophobia (,klɔs·trə'fo·bi·ə) *n.* claustrofobia.

clavichord ('klæv·ə,kɔrd) *n.* clavicordio.

clavicle ('klæv·ɪ·kəl) *n.* clavícula.

claw (klɔː) *n.* **1,** *anat.* garra. **2,** (tool) garfio; gancho; diente. —*v.t. & i.* desgarrar; arañar; despedazar.

clay (klei) *n.* **1,** (earth) arcilla; barro. **2,** *fig.* (human body) barro; el cuerpo humano. —**potter's clay,** barro de alfarero.

clayey ('kle·i) *adj.* arcilloso.

clean (kliːn) *adj.* **1,** (free from dirt) limpio; nítido; aseado. **2,** *fig.* (pure) puro; honrado. **3,** (innocent) inocente. **4,** (fastidious) meticuloso. —*v.t.* **1,** (remove dirt from) limpiar; asear. **2,** (rid of superfluous material) depurar. —*adv.* completamente. —**clean up,** *colloq.* **1,** (make clean) limpiar; lavar. **2,** (tidy) arreglar; asear. **3,** (finish) completar; terminar. **4,** (make money) ganar mucho. —**come clean,** *slang* confesar; desahogarse.

clean-cut *adj.* **1,** (shapely)

definido; claro. **2,** *fig.* (neat) agradable; bien portado; límpido.

cleaner ('kli·nər) *n.* limpiador; quitamanchas.

cleanly ('klin·li) *adv.* limpiamente. —*adj.* ('klɛn·li) limpio. —**cleanliness** ('klɛn-) *n.* limpieza.

cleanness ('klin·nəs) *n.* limpieza; aseo.

cleanse (klɛnz) *v.t.* **1,** (clean) limpiar; quitar manchas. **2,** *fig.* (purge) depurar; purificar. —**cleanser,** *n.* limpiador; quitamanchas; *fig.* purificador.

clean-shaven *adj.* apurado; bien afeitado; bien rasurado.

clear (klɪr) *adj.* **1,** (easily understood) claro; evidente; palpable. **2,** (transparent) transparente; claro; lúcido; despejado. **3,** (innocent) inocente; libre; limpio. —*v.t.* **1,** (unburden) desembarazar; limpiar; aclarar. **2,** (make a profit) ganar; sacar. **3,** (jump over) saltar; salvar. **4,** [también, **clear up**] (solve) solucionar; dilucidar. **5,** [también, **clear away** o **off**] (empty) quitar; desembarazar. —*v.i.* **1,** [usu., **clear up**] (brighten) aclararse; despejarse. **2,** (be paid, as a check) pasar. **3,** [usu., **clear out**] (leave) marcharse; escabullirse. —**clearness,** *n.* claridad; limpidez.

clearance ('klɪr·əns) *n.* **1,** *comm.* despacho de aduana; utilidad líquido. **2,** (space) espacio libre; paso. **3,** (for security) acreditación. —**clearance sale,** venta de liquidación.

clearcut ('klɪr,kʌt) *adj.* obvio; claro; definido.

clearing ('klɪr·ɪŋ) *n.* raso; claro. —**clearing house,** cámara de compensación.

cleat (klit) *n.* abrazadera; tojino.

cleavage ('kliv·ɪdʒ) *n.* hendidura; raja.

cleave (kliːv) *v.i.* **1,** (adhere) adherirse; pegarse; unirse. **2,** (split) henderse; rajarse; partirse. —*v.t.* [pret. **cleft** o **clove**; *p.p.* **cloven**] hender; rajar; partir.

cleaver ('kli·vər) *n.* cuchillo; hacha.

clef (klɛf) *n.* clave. —**bass** o **F clef,** clave de fa. —**tenor** o **C clef,** clave de do. —**treble** o **G clef,** clave de sol.

cleft (klɛft) *n.* grieta; rajadura; hendidura. —*v., pret. & p.p. de*

cleave. —*adj.* agrietado; hendido; rajado.

clematis ('klɛm·ə·tɪs) *n.* clemátide.

clemency ('klɛm·ən·si) *n.* clemencia; indulgencia; piedad. —**clement,** *adj.* clemente; piadoso; indulgente.

clench (klɛntʃ) *v.t.* **1,** (close tightly) apretar. **2,** (grip tightly) asir; agarrar; atenazar.

clergy ('klʌr·dʒi) *n.* clerecía; clero.

clergyman ('klʌr·dʒi·mən) *n.* [*pl.* -**men**] clérigo; eclesiástico; sacerdote; pastor.

cleric ('klɛr·ɪk) *n.* & *adj.* clérigo.

clerical ('klɛr·ə·kəl) *adj.* **1,** *eccles.* clerical; eclesiástico. **2,** (administrative) de oficina.

clerk (klʌrk) *n.* **1,** (shop employee) dependiente. **2,** (office worker) oficinista. —*v.i.* trabajar de oficinista o dependiente. —**clerkship,** *n.* oficio de dependiente u oficinista.

clever ('klɛv·ər) *adj.* listo; inteligente; alerta; hábil; ingenioso. —**cleverness,** *n.* agudeza; listeza.

clew (kluʳ) *n.* **1,** (ball of yarn) madeja; ovillo. **2,** = **clue.**

cliché (kli'ʃei) *n.* frase trillada.

click (klɪk) *n.* golpe seco. —*v.t.* & *i.* (sound) sonar secamente. —*v.i.,* *colloq.* (succeed) triunfar; prosperar.

client ('klai·ənt) *n.* cliente. —**clientele** (kli·ən'tɛl; klai-) *n.* clientela.

cliff (klɪf) *n.* farallón; escarpadura.

climacteric (klai'mæk·tər·ɪk) *adj.* climatérico. —*n.* período climatérico.

climactic (klai'mæk·tɪk) *adj.* culminante.

climate ('klai·mɪt) *n.* clima. —**climatic** (klai'mæt·ɪk) *adj.* climático.

climax ('klai·mæks) *n.* clímax; culminación. —*v.t.* & *i.* culminar.

climb (klaim) *v.t.* & *i.* escalar; trepar; subir. —*n.* ascenso; subida. —**climb down,** descender; bajar.

clime (klaim) *n.,* *poet.* región.

clinch (klɪntʃ) *v.t.* **1,** (fasten) remachar. **2,** (clench) apretar; consolidar. **3,** *fig.* (settle) afirmar; confirmar. —*v.i.* **1,** *colloq.* (hug) abrazar. **2,** *boxing* echar un gancho. —*n.* **1,** (fastening) remache. **2,** *boxing* gancho. **3,** *colloq.* (hug) abrazo.

clincher ('klɪntʃ·ər) *n.* **1,** (person; tool) remachador. **2,** *colloq.* (deci-

sive statement) argumento decisivo; remache.

cling (klɪŋ) *v.i.* [**clung, clinging**] adherirse; pegarse.

clingstone ('klɪŋ·ston) *n.* albérchigo; pavía. *También,* **cling peach.**

clinic ('klɪn·ɪk) *n.* clínica. —**clinical,** *adj.* clínico.

clink (klɪŋk) *n.* **1,** (sharp sound) retintín; sonido agudo. **2,** *slang* (jail) cárcel. —*v.i.* tintinar. —*v.t.* hacer tintinar.

clip (klɪp) *n.* **1,** (fastener) pinza; grapa. **2,** *colloq.* (rapid pace) galope. —*v.t.* [**clipped, clipping**] **1,** (fasten) póner pinzas o grapas a; asegurar; unir. **2,** (shear) cortar; recortar. **3,** (cut short, as hair) esquilar; trasquilar. **4,** *colloq.* (strike) pegar; golpear. —**paper clip,** sujetapapeles.

clipper ('klɪp·ər) *n.* **1,** (cutting tool) recortador; trasquilador; *pl.* tijeras. **2,** (ship) clíper.

clipping ('klɪp·ɪŋ) *n.* recorte.

clique (klik) *n.* camarilla; círculo. —**cliquish,** *adj.* exclusivista.

clitoris ('klɪt·ə·rɪs; 'klai·tə-) *n.* clítoris.

cloaca (klo'ei·kə) *n.* [*pl.* -**cae** (-si)] cloaca.

cloak (klok) *n.* **1,** (garment) capa; manto. **2,** *fig.* (disguise) capa; pretexto; excusa. —*v.t.* **1,** (cover) cubrir; encubrir. **2,** (conceal) ocultar.

clobber ('klab·ər) *v.t.,* *slang* aporrear; golpear.

clock (klak) *n.* **1,** (timepiece) reloj. **2,** (design on hose) cuadrado de medias. —*v.t.* calcular o medir el tiempo de.

clockface ('klak,feis) *n.* esfera del reloj.

clockmaker ('klak,mei·kər) *n.* relojero.

clockwise ('klak,waiz) *adj.* & *adv.* según las manecillas del reloj.

clockwork ('klak,wʌrk) *n.* movimiento de reloj. —**like clockwork,** como un reloj; muy regular.

clod (klad) *n.* **1,** (turf) terrón; tierra. **2,** *fig.* (dolt) estúpido; zoquete; idiota. —**cloddish,** *adj.* estúpido; idiota.

clog (klag) *n.* **1,** (block) obstrucción; obstáculo; traba. **2,** (thick-soled shoe) zueco; chanclo. **3,** (dance) zapateado. —*v.t.* [**clogged, clogging**] **1,** (impede) obstaculizar; entorpecer; embarazar. **2,** (stop up) atorar. —*v.i.* **1,** (become obstructed) atorarse. **2,** (dance) zapatear; bailar el zapateado.

cloister ('klɔis·tər) *n.* **1,** (arcade) claustro. **2,** (religious retreat) monasterio. —**cloistered,** *adj.* enclaustrado.

clone (klon) *n.* clon. —*v.t.* duplicar.

close (kloz) *v.t.* **1,** (shut) cerrar; clausurar. **2,** (fill) cerrar; tapar. **3,** (finish) terminar; concluir; acabar. —*v.i.* **1,** [*usu.,* **close in**] (draw near) acercarse; aproximarse. **2,** (join) unirse; juntarse. **3,** (end) finalizar; concluir. **4,** (complete a transaction) ponerse de acuerdo; saldar. **5,** (grapple) agarrarse; pelearse. —*n.* conclusión; terminación; fin. —**close out,** liquidar. —**close up, 1,** (shut) cerrar por completo; terminar. **2,** (fill a gap in) acercarse más.

close (klos) *adj.* **1,** (near) cercano; junto; inmediato. **2,** (airless) cerrado; sofocante. **3,** (dense) denso; compacto; pesado. **4,** (reticent) reticente; secreto; oculto. **5,** *colloq.* (penurious) tacaño; interesado. —*adv.* cerca. —*n.* cercado; vallado. —**close quarters, 1,** (narrow space) cuchitril; lugar estrecho. **2,** (encounter with an enemy) lucha cuerpo a cuerpo. —**close shave; close call,** *colloq.* escape por un pelo.

closed shop taller de unión obligatoria; taller cerrado.

closefisted (klos'fist·ıd) *adj.* miserable; cicatero; tacaño.

closefitting (klos'fıt·ıŋ) *adj.* ajustado; apretado.

closeness ('klos·nəs) *n.* **1,** (nearness) proximidad. **2,** (airlessness) falta de aire.

closet ('klaz·ıt) *n.* **1,** (place for storage) armario. **2,** (small room) gabinete. **3,** (toilet) excusado; retrete; lavabo. —*v.t.* encerrar. —**closeted,** *adj.* encerrado.

close-up ('klos,ʌp) *n.* vista de cerca.

closure ('klo·ʒər) *n.* **1,** (act) cierre; clausura. **2,** (state) encierro. **3,** (thing that closes) cierre. **4,** (end) conclusión; fin; término.

clot (klat) *n.* coágulo; grumo. —*v.t.* [**clotted, clotting**] coagular; cuajar. —*v.i.* coagularse; cuajarse.

cloth (klɔθ) *n.* **1,** (fabric) tejido; paño; tela. **2,** (clerical robe) traje clerical; sotana. **3,** *fig.* (the clergy) clero. —*adj.* de tejido; de tela.

clothe (kloð) *v.t.* vestir; arropar; trajear.

clothes (kloz) *n.pl.* **1,** (for men) traje. **2,** (for women) vestido. **3,** (for a bed) ropa de cama; cobertor. —**clothes closet,** ropero. —**clothespin,** *n.* pinza (para tender la ropa). —**clothes tree,** perchero.

clotheshorse ('kloz·hors) *n., slang* petimetra; pisaverde.

clothesline ('kloz·lain) *n.* cordel de tender.

clothier ('kloð·jər) *n.* ropero.

cloture ('klo·tʃər) *n.* clausura (de un debate).

clothing ('klo·ðıŋ) *n.* vestuario; ropa. —**clothing shop** o **store,** ropería.

cloud (klaud) *n.* **1,** (sky vapor) nube; nublado. **2,** (dark spot) nube; mancha. **3,** *fig.* (mass) nube; multitud. —*v.t.* & *i.* (obscure) anublar; nublar; oscurecer; empañar. —*v.t.* (sully) difamar; manchar. —**cloudiness,** *n.* nublosidad; obscuridad. —**cloudless,** *adj.* sin nubes; despejado. —**cloudy,** *adj.* nublado.

cloudburst ('klaud·bʌrst) *n.* aguacero; turbión.

clout (klaut) *n.* **1,** (blow) golpe; bofetón. **2,** *slang* (power) poder; influencia. —*v.t.* abofetear; golpear con la mano.

clove (klov) *n.* **1,** (segment, as of garlic) diente. **2,** (spice) clavo. —*v., pret. de* **cleave.**

cloven ('klo·vən) *v., p.p. de* **cleave.** —**cloven hoof** pie hendido. —**cloven-hoofed,** *adj.* bisulco; *fig.* diabólico.

clover ('klo·vər) *n.* trébol.

cloverleaf ('klo·vər,lif) *n.* cruce en forma de trébol.

clown (klaun) *n.* payaso. —*v.i.* payasear; hacer el payaso o el bufón; parodiar. —**clownish,** *adj.* grotesco; apayasado.

cloy (klɔi) *v.t.* & *i.* hartar; saciar. —*v.i.* empalagarse.

club (klʌb) *n.* **1,** (weapon) porra; garrote; palo. **2,** (association) club; círculo. **3,** *cards* trébol (*in the French deck);* basto (*in the Spanish deck).* —*v.t.* [**clubbed, clubbing**] golpear; aporrear. —**club together,** unirse; congregarse.

clubfoot ('klʌb·fut) *n.* [*pl.* **-feet**]

patituerto. —**clubfooted,** `adj.` patituerto.

cluck (klʌk) n. **1,** (of a person) chasquido de la lengua. **2,** (of a hen) cloqueo. —v.i. cloquear.

clue (kluɹ) n. pista; guía; indicio.

clump (klʌmp) n. **1,** (lump) trozo; masa. **2,** (cluster, as of trees) macizo; grupo. —v.i. andar pesadamente.

clumpy ('klʌm·pi) adj. **1,** (heavy) macizo; pesado. **2,** (awkward) desmañado; torpe.

clumsy ('klʌm·zi) adj. zafio; ordinario; tosco; inadaptado. —**clumsiness,** n. zafiedad; ordinariez; desmañamiento.

clung (klʌŋ) v., pret. & p.p. de **cling.**

clunk (klʌŋk) n. golpe o sonido seco. —v.i. golpear o sonar secamente. —**clunker,** n., slang carro destartalado.

cluster ('klʌs·tər) n. **1,** (of persons) grupo; pelotón. **2,** (of things) racimo; ramo. —v.t. agrupar; arracimar. —v.i. arracimarse; agruparse.

clutch (klʌtʃ) v.t. agarrar; asir. —v.i. [usu., **clutch at**] intentar agarrar o apresar. —n. **1,** usu. pl. (grip) control; poder; mando. **2,** mech. embrague. **3,** (brood of chickens) nidada; pollada. —**fall into the clutches of,** caer en las garras de. —**engage the clutch,** embragar.

clutter ('klʌt·ər) n. desorden; confusión. —v.t. [también, **clutter up**] alborotar; desordenar.

coach (kotʃ) n. **1,** (carriage) carruaje; coche; vehículo. **2,** (instructor) instructor; entrenador. —v.t. instruir; entrenar; aconsejar.

coachman ('kotʃ·mən) n. [pl. -men] cochero.

coagulate (ko'æg·jə,leit) v.t. coagular. —v.i. coagularse. —**coagulation,** n. coagulación.

coal (koɹl) n. **1,** (mineral) hulla; carbón de piedra. **2,** (lump) brasa; carbón. —**coal mine,** mina de carbón; mina de hulla. —**coal tar,** alquitrán de hulla.

coalesce (ko·ə'lɛs) v.i. incorporarse; juntarse; integrarse. —**coalescence,** n. coalición; unión. —**coalescent,** adj. integrante.

coalition (ko·ə'lɪʃ·ən) n. coalición.

coarse (kors) adj. **1,** (rough) basto; ordinario. **2,** fig. (vulgar) rudo;

soez; vulgar. —**coarsen** ('kor·sən) v.t. hacer ordinario. —**coarseness,** n. rudeza; ordinariez.

coast (kost) n. costa; litoral. —v.i. deslizarse; correr por la gravedad. —**coastal,** adj. costero. —**coast guard,** cuerpo de guardacostas.

coastline ('kost·lain) n. litoral.

coat (kot) n. **1,** (outer garment) chaqueta; americana; Amer. saco. **2,** (hair; fur) pelo. **3,** (layer, as of paint) mano. —v.t. **1,** (cover) cubrir; vestir. **2,** (paint) dar una mano a. —**coat of mail,** cota de malla.

coating ('ko·tɪŋ) n. **1,** (covering) capa; revestimiento. **2,** (plating) baño.

coax (koks) v.t. & i. engatusar; halagar. —**coaxing,** n. engatusamiento; halago.

coaxial (ko'æk·si·əl) adj. coaxial.

cob (kaɹb) n. **1,** (of corn) mazorca; Amer. tusa. **2,** (horse) jaca. **3,** (male swan) cisne.

cobalt ('ko·bɔlt) n. cobalto. —adj. de cobalto.

cobble ('kab·əl) v.t. & i. remendar (zapatos).

cobbler ('kab·lər) n. **1,** (shoemaker) zapatero remendón. **2,** (fruit pie or drink) postre o bebida con frutas.

cobblestone ('kab·əl·ston) n. guijarro.

COBOL ('ko·bɔl) n., comput., abr. de **common business oriented language.**

cobra ('ko·brə) n. cobra.

cobweb ('kab·wɛb) n. tela de araña; telaraña.

coca ('ko·kə) n., bot. coca.

cocaine (ko'kein) n. cocaína.

coccus ('kak·əs) n. [pl. **cocci** (-sai)] **1,** (bacterium) coco. **2,** bot. carpelo.

coccyx ('kak·siks) n. [pl. **coccyges** (-sɪ,dʒiz)] cóccix; rabadilla.

cochineal ('katʃ·ə'niɹl) n. cochinilla.

cochlea (,kak·li·ə) n. [pl. **cochleae** (-i)] caracol (del oído).

cock (kak) n. **1,** (male fowl) gallo; macho. **2,** (leader) capitán; líder; caudillo. **3,** (conical pile) pajar; henil. **4,** (tilt, as of a hat) vuelta (del ala); inclinación. **5,** (weathercock) veleta. —v.t. **1,** (turn up on one side) ladear; inclinar. **2,** (ready a gun) amartillar; montar. **3,** (raise) levantar. —**cock and bull story,** cuento increíble.

cockatoo (,kak·ə'tuɹ) n. cacatúa.

cockboat ('kak,bot) *n.* barquichuelo.

cocked hat tricornio; sombrero de tres picos.

cockfight ('kak,fait) *n.* pelea de gallos.

cockle ('kak·əl) *n.* 1, (weed) maleza; cizaña. 2, (mollusk) coquina; caracol de mar. 3, (boat) barquichuelo. —*v.t.* & *i.* arrugar; doblar. —**cockles of the heart,** las entrañas.

cockleshell ('kak·əl,ʃel) *n.* coquina.

cockney ('kak·ni) *n.* londinense bajo; lenguaje de éste.

cockpit ('kak·pɪt) *n.* 1, *aero.* carlinga. 2, (place for cockfighting) gallera.

cockroach ('kak·rotʃ) *n.* cucaracha.

cockscomb ('kaks·kom) *n.* cresta de gallo.

cocksure ('kak·ʃur) *adj.* seguro; confiado.

cocktail ('kak·tel) *n.* coctel. —**cocktail shaker,** coctelera.

cocky ('kak·i) *adj.* vanidoso; presumido. —**cockiness,** *n.* presunción.

cocoa ('ko·ko) *n.* cacao; chocolate. —**cocoa butter,** manteca de cacao.

coconut *también,* **cocoanut** ('ko·kə,nʌt) *n.* 1, (fruit) coco. 2, (tree) coco; cocotero. —**coconut grove** o **plantation,** cocotal.

cocoon (kə'kuːn) *n.* capullo (de gusanos).

cod (kad) *n.* bacalao. *También,* **codfish.**

coda ('ko·də) *n.* coda.

coddle ('kad·əl) *v.t.* 1, (pamper) consentir; mimar. 2, (cook) mediococer; mediohervir.

code (kod) *n.* 1, (set of laws or rules) código. 2, (system of signals) código; clave; cifra.

codeine ('ko·din) *n.* codeína.

codex ('ko·deks) *n.* [*pl.* **-dices** (-dɪ·siz)] códice.

codger ('kadʒ·ər) *n., colloq.* vejete.

codicil ('kad·ə·səl) *n.* codicilo.

codify ('kad·ɪ,fai) *v.t.* codificar; compilar. —**codification** (-fɪ'kei·ʃən) *n.* codificación.

coed ('ko·ed) *n., colloq.* alumna de escuela o de universidad coeducativa.

coeducation (,ko·ed·jə'kei·ʃən) *n.* coeducación. —**coeducational,** *adj.* coeducativo.

coefficient (,ko·ə'fɪʃ·ənt) *n.* & *adj.* coeficiente.

coequal (ko'i·kwəl) *adj.* & *n.* igual; semejante.

coerce (ko'ʌrs) *v.t.* coercer; obligar; forzar. —**coercion** (-'ʌr·ʃən) *n.* coerción.

coeval (ko'i·vəl) *adj.* coevo; contemporáneo.

coexist (,ko·eg'zɪst) *v.i.* coexistir; convivir. —**coexistence,** *n.* coexistencia.

coffee ('kɔf·i) 1, (tree) cafeto. 2, (drink) café. —**coffee pot,** cafetera. —**coffee shop,** café.

coffee break pausa para tomar café.

coffeehouse ('kɔf·i,haus) *n.* café.

coffer ('kɔf·ər) *n.* cofre; arca.

coffin ('kɔf·ɪn) *n.* ataúd; féretro; caja.

cog (kag) *n.* diente de rueda. —**cog railway,** ferrocarril de cremallera.

cogent ('ko·dʒənt) *adj.* convincente; poderoso; urgente. —**cogency,** *n.* evidencia; fuerza.

cogitate ('kadʒ·ə·teit) *v.t.* & *i.* pensar; planear; meditar; reflexionar. —**cogitation,** *n.* meditación; reflexión.

cognac ('kon·jæk) *n.* coñac.

cognate ('kag·net) *adj.* & *n.* cognado.

cognition (kag'nɪʃ·ən) *n.* conocimiento; entendimiento. —**cognitive** ('kag·nɪ·tɪv) *adj.* cognoscitivo.

cognizance ('kag·nɪ·zəns) *n.* 1, (awareness) conocimiento; noticia; percepción. 2, (range of knowledge) comprensión. 3, *law* jurisdicción; competencia. 4, *her.* divisa; mote. —**cognizant,** *adj.* sabedor; conocedor; informado. —**take cognizance of,** reconocer oficialmente.

cognomen (kag'no·mən) *n.* 1, (surname) apellido. 2, (nickname) mote; apodo. 3, (Roman family name) cognomen.

cogwheel ('kag,wil) *n.* rueda dentada.

cohabit (ko'hæb·ɪt) *v.i.* cohabitar; vivir maritalmente. —**cohabitation,** *n.* cohabitación.

coheir (ko'eir) *n.* coheredero.

cohere (ko'hɪr) *v.i.* 1, (adhere) unirse; adherirse; pegarse. 2, (conform) conformarse; ajustarse. —**coherence,** *n.* coherencia. —**coherent,** *adj.* coherente.

cohesion (ko'hi·ʒən) *n.* cohesión;

coherencia. —**cohesive** (-sɪv) *adj.* adherente; coherente.

cohort ('ko·hort) *n.* **1,** (group) cohorte; banda. **2,** (companion) compañero.

coif (kɔif) *n.* **1,** (tight cap) cofia. **2,** (nun's cap) toca.

coiffure (kwa'fjʊr) *n.* peinado; tocado. —**coiffeur** (-'fʌr) *n.* peluquero.

coil (kɔil) *v.t. & i.* enrollar; arrollar. —*n.* **1,** (roll) rollo. **2,** *elect.* bobina.

coin (kɔin) *n.* moneda. —*v.t.* **1,** (mint) acuñar. **2,** (invent) acuñar; inventar.

coinage ('kɔin·ɪdʒ) *n.* **1,** (minting) acuñación. **2,** (currency) moneda; dinero; sistema monetario. **3,** (invention) acuñación; invención.

coincide (ˌko·ɪn'said) *v.i.* **1,** (take up the same space) coincidir. **2,** (occur at the same time) coincidir; concurrir. **3,** (agree) convenir; estar o ponerse de acuerdo.

coincidence (ko'ɪn·sɪ·dəns) *n.* coincidencia; casualidad.

coincident (ko'ɪn·sɪ·dənt) *adj.* coincidente.

coincidental (koˌɪn·sɪ'dɛn·təl) *adj.* coincidente; de coincidencia; por casualidad.

coitus ('ko·ɪ·təs) *n.* coito. *También,* **coition** (ko'ɪʃ·ən).

coke (kok) *n.* **1,** (fuel) cok; coque. **2,** *slang* = **cocaine. 3,** *colloq.* Coca-Cola *(T.N.).*

cola ('ko·lə) *n.* **1,** *bot.* cola. **2,** (refresco) bebida hecha con extracto de cola.

colander ('kal·ən·dər) *n.* colador; coladera; escurridor.

cold (kold) *adj.* **1,** (lacking warmth) frío. **2,** *fig.* (unfeeling) frío; tibio; indiferente; insensible. —*n.* **1,** (lack of warmth) frío. **2,** (ailment) catarro; constipado; resfrío. —**catch, take** o **get a cold,** acatarrarse; resfriarse; tomar frío. —**cold feet,** *colloq.* miedo; temor; desánimo. —**cold meat; cold cuts,** fiambre. —**cold shoulder,** *colloq.* indiferencia; frialdad. —**cold storage,** (conservación en) cámara frigorífica. —**cold turkey,** *colloq., en* **quit cold turkey,** renunciar repentinamente. —**talk cold turkey,** *colloq.* hablar cándidamente. —**cold war,** guerra fría.

cold cream colcrén.

cold front frente frío.

coldblooded (ˌkold'blʌd·ɪd) *adj.* inhumano; cruel; de sangre fría; atroz. —**cold-bloodedness,** *n.* sangre fría; crueldad; inhumanidad.

coldhearted (ˌkold'har·tɪd) *adj.* duro; frío; insensible.

coldness ('kold·nəs) *n.* **1,** (lack of warmth) frío; frigidez. **2,** (indifference) frialdad; insensibilidad; indiferencia.

cole (kol) *n.* col; berza.

coleslaw ('kol·slɔ) *n.* ensalada de col.

colic ('kal·ɪk) *n. & adj.* cólico. —**colicky,** *adj.* que padece cólico.

coliseum (kal·ə'si·əm) *n.* coliseo.

colitigant (ˌko'lɪt·ə·gənt) *n., law* consorte.

colitis (ko'lai·tɪs) *n.* colitis.

collaborate (kə'læb·ə·reit) *v.i.* colaborar. —**collaboration,** *n.* colaboración. —**collaborationist,** *n.* colaboracionista. —**collaborator,** *n.* colaborador.

collage (kə'laʒ) *n.* montaje.

collapse (kə'læps) *n.* colapso. —*v.i.* **1,** (become broken) romperse. **2,** (fail) desplomarse; derrumbarse. **3,** (break down physically) debilitarse; prostrarse. —*v.t.* plegar; cerrar. —**collapsible,** *adj.* plegable.

collar ('kal·ər) *n.* **1,** (of a garment) cuello. **2,** (of an animal) collar; collera. —*v.t.* **1,** (put a collar on) poner cuello o collar a. **2,** (grasp by the collar) coger por el cuello. **3,** *slang* (seize; arrest) agarrar; capturar.

collarbone ('kal·ər·bon) *n.* clavícula.

collate (kə'leit) *v.t.* **1,** (compare) comparar; cotejar. **2,** (assemble in order) ordenar.

collateral (kə'læt·ə·rəl) *adj.* **1,** (supplementary) accesorio; subordinado. **2,** (side by side) paralelo; colateral. —*n.* garantía.

collation (ko'lei·ʃən) *n.* **1,** (act of collating) cotejo; comparación. **2,** (light meal) colación.

colleague ('kal·ig) *n.* colega; compañero.

collect (kə'lɛkt) *v.t.* **1,** (assemble) congregar; reunir; juntar. **2,** (obtain payment for) cobrar; recaudar. **3,** (acquire) coleccionar; juntar. —*n.* ('kal·ɛkt) colecta. —**collect oneself,** volver en sí; reponerse; tranquilizarse. —**collectedness,** *n.* calma. —**collectible,** *adj.* cobrable.

collection (kə'lɛk·ʃən) *n.* **1,**

(things collected) colección. **2,** (money collected) colecta. **3,** (mass) conjunto; acumulación.

collective (kə'lɛk·tɪv) *adj.* colectivo. **—collectively,** *adv.* en conjunto. **—collectivism,** *n.* colectivismo. **—collectivity** (,kal·ɛk'tɪv·ə·ti) *n.* colectividad. **—collective bargaining,** negociaciones colectivas.

collector (kə'lɛk·tər) *n.* **1,** (one who collects as a hobby) coleccionista. **2,** (one who collects money due) recaudador.

college ('kal·ɪdʒ) *n.* colegio; universidad.

collegian (kə'liː·dʒən) *n.* colegial; universitario.

collegiate (kə'liː·dʒɪ·ət) *adj.* **1,** (of a college) colegiado; colegial. **2,** *eccles.* colegial.

collide (kə'laid) *v.i.* chocar; topar.

collie ('kal·i) *n.* perro de pastor escocés.

collier ('kal·jər) *n.* **1,** (coal miner) minero de carbón. **2,** (vessel) barco carbonero; carbonero. **—colliery,** *n.* mina de carbón.

collision (kə'lɪʒ·ən) *n.* **1,** (clash) colisión; choque. **2,** (encounter) encuentro.

collodion (kə'lo·di·ən) *n.* colodión.

colloid ('kal·ɔid) *n.* coloide. **—colloidal** (kə'lɔi·dəl) *adj.* coloideo.

colloquial (kə'lo·kwi·əl) *adj.* familiar. **—colloquialism,** *n.* expresión familiar.

colloquium (kə'lo·kwi·əm) *n.* coloquio; conferencia.

colloquy ('kal·ə·kwi) *n.* coloquio; conversación.

collusion (kə'lu·ʒən) *n.* colusión. **—collusive** (-sɪv) *adj.* colusorio.

cologne (kə'loːn) *n.* colonia; agua de colonia.

colon ('ko·lən) *n.* **1,** *anat.* colon. **2,** *gram.* dos puntos (:).

colonel ('kɜr·nəl) *n.* coronel. **—colonelcy** (-si) *n.* coronelía.

colonial (kə'lo·ni·əl) *adj.* colonial. **—n.** colono. **—colonialism,** *n.* colonialismo.

colonist ('kal·ə·nɪst) *n.* colono.

colonize ('kal·ə,naiz) *v.t.* colonizar. **—colonization** (-nɪ'zei·ʃən) *n.* colonización.

colonnade (kal·ə'neid) *n.* columnata.

colony ('kal·ə·ni) *n.* colonia.

colophon ('kal·ə,fan) *n.* colofón.

color *también,* **colour** ('kʌl·ər) *n.* **1,** (hue) color. **2,** *fig.* (appearance) complexión; color de la piel; apariencia; constitución. **3,** *pl.* (flag) colores; bandera. **—v.t. 1,** (dye) teñir; colorar. **2,** (misrepresent) falsear; desfigurar. **—v.i.** enrojecerse; ruborizarse. **—coloration,** *n.* coloración. **—show one's colors,** descubrirse; declararse. **—with flying colors,** con lucimiento; a banderas desplegadas.

color-blind *adj.* daltoniano. **—color blindness,** daltonismo.

color-code *v.t.* identificar mediante distintos colores.

colored ('kʌl·ərd) *adj.* **1,** (having color) de o con color. **2,** (Negro) negro. **3,** (biased) prejuiciado; predispuesto; influenciado.

colorfast ('kʌl·ər,fæst) *adj.* de color fijo o permanente.

colorful ('kʌl·ər·fəl) *adj.* vistoso; lleno de color; pintoresco.

coloring ('kʌl·ər·ɪŋ) *n.* tinte; colorante; colorido.

colorless ('kʌl·ər·ləs) *adj.* **1,** (without color) incoloro; descolorido. **2,** *fig.* (dull) sin atractivo.

colossal (kə'las·əl) *adj.* colosal; gigantesco.

colossus (kə'las·əs) *n.* coloso.

colostomy (kə'las·tə·mi) *n.* colostomía.

colt (kolt) *n.* potro.

columbine ('kal·əm,bain) *n., bot.* aguileña.

columbium (kə'lʌm·bi·əm) *n.* columbio.

column ('kal·əm) *n.* columna. **—columnar** (kə'lʌm·nər) *adj.* columnario.

columnist ('kal·əm·ɪst; -nɪst) *n.* articulista; columnista.

coma ('ko·mə) *n.* coma; letargo. **—comatose** (-tos) *adj.* comatoso; letárgico.

comb (kom) *n.* **1,** (for hair) peine; peineta; *Amer.* peinilla. **2,** (for fibers) carda; cardencha; rastrillo. **3,** (of a rooster) cresta. **4,** (honeycomb) panal. **—v.t. 1,** (dress hair) peinar. **2,** (card fibers) cardar; rastrillar. **3,** (search thoroughly) registrar; revolver.

combat ('kam·bæt) *n.* combate; batalla; lucha. **—v.t. & i.** (kəm'bæt) combatir; pelear; batallar; luchar. **—combatant** (kam·'bæ·tənt) *n. & adj.* combatiente. **—com-**

bative (kəm'bæt·ɪv) *adj.* peleador; luchador.

combination (ˌkam·bɪ'nei·ʃən) *n.* combinación.

combine (kəm'bain) *v.t. & i.* combinar; mezclar; unir. —*n.* ('kam·bain) **1,** (harvesting machine) segadora; trilladora. **2,** *colloq.* (union) combinación; unión de personas o empresas.

combustion (kəm'bʌs·tʃən) *n.* combustión. —**combustible** (-tə·bəl) *n. & adj.* combustible.

come (kʌm) *v.i.* [**came, come, coming**] **1,** (approach) acercarse; aproximarse. **2,** (arrive) llegar; venir; aparecer. **3,** (be derived) provenir; proceder. **4,** (become) convertirse; hacerse. **5,** (happen) ocurrir; acontecer. **6,** (extend to) acercarse; llegar. **7,** (be obtainable) conseguirse; venir. —**come about,** acaecer; suceder; pasar. —**come across, 1,** *colloq.* (meet) encontrarse con. **2,** *slang* (deliver) entregar. —**come apart,** separarse; desmontarse; despegarse. —**come around,** *colloq.* **1,** (recover) recuperar. **2,** (yield) someterse. —**come back, 1,** (recur to mind) recordar; acordarse de. **2,** (return) volver. **3,** *slang* (retort) responder; contestar. —**come between,** interponerse en; separar; desunir. —**come by,** conseguir; obtener. —**come down, 1,** (descend) bajar; descender. **2,** (lose caste) descender. **3,** (be inherited) transmitirse. —**come down with,** enfermarse de. —**come forth,** salir. —**come forward, 1,** (advance) avanzar; adelantarse. **2,** (appear) presentarse. **3,** (volunteer) ofrecerse. —**come in, 1,** (enter) entrar. **2,** (arrive) llegar. **3,** (begin) empezar. —**come in!,** ¡adelante! —**come into, 1,** (enter) entrar en. **2,** (acquire) conseguir; obtener; recibir. **3,** (inherit) heredar. —**come off, 1,** (become separated) separarse; soltarse; salir. **2,** (occur) ocurrir; suceder. **3,** *colloq.* (result) salir; resultar. —**come on, 1,** (make progress) mejorar; adelantar. **2,** (find; meet) encontrar; encontrarse con; hallar. **3,** (attack) caerle encima a uno. —**come on!,** ¡vamos!; ¡vaya!; ¡adelante! —**come out, 1,** (leave; exit) salir. **2,** (be disclosed) salir a luz. **3,** (make a debut) debutar; estrenarse. **4,** (be presented to soci-ety) ponerse de largo. **5,** (result) salir; resultar. **6,** (take a stand) declararse. —**come over, 1,** (happen to) pasarle a uno. **2,** (seize) asir; coger. **3,** (be persuaded) convencerse. —**come through, 1,** (survive) sobrevivir. **2,** (do as expected) acceder; convenir. **3,** (perform well) triunfar. —**come to; come to oneself,** recobrarse; volver en sí. —**come true,** realizarse. —**come up, 1,** (ascend) subir. **2,** (arise; come under consideration) surgir; presentarse. —**come upon, 1,** (meet) tropezar con; encontrarse con. **2,** (attack) atacar. —**come up to, 1,** (reach) alcanzar. **2,** (approach) acercarse a. **3,** (ascend to) subir a. **4,** (be equal to) ser igual a; estar a la altura de. —**come up with, 1,** (overtake) alcanzar. **2,** (propose) proponer. —**how come?,** *slang* ¿cómo pudo?

comeback ('kʌm·bæk) *n., colloq.* **1,** (recovery) rehabilitación. **2,** (return) reaparición; retorno. **3,** (retort) respuesta mordaz.

comedian (kə'mi·di·ən) *n.* actor; cómico; comediante. —**comedienne** (-'ɛn) *n.f.* actriz; cómica; comedianta.

comedown ('kʌm·daun) *n., slang* revés.

comedy ('kam·ə·di) *n.* comedia.

comely ('kʌm·li) *adj.* gracioso; gentil; guapo. —**comeliness,** *n.* gentileza; donosura.

comestible (kə'mɛs·tə·bəl) *adj. & n.* comestible.

comet ('kam·ɪt) *n.* cometa.

comfort ('kʌm·fərt) *v.t.* confortar; animar; consolar. —*n.* **1,** (solace) consuelo; ánimo. **2,** (well-being) bienestar; consuelo; alivio. **3,** (ease) comodidad; satisfacción. **4,** *pl.* (conveniences) comodidades.

comfortable ('kʌm·fərt·ə·bəl) *adj.* **1,** (affording ease; at ease) confortable; cómodo. **2,** (free from distress) tranquilo; sereno.

comforter ('kʌm·fər·tər) *n.* **1,** (bed covering) edredón; cubrecama amohadillado. **2,** (muffler) bufanda; tapado. **3,** (consoler) consolador.

comic ('kam·ɪk) *adj.* cómico; divertido. —*n.* **1,** (comedian) cómico. **2,** *pl.* (cartoon strips) historietas; dibujos; caricaturas. —**comical,** *adj.* cómico; divertido; gracioso. —**comic opera,** ópera bufa.

coming ('kʌm·ɪŋ) *adj.* **1,** (approaching) venidero; futuro. **2,** *colloq.* (progressing) en camino; prometedor. —*n.* venida; llegada; advenimiento.

comity ('kam·ə·ti) *n.* cortesía; deferencia.

comma ('kam·ə) *n.* coma (,).

command (kə'mænd) *v.t.* **1,** (order) ordenar; mandar; dirigir. **2,** (rule) gobernar; regir. **3,** (look down on) dominar. —*v.i.* imponerse; mandar. —*n.* **1,** (order) mandato; mandamiento; orden. **2,** (authority) autoridad; mandato; poder. **3,** (mastery) recursos; habilidad; facilidad. **4,** *mil.* comando. —**command performance,** actuación magistral.

commandant (,kam·ən'dant) *n.* comandante.

commandeer (,kam·ən'dɪr) *v.t.* **1,** (recruit persons) reclutar a la fuerza. **2,** (seize things) requisar; confiscar.

commander (kə'mæn·dər) *n.* **1,** *mil.* comandante. **2,** *naval* teniente de navío. —**commander in chief,** comandante en jefe; jefe supremo.

commanding (kə'mæn·dɪŋ) *adj.* **1,** (in command) que manda. **2,** (dominant) dominante.

commandment (kə'mænd·mənt) *n.* **1,** mandato; orden; precepto. **2,** *cap., Bib.* mandamiento.

commando (kə'mæn·do) *n.* [*pl.* -dos] **1,** (assault group) comando. **2,** (member of group) atacador.

commemorate (kə'mɛm·ə·reit) *v.t.* conmemorar. —**commemoration,** *n.* conmemoración. —**commemorative** (-re·tɪv) *adj.* conmemorativo.

commence (kə'mɛns) *v.t. & i.* comenzar; empezar.

commencement (kə'mɛns·mənt) *n.* **1,** (beginning) principio; comienzo. **2,** (graduation) distribución de diplomas.

commend (kə'mɛnd) *v.t.* **1,** (praise) alabar; elogiar. **2,** (recommend) recomendar; aconsejar. **3,** (entrust) confiar. —**commendable,** *adj.* loable; notable.

commendation (,kam·ən'dei·ʃən) *n.* elogio; loa.

commensurable (kə'mɛn·ʃə·rə·bəl) *adj.* conmensurable.

commensurate (kə'mɛn·ʃə·rət) *adj.* proporcionado; adecuado; conmensurado.

comment ('ka·mɛnt) *n.* comen-

tario; observación. —*v.i.* comentar; glosar.

commentary ('kam·ən,tɛr·i) *n.* comentario; explicación. —**commentator** (-tei·tər) *n.* comentador.

commerce ('ka·mʌrs) *n.* comercio.

commercial (kə'mʌr·ʃəl) *adj.* comercial; mercantil. —*n.* anuncio publicitario. —**commercialism,** *n.* mercantilismo. —**commercialize,** *v.t.* comercializar.

commiserate (kə'mɪz·ə·reit) *v.t. & i.* compadecer. —*v.i.* apiadarse. —**commiseration,** *n.* conmiseración; piedad.

commissar ('kam·ɪ,sar) *n.* comisario. —**commissariat** (-'sɛr·ɪ·ət) *n.* comisariado.

commissary ('kam·ə,sɛr·i) *n.* **1,** (store) comisaría; intendencia. **2,** (deputy) comisario; delegado.

commission (kə'mɪʃ·ən) *n.* **1,** (act of committing) cometido; acción. **2,** (warrant) patente; nombramiento. **3,** (group of persons) comisión; junta; misión. **4,** (assignment) misión; tarea; deber. **5,** (fee) comisión; corretaje. **6,** *mil.; naval* nombramiento. —*v.t.* **1,** (appoint) nombrar. **2,** (give authority) comisionar. **3,** (equip) poner en servicio activo. —**commissioned officer,** oficial; oficial destinado.

commissioner (kə'mɪʃ·ən·ər) *n.* jefe; delegado; comisionado.

commit (kə'mɪt) *v.t.* [**committed, -mitting**] **1,** (entrust) confiar; depositar. **2,** (do) cometer; perpetrar. **3,** (venture) aventurar. **4,** (consign to custody) encerrar; internar. —**commit oneself,** comprometerse; obligarse. —**commit to memory,** aprender de memoria. —**commit to paper,** poner por escrito.

commitment (kə'mɪt·mənt) *n.* **1,** (act of committing) cometido. **2,** (pledge) promesa; obligación; compromiso. **3,** (consignment to custody) encierro; internación.

committee (kə'mɪt·i) *n.* comisión; comité.

commode (kə'mod) *n.* **1,** (chest of drawers) cómoda. **2,** (toilet) retrete; excusado.

commodious (kə'mo·di·əs) *adj.* holgado; amplio; cómodo. —**commodiousness,** *n.* comodidad; amplitud.

commodity (kə'mad·ə·ti) *n.* **1,** *comm.* mercancía. **2,** (useful thing) comodidad.

commodore ('kam·ə·dor) *n.* comodoro.

common ('kam·ən) *adj.* **1,** (shared) común; mutuo. **2,** (public) general; público. **3,** (familiar) familiar; usual; común. **4,** (ordinary) ordinario; corriente. **5,** (coarse) vulgar; bajo. —*n.* **1,** (public land) ejido. **2,** (public square) plaza. **3,** *pl., cap.* (Brit. parliament) los Comunes. —**common law,** derecho común. —**Common Market,** Mercado Común. —**common noun,** nombre común. —**common sense,** sentido común. —**common stock,** acciones ordinarias. —**in common,** en común.

commoner ('kam·ən·ər) *n.* plebeyo.

commonplace ('kam·ən‚pleis) *adj.* ordinario; corriente. —*n.* cosa común.

commonwealth ('kam·ən ‚welθ) *n.* mancomunidad. —**Commonwealth of Puerto Rico,** Estado libre asociado de Puerto Rico.

commotion (kə'mo·ʃən) *n.* **1,** (agitation) conmoción; perturbación. **2,** (public unrest) tumulto; desorden.

communal ('kam·ju·nəl) *adj.* comunal; público.

commune (kə'mjuːn) *v.i.* comunicarse; conversar; hablar. —*n.* ('kam·jun) comuna; comunidad.

communicant (kə'mju·nɪ·kənt) *n.* **1,** (one who communicates) comunicante. **2,** (one who takes Communion) comulgante.

communicate (kə'mju·nɪ·keit) *v.t.* comunicar; notificar. —*v.i.* comunicarse; tener comunicación. —**communicable,** *adj.* comunicable; *med.* contagioso.

communication (kə‚mju·nɪ 'kei·ʃən) *n.* **1,** (act of communicating) comunicación; participación. **2,** (message) comunicación; noticia. **3,** (passage) comunicación; acceso.

communicative (kə'mju·nɪ·kə·tɪv) *adj.* comunicativo; hablador; franco.

communion (kə'mjun·jən) *n.* **1,** (sharing) comunión; contacto. **2,** (fellowship) amistad; confraternidad; trato. **3,** *cap.* (Eucharist) comunión.

communiqué (kə·mju·nɪ'kei) *n.* comunicado o boletín oficial.

communism ('kam·jə·nɪz·əm) *n.* comunismo. —**communist,** *n.* & *adj.* comunista. —**communistic,** *adj.* comunista.

community (kə'mju·nə·ti) *n.* **1,** (group of persons; locality) comunidad; público; colectividad; sociedad. **2,** (joint sharing) comunidad; colectividad. —**community property,** comunidad de bienes.

communize ('kam·jə‚naiz) *v.t.* comunizar.

commutation (‚kam·ju'tei·ʃən) *n.* conmutación; permuta. —**commutation ticket,** billete de abono.

commute (kə'mjut) *v.t.* conmutar; cambiar. —*v.i.* viajar diariamente. —**commuter,** *n.* viajero diario.

compact (kəm'pækt) *adj.* **1,** (solid) compacto; sólido. **2,** (closely packed) apretado; cerrado. **3,** (concise) compacto; breve; conciso. —*n.* ('kam·pækt) **1,** (agreement) convenio; acuerdo. **2,** (cosmetic container) polvera.

companion (kəm'pæn·jən) *n.* **1,** (comrade) compañero; camarada. **2,** (paid attendant) acompañante. —**companionable,** *adj.* sociable; amistoso. —**companionship,** *n.* compañerismo; camaradería.

companionway (kəm'pæn·jən‚wei) *n.* escalera de cámara.

company ('kʌm·pə·ni) *n.* **1,** (group) compañía. **2,** (guest o guests) invitados; visita; visitantes. **3,** *comm.* compañía; sociedad; empresa. **4,** *mil.* compañía. **5,** *naut.; aero.* tripulación. —**have company,** tener visita. —**keep company,** acompañar; *colloq.* cortejar; galantear. —**part company,** separarse; desunirse.

comparable ('kam·pə·rə·bəl) *adj.* comparable; semejante.

comparative (kəm'pær·ə·tɪv) *adj.* comparativo; relativo. —*n., gram.* comparativo.

compare (kəm'peːr) *v.t.* comparar; cotejar. —*v.i.* poder compararse.

comparison (kəm'pær·ɪ·sən) *n.* comparación.

compartment (kəm'part·mənt) *n.* compartimiento; división.

compass ('kʌm·pəs) *n.* **1,** (extent; range) circuito; ámbito. **2,** (instrument) brújula. **3,** *también pl.* (dividers) compás. —*v.t.* **1,** (encircle) circundar. **2,** (accomplish) lograr; obtener; conseguir.

compassion (kəm'pæʃ·ən) *n.* compasión. —**compassionate** (-ət) *adj.* compasivo.

compatible (kəm'pæt·ə·bəl) *adj.* compatible. —**compatibility,** *n.* compatibilidad.

compatriot (kəm'pei·tri·ət) *n.* & *adj.* compatriota.

compel (kəm'pɛl) *v.t.* [**compelled, -pelling**] compeler; forzar; obligar.

compendium (kəm'pɛn·di·əm) *n.* compendio. —**compendious,** *adj.* compendioso.

compensate ('kam·pən,seit) *v.t.* & *i.* 1, (offset) compensar; resarcir. 2, (recompense) remunerar; recompensar. —**compensation,** *n.* compensación; reparación.

compensatory (kəm'pɛns·ə·tor·i) *adj.* compensatorio; compensativo.

compete (kəm'pit) *v.i.* competir; emular.

competence ('kam·pɪ·təns) *n.* 1, (fitness) competencia; habilidad; aptitud. 2, (sufficient means) suficiencia; bienestar.

competent ('kam·pə·tənt) *adj.* hábil; competente.

competition (,kam·pə'tɪʃ·ən) *n.* 1, (rivalry) competición; competencia. rivalidad. 2, (contest) concurso; competición; pugna; contienda.

competitive (kəm'pɛt·ə·tɪv) *adj.* competidor; que compite. —**competitive bid,** oferta en competencia.

competitor (kəm'pɛt·ə·tər) *n.* competidor; rival.

compilation (,kam·pə'lei·ʃən) *n.* compilación; recopilación.

compile (kəm'pail) *v.t.* compilar; recopilar. —**compiler,** *n.* compilador; recopilador.

complacency (kəm'plei·sən·si) *también,* **complacence,** *n.* complacencia; satisfacción. —**complacent,** *adj.* complaciente.

complain (kəm'plein) *v.i.* 1, (express dissatisfaction) quejarse; lamentarse. 2, *law* demandar; querellarse. —**complainant,** *n.* demandante; querellante.

complaint (kəm'pleint) *n.* 1, (expression of discontent) queja; lamento. 2, (ailment) mal; dolencia. 3, *law* querella; demanda.

complaisant (kəm'plei·zənt) *adj.* complaciente; condescendiente.

complement ('kam·plə·mənt) *n.* complemento. —*v.t.* complementar; completar. —**complementary** (-'mɛn·tə·ri) *adj.* complementario.

complete (kəm'plit) *adj.* 1, (whole) completo; total. 2, (fin-ished) completo; terminado. —*v.t.* completar; acabar; terminar. —**completion** (-'pli·ʃən) *n.* terminación; fin.

complex (kəm'plɛks) *adj.* 1, (of many parts) complejo; compuesto. 2, (complicated) complejo; difícil. —*n.* ('kam·plɛks) complejo; conjunto. —**complexity** (kəm'plɛks·ə·ti) *n.* complejidad.

complexion (kəm'plɛk·ʃən) *n.* 1, (skin) tez; complexión. 2, (aspect) complexión; constitución; apariencia.

compliant (kəm'plai·ənt) *adj.* 1, (acquiescent) condescendiente; complaciente. 2, (submissive) sumiso; rendido; servicial. —**compliance,** *n.* obediencia; sumisión. —**in compliance with,** de acuerdo con; según; accediendo a.

complicate ('kam·plɪ·keit) *v.t.* complicar; enredar; embrollar. —**complication,** *n.* complicación.

complicity (kəm'plɪs·ə·ti) *n.* complicidad.

compliment ('kam·plə·mənt) *n.* 1, (praise) elogio; cumplido; fineza. 2, (gallantry) piropo; galantería. 3, *pl.* (greetings) saludos; respetos. —*v.t.* felicitar.

complimentary (,kam·plə'mɛn·tə·ri) *adj.* 1, (laudatory) lisonjero; obsequioso. 2, (free) gratuito; como obsequio; de regalo.

comply (kəm'plai) *v.i.* someterse; cumplir. —**comply with,** acatar; obedecer.

component (kəm'po·nənt) *n.* componente; parte. —*adj.* componente.

comport (kəm'port) *v.t.* proceder; obrar. —*v.i.* convenir; acordar. —**comport oneself,** portarse; comportarse.

comportment (kəm'port·mənt) *n.* comportamiento; conducta.

compose (kəm'porz) *v.t.* 1, (form) componer; formar. 2, (create, esp. music) componer. 3, (calm) calmar; sosegar. 4, (settle differences) apaciguar; sosegar; serenar. 5, (set) arreglar; *print.* ajustar. —*v.i.* componer. —**composed,** *adj.* compuesto; tranquilo; sereno. —**composer,** *n.* compositor.

composite (kəm'paz·ɪt) *n.* & *adj.* compuesto.

composition (kam·pə'zɪʃ·ən) *n.* composición.

compositor (kəm'paz·ɪ·tər) *n.* cajista.

compost ('kam·post) *n.* abono.

composure (kəm'po·ʒər) *n.* compostura; calma; serenidad.

compote ('kam·pot) *n.* **1,** (stewed fruit) compota. **2,** (small dish) compotera.

compound (kəm'paund) *v.t.* componer; combinar. —*n.* ('kam·paund) **1,** (mixture) compuesto. **2,** (enclosure) recinto. —*adj.* compuesto. —**compound fracture,** fractura abierta. —**compound interest,** interés compuesto.

comprehend (,kam·prɪ'hɛnd) *v.t.* **1,** (include) comprender; contener; incluir. **2,** (understand) comprender; entender. —**comprehensible** (-'hɛn·sə·bəl) *adj.* comprensible; inteligible. —**comprehensibility,** *n.* comprensibilidad.

comprehension (,kam·prɪ'hɛn·ʃən) *n.* comprensión. —**comprehensive** (-sɪv) *adj.* comprensivo. —**comprehensiveness,** *n.* comprensión; alcance; perspicacia.

compress (kəm'prɛs) *v.t.* **1,** (press) comprimir; apretar. **2,** (condense) condensar; abreviar. —*n.* ('kam·prɛs) compresa. —**compression** (kəm'prɛʃ·ən) *n.* compresión. —**compressor** (kəm'prɛs·ər) *n.* compresor.

comprise (kəm'praiz) *v.t.* **1,** (include) comprender; abarcar; incluir. **2,** (consist of) consistir de.

compromise ('kam·prə,maiz) *n.* **1,** (settlement) compromiso; convenio; acuerdo. **2,** (middle course) compromiso; termino medio. —*v.t.* **1,** (settle) comprometer; acordar; arreglar. **2,** (expose to suspicion) comprometer; exponer. —*v.i.* comprometerse; convenir; transigir.

comptroller *también,* **controller** (kən'trol·ər) *n.* interventor; *Amer.* contralor. —**comptrollership,** *n.* intervención.

compulsion (kəm'pʌl·ʃən) *n.* **1,** (coercion) impulso; impulsión. coerción. **2,** *law* compulsión. —**compulsive** (-sɪv) *adj.* compulsivo. —**compulsory** (-sə·ri) *adj.* obligatorio.

compunction (kəm'pʌŋk·ʃən) *n.* compunción; remordimiento.

compute (kəm'pjut) *v.t.* computar; calcular; contar. —**computation** (,kam·pju'tei·ʃən) *n.* computación; cómputo; recuento.

computer (kəm'pju·tər) *n.* **1,** (person) calculador. **2,** (machine) calculadora; computadora. —**computer science,** computación.

computerize (kəm'pju·tə,raiz) *v.t.* computarizar. —*v.i.* computarizarse. —**computerization** (-'pju·tə·rɪ'zei·ʃən) *n.* instalación de computadoras; registro computerizado.

comrade ('kam·ræd) *n.* camarada; compañero. —**comradeship,** *n.* camaradería; compañerismo.

con (kaɴn) *v.t.* [**conned, conning**] **1,** (study) estudiar; escudriñar. **2,** *slang* (swindle) estafar; embaucar. **3,** (steer, as a ship) gobernar; dirigir. —*adv.* & *n.* contra. —*n.*, *slang* preso; prisionero. —**con game,** *slang* estafa; fraude. —**con man,** *slang* estafador.

concatenate (kən'kæt·ə,neit) *v.t.* encadenar. —**concatenation,** *n.* encadenamiento.

concave (kan'keiv) *adj.* cóncavo. —**concavity** (kən'kæv·ə·ti) *n.* concavidad; hueco.

conceal (kən'siːl) *v.t.* ocultar; esconder; encubrir.

concealment (kən'sil·mənt) *n.* **1,** (act of concealing) encubrimiento; secreto. **2,** (hiding place) escondite; escondrijo.

concede (kən'sird) *v.t.* **1,** (grant) conceder; otorgar. **2,** (admit) aceptar; admitir. —*v.i.* conceder.

conceit (kən'sit) *n.* **1,** (vanity) presunción; engreimiento. **2,** (quaint idea or object) fantasía; imaginación. —**conceited,** *adj.* presuntuoso; vano; engreído.

conceivable (kən'siv·ə·bəl) *adj.* concebible.

conceive (kən'siːv) *v.t.* **1,** (form in the mind) concebir; inventar; formar. **2,** (believe) creer; comprender; concebir. —*v.i.* concebir. —**conceive of,** imaginar; formar idea de.

concentrate ('kan·sən·treit) *v.t.* reunir; concentrar. —*v.i.* **1,** (meet) concentrarse; encontrarse. **2,** (focus attention) concentrarse; pensar detenidamente; enfocar. —*n.* concentrado.

concentration (,kan·sən'trei·ʃən) *n.* concentración. —**concentration camp,** campo de concentración.

concentric (kən'sɛn·trɪk) *adj.* concéntrico. —**concentricity** (,kan·sən'trɪs·ə·ti) *n.* concentricidad.

concept ('kan·sɛpt) *n.* concepto;

idea; noción. —**conceptual** (kən'sɛp·tʃu·əl) *adj.* conceptual.

conception (kən'sɛp·ʃən) *n.* concepción; concepto; noción.

concern (kən'sʌrn) *v.t.* **1,** (interest) concernir; afectar; interesar; importar. **2,** (disturb) preocupar; inquietar. —*n.* **1,** (matter of interest) asunto; negocio. **2,** (anxiety) preocupación; inquietud. **3,** (business firm) empresa; firma. —**concerning,** *prep.* con referencia a; respecto a.

concert (kan·sərt) *n.* **1,** (agreement) concierto; convenio. **2,** (musical performance) concierto. **3,** (unison) concierto; armonía. —*v.t.* & *i.* (kən'sʌrt) concertar; aunar; ajustar. —**concerted** (kən'sʌr·tɪd) *adj.* concertado; armonioso.

concertina (ˌkan·sər'ti·nə) *n.* concertina.

concerto (kən'tʃɛr·to) *n.* [*pl.* **-tos**] concierto.

concession (kən'sɛʃ·ən) *n.* concesión. —**concessionaire** (-'ɛːr) *n.* concesionario.

conch (kantʃ; kaŋk) *n.* concha; caracol de mar.

concierge (kan'sjɛrʒ) *n.* conserje; portero.

conciliate (kən'sɪl·i·eit) *v.t.* conciliar; pacificar. —**conciliation,** *n.* conciliación. —**conciliatory** (-ə·tor·i) *adj.* conciliatorio; conciliador.

concise (kən'sais) *adj.* conciso. —**conciseness; concision** (kən·'sɪʒ·ən) *n.* concisión.

conclave (kan'kleiv) *n.* cónclave.

conclude (kən'kluːd) *v.t.* **1,** (finish) concluir; terminar; acabar. **2,** (deduce) inferir; deducir. **3,** (decide) settle) decidir; determinar. —*v.i.* **1,** (finish) finalizar; acabarse. **2,** (decide) resolver; decidir.

conclusion (kən'kluː·ʒən) *n.* conclusión; final; resultado. —**conclusive** (-sɪv) *adj.* concluyente; conclusivo.

concoct (kən'kakt) *v.t.* **1,** (combine and cook) preparar mezclando; combinar. **2,** (devise) planear; proyectar.

concoction (kən'kak·ʃən) *n.* **1,** (thing prepared) preparación; combinación. **2,** (thing devised) trama; maquinación.

concomitant (kan'kam·ə·tənt) *adj.* & *n.* concomitante. —**concomitance,** *n.* concomitancia.

concord ('kan·kord) *n.* **1,** (har-mony) concordia; armonía; unanimidad. **2,** (agreement) acuerdo; paz; convenio.

concordance (kən'kor·dəns) *n.* **1,** (agreement) concordancia; concordia. **2,** (word index) concordancias.

concordant (kən'kor·dənt) *adj.* concordante; armonioso; conforme.

concourse ('kan·kors) *n.* **1,** (throng) concurso; concurrencia; gentío. **2,** (thoroughfare) bulevar; avenida. **3,** (flowing together) confluencia.

concrete (kan'krit) *adj.* **1,** (real; specific) concreto; definido. **2,** (made of concrete) de cemento; de hormigón. —*n.* ('kan·krit) cemento; hormigón. —**concreteness,** *n.* calidad de concreto. —**concretion** (kən'kri·ʃən) *n.* concreción.

concubine ('kaŋ·kju·bain) *n.* concubina. —**concubinage** (kən·'kju·bɪ·nɪdʒ) *n.* concubinato.

concupiscent (kan'kju·pə·sənt) *adj.* concupiscente. —**concupiscence,** *n.* concupiscencia.

concur (kən'kʌr) *v.i.* [**concurred, concurring**] **1,** (coincide) concurrir; coincidir. **2,** (agree) convenir; ponerse de acuerdo. —**concurrence,** *n.* concurrencia; coincidencia. —**concurrent,** *adj.* concurrente; coincidente; simultáneo.

concussion (kən'kʌʃ·ən) *n.* concusión; golpe.

condemn (kən'dɛm) *v.t.* **1,** (censure) condenar; censurar; reprobar. **2,** (sentence) condenar; castigar; sentenciar. **3,** (declare unfit) condenar; cerrar. **4,** (claim for public use) expropiar. —**condemnation** (ˌkan·dɛm'nei·ʃən) *n.* condenación.

condense (kən'dɛns) *v.t.* **1,** (compress) condensar; comprimir. **2,** (abridge) condensar; resumir; compendiar. —*v.i.* condensarse. —**condensation** (ˌkan·dən'sei·ʃən) *n.* condensación. —**condenser,** *n.* condensador.

condescend (ˌkan·dɪ'sɛnd) *v.i.* **1,** (adjust) condescender; avenirse; transigir. **2,** (deign) dignarse. **3,** (deal patronizingly) prestarse; contemporizar. —**condescension** (-'sɛn·ʃən) *n.* condescendencia.

condign (kən'dain) *adj.* condigno; adecuado; merecido.

condiment ('kan·də·mənt) *n.* condimento.

condition (kən'dɪʃ·ən) *n.* **1,** (state

of being) condición; circunstancia. **2,** (social rank) condición; categoría; clase. **3,** (state of health) salud. **4,** (stipulation) condición; requisito; estipulación. —*v.i.* poner condiciones. —*v.t.* **1,** (limit) condicionar; estipular. **2,** (put into condition) subordinar; supeditar. —**conditional,** *adj.* condicional. —**on condition that,** a condición de; a condición que; con la condición de que.

condole (kən'doʊl) *v.i.* condolerse. —**condolence,** *n.* condolencia.

condom ('kan·dəm) *n.* condón; preservativo.

condominium (,kan·də'mɪn·i·əm) *n.* condominio.

condone (kən'doʊn) *v.t.* condonar; perdonar; olvidar. —**condonement; condonation** (,kan·də'nei·ʃən) *n.* condonación; perdón.

condor ('kan·dər) *n.* cóndor.

conduce (kən'dus) *v.i.* conducir; llevar; tender. —**conducive,** *adj.* conducente; tendente.

conduct (kən'dʌkt) *v.t.* **1,** (guide; lead) conducir; dirigir. **2,** (manage) dirigir; administrar; manejar. —*n.* ('kan·dʌkt) **1,** (behavior) comportamiento. **2,** (management) dirección. —**conduct oneself,** portarse; comportarse.

conductible (kən'dʌk·tə·bəl) *adj.* conductible. —**conductibility,** *n.* conductibilidad.

conduction (kən'dʌk·ʃən) *n.* conducción.

conductive (kən'dʌk·tɪv) *adj.* conductivo. —**conductivity** (,kan·dʌk'tɪv·ə·ti) *n.* conductividad.

conductor (kən'dʌk·tər) *n.* **1,** (orchestra leader) director. **2,** *R.R.* revisor; cobrador. **3,** *elect.* conductor. —**conductress,** *n.f.* directora; cobradora.

conduit ('kan·dʊɪt) *n.* **1,** (channel for fluids) conducto. **2,** *elect.* tubo.

cone (kon) *n.* cono.

confect (kən'fɛkt) *v.t.* confeccionar; preparar; hacer.

confection (kən'fɛk·ʃən) *n.* **1,** (a sweet) confitura; dulce. **2,** *fig.* (dress) confección. —**confectioner,** *n.* confitero; dulcero. —**confectionery,** *n.* confitería; dulcería.

confederacy (kən'fɛd·ə·rə·si) *n.* confederación.

confederate (kən'fɛd·ə·reit) *v.t. & i.* confederar. —*adj.* (-rət) confederado. —*n.* (-rət) **1,** (ally) confede-

rado. **2,** (accomplice) socio; compinche. —**confederation,** *n.* confederación; liga.

confer (kən'fʌr) *v.t.* [**conferred, -ferring**] conferir; otorgar. —*v.i.* conferenciar; consultar.

conference ('kan·fər·əns) *n.* **1,** (meeting) conferencia; consulta. **2,** (league) conferencia; junta; asamblea.

confess (kən'fɛs) *v.t.* **1,** (acknowledge) confesar; admitir; reconocer. **2,** *eccles.* confesar. —*v.i.* confesarse. —**confessedly** (-ɪd·li) *adv.* reconocidamente.

confession (kən'fɛʃ·ən) *n.* confesión.

confessional (kən'fɛʃ·ən·əl) *n.* **1,** (enclosure) confesonario; confesionario. **2,** (book of confession) confesionario. **3,** (act of confessing) confesión. —*adj.* confesional.

confessor (kən'fɛs·ər) *n.* confesor.

confetti (kən'fɛt·i) *n.* confeti.

confidant (,kan·fɪ'dant) *n.* confidente. —**confidante** (-'dant) *n. f.* confidente.

confide (kən'faid) *v.t.* confiar. —*v.i.* **1,** (have trust) tener confianza. **2,** (entrust a secret) confiarse; fiarse.

confidence ('kan·fɪ·dəns) *n.* **1,** (faith) confianza; fe; seguridad. **2,** (self-assurance) ánimo; creencia. **3,** (state of mind) tranquilidad; certeza. **4,** (intimacy) intimidad; familiaridad. **5,** (secret) confidencia. —**confidence man,** estafador; timador.

confident ('kan·fɪ·dənt) *adj.* confiado; seguro.

confidential (,kan·fɪ'dɛn·ʃəl) *adj.* **1,** (secret) confidencial; secreto; privado. **2,** (intimate) íntimo; privado. **3,** (trusted) confidencial; de confianza.

configuration (kən,fɪg·jə'rei·ʃən) *n.* configuración; forma; aspecto.

confine (kən'fain) *v.t.* **1,** (restrict) limitar. **2,** (put to bed, as in illness or childbirth) confinar. **3,** (shut in) encerrar. **4,** (imprison) encarcelar. —**be confined,** estar de parto.

confinement (kən'fain·mənt) *n.* **1,** (restriction) limitación. **2,** (childbirth) parto. **3,** (imprisonment) encarcelamiento.

confines ('kan·fainz) *n.pl.* confines; límites.

confirm (kən'fʌrm) *v.t.* **1,** (strengthen) confirmar; afirmar. **2,**

(verify) verificar; corroborar. **3,** (make valid) confirmar; sancionar; ratificar. **4,** *eccles.* confirmar. —**confirmation** (‚kan·fər'mei·ʃən) *n.* confirmación. —**confirmatory** (kən'fʌr·mə·tor·i) *adj.* confirmatorio; confirmativo.

confirmed (kən'fʌrmd) *adj.* **1,** (settled) confirmado; comprobado; demostrado. **2,** (chronic) inveterado; crónico; consumado.

confiscate ('kan·fɪs‚keit) *v.t.* confiscar; expropiar. —**confiscation,** *n.* confiscación.

conflagration (‚kan·flə'grei·ʃən) *n.* conflagración.

conflict (kən'flɪkt) *v.i.* chocar; estar en pugna. —*n.* ('kan·flɪkt) **1,** (combat) conflicto; lucha; combate. **2,** *fig.* (opposition) discordia; contradicción.

confluence ('kan·flu·əns) *n.* **1,** (of rivers) confluente. **2,** (of a crowd) concurrencia; concurso. —**confluent,** *adj.* confluente.

conform (kən'form) *v.t.* conformar; concordar; adaptar. —*v.i.* obedecer; conformarse; acatar.

conformable (kən'for·mə·bəl) *adj.* conforme.

conformation (‚kan·fər'mei·ʃən) *n.* **1,** (structure) configuración; forma; estructura. **2,** (adaptation) conformación; adaptación.

conformist (kən'for·mɪst) *n.* conformista.

conformity (kən'for·mə·ti) *n.* conformidad.

confound (kan'faund) *v.t.* **1,** (perplex) aturdir; embrollar; desordenar. **2,** (mistake for another) confundir; equivocar. —**confounded,** *adj.‚ colloq.* endemoniado; maldito. —**confound it!,** ¡diablo!

confraternity (‚kan·frə'tʌr·nə·ti) *n.* confraternidad; cofradía.

confront (kən'frʌnt) *v.t.* **1,** (face) confrontar; encontrar. **2,** (meet boldly) afrontar; hacer frente a; desafiar. **3,** [*usu.,* **confront with**] (face to face) carear. **4,** (compare) cotejar; comparar. —**confrontation** (‚kan·frən'tei·ʃən) *n.* confrontación; careo.

confuse (kən'fjuːz) *v.t.* **1,** (confound) confundir; desordenar; embrollar. **2,** (mistake) confundir; equivocar. —**confusion** (-'fju·ʒən) *n.* confusión.

confutation (‚kan·fju'tei·ʃən) *n.*

confutación; desaprobación; refutación.

confute (kən'fjut) *v.t.* confutar; desaprobar; refutar.

congeal (kən'dʒiːl) *v.t.* congelar. —*v.i.* congelarse.

congenial (kən'dʒin·jəl) *adj.* **1,** (kindred) semejante; parecido; congénere. **2,** (agreeable) congenial; simpático; afable.

congeniality (kən‚dʒi·ni'æl·ə·ti) *n.* **1,** (likeness) parecido; semejanza. **2,** (affability) afabilidad; simpatía.

congenital (kən'dʒen·ɪ·təl) *adj.* congénito.

congest (kən'dʒest) *v.t.* **1,** (overcrowd) amontonar; apiñar. **2,** (overfill, as with blood) congestionar. —**congestion** (-'dʒɛs·tʃən) *n.* congestión.

conglomerate (kən'glam·ər·ət) *n.* & *adj.* conglomerado. —*v.t.* & *i.* (-'reit) conglomerar; aglomerar. —**conglomeration,** *n.* conglomeración.

Congolese (‚kaŋ·go'liːz) *adj.* & *n.* congoleño; congolés.

congratulate (kən'grætʃ·ə‚leit) *v.t.* congratular; felicitar. —**congratulation,** *n.* congratulación; felicitación. —**congratulations!,** ¡enhorabuena!; ¡felicidades!

congregate ('kaŋ·grɪ‚geit) *v.t.* & *i.* congregar; juntar; reunir; convocar.

congregation (‚kaŋ·grɪ'gei·ʃən) *n.* reunión; asamblea; *relig.* congregación.

congregational (‚kaŋ·grɪ'gei·ʃən·əl) *adj.* congregacionalista.

congress ('kaŋ·grəs) *n.* **1,** (meeting) congreso; asamblea. **2,** *cap.* (U.S. legislative body) Congreso. —**congressional** (kən'greʃ·ə·nəl) *adj.* del congreso.

congressman ('kaŋ·grəs·mən) *n.* [*pl.* **-men**] diputado; *U.S.* congresista. —**congresswoman,** *n.* [*pl.* **-women**] diputada; *U.S.* congresista.

congruent ('kaŋ·gru·ənt) *adj.* congruente. —**congruence,** *n.* congruencia.

congruity (kəŋ'gru·ə·ti) *n.* congruidad.

congruous ('kaŋ·gru·əs) *adj.* congruente; congruo; apropiado. —**congruousness,** *n.* congruencia; congruidad; armonía.

conic ('kan·ɪk) *también,* **conical,** *adj.* cónico.

conifer ('kan·ɪ·fər) *n.* conífera.

—**coniferous** (kə'nɪf·ər·əs) *adj.* conífero.

conjecture (kən'dʒɛk·tʃər) *n.* conjetura; presunción. —*v.t. & i.* conjeturar; presumir. —**conjectural,** *adj.* conjetural.

conjoin (kən'dʒɔin) *v.t. & i.* asociar; unir; federarse. —**conjoint** (-'dʒɔint) *adj.* conjunto; unido; asociado.

conjugal ('kan·dʒə·gəl) *adj.* conyugal; matrimonial.

conjugate ('kan·dʒə‚geit) *v.t.* conjugar. —*adj.* (-gət) apareado; en pares; a pares.

conjugation (‚kan·dʒə'gei·ʃən) *n.* **1,** *gram.* conjugación. **2,** (conjunction) unión; conjunción.

conjunct (kən'dʒʌŋkt) *adj.* conjunto; unido. —**conjunctive,** *adj.* conjuntivo; conjunto.

conjunction (kən'dʒʌŋk·ʃən) *n.* **1,** (act of joining) conjunción. **2,** (union) unión; conexión; liga. **3,** *gram.* conjunción.

conjunctivitis (kən‚dʒʌŋk·tə'vai·tɪs) *n.* conjuntivitis.

conjuncture (kən'dʒʌŋk·tʃər) *n.* **1,** (concurrence) coyuntura; oportunidad. **2,** (crisis) crisis.

conjure ('kan·dʒər) *v.t. & i.* **1,** (practice magic) conjurar; imprecar. **2,** (entreat) conjurar; conspirar. —**conjuration** (‚kan·dʒə'rei·ʃən) *n.* conjuración. —**conjurer** *también,* **conjuror** *n.* mago; brujo.

connect (kə'nɛkt) *v.t.* **1,** (associate mentally) conectar; coordinar; relacionar. **2,** (join) unir; reunir; conectar. —*v.i.* **1,** (join; be joined) unirse; conectarse; juntarse. **2,** (be related) relacionarse. **3,** (meet, as trains) empalmar. **4,** *slang* (hit the mark; succeed) dar en el blanco; tener éxito.

connecting rod biela.

connection (kə'nɛk·ʃən) *n.* **1,** (union) conexión; unión; enlace. **2,** (kin) parentesco. **3,** (relation o coherence) ilación; coherencia. **4,** *pl.* (associates) asociados; compañía. **5,** *usu. pl.* (meeting, as of trains) conexiones; empalme.

connective (kə'nɛk·tɪv) *n.* conjunción. —*adj.* conectivo.

conning tower *n.* torre de mando.

connive (kə'naive) *v.i.* **1,** (tolerate) tolerar; disimular; permitir. **2,** (conspire) conspirar; atentar. —**connivance,** *n.* connivencia.

connoisseur (kan·ə'sʌr) *n.* experto; conocedor; crítico.

connotation (‚kan·ə'tei·ʃən) *n.* connotación.

connote (kə'not) *v.t.* connotar; sugerir; implicar.

connubial (kə'nu·bi·əl) *adj.* conyugal.

conquer ('kaŋ·kər) *v.t.* **1,** (defeat) conquistar; vencer. **2,** *fig.* (overcome) triunfar; superar. —**conqueror** *n.* conquistador; vencedor.

conquest ('kan·kwɛst; 'kaŋ-) *n.* conquista; triunfo; victoria.

consanguineous (‚kan·sæŋ·'gwin·i·əs) *adj.* consanguíneo. —**consanguinity** (-ə·ti) *n.* consanguinidad.

conscience ('kan·tʃəns) *n.* conciencia. —**clear conscience,** conciencia limpia; manos limpias. —**guilty conscience,** complejo de culpabilidad. —**have a guilty conscience,** sentirse culpable. —**on one's conscience,** en la conciencia.

conscientious (‚kan·ʃi'ɛn·ʃəs) *adj.* concienzudo; recto; justo. —**conscientiousness,** *n.* escrupulosidad; rectitud.

consionable ('kan·ʃən·ə·bəl) *adj.* razonable; prudente.

conscious ('kan·ʃəs) *adj.* **1,** (aware) consciente. **2,** (awake) despierto. —*n.* consciente. —**be conscious of,** darse cuenta de. —**become conscious,** recobrar el sentido.

consciousness ('kan·ʃəs·nəs) *n.* **1,** (awareness) conocimiento. **2,** *psychol.* (self-awareness) consciencia. —**lose consciousness,** perder el sentido; desvanecerse. —**regain consciousness,** volver en sí.

conscript ('kan·skrɪpt) *n.* conscripto; recluta. —*v.t.* (kən'skrɪpt) reclutar. —**conscription** (kən'skrɪp·ʃən) *n.* conscripción; reclutamiento.

consecrate ('kan·sɪ·kreit) *v.t.* consagrar. —**consecration,** *n.* consagración.

consecutive (kən'sɛk·jə·tɪv) *adj.* consecutivo; sucesivo.

consensus (kən'sɛn·səs) *n.* consenso; asentimiento; opinión.

consent (kən'sɛnt) *v.i.* consentir; aceptar; acceder. —*n.* consentimiento; permiso.

consequence ('kan·sɪ‚kwɛns) *n.* **1,** (result) consecuencia; derivación; efecto. **2,** (importance) importancia; valor.

constitutivo. —**constituency,** *n.* distrito electoral.

constitute ('kan·stɪ,tut) *v.t.* **1,** (form) constituir; establecer; formar. **2,** (appoint) nombrar; dar poder a.

constitution (,kan·stɪ'tu·ʃən) *n.* constitución. —**constitutional,** *adj.* constitucional; básico; esencial. —**take a constitutional,** dar un paseo (de salud).

constrain (kən'strein) *v.t.* **1,** (oblige) constreñir; compeler. **2,** (bind) apretar; estrechar. **3,** (restrain) impedir; restringir. —**constraint** (-'streint) *n.* coerción; impedimento; restricción.

constrict (kən'strɪkt) *v.t.* **1,** (shrink) encoger. **2,** (bind) apretar; reducir. —**constriction** (-'strɪk·ʃən) *n.* constricción; encogimiento.

constrictive (kən'strɪk·tɪv) *adj.* constrictor.

constrictor (kən'strɪk·tər) *n.* **1,** (binder) constrictor. **2,** (snake) boa.

construct (kən'strʌkt) *v.t.* **1,** (build) construir; fabricar. **2,** (contrive) idear; planear; imaginar. —**constructor,** *n.* constructor.

construction (kən'strʌk·ʃən) *n.* **1,** (building) construcción; obra; estructura. **2,** (explanation) interpretación; sentido. **3,** *gram.* construcción.

constructive (kən'strʌk·tɪv) *adj.* constructivo.

construe (kən'struɹ) *v.t.* **1,** *gram.* construir. **2,** (translate) traducir. **3,** (interpret) interpretar.

consubstantiation (,kan·sʌb,stæn·ʃi'ei·ʃən) *n.* consubstanciación.

consul ('kan·səl) *n.* cónsul. —**consular,** *adj.* consular. —**consulate,** *n.* consulado. —**consulship,** *n.* consulado.

consult (kən'sʌlt) *v.t.* **1,** (ask advice from) consultar. **2,** (consider) considerar. —*v.i.* asesorarse.

consultant (kən'sʌl·tənt) *n.* **1,** (person asking advice) consultante. **2,** (advisor) asesor; consultor.

consultation (,kan·səl'tei·ʃən) *n.* **1,** (act of consulting) consulta. **2,** (conference) consultación; deliberación; conferencia. —**consultative** (kən'sʌlt·ə·tɪv) *adj.* consultivo.

consume (kən'suːm) *v.t.* **1,** (eat) consumir. **2,** (waste) desperdiciar. —**consumer,** *n.* consumidor.

consummate ('kan·sə·meit) *v.t.*

consumar; completar; perfeccionar. —*adj.* (kən'sʌm·ət) consumado; excelente; perfecto. —**consummation** (,kan·sə'mei·ʃən) *n.* consumación; final; término.

consumption (kən'sʌmp·ʃən) *n.* **1,** (using up) consunción; extinción. **2,** *econ.* consumo. **3,** *pathol.* tuberculosis; tisis.

consumptive (kən'sʌmp·tɪv) *n.* & *adj.* tuberculoso; tísico.

contact ('kan,tækt) *n.* **1,** (meeting; touching) contacto. **2,** *colloq.* (personal connection) relación; *Mex.* palancas. —*v.t.* & *i.* relacionarse (con); ponerse en contacto (con). —**contact lens,** lente de contacto. —**contact man,** *colloq.* intermediario.

contagion (kən'tei·dʒən) *n.* contagio; contaminación. —**contagious,** *adj.* contagioso. —**contagiousness,** *n.* contagiosidad.

contain (kən'tein) *v.t.* **1,** (hold) contener; encerrar; incluir. **2,** (have capacity) contener; tener cabida. **3,** *math.* ser divisible por. —**container,** *n.* envase; receptáculo; caja.

contaminate (kən'tæm·ɪ·neit) *v.t.* **1,** (taint) contaminar; corromper. **2,** (corrupt) pervertir; depravar. —**contaminant** (-nənt) *n.* contaminante. —**contamination,** *n.* contaminación.

contemplate ('kan·təm,pleit) *v.t.* **1,** (study) contemplar; considerar; estudiar. **2,** (intend) planear; esperar. —*v.i.* meditar; contemplar.

contemplation (,kan·təm'plei·ʃən) *n.* **1,** (study) contemplación; meditación. **2,** (intention) esperanza; intención.

contemplative ('kan·təm,ple·tɪv) *adj.* contemplativo.

contemporaneous (kən,təm·pə'rei·ni·əs) *adj.* contemporáneo.

contemporary (kən'təm·pə·rer·i) *n.* & *adj.* contemporáneo; coetáneo.

contempt (kən'tempt) *n.* **1,** (scorn) desprecio; desdén; menosprecio. **2,** *law* rebeldía; contumacia; desacato. —**contemptible,** *adj.* despreciable; menospreciable. —**contemptibility,** *n.* desprecio; menosprecio.

contemptuous (kən'temp·tʃu·əs) *adj.* desdeñoso; despectivo; altivo. —**contemptuousness,** *n.* desdén; altanería; altivez.

contend (kən'tend) *v.i.* **1,** (struggle) contender; luchar; pelear. **2,** (assert) afirmar; asentir. —**contender,** *n.* contendiente.

content (kən'tɛnt) *adj.* [*también,* **contented**] contento; satisfecho; tranquilo. —*v.t.* satisfacer; contentar.

content ('kan·tɛnt) *n.* **1,** (gist; substance) tema; asunto; objeto. **2,** (capacity) volumen; capacidad. **3,** *pl.* (of a receptacle) contenido; cabida. **4,** *pl.* (of a book) asunto; materia.

contention (kən'tɛn·ʃən) *n.* **1,** (oral strife) contienda; disputa; debate. **2,** (struggle) contienda; lucha; pelea.

contentious (kən'tɛn·ʃəs) *adj.* contencioso; litigioso. —**contentiousness,** *n.* tendencia a litigar.

contentment (kən'tɛnt·mənt) *n.* contentamiento; satisfacción.

contest ('kan·tɛst) *n.* **1,** (fight) encuentro; lucha; pugna; pelea. **2,** (competition) concurso; competición. —*v.t.* (kən'tɛst) desafiar; disputar; oponer; *law* rebatir. —**contestant** (kən'tɛs·tənt) *n.* contendiente; contrincante; concursante.

context ('kan·tɛkst) *n.* contexto; contenido. —**contextual** (kən'tɛkst·ju·el) *adj.* perteneciente al contexto.

contiguity (,kan·tɪ'gju·ə·ti) *n.* contigüidad; inmediación.

contiguous (kən'tɪg·ju·əs) *adj.* contiguo; inmediato.

continence ('kan·tɪ·nəns) *n.* continencia.

continent ('kan·tɪ·nənt) *n.* continente. —*adj.* continente; casto; puro. —**continental** (-'nɛnt·əl) *adj.* continental.

contingency (kən'tɪn·dʒən·si) *n.* contingencia; casualidad; circunstancia.

contingent (kən'tɪn·dʒənt) *adj.* contingente; accidental. —*n.* contingente; cuota.

continual (kən'tɪn·ju·əl) *adj.* **1,** (continuing) continuo **2,** (repeated) reiterado. **3,** (unceasing) incesante.

continuance (kən'tɪn·ju·əns) *n.* continuación; *law* aplazamiento.

continuation (kən,tɪn·ju'ei·ʃən) *n.* continuación; prolongación.

continue (kən'tɪn·ju) *v.t.* **1,** (prolong) continuar; prolongar; extender. **2,** (resume) continuar; proseguir. **3,** (retain, as in office) continuar; retener. —*v.i.* **1,** (persist) persistir; perseverar. **2,** (resume) proseguir; seguir. **3,** (stay)

permanecer; quedarse. **4,** (endure) prolongarse; durar.

continuity (,kan·tɪ'nju·ə·ti) *n.* **1,** (unbroken sequence) continuidad. **2,** (script, as for radio) guión.

continuous (kən'tɪn·ju·əs) *adj.* continuo; ininterrumpido; incesante. —**continuously,** *adv.* continuamente; de continuo.

continuum (kən'tɪn·ju·əm) *n.* continuo.

contort (kən'tort) *v.t.* retorcer. —**contortion** (-'tor·ʃən) *n.* contorsión; retorcimiento. —**contortionist,** *n.* contorsionista.

contour ('kan·tur) *n.* contorno; perímetro.

contraband ('kan·trə·bænd) *n.* contrabando. —*adj.* de contrabando; prohibido.

contraception (kan·trə'sɛp·ʃən) *n.* prevención del embarazo; anticoncepción. —**contraceptive** (-tɪv) *n. & adj.* anticonceptivo.

contract ('kan·trækt) *n.* **1,** contrato; escritura. **2,** *cards* mayor apuesta. —*v.t.* (kən'trækt) **1,** (condense) contraer; condensar; encoger. **2,** (acquire; incur) contraer; incurrir. —*v.i.* **1,** (shrink) encogerse; contraerse. **2,** (agree formally) comprometerse; hacer contrato.

contraction (kən'træk·ʃən) *n.* **1,** (shrinkage) encogimiento; contracción. **2,** *gram.* contracción.

contractor (kən'træk·tər) *n.* contratista.

contractual (kən'træk·tʃu·əl) *adj.* contractual.

contradict (kan·trə'dɪkt) *v.t.* **1,** (deny) contradecir; negar. **2,** (be contrary to) oponerse a. —**contradiction** (-'dɪk·ʃən) *n.* contradicción. —**contradictory,** *adj.* contradictorio.

contralto (kən'træl·to) *n.* contralto. —*adj.* de o para contralto.

contraption (kən'træp·ʃən) *n.,* *colloq.* aparato; artefacto.

contrapuntal (kan·trə'pʌnt·əl) *adj., mus.* referente al contrapunto.

contrary ('kan·trɛr·i) *adj.* **1,** (opposite) contrario; opuesto. **2,** (conflicting) contradictorio. **3,** (perverse) terco; porfiado. —*n.* lo contrario; lo opuesto. —**contrariness,** *n.* terquedad; oposición.

contrast (kən'træst) *v.t. & i.* contrastar. —*n.* ('kan·træst) contraste; diferencia.

contravene (ˌkan·trə'viːn) *v.t.*
contravenir; infringir; romper.
—**contravention** (-'ven·ʃən) *n.*
contravención.
contretemps ('kan·trə‚taN) *n.*
contratiempo; *Amer.* broma.
contribute (kən'trɪb·jut) *v.t.* contribuir. —*v.i.* cooperar; colaborar.
—**contributor**, *n.* contribuyente;
contribuidor; colaborador. —**contributory** (-jə·tor·i) *adj.* cooperante;
que contribuye; contribuidor.
contribution (ˌkan·trɪ'bju·ʃən) *n.*
contribución; colaboración.
contrite (kən'trait) *adj.* contrito;
arrepentido. —**contrition** (-'trɪʃ·ən)
n. contrición.
contrivance (kən'trai·vəns) *n.* 1,
(device) artefacto; aparato; utensilio. 2, (scheme) plan; estratagema.
contrive (kən'traiv) *v.t.* planear;
imaginar; maquinar; tramar. —*v.i.*
1, (scheme) urdir; idear. 2, *con inf.*
(manage) ingeniarse para; darse
maña para.
control (kən'trol) *v.t.* [**controlled,
-trolling**] 1, (govern) dominar;
gobernar. 2, (regulate) inspeccionar; revisar. 3, (restrain) refrenar;
cohibir. —*n.* 1, (authority) dominio;
supremacía; dirección. 2, *mech.*
regulador; control. 3, (restraint)
freno; limitación. —**controllable,**
adj. sujeto a dirección o registro.
controller (kən'tro·lər) *n.* =
comptroller.
controversial (ˌkan·trə'vʌr·ʃəl)
adj. controversial; discutible; polémico.
controversy ('kan·trə‚vʌr·si) *n.*
controversia; polémica.
controvert (ˌkan·trə'vʌrt) *v.t.*
controvertir; debatir. —**controvertible,** *adj.* controvertible.
contumacy ('kan·tju·mə·si) *n.*
contumacia. —**contumacious**
(-'me·ʃəs) *adj.* contumaz.
contumely ('kan·tju·mə·li) *n.*
contumelia; injuria; ultraje.
—**contumelious** (-'mi·li·əs)
adj. contumelioso; injurioso;
ultrajante.
contusion (kən'tu·ʒən) *n.*
contusión.
conundrum (kə'nʌn·drəm) *n.*
adivinanza, esp. la que termina con
juego de palabras.
convalesce (ˌkan·və'les) *v.i.* convalecer; recuperarse. —**convalescence,** *n.* convalecencia. —**convalescent,** *n. & adj.* convaleciente.

convection (kən'vek·ʃən) *n.*
convección.
convene (kən'viːn) *v.t.* convocar;
congregar. —*v.i.* congregarse;
reunirse; juntarse.
convenience (kən'vin·jəns) *n.* 1,
(suitability; advantage) conveniencia; comodidad; oportunidad. 2,
usu. pl. (comforts) comodidades.
—**convenient,** *adj.* conveniente;
adecuado.
convent ('kan·vənt) *n.* convento.
convention (kən'ven·ʃən) *n.* 1,
(meeting) asamblea; convención. 2,
(agreement) convención. 3, (custom) conformidad; conveniencia;
regla.
conventional (kən'ven·ʃən·əl)
adj. 1, (customary) convencional. 2,
(stipulated) estipulado; convenido.
—**conventionality** (-'æl·ə·ti) *n.*
convencionalismo.
converge (kən'vʌrdʒ) *v.i.* converger. —**convergence,** *n.* convergencia. —**convergent,** *adj.* convergente.
conversant (kən'vʌr·sənt) *adj.* 1,
(acquainted with) versado. 2, (informed) enterado.
conversation (ˌkan·vər'sei·ʃən) *n.*
conversación; charla. —**conversational,** *adj.* de conversación.
converse (kən'vʌrs) *v.i.* conversar;
platicar; charlar. —*n.* ('kan·vʌrs)
charla; plática.
converse ('kan·vʌrs) *adj.*
traspuesto; inverso. —*n.* 1, (the opposite) lo opuesto; lo contrario. 2,
philos. (a proposition) recíproca.
conversion (kən'vʌr·ʒən) *n.* 1,
(act of converting) conversión. 2,
(change) transformación; cambio. 3,
fin. (exchange) cambio.
convert (kən'vʌrt) *v.t.* 1, (change)
convertir; transformar. 2, *comm.*
(exchange) convertir; cambiar. 3,
law apropiar ilícitamente. —*n.*
('kan·vʌrt) converso. —**converter;
convertor,** *n.* convertidor.
convertible (kən'vʌrt·ə·bəl) *adj.*
1, (alterable) convertible; transformable. 2, (automobile) descapotable. —*n.* descapotable. —**conver-
tibility,** *n.* condición de convertible;
capacidad de transformación.
convex (kan'veks) *adj.* convexo.
—**convexity** (-ə·ti) *n.* convexidad.
convey (kən'vei) *v.t.* 1, (carry)
transportar; llevar. 2, (send)
transmitir; transferir. 3, (communi-

cate) comunicar; impartir. **4,** *law* traspasar; transferir.

conveyance (kən'vei·əns) *n.* **1,** (transportation) transporte; conducción. **2,** (vehicle) vehículo. **3,** (transfer of ownership) cesión de propiedad. **4,** (deed) escritura de traspaso.

conveyor (kən'vei·ər) *n.* transportador; correa de transmisión.

convict (kən'vɪkt) *v.t.* condenar. —*n.* ('kɑn·vɪkt) convicto; reo. —**convicted,** *adj.* convicto.

conviction (kən'vɪk·ʃən) *n.* **1,** (act of convincing) convencimiento. **2,** (act of convicting) convicción. **3,** (belief) convicción; creencia.

convince (kən'vɪns) *v.t.* convencer; persuadir. —**convincing,** *adj.* convincente.

convivial (kən'vɪv·i·əl) *adj.* convival; alegre; divertido; jovial. —**conviviality** (-'æl·ə·ti) *n.* jovialidad.

convocation (,kɑn·vo'kei·ʃən) *n.* **1,** (summons) convocación; convocatoria. **2,** (assembly) asamblea.

convoke (kən'vok) *v.t.* convocar; llamar.

convoy (kən'vɔi) *v.t.* convoyar. —*n.* ('kɑn·vɔi) convoy.

convulse (kən'vʌls) *v.t.* & *i.* **1,** (cause spasms) producir convulsiones; convulsionar; crispar. **2,** (agitate) agitar; trastornar; disturbar. —*v.i.* (shake with laughter) morirse de risa; reír con convulsiones.

convulsion (kən'vʌl·ʃən) *n.* **1,** *pathol.* convulsión; espasmo. **2,** *fig.* (agitation) conmoción; alboroto. —**convulsive** (-sɪv) *adj.* convulsivo; espasmódico.

coo (kuɹ) *v.i.* arrullar. —*n.* [*también,* **cooing**] arrullo; mimo.

cook (kuk) *v.t.* & *i.* cocer; cocinar. —*n.* cocinero. —**cookery** (-ər·i) *n.* arte de cocinar; cocina. —**cook up,** *slang,* fraguar; planear; tramar.

cookie *también,* **cooky** ('kuk·i) *n.* **1,** (pastry) galleta; pasta. **2,** *slang* (person) tipo; sujeto.

cool (kuɹl) *adj.* **1,** (not very cold) frío; fresco. **2,** (calm) sereno; tranquilo. **3,** (not cordial) frío; tibio; indiferente. —*v.t.* **1,** (make cool) enfriar; refrescar. **2,** (calm) calmar; sosegar. —*v.i.* **1,** (become cool) enfriarse. **2,** (calm down) apaciguarse.

cooler ('kuɹ·lər) *n.* **1,** enfriadera;

refrigerador. **2,** *slang* (prison) cárcel; prisión.

cool-headed *adj.* sereno; sensato.

coolie ('kuɹ·li) *n.* peón chino.

coolness ('kul·nəs) *n.* **1,** (of temperature) frescura. **2,** (calmness) calma; tranquilidad. **3,** (indifference) frialdad; indiferencia.

coop (kup) *n.* **1,** (for fowl) pollera; jaula. **2,** (cramped place) jaula; ratonera; cárcel. —*v.t.* [*usa.,* **coop up**] confinar; encerrar.

co-op (ko'ap) *n., slang* = **cooperative.**

cooper ('ku·pər) *n.* barrilero; tonelero.

cooperate (ko'ap·ə,reit) *v.i.* cooperar; colaborar. —**cooperation,** *n.* cooperación; ayuda; colaboración.

cooperative (ko'ap·ə·rə·tɪv) *adj.* cooperante; cooperativo. —*n.* [*también, slang,* **co-op**] cooperativa.

co-opt (ko'apt) *v.t.* elegir o nombrar como miembro.

coordinate (ko'or·də,neit) *v.t.* coordinar. —*adj.* (-nət) coordinado; *math.* coordenado. —*n., math.* coordenada. —**coordination,** *n.* coordinación. —**coordinator,** *n.* coordinador.

coot (kut) *n.* **1,** *ornith.* fúlica. **2,** *colloq.* bobo.

cootie ('ku·ti) *n., slang* piojo.

cop (kap) *n., slang* policía. —*v.t.* [**copped, copping**] *slang* **1,** (steal) robar. **2,** (catch) atrapar; coger. —**cop a plea,** *slang* declararse culpable de delito menor para evitar otro mayor. —**cop out,** *slang* echarse atrás. —**cop-out,** *n., slang* rendición.

cope (kop) *n.* **1,** *eccles.* capa pluvial. **2,** (arch, as of the sky) bóveda; arco. **3,** [*también,* **coping**] (sloping ridge) albardilla. —*v.t.* cubrir. —*v.i.* competir; hacer frente. —**cope with,** hacer frente a; competir con.

copier ('kap·i·ər) *n.* copiadora.

copious ('ko·pi·əs) *adj.* copioso; abundante. —**copiousness,** *n.* abundancia; profusión.

copper ('kap·ər) *n.* **1,** (metal) cobre. **2,** *fig.* (coin) cobre; centavo. **3,** *slang* (policeman) policía; guardia. —*adj.* de cobre; cobrizo. —**coppery; copperish,** *adj.* de cobre; cobrizo.

copperhead ('kap·ər·hɛd) *n., zoöl.* víbora norteamericana muy venenosa, con cabeza de color cobrizo.

coppersmith ('kap·ər·smiθ) *n.* calderero.

coppice ('kap·ɪs) *n.* = copse.

copse (kaps) *n.* matorral; soto.

Coptic ('kap·tɪk) *adj.* cóptico; copto. —*n.* copto. —**Copt** (kapt) *n.* copto.

copula ('kap·jə·lə) *n.* cópula.

copulate ('kap·jə·leit) *v.i.* copular; copularse; unirse. —**copulation**, *n.* copulación; unión. —**copulative** (-lə·tɪv) *adj.* copulativo.

copy ('kap·i) *n.* 1, (reproduction) copia; imitación; reproducción. 2, (magazine, book, etc.) ejemplar; número. 3, *print.* original. —*v.t.* 1, (reproduce) copiar; reproducir. 2, (imitate) imitar. —**copyist**, *n.* copista.

copyright ('kap·i·rait) *n.* propiedad literaria o artística. —*v.t.* patentar; registrar.

coquette (ko'kɛt) *n.* coqueta. —**coquettish**, *adj.* coquetón. —**coquetry** (-ri) *n.* coquetería.

coral ('kor·əl) *n.* coral. —*adj.* 1, (of or like coral) coralino. 2, (of coral color) acoralado. —**coral snake**, coral.

cord (kord) *n.* 1, (string) cordón; cordel. 2, *anat.* tendón. 3, (cubic measure) cuerda. 4, (rib in fabric) pana; cordoncillo. —*v.t.* encordelar. —**cordage** ('kor·dɪdʒ) *n.* cordaje; cordelería.

cordial ('kor·dʒəl) *adj.* cordial; abierto; afable. —*n.* cordial; licor. —**cordiality** (-'dʒæl·ə·ti) *n.* cordialidad; afabilidad.

cordillera (kor·dɪ'lɛr·ə) *n.* cordillera.

cordon ('kord·ən) *n.* 1, *mil.* (defensive line) cordón. 2, (badge) cíngulo. 3, *archit.* (projection) parapeto.

cordovan ('kor·də·vən) *n.* cordobán. —*adj.* de cordobán.

corduroy ('kor·də·rɔi) *n.* pana.

core (kor) *n.* 1, (pith) corazón; meollo; esencia. 2, (center of fruit) pepita; corazón; hueso. —*v.t.* despepitar.

coreligionist (,ko·rɪ'lɪdʒ·ən·ɪst) *n.* correligionario.

co-respondent (,ko·rə'spon·dənt) *n.* codemandado.

coriander (,kor·i'æn·dər) *n.* cilantro.

cork (kork) *n.* corcho. —*v.t.* encorchar; taponar. —**corking**, *adj.*, *colloq.* excelente.

corkscrew ('kork·skru) *n.* sacacorchos; tirabuzón. —*adj.* retorcido; tortuoso. —*v.i.*, *fig.* zigzaguear; serpentear.

cormorant ('kor·mə·rənt) *n.* cormorán.

corn (korn) *n.* 1, (cereal) maíz. 2, (callus) callo; dureza. 3, *slang* (triteness) trivialidad; vulgaridad. —*v.t.* acecinar; salar; curar.

corncob ('korn,kab) *n.* mazorca de maíz; carozo; *Amer.* tusa.

cornea ('kor·ni·ə) *n.* córnea.

corner ('kor·nər) *n.* 1, (angle; street crossing) esquina; rincón. 2, (nook) escondrijo. 3, (awkward position) aprieto; apuro. 4, (region) región apartada. 5, *comm.* monopolio. —*v.t.* 1, (trap) arrinconar; apretar; acosar. 2, *comm.* monopolizar.

cornerstone ('kor·nər,ston) *n.* piedra angular; primera piedra.

cornet (kor'nɛt) *n.*, *mus.* corneta. —**cornetist**, *n.* corneta.

corn flour también, **corn meal** maicena.

cornflower ('korn,flau·ər) *n.* aciano.

cornice ('kor·nɪs) *n.* cornisa.

cornstarch ('korn,startʃ) *n.* almidón de maíz.

cornucopia (,korn·ju'ko·pi·ə) *n.* cuerno de la abundancia.

corny ('kor·ni) *adj. slang* sensiblero; trillado.

corolla (kə'ro·lə) *n.*, *bot.* corola.

corollary ('kar·ə·lɛr·i) *n.* corolario.

corona (kə'ro·nə) *n.* corona; halo. —**coronal** ('kor·ə·nəl) *adj.*, coronal.

coronary ('kar·ə,nɛr·i) *adj.* coronario.

coronation (,kar·ə'nei·ʃən) *n.* coronación.

coroner ('kar·ə·nər) *n.* pesquisidor (en una encuesta).

coronet (kar·ə·nɛt) *n.* 1, (crown) corona. 2, (headdress) diadema.

corporal ('kor·pə·rəl) *n.* cabo. —*adj.* corporal; físico. —**corporal punishment**, castigo físico.

corporate ('kor·pə·rət) *adj.* 1, (of or like a corporation) incorporado. 2, (joint; common) colectivo.

corporation (,kor·pə'rei·ʃən) *n.* 1, (company; association) corporación; sociedad. 2, *slang* (paunch) panza; barriga; *Amer.* pipa.

corporeal (kor'por·i·əl) *adj.* corpóreo; físico; material.

corps (kor) *n.* [*pl.* **corps** (kor; korz)] cuerpo.

corpse (korps) *n.* cadáver.

corpulence ('kor·pjə·ləns) *n.* corpulencia; robustez; obesidad. —**corpulent,** *adj.* corpulento; robusto.

corpus ('kor·pəs) *n.* **1,** (body) cuerpo. **2,** (collection, as of laws) cuerpo; conjunto.

corpuscle ('kor·pəs·əl) *n.* **1,** (small particle) corpúsculo. **2,** (blood cell) glóbulo.

corral (kə'ræl) *n.* corral. —*v.t.* acorralar; acosar; cazar.

correct (kə'rɛkt) *v.t.* **1,** (note errors in) corregir. **2,** (rectify) rectificar; enmendar. **3,** (discipline) reprender; castigar. —*adj.* **1,** (true) correcto; exacto; justo. **2,** (ethical) propio; bien hecho. —**corrective,** *adj.* correctivo; correccional. —**correctness,** *n.* corrección; exactitud.

correction (kə'rɛk·ʃən) *n.* **1,** (act of correcting) corrección; rectificación; enmienda. **2,** (rebuke) castigo; escarmiento.

correlate ('kar·ə,leit) *v.t.* correlacionar; relacionar. —**correlation,** *n.* correlación; relación.

correlative (kə'rɛl·ə·tɪv) *n.* & *adj.* correlativo.

correspond (kar·ə'spand) *v.i.* **1,** (match) corresponder; tener proporción (con). **2,** (write) escribirse; tener o mantener correspondencia. —**correspondence** (-əns) *n.* correspondencia.

correspondent (kar·ə'spand·ənt) *n.* corresponsal; correspondiente. —*adj.* correspondiente.

corridor ('kar·ı·dər) *n.* corredor; pasillo; galería.

corroborate (kə'rab·ə·reit) *v.t.* corroborar; confirmar. —**corroboration,** *n.* corroboración. —**corroborative,** *adj.* corroborativo; que corrobora.

corrode (kə'roːd) *v.t.* corroer. —*v.i.* corroerse.

corrosion (kə'ro·ʒən) *n.* corrosión. —**corrosive** (-sıv) *n.* & *adj.* corrosivo.

corrugate ('kar·ə,geit) *v.t.* & *i.* arrugar; acanalar; plegar. —**corrugation,** *n.* acanalamiento. —**corrugated paper,** cartón acanalado.

corrupt (kə'rʌpt) *adj.* **1,** (evil) corrompido; degenerado; depravado. **2,** (tainted) putrefacto; pútrido. —*v.t.* **1,** (pervert) corromper; pervertir. **2,** (bribe) sobornar; cohechar. **3,** (taint) podrir; infectar. —**corruptible,** *adj.* corruptible. —**corruptness; corruption** (kə'rʌp·ʃən) *n.* corrupción.

corsage (kor'saːʒ) *n.* ramillete para llevar al hombro o a la cintura.

corsair (kor'seːr) *n.* corsario.

corset ('kor·sət) *n.* corsé.

cortege (kor'tɛːʒ) *n.* **1,** (procession) cortejo; procesión. **2,** (retinue) comitiva; séquito.

cortex ('kor·tɛks) *n.* [*pl.* **cortices** ('kor·tə,siz)] *anat.; bot.* corteza. —**cortical** (-tı·kəl) *adj.* cortical.

cortisone ('kor·tı,son) *n.* cortisona.

corvette (kor'vɛt) *n.* corbeta.

cosecant (ko'si·kənt) *n.* cosecante.

cosignatory (ko'sɪg·nə·tor·i) *adj.* & *n.* cosignatario. *También,* **cosigner.**

cosine ('ko·sain) *n.* coseno.

cosmetic (kaz'mɛt·ık) *n.* & *adj.* cosmético.

cosmic ('kaz·mık) *adj.* **1,** (pert. to the universe) cósmico. **2,** *fig.* (vast; ordered) vasto; metódico; ordenado. —**cosmic rays,** rayos cósmicos.

cosmogony (kaz'mag·ə·ni) *n.* cosmogonía.

cosmography (kaz'mag·rə·fi) *n.* cosmografía.

cosmology (kaz'mal·ə·dʒi) *n.* cosmología.

cosmonaut ('kaz·mə·nɔt) *n.* cosmonauta; astronauta.

cosmopolitan (kaz·mə'pal·ı·tən) *adj.* cosmopolita. —*n.* [*también,* **cosmopolite** (kaz'map·ə·lait)] cosmopolita.

cosmos ('kaz·məs) *n.* **1,** (universe) cosmos; universo. **2,** *bot.* flor cosmos.

Cossack ('kas·æk) *n.* & *adj.* cosaco.

cost (kɔːst) *n.* **1,** (price) coste; costo; precio. **2,** (expense) expensas; gastos. **3,** (loss; suffering) pérdida; daño. **4,** *pl.,* *law* costas. —*v.t.* & *i.* costar. —**at all costs,** a toda costa. —**cost of living,** costo de la vida.

costly ('kɔst·li) *adj.* **1,** (expensive) costoso; caro. **2,** (very valuable) suntuoso; magnífico. —**costliness,** *n.* lo costoso; suntuosidad; magnificencia.

costume ('kas·tjum) *n.* **1,** (garb) vestido; traje. **2,** (fancy dress) disfraz. **3,** *theat.* (clothes) indumentaria; atavío. —*v.t.* **1,** (dress) vestir.

2, (disguise) disfrazar. —**costumer,** *n.* sastre de teatro. —**costume jewelry,** joyas de poco valor.

cot (kat) *n.* catre; damita.

cotangent (ko'tæn·dʒənt) *n.* cotangente.

coterie ('ko·tə·ri) *n.* grupo; círculo; corrillo.

cotillion (ko'tɪl·jən) *n.* cotillón.

cottage ('kat·ɪdʒ) *n.* 1, (small house) cabaña. 2, (country house) quinta. —**cottage cheese,** requesón.

cotter pin ('kat·ər) chaveta.

cotton ('kat·ən) *n.* 1, (fiber; cloth) algodón. 2, (plant) algodonero. —*adj.* de algodón; algodonero. —**cotton field; cotton plantation,** algodonal.

cottonseed ('kat·ən,sid) *n.* semilla de algodón.

cotyledon (,kat·ə'li·dən) *n.* cotiledón.

couch (kautʃ) *n.* 1, (sofa) poltrona; diván; sofá. 2, (small bed) camita; lecho. —*v.t.* 1, (lay) recostar; reclinar. 2, (express) indicar; expresar. —*v.i.* 1, (to lie down) recostarse; reclinarse. 2, (wait in ambush) agacharse; encorvarse.

cougar ('ku·gər) *n.* cuguar; puma.

cough (kɔf) *v.i.* toser. —*n.* tos. —**cough up,** 1, (expel from the throat) esputar. 2, *slang* (hand over) rendir; entregar.

could (kʊd) *v.*, *pret. de* **can.**

coulomb (kʊ'lam) *n.* culombio.

council ('kaun·səl) *n.* 1, (assembly) consejo; junta. 2, (municipal body) concejo. 3, *eccles.* concilio.

councilman ('kaun·səl·mən) *n.* [*pl.* **-men**] concejal. —**councilwoman,** *n.f.* [*pl.* **-women**] concejala.

councilor *también,* **councillor** ('kaun·səl·ər) *n.* consejero; concejal.

counsel ('kaun·səl) *n.* 1, (consultation) consejo; consulta. 2, (advice) parecer; aviso; guía. 3, (plan) trama; deliberación; plan. 4, *law* abogado; consultor. —*v.t. & i.* aconsejar; consultar; dirigir; asesorar. —**keep one's own counsel,** callarse la boca; reservarse la opinión. —**take counsel,** aconsejarse; pedir consejo.

counselor *también,* **counsellor** ('kaun·sə·lər) *n.* 1, (lawyer) abogado. 2, (adviser) consejero; asesor; confidente.

count (kaunt) *v.t.* 1, (enumerate)

contar; enumerar. 2, (deem) considerar; reputar; estimar. —*v.i.* 1, (enumerate) contar; numerar. 2, (be of value) importar. —*n.* 1, (enumeration) cuenta; enumeración; cálculo. 2, *law* cargo; demanda. 3, *cap.* (title) conde. —**count in,** incluir. —**count off,** contar separado. —**count on o upon,** depender de; contar con. —**count out,** 1, (omit) omitir. 2, *colloq., polit.* falsear una elección. 3, *boxing* declarar vencido.

countdown ('kaunt,daun) *n.* conteo.

countenance ('kaun·tə·nəns) *n.* 1, (face) cara; faz. 2, (facial expression) aspecto; semblante; expresión. 3, (favor) apoyo; favor; protección. —*v.t.* ayudar; apoyar; favorecer; fomentar.

counter ('kaun·tər) *n.* 1, (device) contador. 2, (token) ficha; tanto. 3, (display table) mostrador. 4, (enumerator) contador. 5, (the opposite) lo opuesto; lo contrario. —*adj.* contrario; opuesto. —*adv.* contra; al revés. —*v.t.* & *i.* 1, (oppose) oponer; contradecir. 2, (attack) oponerse; contraatacar.

counteract (,kaun·tər'ækt) *v.t.* contrarrestar; estorbar; neutralizar; impedir.

counterattack ('kaun·tər·ə,tæk) *v.t. & i.* contraatacar. —*n.* contraataque.

counterbalance ('kaun·tər,bæl·əns) *v.t.* contrabalancear. —*n.* contrapeso.

counterclockwise ('kaun·tər·'klak·waiz) *adj. & adv.* contrario a las manecillas del reloj.

counterfeit ('kaun·tər,fɪt) *adj.* falsificado; espurio. —*n.* 1, (imitation) falsificación; imitación. 2, (false money) moneda falsa. —*v.t.* falsificar; falsear. —*v.i.* fingir; pretender; disimular. —**counterfeiter,** *n.* falsario; falsificador.

countermand ('kaun·tər,mænd) *v.t.* contramandar; revocar; cancelar. —*n.* contramandato; contraorden.

countermark ('kaun·tər,mark) *n.* contramarca. —*v.t.* contramarcar.

counteroffensive (,kaun·tər·ə'fɛn·sɪv) *n.* contraofensiva.

counterpane ('kaun·tər,pein) *n.* cubrecama; colcha.

counterpart ('kaun·tər,part) *n.* 1, (complement) contraparte. 2, (copy) duplicado; facsímil.

counterpoint ('kaun·tər‚pɔint) *n.*, *mus.* contrapunto.

counterpoise ('kaun·tər‚pɔiz) *n.* contrapeso.

counterproductive ('kaun·tər‚prə‚dʌk·tɪv) *adj.* contraproducente.

counterrevolution (‚kaun·tər‚rɛv·ə'lu·ʃən) *n.* contrarrevolución. —**counterrevolutionary** (-ɛr·i) *adj.* & *n.* contrarrevolucionario.

countersign ('kaun·tər‚sain) *v.t.* refrendar; visar. —*n.* contraseña; santo y seña.

countersignature ('kaun·tər‚sɪg·nə·tʃər) *n.* refrendata.

countersink ('kaun·tər‚sɪŋk) *v.t.* [*pret.* & *p.p.* -sunk] avellanar. —*n.* 1, (tool) avellanador. 2, (counter-sunk hole) agujero avellanado.

counterspy ('kaun·tər‚spai) *n.* contraespía. —**counterespionage,** *n.* contraespionaje.

counterweight ('kaun·tər‚weit) *n.* contrapeso.

countess ('kaun·tis) *n.* condesa.

countless ('kaunt·ləs) *adj.* incontable; innumerable.

country ('kʌn·tri) *n.* 1, (expanse of land) región; tierra; país. 2, (nation) país; nación. 3, (rural region) campiña; campo. —*adj.* campestre; rústico; rural. —**country club,** club de campo.

countryman ('kʌn·tri·mən) *n.* [*pl.* -men] 1, (compatriot) compatriota. 2, (rustic) campesino.

countryside ('kʌn·tri·said) *n.* paisaje campestre; campiña; campo.

county ('kaun·ti) *n.* condado; distrito. —*adj.* del condado.

coup (kuı) *n.* golpe. —**coup de grâce,** golpe o tiro de gracia. —**coup d'etat** (ku·de'taı) golpe de estado.

coupe *también,* **coupé** (ku'pei) *n.* 1, (automobile) cupé. 2, (closed carriage) berlina.

couple ('kʌp·əl) *n.* 1, (pair) par; pareja. 2, (man and wife) matrimonio. —*v.t.* acoplar; ensamblar; juntar.

couplet ('kʌp·lət) *n.* copla.

coupling ('kʌp·lɪŋ) *n.* acoplamiento; *R.R.* enganche.

coupon ('ku·pan) *n.* cupón.

courage ('kʌr·ɪdʒ) *n.* coraje; valentía; bravura. —**courageous** (kə'rei·dʒəs) *adj.* intrépido; valeroso; bravo.

courier ('kur·i·ər) *n.* 1, (messenger) correo; mensajero; ordinario. 2,

(travel guide) acompañante; encargado.

course (kors) *n.* 1, (passage) vía; pasaje; pasadizo. 2, (direction) recorrido; dirección. 3, *sports* campo; terreno. 4, (progressive phases) curso; marcha; rumbo. 5, (series, as of classes) curso; serie. 6, (behavior) conducta; comportamiento. 7, (succession of acts, procedures, etc.) sistema; método. 8, (part of a meal) plato. 9, *naut.* rumbo. —*v.t.* correr; perseguir; cazar; ir detrás de. —*v.i.* corretear. —**in due course,** a su debido tiempo; oportunamente. —**matter of course,** cosa común o de cajón. —**of course,** desde luego; naturalmente; por supuesto; claro.

courser ('kor·sər) *n.*, *poet.* corcel; caballo de guerra.

court (kort) *n.* 1, (patio) patio; atrio. 2, (sports area) cancha; frontón. 3, (royal) corte; palacio. 4, *law* tribunal; sala de justicia. —*v.t.* 1, (seek the favor of) cortejar. 2, (woo) enamorar; cortejar; galantear. 3, (aspire to) solicitar; buscar; —*v.i.* hacer la corte.

courteous ('kʌr·ti·əs) *adj.* cortés; atento; educado.

courtesan ('kor·tə·zən) *n.* cortesana.

courtesy ('kʌr·tə·si) *n.* 1, (politeness) cortesía; atención; finura. 2, (indulgence) favor.

courthouse ('kort‚haus) *n.* audiencia; tribunal; palacio de justicia.

courtier ('kor·ti·ər) *n.* cortesano; palaciego.

courtly ('kort·li) *adj.* cortesano; cortés.

court-martial (kort'mar·ʃəl) *n.* [*pl.* **courts-martial**] *mil.* consejo de guerra. —*v.t.* someter a consejo de guerra.

courtship ('kort·ʃɪp) *n.* cortejo; corte; noviazgo.

courtyard ('kort‚jard) *n.* atrio; patio.

cousin ('kʌz·ən) *n.* primo; prima.

cove (koıv) *n.* 1, (inlet) caleta; ensenada. 2, *Brit., slang* (fellow) hombre; tipo.

covenant ('kʌv·ə·nənt) *n.* pacto; convenio. —*v.t.* prometer; estipular. —*v.i.* pactar; comprometerse.

cover ('kʌv·ər) *v.t.* 1, (place something on) cubrir; encubrir; proteger; abrigar. 2, (hide) ocultar; tapar. 3, (traverse) andar; recorrer. 4, (include) comprender; incluir. **5,** (aim at) apuntar a; cubrir. **6,** *comm.* remesar o cubrir fondos. **7,** *colloq.* (report on) informar de; cubrir. —*v.i.* **1,** (spread over) correrse; esparcirse. **2,** (put one's hat on) cubrirse; taparse; tocarse. —*n.* **1,** (lid) tapadera; tapa. **2,** (protective layer) funda; forro; tapete. **3,** (envelope) cubierta. **4,** (disguise) pretexto; pretensión; velo. **5,** (shelter) refugio; abrigo; albergue. **6,** (table setting) cubierto. —**cover charge,** precio de admisión. —**from cover to cover,** de cabo a rabo. —**take cover,** ponerse a cubierto; ocultarse. —**under cover, 1,** (sheltered) a cubierto; a seguro. **2,** (hidden) secreto; oculto; escondido. **3,** (by pretense) so pretexto (de); con la excusa (de).

coverage ('kʌv·ər·ɪdʒ) *n.* **1,** (insurance) protección. **2,** (reporting) información; reportaje.

covering ('kʌv·ər·ɪŋ) *n.* cubierta; tapadera; envoltura.

coverlet ('kʌv·ər·lɪt) *n.* colcha; cobertor; cubrecama.

covert ('kʌv·ərt) *adj.* **1,** (hidden) secreto; escondido. **2,** (sheltered) cubierto; tapado; resguardado. —*n.* refugio; guarida; escondite.

covet ('kʌv·ɪt) *v.t.* **1,** (aspire to) ambicionar. **2,** (desire) condiciar. —**covetous** ('kʌv·ə·təs) *adj.* ambicioso; codicioso; envidioso; interesado. —**covetousness,** *n.* codicia.

covey ('kʌv·i) *n.* bandada; nidada.

cow (kau) *n.* vaca. —*v.t.* acobardar; intimidar; amedrentar.

coward ('kau·ərd) *n.* cobarde. —**cowardice** ('kau·ər·dɪs) *n.* cobardía. —**cowardly,** *adj.* cobarde; miedoso. —*adv.* cobardemente.

cowbell ('kau,bɛl) *n.* cencerro.

cowboy ('kau·bɔi) *n.* vaquero. *También,* **cowhand, cowpuncher.** —**cowgirl,** *n.f.* vaquera.

cower ('kau·ər) *v.i.* agacharse; achicarse; derrumbarse.

cowherd ('kau·hʌrd) *n.* boyero.

cowhide ('kau·haid) *n.* cuero o piel de vaca.

cowl (kaul) *n.* **1,** (monk's hood) capucha; capuz; cogulla. **2,** *auto.* cubretablero.

cowling ('kau·lɪŋ) *n., aero.; auto.* cubierta o caja del motor.

cowpox ('kau·paks) *n.* vacuna.

coxcomb ('kaks·kom) *n.* **1,** *lit.*

cresta de gallo. **2,** *fig.* (vain man) farol; presumido; mequetrefe. **3,** (jester's cap) gorro de bufón.

coy (kɔi) *adj.* **1,** (shy) tímido; vergonzoso; recatado. **2,** (feigning shyness) hipócrita; esquivo. —**coyness,** *n.* timidez; recato.

coyote (kai'o·ti; 'kai·ot) *n.* coyote.

cozen ('kʌz·ən) *v.t. & i.* engañar; defraudar; embaucar. —**cozenage** (-ɪdʒ) *n.* engaño; embaucamiento.

cozy ('ko·zi) *adj.* **1,** (of things) cálido; acogedor. **2,** (of persons) cómodo; a gusto. —**coziness,** *n.* comodidad.

CPA *abr. de* **certified public accountant.**

CPR *abr. de* **cardiopulmonary resuscitation.**

CPU *abr. de* **central processing unit.**

crab (kræb) *n.* **1,** (shellfish) cangrejo; *Amer.* jaiba. **2,** *colloq.* (irascible person) iracundo; mal genio; cascarrabias. **3,** *cap., astron.* Cáncer. —*v.i.* [**crabbed, crabbing**] *colloq.* quejarse; culpar. —**crabby,** *adj.* espinoso. —**crabgrass,** *n.* garranchuelo.

crabapple ('kræb,æp·əl) *n.* **1,** (tree) manzano silvestre. **2,** (fruit) manzana silvestre.

crabbed ('kræb·ɪd) *adj.* **1,** (cramped) obscuro; difícil. **2,** (cross) áspero; espinoso. —*v.,* *pret. & p.p. de* **crab.**

crack (kræk) *v.t.* **1,** (split) quebrar; hender; rajar. **2,** (damage) romper; destruir. **3,** (distill) someter a destilación fraccionada. —*v.i.* **1,** (split) quebrarse; rajarse; reventarse. **2,** (break, as a voice) dar chasquidos. **3,** *colloq.* (lose one's effectiveness) desquiciarse; trastornarse. **4,** *colloq.* (tell, as a joke) bromear; hacer chistes. —*n.* **1,** (sound) chasquido; crujido; estallido. **2,** (fissure) grieta; raja; hendura. **3,** *slang* (attempt) golpe; atentado. **4,** *slang* (gibe) escarnio; burla. **5,** (voice break) mudanza o cambio de la voz. —*adj.,* *colloq.* excelente; estupendo; superior. —**crack down on,** *colloq.* castigar; tratar con rigor. —**crack up,** *colloq.* **1,** (crash) estrellarse. **2,** (break down) quebrantarse; enfermarse.

cracked (krækt) *adj.* **1,** (split) roto; quebrado. **2,** *colloq.* (brainless) chiflado; alocado; loco.

cracker ('kræk·ər) *n.* **1,** (biscuit)

galleta. **2,** (firecracker) petardo; cohete.

crackle ('kræk·əl) *v.i.* crujir; dar chasquidos. —*n.* crepitación.

crackpot ('kræk·pat) *n. & adj.*, *slang* chiflado; excéntrico.

crack-up *n.* **1,** (crash) choque. **2,** (collapse) trastorno; agotamiento.

cradle ('krei·dəl) *n.* **1,** (crib) cuna. **2,** *fig.* (origin; infancy) origen; infancia; nacimiento. —*v.t.* acunar; mecer.

craft (kræft) *n.* **1,** [*pl.* **craft**] (vessel) nave; barco; buque. **2,** (trade) profesión; oficio. **3,** (guild) gremio. **4,** (skill) destreza; habilidad; maña. **5,** (guile) astucia; artificio.

craftsman ('kræfts·mən) *n.* (*pl.* **-men**) artesano; artífice. —**craftsmanship,** *n.* artesanía.

crafty ('kræft·i) *adj.* astuto; taimado; avieso. —**craftiness,** *n.* astucia; maña.

crag (kræg) *n.* risco; despeñadero. —**craggy,** *adj.* escarpado; riscoso.

cram (kræm) *v.t.* [**crammed,** **cramming**] **1,** (fill overfull) rellenar; atestar; embutir. **2,** (eat greedily) hartar; atracar. —*v.i.* **1,** (stuff oneself) llenarse; hartarse; atracarse. **2,** *colloq.* (study) empollar; darse un atracón.

cramp (kræmp) *n.* **1,** (of a muscle) calambre. **2,** *pl.* (in the abdomen) retortijones. **3,** (clamp) grapa; abrazadera. **4,** (hindrance) traba; impedimento. —*v.t.* **1,** (give cramps to) dar calambres. **2,** (fasten) sujetar; trabar. **3,** (constrict) constreñir; apretar. **4,** (hinder) impedir; estorbar. —**cramped,** *adj.* dificultoso; apretado; diminuto.

cranberry ('kræn,bɛr·i) *n.* arándano agrio.

crane (krein) *n.* **1,** (bird) grulla. **2,** (derrick) grúa. —*v.t.* **1,** (stretch, as the neck) estirar; alargar. **2,** (raise or move by crane) levantar con grúa.

cranium ('krei·ni·əm) *n.* cráneo. —**cranial,** *adj.* craneal.

crank (kræŋk) *n.* **1,** (device) manivela; manubrio. **2,** *colloq.* (zealot) maniático; extravagante. —*v.t. & i.* dar a o voltear (la manivela).

crankshaft *n.* cigüeñal.

cranky ('kræŋ·ki) *adj.* irritable; maniático; caprichoso. —**crankiness,** *n.* manía; chifladura.

cranny ('kræn·i) *n.* grieta; raja; hendedura.

craps (kræps) *n.* juego de dados.

crash (kræʃ) *n.* **1,** (sound) estampido; estallido. **2,** (collision) choque; colisión. **3,** (financial failure) fracaso; quiebra; bancarrota. **4,** (rough fabric) cutí; tela basta. **5,** *comput.* parada; derrumbamiento. —*v.t.* **1,** (smash) estallar; despedazar. **2,** *slang* (burst into) irrumpir; abrirse paso. —*v.i.* chocar; estrellarse.

crass (kræs) *adj.* craso; torpe; tosco; obtuso. —**crassness,** *n.* crasitud.

crate (kreit) *n.* banasta; envase o embalaje de madera; *Amer.* guacal. —*v.t.* poner en banasta; embalar con tablas de madera.

crater ('krei·tər) *n.* cráter.

cravat (krə'væt) *n.* corbata; *W.I.* chalina.

crave (kreiv) *v.t.* **1,** (desire) anhelar; desear; ambicionar. **2,** (beg for) pedir humildemente.

craven ('krei·vən) *adj. & n.* cobarde.

craving ('krei·viŋ) *n.* deseo; ansia; anhelo.

crawfish ('krɔ·fiʃ) *n.* langostino. *También,* **crayfish** ('krei-).

crawl (krɔl) *v.i.* **1,** (creep) arrastrarse; gatear; serpentear. **2,** (advance slowly) andar a paso de tortuga. **3,** (humiliate oneself) rebajarse; humillarse. —*n.* **1,** (creeping movement) gateo. **2,** (slow progress) marcha lenta; paso de tortuga. **3,** (swimming stroke) crawl.

crayon ('krei·an) *n.* clarión; tiza de color.

craze (kreiz) *v.t. & i.* enloquecer. —*n.* manía; capricho; moda.

crazy ('krei·zi) *adj.* **1,** (insane) loco; demente; enfurecido. **2,** *slang* (excited) extravagante; insensato. —**craziness,** *n.* locura; demencia; extravío. —**be crazy about,** *colloq.* sorber los vientos por. —**crazy bone,** nervio ulnar. —**crazy quilt,** centón.

creak (krik) *v.i.* rechinar; chirriar. —*n.* chirrido; rechinamiento. —**creakiness** ('kri·ki·nəs) *n.* rechinamiento. —**creaky,** *adj.* rechinante.

cream (krim) *n.* **1,** (of milk) crema; nata. **2,** *fig.* (the best part) la flor y nata; lo mejor. —*v.t.* desnatar; hacer nata. —**creamy,** *adj.* de o con

crema o nata. —**cream of tartar,**
crémor; crémor tártaro.
creamer ('kri·mər) n. cremera.
creamery ('kri·mə·ri) n. lechería;
granja.
crease (kris) n. 1, (pressed fold)
pliegue; doblez. 2, (trouser fold)
raya. 3, (wrinkle) arruga. —v.t. 1,
(make a crease in) sacar la raya a.
2, (wrinkle) plegar; arrugar. —v.i.
arrugarse; plegarse.
create (kri'eit) v.t. 1, (bring into being) crear; engendrar; hacer;
producir. 2, (give a new rank)
constituir; elegir. 3, (originate)
causar; ocasionar.
creation (kri'ei·ʃən) n. creación.
creative (kri'ei·tɪv) adj. creador;
inventor. —**creativeness**, n. genio;
capacidad de crear.
creator (kri'ei·tər) n. creador.
creature ('kri·tʃər) n. criatura.
creche (krɛʃ) n. belén; nacimiento;
pesebre.
credence ('kri·dəns) n. creencia;
crédito; fe.
credentials (krɪ'dɛn·ʃəlz) n.pl.
credenciales.
credible ('krɛd·ə·bəl) adj. creíble;
verosímil. —**credibility**, n. credibilidad; verosimilitud.
credit ('krɛd·ɪt) n. 1, (belief)
crédito; fe. 2, (credibility)
credibilidad. 3, (acknowledgment)
mérito; reconocimiento. 4, comm.
crédito. 5, bookkeeping haber. —v.t.
1, (believe) creer; tener fe. 2, (acknowledge) reconocer; atribuir;
acreditar. 3, comm. acreditar;
abonar. —**creditable**, adj creíble;
fidedigno; loable. —**creditor**, n.
acreedor. —**credit (someone) with,**
hacer justicia a; atribuir el mérito a.
—**do credit to,** acreditar. —**give
credit for,** conceder el mérito de o
por. —**letter of credit,** carta de
crédito. —**on credit,** comm. a
crédito; fiado. —**to the credit of,**
para mérito de.
credo ('kre·do) n. [pl. -dos] credo;
creencia.
credulity (krɛ'dju·lə·ti) n. credulidad. —**credulous** ('krɛd·jə·ləs) adj.
crédulo.
creed (krird) n. 1, (belief) credo;
doctrina. 2, (sect) creencia; secta.
creek (krik) n. riachuelo; arroyo.
creel (kriːl) n. cesta para pescados;
chistera.
creep (krip) v.i. [pret. & p.p. **crept**]
1, (crawl) gatear; arrastrarse;

deslizarse. 2, (move slowly)
moverse a paso de tortuga. 3, fig.
(debase oneself) humillarse. 4,
(grow along a surface) trepar;
correrse; expandirse. —n. 1, (crawl)
arrastramiento. 2, (slow pace) paso
de tortuga. 3, slang (repulsive person) pendejo. —**creep up (on),**
acercarse furtivamente (a).
creeper ('kri·pər) n. 1, (vine)
enredadera; planta trepadora. 2, (infant's garment) traje de niño hecho
todo de una pieza.
creeps (krips) n.pl., colloq. pavor;
crispamiento.
creepy ('kri·pi) adj. pavoroso;
horroroso. —**creepiness**, n. pavor;
horror.
cremate ('kri·meit) v.t. incinerar.
—**cremation**, n. incineración.
—**crematory** (-mə,tor·i) [también,
crematorium (-mə'tor·i·əm)] n.
crematorio.
crenelated ('krɛn·ə,le·tɪd) adj.
almenado.
creole ('kri·ol) adj. & n. criollo.
creosote ('kri·ə·sot) n. creosota.
crêpe (krəp) también, **crape** (kreip)
n. crepé; crespón. —**crêpe de chine**
(-də'ʃiːn) crepé; crespón; burato.
—**crêpes Suzette** (,kreip·su'zɛt)
panqueques Suzette.
crept (krɛpt) v., pret. & p.p. de
creep.
crepuscular (krə'pʌs·kjə·lər) adj.
crepuscular.
crescendo (krə'ʃɛn·do) n., adj. &
adv., mus. crescendo.
crescent ('krɛs·ənt) adj. creciente.
—n. media luna; luneta.
cress (krɛs) n. mastuerzo.
crest (krɛst) n. 1, (of fowl) cresta;
copete. 2, her. cimera; timbre. 3,
(the top) cima; cumbre. —v.t.
coronar. —v.i. formar cresta.
crestfallen ('krɛst,fɔl·ən) adj.
abatido; amilanado; caído.
cretin ('kri·tɪn) n. cretino.
—**cretinism**, n. cretinismo.
cretonne (krɪ'taɪn) n. cretona.
crevasse (krə'væs) n. brecha;
hendidura.
crevice ('krɛv·ɪs) n. raja; hendedura; grieta.
crew (kruː) n. personal; naut. tripulación; dotación; aero. tripulación.
—v., pret. alt. de **crow.**
crib (krɪb) n. 1, (infant's bed) cuna.
2, (bin) arca; pesebre; granero.
—v.t. [**cribbed, cribbing**] 1, (confine) confinar; enjaular; encerrar. 2,

colloq. (plagiarize) plagiar; (for an examination) hurtar. **—cribber** (-ər) *n.* plagiario.

cribbage ('krɪb·ɪdʒ) *n.* un juego inglés de naipes.

crick (krɪk) *n.* **1,** calambre; espasmo; (in the neck) tortícolis. **2,** *dial.* = **creek.**

cricket ('krɪk·ɪt) *n.* **1,** (insect) grillo. **2,** (game) cricket.

crier ('kraɪ·ər) *n.* pregonero.

crime (kraim) *n.* crimen.

criminal ('krɪm·ɪ·nəl) *n.* & *adj.* criminal. **—criminality** (-'næl·ə·ti) *n.* criminalidad.

criminology (ˌkrɪ·mɪ'na·lə·dʒi) *n.* criminología. **—criminologist** (-dʒɪst) *n.* criminalista.

crimp (krɪmp) *v.t.* rizar; plegar; ondear. **—n.** rizo; onda; ondulación.

crimson ('krɪm·zən) *n.* & *adj.* carmesí.

cringe (krɪndʒ) *v.i.* rebajarse; encogerse; adular. **—cringing** ('krɪn·dʒɪŋ) *adj.* bajo; rastrero.

crinkle ('krɪŋ·kəl) *v.t.* & *i.* **1,** (ripple) rizar; arrugar; ondular. **2,** (twist) retorcerse; serpentear. **—crinkly,** *adj.* arrugado; rizo.

crinoline ('krɪn·ə·lɪn) *n.* **1,** (fabric) crinolina; **2,** (hoop skirt) miriñaque.

cripple ('krɪp·əl) *n.* inválido; lisiado. **—v.t.** lisiar; baldar; tullir.

crisis ('kraɪ·sɪs) *n.* crisis.

crisp (krɪsp) *adj.* **1,** (brittle) crespo; quebradizo; tostado. **2,** (fresh) fresco; lozano. **3,** *fig.* (terse) terso. **4,** (pithy) enérgico; eficaz. **5,** (tightly curled) rizado. **—v.t.** rizar. **—crispness,** *n.* frescura; lozanía.

crisscross ('krɪs,krɔs) *adj.* cruzado. **—adv.** en cruz. **—n.** cruz. **—v.t.** rayar o marcar con líneas cruzadas. **—v.i.** entrecruzarse.

criterion (kraɪ'tɪr·i·ən) *n.* [*pl.* **criteria** (-ə)] criterio.

critic ('krɪt·ɪk) *n.* crítico. **—critical** (-ɪ·kəl) *adj.* crítico.

criticism ('krɪt·ɪ·sɪz·əm) *n.* crítica.

criticize ('krɪt·ɪ,saɪz) *v.t.* & *i.* criticar; censurar.

critique (krɪ'tik) *n.* crítica.

croak (krok) *n.* **1,** (of a frog) canto de rana. **2,** (of a raven) graznido. **—v.i. 1,** (utter a hoarse cry) croar; graznar. **2,** *slang* (die) morirse.

Croat ('kro·æt) *n.* croata. **—Croatian** (kro'ei·ʃən) *n.* & *adj.* croata.

crochet (kro'ʃei) *n.* gancho; ganchillo; punto o labor de croché.

—v.t. & i. hacer ganchillo; hacer punto o labor de croché.

crock (krak) *n.* olla o cazuela de barro; cacharro.

crockery ('krak·ə·ri) *n.* loza; vasijas de barro; loza vidriada.

crocodile ('krak·ə,dail) *n.* cocodrilo. **—crocodile tears,** lágrimas de cocodrilo.

crocus ('kro·kəs) *n.* azafrán.

crone (kron) *n.* vieja marchita.

crony ('kro·ni) *n.* compadre; compinche.

crook (kruk) *n.* **1,** (a bend) curva; curvatura; doble. **2,** (hook) gancho; garfio. **3,** (bent staff) cayado; báculo. **4,** *slang* (a cheat) pícaro; fullero; tramposo. **—v.t.** curvar; doblar. **—v.i.** curvarse; doblarse.

crooked ('kruk·ɪd) *adj.* **1,** (bent) doblado; torcido; sinuoso. **2,** *slang* (dishonest) tramposo; fullero; deshonesto. **—crookedness** ('kruk·ɪd·nəs) *n.* **1,** curvatura; corvadura. **2,** *slang* (dishonesty) picardía; perversión; deshonestidad.

croon (kruːn) *v.t.* & *i.* canturrear.

crop (krap) *n.* **1,** (harvest) cosecha; producción. **2,** (plants growing) siembra. **3,** (riding whip) fusta. **4,** (bird's gullet) buche. **5,** (haircut) cabello corto. **—v.t. [cropped, cropping] 1,** (trim; pare) cortar; recortar. **2,** (bite off) mordisquear; roer (la hierba); pacer. **3,** (cut short) trasquilar. **4,** (reap) segar; cosechar. **—crop up,** surgir; aparecer; aflorar.

cropper ('krap·ər) *n., usu. in* come a cropper, fracasar; caerse.

croquet (kro'kei) *n.* argolla.

croquette (kro'kɛt) *n.* croqueta.

crosier ('kro·ʒər) *n.* = **crozier.**

cross (krɔs) *n.* **1,** (symbol) cruz. **2,** *fig.* (burden) carga; peso; revés; desgracia. **3,** (crossing of breeds) cruce. **—adj. 1,** (intersecting) cruzado; atravesado; transversal. **2,** (contrary) contrario; opuesto. **3,** (peevish) malhumorado; serio. **4,** (hybrid) cruzado; híbrido. **—v.t. & i. 1,** (intersect) cruzar. **2,** (go across) cruzar; atravesar. **3,** (meet and pass) encontrar. **4,** (crossbreed) cruzar. **—v.t.** (thwart) oponer; contradecir; frustrar. **—crossly,** *adv.* con enfado. **—crossness,** *n.* enfado; enojo. **—cross fire,** fuego cruzado. **—cross off** o **out,** borrar; tachar; cruzar. **—cross oneself,** cruzarse; santiguarse. **—cross reference,**

comprobación; contrarreferencia.
—**cross section,** corte o sección
transversal.

crossbar ('krɔs·bar) *n.* travesaño;
tranca.

crossbeam ('krɔs,bim) *n.* travesaño; balancín.

crossbones ('krɔs,bonz) *n.* huesos
cruzados; bandera pirata.

crossbow ('krɔs,boʊ) *n.* ballesta.

crossbreed ('krɔs,brid) *v.t.* [*pret.*
& *p.p.* **-bred** (-bred)] cruzar. —*v.i.*
cruzarse. —*n.* híbrido; mestizo.

cross-country *adj.* & *adv.* a
campo traviesa.

cross-examine *v.t.* interrogar.
—**cross-examination,** *n.* interrogatorio.

crosseyed ('krɔs,aid) *adj.* bizco;
bisojo.

crossing ('krɔs·ɪŋ) *n.* **1,** (intersection) cruce; intersección. **2,** (place
to cross) travesía; paso; cruce. **3,**
(ford) vado. **4,** (act of opposing)
oposición; resistencia.

cross-purpose *n.* propósito contrario. —**at cross-purposes,** por caminos opuestos; en pugna
involuntaria.

cross-question *v.t.* interrogar.

crossroads ('krɔs·rodz) *n.* encrucijada; cuatro caminos.

crosswise ('krɔs·waiz) *adv.* en
cruz; a, al, o de través. *También,*
crossways (-weiz):

crossword puzzle ('krɔs·wərd)
n. crucigrama.

crotch (kratʃ) *n.* **1,** (juncture, as of
branches) bifurcación; cruz. **2,** *anat.*
ingle. **3,** (of trousers) entrepierna.

crotchety ('kratʃ·ɪt·i) *adj.* excéntrico; chiflado; extravagante.

crouch (krautʃ) *v.i.* agacharse;
ponerse en cuclillas. —*n.*
inclinación de cuerpo; posición
agachada.

croup (krup) *n.* **1,** (ailment) tos
ferina. **2,** (rump) anca; grupa.
—**croupy,** *adj.* con o de tos ferina.

croupier ('kru·pi·ər) *n.* crupié.

crouton ('kru·tan) *n.* cuscurro.

crow (kroʊ) *v.i.* **1,** [*pret.* **crowed** o
crew] (cry, as a rooster) cantar el
gallo; cacarear. **2,** (brag) gallear;
alardear; presumir. —*n.* **1,** (rooster's cry) canto del gallo; cacareo. **2,**
(bird) cuervo; corneja.

crowbar ('kro·bar) *n.* palanca de
hierro.

crowd (kraud) *n.* **1,** (throng)
muchedumbre; gentío; multitud. **2,**

(the populace) populacho; plebe. **3,**
colloq. (coterie) círculo; pandilla;
grupo. —*v.t.* **1,** (cram) apretar;
estrechar. **2,** (fill to excess)
amontonar; agolpar; apiñar. —*v.i.*
pulular; amontonarse; agolparse.
—**be crowded,** estar de bote en
bote.

crown (kraun) *n.* **1,** (of a monarch)
corona. **2,** (wreath for the head) diadema. **3,** (summit) corona; cima;
cumbre. **4,** (of a tooth) colmo o corona del diente. **5,** (English coin)
corona. —*v.t.* **1,** (put a crown on)
coronar. **2,** (confer honor upon)
premiar; recompensar; honrar. **3,**
(finish) coronar; culminar;
completar. **4,** *colloq.* (hit on the
head) golpear en la cabeza.
—**crown jewels,** joyas de la corona.
—**crown prince,** príncipe heredero.
—**crown princess,** princesa heredera.

crozier ('kro·ʒər) *n., eccles.*
cayado.

crucial ('kru·ʃəl) *adj.* crucial;
decisivo; crítico.

crucible ('kru·sə·bəl) *n.* crisol.

crucifer ('kru·sɪ·fər) *n.* crucero.

crucifix ('kru·sɪ·fɪks) *n.* crucifijo.
—**crucifixion** (-'fɪk·ʃən) *n.*
crucifixión.

crucify ('kru·sɪ,fai) *v.t.* **1,** (nail to a
cross) crucificar; clavar en la cruz.
2, *fig.* (mortify) mortificar.

crude (kruːd) *adj.* **1,** (raw) crudo;
bruto. **2,** (unrefined) tosco; sin
refinar. —**crudeness; crudity,** *n.*
crudeza; aspereza; tosquedad.

cruel ('kru·əl) *adj.* cruel; implacable. —**cruelty,** *n.* crueldad.

cruet ('kru·ɪt) *n.* vinagrera.

cruise (kruːz) *v.i.* vagar; navegar.
—*n.* crucero; viaje marítimo de
placer.

cruiser ('kru·zər) *n.* crucero.

cruller ('krʌl·ər) *n.* buñuelo;
churro.

crumb (krʌm) *n.* **1,** (particle)
migaja; miga. **2,** *slang* (insignificant
person) don nadie; don pizca.
—**crumby,** *adj.* de migajas.

crumble ('krʌm·bəl) *v.t.*
desmigajar; desmenuzar; hacer
migas. —*v.i.* desmigajarse; desmenuzarse; desmoronarse. —**crumbly**
(-bli) *adj.* susceptible de desmigajarse.

crummy ('krʌm·i) *adj., slang*
asqueroso; despreciable.

crumpet ('krʌm·pɪt) *n.* mollete.

crumple ('krʌm·pəl) *v.t.* arrugar; ajar; encoger. —*v.i.* arrugarse; encogerse.

crunch (krʌntʃ) *v.t. & i.* mascar; tascar; cascar.

crusade (kru'seid) *n.* cruzada. —*v.i.* participar en una cruzada. —**crusader**, *n.* cruzado.

crush (krʌʃ) *v.t.* 1, (mash) majar. 2, (grind) moler; triturar. 3, (conquer) arrollar; aplastar; vencer. —*v.i.* aplastarse; triturarse. —*n.* 1, (pressure) trituración; aplastamiento. 2, (crowd) agolpamiento; apiñamiento. 3, *slang* (infatuation) apasionamiento.

crust (krʌst) *n.* 1, (outer coating, as of bread or pie) costra; corteza. 2, *slang* (insolence) nervio; descaro; insolencia.

crustacean (krʌs'tei·ʃən) *n. & adj.* crustáceo.

crusty ('krʌs·ti) *adj.* 1, (having a crust) costroso; cortezoso. 2, *fig.* (hard) duro; rudo; brusco.

crutch (krʌtʃ) *adj.* 1, (staff) muleta. 2, *fig.* (support) ayuda; soporte.

crux (krʌks) *n.* 1, (puzzling thing) enigma; misterio. 2, (essential part) esencial; meollo.

cry (krai) *v.i.* 1, (call loudly) gritar; exclamar; vocear. 2, (weep) llorar; lamentarse. 3, (call, as an animal) chillar; aullar; bramar. —*v.t.* 1, (proclaim) promulgar; proclamar. 2, (hawk wares) pregonar; vocear. —*n.* 1, (outcry) grito; exclamación; alarido. 2, (fit of weeping) lamento; lloro; clamor. —**a far cry**, mucho; lejos.

crybaby ('krai,bei·bi) *n., colloq.* llorón.

crypt (krɪpt) *n.* 1, (cave) cripta; gruta. 2, (secret code) clave; cifra.

cryptic ('krɪp·tɪk) *adj.* secreto; misterioso; oculto.

cryptograph ('krɪp·tə·græf) *n.* 1, (device) criptógrafo. 2, [*también,* **cryptogram** (-græm)] (message) criptograma.

cryptographer (krɪp'tag·rə·fər) *n.* criptógrafo.

cryptographic (,krɪp·tə'græf·ɪk) *adj.* criptográfico.

cryptography (krɪp'tag·rə·fi) *n.* criptografía.

crystal ('krɪs·təl) *n.* cristal. —**crystalline** (-tə·lɪn) *adj.* cristalino.

crystallize ('krɪs·tə,laiz) *v.t. & i.* cristalizar. —**crystallization** (-lɪ'zei·ʃən) *n.* cristalización.

cub (kʌb) *n.* 1, (young animal) cachorro. 2, *fig.* (child) cachorro; criatura. 3, *colloq.* (tyro) novato; principiante. —*adj.* sin experiencia.

cubbyhole ('kʌb·i,hoɪl) *n.* 1, (small room) cubículo; aposento. 2, (compartment) casilla; compartimiento.

cube (kjuːb) *n.* cubo. —*v.t.* 1, *math.* cubicar; elevar al cubo. 2, (cut into cubes) hacer o cortar en cubos. 3, (measure) cubicar. —**cube root**, raíz cúbica.

cubic ('kju·bɪk) *adj.* cúbico.

cubicle ('kju·bə·kəl) *n.* cubículo.

cubism ('kju·bɪz·əm) *n.* cubismo. —**cubist**, *n. & adj.* cubista.

cuckold ('kʌk·əld) *n. & adj.* cornudo. —*v.t.* poner cuernos a.

cuckoo ('ku·ku) *n.* cuco. —*adj., slang* alocado; loco. —**cuckoo clock**, reloj de cuco.

cucumber ('kju·kʌm·bər) *n.* pepino; cohombro.

cud (kʌd) *n.* bolo de alimento a medio mascar. —**chew the cud**, rumiar.

cuddle ('kʌd·əl) *v.t.* abrazar; acariciar; acunar. —*v.i.* estar abrazado. —**cuddly** (-li) [*también,* **cuddlesome** (-səm)] *adj.* querendón.

cudgel ('kʌdʒ·əl) *n.* porra. —*v.t.* aporrear; dar golpes de o con porra. —**cudgel one's brains**, devanarse los sesos.

cue (kjuː) *n.* 1, (hint) sugerencia; idea. 2, *theat.* apunte. 3, *billiards* taco. 4, (pigtail) rabo; cola. 5, = **queue.** —*v.t., theat.* apuntar.

cuff (kʌf) *n.* 1, (end, as of a sleeve) puño; bocamanga. 2, (slap) bofetón; bofetada; puñetazo. —*v.t.* abofetear. —**on the cuff**, *slang* a plazos; a crédito.

cuff links gemelos.

cuirass (kwɪ'ræs) *n.* coraza.

cuisine (kwɪ'ziːn) *n.* cocina.

cul-de-sac ('kʌl·də,sæk) *n.* callejón sin salida.

culinary ('kju·lə·ner·i) *adj.* culinario.

cull (kʌl) *n.* desperdicio. —*v.t.* escoger; elegir lo mejor.

culminate ('kʌl·mɪ·neit) *v.i.* culminar. —**culmination**, *n.* culminación.

culottes (kju'lats) *n.pl.* falda pantalón.

culpable ('kʌl·pə·bəl) *adj.* culpable. —**culpability**, *n.* culpabilidad.

culprit ('kʌl·prɪt) *n.* ofensor; reo; delincuente.

cult (kʌlt) *n.* culto.

cultivate ('kʌl·tə·veit) *v.t.* 1, (till) cultivar; labrar. 2, (foster) cultivar; promover; favorecer; impulsar. 3, (refine) cultivar; estudiar. 4, (develop) desarrollar; perfeccionar. —**cultivation**, *n.* cultivo; educación.

cultivated ('kʌl·tə,ve·tɪd) *adj.* 1, (tilled) cultivado. 2, (trained; refined) educado; instruido.

cultivator ('kʌl·tə,ve·tər) *n.* 1, (grower) cultivador. 2, (machine) cultivadora.

culture ('kʌl·tʃər) *n.* 1, (civilization) cultura. 2, (growth of bacteria) cultivo. 3, (tillage) cultivo; labranza; labor. 4, (refinement) cultura; conocimiento; educación. —**cultural**, *adj.* cultural.

cultured ('kʌl·tʃərd) *adj.* 1, (tilled) cultivado. 2, (refined) culto; instruido.

culvert ('kʌl·vərt) *n.* alcantarilla.

cumbersome ('kʌm·bər·səm) *adj.* pesado; incómodo; fastidioso; molesto. *También,* **cumbrous** (-brəs).

cumin ('kʌ·mən) *n., bot.* comino.

cumulative ('kju·mjə·le,tiv) *adj.* acumulativo.

cumulus ('kju·mje·ləs) *n.* [*pl.* **cumuli** (-lai)] cúmulo.

cuneiform (kju'ni·ə·form) *n. & adj.* cuneiforme.

cunning ('kʌn·ɪŋ) *adj.* ingenioso; astuto; socarrón. —*n.* astucia; ardid; marrullería.

cup (kʌp) *n.* 1, (vessel) copa; taza; jícara. 2, (chalice) cáliz. —**cupful**, *n.* una taza. —**cupped** (kʌpt) *adj.* en forma de copa. —**in one's cups**, ebrio.

cupboard ('kʌb·ərd) *n.* aparador; chinero.

cupid ('kju·pɪd) *n.* cupido; Cupido.

cupidity (kju'pɪd·ə·ti) *n.* codicia; avaricia.

cupola ('kju·pə·lə) *n.* cúpula.

cur (kʌr) *n.* 1, (dog) perro de mala casta. 2, *colloq.* (evil man) perro; canalla.

curable ('kjur·ə·bəl) *adj.* curable.

curate ('kjur·ɪt) *n.* cura. —**curacy** (-ə·si) *n.* curato.

curative ('kjur·ə·tiv) *adj.* curativo. —*n.* curativa.

curator (kju'rei·tər) *n.* curador; conservador.

curb (kʌrb) *v.t.* refrenar; poner freno; contener; sujetar. —*n.* 1, (restraint) sujeción; freno; restricción. 2, (bridle) freno; barbada. 3, [*también,* **curbstone**] bordillo o borde de acera. 4, (minor securities market) lonja; bolsín.

curd (kʌrd) *n.* cuajada; requesón.

curdle ('kʌr·dəl) *v.t.* cuajar; coagular. —*v.i.* cuajarse; coagularse. —**curdle one's blood**, helarse la sangre.

cure (kjur) *n.* 1, (healing) curación. 2, (treatment) cura. 3, (remedy) remedio. —*v.t.* 1, (heal) curar; sanar. 2, (remedy) remediar. 3, (dry or salt, as meat) curar.

curé (kju'rei) *n.* cura; párroco.

cure-all *n.* cúralotodo.

curfew ('kʌr·fju) *n.* toque de queda.

curie (kju'ri) *n., physics* curie.

curio ('kju·ri·o) *n.* [*pl.* -**os**] objeto curioso; curiosidad.

curiosity (,kjur·i'as·ə·ti) *n.* curiosidad; rareza.

curious ('kjur·i·əs) *adj.* 1, (inquisitive) curioso; deseoso. 2, (strange) raro; curioso; extraño.

curium ('kjur·i·əm) *n.* curio.

curl (kʌrl) *n.* 1, (of hair) rizo; bucle; *Amer.* crespo. 2, (spiral) rollo; espiral; ondulación; sinuosidad. —*v.t. & i.* rizar; enrollar; ondular. —**curler**, *n.* rizador. —**curly**, *adj.* rizado; enrollado; rizo.

curlew (kʌr'lu:) *n.* chorlito.

curlicue ('kʌr·lɪ,kju) *n.* rasgo; plumada.

curmudgeon (kər'mʌdʒ·ən) *n.* erizo; cicatero; camorrista.

currant ('kʌr·ənt) *n.* 1, (bush) grosellero. 2, (berry) grosella. 3, (raisin) pasa de Corinto.

currency ('kʌr·ən·si) *n.* 1, (currentness) circulación; uso corriente. 2, (money) moneda en circulación.

current ('kʌr·ənt) *adj.* 1, (prevalent) corriente; común; ordinario. 2, (contemporary) actual; presente. —*n.* 1, (stream) corriente. 2, (trend) corriente; curso; marcha.

curriculum (kə'rɪk·jə·ləm) *n.* 1, (study plan) plan de estudios. 2, (routine) plan; programa. —**curriculum vitae** ('vai·ti) historial. —**curricular** (-lər) *adj.* de un plan de estudios.

curry ('kʌr·i) *v.t.* **1,** (comb) almohazar. **2,** (dress leather) curtir; adobar. —*n.* cari. —**curry favor,** pedir favores adulando.

currycomb ('kʌr·i,kom) *n.* almohaza. —*v.t.* almohazar.

curse (kʌrs) *n.* **1,** (invocation of evil) maldición; anatema. **2,** (profane oath) imprecación; blasfemia. **3,** (bane) aflicción; azote; castigo; ruina. —*v.t.* **1,** (invoke evil on) maldecir; anatematizar. **2,** (swear at) renegar de. **3,** (blaspheme) blasfemar. **4,** (harm) dañar; ofender. —*v.i.* jurar en vano; blasfemar. —**cursed** ('kʌr·sɪd) *adj.* maldecido; maldito; abominable. —**cursedness,** *n.* maldición.

cursive ('kʌr·sɪv) *adj.* cursivo.

cursor ('kʌr·sər) *n.* cursor.

cursory ('kʌr·sə·ri) *adj.* precipitado; rápido; superficial.

curt (kʌrt) *adj.* **1,** (short) corto; sucinto; breve. **2,** (abrupt) rudo; abrupto; tosco.

curtail (kər'teil) *v.t.* **1,** (cut short) cortar; abreviar; reducir. **2,** (deprive of) privar de; restringir; circunscribir. —**curtailment,** *n.* abreviación; reducción.

curtain ('kʌr·tən) *n.* **1,** (drape) cortina. **2,** *theat.* telón. —*v.t.* **1,** (drape) poner cortinas a. **2,** (conceal) ocultar; encubrir. —**curtain call,** salida o llamada a las candilejas. —**curtain off,** separar con cortinas. —**curtain raiser,** entremés.

curtness ('kʌrt·nəs) *n.* **1,** (shortness) brevedad; concisión. **2,** (abruptness) tosquedad; rudeza.

curtsy también, **curtsey** ('kʌrt·si) *n.* reverencia; cortesía.

curvature ('kʌr·və·tʃur) *n.* curvatura.

curve (kʌrv) *n.* curva. —*v.t.* & *i.* curvar; torcer.

cushion ('kuʃ·ən) *n.* **1,** (pillow) cojín; almohadón; almohadilla. **2,** (rim of billiard table) banda. —*v.t.* **1,** (pillow) poner cojines a; cubrir con cojines. **2,** (absorb the shock of) amortiguar; suavizar.

cusp (kʌsp) *n.* cúspide.

cuspid ('kʌs·pɪd) *n.* cúspide.

cuspidor ('kʌs·pɪ·dor) *n.* escupidera.

cuss (kʌs) *v.t.* & *i.* = **curse.** —*n.* **1,** = **curse. 2,** (mean person) cascarra-

bias. —**cussed** ('kʌs·ɪd) *adj., colloq.* maldito; abominable.

custard ('kʌs·tərd) *n.* flan.

custard apple anón; anona.

custodian (kəs'to·di·ən) *n.* custodio; guardián; encargado.

custody ('kʌs·tə·di) *n.* **1,** (guardianship) custodia; cuidado; guardia. **2,** *law* (arrest) seguridad; prisión; arresto. —**custodial** (-'to·di·əl) *adj.* bajo custodia.

custom ('kʌs·təm) *n.* **1,** (habit) costumbre; usanza; uso. **2,** (patronage) clientela; parroquia. **3,** *pl.* (import taxes) derechos de aduana. —**customhouse,** *n.* aduana. —**custom-made,** *adj.* hecho a la medida.

customary ('kʌs·tə,mɛr·i) *adj.* acostumbrado; usual; sólito.

customer ('kʌs·tə·mər) *n.* cliente; parroquiano.

cut (kʌt) *v.t.* [**cut, cutting**] **1,** (sever) cortar; partir. **2,** (trim) recortar; desbastar. **3,** (reap) segar. **4,** (intersect) cortar; cruzar. **5,** (divide into parts) cortar; dividir. **6,** (insult) lastimar; herir; insultar. **7,** *slang* (hit) golpear. **8,** (abridge) reducir; abreviar. **9,** (ignore) extrañar; ignorar; negar el saludo a. **10,** *colloq.* (fail to attend) faltar a; dejar de ir. —*v.i.* **1,** (slit) hacer corte o incisión; cortar. **2,** (admit of being cut) cortarse; poderse cortar. **3,** (go by a shorter route) atajar. —*n.* **1,** (incision) corte; cortadura; *Amer.* cortada. **2,** *print.* grabado. —*adj.* **1,** (made by cutting) cortado. **2,** (carved) tallado. **3,** (lessened) rebajado; reducido. —**cut and dried,** preparado. —**cut back, 1,** (turn back) cambiar; volver. **2,** (shorten) acortar. —**cut down, 1,** (kill) matar. **2,** (fell) talar; derribar. **3,** (abridge) condensar; resumir. —**cut in, 1,** (move in sharply) cortar; introducirse rápidamente. **2,** (interrupt) intercalar; introducir. —**cut off, 1,** (intercept) cortar; interrumpir; interceptar. **2,** (shut out) excluir; abandonar; olvidar. **3,** (halt suddenly) parar repentinamente; suspender. **4,** (disinherit) desheredar. —**cut out, 1,** ' (apt; suited) adecuado; apto. **2,** (cease) dejar; dejarse de. —**cut up,** *slang* hacer el tonto; bromear.

cutaneous (kju'tei·ni·əs) *adj.* cutáneo.

cutaway ('kʌt·ə·we) *n.* chaqué. También, **cutaway coat.**

cute (kjut) *adj., colloq.* mono; lindo; atractivo. —**cuteness,** *n.* monería; lindeza; atractivo.

cuticle ('kju·tə·kəl) *n.* cutícula.

cutlass ('kʌt·ləs) *n.* alfanje.

cutler ('kʌt·lər) *n.* cuchillero.

cutlery ('kʌt·lə·ri) *n.* cuchillería.

cutlet ('kʌt·lət) *n.* **1,** (slice of meat) chuleta. **2,** (croquette) croqueta.

cut-rate *adj.* de descuento; de rebaja.

cutter ('kʌt·ər) *n.* **1,** (person or thing that cuts) cortador. **2,** *naval* cúter. **3,** (sleigh) trineíllo.

cutthroat ('kʌt·θrot) *n.* asesino; criminal. —*adj.* implacable; criminal; asesino.

cutting ('kʌt·ɪŋ) *n.* recorte. —*adj.* cortante; mordaz.

cuttlefish ('kʌt·əl·fɪʃ) *n.* jibia; calamar.

cutwater ('kʌt·wɔtər) *n.* tajamar.

cyanide ('sai·ə‚naid) *n.* cianuro.

cyanogen (sai'æn·ə·dʒən) *n.* cianógeno.

cyanosis (‚sai·ə'no·sɪs) *n.* cianosis.

cybernetics (‚sai·bər'nɛt·ɪks) *n., sing.* cibernética. —**cybernetic,** *adj.* cibernético.

cyclamen ('sɪk·lə·mən) *n., bot.* ciclamino; pamporcino.

cycle ('sai·kəl) *n.* **1,** (era) ciclo; período. **2,** (series) curso. —*v.i.* montar en bicicleta. —**cycling** (-klɪŋ) *n.* ciclismo.

cyclic ('sai·klɪk; 'sɪ-) *adj.* cíclico. *También,* **cyclical.**

cyclist ('sai·klɪst) *n.* ciclista.

cycloid ('sai·klɔid) *n.* cicloide. —**cycloidal** (-'klɔi·dəl) *adj.* cicloidal; cicloideo.

cyclone ('sai·klon) *n.* ciclón; huracán. —**cyclonic** (-'klan·ɪk) *adj.* ciclónico; ciclonal.

cyclopedia (‚sai·klə'pi·di·ə) *n.* enciclopedia. —**cyclopedic,** *adj.* encyclopédico.

Cyclops ('sai·klaps) *n.* Cíclope.

—**Cyclopean** (-klə'pi·ən) *adj.* ciclópeo.

cyclorama (‚sai·klə'ræm·ə) *n.* ciclorama.

cyclotron ('sai·klə‚tran) *n.* ciclotrón.

cygnet ('sɪg·nət) *n.* pichón de cisne.

cylinder ('sɪl·ɪn·dər) *n.* cilindro. —**cylindrical** (sə'lɪn·drɪ·kəl) *adj.* cilíndrico.

cymbal ('sɪm·bəl) *n.* címbalo. —**cymbalist,** *adj.* cimbalista; cimbalero.

cynic ('sɪn·ɪk) *n.* cínico. —**cynicism** (-ɪ‚sɪz·əm) *n.* cinismo. —**cynical** (-ɪ·kəl) *adj.* cínico.

cynosure ('sai·nə‚ʃur) *n.* **1,** (center of attention) cinosura; centro de atracción. **2,** *cap., astron.* Osa Menor.

cypher ('sai·fər) *n. & v.t. & i.* = **cipher.**

cypress ('sai·prəs) *n.* ciprés.

Cyrillic (sɪ'rɪl·ɪk) *adj. & n.* cirílico.

cyst (sɪst) *n.* quiste. —**cystic,** *adj.* cístico; del quiste.

cystitis (sɪs'tai·tɪs) *n.* cistitis.

cystology (sɪs'tal·ə·dʒi) *n.* cistología.

cystoscope ('sɪs·tə‚skop) *n.* cistoscopio.

cytology (sai'tal·ə·dʒi) *n.* citología. —**cytological** (-tə'ladʒ·ɪ·kəl) *adj.* citológico. —**cytologist,** *n.* citólogo.

cytoplasm ('sai·tə‚plæz·əm) *n.* citoplasma.

czar *también,* **tsar** (zaɪr; tsaɪr) *n.* **1,** (emperor) zar. **2,** *fig.* (dictator) déspota; autócrata. —**czarevitch** (-ə·vɪtʃ) *n.* zarevitz. —**czarevna** (zar'ɛv·nə) *n.* zarevna. —**czarina** (zar'i·nə) *n.* zarina.

Czech (tʃɛk) *n. & adj.* checo.

Czechoslovak (‚tʃɛk·o'slo·vak) *n. & adj.* [*también,* **Czechoslovakian** (‚tʃɛk·ə·slo'vak·i·ən)] checoslovaco; checoeslovaco.

D

D, d (diɪ) cuarta letra del alfabeto inglés. —*n., mus.* re.

dab (dæb) *v.t. & i.* [**dabbed, dabbing**] **1,** (pat) frotar suavemente; golpear levemente. **2,** (moisten) humedecer. —*n.* **1,** (pat) golpe

suave; sopapo. **2,** (bit) trocito; salpicadura.

dabble ('dæb·əl) *v.i.* **1,** (splash in water) salpicar; rociar. **2,** (do in a superficial way) chapucear. —**dabbler** (-lər) *n.* chapucero.

dachshund ('daks·hʊnd) *n.* perro pachón.

dactyl ('dæk·təl) *n.* dáctilo. —**dactylic** (-'tɪl·ɪk) *adj.* dactílico.

dad (dæːd) *n., colloq.* papá; padre. *También,* **daddy** ('dæd·i).

daddy longlegs ('lɔŋ·lɛgz) *n.sing. & pl.* segador.

dado ('dei·do) *n.* friso; zócalo.

daffodil ('dæf·ə·dɪl) *n.* narciso.

daffy ('dæf·i) *adj., slang* loco; tonto; bobo. —**daffiness,** *n., slang* bobería; tontería.

daft (dæft) *adj.* loco; tonto.

dagger ('dæg·ər) *n.* **1,** (knife) daga; estilete; puñal. **2,** *print.* (†) cruz.

daguerreotype (də'gɛr·ə,taip) *n.* daguerrotipo.

dahlia ('dæl·ja; 'dal-) *n.* dalia.

daily ('dei·li) *adj.* diario; cotidiano. —*adv.* diariamente; todos los días. —*n.* diario; periódico.

dainty ('dein·ti) *adj.* **1,** (delicate) delicado; fino; precioso. **2,** (of refined taste) gustoso; sabroso; exquisito. **3,** (fastidious) melindroso; afectado. —*n.* confitura; golosina. —**daintiness,** *n.* exquisitez.

dairy ('dɛr·i) *n.* **1,** (milk farm) granja; vaquería. **2,** (enterprise) compañía de productos lácteos.

dairymaid ('dɛr·i,meid) *n.* lechera.

dairyman ('dɛr·i·mən) *n.* [*pl.* -men] lechero.

dais ('dei·ɪs) *n.* tribuna; estrado.

daisy ('dei·zi) *n.* margarita.

dale (deil) *n.* valle.

dally ('dæl·i) *v.i.* **1,** (trifle) juguetear; entretener. **2,** (idle) tardar; dilatar. **dalliance** (-i·əns) *n.* **1,** (play) entretenimiento **2,** (delay) dilatación; demora.

Dalmatian (dæl'mei·ʃən) *adj. & n.* dálmata. —*n.* (dog) perro dálmata.

Daltonism ('dɔl·tə,nɪz·əm) *n.* daltonismo.

dam (dæːm) *n.* **1,** (wall to stop water) persa; pantano. **2,** (mare) yegua. —*v.t.* [**dammed, damming**] **1,** (build a dam) estancar; represar. **2,** confine) detener; contener. **3,** (shut up) cerrar.

damage ('dæm·ɪdʒ) *n.* **1,** (injury) daño; estropeo. **2,** *pl., law* indemnización; daños y perjuicios. —*v.t.* perjudicar; ofender.

damask ('dæm·əsk) *n.* damasco. —*adj.* adamascado.

dame (deim) *n.* **1,** (lady) dama; señora. **2,** *slang* (woman) mujer; moza. **3,** *cap., Brit.* (female peer) baronesa.

damn (dæːm) *v.t.* **1,** (condemn) condenar. **2,** (curse) maldecir. **3,** (censure) vituperar. —*n.* juramento; maldición. —*interj.* ¡maldito sea! —**damnable** ('dæm·nə·bəl) *adj.* condenable; detestable. —**damned** (dæːmd) *adj.* maldito; condenado.

damnation (dæm'nei·ʃən) *n.* condenación.

damp (dæmp) *adj.* húmedo; mojado. —*n.* **1,** (moisture) humedad. **2,** (poisonous vapor) emanación. —*v.t.* **1,** (moisten) humedecer; remojar. **2,** (dispirit) desanimar; enfriar. **3,** (smother) extinguir; apagar. —**dampness,** *n.* humedad.

dampen ('dæm·pən) *v.t.* **1,** (wet) humedecer; remojar. **2,** (dishearten) desanimar; desalentar.

damper ('dæm·pər) *n.* **1,** (of a flue) regulador de tiro. **2,** (of a piano) sordina. **3,** *fig.* (disheartening person or thing) desalentador; aguafiestas.

damsel ('dæm·zəl) *n.* damisela; señorita.

damson ('dæm·zən) *n.* damasco. *También,* **damson plum.**

dance (dæns) *v.i.* **1,** (move rhythmically) danzar; bailar. **2,** (quiver) saltar; brincar. **3,** (bounce) botar; brincar. —*v.t.* **1,** (make dance) hacer bailar; llevar a bailar. **2,** (perform, as a dance) bailar. **3,** (bounce up and down) balancear; hacer saltar. —*n.* danza; baile. —**dancer,** *n.* bailarín; *fem.* bailarina.

dandelion ('dæn·də,lai·ən) *n.* diente de león.

dandruff ('dæn·drəf) *n.* caspa.

dandy ('dæn·di) *n.* **1,** (fop) petimetre; presumido. **2,** *colloq.* (an excellent thing) belleza; primor. —*adj., colloq.* perfecto; estupendo.

Dane (dein) *n.* danés; dinamarqués.

danger ('dein·dʒer) *n.* peligro; riesgo. —**dangerous,** *adj.* peligroso; arriesgado. —**be in danger,** correr peligro.

dangle ('dæŋ·gəl) *v.t.* colgar; suspender. —*v.i.* colgarse; bambolearse; quedar o estar colgado.

Danish ('dei·nɪʃ) *adj. & n.* danés; dinamarqués.

dank (dæŋk) *adj.* viscoso; húmedo; mojado. —**dankness,** *n.* viscosidad; humedad.

dapper ('dæp·ər) *adj.* **1,** (trim) impecable; nítido; apuesto. **2,** (small and lively) vivaracho; vivaz.

dapple ('dæp·əl) *v.t.* motear; salpicar. —**dappled,** *adj.* rodado.

dare (deɪr) *v.t.* **1,** (challenge) desafiar; retar. **2,** (face boldly) enfrentar; hacer frente a. —*v.i.* [*pret.* **dared** o **durst** (dʌrst) atreverse; arriesgarse.

daredevil ('deɪr‚dev·əl) *n.* atrevido; aventurero; temerario. —*adj.* intrépido; valeroso; aventurado. —**daredeviltry** (-tri) *n.* intrepidez; temeridad.

daring ('deɪr·ɪŋ) *n.* valentía; intrepidez. —*adj.* intrépido; temerario.

dark (dark) *adj.* **1,** (unlighted) oscuro; apagado. **2,** (deep in color, as skin) moreno; oscuro; trigueño. **3,** (dreary) desconsolador; triste. **4,** (concealed) oscuro; oculto. **5,** (sinister) difícil; siniestro; amenazador. —*n.* **1,** (absence of light) oscuridad; tenebrosidad. **2,** (nightfall) noche. **3,** (secrecy) secreto; enigma. **4,** (ignorance) oscuridad; ignorancia; desconocimiento. **5,** *paint.* (shadow) sombra. —**be in the dark,** ofuscarse. —**become** o **get dark,** anochecer.

darken ('dar·kən) *v.t.* **1,** (make dark) oscurecer. **2,** (shut off) apagar. **3,** (blacken) ennegrecer. **4,** (conceal) ocultar. **5,** (sadden) contristar; deprimir. **6,** (harm) manchar; denigrar. **7,** (confound) confundir; ofuscar. —*v.i.* **1,** (become dark) oscurecerse. **2,** (be shut off) apagarse. **3,** (become blackened) ennegrecerse. **4,** (be concealed) no verse claro; estar oculto. **5,** (become dreary) deprimirse; desfallecer. **6,** (be harmed) mancharse. **7,** (be confused) ofuscarse; confundirse.

dark horse 1, (candidate) candidato inesperado. **2,** (winner) vencedor inesperado.

darkness ('dark·nɪs) *n.* oscuridad.

darkroom ('dark‚rum) *n.* cámara oscura.

darling ('dar·lɪŋ) *n.* querido; cariño. —*adj.* querido; amado; favorito.

darn (darn) *v.t.* **1,** (mend) zurcir; repasar. **2,** *colloq.* (damn) maldecir. —*adj., colloq.* [*también,* **darned**] maldito; condenado. —*n.* **1,** (mend) zurcido; cosido. **2,** (oath) juramento y maldición leve.

darnel ('dar·nəl) *n., bot.* cizaña.

darning needle *n.* **1,** (for sewing) aguja para zurcir. **2,** *entom.* caballito del diablo.

dart (dart) *n.* **1,** (missile) dardo; flecha. **2,** *pl.* (game) dardos. **3,** (dash) salpicadura; rociadura. —*v.t.* **1,** (thrust) echar; tirar. **2,** (start) arrancar; flechar. —*v.i.* disparar como dardo.

dash (dæʃ) *v.t.* **1,** (smash) disparar. **2,** (sprinkle) rociar; salpicar. **3,** (season lightly) sazonar. **4,** (frustrate) malograr; frustrar. —*v.i.* **1,** (crash) chocar; estrellarse. **2,** (rush) lanzarse; abalanzarse. —*n.* **1,** (sudden thrust) arranque; embestida. **2,** (bit, as a flavor) condimento; *W.I.; C.A.; Mex.* sazón. **3,** *slang* (vigorous or dramatic behavior) gran papel. **4,** (punctuation) guión. **5,** *teleg.* raya. **6,** (rush) embestida; arranque. —**cut a dash,** *colloq.* hacer un gran papel. —**dash off** (a letter, etc.) escribir rápidamente; (a sketch) esbozar. —**dash one's hopes to the ground,** dejar a uno con un palmo de narices. —**dash to pieces,** estrellar; estrellarse.

dashboard ('dæʃ·bord) *n.* **1,** (splashboard) guardafangos; cristal. **2,** (in a vehicle) tablero de instrumentos.

dasher ('dæʃ·ər) *n., mech.* agitador.

dashing ('dæʃ·ɪŋ) *adj.* atrayente; vistoso.

dastard ('dæs·tərd) *n.* cobarde. —**dastardly,** *adj.* cobarde.

data ('deɪ·tə) *n.pl.* [*sing.* **datum** (-təm)] hechos; datos. —**data bank,** banco de datos. —**database,** *n.* base de datos. —**data processing,** procesamiento de datos. —**data processor,** ordenador.

datamation (deɪ·tə'meɪ·ʃən) *n., comput.* procesamiento automático de datos.

date (deɪt) *n.* **1,** (point in time) fecha; día. **2,** *law* fecha; plazo. **3,** *colloq.* (engagement) cita. **4,** (a fruit) dátil. —*v.t.* **1,** (mark with a time) fechar; poner fecha a. **2,** (note the date of) computar; contar. **3,** *colloq.* (meet with) salir con. —*v.i.* datar. —**out of date,** antiguo; pasado. —**to date,** hasta la fecha; hasta hoy. —**up to date, 1,** (current; informed) al día. **2,** (in vogue) del día.

dated ('deɪ·tɪd) *adj.* **1,** (marked with a date) fechado. **2,** *colloq.* (old-fashioned) pasado; antiguo.

dative ('dei·tɪv) *n. & adj.* dativo.

datum ('dei·təm) *n.* [*pl.* **data**] dato.

daub (dɔːb) *v.t.* **1,** (smear) embarrar; manchar. **2,** (paint coarsely) pintorrear; pintarrajar. —*n.* **1,** (smear) mancha; embarradura. **2,** (inartistic painting) mamarracho; mamarrachada. —**dauber,** *n.* pintor de brocha gorda.

daughter ('dɔ·tər) *n.* hija.

daughter-in-law *n.* [*pl.* **daughters-in-law**] nuera; hija política.

daughterly ('dɔ·tər·li) *adj.* filial; de o como hija.

daunt (dɔnt) *v.t.* **1,** (make afraid) amedrentar; intimidar. **2,** (discourage) desalentar; desanimar. —**dauntless,** *adj.* intrépido; valiente.

dauphin ('dɔ·fɪn) *n.* delfín.

davenport ('dæv·ən‚port) *n.* sofá cama; canapé.

davit ('dæv·ɪt) *n.* pescante de bote.

dawdle ('dɔ·dəl) *v.t. & i.* holgazanear; perder el tiempo; tontear.

day (dei) *n.* **1,** (division of time) día. **2,** *usu. pl.* (epoch) tiempos; días; época. **3,** *slang* (a hard time) lid; jornada. —**by day,** de día. —**day after day,** día tras día. —**day after tomorrow,** pasado mañana. —**day before,** víspera. —**day before yesterday,** anteayer. —**day by day,** día a día. —**every other day,** un día sí y otro no. —**from day to day,** de día en día. —**the next day,** el día siguiente.

day bed sofá cama.

daybreak ('dei‚breik) *n.* amanecer; aurora.

daydream ('dei‚drim) *n.* sueño. —*v.i.* soñar despierto.

daylight ('dei‚lait) *n.* luz natural; luz diurna. —**daylight saving time,** hora de verano.

day nursery guardería infantil.

day school 1, (school with daytime hours) escuela diurna. **2,** (school whose pupils live at home) externado.

daytime ('dei‚taim) *n.* día. —**in the daytime,** de día.

daze (deiz) *n.* ofuscación; ofuscamiento; aturdimiento. —*v.t.* ofuscar; aturdir.

dazzle ('dæz·əl) *v.t.* deslumbrar; ofuscar.

deacon ('di·kən) *n.* diácono. —**deaconess,** *n.* diaconisa.

deactivate (di'æk·tɪ·veit) *v.t.* desactivar. —**deactivation,** *n.* desactivación.

dead (dɛd) *adj.* **1,** (deceased) muerto; fallecido; difunto. **2,** (numb) insensible. **3,** (inert) inerte; inmóvil. **4,** (complete) completo; total; absoluto. **5,** (useless) inútil; inactivo; inservible. **6,** (unprofitable) improductivo; baldío. **7,** *slang* (tired) cansado; entregado; exhausto. —*adv.* por completo; totalmente. —*n.* **1,** (that which no longer exists) muerto; fallecido; difunto. **2,** (culminating point) profundidad. —**dead reckoning,** estima. —**dead weight,** peso muerto; *fig.* (heavy burden) carga onerosa.

deaden ('dɛd·ən) *v.t.* **1,** (muffle) amortiguar; parar. **2,** (retard) retardar; restrasar. **3,** (dull) apagar; embotar.

dead end 1, (street without an exit) camino sin salida. **2,** *colloq.* (impasse) punto muerto. —**deadend,** *adj.* sin salida.

dead letter carta no reclamada; *fig.* costumbre o ley desusada.

deadline ('dɛd·lain) *n.* límite; término; plazo.

deadlock ('dɛd·lak) *n.* punto muerto; estancamiento. —*v.t.* estancar. —*v.i.* estancarse.

deadly ('dɛd·li) *adj.* **1,** (lethal) mortal; letal. **2,** *fig.* (relentless) implacable. **3,** *colloq.* (dull) pesado; soso; aburrido. —**deadliness,** *n.* calidad de mortífero; peligro mortal. —**deadly sins,** pecados capitales.

deadpan ('dɛd‚pæn) *adj., slang* inmutable; inescrutable. —*n., slang* cara inexpresiva.

deadwood ('dɛd·wʊd) *n.* rama muerta; *fig.* persona o cosa inútil.

deaf (dɛf) *adj.* sordo. —**deafness,** *n.* sordera.

deafen ('dɛf·ən) *v.t.* **1,** (make deaf) ensordar. **2,** (seem too loud) ensordecer. —**deafening,** *adj.* ensordecedor.

deafmute ('dɛf‚mjut) *n.* sordomudo.

deal (diːl) *v.t.* [*pret. & p.p.* **dealt**] **1,** (apportion; distribute) distribuir; repartir. **2,** (administer, as a blow) asestar. **3,** (distribute, as cards) dar. —*v.i.* **1,** [*usu.,* **deal with**] (negotiate) entenderse (con); (transact business) tratar (con). **2,** [*usu.,* **deal with**] (cope) ocuparse (de o en);

tratar (con o de). **3,** (comport one-self) comportarse; portarse. **4,** [*usu.*, **deal in**] (trade; conduct a business) comerciar; negociar; traficar. **5,** (distribute cards) dar cartas. —*n.* **1,** (portion) porción; parte; trozo. **2,** (transaction) trato; negocio. **3,** *colloq.* (private pact) acuerdo. **4,** (distribution of cards) reparto de cartas. **5,** (wood) madero de pino o abeto. —**deal dishonestly with,** abusar de; engañar. —**a good deal** (a large quantity) bastante. —**a great deal** (a very large quantity) mucho.

dealer ('di·lər) *n.* **1,** *comm.* (tradesman) comerciante; negociante. **2,** (distributor) repartidor. —**dealership,** *n.* exclusiva.

dealing ('di·liŋ) *n.* **1,** (treatment of others) comportamiento; proceder; trato. **2,** *comm.* (distribution) distribución. **3,** *comm., usu.pl.* (transactions) transacciones.

dealt (dɛlt) *v.,* pret. & p.p. de **deal.**

dean (din) *n.* **1,** *eccles.* deán. **2,** (senior member of a group) decano. —**deanship,** *n.* decanato.

dear (dɪr) *adj.* **1,** (beloved) querido; caro; estimado. **2,** (valuable) valioso; estimable. **3,** (costly) caro; costoso. —*n.* querido; persona querida. —**Dear Sir,** Muy señor mío; Estimado señor. —**oh dear!**; **dear me!,** ¡válgame Dios!

dearness ('dɪr·nəs) *n.* **1,** (closeness) cariño; afecto. **2,** (kindness) benevolencia. **3,** (value) costo; valor; precio alto.

dearth (dʌrθ) *n.* carestía; escasez.

death (dɛθ) *n.* **1,** (dying) muerte; fallecimiento. **2,** (plague) estrago; plaga. —**deathless,** *adj.* inmortal. —**deathly,** *adj.* **1,** (like one dead) cadavérico. **2,** (mortal) fatal. —*adv.* (very) gravemente. —**death house,** capilla. —**death rate,** mortalidad; índice de mortalidad. —**be at death's door,** estar a la muerte. —**on pain of death,** bajo pena de muerte.

deb (dɛb) *n., colloq.* = **debutante.**

debacle (de'ba·kəl) *n.* **1,** (disaster; rout) desastre; derrota. **2,** (ice-breaking) deshielo. **3,** (rush of waters) inundación.

debar (dɪ'bar) *v.t.* [**debarred, -barring**] **1,** (shut out) expulsar; despedir. **2,** (exclude) excluir; prohibir. —**debarment,** *n.* expulsión; exclusión.

debark (di'bark) *v.t. & i.* desembarcar.

debarkation (,di·bar'kei·ʃən) *n.* **1,** (of passengers) desembarco. **2,** (of cargo) desembarque.

debase (di'beis) *v.t.* **1,** (degrade) degradar; rebajar; **2,** (adulterate) degenerar; envilecer. **3,** (lower in value) depreciar. —**debasement,** *n.* degradación; envilecimiento; depreciación.

debate (di'beit) *v.t. & i.* **1,** (argue) debatir; discutir; disputar. **2,** (consider) considerar; reflexionar; deliberar. —*n.* debate; discusión; controversia. —**debatable,** *adj.* debatible; disputable.

debauch (di'bɔtʃ) *v.t.* corromper; destruir; pervertir. —*v.i.* entregarse al vicio o al libertinaje. —*n.* libertinaje; corrupción; licencia. —**debauchee** (,di·bɔ'tʃiz) *n.* libertino. —**debaucher,** *n.* seductor. —**debauchery** (-ɚ·ri) *n.* libertinaje; licencia; corrupción.

debenture (di'bɛn·tʃər) *n.* obligación.

debilitate (dɪ'bɪl·ə·teit) *v.t.* debilitar. —**debilitation,** *n.* debilitación.

debility (dɪ'bɪl·ə·ti) *n.* debilidad.

debit ('dɛb·ɪt) *n., fin.* **1,** (a charge) debe. **2,** (entry) cargo; adeudo. —*v.t.* adeudar; cargar.

debonair (,dɛb·ə'nɛr) *adj.* **1,** (gay) alegre; vivaz. **2,** (courteous) afable; cortés; educado.

debris (də'briz) *n.* partícula; fragmento; residuo; *geol.* despojos.

debt (dɛt) *n.* deuda; obligación. —**debtor,** *n.* deudor. —**bad debt,** deuda incobrable.

debug (di'bʌg) *v.t., slang* **1,** *elect.* sacar los micrófonos ocultos de (un lugar). **2,** *mech.; elect.; comput.* eliminar los defectos mecánicos de (un aparato).

debunk (di'bʌŋk) *v.t., colloq.* exponer las falsedades de.

debut (dɪ'bju) *n.* debut; estreno; primera presentación. —**debutante** (,dɛb·ju'tant) *n.* presentada en sociedad; puesta de largo; debutante.

decade ('dɛk·eid) *n.* década.

decadence (dɪ'kei·dəns; 'dɛk·ə-) *n.* decadencia. —**decadent,** *adj.* decadente.

decaffeinate (di'kæf·ɪ·neit) *v.t.* descafeinar.

decagon ('dɛk·ə,gan) *n.* decágono.

decagram ('dɛk·ə·græm) *n.* decagramo.

decahedron (dɛk·ə'hi·drən) *n.* decaedro.

decalcomania (dɪˌkæl·kə'mein·jə) *también, colloq.,* **decal** (di'kæl) *n.* calcomanía.

decaliter ('dɛk·ə,li·tər) *n.* decalitro.

decalogue ('dɛk·ə,lɔg) *n.* decálogo.

decameter ('dɛk·ə,mi·tər) *n.* decámetro.

decamp (di'kæmp) *v.i.* **1,** (break camp) decampar. **2,** *slang* (depart) despedirse a la francesa.

decant (dɪ'kænt) *v.t.* decantar. —**decanter,** *n.* frasco; botella.

decapitate (dɪ'kæp·ɪ·teit) *v.t.* decapitar. —**decapitation,** *n.* decapitación.

decare ('dɛk·ɛr) *n.* decárea.

decastere ('dɛk·ə,stɪr) *n.* decastéreo.

decasyllable ('dɛk·ə,sɪl·ə·bəl) *n.* decasílabo. —**decasyllabic,** *adj.* decasílabo.

decathlon (dɪ'kæθ·lan) *n.* decatlon.

decay (dɪ'kei) *v.t.* podrir; corromper. —*v.i.* **1,** (decline) decaer; declinar. **2,** (rot) podrirse. **3,** *dent.* cariarse. —*n.* **1,** (decline) decaimiento. **2,** (rottenness) podredumbre. **3,** *dent.* caries.

decease (dɪ'sis) *n.* fallecimiento; muerte; óbito. —*v.i.* fallecer; morir. —**deceased** (-'sist) *n.* & *adj.* muerto; fallecido.

deceit (dɪ'sit) *n.* fraude; mentira; engaño. —**deceitful,** *adj.* mentiroso; fraudulento; engañoso. —**deceitfulness,** *n.* falsedad; duplicidad.

deceive (dɪ'siːv) *v.t.* engañar. —*v.i.* mentir.

decelerate (ˌdi'sɛl·ə·reit) *v.t.* retardar; disminuir. —*v.i.* retardarse. —**deceleration,** *n.* retardación; disminución.

December (di'sɛm·bər) *n.* diciembre.

decency ('di·sən·si) *n.* decencia.

decennial (dɪ'sɛn·i·əl) *n.* decenio. —*adj.* decenal.

decent ('di·sənt) *adj.* **1,** (proper) decente; honesto. **2,** (honest) honorado. **3,** (fair) razonable.

decentralize (ˌdi'sɛn·trə,laiz) *v.t.* descentralizar. —*v.i.* descentralizarse. —**decentralization** (-lɪ'zei·ʃən) *n.* descentralización.

deception (dɪ'sɛp·ʃən) *n.* **1,** (act of deceiving) decepción; engaño. **2,** (misrepresentation) fraude. —**deceptive** (-tɪv) *adj.* engañoso; falaz.

decibel ('dɛs·ə·bɛl) *n.* decibel; decibelio.

decide (dɪ'said) *v.t.* & *i.* decidir; determinar; resolver.

decided (dɪ'sai·dɪd) *adj.* **1,** (unmistakable) decidido. **2,** (determined) determinado; resuelto. —**decidedly,** *adv.* indudablemente.

deciduous (dɪ'sɪd·dʒu·əs) *adj.* deciduo.

decigram ('dɛs·ɪ·græm) *n.* decigramo.

deciliter ('dɛs·ɪ,li·tər) *n.* decilitro.

decillion (dɪ'sɪl·jən) *n. (U.S.)* mil quintillones; *(Brit.)* un millón de nonillones; decillón.

decimal ('dɛs·ɪ·məl) *n.* & *adj.* cimal. —**decimal point,** coma de decimal.

decimate ('dɛs·ɪ,meit) *v.t.* diezmar. —**decimation,** *n.* gran mortandad.

decimeter ('dɛs·ɪ,mi·tər) *n.* decímetro.

decipher (di'sai·fər) *v.t.* descifrar. —**decipherable,** *adj.* descifrable. —**decipherment,** *n.* descifre.

decision (dɪ'sɪʒ·ən) *n.* **1,** (selection) decisión. **2,** (determination) determinación; resolución. **3,** *law* (judgment) decisión; sentencia.

decisive (dɪ'sai·sɪv) *adj.* decisivo. —**decisiveness,** *n.* fuerza decisiva.

deck (dɛk) *n.* **1,** *naut.* cubierta. **2,** *cards* baraja. —*v.t.* [*también,* **deck out**] adornar; engalanar.

declaim (dɪ'kleim) *v.t.* & *i.* declamar; recitar.

declamation (ˌdɛk·lə'mei·ʃən) *n.* declamación. —**declamatory** (dɪ'klæm·ə·tor·i) *adj.* declamatorio.

declaration (ˌdɛk·lə'rei·ʃən) *n.* declaración.

declarative (dɪ'klær·ə·tɪv) *adj.,* *gram.* aseverativo.

declare (dɪ'klɛr) *v.t.* & *i.* declarar.

declassify (di'klæs·ɪ,fai) *v.t.* hacer público.

declension (dɪ'klɛn·ʃən) *n.* **1,** (descent) declive. **2,** (deterioration) decadencia; deterioro. **3,** *gram.* declinación.

declination (ˌdɛk·lɪ'nei·ʃən) *n.* **1,** (bending) declive; inclinación. **2,** (refusal) excusa; rechazamiento.

decline (dɪ'klain) *v.t.* & *i.* **1,** (bend) inclinar; descender; bajar. **2,** (refuse) declinar; rehusar. —*v.t.,* *gram.*

declinar. —*v.i.* **1**, (approach the end) ponerse. **2**, (deteriorate) desmejorarse; decaer. —*n.*, **1**, (slope) declinación. **2**, (decay) decadencia. **3**, (deterioration) menoscabo.

declining (dɪ'klai·nɪŋ) *adj.* **1**, (bending) pendiente. **2**, (ending) final. **3**, (refusing) rehusante.

declivity (dɪ'klɪv·ə·ti) *n.* declive; pendiente.

decoct (dɪ'kakt) *v.t.* extraer por decocción. —**decoction** (-'kak·ʃən) *n.* decocción.

decode (di'koːd) *v.t.* descifrar. —**decoding,** *n.* descifre.

décolleté (ˌde·kal'teɪ) *adj.* descotado; escotado. —**décolletage** (-'taːʒ) *n.* descote; escote.

decompose (ˌdi·kəm'poːz) *v.t.* descomponer. —*v.i.* descomponerse. —**decomposition** (ˌdi·kam·pə'zɪʃ· ən) *n.* descomposición.

decongestant (di·kən'dʒɛs·tənt) *n.* descongestionante.

decontaminate (ˌdi·kən'tæm· ɪˌneit) *v.t.* purificar. —**decontamination,** *n.* purificación.

decontrol (di·kən'trol) *n.* descontrol. —*v.t.* descontrolar.

decor (de'koːr) *n.* decoración.

decorate ('dɛk·ə·reit) *v.t.* **1**, (ornament) decorar; adornar; engalanar. **2**, (award a medal, etc., to) condecorar. **3**, (paint) pintar. **4**, (furnish) decorar. —**decorator,** *n.* decorador.

decoration (ˌdɛk·ə'rei·ʃən) *n.* **1**, (ornament) decoración. **2**, (award) condecoración.

decorative ('dɛk·ə·reˌtɪv) *adj.* decorativo; adornante.

decorum (dɪ'kor·əm) *n.* decoro. —**decorous** ('dɛk·ə·rəs) *adj.* decoroso.

decoy (di'kɔi) *n.* **1**, (a lure) trampa. **2**, *hunting* reclamo. **3**, (stratagem) añagaza; estratagema. **4**, (person used as lure) entruchón. —*v.t. & i.* atraer; entruchar.

decrease (dɪ'kris) *v.i.* decrecer; reducirse; bajar. —*v.t.* disminuir; reducir. —*n.* ('di·kris) reducción; disminución.

decree (dɪ'kriː) *n.* decreto; ley; edicto; orden. —*v.t. & i.* decretar; ordenar; mandar.

decrement ('dɛk·rə·mənt) *n.* decremento.

decrepit (dɪ'krɛp·ɪt) *adj.* decrépito; viejo. —**decrepitude** (-ˌtud) *n.* decrepitud.

decry (di'krai) *v.t.* **1**, (blame) vituperar; acusar. **2**, (deplore) deplorar; lamentar.

decuple ('dɛk·ju·pəl) *adj.* décuplo. —*v.t* decuplicar; decuplar.

dedicate ('dɛd·ɪˌkeit) *v.t.* dedicar. —**dedication,** *n.* dedicación. —**dedicatory** (-kəˌtor·i) *adj.* dedicatorio.

deduce (di'dus) *v.t.* deducir; colegir. —**deducible,** *adj.* deducible; colegible.

deduct (dɪ'dʌkt) *v.t.* deducir; substraer; descontar. —**deductible,** *adj.* deducible; descontable.

deduction (dɪ'dʌk·ʃən) *n.* **1**, (subtraction) substracción. **2**, (reasoning) deducción. —**deductive** (-tɪv) *adj.* deductivo.

deed (diːd) *n.***1**, (act) hecho; acción; acto. **2**, (exploit) proeza; gesta. **3**, *law* (title) escritura. —*v.t.* hacer escritura de cesión o traspaso; ceder o traspasar por escritura.

deem (diːm) *v.t. & i.* estimar; creer; juzgar.

deep (dip) *adj.* **1**, (extending far down, back, or into) hondo; profundo. **2**, (absorbed) embebecido; absorto. **3**, (abstruse) oscuro; difícil; complicado. **4**, (extreme) tremendo; grande. **5**, *mus.* (low-pitched) grave; profundo. **6**, (intense) subido; intenso. **7**, (heartfelt) sentido; profundo. —*n.* **1**, (the sea) el mar. **2**, (hell) abismo; infierno. **3**, (the farthest point) lo profundo. —**deepness,** *n.* profundidad; hondura; intensidad.

deepen ('di·pən) *v.t.* **1**, (make deeper) profundizar; ahondar. **2**, (intensify) intensificar. —*v.i.* **1**, (grow deeper) profundizarse. **2**, (grow more intense) intensificarse.

deepseated ('dip,sit·əd) *adj.* incrustado; firmemente fijo.

deer (dɪːr) *n.sing. & pl.* ciervo; venado. —**deerskin,** *n.* gamuza.

deface (di'feis) *v.t.* desfigurar; estropear. —**defacement,** *n.* desfiguración; estropeo; mutilación.

de facto (di'fæk·to) *adv.* de hecho.

defalcate (dɪ'fæl·ket) *v.i.* desfalcar. —**defalcation,** *n.* desfalco.

defame (di'feim) *v.t.* difamar; calumniar. —**defamation** (ˌdɛf· ə'me·ʃən) *n.* difamación; calumnia.

—**defamatory** (dɪ'fæm·ə·tor·i) *adj.* difamatorio.

default (dɪ'fɔlt) *v.t.* 1, (fail to do) faltar; no cumplir. 2, *sports* perder por incomparecencia. 3, *law* condenar en rebeldía. —*v.i.* 1, (fail to appear) no aparecer; no presentarse. 2, (lose) perder por incomparecencia. 3, *law* caer en rebeldía. —*n.* 1, (voluntary failure) falta; incumplimiento. 2, (involuntary failure) omisión; descuido; falta. 3, *law* rebeldía. —**in default of,** 1, *law* en rebeldía. 2, (through lack of) por ausencia de.

defeat (dɪ'fit) *v.t.* 1, (overcome) derrotar; vencer; ganar. 2, (thwart) frustrar; impedir. —*n.* derrota. —**defeatism,** *n.* derrotismo. —**defeatist,** *adj. & n.* derrotista.

defecate ('def·ə·keit) *v.t. & i.* defecar. —**defecation,** *n.* defecación.

defect (dɪ'fɛkt) *n.* 1, (imperfection) defecto; imperfección. 2, (deficiency) omisión. —*v.i.* desertar. —**defector,** *n.* desertor.

defection (dɪ'fɛk·ʃən) *n.* deserción; defección.

defective (dɪ'fɛk·tɪv) *adj.* defectuoso; deficiente; *gram.* defectivo. —*n.* persona anormal o de inteligencia poco desarrollada.

defend (dɪ'fɛnd) *v.t.* 1, (protect) defender. 2, (uphold) mantener; sostener. —**defender,** *n.* defensor.

defendant (dɪ'fɛn·dənt) *n.* 1, (in criminal proceedings) acusado; reo. 2, (in civil proceedings) demandado.

defense también, **defence** (dɪ'fɛns) *n.* defensa. —**defenseless,** *adj.* indefenso; inerme.

defensible (dɪ'fɛns·ə·bəl) *adj.* 1, (that can be defended) defendible. 2, (that can be upheld) sostenible.

defensive (dɪ'fɛn·sɪv) *adj.* defensivo. —*n.* defensiva.

defer (dɪ'fʌr) *v.t.* [**deferred,** -**ferring**] diferir; aplazar; retrasar. —*v.i.* ceder; acceder; deferir.

deference ('def·ə·rəns) *n.* deferencia; acatamiento.

deferent ('def·ə·rənt) *adj.* deferente.

deferential (def·ə'rɛn·ʃəl) *adj.* deferente; respetuoso.

deferment (dɪ'fʌr·mənt) *n.* aplazamiento.

defiance (dɪ'fai·əns) *n.* 1, (resistance) desafío; oposición. 2, (contempt) contumacia; obstinación. —**defiant,** *adj.* desafiador; provocador.

deficient (dɪ'fɪʃ·ənt) *adj.* 1, (incomplete) defectuoso. 2, (insufficient) deficiente. —**deficiency,** *n.* deficiencia.

deficit ('def·ə·sɪt) *n.* déficit.

defile (dɪ'fail) *v.t.* manchar; corromper; profanar. —*v.i.* desfilar; marchar. —*n.* desfiladero. —**defilement,** *n.* corrupción; profanación; violación.

define (dɪ'fain) *v.t.* 1, (limit) definir; prescribir. 2, (explain) explicar; definir; describir. —**definable,** *adj.* definible.

definite ('def·ə·nɪt) *adj.* definido; cierto; preciso. —**definiteness,** *n.* exactitud; precisión.

definition (def·ə'nɪʃ·ən) *n.* definición.

definitive (dɪ'fɪn·ə·tɪv) *adj.* definitivo; final. —**definitiveness,** *n.* lo definitivo.

deflate (dɪ'fleit) *v.t.* 1, (remove gas or air from) desinflar. 2, (lower, as prices) rebajar; disminuir.

deflation (dɪ'flei·ʃən) *n.* 1, (act of deflating) desinflación. 2, (devaluation of currency) disminución; desinflación.

deflect (dɪ'flɛkt) *v.t.* desviar; apartar. —*v.i.* desviarse; apartarse.

deflection (dɪ'flɛk·ʃən) *n.* desviación; deflexión.

deflective (dɪ'flɛk·tɪv) *adj.* desviador.

deflector (dɪ'flɛk·tər) *n.* deflector.

defloration (,def·lə'rei·ʃən) *n.* desfloración.

deflower (dɪ'flau·ər) *v.t.* desflorar.

defog (dɪ'fɑːg) *v.t.* [-**fogged,** -**fogging**] desempañar.

defoliate (dɪ'fo·li,et) *v.t.* deshojar. —**defoliant,** *adj. & n.* defoliante. —**defoliation,** *n.* defoliación.

deform (di'form) *v.t.* deformar; estropear. —**deformation** (,di·for'mei·ʃən) *n.* deformación.

deformed (di'formd) *adj.* 1, (misshapen) deformado. 2, (ugly) deforme.

deformity (di'form·ə·ti) *n.* deformidad.

defraud (di'frɔːd) *v.t.* defraudar; estafar.

defray (dɪ'frei) *v.t.* sufragar; costear. —**defrayal,** *n.* pago; sufragación.

defrost (di'frɔst) *v.t.* descongelar;

deshelar. —**defroster,** *n.* descongelador.

deft (dɛft) *adj.* diestro; apto; hábil. —**deftness,** *n.* destreza; habilidad.

defunct (di'fʌŋkt) *adj.* difunto; fallecido; muerto.

defy (dɪ'fai) *v.t.* **1,** (challenge) desafiar; retar. **2,** (show contempt for) despreciar; resistir.

degenerate (di'dʒɛn·ə·reit) *v.i.* degenerar; degradar. —*adj.* & *n.* (-rət) degenerado. —**degeneracy,** *n.* degeneración. —**degeneration,** *n.* degeneración.

degrade (di'greid) *v.t.* **1,** (demote) degradar; deponer. **2,** (debase) reducir; rebajar. **3,** (corrupt) degradar; depravar. —**degradable,** *adj.* degradable. —**degradation** (dɛg·rə'dei·ʃən) *n.* degradación. —**degrading,** *adj.* degradante.

degree (dɪ'griː) *n.* **1,** (stage in a series; unit of temperature; *mil., geom., physics*) grado. **2,** (condition) estado. **3,** (academic rank won by study) licencia. —**by degrees,** poco a poco. —**take a degree,** licenciarse.

dehumanize (di'hju·mə·naiz) *v.t.* deshumanizar. —**dehumanization,** *n.* deshumanización.

dehydrate (di'hai·dreit) *v.t.* deshidratar. —*v.i.* deshidratarse. —**dehydration** (ˌdi·hai'drei·ʃən) *n.* deshidratación.

deicer (di'ai·sər) *n.* anticongelante.

deify ('di·ə·fai) *v.t.* deificar; endiosar. —**deification** (-fɪ'kei·ʃən) *n.* endiosamiento; deificación.

deign (dein) *v.i.* dignarse; condescender. —*v.t.* conceder; dar.

deism ('diː·ɪz·əm) *n.* deísmo. —**deist,** *n.* deísta. —**deistic,** *adj.* deísta.

deity ('di·ə·ti) *n.* deidad; *cap.* Dios.

deject (dɪ'dʒɛkt) *v.t.* abatir; desanimar; descorazonar. —**dejected,** *adj.* abatido; descorazonado.

dejection (dɪ'dʒɛk·ʃən) *n.* **1,** (gloom) melancolía; desánimo. **2,** *med.* (evacuation) deposición.

delay (dɪ'lei) *v.t.* dilatar; retrasar; hacer esperar. —*v.i.* dilatarse; tardar; demorarse. —*n.* dilación; tardanza; retraso.

delectable (dɪ'lɛk·tə·bəl) *adj.* deleitable; delicioso. —**delectability,** *n.* delectación.

delectation (ˌdi·lɛk'tei·ʃən) *n.* delectación.

delegate ('dɛl·ɪ·gət) *n.* delegado.

—*v.t.* (-geit) **1,** (empower) autorizar; comisionar. **2,** (send as a representative) delegar. —**delegation,** *n.* delegación; comisión.

delete (dɪ'lit) *v.t.* borrar; suprimir. —**deletion** (-'li·ʃən) *n.* supresión.

deleterious (del·ə'tɪr·i·əs) *adj.* deletéreo. —**deleteriousness,** *n.* daño; agravio.

deliberate (dɪ'lɪb·ər·eit) *v.t.* & *i.* deliberar. —*adj.* (-ət) **1,** (careful) cauto; circunspecto. **2,** (unhurried) lento; calmo. **3,** (intentional) reflexionado; pensado; premeditado. —**deliberation,** *n.* deliberación.

deliberative (dɪ'lɪb·ə·re·tɪv) *adj.* **1,** (discussing) deliberante. **2,** (considered) deliberado.

delicacy ('del·ɪ·kə·si) *n.* **1,** (fineness) delicadeza; sensibilidad. **2,** (fragility) fragilidad; cuidado. **3,** (food) golosina; exquisitez.

delicate ('dɛl·ɪ·kət) *adj.* **1,** (fragile; requiring care) delicado. **2,** (tactful; sensitive) fino; sensible. **3,** (choice, as food) exquisito; de buen gusto o sabor.

delicatessen (ˌdɛl·ɪ·kə'tɛs·ən) *n.* **1,** (delicacies) ultramarinos; gollerías. **2,** (store) tienda de ultramarinos.

delicious (dɪ'lɪʃ·əs) *adj.* delicioso; sabroso. —**deliciousness,** *n.* lo delicioso; lo sabroso.

delight (dɪ'lait) *n.* delicia; deleite. —*v.t.* & *i.* deleitar; encantar; agradar. —**delightful,** *adj.* delicioso; deleitoso.

delimit (dɪ'lɪm·ɪt) *v.t.* delimitar.

delineate (dɪ'lɪn·i·eit) *v.t.* **1,** (outline) delinear; esbozar. **2,** (describe) describir. —**delineation,** *n.* delineación; esbozo.

delinquent (dɪ'lɪŋ·kwənt) *adj.* **1,** (tardy) delincuente. **2,** (failing in duty) culpable; reo. —*n.* delincuente. —**delinquency,** *n.* delincuencia.

deliquesce (ˌdɛl·ɪ'kwɛs) *v.i.* derretirse; licuarse. —**deliquescence,** *n.* licuación; delicuescencia. —**deliquescent,** *adj.* delicuescente.

delirious (də'lɪr·i·əs) *adj.* delirante. —**deliriousness,** *n.* delirio.

delirium (də'lɪr·i·əm) *n.* delirio. —**delirium tremens,** delirium tremens.

deliver (dɪ'lɪv·ər) *v.t.* **1,** (transmit; send) entregar; repartir. **2,** (deal, as a blow) dar; asestar. **3,** throw, as a ball) tirar; lanzar. **4,** (give birth to) parir. **5,** *obstetrics* asistir en el nacimiento de. **6,** (utter) pronunciar. **7,** (set free) liberar; librar; libertar.

deliverance (dɪ'liv·ər·əns) *n.* **1,** (rescue) rescate; liberación. **2,** (pronouncement) discurso; alocución.

delivery (dɪ'lɪv·ə·ri) *n.* **1,** (handing over) entrega; reparto. **2,** *obstetrics* parto. **3,** (rescue) liberación. **4,** (manner of speaking) estilo. **5,** (act of throwing) tiro; lanzamiento.

dell (del) *n.* vallecito.

delouse (di'laus) *v.t.* espulgar.

delta ('del·tə) *n.* delta.

delude (dɪ'luːd) *v.t.* deludir; burlar; engañar.

deluge ('del·juːdʒ) *n.* **1,** (heavy rain) diluvio. **2,** (flood) inundación. —*v.t.* inundar.

delusion (dɪ'luː·ʒən) *n.* **1,** (mistaken belief) error. **2,** (false conception) ilusión; engaño. —**delusive** (-sɪv) [también, **delusory** (-sə·ri)] *adj.* ilusorio; engañoso.

de luxe (də'lʌks; -'lʊks) de lujo.

delve (delv) *v.i.* cavar; ahondar. —**delve into,** profundizar; sondear.

demagnetize (di'mæg·nə,taiz) *v.t.* desimantar.

demagogue *también,* **demagog** ('dem·ə·gɔg) *n.* demagogo. —**demagoguery** (-,gɔg·ər·i) *n.* demagogia. —**demagogic** (-'gadʒ·ɪk) *adj.* demagógico.

demand (dɪ'mænd) *v.t.* **1,** (ask) demandar; preguntar. **2,** (request urgently) pedir. **3,** (claim by right) reclamar. **4,** (require) exigir. —*n.* **1,** (request) demanda. **2,** (requirement) exigencia. **3,** *comm.* (sales potential) demanda. **4,** *law* (claim) petición jurídica. —**in demand,** en demanda; solicitado. —**on demand,** a instancia; a solicitud; a la presentación.

demanding (dɪ'mæn·dɪŋ) *adj.* **1,** (difficult) perentorio; apremiante. **2,** (exacting) exigente.

demarcate (dɪ'mar·ket) *v.t.* demarcar; deslindar. —**demarcation,** *n.* demarcación; deslinde.

demarche (di'marʃ) *n.* gestión.

demean (dɪ'min) *v.t. & i.* rebajar; degradar.

demeanor (dɪ'min·ər) *n.* comportamiento; conducta.

demented (dɪ'men·tɪd) *adj.* demente; loco. —**dementia** (-ʃə) *n.* demencia; locura. —**dementia praecox,** ('pri·kaks) demencia precoz.

demerit (di'mer·ɪt) *n.* demérito.

demigod ('dem·ɪ,gad) *n.* semidiós.

demijohn ('dem·ɪ,dʒan) *n.* garrafa; garrafón; damajuana.

demilitarize (di'mɪl·ɪ·tə,raiz) *v.t.* desmilitarizar. —**demilitarization** (-rɪ'zei·ʃən) *n.* desmilitarización.

demimonde ('dem·i,mond) *n.* mujeres mundanas. —**demimondaine** (-mon'dein) *n.* mujer mundana.

demise (dɪ'maiz) *n.* **1,** (death) fallecimiento; muerte. **2,** *law* (transfer) traslación de dominio, poderes o soberanía. —*v.t.* **1,** (transfer) transferir; pasar. **2,** (yield) ceder.

demitasse ('dem·i,tæs) *n.* tacita.

demobilize (di'mo·bə,laiz) *v.t. & i.* desmovilizar. —**demobilization** (-lɪ'zei·ʃən) *n.* desmovilización.

democracy (dɪ'mak·rə·si) *n.* democracia.

democrat ('dem·ə·kræt) *n.* demócrata. —**democratic** (-'kræt·ɪk) *adj.* demócrata; democrático.

democratize (dɪ'mak·rə,taiz) *v.t.* democratizar. —**democratization** (-tɪ'zei·ʃən) *n.* democratización.

demography (dɪ'mag·rə·fi) *n.* demografía. —**demographer** (-fər) *n.* demógrafo. —**demographic** (,di·mə'græf·ik) demográfico.

demolish (di'mal·ɪʃ) *v.t.* demoler; destruir; arruinar. —**demolition** (dem·ə'lɪʃ·ən) *n.* demolición.

demon ('di·mən) *n.* demonio; diablo. —**demoniac** (dɪ'mo·ni·æk) [también, **demoniacal** (,di·mə'nai·ə·kəl)] *adj.* demoníaco.

demonstrable (dɪ'man·strə·bəl) *adj.* demostrable.

demonstrate ('dem·ən·streit) *v.t.* demostrar; probar. —*v.i.* demostrarse.

demonstration (,dem·ən'strei·ʃən) *n.* **1,** (act of demonstrating) demostración; prueba. **2,** (display) prueba; exhibición. **3,** *mil.* (show of force) alarde. **4,** (protest) manifestación.

demonstrative (dɪ'man·strə·tɪv) *adj.* demostrativo.

demonstrator ('dem·ən·stre·tər) *n.* **1,** (person or thing that displays) demostrador. **2,** (noisy person) alborotador. **3,** *colloq.* (automobile) vehículo de demostración.

demoralize (di'mar·ə,laiz) *v.t.* desmoralizar. —**demoralization** (-lɪ'zei·ʃən) *n.* desmoralización.

demote (di'mot) *v.t.* degradar.

—**demotion** (-'moˑʃən) *n.* degradación.

demur (dɪ'mʌr) *v.i.* [**demurred, -murring**] **1,** (object) objetar; poner dificultades. **2,** (hesitate) dudar; vacilar. **3,** *law* (enter a demurrer) aceptar con excepciones. —*n.* **1,** (objection) objeción. **2,** (hesitation) duda; vacilación.

demure (dɪ'mjuːr) *adj.* **1,** (prim) gazmoño; relamido. **2,** (sedate) formal; grave; serio.

demureness (dɪ'mjuːr·nəs) *n.* **1,** (primness) gazmoñería. **2,** (sedateness) seriedad.

demurrage (dɪ'mʌr·ɪdʒ) *n.*, *comm.* estadía.

demurrer (dɪ'mʌr·ər) *n.* **1,** (irresolute person) persona irresoluta. **2,** *law* excepción perentoria.

den (dɛn) *n.* **1,** (cave) madriguera; guarida. **2,** (retreat) guarida; cuchitril. **3,** (room) estudio; cuartito.

denaturalize (di'næt̮ʃ·ə·rə,laiz) *v.t.* desnaturalizar.

denature (ˌdi'nei·tʃər) *v.t.* adulterar; desnaturalizar.

dendrite ('dɛn·drait) *n.* dendrita.

dengue ('dɛŋ·gei) *n.* dengue.

denial (dɪ'nai·əl) *n.* **1,** (refusal) negativa. **2,** (contradiction) negación. **3,** (self-restraint) abnegación.

denigrate ('dɛn·ə,gret) *v.t.* denigrar. —**denigration**, *n.* denigración.

denim ('dɛn·əm) *n.* tela de mono; dril; mezclilla.

denizen ('dɛn·ɪ·zən) *n.* **1,** (inhabitant) habitante. **2,** (naturalized foreigner) ciudadano naturalizado. **3,** (naturalized thing) naturalizado.

denominate (dɪ'nam·ɪ,neit) *v.t.* denominar; designar; nombrar.

denomination (dɪ,nam·ɪ'nei·ʃən) *n.* **1,** (type) denominación; nombre. **2,** (sect) denominación; secta.

denominative (dɪ'nam·ə,ne·tɪv) *adj.* denominativo.

denominator (dɪ'nam·ɪ,ne·tər) *n.*, *math.* denominador.

denote (dɪ'not) *v.t.* **1,** (designate) señalar; marcar. **2,** (mean) significar; denotar; indicar. —**denotation** (ˌdi·no'tei·ʃən) *n.* denotación; indicación.

denouement (ˌde·nu'mant; -'mɔn) *n.* desenlace.

denounce (dɪ'nauns) *v.t.* **1,** (stigmatize) denunciar; censurar. **2,** (inform against) delatar. **3,** (repudiate, as a treaty) denunciar. —**denouncement**, *n.* = **denunciation.**

dense (dɛns) *adj.* **1,** (compact) denso; espeso; compacto. **2,** (stupid) torpe. —**denseness** [*también*, **density** (-ə·ti)] *n.* densidad; opacidad.

dent (dɛnt) *n.* abolladura. —*v.t.* abollar. —*v.i.* abollarse.

dental ('dɛn·təl) *adj.* dental.

dentifrice ('dɛn·tɪ·frɪs) *n.* dentífrico; pasta dentífrica.

dentine ('dɛn·tin) *también*, **dentin** (-tɪn) *n.* dentina.

dentist ('dɛn·tɪst) *n.* dentista; odontólogo. —**dentistry**, *n.* odontología.

dentition (dɛn'tɪʃ·ən) *n.* dentición.

denture ('dɛn·tʃər) *n.* dentadura postiza.

denude (di'nuːd) *v.t.* **1,** (strip of clothing) desnudar; desvestir. **2,** (despoil) despojar; privar. —**denudation**, *n.* denudación.

denunciation (dɪ,nʌn·si'ei·ʃən) *n.* denuncia; acusación.

deny (dɪ'nai) *v.t. & i.* **1,** (contradict) negar; contradecir. **2,** (refuse; reject) rehusar. **3,** (renounce) abjurar; renunciar.

deodorant (di'o·də·rənt) *n. & adj.* desodorante.

deodorize (di'o·də·raiz) *v.t.* desodorizar. —**deodorization** (-rɪ'zei·ʃən) *n.* desodorización.

depart (dɪ'part) *v.i.* **1,** (leave) partir; marchar; irse. **2,** (deviate) apartarse; desviarse. **3,** (die) morir. —**departed**, *adj. & n.* difunto; fallecido; muerto.

department (dɪ'part·mənt) *n.* **1,** (section) departamento; sección. **2,** (government bureau) ministerio. **3,** (area) distrito; provincia. —**departmental** (-'men·təl) *adj.* departamental; ministerial. —**department store**, galerías; almacén.

departure (dɪ'par·tʃər) *n.* **1,** (leaving) partida; salida; marcha. **2,** (deviation) desviación.

depend (dɪ'pɛnd) *v.i.* pender; colgar. —**depend on** o **upon**, **1,** (trust in) contar con; confiar en. **2,** (rely on) depender de; descansar en. **3,** (be contingent on) depender de.

dependable (dɪ'pɛn·də·bəl) *adj.* confiable; seguro; digno de confianza.

dependence (dɪ'pɛn·dɛns) *n.* dependencia; pertenencia.

dependency (dɪ'pɛn·dən·si) *n.* **1,** = **dependence. 2,** (dependent territory) dependencia; posesión.

dependent (dɪ'pɛn·dənt) *adj.* **1,**

(hanging) pendiente; colgante. **2,** (contingent) dependiente; contingente; condicional. **3,** (subordinate) dependiente; subordinado; subalterno. —*n.* dependiente; carga de familia. —**dependent** *or* **depending upon, 1,** (according to) según. **2,** (contingent on) si ... permite.

depict (dɪ'pɪkt) *v.t.* describir; representar; pintar. —**depiction** (-'pɪk·ʃən) *n.* descripción; representación; pintura.

depilate ('dɛp·ə,let) *v.t.* depilar. —**depilation**, *n.* depilación. —**depilatory** (dɪ'pɪl·ə,tor·i) *adj. & n.* depilatorio.

deplete (dɪ'plit) *v.t.* consumir; agotar; depauperar. —**depletion** (-'pli·ʃən) *n.* agotamiento; depauperación.

deplore (dɪ'plor) *v.t.* deplorar; lamentar. —**deplorable**, *adj.* deplorable; lamentable.

deploy (dɪ'plɔɪ) *v.t.* desplegar. —*v.i.* desplegarse. —**deployment**, *n.* despliegue.

deponent (dɪ'po·nənt) *n. & adj.* deponente.

depopulate (di'pap·jə,let) *v.t.* despoblar.

deport (di'port) *v.t.* (exile) deportar; desterrar. —**deportee** (di'por·ti) *n.* deportado. —**deport oneself,** comportarse; conducirse.

deportation (,di·por'tei·ʃən) *n.* deportación.

deportment (di'port·mənt) *n.* comportamiento; conducta; modales.

depose (di'poᵣz) *v.t.* **1,** (unseat) deponer. **2,** *law* (testify) atestiguar. —*v.i.,* *law* (bear witness) ser testigo.

deposit (dɪ'paᵣ·ɪt) *v.t.* **1,** (put) depositar; poner; colocar. **2,** (pledge) dar como señal. —*n.* **1,** (deposited thing) depósito. **2,** *banking* ingreso. **3,** (part payment) señal. **4,** *geol.* (residue) depósito; residuo.

depositary (dɪ'paz·ə,ter·i) *adj.* depositario. —*n.* **1,** (trustee) depositario. **2,** = **depository.**

deposition (,dɛp·ə'zɪʃ·ən) *n.* **1,** (displacement) deposición. **2,** *law* (testimony) declaración; testimonio; deposición.

depositor (dɪ'paz·ə·tər) *n.* depositador.

depository (dɪ'paz·ɪ,tor·i) *n.* **1,** (storage place) depósito; almacén;

depositaria. **2,** = **depositary.** —*adj.* depositario.

depot ('di·po) *n.* **1,** (warehouse) depósito; almacén. **2,** *R.R.* estación. **3,** *mil.* depósito.

deprave (dɪ'preiv) *v.t.* depravar; degenerar; pervertir.

depravity (dɪ'præv·ə·ti) *n.* depravación; perversión.

deprecate ('dɛp·rə·keit) *v.t.* desaprobar; lamentar; rechazar. —**deprecation**, *n.* desaprobación.

deprecatory ('dɛp·rə·kə,tor·i) *adj.* desaprobante; desaprobador.

depreciate (dɪ'pri·ʃi·eit) *v.i.* depreciarse. —*v.t.* **1,** (lessen value of) depreciar. **2,** (belittle) desestimar; despreciar. —**depreciation**, *n.* depreciación.

depredate ('dɛp·rə,deit) *v.t. & i.* depredar. —**depredation**, *n.* depredación.

depress (dɪ'prɛs) *v.t.* **1,** (press or move down) bajar; rebajar. **2,** (sadden) deprimir; abatir; desanimar. **3,** (weaken) desalentar; descorazonar. —**depressive** (-ɪv) *adj.* depresivo; deprimente. —**depressor**, *n.* depresor. —**depressant** (-ənt) *n. & adj.* sedante.

depression (dɪ'prɛʃ·ən) *n.* **1,** (concavity) concavidad; depresión. **2,** (melancholy) desánimo; melancolía. **3,** (market decline) depresión; crisis.

deprivation (,dɛp·rɪ'vei·ʃən) *n.* **1,** (removal) privación. **2,** (loss) pérdida. **3,** (poverty) carencia.

deprive (dɪ'praiv) *v.t.* **1,** (divest) privar. **2,** (strip) despojar. **3,** (withhold) retener; impedir; excluir.

depth (dɛpθ) *n.* **1,** (deepness) profundidad; hondura; hondo. **2,** (intensity) intensidad; fuerza; viveza. **3,** (profundity) gravedad. —**depth charge,** carga o bomba de profundidad. —**in the depths of,** (winter, etc.) en pleno (invierno, etc.) —**out of one's depth,** en honduras.

deputation (,dɛp·ju'tei·ʃən) *n.* **1,** (mission) delegación; comisión. **2,** (group of emissaries) diputación.

depute (dɪ'pjut) *v.t.* diputar.

deputize ('dɛp·jə,taiz) *v.t.* diputar; delegar.

deputy ('dɛp·jə·ti) *n.* diputado; delegado. —*adj.* teniente.

derail (di'reil) *v.t.* hacer descarrilar. —*v.i.* descarrilar. —**derailment**, *n.* descarrilamiento.

derange (dɪ'reindʒ) *v.t.* **1,** (disarrange) descomponer; desordenar. **2,** (make insane) volver loco; enloquecer. —**deranged,** *adj.* loco.

derangement (dɪ'reindʒ·mənt) *n.* **1,** (disorder) desarreglo. **2,** (insanity) locura.

derby ('dɑr·bi) *n.* **1,** (hat) hongo. **2,** *cap.* (a race) derby.

deregulate (di'rɛg·jə,leit) *v.t.* eximir de reglamentaciones. —**deregulation,** *n.* exención de reglamentaciones.

derelict ('dɛr·ə,lɪkt) *adj.* **1,** (forsaken) derrelicto; abandonado; desamparado. **2,** (remiss) negligente; remiso. —*n.* **1,** *naut.* (abandoned ship) derrelicto. **2,** (outcast) desecho.

dereliction (dɛr·ə'lɪk·ʃən) *n.* derrelicción; abandono; negligencia.

deride (dɪ'raid) *v.t.* ridiculizar; hacer burla de.

derision (dɪ'rɪʒ·ən) *n.* irrisión; burla.

derisive (dɪ'rai·sɪv) *adj.* irrisorio.

derivation (,dɛr·ɪ'vei·ʃən) *n.* **1,** (act of deriving) derivación. **2,** (source) fuente; origen. **3,** (etymology) etimología.

derivative (də'rɪv·ə·tɪv) *adj.* derivativo; derivado. —*n.* derivado.

derive (dɪ'raiv) *v.t.* **1,** (receive) derivar. **2,** (deduce) inferir; deducir. —*v.i.* derivarse.

dermatitis (,dɑr·mə'tai·tɪs) *n.* dermatitis.

dermatology (,dɑr·mə'tal·ə·dʒi) *n.* dermatología. —**dermatological** (-tə'ladʒ·ɪ·kəl) *adj.* dermatológico. —**dermatologist,** *n.* dermatólogo.

dermis ('dɑr·mɪs) *n.* dermis; piel; cutis.

derogate ('dɛr·ə,geit) *v.t.* derogar. —*v.i.* [*usu.,* **derogate from**] **1,** (detract) disminuir; desmerecer; menospreciar. **2,** (degenerate) degenerar; quitar mérito (a). —**derogation,** *n.* derogación; desmerecimiento; menosprecio.

derogatory (dɪ'rag·ə,tor·i) *adj.* despectivo; menospreciativo. *También,* **derogative** (-tɪv).

derrick ('dɛr·ɪk) *n.* **1,** (crane) grúa. **2,** (oil rig) torre de perforación.

dervish ('dɑr·vɪʃ) *n.* derviche.

desalt (di'sɔːlt) *v.t.* [*también,* **desalinate** (di'sæl·ə·neit)] desalar; desalinizar. —**desalination** (-'nei·ʃən) *n.* desalinización; desalación.

descant ('dɛs·kænt) *n.* discante. —*v.t.* (dəs'kænt) discantar.

descend (dɪ'sɛnd) *v.t. & i.* descender; bajar. —*v.i.* **1,** (lower oneself) rebajarse. **2,** *mus.* (lower) bajar. **3,** (derive from) descender; provenir; venir. —**descendant,** *n.* descendiente. —**descendent,** *adj.* descendiente.

descent (dɪ'sɛnt) *n.* **1,** (downward progress) descenso. **2,** (downward slope) bajada; declive. **3,** (ancestry) descendencia; origen; alcurnia.

describe (dɪ'skraib) *v.t.* **1,** (portray) describir; representar. **2,** (explain) definir; explicar. **3,** (delineate) trazar; delinear.

description (dɪ'skrɪp·ʃən) *n.* **1,** (a describing) descripción; representación. **2,** (kind) clase; género. —**descriptive** (-tɪv) *adj.* descriptivo.

desecrate ('dɛs·ɪ,kreit) *v.t.* violar; profanar. —**desecration,** *n.* profanación.

desegregate (di'sɛg·rə·geit) *v.t.* quitar la segregación en o de. —**desegregation,** *n.* falta de segregación.

desensitize (di'sɛn·sɪ,taiz) *v.t.* desensibilizar.

desert ('dɛz·ərt) *n. & adj.* desierto.

desert (dɪ'zɑrt) *v.t.* desertar; abandonar; desamparar. —*v.i.* desertar. —*n., usu. pl.* merecido. —**deserted,** *adj.* despoblado; desierto. —**deserter,** *n.* desertor.

desertion (dɪ'zɑr·ʃən) *n.* **1,** (dishonorable departure) deserción. **2,** (abandonment) abandono.

deserve (dɪ'zɑrv) *v.t.* merecer. —*v.i.* tener merecimientos. —**deserved** (-'zɑrvd) *adj.* merecido. —**deservedly** (-'zɑr·vəd·li) *adv.* merecidamente; justamente. —**deserving** (-'zɑr·vɪŋ) *adj.* meritorio; valioso; digno; merecedor.

desiccate ('dɛs·ə,ket) *v.t.* desecar. —*v.i.* desecarse. —**desiccant,** *adj. & n.* desecante. —**desiccation,** *n.* desecación.

design (dɪ'zain) *v.t.* **1,** (sketch) diseñar; trazar. **2,** (contrive) proyectar; planear. **3,** (intend) intentar; tener intención de. —*n.* **1,** (art work) diseño; trazado; bosquejo. **2,** *pl.* (scheme) planes; designios; intenciones. **3,** (decorative arrangement) diseño; composición.

designate ('dɛz·ɪg,neit) *v.t.* **1,** (point out) indicar; señalar. **2,**

(name) denominar. 3, (appoint) designar; elegir. —*adj.* designado.

designation (ˌdɛz·ɪgˈnei·ʃən) *n.* 1, (indication) indicación; señalamiento. 2, (name; naming) denominación. 3, (appointing) designación; elección.

designer (dɪˈzai·nər) *n.* 1, (one who designs) diseñador; (of machinery) proyectista. 2, (plotter) maquinador.

designing (dɪˈzai·nɪŋ) *adj.* 1, (making a design) del diseño. 2, (crafty) intrigante; astuto. —*n.* (art work) diseño.

desire (dɪˈzair) *v.t.* 1, (want) desear; anhelar. 2, (request) suplicar; rogar. —*n.* deseo. —**desirable**, *adj.* deseable; apetecible. —**desirous**, *adj.* deseoso; anhelante.

desist (dɪˈzist) *v.i.* desistir; cesar. —**desistance**, *n.* desistimiento.

desk (dɛsk) *n.* 1, (writing table) escritorio. 2, (for messages) mesa (de despacho). 3, (school desk) pupitre. 4, (editorial office) redacción. —**desk work**, trabajo de oficina.

desolate (ˈdɛs·ə·lət) *adj.* 1, (forlorn) desolado. 2, (solitary) solitario. 3, (miserable) infeliz; triste. 4, (deserted) desierto; despoblado. 5, (ravaged) asolado. —*v.t.* (-ˌleit) 1, (make desolate) desolar. 2, (depopulate) despoblar. 3, (devastate) asolar; devastar; arrasar.

desolation (ˌdɛs·əˈlei·ʃən) *n.* 1, (barren waste) desolación. 2, (loneliness) soledad.

despair (dɪˈspɛɪr) *v.i.* desesperar. —*n.* desesperación. —**despairing**, *adj.* desesperanzado.

despatch (dɪˈspætʃ) *n.* & *v.* = **dispatch**.

desperado (dɛs·pəˈra·do) *n.* criminal desesperado; bandido.

desperate (ˈdɛs·pər·ət) *adj.* 1, (impelled by despair) desesperado; perdido. 2, (reckless) violento; terrible. 3, (hopeless) irremediable. 4, (drastic) heroico. 5, (brutal; bloody) encarnizado.

desperation (ˌdɛs·pəˈrei·ʃən) *n.* desesperación.

despicable (ˈdɛs·pɪ·kə·bəl) *adj.* despreciable; bajo; vil.

despise (dɪˈspaiz) *v.t.* 1, (scorn) despreciar. 2, (hate) detestar.

despite (dɪˈspait) *n.* 1, (insult) insulto; afrenta. 2, (malice) malicia. —*prep.* a pesar de; a despecho de; no obstante. —**in despite of,** a pesar de; a despecho de; no obstante.

despoil (dɪˈspɔil) *v.t.* despojar; robar; saquear. —**despoilment**, *n.* despojo.

despond (dɪˈspand) *v.i.* desanimarse; desesperarse. —**despondent,** *adj.* desanimado; abatido. —**despondency,** *n.* desánimo.

despot (ˈdɛs·pət) *n.* déspota. —**despotic** (deˈspat·ɪk) *adj.* despótico. —**despotism** (ˈdɛs·pə·tɪz·əm) *n.* despotismo.

dessert (dɪˈzʌrt) *n.* postre; dulces.

destination (ˌdɛs·tɪˈnei·ʃən) *n.* 1, (aim; goal) destinación. 2, (place or condition to be reached) destino.

destine (ˈdɛs·tɪn) *v.t.* 1, (intend) destinar; dedicar. 2, (predetermine unalterably) predeterminar.

destiny (ˈdɛs·tə·ni) *n.* destino.

destitute (ˈdɛs·tɪˌtut) *adj.* 1, [*con of*] (lacking) desprovisto de. 2, (indigent) destituido; pobre; indigente. —**destitution** (-ˈtu·ʃən) *n.* pobreza; indigencia.

destroy (dɪˈstrɔi) *v.t.* destruir; aniquilar.

destroyer (dɪˈstrɔi·ər) *n.* 1, (demolisher) destructor. 2, *naval* cazatorpedero; destructor.

destructible (dɪˈstrʌk·tə·bəl) *adj.* destruible.

destruction (dɪˈstrʌk·ʃən) *n.* destrucción. —**destructive** (-trɪv) *adj.* destructivo.

desultory (ˈdɛs·əlˌtor·i) *adj.* deshilvanado; incoherente; inconexo.

detach (dɪˈtætʃ) *v.t.* 1, (unfasten) despegar; desprender; separar 2, *mil.* (send on a mission) destacar. —**detachable**, *adj.* separable; despegable; desmontable.

detached (dɪˈtætʃt) *adj.* 1, (separate) separado; suelto. 2, (impartial) imparcial; desinteresado. 3, (aloof) despreocupado.

detachment (dɪˈtætʃ·mənt) *n.* 1, (separation) despegadura. 2, (aloofness) separación. 3, *mil.* destacamento.

detail (dɪˈteil) *v.t.* 1, (describe minutely) detallar. 2, *mil.* (assign) destacar. —*n.* 1, (item) detalle. 2, *mil.* (assigned group) destacamento. —**detailed,** *adj.* detallado; completo.

detain (dɪ'tein) v.t. **1,** (delay)
detener. **2,** (arrest) arrestar.
—**detainer,** n., law orden de arresto.

detect (dɪ'tɛkt) v.t. **1,** (discover)
percibir; descubrir. **2,** radio
detectar; rectificar. —**detectable,**
adj. averiguable. —**detector,** n. detector.

detection (di'tɛk·ʃən) n. **1,** (discovery) descubrimiento. **2,** radio
detección.

detective (dɪ'tɛk·tɪv) n. detective.

detente (de'tɑnt) n. relajación de
enemistad.

detention (dɪ'tɛn·ʃən) n. detención.

deter (dɪ'tʌr) v.t. [**deterred,**
-terring] detener; refrenar. —**deter-
ment,** n. freno; impedimento.

detergent (dɪ'tʌr·dʒənt) n. & adj.
detergente; limpiador.

deteriorate (dɪ'tɪr·i·ə,reit) v.t.
deteriorar. —v.i. deteriorarse.
—**deterioration,** n. deterioración;
deterioro.

determinate (dɪ'tʌr·mə·nət) adj.
determinado.

determination (dɪ,tʌr·mɪ'neiʃən) n. determinación.

determine (dɪ'tʌr·mɪn) v.t. **1,** (resolve) determinar; resolver;
solucionar. **2,** (end) terminar;
acabar; law concluir. **3,** (restrict)
limitar. **4,** (ordain) decretar. —v.i.
determinarse; resolverse. —**determined,** adj. determinado.

deterrent (dɪ'tʌr·ənt) adj.
impeditivo; disuasivo. —n. freno;
impedimento.

detest (dɪ'tɛst) v.t. detestar;
aborrecer; odiar. —**detestable,** adj.
detestable.

detestation (,di·tɛs'tei·ʃən) n. **1,**
(hatred) detestación; aborrecimiento. **2,** (object of hatred) lo de-
testado; persona o cosa detestada.

dethrone (di'θron) v.t. destronar.
—**dethronement,** n. destronamiento.

detonate ('dɛt·ə,neit) v.i. detonar.
—v.t. hacer detonar. —**detonation,**
n. detonación. —**detonator,** n.
detonador.

detour ('di·tur) n. desvío; rodeo.
—v.t. desviar. —v.i. desviarse; dar
rodeos.

detoxify (di'tɑk·sɪ,fai) v.t. desintoxicar. —**detoxification** (-fɪ'kei-
ʃən) n. desintoxicación.

detract (dɪ'trækt) v.t. & i. [usu.,

detract from] detraer; reducir;
disminuir; denigrar. —**detractor,** n.
detractor; enemigo; denigrador.

detraction (dɪ'træk·ʃən) n.
detracción; maledicencia. —**detrac-
tive** (-tɪv) adj. difamatorio.

detriment ('dɛt·rɪ·mənt) n. detrimento. —**detrimental** (-'mɛn·təl)
adj. perjudicial; nocivo.

detritus (dɪ'trai·təs) n. detritus.

deuce (dus) n. **1,** cards; dice dos;
tennis a dos. **2,** (in exclamations)
¡diablo!

deuced (dust; 'du·sɪd) adj., slang
diabólico, excesivo. —adv. [tam-
bién, **deucedly** ('dus·əd·li)] diabóli-
camente; en demasía.

deuterium (dju'tɪr·i·əm) n.
deuterio.

deuteron ('du·tə·ran) n. deuterión.

devaluate (di'væl·ju,eit) v.t.
desvalorar; desvalorizar. También,
devalue. —**devaluation,** n. devaluación; desvalorización.

devastate ('dɛv·ə·steit) v.t.
devastar; asolar; arrasar. —**devastation,** n. devastación.

develop (dɪ'vɛl·əp) v.t. **1,** (expand)
desarrollar. **2,** (train) entrenar;
adiestrar. **3,** (disclose) desplegar;
revelar; descubrir. **4,** (improve)
perfeccionar; mejorar. **5,** photog.
revelar. **6,** (real estate) urbanizar.
—v.i. **1,** (evolve) desarrollarse. **2,**
(grow) crecer. **3,** (be disclosed)
revelarse; descubrirse.

development (dɪ'vɛl·əp·mənt) n.
1, (growth; expansion) desarrollo;
desenvolvimiento. **2,** photog.
revelado. **3,** (real estate) urbanización. **4,** (undertaking; venture)
empresa. **5,** (accomplishment) creación; realización.

deviate ('di·vi,eit) v.t. desviar.
—v.i. desviarse; dar vueltas. —n.
(-ət) excéntrico. —**deviation,** n.
desviación.

device (dɪ'vais) n. **1,** (apparatus)
artefacto; dispositivo; utensilio. **2,**
(scheme) treta; ardid. **3,** her. mote;
blasón; lema. **4,** pl. (desires) deseos;
antojos.

devil ('dɛv·əl) n. **1,** (evil spirit)
demonio; diablo. **2,** cap. el Diablo;
Satán. —v.t. **1,** (torment) atormentar; martirizar; molestar. **2,**
(season) condimentar.

devilfish ('dɛv·əl,fɪʃ) n. **1,** (octopus) octópodo; pulpo. **2,** (ray)
manta.

devilish ('dɛv·əl·ɪʃ) adj. **1,** (fiend-

ish) diabólico; perverso. **2,** (roguish) excesivo.

devilment ('dɛv·əl·mənt) *también,* **deviltry,** (-tri) *n.* **1,** (evil act) perversidad. **2,** (mischief) diablura.

devious ('di·vi·əs) *adj.* desviado; tortuoso. **—deviousness,** *n.* desviación; extravío.

devise (dɪ'vaiz) *v.t.* **1,** (concoct) proyectar; planear. **2,** *law* (bequeath) legar. **—v.i.** hacer planes o proyectos. **—n.,** *law* **1,** (bequest) legado; manda. **2,** (will) testamento. **—devisee** (-,vai'ziː) *n.* legatorio. **—deviser,** *n.* autor; inventor. **—devisor,** *n., law* testador.

devoid (dɪ'vɔid) *adj.* vacío; desprovisto; carente.

devolution (dɛv·ə'lu·ʃən) *n.* **1,** (transmission) traspaso; transmisión. **2,** *biol.* degeneración.

devolve (dɪ'valv) *v.t.* transferir; traspasar; transmitir. **—v.i.** pasar (a); incumbir (a).

devote (dɪ'vot) *v.t.* **1,** (give) dedicar; aplicar. **2,** (consecrate) consagrar. **—devoted** (-ɪd) *adj.* dedicado; devoto; ferviente. **—devotee** (dɛv·ə'ti) *n.* devoto.

devotion (dɪ'vo·ʃən) *n.* **1,** (affection) devoción; dedicación. **2,** *pl.* (prayers) oraciones; preces; plegarias. **—devotional,** *adj.* devoto; piadoso.

devour (dɪ'vaur) *v.t.* devorar; destruir.

devout (dɪ'vaut) *adj.* **1,** (pious) devoto; piadoso. **2,** (heartfelt) sincero; cordial. **—devoutness,** *n.* devoción; piedad.

dew (djuː) *n.* rocío.

dewberry ('du,bɛr·i) *n.* zarza.

dewdrop ('dju,drap) *n.* gota de rocío.

dewy ('dju·i) *adj.* **1,** (moist) rociado. **2,** *fig.* (fresh) fresco; joven; hermoso.

dexterity (dɛk'stɛr·ə·ti) *n.* destreza; habilidad; **—dexterous** ('dɛks·tər·əs) *adj.* diestro; hábil.

dextrose ('dɛks·tros) *n.* dextrosa.

diabetes (,dai·ə'bi·tɪs) *n.* diabetes. **—diabetic** (-'bɛt·ɪk) *n. & adj.* diabético.

diabolic (,dai·ə'bal·ɪk) *adj.* diabólico; infernal; demoníaco. *También,* **diabolical.**

diacritical (,dai·ə'krɪt·ɪ·kəl) *adj.* diacrítico. **—diacritical mark,** signo diacrítico.

diadem ('dai·ə,dɛm) *n.* diadema.

diagnose (,dai·əg'nos) *v.t.* diagnosticar.

diagnosis (,dai·əg'no·sɪs) [*pl* -ses (-siz)] *n.* diagnosis; diagnóstico.

diagnostic (,dai·əg'nas·tɪk) *adj.* diagnóstico. **—diagnostician** (-nas'tɪʃ·ən) *n.* médico experto en diagnosticar.

diagonal (dai'æg·ə·nəl) *adj. & n.* diagonal.

diagram ('dai·ə,græm) *n.* diagrama. **—v.t.** esquematizar. **—diagrammatic** (-grə'mæt·ɪk) *adj.* diagramático.

dial ('dai·əl) *n.* **1,** (clock face) esfera. **2,** (sundial) cuadrante. **3,** (telephone device) disco. **4,** *radio; TV* (station finder) cuadrante; dial. **—v.t.** **1,** (use telephone device) marcar. **2,** *radio; TV* (tune in) sintonizar. **—dial tone,** señal para marcar.

dialect ('dai·ə,lɛkt) *n.* dialecto. **—dialectal** (-'lɛk·təl) *adj.* dialectal.

dialectic (,dai·ə'lɛk·tɪk) *adj.* [*también,* **dialectical**] dialéctico. **—n.** [*también,* **dialectics**] dialéctica.

dialectician (,dai·ə·lɛk'tɪʃ·ən) *n.* dialéctico.

dialogue *también,* **dialog** ('dai·ə,lɔg) *n.* diálogo.

dialysis (dai'æl·ə·sɪs) *n.* [*pl.* -ses (-siz)] diálisis.

diameter (dai'æm·ɪ·tər) *n.* diámetro. **—diametrical** (,dai·ə'mɛt·rɪ·kəl) *adj.* diametral.

diamond ('dai·mənd) *n.* **1,** (gem) diamante. **2,** (rhombus or lozenge [◇]) rombo; losange. **3,** (playing-card symbol), *in the French deck,* rombo; diamante; *in Amer.* carró; *in the Spanish deck,* oro. **4,** (baseball field) losange.

diapason (,dai·ə'pei·zən) *n.* diapasón.

diaper ('dai·pər) *n.* **1,** (infant's breech cloth) pañal. **2,** (pattern) adamasca. **3,** (patterned cloth) lienzo adamascado.

diaphanous (dai'æf·ə·nəs) *adj.* diáfano.

diaphragm ('dai·ə,fræm) *n.* diafragma.

diarrhea (dai·ə'ri·ə) *n.* diarrea.

diarrhetic (dai·ə'rɛt·ɪk) *adj.* diarreico. **—n.** purgante.

diary ('dai·ə·ri) *n.* diario.

Diaspora (dai'æs·pə·rə) *n.* Diáspora.

diastole (dai'æs·tə·li) *n.* diástole.
—**diastolic** (,dai·ə'stal·ık) *adj.*
diastólico.
diathermy ('dai·ə,θʌr·mi) *n.*
diatermia. —**diathermic** (-θʌr·mık)
adj. diatérmico.
diatom ('dai·ə·təm) *n.* diatomea.
diatonic (,dai·ə'tan·ık) *adj.*
diatónico.
diatribe ('dai·ə,traib) *n.* diatriba.
dice (dais) *n.* 1, (game) dados. 2, *pl.*
de **die.** —*v.i.* cortar en cubitos.
—*v.i.* jugar a los dados. —**dicey**
('dais·i) *adj., colloq.* peligroso;
arriesgado.
dichotomy (dai'kat·ə·mi) *n.* dicotomía.
dick (dık) *n., slang* detective.
dickens ('dık·ənz) *interj.* ¡diablo!
dicker ('dık·ər) *v.t. & i., colloq.*
regatear. —*n.* regateo.
dickey ('dık·i) *n.* 1, (child's bib)
babero; (shirt front) pechera. 2,
(bird) pajarito. 3, (backseat) asiento
trasero. 4, (driver's seat) asiento del
conductor.
dicta ('dık·tə) *n., pl. de* dictum.
Dictaphone ('dık·tə,fon) *n., T.N.*
dictáfono.
dictate ('dık·teit) *v.t. & i.* 1, (tell
what to write) dictar. 2, (decree;
command) ordenar; mandar; dictar.
—*n.* dictado; mandato. —**dictation**,
n. dictado.
dictator ('dık·tei·tər) *n.* dictador.
—**dictatorship**, *n.* dictadura.
dictatorial (dık·tə'tor·i·əl) *adj.*
dictatorial.
diction ('dık·ʃən) *n.* dicción.
dictionary ('dık·ʃə·nɛr·i) *n.*
diccionario.
dictum ('dık·təm) *n. [pl.* **-ta** (-tə)]
1, (order) dictamen; sentencia. 2,
(saying) dicho; máxima; aforismo.
did (dıd) *v., pret. de* do.
didactic (dai'dæk·tık) *adj.*
didáctico. —**didactics**, *n.* didáctica.
diddle ('dıd·əl) *v.t., colloq.* 1, (dawdle) perder el tiempo. 2, (swindle)
estafar; engañar.
didymium (dı'dım·i·əm) *n.*
didimio.
die (dai) *v.i.* [**died, dying**] 1, (cease
living) morir; fallecer. 2, *fig.* (come
to an end) acabarse; terminarse. 3,
[*usu.*, **die away** o **out**] (fade away)
desaparecer lentamente; morir poco
a poco. 4, (lose sparkle, as wine)
desvirtuarse. 5, *colloq.* (desire)
morirse. —*n.* 1, (engraving stamp)
troquel; plancha; matriz. 2, *sing. de*

dice, dado. 3, *mech.* (various tools)
tuerca; cojinete o hembra de terraja.
4, *archit.* (dado) cubo.
diehard ('dai·hard) *n. & adj.* intransigente.
dielectric (,dai·ə'lɛk·trık) *adj. &*
n. dieléctrico.
dieresis (dai'ɛr·ə·sıs) *n.* [*pl.* **-ses**
(-siz)] diéresis; crema.
die-stamp *v.t.* troquelar; acuñar.
diet ('dai·ət) *n.* 1, (food intake)
dieta; régimen. 2, (assembly) dieta.
—*v.i.* adietar; estar a dieta. —**put**
on a diet, poner a dieta.
dietary ('dai·ə·tɛr·i) *adj.* dietético.
dietetic (,dai·ə'tɛt·ık) *adj.* dietético. —**dietetics**, *n.* dietética.
dietician (,dai·ə'tıʃ·ən) *n.*
especialista en dietética.
differ ('dıf·ər) *v.i.* 1, [**differ from**]
(be dissimilar) diferir; no parecerse
a. 2, [**differ with**] (disagree) diferir
de; no estar de acuerdo; discutir.
difference ('dıf·ər·əns) *n.*
diferencia. —**what difference does**
it make?, ¿qué más da?
different ('dıf·ər·ənt) *adj.*
diferente; distinto.
differential (dıf·ə'rɛn·ʃəl) *adj. &*
n. diferencial.
differentiate (,dıf·ə'rɛn·ʃi,et) *v.t.*
diferenciar —*v.i.* diferenciarse.
—**differentiation**, *n.* diferenciación.
difficult ('dıf·ı·kəlt) *adj.* difícil.
difficulty ('dıf·ı,kʌl·ti) *n.* 1, (obstacle) dificultad. 2, *pl.* (troubles,
esp. economic) aprietos; apuros
económicos. —**be in difficulties**,
hallarse en un apuro.
diffidence ('dıf·ı·dəns) *n.*
apocamiento; vergüenza; timidez.
—**diffident**, *adj.* apocado;
vergonzoso; tímido.
diffract (dı'frækt) *v.t.* difractar; descomponer. —**diffraction**
(-'fræk·ʃən) *n.* difracción.
diffuse (dı'fjuz) *v.t.* difundir;
esparcir; derramar. —*v.i.* difundirse;
esparcirse; derramarse. —*adj.*
(-'fjus) 1, (scattered) difundido;
extendido. 2, (verbose) difuso;
prolijo.
diffusion (dı'fju·ʒən) *n.* difusión.
—**diffusive** (-sıv) *adj.* difusor.
dig (dıg) *v.t.* [**dug, digging**] 1, (excavate) cavar; excavar. 2, *colloq.*
(work hard) ahondar; trabajar
mucho. 3, *slang* (understand)
comprender. —*v.i.* 1, (excavate)
cavar. 2, *colloq.* (work hard) sudar
la gota gorda. 3, *mil.* (dig trenches)

abrir trincheras. **4,** [**dig through** o **into**] (penetrate) abrirse camino. —*n., colloq.* **1,** (hole) cava. **2,** (poke) empuje; empellón. **3,** *colloq.* (jeer) pulla; puya. —**dig in,** (entrench) atrincherar.

digest (dɪ'dʒɛst) *v.t.* **1,** (absorb) digerir. **2,** (assimilate) digerir; meditar. **3,** (epitomize) condensar. —*n.* ('dai·dʒɛst) compendio; resumen; *law* digesto. —**digestible** (dɪ'dʒɛs·tə·bəl) *adj.* digestible; digerible. —**digestion** (-'dʒɛs·tʃən) *n.* digestión. —**digestive,** *adj.* digestivo.

digger ('dɪg·ər) *n.* **1,** (person digging) excavador; cavador. **2,** (tool) azada; azadón. **3,** (machine) excavadora.

diggings ('dɪg·ɪŋz) *n.pl.* **1,** (excavations) excavaciones. **2,** *slang* (abode) domicilio; morado.

digit ('dɪdʒ·ɪt) *n.* **1,** (finger; toe) dedo. **2,** (number) dígito. —**digital,** *adj.* dígito; digital.

digitalis (dɪdʒ·ə'tæl·ɪs) *n., bot.; pharm.* digital.

dignify ('dɪg·nɪ,fai) *v.t.* dignificar; ennoblecer; honrar. —**dignified,** *adj.* digno; grave; noble.

dignitary ('dɪg·nɪ,tɛr·i) *n.* dignatario.

dignity ('dɪg·nə·ti) *n.* **1,** (worthiness) dignidad. **2,** (rank) ocupación; cargo. **3,** (stateliness) gravedad; nobleza.

digress (dɪ'grɛs) *v.i.* desviarse; divagar. —**digression** (-'grɛʃ·ən) *n.* digresión. —**digressive** (-'grɛs·ɪv) *adj.* digresivo.

dihedral (dai'hi,·drəl) *adj.* diedro.

dike (daik) *n.* dique; represa.

dilapidate (dɪ'læp·ə·deit) *v.t.* dilapidar. —*v.i.* arruinarse; desmantelarse. —**dilapidated,** *adj.* arruinado; destartalado.

dilapidation (dɪ,læp·ə'dei·ʃən) *n.* dilapidación; derroche.

dilate ('dai·leit) *v.t. & i.* dilatar; extender. —**dilation** [*también,* **dilatation** (,dɪl·ə'tei·ʃən)] *n.* dilatación. —**dilator,** *n.* dilatador.

dilatory ('dɪl·ə·tor·i) *adj.* dilatorio; tardo; lento; *law* dilatorio.

dilemma (dɪ'lɛm·ə) *n.* dilema; alternativa; disyuntiva.

dilettante (,dɪl·ə'tan·ti; -'tant) *n.* diletante; aficionado; entusiasta.

diligence ('dɪl·ɪ·dʒəns) *n.* diligencia. —**diligent,** *adj.* diligente.

dill (dɪl) *n.* eneldo.

dilly ('dɪl·i) *n., colloq.* curiosidad; persona o cosa extravagante.

dillydally ('dɪl·i'dæl·i) *v.i.* malgastar el tiempo.

dilute (dɪ'lut) *v.t.* diluir; desleír. —*adj.* diluido; desleído.

dilution (dɪ'lu·ʃən) *n.* dilución; desleimiento.

diluvial (dɪ'lu·vi·əl) *adj.* diluvial; diluviano.

dim (dɪm) *adj.* **1,** (almost dark) mortecino; difuso; débil. **2,** (vague) oscuro; confuso. **3,** (dull) tardo; torpe; lento. —*v.t.* [**dimmed, dimming**] amortiguar; oscurecer. —*v.i.* amortiguarse; oscurecerse.

dime (daim) *n., U.S.* moneda de 10 centavos.

dimension (dɪ'mɛn·ʃən) *n.* dimensión. —**dimensional,** *adj.* dimensional.

diminish (dɪ'mɪn·ɪʃ) *v.t. & i.* disminuir; rebajar.

diminuendo (dɪ,mɪn·ju'ɛn·do) *n., adj. & adv., mus.* diminuendo.

diminution (,dɪ·mɪ'nju·ʃən) *n.* disminución; diminución.

diminutive (dɪ'mɪn·ju·tɪv) *adj.* diminutivo; diminuto. —*n.* **1,** (small thing) cosa diminuta. **2,** *gram.* diminutivo.

dimmer ('dɪm·ər) *n.* reductor de luz.

dimness ('dɪm·nəs) *n.* oscuridad.

dimple ('dɪm·pəl) *n.* hoyuelo. —*v.i.* formarse hoyuelos.

dimwit ('dɪm·wɪt) *n., slang* lerdo; tonto.

din (dɪn) *n.* clamor; estrépito.

dine (dain) *v.i.* cenar; comer. —*v.t.* dar de comer; ofrecer una comida a.

diner ('dai·nər) *n.* **1,** (person who dines) comensal. **2,** (eating place) restaurante; café. **3,** *R.R.* coche-comedor; coche-restaurante.

dinette (dai'nɛt) *n.* comedor pequeño; conjunto de muebles para éste.

ding (dɪŋ) *n.* **1,** (sound) repique; sonido. **2,** *slang* (dent) abolladura —*v.t.* **1,** (clang) repicar; sonar. **2,** *slang* (repeat) insistir; repetir insistentemente. —*v.i., slang* (dent) abollar. —**ding dong** ('dɪŋ'dɑŋ) *n.* din-dán; tintín.

dingbat ('dɪŋ,bæt) *n., slang* loco; chiflado.

dinghy ('dɪŋ·gi) *n.* bote de remos.

dingy ('dɪn·dʒi) *adj.* deslucido; manchado. —**dinginess,** *n.* deslustre; suciedad.

dining room ('dai·nɪŋ) *n.* comedor.

dinky ('dɪŋ·ki) *adj.* diminuto; pequeño. —*n.* [*también,* **dinkey**] locomotora de maniobras.

dinner ('dɪn·ər) *n.* 1, (meal) cena; comida. 2, (banquet) banquete. —**dinner coat**, smoking. —**dinner napkin**, servilleta. —**dinner party**, convite.

dinosaur ('dai·nə,sor) *n.* dinosauro.

dint (dɪnt) *n.* 1, (dent) abolladura. 2, (power) fuerza. —**by dint of**, a fuerza de.

diocese ('dai·ə·sis) *n.* diócesis. —**diocesan** (dai'as·ɪ·sən) *adj.* diocesano.

diode ('dai·od) *n.* díodo.

diorama (,dai·ə'ræm·ə) *n.* diorama. —**dioramic,** *adj.* diorámico.

dioxide (dai'ak·said) *n.* dióxido.

dip (dɪp) *v.t.* [**dipped, dipping**] 1, (immerse) sumergir. 2, (lower and raise) subir y bajar rápidamente. 3, (scoop up) sacar. —*v.i.* 1, (plunge) sumergirse; zambullirse. 2, [*usu.,* **dip into**] (investigate) investigar; buscar; (be interested in) empeñarse en; interesarse en; (browse) hojear. 3, (bend down) inclinarse hacia abajo. 4, *fig.* (sink) hundirse; penetrar. 5, *geol.; mining* buzar. —*n.* 1, (immersion) inmersión; zambullida. 2, (downward slope) inclinación; declive; *aero.* bache. 3, (bath, to dye or disinfect) tinte. 4, *geol.; mining* buzamiento. —**dip the flag**, saludar con la bandera.

diphtheria (dɪf'θɪr·i·ə) *n.* difteria.

diphthong ('dɪf·θaŋ) *n.* diptongo.

diploma (dɪ'plo·mə) *n.* diploma.

diplomacy (dɪ'plo·mə·si) *n.* 1, (international relations) diplomacia. 2, (tact) tacto.

diplomat ('dɪp·lə·mæt) *n.* diplomático. —**diplomatic** (-'mæt·ɪk) *adj.* diplomático.

diplomatist (dɪ'plo·mə·tɪst) *n.* diplomático.

dipper ('dɪp·ər) *n.* 1, (ladle) cucharón; cazo; (of a machine) cuchara; pala. 2, *cap., astron.* Carro.

dippy ('dɪp·i) *adj., slang* loco; excéntrico.

dipsomania (,dɪp·sə'mei·ni·ə) *n.* dipsomanía. —**dipsomaniac** (-,æk) *n. & adj.* dipsomaníaco.

diptych ('dɪp·tɪk) *n.* díptico.

dire (dair) *adj.* horrible; horroroso;

lamentable. —**direful** (-fəl) *adj.* horrendo; deplorable.

direct (dɪ'rɛkt) *v.t.* 1, (aim) dirigir. 2, (guide) guiar; ordenar. 3, (command) mandar. —*adj.* 1, (straightforward) directo; franco; abierto. 2, (firsthand) personal; fidedigno.

direct current corriente continua.

direction (dɪ'rɛk·ʃən) *n.* 1, (relative position) dirección. 2, (regulation) orden; mandato. 3, *usu.pl.* (instruction) instrucción. —**directional,** *adj.* direccional.

directive (dɪ'rɛk·tɪv) *n.* directiva. —*adj.* directivo.

directly (dɪ'rɛkt·li) *adv.* 1, (without deviating) derecho. 2, (immediately) en seguida.

direct object *gram.* complemento directo.

director (dɪ'rɛk·tər) *n.* director. —**directorate** (-ət) [*también,* **directorship**] *n.* dirección; directorio.

directory (dɪ'rɛk·tə·ri) *n.* 1, (list of names, etc.) directorio. 2, (telephone book) guía telefónica. 3, *cap., hist.* Directorio.

dirge (dʌrdʒ) *n.* 1, (sad music or poem) endecha. 2, *eccles.* (hymn) canto fúnebre; (mass) oficio de difuntos.

dirigible ('dɪr·ɪ·dʒə·bəl) *adj. & n.* dirigible.

dirt (dʌrt) *n.* 1, (dust) polvo; (mud) lodo; barro. 2, (earth; soil) tierra; suelo; terreno. 3, (filth) suciedad; porquería. 4, *slang* (gossip) chisme. —*adj.* de tierra. —**dirt cheap,** *colloq.* muy barato.

dirtiness ('dʌr·ti·nəs) *n.* 1, (uncleanliness) suciedad; porquería. 2, (baseness) bajeza; vileza.

dirty ('dʌr·ti) *adj.* 1, (soiled) enlodado; sucio; con polvo. 2, (base) bajo; vil; menospreciable. —*v.t.* ensuciar. —**dirty look,** *slang* mirada despectiva.

disable (dɪs'ei·bəl) *v.t.* inhabilitar; incapacitar. —**disability** (dɪs·ə'bɪl·ə·ti) *n.* incapacidad; impedimento.

disabuse (dɪs·ə'bjuːz) *v.t.* desengañar.

disaccord (,dɪs·ə'kord) *n.* desacuerdo. —*v.i.* estar en desacuerdo.

disadvantage (,dɪs·əd'væn·tɪdʒ) *n.* 1, (unfavorable condition) desventaja. 2, (drawback) detrimento; menoscabo. —*v.t.* perjudicar. —**dis-**

advantageous (ˌdɪs·æd·væn'tei·dʒəs) adj. desventajoso.

disaffect (dɪs·ə'fɛkt) v.t. enemistar; indisponer. —**disaffection** (-'fɛk·ʃən) n. desafección; desafecto; descontento.

disaffirm (dɪs·ə'fʌrm) v.t. negar; contradecir; law impugnar; anular.

disagree (dɪs·ə'griː) v.i. 1, (have different opinions) no estar de acuerdo; diferir; disentir. 2, (be incompatible or unsuitable) no sentar bien (a); no ir bien (con).

disagreeable (ˌdɪs·ə'griː·ə·bəl) adj. desagradable.

disagreement (ˌdɪs·ə'griː·mənt) n. 1, (difference of opinion) desacuerdo; disensión. 2, (quarrel) contienda; altercado. 3, (discrepancy) discrepancia; diferencia.

disallow (dɪs·ə'lau) v.t. 1, (disapprove) desaprobar. 2, (deny; reject) denegar; rechazar.

disappear (dɪs·ə'pɪr) v.i. desaparecer. —**disappearance**, n. desaparición.

disappoint (dɪs·ə'pɔint) v.t. 1, (fail to satisfy) defraudar; decepcionar; desilusionar. 2, (thwart) chasquear; frustrar; desbaratar. —**disappointing**, adj. desilusionante. —**disappointment**, n. decepción; desilusión; chasco.

disapprove (dɪs·ə'pruv) v.t. & i. desaprobar. —**disapproval**, n. desaprobación.

disarm (dɪs'arm) v.t. & i. desarmar. —**disarming**, adj. conciliador; amistoso.

disarmament (dɪs'ar·mə·mənt) n. desarme.

disarrange (dɪs·ə'reindʒ) v.t. desarreglar; descomponer.

disarray (dɪs·ə'rei) v.t. 1, (disrobe) desnudar; desvestir. 2, (rout) derrotar; desordenar. —n. 1, (confusion) desorden; desarreglo; confusión. 2, (slovenly dress) desatavío; descompostura.

disassemble (dɪs·ə'sɛm·bəl) v.t. desarmar; desmontar; desacoplar.

disassociate (dɪs·ə'so·si·eit; -ʃi·eit) v.t. disociar; desunir; separar.

disaster (dɪ'zæs·tər) n. desastre. —**disastrous** (-trəs) adj. desastroso.

disavow (dɪs·ə'vau) v.t. 1, (deny approval of) desautorizar; repudiar. 2, (disown) negar; repudiar. 3, (deny knowledge of) desconocer; ignorar. —**disavowal**, n. negación; desconocimiento; repudiación.

disband (dɪs'bænd) v.t. 1, (dissolve, as a group) disolver. 2, mil. (dismiss) licenciar. —v.i. desbandarse. —**disbandment**, n. desbandada; disolución; mil. licenciamiento.

disbar (dɪs'bar) v.t. expulsar de la abogacía. —**disbarment**, n. expulsión de la abogacía.

disbelief (dɪs·bə'lif) n. incredulidad.

disbelieve (dɪs·bə'liːv) v.t. & i. descreer; dudar.

disburse (dɪs'bʌrs) v.t. desembolsar. —**disbursement**, n. desembolso.

disc (dɪsk) n. = **disk**.

discard (dɪs'kard) v.t. & i. descartar. —n. ('dɪs·kard) descarte.

discern (dɪ'sʌrn) v.t. & i. discernir; distinguir; percibir. —**discernible**, adj. discernible; perceptible. —**discerning**, adj. perspicaz; sagaz. —**discernment**, n. discernimiento; percepción.

discharge (dɪs'tʃardʒ) n. 1, (act of unloading; shooting) descarga. 2, (payment, as of a debt) descargo; cumplimiento. 3, (release, as of a prisoner) liberación; absolución; (as of a defendant) exoneración; (as of a soldier) licenciamiento; licencia; (as of a patient) alta; (as from a duty) descargo. 4, (dismissal) despedida; remoción. 5, (emission) derrame. 6, (performance) desempeño; cumplimiento. 7, elect. descarga. —v.t. 1, (unload) descargar. 2, (emit, as water) desaguar; (suppurate) arrojar; echar; emitir. 3, (release) libertar; absolver; (as from suspicion) exonerar; (as from obligations) eximir; (as from the army) licenciar; (as a patient) dar de alta. 4, (dismiss) despedir; echar. 5, (perform) desempeñar; cumplir. 6, (fire) disparar; descargar. 7, (pay a debt) saldar; cancelar. 8, elect. descargar. —v.i. descargar; descargarse.

disciple (dɪ'sai·pəl) n. discípulo.

discipline ('dɪs·ə·plɪn) n. 1, (training; obedience) disciplina. 2, (punishment) disciplina; corrección; castigo. —v.t. 1, (train) disciplinar. 2, (punish) castigar; disciplinar. —**disciplinarian** (-plɪ'nɛr·i·ən) n. ordenancista. —adj. disciplinario. —**disciplinary**, adj. disciplinario.

disclaim (dɪs'kleim) *v.t.* **1**, (disown) renunciar; rehusar. **2**, (refuse to acknowledge) rechazar; repudiar. **3**, (deny) negar. **4**, *law* renunciar. —**disclaimer,** *n.* renuncia; rechazo; repudio.

disclose (dɪs'kloːz) *v.t.* descubrir; revelar; exponer. —**disclosure** (-'kloː·ʒər) *n.* revelación; descubrimiento.

discolor (dɪs'kʌl·ər) *v.t.* descolorar; desteñir. —*v.i.* descolorarse; desteñirse. —**discoloration,** *n.* decoloración.

discomfit (dɪs'kʌm·fɪt) *v.t.* frustrar; desconcertar. —**discomfiture** (-fɪ·tʃər) *n.* desconcierto; frustración.

discomfort (dɪs'kʌm·fərt) *n.* incomodidad; malestar. —*v.t.* incomodar; molestar.

discompose (ˌdɪs·kʌm'poːz) *v.t.* descomponer; desconcertar. —**discomposure** (-'po·ʒər) *n.* descomposición; desconcierto.

disconcert (dɪs·kən'sʌrt) *v.t.* **1**, (confuse) desconcertar; confundir; perturbar. **2**, (throw into disorder) desconcertar; desordenar.

disconnect (dɪs·kə'nɛkt) *v.t.* desconectar; desunir; desenchufar.

disconsolate (dɪs'kan·sə·lət) *adj.* desconsolado; inconsolable.

discontent (dɪs·kən'tɛnt) *n.* descontento. —*v.t.* descontentar. —**discontented,** *adj.* descontento.

discontinue (dɪs·kən'tɪn·ju) *v.t. & i.* descontinuar o discontinuar; interrumpir. —**discontinuation,** *n.* descontinuación. —**discontinuance,** *n.* descontinuación. —**discontinuous,** *adj.* discontinuo; interrumpido.

discontinuity (dɪsˌkan·tə'nju·ə·ti) *n.* discontinuidad.

discord ('dɪs'kord) *n.* **1**, (disagreement) desacuerdo; discordia. **2**, *mus.* discordancia; disonancia.

discordant (dɪs'kor·dənt) *adj.* discordante; discorde; desacorde; *mus.* disonante. —**discordance,** *n.* discordancia; discordia; desacuerdo; *mus.* disonancia.

discotheque ('dɪs·kə̩tɛk) *n.* discoteca.

discount ('dɪs'kaunt) *v.t.* **1**, (deduct) descontar. **2**, (disregard) considerar exagerado; desestimar. **3**, *comm.* descontar; deducir; rebajar. —*n.* descuento; rebaja.

discountenance (dɪs'kaun·tə·nəns) *v.t.* **1**, (abash) avergonzar;

humillar. **2**, (discourage) desaprobar; desanimar.

discourage (dɪs'kʌr·ɪdʒ) *v.t.* **1**, (lessen one's hopes) desanimar; desalentar. **2**, (urge to refrain) disuadir. **3**, (try to prevent) oponerse a. —**discouraging,** *adj.* desalentador.

discouragement (dɪs'kʌr·ɪdʒ·mənt) *n.* **1**, (dejection) desánimo; desaliento. **2**, (dissuasion) disuasión. **3**, (hindrance) oposición.

discourse ('dɪs·kors) *n.* discurso. —*v.i.* (dɪs'kors) discurrir.

discourteous (dɪs'kʌr·ti·əs) *adj.* descortés; mal educado. —**discourtesy** (-tə·si) *n.* descortesía.

discover (dɪs'kʌv·ər) *v.t.* descubrir. —**discoverer,** *n.* descubridor. —**discovery,** *n.* descubrimiento.

discredit (dɪs'krɛd·ɪt) *v.t.* **1**, (destroy the reputation of) desacreditar. **2**, (mistrust) descreer. —*n.* descrédito; deshonra. —**discreditable,** *adj.* deshonroso; vergonzoso.

discreet (dɪs'krit) *adj.* discreto; comedido. —**discreetness,** *n.* discreción; comedimiento.

discrepancy (dɪs'krɛp·ən·si) *n.* discrepancia; contradicción.

discrete (dɪs'krit) *adj.* distinto; descontinuo; discreto. —**discreteness,** *n.* distinción.

discretion (dɪs'krɛʃ·ən) *n.* **1**, (prudence) discreción. **2**, (power to decide) albedrío. —**discretionary** (-ə·nɛr·i) *adj.* discrecional.

discriminate (dɪs'krɪm·ɪ·neit) *v.t.* distinguir; separar; discriminar. —*v.i.* diferenciarse. —**discriminating,** *adj.* discerniente; de buen gusto. —**discrimination,** *n.* distinción; diferencia; discriminación. —**discriminative** (-ˌne·trv); **discriminatory** (-nə̩tor·i) *adj.* injusto; parcial.

discursive (dɪs'kʌr·sɪv) *adj.* digresivo; divagante.

discus ('dɪs·kəs) *n.* disco.

discuss (dɪs'kʌs) *v.t.* discutir; debatir; tratar de. —**discussion** (-'kʌʃ·ən) *n.* discusión.

disdain (dɪs'dein) *v.t. & i.* desdeñar. —*n.* desdén. —**disdainful** (-fəl) *adj.* desdeñoso.

disease (dɪ'ziːz) *n.* enfermedad. —*v.t.* enfermar.

disembark (ˌdɪs·ɛm'bark) *v.i.* desembarcar.

disembarrass (dɪs·əm'bær·əs) *v.t.* desembarazar.

disembody (dɪs·ɛm'ba·di) *v.t.*
libertar; desencarnar.
disembowel (ˌdɪs·ɛm'bau·əl) *v.t.*
destripar; desentrañar.
disenchant (dɪs·ɛn'tʃænt) *v.t.*
desencantar; desilusionar. —**disenchantment,** *n.* desencantamiento;
desilusión.
disencumber (dɪs·ɛn'kʌm·bər)
v.t. descombrar; liberar. —**disencumbrance** (-brəns) *n.* descombro.
disenfranchise (ˌdɪs·ən'fræn·
tʃaɪz) *v.t.* = **disfranchise**.
disengage (ˌdɪs·ɛn'geidʒ) *v.t.* 1,
(free) librar; soltar. 2, (detach)
desunir. 3, (disentangle) desenredar.
4, *mech.* desembragar; desengranar.
disentangle (ˌdɪs·ɛn'tæŋ·gəl) *v.t.*
desenredar. —**disentanglement,** *n.*
desenredo.
disestablish (ˌdɪs·ɛs'tæb·lɪʃ) *v.t.*
separar (la Iglesia) del Estado.
disfavor (dɪs'fei·vər) *v.t.*
desfavorecer; desairar. —*n.* disfavor; desgracia.
disfigure (dɪs'fɪg·jər) *v.t.* desfigurar. —**disfigurement,** *n.* desfiguración; desfiguramiento.
disfranchise (dɪs'fræn·tʃaɪz) *v.t.*
privar de derechos (de ciudadanía o
de franquicia).
disgorge (dɪs'gordʒ) *v.t.* arrojar;
vomitar. —*v.i.* vaciarse. —**dis-
gorgement,** *n.* vómito.
disgrace (dɪs'greis) *n.* desgracia;
deshonra. —*v.t.* deshonrar. —**disgraceful** (-fəl) *adj.* deshonroso;
lamentable.
disgruntled (dɪs'grʌn·təld) *adj.*
disgustado; descontento; enfadado.
—**disgruntle,** *v.t.* disgustar;
descontentar. —**disgruntlement,** *n.*
disgusto; enfado; descontento.
disguise (dɪs'gaiz) *v.t.* 1, (mask)
disfrazar. 2, (hide) encubrir; ocultar.
3, (obscure) desfigurar. —*n.* disfraz;
falsa apariencia.
disgust (dɪs'gʌst) *n.* asco; repugnancia. —*v.t.* asquear; repugnar.
—**disgusting,** *adj.* repugnante;
asqueroso.
dish (dɪʃ) *n.* 1, (plate) plato. 2, *pl.*
(set of dishes) vajilla. —*v.t.* 1,
(serve) servir. 2, (shape like a dish)
formar una concavidad en. —**dish
out,** 1, [*también,* **dish up**] (serve)
servir. 2, *slang* (administer; inflict)
echar (una afrenta); pegar (un
castigo) —**do the dishes,** lavar o
fregar los platos.
disharmony (dɪs'har·mə·ni) *n.* 1,

(discord) discordancia; discordia. 2,
mus. disonancia.
dishcloth ('dɪʃˌklɔθ) *n.* paño de
cocina.
dishearten (dɪs'har·tən) *v.t.*
descorazonar; desanimar.
dishevel (dɪ'ʃɛv·əl) *v.t.*
desmelenar; desgreñar. —**dishevel-
ment,** *n.* desmelenamiento.
dishonest (dɪs'an·əst) *adj.*
fraudulento; engañador; deshonesto;
ímprobo. —**dishonesty,** *n.*
deshonestidad; improbidad.
dishonor (dɪs'an·ər) *v.t.* 1, (shame)
deshonrar. 2, *comm.* (refuse to pay)
no aceptar; no pagar. —*n.* deshonra;
deshonor.
dishonorable (dɪs'an·ər·ə·bəl)
adj. 1, (not honorable) deshonoroso;
vergonzoso. 2, (disgraceful) des-
honrado.
dishpan ('dɪʃˌpæn) *n.* paila para
lavar platos.
dishtowel ('dɪʃˌtau·əl) *n.* paño de
secar; albero.
dishwasher ('dɪʃˌwɔʃ·ər) *n.* 1,
(person) lavaplatos. 2, (machine)
lavadora de platos; máquina de
lavar platos.
dishwater ('dɪʃˌwɔ·tər) *n.* agua de
cocina.
disillusion (dɪs·ɪ'lu·ʒən) *n.*
desilusión; desencantamiento. —*v.t.*
desilusionar; desencantar. —**disillusionment,** *n.* desilusión.
disinclination (dɪsˌɪn·klɪ'nei·
ʃən) *n.* mala gana; repugnancia;
aversión.
disincline (ˌdɪs·ɪn'klain) *v.t.*
desinclinar. —*v.i.* desinclinarse.
disinfect (dɪs·ɪn'fɛkt) *v.t.*
desinfectar. —**disinfectant,** *n.* &
adj. desinfectante. —**disinfection,**
(-'fɛk·ʃən) *n.* desinfección.
disingenuous (dɪs·ɪn'dʒɛn·ju·əs)
adj. falso; disimulado. —**disingen-
uousness,** *n.* disimulación; mala fe.
disinherit (dɪs·ɪn'hɛr·ɪt) *v.t.*
desheredar. —**disinheritance,** *n.*
desheredación.
disintegrate (dɪs'ɪn·tə·greit) *v.t.*
desintegrar. —*v.i.* desintegrarse.
—**disintegration,** *n.* desintegración.
disinter (ˌdɪs·ɪn'tʌr) *v.t.* [**-interred,
-terring**] 1, (dig up) desenterrar. 2,
fig. (bring to light) descubrir.
—**disinterment,** *n.* desenterramiento.
disinterest (dɪs'ɪn·tə·rist) *n.*
desinterés. —**disinterested** (-res·
tɪd) *adj.* desinteresado; imparcial.

disjoin (dıs'dʒɔin) *v.t.* desunir; separar.

disjoint (dıs'dʒɔint) *v.t.* **1,** (dislocate) dislocar; desarticular. **2,** (dismember) descoyuntar; desmembrar.

disjointed (dıs'dʒɔin·tıd) *adj.* **1,** (dislocated) descoyuntado; dislocado. **2,** (disconnected) desarticulado.

disjunction (dıs'dʒʌŋk·ʃən) *n.* disyunción.

disjunctive (dıs'dʒʌŋk·tıv) *adj.* disyuntivo. —*n.* **1,** *gram.* conjunción disyuntiva. **2,** *logic* disyuntiva.

disk también, **disc** (dısk) *n.* disco.

diskette (dıs'kɛt) *n.* disquete; disco flexible.

disk jockey radiolocutor (que toca discos).

dislike (dıs'laik) *v.t.* disgustar; no gustar de. —*n.* aversión; antipatía. —**dislikable,** *adj.* antipático.

dislocate (dıs·lo'keit) *v.t.* dislocar. —**dislocation,** *n.* dislocación.

dislodge (dıs'ladʒ) *v.t.* desalojar. —**dislodgment,** *n.* desalojamiento.

disloyal (dıs'lɔi·əl) *adj.* desleal. —**disloyalty** (-ti) *n.* deslealtad.

dismal ('dız·məl) *adj.* **1,** (miserable) triste; oscuro; miserable. **2,** (dreary) tenebroso. —**dismalness,** *n.* tristeza; melancolía.

dismantle (dıs'mæn·təl) *v.t.* desmantelar. —**dismantlement,** *n.* desmantelamiento.

dismay (dıs'mei) *v.t.* **1,** (cause unexpected alarm) consternar; desanimar. **2,** (frighten) espantar. —*n.* miedo; desánimo; consternación.

dismember (dıs'mɛm·bər) *v.t.* desmembrar. —**dismemberment,** *n.* desmembramiento.

dismiss (dıs'mıs) *v.t.* **1,** (send away) despedir. **2,** (order or permit to depart) autorizar para marcharse. **3,** (remove from office) destituir. **4,** (discard) descartar. **5,** (put out of mind) echar en olvido. **6,** *law* (discontinue; reject) rechazar.

dismissal (dıs'mıs·əl) *n.* **1,** (act of dismissing) despido; despedida. **2,** (order to depart) autorización; permiso. **3,** (removal from office) destitución; deposición. **4,** *law* rechazamiento. **5,** *mil.* licenciamiento.

dismount (dıs'maunt) *v.t. & i.* desmontar. —**dismountable,** *adj.* desmontable.

disobedience (dıs·ə'bi·di·əns) *n.* desobediencia. —**disobedient,** *adj.* desobediente.

disobey (dıs·ə'bei) *v.t. & i.* desobedecer.

disoblige (,dıs·ə'blaidʒ) *v.t.* desobligar.

disorder (dıs'or·dər) *n.* **1,** (disarray) desorden; confusión. **2,** (riot) alboroto; tumulto. **3,** (irregularity) desarreglo; irregularidad. **4,** (disease) enfermedad; (mental) enajenación mental. —*v.t.* desordenar; revolver; desarreglar. —**disordered** (-dərd) *adj.* desordenado; desarreglado; revuelto.

disorderly (dıs'or·dər·li) *adj.* **1,** (irregular; illegal) desordenado. **2,** (untidy) desarreglado. **3,** (unruly) violento; turbulento. **4,** (immoral) inmoral; escandaloso. —**disorderly conduct,** perturbación del orden público; *Amer.* conducta escandalosa. —**disorderly house,** burdel.

disorganize (dıs'or·gə,naiz) *v.t.* desorganizar. —**disorganization** (-nı'zei·ʃən) *n.* desorganización.

disorient (dıs'or·i·ɛnt) *v.t.* [también, **disorientate**] desorientar. —**disorientation,** *n.* desorientación.

disown (dıs'on) *v.t.* repudiar; desconocer; negar.

disparage (dıs'pær·ıdʒ) *v.t.* desacreditar. —**disparagement,** *n.* descrédito; infamia; desprecio.

disparate ('dıs·pə·rət) *adj.* disparejo; dispar. —**disparity** (-'pær·ə·ti) *n.* disparidad.

dispassion (dıs'pæʃ·ən) *n.,* desapasionamiento; imparcialidad. —**dispassionate** (-ət) *adj.* desapasionado; imparcial.

dispatch también, **despatch** (dıs'pætʃ) *v.t.* **1,** (send off or away) despachar; expedir; remitir. **2,** (transact) despachar; apresurar. **3,** (kill) concluir; rematar; acabar. —*n.* **1,** (sending away) despacho; envío; expedición. **2,** (message) despacho; parte; comunicación. **3,** (speed) prontitud; celeridad. —**dispatcher,** *n.* despachador.

dispel (dıs'pɛl) *v.t.* [**dispelled, -pelling**] hacer desaparecer.

dispensable (dıs'pɛn·sə·bəl) *adj.* dispensable.

dispensary (dıs'pɛns·ər·i) *n.* dispensario.

dispensation (dıs·pən'sei·ʃən) *n.* **1,** (distribution) dispensación. **2,** *law; eccles.* (release) dispensa. **3,**

(divine act) decreto o designio divino.

dispense (dɪsˈpɛns) *v.t.* **1,** (distribute) dispensar; distribuir. **2,** (administer) administrar. **3,** (excuse) eximir. —**dispenser,** *n.* dispensador. —**dispense with,** pasar sin; hacer caso omiso de.

disperse (dɪsˈpʌrs) *v.t.* **1,** (scatter) dispersar; difundir. **2,** (cause to vanish) disipar. **3,** *opt.* descomponer. —*v.i.* desbandarse. —**dispersion** (-ˈpʌrˈʒən) *n.* dispersión.

dispirit (dɪsˈpɪrˈɪt) *v.t.* desanimar; desalentar.

displace (dɪsˈpleis) *v.t.* **1,** (put out) desplazar; **2,** (replace) reemplazar. **3,** (remove from office) destituir. —**displaced person,** persona sin hogar.

displacement (dɪsˈpleisˈmənt) *n.* **1,** (dislocation) desalojamiento; mudanza. **2,** (removal) destitución. **3,** (weight or volume displaced) desplazamiento. **4,** *chem.* (filtration) coladura. **5,** *geol.* (slide) falla.

display (dɪsˈplei) *v.t.* **1,** (spread out) desplegar; abrir. **2,** (show) mostrar; exhibir. **3,** (show off) ostentar. —*v.i.* desplegarse; exhibirse. —*n.* **1,** (array) despliegue; presentación. **2,** (exhibition) exposición; exhibición. **3,** (ostentatious show) espectáculo; manifestación. **4,** *mil.* (parade) parada. —**display the flag,** enarbolar la bandera.

displease (dɪsˈpliːz) *v.t.* desplacer; desagradar; disgustar. —**displeasure** (-ˈplɛʒˈər) *n.* desplacer; desagrado; disgusto.

disport (dɪsˈport) *v.i.* divertirse; juguetear.

disposable (dɪsˈpoˈzəˈbəl) *adj.* **1,** (available) disponible. **2,** (expendable) gastable.

disposal (dɪsˈpozˈəl) *n.* **1,** (arrangement) disposición; posición; arreglo. **2,** (settlement) ajuste; arreglo. **3,** *comm.* (transfer) venta; distribución. **4,** (bestowal) cesión; donación. —**at one's disposal,** a la disposición de uno. —**have at one's disposal,** disponer de; poder disponer de.

dispose (dɪsˈpoz) *v.t.* **1,** (arrange) disponer; componer; arreglar. **2,** (regulate) decidir; mandar. **3,** (make willing) inducir; mover. —**dispose of, 1,** (get rid of) deshacerse; disponer de. **2,** (con-

trol) disponer de. **3,** (pass on, as by gift or sale) traspasar; ceder.

disposition (dɪsˈpəˈzɪʃˈən) *n.* **1,** (arrangement) disposición; orden. **2,** settlement) arreglo; acuerdo. **3,** (innate temper) natural; índole; genio. **4,** (tendency) propensión; disposición; tendencia.

dispossess (dɪsˈpəˈzɛs) *v.t.* desposeer; desalojar; *law* desahuciar. —**dispossession** (-ˈzɛʃˈən) *n.* desposeimiento; *law* desahucio.

disproof (dɪsˈpruf) *n.* refutación.

disproportion (dɪsˈprəˈporˈʃən) *n.* desproporción; disparidad. —*v.t.* desproporcionar. —**disproportionate** (-ət) *adj.* desproporcionado.

disprove (dɪsˈpruv) *v.t.* refutar.

disputation (ˌdɪsˈpjuˈteiˈʃən) *n.* disputa; debate. —**disputatious** (-ʃəs) *adj.* disputador.

dispute (dɪsˈpjut) *v.t. & i.* disputar; argüir. —*n.* disputa. —**disputable,** *adj.* disputable. —**disputant** (ˈdɪsˈpjuˈtənt) *n. & adj.* disputador.

disqualify (dɪsˈkwalˈɪˌfai) *v.t.* descalificar. —**disqualification** (-frˈkeiˈʃən) *n.* descalificación.

disquiet (dɪsˈkwaiˈət) *v.t.* inquietar; desasoegar. —*n.* [*también,* **disquietude** (-əˈtud)] inquietud; desasosiego.

disquisition (dɪsˈkwɪˈzɪʃˈən) *n.* disquisición.

disregard (ˌdɪsˈrɪˈgard) *v.t.* **1,** (ignore) pasar por alto. **2,** (disdain) desairar; desatender. —*n.* omisión; desaire. —**disregardful,** *adj.* desatento; negligente.

disrepair (ˌdɪsˈrɪˈpeːr) *n.* desconcierto; estado destartalado.

disrepute (ˌdɪsˈrɪˈpjut) *n.* descrédito; mala fama. —**disreputable** (dɪsˈrɛpˈjəˈtəˈbəl) *adj.* desacreditado; deshonroso.

disrespect (ˌdɪsˈrɪˈspɛkt) *v.t.* desacatar. —*n.* desacato. —**disrespectful** (-fəl) *adj.* irrespetuoso.

disrobe (dɪsˈrozb) *v.t.* desnudar; desvestir. —*v.i.* desnudarse; desvestirse.

disrupt (dɪsˈrʌpt) *v.t. & i.* romper; desbaratar.

disruption (dɪsˈrʌpˈʃən) *n.* **1,** (break-up) rompimiento; ruptura; separación. **2,** (turmoil) desorganización. **3,** *elect.* interrupción.

disruptive (dɪsˈrʌpˈtiv) *adj.* **1,** (destructive) rompedor. **2,** (disturbing) desorganizador. **3,** *elect.* disruptivo.

dissatisfy (dɪs'sæt·ɪs,fai) v.t. desagradar; descontentar. —**dissatisfaction** (-'fæk·ʃən) n. desagrado; descontento.

dissect (dɪ'sɛkt) v.t. **1,** (divide) disecar. **2,** fig. (analyze) analizar.

dissection (dɪ'sɛk·ʃən) n. **1,** (division) disección; anat. anatomía. **2,** (analysis) análisis.

dissector (dɪ'sɛk·tər) n. disector.

dissemble (dɪ'sɛm·bəl) v.t. & i. disimular; encubrir; fingir. —**dissemblance** (-bləns) n. disimulo; fingimiento.

disseminate (dɪ'sɛm·ɪ·neit) v.t. diseminar. —**dissemination,** n. diseminación.

dissent (dɪ'sɛnt) v.i. disentir. —n. disensión; desavenencia. —**dissenter,** n. disidente. —**dissension** (-'sɛn·ʃən) n. disensión.

dissertation (,dɪs·ər'tei·ʃən) n. disertación.

disservice (dɪs'sʌr·vɪs) n. deservicio.

dissidence ('dɪs·ɪ·dəns) n. disidencia. —**dissident,** n. & adj. disidente.

dissimilar (dɪ'sɪm·ɪ·lər) adj. disímil; disparejo; diferente. —**dissimilarity** (-'lær·ə·ti) n. disimilitud; disparidad.

dissimilate (dɪ'sɪm·ə,leit) v.t. disimilar. —v.i. disimilarse. —**dissimilation,** n. disimilación.

dissimilitude (,dɪs·sɪ'mɪl·ɪ·tud) n. disimilitud; disparidad.

dissimulate (dɪ'sɪm·ju,leit) v.t. & i. disimular. —**dissimulation,** n. disimulación; disimulo.

dissipate ('dɪs·ɪ·peit) v.t. disipar. —v.i. disiparse; desvanecerse. —**dissipation,** n. disipación.

dissociate (dɪ'so·ʃi·eit) v.t. disociar; separar. —**dissociation,** n. disociación.

dissolute ('dɪs·ə·lut) adj. disoluto; depravado; relajado. —**dissoluteness,** n. disipación; relajación.

dissolution (,dɪs·ə'lu·ʃən) n. disolución.

dissolve (dɪ'salv) v.t. **1,** (melt; terminate) disolver. **2,** law (revoke) anular; revocar. **3,** photog. (fade out) disolver; mezclar. —v.i. disolverse. —**dissoluble,** adj. disoluble. —**dissolvent,** adj. & n. disolvente.

dissonance ('dɪs·ə·nəns) n. **1,** (disharmony) disonancia. **2,** (discord) discordia; desacuerdo. —**dissonant,** adj. disonante.

dissuade (dɪ'sweid) v.t. disuadir. —**dissuasion** (-'swei·ʒən) n. disuasión. —**dissuasive** (-sɪv) adj. disuasivo.

dissymmetry (dɪs'sɪm·ə·tri) n. disimetría. —**dissymmetrical** (,dɪs·ɪ'mɛt·rɪ·kəl) adj. disimétrico.

distaff ('dɪs·tæf) n. **1,** (rod for flax) rueca. **2,** (woman's work) labores femeninas. **3,** (the female sex) el sexo femenino. —**distaff side,** lado materno.

distance ('dɪs·təns) n. **1,** (intervening space) distancia. **2,** (remoteness) lontananza. **3,** mus. (interval) intervalo. **4,** fig. (haughtiness) esquivez. —**at a distance,** a lo lejos. —**from a distance,** desde lejos. —**keep at a distance,** tratar con indiferencia; mantener a distancia. —**keep one's distance,** mantenerse a distancia; mantenerse en su lugar.

distant ('dɪs·tənt) adj. **1,** (remote) distante; lejano; remoto. **2,** (cold; indifferent) esquivo; reservado; frío.

distaste (dɪs'teist) n. **1,** (dislike) disgusto. **2,** (aversion) antipatía; aversión. —**distasteful,** adj. desagradable.

distemper (dɪs'tɛm·pər) n. **1,** (bad humor) destemplanza. **2,** vet. moquillo. **3,** (disorder) alboroto; tumulto. **4,** paint. temple. —v.t. **1,** (disorder) destemplar; desconcertar; desordenar. **2,** paint. pintar al temple.

distend (dɪs'tɛnd) v.t. distender; dilatar. —v.i. distenderse; inflamarse. —**distensible,** adj. dilatable; distensible. —**distention; distension** (-'tɛn·ʃən) n. distensión.

distill (dɪs'tɪl) v.t. & i. destilar. —**distillate** ('dɪs·tɪ,leit) n. destilado.

distillation (,dɪs·tɪ'lei·ʃən) n. destilación. —**fractional distillation,** destilación fraccionada.

distillery (dɪs'tɪl·ə·ri) n. destilería.

distinct (dɪs'tɪŋkt) adj. **1,** (different) distinto; diferente. **2,** (well-defined) claro; preciso. **3,** (unmistakable) inequívoco; indudable. —**distinctness,** n. distinción; claridad.

distinction (dɪs'tɪŋk·ʃən) n. **1,** (differentiation); characteristic) diferencia; distintivo. **2,** (honor) distinción.

distinctive (dɪs'tɪŋk·tɪv) adj. **1,**

(different) distintivo; diferente. **2,** (characteristic) característico.

distinctiveness (dɪsˈtɪŋk·tɪv·nəs) *n.* **1,** (difference) diferencia. **2,** (characteristic quality) característica.

distinguish (dɪsˈtɪŋ·gwɪʃ) *v.t.* **1,** (mark; recognize) distinguir; diferenciar. **2,** (discern) discernir; distinguir. **3,** (honor) distinguir; honrar. —*v.i.* [*usu. seg. de* between o among] distinguir; diferenciar. —*v.r.* distinguirse; destacarse. —**distinguishable,** *adj.* distinguible; destacable. —**distinguished,** *adj.* distinguido; destacado; eminente.

distort (dɪsˈtɔrt) *v.t.* **1,** (twist) retorcer; distorsionar. **2,** (falsify) falsear; pervertir. —**distortion** (-ˈtɔr·ʃən) *n.* distorsión; falseamiento.

distract (dɪsˈtrækt) *v.t.* **1,** (divert) distraer; interrumpir. **2,** (bewilder) aturullar; alborotar. **3,** (derange) enloquecer.

distracted (dɪsˈtræk·tɪd) *adj.* **1,** (diverted) distraído. **2,** (bewildered) aturullado.

distraction (dɪsˈtræk·ʃən) *n.* **1,** (diversion) distracción. **2,** (bewilderment) alboroto. **3,** *colloq.* (madness) locura; frenesí.

distrait (dɪsˈtreit) *adj.* distraído.

distraught (dɪsˈtrɔt) *adj.* **1,** (bewildered) aturdido; perplejo. **2,** (irrational) demente.

distress (dɪsˈtres) *n.* **1,** (pain; suffering) dolor; pena; angustia. **2,** (adversity) revés; infortunio; apuro. **3,** (danger) peligro. **4,** *law* (property seizure) embargo. —*v.t.* afligir; angustiar. —**distressful,** *adj.* penoso; angustioso.

distribute (dɪsˈtrɪb·jut) *v.t.* **1,** (apportion) distribuir. **2,** (classify) clasificar. **3,** (spread out) esparcir. —**distribution,** *n.* distribución. —**distributive** (-ju·tɪv) *n. & adj.* distributivo. —**distributor,** *n.* distribuidor; distribuidor.

district (ˈdɪs·trɪkt) *n.* distrito. —**district attorney,** fiscal de distrito.

distrust (dɪsˈtrʌst) *n.* desconfianza; recelo. —*v.t.* desconfiar; recelar. —**distrustful** (-fəl) *adj.* desconfiado; receloso; sospechoso.

disturb (dɪsˈtɜrb) *v.t.* **1,** (disquiet) turbar; perturbar; alborotar. **2,** (disarrange) desordenar; revolver. **3,**

(molest) molestar. —**disturbance,** *n.* disturbio; perturbación; alboroto. —**disturbed,** *adj., psychol.* desordenado; loco.

disunion (dɪsˈjun·jən) *n.* desunión.

disunite (ˌdɪs·juˈnait) *v.t.* desunir; separar. —*v.i.* desunirse; separarse. —**disunity** (dɪsˈju·nə·ti) *n.* desunión.

disuse (dɪsˈjus) *n.* desuso. —*v.t.* (dɪsˈjuːz) desusar.

disyllable (dɪˈsɪl·ə·bəl) *n.* disílabo; bisílabo. —**disyllabic** (ˌdɪs·ɪˈlæb·ɪk) *adj.* disílabo; bisílabo.

ditch (dɪtʃ) *n.* **1,** (channel) zanja. **2,** (gutter) cuneta. **3,** *mil.* (trench) foso. **4,** (channel for drainage) badén. **5,** *slang* (the sea) charco. —*v.t.* **1,** (surround or drain by a ditch) zanjar. **2,** (throw into a ditch) echar en una zanja. **3,** (run, as a vehicle into a ditch) embarrancar. **4,** (land, as an aircraft in the sea) amerizar por emergencia. **5,** *slang* (abandon) sacudir; desembarazarse de.

ditto (ˈdɪt·o) *n.* [*pl.* -os] **1,** (the same) dicho; ídem. **2,** (duplicate) copia; duplicado. —*v.t.* copiar; duplicar. —*adv., colloq.* igualmente; así como.

ditty (ˈdɪt·i) *n.* cancioncilla.

diuretic (ˌdai·juˈret·ɪk) *adj. & n.* diurético. —**diuresis** (-ˈri·sɪs) *n.* diuresis.

diurnal (daiˈʌr·nəl) *adj.* diurno; diario.

diva (ˈdi·va; -və) *n.* diva.

divalent (daiˈvei·lənt) *adj.* bivalente.

divan (ˈdai·væn) *n.* diván.

dive (daiv) *v.i.* **1,** (plunge) bucear; zambullirse. **2,** *fig.* (interest oneself) enfrascarse; sumergirse. **3,** *naut.* (submerge) sumergirse. **4,** *aero.* (descend) picar. —*v.t.* zambullir; sumergir. —*n.* **1,** (plunge) zambullida; inmersión. **2,** *colloq.* (disreputable place) tasca; garito. **3,** (plunge) *naut.* inmersión; *aero.* picado. —**dive bomber,** bombardero en picado.

diver (ˈdai·vər) *n.* **1,** (swimmer) zambullidor. **2,** (skindiver; deepsea diver) buzo; buceador. **3,** (diving bird) somorgujo.

diverge (dɪˈvʌrdʒ) *v.i.* divergir. —**divergence; divergency,** *n.* divergencia. —**divergent,** *adj.* divergente.

diverse (dɪ'vʌrs; 'dai·vərs) *también*, **divers** ('dai·vərz) *adj.* diverso; vario. —**diverseness**, *n.* diversidad; variedad.

diversify (dɪ'vʌrs·ə‚fai) *v.t.* diversificar. —*v.i.* diversificarse. —**diversification** (-ɪ·fɪ'kei·ʃən) *n.* diversificación.

diversion (dɪ'vʌr·ʒən) *n.* **1,** (change of direction) desvío; desviación. **2,** (amusement) diversión; entretenimiento. —**diversionary**, *adj.* de diversión.

diversity (dɪ'vʌrs·ə·ti) *n.* diversidad; variedad.

divert (dɪ'vʌrt) *v.t.* **1,** (turn away) desviar; apartar. **2,** (amuse) divertir; entretener.

divest (dɪ'vɛst) *v.t.* **1,** (strip) desvestir; desnudar. **2,** (deprive) despojar; desposeer. —**divestment**, *n.* despojo.

divestiture (dɪ'vɛs·tɪ·tʃər) *n.* despojo; desposeimiento.

divide (dɪ'vaid) *v.t.* **1,** (separate) dividir. **2,** (sever) desunir. **3,** (apportion) compartir. —*v.i.* dividirse; separarse. —*n.* (watershed) vertiente; línea divisoria. —**dividers**, *n.pl.* compás.

dividend ('dɪv·ə·dend) *n.* dividendo.

divination (‚dɪv·ə'nei·ʃən) *n.* adivinación.

divine (dɪ'vain) *adj.* divino. —*n.* clérigo. —*v.t.* & *i.* adivinar. —**divine right**, derecho divino. —**divining rod**, vara de adivinar.

diviner (dɪ'vai·nər) *n.* **1,** (clairvoyant) adivinador. **2,** (magical device) vara mágica. **3,** (divining rod) buscador.

diving ('dai·vɪŋ) *adj.* zambullidor; sumergible. —*n.* zambullida; buceo. —**diving suit**, escafandra.

divinity (dɪ'vɪn·ə·ti) *n.* **1,** (divine nature; deity) divinidad. **2,** (study of religion) teología. **3,** *cap.* (God) Dios.

divisible (dɪ'vɪz·ə·bəl) *adj.* divisible. —**divisibility**, *n.* divisibilidad.

division (dɪ'vɪʒ·ən) *n.* división. —**divisional**, *adj.* divisional.

divisive (dɪ'vai·sɪv) *adj.* divisivo.

divisor (dɪ'vai·zər) *n.* divisor.

divorce (dɪ'vors) *n.* divorcio. —*v.t.* divorciar. —*v.i.* divorciarse. —**divorcé** [*fem.* **divorcée**] (-'sei) *n.* divorciado; *fem.* divorciada. —**divorcement**, *n.* divorcio.

divulge (dɪ'vʌldʒ) *v.t.* divulgar;

revelar; publicar. —**divulgence**, *n.* divulgación.

Dixie ('dɪk·si) *n.* el sur de EE.UU.

dizzy ('dɪz·i) *adj.* **1,** (giddy) vertiginoso; mareado; aturdido. **2,** (causing dizziness) mareante. **3,** *slang* (silly) atontado; mentecato; tonto. —*v.t.* marear; aturdir —**dizziness**, *n.* mareo; vértigo; aturdimiento.

DNA *abr. de.* **deoxyribonucleic acid**, ácido desoxirribonucleico.

do (duː) *v.t.* **[did, done, doing] 1,** (carry out) hacer; (perform) realizar; ejecutar. **2,** (cause) hacer; causar. **3,** (render) tributar; rendir. **4,** (work at) trabajar en; ocuparse de o en. **5,** (finish) terminar; acabar. **6,** (solve) solucionar; resolver. **7,** *slang* (tour) ver; visitar. **8,** (cover, as distance) recorrer. **9,** (translate) traducir. **10,** *colloq.* (cheat; swindle) chasquear; engañar. **11,** *colloq.* (serve, as a jail term) cumplir (una condena). —*v.i.* **1,** (behave) comportarse; conducirse. **2,** (fare) estarse; ir; hallarse. **3,** (suffice; be suitable) servir; bastar. —*v. aux.* **1,** *formando preguntas: Do you like this?,* ¿Le gusta a Vd. esto? **2,** *formando oraciones negativas: I do not like this,* No me gusta esto. **3,** *dando énfasis: I do like this,* Esto sí me gusta. **4,** *reemplazando un verbo ya expresado o sobrentendido: Work hard; if you do, you will succeed,* Trabaja; si lo haces, triunfarás. **5,** *en orden invertido tras adverbio: Rarely do things turn out as we expect,* Es raro que salgan las cosas tal cual se espera. —**do away with**, **1,** (get rid of) suprimir; desembarazarse de. **2,** (destroy) matar; destrozar. —**do for,** *colloq.* **1,** (destroy) destrozar; arruinar. **2,** (provide for) tratar; cuidar. —**do in,** *slang* **1,** (kill) matar. **2,** (swindle) engañar; timar. —**do up,** *colloq.* **1,** (wrap) envolver; atar. **2,** (dress) arreglar; componer. —**do without**, prescindir de; pasar sin.

do (do) *n., mus.* do.

docile ('das·əl) *adj.* dócil; sumiso. —**docility** (da'sɪl·ə·ti) *n.* docilidad; sumisión.

dock (dak) *n.* **1,** (pier) dársena; muelle. **2,** (prisoner's stand) banquillo de los acusados. **3,** (plant) romaza. **4,** (cut tail) muñón de la cola. —*v.t.* **1,** (cut, as a tail) derrabar; cercenar. **2,** (deduct from, as wages) reducir; descontar. **3,** (settle at a pier) atracar. —*v.i.* (arrive at a pier) entrar en muelle.

dockage ('dak·ɪdʒ) *n.* **1,** *naut.* (docking) entrada en muelle; (docking fee) muellaje; (docking rights) derecho de dique. **2,** (curtailment) rebaja; reducción.

docket ('dak·ɪt) *n., law* **1,** (agenda) orden del día; lista de causas pendientes. **2,** (registry of judgments) sumario; lista. —*v.t.* poner en el orden del día.

dockyard ('dak·jard) *n.* arsenal; dársena.

doctor ('dak·tər) *n.* doctor; (physician) médico. —*v.t.* **1,** (treat medicinally) medicinar; recetar. **2,** *colloq.* (patch up) componer; reparar. **3,** (adulterate) adulterar. —**doctorate,** *n.* doctorado.

doctrine ('dak·trɪn) *n.* doctrina. —**doctrinal,** *adj.* doctrinal. —**doctrinaire** (,dak·trɪ'neːr) *n.* & *adj.* doctrinario.

document ('dak·jə·mənt) *n.* documento. —*v.t.* documentar. —**documental** (-'mɛn·təl) *adj.* documental. —**documentation** (-mɛn'teɪ·ʃən) *n.* documentación. —**documentary** (-'mɛn·tə·ri) *n.* & *adj.* documental.

dodder ('dad·ər) *v.i.* **1,** (tremble) temblar. **2,** (totter) tambalear.

dodge (dadʒ) *v.t.* escapar; evadir. —*v.i.* escabullirse; regatear; zafarse. —*n.* **1,** (evasion) regate; evasión. **2,** *colloq.* (trick) esquinazo; evasiva.

dodo ('do·do) *n.* **1,** (extinct bird) dodo; dodó. **2,** (simpleton) necio; bodoque. **3,** (fogy) vejestorio; vejete.

doe (doː) *n.* **1,** (deer) cierva. **2,** (antelope) antílope hembra. **3,** (hare) liebre. **4,** (rabbit) coneja.

doer ('du·ər) *n.* **1,** (performer) hacedor. **2,** (effective person) persona activa.

does (dʌz) *v., tercera persona del sing. del pres. de ind. de* **do.**

doeskin ('do,skɪn) *n.* **1,** (leather) piel de ante. **2,** (woolen cloth) tejido fino de lana.

doff (daf) *v.t.* quitar; quitarse.

dog (dɔg) *n.* **1,** (canine) perro. **2,** (mechanical device) fiador. **3,** (andiron) morillo. **4,** (mean fellow) perro; tunante. **5,** *cap., astron.* Can. —*v.t.* [**dogged** (dɔgd), **dogging**] *colloq.* (track; pursue) rastrear; perseguir; seguir las huellas de. —a

dog's age, una eternidad. —**a dog's life,** vida de perros. —**dog days,** días de perros. —**dog in the manger,** perro de hortelano. —**dog Latin,** latinajo. —**dog tag,** placa. —**dog tired,** cansado como perro; extenuado. —**go to the dogs,** arruinarse; estar perdido. —**house dog,** perro guardián. —**lap dog,** perrito faldero. —**put on the dog,** *slang* presumir; darse ínfulas. —**rain cats and dogs,** llover a cántaros.

dogcatcher ('dɔg,kætʃ·ər) *n.* cazaperros.

dog collar dogal.

dogear ('dɔg,ɪr) *n.* orejón. —*v.t.* doblar la punta de.

dogfight ('dɔg,fait) *n.* **1,** (fight of dogs) lucha de perros. **2,** (any violent fight) refriega. **3,** *aero.* combate de cazas.

dogfish ('dɔg,fɪʃ) *n.* cazón; tollo.

dogged ('dag·ɪd) *adj.* emperrado; terco. —**doggedness,** *n.* emperramiento; terquedad.

doggerel ('dag·ər·əl) *n.* aleluyas; coplas de ciego.

doggone ('dɔg'gɔn) *adj., colloq.* maldito. —*interj., colloq.* ¡maldición!

doggy ('dɔg·i) *n., colloq.* perrito. —*adj.* de o como perro. —**doggy bag,** saco o cajetilla para llevarse los restos de comida de un restaurante.

doghouse ('dɔg,haus) *n.* perrera. —**in the doghouse,** *slang* en desgracia.

dogma ('dɔg·mə) *n.* dogma. —**dogmatism** (-tɪz·əm) *n.* dogmatismo. —**dogmatic** (-'mæt·ɪk) *adj.* dogmático.

Dog Star Sirio.

dogtooth ('dɔg,tuθ) *n.* [*pl.* -**teeth**] **1,** (eyetooth) colmillo. **2,** *archit.* diente de perro. —**dogtooth violet,** *n.* diente de perro.

dog track canódromo.

dogtrot ('dɔg,trat) *n.* trote lento.

dogwatch ('dɔg,watʃ) *n., naut.* guardia de cuartillo.

dogwood ('dɔg·wʊd) *n.* cornejo.

doily ('dɔi·li) *n.* pañito de adorno.

doings ('du·ɪŋs) *n.pl.* **1,** (actions) acciones; actos; hechos. **2,** (behavior) conducta; proceder.

doldrums ('dal·drəmz) *n.pl.* **1,** *naut.* (calm) zona de calmas tropicales. **2,** *fig.* (low spirits) abatimiento.

dole (do:l) *n.* dádiva; limosna; *Brit.* subsidio o socorro de desempleo. —*v.t.* [*usu.,* **dole out**] distribuir; repartir.

doleful ('do:l·fəl) *adj.* triste. —**dolefulness,** *n.* tristeza.

doll (da:l) *n.* muñeca. —*v.t.* [*usu.,* **doll up**] engalanar; ataviar.

dollar ('da·lər) *n.* dólar.

dolly ('da·li) *n.* **1,** (doll) muñequita. **2,** (truck) plataforma de rodillos.

dolor ('do·lər) *n.* dolor. —**dolorous,** *adj.* doloroso; triste. —**dolorousness,** *n.* dolor; tristeza.

dolphin ('dal·fɪn) *n.* delfín.

dolt (do:lt) *n.* mentecato; bobo.

domain (do'mein) *n.* **1,** (territory) dominio. **2,** (scope) campo.

dome (dom) *n.* **1,** (cupola) domo; cúpula. **2,** *slang* (head) cabeza.

domestic (də'mɛs·tɪk) *adj.* **1,** (of the home) doméstico. **2,** (internal) interno. —*n.* doméstico; criado. —**domesticate** (-tɪˌkeit) *v.t.* domesticar. —**domesticity** (ˌdo·mɛs·'tɪs·ə·ti) *n.* domesticidad; *pl.* asuntos domésticos.

domicile ('dom·ə·sɪl; -sail) *n.* domicilio. —*v.t.* domiciliar.—*v.i.* domiciliarse.

dominate ('dam·ə·neit) *v.t. & i.* dominar; mandar. —**dominance;** **domination,** *n.* dominación. —**dominant,** *adj.* dominante.

domineer (da·mɪ'nɪːr) *v.t. & i.* dominar; tiranizar. —**domineering,** *adj.* dominante; tiránico.

dominical (də'mɪn·ə·kəl) *adj.* dominical.

Dominican (də'mɪn·ɪ·kən) *adj. & n.* **1,** (of the Dominican Republic) dominicano. **2,** (of the order of St. Dominic) dominico.

dominion (də'mɪn·jən) *n.* dominio.

domino ('dam·ɪ·no) *n.* **1,** (masquerade costume) máscara; dominó. **2,** *pl.* (game) dominós; dominó. **3,** (tile used in game) dominó; ficha.

don (dan) *v.t.* [**donned, donning**] vestir; poner. —*n.* **1,** *cap.* (Spanish title) don; señor. **2,** *Brit.* (fellow) socio; (tutor) preceptor.

doña ('do·ɲa) *n., fem. of* **don.**

donate ('do·neit) *v.t.* donar; dar; regalar. —**donation,** *n.* donativo; donación.

done (dʌn) *v., p.p. de* **do.** —*adj., cooking* cocinado; cocido; hecho.

donee (do'ni:) *n.* donatario.

donkey ('daŋ·ki) *n.* burro; asno.

donor ('do·nər) *n.* donador; donante.

doodle ('du·dəl) *v.i.* borrajear; borronear; garabatear. —*n.* garabato; borrón.

doom (dum) *n.* **1,** (destiny) destino; hado; ruina. **2,** (judgment) juicio; condena; sentencia. —*v.t.* predestinar a la ruina; condenar.

doomsday ('dumʒ·de) *n.* día del juicio final o universal.

door (do:r) *n.* puerta; entrada. —**back door,** puerta trasera. —**street door,** puerta de entrada. —**throw open one's doors,** dar hospitalidad.

doorbell ('do:rˌbɛl) *n.* campanilla; timbre.

doorkeeper ('do:rˌkip·ər) *n.* portero.

doorknob ('do:rˌnab) *n.* tirador; pomo.

doorman ('do:rˌmæn) *n.* [*pl.* **-men**] portero.

doorsill ('do:rˌsɪl) *n.* umbral.

doorstep ('do:rˌstɛp) *n.* escalón.

doorway ('do:rˌwei) *n.* portal; jamba.

dope (dop) *n.* **1,** (viscous substance) pasta; lubricante. **2,** (narcotic) narcótico; droga. **3,** *slang* (information) informe. **4,** *slang* (stupid person) idiota; bobo. —*v.t.* **1,** *colloq.* = **drug. 2,** *slang.* [*usu.,* **dope out**] (solve) solucionar; (predict) pronosticar. —**dopey; dopy** ('do·pi) *adj.* atontado.

Doric ('dor·ɪk) *adj.* dórico.

dormant ('dor·mənt) *adj.* adormilado; inactivo; latente. —**dormancy** ('dor·mən·si) *n.* adormilamiento; letargo.

dormer ('dor·mər) *n.* buhardilla; buharda.

dormitory ('dor·məˌtor·i) *n.* dormitorio; residencia estudiantil.

dormouse ('dorˌmaus) *n.* [*pl.* **-mice**] lirón.

dorsal ('dor·səl) *adj.* dorsal.

dory ('dor·i) *n.* **1,** (dinghy) bote. **2,** (fish) gallo; dorado.

dosage ('do·sɪdʒ) *n.* **1,** (act of dosing) dosificación. **2,** (dose) dosis.

dose (dos) *n.* dosis. —*v.t.* **1,** (give a dose to) dar o administrar una dosis; medicinar. **2,** (give in doses) dosificar.

dossier (do'sje) *n.* expediente.

dot (dat) *n.* **1,** *print.* (period) punto. **2,** (speck) lunar. **3,** (dowry) dote. —*v.t.* [**dotted, dotting**] **1,** (mark with a dot) puntear. **2,** (cover with dots) motear; salpicar. **—on the dot,** puntualmente; con exactitud; preciso.

dote (dot) *v.i.* chochear. **dotage** ('do·tɪdʒ) *n.* chochez. **—dotard** ('do·tərd) *n.* viejo chocho.

double ('dʌb·əl) *adj.* doble. **—v.t.** doblar. **—v.i.** doblarse. **—n.** doble; copia. **—doubly** (-li) *adv.* doblemente; dos al mismo tiempo. **—double chin,** papada. **—double meaning,** doble intención.

double bass *mus.* contrabajo.

double-breasted *adj.* cruzado.

double-cross *v.t., slang* traicionar. **—n., slang** traición.

double-dealing *n.* doblez; trato de dos caras. **—adj.** doblado; de dos caras.

double-entry *adj.* a partida doble.

double-header *n.* **1,** *baseball* doble encuentro. **2,** *R.R.* tren con dos locomotoras.

double-jointed *adj.* que tiene articulaciones dobles; contorsionista.

doubles ('dʌb·əlz) *n.pl., games* juego de dobles.

doublet ('dʌb·lɪt) *n.* **1,** (jacket) jubón. **2,** (couple; one of a pair) par; pareja.

doubletalk ('dʌb·əl,tɔk) *n* jerga; jerigonza.

doubloon (dʌ'blu:n) *n.* doblón.

doubt (daut) *n.* duda. **—v.t. & i.** dudar. **—doubtful** (-fəl) *adj.* dudoso. **—doubtless** (-ləs) *adj.* indudable; cierto.

douche (duʃ) *n.* **1,** (spray) ducha; irrigación. **2,** (syringe) ducha; bolsa; jeringa. **—v.t.** duchar. **—v.i.** darse una ducha.

dough (doʊ) *n.* **1,** (flour paste) pasta; masa. **2,** *slang* (money) pasta; dinero; parné.

doughnut ('do·nʌt) *n.* buñuelo; *Amer.* dona.

doughty ('dau·ti) *adj.* valiente. **—doughtiness,** *n.* valentía.

dour (dʊr) *adj.* hosco. **—dourness,** *n.* hosquedad.

douse (daus) *v.t.* **1,** (immerse) zambullir. **2,** (soak) empapar. **3,** *colloq.* (extinguish) apagar. **—v.i. 1,** (dive) zambullirse. **2,** (soak) empaparse.

dove (dʌv) *n.* paloma.

dove (doʊv) *v., pret. & p.p. de* **dive.**

dovecot ('dʌv,kat) *n.* palomar. *También,* **dovecote** (-,kot).

dovetail ('dʌv,teil) *v.t.* ensamblar; ajustar; machihembrar. **—v.i.** ajustarse.

dowager ('dau·ə·dʒər) *n.* **1,** (widow) viuda. **2,** *colloq.* (elderly lady) matrona; anciana.

dowdy ('dau·di) *adj.* descuidado; desaliñado. **—dowdiness,** *n.* descuido; desaliño.

dowel ('dau·əl) *n.* clavija.

dower ('dau·ər) *n.* **1,** (dowry) dote. **2,** (widow's inheritance) viudedad. **3,** (endowment) prenda. **—v.t. 1,** (give a dowry to) dotar. **2,** (endow, as a widow) señalar o dar viudedad a.

down (daun) *adv.* **1,** (descending) para abajo; hacia abajo. **2,** (at the bottom) abajo. **3,** (in written form) por escrito; en papel. **4,** (at a lower rate) a precio reducido. **5,** (as the first payment) al contado; de pronto; *Mex.* pronto. **6,** (completely) por completo. **—adj. 1,** (downward) descendente; pendiente. **2,** (lower) de abajo. **3,** *colloq.* (dejected) desanimado; abatido; desalentado. **4,** *colloq.* (prostrate; ill) enfermo; agotado. **—prep.** bajo; bajo de. **—n. 1,** (downward movement) bajada; descenso. **2,** *football* colocación de pelota. **3,** (fuzz, as of birds) plumón; (of fruits) pelusa; pelusilla; (of persons) vello. **4,** *usu.pl.* (hill; dune) colina; duna. **—v.t.** derribar; hacer caer. **—v.i.** caerse; bajarse. **—down and out,** *boxing* fuera de combate. **2,** (in bad shape) arruinado; vencido. **—down-to-earth,** *adj.* práctico; realista. **—down with . . . !,** ¡muera!; ¡abajo!

downcast ('daun,kæst) *adj.* abatido; desanimado.

downfall ('daun·fɔl) *n.* caída; derrota.

downfallen ('daun·fɔl·ən) *adj.* caído; arruinado.

downgrade ('daun,greid) *n.* pendiente; declive; bajada. **—adj.** pendiente; inclinado. **—adv.** en pendiente; en declive. **—v.t.** degradar.

downhearted ('daun'har·tɪd) *adj.* deprimido; desalentado.

downhill ('daun·hɪl) *adj.* inclinado; pendiente. **—adv.** en pendiente; cuesta abajo.

download ('daun·lod) *v.t.*

transferir (datos) del CPU o del modem a un disco.

down payment pago inicial.

downpour ('daun·por) *n.* aguacero; chaparrón.

downright ('daun,rait) *adj.* **1,** (absolute) categórico; absoluto. **2,** (clear; complete) claro; patente; completo. —*adv.* completamente; directamente.

downsize ('daun,saiz) *v.t.* reducir; disminuir.

downstairs ('daun,sterz) *adj.* de abajo. —*adv.* abajo; en o al piso de abajo. —*n.* piso inferior; piso bajo.

downstream ('daun,strim) *adv.* río abajo; aguas abajo. —*adj.* de río abajo; que va río abajo; descendente.

downtime ('daun,taim) *n.* tiempo muerto.

downtown ('daun·taun) *adj.* del sector comercial de la ciudad; céntrico. —*adv.* en, al o del centro. —*n.* centro de la ciudad.

downtrodden ('daun,trad·ən) *adj.* **1,** (trampled) pisoteado. **2,** (oppressed) oprimido.

downturn ('daun,tʌrn) *n.* baja; (*econ.*) receso económico.

downward ('daun·wərd) *adv.* [*también,* **downwards** (-wərdz)] **1,** (going lower) hacia abajo. **2,** (more recent) más atrás. —*adj.* descendente.

downy ('dau·ni) *adj.* **1,** (covered with down) velloso. **2,** (soft) blando; suave. **3,** (fluffy) felpudo. —**downiness,** *n.* vellosidad; suavidad.

dowry ('dau·ri) *n.* dote.

dowse (daus) *v.t. & i.* **1,** = **douse. 2,** buscar depósitos de agua o de minerales con una vara de adivinar.

doxology (dak'sal·ə·dʒi) *n.* doxología.

doze (doz) *n.* sueño ligero; sopor. —*v.i.* dormitar.

dozen ('dʌz·ən) *n.* docena. —**baker's dozen,** docena del fraile.

drab (dræb) *adj.* **1,** (yellow-gray) parduzco. **2,** (dull) monótono; soso. —*n.* **1,** (color) gris amarillento; parduzco. **2,** (slattern) puta; ramera. —**drabness,** *n.* monotonía.

drachma ('dræk·mə) *n.* dracma.

draft (dræft; draft) *n.* **1,** (hauling) tiro; tirón. **2,** (load) carga. **3,** (drink) trago; bebida. **4,** (heavy demand) demanda. **5,** (conscription) llamamiento a filas; quinta. **6,**

comm. giro; libranza; letra de cambio. **7,** *naut.* calado. **8,** (current of air) corriente (de aire). **9,** (device to regulate air intake) tiro. **10,** (outline; preliminary copy) borrador; bosquejo; apunte. —*adj.* **1,** (for hauling) de tiro; de arrastre. **2,** (drawn from a cask) de grifo; de barril. —*v.t.* **1,** (conscript) llamar a quintas o al servicio. **2,** (sketch; outline) bosquejar; hacer un borrador de. *También, Brit.,* **draught.** —**draftee,** *n.* conscripto; recluta. —**on draft,** de barril.

draftsman ('dræfts·mən) *n.* [*pl.* **-men**] delineante; dibujante.

drafty ('dræf·ti) *adj.* con o de corrientes de aire.

drag (dræg) *v.t.* [**dragged, dragging**] **1,** (haul) arrastrar; tirar. **2,** (dredge) rastrear; dragar. **3,** (harrow) rastrillar. —*v.i.* **1,** (trail) arrastrarse. **2,** (move slowly) avanzar lentamente. **3,** (lag) retrasarse. **4,** (decline) decaer. —*n.* **1,** (harrow) rastrillo. **2,** (carriage) narria. **3,** (hindrance) carga; impedimento; freno; obstáculo. **4,** (act of dragging) arrastre; tirón. **5,** *naut.* (slipping of the anchor) rastra; dragado. **6,** *aero.* resistencia al aire. **7,** *slang* (influence) poder; influencia. **8,** *slang* (draw, as on a cigarette) vaharada; fumada. **9,** *slang* (street; district) calle; barrio.

dragnet ('dræg,nɛt) *n.* red barredera.

dragon ('dræg·ən) *n.* dragón.

dragonfly ('dræg·ən,flai) *n.* caballito del diablo.

dragoon (drə'gun) *n.* dragón. —*v.t.* acosar.

drain (drein) *v.t.* **1,** (draw off) desaguar; escurrir; vaciar. **2,** *surg.* drenar; desangrar. **3,** (empty) vaciar; disipar. **4,** *fig.* (exhaust gradually) consumir. —*v.i.* **1,** (run; flow out or into) desaguarse; escurrirse. **2,** (be exhausted gradually) escaparse. —*n.* **1,** (channel; pipe) desaguadero; desagüe. **2,** *surg.* drenaje; desangre. **3,** (drawing off of resources) desangramiento; agotamiento.

drainage ('drei·nidʒ) *n.* **1,** (draining) desagüe; desaguadero. **2,** *surg.* drenaje. **3,** (sewerage) alcantarillado. **4,** (area drained) arroyada.

drake (dreik) *n.* pato.

dram (dræm) *n.* **1,** ($\frac{1}{16}$ ounce) dracma. **2,** (small drink) trago de licor.

drama ('dræ·mə; 'dra-) *n.* drama. —**dramatist** (-tɪst) *n.* dramaturgo.
dramatic (drə'mæt·ɪk) *adj.* dramático. —**dramatics**, *n.* dramática.
dramatize ('dræm·ə,taiz) *v.t.* dramatizar. —**dramatization** (-tɪ'zei·ʃən) *n.* dramatización.
drank (dræŋk) *v.*, *pret. de* **drink**.
drape (dreip) *v.t.* **1**, (cover with fabric) engalanar; ornar. **2**, (arrange in folds) adornar con pliegues; arreglar los pliegues de. —*n.* colgadura; *pl.* = **drapery**. —**draper**, *n.* tapicero; pañero.
drapery ('drei·pə·ri) *n.* paño; tejido; *pl.* [*también*, **drapes**] cortinas; colgaduras.
drastic ('dræs·tɪk) *adj.* drástico.
draught (dræft; draft) *n.* = **draft**.
draughts (drafts) *n.pl.* (game) juego de damas.
draw (drɔː) *v.t.* [**drew, drawn, drawing**] **1**, (pull) tirar; arrastrar. **2**, (take out) sacar; retirar. **3**, (derive) obtener; conseguir. **4**, (induce; attract) incitar; mover; atraer. **5**, (infer) deducir; derivar. **6**, (inhale) inspirar; aspirar; respirar. **7**, (suck) chupar; mamar. **8**, (drain) desaguar; vaciar. **9**, *sports* (tie) empatar. **10**, (lengthen) estirar; alargar; extender. **11**, (attenuate) atenuar. **12**, (obtain, as salary) cobrar. **13**, (sketch; outline) trazar; dibujar; esbozar. **14**, *comm.* (write, as a check or draft) librar; girar; extender. **15**, *comm.* (earn, as interest) devengar. **16**, (pull, as curtains) correr; descorrer. **17**, *naut.* calar. **18**, (win in a lottery) ganar. **19**, *cards* robar. —*v.i.* **1**, (move nearer) acercarse; venir. **2**, (move away) alejarse; irse. **3**, (attract an audience) atraer público. **4**, (sketch) dibujar; esbozar. **5**, *comm.* girar. **6**, (create an air current) tirar bien. **7**, (unsheathe a weapon) desenvainar; sacar. **8**, (tie the score) empatar; (in chess or checkers) hacer tablas. **9**, (shrink) encogerse; contraerse. —*n.* **1**, (pulling) tirada; tiro; (tugging) tracción; arrastre. **2**, (tie score) empate; (in chess or checkers) tablas. **3**, (lift of a drawbridge) compuerta; piso. —**draw back**, echarse para atrás; retroceder. —**draw out**, **1**, (encourage to talk) sonsacar; sacar. **2**, = **draw**, *v.t.* **10**.
drawback ('drɔː·bæk) *n.* desventaja; inconveniente.
drawbridge ('drɔː,brɪdʒ) *n.* (bridge with rising section) puente levadizo; (with turning section) puente giratorio.
drawer (dror; 'drɔː·ər) *n.* **1**, (sliding tray) cajón; gaveta. **2**, (draftsman) dibujante; delineante. **3**, *comm.* librador. **4**, *pl.* (undergarment) calzoncillos; *Amer.* pantaloncillos.
drawing ('drɔː·ɪŋ) *n.* **1**, (art) dibujo. **2**, (plan) esbozo; plan. **3**, (selection by lot) sorteo.
drawing room *n.* sala; recibidor; recibimiento.
drawl (drɔːl) *v.i.* arrastrar las palabras. —*v.t.* pronunciar lentamente. —*n.* arrastre de palabras; pronunciación lenta.
drawn (drɔːn) *adj.* **1**, (disemboweled) destripado; desentrañado. **2**, (pulled out) desenvainado; sacado. **3**, (tied) empatado. **4**, (strained) agotado; cansado. **5**, (melted, as butter) fundido; derretido. —*v.*, *p.p. de* **draw**.
dray (drei) *n.* carro; carreta. —**drayage** (-ɪdʒ) *n.* acarreo.
drayhorse ('drei,hors) *n.* caballo de tiro.
drayman ('drei·mən) *n.* [*pl.* **-men**] acarreador; carretero.
dread (drɛd) *v.t.* temer. —*v.i.* tener miedo. —*n.* pavor; temor; sobrecogimiento. —*adj.* **1**, (frightening) espantoso. **2**, (awesome) impresionante.
dreadful ('drɛd·fəl) *adj.* **1**, (horrible) terrible; horrible; espantoso. **2**, (awesome) impresionante. **3**, *colloq.* (extreme) desagradable. —**dreadfulness**, *n.* horror.
dreadnought ('drɛd·nɔːt) *n.* acorazado grande.
dream (driːm) *n.* **1**, (thoughts while asleep) sueño. **2**, (fancy) ensueño. —*v.i. & t.* [*pret. & p.p.* **dreamed** o **dreamt**] soñar. —**dream of** o **about**, soñar con.
dreamer ('dri·mər) *n.* soñador; *fig.* visionario.
dreamland ('drim,lænd) *n.* tierra de hadas; región de los sueños.
dreamt (drɛmt) *v.*, *pret. & p.p. de* **dream**.
dreamy ('dri·mi) *adj.* **1**, (vague) desvariado; vago. **2**, (fanciful) soñador; lleno de sueños. **3**, *colloq.* (delightful) encantador; delicioso.
dreary ('drɪr·i) *adj.* triste; cansado; fastidioso. *También*, **drear**. —**dreariness**, *n.* tristeza; fastidio; cansancio.

dredge (drɛdʒ) *n.* draga; rastra.
—*v.t.* & *i.* **1,** (drag) dragar; rastrear.
2, (cover with flour) espolvorear.

dregs (drɛgz) *n.pl.* **1,** (residue)
heces; poso; impurezas. **2,** *fig.*
(worst portion) heces; escoria.

drench (drɛntʃ) *v.t.* **1,** (soak)
ensopar; empapar. **2,** *vet.* purgar.
—*n.* **1,** (large dose) tragantada;
purgante. **2,** (soaking) mojada.

dress (drɛs) *v.t.* **1,** (clothe) vestir;
trajear; (adorn) adornar; engalanar.
2, *med.* (bandage) vendar. **3,** (prepare for cooking) preparar;
aderezar; adobar. **4,** (put in order)
arreglar. —*v.i.* **1,** (clothe oneself)
vestirse; (wear clothes) vestir. **2,**
mil. (come into alignment)
alinearse. —*n.* **1,** (garment) vestido;
traje. **2,** (apparel) indumentaria.
—**dress coat,** frac. —**dress down,**
colloq. **1,** (reprimand) reñir;
amonestar. **2,** (thrash) azotar; zurrar.
—**dress parade,** desfile. —**dress
rehearsal,** ensayo general. —**dress
suit,** traje de etiqueta.

dresser ('drɛs·ər) **1,** (one who
dresses another person) ayuda de
cámara; camarera; doncella. **2,** (pre-
parer, as of meat, leather, etc.)
aliñador; adobador. **3,** (furniture)
cómoda; tocador; *Amer.* gaveteo.

dressing ('drɛs·ɪŋ) *n.* **1,** (act of
clothing) aderezo; adorno. **2,** (bandage) venda; hila. **3,** (sauce)
aderezo; aliño; condimento; (stuffing) relleno. **4,** (sizing for leather)
adobo; (for fabrics) aderezo.
—**dressing gown,** bata; peinador.
—**dressing room,** tocador; *theat.*
camarín; camerino.

dressing-down *n., colloq.* **1,**
(reprimand) regaño; reprimenda. **2,**
(thrashing) zurra; aporreo.

dressmaker ('drɛs,mei·kər) *n.*
modista; sastre (*fem.* sastresa).

dressy ('drɛs·i) *adj., colloq.* **1,**
(formal; stylish) elegante; de gala.
2, (showy) acicalado.

drew (dru) *v., pret. de* **draw.**

dribble ('drɪb·əl) *v.i.* **1,** (drip)
gotear. **2,** (drool) babear. —*v.t.* **1,**
(let fall in drops) derramar gota a
gota. **2,** *sports* (bounce, as a ball)
driblar. —*n.* **1,** (dripping) goteo. **2,**
colloq. (drizzle) llovizna. **3,** *sports*
dribling.

driblet ('drɪb·lɪt) *n.* gota; trozo;
pedacito; (of money) pico.

drier *también,* **dryer** ('drai·ər) *n.* **1,**
(person; device) secador. **2,** (sub-

stance) secante. —*adj., comp. de*
dry.

driest ('drai·ɪst) *adj., superl. de*
dry.

drift (drɪft) *n.* **1,** (direction)
corriente; rumbo. **2,** (snow, etc.,
driven by wind) ventisquero; alud.
3, (trend) inclinación; impulso;
tendencia. **4,** *naut.; aero.* deriva. **5,**
colloq. (meaning) intención;
sentido. **6,** *geol.* terrenos de acarreo.
7, *mech.* (tool) mandril de
ensanchar. **8,** *mining* galería;
socavón. —*v.i.* **1,** *naut.; aero.* ir a la
deriva. **2,** (be heaped up)
amontonarse. **3,** *fig.* (move aimlessly) vagar; ir sin rumbo.
—**drifter** *n.* vagabundo.

driftwood ('drɪft,wʊd) *n.* despojo
del mar.

drill (drɪl) *n.* **1,** (tool) taladro;
barrena. **2,** (training exercise)
instrucción. **3,** (teaching) disciplina;
repetición; (test) ejercicio;
simulacro. **4,** (agricultural machine)
sembradora mecánica. **5,** (fabric)
dril. **6,** = **mandrill.** —*v.t.* **1,** (pierce)
taladrar; barrenar. **2,** *mil.* enseñar la
instrucción a. **3,** (train) insistir;
repetir. **4,** (sow in rows) plantar en
hileras.

drillmaster ('drɪl,mæs·tər) *n.*
maestro de ejercicios o en instrucción.

drink (drɪŋk) *v.t.* [**drank, drunk,
drinking**] **1,** (swallow) beber;
tragar. **2,** *fig.* [*usu.,* **drink in**] (absorb) embeber; empapar. —*v.i.* **1,**
(imbibe) beber. **2,** (drink a toast)
brindar. —*n.* **1,** (beverage; liquor)
bebida; trago. **2,** *slang* (body of water) océano; charco. —**drinkable,**
adj. potable; bebible.

drinker ('drɪŋk·ər) *n.* **1,** (one who
drinks) bebedor. **2,** (drunkard)
borrachín.

drip (drɪp) *v.i.* [**dripped, dripping**]
gotear; chorrear. —*v.t.* verter gota a
gota; hacer gotear. —*n.* **1,** (dropping) goteo. **2,** (roof leak) gotera. **3,**
archit. (rain catch) alero. **4,** *slang*
(unattractive person) mastuerzo;
pelma. —**drippings,** *n.pl.* (juices
from roasting) pringue; grasa.

drive (draiv) *v.t.* [**drove, driven,
driving**] **1,** (impel) impulsar;
impeler. **2,** (urge) empujar; forzar.
3, (direct, as a vehicle) conducir;
guiar; *Amer.* manejar. **4,** (transport
in a vehicle) transportar; acarrear;
llevar. **5,** (carry forward) ejecutar;

actuar. **6,** (chase, as game; hunt) acosar; acorralar. **7,** (lead, as animals) acarrear; conducir. **8,** (force to work) forzar; empujar. **9,** *sports* (hit; cast) lanzar; golpear fuerte. **10,** (cause to go through or penetrate) atornillar (a screw); clavar (a nail); hincar (a stick). —*v.i.* **1,** (dash) lanzarse; arrojarse. **2,** (go in a vehicle) ir en coche o auto. **3,** (operate a vehicle) guiar; conducir; *Amer.* manejar. **4,** (aim; tend) pretender; proponerse. **5,** (work energetically) afanarse. —*n.* **1,** (trip, as by car) paseo o viaje en auto. **2,** (road; driveway) calzada para autos. **3,** (animal roundup) manada. **4,** (campaign) campaña. **5,** (extreme haste) urgencia; exigencia. **6,** (energy; ambition) energía; vigor; ambición. **7,** *mech.* mecanismo de transmisión o dirección.

drive-in *adj.* para automovilistas. —*n.* cine, restaurante, ventanilla de banco, etc., para automovilistas.

drivel ('drɪv·əl) *v.i.* **1,** (drool) babear; babosear. **2,** (talk foolishly) bobear; hablar tonterías. —*n.* baba.

driven ('drɪv·ən) *v., p.p. de* **drive.**

driver ('draɪ·vər) *n.* **1,** (one who drives) conductor. **2,** (golf club) conductor. **3,** *mech.* pieza o rueda motriz.

driveshaft ('draɪv·ʃæft) *n.* eje motor; árbol de mando.

driveway ('draɪv·weɪ) *n.* entrada de coches.

driving ('draɪ·vɪŋ) *v., p.pr. de* **drive.** —*n.* conducción; *Amer.* manejo. —*adj.* **1,** (compelling) impulsor; motriz. **2,** (moving forcefully) devastador; violento.

drizzle ('drɪz·əl) *v.i.* lloviznar. —*n.* llovizna.

droll (droʊl) *adj.* gracioso; chocante; festivo; jocoso. —**drollery** ('droʊ·lə·ri) *n.* chocarrería; bufonería.

dromedary ('drɑm·ə·dɛr·i) *n.* dromedario.

drone (droʊn) *v.i.* **1,** (hum) zumbar. **2,** (speak monotonously) salmodiar. **3,** (idle) haraganear; zanganear. —*n.* **1,** (sound) zumbido. **2,** (bee) zángano. **3,** (idler) zángano; haragán. **4,** aeroplano de control remoto.

drool (druːl) *v.i.* **1,** (slobber) babear. **2,** (talk nonsense) bobear. —*n.* **1,** (slobbering) baba. **2,** (nonsense) bobería.

droop (druːp) *v.t.* hundir; inclinar. —*v.i.* **1,** (sag) caer; desplomarse. **2,** (languish) desanimarse; consumirse. —*n.* **1,** (sagging) hundimiento **2,** (languor) decaimiento. **3,** *slang* (killjoy) aguafiestas. —**droopy,** *adj.* inclinado; caído; abatido.

drop (drɑp) *n.* **1,** (liquid globule) gota. **2,** (small quantity) gota; poquito; pizca. **3,** (fall) caída; bajada; (from an airplane) lanzamiento. **4,** (decrease) baja. **5,** *theat.* (curtain) telón de boca. **6,** (mailbox) buzón. **7,** (trapdoor) escotillón. —*v.t.* **1,** (let fall) dejar caer. **2,** (lower) bajar. **3,** (drip) echar; tirar. **4,** (let drip) poner o echar a gotas. **5,** *colloq.* (utter, as a hint) indicar; sugerir. **6,** (send, as a note) mandar; enviar. **7,** (put aside; dismiss) descartar. **8,** (let off, as from a conveyance) dejar. **9,** (knock down) derribar; abatir. **10,** (omit) omitir; suprimir. —*v.i.* **1,** (fall; descend) caer; bajar; descender. **2,** (drip) gotear. **3,** (cease) parar; cesar. —**drop by drop,** gota a gota. —**drop in,** visitar de paso; entrar al pasar. —**drop in the bucket,** nada; pelillos a la mar. —**drop off, 1,** (diminish) disminuir. **2,** (fall asleep) caer dormido; quedarse dormido. —**drop out,** retirarse; darse de baja.

dropper ('drɑp·ər) *n.* cuentagotas.

droppings ('drɑp·ɪŋz) *n.pl.* excrementos; heces.

dropsy ('drɑp·si) *n.* hidropesía. —**dropsical** (-sɪ·kəl) *adj.* hidrópico.

dross (drɔs) *n.* **1,** (waste from metal) escoria. **2,** *fig.* (refuse) desecho; hez.

drought (draʊt) *n.* **1,** (dryness) sequedad; aridez. **2,** (prolonged dry weather) sequía. *También,* **drouth** (draʊθ).

drove (droʊv) *n.* (of cattle or horses) manada; (of sheep) rebaño; (of mules) recua; (of pigs) piara. —*v., pret. de* **drive.** —**in droves,** en masa.

drover ('droʊ·vər) *n.* ganadero.

drown (draʊn) *v.t.* **1,** (suffocate with water) ahogar. **2,** (drench) inundar; anegar. **3,** [*también,* **drown out**] (deaden) sofocar; apagar. **4,** *fig.* (dispel, as sorrow) ahogar; olvidar. —*v.i.* **1,** (be suffocated) ahogarse. **2,** (be soaked) anegarse; inundarse.

drowse (draʊz) *v.i.* amodorrarse;

adormecerse. —*n.* siestita; siestecita.

drowsy ('drau·zi) *adj.* amodorrado; adormilado; adormecido. —**drowsiness,** *n.* modorra; somnolencia.

drub (drʌb) *v.t.* [**drubbed, drubbing**] 1, (beat) golpear; sacudir; apalear. 2, (defeat) ganar; vencer; derrotar. —**drubbing** (-ɪŋ) *n.* paliza; zurra; derrota.

drudge (drʌdʒ) *v.i.* afanarse. —*n.* esclavo (del trabajo). —**drudgery,** *n.* faena; afán; trabajo penoso.

drug (drʌg) *n.* 1, *pharm.* medicina. 2, (narcotic) droga; narcótico. —*v.t.* 1, (add a drug to) poner narcótico en. 2, (administer a drug to) narcotizar. —**drug on the market,** artículo difícil de vender.

druggist ('drʌg·ɪst) *n.* farmacéutico; boticario.

drugstore ('drʌg,stor) *n.* farmacia; botica.

druid ('dru·ɪd) *n.* druida.

drum (drʌm) *n.* tambor. —*v.i.* [**drummed, drumming**] 1, (play a drum) tocar el tambor. 2, (tap with the fingers) teclear; tamborilear. 3, (resound) resonar. —*v.t.* 1, *mil.* [*usu.,* **drum out**] expulsar a tambor batiente. 2, [*usu.,* **drum into**] (instill) machacar; repetir. —**drum major,** tambor mayor. —**drum up,** fomentar; avivar.

drumbeat ('drʌm,bit) *n.* redoble; toque de tambor.

drumhead ('drʌm,hɛd) *n.* piel de tambor; parche.

drummer ('drʌm·ər) *n.* 1, (drum player) tambor. 2, (traveling salesman) viajante.

drumstick ('drʌm·stɪk) *n.* 1, (baton) palillo. 2, (leg of fowl) muslo.

drunk (drʌŋk) *v., p.p. de* **drink**. —*n.* = **drunkard**. —*adj.* borracho; ebrio; beodo.

drunkard ('drʌŋk·ərd) *n.* borracho; borrachón; beodo.

drunken ('drʌŋk·ən) *adj.* *atributivo* = **drunk**. —**drunkenness,** *n.* embriaguez; borrachera.

drupe (drup) *n.* drupa.

dry (drai) *adj.* 1, (not wet) seco. 2, (sterile) estéril. 3, (thirsty) seco; sediento. 4, (arid) árido; sediento. 5, (dull) monótono; árido; aburrido. 6, (grave but humorous) incisivo; satírico; agudo. 7, (not sweet, as wine) seco. 8, (plain) escueto; frío. —*v.t.* secar. —*v.i.* secarse. —**dry**

cell, pila seca. —**dry dock,** dique seco o de carena. —**dry goods,** telas; tejidos. —**dry ice,** hielo seco; nieve carbónica. —**dry measure,** medida para áridos. —**dry up,** 1, secarse totalmente. 2, *colloq.* (be quiet) callarse.

dryad ('drai·æd) *n.* dríada.

dry-clean *v.t.* limpiar en seco. —**dry cleaning,** limpieza en seco.

dry-cleaner *n.* quitamanchas. —**dry-cleaner's,** *n.sing.* tintorería; quitamanchas.

dryness (drai·nəs) *n.* sequedad; aridez.

dual ('du·əl) *adj.* binario; dual; *gram.* dual.

dualism ('du·ə,lɪz·əm) *n.* dualismo. —**dualistic** (-'lɪs·tɪk) *adj.* dualístico.

duality (du'æl·ə·ti) *n.* dualidad.

dub (dʌb) *v.t.* [**dubbed, dubbing**] 1, (knight) armar caballero a. 2, (name) apellidar. 3, (confer a title on) dar título a. 4, (make smooth) alisar. 5, (in sound recording) doblar. —*n.,* *colloq.* (inept person) desmañado; torpe.

dubiety (du'bai·ə·ti) *n.* incertidumbre; duda.

dubious ('du·bi·əs) *adj.* 1, (doubtful) dudoso; incierto. 2, (of doubtful value) sospechoso; ambiguo. —**dubiousness,** *n.* duda; incertidumbre.

ducal ('du·kəl) *adj.* ducal.

ducat ('dʌk·ət) *n.* 1, (old coin) ducado. 2, *slang* (money) dinero; pasta.

duchess ('dʌtʃ·əs) *n.* duquesa.

duchy ('dʌtʃ·i) *n.* ducado.

duck (dʌk) *n.* 1, (fowl) pato. 2, (fabric) dril; *pl.,* pantalones de dril. 3, (evasive action) agachada. 4, (dip; immersion) zambullida —*v.t.* 1, (immerse) sumergir. 2, (bow) agachar rápidamente. 3, (dodge) evitar agachándose. 4, (avoid) evadir; evitar. —*v.i.* 1, (submerge) zambullirse. 2, (lower the head or body) agacharse. 3, *colloq.* (escape) evadirse; escaparse.

duckling ('dʌk·lɪŋ) *n.* anadeja.

ducky ('dʌk·i) *adj., colloq.* excelente. —*n.* querido [*fem.* querida].

duct (dʌkt) *n.* conducto; canal; tubo. —**ductless gland,** glándula cerrada. —**duct tape,** cinta adhesiva para tubos.

ductile ('dʌk·təl) *adj.* dúctil;

maleable. —**ductility** (-'tɪl·ə·ti) *n.* ductilidad.

dud (dʌd) *n., colloq.* **1,** (false coin) ochavo falso. **2,** (faulty explosive) bomba, granada o cohete que no estalla. **3,** (failure) fracaso; calamidad. **4,** *pl.* (clothes) trapos. —*adj.* falso; inútil.

dude (du:d) *n.* caballerete. —**dude ranch,** rancho de veraneo.

due (dju; du:) *adj.* **1,** (owed) debido; vencido; (payable) pagadero. **2,** (expected) esperado. **3,** (attributable) debido. **4,** (suitable) propio; apto. —*n.* **1,** (debt) deuda. **2,** *pl.* (fee) derechos. —**due bill,** pagaré. —**due to,** debido a. —**give (someone) his due,** ser justo hacia o con. —**in due time,** a su debido tiempo.

duel ('du·əl) *n.* duelo; desafío. —*v.t.* desafiar; combatir en duelo. —*v.i.* tener un duelo; batirse. —**duelist,** *n.* duelista.

duenna (dju'en·ə) *n.* dueña; doña; acompañante de señoritas.

duet (du'et) *n.* dueto.

duffel ('dʌf·əl) *n.* **1,** (woolen cloth) paño de lana basta. **2,** (outfit) equipo; pertrechos. —**duffel bag,** talego.

duffer ('dʌf·ər) *n.* **1,** (peddler) buhonero. **2,** (inept person) desmañado; torpe.

dug (dʌg) *v., pret. & p.p. de* **dig.** —*n.* teta; pezón.

dugout ('dʌg·aut) *n.* **1,** (boat) canoa; piragua. **2,** (shelter) refugio subterráneo.

duke (duk) *n.* duque. —**dukedom** (-dəm) *n.* ducado.

dulcet ('dʌl·sət) *adj.* dulce; suave; armonioso; melodioso.

dull (dʌl) *adj.* **1,** (stupid) estúpido; lerdo. **2,** (tedious; boring) árido; tedioso; fastidioso; aburrido. **3,** (dismal) lánguido; triste; desanimado. **4,** (dim) empañado; nebuloso. **5,** (blunt) obtuso; romo. **6,** (slack) inactivo; muerto; paralizado. —*v.t.* **1,** (blunt) embotar. **2,** (benumb) entorpecer. —**dullness,** *n.* **1,** (stupidity) estupidez. **2,** (tediousness) aburrimiento; pesadez.

dullard ('dʌl·ərd) *n.* lerdo; estúpido; idiota.

dullwitted ('dʌl,wɪt·ɪd) *adj.* boto; estúpido; lerdo.

duly ('du·li) *adv.* **1,** (as owed) debidamente; propiamente. **2,** (on time) puntualmente. **3,** (as required) exactamente.

dumb (dʌm) *adj.* **1,** (mute) mudo. **2,** (silent) callado; silencioso. **3,** *colloq.* (moronic) estúpido; lerdo. —**dumbness,** *n.* mudez; silencio; estupidez. —**dumb show,** pantomima.

dumbbell ('dʌm·bɛl) *n.* **1,** (weight for exercise) bola gimnástica. **2,** *slang* (dolt) estúpido. .

dumbwaiter ('dʌm,wei·tər) *n.* montacargas.

dumfound *también,* **dumbfound** (dʌm'faund) *v.t.* dejar mudo; confundir; pasmar.

dummy ('dʌm·i) *n.* **1,** (mute) mudo. **2,** (model) maniquí; (figurehead) testaferro; figurón. **3,** (effigy) efigie; imagen. **4,** *cards* muerto. **5,** *print.* modelo o copia (en blanco). **6,** (sham) imitación; remedo. —*adj.* falso; de imitación; fingido.

dump (dʌmp) *v.t.* **1,** (unload) descargar. **2,** (spill) verter. **3,** (throw away) tirar; arrojar. **4,** *comm.* vender (exceso de productos) al extranjero más barato que en el mercado nacional. —*n.* **1,** (field for rubbish) vertedero; basurero. **2,** *mil.* (storage place) depósito de municiones o de materiales. **3,** *slang* (hovel; shack) cuchitril. —**in the dumps,** melancólico; desanimado.

dumpling ('dʌmp·liŋ) *n.* relleno; bola de pasta rellena de fruta o carne.

dumpy ('dʌm·pi) *adj., colloq.* regordete; rechoncho.

dun (dʌn) *v.t.* [**dunned, dunning**] importunar; apremiar. —*n.* apremio. —*adj. & n.* (color) pardo; bruno.

dunce (dʌns) *n.* torpe; ignorante; zopenco. —**dunce cap,** gorro de tonto.

dune (dun) *n.* duna.

dung (dʌŋ) *n.* estiércol; excremento; slang caca. —**dung caca.**

dungaree (,dʌŋ·gə'ri:) *n.* **1,** (coarse fabric) tela de mono. **2,** *pl.* (work clothes) mono; traje de faena.

dungeon ('dʌn·dʒən) *n.* calabozo; mazmorra.

dunghill ('dʌŋ,hɪl) *n.* estercolar; estercolero.

dunk (dʌŋk) *v.t.* ensopar; empapar; remojar.

duo ('du·o) *n.* dúo; dueto; pareja.

duodecimal (,du·o'dɛs·ɪ·məl) *adj.* duodecimal.

duodenum (,du·o'di·nəm) *n.*

duodeno. —**duodenal** (-nəl) *adj*. duodenal.

dupe (dup) *v.t.* engañar; embaucar. —*n.* primo; incauto; bobo. —**dupery** ('du·pə·ri) *n.* engaño; embaucamiento.

duplex ('du·plɛks) *adj*. doble; duplo. —*n.* apartamento de dos pisos.

duplicate ('du·pli·kət) *n. & adj.* duplicado. —*v.t.* (-,keit) duplicar. —**duplication** (-'kei·ʃən) *n.* duplicación. —**duplicator** (-,ke·tər) *n.* multicopista.

duplicity (du'plis·ə·ti) *n.* doblez; duplicidad.

durable ('dʊr·ə·bəl) *adj*. durable; duradero. —**durability**, *n.* durabilidad.

dura mater ('djʊr·ə'mei·tər) duramadre.

duration (dʊ'rei·ʃən) *n.* duración.

duress (dʊ'rɛs; 'djʊr·əs) *n.* 1, (imprisonment) encierro; prisión. 2, (coercion) coacción.

during ('dʊr·iŋ) *prep.* durante; mientras.

durst (dʌrst) *v., archaic, pret. de* **dare**.

durum ('dʊr·əm) *n.* trigo duro.

dusk (dʌsk) *n.* 1, (twilight) anochecida; crepúsculo. 2, (partial darkness) penumbra.

dusky ('dʌsk·i) *adj*. 1, (dim) oscuro. 2, (swarthy) moreno; atezado. —**duskiness**, *n.* atezamiento.

dust (dʌst) *n.* 1, (tiny bits, as of earth) polvo. 2, *fig.* (remains) cenizas; restos. —*v.i.* 1, (rid of dust) quitar el polvo a; desempolvar. 2, (sprinkle) empolvar; espolvorear. —**dust bowl**, cuenca polvorienta. —**dust jacket**, sobrecubierta.

duster ('dʌs·tər) *n.* 1, (cloth for dusting) paño del polvo; (feather duster) plumero. 2, (protective coat) guardapolvo.

dustpan ('dʌst,pæn) *n.* pala de recoger la basura.

dusty ('dʌs·ti) *adj*. polvoriento.

Dutch (dʌtʃ) *n. & adj.* 1, (of Holland) holandés. 2, *U.S. slang* (German) alemán. —**Dutch oven**, horno portátil. —**Dutch treat**, *colloq.* convite a escote. —**Dutch uncle**, mentor severo. —**in Dutch**, *slang* 1, (in disfavor) en desgracia. 2, (in trouble) en apuros.

duteous ('du·ti·əs) *adj*. = **dutiful**.

dutiable ('du·ti·ə·bəl) *adj*. sujeto a derechos de aduana.

dutiful ('du·tɪ·fəl) *adj*. 1, (obedient) obediente; respetuoso. 2, (diligent) meticuloso; diligente.

duty ('du·ti) *n.* 1, (obligation) deber; obligación. 2, (responsibility) faena; tarea; obligación. 3, (tax) impuesto; derecho. —**duty free**, exento de impuestos. —**off duty**, libre (de servicio). —**on duty**, de servicio.

dwarf (dworf) *n. & adj.* enano. —*v.t.* 1, (stunt the growth of) impedir crecer; parar. 2, (make to seem smaller) empequeñecer; achicar. —**dwarfish**, *adj*. enano; diminuto.

dwell (dwɛl) *v.i.* [*pret. & p.p.* **dwelt** o **dwelled**] 1, (remain) estar. 2, (reside) vivir; morar. —**dweller**, *n.* habitante; morador; residente. —**dwelling**, *n.* morada; vivienda. —**dwell on** o **upon**, explayarse en.

dwindle ('dwin·dəl) *v.i.* disminuirse; achicarse; encogerse. —*v.t.* disminuir; acortar; encoger.

dyad ('dai·æd) *n.* elemento bivalente. —*adj*. bivalente.

dye (dai) *n.* tinte; colorante. —*v.t.* [dyed, dyeing] teñir; tintar. —**dyer**, *n.* tintorero. —**dyeing**, *n.* tinte; tintura.

dyestuff ('dai,stʌf) *n.* materia colorante.

dying ('dai·iŋ) *v., p.pr. de* **die**. —*adj*. moribundo; agonizante. —*n.* (death) muerte.

dynamic (dai'næm·ik) *adj*. dinámico; enérgico.

dynamics (dai'næm·iks) *n.* dinámica; *pl.* fuerzas dinámicas.

dynamism ('dai·nə,miz·əm) *n.* dinamismo.

dynamite ('dai·nə,mait) *n.* dinamita. —*v.t.* dinamitar.

dynamo ('dai·nə·mo) *n.* [*pl.* -**mos**] dínamo. —**dynamometer** (-'mam·i·tər) *n.* dinamómetro.

dynasty ('dai·nəs·ti) *n.* dinastía. —**dynast** (-,næst) *n.* dinasta. —**dynastic** (-'næs·tik) *adj*. dinástico.

dyne (dain) *n., physics* dina.

dysentery ('dis·ən·tɛr·i) *n.* disentería.

dysfunction (dis'fʌŋk·ʃən) *n.* disfunción.

dyslexia (dis'lɛk·si·ə) *n.* dislexia. —**dyslexic**, *adj*. disléxico.

dyspepsia (dis'pɛp·ʃə) *n.* dispepsia.

dyspeptic (dıs'pɛp·tık) *adj.* **1**, (suffering from indigestion) dispéptico. **2**, (irritable) melancólico; irritable.

dysprosium (dis'pro·si·əm) *n.* disprosio.

dystrophy ('dıs·trə·fi) *n.* distrofia.

E

E, e (iː) quinta letra del alfabeto inglés. —*n.*, *mus.* mi.

each (itʃ) *adj.* cada; todo. —*pron.* cada uno; cada cual. —*adv.* por persona; por cabeza; por pieza. —**each other**, mutuamente; uno a otro.

eager ('i·gər) *adj.* ansioso; anhelante; afanoso. —**eagerness**, *n.* ansia; anhelo; afán.

eagle ('i·gəl) *n.* águila. —**eaglet** (-glət) *n.* aguilucho.

ear (ır) *n.* **1**, (outer ear) oreja. **2**, (inner ear) oído. **3**, (hearing) oído. **4**, (of corn) mazorca. **5**, (of wheat, etc.) espiga. —*v.i.* espigar. —**turn a deaf ear**, hacerse sordo.

eardrum ('ır,drʌm) *n.* tímpano.

earl (ʌrl) *n.* conde. —**earldom** (-dəm) *n.* condado.

earliness ('ʌr·li·nəs) *n.* **1**, (punctualness) prontitud. **2**, (prematureness) precocidad.

early ('ʌr·li) *adj. & adv.* (near the beginning of a stated time) temprano. —*adj.* **1**, (ancient) primitivo; antiguo. **2**, (before expected) precoz; prematuro. **3**, (in the near future) próximo; cercano. —*adv.* **1**, (soon) pronto. **2**, (at an early time) temprano. **3**, (before expected) temprano; con anticipación; precozmente. —**early bird; early riser**, madrugador. —**early in the morning**, muy de mañana. —**rise early**, madrugar.

early-rising *adj.* madrugador; madrugón.

earmark ('ır·mark) *n.* señal de identificación. —*v.t.* asignar; señalar.

earn (ʌrn) *v.t.* **1**, (as wages) ganar. **2**, (as interest) devengar. **3**, (deserve) merecer; ganar. —**earnings**, *n.pl.* sueldo; salario; jornal.

earnest ('ʌr·nəst) *adj.* **1**, (serious) serio; formal; sincero. **2**, (diligent) activo; celoso. —*n.* prenda; señal; arras. —**earnestness**, *n.* formalidad; seriedad. —**in earnest**, en serio.

earphone ('ır,fon) *n.* auricular; audífono.

earring ('ır,rıŋ) *n.* pendiente; arete; zarcillo.

earshot ('ır·ʃat) *n.* alcance del oído.

earth (ʌrθ) *n.* **1**, *often cap.* (planet) tierra; globo terráqueo; orbe. **2**, (soil) suelo. **3**, (people of the world) gente; mundo. —**earth science**, ciencia ecológica.

earthen ('ʌrθ·ən) *adj.* térreo; terrizo. —**earthenware**, *n.* loza de barro; alfarería.

earthiness ('ʌr·θi·nəs) *n.* **1**, (quality of earth) terrosidad. **2**, (coarseness) tosquedad.

earthling ('ʌrθ·lıŋ) *n.* habitante de la tierra; mortal; mundano.

earthly ('ʌrθ·li) *adj.* terreno; terrestre; terrenal; mundano. —**earthliness**, *n.* terrenidad; mundanalidad.

earthquake ('ʌrθ,kweik) *n.* terremoto; temblor de tierra.

earthworks ('ʌrθ,wʌrks) *n.pl.* terraplén.

earthworm ('ʌrθ,wʌrm) *n.* lombriz de tierra.

earthy ('ʌr·θi) *adj.* **1**, (of earth) terrizo; terroso. **2**, (coarse) grosero; tosco.

earwax ('ır,wæks) *n.* cerumen; cerilla.

ease (iːz) *n.* **1**, (comfort) comodidad. **2**, (mental calm) tranquilidad; sosiego. **3**, (facility) facilidad. **4**, (unaffectedness) naturalidad; desenvoltura. —*v.t.* **1**, (put at ease) aliviar; descansar. **2**, (mitigate) aligerar; descargar. **3**, (facilitate) facilitar. —*v.i.* **1**, (be mitigated) aliviarse; disminuir. **2**, (move slowly) moverse lentamente. —**at ease**, cómodo; *mil.* ¡en su lugar descansen! —**take one's ease**, descansar.

easel ('iː·zəl) *n.* caballete de pintor.

easement ('iːz·mənt) *n.* **1**, (easing) alivio; descarga. **2**, *law* servidumbre.

east (ist) *n.* este; oriente. —*adj.*

este; del este; oriental. —*adv.* hacia el este; al este.

Easter ('is·tər) *n.* Pascua de Resurrección. —**Easter Day,** día de Pascua; domingo de gloria. —**Easter Eve,** sábado santo.

easterly ('irs·tər·li) *adj.* este; del este; hacia el este. —*adv.* hacia el este.

eastern ('irs·tərn) *adj.* este; del este; oriental. —**easterner,** *n.* oriental; habitante del este.

eastward ('ist·wərd) *adj.* en o de dirección este. —*adv.* hacia el este.

easy ('iz·zi) *adj.* **1,** (not difficult) fácil. **2,** (comfortable; tranquil) cómodo; tranquilo. **3,** (not oppressive) complaciente; condescendiente; razonable. —**easiness,** *n.* facilidad; comodidad; tranquilidad; soltura. —**easy chair,** butaca; sillón; poltrona. —**go easy on,** tratar suavemente. —**on easy street,** *slang* en situación acomodada.

easygoing ('iz·zi,go·ıŋ) *adj.* lento; tranquilo; despreocupado.

eat (it) *v.t.* [**ate, eaten, eating**] **1,** (consume) comer. **2,** (corrode) corroer; consumir. —*v.i.* comer; alimentarse; sustentarse. —**eatables,** *n.pl., colloq.* comestibles; víveres; vituallas. —**eat crow,** humillarse; rendirse. —**eat humble pie,** ceder; admitir la derrota. —**eat one's words,** desdecirse. —**eat out,** comer fuera. —**eats,** *n.pl., slang* alimentos.

eaves (izvz) *n.pl.* alero.

eavesdrop ('izvz,drap) *v.i.* [**-dropped, -dropping**] escuchar a las puertas; escuchar a escondidas. —**eavesdropper,** *n.* escucha. —**eavesdropping,** *n.* escucha.

ebb (eb) *v.i.* **1,** (recede) bajar. **2,** *fig.* (decline) decaer; disminuir. —*n.* decaimiento; disminución. —**ebb tide,** marea menguante; bajamar.

ebony ('eb·ə·ni) *n.* ébano. —*adj.* **1,** (made of ebony) de ébano. **2,** (black) negro.

ebullient (ı'bʌl·jənt) *adj.* **1,** (boiling) hirviente. **2,** (excited) apasionado; entusiasta. —**ebullience,** *n.* entusiasmo; alegría.

ebullition (,eb·ə'lıʃ·ən) *n.* **1,** (boiling) ebullición. **2,** *fig.* (excitement) agitación; conmoción.

eccentric (ɛk'sɛn·trık) *adj.* **1,** (off center) excéntrico. **2,** (unusual) extraño; extravagante; excéntrico;

estrafalario; raro. —*n.* **1,** (eccentric person) excéntrico; persona excéntrica. **2,** (device) excéntrica. —**eccentricity** (,ɛk·sən'trıs·ə·ti) *n.* excentricidad.

ecclesiastic (ɛ,kli·zi'æs·tık) *n.* eclesiástico; clérigo. —*adj.* [*también,* **ecclesiastical**] eclesiástico.

echelon ('ɛʃ·ə,lan) *n., mil.* **1,** (level of command) escalón. **2,** (deployment) despliegue escalonado.

echo ('ɛk·oʒ) *n.* eco. —*v.i.* hacer eco; repercutir; reverberar; resonar. —*v.t.* repetir. —**echoic,** *adj.* onomatopéyico.

eclectic (ɛk'lɛk·tık) *adj. & n.* ecléctico. —**eclecticism** (-sız·əm) *n.* eclecticismo.

eclipse (ı'klıps) *n.* eclipse. —*v.t.* eclipsar. —**ecliptic** (ı'klıp·tık) *n.* eclíptica. —*adj.* eclíptico.

eclogue ('ɛk·lag) *n.* égloga.

ecology (ı'kal·ə·dʒi) *n.* ecología. —**ecological** (-'ladʒ·ı·kəl) ecológico. —**ecologist,** *n.* ecólogo.

economic (,i·kə'nam·ık; ,ɛk·ə-) *adj.* económico. —**economics,** *n.pl.* economía.

economical (,i·kə'nam·ı·kəl; ,ɛk·ə-) *adj.* económico; ahorrativo; frugal; parco.

economy (ı'ka·nə·mi) *n.* economía; ahorro. —**economist** (-mıst) *n.m. & f.* economista. —**economize** (-maiz) *v.i.* economizar; ahorrar.

ecosystem ('ɛk·o,sıs·təm) *n.* ecosistema.

ecru ('ɛk·ru;) *adj.* amarillento.

ecstasy ('ɛk·stə·si) *n.* éxtasis; rapto; transporte. —**ecstatic** (ɛk·'stæt·ık) *adj.* extático.

ectoplasm ('ɛk·tə,plæz·əm) *n.* ectoplasma.

Ecuadoran (ɛk·wə'dor·ən) *also,* **Ecuadorian** (-i·ən) *n. & adj.* ecuatoriano.

ecumenical (,ɛk·ju'mɛn·ı·kəl) *adj.* ecuménico.

eczema ('ɛk·sə·mə; 'ɛg·zə-) *n.* eczema.

eddy ('ɛd·i) *n.* remolino. —*v.t.* arremolinar. —*v.i.* arremolinarse.

edema (ı'di·mə) *n.* edema.

Eden ('i·dən) *n.* Edén.

edge (ɛdʒ) *n.* **1,** (border) borde; orilla; margen. **2,** (sharp side) filo; corte; canto. **3,** *geom.* arista. **4,** *colloq.* (advantage) ventaja. —*v.t.* **1,** (trim) orlar; ribetear; bordear. **2,** (sharpen) afilar; aguzar. —*v.i.*

avanzar de lado. —**edgy,** *adj.* impaciente; irritable; nervioso.

edging ('ɛdʒ·ɪŋ) *n.* orilla; ribete; pestaña.

edgewise ('ɛdʒ·waiz) *adj. & adv.* de filo; de canto.

edible ('ɛd·ə·bəl) *adj. & n.* comestible. —**edibility,** *n.* calidad de comestible.

edict ('i·dɪkt) *n.* edicto.

edifice ('ɛd·ə·fɪs) *n.* edificio.

edify ('ɛd·ɪ,fai) *v.t. & i.* edificar. —**edification** (-fɪ'kei'ʃən) *n.* edificación.

edit ('ɛ·dɪt) *v.t.* **1,** (revise) redactar; revisar; corregir. **2,** (supervise publication of) dirigir.

edition (ɪ'dɪʃ·ən) *n.* edición; tirada.

editor ('ɛd·ɪ·tər) *n.* redactor; compilador; director (de un periódico).

editorial (,ɛd·ɪ'tor·i·əl) *adj.* editorial. —*n.* editorial; artículo de fondo. —**editorialize** (-ə,laiz) *v.i.* escribir editoriales.

educate ('ɛd·ju,keit) *v.t.* educar; instruir; enseñar. —**educated** (-,ke·tɪd) *adj.* culto; instruido. —**educator** (-,ke·tər) *n.* educador; pedagogo.

education (,ɛd·ju'kei·ʃən) *n.* educación; instrucción; enseñanza. —**educational,** *adj.* educativo.

eel (i:l) *n.* anguila.

e'en (ɪn) *adv., poet.* = **even.** —*n., poet.* = **even** (evening).

e'er (ɛɪr) *adv., poet.* = **ever.**

eerie ('ɪr·i) *adj.* espectral; misterioso.

efface (ɛ'feis) *v.t.* **1,** (erase) borrar; raspar; tachar. **2,** (make inconspicuous) apagar. —**effacement,** *n.* tachadura; raspadura; destrucción.

effect (ɛ'fɛkt) *n.* **1,** (result) efecto; resultado; impresión. **2,** (force) efecto; eficacia; eficiencia; validez. **3,** *pl.* (personal property) efectos; bienes muebles. —*v.t.* efectuar. —**effective,** *adj.* eficaz; válido; fuerte. —**effectiveness,** *n.* eficacia.

effectual (ɛ'fɛk·tʃu·əl) *adj.* eficaz.

effectuate (ɛ'fɛk·tʃu·eit) *v.t.* efectuar.

effeminate (ə'fɛm·ɪ·nət) *adj.* afeminado. —**effeminacy** (-ɪ·nə·si) *n.* afeminamiento; afeminación.

effervesce (ɛf·ər'vɛs) *v.i.* fermentar; estar en efervescencia. —**effervescence,** *n.* efervescencia. —**effervescent,** *adj.* efervescente.

effete (ə'fit) *adj.* usado; gastado; agotado.

efficacious (,ɛf·ɪ'kei·ʃəs) *adj.* eficaz. —**efficacy** ('ɛf·ɪ·kə·si) *n.* fuerza; validez; eficacia.

efficiency (ɪ'fɪʃ·ən·si) *n.* eficiencia; competencia.

efficient (ɪ'fɪʃ·ənt) *adj.* **1,** (competent) eficiente; competente. **2,** *mech.* (productive) de buen rendimiento.

effigy ('ɛf·ə·dʒi) *n.* efigie.

efflorescence (,ɛf·lo'rɛs·əns) *n.* eflorescencia. —**efflorescent,** *adj.* eflorescente.

effluence ('ɛf·lu·əns) *n.* **1,** efluvio; chorro. **2,** emanación.

effluent (-ənt) *adj.* corriente. —*n.* chorro.

effluvium (ɪ'flu·vi·əm) *n.* efluvio.

effort ('ɛf·ərt) *n.* **1,** (exertion) esfuerzo. **2,** (achievement) obra. —**effortless,** *adj.* sin esfuerzo. —**effortlessly,** *adv.* fácilmente.

effrontery (ɪ'frʌn·tə·ri) *n.* desfachatez; descaro; desvergüenza.

effulgent (ɪ'fʌl·dʒənt) *adj.* fulgente; resplandeciente. —**effulgence,** *n.* fulgor; fulgencia.

effuse (ɛ'fjuːz) *v.t.* derramar; verter. —*v.i.* emanar; exudar. —*adj.* (ɛ'fjus) esparcido. —**effusion** (ɪ'fju·ʒən) *n.* efusión; derrame. —**effusive** (ɪ'fju·sɪv) *adj.* efusivo; expansivo; comunicativo.

egad (i'gæd) *interj.* ¡Dios mío!

egalitarian (i,gæl·ə'tɛr·i·ən) *adj.* igualitario. —*n.* persona que favorece ideas igualitarias.

egg (ɛg) *n.* huevo; *Mex.* postura; blanquillo. —*v.t.* incitar; provocar.

eggplant ('ɛg,plænt) *n.* berenjena.

eggshell ('ɛg,ʃɛl) *n.* cáscara de huevo; cascarón.

egis *también,* **aegis** ('iː·dʒɪs) *n.* égida.

eglantine ('ɛg·lən,tain) *n.* eglantina.

ego ('i·go) *n.* **1,** [*pl.* -gos] (self) ego; yo. **2,** *colloq.* = **egotism.**

egocentric (,i·gə'sɛn·trɪk) *adj.* egocéntrico.

egoism ('i·go,ɪz·əm) *n.* egoísmo. —**egoist,** *n.* egoísta. —**egoistic,** *adj.* egoísta.

egomania (,i·gə'mei·ni·ə) *n.* egotismo excesivo. —**egomaniac** (-'mei·ni·æk) *n.* persona excesivamente egotista.

egotism ('i·gə,tɪz·əm) *n.* egotismo. —**egotist,** *n.* egotista. —**egotistic; egotistical,** *adj.* egotista.

egregious (ɪ'griː·dʒəs) *adj.* **1**, (utter; complete) perfecto; cabal. **2**, (flagrant) atroz; escandaloso; enorme.

egress ('iː·grɛs) *n.* salida.

egret ('iː·grɛt) *n.* airón.

Egyptian (ɪ'dʒɪp·ʃən) *adj. & n.* egipcio.

eh (ei) *interj.* ¡eh! —**eh?**, ¿qué?; ¿eh?; ¿no?

eider ('ai·dər) *n.* [también, **eider duck**] eíder; pato de flojel. —**eider down**, edredón.

eight (eit) *n. & adj.* ocho.

eighteen ('e'tin) *n. & adj.* diez y ocho; dieciocho. —**eighteenth** (-tinθ) *n. & adj.* décimoctavo; dieciochavo.

eightfold ('eit,fold) *adj. & n.* óctuple; ocho veces (más). —*adv.* ocho veces; en un óctuple.

eighth (eitθ) *adj.* octavo. —*n.* octavo; octava parte; *mus.* octava.

eight hundred ochocientos. —**eight-hundredth**, *adj. & n.* octingentésimo.

eighty ('e·ti) *n. & adj.* ochenta. —**eightieth** (-əθ) *n. & adj.* octogésimo; ochentavo.

einsteinium ('ain,stain·i·əm) *n.* einsteinio.

either ('iː·ðer; 'ai-) *adj. & pron.* uno u otro; cualquiera de los dos; uno y otro. —*conj.* o —*adv.* tampoco. —**either ... or**, o ... o.

ejaculate (ɪ'dʒæk·jə·leit) *v.t.* **1**, (exclaim) exclamar; proferir. **2**, (emit forcibly) eyacular.

ejaculation (ɪ,dʒæk·jə'lei·ʃən) **1**, (exclamation) exclamación. **2**, (discharge) eyaculación. **3**, (short prayer) jaculatoria.

eject (ɪ'dʒɛkt) *v.t.* echar; arrojar; expeler; expulsar. —**ejection** (ɪ'dʒɛk·ʃən) *n.* expulsión. —**ejector**, *n.* eyector; expulsor.

eke (ik) *v.t.* [*usu.*, **eke out**] **1**, (obtain with difficulty) ganar a duras penas. **2**, (supplement) suplementar; suplir.

elaborate (ɪ'læb·ə·rət) *adj.* **1**, (carefully worked out) detallado; primoroso. **2**, (intricate; involved) complicado; intrincado. —*v.t.* (-reit) elaborar; complicar; detallar. —*v.i.* dar detalles. —**elaborateness**, *n.* primor; complicación. —**elaboration** (-'rei·ʃən) *n.* elaboración.

elapse (ɪ'læps) *v.i.* mediar; pasar; transcurrir.

elastic (ɪ'læs·tɪk) *adj. & n.* elástico. —**elasticity** (,ɪ·læs'tɪs·ə·ti) *n.* elasticidad.

elate (ɪ'leit) *v.t.* regocijar. —**elation**, *n.* júbilo; alborozo; regocijo.

elbow ('ɛl·boʊ) *n.* **1**, *anat.* codo. **2**, (angle) recodo; ángulo. —*v.t.* dar codazos a; dar con el codo a. —*v.i.* abrirse paso con el codo; codear. —**elbow grease**, *colloq.* trabajo físico. —**elbow room**, *colloq.* amplio espacio; libertad de acción.

elder ('ɛl·dər) *adj.* mayor; de más edad. —*n.* **1**, (older person) mayor; anciano. **2**, (person of authority) dignatario. **3**, (shrub) saúco. —**elderly** (-li) *adj.* mayor; de edad madura. —**elderliness**, *n.* ancianidad. —**eldest** (-dəst) *adj.* el mayor.

elect (ɪ'lɛkt) *v.t.* **1**, (select by vote) elegir. **2**, (choose) elegir; escoger. —*adj.* **1**, (elected) electo; elegido. **2**, (chosen) escogido. —*n.* elegido; electo; *theol.* predestinado.

election (ɪ'lɛk·ʃən) *n.* elección. —**electioneer** (-ʃə'nɪr) *v.i.* solicitar votos.

elective (ɪ'lɛk·tɪv) *adj.* **1**, (chosen by election) electivo. **2**, (optional) facultativo; potestativo.

elector (ɪ'lɛkt·ər) *n.* elector.

electoral (ɪ'lɛk·tə·rəl) *adj.* electoral.

electorate (ɪ'lɛk·tə·rət) *n.* electorado.

electric (ɪ'lɛk·trɪk) *adj.* **1**, [también, **electrical**] eléctrico. **2**, *fig.* (exciting) vivo; ardiente.

electrician (ɪ,lɛk'trɪʃ·ən) *n.* electricista.

electricity (ɪ,lɛk'trɪs·ə·ti) *n.* electricidad.

electrification (ɪ,lɛk·trə·fɪ'kei·ʃən) *n.* **1**, (providing with electricity) electrificación. **2**, (stimulation) electrización.

electrify (ɪ'lɛk·trɪ,fai) *v.t.* **1**, (charge with electricity) electrizar. **2**, (equip for electricity) electrificar. **3**, (startle; thrill) avivar; inflamar.

electrocute (ɪ'lɛk·trə·kjut) *v.t.* electrocutar. —**electrocution** (-'kju·ʃən) *n.* electrocución. —**electrocutionist**, *n.* electrocutor.

electrode (ɪ'lɛk·trod) *n.* electrodo.

electrolysis (ɪ,lɛk'tral·ə·sɪs) *n.* electrólisis. —**electrolytic** (-trə'lɪt·ɪk) *adj.* electrolítico.

electrolyte (ɪ'lɛk·trə·lait) *n.* electrólito.

electrolyze (ɪˈlɛk·trəˌlaiz) *v.t.* electrolizar.

electromagnet (ɪˈlɛk·trəˌmæg·nət) *n.* electroimán. —**electromagnetic** (-mægˈnɛt·ɪk) *adj.* electromagnético. —**electromagnetism** (-ˈmæg·nəˌtɪz·əm) *n.* electromagnetismo.

electromotive (ɪˌlɛk·trəˈmo·tɪv) *adj.* electromotriz.

electron (ɪˈlɛk·tran) *n.* electrón.

electronic (ɪˌlɛkˈtran·ɪk) *adj.* electrónico. —**electronics,** *n.* electrónica.

electrostatic (ɪˌlɛk·trəˈstæt·ɪk) *adj.* electrostático. —**electrostatics,** *n.* electrostática.

electrotype (ɪˈlɛk·trə·taip) *n.* electrotipo.

elegant (ˈɛl·ɪ·gənt) *adj.* elegante. —**elegance,** *n.* elegancia.

elegiac (ɛˈliː·dʒi·æk) *adj.* elegíaco.

elegy (ˈɛl·ə·dʒi) *n.* elegía. —**elegize** (-dʒaiz) *v.t. & i.* lamentar.

element (ˈɛl·ə·mənt) *n.* **1,** *chem.* cuerpo simple; elemento. **2,** (component) elemento; componente; ingrediente. **3,** (environment) medio; ambiente. **4,** *pl.* (fundamentals) nociones; elementos; principios. **5,** *pl.* (weather) elementos; fuerzas naturales. —**elemental** (ɛl·əˈmɛn·təl) *adj.* elemental.

elementary (ˌɛl·ɪˈmɛn·tə·ri) *adj.* elemental; rudimentario. —**elementary school,** escuela primaria.

elephant (ˈɛl·ə·fənt) *n.* elefante. —**elephantine** (-ˈfæn·tɪn) *adj.* elefantino.

elephantiasis (ˌɛl·ə·fənˈtai·ə·sɪs) *n.* elefancía; elefantiasis.

elevate (ˈɛl·ə·veit) *v.t.* elevar; alzar; levantar. —**elevated,** *adj. & n.* elevado.

elevation (ˌɛl·ɪˈvei·ʃən) *n.* **1,** (raising) elevación. **2,** (altitude) altura; altitud. **3,** (high place) altura; eminencia. **4,** (in mechanical drawing) alzado; proyección vertical.

elevator (ˈɛl·ɪˌve·tər) *n.* **1,** (conveyance) ascensor; montacargas; elevador. **2,** (storehouse for grain) depósito de granos. **3,** *aero.* timón de profundidad; elevador.

eleven (ɪˈlɛv·ən) *n. & adj.* once. —**eleventh** (-ənθ) *n. & adj.* undécimo; onceno; onceavo. —**eleventh hour,** el último momento.

elf (ɛlf) *n.* [*pl.* **elves**] elfo; duende. —**elfin** (ˈɛl·fɪn) *adj.* de duende.

elicit (ɪˈlɪs·ɪt) *v.t.* sonsacar; evocar. —**elicitation,** *n.* sonsacamiento; evocación.

elide (ɪˈlaid) *v.t.* elidir. —**elision** (ɪˈlɪʒ·ən) *n.* elisión.

eligible (ˈɛl·ə·dʒə·bəl) *adj.* elegible. —**eligibility** (-ˈbɪl·ə·ti) *n.* elegibilidad.

eliminate (ɪˈlɪm·əˌneit) *v.t.* eliminar. —**elimination,** *n.* eliminación.

elite (eˈlit) *n.* flor y nata; lo selecto; lo escogido. —**elitism,** *n.* dominio de un grupo selecto. —**elitist,** *n.* miembro de un grupo selecto.

elixir (ɪˈlɪk·sər) *n.* elíxir; elixir.

elk (ɛlk) *n.* anta; alce.

ell (ɛl) *n.* **1,** (wing) ala. **2,** (measure) ana.

ellipse (ɪˈlɪps) *n.* elipse.

ellipsis (ɪˈlɪp·sɪs) *n.* [*pl.* **-ses** (siz)] elipsis.

elliptical (ɪˈlɪp·tɪ·kəl) *adj.* elíptico.

elm (ɛlm) *n.* olmo.

elocution (ɛl·əˈkjuː·ʃən) *n.* elocución; declamación. —**elocutionary** (-ʃəˌnɛ·ri) *adj.* declamatorio. —**elocutionist** (-ɪst) *n.* declamador.

elongate (ɪˈlɔŋ·geit) *v.t.* alargar; extender. —*v.i.* alargarse; prolongarse. —**elongation,** *n.* alargamiento.

elope (ɪˈlop) *v.i.* escaparse; fugarse. —**elopement,** *n.* fuga.

eloquent (ˈɛl·ə·kwənt) *adj.* elocuente. —**eloquence,** *n.* elocuencia.

else (ɛls) *adj.* otro; diferente; más. —*adv.* **1,** (more) más. **2,** (also) además. **3,** (otherwise) de otro modo; de otra manera.

elsewhere (ˈɛls·hwɛr) *adv.* en, a o de otra parte.

elucidate (ɪˈlu·sɪˌdeit) *v.t.* elucidar; dilucidar; aclarar. —**elucidation,** *n.* elucidación; dilucidación; aclaración.

elude (ɪˈluːd) *v.t.* eludir; esquivar; evitar; evadir.

elusion (ɪˈluːʃən) *n.* evasión.

elusive (ɪˈluːsɪv) *adj.* evasivo. *También,* **elusory** (-sə·ri).

elves (ɛlvz) *n., pl. de* **elf.**

emaciate (ɪˈmeiˈʃiˌeit) *v.t.* adelgazar; enflaquecer; extenuar. —**emaciation,** *n.* adelgazamiento; enflaquecimiento; extenuación.

emanate (ˈɛm·əˌneit) *v.i.* emanar; derivar; proceder. —**emanation,** *n.* emanación; exhalación.

emancipate (ɪˈmæn·sɪˌpeit) *v.t.*

emancipar; libertar. —**emancipation,** *n.* emancipación. —**emancipator,** *n.* emancipador; libertador.

emasculate (ɪ'mæs·kju,leit) *v.t.* castrar; capar; mutilar. —**emasculation,** *n.* castradura; castración; mutilación.

embalm (ɛm'baːrm) *v.t.* embalsamar. —**embalmer,** *n.* embalsamador. —**embalmment,** *n.* embalsamamiento.

embank (ɛm'bæŋk) *v.t.* represar; terraplenar. —**embankment,** *n.* malecón; dique; terraplén.

embargo (ɛm'baːr,go) *v.t.* embargar. —*n.* embargo.

embark (ɛm'bark) *v.i.* embarcarse. **embarkation** (,ɛm·bar'kei·ʃən) *n.* **1,** (of passengers) embarco; embarcación. **2,** (of freight) embarque.

embarrass (ɛm'bær·əs) *v.t.* **1,** (abash) turbar; desconcertar. **2,** (perplex) desconcertar. **3,** (hamper; impede) estorbar; poner en un aprieto.

embarrassment (ɛm'bær·əs·mənt) *n.* **1,** (abashment) turbación; desconcierto. **2,** (perplexity) desconcierto; perplejidad. **3,** (impediment) estorbo; embarazo.

embassy ('ɛm·bə·si) *n.* embajada.

embattled (ɛm'bæt·əld) *adj.* **1,** (engaged in battle) empeñado en la lucha. **2,** (fortified) almenado.

embed (ɛm'bɛd) *v.t.* = **imbed.**

embellish (ɛm'bɛl·ɪʃ) *v.t.* **1,** (beautify) hermosear; embellecer. **2,** (exaggerate) adornar. —**embellishment,** *n.* embellecimiento.

ember ('ɛm·bər) *n.* ascua; pavesa. —**embers,** *n.pl.* rescoldo.

embezzle (ɛm'bɛz·əl) *v.t.* desfalcar. —**embezzlement,** *n.* desfalco. —**embezzler** (-lər) *n.* desfalcador.

embitter (ɛm'bɪt·ər) *v.t.* amargar; agriar. —**embitterment,** *n.* resentimiento; enojo.

emblem ('ɛm·bləm) *n.* emblema; símbolo; insignia. —**emblematic** (ɛm·blə'mæt·ɪk) *adj.* emblemático.

embodiment (ɛm'ba·di·mənt) *n.* **1,** (incarnation) encarnación. **2,** (expression) personificación. **2,** (expression) expresión; fórmula. **3,** (inclusion) inclusión.

embody (ɛm'ba·di) *v.t.* **1,** (incarnate) encarnar; personificar. **2,** (express concretely) formular; fijar. **3,** (comprise) incluir; comprender; englobar.

embolden (ɛm'bol·dən) *v.t.* animar; alentar.

embolism ('ɛm·bə·lɪz·əm) *n.* embolia.

embolus ('ɛm·bə·ləs) *n.* émbolo.

emboss (ɛm'bɔs) *v.t.* abollonar; repujar; realzar; imprimir en relieve. —**embossment,** *n.* abolladura; realce; relieve.

embrace (ɛm'breis) *v.t.* **1,** (hug) abrazar. **2,** (enclose; comprise) abarcar; contener; comprender; encerrar. **3,** (accept) admitir; aceptar; adoptar. —*n.* abrazo.

embroider (ɛm'brɔi·dər) *v.t.* **1,** (decorate with needlework) bordar; recamar. **2,** (embellish) adornar; embellecer. —**embroiderer,** *n.* bordador. —**embroidery,** *n.* bordado; recamado.

embroil (ɛm'brɔil) *v.t.* embrollar; enredar. —**embroilment,** *n.* embrollo; intriga; lío.

embryo ('ɛm·bri·o) *n.* **1,** *biol.* embrión. **2,** (rudimentary stage) rudimento; germen; principio. —**embryonic** (-'an·ɪk) *adj.* embrionario; rudimentario.

embryology (,ɛm·bri·'al·ə·dʒi) *n.* embriología. —**embryologist,** *n.* embriólogo.

emcee (,ɛm'siː) *n.* representación fonética de *M.C.,* abr. de **master** o **mistress of ceremonies.**

emend (i'mɛnd) *v.t.* enmendar; corregir. —**emendation** (,ɛm·ən·'dei·ʃən) *n.* enmienda; corrección.

emerald ('ɛm·ər·əld) *n.* esmeralda. —*adj.* de esmeralda; esmeraldino.

emerge (ɪ'mʌrdʒ) *v.i.* **1,** (rise, as from water) emerger. **2,** (come out) salir; surgir. **3,** (grow out) brotar. **4,** (appear) aparecer. —**emergent** (-dʒənt) *adj.* emergente; naciente.

emergence (ɪ'mʌr·dʒəns) *n.* emergencia; salida; surgimiento; aparición.

emergency (ɪ'mʌr·dʒən·si) *n.* emergencia. —*adj.* **1,** (of or for extremity) de emergencia. **2,** (of or for rescue) de socorro; de auxilio.

emeritus (ɪ'mɛr·ɪ·təs) *adj.* emérito; retirado; jubilado.

emery ('ɛm·ə·ri) *n.* esmeril.

emetic (ɪ'mɛt·ɪk) *n.* & *adj.* emético; vomitivo.

emigrate ('ɛm·ɪ,greit) *v.i.* emigrar; expatriarse. —**emigrant** (-grənt) *n.* emigrante; expatriado. —**emigration,** *n.* emigración.

emigré ('ɛm·ɪ,gre) *n.* emigrado.

eminence ('ɛm·ɪ·nəns) *n.* **1,** (high repute) eminencia; encumbramiento; distinción. **2**, (hill) altura; cima. **3**, *cap.* (title of a cardinal) eminencia.

eminent ('em·i·nənt) *adj.* **1**, (distinguished) eminente. **2**, (conspicuous) sobresaliente; relevante; supremo. —**eminent domain**, dominio eminente.

emir (ε'mɪr) *n.* emir; amir.

emissary ('em·i·ser·i) *n.* emisario.

emission (ɪ'mɪʃ·ən) *n.* emisión.

emit (ɪ'mɪt) *v.t.* [**emitted, -mitting**] emitir; arrojar; despedir; exhalar.

emollient (ɪ'mal·jənt) *adj. & n.* emoliente.

emolument (ɪ'mal·jə·mənt) *n.* emolumento.

emotion (ɪ'mo·ʃən) *n.* emoción.

emotional (ɪ'mo·ʃən·əl) *adj.* **1**, (showing emotion) emocional; emotivo. **2**, (easily stirred) impresionable; sensible.

emotive (ɪ'mo·tɪv) *adj.* emotivo.

empathy ('em·pə·θi) *n.* empatía.

emperor ('em·pər·ər) *n.* emperador.

emphasis ('em·fə·sɪs) *n.* [*pl.* **-ses** (siz)] énfasis; relieve; realce.

emphasize ('em·fə‚saiz) *v.t.* recalcar; acentuar; poner de relieve; insistir en; subrayar.

emphatic (em'fæt·ɪk) *adj.* enfático; categórico.

emphysema (‚em·fə'si·mə) *n.* enfisema.

empire ('em·pair) *n.* imperio.

empiric (em'pɪr·ɪk) *n. & adj.* empírico. —**empirical,** *adj.* empírico. —**empiricism** (-ɪ‚sɪz·əm) *n.* empirismo.

emplacement (em'pleis·mənt) *n., mil.* colocación; emplazamiento.

employ (em'plɔi) *v.t.* **1**, (use) usar; aplicar; dedicar. **2**, (hire) emplear; encargar; dar trabajo a. —*n.* empleo. —**employee** (-iː) *n.* empleado; obrero; dependiente. —**employer,** *n.* amo; dueño; jefe; patrón; patrono; empresario.

employment (em'plɔi·mənt) *n.* **1**, (use) uso; aplicación. **2**, (work; occupation) empleo.

emporium (em'por·i·əm) *n.* [*pl.* **-a** (-ə)] emporio.

empower (em'pau·ər) *v.t.* **1**, (authorize) autorizar. **2**, (enable) habilitar; dar poderes. —**empowerment,** *n.* autorización; facultad; apoderamiento.

empress ('em·prəs) *n.* emperatriz.

empty ('emp·ti) *adj.* **1**, (unfilled) vacío; desocupado; vacante. **2**, (futile) vano; inútil. —*v.t. & i.* vaciar; evacuar; desocupar; descargar. —*v.i.* desaguar; desembocar. —**emptiness,** *n.* vacío; vacuidad; vaciedad.

empty-headed *adj.* tonto; casquivano.

emulate ('em·ju·leit) *v.t.* emular; rivalizar con;∘imitar. —**emulation,** *n.* emulación; rivalidad. —**emulous** (-ləs) *adj.* émulo; rival.

emulsify (ɪ'mʌl·sɪ‚fai) *v.t.* emulsionar. —**emulsification** (-fɪ'kei·ʃən) *n.* emulsionamiento. —**emulsifier,** *n.* emulsor.

emulsion (ɪ'mʌl·ʃən) *n.* emulsión.

enable (en'ei·bəl) *v.t.* habilitar; capacitar; permitir.

enact (en'ækt) *v.t.* **1**, (make into law) establecer; realizar; estatuir; promulgar; decretar. **2**, (perform) representar; desempeñar (un papel). —**enactment,** *n.* estatuto; promulgación.

enamel (ɪ'næm·əl) *n.* esmalte. —*v.t.* esmaltar.

enamor (ɪ'næm·ər) *v.t.* enamorar; encantar; cautivar.

encamp (en'kæmp) *v.i.* acampar.

encampment (en'kæmp·mənt) *n.* **1**, (act of camping) acampamiento. **2**, (camp) campamento.

encase (en'keis) *v.t.* encajar; encajonar.

encephalitis (en‚sef·ə'lai·tɪs) *n.* encefalitis.

enchant (en'tʃænt) *v.t.* **1**, (put under a spell) hechizar; encantar; ensalmar. **2**, (charm) encantar; deleitar; embelesar. —**enchantment,** *n.* encantamiento; hechicería; encanto.

enchantress (en'tʃænt·rɪs) *n.* **1**, (witch) bruja; hechicera. **2**, (charmer) encantadora.

enchilada (‚en·tʃɪ'la·də) *n.* enchilada.

encircle (en'sʌr·kəl) *v.t.* **1**, (surround) cercar; circuir; circundar. **2**, (move around) rodear; circunvalar; circunscribir. —**encirclement,** *n.* circunvalación; encerramiento.

enclave ('en·kleiv) *n.* enclavado; enclave.

enclose (en'kloːz) *v.t.* **1**, (surround) cercar; rodear; circundar. **2**, (confine) encerrar. **3**, (include) incluir; adjuntar. *También,* **inclose.**

enclosure (en'klo·ʒər) *n.* **1**, (act of enclosing) cercamiento. **2**, (en-

encode (ɛn'koɹd) *v.t.* codificar.

encomium (ɛn'ko·mi·əm) *n.* encomio.

encompass (ɛn'kʌm·pəs) *v.t.* **1,** (encircle) cercar; circundar; rodear. **2,** (include) encerrar; abarcar; incluir. —**encompassment,** *n.* cerco; rodeo; encierro.

encore ('an·kor) *interj., theat.* ¡bis!; ¡que se repita! —*n., theat.* repetición.

encounter (ɛn'kaun·tər) *v.t.* **1,** (meet) encontrar; topar con; tropezar con. **2,** (engage) batirse con. —*n.* encuentro; choque; combate.

encourage (ɛn'kʌr·ɪdʒ) *v.t.* **1,** (incite) animar; alentar; estimular. **2,** (support) fortalecer; estimular; aprobar. —**encouraging,** *adj.* animador; alentador; favorable. —**encouragement,** *n.* aliento; estímulo; ánimo; incentivo.

encroach (ɛn'kroɹtʃ) *v.i.* [*usu.,* **encroach on** o **upon**] **1,** (trespass; make inroads) adentrarse; meterse; invadir. **2,** (violate) violar; abusar. —**encroachment,** *n.* intrusión; invasión; abuso.

encumber (ɛn'kʌm·bər) *v.t.* **1,** (hinder) impedir; embarazar; estorbar. **2,** (burden) cargar; gravar.

encumbrance (ɛn'kʌm·brəns) *n.* **1,** (hindrance) impedimento; estorbo. **2,** (burden) carga. **3,** (financial obligation) gravamen.

encyclical (ɛn'sɪk·lɔ·kəl) *adj.* encíclico. —*n.* encíclica.

encyclopedia *también,* **encyclopaedia** (ɛn,saɪ·klə'piɹ·di·ə) *n.* enciclopedia. —**encyclopedic** (-dɪk) *adj.* enciclopédico. —**encyclopedist** (-dɪst) *n.* enciclopedista.

end (ɛnd) *n.* **1,** (finish) final; extremidad; punta; cola. **2,** (boundary) remate; final. **3,** (final moment) conclusión; desenlace; final. **4,** (death; extinction) fin; muerte. **5,** (purpose) finalidad; objeto; propósito. **6,** (outcome; result) resultado; desenlace. —*v.t.* & *i.* acabar; concluir; terminar; cesar; morir. —*adj.* final; terminal; último; de cola. —**at loose ends,** en desorden; desarreglado. —**come to an end,** acabarse; terminarse. —**come to a bad end,** acabar mal. —**end over end,** de cabeza; dando traspiés o

volatines. —**end to end,** punta a punta; cabeza con cabeza. —**end up,** **1,** (upright) de cabeza; de pie; derecho; *Amer.* parado. **2,** (finish) acabar. —**in the end,** al fin; a la larga; al fin y al cabo. —**make an end of,** acabar con. —**make ends meet,** pasar con lo que se tiene. —**on end,** **1,** (upright) de pie; de punta; derecho. **2,** (one after the other) sucesivamente; uno después de otro. —**put an end to,** acabar con; poner fin a.

endanger (ɛn'dein·dʒər) *v.t.* poner en peligro; arriesgar; comprometer. —**endangerment,** *n.* arriesgo; compromiso.

endear (ɛn'dɪr) *v.t.* hacer querer. —**endearing,** *adj.* cariñoso. —**endearment,** *n.* encariñamiento; cariño.

endeavor (ɛn'dɛv·ər) *v.i.* intentar; probar (a o de); tratar (de); esforzarse (a, en o por). —*n.* esfuerzo.

endemic (ɛn'dɛm·ɪk) *adj.* endémico.

ending ('ɛn·dɪŋ) *n.* **1,** (termination) fin; conclusión; cesación; suspensión. **2,** (final part) desenlace; final.

endive ('ɛn·daɪv) *n.* endibia.

endless ('ɛnd·ləs) *adj.* sin fin; infinito; perpetuo; interminable; continuo. —**endlessness,** *n.* perpetuidad.

endmost *adj.* extremo; último.

endocrine ('ɛn·do,krɪn) *adj.* & *n.* endocrino.

endorse (ɛn'dors) *v.t.* **1,** (sign) endosar. **2,** (support) apoyar; aprobar. —**endorsee,** *n.* endosatario. —**endorser,** *n.* endosante.

endorsement (ɛn'dors·mənt) *n.* **1,** (signature)· endoso. **2,** (support) apoyo; aprobación.

endow (ɛn'dau) *v.t.* dotar; fundar. —**endowment,** *n.* dote; dotación; fundación. —**endowment policy,** póliza dotal.

endurance (ɛn'djur·əns) *n.* paciencia; resistencia; perduración. —**beyond endurance,** insoportable.

endure (ɛn'djur) *v.t.* **1,** (bear; suffer) sufrir; soportar; sobrellevar. **2,** (sustain without harm) resistir; aguantar; tolerar. —*v.i.* durar; perdurar.

endways ('ɛnd·weiz) *adv.* **1,** (erect) de punta; de pie; *Amer.* parado. **2,** (lengthwise) a lo largo; de largo; longitudinalmente. **3,** (end to end) punta a punta; cabeza con cabeza. *También,* **endwise** (-waiz).

enema ('ɛn·ə·mə) *n.* enema.

enemy ('ɛn·ə·mi) *n. & adj.* enemigo; adversario; antagonista.

energetic (ɛn·ər'dʒɛt·ɪk) *adj.* enérgico; vigoroso.

energy ('ɛn·ər·dʒi) *n.* **1,** (vigor) energía; vigor. **2,** (activity) energía; acción; actividad. **3,** *mech.* (power) energía; fuerza; potencia. —**energize** (-dʒaiz) *v.t.* excitar; dar energía a.

enervate ('ɛn·ər,veit) *v.t.* enervar; debilitar; desvirtuar. —**enervation,** *n.* enervación; debilidad.

enfilade (,ɛn·fə'leid) *n., mil.* enfilada. —*v.t., mil.* enfilar.

enforce (ɛn'fors) *v.t.* ejecutar; dar fuerza o vigor a; poner en vigor; cumplimentar; hacer cumplir. —**enforceable,** *adj.* ejecutable. —**enforcement,** *n.* ejecución; coacción; compulsión.

enfranchise (ɛn'fræn·tʃaiz) *v.t.* **1,** (grant a franchise to) conceder franquicia. **2,** (accord voting rights to) conceder sufragio. **3,** (liberate) emancipar.

enfranchisement (ɛn'fræn·tʃaiz·mənt) *n.* **1,** (franchise) franquicia. **2,** (voting) concesión del sufragio. **3,** (emancipation) emancipación.

engage (ɛn'geidʒ) *v.t.* **1,** (hire) emplear; contratar; tomar a su servicio. **2,** (bind by a pledge) apalabrar; comprometer. **3,** (attract) atraer. **4,** (meet in conflict) trabar con; entrar en lucha con. **5,** *mech.* (interlock) engranar.

engaged (ɛn'geidʒd) *adj.* **1,** (busy) ocupado. **2,** (betrothed) prometido; comprometido. —**become engaged (to),** comprometerse (con); prometerse (a).

engagement (ɛn'geidʒ·mənt) *n.* **1,** (pledge) ajuste; contrato; obligación. **2,** (betrothal) compromiso; noviazgo. **3,** *mech.* engranaje; ajuste. **4,** (conflict) acción; batalla.

engaging (ɛn'geidʒ·ɪŋ) *adj.* atractivo; agraciado; simpático.

engender (ɛn'dʒɛn·dər) *v.t.* **1,** (generate) engendrar; producir. **2,** (beget) procrear. **3,** (cause) causar.

engine ('ɛn·dʒən) *n.* **1,** (machine) máquina; motor; ingenio. **2,** *R.R.* locomotora.

engineer (ɛn·dʒə'nɪ,r) *n.* **1,** (engine operator) maquinista; mecáni-

co. **2,** (graduate in engineering) ingeniero. —*v.t.* **1,** (act as engineer for) hacer de ingeniero o maquinista de. **2,** *colloq.* (contrive) ingeniar; gestionar; manejar; dirigir. —**engineering,** *n.* ingeniería.

English ('ɪŋ·glɪʃ) *n. & adj.* inglés.

Englishman ('ɪŋ·glɪʃ·mən) *n.* [*pl.* **-men**] inglés. —**Englishwoman,** *n.* [*pl.* **-women**] inglesa.

engrave (ɛn'greiv) *v.t.* **1,** (carve) esculpir; cincelar; burilar. **2,** (etch) grabar. —**engraver,** *n.* esculpidor. —**engraving,** *n.* grabado; lámina; estampa.

engross (ɛn'gros) *v.t.* **1,** (absorb) absorber; abstraer. **2,** (write) transcribir caligráficamente.

engrossing (ɛn'gro·sɪŋ) *adj.* muy interesante; fascinante. —*n.* = **engrossment.**

engrossment (ɛn'gros·mənt) *n.* **1,** (absorption) abstracción; ensimismamiento. **2,** (writing) transcripción caligráfica.

engulf (ɛn'gʌlf) *v.t.* **1,** (swallow) tragar. **2,** (submerge) sumergir; hundir. **3,** (overwhelm) abrumar.

enhance (ɛn'hæns) *v.t.* realzar; mejorar; acrecentar; aumentar el valor de. —**enhancement,** *n.* realce; acrecentamiento; mejoría.

enigma (ɪ'nɪg·mə) *n.* enigma. —**enigmatic** (,ɛn·ɪg'mæt·ɪk) *adj.* enigmático.

enjoin (ɛn'dʒɔin) *v.t.* **1,** (command; prescribe) mandar; ordenar; prescribir. **2,** (restrain by injunction) prohibir.

enjoy (ɛn'dʒɔi) *v.t.* **1,** (take pleasure in) gozar de; gozarse en; gustar de. **2,** (possess) disfrutar de; tener; poseer. —**enjoyable,** *adj.* deleitable; agradable.

enjoyment (ɛn'dʒɔi·mənt) *n.* **1,** (pleasure) goce; disfrute; placer. **2,** (possession) uso; usufructo.

enlace (ɛn'leis) *v.t.* enlazar.

enlarge (ɛn'lardʒ) *v.t.* **1,** (make larger) agrandar; aumentar; ensanchar; ampliar. **2,** (amplify) ampliar; amplificar. —*v.i.* **1,** (become larger) ensancharse; agrandarse. **2,** (expatiate) explayarse; tratar detalladamente.

enlargement (ɛn'lardʒ·mənt) *n.* **1,** (enlarging) agrandamiento; ensanchamiento. **2,** (expansion) aumento; dilatación; expansión. **3,** *photog.* ampliación.

enlighten (ɛn'lai·tən) *v.t.* **1,** (give

knowledge to) ilustrar; iluminar; instruir. **2,** (inform) informar.

enlightenment (ɛn'lai·tən·mənt) *n.* **1,** (knowledge) instrucción; civilización; cultura. **2,** (information) información. **3,** *cap., hist.* el siglo de las luces.

enlist (ɛn'lɪst) *v.t.* alistar; enrolar; *mil.* reclutar. —*v.i.* alistarse; enrolarse; *mil.* sentar plaza. —**enlistment,** *n.* alistamiento; enganche; enrolamiento. —**enlisted man,** recluta; soldado.

enliven (ɛn'laiv·ən) *v.t.* **1,** (give life to) vivificar; animar. **2,** (in spirit) alegrar; regocijar.

enmesh (ɛn'mɛʃ) *v.t.* enredar.

enmity ('ɛn·mə·ti) *n.* enemistad.

ennoble (ɛn'no·bəl) *v.t.* ennoblecer. —**ennoblement,** *n.* ennoblecimiento.

enormity (ɪ'nɔr·mə·ti) *n.* atrocidad; enormidad.

enormous (ɪ'nɔr·məs) *adj.* enorme; descomunal. —**enormousness,** *n.* demasía; exceso.

enough (ɪ'nʌf) *adj.* bastante; suficiente. —*adv.* suficientemente; bastante. —*n.* (lo) suficiente. —*interj.* ¡basta!

enquire (ɪn'kwair) *v.i. & t.* = **inquire.** —**enquiry,** *n.* = **inquiry.**

enrage (ɛn'reidʒ) *v.t.* enfurecer; encolerizar.

enrapture (ɛn'ræp·tʃər) *v.t.* arrebatar; embelesar; extasiar.

enrich (ɛn'rɪtʃ) *v.t.* **1,** (make rich) enriquecer. **2,** (improve, as soil) abonar; fertilizar; beneficiar. —**enrichment,** *n.* enriquecimiento; abono; beneficio.

enroll *también,* **enrol** (ɛn'roul) *v.t.* alistar. —*v.i.* alistarse; inscribirse; matricularse. —**enrollment; enrolment,** *n.* alistamiento; inscripción; matriculación; registro.

ensconce (ɛn'skɑns) *v.i.* **1,** (settle firmly) acomodar; situar. **2,** (cover; hide) ocultar; esconder; poner en seguro.

ensemble (ɑn'sɑm·bəl) *n.* **1,** (group) conjunto; grupo. **2,** (costume) traje.

enshrine (ɛn'ʃrain) *v.t.* **1,** (place in a shrine) guardar como reliquia. **2,** *fig.* (cherish) apreciar; estimar.

enshroud (ɛn'ʃraud) *v.t.* **1,** (wrap) amortajar; envolver. **2,** (conceal) ocultar; tapar.

ensign ('ɛn·sain) *n.* **1,** (flag) bandera; pabellón; enseña. **2,** (emblem) insignia; divisa. **3,** (-sɪn) *mil.; naval* alférez.

ensile (ɛn'sail) *v.t.* ensilar. —**ensilage** ('ɛn·sə·lɪdʒ) *n.* ensilaje.

enslave (ɛn'sleiv) *v.t.* esclavizar; avasallar. —**enslavement,** *n.* esclavitud; esclavización.

ensnare (ɛn'sneɪr) *v.t.* atrapar; enredar; engañar. —**ensnarement,** *n.* atrapamiento; enredo; engaño.

ensue (ɛn'su) *v.i.* **1,** (follow) seguir; suceder. **2,** (result) sobrevenir.

ensure (ɛn'ʃʊr) *v.t.* asegurar.

entail (ɛn'teil) *v.t.* **1,** (bring about) ocasionar. **2,** (involve) envolver. **3,** (impose as a burden) imponer. **4,** *law* vincular. —**entailment,** *n., law* vinculación.

entangle (ɛn'tæŋ·gəl) *v.t.* **1,** (involve in difficulties) enredar; embrollar; enmarañar. **2,** (complicate) intrincar; implicar. —**entanglement,** *n.* enredo; embrollo; complicación.

entente (ɑn'tɑrnt) *n.* pacto; alianza.

enter ('ɛn·tər) *v.t.* **1,** (come into) entrar en o a; penetrar. **2,** (insert) introducir; insertar. **3,** (join, as a class or club) ingresar en; alistarse en; matricularse en; afiliarse a. **4,** (record) asentar; anotar; registrar. —*v.i.* **1,** (come or go in) entrar; introducirse; ingresar. **2,** (take part) participar; interesarse.

enteric (ɛn'tɛr·ɪk) *adj.* entérico. —**enteritis** (ɛn·tə'rai·tɪs) *n.* enteritis.

enterprise ('ɛn·tər·praiz) *n.* **1,** (project; business) empresa. **2,** (boldness; initiative) arresto; actividad. —**enterprising,** *adj.* emprendedor; acometedor; esforzado.

entertain (ɛn·tər'tein) *v.t.* **1,** (amuse) festejar; agasajar; entretener; divertir. **2,** (have as a guest) hospedar. **3,** (have in mind) tomar en consideración; acariciar; abrigar. —*v.i.* invitar; dar fiestas, comidas, etc. —**entertaining,** *adj.* divertido; entretenido.

entertainment (ˌɛn·tər'tein·mənt) *n.* **1,** (receiving of guests) recepción; recibimiento. **2,** (amusement) entretenimiento; diversión. **3,** (show) espectáculo.

enthrall (ɛn'θrɔl) *v.t.* **1,** (captivate; charm) dominar; cautivar. **2,** (enslave) esclavizar; sojuzgar. —**en-**

thrallment, *n.* dominación; esclavización; sojuzgación.

enthrone (ɛn'θroːn) *v.t.* entronar; entronizar. —**enthronement,** *n.* entronización.

enthuse (ɛn'θuːz) *v.i.* entusiasmarse.

enthusiasm (ɛn'θuː·zi·æz·əm) *n.* entusiasmo. —**enthusiast** (-,æst) *n.* entusiasta; aficionado. —**enthusiastic** (-'æs·tɪk) *adj.* entusiástico.

entice (ɛn'tais) *v.t.* tentar; seducir; atraer. —**enticement,** *n.* tentación; seducción; añagaza.

entire (ɛn'tair) *adj.* entero; completo; íntegro; total. —**entireness,** *n.* entereza. —**entirety** (-ti) *n.* entereza; totalidad; integridad; todo.

entirely (ɛn'tair·li) *adv.* **1,** (wholly) del todo; enteramente. **2,** (solely) solamente; exclusivamente.

entitle (ɛn'tai·təl) *v.t.* **1,** (authorize) dar derecho; habilitar; autorizar. **2,** (name) titular. —**entitlement,** *n.* derecho; autorización.

entity ('ɛn·tə·ti) *n.* **1,** (individual reality) entidad. **2,** (being) ser; ente.

entomb (ɛn'tuːm) *v.t.* enterrar; sepultar. —**entombment,** *n.* entierro; sepultura.

entomology (ɛn·tə'mɑl·ə·dʒi) *n.* entomología. —**entomological** (-mə'lɑ·dʒɪ·kəl) *adj.* entomológico. —**entomologist,** *n.* entomólogo.

entourage (an·tu'raːʒ) *n.* compañía; cortejo; séquito.

entr'acte (an'trækt) *n.* entreacto.

entrails ('ɛn·trəlz; -treilz) *n.pl.* entrañas; vísceras.

entrance ('ɛn·trəns) *n.* **1,** (the act of entering) entrada; ingreso. **2,** (place to enter) entrada; puerta; portal; embocadura.

entrance (ɛn'træns) *v.t.* extasiar; fascinar; embelesar; hechizar.

entrant ('ɛn·trənt) *n.* principiante; *sports* competidor.

entrap (ɛn'træp) *v.t.* [**entrapped, -trapping**] atrapar con trampa; entrampar. —**entrapment,** *n.* entrampamiento.

entreat (ɛn'trit) *v.t.* rogar; suplicar; implorar; impetrar.

entreaty (ɛn'tri·ti) *n.* **1,** (request) ruego; súplica. **2,** (petition) rogación; rogativa.

entrée (an'tre) *n.* **1,** (right of entering) entrada; privilegio de entrar. **2,** (main dish) principio; entrada.

entrench (ɛn'trɛntʃ) *v.t.* atrincherar. —*v.i.* invadir; infringir.

—**entrenchment,** *n.* atrincheramiento.

entrepreneur (,an·trə·prə'nʌːr) *n.* empresario.

entropy ('ɛn·trə·pi) *n.* entropía.

entrust (ɛn'trʌst) *v.t.* confiar; encomendar; encargar.

entry ('ɛn·tri) *n.* **1,** (act of entering; entrance) entrada; acceso; ingreso. **2,** (opening) vestíbulo; portal; zaguán. **3,** (item recorded) asiento; anotación; inscripción; *comm.* partida.

entwine (ɛn'twain) *v.t.* & *i.* entrelazar.

enumerate (ɪ'nu·mə·reit) *v.t.* **1,** (name one by one) enumerar. **2,** (count) enumerar; contar. —**enumeration,** *n.* enumeración; recuento.

enunciate (ɪ'nʌn·si·eit) *v.t.* & *i.* pronunciar; enunciar; articular. —**enunciation,** *n.* pronunciación; enunciación; articulación.

envelop (ɛn'vɛl·əp) *v.t.* envolver; cubrir. —**envelopment,** *n.* envolvimiento.

envelope ('ɛn·və·lop) *n.* **1,** (covering) cubierta; envolvedor. **2,** (for a letter) sobre.

envenom (ɛn'vɛn·əm) *v.t.* envenenar.

enviable ('ɛn·vi·ə·bəl) *adj.* envidiable.

envious ('ɛn·vi·əs) *adj.* envidioso. —**enviousness,** *n.* envidia.

environment (ɛn'vai·rən·mənt) *n.* cercanía; medio ambiente. —**environmental** (-'mɛn·təl) *adj.* ambiente.

environs (ɛn'vai·rənz) *n.pl.* **1,** (surroundings) alrededores; cercanías; inmediaciones. **2,** (outlying areas) afueras.

envisage (ɛn'vɪz·ədʒ) *v.t.* imaginarse; representarse.

envision (ɛn'vɪʒ·ən) *v.t.* imaginar.

envoy ('ɛn·vɔi) *n.* **1,** (representative) enviado; agente diplomático; mensajero. **2,** (postscript) despedida.

envy ('ɛn·vi) *v.t.* envidiar; codiciar. —*n.* envidia.

enzyme ('ɛn·zaim) *n.* enzima.

eon ('i·ən; 'i·an) *n.* eón.

epaulet *también,* **epaulette** ('ɛp·ə·lɛt) *n., mil.* charretera.

ephemeral (ɪ'fɛm·ər·əl) *adj.* efímero; transitorio.

epic ('ɛp·ɪk) *adj.* épico. —*n.* poema épico; epopeya.

epicenter ('ɛp·ə‚sɛn·tər) *n.* epicentro.

epicure ('ɛp·ɪ‚kjʊr) *n.* **1,** (gourmet) epicúreo; gastrónomo. **2,** (sensualist) epicúreo; sibarita. —**epicurean** (-kju'ri·ən) *adj.* epicúreo.

epidemic (‚ɛp·ɪ'dɛm·ɪk) *adj.* epidémico. —*n.* epidemia; plaga; peste.

epidermis (‚ɛp·ə'dʌr·mɪs) *n.* epidermis; cutícula; piel.

epiglottis (‚ɛp·ə'glat·ɪs) *n.* epiglotis; lengüeta.

epigram ('ɛp·ɪ‚græm) *n.* epigrama. —**epigrammatic** (-græ'mæt·ɪk) *adj.* epigramático. —**epigrammatist** (-'græm·ə·tɪst) *n.* epigramista; epigramatista.

epigraph ('ɛp·ə‚græf) *n.* epígrafe. —**epigraphy** (ɪ'pɪg·rə·fi) *n.* epigrafía.

epilepsy ('ɛp·ə·lɛp·si) *n.* epilepsia. —**epileptic** (-'lɛp·tɪk) *adj. & n.* epiléptico.

epilogue ('ɛp·ə·lɔg) *n.* epílogo.

Epiphany (ɪ'pɪf·ə·ni) *n.* Epifanía; día de los Reyes.

episcopacy (ɪ'pɪs·kə·pə·si) *n.* episcopado.

episcopal (ɪ'pɪs·kə·pəl) *adj.* episcopal; obispal.

Episcopalian (ɪ‚pɪs·kə'peil·jən) *adj. & n.* episcopalista; episcopaliano.

episcopate (ɪ'pɪs·kə·pɪt; -‚peit) *n.* episcopado.

episode ('ɛp·ɪ·sod) *n.* **1,** (event) episodio; lance; peripecia. **2,** *mus.* (digressive passage) digresión. —**episodic** (-'sad·ɪk) *adj.* episódico.

epistemology (ɪ‚pɪs·tə'mal·ə·dʒi) *n.* epistemología.

epistle (ɪ'pɪs·əl) *n.* epístola; carta. —**epistolary** (-tə·lɛr·i) *adj.* epistolar. —*n.* epistolario.

epitaph ('ɛp·ɪ‚tæf) *n.* epitafio.

epithelium (‚ɛp·ə'θi·li·əm) *n.* epitelio.

epithet ('ɛp·ə·θɛt) *n.* epíteto.

epitome (ɪ'pɪt·ə·mi) *n.* epítome; sumario; compendio. —**epitomize** (-‚maiz) *v.t.* epitomar; compendiar.

epoch ('ɛp·ək) *n.* época; edad; período; era. —**epochal,** *adj.* trascendental; memorable.

equable ('ɛk·wə·bəl) *adj.* **1,** (uniform) igual; uniforme; ecuable. **2,** (stable) estable. **3,** (calm) tranquilo. —**equability** [*también,* **equableness**] *n.* igualdad; uniformidad.

equal ('i·kwəl) *adj.* **1,** (same) igual.

2, (balanced; level) igual; parejo. —*n.* igual. —*v.t.* **1,** (be equal to) ser igual a; equivaler; valer. **2,** (make equal) igualar. **3,** (become equal to) igualarse a. **4,** (adjust) compensar. —**equal to, 1,** (sufficient for) suficiente para. **2,** (competent for) con fuerzas para. —**equal out,** igualar; igualarse. —**feel equal to,** sentirse con fuerzas para.

equality (i'kwal·ə·ti) *n.* igualdad; uniformidad; paridad.

equalize ('i·kwə·laiz) *v.t.* igualar; compensar. —**equalization** (‚i·kwə·lɪ'zei·ʃən) *n.* igualamiento; igualación; compensación.

equanimity (i·kwə'nɪm·ə·ti) *n.* ecuanimidad.

equate (ɪ'kweit) *v.t.* igualar; poner en ecuación.

equation (ɪ'kwei·ʃən) *n.* ecuación.

equator (ɪ'kwei·tər) *n.* ecuador. —**equatorial** (i·kwə'tor·i·əl) *adj.* ecuatorial.

equestrian (ɪ'kwɛs·tri·ən) *adj.* ecuestre. —*n.* jinete. —**equestrienne** (-'ɛn) *n.* amazona.

equidistant (i·kwə'dɪs·tənt) *adj.* equidistante.

equilateral (i·kwə'læt·ər·əl) *adj.* equilátero.

equilibrate (‚i·kwɪ'lɪ·bret) *v.t.* equilibrar.

equilibrist (ɪ'kwɪl·ə·brɪst) *n.* equilibrista.

equilibrium (i·kwə'lɪb·ri·əm) *n.* equilibrio; balance.

equine ('i·kwain) *adj.* equino.

equinox ('i·kwə‚naks) *n.* equinoccio. —**equinoctial** (-'nak·ʃəl) *adj.* equinoccial.

equip (ɪ'kwɪp) *v.t.* [**equipped, equipping**] **1,** (fit out) equipar; pertrechar. **2,** *naut.* (fit) aprestar.

equipment (ɪ'kwɪp·mənt) *n.* equipo; aparatos; material.

equipoise ('i·kwə‚poiz) *n.* equilibrio; contrapeso.

equitable ('ɛk·wɪ·tə·bəl) *adj.* equitativo; justo. —**equitableness,** *n.* equidad; imparcialidad; justicia.

equitation (‚ɛk·wə'tei·ʃən) *n.* equitación.

equity ('ɛk·wə·ti) *n.* **1,** (fairness) equidad; imparcialidad. **2,** *law* equidad; justicia. **3,** *fin.* valor; título; acción.

equivalent (ɪ'kwɪv·ə·lənt) *n. & adj.* equivalente. —**equivalence,** *n.* equivalencia.

equivocal (ɪ'kwɪv·ə·kəl) *adj.* equívoco; ambiguo.

equivocate (ɪ'kwɪv·ə,keit) *v.t. & i.* tergiversar. —**equivocation,** *n.* equívoco.

era ('ɪr·ə) *n.* era; época; edad.

eradicate (ɪ'ræd·ɪ·keit) *v.t.* desarraigar; erradicar; extirpar. —**eradication,** *n.* erradicación; desarraigo; extirpación. —**eradicator,** *n.* desarraigador; erradicador; extirpador.

erase (ɪ'reis) *v.t.* borrar; tachar; raer. —**eraser,** *n.* borrador; goma de borrar.

erasure (ɪ'rei·ʃər) *n.* borradura.

erbium ('ʌr·bi·əm) *n.* erbio.

ere (ɛɪr) *prep., poet.* antes de. —*conj.* antes que.

erect (ɪ'rɛkt) *v.t.* **1,** (build) erigir; edificar; construir; levantar. **2,** (establish) montar; instalar. **3,** (place upright) erguir; poner de pie; *Amer.* parar. —*adj.* erguido; enhiesto; de pie; *Amer.* parado. —**erection** (ɪ'rɛk·ʃən) *n.* erección; montaje; instalación.

erg (ʌrg) *n.* erg; ergio.

ergot ('ʌr·gət) *n.* **1,** *bot.; pharm.* cornezuelo. **2,** (plant disease) ergotismo. —**ergotism,** *n.* ergotismo.

ergotine ('ʌr·gət·ɪn) *n.* ergotina.

ermine ('ʌr·mɪn) *n.* **1,** (animal; fur) armiño. **2,** *fig.* (judge's office or dignity) toga; judicatura.

erode (ɪ'roɪd) *v.t.* corroer; roer; comer. —*v.i.* desgastarse.

erogenous (ɪ'radʒ·ə·nəs) *adj.* erógeno.

erosion (ɪ'roɪ·ʒən) *n.* corrosión; desgaste; *geol.* erosión. —**erosive** (-sɪv) *adj.* erosivo.

erotic (ɪ'rat·ɪk) *adj.* erótico. —**eroticism** (-ə,sɪz·əm) *n.* eroticismo. —**erotism** ('ɛr·ə,tɪz·əm) *n.* erotismo.

err (ʌr) *v.t.* **1,** (blunder) errar; equivocarse. **2,** (go astray) descarriarse. **3,** (sin) pecar.

errand ('ɛr·ənd) *n.* encargo; recado; mandado.

errant ('ɛr·ənt) *adj.* **1,** (roving) errante; andante. **2,** (erring) errado.

erratic (ə'ræt·ɪk) *adj.* excéntrico; irregular.

erratum (ɪ'rat·əm) *n.* [*pl.* **-ta** (-tə)] errata.

erroneous (ɪ'roɪ·ni·əs) *adj.* errado; erróneo; falso. —**erroneousness,** *n.* error; falsedad.

error ('ɛr·ər) *n.* **1,** (mistake) error; equivocación; yerro. **2,** (sin) engaño; pecado. **3,** (deviation) error.

Erse (ʌrs) *n. & adj.* gaélico; erso.

erstwhile ('ʌrst·hwail) *adj.* antiguo; de otro tiempo. —*adv.* antes; primeramente.

eruct (ɪ'rʌkt) *v.t. & i.* eructar; regoldar. *También,* **eructate** (ɪ'rʌk·teit). —**eructation** (ɪ,rʌk'tei·ʃən) *n.* eructación; eructo; regüeldo.

erudition (,ɛr·u'dɪʃ·ən) *n.* erudición; conocimientos. —**erudite** (-dait) *adj.* erudito.

erupt (ɪ'rʌpt) *v.i.* erumpir; hacer erupción. —**eruption** (ɪ'rʌp·ʃən) *n.* erupción. —**eruptive** (-tɪv) *adj.* eruptivo.

erysipelas (,ɛr·ə'sɪp·ə·ləs) *n.* erisipela.

escalate ('ɛs·kə,leit) *v.t.* extender; intensificar; subir. —*v.i.* extenderse; intensificarse; subir. —**escalation,** *n.* extensión; intensificación; subida.

escalator ('ɛs·kə·le·tər) *n.* escalera móvil. —*adj., law* de ajuste automático.

escallop *también,* **escalop** (ɛs'kal·əp) *v.t.* **1,** *cookery* cocer en salsa. **2,** (serrate) ondear. —*n.* = **scallop.**

escapade ('ɛs·kə·peid) *n.* escapada; travesura; aventura.

escape (ɛs'keip) *v.i.* **1,** (flee) escaparse; fugarse; huir. **2,** (leak out) escaparse; salirse; filtrarse. —*v.t.* evadir; evitar; eludir. —*n.* escapada; huída; fuga; evasión. —**escape hatch,** escotilla de emergencia. —**have a narrow escape,** salvarse por un pelo.

escapism (ɛs'kei·pɪz·əm) *n.* escapismo. —**escapist,** *adj. & n.* escapista.

escapement (ɛs'keip·mənt) *n.* escape.

escarole ('ɛs·kə,rol) *n.* escarola.

escarpment (ɛs'karp·mənt) *n.* escarpa; escarpadura; frontón.

eschatology (,ɛs·kə'tal·ə·dʒi) *n.* escatología. —**eschatological** (ɛs,kæt·ə'ladʒ·ə·kəl) *adj.* escatológico.

eschew (ɛs'tʃuɪ) *v.t.* huir de; evitar.

escort (ɛs'kort) *v.t.* escoltar; acompañar; convoyar. —*n.* ('ɛs·kort) escolta; acompañante; convoy.

escrow ('ɛs·kroɪ) *n.* plica.

escudo (ɛs'ku·do) *n.* escudo.

escutcheon (ɛs'kʌtʃ·ən) n. escudo de armas.

Eskimo ('ɛs·kə·mo) n. [pl. -mos] & adj. esquimal.

esophagus (ɪ'saf·ə·gəs) n. [pl. -gi (-dʒai)] esófago.

esoteric (ɛs·ə'tɛr·ɪk) adj. esotérico; secreto; oculto.

ESP abr. de **extrasensory perception**.

esparto (ɛs'par·to) n. esparto.

especial (ɛs'pɛʃ·əl) adj. 1, (particular) especial; particular. 2, (exceptional) notable; sobresaliente. También, **special**.

espionage (ˌɛs·pi·ə'naʒ) n. espionaje.

esplanade (ɛs·plə'nad; -'neid) n. explanada.

espouse (ɛs'pauz) v.t. 1, (wed) casarse con; contraer matrimonio con. 2, (advocate) defender; abogar por; abrazar.

esprit de corps (ɛs,pri·də'kɔrr) compañerismo.

espy (ɛs'pai) v.t. divisar; alcanzar a ver; columbrar.

esquire (ɛs'kwair) n. 1, (courtesy title) señor; don. 2, (knight's attendant) escudero.

essay ('ɛs·ei) n. 1, (composition) ensayo. 2, (attempt) conato; esfuerzo. —v.t. (ɛ'sei) ensayar; tratar. —**essayist** ('ɛs·e·jɪst) n. ensayista.

essence ('ɛs·əns) n. 1, (characteristic) esencia. 2, (nature) ser; substancia; médula. 3, (distillate) esencia; perfume. —**in essence**, en el fondo.

essential (ə'sɛn·ʃəl) adj. 1, (indispensable) esencial; vital; indispensable; imprescindible. 2, (basic) esencial; constitutivo; substancial. 3, chem. esencial. —n. parte o elemento esencial.

establish (ɛs'tæb·lɪʃ) v.t. 1, (set up; found) establecer; fundar; crear; constituir. 2, (install) establecer; instalar; radicar. 3, (prove) establecer; determinar; dejar sentado. —**establishment**, n. establecimiento.

estate (ɛs'teit) n. 1, (residence) hacienda; heredad. 2, (possessions) propiedad; bienes. 3, (inheritance) herencia. 4, (class; condition) estado; clase; condición.

esteem (ɛs'tiːm) v.t. 1, (respect) estimar; apreciar. 2, (rate) juzgar; reputar. —n. 1, (respect) estima;

aprecio. 2, (estimate) juicio; opinión.

ester ('ɛs·tər) n. éster.

esthete también, **aesthete** ('ɛs·θit) n. esteta. —**esthetic; aesthetic** (ɛs'θɛt·ɪk) adj. estético. —**esthetics; aesthetics**, n.pl. estética.

estimable ('ɛs·tɪ·mə·bəl) adj. 1, (worthy of esteem) benemérito; estimable. 2, (calculable) calculable.

estimate ('ɛs·tə·meit) v.t. apreciar; computar; calcular aproximadamente. —n. (-mət) estimación; tasación; cálculo aproximado; comm. presupuesto. —**estimation**, n. cálculo; opinión; suposición.

estop (ɛs'tap) v.t., law impedir; evitar. —**estoppel** (-'tap·əl) n. impedimento; prevención.

estrange (ɛs'treindʒ) v.t. alejar; malquistar; enajenar. —**estrangement**, n. desvío; alejamiento; enajenamiento.

estrogen ('ɛs·trə·dʒən) n. estrógeno.

estrus ('ɛs·trəs) n. estro; celo.

estuary ('ɛs·tju,ɛr·i) n. estuario; ría.

et cetera (ɛt 'sɛt·ər·ə) etcétera.

etch (ɛtʃ) v.t. 1, (cut with acid) grabar al aguafuerte. 2, (cut with stylus) cincelar. —**etching**, n. aguafuerte; grabado al aguafuerte.

eternal (ɪ'tʌr·nəl) adj. eterno; eternal; inmortal.

eternity (ɪ'tʌr·nə·ti) n. eternidad.

ethane ('ɛθ·ein) n. etano.

ethanol ('ɛθ·ə·nɒl; -nal) n. etanol.

ether ('i·θər) n. éter.

ethereal también, **aethereal** (ɪ'θɪr·i·əl) adj. etéreo.

ethical ('ɛθ·ɪ·kəl) también, **ethic** ('ɛθ·ɪk) adj. ético; moral.

ethics ('ɛθ·ɪks) n.pl., también, **ethic**, n.sing. ética; moral.

Ethiopian (ˌi·θi'o·pi·ən) adj. etíope; etiópico. —n. etíope.

Ethiopic (ˌi·θi'ap·ɪk) adj. etiópico. —n. lengua etiópica.

ethnic ('ɛθ·nɪk) adj. étnico. También, **ethnical**.

ethnology (ɛθ'nal·e·dʒi) n. etnología. —**ethnological** (ɛθ·nə'ladʒ·ɪ·kəl) adj. etnológico. —**ethnologist** (-dʒɪst) n. etnólogo.

ethos ('i·θas) n. carácter, costumbres y modales de un grupo étnico.

ethyl ('ɛθ·əl) n. etilo.

ethylene ('ɛθ·ə,lin) n. etileno.

etiology (ˌi·ti'al·ə·dʒi) n. etiología.

etiquette ('ɛt·ɪ·kɛt) *n.* etiqueta.
etymology (ɛt·ɪ'mal·ə·dʒi) *n.* etimología. —**etymological** (-məˈladʒ·ɪ·kəl) *adj.* etimológico. —**etymologist** (-dʒɪst) *n.* etimologista; etimólogo.
eucalyptus (ju·kə'lɪp·təs) *n.* eucalipto.
Eucharist ('ju·kə·rɪst) *n.* eucaristía. —**Eucharistic** (-'rɪs·tɪk) *adj.* eucarístico.
eugenics (ju'dʒɛn·ɪks) *n.pl.* eugenesia. —**eugenic,** *adj.* eugenésico.
eulogy ('ju·lə·dʒi) *n.* elogio; encomio; panegírico; apología. —**eulogistic** (-'dʒɪs·tɪk) *adj.* laudatorio; encomiástico. —**eulogize** (-dʒaiz) *v.t.* elogiar; loar; encomiar; ensalzar.
eunuch ('ju·nək) *n.* eunuco.
euphemism ('ju·fə·mɪz·əm) *n.* eufemismo. —**euphemistic** (-'mɪs·tɪk) *adj.* eufemístico.
euphonious (ju'foː·ni·əs) *adj.* eufónico. —**euphoniousness,** *n.* eufonía.
euphony ('ju·fə·ni) *n.* eufonía. —**euphonic** (ju'fan·ɪk) *adj.* eufónico.
euphoria (ju'for·i·ə) *n.* euforia. —**euphoric** (-ɪk) *adj.* eufórico.
Eurasian (ju'rei·ʒən) *n. & adj.* eurásico.
European (ˌjur·ə'pi·ən) *n. & adj.* europeo. —**European plan,** hospedaje o habitación sin comidas.
europium (ju'ro·pi·əm) *n.* europio.
Eustachian (ju'stei·ʃən; -'stei·ki·ən) **tube,** tubo de Eustaquio.
euthanasia (ju·θə'nei·ʒə) *n.* 1, (mercy-killing) eutanasia. 2, (painless death) muerte tranquila.
evacuate (ɪ'væk·ju·eit) *v.t.* 1, (empty) evacuar; vaciar. 2, (withdraw from) desocupar; sacar. 3, (excrete) evacuar; excretar. —**evacuation,** *n.* evacuación; desocupación. —**evacuee** (-iː) *n.* evacuado.
evade (ɪ'veid) *v.t. & i.* evadir; eludir; huir.
evaluate (ɪ'væl·ju·eit) *v.t.* evaluar; valorar; tasar. —**evaluation,** *n.* evaluación; valoración; tasación.
evanesce (ɛv·ə'nɛs) *v.i.* desaparecer; disiparse; desvanecerse. —**evanescence,** *n.* disipación; desvanecimiento; evanescencia. —**evanescent,** *adj.* evanescente.
evangel (ɪ'væn·dʒəl) *n.* evangelio.

evangelical (ˌi·væn'dʒel·ɪ·kəl) *adj.* evangélico.
evangelism (ɪ'væn·dʒə·lɪz·əm) *n.* evangelismo. —**evangelist,** *n.* evangelista. —**evangelize,** *v.t.* evangelizar.
evaporate (ɪ'væp·ə·reit) *v.t.* evaporar; vaporizar. —*v.i.* evaporarse; disiparse; desvanecerse. —**evaporation,** *n.* evaporación; vaporización.
evasion (ɪ'vei·ʒən) *n.* 1, (avoidance) evasión; fuga; escape. 2, (subterfuge; equivocation) evasiva; equívoco. —**evasive** (-sɪv) *adj.* evasivo; ambiguo.
eve (iːv) *n.* 1, (night before) vigilia; víspera. 2, (time preceding an event) víspera. 3, *poet.* (evening) noche.
even ('i·vən) *adj.* 1, (level; smooth) llano; plano; nivelado. 2, (uniform) igual; uniforme; inmutable. 3, (equal) igual; parejo; al mismo nivel. 4, (divisible by 2) par. 5, *math.* (having no fraction) justo. 6, (placid) apacible; ecuánime. —*adv.* 1, (equally; wholly) uniformemente; precisamente; llanamente; inmutablemente. 2, (exactly; moreover) exactamente; aún; hasta; incluso; siquiera. —*v.t.* 1, (make equal) igualar; emparejar. 2, (make smooth) allanar; nivelar. 3, (adjust evenly) ajustar cuentas. —*n., poet.* = **evening.** —**break even,** salir en paz; cubrir los gastos. —**even if** o **though,** aun cuando; aunque. —**even so,** no obstante. —**even with,** al nivel de. —**get even with,** vengarse de. —**not even,** ni siquiera.
evenhanded ('i·vən,hæn·dɪd) *adj.* imparcial; equitativo.
evening ('iːv·nɪŋ) *n.* 1, (late day; early night) tarde; noche; vísperas. 2, *fig.* (decline) terminación. —*adj.* vespertino. —**evening clothes** o **dress,** traje o vestido de etiqueta. —**good evening!** (before sundown) buenas tardes; (after dark) buenas noches.
evenness ('i·vən·nəs) *n.* 1, (uniformity) igualdad; uniformidad. 2, (smoothness) llanura; lisura. 3, (fairness) imparcialidad.
event (ɪ'vɛnt) *n.* 1, (occurrence) suceso; ocurrencia. 2, (notable occasion) acontecimiento; acaecimiento. 3, (result) éxito; consecuencia; resultado. —**at all events; in any event,** en todo caso; de cual-

quier modo; sea lo que fuere. —**in the event of,** en caso de.

even-tempered *adj.* tranquilo; apacible; ecuánime.

eventful (ɪ'vɛnt·fəl) *adj.* lleno de acontecimientos; memorable.

eventide ('i·vən·taid) *n., poet.* crepúsculo; caída de la tarde.

eventual (ɪ'vɛn·tʃu·əl) *adj.* **1,** (ultimate) consiguiente; eventual. **2,** (contingent) contingente; fortuito. —**eventuality** (-'æl·ə·ti) *n.* eventualidad.

eventuate (ɪ'vɛn·tʃu·eit) *v.i.* acontecer; acaecer.

ever ('ɛv·ər) *adv.* **1,** (always) siempre; constantemente. **2,** (at any time) en cualquier tiempo. **3,** (in any degree) nunca; jamás; en la, mi, o su vida.

evergreen ('ɛv·ər·grin) *adj.* de hojas perennes. —*n.* árbol o planta de hojas perennes.

evergreen oak encina.

everlasting (,ɛv·ər'læs·tɪŋ) *adj.* eterno; perdurable; perpetuo. —*n., bot.* perpetua; siempreviva.

evermore (,ɛv·ər'mor) *adv.* eternamente; de todo tiempo.

evert (i'vʌrt) *v.t.* volver al revés. —**eversion** (-'vʌr·ʒən) *n.* acción de volver al revés.

every ('ɛv·ri) *adj.* **1,** (each) cada. **2,** (all) todos los . . . —**every now and then,** de vez en cuando. —**every once in a while,** una que otra vez. —**every other,** cada dos; uno sí y otro no. —**every which way,** en toda dirección.

everybody ('ɛv·ri,ba·di) *n.* todos; todo el mundo; cada uno; cada cual.

everyday ('ɛv·ri·dei) *adj.* de cada día; cotidiano; diario.

everyone ('ɛv·ri·wʌn) *n.* todo el mundo; todos.

everything ('ɛv·ri·θɪŋ) *n.* todo; toda cosa.

everywhere ('ɛv·ri·hwɛr) *adv.* en, a o por todas partes; por dondequiera.

evict (ɪ'vɪkt) *v.t.* desahuciar; desalojar; expulsar. —**eviction** (ɪ'vɪk·ʃən) *n.* desahucio; desalojamiento; expulsión.

evidence ('ɛv·ɪ·dəns) *n.* **1,** (manifestness) evidencia. **2,** *law* prueba; *Amer.* evidencia. —*v.t.* evidenciar; patentizar. —**give evidence,** deponer. —**in evidence,** a la vista; manifiesto.

evident ('ɛv·ɪ·dənt) *adj.* evidente;

claro; manifiesto; patente. —**be evident,** resaltar.

evil ('iː·vəl) *adj.* **1,** (wicked) malo; maligno; perverso. **2,** (harmful) nocivo; perjudicial. —*n.* **1,** (improper conduct) maldad; perversidad. **2,** (harm) mal; desgracia. —**evilness,** *n.* maldad. —**evil eye,** aojo; mal de ojo.

evildoing ('i·vəl,du·ɪŋ) *n.* maldad. —**evildoer,** *n.* malhechor.

evil-minded ('i·vəl,main·dɪd) *adj.* malicioso; mal intencionado.

evince (ɪ'vɪns) *v.t.* hacer patente; revelar; indicar. —**evincible,** *adj.* demostrable.

eviscerate (ɪ'vɪs·ə·reit) *v.t.* destripar; desentrañar; eviscerar. —**evisceration,** *n.* destripamiento; evisceración.

evocation (ɛv·ə'kei·ʃən) *n.* evocación; llamamiento. —**evocative** (ɪ'vak·ə·tɪv) *adj.* evocador.

evoke (i'vork) *v.t.* evocar; llamar.

evolution (ɛv·ə'lu·ʃən) *n.* **1,** (natural growth) evolución; desarrollo. **2,** (progress) progreso; marcha. —**evolutionary,** *adj.* evolucionista; evolutivo. —**evolutionism,** *n.* evolucionismo. —**evolutionist,** *n.* evolucionista.

evolve (ɪ'valv) *v.t.* **1,** (develop) desenvolver; desarrollar. **2,** (emit, as a gas) despedir; emitir. —*v.i.* desarrollarse; evolucionar.

ewe (juː) *n.* oveja.

exacerbate (ɛg'zæs·ər,beit) *v.t.* exacerbar; irritar. —**exacerbation,** *n.* exacerbación; irritación; exasperación.

exact (ɛg'zækt) *v.t.* exigir; imponer. —*adj.* (ig-) **1,** (accurate) exacto; cabal; correcto. **2,** (strict) estrecho; estricto; riguroso. —**exacting,** *adj.* exigente. —**exactness,** *n.* = **exactitude.**

exaction (ɪg'zæk·ʃən) *n.* exacción; extorsión.

exactitude (ɪg'zæk·tɪ,tuːd) *n.* exactitud; precisión; rectitud.

exactly (ɪg'zækt·li) *adv.* exactamente; precisamente. —*interj.* ¡justo!; ¡exacto!

exaggerate (ɛg'zædʒ·ə,reit) *v.t. & i.* exagerar. —**exaggeration,** *n.* exageración.

exalt (ɛg'zɔlt) *v.t.* **1,** (elevate) exaltar; elevar. **2,** (praise; extol) exaltar; enaltecer; ensalzar; sublimar. **3,** (inspire; elate) alegrar; regocijar.

exaltation (ˌɛg·zɔl'tei·ʃən) *n.* **1,** (elevation) exaltación; enaltecimiento. **2,** (praise) ensalzamiento; sublimación. **3,** (elation) regocijo.

examination (ɛgˌzæm·ɪ'nei·ʃən) *n.* examen; investigación; inspección; *law* interrogatorio.

examine (ɛg'zæm·ɪn) *v.t.* **1,** (inspect) inspeccionar; revisar; explorar. **2,** (inquire into) inquirir; interrogar. **3,** (test) examinar.

example (ɪg'zæm·pəl) *n.* **1,** (sample) ejemplo; dechado. **2,** (illustration) ejemplo; paradigma. **3,** (model) modelo; muestra. **4,** (precedent; analogy) ejemplar. **5,** (warning; lesson) ejemplar; escarmiento.

exasperate (ɛg'zæs·pə·reit) *v.t.* exasperar. —**exasperation,** *n.* exasperación.

excavate ('ɛks·kə·veit) *v.t.* **1,** (dig into) excavar; cavar. **2,** (form by digging) ahondar; vaciar. **3,** (unearth) desenterrar. —**excavation,** *n.* excavación. —**excavator,** *n.* excavador *(person);* excavadora *(machine).*

exceed (ɛk'siːd) *v.t.* **1,** (go beyond) exceder; aventajar; rebasar. **2,** (surpass) sobrepasar; superar. —**exceedingly,** *adv.* excesivamente; sumamente; muy.

excel (ɛk'sɛl) *v.t.* [**excelled, -celling**] aventajar; superar. —*v.i.* sobresalir.

excellence ('ɛk·sə·ləns) *n.* excelencia. —**excellent** (-lənt) *adj.* excelente; sobresaliente.

excellency ('ɛk·sə·lən·si) *n., usu. con mayúscula* Excelencia.

except (ɪk'sɛpt) *prep.* [*también,* ex**cepting**] excepto; con excepción de; salvo; menos. —*conj.* sino; fuera de que. —*v.t.* exceptuar; excluir; omitir. —*v.i., law* recusar. —**except for,** si no fuera porque; salvo.

exception (ɪk'sɛp·ʃən) *n.* **1,** (exclusion) excepción; salvedad. **2,** (objection) objeción; *law* recusación. —**take exception, 1,** (object) oponerse; objetar. **2,** (be offended) ofenderse.

exceptionable (ɪk'sɛp·ʃə·nə·bəl) *adj.* recusable; objetable; tachable.

exceptional (ɪk'sɛp·ʃə·nəl) *adj.* excepcional.

excerpt ('ɛk·sərpt) *n.* extracto; excerta. —*v.t.* (ɛk'sʌrpt) extractar.

excess (ɛk'sɛs) *n.* **1,** (superfluity) exceso; demasía. **2,** (surplus; remainder) excedente; sobrante;

superávit. **3,** (immoderation) inmoderación; destemplanza. —*adj.* excesivo; desmedido.

excessive (ɛk'sɛs·ɪv) *adj.* excesivo; inmoderado; superfluo. —**excessiveness,** *n.* demasía; inmoderación; destemplanza.

exchange (ɛks'tʃeindʒ) *v.t. & i.* **1,** (give and take) cambiar; canjear. **2,** (barter; trade) permutar; trocar. —*n.* **1,** (act of exchanging) cambio; permuta; (of prisoners, etc.) canje. **2,** (thing exchanged) cambio. **3,** (stock exchange) bolsa. **4,** (telephone exchange) central telefónica.

exchequer (ɛks'tʃɛk·ər) *n.* tesoro público; fisco; fondos; *Brit.* Ministerio de Hacienda.

excise ('ɛk·saiz) *n.* impuesto sobre consumos. —*v.t.* **1,** (cut out) extirpar. **2,** (tax) someter a impuesto. —**excision** (ɛk'sɪʒ·ən) *n.* excisión.

excitable (ɛk'sai·tə·bəl) *adj.* excitable. —**excitability,** *n.* excitabilidad.

excitation (ˌɛk·sai·tei·ʃən) *n.* excitación.

excite (ɛk'sait) *v.t.* excitar. —**excited,** *adj.* excitado; agitado. —**exciter,** *n.* excitante.

excitement (ɛk'sait·mənt) *n.* excitación; agitación; conmoción.

exciting (ɛk'sai·tɪŋ) *adj.* excitante; estimulante; emocionante.

exclaim (ɛk'skleim) *v.i.* exclamar; clamar. —*v.t.* gritar; proferir.

exclamation (ˌɛks·klə'mei·ʃən) *n.* exclamación; grito. —**exclamation point,** signo de admiración (!).

exclamatory (ɛk'sklæm·ə·tor·i) *adj.* **1,** (spoken vehemently) exclamativo; exclamatorio. **2,** *gram.* admirativo.

exclude (ɛk'skluːd) *v.t.* **1,** (shut out) excluir. **2,** (omit) omitir. —**exclusion** (ɪk'skluː·ʒən) *n.* exclusión; eliminación.

exclusive (ɪk'sklu·sɪv) *adj.* exclusivo; exceptuado; privativo. —**exclusiveness,** *n.* exclusividad; —**exclusive of,** exclusive; con exclusión de.

excommunicate (ˌɛks·kə'mju·nɪ·keit) *v.t.* excomulgar. —**excommunication,** *n.* excomunión.

excoriate (ɛk'skor·i·eit) *v.t.* **1,** (denounce) excoriar; flagelar. **2,** (strip the skin off) desollar; despellejar. —**excoriation,** *n.* desolladura; excoriación.

excrement ('ɛks·krə·mənt) *n.* excremento; heces.

excrescence (ɪk'skrɛs·əns) *n.* excrecencia. —**excrescent**, *adj.* excrecente; superfluo.

excrete (ɛk'skrit) *v.t.* excretar. —**excretion** (-'skri·ʃən) *n.* excreción.

excruciating (ɪk'skru·ʃi‚ei·tɪŋ) *adj.* agudísimo; penosísimo. —**excruciation** (-'ei·ʃən) *n.* tormento.

exculpate (ɛk'skʌl·peit) *v.t.* disculpar; justificar; exonerar. —**exculpation** (‚ɛks·kəl'pei·ʃən) *n.* disculpa; exoneración. —**exculpatory** (ɛk'skʌlp·ə·tor·i) *adj.* disculpador; justificador.

excursion (ɪk'skʌr·ʒən) *n.* 1, (journey) excursión. 2, (digression) digresión; desviación. —**excursionist** (-ɪst) *n.* excursionista.

excuse (ɛk'skjuz) *v.t.* 1, (forgive) excusar; dispensar; disculpar. 2, (justify) sincerar; justificar. 3, (release from a duty) excusar; exentar. 4, (refrain from exacting; remit) perdonar; condonar. —*n.* (ɛk'skjus) 1, (plea; reason) excusa; justificación. 2, (pretext) disculpa; pretexto. —**excusable**, *adj.* excusable; disculpable.

execrable ('ɛk·sɪ·krə·bəl) *adj.* execrable; aborrecible; abominable.

execrate ('ɛk·sɪ·kreit) *v.t.* 1, (detest) execrar; aborrecer. 2, (denounce) execrar; abominar; maldecir. —**execration**, *n.* execración; aborrecimiento; maldición.

execute ('ɛk·sɪ·kjut) *v.t.* 1, (perform) ejecutar; realizar; llevar a cabo. 2, (effect) legalizar; formalizar; otorgar (un documento). 3, (put to death) ejecutar; ajusticiar.

execution (‚ɛk·sɪ'kju·ʃən) *n.* ejecución. —**executioner**, *n.* verdugo; ejecutor de la justicia.

executive (ɪg'zɛk·jə·tɪv) *adj.* ejecutivo. —*n.* ejecutivo; director; administrador; *U.S.,* con **the,** poder ejecutivo; el ejecutivo. —**Chief Executive,** jefe de estado; *U.S.* Presidente.

executor (ɪg'zɛk·jə·tər) *n.* 1, (administrator) ejecutivo; ejecutor. 2, *law* albacea. —**executorship,** *n.,* *law* albaceazgo.

executory (ɪg'zɛk·jə‚tor·i) *adj.* 1, (administrative) ejecutivo; administrativo. 2, *law* (in force) ejecutorio.

executrix (ɪg'zɛk·jə‚trɪks) *n.* 1, (administrator) ejecutora. 2, *law* albacea.

exegesis (ɛk·sə'dʒi·sɪs) *n.* [*pl.* -ses] exégesis. —**exegete** ('ɛk·sə·dʒit) *n.* exégeta. —**exegetic** (-dʒɛt·ɪk) *adj.* [también, **exegetical**] exegético.

exemplar (ɛg'zɛm·plər) *n.* ejemplar; modelo.

exemplary (ɪg'zɛm·plə·ri) *adj.* ejemplar.

exemplify (ɛg'zɛm·plɪ·fai) *v.t.* ejemplificar. —**exemplification** (-fɪ'kei·ʃən) *n.* ejemplificación.

exempt (ɛg'zɛmpt) *v.t.* eximir; franquear. —*adj.* exento; libre; franco; inmune. —**exemption** (ɛg·'zɛmp·ʃən) *n.* exención; franquicia; dispensa; inmunidad.

exercise ('ɛk·sər‚saiz) *n.* 1, (exertion; drill) ejercicio. 2, (performance; use) ejercicio; uso. 3, *usu.pl.* (ceremonies) ceremonia. —*v.t.* 1, (perform; use) ejercer; ejercitar. 2, (train) adiestrar; ejercitar. —*v.i.* hacer ejercicios.

exert (ɛg'zʌrt) *v.t.* esforzar; ejercer. —**exert oneself,** empeñarse; esforzarse; hacer esfuerzo. —**exertion** (ɪg'zʌr·ʃən) *n.* esfuerzo; ejercicio.

exhalation (ɛks·ə'lei·ʃən) *n.* 1, *physiol.* (act of exhaling) exhalación; espiración; evaporación. 2, (what is exhaled) exhalación; efluvio; emanación; vapor.

exhale (ɛks'heil) *v.t.* exhalar; emitir; espirar. —*v.i.* vahear; disiparse.

exhaust (ɛg'zɔst) *v.t.* 1, (empty) vaciar. 2, (consume) agotar; consumir. 3, (fatigue) fatigar; agotar. —*n.* escape. —**exhaustible,** *adj.* agotable. —**exhaustive,** *adj.* cabal; completo.

exhaustion (ɛg'zɔs·tʃən) *n.* 1, (depletion) agotamiento. 2, (fatigue) extenuación.

exhibit (ɛg'zɪb·ɪt) *v.t.* 1, (display) exhibir; presentar. 2, (manifest) manifestar; mostrar. —*v.i.* dar una exhibición. —*n.* 1, (display) exhibición. 2, *law* (item of evidence) prueba material.

exhibition (‚ɛk·zə'brɪʃ·ən) *n.* exhibición; exposición. —**exhibitionism,** *n.* exhibicionismo. —**exhibitionist,** *n.* exhibicionista.

exhibitor (ɛg'zɪb·ɪ·tər) *n.* 1, (one who exhibits) expositor. 2, *motion pictures* empresario de teatro.

exhilarate (ɛg'zɪl·ə·reit) *v.t.*

regocijar; alborozar. **—exhilaration,** n. regocijo; alborozo.

exhort (ɛg'zort) v.t. exhortar; dar amonestación o consejo a. **—exhortation** (,ɛk·sor'tei·ʃən) n. exhortación; consejo. **—exhortative** (ɛg'zor·tə·tɪv) [también, **exhortatory** (-tor·i)] adj. exhortatorio.

exhume (ɛks'hjuːm) v.t. exhumar; desenterrar. **—exhumation** (,ɛk·sju·'mei·ʃən) n. exhumación.

exigency ('ɛk·sɪ·dʒən·si) n. exigencia; requisito urgente. **—exigent,** adj. exigente; urgente.

exiguous (ɪg'zɪg·ju·əs) adj. exiguo. **—exiguousness,** n. exigüidad.

exile ('ɛg·zail; 'ɛk·sail) n. 1, (expatriation) destierro; expatriación. 2, (expatriate) desterrado; expatriado. **—**v.t. desterrar; expatriar.

exist (ɛg'zɪst) v.i. existir; subsistir; encontrarse. **—existence,** n. existencia; ser; vida. **—existent,** adj. existente.

existential (,ɛg·zɪs'tɛn·ʃəl) adj. existencial. **—existentialism,** n. existencialismo. **—existentialist,** n. & adj. existencialista.

exit ('ɛk·sɪt; 'ɛg·zɪt) n. 1, (avenue of departure) salida. 2, (departure) partida; marcha; salida. 3, fig. (death) muerte. **—**v.i. salir.

exodus ('ɛk·sə·dəs) n. 1, (a going out) éxodo; salida; emigración. 2, cap., Bib. Éxodo.

exonerate (ɛg'zan·ə·reit) v.t. exonerar; descargar; disculpar. **—exoneration,** n. exoneración; exculpación; descargo.

exorbitant (ɪg'zor·bɪ·tənt) adj. exorbitante; excesivo. **—exorbitance,** n. exorbitancia; exceso.

exorcise ('ɛk·sor·saiz) v.t. exorcisar; conjurar. **—exorcism** (-sɪz·əm) n. exorcismo; conjuro. **—exorcist** (-sɪst) n. exorcista.

exoteric (,ɛk·sə'tɛr·ɪk) adj. exotérico.

exotic (ɪg'zat·ɪk) adj. 1, (foreign; strange) exótico; forastero; extraño. 2, colloq. (striking in appearance) extraño; raro. **—exoticism** (ɪg'zat·ə,sɪz·əm) n. exotismo.

expand (ɛk'spæːnd) v.t. 1, (increase) dilatar; ensanchar; agrandar; ampliar. 2, (spread; unfold) extender; tender; desarrollar.

expanse (ɪk'spæns) n. extensión; espacio.

expansible (ɪk'spæn·sə·bəl) adj. expansible.

expansile (ɪk'spæn·sɪl) adj. expansivo.

expansion (ɪk'spæn·ʃən) n. expansión. **—expansive** (-sɪv) adj. expansivo.

expatiate (ɪk'spei·ʃi,et) v.i. espaciarse; explayarse; extenderse.

expatriate (ɛks'pei·tri·ət) n. & adj. expatriado; exiliado; desnaturalizado; proscrito. **—**v.t. (-eit) desnaturalizar; desterrar; expatriar. **—expatriation,** n. expatriación.

expect (ɛk'spekt) v.t. 1, (anticipate; await) esperar; aguardar. 2, (rely on) contar con. 3, colloq. (suppose) suponer.

expectancy (ɛk'spɛk·tən·si) n. 1, (expectation) expectativa; expectación; esperanza. 2, (contingency) contingencia; eventualidad; casualidad.

expectant (ɛk'spɛk·tənt) adj. 1, (awaiting) expectante. 2, (pregnant) preñada; encinta. **—expectant mother,** madre en cierne.

expectation (,ɛk·spɛk'tei·ʃən) n. expectación; expectativa; esperanza.

expectorate (ɛk'spɛk·tə,reit) v.t. & i. expectorar; esputar. **—expectorant,** adj. & n. expectorante. **—expectoration,** n. expectoración; esputo.

expedient (ɪk'spiː·di·ənt) adj. oportuno; conveniente; propio. **—**n. expediente; medio; recurso. **—expediency** [también, **expedience**] n. propiedad; conveniencia; comodidad; oportunidad.

expedite ('ɛks·pə,dait) v.t. 1, (accelerate) acelerar; apresurar; dar prisa a. 2, (dispatch) facilitar; despachar; expedir. **—expediter,** n. despachador; expedidor.

expedition (ɛks·pə'dɪʃ·ən) n. expedición. **—expeditionary** (-ə·ner·i) adj. expedicionario.

expeditious (ɛks·pə'dɪʃ·əs) adj. pronto; expeditivo. **—expeditiousness,** n. prontitud; despacho.

expel (ɛk'spɛl) v.t. [**expelled, -pelling**] expeler; expulsar; echar. **—expellant** (-ənt) adj. & n. expelente; expulsivo.

expend (ɛk'spɛnd) v.t. expender; gastar.

expenditure (ɛk'spɛn·dɪ·tʃər) n. desembolso; gasto; salida.

expense (ɪk'spɛns) n. 1, (cost) costo; coste. 2, (expenditure) gasto.

3, (loss) detrimento; pérdida. —**at any expense,** a toda costa. —**at the expense of,** a costa de. —**expense account,** cuenta de gastos.

expensive (ɪkˈspɛnˑsɪv) *adj.* costoso; caro.

experience (ɪkˈspɪrˑiˑəns) *n.* experiencia. —*v.t.* experimentar; sufrir. —**experienced,** *adj.* experimentado.

experiment (ɪkˈspɛrˑəˑmənt) *n.* experimento; ensayo. —*v.i.* experimentar; hacer una prueba. —**experimental** (-ˈmɛnˑtəl) *adj.* experimental; de prueba. —**experimentation** (-mɛnˈteiˑʃən) *n.* experimento; experimentación.

expert (ˈɛksˑpʌrt) *adj.* experimentado; experto; diestro; hábil. —*n.* experto; perito; juez. —**expertness,** *n.* destreza; habilidad; pericia.

expiate (ˈɛksˑpiˑeit) *v.t.* expiar; purgar; reparar. —**expiation,** *n.* expiación.

expiration (ˌɛkˑspəˈrəiˑʃən) *n.* 1, (termination) expiración; terminación; cumplimiento. 2, (exhalation) espiración.

expire (ɛkˈspair) *v.i.* 1, (come to an end) expirar; acabarse; cumplirse; terminar. 2, (die) fallecer; morir. 3, (exhale) espirar; exhalar.

explain (ɛkˈsplein) *v.t. & i.* explicar.

explanation (ˌɛkˑspləˈneiˑʃən) *n.* explicación.

explanatory (ɛkˈsplænˑəˑtorˑi) *adj.* explicativo.

expletive (ˈɛksˑpləˑtiv) *adj.* expletivo. —*n.* interjección; reniego.

explicable (ˈɛksˑplɪˑkəˑbəl) *adj.* explicable.

explicate (ˈɛksˑpləˌkeit) *v.t.* explicar. —**explication,** *n.* explicación.

explicit (ɪkˈsplɪsˑɪt) *adj.* 1, (definite) explícito; claro; inequívoco. 2, (outspoken) franco; abierto. —**explicitness,** *n.* claridad; franqueza.

explode (ɛkˈsplod) *v.i.* volar; estallar; detonar; hacer explosión; reventar. —*v.t.* 1, (cause to burst) hacer estallar; fulminar. 2, *fig.* (disprove) refutar; desbaratar; confundir.

exploit (ˈɛksˑploit) *n.* hazaña; proeza. —*v.t.* (ɛkˈsploit) explotar; aprovechar. —**exploitation** (ˌɛksˑploiˈteiˑʃən) *n.* explotación; aprovechamiento.

exploration (ˌɛksˑpləˈreiˑʃən) *n.* exploración. —**exploratory** (ɪkˈsplorˑəˑtorˑi) *adj.* exploratorio; explorador.

explore (ɛkˈsplor) *v.t. & i.* 1, (traverse, for discovery) explorar. 2, (investigate) averiguar. —**explorer,** *n.* explorador.

explosion (ɛksˈplorˑʒən) *n.* explosión; reventón.

explosive (ɛksˈplosˑɪv) *n. & adj.* explosivo; fulminante.

exponent (ɛkˈsporˑnənt) *n.* 1, (expounder) exponente; expositor. 2, (representative; symbol) representante; símbolo. 3, *math.* (power) exponente.

export (ɛkˈsport) *v.t.* exportar. —*n.* (ˈɛksˑport) 1, [*también,* **exportation**] (shipment) exportación. 2, (something exported) artículo de exportación. —**exportable,** *adj.* exportable. —**exporter,** *n.* exportador. —**exporting,** *adj.* exportador. —**export trade,** comercio exterior.

expose (ɛkˈspoz) *v.t.* 1, (exhibit) exponer; mostrar; descubrir; revelar. 2, (reveal the truth about) desenmascarar; descubrir. 3, (leave unprotected) exponer; arriesgar; poner en peligro.

exposé (ˌɛkˑspoˈze) *n.* revelación; descubrimiento; desenmascaramiento.

exposition (ɛksˑpəˈzɪʃˑən) *n.* exposición; exhibición.

expositor (ɪkˈspazˑəˑtər) *n.* comentador; expositor.

expository (ɛkˈspazˑəˑtorˑi) *adj.* expositivo; explicativo.

expostulate (ɛkˈspasˑtʃəˑleit) *v.i.* protestar; altercar; contender. —**expostulation,** *n.* protesta; reconvención; disuasión.

exposure (ɛkˈsporˑʒər) *n.* 1, (act or effect of exposing) exposición. 2, (direction faced) orientación. 3, *photog.* exposición; toma. 4, (lack of shelter or cover) desabrigo. 5, (unmasking) desenmascaramiento. —**exposure meter,** fotómetro.

expound (ɛkˈspaund) *v.t.* exponer; explicar.

express (ɛkˈsprɛs) *v.t.* 1, (reveal in words, etc.) expresar; representar. 2, (manifest) expresar; manifestar; explicar. 3, (press) exprimir; prensar; extraer el jugo de. 4, (send by express) enviar o expedir por expreso. —*adj.* 1, (clear; explicit) expreso; claro; explícito. 2, (special; fast) especial; pronto; rápido. —*n.* expreso; tren expreso. —**expres-**

sible, *adj.* expresable; exprimible. **—expressly,** *adv.* expresamente.

expression (ɛk'sprɛʃ·ən) *n.* **1,** (act or manner of expressing) expresión. **2,** (word or phrase) vocablo; palabra; voz; locución. **3,** (manifestation) expresión; gesto; cara.

expressive (ɛk'sprɛs·ɪv) *adj.* expresivo. **—expressiveness,** *n.* significación; expresión; energía.

expressway (ɛk'sprɛs,wei) *n.* autopista.

expropriate (ɛks'pro·pri·eit) *v.t.* expropiar. **—expropriation,** *n.* expropiación. **—expropriator,** *n.* expropiador.

expulsion (ɪk'spʌl·ʃən) *n.* expulsión.

expunge (ɛks'pʌndʒ) *v.t.* **1,** (strike out) borrar; cancelar. **2,** (destroy) aniquilar; destruir.

expurgate ('ɛks·pər,geit) *v.t.* expurgar; purificar. **—expurgation,** *n.* expurgación; expurgo; purificación.

exquisito ('ɛks·kwi·zɪt) *adj.* **1,** (dainty; elegant) exquisito; delicado; primorosó. **2,** (intense; keen) vivo; agudo; excesivo. **—exquisiteness,** *n.* exquisitez; primor; delicadeza; perfección.

extant ('ɛks·tənt) *adj.* existente; viviente.

extemporaneous (ɛk,stɛm·pə·'rei·ni·əs) *adj.* improvisado. *También,* **extemporary** (-,rɛr·i). **—extemporaneousness,** *n.* improvisación.

extemporize (ɛk'stɛm·pə·raiz) *v.t. & i.* improvisar; repentizar.

extend (ɛk'stɛnd) *v.t.* **1,** (stretch) extender. **2,** (enlarge) ampliar. **3,** (extend in time) prorrogar. **4,** (defer; postpone) diferir. **5,** (offer; bestow) ofrecer. **—v.i.** extenderse. **—extend to,** llegar a; alcanzar a.

extensible (ɛk'stɛn·sə·bəl) *adj.* extensible.

extension (ɛk'stɛn·ʃən) *n.* **1,** (extending) extensión; dilatación; expansión; ensanche. **2,** (addition) aumento; adición; prolongación; anexo. **3,** (scope; extent) alcance; proporción; grado.

extensive (ɛk'stɛn·sɪv) *adj.* extendido; dilatado; amplio. **—extensiveness,** *n.* extensión; amplitud; grado; alcance.

extent (ɪk'stɛnt) *n.* **1,** (expanse) extensión. **2,** (limit) alcance; límite. **3,** (degree) grado. **—to a certain**

extent, hasta cierto punto. **—to the full extent,** en toda su extensión. **—to a great extent,** en sumo grado.

extenuate (ɛk'stɛn·ju·eit) *v.t.* **1,** (attenuate) atenuar. **2,** (mitigate) mitigar; paliar. **—extenuated,** *adj.* mermado; delgado. **—extenuating,** *adj.* paliativo; atenuante. **—extenuation,** *n.* atenuación; paliación; mitigación.

exterior (ɪk'stɪr·i·ər) *adj.* exterior; externo. **—n.** exterior; aspecto; exterioridad.

exterminate (ɛk'stʌr·mɪ·neit) *v.t.* exterminar. **—extermination,** *n.* exterminio; extirpación. **—exterminator,** *n.* exterminador.

external (ɪk'stʌr·nəl) *adj.* **1,** (exterior) externo; exterior. **2,** (outside and apart) extraño; extranjero.

extinct (ɪk'stɪŋkt) *adj.* **1,** (extinguished) extinto; extinguido; apagado. **2,** (no longer existing) extinto; desaparecido. **—extinction,** *n.* extinción; desaparición. **—become extinct,** extinguirse.

extinguish (ɛk'stɪŋ·gwɪʃ) *v.t.* **1,** (quench) extinguir; apagar; sofocar. **2,** (put an end to) extinguir; suprimir; destruir. **—extinguishment,** *n.* extinción; apagamiento. **—fire extinguisher,** extintor.

extirpate ('ɛks·stər·peit) *v.t.* extirpar; desarraigar; arrancar. **—extirpation,** *n.* extirpación; arrancamiento.

extol (ɛk'stoʊl) *v.t.* [**extolled, -tolling**] ensalzar; enaltecer; exaltar.

extort (ɛk'stort) *v.t.* extorsionar; sacar u obtener por fuerza; arrancar. **—extortion** (ɛk'stor·ʃən) *n.* extorsión; exacción; concusión. **—extortionate** (-ət) *adj.* opresivo; injusto; gravoso.

extra ('ɛks·trə) *adj.* extraordinario; suplementario; adicional; de más; de sobra; sobrante; de repuesto; de recambio; de reserva. **—adv.** excepcionalmente. **—n.** **1,** (addition) exceso; recargo. **2,** (additional cost) gasto extraordinario. **3,** (newspaper) extra; edición o número extraordinario. **4,** *theat.* (supernumerary) extra. **5,** (spare) repuesto.

extract (ɛk'strækt) *v.t.* **1,** (remove) extraer; sacar; arrancar. **2,** (separate) extraer; separar. **3,** (select) seleccionar; extractar; compendiar. **—n.** ('ɛks·trækt) **1,** (thing extracted) extracto. **2,** (excerpt) excerta.

extraction (ɛk'stræk·ʃən) n. 1, (removal) extracción; saca. 2, (derivation) descendencia; origen.

extractor (ɛk'stræk·tər) n. 1, (abstractor) extractador. 2, (device) exprimidera; extractor.

extracurricular ('ɛk·strə·kə'rɪk·jə·lər) adj. extracurricular; fuera del plan de estudios.

extradite ('ɛks·trə·dait) v.t. entregar por extradición; obtener la extradición de. —**extradition** (-'dɪ·ʃən) n. extradición.

extraneous (ɛk'strei·ni·əs) adj. extraño; externo; extranjero; ajeno.

extraordinary (ɛk'strɔr·də·nɛr·i) adj. extraordinario; raro; singular; especial; descomunal.

extrapolate (ɛk'stræp·ə‚leit) v.t. extrapolar. —**extrapolation**, n. extrapolación.

extrasensory (‚ɛk·strə'sɛn·sə·ri) adj. extrasensible. —**extrasensory perception,** percepción por medios extrasensibles.

extraterritorial (‚ɛks·trə‚ter·ɪ·'tor·i·əl) adj. extraterritorial.

extravagant (ɪk'stræv·ə·gənt) adj. 1, (wasteful) pródigo; manirroto; gastador. 2, (high priced) exorbitante; disparado. 3, (irregular; fantastic) extravagante; estrafalario. —**extravagance**, n. lujo exagerado; derroche; profusión; extravagancia.

extravaganza (ɪk·stræv·ə'gæn·zə) n., theat. obra o composición extravagante.

extreme (ɪk'striːm) adj. 1, (utmost) extremo; extremado. 2, (final) último; postrero. 3, (exact; strict) riguroso; estricto; severo. 4, (immoderate) extremado; extremoso. —n. 1, (greatest degree) extremo. 2, (something immoderate) extremosidad. 3, (the first or last) extremidad; ápice; fin; cabo. 4, (exactness) rigurosidad; severidad. —**extremely,** adv. extremadamente; sumamente. —**extremeness**, n. extremosidad; rigurosidad; severidad. —**extreme unction,** extremaunción.

extremist (ɛk'striː·mɪst) n. extremista; radical.

extremity (ɛk'strɛm·ə·ti) n. 1, (terminal) extremidad. 2, a veces pl. (distress) necesidad; apuro.

extricable ('ɛks·trɪ·kə·bəl) adj. fácil de desenredar.

extricate ('ɛks·trɪ·keit) v.t. desenredar; desembrollar; sacar. —**extrication**, n. desembarazo; desenredo.

extrinsic (ɛk'strɪn·zɪk) adj. extrínseco.

extroversion (‚ɛks·trə'vʌr·ʒən) n. extraversión; extroversión.

extrovert ('ɛks·trə·vʌrt) n. & adj. extrovertido. —**extroverted,** adj. extrovertido.

extrude (ɛk'struːd) v.t. 1, (eject) forzar hacia fuera; echar; arrojar. 2, metall.; plastics fabricar por extrusión. —v.i. salir fuera; sobresalir.

extrusion (ɛk'struː·ʒən) n. 1, (extruding) expulsión; resalto. 2, metall.; plastics extrusión. 3, geol. efusión de lava por grietas de rocas.

exuberant (ɛg'zu·bə·rənt) adj. exuberante; lujuriante; profuso. —**exuberance**, n. exuberancia.

exude (ɛg'zuːd) v.t. exudar; sudar; transpirar. —v.i. rezumarse; revenirse. —**exudation** (‚ɛks·ju'dei·ʃən) n. exudación; exudado.

exult (ɛg'zʌlt) v.i. exultar; regocijarse; alegrarse. —**exultant,** adj. triunfante; regocijado; alborozado. —**exultation** (‚ɛks·əl'tei·ʃən) n. exultación; regocijo; transporte.

eye (ai) n. 1, (organ of vision) ojo. 2, (view) vista; aspecto. 3, (opinion) talante; juicio; discernimiento. 4, mech. (hole) anillo; aro. 5, bot. (bud; shoot) yema; botón. 6, (hurricane's center) vórtice. —v.t. mirar de hito en hito; observar. —**an eye for an eye,** ojo por ojo. —**black eye,** ojo amoratado. —**blind in one eye,** tuerto. —**have a cast in one eye,** ser bisojo. —**have an eye on,** echar el ojo a. —**have an eye to,** intentar; proponerse. —**keep an eye on,** vigilar. —**keep one's eyes open,** abrir el ojo. —**make eyes at,** mirar amorosamente o con codicia. —**see eye to eye,** estar de acuerdo; ver con el mismo ojo. —**with an eye to,** con la intención de.

eyeball ('ai·bɔl) n. globo del ojo.

eyebrow ('ai‚brau) n. ceja.

eyecup ('ai‚kʌp) n. ojera; lavaojos.

eyeful ('ai·fʊl) n., slang cuadro completo.

eyeglass ('ai‚glæs) n. 1, (lens) ocular; anteojo. 2, pl. (spectacles) lentes; anteojos; gafas; quevedos.

eyelash ('ai·læʃ) n. pestaña.

eyeless ('ai·ləs) adj. sin ojos; ciego.

eyelet ('ai·lət) n. resquicio; abertura; ojete.

eyelid ('ai·lɪd) n. párpado.

eye opener 1, (surprise) revelación; sorpresa. **2,** (drink) copa temprana; trago temprano.

eyepiece ('ai·pis) *n.* ocular.

eyeshade ('ai‚ʃeid) *n.* visera.

eyesight ('ai‚sait) *n.* vista; alcance de la vista.

eyesore ('ai·sor) *n.* cosa que ofende a la vista; esperpento.

eyestrain ('ai‚strein) *n.* vista cansada.

eyetooth ('ai‚tuθ) *n.* colmillo; diente canino.

eyewash ('ai‚wɔʃ) *n.* **1,** (fluid) loción para los ojos. **2,** (obfuscation) embuste; prevaricación.

eyewitness ('ai‚wɪt·nis) *n.* testigo ocular o presencial.

eyrie *también,* **aerie** ('ei·ri; 'ai·ri) *n.* **1,** (eagle's nest) nido de águila; aguilera. **2,** (dwelling on a height) vivienda elevada.

F

F, f (ɛf) sexta letra del alfabeto inglés. —*n., mus.* fa.

fa (faɹ) *n., mus.* fa.

fable ('fei·bəl) *n.* fábula; cuento. —**fabled,** *adj.* legendario; ficticio.

fabric ('fæb·rɪk) *n.* **1,** (frame; structure) estructura; trama; fábrica. **2,** (cloth) tejido; tela; género.

fabricate ('fæb·rɪ·kelt) *v.t.* **1,** (build; manufacture) fabricar. **2,** (invent) inventar; elaborar.

fabrication (‚fæb·rɪ'kei·ʃən) *n.* **1,** (manufacture) fabricación; manufactura. **2,** (invention) invención; mentira.

fabulist ('fæb·ju·lɪst) *n.* fabulista.

fabulous ('fæb·ju·ləs). *adj.* fabuloso.

façade (fə'saɹd) *n.* fachada; frente.

face (feis) *n.* **1,** (front of the head; countenance) cara; faz; rostro. **2,** (expression; look) expresión; cara. **3,** (outward aspect) aspecto; cariz. **4,** (reputation) prestigio. **5,** (effrontery) descaro; desfachatez. **6,** (surface) superficie; lado; cara. **7,** (front) fachada; frente. **8,** *typog.* carácter. —*v.t.* **1,** (have the face or front toward) dar a; mirar a o hacia. **2,** (meet boldly) afrontar; enfrentar; encarar. **3,** (cover the surface of) revestir; cubrir. —*v.i.* mirar. —**face card,** figura. —**face down,** boca abajo; cara abajo. —**to face down,** apocar; desconcertar. —**face lifting, 1,** *surg.* cirugía plástica de la cara. **2,** (refurbishing) arreglo. —**face the music,** afrontar las consecuencias. —**face up,** boca arriba; cara arriba. —**face up to, 1,** (confront boldly) arrostrar; dar cara a; enfrentar. **2,** (resign oneself to) amoldarse a; avenirse a. —**face value,** *comm.* valor nominal. —**at face value,** como tal; en su valor; por lo que vale. —**in the face of,** encarando; en presencia de. —**lose face,** desprestigiarse. —**on the face of it,** por lo manifiesto; por lo que se ve. —**save face,** salvar las apariencias.

face-off ('feis‚ɔf) *n.* confrontación.

facet ('fæs·ɪt) *n.* faceta.

facetious (fə'si·ʃəs) *adj.* gracioso; chistoso. —**facetiousness,** *n.* chiste; gracia.

facial ('fei·ʃəl) *adj.* facial.

facile ('fæs·əl) *adj.* **1,** (ready; quick; easy) fácil; vivo. **2,** (affable) agradable.

facilitate (fə'sɪl·ə‚teit) *v.t.* facilitar. —**facilitation,** *n.* facilitación.

facility (fə'sɪl·ə·ti) *n.* **1,** (ease) facilidad. **2,** (talent; skill) facilidad; destreza. **3,** *pl.* (conveniences) comodidades; acomodaciones.

facing ('fei·sɪŋ) *n.* **1,** (outer covering) paramento. **2,** (trim) guarnición. **3,** *sewing* falso. —*prep.* frente a; en frente de. —*adv.* enfrente.

facsimile (fæk'sɪm·ə·li) *n.* facsímile.

fact (fækt) *n.* **1,** (something done or known) hecho. **2,** (reality) realidad. —**in fact,** en realidad; de hecho.

faction ('fæk·ʃən) *n.* facción. —**factional,** *adj.* faccioso. —**factionalism,** *n.* faccionalismo. —**factious** (-ʃəs) *adj.* faccioso.

factitious (fæk'tɪʃ·əs) *adj.* facticio.

factor ('fæk·tər) *n.* **1,** *comm.* factor; corredor. **2,** (contributing element) elemento; factor. **3,** *math.* factor. —*v.t., math.* descomponer en factores. —**factorial** (fæk'tor·i·əl) *adj.* factorial. —**factoring,** *n.,* *comm.* factoraje; factoría.

factory ('fæk·tə·ri) *n.* fábrica; taller.

factual ('fæk·tʃu·əl) *adj.* **1,** (of facts) basado en hechos; objetivo. **2,** (real; actual) real; verdadero.

facultative ('fæk·əl,tei·tiv) *adj.* facultativo; *law* potestativo.

faculty ('fæk·əl·ti) *n.* **1,** (aptitude; ability) facultad; aptitud. **2,** (academic) facultad; claustro.

fad (fæd) *n.* novedad; moda; manía. —**faddish,** *adj.* novelero. —**faddishness,** *n.* novelería. —**faddist,** *n.* novelero; aficionado a novedades.

fade (feid) *v.i.* **1,** (lose color) descolorarse; desteñirse. **2,** (wither) marchitarse. **3,** (grow dim; die gradually) disminuir; apagarse; desvanecerse. —*v.t.* **1,** (cause to fade) descolorar; desteñir. **2,** (wither) marchitar. **3,** (accept, as a bet) cubrir (una apuesta). —**fadeless,** *adj.* inmarchitable. —**fade in,** aclararse gradualmente. —**fade out,** borrarse gradualmente; desvanecerse.

fag (fæg) *v.t.* [**fagged, fagging**] fatigar; cansar. —*v.i.* trabajar como esclavo; fatigarse; cansarse. —*n., slang* cigarrillo.

fagot *también,* **faggot** ('fæg·ət) *n.* haz de leña.

fagoting *también,* **faggoting** ('fæg·ət·iŋ) *n.* vainicas.

Fahrenheit ('fær·ən·hait) *adj.* Fahrenheit.

fail (feil) *v.i.* **1,** (fall short; be deficient or lacking) faltar. **2,** (weaken; diminish) decaer; menguar. **3,** (be exhausted or spent) acabarse. **4,** (be unsuccessful) fallar; fracasar. **5,** (cease to function) fallar. **6,** (go bankrupt) quebrar; arruinarse. **7,** *educ.* ser suspendido; ser desaprobado. —*v.t* **1,** (disappoint) desilusionar; decepcionar; defraudar. **2,** *educ.* suspender; desaprobar; *Amer.* aplazar. —**without fail,** sin falta.

failing ('fei·liŋ) *n.* falta; defecto. —*prep.* a falta de; sin.

failure ('feil·jər) *n.* **1,** (unsuccessful deed or attempt) fracaso. **2,** (unsuccessful person) fracasado; fracaso. **3,** (bankruptcy) quiebra; bancarrota. **4,** (nonperformance; neglect) omisión. **5,** (ceasing of function) falla. **6,** *educ.* suspenso; desaprobado; *Amer.* aplazado.

faint (feint) *adj.* **1,** (feeble; weak) débil. **2,** (dim; subdued) pálido; apagado; tenue. **3,** (dizzy) desfallecido; desfalleciente. —*n.* desmayo;

desvanecimiento. —*v.i.* desmayarse; privarse; desvanecerse.

fainthearted ('feint,har·tid) *adj.* medroso; apocado; pusilánime.

faintness ('feint·nəs) *n.* **1,** (weakness) debilidad. **2,** (dimness) tenuidad; palidez. **3,** (dizziness) desfallecimiento; languidez; desmayo.

fair (feᵣr) *adj.* **1,** (handsome; comely) hermoso; bello. **2,** (blond) rubio. **3,** (light-skinned) blanco; de tez blanca. **4,** (unblemished) intachable; limpio. **5,** (just; honest) justo; recto. **6,** (valid) legal; válido. **7,** (clear; sunny) claro; despejado. **8,** (good; of good size or quality) buen; bueno. **9,** (average) regular; pasable. —*n.* **1,** (exposition) feria; exposición. **2,** (sale; bazaar) bazar. **3,** (market) mercado; feria. —*adv.* **1,** (according to rule) imparcialmente; justamente; legalmente. **2,** (favorably) bien. **3,** (squarely) justo; redondamente. —**bid fair,** tener buen cariz; prometer. —**fair and square,** *colloq.* muy justo o justamente; limpio o. limpiamente. —**fair play,** juego limpio. —**fair sex,** sexo débil; sexo bello. —**fair to middling,** *colloq.* regular; pasable.

fairhaired ('feᵣ,herd) *adj.* **1,** (having blond hair) rubio. **2,** *slang* (unduly favored) favorito; preferido.

fairly ('feᵣ·li) *adv.* **1,** (according to rule) imparcialmente; justamente; legalmente. **2,** (moderately; somewhat) moderadamente; bastante. **3,** (squarely) justo; redondamente.

fairness ('feᵣ·nəs) *n.* **1,** (handsomeness) hermosura; belleza. **2,** (justness) justicia; imparcialidad. **3,** (light color) blancura.

fairspoken ('feᵣ,spo·kən) *adj.* bien hablado; comedido.

fairway ('feᵣ·wei) *n.* **1,** *golf* calle; pista. **2,** *naut.* canal navegable.

fairy ('feᵣ·i) *n.* hada. —**fairy tale,** cuento de hadas.

fairyland ('feᵣ·i,lænd) *n.* país de las hadas.

faith (feiθ) *n.* fe. —**in faith,** en realidad; realmente. —**in good (o bad) faith,** de buena (o mala) fe.

faithful ('feiθ·fəl) *adj.* fiel. —**faithfulness,** *n.* fidelidad.

faithless ('feiθ·ləs) *adj.* **1,** (not keeping faith) desleal; infiel. **2,** (untrustworthy) falaz; falso. **3,** (unbelieving) descreído; incrédulo; sin fe.

—**faithlessness,** *n.* infidelidad; deslealtad.

fake (feik) *v.t. & i.* **1,** (feign) fingir. **2,** (falsify) falsificar. —*adj.* **1,** (feigned) fingido. **2,** (false) falso; falsificado. —*n.* **1,** (counterfeit) falsificación. **2,** (deception) engaño; mentira. **3,** (impostor) farsante; impostor.

faker ('fei·kər) *n.* **1,** (one who fakes) falsario; farsante; impostor. **2,** (swindler) estafador; engañabobos.

fakir (fə'kɪr) *n.* faquir.

Falange (fə'landʒ) *n.* Falange. —**Falangist,** *n.* falangista.

falcon ('fɔl·kən) *n.* halcón. —**falconry,** *n.* halconería; cetrería.

fall (fɔl) *v.i.* [**fell, fallen, falling**] **1,** (drop) caer. **2,** (come down; tumble) caerse. **3,** (descend) bajar. **4,** (occur; take place) caer. —*n.* **1,** (drop; dropping) caída. **2,** (autumn) otoño. **3,** (waterfall) salto de agua; catarata. —**fall away, 1,** (become estranged) alejarse; apartarse. **2,** (decline) debilitarse; desintegrarse. —**fall back,** echarse atrás; retroceder. —**fall back on o upon, 1,** (count on) contar con; apoyarse en. **2,** (retreat to) retroceder a; replegarse a. —**fall behind, 1,** (lag; drop back) quedarse atrás; rezagarse. **2,** (be in arrears) atrasarse. —**fall flat,** fallar; fracasar; no surtir efecto. —**fall for,** *slang* **1,** (fall in love with) enamorarse de; prendarse de; estar colado por. **2,** (be taken in by) engañarse con; ser engañado por. —**fall in, 1,** (line up) alinearse; ponerse en línea. **2,** (agree) ajustarse; concordar. **3,** (cave in) desplomarse; hundirse. —**fall off, 1,** (drop) declinar; caer. **2,** (fade) debilitarse; decaer. —**fall out, 1,** (quarrel) reñir; pelearse; enemistarse. **2,** (break ranks) romper filas; salirse de la fila. —**fall short,** quedarse corto; faltar; ser insuficiente. —**fall through,** fracasar; quedar en nada. —**fall to, 1,** (begin) comenzar; partir; empezar. **2,** (move into position) caer o entrar en marco. —**fall to one's lot,** tocar o venir en suerte. —**falling out,** desavenencia; desacuerdo. —**falling star,** estrella fugaz.

fallacious (fə'lei·ʃəs) *adj.* falaz.

fallacy ('fæl·ə·si) *n.* falacia.

fallible ('fæl·ə·bəl) *adj.* falible. —**fallibility,** *n.* falibilidad.

Fallopian tube (fə'lo·pi·ən) tubo de Falopio.

fallout ('fɔl,aut) *n.* resultado; lluvia radioactiva. —**fallout shelter,** refugio atómico.

fallow ('fæl·o) *adj.* **1,** (plowed but unseeded) barbechado. **2,** (idle; untended) eriazo; sin cultivo. **3,** (color) melado; amarillo pálido. —*n.* barbecho. —*v.t.* barbechar. —**fallow deer,** gamo.

false (fɔls) *adj.* **1,** (untrue) falso. **2,** (artificial) postizo. —**falseness,** *n.* falsedad. —**false front,** fachada engañosa. —**false step,** paso en falso.

falsehood ('fɔls·hʊd) *n.* falsedad; embuste; mentira.

falsetto (fɔl'sɛt·o) *n.* [*pl.* **-tos**] falsete.

falsify ('fɔl·sɪ,fai) *v.t.* falsear; falsificar. —**falsification** (-fɪ'kei·ʃən) *n.* falsificación.

falsity ('fɔl·sə·ti) *n.* falsedad; falsía.

falter ('fɔl·tər) *v.i.* vacilar; titubear.

fame (feim) *n.* fama. —**famed,** *adj.* afamado; famoso.

familiar (fə'mɪl·jər) *adj.* **1,** (friendly; intimate) familiar; íntimo; amistoso. **2,** (overfree; presuming) confianzudo; presuntuoso. **3,** (well-known) familiar; muy conocido. **4,** (well versed) familiarizado. —*n.* familiar; íntimo.

familiarity (fə,mɪl'jær·ə·ti) *n.* **1,** (quality of being well-known) familiaridad. **2,** (knowledge) conocimiento.

familiarize (fə'mɪl·jə,raiz) *v.t.* familiarizar.

family ('fæm·ə·li) *n.* familia. —**family tree,** árbol genealógico.

famine ('fæm·ɪn) *n.* hambre; *Amer.* hambruna.

famish ('fæm·ɪʃ) *v.t.* matar de hambre; hacer pasar hambre. —*v.i.* morirse de hambre; pasar hambre. —**famished,** *adj.* famélico; hambriento; muerto de hambre. —**famishment,** *n.* hambre.

famous ('fei·məs) *adj.* famoso; célebre.

fan (fæn) *n.* **1,** (manual device) abanico. **2,** (machine) ventilador. **3,** *slang* (devotee) entusiasta; aficionado; hincha. —*v.t.* [**fanned, fanning**] **1,** (drive air into o upon) abanicar; soplar. **2,** (rouse; excite) atizar. **3,** (spread out) desplegar en abanico.

fanatic (fə'næt·ık) *n.* fanático. —*adj.* [*también,* **fanatical**] fanático. —**fanaticism** (-ı‚sız·əm) *n.* fanatismo.

fancied ('fæn·sid) *adj.* imaginado; imaginario.

fanciful ('fæn·sı·fəl) *adj.* fantástico; extravagante; caprichoso.

fancy ('fæn·si) *n.* **1,** (imagination) fantasía; imaginación. **2,** (whim) antojo; capricho. **3,** (fondness; liking) inclinación; afecto. —*adj.* **1,** (imaginative; whimsical) fantástico; imaginativo; caprichoso. **2,** (of best quality) fino; de calidad. **3,** (extravagant) extravagante; rebuscado. **4,** (done with skill) primoroso; refinado. —*v.t.* **1,** (imagine) imaginar. **2,** (like; wish for) gustar; gustar de. —**fancy dress,** traje de máscara. —**fancy free,** libre; desembarazado.

fandango (fæn'dæŋ·go) *n.* [*pl.* **-gos**] fandango.

fanfare ('fæn·fer) *n.* **1,** (ceremony; ostentation) fanfarria. **2,** (trumpet flourish) toque de clarines; fanfarria.

fang (fæŋ) *n.* colmillo.

fanny ('fæn·i) *n., slang* trasera; nalgas.

fantastic (fæn'tæs·tık) *adj.* fantástico.

fantasy *también,* **phantasy** ('fæn·tə·si) *n.* fantasía.

far (faːr) *adj.* lejano; remoto; distante. —*adv.* **1,** (a long way) lejos. **2,** *in comparisons* (by a great deal) mucho; por mucho; *Amer.* lejos. —**a far cry,** muy lejos; muy diferente. —**as far as; so far as,** hasta. —**by far,** mucho; por mucho; *Amer.* lejos. —**far and away,** muchísimo; por un mucho. —**far and near; far and wide,** por o en todas partes. —**far off,** a lo lejos; muy lejos. —**in so far as,** en lo que; en cuanto. —**not by far,** ni con mucho. —**so far, 1,** (up to now) hasta este momento; hasta ahora. **2,** (to that point) hasta ese punto; hasta allá.

farad ('fær·əd) *n.* faradio; farad.

faraway ('far·ə‚wei) *adj.* **1,** (distant) lejano. **2,** (dreamy) abstraído.

farce (fars) *n.* farsa; sainete. —**farcical** ('far·sı·kəl) *adj.* burlesco; de reír; de farsa.

fare (feːr) *v.i.* **1,** (proceed; go; travel) ir; viajar. **2,** (get along) pasarlo (bien o mal); irle a uno (bien o mal). —*n.* **1,** (charge; rate) pasaje; tarifa. **2,** (paying passenger) pasajero. **3,** (food) comida.

Far East *n.* Lejano Oriente; Extremo Oriente.

farewell (fɛr'wel) *interj.* adiós; que (le) vaya bien. —*n.* despedida.

farfetched ('far‚fetʃd) *adj.* rebuscado; traído por los cabellos.

farflung ('far‚flʌŋ) *adj.* muy extenso; vasto.

farina (fə'ri·nə) *n.* harina.

farinaceous (‚fær·ə'nei·ʃəs) *adj.* farináceo.

farm (farm) *n.* hacienda; cortijo; granja; *S.A.* estancia; *Mex.* rancho. —*v.t. & i.* cultivar o labrar (la tierra). —**farmhand,** campesino; peón. —**farm out,** dar o ceder (un contrato, trabajo, etc.) a consignación.

farmer ('far·mər) *n.* **1,** (small farm owner or operator) agricultor; granjero; labrador; *Mex.* ranchero. **2,** (large landowner) latifundista; *S.A.* estanciero. **3,** (rustic) rústico; campesino.

farmhouse ('farm‚haus) *n.* alquería; cortijo; casa de una granja.

farming ('far·mıŋ) *n.* agricultura; cultivo; labranza.

farmyard ('farm·jard) *n.* corral.

faro ('fɛr·o) *n.* faraón; faro.

far-off *adj.* lejano; remoto.

far-reaching *adj.* de gran alcance; de vasta proyección.

farsighted ('far‚sai·tıd) *adj.* **1,** *opt.* présbita. **2,** [*también,* **farseeing**] (having foresight) de visión; previsor.

farsightedness ('far‚sai·tıd·nəs) *n.* **1,** *opt.* presbicia. **2,** (foresight) visión.

farther ('far·ðər) *comp. de* **far.** —*adj.* más lejano; más alejado. —*adv.* más lejos; más allá; más adelante.

farthermost ('far·ðər·most) *adj.* más lejano; más alejado.

farthest ('far·ðəst) *superl. de* **far.** —*adj.* **1,** (most distant) más lejano; más alejado. **2,** (longest) más largo. —*adv.* más lejos.

farthing ('far·ðıŋ) *n.* **1,** (coin) cuarto de penique. **2,** *fig.* (trifle) ardite; bagatela.

fascicle ('fæs·ı·kəl) *n.* fascículo.

fascinate ('fæs·ı‚neit) *v.t.* fascinar. —**fascination,** *n.* fascinación.

fascism ('fæʃ·ɪz·əm) *n.* fascismo.
fascist ('fæʃ·ɪst) *n.* fascista. —*adj.*
[*también,* **fascistic** (fə'ʃɪs·tɪk)] fascista.
fashion ('fæʃ·ən) *n.* **1,** (prevailing mode or custom) moda. **2,** (kind; sort) clase; suerte. **3,** (manner; way) manera; forma. **4,** (shape; form) forma; estilo. —*v.t.* formar; hacer. —**fashion plate,** figurín. —**high fashion,** alta costura.
fashionable ('fæʃ·ən·ə·bəl) *adj.* **1,** (stylish) de moda; a la moda; en boga. **2,** (favored by society) elegante; de buen tono.
fast (fæst; fast) *adj.* **1,** (swift) veloz; ligero; rápido. **2,** (of a clock) adelantado. **3,** (morally lax) disoluto. **4,** (firmly fixed; tight) firme; seguro; fijo; sólido; permanente. —*adv.* **1,** (rapidly) rápidamente; *Amer.* ligero. **2,** (firmly) fuertemente; firmemente; seguro. **3,** (soundly) profundamente. —*n.* ayuno. —*v.i.* ayunar. —**fasting,** *adj. & n.* ayuno.
fasten ('fæs·ən) *v.t. & i.* asegurar; sujetar; abrochar. —**fastener,** *n.* cierre; broche. —**fastening,** *n.* cierre; atadura; sujetador.
fastidious (fæs'tɪd·i·əs) *adj.* quisquilloso; prolijo; nimio; difícil de complacer. —**fastidiousness,** *n.* prolijidad; nimiedad.
fastness ('fæst·nəs) *n.* **1,** (firmness) firmeza; seguridad. **2,** (of colors) solidez. **3,** (speed) celeridad; rapidez; velocidad. **4,** (stronghold) fortaleza; plaza fuerte.
fast-track *adj.* muy agresivo; muy competitor.
fat (fæt) *adj.* **1,** (plump) gordo; grueso; obeso. **2,** (fatty; greasy) grasoso; mantecoso. **3,** (rich; fertile) fértil; abundante; rico. —*n.* **1,** (fat part) gordo. **2,** (grease; fatty substance) grasa. —**fatness,** *n.* gordura; grasa.
fatal ('fei·təl) *adj.* fatal.
fatalism ('fei·tə·lɪz·əm) *n.* fatalismo. —**fatalist,** *n.* fatalista. —**fatalistic,** *adj.* fatalístico; fatalista.
fatality (fə'tæl·ə·ti) *n.* fatalidad.
fate (feit) *n.* destino; suerte; sino; estrella. —**fated,** *adj.* predestinado.
fateful ('feit·fəl) *adj.* **1,** (momentous) trascendente; decisivo. **2,** (predestined) fatal; inevitable. **3,** (ominous) fatídico. **4,** (disastrous) funesto; aciago.

fathead ('fæt·hɛd) *n., colloq.* lerdo; torpe; tardo.
father ('fa·ðər) *n.* **1,** (male parent; creator) padre. **2,** *pl.* (ancestors) antepasados. —*v.t.* **1,** (beget) engendrar; procrear. **2,** (foster) servir de padre; tratar como hijo. **3,** (found; originate) fundar; crear. —**fatherhood,** *n.* paternidad. —**fatherly,** *adj.* paternal; paterno.
father-in-law *n.* [*pl.* **fathers-in-law**] suegro; padre político.
fatherland ('fa·ðər·lænd) *n.* patria.
fathom ('fæð·əm) *n.* braza. —*v.t.* **1,** (measure in fathoms; reach the bottom of) sondar; sondear. **2,** (understand thoroughly) profundizar; penetrar. —**fathomless,** *adj.* insondable; impenetrable.
fatigue (fə'ti:g) *n.* fatiga; cansancio. —*v.t.* fatigar; cansar; rendir.
fatten ('fæt·ən) *v.t.* **1,** (feed to make fat) cebar; engordar. **2,** (enrich; increase) enriquecer. —*v.i.* engordar.
fatty ('fæt·i) *adj.* grasoso; graso; grasiento. —*n., slang* gordinflón; gordito.
fatuous ('fætʃ·u·əs) *adj.* fatuo. —**fatuity** (fə'tu·ə·ti); **fatuousness,** *n.* fatuidad.
faucet ('fɔ·sɪt) *n.* espita; canilla; grifo; llave.
fault (fɔːlt) *n.* **1,** (defect; flaw) falta; defecto; tacha. **2,** (blame) culpa. **3,** *geol.* falla. **4,** *sports* falta. —**faultless,** *adj.* perfecto; cabal; intachable. —**faulty,** *adj.* defectuoso; imperfecto.
faultfinding ('fɔlt,fain·dɪŋ) *adj.* criticón.
faun (fɔːn) *n.* fauno.
fauna ('fɔ·nə) *n.* fauna.
favor ('fei·vər) *n.* **1,** (preferment) favor; gracia. **2,** (act of kindness) favor. **3,** (acceptance; approval) aceptación; aprobación. **4,** (small gift; token) obsequio; agasajo. **5,** *comm.* atenta; estimada. —*v.t.* **1,** (prefer; advocate) favorecer; preferir. **2,** *colloq.* (resemble) parecerse a. —**favored,** *adj.* favorecido. —**find favor,** tener aceptación o aprobación. —**out of favor,** caído en desgracia.
favorable ('fei·vər·ə·bəl) *adj.* favorable; propicio. —**favorableness,** *n.* lo favorable.
favorite ('fei·vər·ɪt) *adj. & n.* favorito; preferido; predilecto.

—**favoritism** (-ə‚tɪz·əm) *n.* favoritismo.

fawn (fɔːn) *n.* **1,** (young deer) cervato. **2,** (color) color ciervo o cervato. —*v.i.* arrastrarse. —**fawn on** o **upon,** adular.

fax (fæks) *n., elect.* facsímile. —*v.t.* facsimilar.

faze (feiz) *v.t., colloq.* **1,** (disturb) perturbar; molestar. **2,** (daunt) desanimar.

fealty ('fi·əl·ti) *n.* lealtad.

fear (fɪr) *n.* **1,** (fright) miedo; terror. **2,** (anxiety) aprensión; temor; recelo. **3,** (awe) respeto; temor. —*v.t. & i.* temer; recelar; tener miedo o aprensión. —**fearless,** *adj.* sin temor; sin miedo.

fearful ('fɪr·fəl) *adj.* **1,** (timid; apprehensive) tímido; temeroso. **2,** = **fearsome.** —**fearfulness,** *n.* temor; miedo.

fearsome ('fɪr·səm) *adj.* temible; espantoso.

feasible ('fiz·ə·bəl) *adj.* **1,** (possible) factible; posible. **2,** (suitable) apropiado; adecuado. —**feasibility,** *n.* factibilidad; posibilidad.

feast (fist) *n.* **1,** (sumptuous meal) banquete; festín. **2,** (festival) fiesta. —*v.t.* **1,** (entertain) festejar; agasajar. **2,** (gratify; delight) regalar; recrear. —*v.i.* **1,** (have a feast) darse un banquete. **2,** (dwell with delight) gozarse; deleitarse.

feat (fit) *n.* hazaña; proeza.

feather ('fɛð·ər) *n.* **1,** (of a bird) pluma. **2,** *fig.* (kind) clase; condición. —*v.t.* **1,** (put feathers on) emplumar. **2,** *aero.* emplumar; poner (la hélice) vertical. **3,** *naut.* poner (el remo) horizontal. —*v.i.* pelechar. —**feathery,** *adj.* plumoso. —**in fine** (también, **good** o **high**) **feather,** en buena condición; de muy buen ánimo.

feather duster plumero.

featherweight ('fɛð·ər‚weit) *n.* peso pluma.

feature ('fi·tʃər) *n.* **1,** (part of the face) rasgo; facción. **2,** (distinctive characteristic) rasgo; característica. **3,** *journalism* artículo, noticia o sección especial. **4,** *motion pictures* película principal; película de largo metraje. —*v.t.* **1,** (give prominence to) hacer resaltar; destacar; ofrecer principalmente. **2,** *motion pictures* presentar como estrella.

febrifuge ('fɛb·rɪ·fjudʒ) *n.* febrífugo.

febrile ('fi·brəl) *adj.* febril.

February ('fɛb·ru‚ɛr·i) *n.* febrero.

feces también, **faeces** ('fi·siz) *n.pl.* heces. —**fecal** (-kəl) *adj.* fecal.

fecund ('fi·kʌnd) *adj.* fecundo. —**fecundity** (fɪ'kʌn·də·ti) *n.* fecundidad.

fecundate ('fi·kən‚deit) *v.t.* fecundar. —**fecundation,** *n.* fecundación.

fed (fɛd) *v., pret. & p.p. de* **feed.**

federal ('fɛd·ə·rəl) *adj.* federal. —**federalism,** *n.* federalismo. —**federalist,** *n.* federalista.

federate ('fɛd·ə‚reit) *v.t.* federar. —*v.i.* federarse. —**federation,** *n.* federación.

fedora (fə'dor·ə) *n.* sombrero de fieltro; fieltro.

fee (fiː) *n.* **1,** (charge for services, privileges, etc.) pago; abono; derechos; (esp. for professional services) honorarios. **2,** (tip; gratuity) gratificación; regalía; propina. **3,** (fief) feudo. **4,** *law* (property; estate) heredad; hacienda; (ownership) feudo. —**fee simple,** dominio absoluto.

feeble ('fi·bəl) *adj.* **1,** (weak; ineffective) débil; vacilante. **2,** (frail) endeble. —**feebleness,** *n.* debilidad.

feebleminded ('fi·bəl‚main·dɪd) *adj.* imbécil; falto de seso.

feed (fiːd) *v.t.* [pret. & p.p. **fed**] **1,** (give food to) dar de comer a; alimentar. **2,** (to provide as food) dar de comer; alimentar con o de. **3,** (nourish) nutrir; alimentar. **4,** (supply, as with fuel or material) surtir; proveer. **5,** (satisfy; gratify) dar pábulo a; nutrir. —*v.i.* alimentarse; comer. —*n.* **1,** (food for cattle) forraje; pienso; alimento. **2,** *colloq.* (meal) comida.

feedback ('fid·bæk) *n.* regeneración; retroalimentación. —**feedback,** *adj.* regenerativo.

feedbag ('fid·bæg) *n.* morral; caparazón.

feeder ('fi·dər) *n.* **1,** (mechanism) mecanismo de alimentación; alimentador. **2,** (tributary) tributario; afluente. **3,** (branch line) ramal; ensamble.

feedline ('fid·lain) *n.* línea o fuente de alimentación. *También,* **feeder line.**

feel (fiːl) *v.t.* [pret. & p.p. **felt**] **1,** (perceive; be aware of) sentir. **2,** (touch; handle) tocar; palpar. **3,** (be moved or affected by) sentir. **4,** (believe) pensar; intuir; considerar. **5**, (grope) tentar; tantear. —*v.i.* **1**, (have physical sensation) percibir; sentir. **2**, (seem, as to the touch) sentirse; parecer. **3**, (grope) tantear. **4**, (perceive oneself to be) sentirse. —*n.* **1**, (touch) tacto. **2**, (sensation) sensación. **3**, (understanding) percepción.

feeler ('fi·lər) *n., lit. & fig.* tiento.

feeling ('fi·lɪŋ) *n.* **1**, (sense of touch) tacto. **2**, (sensation) sensación. **3**, (emotion) sentimiento; emoción; sensibilidad. **4**, (premonition) presentimiento. —*adj.* sensible; sensitivo.

feet (fit) *n., pl. de* **foot.**

feign (fein) *v.i. & t.* fingir.

feint (feint) *n.* amago; finta. —*v.t. & i.* amagar.

feldspar ('feld·spar) *n.* feldespato.

felicitate (fə'lɪs·ɪˌteit) *v.t.* felicitar. —**felicitation,** *n.* felicitación.

felicitous (fə'lɪs·ə·təs) *adj.* feliz; acertado; apropiado; oportuno. —**felicitousness,** *n.* felicidad.

felicity (fə'lɪs·ə·ti) *n.* **1**, (bliss) felicidad; dicha. **2**, (aptness; grace) gracia; felicidad.

feline ('fi·lain) *n. & adj.* felino.

fell (fel) *v.t.* derribar; talar. —*v.i., pret. de* **fall.** —*adj.* cruel; fiero.

fellow ('fel·o) *n.* **1**, (comrade) compañero; camarada; colega; compadre. **2**, (one of a pair; mate) pareja; compañero. **3**, *colloq.* (person) hombre; sujeto; tipo. **4**, (member of a society) socio; compañero. **5**, (graduate student) becario. —*adj.* asociado; compañero.

fellowship ('fel·oˌʃip) *n.* **1**, (body of associates) cuerpo; sociedad. **2**, (comradeship) fraternidad; confraternidad; compañerismo. **3**, (grant of money for further study) beca.

felon ('fel·ən) *n.* **1**, (criminal) criminal; felón. **2**, *pathol.* panadizo. —**felony,** *n.* crimen; delito mayor. —**felonious** (fə'lo·ni·əs) *adj.* criminal.

felt (felt) *n.* fieltro. —*v., pret. & p.p. de* **feel.**

female ('fi·meil) *adj.* **1**, (of women) femenino. **2**, (of animals) hembra; de hembra. **3**, *mech.* hembra. —*n.* hembra.

feminine ('fem·ɪ·nɪn) *adj.* femenino. —**femininity,** *n.* feminidad; feminidad.

feminism ('fem·ɪ·nɪzˈəm) *n.*

feminismo. —**feminist,** *n.* feminista.

femur ('fi·mər) *n.* fémur. —**femoral** ('fem·ər·əl) *adj.* femoral.

fen (fen) *n.* marjal; fangal.

fence (fens) *n.* **1**, (enclosure) cerca; valla; empalizada. **2**, *slang* (receiver of stolen goods) traficante en efectos robados. —*v.t.* cercar; vallar; empalizar. —*v.i.* **1**, (practice fencing) conocer o practicar la esgrima. **2**, *fig.* (parry; avoid argument) hacer el quite. —**fencer,** *n.* esgrimidor; *S.A.* esgrimista. —**on the fence,** *colloq.* indeciso; entre dos fuegos.

fencing ('fen·sɪŋ) *n.* **1**, (swordplay) esgrima. **2**, (system of fences) cercados; vallados. **3**, (material for fences) cercado.

fend (fend) *v.t.* [*también,* **fend off**] rechazar; parar; defenderse de. —*v.i.* defenderse. —**fend for oneself,** componérselas; arreglárselas.

fender ('fen·dər) *n.* **1**, (of an automobile) guardabarros; guardafango. **2**, (of a fireplace) guardafuegos.

fenestra (fɪ'nes·trə) *n., anat.* [*pl.* **-trae** (-tri)] ventana.

fennel ('fen·əl) *n.* hinojo.

feral ('fi·rəl) *adj.* salvaje; feral.

fermata (fer'ma·ta) *n., mus.* calderón (⌢).

ferment ('fɑr·ment) *n.* fermento. —*v.t. & i.* (fər'ment) fermentar. —**fermentation** (ˌfɑr·men'tei·ʃən) *n.* fermentación.

fermium ('fer·mi·əm) *n.* fermio.

fern (fɑrn) *n.* helecho.

ferocious (fə'ro·ʃəs) *adj.* feroz; fiero. —**ferocity** (fə'ras·ə·ti) *n.* ferocidad.

ferret ('fer·ɪt) *n.* hurón. —*v.t.* **1**, (seek by searching) buscar; andar tras de. **2**, (find by searching) encontrar; capturar. **3**, (elicit, as information) sonsacar; extraer.

ferrotype ('fer·o·taip) *n.* ferrotipo.

ferrous ('fer·əs) *adj.* ferroso.

ferruginous (fə'ru·dʒɪ·nəs) *adj.* ferruginoso.

ferrule ('fer·əl; -ul) *n.* contera; virola.

ferry ('fer·i) *n.* transbordador; barco de transbordo. —*v.t. & i.* transbordar.

fertile ('fɑr·tɪl) *adj.* fértil; feraz. —**fertility** (fər'tɪl·ə·ti) *n.* fertilidad; feracidad.

fertilize ('fɑr·tɪ·laiz) *v.t.* **1**, (make

fertile) fertilizar. **2**, (spread fertilizer on) abonar; fertilizar con abono. **3**, *biol.* fecundar. —**fertilization** (-lɪ'zei·ʃən) *n.* fertilización; fecundación. —**fertilizer,** *n.* abono; fertilizante.

ferule ('fɛr·əl) *n.* palmeta; férula.

fervent ('fɅr·vənt) *adj.* fervoroso; ferviente. —**fervency,** *n.* fervor.

fervid ('fɅr·vɪd) *adj.* férvido. —**fervidness,** *n.* fervor.

fervor ('fɅr·vər) *n.* fervor.

festal ('fɛs·təl) *adj.* festivo; de gala.

fester ('fɛs·tər) *v.t.* enconar. —*v.i.* enconarse.

festival ('fɛs·tɪ·vəl) *n.* festival; fiesta.

festive ('fɛs·tɪv) *adj.* festivo. —**festivity** (fɛs'tɪv·ɔ·ti) *n.* fiesta; festividad.

festoon (fɛs'tuːn) *n.* festón. —*v.t.* festonear.

fetal ('fi·təl) *adj.* fetal.

fetch (fɛtʃ) *v.t.* **1**, (bring) traer; ir por. **2**, (deal, as a stroke or blow) dar; pegar. **3**, (sell for) traer; venderse por.

fetching ('fɛtʃ·ɪŋ) *adj., colloq.* atrayente; atractivo.

fête (feit) *n.* fiesta. —*v.t.* festejar.

fetid ('fɛt·ɪd) *adj.* fétido; hediondo. —**fetidness,** *n.* fetidez; hediondez.

fetish ('fɛt·ɪʃ) *n.* fetiche. —**fetishism,** *n.* fetichismo. —**fetishist,** *n.* fetichista. —**fetishistic,** *adj.* fetichista.

fetlock ('fɛt·lak) *n.* espolón.

fetter ('fɛt·ər) *n.* **1**, *usu.pl.* (shackle) grilletes; grillos; cadenas. **2**, (check; restraint) traba; freno. —*v.t.* engrillar; encadenar; trabar.

fettle ('fɛt·əl) *n.* condición; disposición.

fetus ('fi·təs) *n.* feto.

feud (fjuːd) *n.* riña; pelea; vendetta. —*v.i.* reñir; pelear. —**feudist,** *n.* disputante.

feudal ('fju·dəl) *adj.* feudal. —**feudalism,** *n.* feudalismo.

fever ('fi·vər) *n.* fiebre; calentura.

feverish ('fi·vər·ɪʃ) *adj.* **1**, (having fever) afiebrado; calenturiento. **2**, (excited; hectic) febril. —**feverishness,** *n.* fiebre; estado febril.

few (fjuː) *adj. & pron.* pocos. —**a few,** unos pocos; unos cuantos; algunos. —**quite a few,** *colloq.* bastantes; una buena cantidad.

fez (fɛz) *n.* fez.

fiancé (ˌfi·an'sei) *n.* prometido;

novio. —**fiancée,** *n.f.* prometida; novia.

fiasco (fi'æs·ko) *n.* fiasco; fracaso.

fiat ('fai·ət) *n.* mandato; decreto.

fib (fib) *n.* mentirilla; embuste; bola. —*v.i.* [**fibbed, fibbing**] mentir; decir embustes. —**fibber,** *n.* mentiroso; embustero.

fiber ('fai·bər) *n.* fibra. —**fibrous** (-brəs) *adj.* fibroso.

fiberboard ('fai·bər,bord) *n.* tablero de fibra.

fiberglass ('fai·bər·glæs) *n.* fibra de vidrio.

fibrosis (fai'bro·sɪs) *n.* fibrosis.

fibula ('fib·ju·lə) *n., anat.* [*pl.* **-lae** (-li)] peroné.

fickle ('fɪk·əl) *adj.* voluble; inconstante; veleidoso. —**fickleness,** *n.* volubilidad; inconstancia; veleidad.

fiction ('fɪk·ʃən) *n.* **1**, (literature) novelística; novela. **2**, (statement contrary to fact) ficción. —**fictional,** *adj.* ficticio; imaginario; de novela.

fictitious (fɪk'tɪʃ·əs) *adj.* ficticio.

fiddle ('fɪd·əl) *n.* violín. —*v.i.* **1**, (play the fiddle) tocar el violín. **2**, (trifle) jugar; enredar. —*v.t.* **1**, (play on the fiddle) tocar en el violín. **2**, (waste) fritter, as time) perder; desperdiciar. —**fiddler** (-lər) *n.* violinista. —**fit as a fiddle,** en forma; en perfecta condición. —**play second fiddle,** tener un papel secundario.

fidelity (fɪ'dɛl·ɪ·ti) *n.* **1**, (faithfulness) fidelidad. **2**, (accuracy) fidelidad; exactitud.

fidget ('fɪdʒ·ət) *v.i.* **1**, (move restlessly) moverse nerviosamente. **2**, (be nervously uneasy) estar inquieto o nervioso. —**fidgety,** *adj.* nervioso; desasosegado. —**to have the fidgets,** estar inquieto.

fiduciary (fɪ'du·ʃi·e·ri) *adj. & n.* fiduciario.

fie (fai) *interj.* ¡vergüenza!

fief (fif) *n.* feudo.

field (fiːld) *n.* **1**, (open space or area; sphere or scope) campo. **2**, (background) fondo; campo. **3**, (group of competitors, as in a race) participantes. —*v.t.* **1**, (put into competition or combat) entrar (un equipo); situar (un ejército). **2**, (catch and return, as a ball) parar y devolver (la pelota). —**field day,** día de ejercicios (atléticos); *fig.* día de gran actividad. —**field glass,** prismáticos de campaña.

fiend (fi:nd) *n.* demonio; diablo. —**fiendish,** *adj.* diabólico; perverso.

fierce (firs) *adj.* fiero; feroz. —**fierceness,** *n.* ferocidad; fiereza.

fiery ('fai:·ri) *adj.* 1, (glowing; burning; hot) ardiente. 2, (spirited) ardiente; fogoso. —**fieriness,** *n.* ardor; fogosidad.

fiesta (fi'ɛs·tə) *n.* fiesta.

fife (faif) *n.* pífano.

fifteen (,fif'tin) *adj. & n.* quince.

fifteenth (,fif'tinθ) *adj.* décimoquinto. —*n.* quinzavo; décimoquinta parte.

fifth (fifθ) *adj.* quinto. —*n.* quinto; quinta parte; *mus.* quinta. —**fifth wheel,** *colloq.* persona superflua.

fiftieth ('fif·ti·əθ) *n. & adj.* quincuagésimo; cincuentavo.

fifty ('fif·ti) *n. & adj.* cincuenta.

fig (fig) *n.* 1, (tree) higuera. 2, (fruit) higo. 3, (bit; small amount) ardite; bledo.

fight (fait) *v.i.* [*pret. & p.p.* **fought**] luchar; pelear; batirse. —*v.t.* 1, (oppose; struggle against) combatir. 2, (wage; carry on) sostener (una guerra); librar (una batalla). —*n.* 1, (struggle; battle) pelea; lucha; contienda. 2, (fighting spirit) espíritu combativo. —**fight it out,** resolverlo luchando. —**fight off,** deshacerse de. —**fight one's way,** abrirse paso o camino.

fighter ('fai·tər) *n.* 1, (warrior) guerrero. 2, (combative person) luchador; combatiente. 3, (boxer) boxeador; pugilista. 4, (fighter plane) avión de caza.

figment ('fig·mənt) *n.* invención; ficción.

figurative ('fig·jə·rə·tiv) *adj.* figurativo; figurado.

figure ('fig·jər) *n.* 1, (form; shape) figura; forma. 2, (bodily form) talle; cuerpo; tipo. 3, *rhet.* figura. 4, (personage) figura; personaje. 5, (number) cifra; número. 6, (price) precio. —*v.t.* 1, (calculate) calcular; computar. 2, (portray) representar. 3, (visualize) imaginar; suponer. 4, (ornament) adornar con figuras. —*v.i.* 1, (take prominent part) figurar. 2, *colloq.* (deduce) suponer; deducir; inferir.

figurehead ('fig·jər,hɛd) *n.* figurón; *naut.* mascarón de proa.

figurine (,fig·ju'ri:n) *n.* estatuilla; estatuita.

filament ('fil·ə·mənt) *n.* filamento.

filbert ('fil·bərt) *n.* avellana.

filch (filtʃ) *v.t.* ratear; escamotear.

file (fail) *n.* 1, (folder) carpeta; ficha; pliego. 2, (case or cabinet) archivador; fichero. 3, (dossier; record) ficha; expediente; archivo. 4, (classified collection) archivo. 5, (row; line) fila; hilera; columna. 6, (tool) lima; escofina. —*v.t.* 1, (put in a file; record) archivar; registrar. 2, (present formally or officially) presentar; registrar. 3, (smooth or cut with a file) limar. —*v.i.* 1, (march in file) marchar en fila. 2, (apply) solicitar; presentar solicitud.

filet (fi'lei; 'fil·ət) *n.* filete. —**filet mignon** (fi,lei·mi'njan) filete de solomillo.

filial ('fil·i·əl) *adj.* filial.

filibuster ('fil·ə,bʌs·tər) *n.* 1, *polit.* táctica de obstruir la aprobación de un proyecto de ley con discursos prolongados. 2, = **freebooter.** —*v.i.* 1, *polit.* emplear la táctica del *filibuster.* 2, (be a freebooter) piratear.

filigree ('fil·ə·gri) *n.* filigrana. —*v.t.* afiligranar. —*adj.* afiligranado.

filing ('fai·liŋ) *n., usu. pl.* limaduras.

filing cabinet archivo; fichero.

fill (fil) *v.t.* 1, (make full) llenar. 2, (puff; swell) henchir; hinchar. 3, (plug up; close, as cracks, ruts, etc.) rellenar; tapar. 4, (satisfy the hunger of) llenar; saciar. 5, (occupy, as a position) ocupar; desempeñar. 6, (supply or satisfy, as an order for merchandise) llenar; despachar. 7, (put a filling in, as a tooth) empastar; *S.A.* tapar. —*v.i.* llenarse. —*n.* 1, (full supply) carga. 2, (filling; filling material) relleno. 3, (dental filling) empaste; *S.A.* tapadura. —**filler,** *n.* relleno. —**fill in,** 1, (fill or complete) llenar. 2, (substitute) substituir. —**fill one in on,** *colloq.* informar a uno sobre. —**fill out,** 1, (become fuller) llenarse. 2, (complete, as a document) llenar. —**have (eat, drink) one's fill,** hartarse, saciarse, darse un hartazgo (de).

fillet ('fil·ət) *n.* 1, (band for the hair) banda para el pelo. 2, (molding; strip) filete; orla. 3, [también,

filet] (cut of meat or fish) filete. —*v.t.* cortar en filetes.

filling ('fɪl·ɪŋ) *n.* relleno; (of a tooth) empaste; *S.A.* tapadura.

filling station puesto o estación de gasolina.

fillip ('fɪl·əp) *n.* capirotazo; papirotazo.

filly ('fɪl·i) *n.* potra; potranca.

film (fɪlm) *n.* 1, (thin layer or coating) película; capa. 2, *photog.* película; film. 3, (mist; haze) nube. —*v.t. & i.* filmar; rodar.

filmy ('fɪl·mi) *adj.* 1, (thin; light) delgado; delicado; leve. 2, (misty) empañado.

filter ('fɪl·tər) *n.* filtro. —*v.t. & i.* filtrar.

filth (fɪlθ) *n.* suciedad; inmundicia. —**filthy,** *adj.* sucio; inmundo.

fin (fɪn) *n.* aleta. —**finned; finny,** *adj.* con aletas.

final ('fai·nəl) *adj.* 1, (last; ultimate) último; final. 2, (conclusive) definitivo; terminante. —*n.pl.* finales. —**finalist,** *n.* finalista. —**finally,** *adv.* finalmente; por fin; al fin; por último.

finale (fɪ'na·li) *n.* final.

finality (fɪ'næl·ə·ti) *n.* ultimidad. —**with finality,** en forma concluyente.

finalize ('fai·nə·laiz) *v.t., colloq.* finalizar. —**finalization** (-lɪ'zei·ʃən) *n.* finalización.

finance (fɪ'næns; 'fai-) *n.* finanzas; *(in government)* hacienda; hacienda pública. —*v.t.* costear; financiar.

financial (fɪ'næn·ʃəl) *adj.* financiero.

financier (fɪ·næn'sir) *n.* financiero.

finch (fɪntʃ) *n.* pinzón.

find (faind) *v.t.* [*pret. & p.p.* **found**] 1, (locate; discover) encontrar; hallar. 2, *law* declarar. —*v.i., law* fallar. —*n.* hallazgo. —**finder,** *n.* visor; enfocador. —**find out,** averiguar; enterarse de.

finding ('fain·dɪŋ) *n.* 1, *usu. pl.* (results, as of study or inquiry) conclusiones; resultado. 2, (verdict) fallo; decisión. 3, *pl.* (accessories) accesorios.

fine (fain) *adj.* 1, (excellent; superior) muy bueno; excelente; fino. 2, (thin; slender; delicate) fino. 3, (sharp; keen) afilado; fino. 4, (discriminating; subtle) fino. 5, (goodlooking; handsome) hermoso; guapo. 6, (pure; refined; unalloyed)

fino. —*n.* multa. —*v.t.* multar. —*adv., colloq.* bien; muy bien. —**fine arts,** bellas artes.

fineness ('fain·nəs) *n.* fineza; finura; *(of metals)* ley.

finery ('fai·nə·ri) *n.* adornos; galas.

finesse (fɪ'nɛs) *n.* 1, (delicacy of execution; subtlety) finura. 2, (tact) tino; tacto; habilidad. 3, *cards* jugada por bajo; *Amer.* fineza.

finger ('fɪŋ·gər) *n.* dedo. —*v.t.* tocar; palpar; manosear. —**fingering,** *n., mus.* digitación. —**finger board,** *(of a stringed instrument)* diapasón; *(of a piano)* teclado. —**finger bowl,** lavafrutas; aguamanil.

fingernail ('fɪŋ·gər,neil) *n.* uña (del dedo).

fingerprint ('fɪŋ·gər,prɪnt) *n.* huella dactilar o digital.

fingertip ('fɪŋ·ger,tɪp) *n.* punta del dedo. —**have at one's fingertips,** saber al dedillo; tener muy a mano.

finical ('fɪn·ə·kəl) *adj.* melindroso; quisquilloso. También, **finicky** (-ki).

finish ('fɪn·ɪʃ) *v.t. & i.* acabar; terminar. —*n.* 1, (end) fin. 2, (final work done upon an object) acabado; terminado. 3, (social polish) refinamiento. —**finished,** *adj.* acabado; terminado.

finite ('fai·nait) *adj.* finito; limitado. —**finiteness,** *n.* limitación; lo finito; lo limitado.

fink (fɪŋk) *n., slang* 1, (strikebreaker) esquirol. 2, (informer) delator. —*v.i.* 1, *con* **out** (quit) rendirse. 2, *con* **on** (inform against) delatar.

fiord también, **fjord** (fjord) *n.* fiordo.

fir (fʌr) *n.* abeto.

fire (fair) *n.* 1, (heat and light caused by burning) fuego. 2, (conflagration) incendio; fuego. 3, (shooting) fuego. 4, *fig.* (zeal) fuego; ardor. —*v.t.* 1, (set ablaze; ignite) encender. 2, (excite; inflame) enardecer; inflamar. 3, (shoot) disparar; descargar. 4, *colloq.* (dismiss from a job) despedir; echar. —**catch fire,** encenderse. —**catch on fire,** incendiarse. —**fire department,** servicio de bomberos; cuerpo de bomberos. —**fire drill,** simulacro de incendio. —**fire engine,** bomba de incendios. —**fire escape,** escalera de incendios. —**firing squad,** piquete o pelotón de fusilamiento. —**on fire,** ardiendo. —**set**

fire to; set on fire, encender; pegar fuego a; quemar. —**under fire,** bajo fuego; *fig.* acosado.

firearm ('fair,arm) *n.* arma de fuego.

firebomb ('fair,bam) *n.* bomba incendiaria. —*v.t.* atacar o destruir con bomba incendiaria.

firebrand ('fair,brænd) *n. lit.* & *fig.* tea.

firebreak ('fair,breik) *n.* corta-fuego.

firebug ('fair·bʌg) *n., colloq.* pirómano.

firecracker ('fair,kræk·ər) *n.* petardo; triquitraque; *Amer.* cohete.

firefight ('fair·fait) *n.* combate a armas de fuego.

firefighter ('fair·fait·ər) *n.* bombero.

firefly ('fair·flai) *n.* luciérnaga; *Amer.* cocuyo.

firelight ('fair·lait) *n.* luz de fuego; flama.

fireman ('fair·mən) *n.* [*pl.* -men] 1, (one employed to prevent or extinguish fires) bombero. 2, (stoker) fogonero.

fireplace ('fair·ples) *n.* hogar; chimenea.

fireplug ('fair,plʌg) *n.* boca de agua.

fireproof ('fair,pruf) *adj.* a prueba de incendios; refractario; incombustible.

fireside ('fair·said) *n.* hogar.

firetrap ('fair,træp) *n.* edificio que puede incendiarse facilmente o que carece de medios adecuados de escape.

firewater ('fair,wɔ·tər) *n., colloq.* aguardiente; licor fuerte barato.

firewood ('fair,wʊd) *n.* leña.

fireworks ('fair,wʌrks) *n.pl.* fuegos artificiales.

firm (farm) *adj.* 1, (steady; rigid) firme; fuerte; fijo. 2, (staunch; loyal) firme; fiel. 3, (positive; unalterable) tenaz; inflexible. —*n.* firma; razón social. —**firmness,** *n.* firmeza; consistencia.

firmament ('fʌr·mə·mənt) *n.* firmamento.

first (fʌrst) *adj.* primero; anterior; delantero. —*adv.* primero; en primer lugar; al principio; antes. —*n.* el primero; el principio. —**first aid,** primeros auxilios; primer socorro. —**first finger,** (dedo) índice. —**First Lady,** primera dama. —**first lieutenant,** teniente

primero. —**first off,** primero; en primer lugar. —**first water,** mejor calidad.

first-class *adj.* de primera clase; de calidad.

firsthand ('fʌrst·hænd) *adj.* directo; personal.

first-rate *adj.* excelente; de primera clase. —*adv., colloq.* muy bien.

fiscal ('fɪs·kəl) *adj.* fiscal. —**fiscal year,** ejercicio o año económico.

fish (fɪʃ) *n.* [*pl.* **fishes** o **fish**] 1, *zoöl.* pez. 2, (fish caught) pescado. 3, *slang* (dupe) primo. —*v.i.* & *t.* 1, (catch, as fish) pescar. 2, (search) buscar. 3, (seek indirectly) sonsacar. —**fish bowl; fish tank,** pecera. —**fish market,** pescadería. —**fish story,** mentira o cuento de marca mayor.

fisherman ('fɪʃ·ər·mən) *n.* [*pl.* -men] 1, (man) pescador. 2, (ship; vessel) barca de pesca.

fishery ('fɪʃ·ə·ri) *n.* 1, (business of fishing) pesca. 2, (fishing ground) pesquería.

fishhook ('fɪʃ·hʊk) *n.* anzuelo.

fishing ('fɪʃ·ɪŋ) *adj.* pesquero; pescador; de pescar. —*n.* pesca; pesquería. —**fishing grounds,** pesquera; pesquería. —**fishing rod,** caña de pescar.

fishline ('fɪʃ·lain) *n.* sedal.

fishmonger ('fɪʃ,maŋ·gər) *n.* pescadero.

fishy ('fɪʃ·i) *adj.* 1, (of or like fish) de, a o como pescado. 2, *colloq.* (suspect) sospechoso; increíble; que huele a chamusquina. 3, (expressionless) pasmado; sin expresión. —**fishiness,** *n.* suspicacia.

fission ('fɪʃ·ən) *n.* fisión. —**fissionable,** *adj.* fisionable.

fissure ('fɪʃ·ər) *n.* fisura; grieta.

fist (fɪst) *n.* puño. —**fistfight,** *n.,* riña a puñadas o puñetazos. —**fistful,** *n.* puño.

fisticuffs ('fɪs·tɪ·kʌfs) *n.pl.* lucha a puñetazos.

fistula ('fɪs·tʃu·lə) *n.* fístula.

fit (fɪt) *adj.* 1, (proper; suitable) apto; adecuado; apropiado; conveniente. 2, (ready; prepared) dispuesto; listo; en forma. —*v.t.* [**fitted, fitting**] 1, (adapt) adaptar; ajustar; acomodar. 2, (equip; supply) surtir; proveer; equipar. 3, (adjust to shape, as a garment) entallar; ajustar. 4, (agree with) cuadrar con. 5, (be suitable for) servir para. 6, (be of the right shape, size, etc., for) servirle a uno; venirle bien a uno, —*v.i.* **1**, (be proper) convenir; venir bien; corresponder. **2**, (be of the right shape, size, etc.) ajustar; encajar; *(esp. of garments)* servir; venir bien. **3**, (be able to be contained) caber. —*n.* **1**, (manner of fitting) ajuste; encaje; *(esp. of garments)* corte; caída. **2**, (something that fits) lo que viene bien; lo apropiado. **3**, (convulsion; outburst) acceso; ataque. —**fitness,** *n.* aptitud; conveniencia; buena condición. —**by fits and starts,** a empujones; a tropezones. —**throw** o **have a fit,** darle a uno una paleta.

fitful ('fɪt·fəl) *adj.* irregular; vacilante. —**fitfulness,** *n.* irregularidad.

fitter ('fɪt·ər) *n.* ajustador; *(esp. of garments)* entallador.

fitting ('fɪt·ɪŋ) *adj.* propio; adecuado; conveniente. —*n.* **1**, (act of fitting) ajuste; *(esp. of garments)* prueba. **2**, *pl.* (furnishings) accesorios.

five (faiːv) *n.* & *adj.* cinco.

fivefold ('faiv,fold) *adj.* quíntuplo; cinco veces (más). —*adv.* cinco veces; en un quíntuplo.

five hundred quinientos. —**five-hundredth,** *adj.* & *n.* quingentésimo.

fix (fɪks) *v.t.* **1**, (fasten) sujetar; asegurar; fijar. **2**, (settle; establish, as a time or place) precisar; señalar. **3**, *chem.; photog.* fijar. **4**, (arrange; repair) arreglar. **5**, *slang* (bribe) arreglar *(mediante soborno o influencia)*. —*n.* **1**, *colloq.* (predicament) apuro; aprieto. **2**, *slang* (bribery) chanchullo. —**fixings,** *n.pl.*, *colloq.* accesorios; *(of foods)* aderezos. —**fix up,** arreglar.

fixation (fɪk'sei·ʃən) *n.* **1**, (act or result of fixing) fijación. **2**, *psychoanal.* idea fija. **3**, *photog.* fijado.

fixative ('fɪks·ə·tɪv) *n., photog.* fijador.

fixed (fɪkst) *adj.* **1**, (fast; firm; rigid) fijo. **2**, (resolved) decidido; resuelto. **3**, *chem.; photog.* fijado. **4**, (put in order; arranged) arreglado.

fixity ('fɪk·sə·ti) *n.* fijeza.

fixture ('fɪks·tʃər) *n.* **1**, (attached article of furniture) artículo; accesorio. **2**, (person or thing that cannot be removed) institución.

fizz (fɪz) *v.i.* efervescer. —*n.* **1**, (ef-

fervescence) efervescencia. **2**, (drink) gaseosa.

fizzle ('fɪz·əl) *v.i.* **1**, (make a hissing sound) chisporrotear. **2**, *colloq.* (fail) fallar; fracasar. —*n.* **1**, (hissing sound) chisporroteo. **2**, *colloq.* (failure) fracaso; fiasco.

fjord (fjord) *n.* = **fiord.**

flab (flæb) *n., colloq.* exceso de peso.

flabbergast ('flæb·ər·gæst) *v.t., colloq.* confundir; pasmar; dejar mudo.

flabby ('flæb·i) *adj.* blando; flojo; débil. —**flabbiness,** *n.* blandura; flojedad; debilidad.

flaccid ('flæk·sɪd) *adj.* fláccido. —**flaccidity** (flæk'sɪd·ə·ti) [*también,* **flaccidness**] *n.* flaccidez.

flag (flæg) *n.* **1**, (banner) bandera; estandarte; pabellón. **2**, *bot.* lirio. —*v.t.* [**flagged flagging**] **1**, (signal to) hacer señales a. **2**, (pave with flagstones) pavimentar. —*v.i.* flaquear; decaer. —**flag officer,** jefe de escuadra.

flagellate ('flædʒ·ə·leit) *v.t.* flagelar. —**flagellant** (-lənt) *n.* flagelante. —**flagellation,** *n.* flagelación.

flagon ('flæg·ən) *n.* frasco; pomo.

flagpole ('flæg,pol) *n.* asta; mástil.

flagrant ('flei·grənt) *adj.* flagrante. —**flagrancy,** *n.* flagrancia.

flagship ('flæg,ʃɪp) *n.* buque bandera.

flagstaff ('flæg,stæf) *n.* asta; mástil.

flagstone ('flæg,ston) *n.* losa; laja.

flail (fleil) *n.* mayal; mangual. —*v.t.* **1**, (thresh) desgranar con mayal. **2**, (beat) batir; sacudir.

flair (fleːr) *n.* **1**, (talent) instinto; talento. **2**, (liking; bent) afición; inclinación.

flak (flæk) *n.* **1**, fuego antiaéreo. **2**, *slang* (complaint) queja.

flake (fleik) *n.* escama; hojuela. —*v.t.* cortar en hojuelas; desmenuzar. —*v.i.* formar escamas u hojuelas; descascararse. —**flaky,** *adj.* **1**, escamoso. **2**, curioso.

flam (flæm) *v.t.* defraudar; estafar. —*n.* fraude; estafa.

flamboyant (flæm'bɔi·ənt) *adj.* ostentoso; vistoso. —**flamboyance,** *n.* ostentación.

flame (fleim) *n.* **1**, (light produced by burning) llama; candela. **2**, (burning zeal; ardor) vehemencia; ardor; llama. **3**, *slang* (sweetheart) pasión. —*v.i.* **1**, (blaze) llamear. **2**, (shine) brillar; fulgurar. **3**, (break out in anger or passion) inflamarse; apasionarse.

flaming ('flei·mɪŋ) *adj.* **1**, (blazing) llameante. **2**, (passionate; violent) ardiente; vehemente.

flamingo (flə'mɪŋ·go) *n.* flamenco.

flammable ('flæm·ə·bəl) *adj.* = **inflammable.**

flange (flændʒ) *n.* pestaña; borde; reborde.

flank (flæŋk) *n.* flanco. —*v.t.* flanquear.

flannel ('flæn·əl) *n.* franela.

flap (flæp) *n.* **1**, (broad hanging piece) falda; faldilla; aleta; *(of a pocket)* cartera. **2**, (flapping motion or sound) aleteo; aletazo. **3**, (slap) bofetada; cachetada. **4**, *slang* (altercation) disputa; lío. —*v.t.* [**flapped, flapping**] batir; sacudir; golpear. —*v.i.* colgar suelto; alatear; golpear.

flapjack ('flæp,dʒæk) *n.* hojuela; *Amer.* panqueque.

flapper ('flæp·ər) *n.* **1**, (thing that flaps) aleta. **2**, (young bird) pollo; polluelo. **3**, *colloq.* (brash girl) polla; pollita.

flare (fleɪr) *n.* **1**, (glaring light) llamarada; fulgor; destello. **2**, (signal) cohete luminoso; bengala. **3**, [*también,* **flare-up**] (outburst) explosión; arrebato (de ira). **4**, (of a garment) vuelo. —*v.i.* **1**, (burst into flame) encenderse; echar llamaradas. **2**, (spread out, as a garment) tener vuelo. —**flare up, 1**, (burst into flames) encenderse; prender fuego. **2**, (become angry) arrebatarse de ira; encenderse.

flash (flæʃ) *n.* **1**, (blaze of light) golpe de luz; relumbrón. **2**, (gun flash; camera flash) fogonazo. **3**, (lightning) rayo. **4**, (gleam) destello. **5**, (glimpse) golpe de vista; ojeada. **6**, (instant) momento; instante. **7**, (burst; spurt; brief display) arranque; golpe; destello. **8**, (ostentation) ostentación; relumbrón. **9**, (brief bulletin) noticia de último momento; noticia súbita; fogonazo. —*v.i.* **1**, (shine; sparkle) destellar; fulgurar. **2**, (move quickly) pasar como un rayo. —*v.t.* **1**, (make gleam; shine) hacer destellar. **2**, (send, as a signal) transmitir; telegrafiar. **3**, *colloq.* (show off) ostentar; hacer alarde de. —**flash bulb,** bombilla de magnesio.

—**flash flood,** torrentada. —**flash gun,** lámpara de magnesio. —**flash in the pan,** relumbrón.

flashback ('flæʃ,bæk) *n.* mirada atrás; retrospección.

flashlight ('flæʃ·lait) *n.* linterna.

flashy ('flæʃ·i) *adj.* ostentoso; llamativo; de relumbrón. —**flashiness,** *n.* ostentación; relumbrón.

flask (flæsk; flask) *n.* frasco; pomo.

flat (flæt) *adj.* **1**, (level; smooth) plano; llano. **2**, (spread out) extendido; tendido; plano. **3**, (categorical; positive) categórico; tajante. **4**, (deflated, as a tire) reventado; desinflado. **5**, (dull; insipid) insulso; insípido. **6**, *slang* (penniless) pelado; sin blanca; *Amer.* planchado. **7**, *mus.* (below pitch) desentonado; desafinado; (lowered in pitch) bemol. —*adv.* **1**, (extended; spread out) tendido. **2**, (categorically) de plano; categóricamente. **3**, *mus.* bajo tono. —*n.* **1**, (plain) planicie; llanura. **2**, (shoal) bajo; bajío. **3**, (flat part) parte plana o llana. **4**, (apartment) apartamento. **5**, *colloq.* (deflated tire) reventón; llanta desinflada. —*v.t.* bajar en o de tono. —*v.i.* bajar el tono; cantar o tocar bajo tono.

flatboat ('flæt·bot) *n.* chalana.

flat-bottomed ('flæt,ba·təmd) *adj.* planudo.

flatcar *n.* vagón de plataforma; batea; *Amer.* chata.

flatfish ('flæt,fɪʃ) *n.* pez plano, como el lenguado.

flatfoot ('flæt,fʊt) *n.* [*pl.* **-feet**] **1**, (deformity of the foot) pie plano **2**, *slang* (policeman) policía. —**flatfooted,** *adj.* de pies planos.

flatiron ('flæt,ai·ərn) *n* plancha.

flatness ('flæt·nəs) *n.* **1**, (evenness) calidad de plano; llanura. **2**, (dullness) insulsez; insipidez.

flatten ('flæt·ən) *v.t.* **1**, (make flat) aplanar; aplastar. **2**, (crush) apabullar; aplastar. **3**, (knock down) tirar al suelo; derribar. —*v.i.* aplanarse; aplastarse.

flatter ('flæt·ər) *v.t.* **1**, (praise excessively) adular; lisonjear; halagar. **2**, (show to advantage) favorecer; dar realce; lucir. —**flattering,** *adj.* adulador; lisonjero; halagüeño; favorecedor. —**flattery,** *n.* adulación; lisonja; halago.

flattop ('flæt,tap) *n.* portaaviones.

flatulent ('flæ·tʃə·lənt) *adj.* flatulento. —**flatulence,** *n.* flatulencia.

flaunt (flɔnt) *v.t.* hacer ostentación de; hacer alarde de. —*v.i.* hacer alarde; pavonearse. —*n.* alarde; gesto desafiante.

flavor ('flei·vər) *n.* **1,** (taste) sabor; gusto. **2,** = **flavoring.** —*v.t.* sazonar; dar sabor o gusto a. —**flavoring,** *n.* condimento; sazón; sabor.

flaw (flɔr) *n.* **1,** (fault) falta; defecto; tacha; falla. **2,** (crack) grieta; raja; rajadura. —**flawless,** *adj.* sin tacha; sin falla; intachable; perfecto.

flax (flæks) *n.* lino. —**flaxseed,** *n.* linaza.

flaxen ('flæk·sən) *adj.* **1,** (made of flax) de lino. **2,** (light yellow) blondo.

flay (flei) *v.t.* despellejar; desollar.

flea (fliː) *n.* pulga. —**flea-ridden,** *adj.* pulgoso; *Amer.* pulguiento. —**flea market,** mercado para artículos baratos.

fleabite ('fliˌbait) *n.* picadura de pulga. —**fleabitten,** *adj.* picado de pulgas; *Amer.* pulguiento.

fleck (flɛk) *n.* mancha; salpicón —*v.t.* manchar; salpicar; vetear.

fledgling *también,* **fledgeling** ('flɛdʒ·lɪŋ) *n.* **1,** (young bird) pajarito. **2,** (novice) novato.

flee (fliː) *v.t.* [*pret.* & *p.p.* **fled** (flɛd)] huir de; escaparse de. —*v.i.* huir; fugarse; escaparse.

fleece (flis) *n.* vellón; vedija; lana. —*v.t.* esquilar; pelar. —**fleecy,** *adj.* lanudo.

fleet (flit) *adj.* veloz; rápido; ligero. —*n.* flota; armada; escuadra. —**fleeting,** *adj.* fugaz; transitorio. —**fleetness,** *n.* velocidad; rapidez; ligereza.

Fleming ('flem·ɪŋ) *n.* flamenco. —**Flemish** (-ɪʃ) *adj.* & *n.* flamenco.

flesh (flɛʃ) *n.* carne. —*adj.* de color carne. —**fleshless,** *adj.* descarnado. —**fleshly,** *adj.* carnal. —**fleshy,** *adj.* carnoso.

fleur-de-lis (ˌflʌr·də'liː) *n.* [*pl.* **fleurs-de-lis** (ˌflʌr·də'liːz)] **1,** (royal emblem of France) flor de lis. **2,** *bot.* (iris) lirio.

flew (fluː) *v.,* *pret. de* **fly.**

flex (flɛks) *v.t.* flexionar; doblar. —**flexion** ('flɛk·ʃən) *n.* flexión.

flexible ('flɛk·sɪ·bəl) *adj.* flexible. —**flexibility,** *n.* flexibilidad.

flick (flɪk) *n.* **1,** golpe o movimien-to ligero; sacudida. **2,** *slang* (motion picture) película. —*v.t.* **1,** (strike lightly) dar un golpe ligero. **2,** (move or remove with a flick) sacudir.

flicker ('flɪk·ər) *v.i.* **1,** (quiver) oscilar; temblar; vacilar. **2,** (blink) parpadear. —*n.* **1,** (flickering) parpadeo. **2,** (wavering light) luz trémula. **3,** (large woodpecker) picamaderos norteamericano.

flier *también,* **flyer** ('flai·ər) *n.* **1,** (aviator) aviador. **2,** (handbill) volante. **3,** *colloq.* (risk; financial venture) albur.

flies (flaiz) *n., pl. de* **fly.**

flight (flait) *n.* **1,** (act of flying) vuelo. **2,** (unit of aircraft) escuadrilla. **3,** (number of creatures flying together) bandada. **4,** (imaginative excursion or soaring) vuelo. **5,** (hasty departure) huída; fuga. **6,** (series of steps or stairs) tramo (de escaleras). **7,** (story; floor) piso. —**flightless,** *adj.* incapaz de volar.

flighty ('flai·ti) *adj.* veleidoso; inconstante. —**flightiness,** *n.* veleidad; inconstancia.

flimsy ('flɪm·zi) *adj.* débil; endeble; insubstancial. —**flimsiness,** *n.* endeblez; inconsistencia.

flinch (flɪntʃ) *v.i.* dar un respingo; respingar; arrugarse; echarse atrás.

fling (flɪŋ) *v.t.* [*pret.* & *p.p.* **flung**] arrojar; tirar; lanzar. —*n.* **1,** (act of flinging) lanzamiento; tiro. **2,** *colloq.* (try) prueba; lance. —**go on a fling,** echar una cana al aire. —**have a fling at,** probar; ensayar; tirarse un lance con.

flint (flɪnt) *n.* pedernal; *(of a lighter)* piedra. —**flinty,** *adj.* empedernido; duro.

flintlock ('flɪnt·lak) *n.* fusil de chispa.

flip (flɪp) *n.* **1,** (flick; snap) tirón; golpe seco. **2,** (mixed drink) vino, sidra o cerveza con ron y azúcar. —*v.t.* [**flipped, flipping**] **1,** (toss) lanzar o tirar con un golpe seco. **2,** (tap; shove) dar un golpe seco a. —*adj., colloq.* descarado; impertinente; fresco.

flippant ('flɪp·ənt) *adj.* petulante; impertinente; frívolo. —**flippancy,** *n.* petulancia; impertinencia; frivolidad.

flipper ('flɪp·ər) *n.* **1,** (limb of turtles, whales, etc.) aleta. **2,** *slang* (hand) mano.

flirt (flʌrt) *v.i.* **1,** (play at being in

love) coquetear; flirtear. **2,** (trifle, as with an idea) acariciar (una idea). —*n.* coqueta; galanteador.

flirtation (flʌr'tei·ʃən) *n.* coqueteo; flirteo.

flirtatious (flʌr'tei·ʃəs) *adj.* galanteador; coquetón. —**flirtatiousness,** *n.* coquetería.

flit (flɪt) *v.i.* [**flitted, flitting**] volar; revolotear.

flitter ('flɪt·ər) *v.i.* = **flutter.**

float (flot) *v.i.* flotar. —*v.t.* **1,** (cause to float) poner a flote; poner a flotar. **2,** (start; launch) lanzar. **3,** *comm.* (offer for sale) emitir. —*n.* **1,** (something that floats) flotador. **2,** (decorated vehicle in a parade) carroza alegórica.

floater ('flo·tər) *n.* **1,** (person that floats) persona sin meta fija; vagabundo. **2,** (insurance policy) póliza flotante.

floating ('flo·tɪŋ) *adj.* flotante; *comm.* en circulación.

flock (flak) *n.* **1,** (of animals) manada; rebaño; (of birds) bandada. **2,** (congregation) rebaño; grey. **3,** (crowd) muchedumbre; multitud. **4,** (tuft) copo; vedija. **5,** (fibers of wool, etc.) borra; pelusilla. —*v.i.* congregarse; reunirse.

floe (floɹ) *n.* témpano.

flog (flʌg) *v.t.* [**flogged, flogging**] azotar. —**flogging,** *n.* azotamiento.

flood (flʌd) *n.* **1,** (overflowing) riada; desbordamiento. **2,** (inundation) inundación; diluvio. **3,** (superfluity) abundancia; exceso. **4,** (inflow of the tide) pleamar. —*v.t.* inundar; anegar. —*v.i.* inundarse; anegarse; desbordarse.

floodgate ('flʌd,geit) *n.* compuerta; esclusa.

floodlight ('flʌd·lait) *n.* reflector.

floor (flor) *n.* **1,** (bottom surface) suelo; piso. **2,** (bottom of the sea) fondo. **3,** (story of a building) piso. **4,** (right to speak) palabra. —*v.t.* **1,** (furnish with a floor) solar; poner suelo o piso a. **2,** *colloq.* (knock down) derribar; echar al suelo. —**flooring,** *n.* (of wood) entablado; piso; entarimado; (of tile) embaldosado. —**floor show,** espectáculo de cabaret; show.

floorwalker ('flor,wɔk·ər) *n.* encargado o jefe de sección.

floozy ('flu·zi) *n., slang* mujercilla; mujerzuela.

flop (flap) *v.i.* [**flopped, flopping**] **1,** (flap) aletear; sacudir. **2,** (fall

clumsily) caer como saco. **3,** *slang* (fail) fracasar. —*n., slang* fracaso. —**floppy,** *adj.* flojo; colgante.

floppy disc *n., comput.* disco flexible.

flora ('flo·rə) *n.* flora.

floral ('flo·rəl) *adj.* floral.

floriculture ('flo·rə,kʌl·tʃər) *n.* floricultura. —**floriculturist** (-'kʌl·tʃər·ist) *n.* floricultor.

florid ('flor·id) *adj.* **1,** (ruddy) encarnado; rojo. **2,** (highly ornate) florido.

florist ('flor·ist) *n.* florista.

floss (flɔs) *n.* seda floja; seda.

flossy ('flɔs·i) *adj.* **1,** (like floss) sedoso. **2,** *slang* (ornate) historiado; recargado.

flotation (flo'tei·ʃən) *n.* flotación; *comm.* lanzamiento.

flotilla (flo'tɪl·ə) *n.* flotilla.

flotsam ('flat·səm) *n.* restos de naufragio; despojos flotantes.

flounce (flauns) *n.* **1,** (ruffle) volante; fleco. **2,** (abrupt twist or jerk of the body) salto; bote. —*v.i.* saltar; ir o salir de un bote.

flounder ('flaun·dər) *v.i.* **1,** (move or speak awkwardly) desorientarse; desconcertarse; andar a tropezones. **2,** (struggle helplessly) forcejear; debatirse. —*n.* lenguado.

flour ('flau·ər) *n.* harina. —*v.t.* enharinar. —**floury,** *adj.* harinoso.

flourish ('flʌr·iʃ) *v.i.* florecer; prosperar. —*v.t.* **1,** (brandish; wave about) hacer molinetes con. **2,** (flaunt) hacer alarde de. —*n.* **1,** (brandishing; waving) floreo; molinete. **2,** (pen stroke) rasgo; rúbrica. **3,** (fanfare) toque de clarines; fanfarria.

flout (flaut) *v.t.* burlar; burlarse de; mofarse de; escarnecer. —*n.* burla; mofa; escarnio.

flow (floɹ) *v.i.* **1,** (move as a stream) correr; fluir. **2,** (issue forth) manar. **3,** (fall in waves, as the hair) caer en ondas; caer con soltura. —*n.* corriente; flujo; caudal. —**flow chart,** diagrama de flujo; diagrama de fabricación.

flower ('flau·ər) *n.* flor. —*v.i.* florecer. —**flowered,** *adj.* floreado. —**flowering,** *adj.* floreciente. —*n.* florecimiento.

flowerpot ('flau·ər,pat) *n.* tiesto; maceta.

flowery ('flau·ə·ri) *adj.* florido. —**floweriness,** *n.* abundancia de flores; floreo *(de palabras)*.

flown (flo:n) v., p.p.de **fly.**

flu (fluː) n. influenza; gripe.

fluctuate ('flʌk·tʃu·et) v.i. fluctuar. —**fluctuation,** n. fluctuación.

flue (fluː) n. cañón o tubo de chimenea.

fluent ('flu·ənt) adj. fluido; suelto. —**fluency,** n. fluidez; soltura; facilidad. —**fluently,** adv. con soltura; con fluidez.

fluff (flʌf) n. 1, (light down) plumón; mullido. 2, (puff of dust, nap, etc.) pelusa; pelusilla. 3, slang (mistake; bungle) equivocación; chapuz; desatino. —v.t. 1, (make fluffy) mullir. 2, slang (mistake; bungle) equivocar; chapucear. —v.i. 1, (become fluffy) mullirse. 2, (blunder) cometer un chapuz; desatinar. —**fluffy,** adj. blando; mullido.

fluid ('flu·id) adj. & n. flúido. —**fluidity** (flu'id·ə·ti) n. fluidez.

fluke (fluk) n. 1, (anchor blade; barb of an arrow, harpoon, etc.) uña; punta. 2, (lobe of a whale's tail) aleta (de la cola de una ballena). 3, (fish) especie de lenguado. 4, (parasitic worm) lombriz intestinal. 5, slang (lucky chance) chiripa. —**fluky,** adj., slang de o por chiripa.

flung (flʌŋ) v., pret. & p.p. de fling.

flunk (flʌŋk) v.t., colloq. colgar; catear. —v.i., colloq. colgarse; salir mal.

flunky también, **flunkey** ('flʌŋ·ki) n. 1, (manservant) lacayo. 2, (toady) adulón; sicofante.

fluorescence (ˌflu·ə'rɛs·əns) n. fluorescencia. —**fluorescent,** adj. fluorescente.

fluorine ('flu·ə·rin) n. flúor. **fluoridate** (rı·deit) v.t. tratar con fluoruros. —**fluoride** (-ˌraid) n. fluoruro. —**fluoridation** (-rı'dei·ʃən) n. fluorización.

fluoroscope ('flur·ə·skop) n. fluoroscopio. —**fluoroscopic** (-'skap·ık) adj. fluoroscópico. —**fluoroscopy** (flu'ras·kə·pi) n. fluoroscopía.

flurry ('flʌr·i) n. 1, (sudden gust of wind) ráfaga; racha. 2, (whir, as of activity; commotion) remolino; conmoción. —v.t. confundir; turbar; aturullar.

flush (flʌʃ) v.t. 1, (blush) sonrojarse; ruborizarse; ponerse colorado. 2, (flow rapidly; rush sud-

denly) afluir; fluir. 3, (fly off, as game) saltar; levantarse; espantarse. —v.t. 1, (cause to blush) sonrojar; ruborizar. 2, (cause to glow) iluminar; hacer brillar. 3, (wash; cleanse) enjuagar. 4, (empty out) pasar; vaciar. 5, (infuse, as with emotion) llenar (de gozo o excitación). 5, (drive from cover) levantar; espantar; hacer saltar. —n. 1, (blush) sonrojo; rubor. 2, (glow) brillo; fulgor. 3, (sudden rush; rapid flow) aflujo; flujo. 4, (washing; cleansing) irrigación; riego; enjuague. 5, (excitement) excitación; animación 6, (heat; fever) calor; fiebre. 7, cards color; flux. —adj. 1, (even; level) al ras; parejo. 2, (full; filled) lleno; rebosante. 3, (glowing; rosy) sonrosado; colorado. 4, colloq. (well supplied, as with money) bien provisto. —adv. 1, (level; in alignment) al ras. 2, (directly; squarely) directamente; al centro.

fluster ('flʌs·tər) v.t. confundir; aturullar; descompaginar. —n. aturullamiento; confusión.

flute (flut) n. 1, (musical instrument) flauta. 2, (groove) estría; acanaladura. —**fluted,** adj. estriado; acanalado. —**flutist,** n. flautista.

flutter ('flʌt·ər) v.i. 1, (flap, as wings) aletear; batir rapidamente. 2, (move or beat irregularly) batir o latir descompasadamente. 3, (wave, flap, as a flag) tremolar; ondear. 4, (quiver, as with excitement) estar trémulo. 5, (dash about; bustle) revolotear. —v.t. batir; agitar; sacudir. —n. 1, (fluttering movement) aleteo; movimiento trémulo. 2, (agitation; stir) agitación; conmoción. 3, (condition of the heart) palpitación acelerada. —**fluttery,** adj. trémulo.

fluvial ('flu·vi·əl) adj. fluvial.

flux (flʌks) n. 1, (flow; continual change) flujo. 2, metall. fundente.

fly (flai) v.i. [flew, flown, flying] 1, (move through or in the air; move or pass swiftly) volar. 2, (flee) huir; volar; escaparse. 3, baseball [pret. & p.p. flied] usu. fly out, batear en alto una pelota que se recoge al vuelo. —v.t. 1, (cause to fly) volar; hacer volar. 2, (travel over) volar; volar por. 3, (flee from) huir de; volarse de; escaparse de. —n. [pl. flies] 1, (insect) mosca. 2, (fishing lure) mosca artificial; señuelo. 3, (flap in a pair of trousers) bragueta. **4,** (flap or roof of a tent) toldo; capota; volante. **5,** *pl., theat.* bambalina. **6,** *baseball* pelota recogida al vuelo. —**flying fish,** pez volador. —**flying saucer,** platillo volador. —**fly at,** atacar; abalanzarse contra. —**fly in the face of,** encarar desafiante o atrevidamente. —**fly into (a rage),** montar en (cólera). —**fly off,** huir. —**let fly,** soltar; mandar; tirar. —**on the fly,** al vuelo. —**with flying colors,** triunfante.

flycatcher ('flai,kætʃ·ər) *n.* papamoscas.

flyer ('flai·ər) *n.* = **flier.**

flyleaf ('flai·lif) *n.* [*pl.* -**leaves** (-livz)] guarda.

fly swatter *n.* matamoscas.

flyweight ('flai·weit) *n.* peso mosca.

flywheel ('flai,hwil) *n.* volante.

foal (fo:l) *n.* **1,** (young horse) potro; potrillo. **2,** (young ass) pollino. —*v.t. & t.* parir (una yegua o burra).

foam (fo:m) *n.* espuma. —*v.t.* hacer espuma. —*v.i.* espumar. —**foamy,** *adj.* espumoso. —**foam at the mouth,** echar espumarajos. —**foam rubber,** caucho esponjoso.

fob (fa:b) *n.* **1,** (watch pocket) bolsillo del reloj. **2,** (watch charm) leopoldina; *Amer.* leontina. —*v.t.* **1,** (palm off) encajar. **2,** (cheat) engañar.

foci ('fo·sai) *n., pl. de* **focus.**

focus ('fo·kəs) *n.* [*pl.* **focuses** o **foci**] foco. —*v.t. & i.* enfocar. —**focal,** *adj.* focal.

fodder ('fad·ər) *n.* forraje.

foe (fo:) *n.* enemigo; antagonista; adversario. —**foeman** (-mən) *n.* enemigo.

fog (fo:g; fa:g) *n.* **1,** (mist) niebla; neblina; bruma. **2,** *fig.* (confusion; muddle) confusión; perplejidad; niebla. —*v.t.* [**fogged, fogging**] **1,** (surround by fog) nublar. **2,** (cover with a fog or vapor) empañar. **3,** *fig.* (obscure; muddle) obscurecer; nublar. **4,** *photog.* velar.

foggy ('fo:g·i; 'fag·i) *adj.* **1,** (full of fog; misty) nublado. **2,** (dim; murky) nebuloso. **3,** (confused; muddled) confuso; perplejo. **4,** *photog.* velado.

foghorn ('fo:g·horn; 'fag-) *n.* sirena o bocina de niebla.

fogy ('fo·gi) *n.* vejestorio; vejete.

foible ('foi·bəl) *n.* debilidad; flaqueza.

foil (foil) *v.t.* frustrar. —*n.* **1,** (thin sheet of metal) papel metálico; hoja metálica. **2,** (person or thing furnishing contrast) persona o cosa que da realce; marco. **3,** (fencing sword) espada de esgrima; florete.

foist (foist) *v.t.* pasar (con maña); colar; endosar.

fold (fo:ld) *v.t.* **1,** (bend double) plegar; doblar. **2,** (draw together and cross, as the arms) cruzar. **3,** (draw close to the body, as wings) plegar. **4,** (envelop; embrace) envolver. —*v.i.* **1,** (double together) plegarse; doblarse. **2,** *slang* (fail; cease to function) fracasar; venirse abajo. —*n.* **1,** (crease; folded layer) pliegue; doblez. **2,** (pen for sheep) redil. **3,** (flock) rebaño.

folder ('fol·dər) *n.* **1,** (booklet) folleto. **2,** (holder for papers or records) carpeta; ficha; pliego.

folding ('fol·diŋ) *adj.* plegable; plegadizo.

foliage ('fol·i·idʒ) *n.* follaje.

folic ('fo·lik) **acid** *n.* ácido fólico.

folio ('fo·li·o) *n.* [*pl.* -**os**] **1,** (sheet of paper; page number) folio. **2,** (book) libro en folio.

folk (fo:k) *n.* **1,** (people) gente. **2,** *pl., colloq.* (relatives) parientes; familiares; (parents) padres. —*adj.* popular; del pueblo.

folklore ('fok,lor) *n.* folclor. —**folkloristic,** *adj.* folclórico.

folksy ('fok·si) *adj.* campechano; afable.

folkways ('fok,weiz) *n.pl.* costumbres tradicionales.

follicle ('fal·i·kəl) *n.* folículo.

follow ('fa·lo) *v.t.* **1,** (come or go after) seguir; ir detrás de; venir después de. **2,** (pursue) perseguir. **3,** (understand) entender. **4,** (imitate) imitar; copiar. **5,** (adhere or conform to; obey) seguir; obedecer. —*v.i.* **1,** (go or come after another) seguir; ir detrás; venir después. **2,** (result) seguirse; resultar. —**follow through,** seguir; rematar. —**follow up,** continuar; insistir.

follower ('fa·lo·ər) *n.* seguidor; discípulo; secuaz.

following ('fa·lo·iŋ) *n.* **1,** (entourage) séquito; acompañamiento. **2,** (group of followers) partidarios; seguidores. **3,** (clientele) clientela. —*adj.* siguiente.

followthrough ('fa·lo,θru) *n.* remate; continuación.

followup ('fa·lo·ʌp) *n.* continuación; insistencia.

folly ('fal·i) *n.* locura; disparate; desatino.

foment (fo'mɛnt) *v.t.* fomentar. —*n.* ('fo·mɛnt) [*también,* **fomentation** (,fo·mɛn'tei·ʃən)] fomento.

fond (fand) *adj.* **1,** (loving) encariñado; apegado. **2,** (inclined toward) aficionado. **3,** (doting) condescendiente; indulgente.

fondle ('fan·dəl) *v.t.* mimar; acariciar.

fondness ('fand·nəs) *n.* **1,** (affection) afecto; cariño; apego. **2,** (inclination) afición. **3,** (doting) condescendencia; indulgencia.

fondue ('fan·duː) *n.* flan de queso o chocolate.

font (fant) *n.* **1,** *eccles.* pila. **2,** *typog.* fundición; tipo de letra.

food (fuːd) *n.* comida. —**food stamp,** estampilla o cupón para comprar alimentos.

foodstuff ('fud,stʌf) *n., usu.pl.* comestibles; víveres; productos alimenticios.

fool (fuːl) *n.* **1,** (stupid person) tonto; bobo; necio. **2,** (court jester) bufón. —*v.t.* engañar; defraudar; embaucar. —*v.i.* bromear; tontear. —**fool around,** *colloq.* **1,** (jest) bromear; chancear. **2,** (idle) haraganear; zanganear. —**fool away,** malgastar; perder (el tiempo). —**fool with,** *colloq.* meterse en; tontear con; entretenerse con. —**make a fool of,** poner en ridículo.

foolhardy ('ful,har·di) *adj.* temerario. —**foolhardiness,** *n.* temeridad.

foolish ('fu·lɪʃ) *adj.* bobo; tonto; necio. —**foolishness,** *n.* bobería; tontería; necedad.

foolproof ('ful,pruf) *adj.* **1,** (easily understood) muy fácil; inequívoco. **2,** (surely effective) cierto; seguro.

foolscap ('fulz,kæp) *n.* papel de oficio.

foot (fʊt) *n.* [*pl.* **feet**] **1,** *anat.* (of humans) pie; (of animals) pata. **2,** (part resembling a foot) pata. **3,** (bottom or lowest point) pie; base. **4,** [*pl. también* **foot**] (measure of length) pie. **5,** (step; pace) paso; movimiento. **6,** (infantry) infantería. **7,** *poesía* pie. —*v.t.* **1,** (add up) sumar. **2,** *colloq.* (pay, as a bill) pagar. —**on foot,** a pie. —**put one's**

foot down, plantarse en sus trece. —**put one's foot in it,** meter la pata.

footage ('fut·ɪdʒ) *n.* largo (*en pies*); metraje.

football ('fut·bɔl) *n.* **1,** (game) fútbol americano; balompié. **2,** (ball) balón; pelota de fútbol.

footboard ('fut,bord) *n.* **1,** (of a vehicle) estribo. **2,** (of a bed) pie de cama.

footgear ('fut,gɪr) *n.* calzado.

foothill ('fut,hɪl) *n.* estribación; falda.

foothold ('fut·hold) *n.* posición; base.

footing ('fut·ɪŋ) *n.* **1,** (foothold) posición; base. **2,** (foundation) base; fundamento. **3,** (basis; relative standing) pie; relación; —**lose one's footing,** perder el pie.

footlights ('fut·laits) *n.pl.* candilejas; batería.

footloose ('fut·lus) *adj.* libre; desembarazado.

footman ('fut·mən) *n.* [*pl.* **-men**] lacayo.

footnote ('fut·not) *n.* nota (*al pie de página*).

footprint ('fut·prɪnt) *n.* huella; pisada.

footrest *n.* **1,** (footstool) escabel. **2,** (support for the foot) reposapiés.

footsore ('fut·sɔr) *adj.* despeado.

footstep ('fut·stɛp) *n.* paso; pisada.

footstool ('fut·stul) *n.* banqueta; escabel.

foot warmer calientapiés.

footwear ('fut·wɛr) *n.* calzado.

footwork ('fut·wʌrk) *n.* juego de pies.

fop (fap) *n.* petimetre; pisaverde. —**foppery,** *n.* afectación en el vestir. —**foppish,** *adj.* peripuesto; afectado.

for (for) *prep.* **1,** (intended for; for the use of) para: *a book for children,* un libro para niños. **2,** (destined for; to be given to) para: *a gift for Louis,* un regalo para Luis. **3,** (for the purpose of; appropriate to) para: *a box for handkerchiefs,* una caja para pañuelos. **4,** (with inclination or tendency toward) para: *a good ear for music,* buen oído para la música. **5,** (toward, as a destination) para: *He left for Washington,* Salió para Washington. **6,** (with the purpose or goal of) para: *He is training for policeman,* Se prepara para policía. **7,** (for the benefit or advantage of) para: *Wine is good for the digestion,* El vino es bueno para la digestión. **8,** (with reference or relation to) para: *He is tall for his age,* Es alto para su edad. **9,** (in quest of; in order to get) por: *I went for the doctor,* Fui por el médico. **10,** (in request of; requesting) por: *a suit for damages,* un pleito por daños. **11,** (in return for; in compensation for) por: *I paid five dollars for a hat,* Pagué cinco dólares por un sombrero. **12,** (in spite of, notwithstanding) aun con; a pesar de: *He is a fool for all his learning,* Es un idiota aun con toda su ciencia. **13,** (over the space or time of) en; por: *I have not seen him in two years,* No lo he visto en o por dos años. **14,** (in favor of) por: *I vote for an honest policy,* Voto por una política recta. **15,** (in place of; in substitution for) por; en vez de: *The vice-president signed for the president,* El vicepresidente firmó por el presidente. **16,** (on behalf of) por: *I act for my brother,* Actúo por mi hermano. **17,** (for the sake of) por: *I did it for you,* Lo hice por ti. **18,** (corresponding to; in proportion to) por: *mile for mile,* milla por milla. **19,** (in token or recognition of) por: *He was given a medal for bravery,* Le concedieron una medalla por su valentía. **20,** (in honor of) por: *He was named Albert for his uncle,* Se llamó Alberto por su tío. **21,** (because of; by reason of) por: *for having done this,* por haber hecho esto. **22,** (as; in the character or capacity of) por; como: *He took her for his wife,* La tomó por o como esposa. **23,** (mistakenly as or for) por: *He took* (o *mistook*) *me for someone else,* Me tomó por otro. **24,** (denoting a designated time) de: *It is time for lunch,* Es hora de almorzar. —*conj.* porque; pues; puesto que. —**as for me,** por mi parte. —**but for,** a no ser por. —**for hire,** de alquiler. —**for rent,** se alquila. —**for sale,** en venta; se vende.

forage ('for·idz) *n.* forraje. —*v.t. & i.* forrajear.

foray ('for·e) *n.* correría; saqueo; pillaje.

forbear (for'berr) *v.t.* [**forbore, forborne, forbearing**] abstenerse de. —*v.i.* reprimirse; contenerse.

forbearance (for'ber·ɘns) *n.* **1,** (abstinence) abstención. **2,** (patient endurance) paciencia; indulgencia. —**forbearing,** *adj.* paciente; sufrido; indulgente.

forbid (for'bɪd) *v.t.* [**forbade** o **forbid, forbidden, forbidding**] **1,** (prohibit) prohibir; vedar **2,** (prevent) impedir.

forbidding (for'bɪd·ɪŋ) *adj.* **1,** (threatening; dark) amenazante; sombrío **2,** (disagreeable) desagradable; adusto.

force (fors) *n.* **1,** (power; might; strength) fuerza. **2,** (operation; effect, as of laws) vigor; vigencia. **3,** (meaning; import) valor; significado. **4,** (body of men prepared for action) fuerza; tropa. **5,** (staff of workers) personal. —*v.t.* forzar; obligar. —**forceful,** *adj.* fuerte; poderoso; enérgico.

forced (forst) *adj.* **1,** (compulsory) forzoso. **2,** (strained; unnatural) forzado; artificial; afectado. **3,** (caused by an emergency) forzado; obligado.

forceps ('for·sɛps) *n.* fórceps.

forcible ('for·sɘ·bɘl) *adj.* **1,** (powerful) fuerte; poderoso. **2,** (convincing) de peso; concluyente. **3,** (effected by force) forzado. **4,** (marked by force) vigoroso; enérgico.

ford (ford) *n.* vado. —*v.t.* vadear.

fore (for) *n.* frente. —*adv.* de proa. —*adj.* anterior; delantero; *naut.* de proa. —*interj., golf* ¡ojo!; ¡atención!

fore-and-aft *adj.* de popa a proa. —**fore-and-aft sail,** cangreja; vela cangreja.

forearm *n.* antebrazo.

forebear ('for·ber) *n.* antepasado.

forebode (for'bord) *v.t.* **1,** (presage) pronosticar; presagiar. **2,** (have a premonition of) presentir. —**foreboding,** *n.* pronóstico; presagio; presentimiento.

forecast ('for·kæst) *n.* **1,** (prediction) pronóstico. **2,** (foresight) previsión. —*v.t.* (for'kæst) [*pret. & p.p.* también **forecast**] **1,** (predict) pronosticar. **2,** (foresee) prever.

forecastle ('fork·sɘl) *n.* castillo de proa.

foreclose (for'klorz) *v.t. & i.* anular por orden judicial el derecho de redimir (una hipoteca). —**foreclosure** (-'klo·ʒɘr) *n.* anulación del derecho de redimir una hipoteca.

forefather ('for·fa·ðɘr) *n.* antepasado; ascendiente.

forefinger ('for·fɪŋ·gɘr) *n.* (dedo) índice.

forefoot ('for,fʊt) *n.* pata delantera.

forefront ('for,frʌnt) *n.* frente; primer lugar.

forego (for'goɹ) *v.t.* = forgo.

foregoing (for'go·ɪŋ) *adj.* anterior; precedente.

foregone ('for,gɔn) *adj.* **1,** (past) pasado. **2,** (settled in advance) predeterminado; decidido de antemano. —**to be foregone,** darse por sentado.

foreground ('for,graund) *n.* primer plano; frente.

forehead ('for·hɛd; 'for·ɪd) *n.* frente.

foreign ('far·ən) *adj.* **1,** (situated outside one's own land) extranjero. **2,** (relating to or dealing with other countries) exterior **3,** (alien; strange) extraño; exótico. **4,** (extraneous; external) extraño; ajeno. —**foreigner,** *n.* extranjero.

foreleg ('for,lɛg) *n.* pata delantera.

forelock ('for·lak) *n.* **1,** (lock of hair on the forehead) mechón. **2,** (of a horse) copete. **3,** *mech.* chaveta.

foreman ('for·mən) *n.* [*pl.* -men] **1,** (person in charge) encargado. **2,** (overseer) capataz. **3,** (field boss) mayoral. **4,** (spokesman of a jury) portavoz del jurado.

foremost ('for·most) *adj.* **1,** (in place) delantero; más avanzado. **2,** (in rank or importance) primero; principal. —*adv.* primero; principalmente.

forenoon ('for·nun) *n.* mañana.

forensic (fə'rɛn·sɪk) *adj.* forense.

forerunner ('for,rʌn·ər) *n.* antecesor; precursor.

foresee (for'siɹ) *v.t.* [**foresaw, foreseen**] prever. —**foreseeable,** *adj.* previsible.

foreshadow (for,ʃæ·do) *v.t.* presagiar; pronosticar.

foresight ('for·sait) *n.* previsión.

foreskin ('for·skɪn) *n.* prepucio.

forest ('far·əst) *n.* bosque; selva; floresta. —**forestation,** *n.* forestación. —**forester,** *n.* guardabosque. —**forestry,** *n.* silvicultura.

forestall (for'stɔl) *v.t.* prevenir; precaver; anticipar; anticiparse a.

foretell (for'tɛl) *v.t.* & *i.* [*pret.* & *p.p.* **foretold**] predecir.

forethought ('for,θɔt) *n.* prevención; providencia; premeditación.

foretoken (for'to·kən) *v.t.* presagiar. —*n.* ('for-) presagio.

forever (for'ɛv·ər) *adv.* siempre; para siempre; por siempre.

forewarn (for'worn) *v.t.* prevenir; advertir. —*v.i.* presagiar. —**forewarning,** *n.* advertencia; presagio.

foreword ('for·wʌrd) *n.* prólogo; introducción.

forfeit ('for·fɪt) *n.* **1,** (something forfeited) pérdida. **2,** (fine; penalty) multa; pena. —*v.t.* & *i.* perder. —*v.t.* perder el derecho a. —*adj.* perdido. —**forfeits,** *n.pl.* juego de prendas. —**forfeiture** ('for·fɪ·tʃər) *n.* pérdida.

forge (fordʒ) *v.t.* **1,** (shape; fashion) forjar; fraguar. **2,** (counterfeit) falsificar —*v.i.* abrirse o labrarse camino; seguir avanzando. —*n.* forja; fragua.

forger ('for·dʒər) *n.* **1,** (counterfeiter) falsificador. **2,** (worker in metals) forjador.

forgery ('for·dʒə·ri) *n.* falsificación.

forget (fər'gɛt) *v.t.* [**forgot, forgotten** o **forgot, forgetting**] olvidar; olvidarse de; olvidársele (a uno) una cosa. —**forget oneself. 1,** (be unselfish) olvidarse de sí. **2,** (act or speak unseemly) olvidarse de lo que uno es.

forgetful (fər'gɛt·fəl) *adj.* **1,** (given to forgetting) olvidadizo. **2,** (unmindful; inconsiderate) desconsiderado; olvidado. —**forgetfulness,** *n.* olvido.

forget-me-not *n.* nomeolvides.

forgive (fər'gɪv) *v.t.* [**forgave, forgiven, forgiving**] perdonar. —**forgiveness,** *n.* perdón; clemencia. —**forgiving,** *adj.* indulgente; clemente; misericordioso.

forgo *también,* **forego** (for'goɹ) *v.t.* [**forwent, forgone, forgoing**] privarse de; renunciar.

fork (fork) *n.* **1,** (utensil for eating) tenedor. **2,** (of a tree) horqueta; horquilla. **3,** (pitchfork) horca; horquilla. **4,** (branching, as of a road or river) bifurcación. **5,** (anything forked or fork-shaped) horquilla; horqueta. —*v.t.* **1,** (pierce or handle with a fork) pinchar, sujetar o mover con tenedor, trinchante u horquilla. **2,** (make fork-shaped) bifurcar; ahorquillar. —*v.i.* bifurcarse; ahorquillarse. —**forked,** *adj.* bifurcado; ahorquillado. —**fork over** o **out,** *slang* entregar; pasar.

forlorn (for'lo:rn) *adj.* **1,** (forsaken) abandonado; desamparado. **2,** (desolate) triste; desolado. **3,**

(hopeless) desesperado. —**forlorn-ness,** *n.* desamparo; desolación; desesperación. —**forlorn hope,** acción o empresa desesperada.

form (form) *n.* 1, (shape; style; pattern) forma. 2, (condition) condición; forma. 3, (blank document) formulario. —*v.t.* formar. —*v.i.* formarse.

formal ('for·məl) *adj.* 1, (of or relating to form) formal. 2, (stiff) formal; ceremonioso; tieso. 3, (ceremonial; gala) de etiqueta —*n., colloq.* función (o vestido) de etiqueta.

formaldehyde (for'mæl·də·haid) *n.* formaldehído.

formalism ('for·mə,lız·əm) *n.* formalismo. —**formalist,** *n.* formalista. —**formalistic,** *adj.* formalista.

formality (for'mæl·ə·ti) *n.* formalidad.

formalize ('for·mə·laiz) *v.t.* formalizar.

format ('for·mæt) *n.* formato; forma. —*v.t., comput.* preparar (un disco) para aceptar datos; organizar; definir (formatos).

formation (for'mei·ʃən) *n.* formación.

formative ('form·ə·tɪv) *adj.* formativo.

former ('for·mər) *adj.* 1, (preceding in time) anterior; pasado; precedente. 2, (first mentioned of two) anterior; primero. —**formerly,** *adv.* antes; anteriormente. —**the former … the latter,** aquél … éste.

formidable ('for·mɪ·də·bəl) *adj.* formidable.

formless ('form·ləs) *adj.* informe; sin forma.

formula ('form·ju·lə) *n.* fórmula.

formulate ('form·ju,leit) *v.t.* formular. —**formulation,** *n.* formulación.

fornicate ('for·nɪ,keit) *v.i.* fornicar. —**fornication,** *n.* fornicación.

forsake (for'seik) *v.t.* [**forsook, forsaken, forsaking**] 1, (abandon) abandonar; desamparar. 2, (renounce) dejar; renunciar.

forswear (for'sweɪr) *v.t.* [*pret.* **forswore;** *p.p.* **forsworn**] renegar. —*v.i.* jurar en falso; perjurar.

fort (fort) *n.* fuerte; fortaleza.

forte ('for·ti; -te) *n.* fuerte. —*adj. & adv., mus.* fuerte.

forth (forθ) *adv.* 1, (onward or forward) adelante; hacia adelante. 2,

(out; away) fuera; afuera; hacia afuera. —**and so forth,** y (lo) demás; etcétera.

forthcoming ('forθ,kʌm·ɪŋ) *adj.* 1, (approaching in time) próximo; que viene. 2, (available) disponible.

forthright ('forθ·rait) *adj.* franco; abierto; directo. —*adv.* 1, (directly) francamente; directamente; abiertamente. 2, (immediately) inmediatamente; en el acto. —**forthright-ness,** *n.* franqueza; sinceridad.

forthwith ('forθ·wɪθ) *adv.* en el acto; en seguida.

fortieth ('for·ti·əθ) *adj. & n.* cuadragésimo; cuarentavo.

fortification (,for·tɪ·fɪ'kei·ʃən) *n.* fortificación.

fortify ('for·tɪ,fai) *v.t.* 1, (provide with defenses) fortificar 2, (strengthen) fortalecer. 3, (reinforce) reforzar.

fortissimo (for'tɪs·ɪ,mo) *adj. & adv.* fortísimo.

fortitude ('for·tɪ·tud; -tjud) *n.* fortaleza; entereza.

fortnight ('fort,nait; -nɪt) *n.* quincena; dos semanas. —**fortnightly,** *adj.* quincenal. —*adv.* quincenalmente.

fortress ('fort·rəs) *n.* fortaleza; fuerte.

fortuitous (for'tu·ɪ·təs) *adj.* fortuito; casual; accidental. —**fortuitousness; fortuity,** *n.* casualidad.

fortunate ('for·tʃə·nət) *adj.* afortunado; feliz.

fortune ('for·tʃən) *n.* 1, (luck) fortuna; suerte. 2, (wealth) caudal; capital.

fortuneteller ('for·tʃən,tel·ər) *n.* vidente; adivino; adivinador.

forty ('for·ti) *n. & adj.* cuarenta.

forum ('for·əm) *n.* foro.

forward ('for·wərd) *adj.* 1, (near or toward the front) delantero; anterior. 2, (well-advanced) adelantado. 3, (eager; ready) entusiasta; emprendedor. 4, (bold) atrevido; descarado. —*adv.* 1, (onward; ahead) toward the front) adelante; hacia delante. 2, (forth; into view) fuera; afuera; hacia fuera. —*v.t.* 1, (send; dispatch) enviar; expedir; transmitir. 2, (send to a further destination) reexpedir. 3, (promote) promover; adelantar.

forwardness ('for·wərd·nəs) *n.* 1, (boldness) audacia; descaro. 2, (drive; energy) empuje; entusiasmo.

fossil ('fas·əl) *n. & adj.* fósil. —**fossilize,** *v.t.* fosilizar. —*v.i.* fosilizarse. —**fossil fuel,** combustible fósil.

foster ('fɔs·tər) *v.t.* **1,** (nourish; bring up) criar. **2,** (cherish) alentar; alimentar. **3,** (promote; sponsor) patrocinar. —*adj.* adoptivo; de crianza.

fought (fɔt) *v., pret. & p.p. de* **fight.**

foul (faul) *adj.* **1,** (filthy) sucio; inmundo; **2,** (of offensive odor) apestoso; pestilente. **3,** (stale, as air) viciado. **4,** (inclement, as weather) malo. **5,** (clogged) atorado; obstruido. **6,** (entangled) enredado; enmarañado. **7,** (in violation of rules) ilegal; inválido. **8,** (base; vicious; scurrilous) sucio; bajo; vil. —*n.* infracción; falta. —*v.t.* **1,** (defile) ensuciar; manchar. **2,** (clog) atorar; obstruir. **3,** (entangle) enredar; enmarañar. —*v.i.* **1,** (become soiled) ensuciarse. **2,** (become clogged) obstruirse; atorarse. **3,** (become entangled) enmarañarse; enredarse. **4,** (violate a rule) cometer una infracción o falta. —**foulness,** *n.* asquerosidad. —**fall foul of; run foul of,** enredarse con; chocarse con; chocar contra. —**foul blow; foul punch,** golpe bajo. —**foul up,** embarrar; embarullar; embrollar.

foulard (fu'lɑrd) *n.* fular.

foul-mouthed *adj.* deslenguado; desbocado.

found (faund) *v.t.* **1,** (lay the foundation of; establish) fundar; establecer. **2,** (support; base) asentar (en); fundar (en); basar (en). **3,** (cast) fundir.

found (faund) *v., pret. & p.p. de* **find.**

foundation (faun'dei·ʃən) *n.* **1,** (base) cimiento. **2,** (basis) base; fundamento; principio. **3,** (endowed institution) fundación. **4,** (act of founding) fundación.

founder ('faun·dər) *v.i.* **1,** (sink) hundirse; irse a pique. **2,** (go lame, as a horse) derrengarse. **3,** (fail) fracasar; hundirse. —*n.* **1,** (originator) fundador. **2,** (caster of metals) fundidor.

founding ('faun·dɪŋ) *n.* fundición.

foundling ('faund·lɪŋ) *n.* (niño) expósito; echadillo. —**foundling hospital; foundling home,** inclusa; hospicio.

foundry ('faun·dri) *n.* fundición.

fountain ('faun·tən) *n.* fuente. —**fountainhead,** *n.* nacimiento; fuente; origen. —**fountain pen,** estilográfica; pluma fuente.

four (for) *n. & adj.* cuatro. —**on all fours,** a o en cuatro patas; gateando.

fourfold ('for·fold) *adj.* cuádruplo; cuatro veces (más). —*adv.* cuatro veces; en un cuádruplo.

four-footed *adj.* cuadrúpedo.

four hundred cuatrocientos. —**four-hundredth,** *adj. & n.* cuadringentésimo.

four-in-hand *n.* **1,** (necktie) corbata de nudo. **2,** (team of horses) tiro de cuatro caballos.

foursome ('for·səm) *n.* grupo de o a cuatro. —*adj.* de a cuatro.

foursquare ('for,skwɛr) *adj.* **1,** (steady) firme; constante. **2,** (frank) franco; abierto.

fourteen (for'tin) *n. & adj.* catorce. —**fourteenth,** *adj.* décimocuarto. —*n.* décimocuarto; décimocuarta parte.

fourth (forθ) *adj.* cuarto. —*n.* cuarto; cuarta parte; *mus.* cuarta.

fowl (faul) *n.* ave; (*collectively*) volatería. —**fowler,** *n.* cazador (de aves). —**fowling,** *n.* caza (de aves). —**fowling piece,** escopeta.

fox (faks) *n.* zorra (*masc.* zorro); raposa. —*v.t., slang* engañar.

foxglove ('faks,glʌv) *n.* digital.

foxhole ('faks·hol) *n., mil.* pozo u hoyo de tirador.

foxhound ('faks,haund) *n.* perro zorrero.

foxy ('fak·si) *adj.* astuto; listo.

foyer ('fɔi·ər) *n.* vestíbulo.

Fra (fra) *n.* fray.

fracas ('frei·kəs) *n.* riña; bronca.

fraction ('fræk·ʃən) *n.* fracción. —**fractional,** *adj.* fraccionario; fraccionado. —**fractional distillation,** destilación fraccionada. —**fractional motor,** motor de menos de un caballo.

fractionate ('fræk·ʃə·neit) *v.t.* fraccionar. —**fractionation,** *n.* fraccionamiento.

fractious ('fræk·ʃəs) *adj.* **1,** (cross; peevish) enojadizo; arisco. **2,** (unruly) reacio; rebelde. —**fractiousness,** *n.* indocilidad; mal genio.

fracture ('fræk·tʃər) *n.* rotura; *surg.* fractura. —*v.t.* fracturar; quebrar; romper.

fragile ('frædʒ·əl) *adj.* frágil.

—**fragility** (fra'dʒɪl·ə·ti) *n.* fragilidad.

fragment ('fræg·mənt) *n.* fragmento; trozo. —*v.t.* fragmentar. —*v.i.* fragmentarse. —**fragmentary**, *adj.* fragmentario. —**fragmentation** (-mən'tei·ʃən) *n.* fragmentación.

fragrant ('frei·grənt) *adj.* fragante; oloroso. —**fragrance**, *n.* fragancia; olor.

frail (freil) *adj.* 1, (fragile) frágil; quebradizo. 2, (weak) débil; delicado; endeble. —**frailty**, *n.* fragilidad; debilidad.

frame (freim) *v.t.* 1, (construct; fit together) armar; fabricar; formar. 2, (compose; devise) componer; inventar; forjar; idear. 3, (surround with a frame) poner marco a. 4, *slang* (incriminate) fraguar; incriminar. —*n.* 1, (ornamental border) marco. 2, (structure for enclosing or holding something) armadura; armazón; bastidor. 3, (bodily structure) esqueleto. 4, (state of mind) talante; disposición. —**frame house**, casa de madera.

frameup ('freim·ʌp) *n., slang* estratagema para incriminar a un inocente.

framework ('freim·wʌrk) *n.* armazón; *fig.* cuadro.

franc (fræŋk) *n.* franco.

franchise ('fræn·tʃaiz) *n.* 1, (right to vote) sufragio. 2, (special right granted) franquicia; exclusiva.

francium ('fræn·si·əm) *n.* francio.

frank (fræŋk) *adj.* franco; abierto. —*n.* franquicia postal; carta franca. —*v.t.* enviar con franquicia. —**frankness**, *n.* franqueza.

frankfurter ('fræŋk,fʌr·tər) *n.* salchicha.

frankincense ('fræŋk·ɪn·sɛns) *n.* incienso.

frantic (fræn·tɪk) *adj.* frenético.

fraternal (frə'tʌr·nəl) *adj.* fraternal.

fraternity (frə'tʌr·nə·ti) *n.* fraternidad; hermandad.

fraternize ('fræt·ər,naiz) *v.i.* fraternizar. —**fraternization** (-nɪ'zei·ʃən) *n.* fraternización.

fratricide ('fræt·rɪ,said) *n.* 1, (act) fratricidio. 2, (agent) fratricida. —**fratricidal**, *adj.* fratricida.

fraud (frɔːd) *n.* 1, (deceit; trick) fraude; engaño; timo. 2, *law* fraude. 3, *colloq.* (cheat) timador; impostor.

fraudulent ('frɔd·jə·lənt) *adj.* fraudulento. —**fraudulence**, *n.* fraude; fraudulencia.

fraught (frɔt) *adj.* lleno; atestado.

fray (frei) *n.* riña; disputa; querella. —*v.t.* deshilachar; desgastar; raer. —*v.i.* deshilacharse; desgastarse; raerse.

frazzle ('fræz·əl) *v.t., colloq.* 1, (fray) rozar; raer; deshilachar. 2, (exhaust) cansar; fatigar; abrumar. —*n.* 1, (shred) hilacha. 2, (exhaustion) cansancio; fatiga; extenuación.

freak (friːk) *n.* 1, (monster) monstruo; aborto; engendro. 2, (whim; odd notion) capricho; rareza. —**freakish** ('fri·kɪʃ) *adj.* 1, (odd; unusual) raro; extravagante. 2, (monstrous) monstruoso.

freckle ('frɛk·əl) *n.* peca. —*v.t.* poner pecoso. —*v.i.* ponerse pecoso. —**freckly** (-li); **freckled**, *adj.* pecoso.

free (friː) *adj.* 1, (independent; self-determining) libre; independiente. 2, (unrestricted; unbound; loose) libre; suelto. 3, (exempt) libre; exento. 4, (free of charge) gratuito; gratis. 5, (not literal or exact) libre. 6, (open to all) abierto. 7, (unoccupied; unengaged) libre; disponible; desocupado. 8, (lavish; profuse) liberal. —*adv.* gratis; de balde. —*v.t.* 1, (release; liberate) liberar; libertar. 2, (save; rescue) librar; rescatar. 3, (exempt) eximir. 4, (loose; let go) soltar. 5, (rid; disencumber) desembarazar. 6, (clear; purify) limpiar. —**free and clear**, libre de hipoteca y cargos. —**free and easy**, desenvuelto; desembarazado. —**free hand**, mano libre; carta blanca. —**free on board**, franco a bordo. —**free port**, puerto franco. —**free will**, propia voluntad; libre albedrío. —**make free with**, tomarse libertades con; abusar de; disponer de.

freebie ('friː·bi) *n., slang* dádiva; obsequio.

freebooter ('friː·bu·tər) *n.* filibustero; pirata.

freeborn ('fri,bɔrn) *adj.* nacido libre.

freedman ('frid·mən) *n.* liberto.

freedom ('fri·dəm) *n.* libertad.

free-for-all *n.* 1, (brawl) trifulca; pelotera. 2, (open contest) carrera o concurso abierto a todos. —*adj.* abierto; general.

freehand ('fri,hænd) *adj. & adv.* a pulso.

freehanded ('fri,hæn·dɪd) *adj.* generoso; liberal; dadivoso.

freehold *n.* feudo franco.

freelance ('fri'læns) *n.* persona que trabaja por su cuenta; contratista independiente. *También,* **free lance; freelancer.** —*v.t.* hacer (un trabajo) por su centa o como contratista independiente. —*v.i.* trabajar por su cuenta o como contratista independiente.

freeman ('fri·mən) *n.* hombre libre; ciudadano.

Freemason ('fri,mei·sən) *n.* masón; francmasón. —**Freemasonic,** *adj.* masónico; francmasónico. —**Freemasonry,** *n.* masonería; francmasonería.

freethinker ('fri,θɪŋ·kər) *n.* librepensador. —**free thought,** libre pensamiento.

freeway ('fri;·wei) *n.* autopista sin peaje.

freewheeling ('fri;·hwi;l·ɪŋ) *adj., colloq.* despreocupado.

freewill ('fri,wil) *adj.* voluntario.

freeze (fri;z) *v.t.* [**froze, frozen, freezing**] **1,** (congeal; chill) congelar; helar. **2,** (block; hinder) bloquear; congelar —*v.i.* helarse; helar; escarchar. —*n.* **1,** helada; escarcha. **2,** (imposed limit; moratorium) congelación; moratoria.

freezer ('fri·zər) *n.* congeladora; congelador.

freight (freit) *n.* **1,** (transportation of goods) transporte. **2,** (cargo; shipment) carga; cargamento. **3,** (charge for handling) flete. **4,** *R.R.* tren de carga o mercancías. —*v.t.* **1,** (load) cargar. **2,** (ship by freight) embarcar. —**freighter,** *n.* buque de carga.

French (frɛntʃ) *adj. & n.* francés. —**Frenchman,** *n.* francés. —**Frenchwoman,** *n.* francesa. —**French doors,** puertas de alas. —**French windows,** ventanas de alas. —**French horn,** trompa. —**French leave,** despedida a la francesa. —**French toast,** torrija.

Frenchify ('frɛn·tʃə·fai) *v.t.* afrancesar.

frenetic (frə'nɛt·ɪk) *adj.* frenético.

frenum ('fri·nəm) *n., anat.* frenillo.

frenzy ('frɛn·zi) *n.* frenesí. —**frenzied,** *adj.* frenético.

Freon ('fri·an) *n., T.N.* freón.

frequency ('fri·kwən·si) *n.* frecuencia. —**frequency modulation,** frecuencia modulada.

frequent ('fri·kwənt) *adj.* frecuente. —*v.t.* (fri'kwɛnt) frecuentar. —**frequentation** (-kwən'tei·ʃən) frecuentación. —**frequentative** (fri'kwɛn·tə·tɪv) *adj.* frecuentativo.

fresco ('frɛs·ko) *n.* fresco.

fresh (frɛʃ) *adj.* **1,** (having its original qualities) fresco. **2,** (not salt, as water) dulce. **3,** (recently made) acabado de hacer; recién hecho; fresco. **4,** (recent; new) reciente; nuevo. **5,** (clean, as clothing) limpio. **6,** (not tired) descansado. **7,** (healthy; youthful) sano; lozano; joven. **8,** (inexperienced) inexperto; novato. **9,** (cool; brisk; refreshing) fresco. **10,** *slang* (impudent) fresco; descarado. —**freshen,** *v.t.* refrescar.

freshet ('frɛʃ·ɪt) *n.* crecida; aluvión.

freshman ('frɛʃ·mən) *n.* [*pl.* -**men**] estudiante de primer año.

freshness ('frɛʃ·nəs) *n.* **1,** (newness) novedad. **2,** (coolness) fresco; frescura; frescor. **3,** (impudence) descaro. **4,** (vigor; vitality) lozanía.

freshwater ('frɛʃ,wɔ·tər) *adj.* **1,** (of inland waters) de agua dulce. **2,** (inexperienced) novato; inexperto. **3,** (rural; rustic) rural; de provincias.

fret (frɛt) *v.i.* [**fretted, fretting**] **1,** (be distressed) atormentarse; desesperarse. **2,** (become worn or corroded) raerse; desgastarse; corroerse. —*v.t.* **1,** (vex; irritate) irritar; desesperar. **2,** (chafe; rub) raer; desgastar. —*n.* **1,** (irritation) irritación; enojo. **2,** (carved pattern) calado; greca. **3,** (of a stringed instrument) traste.

fretful ('frɛt·fəl) *adj.* **1,** (distressing) enojoso; molesto. **2,** (peevish) enojadizo. **3,** (perturbed; restless) inquieto; perturbado.

fretwork ('frɛt·wʌrk) *n.* calado; greca.

friable ('frai·ə·bəl) *adj.* friable.

friar ('frai·ər) *n.* fraile; fray.

fricassee ('frɪk·ə·si) *n.* fricasé. —*v.t.* hacer un fricasé de; preparar al fricasé.

fricative ('frɪk·ə·tɪv) *adj.* fricativo. —*n.* fricativa.

friction ('frɪk·ʃən) *n.* **1,** (a rubbing together) fricción; rozamiento; roce. **2,** (disagreement; conflict) rozamiento; fricción. **3,** *mech.* roza-

miento. —**frictional,** *adj.* de rozamiento.
Friday ('frai·de) *n.* viernes.
—**Good Friday,** viernes santo.
fried (fraid) *v., pret. & p.p. de* **fry.**
—*adj.* frito.
friend (frɛnd) *n.* **1,** (close acquaintance; supporter) amigo. **2,** *cap.*
(Quaker) cuáquero.
friendly ('frɛnd·li) *adj.* **1,** (of or
like a friend) amistoso; amigo. **2,**
(not hostile; amicable) amigable;
cordial. **3,** (supporting; helping; favorable) favorable; amigo. **4,** (desir-
ing friendship) cariñoso; amistoso.
—**friendliness,** *n.* amistad.
friendship ('frɛnd·ʃıp) *n.* amistad.
frieze (friːz) *n.* **1,** *archit.* friso. **2,**
(cloth) frisa.
frigate ('frıg·ət) *n.* fragata.
fright (frait) *n.* **1,** (sudden terror)
espanto; susto. **2,** *colloq.* (grotesque
person or thing) esperpento;
espantajo.
frighten ('frai·tən) *v.t.* **1,** (terrify;
startle) espantar; asustar. **2,** (intimidate) amedrentar; atemorizar. —*v.i.*
asustarse; amedrentarse.
frightful ('frait·fəl) *adj.* **1,** (terrifying; shocking) espantoso; horri-
ble; pavoroso. **2,** *colloq.* (unpleasant) desagradable; atroz; horrible.
—**frightfulness,** *n.* espanto.
frigid ('frıdʒ·ıd) *adj.* frígido; glacial; frío.
frigidity (frı'dʒıd·ə·ti) *n.* frialdad;
frigidez.
frill (frıl) *n.* **1,** (ruffle) faralá; volante. **2,** *usu.pl., colloq.* (affectations) faralá; faramallas. **3,** (fancy
detail) ringorrango; *Amer.* firulete.
—**frilly,** *adj.* alechugado; escaro-
lado.
fringe (frındʒ) *n.* **1,** (trimming)
fleco; orla. **2,** (border; margin)
borde; linde; margen. —*adj.* al
linde; marginal. —**fringe benefits,**
beneficios suplementarios.
frippery ('frıp·ə·ri) *n.* **1,** (cheap
finery) perifollos; cursilerías. **2,** (ostentation) perejil; cursilería.
frisk (frısk) *v.i.* retozar; brincar; dar
cabriolas. —*v.t., slang* cachear; registrar; *Amer.* escular —**frisky,**
adj. vivaracho; retozón; juguetón.
fritter ('frıt·ər) *v.t.* derrochar;
desperdiciar. —*n.* fritura; frito;
fritada.
frivolity (frı'val·ə·ti) *n.* frivolidad.
frivolous ('frıv·ə·ləs) *adj.* frívolo.
—**frivolousness,** *n.* frivolidad.

frizzle ('frız·əl) *v.t.* **1,** (form into
tight curls; crimp) encrespar; rizar.
2, (make crisp, as by frying)
achicharrar; churruscar. —*v.i.* **1,**
(curl; crimp) encresparse; rizarse. **2,**
(become crisp) achicharrarse; chu-
rruscarse. —**frizzly** (-li); **frizzy,**
adj. rizado; encrespado.
fro (froˌ) *adv.* atrás; hacia atrás. —**to
and fro,** de un lado a otro; de aquí
para allí.
frock (frak) *n.* **1,** (dress) vestido;
sayo. **2,** (monk's habit) sayo.
—**frock coat,** levita.
frog (frɔg; frag) *n.* **1,** *zoöl.; R.R.*
rana. **2,** (ornamental fastening)
alamar; recamo. —**frog in the
throat,** carraspera. —**frogs' legs,**
ancas de rana.
frogman ('frɔg·mæn) *n.* buzo;
hombre rana.
frolic ('fral·ık) *v.i.* [**frolicked, frolicking**] **1,** (make merry) jaranear;
divertirse. **2,** (gambol) retozar;
juguetear. —*n.* holgorio; diversión. —**frolicsome,** *adj.* retozón;
juguetón; travieso.
from (frʌm) *prep.* **1,** (distant or separated in time, space, order, etc.)
de: *ten miles from here,* a diez millas de aquí. **2,** (beginning at; starting with) de; desde: *from here to
there,* desde aquí hasta allá. **3,** (out
of; drawn or derived from) de: *This
wine comes from Spain,* Este vino
viene de España. **4,** (coming from;
emanating from, as a message, order, etc.) de; de parte de: *This message comes from the judge,* Este
mensaje viene del (o de parte del)
juez. **5,** (because of; by reason of)
de; por: *suffering from love,*
sufriendo de o por amor. **6,** (removed, released, prevented, absent,
different, etc., from) de: *He took the
money from his savings,* Sacó el dinero de sus ahorros; *This house is
different from the other,* Esta casa es
distinta de la otra.
frond (frand) *n.* fronda.
front (frʌnt) *n.* **1,** (foremost part or
position) frente. **2,** (outward appearance or aspect) fachada; apariencia.
3, *mil.* frente. **4,** *colloq.* (ostentation
of wealth, importance, etc.)
fachenda; ostentación. **5,** (business
firm, noted individual, etc., used as
a cover up) pantalla; tapujo. **6,**
(front part of a shirt) pechera. **7,**
(front part of a book) comienzo;
principio. —*adj.* delantero; de

adelante; de frente; anterior. —*v.t.*
hacer frente a; dar o caer a. —*v.i.*
estar al frente o de frente; dar
frente. —**front door,** puerta de entrada. —**front page,** primera plana.
—**in front of,** al o en frente de;
frente a; delante de.

frontage ('frʌn·tɪdʒ) *n.* frente;
fachada; extensión delantera.

frontal ('frʌn·təl) *adj.* frontal.

frontier (frʌn'tɪr) *n.* frontera.
—*adj.* fronterizo. —**frontiersman**
(-'tɪrz·mən) *n.* hombre de la
frontera; colonizador.

frontispiece ('frʌn·tɪs·pis) *n.*
frontispicio.

frost (frɔst) *n.* **1,** (frozen dew)
escarcha. **2,** (freezing weather)
helada. **3,** (frozen or icy state) hielo.
4, (coldness of manner) hielo;
frialdad. **5,** *slang* (failure) fracaso;
plancha. —*v.t.* **1,** (cover with frost)
cubrir de escarcha. **2,** (injure by
freezing) helar; dañar la helada las
mieses, frutas, etc. **3,** (cover with
frosting) escarchar; garapiñar. **4,**
(give a frosty finish to, as glass)
escarchar; esmerilar.

frostbite ('frɔst·baɪt) *n.* congelación; congelamiento; quemadura.
—**frostbitten,** *adj.* quemado por el
frío.

frosting ('frɔs·tɪŋ) *n.* **1,** (sugar
coating) escarchado; garapiña. **2,**
(finish, as on glass) escarchado;
esmerilado.

frosty ('frɔs·ti) *adj.* **1,** (cold; freezing) helado; frígido; frío. **2,** (covered with or as with frost)
escarchado. **3,** (cold in manner or
feeling) frío. **4,** (gray, as from age)
canoso.

froth (frɔθ) *n.* espuma. —*v.t.* hacer
espumar. —*v.i.* espumar; echar
espuma.

frothy ('frɔθ·i) *adj.* **1,** (foamy)
espumante; espumoso. **2,** (insubstantial) ligero; insubstancial.

froward ('fro·wərd) *adj.* indócil;
díscolo. —**frowardness,** *n.*
indocilidad.

frown (fraun) *n.* ceño. —*v.i.*
fruncirse; arrugar el entrecejo.
—**frown on** o **upon,** desaprobar de;
mirar con malos ojos.

frowzy ('frau·zi) *adj.* desaliñado.
—**frowziness,** *n.* desaliño.

froze (froz) *v., pret. de* **freeze.**

frozen ('fro·zən) *adj.* **1,** (frigid;
cold) helado. **2,** (congealed; preserved by freezing) congelado. **3,**

(stiff; rigid) helado; rígido. **4,** (not
liquid, as assets) congelado. —*v.,
p.p. de* **freeze.**

fructify ('frʌk·tɪˌfaɪ) *v.i.* fructificar.
—*v.t.* hacer fructificar. —**fructifica-
tion** (-fɪ'keɪ·ʃən) *n.* fructificación.

fructose ('frʌk·tos) *n.* fructosa.

frugal ('fru·gəl) *adj.* frugal.
—**frugality** (fru'gæl·ə·ti) *n.* frugalidad.

fruit (frut) *n.* **1,** (yield: seed of a
plant) fruto. **2,** (sweet fruit of certain plants) fruta. **3,** (result; consequence) fruto; resultado. —**fruitful,**
adj. fructífero; fructuoso. —**fruitless,** *adj.* estéril; infructuoso.

fruiterer ('fru·tər·ər) *n.* frutero.

fruition (fru'ɪʃ·ən) *n.* **1,** (state of
bearing fruit) fructificación. **2,** (attainment; realization) realización;
consecución. **3,** (enjoyment of use
or possession) fruición.

frump (frʌmp) *n.* vieja desastrada y
regañona. —**frumpish,** *adj.*
regañón; a mal traer.

frustrate ('frʌs·tret) *v.t.* frustrar.
—**frustration,** *n.* frustración.

frustum ('frʌs·təm) *n.* tronco.

fry (fraɪ) *v.t.* freír. —*v.i.* freírse;
achicharrarse. —*n.* **1,** (young fish)
pececillo; (young frog) renacuajo.
2, (swarm or brood of young) cría;
cardumen de pececillos o
renacuajos. **3,** (children collectively) chiquillería; enjambre de
niños. **4,** (fried food) frito; fritada;
fritura. —**frying pan,** sartén.

fuchsia ('fju·ʃə) *n.* fucsia.

fuddle ('fʌd·əl) *v.t.* **1,** (intoxicate)
emborrachar. **2,** (confuse) confundir; aturdir.

fudge (fʌdʒ) *n.* **1,** (candy)
melcocha. **2,** (nonsense) tontera;
tontería; paja. —*v.t.* **1,** (botch)
chapucear. **2,** (perform dishonestly)
hacer con trampa. —*v.i.* (cheat)
trampear.

fuel ('fju·əl) *n.* **1,** (combustible material) combustible. **2,** (means of increasing passion, etc.) pábulo; leña.
—*v.t.* abastecer de combustible.
—*v.i.* abastecerse de combustible.

fugitive ('fju·dʒə·tɪv) *adj.* **1,** (fleeing) fugitivo; prófugo. **2,** (evanescent; transitory) fugaz; efímero;
fugitivo. —*n.* fugitivo; prófugo.

fugue (fjuɡ) *n., mus.* fuga.

fulcrum ('fʌl·krəm) *n.* [*pl. también*
fulcra (-krə)] fulcro; punto de
apoyo.

fulfill *también,* **fulfil** (fʊl'fɪl) *v.t.* **1,**

(carry out; complete) cumplir; llevar a cabo; consumar. 2, (perform, as a duty) cumplir; desempeñar. 3, (satisfy, as a desire) colmar; satisfacer. —**fulfillment** [también, **fulfilment**] n. cumplimiento; realización; consumación.

fulgent ('fʌl·dʒənt) adj. fulgente; resplandeciente.

full (ful) adj. 1, (filled to capacity; filled or rounded out; rich; abounding; sated) lleno. 2, (complete; entire) completo; entero; cabal. 3, (with loose, wide folds; ample) lleno; amplio; de mucho vuelo. 4, (having reached full development, size, intensity, etc.) pleno; máximo; todo. 5, (entirely visible) pleno; completo. 6, (sonorous) lleno; sonoro. 7, (filled, as with emotions, thoughts, ideas) lleno; pleno; colmado. —adv. 1, (entirely) enteramente; del todo. 2, (directly) de pleno; de lleno. 3, (very) muy. —n. tope; plenitud. —v.t. abatanar; enfurtir. —**at the full,** pleno; lleno; en (su) plenitud. —**full blast,** con toda fuerza; a todo volumen. —**full dress,** vestido o traje de etiqueta. —**full house,** poker fulján. —**full stop,** 1, (of a vehicle) parada; alto. 2, gram. punto aparte; punto final. —**in full,** por completo; por entero; en (su) totalidad; sin abreviar —**to the full,** completamente; enteramente; de pleno.

full-blooded adj. 1, (of unmixed ancestry) de pura raza. 2, (virile) vigoroso; robusto.

full-blown adj. 1, (in full bloom) en (plena) flor. 2, (fully developed) cabal; pleno.

full-bodied (-'ba·did) adj. de (mucho) cuerpo; que tiene cuerpo; rico.

fuller ('ful·ər) n. 1, (one who treats cloth) batanero. 2, (hammer) mazo de batán. —**fuller's earth,** tierra de batán; greda.

full-fledged ('ful,fledʒd) adj. acabado; cabal; completo; hecho y derecho.

full-grown adj. maduro; completamente desarrollado.

fullness ('ful·nəs) n. 1, (state of being full) plenitud. 2, (satiety) hartura; llenura. 3, (completeness; entirety) integridad; totalidad.

fully ('ful·i) adv. 1, (completely) completamente; enteramente. 2, (copiously) llenamente; abundantemente.

fulminate ('fʌl·mɪ,neit) v.t. & i. 1, (detonate) detonar. 2, (denounce; thunder forth) fulminar. —n. fulminante. —**fulmination,** n. fulminación.

fulsome ('ful·səm) adj. burdo; torpe; grosero. —**fulsomeness,** n. torpeza; grosería.

fumble ('fʌm·bəl) v.t. & i. 1, (grope clumsily) tentar o tantear a ciegas; buscar a tientas. 2, (bungle) chapucear. 3, sports perder (la pelota). —n. 1, (bungle) chapuz. 2, sports pérdida (de la pelota). —**fumbling** (-blɪŋ) adj. chapucero. —n. tanteo; tentativa.

fume (fjum) n., usu.pl. humo; gas; vapor; vaho. —v.i. 1, (emit fumes) humear; exhalar vahos o vapores. 2, (be vexed; fret) echar humo; encolerizarse; enojarse. —v.t. ahumar; sahumar; fumigar. —**fumed,** adj. ahumado.

fumigate ('fju·mɪ,geit) v.t. fumigar; sahumar. —**fumigant** (-gənt) n. fumigante. —**fumigation,** n. fumigación. —**fumigator,** n. fumigador.

fun (fʌn) n. diversión. —**in fun,** en o de broma; por o como chiste. —**make fun of; poke fun at,** burlarse de; mofarse de.

function ('fʌŋk·ʃən) n. función —v.i. funcionar. —**functional,** adj. funcional. —**functioning,** n. funcionamiento.

functionary ('fʌŋk·ʃə,ner·i) n. funcionario.

fund (fʌnd) n. 1, (stock or supply, esp. of money) fondo; caudal. 2, (store of anything, as of knowledge) acopio; reserva. —v.t. subvencionar; consolidar (una deuda).

fundamental (,fʌn·də'men·təl) adj. fundamental. —n. fundamento.

funeral ('fju·nə·rəl) n. funeral; funerales; exequias. —adj. funerario; fúnebre. —**funeral director,** funerario. —**funeral parlor,** funeraria.

funereal (fju'nɪr·i·əl) adj. fúnebre; funeral.

fungicide ('fʌn·dʒɪ,said) n. fungicida. —**fungicidal,** adj. fungicida.

fungous ('fʌŋ·gəs) adj. fungoso.

fungus ('fʌŋ·gəs) n. [pl. **fungi** ('fʌn·dʒai)] fungo; hongo.

funicular (fju'nɪk·ju·lər) adj. & n. funicular.

funk (fʌŋk) *n., colloq.* **1,** (fear) temor; miedo; pánico. **2,** (coward) miedoso; cobarde. —*v.i., colloq.* acobardarse; amilanarse. —*v.t., colloq.* sacar el cuerpo a; hacer el quite a. —**funky,** *adj., colloq.* miedoso; cobarde.

funnel ('fʌn·əl) *n.* **1,** (device for pouring) embudo. **2,** (smokestack) chimenea. **3,** (shaft for ventilation) tubo o caño de ventilación. —*v.t.* enfocar; concentrar; hacer converger. —*v.i.* enfocarse; concentrarse; converger.

funny ('fʌn·i) *adj.* **1,** (amusing) cómico; divertido; gracioso. **2,** *colloq.* (odd) extraño; raro; curioso. —*n., usu. pl., colloq.* (comic strips) historietas; dibujos. —**funniness,** *n.* comicidad; gracia.

funnybone ('fʌn·i,bon) *n.* **1,** (nerve in the elbow) nervio ulnar. **2,** (sense of humor) sentido del humor.

fur (fʌr) *n.* **1,** (animal hide) piel; pelaje. **2,** (coating on the tongue) saburra; sarro. —**fur shop,** peletería.

furbelow ('fʌr·bə·lo) *n.* **1,** (ruffle) fleco; orla. **2,** (fancy detail) ringorrango; *Amer.* firulete.

furbish ('fʌr·bɪʃ) *v.t.* acicalar; pulir.

furious ('fjʊr·i·əs) *adj.* furioso; violento. —**furiousness,** *n.* furia; violencia.

furl (fʌrl) *v.t.* plegar; recoger (una bandera o vela).

furlong ('fʌr·lɔŋ) *n.* medida de longitud de 220 yardas o ⅛ de milla.

furlough ('fʌr·lo) *n.* licencia.

furnace ('fʌr·nɪs) *n.* horno; calorífero.

furnish ('fʌr·nɪʃ) *v.t.* **1,** (supply; provide; give) surtir; suministrar; proporcionar. **2,** (equip) equipar. **3,** (put furniture into) amueblar; amoblar.

furnishings ('fʌr·nɪʃ·ɪŋz) *n.pl.* **1,** (furniture) moblaje; mobiliario. **2,** (equipment) avíos; enseres **3,** (accessories) accesorios. **4,** (house furnishings) ajuar doméstico; enseres domésticos.

furniture ('fʌr·nɪ·tʃər) *n.* muebles; mobiliario.

furor ('fjʊr·or) *n.* furor.

furred (fʌrd) *adj.* **1,** (made, trimmed, or lined with fur) de piel. **2,** (having fur) que tiene piel o

pelaje; peludo. **3,** (coated, as the tongue) sucio; saburroso; sarroso.

furrier ('fʌr·i·ər) *n.* peletero. —**furriery,** *n.* peletería.

furring ('fʌr·ɪŋ) *n.* **1,** (fur for a garment) piel; pieles. **2,** (in building) enlistonado.

furrow ('fʌr·o) *n.* surco. —*v.t.* surcar.

furry ('fʌr·i) *adj.* peludo; velludo; velloso. —**furriness,** *n.* vellosidad.

further ('fʌr·ðər) *adj.* **1,** (more remote or extended) más lejano; más distante. **2,** (additional) adicional; otro; mayor; más. —*adv.* **1,** (to a greater distance or extent) más lejos; más allá; más adelante. **2,** (also) además; aún; por añadidura. —*v.t.* promover; adelantar; ayudar. —**furtherance,** *n.* adelantamiento; promoción; medra.

furthermore ('fʌr·ðər·mor) *adv.* además.

furthermost ('fʌr·ðər·most) *adj.* más lejano.

furthest (fʌr·ðɪst) *adj.* más lejano; más distante. —*adv.* más lejos; más allá.

furtive ('fʌr·tɪv) *adj.* furtivo. —**furtiveness,** *n.* sigilo; secreto.

furuncle ('fjʊr·ʌŋ·kəl) *n.* furúnculo.

fury ('fjʊ·ri) *n.* furia.

furze (fʌrz) *n.* tojo; aulaga.

fuse (fjuz) *n.* **1,** (powder wick) mecha. **2,** (detonating device) espoleta. **3,** *elect.* fusible; cortacircuitos. —*v.t.* fundir. —*v.i.* fundirse.

fuselage ('fju·sə·lɪdʒ) *n.* fuselaje.

fusible ('fju·zɪ·bəl) *adj.* fusible; fundible. —**fusibility,** *n.* fusibilidad.

fusilier (,fju·zə'lɪr) *n.* fusilero.

fusillade (,fju·zə'leid) *n.* descarga de fusilería.

fusion ('fju·ʒən) *n.* fusión.

fuss (fʌs) *n.* **1,** (bustle; ado) aspavientos; bulla; alharacas. **2,** *colloq.* (petty quarrel) riña; reyerta; pleito. —*v.i.* agitarse; hacer aspavientos o alharacas. —*v.t.* turbar; fastidiar.

fussy ('fʌs·i) *adj.* **1,** (fretful; peevish) quisquilloso. **2,** (bustling) aspaventero; alharaquiento. **3,** (fastidious) prolijo; nimio; difícil de complacer. **4,** (bothersome) fastidioso; molesto.

fustian ('fʌs·tʃən) *n.* **1,** (coarse cotton fabric) fustán. **2,** (high-flown language) altisonancia; grandilocuencia.

fusty ('fʌs·ti) *adj.* 1, (musty; stuffy) rancio. 2, (old-fashioned) anticuado; del tiempo de Maricastaña. —**fustiness,** *n.* 1, ranciedad. 2, antigüedad.

futile ('fju·təl) *adj.* fútil. —**futility** (fju·tɪl·ə·ti) *n.* futilidad.

future ('fju·tʃər) *adj.* futuro. —*n.* futuro; porvenir; *pl.*, *comm.* futuros.

futurism ('fju·tʃər·ɪz·əm) *n.* futurismo. —**futuristic,** *adj.* futurista.

futurity (fju·tjʊr·ə·ti) *n.* futuro; porvenir.

fuzz (fʌz) *n.* 1, pelusa; pelusilla; vello. 2, *slang* (police; police officer) policía. —**fuzzy,** *adj.* velloso; cubierto de pelusa. —**fuzziness,** *n.* vellosidad.

G

G, g (dʒi) séptima letra del alfabeto inglés. —*n.* 1, *mus.* sol. 2, gravedad. 3, fuerza atractiva de la gravedad. 4, *slang* = **grand** (mil dólares).

gab (gæb) *n.*, *colloq.* parloteo; locuacidad. —*v.i.*, *colloq.* [**gabbed, gabbing**] parlotear. —**gabby,** *adj.*, *colloq.* parlanchín. —**gift of gab,** labia; elocuencia.

gabardine ('gæb·ər‚din) *n.* garbardina. —*adj.* de garbardina.

gabble ('gæb·əl) *n.* parloteo; cotorreo; cháchara. —*v.i.* parlotear; cotorrear.

gable ('gei·bəl) *n.* gablete; faldón. —**gable roof,** tejado a dos aguas.

gad (gæd) *n.* aguijón; aguijada; rejo. —*v.i.* [**gadded, gadding**] vagar; callejear. —*interj.*, *slang* ¡Dios! —**gadder** [*también,* **gadabout**] *n.* callejero; vagabundo.

gadfly ('gæd·flai) *n.* tábano; moscardón.

gadget ('gædʒ·ɪt) *n.* artefacto.

gadolinium (‚gæd·ə'lɪn·i·əm) *n.* gadolinio.

Gaelic ('gei·lɪk) *adj.* & *n.* gaélico.

gaff (gæf) *n.* 1, (hook) garfio. 2, *naut.* (spar) cangrejo; botavara; pico. 3, *slang* (nuisance) vaina; *Amer.* friega. —**stand the gaff,** *slang* ser de aguante.

gag (gæg) *n.* 1, (silencer) mordaza. 2, *slang* (joke) broma; burla; chiste. —*v.t.* [**gagged, gagging**] 1, (silence) amordazar; silenciar. 2, (cause to retch) atragantar. —*v.i.* atragantarse.

gaiety *también,* **gayety** ('gei·ə·ti) *n.* alegría; alborozo; júbilo.

gaily *también,* **gayly** ('gei·li) *adv.* 1, (merrily) alegremente. 2, (showily) vistosamente.

gain (gein) *n.* 1, (profit) ganancia. 2, (improvement); adelanto; mejora. 3, (benefit) beneficio;

provecho; utilidad. 4, (increase) aumento; acrecentamiento. —*v.t.* 1, (get; obtain) ganar; obtener. 2, (win; earn) ganar. 3, (reach; achieve) ganar; alcanzar. 4, (acquire as an increase or addition) aumentar (en). —*v.i.* 1, (benefit) aprovechar; ganar. 2, (progress; improve) adelantar; mejorar. 3, (put on weight) aumentar de peso. 4, (run fast, as a watch) adelantarse. —**gain on** o **upon,** ir alcanzando a; ganar terreno; acercarse a.

gainful ('gein·fəl) *adj.* remunerativo; útil; provechoso.

gainsay ('gein'sei) *v.t.* [*pret.* & *p.p.* **gainsaid**] contradecir; negar; desmentir.

gait (geit) *n.* paso; andar; modo de andar.

gaiter ('gei·tər) *n.* polaina corta.

gal (gæl) *n.*, *colloq.* mujer; muchacha.

gala ('gei·lə; 'gæl·ə) *n.* fiesta; gala. —*adj.* festivo; de gala; de fiesta.

galaxy ('gæl·ək·si) *n.* galaxia. —**galactic** (gə'læk·tɪk) *adj.* galáctico.

gale (geil) *n.* 1, (strong wind) ventarrón. 2, (outburst, as of laughter) explosión.

gall (gɔl) *n.* 1, (liver secretion) bilis; hiel. 2, (something bitter or distasteful) hiel. 3, (rancor; bitter feeling) rencor; inquina. 4, (sore, as on a horse) matadura. 5, *bot.* agalla. 6, *colloq.* (impudence) desfachatez; descaro; agallas. —*v.t.* & *i.* 1, (chafe) irritar; desollar. 2, (annoy; vex) irritar; molestar; *Amer.* fregar. —**gall bladder,** vesícula biliar.

gallant ('gæl·ənt) *adj.* 1, (brave; daring) gallardo; bizarro. 2, (courtly) galante; galán. 3, (stately; impressive) impresionante; fastuoso. —*n.* (gə'lænt) galán.

gallantry ('gæl·ən·tri) n. **1,** (bravery) gallardía; bizarría. **2,** (courtly act or manner) galantería; galanteo.

galleon ('gæl·i·ən) n. galeón.

gallery 'gæl·ə·ri) n. galería.

galley ('gæl·i) n. **1,** (ship) galera. **2,** (ship's kitchen) cocina de un barco. **3,** print. galera. —**galley slave,** galeote.

Gallic ('gæl·ɪk) adj. galo.

Gallicism ('gæl·ə·sɪz·əm) n. galicismo. —**Gallicize,** v.t. afrancesar.

gallinaceous (gæl·ə'nei·ʃəs) adj. gallináceo.

gallium ('gæl·i·əm) n. galio.

gallivant ('gæl·ɪ,vænt) v.i. callejear; vagar.

gallon ('gæl·ən) n. medida para líquidos equivalente a 4.5 litros; galón.

gallop ('gæl·əp) n. galope. —v.i. galopar.

gallows ('gæl·oz) n. horca; patíbulo.

gallstone (gɔl,ston) n. cálculo biliar.

galore (gə'lo:r) adv. en abundancia; por montones.

galosh (gə'laʃ) n. chanclo; galocha.

galvanic (gæl'væn·ɪk) adj. **1,** elect. galvánico. **2,** fig. (startling) electrizante.

galvanism ('gæl·və·nɪz·əm) n. galvanismo.

galvanize ('gæl·və,naiz) v.t. galvanizar. —**galvanization** (-nɪ'zei·ʃən) n. galvanización.

galvanometer (,gæl·və'nam·ə·tər) n. galvanómetro.

gambit ('gæm·bɪt) n. gambito.

gamble ('gæm·bəl) v.i. **1,** (play games of chance) jugar. **2,** (take a risk) arriesgarse. —v.t. **1,** (bet; wager) apostar; jugar. **2,** [también, **gamble away**] (lose in gambling) perder; jugarse. —n. albur; riesgo. —**gambler** (-blər) n. jugador. —**gambling** (-blɪŋ) n. juego. —**gambling den,** casa de juego; garito.

gambol ('gæm·bəl) n. retozo; cabriola. —v.i. retozar; dar cabriolas.

game (geim) n. **1,** (play; sport) juego. **2,** (contest) partido. **3,** (trick; scheme) jugada. **4,** (in hunting) caza. —adj. **1,** (of animals) de caza. **2,** (plucky; willing) animoso; resuelto. **3,** (lame) cojo. —**gameness,** n. ánimo; resolución. —**game bag,** morral. —**game plan,**

estrategia de juego. —**make game of,** reírse de; burlarse de. —**play the game,** seguir el juego.

gamecock ('geim,kak) n. gallo de pelea.

gamekeeper ('geim,ki·pər) n. guardabosque.

gamete ('gæm·it) n. gameto

gamin ('gæm·ɪn) n. pilluelo; golfillo.

gaming ('gei·mɪŋ) n. juego.

gamma ('gæm·ə) n. gamma. —**gamma rays,** rayos gamma.

gammon ('gæm·ən) n. **1,** (smoked ham) jamón ahumado; pernil. **2,** (trickery) engaño; añagaza.

gamut ('gæm·ət) n. gama.

gamy ('gei·mi) adj. **1,** (of meat) que sabe o huele a carne de caza. **2,** (plucky) valeroso; osado.

gander ('gæn·dər) n. **1,** ganso. **2,** slang mirada; escrutinio.

gang (gæŋ) n. cuadrilla; pandilla. —v.i. **1,** (band together) unirse; organizarse. **2,** (pile up) amontonarse. —**gangland,** n. hampa; mundo de vicio. —**gang up on,** unirse u organizarse contra.

gangling ('gæŋ·glɪŋ) adj. desgarbado.

ganglion ('gæŋ·gli·ən) n. ganglio.

gangplank ('gæŋ·plæŋk) n. pasarela; plancha.

gangrene ('gæŋ·grin) n. gangrena. —**gangrenous** (-grə·nəs) adj. gangrenoso.

gangster ('gæŋ·stər) n. pistolero; gangster.

gangue (gæŋ) n. ganga.

gangway ('gæŋ·wei) n. **1,** (passageway) paso; pasadizo. **2,** naut. pasarela; portalón. —interj. ¡a un lado!; ¡abran paso!; ¡paso!

gannet ('gæn·ɪt) n. bubia.

gantlet ('gɔnt·lət; 'gænt-) n. (punishment) baqueta. También, **gauntlet.** —**run the gantlet,** correr la baqueta.

gantry ('gæn·tri) n. **1,** (framework) armazón. **2,** (movable bridge of a crane) puente corredizo de grúa. También, **gauntry** ('gɔn·tri).

gaol (dʒeil) n. Brit. = **jail.**

gap (gæp) n. **1,** (opening; breach) brecha; boquete; hendidura. **2,** (interruption of continuity) hueco; vacío; laguna. **3,** (difference) diferencia; discrepancia; laguna. **4,** (distance that separates) distancia; luz.

gape (geip) v.i. **1,** (yawn; open the

mouth) bostezar; abrir la boca. **2,** (open wide) abrirse. **3,** (stare open-mouthed) quedarse boquiabierto; embobarse. —*n.* **1,** (yawn) bostezo. **2,** (openmouthed stare) boca abierta. **3,** (breach; gap) brecha; hendidura.

gar (ga:r) *n.* pez aguja. *También,* **garfish.**

garage (gə'ra:ჳ) *n.* garaje. —*v.t.* meter en garaje.

garb (garb) *n.* **1,** (clothing) vestido; indumentaria. **2,** *fig.* (guise) aspecto; apariencia. —*v.t.* vestir; ataviar.

garbage ('gar·bɪdჳ) *n.* basura.

garble ('gar·bəl) *v.t.* **1,** (jumble) hacer confuso; hacer un revoltijo de. **2,** (distort; misrepresent) torcer; tergiversar. —*n.* confusión; revoltijo.

garden ('gar·dən) *n.* jardín. —*v.i.* cuidar un jardín. —**gardener,** *n.* jardinero. —**gardening,** *n.* jardinería.

gardonia (gar'di·njə) *n.* gardenia.

garfish *n.* = **gar.**

Gargantuan (gar'gænt·ju·ən) *adj.* enorme; gigantesco.

gargle ('gar·gəl) *n.* gárgara; gargarismo. —*v.i.* gargarizar; hacer gárgaras.

gargoyle ('gar·gɔil) *n.* gárgola.

garish ('gɛr·ɪʃ) *adj.* llamativo; chillón. —**garishness,** *n.* lo llamativo; lo chillón.

garland ('gar·lənd) *n.* guirnalda. —*v.t.* enguirnaldar; adornar con guirnaldas.

garlic ('gar·lɪk) *n.* ajo. —**garlicky,** *adj.* de o con ajo.

garment ('gar·mənt) *n.* vestido; traje. —**garments,** *n.pl.* ropa.

garner ('gar·nər) *v.t.* **1,** (gather; reap) cosechar; recoger. **2,** (store) almacenar. —*n.* **1,** (granary) granero. **2,** (storage place) depósito; almacén.

garnet ('gar·nɪt) *n.* granate.

garnish ('gar·nɪʃ) *n.* adorno; aderezo. —*v.t.* **1,** (adorn) adornar; aderezar. **2,** *law* = **garnishee.** —**garnishment,** *n., law* embargo.

garnishee (,gar·nɪ'ʃiː) *v.t.* [-**sheed,** -**sheeing**] *law* embargar.

garret ('gɛr·ət) *n.* desván; buhardilla.

garrison ('gær·ə·sən) *n.* guarnición. —*v.t.* **1,** (provide with a garrison) guarnecer. **2,** (station, as troops) acuartelar.

garrote *también,* **garotte, garrotte** (gə'rot) *n.* garrote. —*v.t.* agarrotar.

garrulity (gə'ru·lə·ti) *n.* garrulidad; locuacidad. *También,* **garrulousness.**

garrulous ('gær·jə·ləs) *adj.* gárrulo; locuaz.

garter ('gar·tər) *n.* liga. —**Order of the Garter,** Orden de la Jarretera.

gas (gæs) *n.* **1,** (vapor) gas. **2,** *colloq.* (gasoline) gasolina. **3,** *slang* (idle talk) vaciedad. —*v.t.* [**gassed, gassing**] **1,** (supply with gas) suministrar gas a. **2,** (attack, poison or kill by gas) atacar, envenenar o matar con gases. —*v.i., slang* (talk idly) decir vaciedades. —**gas burner,** mechero o quemador de gas. —**gas chamber,** cámara de gas. —**gas mask,** careta antigás.

gaseous ('gæs·i·əs) *adj.* gaseoso.

gash (gæʃ) *n.* tajo. —*v.t.* dar un tajo o tajos a.

gasket ('gæs·kɪt) *n.* empaquetadura.

gasoline *también,* **gasolene** (,gæs·ə'lin) *n.* gasolina.

gasp (gæsp) *n.* **1,** (labored breath) jadeo; boqueada. **2,** (convulsive utterance) grito sofocado. —*v.t.* **1,** (breathe out) exhalar. **2,** (utter convulsively) decir jadeando. —*v.i.* jadear; dar boqueadas.

gastric ('gæs·trɪk) *adj.* gástrico.

gastritis (gæs'trai·tɪs) *n.* gastritis.

gastronomy (gæs'tran·ə·mi) *n.* gastronomía. —**gastronomic** (,gæs·trə'nam·ɪk) [*también,* **gastronomical**] *adj.* gastronómico. —**gastronome** ('gæs·trə,nom) *n.* gastrónomo.

gate (geit) *n.* **1,** (opening; entrance) portón; puerta. **2,** (barrier) barrera. **3,** *slang* (gate receipts) entrada; taquilla. **4,** *slang* (dismissal) despedida. —**give the gate to,** *slang* largar; mandar a paseo.

gatehouse ('geit,haus) *n.* portería.

gatekeeper ('geit,ki·pər) *n.* portero; *R.R.* guardabarreras.

gateway ('geit·wei) *n.* entrada; puerta.

gather ('gæð·ər) *v.t.* **1,** (pick; cull; pick up) recoger. **2,** (accumulate; amass) acumular; amasar. **3,** (assemble) juntar; reunir. **4,** (infer) deducir; inferir. **5,** (pleat; draw into folds) plegar; recoger. **6,** (prepare or collect, as oneself) aprestarse; aprontarse. **7,** (regain one's composure) reponerse; recobrarse. **8,** (gain, as speed) coger; cobrar; tomar (velocidad, vuelo, etc.). **9,** (wrinkle, as the brow) arrugar. —*v.i.* **1,** (assemble) reunirse; congregarse. **2,** (accumulate) acumularse; amontonarse. —*n.* pliegue.

gathering ('gæð·ər·ɪŋ) *n.* **1,** (meeting; assembly) reunión. **2,** (collection) recogida; recolección. **3,** (heap; crowd) amontonamiento; montón.

gauche (goʃ) *adj.* torpe; desmañado.

gaucho ('gau·tʃo) *n.* [*pl.* **-chos**] gaucho. —*adj.* gauchesco.

gaudy ('gɔ·di) *adj.* charro; llamativo. —**gaudiness,** *n.* charrada.

gauge (geidʒ) *n.* **1,** (measure) medida; tamaño; dimensión. **2,** (caliber) calibre. **3,** (thickness, as of wire) grosor; calibre. **4,** *R.R.* vía. **5,** (calibrator) calibrador. **6,** (indicator) indicador. —*v.t.* medir; calibrar; estimar; calcular.

Gaul (gɔl) *n.* **1,** (country) Galia. **2,** (person) galo.

gaunt (gɔnt) *adj.* **1,** (thin; emaciated) flaco; demacrado. **2,** (desolate; grim) desolado; sombrío. —**gauntness,** *n.* flacura.

gauntlet ('gɔnt·lət) *n.* **1,** (glove) guantelete; manopla. **2,** *fig.* (challenge) reto. **3,** = **gantlet.** —**throw down the gauntlet,** retar. —**take up the gauntlet,** recoger el guante; aceptar el reto.

gauze (gɔz) *n.* gasa; cendal.

gave (geiv) *v., pret. de* **give.**

gavel ('gæv·əl) *n.* mazo o martillo (*de quien preside una asamblea, un tribunal, etc.*).

gavotte (gə'vat) *n.* gavota.

gawk (gɔk) *n.* ganso; bobo. —*v.i.* papar moscas; mirar como bobo. —**gawky,** *adj.* desmañado; desgarbado.

gay (gei) *adj.* **1,** alegre; jovial; festivo. **2,** homosexual. —*n.* homosexual. —**gayety** (-ə·ti) *n.* = **gaiety.** —**gayly,** *adv.* = **gaily.** —**gayness,** *n.* jovialidad; viveza; alegría.

gaze (geiz) *v.i.* mirar. —*n.* mirada. —**gaze at o on,** mirar; contemplar.

gazelle (gə'zɛl) *n.* gacela.

gazette (gə'zɛt) *n.* gaceta. —*v.t.* publicar en la gaceta.

gazetteer (ˌgæz·ə'tir) *n.* diccionario o índice geográfico.

gear (gɪr) *n.* **1,** (apparel) atavío;

indumentaria. **2,** (equipment; rigging) equipo; avíos; aparejo; aparejos. **3,** (harness) arneses; arreos. **4,** *mech.* (gear system) engranaje; sistema de engranaje; *auto.* embrague; cambio; cambio de velocidades. **5,** *mech.* (specific gear adjustment) velocidad; cambio. **6,** *mech.* (gearwheel) rueda dentada o de engranaje. **7,** *mech.* (mechanism) mecanismo; aparato; sistema. —*v.t.* **1,** (equip; fit out) equipar. **2,** (adapt) ajustar; adaptar; acomodar. **3,** *mech.* (furnish with gears) poner engranajes a. **4,** *mech.* (put into gear) hacer engranar; embragar. —*v.i.* engranar. —**high gear,** tercera o alta (velocidad). —**in high gear,** en tercera o alta (velocidad); *fig.,* *colloq.* embalado; a toda máquina. —**in gear,** embragado. —**low gear,** primera (velocidad). —**in low gear,** en primera (velocidad); *fig., colloq.* lentamente; despacio. —**out of gear,** desembragado, desengranado; *fig., colloq.* desajustado; en desajuste. —**reverse gear,** marcha atrás. —**shift gears,** cambiar (de velocidad). —**throw into gear,** embragar; hacer engranar. —**throw out of gear,** desembragar; desengranar.

gearbox ('gɪrˌbaks) *n.* caja de cambios; caja de engranajes.

gearing ('gɪr·ɪŋ) *n.* engranaje.

gearshift ('gɪrˌʃɪft) *n.* embrague; cambio de velocidades. —**gearshift lever,** palanca de cambios.

gearwheel ('gɪrˌhwil) *n.* rueda dentada.

gee (dʒiː) *v.t. & i.* [**geed, geeing**] volver a derecha. —*interj., colloq.* ¡cielos!; ¡Jesús! —**gee up!,** ¡arre!

geese (giːs) *n., pl. de* **goose.**

geisha ('gei·ʃə) *n.* geisha.

gel (dʒɛl) *n.* materia gelatinosa, producida por la coagulación. —*v.i.* cuajarse.

gelatine ('dʒɛl·ə·tɪn) *n.* gelatina. —**gelatinous** (dʒə'læt·ɪ·nəs) *adj.* gelatinoso.

geld (gɛld) *v.t.* castrar; capar. —**gelding,** *n.* caballo castrado.

gelid ('dʒɛl·ɪd) *adj.* gélido; helado. —**gelidity** (dʒə'lɪd·ə·ti); **gelidness,** *n.* frialdad.

gem (dʒɛm) *n.* gema; joya. —*v.t.* enjoyar; engastar de joyas.

geminate ('dʒɛm·ə·nət) *adj. & n.* geminado. —*v.t.* (-ˌneit) geminar.

—*v.i.* geminarse. —**gemination,** *n.* geminación.

Gemini ('dʒɛm·ə,nai) *n.* Géminis.

gendarme ('ʒan·darm) *n.* gendarme.

gender ('dʒɛn·dər) *n.* género.

gene (dʒiːn) *n.* gen; gene.

genealogy (,dʒi·ni'æl·ə·dʒi) *n.* genealogía. —**genealogical** (-ə·'ladʒ·ɪ·kəl) *adj.* genealógico. —**genealogist,** *n.* genealogista.

genera ('dʒɛn·ə·rə) *n.,* *pl.* de **genus.**

general ('dʒɛn·ər·əl) *adj.* & *n.* general. —**in general,** en general; por lo general. —**general delivery,** lista de correos. —**general staff,** estado mayor. —**general store,** tienda de comestibles y ultramarinos; *Amer.* pulpería; *Amer.* almacén.

generalissimo (,dʒən·ə·rə'lɪs·ɪ·moʊ) *n.* generalísimo.

generality (,dʒɛn·ər'æl·ə·ti) *n.* generalidad.

generalize ('dʒɛn·ər·ə,laiz) *v.i.* generalizar. —**generalization** (-lɪ'zei·ʃən) *n.* generalización.

generalship ('dʒɛn·ər·əl,ʃɪp) *n.* **1,** (rank) generalato. **2,** (leadership) capacidad directiva; dotes de general. **3,** (tactics) táctica.

generate ('dʒɛn·ə,reit) *v.t.* generar; engendrar. —**generative,** *adj.* generativo.

generation (,dʒɛn·ə'rei·ʃən) *n.* generación.

generator ('dʒɛn·ə,rei·tər) *n.* generador.

generic (dʒɪ'nɛr·ɪk) *adj.* genérico.

generous ('dʒɛn·ər·əs) *adj.* generoso. —**generosity** (-ə'ras·ə·ti) *n.* generosidad.

genesis ('dʒɛn·ə·sɪs) *n.* [*pl.* -ses (-siz)] génesis.

genetic (dʒɪ'nɛt·ɪk) *adj.* **1,** (of genetics or reproduction) genésico. **2,** (of genesis or origin) genético.

genetics (dʒɪ'nɛt·ɪks) *n.* genética.

genial ('dʒin·jəl) *adj.* **1,** (amiable) afable; cordial. **2,** (mild, as a climate) suave; agradable.

genie ('dʒi·ni) *n.* genio.

genital ('dʒɛn·ə·təl) *adj.* genital. —**genitals,** *n.pl.* genitales.

genitive ('dʒɛn·ə·tɪv) *n.* & *adj.* genitivo.

genius ('dʒin·jəs) *n.* genio.

genocide ('dʒɛn·ə·said) *n.* genocidio. —**genocidal,** *adj.* genocida.

genre ('ʒan·rə) *n.* género; clase.

gent (dʒɛnt) *n., colloq., contr. de* **gentleman.**

genteel (dʒɛn'til) *adj.* **1,** (wellbred; refined) gentil. **2,** (elegant; fashionable) elegante; distinguido. **3,** (affected) afectado; cursi.

gentian ('dʒɛn·ʃən) *n.* genciana.

gentile ('dʒɛn·tail) *adj.* & *n.* **1,** (pagan) gentil. **2,** (non-Jewish) no judío; cristiano. **3,** *gram.* gentilicio.

gentility (dʒɛn'tɪl·ə·ti) *n.* **1,** (nobility) nobleza. **2,** (gentleness) gentileza.

gentle ('dʒɛn·təl) *adj.* **1,** (wellborn) noble. **2,** (well-bred; refined) gentil; fino; delicado. **3,** (light) leve; ligero; liviano. **4,** (kind; generous) gentil; amable. **5,** (tame) manso; dócil. **6,** (mild; soft) apacible; suave.

gentleman ('dʒɛn·təl·mən) *n.* [*pl.* -men] caballero; señor. —**gentlemanly,** *adj.* caballeroso. —**gentlewoman,** *n.* dama; señora.

gentleness ('dʒɛn·təl·nəs) *n.* **1,** (lightness; mildness) suavidad; delicadeza. **2,** (kindness) gentileza. **3,** (tameness) docilidad; mansedumbre.

gentry ('dʒɛn·tri) *n.* clase acomodada; alta burguesía.

genuflect ('dʒɛn·ju,flɛkt) *v.i.* hacer genuflexión. —**genuflection; genuflexion** (-'flɛk·ʃən) *n.* genuflexión.

genuine ('dʒɛn·ju·ɪn) *adj.* genuino.

genuineness ('dʒɛn·ju·ɪn·nəs) *n.* **1,** (authenticity) legitimidad; autenticidad. **2,** (sincerity) sinceridad; pureza.

genus ('dʒi·nəs) *n.* [*pl.* **genera**] género.

geocentric (,dʒi·o'sɛn·trɪk) *adj.* geocéntrico.

geode ('dʒi·oʊd) *n.* geoda.

geodesy (dʒi'ad·ə·si) *n.* geodesia. —**geodetic** (,dʒi·ə'dɛt·ɪk) *adj.* geodésico. —**geodesic** (-'dɛs·ɪk) *adj.* geodésico.

geography (dʒi'ag·rə·fi) *n.* geografía. —**geographer,** *n.* geógrafo. —**geographic** (,dʒi·ə'græf·ɪk); **geographical,** *adj.* geográfico.

geology (dʒi'al·ə·dʒi) *n.* geología. —**geological** (,dʒi·ə'ladʒ·ɪ·kəl) *adj.* geológico. —**geologist,** *n.* geólogo.

geometry (dʒi'am·ə·tri) *n.* geometría. —**geometric** (,dʒi·ə'mɛt·rɪk); **geometrical,** *adj.* geométrico. —**geometrician** (,dʒi·ə·mə'trɪʃ·ən) *n.* geómetra.

geophysics (,dʒi·o'fɪz·ɪks) n. geofísica. —**geophysical,** adj. geofísico. —**geophysicist,** n. geofísico.

geopolitics (,dʒi·o'pal·ə·tɪks) n.pl. geopolítica. —**geopolitical,** adj. geopolítico.

geranium (dʒə'rei·ni·əm) n. geranio.

geriatrics (,dʒer·i'æt·rɪks) n. geriatría. —**geriatric,** adj. geriátrico.

germ (dʒʌrm) n. germen; embrión. —**germ cell,** célula embrionaria.

German ('dʒʌr·mən) n. & adj. alemán; germano. —**Germanic** (dʒər'mæn·ɪk) adj. germánico. —**German measles,** viruelas locas; rubéola.

germane (dʒər'mein) adj. relacionado; afín.

germanium (dʒər'mei·ni·əm) n. germanio.

germicide ('dʒʌr·mɪ·said) n. germicida. —**germicidal,** adj. germicida.

germinal ('dʒʌr·mə·nəl) adj. germinal.

germinate ('dʒʌr·mə,neit) v.i. germinar. —**germination,** n. germinación.

gerontology (,dʒer·ən'tal·ə·dʒi) n. gerontología. —**gerontologist,** n. gerontólogo.

gerund ('dʒer·ənd) n. gerundio.

gest (dʒest) n. gesta.

gestate ('dʒes·teit) v.t. gestar. —**gestation,** n. gestación.

gesticulate (dʒes'tɪk·jə,leit) v.i. gesticular. —**gesticulation,** n. gesticulación.

gesture ('dʒes·tʃər) n. gesto; ademán. —v.i. gesticular; hacer gestos. —v.t. indicar por o con gestos.

get (get) v.t. [**got** o **gotten, getting**] **1,** (receive) recibir. **2,** (obtain; acquire) conseguir; lograr; obtener. **3,** (gain; earn) ganar. **4,** (reach; contact) comunicarse con; ponerse en contacto con. **5,** radio; TV (tune in) sintonizar; captar. **6,** (fetch; bring) traer. **7,** (catch; seize; take hold of) agarrar; coger. **8,** (learn; commit to memory) aprender. **9,** (obtain as a result) tener; obtener (como resultado): When you add one and one you get two, Cuando sumas uno y uno, tienes dos. **10,** (cause to do or be done; bring about) hacer (que); conseguir (que); lograr (que); componérselas (para que): Can you

get the door to close?, ¿Puedes hacer que la puerta se cierre? **11,** (cause to be or become) poner; volver: The smoke gets your face dirty, El humo te pone sucia la cara. **12,** (carry; take; convey) llevar: Get him to the doctor, Llévelo al médico. **13,** (cause to go; send) enviar; mandar: I will get the bill to you tomorrow, Le enviaré la cuenta mañana. **14,** (cause to be carried or conveyed; cause to arrive) hacer llegar; hacer que llegue: Get this letter to the manager, Haz llegar esta carta a manos del gerente. **15,** (prepare) preparar: Will you get dinner for us?, ¿Puedes prepararnos la comida? **16,** archaic = beget. **17,** colloq. (overpower; get control of) dominar; esclavizar; hacer un esclavo de: Liquor will get him, El trago hará de él un esclavo. **18,** colloq. (puzzle; baffle) confundir; dejar confuso. **19,** colloq. (kill; destroy; finish off) acabar con; aniquilar; matar. **20,** slang (perceive) captar; coger: Did you get his expression?, ¿Captaste su expresión? **21,** colloq. (irritate) irritar; molestar; Amer. fregar. **22,** colloq. (strike; hit) dar; pegar: He got him in the nose, Le dio (o pegó) en la nariz. **23,** colloq. (understand; comprehend) comprender; entender. —v.i. **1,** (come; arrive) llegar: When will we get to Lima?, ¿Cuándo llegaremos a Lima? **2,** (be; become; come to be) ponerse; volverse: He got angry, Se puso furioso; se enfureció. Los modismos consistiendo de get y un adjetivo se expresan muchas veces en español por un verbo intransitivo o reflexivo: get married, casarse; get sick, enfermarse; get old, envejecer. **3,** en la voz pasiva (be; become): I got caught in the rain, Me cogió la lluvia; My suit got wet, Se me mojó el traje. **4,** (begin, as to acquire skills, knowledge, attitudes, habits, etc.) empezar a; comenzar a; llegar a: He is getting to dance well, Empieza a bailar bien; He has got to be a big chatterbox, Ha llegado a ser un gran parlanchín. **5,** (manage; contrive) lograr; conseguir; arreglárselas para: Could I get to see the president?, ¿Podría arreglármelas para ver al presidente? —n. prole; cría. —**get about, 1,** (move from place to place) andar;

moverse; andar por aquí y por allá. **2,** (circulate; spread) circular; difundirse. —**get across, 1,** (cross; reach the opposite side) cruzar; atravesar; pasar. **2,** *colloq.* (transmit; impart) hacer comprender o entender. **3,** *colloq.* (be clear; be understood) comprenderse; entenderse; estar claro. **4,** *colloq.* (succeed; gain acceptance) tener aceptación; tener éxito. —**get ahead,** tener éxito; progresar. —**get ahead of,** adelantarse a. —**get along, 1,** (proceed; move on) seguir adelante. **2,** (fare; progress) seguir; irle a uno. **3,** (manage) arreglárselas; componérselas; manejárselas. **4,** (agree) llevarse; entenderse. **5,** (grow older) envejecer; entrar en años. —**get around, 1,** (move about) andar; moverse; andar por aquí y por allá. **2,** (circumvent; avoid) eludir; hacer el quite a; evitar. **3,** (influence; cajole) engatusar; manejar. —**get around to, 1,** (reach) llegar a. **2,** (be ready for) estar listo para. **3,** (attend to) ocuparse de; atender. —**get at, 1,** (reach; approach) alcanzar. **2,** (find out; ascertain) averiguar; llegar a conocer. **3,** *colloq.* (imply; hint) pretender; implicar. **4,** (apply oneself to; attend to) aplicarse a; ocuparse de. **5,** *colloq.* (influence, as by bribery or intimidation) sobornar; intimidar. —**get away, 1,** (leave; start) salir; partir. **2,** (escape) escaparse. **3,** (slip out) zafarse. —**get away with,** *slang* salirse con (la suya); zafarse de; escaparse de. —**get back, 1,** (return) volver; regresar. **2,** (move back) retroceder; echarse atrás. **3,** (recover) recobrar. **4,** *slang* [*usu.* **get back at**] (get revenge) vengarse (de); desquitarse (con). —**get behind, 1,** (give support to) apoyar; prestar apoyo a; ayudar. **2,** = **fall behind.** —**get by, 1,** (pass) pasar. **2,** *colloq.* (escape notice; sneak past) colarse; pasarse; pasar desapercibido. **3,** *colloq.* (survive; manage) arreglárselas; manejárselas; componérselas. —**get down,** bajar; descender. —**get down to,** considerar; abocar; enfrentarse con. —**get even, 1,** (recover one's losses) recuperar; desquitarse. **2,** (retaliate) desquitarse (con). —**get in, 1,** (enter) entrar. **2,** (arrive) llegar. **3,** *colloq.* [*usu.* **get in with**] (ingratiate

oneself) hacer amistad con; ganarse la voluntad de. —**get lost!,** *slang* ¡lárgate!; ¡mándate cambiar! —**get nowhere,** *colloq.* no llegar (o llevar) a ninguna parte. —**get off, 1,** (come down from) bajar de; apearse de. **2,** (leave; go away) marcharse. **3,** (take off; remove) sacar; quitar. **4,** (escape) escaparse; zafarse. **5,** (start; commence) partir; salir; arrancar; comenzar. **6,** (utter, as a joke) salir con o decir (un chiste); tener (una ocurrencia o salida). —**get on, 1,** (go on o into) subir (a); montar (en). **2,** = **get along.** —**get out, 1,** (go out) salir. **2,** (go away) irse; marcharse. **3,** (take out) sacar. **4,** (become known, as a secret) salir a la luz; descubrirse. **5,** (publish) dar a luz; publicar. —**get out of, 1,** (go out from) salir de. **2,** (escape from; avoid) salir de; escapar de; evitar; zafarse de. **3,** (go beyond the reach of, as of sight, hearing, etc.) perderse de; ponerse fuera del alcance de: *to get out of sight,* perderse de vista. **4,** (elicit from) sonsacar de; sacar de. —**get over, 1,** (recover from) recobrarse de; recuperarse de. **2,** = **get across.** **3,** (forget) olvidarse de. —**get ready,** preparar; disponer. —**get rid of,** deshacerse de; zafarse de; sacarse de encima (una cosa o persona). —**get round** = **get around.** —**get there,** *colloq.* triunfar; tener éxito. —**get through, 1,** (finish) terminar. **2,** (manage to survive) sobrevivir; arreglárselas (en); pasar. **3,** *colloq.* = **get across. 4,** (make contact) ponerse en contacto; establecer comunicación. —**get to, 1,** (make contact with) comunicarse con; ponerse en contacto con. **2,** (influence; persuade) convencer; persuadir; influir en el ánimo de. **3,** = **get at.** —**get together, 1,** (bring together; accumulate) acumular; juntar. **2,** (come together) juntarse; reunirse. **3,** *colloq.* (reach agreement) ponerse de acuerdo. —**get up, 1,** (rise) levantarse. **2,** (raise) levantar. **3,** (assemble; organize) levantar; organizar. **4,** (dress up) vestir; ataviar. **5,** (advance; make progress) avanzar; adelantar. **6,** (climb; mount) subir; montar.

getaway ('get·ə·wei) *n., colloq.* **1,** (escape) fuga; huída; escapada. **2,** (start) partida; arranque.

get-together n., colloq. reunión; tertulia.

getup también, **get-up** ('gɛt·ʌp) n., colloq. **1,** (makeup; appearance) apariencia; hechura; facha. **2,** (costume) ropaje; vestimenta.

geyser ('gai·zər) n. géiser.

ghastly ('gæst·li; 'gast-) adj. **1,** (horrible; frightful) horrible; espantoso. **2,** (ghostlike; haggard) cadavérico; lívido. **3,** colloq. (very bad) horrible; pésimo. —adv. horriblemente.

gherkin ('gɑr·kɪn) n. pepinillo.

ghetto ('gɛt·o) n. [pl. **ghettos**] judería; ghetto.

ghost (gost) n. fantasma; espectro. —**ghostly,** adj. espectral. —**ghost writer,** autor de escritos que aparecen con firma de otro; escritor anónimo.

ghoul (guːl) n. vampiro. —**ghoulish,** adj. vampiresco.

G.I. ('dʒi'ai) n., slang soldado del ejército de los EE.UU.

giant ('dʒai·ənt) n. gigante. —adj. gigante; gigantesco. —**giantess,** n.f. giganta. —**giantism,** n. gigantez; gigantismo. También, **gigantism.**

gibber ('dʒɪb·ər) v.i. chapurrear. —**gibberish,** n. jerigonza; cháchara; chapurreo.

gibbet ('dʒɪb·ət) n. horca; patíbulo. —v.t. ahorcar.

gibbon ('gɪb·ən) n. gibón.

gibbous ('gɪb·əs) adj. giboso.

gibe (dzaib) v.t. burlarse de; mofarse de; tirar pullas a. —v.i. burlarse; mofarse. —n. mofa; burla; pulla.

giblets ('dʒɪb·ləts) n.pl. menudillos.

giddap (gɪ'dæp) interj. ¡arre!

giddiness ('gɪd·i·nəs) n. **1,** (dizziness) mareo; vértigo. **2,** (frivolity) frivolidad; atolondramiento.

giddy ('gɪd·i) adj. **1,** (dizzy; dazed) mareado; aturdido. **2,** (causing giddiness, as a height) que da mareo o vértigo. **3,** (frivolous) alocado; atolondrado; frívolo.

gift (gɪft) n. **1,** (present) regalo; obsequio. **2,** (donation) donación; donativo. **3,** (talent) don; talento. —**gifted,** adj. de talento; talentoso. —**gift wrap,** papel de regalo. —**gift-wrap,** v.t. envolver como regalo.

gig (gɪg) n. **1,** (carriage) calesa; cabriolé. **2,** naut. lancha; falúa. **3,**

(toy) trompo; peonza. **4,** slang (demerit) demérito; falta.

gigantic (dʒai'gæn·tɪk) adj. gigantesco; gigante. —**gigantism** (dʒai'gæn·tɪz·əm) n. = **giantism.**

giggle ('gɪg·əl) v.i. reír tontamente o nerviosamente. —n. risita; risa tonta o nerviosa.

gigolo ('dʒɪg·ə·lo) n. [pl. **-los**] gígolo.

gigot ('dʒɪg·ət) n. **1,** (leg of mutton) pierna de carnero. **2,** [también, **gigot sleeve**] (puffed sleeve) manga ajamonada.

gigue (ʒig) n. giga.

gild (gɪld) v.t. [pret. & p.p. **gilded** o **gilt**] dorar. —**gilding,** n. dorado.

gill (gɪl) n. **1,** (fish organ) agalla; branquia. **2,** (dʒɪl) (liquid measure) cuarto de pinta.

gillyflower ('dʒɪl·i,flau·ər) n. alhelí; alelí.

gilt (gɪlt) adj. & n. dorado. —v., pret. & p.p. alt. de **gild.**

gimlet ('gɪm·lɪt) n. barrena; barrena de mano.

gimmick ('gɪm·ɪk) n., slang treta; truco; martingala.

gin (dʒɪn) n. **1,** (liquor) ginebra. **2,** (trap; snare) trampa. **3,** = **cotton gin.** —v.t. [**ginned, ginning**] alijar; desmotar (algodón). —**gin fizz,** ginebra con gaseosa. —**gin rummy,** cierto juego de cartas. —**cotton gin,** alijadora; desmotadora.

ginger ('dʒɪn·dʒər) n. **1,** (spice) jengibre. **2,** colloq. (vigor) vivacidad; energía. —**ginger ale,** gaseosa de jengibre.

gingerbread ('dʒɪn·dʒər,brɛd) n. **1,** (cake) pan de jengibre. **2,** (fancy decoration) decorado excesivo.

gingerly ('dʒɪn·dʒər·li) adj. tímido; cuidadoso. —adv. tímidamente; cuidadosamente. —**gingerliness,** n. cuidado.

gingham ('gɪŋ·əm) n. guinga.

gingivitis (,dʒɪn·dʒə'vai·tɪs) n. gingivitis.

gipsy ('dʒɪp·si) n. & adj. = **gypsy.**

giraffe (dʒə'ræf) n. jirafa.

gird (gʌrd) v.t. [pret. & p.p. **girt** o **girded**] **1,** (fasten with a belt) ceñir. **2,** (encircle; enclose) circundar; rodear. **3,** (prepare for action) preparar; aprestar.

girder ('gʌr·dər) n. viga; durmiente.

girdle ('gʌr·dəl) n. faja; ceñidor. —v.t. ceñir; rodear; circundar.

girl (gʌrl) n. **1,** (young lady) niña;

muchacha; chica. **2,** (servant) moza; criada; sirvienta. **3,** (female assistant) [*también,* **girl Friday**] asistenta. —**girlfriend,** *colloq.* **1,** (consort) amiga íntima. **2,** (sweetheart) novia. —**girlhood,** *n.* niñez; mocedad. —**girlish,** *adj.* de niña; de muchacha.

Girl Scout exploradora.

girt (gʌrt) *v., pret.* & *p.p. de* **gird.**

girth (gʌrθ) *n.* **1,** (cinch) cincha; cinto. **2,** (circumference) circunferencia; *(of the waist)* talle. —*v.t.* ceñir.

gist (dʒɪst) *n.* sustancia; esencia; médula; quid; meollo.

give (gɪv) *v.t.* [**gave, given, giving**] dar. —*v.i.* **1,** (make gifts) hacer regalos; dar. **2,** (yield) ceder; dar; dar de sí. **3,** (be soft or resilient) tener elasticidad; ser muelle. —*n.* elasticidad. —**give away, 1,** (give freely) donar; regalar; dar de balde. **2,** (give in marriage) dar en matrimonio. **3,** (reveal) revelar; dar a conocer. **4,** (betray) traicionar; vender. —**give back,** devolver; restituir. —**give birth,** dar a luz; parir. —**give ear,** escuchar; prestar oídos. —**give forth,** emitir; dar. —**give ground,** retroceder. —**give heed,** atender; hacer caso. —**give in, 1,** (hand in) entregar; presentar. **2,** (yield) ceder; rendirse. —**give it to,** *colloq.* dar una paliza a; zurrarle una a. —**give leave,** dar permiso. —**give off,** emitir; dar. —**give out, 1,** (send forth; emit) emitir; dar. **2,** (make public) dar a conocer. **3,** (distribute) dar; distribuir. **4,** (fail; cease; be exhausted or worn out) terminarse; acabarse; agotarse. —**give over,** entregar. —**give the lie to,** dar (el) mentís a. —**give up, 1,** (hand over; relinquish) entregar; dar. **2,** (surrender) rendirse; darse por vencido. **3,** (cease; stop) dejar; desistir de. **4,** (abandon) abandonar. **5,** (devote wholly) dedicar. **6,** (sacrifice) sacrificar; renunciar. —**give warning,** avisar; advertir. —**give way,** ceder.

give-and-take *n.* toma y daca; tira y afloja.

giveaway ('gɪv·ə·wei) *n., colloq.* **1,** (unintentional betrayal) indicio revelador; revelación. **2,** (gift; premium) obsequio; regalo. —*adj., colloq.* de regalo; de cesión.

given ('gɪv·ən) *p.p. de* **give.** —*adj.* **1,** (bestowed; presented) dado;

regalado. **2,** (prone; accustomed) dado; adicto; inclinado. **3,** (stated; specified) dado; determinado; especificado. **4,** *math.; logic* dado; supuesto. —**given name,** nombre de pila.

giver ('gɪv·ər) *n.* dador; donador. —**giving,** *n.* donación; presentación.

gizzard ('gɪz·ərd) *n.* molleja.

glacé (glæ'sei) *adj.* **1,** (having a glossy surface) lustroso; pulido; glaseado. **2,** (candied) acaramelado; garapiñado.

glacial ('glei·ʃəl) *adj.* glacial.

glacier ('glei·ʃər) *n.* glaciar; ventisquero.

glad (glæd) *adj.* **1,** (happy; pleased) alegre; contento; dichoso. **2,** (pleasing; bright) alegre. —**gladden,** *v.t.* regocijar; alegrar. —*v.i.* regocijarse; alegrarse. —**gladness,** *n.* alegría; gozo; regocijo. —**gladly,** *adv.* alegremente; con (mucho) gusto; gustosamente. —**be glad,** alegrarse; tener mucho gusto; estar gustoso.

glade (gleid) *n.* claro *(de un bosque o floresta).*

gladiator ('glæd·i,ei·tər) *n.* gladiador.

gladiolus (glæd·i'o·ləs) *n.* estoque; gladiolo; *Amer.* gladiola. *También,* **gladiola** (-lə).

gladsome ('glæd·səm) *adj.* alegre; festivo.

glamour *también,* **glamor** ('glæm·ər) *n.* encanto; fascinación; embrujo. —**glamorous,** *adj.* encantador; fascinador; hechicero. —**glamour girl,** *slang* moza maja y bien puesta; *Amer.* mujer chula. —**glamorize,** *v.t.* prestar atracción o atractivo a; embellecer; acicalar.

glance (glæns) *n.* mirada; vistazo; ojeada. —*v.i.* **1,** (strike and be deflected) dar o pegar de refilón. **2,** (give a quick look) echar una ojeada o vistazo. **3,** (flash; gleam) destellar; centellear. —**glancing,** *adj.* de refilón. —**glance off,** rebotar; salir de refilón.

gland (glænd) *n.* glándula. —**glandular** ('glæn·dʒə·lər) *adj.* glandular.

glans (glænz) *n., anat.* bálano; glande.

glare (gleɪr) *n.* **1,** (dazzling light) destello; reflejo; brillo deslumbrante. **2,** (fierce stare) mirada furiosa. —*adj.* lustroso; vidrioso. —*v.i.* **1,** (shine) destellar; relumbrar; brillar. **2,** (look fiercely) mirar con enojo o furiosamente.

glaring ('glɛr·ɪŋ) *adj.* **1,** (dazzlingly bright) destellante; deslumbrante. **2,** (flagrant; obvious) muy evidente; que salta a la vista.

glass (glæs) *n.* **1,** (material) vidrio; cristal. **2,** (container) vaso. **3,** (pane or sheet of glass) luna; vidrio; cristal. **4,** *pl.* (eyeglasses; binoculars) anteojos. —*adj.* de vidrio; de cristal. —*v.t.* encerrar entre vidrios; poner vidrios a. —**glassful** (-ful) *n.* vaso; vaso lleno. —**cut glass,** cristal tallado. —**glass blower,** soplador de vidrio. —**glass case,** vitrina.

glasshouse ('glæs‚haus) *n.* invernáculo; invernadero.

glassware ('glæs·wɛr) *n.* vajilla de cristal; cristalería.

glassy ('glæs·i) *adj.* vidrioso. —**glassiness,** *n.* vidriosidad.

glaucoma (glɔ'ko·ma) *n.* glaucoma.

glaze (gleiz) *n.* **1,** [*también,* **glazing**] (glassy coating) vidriado; lustre. **2,** (film, as on the eyes) vidriosidad. **3,** (sugar coating) garapiña. —*v.t.* **1,** (furnish with glass) encristalar; poner vidrios a. **2,** (put a glaze on or in) vidriar. **3,** (coat with sugar) acaramelar; garapiñar; confitar. —*v.i.* vidriarse.

glazier ('glei·ʒər) *n.* vidriero.

gleam (gliːm) *n.* destello. —*v.i.* destellar; fulgurar; centellear.

glean (gliːn) *v.t. & i.* **1,** (collect, as grain) espigar. **2,** (gather, as information) colegir; recoger; espigar. —**gleaner,** *n.* espigadora. —**gleanings,** *n.pl.* espigaduras.

glee (gliː) *n.* **1,** (gaiety) regocijo; júbilo; alegría. **2,** *mus.* especie de canción para tres o más voces sin acompañamiento. —**gleeful,** *adj.* alegre; gozoso; jubiloso. —**glee club,** grupo coral; coral.

glen (glɛn) *n.* cañada; vallecito.

glib (glɪb) *adj.* desenvuelto; despapajado; desembarazado. —**glibness,** *n.* desenvoltura; desparpajo; desenfado; facilidad.

glide (glaid) *n.* **1,** (sliding) deslizamiento; desliz; movimiento gracioso y fluido. **2,** (in flight) planeo. **3,** *mus.* ligadura. —*v.i.* **1,** (slide) deslizarse. **2,** (in flight) planear. —*v.t.* deslizar; resbalar. —**glider,** *n.* planeador.

glimmer ('glɪm·ər) *n.* **1,** (faint, flickering light) centelleo; titileo;

luz trémula. **2,** (glimpse) vislumbre. —*v.i.* **1,** (shine faintly) centellear; titilar; dar una luz trémula. **2,** (be seen dimly) vislumbrarse.

glimmering ('glɪm·ər·ɪŋ) *n.* = **glimmer**.

glimpse (glɪmps) *n.* vislumbre; vistazo. —*v.t.* vislumbrar.

glint (glɪnt) *n.* destello; centelleo. —*v.i.* destellar; centellear.

glisten ('glɪs·ən) *v.i.* relucir; brillar; tener lustre.

glitch (glɪtʃ) *n., colloq.* leve defecto en un aparato o en un procedimiento.

glitter ('glɪt·ər) *n.* **1,** (sparkling light; brightness) brillo; resplandor; lustre. **2,** (showiness) splendor) brillo; oropel; esplendor. —*v.i.* brillar; resplandecer.

glitz (glɪts) *n., colloq.* brillo; esplendor. —**glitzy,** *adj.* brillante; espléndido.

gloaming ('glo·mɪŋ) *n.* anochecer; anochecida.

gloat (glot) *v.i.* gozar con malicia; relamerse.

glob (glab) *n.* gota; masa

global ('glo·bəl) *adj.* global.

globe (glob) *n.* globo.

globetrotter ('glob‚trat·ər) *n.* trotamundos.

globular ('glab·jə·lər) *adj.* globular. —**globularity** (-'lær·ə·ti) *n.* redondez; esfericidad.

globule ('glab·jul) *n.* glóbulo.

gloom (gluːm) *n.* **1,** (darkness) oscuridad; sombra; lobreguez. **2,** (melancholy feeling) abatimiento; melancolía; tristeza.

gloomy ('glu·mi) *adj.* **1,** (dark; dim) oscuro; sombrío; lóbrego. **2,** (sad; morose) abatido; melancólico; triste. —**gloominess,** *n.* = **gloom**.

glorify ('glor·ɪ‚fai) *v.t.* glorificar. —**glorification** (-fɪ'kei·ʃən) *n.* glorificación.

glorious ('glor·i·əs) *adj.* glorioso.

glory ('glor·i) *n.* gloria. —*v.i.* gloriarse.

gloss (glɔs) *n.* **1,** (shine) lustre; brillo. **2,** (specious appearance) barniz; pátina. **3,** (comment; explanation) glosa. —*v.t.* **1,** (make lustrous) lustrar; dar lustre a. **2,** [*usu.* **gloss over**] (cover up, as by a specious argument) arreglar; adornar; disfrazar. **3,** (comment on; explain) glosar.

glossary ('glas·ə·ri) *n.* glosario.

glossy ('glɔs·i) *adj.* lustroso; brillante; satinado.

glottis ('glat·ɪs) *n.* glotis. —**glottal,** *adj.* glotal.

glove (glʌv) *n.* guante. —*v.t.* enguantar. —**glover,** *n.* comerciante en guantes. —**handle with kid gloves,** tratar con delicadeza.

glow (gloɪ) *v.i.* **1,** (shine; gleam) brillar; lucir; resplandecer. **2,** (be flushed; redden) encenderse; ruborizarse. **3,** *fig.* (radiate health or high spirits) resplandecer; brillar. —*n.* **1,** (luminosity) brillo; luz. **2,** (vividness) brillo; viveza. **3,** (ardor) calor; ardor. **4,** (flush; redness) rubor; color. **5,** (pervading feeling) calor; euforia.

glower ('glau·ər) *v.i.* poner mala cara; fruncir el ceño. —*n.* mala cara; ceño.

glowworm ('glo,wʌrm) *n.* luciérnaga.

glucinium (glu'sɪn·i·əm) *n.* glucinio.

glucose ('glu·kos) *n.* glucosa.

glue (glu) *n.* goma; cola. —*v.t.* encolar; pegar. —**gluey,** *adj.* pegajoso.

glum (glʌm) *adj.* hosco; triste; sombrío. —**glumness,** *n.* hosquedad; tristeza.

glut (glʌt) *n.* **1,** (surfeit) hartura; saciedad. **2,** (supply exceeding demand) saturación; inundación. —*v.t.* [**glutted, glutting**] **1,** (surfeit) hartar; saciar; llenar. **2,** *comm.* saturar; inundar; *Amer.* abarrotar. —*v.i.* hartarse; saciarse; llenarse.

gluten ('glu·tən) *n.* gluten. —**glutinous,** *adj.* glutinoso.

glutton ('glʌt·ən) *n.* glotón; tragón; *zoöl.* glotón. —**gluttonous,** *adj.* glotón. —**gluttony,** *n.* gula; glotonería.

glycerin ('glɪs·ər·ɪn) *n.* glicerina.

glycogen ('glai·kə·dʒən) *n.* glicógeno.

glycol ('glai·kɔl) *n.* glicol.

glyph (glɪf) *n.* **1,** *archit.; sculp.* glifo. **2,** (sign) símbolo.

G-man ('dʒi,mæn) *n., slang* agente federal.

gnarl (narl) *n.* nudo; nudosidad. —*v.t.* retorcer. —*v.i.* gruñir. —**gnarled,** *adj.* nudoso; retorcido; deforme.

gnash (næʃ) *v.t.* rechinar; hacer crujir (los dientes).

gnat (næt) *n.* mosquito; *Amer.* jején.

gnaw (nɔɪ) *v.t.* & *i.* roer. —**gnawing,** *n.* roedura; *fig.* carcoma.

gnome (noɪm) *n.* gnomo.

gnostic ('nas·tɪk) *adj.* & *n.* gnóstico. —**gnosticism** (-tɪ,sɪz·əm) *n.* gnosticismo.

gnu (nu) *n.* ñu.

go (go) *v.i.* [**went, gone, going**] **1,** (move off or along; proceed; be moving) ir. **2,** (operate; work) marchar; funcionar; caminar. **3,** (behave in a specified way) hacer: *The bottle went "pop,"* La botella hizo "pop." **4,** (result; turn out) salir; resultar: *All went well,* Todo salió bien. **5,** (be guided or regulated) guiarse (por); sujetarse (a); ir de acuerdo (con): *I will go by what you say,* Me guiaré por lo que digas. **6,** (take its course; proceed) ir: *How is the work going?,* ¿Cómo va el trabajo? **7,** (pass, as time) pasar; irse: *Time went quickly,* El tiempo pasó rápidamente. **8,** (circulate; get around) circular; correr: *The news went through the town,* Las noticias circularon por el pueblo. **9,** (be known or named) conocerse; llevar el nombre (de): *He goes by the name of González,* Se le conoce como González. **10,** (move about; be in a certain condition or state) andar; ir; estar: *He goes in rags,* Anda en harapos. **11,** (become; turn or change to) volverse: *He went mad,* Se volvió loco. **12,** (follow a certain plan or arrangement) ir; ser: *How does the story go?,* ¿Cómo va el cuento? **13,** (be fitting or suitable) ir: *This goes well with that,* Esto va bien con aquello. **14,** (put oneself) meterse; pasar; verse: *He went to a lot of trouble to do it,* Pasó (o se vio en) muchas dificultades para hacerlo. **15,** (leave; depart) ir; salir; partir. **16,** (cease) cesar; pasar; irse: *The pain went,* Se fue el dolor. **17,** (die) morir: *His wife went first,* Su esposa murió primero. **18,** (be done away with; be eliminated) terminarse; acabarse. **19,** (break away; be carried away or broken off) perderse; romperse; irse: *The oars went in the storm,* Los remos se perdieron en la tormenta. **20,** (fail; give way) fallar; perderse: *His eyesight is going,* Le está fallando la vista. **21,** (be allotted or given) tocar; corresponder: *The medal goes*

to John, La medalla le toca a Juan.
22, (be sold) venderse: *The chair
went for ten dollars,* La silla se
vendió por diez dólares. **23,** (extend; lead) ir; llevar: *This road goes
to Mexico,* Este camino va a
México. **24,** (reach; extend)
alcanzar; llegar: *The carpet didn't
go to the wall,* La alfombra no llegó
a la pared. **25,** (enter; attend; engage in) ir: *They have gone fishing,*
Han ido a pescar. **26,** (resort; have
recourse) ir; dirigirse (a): *You must
go to the judge,* Tienes que dirigirte
al juez. **27,** (carry one's activity to
certain lengths) ir; llegar; alcanzar:
*How far will you go with this
plan?,* ¿Hasta dónde llegarás con
este plan? **28,** (endure; last; hold
out) ir: *I can go no further,* No
puedo ir más lejos. **29,** (have a particular place or position; belong) ir:
The ties go in this box, Las corbatas
van en esta caja. **30,** (fit; be contained) caber; ir. **31,** (count; be
valid; be acceptable) valer; contar;
ir. **32,** (be accepted; be successful)
tener aceptación; tener éxito. —*v.t.,*
colloq. **1,** (bet; wager) apostar; ir. **2,**
colloq. (put up with) tolerar;
soportar; aguantar. —*n.* **1,** (act of
going) ida; partida; salida. **2,** *colloq.*
(success) éxito. **3,** *colloq.* (animation; energy) empuje; energía. **4,**
colloq. (state of affairs) estado de
cosas; situación. **5,** *colloq.* (try; attempt) tentativa; intentona. —**go
about, 1,** (be busy at; do) ocuparse
de; atender. **2,** (move from place to
place) ir por aquí y por allí; dar
vueltas. **3,** (circulate) circular;
correr. **4,** *naut.* (turn) virar; cambiar
de bordada. —**go after,** *colloq.*
perseguir; ir detrás de. —**go along,**
1, (proceed) seguir; proseguir. **2,**
(agree) estar de acuerdo; avenirse.
3, (cooperate) cooperar. **4,** (accompany) ir (con); acompañar. —**go
around, 1,** (enclose; surround)
circundar; rodear; circunvalar. **2,**
(provide a share for each) alcanzar;
bastar. **3,** (move from place to
place; circulate) circular; ir por aquí
y por allí; dar vueltas. —**go at,**
atacar. —**go away,** irse; marcharse.
—**go back, 1,** (return) volver;
regresar. **2,** (move back) retroceder;
echarse atrás. —**go back on,** *colloq.*
1, (break, as a promise) quebrar;
quebrantar; faltar a. **2,** (betray)
traicionar. —**go beyond, 1,** (go

past) pasar; ir más allá de. **2,** (exceed) exceder. —**go by, 1,** (pass)
pasar; pasar por; pasar de largo por.
2, (be overlooked; slip past) pasar
por alto; pasar desapercibido. —**go
down, 1,** (descend) descender;
bajar. **2,** (sink) hundirse. **3,** (set, as
the sun) ponerse. **4,** (fall; suffer defeat) caer. **5,** (be put on record)
inscribirse; anotarse. —**go for, 1,**
(try to get) ir por; tratar de
conseguir. **2,** *colloq.* (attack) atacar;
cargar contra. **3,** *slang* (regard with
favor) gustar; entusiasmarse de o
con o por. —**go halves,** *colloq.* ir a
medias. —**go in, 1,** (enter) entrar. **2,**
(be contained) caber. —**go in for,**
colloq. gustar de; ser aficionado a.
—**go into, 1,** (enter) entrar en. **2,**
(inquire into) investigar; indagar. **3,**
(take up, as a study or occupation)
tomar; seguir. **4,** (be contained in)
caber en. —**go in with,** asociarse
con. —**go off, 1,** (leave; depart)
irse; marcharse; salir. **2,** (explode)
explotar; detonar. **3,** (happen) pasar;
ocurrir; suceder. **4,** (be extinguished) apagarse. —**go on, 1,**
(continue) continuar; seguir. **2,** (behave) comportarse. **3,** (happen) pasar; tener lugar. **4,** *theat.* (come on
stage) entrar (en escena). **5,** (be
turned on, as a light) prenderse;
encenderse. —**go (someone) one
better,** superar; aventajar. —**go out,**
1, (leave; go out of doors) salir. **2,**
(be extinguished) apagarse. **3,** (be
outdated) pasar (de moda). **4,** (go
on strike) declararse (en huelga)
—**go over, 1,** (examine thoroughly)
examinar; escudriñar. **2,** (do again)
rehacer; volver a hacer. **3,** (review) repasar. —**go through, 1,**
(carry out; perform) actuar; desempeñar. **2,** (suffer; undergo) sufrir;
experimentar. **3,** (search; look
through) examinar; investigar. **4,**
(win approval) pasar; aprobarse. **5,**
(spend) gastar; dilapidar. —**go
through with,** concluir; terminar.
—**go together, 1,** (combine suit-
ably) combinar; ir bien. **2,** *colloq.*
(be sweethearts) salir o ir juntos.
—**go under,** hundirse. —**go up,**
subir. —**go without,** pasar sin;
arreglárselas sin. —**it's no go,**
colloq. es imposible; no hay tu tía.
—**let go, 1,** (set free; release) soltar.
2, (give up) dejar pasar; abandonar.
—**let oneself go,** dejarse;
abandonarse. —**on the go,** en

movimiento; activo; atareado. **—to go,** *slang* para llevar.

goad (goːd) *n.* aguijón; aguijada; rejo. **—***v.t.* aguijonear.

goal (goːl) *n.* **1,** *sports* gol; meta. **2,** (aim) gol; meta; objetivo. **—goalie** (-i) *n.* = **goalkeeper.**

goalkeeper ('gol,kiˑpər) *n.* guardameta. *También,* **goaltender.**

goat (got) *n.* **1,** (she-goat) cabra; chiva. **2,** (male goat) chivo; macho cabrío; *Amer.* cabro. **3,** *slang* (scapegoat) pagano; víctima. **—be the goat,** *colloq.* ser la víctima; ser el pagano; pagar el pato. **—get one's goat,** *colloq.* molestar; enojar. **—wild goat,** cabra montés.

goatee (go'tiː) *n.* perilla; pera; *Amer.* chiva.

goatherd ('got,hʌrd) *n.* cabrero.

goatish ('got·ɪʃ) *adj.* cabrío.

goatskin ('got,skɪn) *n.* cabritilla.

goatsucker ('got,sʌk·ər) *n.* chota-cabras.

gob (gaːb) *n.* **1,** (mass; lump) mazacote; pelmazo. **2,** *colloq.* (sailor) marinero.

gobble ('gab·əl) *n.* voz del pavo; gluglú. **—***v.t.* tragar; engullir; devorar. **—***v.i.* gluglutear.

gobbledygook ('gab·əl·di,guk) *n.* jerga; jerigonza.

gobbler ('gab·lər) *n.* **1,** (male turkey) pavo. **2,** *colloq.* (glutton) tragón; glotón; engullidor.

go-between *n.* **1,** (mediator) intermediario; mediador. **2,** (between lovers) alcahuete.

goblet ('gab·lɪt) *n.* copa.

goblin ('gab·lɪn) *n.* duende.

god (gaːd) *n.* dios. **—goddess,** *n.f.* diosa.

godchild ('gad,tʃaild) *n.* ahijado.

goddaughter ('gad,dɔˑtər) *n.* ahijada.

godfather ('gad,faˑðər) *n.* padrino.

godhead ('gad·hed) *n.* divinidad; deidad.

godless ('gad·ləs) *adj.* sindiós; impío. **—godlessness,** *n.* impiedad.

godlike ('gad·laik) *adj.* divino.

godly ('gad·li) *adj.* piadoso; devoto. **—godliness,** *n.* piedad.

godmother ('gad,mʌð·ər) *n.* madrina.

godsend ('gad·send) *n.* bendición de Dios.

godson ('gad·sʌn) *n.* ahijado.

Godspeed ('gad'spiːd) *interj.* ¡buena suerte!; ¡Vaya con Dios!

gofer ('go·fər) *n.,* *slang* asistente, esp. joven que lleva recados.

go-getter (go'get·ər) *n.,* *slang* buscavidas; hombre o mujer de empuje.

goggle ('gag·əl) *v.i.* saltársele a uno los ojos; poner los ojos saltones; mirar con ojos saltones. **—goggles,** *n.pl.* anteojos de protección o seguridad.

going ('go·ɪŋ) *n.* **1,** (departure) ida; salida; partida. **2,** (manner or conditions of movement) camino; marcha. **3,** *colloq.* (circumstances) estado o marcha de las cosas. **—***adj.* en marcha. **—be going to,** ir a; estar por o para. **—get going,** *colloq.* marcharse; irse. **—goings on,** *colloq.* enredos; pasos.

goiter ('gɔi·tər) *n.* papera; bocio.

gold (goːld) *n.* oro. **—***adj.* de oro; dorado; áureo.

gold brick 1, (worthless object) gato por liebre. **2,** *slang* (shirker of duty) zángano.

goldbrick ('gold,brɪk) *v.t.* (swindle) dar o vender gato por liebre. **—***v.i.* (loaf) escurrir el bulto; hacer el zángano. **—***n.* [también, **goldbricker**] zángano.

gold digger *slang* vampiresa.

golden ('gol·dən) *adj.* de oro; dorado; áureo.

goldenrod ('gol·dən,rad) *n.* vara de oro; vara de San José.

golden rule norma o regla de conducta.

gold-filled *adj.* chapado o enchapado en oro.

goldfinch ('gold·fɪntʃ) *n.* cardelina.

goldfish ('gold·fɪʃ) *n.* carpa dorada; pez de color.

gold leaf pan de oro.

gold plate 1, (coating of gold) dorado. **2,** (tableware) vajilla de oro. **—gold-plated,** *adj.* dorado.

goldsmith ('gold·smɪθ) *n.* orfebre.

gold standard patrón oro.

golf (galf) *n.* golf. **—***v.i.* jugar al golf.

golly ('gal·i) *interj.* ¡cielos!; ¡caramba!

gonad ('go·næd) *n.* gonado; gónada.

gondola ('gan·də·lə) *n.* **1,** (boat) góndola. **2,** *aero.* barquilla. **3,** *R.R.* (open freight car) vagón descubierto.

gondolier (,gan·də'lɪr) *n.* gondolero.

gone (gɔɪn) *v., p.p. de* go. —*adj.* 1, (departed) ido. 2, (ruined; lost) arruinado; perdido. 3, (dying; dead) muerto. 4, (used up) agotado; consumido. 5, (past) pasado; ido. —**goner**, *n., slang* persona o cosa perdida o acabada. —**far gone,** 1, (deeply involved) muy comprometido o envuelto. 2, (far advanced) muy avanzado. 3, (exhausted) exhausto; agotado. —**gone on,** *colloq.* loco por; chalado por.

gong (gɔŋ) *n.* gong; batintín.

gonococcus (ˌga·nə'ka·kəs) *n.* gonococo.

gonorrhea (ˌgan·ə'ri·ə) *n.* gonorrea; blenorragia.

goo (guɪ) *n., slang* masa pegajosa; mazacote; pegote.

good (gud) *adj.* [**better, best**] bueno. —*n.* 1, (virtue; merit) bondad; bien. 2, (benefit; advantage) bien. —*interj.* ¡bien!; ¡bueno! —**come to no good,** terminar mal; fracasar. —**for good; for good and all,** para siempre; por siempre. —**good afternoon,** buenas tardes. —**good and . . . ,** *colloq.* bien; muy. —**good evening,** buenas noches. —**good for,** 1, (able to last or hold out for) que puede durar o servir por. 2, (worth; valid for) válido por. 3, (able to give or repay) capaz de dar o pagar. —**Good Friday,** Viernes Santo. —**good morning,** buenos días. —**good night,** buenas noches. —**good will,** buena voluntad. —**have a good time,** divertirse; pasar un buen rato. —**in good time,** a tiempo; a su tiempo. —**make good,** 1, (be successful) tener éxito. 2, (fulfill) cumplir. 3, (repay; replace) reponer; pagar. 4, (prove) demostrar; probar. —**no good,** 1, (bad) malo. 2, (worthless) sin valor. 3, (useless) inútil; que no sirve. —**to the good,** 1, (to advantage) para bien. 2, (representing credit or profit) de ganancia; sobrante.

good-bye *también,* **goodby** (gud'bai) *n. & interj.* adiós.

good-for-nothing *adj. & n.* inútil; zángano.

good-hearted *adj.* de buen corazón; bondadoso.

goodies (gud·iz) *n.pl.* golosinas.

good-looking *adj.* bien parecido; guapo; hermoso.

goodly ('gud·li) *adj.* 1, (good-looking) bien parecido; hermoso. 2,

(of good quality) excelente; bueno. 3, (pleasing) atractivo; agradable. 4, (rather large) considerable; bueno.

good-natured *adj.* afable; bondadoso; benévolo.

goodness ('gud·nəs) *n.* bondad. —*interj.* ¡Dios mío!

goods (gudz) *n.pl.* 1, (personal property) bienes. 2, (merchandise; wares) artículos; mercancías; efectos. 3, (fabric) géneros.

goody ('gud·i) *interj.* ¡bueno!; ¡muy bien! —*n.* golosina. —**goody-goody,** *adj. & n.* mojigato; santurrón.

gooey ('gu·i) *adj.* pegajoso; mazacotudo.

goof (guf) *n., slang* bobo; tonto; mentecato. —*v.i., slang* meter la pata. —**goofy,** *adj., slang* tonto; necio; disparatado. —**goof off,** *slang* holgazanear.

goon (guɪn) *n., slang* 1, matón; rufián. 2, bobo.

goose (gus) *n.* [*pl.* **geese**] ganso. —**goose flesh; goose pimples,** carne de gallina. —**goose step,** paso de ganso.

gooseberry ('gus,bɛr·i; -bə·ri) *n.* grosella blanca o silvestre.

gooseneck ('gus·nɛk) *n.* herramienta o soporte en forma de cuello de ganso.

gopher ('go·fər) *n.* 1, tuza; taltuza. 2, *slang* = gofer.

gore (gɔɪr) *n.* 1, (blood) cuajo de sangre; sangre. 2, *sewing* nesga. —*v.t.* 1, (pierce, as with a horn or tusk) acornear; cornear; dar cornadas o colmillazos a. 2, *sewing* poner nesgas a.

gorge (gordʒ) *n.* 1, (ravine) garganta; cañón; barranco. 2, (gluttonous eating; feast) atracón; empacho. 3, (disgust; revulsion) bilis; asco. —*v.t.* 1, (stuff with food; glut) atracar; atiborrar. 2, (swallow greedily) engullir. —*v.i.* atracarse; atiborrarse.

gorgeous ('gor·dʒəs) *adj.* espléndido; magnífico; hermosísimo. —**gorgeousness,** *n.* esplendor; magnificencia; hermosura.

gorilla (gə'rɪl·ə) *n.* gorila.

gorse (gors) *n.* aulaga; tojo.

gory ('gor·i) *adj.* 1, (covered with blood) sangriento; ensangrentado; sanguinolento. 2, (involving bloodshed) cruento; sangriento. —**goriness,** *n.* sanguinolencia; sangre.

gosh (gaʃ) *interj.* ¡caramba!; ¡Dios mío!

goshawk ('gas,hɔk) *n.* azor.

gosling ('gaz·lɪŋ) *n.* ganso joven; ansarino.

gospel ('gas·pəl) *n.* evangelio. —*adj.* evangélico.

gossamer ('gas·ə·mər) *n.* **1,** (cobweb) telaraña. **2,** (fabric) gasa; tul. —*adj.* sutil; delicado; tenue.

gossip ('gas·ɪp) *n.* **1,** (chatter; rumor) chisme; murmuración; habladuría. **2,** [*también,* **gossiper**] (person who chatters) chismoso; murmurador. —*v.i.* chismear; murmurar. —**gossipy,** *adj.* chismoso.

got (gat) *v.* **1,** *pret.* & *p.p. de* **get. 2,** *U.S. colloq.* & *Brit.,* con el *v.aux.* **have** (hold; own; possess) tener: *Have you got a pencil?,* ¿Tiene Vd. un lápiz?

Goth (gaθ) *n.* godo.

Gothic ('gaθ·ɪk) *adj.* gótico; godo. —*n.* gótico.

gotten ('gat·ən) *v., p.p. de* **get.**

gouge (gaudʒ) *v.t.* **1,** (make grooves in) acanalar; hacer surcos en. **2,** (remove; scoop out) vaciar; sacar. **3,** (rip or tear out) arrancar. **4,** (nick; notch) mellar; hacer muescas en. **5,** *colloq.* (swindle; cheat) estafar; robar. —*n.* **1,** (tool) gubia; escoplo. **2,** (groove) estría; surco; escopladura. **3,** (nick; notch) mella; muesca. **4,** *colloq.* (swindle) estafa; robo.

goulash ('gu·laʃ) *n.* estofado; guiso de carne; guisado.

gourd (gord) *n.* calabaza.

gourmand ('gur·mand) *n.* **1,** (glutton) glotón; comilón. **2,** = **gourmet.**

gourmet (gur'mei) *n.* gastrónomo; gourmet; epicúreo.

gout (gaut) *n.* gota. —**gouty,** *adj.* gotoso.

govern ('gʌv·ərn) *v.t.* **1,** (rule) gobernar; regir. **2,** *gram.* regir. —*v.i.* gobernar.

governess ('gʌv·ər·nəs) *n.* institutriz; aya.

government ('gʌv·ərn·mənt) *n.* **1,** (rule) gobierno; régimen. **2,** *gram.* régimen. —**governmental** (-'mɛn·təl) *adj.* gubernativo; gubernamental.

governor ('gʌv·ər·nər) *n.* **1,** *polit.* gobernador. **2,** *mech.* regulador.

gown (gaun) *n.* **1,** (woman's garment) vestido; traje. **2,** (nightgown; dressing gown) bata; salto de cama.

3, *law; educ.* toga. **4,** *eccles.* sotana; traje talar. —*v.t.* vestir.

grab (græb) *v.t.* [**grabbed, grabbing**] **1,** (seize) agarrar; coger; asir; empuñar. **2,** (snatch) arrebatar; arrancar; *Amer.* arranchar. —*n.* **1,** (act of grabbing) tirón; agarrón. **2,** (something grabbed) presa; botín. **3,** (hook; grapple) gancho; garfio. —**up for grabs,** *slang* para disputar; para quien lo coja.

grace (greis) *n.* **1,** (favor) gracia; favor. **2,** (charm) gracia; garbo; donaire. **3,** (prayer at meals) bendición de la mesa. **4,** *cap.* (title of respect) Señoría. —*v.t.* adornar; agraciar. —**fall from grace,** caer en desgracia. —**grace period,** aplazamiento; plazo. —**say grace,** bendecir la mesa.

graceful ('greis·fəl) *adj.* agraciado; gracioso; donoso.

gracious ('grei·ʃəs) *adj.* **1,** (affable; courteous) afable; grato. **2,** (merciful) indulgente; benévolo. —*interj.* ¡válgame Dios!

grad (græd) *n., colloq.* graduado.

gradate ('grei·deit) *v.t.* graduar; ordenar en grados. —*v.i.* graduarse. —**gradation,** *n.* gradación.

grade (greid) *n.* **1,** (degree) grado. **2,** (rank; class) grado; rango; categoría. **3,** *educ.* nota; calificación. **4,** (slope) cuesta; pendiente; declive. —*v.t.* **1,** (classify) clasificar. **2,** (give a grade to) calificar. **3,** (graduate) graduar. **4,** (level) aplanar; nivelar. —**grade crossing,** paso o cruce a nivel. —**grade school,** escuela primaria.

gradient ('grei·di·ənt) *n.* **1,** (slope) pendiente; declive. **2,** (degree of slope) inclinación.

gradual ('græ·dʒu·əl) *adj.* gradual.

graduate ('græ·dʒu·ət) *n.* **1,** *educ.* graduado. **2,** *chem.* probeta graduada. —*adj.* graduado. —*v.t.* (-et) **1,** *educ.* conferir un grado o diploma a; graduar. **2,** (calibrate) calibrar; graduar. —*v.i.* **1,** *educ.* graduarse. **2,** (change by degrees) cambiar gradualmente; ir en graduaciones. —**graduation,** *n.* graduación.

graft (græft) *n.* **1,** (transplant) injerto. **2,** (political corruption) malversación; soborno; *Amer.* coima. **3,** (extortion by a public official) concusión; *Amer.* mordida. —*v.t.* & *i.* **1,** (transplant) injertar. **2,**

(gain dishonestly) malversar; obtener ilícitamente; *Amer.* coimear.

grail (greil) *n.* grial.

grain (grein) *n.* **1,** (seed) grano. **2,** (texture) vena; veta; veteado. **3,** (particle) pizca; grano. **4,** (unit of weight) grano. **5,** (of leather) grano. —*v.t.* vetear. —**against the grain,** a contrapelo.

grainy ('grei·ni) *adj.* **1,** (streaked; veined) veteado. **2,** (granular) granular; granoso.

gram (græm) *n.* gramo.

grammar ('græm·ər) *n.* gramática. —**grammar school,** escuela primaria.

grammarian (grə'mɛr·i·ən) *n.* gramático.

grammatical (grə'mæt·ɪ·kəl) *adj.* gramatical; gramático.

gramophone ('græm·ə·fon) *n.* gramófono.

granary ('græn·ə·ri) *n.* granero.

grand (grænd) *adj.* **1,** (great) grande; gran. **2,** (principal; chief) principal. **3,** (magnificent; grandiose) grandioso; grande; gran. **4,** (complete; comprehensive) grande; gran; general. **5,** (pretentious; haughty) pomposo; ostentoso. —*n.,* *slang* mil dólares. —**grandness,** *n.* grandeza.

grandaunt ('grænd'ænt) *n.* tía abuela.

grandchild ('grænd₁tʃaild) *n.* nieto.

granddad ('græn·dæd) *n., colloq.* abuelo.

granddaughter ('græn₁dɔ·tər) *n.* nieta.

grand duke gran duque. —**grand duchess,** gran duquesa. —**grand duchy,** gran ducado.

grandee (græn'di) *n.* grande (*de España o Portugal*).

grandeur ('græn·dʒər) *n.* grandeza; grandiosidad.

grandfather ('grænd₁fa·ðər) *n.* abuelo.

grandiloquent (græn'dɪl·ə·kwənt) *adj.* grandilocuente. —**grandiloquence,** *n.* grandilocuencia.

grandiose ('græn·di·os) *adj.* grandioso. —**grandiosity** (-'as·ə·ti) *n.* grandiosidad.

grand jury gran jurado.

grand larceny robo de mayor cuantía.

grandma ('grænd·ma) *n., colloq.* abuela; abuelita. *También,* **grandmamma.**

grandmother ('grænd₁mʌð·ər) *n.* abuela.

grandnephew ('grænd₁nɛf·ju) *n.* resobrino. —**grandniece,** *n.* resobrina.

grand opera ópera.

grandpa ('grænd₁pa; 'græm-) *n., colloq.* abuelo; abuelito. *También,* **grandpapa** (-₁pa·pə; -pə₁paɪ).

grandparent ('grænd₁pɛr·ənt) *n.* abuelo.

grand piano piano de cola.

grand slam *cards* bola.

grandson ('grænd₁sʌn) *n.* nieto.

grandstand ('grænd·stænd) *n.* tribuna. —**grandstand play,** *slang* jugada llamativa; lance ostentoso.

granduncle ('grænd₁ʌŋ·kəl) *n.* tío abuelo.

grange (greindʒ) *n.* granja.

granite ('græn·ɪt) *n.* granito.

granny ('græn·i) *n., colloq.* **1,** (grandmother) abuela; abuelita. **2,** (old woman) viejita; viejecita; anciana. **3,** (fussy person) melindroso; remilgado.

grant (grænt) *n.* donación; concesión. —*v.t.* **1,** (give; bestow) dar; otorgar; conceder. **2,** (convey by deed) ceder; transferir. **3,** (concede; allow) conceder. —**take for granted,** dar por descontado o seguro.

grantee (græn'ti) *n.* cesionario; donatario.

grantor (græn'tor) *n.* cesionista; donante; otorgante.

granular ('græn·jə·lər) *adj.* granular.

granulate ('græn·jə₁leit) *v.t.* granular. —**granulation,** *n.* granulación.

granule ('græn·jul) *n.* gránulo.

grape (greip) *n.* uva.

grapefruit ('greip₁frut) *n.* toronja; pomelo.

grapeshot ('greip·ʃat) *n.* metralla.

grapevine ('greip·vain) *n.* **1,** (plant) vid; parra. **2,** *colloq.* (secret channel of communication) fuente o vía de rumores; correo de las brujas.

graph (græf) *n.* gráfica. —*v.t.* hacer una gráfica de. —**graph paper,** papel cuadriculado.

graphic ('græf·ɪk) *adj.* gráfico. *También,* **graphical.**

graphite ('græf·ait) *n.* grafito.

grapple ('græp·əl) *n.* arpeo; gancho. —*v.i.* luchar. —*v.t.* agarrar;

asir; aferrar. —**grappling iron** ('græp·lɪŋ) arpeo.

grasp (græsp) n. **1**, (grip; clasp) apretón; agarrón. **2**, (reach) alcance. **3**, (grab; attempt to seize) agarrón. **4**, (hold; possession) posesión; poder; mano. **5**, (understanding) comprensión. —v.t. **1**, (seize) agarrar; coger; asir; empuñar. **2**, (grip; clasp) apretar. **3**, (understand) comprender. —**grasping**, adj. codicioso.

grass (græs) n. **1**, (plant; greenery) hierba. **2**, (lawn) césped. **3**, (pasture) pasto. **4**, slang marihuana.

grasshopper ('græs·hap·ər) n. saltamontes; grillo.

grass widow mujer divorciada o separada.

grassy ('græs·i) adj. **1**, (covered with grass) herboso; con o de hierba. **2**, (like grass) herbáceo.

grate (greit) n. **1**, (grating) reja; verja; enrejado. **2**, (fireplace) parrilla. —v.t. **1**, (reduce to particles) rallar. **2**, (rub harshly) crujir; rechinar. —v.i. **1**, (creak) crujir; rechinar. **2**, [usu. **grate on** o **upon**] (annoy) enojar; irritar.

grateful ('greit·fəl) adj. agradecido.

grater ('grei·tər) n. rallador; raspador; rallo.

gratify ('græt·ɪ·fai) v.t. agradar; complacer; satisfacer. —**gratification** (-fɪ'kei·ʃən) n. agrado; satisfacción; placer.

grating ('grei·tɪŋ) n. reja; enrejado; verja. —adj. irritante; áspero.

gratis ('grei·tɪs; 'græt·ɪs) adv. gratis; de balde.

gratitude ('græt·ɪ·tud) n. gratitud; reconocimiento; agradecimiento.

gratuitous (grə'tu·ɪ·təs) adj. gratuito.

gratuity (grə'tu·ɪ·ti) n. gratificación; propina.

grave (greiv) n. **1**, (excavation) fosa. **2**, (tomb) tumba; sepultura. —adj. grave; serio. —v.t. & i. = **engrave**. —**graveness**, n. seriedad; gravedad.

gravedigger ('greiv,dɪg·ər) n. sepulturero.

gravel ('græv·əl) n. grava; cascajo. —v.t. enarenar; cubrir con grava.

graven ('grei·vən) v., p.p. var. de **grave**. —adj. grabado.

gravestone ('greiv,ston) n. lápida.

graveyard ('greiv·jard) n. cemen-

terio; camposanto. —**graveyard shift**, turno nocturno.

gravitate ('græv·ɪ,teit) v.i. gravitar. —**gravitation**, n. gravitación.

gravity ('græv·ə·ti) n. gravedad. —**specific gravity**, peso específico; gravedad específica.

gravy ('grei·vi) n. **1**, (sauce) salsa. **2**, (juice given off by meat) jugo. **3**, slang (unearned profit) extra; miel sobre buñuelos.

gray también, **grey** (grei) adj. & n. gris. —v.t. encanecer. —v.i. encanecer. —**grayish**, adj. grisáceo. —**gray matter**, lit. & fig. materia gris.

grayhaired ('grei,herd) adj. cano; canoso.

graze (greiz) n. **1**, (light touch; brush) roce; rozamiento. **2**, (scratch; scrape) raspadura; rasguño. —v.t. **1**, (brush lightly) rozar. **2**, (scratch; scrape) raspar; arañar. **3**, (put to pasture) pastorear; apacentar. —v.i. pacer; pastar. —**grazing**, n. pasto.

grease (gris) n. grasa. —v.t. engrasar. —**grease the palm**, slang untar la mano.

greasy ('gri·zi; -si) adj. grasiento; grasoso. —**greasiness**, n. lo grasiento; calidad de grasiento; grasa.

great (greit) adj. **1**, (large) grande. **2**, (eminent) grande; gran; eminente. **3**, colloq. (fine; excellent) magnífico; estupendo. —**greatness**, n. grandeza.

greatcoat ('greit·kot) n. paletó.

great-grandchild n. bisnieto. —**great-granddaughter**, n. bisnieta. —**great-grandfather**, n. bisabuelo. —**great-grandmother**, n. bisabuela. —**great-grandparent**, n. bisabuelo. —**great-grandson**, n. bisnieto.

great-great-grandfather n. tatarabuelo; rebisabuelo. —**great-great-grandmother**, n. tatarabuela; rebisabuela.

great-great-grandson n. rebisnieto. —**great-great-granddaughter**, n. rebisnieta.

great-nephew n. resobrino. —**great-niece**, n. resobrina.

Grecian ('gri·ʃən) adj. & n. griego.

Greco-Roman adj. grecorromano.

greed (grid) n. codicia; avaricia. —**greedy**, adj. codicioso; avariento.

Greek (grik) n. & adj. griego.

green (grin) adj. **1**, (color) verde. **2**, (unripe; inexperienced) verde. **3**, (new, fresh) reciente; fresco. **4**, (wan) demudado; verde. **5,** [*también,* **green-eyed**] *colloq.* (envious) amarillo de envidia. —*n.* **1,** (color) verde. **2,** (common) prado; pradera. **3,** *pl.* (evergreens) ramos verdes. **4,** *pl.* (green vegetables) verduras; hortalizas. **5,** *golf* césped. —**greenish,** *adj.* verdoso. —**green light, 1,** señal verde. **2,** *fig.* autorización para proceder. —**green thumb,** habilidad de jardinero.

greenback ('grin·bæk) *n., U.S.* papel moneda.

greenery ('gri·nə·ri) *n.* verde; verdura.

greenhorn ('grin·hɔrn) *n., colloq.* novato; bisoño.

greenhouse ('grin·haus) *n.* invernadero.

greenness ('grin·nəs) *n.* **1,** (green color) verdor. **2,** (immaturity; inexperience) inmadurez; inexperiencia.

greensward ('grin·swɔrd) *n.* césped.

greet (grit) *v.t.* saludar; recibir.

greeting ('gri·tɪŋ) *n.* saludo; salutación; bienvenida. —**greetings,** *n.pl.* saludos. —**greeting card,** tarjeta de saludo o felicitación.

gregarious (grɪ'gɛr·i·əs) *n.* gregario. —**gregariousness,** *n.* gregarismo.

gremlin ('grɛm·lɪn) *n.* duende; diablillo.

grenade (grɪ'neid) *n.* granada.

grenadier (,grɛn·ə'dɪr) *n.* granadero.

grenadine (,grɛn·ə'din) *n.* granadina.

grew (gruɹ) *v., pret. de* **grow.**

grey (grei) *n., adj. & v.* = **gray.**

greyhound ('grei,haund) *n.* galgo.

grid (grɪd) *n.* **1,** (grate; gridiron) reja; enrejado. **2,** *elect.* rejilla; grilla.

griddle ('grɪd·əl) *n.* tortera; plancha.

gridiron *n.* **1,** *cookery* parrilla. **2,** (football field) campo; cancha.

gridlock ('grɪd,lak) *n.* embotellamiento; empate.

grief (grif) *n.* dolor; pesar; pesadumbre. —**come to grief,** venir a menos; parar mal.

grievance ('gri·vəns) *n.* queja; querella.

grieve (griɹv) *v.t.* afligir; apenar; acongojar. —*v.i.* estar apenado o afligido. —**grieve for** o **over,** lamentar; llorar.

grievous ('gri·vəs) *adj.* **1,** (causing pain or grief) doloroso; penoso. **2,** (severe; serious) grave.

griffin ('grɪf·ɪn) *n.* grifo.

grifter ('grɪf·tər) *n., slang* estafador.

grill (grɪl) *n.* **1,** (gridiron) parrilla. **2,** (grilled food) asado; *S.A.* parrillada. **3,** (grillroom) parrilla. —*v.t.* **1,** (broil) asar a la parrilla. **2,** *colloq.* (question) asar o acribillar a preguntas.

grille (grɪl) *n.* reja; verja; enrejado; *auto.* parrilla.

grillwork ('grɪl,wʌrk) *n.* enrejado.

grim (grɪm) *adj.* **1,** (forbidding) torvo; hosco. **2,** (frightful; cruel) siniestro; cruel. —**grimness,** *n.* hosquedad; crueldad.

grimace (grɪ'meis, 'grɪ·məs) *n.* mueca; gesto. —*v.i.* hacer muecas; hacer gestos.

grime (graim) *n.* mugre. —**grimy,** *adj.* mugriento.

grin (grɪn) *n.* sonrisa. —*v.i.* [**grinned, grinning**] sonreír.

grind (graind) *v.t.* [*pret. & p.p.* **ground**] **1,** (crush; pulverize) moler; triturar. **2,** (sharpen) afilar; amolar. **3,** (polish) pulir. **4,** (grate) rallar. **5,** (rub harshly) refregar; restregar. **6,** (crush; oppress) aplastar; oprimir. **7,** (grate together; grit, as the teeth) rechinar. **8,** (operate by turning) dar vueltas a. —*v.i.* *slang* (work hard) echar los bofes; sudar. —*n.* **1,** (act or result of grinding) molienda. **2,** (tedious routine) rutina; matraca; monotonía. **3,** *slang* (industrious student) empollón; machacón. —**grind to a stop** o **halt,** frenar o parar en seco.

grinder ('grain·dər) *n.* **1,** (machine for sharpening) amoladera; (for coffee) molino o molinillo. **2,** (person that sharpens) amolador; afilador.

grindstone ('graind,ston) *n.* piedra de amolar.

gringo ('grɪŋ·go) *n.* gringo.

grip (grɪp) *n.* **1,** (handle) mango; agarradero; *Amer.* agarradera. **2,** (secure grasp) agarrón; apretón. **3,** (power of one's clasp) fuerza en la mano; pulso. **4,** (control; command) control; dominio. **5,** *colloq.* (valise) maletín; valija. —*v.t.* [**gripped, gripping**], **1,** (grasp firmly) agarrar; aferrar; sujetar; apretar. **2,** (take hold upon, as the emotions, attention, etc.) coger; dominar. —**come to grips,** agarrarse; llegar a las manos. —**come to grips with,**

atacar; tratar de resolver. **—get a grip on oneself,** dominarse.

gripe (graip) *v.t.* **1,** (grip; squeeze) apretar; oprimir. **2,** (distress; oppress) afligir; oprimir; acongojar. **—v.i. 1,** (have pain in the bowels) tener cólico. **2,** *slang* (complain) quejarse; lamentarse. **—n. 1,** (colic) cólico. **2,** *slang* (complaint) queja; querella. **—griper,** *n., slang* gruñón.

grippe (grɪp) *n.* gripe; influenza.

grisly ('grɪz·li) *adj.* **1,** (somewhat gray) grisáceo; entregris. **2,** (gruesome) horripilante; espantoso.

grist (grɪst) *n.* molienda. **—be grist to one's mill,** ser de provecho propio; servir de experiencia.

gristle ('grɪs·əl) *n.* cartílago. **—gristly** (-li) *adj.* cartilaginoso; correoso.

grit (grɪt) *n.* **1,** (sand; tiny particles) arena; polvillo áspero. **2,** (courage; pluck) valor; aguante; firmeza. **3,** *pl.* (ground corn) sémola; maíz molido. **—v.t. & i.** [**gritted, gritting**] crujir; rechinar.

gritty ('grɪt·i) *adj.* **1,** (coarse) áspero; rasposo. **2,** (plucky) valeroso; firme; de aguante.

grizzled ('grɪz·əld) *adj.* canoso; cano.

grizzly ('grɪz·li) *adj.* grisáceo; pardusco. **—grizzly bear,** oso pardo o gris.

groan (groːn) *n.* gemido; quejido. **—v.i.** gemir; quejarse.

groats (grots) *n.pl.* sémola; avena o trigo molido.

grocer ('groː·sər) *n.* abacero; *Amer.* bodeguero; *Amer.* almacenero; *Amer.* abarrotero. **—grocery,** *n.* abacería; *Amer.* bodega; *Amer.* almacén; *Amer.* tienda de abarrotes. **—groceries,** *n.pl.* comestibles; *Amer.* abarrotes.

grog (graːg) *n.* bebida de ron y agua; brebaje. **—groggy,** *adj.* mareado; turulato; atontado.

groin (grɔɪn) *n.* **1,** *anat.* ingle. **2,** *archit.* arista de bóveda.

grommet ('gram·ɪt) *n.* ojete; hembrilla; *naut.* estrobo; amura.

groom (gruːm) *n.* **1,** (stableman) caballerizo; mozo de cuadra; palafrenero. **2,** (bridegroom) novio. **3,** (attendant in a royal household) encargado de palacio. **—v.t. 1,** (tend, as horses) atender; cuidar de. **2,** (make neat) arreglar; acicalar. **3,** (train) adiestrar; preparar. **—grooming,** *n.* arreglo; acicalado.

groomsman ('grumz·mən) *n.* padrino de boda.

groove (gruːv) *n.* **1,** (notch) muesca. **2,** (furrow) surco. **3,** (hollow cut) acanaladura; estría. **4,** (slit) ranura; hendidura. **—v.t.** acanalar; estriar. **—in the groove,** en las mismas de siempre.

grope (grop) *v.i. & t.* tantear; tentar. **—grope for,** buscar a ciegas o a tientas; tantear.

grosgrain ('gro·gren) *n.* gro.

gross (gros) *adj.* **1,** (fat; heavy) grueso; gordo. **2,** (thick; dense) espeso; denso. **3,** (coarse) burdo; tosco. **4,** (vulgar) grosero; vulgar; rudo. **5,** (stupid) bruto. **6,** (flagrant; glaring) grande; tremendo; enorme. **7,** (total) total. **8,** (without deductions) bruto. **9,** (raw; unfinished) en bruto. **—n.** gruesa. **—v.t.** sacar o hacer en total o en bruto. **—gross national product,** producto bruto nacional. **—gross profit,** utilidad bruta. **—gross weight,** peso bruto.

grossness ('gros·nəs) *n.* **1,** (vulgarity) vulgaridad; rudeza. **2,** (thickness) espesor; densidad. **3,** (fatness) heaviness) gordura.

grotesque (gro'tɛsk) *adj.* grotesco. **—grotesqueness,** *n.* extravagancia; lo grotesco.

grotto ('grat·o) *n.* gruta.

grouch (grautʃ) *n., colloq.* **1,** (morose person) gruñón; refunfuñón; cascarrabias. **2,** (sullen mood) mal humor. **3,** (complaint) queja. **—v.i.** quejarse; gruñir; refunfuñar. **—grouchy,** *adj.* gruñón; refunfuñón; malhumorado.

ground (graund) *n.* **1,** (earth; soil) tierra; suelo. **2,** (area) terreno. **3,** *usu. pl.* (basis; justification) fundamento; base; razón. **4,** *usu. pl.* (plot of land) tierra; solar; terreno. **5,** *usu. pl.* (land used for a special purpose) terreno; terrenos; campo. **6,** *pl.* (meal; coarse particles) harina; polvo. **7,** *pl.* (dregs; sediment) poso; posos. **8,** *elect.* tierra; conductor a tierra. **—adj. 1,** (prepared by grinding) molido. **2,** (at ground level) a nivel del terreno o de tierra. **—v.t. 1,** (set on the ground) poner en tierra. **2,** (base; found) basar; cimentar; fundar. **3,** *aero.* prohibir o detener el vuelo de; detener en tierra. **4,** *elect.* conectar a tierra. **5,** (run aground) varar. **6,** *pret. & p.p. de* **grind. —v.i. 1,** (run aground) encallar; embarrancar; varar. **2,** (alight; land) aterrizar. **—above ground,** vivo; vivito y coleando. **—break ground, 1,** (begin digging) comenzar una obra. **2,** (plow) arar. **3,** (prepare the way) preparar el camino. **—cut the ground from under one's feet,** echar la zancadilla a. **—give ground,** ceder. **—ground floor, 1,** lit. planta baja; piso bajo. **2,** fig. posición ventajosa; ventaja. **—ground swell,** marejada; mar de fondo. **—hold o stand one's ground,** mantener o sostener su posición. **—lose ground,** perder terreno. **—on the grounds of,** basado en; por razón de. **—run into the ground,** colloq. agotar; acabar (con). **—shift one's ground,** cambiar de actitud or posición.

ground hog marmota de América.

groundless ('graund·ləs) adj. infundado; sin base o fundamento.

groundwork ('graund·wʌrk) n. base; fundamento.

group (grup) n. grupo. **—v.t.** agrupar. **—v.i.** agruparse.

grouper ('gru·pər) n., ichthy. cabrilla.

grouse (graus) n. **1,** [pl. **grouse**] (bird) ave silvestre (perdiz, faisán, etc.). **2,** [pl. **grouses**] slang (complaint) queja. **—v.i.,** slang refunfuñar; gruñir; quejarse.

grout (graut) n. lechada; argamasa clara.

grove (groːv) n. arboleda.

grovel ('grʌv·əl) v.i. arrastrarse; humillarse.

grow (groː) v.i. [grew, grown, growing] **1,** (sprout; spring up) brotar. **2,** (develop) crecer; desarrollarse. **3,** (increase) crecer. **4,** (become) ponerse; volverse. **—v.t. 1,** (cultivate; raise) cultivar; producir. **2,** (cause or allow to grow) hacer crecer; dejar(se) crecer. **—grow old,** envejecer. **—grow on,** conquistar; apoderarse de. **—grow out of, 1,** (develop from) provenir de; surgir de. **2,** (outgrow) dejar atrás; perder (la costumbre de). **—grow up, 1,** (reach maturity) crecer; llegar a la madurez. **2,** (develop; arise) brotar; surgir. **—grow young,** rejuvenecerse.

growl (graul) n. gruñido; ronquido. **—v.i.** gruñir; roncar. **—v.t.** proferir gruñendo. **—growler,** n. gruñón.

grown (groːn) v., p.p. de **grow**. **—adj. 1,** (mature) crecido;

desarrollado. **2,** (covered over) lleno; cubierto.

grownup ('groːn‚ʌp) n. adulto; persona mayor. **—grown-up,** adj. crecido; adulto; juicioso.

growth (groːθ) n. **1,** (development) crecimiento; desarrollo. **2,** (increase) aumento. **3,** (something growing or grown) brote; cultivo; vegetación. **4,** med. tumor.

grub (grʌb) v.t. [**grubbed, grubbing**] **1,** (dig up by the roots) sacar de raíz; arrancar; desarraigar. **2,** (clear, as earth) quitar la maleza de; Amer. desmalezar. **3,** slang (sponge; beg) gorrear. **—v.i. 1,** (dig) escarbar. **2,** (toil) afanarse; trabajar asiduamente. **—n. 1,** (larva) larva; gorgojo. **2,** slang (food) comida; manducatoria.

grubby ('grʌb·i) adj. **1,** (dirty) sucio; mugriento. **2,** (covered with vermin) piojento; piojoso. **3,** (ragged; shabby) desaliñado; desharrapado.

grudge (grʌdʒ) n. rencor; ojeriza. **—v.t. 1,** (envy) envidiar. **2,** (grant reluctantly) escatimar; escasear. **—grudging,** adj. dado o hecho de mala gana o con repugnancia.

gruel ('gru·əl) n. gachas; puches. **—v.t.** cansar; agotar. **—grueling,** adj. arduo; agotador.

gruesome ('gru·səm) adj. repulsivo; horrible; horripilante.

gruff (grʌf) adj. **1,** (hoarse) ronco; áspero. **2,** (surly; rude) hosco; rudo. **—gruffness,** n. aspereza; sequedad; hosquedad.

grumble ('grʌm·bəl) n. refunfuño; gruñido; queja. **—v.i.** refunfuñar; gruñir; quejarse.

grumpy ('grʌm·pi) adj. malhumorado; gruñón.

grunt (grʌnt) n. gruñido. **—v.i.** gruñir.

guanaco (gwə'na·ko) n. guanaco.

guano ('gwa·no) n. [pl. **-nos**] guano.

guarantee (‚gær·ən'tiː) n. garantía. **—v.t.** [**-teed, -teeing**] garantizar; garantir.

guarantor ('gær·ən‚tor; -tər) n. fiador; garante; garantizador.

guaranty ('gær·ən·ti) n. **1,** = **guarantee**. **2,** = **guarantor**. **—v.t.** = **guarantee**.

guard (gard) v.t. **1,** (defend; protect) proteger; guardar; defender. **2,** (keep watch on; keep in check) cuidar; atender. **3,** (keep watch

over) custodiar; guardar; vigilar. **4,**
(provide with a safeguard) cubrir;
resguardar; poner resguardo a. —*v.i.*
1, (take precautions) resguardarse
(de o contra); precaverse (de o contra). **3,** (keep watch) hacer guardia;
velar. —*n.* **1,** (act or duty of
guarding) guardia. **2,** (precaution;
safeguard) resguardo; protección. **3,**
(defensive posture) guardia. **4,** (protective device) protector; resguardo;
guarda; guarnición. **5,** (sentry)
guardia; guarda. **6,** *sports* defensa.
—**mount guard,** montar guardia.
—**off guard,** desprevenido. —**on
(one's) guard,** en guardia;
prevenido. —**stand guard,** hacer
guardia.

guarded ('gar·dɪd) *adj.* **1,** (protected; defended) protegido;
resguardado; defendido. **2,** (super-
vised; watched) cuidado; vigilado.
3, (cautious; careful; restrained)
cuidadoso; comedido; receloso.

guardhouse ('gard,haus) *n.* prevención; cuartel de guardia.

guardian ('gar·di·ən) *n.* **1,** (person
who guards) guardián. **2,** *law* tutor;
encargado. —*adj.* custodio; de la
guarda.

guardroom ('gard·rum) *n.* calabozo; prevención.

guava ('gwa·və) *n.* **1,** (fruit) guayaba. **2,** (tree) guayabo.

gubernatorial (,gu·bər·nə'tor·i·
əl) *adj.* de o del gobernador.

gudgeon ('gʌdʒ·ən) *n.* **1,** *ichthy.*
gobio. **2,** (bait) cebo. **3,** *mech.*
gorrón; espiga. **4,** (dupe; gull)
cándido; inocentón; pazguato. —*v.t.*
engatusar; engañar.

guerrilla *también,* **guerilla**
(gə'rɪl·ə) *n.* (guerrilla fighter) guerrillero. —*adj.* de guerrillas.
—**guerrilla band,** guerrilla.

guess (ges) *v.t. & i.* conjeturar;
adivinar. —*n.* [*también,* **guess-
work**] conjetura; adivinación.

guest (gest) *n.* **1,** (visitor) visita;
invitado; convidado. **2,** (lodger, as
at a hotel) huésped.

guffaw (gʌ'fɔ) *n.* risotada;
carcajada. —*v.i.* dar risotadas; reír a
carcajadas.

guidance ('gai·dəns) *n.* guía;
dirección.

guide (gaid) *v.t.* guiar; dirigir. —*n.*
guía. —**guided missile,** proyectil
dirigido.

guidebook ('gaid,buk) *n.* guía.

guidepost ('gaid,post) *n.* hito;
poste indicador.

guild (gɪld) *n.* gremio.

guile (gail) *n.* astucia; maña;
engaño. —**guileful,** *adj.* astuto;
mañoso. —**guileless,** *adj.* inocente;
sincero; cándido.

guillotine ('gɪl·ə,tin) *n.* guillotina. —*v.t.* guillotinar.

guilt (gɪlt) *n.* culpa; delito.
—**guiltless,** *adj.* inocente; sin culpa.

guilty ('gɪl·ti) *adj.* culpable.
—**guiltiness,** *n.* culpabilidad.

guinea ('gɪn·i) *n.* guinea. —**guinea
hen,** gallina de guinea; guinea.
—**guinea pig,** conejillo de Indias;
S.A. cuy.

guise (gaiz) *n.* **1,** (attire; dress)
vestido; traje. **2,** (appearance)
aspecto; apariencia.

guitar (gɪ'taɹ) *n.* guitarra.
—**guitarist,** *n.* guitarrista.

gulch (gʌltʃ) *n.* barranca; quebrada.

gulden ('gul·dən) *n.* florín.

gulf (gʌlf) *n.* **1,** *geog.* golfo. **2,**
(chasm) abismo.

gull (gʌl) *n.* **1,** (bird) gaviota. **2,**
(dupe) bobo; pazguato. —*v.t.*
embaucar; engatusar.

gullet ('gʌl·ɪt) *n.* gaznate; garganta.

gullible ('gʌl·ə·bəl) *adj.* crédulo;
simplón. —**gullibility,** *n.* credulidad; simplonería.

gully ('gʌl·i) *n.* barranca; garganta;
quebrada.

gulp (gʌlp) *v.t.* tragar; engullir;
echarse (algo) al coleto. —*v.i.*
atragantarse. —*n.* trago.

gum (gʌm) *n.* **1,** *anat.* encía. **2,**
(sticky substance) goma; pegamen-
to. —*v.t.* [**gummed, gumming**]
engomar; pegar. —*v.i.* ponerse pegajoso. —**chewing gum,** goma de
mascar; chicle. —**gum arabic,**
goma arábiga. —**gum up,** *colloq.*
estropear; *Amer.* embarrar.

gumbo ('gʌm·bo) *n.* [*pl.* **-bos**]
quingombó.

gumdrop ('gʌm·drap) *n.* pastilla
de goma.

gummy ('gʌm·i) *adj.* **1,** (of or like
gum) gomoso. **2,** (sticky) pegajoso.
—**gumminess,** *n.* pegajosidad.

gumption ('gʌmp·ʃən) *n., colloq.*
1, (initiative) iniciativa; empuje;
nervio. **2,** (common sense) sentido
común.

gumshoe ('gʌm,ʃu) *n.* **1,** *colloq.*
(overshoe) chanclo. **2,** *slang* (detective) detective.

gun (gʌn) *n.* **1,** (weapon) arma de fuego (pistola, escopeta, cañón, etc.). **2,** (discharge of a gun, as in a salute) cañonazo. —*v.t.* [**gunned, gunning**] **1,** (shoot) disparar. **2,** [*usu.* **gun for**] (pursue) cazar; perseguir; ir en busca de. **3,** (accelerate) acelerar. —**stick to one's guns,** mantenerse en sus trece.

gunboat ('gʌn·bot) *n.* cañonero; lancha cañonera.

guncotton ('gʌn,kat·ən) *n.* pólvora de algodón; algodón pólvora.

gunfire ('gʌn·fair) *n.* fuego; tiros *(de armas de fuego).*

gung ho ('gʌŋ'hoʊ) *adj., colloq.* entusiástico; ansioso.

gunman ('gʌn·mən) *n.* [*pl.* **-men**] pistolero.

gunner ('gʌn·ər) *n.* artillero.

gunnery ('gʌn·ər·i) *n.* artillería.

gunpowder ('gʌn,pau·dər) *n.* pólvora.

gunrunning ('gʌn,rʌn·ɪŋ) *n.* tráfico de armas. —**gunrunner,** *n.* traficante de armas.

gunshot ('gʌn·ʃat) *n.* balazo; escopetazo. —**gunshot wound,** balazo; escopetazo.

gunsmith ('gʌn·smɪθ) *n.* armero.

gunwale ('gʌn·əl) *n.* borda.

gurgle ('gʌr·gəl) *v.i.* **1,** (flow noisily) gluglutear. **2,** (utter inarticulate sounds) hacer gorgoritos; gorjear. —*n.* **1,** (noise of flowing) gluglú; gorgoteo. **2,** (inarticulate sound) gorgorito; gorjeo.

gush (gʌʃ) *n.* **1,** (flow) chorro; borbotón; borbollón. **2,** *colloq.* (effusiveness) efusión; sensiblería. —*v.i.* borbollar; hacer borbollones; manar a borbotones. —*v.t.* echar a borbollones o borbotones.

gusher ('gʌʃ·ər) *n.* **1,** (oil well) pozo surgente. **2,** (effusive person) persona efusiva.

gushy ('gʌʃ·i) *adj., colloq.* efusivo. —**gushiness,** *n., colloq.* efusividad.

gusset ('gʌs·ɪt) *n.* **1,** *sewing* escudete. **2,** (connecting metal plate) codo de metal; escuadra metálica.

gussy ('gʌs·i) *v.t.* (*with* **up**) embellecer; acicalar. —*v.i.* (*with* **up**) embellecerse; acicalarse.

gust (gʌst) *n.* **1,** (blast of wind) ráfaga; racha. **2,** (outburst) arrebato; explosión.

gustatory ('gʌs·tə,tor·i) *adj.* gustativo; del gusto.

gusto ('gʌs·to) *n.* gusto; placer; satisfacción.

gusty ('gʌs·ti) *adj.* ventoso; impetuoso; de o con ventoleras.

gut (gʌt) *n.* **1,** *usu.pl.* (intestine) intestino; tripas. **2,** *naut.* (channel) canal; estrecho; paso. **3,** *pl., slang* (courage) agallas. **4,** *slang* (belly) barriga; panza. **5,** = **catgut.** —*v.t.* [**gutted, gutting**] destripar; desentrañar. —**gutsy,** *adj., slang* valeroso; osado.

gutta-percha ('gʌt·ə'pʌr·tʃə) *n.* gutapercha.

gutter ('gʌt·ər) *n.* **1,** (of a road) cuneta. **2,** (of a roof) canal; canalón.

guttersnipe ('gʌt·ər,snaip) *n.* pillo; pilluelo; granuja.

guttural ('gʌt·ər·əl) *n.* gutural.

guy (gai) *n.* **1,** (rope or cable for steadying something) tirante. **2,** *slang* (fellow) tipo; sujeto; individuo. —*v.t., colloq.* burlarse de; mofarse de.

guzzle ('gʌz·əl) *v.t. & i.* beber mucho o con rapidez; tragar.

gym (dʒɪm) *n., colloq.* = **gymnasium.**

gymnasium (dʒɪm'nei·zi·əm) *n.* gimnasio.

gymnast ('dʒɪm·næst) *n.* gimnasta. —**gymnastic** (dʒɪm'næs·tɪk) *adj.* gimnástico. —**gymnastics,** *n.pl.* gimnasia; gimnástica.

gynecology (,dʒai·nə'kal·ə·dʒi; ,gai-) *n.* ginecología. —**gynecological** (-kə'ladʒ·ɪ·kəl) *adj.* ginecológico. —**gynecologist,** *n.* ginecólogo.

gyp (dʒɪp) *n., slang* **1,** (swindler) tramposo; estafador. **2,** (swindle) estafa; timo. —*v.t., slang* estafar; timar.

gypsum ('dʒɪp·səm) *n.* yeso.

gypsy *también* **gipsy** ('dʒɪp·si) *n.* gitano. —*adj.* gitano; gitanesco.

gyrate ('dʒai·ret) *v.i.* girar; dar vueltas. —**gyration,** *n.* giro; vuelta.

gyrocompass ('dʒai·ro,kam·pəs) *n.* brújula giroscópica.

gyroscope ('dʒai·rə·skop) *n.* giroscopio; giróscopo.

H

H, h (eitʃ) octava letra del alfabeto inglés.

ha (ha) *interj.* ¡ja!

haberdasher ('hæb·ər͵dæʃ·ər) *n.* camisero. —**haberdashery**, *n.* camisería.

habilitate (hə'bɪl·ə͵teit) *v.t.* habilitar.

habit ('hæb·ɪt) *n.* hábito. —*v.t.* vestir. —**be in the habit of**, tener el hábito de; acostumbrar; soler. —**get into the habit of**, habituarse a; coger el hábito de.

habitable ('hæb·ɪt·ə·bəl) *adj.* habitable.

habitat ('hæb·ə͵tæt) *n.* habitat; habitación; medio; elemento.

habitation (͵hæb·e'tei·ʃən) *n.* residencia; habitación.

habitual (hæ'bɪtʃ·u·əl) *adj.* habitual; acostumbrado.

habituate (hæ'bɪtʃ·u͵eit) *v.t.* habituar; acostumbrar. —**habituation**, *n.* costumbre; hábito.

habitué (hə'bɪtʃ·u͵ei) *n.* parroquiano o concurrente asiduo; habitué.

hacienda (͵ha·si'ɛn·də) *n.* hacienda.

hack (hæk) *n.* **1,** (gash) tajo; corte. **2,** (tool) azuela; hacha. **3,** (cough) tos seca. **4,** (old horse) jamelgo. **5,** (car for hire) taxi. **6,** (hired writer) escritor mercenario; rutinero. —*adj.* **1,** (hired) alquilado; de alquiler. **2,** = **hackneyed.** —*v.t.* **1,** (chop) dar tajos a. **2,** = **hackney.** —*v.i.* **1,** (chop) dar o hacer tajos. **2,** (cough) tener una tos seca; toser. **3,** (drive a taxicab) conducir o manejar un taxi. **4,** (write for hire) escribir por un precio. —**hack out**, producir por rutina.

hackie ('hæk·i) *n.* = **hackman.**

hackle ('hæk·əl) *n.* **1,** (comb for dressing flax, hemp, etc.) rastrillo. **2,** *usu.pl.* (bristling hair) pelo erizado. —*v.t. & i.* **1,** (dress flax, hemp, etc.) rastrillar. **2,** (hack roughly) hacer pedazos; cortar a machetazos o hachazos.

hackman ('hæk·mən) *n.* [*pl.* **-men**] taxista; chofer.

hackney ('hæk·ni) *n.* **1,** (horse) caballo. **2,** (hired horse or carriage) caballo o carruaje de alquiler. —*v.t.* **1,** (hire out) alquilar. **2,** (make trite)

repetir hasta el cansancio; usar demasiado. —*adj.* alquilado; de alquiler. —**hackneyed**, *adj.* trillado; manoseado; gastado.

hacksaw ('hæk͵sɔ) *n.* sierra para metales.

had (hæd) *v., pret. & p.p. de* **have.**

haddock ('hæd·ək) *n.* bacalao de Escocia; merluza.

Hades ('hei·diz) *n.* infierno; averno.

hafnium ('hæf·ni·əm) *n.* hafnio.

haft (hæft) *n.* empuñadura; puño.

hag (hæg) *n.* **1,** (ugly woman; witch) vieja fea; bruja. **2,** = **hagfish.**

hagfish ('hæg·fɪʃ) *n.* lamprea glutinosa.

haggard ('hæg·ərd) *adj.* demacrado; ojeroso; extenuado. —**haggardness**, *n.* fatiga; demacración.

haggle ('hæg·əl) *v.i. & t.* **1,** (bargain) regatear. **2,** (wrangle) disputar; altercar. —*n.* **1,** (bargaining) regateo. **2,** (wrangle) disputa; altercado. —**haggler** (-lər) *n.* regatero.

haha (ha'ha) *interj.* ¡ja, ja! —*n.* risa; risoteo.

hail (heil) *v.t.* **1,** (acclaim) aclamar. **2,** (call to) llamar de un grito a; dar una voz a; llamar. **3,** (salute) saludar; dar la bienvenida a. **4,** (shower; pour) llover; granizar; dar a granel. —*v.impers.* granizar. —*n.* **1,** (shout) grito; llamada. **2,** (greeting; salutation) saludo; bienvenida. **3,** (hailstone) granizo. **4,** (downpour) granizada. **5,** (hailing distance) grito. —*interj.* ¡salud!; ¡salve! —**hail from**, venir de; ser de. —**Hail Mary**, Ave María. —**within hail**, a un grito (de aquí o allí); al habla.

hailstone ('heil͵ston) *n.* granizo; piedra.

hailstorm ('heil͵storm) *n.* granizada.

hair (hɛr) *n.* **1,** (on the head) pelo; cabello. **2,** (on the body) vello; pelo. **3,** (covering or coat of hair) pelambre; pelaje; pelo. **4,** (head of hair) cabellera. **5,** *bot.* filamento. **6,** (bit; small amount) pelo; cabello. —*adj.* de, del o para el pelo. —**get in one's hair**, *slang* fastidiar; disgustar; *Amer.* fregar. —**let one's**

hair down, *slang* andar sin formalidades; ponerse a sus anchas. —**make one's hair stand on end,** ponérsele a uno el pelo de punta. —**not turn a hair,** no inmutarse. —**split hairs,** pararse en pelillos. —**to a hair,** exactamente; perfectamente.

hairbreadth ('hɛr,brɛdθ) *n.* pelo; suspiro; tris. —*adj.* estrecho; de o por un pelo.

hairbrush ('hɛr·brʌʃ) *n.* cepillo para el pelo.

haircut ('hɛr·kʌt) *n.* corte del pelo.

hairdo ('hɛr·du) *n., colloq.* peinado; tocado.

hairdresser ('hɛr,drɛs·ər) *,n.* peluquero [*fem.* -ra].

hairless ('hɛr·ləs) *adj.* pelón; pelado.

hairline ('hɛr·lain) *n.* raya.

hairnet ('hɛr·nɛt) *n.* redecilla; cofia.

hairpiece ('hɛr·pis) *n.* tupé; peluca.

hairpin ('hɛr·pɪn) *n.* horquilla; gancho. —*adj.* con vueltas y revueltas.

hair-raising ('hɛr,rei·zɪŋ) *adj.* espeluznante.

hairsbreadth también, **hair's-breadth** ('hɛrz,brɛdθ) *n. & adj.* = hairbreadth.

hairsplitting ('hɛr,splɪt·ɪŋ) *n.* un pararse en pelillos; nimiedades. —*adj.* nimio; que repara en pelillos.

hairspring ('hɛr,sprɪŋ) *n.* muelle; espiral.

hairy ('hɛr·i) *adj.* peludo; piloso; velludo; velloso. —**hairiness,** *n.* vellosidad; pelambre.

hake (heik) *n.* merluza; pescada.

halberd ('hæl·bərd) *n.* alabarda. —**halberdier** (-bər'dɪr) *n.* alabardero.

halcyon ('hæl·si·ən) *n., ornith.* martín pescador. —*adj.* tranquilo; quieto; apacible.

hale (heil) *adj.* sano; saludable; robusto. —*v.t.* tirar; halar; arrastrar. —**hale and hearty,** sano y fuerte.

half (hæf) *n.* [*pl.* **halves**] mitad; medio. —*adj.* medio. —*adv.* medio; a medio; a medias. —**better half,** *colloq.* cara mitad. —**by half,** por un mucho. —**in half,** por la mitad.

half-and-half *adj., adv. & n.* mitad y mitad.

halfback ('hæf,bæk) *n., sports* medio.

half-baked *adj.* a medio cocer.

halfblood ('hæf,blʌd) *adj. & n.* = halfbreed.

halfbreed ('hæf,brid) *n. & adj.* mestizo.

half brother hermanastro.

half-caste *adj. & n.* mestizo.

half-cocked *adj.* **1,** (of a firearm) a medio amartillar. **2,** (harebrained) descabellado.

halfhearted ('hæf,har·tɪd) *adj.* sin entusiasmo; desganado. —**half-heartedly,** *adv.* de mala gana; sin ánimo.

half-length *adj.* de medio cuerpo. —*n.* retrato de medio cuerpo.

half life período medio.

half-mast *n.* media asta. —*v.t.* poner a media asta.

half moon media luna.

half note mínima.

halfpenny ('hei·pə·ni) *n.* medio penique.

half sister hermanastra.

half sole media suela. —**half-sole,** *v.t.* poner media suela a.

half-staff *n. & v.t.* = half-mast.

half step 1, *mus.* semitono; medio tono. **2,** *mil.* paso corto.

halftone ('hæf,ton) *n.* media tinta. —*adj.* de media tinta.

half tone *mus.* semitono; medio tono.

half-truth *n.* verdad a medias.

halfway ('hæf·wei) *adv.* **1,** (to or at the midpoint) hasta la mitad; hasta el medio; a mitad de camino; a medio camino. **2,** (partially) medio; a medio; a medias; en parte. —*adj.* **1,** (situated at the midpoint) medio; a mitad del camino. **2,** (partial) parcial; medio; a medio hacer.

half-wit *n.* imbécil; tonto de capirote. —**half-witted,** *adj.* imbécil; tonto.

halibut ('hæl·ə·bət) *n.* halibut.

halitosis (,hæl·ə'to·sɪs) *n.* halitosis; mal aliento.

hall (hɔl) *n.* **1,** (large or principal room) sala; salón **2,** (building) edificio. **3,** (mansion) mansión. **4,** (vestibule) vestíbulo. **5,** (corridor) pasillo; corredor. —**town** o **city hall,** ayuntamiento; alcaldía.

hallelujah (,hæl·e'lu·ja) *n. & interj.* aleluya.

hallmark ('hɔl·mark) *n.* sello de calidad; sello distintivo.

halloo (hæ'luʒ) *interj.* ¡busca!; ¡sus! —*n.* grito; llamada. —*v.t. & i.* **1,** (call; shout) dar voces; llamar a voces. **2,** (incite) azuzar.

hallow ('hæl·o) *v.t.* santificar; consagrar.

Halloween (ˌhæl·ə'wiːn) *n.* víspera de Todos los Santos.

hallucinate (hə'lu·sə,neit) *v.t.* alucinar. —**hallucination,** *n.* alucinación. —**hallucinatory,** *adj.* alucinante; alucinador.

hallway ('hɔl·wei) *n.* 1, (vestibule) vestíbulo. 2, (corridor) corredor; pasillo.

halo ('hei·lo) *n.* [*pl.* **halos**] halo.

halogen ('hæl·ə·dʒən) *n.* halógeno.

halt (hɔlt) *v.i.* 1, (stop) pararse; detenerse. 2, (waver; hesitate) vacilar; titubear. —*v.t.* parar; detener. —*n.* parada; alto; pausa. —*adj., archaic* cojo. —**halting,** *adj.* vacilante; entrecortado.

halter ('hɔl·tər) *n.* 1, (rope or strap for tying or leading) cabestro; ronzal. 2, (hangman's noose) dogal. 3, (garment) especie de corpiño que deja la espalda al descubierto. —*v.t.* encabestrar; poner cabestro a

halve (hæv) *v.t.* dividir en dos o por mitad.

halves (hævz) *n., pl. de* **half.** —**by halves,** por mitad. —**go halves,** ir a medias.

halyard ('hæl·jərd) *n.* driza.

ham (hæm) *n.* 1, (cut of meat) jamón; pernil. 2, (part behind the knee) corva. 3, (buttock) anca; nalga. 4, *slang* (actor who overacts) actor exagerado; aspaventero. 5, *slang* (amateur, esp. in radio) aficionado.

hamburger ('hæm·bʌr·gər) *n.* 1, carne molida o picada. 2, sandwich o emparedado de carne molida; *Amer.* hamburguesa.

Hamite ('hæm·ait) *n. & adj.* camita. —**Hamitic** (hæ'mɪt·ɪk) *adj.* camítico.

hamlet ('hæm·lɪt) *n.* caserío; aldea; villorrio.

hammer ('hæm·ər) *n.* 1, (tool) martillo. 2, (of a firearm) percusor. 3, (of a piano) macillo. 4, *anat.* martillo. 5, (gavel; mallet) mazo; martillo. 6, (drop hammer) maza; martinete; martillo pilón. —*v.t. & i.* martillear; martillar. —*v.t.* 1, (drive with or as with a hammer) clavar; meter. 2, (shape with a hammer) batir; formar a martillazos. —**hammering,** *n.* martilleo. —**hammer and tongs,** con vehemencia; con energía.

—**hammer (away) at,** 1, (work diligently at) trabajar con empeño en. 2, (insist on) esforzarse en; insistir en. —**hammer out,** 1, (remove dents from) desabollar. 2, (fashion laboriously) crear trabajosamente; conseguir con esfuerzo.

hammerhead ('hæm·ər,hed) *n.,* *ichthy.* cornuda; cornudilla; pez martillo.

hammock ('hæm·ək) *n.* hamaca.

hamper ('hæm·pər) *v.t.* estorbar; impedir. —*n.* canasta; cesto.

hamster ('hæm·stər) *n.* hámster.

hamstring ('hæm,strɪŋ) *n.* tendón de la corva. —*v.t.* [*pret. & p.p.* **hamstrung**] desjarretar; *fig.* incapacitar.

hand (hænd) *n.* 1, (part of the body) mano. 2, (side) lado; mano. 3, (manner of doing or dexterity) mano. 4, (handwriting) caligrafía; escritura; letra. 5, (applause) aplauso. 6, (help; aid) ayuda; mano. 7, (employee; laborer) obrero; trabajador. 8, (pointer; indicator) manecilla; aguja. 9, (handbreadth) mano. 10, *cards* mano. —*adj.* 1, (of or with the hand) de mano; a mano. 2, (manual) manual. —*v.t.* 1, (pass; give) pasar; dar. 2, (deliver) entregar. 3, (help; conduct; steady) ayudar; asistir. —**all hands,** todos; todo el mundo. —**at first hand,** directamente. —**at hand,** a mano. —**at the hand (o hands) of,** a las manos de. —**by hand,** a mano. —**eat out of one's hand,** ser manso o dócil. —**from hand to hand,** de mano en mano. —**hand and foot,** 1, (securely tied) de pies y manos. 2, (diligently) con diligencia. —**hand down,** 1, (bequeath; pass on) legar; transmitir. 2, (announce, as an order or decision) dar; emitir. —**hand in,** entregar; presentar. —**hand in glove; hand and glove,** uña y carne. —**hand in hand,** 1, (holding hands) cogidos de la mano. 2, (together) de la mano. —**hand it to (someone)** *slang* reconocérselo (a uno). —**hand on,** transmitir; legar. —**hand out,** distribuir; dar. —**hand over,** pasar; dar; entregar. —**hand over fist,** *colloq.* a manos llenas. —**hands down,** sin dificultad; sin esfuerzo. —**hands off,** no tocar; no meterse. —**hands up!,** ¡manos arriba!; ¡arriba las manos! —**hand to hand,** cuerpo a cuerpo. —**in hand,** 1, (under control) dominado; controlado; bajo rienda. **2**, (in possession) en poder. **3**, (being attended to) entre manos. —**join hands**, unirse. —**lay hands on**, **1**, (get hold of) echar la mano a; poner las manos en. **2**, (attack) caer encima. **3**, (find) encontrar. **4**, (touch, as in blessing) imponer las manos. —**live from hand to mouth**, ir tirando. —**not lift a hand**, no levantar un dedo. —**on every hand**, por todas partes; por todos lados. —**on hand**, a mano. —**on one's hands**, a cargo de uno. —**on the one hand**, por un lado. —**on the other hand**, por otro lado. —**out of hand**, **1**, (out of control) imposible; fuera de control. **2**, (immediately) de súbito; sin más ni más. —**shake hands**, dar(se) la mano; estrechar(se) la mano. —**take in hand**, encargarse de. —**take (o get) off one's hands**, quitar de encima. —**throw up one's hands**, darse por vencido; rendirse; entregarse. —**to hand**, a mano. —**turn (o put) one's hand to**, dedicarse a. —**upper hand**, ventaja; posición ventajosa. —**have a hand in**, tener que ver con; tener que hacer con.

handbag ('hænd,bæg) *n.* **1**, (purse) bolso; *Amer.* cartera. **2**, (case; satchel) maletín; bolsa o saco de mano.

handball ('hænd,bɔl) *n.* pelota; juego de frontón.

handbill ('hænd,bɪl) *n.* volante; impreso.

handbook ('hænd,bʊk) *n.* manual; guía; prontuario.

handcar ('hænd,kar) *n.*, *R.R.* vagoneta; zorra.

handclasp ('hænd,klæsp) *n.* apretón de mano.

handcuff ('hænd,kʌf) *v.t.* esposar; maniatar. —**handcuffs**, *n.pl.* esposas; manillas.

handful ('hænd,fʊl) *n.* [*pl.* **handfuls**] **1**, (fistful) puñado. **2**, *slang* (difficult task) hueso.

handicap ('hæn·di,kæp) *n.* **1**, (hindrance; disadvantage) desventaja; handicap. **2**, (race or contest) handicap. **3**, (advantage given to an inferior contestant) ventaja; margen. —*v.t.* [-**capped**, -**capping**] **1**, (impede) estorbar; impedir; poner trabas a; poner en desventaja. **2**,

(put a handicap on) poner handicap a.

handicraft ('hæn·di·kræft) *n.* artesanía. *También,* **handcraft**. —**handcraftsman**, *n.* artesano.

handily ('hæn·dɪ·li) *adv.* con soltura; con facilidad.

handiness ('hæn·di·nəs) *n.* **1**, (convenience) comodidad; conveniencia. **2**, (skill) facilidad; destreza.

handiwork ('hæn·di,wʌrk) *n.* **1**, (hand work) labor manual. **2**, (work; creation) obra.

handkerchief ('hæŋ·kər·tʃɪf; -tʃif) *n.* pañuelo.

handle ('hæn·dəl) *v.t.* **1**, (touch) tocar; manosear. **2**, (manipulate) manipular; manejar. **3**, (have charge of) encargarse de; ocuparse de; atender. **4**, (treat; deal with) tratar. **5**, (manage; control) dirigir; manejar. **6**, *comm.* (deal in) negociar en; tener negocios de; vender. —*v.i.* trabajar; manejarse. —*n.* **1**, (of a tool or utensil) mango; asa. **2**, (of a door) tirador. **3**, (lever) manubrio. —**fly off the handle**, *colloq.* salirse (uno) de sus casillas; perder los estribos. —**handle with care**, trátese con cuidado.

handlebar ('hæn·dəl·bar) *n.* manillar; *Amer.* manubrio.

handler ('hæn·dlər) *n.* **1**, (person or thing that handles) persona o cosa que maneja o controla. **2**, (trainer; coach) entrenador.

handmade ('hænd,meid) *adj.* hecho a mano.

handmaid ('hænd,meid) *n.* sirvienta; criada; moza.

hand-me-down *n.*, *colloq.* prenda o cosa usada. —*adj.* de segunda mano.

hand organ organillo.

handout ('hænd·aut) *n.* **1**, *slang* (gift) limosna. **2**, *slang* (favor; reward) favor; premio. **3**, (handbill) volante. **4**, (press release) comunicado.

hand-picked *adj.* escogido; seleccionado.

handsaw ('hænd,sɔ) *n.* serrucho.

handset ('hænd·sɛt) *n.* microteléfono.

handshake ('hænd,ʃeik) *n.* apretón de manos.

handsome ('hæn·səm) *adj.* **1**, (large; considerable) importante; considerable. **2**, (gracious; seemly) gentil; generoso. **3**, (good-looking) hermoso; guapo; apuesto; buen mozo. **4**, (impressive; pleasing) hermoso; atractivo. —**handsomeness**, *n.* belleza; hermosura.

handspring ('hænd,sprɪŋ) *n.* voltereta sobre las manos.

handwriting ('hænd,raɪ·tɪŋ) *n.* escritura; caligrafía; letra.

handy ('hæn·di) *adj.* **1**, (accessible) cerca; a (la) mano. **2**, (skillful) hábil; diestro. **3**, (adaptable) cómodo; fácil de uso.

handyman ('hænd·di,mæn) *n.* [*pl.* **-men**] ayudante; persona que en una casa o establecimiento desempeña oficios menudos.

hang (hæŋ) *v.t* [*pret.* & *p.p.* **hung**] **1**, (suspend from a support) colgar. **2**, (attach, as to a hinge) suspender. **3**, [*pret.* & *p.p.* **hanged**] (put to death by hanging) ahorcar; colgar. **4**, (decorate or cover with hangings) decorar; adornar o cubrir (con cuadros o colgaduras). **5**, (deadlock, as a jury) inmovilizar; obstruir (un jurado). —*v.i.* **1**, (be suspended) pender; colgar. **2**, (fall or flow, as a coat) caer. **3**, (lean; droop) inclinarse. **4**, [*pret.* & *p.p.* **hanged**] (die by hanging) morir ahorcado. **5**, (hesitate) vacilar. **6**, (come to a standstill) estar suspendido. —*n.* **1**, (way that a thing hangs) caída; vuelo. **2**, (way of doing or using) manera; forma. **3**, (significance) significado. **4**, (pause in motion) pausa; alto. —**hang around** (o **about**), **1**, (cluster around) agruparse alrededor (de). **2**, *colloq.* (loiter) rondar; vagar. —**hang back**, echarse para atrás; amilanarse. —**hang fire**, **1**, (be slow in firing, as a gun) retardarse en disparar. **2**, (be slow in acting) retrasarse; demorarse; quedar en ciernes. **3**, (be undecided) estar o quedar en duda. —**hang it!**, ¡al diablo! —**hang on**, **1**, (keep hold) agarrarse; sujetarse. **2**, (go on doing; persevere) seguir; continuar; perseverar. **3**, (depend on) depender de. **4**, (lean on) apoyarse en; recostarse contra. **5**, (listen attentively to) estar pendiente a. —**hang on to**, no soltar; guardar. —**hang out**, **1**, (lean out) asomarse. **2**, *slang* (reside; frequent) residir; parar. **3**, (loiter) holgazanear. —**hang over**, **1**, (project; overhang) extenderse sobre; proyectarse sobre. **2**, (hover or loom over) cernirse sobre. **3**, (be left

over; remain) quedar. —**hang together**, **1**, (be united) estar o ir unidos. **2**, (be coherent) concordar; tener coherencia. —**hang up**, **1**, (put on a hook, hanger, etc.) colgar. **2**, (delay; suspend) demorar; dilatar; suspender.

hangar ('hæŋ·ər) *n.* hangar.

hangdog ('hæŋ·dɔg) *adj.* abyecto; ruin; abatido.

hanger ('hæŋ·ər) *n.* percha; colgador; *Amer.* gancho.

hanger-on *n.* [*pl.* **hangers-on**] pegote; gorrón; *Amer.* lapa.

hangfire ('hæŋ·faɪr) *n.* tiro retardado.

hanging ('hæŋ·ɪŋ) *adj.* **1**, (suspended; pendulous) colgante. **2**, (overhanging) sobresaliente; salido. **3**, (unsettled; inconclusive) en ciernes; en suspenso; pendiente. **4**, (deserving the death penalty) que merece la horca. —*n.* **1**, (a suspending or being suspended) colgamiento; colgado. **2**, (execution) ahorcadura; horca; muerte en la horca. **3**, *usu.pl.* (drapings) colgaduras.

hangman ('hæŋ·mən) *n.* [*pl.* **-men**] verdugo.

hangnail ('hæŋ·neɪl) *n.* padrastro.

hangout ('hæŋ·aut) *n.*, *slang* guarida; paraje.

hangover ('hæŋ·o·vər) *n.* **1**, (carryover; survival) remanente; sobreviviente. **2**, *colloq.* (aftereffect of intoxication) resaca; *Amer.* flato; *Amer.* perseguidora.

hangup ('hæŋ·ʌp) *n.*, *slang* **1**, (obstacle) obstáculo; traba. **2**, (obsession) obsesión.

hank (hæŋk) *n.* madeja; ovillo.

hanker ('hæŋ·kər) *v.i.* [*usu.* **hanker after** o **for**] ansiar; apetecer; anhelar. —**hankering**, *n.* ansia; anhelo.

hankie ('hæŋ·ki) *n.*, *colloq., also* **hanky**, pañuelo.

hanky-panky ('hæŋ·ki'pæŋ·ki) *n., colloq.* escamoteo; tramoya; manipuleo; enredo.

hansom ('hæn·səm) *n.* cabriolé Hansom.

haphazard (hæp'hæz·ərd) *adj.* casual; accidental; fortuito. —*adv.* al azar; a lo loco; a la diabla. —*n.* suerte; casualidad.

hapless ('hæp·ləs) *adj.* desafortunado; infeliz; desgraciado. —**haplessness**, *n.* desventura; desgracia.

happen 854 harlequin

happen ('hæp·ən) *v.i.* suceder; acaecer; acontecer; ocurrir. —**happening**, *n.* acontecimiento; suceso.

happenstance ('hæp·ən,stæns) *n.* casualidad.

happy ('hæp·i) *adj.* feliz. —**happiness**, *n.* felicidad; dicha. —**happy-go-lucky**, *adj.* despreocupado; alegre.

harakiri ('ha·rə'kɪr·i) *n.* harakiri.

harangue (hə'ræŋ) *n.* arenga. —*v.t. & i.* arengar.

harass ('hær·əs; hə'ræs) *v.t.* acosar; hostigar. —**harassment**, *n.* acosamiento; hostigamiento.

harbinger ('har·bɪn·dʒər) *n.* precursor; heraldo; nuncio. —*v.t.* anunciar; presagiar.

harbor *también,* **harbour** ('har·bər) *n.* 1, (shelter) albergue; refugio; asilo. 2, (inlet; port) rada; bahía; puerto. —*v.t.* 1, (shelter) albergar; refugiar; asilar. 2, (hold, as in the mind) albergar; guardar. —*v.i.* refugiarse.

harborage ('har·bər·ɪdʒ) *n.* 1, (port; anchorage) puerto; fondeadero. 2, (shelter) albergue.

hard (hard) *adj.* 1, (stiff; strong; harsh) duro. 2, (difficult) difícil. 3, (callous; unfeeling) duro. 4, (arduous) arduo; duro. 5, (steady; persistent) asiduo; empeñoso. 6, (containing much alcohol) fuerte. 7, *phonet.* sordo. —*adv.* duro; fuerte. —**be hard on**, ser duro para (con). —**go hard with**, irle mal a. —**hard and fast**, estricto; inflexible; inamovible. —**hard by**, cerca; muy cerca. —**hard cash** (o **money**), efectivo. —**hard of hearing**, medio sordo; duro de oído. —**(be) hard put to it**, vérselas difíciles; verse en apuros. —**hard up**, *colloq.* en apuros; en trances apurados; arrancado.

hardbitten ('hard,bɪt·ən) *adj.* endurecido.

hard-boiled *adj.* 1, (of eggs) duro. 2, *colloq.* (unfeeling) duro; endurecido.

hardbound ('hard,baund) *adj.* encuadernado en pasta. *También,* **hardcover**.

hard core *n.* núcleo arraigado. —**hardcore**; **hard-core**, *adj.* 1, (inveterate) empedernido; endurecido. 2, (all-out) extremo; explícito.

harden ('har·dən) *v.t.* endurecer; *(of metals)* templar. —*v.i.* endurecerse.

hardening ('har·dən·ɪŋ) *n.* endurecimiento; *(of metals)* templado.

hardhead ('hard,hɛd) *n.* cabeza dura.

hardheaded ('hard,hɛd·ɪd) *adj.* obstinado; terco.

hardhearted ('hard,har·tɪd) *adj.* empedernido; de corazón duro.

hardihood ('har·di·hud) *n.* audacia; temeridad; atrevimiento.

hardily ('har·də·li) *adv.* sufridamente; con entereza.

hardiness ('har·di·nəs) *n.* 1, (endurance) vigor; aguante; vigor. 2, = **hardihood**.

hard labor trabajo forzado.

hard line *n.* actitud intransigente. —**hardline**; **hard-line**, *adj.* intransigente.

hardly ('hard·li) *adv.* 1, (with difficulty) con dificultad; penosamente. 2, (severely) severamente; ásperamente. 3, (scarcely) apenas; a duras penas; difícilmente.

hardness ('hard·nəs) *n.* dureza.

hard-set *adj.* 1, (in trouble) en apuros. 2, (rigid; fixed; firm) fijo; firme. 3, (stubborn) obstinado; emperrado.

hardship ('hard·ʃɪp) *n.* adversidad; desgracia; penalidad; privación.

hardtack ('hard,tæk) *n.* galleta de munición; pan de tropa; rosca.

hardware ('hard·wer) *n.* 1, (tools, nails, fittings, etc.) ferretería; herraje; utensilios de metal. 2, (gear; equipment) equipo. 3, *elect.; comput.* equipo; maquinaria; material. —**hardware store**, ferretería.

hard water agua cruda; agua dura.

hardwood ('hard·wud) *n.* madera dura; árbol de madera dura.

hardy ('har·di) *adj.* robusto; resistente; de aguante.

hare (her) *n.* liebre.

harebrained ('her,breind) *adj.* atolondrado; atronado; sin pies ni cabeza.

harelip ('her·lɪp) *n.* labio leporino. —**harelipped**, *adj.* labihendido.

harem ('her·əm) *n.* harén.

hark (hark) *v.i.* escuchar; oír atentamente; atender. —*interj.* ¡oiga!; ¡escuche!; ¡atienda! —**hark back**, revertir; volver.

harken ('har·kən) *v.i.* = **hearken**.

harlequin ('har·lə·kwɪn) *n.* arlequín.

harlequinade (ˌhar·lə·kwɪ'neid) *n.* arlequinada.

harlot ('har·lət) *n.* prostituta; ramera; meretriz. —**harlotry,** *n.* prostitución.

harm (harm) *n.* daño; mal; perjuicio. —*v.t.* dañar; hacer daño a; perjudicar.

harmful ('harm·fəl) *adj.* dañino; perjudicial; nocivo. —**harmfulness,** *n.* lo malo; lo dañino; nocividad.

harmless ('harm·ləs) *adj.* inofensivo; innocuo. —**harmlessness,** *n.* innocuidad.

harmonic (har'man·ɪk) *adj. & n.* armónico. —**harmonics,** *n.pl.* armonía.

harmonica (har'man·ɪ·kə) *n.* armónica.

harmonious (har'mo·ni·əs) *adj.* armonioso. —**harmoniousness,** *n.* armonía.

harmonize ('har·mə‚naiz) *v.t. & i.* armonizar.

harmony ('har·mə·ni) *n.* armonía.

harness ('har·nəs) *n.* arneses; arreos; *Amer.* aperos; aparejo. —*v.t.* 1, (put harness on) aparejar; *Amer.* aperar. 2, (bring into fruitful control) controlar; dominar. —**in harness,** empleado; activo.

harp (harp) *n.* arpa. —*v.i.* 1, (play the harp) tocar el arpa. 2, [*usu.* **harp on** o **upon**] (insist; persist) insistir; machacar. —**harpist,** *n.* arpista.

harpoon (har'puːn) *n.* arpón. —*v.t.* arponear.

harpsichord ('harp·sɪ·kord) *n.* clavicémbalo.

harpy ('har·pi) *n.* arpía.

harquebus ('har·kwə·bəs) *n.* arcabuz.

harridan ('hær·ə·dən) *n.* bruja; vieja taimada.

harrow ('hær·o) *n.* grada; rastro; rastra. —*v.t.* 1, (draw a harrow over) gradar; pasar el rastro a. 2, (wound; lacerate) herir; desgarrar; lacerar. 3, (distress; torment) perturbar; atormentar.

harrowing ('hær·o·ɪŋ) *adj.* angustioso; desgarrador.

harry ('hær·i) *v.t.* acosar; hostigar.

harsh (harʃ) *adj.* 1, (strident) estridente; chillón. 2, (glaring) intenso; crudo. 3, (rough; unpleasant) áspero. 4, (severe; rigorous) severo; riguroso; inclemente.

harshness ('harʃ·nəs) *n.* 1, (stridency) estridencia. 2, (glare)

intensidad; crudeza. 3, (roughness; unpleasantness) aspereza. 4, (severity) severidad; rigor; inclemencia.

hart (hart) *n.* ciervo; venado.

harum-scarum ('hɛr·əm'skɛr·əm) *adj.* atolondrado; desordenado. —*adv.* a la diabla; a lo loco; desordenadamente; atolondradamente. —*n.* atolondrado; desordenado; tarambana.

harvest ('har·vɪst) *n.* cosecha; recogida; recolección; siega. —*v.t. & i.* cosechar; recoger; segar.

harvester ('har·vɪs·tər) *n.* 1, (worker) jornalero; (of grain) segador. 2, (machine) segadora; trilladora.

has (hæz) *v.,* tercera pers. del sing. del pres. de ind. de **have.**

has-been *n., colloq.* persona que ha visto mejores tiempos.

hash (hæʃ) *n.* 1, (food) picadillo; salpicón. 2, (mess) lío; enredo; *Amer.* sancocho. —*v.t.* 1, (mince) picar; hacer picadillo. 2, [*también,* **hash up; make a hash of**] (bungle) enredar; embrollar. —**make hash of,** (defeat; crush) triturar; pulverizar.

hashish ('hæʃ·iʃ) *n.* haxix.

hasp (hæsp) *n.* aldaba; (of a book) broche. —*v.t.* cerrar con aldaba.

hassle ('hæs·əl) *n., colloq.* lío; bronca; agarrada. —*v.i., colloq.* pelearse; armar bronca.

hassock ('hæs·ək) *n.* 1, (stool) banqueta almohadillada. 2, (clump of grass) mata.

hast (hæst) *v., arcaico, segunda pers. del sing. del pres. de ind. de* **have.**

haste (heist) *n.* prisa. —**be in haste,** tener prisa. —**make haste,** apresurarse; darse prisa.

hasten ('hei·sən) *v.t.* apresurar; acelerar. —*v.i.* apresurarse; darse prisa.

hasty ('heis·ti) *adj.* apresurado; precipitado. —**hastily,** *adv.* de prisa; apresuradamente. —**hastiness,** *n.* apresuramiento; precipitación.

hat (hæt) *n.* sombrero. —*v.t.* cubrir con sombrero. —**hat shop,** sombrerería. —**take one's hat off to,** descubrirse ante. —**talk through one's hat,** *colloq.* decir tonterías; hablar sandeces. —**throw one's hat into the ring,** entrar en la lid.

hatband ('hæt·bænd) *n.* cintillo.

hatbox ('hæt·baks) *n.* sombrerera.

hatch (hætʃ) *v.t.* **1,** (incubate)
empollar; incubar. **2,** (devise; plan;
plot) idear; maquinar. **3,** (mark with
lines, as for shading) sombrear.
—*v.i.* **1,** (bring forth young, as an
egg) empollar. **2,** (come forth, as
from the egg) salir del cascarón;
empollar. **3,** (take shape; be realized) resultar; cuajar. —*n.* **1,**
(brood) cría; pollada. **2,** *naut.*
(hatchway) escotilla. **3,** (trapdoor)
escotillón. **4,** (floodgate) compuerta.
5, (small door) portillo; portezuela.
6, (outcome; result) resultado; fruto.
—**hatchery,** *n.* criadero.

hatchet ('hætʃ·ɪt) *n.* hacha.
—**bury the hatchet,** hacer las
paces. —**hatchet job,** *colloq.*
ataque malicioso; aniquilación.

hatchetman ('hætʃ·ɪt·mæn) *n.,*
slang pistolero; asesino.

hatchway ('hætʃ·weɪ) *n.* **1,** (trapdoor) trampa; escotillón **2,** *naut.*
escotilla.

hate (heɪt) *v.t. & i.* odiar; aborrecer;
detestar. —*n.* odio; aborrecimiento.

hateful ('heɪt·fəl) *adj.* detestable;
odioso; aborrecible. —**hatefulness,**
n. odio; inquina.

hath (hæθ) *v., arcaico, tercera*
pers. del sing. del pres. de ind. de
have.

hatrack ('hæt·ræk) *n.* percha.

hatred ('heɪ·trəd) *n.* odio; inquina.

hatter ('hæt·ər) *n.* sombrerero.

haughty ('hɔ·ti) *adj.* altanero;
altivo; orgulloso. —**haughtiness,** *n.*
altanería; altivez; orgullo.

haul (hɔl) *v.t.* **1,** (tug; drag) tirar
de; arrastrar; halar. **2,** (transport)
acarrear; transportar. —*v.i.* **1,** (pull)
tirar. **2,** *naut.* (change course) virar.
—*n.* **1,** (pull; tug) tirón. **2,** (catch;
gain) redada; cosecha; ganancia. **3,**
(distance   covered)   trayecto;
recorrido; *Amer.* tiro. **4,** (load transported) carga; cargamento. **5,** *slang*
(booty) botín; tajada. —**haulage,** *n.*
acarreo; transporte. —**hauler,** *n.*
acarreador; porteador. —**haul off,**
1, (retreat) retirarse; largarse. **2,**
naut. (change direction) virar. **3,**
colloq. (prepare to strike a blow)
aprestarse a pegar un golpe.

haunch (hɔntʃ) *n.* **1,** (human)
cadera. **2,** (animal) anca.

haunt (hɔnt) *v.t.* **1,** (visit or inhabit
as a ghost) rondar como alma en
pena. **2,** (recur too persistently; obsess) perseguir; obsesionar. **3,** (visit
frequently) frecuentar. —*n.* cubil;

guarida. —**haunted,** *adj.* embru-
jado.

have (hæv) *v.t.* [*pres.ind. I* **have,**
you **have** (*arcaico, thou* **hast**), *he,*
she, it **has** *we, you, they* **have**; *pret.*
& p.p. **had**; *ger.* **having**] **1,** (hold;
possess; contain) tener. **2,** (experience; undergo) tener: *She has a*
cold, Tiene un resfrío. **3,** (believe;
maintain) mantener; sostener: *Pub-*
lic opinion has it that business is
good, La opinión pública mantiene
que los negocios van bien. **4,** (engage in; carry on) tener: *We had a*
fight, Tuvimos una pelea. **5,** (cause
to do or be done) hacer: *I had the*
roof fixed, Hice arreglar el techado.
6, *colloq.* (perform; realize in action) echar; dar: *Have a look at this,*
Échele una ojeada a esto. **7,** (bear;
beget) tener: *She had a baby boy,*
Tuvo un niño. **8,** (permit; tolerate;
admit) permitir; tolerar; soportar;
admitir. **9,** (take; get) tomar: *Have a*
cigarette, Tome un cigarrillo. **10,**
(hold at a disadvantage) tener; tener
dominado; tener aviado: *I have you*
now, Ya te tengo; *This problem has*
me, Este problema me tiene aviado.
11, [*usu.* **have on**] (wear) tener
puesto. **12,** *slang* (cheat; deceive)
estafar; embaucar; engañar: *I've*
been had, Me han estafado.
—*v.aux.* **1,** (con el *p.p.,* formando
los tiempos pasados) haber: *I have*
finished, He terminado. **2,** (con el
inf., expresa obligación o necesidad) tener que: *I have to write to*
him, Tengo que escribirle. —*n.,*
usu.pl. ricos; los que tienen. —**had**
as good (o **well**), valerle tanto a
uno; dar lo mismo: *I had as well*
lost the money as spent it that way,
Me hubiera dado lo mismo perder
el dinero que gastarlo en esa forma.
—**had as soon; had sooner,** valerle
más a uno; preferir; ser mejor: *I had*
as soon die as face him, Prefiero
morir a enfrentarme con él. —**had**
better (o **best**), ser mejor (que);
convenir (que): *We had better* (o
best) *consent,* Conviene que
consintamos. —**had   rather,**
preferir: *I had rather leave at once,*
Prefiero salir en seguida. —**have at,**
atacar; acometer. —**have done,**
terminar: *Let's have done with it,*
Terminemos con esto. —**have it**
coming, merecérselo. —**have it in**
for, *colloq.* tenérsela jurada a;
tenerle tirria a. —**have it out,**

decidir; resolver; zanjar (la cuestión, el problema, etc.). —**have none of,** no tolerar; no aguantar. —**have to do with,** tener que ver con.

haven ('hei·vən) *n.* **1,** (shelter) asilo; refugio. **2,** (harbor) puerto.

have-not *n., colloq.* pobre; desposeído; destituído.

haversack ('hæv·ər·sæk) *n.* mochila; alforja.

havoc ('hæv·ək) *n.* estrago; devastación. —**play havoc with,** perjudicar; estropear. —**wreak havoc (on** u **upon),** devastar; hacer estragos (en).

haw (hɔ) *v.t. & i.* (turn left) tirar o virar a la izquierda. —*v.i.* (hesitate) vacilar; titubear. —*n.* **1,** (hesitation) titubeo. **2,** (laugh) risa; carcajada. **3,** = **hawthorn berry.** —*interj.* ¡riá!

hawk (hɔk) *n.* **1,** (bird) ave de presa; halcón. **2,** (cough) carraspeo. —*v.t. & i.* (hunt) cazar con halcones. —*v.t.* (peddle) pregonar; ofrecer. —*v.i.* (clear the throat) carraspear.

hawker ('hɔ·kər) *n.* **1,** (falconer) halconero. **2,** (peddler) buhonero; vendedor ambulante.

hawk-eyed *adj.* que tiene ojos de lince.

hawking ('hɔ·kɪŋ) *n.* halconería; cetrería.

hawser ('hɔ·zər) *n.* maroma; cable.

hawthorn ('hɔ·θɔrn) *n.* acerolo; espino. —**hawthorn berry,** acerola.

hay (hei) *n.* heno; forraje. —**hay fever,** fiebre del heno; alergia. —**hit the hay,** *colloq.* irse a dormir; tumbarse. —**that's not hay,** *colloq.* no es paja; no es ardite.

hayfield ('hei·fild) *n.* henar.

hayloft ('hei·lɔft) *n.* henil.

haymaker ('hei,mei·kər) *n.* puñetazo decisivo.

hayseed ('hei·sid) *adj. & n.* rústico; patán.

haystack ('hei·stæk) *n.* almiar; montón de heno; parva de paja. *También,* **hayrick.**

haywire ('hei·wair) *adj., slang* **1,** (out of order) malogrado; descompuesto. **2,** (crazy) loco; fuera de sus casillas.

hazard ('hæz·ərd) *n.* **1,** (peril) riesgo; peligro. **2,** (chance) azar; suerte. **3,** (hindrance) obstáculo. **4,** (game) juego de azar. —*v.t.* arriesgar. —**hazardous,** *adj.*

peligroso; azaroso; arriesgado. —**at all hazards,** a toda costa.

haze (heiz) *n.* bruma; neblina. —*v.i.* [*usu.* **haze over**] empañarse.

haze (heiz) *v.t.* dar *o* hacer novatadas a. —**hazing,** *n.* novatada.

hazel ('hei·zəl) *n.* **1,** (tree and wood) avellano. **2,** (nut; color) avellana. —*adj.* de avellano; de color avellana.

hazelnut ('hei·zəl,nʌt) *n.* avellana.

hazy ('hei·zi) *adj.* brumoso; nebuloso. —**haziness,** *n.* nebulosidad.

H-bomb *n.* bomba de hidrógeno.

he (hi) *pron. pers.* él. —*adj. & n.* varón; macho.

head (hɛd) *n.* **1,** *anat.* cabeza. **2,** (intelligence; aptitude) cabeza. **3,** (unit; individual) cabeza. **4,** (chief; director) jefe; cabeza. **5,** (top, as of a page, article, etc.) tope; cabecera. **6,** (heading) encabezamiento; título. **7,** (headline) titular. **8,** (of a coin) cara. **9,** (of a bed) cabecera. **10,** (front; lead) cabeza. **11,** (extremity; end) punta; cabeza; extremo. **12,** (headland) cabo; punta. **13,** (source) fuente. **14,** (pressure) presión; nivel de presión. **15,** (froth, as on a liquid) espuma. **16,** (handle of a cane, umbrella, etc.) puño. —*adj.* **1,** (main; principal) principal; primero. **2,** (at the top or front) primero; delantero. **3,** (striking against the front) de frente; *naut.* de proa. —*v.t.* **1,** (command; lead) encabezar. **2,** (direct) dirigir. —*v.i.* **1,** (travel; set out) dirigirse; encaminarse. **2,** (originate) nacer. —**come to a head, 1,** (reach the bursting point) estar para reventar o estallar. **2,** (culminate) culminar. —**give one his head,** soltarle a uno las riendas; dejarle hacer. —**go to one's head,** irse o subirse a la cabeza. —**hang one's head,** bajar la cabeza. —**head first,** la cabeza primero. —**head off, 1,** (overtake) interceptar; atrapar. **2,** (prevent) prevenir; evitar. —**head on,** de frente. —**head over heels, 1,** (tumbling) patas arriba; dando traspiés o volatines. **2,** (completely) locamente; perdidamente. —**heads up!,** ¡cuidado!; ¡alerta! —**hit the nail on the head,** dar en el clavo. —**keep one's head,** mantener la cabeza. —**lose one's head,** perder la cabeza. —**make head,** avanzar; adelantar. —**make head or tail of,** comprender; en-

tender. —**out of** (o **off**) **one's head,**
fuera de sí. —**over one's head, 1,**
(too difficult) fuera del alcance. **2,**
(without consulting one) por
encima de uno. —**take it into one's
head,** metérsele a uno en la cabeza;
darle a uno (por). —**talk** (**yell,** *etc.*)
one's head off, hablar (gritar, *etc.*)
hasta el cansancio. —**turn one's
head, 1,** (make dizzy) marear. **2,**
(make vain) trastornar. **3,** (inveigle)
cajole) engatusar.

headache ('hɛd·ek) *n.* dolor de cabeza; jaqueca.

headband ('hɛd·bænd) *n.* cinta o
banda para el pelo; cintillo.

headboard ('hɛd·bord) *n.* cabecera.

headdress ('hɛd·drɛs) *n.* tocado.

headfirst ('hɛd'fʌrst) *adv.* de cabeza.

headgear ('hɛd·gir) *n.* **1,** (head
covering) tocado. **2,** (for a horse)
cabezada. **3,** (protective helmet)
casco.

headiness ('hɛd·i·nəs) *n.* **1,** (recklessness) impetuosidad; temeridad.
2, (intoxicating quality) lo espirituoso.

heading ('hɛd·ɪŋ) *n.* **1,** encabezamiento; título. **2,** (direction) rumbo.

headless ('hɛd·ləs) *adj.* sin cabeza.

headlight ('hɛd,lait) *n.* farol; faro.

headline ('hɛd,lain) *n.* titular; cabecera. —*v.t.* anunciar; poner en tit-
ulares

headlong ('hɛd,lɔŋ) *adj.* **1,** (rash)
temerario; impetuoso; arriesgado. **2,**
(with head forward) de cabeza.
—*adv.* **1,** (rashly) temerariamente;
impetuosamente. **2,** (headfirst; violently) de cabeza.

headman ('hɛd·mən) *n.* [*pl.* **-men**]
cacique; caudillo; jefe.

headmaster ('hɛd,mæs·tər) *n.* director. —**headmistress,** *n.*
directora.

head-on *adj.* de frente.

headphone ('hɛd·fon) *n.* = **headset.**

headpiece ('hɛd·pis) *n.* **1,** = **headgear. 2,** = **headset. 3,** *print.* cabecera.

headquarters ('hɛd,kwor·tərz) *n.*
1, (center of operations) jefatura;
esp.mil. cuartel general. **2,** (main office) oficina principal.

headroom ('hɛd·rum) *n.* espacio
libre; luz.

headset ('hɛd·sɛt) *n.* auricular;
audífono.

headsman ('hɛdz·mən) *n.* [*pl.*
-men] verdugo.

headstone ('hɛd·ston) *n.* **1,** (tombstone) lápida. **2,** (cornerstone) piedra fundamental; primera piedra.

headstrong ('hɛd·strɔŋ) *adj.*
obstinado; terco; testarudo.

headwaiter ('hɛd,wei·tər) *n.* jefe
de camareros.

headwaters ('hɛd,wɔ·tərz) *n.pl.*
manantiales; fuentes.

headway ('hɛd·wei) *n.* **1,** (progress) avance; adelanto. **2,** (headroom) espacio libre; luz. **3,** *R.R.*
intervalo entre dos trenes. —**make
headway,** avanzar; adelantar.

heady ('hɛd·i) *adj.* **1,** (impetuous;
reckless) impetuoso; osado; temerario. **2,** (intoxicating) intoxicante;
turbador; espirituoso.

heal (hi:l) *v.t.* **1,** (make sound; cure)
sanar; curar. **2,** (free from troubles)
sanear; remediar. **3,** (reconcile)
reconciliar; reparar. —*v.i.* sanar;
curar; *(of a wound)* cicatrizar.

healer ('hi·lər) *n.* **1,** (person)
curandero. **2,** (remedy) curativo.

healing ('hi·lɪŋ) *adj.* curativo. —*n.*
curación; cura; *(of a wound)*
cicatrización.

health (hɛlθ) *n.* salud; sanidad;
salubridad. —**bill of health,**
certificado de salud. —**health officer,** oficial de sanidad. —**to your
health!,** ¡a su salud!

healthful ('hɛlθ·fəl) *adj.* sano;
saludable; salubre. —**healthfulness,**
n. salubridad; sanidad.

healthy ('hɛl·θi) *adj.* saludable;
sano. —**healthiness,** *n.* estado sano;
buena salud.

heap (hip) *n.* montón; pila. —*v.t.*
amontonar; apilar. —**heaping,** *adj.*
lleno hasta el borde; rebozante.

hear (hir) *v.t.* [*pret. & p.p.* **heard**
(hʌrd)] **1,** (perceive by the ear) oír.
2, (listen) escuchar; oír. —*v.i.* oír.
—**hearer,** *n.* oyente.

hearing ('hɪr·ɪŋ) *n.* **1,** (sense) oído.
2, (earshot) alcance del oído. **3,** (opportunity to be heard) audiencia. **4,**
law vista.

hearing aid audífono.

hearken también, **harken** ('har·
kən) *v.i.* escuchar; atender.

hearsay ('hɪr·sei) *n.* rumor; habladuría. —**by hearsay,** de o por
oídas.

hearse (hʌrs) *n.* carroza fúnebre.

heart (hart) *n.* corazón. —**after one's own heart,** que llena los deseos del corazón. —**at heart,** en el fondo. —**by heart,** de memoria. —**change of heart,** cambio de parecer. —**do one's heart good,** halagar; contentar; agradar. —**eat one's heart out,** atormentarse; remorderse. —**have a heart,** ser bueno; ser compasivo. —**in one's heart of hearts,** en lo más recóndito de uno. —**lose heart,** desanimarse; descorazonarse. —**set one's heart at rest,** sosegarse; calmarse; perder la ansiedad. —**set one's heart on,** ansiar; apetecer; desear con ansia. —**take heart,** animarse; alentarse. —**take to heart,** tomar a pecho. —**to one's heart's content,** hasta la saciedad; a la completa satisfacción de uno. —**wear one's heart on one's sleeve,** tener el corazón en la mano; ser sincero o abierto. —**with half a heart,** de mala gana; sin ánimo.

heartache ('hart·eik) *n.* pesar; congoja; aflicción.

heartbreak ('hart·breik) *n.* gran pena; pena honda. —**heartbreaking,** *adj.* doloroso; angustioso; acongojante. —**heartbroken** (-'bro·kən) *adj.* apenado; acongojado.

heartburn ('hart·bʌrn) *n.* acedía; acidez estomacal.

hearten ('hart·ən) *v.t.* animar; alentar.

heartfelt ('hart·felt) *adj.* sincero; cordial; sentido.

hearth (harθ) *n.* hogar; chimenea.

heartland ('hart·lænd) *n.* centro; región de suma importancia.

heartless ('hart·ləs) *adj.* cruel; insensible; sin corazón. —**heartlessness,** *n.* crueldad; insensibilidad; falta de corazón.

heartrending ('hart,rɛn·dɪŋ) *adj.* desgarrador; conmovedor.

heartsick ('hart·sɪk) *adj.* afligido; acongojado.

heartstrings ('hart·strɪŋz) *n.pl.* entrañas; compasión. —**tug at the (o one's) heartstrings,** conmover; ser conmovedor.

heart-to-heart *adj.* íntimo; confidencial.

hearty ('har·ti) *adj.* 1, (sincere; cordial) sincero; cordial; sentido. 2, (unrestrained) abierto; franco. 3, (healthy; healthful) sano; saludable. 4, (nourishing; satisfying)

substancioso; nutritivo; reconfortante. 5, (large; substantial) grande; substancial; de consideración.

heat (hit) *n.* 1, (hotness) calor. 2, (heating system) calefacción. 3, (excitement; ardor) ardor; vehemencia; calor. 4, (burning sensation) ardor; quemazón. 5, *sports* prueba. 6, (sexual excitement) excitación sexual; celo. 7, *slang* (pressure; coercion) presión; coerción. —*v.t.* calentar. —*v.i.* calentarse.

heated ('hi·tɪd) *adj.* 1, (made hot; warmed) calentado. 2, (angry; vehement) acalorado.

heater ('hi·tər) *n.* calentador; calefactor.

heath (hiθ) *n.* brezal; páramo.

heathen ('hi·ðən) *n. & adj.* pagano.

heather ('hɛð·ər) *n.* brezo.

heating ('hi·tɪŋ) *n.* 1, (act of heating) calentamiento. 2, (warming, as by a stove, furnace, etc.) calefacción. —*adj.* de calentamiento; calentador; calefactor. **heating pad,** almohadilla eléctrica.

heave (hiːv) *v.t.* [*pret. & p.p.* **heaved** o **hove;** *ger.* **heaving**] 1, (lift; raise) levantar pesadamente; levantar con esfuerzo. 2, (throw) lanzar; arrojar. 3, (throw up) vomitar; arrojar; vomitar. 4, (utter, as a sigh or groan) lanzar (un quejido, suspiro, etc.) 5, (pull; haul) tirar de; halar de. 6, *naut.* (turn, as a ship) virar. —*v.i.* 1, (lift; swell up) solevarse; levantarse. 2, (pant; gasp) acezar; jadear. 3, (retch; vomit) tener bascas; dar o tener arcadas. 4, (tug, as on a cable) tirar; halar. 5, *naut.* (move; proceed) avanzar. —*n.* 1, (effort or act of throwing or lifting) tirón; tiro; empujón; esfuerzo. 2, *usu. pl.* (retch; vomit) bascas; arcadas. 3, (upheaval) levantamiento. 4, *geol.* desplazamiento horizontal de una falla. —**heave ho!,** ¡halen fuerte! ¡tiren fuerte! —**heave to,** ponerse al pairo; detenerse.

heaven ('hɛv·ən) *n.* cielo. —**heavens!,** *interj.* ¡cielos!

heavenly ('hɛv·ən·li) *adj.* 1, (of the heavens) celeste. 2, (divine; sublime) celestial; divino. —**heavenliness,** *n.* felicidad suprema; hermosura divina.

heavenward ('hɛv·ən·wərd) *adj. & adv.* hacia el cielo; en alto.

heaviness ('hɛv·i·nəs) *n.* 1,

(weightiness) · peso; pesadez; pesantez. 2, (forcefulness) fuerza; peso. 3, (thickness; denseness) densidad; espesor. 4, (coarseness) dureza. 5, (stoutness) peso. 6, (burdensomeness; burden) pesadez; peso. 7, (clumsiness) pesadez. 8, (gloominess) pesadez. 9, (languidness) languidez. 10, (drowsiness) modorra.

heavy ('hɛv·i) *adj.* 1, (weighty) pesado. 2, (forceful; intense) pesado; fuerte; recio; duro. 3, (resounding) estruendoso; pesado. 4, (rough, as the sea) grueso. 5, (thick; dense) espeso. 6, (coarse; rough) grueso; duro. 7, (stout) grueso; gordo; de peso. 8, (grave; important) grave; de peso; importante. 9, (burdened) cargado. 10, (burdensome; difficult) pesado. 11, (clumsy; unwieldly) pesado. 12, (somber; gloomy) pesado; sombrío. 13, (slow; languid) lánguido. 14, (drowsy) amodorrado. —*n., theat.* villano. —*adv.* pesadamente; fuerte. —**hang heavy**, pesar; aplastar; abrumar. —**heavy fire**, fuego nutrido o pesado. —**heavy hydrogen**, hidrógeno pesado. —**heavy water**, agua pesada. —**heavy with child**, encinta; embarazada; grávida.

heavy-duty *adj.* extrafuerte; de gran resistencia.

heavy-handed *adj.* pesado; opresivo.

heavy-hearted *adj.* apesadumbrado; acongojado.

heavy-set *adj.* rehecho; fornido.

heavyweight ('hɛv·i,weit) *n.* 1, (boxer) peso pesado. 2, (VIP) alto personaje.

Hebraic (hi'brei·ɪk) *adj.* hebreo; hebraico.

Hebrew ('hi·bru) *n.* hebreo. —*adj.* hebraico; hebreo.

hecatomb ('hɛk·ə,tom) *n.* hecatombe.

heck (hɛk) *interj., slang* ¡al diablo! —**what the heck!** ¡qué diablos!

heckle ('hɛk·əl) *v.t.* importunar; acosar.

hectare ('hɛk·tər) *n.* hectárea.

hectic ('hɛk·tɪk) *adj.* 1, (turbulent) arrebatado; tumultuoso. 2, (feverish) febril.

hectogram ('hɛk·tə,græm) *n.* hectogramo.

hectoliter ('hɛk·tə,li·tər) *n.* hectolitro.

hectometer ('hɛk·tə,mi·tər) *n.* hectómetro.

he'd (hi:d) *contr.* de **he had** o **he would.**

hedge (hɛdʒ) *n.* 1, (closely planted shrubs) seto; seto vivo. 2, (evasion) rodeo. —*v.t.* 1, (place a hedge around or along) poner un seto a. 2, (surround with a barrier) cercar; rodear; limitar. 3, (protect; cover against loss) cubrir; proteger; asegurar. —*v.i.* 1, (hide or protect oneself) protegerse; cubrirse; esconderse. 2, (practice evasions) andarse con rodeos; eludir la cuestión. 3, (cover oneself, as against loss) cubrirse; protegerse; asegurarse.

hedgehog ('hɛdʒ,hag) *n.* erizo; puerco espín.

hedonism ('hi·də,nɪz·əm) *n.* hedonismo. —**hedonist,** *n.* hedonista. —**hedonistic,** *adj.* hedonista.

heed (hi:d) *v.t. & i.* atender; escuchar; hacer caso (de o a). —*n.* atención; caso.

heedful ('hid·fəl) *adj.* atento. —**heedfulness,** *n.* atención.

heedless ('hid·ləs) *adj.* descuidado. —**heedlessness,** *n.* descuido; falta de atención.

heehaw ('hi,hɔ) *n.* rebuzno. —*v.i.* rebuznar.

heel (hi:l) *n.* 1, *anat.* talón. 2, (of hose) talón. 3, (of a shoe) tacón; *Amer.* taco. 4, (tilt) inclinación; ladeo. 5, *slang* (cad) canalla; sinvergüenza. —*v.t.* 1, (put heels on) poner tacones o tacos a. 2, (follow) seguir; perseguir; pisar los talones a. 3, *slang* (furnish, esp. with money) pertrechar. —*v.i.* 1, (follow closely) seguir. 2, (list; tilt) inclinarse; ladearse; *naut.* escorar. —**at heel,** a un paso; pisando los talones. —**cool one's heels,** quedarse esperando. —**down (o out) at the heels,** hecho un pordiosero. —**drag one's heels,** estar irresoluto; vacilar; roncear. —**kick up one's heels,** saltar de contento; estar de fiesta. —**lay by the heels,** 1, (arrest) arrestar; encarcelar. 2, (overcome) superar. —**on (o upon) the heels of,** pisando los talones a. —**show one's heels; take to one's heels,** poner pies en polvorosa. —**to heel,** 1, (close; just behind) pisando los talones; un paso detrás. 2, (under control) bajo rienda; dominado.

heel-dragging *n.* vacilación; irresolución; roncería.

heft (heft) *v.t., colloq.* **1,** (lift; heave) levantar; alzar. **2,** (try the weight of) pesar; sopesar. —*n., colloq.* **1,** (weight) peso. **2,** (larger part) mayor parte; gran parte.

hefty ('hɛf·ti) *adj.* **1,** (weighty) grueso; pesado. **2,** (brawny) musculoso; membrudo.

hegemony (hɪ'dʒɛm·ə·ni; 'hɛdz·ə,mo·ni) *n.* hegemonía.

hegira (hɛ'dʒaɪ·rə) *n.* huída; fuga.

heifer ('hɛf·ər) *n.* novilla.

heigh (hei; hai) *interj.* ¡eh!; ¡ea!; ¡oiga! —**heigh-ho,** *interj.* ¡ay!; ¡ea!

height (hait) *n.* **1,** (of a person) estatura; talla. **2,** (tallness) altura; alto. **3,** *a veces pl.* (high place or position) altura; eminencia; cumbre. **4,** (elevation; altitude) altura; elevación. **5,** (top) lo alto; tope; cima. **6,** (greatest degree; highest limit) colmo; cumbre. —**at its height,** en su apogeo.

heighten ('hai·tən) *v.t.* **1,** (raise) levantar; elevar. **2,** (intensify) aumentar; intensificar; acrecentar. —*v.i.* **1,** (rise) levantarse; elevarse. **2,** (increase; intensify) crecer; aumentar; intensificarse.

heinous ('hei·nəs) *adj.* odioso; aborrecible. —**heinousness,** *n.* lo odioso; lo aborrecible.

heir (ɛr) *n.* heredero. —**heiress,** *n.* heredera. —**heir apparent,** heredero forzoso. —**heir presumptive,** presunto heredero.

heirloom ('ɛr,lum) *n.* reliquia o herencia de familia.

heist (haist) *n., slang* hurto; robo. —*v.t.* hurtar; robar.

held (hɛld) *v., pret. & p.p. de* **hold.**

helical ('hɛl·ɪ·kəl) *adj.* espiral; en espiral.

helicopter ('hɛl·ə,kap·tər) *n.* helicóptero.

heliocentric (,hi·li·o'sɛn·trɪk) *adj.* heliocéntrico.

heliograph ('hi·li·ə,græf) *n.* heliógrafo.

heliotrope ('hi·li·ə,trop) *n.* heliotropo.

heliport ('hɛl·ə·port) *n.* helipuerto.

helium ('hi·li·əm) *n.* helio.

helix ('hi·lɪks) *n.* hélice; espiral.

held (hɛld) *v., pret. & p.p. de* **hold.**

he'll (hil) *contr. de* **he will** *o* **he shall.**

hell (hɛl) *n.* infierno. —*interj.* ¡cuernos!; ¡diantre!

hellbent ('hɛl,bɛnt) *adj., slang* empeñado; embestido; desenfrenado.

hellcat ('hɛl·kæt) *n.* bruja; furia.

Hellene ('hɛl·in) *n.* heleno; griego.

Hellenic (hɛ'lɛn·ɪk) *adj.* helénico; griego.

hellfire ('hɛl·fair) *n.* fuego del infierno.

hellhound ('hɛl·haund) *n.* demonio.

hellion ('hɛl·jən) *n., colloq.* enredador; alborotador.

hellish ('hɛl·ɪʃ) *adj.* infernal; diabólico. —**hellishness,** *n.* infierno; lo infernal.

hello (hɛ'loɪ) *interj.* ¡hola!; *(in answering the telephone)* ¡diga!; ¡qué hay!; *Amer.* ¡bueno!

helm (hɛlm) *n.* timón; gobierno.

helmet ('hɛl·mɪt) *n.* casco; *hist.* yelmo; celada.

helmsman ('hɛlmz·mən) *n.* [*pl.* **-men**] timonel; timonero.

help (hɛlp) *v.t.* **1,** (aid; assist) ayudar. **2,** (further) favorecer; facilitar. **3,** (alleviate; relieve) aliviar; mejorar. **4,** (avoid; prevent) evitar; remediar. **5,** (attend; minister to the needs of) asistir; atender. **6,** (serve; wait on) servir; atender. **7,** (serve; give a helping of, as food or drink) servirle u ofrecerle algo a uno. **8,** (come to the aid of) socorrer; asistir. —*v.i.* **1,** (aid; be useful) ayudar; contribuir. **2,** (serve) servir. —*n.* **1,** (aid) ayuda; socorro. **2,** (remedy) remedio. **3,** (relief) alivio. **4,** (employee; employees) empleado(s); obrero(s); sirviente(s). **5,** (service, esp. domestic) servicio; servidumbre. —*interj.* ¡socorro! —**be unable to help** no poder dejar de; no poder remediar o evitar. —**be unable to help but** no poder menos que. —**cry for help,** pedir socorro. —**help oneself to, 1,** (serve oneself with) servirse; tomar. **2,** (take without asking) tomar o usar sin permiso. —**help out,** ayudar. —**it can't be helped,** no hay remedio. —**so help me God,** por Dios; *(in swearing an oath)* que Dios me ayuda.

helper ('hɛl·pər) *n.* **1,** (assistant) ayudante; asistente. **2,** (supporter) apoyo; auxilio.

helpful ('hɛlp·fəl) *adj.* **1,** (useful; beneficial) útil; provechoso. **2,** (inclined to help) servicial. —**helpfulness,** *n.* utilidad; ayuda.

helping ('hɛl·pɪŋ) *n.* porción.

helpless ('hɛlp·ləs) *adj.* **1,** (feeble; powerless) incapacitado; impotente. **2,** (defenseless) desamparado; desvalido; indefenso. **3,** (incompetent) incompetente; incapaz. —**helplessness,** *n.* impotencia; incapacidad.

helpmate ('help,meit) *n.* **1,** (companion; helper) compañero de trabajos; auxiliar. **2,** (wife) cónyuge. *También,* **helpmeet** ('help,mit).

helter-skelter ('hɛl·tər'skɛl·tər) *adv.* desordenadamente; sin ton ni son; sin orden ni concierto. —*adj.* desordenado. —*n.* confusión; desorden.

hem (hɛm) *n.* **1,** (border, as on a garment) doble; dobladillo; bastilla; *Amer.* ruedo. **2,** (edge) borde. —*v.t.* [**hemmed, hemming**] **1,** (put a hem on) hacer el doble a; bastillar. **2,** (encircle) cercar; rodear. **3,** [*usu.,* **hem in, about** o **around**] (confine; restrain) confinar; limitar. —*interj.* ¡ejem! —**hem and haw,** vacilar; andar con rodeos.

hemiplegia (,hɛm·ɪ'pliː·dʒi·ə) *n.* hemiplejía. —**hemiplegic,** *n. & adj.* hemipléjico.

hemisphere ('hɛm·ə·sfɪr) *n.* hemisferio. —**hemispheric** (-'sfɛr·ɪk); **hemispherical** (-'sfɛr·ə·kəl) *adj.* hemisférico.

hemlock ('hɛm·lak) *n.* **1,** (poisonous herb) cicuta. **2,** (evergreen tree) abeto americano.

hemoglobin (,hi·mə'glo·bɪn) *n.* hemoglobina.

hemophilia (,hi·mə'fɪl·i·ə) *n.* hemofilia. —**hemophiliac** (-æk) *n.* hemofílico. —**hemophilic,** *adj.* hemofílico.

hemorrhage ('hɛm·ə·rɪdʒ) *n.* hemorragia.

hemorrhoid ('hɛm·ə,rɔid) *n., usu.pl.* hemorroides; almorranas.

hemp (hɛmp) *n.* cáñamo.

hemstitch ('hɛm,stɪtʃ) *n.* vainica. —*v.t.* hacer vainica en.

hen (hɛn) *n.* gallina.

henbane ('hɛn·bein) *n.* beleño.

hence (hɛns) *adv.* **1,** (away; from this place) fuera de aquí; fuera. **2,** (from this time) de aquí a; cuando pase. **3,** (from this life) de ⊖ desde aquí. **4,** (therefore) por tanto; por lo tanto; por consiguiente. **5,** (from this origin or source) de aquí; de donde.

henceforth ('hɛns,forθ) *adv.* de aquí en adelante; en lo futuro.

henchman ('hɛntʃ·mən) *n.* [*pl.* **-men**] secuaz; sicario.

henna ('hɛn·ə) *n.* alheña. —*v.t.* alheñar.

hennery ('hɛn·ə·ri) *n.* gallinero. *También,* **hencoop, henhouse.**

henpeck ('hɛn,pɛk) *v.t.* dominar; tiranizar (al marido).

hep (hɛp) *adj., slang* experimentado; corrido.

hepatic (hɪ'pæt·ɪk) *adj.* hepático. —**hepatitis** (,hɛp·ə'tai·təs) *n.* hepatitis.

hepatica (hɪ'pæt·ɪ·kə) *n.* hepática.

her (hɑr) *pron.pers.fem.sing.* **1,** *(complemento directo de verbo)* la; a ella. **2,** *(complemento indirecto de verbo)* le; a ella. **3,** *(complemento de prep.)* ella. **4,** *(tras* **than,** *en comparaciones)* ella; a ella. —*adj.pos.* su *(pl.* sus); de ella.

herald ('hɛr·əld) *n.* heraldo. —*v.t.* anunciar; preconizar. —**heraldic** (he'ræl·dɪk) *adj.* heráldico. —**heraldry,** *n.* heráldica.

herb (ʌrb; hʌrb) *n.* hierba. —**herbaceous** (hʌr'bei·ʃəs) *adj.* herbáceo. —**herbage,** *n.* herbaje; pasto; hierba.

herbal ('ʌr·bəl; 'hʌr-) *adj. & n.* herbario.

herbarium (hʌr'bɛr·i·əm) *n.* [*pl.* **-ums** o **-a** (ə)] herbario.

herbicide ('hʌr·bə·said) *n.* herbicida.

herbivorous (hər'bɪv·ə·rəs) *adj.* herbívoro. —**herbivore** ('hʌr·bə·vor) *n.* herbívoro.

herb tea tisana.

Herculean (hər'kju·li·ən) *adj.* hercúleo.

herd (hʌrd) *n.* **1,** (of cattle) manada; (of sheep) hato; rebaño; (of swine) piara. **2,** (throng) hato; manada; muchedumbre. —*v.t.* reunir; juntar. —*v.i.* ir juntos; ir en manada.

herdsman ('hʌrdz·mən) *n.* [*pl.* **-men**] vaquero; pastor; porquerizo.

here (hɪr) *adv.* aquí; acá. —*interj.* ¡presente!; ¡aquí!; *(in handing something)* ¡tenga! —**here's to you!,** ¡a su salud!

hereabout ('hɪr·ə,baut) *adv.* aquí cerca; por aquí. *También,* **hereabouts.**

hereafter (hɪr'æf·tər) *adv.* en lo futuro; de aquí en adelante. —*n.* el más allá; la otra vida.

hereat (hɪr'æt) *adv.* a esto.

hereby ('hɪr,bai) *adv.* por éstas; por la(s) presente(s); con o por esto.

hereditary (hə'rɛd·ə,tɛr·i) *adj.* hereditario.

heredity (hə'rɛd·ə·ti) *n.* herencia.

herein (hɪr'ɪn) *adv.* **1,** (enclosed, as in a letter) adjunto. **2,** (in this place) aquí. —**hereinafter,** *adv.* en adelante.

hereof (hɪr'ʌv) *adv.* de esto; de eso.

hereon (hɪr'an) *adv.* sobre esto; en esto.

heresy ('hɛr·ə·si) *n.* herejía.

heretic ('hɛr·ə·tɪk) *n.* hereje. —**heretical** (hə'rɛt·ɪ·kəl) *adj.* herético.

hereto (hɪr'tu) *adv.* a esto.

heretofore (,hɪr·tə'for) *adv.* antes; hasta ahora; hasta hoy; hasta aquí.

hereunder (hɪr'ʌn·dər) *adv.* **1,** (below) más abajo; más adelante. **2,** (by this authority) en virtud de esto.

hereupon ('hɪr·ə·pan) *adv.* sobre esto; en esto.

heritable ('hɛr·ə·tə·bəl) *adj.* heredable.

heritage ('hɛr·ə·tɪdʒ) *n.* herencia.

hermaphrodite (hər'mæf·rə,dait) *n.* hermafrodita. —**hermaphroditic** (-'dɪt·ɪk) *adj.* hermafrodita.

hermetic (hər'mɛt·ɪk) *adj.* hermético.

hermit ('hʌr·mɪt) *n.* eremita; ermitaño.

hermitage ('hʌr·mɪ·tɪdʒ) *n.* ermita.

hernia ('hʌr·ni·ə) *n.* hernia.

hero ('hɪr·o) *n.* héroe.

heroic (hɪ'ro·ɪk) *adj.* heroico.

heroics (hɪ'ro·ɪks) *n.pl.* rimbombancia; lenguaje rimbombante.

heroin ('hɛr·o·ɪn) *n.* heroína.

heroine ('hɛr·o·ɪn) *n.* heroína.

heroism ('hɛr·o·ɪz·əm) *n.* heroísmo.

heron ('hɛr·ən) *n.* garza.

herpes ('hʌr·piz) *n.* herpe; herpes.

herpetology (,hʌr·pə'tal·ə·dʒi) *n.* herpetología. —**herpetologist,** *n.* herpetólogo.

herring ('hɛr·ɪŋ) *n.* arenque.

hers (hʌrz) *pron.pos.* el suyo; la suya; lo suyo; los suyos; las suyas; el, la, lo, los o las de ella.

herself (hʌr'sɛlf) *pron.pers. fem. sing.* ella; ella misma. —*pron.refl.* **1,** (complemento directo o indirecto de verbo) se: *She washed herself,* Se lavó; *She put it on herself,* Se lo puso. **2,** (complemento de prep.) sí; sí misma: *She bought it for herself,* Se lo compró para sí. —**to herself,**

para sí: *She said to herself, "I'm not going,"* Dijo para sí: no voy. —**with herself,** consigo.

he's (his) *contr. de* **he is** *o* **he has.**

hesitant ('hɛz·ɪ·tənt) *adj.* vacilante; titubeante; indeciso; irresoluto. —**hesitancy,** *n.* vacilación; indecisión; irresolución.

hesitate ('hɛz·ɪ,teit) *v.i.* vacilar; titubear. —**hesitation,** *n.* vacilación; titubeo.

heterodox ('hɛt·ər·ə,daks) *adj.* heterodoxo. —**heterodoxy,** *n.* heterodoxia.

heterogeneous (,hɛt·ər·ə'dʒi·ni·əs) *adj.* heterogéneo.

heterosexual (,hɛt·ə·ro'sɛk·ʃu·əl) *adj. & n.* heterosexual.

heuristic (hjʊ'rɪs·tɪk) *adj.* heurístico. —**heuristic,** *n.sing.;* **heuristics,** *n.pl.* heurística.

hew (hju) *v.t. & i.* [*p.p.* hewed *o* hewn] **1,** (sever) tajar; hender; partir. **2,** (carve) tallar; esculpir; cincelar.

hex (hɛks) *v.t., colloq.* embrujar; maleficiar. —*n., colloq.* hechizo; maleficio.

hexagon ('hɛks·ə·gan) *n.* hexágono. —**hexagonal** (hɛks'æg·ə·nəl) *n. adj.* hexagonal.

hexagram ('hɛks·ə·græm) *n.* hexagrama.

hey (hei) *interj.* ¡eh!; ¡oiga!; ¡ea!; *Amer.* ¡epa!

heyday ('hei,dei) *n.* apogeo; cúspide; momento cumbre.

hiatus (hai'ei·təs) *n.* **1,** (lacuna) laguna; hueco; omisión. **2,** (pause) pausa; hiato.

hibernal (hai'bʌr·nəl) *adj.* hibernal; invernal.

hibernate ('hai·bər,neit) *v.i.* hibernar; invernar. —**hibernation,** *n.* hibernación.

hibiscus (hai'bɪs·kəs) *n.* hibisco.

hiccup ('hɪk·ʌp) *n.* hipo. —*v.i.* hipar. *También,* **hiccough** ('hɪk·ʌp).

hick (hɪk) *n.* rústico; palurdo; *Amer.* jíbaro. —*adj., colloq.* rústico; de campo.

hickory ('hɪk·ə·ri) *n.* nogal americano.

hid (hɪd) *v., pret. & p.p. de* **hide.**

hidden ('hɪd·ən) *v., p.p. de* **hide.** —*adj.* escondido; oculto.

hide (haid) *v.t.* [**hid,** hid *o* **hidden,** **hiding**] **1,** (put or keep out of sight) esconder; ocultar. **2,** (conceal; keep secret) ocultar; encubrir; disimular.

—v.i. esconderse; ocultarse. **—n.** cuero; piel; pellejo. **—neither hide nor hair,** ni señal; nada.

hide-and-seek *n.* juego del escondite. **—play hide-and-seek,** jugar al escondite.

hideaway ('haid·ə·wei) *n.* escondite.

hidebound ('haid,baund) *adj.* cerrado; rígido; inveterado; empedernido.

hideous ('hɪd·i·əs) *adj.* horrendo; espantoso; deforme. **—hideousness,** *n.* horror; deformidad.

hideout ('haid·aut) *n.* escondite; refugio; guarida.

hiding ('hai·dɪŋ) *n.* **1,** (concealment) ocultación. **2,** *slang* (whipping) zurra; paliza. **—in hiding,** escondido. **—hiding place,** escondite; escondrijo.

hie (hai) *v.i.* apurarse; correr; precipitarse.

hierarch ('hai·ər·ark) *n.* jerarca. **—hierarchal,** *adj.* jerárquico. **—hierarchic; hierarchical,** *adj.* jerárquico. **—hierarchy,** *n.* jerarquía.

hieroglyphic (,hai·ər·ə'glɪf·ɪk) *n.* & *adj.* jeroglífico.

high (hai) *adj.* **1,** (lofty; elevated) alto. **2,** (having a specified height) de alto; de altura: *a tree fifty feet high,* un árbol de cincuenta pies de alto; *That tree is fifty feet high,* Ese árbol tiene cincuenta pies de alto. **3,** (situated at a specified height) a una altura de . . . : *Mexico City is 7400 feet high;* La Ciudad de México está a una altura de 7400 pies. **4,** (great; greater than usual in size, amount, price, importance, etc.) alto; grande. **5,** (sharp; shrill) alto; agudo. **6,** (superior; excellent) alto; superior. **7,** (haughty; overbearing) altanero; arrogante. **8,** (fully advanced or developed) pleno. **9,** (smelly; tainted) pasado; rancio. **10,** *slang* (exhilarated; slightly intoxicated) borracho; alegre. **—adv. 1,** (in a high manner) a lo grande. **2,** (at or to a high level) alto. **3,** (at a high price) caro. **—n. 1,** (high level or point) altura; lo alto. **2,** (highest level or point) tope; cumbre. **3,** (high gear) tercera o alta (velocidad). **4,** (center of high pressure) presión; centro de alta presión. **—fly high,** ambicionar mucho. **—high and dry, 1,** (beached) varado. **2,** (in the lurch)

plantado. **—high and low,** por todas partes. **—high and mighty,** *colloq.* altanero; arrogante. **—high command,** alto mando; alto comando. **—high days,** festividades; días de fiesta. **—high explosive,** explosivo fulminante o de alta potencia. **—high hat,** sombrero de copa. **—high life; high society,** gran mundo; alta sociedad. **—high living,** la buena vida; la gran vida; el buen vivir. **—High Mass,** misa mayor. **—high priest,** gran sacerdote; sumo sacerdote. **—high sea** o **seas,** alta mar. **—high spirits,** buen humor; contento. **—high tide,** pleamar; marea alta. **—the Most High,** el Altísimo.

highball ('hai,bɔl) *n.* **1,** (drink) highball; jaibol. **2,** *R.R.* vía libre. **—v.i., colloq.** ir disparado o embalado.

highborn ('hai·born) *adj.* noble; de noble alcurnia.

highbred ('hai·brɛd) *adj.* de buena familia; refinado.

highbrow ('hai·brau) *n.* & *adj., colloq.* intelectual; erudito.

high chair sillita para niños.

high-class *adj.* de calidad; de alto copete.

higher education educación o instrucción superior; educación universitaria.

higher-up *n., colloq.* superior; jefe.

highfalutin (,hai·fə'lu·tən) *adj., colloq.* pretencioso; fachendoso; *(of language)* altisonante.

high-flown *adj.* **1,** (ambitious) ambicioso; desmedido. **2,** (bombastic) altisonante.

high-grade *adj.* de calidad; superior.

high-handed *adj.* arbitrario; despótico; tiránico. **—highhandedness,** *n.* arbitrariedad.

high-hat *adj., slang* de alto copete; encopetado. **—n., slang** esnob. **—v.t. & i., slang** menospreciar; mirar con menosprecio o condescendencia.

highjack ('hai,dʒæk) *v.t. & i., slang* = **hijack.**

highland ('hai·lənd) *adj.* serrano; montañés; de las montañas. **—n., usu.pl.** montañas; serranías. **—highlander,** *n.* montañés; serrano.

highlight ('hai·lait) *n.* [*también,* **high light**] **1,** (outstanding part; feature) punto culminante; punto más destacado. **2,** (brightly lighted part) toque de luz; matiz de resalte. —*v.t.* hacer resaltar; dar énfasis a.

highly ('hai·li) *adv.* altamente; extremadamente; muy; muy bien.

high-minded *adj.* de miras elevadas; idealista.

highness ('hai·nəs) *n.* **1,** (loftiness) altura; elevación. **2,** *cap.* (title of honor) Alteza.

high-pressure *adj.* **1,** (of or for high pressure) de alta presión. **2,** (strongly persuasive) insistente; enérgico; persuasivo. —*v.t.*, *colloq.* empujar; apretar; hacer presión (a o en); *Amer.* presionar.

high-priced *adj.* caro; costoso.

high-rise *adj.* & *n.* (edificio) de muchos pisos.

high road *n.* camino principal; camino real.

high school escuela superior o secundaria; instituto de segunda enseñanza.

high-sounding *adj.* altisonante.

high-spirited *adj.* animoso; fogoso.

high-strung *adj.* nervioso; tenso; excitable.

high time 1, *slang* (revel; spree) fiesta; juerga. **2,** (late hour) hora; *It's high time you were in bed,* (Ya) es hora de que estés en cama.

high-toned *adj.* **1,** (high-pitched) agudo; de tono alto. **2,** *fig.* (lofty) de mucho tono; de alto copete. **3,** *colloq.* (stylish) de buen tono; elegante.

high water 1, (of a river or stream) nivel superior de las aguas. **2,** (high tide) pleamar; marea alta. —**high-water mark,** *lit.* cota superior de las aguas. **2,** *fig.* apogeo; punto culminante.

highway ('hai·wei) *n.* carretera; camino.

highwayman ('hai·we·mən) *n.* [*pl.* **-men**] salteador; bandolero.

hijack también, **highjack** ('hai,dʒæk) *v.t.* & *i.*, *slang* asaltar o robar en tránsito.

hike (haik) *v.i.* dar un paseo; dar o echar una caminata. —*v.t.*, *colloq.* levantar; subir. —*n.* caminata; paseo.

hilarious (hɪ'lɛr·i·əs) *adj.* hilarante; divertido; alegre. —**hilarity,** *n.* hilaridad; alegría; risa.

hill (hɪl) *n.* cerro; colina; loma. —*v.t.* apilar; amontonar. —**down-**

hill, cuesta abajo. —**uphill,** cuesta arriba.

hillbilly ('hɪl,bɪl·i) *n.* & *adj.* patán; rústico.

hillock ('hɪl·ək) *n.* montecillo; loma.

hillside ('hɪl·said) *n.* ladera; falda.

hilltop ('hɪl·tap) *n.* cima; cumbre.

hilly ('hɪl·i) *adj.* con o de muchas colinas o lomas. —**hilliness,** *n.* abundancia de colinas o lomas.

hilt (hɪlt) *n.* empuñadura; puño.

him (hɪm) *pron.pers. masc.sing.* **1,** (complemento directo de verbo) lo; le; a él. **2,** (complemento indirecto de verbo) le; a él. **3,** (complemento de prep.) él. **4,** (tras **than,** en comparaciones) él; a él.

himself (hɪm'sɛlf) *pron.pers. masc.sing.* él; él mismo. —*pron. refl.* **1,** (complemento directo o indirecto de verbo) se: *He washed himself,* Se lavó; *He put it on himself,* Se lo puso. **2,** (complemento de prep.) sí; sí mismo: *He bought it for himself,* Se lo compró para sí. **to himself,** para sí: *He said to himself, "I'm not going,"* Dijo para sí: no voy. —**with himself,** consigo.

hind (haind) *adj.* de atrás; trasero; posterior. —*n.* cierva; venado hembra.

hinder ('hɪn·dər) *v.t.* & *i.* impedir; obstruir; estorbar.

hinder ('hain·dər) *adj.* trasero; posterior.

hindmost ('haind·most) *adj.* último; postrero. *También,* **hindermost** ('hain·dər-).

hindrance ('hɪn·drəns) *n.* impedimento; obstáculo; estorbo.

hindsight ('haind·sait) *n.* mirada retrospectiva; mirada atrás; retrospección.

Hindu ('hɪn·du) *n.* & *adj.* hindú. —**Hinduism,** *n.* hinduismo.

hinge (hɪndʒ) *n.* **1,** (joint) bisagra; charnela; gozne. **2,** *fig.* (controlling principle) fundamento; base; punto cardinal. —*v.t.* poner bisagras o goznes a; engoznar. —*v.i.* girar; depender.

hint (hɪnt) *n.* **1,** (clue; indication) indicación; sugerencia. **2,** (intimation; innuendo) indirecta; insinuación; alusión. —*v.t.* indicar; sugerir. —*v.i.* aludir; hacer alusión. —**hint at,** insinuar; hacer alusión a.

hinterland ('hɪn·tər,lænd) *n.* tierra adentro; interior.

hip (hɪp) *n.* **1,** *anat.* cadera. **2,** *zoöl.*

anca. **3**, *archit.* caballete. —*adj.*, *slang* = **hep.**

hipbone ('hɪp,bon) *n.* cía.

hippodrome ('hɪp·ə,drom) *n.* hipódromo.

hippopotamus (,hɪp·ə'pat·ə·məs) *n.* hipopótamo.

hire (hair) *v.t.* **1**, (employ) emplear. **2**, (rent) alquilar. —*n.* **1**, (salary) salario; paga. **2**, (rental) alquiler. **3**, (act of hiring or being hired) empleo. —**for hire**, de alquiler. —**hire out**, emplearse.

hireling ('hair·lɪŋ) *n.*, *derog.* alquiladizo.

hirsute (hʌr'sut) *adj.* hirsuto.

his (hɪz) *adj.pos.* su (*pl.* sus); de él. —*pron.poss.* el suyo; la suya; lo suyo; los suyos; las suyas; el, la, lo, los o las de él.

Hispanic (hɪs'pæn·ɪk) *adj.* hispánico.

hiss (hɪs) *v.i.*[*] & *t.* sisear; silbar. —*n.* siseo; silbido.

hist (hɪst) *interj.* ¡chito!; ¡chitón!; ¡silencio!

histamine ('hɪs·tə,min) *n.* histamina.

histology (hɪs'tal·ə·dʒi) *n.* histología. —**histological** (hɪs·tə'ladʒ·ɪ·kəl) *adj.* histológico. —**histologist**, *n.* histólogo.

historian (hɪs'tor·i·ən) *n.* historiador.

historic (hɪs'tor·ɪk) *adj.* histórico. *También,* **historical.** —**historicity** (,hɪs·tə'rɪs·e·ti) *n.* historicidad.

history ('hɪs·tə·ri) *n.* historia. —**case history**, historial.

histrionic (,hɪs·tri'an·ɪk) *adj.* histriónico; teatral. —**histrionics,** *n.pl.* histrionismo; teatro.

hit (hɪt) *v.t.* [**hit, hitting**] **1**, (strike against) chocar contra; pegar contra. **2**, (give a blow to) golpear; pegar. **3**, (give, as a blow) dar; pegar; asestar. **4**, (strike as a mark) pegar en; dar en. **5**, [*también,* **hit on** o **against**] (cause to bump) golpearse (la cabeza, el pie, etc.) contra. **6**, *fig.* (affect strongly) afectar; impresionar. **7**, (come upon; find) encontrar; hallar. **8**, (reach; come to or upon) llegar a. **9**, *baseball* batear; conseguir. —*v.i.* **1**, (strike) golpear; chocar. **2**, [*usu.* **hit on** o **upon**] (find) encontrar; hallar. **3**, *baseball* conseguir una base. —*n.* **1**, (blow; stroke) golpe. **2**, (collision) choque. **3**, *colloq.* (success; successful event) éxito. **4**, *baseball*

bola bateada con éxito. —**be a hit,** *colloq.* ser un éxito; hacer sensación. —**hit it off,** *colloq.* llevarse bien; congeniar. —**hit or miss,** a la diabla; a la buena de Dios. —**hit the nail on the head,** dar en el clavo. —**hit (out) at,** atacar.

hitch (hɪtʃ) *v.t.* **1**, (fasten) sujetar; atar; amarrar. **2**, [*usu.* **hitch up**] (raise) subir; levantar. **3**, (harness) enganchar. —*v.i.* **1**, (become caught or entangled) engancharse; enredarse. **2**, (move jerkily) andar a saltos o tropezones. **3**, (limp) cojear. —*n.* **1**, (fastening) enganche. **2**, (kind of knot) vuelta de cabo. **3**, (obstacle) dificultad; obstáculo. **4**, (jerk; limping gait) tropezón; tirón. **5**, *colloq.* (period, as of duty, imprisonment, etc.) estancia.

hitchhike ('hɪtʃ,haik) *v.i.*, *colloq.* gorrear un viaje en automóvil; viajar de gorra en un auto.

hitching post atadero.

hither ('hɪð·ər) *adv.* aquí; hacia aquí. —*adj.* más cercano. —**hithermost,** *adj.* más cercano.

hitherto ('hɪð·ər·tu) *adv.* hasta ahora; hasta aquí; hasta hoy.

hive (haiv) *n.* **1**, (beehive) colmena. **2**, (swarm) enjambre.

hives (haivz) *n.pl.* urticaria.

ho (ho) *interj.* **1**, (calling attention) ¡eh!; ¡ea!; ¡oiga! **2**, (expressing surprise, exultation, etc.) ¡oh!; ¡ay!; ¡ja!

hoar (hor) *adj.* **1**, (whitish; gray) blanquecino; blancuzco. **2**, (grayhaired) cano; canoso.

hoard (hord) *n.* cúmulo; montón. —*v.t. & i.* **1**, (accumulate) acumular; amontonar. **2**, (monopolize) acaparar.

hoarfrost *n.* escarcha.

hoarhound *n.* = **horehound.**

hoariness ('hor·i·nəs) *n.* **1**, (whitishness) blancura. **2**, (grayness of hair) canicie. **3**, (antiquity) vejez.

hoarse (hors) *adj.* ronco; bronco; áspero. —**hoarseness,** *n.* ronquera; bronquedad; aspereza. —**make hoarse,** enronquecer; poner ronco.

hoary ('hor·i) *adj.* **1**, = **hoar. 2**, (ancient) viejo.

hoax (hoks) *n.* decepción; engaño; burla. —*v.t.* engañar; burlar.

hob (harb) *n.* **1**, (ledge of a fireplace) anaquel o repisa de chimenea. **2**, (elf) duende. —**play**

(o **raise**) **hob with**, *colloq.* dar al traste con; trastornar.

hobble ('hab·əl) *n.* **1**, (limp) cojera; renquera. *Amer.* renguera. **2**, (fetter) maniota; traba. —*v.i.* **1**, (move haltingly) moverse a duras penas; avanzar con dificultad. **2**, (limp) cojear; renquear; *Amer.* renguear. —*v.t.* poner maniota a; trabar.

hobby ('hab·i) *n.* afición; pasatiempo; manía. —**hobbyist**, *n.* aficionado.

hobbyhorse ('hab·i,hors) *n.* caballito mecedor; caballito de palo.

hobgoblin ('hab,gab·lin) *n.* duende.

hobnail ('hab·neil) *n.* tachuela; tachón.

hobnob ('hab·nab) *v.i., colloq.* tratarse con familiaridad; codearse.

hobo ('ho·bo) *n., colloq.* [*pl.* **-bos** o **-boes**] vagabundo.

hock (hak) *n.* **1**, (joint above the hoof) jarrete; corvejón. **2**, *slang* (pawn) empeño. —*v.t.* **1**, (hamstring) desjarretar. **2**, *slang* (pawn) empeñar.

hockey ('hak·i) *n.* hockey.

hockshop ('hak·ʃap) *n., slang* = **pawnshop**.

hocus ('ho·kəs) *v.t.* **1**, (to fool) engañar. **2**, (to drug) narcotizar.

hocus-pocus ('ho·kəs'po·kəs) *n.* **1**, (incantation) palabras cabalísticas; abracadabra; cábala. **2**, (meaningless jargon) jerigonza. **3**, (trickery) cábala; engañifa. —*v.t., colloq.* engañar; engatusar.

hod (had) *n.* **1**, (device for carrying bricks or mortar) capacho. **2**, (coal scuttle) cubo para carbón.

hodgepodge ('had3,pad3) *n.* mescolanza; baturrillo. *También,* **hotchpotch**.

hoe (ho) *n.* azada; azadón. —*v.t. & i.* azadonar; cavar o escardar con azada.

hog (harg) *n.* puerco; cerdo; cochino. —*v.t., slang* [**hogged, hogging**] cogerse lo mejor de; acaparar; tragar. —**go the whole hog**, *slang* ir o seguir hasta el fin; entregarse sin reservas. —**hog wild**, *slang* fuera de sí; loco.

hoggish ('hag·iʃ) *adj.* **1**, (hoglike) porcino. **2**, (selfish; gluttonous) puerco; cerdo; glotón; *Amer.* angurriento. —**hoggishness**, *n.* glotonería; *Amer.* angurria.

hogshead ('hagz,hed) *n.* tonel; pipa; bocoy.

hogtie ('hag,tai) *v.t.* atar de pies y manos.

hogwash ('hag,waʃ) *n.* bazofia.

hoi polloi (,hɔi·pə'lɔi) plebe; vulgo.

hoist (hɔist) *v.t.* alzar; levantar; izar. —*n.* **1**, (a hoisting) tirón; esfuerzo hacia arriba; alzamiento. **2**, (elevator) elevador. **3**, (lifting apparatus) cabria; pescante.

hoity-toity ('hɔi·ti'tɔi·ti) *adj.* altanero; presumido.

hokum ('ho·kəm) *n., slang* **1**, (mawkishness) ñoñerías; sensibilería. **2**, (nonsense) tontería; boberías.

hold (hold) *v.t.* [*pret. & p.p.* **held**] **1**, (grasp; seize) coger; agarrar. **2**, (clutch; keep fast) tener; sujetar; apretar. **3**, (detain; delay) retener; detener. **4**, (keep; save) guardar. **5**, (keep in a certain place or condition) tener; mantener. **6**, (possess; own) poseer; tener. **7**, (occupy, as a job) desempeñar; ocupar. **8**, (support; bear the weight of) sostener; soportar; aguantar. **9**, (restrain) contener; reprimir; refrenar. **10**, (have or keep control of) sujetar; mantener. **11**, (have; carry on, as a meeting, social function, etc.) tener; dar; celebrar. **12**, (consider) considerar; estimar. **13**, (maintain) sostener; mantener. **14**, (contain; have within) contener; tener. **15**, (contain; have room for) poder contener; tener capacidad para; acomodar. —*v.i.* **1**, (keep on; continue) mantenerse; continuar; seguir. **2**, (remain unyielding) aguantar; resistir; no ceder. **3**, (be true or valid) ser válido; tener fuerza. **4**, (halt; stop) aguantarse; detenerse; parar. —*n.* **1**, (act or manner of holding) agarrón; apretón. **2**, (handle) agarradera; mango. **3**, (of a ship) bodega. **4**, (influence; control) influencia; poder; mano. **5**, *wrestling* llave. —*interj.* ¡para!; ¡pare! —**catch hold of**, agarrar. —**get hold of**, **1**, (grasp) agarrar. **2**, (acquire; attain; reach) conseguir. —**hold down**, **1**, (restrain; keep down) sujetar; reprimir. **2**, *colloq.* (keep, as a job) mantenerse en; ocupar. —**hold forth**, **1**, (speak; preach) hablar; perorar. **2**, (offer; propose) proponer; ofrecer. —**hold in**, contener; sujetar. —**hold off**, **1**, (keep at bay) contener; mantener a distancia. **2,** (refrain) contenerse; aguantarse. —**hold on, 1,** (keep one's hold) mantenerse; afirmarse. **2,** (persist) persistir. **3,** *colloq., usu.impve.* (stop; wait) parar. —**hold one's own,** mantenerse; mantenerse firme; no quedarse atrás. —**hold out, 1,** (last; endure) aguantar; durar. **2,** (stand firm) aguantar; resistir. **3,** (offer) ofrecer. **4,** *slang* (refuse to give) resistirse o negarse a dar. —**hold over, 1,** (postpone) aplazar; posponer. **2,** (stay or keep for an additional period) continuar; seguir. **3,** (keep as a threat) amenazar (con). —**hold up, 1,** (support) soportar; aguantar. **2,** (show; exhibit) mostrar; exhibir. **3,** (last; endure; continue) durar; aguantar; resistir. **4,** (stop; delay; impede) demorar; detener. **5,** (rob) asaltar; atracar; robar. —**hold with,** estar de acuerdo con. —**lay hold of, 1,** (seize) agarrar. **2,** (get possession or control of) apoderarse de. **3,** (acquire; attain) conseguir. —**take hold (of), 1,** (grasp) coger; agarrar. **2,** (get control of) apoderarse de. **3,** (take root) arraigar.

holder ('hol·dər) *n.* **1,** (possessor, as of a title or record in sports) poseedor. **2,** (bearer, as of a title, passport, etc.) titular. **3,** (tenant; lessee) arrendatario. **4,** *comm.* tenedor; portador. **5,** (handle) agarradera; mango. **6,** (base; support) pie; base; soporte. **7,** (case; container) caja; estuche. *Muchas veces* **holder** *se expresa en español por el prefijo* porta- *en los compuestos:* pen-holder, portaplumas.

holding ('hol·dɪŋ) *n.* **1,** *usu.pl.* (property) bienes; posesiones. **2,** (lease; tenure) arrendamiento; tenencia. —**holding company,** compañía tenedora o matriz.

holdover ('hold,o·vər) *n.* persona o cosa que queda; resto; remanente.

holdup ('hold·ʌp) *n., colloq.* **1,** (robbery) atraco; robo. **2,** (delay) demora; retraso.

hole (hoʊl) *n.* **1,** (pit; hollow) hoyo; cavidad. **2,** (pool; deep place in water) pozo; hoya. **3,** (den; lair) madriguera; guarida. **4,** (opening) vano; hueco. **5,** (tear; rent) roto; agujero. **6,** *colloq.* (flaw; defect) fallo; defecto. **7,** *colloq.* (predicament) aprieto; apuro. **8,** *golf* hoyo. **9,** (prison cell) calabozo. —*v.t.* **1,** (pierce; perforate) agujerear;

perforar. **2,** (put or drive into a hole) meter; introducir. **3,** (make by digging a hole) cavar; excavar. —*v.i.* meterse; encerrarse. —**be in the hole,** *colloq.* estar o quedar en deuda. —**hole up, 1,** (hibernate) invernar; hibernar. **2,** (shut oneself in) enclaustrarse; recluirse. **3,** *slang* (find lodgings) meterse; alojarse.

holiday ('hal·ə·dei) *n.* **1,** (special day) fiesta; día de fiesta. **2,** *often pl.* (vacation) vacaciones. —*adj.* festivo.

holiness ('ho·li·nəs) *n.* santidad.

holistics (ho'lɪs·tɪks) *n.sing. & pl.* holismo. —**holistic,** *adj.* holístico.

holler ('hal·ər) *v.i. & t., colloq.* gritar. —*n., colloq.* grito.

hollow ('hal·o) *adj.* **1,** (empty) vacío; hueco. **2,** (concave) cóncavo. **3,** (insincere) falso; vacío; hueco. **4,** (deep-toned) hueco. —*n.* **1,** (pit) hueco; hoyo; cavidad. **2,** (valley; depression) hondonada; hoya. —*v.t.* [*también,* **hollow out**] ahuecar; excavar. —*v.i.* ahuecarse. —**beat all hollow,** *colloq.* ganar o superar por mucho; *Amer.* ganar lejos.

hollow-eyed *adj.* de o con ojos hundidos; ojeroso; demacrado.

hollowness ('hal·o·nəs) *n.* **1,** (emptiness) vacío. **2,** (empty place or space) hueco. **3,** (insincerity) vacuidad; falsedad; falsía.

holly ('hal·i) *n.* acebo.

hollyhock ('hal·i,hak) *n.* malva loca.

holmium ('hol·mi·əm) *n.* holmio.

holocaust ('hal·ə·kɔst) *n.* holocausto.

hologram ('hal·ə·græm) *n.* holograma.

holograph ('hal·ə,græf) *n. & adj.* ológrafo; hológrafo. —**holographic,** *adj.* ológrafo. —**holography** (ho'lag·rə·fi) *n.* olografía.

holster ('hol·stər) *n.* pistolera.

holy ('ho·li) *adj.* sagrado; santo; sacro. —**Holy day,** fiesta; día de fiesta. —**Holy Ghost; Holy Spirit,** Espíritu Santo. —**Holy Office,** Santo Oficio. —**holy oil,** crisma. —**holy water,** agua bendita. —**Holy Week,** Semana Santa.

homage ('ham·ɪdʒ) *n.* homenaje.

homburg ('ham·bʌrg) *n.* cierto sombrero de fieltro.

home (hoʊm) *n.* **1,** (house) casa. **2,** (residence) casa; domicilio. **3,** (family abode) hogar. **4,** (dwelling) vivienda; habitación. **5,** (place or country of origin) lugar de origen; patria; país o pueblo natal. **6,** (asylum; poorhouse; orphanage) asilo; hospicio. **7,** (habitat) medio; habitat; habitación. **8,** (focal point; center) capital; centro. **9,** (place of initial development; cradle) cuna; fuente; lugar de origen. **10,** (finish line; goal) meta. **11,** *baseball* base. —*adj.* **1,** (of the house; domestic) doméstico; casero. **2,** (of one's own country) nacional; interno. **3,** (local) local. **4,** (effective; to the point) efectivo; certero. —*adv.* **1,** (to or toward home) a casa. **2,** (at home) en casa. **3,** (to the mark) en el blanco; a su meta; a o en su lugar. **4,** (deeply; directly) a fondo; en lo vivo; de pleno. —*v.i.* **1,** (go to or toward home) dirigirse a casa; orientarse hacia su destino. **2,** (reside) vivir; habitar. —**at home,** en casa; como en su casa. —**be at home (in),** conocer bien o a fondo; estar en su elemento. —**bring home to,** hacer comprender; hacer darse cuenta de. —**home office,** oficina central. —**home rule,** gobierno autónomo; autonomía. —**home run,** *baseball* cuadrangular; jonrón. —**home town,** ciudad o pueblo natal. —**strike home,** *colloq.* dar en el blanco.

home-bred *adj.* **1,** (native; peculiar to a given locality) casero; propio o característico del lugar. **2,** (unsophisticated; crude) burdo; basto; poco refinado.

home brew preparación casera.

homecoming ('hom,kʌm·ɪŋ) *n.* vuelta (a casa); retorno; regreso.

homeland ('hom·lænd) *n.* patria.

homeless ('hom·ləs) *adj.* sin hogar; desamparado.

homely ('hom·li) *adj.* **1,** (domestic) casero. **2,** (plain; simple) simple; familiar; sencillo. **3,** (ugly) feo; basto.

homemade ('hom,meid) *adj.* casero; hecho en casa; de fabricación casera.

homemaker ('hom,mei·kər) *n.* ama de casa.

homeopathy (,ho·mi'ap·ə·θi) *n.* homeopatía. —**homeopath** ('ho·mi·ə,pæθ) *n.* homeópata. —**homeopathic** (-ə'pæθ·ɪk) *adj.* homeopático.

homer ('ho·mər) *n.* **1,** = **homing pigeon. 2,** = **home run.**

homesick ('hom·sɪk) *adj.* nostálgico; que tiene morriña. —**homesick-**

ness, *n.* nostalgia; morriña. —**be homesick (for),** añorar; tener nostalgia o morriña (por); *Amer.* extrañar.

homespun ('hom,spʌn) *adj.* **1,** (made at home) casero; de fabricación casera. **2,** (simple; crude) burdo; tosco. —*n.* tela casera.

homestead ('hom,stɛd) *n.* heredad; casa solariega.

homework ('hom·wʌrk) *n.* tarea; trabajo en la casa.

homey *también,* **homy** ('ho·mi) *adj., colloq.* hogareño.

homicide ('ham·ə·said) *n.* **1,** (act) homicidio. **2,** (agent) homicida. —**homicidal** (-'sai·dəl) *adj.* homicida.

homiletic (,ham·ə'lɛt·ɪk) *adj.* homilético. —**homiletics,** *n.pl.* homilética.

homily ('ham·ə·li) *n.* homilía.

homing ('ho·mɪŋ) **pigeon** paloma mensajera.

hominy ('ham·ə·ni) *n.* maíz molido.

homogamous (ho'mag·ə·məs) *adj.* homógamo.

homogeneous (,ho·mə'dʒi·ni·əs) *adj.* homogéneo. —**homogeneity** (-dʒə'ni·ə·ti) *n.* homogeneidad.

homogenize (ho'madʒ·ə,naiz) *v.t.* homogeneizar. —**homogenization** (-nɪ'zei·ʃən) *n.* homogeneización.

homologous (ho'mal·ə·gəs) *adj.* homólogo. —**homology** (-dʒi) *n.* homología.

homonym ('ham·ə·nɪm) *n.* homónimo. —**homonymous** (ho'man·ə·məs) *adj.* homónimo. —**homonymy** (ho'man·ə·mi) *n.* homonimia.

homophone ('ham·ə,fon) *n.* homófono. —**homophonic** (-'fan·ɪk) *adj.* homófono. —**homophonous** (hə'maf·ə·nəs) *adj.* homófono. —**homophony** (hə'maf·ə·ni) *n.* homofonía.

homosexual (,hom·ə'sɛk·su·əl) *n.* & *adj.* homosexual. —**homosexuality** (-,sɛk·su'æl·ə·ti) *n.* homosexualidad.

homunculus (ho'mʌŋ·kjə·ləs) *n.* homúnculo.

homy ('ho·mi) *adj.* = **homey.**

honcho ('han·tʃo) *n., slang* jefe.

hone (hoːn) *n.* piedra de afilar. —*v.t.* afilar. —*v.i., dial.* anhelar; ansiar.

honest ('an·ɪst) *adj.* honrado; honesto; justo.

honesty ('an·ıs·ti) *n.* honradez; honestidad.

honey ('hʌn·i) *n.* **1,** (sweet substance) miel. **2,** *colloq.* (term of endearment) querido; querida; mi amor. **—honeyed,** *adj.* dulce; meloso; melifluo.

honeybee ('hʌn·i,biz) *n.* abeja de miel.

honeycomb ('hʌn·i,kom) *n.* **1,** (beehive) panal; bresca. **2,** (maze) laberinto; red. **—v.t. 1,** (riddle, as with tunnels) llenar o tupir de perforaciones, canales, etc.; atravesar; calar. **2,** (permeate; undermine) penetrar; llenar; saturar; minar. **—v.i.** volverse un laberinto. **—adj.** de o como un panal; laberíntico.

honeydew ('hʌn·i,dju) *n.* exudación o secreción dulce. **—honeydew melon,** cierto melón muy dulce.

honeymoon ('hʌn·i,mun) *n.* luna de miel.

honeysuckle ('hʌn·i,sʌk·əl) *n.* madreselva.

honk (haŋk) *n.* **1,** (call of the goose) grito del ganso; trompetazo. **2,** (sound of a horn) toque de sirena o bocina; bocinazo. **—v.t. & i. 1,** (cry, as a goose) gritar el ganso. **2,** (sound, as a horn) tocar (la bocina).

honor *también,* **honour** ('an·ər) *n.* **1,** (quality or distinction) honor; honra. **2,** *cap.* (title of respect) señoría. **—v.t. 1,** (respect greatly; confer honor upon) honrar. **2,** (accept; credit) aceptar; dar buena acogida a. **3,** *comm.* aceptar; pagar. **—do honor to,** honrar. **—do the honors,** hacer los honores. **—on (o upon) one's honor,** por el honor de uno.

honorable ('an·ər·ə·bəl) *adj.* **1,** (noble; illustrious) honorable; noble; ilustre. **2,** *cap.* (title of respect) honorable. **3,** (upright; honest) honrado; honesto; pundonoroso. **4,** (conferring honor) honroso.

honorarium (,an·ə'rɛr·i·əm) *n.* [*pl.* **honoraria** (-i·ə)] honorarios.

honorary ('an·ər·ɛr·i) *adj.* honorario; honorífico.

hooch (hutʃ) *n., slang* licor; whisky.

hood (hʊd) *n.* **1,** (head covering) caperuza; capucha; capirote; capilla. **2,** (cover of an engine) cubierta; capota. **3,** (folding cover, as of a carriage) toldo; capota. **4,** *zoöl.* (crest) cresta. **5,** (chimney cowl) sombrerete; caperuza. **6,** *slang =* **hoodlum. —v.t. 1,** (cover with a hood, as the head or body) encapuchar. **2,** (put a hood on or over) entoldar; proveer de capota. **3,** (hide) encubrir; ocultar; esconder.

hoodlum ('hud·ləm) *n., colloq.* rufián; maleante; matón de barrio.

hoodoo ('hu·du) *n.* **1,** (voodoo) magia negra; brujería. **2,** *colloq.* (bad luck) aojo; mala suerte. **3,** *colloq.* (jinx) pájaro de mal agüero; persona o cosa que trae mala suerte. **—v.t.** maldecir; embrujar; aojar.

hoodwink ('hud,wiŋk) *v.t.* engatusar; engañar; pasar gato por liebre.

hooey ('hu·i) *n., slang* tontería; farfolla; pamplinas.

hoof (huf) *n.* [*pl.* **hoofs** o **hooves**] casco; uña; pezuña. **—v.t. & i. 1,** (trample) pisotear; patear. **2,** *colloq.* (walk) andar; caminar; ir a pie. **3,** *slang* (dance) bailar. **—hoofer,** *n., slang* bailarín. **—on the hoof,** en pie; vivo.

hoof-and-mouth disease fiebre aftosa.

hoofbeat ('huf·bit) *n.* ruido de cascos.

hook (hʊk) *n.* **1,** (device for catching, pulling, etc.) gancho. **2,** (gaff) garfio. **3,** (part of a hook and eye) corchete. **4,** (bend) turn) curva; recodo; vuelta. **5,** (fishhook) anzuelo. **6,** (curved course, as of a ball) curva. **7,** *boxing* gancho. **—v.t. 1,** (attach; catch) enganchar. **2,** (gore) acornear. **3,** (bend) doblar; curvar. **4,** (hit or throw in a curve, as a ball) dar curva a. **5,** *boxing* dar un gancho a. **6,** *slang* (filch) birlar. **—v.i. 1,** (curve) curvarse; doblarse. **2,** (be fastened or caught) engancharse. **—by hook or by crook,** de todos modos; de cualquier manera; a toda costa. **—hook it,** *slang* huir; salir corriendo. **—hook, line, and sinker,** *colloq.* completamente; todo. **—hooks and eyes,** corchetes. **—hook up, 1,** (attach, as with hooks) enganchar. **2,** (connect; assemble) conectar; montar. **—on one's own hook,** por cuenta propia.

hooked (hʊkt) *adj.* **1,** (shaped like a hook) ganchudo; corvo. **2,** (having a hook or hooks) con gancho o ganchos. **3,** (caught) cogido; enganchado.

hooker ('hʊk·ər) *n., slang* prostituta; puta; ramera.

hook-nosed *adj.* de nariz ganchuda, corva o aguileña.

hookup ('hʊkˌʌp) *n.* **1,** (assembly) montaje; conexiones. **2,** (connection, in communications) conexión; conexión en cadena. **3,** *colloq.* (alliance) alianza; acuerdo.

hookworm ('hʊkˌwʌrm) *n.* lombriz intestinal.

hooky ('hʊk·i) *n., in* **play hooky,** hacer novillos; hacerse la rabona.

hooligan ('hu·lə·gən) *n. & adj.* rufián; matón de barrio; camorrista.

hoop (hup) *n.* aro; argolla; zuncho. —*v.t.* **1,** (provide with hoops) poner aros a; enzunchar. **2,** (encircle) cercar; rodear.

hoopla ('hup·la) *n., colloq.* baraúnda. —*interj.* ¡upa!

hoopskirt ('hup,skʌrt) *n.* miriñaque.

hooray (hə'rei) *interj., n. & v.* = **hurrah.**

hoosegow ('hus·gau) *n., slang* cárcel; calabozo.

hoot (hut) *n.* **1,** (cry, esp. of an owl) grito (del buho); alarido. **2,** (shout of disapproval) pitido; chifla; rechifla; *Amer.* pifia. **3,** (thing of no value) ardite. —*v.i.* **1,** (cry, esp. as an owl) gritar; ulular. **2,** (shout in disapproval) dar pitidos; rechiflar; *Amer.* pifiar. —*v.t.* pitar; rechiflar; *Amer.* pifiar.

hooves (huːvz) *n., pl. de* **hoof.**

hop (hap) *v.i.* [**hopped, hopping**] **1,** (jump) saltar; brincar. **2,** (leap on one foot) saltar a la pata coja o en un pie. **3,** *colloq.* (dance) bailotear. —*v.t.* **1,** (jump) saltar. **2,** (get on; jump on) subirse a; saltar a. —*n.* **1,** (a hopping) salto; brinco. **2,** *colloq.* (dance) bailoteo. **3,** *bot.* lúpulo. —**hop off,** *colloq.* **1,** (take off) despegar; salir volando. **2,** (get down, jump down) bajarse; saltar de.

hope (hop) *v.t. & i.* esperar. —*n.* esperanza.

hopeful ('hop·fəl) *adj.* **1,** (feeling hope) esperanzado. **2,** (giving hope) prometedor. —**hopefully,** *adv.* con esperanza. —**hopefulness,** *n.* esperanza; promesa.

hopeless ('hop·ləs) *adj.* **1,** (without hope) desesperanzado; desilusionado. **2,** (beyond hope) desesperado. —**hopelessly,** *adv.* sin esperanza. —**hopelessness,** *n.* desesperación.

hophead ('hap,hɛd) *n., slang* morfinómano; narcómano.

hopped up *slang* **1,** (drugged) embriagado; eufórico. **2,** (supercharged) hecho más potente; de mayor potencia.

hopper ('hap·ər) *n.* **1,** (jumper) saltarín; saltador. **2,** (bin) tolva.

hops (haps) *n.pl.* lúpulo.

hopscotch ('hap,skatʃ) *n.* juego a la pata coja; rayuela.

horde (hord) *n.* horda. —*v.i.* reunirse en hordas.

horehound *también,* **hoarhound** ('hor,haund) *n.* marrubio.

horizon (hə'rai·zən) *n.* horizonte.

horizontal (ˌhar·ɪ'zan·təl) *adj. & n.* horizontal.

hormone ('hor·mon) *n.* hormona.

horn (horn) *n.* **1,** (bonelike growth) cuerno; asta. **2,** (anything made of or shaped like a horn) cuerno. **3,** *mus.* trompa. **4,** (sounding device) bocina. **5,** (loudspeaker) altavoz; *Amer.* altoparlante. **6,** *slang* teléfono. *v.t.* **1,** (put horns on) poner cuernos a. **2,** (gore) acornear. —*adj.* de cuerno; de asta. —**horned,** *adj.* con cuerno o cuernos. —**blow one's horn,** *colloq.* alabarse; jactarse. —**horn in,** *slang* entremeterse. —**on the horns of a dilemma,** entre la espada y la pared. —**pull, draw o haul in one's horns,** echarse para atrás.

hornet ('hor·nɪt) *n.* avispón.

hornpipe ('horn,paip) *n.* chirimía.

hornswoggle ('horn,swag·əl) *v.t., slang* engañar; engatusar.

horny ('hor·ni) *adj.* **1,** (made of or resembling horn) de cuerno; de asta. **2,** (having horns) con cuerno o cuernos. **3,** (hard like horn) calloso; duro. **4,** *slang* (passionate) cachondo.

horology (ho'ral·ə·dʒi) *n.* horología. —**horologist,** *n.* horólogo.

horoscope ('hor·ə,skop) *n.* horóscopo.

horrendous (hə'rɛn·dəs) *adj.* horrendo.

horrible ('har·ə·bəl) *adj.* horrible.

horrid ('har·ɪd) *adj.* horroroso; horrendo; espantoso.

horrify ('har·ɪ·fai) *v.t.* horrorizar; horripilar. —**horrific** (ho'rɪf·ɪk) *adj.* espantoso; horrible. —**horrifying,** *adj.* horripilante; horroroso.

horror ('har·ər) *n.* horror.

hors d'oeuvres (or'dʌrvr) *n.pl.* entremeses.

horse (hors) *n.* 1, (animal) caballo. 2, (frame) caballete. 3, *gymnastics* potro. —*v.t.* equipar con caballos o monturas; montar. —*v.i.* montar o ir a caballo. —*adj.* 1, (of a horse or horses) de caballo o caballos; hípico. 2, (mounted) a caballo; *mil.* de caballería. 3, muchas veces en los compuestos (large; coarse) grande; basto. —**back (o bet on) the wrong horse,** jugar al caballo que pierde; *fig.* respaldar al que pierde. —**be o get on one's high horse,** *colloq.* dárselas de mucho. —**hold one's horses,** *colloq.* contenerse; aguantarse. —**horse around,** *slang* hacer el zángano; zanganear. —**horse of another (o different) color,** *colloq.* otro asunto; otra cosa; harina de otro costal.

horseback ('hors,bæk) *n.* lomo del caballo. —*adv.* a caballo.

horsecar ('hors,kar) *n.* carruaje tirado por caballos.

horse chestnut 1, (tree) castaño de Indias. 2, (nut) castaña de Indias.

horsefeathers ('hors,feð·ərz) *interj., slang* tontería; disparate.

horsefly ('hors,flai) *n.* tábano; moscardón.

horsehair ('hors,hɛr) *n.* crin; tejido de crin.

horselaugh ('hors,læf) *n.* carcajada; risotada.

horseman ('hors·mən) *n.* [*pl.* **-men**] jinete. —**horsemanship,** *n.* 1, (art of riding) equitación. 2, (skill in handling horses) dotes de jinete.

horse opera *colloq.* película que trata de vaqueros.

horseplay ('hors·plei) *n.* chacota; chacoteo; payasada.

horsepower ('hors,pau·ər) *n.* caballo de fuerza.

horseradish *n.* rábano picante.

horse sense *colloq.* sentido común.

horseshoe ('hors·ʃu) *n.* herradura; *pl.* juego de herraduras. —**horseshoe crab,** cangrejo bayoneta o de las Molucas.

horsewhip ('hors,hwɪp) *n.* fusta; látigo; *Amer.* fuete. —*v.t.* dar o pegar con la fusta o el látigo.

horsewoman ('hors,wʊm·ən) *n.* [*pl.* **-women**] amazona.

horsy ('hor·si) *adj.* 1, (of or like a horse or horses) de caballo o caba-

llos. 2, (concerned with or fond of horses) hípico; de caballos.

hortatory ('hor·tə,tor·i) *adj.* exhortatorio.

horticulture ('hor·tɪ,kʌl·tʃər) *n.* horticultura. —**horticultural** (-'kʌl·tʃər·əl) *adj.* hortícola; de horticultura. —**horticulturist** (-'kʌl·tʃər·ɪst) *n.* horticultor.

hosanna (ho'zæn·ə) *interj.* & *n.* hosanna.

hose (hoz) *n.* 1, (pipe) manguera. 2, [*pl.* **hose**] (stockings; socks) medias; calcetines. —*v.t.* regar con manguera.

hosier ('ho·ʒər) *n.* calcetero. —**hosiery,** *n.* calcetería; medias; calcetines.

hospice ('has·pɪs) *n.* hospicio.

hospitable ('has·pɪ·tə·bəl) *adj.* hospitalario. —**hospitableness,** *n.* hospitalidad.

hospital ('has·pɪ·təl) *n.* hospital.

hospitality (,has·pə'tæl·ə·ti) *n.* hospitalidad.

hospitalize ('has·pɪ·tə,laiz) *v.t.* hospitalizar. —**hospitalization** (-lɪ'zei·ʃən) *n.* hospitalización.

host (host) *n.* 1, (one who entertains or presides) anfitrión. 2, (innkeeper) posadero; mesonero; hostelero. 3, (army) hueste; ejército. 4, (crowd) multitud; muchedumbre. 5, *cap., eccles.* hostia. 6, *biol.* huésped.

hostage ('has·tɪdʒ) *n.* rehén.

hostel ('has·təl) *n.* hostería; albergue. *También,* **hostelry.**

hostess ('hos·tɪs) *n.* 1, (one who entertains or presides) anfitriona; (in a restaurant) encargada de mesas. 2, (stewardess) camarera; azafata; auxiliar de a bordo; *Amer.* aeromoza.

hostile ('has·təl) *adj.* hostil. —**hostility** (has'tɪl·ə·ti) *n.* hostilidad.

hot (hat) *adj.* 1, (very warm) caliente; caluroso. 2, (pungent) picante; acre. 3, (violent) violento; furioso. 4, (impassioned; excited) apasionado; vehemente. —**hotness,** *n.* calentura; lo caliente. —**be in hot water,** estar con el agua al cuello. —**hot air,** *slang* palabrería. —**hot line,** línea de emergencia. —**hot plate,** hornillo; plancha. —**hot rod,** *slang* automóvil sobrealimentado.

hotbed ('hat·bɛd) *n.* vivero; *fig.* foco.

hotblooded ('hat,blʊd·ɪd) *adj.* ardiente; impetuoso.

hotcake ('hat·keik) *n.* = **pancake.** —**sell like hotcakes,** venderse como pan bendito.

hotchpotch ('hatʃ,patʃ) *n.* = **hodgepodge.**

hot dog *colloq.* perro caliente; salchicha.

hotel (ho'tɛl) *n.* hotel. —*adj.* hotelero. —**hotel manager,** hotelero.

hotfoot ('hat·fʊt) *adv.* a toda prisa. —*v.i., colloq.* ir a toda prisa; correr.

hotheaded ('hat,hɛd·ɪd) *adj.* vehemente; excitable; arrebatado. —**hothead,** *n.* persona impetuosa. —**hotheadedness,** *n.* vehemencia; excitabilidad.

hothouse ('hot,haus) *n.* invernáculo.

hot-wire *adj.* de alambre caliente. —*v.t., slang* encender mediante alambre caliente.

hound (haund) *n.* 1, (dog) perro; can. 2, (hunting dog) perro de caza; sabueso. 3, *slang* pícaro. 4, *slang* aficionado. —*v.t.* 1, (pursue; harass) perseguir; acosar; importunar. 2, (urge on) urgir; azuzar.

hour (aur) *n.* hora. —**hour by hour,** de hora en hora; cada hora. —**hour hand,** horario. —**keep late hours,** trasnochar; acostarse tarde. —**late hours,** altas horas de la noche. —**man of the hour,** hombre del momento. —**strike the hour,** dar la hora. —**small (o wee) hours,** primeras horas de la mañana; la madrugada.

hourglass ('aur,glæs) *n.* reloj de arena; clepsidra.

hourly ('aur·li) *adj.* 1, (occurring every hour) cada hora; de cada hora; de hora en hora. 2, (per hour; occupying an hour) por hora; en cada hora. 3, (often; continual) frecuente; continuo. —*adv.* 1, (once an hour; every hour) cada hora. 2, (at any hour) a toda hora; de hora en hora. 3, (often; continually) a todas horas; continuamente.

house (haus) *n.* [*pl.* **houses** ('hau·zɪz)] 1, (dwelling; abode) casa. 2, (building; residence) casa; residencia; edificio. 3, (family; lineage) casa. 4, (chamber; assembly) cámara; asamblea. 5, (assembly room; hall) cámara; sala de asambleas. 6, (theater) teatro; sala de espectáculos. 7, (audience) concurrencia; entrada. 8, (business establishment) establecimiento; firma; casa. 9, (small shelter or building) caseta. —*v.t.* (hauz) 1, (provide lodgings for) alojar; proveer de casa o vivienda. 2, (store) almacenar; acomodar. 3, (shelter) albergar. 4, (cover; enclose) cubrir; encerrar. —*adj.* de casa; de la casa. —**clean house,** 1, (do housecleaning) limpiar la casa; hacer la limpieza. 2, (get rid of undesirable persons or things) hacer una limpieza; hacer un barrido. —**keep house,** cuidar de la casa; hacer los oficios domésticos. —**on the house,** a expensas del dueño o establecimiento. —**play house,** *colloq.* jugar a ser dueños de casa; jugar al papá y a la mamá.

houseboy ('haus·bɔi) *n.* joven doméstico.

housebreaker ('haus,breik·ər) *n.* ladrón; escalador. —**housebreaking,** *n.* robo; escalo.

housebroken ('haus,brok·ən) *adj.* enseñado (a comportarse en casa).

housecoat ('haus,kot) *n.* bata (de entrecasa).

housefly ('haus,flai) *n.* mosca doméstica.

household ('haus·hold) *n.* casa; familia. —*adj.* casero; doméstico; de familia; de casa; para la casa. —**householder,** *n.* dueño de casa; jefe de familia.

housekeeper ('haus,ki·pər) *n.* 1, (housewife) ama de casa. 2, (person in charge of a house) ama de llaves.

housekeeping ('haus,ki·pɪŋ) *n.* quehaceres domésticos; manejo de la casa. —*adj.* doméstico.

housemaid ('haus·meid) *n.* sirvienta; criada.

housetop ('haus·tap) *n.* techo; tejado.

housewares ('haus·weɪrz) *n.pl.* enseres domésticos.

housewarming ('haus,worm·ɪŋ) *n.* tertulia para estrenar un nuevo domicilio.

housewife ('haus,waif) *n.* [*pl.* **-wives** (-waivz)] ama de casa.

housework ('haus,wʌrk) *n.* faenas domésticas.

housing ('hau·zɪŋ) *n.* 1, lodging; sheltering) alojamiento. 2, (houses collectively) casas; viviendas. 3, *archit.* nicho; empotrado. 4, (cover) cubierta; *mech.* cárter; 5, (frame) bastidor; armazón. **6,** (covering for a horse; caparison) caparazón.

hove (ho:v) *v., pret. & p.p. de* **heave.**

hovel ('hʌv·əl) *n.* casucha; choza; cuchitril.

hover ('hʌv·ər) *v.i.* **1,** (stay suspended; flutter in the air) cernerse. **2,** (linger about) revolotear; rondar. **3,** (waver; be uncertain) vacilar.

how (hau) *adv.* **1,** (in what way or manner; by what means) cómo; de qué manera o modo; en qué forma. **2,** (in what state or condition) cómo; qué tal. **3,** (at what price) a cuánto; a cómo: *How do you sell these oranges?,* ¿A cómo vende estas naranjas? **4,** (for what reason or purpose) cómo: por qué: *How is it that you arrived late?,* ¿Cómo es que llegaste tarde? **5,** (with what meaning; to what effect) cómo; en qué forma; en qué sentido. **6,** *(en cláusulas relativas, en expresiones de admiración y como intensivo)* cuán; cuánto; qué: *How pretty she looks!,* ¡Cuán linda se ve! —*n.* cómo. —**how do you do?,** ¿Cómo está Vd.? —**how many?,** ¿cuántos? —**how much?,** ¿cuánto? —**how now?,** ¿cómo así? —**how so?,** ¿cómo así?; ¿por qué? —**how then?** **1,** (what is the meaning of this) ¿Qué es esto?; ¿Qué significa esto? **2,** (how else) ¿Cómo entonces?

howdy ('hau·di) *interj., colloq.* ¡Qué tal!; ¡hola!

however (hau'ɛv·ər) *conj.* sin embargo; no obstante; empero; pero. —*adv.* **1,** (no matter how) de cualquier modo; en todo caso; pese a todo. **2,** (to whatever degree or extent) por muy; por mucho; como quiera que.

howitzer ('hau·ɪt·sər) *n.* obús; mortero.

howl (haul) *v.i.* **1,** (wail) aullar; ulular *(esp. of the wind).* **2,** (laugh or shout in scorn, mirth, etc.) dar risotadas; morirse de risa. —*v.t.* **1,** (utter with howls) aullar; gritar. **2,** (drive or force by howling) sacar a gritos. —*n.* **1,** (wail) aullido; alarido; el ular *(esp. of the wind).* **2,** (loud laugh) risotada. **3,** (shouting) griterío. —**howl down,** ahogar a gritos; hacer callar.

howler ('hau·lər) *n.* **1,** (person or thing that howls) gritón; chillón. **2,** (howling monkey) mono aullador.

3, *colloq.* (boner) plancha; error ridículo.

howsoever (ˌhau·so'ɛv·ər) *adv.* **1,** (to whatever degree or extent) por muy; por mucho; como quiera que. **2,** (in whatever manner) como quiera que.

hoyden ('hɔi·dən) *n.* marimacho.

hub (hʌb) *n.* **1,** (of a wheel) cubo. **2,** (center; focal point) centro; foco.

hubbub ('hʌb·ʌb) *n.* tumulto; barullo; alboroto.

hubby ('hʌb·i) *n., colloq.* maridito.

hubcap ('hʌb,kæp) *n.* plato o platillo del cubo.

huckleberry ('hʌk·əl,bɛr·i) *n.* arándano.

huckster ('hʌk·stər) *n.* **1,** (hawker) buhonero; vendedor ambulante. **2,** (peddler of produce) verdulero. **3,** (petty dealer; haggler) mercachifle. —*v.t. & i.* vender.

huddle ('hʌd·əl) *v.i.* **1,** (crowd together) apelotonarse; amontonarse. **2,** (hunch into a heap) encogerse; acurrucarse. —*v.t.* **1,** (crowd or jumble together) apelotonar; amontonar. **2,** (hunch) encoger. —*n.* **1,** (crowd; heap) pelotón; montón; masa. **2,** (confusion; muddle) confusión; baraúnda. **3,** *slang* (private conference) conferencia privada.

hue (hju:) *n.* **1,** (color) color. **2,** (shade) matiz. —**hue and cry,** clamor; griterío.

huff (hʌf) *v.t.* **1,** (make angry) enojar; enfadar; ofender. **2,** (bully; hector) abusar; atropellar. —*v.i.* soplar; bufar; dar resoplidos. —*n.* bufido; resoplido. —**in a huff,** disgustado; enfadado.

huffy ('hʌf·i) *adj.* **1,** (touchy) susceptible. **2,** (sulky) resentido.

hug (hʌg) *v.t.* [**hugged, hugging**] **1,** (embrace) abrazar; apretar. **2,** (go or get close to) arrimarse a. —*v.i.* abrazarse. —*n.* abrazo.

huge (hju:dʒ) *adj.* enorme; inmenso. —**hugeness,** *n.* enormidad; inmensidad.

hulk (hʌlk) *n.* **1,** (shell; skeleton) esqueleto; armazón. **2,** (clumsy person or thing) armatoste. —*v.i.* [*usu.* **hulk up**] levantarse; abultar. —**hulking,** *adj.* tosco; pesado.

hull (hʌl) *n.* **1,** (shell; husk) cáscara; vaina; hollejo. **2,** (outer covering) envoltura; cubierta; corteza. **3,** (body of a ship) casco. **4,** *aero.* (frame) armazón. —*v.t.* descascarar; mondar.

hullabaloo ('hʌl·ə·bə‚lu) *n.* alboroto; algarabía.

hum (hʌm) *v.i.* [**hummed, humming**] **1,** (drone; buzz; murmur) zumbar; ronronear. **2,** (sing without words) tararear. **3,** *colloq.* (be full of activity or excitement) vibrar; zumbar con actividad; parecer una colmena. —*v.t.* tararear. —*n.* **1,** (drone; buzz; murmur) zumbido; runrún. **2,** (singing without words) tarareo. —*interj.* ¡ejem! —**hum to sleep,** arrullar.

human ('hju·mən) *adj.* humano. —*n.* [*también*, **human being**] ser humano.

humane (hju'mein) *adj.* humano; compasivo; generoso. —**humaneness,** *n.* humanidad; benevolencia; compasión.

humanism ('hju·mə·nɪz·əm) *n.* humanismo. —**humanist,** *n.* humanista. —**humanistic,** *adj.* humanista.

humanitarian (hju‚mæn·ə'tɛr·ɪ·ən) *adj.* humanitario. —*n.* filántropo; persona humanitaria.

humanity (hju'mæn·ə·ti) *n.* humanidad. —**humanities,** *n.pl.* humanidades; letras humanas.

humanize ('hju·mə‚naiz) *v.t.* humanizar.

humankind ('hju·mən‚kaind) *n.* humanidad; género humano.

humanoid ('hju·mə·noid) *adj.* humanoide. —*n.* androide.

humble ('hʌm·bəl) *adj.* humilde. —*v.t.* humillar; hacer sentir humilde. —**humbleness,** *n.* humildad.

humbug ('hʌm·bʌg) *n.* **1,** (deception) patraña; embuste; farsa. **2,** (charlatan) charlatán; farsante; embustero. —*v.t.* [**-bugged, -bugging**] engañar; embaucar.

humdinger (hʌm'dɪŋ·ər) *n., slang* maravilla; fenómeno.

humdrum ('hʌm‚drʌm) *adj.* monótono; rutinario; banal. —*n.* **1,** (monotony) monotonía; rutina; matraca. **2,** (dull, boring person) persona rutinaria; plomo.

humerus ('hju·mər·əs) *n.* húmero.

humid ('hju·mɪd) *adj.* húmedo.

humidify (hju'mɪd·ə·fai) *v.t.* humidificar. —**humidification** (-fɪ'kei·ʃən) *n.* humidificación.

humidity (hju'mɪd·ə·ti) *n.* humedad.

humidor ('hju·mə‚dor) *n.* caja humedecida para guardar tabaco.

humiliate (hju'mɪl·i‚eit) *v.t.* hu-

millar. —**humiliation,** *n.* humillación.

humility (hju'mɪl·ə·ti) *n.* humildad.

humming ('hʌm·ɪŋ) *adj.* **1,** (buzzing; droning) zumbante; ronroneante. **2,** *colloq.* (active; brisk) activo; furioso; febril. —*n.* = **hum.**

hummingbird ('hʌm·ɪŋ‚bʌrd) *n.* colibrí; picaflor.

hummock ('hʌm·ək) *n.* mogote; loma.

humor ('hju·mər) *n.* **1,** (mood; disposition) humor; disposición. **2,** (body fluid) humor. **3,** (comicality) humor; comicidad; gracia. **4,** (humorous style or works) humorismo. —*v.t.* complacer; seguirle la cuerda a. —**out of humor,** malhumorado; destemplado.

humorist ('hju·mər·ɪst) *n.* humorista. —**humoristic,** *adj.* humorístico.

humorous ('hju·mər·əs) *adj.* cómico; gracioso; chistoso; humorístico.

hump (hʌmp) *n.* **1,** (fleshy protuberance) joroba; giba. **2,** (mound) loma; montículo; corcovo. —*v.t.* arquear; encorvar. —*v.i.* combarse; arquearse.

humpback ('hʌmp‚bæk) *n.* **1,** (hump on the back) joroba; giba; corcova. **2,** (person with a hump) jorobado. **3,** (whale) ballena jorobada. —**humpbacked,** *adj.* jorobado; giboso; corcovado.

humph (hʌmf) *interj.* ¡uf!; ¡quia!

humus ('hju·məs) *n.* humus.

hunch (hʌntʃ) *n.* **1,** (hump) joroba; giba. **2,** *colloq.* (intuition) presentimiento; corazonada. —*v.t.* encorvar; arquear. —*v.i.* andar a empujones o empellones.

hunchback ('hʌntʃ‚bæk) *n.* = **humpback.**

hundred ('hʌn·drɪd) *adj.* cien; ciento. —*n.* ciento; centena; centenar. —**hundredth,** *adj. & n.* centésimo.

hundredfold ('hʌn·drɪd‚fold) *adj.* céntuplo; cien veces (más). —*adv.* cien veces; en un céntuplo.

hundredweight ('hʌn·drɪd‚weit) *n.* quintal.

hung (hʌŋ) *v., pret. & p.p. de* **hang.**

hunger ('hʌŋ·gər) *n.* **1,** (craving for food) hambre. **2,** (strong desire) deseo intenso; hambre; anhelo. —*v.i.* tener hambre. —**hunger for** o

after, desear con ansia; anhelar; ansiar.

hungry ('hʌŋ·gri) *adj.* hambriento. —**be** o **feel hungry,** tener hambre. —**go hungry,** pasar hambre.

hunk (hʌŋk) *n., colloq.* pedazo grande; buen pedazo; lonja.

hunky ('hʌŋ·ki) *adj., slang* magnífico; bonísimo. *También,* **hunky-dory** (-'dor·i).

hunt (hʌnt) *v.t. & i.* **1,** (chase, as game) cazar. **2,** (search) buscar. **3,** (pursue) perseguir; ir en búsqueda (de). —*n.* **1,** (chase; hunting) caza; cacería. **2,** (search) búsqueda; busca. **3,** (pursuit) persecución; búsqueda. **4,** (hunting party) partida de caza; cazadores. —**go hunting (for),** ir de caza; ir a la caza (de). —**hunt down,** buscar o perseguir hasta encontrar. —**hunt up,** buscar.

hunter ('hʌn·tər) *n.* **1,** [*también,* **huntsman** ('hʌnts·mən)] (one who hunts game) cazador. **2,** (pursuer) perseguidor.

hunting ('hʌn·tɪŋ) *n.* **1,** (sport or occupation) caza; montería. **2,** = **hunt.**

hurdle ('hʌr·dəl) *n.* **1,** (fence; barrier, as used in sports) valla; barrera. **2,** (obstacle; difficulty) obstáculo; dificultad. —*v.t.* **1,** (jump over) saltar sobre. **2,** (overcome, as a difficulty) superar. —**hurdler** (-dlər) *n.* saltador de vallas.

hurdy-gurdy ('hʌr·di,gʌr·di) *n.* organillo.

hurl (hʌrl) *v.t.* lanzar; arrojar. —*n.* tiro.

hurly-burly (,hʌr·li'bʌr·li) *n.* tumulto; alboroto; batahola. —*adj.* confuso; tumultuoso; alborotado.

hurrah (hə'rɑ;) *interj. & n.* viva; hurra. —*v.t. & i.* aclamar; dar vivas o hurras. *También,* **hurray** (hə'rei).

hurricane ('hʌr·ə,kein) *n.* huracán. —**hurricane lamp,** quinqué.

hurry ('hʌr·i) *v.i.* [*también,* **hurry up**] apresurarse; darse prisa; *Amer.* apurarse. —*v.t.* acelerar; apurar; apresurar; meter prisa a. —*n.* prisa; *Amer.* apuro. —**be in a hurry,** tener prisa; estar de prisa.

hurry-scurry *también,* **hurry-skurry** ('hʌr·i'skʌr·i) *n.* pelotera; baraúnda; idas y venidas. —*v.i.* ir o correr de un lado para otro; precipitarse; andar como loco. —*adj.* confuso y precipitado. —*adv.* confusa y precipitadamente.

hurt (hʌrt) *v.t.* [**hurt, hurting**] **1,**

(wound) herir; lastimar. **2,** (be detrimental to; damage) perjudicar; estropear; dañar. **3,** (wound the feelings of; offend) herir; ofender. —*v.t. & i.* (cause pain) doler; hacer daño. —*n.* **1,** (pain) dolor. **2,** (wound) herida. **3,** (damage; harm) daño; perjuicio. —**hurtful,** *adj.* perjudicial; nocivo.

hurtle ('hʌr·təl) *v.i.* **1,** [*usu.* **hurtle against** o **together**] (collide; crash) chocar; estrellarse. **2,** (clatter; resound) retumbar; resonar. **3,** (rush violently) ir disparado; ir como bólido. —*v.t.* arrojar; lanzar.

husband ('hʌz·bənd) *n.* marido; esposo. —*v.t.* conservar; cuidar de. —**husbandman** (-mən) *adj.* agricultor; granjero.

husbandry ('hʌz·bən·dri) *n.* **1,** (thrift; economy) economía. **2,** (farming) labranza; labores agrícolas. **3,** (management) manejo; cuidado.

hush (hʌʃ) *v.t.* **1,** (silence) silenciar; hacer callar. **2,** (calm; quiet) acallar; aquietar. —*v.i.* enmudecer; callarse; aquietarse. —*n.* silencio; quietud. —*interj.* ¡silencio!; ¡chito!

hush-hush ('hʌʃ,hʌʃ) *adj.* secreto.

husk (hʌsk) *n.* **1,** (outer covering, as of fruits or seeds) corteza; cáscara; vaina; hollejo. **2,** (any dry, hard covering) corteza; cáscara. —*v.t.* descascarar; pelar; mondar.

huskiness ('hʌs·ki·nəs) *n.* **1,** (hoarseness) ronquera; aspereza. **2,** (strength; robustness) fuerza; robustez.

husky ('hʌs·ki) *adj.* **1,** (hoarse) ronco; áspero. **2,** (robust) fornido; robusto. —*n.* perro esquimal.

hussar (hʊ'zɑ;r) *n.* húsar.

hussy ('hʌz·i; 'hʌs-) *n.* pícara; buena pieza.

hustle ('hʌs·əl) *v.t.* **1,** (shove; jostle) empujar; dar empujones. **2,** *colloq.* (hurry; press) empujar; apurar. —*v.i.* **1,** (move hurriedly) apresurarse; *Amer.* apurarse. **2,** (act or work energetically) ajetrearse; afanarse; trabajar afanosamente. —*n.* **1,** (a shoving; a pushing) empujón. **2,** *colloq.* (drive; push) empuje. —**hustler** (-lər) *n.* buscavidas.

hut (hʌt) *n.* choza; barraca; cabaña; *Amer.* bohío.

hutch (hʌtʃ) *n.* **1,** (bin; chest) arca; cofre. **2,** (cupboard) alacena; apara-

dor. **3,** (pen; coop) pollera; conejera. **4,** (hut) choza; barraca.
huzza (hə'zaȝ) *interj., n. & v.* =
hurrah.
hyacinth ('hai·ə·sɪnθ) *n.* jacinto.
hybrid ('hai·brɪd) *n. & adj.*
híbrido. —**hybridism,** *n.* hibridismo. —**hybridize,** *v.t.* cruzar. —*v.i.*
producir híbridos.
hydrangea (hai'drein·dȝə) *n.*
hortensia.
hydrant ('hai·drənt) *n.* boca de
riego; boca de agua; toma de agua.
hydrate ('hai·dreit) *n.* hidrato.
—*v.t.* hidratar. —**hydration,** *n.*
hidratación.
hydraulic (hai'drɔ·lɪk) *adj.* hidráulico. —**hydraulics,** *n.* hidráulica.
hydrocarbon (,hai·drə'kar·bən) *n.*
hidrocarburo.
hydrocephaly (,hai·drə'sɛf·ə·li)
n. hidrocefalia. —**hydrocephalic**
(-'fæl·ɪk) *adj.* hidrocéfalo.
hydrodynamic (,hai·dro·dai·
'næm·ɪk) *adj.* hidrodinámico.
—**hydrodynamics,** *n.* hidrodinámica.
hydroelectric (,hai·dro·ə'lɛk-
trɪk) *adj.* hidroeléctrico. —**hydroelectrics,** *n.* hidroeléctrica.
hydrogen ('hai·drə·dȝən) *n.*
hidrógeno.
hydrogenate ('hai·drə·dȝə,neit)
v.t. hidrogenar. —**hydrogenation,**
n. hidrogenación.
hydrolysis (hai'drɑl·ə·sɪs) *n.*
hidrólisis.
hydrometer (hai'drɑm·ɪ·tər) *n.*
hidrómetro.
hydrophobia (,hai·drə'fo·bi·ə) *n.*
hidrofobia; rabia. —**hydrophobe**
('hai·drə,fob) *n.* hidrófobo.
—**hydrophobic,** *adj.* hidrófobo.
hydroplane ('hai·drə,plein) *n.*
hidroavión; hidroplano.
hydroponics (,hai·drə'pɑn·ɪks)
n.sing. & pl. hidroponía; hidropónica. —**hydroponic,** *adj.* hidropónico.
hydrous ('hai·drəs) *adj.* acuoso.
hydroxide (hai'drɑk·said) *n.*
hidróxido.
hyena (hai'i·na) *n.* hiena.
hygiene ('hai·dȝin) *n.* higiene.
hygienic (,hai·dȝi'en·ɪk) *adj.*
higiénico. —**hygienics,** *n.* higiene.
hygienist ('hai·dȝi·ən·ɪst) *n.*
higienista.
hygrometer (hai'grɑm·ə·tər) *n.*

higrómetro. —**hygrometric** (,hai·
grə'mɛt·rɪk) *adj.* higrométrico.
hymen ('hai·mən) *n.* **1,** *anat.*
himen. **2,** (marriage) himeneo.
—**hymeneal** (-mə'ni·əl) *adj.*
nupcial.
hymn (hɪm) *n.* himno.
hymnal ('hɪm·nəl) *n.* himnario.
hype (haip) *n., colloq.* publicidad
extravagante. —*v.t.* promover;
estimular.
hyperbola (hai'pʌr·bə·lə) *n.*
hipérbola.
hyperbole (hai'pʌr·bə·li) *n.* hipérbole.
hyperbolic (,hai·pər'bɑl·ɪk) *adj.*
hiperbólico.
hypersensitive (,hai·pər'sɛn·sə-
tɪv) *adj.* hipersensible.
hypertension (,hai·pər'tɛn·ʃən)
n. hipertensión. —**hypertensive,**
adj. hipertenso.
hypertrophy (hai'pʌr·trə·fi) *n.*
hipertrofia. —*v.i.* hipertrofiarse.
hyphen ('hai·fən) *n.* guión.
hyphenate ('hai·fə,neit) *v.t.*
separar con guión. —**hyphenation,**
n. separación con guiones.
hypnosis (hɪp'no·sis) *n.* hipnosis.
—**hypnotic** (-'nɑt·ɪk) *adj.* hipnótico.
hypnotism ('hɪp·nə·tɪz·əm) *n.*
hipnotismo. —**hypnotist,** *n.* hipnotizador.
hypnotize ('hɪp·nə,taiz) *v.t.*
hipnotizar.
hypo ('hai·po) *n.* **1,** *photog.* (fixative) fijador, **2,** *slang* = **hypodermic. 3,** *slang* = **hypochondriac.**
hypochondriac (hai·pə'kan-
dri·æk) *n. & adj.* hipocondríaco.
—**hypochondria** (-ə) *n.* hipocondría.
hypocrisy (hɪ'pak·rə·si) *n.* hipocresía.
hypocrite ('hɪp·ə·krɪt) *n.* hipócrita.
—**hypocritical** (-'krɪt·ɪ·kəl) *adj.*
hipócrita.
hypodermic (,hai·pə'dʌr·mɪk) *adj.*
& *n.* hipodérmico.
hypoglycemia (,hai·pə·glai'si·
mi·ə) *n.* hipoglucemia.
hypotenuse (hai'pat·ə·nus) *n.*
hipotenusa.
hypothesis (hai'paθ·ə·sɪs) *n.*
hipótesis.
hypothesize (hai'paθ·ə,saiz) *v.i.*
asumir una hipótesis. —*v.t.*
postular; asumir.
hypothetical (,hai·pə'θɛt·ɪ·kəl)
adj. hipotético.

hyssop ('hɪs·əp) *n.* hisopo.
hysterectomy (ˌhɪs·tə'rɛk·tə·mi) *n.* histerectomía.
hysteria (hɪs'tɪr·i·ə) *n.* histeria; histerismo.

hysteric (hɪs'tɛr·ɪk) *n.* **1,** (person) histérico. **2,** *pl.* (attack) histerismo; histeria. —**hysterical,** *adj.* histérico.

I

I, i (ai) novena letra del alfabeto inglés.
I (ai) *pron.pers.* yo.
iambic (ai'æm·bɪk) *n.* yambo. —*adj.* yámbico.
Iberian (ai'bɪr·i·ən) *adj.* ibérico. —*adj. & n.* ibero.
ibex ('ai·bɛks) *n.* íbice.
ibis ('ai·bɪs) *n.* ibis.
ice (ais) *n.* **1,** (frozen water) hielo. **2,** (sherbet) helado de agua; sorbete. **3,** = **icing. 4,** (reserve; formality) frialdad. —*v.t.* **1,** (cool with ice) poner en hielo; enfriar. **2,** (freeze) helar. **3,** *cooking* (frost) garapiñar; acaramelar: confitar. —*v.i.* helarse. —*adj.* [*también*, **iced**] helado; congelado; de o como hielo. —**ice box,** nevera. —**ice cream,** helado. —**ice cream parlor,** salón de refrescos; *Amer.* heladería. —**ice water,** agua fría o helada.
Ice Age la época glaciar.
iceberg ('ais,bʌrg) *n.* iceberg; témpano de hielo.
icebound ('ais,baund) *adj.* rodeado por el hielo.
icebreaker ('ais,breik·ər) *n.* rompehielos.
iceman ('ais·mæn) *n.* [*pl.* **-men**] vendedor o repartidor de hielo.
ichthyology (ˌɪk·θi'al·ə·dʒi) *n.* ictiología. —**ichthyological** (-ə'la·dʒə·kəl) *adj.* ictiológico. —**ichthyologist,** *n.* ictiólogo.
icicle ('ai·sɪ·kəl) *n.* carámbano.
icing ('ai·sɪŋ) *n.* baño o capa de pasta confitada; escarchado.
icon ('ai·kan) *n.* icono.
iconoclast (ai'kan·ə,klæst) *n.* iconoclasta. —**iconoclasm,** *n.* iconoclasia. —**iconoclastic** (-'klæs·tɪk) *adj.* iconoclasta.
iconography (ai·kə'nag·rə·fi) *n.* iconografía.
icy ('ai·si) *adj.* **1,** (cold; frozen) helado; frío; frígido. **2,** (slippery) resbaladizo.
id (ɪd) *n., psychol.* id.

I'd (aid) *contr. de* **I should, I would** o **I had.**
idea (ai'di·ə) *n.* idea.
ideal (ai'di·əl) *n. & adj.* ideal. —**idealism,** *n.* idealismo. —**idealist,** *n.* idealista. —**idealistic,** *adj.* idealista.
idealize (ai'di·ə·laiz) *v.t.* idealizar. —**idealization** (-lɪ'zei·ʃən) *n.* idealización.
ideate (ai'di·eit) *v.t.* idear; imaginar. —**ideation,** *n.* ideación.
idem ('ɪd·əm) *pron.* ídem.
identical (ai'dɛn·tɪ·kəl) *adj.* idéntico.
identify (ai'dɛn·tɪ·fai) *v.t.* identificar. —**identifiable,** *adj.* identificable. —**identification** (-fɪ'kei·ʃən) *n.* identificacion.
identity (ai'dɛn·tə·ti) *n.* identidad.
ideogram ('ai·di·ə,græm) *n.* ideograma. *También,* **ideograph** (-,græf).
ideology (ˌai·di'al·ə·dʒi) *n.* ideología. —**ideological** (-ə'ladʒ·ɪ·kəl) *adj.* ideológico.
ides (aidz) *n.pl.* idus.
idiocy ('ɪd·i·ə·si) *n.* idiotez.
idiom ('ɪd·i·əm) *n.* **1,** (idiomatic expression) modismo. **2,** (language) lenguaje; idioma. **3,** (style) estilo. —**idiomatic** (-ə'mæt·ɪk) *adj.* idiomático.
idiosyncrasy (ˌɪd·i·ə'sɪn·krə·si) *n.* idiosincrasia. —**idiosyncratic** (-'kræt·ɪk) *adj.* idiosincrásico.
idiot ('ɪd·i·ət) *n.* idiota. —**idiotic** (-'at·ɪk) *adj.* idiota.
idle ('ai·dəl) *adj.* **1,** (useless; futile) ocioso; inútil; fútil. **2,** (baseless; unfounded) sin fundamento; sin base. **3,** (unemployed; without work) desempleado; sin trabajo. **4,** (inactive) inactivo. **5,** (not filled with activity) de ocio. **6,** (lazy) ocioso; holgazán. —*v.i.* **1,** (loaf) holgazanear. **2,** (operate without transmitting power) dar vueltas o funcionar sin efectuar trabajo; funcionar desconectado o en neutro.

—*v.t.* **1,** (waste; squander) perder; malgastar. **2,** (cause to idle, as a motor) desconectar; poner en neutro; hacer funcionar en neutro. —**idleness,** *n.* ociosidad.

idler ('ai·dlər) *n.* **1,** (loafer) ocioso; holgazán. **2,** *mech.* rueda o polea loca.

idling ('ai·dlɪŋ) *n.* **1,** (loafing) holgazanería. **2,** *mech.* funcionamiento o marcha en neutro.

idly ('ai·dli) *adv.* ociosamente.

idol ('ai·dəl) *n.* ídolo. —**idolize,** *v.t.* idolatrar.

idolater (ai'dal·ə·tər) *n.* idólatra.

idolatry (ai'dal·ə·tri) *n.* idolatría. —**idolatrous,** *adj.* idólatra.

idyl *también,* **idyll** ('ai·dəl) *n.* idilio. —**idyllic** (ai'dɪl·ɪk) *adj.* idílico.

if (ɪf) *conj.* si. —*n.* punto dudoso; supuesto. —**as if,** como si. —**even if,** aun cuando; aunque; aun si. —**if so,** si es así.

igloo ('ɪg·lu) *n.* iglú.

igneous ('ɪg·ni·əs) *adj.* ígneo.

ignite (ɪg'naɪt) *v.t. & i.* encender; prender.

ignition (ɪg'nɪʃ·ən) *n.* **1,** (burning) ignición. **2,** *mech.* encendido; ignición.

ignoble (ɪg'no·bəl) *adj.* innoble; bajo. —**ignobility; ignobleness,** *n.* bajeza.

ignominious (ˌɪg·nə'mɪn·i·əs) *adj.* ignominioso. —**ignominy** ('ɪg·nə,mɪn·i) *n.* ignominia.

ignoramus (ˌɪg·nə'rei·məs; -'ræm·əs) *n.* ignorante.

ignorant ('ɪg·nə·rənt) *adj.* **1,** (untutored) ignorante. **2,** (of or through ignorance) de ignorancia; torpe. —**ignorance,** *n.* ignorancia.

ignore (ɪg'noɹr) *v.t.* no hacer caso de; no tener en cuenta; pasar por alto.

iguana (ɪ'gwa·nə) *n.* iguana.

ileum ('ɪl·i·əm) *n., anat.* íleon.

iliac ('ɪl·i·æk) *adj.* ilíaco; iliaco.

ilk (ɪlk) *n.* jaez; clase; especie.

I'll (ail) *contr. de* I shall o I will.

ill (ɪl) *adj.* **1,** (evil; bad) malo. **2,** (sick) enfermo; malo. **3,** (faulty; poor) malo; inadecuado. —*n.* mal. —*adv.* **1,** (badly) malamente; mal. **2,** (scarcely) difícilmente; mal. —**go ill with,** irle mal; venirle o caerle mal. —**ill at ease,** incómodo; desasosegado. —**take ill, 1,** (take offense at) tomar a mal. **2,** (take sick) enfermarse; caer enfermo.

ill-advised (ˌɪl·æd'vaizd) *adj.* imprudente.

ill-bred ('ɪl,brɛd) *adj.* malcriado; mal educado. —**ill breeding,** mala educación.

ill-considered *adj.* poco prudente; de incauto.

ill-defined *adj.* obscuro; indefinido.

ill-disposed *adj.* maldispuesto.

illegal (ɪ'li·gəl) *adj.* ilegal. —**illegality** (ˌɪl·li'gæl·ə·ti) *n.* ilegalidad.

illegible (ɪ'lɛdʒ·ə·bəl) *adj.* ilegible. —**illegibility,** *n.* lo ilegible.

illegitimate (ˌɪl·ɪ'dʒɪt·ə·mət) *adj.* ilegítimo. —**illegitimacy** (-mə·si) *n.* ilegitimidad.

ill-fated *adj.* desgraciado; infausto; aciago.

ill-favored *adj.* feo; malcarado.

ill-fed *adj.* desnutrido; hambriento.

ill-founded *adj.* mal fundado.

ill-gotten *adj.* mal adquirido.

ill-humored *adj.* malhumorado. —**ill humor,** mal humor.

illiberal (ɪ'lɪb·ə·rəl) *adj.* iliberal. —**illiberality** (ɪ,lɪb·ə'ræl·ə·ti) *n.* iliberalidad.

illicit (ɪ'lɪs·ɪt) *adj.* ilícito.

illimitable (ɪ'lɪm·ɪ·tə·bəl) *adj.* ilimitable.

ill-intentioned *adj.* malintencionado.

illiterate (ɪ'lɪt·ə·rət) *adj.* analfabeto. —**illiteracy** (-ər·ə·si) *n.* analfabetismo.

ill-kept *adj.* desatendido; desaseado.

ill-looking *adj.* malcarado; feo.

ill-mannered *adj.* de malos modales; descortés.

ill-natured *adj.* maldispuesto; atravesado.

illness ('ɪl·nəs) *n.* enfermedad.

illogical (ɪ'ladʒ·ɪ·kəl) *adj.* ilógico. —**illogicality** (-'kæl·ə·ti) *n.* falta de lógica; lo ilógico.

ill-omened *adj.* de mal agüero.

ill-spent *adj.* malgastado.

ill-starred *adj.* desastrado; malaventurado.

ill-tempered *adj.* de mal genio; malhumorado. —**ill temper,** mal genio; mal humor.

ill-timed *adj.* inoportuno.

ill-treat *v.t.* maltratar. —**ill-treatment,** *n.* maltrato.

illuminate (ɪ'lu·mə,neit) *v.t.* iluminar. —**illumination,** *n.*

iluminación. —**illuminator,** *n.* lámpara; fuente de iluminación.

ill-use (ɪl'juːz) *v.t.* maltratar. —**ill-use** (ɪl'jus) *n.* maltrato. *También,* **illusage.**

illusion (ɪ'luː·ʒən) *n.* ilusión. —**illusive** (-sɪv) *adj.* ilusivo. —**illusory** (-sə·ri) *adj.* ilusorio.

illustrate ('ɪl·ə,streit) *v.t.* ilustrar. —**illustration,** *n.* ilustración. —**illustrative** (ɪ'lʌs·trə·tɪv) *adj.* ilustrativo. —**illustrator,** *n.* ilustrador.

illustrious (ɪ'lʌs·tri·əs) *adj.* ilustre. —**illustriousness,** *n.* fama; grandeza.

ill will mala voluntad; ojeriza; malquerencia.

ill-wisher *n.* malintencionado.

I'm (aim) *contr. de* **I am.**

image ('ɪm·ɪdʒ) *n.* imagen. —*v.t.* **1,** (portray; depict) representar; describir. **2,** (reflect; mirror) reflejar. **3,** (image) imaginar. —**imagery,** *n.* imágenes.

imaginary (ɪ'mædʒ·ɪ·ner·i) *adj.* imaginario.

imagination (ɪ,mædʒ·ɪ'nei·ʃən) *n.* imaginación.

imaginative (ɪ'mædʒ·ɪ·nə·tɪv) *adj.* imaginativo.

imagine (ɪ'mædʒ·ɪn) *v.t. & i.* imaginar. —**imaginable,** *adj.* imaginable.

imbalance (ɪm'bæl·əns) *n.* desequilibrio.

imbecile ('ɪm·bə·sɪl) *n. & adj.* imbécil. —**imbecilic** (-'sɪl·ɪk) *adj.* imbécil. —**imbecility** (-'sɪl·ə·ti) *n.* imbecilidad.

imbed (ɪm'bɛd) *v.t.* [-bedded, -bedding] **1,** (encase; inlay) encajar; incrustar; embutir; empotrar. **2,** (plant; fix) plantar; fijar.

imbibe (ɪm'baib) *v.t.* **1,** (drink) beber. **2,** (absorb) absorber; embeber.

imbroglio (ɪm'brol·jo) *n.* embrollo; enredo; lío.

imbue (ɪm'bjuː) *v.t.* **1,** (dye) teñir. **2,** (infuse) imbuir. —**imbuement,** *n.* imbuimiento.

imitate ('ɪm·ə,teit) *v.t.* imitar. —**imitable,** *adj.* imitable. —**imitation,** *n.* imitación; copia. —*adj.* imitado; de imitación. —**imitative,** *adj.* imitativo. —**imitator,** *n.* imitador.

immaculate (ɪ'mæk·jə·lɪt) *adj.* inmaculado. —**immaculateness,** *n.* pureza; perfección.

immanent ('ɪm·ə·nənt) *adj.* inmanente. —**immanence,** *n.* inmanencia.

immaterial (,ɪm·ə'tɪr·i·əl) *adj.* **1,** (incorporeal) inmaterial. **2,** (unimportant) sin importancia; indiferente. —**immaterialness; immateriality** (-'æl·ə·ti) *n.* inmaterialidad.

immature (,ɪm·ə'tjur) *adj.* inmaduro; sin madurez. —**immaturity,** *n.* inmadurez; falta de madurez.

immeasurable (ɪ'mɛʒ·ər·ə·bəl) *adj.* inmensurable.

immediacy (ɪ'mi·di·ə·si) *n.* urgencia.

immediate (ɪ'mi·di·ət) *adj.* inmediato. —**immediateness,** *n.* lo inmediato.

immediately (ɪ'mi·di·ət·li) *adv.* inmediatamente; en seguida.

immemorial (,ɪm·ə'mor·i·əl) *adj.* inmemorial.

immense (ɪ'mɛns) *adj.* inmenso. —**immenseness; immensity,** *n.* inmensidad; lo inmenso.

immerse (ɪ'mʌrs) *v.t.* sumergir. —**immersion** (ɪ'mʌr·ʃən) *n.* inmersión; sumersión.

immigrant ('ɪm·ə·grənt) *n. & adj.* inmigrante.

immigrate ('ɪm·ə,greit) *v.i.* inmigrar. —**immigration,** *n.* inmigración.

imminent ('ɪm·ə·nənt) *adj.* inminente. —**imminence,** *n.* inminencia.

immobile (ɪ'mo·bɪl) *adj.* inmóvil. —**immobility,** *n.* inmovilidad.

immobilize (ɪ'mo·bə,laiz) *v.t.* inmovilizar. —**immobilization** (-lɪ'zei·ʃən) *n.* inmovilización.

immoderate (ɪ'mad·ər·ət) *adj.* inmoderado. —**immoderation** (-ə'rei·ʃən) *n.* inmoderación.

immodest (ɪ'mad·ɪst) *adj.* inmodesto. —**immodesty,** *n.* inmodestia.

immolate ('ɪm·ə,leit) *v.t.* inmolar. —**immolation,** *n.* inmolación.

immoral (ɪ'mor·əl) *adj.* inmoral. —**immorality** (,ɪm·ə'ræl·ə·ti) *n.* inmoralidad.

immortal (ɪ'mor·təl) *adj. & n.* inmortal. —**immortality** (-'tæl·ə·ti) *n.* inmortalidad.

immortalize (ɪ'mor·tə,laiz) *v.t.* inmortalizar. —**immortalization** (-lɪ'zei·ʃən) *n.* inmortalización.

immortelle (,ɪm·or'tɛl) *n.* perpetua.

immovable (ɪˈmuv·ə·bəl) *adj.*
inamovible; inmovible.
immune (ɪˈmjuːn) *adj.* inmune.
—**immunity** (ɪˈmjuː·nə·ti) *n.*
inmunidad.
immunize (ˈɪm·jəˌnaiz) *v.t.* inmunizar. —**immunization** (-nɪˈzei·ʃən)
n. inmunización.
immunology (ɪm·juˈna·lə·dʒi) *n.*
inmunología.
immutable (ɪˈmjuː·tə·bəl) *adj.*
inmutable. —**immutability**, *n.*
inmutabilidad.
imp (ɪmp) *n.* diablillo.
impact (ˈɪm·pækt) *n.* impacto.
—*v.t.* (ɪmˈpækt) encajar; embutir.
—**impacted**, *adj.* embutido; apretado; *dent.* impactado.
impair (ɪmˈpeɪr) *v.t.* 1, (spoil; damage) dañar; malograr; perjudicar. 2,
(hinder) dificultar; estorbar.
impairment (ɪmˈpeɪr·mənt) *n.* 1,
(damage) daño; perjuicio. 2, (hindrance) dificultad; estorbo; traba.
impale (ɪmˈpeil) *v.t.* 1, (transfix)
empalar. 2, (fence in) cercar.
—**impalement**, *n.* empalamiento.
impalpable (ɪmˈpæl·pə·bəl) *adj.*
impalpable. —**impalpability**, *n.*
impalpabilidad.
impanel (ɪmˈpæn·əl) *v.t.* convocar
como jurado. —**impanelment**, *n.*
convocación.
imparity (ɪmˈpær·ə·ti) *n.* desigualdad.
impart (ɪmˈpart) *v.t.* impartir.
impartial (ɪmˈpar·ʃəl) *adj.*
imparcial. —**impartiality** (-ʃiˈæl·
ə·ti) *n.* imparcialidad.
impassable (ɪmˈpæs·ə·bəl) *adj.*
impasable; intransitable. —**impass-
ability**, *n.* calidad de impasable o
intransitable.
impasse (ɪmˈpæs) *n.* atolladero;
estancamiento.
impassion (ɪmˈpæʃ·ən) *v.t.*
apasionar. —**impassioned**, *adj.*
apasionado.
impassive (ɪmˈpæs·ɪv) *adj.*
impasible. —**impassiveness**, *n.*
impasibilidad.
impaste (ɪmˈpeist) *v.t.* empastar.
—**impasto** (ɪmˈpas·to) *n.* empaste.
impatient (ɪmˈpei·ʃənt) *adj.*
impaciente. —**impatience**, *n.*
impaciencia.
impeach (ɪmˈpitʃ) *v.t.* 1, (call in
question) disputar; poner en duda;
poner en tela de juicio. 2, (accuse)
acusar; procesar. —**impeachable**,
adj. censurable; disputable.

impeachment (ɪmˈpitʃ·mənt) *n.*
1, (public accusation) acusación;
procesamiento. 2, (discredit) descrédito.
impeccable (ɪmˈpek·ə·bəl) *adj.*
impecable. —**impeccability**, *n.*
impecabilidad.
impecunious (ˌɪm·pəˈkjuː·ni·əs)
adj. sin recursos; pobre. —**impe-
cuniousness**, *n.* falta de recursos;
pobreza.
impedance (ɪmˈpiːd·əns) *n., elect.*
impediencia; impedancia.
impede (ɪmˈpiːd) *v.t.* impedir.
—**impediment** (ɪmˈped·ə·mənt) *n.*
impedimento.
impedimenta (ɪmˌped·ɪˈmen·tə)
n.pl. impedimenta.
impel (ɪmˈpel) *v.t.* [-**pelled**,
-**pelling**] impeler.
impend (ɪmˈpend) *v.i.* 1, (be suspended) pender; cernerse. 2, (be imminent) amenazar; ser inminente.
impenetrable (ɪmˈpen·ə·trə·bəl)
adj. impenetrable. —**impenetrability**, *n.* impenetrabilidad.
impenitent (ɪmˈpen·ɪ·tənt) *adj.*
impenitente. —**impenitence**, *n.*
impenitencia. —**impenitently**, *adv.*
sin contrición.
imperative (ɪmˈper·ə·tɪv) *adj.* &
n. imperativo.
imperceptible (ˌɪm·pərˈsep·tə·
bəl) *adj.* imperceptible. —**imperceptibility**, *n.* imperceptibilidad.
imperfect (ɪmˈpɑr·fɪkt) *adj.* & *n.*
imperfecto. —**imperfection** (ˌɪm·
pərˈfek·ʃən) *n.* defecto; imperfección.
imperial (ɪmˈpɪr·i·əl) *adj.* 1, (of an
empire or emperor) imperial. 2, (superior) superior; de primera. —*n.* 1,
(beard) barba estilo imperio; perilla.
2, (top of a bus, carriage, etc.) imperial.
imperialism (ɪmˈpɪr·i·əˌlɪz·əm) *n.*
imperialismo. —**imperialist**, *n.*
imperialista. —**imperialistic**, *adj.*
imperialista.
imperil (ɪmˈper·əl) *v.t.* hacer
peligrar; poner en peligro. —**imper-
ilment**, *n.* peligro; el poner en peligro.
imperious (ɪmˈpɪr·i·əs) *adj.*
imperioso. —**imperiousness**, *n.*
imperiosidad.
imperishable (ɪmˈper·ɪʃ·ə·bəl)
adj. imperecedero. —**imperishabil-
ity**, *n.* indestructibilidad; durabilidad.
impermanent (ɪmˈpɑr·mə·nənt)

adj. transitorio; efímero. —**impermanence,** *n.* transitoriedad; lo efímero.

impermeable (ɪm'pʌr·mi·ə·bəl) *adj.* impermeable. —**impermeability,** *n.* impermeabilidad.

impersonal (ɪm'pʌr·sə·nəl) *adj.* impersonal; *gram.* unipersonal; impersonal.

impersonate (ɪm'pʌr·sə‚neit) *v.t.* 1, (represent) representar; personificar. 2, (imitate; pretend to be) imitar; hacerse pasar por.

impersonation (ɪm‚pʌr·sə'nei·ʃən) *n.* 1, (representation) representación; personificación. 2, (imitation) imitación. 3, (imposture) impostura.

impersonator (ɪm'pʌr·sə‚nei·tər) *n.* 1, (actor) actor. 2, (imitator) imitador. 3, (impostor) impostor.

impertinent (ɪm'pʌr·tə·nənt) *adj.* impertinente. —**impertinence,** *n.* impertinencia.

imperturbable (‚ɪm·pər'tʌrb·ə·bəl) *adj.* imperturbable. —**imperturbability,** *n.* imperturbabilidad.

impervious (ɪm'pʌr·vi·əs) *adj.* 1, (impermeable) impermeable; impenetrable. 2, (resistant) resistente. 3, (unheeding; insensible) sordo; ciego. —**imperviousness,** *n.* impermeabilidad; impenetrabilidad.

impetigo (‚ɪm·pə'tai·go) *n.* impétigo.

impetuous (ɪm'pɛtʃ·u·əs) *adj.* impetuoso. —**impetuousness; impetuosity** (-'as·ə·ti) *n.* impetuosidad.

impetus (ɪm'pə·təs) *n.* ímpetu.

impiety (ɪm'pai·ə·ti) *n.* impiedad.

impinge (ɪm'pɪndʒ) *v.i.* 1, (touch) tocar; incidir; hacer contacto. 2, (encroach; invade) invadir; estar o caer dentro.

impingement (ɪm'pɪndʒ·mənt) *n.* 1, (incidence) incidencia. 2, (encroachment) invasión; transgresión.

impious (ɪm'pi·əs) *adj.* impío. —**impiousness,** *n.* impiedad.

impish ('ɪmp·ɪʃ) *adj.* travieso; malicioso; de diablillo.

implacable (ɪm'plei·kə·bəl) *adj.* implacable. —**implacableness; implacability,** *n.* implacabilidad.

implant (ɪm'plænt) *v.t.* 1, (fix; set) implantar. 2, (imbed) plantar; enterrar. 3, (graft) injertar. —*n.* ('ɪm·plænt) injerto.

implausible (ɪm'plɔz·ə·bəl) *adj.* improbable; increíble.

implement ('ɪm·plə·mənt) *n.* 1,

(tool) herramienta; utensilio. 2, (means) medio; instrumento. —*v.t.* (-‚mɛnt) 1, (carry out) realizar; llevar a cabo; efectuar. 2, (provide with means) ayudar; secundar.

implicate ('ɪm·plɪ‚keit) *v.t.* implicar.

implication (‚ɪm·plɪ'kei·ʃən) *n.* 1, (involvement) complicidad; implicación. 2, (meaning; intimation) intimación; significación.

implicit (ɪm'plɪs·ɪt) *adj.* implícito. —**implicitness,** *n.* calidad de implícito.

implied (ɪm'plaid) *adj.* implícito.

implode (ɪm'plɔːd) *v.t.* & *i.* implosionar. —**implosion,** *n.* implosión.

implore (ɪm'plɔːr) *v.t.* implorar.

imply (ɪm'plai) *v.t.* 1, (involve; entail) implicar. 2, (suggest) sugerir; intimar.

impolite (‚ɪm·pə'lait) *adj.* descortés. —**impoliteness,** *n.* descortesía; falta de cortesía.

impolitic (ɪm'pal·ə·tɪk) *adj.* impolítico.

imponderable (ɪm'pan·dər·ə·bəl) *adj.* imponderable.

import (ɪm'port) *v.t.* importar. —*v.i.* importar; tener importancia. —*n.* ('ɪm·port) 1, (importation) importación. 2, (importance) importancia. 3, (significance) significado; significación. —**importation** (‚ɪm·por'tei·ʃən) *n.* importación. —**importer,** *n.* importador.

important (ɪm'por·tənt) *adj.* importante. —**importance,** *n.* importancia.

importune (‚ɪm·por'tjuːn) *v.t.* importunar. —**importunate** (ɪm'port·ju·nət) *adj.* importuno. —**importunity** (-tʃər) *n.* importunidad.

impose (ɪm'pɔːz) *v.t.* 1, (lay on or upon) imponer. 2, (palm off) pasar (con maña); colar; endosar. —**imposing,** *adj.* imponente. —**imposition** (‚ɪm·pə'zɪʃ·ən) *n.* imposición. —**impose on o upon** (trouble; annoy) molestar; importunar; incomodar.

impossible (ɪm'pas·ə·bəl) *adj.* imposible. —**impossibility,** *n.* imposibilidad.

impost ('ɪm·post) *n.* impuesto.

impostor (ɪm'pas·tər) *n.* impostor. —**imposture** (-tʃər) *n.* impostura.

impotent ('ɪm·pə·tənt) *n.* impotente. —**impotence; impotency,** *n.* impotencia.

impound (ɪm'paund) *v.t.* 1, (shut in

a pen) encerrar; encorralar; meter en perrera. **2,** (seize; keep in custody) embargar; retener. **—impoundage; impoundment,** *n.* embargo.

impoverish (ım'pav·ər·ıʃ) *v.t.* empobrecer. **—impoverishment,** *n.* empobrecimiento.

impracticable (ım'præk·tı·kə·bəl) *adj.* impracticable. **—impracticability,** *n.* impracticabilidad.

impractical (ım'præk·tı·kəl) *adj.* impráctico. **—impracticalness; impracticality** (-'kæl·ə·ti) *n.* lo impráctico; impractibilidad.

imprecate (‘ım·prə,keit) *v.t.* imprecar. **—imprecation,** *n.* imprecación.

impregnable (ım'prɛg·nə·bəl) *adj.* **1,** (unassailable) inexpugnable. **2,** (fecund) fecundable. **3,** (saturable) impregnable; saturable.

impregnate (ım'prɛg·net) *v.t.* **1,** (fecundate) fecundar; preñar. **2,** (saturate) impregnar; saturar.

impregnation (,ım·prɛg'nei·ʃən) *n.* **1,** (fecundation) fecundación. **2,** (saturation) impregnación; saturación.

impresario (,ım·prə'sar·i·o) *n.* empresario.

impress (ım'prɛs) *v.t.* **1,** (affect deeply) impresionar. **2,** (stamp; fix firmly) imprimir; estampar. **3,** (urge) urgir. **4,** (recruit) reclutar. **5,** (requisition) requisar; requisicionar. **—n.** (‘ım·prɛs) impresión.

impression (ım'prɛʃ·ən) *n.* impresión. **—impressionable,** *adj.* impresionable.

impressionism (ım'prɛʃ·ə·nız·əm) *n.* impresionismo. **—impressionist,** *n.* impresionista. **—impressionistic,** *adj.* impresionista.

impressive (ım'prɛs·ıv) *adj.* impresionante. **—impressiveness,** *n.* lo impresionante.

impressment (ım'prɛs·mənt) *n.* **1,** (recruiting) reclutamiento. **2,** (requisition) requisición.

imprint (ım'prınt) *v.t.* imprimir; estampar. **—n.** (‘ım·prınt) **1,** (publisher's mark) pie de imprenta. **2,** (impression) impresión. **3,** (distinctive sign) marca; señal; huella.

imprison (ım'prız·ən) *v.t.* encarcelar. **—imprisonment,** *n.* encarcelamiento.

improbable (ım'prab·ə·bəl) *adj.* improbable. **—improbability,** *n.* improbabilidad.

improbity (ım'pro·bə·ti) *n.* improbidad.

impromptu (ım'pramp·tu) *adj.* improvisado; extemporáneo. **—adv.** improvisadamente; extemporáneamente. **—n., mus.** improvisación.

improper (ım'prap·ər) *adj.* impropio. **—impropriety** (,ım·prə'prai·ə·ti) *n.* impropiedad.

improve (ım'pruːv) *v.t.* mejorar. **—v.i.** mejorarse. **—improvement,** *n.* mejora; mejoramiento; *(esp. of health)* mejoría.

improvident (ım'prav·ı·dənt) *adj.* impróvido. **—improvidence,** *n.* improvidencia.

improvise (‘ım·prə,vaiz) *v.t.* improvisar. **—improvisation** (ım,prav·ı'zei·ʃən) *n.* improvisación.

imprudent (ım'pru·dənt) *adj.* imprudente. **—imprudence,** *n.* imprudencia.

impudent (‘ım·pjə·dənt) *adj.* insolente; atrevido; impudente. **—impudence,** *n.* insolencia; atrevimiento; impudicia.

impugn (ım'pjuːn) *v.t.* impugnar; poner en tela de juicio. **—impugnment,** *n.* impugnación.

impulse (‘ım·pʌls) *n.* impulso. **—impulsive** (ım'pʌl·sıv) *adj.* impulsivo. **—impulsiveness,** *n.* impulsividad.

impunity (ım'pju·nə·ti) *n.* impunidad.

impure (ım'pjur) *adj.* impuro. **—impureness,** *n.* impureza. **—impurity,** *n.* impureza.

impute (ım'pjut) *v.t.* imputar. **—imputable,** *adj.* imputable. **—imputation** (,ım·pju'tei·ʃən) *n.* imputación.

in (ın) *prep.* **1,** *(expresando inclusión o localidad)* en: *in the room,* en el cuarto. **2,** *(expresando estado o condición)* en; de; con: *in good spirits,* en, de o con buen humor. **3,** *(con el gerundio, expresando acción)* al (+ inf.) o el mero gerundio español: *in writing this,* al escribir esto; escribiendo esto. **4,** *(expresando modo o manera)* en; de; con: *in silence,* en silencio; *in good faith,* de o con buena fe. **5,** *(expresando tiempo o época en que o al fin de que sucede algo)* en; dentro de: *in these times,* en estos tiempos; *in a little while,* dentro de poco. **6,** *(expresando movimiento, dirección o cambio)* en: *set in motion,* poner en movimiento; *break in two,* partir en dos. **7,** (during) en: *in the day-time,* de día; *in the summer,* en el verano. **8,** (wearing; clothed in) de; con; en: *the lady in red,* la dama de rojo. **9,** *(expresando relación o respecto)* de; en: *a change in policy,* un cambio de política; *We agreed in this matter,* Convinimos en este asunto. **10,** *(expresando colocación o disposición)* en: *in a group,* en grupo. **11,** *(expresando distribución)* por; a: *in dozens,* por docenas. **12,** (made of or with) en; de: *in marble,* en o de mármol. **13,** (because of) de: *She sighed in relief,* Suspiró de alivio. **14,** (into) en; a; dentro de: *come in the house,* entra en o a casa. —*adv.* dentro; adentro; hacia dentro. —*adj.* de dentro; de adentro. —*n.* **1,** *usu.pl.* (persons in power or favor) los de arriba; los de adentro. **2,** *colloq.* (influence) mano. —**be in for,** buscarse (algo); merecer; no poder escapar. —**be in with,** tener intimidad con; ser íntimo de. —**ins and outs,** pormenores; minucias. —**in that,** porque; puesto que.

inability (ˌɪn·ə'bɪl·ə·ti) *n.* incapacidad.

inaccessible (ˌɪn·æk'sɛs·ə·bəl) *adj.* inaccesible. —**inaccessibility,** *n.* inaccesibilidad.

inaccurate (ɪn'æk·jə·rət) *adj.* inexacto. —**inaccuracy,** *n.* inexactitud.

inaction (ɪn'æk·ʃən) *n.* inacción.

inactive (ɪn'æk·tɪv) *adj.* inactivo. —**inactivity** (ˌɪn·æk'tɪv·ə·ti) *n.* inactividad.

inadequate (ɪn'æd·ə·kwət) *adj.* inadecuado; insuficiente. —**inadequacy,** *n.* insuficiencia.

inadmissible (ɪn·æd'mɪs·ə·bəl) *adj.* inadmisible. —**inadmissibility,** *n.* inadmisibilidad.

inadvertent (ɪn·əd'vʌr·tənt) *adj.* inadvertido. —**inadvertence; inadvertency,** *n.* inadvertencia.

inadvisable (ɪn·əd'vaiz·ə·bəl) *adj.* no aconsejable; imprudente. —**inadvisability,** *n.* imprudencia.

inalienable (ɪn'eil·i·ən·ə·bəl) *adj.* inalienable; inajenable.

inane (ɪn'ein) *adj.* inane; vacío; huero. —**inanity** (ɪn'æn·ə·ti) *n.* inanidad.

inanimate (ɪn'æn·ɪ·mət) *adj.* inanimado; inánime. —**inanimate-**

ness; inanimation (-'mei·ʃən) *n.* calidad de inanimado o inánime.

inanition (ˌɪn·ə'nɪʃ·ən) *n.* inanición.

inapplicable (ɪn'æp·lɪk·ə·bəl) *adj.* inaplicable. —**inapplicability,** *n.* inaplicabilidad.

inappreciable (ˌɪn·ə'priʃ·ə·bəl) *adj.* inapreciable.

inappropriate (ˌɪn·ə'pro·pri·ət) *adj.* inadecuado; impropio; improcedente. —**inappropriateness,** *n.* impropiedad; improcedencia.

inapt (ɪn'æpt) *adj.* inepto.

inaptitude (ɪn'æp·tə·tud) *n.* ineptitud.

inarticulate (ˌɪn·ɑr'tɪk·jə·lət) *adj.* **1,** (not articulated) inarticulado. **2,** (unable to articulate) balbuciente.

inartistic (ˌɪn·ɑr'tɪs·tɪk) *adj.* inartístico.

inasmuch as (ˌɪn·əz'mʌtʃ) **1,** (since) en vista de que; ya que; puesto que. **2,** (insofar as; to such a degree that) en cuanto; tanto como; hasta donde.

inattention (ˌɪn·ə'tɛn·ʃən) *n.* desatención; falta de atención. —**inattentive** (-tɪv) *adj.* desatento.

inaudible (ɪn'ɔ·də·bəl) *adj.* inaudible. —**inaudibleness; inaudibility,** *n.* calidad de inaudible.

inaugurate (ɪn'ɔ·gjə,reit) *v.t.* inaugurar. —**inaugural** (-gjʊ·rəl) *adj.* inaugural. —**inauguration,** *n.* inauguración.

inauspicious (ˌɪn·ɔ'spɪʃ·əs) *adj.* desfavorable; poco propicio.

inboard ('ɪn·bord) *adj. & adv.* en o hacia el interior.

inborn ('ɪn·born) *adj.* innato.

inbred ('ɪn·brɛd) *adj.* **1,** (inborn) ingénito. **2,** (produced by inbreeding) resultado de o producido por uniones de consanguinidad.

inbreeding ('ɪn,bri·dɪŋ) *n.* procreación por uniones de consanguinidad.

Inca ('ɪŋ·kə) *adj. & n.* inca. —**Incan** ('ɪŋ·kən) *adj.* incaico.

incalculable (ɪn'kæl·kjə·lə·bəl) *adj.* incalculable.

incandescent (ˌɪn·kən'dɛs·ənt) *adj.* incandescente. —**incandescence,** *n.* incandescencia.

incantation (ˌɪn·kæn'tei·ʃən) *n.* encantamiento; conjuro.

incapable (ɪn'kei·pə·bəl) *adj.* incapaz. —**incapability,** *n.* incapacidad.

incapacitate (ˌɪn·kə'pæs·ə,teit)

v.t. incapacitar; inhabilitar. —**inca-pacitation,** *n.* inhabilitación.

incapacity (,ɪn·kə'pæs·ə·ti) *n.* incapacidad; inutilidad.

incarcerate (ɪn'kar·sə,reit) *v.t.* encarcelar. —**incarceration,** *n.* encarcelación.

incarnate (ɪn'kar·nət) *adj.* encarnado. —*v.t.* (-,neit) encarnar. —**incarnation,** *n.* encarnación.

incautious (ɪn'kɔ·ʃəs) *adj.* incauto. —**incautiousness,** *n.* imprudencia.

incendiary (ɪn'sɛn·di·ɛr·i) *adj.* & *n.* incendiario. —**incendiarism** (-ə·rɪz·əm) *n.* condición o acto de incendiario.

incense ('ɪn·sɛns) *n.* incienso.

incense (ɪn'sɛns) *v.t.* enfurecer; encolerizar; enojar.

incentive (ɪn'sɛn·tɪv) *n.* incentivo; aliciente. —*adj.* estimulante; alentador.

inception (ɪn'sɛp·ʃən) *n.* comienzo; principio; iniciación. —**inceptive** (-tɪv) *adj.* inicial; *gram.* incoativo.

incertitude (ɪn'sʌr·tə,tud) *n.* incertidumbre.

incessant (ɪn'sɛs·ənt) *adj.* incesante. —**incessancy,** *n.* calidad de incesante; persistencia.

incest ('ɪn·sɛst) *n.* incesto. —**incestuous** (ɪn'sɛs·tʃu·əs) *adj.* incestuoso.

inch (ɪntʃ) *n.* **1,** (measure) pulgada. **2,** (small amount) tris; pelo. —*v.t.* & *i.* avanzar poquito a poco; avanzar de a poquitos. —**by inches; inch by inch,** de a poquitos. —**every inch,** todo; en todo; enteramente.

inchoate (ɪn'ko·ət) *adj.* incipiente. —**inchoative,** *adj., gram.* incoativo.

incidence ('ɪn·sɪ·dəns) *n.* incidencia.

incident ('ɪn·sɪ·dənt) *n.* & *adj.* incidente.

incidental (,ɪn·sɪ'dɛn·təl) *adj.* incidental; incidente. —*n.* accidente. —**incidentals,** *n.pl.* imprevistos; gastos contingentes.

incinerate (ɪn'sɪn·ə,reit) *v.t.* incinerar. —**incineration,** *n.* incineración. —**incinerator,** *n.* incinerador.

incipient (ɪn'sɪp·i·ənt) *adj.* incipiente. —**incipience; incipiency,** *n.* principio; comienzo.

incise (ɪn'saiz) *v.t.* **1,** (cut into) cortar. **2,** (engrave) grabar. —**inci-**

sion (ɪn'sɪʒ·ən) *n.* incisión. —**incisor,** *n.* incisivo.

incisive (ɪn'sai·sɪv) *adj.* incisivo. —**incisiveness,** *n.* calidad de incisivo.

incite (ɪn'sait) *v.t.* incitar. —**incitement,** *n.* incitación.

incivility (,ɪn·sə'vɪl·ə·ti) *n.* descortesía; incivilidad.

inclement (ɪn'klɛm·ənt) *adj.* inclemente. —**inclemency,** *n.* inclemencia.

inclination (,ɪn·klə'nei·ʃən) *n.* inclinación.

incline (ɪn'klain) *v.t.* & *i.* inclinar. —*n.* ('ɪn·klain) declive; cuesta; gradiente.

inclose (ɪn'kloːz) *v.t.* = **enclose.** —**inclosure** (-ʒər) *n.* = **enclosure.**

include (ɪn'kluːd) *v.t.* incluir; comprender; abarcar. —**inclusion** (ɪn'klu·ʒən) *n.* inclusión; comprensión.

inclusive (ɪn'klu·sɪv) *adj.* inclusivo; comprensivo. —**inclusiveness,** *n.* comprensión; calidad de inclusivo o comprensivo. —**inclusive of,** incluso.

incognito (ɪn'kag·nɪ·to) *adj.* incógnito. —*adv.* de incógnito.

incognizant (ɪn'kag·nɪ·zant) *adj.* inconsciente. —**incognizance,** *n.* inconsciencia.

incoherent (,ɪn·ko'hɪr·ənt) *adj.* incoherente. —**incoherence,** *n.* incoherencia.

incombustible (,ɪn·kəm'bʌst·ə·bəl) *adj.* incombustible.

income ('ɪn·kʌm) *n.* entrada; ingreso. —**income tax,** impuesto sobre la renta; impuesto de utilidades. —**income tax return,** declaración de utilidades o de ingresos.

incoming ('ɪn,kʌm·ɪŋ) *adj.* que llega; que entra.

incommensurable (,ɪn·kə·'mɛn·ʃə·rə·bəl) *adj.* inconmensurable. —**incommensurability,** *n.* inconmensurabilidad.

incommensurate (,ɪn·kə'mɛn·ʃə·rət) *adj.* desproporcionado.

incommode (,ɪn·kə'moːd) *v.t.* incomodar; fastidiar. —**incommodious** (-'mo·di·əs) *adj.* incómodo. —**incommodiousness,** *n.* incomodidad.

incommunicable (,ɪn·kə'mju·nɪ·kə·bəl) *adj.* incomunicable.

incommunicado (,ɪn·kə,mju·nɪ'ka·do) *adj.* incomunicado.

incomparable (ɪn'kam·pə·rə·bəl)
adj. incomparable. —**incompara-
bility,** *n.* excelencia.

incompatible (,ɪn·kəm'pæt·ə·
bəl) *adj.* incompatible. —**incompatibility,** *n.* incompatibilidad.

incompetent (ɪn'kam·pə·tənt)
adj. incompetente. —**incompetence; incompetency,** *n.* incompetencia.

incomplete (,ɪn·kəm'plit) *adj.*
incompleto. —**incompleteness,** *n.*
calidad de incompleto.

incomprehensible (ɪn,kam·
prɪ'hɛn·sə·bəl) *adj.* incomprensible.

incomprehensive (ɪn,kam·prɪ·
'hɛn·sɪv) *adj.* limitado; restringido.

incompressible (ɪn·kəm'prɛs·ə·
bəl) *adj.* incompresible.

inconceivable (,ɪn·kən'si·və·bəl)
adj. inconcebible.

inconclusive ('ɪn·kən'klu·sɪv)
adj. no concluyente; no definitivo;
sin fuerza.

incongruent (ɪn'kaŋ·gru·ənt) *adj.*
incongruente. —**incongruence,** *n.*
incongruencia.

incongruous (ɪn'kaŋ·gru·əs) *adj.*
incongruente; incongruo. —**incongruousness,** *n.* incongruencia; incongruidad. —**incongruity**
(,ɪn·kən'gru·ə·ti) *n.* incongruidad.

inconsequent (ɪn'kan·sə·kwənt)
adj. inconsecuente. —**inconsequence,** *n.* inconsecuencia.

inconsequential (ɪn,kan·sə·
'kwɛn·ʃəl) *adj.* sin importancia;
insignificante.

inconsiderable (,ɪn·kən'sɪd·
ər·ə·bəl) *adj.* insignificante.

inconsiderate (,ɪn·kən'sɪd·ər·ət)
adj. inconsiderado. —**inconsiderateness,** *n.* inconsideración.

inconsistent (,ɪn·kən'sɪs·tənt)
adj. inconsistente. —**inconsistency,**
n. inconsistencia.

inconsolable (,ɪn·kən'sol·ə·bəl)
adj. inconsolable.

inconspicuous (,ɪn·kən'spɪk·
ju·əs) *adj.* poco llamativo; poco
aparente; obscuro. —**inconspicu-
ousness,** *n.* obscuridad.

inconstant (ɪn'kan·stənt) *adj.* inconstante. —**inconstancy,** *n.* inconstancia.

incontestable (,ɪn·kən'tɛst·ə·bəl)
adj. incontestable.

incontinent (ɪn'kan·tə·nənt) *adj.*
incontinente. —**incontinence,** *n.*
incontinencia.

incontrovertible (,ɪn·kan·trə·
'vʌrt·ə·bəl) *adj.* incontrovertible.
—**incontrovertibility,** *n.* incontrovertibilidad.

inconvenience (ɪn·kən'vin·jəns)
n. inconveniencia; molestia. —*v.t.*
molestar; incomodar. —**inconvenient,** *adj.* inconveniente; molesto.

incorporate (ɪn'kor·pə,reit) *v.t.*
incorporar; constituir (una sociedad). —*v.i.* asociarse; incorporarse.
—**incorporation,** *n.* incorporación;
formación (de una sociedad).

incorporeal (,ɪn·kor'por·i·əl) *adj.*
incorpóreo.

incorrect (,ɪn·kə'rɛkt) *adj.* incorrecto. —**incorrectness,** *n.* incorrección.

incorrigible (ɪn'kar·ɪ·dʒə·bəl)
adj. incorregible. —**incorrigibility,**
n. incorregibilidad.

incorruptible (,ɪn·kə'rʌp·tə·bəl)
adj. incorruptible. —**incorruptibility,** *n.* incorruptibilidad.

increase (ɪn'kris) *v.t* & *i.* aumentar. —*n.* ('ɪn·kris) aumento; incremento. —**increasingly,** *adv.* cada
vez más; progresivamente. —**on
the increase,** en aumento.

incredible (ɪn'krɛd·ə·bəl) *adj.*
increíble. —**incredibility,** *n.* incredibilidad.

incredulous (ɪn'krɛdʒ·ə·ləs) *adj.*
incrédulo. —**incredulity** (,ɪn·
krə'dju·lə·ti) *n.* incredulidad.

increment ('ɪn·krə·mənt) *n.* incremento.

incriminate (ɪn'krɪm·ə,neit) *v.t.*
incriminar. —**incrimination,** *n.*
incriminación.

incrust (ɪn'krʌst) *v.t.* incrustar.
—**incrustation** (,ɪn·krʌs'tei·ʃən) *n.*
incrustación.

incubate ('ɪn·kjə,beit) *v.t.* & *i.*
incubar. —**incubation,** *n.* incubación. —**incubator,** *n.* incubadora.

incubus ('ɪn·kjə·bəs) *n.* íncubo.

inculcate (ɪn'kʌl,keit) *v.t.* inculcar.
—**inculcation,** *n.* inculcación.

inculpable (ɪn'kʌl·pə·bal) *adj.* inculpable; inocente.

inculpate (ɪn'kʌl,peit) *v.t.* inculpar.
—**inculpation,** *n.* inculpación.

incumbency (ɪn'kʌm·bən·si) *n.* 1,
(obligation) incumbencia. 2, (tenure
of office) tenencia.

incumbent (ɪn'kʌm·bənt) *adj.* 1,
(obligatory) obligatorio. 2, (leaning)
apoyado. —*n.* titular. —**be incumbent (upon),** incumbir (a).

incur (ɪn'kʌr) *v.t.* incurrir en. —**in-
currence,** *n.* obligación.

incurable (ın'kjυr·ə·bəl) *adj.* incurable.

incurious (ın'kjυr·i·əs) *adj.* indiferente.

incursion (ın'kʌr·ʒən) *n.* incursión. —**incursive** (-sıv) *adj.* invasor.

indebted (ın'dɛt·ıd) *adj.* **1,** (in debt) endeudado. **2,** (owing gratitude) en deuda; obligado. —**indebtedness,** *n.* deuda.

indecent (ın'di·sənt) *adj.* indecente. —**indecency,** *n.* indecencia.

indecipherable (ın·di'sai·fər·ə·bəl) *adj.* indescifrable.

indecision (ın·dı'sıʒ·ən) *n.* indecisión.

indecisive (ın·dı'sai·sıv) *adj.* indeciso. —**indecisiveness,** *n.* indecisión.

indecorous (ın'dɛk·ə·rəs) *adj.* indecoroso. —**indecorousness; indecorum** (ın·dı'kor·əm) *n.* indecoro; falta de decoro.

indeed (ın'di:d) *adv.* claro; desde luego; de veras. —*interj.* ¡de veras!

indefatigable (ın·dı'fæt·ə·gə·bəl) *adj.* infatigable. —**indefatigability,** *n.* calidad de infatigable.

indefensible (ın·dı'fɛn·sə·bəl) *adj.* indefendible.

indefinable (ın·dı'fain·ə·bəl) *adj.* indefinible.

indefinite (ın'dɛf·ə·nıt) *adj.* indefinido. —**indefiniteness,** *n.* lo indefinido.

indelible (ın'dɛl·ə·bəl) *adj.* indeleble. —**indelibility,** *n.* lo indeleble.

indelicate (ın'dɛl·ə·kət) *adj.* falto de delicadeza. —**indelicacy,** *n.* falta de delicadeza.

indemnify (ın'dɛm·nə,fai) *v.t.* indemnizar. —**indemnification** (-fı'kei·ʃən) *n.* indemnización.

indemnity (ın'dɛm·nə·ti) *n.* **1,** (compensation) indemnización. **2,** (security against loss; exemption from liability) indemnidad.

indent (ın'dɛnt) *v.t.* **1,** (notch) dentar; cortar muescas en; mellar. **2,** (space in from the regular margin) empezar más adentro; *print.* sangrar. —*n.* mella; diente; muesca.

indentation (ın·dɛn'tei·ʃən) *n.* **1,** (notch) muesca. **2,** (additional margin) margen adicional; *print.* sangría.

indenture (ın'dɛn·tʃər) *n.* contrato. —*v.t.* contratar.

independent (ın·dı'pɛn·dənt) *adj.* independiente. —**independence,** *n.* independencia.

indescribable (ın·dı'skraib·ə·bəl) *adj.* indescriptible.

indestructible (ın·dı'strʌkt·ə·bəl) *adj.* indestructible.

indeterminable (ın·dı'tʌr·mə·nə·bəl) *adj.* indeterminable.

indeterminate (ın·dı'tʌr·mə·nət) *adj.* indeterminado.

index ('ın·dɛks) *n.* índice. —*v.t.* **1,** (list the contents of) poner índice a. **2,** (put in the index) poner en el índice. **3,** (indicate) indicar; señalar. —**card index,** fichero. —**index card,** ficha. —**index finger,** (dedo) índice.

India ink ('ın·di·ə) tinta china.

Indian ('ın·di·ən) *adj. & n.* indio. —**Indian corn,** maíz. —**Indian file,** fila india. —**Indian summer,** veranillo.

India paper papel de China.

India rubber caucho.

indicate ('ın·dı,keit) *v.t.* indicar. —**indication,** *n.* indicación. —**indicative** (ın'dık·ə·tıv) *adj.* indicativo. —**indicator,** *n.* indicador.

indict (ın'dait) *v.t.* acusar. —**indictment,** *n.* acusación.

indifferent (ın'dıf·ər·ənt) *adj.* indiferente. —**indifference,** *n.* indiferencia.

indigenous (ın'dıdʒ·ə·nəs) *adj.* indígena; nativo.

indigent ('ın·dı·dʒənt) *adj.* indigente. —**indigence,** *n.* indigencia.

indigestible (ın·dı'dʒɛs·tə·bəl) *adj.* indigestible.

indigestion (ın·dı'dʒɛs·tʃən) *n.* indigestión.

indignant (ın'dıg·nənt) *adj.* indignado. —**indignation** (ın·dıg'nei·ʃən) *n.* indignación.

indignity (ın'dıg·nə·ti) *n.* indignidad.

indigo ('ın·dı·go) *n.* índigo; añil.

indirect (ın·dı'rɛkt) *adj.* indirecto. —**indirectness,** *n.* rodeos; lo indirecto.

indirection (ın·dı'rɛk·ʃən) *n.* indirecta; rodeo.

indiscernible (ın·dı'sʌrn·ə·bəl) *adj.* indiscernible.

indiscreet (ın·dıs'krit) *adj.* indiscreto. —**indiscreetness,** *n.* indiscreción.

indiscretion (ın·dıs'krɛʃ·ən) *n.* indiscreción.

indiscriminate (ın·dıs'krım·

ə·nət) *adj.* 1, (random; haphazard) indistinto; sin discriminación. 2, (promiscuous) promiscuo; poco exigente. —**indiscriminateness,** *n.* lo indistinto. —**indiscrimination** (-'nei·ʃən) *n.* falta de discriminación.

indispensable (ˌɪn·dɪ'spɛn·sə·bəl) *adj.* indispensable.

indispose (ˌɪn·dɪ'spoz) *v.t.* indisponer. —**indisposed,** *adj.* indispuesto. —**indisposition** (ˌɪn·dɪs·pə'zɪʃ·ən) *n.* indisposición.

indisputable (ˌɪn·dɪs'pju·tə·bəl) *adj.* indisputable.

indissoluble (ˌɪn·dɪ'sal·jə·bəl) *adj.* indisoluble. —**indissolubility,** *n.* indisolubilidad.

indistinct (ˌɪn·dɪ'stɪŋkt) *adj.* indistinto; impreciso. —**indistinctness,** *n.* imprecisión.

indistinguishable (ˌɪn·dɪ'stɪŋ·gwɪʃ·ə·bəl) *adj.* indistinguible.

indium (ˌɪn·di·əm) *n.* indio.

individual (ˌɪn·dɪ'vɪdʒ·u·əl) *adj.* individual. —*n.* individuo. —**individualism,** *n.* individualismo. —**individualist,** *n.* individualista. —**individualistic,** *adj.* individualista. —**individuality** (-'æl·ə·ti) *n.* individualidad. —**individualize,** *v.t.* individualizar.

indivisible (ɪn·dɪ'vɪz·ə·bəl) *adj.* indivisible. —**indivisibility,** *n.* indivisibilidad.

indoctrinate (ɪn'dak·trɪˌneit) *v.t.* adoctrinar. —**indoctrination,** *n.* adoctrinamiento; saturación.

Indo-European *adj. & n.* indoeuropeo.

indolent (ˈɪn·də·lənt) *adj.* indolente. —**indolence,** *n.* indolencia.

indomitable (ɪn'dam·ɪ·tə·bəl) *adj.* indómito; bravo. —**indomitability,** *n.* lo indómito.

indoor (ˈɪn·dor) *adj.* interior; de casa. —**indoors,** *adv.* adentro; a o en casa.

indorse (ɪn'dors) *v.t.* = endorse. —**indorsee,** *n.* = endorsee. —**indorsement,** *n.* = endorsement. —**indorser,** *n.* = endorser.

indubitable (ɪn'du·bɪ·tə·bəl) *adj.* indudable. —**indubitableness,** *n.* certeza.

induce (ɪn'djus) *v.t.* inducir.

inducement (ɪn'djus·mənt) *n.* 1, (persuasion) inducción; inducimiento. 2, (incentive) incentivo.

induct (ɪn'dʌkt) *v.t.* instalar; iniciar; *mil.* alistar.

induction (ɪn'dʌk·ʃən) *n.* 1, (installation) instalación; *mil.* alistamiento. 2, *physics; logic* inducción. —**inductive** (-tɪv) *adj.* inductivo.

indulge (ɪn'dʌldʒ) *v.t.* 1, (gratify) satisfacer. 2, (allow) permitir. 3, (yield to; humor) consentir. —**indulge in,** 1, (take pleasure in) recrearse en. 2, (allow oneself) permitirse.

indulgence (ɪn'dʌl·dʒəns) *n.* 1, (gratification) satisfacción. 2, (leniency) complacencia; indulgencia. 3, *comm.* (extension of time) moratoria. 4, *eccles.* indulgencia.

indulgent (ɪn'dʌl·dʒənt) *.adj.* condescendiente; indulgente.

induration (ˌɪn·dju'rei·ʃən) *n.* induración.

industrial (ɪn'dʌs·tri·əl) *adj.* industrial.

industrialism (ɪn'dʌs·tri·əˌlɪz·əm) *n.* industrialismo. —**industrialist,** *n.* industrial; *Amer.* industrialista.

industrialize (ɪn'dʌs·tri·əˌlaiz) *v.t.* industrializar. —**industrialization** (-lɪ'zei·ʃən) *n.* industrialización.

industrious (ɪn'dʌs·tri·əs) *adj.* diligente; industrioso. —**industriousness,** *n.* diligencia.

industry (ˈɪn·dəs·tri) *n.* 1, (business; trade) industria. 2, (diligence) diligencia.

inebriate (ɪn'i·bri,eit) *v.t.* embriagar; emborrachar. —**inebriation,** *n.* embriaguez. —**inebriety** (ˌɪn·ɪ'brai·ə·ti) *n.* embriaguez.

inedible (ɪn'ed·ə·bəl) *adj.* no comestible; incomible.

ineffable (ɪn'ef·ə·bəl) *adj.* inefable. —**ineffability,** *n.* inefabilidad.

ineffective (ˌɪn·ɪ'fek·tɪv) *adj.* ineficaz. —**ineffectiveness,** *n.* ineficacia.

ineffectual (ˌɪn·ɪ'fek·tʃu·əl) *adj.* ineficaz.

inefficacy (ɪn'ef·ɪ·kə·si) *n.* ineficacia. —**inefficacious** (-'kei·ʃəs) *adj.* ineficaz.

inefficient (ˌɪn·ə'fɪʃ·ənt) *adj.* ineficiente. —**inefficiency,** *n.* ineficiencia; ineficacia.

inelastic (ˌɪn·ə'læs·tɪk) *adj.* sin elasticidad. —**inelasticity** (-'tɪs·ə·ti) *n.* falta de elasticidad.

inelegant (ɪn'el·ɪ·gənt) *adj.* sin

elegancia; inelegante. —**inelegance; inelegancy,** *n.* inelegancia.

ineligible (ɪn'ɛl·ɪ·dʒə·bəl) *adj.* ineligible. —**ineligibility,** *n.* inelegibilidad.

ineluctable (ɪn·ɪ'lʌk·tə·bəl) *adj.* ineluctable.

inept (ɪn'ɛpt) *adj.* inepto. —**ineptness; ineptitude** (,ɪn'ɛp·tə·tud) *n.* ineptitud.

inequality (,ɪn·i'kwal·ə·ti) *n.* desigualdad.

inequitable (ɪn'ɛk·wɪ·tə·bəl) *adj.* injusto; no equitativo.

inequity (ɪn'ɛk·wə·ti) *n.* injusticia.

ineradicable (,ɪn·ɪ'ræd·ɪ·kə·bəl) *adj.* inextirpable.

inert (ɪn'ʌrt) *adj.* inerte. —**inertness,** *n.* inercia.

inertia (ɪn'ʌr·ʃə) *n.* inercia.

inescapable (,ɪn·ɛs'kei·pə·bəl) *adj.* ineludible.

inestimable (ɪn'ɛs·tə·mə·bəl) *adj.* inestimable.

inevitable (ɪn'ɛv·ɪ·tə·bəl) *adj.* inevitable. —**inevitability,** *n.* inevitabilidad.

inexact (,ɪn·ɛg'zækt) *adj.* inexacto. —**inexactness,** *n.* inexactitud.

inexcusable (,ɪn·ɛk'skjuz·ə·bəl) *adj.* inexcusable.

inexhaustible (,ɪn·ɛg'zɔs·tə·bəl) *adj.* inagotable.

inexorable (ɪn'ɛk·sə·rə·bəl) *adj.* inexorable. —**inexorableness; inexorability,** *n.* inexorabilidad.

inexpedient (,ɪn·ɪk'spi·di·ənt) *adj.* inconveniente; inoportuno. —**inexpediency,** *n.* inconveniencia; inoportunidad.

inexpensive (,ɪn·ɪk'spɛn·sɪv) *adj.* barato.

inexperience (,ɪn·ɪk'spɪr·i·əns) *n.* inexperiencia. —**inexperienced,** *adj.* inexperto.

inexpert (ɪn'ɛk·spʌrt) *adj.* inexperto.

inexpiable (ɪn'ɛk·spi·ə·bəl) *adj.* inexpiable.

inexplicable (ɪn'ɛk·splɪk·ə·bəl) *adj.* inexplicable.

inexpressible (,ɪn·ɪk'sprɛs·ə·bəl) *adj.* inexplicable.

inexpressive (,ɪn·ɪk'sprɛs·ɪv) *adj.* inexpresivo.

inextinguishable (,ɪn·ɪk'stɪŋ·gwɪʃ·ə·bəl) *adj.* inextinguible.

inextricable (ɪn'ɛks·trɪ·kə·bəl) *adj.* inextricable.

infallible (ɪn'fæl·ə·bəl) *adj.*

infalible. —**infallibility,** *n.* infalibilidad.

infamous ('ɪn·fə·məs) *adj.* infame. —**infamy,** *n.* infamia.

infancy ('ɪn·fən·si) *n.* infancia.

infant ('ɪn·fənt) *n.* **1,** (child) niño (*fem.* niña); nene (*fem.* nena); criatura. **2,** *law* menor de edad.

infanta (ɪn'fæn·tə) *n.* infanta.

infante (ɪn'fæn·te) *n.* infante.

infanticide (ɪn'fæn·tə,said) *n.* **1,** (act) infanticidio. **2,** (agent) infanticida.

infantile ('ɪn·fən,tail) *adj.* infantil. —**infantile paralysis,** poliomielitis.

infantry ('ɪn·fən·tri) *n.* infantería. —**infantryman** (-mən) *n.* infante; soldado de infantería.

infatuate (ɪn'fætʃ·u,eit) *v.t.* infatuar. —**infatuation,** *n.* infatuación.

infect (ɪn'fɛkt) *v.t.* **1,** *pathol.* infectar. **2,** *fig.* (contaminate) contaminar; inficionar.

infection (ɪn'fɛk·ʃən) *n.* infección. —**infectious** (-ʃəs) *adj.* infeccioso. —**infectiousness,** *n.* calidad de infeccioso.

infecund (ɪn'fi·kund) *adj.* infecundo. —**infecundity** (,ɪn·fɪ'kʌn·də·ti) *n.* infecundidad.

infer (ɪn'fʌr) *v.t. & i.* inferir.

inference ('ɪn·fə·rəns) *n.* inferencia; ilación.

inferior (ɪn'fɪr·i·ər) *adj. & n.* inferior. —**inferiority** (-'ar·ə·ti) *n.* inferioridad.

inferno (ɪn'fʌr·no) *n.* infierno. —**infernal** (-nəl) *adj.* infernal.

infertile (ɪn'fʌr·təl) *adj.* infecundo; estéril. —**infertility** (,ɪn·fər'tɪl·ə·ti) *n.* infecundidad; esterilidad.

infest (ɪn'fɛst) *v.t.* infestar.

infestation (,ɪn·fɛs'tei·ʃən) *n.* infestación.

infidel ('ɪn·fə·dəl) *adj. & n.* infiel. —**infidelity** (-'dɛl·ə·ti) *n.* infidelidad.

infield ('ɪn·fild) *n., baseball* diamante; losange.

infighting ('ɪn,fai·tɪŋ) *n.* lucha cuerpo a cuerpo.

infiltrate (ɪn'fɪl,treit) *v.t.* infiltrar. —*v.i.* infiltrarse. —**infiltration,** *n.* infiltración.

infinite ('ɪn·fə·nɪt) *adj. & n.* infinito.

infinitesimal (,ɪn·fɪn·ɪ'tɛs·ə·məl) *adj.* infinitesimal.

infinitive (ɪnˈfɪn·ə·tɪv) *adj.* & *n.* infinitivo.

infinity (ɪnˈfɪn·ə·ti) *n.* **1,** (quality or state of being infinite) infinito. **2,** (infinite or great amount) infinidad.

infirm (ɪnˈfʌrm) *adj.* **1,** (of feeble health) achacoso; enfermizo. **2,** (weak; unsound) enfermizo; débil.

infirmary (ɪnˈfʌr·mə·ri) *n.* enfermería.

infirmity (ɪnˈfʌr·mə·ti) *n.* **1,** (ailment) achaque. **2,** (weakness) debilidad; calidad de enfermizo. **3,** (moral weakness or defect) flaqueza.

infix (ɪnˈfɪks) *v.t.* plantar; implantar; fijar. —*n.* (ˈɪn·fɪks) afijo.

inflame (ɪnˈfleim) *v.t.* inflamar.

inflammable (ɪnˈflæm·ə·bəl) *adj.* inflamable.

inflammation (ˌɪn·fləˈmei·ʃən) *n.* inflamación.

inflammatory (ɪnˈflæm·ə·tor·i) *adj.* inflamatorio.

inflate (ɪnˈfleit) *v.t.* inflar. —*v.i.* inflarse.

inflation (ɪnˈflei·ʃən) *n.* inflación. —**inflationary,** *adj.* inflacionista.

inflect (ɪnˈflɛkt) *v.t.* dar inflexión a.

inflection (ɪnˈflɛk·ʃən) *n.* inflexión. —**inflectional,** *adj.,* *gram.* desinencial.

inflexible (ɪnˈflɛk·sə·bəl) *adj.* inflexible. —**inflexibility,** *n.* inflexibilidad.

inflict (ɪnˈflɪkt) *v.t.* infligir.

infliction (ɪnˈflɪk·ʃən) *n.* **1,** (act of inflicting) imposición. **2,** (something inflicted) pena; castigo.

inflorescence (ˌɪn·fləˈrɛs·əns) *n.* florescencia. —**inflorescent,** *adj.* floreciente.

inflow (ˈɪn·flo) *n.* flujo (que entra); afluencia; entrada.

influence (ˈɪn·flu·əns) *n.* influencia. —*v.t.* influir en. —**influential** (-ˈɛn·ʃəl) *adj.* influyente.

influenza (ˌɪn·fluˈɛn·zə) *n.* influenza.

influx (ˈɪn·flʌks) *n.* **1,** (inflow) flujo (que entra); afluencia; entrada. **2,** (point of inflow) entrada; punto o boca de entrada.

inform (ɪnˈfor) *v.t.* & *i.* informar. —**inform on** o **against,** delatar; denunciar. —**informer,** *n.* delator; soplón.

informal (ɪnˈfor·məl) *adj.* informal. —**informality** (ˌɪn·forˈmæl·ə·ti) *n.* informalidad.

informant (ɪnˈfor·mənt) *n.* informante; informador.

information (ˌɪn·forˈmei·ʃən) *n.* información.

informative (ɪnˈfor·mə·tɪv) *adj.* informativo.

infraction (ɪnˈfræk·ʃən) *n.* infracción.

infrangible (ɪnˈfræn·dʒə·bəl) *adj.* infrangible.

infrared (ˌɪn·frəˈrɛd) *adj.* infrarrojo.

infrastructure (ˈɪn·frə·strʌk·tʃər) *n.* infraestructura.

infrequent (ɪnˈfri·kwənt) *adj.* infrecuente. —**infrequency,** *n.* infrecuencia.

infringe (ɪnˈfrɪndʒ) *v.t.* infringir; violar. —**infringe on** o **upon,** invadir; disturbar. —**infringement,** *n.* infracción; violación; invasión.

infuriate (ɪnˈfjur·i·eit) *v.t.* enfurecer; irritar.

infuse (ɪnˈfjuz) *v.t.* **1,** (instill; imbue) instilar; infundir; imbuir. **2,** (steep) poner en infusión; infundir. —**infusion** (ɪnˈfju·ʒən) *n.* infusión.

ingenious (ɪnˈdʒin·jəs) *adj.* ingenioso. —**ingeniousness,** *n.* ingeniosidad.

ingenuity (ˌɪn·dʒəˈnju·ə·ti) *n.* inventiva; ingenio; ingeniosidad.

ingenuous (ɪnˈdʒɛn·ju·əs) *adj.* ingenuo. —**ingenuousness,** *n.* ingenuidad.

ingest (ɪnˈdʒɛst) *v.t.* ingerir. —**ingestion** (ɪnˈdʒɛs·tʃən) *n.* ingestión.

inglorious (ɪnˈglor·i·əs) *adj.* ignominioso; innoble.

ingoing (ˈɪnˌgo·ɪŋ) *adj.* entrante; que entra; que llega.

ingot (ˈɪŋ·gət) *n.* lingote.

ingrain (ɪnˈgrein) *v.t.* arraigar; fijar profundamente.

ingrate (ˈɪn·greit) *n.* ingrato.

ingratiate (ɪnˈgrei·ʃi·eit) *v.t.* congraciar. —**ingratiating,** *adj.* atractivo; congraciador.

ingratitude (ɪnˈgræt·ɪ·tud) *n.* ingratitud.

ingredient (ɪnˈgri·di·ənt) *n.* ingrediente.

ingrown (ˈɪn·gron) *adj.* **1,** (grown into the flesh) encarnado. **2,** (inborn) congénito; ingénito.

inhabit (ɪnˈhæb·ɪt) *v.t.* habitar. —**inhabitable,** *adj.* habitable. —**inhabitant** (-ə·tənt) *n.* habitante.

inhalant (ɪnˈhei·lənt) *n.* **1,** (inhalator) inhalador. **2,** (medicinal vapor) inhalante; inhalación.

inhalation (ˌɪn·hə'lei·ʃən) *n.* inhalación.

inhalator ('ɪn·hə,lei·tər) *n.* inhalador.

inhale (ɪn'heil) *v.t. & i.* inhalar; aspirar. —**inhaler**, *n.* inhalador.

inharmonious (ˌɪn·har'mo·ni·əs) *adj.* inarmónico.

inhere (ɪn'hɪr) *v.i.* ser inherente; ser innato o intrínseco. —**inherence**, *n.* inherencia. —**inherent**, *adj.* inherente.

inherit (ɪn'hɛr·ɪt) *v.t. & i.* heredar. —**inheritance**, *n.* herencia. —**inheritor**, *n.* heredero.

inhibit (ɪn'hɪb·ɪt) *v.t.* inhibir. —**inhibition** (ˌɪn·ə'bɪʃ·ən) *n.* inhibición.

inhospitable (ɪn'has·pɪt·ə·bəl) *adj.* inhospitalario. —**inhospitability**, *n.* inhospitalidad.

inhuman (ɪn'hju·mən) *adj.* inhumano. —**inhumanity** (ˌɪn·hju·'mæn·ə·ti) *n.* inhumanidad.

inhumane (ˌɪn·hju'mein) *n.* inhumano; cruel.

inimical (ɪn'ɪm·ɪ·kəl) *adj.* 1, (harmful) perjudicial. 2, (hostile) hostil.

inimitable (ɪn'ɪm·ə·tə·bəl) *adj.* inimitable.

iniquitous (ɪ'nɪk·wə·təs) *adj.* inicuo. —**iniquity**, *n.* iniquidad.

initial (ɪ'nɪʃ·əl) *adj. & n.* inicial. —*v.t.* poner sus iniciales a o en.

initiate (ɪ'nɪʃ·iˌeit) *v.t.* iniciar. —*adj. & n.* (-ət) iniciado —**initiating**, *adj.* iniciador; iniciativo. —**initiation**, *n.* iniciación.

initiative (ɪ'nɪʃ·i·ə·tɪv) *n.* iniciativa.

inject (ɪn'dʒɛkt) *v.t.* inyectar. —**injection** (ɪn'dʒɛk·ʃən) *n.* inyección. —**injector** *n.* inyector.

injudicious (ˌɪn·dʒu'dɪʃ·əs) *adj.* indiscreto; imprudente; poco juicioso. —**injudiciousness**, *n.* falta de discreción o juicio.

injunction (ɪn'dʒʌŋk·ʃən) *n.* mandato; *law* prohibición judicial.

injure ('ɪn·dʒər) *v.t.* 1, (wound; hurt) herir; lastimar. 2, (do wrong or injustice to) perjudicar. 3, (offend) ofender.

injurious (ɪn'dʒʊr·i·əs) *adj.* dañino; dañoso; perjudicial. —**injuriousness**, *n.* calidad de dañino.

injury ('ɪn·dʒə·ri) *n.* 1, (lesion) lesión. 2, (harm) daño. 3, (wrong) perjuicio; daño.

injustice (ɪn'dʒʌs·tɪs) *n.* injusticia.

ink (ɪŋk) *n.* tinta. —*v.t.* 1, (spread ink on) entintar. 2, (mark or draw in ink) hacer o trazar en tinta.

inkling ('ɪŋk·lɪŋ) *n.* indicio; intimación; indicación.

inkstand ('ɪŋk,stænd) *n.* tintero; base para tintero.

inkwell ('ɪŋk·wɛl) *n.* tintero.

inky ('ɪŋk·i) *adj.* 1, (dark; black) negro; de o como tinta. 2, (covered or stained with ink) entintado.

inlaid ('ɪn,leid) *v., pret. & p.p. de* **inlay.** —*adj.* embutido; encajado; incrustado.

inland ('ɪn·lənd) *adj.* del interior; de tierra adentro. —*adv.* tierra adentro. —*n.* interior. —**inlander**, *n.* habitante del interior.

in-law *n.* pariente por afinidad; afín.

inlay (ɪn'lei) *v.t.* [**inlaid, inlaying**] embutir; incrustar; taracear. —*n.* ('ɪn·lei) 1, (inlaid work) incrustación; embutido; taracea. 2, *dent.* empaste; *Amer.* tapadura.

inlet ('ɪn·lɛt) *n.* 1, (small bay) cala; caleta; ensenada. 2, (entrance; mouth) entrada; boca.

inmate ('ɪn,meit) *n.* 1, (resident) residente; ocupante. 2, (confined person, as in a prison) preso; recluso; (in an asylum) asilado; (in a hospital) enfermo.

inmost ('ɪn,most) *adj.* más íntimo; más recóndito; más profundo.

inn (ɪn) *n.* posada; mesón; fonda.

innards ('ɪn·ərdz) *n.pl.* vísceras; entrañas.

innate (ɪ'neit) *adj.* innato. —**innateness**, *n.* lo innato.

inner ('ɪn·ər) *adj.* 1, (interior) interior. 2, (private; intimate) privado; íntimo. —**inner tube**, cámara; tubo.

innermost ('ɪn·ər·most) *adj.* = **inmost.**

innervate ('ɪn·ər·veit) *v.t.* estimular; animar. —**innervation**, *n.* estímulo; aliento.

inning ('ɪn·ɪŋ) *n.* 1, *baseball* inning; turno de juego. 2, (turn) chance) turno; oportunidad.

innkeeper ('ɪn,ki·pər) *n.* posadero; mesonero.

innocent (ɪn·ə·sənt) *adj. & n.* inocente. —**innocence**, *n.* inocencia.

innocuous (ɪ'nak·ju·əs) *adj.* innocuo. —**innocuousness**, *n.* inocuidad.

innominate (ɪ'nam·ə·nɪt) *adj.* innominado.

innovate ('ɪn·ə,veit) *v.t. & i.* inno-

var. —**innovation,** *n.* innovación.
—**innovator,** *n.* innovador.

innuendo (ˌɪn·juˈɛn·do) *n.* indirecta; insinuación.

innumerable (ɪˈnum·ər·ə·bəl) *adj.* innumerable.

inobservant (ˌɪn·əbˈzʌr·vənt) *adj.* desatento.

inoculate (ɪˈnak·jə,leit) *v.t.* inocular. —**inoculation,** *n.* inoculación.

inoffensive (ˌɪn·əˈfɛn·sɪv) *adj.* innocuo; inofensivo. —**inoffensiveness,** *n.* innocuidad.

inoperable (ɪnˈap·ər·ə·bəl) *adj.* inoperable.

inoperative (ɪnˈap·ər·ə·tɪv) *adj.* inoperante.

inopportune (ɪnˌap·ərˈtjun) *adj.* inoportuno. —**inopportuneness,** *n.* inoportunidad.

inordinate (ɪnˈor·də·nət) *adj.* excesivo; inmoderado; desmesurado. —**inordinateness; inordinacy,** *n.* exceso; inmoderación.

inorganic (ˌɪn·orˈgæn·ɪk) *adj.* inorgánico.

inpatient (ˈɪn,pei·ʃənt) *n.* (paciente) internado.

input (ˈɪn·pʊt) *n.* suministro; inversión.

inquest (ˈɪn·kwɛst) *n.* encuesta.

inquietude (ɪnˈkwai·ə·tud) *n.* inquietud.

inquire (ɪnˈkwair) *v.t. & i.* **1,** (ask) preguntar; indagar. **2,** (investigate) investigar; inquirir; indagar.

inquiry (ɪnˈkwai·ri; ˈɪn·kwə·ri) *n.* **1,** (question) pregunta; indagación. **2,** (investigation) investigación; encuesta; indagación.

inquisition (ˌɪn·kwəˈzɪʃ·ən) *n.* inquisición.

inquisitive (ɪnˈkwɪz·ə·tɪv) *adj.* inquisitivo; curioso. —**inquisitiveness,** *n.* curiosidad.

inquisitor (ɪnˈkwɪz·ɪ·tər) *n.* inquisidor.

in re (ɪnˈri) *prep.* acerca de; concerniente a.

inroad (ˈɪn·rod) *n.* **1,** (incursion) incursión. **2,** *usu.pl.* (encroachment) mella.

insalubrious (ˌɪn·səˈlu·bri·əs) *adj.* insalubre.

insane (ɪnˈsein) *adj.* insano; loco. —**insane asylum,** manicomio.

insanitary (ɪnˈsæn·ə,ter·i) *adj.* insaluble.

insanity (ɪnˈsæn·ə·ti) *n.* locura.

insatiable (ɪnˈsei·ʃə·bəl) *adj.*

insaciable. —**insatiability,** *n.* insaciabilidad.

inscribe (ɪnˈskraib) *v.t.* inscribir.

inscription (ɪnˈskrɪp·ʃən) *n.* inscripción.

inscrutable (ɪnˈskru·tə·bəl) *adj.* inescrutable. —**inscrutability,** *n.* inescrutabilidad.

insect (ˈɪn·sɛkt) *n.* insecto.

insecticide (ɪnˈsɛk·tɪ,said) *n.* insecticida.

insectivorous (ɪn·sɛkˈtɪv·ə·rəs) *adj.* insectívoro. —**insectivore** (ɪnˈsɛk·tə·vor) *n.* insectívoro.

insecure (ˌɪn·sɪˈkjur) *adj.* inseguro. —**insecurity,** *n.* inseguridad.

inseminate (ɪnˈsem·ə·neit) *v.t.* sembrar; inseminar. —**insemination,** *n.* siembra; inseminación.

insensate (ɪnˈsɛn·set) *adj.* **1,** (insensible; insensitive) insensible. **2,** (unreasoning) insensato.

insensible (ɪnˈsɛn·sə·bəl) *adj.* insensible. —**insensibility,** *n.* insensibilidad.

insensitive (ɪnˈsɛn·sɪ·tɪv) *adj.* insensible.

inseparable (ɪnˈsɛp·ər·ə·bəl) *adj.* inseparable.

insert (ɪnˈsʌrt) *v.t.* insertar. —*n.* (ˈɪn·sʌrt) inserción. —**insertion** (ɪnˈsʌr·ʃən) *n.* inserción.

inset (ˈɪn·sɛt) *n.* inserción. —*v.t.* insertar.

inside (ɪnˈsaid) *prep.* en; dentro de. —*adv.* dentro; adentro. —*n.* **1,** (inner part; interior) parte o lado de adentro; interior. **2,** *pl., colloq.* (viscera) entrañas. —*adj.* **1,** (interior; internal) de adentro; interno; interior. **2,** (private; secret) privado; íntimo; secreto. **3,** (specially privileged) confidencial. —**insider,** *n., colloq.* privilegiado. —**inside out,** al revés. —**inside track,** *colloq.* ventaja.

insidious (ɪnˈsɪd·i·əs) *adj.* insidioso. —**insidiousness,** *n.* insidia.

insight (ˈɪn·sait) *n.* **1,** (perspicacity) perspicacia. **2,** (sudden awareness) visión.

insignia (ɪnˈsɪg·ni·ə) *n.sing. & pl.* [*sing.*, también, **insigne** (-ni)] insignia; insignias.

insignificant (ˌɪn·sɪgˈnɪf·ə·kənt) *adj.* insignificante. —**insignificance,** *n.* insignificancia.

insincere (ˌɪn·sɪnˈsɪr) *adj.* insincero. —**insincerity** (-ˈsɛr·ə·ti) *n.* insinceridad.

insinuate (ɪnˈsɪn·ju,eit) *v.t.*

insinuar. **—insinuation,** _n._ insinuación.

insipid (ɪnˈsɪp·ɪd) _adj._ insípido. **—inspidity** (ˌɪn·sɪˈpɪd·ə·ti) _n._ insipidez.

insist (ɪnˈsɪst) _v.i._ insistir. **—insistence,** _n._ insistencia. **—insistent,** _adj._ insistente.

insobriety (ˌɪn·soˈbraɪ·ə·ti) _n._ falta de sobriedad; embriaguez.

insofar (ˌɪn·səˈfar) _adv._ hasta ahí o allí. _También,_ **in so far. —insofar as,** en cuanto.

insole (ˈɪn·sol) _n._ plantilla.

insolent (ˈɪn·sə·lənt) _adj._ insolente. **—insolence,** _n._ insolencia.

insoluble (ɪnˈsal·jə·bəl) _adj._ insoluble. **—insolubility,** _n._ insolubilidad.

insolvent (ɪnˈsal·vənt) _adj._ insolvente. **—insolvency,** _n._ insolvencia.

insomnia (ɪnˈsam·ni·ə) _n._ insomnio. **—insomniac** (-æk) _n._ quien padece de insomnio.

insomuch (ˌɪn·soˈmʌtʃ) _adv._ **1,** (to such an extent or degree) tanto; de tal manera. **2,** = **inasmuch.**

insouciant (ɪnˈsu·si·ənt) _adj._ despreocupado. **—insouciance,** _n._ despreocupación.

inspect (ɪnˈspɛkt) _v.t._ inspeccionar. **—inspection** (ɪnˈspɛk·ʃən) _n._ inspección. **—inspector,** _n._ inspector [_fem._ -tora].

inspire (ɪnˈspair) _v.t._ inspirar. **—inspiration** (ˌɪn·spəˈrei·ʃən) _n._ inspiración. **—inspirational,** _adj._ que inspira.

instability (ˌɪn·stəˈbɪl·ə·ti) _n._ inestabilidad.

install (ɪnˈstɔːl) _v.t._ instalar. **—installation** (ˌɪn·stəˈlei·ʃən) _n._ instalación.

installment _también,_ **instalment** (ɪnˈstɔl·mənt) _n._ **1,** (periodic payment) plazo. **2,** (chapter in a serial) serie; entrega. **3,** (installation) instalación.

instance (ˈɪn·stəns) _n._ **1,** (case; example) caso; ejemplo. **2,** (occasion) momento; ocasión. **—for instance,** por ejemplo.

instant (ˈɪn·stənt) _n._ instante. **—adj. 1,** (immediate) inmediato. **2,** (of present time) actual; corriente. **3,** (quickly prepared) al instante; instantáneo. **—instantaneous** (ˌɪn·stənˈtei·ni·əs) _adj._ instantáneo.

instead (ɪnˈstɛd) _adv._ **1,** (in place [of]) en lugar (de); en vez (de). **2,** (contrary to expectation) en cambio.

instep (ˈɪn·stɛp) _n._ empeine.

instigate (ˈɪn·stɪˌgeit) _v.t._ instigar. **—instigation,** _n._ instigación. **—instigator,** _n._ instigador.

instill (ɪnˈstɪl) _v.t._ instilar. **—instillation** (ˌɪn·stɪˈlei·ʃən) _n._ instilación.

instinct (ˈɪn·stɪŋkt) _n._ instinto. **—adj.** (ɪnˈstɪŋkt) cargado; lleno. **—instinctive** (ɪnˈstɪŋk·tɪv) _adj._ instintivo.

institute (ˈɪn·stɪ·tut) _v.t._ instituir. **—n.** instituto.

institution (ˌɪn·stɪˈtu·ʃən) _n._ institución. **—institutional,** _adj._ institucional. **—institutionalize,** _v.t._ **1,** dar forma de institución a. **2,** internar (en un asilo, en la cárcel, etc.).

instruct (ɪnˈstrʌkt) _v.t._ instruir. **—instructor,** _n._ instructor [_fem._ -tora].

instruction (ɪnˈstrʌk·ʃən) _n._ instrucción.

instructive (ɪnˈstrʌk·tɪv) _adj._ instructivo. **—instructiveness,** _n._ lo instructivo.

instrument (ˈɪn·strə·mənt) _n._ instrumento. **—instrumental** (ˌɪn·strə·mən·təl) _adj._ instrumental. **—instrumentalist,** _n._ instrumentista. **—instrumentality** (-mənˈtæl·ə·ti) _n._ agencia. **—instrumentation** (-mənˈtei·ʃən) _n._ instrumentación.

insubordinate (ˌɪn·səˈbor·də·nət) _adj. & n._ insubordinado. **—insubordination** (-ˈnei·ʃən) _n._ insubordinación.

insubstantial (ˌɪn·səbˈstæn·ʃəl) _adj._ insubstancial.

insufferable (ɪnˈsʌf·ər·ə·bəl) _adj._ insufrible; intolerable.

insufficient (ˌɪn·səˈfɪʃ·ənt) _adj._ insuficiente. **—insufficiency,** _n._ insuficiencia.

insular (ˌɪn·sju·lər) _adj._ **1,** (of or pert. to an island) insular. **2,** (narrow-minded) estrecho de miras.

insularity (ˌɪn·sjuˈlær·ə·ti) _n._ **1,** (being or living on an island) insularidad. **2,** (narrow-mindedness) estrechez de miras.

insulate (ˈɪn·sə·leit) _v.t._ aislar. **—insulation,** _n._ aislamiento. **—insulator,** _n._ aislador.

insulin (ˈɪn·sə·lɪn) _n._ insulina.

insult (ɪnˈsʌlt) _v.t._ insultar. **—n.** (ˈɪn·sʌlt) insulto.

insuperable (ɪnˈsu·pər·ə·bəl) _adj._

insuperable. —**insuperability,** n. calidad de insuperable.

insupportable (ˌɪn·səˈpor·tə·bəl) adj. insoportable.

insurance (ɪnˈʃur·əns) n. 1, (protection against loss) seguro. 2, (insurance business) seguros.

insure (ɪnˈʃur) v.t. asegurar. —**insurable,** adj. asegurable.

insurgent (ɪnˈsʌr·dʒənt) n. & adj. insurgente. —**insurgence; insurgency,** n. insurgencia.

insurmountable (ˌɪn·sərˈmaunt·ə·bəl) adj. insuperable; infranqueable.

insurrection (ˌɪn·səˈrɛk·ʃən) n. insurrección. —**insurrectionist,** n. insurrecto.

intact (ɪnˈtækt) adj. intacto; íntegro.

intake (ˈɪn,teik) n. 1, (place of intake) toma. 2, (quantity or thing taken in) consumo; toma. 3, (a taking in) toma; admisión.

intangible (ɪnˈtæn·dʒə·bəl) adj. intangible. —**intangibility,** n. intangibilidad.

integer (ˈɪn·tə·dʒər) n. entero; número entero.

integral (ˈɪn·tə·grəl) adj. & n. integral.

integrate (ˈɪn·tə,greit) v.t. integrar. —v.i. integrarse. —**integration,** n. integración.

integrated circuit n., elect.; comput. circuito integrado.

integrity (ɪnˈtɛg·rə·ti) n. integridad.

integument (ɪnˈtɛg·jə·mənt) n. integumento.

intellect (ˈɪn·tə·lɛkt) n. intelecto. —**intellectual** (-ˈlɛk·tʃu·əl) adj. & n. intelectual. —**intellectualize,** v.t. intelectualizar.

intelligence (ɪnˈtɛl·ɪ·dʒəns) n. 1, (mind; understanding) inteligencia. 2, (news; information) información; datos. 3, (gathering of secret information) servicio secreto; servicio de inteligencia. —**intelligence quotient,** cociente intelectual.

intelligent (ɪnˈtɛl·ɪ·dʒənt) adj. inteligente.

intelligentsia (ɪn,tɛl·ɪˈdʒɛn·si·ə) n.pl. intelectualidad.

intelligible (ɪnˈtɛl·ə·dʒə·bəl) adj. inteligible. —**intelligiblity,** n. inteligibilidad.

intemperate (ɪnˈtɛm·pər·ət) adj. intemperante. —**intemperance; intemperateness,** n. intemperancia.

intend (ɪnˈtɛnd) v.t. 1, (have in mind; plan) pensar; proponerse; tener la intención (de). 2, (destine; design; mean) destinar; señalar.

intended (ɪnˈtɛn·dɪd) adj. 1, (intentional) de propósito; intencional. 2, (prospective; future) futuro. —n., colloq. prometido; futuro.

intense (ɪnˈtɛns) adj. intenso. —**intensity,** n. intensidad. —**intensive,** adj. intensivo.

intensify (ɪnˈtɛn·sɪ,fai) v.t. intensificar. —v.i. intensificarse. —**intensification** (-fɪˈkei·ʃən) n. intensificación.

intent (ɪnˈtɛnt) n. intento; intención. —adj. 1, (firm; earnest) atento; firme; fijo. 2, (engrossed) preocupado; absorto; ensimismado. 3, (firmly resolved) decidido. —**to all intents and purposes,** en todo caso; de cualquier manera.

intention (ɪnˈtɛn·ʃən) n. intención. —**intentional,** adj. intencional.

inter (ɪnˈtʌr) v.t. enterrar.

interact (ˌɪn·tərˈækt) v.i. actuar entre sí; afectarse mutuamente; reaccionar entre sí. —**interaction,** n. acción recíproca; interacción.

intercalate (ɪnˈtʌr·kə,leit) v.t. intercalar. —**intercalation,** n. intercalación.

intercede (ˌɪn·tərˈsiːd) v.i. interceder.

intercept (ˌɪn·tərˈsɛpt) v.t. interceptar. —**interception** (-ˈsɛp·ʃən) n. interceptación; intercepción. —**interceptor,** n. interceptor; aero. avión de caza; avión interceptor.

intercession (ˌɪn·tərˈsɛʃ·ən) n. intercesión. —**intercessor** (-ˈsɛs·ər) n. intercesor.

interchange (ˌɪn·tərˈtʃeindʒ) v.t. 1, (exchange; transpose) intercambiar; trocar. 2, (alternate) alternar. —v.i. 1, (alternate) alternarse. 2, (change places) trocarse. —n. (ˈɪn·tər·tʃeindʒ) 1, (exchange; transposition) intercambio; trueque. 2, (alternation) alternación. 3, (highway ramp system) intercambio. —**interchangeable,** adj. intercambiable.

intercollegiate (ˌɪn·tər·kəˈli·dʒət) adj. entre universidades o universitarios; universitario.

intercom (ˈɪn·tər,kam) n., colloq. sistema de intercomunicación.

intercommunicate (ˌɪn·tər·kəˈmju·nɪ,keit) v.i. intercomunicarse.

—intercommunication, *n.* intercomunicación.

interconnect (ˌɪn·tər·kəˈnɛkt) *v.t.* & *i.* conectar entre sí. **—interconnection** (-ˈnɛk·ʃən) *n.* conexión mutua; interdependencia.

intercourse (ˈɪn·tər·kors) *n.* 1, (exchange; communication) intercambio. 2, (copulation) cópula; coito. 3, (trade; dealings) trato.

interdenominational (ˈɪn·tər·dɪ·nam·ɪˈnei·ʃən·əl) *adj.* intersectario.

interdependent (ˌɪn·tər·diˌpɛndənt) *adj.* interdependiente. **—interdependence,** *n.* interdependencia.

interdict (ˈɪn·tərˌdɪkt) *v.t.* prohibir; vedar; interdecir. **—n.** entredicho; interdicto. **—interdiction** (-ˈdɪkʃən) *n.* interdicción.

interest (ˈɪn·tər·ɪst) *n.* interés. **—v.t.** interesar. **—interesting,** *adj.* interesante. **—lose interest (in),** desinteresarse (de).

interface (ˈɪn·tər·feɪs) *n.* 1, *physics; chem.* entrecara. 2, *comput.* conectador entre las piezas del sistema.

interfaith (ˈɪn·tər·feɪθ) *adj.* ecuménico.

interfere (ˌɪn·tərˈfɪr) *v.i.* interferir; *fig.* entremeterse. **—interference,** *n.* interferencia; *fig.* entremetimiento. **—interfering,** *adj.* entremetido.

interferon (ˌɪn·tərˈfɪr·ən) *n.* interferona.

interim (ˈɪn·tər·ɪm) *n.* ínterin. **—adj.** provisional; interino.

interior (ɪnˈtɪr·i·ər) *n.* & *adj.* interior.

interject (ˌɪn·tərˈdʒɛkt) *v.t.* & *i.* interponer; insertar; interpolar.

interjection (ˌɪn·tərˈdʒɛk·ʃən) *n.* 1, (act of interjecting) interposición. 2, *gram.* interjección.

interlace (ˈɪn·tərˈleɪs) *v.t.* entrelazar.

interlard (ˈɪn·tərˌlard) *v.t.* entreverar; entremezclar.

interline (ɪn·tərˈlaɪn) *v.t.* 1, (write between) interlinear. 2, (put interlining in) poner entretela a. **—interlining,** *n.* entretela.

interlinear (ˌɪn·tərˈlɪn·i·ər) *adj.* interlineal.

interlock (ˌɪn·tərˈlak) *v.t.* & *i.* trabar; ensamblar; *mech.* engranar. **—n.** engranaje.

interlocution (ˌɪn·tər·loˈkju·ʃən) *n.* interlocución; diálogo.

interlocutor (ˌɪn·tərˈlak·ju·tər) *n.* interlocutor.

interlocutory (ˌɪn·tərˈlak·ju·tor·i) *adj.* 1, (conversational) de o en el diálogo. 2, (interpolated) interpolado; interpuesto. 3, *law* interlocutorio.

interlope (ˌɪn·tərˈlop) *v.i.* inmiscuirse; entremeterse. **—interloper,** *n.* intruso; advenedizo; entremetido.

interlude (ˈɪn·tər,lud) *n.* 1, (intervening time) intervalo. 2, *theat.* entremés. 3, *mus.* interludio.

intermarry (ˌɪn·tərˈmær·i) *v.i.* casarse entre sí. **—intermarriage** (-ˈmær·ɪdʒ) *n.* casamiento entre parientes o entre personas de distintas razas.

intermediary (ˌɪn·tərˈmi·di·ɛr·i) *adj.* & *n.* intermediario.

intermediate (ˌɪn·tərˈmi·di·ət) *adj.* intermedio. **—v.i.** (-eit) mediar; intermediar.

interment (ɪnˈtɑr·mənt) *n.* entierro.

intermezzo (ˌɪn·tərˈmɛt·so) *n.* interludio.

interminable (ɪnˈtɑr·mə·nə·bəl) *adj.* interminable; inacabable.

intermingle (ˌɪn·tərˈmɪŋ·gəl) *v.t.* mezclar; entremezclar. **—v.i.** mezclarse; entremezclarse.

intermission (ˌɪn·tərˈmɪʃ·ən) *n.* intermisión; descanso; *theat.* entreacto.

intermittent (ˌɪn·tərˈmɪt·ənt) *adj.* intermitente. **—intermittence; intermittency,** *n.* intermitencia.

intermix (ˌɪn·tərˈmɪks) *v.t.* mezclar; entremezclar. **—v.i.** mezclarse; entremezclarse.

intern (ɪnˈtɑrn) *v.t.* internar. **—n.** (ˈɪn·tɑrn) = **interne**. **—internee** (ɪnˈtɑr·ni) *n.* internado; recluído. **—internment,** *n.* reclusión; internamiento.

internal (ɪnˈtɑr·nəl) *adj.* interno.

international (ˌɪn·tərˈnæʃ·ən·əl) *adj.* internacional. **—internationalism,** *n.* internacionalismo. **—internationalist,** *n.* internacionalista. **—internationalistic,** *adj.* internacionalista.

interne (ˈɪn·tɑrn) *n.* ́interno; médico interno. **—interneship,** *n.* internado.

internecine (ˌɪn·tərˈni·sɪn) *adj.* encarnizado; sanguinario.

internist (ɪnˈtɑr·nɪst) *n.,* *med.* internista.

interplanetary (,ɪn·tər'plæn·ɪ·ter·i) *adj.* interplanetario.

interplay ('ɪn·tər·plei) *n.* interacción; juego.

interpolate (ɪn'tʌr·pə,leit) *v.t.* interpolar. —**interpolation,** *n.* interpolación.

interpose (,ɪn·tər'poːz) *v.t.* interponer. —*v.i.* interponerse. —**interposition** (-pə'zɪʃ·ən) *n.* interposición.

interpret (ɪn'tʌr·prɪt) *v.t.* interpretar.

interpretation (ɪn,tʌr·prə'tei·ʃən) *n.* interpretación.

interpretative (ɪn'tʌr·prə,tei·tɪv) *también,* **interpretive** (-tɪv) *adj.* interpretativo.

interpreter (ɪn·tʌr·prɪ·tər) *n.* intérprete.

interracial (,ɪn·tər'rei·ʃəl) *adj.* interracial; que comprende varias razas.

interrogate (ɪn'tɛr·ə,geit) *v.t. & i.* interrogar. —**interrogation,** *n.* interrogación; interrogatorio. —**interrogator,** *n.* interrogador.

interrogative (,ɪn·tə'rag·ə·tɪv) *adj.* interrogativo.

interrogatory (,ɪn·tə'rag·ə·tor·i) *adj.* interrogativo. —*n.* interrogatorio.

interrupt (,ɪn·tə'rʌpt) *v.t.* interrumpir. —**interruption** (-'rʌp·ʃən) *n.* interrupción.

interscholastic (,ɪn·tər·sko'læs·tik) *adj.* entre escuelas; escolar.

intersect (,ɪn·tər'sɛkt) *v.t.* cortar. —*v.i.* cortarse; cruzarse; intersecarse. —**intersection** (-'sɛk·ʃən) *n.* intersección.

intersperse (,ɪn·tər'spʌrs) *v.t.* diseminar; esparcir.

interstate ('ɪn·tər,steit) *adj.* entre estados. —*n.* carretera nacional.

interstellar (,ɪn·tər'stɛl·ər) *adj.* interestelar.

interstice (ɪn'tʌr·stɪs) *n.* intersticio.

intertribal (,ɪn·tər'trai·bəl) *adj.* entre tribus; que comprende varias tribus.

intertwine (,ɪn·tər'twain) *v.t.* entrelazar; entretejer. —*v.i.* entrelazarse; entretejerse.

interurban (,ɪn·tər'ʌr·bən) *adj. & n.* interurbano.

interval ('ɪn·tər·vəl) *n.* intervalo.

intervene (,ɪn·tər'viːn) *v.i.* intervenir. —**intervention** (-'vɛn·ʃən) *n.* intervención.

interview ('ɪn·tər·vju) *n.* entrevista; interviú. —*v.t.* entrevistar.

interweave (,ɪn·tər'wiːv) *v.t.* entretejer. —*n.* [*también,* **interweaving**] entretejido. —**interwoven,** *adj.* entretejido.

intestate (ɪn'tɛs·teit) *n. & adj.* intestado. —**intestacy** (-tə·si) *n.* falta de testamento.

intestine (ɪn'tɛs·tɪn) *n.* intestino. —**intestinal,** *adj.* intestinal.

intimate ('ɪn·tə·mət) *n. & adj.* íntimo. —**intimacy,** *n.* intimidad.

intimate ('ɪn·tə,meit) *v.t.* insinuar; intimar. —**intimation,** *n.* insinuación; intimación.

intimidate (ɪn'tɪm·ə,deit) *v.t.* intimidar. —**intimidation,** *n.* intimidación.

into ('ɪn·tu) *prep.* en; a; dentro de.

intolerable (ɪn'tal·ər·ə·bəl) *adj.* intolerable. —**intolerability; intolerableness,** *n.* intolerabilidad.

intolerant (ɪn'tal·ər·ənt) *adj.* intolerante. —**intolerance,** *n.* intolerancia.

intone (ɪn'toːn) *v.t. & i.* entonar. —**intonation** (,ɪn·tə'nei·ʃən) *n.* entonación.

intoxicant (ɪn'tak·sɪ·kənt) *n.* tóxico.

intoxicate (ɪn'tak·sɪ,keit) *v.t.* **1,** (inebriate; elate) embriagar; emborrachar. **2,** (poison) intoxicar. —**intoxicated,** *adj.* borracho.

intoxication (ɪn,tak·sɪ'kei·ʃən) *n.* **1,** (drunkenness) embriaguez. **2,** (poisoning) intoxicación.

intractable (ɪn'træk·tə·bəl) *adj.* intratable. —**intractability,** *n.* intratabilidad.

intramural (,ɪn·trə'mjur·əl) *adj.* interior.

intransigent (ɪn'træn·sə·dʒənt) *n. & adj.* intransigente. —**intransigence,** *n.* intransigencia.

intransitive (ɪn'træn·sə·tɪv) *adj.* intransitivo.

intrauterine (,ɪn·trə'ju·tər·ɪn) *adj.* intrauterino. —**intrauterine device,** dispositivo intrauterino.

intravenous (,ɪn·trə'vi·nəs) *adj.* intravenoso.

intrench (ɪn'trɛntʃ) *v.t. & i.* = **entrench.** —**intrenchment,** *n.* = **entrenchment.**

intrepid (ɪn'trɛp·ɪd) *adj.* intrépido. —**intrepidity** (,ɪn·trə'prɪd·ə·ti) *n.* intrepidez.

intricate ('ɪn·trɪ·kət) *adj.* intrin-

cado. —**intricacy,** *n.* intrincación;
lo intrincado; complejidad.
intrigue (ɪn'triːg) *v.t.* & *i.* intrigar.
—*n.* intriga.
intrinsic (ɪn'trɪn·zɪk) *adj.* intrínseco.
introduce (ˌɪn·trə'djus) *v.t.* **1,**
(bring in; begin) introducir. **2,**
(present) presentar.
introduction (ˌɪn·trə'dʌk·ʃən) *n.*
1, (act or result of beginning)
introducción. **2,** (presentation)
presentación. **3,** (foreword) prólogo;
introducción. —**introductory**
(-tə·ri) *adj.* preliminar.
introspection (ˌɪn·trə'spɛk·ʃən)
n. introspección. —**introspective**
(-tɪv) *adj.* introspectivo.
introversion (ˌɪn·trə'vʌr·ʒən) *n.*
introversión.
introvert ('ɪn·trə,vʌrt) *n.*
introvertido. —*v.t.* volver hacia
adentro; volver sobre sí.
—**introverted,** *adj.* introvertido.
intrude (ɪn'truːd) *v.t.* insertar;
introducir; entremeter. —*v.i.*
[*también v.r.* **intrude oneself**]
molestar; estorbar; entremeterse; ser
intruso.
intruder (ɪn'truː·dər) *n.* intruso.
intrusion (ɪn'truː·ʒən) *n.* intrusión.
—**intrusive** (-sɪv) *adj.* intruso.
intrust (ɪn'trʌst) *v.t.* = **entrust.**
intuition (ˌɪn·tu'ɪʃ·ən) *n.* intuición.
—**intuitive** (ɪn'tu·ə·tɪv) *adj.*
intuitivo.
inundate ('ɪn·ʌn,deit) *v.t.* inundar.
—**inundation,** *n.* inundación.
inure (ɪn'jur) *v.t.* endurecer;
acostumbrar. —*v.i.* **1,** (take effect)
tener efecto. **2,** (accrue) pasar;
redundar. —**inurement,** *n.* **1,** (hardening) endurecimiento. **2,** (habituation) habituación.
invade (ɪn'veid) *v.t.* invadir.
—**invader,** *n.* invasor.
invalid ('ɪn·və·lɪd) *n.* & *adj.*
inválido.
invalid (ɪn'væl·ɪd) *adj.* inválido.
invalidate (ɪn'væl·ɪ,deit) *v.t.*
invalidar. —**invalidation,** *n.*
invalidación. —**invalidity** (ˌɪnvə'lɪd·ə·ti) *n.* invalidez.
invaluable (ɪn'væl·ju·ə·bəl) *adj.*
inestimable; inapreciable.
invariable (ɪn'vɛr·i·ə·bəl) *adj.* invariable. —**invariability,** *n.*
invariabilidad.
invasion (ɪn'vei·ʒən) *n.* invasión.
—**invasive** (-sɪv) *adj.* agresivo; de
invasión.

invective (ɪn'vɛk·tɪv) *n.* invectiva.
—*adj.* vituperativo.
inveigh (ɪn'vei) *v.i.* lanzar
invectivas.
inveigle (ɪn'vei·gəl) *v.t.* engatusar;
embaucar. —**inveiglement,** *n.*
engañifa; embaucamiento. —**inveigler** (-glər) *n.* embaucador.
invent (ɪn'vɛnt) *v.t.* inventar.
—**inventor,** *n.* inventor.
invention (ɪn'vɛn·ʃən) *n.*
invención; invento.
inventive (ɪn'vɛn·tɪv) *adj.*
inventivo. —**inventiveness,** *n.*
inventiva.
inventory ('ɪn·vən,tor·i) *n.*
inventario. —*v.t.* inventariar.
inverse (ɪn'vʌrs) *adj.* inverso.
—**inversion** (ɪn'vʌr·ʒən) *n.*
inversión.
invert (ɪn'vʌrt) *v.t.* invertir. —*adj.*
& *n.* ('ɪn·vʌrt) invertido.
invertebrate (ɪn'vʌr·tə·brət) *adj.*
& *n.* invertebrado.
invest (ɪn'vɛst) *v.t.* **1,** (install in office; endow, as with authority)
investir. **2,** (put to use, as money)
invertir. **3,** (cover; surround) cubrir;
envolver. **4,** (besiege) sitiar. —*v.i.*
invertir dinero; hacer inversión.
—**investment,** *n.* inversión. —**investor,** *n.* inversionista.
investigate (ɪn'vɛs·tɪ,geit) *v.t.*
investigar. —**investigation,** *n.*
investigación. —**investigator,** *n.*
investigador (*fem.* -dora).
investiture (ɪn'vɛs·tɪ·tʃər) *n.*
investidura.
inveterate (ɪn'vɛt·ər·ət) *adj.*
inveterado. —**inveteracy,** *n.* calidad
de inveterado; hábito inveterado.
invidious (ɪn'vɪd·i·əs) *adj.* **1,** (malicious) malicioso; envidioso. **2,**
(odious) odioso.
invidiousness (ɪn'vɪd·i·əs·nəs)
n. **1,** (maliciousness) malicia;
envidia. **2,** (odiousness) odiosidad.
invigorate (ɪn'vig·ə,reit) *v.t.*
vigorizar; dar vigor; tonificar.
—**invigoration,** *n.* vigorización;
tonificación.
invincible (ɪn'vɪn·sə·bəl) *adj.*
invencible. —**invincibility,** *n.*
invencibilidad.
inviolable (ɪn'vai·ə,lə·bəl) *adj.* inviolable.
inviolate (ɪn'vai·ə·lət) *adj.* **1,** (not
violated) inviolado. **2,** = **inviolable.**
invisible (ɪn'vɪz·ə·bəl) *adj.* & *n.*
invisible. —**invisibility,** *n.* invisibilidad.

invite (ɪn'vait) *v.t.* invitar. —**invitation** (ˌɪn·vɪ'tei·ʃən) *n.* invitación. —**inviting,** *adj.* atrayente; invitante; provocativo.

invoice ('ɪn·vɔis) *n.* factura. —*v.t.* facturar.

invoke (ɪn'vok) *v.t.* invocar. —**invocation** (ˌɪn·və'kei·ʃən) *n.* invocación.

involute ('ɪn·və,lut) *adj.* **1,** (spiral) enrollado en espiral. **2,** (intricate) intrincado. —**involution** (-'lu·ʃən) *n.* involución.

involve (ɪn'vaɪlv) *v.t.* **1,** (complicate) complicar; embrollar. **2,** (entangle; implicate) enredar; implicar; comprometer. **3,** (include; entail) comprender; implicar; envolver. **4,** (occupy the attention of) enfrascar; ocupar; preocupar.

involvement (ɪn'valv·mənt) *n.* **1,** (an involving or being involved) compromiso; implicación; envolvimiento. **2,** (complicated state of affairs) enredo; embrollo; complicación.

invulnerable (ɪn'vʌl·nər·ə·bəl) *adj.* invulnerable. —**invulnerability,** *n.* invulnerabilidad.

inward ('ɪn·wərd) *adj.* **1,** (situated within; internal) de adentro; interno; interior. **2,** (ingoing) hacia dentro. —*adv.* [*también,* **inwards** (-wərdz)] hacia dentro; hacia el interior. —**inwardly,** *adv.* interiormente.

iodide ('ai·ə,daid) *n.* yoduro.

iodine ('ai·ə,dain) *n.* yodo.

iodize ('ai·ə,daiz) *v.t.* yodurar; tratar con yodo o yoduro.

iodoform (ai'o·də,form) *n.* yodoformo.

ion ('ai·ən) *n.* ión.

Ionic (ai'an·ɪk) *adj.* jónico.

ionium (ai'o·ni·əm) *n.* ionio.

ionosphere (ai'an·ə·sfɪr) *n.* ionosfera.

iota (ai'o·tə) *n.* ápice; jota.

I.O.U. (ˌai·o'juː) *n., abr. de* I owe you, pagaré.

ipecac ('ɪp·ə,kæk) *n.* ipecacuana.

I.Q. ('ai'kjuː) *n., abr. de* **intelligence quotient,** cociente intelectual.

irascible (ɪ'ræs·ə·bəl) *adj.* irascible. —**irascibility,** *n.* irascibilidad.

irate ('ai·ret) *adj.* airado; irritado.

ire (air) *n.* ira. —**ireful,** *adj.* iracundo.

iridescent (ˌɪr·ə'dɛs·ənt) *adj.* iridiscente. —**iridescence,** *n.* iridiscencia.

iridium (ɪ'rɪd·i·əm) *n.* iridio.

iris ('ai·rɪs) *n.* **1,** *anat.; opt.* iris. **2,** *bot.* flor de lis; iris. **3,** (rainbow) iris; arco iris.

Irish ('ai·rɪʃ) *adj. & n.* irlandés. —**Irishman** (-mən) *n.* irlandés. —**Irishwoman,** *n.* irlandesa.

irk (ʌrk) *v.t.* fastidiar; molestar; enfadar. —**irksome** ('ʌrk·səm) *adj.* fastidioso; molesto; enfadoso.

iron ('ai·ərn) *n.* **1,** (metal) hierro. **2,** (iron object, device, etc.) instrumento de hierro; herramienta. **3,** *pl.* (shackles) grillos; grilletes. **4,** (flatiron) plancha. **5,** (strength; power) hierro; acero. —*adj.* de hierro; férreo. —*v.t. & i.* planchar. —**have (too) many irons in the fire,** *colloq.* abarcar mucho; traer muchos asuntos entre manos. —**iron out,** allanar. —**strike while the iron is hot,** aprovechar la ocasión.

Iron Age Edad de Hierro.

ironclad ('ai·ərn,klæd) *adj.* **1,** (armored) acorazado; blindado. **2,** (unassailable) irrefutable. **3,** (inviolable) inviolable.

Iron Curtain telón de acero.

iron horse *colloq.* locomotora.

ironing ('ai·ər·nɪŋ) *n.* planchado. —**ironing board,** tabla de planchar.

iron lung respirador.

ironwork ('ai·ərn·wʌrk) *n.* herraje. —**ironworks,** *n.pl.* talleres metalúrgicos.

irony ('ai·rə·ni) *n.* ironía. —**ironic** (ai'ran·ɪk); **ironical** (ai'ran·ə·kəl) *adj.* irónico.

irradiate (ɪ'rei·di·et) *v.t.* irradiar. —**irradiation,** *n.* irradiación.

irrational (ɪ'ræʃ·ən·əl) *adj.* irracional. —**irrationality** (-ə'næl·ə·ti) *n.* irracionalidad.

irreconcilable (ɪˌrɛk·ən'sail·ə·bəl) *adj.* irreconciliable.

irrecoverable (ˌɪr·i'kʌv·ər·ə·bəl) *adj.* irrecuperable.

irredeemable (ˌɪr·ɪ'dim·ə·bəl) *adj.* **1,** *comm.* irredimible. **2,** *fin.* inconvertible.

irreducible (ˌɪr·i'djus·ə·bəl) *adj.* irreducible; irreductible.

irrefutable (ɪ'rɛf·ju·tə·bəl) *adj.* irrefutable; irrebatible.

irregardless (ɪ·rɪ'gard·ləs) *adj.* (erróneo) = **regardless.**

irregular (ɪ'rɛg·jə·lər) *adj.* irregular. —**irregularity** (-'lær·ə·ti) *n.* irregularidad.

irrelevant (ɪ'rɛl·ə·vənt) *adj.* ajeno o extraño al caso; fuera de propósito. **—irrelevance; irrelevancy,** *n.* lo ajeno o extraño; cosa ajena o extraña.

irreligious (,ɪr·ɪ'lɪdʒ·əs) *adj.* irreligioso. **—irreligiousness,** *n.* irreligiosidad.

irremediable (,ɪr·ɪ'miː·di·ə·bəl) *adj.* irremediable.

irremovable (,ɪr·ɪ'muv·ə·bəl) *adj.* irremovible.

irreparable (ɪ'rɛp·ə·rə·bəl) *adj.* irreparable.

irreplaceable (,ɪr·ɪ'plei·sə·bəl) *adj.* irreemplazable.

irrepressible (,ɪr·ɪ'prɛs·ə·bəl) *adj.* irreprimible.

irreproachable (,ɪr·ɪ'pro·tʃə·bəl) *adj.* irreprochable.

irresistible (,ɪr·ɪ'zɪs·tə·bəl) *adj.* irresistible.

irresolute (ɪ'rɛz·ə·lut) *adj.* irresoluto. **—irresoluteness; irresolution** (-'lu·ʃən) *n.* irresolución.

irrespective (,ɪr·ɪ'spɛk·tɪv) *adj.* independiente; imparcial. **—irrespective of,** independiente de; sin fijarse en; sin hacer caso de.

irresponsible (,ɪr·ɪ'span·sə·bəl) *adj.* irresponsable. **—irresponsibility,** *n.* irresponsabilidad.

irresponsive (,ɪr·ɪ'span·sɪv) *adj.* irresponsivo.

irretrievable (,ɪr·ɪ'tri·və·bəl) *adj.* irrecuperable.

irreverent (ɪ'rɛv·ər·ənt) *adj.* irreverente. **—irreverence,** *n.* irreverencia.

irreversible (,ɪr·ɪ'vʌr·sa·bəl) *adj.* irreversible; irremediable.

irrevocable (ɪ'rɛv·ə·kə·bəl) *adj.* irrevocable. **—irrevocability,** *n.* irrevocabilidad.

irrigate ('ɪr·ə,geit) *v.t.* **1,** (provide with water) regar. **2,** *med.* irrigar. **—irrigable,** *adj.* regadío.

irrigation (,ɪr·ə'gei·ʃən) *n.* **1,** (watering) riego. **2,** *med.* irrigación.

irritable ('ɪr·ə·tə·bəl) *adj.* irritable. **—irritability,** *n.* irritabilidad.

irritant ('ɪr·ə·tənt) *n. & adj.* irritante.

irritate ('ɪr·ə,teit) *v.t.* irritar. **—irritation,** *n.* irritación.

is (ɪz) *v., tercera pers. del sing. del pres. de ind. de* **be.**

isinglass ('ai·zɪŋ,glæs) *n.* **1,** (gelatin) cola de pescado. **2,** (mica) mica.

Islam ('ɪs·ləm) *n.* Islam. **—Islamic** (ɪs'læm·ɪk) *adj.* islámico.

island ('ai·lənd) *n.* isla. **—islander,** *n.* isleño.

isle (ail) *n.* isla; ínsula.

islet ('ai·lət) *n.* pequeña isla; islote.

ism ('ɪz·əm) *n.* ismo.

isolate ('ai·sə,leit) *v.t.* aislar.

isolation (,ai·sə'lei·ʃən) *n.* aislamiento. **—isolationism,** *n.* aislacionismo. **—isolationist,** *n.* aislacionista.

isometric (,ai·sə'mɛt·rɪk) *adj.* isométrico.

isosceles (ai'sas·ə·liz) *adj.* isósceles.

isotope ('ai·sə,top) *n.* isótopo.

Israeli (ɪz'rei·li) *adj. & n.* israelí. **—Israelite** ('ɪz·ri·ə,lait) *adj. & n.* israelita.

issuance ('ɪʃ·u·əns) *n.* emisión.

issue ('ɪʃ·u) *n.* **1,** (sending out; putting forth) emisión. **2,** (result; outcome) producto; resultado. **3,** (outlet; exit) salida. **4,** (point in question) disputa; controversia. **5,** (matter of importance) problema; punto. **6,** (publication; edition) número; edición. **7,** (progeny) sucesión; prole; hijos. **—v.t. 1,** (put or send forth) emitir. **2,** (publish) publicar. **—v.i.** emanar; salir. **—at issue,** en disputa. **—join issue,** tomar posiciones opuestas. **—take issue (with),** oponerse (a).

isthmus ('ɪs·məs) *n.* istmo.

it (ɪt) *pron.pers. neutro* **1,** (*sujeto de verbo*) él; ella; ello. **2,** (*complemento directo de verbo*) lo; la. **3,** (*complemento indirecto de verbo*) le. **4,** (*complemento de prep.*) él; ella; ello. **5,** *como sujeto en las construcciones impersonales* (*no se expresa en español*): *It is raining,* Llueve. **—n.,** *colloq.* **1,** (person singled out, as in games) a quien le toca: *You're it,* A ti te toca; Tú eres. **2,** (center of attraction) persona o cosa que da el golpe. **3,** (indefinable appeal) eso.

Italian (ɪ'tæl·jən) *adj. & n.* italiano.

Italic (ɪ'tæl·ɪk) *adj.* itálico.

italic (ɪ'tæl·ɪk) *n. & adj.* bastardilla. **—italicize** (-ə,saiz) *v.t.* poner en bastardilla.

itch (ɪtʃ) *v.t. & v.i.* picar. **—v.i.** (yearn) desear; anhelar. **—n. 1,** (tingling sensation) picazón; comezón. **2,** (skin disease) sarna. **3,** (yearning) deseo; anhelo. **—itchy,** *adj.* picante.

it'd ('ɪt·əd) *contr. de* **it had** *o* **it would.**

item ('ai·təm) *n.* artículo; ítem; *bookkeeping* partida. —**itemize,** *v.t.* detallar.

iterate ('ıt·ə‚reit) *v.t.* iterar; reiterar; repetir. —**iteration,** *n.* iteración; reiteración; repetición.

itinerant (ai'tın·ə·rənt) *adj.* & *n.* ambulante. —**itinerancy,** *n.* rotación.

itinerary (ai'tın·ə·rər·i) *n.* & *adj.* itinerario.

it'll ('ıt·əl) *contr. de* **it will** o **it shall.**

it's (ıts) *contr. de* **it is** o **it has.**

its (ıts) *adj.pos.* concordándose en género y en número con el poseedor su (*pl.* sus); de él, ella o ello.

—*pron.pos.,* concordándose en género y en número con el poseedor el suyo; la suya; lo suyo; los suyos; las suyas; el, la, lo, los o las de él, ella o ello.

itself (ıt'sɛlf) *pron.pers.* neutro el mismo; la misma. —*pron.refl.* de verbo) se. **2,** (complemento de prep.) sí; sí mismo; sí misma.

I've (aiv) *contr. de* **I have.**

ivory ('ai·və·ri) *n.* marfil. —*adj.* de marfil; marfileño. —**ivory tower,** torre de marfil; mundo de fantasía.

ivy ('ai·vi) *n.* hiedra.

izzard ('ız·ərd) *n.,* *colloq.* la letra z.

J

J, j (dʒei) décima letra del alfabeto inglés.

jab (dʒæb) *v.t.* & *i.* **1,** (thrust; poke) hincar; clavar. **2,** (pierce; stab) punzar; picar. **3,** (punch; strike short blows) dar golpes cortos. —*n.* **1,** (stab; thrust) punzada; piquete. **2,** (blow) golpe corto.

jabber ('dʒæb·ər) *v.t.* & *i.* chapurrear. —*n.* chapurreo; cháchara.

jack (dʒæk) *n.* **1,** *mech.* gato. **2,** *cards* sota. **3,** *colloq.* (fellow) sujeto; tipo; fulano. **4,** (sailor) marinero. **5,** *elect.* enchufe; jack. **6,** (flag) bandera; pabellón. **7,** *slang* (money) dinero; parné. —*v.t.* [*usu.* **jack up**] levantar; subir.

jackal ('dʒæk·əl) *n.* chacal.

jackass ('dʒæk·æs) *n.* asno; burro; jumento.

jackboot ('dʒæk‚but) *n.* bota grande.

jackdaw ('dʒæk‚dɔ) *n.* **1,** (crow) corneja. **2,** (grackle) estornino.

jacket ('dʒæk·ıt) *n.* **1,** (coat) chaqueta. **2,** (covering) cubierta; funda. —*v.t.* poner cubierta o funda a.

jack-in-the-box *n.* caja de sorpresa; muñeco en cajón.

jackknife ('dʒæk·naif) *n.* **1,** (large knife) cuchilla; navaja. **2,** (kind of dive) salto de carpa. —*v.i.* doblarse en dos.

jack-of-all-trades *n.* aprendiz de todo y oficial de nada.

jack-o'-lantern ('dʒæk·o‚læn·tərn) *n.* linterna hecha de una calabaza hueca.

jackpot ('dʒæk·pat) *n.* **1,** *cards* pozo. **2,** *colloq.* (large prize) premio mayor; premio gordo.

jackrabbit ('dʒæk‚ræb·ıt) *n.* liebre grande norteamericana.

jade (dʒeid) *n.* **1,** (mineral) jade. **2,** (color) color jade. **3,** (dissolute woman) mujerzuela. **4,** (old horse) jaco; jamelgo. —*adj.* de jade. —*v.t.* **1,** (exhaust; wear out) cansar; agotar; desgastar. **2,** (surfeit) saciar; embotar.

jaded ('dʒei·dıd) *adj.* **1,** (tired; worn-out) cansado; agotado; gastado. **2,** (surfeited) satiated) saciado; embotado.

jag (dʒæg) *n.* **1,** (notch; nick) muesca; recorte. **2,** (toothlike projection) diente; saliente; pico. **3,** *slang* (drunk) borrachera. —**jagged** ('dʒæg·ıd) *adj.* dentado; serrado; quebrado.

jaguar ('dʒæg·war) *n.* jaguar.

jai alai (‚hai·ə'lai) *n.* pelota; jai alai.

jail (dʒeil) *n.* cárcel. —*v.t.* encarcelar. —**jailer,** *n.* carcelero.

jailbird ('dʒeil·bʌrd) *n.,* *slang* **1,** (prisoner) preso. **2,** (habitual law-breaker) delincuente empedernido.

jalopy (dʒə'lap·i) *n.,* *slang* automóvil desvencijado.

jalousie ('dʒæl·ə·si) *n.* celosía.

jam (dʒæm) *v.t.* **1,** (squeeze; press) apretar; apiñar. **2,** (crowd into; fill up) atestar; atiborrar. **3,** (clog; choke) atascar; obstruir. **4,** (cause to stick) atascar; trancar. **5,** (catch fast;

crush) coger; pillar. **6,** *radio* interferir; perturbar. —*v.i.* **1,** (become stuck) atascarse; encajarse; trancarse. **2,** (crowd together) apiñarse; aglomerarse. **3,** (improvise) improvisar. —*n.* **1,** (congestion) congestión; *W.I.* tapón; *S.A.* taco. **2,** *colloq.* (predicament) apuro; lío; aprieto. **3,** (preserve) compota; mermelada. —**jam session,** tertulia de músicos para improvisar.

jamb (dʒæm) *n.* jamba; quicio.

jamboree (ˌdʒæm·bə'riː) *n., slang* holgorio; fiesta; verbena.

jam-packed *adj., colloq.* apiñado; lleno de bote en bote.

Jane Doe ('dʒein'do) Fulana de Tal; mujer no identificada.

jangle ('dʒæŋ·gəl) *v.i.* cencerrear. —*v.t.* **1,** (cause to sound harshly) hacer sonar destempladamente. **2,** (jar, as the nerves) destemplar. —*n.* sonido estridente; estridencia.

janitor ('dʒæn·ə·tər) *n.* portero; conserje.

January ('dʒæn·ju,ɛr·i) *n.* enero.

japan (dʒə'pæn) *n.* laca; barniz.

Japanese (ˌdʒæp·ə'niːz) *adj. & n.* japonés [*fem.* japonesa].

jar (dʒɑːr) *v.t. & i.* **1,** (jolt; rattle) sacudir. **2,** (grate; sound harshly) destemplar. **3,** (upset; disturb) turbar; desconcertar. —*n.* **1,** (jolt) sacudida. **2,** (vessel) jarra; pote; vasija; frasco.

jardinière (ˌdʒɑr·də'nɪr) *n.* jardinera.

jargon ('dʒɑr·gən) *n.* jerga; jerigonza.

jasmine ('dʒæs·mɪn) *n.* jazmín.

jasper ('dʒæs·pər) *n.* jaspe.

jaundice ('dʒɒn·dɪs) *n.* **1,** *pathol.* ictericia. **2,** (embitterment) resentimiento; amargura.

jaundiced ('dʒɒn·dɪst) *adj.* **1,** *pathol.* que tiene o padece ictericia; ictérico. **2,** (embittered) resentido; amargado.

jaunt (dʒɒnt) *n.* paseo; excursión.

jaunty ('dʒɒn·ti) *adj.* **1,** (sprightly) vivo; animado. **2,** (stylish) elegante; de buen gusto.

javelin ('dʒæv·lɪn) *n.* jabalina.

jaw (dʒɔː) *n.* mandíbula; (*esp. of animals*) quijada.

jawbone ('dʒɔ·bon) *n.* mandíbula; quijada.

jawbreaker ('dʒɔ,brei·kər) *n., colloq.* **1,** (tongue-twister) trabalen-

guas. **2,** (hard candy) rompemuelas; pirulí; caramelo.

jay (dʒei) *n.* arrendajo.

jaywalk ('dʒei,wɔk) *v.i., colloq.* cruzar una calle en contravención a las ordenanzas. —**jaywalker,** *n.* peatón imprudente.

jazz (dʒæz) *n.* **1,** *mus.* jazz. **2,** *slang* (liveliness) animación. **3,** *slang* (rumpus; tumult) jaleo; bochinche. **4,** *slang* (nonsense) tontería. —*v.t.* [*también,* **jazz up**] **1,** *mus.* arreglar, tocar o cantar en estilo de jazz. **2,** *slang* (enliven) animar; dar animación.

jealous ('dʒɛl·əs) *adj.* **1,** (possessive) celoso. **2,** (envious) envidioso.

jealousy ('dʒɛl·ə·si) *n.* **1,** (possessiveness) celos. **2,** (envy) envidia.

jean (dʒiːn) *n.* **1,** (fabric) dril. **2,** *pl.* (trousers or overalls) pantalones de dril; overoles; mono.

jeep (dʒiːp) *n.* jeep.

jeer (dʒɪr) *v.i.* [*usu.* **jeer at**] mofarse (de); burlarse (de). —*n.* befa; mofa.

Jehovah (dʒə'ho·və) *n.* Jehová.

jejune (dʒɪ'dʒuːn) *adj.* insípido; insulso.

jell (dʒɛl) *v.i.* cuajar.

jelly ('dʒɛl·i) *n.* jalea; gelatina. —**jellied,** *adj.* con gelatina; convertido en gelatina.

jellyfish ('dʒɛl·i,fɪʃ) *n.* medusa; aguamala; *Amer.* malagua.

jenny ('dʒɛn·i) *n.* **1,** (spinning machine) máquina de hilar. **2,** (female ass) burra; asna. —*adj.* hembra.

jeopardy ('dʒɛp·ər·di) *n.* riesgo; peligro. —**jeopardize,** *v.t.* arriesgar; hacer peligrar; comprometer.

jeremiad (ˌdʒɛr·ə'mai·æd) *n.* jeremiada.

jerk (dʒʌrk) *v.t.* **1,** (pull sharply) tirar o mover bruscamente; tironear. **2,** [*usu.* **jerk out**] (gasp; ejaculate) exclamar; decir bruscamente. —*v.i.* **1,** (move abruptly) moverse bruscamente; sacudirse. **2,** (twitch) saltar; dar un tic. —*n.* **1,** (quick pull) tirón. **2,** (jar; jolt) sacudida. **3,** (twitch) tic; espasmo. **4,** *slang* (fool) tonto; imbécil; cretino. —**jerky,** *adj.* irregular; espasmódico; abrupto. —**jerkiness,** *n.* irregularidad; calidad de espasmódico.

jerked beef cecina; tasajo; *Amer.* charqui.

jerkin ('dʒʌr·kɪn) *n.* jubón.

jerry-built ('dʒɛr·i,bɪlt) *adj.* mal construido.

jersey ('dʒʌr·zi) *n.* jersey.

Jesuit ('dʒɛʒ·ju·ɪt) *n. & adj.* jesuita.

jest (dʒɛst) *v.i.* burlarse; bromear; chancearse. —*n.* broma; chanza; chiste. —**jester**, *n.* bufón. —**jesting**, *n.* bufonería.

jet (dʒɛt) *n.* 1, (gush) chorro. 2, (spout) pitón; caño; surtidor. 3, (mineral) azabache. 4, (plane) avión a o de reacción. —*v.t.* lanzar con fuerza o a chorros. —*v.i.* salir a chorros. —*adj.* 1, (of or like jet) de azabache; azabachado. 2, (jet-propelled) a o de chorro; de propulsión a chorro; a o de reacción. —**jet lag**, cansancio de viajeros después de atravesar varios husos horarios. —**jet propulsion**, propulsión a chorro o a reacción. —**jet set**, *colloq.* personas que hacen frecuentes viajes aéreos. —**jet stream**, corriente de aire fuerte y veloz.

jet-black *adj.* azabachado.

jetsam ('dʒɛt·səm) *n.* echazón; desechos.

jetty ('dʒɛt·i) *n.* 1, (breakwater) escollera; rompeolas. 2, (wharf) muelle.

jettison ('dʒɛt·ə·sən) *v.t.* arrojar al mar. —*n.* echazón.

Jew (dʒuː) *n.* judío. —**Jewish**, *adj.* judío. —**Jewry**, *n.* judíos; pueblo judío.

jewel ('dʒuː·əl) *n.* joya. —*v.t.* adornar con joyas; enjoyar. —**jeweler**, *n.* joyero.

jewelry ('dʒuː·əl·ri) *n.* joyas; pedrería. —**jewelry shop**, joyería. —**jewelry trade**, joyería.

jewfish ('dʒuː·fɪʃ) *n.* mero.

jew's-harp ('dʒuːz,harp) *n.* birimbao.

jib (dʒɪb) *n.* 1, (sail) foque. 2, (boom) brazo de grúa; pescante.

jibe (dʒaib) *v.t. & i., naut.* virar. —*v.i.* 1, *colloq.* (agree) concordar. 2, = gibe. —*n.* = gibe.

jiffy ('dʒɪf·i) *n., colloq.* instante; santiamén.

jig (dʒɪg) *n.* 1, *mech.* guía. 2, (dance) giga. —*v.i.* bailar la giga.

jiggle ('dʒɪg·əl) *v.t.* zangolotear; zarandear. —*v.i.* zarandearse; zangolotearse. —*n.* zangoloteo.

jigsaw ('dʒɪg,sɔ) *n.* sierra de vaivén. —**jigsaw puzzle**, rompecabezas.

jilt (dʒɪlt) *v.t.* dejar plantado; plantar; dar calabazas.

jimmy ('dʒɪm·i) *n.* palanqueta. —*v.t.* forzar.

jingle ('dʒɪŋ·gəl) *v.i. & t.* tintinar; retiñir. —*n.* 1, (sound) tintineo; retintín; cascabeleo. 2, (ditty) estribillo; sonsonete. —**jingle bell**, cascabel.

jingo ('dʒɪŋ·go) *n.* jingo. —**jingoism**, *n.* jingoísmo. —**jingoist**, *n. & adj.* jingoísta.

jinks (dʒɪŋks) *n.pl., colloq.* travesuras; bromas.

jinrikisha (dʒɪnˈrɪk·ʃə) *n.* jinrikisha.

jinx (dʒɪŋks) *n., colloq.* cenizo; gafe. —*v.t., colloq.* traer mala suerte; dar cenizo.

jitney ('dʒɪt·ni) *n.* 1, *colloq.* (small bus) vehículo de pasajeros con trayecto fijo. 2, *slang* (U.S. nickel) níquel; moneda de cinco centavos.

jitter ('dʒɪt·ər) *v.i., slang* estar nervioso. —*n., usu. pl.* nerviosidad. —**jittery**, *adj., slang* agitado; nervioso.

jitterbug ('dʒɪt·ər·bʌg) *n.* persona que baila jazz con movimientos exagerados. —*v.i.* bailar de esta forma.

jive (dʒaiv) *n., slang* 1, (rhythm) ritmo de jazz o de swing. 2, (jargon) jerga de músicos.

job (dʒɑːb) *n.* 1, (piece of work) obra; labor; trabajo. 2, (task; chore) tarea; trabajo. 3, (duty) obligación; tarea; deber. 4, (employment; work) trabajo; empleo. 5, (office; post) puesto; cargo. 6, *colloq.* (matter) asunto; cosa. —*v.i.* [**jobbed, jobbing**] trabajar a destajo. —*v.t.* 1, (portion out, as an order or contract) repartir. 2, (buy or sell wholesale) comprar o vender al por mayor. —**jobber**, *n.* mayorista. —**by the job**, a destajo. —**odd jobs**, trabajos menudos. —**on the job**, *colloq.* en el trabajo; en su sitio.

jock (dʒɑk) *n., slang* atleta masculino. —**jockstrap**, *n.* suspensorio *(para sostener el escroto)*.

jockey ('dʒɑk·i) *v.t. & i.* 1, (maneuver) componérselas; maniobrar para obtener ventaja. 2, (swindle) embaucar. —*n.* jockey. —**disk jockey**, locutor musical.

jocose (dʒoˈkos) *adj.* jocoso. —**jocosity** (-ˈkɑs·ə·ti) *n.* jocosidad.

jocular ('dʒɑk·jə·lər) *adj.* jocoso. —**jocularity** (-ˈlær·ə·ti) *n.* jocosidad.

jocund ('dʒɑk·ənd) *adj.* jocundo.

—**jocundity** (dʒo'kʌn·də·ti) *n.* jocundidad.

jodhpurs ('dʒad·pərz) *n.pl.* pantalones de equitación.

jog (dʒag) *v.t.* [**jogged, jogging**] 1, (shove; push) empujar; mover de un empujón o tirón. 2, (shake) sacudir; remecer. 3, (stimulate) estimular; despertar. —*v.i.* 1, (shake; jolt) remecerse; dar una sacudida; sacudirse. 2, (move or travel joltingly) moverse dando sacudidas; traquetear. 3, (trudge; plod) ir pausadamente; ir a paso de buey. —*n.* 1, (shove; nudge) empujoncito. 2, (shake) sacudida. 3, (trot) trote lento. 4, (projection) saliente. 5, (recessed part) entrante.

joggle ('dʒag·əl) *v.t.* sacudir; traquetear. —*v.i.* sacudirse; traquetearse. —*n.* sacudida; traqueteo.

John (dʒan) *n., slang* 1, cliente de una prostituta. 2, retrete; excusado.

John Bull 1, un inglés. 2, apodo del pueblo británico.

John Doe Fulano de Tal; Juan Pérez.

join (dʒɔin) *v.t.* 1, (bring together; unite) unir. 2, (fasten; fit together) juntar; unir; *carp.* ensamblar. 3, (become a member of) ingresar en; hacerse socio de; *mil.* alistarse en. 4, (ally or associate oneself with) unirse o asociarse a o con. 5, (accompany) acompañar. 6, (connect with) unirse o juntarse a o con. 7, (meet) encontrar; alcanzar. 8, (return to) volver o reunirse a o con. —*v.i.* 1, (come together; unite) unirse. 2, (become a member) ingresar. 3, (take part) tomar parte; participar. —*n.* unión; juntura.

joiner ('dʒɔi·nər) *n.* 1, (person or thing that joins) persona o cosa que une. 2, (woodworker) ensamblador. 3, *colloq.* (person given to joining organizations) persona muy dada a pertenecer a distintas asociaciones.

joint (dʒɔint) *n.* 1, *anat.; zoöl.* articulación; coyuntura. 2, *bot.* articulación; nudo. 3, (place or manner of joining) juntura; empalme. 4, (coupling) articulación; unión. 5, (section) parte; sección. 6, (cut of meat) cuarto; sección. 7, *slang* (place) cuchitril. 8, *slang* (cheap restaurant) figón. —*adj.* 1, (done or executed in common) conjunto; colectivo; común. 2, (held or shared in common) común; en común. 3, (concurrent) concurrente.

—*v.t.* 1, (fasten with joints) juntar; empalmar; *carp.* ensamblar. 2, (form into joints) articular. 3, (cut into joints) descoyuntar; desmembrar. —**joint account**, cuenta indistinta; *Amer.*, cuenta conjunta; común o en común. —**joint session**, sesión plenaria. —**joint-stock company**, sociedad anónima.

joist (dʒɔist) *n.* viga; cabio.

joke (dʒok) *n.* broma; chiste. —*v.i.* bromear; chancear. —**bad joke**, broma pesada. —**crack a joke**, soltar un chiste. —**practical joke**, bromazo.

joker ('dʒo·kər) *n.* 1, (one who jokes) bromista. 2, *cards* comodín. 3, (insidious clause in a document) cláusula capciosa.

jolly ('dʒal·i) *adj.* alegre; jovial. —**jolliness; jollity**, *n.* alegría; jovialidad. —**Jolly Roger**, bandera de piratas.

jolt (dʒolt) *v.t.* sacudir bruscamente. —*v.i.* sacudirse; moverse dando sacudidas; traquetear. —*n.* sacudida.

jonquil ('dʒaŋ·kwil) *n.* junquillo.

josh (dʒaʃ) *v.t. & i., slang* tomar el pelo (a); gastar bromas (a).

jostle ('dʒas·əl) *v.t.* empujar. —*v.i.* moverse a empujones. —*n.* empujón.

jot (dʒat) *n.* jota; ápice. —*v.t.* anotar; apuntar.

joule (dʒaul) *n.* julio; joule.

jounce (dʒauns) *v.t. & i.* traquetear. —*n.* traqueteo.

journal ('dʒʌr·nəl) *n.* 1, (daily record; diary) diario. 2, (newspaper) diario; periódico. 3, (periodical) revista; gaceta. —**journalese**, *n.* estilo periodístico. —**journalism**, *n.* periodismo. —**journalist**, *n.* periodista. —**journalistic**, *adj.* periodístico.

journey ('dʒʌr·ni) *n.* viaje. —*v.i.* viajar.

journeyman ('dʒʌr·ni·mən) *n.* [*pl.* **-men**] oficial.

joust (dʒaust) *n.* justa; torneo. —*v.i.* pelear; luchar.

jovial ('dʒo·vi·əl) *adj.* jovial; alegre. —**joviality** (-'æl·ə·ti) *n.* jovialidad.

jowl (dʒaul) *n.* cachete; carrillo.

joy (dʒɔi) *n.* gozo; júbilo; alegría. —**joyful; joyous**, *adj.* jubiloso; alegre; gozoso. —**joyfulness; joyousness**, *n.* gozo; júbilo; alegría. —**joy ride**, paseo de placer, esp. en vehículo robado o tomado sin permiso.

joyless ('dʒɔi·ləs) *adj.* triste. —**joylessness**, *n.* tristeza.

jubilant ('dʒu·bə·lənt) *adj.* jubiloso. —**jubilation** (-'lei·ʃən) *n.* júbilo.

jubilee ('dʒu·bə·li) *n.* jubileo.

Judaism ('dʒu·də·ɪz·əm) *n.* judaísmo. —**Judaic** (dʒu'dei·ɪk) *adj.* judaico.

judge (dʒʌdʒ) *v.t. & i.* juzgar. —*n.* juez. —**judgeship**, *n.* magistratura.

judge advocate auditor (de guerra o de marina).

judgment ('dʒʌdʒ·mənt) *n.* 1, (act or ability of judging) juicio. 2, (decision) fallo; sentencia.

judicature ('dʒu·də·kə·tʃər) *n.* judicatura.

judicial (dʒu'dɪʃ·əl) *adj.* judicial.

judiciary (dʒu'dɪʃ·i·ɛr·i) *n.* judicatura. —*adj.* judicial.

judicious (dʒu'dɪʃ·əs) *adj.* juicioso. —**judiciousness**, *n.* juicio.

judo ('dʒu·do) *n.* judo; yudo.

jug (dʒʌg) *n.* 1, (vessel) jarro; cántaro. 2, *slang* (jail) cárcel. —*v.t.*, *slang* (imprison) encarcelar.

juggernaut ('dʒʌg·ər·nɔt) *n.* cosa o fuerza ineluctable.

juggle ('dʒʌg·əl) *v.i.* 1, (perform tricks) hacer juegos malabares. 2, (practice deception) engañar; embaucar. —*v.t.* 1, (perform tricks with) hacer juegos malabares con. 2, (manipulate) manipular. —**juggler** (-lər) *n.* malabarista. —**jugglery** (-lə·ri); **juggling** (-lɪŋ) *n.* malabarismo; juegos malabares.

jugular ('dʒʌg·jə·lər) *adj.* yugular.

juice (dʒus) *n.* 1, (liquid) jugo; zumo. 2, *slang* (gasoline) gasolina. 3, *slang* (electricity) electricidad. —**juicy**, *adj.* jugoso.

jujitsu (dʒu'dʒɪt·su) *n.* jiu-jitsu.

jujube ('dʒu·dʒub) *n.* 1, (tree) azufaifo. 2, (fruit) azufaifa. 3, (jellybean) pastilla de pasta de azufaifas.

jukebox ('dʒuk,bɑks) *n.* tocadiscos; tragamonedas; *W.I.* vellonera.

julep ('dʒu·lɪp) *n.* julepe.

July (dʒu'lai) *n.* julio.

jumble (dʒʌm·bəl) *v.t.* mezclar; revolver. —*v.i.* mezclarse; revolverse. —*n.* revoltijo.

jumbo (dʒʌm·bo) *n.* [*pl.* -**bos**] persona o cosa muy grande; coloso. —*adj.* grande.

jump (dʒʌmp) *v.i. & t.* saltar. —*v.t.*

hacer saltar. —*n.* salto. —**jumpy**, *adj.* nervioso; excitado. —**jumpiness**, *n.* nerviosidad. —**jump rope**, comba. —**jumpsuit**, *n.*, vestido de paracaidistas; mono; traje de faena.

jumper ('dʒʌm·pər) *n.* 1, (person or thing that jumps) saltador. 2, *elect.* alambre de cierre. 3, (loose garment) guardapolvo. 4, (sleeveless dress) vestido sin mangas. 5, *pl.* = **rompers**.

junction ('dʒʌŋk·ʃən) *n.* 1, (act or result of joining) unión; juntura. 2, (place of joining) empalme; *(of rivers)* confluencia.

juncture ('dʒʌŋk·tʃər) *n.* 1, (place of joining; seam) juntura. 2, (point of time) coyuntura.

June (dʒun) *n.* junio.

jungle ('dʒʌŋ·gəl) *n.* jungla.

junior ('dʒun·jər) *n.* 1, (younger person) persona más joven que otra. 2, (namesake son) hijo. 3, (subordinate) subalterno. 4, (third-year college student) estudiante de penúltimo año. —*adj.* 1, (younger) menor. 2, (of lower rank) de grado inferior; de menor grado. 3, (more recent) más reciente. 4, [*abr.* **Jr.**] (designating the son of the same name) hijo: *David Jones, Jr.*, David Jones, hijo. —**junior high school**, escuela intermedia. —**junior college**, colegio que enseña los dos primeros años universitarios.

juniper ('dʒu·nə·pər) *n.* 1, (shrub) enebro. 2, (fruit) enebrina.

junk (dʒʌŋk) *n.* 1, (trash) basura. 2, (worthless objects) trastos; trastos viejos. 3, (scrap metal) chatarra; hierro viejo. 4, (boat) junco. 5, *slang* (narcotics) narcóticos. —*v.t.*, *colloq.* 1, (throw away) descartar; desechar; tirar. 2, (sell for scrap) vender por chatarra. —**junk food**, *colloq.* comida de poco valor nutritivo. —**junk mail**, *colloq.* publicidad comercial expedida por los correos. —**junk yard**, chatarrería.

junket ('dʒʌŋ·kɪt) *n.* 1, (dessert) especie de cuajada. 2, (excursion) jira. —*v.i.* ir o andar de jira.

junkie ('dʒʌŋ·ki) *n.*, *slang* drogadicto.

junta ('dʒʌn·tə) *n.* junta.

junto ('dʒʌn·to) *n.* [*pl.* -**tos**] camarilla; facción.

Jupiter ('dʒu·pɪ·tər) *n.* Júpiter.

juridical (dʒu'rɪd·ə·kəl) *adj.* jurídico.

jurisdiction (ˌdʒur·ɪs'dɪk·ʃən) *n.* jurisdicción. —**jurisdictional,** *adj.* jurisdiccional.

jurisprudence (ˌdʒur·ɪs'pru·dəns) *n.* jurisprudencia.

jurist ('dʒur·ɪst) *n.* jurista.

juror ('dʒur·ər) *también,* **juryman** ('dʒur·i·mən) *n.* jurado.

jury (dʒur·i) *n.* jurado. —*adj., naut.* provisional.

just (dʒʌst) *adj.* justo. —*adv.* **1,** (precisely) justamente; precisamente; exactamente. **2,** (barely) apenas; casi no. **3,** (only; merely) simplemente; sólo. **4,** *colloq.* (completely) completamente; absolutamente. —**justness,** *n.* justicia. —**have just,** acabar de: *I have just*

arrived, Acabo de llegar. —**just now,** ahora mismo.

justice ('dʒʌs·tɪs) *n.* justicia. —**justice of the peace,** juez de paz; juez municipal.

justify ('dʒʌs·tə,fai) *v.t.* justificar. —*v.i.* justificarse. —**justifiable,** *adj.* justificable. —**justification** (-fɪ'kei·ʃən) *n.* justificación.

jut (dʒʌt) *v.i.* sobresalir; proyectarse. —*n.* saliente.

jute (dʒut) *n.* yute.

juvenile ('dʒu·və·nəl) *adj.* juvenil. —*n.* joven. —**juvenility** (-'nɪl·ə·ti) *n.* juventud; mocedad.

juxtapose (ˌdʒʌks·tə'poːz) *v.t.* yuxtaponer. —**juxtaposition** (-pə'zɪʃ·ən) yuxtaposición.

K

K, k (kei) **1,** undécima letra del alfabeto inglés. **2,** *comput.* = 1,000.

Kaiser ('kai·zər) *n.* káiser.

kale (keil) *n.* berza; col.

kaleidoscope (kə'lai·də,skop) *n.* calidoscopio. —**kaleidoscopic** (-'skap·ik) *adj.* calidoscópico.

kalsomine ('kæl·sə,main) *n.* lechada. —*v.t.* blanquear.

kangaroo (ˌkæŋ·gə'ruː) *n.* canguro. —**kangaroo court,** tribunal anómalo y arbitrario.

kapok ('kei·pak) *n.* kapok; algodón de ceiba.

kaput (kə'put) *adj., slang* perdido; arruinado.

katydid ('kei·ti·dɪd) *n.* saltamontes americano.

kayak ('kai·æk) *n.* kajak; kayak.

kayo ('kei·o) *v.t., slang* noquear; poner fuera de combate. —*n.* knockout.

kedge (kedʒ) *v.t. & i., naut.* halar (una embarcación) por el anclote. —*n.* anclote.

keel (kiːl) *n.* quilla. —**keel over,** *colloq.* **1,** (upset; turn over) dar(se) vuelta; volcar; voltear. **2,** (fall down, as in a faint) desplomarse. —**on an even keel,** estable.

keelhaul ('kiːl·hɔːl) *v.t., naut.* castigar a uno haciéndolo pasar por debajo de la quilla; *(fig.)* reprender fuertemente.

keen (kiːn) *adj.* **1,** (sharp; acute) agudo. **2,** (eager; enthusiastic) entusiasmado; muy interesado. **3,**

slang (excellent) excelente. —**keenness,** *n.* agudeza.

keep (kip) *v.t.* [*pret. & p.p.* **kept**] **1,** (observe; pay regard to) guardar; observar. **2,** (fulfill, as a promise) cumplir. **3,** (guard; watch over) guardar; cuidar. **4,** (maintain) mantener. **5,** (preserve) preservar. **6,** (maintain, as a record) llevar; llevar apuntes en. **7,** (have; hold) tener. **8,** (retain in one's possession) quedarse con; guardar. **9,** (detain; delay) detener; retener; demorar. **10,** (hold back; restrain) contener; aguantar. **11,** (prevent) impedir. **12,** (care for; support) mantener; cuidar de. —*v.i.* **1,** (stay) mantenerse. **2,** (continue) continuar; seguir. **3,** (abstain; refrain) abstenerse. **4,** (stay in good condition; last) conservarse; preservarse; durar. **5,** *colloq.* (wait; remain in abeyance) esperar; guardarse. —*n.* **1,** (livelihood; support) sustento; manutención; subsistencia. **2,** (stronghold of a castle) torre del homenaje. —**for keeps,** *colloq.* **1,** (in earnest) en serio; de veras. **2,** (forever) para siempre. —**keep at,** continuar en; seguir con. —**keep back, 1,** (contain; restrain) contener; sujetar; mantener apartado. **2,** (conceal) ocultar. —**keep down, 1,** (repress) reprimir. **2,** (limit) limitar. —**keep from** (+ *ger.*) evitar (+ *inf.*); abstenerse de. —**keep (someone** o **something) from** (+ *ger.*) evitar que; prevenir que; cuidar de que no. —**keep in with,** *colloq.* llevarse bien con. —**keep off,** mantener(se) a distancia; apartar(se). —**keep on,** continuar; seguir. —**keep out,** impedir la entrada a o de; apartar(se). —**keep to oneself, 1,** (avoid company) ser retraído; andar solo. **2,** (not divulge) guardar; ocultar; no contar. —**keep up, 1,** (maintain) mantener. **2,** (continue) seguir con; continuar con. **3,** (maintain the pace; not lag behind) ir a la par; no rezagarse. —**keep up with the Joneses,** llevar el mismo tren de vida que los vecinos.

keeper ('ki·pər) *n.* cuidador; guarda; guardián; encargado.

keeping ('ki·pɪŋ) *n.* **1,** (observance) observancia. **2,** (care; custody) cargo; custodia; cuidado. **3,** (maintenance; keep) manutención; subsistencia. **4,** (agreement; conformity) acuerdo; conformidad. **5,** (preservation) preservación.

keepsake ('kip,seik) *n.* recuerdo.

keg (kɛg) *n.* barril pequeño; barrilito.

kelp (kɛlp) *n.* alga marina grande.

Kelt (kɛlt) *n.* = **Celt.** —**Keltic,** *n.* & *adj.* = **Celtic.**

ken (kɛn) *n.* alcance del conocimiento; visión.

kennel ('kɛn·əl) *n.* perrera. —*v.t.* meter o tener en una perrera.

kepi ('kɛp·i) *n.* kepis; quepis.

kept (kɛpt) *v., pret. & p.p. de* **keep.**

keratin ('kɛr·ə·tɪn) *n., biol.* queratina.

kerb (kʌrb) *v.t. & n., Brit.* = **curb.**

kerchief ('kʌr·tʃɪf) *n.* pañuelo.

kernel ('kʌr·nəl) *n.* **1,** (seed) semilla. **2,** (essence; core) esencia; meollo; médula.

kerosene ('kɛr·ə,sin) *n.* kerosina; *Amer.* kerosén; keroseno.

ketch (kɛtʃ) *n.* queche.

ketchup ('kɛtʃ·əp) *n.* = **catchup.**

ketone ('ki·ton) *n.* cetona.

kettle ('kɛt·əl) *n.* caldero; perol; *(teakettle)* tetera. —**kettle of fish,** enredo; embrollo; lío.

kettledrum ('kɛt·əl,drʌm) *n.* atabal; timbal.

kewpie ('kju·pi) *n., T.N.* muñeca en forma caricaturizada de querube.

key (ki꞉) *n.* **1,** (device to turn a lock, bolt, etc.) llave. **2,** (lever, as of a piano, accordion, typewriter, etc.) tecla. **3,** (lever of wind instruments) llave. **4,** (peg; pin) clavija; chaveta

cuña. **5,** (controlling factor) clave. **6,** (clue; explanation) clave. **7,** (code; reference system) clave. **8,** (pitch; tone) tono. **9,** *mus.* clave. **10,** (reef; low island) cayo. —*v.t.* **1,** (adjust; regulate) ajustar; arreglar; regular. **2,** (regulate the pitch of) templar; afinar. **3,** (relate to a reference system) clasificar o relacionar con o por clave. —*adj.* clave. —**key up,** excitar; acalorar.

keyboard ('ki·bord) *n.* teclado.

keyhole ('ki·hol) *n.* bocallave; ojo de la cerradura.

keynote ('ki·not) *n.* **1,** *mus.* (tonic) clave; llave. **2,** (basic idea) punto o tema principal; tenor.

keystone ('ki·ston) *n.* clave.

khaki ('kæk·i) *n.* caqui; kaki.

khan (kan) *n.* kan. —**khanate** (-eit) *n.* kanato.

khedive (kə'diːv) *n.* jedive.

kibitzer ('kɪb·ɪt·sər) *n.* mirón; entremetido. —**kibitz** (-ɪts) *v.t. & i.* hacer de mirón (en).

kibosh ('kai·baʃ) *n., slang* maldición. —**put the kibosh on,** ponerle fin a algo.

kick (kɪk) *v.i.* **1,** (strike out with the foot or feet) dar puntapiés o patadas; *Amer.* patear. **2,** (thrash about with the feet) patalear. **3,** (recoil) retroceder; recular; *Amer.* patear. **4,** *colloq.* (complain; grumble) rezongar; patalear; refunfuñar. —*v.t.* **1,** (strike or drive with the foot or feet) dar puntapiés o patadas; *Amer.* patear. **2,** (recoil against) retroceder contra; dar un culatazo a o en; recular contra; *Amer.* patear. **3,** (force, as one's way, by kicking) abrir a patadas. —*n.* **1,** (blow with the foot) puntapié; coz. **2,** (recoil) culatazo; coz; *Amer.* patada. **3,** *colloq.* (complaint) queja; motivo de queja. **4,** *slang* (thrill) gusto; placer. —**kick around** (o **about**) **1,** (treat roughly) maltratar; castigar; patear. **2,** (move about) ir de aquí para allí; vagar. **3,** (think about; discuss) considerar; discutir. —**kick back,** *colloq.* (recoil unexpectedly) rebotar; dar de rechazo. **2,** *slang* (give back, as part of money received) devolver. —**kick in,** *slang* **1,** (pay, as one's share) pagar; pagar a escote. **2,** (die) estirar la pata; morirse. —**kick off, 1,** (put a football into play) hacer el saque. **2,** *slang* [*también,* **kick the bucket**] (die) estirar la pata; morirse. —**kick up, 1**, (raise by kicking) levantar a puntapiés o patadas. **2**, *slang* (stir up, as trouble) armar (un bochinche). **3**, *slang* (flare up) reventar.

kickback ('kık·bæk) *n*. **1**, *colloq.* (reaction) coz; reacción violenta. **2**, *slang* (return, as of money from one's earnings) devolución.

kid (kıd) *n*. **1**, (young goat) cabrito. **2**, (leather) cabritilla. **3**, *colloq.* (child) niño; chiquillo; muchacho. **4**, *slang* (hoax) broma; burla. —*adj*. **1**, (made of kidskin) de cabritilla. **2**, *colloq.* (younger) menor; más joven. —*v.t.* [**kidded, kidding**] *slang* **1**, (deceive; fool) engañar; embaucar. **2**, (tease) reírse de; tomar el pelo a; chacotear con. —*v.i.* bromear; chancear; chacotear.

kidnap ('kıd·næp) *v.t.* secuestrar; raptar. —**kidnaper**, *n*. secuestrador; raptor. —**kidnaping**, *n*. secuestro; rapto.

kidney ('kıd·ni) *n*. riñón. —**kidney bean**, judía; habichuela; frijol; fréjol; *S.A.* poroto.

kidskin ('kıd,skın) *n*. cabritilla. —*adj*. de cabritilla.

kill (kıl) *v.t.* **1**, (slay) matar. **2**, (put out; turn off) apagar; matar. **3**, (put an end to; ruin) destrozar; arruinar. **4**, (spend, as time) pasar; perder; matar. **5**, (veto; defeat) vetar; derrotar. **6**, (suppress; cancel) suprimir; cancelar. —*n*. **1**, (act of killing) matanza. **2**, (animal or animals killed) caza; piezas. —**be in at the kill**, estar presente en el momento crítico; ser testigo presencial.

killer ('kıl·ər) *n*. asesino.

killing ('kıl·ıŋ) *adj*. **1**, (deadly) mortal. **2**, (exhausting; fatiguing) agotador; extenuante; matador. **3**, *colloq.* (very comical) de morirse de risa; muy divertido. **4**, *colloq.* (very attractive) guapísimo. —*n*. **1**, (slaughter) matanza. **2**, (murder) asesinato. **3**, *colloq.* (quick profit) golpe; negocio redondo.

killjoy ('kıl,dʒɔı) *n*. aguafiestas.

kiln (kıl) *n*. horno. —*v.t.* cocer o secar al horno.

kilo ('kıl·o) *n*. = **kilogram**.

kilobyte ('kıl·ə,bait) *n*. kilobyte; kiloocteto.

kilocycle ('kıl·ə,sai·kəl) *n*. kilociclo.

kilogram ('kıl·ə,græm) *n*. kilogramo.

kiloliter ('kıl·ə,li·tər) *n*. kilolitro.

kilometer ('kıl·ə,mi·tər; kı·'lam·ə·tər) *n*. kilómetro. —**kilometric** (,kıl·ə'met·rık) *adj*. kilométrico.

kilowatt ('kıl·ə,wat) *n*. kilovatio.

kilt (kılt) *n*. falda escocesa.

kilter ('kıl·tər) *n., en* **in** o **out of kilter**, en o fuera de quicio; en buena (o mala) condición.

kimono (kə'mo·nə) *n*. quimono; kimono.

kin (kın) *n*. **1**, (family; relatives) parientes; familia; parentela. **2**, (family relationship) parentesco. —*adj*. emparentado. —**of kin**, emparentado; pariente.

kind (kaind) *n*. clase. —*adj*. **1**, (gentle; friendly) bondadoso; bueno; benévolo. **2**, (cordial) cordial. —**be kind enough to; be so kind as to**, tener la bondad de. —**in kind, 1**, (in goods) en especie; en géneros. **2**, (in like manner) con la misma moneda; en la misma forma. —**kind of**, *colloq.* como; algo. —**of a kind, 1**, (alike) de la misma clase. **2**, (mediocre) mediocre; de poca monta.

kindergarten ('kın·dər,gar·tən) *n*. jardín de infancia; kindergarten.

kindhearted ('kaind,hart·ıd) *adj*. bondadoso. —**kindheartedness**, *n*. bondad.

kindle ('kın·dəl) *v.t.* encender. —*v.i.* encenderse. —**kindling** (-dlıŋ) *n*. leña menuda.

kindly ('kaind·li) *adj*. **1**, (kind; benevolent) bondadoso; benévolo; bueno. **2**, (agreeable; pleasant) agradable; cordial. —*adv*. **1**, (in a kind manner) con bondad; bondadosamente. **2**, (agreeably; cordially) agradablemente; cordialmente. **3**, (please) por favor; sírvase. —**kindliness**, *n*. bondad; benevolencia. —**take kindly to**, adaptarse a; aceptar; ver con buenos ojos.

kindness ('kaind·nəs) *n*. bondad.

kindred ('kın·drəd) *n*. = **kin**. —*adj*. **1**, (related by blood) emparentado. **2**, (like; similar) afín; parecido; similar.

kinescope ('kın·ə,skop) *n*. kinescopio.

kinesthesia (,kın·əs'θi·ʒə) *n., physiol.* quinestesia.

kinetic (kı'net·rık; kai-) *adj*. cinético. —**kinetics**, *n*. cinética.

kinfolk ('kın,fok) *n.pl.* parientes; familia; parentela.

king (kıŋ) *n.* rey. —**kingdom,** *n.* reino.

kingfisher ('kıŋ,fıʃ·ər) *n.* martín pescador.

kinglet ('kıŋ·lət) *n.* reyezuelo; régulo.

kingly ('kıŋ·li) *n.* **1,** (royal) real. **2,** (resembling or befitting a king) majestuoso; de rey; digno de un rey. —**kingliness,** *n.* majestad.

kingpin ('kıŋ·pın) *n.* **1,** *mech.* pivote de dirección; gorrón; espiga. **2,** *slang* (chief) jefe; el que manda.

kingship ('kıŋ·ʃıp) *n.* majestad.

king-size ('kıŋ·saiz) *adj., colloq.* grande.

kink (kıŋk) *n.* **1,** (crimp; crinkle) pliegue; torcedura. **2,** (twist; knot) vuelta; nudo. **3,** (curl) rizo; *S.A.* mota. **4,** (cramp; crick) calambre. **5,** (eccentricity) rareza. **6,** (difficulty) problema; dificultad. —*v.t. & i.* **1,** (crimp) doblar(se); plegar(se). **2,** (twist; knot) enmarañar(se); enredar(se). **3,** (curl) encrespar(se); rizar(se). —**kinky,** *adj.* ensortijado; rizado.

kinsfolk (kınz,fok) *n.pl.* = kinfolk.

kinship ('kın·ʃıp) *n.* **1,** (family relationship) parentesco. **2,** (affinity) afinidad.

kinsman ('kınz·mən) *n.* [*pl.* **-men**] pariente. —**kinswoman,** *n.* [*pl.* **-women**] pariente.

kiosk (ki'ask) *n.* quiosco; kiosco.

kipper ('kıp·ər) *v.t.* curar; ahumar. —*n.* pescado ahumado.

kismet ('kız·mɛt) *n.* suerte; destino; sino.

kiss (kıs) *v.t. & i.* besar. —*n.* **1,** (caress) beso. **2,** (candy) dulce; confite. —**kisser,** *n., slang* trompa; hocico.

kit (kıt) *n.* **1,** (equipment) equipo. **2,** (case) estuche; caja. **3,** (kitten) gatito. —**kit and caboodle** (,kıt·ən·kə'bu·dəl) *colloq.* todo; todos.

kitchen ('kıtʃ·ən) *n.* cocina. —**kitchenette** (-ə'nɛt) *n.* cocina pequeña.

kite (kait) *n.* **1,** (toy) cometa; *Amer.* volantín. **2,** *ornith.* milano. **3,** *fin.* cheque inválido. —*v.t. & i.* cobrar (un cheque inválido).

kith (kıθ) *n.* amigos.

kitten ('kıt·ən) *n.* gatito; minino. —**kittenish,** *adj.* travieso; juguetón.

kitty ('kıt·i) *n.* **1,** (stakes; pool) pozo; puestas; posta. **2,** (kitten) gatito; minino.

kiwi ('ki·wi) *n.* kiwi.

kleptomania (,klɛp·tə'mei·ni·ə) *n.* cleptomanía. —**kleptomaniac** (-æk) *n.* cleptómano; cleptomaníaco.

knack (næk) *n.* aptitud; habilidad; destreza.

knapsack ('næp,sæk) *n.* mochila; morral.

knave (neiv) *n.* **1,** (rascal) bribón; pícaro. **2,** *cards* sota. —**knavery,** *n.* bribonería; bribonada. —**knavish,** *adj.* pícaro; picaresco; de bribón.

knead (niːd) *v.t.* amasar; sobar. —**kneading,** *n.* amasijo.

knee (niː) *n.* **1,** (part of the body, of a garment, etc.) rodilla. **2,** (bend) codo; curva. —*v.t.* dar un rodillazo a; dar con la rodilla a.

kneecap ('ni·kæp) *n.* **1,** *anat.* rótula. **2,** (knee protector) rodillera.

kneel (niːl) *v.i.* [*pret. & p.p.* **knelt** o **kneeled**] arrodillarse.

knell (nɛl) *n.* tañido; toque; doble. —*v.t. & i.* doblar; tañer; tocar.

knelt (nɛlt) *v., pret. & p.p. de* **kneel.**

knew (nuː) *v., pret. de* **know.**

knickers ('nık·ərz) *n.pl.* pantalones bombachos; *Amer.* bombachas. *También,* **knickerbockers** (-,bak·ərz).

knickknack ('nık,næk) *n.* chuchería.

knife (naif) *n.* cuchillo; cuchilla. —*v.t.* acuchillar; apuñalar.

knight (nait) *n.* caballero; *chess* caballo. —*v.t.* armar o nombrar caballero. —**knightly,** *adj.* caballeresco.

knight-errant ('nait,ɛr·ənt) *n.* [*pl.* **knights-errant**] caballero andante. —**knight-errantry,** *n.* caballería andante.

knighthood ('nait·hud) *n.* **1,** (rank of a knight) rango de caballero. **2,** (knights collectively) caballeros; caballería.

knit (nıt) *v.t. & i.* [**knitted, -ing**] **1,** (weave) tejer. **2,** (join closely) unir; ligar; trabar. **3,** (wrinkle; contract) arrugar; fruncir. —*n.* tejido de punto. —*adj.* de punto. —**knitting,** *n.* tejido de punto.

knitwear ('nıt·wer) *n.* géneros de punto.

knob (nazb) *n.* **1,** (lump; protuberance) bulto; protuberancia. **2,** (handle of a door, drawer, etc.) pomo; *Amer.* perilla. **3,** (controlling or regulating device) botón. **4,** (hill; knoll) loma; mota.

knobby ('nab·i) *adj.* **1,** (covered with knobs) nudoso; con bultos o protuberancias. **2,** (like a knob) redondo; redondeado.

knock (nak) *v.t.* **1,** (hit; strike) golpear; pegar. **2,** [*usu.* **knock down** o **off**] (strike down) derribar; tumbar. **3,** *colloq.* (criticize) criticar; rebajar. —*v.i.* **1,** (strike; pound) dar un golpe; dar golpes; golpear. **2,** (rap on the door) tocar o llamar a la puerta. **3,** (collide; clash) golpearse; chocar. —*n.* **1,** (blow) golpe; porrazo. **2,** (rap, as on a door) golpe; llamada; toque. **3,** (thump; pounding) golpe; golpeteo. **4,** *colloq.* (censure) crítica; censura. —**knock about** o **around,** *colloq.* **1,** (wander about; roam) vagar; andar. **2,** (treat roughly) golpear; maltratar. —**knock down, 1,** (dismount; take apart) desmontar; desarmar. **2,** (sell, as at auction) rematar; adjudicar (en subasta). —**knock off, 1,** *colloq.* (stop working) dejar o parar de trabajar. **2,** *colloq.* (deduct) rebajar; descontar. **3,** *colloq.* (do; accomplish) hacer; acabar; terminar. **4,** *slang* (kill) matar; asesinar. **5,** *slang* (cease; desist from) dejar; acabar; parar. —**knock out, 1,** *boxing* noquear. **2,** (defeat; destroy) poner fuera de combate; aniquilar. **3,** *colloq.* (do; make) hacer. —**knock up,** *colloq.* **1,** (exhaust) cansar; extenuar. **2,** *Brit.* (wake up) despertar. **3,** (make pregnant) preñar.

knockabout ('nak·ə·baut) *n.* balandro. —*adj.* **1,** (rough; boisterous) vocinglero; escandaloso. **2,** (suitable for rough use) de o para uso diario.

knockdown ('nak,daun) *adj.* **1,** (overwhelming) terrible; violento. **2,** (easily taken apart) desarmable; desmontable. —*n.* tumbo; golpe.

knocker ('nak·ər) *n.* aldaba; llamador.

knockkneed ('nak·niːd) *adj.* patizambo.

knockout *n.* **1,** *boxing* knockout. **2,** *slang* (sensation) sensación. —*adj.* terrible; violento.

knoll (noːl) *n.* loma; mota.

knot (nat) *n.* **1,** (enlacement; entanglement) nudo. **2,** (lump; protuberance) bulto. **3,** (tough grain in wood) nudo. **4,** (tie; bond) lazo. **5,** *naut.* nudo. **6,** (muscular spasm) calambre. **7,** (bunch; cluster) puñado; grupo. —*v.t.* anudar. —*v.i.* anudarse; formar nudo o nudos.

knothole ('nat·hoːl) *n.* agujero (del nudo).

knotty ('nat·i) *adj.* **1,** (full of knots) nudoso; con nudos. **2,** (difficult) difícil; complicado.

knout (naut) *n.* knut.

know (noː) *v.t.* [**knew; known**] **1,** (be cognizant of; have knowledge of) saber; saber de. **2,** (be acquainted with; discern) conocer. —*v.i.* saber; estar enterado. —**in the know,** *colloq.* enterado; informado; *Amer.* interiorizado.

knowable ('noː·ə·bəl) *adj.* conocible.

know-all *adj., colloq.* sabihondo. —*n., colloq.* sábelotodo. *También,* **know-it-all.**

know-how *n., colloq.* **1,** (knowledge) conocimiento. **2,** (skill) habilidad; destreza.

knowing ('noː·iŋ) *adj.* **1,** (well-informed) entendido; informado. **2,** (shrewd; understanding) ducho; astuto; inteligente. **3,** (deliberate; intentional) deliberado; intencional. —**knowingly,** *adv.* a sabiendas; con conocimiento de causa.

knowledge ('nal·idʒ) *n.* conocimiento; saber. —**knowledgeable,** *adj.* inteligente; de conocimientos. —**to (the best of) one's knowledge,** al entender de uno; en cuanto uno sabe; por lo que uno sabe.

known (noːn) *v., p.p. de* **know.**

know-nothing *n. & adj.* ignorante.

knuckle ('nʌk·əl) *n.* **1,** (joint of the finger) nudillo. **2,** (animal joint used as food) pata; patita. **3,** (hinge) charnela. —**knuckle down, 1,** (work energetically) afanarse; esmerarse. **2,** [*también,* **knuckle under**] (submit) someterse; rendirse.

knurl (nʌrl) *n.* **1,** (knot; knob) nudo. **2,** (milling, as on a coin) cordoncillo. —*v.t.* acordonar; cerrillar.

KO ('keiˌoː) *n., slang* knockout. —*v.t.* noquear. *Also,* **K.O.;** kayo.

koala (koˈaˈlə) *n.* koala.

kohlrabi ('kolˌraˈbi) *n.* colinabo.

kopeck ('koˈpɛk) *n.* copec; kopek.

Koran (koˈraːn) *n.* Corán; Alcorán.

kosher ('koˈʃər) *adj.* **1,** *relig.*

hecho o preparado conforme a la ley dietética judía. **2,** *slang* (authentic) genuino: legítimo.

kowtow (ˌkauˈtau) *v.i.* humillarse. —*n.* reverencia.

kraal (kraˌl) *n.* **1,** (So. Afr. village) craal. **2,** (cattle pen) redil; corral.

Kremlin (ˈkrɛm·lɪn) *n.* kremlin.

krona (ˈkro·nə) *n.* moneda sueca; corona.

krone (ˈkro·nə) *n.* moneda de varios países; corona.

krypton (ˈkrɪp·tan) *n.* criptón.

kulak (kuˈlak) *n.* kulak.

L

L, l (ɛl) duodécima letra del alfabeto inglés.

la (laˌ) *n., mus.* la. —*interj.* ¡ah!; ¡oh!; ¡mira!

lab (læb) *n., colloq.* laboratorio.

label (ˈlei·bəl) *n.* **1,** (tag; tab) etiqueta; marbete. **2,** (appellation; name) apelativo; nombre; clasificación; (*usu. despectivo*) mote. —*v.t.* **1,** (attach a label to) poner etiqueta o marbete a. **2,** (classify as; call) clasificar de o como; llamar; motejar.

labial (ˈlei·bi·əl) *adj.* labial.

labor *también,* **labour** (lei·bər) *n.* **1,** (work; toil) trabajo; labor. **2,** (piece of work; task) labor; trabajo; faena. **3,** (working class) trabajo. **4,** (manual work or workers) mano de obra. **5,** (childbirth) parto. —*v.i.* **1,** (work; toil) trabajar; laborar. **2,** (strive; work hard) laborar; pujar; esforzarse. **3,** (undergo childbirth) estar de parto. —*v.t.* insistir demasiado en o sobre; elaborar mucho. —**Labor Day,** día del trabajo.

laboratory (ˈlæb·rə·torˌi) *n.* laboratorio.

labored (ˈlei·bərd) *adj.* **1,** (elaborate) muy elaborado; complicado; rebuscado. **2,** (requiring great effort) trabajoso; pesado; penoso.

laborer (ˈlei·bər·ər) *n.* trabajador; obrero.

laborious (lə·bor·i·əs) *adj.* laborioso. —**laboriousness,** *n.* laboriosidad.

Laborite (ˈlei·bər,ait) *n.* laborista. —**Labor party,** partido laborista.

labor union sindicato; gremio; unión de trabajadores.

labyrinth (ˈlæb·ə·rɪnθ) *n.* laberinto. —**labyrinthine** (-ˈrɪn·θɪn) *adj.* laberíntico.

lac (læk) *n.* laca.

lace (leis) *n.* **1,** (openwork fabric) encaje. **2,** (ornamental braid) galón.

3, (cord; fastening) cordón; lazo; atadura. —*v.t.* **1,** (bind; tie) atar; anudar; amarrar. **2,** (entwine) enlazar; entrelazar. **3,** *colloq.* (thrash; whip) azotar; dar de azotes. **4,** (put liquor in; spike) añadir licor a. —**lace into,** *colloq.* arremeter contra; atacar.

lacerate (ˈlæs·ə,reit) *v.t.* lacerar. —**laceration,** *n.* laceración.

lacework (ˈleis·wʌrk) *n.* **1,** (lace) encaje. **2,** (fretwork; openwork) calado.

lachrymal *también,* **lacrimal** (ˈlæk·rə·məl) *adj.* lacrimal; *anat.* lagrimal.

lachrymose (ˈlæk·rə,mos) *adj.* lacrimoso; lagrimoso.

lacing (ˈlei·sɪŋ) *n.* **1,** (act of fastening) atadura. **2,** (cord; binding) cordón; lazo. **3,** *colloq.* (thrashing) azotaina; zurra. **4,** *colloq.* (scolding) reprimenda. **5,** (ornamental braid) galón.

lack (læk) *n.* **1,** (shortage) falta; escasez. **2,** (absence) falta; carencia. **3,** (what is needed) lo que falta; falta. —*v.t.* **1,** (have not enough; need) no tener suficiente; necesitar. **2,** (be without; have no) carecer de; no tener. —*v.i.* **1,** (be wanting or missing) faltar; hacer falta; no haber. **2,** (be short; be in need) necesitar; tener necesidad. **3,** (be in short supply) escasear.

lackadaisical (ˌlæk·əˈdei·zɪ·kəl) *adj.* lánguido; indiferente; apático.

lackey (ˈlæk·i) *n.* lacayo.

lackluster (ˈlæk,lʌs·tər) *adj.* insípido; insulso.

laconic (lə·kanˈɪk) *adj.* lacónico.

lacquer (ˈlæk·ər) *n.* laca; barniz. —*v.t.* laquear; barnizar.

lacrosse (lə·krɔs) *n.* juego de pelota canadiense; lacrosse.

lactation (læk·teiˈʃən) *n.* lactación; lactancia.

lacteal (ˈlæk·ti·əl) *adj.* lácteo.

lactic ('læk·tık) *adj.* láctico.
lactose ('læk‚tos) *n.* lactosa; lactina.
lacuna (lə'kju·nə) *n.* laguna.
lacy ('lei·si) *adj.* de o como encaje.
lad (læd) *n.* muchacho; niño; mozo.
ladder ('læd·ər) *n.* **1,** (frame with rungs) escalera; escalera de mano. **2,** (way, as to fame) escalones; escala. **3,** (run, as in hose) carrera.
laddie ('læd·i) *n., dim. de* **lad**.
lade (leid) *v.t.* **1,** (load) cargar; *fig.* abrumar. **2,** (ladle) servir o sacar con cucharón. **3,** (bail) achicar.
laden ('lei·dən) *v., p.p. de* **lade**.
lading ('lei·dıŋ) *n.* carga. —**bill of lading,** conocimiento o manifiesto de embarque.
ladle ('lei·dəl) *n.* cucharón; cazo. —*v.t.* servir o sacar con cucharón.
lady ('lei·di) *n.* **1,** (any woman) mujer. **2,** (woman of good breeding or standing) dama; señora. **3,** (title of nobility or respect) dama. **4,** (wife) señora; esposa. **5,** (mistress) señora. —*adj.* mujer; hembra. —**Our Lady,** Nuestra Señora.
ladybug ('lei·di‚bʌg) *n.* mariquita. *También,* **ladybird.**
ladyfinger ('lei·di‚fıŋ·gər) *n.* melindre.
lady in waiting azafata; camarera.
lady-killer *n., slang* tenorio; don Juan.
ladylike ('lei·di‚laik) *adj.* femenino; delicado.
ladylove ('lei·di‚lʌv) *n.* novia; amada; amor.
ladyship ('lei·di‚ʃıp) *n.* señoría.
lag (læg) *v.i.* atrasarse; retrasarse. —*n.* atraso; retraso.
lager ('la·gər) *n.* cerveza reposada.
laggard ('læg·ərd) *adj.* moroso; lento; perezoso. —*n.* posma; perezoso.
lagoon (lə'guːn) *n.* laguna.
laic ('lei·ık) *adj.* laico.
laid (leid) *v., pret. & p.p. de* **lay**.
lain (lein) *v., p.p. de* **lie**.
lair (leːr) *n.* cubil; guarida.
laity ('lei·ə·ti) *n.* **1,** (laymen) seglares. **2,** (lay brothers) legos. **3,** (nonprofessionals) legos.
lake (leik) *n.* lago.
lam (læm) *v.t.* **[lammed, lamming]** *slang* azotar; pegar. —*v.i., slang* escapar; largarse. —**on the lam,** *slang* huyendo; escapando. —**take it on the lam,** *slang* poner pies en polvorosa.

lama ('la·mə) *n.* lama. —**Lamaism,** *n.* lamaísmo. —**Lamaist,** *n.* & *adj.* lamaísta. —**lamasery** (-sɛr·i) *n.* lamasería.
lamb (læm) *n.* cordero. —**lambkin,** *n.* corderito. —**lambskin,** *n.* piel de cordero.
lambaste (læm'beist) *v.t., slang* zurrar; dar una zurra a; vapulear.
lame (leim) *adj.* **1,** (crippled) lisiado; cojo. **2,** (ineffectual) débil; ineficaz; flaco. —*v.t.* lisiar; volver cojo. —**lame duck,** *colloq.* **1,** (ineffectual person) pelma; inútil. **2,** *polit.* funcionario sin influencia por estar próximo su reemplazo.
lamé (læ'mei) *n.* lamé; lama.
lameness ('leim·nəs) *n.* **1,** (disability) cojera. **2,** (weakness) debilidad; ineficacia.
lament (lə'mɛnt) *v.t. & i.* lamentar. —*n.* lamento. —**lamentable** ('læm·ən·tə·bəl) *adj.* lamentable. —**lamentation** (‚læm·ən'tei·ʃən) *n.* lamentación.
lamina ('læm·ə·nə) *n.* [*pl.* -**nae** (-ni) o -**nas**] lámina; hoja. —**laminate** (-neit) *v.t.* laminar. —*adj.* (-nət) laminado. —**lamination,** *n.* laminado; laminación.
lamp (læmp) *n.* **1,** (lighting device) lámpara. **2,** *slang, usu. pl.* (eyes) ojos; faroles.
lampblack ('læmp‚blæk) *n.* negro de humo.
lampoon (læm'puːn) *n.* pasquín; sátira. —*v.t.* pasquinar; satirizar.
lamppost ('læmp‚post) *n.* poste de farol.
lamprey ('læm·pri) *n.* lamprea.
lampshade ('læmp‚ʃeid) *n.* pantalla de lámpara.
lance (læns) *n.* lanza; *surg.* lanceta. —*v.t.* lancear; *surg.* abrir con lanceta; dar una lancetada. —**lancer,** *n.* lancero.
lancet ('læn·sıt) *n.* lanceta.
land (lænd) *n.* tierra. —*v.t.* **1,** (put ashore) desembarcar. **2,** (take, as to a destination) llevar (a); dejar (en). **3,** (put or cause to get into) meter; poner de patitas en. **4,** (set down, as an aircraft) hacer aterrizar. **5,** (catch, as a fish) coger; pescar. **6,** *colloq.* (get; secure) obtener; conseguir. **7,** *colloq.* (deliver, as a blow) dar; asestar. —*v.i.* **1,** (go ashore) desembarcar. **2,** (arrive; reach port) llegar; arribar. **3,** *colloq.* (end up; wind up) terminar;

encontrarse; ir a parar. **4,** (alight; come to rest) aterrizar.

landed ('lænd·dɪd) *adj.* **1,** (owning land) latifundista; terrateniente. **2,** (consisting of land) de tierras; inmueble.

landfall ('lænd·fɔl) *n.* **1,** (sight of land) recalada; vista de tierra. **2,** (land sighted) tierra avistada. **3,** (arrival in port) arribo; llegada. **4,** (alighting) aterrizaje.

landfill ('lænd·fɪl) *n.* tierra, grava, etc., que sirve para rellenar hoyas, pantanos, etc.; la tierra así reconstruída.

landholder ('lænd,hol·dər) *n.* terrateniente.

landing ('læn·dɪŋ) *n.* **1,** (debarkation) desembarco; desembarque. **2,** (place for unloading or loading) embarcadero. **3,** (platform, as on stairs) descanso; descansillo. **4,** (act of alighting) aterrizaje. —**landing gear,** tren de aterrizaje. —**landing strip,** pista de aterrizaje.

landlady ('lænd,lei·di) *n.* **1,** (landowner) propietaria; dueña; *Amer.* patrona. **2,** (owner of a hotel, rooming house, etc.) patrona; dueña.

landlocked ('lænd,lakt) *adj.* sin acceso al mar.

landlord ('lænd·lord) *n.* **1,** (landowner) propietario; dueño; *Amer.* patrón. **2,** (owner of a hotel, rooming house, etc.) patrón; dueño.

landlubber ('lænd,lʌb·ər) *n.* marinero de agua dulce.

landmark *n.* **1,** (boundary mark; milestone) hito; mojón. **2,** (conspicuous object on land) marca; guía. **3,** (point of interest) sitio destacado; sitio de interés. **4,** (memorable event) hito; momento culminante.

land office oficina del catastro. —**land-office business,** negocio muy vivo.

landowner ('lænd,o·nər) *n.* terrateniente; propietario.

landscape ('lænd,skeip) *n.* paisaje. —*v.t. & i.* arreglar como jardín; arreglar el paisaje (de).

landslide ('lænd,slaid) *n.* avalancha; alud.

lane (lein) *n.* **1,** (byroad) callejón; callejuela. **2,** (path; opening) paso; senda; vereda. **3,** *naut.; aero.* (fixed route) derrotero; ruta. **4,** (designated path, as for traffic) vía; pista; *Amer.* carril.

language ('læŋ·gwɪdʒ) *n.* **1,** (idiom; tongue) idioma; lengua. **2,** (form or manner of expression) lenguaje.

languid ('læŋ·gwɪd) *adj.* lánguido. —**languidness,** *n.* languidez.

languish ('læŋ·gwɪʃ) *v.i.* languidecer. —**languishment,** *n.* languidecimiento.

languor ('læŋ·gər) *n.* languidez. —**languorous,** *adj.* lánguido.

lank (læŋk) *adj.* **1,** (lean; gaunt) delgado; flaco; enjuto. **2,** (straight, as hair) lacio. —**lanky,** *adj.* larguirucho; desgarbado.

lanolin ('læn·ə·lɪn) *n.* lanolina.

lantern ('læn·tərn) *n.* **1,** (lamp; globe) linterna; farol. **2,** (skylight) tragaluz. —**lantern-jawed,** *adj.* chupado de cara.

lanthanum ('læn·θə·nəm) *n.* lantano.

lanyard *también,* **laniard** ('læn·jərd) *n.* trinca.

lap (læp) *n.* **1,** (portion between waist and knees) rodillas; regazo; *W.I.* falda. **2.** (hollow; fold) regazo; seno. **3,** (flap, as of clothing) falda; faldón; faldillas. **4,** (overlap) traslapo; solapo. **5,** (single turn; circuit) vuelta. **6,** (lick) lengüetada. **7,** (sound of lapping) golpeteo; batido. —*v.t.* **1,** (fold over or about; wind) envolver; dar una vuelta o vueltas a. **2,** (wrap; enfold) envolver. **3,** (cause to overlap) traslapar; solapar. **4,** (get a turn ahead of) llevar una vuelta de ventaja a. **5,** (polish; grind) pulir; labrar. **6,** (wash against, as waves) lamer. —*v.i.* **1,** (overlap) traslaparse; solaparse. **2,** (extend beyond) extenderse en parte; incluir parcialmente; proyectarse. —**lap dog,** perro faldero. —**lap up, 1,** (lick up, as food) tomar o comer a lengüetadas. **2,** *colloq.* (eat or drink greedily) comer a dos carrillos; engullir; tragar de golpe. **3,** *colloq.* (absorb eagerly) absorber; embeber.

lapel (lə'pɛl) *n.* solapa.

lapidary ('læp·ə·dɛr·i) *n. & adj.* lapidario.

lapin ('læp·ɪn) *n.* conejo; piel de conejo.

lapis lazuli ('læp·ɪs'læz·ju,li; -,lai) lapislázuli.

Lapp (læp) *n. & adj.* lapón.

lappet ('læp·ɪt) *n.* **1,** (flap) faldillas; faldón. **2,** (wattle) papo; carnosidad. **3,** (lobe of the ear) lóbulo.

lapse (læps) *n.* lapso; *comm.; law*

caducidad. —*v.i.* **1,** (slip; fall) caer; recaer. **2,** (pass away; elapse) pasar; correr; transcurrir. **3,** (retrogress) retroceder; recaer. **4,** *comm.; law* (expire) caducar; vencer; vencerse.

larboard ('lar·bərd) *n.* babor. —*adj.* de babor. —*adv.* a babor.

larceny ('lar·sə·ni) *n.* robo; hurto. —**larcenist,** *n.* ladrón. —**larcenous,** *adj.* ladrón; de ladrón.

larch (lartʃ) *n.* alerce.

lard (lard) *n.* manteca. —*v.t.* **1,** (grease) poner manteca a o en. **2,** (stuff with bacon strips) mechar. **3,** (garnish) adornar.

larder ('lar·dər) *n.* despensa.

large (lardʒ) *adj.* grande. —**largeness,** *n.* extensión; amplitud. —**at large, 1,** (not confined) libre; en libertad. **2,** (fully) extensamente; sin limitación. **3,** *polit.* general; de representación general.

largely ('lardʒ·li) *adv.* **1,** (in great amount) grandemente; ampliamente; mucho. **2,** (mainly) por la mayor parte; en su mayor parte; en gran parte.

large-scale *adj.* en o a gran escala.

largess (lar'dʒɛs) *n.* largueza.

largo ('lar·go) *adj.* & *adv.* largo.

lariat ('lær·i·ət) *n.* reata.

lark (lark) *n.* **1,** (bird) alondra. **2,** (frolic) juerga; parranda. —*v.i.* ir de parranda o juerga.

larkspur ('lark·spʌr) *n.* espuela de caballero.

larva ('lar·və) *n.* [*pl.* **larvae** (-vi)] larva. —**larval,** *adj.* larval.

larynx ('lær·ɪŋks) *n.* laringe. —**laryngeal** (lə'rɪn·dʒi·əl) *adj.* laríngeo. —**laryngitis** (ˌlær·ɪn'dʒai·tɪs) *n.* laringitis.

lascivious (lə'sɪv·i·əs) *adj.* lascivo. —**lasciviousness,** *n.* lascivia.

laser ('lei·zər) *n.* láser. —**laser beam,** rayo láser.

lash (læʃ) *n.* **1,** (whip) látigo. **2,** (blow with a whip) latigazo. **3,** *fig.* (censure; sarcasm) latigazo. **4,** (eyelash) pestaña. —*v.t.* **1,** (flog) azotar. **2,** (beat or dash against) golpear. **3,** (move or switch sharply) sacudir; agitar. **4,** (assail) fustigar. **5,** (tie) atar; amarrar. —*v.i.* [*usu.* **lash out**] arremeter; embestir; desatarse.

lashing ('læʃ·ɪŋ) *n.* **1,** (binding) atadura; *naut.* amarra. **2,** (strong rebuke) invectiva. **3,** (beating) latigazos; azotes.

lass (læs) *n.* moza; muchacha; niña. *También,* **lassie.**

lassitude ('læs·ɪ·tjud) *n.* lasitud.

lasso ('læs·o) *n.* lazo. —*v.t.* lazar.

last (læst) *v.i.* **1,** (endure) durar. **2,** (continue) continuar; seguir. —*n.* **1,** (person or thing coming latest or at the end) el, la o lo último; el fin. **2,** (shoe mold) horma. —*adj.* **1,** (latest; hindmost; final) último. **2,** (immediately before the present) pasado. —*adv.* **1,** (after all others; at the end) al final; a lo último. **2,** (finally) finalmente. **3,** (on the most recent occasion) por última vez; la última vez. —**lasting,** *adj.* duradero; permanente. —**at last,** al fin; por fin. —**before (the) last, 1,** (before the most recent) antepasado. **2,** (just preceding the endmost) penúltimo. —**breathe one's last,** expirar; exhalar el último suspiro. —**last but not least,** lo último pero no menos importante. —**last name,** apellido. —**last night,** anoche. —**last quarter,** cuarto menguante. —**last straw,** el colmo. —**last word,** *colloq.* lo último. —**next to (the) last,** penúltimo. —**of the last importance,** trascendental; de máxima importancia.

lastly ('læst·li) *adv.* finalmente; por último.

latch (lætʃ) *n.* pestillo; aldaba. —*v.t.* echar o correr el pestillo o aldaba a. —**latch on to,** *slang* agarrar; coger.

late (leit) *adj.* **1,** (tardy; delayed) retrasado; atrasado. **2,** (protracted in time) prolongado; que dura hasta tarde. **3,** (coming near the end) de fines (de); de finales (de). **4,** (recent) último; reciente. **5,** (occurring after the expected time) tardío. **6,** (occurring at the last moment) de último momento; postrero. **7,** (former) ex; que ha sido. **8,** (bygone) pasado. **9,** (deceased) difunto. **10,** (advanced, as the hour) avanzado; entrado. —*adv.* **1,** (tardily) tarde. **2,** (toward the end of a stated period of time) a fines (de); en las últimas horas (de); tarde (en). **3,** (at or until an advanced hour) tarde; hasta tarde; a o hasta hora avanzada. **4,** = **lately.** —**lately,** *adv.* recientemente; últimamente; poco ha. —**later,** *adv.* luego; más tarde. —**be late, 1,** (of the hour) ser tarde. **2,** (of arrival) llegar tarde; llegar con atraso o retraso; estar atrasado o retrasado. **—of late,** recientemente; últimamente.

lateen sail (lə'tiːn) *n.* vela latina.

lateness ('leit·nəs) *n.* **1,** (delay) atraso; retraso. **2,** (advanced time) lo avanzado. **3,** (tardiness) lo tardío.

latent ('lei·tənt) *adj.* latente. **—latency,** *n.* lo latente; estado latente.

lateral ('læt·ər·əl) *adj.* lateral.

latex ('lei·teks) *n.* látex.

lath (læθ) *n.* listón. **—***v.t.* poner listones a o en. **—lathing,** *n.* enlistonado; listonado.

lathe (leið) *n.* torno. **—***v.t.* tornear.

lather ('læð·ər) *n.* espuma. **—***v.t.* **1,** (cover with foam) enjabonar; jabonar. **2,** (cause to foam) hacer espumar. **3,** *colloq.* (flog) zurrar; dar una zurra. **—lathery,** *adj.* espumoso.

lathwork ('læθˌwʌrk) *n.* enlistonado; listonado.

Latin ('læt·in) *n.* **1,** (language) latín. **2,** (person) latino. **—***adj.* latino. **—Latinization,** *n.* latinización. **—Latinity,** *n.* latinidad. **—Latinize,** *v.t. & i.* latinizar.

Latin American *adj. & n.* latinoamericano.

latitude ('læt·ɪ·tjud) *n.* latitud. **—latitudinal** (-'tju·dɪ·nəl) *adj.* latitudinal.

latrine (lə'triːn) *n.* letrina.

latter ('læt·ər) *adj.* **1,** (last mentioned of two) último; segundo. **2,** (more recent) más reciente. **3,** (near or nearer to the end) último; final. **—the former . . . the latter,** aquél . . . éste.

latter-day *adj.* actual; de hoy; moderno. **—Latter-day Saints,** santos de los últimos días; mormones.

latterly ('læt·ər·li) *adv.* **1,** (recently) últimamente; recientemente. **2,** (toward the end) hacia el fin; a lo último.

lattice ('læt·is) *n.* enrejado; rejilla; celosía. **—***v.t.* enrejar con listones; poner celosías a; hacer un enrejado de.

laud (lɔːd) *v.t.* alabar; elogiar. **—laudable,** *adj.* laudable. **—laudatory** (-ə·tor·i) *adj.* laudatorio.

laudanum ('lɔ·də·nəm) *n.* láudano.

laugh (læf) *v.i.* reír; reírse. **—***v.t.* reírse de; mover con risa; sacar a risotadas; decir o expresar riendo. **—***n.* risa. **—laughable,** *adj.* risible.

—laugh at, reírse de. **—laughing gas,** gas hilarante.

laughingstock ('læf·iŋˌstak) *n.* hazmerreír.

laughter ('læf·tər) *n.* risa; risas.

launch (lɔntʃ) *v.t.* **1,** (set afloat) botar. **2,** (begin) iniciar; inaugurar. **3,** (hurl) lanzar; arrojar. **—***v.i.* lanzarse. **—***n.* lancha. **—launching,** *n.* botadura.

launder ('lɔn·dər) *v.t. & i.* lavar. **—launderer,** *n.* lavandero. **—laundress** (-drɪs) *n.* lavandera.

laundry ('lɔn·dri) *n.* **1,** (establishment) lavandería. **2,** (what is laundered) lavado.

laureate ('lɔ·ri·ət) *adj. & n.* laureado.

laurel ('lɔr·əl) *n.* laurel.

lava ('la·və) *n.* lava.

lavatory ('læv·ə·tor·i) *n.* lavabo; excusado; retrete.

lave (leiv) *v.t.* lavar; bañar. **—***v.i.* lavarse; bañarse.

lavender ('læv·ən·dər) *n.* **1,** *bot.* espliego; lavanda. **2,** (color; scent) lavanda.

lavish ('læv·iʃ) *adj.* pródigo; suntuoso. **—***v.t.* prodigar. **—lavishness,** *n.* prodigalidad; suntuosidad.

law (lɔ) *n.* **1,** (rule; set of rules) ley. **2,** (jurisprudence) derecho; jurisprudencia. **3,** *colloq.* (police) policía; justicia. **—law-abiding,** *adj.* que respeta la ley. **—lawful,** *adj.* legal; lícito. **—lawfulness,** *n.* legalidad. **—go to law,** ir a juicio; litigar.

lawless ('lɔ·ləs) *adj.* **1,** (contrary to law) ilegal. **2,** (without law; defiant of law) sin ley. **—lawlessness,** *n.* desorden.

lawmaker ('lɔˌmei·kər) *n.* legislador.

lawn (lɔn) *n.* **1,** (grass) césped. **2,** (fabric) linón.

lawn mower segadora.

lawrencium (lɔ'ren·si·əm) *n.* laurencio.

lawsuit ('lɔ·sut) *n.* juicio; pleito; demanda.

lawyer ('lɔi·jər) *n.* abogado; *Amer.* licenciado.

lax (læks) *adj.* **1,** (loose; relaxed) laxo; flojo. **2,** (careless; remiss) descuidado. **3,** (not strict) relajado. **4,** (vague) vago; indeterminado. **—laxity; laxness,** *n.* laxitud.

laxative ('læk·sə·tiv) *n. & adj.* laxante; purgante.

lay (lei) *v.t.* [*pret. & p.p.* **laid**] **1,**

(put; set) poner. **2,** (allay; appease) calmar; apaciguar. **3,** (overcome) vencer; superar. **4,** (devise) hacer; trazar. **5,** (locate; situate) situar. **6,** (bet) apostar. **7,** (impute; ascribe) imputar; atribuir. —*v.i.* poner (huevos). —*v., pret. de* lie. —*n.* **1,** (arrangement) disposición; situación. **2,** (poem; song) lay. —*adj.* **1,** (secular) secular; seglar. **2,** (nonclerical; nonprofessional) lego. —**lay about (one),** dar golpes a diestra y siniestra. —**lay an egg,** *slang* fracasar. —**lay aside, away o by,** poner a un lado; guardar. —**lay claim to,** reclamar. —**lay down, 1,** (place in a reclining position) acostar; recostar. **2,** (give up, as one's life) dar u ofrecer (la vida). **3,** (surrender) rendir; entregar. **4,** (set; establish) fijar; establecer. **5,** (store) guardar; reservar. —**lay for,** acechar. —**lay hold of,** aferrar; asir. —**lay in,** almacenar; guardar. —**lay off, 1,** (take off) quitar; quitarse. **2,** (discharge) despedir. **3,** (mark off) marcar. **4,** (cease; desist) parar; dejar. —**lay oneself open,** arriesgarse; exponerse. —**lay out, 1,** (arrange) arreglar; disponer. **2,** (spend) gastar. **3,** (advance, as funds) adelantar. —**lay over,** hacer alto; detenerse. —**lay the blame,** culpar; echar la culpa. —**lay up, 1,** (store up) amontonar; almacenar. **2,** (make inactive) inutilizar. **3,** (incapacitate) inhabilitar; incapacitar.

layer ('leiꞏər) *n.* **1,** (thickness of some material laid on another) capa. **2,** (stratum) estrato; cama. **3,** (egg-producing fowl) ave ponedora.

layette (lei'ɛt) *n.* canastilla; ajuar de niño.

layman ('leiꞏmən) *n.* [*pl.* **-men**] **1,** (nonprofessional) lego. **2,** (nonclerical) seglar.

layoff ('leiꞏɔf) *n.* **1,** (suspension of employment) suspensión; despido. **2,** (period of suspension) cesantía.

layout ('leiꞏaut) *n.* **1,** (plan) plan. **2,** (arrangement) arreglo; disposición. **3,** (equipment) equipo; aparatos. **4,** (format) formato; presentación.

laze (leiz) *v.i.* holgazanear; flojear.

lazy ('leiꞏzi) *adj.* perezoso; flojo. —**laziness,** *n.* pereza; flojedad; flojera. —**lazybones,** *n.* holgazán.

leach (litʃ) *v.t. & i.* filtrar; pasar; colar.

lead (lɛd) *n.* **1,** (metal, or something made of it) plomo. **2,** (graphite)

grafito; (of a pencil) mina. **3,** *print.* regleta. **4,** *naut.* sonda. —*v.t.* **1,** (fill or line with lead) emplomar. **2,** *print.* regletear. **3,** (weight with lead) cargar con pesas de plomo. —*adj.* de plomo.

lead (liːd) *v.t. & i.* [*pret. & p.p.* **led**] **1,** (guide) guiar. **2,** (conduct) llevar; conducir. **3,** (direct; control) dirigir. **4,** (command) mandar. —*v.t.* **1,** (go or be first in; head) encabezar. **2,** *cards* salir con. —*v.i.* **1,** (go or be first) ir o ser primero; preceder. **2,** *en* lead to (be the cause of) llevar a; resultar en; traer como consecuencia. **3,** *cards* salir. —*n.* **1,** (role of a leader) posición de mando; dirección. **2,** (initiative) iniciativa. **3,** (example) ejemplo. **4,** (first or front place) delantera. **5,** (distance ahead) ventaja; delantera. **6,** (clue) indicio; pista. **7,** (indication; suggestion) indicación; dato. **8,** *cards* salida. **9,** *boxing* golpe. **10,** *elect.* conductor. **11,** *theat.* papel principal. **12,** *journalism* primer párrafo. —*adj.* primero; principal. —**lead off o out,** comenzar; empezar; iniciar. —**lead on, 1,** (go ahead) seguir adelante; continuar. **2,** (lure) dar cuerda a; embelecar. —**lead the way,** mostrar el camino; tomar la delantera. —**lead up to,** conducir o llevar a.

leaden ('lɛd·ən) *adj.* **1,** (made of lead) de plomo. **2,** (color) plomizo. **3,** (heavy) pesado; de o como plomo.

leader ('li·dər) *n.* **1,** (chief) jefe; líder. **2,** (ringleader) cabecilla. **3,** (director) director. **4,** (editorial) artículo de fondo.

leadership ('li·dər·ʃɪp) *n.* **1,** (position or function of a leader) dirección; jefatura; mando. **2,** (ability to lead) cualidades de mando.

leading lady primera dama; primera actriz. —**leading man,** galán; primer actor.

leaf (lif) *n.* [*pl.* **leaves**] hoja. —*v.i.* echar hojas. —*v.t.* [*también,* **leaf through**] hojear. —**leafage,** *n.* follaje. —**leafy,** *adj.* frondoso; con hojas.

leaflet ('lif·lət) *n.* volante; folleto.

league (liːg) *n.* **1,** (alliance) liga. **2,** (distance) legua. —*v.t. & i.* ligar(se); unir(se).

leak (lik) *n.* gotera; escape; *naut.* vía de agua. —*v.i.* gotear;

escaparse; rezumar; (*esp. of news*) trascender; *naut.* hacer agua. —*v.t.* divulgar. —**leakage,** *n.* goteo; escape; *comm.* merma. —**leaky,** *adj.* con goteras o escapes; llovedizo; *naut.* que hace agua.

lean (liːn) *v.i.* **1,** (incline) inclinarse. **2,** (rest on) descansar; apoyarse. —*v.t.* apoyar. —*n.* **1,** (inclination) inclinación. **2,** (lean part of meat) molla. —*adj.* **1,** (thin) flaco; magro. **2,** (scanty) pobre. **3,** (not fatty, as meat) magro. —**leaning,** *adj.* inclinado. —*n.* inclinación; tendencia. —**lean over backward,** exagerar la imparcialidad; esmerarse hasta la exageración.

leanness ('lin·nəs) *n.* **1,** (thinness) magrez; flacura. **2,** (scarcity) pobreza.

lean-to ('lin,tu) *n.* [*pl.* **-tos**] colgadizo.

leap (lip) *v.i.* brincar; saltar. —*v.t.* saltar. —*n.* salto. —**leap year,** año bisiesto.

leapfrog ('lip,frɔg) *n.* la una la mula.

learn (lʌrn) *v.t.* & *i.* **1,** (acquire knowledge [of] or skill [in]) aprender. **2,** (become aware [of]) saber; enterarse (de). —**learned** ('lʌr·nɪd) *adj.* erudito. —**learner,** *n.* principiante; estudiante; aprendiz.

learning ('lʌr·nɪŋ) *n.* **1,** (acquiring knowledge or skill) estudios; el aprender. **2,** (erudition) erudición.

lease (lis) *v.t.* arrendar. —*n.* arrendamiento; arriendo. —**take (o get) a new lease on life,** volver a vivir.

leasehold ('lis·hold) *n.* arrendamiento; arriendo.

leash (liʃ) *n.* traílla. —*v.t.* sujetar con traílla.

least (list) *adj.* menor; mínimo. —*adv.* menos. —*n.* (lo) menos; (el) menor. —**at least,** al menos; por lo menos. —**not in the least,** de ningún modo; de ninguna manera.

leather ('lɛð·ər) *n.* cuero; piel. —*v.t.* forrar con cuero. —*adj.* [*también,* **leathern** (-ərn)] de cuero. —**leatherette** (-ɛt) *n.* cuero artificial; imitación cuero. —**leathery,** *adj.* como cuero.

leave (liːv) *v.t.* [*pret.* & *p.p.* **left**] dejar. —*v.i.* irse; marcharse; salir. —*n.* permiso; licencia. —**leave off,** dejar (de); dejarse de. —**take leave,** despedirse.

leaven ('lɛv·ən) *n.* **1,** (dough)

levadura. **2,** (stimulating influence) fermento. —*v.t.* fermentar. —**leavening,** *n.* fermento; levadura.

leaves (liːvz) *n., pl. de* **leaf.**

leave-taking *n.* despedida.

leavings ('li·vɪŋz) *n.pl.* restos; residuos.

lecher ('lɛtʃ·ər) *n.* libertino. —**lecherous,** *adj.* lascivo; lujurioso. —**lechery,** *n.* lascivia; lujuria.

lecithin ('lɛs·ə·θɪn) *n.* lecitina.

lectern ('lɛk·tərn) *n.* atril.

lecture ('lɛk·tʃər) *n.* **1,** (discourse) conferencia; disertación. **2,** (reprimand) lección; reprensión. —*v.t.* & *i.* **1,** (teach; instruct) dar una conferencia; explicar. **2,** (scold) dar una lección; amonestar. —**lecturer,** *n.* conferenciante.

led (lɛd) *v., pret.* & *p.p. de* **lead.**

ledge (lɛdʒ) *n.* repisa; borde.

ledger ('lɛdʒ·ər) *n.* libro mayor. —**ledger line,** línea suplementaria del pentagrama.

lee (liː) *n.* **1,** (shelter) abrigo; socaire. **2,** *naut.* sotavento. —*adj.* de sotavento.

leech (litʃ) *n.* sanguijuela.

leek (lik) *n.* puerro.

leer (lɪr) *v.i.* mirar de reojo. —*n.* mirada de reojo. —**leery,** *adj., slang* suspicaz.

lees (liz) *n.pl.* poso; heces.

leeward ('li·wərd) *n.* sotavento. —*adj.* de sotavento. —*adv.* a sotavento.

leeway ('li,wei) *n.* **1,** *naut.* deriva. **2,** *fig.* (margin) margen; espacio.

left (lɛft) *v., pret.* & *p.p. de* **leave.** —*adj.* izquierdo. —*n.* izquierda.

lefthand ('lɛft·hænd) *adj.* izquierdo; de o a la izquierda.

lefthanded ('lɛft,hæn·dɪd) *adj.* **1,** (preferring the left hand) zurdo. **2,** (done with the left hand) con la zurda o izquierda. **3,** (toward the left) a la izquierda. **4,** *colloq.* (insincere) insincero; malicioso. —*adv.* con la zurda o izquierda.

leftist ('lɛf·tɪst) *adj.* & *n.* izquierdista.

leftover ('lɛft,o·vər) *adj.* & *n.* sobrante; residuo. —**leftovers,** *n.pl.* sobras; restos; residuos.

leftwing ('lɛft·wɪŋ) *adj.* izquierdista.

leg (lɛg) *n.* **1,** (limb) pierna; (*esp. of animals*) pata. **2,** (furniture support) pata. **3,** (part of a garment) pernera; pierna. **4,** *geom.* cateto. **5,** (stage, as of a journey or course) etapa.

—**have not a leg to stand on**, no tener fundamento. —**leg it**, *colloq.* andar; caminar. —**on one's last legs**, en las últimas. —**pull one's leg**, tomar el pelo a. —**shake a leg**, darse prisa; *Amer.* apurarse.

legacy ('lɛg·ə·si) *n.* legado; herencia.

legal ('li·gəl) *adj.* legal. —**legalize**, *v.t.* legalizar. —**legal tender**, moneda de curso legal.

legality (lɪ'gæl·ə·ti) *n.* legalidad.

legate ('lɛg·ət) *n.* legado. —**legateship**, *n.* legacía.

legatee (lɛg·ə·ti) *n.* legatario.

legation (lɪ'gei·ʃən) *n.* legación.

legato (lɪ'ga·to) *adj.* & *adv.* ligado.

legend ('lɛdʒ·ənd) *n.* leyenda. —**legendary**, *adj.* legendario.

legerdemain (ˌlɛdʒ·ər·də'mein) *n.* prestidigitación; juego de manos.

leggings ('lɛg·ɪŋz) *n.pl.* polainas.

leggy ('lɛg·i) *adj.* **1**, (long-legged) zanquilargo. **2**, (having shapely legs) de piernas torneadas.

legible ('lɛdʒ·ə·bəl) *adj.* legible. —**legibility**, *n.* legibilidad.

legion ('li·dʒən) *n.* legión. —**legionary**, *adj.* legionario.

legionnaire (ˌli·dʒə'neɪr) *n.* legionario.

legislate ('lɛdʒ·ɪs·leit) *v.t.* & *i.* legislar; decretar. —**legislation**, *n.* legislación. —**legislative**, *adj.* legislativo. —**legislator**, *n.* legislador.

legislature ('lɛdʒ·ɪs·lei·tʃər) *n.* cuerpo legislativo; legislatura.

legitimate (lə'dʒɪt·ɪ·mət) *adj.* legítimo. —*v.t.* (-ˌmeit) legitimar. —**legitimacy**, *n.* legitimidad. —**legitimation**, *n.* legitimación.

legitimize (lə'dʒɪt·ə·maiz) *v.t.* [*también*, **legitimatize** (-məˌtaiz)] legitimar. —**legitimization** (-mə·'zei·ʃən) *n.* legitimación.

legume ('lɛg·jum) *n.* legumbre. —**leguminous** (lɛ'gju·mɪ·nəs) *adj.* leguminoso.

leisure ('li·ʒər; 'lɛʒ·ər) *n.* tiempo libre; ocio. —*adj.* libre; ocioso; desocupado. —**at leisure**, **1**, (free; not busy) libre; desocupado. **2**, (without hurry) sin prisa o apuro; descansadamente. —**at one's leisure**, a su conveniencia.

leisurely ('li·ʒər·li) *adj.* reposado; pausado; tranquilo. —*adv.* reposadamente; despacio.

lemming ('lɛm·ɪŋ) *n.* conejo de Noruega.

lemon ('lɛm·ən) *n.* **1**, (fruit) limón. **2**, (tree) limonero. **3**, *slang* (failure) clavo. **4**, *slang* (defective article) maula. —*adj.* **1**, (color) limón. **2**, (made of or with lemon) de limón. —**lemonade** (-'eid) *n.* limonada.

lemur ('li·mər) *n.* lémur.

lend (lɛnd) *v.t.* [*pret.* & *p.p.* **lent**] **1**, (let have, as for use) prestar; hacer un préstamo o empréstito de. **2**, (give; impart) dar; impartir. —*v.i.* prestar; hacer préstamos o empréstitos. —**lend a hand (to)**, ayudar; echar una mano. —**lend oneself** (o **itself**), prestarse.

lender ('lɛn·dər) *n.* prestador; quien presta.

length (lɛŋθ) *n.* **1**, (dimension) largo; longitud; extensión. **2**, (duration) espacio; tiempo. **3**, (distance ahead, as in a horse race) cuerpo. **4**, (extreme) extremo; punto. —**at length**, **1**, (finally) por fin; finalmente. **2**, (in detail) con gran detalle; por completo. —**keep at arm's length**, mantener a distancia.

lengthen ('lɛŋ·θən) *v.t.* alargar; extender; prolongar. —*v.i.* alargarse; extenderse; prolongarse.

lengthwise ('lɛŋθˌwaiz) *adj.* longitudinal. —*adv.* longitudinalmente; a lo largo; a la larga.

lengthy ('lɛŋ·θi) *adj.* muy largo. —**lengthiness**, *n.* lo largo.

lenient ('li·ni·ənt) *adj.* blando; indulgente. —**leniency**; **lenity** ('lɛn·ə·ti) *n.* lenidad.

lens (lɛnz) *n.* **1**, (glass) lente. **2**, *anat.* cristalino.

Lent (lɛnt) *n.* cuaresma. —**Lenten** ('lɛn·tən) *adj.* de cuaresma.

lent (lɛnt) *v.*, *pret.* & *p.p.* de **lend**.

lenticular (lɛn'tɪk·jə·lər) *adj.* lenticular.

lentil ('lɛn·təl) *n.* lenteja.

lento ('lɛn·to) *adj.* & *adv.* lento.

Leo ('li·o) *n.*, *astron.* Leo.

leonine ('li·ə·nain) *adj.* leonino.

leopard ('lɛp·ərd) *n.* leopardo.

leotard ('li·ə·tard) *n.* leotardo.

leper ('lɛp·ər) *n.* leproso. —**leprosy** (-rə·si) *n.* lepra. —**leprous** (-rəs) *adj.* leproso.

leporine ('lɛp·əˌrain) *adj.* lebruno; leporino.

leprechaun ('lɛp·rəˌkɔn) *n.* duende; gnomo (*esp. de Irlanda*).

Lesbian ('lɛz·bi·ən) *n.* & *adj.* **1**, (of Lesbos) lesbiano. **2**, *l.c.* (homosexual woman) lesbia.

lese majesty (liz) lesa majestad.

lesion ('li·ʒən) *n.* lesión.
less (lɛs) *adv., prep. & n.* menos.
—*adj.* [**lesser, least**] menor.
lessee (lɛ'siː) *n.* arrendatario.
lessen ('lɛs·ən) *v.t. & i.* disminuir.
lesser ('lɛs·ər) *adj.* menor.
lesson ('lɛs·ən) *n.* lección.
lessor ('lɛs·ɔr) *n.* arrendador.
lest (lɛst) *conj.* **1,** (that ... not; so
that ... not) para que no; no sea
que. **2,** (for fear that) de o por
miedo que. **3,** *tras expresiones de
temor, duda, peligro, etc.* (that) que:
I fear lest he is lost, Temo que se
haya perdido.
let (lɛt) *v.t.* [**let, letting**] **1,** (leave)
dejar. **2,** (rent; lease) alquilar;
arrendar. **3,** (assign) asignar. **4,**
(draw, as blood) sangrar; sacar. **5,**
(allow; permit) permitir; dejar.
—*v.i.* alquilarse; arrendarse.
—*v.aux., úsase en las exhorta-
ciones; se expresa en el español
con el subjuntivo: let us drink,* be-
bamos; *let him come in,* que entre.
—*n., usu. en* **without let or hindrance,** sin estorbo ni embarazo.
—**let alone, 1,** [*también,* **let be**]
(not interfere with) dejar tranquilo;
dejar en paz; no molestar. **2,** (not to
mention; much less) para qué decir;
aún menos. —**let by,** dejar pasar.
—**let down, 1,** (lower) bajar. **2,**
(slacken; relax) no pujar tanto;
andar más despacio. **3,** (disappoint)
desilusionar; decepcionar. —**let go,**
soltar; aflojar; dejar escapar. —**let
in,** dejar entrar. —**let in for,** exponer; comprometer. —**let loose,**
soltar. —**let know,** advertir; enterar;
hacer saber. —**let off, 1,** (emit)
lanzar; soltar. **2,** (release) dejar
salir; soltar. **3,** (deal leniently with)
soltar; dejar escapar; perdonar.
—**let on,** *colloq.* **1,** (pretend) fingir.
2, (give to understand) dar a entender. **3,** (divulge) dar a conocer; divulgar. —**let oneself go,** dejarse ir;
abandonarse. —**let out, 1,** (release)
soltar. **2,** (rent out) alquilar; arrendar. —**let up, 1,** (slacken; relax)
cejar; dejar de pujar. **2,** (cease)
cesar; desistir. —**let well** (o **bad**)
enough alone, más vale no menea-
allo (= menearlo).
letdown ('lɛt·daun) *n.* **1,** (decrease
in tension) relajamiento. **2,** *colloq.*
(disappointment) desilusión;
decepción.
lethal ('li·θəl) *adj.* letal.
lethargy ('lɛθ·ər·dʒi) *n.* letargo.

—**lethargic** (lə'θar·dʒɪk) *adj.*
letárgico.
letter ('lɛt·ər) *n.* **1,** (written character) letra. **2,** (missive) carta. **3,**
print. carácter; letra. **4,** (literal
meaning) letra. **5,** *pl.* (literature)
letras. —*v.t. & i.* **1,** (inscribe)
escribir o inscribir (con letras). **2,**
(mark with letters) poner
inscripción en. —**letter bomb,** carta
explosiva. —**letter carrier,** cartero.
—**letter of credit,** letra; carta de
crédito. —**letter of exchange,** letra
de cambio. —**letter box,** buzón.
—**to the letter,** al pie de la letra.
lettered ('lɛt·ərd) *adj.* **1,** (literate)
que sabe leer y escribir. **2,** (learned)
instruido; letrado. **3,** (marked with
letters) rotulado; marcado con
letras.
letterhead ('lɛt·ər·hɛd) *n.* membrete.
lettering ('lɛt·ər·ɪŋ) *n.* inscripción; letras.
letter-perfect *adj.* exacto; correcto; al pie de la letra.
letterpress ('lɛt·ər‚prɛs) *n.*
imprenta tipográfica. —*adj.* tipográfico.
lettuce ('lɛt·əs) *n.* lechuga.
letup ('lɛt·ʌp) *n., colloq.* descanso;
pausa.
leucocyte ('lu·kə‚sait) *n.* leucocito.
leukemia (lu'ki·mi·ə) *n.* leucemia.
Levant (lɪ'vænt) *n.* levante.
—**Levantine** (lɪ'væn·tɪn; -tain;
'lɛv·ən·tin; -tain) *adj. & n.* levantino.
levee ('lɛv·i) *n.* **1,** (dike) ribero. **2,**
(reception) recepción.
level ('lɛv·əl) *adj.* **1,** (flat; even)
llano; plano; raso; igual. **2,** (not
sloping) nivelado. **3,** (even; on the
same plane) a nivel; igual; nivelado.
—*n.* nivel. —*adv.* al mismo nivel; a
la par. —*v.t.* **1,** (make level or even)
nivelar. **2,** (knock down; raze)
arrasar. **3,** (direct; aim) dirigir;
apuntar. —*v.i.* **1,** (become level)
nivelarse. **2,** (take aim) apuntar. **3,**
colloq. (be candid) ser franco;
abrirse. —**levelness,** *n.* igualdad.
levelheaded ('lɛv·əl‚hɛd·ɪd) *adj.*
juicioso; sensato.
lever ('lɛv·ər) *n.* palanca.
leverage ('lɛv·ər·ɪdʒ) *n.* **1,** (action
of a lever) acción de palanca. **2,**
(mechanical advantage) brazo de
palanca. **3,** (influence) palanca.
leviathan (lɪ'vai·ə·θən) *n.* leviatán.

Levi's ('li·vaiz) *n.pl., T.N.* overoles; pantalones de trabajo; jeans.

levitate ('lɛv·ə‚teit) *v.t.* suspender en el aire. —*v.i.* flotar en el aire. —**levitation,** *n.* levitación.

Levite ('li·vait) *n.* levita. —**Levitical** (lɪ'vɪt·ə·kəl) *adj.* levítico.

levity ('lɛv·ə·ti) *n.* frivolidad; ligereza.

levy ('lɛv·i) *n.* 1, (assessment; collection) recaudación. 2, (conscription) leva; recluta. 3, *law* embargo. —*v.t.* 1, (assess; collect) recaudar. 2, (conscript) reclutar; enganchar. 3, (demand; exact) exigir. 4, *law* embargar; poner embargo sobre.

lewd (luːd) *adj.* indecente; lascivo; lujurioso. —**lewdness,** *n.* lujuria; lascivia.

lexicography (‚lɛk·sɪ'kag·rə·fi) *n.* lexicografía. —**lexicographer,** *n.* lexicógrafo. —**lexicographic** (-ko'græf·ɪk) *adj.* lexicográfico.

lexicon ('lɛk·sɪ·kən) *n.* léxico. —**lexical,** *adj.* léxico.

liability (‚lai·ə'bɪl·ə·ti) *n.* 1, (responsibility) responsabilidad. 2, (risk) riesgo. 3, *usu.pl.* (debts; obligations) deudas; obligaciones; debe. 4, (disadvantage) desventaja; tara.

liable ('lai·ə·bəl) *adj.* 1, (responsible) responsable. 2, (susceptible) susceptible; propenso. 3, (vulnerable; exposed) expuesto; sujeto. 4, *colloq.* (likely) capaz (de).

liaison ('li·ə‚zan) *n.* 1, (intercommunication) enlace. 2, (link) lazo; relación; vínculo. 3, *colloq.* (love affair) amorío; lío.

liar ('lai·ər) *n.* mentiroso; embustero.

libation (lai'bei·ʃən) *n.* libación.

lib (lɪb) *n., slang* liberación. —**libber** ('lɪb·ər) *n., slang* persona, esp. mujer, que fomenta la liberación social y económica.

libel ('lai·bəl) *n.* libelo; difamación; calumnia. —*v.t.* difamar; calumniar. —**libeler,** *n.* libelista; difamador; calumniador. —**libelous,** *adj.* difamatorio.

liberal ('lɪb·ə·rəl) *adj.* 1, (generous) liberal; generoso. 2, *polit.* liberal. —*n., polit.* liberal. —**liberalism,** *n.* liberalismo. —**liberal arts,** artes liberales; humanidades.

liberality (‚lɪb·ə'ræl·ə·ti) *n.* liberalidad.

liberalize ('lɪb·ər·ə‚laiz) *v.t.* liberalizar. —**liberalization** (-lɪ'zei·ʃən) *n.* liberalización.

liberate ('lɪb·ə‚reit) *v.t.* libertar; liberar. —**liberation,** *n.* liberación. —**liberator,** *n.* libertador.

libertarian (‚lɪb·ər'tɛːr·i·ən) *adj.* & *n.* libertario.

libertine ('lɪb·ər‚tin) *n.* & *adj.* libertino.

liberty ('lɪb·ər·ti) *n.* libertad. —**at liberty,** en libertad; libre; desocupado.

libido (lɪ'bi·do) *n.* libido. —**libidinous** (lɪ'bɪd·ə·nəs) *adj.* libidinoso.

Libra ('lai·brə) *n., astron.* Libra.

library ('lai‚brɛr·i) *n.* biblioteca. —**librarian** (lai'brɛr·i·ən) *n.* bibliotecario.

libretto (lɪ'brɛt·o) *n.* libreto. —**librettist,** *n.* libretista.

lice (lais) *n., pl. de* **louse.**

license ('lai·səns) *n.* licencia. —*v.t.* licenciar; dar licencia. —**licensee** (-sən'siː) *n.* concesionario. —**licenser,** *n.* persona u organismo que expide licencias.

licentiate (lai'sɛn·ʃi‚eit) *n.* 1, (person) licenciado. 2, (degree) licenciatura.

licentious (lɪ'sɛn·ʃəs) *adj.* licencioso. —**licentiousness,** *n.* libertinaje; licencia.

lichen ('lai·kən) *n.* liquen.

licit ('lɪs·ɪt) *adj.* lícito.

lick (lɪk) *v.t.* 1, (lap) lamer. 2, *colloq.* (whip; thrash) dar una zurra; dar una tunda. 3, *colloq.* (overcome) vencer; derrotar. —*n.* 1, (stroke with the tongue) lamedura; lengüetada; lengüetazo. 2, *colloq.* (blow) golpe. 3, (salt deposit) salobral; saladar. 4, (small quantity) pizca. 5, *colloq.* (gait) paso; marcha. —**give a lick and a promise,** hacer mal y pronto.

lickety-split ('lɪk·ə·ti'splɪt) *adv., colloq.* a todo correr; a toda marcha.

licorice ('lɪk·ə·rɪs) *n.* regaliz.

lid (lɪd) *n.* 1, (cover) tapa. 2, (eyelid) párpado. 3, *slang* (hat) sombrero. 4, *fig., colloq.* (curb; restraint) freno.

lie (lai) *v.i.* [**lay, lain, lying**] 1, (recline; rest) estar echado; descansar. 2, [también, **lie down**] (put oneself in a reclining position) echarse; acostarse; tenderse. 3, (be; remain) estar. 4, (be situated) estar; estar situado; hallarse; encontrarse. 5, (extend; stretch) extenderse. 6, (be buried) descansar; yacer. 7, [**lied, lying**] (make false statements; deceive) mentir. —*n.* **1,** (disposition; arrangement) disposición; situación; posición. **2,** (deception) mentira. —**give the lie to, 1,** (deny; belie) dar el mentís a. **2,** (accuse of lying) acusar de mentiroso. —**lie down on the job,** *colloq.* flojear; remolonear. —**lie in,** estar de parto. —**lie in wait (for),** acechar. —**lie over,** aplazarse; demorarse; quedar en suspenso. —**lie to,** *naut.* ponerse al pairo. —**take lying down,** *colloq.* aceptar o someterse sin protestar.

liege (lï:з) *adj.* & *n.* vasallo.

lien (lï:n) *n.* gravamen; obligación.

lieu (lu:) *n.* lugar. —**in lieu of,** en lugar de; en vez de.

lieutenant (lu'tɛn·ənt) *n.* **1,** (deputy) lugarteniente. **2,** (military officer) teniente. —**lieutenancy,** *n.* tenencia. —**lieutenant colonel,** teniente coronel. —**lieutenant commander,** capitán de corbeta. —**lieutenant general,** teniente general. —**lieutenant governor,** vicegobernador.

life (laif) *n.* [*pl.* **lives**] vida. —**lifeless,** *adj.* sin vida; muerto. —**lifelessness,** *n.* falta de vida; muerte.

lifeboat ('laif,bot) *n.* lancha o bote salvavidas.

life buoy boya salvavidas.

life expectancy *n.* expectación de vida.

lifeguard ('laif·gard) *n.* guardia de piscina.

life insurance seguro sobre la vida.

lifelike ('laif,laik) *adj.* natural; real.

lifeline ('laif·lain) *n.* **1,** (cable or rope) cable o cuerda salvavidas. **2,** *palmistry* línea de la vida. **3,** (vital route) ruta vital; línea vital.

lifelong ('laif·lɔŋ) *adj.* de o para toda la vida.

life net red de bomberos.

life preserver salvavidas.

life-size (de) tamaño natural.

life span duración de vida; vida.

lifestyle ('laif,stail) *n.* nivel de vida; tren de vida.

lifetime ('laif·taim) *n.* **1,** (life span) vida. **2,** *colloq.* (long time) mucho tiempo; eternidad. —*adj.* de toda la vida; de por vida.

lifework ('laif·wʌrk) *n.* obra de toda la vida; obra de una vida; carrera.

lift (lɪft) *v.t.* **1,** (raise) levantar; alzar. **2,** (elevate; exalt) elevar;

exaltar. **3,** *colloq.* (plagiarize) plagiar. **4,** *slang* (steal) robar; alzarse con. —*v.i.* **1,** (rise; go up) levantarse; elevarse. **2,** (be dispelled) disiparse. **3,** (tug upward) tirar hacia arriba. —*n.* **1,** (act of raising) levantamiento; alzamiento. **2,** (elevation) elevación. **3,** (uplift; encouragement) ánimo; aliento. **4,** (lifting force) fuerza de sustentación. **5,** (help) ayuda. **6,** (free ride) viaje gratis o de gorra; *W.I.* pon. **7,** (heel wedge) tapa. **8,** (cargo elevator) montacargas; elevador. **9,** *Brit.* (elevator) ascensor; elevador. —**give (someone) a lift,** llevar; *W.I.* dar pon.

liftoff ('lɪft·ɔf) *n.* despegue.

ligament ('lɪg·ə·mənt) *n.* ligamento.

ligature ('lɪg·ə,tʃur) *n.* **1,** (binding) ligadura. **2,** *mus.* (slur) ligadura; (tie; bind) ligado. **3,** *print.* ligado.

light (lait) *n.* **1,** (illumination or source) luz. **2,** (means of igniting) fuego; candela; lumbre. **3,** *usu.pl.* (understanding) luces. —*adj.* **1,** (having light; bright) bien iluminado; claro. **2,** (pale; not dark) claro; pálido. **3,** (fair; whitish) blanco; claro. **4,** (not heavy) ligero; liviano; leve. **5,** (gay; buoyant) alegre. **6,** (fickle; frivolous) inconstante; ligero. **7,** (morally loose) libre; inmoral; ligero. **8,** (soft; spongy) esponjoso; ligero. **9,** (swift; nimble) ligero; ágil. **10,** (not serious) ligero; poco serio. **11,** (graceful; delicate) delicado; gracioso; fino. —*adv.* = **lightly.** —*v.t.* [*pret.* & *p.p.* **lighted** o **lit**] **1,** (ignite; turn on) encender; prender. **2,** (illuminate) iluminar; dar luz. **3,** [*usu.* **light up**] (animate, brighten) animar; iluminar. **4,** (guide, as by a beacon) mostrar el camino a; guiar. —*v.i.* **1,** (catch fire) prenderse; encenderse. **2,** [*usu.* **light up**] (brighten; be animated) animarse; iluminarse. **3,** (alight) aterrizar; posarse. **4,** [*usu.* **light on** o **upon**] (come upon; find) encontrar; dar con. **5,** (fall; strike suddenly) caer; golpear; dar. —**light in the head, 1,** (dizzy) mareado. **2,** (simple; foolish) tonto; zonzo. —**light into,** *colloq.* arremeter contra; atacar. —**light out,** *slang,* salir corriendo; largarse. —**light up, 1,** (make or become light) iluminar(se). **2,**

(make or become cheerful; brighten) animar(se); iluminar(se). 3, (ignite; set to burning; begin smoking) encender; prender. —**make light of,** tratar con ligereza; no parar muchas mientes en; no dar importancia a.

lighten ('lai·tən) *v.t.* 1, (illuminate; shed light on) aclarar; iluminar. 2, (make paler) aclarar; hacer más pálido. 3, (make less heavy) aligerar. 4, (relieve) aliviar. 5, (gladden) alegrar. —*v.i.* 1, (become light; grow brighter) aclararse; iluminarse. 2, (grow paler) palidecer; aclararse. 3, (flash, as lightning) relampaguear. 4, (become less heavy) aligerarse.

lighter ('lai·tər) *n.* 1, (igniting device) encendedor. 2, (barge) lanchón; barcaza; chalana; gabarra.

lightface ('lait·feis) *n.* letra fina.

light-footed *adj.* ligero de pies; ágil.

light-headed ('lait‚hed·ɪd) *adj.* 1, (dizzy) mareado. 2, (delirious) delirante; desatado. 3, (thoughtless; frivolous) frívolo; tarambana; ligero de cascos.

lighthearted ('lait‚har·tɪd) *adj.* alegre; despreocupado.

light heavyweight *n.* peso semipesado.

lighthouse ('lait·haus) *n.* faro.

lighting ('lai·tɪŋ) *n.* alumbrado; iluminación.

lightly ('lait·li) *adv.* 1, (with little pressure; gently) ligeramente. 2, (to a small degree or amount) poco. 3, (cheerfully) alegremente. 4, (indifferently; frivolously) con despego; con indiferencia.

lightness ('lait·nəs) *n.* 1, (lack of weight; insubstantiality) ligereza. 2, (delicacy) delicadeza; finura. 3, (mildness) suavidad. 4, (cheerfulness) alegría. 5, (nimbleness) agilidad. 6, (brightness) luz; iluminación. 7, (paleness) palidez. 8, (whiteness) blancura.

lightning ('lait·nɪŋ) *n.* rayo; relámpago. —**lightning bug,** luciérnaga. —**lightning rod,** pararrayos.

lightweight ('lait·weit) *n.* peso ligero.

light year año luz.

ligneous ('lɪg·ni·əs) *adj.* leñoso.

lignite ('lɪg·nait) *n.* lignito.

likable ('lai·kə·bəl) *adj.* simpático; agradable.

like (laik) *v.t.* 1, (wish; desire) querer; desear. 2, (have a taste or fondness for) gustarle a uno; placerle a uno. —*v.i.* querer; desear. —*adj.* 1, (similar) similar; parecido; semejante. 2, (characteristic of) propio de; característico de. —*adv., colloq.* 1, (as though) como; igual que. 2, (likely) probablemente; con toda probabilidad. 3, (nearly) como. —*prep.* 1, (similar to; similarly to) como. 2, (in the mood of; desirous of) con ganas de. —*conj., colloq.* 1, (as) tal como; tal cual; como. 2, (as if) como si; como que. —*n.* 1, (something equal) cosa semejante o parecida; cosa o persona igual. 2, *pl.* (preferences) gustos. —**feel like,** tener ganas (de). —**like as not,** con toda probabilidad. —**look like,** 1, (resemble) parecerse a. 2, (seem as if) parecer que.

likely ('laik·li) *adj.* 1, (credible) creíble; verosímil. 2, (probable) probable. 3, (due; apparently destined) supuesto; destinado. 4, (promising) prometedor; que promete. 5, (suitable) apropiado; adecuado. —*adv.* probablemente. —**likelihood,** *n.* probabilidad.

liken ('lai·kən) *v.t.* comparar; asemejar.

likeness ('laik·nəs) *n.* 1, (similarity) similitud; parecido; semejanza. 2, (semblance) figura; apariencia. 3, (copy; image) copia fiel; vivo retrato.

likewise ('laik‚waiz) *adv.* 1, (in the same manner) lo mismo; igualmente; del mismo modo. 2, (too; also) también; asimismo.

liking ('lai·kɪŋ) *n.* 1, (preference; taste) gusto; preferencia; predilección. 2, (fondness) cariño; afecto. —**take a liking to,** inclinarse a; aficionarse a; enamorarse de.

lilac ('lai·lək; -læk) *n.* lila.

lilt (lilt) *n.* ritmo; ritmo alegre.

lily ('lɪl·i) *n.* lirio; azucena. —*adj.* de lirio; de azucena. —**lily-livered,** *adj.* cobarde. —**lily of the valley,** lirio de los valles; muguete. —**lily pad,** hoja de nenúfar. —**water lily,** nenúfar.

Lima bean ('lai·mə) haba de Lima.

limb (lim) *n.* 1, (leg; arm) miembro; extremidad. 2, (branch) rama. 3, (offshoot; outgrowth) vástago; brazo. —**out on a limb,** en situación arriesgada.

limber ('lɪm·bər) *adj.* 1, (flexible)

flexible. **2,** (agile) ágil. —*v.t.* & *i.* poner(se) o hacer(se) flexible o ágil; entonar(se).

limbo ('lɪm·bo) *n.* limbo.

lime (laim) *n.* **1,** (fruit tree) limero. **2,** (fruit) lima; lima agria. **3,** (calcium oxide) cal. **4,** (linden tree) tilo. —*adj.* **1,** (of limes) de lima. **2,** (of quicklime) de cal. —**limeade,** *n.* bebida hecha con agua, azúcar y zumo de lima agria.

limelight ('laim,lait) *n.* luz (de un reflector). —**be in the limelight,** estar en el candelero.

limestone ('laim·ston) *n.* piedra caliza.

limewater ('laim,wɔ·tər) *n.* agua de cal.

limey ('lai·mi) *n., slang, usu. derog.* **1,** marinero británico. **2,** inglés; británico. —*adj.* inglés; británico.

limit ('lɪm·ɪt) *n.* límite. —*v.t.* limitar. —**limitless,** *adj.* sin límites; ilimitado.

limitation (,lɪm·ə'tei·ʃən) *n.* limitación.

limited ('lɪm·ɪt·ɪd) *adj.* limitado. —*n.* tren expreso.

limousine ('lɪm·ə,zin) *n.* automóvil cerrado; limousine; limosina. *También, slang* **limo** ('lɪm·o).

limp (lɪmp) *v.i.* **1,** (walk lamely) cojear. **2,** (move laboriously) avanzar o moverse con dificultad. —*n.* cojera. —*adj.* **1,** (flaccid) fláccido; lacio. **2,** (wilted) mustio; marchito; ajado. **3,** (lacking vigor) flojo; inerte; sin vigor.

limpet ('lɪm·pət) *n.* lapa.

limpid ('lɪm·pɪd) *adj.* límpido. —**limpidity** (lɪm'pɪd·ə·ti); **limpidness,** *n.* limpidez.

limpness ('lɪmp·nəs) *n.* **1,** (lameness) cojera. **2,** (flaccidity) flaccidez; laxitud. **3,** (wilted condition) lo mustio; marchitez. **4,** (lack of vigor) flojedad; inercia; languidez.

limy ('lai·mi) *adj.* **1,** (of or resembling lime) calizo; de cal. **2,** (sticky) pegajoso.

linden ('lɪn·dən) *n.* tilo.

line (lain) *n.* **1,** (cord; rope) cordel; cuerda; *naut.* cabo; *fishing* sedal. **2,** (length of wire) alambre. **3,** (means or agency of communication or transportation) línea. **4,** (pipe; tubing) tubería; cañería. **5,** (thin mark or crease) línea. **6,** (limit; border) línea de demarcación. **7,** (delineation; outline) figura; delineación. **8,**

(path; course) línea. **9,** (occupation) ocupación; profesión. **10,** (stock of goods) renglón; línea. **11,** (specialty) especialidad. **12,** (row; file) línea. **13,** (series; succession) serie; sucesión. **14,** (lineage) línea; linaje. —*v.t.* **1,** (draw lines on or in) trazar líneas sobre o en; linear; regular; rayar. **2,** [*usu.* **line up**] (align) alinear. **3,** (put a lining in) forrar; revestir. **4,** (form a line along; edge) bordear; formar línea a lo largo de. —*v.i.,* [*usu.* **line up**] alinearse; colocarse en fila. —**all along the line, 1,** (throughout) en toda la línea; en todas partes. **2,** (at every turn) a cada paso. —**bring into line, 1,** (align) alinear. **2,** (make conform) hacer conformar; hacer entrar en línea. —**come into line, 1,** (line up) alinearse. **2,** *colloq.* (correspond; agree) concordar; corresponder. **3,** *colloq.* (behave properly) encarrilarse; *Amer.* enrielarse. —**draw the** (o **a**) **line,** poner límite. —**get a line on,** *colloq.* inquirir o indagar sobre. —**hold the line, 1,** (stand firmly) aguantar; mantenerse firme. **2,** (wait; keep the line open) esperar; no cortar; mantener la línea abierta. —**in line, 1,** (in alignment) en línea. **2,** (in harmony) de acuerdo; conforme. **3,** (in readiness) listo; pronto; preparado. —**line up, 1,** (form a line) alinearse. **2,** (organize effectively) organizar; encarrilar. —**on a line,** en línea; alineado; nivelado. —**out of line, 1,** (not aligned) fuera de línea. **2,** (not in agreement) en desacuerdo. **3,** (behaving improperly) en falta; errado; portándose mal. —**stand in line,** hacer cola. —**toe the line,** andar derecho; seguir la norma; ajustarse a la norma.

lineage ('lɪn·i·ɪdʒ) *n.* linaje.

lineal ('lɪn·i·əl) *adj.* **1,** (in direct line of descent) en línea recta; lineal. **2,** (linear) lineal. —**lineally,** *adv.* en línea recta.

lineament ('lɪn·i·ə·mənt) *n.* lineamento; rasgo.

linear ('lɪn·i·ər) *adj.* lineal. —**linear measure,** medida de longitud.

lineman ('lain·mən) *n.* [*pl.* **-men**] **1,** *R.R.* inspector o reparador de vías. **2,** (telephone repairman) reparador de líneas. **3,** *sports* jugador de línea.

linen ('lɪn·ən) *n.* **1,** (yarn or fabric)

lino. **2,** (bedclothes) ropa de cama. **3,** (shirts, underwear, etc.) ropa blanca. **4,** (table coverings) mantelería. —*adj.* de lino. —**linen shop,** lencería.

liner ('lai·nər) *n.* **1,** (ship) transatlántico. **2,** (aircraft) avión comercial. **3,** (drawing instrument) tiralíneas. **4,** (lining) forro.

linesman ('lainz·mən) *n.* [*pl.* -men] **1,** *sports* juez de línea. **2,** = **lineman.**

lineup ('lain‚ʌp) *n.* **1,** (order; array) formación. **2,** (grouping) agrupación; composición. **3,** *sports* formación. **4,** (display of suspects) rueda (de sospechosos).

ling (lɪŋ) *n., ichthy.* abadejo.

linger ('lɪŋ·gər) *v.i.* **1,** (stay on) quedarse; detenerse; demorarse. **2,** [*también*, **linger on**] (continue) durar; persistir. **3,** (delay; loiter) demorarse; remolonear.

lingerie (‚læn·ʒə'riː) *n.* ropa interior femenina.

lingo ('lɪŋ·go) *n., colloq.* lenguaje; jerga.

lingual ('lɪŋ·gwəl) *adj.* lingual.

linguist ('lɪŋ·gwɪst) *n.* lingüista. —**linguistic** (lɪŋ'gwɪs·tɪk) *adj.* lingüístico. —**linguistics,** *n.* lingüística.

liniment ('lɪn·ə·mənt) *n.* linimento.

lining ('lai·nɪŋ) *n.* forro; revestimiento.

link (lɪŋk) *n.* **1,** (part of a chain) eslabón. **2,** (connection; tie) vínculo; lazo. **3,** *mech.* biela; conexión. **4,** (measure) medida de longitud de unos 201 mm. —*v.t.* unir; conectar; acoplar. —*v.i.* unirse; conectarse. —**linkage,** *n.* eslabonamiento; conexión. —**links,** *n.pl.* campo o cancha de golf.

linnet ('lɪn·ɪt) *n.* jilguero; pardillo.

linoleum (lɪ'no·li·əm) *n.* linóleo.

linotype ('lai·nə‚taip) *T.N., n.* **1,** (machine) linotipia. **2,** (plate) linotipo. —**linotypist,** *n.* linotipista.

linseed ('lɪn‚sid) *n.* linaza.

lint (lɪnt) *n.* pelusa; hilachas.

lintel ('lɪn·təl) *n.* dintel.

lion ('lai·ən) *n.* **1,** (animal; person of courage) león. **2,** (celebrity) celebridad. —**lioness,** *n.* leona. —**lionize,** *v.t.* poner por las alturas; agasajar.

lionhearted ('lai·ən‚har·tɪd) *adj.* valiente; bravo.

lip (lɪp) *n.* **1,** *anat.* labio. **2,** (rim) borde. **3,** *slang* (impertinence) insolencia; impertinencia. —**lip service,** sólo palabras. —**lip-read,** *v.t.* & *i.* leer (en) los labios.

lipstick ('lɪp·stɪk) *n.* lápiz para los labios o de labios; lápiz labial.

liquefy ('lɪk·wɪ‚fai) *v.t.* licuar. —*v.i.* licuarse. —**liquefaction** (-'fæk·ʃən) *n.* licuación; licuefacción.

liquescent (lɪ'kwɛs·ənt) *adj.* licuescente. —**liquescence,** *n.* licuescencia.

liqueur (lɪ'kʌr) *n.* licor.

liquid ('lɪk·wɪd) *n.* & *adj.* líquido. —**liquidity** (lɪ'kwɪd·ə·ti) liquidez. —**liquid assets,** valores realizables.

liquidate ('lɪk·wɪ‚deit) *v.t.* & *i.* liquidar. —**liquidation,** *n.* liquidación.

liquor ('lɪk·ər) *n.* licor.

lira ('li·ra) *n.* lira.

lisle (lail) *n.* hilo de Escocia.

lisp (lɪsp) *n.* ceceo. —*v.i.* cecear. —*v.t.* pronunciar ceceando o con ceceo. —**lisper,** *n.* ceceoso. —**lisping,** *adj.* ceceoso. —*n.* ceceo.

lissome ('lɪs·əm) *adj.* esbelto.

list (lɪst) *n.* **1,** (roll; roster) lista. **2,** (slant) inclinación; *naut.* escora. **3,** (selvage) orillo. **4,** (ridge of a furrow) lomo. **5,** *pl.* (jousting arena) liza. —*v.t.* alistar; incluir en una lista; hacer una lista de. —*v.i.* **1,** *naut.* escorar. **2,** *poet.* = **listen. 3,** *archaic* (wish) desear; querer. —**be listed,** figurar o aparecer inscrito. —**list price,** precio alistado o anunciado.

listen ('lɪs·ən) *v.i.* **1,** (attend closely) escuchar. **2,** (pay heed) hacer caso; escuchar. —**listen in,** escuchar a hurtadillas. —**listener,** *n.* oyente.

listing ('lɪs·tɪŋ) *n.* alistamiento; inclusión o aparición en una lista.

listless ('lɪst·ləs) *adj.* sin ánimo; indiferente. —**listlessness,** *n.* falta de ánimo; indiferencia.

lit (lɪt) *v., pret. & p.p. de* **light.**

litany ('lɪt·ə·ni) *n.* letanía.

liter *también,* **litre** ('li·tər) *n.* litro.

literacy ('lɪt·ə·rə·si) *n.* capacidad de leer y escribir.

literal ('lɪt·ər·əl) *adj.* literal. —**literally,** *adv.* al pie de la letra.

literal-minded *adj.* sin imaginación; prosaico.

literary ('lɪt·ə‚rɛr·i) *adj.* literario; de letras; de literatura.

literate ('lɪt·ər·ət) *adj.* **1,** (able to

read and write) capaz de leer y escribir. 2, (learned) literato.

literati (‚lɪt·ə'ra·ti) n.pl. eruditos; literatos.

literature ('lɪt·ər·ə‚tʃur) n. literatura.

lithe (laɪð) adj. 1, (flexible) flexible; cimbreante. 2, (agile) ágil. *También,* **lithesome.** —**litheness,** n. flexibilidad; agilidad.

lithium ('lɪθ·i·əm) n. litio.

lithograph ('lɪθ·ə·græf) n. litografía. —v.t. litografiar. —**lithographic,** adj. litográfico. —**lithography** (lɪ'θag·rə·fi) n. litografía. —**lithographer** (lɪ'θag·rə·fər) n. litógrafo.

lithosphere ('lɪθ·ə·sfɪr) n. litosfera.

litigate ('lɪt·ɪ‚geit) v.t. & i. litigar. —**litigant,** n. & adj. litigante. —**litigation,** n. litigación; litigio.

litigious (lɪ'tɪdʒ·əs) adj. litigioso.

litmus paper ('lɪt·məs) n. papel de tornasol.

litter ('lɪt·ər) n. 1, (animals born at one time) camada; lechigada. 2, (stretcher) camilla. 3, (straw bedding) mullido; cama; lecho. 4, (kind of palanquin) litera. 5, (rubbish) basura; desperdicio. 6, (disorder; disarray) desorden; confusión. —v.t. 1, [*también,* **litter up**] (make untidy) tirar basura en; cubrir de basura; ensuciar. 2, (scatter; throw about) esparcir; tirar. —v.i. parir; dar cría.

little ('lɪt·əl) adj. 1, (small in size) pequeño; chico. 2, (small in amount or degree) poco. 3, (short in duration or distance) corto. 4, (trifling; trivial) nimio; pequeño; trivial. —adv. 1, (not much) poco. 2, (scarcely) apenas; escasamente. —n. poco. —**littleness,** n. pequeñez; lo pequeño. —**little by little,** poco a poco; poquito a poco. —**little finger,** (dedo) meñique. —**make little of,** no dar mayor importancia a; tomar a la ligera. —**not a little,** no poco; bastante; muy; mucho. —**think little of,** 1, (despise) tener a menos; mirar en menos. 2, (have no hesitancy about) no vacilar en.

littoral ('lɪt·ə·rəl) n. & adj. litoral.

liturgy ('lɪt·ər·dʒi) n. liturgia. —**liturgical** (lɪ'tʌr·dʒɪ·kəl) adj. litúrgico.

livable *también,* **liveable** ('lɪv·ə·bəl) adj. 1, (habitable) habi-

table. 2, (endurable) soportable. 3, (pleasant to live with) agradable; amistoso; cordial.

live (lɪv) v.i. & t. vivir. —adj. (laiv) 1, (alive; living) vivo. 2, (alert; wide-awake) alerta; despierto; vivo. 3, (charged, as with explosives, electricity, etc.) cargado. 4, (burning) candente; encendido. 5, (bright; vivid) vivo. 6, (filled with activity) lleno de vida; animado. 7, (fresh; refreshing) fresco. 8, (of immediate interest) de actualidad. 9, *radio; TV* simultáneo. —adv., *radio; TV* simultáneamente. —**live down,** hacer enmiendas por; recobrarse de; borrar. —**live high,** vivir como rey; darse buena vida. —**live out,** durar; pasar de. —**live steam,** vapor a presión. —**live through,** soportar; sobrellevar. —**live up to,** vivir de acuerdo a o con; cumplir con.

livelihood ('laiv·li·hud) n. subsistencia; vida.

livelong ('lɪv‚lɔŋ) adj. todo; entero. —**all the livelong day,** todo el santo día (de Dios).

lively ('laiv·li) adj. vivaz. —adv. vivazmente; vivamente. —**liveliness,** n. vivacidad; vida.

liven ('lai·vən) v.t. animar; avivar. —v.i. animarse; avivarse.

liver ('lɪv·ər) n. hígado. —**liverish,** adj. bilioso.

liverwurst ('lɪv·ər‚wʌrst) n. embutido de hígado.

livery ('lɪv·ə·ri) n. 1, (uniform) librea. 2, (uniformed help) criados de librea. 3, (livery stable) caballeriza. 4, (keeping of vehicles for hire; rental company) alquiler de vehículos; *S.A.* cochería. —**liveried,** adj. de librea; en librea.

lives (laivz) n., *pl. de* **life.**

livestock ('laiv‚stak) n. ganado; animales de cría.

live wire (laiv) 1, *elect.* alambre cargado. 2, *slang* (go-getter) buscavidas.

livid ('lɪv·id) adj. lívido. —**lividness,** n. lividez.

living ('lɪv·ɪŋ) n. vida; subsistencia. —adj. 1, (alive) vivo; viviente. 2, (for the maintenance of life) de subsistencia; para poder vivir. —**living quarters,** habitación; vivienda. —**living room,** sala; salón.

lizard ('lɪz·ərd) n. lagarto.

llama ('la·mə) n. llama.

llano ('la·no) n. [*pl.* **-nos**] llano.

lo (loː) *interj.* ¡he aquí!; ¡he allí!; ¡mira!

load (loːd) *n.* **1,** (charge; burden) carga. **2,** *slang* (drunk) borrachera. —*v.t. & i.* cargar. —**loaded,** *adj. slang* borracho. —**get a load of,** *slang* mirar; escuchar.

loadstar ('lod·star) *n.* = **lodestar.**

loadstone ('lod·ston) *n.* = **lodestone.**

loaf (lof) *n.* [*pl.* **loaves**] pan; bollo. —*v.i.* haraganear; holgazanear.

loafer ('lo·fər) *n.* **1,** (idler) holgazán. **2,** (casual shoe) zapato de sport.

loam (loːm) *n.* **1,** (soil) marga. **2,** (material for making molds) tierra de moldeo. —**loamy,** *adj.* margoso.

loan (loːn) *n.* préstamo; empréstito. —*v.t.* prestar; hacer un préstamo o empréstito (de). —**loan shark,** *colloq.* usurero; *Amer.* garrotero.

loath (loθ) *adj.* poco dispuesto; desinclinado.

loathe (loːð) *v.t.* odiar; detestar; aborrecer. —**loathing,** *n.* aversión; repugnancia; aborrecimiento. —**loathsome,** *adj.* repugnante; aborrecible. —**loathsomeness,** *n.* repugnancia; aborrecimiento.

loaves (loːvz) *n.*, *pl. de* **loaf.**

lob (laːb) *v.t.* volear; arrojar al voleo. —*n.* voleo.

lobby ('lab·i) *n.* **1,** (building entrance) vestíbulo; sala de entrada. **2,** (political pressure group) cabilderos. —*v.i.* cabildear. —**lobbying,** *n.* cabildeo. —**lobbyist,** *n.* cabildero.

lobe (loːb) *n.* lóbulo.

lobotomy (lə'bat·ə·mi) *n.* lobotomía.

lobster ('lab·stər) *n.* langosta.

lobule ('lab·jul) *n.* lóbulo.

local ('lo·kəl) *adj.* local. —*n.* **1,** (train, bus, etc.) tren ómnibus; tren, autobús, etc., que hace todas las paradas. **2,** (chapter; branch) junta u organización local.

locale (lo'kæl) *n.* local; sitio.

locality (lo'kæl·ə·ti) *n.* localidad.

localize ('lo·kə,laiz) *v.t.* localizar. —**localization** (-lɪ'zei·ʃən) *n.* localización.

locate ('lo·keit; lo'keit) *v.t.* **1,** (situate) situar; localizar; *Amer.* ubicar. **2,** (find; discover) localizar; encontrar. **3,** (assign; place) asignar; poner; colocar.

location (lo'kei·ʃən) *n.* **1,** (act of locating) emplazamiento; colocación; localización. **2,** (position; situation) ubicación; situación; posición. **3,** (site) sitio.

loci ('lo·sai) *n.*, *pl. de* **locus.**

lock (lak) *n.* **1,** (device for closing) cerradura. **2,** (bolt) cerrojo. **3,** (safety lock) seguro. **4,** (padlock) candado. **5,** (barring or stopping device) traba. **6,** (sluice; canal lock) esclusa. **7,** (curl of hair) bucle; rizo; mechón. **8,** (wrestling hold) llave. **9,** (a locking together) trabazón; enganche. —*v.t.* **1,** (secure with a key) cerrar con llave; echar llave a. **2,** [*también,* **lock up**] (close) cerrar. **3,** [*usu.* **lock up**] (put in safekeeping) guardar bajo llave. **4,** (shut in) encerrar. **5,** [*usu.* **lock up**] (jail) encarcelar. **6,** (grip; embrace) aprisionar; encerrar. **7,** *en* **lock out** (shut out) dejar afuera; cerrar la puerta a; dejar en la calle. **8,** (join or link together) enganchar; unir. **9,** (bar or stop from moving) trabar. **10,** (jam) trabar; atrancar. —*v.i.* **1,** (become locked) cerrarse. **2,** (become fixed) clavarse; trancarse; trabarse. —**lock on,** fijarse en; centrarse en. —**lock, stock and barrel,** entero; todo. —**under lock and key,** bajo llave.

locker ('lak·ər) *n.* **1,** (closet) ropero; armario. **2,** (filing cabinet) casillero; clasificador. **3,** (compartment with a lock) compartimento con llave; casillero; casilla. **4,** (drawer) gaveta; cajón.

locket ('lak·ɪt) *n.* relicario; medallón.

lockjaw ('lak·dʒɔ) *n.* tétano.

lockout ('lak·aut) *n.* paro.

locksmith ('lak·smɪθ) *n.* cerrajero.

lockup ('lak·ʌp) *n.*, *colloq.* cárcel; calabozo.

loco ('lo·ko) *adj.*, *slang* loco.

locomotion (,lo·kə'mo·ʃən) *n.* locomoción.

locomotive (,lo·kə'mo·tɪv) *adj.* locomotor. —*n.* locomotora.

locomotor (,lo·kə'mo·tər) *adj.* locomotor; locomotriz. —**locomotor ataxia,** (ə'tæk·si·ə) ataxia locomotriz.

locus ('lo·kəs) *n.* [*pl.* **loci**] lugar; *geom.* lugar geométrico.

locust ('lo·kəst) *n.* **1,** *entom.* langosta; *U.S.* cicada. **2,** *bot.* acacia falsa.

locution (lo'kju·ʃən) *n.* locución.

lode (loːd) *n.* veta; filón.

lodestar ('lod,star) *n.* estrella (de guía); *fig.* norte.

lodestone ('lod,ston) *n.* piedra imán.

lodge (ladʒ) *n.* **1,** (gatehouse; porter's lodge) garita; portería. **2,** (small adjoining house) casita; pabellón. **3,** (country or summer cottage) casa de campo; casa de veraneo; chalet. **4,** (cabin; hut) cabaña. **5,** (boarding house) casa de huéspedes; pensión. **6,** (fraternal society) logia. —*v.t.* **1,** (provide lodging for) alojar; hospedar. **2,** (deposit, as for safekeeping) depositar; confiar. **3,** (place; insert) alojar; meter. **4,** (present formally) presentar formalmente. —*v.i.* **1,** (have lodging) alojarse; hospedarse; aposentarse. **2,** (be or remain fixed) alojarse. —**lodger,** *n.* huésped.

lodging ('ladʒ·ɪŋ) *n.* [*también pl.* **lodgings**] alojamiento; habitación.

loft (lɔft) *n.* **1,** (attic) desván; mansarda. **2,** (hayloft) pajar. **3,** (floor space in a warehouse or factory) piso; local. **4,** (lifting stroke) tiro por lo alto. —*v.t.* tirar por lo alto. —*v.i.* elevarse; remontarse.

lofty ('lɔf·ti) *adj.* alto; elevado. —**loftiness,** *n.* altura; elevación.

log (lɔg) *n.* **1,** (piece of timber) tronco; madero; leño. **2,** (record) anotación; crónica; registro; *naut.* diario de navegación; cuaderno de bitácora. **3** = **logarithm.** —*v.t.* [**logged logging**] **1,** (cut into logs) aserrar; serrar. **2,** (record) hacer crónica de; registrar; anotar. —*v.i.* serrar y transportar maderos. —**logger,** *n.* cortador de árboles; maderero; leñador. —**logging,** *n.* extracción de maderas.

logarithm ('lag·ə·rɪð·əm) *n.* logaritmo. —**logarithmic** (-'rɪð·mɪk) *adj.* logarítmico.

loge (loʒ) *n.* palco.

loggerhead ('lɔg·ər,hɛd) *n.* zopenco; mentecato. —**at loggerheads,** en riña; en disputa.

loggia ('ladʒ·ə) *n.* logia; galería.

logic ('ladʒ·ɪk) *n.* lógica. —**logical,** *adj.* lógico.

logician (lo'dʒɪʃ·ən) *n.* lógico.

logistics (lo'dʒɪs·tɪks) *n.* logística. —**logistic; logistical,** *adj.* logístico.

logjam ('lɔg·dʒæm) *n.* atasco de troncos apretados por la corriente.

logotype ('lo·gə·taip) *n.*, *print.* logotipo. Also, **logo** ('loɪ·go).

logy ('lo·gi) *adj.* lerdo; torpe; pesado.

loin (lɔin) *n.* lomo. —**loins,** *n.pl.* riñones.

loincloth ('lɔin·klɔθ) *n.* taparrabos.

loiter ('lɔi·tər) *v.i.* **1,** (linger idly) holgazanear; perder el tiempo. **2,** (dally) remolonear.

loiterer ('lɔi·tər·ər) *n.* holgazán; remolón; vago.

loitering ('lɔi·tər·ɪŋ) *n.* holgazanería; remoloneo; vagancia. —*adj.* holgazán; remolón; vago.

loll (lal) *v.i.* **1,** (recline; lounge) arrellanarse; tenderse; recostarse. **2,** (hang; droop) caer; pender; colgar. —*v.t.* dejar caer o colgar.

lollipop ('lal·i,pap) *n.* pirulí; *Amer.* chupete.

lone (lon) *adj.* **1,** (solitary) solitario; solo. **2,** (single; unwed) soltero.

lonely ('lon·li) *adj.* **1,** (isolated) solitario; aislado. **2,** [*también,* **lonesome**] (alone) solo; solitario. —**loneliness; lonesomeness,** *n.* soledad.

loner ('lo·nər) *n.*, *colloq.* solitario.

long (lɔŋ) *adj.* **1,** (of great extent) largo. **2,** (of a specified length) de largo. **3,** (far-reaching) amplio; extenso. **4,** (large; big) grande. **5,** (tall) largo; alto. **6,** *en* **long on,** *in o* **of,** (well provided with) que tiene mucho ...; de mucho ...; luengo en.... —*adv.* **1,** (for a long time) mucho; mucho tiempo; en o por mucho tiempo. **2,** (for the duration of) todo el ...; en todo el ...: *all day long,* (en) todo el día. —*n.* largo; longitud. —*v.i.* ansiar; desear; anhelar. —**as** (*o* **so**) **long as, 1,** (since) puesto que; ya que. **2,** (provided that) con tal que; siempre que. **3,** (while) mientras. —**be long,** tardar mucho. —**before long,** pronto. —**how long,** cuánto tiempo; cuánto. —**long ago,** hace mucho (tiempo). —**long for,** morirse por. —**long shot,** contendiente que tiene poca probabilidad de ganar. —**long since,** mucho antes. —**the long and the short of** (it), en dos palabras.

longboat ('lɔŋ·bot) *n.* chalupa; lancha.

long-distance *adj.* de larga distancia; interurbano.

long-drawn *adj.* prolongado; largo.

longevity (lɔn'dʒɛv·ə·ti) *n.* longevidad.

longhair ('lɔŋ·her) *n., colloq.* bohemio; hippie; músico.

longhand ('lɔŋ·hænd) *n.* escritura a mano.

longing ('lɔŋ·ɪŋ) *n.* anhelo; ansia. —**longingly,** *adv.* con anhelo; con ansia.

longitude ('lɔn·dʒə,tjud) *n.* longitud. —**longitudinal** (-'tju·dɪ·nəl) *adj.* longitudinal.

long-lived ('lɔŋ'laivd) *adj.* longevo.

long-range *adj.* de largo alcance.

longshoreman ('lɔŋ,ʃor·mən) *n.* [*pl.* **-men**] estibador; cargador de muelle.

long ton tonelada grande (*2,240 libras*).

longwinded ('lɔŋ,wɪn·dɪd) *adj.* palabrero. —**longwindedness,** *n.* palabrería.

look (luk) *v.i.* **1,** [*usu. en* **look at** *o* **upon**] (see; behold) mirar; ver. **2,** (search) buscar; mirar. **3,** (seem; appear) parecer; tener apariencia. **4,** (face or be turned in a given direction) dar (a); mirar (a). **5,** [*en* **look to** *o* **for**] (hope; expect) esperar; confiar. **6,** (keep watch; take heed) mirar; tener cuidado. —*v.t.* **1,** [*en* **look up**] (try to find) buscar. **2,** (suggest by appearance) parecer; parecer tener (cierta edad). —*n.* **1,** (act of looking) mirada. **2,** [*también pl.* **looks**] (appearance; aspect) apariencia; aspecto. —**look after,** cuidar (de); encargarse de. —**look alive,** *colloq.* estar alerta; despabilarse. —**look daggers,** mirar con ira; echar rayos por los ojos. —**look down on** (o **upon**), tener a menos; menospreciar. —**look for, 1,** (seek) buscar. **2,** (expect; hope for) esperar; confiar. —**look forward to,** esperar; confiar; esperar gozar de. —**look in** (on), hacer una visita corta (a). —**look into,** investigar; examinar. —**look like, 1,** (resemble) parecerse a. **2,** (seem to be) parecer. **3,** *colloq.* (seem as if) parecer que: *It looks like rain,* Parece que va a llover. —**look on,** observar; mirar; ver. —**look oneself,** parecerse uno; parecer él mismo. —**look out,** tener cuidado. —**look out for,** cuidar (de); encargarse de. —**look over,** examinar; repasar. —**look through,** repasar; mirar por. —**look to, 1,**

(take care of; give attention to) mirar por; cuidar de. **2,** (resort to) acudir a. **3,** (expect; look forward to) esperar; confiar. —**look up, 1,** (try to find) buscar. **2,** (consult) consultar. **3,** *colloq.* (call on; visit) ir a visitar. **4,** *colloq.* (improve) mejorar; tomar buen cariz. —**look up to,** admirar.

looker ('luk·ər) *n.* **1,** (watcher) espectador. **2,** *slang* (handsome person) bombón.

looker-on *n.* espectador; mirón.

looking glass espejo.

lookout ('luk·aut) *n.* **1,** (watch) guardia; vigilancia. **2,** (person who keeps watch) vigía; centinela. **3,** (vantage point) puesto de observación. **4,** *colloq.* (care; concern) problema; asunto. —**on the lookout (for),** alerta (para); a la mira (de).

loom (lurm) *n.* telar; *fig.* urdimbre. —*v.i.* **1,** (appear dimly) vislumbrarse. **2,** *fig.* (impend) cernerse. —**loom large,** proyectarse ampliamente.

loon (lurn) *n.* **1,** *ornith.* somorgujo. **2,** *slang* (dolt) bobo.

loony ('lu·ni) *adj. & n., slang* lunático. —**loony bin,** *slang* manicomio.

loop (lup) *n.* **1,** (doubled cord) lazo. **2,** (fastening) alamar; presilla. **3,** (turn; bend) recodo; vuelta. **4,** *aero.* rizo. —*v.t.* **1,** (fasten) enlazar. **2,** (form loops) hacer lazos. —*v.i.* dar vueltas. —**looped** (lupt) *adj., slang* borracho. —**loopy,** *adj., slang* loco; chiflado. —**loop the loop,** hacer el rizo.

loophole ('lup·hol) *n.* escapatoria; salida.

loose (lus) *adj.* **1,** (free; unattached) libre; suelto. **2,** (roomy; loose-fitting) holgado. **3,** (not tight; slack) flojo. **4,** (diffuse) difuso; impreciso. **5,** (morally lax) relajado; libertino. —*v.t.* **1,** (set free; release) soltar; dejar escapar o ir. **2,** (unfasten; slacken) desatar; aflojar. **3,** (let fly; fire) disparar; lanzar. —**at a loose end,** sin nada que hacer. —**at loose ends,** en desorden. —**break loose,** soltarse; escaparse. —**cast loose,** soltar; dejar suelto. —**cut loose, 1,** (make or become unfastened) romper los lazos; soltar las amarras. **2,** (make or become free) librar(se); soltar(se). **3,** *colloq.* (go on a spree) ir o estar de juerga.

—**loose ends,** cabos sueltos. —**on the loose,** suelto; libre. —**turn, let o set loose,** soltar; dejar suelto.

loose-leaf *adj.* de hojas sueltas.

loosen ('lu·sən) *v.t.* aflojar; soltar. —*v.i.* aflojarse; soltarse.

looseness ('lus·nəs) *n.* **1,** (roominess) holgura. **2,** (diffuseness) imprecisión. **3,** (slackness) flojedad. **4,** (moral laxity) relajación; libertinaje.

loot (lut) *n.* botín. —*v.t.* saquear. —**looter,** *n.* saqueador.

lop (lap) *v.t.* [**lopped, lopping**] **1,** (trim; cut off) cortar; cercenar. **2,** (let droop) inclinar; dejar colgar. —*v.i.* pender; colgar.

lope (lop) *v.i.* andar a paso largo. —*n.* medio galope; paso largo.

lopsided ('lap,sai·dɪd) *adj.* desequilibrado. —**lopsidedness,** *n.* desequilibrio.

loquacious (lo'kwei·ʃəs) *adj.* locuaz. —**loquacity** (lo'kwæs·ə·ti); **loquaciousness,** *n.* locuacidad.

loran ('lor·ən; -æn) *n.* lorán.

lord (lord) *n.* señor. —**lord it over,** imponerse a; dominar. —**Lord's Prayer,** padrenuestro. —**Lord's Supper,** Eucaristía.

lordly ('lord·li) *adj.* **1,** (of or befitting a lord) de señor; señorial. **2,** (imperious) imperioso. **3,** (haughty) altivo; altanero. —**lordliness,** *n.* señorío.

lordship ('lord·ʃɪp) *n.* señoría.

lore (lor) *n.* ciencia; saber.

lorelei ('lor·ə,lai) *n.* sirena.

lorgnette (lor'njet) *n.* impertinentes.

lorry ('lor·i) *n., Brit.* camión.

lose (luz) *v.t. & i.* [*pret. & p.p.* **lost**] perder. —*v.i.* (run slow, as a watch) atrasarse. —**loser,** *n.* perdedor.

loss (lɔs) *n.* pérdida. —**at a loss,** perplejo; confundido.

lost (lɔst) *v., pret. & p.p. de* **lose.** —*adj.* perdido.

lot (lat) *n.* **1,** (chance; destiny) suerte. **2,** (parcel of land) solar; parcela; *Amer.* lote. **3,** (unit quantity) cantidad. **4,** *colloq.,* [*también pl.* **lots**] (much; many) gran cantidad o número; mucho o muchos. —**cast lots,** echar suertes.

lotion ('lo·ʃən) *n.* loción.

lottery ('lat·ə·ri) *n.* lotería.

lotus ('lo·təs) *n.* loto.

loud (laud) *adj.* **1,** (strongly audible) fuerte; (esp. of the voice) alto.

2, (noisy; clamorous) ruidoso; fuerte. **3,** *colloq.* (garish) chillón. **4,** *colloq.* (vulgar) bullanguero. —*adv.* fuerte; alto. —**loudness,** *n.* volumen; intensidad; fuerza.

loudmouth ('laud,mauθ) *n.m.* barbullón. —**loudmouthed** (-mauðd) *adj.* barbullón; vocinglero.

loudspeaker ('laud,spi·kər) *n.* altavoz; *Amer.* altoparlante.

lounge (laundʒ) *v.i.* **1,** (loll) arrellanarse; ponerse o estar a sus anchas. **2,** (rest; idle) descansar. **3,** (loiter) holgazanear; estar de vago. —*n.* **1,** (public room) salón (de fumar, de espera, etc.). **2,** (sofa) canapé. **3,** (slovenly gait or posture) holgazanería; descuido. —**lounger,** *n.* ocioso; holgazán.

louse (laus) *n.* **1,** [*pl.* **lice**] piojo. **2,** *slang* (mean person) canalla. —**louse up,** *slang* estropear; chapucear.

lousy ('lau·zi) *adj.* **1,** (infested with lice) piojoso. **2,** *slang* (mean; contemptible) asqueroso; horrible. **3,** *slang, en* **lousy with** (well supplied) colmado (de); nadando (en). —**lousiness,** *n.* piojería; asquerosidad.

lout (laut) *n.* patán; zafio. —**loutish,** *adj.* patán; zafio.

louver ('lu·vər) *n.* lumbrera (de tablillas); persiana.

lovable *también,* **loveable** ('lʌv·ə·bəl) *adj.* encantador; simpático.

love (lʌv) *n.* **1,** (affection; object of affection) amor; cariño. **2,** (sports) (no score) cero; nada. —*v.t.* **1,** (have affection for) amar; querer. **2,** (like; enjoy) encantarle a uno. —*v.i.* amar; querer; estar enamorado. —**be in love (with),** estar enamorado (de). —**fall in love (with),** enamorarse (de). —**love potion,** filtro (de amor).

lovebird ('lʌv·bʌrd) *n.* **1,** (bird) periquito. **2,** *pl.* (lovers) tórtolos.

lovelorn ('lʌv,lorn) *adj.* suspirando de amor.

lovely ('lʌv·li) *adj.* encantador; bonito. —**loveliness,** *n.* encanto; belleza.

lover ('lʌv·ər) *n.* amante.

love seat confidente; canapé de dos asientos.

lovesick ('lʌv·sɪk) *adj.* enamorado; chalado. —**lovesickness,** *n.* mal de amor o amores.

loving ('lʌv·ɪŋ) *adj.* **1,** (feeling love; devoted) cariñoso; amoroso.

2, (expressing love) de cariño; de amor. —*n.* amor; cariño. —**loving cup,** copa de la amistad.

low (lo:) *adj.* **1,** (not high) bajo. **2,** (inferior) inferior. **3,** (base; mean) bajo; vil. **4,** (not loud; soft) bajo. **5,** (deep) profundo. **6,** (vulgar; coarse) vulgar. **7,** (humble) humilde. **8,** (not many in number) pocos. **9,** (short; in short supply) poco; escaso. **10,** (dejected) abatido; desanimado. **11,** (weak; enfeebled) postrado; débil. —*adv.* **1,** (in a low position, manner, degree, etc.) bajo. **2,** (cheaply) barato. —*n.* **1,** (something low) bajo. **2,** (low point or degree) mínimo. **3,** (low gear) primera (velocidad). **4,** *meteorol.* depresión. **5,** (sound of cattle) mugido. —*v.i.* mugir. —**lay low, 1,** (fell) derribar; derrotar. **2,** (kill) matar. —**lie low,** esconderse; estar o quedarse escondido. —**Low Mass,** misa rezada. —**low spirits,** abatimiento; falta de ánimo. —**low tide,** bajamar; marea baja.

lowborn ('lo·born) *adj.* de origen humilde; plebeyo.

lowbred ('lo,brɛd) *adj.* tosco; grosero.

lowbrow ('lo,brau) *n.* & *adj.*, *colloq.* ignorante; poco refinado.

low-class *adj.* de clase baja.

low-down *n.*, *slang* datos; información. —*adj.*, *colloq.* bajo; vil; despreciable.

lower ('lo·ər) *v.t.* **1,** (move or let down) bajar. **2,** (reduce) bajar; rebajar; disminuir. **3,** (degrade) humillar; rebajar. —*v.i.* bajar; menguar; disminuir. —*adj.* más bajo; inferior. —*adv.* más bajo; más abajo.

lower ('lau·ər) *v.i.* **1,** (scowl) fruncir el ceño; mirar con mal ceño. **2,** (become overcast) encapotarse. —**lowering,** *adj.* ceñudo; encapotado.

lower berth litera baja.

lower case caja baja; (letra) minúscula; letra de caja baja. —**lowercase,** *adj.* de caja baja; minúscula; de o con minúsculas.

lowerclassman ('lo·ər'klæs·mən) *n.* [*pl.* -**men**] alumno universitario de los dos primeros años.

lower house cámara baja.

low-grade *adj.* de poca calidad; de calidad inferior.

lowland ('lo·lənd) *n.* tierra baja.

—**lowlander,** *n.* habitante de tierras bajas.

lowly ('lo·li) *adj.* humilde. —*adv.* con humildad; humildemente. —**lowliness,** *n.* humildad.

low-necked *adj.* escotado.

low-pressure *adj.* **1,** (of or for low pressure) de baja presión. **2,** (subdued; mild) suave; de o con poca insistencia.

low-priced *adj.* barato.

low-spirited *adj.* desanimado; sin humor.

low water 1, (of a river or stream) estiaje. **2,** (low tide) bajamar. —**low-water mark, 1,** *lit.* nivel de bajamar o estiaje. **2,** *fig.* punto más bajo.

loyal ('lɔi·əl) *adj.* leal. —**loyalty,** *n.* lealtad.

loyalist ('lɔi·əl·ɪst) *n.* **1,** (monarchist) realista. **2,** (republican) republicano.

lozenge ('laz·əndʒ) *n.* **1,** (pastille) pastilla. **2,** (diamond-shaped figure) rombo; losange.

lubber ('lʌb·ər) *n.* tonto; marinero de agua dulce. —**lubberly,** *adj.* tonto; zafio.

lube (lu:b) *n.*, *slang* = **lubrication**. —*v.t.*, *slang* = **lubricate**.

lubricate ('lu·brɪ,keit) *v.t.* lubricar; engrasar. —**lubricant,** *n.* & *adj.* lubricante. —**lubrication,** *n.* lubricación; engrase.

lucerne (lu'sʌrn) *n.*, *Brit.* alfalfa.

lucid ('lu·sɪd) *adj.* lúcido.

lucidity (lu'sɪd·ə·ti) *n.* lucidez.

Lucite ('lu·sait) *n.*, *T.N.* lucita.

luck (lʌk) *n.* suerte; fortuna. —**luckless,** *adj.* desafortunado. —**lucky,** *adj.* afortunado. —**luckiness,** *n.* buena suerte; buena fortuna.

lucrative ('lu·krə·tɪv) *adj.* lucrativo.

lucre ('lu·kər) *n.* lucro.

lucubrate ('lu·kju,breit) *v.i.* lucubrar. —**lucubration,** *n.* lucubración.

ludicrous ('lu·dɪ·krəs) *adj.* ridículo; risible. —**ludicrousness,** *n.* ridiculez; lo risible.

lug (lʌg) *v.t.* [**lugged, lugging**] arrastrar; tirar (de); cargar con. —*n.* **1,** (tug) tirón. **2,** (projecting part) saliente. **3,** *colloq.* (sluggish fellow) zángano; posma.

luggage ('lʌg·ɪdʒ) *n.* equipaje; maletas.

lugubrious (lu'gu·bri·əs) *adj.*

lúgubre. **—lugubriousness,** *n.* lo lúgubre.

lukewarm ('luk,worm) *adj.* tibio. **—lukewarmness,** *n.* tibieza.

lull (lʌl) *v.t.* arrullar; adormecer. **—v.i.** calmarse; sosegarse. **—n.** momento de calma o de silencio.

lullaby ('lʌl·ə·bai) *n.* arrullo.

lumbago (lʌm'bei·go) *n.* lumbago.

lumbar ('lʌm·bər) *adj.* lumbar.

lumber ('lʌm·bər) *n.* madera. **—v.i.** andar o moverse pesadamente.

lumbering ('lʌm·bər·ɪŋ) *adj.* 1, (clumsy) pesado; tardo. 2, (pert. to the lumber industry) maderero; de la madera. **—n.** industria de la madera; industria maderera.

lumberjack ('lʌm·bər,dʒæk) *n.* leñador.

lumberman ('lʌm·bər·mən) *n.* [*pl.* **-men**] 1, = **lumberjack.** 2, (lumber dealer) maderero.

lumberyard ('lʌm·bər,jard) *n.* almacén de maderas.

luminary ('lu·mə·nɛr·i) *n.* lumbrera; luminaria.

luminescence (,lu·mə'nɛs·əns) *n.* luminiscencia. **—luminescent,** *adj.* luminiscente.

luminosity (lu·mɪ'nas·ə·ti) *n.* luminosidad.

luminous ('lu·mə·nəs) *adj.* luminoso.

lummox ('lʌm·əks) *n., colloq.* tonto; bobo.

lump (lʌmp) *n.* 1, (shapeless mass) pedazo; masa. 2, (lump of sugar; clod of earth) terrón. 3, (swelling; bump) bulto; chichón; hinchazón. 4, (clot) grumo. 5, (dolt) bobo. **—adj.** en forma de terrón. **—v.t.** poner junto; agrupar. **—v.i.** 1, (swell) hincharse. 2, (form lumps) hacer grumos. 3, (move heavily) andar pesadamente. **—lump it,** *colloq.* tragarlo. **—lump sum,** suma total.

lumpy ('lʌm·pi) *adj.* 1, (swollen) hinchado. 2, (bumpy) abollado. 3, (containing lumps) con grumos; que tiene grumos. 4, [*también,* **lumpish**] (doltish) bobo; necio.

lunacy ('lu·nə·si) *n.* locura.

lunar ('lu·nər) *adj.* lunar.

lunatic ('lu·nə·tɪk) *n. & adj.* lunático; loco.

lunch (lʌntʃ) *n.* 1, (midday meal) almuerzo. 2, (any light meal) refrigerio. **—v.i.** almorzar.

luncheon ('lʌn·tʃən) *n.* almuerzo. **—luncheonette** (-'ɛt) *n.* cantina.

lunchroom ('lʌntʃ·rum) *n.* comedor.

lung (lʌŋ) *n.* pulmón. **—at the top of one's lungs,** a grito pelado; a pulmón tendido. **—iron lung,** pulmón artificial.

lunge (lʌndʒ) *n.* 1, (thrust) estocada; golpe a fondo. 2, (onslaught) acometida; arremetida. 3, (forward plunge) impulso; movimiento brusco. **—v.i.** 1, (thrust) irse a fondo; dar una estocada. 2, (attack; charge) acometer; arremeter. 3, (plunge forward) abalanzarse; tirarse.

lupine ('lu·pain) *adj.* lupino.

lupus ('lu·pəs) *n., pathol.* lupus.

lurch (lʌrtʃ) *v.i.* dar sacudidas o tirones; *naut.* dar bandazos. **—n.** sacudida; tirón; *naut.* bandazo. **—in the lurch,** 1, (far behind) a la cola. 2, (forsaken) colgado; plantado.

lure (lur) *n.* 1, (bait) cebo; anzuelo; señuelo. 2, (decoy) reclamo. 3, (enticement) atracción; atractivo. **—v.t.** atraer; tentar.

lurid ('lur·ɪd) *adj.* 1, (glowing) ardiente. 2, (sensational) sensacional; escandaloso.

lurk (lʌrk) *v.i.* 1, (be concealed) estar escondido u oculto. 2, (lie in wait) acechar; estar en acecho.

luscious ('lʌʃ·əs) *adj.* delicioso; exquisito; sabroso. **—lusciousness,** *n.* exquisitez.

lush (lʌʃ) *adj.* 1, (fresh; juicy) lozano; jugoso. 2, (luxuriant) exuberante. **—n.,** *slang* (drunkard) borrachón. **—lushness,** *n.* lozanía; exuberancia.

lust (lʌst) *n.* 1, (strong desire) deseo; ansia. 2, (carnal appetite) lujuria; concupiscencia. **—v.i.** codiciar; desear. **—lustful,** *adj.* lujurioso. **—lusty,** *adj.* fuerte; vigoroso. **—lustiness,** *n.* fuerza; vigor.

luster ('lʌs·tər) *n.* lustre. **—lustrous** (-trəs) *adj.* lustroso.

lute (lut) *n.* laúd.

lutecium (lu'ti·ʃi·əm) *n.* lutecio.

Lutheran ('lu·θə·rən) *n. & adj.* luterano. **—Lutheranism,** *n.* luteranismo.

luxuriate (lʌg'ʒur·i,eit) *v.i.* 1, (grow profusely) abundar; crecer con abundancia. 2, [*usu.* **luxuriate in**] (enjoy) deleitarse (en); disfrutar (de). **—luxuriant,** *adj.* abundante; lujuriante; *fig.* recargado. **—luxuriance,** *n.* abundancia; profusión.

luxury ('lʌk·ʃə·ri) *n.* lujo. —**luxurious** (lʌg'ʒur·i·əs) *adj.* lujoso. —**luxuriousness,** *n.* lujo; lo lujoso.

lycanthrope ('lai·kən,θrop) *n.* licántropo. —**lycanthropy** (lai'kæn·θrə·pi) *n.* licantropía.

lyceum (lai'si·əm) *n.* liceo; ateneo.

lye (lai) *n.* lejía.

lying ('lai·ɪŋ) *v.,* *ger. de* **lie.** —*n.* mentira. —*adj.* **1,** (recumbent) recostado; acostado. **2,** (located) situado. **3,** (false) mentiroso.

lying-in *n.* parto. —**lying-in hospital,** clínica de maternidad.

lymph (lɪmf) *n.* linfa. —**lymphatic** (lɪm'fæt·ɪk) *adj.* linfático.

lynch (lɪntʃ) *v.t.* linchar. —**lynching,** *n.* linchamiento.

lynx (lɪŋks) *n.* lince.

lyre (lair) *n.* lira.

lyric ('lɪr·ɪk) *adj.* lírico. —*n.* **1,** (lyric poem) poema lírico. **2,** (lyric poetry) lírica. **3,** *colloq.* (words of a song) letra. —**lyrical,** *adj.* lírico. —**lyricism** ('lɪr·ɪ·sɪz·əm) *n.* lirismo.

M

M, m (ɛm) decimotercera letra del alfabeto inglés.

ma (mɑɪ) *n., colloq.* mamá.

ma'am (mæm) *n., colloq.* = **madam.**

macabre (mə'ka·brə) *también,* **macaber** (-bər) *adj.* macabro.

macadam (mə'kæd·əm) *n.* macadán; macádam. —**macadamize,** *v.t.* macadamizar.

macaque (mə'kak) *n.* macaco.

macaroni (,mæk·ə'ro·ni) *n.* macarrón; macarrones.

macaroon (,mæk·ə'ruːn) *n.* almendrado; macarrón.

macaw (mə'kɔː) *n.* guacamayo; papagayo.

mace (meis) *n.* **1,** (club; staff) maza; clava; porra. **2,** (spice) macias; macis.

macerate ('mæs·ə,reit) *v.t.* macerar. —**maceration,** *n.* maceración.

machete (ma'tʃe·te; mə'ʃet; mə'ʃɛt·i) *n.* machete.

Machiavellian (,mæk·i·ə'vɛl·i·ən) *adj.* maquiavélico; maquiavelista. —*n.* maquiavelista. —**Machiavellism,** *n.* maquiavelismo.

machinate ('mæk·ə,neit) *v.t. & i.* maquinar. —**machination,** *n.* maquinación.

machine (mə'ʃiːn) *n.* **1,** (mechanical device) máquina; aparato. **2,** *polit.* camarilla. **3,** = **automobile.** —*v.t.* trabajar a máquina. —**machine gun,** ametralladora. —**machine-gun,** *v.t.* [-gunned, -gunning] ametrallar. —**machine gunner,** ametrallador.

machinery (mə'ʃiː·nə·ri) *n.* maquinaria; mecanismo.

machinist (mə'ʃiː·nɪst) *n.* maquinista.

mackerel ('mæk·ər·əl) *n.* caballa; escombro.

mackinaw ('mæk·ə·nɔ) *n.* chaquetón; chamarra.

mackintosh ('mæk·ɪn,tɑʃ) *n.* impermeable.

macrocosm ('mæk·rə,kaz·əm) *n.* macrocosmo.

macroeconomics (,mæk·ro·ɛk·ə'nam·ɪks) *n.* macroeconomía.

macron ('mei·kran) *n.* signo de vocal larga: ā.

macroscopic (,mæk·rə'skap·ɪk) *adj.* macroscópico.

mad (mæd) *adj.* **1,** (insane) loco. **2,** (rabid) rabioso. **3,** *colloq.* (angry) furioso. —**be mad about,** *colloq.* estar loco por. —**get mad,** *colloq.* enfadarse. —**go mad,** enloquecer.

madam ('mæd·əm) *n.* señora. *También,* **madame** (ma'daɪm).

madcap ('mæd,kæp) *n. & adj.* tarambana.

madden ('mæd·ən) *v.t.* **1,** (drive mad) enloquecer. **2,** (make furious) enfurecer. —**maddening,** *adj.* exasperante; enloquecedor.

madder ('mæd·ər) *n.* rubia. —*adj., comp. de* **mad.**

made (meid) *v., pret. & p.p. de* **make.** —*adj.* **1,** (artificially produced) hecho; fabricado. **2,** *colloq.* (assured of success) hecho; asegurado.

mademoiselle (,mæd·mwə'zɛl) *n.* [*pl.* **mesdemoiselles** (,med·mwə'zɛl)] señorita.

made-to-order *adj.* hecho a la medida.

made-up *adj.* **1,** (contrived) artificial; ficticio. **2,** (assembled) compuesto. **3,** (with cosmetics applied) maquillado.

madhouse ('mæd,haus) *n.* manicomio.

madman ('mæd·mæn) *n.* [*pl.* -men] loco. —**madwoman,** *n.* [*pl.* -women] loca.

madness ('mæd·nɪs) *n.* **1,** (insanity; folly; excitement) locura. **2,** (fury) furor; ira. **3,** (rabies) rabia.

Madonna (mə'dan·ə) *n.* madona; Nuestra Señora.

madrigal ('mæd·rɪ·gəl) *n.* madrigal.

Madrilenian (,mæd·rə'li·ni·ən) *adj.* & *n.* madrileño. *Also,* **Madrilene** ('mæd·rə,lin).

maelstrom ('meil·strəm) *n.* maelstrom; remolino; vorágine.

maestro ('mai·stro) *n.* [*pl.* -tros] maestro.

magazine (,mæg·ə'ziːn) *n.* **1,** (publication) revista. **2,** (supply receptacle, as of a firearm) cargador. **3,** (depository for powder) polvorín. **4,** (storage place) almacén.

magenta (mə'dʒɛn·tə) *n.* & *adj.* magenta.

maggot ('mæg·ət) *n.* cresa; gusano. —**maggoty,** *adj.* gusanoso.

Magi ('mei·dʒai) *n.pl.* magos; *Bib.* reyes magos.

magic ('mædʒ·ɪk) *n.* magia. —*adj.* [*también,* **magical**] mágico. —**magician** (mə'dʒɪʃ·ən) *n.* mago; brujo. —**by magic,** por ensalmo; por arte de magia.

magisterial (,mædʒ·ɪs'tir·i·əl) *adj.* **1,** (masterly; authoritative) magistral. **2,** (of or pert. to a magistrate) de magistrado. **3,** (pompous) magisterial.

magistrate ('mædʒ·ɪs,treit) *n.* magistrado. —**magistracy** (-trə·si) *n.* magistratura.

magma ('mag·mə) *n., geol.* [*pl.* -mas o -mata (-ma·tə)] magma.

Magna Charta o **Carta** ('mæg·nə'kar·tə) *n.* Carta Magna.

magnanimous (mæg'næn·ə·məs) *adj.* magnánimo. —**magnanimity** (,mæg·nə'nɪm·ə·ti) *n.* magnanimidad.

magnate ('mæg·neit) *n.* magnate.

magnesia (mæg'ni·ʒə) *n.* magnesia.

magnesium (mæg'ni·ʒi·əm) *n.* magnesio.

magnet ('mæg·nɪt) *n.* imán. —**magnetic** (mæg'nɛt·ɪk) *adj.* mag-

nético. —**magnetism,** *n.* magnetismo. —**magnetize,** *v.t.* magnetizar.

magnetite ('mag·nə,tait) *n.* magnetita.

magneto (mæg'ni·to) *n.* magneto.

magnificent (mæg'nɪf·ə·sənt) *adj.* magnífico. —**magnificence,** *n.* magnificencia.

magnify ('mæg·nə,fai) *v.t.* magnificar; agrandar. —**magnification** (-fɪ'kei·ʃən) *n.* magnificación. —**magnifier,** *n.* lente de aumento. —**magnifying,** *adj.* de aumento. —**magnifying glass,** lupa; vidrio o luna de aumento.

magniloquent (mæg'nɪl·ə·kwənt) *adj.* grandilocuente. —**magniloquence,** *n.* grandilocuencia.

magnitude ('mæg·nə,tjud) *n.* magnitud.

magnolia (mæg'no·li·ə) *n.* magnolia.

magnum ('mæg·nəm) *n.* botella grande; botellón.

magpie ('mæg,pai) *n.* **1,** (bird) urraca; cotorra. **2,** (chatterbox) cotorra; parlanchín.

Magyar ('ma·gjar) *n.* & *adj.* magiar.

maharajah (,ma·hə'ra·dʒə) *n.* maharajá. —**maharanee** (-ni) *n.* maharaní.

mahogany (mə'hag·ə·ni) *n.* **1,** (tree) caobo; caoba. **2,** (wood) caoba.

Mahometan (mə'ham·ə·tən) *n.* & *adj.* = **Mohammedan.**

maid (meid) *n.* **1,** (young woman) doncella; moza. **2,** [*también,* **maidservant**] criada; sirvienta. —**maid-in-waiting** [*pl.* **maids-in-waiting**] dama de compañía. —**maid of honor,** madrina de boda.

maiden ('mei·dən) *n.* virgen; doncella; joven soltera. —*adj.* **1,** (virginal) virginal. **2,** (unmarried) soltera. **3,** (first) inicial. —**maidenhood,** *n.* doncellez; virginidad. —**maidenly,** *adj.* virginal; modesto; pudoroso. —**maiden name,** apellido de soltera.

maidenhead ('mei·dən·hɛd) *n.* **1,** = **maidenhood.** **2,** (hymen) virgo; himen.

mail (meil) *n.* **1,** (post) correo. **2,** (letters) correspondencia. **3,** (armor) malla. —*v.t.* enviar por correo; echar al correo.

mailbag ('meil,bæg) *n.* portacartas. *También,* **mail pouch.**

mailbox ('meil·baks) *n.* buzón.

mailman ('meil·mæn) *n.* [*pl.* -men] cartero.

mail order pedido postal. —**mail-order,** *adj.* pedido por correo. —**mail-order house,** casa de ventas por correo; casa de pedidos postales.

maim (meim) *v.t.* **1,** (mutilate) mutilar. **2,** (cripple; damage) estropear; lisiar.

main (mein) *adj.* **1,** (chief) principal. **2,** (sheer) puro. —*n.* **1,** (pipe) cañería maestra. **2,** (ocean) alta mar; piélago. **3,** (strength) fuerza. —**mainly,** *adv.* principalmente; sobre todo. —**by main force** (o **strength**), a puro pulso; a pura fuerza. —**main drag,** *slang* calle mayor; calle principal. —**mainframe,** *n., comput.* computadora principal. —**main line, 1,** carretera o vía férrea principal. **2,** *slang* vena principal. —**mainline,** *v.i., slang* inyectarse drogas directamente en una vena. —**with might and main,** con toda fuerza.

mainland ('mein·lənd) *n.* continente; tierra firme.

mainmast ('mein,mæst; -məst) *n.* palo mayor.

mainsail ('mein,seil; -səl) *n.* vela mayor.

mainspring ('mein,spriŋ) *n.* **1,** (of a watch) muelle real. **2,** (chief source or motive) móvil o causa principal; fuente.

mainstay ('mein·ste) *n.* base; soporte principal.

mainstream ('mein·strim) *n.* corriente común; corriente principal.

maintain (mein'tein) *v.t.* mantener. —**maintenance** ('mein·tə·nəns) *n.* mantenimiento; manutención.

maize (meiz) *n.* maíz.

majesty ('mædʒ·ıs·ti) *n.* majestad. —**majestic** (mə'dʒɛs·tık) adj. majestuoso.

major ('mei·dʒər) *adj.* mayor. —*n.* **1,** (army officer) comandante. **2,** (principal field of study) especialidad. —*v.i.* especializarse. —**major general,** general de división.

majordomo (,mei·dʒər'do·mo) *n.* mayordomo.

majority (mə'dʒar·ə·ti) *n.* mayoría.

make (meik) *v.t.* [*pret. & p.p.* made] **1,** (bring into being; shape; build) hacer. **2,** (cause; bring about) traer; ocasionar; causar: *This made*

trouble, Esto trajo dificultades. **3,** (cause to; force to) hacer; obligar. **4,** (establish, as a rule) establecer; imponer. **5,** (cause to be or become) hacer; poner: *That noise makes me nervous,* Ese ruido me pone nervioso. **6,** (turn out to be; become) ser; hacer: *He will make a good hunter,* Hará un buen cazador. **7,** (arrange, as a bed) hacer; arreglar. **8,** (cause to seem) hacer aparecer; hacer: *This picture makes her younger,* Este retrato la hace (aparecer) más joven. **9,** (get; acquire) hacer; hacerse de: *He made many enemies,* Se hizo de muchos enemigos. **10,** (earn) ganar. **11,** (do; perform) hacer. **12,** (amount to; add up to) sumar. **13,** [*en* **make of**] (understand; infer) sacar; sacar en limpio; pensar. **14,** (estimate to be; regard as) tener por; considerar (como). **15,** (deliver, as a speech) pronunciar. **16,** (utter) proferir; emitir. **17,** (traverse, as a distance) cubrir; recorrer. **18,** (go or move to a certain speed) hacer; correr: *This train makes 60 miles an hour,* Este tren corre 60 millas por hora. **19,** (arrive at; reach) llegar a. **20,** (arrive in time for; catch) llegar a tiempo a o para. **21,** *games* (score) hacer. **22,** *slang* (win; succeed in getting) lograr; conseguir. **23,** *colloq.* (gain admission or acceptance in) figurar en. —*v.i.* **1,** *con inf.* (start; attempt) hacer además de. **2,** (head; proceed) ir; dirigirse. **3,** (behave) portarse; comportarse. —*n.* **1,** (manufacture) manufactura. **2,** (brand) marca. —**make after,** seguir; perseguir. —**make as if** (o **as though**) hacer como que; hacer además de. —**make away with, 1,** (steal) robar; birlar. **2,** (get rid of) eliminar; sacar de en medio. —**make believe,** hacer creer. —**make for, 1,** (head for; go toward) ir a o hacia; dirigirse a o hacia. **2,** (tend toward; promote) fomentar; promover; contribuir a. —**make good, 1,** (succeed) tener éxito; triunfar. **2,** (fulfill) cumplir. **3,** (accept responsibility) responder (por). **4,** (recoup) recobrar. **5,** (compensate; overcome) vencer; superar. **6,** (pay) pagar. —**make it,** *colloq.* conseguirlo; triunfar. —**make off,** salir corriendo. —**make out, 1,** (discern; distinguish) poder ver; distinguir. **2,** (understand) comprender. **3,** (write out; draw up) hacer; extender. **4,** (pretend to be; pass off as) hacer; pasar por. **5,** *colloq.* (manage; get along) arreglárselas. —**make over, 1,** (renovate) renovar; cambiar. **2,** (transfer; sign over) transferir; traspasar. —**make up, 1,** (put together; compose) componer; hacer. **2,** (invent; concoct) inventar; imaginar. **3,** (supply what is lacking) completar; suplir. **4,** (compensate) compensar; pagar. **5,** (arrange) arreglar; hacer. **6,** (recover) recobrar; ganar. **7,** (be reconciled) arreglarse; hacer las paces. **8,** (apply cosmetics) arreglar; maquillar. **9,** (resolve, as one's mind) resolver(se); decidir(se). **10,** (take again, as an examination) volver a examinarse (de). —**make up to,** halagar.

make-believe *adj.* fingido; ficticio; de mentirijillas. —*n.* artificio; pretexto.

maker ('mei·kər) *n.* **1,** (creator; designer) creador; modelador. **2,** (manufacturer) fabricante. **3,** *cap.* (God) Creador; Hacedor.

makeshift ('meik·ʃɪft) *adj.* provisional; interino. —*n.* expediente.

makeup ('meik·ʌp) *n.* **1,** (composition) composición; construcción; arreglo. **2,** (nature; disposition) carácter; disposición; naturaleza. **3,** (cosmetics) maquillaje. **4,** *print.* imposición.

malachite ('mæl·ə·kait) *n.* malaquita.

maladjusted (ˌmæl·ə'dʒʌs·tɪd) *adj.* desajustado; *psychol.* inadaptado. —**maladjustment** (-'dʒʌst·mənt) *n.* desajuste; inadaptación.

maladroit (ˌmæl·ə'drɔit) *adj.* torpe; desmañado.

malady ('mæl·ə·di) *n.* enfermedad; mal.

malaise (mæ'leiz) *n.* malestar; desazón.

malapropism ('mæl·ə,prap·ɪz·əm) *n.* despropósito.

malapropos (ˌmæl·æp·rə'por) *adj.* impropio; inoportuno; inapropiado.

malar ('mei·lər) *adj.* malar. —*n.* pómulo.

malaria (mə'lɛr·i·ə) *n.* malaria.

Malay (mə'lei; 'mei-) *n. & adj.* malayo. **Malayan, Malayan.**

malcontent ('mæl·kən,tɛnt) *n. & adj.* malcontento; descontento.

male (meil) *adj.* **1,** (of or pert. to the masculine sex) masculino; (*chiefly of animals*) macho; (*of persons*) varón. **2,** *mech.* macho. **3,** (composed of males) de hombres; masculino. —*n.* **1,** (male person) hombre; varón. **2,** (male animal) macho.

malediction (ˌmæl·ə'dɪk·ʃən) *n.* maldición.

malefactor ('mæl·ə,fæk·tər) *n.* malhechor. —**malefaction** (-'fæk·ʃən) *n.* delito.

malefic (mə'lɛf·ɪk) *adj.* maléfico.

maleficent (mə'lɛf·ə·sənt) *adj.* maléfico. —**maleficence,** *n.* maleficencia.

malevolent (mə'lɛv·ə·lənt) *adj.* malévolo. —**malevolence,** *n.* malevolencia.

malfeasance (mæl'fi·zəns) *n.* mal proceder; mala conducta; corrupción.

malformation (ˌmæl·fɔr'mei·ʃən) *n.* malformación. —**malformed,** *adj.* mal formado.

malfunction (mæl'fʌŋk·ʃən) *v.i.* funcionar mal. —*n.* funcionamiento defectuoso.

malic ('mæl·ɪk) *adj.* málico. —**malic acid,** ácido málico.

malice ('mæl·ɪs) *n.* malicia. —**malicious** (mə'lɪʃ·əs) *adj.* malicioso.

malign (mə'lain) *v.t.* calumniar; difamar. —*adj.* maligno; pernicioso.

malignancy (mə'lɪg·nən·si) *n.* malignidad.

malignant (mə'lɪg·nənt) *adj.* maligno.

malignity (mə'lɪg·nə·ti) *n.* malignidad.

malinger (mə'lɪŋ·gər) *v.i.* fingirse enfermo; hacerse el (o la) calandria. —**malingerer,** *n.* calandria.

malingering (mə'lɪŋ·gər·ɪŋ) *n.* enfermedad fingida. —*adj.* remolón.

mall (mɔːl) *n.* **1,** (mallet) mazo. **2,** (public walk) alameda. **3,** (shopping center) centro comercial; galería.

mallard ('mæl·ərd) *n.* pato silvestre; ánade común.

malleable ('mæl·i·ə·bəl) *adj.* maleable. —**malleability,** *n.* maleabilidad.

mallet ('mæl·ɪt) *n.* mazo.

mallow ('mæl·o) *n.* malva.

malnutrition (ˌmæl·nu'trɪʃ·ən) *n.* desnutrición.

malodorous (mæl'o·dər·əs) *adj.* maloliente; hediondo.

malpractice (mæl'præk·tɪs) *n.* descuido o inmoralidad profesional.

malt (mɔlt) *n.* malta.

Maltese (mɔl'tiːz) *adj. & n.* maltés [*fem.* -esa].

maltose ('mɔl·tos) *n.* maltosa.

maltreat (mæl'trit) *v.t.* maltratar. —**maltreatment,** *n.* maltrato.

mama ('ma·mə; mə'ma) *n.* mamá. *También,* **mamma.**

mambo ('mam·bo) *n.* mambo.

mamma ('ma·mə; mə'ma) *n.* **1,** (mother) mamá. **2,** *anat.* ('mæm·ə) [*pl.* -mae (-mi)] mama.

mammal ('mæm·əl) *n.* mamífero. —**mammalian** (mæ'mei·li·ən) *adj.* mamífero.

mammary ('mæm·ə·ri) *adj.* mamario.

mammography (mæ'mag·rə·fi) *n.* mamografía. —**mammogram** ('mæm·ə‚græm) *n.* mamografía.

mammon ('mæm·ən) *n.* **1,** (wealth) dinero; riquezas. **2,** *cap.* (personification of riches) mammón.

mammoth ('mæm·əθ) *adj.* enorme; gigantesco. —*n.* mamut.

mammy ('mæm·i) *n., colloq.* **1,** (mother) mamita. **2,** (nursemaid) niñera; nana.

man (mæn) *n.* [*pl.* **men**] **1,** (human being) hombre. **2,** (servant) criado. **3,** *chess* pieza. —*adj.* varón. —*v.t.* [**manned, manning**] **1,** (furnish with men) dotar de hombres; *mil.* guarnecer; *naut.; aero.* tripular. **2,** (make up the crew or staff of) constituir la dotación, el personal, etc., de. **3,** (tend; have charge of) atender; tomar o hacerse cargo de. **4,** *usu. refl.* (brace; fortify) aprestar(se); aprontar(se); hacer acopio de fuerzas. —**be one's own man,** campar por sus respetos; ser libre; ser independiente. —**man in the street,** hombre común; hombre corriente. —**man Friday,** criado de confianza; mano derecha. —**to a man,** todos a una; como un solo hombre.

manacle ('mæn·ə·kəl) *n.* manilla; esposas. —*v.t.* maniatar; esposar.

manage ('mæn·ɪdʒ) *v.t.* **1,** (handle) manejar. **2,** (have charge of) dirigir; administrar. **3,** (arrange; contrive) arreglar; tramitar. —*v.i.* arreglárselas. —**manageable,** *adj.* manejable; dócil. —**management,** *n.* administración; dirección.

manager ('mæn·ɪdʒ·ər) *n.*

administrador; director; gerente. —**managerial** (‚mæn·ə'dʒɪr·i·əl) *adj.* administrativo; de gerente.

man-at-arms *n.* [*pl.* **men-at-arms**] soldado; hombre de guerra.

manatee (‚mæn·ə'ti) *n.* manatí; vaca marina.

Manchu (mæn'tʃuː) *n. & adj.* manchú.

mandarin ('mæn·də·rɪn) *n.* **1,** (official; language) mandarín. **2,** (citrus fruit) naranja mandarina. **3,** (long coat) traje mandarín. **4,** (color) color mandarín.

mandate ('mæn·deit) *n.* mandato. —**mandatary** (-də·ter·i) *n.* mandatario. —**mandatory** (-də·tor·i) *adj.* preceptivo; obligatorio.

mandible ('mæn·də·bəl) *n.* mandíbula.

mandibular (mæn'dɪb·jə·lər) *adj.* mandibular.

mandolin ('mæn·də‚lɪn) *n.* mandolina; bandola.

mandrake ('mæn·dreik) *n.* mandrágora.

mandrel ('mæn·drəl) *n.* mandril.

mandrill ('mæn·drɪl) *n.* mandril.

mane (mein) *n.* melena; (*esp. of horses*) crin.

man-eater *n.* **1,** (cannibal) caníbal; antropófago. **2,** (animal dangerous to man) devorador de hombres.

maneuver *también,* **manoeuvre** (mə'nu·vər) *n.* maniobra. —*v.t. & i.* maniobrar. —**maneuverable,** *adj.* maniobrable. —**maneuverability,** *n.* maniobrabilidad.

manful ('mæn·fəl) *adj.* bravo; varonil; resuelto. —**manfulness,** *n.* valor; resolución.

manganese ('mæŋ·gə‚nis) *n.* manganeso. —**manganic** (mæn·'gæn·ɪk) *adj.* mangánico.

mange (meindʒ) *n.* sarna; roña. —**mangy,** *adj.* sarnoso; roñoso.

manger ('mein·dʒər) *n.* pesebre.

mangle ('mæŋ·gəl) *v.t.* destrozar; estropear; mutilar. —*n.* calandria; planchadora.

mango ('mæŋ·go) *n.* mango.

mangrove ('mæn·grov) *n.* mangle.

manhandle ('mæn‚hæn·dəl) *v.t.* **1,** (treat roughly) maltratar. **2,** (move by hand) mover a brazo.

manhole ('mæn·hol) *n.* boca de alcantarillado.

manhood ('mæn‚hʊd) *n.* **1,** (manliness) hombría. **2,** (age of maturity) edad viril. **3,** (men collectively) los hombres.

manhunt ('mæn·hʌnt) *n.* persecución; búsqueda *(de un criminal).*

mania ('mei·ni·ə) *n.* manía. —**maniac**, *n.* maniático; loco.

maniacal (mə'nai·ə·kəl) *adj.* maníaco.

manic ('mæn·ɪk) *adj.* maníaco. —**manic depressive**, maníacodepresivo.

manicure ('mæn·ə·kjur) *n.* manicura. —*v.t.* hacer la manicura a. —**manicurist**, *n.* manicuro [*fem.* -cura]; *Amer.* manicurista.

manifest ('mæn·ə·fɛst) *v.t.* manifestar. —*adj.* manifiesto; claro. —*n.* manifiesto. —**manifestation** (-fɛs'tei·ʃən) *n.* manifestación. —**make manifest**, poner de manifiesto.

manifesto (,mæn·ə'fɛs·to) *n.* manifiesto; proclama.

manifold ('mæn·ə·fold) *adj.* múltiple; amplio; diverso; variado. —*n.* **1,** (something complex) complejo. **2,** (copy) copia. **3,** (onionskin) papel cebolla. **4,** *mech.* tubo múltiple. —*v.t.* **1,** (multiply) multiplicar. **2,** (make copies of) sacar copias de.

manikin ('mæn·ə·kɪn) *n.* **1,** (model) maniquí; modelo. **2,** (dwarf) enano.

manila (mə'nɪl·ə) *n.* **1,** (hemp) cáñamo de Manila. **2,** (paper) papel (de) Manila.

manioc ('mæn·i·ak) *n.* mandioca.

manipulate (mə'nɪp·jə,leit) *v.t.* manipular. —**manipulation**, *n.* manipulación. —**manipulator**, *n.* manipulador.

mankind ('mæn,kaind) *n.* humanidad; género humano.

manlike ('mæn·laik) *adj.* **1,** (resembling a man) parecido al hombre; casi humano. **2,** = **manly**.

manly ('mæn·li) *adj.* de hombre; varonil; viril. —**manliness**, *n.* hombría; virilidad.

manna ('mæn·ə) *n.* maná.

mannequin ('mæn·ə·kɪn) *n.* maniquí; modelo.

manner ('mæn·ər) *n.* **1,** (way of doing or being) manera; modo; forma. **2,** (custom; usage) costumbre; usanza. **3,** (sort) clase; género. **4,** *pl.* (social ways) modales. —**by all manner of means**, de todos modos.

mannered ('mæn·ərd) *adj.* amanerado.

mannerism ('mæn·ə,rɪz·əm) *n.* **1,** (affectation) amaneramiento. **2,** (idiosyncrasy) costumbre; hábito; *derog.* vicio.

mannerly ('mæn·ər·li) *adj.* cortés; educado. —**mannerliness**, *n.* urbanidad.

mannish ('mæn·ɪʃ) *adj.* masculino; varonil.

manoeuvre (mə'nu·vər) *n.* & *v.* = **maneuver**.

man-of-war *n.* [*pl.* **men-of-war**] buque de guerra.

manometer (mə'nam·ə·tər) *n.* manómetro. —**manometric** (,mæn·ə'mɛt·rɪk) *adj.* manométrico.

manor ('mæn·ər) *n.* finca o casa solariega. —**manorial** (mə,nor·i·əl) *adj.* señorial; solariego.

manpower ('mæn,pau·ər) *n.* **1,** (human resources) recursos humanos. **2,** *mil.* fuerzas disponibles. **3,** (manual power) mano de obra; brazo.

mansard ('mæn·sard) *n.* mansarda.

manse (mæns) *n.* rectoría.

manservant ('mæn,sʌr·vənt) *n.* [*pl.* **menservants**] criado; sirviente.

mansion ('mæn·ʃən) *n.* mansión.

manslaughter ('mæn,slɔ·tər) *n.* homicidio casual o involuntario.

manta ('mæn·tə) *n.* manta.

mantel ('mæn·təl) *n.* manto; chimenea. —**mantelpiece**, *n.* repisa de chimenea.

mantilla (mæn'tɪl·ə) *n.* mantilla.

mantis ('mæn·tɪs) *n.* mantis.

mantissa (mæn'tɪs·ə) *n.* mantisa.

mantle ('mæn·təl) *n.* **1,** (cloak; covering) capa; manto. **2,** (incandescent hood) manguito. —*v.t.* cubrir.

manual ('mæn·ju·əl) *adj.* & *n.* manual.

manufacture (,mæn·jə'fæk·tʃər) *n.* manufactura. —*v.t.* manufacturar; fabricar. —**manufacturer**, *n.* fabricante; manufacturero.

manufacturing (,mæn·jə'fæk·tʃər·ɪŋ) *n.* fabricación; manufactura. —*adj.* manufacturero.

manumission (,mæn·jə'mɪʃ·ən) *n.* manumisión. —**manumit** (-'mɪt) *v.t.* manumitir.

manure (mə'njur) *n.* abono; estiércol. —*v.t.* abonar; estercolar.

manuscript ('mæn·jə,skrɪpt) *n.* & *adj.* manuscrito; *print.* original.

Manx (mæŋks) *adj. & n.* manés [*fem.* manesa].

many ('mɛn·i) *adj. & pron.* muchos. —*n.* gran número. —**a good many,** un buen número. —**a great many,** muchos; gran número. —**as many as,** tantos como; (*ante un número*) hasta. —**as many more,** otros tantos. —**be one too many,** ser uno más de la cuenta. —**how many,** cuántos. —**many a,** muchos. —**so many,** tantos. —**the many,** los más. —**too many,** demasiados; (*precedido de un número*) de más: *ten too many,* diez de más.

many-sided *adj.* **1,** (having many sides or faces) poligonal. **2,** (complex) de muchos aspectos. **3,** (having many talents) versátil.

map (mæp) *n.* mapa. —*v.t.* [**mapped, mapping**] **1,** (chart the geography of) trazar o dibujar el mapa de. **2,** (plan) planear; proyectar. —**map maker,** cartógrafo. —**map making,** cartografía.

maple ('mei·pəl) *n.* arce.

mar (maːr) *v.t.* [**marred, marring**] desfigurar; estropear.

marabou ('mær·ə,bu) *n.* marabú.

maraschino (,mær·ə'ski·no) *n.* marrasquino.

marasmus (mə'ræz·məs) *n., pathol.* marasmo.

marathon ('mær·ə,θan) *n.* maratón.

maraud (mə'rɔːd) *v.t. & i.* merodear. —**marauder,** *n.* merodeador. —**marauding,** *n.* merodeo. —*adj.* merodeador.

marble ('mar·bəl) *n.* **1,** (mineral) mármol. **2,** (little ball) bola; bolita; pepa; canica. —*adj.* marmóreo; de o como mármol. —*v.t.* jaspear. —**marbled,** *adj.* jaspeado. —**marbling** (-blɪŋ) *n.* jaspeado.

marblework ('mar·bəl,wʌrk) *n.* marmolería. —**marbleworker,** *n.* marmolista.

marcasite ('mar·kə,sait) *n.* marcasita.

marcel (mar'sɛl) *n.* ondulación Marcel. —*v.t.* ondular (el pelo).

march (martʃ) *v.i.* marchar. —*v.t.* hacer marchar. —*n.* marcha. —**marches,** *n.pl.* distritos fronterizos. —**marching,** *n.* marcha; paso de tropas. —*adj.* de o en marcha. —**march in,** entrar. —**march off,** marcharse. —**march out,** marcharse; salir. —**march up,** avanzar. —**steal a march on,** ganarle el quien vive a; *Amer.* madrugarse a.

March (martʃ) *n.* marzo.

marchioness ('mar·ʃə,nɛs) *n.* marquesa.

marchpane ('martʃ,pein) *n.* mazapán.

Mardi Gras ('mar·di'gra) *n.* carnaval.

mare (meːr) *n.* yegua.

margarine ('mar·dʒə·rin) *n.* margarina.

margin ('mar·dʒɪn) *n.* margen. —**marginal,** *adj.* marginal.

marguerite (,mar·gə'rit) *n.* margarita.

marigold ('mær·ɪ,gold) *n.* maravilla; flor de muerto.

marijuana (,mær·ə'hwa·nə) *n.* marijuana.

marimba (mə'rɪm·bə) *n.* marimba.

marina (mə'ri·nə) *n.* atracadero; dársena.

marinade (,mær·ə'neid) *n.* escabeche.

marinate ('mær·ə,neit) *v.t.* escabechar; marinar. —**marinated,** *adj.* en escabeche.

marine (mə'riːn) *adj.* marino; marinero; marítimo. —*n.* **1,** (seagoing soldier) marino; soldado de marina. **2,** (fleet; shipping) marina. **3,** (seascape) marina. —**mariner** ('mær·ə·nər) *n.* marinero; marino.

marionette (,mær·i·ə'nɛt) *n.* marioneta.

marital ('mær·ɪ·təl) *adj.* marital; matrimonial.

maritime ('mær·ɪ,taim) *adj.* marítimo.

marjoram ('mar·dʒə·rəm) *n.* mejorana. —**wild marjoram,** orégano.

mark (mark) *v.t.* marcar; señalar. —*v.i.* advertir; notar. —*n.* **1,** (sign; trace) marca; señal. **2,** (monetary unit) marco. —**hit the mark,** dar en el blanco. —**mark down,** rebajar (de precio). —**mark time,** marcar el paso; *fig.* hacer tiempo. —**mark up,** aumentar de precio. —**toe the mark,** entrar o ponerse en vereda; andar derecho.

markdown ('mark,daun) *n.* rebaja (de precio).

marked (markt) *adj.* **1,** (having a mark; singled out) marcado; señalado. **2,** (doomed) condenado. **3,** (notable) notable; considerable.

marker ('mar·kər) *n.* **1,** (instrument or device for marking)

marcador. **2,** (indicator; sign) indicador; señal. **3,** (chip; counter) ficha. **4,** *slang* = **I.O.U.**
market ('mar·kɪt) *n.* mercado. —*v.t.* vender. —*v.i.* comprar o vender en el mercado. —**marketable,** *adj.* vendible; comerciable. —**marketing,** *n.* mercadeo; mercados. —**be in the market for,** pensar o querer comprar. —**market dealer,** placero.
marksman ('marks·mən) *n.* [*pl.* -men] tirador. —**marksmanship,** *n.* puntería.
markup ('mark·ʌp) *n.* beneficio bruto; monto de la diferencia entre el precio de costo y el de venta.
marlin ('mar·lɪn) *n.* marlín.
marline ('mar·lɪn) *n.* merlín. —**marlinespike,** *n.* pasador.
marmalade ('mar·mə,leid) *n.* mermelada.
marmoreal (mar'mor·i·əl) *adj.* marmóreo.
marmoset ('mar·mə,zɛt) *n.* mono pequeño de la América del Sur.
marmot ('mar·mət) *n.* marmota.
maroon (mə'ruːn) *v.t.* abandonar (en una costa desierta). —*n.* color castaño. —*adj.* castaño.
marquee (mar'kiː) *n.* marquesina.
marquetry ('mar·kə·tri) *n.* marquetería.
marquis *también, Brit.,* **marquess** ('mar·kwɪs) *n.* marqués. —**marquisate** (-kwɪz·ɪt) *n.* marquesado. —**marquise** (mar'kiz) *n.* marquesa.
marriage ('mær·ɪdʒ) *n.* matrimonio. —*adj.* matrimonial. —**marriageable,** *adj.* casadero.
married ('mær·id) *adj.* **1,** (wedded) casado. **2,** (of or pert. to marriage) matrimonial; conyugal. —**married couple,** casados; esposos; cónyuges.
marron ('mær·ən) *n.* marrón.
marrow ('mær·o) *n.* médula; tuétano.
marry ('mær·i) *v.t.* **1,** (wed) casarse con. **2,** (give or join in marriage) casar. —*v.i.* casarse.
Mars (marz) *n.* Marte.
Marseillaise (,mar·sə'leiz) *n.* Marsellesa.
marsh (marʃ) *n.* pantano; ciénaga. —**marshy,** *adj.* pantanoso.
marshal ('mar·ʃəl) *n.* **1,** *mil.* mariscal. **2,** *U.S.* (law-enforcement officer) alguacil; ministril. —*v.t.* ordenar; poner en orden; disponer.

—**marshalship,** *n., mil.* mariscalato; mariscalía.
marshmallow ('marʃ,mæl·o) *n.* confite de malvavisco. —**marsh mallow,** malvavisco; altea.
marsupial (mar'su·pi·əl) *n.* & *adj.* marsupial.
mart (mart) *n.* mercado.
marten ('mar·tən) *n.* marta.
martial ('mar·ʃəl) *adj.* marcial. —**martial arts,** artes marciales.
Martian ('mar·ʃən) *adj.* & *n.* marciano.
martin ('mar·tən) *n.* vencejo.
martinet (,mar·tə'nɛt) *n.* ordenancista.
martingale ('mar·tən,geil) *n.* **1,** (harness) gamarra. **2,** *naut.* moco del bauprés. **3,** (betting system) martingala.
martini (mar'ti·ni) *n.* martini.
martyr ('mar·tər) *n.* mártir. —*v.t.* martirizar. —**martyrdom,** *n.* martirio. —**martyrize,** *v.t.* martirizar.
marvel ('mar·vəl) *n.* maravilla. —*v.i.* maravillarse. —**marvelous,** *adj.* maravilloso.
Marxism ('mark·sɪz·əm) *n.* marxismo. —**Marxist,** *n.* & *adj.* marxista. —**Marxian,** *adj.* marxista.
marzipan ('mar·zə,pæn) *n.* mazapán.
mascara (mæs'kær·ə) *n.* tinte para las pestañas.
mascot ('mæs·kət) *n.* mascota.
masculine ('mæs·kjə·lɪn) *adj.* masculino. —**masculinity** (-'lɪn·ə·ti) *n.* masculinidad.
mash (mæʃ) *n.* masa. —*v.t.* majar; machacar; macerar.
masher ('mæʃ·ər) *n.* **1,** (crushing device) majador. **2,** *slang* (flirt) galanteador.
mask (mæsk) *n.* **1,** (covering for the face) máscara. **2,** (disguise) disfraz. **3,** (death mask) mascarilla. —*v.t.* **1,** (cover with a mask) enmascarar. **2,** (disguise; conceal) disfrazar; disimular. —*v.i.* enmascararse.
masochism ('mæs·ə·kɪz·əm) *n.* masoquismo. —**masochist,** *n.* masoquista. —**masochistic,** *adj.* masoquista; masoquístico.
mason ('mei·sən) *n.* **1,** (worker in stone) albañil. **2,** *cap.* = **Freemason.**
Masonic (mə'san·ɪk) *adj.* masónico.

Masonite ('mei·sə,nait) *n., T.N.* masonita.

masonry ('mei·sən·ri) *n.* 1, (work in stone) albañilería; mampostería. 2, *cap.* = **Freemasonry**.

masque (mæsk) *n.* 1, *hist.* (dramatic form) representación dramática alegórica. 2, (revel) mascarada; máscaras. 3, = **mask**.

masquerade (,mæs·kə'reid) *n.* 1, (masked ball) mascarada; máscaras. 2, (disguise) disfraz. —*v.i.* disfrazarse; enmascararse. —**masquerader**, *n.* máscara.

mass (mæs) *n.* 1, (body of matter) masa. 2, (aggregation) masa; montón. 3, *cap., eccles.* misa. —*adj.* en masa. —*v.t.* juntar; agrupar; reunir. —*v.i.* agruparse; reunirse; apiñarse. —**in the mass,** en conjunto. —**mass media,** los medios públicos de comunicación. —**mass production,** fabricación en serie.

massacre ('mæs·ə·kər) *n.* matanza; masacre. —*v.t.* hacer una matanza de; masacrar.

massage (mə'saɪʒ) *n.* masaje; soba. —*v.t.* dar masaje; sobar. *Amer.* masajear.

masseur (mæ'sʌr) *n.* masajista. —**masseuse** (-'suz) *n.* masajista.

massive ('mæs·ɪv) *adj.* 1, (bulky; heavy) macizo; sólido. 2, (imposing) imponente. —**massiveness,** *n.* masa; lo macizo.

mast (mæst) *n.* mástil; palo.

master ('mæs·tər) *n.* 1, (lord; ruler; owner) amo; dueño; patrón; señor. 2, (head: chief) maestro; jefe. 3, (skilled workman or practitioner) maestro; perito. 4, (teacher) maestro; profesor. 5, (holder of a master's degree) licenciado; doctor. 6, *naut.* capitán. —*v.t.* 1, (subdue) dominar; vencer. 2, (rule) señorear. 3, (know thoroughly) saber a fondo; dominar. —*adj.* maestro. —**master's degree,** grado de maestro; licenciatura; doctorado. —**master mind,** inteligencia superior. —**master** [*fem.* **mistress**] **of ceremonies,** maestro (*fem.* maestra) de ceremonias. —**master stroke,** golpe maestro. —**meet one's master,** encontrar la horma de su zapato.

masterful ('mæs·tər·fəl) *adj.* 1, (domineering) imperioso; dominante. 2, (expert) perito; experto.

—masterfulness, *n.* maestría; dominio.

masterly ('mæs·tər·li) *adj.* maestro; magistral. —*adv.* con maestría; magistralmente. **—masterliness,** *n.* maestría.

mastermind ('mæs·tər·maind) *n.* mente creadora y directora. —*v.t.* crear y dirigir.

masterpiece ('mæs·tər·pis) *n.* obra maestra. *También,* **masterwork** (-wʌrk).

mastership ('mæs·tər·ʃɪp) *n.* 1, (mastery) maestría. 2, (position of a teacher) magisterio.

mastery ('mæs·tə·ri) *n.* 1, (control; authority) dominio; control; poder. 2, (expertness) maestría; dominio.

masthead ('mæst·hɛd) *n.* 1, *naut.* tope del mástil; espiga. 2, *journalism* membrete de periódico.

mastic ('mæs·tɪk) *n.* almáciga; mástique. —**mastic tree,** almácigo.

masticate ('mæs·tə,keit) *v.t. & i.* 1, (chew) masticar; mascar. 2, (crush to pulp) hacer pulpa de; machacar. —**mastication,** *n.* masticación.

mastiff ('mæs·tɪf) *n.* mastín.

mastitis (mæs'tai·tɪs) *n., med.* mastitis.

mastodon ('mæs·tə,dan) *n.* mastodonte.

mastoid ('mæs·tɔid) *n. & adj.* mastoides. —**mastoidal** (mæs'tɔi·dəl) *adj.* mastoideo. —**mastoiditis** (-tɔi'dai·tɪs) *n.* mastoiditis.

masturbate ('mæs·tər,beit) *v.i.* masturbarse. —**masturbation,** *n.* masturbación.

mat (mæt) *n.* 1, (small rug) estera; esterilla; *Amer.* felpudo. 2, (place mat) salvamanteles. 3, (border for a picture) orla; marco. 4, (for gymnastics) colchoneta. 5, (tangled mass, as of hair) mata de pelo; greña. 6, (dull finish) terminado o acabado mate. —*adj.* mate. —*v.t.* [**matted, matting**] 1, (cover with a mat) poner estera o felpudo en. 2, (tangle) enmarañar. 3, (put a dull finish on) matar. —*v.i.* enmarañarse.

matador ('mæt·ə·dor) *n.* matador [*fem.* -dora].

match (mætʃ) *n.* 1, (equal; peer) igual; par; rival. 2, (counterpart; facsimile) réplica. 3, (companion; one of a pair) compañero; pareja. 4, (pair) par; pareja. 5, (set; combination) juego; combinación. 6, (contest; bout) partido; partida; encuentro. **7,** (partido; partida; mate) partido. **8,** (alliance) alianza. **9,** (device for igniting) fósforo; cerilla. —*v.t.* **1,** (give or join in marriage) casar. **2,** (mate; pair) hacer pareja de o con; poner juntos; unir. **3,** (compete with successfully) competir con; rivalizar con. **4,** (compare) comparar. **5,** (provide or obtain a counterpart or equivalent to) dar o conseguir el igual de o el mismo que. **6,** (pit; oppose) enfrentar; poner frente a frente; oponer. **7,** (fit or go together with) hacer juego con; combinar con. **8,** (be equal to) ser igual a. —*v.i.* **1,** (get married; mate) casarse; aparejarse. **2,** (harmonize) armonizar; hacer juego. **3,** (be equal) ser iguales.

matchless ('mætʃ·ləs) *adj.* sin par; incomparable.

matchmaker ('mætʃ,mei·kər) *n.* **1,** (arranger of marriages) casamentero. **2,** (sports promoter) promotor.

mate (meit) *n.* **1,** (spouse; companion; one of a pair or set) compañero; pareja. **2,** *chess* mate. **3,** *naut.* piloto; segundo de a bordo. —*v.t.* **1,** (couple; join as a pair) casar; unir. **2,** *chess* dar mate. —*v.i.* casarse; unirse.

maté ('ma·te; 'mæt·e) *n.* mate; yerba mate.

material (mə'tɪr·i·əl) *adj.* **1,** (physical) material. **2,** (important; essential) esencial; substancial. —*n.* material. —**material witness,** testigo de causa. —**raw material,** materia prima.

materialism (mə'tɪr·i·ə·lɪz·əm) *n.* materialismo. —**materialist,** *n.* materialista. —**materialistic,** *adj.* materialista.

materiality (mə,tɪr·i·'æl·ə·ti) *n.* materialidad.

materialize (mə'tɪr·i·ə,laiz) *v.t.* materializar. —*v.i.* **1,** (be realized) llevarse a cabo; realizarse. **2,** (assume physical form) materializarse; hacerse palpable o visible; tomar cuerpo. —**materialization** (-lɪ'zei·ʃən) *n.* materialización; realización.

materially (mə'tɪr·i·ə·li) *adv.* materialmente.

matériel (mə·tɪr·i'ɛl) *n.* material; materiales; pertrechos.

maternal (mə'tʌr·nəl) *adj.* maternal.

maternity (mə'tʌr·nə·ti) *n.* maternidad. —*adj.* de maternidad.

mathematical (,mæθ·ə·'mæt·ɪ·kəl) *adj.* matemático.

mathematics (,mæθ·ə'mæt·ɪks) *n.* matemática; matemáticas. —**mathematician** (-mə'tɪʃ·ən) *n.* matemático.

matinal ('mæt·ə·nəl) *adj.* matinal.

matinee (,mæt·ə'nei) *n.* matiné.

matins ('mæt·ɪnz) *n.pl.* maitines.

matriarch ('mei·tri·ark) *n.* matriarca. —**matriarchal** (-'ar·kəl) *adj.* matriarcal. —**matriarchy,** *n.* matriarcado.

matricide ('mæ·trə,said) *n.* **1,** (act) matricidio. **2,** (agent) matricida. —**matricidal** (-'sai·dəl) *adj.* matricida.

matriculate (mə'trɪk·jə,leit) *v.t.* matricular. —*v.i.* matricularse. —**matriculation,** *n.* matrícula.

matrimony ('mæt·rə,mo·ni) *n.* matrimonio. —**matrimonial** (-'mo·ni·əl) *adj.* matrimonial.

matrix ('mei·trɪks) *n.* [*pl.* **-trices** (-trɪ·siz)] matriz.

matron ('mei·trən) *n.* matrona. —**matronly,** *adj.* matronal; de matrona.

matted ('mæt·ɪd) *adj.* **1,** (covered with a mat) esterado. **2,** (tangled) enmarañado.

matter ('mæt·ər) *n.* **1,** (material) materia. **2,** (affair) asunto; cosa; cuestión. **3,** (importance; moment) importancia. **4,** (pus) pus. —*v.i.* **1,** (be important) importar. **2,** (form pus) formar pus; supurar. —**as a matter of fact,** a decir verdad; en realidad. —**for that matter,** en cuanto a eso; respecto a eso. —**no matter,** no importa. —**no matter how,** por mucho que. —**What is the matter?,** ¿Qué pasa?; ¿Qué hay? —**What is the matter with you?,** ¿Qué tienes?; ¿Qué te pasa?

matter of course cosa natural; cosa de cajón. —**matter-of-course,** *adj.* de cajón; natural. —**as a matter of course,** como o por rutina.

matter of fact cosa positiva; hecho; realidad. —**matter-of-fact,** *adj.* prosaico; sin imaginación. —**as a matter of fact,** en realidad; de hecho.

matting ('mæt·ɪŋ) *n.* esterado.

mattock ('mæt·ək) *n.* piqueta; pico.

mattress ('mæt·rɪs) *n.* colchón.

maturation (ˌmætʃ·ʊ'rei·ʃən) *n.* maduración; *med.* supuración.

mature (mə'tjur) *adj.* **1,** (full-grown) maduro. **2,** *comm.* vencido. —*v.t.* madurar. —*v.i.* madurarse; *comm.* vencerse. —**maturity,** *n.* madurez; *comm.* vencimiento.

matutinal (mə'tju·tə·nəl) *adj.* matutino; matinal.

maudlin ('mɔd·lɪn) *adj.* sensiblero.

maul (mɔːl) *n.* mazo. —*v.t.* maltratar; magullar.

maunder ('mɔn·dər) *v.i.* hablar u obrar sin ton ni son.

Maundy Thursday ('mɔn·di) Jueves Santo.

mausoleum (ˌmɔ·sə'li·əm) *n.* mausoleo.

mauve (moᵓv) *n. & adj.* malva.

maverick ('mæv·ər·ɪk) *n.* **1,** (unbranded animal) animal mostrenco. **2,** (dissenter) rebelde; independiente.

mavis ('mei·vɪs) *n.* malvís.

maw (mɔː) *n.* buche; gaznate.

mawkish ('mɔ·kɪʃ) *adj.* **1,** (nauseating) asqueroso. **2,** (maudlin) sensiblero. —**mawkishness,** *n.* sensiblería.

maxilla (mæk'sɪl·ə) *n.* [*pl.* **-lae** (-i)] (*of persons*) mandíbula; (*of animals*) quijada. —**maxillary** ('mæk·sə·lɛr·i) *adj. & n.* maxilar.

maxim (mæk·sɪm) *n.* máxima.

maximal ('mæk·sɪ·məl) *adj.* máximo.

maximize ('mæk·sə,maiz) *v.t.* llevar al máximo; exagerar.

maximum ('mæk·sə·məm) *adj.* máximo. —*n.* máximo; máximum.

may (mei) *v.aux.* [*pret.* **might**] **1,** *expresando posibilidad o contingencia,* poder; ser posible: *I may do it now,* Puedo hacerlo ahora; Es posible que lo haga ahora; Puede que lo haga ahora. **2,** *expresando permiso,* poder: *You may come out now,* Puedes salir ahora. **3,** *denotando deseo, esperanza o súplica; se expresa en español con el subjuntivo: May you be happy,* Que seas feliz. —**come what may,** pase lo que pase. —**I may go,** puede que vaya. —**who may he be?,** ¿quién será?

May (mei) *n.* mayo. —**May Day, 1,** primero de mayo. **2,** (call of distress) ¡socorro!

Maya ('ma·jə) *n.* maya. —**Mayan** ('ma·jən) *n. & adj.* maya.

maybe ('mei·bi) *adv.* tal vez; acaso; quizá; a lo mejor.

mayflower ('mei,flau·ər) *n.* nombre de varias plantas que florecen en mayo; *en los EE.UU.,* hepática; anémona; *en las Islas Británicas,* espino majuelo.

May fly mosca de mayo.

mayhem ('mei·hɛm) *n.* **1,** *law* mutilación o lesión criminal. **2,** (violence) violencia; tropelía.

mayonnaise (ˌmei·ə'neiz) *n.* mayonesa.

mayor ('mei·ər) *n.* alcalde. —**mayoralty,** *n.* alcaldía. —**mayoress,** *n.* alcaldesa.

Maypole ('mei,pol) *n.* mayo; árbol de mayo.

maze (meiz) *n.* laberinto. —**be in a maze,** estar perplejo.

mazurka (mə'zʌr·kə) *n.* mazurca.

me (miː) *pron.pers.* **1,** *complemento directo o indirecto de verbo* me. **2,** *complemento de prep.* mí. **3,** *tras* than, *en las comparaciones* yo. —**with me,** conmigo.

mead (miːd) *n.* **1,** (drink) aguamiel; hidromiel. **2,** = **meadow.**

meadow ('mɛd·o) *n.* pradera; prado. —**meadowland,** *n.* pradera.

meager ('mi·gər) *adj.* **1,** (lean) flaco; magro; enjuto. **2,** (poor; scarce) escaso; mezquino. —**meagerness,** *n.* escasez; mezquindad.

meal (miːl) *n.* **1,** (repast) comida. **2,** (ground grain) harina.

mealy ('mi·li) *adj.* **1,** (of or containing meal) harinoso; farináceo. **2,** (like meal; pasty) pastoso.

mealymouthed ('mi·li,mauðd) *adj.* pacato; timorato; apocado en el hablar.

mean (miːn) *v.t.* [*pret. & p.p.* **meant**] **1,** (intend; have as a purpose) pensar; intentar; pretender; tener intención (o intenciones) de. **2,** (intend; destine) destinar: *She was meant for the stage,* Estaba destinada para el escenario. **3,** (signify; indicate) significar; indicar. **4,** (intend to express) querer decir. —*v.i.* tener intención o intenciones. —*adj.* **1,** (low; small; base; poor; miserly) mezquino. **2,** (of low estate) humilde. **3,** *colloq.* (illnatured) malo; avieso; cruel. **4,** *colloq.* (unpleasant; distasteful) malo; desagradable. **5,** *colloq.* (ashamed) abochornado. **6,** (middle; average) medio; del medio. —*n.* **1,** (average) promedio. **2,** *math.* (middle term) media. **3,** *pl.* (resources) medios; recursos; posibilidades. —**by all means, 1,** (without fail) sin falta; de todos modos. **2,** (of course) por supuesto. —**by any means,** de cualquier modo o manera; a toda costa. —**by means of,** por medio de. —**by no (manner of) means,** de ninguna manera; de ningún modo. —**mean well** (o **ill),** tener buena (o mala) intención. —**no mean . . . ,** un . . . de cierta importancia o de cierto valor. —**not by any means,** ni pensarlo; ni por pienso. —**to mean business,** hacer o decir (algo) en serio; hablar en serio.

meander (mi'æn·dər) *v.i.* **1,** (take a winding course) serpentear. **2,** (ramble; wander) dar vueltas. —*n.* [*también,* **meandering**] **1,** (bend; turn) meandro; vuelta; recodo. **2,** (a ramble) vueltas. —**meandering,** *adj.* serpenteante; tortuoso.

meaning ('mi·nɪŋ) *n.* significado; sentido. —*adj.* expresivo; significativo.

meaningful ('mi·nɪŋ·fəl) *adj.* **1,** (having significance) significativo; expresivo. **2,** (understandable) comprensible; inteligible. **3,** (useful; productive) útil; provechoso.

meaningless ('mi·nɪŋ·ləs) *adj.* sin sentido.

meanness ('min·nɪs) *n.* **1,** (baseness; shabbiness; miserliness) mezquindad. **2,** (ill nature) maldad; crueldad.

mean-spirited *adj.* pequeño; estrecho de miras.

meant (mɛnt) *v.,* *pret.* & *p.p. de* **mean.**

meantime ('min,taim) *adv.* mientras tanto; entretanto; a todo esto. —*n.* ínterin. *También,* **meanwhile** (-,hwail).

measles ('mi·zəlz) *n.* sarampión.

measly ('mi·zli) *adj.* mezquino; insignificante; despreciable. —**measliness,** *n.* insignificancia; mezquindad.

measurable ('mɛʒ·ər·ə·bəl) *adj.* **1,** (allowing of measurement) mensurable. **2,** (perceptible) perceptible.

measure ('mɛʒ·ər) *n.* **1,** (size; extent; capacity) medida. **2,** (unit or standard of measurement) medida. **3,** (system of measurement) sistema de medidas. **4,** (criterion) criterio. **5,** (action; step; means) medida. **6,** (quantity; degree) parte; proporción.

7, (meter) metro; medida. **8,** *mus.* compás. —*v.t.* **1,** (determine the size or extent of) medir. **2,** (bring into comparison) comparar; cotejar. —*v.i.* medir. —**beyond measure,** fuera de toda medida; sin tasa. —**for good measure,** para mayor seguridad o comodidad; por lo que toque. —**full measure,** el todo; el total. —**in full measure,** enteramente; todo. —**in a** (o **some) measure,** hasta cierto punto; en parte. —**in great measure,** en sumo grado; en gran parte. —**made to measure,** hecho a (la) medida. —**measure one's length,** medir el suelo; caerse. —**measure up to,** estar, llegar o ponerse a la altura de. —**tread a measure,** bailar.

measured ('mɛʒ·ərd) *adj.* **1,** (ascertained; determined) medido. **2,** (regular; steady; uniform) regular; uniforme. **3,** (slow; deliberate) mesurado. **4,** (restrained; calculated) medido; comedido; moderado.

measureless ('mɛʒ·ər·ləs) *adj.* sin límites; inmensurable.

measurement ('mɛʒ·ər·mənt) *n.* **1,** (measuring) medición. **2,** (dimension) medida.

meat (mit) *n.* **1,** (flesh) carne. **2,** (substance; pith) sustancia.

meatball ('mit·bɔl) *n.* albóndiga.

meat pie empanada; pastel de carne.

meaty ('mi·ti) *adj.* **1,** (fleshy) carnoso. **2,** (pithy) sustancioso.

mechanic (mə'kæn·ɪk) *adj.* & *n.* mecánico.

mechanical (mə'kæn·ə·kəl) *adj.* **1,** (of machinery or tools) mecánico. **2,** (automatic; reflex) maquinal; automático.

mechanics (mə'kæn·ɪks) *n.* mecánica.

mechanism ('mɛk·ə·nɪz·əm) *n.* mecanismo.

mechanize ('mɛk·ə,naiz) *v.t.* mecanizar. —**mechanization** (-nɪ'zei·ʃən) *n.* mecanización.

medal ('mɛd·əl) *n.* medalla.

medallion (mə'dæl·jən) *n.* medallón.

meddle ('mɛd·əl) *v.i.* entremeterse; inmiscuirse. —**meddler** (-lər) *n.* entremetido. —**meddlesome; meddling** (-lɪŋ) *adj.* entremetido; *Amer.* metido.

media ('mi·di·ə) *n., pl. de* **medium.**

medial ('mi·di·əl) *adj.* medio; del centro.

median ('mi·di·ən) *adj.* medio; del medio; intermedio. —*n.* punto o plano intermedio; *geom.* mediana.

mediate ('mi·di,eit) *v.i.* mediar. —*v.t.* **1,** (intervene in) mediar en; terciar en. **2,** (settle; adjust) dirimir. **3,** (effect by mediation) mediar en la promoción de. —**mediation,** *n.* mediación. —**mediator,** *n.* mediador [*fem.* -dora].

medic ('mɛd·ɪk) *n., colloq.* **1,** médico. **2,** (paramedic) médico auxiliar

medical ('mɛd·ɪ·kəl) *adj.* médico. —**medical examiner,** médico forense.

medicament (mə'dɪk·ə·mənt) *n.* medicamento.

medicate ('mɛd·ɪ,keit) *v.t.* medicinar. —**medication,** *n.* **1,** (treatment) medicación. **2,** (remedy) medicamento.

medicine ('mɛd·ə·sən) *n.* medicina. —**medicinal** (mə'dɪs·ə·nəl) *adj.* medicinal. —**medicine ball,** pelota o balón de fisioterapia. —**medicine chest,** botiquín. —**medicine man,** curandero; médico brujo. —**take one's medicine,** *colloq.* hacer(se) espaldas.

medico ('mɛd·ɪ·koɪ) *n., slang* médico; doctor.

medieval *también,* **mediaeval** (,mi·di'i·vəl) *adj.* medieval; medioeval.

mediocre ('mi·di,o·kər) *adj.* mediocre. —**mediocrity** (-'ak·rə·ti) *n.* mediocridad.

meditate ('mɛd·ɪ,teit) *v.t. & i.* meditar. —**meditation,** *n.* meditación. —**meditative,** *adj.* meditabundo; *Amer.* meditativo.

Mediterranean (,mɛd·ɪ·tə'rei·ni·ən) *n. & adj.* mediterráneo.

medium ('mi·di·əm) *n.* [*pl.* **media**] **1,** (mean) medio; punto medio. **2,** (means; agency) medio. **3,** (spiritualist) médium. —*adj.* medio; intermedio; mediano. —*adv.* a medias; a medio hacer; medianamente.

medlar ('mɛd·lər) *n.* níspero.

medley ('mɛd·li) *n.* mescolanza; popurrí. —*adj.* mezclado; mixto.

medulla (mɪ'dʌl·ə) *n.* médula. —**medullar,** *adj.* medular.

meek (mik) *adj.* manso; sumiso. —**meekness,** *n.* mansedumbre.

meerschaum ('mɪr·ʃəm) *n.* espuma de mar.

meet (mit) *v.t.* [*pret. & p.p.* **met**] **1,** (come into contact with; join) encontrarse con. **2,** (receive; greet) recibir; acoger. **3,** (conform to; satisfy) cumplir con; satisfacer. **4,** (face; deal with) hacer frente a. **5,** (make the acquaintance of) conocer. —*v.i.* **1,** (gather) reunirse. **2,** (come into contact) juntarse; encontrarse. —*n.* **1,** (gathering) reunión; encuentro. **2,** (contest) concurso. —*adj.* adecuado; a propósito. —**have (someone) meet (someone),** presentarle a uno (una persona): *I would like to have you meet my wife,* Me gustaría presentarle a mi esposa.

meeting ('mi·tɪŋ) *n.* **1,** (encounter) encuentro. **2,** (gathering) reunión. —**meeting of minds,** acuerdo.

megabyte ('mɛg·ə,bait) *n.* megabyte; megaocteto.

megacycle ('mɛg·ə,sai·kəl) *n.* megaciclo.

megalomania (,mɛg·ə·lə'mei·ni·ə) *n.* megalomanía. —**megalomaniac,** *n. & adj.* megalómano.

megaphone ('mɛg·ə,fon) *n.* megáfono.

megaton ('mɛg·ə,tʌn) *n.* megatón.

meiosis (mai'o·sɪs) *n.* [*pl.* **-ses** (-siːz)] meiosis.

melancholia (,mɛl·ən'ko·li·ə) *n.* melancolía.

melancholy ('mɛl·ən,kal·i) *n.* melancolía. —*adj.* melancólico. —**melancholic** (-'kal·ɪk) *adj.* melancólico.

Melanesian (,mɛl·ə'ni·ʒən) *adj. & n.* melanesio.

melange (mɛ'laɪŋʒ) *n.* mezcla; mescolanza; mejunje.

melanoma (mɛl·ə'no·mə) *n., med.* melanoma.

meld (mɛld) *v.t.* **1,** (blend) combinar. **2,** *cards* exhibir. —*n., cards* combinación de naipes; tanteo de éstos.

melée ('mei·lei; 'mɛl·ei) *n.* pelotera; trifulca.

meliorate ('mil·jə,reit) *v.t.* mejorar. —*v.i.* mejorarse. —**melioration,** *n.* mejoramiento; mejoría.

mellifluous (mə'lɪf·lu·əs) *adj.* melifluo. —**mellifluousness,** *n.* melifluidad.

mellow ('mɛl·o) *adj.* **1,** (soft; tender) dulce; tierno. **2,** (smooth) suave. **3,** (ripe) maduro. **4,** *colloq.* (jovial) jovial; genial. —*v.t. & i.* **1,**

(soften) suavizar. **2,** (sweeten) endulzar. **3,** (ripen) madurar.

melodic (mə'lad·ık) *adj.* melódico.

melodious (mə'lo·di·əs) *adj.* melodioso. —**melodiousness,** *n.* lo melodioso; melodía.

melodrama ('mɛl·ə,dra·ma) *n.* melodrama. —**melodramatic** (-drə·'mæt·ık) *adj.* melodramático.

melody ('mɛl·ə·di) *n.* melodía.

melon ('mɛl·ən) *n.* melón.

melt (mɛlt) *v.t.* **1,** (liquefy by heating) fundir; derretir. **2,** (dissolve) deshacer; disolver. **3,** (soften emotionally) ablandar; deshacer. —*v.i.* **1,** (become liquid) fundirse; derretirse. **2,** (dissolve) deshacerse; disolverse. **3,** (fade away; dwindle) esfumarse; desaparecer. **4,** (become softened in feeling) ablandarse; deshacerse. —**melting pot,** crisol; *fig.* lugar de fusión de pueblos o razas.

meltdown ('mɛlt,daun) *n.* fusión del núcleo (*de un reactor nuclear*).

member ('mɛm·bər) *n.* miembro.

membership ('mɛm·bər·ʃıp) *n.* **1,** (status as a member) membresía; afiliación. **2,** (members collectively) miembros; socios.

membrane ('mɛm·brein) *n.* membrana. —**membranous** ('mɛm·brə·nəs) *adj.* membranoso.

memento (mə'mɛn·to) *n.* recuerdo; memento.

memo ('mɛm·o) *n.* [*pl.* -os] *colloq.* = **memorandum.**

memoir ('mɛm·war) *n.* memoria.

memorable ('mɛm·ə·rə·bəl) *adj.* memorable.

memorandum (,mɛm·ə'ræn·dəm) *n.* memorándum; minuta.

memorial (mə'mor·i·əl) *n.* **1,** (monument) monumento. **2,** (remembrance) memoria; recuerdo. **3,** (petition) memorial; instancia; petición. —*adj.* conmemorativo.

memorialize (mə'mor·i·ə,laiz) *v.t.* **1,** (commemorate) conmemorar. **2,** (petition) presentar un memorial a o ante.

memorize ('mɛm·ə,raiz) *v.t.* aprender de memoria; memorizar.

memory ('mɛm·ə·ri) *n.* memoria.

men (mɛn) *n., pl. de* **man.**

menace ('mɛn·ıs) *n.* amenaza. —*v.t. & i.* amenazar.

ménage *también,* **menage** (me·'naʒ) *n.* **1,** (household) casa; hogar. **2,** (housekeeping) economía doméstica.

menagerie (mə'nædʒ·ə·ri) *n.* colección de fieras; casa de fieras.

mend (mɛnd) *v.t.* **1,** (repair) componer; arreglar. **2,** (correct; improve) corregir; mejorar. —*v.i.* mejorar. —*n.* arreglo. —**mend one's ways,** reformarse; corregirse. —**on the mend,** mejorando.

mendacious (mɛn'dei·ʃəs) *adj.* mendaz; mentiroso. —**mendacity** (mɛn'dæs·ə·ti) *n.* mendacidad.

mendelevium (,mɛn·də'li·vi·əm) *n.* mendelevio.

mendicant ('mɛn·di·kənt) *adj. & n.* mendicante. —**mendicancy,** *n.* mendicidad.

menhir (mɛn'hir) *n.* menhir.

menial ('mi·ni·əl) *n.* sirviente; criado. —*adj.* servil; bajo; de criado.

meningitis (,mɛn·ın'dʒai·tıs) *n.* meningitis.

Mennonite ('mɛn·ə,nait) *adj. & n.* menonita.

menopause ('mɛn·ə,pɔz) *n.* menopausia.

menses ('mɛn·siz) *n.pl.* menstruación; regla.

menstruate ('mɛn·stru,eit) *v.i.* menstruar. —**menstruation,** *n.* menstruación. —**menstrual,** *adj.* menstrual.

mensurable ('mɛn·ʃər·ə·bəl) *adj.* mensurable.

mensuration (,mɛn·ʃə'rei·ʃən) *n.* medida; medición.

mental ('mɛn·təl) *adj.* mental. —**mentality** (mɛn'tæl·ə·ti) *n.* mentalidad.

menthol ('mɛn·θal) *n.* mentol. —**mentholated** (-θə,leit·ıd) *adj.* mentolado.

mention ('mɛn·ʃən) *v.t.* mencionar. —*n.* mención; alusión. —**don't mention it,** no hay de qué; de nada.

mentor ('mɛn·tor) *n.* mentor.

menu ('mɛn·ju) *n.* menú.

meow (mi'au) *v.i.* maullar. —*n.* miau; maullido.

mephitis (mı'fai·tıs) *n.* vapor fétido. —**mephitic** (mı'fıt·ık) *adj.* mefítico.

mercantile ('mʌr·kən·tıl) *adj.* mercantil. —**mercantilism,** *n.* mercantilismo.

mercenary ('mʌr·sə,nɛr·i) *adj. & n.* mercenario.

mercer ('mʌr·sər) *n.* mercero.

mercerize ('mʌr·sə,raiz) *v.t.* mercerizar.

merchandise ('mʌr·tʃən,daiz) *n.*

mercadería; mercancía(s). —*v.t.* & *i.* traficar (en); comerciar (en). —**merchandising,** *n.* ventas.

merchant ('mʌr·tʃənt) *n.* comerciante; mercader. —**merchant marine,** marina mercante.

merchantman ('mʌr·tʃənt·mən) *n.* [*pl.* **-men**] barco o buque mercante.

merciful (,mʌr·sɪ·ʃəl) *adj.* clemente; misericordioso. —**mercifulness,** *n.* clemencia; misericordia.

merciless ('mʌr·sɪ·ləs) *adj.* despiadado; inclemente; cruel. —**mercilessness,** *n.* crueldad; falta de compasión.

mercurial (mər'kjur·i·əl) *adj.* **1,** [*también,* **mercuric** (-ɪk)] (of mercury) mercurial; mercúrico. **2,** (changeable) volátil; mudable.

mercurochrome (mər'kjur·ə,krom) *n., T.N.* mercurocromo.

mercury ('mʌr·kjə·ri) *n.* mercurio; *cap.* Mercurio.

mercy ('mʌr·si) *n.* clemencia; misericordia; piedad; compasión. —*interj.* ¡Dios santo!; ¡Dios mío! —**mercy seat,** trono de Dios.

mere (mɪr) *adj.* mero; simple; solo; puro. —*n., poet.* lago; mar. —**merely,** *adv.* meramente; simplemente.

merengue (mə'rɛn·ge) *n.* merengue.

meretricious (,mɛr·ə'trɪʃ·əs) *adj.* meretricio; interesado. —**meretriciousness,** *n.* lo meretricio.

merganser (mər'gæn·sər) *n.* mergo; mergánsar; somorgujo.

merge (mʌrdʒ) *v.t.* & *i.* unir(se); fundir(se); fusionar(se).

merger ('mʌr·dʒər) *n.* fusión. —**form a merger,** fusionarse.

meridian (mə'rɪd·i·ən) *n.* & *adj.* meridiano. —**meridional,** *adj.* meridional; meridiano.

meringue (mə'ræŋ) *n.* merengue.

merino (mə'ri·no) *n.* & *adj.* merino.

merit ('mɛr·ɪt) *n.* mérito. —*v.t.* merecer; ser digno de.

meritorious (,mɛr·ɪ'tor·i·əs) *adj.* meritorio. —**meritoriousness,** *n.* mérito.

merle (mʌrl) *n.* mirlo; merla.

merlin ('mʌr·lɪn) *n.* esmerejón.

mermaid ('mʌr,meid) *n.* sirena.

merman ('mʌr,mæn; -mən) *n.* [*pl.* **-men**] tritón.

merry ('mɛr·i) *adj.* alegre; festivo; risueño. —**merriment,** *n.* alegría;

júbilo. —**make merry,** regodearse; jaranear.

merry-andrew (,mɛr·i'æn·dru) *n.* bufón; chocarrero; payaso.

merry-go-round ('mɛr·i·go,raund) *n.* tiovivo; caballitos; *Amer.* carrusel.

merrymaker ('mɛr·i,mei·kər) *n.* parrandero; fiestero. —**merrymaking,** *n.* parranda; jarana.

mesa ('mei·sə) *n.* meseta; mesa.

mesalliance (mei'zæl·i·əns) *n.* matrimonio desigual.

mescal (mɛs'kæl) *n.* mezcal.

mesdemoiselles (,med·mwə'zɛl) *n., pl. de* **mademoiselle,** señoritas.

mesh (mɛʃ) *n.* **1,** (open space of a net) malla; ojo de red. **2,** (net; network) red. —*v.t.* & *i.* **1,** (tangle) enredar(se). **2,** *mech.* (engage) engranar.

mesmerism ('mɛs·mə·rɪz·əm) *n.* mesmerismo. —**mesmeric** (mɛs·'mɛr·ɪk) *adj.* mesmeriano. —**mesmerist,** *n.* hipnotizador. —**mesmerize,** *v.t.* hipnotizar.

mesolithic (,mɛz·ə'lɪθ·ɪk) *adj.* mesolítico.

meson ('mei·san) *n.* mesón.

mesotron ('mɛs·ə,tran) *n.* mesotrón.

Mesozoic (,mɛs·ə'zo·ɪk) *adj.* mesozoico.

mesquite (mɛs'kit) *n.* mezquite.

mess (mɛs) *n.* **1,** (disorder) desorden; revoltijo. **2,** (trouble; entanglement) embrollo; lío. **3,** (dirt; filth) suciedad; porquería. **4,** (sticky mass) plasta; mazamorra; mazacote. **5,** *colloq.* (bunch; group) montón. **6,** (group taking meals together; a meal so taken) rancho. —*v.t.* **1,** (make untidy) desordenar; desarreglar. **2,** (confuse) embrollar; complicar. **3,** (spoil; ruin) estropear; dañar. **4,** (dirty) ensuciar. —*v.i.* **1,** (take meals together) comer o tomar rancho. **2,** (cause dirt or filth) ensuciarse. **3,** *colloq.* (putter; bungle) chapucear.

message ('mɛs·ɪdʒ) *n.* mensaje.

messenger ('mɛs·ən·dʒər) *n.* mensajero.

Messiah (mə'sai·ə) *n.* Mesías. —**Messianic** (,mɛs·i'æn·ɪk) *adj.* mesiánico.

messieurs ('mɛs·ərz; me'sju) *n., pl. de* **monsieur,** señores.

messmate ('mɛs,meit) *n.* compañero de mesa o rancho.

messy ('mɛs·i) *adj.* **1,** (untidy)

desarreglado; desaliñado; desbarajustado. **2,** (dirty) sucio. **3,** (muddled) embrollado; enredado. **4,** (gooey) mazacotudo; apelmazado.

mestizo (mɛs'ti·zo) *n.* & *adj.* mestizo.

met (mɛt) *v., pret.* & *p.p. de* meet.

metabolism (mə'tæb·ə·lɪz·əm) *n.* metabolismo. —**metabolic** (,mɛt·ə'bal·ɪk) *adj.* metabólico.

metacarpus (,mɛt·ə'kar·pəs) *n.* metacarpo. —**metacarpal,** *adj.* metacarpiano.

metal ('mɛt·əl) *n.* metal. —**metallic** (mə'tæl·ɪk) *adj.* metálico.

metalliferous (,mɛt·ə'lɪf·ə·rəs) *adj.* metalífero.

metalloid ('mɛt·ə,lɔid) *n.* & *adj.* metaloide.

metallurgy ('mɛt·ə,lʌr·dʒi) *n.* metalurgia. —**metallurgic** (-'lʌr·dʒɪk) *también,* **metallurgical,** *adj.* metalúrgico. —**metallurgist,** *n.* metalúrgico.

metamorphosis (,mɛt·ə'mor·fə·sɪs) *n.* [*pl.* -ses (siz)] metamorfosis. —**metamorphic** (-fɪk) *adj.* metamórfico. —**metamorphose** (-foz) *v.t.* metamorfosear.

metaphor ('mɛt·ə,for; -fər) *n.* metáfora. —**metaphoric** (-'for·ɪk); **metaphorical,** *adj.* metafórico.

metaphysics (,mɛt·ə'fɪz·ɪks) *n.* metafísica. —**metaphysical,** *adj.* metafísico. —**metaphysician** (-fɪ'zɪʃ·ən) *n.* metafísico.

metaplasm ('mɛt·ə,plaez·əm) *n.* metaplasma.

metastasis (mə'tæs·tə·sɪs) *n.* metástasis. —**metastatic** (,mɛt·ə'stæt·ɪk) *adj.* metastático.

metatarsus (,mɛt·ə'tar·sʌs) *n.* metatarso. —**metatarsal,** *adj.* metatarsiano.

Metazoa (,mɛt·ə'zo·ə) *n.pl.* metazoos. —**Metazoan,** *n.* & *adj.* metazoo; metazoario.

mete (mit) *v.t.* asignar; repartir; distribuir.

metempsychosis (mə,tɛmp·sə'ko·sɪs) *n.* [*pl.* -ses (siz)] metempsicosis.

meteor ('mi·ti·ər) *n.* meteoro. —**meteoric** (-'or·ɪk) *adj.* meteórico. —**meteorite,** *n.* meteorito.

meteorology (,mi·ti·ə'ral·ə·dʒi) *n.* meteorología. —**meteorological** (-ər·ə'ladʒ·ɪ·kəl) *adj.* meteorológico. —**meteorologist,** *n.* meteorologista; meteorólogo.

meter ('mi·tər) *n.* **1,** (unit of length) metro. **2,** (measuring instrument) contador; *Amer.* medidor. **3,** metro. **4,** *mus.* compás; tiempo.

methadone ('mɛθ·ə,doːn) *n.* metadona.

methane ('mɛθ·ein) *n.* metano.

methanol ('mɛθ·ə,nal) *n.* metanol.

method ('mɛθ·əd) *n.* método. —**methodical** (mə'θad·ə·kəl) *adj.* metódico. —**methodology** (-'dal·ə·dʒi) *n.* metodología.

Methodist ('mɛθ·ə·dɪst) *n.* & *adj.* metodista. —**Methodism,** *n.* metodismo.

methyl ('mɛθ·ɪl) *n.* metilo. —**methylic** (mə'θɪl·ɪk) *adj.* metílico. —**methyl alcohol,** alcohol metílico.

methylene ('mɛθ·ə,lin) *n.* metileno.

meticulous (mə'tɪk·jə·ləs) *adj.* meticuloso. —**meticulousness,** *n.* meticulosidad.

métier (mɛ'tjei) *n.* oficio; profesión.

metric ('mɛt·rɪk) *adj.* métrico.

metrical ('mɛt·rɪ·kəl) *adj.* métrico.

metrics ('mɛt·rɪks) *n.* métrica.

metronome ('mɛt·rə,nom) *n.* metrónomo.

metropolis (mə'trap·ə·lɪs) *n.* metrópoli.

metropolitan (,mɛt·rə'pal·ə·tən) *adj.* & *n.* metropolitano.

mettle ('mɛt·əl) *n.* temple; fibra. —**mettlesome,** *adj.* de temple; de fibra.

mew (mju) *n.* **1,** (sound of a cat) maullido. **2,** (enclosure) cercado. **3,** (cage) jaula. **4,** (secret place) escondite; refugio. **5,** (sea gull) gaviota. **6,** *pl.* (stables) cuadras; caballerizas. —*v.t.* encerrar. —*v.i.* maullar.

mewl (mjuːl) *v.i.* lloriquear.

Mexican ('mɛk·sɪ·kən) *adj.* & *n.* mexicano; mejicano.

mezzanine ('mɛz·ə,nin) *n.* entresuelo.

mezzo-soprano ('mɛt·so·sə·'præn·o) *n.* mezzo-soprano.

mezzotint ('mɛt·so,tɪnt) *n.* media tinta.

mi (miː) *n., mus.* mi.

miasma (mai'æz·mə) *n.* miasma. —**miasmal; miasmatic** (,mai·æz·'mæt·ɪk) *adj.* miasmático.

mica ('mai·kə) *n.* mica.

mice (mais) *n., pl. de* mouse.

microbe ('mai·krob) *n.* microbio.

—**microbic** (mai'kro·bɪk) *adj.* micróbico.

microchip ('mai·kro,tʃɪp) *n.* microplaqueta.

microcomputer (,mai·kro·kəm'pju·tər) *n.* microordenador; microcomputadora.

microcosm ('mai·krə,kaz·əm) *n.* microcosmo. —**microcosmic**, *adj.* microcósmico.

microeconomics (,mai·kro·ek·ə'nam·ɪks) *n.* microeconomía.

microfiche ('mai·kro,fiʃ) *n.* microficha.

microfilm ('mai·kro,fɪlm) *n.* microfilm.

micrograph ('mai·kro,græf) *n.* micrografía. —**micrography** (mai'krag·rə·fi) *n.* micrografía.

micrometer (mai'kram·ə·tər) *n.* micrómetro.

micron ('mai·kran) *n.* micra; micrón.

Micronesian (,mai·krə'ni·ʒən) *n. & adj.* micronesio.

microorganism (,mai·kro'or·gə·nɪz·əm) *n.* microorganismo.

microphone ('mai·krə,fon) *n.* micrófono.

microphotograph (,mai·kro'fo·tə,græf) *n.* microfotografía. —**microphotography** (-fə'tag·rə·fi) *n.* microfotografía.

microprocessor (,mai·kro'pras·ɛs·ər) *n.* microprocesador.

microscope ('mai·krə,skop) *n.* microscopio. —**microscopic** (-'skap·ɪk) *adj.* microscópico.

microtome ('mai·krə,tom) *n.* micrótomo.

microwave ('mai·kro,weiv) *n.* microonda. —**microwave oven,** horno de microondas.

mid (mɪd) *adj.* medio. —*prep.* entre; en medio de. —**in mid air,** en el aire.

midair (,mɪd'ɛir) *adj.* en medio del aire. —**midair collision,** choque en pleno vuelo.

midday ('mɪd,dei) *n.* mediodía. —*adj.* de o a mediodía; de o a la tarde.

middle ('mɪd·əl) *adj.* **1,** (halfway between; in the center) del medio; del centro; entremedio. **2,** (medium) medio; mediano. **3,** (intermediate; intervening) intermedio; medio. —*n.* **1,** (central point or part) medio; centro; mitad. **2,** (waist) cintura. —**Middle Ages,** edad media; medioevo. —**middle class,**

clase media. —**middle ear,** oído medio. —**Middle East,** Oriente Medio. —**middle finger,** (dedo) corazón. —**middle school,** escuela intermedia. —**Middle West,** parte central del norte de los EE.UU. —**towards** o **about the middle of** *(the month, year, etc.),* a mediados de *(mes, año, etc.).*

middle-aged *adj.* de mediana edad. —**middle age,** edad mediana.

middle-class *adj.* de clase media; burgués.

middleman ('mɪd·əl·mæn) *n.* [*pl.* -men] intermediario.

middle-of-the-road *adj.* moderado; del centro. —**middle-of-the-roader,** *n.* moderado.

middling ('mɪd·lɪŋ) *adj.* regular; pasadero; pasable; mediano.

middy ('mɪd·i) *n.* **1,** (sailor's blouse) marinera. **2,** *colloq.* = **midshipman.**

midge (mɪdʒ) *n.* **1,** (gnat) mosquito; *Amer.* jején. **2,** (midget) enano.

midget ('mɪdʒ·ɪt) *adj. & n.* enano

midland ('mɪd·lənd) *n.* interior. —*adj.* de tierra adentro; del interior.

midlife ('mɪd,laif) *n.* edad mediana. —**midlife crisis,** crisis de la edad mediana.

midnight ('mɪd,nait) *n.* medianoche. —*adj.* de o a medianoche.

midriff ('mɪd·rɪf) *n.* diafragma. —*adj.* con abertura en la parte del diafragma.

midshipman ('mɪd,ʃɪp·mən) *n.* guardia marina.

midst (mɪdst) *n.* medio. —*prep., poet.* entre; en medio de.

midstream ('mɪd,strim) *n.* el medio de una corriente. —**in midstream,** a mitad de camino; a medio camino.

midway ('mɪd,wei) *n.* avenida de atracciones *(de una feria).* —*adj.* a o de medio camino; a o en mitad del camino. —*adv.* (a) medio camino; a o en mitad del camino.

midweek ('mɪd,wik) *n.* mediados de semana. —*adj.* a o de mediados de semana.

Midwest ('mɪd,wɛst) *n., U.S.* el medio oeste.

midwife ('mɪd,waif) *n.* comadrona; partera. —**midwifery,** *n.* partería.

midyear ('mɪd,jir) *n.* mediados de año. —*adj.* a o de mediados de año.

mien (miːn) *n.* semblante; aire.

miff (mɪf) *v.t., colloq.* enfadar; enojar. —*n., colloq.* enfado; enojo.

might (mait) *n.* fuerza; poder; poderío. —**with might and main**, con todas sus fuerzas.

might (mait) *aux.v.* **1**, *pret. de* **may**. **2**, *expresando duda, permiso o posibilidad en el presente o en el futuro; equivalente al condicional en español: Might I go now?*, ¿Podría ir ahora?; *We might arrive in time*, Podríamos llegar a tiempo.

mighty ('mai·ti) *adj.* **1**, (powerful) potente; poderoso. **2**, (great; momentous) importante; grande. —*adv., colloq.* muy.

mignonette (,mɪn·jə'nɛt) *n.* reseda.

migraine ('mai·grein) *n.* jaqueca.

migrant ('mai·grənt) *n. & adj.* emigrante.

migrate ('mai·gret) *v.i.* emigrar. —**migration,** *n.* migración; emigración. —**migratory** (-grə,tor·i) *adj.* migratorio; peregrino; (*of birds*) de paso.

mikado (mɪ'ka·do) *n.* micado.

mike (maik) *n., slang* = **microphone, micrometer,** *etc.*

mil (mɪl) *n.* **1**, (measure of diameter) milésima de pulgada. **2**, *artillery* unidad de medida de ángulos de tiro (1/6400 de la circunferencia).

milch (mɪltʃ) *adj.* lechera; de leche.

mild (maild) *adj.* **1**, (kind; gentle) apacible; dulce. **2**, (not harsh; bland) leve; ligero. **3**, (soft or pleasant to the taste) suave. **4**, (temperate) templado. —**mildness,** *n.* suavidad; lo suave; lo templado.

mildew ('mɪl·du) *v.t. & i.* enmohecer(se); cubrir(se) de moho. —*n.* moho.

mile (mail) *n.* milla.

mileage ('mai·lɪdʒ) *n.* **1**, (distance traversed) distancia en millas o kilómetros; millaje. **2**, (charge per mile) derecho por milla.

milepost ('mail,post) *n.* poste miliar.

miler ('mai·lər) *n.* corredor de una milla.

milestone ('mail,ston) *n.* **1**, = **milepost**. **2**, (important event) hito; acontecimiento.

milfoil ('mɪl,fɔil) *n.* milenrama; milhojas.

miliaria (,mɪl·i'ɛr·i·ə) *n.* erupción miliar.

milieu (mi'ljʊ) *n.* medio; medio ambiente.

militant ('mɪl·ə·tənt) *adj.* militante. —**militancy,** *n.* lo militante.

militarism ('mɪl·ə·tə,rɪz·əm) *n.* militarismo. —**militarist,** *n.* militarista. —**militaristic,** *adj.* militarista.

militarize ('mɪl·ə·tə,raiz) *v.t.* militarizar. —**militarization** (-rɪ'zei·ʃən) *n.* militarización.

military ('mɪl·ə,ter·i) *adj.* militar. —*n.* ejército.

militate ('mɪl·ə,teit) *v.i.* militar.

militia (mɪ'lɪʃ·ə) *n.* milicia; guardia nacional. —**militiaman** (-mən) *n.* [*pl.* **-men**] miliciano.

milk (mɪlk) *n.* leche. —*v.t.* **1**, (extract milk from) ordeñar. **2**, (squeeze out; drain) exprimir; agotar; sacar el jugo de. —*v.i.* dar leche. —**milker,** *n.* ordeñador; ordeñadora. —**milking,** *n.* ordeño; el ordeñar. —**milk fever,** fiebre de lactancia. —**milk leg,** flebitis puerperal. —**milk tooth,** diente de leche; diente mamón.

milkmaid ('mɪlk,meid) *n.* lechera.

milkman ('mɪlk,mæn) *n.* [*pl.* **-men**] lechero.

milk shake batido (de leche).

milksop ('mɪlk·sap) *n.* hombre afeminado.

milkweed ('mɪlk,wid) *n.* hierba lechera.

milkwort ('mɪlk·wʌrt) *n.* polígala.

milky ('mɪl·ki) *adj.* lechoso; como leche; lácteo. —**Milky Way,** Vía Láctea.

mill (mɪl) *n.* **1**, (machine or establishment for grinding) molino. **2**, (factory) fábrica; taller. **3**, (machine for rolling metal) laminadora. **4**, (U.S. monetary unit) milésimo de dólar. —*v.i.* arremolinarse; dar vueltas. —*v.t.* **1**, (grind) moler. **2**, (roll, as metal) laminar. **3**, (shape by grinding, as metal) fresar. **4**, (put grooves on, as coins) acordonar. **5**, (manufacture; process) manufacturar; fabricar. —**go through the mill,** *colloq.* pasar las de San Quintín (o las de Caín); pasarlas todas. —**put through the mill,** *colloq.* hacer pasar las de San Quintín (o las de Caín); poner a prueba.

millenary ('mɪl·ə,nɛr·i) *adj.* milenario.

millennium (mɪ'lɛn·i·əm) *n.* **1**, (period of a thousand years) milenio.

2, (thousandth anniversary) milenario. **—millennial,** *adj.* milenario.

miller ('mɪl·ər) *n.* **1,** (operator of a mill) molinero. **2,** (moth) mariposa nocturna blanquecina.

millet ('mɪl·ɪt) *n.* mijo.

milliard ('mɪl·jərd) *n., Brit.* mil millones.

milligram ('mɪl·ə‚græm) *n.* miligramo.

milliliter ('mɪl·ə‚li·tər) *n.* mililitro.

millimeter ('mɪl·ə‚mi·tər) *n.* milímetro.

milliner ('mɪl·ə·nər) *n.* sombrerero; modista de sombreros.

millinery ('mɪl·ə‚ner·i) *n.* **1,** (women's hats) sombreros de señora. **2,** (milliner's shop or trade) sombrerería (de señoras).

milling ('mɪl·ɪŋ) *n.* **1,** (crushing; grinding) molienda. **2,** (grooves cut in coins) acordonamiento; cordoncillo. **3,** (lamination) laminación. **4,** (processing) manufactura; fabricación.

million ('mɪl·jən) *n.* millón. **—millionth,** *adj. & n.* millonésimo.

millionaire (‚mɪl·jə'ne:r) *n.* millonario.

millipede ('mɪl·ə‚pi:d) *n.* milpiés.

millpond ('mɪl‚pand) *n.* alberca; presa o represa de molino.

millrace ('mɪl‚reis) *n.* canal de molino; caz.

millstone ('mɪl‚ston) *n.* piedra de molino; muela.

milquetoast ('mɪlk‚tost) *n.* pacato.

milt (mɪlt) *n., ichthy.* lecha.

mime (maim) *n.* **1,** (comic actor) pantomimo; cómico; mimo. **2,** (farce) pantomima; farsa. *—v.t. & i.* remedar; imitar.

mimeograph ('mɪm·i·ə‚græf) *n.* mimeógrafo. *—v.t.* copiar a mimeógrafo; mimeografiar.

mimic ('mɪm·ɪk) *v.t.* [**mimicked, mimicking**] remedar; imitar; copiar. *—n.* imitador; pantomimo. *—adj.* **1,** (imitative) mímico; imitativo. **2,** (mock; simulated) simulado; de mentirijillas.

mimicry ('mɪm·ɪk·ri) *n.* mímica; imitación; remedo; *biol.* mimetismo.

mimosa (mɪ'mo·sə) *n.* mimosa; sensitiva.

minaret (‚mɪn·ə'ret) *n.* minarete.

minatory ('mɪn·ə‚tor·i) *adj.* amenazador.

mince (mɪns) *v.t.* **1,** (chop) picar; cortar en pedacitos. **2,** (express or do with affectation) usar de afectación o remilgo en; poner afectación en. **3,** (weaken; soften, as words) comedirse en; medirse o moderarse en. *—v.i.* **1,** (speak or behave daintily) andarse con remilgos o mojigaterías. **2,** (walk daintily or affectedly) moverse con afectación o delicadeza afectada. **—mincing,** *adj.* afectado. **—not to mince words** (o **matters**), no pararse en pelillos; no andar por las ramas; hablar francamente. **—mince pie,** pastel hecho con pasas y especias.

mincemeat ('mɪns‚mit) *n.* **1,** (chopped meat) carne picada. **2,** (anything chopped fine) picadillo. **3,** (pie filling) pasas y especias. **—make mincemeat of,** hacer pedazos.

mind (maind) *n.* **1,** (mental faculty) mente; cerebro. **2,** (opinion) parecer; juicio; opinión. **3,** (reason; sanity) razón; cabeza; juicio. **4,** (intention) propósito; intención; ánimo. *—v.t.* **1,** (pay attention to) fijarse en. **2,** (heed) hacer caso de o a. **3,** (attend to; look after) cuidar; atender; ocuparse de. **4,** (be careful about) tener cuidado con. **5,** (care about; object to) importarle a uno. **6,** *colloq.* (keep in mind) tener presente; tener en cuenta. *—v.i.* **1,** (pay attention; give heed) prestar atención; atender; hacer caso. **2,** (be careful) tener cuidado. **3,** (care; be concerned) importarle a uno. **—bear in mind,** tener presente; tener en cuenta. **—be in one's right mind,** estar en sus cabales. **—be of one mind,** estar de acuerdo; ser de la misma opinión. **—be of two minds,** estar indeciso. **—be out of one's mind,** estar fuera de sí; estar loco. **—call to mind,** recordar; traer a (las) mientes. **—change one's mind,** cambiar de idea o pensamiento. **—give (someone) a piece of one's mind,** decirle a uno lo que piensa. **—go out of one's mind,** perder el juicio; salirse de sus casillas. **—have a good (o great) mind to,** tener muchas ganas de. **—have in mind,** pensar (en); acordarse de. **—keep in mind,** tener presente. **—keep one's mind on,** fijarse en; atender a; prestar atención a. **—make up one's mind,** decidirse; resolverse. **—never**

mind, no importa; no se moleste. —**set one's mind on,** empeñarse en; decidirse a. —**slip one's mind,** olvidársele a uno; escapársele a uno. —**to one's mind,** para uno; en la opinión de uno.

minded ('main·dɪd) *adj.* inclinado; dispuesto.

mindful ('maind·fəl) *adj.* atento; cuidadoso. —**mindfulness,** *n.* atención; cuidado.

mindless ('maind·ləs) *adj.* **1,** (senseless) necio; insensato. **2,** (heedless; unmindful) despreocupado; desatento.

mindset ('maind,sɛt) *n.* disposición mental.

mine (main) *poss.pron.* el mío; la mía; lo mío; los míos; las mías.

mine (main) *n.* mina. —*v.t. & i.* minar. —**minefield,** *n.* campo minado. —**miner,** *n.* minero.

mine-layer *n.* minador.

mineral ('mɪn·ər·əl) *n. & adj.* mineral.

mineralogy (,mɪn·ə'ræl·ə·dʒi) *n.* mineralogía. —**mineralogical** (-ə'ladʒ·ɪ·kəl) *adj.* mineralógico. —**mineralogist,** *n.* mineralogista.

mine sweeper dragaminas; barreminas.

mingle ('mɪŋ·gəl) *v.t.* mezclar; juntar. —*v.i.* mezclarse; juntarse.

miniature ('mɪn·i·ə·tʃər) *n.* miniatura. —*adj.* en miniatura.

minicomputer (,mɪn·i·kəm'pju·tər) *n.* computadora pequeña; mini-ordenador.

minidress ('mɪn·i,drɛs) *n.* mini-vestido; minitraje.

minim ('mɪn·əm) *n.* mínima.

minimal ('mɪn·ə·məl) *adj.* mínimo.

minimize ('mɪn·ə,maiz) *v.t.* **1,** (reduce to a minimum) reducir al mínimo. **2,** (undervalue; belittle) atenuar; menospreciar.

minimum ('mɪn·ə·məm) *n.* mínimo; mínimum. —**minimum wage,** salario mínimo.

mining ('mai·nɪŋ) *n.* minería. —*adj.* minero.

minion ('mɪn·jən) *n.* **1,** (favorite) valido; favorito. **2,** (henchman) esbirro; sicario.

miniskirt ('mɪn·i,skʌrt) *n.* minifalda.

minister ('mɪn·ɪs·tər) *n.* ministro. —*v.i.* servir. —**minister to,** servir; atender; asistir.

ministerial (,mɪn·ɪs'tɪr·i·əl) *adj.* ministerial.

ministration (,mɪn·ə'strei·ʃən) *n.* oficio; servicio; atención.

ministry ('mɪn·ɪs·tri) *n.* ministerio.

mink (mɪŋk) *n.* visón.

minnow ('mɪn·o) *n.* nombre de varios peces de la familia de la carpa.

minor ('mai·nər) *adj. & n.* menor.

minority (mɪ'nar·ə·ti) *n.* minoría. *(of age)* minoridad.

minstrel ('mɪn·strəl) *n.* trovador; juglar; *Amer.* payador. —**minstrelsy** (-si) *n.* juglaría.

mint (mɪnt) *n.* **1,** (plant) menta; hierbabuena. **2,** (place where money is coined) casa de moneda. **3,** *colloq.* (vast amount) mina; montón. —*v.t.* acuñar.

mintage ('mɪnt·ɪdʒ) *n.* acuñación.

minuend ('mɪn·ju·ɛnd) *n.* minuendo.

minuet (,mɪn·ju'ɛt) *n.* minué.

minus ('mai·nəs) *prep.* **1,** (less) menos. **2,** (lacking) sin; falto de. —*adj.* **1,** (denoting subtraction) menos. **2,** (negative) negativo.

minuscule (mɪ'nʌs·kjul) *adj.* minúsculo. —*n.* minúscula.

minute ('mɪn·ɪt) *n.* **1,** (sixtieth part of an hour or degree) minuto. **2,** (moment) minuto; momento. **3,** *pl.* (record) minutas; actas. **4,** (memorandum) minuta. —**minute hand,** minutero. —**up to the minute,** de última hora; de último momento; al corriente.

minute (mai'njut) *adj.* **1,** (very small, tiny) minúsculo; muy menudo. **2,** (exact; attentive to detail) minucioso.

minuteman ('mɪn·ɪt,mæn) *n.,* U.S. *[pl.* **-men]** miliciano listo a tomar armas.

minuteness (mai'njut·nəs) *n.* **1,** (smallness) pequeñez; menudencia. **2,** (exactness) minuciosidad.

minutiae (mɪ'nju·ʃi·i) *n.pl.* minucias; menudencias.

minx (mɪŋks) *n.* tunanta; moza descarada.

miracle ('mɪr·ə·kəl) *n.* milagro.

miraculous (mɪ'ræk·jə·ləs) *adj.* milagroso.

mirage (mɪ'raːʒ) *n.* espejismo.

mire (mair) *n.* cieno; fango; lodo. —*v.t.* **1,** (bog down) atascar; atollar. **2,** (make muddy) enlodar. —*v.i.*

atascarse; atollarse. —**miry,** *adj.* fangoso; barroso.

mirror ('mɪr·ər) *n.* espejo. —*v.t.* reflejar.

mirth (mʌrθ) *n.* alegría; regocijo. —**mirthful,** *adj.* alegre; regocijado. —**mirthless,** *adj.* triste; abatido.

misadventure (,mɪs·əd'vɛn·tʃər) *n.* mala suerte; desgracia; contratiempo.

misanthrope ('mɪs·ən,θrop) *también,* **misanthropist** (mɪs'æn·θrə·pɪst) *n.* misántropo. —**misanthropic** (-'θrap·ɪk) *adj.* misantrópico. —**misanthropy** (mɪs'æn·θrə·pi) *n.* misantropía.

misapprehend (,mɪs·æp·rɪ'hɛnd) *v.t.* entender mal. —**misapprehension,** *n.* error; equivocación.

misappropriate (,mɪs·ə'pro·pri·eit) *v.t.* malversar; distraer (fondos). —**misappropriation,** *n.* malversación.

misbegotten (,mɪs·bi'gat·ən) *adj.* ilegítimo; bastardo.

misbehave (,mɪs·bi'heiv) *v.i.* portarse o conducirse mal. —**misbehavior,** *n.* mala conducta; mal comportamiento.

misbelieve (,mɪs·bi'liːv) *v.i.* estar errado; vivir en el error. —*v.t.* no creer. —**misbeliever,** *n.* infiel; descreído.

miscalculate (mɪs'kæl·kjə,leit) *v.t.* & *i.* calcular mal. —**miscalculation,** *n.* error; mal cálculo.

miscarriage (mɪs'kær·ɪdʒ) *n.* 1, (mismanagement) extravío; desmán. 2, (failure to reach a destination) pérdida; extravío. 3, (abortion) malparto; aborto.

miscarry (mɪs'kær·i) *v.i.* 1, (go wrong; fail) fracasar; abortar. 2, (go astray; fail to arrive) extraviarse; perderse. 3, (abort) abortar; malparir.

miscast (mɪs'kæst) *v.t.* dar (a un actor) un papel inapropiado; hacer un mal reparto de actores en (una obra).

miscegenation (,mɪs·ɪ·dʒə'neiʃən) *n.* mezcla de razas.

miscellaneous (,mɪs·ə'lei·ni·əs) *adj.* misceláneo.

miscellany ('mɪs·ə,lei·ni) *n.* miscelánea.

mischance (mɪs'tʃæns) *n.* percance; desgracia; mala suerte.

mischief ('mɪs·tʃɪf) *n.* 1, (harm; damage; injury) daño; perjuicio; mal. 2, (noxious behavior) maldad;

mal proceder. 3, (naughtiness) travesura; diablura.

mischievous ('mɪs·tʃə·vəs) *adj.* 1, (injurious) dañoso; dañino; malo. 2, (full of tricks) trapacero; embrollón; malicioso. 3, (naughty) travieso; revoltoso.

mischievousness ('mɪs·tʃə·vəs·nəs) *n.* 1, (evil; harmfulness) maldad. 2, (malice; trickery) malicia; trapacería. 3, (naughtiness) travesura; diablura.

miscible ('mɪs·ə·bəl) *adj.* miscible. —**miscibility,** *n.* miscibilidad.

misconceive (,mɪs·kən'siːv) *v.t.* formar concepto erróneo de; entender mal. —**misconception** (-'sɛp·ʃən) *n.* concepto erróneo.

misconduct (mɪs'kan·dʌkt) *n.* desafuero; mal proceder; acción o conducta impropia. —*v.t.* (,mɪs·kən'dʌkt) 1, (mismanage) errar en; proceder sin acierto en. 2, *usu.refl.* (misbehave) conducirse mal.

misconstrue (,mɪs·kən'struː) *v.t.* interpretar mal; torcer el sentido de. —**misconstruction** (-'strʌk·ʃən) *n.* mala interpretación; error.

miscount ('mɪs·kaunt) *v.t.* & *i.* contar mal. —*n.* cuenta errónea.

miscreant ('mɪs·kri·ənt) *adj.* & *n.* malandrín; bribón; sinvergüenza.

miscue (mɪs'kjuː) *n.* 1, *billiards* pifia. 2, *theat.* equivocación en el apunte. —*v.i.* 1, *billiards* pifiar. 2, *theat.* equivocarse de apunte.

misdeal (mɪs'diːl) *v.t.* & *i.* dar *o* repartir mal (las cartas). —*n.* repartición mal hecha.

misdeed (mɪs'diːd) *n.* mala acción; delito.

misdemeanor (,mɪs·də'mi·nər) *n.* 1, (misbehavior) mala conducta. 2, *law* delito menor.

misdirect (,mɪs·dɪ'rɛkt) *v.t.* encaminar mal. —**misdirection,** *n.* mala dirección; malas instrucciones.

misdoing (mɪs'du·ɪŋ) *n.* delito; mala acción.

miser ('mai·zər) *n.* avaro; miserable; tacaño. —**miserliness,** *n.* avaricia; tacañería. —**miserly,** *adj.* avariento; miserable; tacaño.

miserable ('mɪz·ər·ə·bəl) *adj.* miserable.

misery ('mɪz·ə·ri) *n.* miseria.

misfeasance (mɪs'fi·zəns) *n.* abuso de autoridad.

misfire (mɪs'fair) *v.i.* fallar el tiro. —*n.* tiro fallo.

misfit ('mɪs,fɪt) *n.* **1,** (poor fit) mal ajuste o calce. **2,** (badly adjusted person) inadaptado. **3,** (ill-fitting thing) cosa que no ajusta bien; prenda que no calza o queda bien. —*v.t. & i.* (mɪs'fɪt) no ajustar bien; no quedar bien; no calzar.

misfortune (mɪs'for·tʃun) *n.* mala suerte; desgracia; desventura.

misgiving (mɪs'gɪv·ɪŋ) *n.* **1,** (suspicion; doubt) recelo; duda. **2,** (foreboding) mal presentimiento; aprensión.

misguide (mɪs'gaid) *v.t.* descaminar; descarriar.

misguided (mɪs'gai·dɪd) *adj.* **1,** (mistaken) equivocado; erróneo. **2,** (led astray) descaminado; descarriado.

mishandle (mis'hæn·dəl) *v.t.* **1,** (handle badly) manejar mal. **2,** (mistreat) maltratar.

mishap ('mɪs·hæp) *n.* percance; contratiempo.

mishmash ('mɪʃ,mæʃ) *n.* mezcolanza; mejunje; mazacote.

misinform (,mɪs·ɪn'form) *v.t.* informar mal. —**misinformation,** *n.* información equivocada o errónea.

misinterpret (,mɪs·ɪn'tʌr·prɪt) *v.t.* interpretar mal. —**misinterpretation,** *n.* mala interpretación.

misjudge (mɪs'dʒʌdʒ) *v.t.* **1,** (miscalculate) calcular mal. **2,** (judge unfairly) juzgar mal o injustamente. —**misjudgment,** *n.* juicio equivocado.

mislay (mɪs'lei) *v.t.* [*pret. & p.p.* **mislaid**] **1,** (misplace) extraviar. **2,** (place incorrectly) colocar mal.

mislead (mɪs'liːd) *v.t.* **1,** (lead astray) descarriar; extraviar. **2,** (deceive) engañar. —**misleading,** *adj.* engañador.

mismanage (mɪs'mæn·ɪdʒ) *v.t.* manejar o administrar mal. —**mismanagement,** *n.* mal manejo; mala administración.

mismatch (mɪs'mætʃ) *v.t.* unir o emparejar mal. —*n.* unión mal hecha; casamiento mal hecho; casorio.

misnomer (mɪs'no·mər) *n.* nombre inapropiado.

misogamy (mɪ'sag·ə·mi) *n.* misogamia. —**misogamist,** *n.* misógamo. —**misogamous,** *adj.* misógamo.

misogyny (mɪ'sadʒ·ə·ni) *n.*

misoginia. —**misogynist,** *n.* misógino. —**misogynous,** *adj.* misógino.

misplace (mɪs'pleis) *v.t.* **1,** (put in a wrong place) colocar mal; poner fuera de sitio. **2,** (bestow unwisely) entregar o poner equivocadamente. **3,** (mislay; lose) extraviar; perder.

misprint ('mɪs·prɪnt) *n.* errata; error de imprenta. —*v.t.* (mɪs'prɪnt) imprimir con erratas; imprimir o escribir incorrectamente.

mispronounce (,mɪs·prə'nauns) *v.t. & i.* pronunciar mal. —**mispronunciation** (-nʌn·si'ei·ʃən) *n.* pronunciación incorrecta.

misquote (mɪs'kwot) *v.t.* citar falsamente o equivocadamente; torcer las palabras de. —**misquotation** (,mɪs· kwo'tei·ʃən) *n.* cita falsa o equivocada; tergiversación.

misread (mɪs'riːd) *v.t.* leer mal; interpretar mal al leer.

misrepresent (,mɪs·rep·rɪ'zent) *v.t.* tergiversar; falsear. —**misrepresentation** (-zen'tei·ʃən) *n.* tergiversación; falsedad.

misrule (mɪs'ruːl) *v.t.* gobernar mal. —*n.* mal gobierno; desorden.

miss (mɪs) *v.t.* **1,** (fail to hit) errar; marrar; no acertar en. **2,** (fail to meet, reach or find) perder; no alcanzar; no encontrar. **3,** (overlook) pasar por alto; no darse cuenta de. **4,** (feel the absence of) echar de menos; *Amer.* extrañar. **5,** (escape; avoid; as a mishap) escaparse de; evitar; eludir. **6,** (fail to be present at) no asistir a; no estar presente a; perder. **7,** (fail to perceive) no ver; no captar. **8,** (lack) faltar; hacerle falta a uno. —*v.i.* fallar. —*n.* **1,** (failure) falla; tiro fallo; error. **2,** (young lady) señorita. —**a miss is as good as a mile,** tanto da errar por un pelo que por una cuadra. —**misfire,** fallar el tiro. —**miss out,** errar el tiro; fracasar en el intento. —**miss the mark,** errar el tiro; errar el blanco.

missal ('mɪs·əl) *n.* misal.

misshapen (mɪs'ʃei·pən) *adj.* deforme. —**misshapenness,** *n.* deformidad.

missile ('mɪs·əl) *n.* proyectil.

missing ('mɪs·ɪŋ) *adj.* **1,** (lost) extraviado; perdido. **2,** (absent) ausente. **3,** (lacking) falto. —**be missing,** faltar. —**missing link,** eslabón perdido.

mission ('mɪʃ·ən) *n.* misión.

missionary ('mɪʃ·ə·ner·i) *n.*

misionero; misionario. —*adj.* misional.

missis *también,* **missus** ('mɪs·ɪz) *n., colloq.* señora; esposa.

missive ('mɪs·ɪv) *n.* misiva.

misspell (mɪs'spɛl) *v.t.* deletrear mal. —**misspelt** (mɪs'spɛlt) *adj.* mal deletreado. —**misspelling,** *n.* falta de ortografía.

misspend (mɪs'spɛnd) *v.t.* malgastar.

misstate (mɪs'steit) *v.t.* tergiversar; relatar falsamente. —**misstatement,** *n.* tergiversación; relación falsa.

misstep (mɪs'stɛp) *n.* 1, (stumble) paso en falso; tropezón. 2, (mistake in conduct) desliz; falta.

missus ('mɪs·ɪz) *n.* = **missis.**

mist (mɪst) *n.* 1, (haze; fog) neblina; niebla; bruma. 2, (film, as of moisture) vaho. 3, (drizzle) llovizna. 4, (fine spray; vapor) vapor. —*v.t.* nublar; empañar. —*v.i.* nublarse; empañarse.

mistakable *también,* **mistakeable** (mɪs'teik·ə·bəl) *adj.* susceptible de error o equivocación.

mistake (mɪs'teik) *v.t.* [*infl.:* **take**] 1, (take wrongly) equivocar; tomar equivocadamente. 2, (misinterpret) entender o interpretar mal. —*v.i.* equivocarse. —*n.* error; equivocación. —**make a mistake,** equivocarse. —**no mistake about it,** *colloq.* sin duda.

mistaken (mɪs'tei·kən) *adj.* 1, (in error) equivocado. 2, (erroneous) erróneo.

mister ('mɪs·tər) *n.* señor.

mistime (mɪs'taim) *v.t.* decir o hacer a destiempo.

mistletoe ('mɪs·əl,to) *n.* muérdago.

mistook (mɪs'tʊk) *v., pret. de* **mistake.**

mistreat (mɪs'trit) *v.t.* maltratar. —**mistreatment,** *n.* maltrato.

mistress ('mɪs·trɪs) *n.* 1, (lady of the house; owner) señora; ama; dueña. 2, (paramour) querida; amante. 3, (skilled woman) maestra. —**be mistress of,** dominar.

mistrial (mɪs'trai·əl) *n.* causa o juicio anulado.

mistrust (mɪs'trʌst) *n.* desconfianza; recelo. —*v.t.* desconfiar de; recelar de. —**mistrustful,** *adj.* desconfiado; receloso.

misty ('mɪs·ti) *adj.* 1, (covered with or resembling mist) brumoso; nublado. 2, (obscure; vague) nebuloso; indistinto. 3, (filmed over) empañado. —**mistiness,** *n.* nebulosidad; brumosidad.

misunderstand (,mɪs·ʌn·dər'stænd) *v.t. & i.* entender o comprender mal. —**misunderstanding,** *n.* mal entendido.

misunderstood (,mɪs·ʌn·dər'stʊd) *v., pret. & p.p. de* **misunderstand.** —*adj.* mal comprendido; incomprendido.

misusage (mɪs'jus·ɪdʒ) *n.* abuso; mal uso.

misuse (mɪs'juːz) *v.t.* 1, (maltreat) maltratar; abusar. 2, (misapply) emplear mal; desperdiciar. —*n.* (mɪs'jus) mal uso; abuso.

mite (mait) *n.* 1, *zoöl.* ácaro. 2, (bit; small amount) pizca; moto. 3, (small coin) óbolo.

miter ('mai·tər) *n.* 1, *eccles.* mitra. 2, (beveled joint) inglete. —*v.t.* cortar o ensamblar en ingletes. —**miter box,** caja de ingletes. —**miter gear,** engranaje cónico. —**miter joint,** inglete.

mitigate ('mɪt·ə,geit) *v.t.* mitigar. —**mitigation,** *n.* mitigación.

mitosis (mai'to·sɪs) *n., biol.* [*pl.* **-ses** (siːz)] mitosis.

mitt (mɪt) *n.* 1, (glove) mitón; *sports* guante. 2, *slang* (hand) mano.

mitten ('mɪt·ən) *n.* mitón.

mix (mɪks) *v.t.* mezclar; juntar; unir. —*v.i.* mezclarse; juntarse. —*n.* mezcla. —**mix up,** (mix thoroughly) mezclar. 2, (confuse) confundir. 3, (involve) meter; enredar.

mixed (mɪkst) *adj.* 1, (blended) mezclado. 2, (assorted) variado. 3, (heterogeneous) mixto. —**mixed up,** *colloq.* confundido.

mixer ('mɪk·sər) *n.* 1, mezclador; mezcladora. 2, (sociable person) persona sociable. 3, (get-acquainted activity) fiesta o juego de conocimiento.

mixture ('mɪks·tʃər) *n.* mixtura; mezcla; mescolanza.

mix-up *n.* confusión; lío.

mizzen ('mɪz·ən) *n.* mesana. —**mizzenmast** (-mæst; -məst) *n.* palo de mesana.

mnemonic (nɪ'man·ɪk) *adj.* mnemotécnico. —**mnemonics,** *n.* mnemotecnia.

moan (mo:n) *n.* gemido; quejido. —*v.i.* gemir; quejarse.

moat (mot) *n.* foso.

mob (ma:b) *n.* turba; chusma; populacho. —*v.t.* [**mobbed, mobbing**] asaltar; atropellar. —**mobocracy** (mab'ak·rə·si) *n.* gobierno de la chusma.

mobile ('mo·bəl) *adj.* 1, (easily moving; movable) móvil; movible. 2, (changing easily) variable. —*n.* móvil. —**mobility** (mo'bɪl·ə·ti) *n.* movilidad. —**mobile home,** casa rodante.

mobilize ('mo·bə,laiz) *v.t.* movilizar. —*v.i.* movilizarse. —**mobilization** (-lɪ'zei·ʃən) *n.* movilización.

mobster ('mab·stər) *n., slang* gángster; pandillero.

moccasin ('mak·ə·sən) *n.* mocasín.

mocha ('mo·kə) *n.* moca; café moca.

mock (mak) *v.t.* 1, (ridicule; deride) escarnecer; mofarse de; burlarse de. 2, (scoff at) despreciar; no hacer caso de. 3, (mimic) imitar; remedar. 4, (deceive) decepcionar; engañar. —*v.i.* mofarse; burlarse. —*adj.* fingido; falso. —**mock-heroic,** *adj.* épico-burlesco. —**mock turtle soup,** sopa de cabeza de ternera, imitando la de tortuga.

mockery ('mak·ə·ri) *n.* 1, (ridicule; derision) burla; mofa. 2, (laughing-stock) hazmerreír. 3, (travesty) remedo grotesco.

mockingbird ('mak·ɪŋ,bʌrd) *n.* sinsonte; pájaro burlón.

mock-up *n.* modelo; réplica.

modal ('mo·dəl) *adj.* modal. —**modality** (mo'dæl·ə·ti) *n.* modalidad.

mode (mo:d) *n.* 1, (manner; style) modo; manera; forma. 2, (custom) moda. 3, *mus.; gram.* modo.

model ('mad·əl) *n.* modelo. —*adj.* modelo (*indecl.*): model home, casa modelo. —*v.t. & i.* modelar. —**modeling,** *n.* modelado. —**model on** (o **after**), hacer o formar a imitación de.

modem ('mo·dəm) *n., comput.; radio* modem.

moderate ('mad·ər·ɪt) *adj.* 1, (restrained) moderado. 2, (medium) mediano. 3, (reasonable, as of prices) módico; razonable. —*n.* moderado. —*v.t.* ('mad·ə,reit) 1, (restrain) moderar; refrenar; reprimir. 2, (preside over) servir de moderador o árbitro en. —*v.i.* 1, (tone down) moderarse; refrenarse.

2, (act as moderator) servir de moderador o árbitro. —**moderation,** *n.* moderación.

moderator ('mad·ə,rei·tər) *n.* 1, (one who presides) árbitro; moderador. 2, *mech.* regulador; moderador.

modern ('mad·ərn) *adj. & n.* moderno. —**modernism,** *n.* modernismo. —**modernist,** *n.* modernista. —**modernistic,** *adj.* modernista.

modernize ('mad·ər,naiz) *v.t.* modernizar. —**modernization** (-nɪ'zei·ʃən) *n.* modernización.

modest ('mad·ɪst) *adj.* modesto. —**modesty** ('mad·əs·ti) *n.* modestia.

modicum ('mad·ə·kəm) *n.* cantidad módica.

modify ('mad·ə,fai) *v.t.* 1, (change) modificar. 2, (moderate) moderar; atenuar. 3, *gram.* modificar. —**modification** (-fɪ'kei·ʃən) *n.* modificación. —**modifier,** *n.* modificador.

modish ('mo·dɪʃ) *adj.* de moda; elegante. —**modishly,** *adv.* a la moda.

modiste (mo'dist) *n.* modista.

modulate ('madʒ·ə,leit) *v.t.* modular. —**modulation,** *n.* modulación. —**modulator,** *n.* modulador.

module ('madʒ·ul) *n.* módulo. —**modular,** *adj.* modular.

modulus ('madʒ·ə·ləs) *n.* módulo.

mogul ('mo·gəl) *n.* 1, (oriental ruler) mogol. 2, (magnate) magnate.

mohair ('mo,her) *n.* lana o tela de Angora.

Mohammedan (mo'hæm·ə·dən) *n. & adj.* mahometano. —**Mohammedanism,** *n.* mahometismo.

moil (mɔil) *v.i.* bregar; afanarse. —*n.* afán.

moire (mwa:r) *n.* moaré; muaré. —**moiré** (mwa'rei) *adj.* de moaré (o muaré).

moist (mɔist) *adj.* húmedo. —**moistness,** *n.* humedad.

moisten ('mɔis·ən) *v.t.* humedecer.

moisture ('mɔis·tʃər) *n.* humedad. —**moisturize,** *v.t.* humedecer.

molar ('mol·ər) *n.* muela; molar. —*adj.* molar.

molasses (mo'læs·ɪz) *n.* melaza.

mold (mo:ld) *n.* 1, (form; matrix) molde. 2, (fungus) moho. 3, (rich earth) mantillo; humus. —*v.t.* 1, (shape) moldear. 2, (make moldy) enmohecer. —*v.i.* enmohecerse; florecerse (*esp. de alimentos*).

—**moldy,** *adj.* mohoso; enmohecido; florecido *(esp. de alimentos).*

molder ('mol·dər) *v.t.* desmoronar. —*v.i.* desmoronarse. —*n.* moldeador.

molding ('mol·dɪŋ) *n.* moldeado; moldura.

mole (moʊl) *n.* **1,** (blemish) lunar. **2,** *zoöl.* topo. **3,** (breakwater) rompeolas. **4,** (harbor) dársena.

molecule ('mal·ə,kjul) *n.* molécula. —**molecular** (mə'lɛkjə·lər) *adj.* molecular.

molehill ('mol,hɪl) *n.* topinera. —**make a mountain out of a molehill,** hacer una montaña de un grano de arena.

moleskin ('mol,skɪn) *n.* **1,** (fur) piel de topo. **2,** (cloth) especie de fustán.

molest (mə'lɛst) *v.t.* molestar; importunar. —**molestation** (,molɛs'teɪ·ʃən) *n.* importunación; molestias.

moll (mal) *n., slang* pandillera.

mollify ('mal·ə,faɪ) *v.t.* molificar; ablandar; aplacar. —**mollification** (-fɪ'keɪ·ʃən) *n.* molificación.

mollusk ('mal·əsk) *n.* molusco.

mollycoddle ('mal·i,kad·əl) *v.t., colloq.* mimar; engreír. —*n.* hombre o niño engreído.

molt (molt) *v.i.* pelechar.

molten ('mol·tən) *adj.* fundido; derretido.

molybdenum (mə'lɪb·də·nəm) *n.* molibdeno. —**molybdic** (-dɪk) *adj.* molíbdico.

mom (maːm) *n., colloq.* mamá. *También,* **mommy** ('ma·mi).

moment ('mo·mənt) *n.* momento.

momentarily (,mo·mən'tɛr·ə·li) *adv.* **1,** (for a short time) momentáneamente. **2,** (from moment to moment) de un momento a otro.

momentary ('mo·mən,tɛr·i) *adj.* momentáneo.

momentous (mo'mɛn·təs) *adj.* trascendental; de gran momento. —**momentousness,** *n.* trascendencia; importancia.

momentum (mo'mɛn·təm) *n.* ímpetu; fuerza; *mech.* momento.

monad ('man·æd) *n.* mónada.

monarch ('man·ərk) *n.* monarca. —**monarchal** (mə'nar·kəl) *adj.* monárquico.

monarchism ('man·ər,kɪz·əm) *n.* monarquismo. —**monarchist,** *n.* monárquico.

monarchy ('man·ər·ki) *n.* monarquía.

monastery ('man·əs,tɛr·i) *n.* monasterio.

monastic (mə'næs·tɪk) *adj.* monástico; monacal. —**monasticism** (-tə,sɪz·əm) *n.* monacato.

Monday ('mʌn·de) *n.* lunes.

monetary ('man·ə,tɛr·i) *adj.* monetario.

monetize ('man·ə,taɪz) *v.t.* **1,** (legalize as money) monetizar. **2,** (coin into money) acuñar.

money ('mʌn·i) *n.* dinero. —**in the money,** *slang* **1,** (among the winners) entre los primeros; entre los ganadores. **2,** (wealthy) acaudalado; adinerado. —**money broker,** cambista. —**money order,** giro. —**paper money,** papel moneda.

moneybag ('mʌn·i·bæg) *n.* **1,** (sack for money) bolsa; saco. **2,** *pl., slang* (rich man) ricachón.

moneychanger ('mʌn·i,tʃeɪndʒər) *n.* cambista.

moneyed ('mʌn·id) *adj.* adinerado; acaudalado.

moneylender ('mʌn·i,lɛn·dər) *n.* prestamista.

money-maker *n.* persona que gana buen dinero; artículo o negocio lucrativo.

money-making *adj.* lucrativo.

monger ('mʌŋ·gər) *n.* tratante; traficante.

Mongol ('maŋ·gəl) *n.* mogol; mongol. —*adj.* mogólico; mongólico. *También,* **Mongolian** (maŋ'goli·ən). —**Mongolism,** *n.* mongolismo.

mongoose ('maŋ·gus) *n.* mangosta.

mongrel ('maŋ·grəl) *n. & adj.* mestizo; cruzado.

moniker ('man·ə·kər) *n., slang* nombre; apodo; mote.

monism ('man·ɪz·əm) *n.* monismo. —**monist,** *n.* monista. —**monistic** (mo'nɪs·tɪk) *adj.* monista.

monitor ('man·ə·tər) *n.* monitor. —*v.t. & i.* vigilar; escuchar. —**monitoring,** *n.* escucha.

monk (mʌŋk) *n.* monje.

monkey ('mʌŋ·ki) *n.* mono. —*v.i., colloq.* hacer el mono; jugar. —**monkey business,** *slang* artimañas. —**monkey fruit,** fruto del baobab. —**monkey jacket,** chaquetón de marinero. —**monkey nut,** cacahuete; maní. —**monkey wrench,** llave inglesa.

monkeyshine ('mʌn·ki,ʃain) n., slang monería; diablura.

monkshood ('mʌŋks·hud) n. acónito.

monochrome ('man·ə,krom) n. & adj. monocromo. —**monochromatic** (-kro'mæt·ɪk) adj. monocromático.

monocle ('man·ə·kəl) n. monóculo. —**monocular** (mə'nak·jə·lər) adj. monocular.

monogamy (mə'nag·ə·mi) n. monogamia. —**monogamist**, n. monógamo. —**monogamous**, adj. monógamo.

monogram ('man·ə,græm) n. monograma.

monograph ('man·ə,græf) n. monografía. —**monographic** (-'græf·ɪk) adj. monográfico.

monolith ('man·ə,lɪθ) n. monolito. —**monolithic** (-'lɪθ·ɪk) adj. monolítico.

monologue ('man·ə,lɔg) n. monólogo.

monomania (,man·ə'mei·ni·ə) n. monomanía. —**monomaniac** (-æk) n. & adj. monomaníaco.

monometallism (,man·ə'met·ə·lɪz·əm) n. monometalismo.

monomial (mo'no·mi·əl) n. monomio. —adj. de monomio.

mononucleosis (,man·o·nu·kli'o·sɪs) n., med. mononucleosis.

monoplane ('man·ə,plein) n. monoplano.

monopolist (mə'nap·ə·lɪst) n. monopolista.

monopolize (mə'nap·ə,laiz) v.t. monopolizar.

monopoly (mə'nap·ə·li) n. monopolio.

monorail ('man·ə,reil) n. monocarril.

monosyllable ('man·ə,sɪl·ə·bəl) n. monosílabo. —**monosyllabic** (-sɪ'læb·ɪk) adj. monosilábico.

monotheism ('man·ə·θi,ɪz·əm) n. monoteísmo. —**monotheist** (-'θi·ɪst) n. monoteísta. —**monotheistic**, adj. monoteísta.

monotone ('man·ə,ton) n. monotonía. —adj. monótono.

monotonous (mə'nat·ə·nəs) adj. monótono. —**monotony**, n. monotonía.

monotype ('man·ə,taip) n., print. (method) monotipia; (machine) monotipo.

monovalent (,man·ə'vei·lənt) adj. monovalente.

monsieur (mə'sju) n. [pl. **messieurs** (me'sju)] señor.

Monsignor (man'sin·jər) n. monseñor.

monsoon (man'sun) n. monzón.

monster ('man·stər) n. monstruo. —adj. monstruoso; enorme.

monstrosity (man'stras·ə·ti) n. monstruosidad.

monstrous ('man·strəs) adj. monstruoso. —**monstrousness**, n. monstruosidad.

montage (man'taʒ) n. montaje.

Montezuma's revenge, (,man·tə'zu·məz) slang diarrea que padecen los turistas, esp. en México.

month (mʌnθ) n. mes.

monthly ('mʌnθ·li) adj. mensual. —n. publicación mensual. —adv. mensualmente.

monument ('man·jə·mənt) n. monumento. —**monumental** (-'men·təl) adj. monumental.

moo (mu) n. mugido. —v.i. mugir.

mooch (mutʃ) v.i., slang (slink about) rondar; vagar —v.t. & i., slang (cadge; sponge) gorrear.

mood (mud) n. 1, (state of mind) ánimo; talante; disposición; humor. 2, gram. modo. 3, pl. (fits of depression) mal genio; ataques de melancolía. —**be in the mood**, estar en o de vena; tener ganas.

moody ('mu·di) adj. 1, (gloomy; sullen) taciturno; deprimido; sombrío. 2, (subject to changes of mood) de ánimo o humor inestable; raro.

moon (mun) n. luna. —v.i. andar como alma en pena; soñar; estar o andar embobado. —**full moon**, plenilunio; luna llena. —**new moon**, novilunio; luna nueva. —**once in a blue moon**, de higos a brevas.

moonbeam ('mun,bim) n. rayo de luna.

moonlight ('mun,lait) n. luz de la luna; claridad lunar. —v.i., colloq. tener empleo suplementario, esp. de noche. —**moonlighter,** n., colloq. persona que tiene empleo suplementario, esp. de noche. —**moonlighting,** n., colloq. trabajo en un empleo suplementario, esp. de noche. —**moonlit,** adj. iluminado por la luna.

moonshine ('mun·ʃin) n. 1, = **moonlight**. 2, (nonsense) sandeces; disparates. 3, colloq. (illegal liquor) licor destilado clandestinamente.

—**moonshiner,** *n., colloq.* fabricante clandestino de licores.

moonstone ('mun·ston) *n.* adularia.

moon-struck *adj.* 1, (lunatic) lunático; loco. 2, (dazed) alelado; lelo.

moony ('mu·ni) *adj.* 1, = **moonstruck.** 2, (listless) sin ánimo.

moor (mur) *n.* páramo. —*v.t. & i.* amarrar.

Moor (mur) *n.* moro. —**Moorish,** *adj.* moro; morisco; moruno.

moorage ('mur·idʒ) *n.* 1, (place for mooring) amarradero. 2, (charge for mooring) derechos de puerto; amarre.

mooring ('mur·ɪŋ) *n.* 1, (tying up) amarre. 2, *often pl.* (lines, cables, etc.) amarras. 3, *pl.* (mooring place) amarradero.

moose (mus) *n.* [*pl.* **moose**] alce; anta.

moot (mut) *adj.* discutible.

mop (map) *n.* 1, (cleaning tool) bayeta. 2, (mass of hair) copete; mechón. —*v.t.* [**mopped, mopping**] 1, (clean) fregar. 2, (wipe dry) secar. —**mop up,** 1, *colloq.* (finish) acabar con. 2, (clean up) limpiar.

mope (mop) *v.i.* estar desanimado. —**mopish,** *adj.* desanimado.

moppet ('map·ɪt) *n.* 1, (doll) muñeca de trapo. 2, (child) niño; muñeco.

moraine (mə'rein) *n.* morena.

moral ('mar·əl) *adj.* moral. —*n.* 1, *usu.pl.* (behavior) moral; moralidad. 2, (lesson) moraleja.

morale (mə'ræl) *n.* moral.

moralist ('mar·əl·ıst) *n.* moralista. —**moralistic,** *adj.* moralizador.

morality (mə'ræl·ə·ti) *n.* moralidad.

moralize ('mor·ə,laiz) *v.t. & i.* moralizar.

morally ('mar·ə·li) *adv.* moralmente.

morass (mə'ræs) *n.* pantano; marisma.

moratorium (,mor·ə'tor·i·əm) *n.* moratoria. —**moratory** ('mor·ə·tor·i) *adj.* moratorio.

moray ('mor·e) *n.* morena.

morbid ('mor·bɪd) *adj.* mórbido; morboso. —**morbidity** (mor'bɪd·ə·ti); **morbidness,** *n.* morbidez; morbosidad.

mordant ('mor·dənt) *adj.* 1, (caustic) mordaz; mordiente. 2, (for fixing colors) mordiente. —*n.* mor-diente. —**mordancy,** *n.* mordacidad.

more (mor) *adj., adv. & n.* más. —**more and more,** cada vez más; más y más. —**once more,** otra vez; una vez más. —**the more the merrier,** cuanto (o cuantos) más, mejor. —**the more . . . the more** .(o **the less**) . . . cuanto más . . . tanto más (o menos) . . . ; mientras más . . . tanto más (o menos) . . . —**what's more,** además.

morel (mə'rɛl) *n.* colmenilla.

moreover (mor'o·vər) *adv.* además; también; por otra parte.

mores ('mor·ez) *n.pl.* costumbres.

Moresque (mɔ'rɛsk) *adj. & n.* morisco.

morganatic (,mor·gə'næt·ık) *adj.* morganático.

morgue (morg) *n.* 1, (mortuary) depósito de cadáveres; morgue. 2, *journalism* archivos.

moribund ('mor·ə,bʌnd) *adj.* moribundo.

Mormon ('mor·mən) *n. & adj.* mormón. —**Mormonism,** *n.* mormonismo.

morn (morn) *n., poet.* = **morning.**

morning ('mor·nɪŋ) *n.* mañana. —*adj.* de mañana. —**morning sickness,** náuseas del embarazo.

morning coat chaqué.

morning-glory *n.* dondiego.

morning star lucero del alba.

morocco (mə'rak·o) *n.* tafilete; marroquín.

moron ('mor·an) *n.* idiota; tonto. —**moronic** (mə'ran·ık) *adj.* idiota; tonto.

morose (mə'ros) *adj.* hosco; ceñudo; áspero. —**moroseness,** *n.* hosquedad; aspereza; mal humor.

morphine ('mor·fin) *n.* morfina. —**morphine addict,** morfinómano.

morphology (mor'fal·ə·dʒi) *n.* morfología. —**morphological** (,mor·fə'ladʒ·ı·kəl) *adj.* morfológico.

morphosis (mor'fo·sıs) *n.* morfosis.

morris dance ('mɔr·ıs) danza morisca inglesa.

morrow ('mar·o) *n.* 1, (the following day) el día siguiente. 2, (tomorrow) mañana. 3, (morning) mañana.

Morse code (mors) código Morse.

morsel ('mor·səl) *n.* 1, (bite; portion of food) bocado. 2, (bit; small amount) pedacito; pizca; poquito. 3, (delicacy) manjar; delicia.

mortal ('mor·təl) *adj.* & *n.* mortal.

mortality (mor'tæl·ə·ti) *n.* mortalidad.

mortar ('mor·tər) *n.* **1,** (mixing bowl) mortero. **2,** (cement) mortero; argamasa. **3,** (artillery weapon) mortero. —*v.t.* argamasar.

mortarboard ('mor·tər,bord) *n.* birrete.

mortgage ('mor·gɪdʒ) *n.* hipoteca. —*v.t.* hipotecar. —**mortgagee** (,mor·gɪ'dʒiː) *n.* acreedor hipotecario. —**mortgagor** (-'dʒoːr) *n.* deudor hipotecario.

mortician (mor'tɪʃ·ən) *n.* director de pompas fúnebres; funerario.

mortify ('mor·tə,fai) *v.t.* **1,** (cause to feel shame) abochornar; avergonzar. **2,** (bother) molestar; mortificar. **3,** (discipline, as the body) mortificar. —*v.i.* mortificarse. —**mortification** (-fɪ'kei·ʃən) *n.* mortificación.

mortise ('mor·tɪs) *n.* muesca; ensambladura. —*v.t.* hacer muescas en; entallar; ensamblar.

mortuary ('mor·tʃu·er·i) *n.* depósito de cadáveres; morgue. —*adj.* mortuorio; funerario.

mosaic (mo'zei·ɪk) *adj.* & *n.* mosaico.

mosey ('mo·zi) *v.i.,* slang, U.S. vagar; pasearse; andar.

Moslem ('mas·ləm) *n.* musulmán; mahometano. —*adj.* muslime; muslímico.

mosque (mask) *n.* mezquita.

mosquito (məs'ki·to) *n.* mosquito; *Amer.* zancudo. —**mosquito net,** mosquitero.

moss (mɔs) *n.* musgo. —**mossy,** *adj.* musgoso. —**mossiness,** *n.* lo musgoso.

mossback ('mɔs,bæk) *n.,* slang ultraconservador; fósil.

most (most) *adj.* la mayor parte de; casi todo(s); lo más de; los más de. —*n.* **1,** (majority) la mayor parte; la mayoría. **2,** (the greatest extent or degree) lo sumo; lo máximo. —*adv.* **1,** (in or to the greatest extent or degree) más. **2,** (very; greatly) muy; sumamente. —**at most; at the most,** a lo sumo; a lo más. —**at the very most,** a todo tirar. —**for the most part,** en su mayor parte; eminentemente; esencialmente. —**make the most of, 1,** (take fullest advantage of) sacar todo el partido posible de. **2,** (treat with the highest regard) poner por las nubes.

hacer gran encomio de. —**the very most,** lo más que; lo sumo que.

mostly ('most·li) *adv.* en su mayor parte; por la mayor parte; esencialmente.

mote (mot) *n.* mota.

motel (mo'tel) *n.* motel; parador.

moth (mɔθ) *n.* **1,** (clothes moth) polilla. **2,** (night-flying insect) mariposa nocturna.

mothball ('mɔθ·bɔl) *n.* naftalina; bola de naftalina. —**in mothballs,** en conserva; en almacenaje.

motheaten ('mɔθ,i·tən) *adj.* apolillado.

mother ('mʌð·ər) *n.* madre. —*adj.* **1,** (maternal) maternal; materno. **2,** (native) nativo; natural. **3,** (original) matriz; madre. —*v.t.* **1,** (be a mother to) hacer de madre para con; servir de madre. **2,** (give rise to) dar a luz; engendrar. —**mother church,** iglesia matriz. —**mother country,** madre patria. —**mother tongue, 1,** (native language) lengua materna. **2,** (parent language) lengua matriz. —**mother wit,** ingenio; chispa.

motherhood ('mʌð·ər·hud) *n.* maternidad; condición de madre.

mother-in-law *n.* [*pl.* **mothers-in-law**] suegra; madre política.

motherland ('mʌð·ər·lænd) *n.* patria.

motherless ('mʌð·ər·ləs) *adj.* huérfano de madre; sin madre.

motherly ('mʌð·ər·li) *adj.* maternal. —**motherliness,** *n.* maternidad; afecto maternal.

mother-of-pearl *n.* nácar; madreperla.

motif (mo'tif) *n.* motivo; tema.

motile ('mo·təl) *adj.* móvil; movible. —**motility** (mo'tɪl·ə·ti) *n.* movilidad; motilidad.

motion ('mo·ʃən) *n.* **1,** (movement) movimiento. **2,** (gesture) gesto. **3,** (proposal) moción. —*v.t.* señalar. —*v.i.* hacer señas o señales.

motionless ('mo·ʃən·ləs) *adj.* inmóvil.

motion picture *n.* película; *pl.* cine; cinematografía.

motivate ('mo·tə,veit) *v.t.* motivar. —**motivation,** *n.* motivación.

motive ('mo·tɪv) *n.* **1,** (determining impulse) móvil; razón. **2,** (purpose) motivo. **3,** = motif. —*adj.* motor; motriz.

motley ('mat·li) *adj.* **1,** (multicolored; variegated) abigarrado. **2,** (heterogeneous) heterogéneo.

motor ('mo·tər) *n.* motor. —*adj.* motor; motriz; de motor. —*v.i.* ir o viajar en automóvil. —**motoring,** *n.* automovilismo. —**motor home,** casa rodante.

motorbike ('mo·tər,baik) *n.* bicimoto.

motorboat ('mo·tər,bot) *n.* lancha motora; motora; gasolinera.

motorbus ('mo·tər,bʌs) *n.* autobús; ómnibus.

motorcade ('mo·tər,ked) *n.* desfile o caravana de automóviles.

motorcar ('mo·tər,kar) *n.* automóvil.

motor court motel; parador.

motorcycle ('mo·tər,sai·kəl) *n.* motocicleta.

motorist ('mo·tər·ɪst) *n.* automovilista; motorista; conductor.

motorize ('mo·tər·aiz) *v.t.* motorizar.

motorman ('mo·tər·mən) *n.* conductor (de tren, tranvía, etc.); *Amer.* motorista.

motor scooter motoneta.

mottle ('mat·əl) *v.t.* motear; jaspear; salpicar de pintas. —*n.* 1, (speck) mancha; pinta; mota. 2, (variegated coloring) jaspeado; moteado. —**mottled,** *adj.* jaspeado; abigarrado; moteado; mosqueado.

motto ('mat·o) *n.* lema; divisa.

moulage (mu'laჳ) *n.* molde de yeso; enyesadura.

mould (mold) *n.* & *v.* = **mold.**

moult (molt) *v.* = **molt.**

mound (maund) *n.* montículo. —*v.t.* amontonar. —*v.i.* amontonarse.

mount (maunt) *v.t.* 1, (go up; climb up) ascender; subir. 2, (get up on; get on) montar. 3, (put in place; set) montar. 4, *theat.; mil.; naval* montar. —*v.i.* 1, (ascend; climb) subir; ascender; elevarse. 2, (get up on a horse, bicycle, etc.) montar. 3, (increase) aumentar; crecer; incrementarse. —*n.* 1, (mounting) montura; montadura; *mech.* montaje. 2, (horse) montura; cabalgadura. 3, (hill; elevation) monte.

mountain ('maun·tən) *n.* montaña. —*adj.* de montaña. —**mountain goat,** cabra de las Montañas Rocosas. —**mountain lion,** puma; cuguar. —**mountain sickness,** mal de las alturas; *S.A.* soroche.

mountaineer (,maunt·tə'nɪɹr) *n.* 1, (highlander) montañés. 2, (mountain climber) alpinista; montañero. —**mountaineering,** *n.* alpinismo; montañismo. —*adj.* montañero.

mountainous ('maun·tə·nəs) *adj.* 1, (full of mountains) montañoso. 2, (very large) enorme.

mountaintop ('maun·tən,tap) *n.* cumbre (de montaña).

mountebank ('maun·tə,bæŋk) *n.* charlatán; saltimbanqui.

mounted ('maun·tɪd) *adj.* montado.

mountie ('maun·ti) *n., colloq.* agente de policía montado a caballo, esp. en el Canadá.

mounting ('maun·tɪŋ) *n.* montura; montadura; *mech.* montaje.

mourn (morn) *v.t.* lamentar; llorar. —*v.i.* lamentarse; dolerse; afligirse. —**mourner,** *n.* persona presente a un funeral; persona de duelo; llorón (*fem.* llorona).

mournful ('morn·fəl) *adj.* triste; melancólico; lastimero.

mourning ('mor·nɪŋ) *n.* 1, (grief) dolor; duelo; aflicción. 2, (conventional signs of mourning) luto. —*adj.* de luto. —**in mourning,** de luto. —**mourning dove,** paloma triste.

mouse (maus) *n.* [*pl.* **mice**] 1, (small rodent) ratón; *Amer.* laucha. 2, (spiritless person) pacato; timorato. 3, *slang* (black eye) ojo amoratado. —*v.i.* 1, (hunt mice) cazar ratones. 2, (prowl; search stealthily) hurgar; buscar o andar a hurtadillas.

mouse-colored *adj.* pardusco.

mousehole ('maus,hol) *n.* ratonera.

mouser ('mau·zər) *n.* 1, (catcher of mice) cazador de ratones; gato o perro ratonero. 2, (snoop) fisgón.

mousetrap ('maus,træp) *n.* ratonera; trampa para ratones.

mousse (mus) *n.* dulce de crema batida; especie de flan o natillas.

moustache (məs'tæʃ; 'mʌs·tæʃ) *n., Brit.* = **mustache.**

mousy ('mau·si) *adj.* 1, (of or like a mouse) de o como ratón. 2, (timid) timorato; pacato. 3, (drab) descolorido; raído.

mouth (mauθ) *n.* [*pl.* **mouths** (mauðz)] boca. —*v.t.* (mauð) 1, (utter; declaim) proferir; declamar. 2, (seize with the mouth) agarrar con la boca. 3, (rub with the mouth) frotar con la boca; hocicar. —*v.i.* 1, (declaim) declamar; perorar. 2, (grimace) hacer muecas. —**down at** (o **in**) **the mouth**, deprimido; desalentado.

mouthful ('mauθ·fʊl) *n.* **1,** (enough to fill the mouth) .bocado. **2,** *colloq.* (tongue twister) trabalenguas. —**say a mouthful,** *slang* decir verdades como puños.

mouth organ armónica.

mouthpiece ('mauθ·pis) *n.* **1,** (part of an instrument) boquilla. **2,** (horse's bit) bocado. **3,** (spokesman) portavoz; vocero. **4,** *slang* (lawyer) abogado; picapleitos.

mouthy ('mau·θi) *adj.* deslenguado; palabrero.

movable ('muv·ə·bəl) *adj.* **1,** (that can be moved) movible; móvil. **2,** (transportable) transportable. **3,** *law* mueble. —**movables,** *n.pl.,* *law* bienes muebles.

move (muːv) *v.t.* **1,** (change the location or position of) mover; mudar. **2,** (set in motion) mover. **3,** (transfer) trasladar. **4,** (prompt; urge) impulsar; empujar. **5,** (touch the feelings of) conmover; impresionar. **6,** (propose) proponer; sugerir. **7,** (evacuate, as the bowels) desocupar; evacuar. —*v.i.* **1,** (change location or position) moverse. **2,** (change residence) mudarse; trasladarse. **3,** (take action) actuar; tomar medidas. **4,** (advance) avanzar. **5,** *colloq.* [*también;* **move on**] (leave; depart) irse; marcharse. —*n.* **1,** (movement) movimiento. **2,** (measure; action) medida; paso. **3,** (change of residence) mudanza. **4,** (transfer) traslado. **5,** (play, as in games) jugada. —**get a move on,** *slang* **1,** (start moving) moverse. **2,** (go faster) apresurarse; *Amer.* apurarse; *Amer.* avanzar. —**move along. 1,** (proceed; advance) avanzar. **2,** (start moving; leave) irse; marcharse. —**move away, 1,** (depart) apartarse; separarse. **2,** (change residence) mudarse. —**move in** o **into,** instalarse (en). —**move off,** alejarse. —**move up,** adelantar.

movement ('muv·mənt) *n.* movimiento.

mover ('mu·vər) *n.* **1,** (that which moves) motor. **2,** (carrier of furniture, etc.) agente de mudanzas.

movie ('mu·vi) *n., colloq.* **1,** (theater) cine; cinematógrafo. **2,** (film) película. —**the movies,** el cine.

moving ('mu·vɪŋ) *adj.* **1,** (that

moves; in motion) móvil; movible. **2,** (causing motion; impelling) motor; motriz. **3,** (stirring the emotions) conmovedor; emocionante. —*n.* mudanza. —**moving picture,** película.

mow (mor) *v.t.* cortar; segar. —*n.* granero; henil. —**mow down,** arrasar; abatir.

mower ('mo·ər) *n.* segadora.

Mozarab (mo'zær·əb) *n.* mozárabe. —**Mozarabic,** *adj.* mozárabe.

Mr. ('mɪs·tər) *n., abr. de* **Mister,** Sr.; señor.

Mrs. ('mɪz·ɪz) *n., abr. de* **Mistress,** Sra.; señora.

Ms. (mɪz) *n., abr. de* **Mistress** *o de* **Miss,** sin distinción.

much (mʌtʃ) [**more, most**] *adj.* mucho. —*adv.* **1,** (to a great extent or degree) muy; mucho. **2,** (nearly; about) casi; en gran parte. —*n.* mucho. —**as much,** otro tanto; tanto. —**as much . . . as,** tanto . . . como. —**as much more,** tanto más; otro tanto más. —**for as much as,** por cuanto; por cuanto que. —**however much,** por mucho que. —**how much?,** ¿cuánto? —**make much of,** tener en mucho; dar mucha importancia a. —**much ado about nothing,** mucho ruido y pocas nueces. —**much as,** por más que; a pesar de que. —**not much of a,** de poca monta; de poca importancia. —**so much the better** (o **worse**), tanto mejor (o peor). —**this** o **that much,** tanto. —**too much,** demasiado. —**very much,** muy; mucho.

mucilage ('mju·sə·lɪdʒ) *n.* mucílago. —**mucilaginous** (-'lædʒ·ə·nəs) *adj.* mucilaginoso.

muck (mʌk) *n.* **1,** (filth) suciedad; basura. **2,** (manure) estiércol. **3,** (organic soil) humus; mantillo. **4,** (mud) lodo; barro. —*v.t.* estercolar.

muckrake ('mʌk,reik) *v.i.* exponer la corrupción (en política, negocios, etc.). —**muckraker,** *n.* expositor de corrupción.

mucous ('mju·kəs) *adj.* mucoso. —**mucous membrane,** mucosa.

mucus ('mju·kəs) *n.* moco; mucosidad.

mud (mʌd) *n.* barro; lodo.

muddle ('mʌd·əl) *v.t.* **1,** (mix up) embrollar. **2,** (befuddle) confundir; turbar. **3,** (make turbid) enturbiar. —*v.i.* pensar o hacer como chambón. —*n.* embrollo; confusión.

—**muddle through**, *Brit.* salir del paso.

muddler ('mʌd·lər) *n.* **1**, (mixing stick) palillo para mezclar bebidas. **2**, (bungler) chapucero.

muddy ('mʌd·i) *adj.* **1**, (covered with mud) con lodo o barro. **2**, (unclear) turbio. —*v.t.* **1**, (cover with mud) embarrar. **2**, (make unclear) enturbiar.

mudguard ('mʌd,gard) *n.* guardabarros.

mudhole ('mʌd,hol) *n.* lodazal; atolladero; atascadero.

muezzin (mju'ɛz·ɪn) *n.* muecín; almuédano.

muff (mʌf) *n.* **1**, (covering for the hands) manguito. **2**, *colloq.* (bungle) chambonada; chapucería. —*v.t.*, *colloq.* chapucear (con).

muffin ('mʌf·ɪn) *n.* mollete; bollo.

muffle ('mʌf·əl) *v.t.* **1**, (cover up; wrap up) embozar; cubrir; arrebujar. **2**, (mute; deaden the sound of) ahogar; amortiguar. —*n.* **1**, (muted sound) sonido apagado; ruido sordo. **2**, (cover; wrap) rebujo; rebozo. **3**, (silencer) silenciador; amortiguador. —**muffled**, *adj.* sordo; apagado.

muffler ('mʌf·lər) *n.* **1**, (scarf) bufanda. **2**, (silencing device) silenciador; amortiguador.

mufti ('mʌf·ti) *n.* **1**, (civilian garb) traje de paisano o civil. **2**, (Muslim religious officer) muftí.

mug (mʌg) *n.* **1**, (cup) pocillo; jícara. **2**, *slang* (face) hocico. **3**, *slang* (rough, uncouth person) patán. —*v.t. slang* [**mugged, mugging**] **1**, (assault from behind) asaltar por la espalda. **2**, (photograph) fotografiar. —*v.i.*, *slang* hacer muecas.

mugger ('mʌg·ər) *n.* **1**, *zoöl.* cocodrilo de la India. **2**, *slang* (attacker) asaltante; bandido.

muggy ('mʌg·i) *adj.* húmedo; bochornoso; cargado. —**mugginess**, *n.* calor húmedo; humedad sofocante; cargazón.

mulatto (mju'læt·o; mə-) *adj.* & *n.* [*pl.* **-toes**] mulato.

mulberry ('mʌl,bɛr·i) *n.* **1**, (tree) morera. **2**, (fruit) mora.

mulch (mʌltʃ) *n.* cubierta de paja y estiércol. —*v.t.* cubrir con paja y estiércol.

mulct (mʌlkt) *v.t.* **1**, (defraud) defraudar; birlar; escamotear. **2**, (fine) multar. —*n.* multa.

mule (mjuːl) *n.* **1**, (animal) mulo; mula. **2**, (textile machine) máquina hiladora intermitente. **3**, *colloq.* (stubborn person) mula. **4**, (slipper) zapatilla; chancleta; chinela. —**pack mule**, acémila; mula de carga.

muleteer (,mju·lə'tɪr) *n.* mulero.

mulish ('mju·lɪʃ) *adj.* terco; obstinado; mulo.

mull (mʌl) *v.i.* reflexionar; meditar. —*v.t.* calentar con substancias aromáticas. —*n.* muselina clara. —**mull over**, reflexionar sobre; meditar en o sobre.

mullein ('mʌl·ɪn) *n.* candelaria; gordolobo.

mullet ('mʌl·ɪt) *n.* mújol; cabezudo.

multicolored (,mʌl·tɪ'kʌl·ərd) *adj.* multicolor; abigarrado.

multifarious (,mʌl·tɪ'fɛr·i·əs) *adj.* diverso; variado; múltiple. —**multifariousness**, *n.* diversidad; multiplicidad.

multiform ('mʌl·tə,fɔrm) *adj.* multiforme.

multilateral (,mʌl·tɪ'læt·ə·rəl) *adj.* multilátero; *fig.* multilateral.

multimedia (,mʌl·ti'mi·di·ə) *adj.* que engloba varios medios de comunicación.

multimillionaire (,mʌl·tə,mɪl·jən'ɛr) *n.* multimillonario.

multipartite (,mʌl·tɪ'par·tait) *adj.* **1**, (having many parts) compuesto; multipartito. **2**, (of or between three or more parties) multilateral.

multiple ('mʌl·tɪ·pəl) *adj.* múltiple; múltiplo. —*n.* múltiplo. —**multiple sclerosis**, esclerosis múltiple.

multiplex ('mʌl·tə,plɛks) *adj.* múltiple.

multiplicand (,mʌl·tə·plɪ'kænd) *n.* multiplicando.

multiplication (,mʌl·tə·plɪ'kei·ʃən) *n.* multiplicación.

multiplicity (,mʌl·tə'plɪs·ə·ti) *n.* multiplicidad.

multiply ('mʌl·tɪ,plai) *v.t.* & *i.* multiplicar(se) —**multiplier**, *n.* multiplicador.

multiprocessor (,mʌl·tɪ'pras·ɛs·ər) *n.* multiprocesador.

multitude ('mʌl·tɪ,tud) *n.* multitud. —**multitudinous** (-'tu·dɪ·nəs) *adj.* multitudinario.

mum (mʌm) *adj.*, *colloq.* callado;

mudo. —*n.*, *colloq.* **1**, *bot.* crisantemo. **2**, (mother) mamá.

mumble ('mʌm·bəl) *v.t. & i.* mascullar; farfullar. —*n.* farfulla; el mascullar.

mumbo jumbo ('mʌm·bo·'dʒʌm·bo) **1**, (fetish) fetiche. **2**, (senseless incantation) sortilegio; cábala. **3**, (superstition) superstición; supercherería.

mummer ('mʌm·ər) *n.* máscara. —**mummery**, *n.* mascarada; farsa.

mummify ('mʌm·ə‚fai) *v.t.* momificar. —*v.i.* momificarse. —**mummification** (-fɪ'kei·ʃən) *n.* momificación.

mummy ('mʌm·i) *n.* **1**, (desiccated corpse) momia. **2**, *colloq.* (mother) mamá.

mumps (mʌmps) *n.* paperas.

munch (mʌntʃ) *v.t. & i.* mascar; mordiscar.

mundane ('mʌn·dein) *adj.* mundano; mundanal. —**mundaneness** (mun'dein·nəs) *n.* mundanalidad; mundanería.

municipal (mju'nɪs·ɪ·pəl) *adj.* municipal. —**municipality** (-'pæl·ə·ti) *n.* municipalidad.

munificent (mju'nɪf·ɪ·sənt) *adj.* munífico; munificente. —**munificence**, *n.* munificencia.

munition (mju'nɪʃ·ən) *n.*, *usu.pl.* municiones. —*v.t.* municionar.

mural ('mjur·əl) *adj.* mural. —*n.* cuadro o pintura mural. —**muralist**, *n.* muralista.

murder ('mʌr·dər) *n.* asesinato; homicidio. —*v.t.* asesinar. —**murderer**, *n.* asesino. —**murderess**, *n.* asesina.

murderous ('mʌr·dər·əs) *adj.* **1**, (brutal; cruel) sanguinario; brutal. **2**, (homicidal) homicida. —**murderousness**, *n.* intención o calidad homicida.

murk (mʌrk) *n.* **1**, (fog) niebla; bruma. **2**, (darkness) obscuridad; lobreguez.

murky ('mʌr·ki) *adj.* **1**, (foggy) nublado; brumoso. **2**, (dark) obscuro; lóbrego.

murmur ('mʌr·mər) *n.* murmullo; susurro. —*v.t. & i.* susurrar; murmurar. —**murmurous**, *adj.* murmurante; susurrante.

muscat ('mʌs·kət) *n.* moscatel.

muscatel (‚mʌs·kə'tɛl) *adj. & n.* moscatel.

muscle ('mʌs·əl) *n.* músculo.

—*v.i.*, *colloq.* entrar o abrirse paso a viva fuerza.

muscle-bound *adj.* que tiene músculos gruesos e inelásticos.

Muscovite ('mʌs·kə‚vait) *adj. & n.* moscovita.

muscular ('mʌs·kjə·lər) *adj.* **1**, (of or done by the muscles) muscular. **2**, (brawny) musculoso. —**muscularity** (-'lær·ə·ti) *n.* musculosidad. —**musculature** (-lə·tʃər) *n.* musculatura. —**muscular dystrophy** ('dɪs·trə·fi) distrofia muscular.

muse (mjuːz) *v.i.* meditar; cavilar; rumiar. —*v.t.* musitar. —*n.* musa.

museum (mju'zi·əm) *n.* museo.

mush (mʌʃ) *n.* **1**, (gruel; pap) gachas; puches; papilla. **2**, *colloq.* (sentimentality) sensiblería; sentimentalismo. **3**, (journey over snow) viaje sobre la nieve. —*v.i.* viajar sobre la nieve.

mushroom ('mʌʃ‚rum) *n.* hongo; seta. —*v.i.* crecer o multiplicarse rápidamente.

mushy ('mʌʃ·i) *adj.* **1**, (soft; pulpy) blanducho; semilíquido; pulposo. **2**, *colloq.* (sentimental) sensiblero.

music ('mju·zɪk) *n.* música. —**musical**, *adj.* musical. —**musical comedy**, comedia musical. —**music box**, caja de música. —**music hall**, salón de conciertos. —**music paper**, papel de pauta. —**music stand**, atril.

musicale (‚mju·zɪ'kæl) *n.* velada musical.

musician (mju'zɪʃ·ən) *n.* músico.

musicology (‚mju·zɪ'kal·e·dʒi) *n.* musicología. —**musicologist**, *n.* musicólogo.

musing ('mju·zɪŋ) *adj.* meditabundo; contemplativo; soñador. —*n.* meditación; ensueño.

musk (mʌsk) *n.* almizcle.

musk deer almizclero.

musket ('mʌs·kɪt) *n.* mosquete.

musketeer (‚mʌs·kə'tɪr) *n.* mosquetero.

musketry ('mʌs·kɪt·ri) *n.* mosquetería; fusilería.

muskmelon ('mʌsk‚mɛl·ən) *n.* melón almizclero.

musk ox *n.* buey almizclado.

muskrat ('mʌsk·ræt) *n.* (rata) almizclera; ratón almizclero.

musky ('mʌs·ki) *adj.* almizclero; almizcleño.

Muslim ('mʌz·ləm) *n. & adj.* = **Moslem.**

muslin ('mʌz·lɪn) *n.* muselina.

muss (mʌs) *n.* desorden; desarreglo. —*v.t.* desarreglar; desordenar. —**mussy,** *adj.* desordenado; desarreglado.

mussel ('mʌs·əl) *n.* mejillón.

must (mʌst) *aux.v.* deber; tener que. —*n.* **1,** *colloq.* (essential thing) obligación; necesidad. **2,** (new wine) mosto. **3,** (mustiness) moho. —*adj., colloq.* necesario; esencial; imprescindible.

mustache ('mʌs·tæʃ; məs'tæʃ) *n.* bigote; mostacho. *También,* **moustache, mustachio** (məs'ta·ʃo).

mustang ('mʌs·tæŋ) *n.* potro salvaje; *Amer.* mustango.

mustard ('mʌs·tərd) *n.* mostaza. —**mustard gas,** gas mostaza. —**mustard plaster,** sinapismo; cataplasma.

muster ('mʌs·tər) *v.t.* **1,** (assemble) reunir; juntar; congregar. **2,** (summon, as strength, courage, etc.) tomar; cobrar; hacer acopio de. —*n.* **1,** (list; roll) lista; nómina. **2,** (assemblage, as of troops) revista. —**call (the) muster,** pasar lista. —**muster in,** alistar; inscribir. —**muster out,** dar de baja. —**pass muster,** ser aceptable; ser adecuado.

musty ('mʌs·ti) *adj.* **1,** (moldy; dank) mohoso; que tiene olor o sabor a humedad. **2,** (antiquated) anticuado; pasado de moda. —**mustiness,** *n.* moho; humedad.

mutable ('mju·tə·bəl) *adj.* mudable. —**mutability,** *n.* mutabilidad.

mutant ('mju·tənt) *adj. & n.* mutante.

mutate ('mju·teit) *v.t.* transformar; cambiar; producir mutación en. —*v.i.* transformarse; cambiar; sufrir mutación.

mutation (mju'tei·ʃən) *n.* mutación.

mute (mjut) *adj.* mudo. —*n.* **1,** (one incapable of speech) mudo. **2,** *mus.* sordina. **3,** *phonet.* letra muda. —*v.t.* amortiguar; *mus.* poner sordina a.

muteness ('mjut·nəs) *n.* **1,** (inability to speak) mudez. **2,** (silence) mutismo; silencio.

mutilate ('mju·tə,leit) *v.t.* mutilar. —**mutilation,** *n.* mutilación.

mutineer (,mju·tə'nɪr) *n.* amotinado.

mutinous ('mju·tɪ·nəs) *adj.* amotinado; rebelde.

mutiny ('mju·tə·ni) *n.* motín. —*v.i.* amotinarse.

mutt (mʌt) *n., slang* **1,** (stupid person) necio; bobo. **2,** (mongrel dog) perro cruzado.

mutter ('mʌt·ər) *v.t. & i.* (mumble) murmurar; mascullar; farfullar. —*v.i.* (grumble) gruñir; refunfuñar. —*n.* **1,** (mumble) farfulla. **2,** (grumble) gruñido; refunfuño.

mutton ('mʌt·ən) *n.* carnero; carne de carnero. —**mutton chop,** chuleta de carnero. —**mutton chop whiskers,** patillas imperiales.

muttonhead ('mʌt·ən,hɛd) *n.. colloq.* zopenco.

mutual ('mju·tʃu·əl) *adj.* mutuo; recíproco. —**mutuality** (-'æl·ə·ti) *n.* mutualidad. —**mutual fund,** fondo de inversión mutualista.

muzzle ('mʌz·əl) *n.* **1,** (of a firearm) boca. **2,** (snout) hocico; morro. **3,** (covering for an animal's mouth) bozal. —*v.t.* **1,** (put a muzzle on) poner bozal a. **2,** (restrain from speech; gag) no dejar hablar; silenciar; amordazar.

my (mai) *adj.pos.* mi (*pl.* mis); *(hablándole a uno)* mío: *my friends,* amigos míos. —*interj.* ¡hombre!; ¡oh!; ¡ah!

myasthenia (,mai·əs'θi·ni·ə) *n.* miastenia.

myelitis (,mai·ə'lai·tɪs) *n.* mielitis.

myopia (mai'o·pi·ə) *n.* miopía. —**myopic** (-'ap·ɪk) *adj.* miope.

myosis (mai'o·sɪs) *n.* miosis. —**myotic** (-'at·ɪk) *adj.* miótico.

myriad ('mɪr·i·əd) *n.* miríada.

myrrh (mʌr) *n.* mirra.

myrtle ('mʌr·təl) *n.* mirto.

myself (mai'sɛlf) [*pl.* **ourselves**] *pron.pers.* yo; yo mismo. —*pron. refl.* **1,** *(complemento directo o indirecto de verbo)* me: *I washed myself,* Me lavé; *I put it on myself,* Me lo puse. **2,** *(complemento de prep.)* mí; mí mismo: *I bought it for myself,* Me lo compré para mí. —**to myself,** para mí: *I said to myself, "I'm not going,"* Dije para mí: no voy. —**with myself,** conmigo.

mysterious (mɪs'tɪr·i·əs) *adj.* misterioso. —**mysteriousness,** *n.* misterio; lo misterioso.

mystery ('mɪs·tə·ri) *n.* misterio. —**mystery play,** drama o auto sacramental.

mystic ('mɪs·tɪk) *n. & adj.* místico. —**mystical,** *adj.* místico.

mysticism ('mɪs·tə,sɪz·əm) *n.* misticismo; mística.

mystify ('mɪs·tə,faɪ) *v.t.* **1,** (surround with mystery) rodear de misterio. **2,** (puzzle; perplex) confundir; intrigar. **3,** (hoax; deceive) mixtificar. —**mystification** (-fɪ'keɪʃən) *n.* mixtificación.

mystique (mɪs'tik) *n.* mística.
myth (mɪθ) *n.* mito. —**mythical** ('mɪθ·ə·kəl) *adj.* mítico.
mythology (mɪ'θɑl·ə·dʒi) *n.* mitología. —**mythological** (,mɪθ·ə'lɑdʒ·ɪ·kəl) *adj.* mitológico.

N

N, n (ɛn) decimocuarta letra del alfabeto inglés.
nab (næb) *v.t., colloq.* **1,** (grab) agarrar; pillar; coger. **2,** (arrest) arrestar; prender.
nabob ('nei·bab) *n.* nabab.
nacre ('nei·kər) *n.* nácar; madreperla. —*adj.* nacarado. —**nacreous** (-kri·əs) *adj.* nacarado; nacarino.
nadir ('nei·dər) *n.* nadir.
nag (næg) *v.t.* & *i.* regañar; jeringar. —*n.* **1,** (old horse) *colloq.* jamelgo; penco; jaco. **2,** (scold) mujer regañona.
naiad ('nai·æd) *n.* náyade.
nail (neil) *n.* **1,** *anat.* uña. **2,** (metal fastener) clavo. —*v.t.* **1,** (fasten) clavar. **2,** (hold; keep fixed) sujetar. **3,** *colloq.* (catch; nab) agarrar; pillar; coger. —**nail file,** lima para las uñas. —**nail polish,** esmalte para las uñas.
naïve (na'iːv) *adj.* ingenuo; cándido. —**naïveté** (-'tei) *n.* ingenuidad.
naked ('nei·kɪd) *adj.* **1,** (uncovered; exposed) desnudo. **2,** (undisguised; plain) puro; patente. —**nakedness,** *n.* desnudez. —**stark naked,** en cueros; en pelota. —**with the naked eye,** a simple vista.
namby-pamby ('næm·bi'pæm·bi) *adj.* melindroso; remilgado; soso. —*n.* melindroso; cosa o persona sosa.
name (neim) *n.* nombre. —*v.t.* **1,** (mention; designate) nombrar. **2,** (give a name to; call) llamar; dar nombre (de). —*adj.* de nombre; de renombre. —**call names,** insultar; poner o decir motes a. —**Christian name,** nombre de pila o bautismo. —**full name,** nombre y apellido; nombre completo. —**What is your name?,** ¿Cómo se llama? —**My name is . . . ,** Me llamo . . .
nameless ('neim·ləs) *adj.* sin nombre; anónimo; innominado.

namely ('neim·li) *adv.* a saber; esto es; es decir.
namesake ('neim,seik) *n.* tocayo; homónimo.
nanny ('næn·i) *n.* **1,** (nurse) nodriza; nana. **2,** (she-goat) cabra.
nap (næp) *n.* **1,** (fuzzy surface) lanilla; pelusa. **2,** (short sleep) siesta. —*v.i.* **1,** (take a short sleep) dormitar; echar una siesta. **2,** (be off guard) estar desprevenido. —**catch (someone) napping,** cogerle a uno desprevenido.
napalm ('nei,paːm) *n.* napalm. —*v.t.* quemar con napalm.
nape (neip) *n.* nuca; cerviz; cogote.
napery ('nei·pə·ri) *n.* mantelería.
naphtha ('næf·θə) *n.* nafta.
naphthalene ('næf·θə,lin) *n.* naftalina.
napkin ('næp·kɪn) *n.* servilleta.
napoleon (nə'po·li·ən) *n.* **1,** (coin) napoleón. **2,** (pastry) pastel de hojaldre y crema.
narcissism (nar'sɪs·ɪz·əm) *n.* narcisismo. —**narcissist,** *n.* narcisista. —**narcissistic,** *adj.* narcisista.
narcissus (nar'sɪs·əs) *n.* narciso.
narcosis (nar'ko·sɪs) *n.* narcosis.
narcotic (nar'kat·ɪk) *adj.* narcótico. —*n.* **1,** (drug) narcótico. **2,** (addict) narcómano.
narcotism ('nar·kə·tɪz·əm) *n.* narcotismo. —**narcotize,** *v.t.* narcotizar.
nard (nard) *n.* nardo.
nares ('nɛr·iz) *n.pl.* [*sing.* **naris** ('nɛr·ɪs)] ventanas de la nariz; narices.
narrate ('næ·ret) *v.t.* & *i.* narrar; relatar. —**narration,** *n.* narración. —**narrator,** *n.* narrador [*fem.* -dora]; relator [*fem.* -tora].
narrative ('nær·ə·tɪv) *n.* narrativa; relato. —*adj.* narrativo.
narrow ('nær·o) *adj.* estrecho. —*v.t.* **1,** (make less wide) angostar; hacer (más) estrecho. **2,** (limit) limitar; restringir. **3,** (reduce)

reducir. —*v.i.* **1,** (become less wide) angostarse; estrecharse. **2,** (reduce) reducirse. **3,** (become smaller, as the eyes) entornarse. —*n.* **1,** (narrow part) parte estrecha o angosta. **2,** *usu.pl.* (narrow passage) angostura; estrecho. —**have a narrow escape,** escaparse por un pelo.

narrowminded (ˌnær·o'main-dɪd) *adj.* estrecho de miras.

narrowness ('nær·o·nəs) *n.* estrechez.

narwhal ('nar·wəl) *n.* narval.

nasal ('nei·zəl) *adj.* nasal. —**nasality** (ne'zæl·ə·ti) *n.* nasalidad. —**nasalize,** *v.t.* nasalizar.

nascent ('neis·ənt) *adj.* naciente.

nastiness ('næs·ti·nəs) *n.* **1,** (foulness) porquería. **2,** (meanness) odiosidad; maldad. **3,** (ill humor) mal humor; mala disposición; mal genio. **4,** (ugliness) mala cara; mal cariz.

nasturtium (næ'stʌr·ʃəm) *n.* capuchina.

nasty ('næs·ti) *adj.* **1,** (offensive; foul) asqueroso. **2,** (mean) desagradable; odioso; detestable. **3,** (noxious; ugly) malo; feo.

natal ('nei·təl) *adj.* natal.

natant ('nei·tənt) *adj.* natátil; flotante.

natatorium (ˌne·tə'tor·i·əm) *n.* piscina; *Amer.* natatorio. —**natatory** ('nei·tə,tor·i) *n.* natatorio.

nation ('nei·ʃen) *n.* nación.

national ('næʃ·ə·nəl) *adj. & n.* nacional.

nationalism ('næʃ·ə·nə,lɪz·əm) *n.* nacionalismo. —**nationalist,** *n.* nacionalista. —**nationalistic,** *adj.* nacionalista.

nationality (ˌnæʃ·ə'næl·ə·ti) *n.* nacionalidad.

nationalize ('næʃ·ə·nə,laiz) *v.t.* nacionalizar. —**nationalization** (-lɪ'zei·ʃən) *n.* nacionalización.

native ('nei·tɪv) *adj.* **1,** (belonging by birth or origin) nativo; natural. **2,** (of the place of one's birth) natal. **3,** (inborn; innate) natural. **4,** (indigenous) indígena. **5,** (in natural state) natural. —*n.* natural; indígena. —**Native American,** indio americano. —**native land,** patria. —**native tongue,** lengua materna.

native-born *adj.* oriundo; nativo; natural.

nativity (nei'tɪv·ə·ti) *n.* **1,** (birth) nacimiento; natividad. **2,** *cap.* (birth of Christ) Navidad.

NATO ('nei·to) *n., abr. de* **North Atlantic Treaty Organization**.

natty ('næt·i) *adj., colloq.* garboso; elegante. —**nattiness,** *n.* garbo; elegancia.

natural ('nætʃ·ə·rəl) *adj.* natural. —*n.* **1,** (fool; idiot) tonto; idiota. **2,** *colloq.* (apt person or thing) persona de habilidad natural; persona o cosa de éxito aseguardo. **3,** *mus.* **a.** (natural sign) becuadro. **b.** (white key) tecla blanca. **c.** (natural tone) nota o tono natural. —**naturally,** *adv.* naturalmente. —**naturalness,** *n.* naturalidad.

naturalism ('nætʃ·ə·rə,lɪz·əm) *n.* naturalismo. —**naturalist,** *n.* naturalista. —**naturalistic,** *adj.* naturalista.

naturalize ('nætʃ·ə·rə,laiz) *v.t.* naturalizar. —**naturalization** (-lɪ'zei·ʃən) *n.* naturalización.

nature ('nei·tʃər) *n.* naturaleza. —**good nature,** bondad. —**ill (o bad) nature,** mala índole. —**of (o in) the nature of,** como.

naught (nɔt) *n.* **1,** (nothing) nada. **2,** (zero) cero. —**come to naught,** malograrse; fracasar; quedar en nada.

naughtiness ('nɔ·ti·nəs) *n.* **1,** (disobedience) desobediencia; *Amer.* malacrianza. **2,** (mischievousness) travesura; picardía.

naughty ('nɔ·ti) *adj.* **1,** (disobedient) desobediente; malcriado. **2,** (mischievous) travieso; pícaro. **3,** (indecent) indecente; feo.

nausea ('nɔ·ʃə) *n.* náusea.

nauseate ('nɔ·ʃi·eit) *v.t.* dar asco; dar náusea(s). —**nauseated,** *adj.* nauseado.

nauseous ('nɔ·ʃəs) *adj.* asqueroso; nauseabundo. —**nauseousness,** *n.* asquerosidad.

nautical ('nɔ·tɪ·kəl) *adj.* náutico; marino. —**nautical mile,** milla marina.

nautilus ('nɔ·tɪ·ləs) *n.* nautilo.

naval ('nei·vəl) *adj.* naval; de marina.

nave (neiv) *n.* nave.

navel ('nei·vəl) *n.* ombligo. —**navel orange,** naranja de ombligo.

navigable ('næv·ɪ·gə·bəl) *adj.* navegable.

navigate ('næv·ɪ,geit) *v.t. & i.* na-

vegar. —**navigation,** n. navegación.
—**navigator,** n. navegante.

navy ('nei·vi) n. armada; marina de
guerra. —**navy bean,** judía blanca.
—**navy blue,** azul marino.

nay (nei) n. no. —adv. **1,** (no) no;
de ningún modo. **2,** (not only so,
but) no sólo ... sino; y aún.

Nazi ('nat·si) n. & adj. nazi.
—**Nazism** (-sɪz·əm) n. nazismo.

Neanderthal (ni'an·dər,θɔːl) adj.
& n. neandertal.

neap tide (nip) marea muerta.

near (nɪr) adv. **1,** (not far) cerca; no
lejos. **2,** (closely; intimately) de
cerca; íntimamente. **3,** (almost) casi.
—adj. **1,** (not far) cercano;
inmediato; próximo. **2,** (intimate)
íntimo; allegado. **3,** (closely related)
cercano. **4,** (approximating; resembling) casi. **5,** (by a close margin;
narrow) por un pelo. —prep. cerca
de; junto a. —v.t. & i. acercarse (a);
aproximarse (a); llegar (a). —**come
near** (doing something) casi o por
poco (hacer algo): *I came near killing him,* Casi o por poco lo mato.
—**near at hand, 1,** (within reach) a
mano. **2,** (imminent) al caer; al
llegar.

nearby ('nɪr·bai) adj. cercano;
próximo. —adv. cerca. —prep.,
colloq. cerca de.

Near East n. Cercano o Próximo
Oriente.

nearly ('nɪr·li) adv. **1,** (almost)
casi. **2,** (closely) de cerca.

near miss 1, (shot close to the target) tiro que cae o pasa cerca del
blanco. **2,** (anything falling short of
its mark) acción o esfuerzo que
queda corto. **3,** (narrow escape)
escapada.

nearness ('nɪr·nəs) n. proximidad;
cercanía.

nearsighted ('nɪr,sai·tɪd) adj.
miope; corto de vista. —**nearsightedness,** n. miopía.

neat (nit) adj. **1,** (clean; tidy)
limpio; pulcro; aseado. **2,** (skillful;
clever) hábil. **3,** (pure; unmixed)
puro; solo. **4,** slang (very pleasing)
bueno. **5,** (net; clean) neto.
—**neatness,** n. limpieza; pulcritud;
aseo.

nebula ('nɛb·jə·lə) . [pl. **nebulae**
(-li)] nebulosa. —**nebular,** adj.
nebuloso. —**nebulous,** adj. nebuloso. —**nebulosity** (-'las·ə·ti);
nebulousness, n. nebulosidad.

necessary ('nɛs·ə,sɛr·i) adj.

necesario. —n. necesidad. —**necessarily,** adv. necesariamente.

necessitate (nə'sɛs·ə,teit) v.t.
necesitar; requerir.

necessitous (nə'sɛs·ə·təs) adj.
necesitado; indigente.

necessity (nə'sɛs·ə·ti) n.
necesidad. —**of necessity,** por
necesidad.

neck (nɛk) n. **1,** (part of the body,
of a garment, etc.) cuello. **2,** (point
of land) lengua de tierra. **3,** (strait)
estrecho. —v.i., slang besuquearse.
—**necking,** n. besuqueo. —**neck
and neck,** parejos; lado a lado.
—**stick one's neck out,** arriesgarse;
exponerse. —**stiff neck,** tortícolis.

neckband ('nɛk,bænd) n. cuello
(de camisa, vestido, etc.).

neckerchief ('nɛk·ər·tʃɪf) n.
pañoleta.

necklace ('nɛk·ləs) n. collar.

neckpiece ('nɛk·pis) n. cuello
postizo.

necktie ('nɛk,tai) n. corbata; Amer.
chalina.

neckwear ('nɛk·wer) n. cuellos;
corbatas; bufandas; etc.

necrology (nə'kral·ə·dʒi) n.
necrología.

necromancy ('nɛk·rə,mæn·si) n.
nigromancia; necromancia. —**necromancer,** n. nigromante.

necrophilia (,nɛk·rə'fɪl·i·ə) n.
necrofilia.

necropolis (nɛ'krap·ə·lɪs) n.
necrópolis.

necrosis (nɛ'kro·sɪs) n. necrosis.
—**necrotic** (nɛ'krat·ɪk) adj. necrótico.

nectar ('nɛk·tər) n. néctar.

nectarine (,nɛk·tə'rin) n. variedad
de melocotón.

née (nei) adj. nacida.

need (niːd) n. necesidad. —v.t.
necesitar; tener necesidad de;
requerir. —v.i. ser necesario; tener
necesidad. —**be in need of,** tener
necesidad de. —**have need to,** tener
que; deber; necesitar. —**if need be,**
si necesario.

needful ('nid·fəl) adj. **1,** (necessary; needed) necesario. **2,** (needy)
necesitado.

neediness ('ni·di·nəs) n. necesidad; pobreza; indigencia.

needle ('ni·dəl) n. aguja. —v.t.,
colloq. **1,** (prod; incite) estimular;
incitar. **2,** (tease; bother) pinchar;
jeringar.

needlepoint ('ni·dǝl,pɔint) *n.* punto de cruz.

needless ('nid·lǝs) *adj.* superfluo; innecesario. —**needlessness,** *n.* superfluidad; inutilidad. —**needless to say,** se excusa decir.

needlework ('ni·dǝl·wʌrk) *n.* **1,** (sewing) costura. **2,** (embroidery) bordado.

needs (niːdz) *adv.* por fuerza; por necesidad.

needy ('ni·di) *adj.* necesitado; indigente; pobre.

ne'er (neːr) *adj., poet.* = **never.**

ne'er-do-well ('nɛr·du,wɛl) *n.* haragán; perdido.

nefarious (nɪ'fɛr·i·ǝs) *adj.* nefando; nefario. —**nefariousness,** *n.* maldad; iniquidad.

negate (nɛ'geit) *v.t.* **1,** (deny) negar. **2,** (nullify) invalidar. —**negation,** *n.* negación.

negative ('nɛg·ǝ·tɪv) *adj.* negativo. —*n.* **1,** (denial) negativa. **2,** *photog.; elect.* negativo. **3,** *gram.* negación. —**negativity,** *n.* negatividad.

neglect (nɪ'glɛkt) *v.t.* descuidar; desatender; olvidar. —*n.* descuido; negligencia; desatención. —**neglectful,** *adj.* negligente; descuidado.

negligee (,nɛg·lǝ'ʒei) *n.* bata de mujer.

negligence ('nɛg·lǝ·dʒǝns) *n.* negligencia. —**negligent,** *adj.* negligente.

negligible ('nɛg·lɪ·dʒǝ·bǝl) *adj.* insignificante. —**negligibility,** *n.* insignificancia.

negotiable (nɪ'go·ʃɪ·ǝ·bǝl) *adj.* negociable.

negotiate (nɪ'go·ʃi,eit) *v.t. & i.* negociar. —**negotiation,** *n.* negociación. —**negotiator,** *n.* negociador [*fem.* -dora].

negro ('ni·gro) *n.* [*pl.* **-groes**] & *adj.* negro. —**negress,** *n.* negra.

negroid ('ni·grɔid) *adj.* negroide.

neigh (nei) *v.t.* relinchar. —*n.* relincho.

neighbor ('nei·bǝr) *n.* **1,** (near-by person or thing) vecino. **2,** (fellow being) prójimo. —*adj.* vecino. —*v.i. & t.* ser vecino (de); limitar (con); colindar (con).

neighborhood ('nei·bǝr,hud) *n.* vecindario; vecindad.

neighboring ('nei·bǝr·ɪŋ) *adj.* vecino; contiguo; próximo.

neighborly ('nei·bǝr·li) *adj.* como

o de buen vecino; sociable. —**neighborliness,** *n.* calidad de buen vecino.

neither ('ni·ðǝr; 'nai-) *conj.* **1,** (not either) ni. **2,** (nor yet) tampoco; ni . . . tampoco. —*adv.* tampoco. —*adj.* ninguno (de los dos). —*pron.* ninguno; ni el uno ni el otro. —**neither . . . nor,** ni . . . ni.

nematode ('nɛm·ǝ,toːd) *n.* nematoda.

nemesis ('nɛm·ǝ·sɪs) *n.* némesis.

Neocene ('ni·ǝ,sin) *adj.* neoceno.

neodymium (,ni·o'dɪm·i·ǝm) *n.* neodimio.

neolithic (,ni·o'lɪθ·ɪk) *adj.* neolítico.

neologism (ni'al·ǝ·dʒɪz·ǝm) *n.* neologismo.

neon ('ni·an) *n.* neón.

neonate ('ni·ǝ,neit) *adj. & n.* neonato; recién nacido.

neophyte ('ni·ǝ,fait) *n.* neófito.

neoplasm ('ni·ǝ,plæz·ǝm) *n.* neoplasma.

nephew ('nɛf·ju) *n.* sobrino.

nephrite ('nɛf·rait) *n.* nefrita.

nephritis (nɪ'frai·tɪs) *n.* nefritis. —**nephritic** (nɪ'frɪt·ɪk) *adj.* nefrítico.

nepotism ('nɛp·ǝ·tɪz·ǝm) *n.* nepotismo.

Neptune ('nɛp·tjun) *n.* Neptuno.

neptunium (nɛp'tju·ni·ǝm) *n.* neptunio.

nerd (nʌrd) *n., slang* persona de mente estrecha, inocente y poco corrido.

nereid ('nɪr·i·ɪd) *n.* nereida.

nervation (nʌr'vei·ʃǝn) *n.* nervadura.

nerve (nʌrv) *n.* **1,** (fiber) nervio. **2,** (courage) valor; fuerzas. **3,** *slang* (audacity) atrevimiento; desfachatez; tupé. —*v.t.* dar valor o fuerzas a; animar. —**get on one's nerves,** atacarle a uno los nervios. —**nerve cell,** neurona. —**nerve gas,** gas neurotóxico. —**nerve oneself,** hacer acopio de valor o fuerzas.

nerveless ('nʌrv·lǝs) *adj.* **1,** (unnerved; weak) enervado. **2,** (cowardly) cobarde. **3,** *zoöl.; bot.* sin nervios.

nervous ('nʌrv·ǝs) *adj.* nervioso. —**nervousness,** *n.* nerviosidad.

nervure ('nʌr·vjur) *n.* nervadura; nervio.

nervy ('nʌr·vi) *adj., slang* atrevido.

nescience ('nɛʃ·ǝns) *n.* nesciencia;

ignorancia. **—nescient,** *adj.*
nesciente; ignorante.

nest (nɛst) *n.* nido. —*v.i.* anidar.
—nest egg, nida; *fig.* ahorro para
emergencias; ahorrito.

nestle ('nɛs·əl) *v.i.* **1,** (snuggle)
acurrucarse; anidarse; *Amer.*
aparragarse. **2,** (lie hidden; be sheltered) anidar; estar anidado. —*v.t.*
anidar; abrigar.

nestling ('nɛst·lɪŋ) *n.* polluelo;
pollito; *Amer.* pichón.

net (nɛt) *n.* **1,** (mesh) malla; red. **2,**
(network) red. —*adj.* neto. —*v.t.*
[**netted, netting**] **1,** (catch, as with
a net) atrapar en la red. **2,** (gain)
sacar o dar de ganancia. **—net
worth,** capital neto o contable.

nether ('nɛð·ər) *adj.* **1,** (infernal)
infernal. **2,** (lower) inferior; de
abajo. **—nethermost,** *adj.* más
bajo. **—netherward,** *adv.* hacia
abajo. **—netherworld,** el infierno;
el otro mundo.

netting ('nɛt·ɪŋ) *n.* red; obra de
malla; redecilla.

nettle ('nɛt·əl) *n.* ortiga. —*v.t.*
irritar; provocar. **—nettlesome,** *adj.*
irritante; provocante.

network ('nɛt,wʌrk) *n.* red; cadena
(de radiodifusión).

neural ('njur·əl) *adj.* nérveo;
nervioso.

neuralgia (nju'ræl·dʒə) *n.* neuralgia. **—neuralgic,** *adj.* neurálgico.

neurasthenia (,njur·əs'θi·ni·ə) *n.*
neurastenia. **—neurasthenic**
(-'θɛn·ɪk) *adj. & n.* neurasténico.

neuritis (nju'rai·tɪs) *n.* neuritis.

neurology (nju'ral·ə·dʒi) *n.*
neurología. **—neurological** (,njur·
ə'ladʒ·ɪk·əl) *adj.* neurológico.
—neurologist, *n.* neurólogo.

neuron ('njur·an) *n.* neurona.

neurosis (nju'ro·sɪs) *n.* neurosis.
—neurotic (-'rat·ɪk) *adj. & n.*
neurótico.

neuter ('nu·tər) *adj.* neutro. —*v.t.*
castrar; capar.

neutral ('nu·trəl) *adj. & n.* **1,** (not
taking sides) neutral. **2,** (inactive,
inert; without definite quality)
neutro.

neutrality (nu'træl·ə·ti) *n.* neutralidad.

neutralize ('nu·trə·laiz) *v.t.*
neutralizar. **—neutralization**
(-lɪ'zei·ʃən) *n.* neutralización.

neutrino (nu'tri·no) *n.* neutrino.

neutron ('nu·tran) *n.* neutrón.

never ('nɛv·ər) *adv.* **1,** (not ever)

nunca; jamás. **2,** (not at all) no; de
ningún modo. **—never fear,** no
tenga cuidado; no hay cuidado.
*—never mind,** no importa.
—never so ..., por muy ... ; por
mucho ... ; por más que....

never-ceasing *adj.* continuo;
incesante; perpetuo.

neverfailing (,nɛv·ər'fei·lɪŋ) *adj.*
1, (inexhaustible) inagotable. **2,** (infallible) infalible.

nevermore (,nɛv·ər'mo:r) *adv.*
jamás; nunca más.

never-say-die *adj.* indómito;
inconquistable.

nevertheless (nɛv·ər·ðə'lɛs) *adv.*
sin embargo; no obstante; con todo.

new (nu:) *adj.* nuevo. —*adv.* **1,** (recently) recientemente. **2,** (anew)
nuevamente; de nuevo.

newborn ('nu·born) *adj. & n.*
recién nacido; neonato.

newcomer ('nu,kʌm·ər) *n.* recién
llegado.

newel ('nu·əl) *n.* nabo o poste de
escalera.

newfangled (nu'fæŋ·gəld) *adj.*
novedoso; de última moda.

new-fashioned *adj.* novedoso.

newly ('nu·li) *adv.* **1,** (recently)
recién; recientemente. **2,** = **anew**.

newlywed ('nu·li,wɛd) *adj. & n.*
recién casado.

newness ('nu·nəs) *n.* novedad; lo
nuevo.

news (nu:z) *n.* **1,** (reports of hap-
penings) noticias. **2,** (information;
local gossip) nuevas; novedades.
—break the news, dar la noticia.
—news agency, empresa o agencia
noticiera. **—news item,** noticia.

newsboy ('nuz·bɔi) *n.* vendedor de
diarios; *Amer.* canillita. **—newsgirl,**
n. vendedora de diarios.

newscast ('nuz·kæst) *n.* noticiario. **—newscaster,** *n.* cronista;
locutor de noticias; noticiero.

newsdealer ('nuz,dɪ·lər) *n.* vendedor de periódicos.

newsletter ('nuz,lɛt·ər) *n.* boletín.

newsman ('nuz·mæn) *n.* [*pl.*
-men] **1,** = **newsdealer. 2,** (journalist) periodista.

newsmonger ('nuz,mʌŋ·gər) *n.*
novelero.

newspaper ('nuz,pei·pər) *n.*
periódico; diario.

newspeak ('nu,spik) *n.* estilo de
habla equívoco y engañador.

newsprint ('nuz,prɪnt) *n.* papel de
periódico.

newsreel ('nuz͵ril) *n.* noticiario; noticiero.

newsstand ('nuz͵stænd) *n.* puesto de periódicos; quiosco.

newswoman ('nuz͵wʊm·ən) *n.* [*pl.* **-women**] periodista.

newsworthy ('nuz͵wʌr·ði) *adj.* que merece publicar en los medios de comunicación.

newsy ('nu·zi) *adj.* noticioso; noticiero; lleno de novelerías. —**newsiness**, *n.* novelería.

newt (nut) *n.* salamandra acuática; tritón.

New Testament Nuevo Testamento.

New Year año nuevo.

next (nɛkst) *adj.* **1,** (immediately following) siguiente; próximo. **2,** (nearest; adjacent) vecino; inmediato. **3,** (of future time) que viene: *next week (month, year)*, la semana (el mes, el año) que viene. —*adv.* **1,** (in the nearest time or position) luego; después. **2,** (forthwith) en seguida; a continuación. **3,** (on the first subsequent occasion) de nuevo; la próxima vez. —*prep.* al lado de; junto a. —*n.* el próximo; el siguiente. —**be next**, tocarle a uno el turno: *Who's next?*, ¿A quién le toca? —**next door** (**to**), al lado (de). —**next of kin**, pariente inmediato. —**next to, 1,** (beside) al lado de; junto a. **2,** (after) después de. **3,** (almost; nearly) casi. —**what next?**, y ahora ¿qué?; ¿y luego?

next-door *adj.* de al lado.

nexus ('nɛk·səs) *n.* nexo.

nib (nɪb) *n.* **1,** (point) punta. **2,** (beak) pico. —**his** (o **her**) **nibs**, *colloq.* su señoría.

nibble ('nɪb·əl) *v.i.* & *t.* mordiscar; picar; picotear. —*n.* mordisco; bocadito.

nice (nais) *adj.* **1,** (subtle; delicate) fino; sutil; delicado. **2,** (refined; discriminating) refinado; esmerado. **3,** *colloq.* (attractive) bonito; mono; lindo. **4,** *colloq.* (good; gentle) bueno; amable. **5,** *colloq.* (pleasant) agradable; bueno. **6,** *colloq.* (in good taste) de buen gusto. **7,** *colloq.* (proper; suitable) apropiado; adecuado. —**nicely**, *adv., colloq.* muy bien. —**nice and . . .**, *colloq.* muy.

nicety ('nai·sə·ti) *n.* delicadeza; finura; sutileza.

niche (nɪtʃ) *n.* nicho.

nick (nɪk) *n.* **1,** (notch; groove)

muesca; mella. **2,** (small cut; abrasion) rasguño; arañazo. **3,** *cap.* [*usu.* Old Nick] el diablo. —*v.t.* **1,** (cut; chip) hacer muescas en; mellar. **2,** (wound slightly) arañar; rasguñar. —**in the nick of time**, justo a tiempo; a punto.

nickel ('nɪk·əl) *n.* níquel. —**nickel-plate**, *v.t.* niquelar. —**nickel-plating**, *n.* niquelado. —**nickel silver**, metal blanco.

nickelodeon (͵nɪk·ə'loː·di·ən) *n.* máquina de discos.

nickname ('nɪk͵neim) *n.* mote; apodo. —*v.t.* apodar.

nicotine ('nɪk·ə͵tin) *n.* nicotina. —**nicotinic** (-'tɪn·ɪk) *adj.* nicotínico.

niece (nis) *n.* sobrina.

nifty ('nɪf·ti) *adj., slang* elegante; primoroso. —**niftiness**, *n., slang* primor.

niggardly ('nɪg·ərd·li) *adj.* mezquino; tacaño. —**niggardliness**, *n.* mezquindad; tacañería.

nigger ('nɪg·ər) *n.* & *adj., derog.* = negro.

niggle ('nɪg·əl) *v.i.* **1,** (trifle) ajetrearse en nimiedades. **2,** (cheat) defraudar; estafar.

nigh (nai) *adj.* cercano; próximo. —*prep.* cerca de; junto a. —*adv.* **1,** (near) cerca. **2,** (nearly) casi.

night (nait) *n.* noche. —*adj.* nocturno; de noche. —**at o by night**, de noche. —**make a night of it**, pasar la noche en o con algo.

nightcap ('nait͵kæp) *n.* **1,** (cap worn in bed) gorro de dormir. **2,** *colloq.* (drink before retiring) último trago (del día).

nightclub ('nait͵klʌb) *n.* cabaret; sala de fiestas; club nocturno; club de noche.

nightdress ('nait͵drɛs) *n.* camisón; camisa de dormir.

nightfall ('nait·fɔl) *n.* anochecer; caída de la tarde o de la noche.

nightgown ('nait·gaun) *n.* = nightdress.

nighthawk ('nait͵hɔk) *n.* **1,** *ornith.* chotacabras. **2,** = night owl.

nightie ('nai·ti) *n., colloq.* = nightdress.

nightingale ('nait·ən͵geil) *n.* ruiseñor.

night letter telegrama nocturno.

nightly ('nait·li) *adj.* **1,** (of the night; at or by night) nocturno; de noche. **2,** (occurring every night) de todas las noches. —*adv.* **1,** (at or by night) de noche; durante la noche. **2,** (every night) todas las noches.

nightmare ('nait,mɛrr) *n.* pesadilla. —**nightmarish,** *adj.* de pesadilla; horrendo.

night owl *colloq.* trasnochador.

nightshade ('nait,ʃeid) *n.* solano; hierba mora.

nightshirt ('nait,ʃʌrt) *n.* camisa de dormir.

nightspot ('nait·spat) *n.* = **nightclub.**

night stick porra; cachiporra; bastón de policía.

nighttime ('nait·taim) *n.* noche; horas de la noche.

night watch 1, (vigil; period of duty) guardia o ronda nocturna; vigilia. **2,** (guard) ronda nocturna; guardia.

nihilism ('nai·ə·lɪz·əm) *n.* nihilismo. —**nihilist,** *n.* nihilista. —**nihilistic,** *adj.* nihilista.

nil (nɪl) *n.* nada.

nimble ('nɪm·bəl) *adj.* ágil. —**nimbleness,** *n.* agilidad.

nimbus ('nɪm·bəs) *n.* nimbo.

nincompoop ('nɪn·kəm,pup) *n.* badulaque; simplón.

nine (nain) *n.* & *adj.* nueve.

ninefold ('nain,fold) *adj.* & *n.* nueve veces (más). —*adv.* nueve veces.

nine hundred novecientos. —**nine-hundredth,** *adj.* & *n.* noningentésimo.

ninepins ('nain,pɪnz) *n.sing.* juego de bolos. —**ninepin,** *n.* bolo.

nineteen ('nain,tin) *n.* & *adj.* diecinueve; diez y nueve. —**nineteenth,** *adj.* & *n.* decimonono; diecinueveavo.

ninety ('nain·ti) *n.* & *adj.* noventa. —**ninetieth,** *adj.* & *n.* nonagésimo; noventavo.

ninth (nainθ) *adj.* noveno; nono. —*n.* noveno; novena parte; *mus.* novena.

ninny ('nɪn·i) *n.* lelo; mentecato.

niobium (nai'o·bi·əm) *n.* niobio; columbio.

nip (nɪp) *v.t.* [nipped, nipping] **1,** (pinch; bite) pellizcar; morder. **2,** (snip; cut off) cortar. —*n.* **1,** (pinch) pellizco. **2,** (bite) mordedura; mordisco. **3,** (chill) frío. **4,** *colloq.* (small drink) traguito; chispo. **5,** *colloq.* (little bit) poquito; bocadito. —**nip and tuck,** *colloq.* empatado; parejo; porfiado. —**nip in the bud,** destruir en germen; cortar en flor.

nipper ('nɪp·ər) *n.* pinza. —**nippers,** *n.pl.* tenazas.

nipple ('nɪp·əl) *n.* **1,** *anat.; zoöl.* pezón; tetilla. **2,** (mouthpiece of a nursing bottle) chupete. **3,** (threaded pipe) tubo roscado de unión.

Nipponese (,nɪp·ə'niz) *adj.* & *n.* nipón; japonés.

nippy ('nɪp·i) *adj., colloq.* **1,** (chilly) helado; frío. **2,** (irritable) áspero; mordaz. **3,** (sharp; biting) picante; mordaz.

nirvana (nɪr'va·na; nɪr-) *n.* nirvana.

nit (nɪt) *n.* liendre.

niter *también,* **nitre** ('nai·tər) *n.* nitro.

niton ('nai·tan) *n.* = **radon.**

nitpick ('nɪt·pɪk) *v.i.* sutilizar.

nitrate ('nai·treit) *n.* nitrato; azoato.

nitric ('nai·trɪk) *adj.* nítrico; azoico.

nitrocellulose (,nai·tro'sɛl·jə·los) *n.* nitrocelulosa.

nitrogen ('nai·trə·dʒən) *n.* nitrógeno; ázoe. —**nitrogenous** (nai'tradʒ·ə·nəs) *adj.* nitrogenado; azoado.

nitroglycerin (,nai·tro'glɪs·ər·ɪn) *n.* nitroglicerina.

nitrous ('nai·trəs) *adj.* nitroso.

nitty-gritty (,nɪt·i'grɪt·i) *n., slang* lo mero mero.

nitwit ('nɪt,wɪt) *n., slang* mentecato.

nix (nɪks) *n., slang* nada; nones. —*adv.* no; ni por pienso; nitos. —*interj.* ¡alto!; ¡para! —*v.t.* negar; prohibir.

no (no) *adv.* no. —*adj.* ninguno. —*n.* no. —**no longer,** ya no. —**no one,** nadie; ninguno. —**no sooner,** apenas.

nob (nab) *n., slang* **1,** (head) cabeza. **2,** (important person) personaje.

nobelium (no'bi·li·əm) *n.* nobelio.

nobility (no'bɪl·ə·ti) *n.* nobleza.

noble ('no·bəl) *adj.* & *n.* noble.

nobleman ('no·bəl·mən) *n.* [*pl.* -men] noble; hidalgo. —**noblewoman,** *n.* [*pl.* -women] dama; mujer noble; hidalga.

nobody ('no,bad·i; -bəd·i) *pron.* nadie; ninguno. —*n.* nadie; don nadie.

nocturnal (nak'tʌr·nəl) *adj.* nocturno; de noche.

nocturne ('nak·tʌrn) *n.* nocturno.

nod (nad) *n.* **1,** (greeting)

inclinación de cabeza. **2,** (signal) seña (con la cabeza). **3,** (approval) aprobación; asentimiento. —*v.t.* inclinar (la cabeza); indicar (con la cabeza). —*v.i.* dar cabezadas.

node (no:d) *n.* nodo. —**nodal,** *adj.* nodal.

nodule ('nad·jul) *n.* nódulo. —**nodular** ('nad·jə·lər) *adj.* nodular.

Noel (no'ɛl) *n.* Navidad; *l.c.* villancico de Navidad.

noggin ('nag·ɪn) *n.* **1,** (small mug) pichel; taza. **2,** *slang* (head) cabeza.

noise (nɔiz) *n.* ruido. —*v.t.* divulgar; vocear.

noiseless ('nɔiz·ləs) *adj.* silencioso. —**noiselessness,** *n.* silencio.

noisemaker ('nɔiz,mei·kər) *n.* **1,** (person) escandaloso. **2,** (instrument) matraca.

noisome ('nɔi·səm) *adj.* **1,** (ill-smelling) apestoso. **2,** (injurious) dañino; nocivo.

noisy ('nɔi·zi) *adj.* ruidoso; estrepitoso. —**noisiness,** *n.* ruido; estrépito.

nomad ('no·mæd) *n.* nómada. —**nomadic** (no'mæd·ɪk) *adj.* nómada.

no man's land tierra de nadie.

nomenclature ('no·mən,klei·tʃər) *n.* nomenclatura.

nominal ('nam·ə·nəl) *adj.* nominal.

nominate ('nam·ə,neit) *v.t.* nominar. —**nomination,** *n.* nominación.

nominative ('nam·ɪ·nə·tɪv) *adj.* & *n.* nominativo.

nominee (,nam·ɪ'ni:) *n.* candidato.

nonage ('nan·ɪdʒ) *n.* minoría de edad; minoridad.

nonagenarian (,nan·ə·dʒə-'nɛr·i·ən) *n.* & *adj.* nonagenario; noventón.

nonagon ('nan·ə,gan) *n.* nonágono.

nonbelligerent (,nan·bə'lɪdʒ·ə·rənt) *n.* & *adj.* no beligerante.

nonce (nans) *n.* tiempo presente. —**for the nonce,** por el momento.

nonchalance ('nan·ʃə·ləns) *n.* despreocupación. —**nonchalant,** *adj.* despreocupado.

noncom ('nan,kam) *n., colloq.* = **noncommissioned officer.**

noncombatant (nan'kam·bə·tənt) *n.* & *adj.* no combatiente.

noncommissioned officer (,nan·kə'mɪʃ·ənd) suboficial.

noncommittal (,nan·kə'mɪt·əl) *adj.* reservado; evasivo.

noncompliance (,nan·kəm'plai·əns) *n.* falta de cumplimiento.

nonconducive (,nan·kən'du·sɪv) *adj.* inconducente.

nonconductor (,nan·kən'dʌk·tər) *n.* mal conductor.

nonconformity (,nan·kən'for·mə·ti) *n.* desconformidad; disidencia. —**nonconformist,** *n.* disidente.

noncooperation (,nan·ko·ap·ə'rei·ʃən) *n.* falta de cooperación.

nondescript ('nan·də,skrɪpt) *adj.* inclasificable; indefinido; ordinario.

none (nʌn) *pron.* **1,** (no one) nadie; ninguno. **2,** (not any) ninguno; nada. —*adv.* no; en absoluto; de ningún modo. —**nonetheless,** *adv.* sin embargo; no obstante.

noneffective (,nan·ɛ'fɛk·tɪv) *n.* & *adj.* inútil.

nonentity (nan'ɛn·tə·ti) *n.* **1,** (person of little importance) don nadie; cero a la izquierda. **2,** (something nonexistent) mito; ente imaginario.

nones (no:nz) *n.pl.* **1,** (*in the ancient calendar*) nonas. **2,** (canonical hour) nona.

nonessential (,nan·ɛ'sɛn·ʃəl) *adj.* no esencial.

nonesuch (,nʌn'sʌtʃ) *n.* sin igual; sin par.

nonexistence (,nan·ɛg'zɪs·təns) *n.* inexistencia. —**nonexistent,** *adj.* inexistente.

nonfeasance (nan'fi·zəns) *n.* falta de cumplimiento.

nonfiction (nan'fɪk·ʃən) *n.* literatura seria o no ficticia.

nonillion (no'nɪl·jən) *n. (U.S.)* un millón de cuatrillones; quintillón; *Brit.* un millón de octillones; nonillón.

nonintervention (,nan·ɪn·tər-'vɛn·ʃən) *n.* no intervención.

nonpareil (,nan·pə'rel) *n.* & *adj.* sin par; sin rival. —*n.* **1,** *ornith.* especie de pinzón. **2,** (candy) dulce de chocolate con pizcas de azucar.

nonpartisan (nan'par·tɪ·zən) *adj.* sin partidismo.

nonperson (nan'pʌr·sən) *n.* persona no reconocida.

nonplus (nan'plʌs) *v.t.* confundir; dejar estupefacto.

nonprofit (nan'praf·ɪt) *adj.* que no ofrece ganancias; no comercial.

nonresident (nan'rɛz·ɪ·dənt) *adj.* & *n.* no residente.

nonsectarian (,nan·sɛk'tɛr·i·ən) *adj.* no sectario.

nonsense ('nan·sɛns) *n.* tontería; disparate. —**nonsensical** (nan'sɛn·sɪ·kəl) *adj.* disparatado; absurdo.

nonstop (,nan'stap) *adj.* directo; expreso. —*adv.* directamente; sin paradas; sin parar.

nonsupport (,nan·sə'port) *n.* falta de manutención.

nontoxic (nan'tak·sɪk) *adj.* atóxico.

nonunion (nan'jun·jən) *adj.* **1**, (not conforming to union requirements) no conforme con los requisitos del sindicato. **2**, (not unionized) no sindicado; no agremiado.

nonviolence (nan'vai·ə·ləns) *n.* abstinencia de medios violentos. —**nonviolent**, *adj.* sin empleo de medios violentos.

noodle ('nu·dəl) *n.* **1**, (spaghetti) tallarín. **2**, *slang* (head) cabeza.

nook (nʊk) *n.* rincón.

noon (nuːn) *n.* mediodía. —**noonday**, *adj.* de mediodía. —**noontime**, *n.* mediodía.

noose (nus) *n.* **1**, (running knot) nudo corredizo. **2**, (execution by hanging) horca.

nope (nop) *adv., slang* = **no**.

nor (nor) *conj.* ni.

Nordic ('nor·dɪk) *adj. & n.* nórdico.

norm (norm) *n.* norma. —**normative**, *adj.* normativo.

normal ('nor·məl) *adj. & n.* normal. —**normalcy** (-si); **normality** (nor'mæl·ə·ti) *n.* normalidad. —**normalize**, *v.t.* normalizar. —**normal school**, escuela normal.

Norman ('nor·mən) *n. & adj.* normando.

Norse (nors) *adj.* nórdico; escandinavo; normando. —*n.* **1**, (language) nórdico. **2**, *pl.* (Norsemen) normandos; escandinavos.

Norseman ('nors·mən) *n.* [*pl.* -men] escandinavo; normando.

north (norθ) *n.* norte. —*adj.* norte; del norte; septentrional. —*adv.* hacia el norte; al norte.

northeast (,norθ'ist) *n.* nordeste; noreste. —*adj.* del o hacia el nordeste. —*adv.* al o hacia el nordeste.

northeaster (,norθ'is·tər) *n.* viento (del) nordeste.

northeasterly (,norθ'is·tər·li) *adj.* (del) nordeste. —*adv.* hacia el nordeste.

northeastern (,norθ'is·tərn) *adj.* (del) nordeste.

northerly ('nor·ðər·li) *adj.* norte; del norte; hacia el norte. —*adv.* hacia el norte.

northern ('nor·ðərn) *adj.* norte; del norte; septentrional; norteño. —**northerner**, *n.* norteño; habitante del norte. —**northern lights**, aurora boreal.

northland ('norθ·lənd) *n.* **1**, (northern region) tierras del norte; norte. **2**, *cap.* Escandinavia.

Northman ('norθ·mən) *n.* [*pl.* -men] = **Norseman**.

North Pole polo norte.

North Star estrella polar.

northward ('norθ·wərd) *adj.* en o de dirección norte. —*adv.* hacia el norte.

northwest (,norθ'wɛst) *n. & adj.* noroeste. —*adv.* al o hacia el noroeste.

northwester (,norθ'wɛs·tər) *n.* viento (del) noroeste.

northwesterly (,norθ'wɛs·tər·li) *adj.* (del) noroeste. —*adv.* hacia el noroeste.

northwestern (,norθ'wɛs·tərn) *adj.* (del) noroeste.

nose (noːz) *n.* **1**, (olfactory organ) nariz. **2**, (sense of smell) olfato. **3**, (something resembling a nose) proa; punta; nariz. —*v.t. & i.* **1**, (scent; sniff) olfatear. **2**, (nuzzle) frotar la nariz (contra); hocicar. **3**, (push forward) avanzar. —*v.i.* (pry) husmear. —**blow one's nose**, sonarse las narices. —**follow one's nose**, seguir en línea recta. —**lead (someone) by the nose**, traer del cabestro. —**look down one's nose**, mirar con desprecio; desdeñar. —**nose out**, ganar por una nariz. —**under one's nose**, en las (propias) barbas de uno.

nosebleed ('noz,blid) *n.* hemorragia nasal.

nose cone *n.* morro.

nosedive ('noz,daiv) *n.* picada. —*v.i.* picar; irse en picada.

nosegay ('noz·gei) *n.* ramillete de flores.

nosey ('no·zi) *adj.* = **nosy**.

no-show ('no,ʃo) *adj. & n.* (persona) que no se presenta para servirse de una reservación, aunque pagada.

nostalgia (nas'tæl·dʒə) *n.* nostalgia. —**nostalgic**, *adj.* nostálgico.

nostril ('nas·trəl) *n.* ventana de la nariz; *pl.* narices.

nostrum ('nas·trəm) *n.* cúralotodo; panacea.

nosy *también,* **nosey** ('no·zi) *adj., colloq.* preguntón; entremetido; curioso.

not (nat) *adv.* no. —**not at all,** de ningún modo; nada. —**not even,** ni; ni siquiera. —**not ever,** nunca; jamás. —**not in any wise,** de ningún modo. —**not ... nor,** no ... ni; ni ... ni. —**not so much as,** ni siquiera. —**not to say,** por no decir.

notable ('no·tə·bəl) *adj. & n.* notable. —**notability,** *n.* notabilidad.

notarial (no'ter·i·əl) *adj.* notarial.

notarize ('no·tə,raiz) *v.t.* autorizar ante notario; *Amer.* notarizar.

notary ('no·tə·ri) *n.* [*también,* **notary public**] notario.

notation (no'tei·ʃən) *n.* 1, (act or result of noting) anotación; notación; apunte. 2, (set of symbols) notación.

notch (natʃ) *n.* 1, (nick; slot) muesca; mella. 2, (defile) desfiladero. —*v.t.* mellar; cortar muescas en.

note (not) *n.* nota. —*v.t.* 1, (notice; observe) notar. 2, (make a note of) anotar; apuntar. 3, (mention particularly) mencionar; indicar. 4, (denote; signify) denotar; indicar.

notebook ('not,bʊk) *n.* libreta; libreta de apuntes; cuaderno.

noted ('no·tɪd) *adj.* notable; célebre; famoso.

noteworthy ('not,wʌr·ði) *adj.* digno de nota; notable.

nothing ('nʌθ·ɪŋ) *n.* 1, (not anything) nada. 2, (trifle) nadería. 3, (zero) cero. —*adv.* de ningún modo; nada. —**be good for nothing,** no servir para nada. —**for nothing,** 1, (free; at no cost) por nada; gratis. 2, (in vain) para nada; en vano. 3, (without reason) por nada; sin motivo. —**make nothing of,** 1, (belittle) tomar a la ligera; no dar importancia a. 2, (fail to understand) no sacar nada en limpio de; no poder comprender. 3, (fail to use) no aprovecharse de. —**nothing but,** nada más que; solamente. —**nothing doing,** *colloq.* no hay caso. —**think nothing of,** no dar importancia a; no importarle nada a uno.

notice ('no·tɪs) *n.* 1, (information; announcement) aviso. 2, (warning) aviso; advertencia. 3, (brief article) artículo; suelto. 4, (attention; heed) atención. —*v.t.* 1, (perceive) notar; advertir; apercibirse de. 2, (give attention to) prestar atención a; hacer caso de. 3, (mention; acknowledge) mencionar; hacer mención de. —**noticeable,** *adj.* perceptible; que se nota; que llama atención. —**serve notice,** anunciar; informar; dar aviso formal. —**take notice (of),** notar; apercibirse (de); hacer caso (de).

notify ('no·tɪ·fai) *v.t.* notificar. —**notification** (-fɪ'kei·ʃən) *n.* notificación.

notion ('no·ʃən) *n.* noción. —**notions,** *n.pl.* artículos de mercería; novedades.

notorious (no'tor·i·əs) *adj.* notorio. —**notoriety** (,no·tə'rai·ə·ti) *n.* notoriedad.

no-trump *adj. & n., cards* sin triunfo.

notwithstanding (,nat'wɪθ·'stæn·dɪŋ) *adv.* no obstante; sin embargo; con todo. —*prep.* a pesar de. —*conj.* aun cuando; aunque; pese a que.

nougat ('nu·gət) *n.* turrón; nuégado. —**nougatine** (,nu·gə'tin) *n.* chocolate de almendras.

nought (nɔt) *n.* = **naught.**

noun (naun) *n.* nombre; substantivo.

nourish ('nʌr·ɪʃ) *v.t.* nutrir; alimentar. —**nourishing,** *adj.* nutritivo; alimenticio. —**nourishment,** *n.* alimento.

nova ('no·və) *n., astron.* nova.

novel ('nav·əl) *adj.* nuevo; original. —*n.* novela. —**novelette** (-ɛt) *n.* novela corta. —**novelist,** *n.* novelista. —**novelize,** *v.t.* novelizar. —**novelization,** *n.* novelización.

novelty ('nav·əl·ti) *n.* 1, (newness; something new) novedad. 2, *usu.pl.* (trinkets) baratijas.

November (no'vɛm·bər) *n.* noviembre.

novena (no'vi·nə) *n.* novena.

novice ('nav·ɪs) *n.* novicio.

novitiate *también,* **noviciate** (no'vɪʃ·i·ət) *n.* noviciado.

novocaine ('no·və,kein) *n.* novocaína.

now (nau) *adv.* ahora; ya. —*conj.* pues (que); ahora que; ya que. —*n.* presente; actualidad. —**now and then,** de cuando en cuando; de vez en cuando. —**now ... now,** ya ... ya; ora ... ora: *now rich, now poor,* ora rico, ora pobre. —**now then,** ahora bien; pues; pues bien.

nowadays ('nau·ə,deiz) *adv.* hoy día; hoy en día.

noway ('no,wei) *adv.* de ningún modo. *También,* **noways.**

nowhere ('no·hwɛr) *adv.* a, en o por ninguna parte. —**be** (o **get**) **nowhere,** no tener éxito. —**get** (**someone**) **nowhere,** no servir de nada. —**nowhere else,** a, en o por ninguna otra parte. —**nowhere near,** ni cerca.

nowise ('no,waiz) *adv.* de ningún modo.

noxious ('nak·ʃəs) *adj.* nocivo. —**noxiousness,** *n.* nocividad.

nozzle ('naz·əl) *n.* pitón; boquilla.

nth (ɛnθ) *adj.* enésimo.

nuance (nu'ans) *n.* matiz.

nub (nʌb) *n.* **1,** (knob; lump) protuberancia; nudo. **2,** *colloq.* (gist) meollo; quid.

Nubian ('nu·bi·ən) *adj. & n.* nubio.

nubile ('nu·bɪl) *adj.* núbil.

nuclear ('nuk·li·ər) *adj.* nuclear.

nucleic acid (nu'kli·ɪk) *n.* ácido nucleico.

nucleolus (nu'kli·ə·ləs) *n.* nucléolo.

nucleon ('nu·kli·an) *n.* nucleón.

nucleus ('nu·kli·əs) *n.* núcleo.

nude (nurd) *adj. & n.* desnudo. —**nudeness,** *n.* desnudez. —**in the nude,** desnudo; al desnudo.

nudge (nʌdʒ) *v.t.* empujar levemente; dar un codazo. —*n.* codazo; leve empujón.

nudism ('nu·dɪz·əm) *n.* nudismo. —**nudist,** *n. & adj.* nudista.

nudity ('nu·də·ti) *n.* desnudez.

nugatory ('nu·gə,tor·i) *adj.* nulo; ineficaz.

nugget ('nʌg·ət) *n.* pedazo; pepita.

nuisance ('nu·səns) *n.* **1,** (child's annoyance) molestia; fastidio. **2,** (annoying person) pelmazo; cataplasma.

null (nʌl) *adj.* nulo. —**null and void,** anulado; nulo.

nullify ('nʌl·ɪ·fai) *v.t.* anular; invalidar. —**nullification** (-fɪ'kei·ʃən) *n.* anulación; invalidación.

nullity ('nʌl·ə·ti) *n.* nulidad.

numb (nʌm) *adj.* entumecido; paralizado. —*v.t.* entumecer; paralizar. —**numbness,** *n.* entumecimiento.

number ('nʌm·bər) *n.* número. —*v.t.* **1,** (designate by number) numerar. **2,** (reckon; classify) contar; enumerar. **3,** (have in number; comprise) contar con; tener. **4,** (amount to) sumar; ser (en total). —**numbers,** *n.pl.* **1,** (many; great number) multitud; gran número. **2,** (numerical superiority) superioridad en número. **3,** (arithmetic) números. —**a number of,** (un) cierto número de. —**be numbered among,** encontrarse o hallarse en. —**beyond number,** sin número; innumerable. —**get one's number,** *slang* calar; fichar. —**one's number is up,** llegarle o tocarle a uno la hora. —**without number,** sin número.

numbering ('nʌm·bər·ɪŋ) *n.* numeración.

numberless ('nʌm·bər·ləs) *adj.* sin número; innumerable.

numeral ('nu·mər·əl) *adj.* numeral. —*n.* número.

numerate ('nu·mə·reit) *v.t.* numerar. —**numeration,** *n.* numeración.

numerator ('nu·mə,rei·tər) *n.* numerador.

numerical (nu'mɛr·ɪ·kəl) *adj.* numérico.

numerology (,nu·mə'ral·ə·dʒi) *n.* numerología. —**numerologist,** *n.* numerólogo.

numerous ('nu·mər·əs) *adj.* numeroso. —**numerousness,** *n.* numerosidad.

numismatics (,nu·mɪs'mæt·ɪks) *n.* numismática. —**numismatic,** *adj.* numismático. —**numismatist** (nu'mɪs·mə·tɪst) *n.* numismático.

numskull ('nʌm,skʌl) *n.* zoquete; zote.

nun (nʌn) *n.* monja; religiosa. —**nunnery,** *n.* convento de monjas.

nuncio ('nʌn·ʃi·o) *n.* nuncio.

nuptial ('nʌp·ʃəl) *adj.* nupcial. —**nuptials,** *n.pl.* nupcias.

nurse (nʌrs) *n.* **1,** (child's attendant) niñera; ama. **2,** (one who tends the sick) enfermero (*fem.* enfermera). **3,** (wet nurse) nodriza. —*v.t.* **1,** (take care of) cuidar; cuidar de. **2,** (suckle) amamantar; dar de mamar. **3,** (nourish; foster) criar; alimentar. **4,** (drink slowly) tomar o beber con calma; beber despacio.

nursery ('nʌr·sə·ri) *n.* **1,** (children's room) cuarto de los niños; cuarto de juegos. **2,** (place where plants or animals are raised) criadero; vivero. **3,** (place where children are cared for) guardería.

nursing ('nʌrs·ɪŋ) *n.* profesión de enfermera o enfermero. —**nursing home,** clínica para convalecientes o ancianos.

nursemaid ('nʌrs,meid) *n.* niñera.

nurture ('nʌr·tʃər) *v.t.* **1,** (feed) alimentar. **2,** (rear; train) criar; educar. —*n.* crianza; educación.

nut (nʌt) *n.* **1,** (fruit) nuez. **2,** *mech.* tuerca. **3,** *slang* (head) cabeza. **4,** *slang* (fixed expenses) gastos fijos. **5,** *slang* (lunatic; eccentric) chiflado; loco.

nutcracker ('nʌt,kræk·ər) *n.* cascanueces.

nutmeg ('nʌt,mɛg) *n.* nuez moscada.

nutria ('nu·tri·ə) *n.* nutria.

nutrient ('nu·tri·ənt) *adj.* nutritivo; alimenticio. —*n.* alimento; nutrimento.

nutriment ('nu·trɪ·mənt) *n.* nutrimento; alimento.

nutrition (nu'trɪʃ·ən) *n.* nutrición.

—**nutritional,** *adj.* de nutrición; nutritivo. —**nutritionist,** *n.* especialista en nutrición. —**nutritious,** *adj.* nutritivo; alimenticio.

nutritive ('nu·trə·tɪv) *adj.* nutritivo; alimenticio.

nuts (nʌts) *adj., slang* chiflado; loco. —*interj.* ¡cuernos!

nutshell ('nʌt,ʃɛl) *n.* cáscara de nuez. —**in a nutshell,** en una palabra; en pocas palabras.

nutty ('nʌt·i) *adj.* **1,** (tasting of nuts) que sabe a nueces. **2,** (full of nuts) lleno de nueces. **3,** *slang* (lunatic; eccentric) chiflado; loco.

nuzzle ('nʌz·əl) *v.t. & i.* (rub with the nose) frotar la nariz (contra); hocicar. —*v.i.* (nestle; snuggle) acurrucarse; *Amer.* aparragarse.

nylon ('nai·lan) *n.* nilón.

nymph (nɪmf) *n.* ninfa.

nymphomania (,nɪm·fə'mei·ni·a) *n.* ninfomanía; fiebre uterina. —**nymphomaniac** (-æk) *n.* ninfomaníaca.

O

O, o (oː) decimoquinta letra del alfabeto inglés. —*n.* cero. —*interj.* ¡oh!

oaf (of) *n.* bobo; bobalicón. —**oafish,** *adj.* lerdo; torpe.

oak (ok) *n.* roble. —**oaken,** *adj.* de roble. —**evergreen oak,** encina. —**oak grove,** robledal; robledo.

oakum ('o·kəm) *n.* estopa.

oar (oːr) *n.* remo. —*v.i.* remar. —*v.t.* mover a remo. —**oar blade,** pala de remo. —**oar stroke,** remada.

oarlock ('oːr·lak) *n.* chumacera.

oarsman ('oːrz·mən) *n.* [*pl.* **-men**] remero.

oasis (o'ei·sɪs) *n.* [*pl.* **-ses** (si:z)] oasis.

oat (ot) *n., usu.pl.* avena. —**oaten,** *adj.* de avena. —**feel one's oats,** *slang* darse importancia; sentirse otra persona. —**sow one's wild oats,** *slang* calaverear; correrla; correr sus mocedades.

oath (oθ) *n.* [*pl.* **oaths** (oːðz)] juramento. —**take (an) oath,** prestar juramento; jurar.

oatmeal ('ot·mil) *n.* avena; harina de avena.

obdurate ('ab·djə·rət) *adj.* **1,** (obstinate) obstinado; terco. **2,** (hard-

hearted) duro; empedernido. —**obduracy,** *n.* obstinación; terquedad.

obedient (o'bi·di·ənt) *adj.* obediente. —**obedience,** *n.* obediencia.

obeisance (o'bei·səns) *n.* cortesía; reverencia.

obelisk ('ab·ə·lɪsk) *n.* obelisco.

obese (o'bis) *adj.* obeso. —**obesity,** *n.* obesidad.

obey (o'bei) *v.t. & i.* obedecer.

obfuscate (ob'fʌs·keit) *v.t.* ofuscar. —**obfuscation,** *n.* ofuscación.

obituary (o'bɪtʃ·u,ɛr·i) *n.* obituario; necrología. —*adj.* necrológico.

object ('ab·dʒɪkt) *n.* **1,** (material thing) objeto. **2,** (person or thing aimed at) objeto; objetivo. **3,** (purpose; aim) objetivo. **4,** *gram.* complemento.

object (əb'dʒɛkt) *v.i.* oponerse. —*v.t.* objetar.

objection (əb'dʒɛk·ʃən) *n.* objeción; reparo.

objectionable (əb'dʒɛk·ʃən·ə·bəl) *adj.* **1,** (censurable) reprobable; censurable. **2,** (unpleasant) molesto; incómodo.

objective (əb'dʒɛk·tɪv) *n. & adj.* objetivo. —**objectivity** (,ab·

dʒek'tɪv·ə·ti) *n.* objetividad. —**objective case,** caso acusativo.

oblate ('ab·let) *adj., geom.* achatado (por los polos). —*n.* oblato.

oblation (ab'lei·ʃən) *n.* oblación.

obligate ('ab·lə,geit) *v.t.* obligar. —**obligation,** *n.* obligación.

obligatory (ab'lɪg·ə,tor·i) *adj.* obligatorio.

oblige (ə'blaidʒ) *v.t.* **1,** (bind; compel) obligar; forzar. **2,** (treat; regale) obsequiar. **3,** (do a favor for) complacer. —**obliging,** *adj.* servicial; solícito; atento. —**much obliged,** muy agradecido.

oblique (ə'blik) *adj.* **1,** (slanting) oblicuo; inclinado. **2,** (indirect) indirecto; torcido. —**obliquity** (ə'blɪk·wə·ti) *n.* oblicuidad.

obliterate (ə'blɪt·ə,reit) *v.t.* **1,** (blot out) borrar. **2,** (destroy) arrasar; destruir. —**obliteration,** *n.* destrucción.

oblivion (ə'blɪv·i·ən) *n.* olvido. —**oblivious,** *adj.* inconsciente; insensible.

oblong ('ab·lɔŋ) *adj.* oblongo. —*n.* figura oblonga.

obloquy ('ab·lə·kwi) *n.* **1,** (abusive language) vituperación; vejámenes. **2,** (disgrace) deshonra; baldón; mala fama.

obnoxious (əb'nak·ʃəs) *adj.* odioso; ofensivo; molesto. —**obnoxiousness,** *n.* odiosidad.

oboe ('o·bo) *n.* oboe. —**oboist,** *n.* oboe.

obscene (əb'siːn) *adj.* obsceno. —**obscenity** (əb'sɛn·ə·ti) *n.* obscenidad.

obscure (əb'skjʊr) *adj.* obscuro. —*v.t.* **1,** (darken; make dim) obscurecer. **2,** (conceal) ocultar. —**obscurant; obscurantist,** *adj.* & *n.* oscurantista. —**obscurantism,** *n.* oscurantismo. —**obscurity,** *n.* obscuridad.

obsequies ('ab·sə,kwiːz) *n.pl.* exequias; funerales.

obsequious (əb'si·kwi·əs) *adj.* obsequioso. —**obsequiousness,** *n.* obsequiosidad.

observable (əb'zʌr·və·bəl) *adj.* observable.

observance (əb'zʌr·vəns) *n.* **1,** (compliance) observancia; acatamiento. **2,** (custom) costumbre; práctica. **3,** (ceremony) ceremonia. **4,** (celebration) celebración.

observant (əb'zʌr·vənt) *adj.* observador.

observation (,ab·zər'vei·ʃən) *n.* observación.

observatory (ab'zʌr·və·tor·i) *n.* observatorio.

observe (əb'zʌrv) *v.t.* **1,** (watch; look at) observar. **2,** (celebrate) celebrar. **3,** (keep, as mourning, silence, etc.) guardar. —**observer,** *n.* observador [*fem.* -dora].

obsess (əb'sɛs) *v.t.* obsesionar. —**obsession** (əb'sɛʃ·ən) *n.* obsesión. —**obsessive,** *adj.* obsesivo.

obsidian (ab'sɪd·i·ən) *n.* obsidiana.

obsolescent (,ab·sə'lɛs·ənt) *adj.* que va cayendo en desuso; que va desapareciendo. —**obsolescence,** *n.* desuso.

obsolete (,ab·sə'lit) *adj.* desusado; anticuado. —**obsoleteness,** *n.* desuso.

obstacle ('ab·stə·kəl) *n.* obstáculo.

obstetrics (əb'stɛt·rɪks) *n.* obstetricia; tocología. —**obstetric; obstetrical,** *adj.* obstétrico. —**obstetrician** (,ab·stə'trɪʃ·ən) *n.* tocólogo.

obstinate ('ab·stɪ·nət) *adj.* obstinado. —**obstinacy,** *n.* obstinación.

obstreperous (əb'strɛp·ər·əs) *adj.* estrepitoso; bullicioso; ruidoso. —**obstreperousness,** *n.* lo ruidoso; lo estrepitoso.

obstruct (əb'strʌkt) *v.t.* obstruir —**obstruction** (əb'strʌk·ʃən) *n.* obstrucción. —**obstructive,** *adj.* obstructor; obstructivo.

obstructionism (ab'strʌk·ʃən·ɪz·əm) *n.* obstruccionismo. —**obstructionist,** *adj.* & *n.* obstruccionista.

obtain (əb'tein) *v.t.* obtener; adquirir; conseguir. —*v.i.* prevalecer; estar en vigor o en boga. —**obtainable,** *adj.* obtenible.

obtrude (əb'truːd) *v.t.* **1,** (push out; thrust forward) empujar o proyectar hacia afuera. **2,** (intrude) meter; entremeter. —*v.i.* entremeterse; hacer intrusión; ser importuno. —**obtrusive** (əb'tru·sɪv) *adj.* intruso; importuno.

obtuse (əb'tus) *adj.* obtuso. —**obtuseness,** *n.* calidad de obtuso.

obverse (əb'vʌrs) *n.* anverso. —*adj.* (ab'vʌrs) del anverso.

obviate ('ab·vi,eit) *v.t.* obviar.

obvious ('ab·vi·əs) *adj.* obvio; evidente. —**obviousness,** *n.* lo obvio; lo evidente.

occasion (ə'kei·ʒən) *n.* ocasión.

—*v.t.* causar; ocasionar; dar ocasión para. —**on occasion,** a veces; de vez en cuando. —**on the occasion of,** con ocasión de. —**rise to the occasion,** ponerse a la altura de las circunstancias.

occasional (ə'kei·ʒə·nəl) *adj.* 1, (occurring now and then) raro; poco frecuente. 2, (of or befitting an occasion) de o para la ocasión. 3, (casual; fortuitous) ocasional; imprevisto. 4, (random; odd) suelto. —**occasionally,** *adv.* de vez en cuando.

occident ('ak·sı·dənt) *n.* occidente. —**occidental** (-'dɛn·təl) *adj. & n.* occidental.

occiput ('ak·sı·pʌt) *n.* occipucio. —**occipital** (ak'sıp·ə·təl) *adj.* occipital.

occlude (ə'kluːd) *v.t.* occluir. —**occlusion** (ə'kluː·ʒən) *n.* oclusión. —**occlusive** (ə'kluː·sıv) *adj.* oclusivo.

occult (a'kʌlt) *adj.* oculto. —**occultism,** *n.* ocultismo. —**occultist,** *adj. & n.* ocultista.

occultation (,ak·ʌl'tei·ʃən) *n.* ocultación.

occupancy ('ak·jə·pən·si) *n.* tenencia; ocupación.

occupant ('ak·jə·pənt) *n.* 1, (one that occupies) ocupante. 2, (tenant) inquilino.

occupation (,ak·jə'pei·ʃən) *n.* ocupación. —**occupational,** *adj.* relativo a una ocupación o empleo. —**occupational hazards,** gajes del oficio.

occupy ('ak·jə·pai) *v.t.* ocupar. —**be occupied with** o **in,** ocuparse de o en; estar ocupado con.

occur (ə'kʌr) *v.i.* 1, (happen) ocurrir; acontecer; suceder. 2, (exist; be found) existir; encontrarse. 3, (come to mind) ocurrírsele a uno.

occurrence (ə'kʌr·əns) *n.* 1, (happening) acontecimiento; suceso; ocurrencia. 2, (appearance; presence) presencia; aparición.

ocean ('o·ʃən) *n.* océano. —**oceanic** (,o·ʃi'æn·ık) *adj.* oceánico.

oceanography (,o·ʃi·ə'nag·rə·fi) *n.* oceanografía. —**oceanographic** (-nə'græf·ık) *adj.* oceanográfico. —**oceanographer,** *n.* oceanógrafo.

ocelot ('o·sə,lat; 'as·ə-) *n.* ocelote.

ocher también, **ochre** ('o·kər) *n.* ocre.

o'clock (ə'klak) *adv.* por o según el reloj. —(**it is**) **one o'clock;** (**it is**) **two o'clock,** etc., (es) la una; (son) las dos, *etc.*

octagon ('ak·tə,gan) *n.* octágono. —**octagonal** (ak'tæg·ə·nəl) *adj.* octagonal.

octahedron (,ak·tə'hi·drən) *n.* octaedro. —**octahedral,** *adj.* octaédrico.

octane ('ak·tein) *n.* octano.

octant ('ak·tənt) *n.* octante.

octave ('ak·tıv) *n.* octava.

octavo (ak'tei·vo) *adj.* en octavo. —*n.* tamaño de octavo; libro en octavo.

octet (ak'tɛt) *n.* octeto.

octillion (ak'tıl·jən) *n. U.S.* mil cuatrillones; *Brit.* un millón de septillones; octillón.

October (ak'to·bər) *n.* octubre.

octogenarian (,ak·tə·dʒə'nɛr·i·ən) *n. & adj.* octogenario.

octopus ('ak·tə·pəs) *n.* [*pl.* **-puses** o **-pi** (pai)] pulpo.

octoroon (,ak·tə'ruːn) *n. & adj.* ochavón.

octuple (ak'tu·pəl; 'ak·tu-) *adj. & n.* óctuple; óctuplo. —*v.t.* octuplicar. —*v.i.* octuplicarse.

ocular ('ak·jə·lər) *adj.* ocular.

oculist ('ak·jə·lıst) *n.* oculista.

OD ('o'di) *n. & v.t. & i., abr. de* **overdose.**

odalisque ('o·də·lısk) *n.* odalisca.

odd (aːd) *adj.* 1, (strange) raro; extraño. 2, (not paired) suelto; sin pareja. 3, (not even) impar. 4, (little more) y pico; y tantos; y poco más. 5, (extra) extra; sobrante. 6, (occasional) ocasional; incidental. —**oddball,** *adj. & n., slang* excéntrico. —**oddment,** *n.* retal; retazo. —**oddness,** *n.* rareza; lo raro.

oddity ('ad·ə·ti) *n.* 1, (strangeness) rareza; lo raro. 2, (strange person or thing) persona o cosa rara; curiosidad; rareza.

odds (aːdz) *n.pl.* 1, (advantage) ventaja. 2, (probability) probabilidades. 3, (superiority) superioridad; fuerzas superiores. —**at odds,** en desacuerdo; en pugna. —**by** (**all**) **odds,** por seguro; con mucho. —**give odds,** dar ventaja; dar tantos de ventaja. —**odds and ends,** cosas sueltas; zarandajas. —**odds-on,** *adj.* que tiene la mayor ventaja.

ode (oːd) *n.* oda.

odious ('o·di·əs) *adj.* odioso. —**odiousness,** *n.* odiosidad.

odium ('o·di·əm) *n.* odio.

odometer (o'dam·ə·tər) *n.* odómetro.

odontology (ˌo·dan'tal·ə·dʒi) *n.* odontología. —**odontological** (-tə'ladʒ·ɪ·kəl) *adj.* odontológico. —**odontologist,** *n.* odontólogo.

odor ('o·dər) *n.* olor. —**in bad odor,** de mala fama; desacreditado.

odoriferous (ˌo·də'rɪf·ər·əs) *adj.* odorífero. —**odoriferousness,** *n.* olor; fragancia.

odorless ('o·dər·ləs) *adj.* inodoro.

odorous ('o·dər·əs) *adj.* oloroso; fragante.

odyssey ('ad·ə·si) *n.* odisea.

oenology (i'nal·ə·dʒi) *n.* enología.

o'er (oɹr) *adv. & prep., poet.* = **over.**

of (ʌv) *prep.* de; *(in telling time)* para: *twenty of twelve,* veinte para las doce.

off (ɔf) *prep.* **1,** (not on; out of) fuera de. **2,** (not fixed to; removed from) despegado de; suelto de. **3,** (out of; from) de. **4,** (coming out from) que sale de. **5,** (close to; adjacent to) cerca de. **6,** (free from) libre de; exento de; sin. **7,** (deprived of) privado de. **8,** (not up to the standard of) no a la altura de. **9,** *colloq.* (abstaining from) absteniéndose de; curado de. —*adj.* **1,** (not on; removed) no puesto. **2,** (loose; not attached) suelto; despegado. **3,** (not in operation) apagado; desconectado. **4,** (cut off) cortado. **5,** (canceled; suspended) suspendido. **6,** (on the way) en marcha; en camino. **7,** (absent) ausente; fuera. **8,** (less; smaller; fewer) menor; menos. **9,** (more remote; further) más lejano; más remoto. **10,** (wrong; in error) errado; equivocado. **11,** (not usual) raro; extraordinario. **12,** (free; devoted to leisure) libre. **13,** *colloq.* (below par) flojo; anormal; destemplado. —*adv.* **1,** (away) fuera; afuera. **2,** (so as to end entirely) del todo; enteramente. **3,** (from here, or a specified place) de aquí; de allí. **4,** (from the present, or a specified time) faltando (cierto tiempo) para: *Christmas is ten days off,* Faltan diez días para Navidad. —*interj.* ¡fuera! ¡afuera! —**be off,** salir; irse. —**off and on,** de cuando en cuando; de vez en cuando. —**off the cuff,** improvisado. —**off the wall,** extraño; raro. —**off with ...,** a fuera (con) ... —**off with you,** ¡fuera!; ¡márchate!

offal ('ɔf·əl) *n.* desechos; desperdicios; basura; bazofia.

offcast *adj. & n.* = **castoff.**

off-center *adj.* descentrado; eccéntrico.

off-chance *n.* casualidad; improbabilidad. —*adj.* improbable.

off-color *adj.* **1,** (defective in color) de mal color; de matiz imperfecto. **2,** (risqué) verde; obsceno; de mal tono.

offend (ə'fɛnd) *v.t.* ofender. —*v.i.* **1,** (be offensive) ofender. **2,** (transgress) pecar; transgredir. —**offender,** *n.* culpable; delincuente.

offense (ə'fɛns) *n.* **1,** (transgression) falta; pecado; transgresión. **2,** (affront) ofensa; afrenta. **3,** (attack) ataque; acometida. **4,** (attacking side) atacante. —**give offense,** ofender. —**no offense,** sin querer ofender. —**take offense,** ofenderse.

offensive (ə'fɛn·sɪv) *adj.* ofensivo. —*n.* ofensiva. —**offensiveness,** *n.* lo ofensivo.

offer ('af·ər; 'ɔf-) *v.t.* **1,** (present; proffer) ofrecer. **2,** (propose; suggest) proponer; presentar; sugerir. **3,** (give, as violence, resistance, etc.) ofrecer. **4,** (make an offering of) ofrendar. **5,** (show intention of) ofrecerse a; hacer ademán de. —*v.i.* **1,** (present itself; occur) ofrecerse; presentarse. **2,** (make an offering) hacer ofrenda. —*n.* oferta.

offering ('af·ər·ɪŋ; 'ɔf-) *n.* **1,** (act of offering; thing offered) ofrecimiento; presentación. **2,** (tribute; contribution) ofrenda.

offertory ('af·ər,tor·i; 'ɔf-) *n.* ofertorio.

offhand ('ɔf,hænd) *adv.* sin mayor estudio. —*adj.* **1,** (impromptu) poco estudiado; improvisado. **2,** (casual; informal) casual; informal; sin ceremonia.

office ('af·ɪs; 'ɔf-) *n.* **1,** (position) cargo. **2,** (place of business) oficina; despacho. **3,** (service; duty) oficio; función. **4,** *usu.pl.* (influence) oficios. **5,** (administrative body) dirección; ministerio. —**office worker,** oficinista.

officeholder ('af·ɪs,hol·dər; 'ɔf-) *n.* funcionario; empleado público.

officer ('af·ə·sər; 'ɔf-) *n.* **1,** (official) oficial; funcionario. **2,** *mil.* oficial. **3,** (policeman) agente de policía; guardia.

official (ə'fɪʃ·əl) *n.* oficial; funcionario. —*adj.* oficial.

officialdom (ə'fɪʃ·əl·dəm) *n.* las autoridades; burocracia.

officiate (ə'fɪʃ·i·eit) *v.i.* oficiar.

officious (ə'fɪʃ·əs) *adj.* oficioso; entremetido. **—officiousness,** *n.* oficiosidad.

offing ('ɔf·ɪŋ) *n.* lontananza. **—in the offing,** cerca; a la vista.

offish ('ɔf·ɪʃ) *adj., colloq.* reservado; huraño. **—offishness,** *n.* reserva.

off-key *adj.* discordante.

off-limits *adj.* prohibido.

off-line ('ɔf,lain) *adj., elect.; comput.* fuera de línea; desconectado; autónomo.

off-load *v.t.* descargar; desembarcar.

offprint ('ɔf,prɪnt) *n.* tirada aparte. **—v.t.** imprimir aparte.

off-season *n.* temporada de poca actividad.

offset ('ɔf·sɛt) *n.* **1,** (compensation) compensación. **2,** (offshoot) ramal. **3,** (perpendicular distance) distancia perpendicular. **4,** *mech.* codo. **5,** *print.* offset. **—v.t.** (ɔf'sɛt) **1,** (compensate) compensar. **2,** (displace, as from the straight line) desplazar.

offshoot ('ɔf,ʃut) *n.* rama; ramal.

offshore (ɔf'ʃɔːr) *adj. & adv.* a distancia de la costa; mar afuera.

offside (,ɔf'said) *adj. & adv., sports* fuera de juego.

offspring ('ɔf,sprɪŋ) *n.* descendiente; progenie; vástago.

off-the-record *adj. & adv.* en confianza; a no divulgar.

off-white *adj. & n.* blancuzco; blanquecino.

often ('ɔf·ən) *adv.* frecuentemente; muchas veces: a menudo. *También, poet.,* **oft** (ɔft).

oftentimes ('ɔf·ən,taimz) *adv.* = **often.** *También,* **ofttimes.**

ogive (o'dʒaiv) *n.* ojiva.

ogle ('o·gəl) *v.t. & i.* mirar con cariño o deseo; ojear. **—n.** ojeada; mirada.

ogre ('o·gər) *n.* ogro.

oh (oː) *interj.* ¡oh!

ohm (oːm) *n.* ohmio; ohm.

oil (ɔil) *n.* **1,** (viscous substance) aceite. **2,** *paint.* óleo. **—v.t.** **1,** (lubricate) lubricar; aceitar. **2,** *colloq.* (bribe) sobornar; untar la mano a. **—oil can,** aceitera. **—oil painting,** pintura al óleo. **—oil well,** pozo de petróleo.

oilcloth ('ɔil,klɔθ) *n.* hule; encerado.

oiler ('ɔi·lər) *n.* **1,** (person or device for lubricating) engrasador. **2,** (ship) barco petrolero.

oilskin ('ɔil,skɪn) *n.* hule.

oily ('ɔi·li) *adj.* **1,** (of, like, or containing oil) aceitoso; oleaginoso. **2,** (greasy) grasoso. **3,** *fig.* (unctuous) untuoso.

oink (oiŋk) *n.* gruñido del cerdo. **—v.i.** gruñir como cerdo.

ointment (ɔint·mənt) *n.* ungüento.

O.K. (o'kei) *adv., colloq.* muy bien. **—adj., colloq.,** bueno. **—v.t., colloq.** aprobar. *También,* **okay.**

okra ('o·krə) *n.* quingombó.

old (oːld) *adj.* **1,** (of great age) viejo. **2,** (of a specified age) de edad. **3,** (ancient) antiguo; viejo; vetusto. **4,** (antique) antiguo. **5,** (former) previo; anterior. **6,** (aged, as wine) añejo. **7,** (antiquated) anticuado; pasado. **—n.** ayer; tiempo pasado. **—of old,** antaño; de antaño. **—How old is he?,** ¿Cuántos años tiene? **—He is ten years old,** Tiene diez años.

old age vejez; ancianidad.

olden ('ol·dən) *adj.* antiguo.

old-fashioned (old'fæʃ·ənd) *adj.* **1,** (holding to the past) chapado a la antigua; anticuado. **2,** (out of style) fuera de moda; pasado de moda.

Old Glory bandera de los Estados Unidos de América.

old hat anticuado.

old maid solterona.

oldness ('old·nəs) *n.* antigüedad.

Old Nick patillas; el Diablo.

oldster ('old·stər) *n., colloq.* viejo; *fem.* vieja.

Old Testament Antiguo Testamento.

old-time *adj.* antiguo; del pasado. **—old-timer,** *n.* anciano; veterano.

Old World Viejo Mundo.

oleaginous (,o·li'ædʒ·ə·nəs) *adj.* oleaginoso.

oleander (,o·li'æn·dər) *n.* adelfa.

oleomargarine (,o·li·o'mar·dʒə,rin; -rɪn) *n.* oleomargarina. *También,* **oleo.**

olfactory (al'fæk·tə·ri) *adj.* olfatorio.

oligarchy ('al·ə,gar·ki) *n.* oligarquía. **—oligarch** (-,gark) *n.* oligarca. **—oligarchic; oligarchical,** *adj.* oligárquico.

olio ('o·li·o) *n.* **1,** (stew) especie de chanfaina. **2,** (miscellany) miscelánea; mescolanza.

olive ('al·ɪv) *n.* **1,** (tree) olivo. **2,**

(fruit) aceituna; oliva. **3,** (color) olivo. —*adj.* oliváceo. —**olive branch,** rama de olivo. —**olive drab, 1,** (color) verde oliva. **2,** (cloth) caqui. —**olive grove,** olivar. —**olive oil,** aceite de oliva.

Olympiad (o'lɪm·pi‚æd) *n.* olimpíada.

Olympus (o'lɪm·pəs) *n.* Olimpo.

Olympic (o'lɪm·pɪk) *adj.* olímpico.

ombre ('am·bər) *n.* tresillo; renegado; calzón.

ombudsman (am'bʌdz·mən) *n.* [*pl.* **-men**] mediador entre el público y el gobierno.

omega (o'me·gə) *n.* omega.

omelet ('am·lɪt) *n.* tortilla (de huevo).

omen ('o·mən) *n.* augurio; agüero; presagio.

ominous ('am·ɪ·nəs) *adj.* ominoso. —**ominousness,** *n.* ominosidad.

omission (o'mɪʃ·ən) *n.* omisión.

omit (o'mɪt) *v.t.* omitir.

omnibus ('am·nə‚bʌs) *n.* **1,** (vehicle) ómnibus; autobús; *W.I.* guagua. **2,** (anthology) antología; colección. —*adj.* general.

omnipotent (am'nɪp·ə·tənt) *adj.* omnipotente. —**omnipotence,** *n.* omnipotencia.

omnipresent (‚am·nə'prɛz·ənt) *adj.* omnipresente. —**omnipresence,** *n.* omnipresencia.

omniscient (am'nɪʃ·ənt) *adj.* omnisciente. —**omniscience,** *n.* omnisciencia.

omnivorous (am'nɪv·ə·rəs) *adj.* omnívoro.

on (an) *prep.* **1,** (on top of) en; sobre; encima de. **2,** (upon) en. **3,** (in) en. **4,** (by; at) a: *on the right,* a la derecha. **5,** (close to; beside) cerca de; al lado de. **6,** (toward) sobre; hacia. **7,** (against) contra. **8,** (by means of) por: *on the telephone,* por teléfono. **9,** (in the condition or manner of) a; en: *on half pay,* a media paga; *on purpose,* a propósito; *on sale,* en venta. **10,** (about, concerning) sobre; de; acerca de. **11,** (on the ground or basis of) por; a través de; basado en. **12,** (at the moment of) a: *They greeted us on our arrival,* Nos festejaron a nuestra llegada. **13,** (during) durante; en. **14,** (for the purpose of) a; para: *He went on an errand,* Fue a un mandado. **15,** (in addition to) sobre: *victory on victory,* victoria sobre victoria. **16,** (among) en: *on the committee,* en la comisión. **17,** (indicating risk or liability) bajo; so: *on pain of death,* bajo (o so) pena de muerte. **18,** *colloq.* (at the expense of) a costa de; por cuenta de. **19,** *indicando la fecha,* **on** *no se expresa en español: on the fourth of July,* el cuatro de julio; *on Sunday,* el domingo; *on Sundays,* los domingos. **20,** *con el ger.* (upon; at the time of) al (+ *inf.*): *on arriving,* al llegar. —*adv.* **1,** (forward) adelante; hacia adelante. **2,** (continuously) continuamente; sin parar. **3,** (henceforth) en adelante. —*adj.* **1,** (in place) puesto. **2,** (in operation or use) encendido; prendido; conectado. **3,** (working; functioning) trabajando; funcionando. **4,** (in progress) en marcha; corriendo; realizándose; pasando. —**and so on,** y así sucesivamente; etcétera. —**on and off,** a intervalos; intermitentemente. —**on and on,** sin parar; continuamente; sin descanso. —**on to,** *slang* al tanto de; enterado de. —**be on to someone,** *slang* tenerlo calado o fichado.

onanism ('o·nə‚nɪz·əm) *n.* onanismo; masturbación.

once (wʌns) *adv.* **1,** (one time) una vez. **2,** (formerly) una vez; en otro tiempo. —*conj.* una vez que. —*n.* vez; una vez. —**all at once, 1,** (all simultaneously) todos a una; todos de una vez. **2,** (suddenly) súbitamente; repentinamente; de pronto. —**at once, 1,** (immediately) inmediatamente; en seguida. **2,** (at the same time) de una vez; a la vez. —**for once,** una vez al menos. —**once and again,** una y otra vez. —**once (and) for all,** por última vez; de una vez (por todos); por fin. —**once in a while,** de vez en cuando; una que otra vez. —**once upon a time,** una vez; tiempo ha.

once-over *n., slang* vistazo; examen rápido.

one (wʌn) *adj.* **1,** (single) un; uno; una. **2,** (any) cierto; un tal. **3,** (some) uno; alguno. **4,** (same) igual; mismo. **5,** (united) uno; uno solo. **6,** (only; sole) único. —*n.* **1,** (number) uno; una. **2,** (single person or thing) uno; una. —*pron.* uno; una. —**all one, 1,** (united or agreed) todos uno. **2,** (of no significance) todo lo mismo. —**at one,** de acuerdo. —**one and all,** todo el mundo. —**one another**, el uno al otro; los unos a los otros. —**one by one**, uno por uno; uno a uno. —**one's self** = **oneself**.

one-horse *adj.* **1,** (using one horse) de un caballo. **2,** *colloq.* (unimportant) de poca monta. —**one-horse town**, villorrio.

oneness ('wʌn·nəs) *n.* unidad.

onerous ('on·ər·əs) *adj.* oneroso. —**onerousness,** *n.* onerosidad.

oneself (wʌn'sɛlf) *pron.pers.* uno; uno mismo. —*pron.refl.* **1,** (complemento directo o indirecto de verbo) se: *One washes oneself,* Uno se lava; *One puts it on oneself,* Uno se lo pone. **2,** (complemento de prep.) sí; sí mismo; uno mismo: *One buys it for oneself,* Uno lo compra para sí. —**be oneself,** estar sobre sí; estar en sus cabales. —**by oneself,** solo; sin ayuda; sin compañía. —**to oneself,** para sí: *One says to oneself, "It cannot be,"* Uno dice para sí: no puede ser. —**with oneself,** consigo.

one-sided *adj.* **1,** (unequal) desigual. **2,** (partial) parcial; injusto. **3,** (unilateral) unilateral.

one-to-one *adj.* cara a cara; uno con otro.

one-track *adj.* **1,** (having one track) de una vía. **2,** *colloq.* (restricted) limitado; que insiste en una sola cosa.

one-way *adj.* de dirección única; de un solo sentido.

ongoing ('an,go·ɪŋ) *adj.* en curso; en marcha.

onion ('ʌn·jən) *n.* cebolla. —**know one's onions,** *slang* conocérselas; sabérselas todas.

onionskin ('ʌn·jən,skɪn) *n.* papel cebolla.

on-line ('an'lain) *adj., elect.; comput.* en línea; conectado.

onlooker ('an,lʊk·ər) *n.* espectador; observador.

only ('on·li) *adj.* único; solo. —*adv.* tan sólo; solamente; únicamente; no más que. —*conj.* sólo que; excepto que. —**only begotten,** unigénito.

onomatopoeia (,an·ə,mæt·ə'pi·ə) *n.* onomatopeya. —**onomatopoeic; onomatopoetic** (-po'ɛt·ɪk) *adj.* onomatopéyico.

onrush ('an,rʌʃ) *n.* embestida; arremetida.

onset ('an·sɛt) *n.* **1,** (attack) ataque. **2,** (start) comienzo; principio.

onside ('an·said) *adj. & adv., sports* conforme a las reglas.

onslaught ('an,slɔt) *n.* ataque furioso; arremetida.

ontology (an'tal·ə·dʒi) *n.* ontología. —**ontological** (,an·tə'ladʒ·ɪ·kəl) *adj.* ontológico. —**ontologist,** *n.* ontólogo.

onus ('o·nəs) *n.* carga; responsabilidad.

onward ('an·wərd) *adj. & adv.* también **onwards.** hacia adelante.

onyx ('an·ɪks) *n.* ónix; ónice.

oodles ('u·dəlz) *n.pl., colloq.* montones.

oomph (umf) *n., colloq.* atracción física; atractivo.

ooze (uːz) *n.* **1,** (exudation) exudación. **2,** (mud; slime) légamo; fango; cieno. —*v.t. & i.* exudar; rezumar.

oozy ('u·zi) *adj.* **1,** (exuding moisture) que exuda o rezuma. **2,** (slimy) legamoso; viscoso.

opacity (o'pæs·ə·ti) *n.* opacidad.

opal ('o·pəl) *n.* ópalo.

opalescent (,o·pə'lɛs·ənt) *adj.* opalescente. —**opalescence,** *n.* opalescencia.

opaline ('o·pə·lɪn) *adj.* opalino.

opaque (o'peik) *adj.* opaco.

open ('o·pən) *adj.* **1,** (not closed) abierto. **2,** (exposed) expuesto. **3,** (receptive) receptivo; susceptible. —*v.t.* abrir. —*v.i.* abrir; abrirse. —*n.* **1,** (outdoors) aire libre; campo raso o abierto. **2,** (public view) atención pública. —**in the open,** al descubierto. —**open air,** aire libre. —**open-air,** *adj.* al aire libre. —**open-end; open-ended,** *adj.* sin término fijo; abierto.

open account *n.* cuenta corriente.

open-and-shut *adj.* evidente; obvio en extremo.

opener ('o·pən·ər) *n.* abridor.

open-eyed *adj.* con los ojos abiertos.

open-handed *adj.* generoso; liberal.

open-hearted *adj.* franco; sincero.

open-hearth furnace horno de hogar abierto.

opening ('o·pən·ɪŋ) *n.* **1,** (act of opening) apertura. **2,** (hole; gap) abertura. **3,** (beginning) comienzo; inauguración; apertura. **4,** (opportunity) oportunidad; ocasión. **5,** (vacancy) vacante. **6,** *theat.* estreno. **7,**

chess apertura. —*adj.* **1,** (that opens) abridor; que abre o se abre. **2,** (beginning; first) de estreno; primero.

open-minded *adj.* amplio; razonable; sin prejuicios. —**open-mindedness,** *n.* amplitud; falta de prejuicios.

open-mouthed ('o·pən,mauðd) *adj.* boquiabierto.

openness ('o·pən·nəs) *n.* franqueza; sinceridad; candor.

open shop taller de unión voluntaria; taller abierto o franco.

openwork ('o·pən,wʌrk) *n.* calado.

opera ('ap·ə·re) *n.* **1,** ('o·pə·rə) *pl. de* **opus. 2,** (musical work) ópera. —**operatic** (,ap·ə'ræt·ɪk) *adj.* operático. —**opera glass; opera glasses,** anteojos de teatro.

operable ('ap·ər·ə·bəl) *adj.* operable.

operate ('ap·ə,reit) *v.i.* operar. —*v.t.* hacer funcionar; manejar; dirigir. —**operate on,** operar. —**operating room,** quirófano; sala de operaciones.

operation (,ap·ə'rei·ʃən) *n.* operación. —**operational,** *adj.* operante; funcional. —**in operation,** funcionando; en funcionamiento; operando. —**out of operation,** fuera de comisión; inoperante.

operative ('ap·ə,rei·tɪv; -ər·ə·tɪv) *adj.* **1,** (in operation) operante. **2,** (effective) eficaz; eficiente. **3,** *surg.* operatorio. —*n.* **1,** (worker) operario. **2,** (detective) detective. **3,** (agent) agente.

operator ('ap·ə,rei·tər) *n.* operador; *comm.* empresario; agente.

operetta (,ap·ə'rɛt·ə) *n.* opereta.

ophthalmic (af'θæl·mɪk) *adj.* oftálmico.

ophthalmology (,af·θəl'mal·ə·dʒi) *n.* oftalmología. —**ophthalmologist,** *n.* oftalmólogo.

opiate ('o·pi·ət) *n.* opiata; opiato. —*adj.* opiado.

opine (o'pain) *v.i.* opinar.

opinion (ə'pɪn·jən) *n.* opinión.

opinionated (ə'pɪn·jə,nei·tɪd) *adj.* obstinado; testarudo; de opiniones estrechas.

opium ('o·pi·əm) *n.* opio.

opossum (o'pas·əm) *n.* zarigüeya.

opponent (ə'po·nənt) *n.* adversario; contrincante; antagonista.

opportune (,ap·ər'tjuːn) *adj.* oportuno. —**opportuneness,** *n.* oportunidad.

opportunism (,ap·ər'tju·nɪz·əm) *n.* oportunismo. —**opportunist,** *n.* oportunista. —**opportunistic,** *adj.* oportunista.

opportunity (,ap·ər'tju·nə·ti) *n.* oportunidad.

oppose (ə'poz) *v.t.* **1,** (set against) oponer. **2,** (object to; contend against) oponerse a. —*v.i.* oponerse.

opposite ('ap·ə·zɪt) *adj.* opuesto; de enfrente. —*adv.* enfrente; al revés; en dirección opuesta. —*prep.* frente a; al lado opuesto de. —*n.* contrario; opuesto. —**opposite number,** persona de rango o de oficio correspondiente.

opposition (,ap·ə'zɪʃ·ən) *n.* oposición. —*adj.* oposicionista. —**oppositionist,** *n.* oposicionista.

oppress (ə'prɛs) *v.t.* oprimir. —**oppression** (ə'prɛʃ·ən) *n.* opresión. —**oppressive,** *adj.* opresivo; opresor. —**oppressor,** *n.* opresor [*fem.* -sora].

opprobrious (ə'pro·bri·əs) *adj.* oprobioso. —**opprobrium** (-əm) *n.* oprobio.

opt (apt) *v.i.* optar.

optic ('ap·tɪk) *adj.* óptico. —*n., usu.pl., colloq.* ojos. —**optical,** *adj.* óptico.

optician (ap'tɪʃ·ən) *n.* óptico.

optics ('ap·tɪks) *n.* óptica.

optimal ('ap·tɪ·məl) *adj.* óptimo.

optimism ('ap·tə·mɪz·əm) *n.* optimismo. —**optimist,** *n.* optimista. —**optimistic,** *adj.* optimista.

optimum ('ap·tɪ·məm) *adj.* óptimo. —*n.* [*pl.* -**mums** o -**ma** (-mə)] punto o grado óptimo.

option ('ap·ʃən) *n.* opción. —**optional,** *adj.* opcional; facultativo.

optometry (ap'tam·ə·tri) *n.* optometría. —**optometer,** *n.* optómetro. —**optometrist,** *n.* optómetra; optometrista.

opulent ('ap·jə·lənt) *adj.* opulento. —**opulence,** *n.* opulencia.

opus ('o·pəs) *n.* [*pl.* **opera** ('o·pə·rə)] obra; composición.

or (or) *conj.* o (*also* u *before words beginning with* o *or* ho). —**either . . . or,** o . . . o; ya . . . ya.

oracle ('ar·ə·kəl) *n.* oráculo. —**oracular** (ɔ'ræk·jə·lər) *adj.* oracular.

oral ('or·əl) *adj.* **1,** (spoken) oral. **2,** (of the mouth) bucal.

orange ('ar·ɪndʒ) *n.* **1,** (fruit) naranja. **2,** (tree) naranjo. **3,** (color) color naranja; anaranjado. —*adj.* de naranja; anaranjado. —**orange blossom,** azahar. —**orange grove,** naranjal.

orangeade (,or·ındȝ'eid) *n.* naranjada.

orangutan (o'ræŋ·ə,tæn) *n.* orangután.

orate (o'reit) *v.i.* perorar.

oration (o'rei·ʃən) *n.* discurso; oración.

orator ('or·ə·tər) *n.* orador [*fem.* -dora].

oratorical (,ar·ə'tor·ə·kəl) *adj.* oratorio.

oratorio (,or·ə'tor·i·o) *n.* oratorio.

oratory ('ar·ə·tor·i) *n.* **1,** (eloquence) oratoria. **2,** *eccles.* oratorio.

orb (orb) *n.* orbe.

orbit ('or·bıt) *n.* órbita. —**orbital,** *adj.* orbital.

orchard ('or·tʃərd) *n.* huerto.

orchestra ('or·kıs·trə) *n.* orquesta. —**orchestral** (or'kɛs·trəl) *adj.* orquestal. —**orchestrate** (-,treit) *v.t. & i.* orquestar. —**orchestration,** *n.* orquestación.

orchid ('or·kıd) *n.* orquídea.

ordain (or'dein) *v.t.* ordenar.

ordeal (or'diːl) *n.* prueba; *hist.* ordalías.

order ('or·dər) *n.* orden. —*v.t. & i.* ordenar. —**by order of,** por orden de. —**in order, 1,** (in proper position or state; according to the rules) en orden; como se debe; en regla. **2,** (appropriate; suitable) apropiado; adecuado. —**in order that,** para que; a fin de que. —**in order to,** para; a fin de; con objeto de. —**in short order,** rápido; sin demora. —**on order,** ordenado; pedido. —**on the order of,** del orden de. —**out of order, 1,** (out of proper place) fuera de sitio; fuera de lugar. **2,** (not functioning) malogrado; descompuesto. **3,** (against the rules) fuera de lugar; en desafuero. **4,** (not suitable) inapropiado; fuera de lugar. —**to order,** a la medida; de encargo; por encargo especial.

orderly ('or·dər·li) *adj.* **1,** (tidy) ordenado. **2,** (peaceable; law-abiding) pacífico; amante del orden. —*n.* **1,** *mil.* ordenanza. **2,** (hospital aide) enfermero; practicante.

ordinal ('or·də·nəl) *adj. & n.* ordinal.

ordinance ('or·də·nəns) *n.* ordenanza.

ordinary ('or·də,ner·i) *adj. & n.* ordinario.

ordinate ('or·də,neit) *n., geom.* ordenada.

ordination (,or·də'nei·ʃən) *n.* ordenación.

ordnance ('ord·nəns) *n.* **1,** (artillery) artillería. **2,** (armaments) armamento; pertrechos de guerra.

ordure ('or·djur) *n.* heces; excrementos; inmundicias.

ore (or) *n.* mineral metalífero.

oregano (o're·gə·no) *n.* orégano.

organ ('or·gən) *n.* órgano. —**barrel organ,** organillo. —**organ grinder,** organillero.

organdy ('or·gən·di) *n.* organdí.

organic (or'gæn·ık) *adj.* orgánico.

organism ('or·gə·nız·əm) *n.* organismo.

organist ('or·gə·nıst) *n.* organista.

organize ('or·gə,naiz) *v.t.* organizar. —*v.i.* organizarse. —**organization** (-nı'zei·ʃən) *n.* organización. —**organizer,** *n.* organizador [*fem.* -dora].

orgasm ('or·gæz·əm) *n.* orgasmo.

orgy ('or·dȝi) *n.* orgía. —**orgiastic** (-'æs·tık) *adj.* orgiástico.

orient ('or·i·ənt) *n.* oriente. —*v.t.* [*también,* **orientate** (-ən,teit)] orientar. —**orientation** (-ən'tei·ʃən) *n.* orientación.

oriental (,or·i'ɛn·təl) *adj. & n.* oriental.

orifice ('or·ə·fıs) *n.* orificio.

origin ('or·ə·dȝın) *n.* origen.

original (ə'rıdȝ·ı·nəl) *adj. & n.* original. —**originality** (-'næl·ə·ti) *n.* originalidad.

originate (ə'rıdȝ·ı·neit) *v.t.* originar; dar origen a. —*v.i.* originarse; nacer. —**origination,** *n.* origen; principio. —**originator,** *n.* originador [*fem.* -dora]; iniciador [*fem.* -dora].

oriole ('or·i,ol) *n.* oriol; oropéndola.

Orion (o'rai·ən) *n.* Orión.

orlon ('or·lan) *n.* orlón.

ormolu ('or·mə,lu) *n.* **1,** (gold for gilding) oro molido. **2,** (imitation gold) similor.

ornament ('or·nə·mənt) *n.* ornamento. —*v.t.* ornamentar; adornar. —**ornamental** (-'men·təl) *adj.* ornamental. —**ornamentation** (-men'tei·ʃən) *n.* ornamentación.

ornate (or'neit) *adj.* ornado; adornado; florido. —**ornateness,** *n.* ornato; aparato; vistosidad.

ornery ('or·nə·ri) *n., dial.* terco; de malos modales.

ornithology (,or·nɪ'θal·ə·dʒi) *n.* ornitología. —**ornithological** (-θə'ladʒ·ɪ·kəl) *adj.* ornitológico. —**ornithologist,** *n.* ornitólogo.

orotund ('or·ə,tʌnd) *adj.* **1,** (sonorous) resonante; sonoro. **2,** (pompous) rimbombante.

orphan ('or·fən) *n.* & *adj.* huérfano. —*v.t.* dejar huérfano. —**orphanhood,** *n.* orfandad.

orphanage ('or·fən·ɪdʒ) *n.* **1,** (orphanhood) orfandad. **2,** (home for orphans) orfanato; orfelinato; asilo de huérfanos.

orthodontia (,or·θə'dan·ʃə) *n.* ortodoncia. —**orthodontic,** *adj.* ortodontista. —**orthodontics,** *n.sing. or pl.* ortodoncia.

orthodox ('or·θə·daks) *adj.* ortodoxo. —**orthodoxy,** *n.* ortodoxia.

orthogonal (or'θag·ə·nəl) *adj.* ortogonal.

orthography (or'θag·rə·fi) *n.* ortografía. —**orthographic** (,or·θə'græf·ɪk) *adj.* ortográfico.

orthopedic (,or·θə'pi·dɪk) *adj.* ortopédico. —**orthopedics,** *n.* ortopedia. —**orthopedist,** *n.* ortopédico; ortopedista.

ortolan ('or·tə·lən) *n.* hortelano.

oscillate ('as·ə,leit) *v.i.* oscilar. —*v.t.* hacer oscilar. —**oscillating,** *adj.* oscilante; oscilatorio. —**oscillation,** *n.* oscilación. —**oscillator,** *n.* oscilador.

oscillograph (ə'sɪl·ə,græf) *n.* oscilógrafo.

oscilloscope (ə'sɪl·ə,skop) *n.* osciloscopio.

osculate ('as·kjə,leit) *v.t.* & *i.* besar. —**osculation,** *n.* beso; ósculo.

osier ('o·ʒər) *n.* **1,** (plant) mimbrera. **2,** (twig of the plant, used for weaving) mimbre.

osmium ('az·mi·əm) *n.* osmio.

osmosis (az'mo·sɪs) *n.* ósmosis; osmosis. —**osmotic** (az'mat·ɪk) *adj.* osmótico.

osseous ('as·i·əs) *adj.* óseo.

osprey ('as·pri) *n.* quebrantahuesos.

ossify ('as·ɪ,fai) *v.i.* osificarse. —**ossification** (-fɪ'kei·ʃən) *n.* osificación.

ossuary ('as·u,ɛr·i) *n.* osario.

ostensible (as'tɛn·sə·bəl) *adj.* ostensible.

ostentation (,as·tɛn'tei·ʃən) *n.*

ostentación. —**ostentatious** (-ʃəs) *adj.* ostentoso.

osteology (as·ti'a·lə·dʒi) *n.* osteología. —**osteologist,** *n.* osteólogo.

osteopathy (,as·ti'ap·ə·θi) *n.* osteopatía. —**osteopath** ('as·ti·ə,pæθ) *n.* osteópata.

ostracize ('as·trə,saiz) *v.t.* condenar al ostracismo. —**ostracism,** *n.* ostracismo.

ostrich ('as·trɪtʃ) *n.* avestruz.

otalgia (o'tæl·dʒi·ə) *n.* dolor de oído.

other ('ʌð·ər) *adj.* & *pron.* otro. —*adv.* más; otra cosa; otramente. —**every other day,** un día sí y otro no; cada dos días. —**other than,** más que; otra cosa que.

otherwise ('ʌð·ər,waiz) *adv.* **1,** (in another manner; differently) de otra manera; de otro modo. **2,** (in all other respects) en todo otro respecto; fuera de eso. **3,** (in other circumstances) en otro caso; de otro modo; de lo contrario. —*adj.* distinto; diferente; otro. —*conj.* de otro modo; si no.

otherworldly (,ʌð·ər'wʌrld·li) *adj.* espiritual.

otiose ('o·ʃi,os) *adj.* ocioso.

otitis (o'tai·tɪs) *n.* otitis.

otology (o'tal·ə·dʒi) *n.* otología. —**otologist,** *n.* otólogo.

otter ('at·ər) *n.* nutria.

ottoman ('at·ə·mən) *n.* **1,** (divan) otomana. **2,** (footstool) escabel. **3,** *cap.* (Turk) otomano. —*adj.* otomano.

ouch (autʃ) *interj.* ¡huy!; ¡ay!

ought (ɔt) *v.aux.* deber. —*n.* = **naught.**

ouija ('wi·dʒə) *n.* tablero usado en prácticas espiritistas.

ounce (auns) *n.* **1,** (unit of weight) onza. **2,** *zoöl.* onza. **3,** (small amount; bit) pizca.

our (aur) *adj. pos.* nuestro (*fem.* nuestra; *pl.* nuestros; nuestras); de nosotros.

ours (aurz) *pron.pos.* el nuestro; la nuestra; lo nuestro; los nuestros; las nuestras; el, la, lo, las o los de nosotros.

ourselves (aur'sɛlvz) *pron.pers.* nosotros; nosotros mismos. —*pron. refl.* **1,** (*complemento directo o indirecto de verbo*) nos: *We washed ourselves,* Nos lavamos; *We put them on ourselves,* Nos los pusimos. **2,** (*complemento de prep.*) nosotros; nosotros mismos: *We* *bought it for ourselves,* Lo compramos para nosotros.

oust (aust) *v.t.* **1,** (dislodge) desalojar. **2,** (remove, as from office) echar fuera; deponer.

ouster ('aus·tər) *n.* **1,** (dispossession) desahucio; desposeimiento. **2,** (removal, as from office) deposición.

out (aut) *adv.* **1,** (not in; outside) fuera; afuera. **2,** (outward) hacia afuera. **3,** (forward; forth) adelante; hacia adelante. **4,** (henceforth) en adelante. **5,** (to the end; completely) hasta el fin; completamente. **6,** (aloud; loudly) en voz alta. —*adj.* **1,** (not in; away) fuera. **2,** (absent) ausente. **3,** (not in fashion) fuera o pasado de moda. **4,** (not in operation) apagado; desconectado; cortado. **5,** (not usual or normal) fuera de lo normal. **6,** (wrong; in error) errado; equivocado. **7,** (missing; suffering loss of) de menos: *I am out ten dollars,* Tengo diez dólares de menos; He perdido diez dólares. —*n.* **1,** (one who is out) el, la, los o las de afuera. **2,** *slang* (excuse; escape) salida; excusa; escapatoria. —*prep.* **1,** (out by way of) por. **2,** (out of or from) de. **3,** (out along) por; a lo largo de. —*v.i.* salir a la luz. —*interj.* ¡fuera! —**at outs; on the outs,** peleado; disgustado; en desavenencia. —**out and away,** por mucho; *Amer.* lejos. —**out for,** en busca de; a la busca de. —**out and out,** a fondo; completamente; sin reserva. —**out of,** **1** (from) de. **2,** (away from; beyond) fuera de; más allá de. **3,** (not having; without) sin; falto de. **4,** (by reason of; because of) por. **5,** (arising from; born of) nacido de. —**out of print,** agotado. —**out of stock,** agotado. —**out of touch,** apartado; alejado. —**out to** (win, kill, etc.), empeñado en (ganar, matar, etc.).

outage ('aut·ɪdʒ) *n.* corte de electricidad o funcionamiento.

out-and-out *adj.* completo; cabal; consumado.

outbalance (aut'bæl·əns) *v.t.* pesar más que; sobreexceder.

outbid (aut'bɪd) *v.t.* [**outbid, -bidding**] pujar más que: mejorar.

outboard ('aut·bord) *adj.* externo a la embarcación; fuera de bordo.

outbound *adj.* que sale; de salida.

outbrave (aut'breiv) *v.t.* arrostrar; enfrentar.

outbreak ('aut,breik) *n.* **1,** (outburst) estallido; ataque violento; acceso. **2,** (riot) tumulto; revuelta. **3,** (epidemic) epidemia.

outbuilding ('aut,bɪl·dɪŋ) *n.* dependencia; anexo; accesoria.

outburst ('aut,bʌrst) *n.* explosión; manifestación violenta.

outcast ('aut,kæst) *n.* paria; proscrito.

outclass (aut'klæs) *v.t.* aventajar; superar.

outcome ('aut·kʌm) *n.* resultado; consecuencia; desenlace.

outcrop ('aut,krap) *n.* afloramiento.

outcry ('aut,krai) *n.* **1,** (shout) grito. **2,** (clamor) griterío; clamor.

outdated (aut'dei·tɪd) *adj.* anticuado; pasado de moda.

outdistance (aut'dɪs·təns) *v.t.* dejar atrás; aventajar.

outdo (aut'du) *v.t.* [*pret.* **outdid**; *p.p.* **outdone**] superar; sobrepujar. —**outdo oneself,** esmerarse; extremarse.

outdoor ('aut,dor) *adj.* al aire libre. —**outdoors,** *adv.* al aire libre; afuera. —*n.* campo; aire libre.

outer ('au·tər) *adj.* exterior; externo. —**outermost,** *adj.* extremo; más de afuera; superior. —**outer space,** espacio exterior.

outface (aut'feis) *v.t.* dominar con una mirada.

outfield ('aut·fild) *n.* campo externo.

outfit ('aut·fɪt) *n.* **1,** (equipment) equipo. **2,** (clothing) conjunto; juego de ropa. **3,** *colloq.* (group) cuerpo; grupo; compañía. —*v.t.* [**outfitted, -fitting**] equipar.

outflank (aut'flæŋk) *v.t.* flanquear.

outflow ('aut·flo) *n.* **1** = outgo. **2,** (a flowing out) salida; flujo (que sale).

outfox (aut'faks) *v.t.* ganar en astucia; burlar.

outgo ('aut,go) *n.* desembolso; gastos; salida.

outgoing ('aut,go·ɪŋ) *adj.* **1,** (going out; leaving) que sale; que parte. **2,** (expansive) abierto; expansivo.

outgrow (aut'gro) *v.t.* [**outgrew, -grown, -growing**] **1,** (surpass in growth) crecer más que. **2,** (grow too old for) dejar atrás; superar. **3,** (grow too large for) quedarle a uno pequeño: *He has outgrown his shoes,* Los zapatos le quedan pequeños.

outgrowth ('aut,groθ) *n.* **1,** (consequence) consecuencia; efecto; fruto. **2,** (excrescence) excrecencia.

outguess (aut'gɛs) *v.t.* anticipar.

outhouse ('aut,haus) *n.* retrete; privada.

outing ('aut·ɪŋ) *n.* paseo; excursión; salida.

outlander ('aut,læn·dər) *n.* extranjero.

outlandish (aut'læn·dɪʃ) *adj.* extraño; exótico; ridículo.

outlast (aut'læst) *v.t.* durar más que; sobrevivir a.

outlaw ('aut·lɔ) *n.* bandido; proscrito. —*v.t.* proscribir. —**outlawry,** *n.* bandidaje.

outlay ('aut·lei) *n.* desembolso; gasto; expendio.

outlet ('aut·lɛt) *n.* **1,** (passage for exit) orificio de salida; escape; desagüe. **2,** *elect.* enchufe. **3,** *comm.* salida.

outline ('aut·lain) *n.* **1,** (shape) contorno; perfil; silueta. **2,** (sketch) bosquejo; esbozo; esquema. —*v.t.* bosquejar; esbozar; delinear.

outlive (aut'lɪv) *v.t.* sobrevivir a; vivir o durar más que (o de).

outlook ('aut·lʊk) *n.* **1,** (view) vista. **2,** (prospect) prospecto; perspectivas. **3,** (mental attitude) actitud; manera de ver las cosas.

outlying ('aut,lai·ɪŋ) *adj.* **1,** (remote) distante; remoto. **2,** (bordering) circundante; adyacente.

outmatch (aut'matʃ) *v.t.* aventajar; superar.

outmoded (aut'mod·ɪd) *adj.* fuera o pasado de moda.

outnumber (aut'nʌm·bər) *v.t.* superar en número.

out-of-date *adj.* anticuado; pasado de moda.

out-of-door *adj.* = **outdoor.** —**out-of-doors,** *n. & adv.* = **outdoors.**

out-of-the-way *adj.* apartado; retirado.

outpatient ('aut,pei·ʃənt) *n.* paciente de hospital que no reside en él.

outpost ('aut,post) *n.* puesto avanzado; puesto de avanzada.

outpouring ('aut,por·ɪŋ) *n.* efusión; emanación; chorro.

output ('aut·pʊt) *n.* producción; *mech.* rendimiento.

outrage ('aut·reidʒ) *n.* **1,** (insult) ultraje; afrenta; injuria. **2,** (violent or vicious act) tropelía; desafuero;

desmán. —*v.t.* **1,** (abuse) ultrajar. **2,** (ravish) violar.

outrageous (aut'rei·dʒəs) *adj.* ultrajante; desaforado; afrentoso.

outrank (aut'ræŋk) *v.t.* exceder en rango o grado.

outreach (,aut'ritʃ) *v.t.* superar; ir más allá de. —*n.* ('aut,ritʃ) alcance; extensión; asistencia especial.

outrider ('aut,rai·dər) *n.* **1,** (attendant on horseback) palafrenero; acompañante de a caballo. **2,** (scout on horseback) batidor de a caballo.

outrigger ('aut,rɪg·ər) *n.* **1,** (stabilizing device) balancín (de canoa). **2,** (boom; spar) botalón.

outright ('aut·rait) *adj.* **1,** (complete) completo; cabal. **2,** (straightforward) franco; abierto. **3,** (downright) rotundo; inequívoco. —*adv.* **1,** (at once) de inmediato. **2,** (completely; entirely) por completo: en su totalidad. **3,** (openly) abiertamente.

outrun (aut'rʌn) *v.t.* [**outran, -run, -running**] **1,** (run faster than) correr más que. **2,** (elude by running) dejar atrás. **3,** (exceed) exceder; sobrepasar.

outset ('aut·sɛt) *n.* comienzo; principio.

outshine (aut'ʃain) *v.t.* [*pret. & p.p.* **outshone**] brillar más que; eclipsar.

outside (aut'said; 'aut-) *adj.* **1,** (outer; external) externo; exterior; de afuera. **2,** (extreme) extremo. —*n.* exterior; parte de afuera. —*adv.* fuera; afuera. —*prep.* **1,** (out from) fuera de. **2,** (beyond) más allá de. **3,** (aside from) fuera de; a o con excepción de. —**at the outside,** a lo más; con mucho.

outsider (aut'sai·dər) *n.* extraño; advenedizo; forastero.

outsize ('aut,saiz) *n.* tamaño poco común. —**outsized,** *adj.* extraordinario; de tamaño poco común.

outskirts ('aut·skʌrts) *n.pl.* afueras; immediaciones; arrabales.

outsmart (aut'smart) *v.t., colloq.* ganar en astucia; ser más listo que; burlar. —**outsmart one's self,** pasarse de listo.

outspoken (aut'spo·kən) *adj.* franco; abierto; atrevido en el hablar.

outspread (aut'sprɛd) *adj.* extendido.

outstanding (aut'stæn·dɪŋ) *adj.* **1,** (prominent) prominente; sobresaliente. 2, (projecting) saliente. 3, (unfulfilled) pendiente. 4, *comm.* (unpaid) sin pagar; en descubierto.

outstay (aut'stei) *v.t.* quedarse más tiempo que; aguantar más que.

outstretched (aut'stretʃd) *adj.* extendido.

outstrip (aut'strip), *v.t.* [**outstripped, -stripping**] dejar atrás; sobrepasar; sobrepujar.

outtalk (aut'tɔk) *v.t.* ganar hablando; hablar más que.

outvote (aut'vot) *v.t.* derrotar en una elección.

outward ('aut·wərd) *adj.* 1, (outer; exterior) exterior; externo. 2, (apparent) aparente. 3, (toward the outside) hacia el exterior; hacia afuera. —*adv.* [*también*, **outwards**] 1, (away; toward the outside) hacia afuera; hacia el exterior. 2, (on the outside; without) afuera; en el exterior. —*n.* parte externa. —**outwardly**, *adv.* aparentemente.

outwear (aut'weɪr) *v.t.* [*pret.* **outwore**; *p.p.* **outworn**] 1, (last longer than) durar más que. 2, (wear out) gastar; consumir.

outweigh (aut'wei) *v.t.* pesar más que.

outwit (aut'wɪt) *v.t.* [**outwitted, -witting**] ganar en astucia; ser más listo que; burlar.

outwore (aut'wɔr) *v.*, *pret. de* **outwear**.

outworn (aut'worn) *adj.* 1, (much used) desgastado; usado. 2, (out of fashion) anticuado. —*v.*, *p.p. de* **outwear**.

ova ('o·və) *n.*, *pl. de* **ovum**.

oval ('o·vəl) *adj.* ovalado; oval. —*n.* óvalo.

ovary ('o·və·ri) *n.* ovario. —**ovarian** (o'veɪr·i·ən) *adj.* ovárico.

ovate (o'veit) *adj.* ovado.

ovation (o'vei·ʃən) *n.* ovación.

oven ('ʌv·ən) *n.* horno.

over ('o·vər) *prep.* 1, (above; on top of) sobre; encima de. 2, (so as to cover) por; por encima de. 3, (so as to pass above) por sobre; por encima de. 4, (during) durante. 5, (to or on the other side of) al otro lado de. 6, (throughout) por; a través de. 7, (more than) más de. 8 (until after) hasta después de. 9, (in preference to) antes que. 10, (because of) por; a causa de. 11, (about; concerning) sobre; acerca de. —*adv.* 1, (above) por encima. 2, (across; to the other side) al otro

lado. 3, (more; beyond) más. 4, (again; anew) otra vez; de nuevo. 5, (so as to be inverted) al otro lado; al revés; boca abajo; boca arriba. 6, (from an upright position) desplomado. 7, (yonder) allá. 8, (from one to another) de uno a otro. —*adj.* 1, (finished) terminado; concluido. 2, (having reached the other side) al otro lado. 3, *colloq.* (in excess) de sobra; de más. —**all over,** 1, (everywhere) por todas partes. 2, (finished) terminado. —**over again,** de nuevo. —**over against,** contra. —**over all,** de punta a punta. —**over and above,** además de. —**over and over,** una y otra vez; repetidamente. —**over here,** acá; aquí. —**over there,** ahí; allá; allí.

overabundant (,o·vər·ə'bʌn·dənt) *adj.* sobreabundante. —**overabundance,** *n.* sobreabundancia.

overact (,o·vər'ækt) *v.t. & i.* exagerar (un papel).

overactive (,o·vər'æk·tiv) *adj.* demasiado activo.

overage ('o·vər·idʒ) *n.* demasía; exceso.

overage (,o·vər'eidʒ) *adj.* anticuado; añejo.

overall ('o·vər,ɔl) *adj.* 1, (comprehensive; total) total; completo. 2, (from end to end) de punta a punta; de cabo a rabo.

overalls ('o·vər,ɔlz) *n.pl.* mono; *Amer.* overol; overoles.

overambitious (,o·vər·æm'biʃ·əs) *adj.* demasiado ambicioso.

overanxious (,o·vər'æŋk·ʃəs) *adj.* demasiado ansioso.

overawe (,o·vər'ɔ) *v.t.* inspirar miedo o respeto.

overbalance (,o·vər'bæl·əns) *v.t.* 1, (outweigh) pesar más que. 2, (tip over) desequilibrar. —*n.* desequilibrio.

overbearing (,o·vər'beɪr·iŋ) *adj.* arrogante; dominante; altanero.

overbid (,o·vər'bid) *v.t. & i.* [**overbid, -bidding**] 1, (offer more than) ofrecer o pujar más (que). 2, (offer more than the worth of) ofrecer demasiado (por). 3, *cards* declarar demasiado. —*n.* ('o·vər,bid) puja exagerada.

overboard ('o·vər·bord) *adv.* al agua; por la borda. —**go overboard,** *colloq.* extremarse; esmerarse.

overbook (,o·vər'bʊk) *v.t.* aceptar exceso (de reservaciones).

overburden (,o·vər'bʌr·dən) *v.t.* sobrecargar; recargar.

overcall (,o·vər'kɔl) *v.t., cards* declarar más que.

overcareful (,o·vər'kɛr·fəl) *adj.* muy cuidadoso.

overcast ('o·vər·kæst) *n.* **1,** (cover of clouds) cielo encapotado. **2,** *sewing* sobrehilado. —*adj.* **1,** (covered, as with clouds) encapotado. **2,** *sewing* sobrehilado. —*v.t.* [*pret. & p.p.* **overcast**] **1,** (cover, as with clouds) encapotar; nublar; anublar. **2,** *sewing* sobrehilar.

overcautious (,o·vər'kɔ·ʃəs) *adj.* muy cauto.

overcharge (,o·vər'tʃardʒ) *v.t.* cobrar de más (por). —*n.* ('o·vər,tʃardʒ) exceso de cobro.

overcloud (,o·vər'klaʊd) *v.t.* anublar; nublar; obscurecer.

overcoat ('o·vər,kot) *n.* abrigo; sobretodo; gabán.

overcome (,o·vər'kʌm) *v.t.* [*pret.* **overcame;** *p.p.* **overcome**] vencer; dominar; sobreponerse a. —*adj.* sobrecogido.

overconfident (,o·vər'kan·fɪ·dənt) *adj.* muy confiado o seguro. —**overconfidence,** *n.* exceso de confianza o seguridad.

overcook (,o·vər'kʊk) *v.t. & i.* cocer(se) demasiado.

overcritical (,o·vər'krɪt·ɪ·kəl) *adj.* criticón; quisquilloso.

overcrowd (,o·vər'kraʊd) *v.t.* llenar demasiado; apiñar.

overdo (,o·vər'du) *v.t.* [*pret.* **overdid;** *p.p.* **overdone**] **1,** (exaggerate) exagerar; extremar. **2,** = **overcook.** —**overdo oneself,** esmerarse; excederse.

overdose ('o·vər,dos) *n.* dosis excesiva. —*v.t.* dar una dosis excesiva. —*v.i.* darse una dosis excesiva.

overdraft ('o·vər,dræft) *n.* sobregiro; giro en descubierto.

overdraw (,o·vər'drɔ) *v.t.* [*pret.* **overdrew;** *p.p.* **overdrawn**] **1,** *comm.* sobregirar; girar en descubierto. **2,** (exaggerate) exagerar.

overdress (,o·vər'drɛs) *v.t. & i.* vestir con exceso.

overdrive (,o·vər'draiv) *v.t.* [*pret.* **overdrove;** *p.p.* **overdriven**] abrumar de trabajo. —*n.* ('o·vər·draiv) sobremarcha.

overdue (,o·vər'du) *adj.* **1,** *comm.* vencido. **2,** (late) atrasado.

retrasado. **3,** (long hoped for) esperado por mucho tiempo.

overeager (,o·vər'i·gər) *adj.* demasiado ansioso.

overeat (,o·vər'it) *v.t. & i.* [*pret.* **overate;** *p.p.* **overeaten**] comer demasiado.

overemotional (,o·vər·ɪ'mo·ʃən·əl) *adj.* demasiado sensible.

overemphasize (,o·vər'ɛm·fə·saiz) *v.t.* exagerar; acentuar demasiado; poner demasiado énfasis en. —**overemphasis,** *n.* exceso de énfasis; exageración.

overenthusiastic (,o·vər·ɛn·θu·zi'æs·tɪk) *adj.* demasiado entusiasta. —**overenthusiasm,** *n.* exceso de entusiasmo.

overestimate (,o·vər'ɛs·tə,meit) *v.t. & i.* exagerar. —*n.* (-mət) presupuesto exagerado.

overexercise (,o·vər'ɛk·sər,saiz) *v.t.* ejercer demasiado. —*v.i.* excederse; hacer exceso de ejercicios. —*n.* exceso de ejercicios.

overexcite (,o·vər·ɛk'sait) *v.t.* sobreexcitar.

overexert (,o·vər·ɛg'zʌrt) *v.t.* ejercer demasiado. —**overexert oneself,** hacer demasiado esfuerzo.

overexpand (,o·vər·ɛk'spænd) *v.t.* extender demasiado. —*v.i.* extenderse demasiado. —**overexpansion,** *n.* extensión excesiva.

overexpose (,o·vər·ɛk'spoz) *v.t.* sobreexponer. —**overexposure,** *n.* sobreexposición.

overfill (,o·vər'fɪl) *v.t.* llenar demasiado; sobrellenar.

overflow (,o·vər'flo) *v.t.* **1,** (flood) cubrir; inundar. **2,** (flow over the brim of) rebosar. **3,** (fill beyond capacity) llenar demasiado; sobrellenar. —*v.i.* rebosar; derramarse; (of a stream) desbordarse; salirse de madre. —*n.* ('o·vər,flo) rebosamiento; derrame; (of a stream) desbordamiento.

overfond (,o·vər'fand) *adj.* **1,** (too affectionate) demasiado encariñado. **2,** (overindulgent) demasiado condescendiente.

overgrow ('o·vər,gro) *v.t.* [*pret.* **overgrew;** *p.p.* **overgrown**] **1,** (cover, as with vegetation) cubrir. **2,** = **outgrow.**

overgrown ('o·vər,gron) *adj.* **1,** (covered, as with vegetation) cubierto (de vegetación, follaje, etc.). **2,** (grown excessively) muy crecido; demasiado grande.

overhand ('o·vər,hænd) *adj.* voleado por alto. —*adv.* al voleo. —*n.* voleo por alto.

overhang (,o·vər'hæŋ) *v.t.* [*pret. & p.p.* **overhung**] **1,** (jut out from) sobresalir de. **2,** (project over) proyectarse por encima de. **3,** (impend; threaten) amenazar. —*v.i.* sobresalir. —*n.* ('o·vər,hæŋ) saliente; proyección; vuelo.

overhasty (,o·vər'heis·ti) *adj.* demasiado apresurado.

overhaul ('o·vər,hɔl) *v.t.* **1,** (examine; check) revisar; examinar. **2,** (repair; adjust) reparar; hacer ajustes en; componer. **3,** (overtake) alcanzar. —*n.* **1,** (examination) revisión; examen minucioso. **2,** (repair) reparación; compostura.

overhead ('o·vər·hɛd) *adv.* por encima; por sobre la cabeza; en alto. —*adj.* **1,** (raised above) elevado; en alto; superior. **2,** (in the sky) en el cielo; en lo alto. **3,** *comm.* fijo; general. —*n.* gastos generales o fijos.

overhear (,o·vər'hɪr) *v.t.* [*pret. & p.p.* **overheard**] alcanzar a oír; acertar a oír.

overheat (,o·vər'hit) *v.t.* recalentar. —*v.i.* recalentarse.

overindulge (,o·vər·ɪn'dʌldʒ) *v.t.* **1,** (gratify to excess) satisfacer descomedidamente. **2,** (be too lenient toward) consentir demasiado. —*v.i.* excederse; propasarse; tomar, comer; etc., descomedidamente.

overindulgence (,o·vər·ɪn'dʌl·dʒəns) *n.* **1,** (immoderation) inmoderación. **2,** (excessive leniency) complacencia o indulgencia exagerada.

overindulgent (,o·vər·ɪn'dʌl·dʒənt) *adj.* **1,** (immoderate) inmoderado. **2,** (too lenient) demasiado condescendiente.

overjoyed (,o·vər'dʒɔid) *adj.* alborozado; desbordante de alegría.

overland ('o·vər·lænd) *adj. & adv.* por tierra.

overlap ('o·vər,læp) *v.t. & i.* [**overlapped, -lapping**] cubrir parcialmente; coincidir en parte. —*n.* área o parte común; área o parte de coincidencia.

overlay (,o·vər'lei) *v.t.* [*pret. & p.p.* **overlaid**] **1,** (place over) superponer; poner sobre. **2,** (coat; cover) cubrir. **3,** (overburden) sobrecargar. **4,** (plate) enchapar. **5,** *pret. de* **overlie.** —*n.* ('o·vər-) **1,** (coating; covering) capa; cubierta. **2,** (plating) enchapado.

overlie (,o·vər'lai) *v.t.* [**overlay, -lain, -lying**] estar o extenderse sobre.

overload (,o·vər'lod) *v.t.* sobrecargar; recargar. —*n.* ('o·vər-) sobrecarga.

overlong (,o·vər'lɔŋ) *adj.* muy largo. —*adv.* mucho tiempo.

overlook (,o·vər'lʊk) *v.t.* **1,** (fail to notice) no notar; escapársele a uno. **2,** (ignore) pasar por alto; no hacer caso de. **3,** (afford a view of from above) mirar a; dar a.

overlord ('o·vər,lord) *n.* soberano; señor supremo.

overly ('o·vər·li) *adv.* demasiado; excesivamente; muy.

overlying (,o·vər'lai·ɪŋ) *adj.* superpuesto; superior. —*v., ger. de* **overlie.**

overmodest (,o·vər'mad·ɪst) *adj.* demasiado modesto.

overmuch ('o·vər,mʌtʃ) *adv.* demasiado; en demasía. —*n.* demasía; exceso.

overnice (,o·vər'nais) *adj.* **1,** (extremely subtle) demasiado fino o sutil. **2,** (extremely fastidious) relamido; melindroso.

overnight ('o·vər,nait) *adv.* durante la noche; por la noche; en una noche. —*adj.* de la noche.

overpass ('o·vər,pæs) *n.* puente sobre un camino o vía; viaducto. —*v.t.* (-'pæs) **1,** (pass above or over) pasar por encima de. **2,** (pass across) atravesar; cruzar. **3,** (exceed) exceder; sobrepasar.

overpay (,o·vər'pei) *v.t. & i.* [*pret. & p.p.* **overpaid**] pagar de más. —**overpayment,** *n.* pago excesivo.

overplay (,o·vər'plei) *v.t.* exagerar; excederse en.

overpleased (,o·vər'plizd) *adj.* muy contento; más que contento.

overpopulate (,o·vər'pap·jə,leit) *v.t.* poblar en exceso. —**overpopulation,** *n.* exceso de población.

overpower (,o·vər'pau·ər) *v.t.* **1,** (subdue) dominar; subyugar; rendir. **2,** (overwhelm) abrumar; anonadar. **3,** (give too much power) dar excesiva potencia o empuje.

overpraise (,o·vər'preiz) *v.t.* sobrealzar; alabar demasiado.

overprice (,o·vər'prais) *v.t.* pedir

demasiado por; poner demasiado caro.

overproduce (‚o·vər·prə'djus) *v.t. & i.* producir en exceso. —**over-production**, *n.* sobreproducción.

overqualified (‚o·vər'kwa·lɪ‚faid) *adj.* demasiado capacitado o preparado (para determinado oficio).

overrate (‚o·vər'reit) *v.t.* sobre-estimar.

overreach (‚o·vər'ritʃ) *v.t.* sobrepasar; llegar más allá de; *fig.* trascender. —**overreach oneself**, pasarse.

override (‚o·vər'raid) *v.t.* [*pret.* **overrode**; *p.p.* **overridden**] 1, (prevail over; vote down) derrotar; rechazar. 2, (outweigh) prevalecer o prevaler sobre; pesar más que. 3, (nullify) anular; invalidar. 4, (trample down) hollar; atropellar. 5, (pass or extend beyond) salirse de; pasarse de.

overripe (‚o·vər'raip) *adj.* pasado.

overrule (‚o·vər'rul) *v.t.* invalidar; anular.

overrun (‚o·vər'run) *v.t.* [**overran, -run, -running**] 1, (rove over; ravage) arrollar; invadir. 2, (infest) plagar; infestar. 3, (spread over) cubrir por completo; inundar. 4, (go beyond) parsarse de.

overscrupulous (‚o·vər'skrup·jə·ləs) *adj.* demasiado escrupuloso; remilgado.

overseas ('o·vər‚siz) *adj.* de ultramar; de allende los mares; del extranjero. —*adv.* (-'siːz) al o en el extranjero.

oversee (‚o·vər'siː) *v.t.* [*pret.* **oversaw**; *p.p.* **overseen**] 1, (supervise) inspeccionar; vigilar; dirigir. 2, (watch) observar. —**overseer**, *n.* capataz; supervisor.

oversensitive (‚o·vər'sɛn·sɪ·tɪv) *adj.* muy susceptible.

overshadow (‚o·vər'ʃæd·o) *v.t.* obscurecer; eclipsar.

overshoe ('o·vər‚ʃu) *n.* chanclo; galocha.

overshoot (‚o·vər'ʃut) *v.t.* [*pret. & p.p.* **overshot**] pasar; pasarse de. —*v.i.* pasarse.

oversight ('o·vər‚sait) *n.* 1, (omission) inadvertencia; omisión. 2, (supervision) supervisión; vigilancia.

oversimplify (‚o·vər'sɪm·plɪ‚fai) *v.t.* simplificar mucho. —**oversimplification**, *n.* exceso de simplificación.

oversize ('o·vər‚saiz) *adj.* muy grande. —*n.* tamaño muy grande.

oversleep (‚o·vər'slip) *v.i.* [*pret. & p.p.* **overslept**] dormir demasiado; pegársele a uno las sábanas.

overspread (‚o·vər'sprɛd) *v.t.* [*pret. & p.p.* **overspread**] extender sobre; cubrir. —*adj.* extendido.

overstate (‚o·vər'steit) *v.t.* exagerar. —**overstatement**, *n.* exageración.

overstay (‚o·vər'stei) *v.t. & i.* quedarse más de lo debido.

overstep (‚o·vər'stɛp) *v.t.* [**overstepped, overstepping**] propasar; propasarse en. —**overstep oneself**, excederse; sobrepasarse.

overstimulate (‚o·vər'stɪm·jə‚leit) *v.t.* estimular excesivamente; sobreexcitar.

overstock (‚o·vər'stak) *v.t.* surtir demasiado (de); sobrellenar. —*n.* ('o·vər-) surtido excesivo; exceso.

overstrict (‚o·vər'strɪkt) *adj.* demasiado estricto; demasiado riguroso.

overstuffed (‚o·vər'stʌft) *adj.* demasiado lleno o relleno; *fig.* sobrecargado.

oversupply (‚o·vər·sə'plai) *v.t.* abarrotar; proveer demasiado. —*n.* exceso.

oversuspicious (‚o·vər·sə'spɪʃ·əs) *adj.* demasiado sospechoso; muy desconfiado.

overt ('o·vʌrt) *adj.* abierto; franco; claro; manifiesto.

overtake (‚o·vər'teik) *v.t.* [*pret.* **overtook**; *p.p.* **overtaken**] 1, (catch up with) alcanzar; sobrecoger. 2, (come upon suddenly) sorprender.

overtax (‚o·vər'tæks) *v.t.* imponer demasiado; pedir demasiado.

over-the-counter *adj.* 1, (stock) que se vende fuera de la bolsa. 2, (drugs) que se vende sin receta autorizada.

overthrow (‚o·vər'θro) *v.t.* [*pret.* **overthrew**; *p.p.* **overthrown**] derribar; derrocar. —*n.* ('o·vər‚θro) derrocamiento.

overtime ('o·vər‚taim) *n.* horas extraordinarias; *sports* tiempo suplementario. —*adv.* en horas extraordinarias; *sports* en tiempo suplementario.

overtire (‚o·vər'tair) *v.t.* cansar mucho.

overtone ('o·vər‚ton) *n.* 1, *mus.*

armónico. 2, *usu.pl.* (implication) implicación; insinuación.

overture ('oᐧvərᐧtʃur) *n.* 1, *mus.* obertura. 2, (proposal) proposición; insinuación.

overturn (ˌoᐧvərˈtɐrn) *v.t. & i.* (upset) volcar. —*v.t.* (overthrow) derribar. —*n.* ('oᐧvər-) vuelco.

overvalue (ˌoᐧvərˈvælᐧju) *v.t.* dar demasiado valor a; valorar en exceso. —**overvaluation,** *n.* valoración excesiva.

overview ('oᐧvərˌvju) *n.* visión general; resumen.

overweening (ˌoᐧvərˈwiᐧnɪŋ) *adj.* presuntuoso; altanero; arrogante.

overweigh (ˌoᐧvərˈwei) *v.t.* 1, (outweigh) pesar más que. 2, (weigh down) abrumar; sobrecargar.

overweight ('oᐧvərˌweit) *n.* sobrepeso; exceso de peso. —*adj.* 1, (obese) grueso; obeso. 2, (having excess weight) que pesa de más.

overwhelm (ˌoᐧvərˈhwelm) *v.t.* 1, (crush) aplastar; arrollar. 2, (overcome, as with emotion, praise, etc.) abrumar; anonadar. —**overwhelming,** *adj.* abrumador.

overwork (ˌoᐧvərˈwɐrk) *v.i.* trabajar demasiado. —*v.t.* 1, (overburden) hacer trabajar mucho; abrumar o recargar de trabajo. 2, (excite excessively) excitar demasiado. 3, (elaborate too much) elaborar demasiado. 4, (make excessive use of) exagerar; abusar de. —*n.* ('oᐧvər-) exceso de trabajo.

overwrought (ˌoᐧvərˈrɔt) *adj.* 1, (excited; upset) muy excitado. 2, (too elaborate) recargado.

overzealous (ˌoᐧvərˈzɛlᐧəs) *adj.* demasiado celoso; muy entregado.

oviduct ('oᐧvɪˌdʌkt) *n.* oviducto.

ovine ('oᐧvain) *adj.* ovino.

oviparous (oˈvɪpᐧəᐧrəs) *adj.* ovíparo.

ovoid ('oᐧvɔid) *adj. & n.* ovoide.

ovulation (ˌoᐧvjəˈleiᐧʃən) *n.* ovulación. —**ovulate** ('oᐧvjəˌleit) *v.i.* desprender óvulos; efectuar ovulación.

ovule ('oᐧvjul) *n.* óvulo.

ovum ('oᐧvəm) *n.* [*pl.* **ova**] óvulo; huevo.

owe (oᵣ) *v.t. & i.* deber. —**owing,** *adj.* debido. —**owing to,** debido a; por causa de; por.

owl (aul) *n.* lechuza; búho. —**owlet** ('auᐧlɪt) *n.* cría de lechuza o búho. —**owlish,** *adj.* semejante a la lechuza; de lechuza.

own (oᵣn) *v.t.* 1, (possess) poseer; tener. 2, (admit) reconocer; admitir. —*adj.* propio. —**come into one's own,** lograr reconocimiento. —**get one's own back,** desquitarse; vengarse. —**hold one's own,** 1, (maintain one's status) no ceder; mantenerse firme. 2, (compete successfully) poder competir. 3, (defend oneself) defenderse. —**on one's own,** por su cuenta.

owner ('oᐧnər) *n.* dueño; propietario. —**ownership,** *n.* propiedad; posesión.

ox (aks) *n.* [*pl.* **oxen** ('akᐧsən)] buey.

oxalic (akˈsælᐧɪk) *adj.* oxálico.

oxalis ('akᐧsəᐧlɪs) *n.* acedera menor.

oxbow ('aksˌboᵣ) *n.* 1, (of oxen) collera de yugo. 2, (of a river) recodo.

oxeye ('aksˌai) *n., bot.* ojo de buey.

oxford ('aksᐧfərd) *n.* 1, (shoe) zapato oxford. 2, (cloth) tela oxford.

oxide ('akˌsaid) *n.* óxido.

oxidize ('akᐧsəˌdaiz) *v.t.* oxidar. —*v.i.* oxidarse. —**oxidation** (-ˈdeiᐧʃən) *n.* oxidación.

oxyacetylene (ˌakᐧsiᐧəˈsɛtᐧəᐧlin) *adj.* oxiacetilénico.

oxygen ('akᐧsəᐧdʒən) *n.* oxígeno.

oxygenate ('akᐧsəᐧdʒəˌneit) *v.t.* oxigenar. —**oxygenation,** *n.* oxigenación.

oxymoron (ˌakᐧsɪˈmorᐧən) *n.* oxímoron.

oyez ('oᐧjɛs; -jɛz) *interj.* ¡escuchen!; ¡atención!

oyster ('ɔisᐧtər) *n.* ostra.

ozone ('oᐧzon) *n.* ozono. —**ozone layer,** capa de ozono; ozonosfera.

P

P, p (piᵣ) decimosexta letra del alfabeto inglés.

pa (pa) *n., colloq.* papá.

PAC (pæk) *abr. de* **political action committee.**

pace (peis) *n.* paso. —*v.t.* 1, (walk

the length of; measure) medir a
pasos. **2,** (set the pace for) dar la
pauta a o para. —*v.i.* pasearse; dar
pasos. —**keep pace with,** ir o
mantenerse con. —**put one
through his paces,** probar; poner a
prueba. —**set the pace,** dar la
pauta.

pacemaker ('peis,mei·kər) *n.* el
que da la pauta; modelo; *med.*
marcapasos.

pacer ('pei·sər) *n.* caballo
amblador.

pachyderm ('pak·ɪ,dʌrm) *n.*
paquidermo.

pacific (pə'sɪf·ɪk) *adj.* pacífico.
—*n., cap.* (Océano) Pacífico.

pacifier ('pæs·ɪ,fai·ər) *n.* chupete;
chupador.

pacifism ('pæs·ɪ·fɪz·əm) *n.*
pacifismo. —**pacifist,** *n.* pacifista.
—**pacifistic,** *adj.* pacifista.

pacify ('pæs·ɪ,fai) *v.t.* pacificar.
—**pacification** (-fɪ'kei·ʃən) *n.*
pacificación.

pack (pæk) *n.* **1,** (package) paquete.
2, (bundle) fardo. **3,** *cards* baraja. **4,**
(bunch of dogs) jauría; (of wolves)
manada; (of mules) recua. **5,** (gang;
band) cuadrilla; pandilla. **6,** (lot;
bunch) sarta; partida. **7,** (mass of
ice) masa de hielo. **8,** (compress)
compresa. **9,** (haversack) mochila.
—*v.t.* **1,** (put in a container)
empacar; empaquetar; encajonar. **2,**
(load) cargar. **3,** (wrap) envolver. **4,**
(compress) apretar; comprimir. **5,**
(fill; stuff) llenar; rellenar. **6,** (cram;
crowd) atestar; apiñar. **7,** *colloq.*
(have; carry) tener; llevar. —*v.i.* **1,**
(prepare luggage) hacer el equipaje
o las maletas; empacar. **2,** (settle
into a compact mass) apretarse;
comprimirse. —*adj.* de carga.
—**packer,** *n.* empacador [*fem.*
-dora]; empaquetador [*fem.* -dora].
—**packing,** *n.* empacado; empaquetadura. —**pack animal,** animal de
carga. —**pack off,** despedir;
despachar; largarse. —**pack rat,**
acumulador; coleccionista. —**send
packing,** despedir.

package ('pæk·ɪdʒ) *n.* paquete.
—*v.t.* empacar; empaquetar.

packet ('pæk·ɪt) *n.* **1,** (small bundle) paquete. **2,** (ship) paquebote.

packsaddle ('pæk,sæd·əl) *n.*
albarda.

pact (pækt) *n.* pacto.

pad (pæd) *n.* **1,** (wad; cushion)
almohadilla. **2,** (writing tablet) bloc;

cuadernillo. **3,** (stamp pad) tampón.
4, (sole) planta. **5,** (lily pad) hoja de
nenúfar. **6,** (launching pad)
plataforma de lanzamiento. **7,** *slang*
(dwelling) morada; vivienda. —*v.t.*
[**padded, padding**] **1,** (fill; stuff)
rellenar. **2,** (line; quilt) acolchar;
poner guata a. **3,** (expand unduly)
abultar. —*v.i.* caminar; (of a horse)
amblar.

padding ('pæd·ɪŋ) *n.* **1,** (stuffing)
relleno. **2,** (lining) guata.

paddle ('pæd·əl) *n.* **1,** (oar) pala;
remo de canoa. **2,** (broad-bladed
implement) pala; paleta. —*v.t. & i.*
1, (row) remar. **2,** (spank) dar una
paliza; dar de azotes. **3,** (dabble;
splash) chapalear; chapotear.
—**paddle boat,** barco o vapor de
ruedas. —**paddle wheel,** rueda de
palas o paletas.

paddock ('pæd·ək) *n.* cercado.

paddy ('pæd·i) *n.* **1,** (rice in the
husk) arroz con cáscara. **2,** (rice
field) arrozal.

paddy wagon coche celular;
camión de policía.

padlock ('pæd,lak) *n.* candado.
—*v.t.* cerrar con candado; echar el
candado a.

padre ('pa·dri) *n.* padre; cura;
capellán.

paella (pə'el·ə) *n.* paella.

pagan ('pei·gən) *adj. & n.* pagano.
—**paganism,** *n.* paganismo.

page (peidʒ) *n.* **1,** (leaf of a book)
página. **2,** (attendant) paje. **3,** (bellboy) botones. —*v.t.* **1,** (arrange in
pages) paginar. **2,** (call) llamar.

pageant ('pædʒ·ənt) *n.* **1,** (parade)
desfile. **2,** (show) espectáculo. **3,**
(tableau) retablo. —**pageantry**
(-ən·tri) *n.* fausto; boato; pompa.

paginate ('pædʒ·ə,neit) *v.t.*
paginar. —**pagination,** *n.* paginación.

pagoda (pə'go·də) *n.* pagoda.

paid (peid) *v., pret. & p.p. de* **pay.**

pail (peil) *n.* cubo; balde.

pain (pein) *n.* dolor. —*v.t.* **1,** (hurt)
doler; causar dolor a. **2,** (grieve)
apenar. —*v.i.* doler. —**be in pain,**
estar con dolor; tener dolor. —**on** (o
under) **pain of,** so (o bajo) pena
de. —**take pains,** esmerarse.
—**take pains not to,** guardarse de;
tener cuidado de.

painful ('pein·fəl) *adj.* **1,** (aching)
doloroso. **2,** (difficult) penoso;
difícil. —**painfulness,** *n.* dolor.

painkiller ('pein,kɪl·ər) *n.* calmante.

painless ('pein·ləs) *adj.* **1,** (not hurtful) sin dolor. **2,** (easy) fácil; sin pena; sin trabajo.

painstaking ('peinz,teik·ɪŋ) *adj.* cuidadoso; esmerado.

paint (peint) *n.* pintura. —*v.t. & i.* pintar.

painter ('pein·tər) *n.* pintor.

painting ('pein·tɪŋ) *n.* pintura.

pair (peɪr) *n.* **1,** (matched set) par. **2,** (couple) pareja. —*v.i.* parear. —*v.i.* parearse. —**pair off,** formarse o irse en parejas.

pajamas (pə'dʒam·əz) *n.pl.* piyamas; pijamas.

pal (pæl) *n., slang* compañero. —*v.i.* [**palled, palling**] ser compañero.

palace ('pæl·ɪs) *n.* palacio. —*adj.* palaciego; del palacio.

paladin ('pæl·ə·dɪn) *n.* paladín.

palanquin (,pæl·ən'kin) *n.* palanquín.

palatable ('pæl·ə·tə·bəl) *adj.* **1,** (tasty) sabroso. **2,** *fig.* (acceptable) aceptable; que se puede pasar.

palate ('pæl·ɪt) *n.* paladar. —**palatal,** *adj.* palatal; palatino.

palatial (pə'lei·ʃəl) *adj.* magnífico; suntuoso.

palatine ('pæl·ə,tain) *adj. & n.* palatino. —**palatinate** (pə'læt·ɪ,neit) *n.* palatinado.

palaver (pə'læv·ər) *n.* palabrería; charla. —*v.i.* charlar.

pale (peil) *adj.* pálido. —*n.* estaca; palo. —*v.i.* perder el color; palidecer. —**paleness,** *n.* palidez.

paleface ('peil,feis) *n.* rostropálido.

paleography (,pei·li'ag·rə·fi) *n.* paleografía. —**paleographer,** *n.* paleógrafo. —**paleographic** (-ə·'græf·ɪk) *adj.* paleográfico.

paleolithic (,pei·li·ə'liθ·ɪk) *adj.* paleolítico.

paleontology (,pei·li·ən'tal·ə·dʒi) *n.* paleontología. —**paleontological** (-,an·tə'ladʒ·ɪ·kəl) *adj.* paleontológico. —**paleontologist,** *n.* paleontólogo.

Paleozoic (,pei·li·ə'zo·ɪk) *adj.* paleozoico.

Palestinian (,pæl·ə'stɪn·i·ən) *adj. & n.* palestino.

palette ('pal·ɪt) *n.* paleta. —**palette knife,** espátula de pintor.

palfrey ('pɔl·fri) *n.* palafrén.

palimony ('pæl·ə,mo·ni) *n.* manutención otorgada por fallo judicial a un(a) ex-amante.

palindrome ('pæl·ɪn·drom) *n.* palíndromo.

paling ('peil·ɪŋ) *n.* estacada; palizada.

palisade (,pæl·ə'seid) *n.* empalizada.

pall (pɔl) *n.* **1,** (coffin cover) paño mortuorio. **2,** (cloud) capa. **3,** (gloomy effect) sombra. —*v.i.* perder su sabor; perder su interés. —**pall on,** hartar; cansar.

palladium (pə'lei·di·əm) *n.* **1,** (metal) paladio. **2,** (safeguard) salvaguardia; garantía.

pallbearer ('pɔl,ber·ər) *n.* pilar.

pallet ('pæl·ɪt) **1,** (straw bed) jergón. **2,** (wooden skid) calzo. **3,** = **palette.**

palliate ('pæl·i,eit) *v.t.* paliar. —**palliation,** *n.* paliación. —**palliative** (-ə,tɪv) *n. & adj.* paliativo.

pallid ('pæl·ɪd) *adj.* pálido.

pallor ('pæl·ər) *n.* palidez.

palm (pɑːm) *n.* **1,** (inner surface of the hand) palma. **2,** (span of the hand) palmo. **3,** *bot.* palmera. **4,** (symbol of victory) palma. —*v.t.* escamotear. —**palmar** ('pal·mər) *adj.* palmar. —**grease the palm,** *colloq.* untar la mano. —**palm grove,** palmar; palmeral. —**palm off,** escamotear.

palmetto (pal'mɛt·o) *n.* palmito.

palmistry ('pɑ·mɪs·tri) *n.* quiromancia. —**palmist,** *n.* quiromántico.

Palm Sunday Domingo de Ramos.

palmy ('pɑ·mi) *adj.* (flourishing) próspero; floreciente.

palomino (,pæl·ə'mi·no) *n.* palomilla.

palooka (pə'lu·kə) *n., slang* bobo; simplón.

palpable ('pæl·pə·bəl) *adj.* palpable.

palpate ('pæl·peit) *v.t. & i.* palpar. —**palpation,** *n.* palpación.

palpitate ('pæl·pə,teit) *v.i.* palpitar. —**palpitation,** *n.* palpitación.

palsy ('pɔl·zi) *n.* parálisis; perlesía. —*v.t.* paralizar.

palter ('pɔl·tər) *v.i.* **1,** (play false) jugar sucio. **2,** (trifle) andar con rodeos.

paltry ('pɔl·tri) *adj.* mezquino. —**paltriness,** *n.* mezquindad.

pampas ('pæm·pəz) *n.pl.* pampas.

pamper ('pæm·pər) *v.t.* mimar; consentir.

pamphlet ('pæm·flɪt) *n.* folleto. —**pamphleteer** (-fləˈtɪr) *n.* folletista.

pan (pæn) *n.* **1,** (saucepan) cacerola; cazuela. **2,** (skillet) sartén. **3,** (baking pan) molde de horno. **4,** (shallow vessel) paila; cubeta. —*v.t. & i.* **1,** (cook in a pan) cocer en cazuela, cacerola, etc. **2,** (sift for gold) cerner en busca de oro. **3,** *slang* (criticize; deride) poner frito. —**pan out,** *colloq.* resultar; tener éxito.

panacea (ˌpæn·əˈsi·ə) *n.* panacea.

panama ('pæn·əˌma) *n.* panamá.

Pan-American *adj.* panamericano. —**Pan-Americanism,** *n.* panamericanismo.

pancake ('pæn·keik) *n.* **1,** (battercake) hojuela; *Amer.* panqueque, **2,** *aero.* aterrizaje a plomo o de plano.

panchromatic ('pæn·kroˈmæt·ɪk) *adj.* pancromático.

pancreas ('pæn·kri·əs) *n.* páncreas. —**pancreatic** (-ˈæt·ɪk) *adj.* pancreático.

panda ('pæn·də) *n.* panda.

pandemic (pænˈdem·ɪk) *adj.* pandémico. —*n.* pandémica.

pandemonium (ˌpæn·dəˈmo·ni·əm) *n.* pandemónium.

pander ('pæn·dər) *v.i.* alcahuetear. —*n.* alcahuete.

pane (pein) *n.* **1,** (sheet of glass) cristal; panel de cristal. **2,** (panel) tablero; cuadro.

panegyric (ˌpæn·əˈdʒɪr·ɪk) *n.* panegírico. —**panegyrical,** *adj.* panegírico.

panel ('pæn·əl) *n.* **1,** (section of a door, wall, etc.) panel. **2,** (group of jurors, judges, experts, etc.) jurado; panel. **3,** (instrument panel; control panel) tablero; cuadro. —**paneled,** *adj.* con o de paneles. —**paneling,** *n.* paneles.

pang (pæŋ) *n.* ramalazo; punzada.

panhandler ('pæn,hæn·dlər) *n.,* *slang* pordiosero. —**panhandle** (-dəl) *v.t. & i., slang* pordiosear.

panic ('pæn·ɪk) *n.* pánico; terror. —*adj.* pánico. —*v.t.* aterrorizar. —*v.i.* aterrorizarse. —**panicky,** *adj.* pánico; que tiene pánico; aterrorizado.

panicle ('pæn·ə·kəl) *n.* panoja.

panic-stricken *adj.* aterrorizado.

pannier ('pæn·jər) *n.* angarillas; serón.

panoply ('pæn·ə·pli) *n.* panoplia.

panorama (ˌpæn·əˈræm·ə) *n.* panorama. —**panoramic,** *adj.* panorámico.

pansy ('pæn·zi) *n.* **1,** *bot.* pensamiento. **2,** *slang* marica.

pant (pænt) *v.i.* **1,** (breathe hard) jadear. **2,** (yearn) anhelar; rabiar (por). —*n.* [*también*, **panting**] jadeo. —**panting,** *adj.* jadeante.

pantaloons (ˌpæn·təˈluːnz) *n.pl.* pantalones.

pantheism ('pæn·θi·ɪz·əm) *n.* panteísmo. —**pantheist,** *n.* panteísta. —**pantheistic,** *adj.* panteísta; panteístico.

pantheon ('pæn·θi,an) *n.* panteón.

panther ('pæn·θər) *n.* pantera.

panties ('pæn·tiz) *n.pl., colloq.* bragas; pantaloncitos de mujer.

pantograph ('pæn·tə,græf) *n.* pantógrafo.

pantomime ('pæn·tə,maim) *n.* pantomima. —**pantomimic** (-ˈmɪm·ɪk) *adj.* pantomímico. —**pantomimist** (-,mɪm·ɪst) *n.* pantomimo.

pantry ('pæn·tri) *n.* despensa.

pants (pænts) *n.pl., colloq.* **1,** (trousers) pantalones. **2,** (drawers) calzoncillos.

pantyhose ('pæn·ti,hoz) *n.* media pantalón.

pantywaist ('pæn·ti,weist) *n., slang* marica.

pap (pæp) *n.* papilla; papa.

papa ('pa·pə) *n.* papá.

papacy ('pei·pə·si) *n.* papado. —**papal** (-pəl) *adj.* papal; del Papa.

papaw ('pɔ·pɔ) *n.* **1,** (tree) papayo. **2,** (fruit) papaya.

papaya (pəˈpa·jə) *n.* **1,** (fruit) papaya; lechosa. **2,** (tree) papayo.

paper ('pei·pər) *n.* **1,** (thin material; sheet) papel. **2,** (newspaper) periódico. **3,** (essay) ensayo; escrito; artículo. **4,** (written exercise) trabajo; composición. **5,** (document) documento. **6,** (paper money) papel moneda; valores. —*adj.* de papel. —*v.t.* empapelar. —**papery,** *adj.* como papel. —**on paper,** por escrito.

paperback ('pei·pər,bæk) *adj.* en rústica. —*n.* libro en rústica.

paper clip sujetapapeles.

paperhanger ('pei·pər,hæŋ·ər) *n.* empapelador. —**paperhanging,** *n.* empapelado.

paperweight ('pei·pər,weit) *n.* pisapapeles.

paperwork ('pei·pər,wʌrk) *n.* papeleo.

papier-maché (,pei·pər·mə'ʃei) *n.* cartón piedra; papel majado; papel maché.

papilla (pə'pɪl·ə) *n.* papila. —**papillary** ('pæp·ə·lɛr·i) *adj.* papilar.

papist ('pei·pɪst) *adj. & n.* papista.

pappy ('pæp·i) *n., colloq.* papá; papito.

paprika ('pa·prɪ·ka; pæ'pri·kə) *n.* pimentón.

papule ('pæp·jul) *n.* pápula.

papyrus (pə'pai·rəs) *n.* papiro.

par (par) *n.* **1,** *fin.* igualdad de cambio; par (*en* a la par). **2,** (equal footing) nivel; altura. **3,** (standard) lo normal; lo corriente. **4,** *golf* tanteo alcanzado por expertos. —*adj.* **1,** (of or at par) igual; a la par. **2,** (normal) normal; corriente. —**at par,** a la par. —**on** o **upon a par,** a la par; al mismo nivel. —**par value,** valor nominal.

parable ('pær·ə·bəl) *n.* parábola.

parabola (pə'ræb·ə·lə) *n.* parábola. —**parabolic** (,pær·ə'bal·ɪk) *adj.* parabólico.

parachute ('pær·ə,ʃut) *n.* paracaídas. —*v.t. & i.* lanzar(se) o tirar(se) en paracaídas. —**parachutist,** *n.* paracaidista.

parade (pə'reid) *n.* **1,** (procession) desfile; *mil.* parada. **2,** (display; ostentation) ostentación; alarde. **3,** (promenade) paseo. **4,** (promenaders) paseantes. —*v.t.* **1,** (cause to march) hacer desfilar. **2,** (march through) desfilar por; recorrer. **3,** (make a display of) hacer ostentación o alarde de. —*v.i.* desfilar; pasear.

paradigm ('pær·ə,dɪm) *n.* paradigma.

paradise ('pær·ə,dais) *n.* paraíso. —**paradisiacal** (-di'sai·ə·kəl); **paradisaical** (-di'sei·ə·kəl) *adj.* paradisíaco.

paradox ('pær·ə,daks) *n.* paradoja. —**paradoxical** (-'dak·sɪ·kəl) *adj.* paradójico.

paraffin ('pær·ə·fɪn) *n.* parafina.

paragon ('pær·ə·gan) *n.* parangón.

paragraph ('pær·ə,græf) *n.* párrafo. —*v.t.* dividir en párrafos.

parakeet ('pær·ə,kit) *n.* perico; periquito.

paralegal (,pæ·rə'li·gəl) *n.* auxiliar en derecho.

parallax ('pær·ə,læks) *n.* paralaje.

parallel ('pær·ə,lɛl) *adj. & n.* paralelo. —*v.t.* **1,** (compare) comparar; parangonar; paralelar. **2,** (run parallel with) ir o correr paralelo a o con. **3,** (be similar or comparable to) parecerse a; que se puede comparar a o con. —**parallel bars,** paralelas; barras paralelas.

parallelepiped (,pær·ə,lɛl·ə 'pai·pɪd) *n.* paralelepípedo.

parallelism ('pær·ə·lɛl,ɪz·əm) *n.* paralelismo.

parallelogram (,pær·ə'lɛl· ə,græm) *n.* paralelogramo.

paralysis (pə'ræl·ə·sɪs) *n.* parálisis. —**paralytic** (,pær·ə'lɪt·ɪk) *adj. & n.* paralítico.

paralyze ('pær·ə,laiz) *v.t.* paralizar. —**paralyzation** (-lɪ'zei·ʃən) *n.* paralización.

paramecium (,pær·ə'mi·si·əm) *n.* paramecio.

paramedic (,pær·ə'mɛd·ɪk) *n.* auxiliar en medicina.

paramedical (,pær·ə'mɛd·ɪ·kəl) *adj.* paramédico.

parameter (pə'ræm·ə·tər) *n.* parámetro.

paramo ('pær·ə,mo) *n.* páramo.

paramount ('pær·ə,maunt) *adj.* sumo; capital.

paramour ('pær·ə,mur) *n.* amante; querido; querida.

paranoia (,pær·ə'nɔi·ə) *n.* paranoia. —**paranoiac** (-æk) *n. & adj.* paranoico.

parapet ('pær·ə·pɛt) *n.* parapeto.

paraphernalia (,pær·ə·fər'neil· jə) *n.pl.* accesorios; atavíos; adornos.

paraphrase ('pær·ə,freiz) *n.* paráfrasis. —*v.t. & i.* parafrasear. —**paraphrastic** (-'fræs·tɪk) *adj.* parafrástico.

paraplegia (,pær·ə'pli·dʒi·ə) *n.* paraplejía. —**paraplegic,** *n. & adj.* parapléjico.

paraprofessional (,pær·ə· prə'fɛʃ·ə·nəl) *n.* auxiliar en determinada profesión.

parapsychology (,pær·ə·sai'kal· ə·dʒi) *n.* parapsicología.

parasite ('pær·ə,sait) *n.* parásito. —**parasitic** (-'sɪt·ɪk) *adj.* parasítico; parásito; parasitario.

parasol ('pær·ə,sɔl) *n.* parasol; quitasol; sombrilla.

paratrooper ('pær·ə,tru·pər) *n.* paracaidista.

paratyphoid (,pær·ə'tai·fɔid) *adj.* paratifoide; paratífico. —*n.* paratifoidea. —**paratyphoid fever**, fiebre paratifoidea.

parboil ('par,bɔil) *v.t.* sancochar.

parcel ('par·səl) *n.* 1, (package) paquete. 2, (piece of land) parcela. —*v.t.* parcelar; dividir. —**parcel post**, paquete postal.

parch (partʃ) *v.t.* agostar; quemar; tostar. —*v.i.* quemarse; abrasarse.

parchment ('partʃ·mənt) *n.* pergamino.

pardon ('par·dən) *v.t.* perdonar. —*n.* perdón. —**pardonable**, *adj.* perdonable.

pare (peɪr) *v.t.* 1, (cut) cortar; recortar. 2, (peel) pelar; mondar. 3, (reduce) recortar.

paregoric (,pær·ə'gor·ɪk) *n.* paregórico.

parent ('pɛr·ənt) *n.* 1, (father) padre. 2, (mother) madre. —**parents**, *n.pl.* padres; progenitores. —**parentage**, *n.* paternidad o maternidad. —**parental** (pə'rɛn·təl) *adj.* paternal. —**parenthood**, *n.* paternidad o maternidad.

parenthesis (pə'rɛn·θə·sɪs) *n.* [*pl.* -ses (-siz)] paréntesis. —**parenthesize** (-,saiz) *v.t.* poner entre paréntesis. —**parenthetical** (,pær·ən·'θɛt·ɪ·kəl) *adj.* entre paréntesis; por paréntesis.

paresis (pə'ri·sɪs) *n.* paresia. —**paretic** (pə'rɛt·ɪk) *adj.* & *n.* parético.

par excellence por excelencia.

parfait (par'fei) *n.* helado de crema suave; parfait.

pariah (pə'rai·ə) *n.* paria.

pari-mutuel (,pær·i'mju·tʃu·əl) *n.* apuesta mutua.

paring ('pɛr·ɪŋ) *n.* cáscara; mondadura. —**paring knife**, cuchillo para mondar.

parish ('pær·ɪʃ) *n.* 1, *eccles.* parroquia; feligresía. 2, (county) condado.

parishioner (pə'rɪʃ·ən·ər) *n.* feligrés; parroquiano.

parity ('pær·ə·ti) *n.* paridad; equidad.

park (park) *n.* parque. —*v.t.* & *i.* estacionar; *Amer.* parquear. —**parking**, *n.* estacionamiento; *Amer.* parqueo. —**parking lot**, estacionamiento; *Amer.* parqueo; parqueadero.

parka ('par·kə) *n.* chaqueta con capucha.

parkway ('park,wei) *n.* carretera; autopista.

parlance ('par·ləns) *n.* lenguaje.

parley ('par·li) *n.* conferencia; parlamento. —*v.i.* conferenciar; parlamentar.

parliament ('par·lə·mənt) *n.* parlamento. —**parliamentarian** (-mɛn'tɛr·i·ən) *n.* parlamentario. —**parliamentarism** (-'mɛn·tə·rɪz·əm) *n.* parlamentarismo. —**parliamentary** (-'mɛn·tə·ri) *adj.* parlamentario.

parlor ('par·lər) *n.* sala; salón.

parlormaid ('par·lər,meid) *n.* camarera.

Parnassus (par'næs·əs) *n.* parnaso; Parnaso.

parochial (pə'ro·ki·əl) *adj.* 1, (of a parish) parroquial. 2, (narrow; provincial) estrecho de miras; limitado.

parody ('pær·ə·di) *n.* parodia. —*v.t.* parodiar.

parole (pə'roʊl) *n.* 1, (prisoner's promise) palabra de honor. 2, (conditional release) libertad provisional. —*v.t.* poner en libertad provisional.

parotid (pə'rat·ɪd) *n.* parótida. —*adj.* parotídeo. —**parotiditis** (-ə'dai·tɪs) *n.* parotiditis.

paroxysm ('pær·ək,sɪz·əm) *n.* paroxismo.

parquet (par'kei) *n.* 1, (flooring) entarimado. 2, *theat.* patio; *Amer.* luneta. —**parquetry** ('par·kɪt·ri) *n.* entarimado.

parricide ('pær·ə,said) *n.* 1, (agent) parricida. 2, (act) parricidio. —**parricidal** (-'sai·dəl) *adj.* parricida.

parrot ('pær·ət) *n.* papagayo; loro; cotorra. —*v.t.* imitar.

parry ('pær·i) *v.t.* & *i.* (ward off) parar; desviar. —*v.t.* (evade) evadir; eludir. —*n.* 1, (a warding off) parada; quite. 2, (evasion) evasiva; evasión.

parse (pars) *v.t.* analizar (una palabra, oración, etc.). —**parsing**, *n.* análisis.

parsimony ('par·sə·mo·ni) *n.* parsimonia. —**parsimonious** (-'mo·ni·əs) *adj.* parsimonioso.

parsley ('pars·li) *n.* perejil.

parsnip ('pars·nɪp) *n.* chirivía; pastinaca.

parson ('par·sən) *n.* párroco; cura.
—**parsonage,** *n.* rectoría.
part (part) *n.* **1,** (portion) parte. **2,**
(rôle) papel. **3,** (component, as of a
mechanism, structure, etc.) pieza. **4,**
usu.pl. (locality) partes. **5,** *pl.* (talent; ability) partes; talento. **6,** (side,
as in a controversy) lado; parte. **7,**
(of the hair) partidura; raya. —*v.t.*
1, (break; divide) partir; dividir. **2,**
(separate) separar. —*v.i.* **1,** (break;
divide) partirse; dividirse. **2,** (separate) separarse. **3,** (depart) salir;
partir; irse. —*adj.* parcial. —*adv.*
parte; en parte. —**for the most
part,** por lo general; en su mayor
parte. —**on one's part,** por su parte
o cuenta. —**part from,** dejar;
separarse de. —**part of speech,**
parte de la oración. —**part with,**
dejar; soltar.
partake (par'teik) *v.i.* participar.
—**partake of, 1,** (have a share in)
participar de. **2,** (eat or drink)
comer o beber. **3,** (have the nature
of) tener de; tener algo de.
parterre (par'te͡ʒr) *n.* parterre.
parthenogenesis (ˌpar·θə·no·
'dʒɛn·ə·sɪs) *n.* partenogénesis.
partial ('par·ʃəl) *adj.* parcial.
—**partiality** (-ʃi'æl·ə·ti) *n.* parcialidad. —**be partial to,** tener debilidad por; sentir simpatía hacia.
participate (par'tɪs·ɪˌpeit)
v.i. participar. —**participant** (-pənt)
n. & *adj.* partícipe; participante.
—**participation,** *n.* participación.
participle ('par·tə,sɪp·əl) *n.*
participio. —**participial** (-'sɪp·i·əl)
adj. participial.
particle ('par·tə·kəl) *n.* partícula.
particolored ('par·ti,kʌl·ərd) *adj.*
abigarrado.
particular (pər'tɪk·jə·lər) *adj.* **1,**
(specific) determinado. **2,** (peculiar;
special) particular; especial;
característico. **3,** (detailed) detallado. **4,** (fastidious) exigente. —*n.*
particular; particularidad.
particularity (pər,tɪk·jə'lær·ə·ti)
n. particularidad.
parting ('par·tɪŋ) *adj.* **1,** (dividing)
divisorio; de separación. **2,** (de-
parting; dying) que se va; que
muere. **3,** (given, done, etc., at parting) de despedida. —*n.* **1,** (division;
separation) división; separación. **2,**
(departure) partida. —**parting of
the ways,** separación.
partisan ('par·tə·zən) *n.* **1,** (adherent) partidario. **2,** (guerrilla) guerri-

llero; *Amer.* montonero. —*adj.*
partidario; partidista. —**partisanship,** *n.* partidismo.
partition (par'tɪʃ·ən) *n.* partición;
división. —*v.t.* dividir.
partitive ('par·tə,tɪv) *adj.* partitivo.
partly ('part·li) *adv.* parcialmente;
en parte.
partner ('part·nər) *n.* **1,** (companion) compañero. **2,** (dancing companion) pareja. **3,** (associate) socio.
4, (spouse) consorte; cónyuge; pareja.
partnership ('part·nər·ʃɪp) *n.* **1,**
(association) asociación. **2,** (business firm) sociedad.
partridge ('par·trɪdʒ) *n.* perdiz.
part-time *adj.* por horas; parcial.
—**part time,** trabajo parcial o por
horas.
parturition (ˌpar·tju'rɪʃ·ən) *n.*
parto. —**parturient** (par'tjur·i·ənt)
adj. parturienta.
party ('par·ti) *n.* **1,** *polit.* partido. **2,**
(social event) fiesta. **3,** (group en-
gaged in sport or play) partida. **4,**
(detachment; detail) grupo; cuerpo.
5, *law* parte; parte contratante.
—**party line, 1,** (of telephones)
línea compartida por dos o más
abonados; línea común. **2,** *polit.*
doctrina o política del partido.
—**party wall,** (pared) medianera.
parvenu ('par·və,nju) *adj.* & *n.*
advenedizo.
paschal ('pas·kəl) *adj.* pascual.
pasha ('pa·ʃə) *n.* bajá; pachá.
pasquinade (ˌpæs·kwɪ'neid) *n.*
pasquinada.
pass (pæs) *v.t.* & *i.* pasar. —*n.* **1,**
(act of passing) pase; paso. **2,** (defile) paso. **3,** (state of affairs)
estado; situación. **4,** (free ticket;
permit) pase. **5,** (movement; gesture) pase. —**bring to pass,** causar;
ocasionar. —**come to pass,** suceder;
ocurrir; pasar. —**let pass,** dejar pasar; pasar por alto. —**make a pass
at, 1,** (attempt to strike) amenazar;
intentar golpear. **2,** *slang* (make amorous advances to) dar un pase a.
—**pass away, 1,** (cease) pasar. **2,**
(spend, as time) pasar. **3,** (die)
morir. —**pass off, 1,** (cease) pasar.
2, (take place; go through)
realizarse. **3,** (be or cause to be accepted) pasar. —**pass out, 1,** (leave)
salir. **2,** *slang* (faint) desmayarse.

—**pass over,** pasar por alto. —**pass the buck.** *slang* escurrir o pasar el bulto. —**pass up,** *slang* dejar pasar; perder; desperdiciar.

passable ('pæs·ə·bəl) *adj.* pasable; pasadero.

passage ('pæs·ɪdʒ) *n.* **1,** (voyage; crossing) travesía; cruce; pasaje. **2,** (road; pass) paso. **3,** (permission to pass) pase; paso. **4,** (right to be conveyed) pasaje. **5,** (change; transition) paso; transición; cambio. **6,** (lapse, as of time) transcurso; lapso. **7,** (occurrence; incident) pasaje. **8,** (excerpt) pasaje. **9,** (enactment) aprobación; pasaje. **10,** = **passageway. 11,** (exchange; reciprocation) intercambio. —**of passage,** migratorio; transeúnte.

passageway ('pæs·ɪdʒ·wei) *n.* **1,** (hall; corridor) pasillo; corredor; pasadizo. **2,** (alley; way) callejón.

passbook ('pæs,bʊk) *n.* **1,** (account book) libro de cuentas. **2,** (bankbook) libreta de banco.

passenger ('pæs·ən·dʒər) *n.* pasajero.

passer-by (,pæs·ər'bai) *n.* [*pl.* **passers-by**] viandante; transeúnte.

passing ('pæs·ɪŋ) *adj.* pasajero; que pasa. —*n.* **1,** paso. **2,** (death) muerte; deceso. **3,** *adv., archaic* muy; sumamente. —**in passing,** de paso. —**passing grade,** aprobación.

passion ('pæʃ·ən) *n.* pasión. —**passionate** (-ɪt) *adj.* apasionado. —**passionless,** *adj.* frío; indiferente.

passionflower ('pæʃ·ən,flau·ər) *n.* pasionaria.

passive ('pæs·ɪv) *adj.* pasivo. —**passivity** (pə'sɪv·ə·ti) *n.* pasividad.

passkey ('pæs,kiː *n.* **1,** (master key) llave maestra. **2,** (private key) llave; llave particular.

Passover ('pæs·o·vər) *n.* pascua; pascua de los hebreos.

passport ('pæs·port) *n.* pasaporte.

password ('pæs·wʌrd) *n.* contraseña.

past (pæst) *adj. & n.* pasado. —*prep.* **1,** (farther on than) más allá de. **2,** (farther in time than; after) después de; más tarde que. **3,** (beyond; in excess of) más allá de; fuera de; más de; en exceso de. **4,** (along the length of) por. **5,** (before; along the front of) por delante de. —*adv.* de largo; por delante.

pasta ('pas·tə) *n.* pastas; fideos.

paste (peist) *n.* **1,** (dough) masa. **2,**

(smooth, malleable substance) pasta. **3,** (adhesive) engrudo; pegote. —*v.t.* **1,** (make adhere) pegar. **2,** (cover with pasted material) cubrir con papel, afiches, etc.; empapelar. **3,** *slang* (hit) pegar; propinar.

pasteboard ('peist,bord) *n.* cartón. —*adj.* de cartón.

pastel (pæs'tel) *n. & adj.* pastel.

pasteurize ('pæs·tə,raiz) *v.t.* pasteurizar. —**pasteurization** (-rɪ·'zei·ʃən) *n.* pasteurización.

pastiche (pæs'tiʃ) *n.* pastiche.

pastille (pæs'tiːl) *n.* **1,** (tablet; lozenge) pastilla; tableta. **2,** (pastel crayon) pastel.

pastime ('pæs,taim) *n.* pasatiempo.

pastor ('pæs·tər) *n.* pastor; ministro. —**pastoral,** *adj.* pastoral. —**pastorale** (-tə'ræl) *n.* pastoral.

pastry ('peis·tri) *n.* **1,** (paste) pasta; pastel. **2,** (baked goods) pastas; pasteles; pastelería. —**pastry cook,** pastelero; repostero. —**pastry shop,** pastelería; repostería.

pasturage ('pæs·tʃər·ɪdʒ) *n.* **1,** = **pasture. 2,** (pasturing) pastoreo.

pasture ('pæs·tʃər) *n.* **1,** (grass; fodder) pasto; hierba. **2,** (ground for grazing) pastadero; apacentadero. —*v.t.* **1,** (put to graze) pastorear; pastar; apacentar. **2,** (graze on) pacer; apacentarse de. —*v.i.* apacentarse; pacer; pastar.

pasty ('peis·ti) *adj.* **1,** (like paste) pastoso. **2,** (pale) pálido. —*n.* pastel; pastelillo. —**pastiness,** *n.* pastosidad.

pat (pæt) *n.* **1,** (tap, as with the hand) palmadita; golpe suave dado de plano. **2,** (light sound) ruido ligero; sonido leve. **3,** (small lump) pedazo de masa; pastilla. —*adj.* **1,** (opportune; timely) oportuno; apto. **2,** (exactly suitable) de perilla. —*adv.* oportunamente; aptamente; de perilla. —*v.t.* [**patted, patting**] **1,** (tap; stroke, as with the hand) dar palmaditas en o contra; dar golpecitos de plano a; palmotear; palmear. **2,** (give shape to by patting) moldear a palmaditas. **3,** (caress) acariciar. —*v.i.* sonar o golpear ligeramente. —**have (o know) pat,** *colloq.* conocer a fondo. —**stand pat,** *colloq.* **1,** (refuse to budge) estar o seguir en sus trece; obstinarse. **2,** *cards* chantarse.

patch (pætʃ) *n.* **1,** (covering, as for

mending) parche; remiendo. **2,** (covering, as a dressing or shield) parche. **3,** (splotch; contrasting area) mancha. **4,** (small area) extensión pequeña; pedazo. **5,** (planted area) sembrado pequeño. **6,** (plot of land) lote de terreno; pequeño lote. **7,** (bit; remnant) retazo. —*v.t.* **1,** (mend) remendar; *Amer.* parchar. **2,** (fix or put together hurriedly) hacer o componer a la diabla; remendar; chapucear. —**patch up,** remediar; poner fin a; resolver.

patchwork ('pætʃ,wʌrk) *n.* **1,** (needlework) labor de retazos. **2,** (jumble) mezcla abigarrada. **3,** (sloppy work) chapucería.

patchy ('pætʃ·i) *adj.* irregular; chapuceado.

pate (peit) *n.* coronilla; mollera.

patent ('pæt·ənt; 'pei·tənt) *adj.* **1,** (obvious; visible) patente. **2,** (open to all) de dominio público. **3,** (patented) patentado. —*n.* patente. —*v.t.* patentar. —**patent leather,** charol. —**patent medicine,** medicina o medicamento de patente.

paternal (pə'tʌr·nəl) *adj.* **1,** (fatherly) paternal. **2,** (inherited) paterno.

paternalism (pə'tʌr·nə·lɪz·əm) *n.* paternalismo. —**paternalistic,** *adj.* paternalista.

paternity (pə'tʌr·nə·ti) *n.* paternidad.

paternoster ('pei·tər,nas·tər) *n.* paternóster; padrenuestro.

path (pæθ) *n.* **1,** (track; trail; walk) senda; sendero; vereda; caminito. **2,** (course; trajectory) curso; trayectoria. **3,** (course of behavior or procedure) camino; senda; curso.

pathetic (pə'θet·ɪk) *adj.* patético.

pathfinder ('pæθ,fain·dər) *n.* explorador; guía; baquiano.

pathogenic (,pæθ·ə'dʒen·ɪk) *adj.* patógeno.

pathology (pə'θal·ə·dʒi) *n.* patología. —**pathological** (,pæθ·ə·'ladʒ·ɪ·kəl) *adj.* patológico. —**pathologist,** *n.* patólogo.

pathos ('pei·θas) *n.* patetismo.

pathway ('pæθ·wei) *n.* senda; sendero; vereda.

patience ('pei·ʃəns) *n.* **1,** (quality or fact of being patient) paciencia. **2,** (card game) solitario.

patient ('pei·ʃənt) *adj.* & *n.* paciente.

patina ('pæt·ə·nə) *n.* pátina.

patio ('pa·ti·o; 'pæt·i·o) *n.* patio.

patois ('pæt·wa) *n.* jerga; dialecto; patuá.

patriarch ('pei·tri·ark) *n.* patriarca. —**patriarchal,** *adj.* patriarcal. —**patriarchate** (-,ar·kɪt) *n.* patriarcado. —**patriarchy,** *n.* patriarcado.

patrician (pə'trɪʃ·ən) *n.* & *adj.* patricio.

patricide ('pæt·rə,said) *n.* **1,** (agent) parricida. **2,** (act) parricidio. —**patricidal** (-'sai·dəl) *adj.* parricida.

patrimony ('pæt·rə,mo·ni) *n.* patrimonio. —**patrimonial** (-'mo·ni·əl) *adj.* patrimonial.

patriot ('pei·tri·ət) *n.* patriota. —**patriotic** (-'at·ɪk) *adj.* patriótico. —**patriotism,** *n.* patriotismo.

patrol (pə'troːl) *v.t.* & *i.* patrullar. —*n.* **1,** (group patrolling) patrulla. **2,** (act of patrolling) patrullaje. —**patroller,** *n.* patrullero. —**patrol boat, car** *or* **plane,** patrullero. —**patrol wagon,** camión de policía; coche celular.

patrolman (pə'trol·mən) *n.* [*pl.* **-men**] agente de policía; policía; guardia municipal.

patron ('pei·trən) *n.* **1,** (protector) protector; patrono. **2,** (sponsor; advocate) patrocinador; patrón. **3,** (customer) cliente. **4,** (patron saint) patrón; patrono. —**patroness,** *n.* patrocinadora; protectora; patrona.

patronage ('pei·trən·ɪdʒ) *n.* **1,** (status or function of a patron) patronato. **2,** (sponsorship) patrocinio. **3,** (condescension) condescendencia. **4,** (clientele) clientela.

patronal ('pei·trən·əl) *adj.* patronal.

patronize ('pei·trə,naiz) *v.t.* **1,** (sponsor; support) patrocinar. **2,** (treat with condescension) mostrarse condescendiente con; tratar o mirar con condescendencia. **3,** (be a regular customer of) ser cliente de; ser parroquiano (asiduo) de. —**patronizing,** *adj.* condescendiente.

patronymic (,pæt·rə'nɪm·ɪk) *adj.* & *n.* patronímico.

patter ('pæt·ər) *v.i.* **1,** (tap) golpetear; tamborilear; repiquetear. **2,** (walk with a tapping sound) caminar con pasito ligero; caminar golpeteando; traquetear. —*v.t.* & *i.* (recite mechanically) recitar mecánicamente; barbotear. —*n.* **1,**

(tapping noise) golpeteo; tamborileo; repiqueteo. **2,** (chatter) charla; parloteo. **3,** (jargon) jerga; jerigonza.

pattern ('pæt·ərn) *n.* **1,** (design) dibujo; diseño. **2,** (model; guide) modelo; patrón. **3,** (arrangement; distribution) arreglo; distribución; configuración. **4,** (norm) pauta; norma. —*v.t.* modelar. —**pattern oneself after,** imitar; modelarse de acuerdo a.

patty ('pæt·i) *n.* pastelillo; empanada; croqueta; torta.

paucity ('pɔ·sə·ti) *n.* parquedad; escasez.

paunch (pɔntʃ) *n.* panza; vientre; barriga. —**paunchy,** *adj.* panzón; barrigón.

pauper ('pɔ·pər) *n.* pobre; indigente; necesitado. —**pauperism,** *n.* pauperismo. —**pauperize,** *v.t.* empobrecer.

pause (pɔːz) *n.* pausa. —*v.i.* hacer pausa; pausar.

pave (peiv) *v.t.* pavimentar. —**pave the way,** allanar el camino.

pavement ('peiv·mənt) *n.* pavimento.

pavilion (pə'vɪl·jən) *n.* pabellón.

paving ('pei·vɪŋ) *n.* **1,** = **pavement. 2,** (act or work of one who paves) pavimentación.

paw (pɔː) *n.* pata; mano o pie de un animal. —*v.t.* **1,** (strike with the paws) manotear. **2,** (handle; stroke) manosear. —*v.i.* piafar.

pawl (pɔl) *n.* trinquete.

pawn (pɔn) *n.* **1,** (chess piece) peón. **2,** (pledge) prenda. —*v.t.* empeñar.

pawnbroker ('pɔn,bro·kər) *n.* prestamista.

pawnshop ('pɔn,ʃap) *n.* casa de empeño; casa de préstamos; monte de piedad.

pay (pei) *v.t. & i.* [*pret. & p.p.* **paid**] **1,** give, as in return; repay) pagar. **2,** (give satisfaction to; be profitable to) convenir (a); ser provechoso (a). **3,** (cover or treat with pitch) embrear. —*n.* paga. —**in the pay of,** al servicio de. —**pay as you go,** pagar a medida que se va comprando. —**pay attention,** poner o prestar atención. —**pay back,** devolver; pagar de vuelta. —**pay down,** pagar al contado. —**pay off, 1,** (discharge a debt) pagar lo debido; pagar en total. **2,** (take revenge on or for)

vengarse de. **3,** (succeed; return a profit) dar resultados; tener éxito. —**pay one's way,** pagar lo que a uno le toca. —**pay out, 1,** (expend) pagar. **2,** (let out, as a rope) soltar; aflojar; dar. —**pay up,** pagar; pagar en total.

payable ('pei·ə·bəl) *adj.* pagadero; por pagar. —*n.* cuenta por pagar.

payday ('pei,dei) *n.* día de paga.

pay dirt terreno o mineral explotable.

payee (pei'iː) *n.* portador; tenedor.

payer ('pei·ər) *n.* pagador.

payload ('pei,lod) *n.* carga útil.

paymaster ('pei,mæs·tər) *n.* pagador. —**paymaster's office,** pagaduría.

payment ('pei·mənt) *n.* **1,** (act of paying; amount paid) pago. **2,** (installment) plazo.

payoff ('pei·ɔf) *n.* **1,** (payment) paga. **2,** (result) éxito; resultado.

payroll ('pei·rol) *n.* **1,** (list) nómina. **2,** (money) paga.

pea (piː) *n.* guisante; *Amer.* arveja.

peace (pis) *n.* paz. —*interj.* ¡paz!; ¡silencio! —**peaceable,** *adj.* pacífico; apacible. —**peaceful,** *adj.* tranquilo; pacífico. —**at peace,** en paz. —**hold** (o **keep**) **one's peace,** mantenerse sereno; quedarse tranquilo. —**keep the peace,** mantener el orden. —**make one's peace with,** hacer las paces con. —**make peace,** hacer las paces.

peacemaker ('pis,mei·kər) *n.* pacificador [*fem.* -dora]. —**peace-making,** *adj.* pacificador.

peace officer guardián del orden público; guardia municipal.

peacetime ('pis,taim) *n.* período de paz; tiempos de paz.

peach (pitʃ) *n.* **1,** (fruit) melocotón; durazno. **2,** (tree) melocotonero; durazno; duraznero. **3,** (color) color de melocotón; color durazno. **4,** *slang* (charming person or thing) encanto; preciosidad. —*v.i., slang* cantar. —**peach on,** *slang* denunciar; delatar.

peachy ('pi·tʃi) *adj.* **1,** (peachlike) como o de melocotón o durazno. **2,** *slang* (excellent) estupendo; precioso.

peacock ('pi,kak) *n.* pavo real. —**peahen** ('pi,hɛn) *n.* pava real.

peak (pik) *n.* **1,** (pointed end) punta; pico. **2,** (crest; summit) cúspide; cima; cumbre. **3,** (mountain) pico; montaña. **4,** (maximum) máximo. **5,** (highest point or degree) cumbre; apogeo; pináculo. —*v.i.* extenuarse; consumirse; enflaquecer.

peaked (pikt) *adj.* **1,** (pointed) puntiagudo. **2,** ('pik·ɪd) *colloq.* (sickly; emaciated) demacrado; pálido; enfermizo.

peal (piːl) *n.* **1,** (loud noise) estruendo; estrépito; fragor. **2,** (ringing of a bell or bells) repique; repiqueteo. —*v.i.* & *t.* resonar; repicar. —**peal of laughter,** carcajada.

peanut ('pi,nʌt) *n.* cacahuete; *Amer.* maní. —**peanut butter,** manteca de maní; crema de cacahuate.

pear (peːr) *n.* pera. —**pear tree,** peral.

pearl (pʌrl) *n.* perla. —**pearly,** *adj.* de perla; perlado.

peasant ('pɛz·ənt) *n.* campesino; rústico. —**peasantry,** *n.* campesinaje; campesinos.

peashooter ('pi,ʃu·tər) *n.* cerbatana.

peat (pit) *n.* turba. —**peat moss,** musgo pantanoso.

pebble ('pɛb·əl) *n.* guija; guijarro. —*v.t.* granular; abollonar. —**pebbled,** *adj.* guijoso; guijarroso.

pecan (pi'kaːn) *n.* **1,** (fruit) pacana. **2,** (tree) pacano.

peccadillo (,pɛk·ə'dɪl·o) *n.* pecadillo.

peccary ('pɛk·ə·ri) *n.* pecarí.

peck (pɛk) *n.* **1,** (measure) medida de áridos (9.09 litros). **2,** (nip) picotazo. **3,** *colloq.* (kiss) besito. —*v.t.* & *i.* picotear.

pectin ('pɛk·tɪn) *n.* pectina.

pectoral ('pɛk·tə·rəl) *adj.* & *n.* pectoral.

peculate ('pɛk·jə,leit) *v.t.* & *i.* malversar. —**peculation,** *n.* desfalco; malversación; peculado.

peculiar (pɪ'kjul·jər) *adj.* peculiar. —**peculiarity** (-'jær·ə·ti) *n.* peculiaridad.

pecuniary (pɪ'kju·ni·ɛr·i) *adj.* pecuniario.

pedagogue ('pɛd·ə,gag) *n.* pedagogo. —**pedagogical** (-'gadʒ·ɪ·kəl) *adj.* pedagógico. —**pedagogy** (-,go·dʒi) *n.* pedagogía.

pedal ('pɛd·əl) *adj.* del pie. —*n.* pedal. —*v.t.* & *i.* pedalear.

pedant ('pɛd·ənt) *n.* pedante. —**pedantic** (pə'dæn·tɪk) *adj.* pe-

dante; pedantesco. —**pedantry,** *n.* pedantería.

peddle ('pɛd·əl) *v.t.* vender de puerta en puerta; vender por las calles o de casa en casa. —*v.i.* vender cosas de buhonería; hacer de mercachifle. —**peddler** (-lər) *n.* buhonero; mercachifle.

pederast ('pɛd·ə,ræst) *n.* pederasta. —**pederasty,** *n.* pederastia.

pedestal ('pɛd·ɪs·təl) *n.* pedestal.

pedestrian (pə'dɛs·tri·ən) *n.* peatón. —*adj.* pedestre.

pediatrics (,pi·di'æt·rɪks) *n.* pediatría. —**pediatric,** *adj.* pediátrico. —**pediatrician** (-ə'trɪʃ·ən) *n.* pediatra; especialista de niños.

pedicure ('pɛd·ə,kjur) *n.* **1,** (treatment) pedicura. **2,** (practitioner) pedicuro [*fem.* -cura].

pedigree ('pɛd·ə,gri) *n.* ascendencia; genealogía; linaje. —**pedigreed,** *adj.* de pura raza.

pediment ('pɛd·ə·mənt) *n.* frontón.

pedometer (pɪ'dam·ə·tər) *n.* podómetro; cuentapasos.

peek (pik) *v.i.* mirar a hurtadillas; atisbar. —*n.* mirada furtiva. —**peekaboo** (-ə'bu) *n.* juego infantil de escondite. —*adj.* transparente.

peel (piːl) *v.t.* **1,** (pare, as a fruit) pelar; mondar; descascarar. **2,** (cut off, as the rind, skin, etc.) quitar la cáscara, el hollejo, etc.). **3,** (unstick) despegar. —*v.i.* **1,** (shed skin, as when sunburnt) despellejarse; pelarse. **2,** (come off, as old paint) descascararse. **3,** *colloq.* (undress) desnudarse. —*n.* cáscara. —**peelings,** *n.pl.* cáscaras; mondaduras.

peen (piːn) *n.* punta o cabeza del martillo.

peep (pip) *v.i.* **1,** (appear) asomar; empezar a mostrarse. **2,** (peek) atisbar. **3,** (chirp) gorjear. —*n.* **1,** (look) mirada furtiva o rápida. **2,** (glimpse) vistazo. **3,** (bird cry) pío; gorjeo.

peephole ('pip,hol) *n.* atisbadero; rendija; portillo.

peer (pir) *n.* **1,** (equal) igual; par. **2,** (nobleman) par; grande. —*v.i.* **1,** (look closely) escrutar con la mirada; mirar. **2,** (come partly into sight) asomar. —**peer pressure,** influencia de los coetáneos.

peerage ('pɪr·ɪdʒ) *n.* **1,** (rank) dignidad de par. **2,** (peers collectively) pares; nobleza. 3, (list of peers) guía de la nobleza.

peeress ('pɪr·ɪs) *n.f.* paresa.

peerless ('pɪr·ləs) *adj.* sin par; incomparable.

peeve (pi:v) *v.t., colloq.* enfadar; enojar. —*v.i. colloq.* enfadarse; enojarse. —*n., colloq.* enfado; enojo.

peevish ('pi·vɪʃ) *adj.* 1, (fretful; irritable) irritable; enojadizo. 2, (illtempered) malhumorado; impaciente. —**peevishness,** *n.* mal humor.

peewee ('pi,wi) *n.* 1, (runt) chiquitín. 2, (small marble) bolita.

peg (pɛg) *n.* 1, (pin; small bolt) clavija; estaca; estaquilla; claveta. 2, (step; degree) escalón; grado. —*v.t.* 1, (fasten with pegs) clavar; sujetar con estacas. 2, (mark with pegs) estacar; marcar con estacas. 3, (fix the price of) fijar; fijar el precio de; estabilizar. —**a peg to hang (something) on,** excusa para; pretexto para; ocasión para. —**peg leg,** pata de palo. —**take (someone) down a peg,** cortarle a uno las alas; quitarle a uno las ínfulas.

peignoir (pen'wa:r) *n.* peinador; bata.

pejorative (pɪ'dʒɔr·ə·tɪv) *adj.* peyorativo; despectivo.

pelagic (pə'lædʒ·ɪk) *adj.* pelágico.

pelf (pɛlf) *n.* vil parné; dinero ruin.

pelican ('pɛl·ə·kən) *n.* pelícano; alcatraz.

pelisse (pə'lis) *n.* pelliza.

pellagra (pə'lei·grə) *n.* pelagra.

pellet ('pɛl·ɪt) *n.* 1, (small round ball) pelotilla; bolita. 2, (pill) píldora. 3, (lead shot) perdigón. 4, (bullet) bala; plomo.

pellicle ('pɛl·ə·kəl) *n.* película; membrana.

pell-mell ('pɛl'mɛl) *adv.* confusamente; atropelladamente; a trochemoche.

pelt (pɛlt) *n.* 1, (hide; fur) piel. 2, (blow) golpe. 3, (speed) velocidad. —*v.t.* 1, (throw things at; assail) acribillar; bombardear. 2, (beat heavily) golpear. 3, (throw) tirar; arrojar; lanzar. —*v.i.* 1, (strike heavily) golpear con fuerza. 2, (speed; rush) correr apresuradamente. —**pelting,** *n.* golpeo. —*adj.* furioso; violento.

pelvis ('pɛl·vɪs) *n.* pelvis. —**pelvic,** *adj.* pelviano.

pen (pɛn) *n.* 1, (enclosure) corral; redil; jaula. 2, (writing implement) pluma. —*v.t.* 1, (enclose) enjaular;

encerrar. 2, (write) escribir; componer. —**fountain pen,** estilográfica. —**pen name,** seudónimo.

penal ('pi·nəl) *adj.* penal. —**penalize,** *v.t.* penalizar; castigar.

penalty ('pɛn·əl·ti) *n.* 1, (punishment) pena; penalidad. 2, (fine) multa. 3, (late charge) recargo. 4, *sports* sanción.

penance ('pɛn·əns) *n.* penitencia.

pence (pɛns) *n.pl.* centavos; peniques.

penchant ('pɛn·tʃənt) *n.* inclinación; gusto; afición.

pencil ('pɛn·səl) *n.* lápiz. —*v.t.* 1, (draw or write with a pencil) trazar con lápiz; escribir con lápiz. 2, (use a pencil on) pasar el lápiz sobre; recalcar con lápiz. —**pencil sharpener,** sacapuntas; cortalápiz.

pend (pɛnd) *v.i.* 1, (hang) colgar; pender. 2, (await settlement) estar pendiente; estar suspendido.

pendant ('pɛn·dənt) *n.* 1, (ornament) pendiente; adorno. 2, (chandelier) araña de luces.

pendent ('pɛn·dɛnt) *adj.* 1, (hanging) colgado; colgante; suspendido. 2, = **pending.** —*n.m.* = **pendant.**

pending ('pɛn·dɪŋ) *adj.* pendiente; indeciso; suspenso. —*prep.* 1, (awaiting) en espera de. 2, (during) durante.

pendulous ('pɛn·dʒə·ləs) *adj.* pendiente; colgante; péndulo.

pendulum ('pɛn·dʒə·ləm) *n.* péndulo.

penetrate ('pɛn·ɪ,treit) *v.t. & i.* penetrar. —**penetrable,** *adj.* penetrable. —**penetrating,** *adj.* penetrante. —**penetration,** *n.* penetración.

penguin ('pɛŋ·gwɪn) *n.* pingüino.

penholder ('pɛn,hol·dər) *n.* portaplumas; *Amer.* plumero.

penicillin (,pɛn·ə'sɪl·ən) *n.* penicilina.

peninsula (pə'nɪn·sə·lə) *n.* península. —**peninsular,** *adj.* peninsular.

penis ('pi·nɪs) *n.* pene.

penitence ('pɛn·ə·təns) *n.* penitencia.

penitent ('pɛn·ə·tənt) *adj.* penitente; arrepentido; contrito. —*n.* penitente. —**penitential** (-'tɛn·ʃəl) *adj.* penitencial.

penitentiary (,pɛn·ə'tɛn·ʃə·ri) *n.* penitenciaria. —*adj.* penitenciario.

penknife ('pɛn,naif) *n.* cortaplumas.

penman ('pɛn·mən) *n.* [*pl.* **-men**] pendolista; calígrafo. —**penman-ship,** *n.* escritura; caligrafía.

pennant ('pɛn·ənt) *n.* gallardete; pendón.

penny ('pɛn·i) *n.* centavo; penique. —**penniless,** *adj.* arruinado; pelado; sin un centavo.

pennyweight ('pɛn·i,weit) *n.* medida de peso de 24 granos.

penology (pi'nal·ə·dʒi) *n.* penología; ciencia penal. —**penologist,** *n.* penalista.

pension ('pɛn·ʃən) *n.* **1,** (payment) pensión; beca. **2,** (pan·si'ɒn) (boarding house) pensión de familia; casa de huéspedes. —*v.t.* pensionar; jubilar. —**pensioner** ('pɛn·ʃən·ər) *n.* pensionado; pensionista.

pensive ('pɛn·sɪv) *adj.* pensativo.

pent (pɛnt) *adj.* acorralado; encerrado; enjaulado.

pentagon ('pɛn·tə·gan) *n.* pentágono. —**pentagonal** (pɛn'tæg·ə·nəl) *adj.* pentagonal.

pentahedron (,pɛn·tə'hi·drən) *n.* pentaedro.

pentameter (pɛn'tæm·ə·tər) *n.* pentámetro.

Pentateuch ('pɛn·tə,tjuk) *n.* Pentateuco.

pentathlon (pɛn'tæθ·lən) *n.* pentatlón.

Pentecost ('pɛn·tə,kɒst) *n.* Pentecostés. —**Pentecostal** (-'kɒs·təl) *adj.* & *n.* pentecostal.

penthouse ('pɛnt,haus) *n.* **1,** (roof house or apartment) apartamento o casa de azotea. **2,** (annex; pavilion) pabellón; anexo. **3,** (outbuilding) colgadizo.

Pentothal ('pɛn·tə,θɒl) *n.*, *T.N.* pentotal.

pent-up ('pɛnt,ʌp) *adj.* contenido; reprimido.

penult ('pi·nʌlt) *n.* penúltima (sílaba).

penultimate (pɪ'nʌl·tɪ·mət) *adj.* penúltimo.

penumbra (pɪ'nʌm·brə) *n.* penumbra. —**penumbral,** *adj.* penumbroso; de penumbra.

penurious (pə'njʊr·i·əs) *adj.* tacaño; ruin; avaro. —**penurious-ness,** *n.* tacañería; ruindad.

penury ('pɛn·jə·ri) *n.* penuria; miseria; pobreza.

peon ('pi·an) *n.* peón. —**peonage** (-ən·ɪdʒ) *n.* peonaje.

peony ('pi·ə·ni) *n.* peonía.

people ('pi·pəl) *n.* **1,** (group; tribe; nation) pueblo; gente. **2,** *pl.* (populace) pueblo; masas; gente. **3,** *pl.*, *colloq.* (persons) personas; gente. —*v.t.* poblar.

pep (pɛp) *n.*, *slang* energía; vigor; fuerza. —*v.t.* [*también*, **pep up**] estimular; animar. —**peppy,** *adj.*, *slang* enérgico; vigoroso; animado. —**pep talk,** exhortación; estímulo.

pepper ('pɛp·ər) *n.* **1,** (spice) pimienta. **2,** (plant) pimentero. —*v.t.* **1,** (season) rociar con pimienta o ají. **2,** (riddle) acribillar. **3,** (dot; sprinkle) salpicar; motear. —**red pepper,** pimiento; ají; *(when ground)* pimentón.

pepper-and-salt *adj.* entrecano.

peppercorn ('pɛp·ər,kɔrn) *n.* grano de pimienta.

peppermint ('pɛp·ər,mɪnt) *n.* **1,** (plant) hierbabuena; menta. **2,** (candy) pastilla de menta.

peppery ('pɛp·ə·ri) *adj.* **1,** (spicy) picante. **2,** (hot-tempered) irascible.

pepsin ('pɛp·sɪn) *n.* pepsina.

peptic ('pɛp·tɪk) *adj.* péptico.

peptide ('pɛp·taid) *n.* péptido.

peptone ('pɛp·ton) *n.* peptona.

per (pʌr) *prep.* **1,** (by means of; through) por; por medio de. **2,** (for each) por; por cada. —**as per,** de acuerdo a.

peradventure (,pʌr·æd'vɛn·tʃər) *adv.* quizás; acaso; por ventura; por casualidad.

perambulate (pər'æm·bjə,leit) *v.i.* ambular; pasear.

perambulator (pər'æm·bjə,lei·tər) *n.* **1,** (promenader) paseante. **2,** (baby carriage) cochecillo de niño.

per annum (pər'æn·əm) *adv.* anualmente; cada año; al año.

percale (pər'keil) *n.* percal.

per capita (pər'kæp·ə·tə) *adv.* por cabeza; por personas.

perceive (pər'siːv) *v.t.* percibir. —**perceivable,** *adj.* perceptible.

percent (pər'sɛnt) *n.* por ciento. —**percentage,** *n.* porcentaje. —**percentile** (-tail; -tɪl) *n.* percentil.

perceptible (pər'sɛp·tə·bəl) *adj.* perceptible. —**perceptibility,** *n.* perceptibilidad.

perception (pər'sɛp·ʃən) *n.* percepción.

perceptive (pər'sɛp·tɪv) *adj.* perceptivo. —**perceptivity,** (,pʌr·sɛp'tɪv·ə·ti) *n.* agudeza; perceptibilidad.

perch (pʌrtʃ) *n.* **1,** (fish) perca. **2,**

(land measure) pértica. **3,** (roost)
percha. —*v.i.* **1,** (alight) posarse;
pararse. **2,** (roost) encaramarse;
estar encaramado. —*v.t.* encaramar.
perchance (pər'tʃæns) *adv.* quizás;
tal vez.
percipient (pər'sɪp·i·ənt) *adj.*
perceptivo; observador.
percolate ('pʌr·kə,leit) *v.t.* colar;
filtrar; pasar. —*v.i.* pasarse; filtrarse; rezumar. —**percolation,** *n.*
filtración. —**percolator,** *n.* colador;
cafetera filtradora.
percussion (pər'kʌʃ·ən) *n.*
percusión. —**percussion cap,**
fulminante. —**percussion instrument,** instrumento de percusión.
per diem (pər'di·əm) *adv.* por día.
—*n.* sustento diario.
perdition (pər'dɪʃ·ən) *n.* perdición.
peregrination (,per·ə·grə'neiʃən) *n.* peregrinación.
peregrine ('per·ə·grin; -grɪn) *adj.*
errante; vagabundo. —*n.,* *ornith.*
halcón peregrino.
peremptory (pə'remp·tə·ri) *adj.*
perentorio.
perennial (pə'ren·i·əl) *adj.*
perenne. —*n.* planta perenne.
perfect ('pʌr·fɪkt) *adj.* perfecto.
—*n., gram.* tiempo perfecto. —*v.t.*
(pər'fɛkt) perfeccionar. —**perfection** (pər'fɛk·ʃən) *n.* perfección.
—**perfectionist,** *n. & adj.* perfeccionista.
perfidy ('pʌr·fə·di) *n.* perfidia.
—**perfidious** (pər'fɪd·i·əs) *adj.*
pérfido.
perforate ('pʌr·fə,reit) *v.t.* perforar. —**perforation,** *n.* perforación.
—**perforator,** *n.* perforador; perforadora.
perforce (pər'fors) *adv.* por fuerza;
por necesidad.
perform (pər'form) *v.t.* **1,** (execute;
carry out) ejecutar; llevar a cabo.
2, (act out; enact) representar. **3,**
(sing) cantar. **4,** (play, as a musical
piece) tocar; ejecutar. —*v.i.* **1,**
(work; function) operar; trabajar;
funcionar. **2,** (act) ser actor;
representar; desempeñar un papel.
3, (sing) cantar. **4,** (play) tocar.
—**performer,** *n.* artista; intérprete; ejecutante; actor; actriz.
—**performing arts,** artes de representación.
performance (pər'for·məns) *n.* **1,**
(execution; accomplishment)
ejecución; desempeño. **2,** (operation; functioning) funcionamiento.

3, (acting of a role) actuación. **4,**
(show; program) representación;
función; programa; espectáculo.
perfume (pər'fjum) *n.* perfume.
—*v.t.* perfumar. —**perfumer,** *n.*
perfumista; perfumero. —**perfumery,** *n.* perfumería.
perfunctory (pər'fʌŋk·tə·ri) *adj.*
perfunctorio; de fórmula.
perhaps (pər'hæps) *adv.* quizás; tal
vez; acaso; a lo mejor.
pericardium (,per·ə'kar·di·əm) *n.*
pericardio.
pericarp ('per·ə,karp) *n.*
pericarpio.
perigee ('per·ə,dʒi) *n.* perigeo.
perihelion (,per·ə'hi·li·ən) *n.*
perihelio.
peril ('per·əl) *n.* peligro; riesgo.
—*v.t.* poner en riesgo; hacer
peligrar. —**perilous,** *adj.* peligroso;
arriesgado.
perimeter (pə'rɪm·i·tər) *n.*
perímetro.
period ('pir·i·əd) *n.* **1,** (time; epoch) período; época; tiempo. **2,** (end
of sentence) punto. **3,** (termination)
terminación; punto final. **4,** (menstruation) menstruación; período. **5,**
rhet.; music; physics período.
periodic (,pir·i'ad·ɪk) *adj.*
periódico.
periodical (,pir·i'ad·ə·kəl) *adj. &
n.* periódico.
peripatetic (,per·ə·pə'tet·ɪk) *adj.
& n.* peripatético.
periphery (pə'rɪf·ə·ri) *n.* periferia.
—**peripheral,** *adj.* periférico.
periphrasis (pə'rɪf·rə·sɪs) *n.*
perífrasis. —**periphrastic** (,per-
ə'fræs·tɪk) *adj.* perifrástico.
periscope ('per·ə,skop) *n.*
periscopio.
perish ('per·ɪʃ) *v.i.* perecer.
—**perish the thought,** ni pensarlo.
perishable ('per·ɪʃ·ə·bəl) *adj.*
perecedero. —*n.* artículo perecedero.
peristalsis (,per·ə'stæl·sɪs) *n.*
peristalsis; perístole. —**peristaltic**
(-tɪk) *adj.* peristáltico.
peristyle ('per·ə,stail) *n.* peristilo.
peritoneum (,per·ə·tə'ni·əm) *n.*
peritoneo. —**peritonitis** (-'nai·tɪs)
n. peritonitis.
periwig ('per·i·wɪg) *n.* peluca.
periwinkle ('per·ə,wɪŋ·kəl) *n.* **1,**
bot. pervinca. **2,** *zoöl.* caracol
marino; litorina.
perjure ('pʌr·dʒər) *v.t.* perjurar.
—**perjured,** *adj.* perjuro; perjurado.

—**perjurer,** *n.* perjuro. —**perjury,** *n.* perjurio. —**commit perjury,** *también,* **perjure oneself,** jurar en falso; perjurar; perjurarse.

perk (pʌrk) *v.t. & i.* [*también,* **perk up**] **1,** (raise in eagerness) levantar(se); erguir(se). **2,** (cheer) animar(se). —*n., slang* = **perquisite.** —**perky,** *adj., colloq.* vivaracho.

permanent ('pʌr·mə·nənt) *adj. & n.* permanente. —**permanence,** *n.* permanencia. —**permanent press,** planchado permanente. —**permanent wave,** ondulación permanente.

permeable ('pʌr·mi·ə·bəl) *adj.* permeable. —**permeability,** *n.* permeabilidad.

permeate ('pʌr·mi,eit) *v.t. & i.* penetrar. —**permeation,** *n.* penetración.

permissible (pər'mɪs·ə·bəl) *adj.* permisible.

permission (pər'mɪʃ·ən) *n.* permiso; permisión.

permissive (pər'mɪs·ɪv) *adj.* permisivo.

permit ('pʌr·mɪt) *n.* permiso; licencia. —*v.t.* (pər'mɪt) permitir.

permute (pər'mjut) *v.t.* permutar. —**permutation** (,pʌr·mju'tei·ʃən) *n.* permutación.

pernicious (pər'nɪʃ·əs) *adj.* pernicioso. —**perniciousness,** *n.* perniciosidad.

peroration (pɛr·ə'rei·ʃən) *n.* peroración.

peroxide (pə'rak·said) *n.* peróxido; agua oxigenada.

perpendicular (,pʌr·pən'dɪk·jə·lər) *adj. & n.* perpendicular.

perpetrate ('pʌr·pə,treit) *v.t.* perpetrar. —**perpetration,** *n.* perpetración. —**perpetrator,** *n.* perpetrador [*fem.* -dora].

perpetual (pər'pɛtʃ·u·əl) *adj.* perpetuo; continuo; eterno.

perpetuate (pər'pɛtʃ·u,eit) *v.t.* perpetuar. —**perpetuation,** *n.* perpetuación.

perpetuity (,pʌr·pə'tju·ə·ti) *n.* perpetuidad.

perplex (pər'plɛks) *v.t.* confundir; dejar perplejo. —**perplexed,** *adj.* perplejo; confuso. —**perplexing,** *adj.* incomprensible. —**perplexity,** *n.* perplejidad; confusión.

perquisite ('pʌr·kwɪ·zɪt) *n.* propina; adehala.

per se (pər'si; -'sei) en o por sí mismo.

persecute ('pʌr·sɪ,kjut) *v.t.* perseguir. —**persecution** (-'kju·ʃən) *n.* persecución. —**persecutor,** *n.* perseguidor.

persevere (,pʌr·sə'vɪr) *v.i.* perseverar. —**perseverance,** *n.* perseverancia. —**persevering,** *adj.* perseverante.

Persian ('pʌr·ʒən) *adj.* persa; pérsico. —*n.* persa.

persiflage ('pʌr·sɪ,flaʒ) *n.* **1,** (lightness; frivolousness) ligereza; frivolidad. **2,** (banter) chanzas.

persimmon (pər'sɪm·ən) *n.* dióspiro; caqui; placaminero.

persist (pər'zɪst) *v.i.* persistir. —**persistence,** *n.* persistencia. —**persistent,** *adj.* persistente.

person ('pʌr·sən) *n.* persona.

personable ('pʌr·sən·ə·bəl) *adj.* presentable; bien parecido.

personage ('pʌr·sən·ɪdʒ) *n.* personaje.

personal ('pʌr·sən·əl) *adj.* personal. —**get personal,** *colloq.* hacer alusiones personales. —**make a personal appearance,** aparecer personalmente.

personality (,pʌr·sə'næl·ə·ti) *n.* **1,** (personal identity or character) personalidad. **2,** *colloq.* (personal charm) atracción; gracia. **3,** *pl.* (personal remarks) alusiones personales.

personalize ('pʌr·sə·nə,laɪz) *v.t.* personalizar.

personalty ('pʌr·sə·nəl·ti) *n.* bienes muebles; propiedad personal.

personify (pər'san·ə·fai) *v.t.* personificar. —**personification** (-fɪ'kei·ʃən) *n.* personificación.

personnel (,pʌr·sə'nɛl) *n.* personal; empleados.

perspective (pər'spɛk·tɪv) *n.* perspectiva.

perspicacious (,pʌr·spə'kei·ʃəs) *adj.* perspicaz. —**perspicacity** (-'kæs·ə·ti) *n.* perspicacia.

perspicuous (pər'spɪk·ju·əs) *adj.* perspicuo. —**perspicuity** (,pʌr·spɪ'kju·ə·ti) *n.* perspicuidad.

perspire (pər'spair) *v.t. & i.* sudar; transpirar. —**perspiration** (,pʌr·spɪ'rei·ʃən) *n.* sudor; transpiración. —**perspiratory** (-ə,tor·i) *adj.* sudorífico.

persuade (pər'sweid) *v.t.* persuadir. —**persuadable,** *adj.* persuasible. —**persuader,** *n.* persuadidor [*fem.* -dora]. —**persuading,** *adj.* persuadidor.

persuasible (pər'swei·sə·bəl) *adj.* persuasible.

persuasion (pər'swei·ʒən) *n.* persuasión.

persuasive (pər'swei·sɪv) *adj.* persuasivo. —**persuasiveness,** *n.* persuasiva.

pert (pʌrt) *adj.* **1,** (lively) vivaracho. **2,** (impudent) atrevido; descarado.

pertain (pər'tein) *v.i.* pertenecer.

pertinacious (ˌpʌr·tɪ'nei·ʃəs) *adj.* pertinaz. —**pertinacity** (-'næs·ə·ti) *n.* pertinacia.

pertinent ('pʌr·tə·nənt) *adj.* pertinente. —**pertinence,** *n.* pertinencia.

perturb (pər'tʌrb) *v.t.* perturbar. —**perturbation** (ˌpʌr·tər'bei·ʃən) *n.* perturbación.

peruke (pə'ruk) *n.* peluca.

peruse (pə'ruːz) *v.t.* examinar; leer atentamente. —**perusal,** *n.* lectura detenida; examen detenido.

Peruvian (pə'ru·vi·ən) *adj. & n.* peruano; peruviano.

pervade (pər'veid) *v.t.* difundirse por; extenderse por; penetrar. —**pervasion** (-'vei·ʒən) *n.* penetración; difusión. —**pervasive** (-'vei·sɪv) *adj.* penetrante.

perverse (pər'vʌrs) *adj.* perverso; depravado; avieso. —**perverseness; perversity,** *n.* perversidad.

perversion (pər'vʌr·ʒən) *n.* perversión.

pervert (pər'vʌrt) *v.t.* pervertir. —*n.* ('pʌr·vʌrt) pervertido.

peseta (pə'sei·tə) *n.* peseta.

pesky ('pɛs·ki) *adj., colloq.* molesto; enfadoso.

peso ('pei·so) *n.* peso.

pessary ('pɛs·ə·ri) *n.* pesario.

pessimism ('pɛs·ə·mɪz·əm) *n.* pesimismo. —**pessimist,** *n.* pesimista. —**pessimistic,** *adj.* pesimista.

pest (pɛst) *n.* **1,** = **pestilence. 2,** (annoying person or thing) pelmazo; cataplasma.

pester ('pɛs·tər) *v.t.* molestar; cansar; importunar.

pesticide ('pɛs·tə,said) *n.* pesticida.

pestiferous (pɛs'tɪf·ər·əs) *adj.* pestífero.

pestilence ('pɛs·tə·ləns) *n.* pestilencia; peste. —**pestilential** (-'lɛn·ʃəl) *adj.* pestilente; pestilencial.

pestilent ('pɛs·tə·lənt) *adj.* pestilente.

pestle ('pɛs·əl) *n.* majador; mano de mortero.

pet (pɛt) *n.* **1,** (animal) animal casero o de la casa. **2,** (favorite) favorito. **3,** (peevishness) mal humor; enfado. —*adj.* **1,** (loved) acariciado; mimado. **2,** (favorite) favorito; preferido; querido. —*v.t.* mimar; acariciar. —*v.i., colloq.* besuquearse. —**be in a pet,** estar enfadado. —**pet name,** apodo cariñoso.

petal ('pɛt·əl) *n.* pétalo.

petard (pɪ'tard) *n.* petardo.

petcock ('pɛt,kak) *n.* llave o válvula de escape; espita.

peter ('pi·tər) *v.i.* [también, **peter out**] *colloq.* agotarse; acabarse.

petiole ('pɛt·i,ol) *n.* pecíolo.

petite (pə'tit) *adj. fem.* pequeña; chiquita.

petit jury ('pɛt·i) jurado; jurado de juicio.

petition (pə'tɪʃ·ən) *n.* petición. —*v.t.* solicitar; pedir; hacer petición a. —**petitioner,** *n.* peticionario; solicitante.

petitionary (pə'tɪʃ·ə,nɛr·i) *adj.* petitorio.

petrel ('pɛt·rəl) *n.* petrel; patín.

petrify ('pɛt·rə·fai) *v.t.* petrificar. —*v.i.* petrificarse. —**petrification** (-fɪ'kei·ʃən) *n.* petrificación.

petrochemistry ('pɛt·ro'kɛm·ɪs·tri) *n.* petroquímica. —**petrochemical,** *adj.* petroquímico.

petrography (pɪ'trag·rə·fi) *n.* petrografía. —**petrographic** (ˌpɛt·rə'græf·ɪk) *adj.* petrográfico.

petrol ('pɛt·rəl) *n., Brit.* gasolina.

petroleum (pə'tro·li·əm) *n.* petróleo. —*adj.* petrolero; de petróleo.

petrous ('pɛt·rəs) *adj.* **1,** (of or like rock) pétreo. **2,** *anat.* petroso.

petticoat ('pɛt·i,kot) *n.* **1,** (skirt) saya; falda. **2,** (underskirt) enaguas.

pettifogger ('pɛt·i,fag·ər) *n.* trapacero; *Amer.* picapleitos; *Amer.* tinterillo. —**pettifoggery,** *n.* trapacería.

pettish ('pɛt·ɪʃ) *adj.* áspero; enojadizo; malhumorado. —**pettishness,** *n.* berrinche; mal humor.

petty ('pɛt·i) *adj.* **1,** (trivial) trivial; insignificante; sin importancia. **2,** (small) pequeño; menor. **3,** (mean) mezquino; estrecho de miras. **4,** *law* menor; de menor cuantía. —**pettiness,** *n.* pequeñez; insignificancia. —**petty cash,** caja de menores.

—petty jury = petit jury. —petty larceny, robo de menor cuantía. —petty officer, suboficial.

petulant ('pɛtʃ·ə·lənt) *adj.* petulante. —**petulance**, *n.* petulancia.

petunia (pə'tju·ni·ə) *n.* petunia.

pew (pjuː) *n.* banco; asiento de iglesia. —*interj.* ¡fo! '

pewter ('pju·tər) *n.* peltre. —*adj.* de peltre.

phaeton ('fei·ə·tən) *n.* faetón.

phagocyte ('fæg·ə,sait) *n.* fagocito.

phalanx ('fei·læŋks) *n.* falange.

phallus ('fæl·əs) *n.* falo. —**phallic,** *adj.* fálico.

phantasm ('fæn·tæz·əm) *n.* espectro; fantasma.

phantasmagoria (fæn,tæs·mə'gor·i·ə) *n.* fantasmagoría. —**phantasmagoric,** *adj.* fantasmagórico.

phantasy ('fæn·tə·si) *n.* = **fantasy.**

phantom ('fæn·təm) *n.* aparición; espectro; fantasma.

Pharaoh ('feːroʊ) *n.* Faraón.

pharisee ('fær·ə,si) *n.* fariseo. —**pharisaic** (-'sei·ɪk) *adj.* farisaico.

pharmaceutical (,far·mə'su·tɪ·kəl) *adj.* farmacéutico.

pharmacist ('far·mə,sɪst) *n.* farmacéutico.

pharmacology (,far·mə'kal·ə·dʒi) *n.* farmacología. —**pharmacological** (-kə'ladʒ·ɪ·kəl) *adj.* farmacológico. —**pharmacologist,** *n.* farmacólogo.

pharmacopeia (,far·mə'ko·pi·ə) *n.f.* farmacopea.

pharmacy ('far·mə·si) *n.* 1, (science of drugs) farmacia; farmacopea. 2, (drugstore) farmacia; botica.

pharyngeal (fə'rɪn·dʒi·əl) *adj.* faríngeo.

pharyngitis (,fær·ɪn'dʒai·tɪs) *n.* faringitis.

pharynx ('fær·ɪŋks) *n.* faringe.

phase (feiz) *n.* fase. —**phase out,** eliminar poco a poco.

pheasant ('fɛz·ənt) *n.* faisán.

phenobarbital (,fi·no'bar·bɪ,tɔl) *n.* fenobárbito.

phenol ('fi·nal) *n.* fenol.

phenomenon (fɪ'nam·ə,nan) *n.* [*pl.* -na (-nə) o -nons] fenómeno. —**phenomenal,** *adj.* fenomenal.

phew! (fju) *interj.* ¡fo!

phial ('fai·əl) *n.* = **vial.**

philander (fɪ'læn·dər) *v.i.* galantear; hacer de tenorio. —*n.* amante.

—**philanderer,** *n.* galanteador; tenorio.

philanthropy (fɪ'læn·θrə·pi) *n.* filantropía. —**philanthropic** (,fɪl·ən'θrap·ɪk) *adj.* filantrópico. —**philanthropist,** *n.* filántropo.

philately (fɪ'læt·ə·li) *n.* filatelia. —**philatelic** (,fɪl·ə'tɛl·ɪk) *adj.* filatélico. —**philatelist,** *n.* filatelista.

philharmonic (,fɪl·har'man·ɪk) *adj.* filarmónico.

Philippine ('fɪl·ə,pin) *adj. & n.* filipino.

Philistine (fɪ'lɪs·tin) *n. & adj.* filisteo.

philology (fɪ'lal·ə·dʒi) *n.* filología. —**philological** (,fɪl·ə'ladʒ·ɪ·kəl) *adj.* filológico. —**philologist,** *n.* filólogo.

philosopher (fɪ'las·ə·fər) *n.* filósofo. —**philosophic** (,fɪl·ə'saf·ɪk); **philosophical** (,fɪl·ə'saf·ɪk·əl) *adj.* filosófico. —**philosophize,** *v.i.* filosofar. —**philosophy,** *n.* filosofía.

philter *también,* **philtre** ('fɪl·tər) *n.* filtro.

phlebitis (flɪ'bai·tɪs) *n.* flebitis.

phlegm (flɛm) *n.* flema. —**phlegmatic** (flɛg'mæt·ɪk) *adj.* flemático.

phlox (flaks) *n.* flox.

phobia ('fo·bi·ə) *n.* fobia.

phoebe ('fi·bi) *n.* **1,** *ornith.* aguador. **2,** *cap., myth.; poet.* Febe.

Phoenician (fə'niʃ·ən) *adj. & n.* fenicio.

phoenix ('fi·nɪks) *n.* fénix.

phone (foːn) *n.* **1,** *colloq.* teléfono. **2,** (speech sound) fon.

phoneme ('fo·nim) *n.* fonema. —**phonemic** (-'ni·mɪk) *adj.* fonémico. —**phonemics,** *n.* fonémica.

phonetic (fo'nɛt·ɪk) *adj.* fonético. —**phonetics,** *n.* fonética.

phonic ('fan·ɪk) *adj.* fónico. —**phonics,** *n.sing. & pl.* fónica; sistema fónico.

phonograph ('fo·nə·græf) *n.* fonógrafo. —**phonographic** (-'græf·ɪk) *adj.* fonográfico. —**phonograph record,** disco.

phony *también,* **phoney** ('fo·ni) *adj., slang* engañado; espúreo; falso. —*n., slang* **1,** (thing or action) engaño; estafa; farsa. **2,** (person) engañador; estafador; farsante.

phooey ('fu·i) *interj.* ¡puf!

phosphate ('fas·feit) *n.* fosfato; sal fosfática o fosfórica.

phosphor ('fas·fər) *n.* materia fosforescente.

phosphorescence (,fas·fə'res· əns) *n.* fosforescencia. —**phospho- rescent,** *adj.* fosforescente.

phosphorus ('fas·fə·rəs) *n.* fósforo.

photo ('fo·to) *n.* foto; fotografía.

photocopy ('fo·to,kap·i) *n.* fotoco- pia. —*v.t.* fotocopiar.

photoelectric (,fo·to·i'lɛk·trɪk) *adj.* fotoeléctrico.

photoengrave (,fo·to·ɛn'greiv) *v.t.* fotograbar. —**photoengraving,** *n.* fotograbado.

photogenic (,fo·tə'dʒɛn·ɪk) *adj.* fotogénico.

photograph ('fo·tə,græf) *n.* fotografía. —*v.t.* & *i* fotografiar. —**photographer** (fə'tag·rə·fər) *n.* fotógrafo. —**photographic** (-'græf· ɪk) *adj.* fotográfico. —**photography** (fə'tag·rə·fi) *n.* fotografía.

photogravure (,fo·tə·grə'vjʊr) *n.* fotograbado.

photometer (fo'tam·ə·tər) *n.* fotómetro.

photon ('fo·tan) *n.* fotón.

photo-offset *n.* litografía foto- gráfica.

photoplay ('fo·to,plei) *n.* drama cinematográfico; película.

photosensitive (,fo·to'sɛn·sɪ·tɪv) *adj.* fotosensible.

photosphere ('fo·to,sfɪr) *n.* fotos- fera.

photostat ('fo·tə,stæt) *n.* fotóstato; copia negativa. —*v.t.* & *i.* fotostatar. —**photostatic** (-'stæt·ɪk) *adj.* fotostático.

photosynthesis (,fo·to'sɪn·θə· sɪs) *n.* fotosíntesis.

phrase (freiz) *n.* **1,** (group of words) frase. **2,** (expression) expresión; dicho. **3,** *mus.* frase mu- sical. —*v.t.* frasear; expresar. —**phrase book,** manual de conversación.

phraseology (,fre·zi'al·ə·dʒi) *n.* fraseología.

phrenetic (frɪ'nɛt·ɪk) *adj.* frenéti- co.

phrenology (frɛ'nal·ə·dʒi) *n.* frenología. —**phrenological** (,frɛn·ə'ladʒ·ɪ·kəl) *adj.* frenológico. —**phrenologist,** *n.* frenólogo.

phthisis ('θai·sɪs) *n.* tisis.

phylactery (fə'læk·tə·ri) *n.* filacteria.

phylogeny (fai'ladʒ·ə·ni) *n.* filogenia.

phylum ('fai·ləm) *n.* fílum; filo.

physic ('fɪz·ɪk) *n.* medicina;

catártico; purgante. —*v.t.* [**phys- icked, physicking**] medicinar.

physical ('fɪz·ɪ·kəl) *adj.* físico.

physician (fə'zɪʃ·ən) *n.* médico; doctor.

physics ('fɪz·ɪks) *n.* física. —**physicist** (-ɪ·sɪst) *n.* físico.

physiognomy (,fɪz·i'ag·nə·mi) *n.* fisonomía. —**physiognomic** (-əg· 'nam·ɪk) *adj.* fisonómico.

physiography (,fɪz·i'ag·rə·fi) *n.* geografía física.

physiology (,fɪz·i'al·ə·dʒi) *n.* fisiología. —**physiological** (-ə'ladʒ· ɪ·kəl) *adj.* fisiológico. —**physiologist,** *n.* fisiólogo.

physiotherapy (,fɪz·i·o'θɛr·ə·pi) *n.* fisioterapia. —**physiotherapist,** *n.* fisioterapeuta.

physique (fi'zik) *n.* físico; cuerpo.

pi (pai) *n.* **1,** (Greek letter; math.) pi. **2,** *print.* mezcla de tipos; pastel. —*v.t.* mezclar (tipos).

pianissimo (,pi·ə'nɪs·ɪ·mo) *adj.* & *adv.* pianísimo.

pianist (pi'æn·ɪst; 'pi·ə·nɪst) *n.* pianista.

piano (pi'æn·o) *n.* piano. —*adj.* & *adv.* piano. —**grand piano,** piano de cola. —**upright piano,** piano vertical o recto.

pianoforte (pi,æn·ə'for·ti; -,fort) *n.* pianoforte.

pianola (,pi·ə'no·lə) *n.* pianola.

piaster (pi'æs·tər) *n.* piastra.

piazza (pi'æz·ə) *n.* **1,** (porch; cov- ered gallery) pórtico; galería. **2,** (pi'æt·sə) (plaza) plaza.

pica ('paj·kə) *n.* cícero; tipo de doce puntos.

picador ('pɪk·ə,dor) *n.* picador.

picaresque (,pɪk·ə'rɛsk) *adj.* picaresco.

picayune (,pɪk·ə'juːn) *adj.* bajo; chico; trivial.

piccolo ('pɪk·ə,lo) *n.* flautín.

pick (pɪk) *n.* **1,** (tool) pico. **2,** (crop) cosecha. **3,** (first choice) escogimiento; derecho de selección. —*v.t.* **1,** (gather) recoger. **2,** (cleanse) mondar; limpiar. **3,** [*también,* **pick out**] (choose) seleccionar; escoger. **4,** (prick) picar. **5,** (pry open, as a lock) abrir con ganzúa. **6,** (pull apart) arrancar; separar. **7,** (provoke) provocar. **8,** [*usu.* **pick on**] (annoy) molestar; fastidiar. —*v.i.* **1,** (use a pick) picotear. **2,** (nibble) mordiscar; picotear. **3,** (select) escoger; seleccionar. —**pick a bone,** *fig.* roer un hueso. —**pick to pieces,** *fig.* criticar. —**pick the pocket of,** limpiar la faltriquera a. —**pick up, 1,** (improve) recuperarse; mejorarse. **2,** (tidy) poner en orden. **3,** (retrieve) recoger. **4,** (acquire; gain) adquirir; ganar. **5,** (lift) levantar; subir. **6,** *colloq.* (call for) buscar. **7,** (meet by chance) conocer por casualidad. —**pick up speed,** acelerar.

pickaback ('pɪk·ə,bæk) *adv.* sobre los hombros; a caballito.

pickax ('pɪk,æks) *n.* pico; azadón.

picker ('pɪk·ər) *n.* **1,** (gatherer) recogedor. **2,** (one who selects) escogedor. **3,** (weeder) escardador.

pickerel ('pɪk·ər·əl) *n.* sollo norteamericano.

picket ('pɪk·ɛt) *n.* **1,** (stake) estaca. **2,** (sentinel) centinela; escucha. **3,** (protesting person) piquete.—*v.t.* **1,** (place stakes around) cercar con estacas. **2,** (post guards) colocar de guardia. **3,** (tether) atar. **4,** (demonstrate against by picketing) poner piquetes a. —*v.i.* hacer manifestación de piquetes.

pickings ('pɪk·ɪŋz) *n.pl.* **1,** (what is gathered) recogida; cosecha. **2,** (selection) surtido; selección.

pickle ('pɪk·əl) *n.* **1,** (brine) salmuera; escabeche. **2,** (food preserved in brine) encurtido. **3,** *slang* (predicament) aprieto; enredo. —*v.t.* encurtir; escabechar. —**pickled,** *adj., slang* borracho.

pickpocket ('pɪk,pak·ɪt) *n.* ratero; cortabolsas.

pickup ('pɪk·ʌp) *n.* **1,** (gathering up; retrieving; collection) recolección; recogida. **2,** (acceleration) aceleración. **3,** (openbody truck) camión. **4,** *colloq.* (improvement) mejora. **5,** *colloq.* (chance acquaintance) persona conocida por casualidad. **6,** (of a phonograph) fonocaptor. —*adj., colloq.* remendado.

picnic ('pɪk·nɪk) *n.* jira; fiesta campestre. —*v.i.* [**picnicked, picnicking**] ir de jira; merendar en el campo. —**picnicker,** *n.* excursionista.

picric ('pɪk·rɪk) *adj.* pícrico.

pictograph ('pɪk·tə,græf) *n.* pictografía.

pictorial (pɪk'tor·i·əl) *adj.* pictórico; gráfico.

picture ('pɪk·tʃər) *n.* **1,** (illustration) cuadro; lámina. **2,** (painting) pintura. **3,** (likeness) retrato; imagen. **4,** (description) descripción; delineación verbal. **5,** *colloq.* (motion picture) película; film. —*v.t.* **1,** (depict) pintar; dibujar. **2,** (visualize) figurar; imaginar. —**picture tube,** tubo de imagen; tubo de televisión. —**picture window,** ventanal.

picturesque (,pɪk·tʃər'ɛsk) *adj.* pintoresco.

piddle ('pɪd·əl) *v.t. & i., colloq.* (dawdle; trifle) desperdiciar; perder (el tiempo). —*v.i.* (urinate) orinar (se usa con niños). —**piddler** (-lər) *n., colloq.* zángano; haragán.

piddling ('pɪd·lɪŋ) *adj.* trivial; de poca monta; de bagatela.

pidgin ('pɪdʒ·ən) *n.* lengua franca.

pie (paɪ) *n.* **1,** (baked dish) pastel; empanada. **2,** *print.* mezcla de tipos; pastel. **3,** (jumble) mescolanza. —*v.t.* mezclar (tipos).

piebald ('paɪ,bɔld) *adj.* coloreado; manchado; pinto. —*n.* animal pinto.

piece (pis) *n.* **1,** (fragment) fragmento; pedazo. **2,** (part of a whole) sección. **3,** (separate article or part) pieza. **4,** (amount of work) cantidad. **5,** (definite quantity) pieza; trozo. **6,** (literary or musical composition) obra; escrito; composición; pieza. **7,** *games* pieza. —*v.t.* **1,** (join) aumentar; juntar; unir. **2,** (patch) remendar; reparar.

piecemeal ('pis,mil) *adj.* fragmentario; en pedazos. —*adv.* a pedacitos; a bocaditos.

piecework ('pis,wʌrk) *n.* trabajo a destajo. —**pieceworker,** *n.* destajero.

pied (paɪd) *adj.* abigarrado; manchado; pintado.

pie-eyed ('paɪ,aɪd) *adj., slang* borracho.

pier (pɪr) *n.* **1,** (breakwater) malecón; rompeolas. **2,** (bridge support) estribo de puente. **3,** (masonry) pilar; pilón. **4,** (dock) embarcadero; muelle. —**pier glass,** espejo de cuerpo entero.

pierce (pɪrs) *v.t.* **1,** (penetrate) agujerear; taladrar. **2,** (stab) punzar; picar; apuñalar. **3,** (affect keenly) penetrar; afectar. —**piercing,** *adj.* agudo; penetrante. —*n.* penetración.

piety ('paɪ·ə·ti) *n.* piedad; reverencia.

piffle ('pɪf·əl) *n., slang* tontería; estupidez. —**piffling** (-lɪŋ) *adj., slang* disparatado.

pig (pɪg) *n.* **1,** (animal) cerdo; cochino; lechón; puerco. **2,** (iron bar) lingote. **3,** *colloq.* (dirty person) sucio; puerco. **4,** *slang* (police officer) perro; chota.

pigeon ('pɪdʒ·ən) *n.* paloma; palomo; pichón. —**carrier pigeon; homing pigeon,** paloma mensajera. —**passenger pigeon,** paloma emigrante. —**pouter pigeon** ('pau·tər) paloma buchona. —**wood pigeon; wild pigeon,** paloma torcaz.

pigeonhole ('pɪdʒ·ən,hol) *n.* **1,** (pigeon house) palomar. **2,** (letter compartment) casilla. —*v.t.* **1,** (file) encasillar. **2,** (put aside) ignorar; olvidar. **3,** (classify) clasificar.

pigeontoed ('pɪdʒ·ən,tod) *adj.* que tiene los pies torcidos hacia dentro.

piggish ('pɪg·ɪʃ) *adj.* **1,** (dirty) sucio; cochino; puerco. **2,** (gluttonous) glotón.

piggy ('pɪg·i) *n.* lechoncillo. —**piggyback,** *adv.* **1,** = **pickaback**. **2,** *R.R.* en vagón plataforma. —**piggy bank,** alcancía.

pigheaded ('pɪg,hɛd·ɪd) *adj.* terco; obstinado; perverso.

pig iron hierro formado en lingotes.

pig Latin modo de hablar empleando vocablos normales, retorciéndolos para ocultar su verdadero sentido; latinajo.

piglet ('pɪg·lɪt) *n.* lechoncillo.

pigment ('pɪg·mənt) *n.* pigmento. —**pigmentation** (-mən'tei·ʃən) *n.* pigmentación.

pigskin ('pɪg·skɪn) *n.* **1,** (leather) piel de cerdo. **2,** *colloq.* (football) balón.

pigsty ('pɪg,stai) *n.* pocilga.

pigtail ('pɪg,teil) *n.* coleta.

pike (paik) *n.* **1,** (weapon) pica; lanza. **2,** (fish) lucio. **3,** (highway) camino real; carretera principal.

piker ('pai·kər) *n., slang* tacaño; mezquino; cicatero.

pikestaff ('paik,stæf) *n.* [*pl.* **-staves**] asta de pica.

pilaster (pɪ'læs·tər) *n.* pilastra.

pile (pail) *n.* **1,** (soft nap) pelusa. **2,** (support) estaca; pilote. **3,** (edifice) edificio macizo. **4,** (mass) montón; pila; rimero. **5,** (pyre) pira; hoguera. **6,** *physics; elect.* pila. **7,** *slang* (fortune) fortuna; caudal. —*v.t.* **1,** (heap) apilar; amontonar. **2,** (load) cargar; echar encima. —**pile up,** amontonar(se); acumular(se).

pile driver martinete.

piles (pailz) *n.pl.* hemorroides; almorranas.

pile-up *n.* accidente que envuelve varios vehículos.

pilfer ('pɪl·fər) *v.t. & i.* ratear; hurtar. —**pilferer,** *n.* ratero; pillo. —**pilferage,** *n.* ratería.

pilgrim ('pɪl·grɪm) *n.* peregrino. —**pilgrimage,** *n.* peregrinación; peregrinaje.

pill (pɪl) *n.* **1,** (tablet) píldora; pastilla; tableta. **2,** *slang* (disagreeable person) cataplasma. **3,** *slang* (ball) pelota. —**bitter pill,** mal trago.

pillage ('pɪl·ɪdʒ) *v.t. & i.* pillar. —*n.* pillaje; saqueo.

pillar ('pɪl·ər) *n.* **1,** (column) columna; pilar. **2,** *fig.* (support; mainstay) sostén.

pillbox ('pɪl,baks) *n.* **1,** (box) caja para píldoras. **2,** *mil.* fortín redondo. **3,** (hat) sombrero redondo y chato.

pillion ('pɪl·jən) *n.* grupera.

pillory ('pɪl·ə·ri) *n.* picota. —*v.t.* **1,** (punish in a pillory) empicotar. **2,** (invoke scorn upon) avergonzar; calumniar.

pillow ('pɪl·o) *n.* **1,** (cushion) cojín; almohada. **2,** *mech.* cojinete. —*v.t.* **1,** (lay on a pillow) acostar sobre una almohada. **2,** (support as a pillow) sostener (como almohada).

pillow block *mech.* chumacera.

pillowcase ('pɪl·o,keis) *n.* funda (de almohada). *También,* **pillowslip** (-,slɪp).

pilose ('pai·los) *adj.* piloso.

pilot ('pai·lət) *n.* **1,** (helmsman; navigator) piloto. **2,** (leader) líder; guía. —*v.t.* pilotar; guiar.

pilotage ('pai·lət·ɪdʒ) *n.* pilotaje.

pilot light 1, (beacon) lámpara testigo; lámpara piloto. **2,** (stove lighter) mechero encendedor.

pimento (pɪ'mɛn·to) *n.* [*pl.* **-tos**] **1,** (tree and berry) pimienta. **2,** = **pimiento.**

pimiento (pɪ'mjɛn·to) *n.* [*pl.* **-tos**] pimiento dulce.

pimp (pɪmp) *n.* alcahuete. —*v.i.* alcahuetear.

pimpernel ('pɪm·pər,nɛl) *n.* murajes.

pimple ('pɪm·pəl) *n.* grano. —**pimply** (-pli); **pimpled,** *adj.* granujoso.

pin (pɪn) *n.* **1,** (pointed piece) alfiler; hebilla; horquilla. **2,** (brooch) broche. **3,** (safety pin) imperdible. **3,** *mech.* pasador; clavija. **4,** *bowls; bowling* bolo. **5,** *slang* (leg) pierna. —*v.t.* asegurar; clavar; fijar; sujetar. —**on pins and needles,** en espinas.

pinball ('pɪn,bɔl) *n.* juego registrado; bagatela.

pince-nez ('pæns'nei) *n.sing. & pl.* quevedos.

pincers ('pɪn·sərz) *n.sing. o pl.* **1,** (tool) pinzas; tenacillas. **2,** (claw) tenaza. **3,** *mil.* ataque de flanco.

pinch (pɪntʃ) *v.t. & i.* **1,** (nip) pinchar; pellizcar. **2,** (press hard upon) apretar; oprimir. **3,** *slang* (arrest) capturar; arrestar. **4,** *slang* (steal) robar; ratear. —*n.* **1,** (nip) pellizco. **2,** (bit) poquito; chispita; pizca. **3,** (stress) dolor; tormento; pena; angustia. **4,** *colloq.* (emergency) apuro; aprieto. **5,** *slang* (arrest) arresto; captura.

pinchers ('pɪn·tʃərz) *n.* = **pincers.**

pinch-hit *v.i.* batear por otro; *fig.* sustituir a otro. —**pinch-hitter,** *n.* bateador sustituto; *fig.* sustituto.

pincushion ('pɪn,kʊʃ·ən) *n.* alfiletero.

pine (pain) *n.* pino. —*v.i.* languidecer; morirse. —**pine for** o **after,** añorar; desear vivamente; morirse por. —**pine cone,** piña. —**pine grove,** pinar. —**pine needle,** pinocha. —**pine seed,** piñón.

pineal ('pɪn·i·əl) *adj.* pineal.

pineapple ('pain,æp·əl) *n.* ananás; piña.

piney ('pai·ni) *adj.* = **piny.**

ping (pɪŋ) *n.* silbido. —*v.i.* silbar.

ping-pong ('pɪŋ,pɑŋ) *n.* ping-pong; pinpón.

pinhead ('pɪn,hɛd) *n.* **1,** (head of a pin) cabecilla de alfiler. **2,** (dot; speck) mote; pizca. **3,** *colloq.* (dolt) estúpido; mentecato.

pinhole ('pɪn,hol) *n.* agujerito.

pinion ('pɪn·jən) *n.* **1,** *mech.* piñón. **2,** *ornith.* huesecillo final; hueso-piñón. —*v.t.* atar o cortar las alas a (un ave); refrenar; maniatar.

pink (pɪŋk) *n.* **1,** (flower) clavel. **2,** (color) rosa; rosado. **3,** *colloq.* (quasi-communist) rojo; comunistoide. **4,** *colloq.* (best condition) mejor estado. —*adj.* rosado. —*v.t.* **1,** (pierce; perforate) agujerear; ojetear; picar con calado. **2,** (adorn) adornar; festonear. **3,** (prick; stab) picar; punzar. **4,** (cut a saw-toothed edge on) ondear.

pinkeye ('pɪŋk,ai) *n.* oftalmía purulenta.

pinkie ('pɪŋ·ki) *n.* dedo meñique.

pinking ('pɪŋ·kɪŋ) *n.* **1,** (perforation) diseño de ojetes; picado; calado. **2,** (adornment) adorno. **3,** (saw-toothed edge) onda.

pin money menudo; alfileres.

pinnacle ('pɪn·ə·kəl) *n.* **1,** (peak; spire) pináculo. **2,** *fig.* (highest point) cumbre; cima.

pinnate ('pɪn·eit) *adj., bot.* pinnado; pinado.

pinochle ('pi,nʌk·əl; -,nak-) *n.* pinocle.

pinpoint ('pɪn·pɔint) *n.* **1,** (point of a pin) punta de alfiler. **2,** (precision) exactitud; precisión. —*adj.* exacto; preciso. —*v.t.* localizar exactamente; puntualizar con precisión.

pinprick ('pɪn,prɪk) *n.* alfilerazo.

pinstripe ('pɪn,straip) *n.* raya fina. —*adj.* de rayas finas.

pint (paint) *n.* pinta.

pinto ('pɪn·to) *n. & adj.* pinto.

pin-up girl sirena; muchacha atractiva; modelo.

pinwheel ('pɪn,hwil) *n.* **1,** (child's toy) molinete; molinillo. **2,** (fireworks) rueda de fuegos.

piny ('pai·ni) *adj.* pinoso.

pioneer (,pai·ə'nɪr) *n.* pionero; iniciador. —*v.t. & i.* explorar; abrir camino (en).

pious ('pai·əs) *adj.* **1,** (godly) devoto; pío. **2,** (pretending piety) piadoso. —**piousness,** *n.* piedad; devoción.

pip (pɪp) *n.* **1,** (disease) pepita. **2,** (seed) pepita; semilla; *Amer.* pepa. **3,** (spot, as on playing cards or dice) punto. **4,** *slang* (excellent thing) fenómeno.

pipe (paip) *n.* **1,** (tube for fluid) tubo. **2,** (smoking) pipa. **3,** (organ tube) tubo o cañón de órgano. **4,** (reed instrument) caramillo; pipa; flauta de Pan. **5,** *pl.* (bagpipe) gaita. **6,** (boatswain's whistle) pito; silbato. **7,** (shrill sound) silbo; silbido. —*v.t.* **1,** (convey by pipes) conducir por tubos o caños. **2,** *naut.* (salute with a pipe) saludar con el pito. **3,** (shrill) soplar. —*v.i.* **1,** (chirp) piar. **2,** (whistle) silbar; pitar. **3,** (play the pipe) flautear; tocar el pito. —**pipe down,** *slang* callarse. —**pipe up,** *slang* hablar; alzar la voz; gritar.

pipe dream vana esperanza; sueño fantástico.

pipeline ('paip,lain) **1,** (conduit) cañería. **2,** (channel, esp. of information) red secreta; fuente o vía de información.

pipe organ órgano de tubos.

piper ('pai·pər) n. flautista; gaitero. **—pay the piper,** sufrir las consecuencias.

pipette (pɪ'pɛt) n. pipeta.

piping ('pai·pɪŋ) n. **1,** (tubing) tubería; cañería. **2,** (music of pipes) música o notas de gaita, flauta, etc. **3,** (shrill sound) silbido; pitido. **4,** sewing cordoncillo. **—adj.** agudo; atiplado. **—piping hot,** muy caliente.

pipsqueak ('pɪp,skwik) n., colloq. pipiolo.

piquant ('pi·kənt) adj. picante; mordaz. **—piquancy,** n. acrimonia; picante.

pique (pik) v.t. **1,** (irritate) ofender. **2,** (interest) excitar; provocar. **—n.** resentimiento; ojeriza; ofensa; pique. **—pique oneself on** o **upon,** jactarse de.

piqué (pi'kei) n. piqué.

piquet (pɪ'kɛt) n. juego de los ciento.

piracy ('pai·rə·si) n. piratería.

piranha (pɪ'ran·ə) n. piraña.

pirate ('pai·rət) n. **1,** (sea marauder) pirata. **2,** (plagiarist) plagiario. **—v.t. 1,** (rob) robar; pillar. **2,** (plagiarize) plagiar. **—v.i.** piratear. **—adj.** pirata. **—pirated,** adj. pirata.

piratical (pai'ræt·ə·kəl) adj. pirático.

pirogue (pɪ'roːg) n. piragua.

pirouette (,pɪr·ə'wɛt) n. pirueta. **—v.i.** hacer piruetas; piruetear.

Pisces ('pɪs·iz; 'pai·siz) n. Piscis.

pisciculture ('pɪs·ə,kʌl·tʃər) n. piscicultura.

pistachio (pɪs'ta·ʃi·o) n. alfóncigo; pistacho.

pistil ('pɪs·tɪl) n. pistilo.

pistol ('pɪs·təl) n. pistola.

pistole (pɪs'tol) n. pistola.

piston ('pɪs·tən) n. émbolo; pistón. **—piston pin,** pasador del pistón. **—piston ring,** aro del pistón. **—piston rod,** biela.

pit (pɪt) n. **1,** (hole) hoyo. **2,** (depression) abismo; hueco. **3,** (well; shaft) pozo. **4,** (small arena) luneta. **5,** comm. parte de una bolsa dedicada a un solo producto. **6,** (fruit stone) hueso; pepita. **7,** (pockmark) hoyuelo. **8,** (trap) trampa. **—v.t.** **[pitted, pitting] 1,** (make holes in) marcar con hoyos. **2,** (scar) formar cicatrices en. **3,** (match against another) oponer; confrontar. **4,** (remove the pit from) deshuesar; despepitar.

pita ('pi·tə) n. pita.

pitch (pɪtʃ) v.t. **1,** (throw) tirar; lanzar. **2,** (set up) plantar. **3,** (fix the tone of) dar el tono de. **4,** (slant) inclinar. **5,** (cover or treat with tar) embrear; alquitranar. **—v.i. 1,** (fall headlong) desplomarse; caerse. **2,** (rise and fall) cabecear. **3,** (slant) inclinarse. **—n. 1,** (throw) lanzamiento. **2,** (headlong fall) desplome; caída. **3,** (plunging of a ship) cabeceo. **4,** fig. (height; extreme) grado; punto; extremo. **5,** (slope) declive. **6,** (slant) inclinación. **7,** (tone) diapasón; altura; grado del tono. **8,** (tar) brea; pez; alquitrán. **—pitch-black; pitch-dark,** tiniéblico; como boca de lobo. **—pitch in,** colloq. poner manos a la obra. **—pitch into,** arremeter a. **—pitch on** o **upon,** decidirse en; escoger.

pitchblende ('pɪtʃ,blɛnd) n. pecblenda.

pitcher ('pɪtʃ·ər) n. **1,** (vessel) cántaro. **2,** baseball lanzador.

pitchfork ('pɪtʃ,fork) n. horca; horquilla.

pitch pipe diapasón de voz.

piteous ('pɪt·i·əs) adj. lastimoso.

pitfall ('pɪt,fɔl) n. **1,** (trap) trampa. **2,** fig. (danger) peligro latente; escollo.

pith (pɪθ) n. **1,** (pulp) médula; meollo; pulpo. **2,** (essential part) médula; parte principal. **3,** (vigor) energía; vigor.

pithecanthropus (,pɪθ·ə'kæn·θrə·pəs) n. pitecántropo.

pithy ('pɪθ·i) adj. **1,** (pulpy) pulposo; meduloso. **2,** fig. (concise; trenchant) enérgico; vivo.

pitiable ('pɪt·i·ə·bəl) adj. **1,** (arousing pity) lastimoso. **2,** (despicable) despreciable; ruin.

pitiful ('pɪt·i·fəl) adj. **1,** (arousing pity) lastimoso. **2,** (paltry; despicable) despreciable. **3,** (compassionate) compasivo.

pitiless ('pɪt·i·ləs) adj. despiadado; duro de corazón. **—pitilessness,** n. dureza de corazón; inhumanidad.

pittance ('pɪt·əns) *n.* pitanza.
pitter-patter ('pɪt·ər,pæt·ər) *n.*
golpeteo; chapaleteo. —*adv.* con
golpeteo; golpeteando.
pituitary (pɪ'tju·ə,ter·i) *adj.*
pituitario.
pity ('pɪt·i) *n.* 1, (compassion)
piedad; compasión. 2, (cause of regret) lástima. —*v.t.* compadecer.
—**for pity's sake,** por piedad.
—**it's a pity,** es (una) lástima.
—**take pity (on),** apiadarse (de);
compadecerse (de).
pivot ('pɪv·ət) *n.* pivote; quicio; eje.
—*v.i.* girar (sobre un eje). —*v.t.*
colocar sobre un eje. —**pivotal,** *adj.*
central; céntrico.
pixy ('pɪk·si) *n.* duende.
placard ('plæk·ərd) *n.* cartel;
cartelón; anuncio. —*v.t.* 1, (place a
placard on) fijar un cartel en. 2,
(announce widely) publicar; pregonar.
placate ('plei·keit) *v.t.* aplacar;
apaciguar. —**placation,** *n.*
aplacamiento; apaciguamiento.
—**placatory** (-kə·tor·i) *adj.* placativo.
place (pleis) *n.* 1, (location) sitio;
lugar; parte. 2, (point in time) lugar.
3, (space; room) espacio; lugar. 4,
(living quarters) residencia. 5,
(short street) callejón. 6, (rank)
rango; grado. 7, (social status)
dignidad; estado. 8, (job)
colocación; puesto. —*v.t.* 1, (arrange) arreglar; ordenar. 2, (find a
home or job for) colocar; establecer.
3, (put; set) poner; meter; echar. 4,
(locate) localizar. —*v.i.,* racing
terminar segundo; colocarse. —**give
place to,** ceder a; hacer lugar a.
—**in place of,** en lugar de; en vez
de. —**out of place,** fuera de lugar;
fuera de propósito; inoportuno.
—**take place,** ocurrir; celebrarse;
tener lugar. —**take the place of,**
sustituir; hacer las veces de.
placebo (plə'si·bo) *n.* placebo.
placement ('pleis·mənt) *n.*
colocación. —**placement agency,**
agencia de colocaciones.
placenta (plə'sɛn·tə) *n.* placenta.
—**placental,** *adj. & n.* placentario.
placid ('plæs·ɪd) *adj.* plácido;
sereno. —**placidity** (plə'sɪd·ə·ti) *n.*
placidez.
plagiarism ('plei·dʒə·rɪz·əm) *n.*
plagio. —**plagiarist,** *n.* plagiario.
—**plagiarize,** *v.t. & i.* plagiar.
plague (pleig) *n.* 1, (disease)

plaga; peste. 2, (trouble) calamidad.
3, *colloq.* (nuisance) molestia. —*v.t.*
1, (afflict with disease) plagar;
apestar. 2, (annoy) molestar; enfadar.
plaguy ('plei·gi) *adj.* 1, (pestilential) apestoso; plagado. 2, *colloq.*
(annoying) molesto; enfadoso.
plaice (pleis) *n.* platija.
plaid (plæd) *n.* tartán; diseño de
cuadros a la escocesa. —*adj.* listado
a la escocesa.
plain (plein) *adj.* 1, (flat) llano. 2,
(easily understood) claro. 3, (sheer)
cabal. 4, (unpatterned) liso. 5, (ordinary) ordinario; sencillo. 6,
(homely) feo; sin atracción. 7, (sincere) franco. 8, (unmixed) puro;
solo. —*n.* llanura; sabana; llano;
vega. —**in plain terms,** en
términos claros. —**plain clothes,**
traje de calle. —**plain cooking,**
cocina casera. —**plain dealing,**
buena fe.
plainclothesman ('plein,kloðz·
mən) *n.* [*pl.* -**men**] agente de policía
que no lleva uniforme; *Amer.*
pesquisa.
plainness ('plein·nəs) *n.* 1, (flatness) llaneza. 2, (simplicity)
sencillez. 3, (clarity) claridad.
plainsman ('pleinz·mən) *n.* [*pl.*
-**men**] llanero.
plainsong ('plein,sɔŋ) *n.* canto
llano.
plain-spoken *adj.* franco.
—**plain-spokenness,** *n.* franqueza.
plaint (pleint) *n.* 1, (lamentation)
plañido; lamento. 2, (complaint)
queja; querella.
plaintiff ('plein·tɪf) *n.* demandante.
plaintive ('plein·tɪv) *adj.* lastimoso; dolorido; plañidero. —**plain-
tiveness,** *n.* lastimosidad.
plait (pleit) *n.* 1, (braid, as of hair)
trenza. 2, (fold) pliegue. —*v.t.* 1,
(braid) trenzar. 2, (fold) plegar. 3,
(weave) tejer.
plan (plæn) *n.* 1, (diagram) plano;
dibujo. 2, (design) diseño; plan. 3,
(scheme) proyecto; esquema. —*v.t.*
& *i.* planear.
plane (plein) *adj.* plano. —*n.* 1,
(level surface) plano. 2, *fig.* (grade;
level) plano; nivel. 3, (airplane)
aeroplano; avión. 4, (tool) cepillo.
5, (tree) plátano. —*v.t.* acepillar.
—**planing,** *n.* acepilladura.
planet ('plæn·ɪt) *n.* planeta.
—**planetary,** *adj.* planetario.

planetarium (ˌplæn·ɪ'tɛr·i·əm) *n.* planetario.

planetoid ('plæn·ɪˌtɔid) *n.* planetoide.

plank (plæŋk) *n.* 1, (long board) tablón; tabla. 2, (political statement) estatuto de plataforma. —*v.t.* 1, (cover) entablillar; entarimar. 2, *slang* (pay) pagar; entregar. 3, *cooking* asar en una tabla. —**planking,** *n.* entablado; entarimado; maderamen.

plankton ('plæŋk·tən) *n.* plancton; plankton.

planner ('plæn·ər) *n.* proyectista.

planning ('plæn·ɪŋ) *n.* planeación; planeamiento.

plant (plænt) *n.* 1, (living organism) planta. 2, (installation) instalación. 3, (factory) fábrica; planta. —*v.t.* 1, (put in the ground) plantar; sembrar. 2, (place firmly; fix) colocar; sentar fijamente; fijar. 3, *colloq.* (secrete maliciously) esconder o meter (una cosa) de manera que se acuse a una persona inocente. 4, *colloq.* (deal, as a blow) plantar; asestar.

plantain ('plæn·tɪn) *n.* 1, (banana tree and fruit) plátano. 2, (weed) llantén; plantaina.

plantation (plæn'tei·ʃən) *n.* finca; plantío; plantación.

planter ('plæn·tər) *n.* 1, (farmer) plantador; cultivador. 2, (machine) sembradora. 3, (pot; box) tiesto.

plaque (plæk) *n.* placa; chapa.

plasma ('plæz·mə) *n.* plasma. *También,* **plasm** ('plæz·əm).

plaster ('plæs·tər) *n.* 1, (paste of lime) yeso. 2, (medicated dressing) emplasto. —*v.t.* 1, (apply paste to) enyesar. 2, (spread on) emplastar. —**plastered,** *adj., slang* borracho. —**mustard plaster,** sinapismo.

plasterboard ('plæs·tərˌbord) *n.* cartón yeso.

plaster cast 1, (model) molde de yeso. 2, *surg.* enyesado.

plaster of Paris ('pær·ɪs) yeso de París.

plastic ('plæs·tɪk) *adj. & n.* plástico. —**plasticity** (plæs'tɪs·ə·ti) *n.* plasticidad. —**plastic arts,** plástica. —**plastic surgery,** cirugía plástica.

plate (pleit) *n.* 1, (sheet; flat piece) plancha; placa; lámina. 2, (dish) vasija; plato. 3, (item of food) plato. 4, (denture) caja; muelle. 5, *print.* (stereotype) clisé; (electroplate) electrotipo. 6, (illustration) grabado. 7, *photog.* placa. 8, (gold or silver table service) cubierto. 9, (armor) blindaje. —*v.t.* 1, (coat with metal) platear; dorar; niquelar. 2, (cover with sheets) chapear; planchear. 3, (cover with armor) blindar. —**plate glass,** vidrio cilindrado.

plateau (plæ'to) *n.* meseta; mesa; altiplano.

platelet ('pleit·lɪt) *n.* plaqueta.

platen ('plæt·ən) *n.* platina.

platform ('plæt·form) *n.* 1, (raised flooring) plataforma. 2, (scaffold) andamio. 3, *R.R.* andén. 4, (political declaration) declaración de principios; plataforma.

platinum ('plæt·ə·nəm) *n.* platino; platina. —*adj.* de platino; platinado.

platitude ('plæt·ɪˌtud) *n.* perogrullada; trivialidad. —**platitudinous** (-'tud·ɪ·nəs) *adj.* trivial.

platonic (plə'tan·ɪk) *adj.* platónico.

platoon (plə'tun) *n.* pelotón.

platter ('plæt·ər) *n.* fuente.

platypus ('plæt·ə·pəs) *n.* ornitorrinco.

plaudit ('plɔ·dɪt) *n.* aplauso.

plausible ('plɔ·zə·bəl) *adj.* plausible. —**plausibility,** *n.* plausibilidad.

play (plei) *v.i.* 1, (engage in a game or sport) jugar. 2, (move) moverse; correr. 3, (behave) comportarse. 4, *theat.* (act) actuar. 5, (ripple, as water) ondear. 6, *mus.* tocar; tañer. 7, (joke) bromear. 8, (pretend) fingir. —*v.t.* 1, (engage in, as a game or sport) jugar a. 2, (compete against) jugar con. 3, *mus.* tocar. 4, (move, in a game) jugar. 5, (act the role of) representar; desempeñar el papel de. 6, (perform, as a show) dar; representar. 7, (put in motion) disparar; tirar; poner en movimiento. 8, (pretend to be) fingir ser; hacerse: *play deaf,* hacerse el sordo. —*n.* 1, (motion) acción; juego. 2, (game) juego. 3, (amusement) diversión. 4, *theat.* drama; comedia; obra de teatro. 5, (turn, as in a game) turno. —**give full** (o **free**) **play to,** dar rienda suelta a. —**play off,** contraponer. —**play on, 1,** (arouse) incitar; provocar. 2, (take advantage of) aprovecharse de. 3, *mus.* tocar (un instrumento); tocar (una pieza) en (un instrumento). —**play on words,** (hacer) juego de palabras. —**play out,** cansar(se); agotar(se). —**play up to,** adular; halagar.

playact ('plei,ækt) v.i. **1,** (act) desempeñar un papel. **2,** (pretend) simular; fingir.

playbill ('plei,bɪl) n. **1,** (poster) cartel. **2,** (program) programa.

playboy ('plei,bɔi) n., slang hombre parrandero. —**playgirl** (-,gʌrl) n., slang mujer parrandera.

player ('plei·ər) n. **1,** (contestant) jugador. **2,** (musician) músico. **3,** (actor) actor; cómico. —**player piano,** pianola.

playful ('plei·fəl) adj. juguetón; travieso.

playgoer ('plei,go·ər) n. aficionado al teatro.

playground ('plei,graund) n. patio de recreo.

playhouse ('plei,haus) n. teatro.

playing card naipe.

playmate ('plei,meit) n. compañero de juegos.

play-off n. revancha; partida adicional para deshacer un empate.

plaything ('plei,θɪŋ) n. juguete.

playwright ('plei,rait) n. dramaturgo.

plaza ('plæz·ə) n. plaza.

plea (pliː) n. **1,** (entreaty) súplica; imploración. **2,** (pretext) pretexto; excusa. **3,** law alegato; contestación.

plead (pliːd) v.i. [pret. & p.p. **pleaded** o **pled**] **1,** (beg) suplicar; implorar. **2,** law abogar. —v.t. **1,** (allege) alegar. **2,** (defend) defender; abogar por. —**plead guilty,** declararse o confesarse culpable. —**plead not guilty,** negar la acusación.

pleader ('pli·dər) n. defensor [fem. -sora]; abogado.

pleadings ('pli·dɪŋz) n.pl., law alegatos; alegaciones.

pleasant ('plɛz·ənt) adj. agradable. —**pleasantness,** n. placer; agrado.

pleasantry ('plɛz·ən·tri) n. chanza; agudeza.

please (pliːz) v.t. & i. placer; gustar; agradar; satisfacer; complacer. —v.impve. por favor; haga el favor de; sírvase (+ inf.); tenga la bondad de; Amer. favor de. —**as you please,** como Vd. quiera. —**be pleased to,** hacer con gusto; tener gusto en; complacerse en. —**if you please,** por favor; si quiere. —**please God,** si Dios quiere.

pleased (pliːzd) adj. contento; satisfecho.

pleasing ('pli·zɪŋ) adj. agradable.

pleasure ('plɛʒ·ər) n. placer; gusto; deleite. —**pleasurable,** adj. divertido; agradable. —**pleasurably,** adv. con gusto. —**take pleasure in,** hacer con gusto en; complacerse en.

pleat (plit) n. pliegue. —v.t. plegar.

plebe (plib) n. cadete o guardia marina de primer año.

plebeian (plɪ'bi·ən) adj. & n. plebeyo.

plebiscite ('plɛb·ə,sait) n. plebiscito.

plectrum ('plɛk·trəm) n. [pl. **plectrums** o **plectra** (-trə)] plectro; púa.

pled (plɛd) v., pret. & p.p. de **plead.**

pledge (plɛdʒ) n. **1,** (security) prenda; fianza. **2,** (promise) promesa. —v.t. **1,** (give as security) empeñar. **2,** (promise) prometer. **3,** (exact a promise from) obligar; exigir promesa (de). **4,** (toast) brindar a o por.

Pleiades ('pli·ə,diz) n.pl. Pléyades; Pléyadas.

Pleistocene ('plais·tə,sin) adj. & n. pleistoceno.

plenary ('plɛn·ə·ri) adj. plenario; lleno.

plenipotentiary (,plɛn·ɪ·po·'tɛn·ʃi·ɛr·i) n. & adj. plenipotenciario.

plenitude ('plɛn·ɪ,tud) n. plenitud.

plenteous ('plɛn·ti·əs) adj. abundante. —**plenteousness,** n. abundancia.

plentiful ('plɛn·tɪ·fəl) adj. **1,** (ample) abundante; amplio; copioso. **2,** (fruitful) fructífero; fértil.

plenty ('plɛn·ti) n. abundancia; copia. —adj. suficiente; bastante. —adv., colloq. muy; bastante.

pleonasm ('pli·ə,næz·əm) n. pleonasmo. —**pleonastic** (-'næs·tɪk) adj. pleonástico.

plethora ('plɛθ·ə·rə) n. plétora. —**plethoric** (plɛ'θɔr·ɪk) adj. pletórico.

pleura ('plur·ə) n. [pl. **-rae** (-ri)] pleura. —**pleural** ('plur·əl) adj. pleural.

pleurisy ('plur·ə·si) n. pleuresía. —**pleuritic** (plu'rɪt·ɪk) adj. pleurítico.

plexus ('plɛk·səs) n. plexo.

pliability (,plai·ə'bɪl·ə·ti) n. **1,** (flexibility) flexibilidad. **2,** (tractability) docilidad.

pliable ('plai·ə·bəl) *adj.* 1, (flexible) flexible. 2, (tractable) dócil.

pliancy ('plai·ən·si) *n.* 1, (suppleness) flexibilidad. 2, (tractability) docilidad.

pliant ('plai·ənt) *adj.* 1, (supple) flexible. 2, (tractable) dócil; manejable.

pliers ('plai·ərz) *n.pl.* alicates.

plight (plait) *n.* embarazo; apuro; aprieto. —*v.t.* 1, (pledge) empeñar. 2, (betroth) prometer en matrimonio. —**plight one's troth,** contraer esponsales.

Pliocene ('pli·ə,sin) *adj. & n.* plioceno.

plod (plaɪd) *v.i.* 1, (trudge) caminar con fatiga. 2, (toil) afanarse. —**plodder,** *n.* trabajador diligente. —**plodding,** *adj.* laborioso.

plop (plap) *n.* ruido seco; paf. —*interj.* ¡paf! —*v.i.* caerse a plomo; hacer paf. —*v.t.* asestar; arrojar.

plot (plat) *n.* 1, (piece of ground) terreno; solar. 2, (plan) trama; plano. 3, (scheme) maquinación; intriga; conjura. 4, (story line) argumento. —*v.t.* 1, (plan) planear. 2, (draw on a chart or map) trazar; delinear. 3, (scheme) maquinar. —*v.i.* conspirar. —**plotter,** *n.* conspirador [*fem.* -dora].

plough (plau) *v. & n.* = **plow.**

plover ('plʌv·ər) *n.* avefría; chorlito.

plow (plau) *n.* arado. —*v.t.* 1, (till) arar; labrar. 2, (move; remove) remover; arrancar; quitar. —*v.i.* (advance forcibly) abrirse o labrarse camino; avanzar enérgicamente. —**plow back,** reinvertir.

plowing ('plau·ɪŋ) *n.* aradura; labranza.

plowland ('plau,lænd) *n.* tierra labrada; labrantío.

plowman ('plau·mən) *n.* [*pl.* -**men**] arador; labrador.

plowshare ('plau,ʃer) *n.* reja de arado.

ploy (plɔi) *n.* truco; estratagema.

pluck (plʌk) *v.t.* 1, (pull off) tirar; arrancar. 2, (strip of feathers) desplumar. 3, (peel; despoil) pelar. 4, (jerk) sacudir. 5, *mus.* (pick) tañer. —*n.* 1, (pull) tirón; arrancada. 2, (courage) valor; ánimo. —**plucky,** *adj.* animoso; valeroso; osado.

plug (plʌg) *n.* 1, (stopper) tapón. 2, *elect.* enchufe. 3, (hydrant) boca de

agua. 4, (cake of tobacco) costra de tabaco. 5, *colloq.* (favorable remark) recomendación; publicidad. 6, (nag; inferior horse) penco; jamelgo; rocín. 7, (fishing lure) anzuelo; señuelo. —*v.t.* [**plugged, plugging**] 1, (stop) tapar; atarugar. 2, *slang* (shoot) disparar; matar. 3, *colloq.* (publicize) recomendar; elogiar. 4, [*usu.* **plug in**] (connect) enchufar; conectar. —*v.i.* trabajar fijamente; afanarse. —**plugger,** *n.,* *colloq.* trabajador industrioso.

plug-ugly *n.,* *slang* rufián; asesino.

plum (plʌm) *n.* 1, (fruit) ciruela. 2, (tree) ciruelo. 3, (color) violáceo; morado. 4, (prize) premio; galardón.

plumage ('plu·mɪdʒ) *n.* plumaje.

plumb (plʌm) *n.* plomo; plomada. —*v.t.* 1, (sound) sondear. 2, (make plumb) aplomar. —*adj.* a plomo; vertical. —*adv.* 1, (vertically) a plomo; verticalmente. 2, (exactly) exactamente. 3, *colloq.* (utterly) totalmente; cabalmente. —**out of plumb,** fuera de plomo. —**plumb bob,** plomo; plomado. —**plumb line,** plomada; cuerda de plomada.

plumber ('plʌm·ər) *n.* fontanero; *Amer.* plomero.

plumbing ('plʌm·ɪŋ) *n.* 1, (trade) fontanería; *Amer.* plomería. 2, (piping) tubería.

plume (plum) *n.* pluma; penacho. —*v.t.* 1, (remove the plumes of) desplumar. 2, (trim with plumes) emplumar. —**plume oneself,** 1, (preen oneself) componerse. 2, (boast) jactarse.

plummet ('plʌm·ɪt) *n.* plomada. —*v.i.* caer a plomo.

plump (plʌmp) *v.t.* 1, (drop suddenly) dejar caer. 2, (puff up) dilatar. —*v.i.* caerse de plomo. —*n.* caída pesada. —*adj.* gordo; rechoncho. —*adv.* de repente. —**plumpness,** *n.* gordura.

plunder ('plʌn·dər) *v.t.* pillar; robar. —*n.* 1, (robbery) pillaje; robo. 2, (booty) botín.

plunge (plʌndʒ) *v.t.* 1, (drop suddenly) dejar caer. 2, (drive in) hundir. —*v.i.* 1, (dive) zambullirse. 2, (fall) caer a plomo. 3, (rush headlong) saltar; precipitarse. 4, (pitch, as a ship) cabecear. 5, (bet or invest rashly) jugarse el todo. —*n.* 1, (dive) zambullida. 2, (leap) salto. 3, (fall) caída a plomo. **4,** (rash bet or investment) juego desenfrenado.

plunger ('plʌn·dʒər) *n.* **1,** (diver) zambullidor. **2,** *mech.* émbolo; chupón. **3,** (rash bettor or investor) jugador desenfrenado.

plunk (plʌŋk) *v.i.* **1,** (make a hollow sound) hacer un ruido seco. **2,** (fall heavily) caerse de plomo. —*v.t.* **1,** (strum) tañer. **2,** (put down heavily) dejar caer pesadamente; arrojar. —*n.* **1,** (hollow sound) ruido seco. **2,** (twang) tañido.

pluperfect (plu'pʌr·fɪkt) *adj. & n.* pluscuamperfecto.

plural ('plʊr·əl) *adj. & n.* plural.

plurality (plu'ræl·ə·ti) *n.* pluralidad.

pluralize ('plʊr·ə,laiz) *v.t.* pluralizar.

plus (plʌs) *adj.* **1,** (added to) más. **2,** (additional) adicional. **3,** (positive) positivo. —*prep.* más. —*n.* **1,** (sign) signo más. **2,** (something added) añadidura. **3,** (bonus; extra) plus. —**plus fours,** pantalones de golf.

plush (plʌʃ) *n.* felpilla; peluche. —*adj.* **1,** (velvety) afelpado. **2,** *slang* (luxurious) de lujo; suntuoso.

Pluto ('plu·to) *n., myth.; astron.* Plutón.

plutocracy (plu'tak·rə·si) *n.* plutocracia.

plutocrat ('plu·tə,kræt) *n.* plutócrata. —**plutocratic** (-'kræt·ɪk) *adj.* plutocrático.

plutonium (plu'to·ni·əm) *n.* plutonio.

pluvial ('plu·vi·əl) *adj.* pluvial.

ply (plai) *n.* estrata; capa; hoja. —*v.t.* **1,** (work; wield) trabajar; manejar. **2,** (practice, as a trade) practicar; ejercer. —*v.i.* **1,** (fold) doblegarse. **2,** (work) trabajar con ahínco. **3,** (go back and forth) ir y venir; recorrer; navegar. —**ply with, 1,** (keep giving) surtirle a uno de; darle a uno abundancia de. **2,** (overwhelm with) acosarle a uno con; importunarle a uno con.

plywood ('plai,wʊd) *n.* madera laminada.

pneumatic (nju'mæt·ɪk) *adj.* neumático. —**pneumatic drill,** perforadora de aire comprimido.

pneumonia (nu'mo·njə) *n.* pulmonía.

poach (potʃ) *v.t.* (cook in water, esp. eggs) escalfar. —*v.t. & i.* **1,** (hunt or fish illegally) cazar o pescar en vedado. **2,** [*usu.* **poach on** o **in**] (trespass) invadir; entrar furtivamente.

poacher ('potʃ·ər) *n.* **1,** (for cooking eggs) olla para escalfar huevos. **2,** (trespasser) intruso; violador. **3,** (illegal hunter or fisherman) cazador o pescador furtivo.

pock (pak) *n.* **1,** (pustule) pústula; viruela. **2,** = **pockmark.**

pocket ('pak·ɪt) *n.* **1,** (pouch) bolsillo; faltriquera. **2,** (cavity) hoyo. **3,** *aero.* bolsa de aire. **4,** *mining* depósito. —*adj.* de bolsillo. —*v.t.* **1,** (put in a pocket) embolsar. **2,** (appropriate) apropiarse. **3,** (suppress) suprimir. **4,** (swallow, as one's pride, an insult, etc.) tragar; tragarse. —**in pocket,** con ganancia. —**out of pocket,** con pérdida; de su bolsillo. —**pick a pocket,** vaciar un bolsillo. —**pocket billiards,** billar de faltriquera. —**pocket veto,** veto de aguante.

pocketbook ('pak·ɪt,bʊk) *n.* portamonedas; bolsa; cartera.

pocketknife ('pak·ɪt,naif) *n.* navaja de bolsillo.

pockmark ('pak,mark) *n.* cicatriz de pústula o viruela; hoyo; hoyuelo. —**pockmarked,** *adj.* marcado de viruelas.

pod (pad) *n.* vaina.

podiatry (po'dai·ə·tri) *n.* podiatría. —**podiatrist,** *n.* podiatra.

podium ('po·di·əm) *n.* podio.

poem ('po·ɪm) *n.* poema; poesía.

poesy ('po·ɪ·si; -zi) *n., arcaico* poesía; poema.

poet ('po·ɪt) *n.* poeta.

poetaster ('po·ɪt,æs·tər) *n.* poetastro.

poetess ('po·ɪt·ɪs) *n.f.* poetisa.

poetic (po'ɛt·ɪk) *también,* **poetical,** *adj.* poético. —**poetics,** *n.sing. & pl.* poética. —**poetic license,** licencia poética.

poet laureate [*pl.* **poets laureate**] poeta laureado.

poetry ('po·ɪt·ri) *n.* **1,** (poetic expression) poesía. **2,** (poems) poemas; poesías.

poignancy ('poin·jən·si) *n.* fuerza conmovedora; intensidad.

poignant ('pɔin·jənt) *adj.* conmovedor; intenso.

poinsettia (pɔin'sɛt·i·ə) *n.* poinsetia; flor de la Pascua.

point (pɔint) *n.* **1,** (sharp end) punta. **2,** (distinctive feature) ras-

go; característica. **3,** (degree) grado;
punto; nivel. **4,** (purpose) objeto;
fin; propósito. **5,** (moment in time)
instante; punto. **6,** (place) sitio;
lugar; paraje. **7,** (score, in games)
tanto; punto. **8,** print. punto. **9,**
(promontory; cape) cabo. **10,** (division of the compass) punto; rumbo.
11, math. punto. **12,** (punctuation
mark) punto. —v.t. **1,** (aim) apuntar.
2, (sharpen) aguzar. **3,** (punctuate;
mark with points) puntuar. —v.i. **1,**
(gesture, as with the finger) hacer
señal; señalar. **2,** (aim or move in a
given direction) dirigirse; volverse.
3, (trend) conducir. **4,** hunting
pararse (el perro de caza). —**beside
the point,** fuera de propósito. —**be
beside the point,** no venir al caso.
—**be to the point,** venir al caso.
—**carry** (o **gain**) **one's point,**
salirse con la suya. —**(a) case in
point,** ejemplo. —**come** (o **get**) **to
the point,** llegar al caso. —**in
point,** a propósito. —**in point of,**
en cuanto a. —**in point of fact,** en
realidad; de veras. —**make a point
of,** insistir en. —**on all points,** de
todos lados. —**on point,** (ballet) de
puntillas. —**on the point of,** a
punto de. —**point at** o **to,** indicar;
señalar. —**point off,** marcar o
medir con puntos. —**point of
view,** punto de vista. —**point out,**
indicar; señalar; enseñar. —**point
up,** destacar; poner de realce. —**see**
(o **get**) **the point,** caer en la cuenta.
—**to the point,** a propósito; al caso.
pointblank ('point'blæŋk) adj.
directo; a quema ropa. —adv. directamente; a quema ropa.
pointed ('pɔin·tid) adj. **1,** (sharp)
puntiagudo. **2,** (pertinent) directo;
intencionado. **3,** (satirical) satírico.
pointer ('pɔin·tər) n. **1,** (hand of a
clock) manecilla o aguja del reloj.
2, (indicator) indicador. **3,** (rod or
wand) puntero. **4,** (dog) perro de
caza; perro braco. **5,** (advice)
consejito; advertencia.
pointless ('pɔint·ləs) adj. sin
sentido; vano. —**pointlessness,** n.
vanidad.
poise (pɔiz) n. **1,** (equilibrium)
equilibrio. **2,** (carriage; bearing)
porte. **3,** (composure) compostura;
serenidad; aplomo. —v.t. equilibrar;
balancear. —v.i. estar suspendido.
poison ('pɔi·zən) n. veneno. —v.t.
envenenar. —**poisoner,** n. envenenador [fem. -dora]. —**poisonous,**

adj. venenoso; tóxico. —**poison
ivy,** hiedra venenosa. —**poison
oak; poison sumac,** zumaque
venenoso.
poke (pok) v.t. **1,** (push; thrust)
empujar. **2,** (prod) impeler. **3,** (put
in) meter; introducir. **4,** (stir, as a
fire) atizar. —v.i. **1,** (search; pry)
buscar; husmear. **2,** (make a thrust)
dar un empujón. **3,** (dawdle)
holgazanear. —n. **1,** (thrust; push)
empujón. **2,** (projecting brim)
borde. **3,** (bag) saco; bolsa. **4,** (daw-
dler) holgazán. —**poke fun at,**
burlarse de. —**poke one's nose in,**
entremeterse en.
poker ('po·kər) n. **1,** (stirrer for a
fire) hurgón; atizador. **2,** (game)
póker.
poky también, **pokey** ('po·ki) adj.
1, (slow) lento; tardo. **2,** (dull)
torpe. **3,** (shabby) desharrapado;
desaliñado. —n., slang calabozo;
cárcel.
polar ('po·lər) adj. polar. —**polar
bear,** oso polar; oso blanco.
Polaris (po'ler·is) n. estrella polar.
polarity (po'lær·ə·ti) n. polaridad.
polarize ('po·lə,raiz) v.t. polarizar. —**polarization** (-rɪ'zei·ʃən) n.
polarización.
pole (pol) n. **1,** geog.; math.;
astron.; elect. polo. **2,** (piece of
wood) poste; palo. **3,** (unit of measure) 5,03 metros; 25,2 metros
cuadrados. **4,** (flagpole) asta; mástil.
5, cap. (inhabitant of Poland)
polaco; polonés [fem. -nesa]. —v.t.
1, (propel) impeler con un palo. **2,**
(support) sostener con palos. —**pole
vault,** salto con garrocha.
poleax; poleaxe ('pol·æks) n.
alabarda.
polecat ('pol,kæt) n. **1,** (European
weasellike animal) veso. **2,** (skunk)
mofeta.
polemic (po'lem·ik) n. polémica.
—**polemical,** adj. polémico.
—**polemics,** n. polémica. —**polemist** ('pal·ə·mist); **polemicist**
(pə'lem·ə·sist) n. polemista.
polestar ('pol,star) n. **1,** (North
Star) estrella polar. **2,** (guide) guía;
norte. **3,** (center of interest)
miradero.
police (pə'lis) n. **1,** sing. & pl.
(law-enforcement body) policía. **2,**
mil. (cleaning) limpieza. —v.t. **1,**
(keep order in) guardar el orden de
o en. **2,** mil. (clean up) limpiar.
—**police dog,** perro policía.

—**police force,** policía; cuerpo de policía. —**police headquarters,** jefatura de policía. —**police officer,** agente de policía. —**police state,** estado-policía. —**police station,** comisaría de policía; prefectura.

policeman (pə'lis·mən) *n.* [*pl.* -**men**] policía; agente de policía; guardia. —**policewoman,** *n.f.* [*pl.* -**women**] agente femenina de policía.

policy ('pal·ə·si) *n.* **1,** (principle) política. **2,** (insurance) póliza. **3,** (lottery) lotería.

poliomyelitis (,pol·i·o,mai·ə'lai·tis) *n.* poliomielitis. *También,* **polio.**

polish ('pal·iʃ) *v.t.* **1,** (shine) pulir; bruñir. **2,** (refine) refinar; adiestrar; perfeccionar. —*v.i.* pulirse. —*n.* **1,** (glossy finish) pulimento. **2,** (polishing material) barniz; cera; laca. **3,** (refinement) urbanidad; elegancia. —**polish off, 1,** (finish; dispose of) acabar con. **2,** (swallow) tragarse.

Polish ('pol·iʃ) *adj.* polaco; polonés [*fem.* -nesa]. —*n.* polaco.

polished ('pal·iʃt) *adj.* **1,** (shiny) pulido; bruñido; brillante. **2,** (refined) refinado; elegante; urbano.

polishing ('pal·iʃ·iŋ) *n.* pulimento; bruñidura.

Politburo (pə'lit,bjur·o) *n.* Politburó.

polite (pə'lait) *adj.* **1,** (courteous) cortés. **2,** (refined) refinado. —**politeness,** *n.* cortesía; cultura.

politic ('pal·ə·tik) *adj.* **1,** (of citizens) político. **2,** (wise) sagaz; astuto.

political (pə'lit·i·kəl) *adj.* político. —**political action committee,** comité para acción política. —**political science,** ciencias políticas.

politician (,pal·ə'tiʃ·ən) *n.* político; *derog.* politicastro.

politicize (pə'lit·ə,saiz) *v.t.* politizar.

politick ('pal·ə·tik) *v.i., colloq.* politiquear. —**politicking,** *n., colloq.* politiqueo.

politics ('pal·ə·tiks) *n.sing.* o *pl.* política.

polity ('pal·ə·ti) *n.* política; gobierno.

polka ('pol·kə) *n.* polca. —**polka dots,** lunares.

poll (pol) *n.* **1,** (votes; voting) votación. **2,** (voting place) caseta o colegio de votación. **3,** (survey) encuesta; conjunto de opinión. **4,** (head) cabeza. —*v.t.* **1,** (register the votes of) escrutar los votos de. **2,** (cast, as one's vote) dar. **3,** (receive, as one's share of votes) recibir. **4,** (survey; canvass) hacer una encuesta de o en. **5,** (clip; cut off) desmochar. —*v.i.* votar. —**poll tax,** capitación. —**polling booth,** cabina de votar.

pollen ('pal·ən) *n.* polen. —**pollinate** (-ə,neit) *v.t.* polinizar. —**pollination,** *n.* polinización.

polliwog *también,* **pollywog** ('pal·i,wag) *n.* renacuajo.

pollster ('pol·stər) *n.* encuestador (*fem.* -dora).

pollute (pə'lut) *v.t.* **1,** (make impure) contaminar. **2,** (soil) ensuciar; manchar. **3,** (defile) profanar; corromper. —**pollutant** (-tənt) *adj. & n.* contaminante. —**polluted,** *adj.* poluto. —**pollution** (pə'lu·ʃən) *n.* polución; contaminación; corrupción.

polo ('po·lo) *n.* polo. —**polo player,** polista.

polonaise (,pal·ə'neiz) *n.* polonesa.

polonium (pə'lo·ni·əm) *n.* polonio.

poltergeist ('pol·tər,gaist) *n.* fantasma travieso.

poltroon (pal'trun) *n.* cobarde. —**poltroonery,** *n.* cobardía.

polyandry ('pal·i,æn·dri) *n.* poliandria. —**polyandrous** (-'æn·drəs) *adj.* poliándrico; *bot.* poliandro.

polychrome ('pal·i,krom) *adj.* policromo. —*n.* policromía. —**polychromy,** *n.* policromía.

polyclinic ('pal·i,klin·ik) *adj.* policlínico. —*n.* policlínica.

polyester (,pal·i'es·tər) *n.* poliéster.

polyethylene (,pal·i'eθ·ə·lin) *n.* polietileno.

polygamy (pə'lig·ə·mi) *n.* poligamia. —**polygamist,** *n.* polígamo. —**polygamous,** *adj.* polígamo.

polyglot ('pal·i,glat) *adj. & n.* políglota; poligloto.

polygon ('pal·i·gan) *n.* polígono. —**polygonal** (pə'lig·ə·nəl) *adj.* poligonal; polígono.

polyhedron (,pal·i'hid·rən) *n.* poliedro. —**polyhedral,** *adj.* poliédrico.

polymer ('pal·i·mər) *n.* polímero.

—**polymeric** (-'mɛr·ɪk) *adj.* polímero.

polymerize ('pal·ɪ·mə,raiz) *v.t.* polimerizar. —**polymerization** (pə,lɪm·ər·ə'zei·ʃən) *n.* polimerización.

Polynesian (,pal·ɪ'ni·ʒən) *adj. & n.* polinesio.

polynomial (,pal·ɪ'no·mi·əl) *n.* polinomio.

polyp ('pal·ɪp) *n.* pólipo.

polyphony (pə'lɪf·ə·ni) *n.* polifonía. —**polyphonic** (-'fan·ɪk) polifónico.

polysyllable (,pal·i'sɪl·ə·bəl) *n.* polisílabo. —**polysyllabic** (-sɪ'læb·ɪk) *adj.* polisílabo.

polytechnic (,pal·i'tɛk·nɪk) *adj.* politécnico. —*n.* instituto politécnico.

polytheism ('pal·i·θi,ɪz·əm) *n.* politeísmo. —**polytheist** (-,θi·ɪst) *n.* politeísta. —**polytheistic; polytheistical** *adj.* politeísta.

polyurethane (,pal·i'jʊr·ə,θein) *n. & adj.* poliuretano.

polyvalent (,pal·i'vei·lənt) *adj.* polivalente.

pomade (po'meid) *n.* pomada.

pome (poₘm) *n.* pomo; poma.

pomegranate ('pam,græn·ɪt) *n.* **1,** (fruit) granada. **2,** (tree) granado.

pommel ('pʌm·əl) *n.* pomo. —*v.t.* golpear; caer encima a puñetazos. —**pommeling**, *n.* paliza.

pomp (pamp) *n.* pompa; ceremonia.

pompadour ('pam·pə·dor) *n.* pompadur; copete.

pompano ('pam·pə,no) *n.* pámpano.

pompon ('pam,pan) *n.* **1,** (fluffy ball) pompón. **2,** (chrysanthemum) crisantemo; *Amer.* pompón.

pompous ('pam·pəs) *adj.* pomposo. —**pomposity** (pam'pas·ə·ti); **pompousness**, *n.* pomposidad.

poncho ('pan·tʃo) *n.* poncho.

pond (pand) *n.* estanque; charco.

ponder ('pan·dər) *v.t.* ponderar. —*v.i.* reflexionar. —**ponderable**, *adj.* ponderable.

ponderous ('pan·dər·əs) *adj.* pesado; macizo; ponderoso.

pontiff ('pan·tɪf) *n.* pontífice. —**pontifical** (pan'tɪf·ɪ·kəl) *adj.* pontifical; pontificio.

pontificate (pan'tɪf·ɪ·kət) *n.* pontificado. —*v.i.* (-keit) pontificar. —**pontification** (-'kei·ʃən) *n.* pontificación.

pontoon (pan'tuːn) *n.* pontón; *aero.*

flotador. —**pontoon bridge**, puente de pontones.

pony ('po·ni) *n.* **1,** (horse) potro; caballito. **2,** *slang* (translation) traducción ilícita que usan los estudiantes. **3,** (liqueur glass) vasillo. —**pony up**, *slang* pagar; entregar; sacar.

ponytail ('po·ni,teil) *n.* coleta.

pooch (putʃ) *n.*, *colloq.* perro.

poodle ('pu·dəl) *n.* perro de lanas.

pooh (puₓ) *interj.* ¡bah!

pooh-pooh (,pu'puₓ) *v.t.* tener a menos; mofarse de. —*v.i.* mofarse. —*interj.* ¡bah!

pool (puːl) *n.* **1,** (pond) estanque; charco. **2,** (tank for swimming) piscina; alberca. **3,** (billiards) billar de faltriquera; trucos. **4,** (combined bets) apuestas; posta. **5,** (community of interests) conjunto; mancomunidad. —*v.t.* mancomunar.

poolroom ('pul,rum) *n.* sala de trucos; sala de billar.

poop (pup) *n.* popa. —**poop deck**, toldilla.

pooped (pupt) *adj.*, *slang* cansado; agotado.

poor (pʊr) *adj.* **1,** (needy) pobre. **2,** (inferior) malo. **3,** (unfortunate) infeliz.

poorbox ('pʊr,baks) *n.* cepillo de limosnas; *Amer.* alcancía.

poorhouse ('pʊr,haus) *n.* casa de caridad.

poorly ('pʊr·li) *adv.* **1,** (badly) mal. **2,** (shabbily) pobremente. **3,** (sparsely) escasamente. —*adj.*, *colloq.* indispuesto; enfermo.

poor-mouth *slang* —*v.i.* fingir pobreza. —*v.t.* despreciar.

pop (pap) *n.* **1,** (sharp sound) estallido; chasquido. **2,** (soft drink) gaseosa. **3,** *colloq.* (papa) papá. —*v.i.* **1,** (make a sharp sound) dar un chasquido; reventarse; estallar. **2,** (appear or disappear suddenly) aparecer o desaparecer de sopetón. **3,** (fire a weapon) tirar; disparar. —*v.t.* **1,** (burst) explotar; reventar. **2,** (fire) tirar; disparar. **3,** (put in or take out quickly) echar o sacar de repente. —*interj.* ¡pum!; ¡paf! —**pop the question (to),** declararse (a); pedir en matrimonio.

popcorn ('pap,korn) *n.* rosetas; rositas; *Amer.* palomitas.

Pope (pop) *n.* Papa. —**popish**, *adj.*, *derog.* papista. —**popery**, *n.*, *derog.* papismo.

popeyed ('pap,aid) *adj.* que tiene los ojos saltones.

popgun ('pap·gʌn) *n.* cerbatana.

popinjay ('pap·ɪn,dʒei) *n.* **1,** (woodpecker) picamaderos. **2,** (vain person) pisaverde.

poplar ('pap·lər) *n.* álamo. —**poplar grove,** alameda.

poplin ('pap·lɪn) *n.* popelina.

poppy ('pap·i) *n.* adormidera; amapola.

poppycock ('pap·i,kak) *n., colloq.* tontería; disparate.

populace ('pap·jə·lɪs) *n.* pueblo; populacho.

popular ('pap·jə·lər) *adj.* popular. —**popularity** (-'lær·ə·ti) *n.* popularidad.

popularize ('pap·jə·lə,raiz) *v.t.* popularizar; vulgarizar. —**popularization** (-rɪ'zei·ʃən) *n.* popularización; vulgarización.

populate ('pap·jə,leit) *v.t.* poblar.

population (,pap·jə'lei·ʃən) *n.* población.

populism ('pap·jə·lɪz·əm) *n.* populismo. —**populist,** *adj. & n.* populista.

populous ('pap·jə·ləs) *adj.* populoso.

porcelain ('por·sə·lɪn) *n.* porcelana. —*adj.* de porcelana.

porch (portʃ) *n.* porche.

porcine ('por·sain) *adj.* porcino.

porcupine ('por·kjə,pain) *n.* puerco espín.

pore (poːr) *n.* poro. —*v.i.* ojear; mirar. —**pore over,** estudiar detalladamente; meditar.

porgy ('por·dʒi; -gi) *n.* pagro; pargo.

pork (pork) *n.* carne de cerdo. —**pork chop,** chuleta de cerdo.

pornography (por'nag·rə·fi) *n.* pornografía. —**pornographic** (,por·nə'græf·ɪk) *adj.* pornográfico.

porous ('por·əs) *adj.* poroso. —**porosity** (pə'ras·ə·ti); **porousness,** *n.* porosidad.

porphyry ('por·fə·ri) *n.* pórfido.

porpoise ('por·pəs) *n.* marsopa.

porridge ('por·ɪdʒ; 'par-) *n.* gachas; puches.

porringer ('por·ɪn·dʒər) *n.* escudilla.

port (port) *n.* **1,** (harbor) puerto. **2,** (opening) abertura. **3,** *naut.* (left) babor. **4,** = **porthole. 5,** (wine) oporto. **6,** *elect.; comput.* puerto; puerta; entrada. —*v.t. & i., naut.* (steer to left) virar a o hacia babor.

—*v.t., mil.* (hold diagonally, as a rifle) terciar; llevar terciado. —**port of call,** escala.

portable ('port·ə·bəl) *adj.* portátil.

portage ('port·ɪdʒ) *n.* porte. —*v.t.* portear.

portal ('por·təl) *n.* portal.

portcullis (port'kʌl·ɪs) *n.* rastrillo.

portend (por'tɛnd) *v.t.* pronosticar; presagiar.

portent ('por·tənt) *n.* augurio; portento.

portentous (por'tɛn·təs) *adj.* **1,** (ominous) ominoso. **2,** (solemn) solemne; portentoso.

porter ('por·tər) *n.* **1,** (bearer) portador; *R.R.* mozo de estación. **2,** (doorkeeper) portero; conserje. **3,** (beer) cerveza tónica.

porterhouse steak ('por·tər,haus) biftec de filete.

portfolio (port'fo·li·o) *n.* **1,** (case) cartera. **2,** (office of minister) cartera. **3,** (list of securities) documentación.

porthole ('port·hol) *n.* tronera; portilla.

portico ('por·tɪ·ko) *n.* pórtico.

portiere (por'tjeːr) *n.* cortinaje de puerta; portier.

portion ('por·ʃən) *n.* **1,** (part; share) porción. **2,** (dowry) dote. —*v.t.* **1,** (allot) dividir; repartir. **2,** (dower) dotar.

portliness ('port·li·nəs) *n.* **1,** (fatness) corpulencia. **2,** (stately bearing) porte majestuoso.

portly ('port·li) *adj.* **1,** (fat) corpulento. **2,** (stately) grave; serio.

portmanteau (port'mæn·to) *n.* valija.

Porto Rican (,por·to'ri·kən) *adj. & n.* = **Puerto Rican.**

portrait ('por·trɪt) *n.* retrato. —**portraiture** (-trɪ·tʃər) *n.* retrato; pintura. —**portrait painter,** retratista.

portray (por'trei) *v.t.* **1,** (picture) retratar. **2,** (describe) describir. **3,** *theat.* representar. —**portrayal,** *n.* representación; retrato.

Portuguese ('por·tjə·giz) *adj. & n.* portugués [*fem.* -guesa].

pose (poːz) *v.t.* **1,** (place) colocar. **2,** (propound) proponer. —*v.i.* **1,** (act as model) posar. **2,** (pretend) fingir; ponerse. —*n.* **1,** (attitude) postura; *art; photog.* pose. **2,** (affectation) postura vana; afectación. —**pose as,** fingir ser; dárselas de.

poser ('po·zər) *n.* **1,** [*también* **po-**

seur (po'zʌr)] (affected person) presuntuoso; afectado. **2,** (baffling question) problema difícil; enigma.
posh (paʃ) adj. elegante; de lujo.
posit ('paz·ıt) v.t. proponer; postular.
position (pə'zıʃ·ən) n. **1,** (place) posición; lugar. **2,** (posture) postura. **3,** (opinion) actitud; posición. **4,** (rank) rango. **5,** (job) puesto; empleo. **6,** (situation) situación; estado. —**in a position to,** en estado de; en condición de.
positive ('paz·ə·tıv) adj. positivo. —n. positivo; photog. positiva. —**positiveness,** n. calidad de positivo. —**positivity** (-'tıv·ə·ti) n. positividad.
positivism ('paz·ə·tıv,ız·əm) n. positivismo. —**positivist,** n. positivista. —**positivistic,** adj. positivista.
positron ('paz·ə,tran) n. positrón.
posse ('pas·i) n. cuerpo de alguaciles.
possess (pə'zɛs) v.t. **1,** (own) poseer. **2,** (obtain power over) apoderarse de.
possessed (pə'zɛst) adj. **1,** (held in possession) en poder (de). **2,** (haunted; crazed) poseído; poseso.
possession (pə'zɛʃ·ən) n. **1,** (ownership; thing possessed) posesión. **2,** pl. (property) bienes; caudal; riquezas. —**take possession of,** entrar en posesión de; apoderarse de.
possessive (pə'zɛs·ıv) adj. & n. posesivo. —**possessiveness,** n. celo posesivo.
possessor (pə'zɛs·ər) n. poseedor [fem. -dora]; posesor [fem. -sora].
possibility (,pas·ə'bıl·ə·ti) n. posibilidad.
possible ('pas·ə·bəl) adj. posible. —**as soon as possible,** cuanto antes.
possum ('pas·əm) n., colloq. = opossum. —**play possum,** colloq. hacer el muerto; fingir la muerte.
post (post) n. **1,** (upright pole) poste. **2,** (position) puesto. **3,** (garrison) puesto. **4,** (mail) correo. **5,** (relay) posta. —v.t. **1,** (fasten; fix) colocar; fijar. **2,** comm. (enter in a ledger) registrar. **3,** Brit. (mail) echar al correo. **4,** colloq. (inform) informar. —v.i. **1,** (hasten) ir de prisa. **2,** (rise to the trot) balancearse. —**by return post,** a vuelta de correo.
postage ('pos·tıdʒ) n. franqueo. —**postage stamp,** sello de correo.
postal ('pos·təl) adj. postal. —n. tarjeta postal. —**postal order,** giro postal.
postboy ('post,bɔi) n. postillón.
postcard ('post,kard) n. tarjeta postal. También, **postal card.**
post chaise silla de posta.
postdate ('post,deit) v.t. posfechar. —n. posfecha.
postdiluvian (,post·dı'lu·vi·ən) adj. & n. postdiluviano.
poster ('pos·tər) n. cartel; cartelón.
posterior (pas'tır·i·ər) adj. posterior. —n. nalga; vulg. trasero. —**posteriority** (-'or·ə·ti) n. posterioridad.
posterity (pas'tɛr·ə·ti) n. posteridad.
postern ('pas·tərn) n. entrada trasera; postigo.
postgraduate (post'græ·dʒu·ıt) adj. & n. postgraduado.
posthaste ('post'heist) adv. a toda prisa; a toda brida.
posthumous ('pas·tju·məs) adj. póstumo.
postillion (pos'tıl·jən) n. postillón.
postlude ('post,lud) n. postludio.
postman ('post·mən) n. cartero.
postmark ('post,mark) n. matasellos. —v.t. timbrar.
postmaster ('post,mæs·tər) n. administrador de correos. —**postmaster general,** director general de correos.
postmeridian (,post·mə'rıd·i·ən) adj. postmeridiano.
post-mortem (post'mor·təm) adj. post mórtem. —n. autopsia.
post office casa de correos; correo. —**post-office box,** apartado de correos.
postpaid ('post,peid) adj. con porte pagado; franco de porte.
postpartum (,post'par·təm) adj. posterior al parto.
postpone (post'poɹn) v.t. posponer; aplazar; diferir. —**postponement,** n. aplazamiento; diferimiento.
postscript ('post,skrıpt) n. posdata.
postulant ('pas·tʃə·lənt) adj. & n. postulante [fem. postulanta].
postulate ('pas·tʃə,leit) v.t. & i. postular. —n. (-lət) **1,** (assumption) postulado. **2,** (prerequisite) requisito.
posture ('pas·tʃər) n. postura. —v.i. posar; pavonearse.

postwar ('post,wor) *adj.* de (la) postguerra. —**postwar period,** postguerra.

posy ('po·zi) *n.* florecilla; ramillete.

pot (pat) *n.* **1,** (cooking vessel) olla; caldera; puchero. **2,** (urn; jar) pote; tiesto; tarro; marmita. **3,** (prize) bolsa. **4,** (pool of bets) posta. —*v.t.* [**potted, potting**] **1,** (cook in a pot) cocer en olla. **2,** (preserve) conservar en marmitas. **3,** (plant in pots) plantar en tiestos. **4,** (shoot) tirar; disparar. —**go to pot,** *colloq.* arruinarse; fracasar. —**pot cheese,** requesón. —**pot roast,** carne asada en olla. —**pot shot,** tiro casual. —**keep the pot boiling,** ganar bastante para vivir.

potable ('po·tə·bəl) *adj.* potable. —*n.* bebida.

potash ('pat,æʃ) *n.* potasa.

potassium (pə'tæs·i·əm) *n.* potasio. —**potassic,** *adj.* potásico.

potato (pə'tei·to) *n.* [*pl.* **-toes**] patata; *Amer.* papa. —**potato chip,** frito de papa. —**small potatoes,** *colloq.* persona o cosa de poca monta.

potbelly ('pat,bɛl·i) *n.,* *colloq.* panza. —**potbellied,** *adj.,* *colloq.* panzudo.

potboiler ('pat,bɔi·lər) *n.* obra hecha únicamente ·para ganar dinero.

potency ('po·tən·si) *n.* potencia.

potent ('po·tənt) *adj.* potente.

potentate ('po·tən,teit) *n.* potentado.

potential (pə'ten·ʃəl) *adj.* **1,** (possible) posible. **2,** (latent) potencial. —*n.* potencial; capacidad. —**potentiality** (-ʃi'æl·ə·ti) *n.* potencialidad.

pothead ('pat,hɛd) *n.,* *slang* persona adicta a marijuana.

pother ('pað·ər) *n.* alboroto; confusión; molestia. —*v.t. & i.* alborotar; molestar.

potholder ('pat,hol·dər) *n.* agarradera.

pothole ('pat,hol) *n.* bache.

pothook ('pat,hʊk) *n.* **1,** (for hanging pots) llares. **2,** (curlicue) garabato. **3,** *pl.* (shorthand symbols) signos taquigráficos.

potion ('po·ʃən) *n.* poción; pócima.

potlatch ('pat·lætʃ) *n.* fiesta para dar y recibir regalos celebrada por ciertos tribus indígenas.

potluck ('pat,lʌk) *n.* cualquier comida que haya. —*adj.* de lo que haya.

potpourri (pat'pʊr·i; po-) *n.* popurrí.

potsherd ('pat·ʃʌrd) *n.* fragmento arqueológico de cerámica.

pottage ('pat·idʒ) *n.* potaje.

potted ('pat·id) *adj.* **1,** (cooked in a pot) cocido en una olla. **2,** *slang* (drunk) borracho.

potter ('pat·ər) *n.* alfarero. —*v.i.* holgazanear; haraganear. —**potter's field,** cementerio de indigentes. —**potter's wheel,** rueda de alfarero.

pottery ('pat·ə·ri) *n.* alfarería.

potty ('pat·i) *n.,* *colloq.* orinal para niños. —*adj.,* *slang* loco; chiflado.

pouch (pautʃ) *n.* bolsa; saco. —*v.t.* embolsar. —*v.i.* formar una bolsa. —**tobacco pouch,** tabaquera; petaca.

poultice ('pol·tis) *n.* cataplasma; bizma. —*v.t.* bizmar.

poultry ('pol·tri) *n.* aves de corral. —**poulterer** (-tər·ər) *n.* traficante de aves caseras. —**poultry breeder,** avicultor. —**poultry breeding,** avicultura.

pounce (pauns) *v.i.* caer a plomo. —*n.* calada; zarpada. —**pounce at, on** o **upon,** agarrar; saltar sobre.

pound (paund) *n.* **1,** (measure of weight) libra. **2,** (monetary unit) libra esterlina. **3,** (enclosure) corral. —*v.t.* **1,** (beat) golpear. **2,** (crush) machacar; moler. —*v.i.* **1,** (hammer) machacar; martillar. **2,** (plod) trabajar fijamente; afanarse. —**poundage** ('paun·didʒ) *n.* tanto por libra.

pour (poɪr) *v.t.* **1,** (cause to flow) verter; echar. **2,** (send forth) emitir. —*v.i.* **1,** (flow) fluir; entrar o salir a chorros. **2,** (rain) llover. **3,** (rush; swarm) precipitarse; arrojarse. —**pour rain,** llover a cántaros.

pout (paut) *v.i.* poner mala cara; hacer pucheros. —*n.* mueca; mala cara; puchero.

pouter ('pau·tər) *n.* **1,** (person) persona ceñuda. **2,** (bird) paloma buchona.

poverty ('pav·ər·ti) *n.* **1,** (lack of money) pobreza; indigencia. **2,** (scarcity) escasez. —**poverty-stricken,** *adj.* empobrecido; indigente.

pow! (pau) *interj.* ¡zas!; ¡paf!

powder ('pau·dər) *n.* **1,** (fine particles) polvo. **2,** (talcum) polvos. **3,** (gunpowder) pólvora. —*v.t.* **1,** (sprinkle) empolvar. **2,** (crush)

pulverizar. —**take a powder,** *slang*
poner pies en polvorosa.

powder box polvera.

powder flask polvorín. *También,*
powder horn.

powder magazine polvorín.

powder puff (pʌf) **1,** (pad) mota.
2, (effeminate man) afeminado;
melindroso.

powder room salón de damas;
tocador.

powdery ('pau·də·ri) *adj.* polvoriento.

power ('pau·ər) *n.* **1,** (ability)
poder. **2,** (strength) fuerza. **3,** (influential person) potestad. **4,** (nation)
potencia. **5,** (lens capacity)
potencia. **6,** *math.* potencia. **7,**
mech.; elect. energía. —*v.t.*
impulsar; accionar. —**power of attorney,** poder legal. —**power
plant,** central eléctrica.

powerboat ('pau·ər‚bot) *n.* lancha
motora; gasolinera.

powerful ('pau·ər·fəl) *adj.* **1,**
(strong) fuerte. **2,** (potent) potente.
3, (mighty) poderoso. —**powerful-
ness,** *n.* fuerza; poderío.

powerhouse ('pau·ər‚haus) *n.* **1,**
(plant) estación generadora. **2,**
colloq. (strong or energetic person)
dínamo.

powerless ('pau·ər·ləs) *adj.*
impotente; sin poder.

powwow ('pau·wau) *n.* ceremonia
de los indios norteamericanos;
colloq. conferencia. —*v.i., colloq.*
conferenciar.

pox (paks) *n.* erupción pustulosa.

practicable ('præk·tɪ·kə·bəl) *adj.*
practicable. —**practicability,** *n.*
posibilidad de hacerse.

practical ('præk·tɪ·kəl) *adj.* **1,**
(useful) práctico; útil. **2,** (advisable)
aconsejable. **3,** (pragmatic) práctico;
pragmático. —**practical joke,**
chasco; broma o burla pesada.

practicality (‚præk·tɪ'kæl·ə·ti) *n.*
calidad de práctico; utilidad.

practically ('præk·tɪk·li) *adv.* **1,**
(actually) de hecho; prácticamente.
2, *colloq.* (nearly) casi.

practice ('præk·tɪs) *n.* **1,** (performance) ejercicio. **2,** (frequent usage) costumbre. **3,** (exercise of a
profession) práctica. **4,** (clientele)
clientela. **5,** (drill) práctica; ejercicio. —*v.t.* practicar. —*v.i.* **1,** (engage in a profession) ejercer (de
abogado, de médico, etc.); practicar

uno su profesión. **2,** (drill) ejercitar-
se; hacer ejercicios.

practitioner (præk'tɪʃ·ən·ər) *n.*
practicante.

praetor *también,* **pretor** ('pri·tər)
n. pretor. —**praetorial; pretorial**
(pri'tor·i·əl) *adj.* pretorial. —**praetorian; pretorian** (pri'tor·i·ən) *adj.*
pretoriano.

pragmatic (præg'mæt·ɪk) *adj.*
pragmático.

pragmatism ('præg·mə·tɪz-
əm) *n.* pragmatismo. —**pragmatist,**
n. pragmatista.

prairie ('prɛr·i) *n.* pradera.

praise (preiz) *v.t.* **1,** (commend)
loar; elogiar; alabar. **2,** (glorify)
glorificar. —*n.* elogio; alabanza.

praiseworthy ('preiz‚wʌr·ði) *adj*
loable. —**praiseworthiness,** *n.*
mérito.

pram (præm) *n., colloq.* = **perambulator.**

prance (præns) *v.i.* cabriolar. —*n.*
cabriola. —**prancer,** *n.* caballo
pisador.

prank (præŋk) *n.* travesura; broma.
—**prankish,** *adj.* travieso.
—**prankster** (-stər) *n.* bromista.

praseodymium (‚prei·zi-
o'dɪm·i·əm) *n.* praseodimio.

prate (preit) *v.t.* & *i.* charlar.
—**prating,** *adj.* charlador. —*n.*
charla.

pratfall ('præt‚fɔl) *n., colloq.* caída
de nalgas.

prattle ('præt·əl) *v.i.* charlar;
parlotear. —*n.* parlería; parloteo;
charlería. —**prattler** (-lər) *n.*
charlador [*fem.* -dora]; parlanchín
[*fem.* -china].

prawn (prɔn) *n.* langostín.

pray (prei) *v.i.* orar; rezar. —*v.t.* **1,**
(beg) rogar; suplicar. **2,** (petition
for) pedir. —**pray tell me,** sírvase
decirme; dígame, por favor.

prayer (prɛr) *n.* **1,** (supplication)
oración; rezo. **2,** (petition) súplica.
3, *usu. pl.* (devotional service)
oficio. —**prayer book,** devocionario.

prayerful ('prɛr·fəl) *adj.* **1,** (devout) devoto. **2,** (entreating) suplicante.

praying mantis mantis
religiosa; predicador.

preach (pritʃ) *v.t.* & *i.* **1,** (deliver a
sermon) predicar. **2,** (exhort)
exhortar. —**preaching,** *n.* predicación. —**preachment,** *n.* prédica;

sermoneo. —**preachy,** *adj.* sermoneador.

preacher ('pritʃ·ər) *n.* 1, (one who
preaches) predicador [*fem.* -dora].
2, (clergyman) pastor; clérigo.

preamble ('pri·æm·bəl) *n.*
preámbulo.

prearrange (ˌpri·ə'reindʒ) *v.t.* predisponer. —**prearrangement,** *n.*
predisposición.

prebend ('prɛb·ənd) *n.* prebenda.

precarious (prɪ'kɛr·i·əs) *adj.*
precario; inseguro. —**precarious-
ness,** *n.* estado precario;
inseguridad.

precaution (prɪ'kɔ·ʃən) *n.* 1, (preventive act) precaución. 2, (foresight) previsión. —**precautionary,**
adj. precautorio.

precede (prɪ'siːd) *v.t.* & *i.* preceder;
anteceder.

precedence ('prɛs·ɪ·dəns) *n.* 1,
(act of going before) precedencia. 2,
(priority) prioridad. —**precedent,** *n.*
precedente; ejemplo.

preceding (pri'si·dɪŋ) *adj.*
precedente; anterior; antecedente.

precept ('pri·sɛpt) *n.* precepto.
—**preceptive** (prɪ'sɛp·tɪv) *adj.*
preceptivo. —**preceptor** (prɪ'sɛp·
tər) *n.* preceptor [*fem.* -tora].

precinct ('pri·sɪŋkt) *n.* recinto;
distrito.

preciosity (ˌprɛʃ·i'as·ə·ti) *n.*
preciosismo.

precious ('prɛʃ·əs) *adj.* 1, (valuable; esteemed; refined) precioso. 2,
(beloved) querido. 3, (affected)
precioso. —*adv., colloq.* bastante;
muy. —**preciousness,** *n.* preciosidad.

precipice ('prɛs·ə·pɪs) *n.* precipicio.

precipitant (prɪ'sɪp·ə·tənt) *adj.*
precipitado. —*n.* precipitante.
—**precipitancy,** *n.* precipitación.

precipitate (prɪ'sɪp·ə·ˌteit) *v.t.*
precipitar. —*v.i.* precipitarse. —*adj.*
& *n.* (-ˌteit; o -tət) precipitado.
—**precipitation,** *n.* precipitación.

precipitous (prɪ'sɪp·ə·təs) *adj.* 1,
(overhasty) precipitado. 2, (steep)
escarpado.

précis (prei'siː) *n.* resumen.

precise (prɪ'sais) *adj.* 1, (definite)
preciso. 2, (punctilious) puntilloso.
3, (exact) exacto. —**preciseness,** *n.*
precisión; exactitud. —**precision**
(-'sɪʒ·ən) *n.* precisión.

preclude (prɪ'kluːd) *v.t.* imposibili-

tar; excluir. —**preclusion** (-'klu·
ʃən) *n.* exclusión.

precocious (prɪ'ko·ʃəs) *adj.*
precoz. —**precociousness; precocity** (-'kas·ə·ti) *n.* precocidad.

precognition (ˌpri·kag'nɪʃ·ən) *n.*
precognición.

pre-Columbian (ˌpri·kə'lʌm·bi·
ən) *adj.* precolombino.

preconceive (ˌpri·kən'siːv) *v.t.*
preconcebir. —**preconception,** *n.*
idea preconcebida; prejuicio.

preconcert (ˌpri·kən'sʌrt) *v.t.*
concertar de antemano.

precondition (ˌpri·kən'dɪʃ·ən) *n.*
condición previa.

precursor (prɪ'kʌr·sər) *n.* precursor [*fem.* -sora].

predator ('prɛd·ə·tər) *n.* 1, (predatory person) depredador. 2, *zoöl.*
ave o bestia de rapiña.

predatory ('prɛd·ə·ˌtor·i) *adj.* 1, (of
or for plunder) de hurto. 2, (preying) rapaz; de rapiña.

predecessor ('prɛd·ɪˌsɛs·ər) *n.*
predecesor [*fem.* -sora]; antecesor
[*fem.* -sora].

predestination (priˌdɛs·tɪ'nei·
ʃən) *n.* predestinación.

predestine (pri'dɛs·tɪn) *v.t.* predestinar.

predetermine (ˌpri·dɪ'tʌr·mɪn)
v.t. predeterminar. —**predetermi-
nate** (-ət) *adj.* predeterminado.
—**predetermination,** *n.* predeterminación.

predicament (prɪ'dɪk·ə·mənt) *n.*
1, (difficult situation) aprieto;
apuro; trance apurado. 2, *logic* (category) predicamento.

predicate ('prɛd·ə·kət) *n.*
predicado. —*v.t.* (-ˌkeit) predicar.
—**predication,** *n.* predicación.

predicative ('prɛd·ɪˌkei·tɪv) *adj.*
predicativo.

predict (prɪ'dɪkt) *v.t.* & *i.* predecir.
—**prediction** (prɪ'dɪk·ʃən) *n.* predicción.

predilection (ˌpri·də'lɛk·ʃən) *n.*
predilección.

predispose (ˌpri·dɪs'poːz) *v.t.*
predisponer. —**predisposition,** *n.*
predisposición.

predominate (prɪ'dam·ɪˌneit)
v.t. & *i.* predominar. —**predominance,** *n.* predominio. —**predominant,** *adj.* predominante.

preemie ('pri·mi) *n., colloq.* niño
prematuro.

preeminent (pri'ɛm·ɪ·nənt) *adj.*

preeminente. **—preeminence,** *n.* preeminencia.

preempt (pri'εmpt) *v.t.* & *i.* **1,** (seize) apoderarse (de). **2,** (take or buy before another) tomar o comprar primero. **—preemption** (-'εmp·ʃən) *n.* derecho de tomar o comprar primero. **—preemptive,** *adj.* sujeto o perteneciente al derecho de tomar o comprar primero. **—preemptor,** *n.* persona que toma o compra por tal derecho.

preen (priːn) *v.t.* **1,** (smooth) suavizar; limpiar. **2,** (adorn) engalanar. **—preen oneself,** componerse.

preexist (ˌpri·ɪgˈzɪst) *v.i.* preexistir. **—preexistence,** *n.* preexistencia. **—preexistent; preexisting,** *adj.* preexistente.

prefabricate (priˈfæb·rɪˌkeit) *v.t.* prefabricar. **—prefabrication,** *n.* prefabricación.

preface (ˈpref·ɪs) *n.* prefacio. **—v.t.** introducir. **—prefatory** (-ə·tor·i) *adj.* preliminar.

prefect (ˈpri·fεkt) *n.* prefecto. **—prefecture** (-fεk·tʃər) *n.* prefectura.

prefer (prɪˈfʌr) *v.t.* preferir. **—preferable** (ˈpref·ər·ə·bəl) *adj.* preferible. **—preferred stocks,** acciones preferidas.

preference (ˈpref·ə·rəns) *n.* preferencia.

preferential (ˌpref·ərˈen·ʃəl) *adj.* preferente.

preferment (prɪˈfʌr·mənt) *n.* preferencia.

prefix (ˈpri·fɪks) *v.t.* prefijar. **—n.** prefijo.

pregnant (ˈpreg·nənt) *adj.* **1,** (carrying unborn young) encinta; preñada; embarazada. **2,** (fertile) preñado; fértil. **3,** (full of significance) profundo. **—pregnancy,** *n.* embarazo; preñez.

prehensile (prɪˈhen·sɪl) *adj.* prensil.

prehistoric (ˌpri·hɪsˈtor·ɪk) *adj.* prehistórico. **—prehistory,** *n.* prehistoria.

prejudge (priˈdʒʌdʒ) *v.t.* prejuzgar. **—prejudgment,** *n.* prejuicio.

prejudice (ˈpredʒ·ə·dɪs) *n.* **1,** (bias) prejuicio. **2,** (harmful effect) daño; perjuicio. **—v.t. 1,** (cause prejudice in) prejuiciar; predisponer. **2,** (damage) perjudicar. **—prejudiced,** *adj.* prejuiciado. **—prejudicial** (-ˈdɪʃ·əl) *adj.* prejudicial.

prelate (ˈprεl·ət) *n.* prelado. **—prelacy,** *n.* prelacía.

preliminary (prɪˈlɪm·ɪ·nεr·i) *adj.* & *n.* preliminar.

prelude (ˈprel·jud) *n.* preludio. **—v.t.** & *i.* preludiar.

premature (ˌpri·məˈtjʊr) *adj.* prematuro.

premedical (priˈmed·ɪ·kəl) *adj.* premédico. **—premedical course,** premédica.

premeditate (priˈmed·ɪˌteit) *v.t.* premeditar. **—premeditation,** *n.* premeditación.

premier (ˈpri·mi·ər) *adj.* primero. **—n.** primer ministro; presidente del consejo.

première (prɪˈmjeir) *n.* debut; estreno. **—v.t.** & *i.* estrenar.

premise (ˈprem·ɪs) *n.* **1,** (previous statement) premisa. **2,** *pl.* (place) local. **—v.t.** exponer o proponer como premisa. **—v.i.** establecer premisas.

premium (ˈpri·mi·əm) *n.* **1,** (award) premio. **2,** *comm.* prima. **—at a premium, 1,** (at increased price) a premio (o a prima). **2,** (in demand) en gran demanda.

premonition (ˌpri·məˈnɪʃ·ən) *n.* presentimiento.

premonitory (prɪˈman·ə,tor·i) *adj.* premonitorio.

prenatal (priˈnei·təl) *adj.* prenatal.

prenuptial (priˈnʌp·ʃal) *adj.* prenupcial.

preoccupy (priˈak·jə,pai) *v.t.* preocupar. **—preoccupancy,** *n.* preocupación. **—preoccupation** (-ˈpei·ʃən) *n.* preocupación.

preordain (ˌpri·orˈdein) *v.t.* preordinar. **—preordination** (-dɪˈnei·ʃən) *n.* preordinación.

prep (prep) *adj., colloq.* preparatorio. **—v.t., slang** preparar. **—prep school, colloq.** escuela preparatoria.

prepaid (priˈpeid) *v., pret.* & *p.p.* de **prepay.** **—adj.** franco de porte; con porte pagado.

preparation (ˌprep·əˈrei·ʃən) *n.* **1,** (making ready) preparación. **2,** (something made ready) preparativo. **3,** (concoction, as medicine) preparado.

preparatory (prɪˈpær·ə,tor·i) *adj.* preparatorio. **—preparatory school,** escuela preparatoria.

prepare (prɪˈpeir) *v.t.* **1,** (make ready) preparar. **2,** (forewarn) prevenir. **—v.i. 1,** (make preparations) hacer preparaciones. **2,** (ready) oneself) prepararse; disponerse. **3,** (take precautions) prevenirse.

preparedness (prɪ'pɛːrd·nəs) *n.* alerta; estado de preparación.

prepay (pri'pei) *v.t.* [*pret.* & *p.p.* -**paid**] pagar por adelantado. —**prepayment,** *n.* pago adelantado.

preponderate (prɪ'pan·də,reit) *v.i.* preponderar. —**preponderance,** *n.* preponderancia. —**preponderant,** *adj.* preponderante.

preposition (,prɛp·ə'zɪʃ·ən) *n.* preposición. **prepositional,** *adj.* preposicional; prepositivo.

prepossess (,pri·pə'zɛs) *v.t.* **1,** (impress favorably) hacer buena impresión en; predisponer favorablemente. **2,** (dominate) preocupar; obsesionar. **3,** (prejudice) prejuiciar; predisponer. —**prepossessing,** *adj.* simpático; impresionante.

prepossession (,pri·pə'zɛʃ·ən) *n.* **1,** (bias) prejuicio; predisposición. **2,** (preoccupation) preocupación; obsesión.

preposterous (prɪ'pas·tər·əs) *adj.* absurdo; ridículo. —**preposterousness,** *n.* absurdidad; ridiculez.

prepuce ('pri·pjus) *n.* prepucio.

prerequisite (prɪ'rɛk·wə·zɪt) *n.* & *adj.* requisito (previo).

prerogative (prɪ'rag·ə·tɪv) *n.* prerrogativa.

presage ('prɛs·ɪdʒ) *n.* presagio. —*v.t.* (prɪ'seidʒ) presagiar.

presbyter ('prɛz·bɪ·tər) *n.* presbítero.

Presbyterian (,prɛz·bɪ'tɪr·i·ən) *adj.* & *n.* presbiteriano.

presbytery ('prɛz·bɪ,tɛr·i) *n.* presbiterio.

preschool ('pri,skul) *adj.* preescolar. —*n.* jardín de infantes.

prescience ('pri·ʃi·əns) *n.* presciencia.

prescribe (prɪ'skraib) *v.t.* & *i.* **1,** (order; advise) prescribir. **2,** *med.* recetar.

prescript ('pri·skrɪpt) *n.* norma; prescripto. —*adj.* prescripto.

prescription (prɪ'skrɪp·ʃən) *n.* **1,** (order; advice) prescripción. **2,** *med.* receta. —**prescriptive** (-tɪv) *adj.* de o por prescripción.

presence ('prɛz·əns) *n.* presencia. —**presence of mind,** serenidad; prescencia de ánimo.

present ('prɛz·ənt) *adj.* **1,** (in a given place) presente. **2,** (of or at this time) actual. —*n.* **1,** (this time) presente. **2,** (gift) regalo. —**at pres-**

ent, ahora; actualmente. —**present participle,** participio activo. —**present perfect,** pretérito perfecto.

present (prɪ'zɛnt) *v.t.* **1,** (give) ofrecer; regalar. **2,** (introduce; exhibit) presentar. **3,** (show) manifestar. —**presentable,** *adj.* presentable.

presentation (,prɛz·ən'tei·ʃən) *n.* presentación.

presentiment (prɪ'zɛn·tə·mənt) *n.* presentimiento.

presently ('prɛz·ənt·li) *adv.* **1,** (soon) pronto. **2,** (at this time) actualmente.

presentment (prɪ'zɛnt·mənt) *n.* **1,** (presentation) presentación. **2,** *law* acusación.

preservation (,prɛz·ər'vei·ʃən) *n.* preservación; conservación.

preservative (prɪ'zɑrv·ə·tɪv) *adj.* & *n.* preservativo.

preserve (prɪ'zɑrv) *v.t.* **1,** (save) preservar. **2,** (retain) guardar. **3,** *cooking* hacer conservas de. —*n.* **1,** (restricted territory) vedado. **2,** *usu.pl.* (confection) confitura; conserva.

preside (prɪ'zaid) *v.i.* presidir. —**presider,** *n.* presidente. —**presiding,** *adj.* que preside; presidente. —**preside over,** presidir.

presidency ('prɛz·ɪ·dən·si) *n.* presidencia.

president ('prɛz·ɪ·dənt) *n.* presidente. —**presidential** (-'dɛn·ʃəl) *adj.* presidencial.

press (prɛs) *v.t.* **1,** (bear heavily on) apretar. **2,** (compress) comprimir. **3,** (clasp in one's arms) abrazar; prensar. **4,** (push) empujar; insistir en. **5,** (harass) acosar; importunar. **6,** (hurry; urge on) apresurar. **7,** (iron) planchar. **8,** (draft) conscribir. —*v.i.* **1,** (weigh heavily) pesar; oprimir. **2,** (crowd) apiñarse. **3,** (hurry) apresurarse. —*n.* **1,** (crowding pressure) presión; turba. **2,** (urgency) urgencia; prisa. **3,** (chest) armario; gavetero. **4,** *print.; publishing* prensa. —**press agent,** agente de publicidad. —**press conference,** entrevista ante la prensa.

presser ('prɛs·ər) *n.* **1,** (person or machine that compresses) prensador. **2,** (ironer) planchador. **3,** (ironing device) planchadora.

pressing ('prɛs·ɪŋ) *adj.* urgente. —*n.* **1,** (pressure) presión. **2,** (mashing, as of grapes) expresión. **3,**

(ironing) planchado. —**pressing iron**, plancha.

pressman ('prɛs·mən) n. [pl. -men] prensista.

pressure ('prɛʃ·ər) n. 1, (bearing down) presión. 2, (burden) opresión. 3, (urgency) urgencia. 4, elect. tensión. —v.t. coercer; influir en. —**pressure-cook**, v.t. cocer en olla de presión. —**pressure cooker**, olla de presión. —**pressure gauge**, manómetro.

pressurized ('prɛʃ·ər·aizd) adj. a prueba de presión.

prestidigitation (ˌprɛs·tə·ˌdɪdʒ·ə'tei·ʃən) n. prestidigitación. —**prestidigitator** (-tər) n. prestidigitador.

prestige (prɛs'tiːʒ) n. prestigio. —adj. prestigioso; de categoría. —**prestigious** (-'tɪdʒ·əs) adj. prestigioso.

presto ('prɛs·to) adv. rápidamente; en seguida; mus. rápido; rápidamente.

presume (prɪ'zuːm) v.t. & i. presumir. —**presumable**, adj. presumible. —**presumably**, adv. por presunción. —**presuming**, adj. presuntuoso.

presumption (prɪ'zʌmp·ʃən) n. presunción.

presumptive (prɪ'zʌmp·tɪv) adj. presuntivo; presunto; supuesto. —**presumptively**, adv. presuntamente.

presumptuous (prɪ'zʌmp·tju·əs) adj. presuntuoso; presumido. —**presumptuousness**, n. presuntuosidad; presunción.

presuppose (ˌpri·sə'poːz) v.t. presuponer. —**presupposition**, n. presuposición.

pretend (prɪ'tɛnd) v.t. & i. 1, (feign) pretender; simular; fingir. 2, (claim falsely) alegar falsamente. —**pretended**, adj. falso; fingido. —**pretender**, n. pretendiente; hipócrita.

pretense ('pri·tɛns) n. 1, (pretext) pretexto. 2, (claim) pretensión.

pretension (prɪ'tən·ʃən) n. pretensión.

pretentious (prɪ'tɛn·ʃəs) adj. presumido; presuntuoso; pretencioso. —**pretentiousness**, n. presunción; pretensión.

preterit ('prɛt·ər·ɪt) adj. & n. pretérito.

preternatural (ˌpri·tər'nætʃ·ə·rəl) adj. preternatural.

pretext ('pri·tɛkst) n. pretexto.

pretor ('pri·tər) n. = **praetor**. —**pretorial** (pri'tor·i·əl) adj. = **praetorial**. —**pretorian** (pri'tor·i·ən) adj. = **praetorian**.

prettify ('prɪt·ə,fai) v.t. [pret. & p.p. **-fied**] embellecer.

pretty ('prɪt·i) adj. bonito; lindo; ironic bueno; menudo. —adv. bastante. —**prettiness**, n. lindeza; gracia. —**pretty well**, colloq. regular; no mal.

pretzel ('prɛt·səl) n. galleta salada tostada en forma de nudo.

prevail (prɪ'veil) v.i. 1, (win) prevalecer. 2, (predominate) predominar. —**prevail on** o **upon**, persuadir.

prevailing (prɪ'vei·lɪŋ) adj. 1, (predominant) prevaleciente; predominante. 2, (general) general; corriente.

prevalent ('prɛv·ə·lənt) adj. general; común; muy extendido. —**prevalence; prevalency**, n. frecuencia; boga.

prevaricate (prɪ'vær·ə,keit) v.i. prevaricar. —**prevaricator**, n. prevaricador [fem. -dora]. —**prevarication**, n. prevaricación.

prevent (prɪ'vɛnt) v.t. impedir; evitar. —**preventable**, adj. evitable.

preventative (prɪ'vɛn·tə·tɪv) adj. & n. preventivo.

prevention (prɪ'vɛn·ʃən) n. prevención.

preventive (prɪ'vɛn·tɪv) adj. & n. preventivo.

preview ('pri·vju) n. 1, (advance view) vista de antemano. 2, (advance showing) previa representación. 3, motion pictures (sample scenes) avance; muestra. —v.t. ver de antemano.

previous ('pri·vi·əs) adj. previo; anterior. —**previously**, adv. anteriormente; antes. —**previousness**, n. anterioridad.

prewar (pri'wor) adj. de (la) preguerra. —**prewar period**, preguerra.

prey (prei) n. 1, (animal killed by another) presa. 2, (victim) víctima. 3, (habit of preying) rapiña. —v.i. [usu. **prey on** o **upon**] 1, (devour) devorar. 2, (plunder) robar; depredar. 3, (oppress) oprimir. —**bird of prey**, ave de rapiña.

price (prais) n. 1, (value) precio. 2, (cost) costo. 3, (reward) recompensa. —v.t. valuar; preciar;

apreciar. —**priceless,** *adj.* inapreciable. —**at any price,** a toda costa. —**cash price,** precio al contado. —**closing price,** precio de cierre. —**list price,** precio de lista. —**market price,** precio corriente. —**price support,** sostenimiento de precios. —**selling price,** precio de venta.

prick (prɪk) *n.* **1,** (hole) agujerito. **2,** (goad) aguijón. **3,** (stinging sensation) punzada. —*v.t.* **1,** (puncture) punzar; aguijerear. **2,** (cause pain) doler. —**pricking,** *n.* picadura. —**prick up one's ears,** aguzar las orejas.

prickle ('prɪk·əl) *n.* púa; pincho; espina. —*v.t. & i.* pinchar; picar.

prickly ('prɪk·li) *adj.* **1,** (thorny) espinoso. **2,** (sharp; biting) agudo; punzante. —**prickly heat,** salpullido. —**prickly pear,** nopal; tuna; higo chumbo. —**prickly pear cactus,** nopal; tunal; chumbera; higuera chumba.

pride (praid) *n.* **1,** (self-respect) orgullo. **2,** (vanity) altivez; engreimiento. **3,** (satisfaction) jactancia. —**prideful,** *adj.* orgulloso. —**pride oneself on o upon,** enorgullecerse de.

prie-dieu (pri'djʊ) *n.* reclinatorio.

prier *también,* **pryer** ('prai·ər) *n.* fisgón; hurón.

priest (prist) *n.* sacerdote; cura. —**priestess,** *n.f.* sacerdotisa. —**priesthood,** *n.* sacerdocio. —**priestly,** *adj.* sacerdotal.

prig (prɪg) *n.* mojigato; remilgado. —**priggery,** *n.* mojigatería; remilgo. —**priggish,** *adj.* mojigato; remilgado.

prim (prɪm) *adj.* relamido; estirado; remilgado.

primacy ('prai·mə·si) *n.* primacía.

prima donna (ˌpri·mə'dan·ə) *n.* [*pl.* **prima donnas**] prima donna.

primal ('prai·məl) *adj.* **1,** (primitive) original; primitivo. **2,** (principal) primero; principal.

primarily (prai'mɛr·ə·li) *adv.* principalmente; sobre todo.

primary ('prai·mɛr·i) *adj.* primario. —*n.* **1,** (first) primero. **2,** *polit.* elección preliminar o primaria. **3,** *elect.* circuito primario.

primate ('prai·met) *n.* **1,** *eccles.* primado. **2,** *zoöl.* primate.

prime (praim) *adj.* **1,** (first) primero. **2,** (most important) principal. **3,** (superior) de primera calidad. **4,**

math. primo. —*n.* **1,** (earliest stage) principio. **2,** (high point) ápice. **3,** (best period) flor. **4,** (best part) flor y nata. —*v.t.* **1,** (prepare) preparar; prevenir. **2,** (charge, as a gun) cebar. **3,** *colloq.* (instruct) dar instrucciones; informar. **4,** (apply the first coat to) dar la primera mano a. —**prime meridian,** primer meridiano. —**prime minister,** primer ministro. —**prime of life,** edad viril. —**prime rate,** tasa preferencial. —**prime time,** horas de máxima sintonización.

primer ('prai·mər) *n.* **1,** (person or device that primes) cebador. **2,** ('prɪm·ər) (elementary textbook) cartilla; abecedario.

primeval (prai'mi·vəl) *adj.* prístino; original.

priming ('prai·mɪŋ) *n.* **1,** (preparation) preparación. **2,** (of a pump or weapon) cebo. **3,** (undercoat) primera mano.

primitive ('prɪm·ə·tɪv) *adj.* **1,** (early in history) primitivo. **2,** (simple) crudo. **3,** (basic) fundamental; básico. —*n.* **1,** (untrained artist) pintor crudo; primitivo. **2,** (basic form) forma original. —**primitiveness,** *n.* estado primitivo.

primness ('prɪm·nəs) *n.* formalidad; precisión; remilgo.

primogeniture (ˌprai·mə'dʒɛn·ə·tʃər) *n.* primogenitura; progenitura.

primordial (prai'mor·di·əl) *adj.* primordial; original.

primp (prɪmp) *v.t.* aliñar; acicalar. —*v.i.* aliñarse; acicalarse.

primrose ('prɪm·roz) *n.* primavera. —*adj.* amarillo claro. —**primrose path,** sendero fácil; vida agradable.

prince (prɪns) *n.* príncipe. —**princedom,** *n.* principado.

prince consort príncipe consorte.

princely ('prɪns·li) *adj.* principesco.

princess ('prɪn·sɪs) *n.* princesa.

principal ('prɪn·sə·pəl) *adj.* principal. —*n.* **1,** (chief person) principal. **2,** (head of a school) director; jefe. **3,** *comm.* principal.

principality (ˌprɪn·sə'pæl·ə·ti) *n.* principado.

principle ('prɪn·sə·pəl) *n.* principio.

prink (prɪŋk) *v.t. & i.* = **primp.**

print (prɪnt) *n.* **1,** (mark) impresión. **2,** (type) tipo; letra. **3,** (seal) sello. **4,** (printed piece) impreso. **5,** (copy) estampa; grabado. **6,** *photog.*

impresión. **7,** (patterned cloth) estampado. —*v.t.* **1,** (produce from type) imprimir. **2,** *photog.* tirar; sacar. —**in print,** impreso. —**out of print,** agotado.

printer ('prɪn·tər) *n.* **1,** (craftsman) impresor. **2,** (machine) impresora. **3,** (copier) copiadora. —**printer's ink,** tinta de imprenta. —**printer's mark,** pie de imprenta.

printing ('prɪn·tɪŋ) *n.* **1,** (process) tipografía; imprenta. **2,** (writing in capitals) molde de imprenta. **3,** (printed piece) impreso. **4,** (quantity printed at one time) tirada. —**printing press,** prensa tipográfica. —**printing shop,** estampería.

printout ('prɪnt,aʊt) *n.* salida impresa.

prior ('praɪ·ər) *adj.* anterior. —*n.* prior. —**prioress,** *n.* priora.

priority (praɪ'ar·ə·ti) *n.* prioridad.

prise (praɪz) *v.t.* levantar con una palanca o cuña.

prism ('prɪz·əm) *n.* prisma. —**prismatic** (prɪz'mæt·ɪk) *adj.* prismático.

prison ('prɪz·ən) *n.* prisión; cárcel. —**prisoner,** *n.* preso; prisionero. —**prison house,** cárcel. —**prison keeper,** carcelero. —**prison van,** coche celular. —**take prisoner,** prender.

prissy ('prɪs·i) *adj., colloq.* afectado; amanerado; melindroso.

pristine ('prɪs·tin) *adj.* prístino.

privacy ('praɪ·və·si) *n.* aislamiento. —**in privacy,** en secreto. —**have (no) privacy,** (no) poder estar tranquilo.

private ('praɪ·vɪt) *adj.* **1,** (personal) privado. **2,** (secret) confidencial. **3,** (retired) retirado. —*n.* soldado raso. —**in private,** en secreto; a solas. —**private eye,** detective privado. —**private first class,** soldado de primera. —**private parts,** partes pudendas.

privateer (ˌpraɪ·və'tɪr) *n.* **1,** (person) corsario. **2,** (ship) buque corsario. —*v.i.* ir a corso; corsear. —**privateering,** *n.* corso. —*adj.* corsario.

privation (praɪ'veɪ·ʃən) *n.* privación.

privative ('prɪv·ə·tɪv) *adj.* privativo.

privet ('prɪv·ɪt) *n.* ligustro.

privilege ('prɪv·ə·lɪdʒ) *n.* privilegio. —*v.t.* privilegiar. —**privileged,** *adj.* privilegiado.

privy ('prɪv·i) *adj.* **1,** (private) privado; secreto. **2,** (knowing) enterado; consabido. —*n.* excusado; letrina; privada. —**privy council,** consejo del rey.

prize (praɪz) *n.* **1,** (reward) premio. **2,** (valued article) joya. **3,** (booty) presa; botín. —*v.t.* **1,** (value highly) estimar o apreciar mucho. **2,** [*también,* **prise**] (pry with a lever) levantar con una palanca o cuña. —*adj.* premiado; superior. —**prize fight,** partido de boxeo. —**prize fighter,** púgil. —**prize ring,** cuadrilátero.

pro (proʊ) *prep.* pro. —*n.* [*pl.* **pros**] **1,** (supporter) proponente. **2,** *colloq.* = **professional.** —**pro forma,** pro forma; por la forma; simulado. —**the pros and cons,** el pro y el contra.

probable ('prab·ə·bəl) *adj.* probable. —**probability,** *n.* probabilidad.

probate ('proʊ·beɪt) *n.* verificación; prueba. —*v.t.* someter a verificación.

probation (proʊ'beɪ·ʃən) *n.* **1,** (trial period) probación; noviciado. **2,** (release from prison) libertad vigilada. —**probationary,** *adj.* probatorio.

probationer (proʊ'beɪ·ʃən·ər) *n.* **1,** (novice) novicio; aprendiz. **2,** (offender released on probation) delincuente en libertad vigilada.

probe (proʊb) *n.* **1,** (instrument) tienta; sonda. **2,** (investigation) investigación; indagación. —*v.t.* & *i.* **1,** (explore with a probe) sondar. **2,** (investigate) investigar; indagar.

probity ('proʊ·bə·ti) *n.* probidad; integridad.

problem ('prab·ləm) *n.* problema. —**problematic** (-lə'mæt·ɪk); **problematical,** *adj.* problemático.

proboscis (proʊ'bas·ɪs) *n.* probóscide.

procedure (prə'si·dʒər) *n.* procedimiento. —**procedural,** *adj.* según los procedimientos.

proceed (prə'siːd) *v.i.* **1,** (go forward) avanzar; seguir. **2,** (continue) seguir; proseguir. —**proceed against,** *law* armar un pleito contra; proceder contra. —**proceed from,** originar de; proceder de.

proceeding (prə'si·dɪŋ) *n., usu. pl.* procedimiento; proceso.

proceeds ('proʊ·sidz) *n.pl.* réditos; ganancia.

process ('pras·ɛs) *n.* **1,** (course; progress) transcurso; progreso. **2,**

(method) método; procedimiento. **3,** *anat.* protuberancia; proceso. **4,** *law* proceso. —*v.t.* **1,** (treat by a special method) someter a un procedimiento especial. **2,** *law* procesar. —*adj.* elaborado; de elaboración. —**processing,** *n.* procesamiento.

procession (prǝ'sɛʃ·ǝn) *n.* procesión. —**processional,** *adj.* procesional.

proclaim (pro'kleim) *v.t.* proclamar.

proclamation (ˌprak·lǝ'mei·ʃǝn) *n.* proclama; proclamación; edicto.

proclivity (pro'klɪv·ǝ·ti) *n.* proclividad.

proconsul (pro'kan·sǝl) *n.* procónsul. —**proconsular,** *adj.* proconsular. —**proconsulate** (-sǝ·lɪt) *n.* proconsulado.

procrastinate (pro'kræs·tǝˌneit) *v.i.* demorar; diferir. —**procrastination,** *n.* tardanza; demora. —**procrastinator,** *n.* moroso.

procreate ('pro·kri,eit) *v.t.* procrear. —**procreation,** *n.* procreación. —**procreative,** *adj.* procreador. —**procreator,** *n.* procreador [*fem.* -dora].

proctor ('prak·tǝr) *n.* **1,** *educ.* censor. **2,** *law* procurador [*fem.* -dora].

procurator ('prak·juˌrei·tǝr) *n.* procurador [*fem.* -dora].

procure (pro'kjur) *v.t.* **1,** (obtain) obtener; lograr; procurar. **2,** (hire for immoral purposes) solicitar (mujeres). —*v.i.* alcahuetear. —**procurable,** *adj.* asequible.

procurement (pro'kjur·mǝnt) *n.* **1,** (acquisition) procuración; obtención. **2,** (hiring of women) alcahuetería.

procurer (pro'kjur·ǝr) *n.* alcahuete. —**procuress,** *n.* alcahueta.

prod (prad) *n.* **1,** (sharp implement) aguijón; aguijada. **2,** (thrust; jab) empujón; pinchada. —*v.t.* aguijar; pinchar.

prodigal ('prad·ɪ·gǝl) *adj. & n.* pródigo. —**prodigality** (-'gæl·ǝ·ti) *n.* prodigalidad.

prodigious (prǝ'dɪdʒ·ǝs) *adj.* **1,** (marvelous) prodigioso; maravilloso. **2,** (huge) inmenso; enorme. —**prodigiousness,** *n.* maravilla; inmensidad.

prodigy ('prad·ǝ·dʒi) *n.* prodigio.

produce (prǝ'djus) *v.t.* **1,** (yield) producir. **2,** (cause) ocasionar. **3,** (show) mostrar. **4,** (manufacture) elaborar; manufacturar. **5,** *theat.*

presentar. **6,** *geom.* extender. **7,** *comm.* rendir. —*v.i.* producir. —*n.* ('pro·djus) **1,** (result) producto; producción. **2,** (natural products) productos. —**producing,** *adj.* productivo.

producer (prǝ'djus·ǝr) *n.* **1,** (maker) productor. **2,** *theat.* director de escena.

product ('prad·ʌkt) *n.* producto.

production (prǝ'dʌk·ʃǝn) *n.* **1,** (act or result of producing) producción. **2,** *theat.* realización; presentación.

productive (prǝ'dʌk·tɪv) *adj.* productivo. —**productivity** (ˌpro·dʌk'tɪv·ǝ·ti) *n.* productividad.

profanation (ˌpraf·ǝ'nei·ʃǝn) *n.* profanación.

profane (prǝ'fein) *adj.* profano. —*v.t.* profanar.

profanity (prǝ'fæn·ǝ·ti) *n.* blasfemia; profanidad.

profess (prǝ'fɛs) *v.t.* profesar. —**professed,** *adj.* profeso; declarado.

profession (prǝ'fɛʃ·ǝn) *n.* **1,** (vocation) profesión. **2,** (avowal) declaración. —**professional,** *adj. & n.* profesional.

professor (prǝ'fɛs·ǝr) *n.* profesor [*fem.* -sora]. —**professorate** (-ɪt) *n.* profesorado. —**professorial** (ˌpro·fɛ'sor·i·ǝl) *adj.* profesoral; de profesor o catedrático. —**professoriate** (ˌpro·fɛ'sor·i·ɪt) *n.* profesorado. —**professorship,** *n.* profesorado.

proffer ('praf·ǝr) *v.t.* ofrecer; proponer. —*n.* oferta; propuesta.

proficient (prǝ'fɪʃ·ǝnt) *adj.* proficiente; hábil. —**proficiency,** *n.* proficiencia; habilidad.

profile ('pro·fail) *n.* **1,** (side view) perfil. **2,** (contour) contorno. —*v.t.* perfilar.

profit ('praf·ɪt) *n.* beneficio; ganancia; provecho. —*v.t.* ser ventajoso para; servir. —*v.i.* ganar; aprovechar; sacar provecho. —**profitable,** *adj.* beneficioso; provechoso; ganancioso. —**profitless,** infructuoso. —**gross profit,** ganancia en bruto. —**profit-and-loss statement,** estado de ganancias y pérdidas.

profiteer (ˌpraf·ɪ'tɪr) *n.* explotador [*fem.* -dora]; usurero. —*v.i.* usurear; explotar; pringarse.

profligate ('praf·lɪ·gǝt) *adj. & n.* libertino. —**profligacy,** *n.* libertinaje.

profound (prə'faund) *adj.* profundo.

profundity (prə'fʌn·də·ti) *n.* profundidad.

profuse (prə'fjus) *adj.* profuso. —**profuseness**; **profusion** (-'fjuʒən) *n.* profusión.

progenitor (pro'dʒɛn·ə·tər) *n.* progenitor.

progeny ('pradʒ·ə·ni) *n.* progenie; prole.

progesterone (pro'dʒɛs·tə,ron) *n.* progesterona.

prognosis (prag'no·sɪs) *n.* pronóstico; prognosis. —**prognostic** (-'nas·tɪk) *adj.* pronosticador.

prognosticate (prag'nas·tə,keit) *v.t.* pronosticar. —**prognostication**, *n.* pronosticación.

program ('pro·græm) *n.* programa. —*v.t.* incluir en el programa; *elect.*; *comput.* programar. —**programmer**, *n.*, *elect.*; *comput.* programador [*fem.* -dora]. —**programming**, *n.*, *elect.*; *comput.* programación.

progress ('prag·rɛs) *n.* **1,** (advance) adelanto. **2,** (development) progreso o progresos. **3,** (improvement) mejoramiento. —*v.i.* (prə'grɛs) **1,** (proceed) adelantar; avanzar. **2,** (develop; grow) progresar. **3,** (improve) mejorar. —**make progress**, hacer progresos.

progression (prə'grɛʃ·ən) *n.* progresión.

progressive (prə'grɛs·ɪv) *adj.* progresivo; *polit.* progresista. —*n.* progresista.

prohibit (pro'hɪb·ɪt) *v.t.* prohibir.

prohibition (,pro·ə'bɪʃ·ən) *n.* prohibición. —**prohibitionist**, *n.* prohibicionista.

prohibitive (prə'hɪb·ɪ·tɪv) *adj.* prohibitivo.

prohibitory (prə'hɪb·ɪ,tor·i) *adj.* prohibitorio.

project ('pradʒ·ɛkt) *n.* proyecto. —*v.t.* (prə'dʒɛkt) proyectar. —*v.i.* sobresalir. —**projecting**, *adj.* saliente.

projectile (prə'dʒɛk·tɪl) *n.* proyectil.

projection (prə'dʒɛk·ʃən) *n.* proyección. —**projectionist**, *n.* operador cinematográfico.

projector (prə'dʒɛk·tər) *n.* proyector.

prolate ('pro·leit) *adj.*, *geom.* elongado (por los polos).

proletariat (,pro·lə'tɛr·i·ət) *n.*

proletariado. —**proletarian**, *adj.* & *n.* proletario.

proliferate (pro'lɪf·ə,reit) *v.t.* multiplicar; reproducir. —*v.i.* multiplicarse; reproducirse. —**proliferation**, *n.* multiplicación; proliferación.

prolific (pro'lɪf·ɪk) *adj.* prolífico.

prolix (pro'lɪks) *adj.* prolijo. —**prolixity**, *n.* prolijidad.

prologue ('pro·lɔg) *n.* prólogo; introducción.

prolong (prə'lɔŋ) *v.t.* prolongar. —**prolongation** (,pro·lɔŋ'gei·ʃən) *n.* prolongación.

prom (pra:m) *n.*, *colloq.* baile de gala, esp. para estudiantes.

promenade (,pram·ə'neid) *n.* **1,** (stroll) paseo. **2,** (wide street) bulevar. **3,** (ball) baile de gala. —*v.i.* pasearse. —**promenader**, *n.* paseante.

Prometheus (prə'mi·θi·əs) *n.* Prometeo. —**Promethean**, *adj.* de o como Prometeo.

promethium (prə'mi·θi·əm) *n.* prometio.

prominent ('pram·ə·nənt) *adj.* prominente; *fig.* eminente. —**prominence**, *n.* prominencia; *fig.* eminencia.

promiscuous (prə'mɪs·kju·əs) *adj.* promiscuo. —**promiscuousness**; **promiscuity** (,pram·ɪs'kju·ə·ti) *n.* promiscuidad.

promise ('pram·ɪs) *n.* promesa. —*v.t.* & *i.* prometer. —**promising**, *adj.* prometedor. —**break one's promise**, faltar a su palabra. —**keep one's promise**, cumplir con su palabra. —**promised land**, tierra de promisión.

promissory ('pram·ɪ·sor·i) *adj.* promisorio.—**promissory note**, pagaré.

promontory ('pram·ən,tor·i) *n.* promontorio.

promote (prə'mot) *v.t.* **1,** (foment) promover. **2,** (advance in grade) adelantar. **3,** *comm.* (develop) agenciar. —**promoter**, *n.* promotor [*fem.* -tora]; *theat.*; *sports* empresario.

promotion (prə'mo·ʃən) *n.* **1,** (advancement) promoción. **2,** (development) desarrollo.

prompt (prampt) *adj.* **1,** (quick; without delay) pronto. **2,** (quick to act; eager) listo; dispuesto. **3,** (on time) puntual. —*v.t.* **1,** (incite) incitar; impulsar; mover. **2,** *theat.*

(cue) apuntar. **—prompter,** *n.,* *theat.* apuntador [*fem.* -dora]. **—promptly,** *adv.* en punto; pronto; prontamente. **—promptness;** **promptitude** ('pramp·tə,tjud) *n.* prontitud.

promulgate (pro'mʌl·geit) *v.t.* promulgar; proclamar. **—promulgation** (,pro·mʌl'gei·ʃən) *n.* promulgación. **—promulgator,** *n.* promulgador [*fem.* -dora].

prone (proːn) *adj.* 1, (prostrate) prono; postrado; acostado boca abajo. 2, (susceptible) inclinado; propenso.

proneness ('pron·nəs) *n.* 1, (prostration) prostración. 2, (inclination) inclinación; propensión.

prong (praːŋ) *n.* diente; punta. **—pronged,** *adj.* dentado.

pronominal (pro'nam·ə·nəl) *adj.* pronominal.

pronoun ('pro·naun) *n.* pronombre.

pronounce (prə'nauns) *v.t.* pronunciar. **—***v.i.* declararse; pronunciarse. **—pronounced,** *adj.* marcado. **—pronouncement,** *n.* declaración; *law* pronunciamiento.

pronto ('pran·to) *adv., colloq.* pronto; en seguida.

pronunciation (prə,nʌn·si'ei·ʃən) *n.* pronunciación.

proof (pruf) *n.* 1, (evidence; test) prueba. 2, *print; photog.* prueba. 3, (alcoholic content) graduación normal. **—***adj.* 1, (strong; durable) de prueba. 2, (impenetrable) a prueba de. 3, (alcoholic) de prueba. 4, (denoting alcoholic content) de graduación normal.

proofread ('pruf,rid) *v.t. & i.* [*pret. & p.p.* **-read** (-,rɛd)] corregir (leyendo). **—proofreader,** *n.* corrector de pruebas. **—proofreading,** *n.* corrección de pruebas.

prop (prap) *v.t.* [**propped, propping**] 1, (hold up; support) sostener. 2, (place against something for support; lean) apoyar. 3, (shore up) apuntalar. **—***n.* 1, (support) sostén. 2, (something to lean against) apoyo. 3, (post; upright) puntal. 4, *colloq.* = **propeller.** 5, *theat.* accesorio.

propaganda (,prap·ə'gæn·də) *n.* propaganda. **—propagandism,** *n.* propagandismo. **—propagandist,** *n.* propagandista. **—propagandize** (-daiz) *v.t. & i.* hacer propaganda (de o con).

propagate ('prap·ə,geit) *v.t.*

propagar. **—***v.i.* propagarse. **—propagation,** *n.* propagación. **—propagator,** *n.* propagador [*fem.* -dora].

propane ('pro·pein) *n.* propano.

propel (prə'pel) *v.t.* impeler; propulsar. **—propellant,** *n.* impulsor; propulsor. **—propellent,** *adj.* impelente; propulsor.

propeller (prə'pɛl·ər) *n.* hélice.

propensity (prə'pɛn·sə·ti) *n.* propensión.

proper ('prap·ər) *adj.* 1, (peculiar; one's own) propio. 2, (appropriate) apropiado; apto. 3, (formal) formal; correcto. 4, (decorous) decente; decoroso. 5, (exact) justo; exacto.

property ('prap·ər·ti) *n.* propiedad; *theat.* accesorio. **—propertied,** *adj.* acaudalado. **—personal property,** bienes muebles. **—real property,** bienes inmuebles; bienes raíces.

prophecy ('praf·ə·si) *n.* profecía.

prophesy ('praf·ə·sai) *v.t. & i.* profetizar.

prophet ('praf·it) *n.* profeta. **—prophetic** (prə'fɛt·ɪk) *adj.* profético. **—prophetess,** *n.* profetisa.

prophylaxis (,praf·fə'læk·sɪs) *n.* profilaxis. **—prophylactic** (-tɪk) *adj. & n.* profiláctico.

propinquity (pro'pɪŋ·kwɪ·ti) *n.* proximidad; propincuidad.

propitiate (pro'pɪʃ·i,eit) *v.t.* propiciar. **—propitiation,** *n.* propiciación. **—propitiatory** (-ə·tor·i) *adj.* propiciatorio.

propitious (prə'pɪʃ·əs) *adj.* propicio; bueno; benigno. **—propitiousness,** *n.* benignidad; calidad de propicio.

proponent (prə'po·nənt) *n.* proponente.

proportion (prə'por·ʃən) *n.* proporción. **—***v.t.* proporcionar. **—proportional,** *adj.* proporcional. **—proportionate** (-ət) *adj.* proporcionado. **—out of proportion,** desproporcionado.

proposal (prə'po·zəl) *n.* 1, (suggestion) propuesta; proposición. 2, (offer of marriage) oferta de matrimonio; declaración de amor.

propose (prə'poːz) *v.t.* proponer; sugerir. **—***v.i.* 1, (plan; intend) proponer o proponerse (+ *inf.*). 2, (make an offer of marriage) declararse; pedir la mano (a).

proposition (,prap·ə'zɪʃ·ən) *n.* proposición. **—***v.t., slang* hacerle a uno una propuesta escandalosa.

propound (prə'paund) *v.t.* proponer.

proprietary (prə'prai·ə,tɛr·i) *adj.* propietario. —*n.* **1,** (owner) dueño. **2,** (ownership) posesión. **3,** (patent medicine) propietario; patentado.

proprietor (prə'prai·ə·tər) *n.* propietario; dueño. —**proprietress,** *n.* propietaria; dueña. —**proprietorship,** *n.* derecho de propiedad.

propriety (prə'prai·ə·ti) *n.* propiedad; conveniencia. —**proprieties,** *n.pl.* convenciones.

propulsion (prə'pʌl·ʃən) *n.* propulsión. —**propulsive** (-sɪv) *adj.* propulsor.

pro rata (pro'rei·tə) a prorrata; a prorrateo.

prorate (pro'reit) *v.t.* prorratear. —**proration,** *n.* prorrateo.

prosaic (pro'zei·ɪk) *adj.* prosaico.

proscenium (pro'si·ni·əm) *n.* **1,** (stage) escenario. **2,** (front of stage) proscenio.

proscribe (pro'skraib) *v.t.* proscribir. —**proscription** (-'skrɪp·ʃən) *n.* proscripción.

prose (proːz) *n.* prosa. —*adj.* en o de prosa. —**prose writer,** prosista.

prosecute ('pras·ə,kjut) *v.t.* **1,** (pursue) proseguir. **2,** *law* procesar. —*v.i.* hacer causa; armar un pleito.

prosecution (,pras·ə'kju·ʃən) *n.* **1,** (pursuit; carrying out) prosecución. **2,** (legal proceedings) procesamiento. **3,** (representative of the state) parte acusadora; prosecución.

prosecutor ('pras·ə,kju·tər) *n.* procurador; fiscal.

proselyte ('pras·ə,lait) *n.* prosélito. —*v.t. & i.* = **proselytize.**

proselytize ('pras·ə·lə,taiz) *v.t.* convertir. —*v.i.* ganar o tratar de ganar prosélitos.

prosody ('pras·ə·di) *n.* prosodia. —**prosodic** (pro'sad·ɪk) *adj.* prosódico.

prospect ('pras·pekt) *n.* **1,** (view) perspectiva; vista. **2,** (outlook; hope; chance) expectativa; esperanza. **3,** (possible customer) cliente o comprador putativo. —*v.t. & i.* explorar (para descubrir minerales, petróleo, etc.).

prospective (prə'spek·tɪv) *adj.* esperado; putativo.

prospector ('pras·pek·tər) *n.* buscador [*fem.* -dora].

prospectus (prə'spek·təs) *n.* prospecto; catálogo.

prosper ('pras·pər) *v.t. & i.* prosperar. —**prosperity** (pras'pɛr·ə·ti) *n.* prosperidad.

prosperous ('pras·pər·əs) *adj.* **1,** (favorable) próspero. **2,** (affluent) rico; adinerado.

prostate ('pras·teit) *n.* próstata. —*adj.* de la próstata; prostático.

prosthesis ('pras·θə·sɪs) *n.* próstesis. —**prosthetic** (-'θɛt·ɪk) *adj.* prostético.

prostitute ('pras·tə,tjut) *v.t.* prostituir. —*n.* prostituta; ramera; puta. —**prostitution** (-'tju·ʃən) *n.* prostitución.

prostrate ('pras·treit) *adj.* postrado. —*v.t.* postrar. —**prostration,** *n.* postración.

protactinium (,pro·tæk'tɪn·i·əm) *n.* protactinio. *También,* **protoactinium.** (,pro·to·æk-)

protagonist (pro'tæg·ə·nɪst) *n.* protagonista.

protean ('pro·ti·ən) *adj.* proteico.

protect (prə'tɛkt) *v.t.* proteger.

protection (prə'tɛk·ʃən) *n.* protección. —**protectionism,** *n.* proteccionismo. —**protectionist,** *adj. & n.* proteccionista.

protective (prə'tɛk·tɪv) *adj.* protector. —**protective coloration,** mimetismo.

protector (prə'tɛk·tər) *n.* protector. —**protectress** (-trɪs) *n.* protectriz; protectora.

protectorate (prə'tɛk·tər·ɪt) *n.* protectorado.

protégé (,pro·tə'ʒei) *n.* protegido. —**protégée,** *n.* protegida.

protein ('pro·tin) *n.* proteína.

protest ('pro·tɛst) *n.* protesta; *comm.* protesto. —*v.t. & i.* (pro'tɛst) protestar.

Protestant ('prat·ɪs·tənt) *n. & adj. también, l.c.* protestante. —**Protestantism,** *n.* protestantismo.

protestation (,prat·əs'tei·ʃən) *n.* protestación; protesta.

protoactinium (,pro·to·æk'tɪn·i·əm) *n.* = **protactinium.**

protocol ('pro·tə,kal) *n.* protocolo. —*adj.* protocolar; protocolario.

proton ('pro·tan) *n.* protón.

protoplasm ('pro·tə,plæz·əm) *n.* protoplasma. —**protoplasmic** (-'plæz·mɪk) *adj.* protoplasmático.

prototype ('pro·tə,taip) *n.* prototipo.

Protozoa (,pro·tə'zo·ə) *n.pl.*

protozoos. —**protozoan**, *n*. & *adj*. protozoo; protozoario.

protract (pro'trækt) *v.t*. **1**, (prolong) prolongar; dilatar. **2**, (extend) alargar; extender. **3**, (draw to scale) planear o trazar usando la escala y el transportador. —**protraction** (-'træk·ʃən) *n*. prolongación.

protractor (pro'træk·tər) *n*. **1**, *anat*. músculo extensor. **2**, (measuring device) transportador.

protrude (pro'truːd) *v.t*. hacer destacar; sacar fuera. —*v.i*. sobresalir; proyectarse. —**protrusion** (-'truː·ʒən) *n*. saliente; proyección.

protuberant (pro'tju·bə·rənt) *adj*. protuberante. —**protuberance**, *n*. protuberancia.

proud (praud) *adj*. **1**, (arrogant) arrogante; engreído. **2**, (self-respecting) orgulloso. **3**, (noble; imposing) noble; altivo. **4**, (spirited) valiente.

proud flesh bezo.

prove (pruːv) *v.t*. **1**, (demonstrate) probar. **2**, *print*. sacar una prueba de. —*v.i*. resultar.

proven ('pruː·vən) *v*., *p.p. de* prove. —*adj*. probado; aprobado; asegurado.

provenance ('prav·ə·nəns) *n*. origen; derivación.

provender ('prav·ən·dər) *n*. **1**, (fodder) forraje. **2**, (food) comida.

proverb ('prav·ɑrb) *n*. proverbio. —**proverbial** (prə'vɑrb·i·əl) *adj*. proverbial; *fig*. notorio.

provide (prə'vaid) *v.t*. proveer; proporcionar; suministrar. —*v.i*. **1**, (supply what is necessary) proporcionar lo necesario. **2**, (prepare) prepararse. **3**, (take precautions) precaverse. **4**, (stipulate) estipular.

provided (prə'vai·dɪd) *v*., *p.p. de* **provide**. —*conj*. [*también*, **providing**] con tal (de) que; dado que.

providence ('prav·ɪ·dəns) *n*. **1**, (foresight) previsión; providencia. **2**, *cap*. (divine care) providencia de Dios.

provident ('prav·ɪ·dənt) *adj*. **1**, (foresighted) providente; próvido; previsor. **2**, (prudent) prudente.

providential (,prav·ɪ'dən·ʃəl) *adj*. providencial.

province ('prav·ɪns) *n*. **1**, (division of a country; rural region) provincia. **2**, (sphere of influence) esfera; campo; pertenencia.

provincial (prə'vɪn·ʃəl) *adj*. provincial; provinciano. —*n*. provinciano. —**provincialism**, *n*. provincialismo.

provision (prə'vɪʒ·ən) *n*. **1**, (preparation) provisión. **2**, *law* (stipulation) estipulación. **3**, *pl*. (food supplies) bastimentos; víveres. —*v.t*. proveer; abastecer; aprovisionar. —**provisional**, *adj*. provisional; provisorio. —**provisioning**, *n*. proveimiento; abastecimiento.

proviso (prə'vai·zo) *n*. estipulación; condición.

provocation (,pra·və'kei·ʃən) *n*. provocación.

provocative (prə'vak·ə·tɪv) *adj*. provocador; provocativo.

provoke (prə'vok) *v.t*. provocar. —**provoking**, *adj*. provocante; provocador.

provost ('prav·əst) *n*. preboste. —**provost marshal** ('pro·vo) preboste; capitán preboste.

prow (prau) *n*. proa.

prowess ('prau·ɪs) *n*. proeza.

prowl (praul) *v.t*. & *i*. rondar; vagar, esp. en busca de presa o pillaje. —*n*. ronda; vagabundeo. —**prowler**, *n*. rondador; ladrón. —**prowl car**, coche de policía.

proximate ('prak·sə·mət) *adj*. próximo.

proximity (prak'sɪm·ə·ti) *n*. proximidad.

proxy ('prak·si) *n*. **1**, (delegated authority) poder. **2**, (authorized person) apoderado. —**by proxy**, por poderes. —**give one's proxy to**, apoderar.

prude (pruːd) *n*. mojigato. —**prudery**, *n*. mojigatería. —**prudish**, *adj*. mojigato.

prudent ('pruː·dənt) *adj*. prudente. —**prudence**, *n*. prudencia.

prudential (pru'dən·ʃəl) *adj*. prudencial.

prune (pruːn) *n*. ciruela pasa. —*v.t*. & *i*. podar. —**pruning**, *n*. poda. —**pruning hook**, podera. —**pruning knife**, podadera.

prurient ('prʊr·i·ənt) *adj*. lascivo. —**prurience; pruriency**, *n*. lascivia.

Prussian ('prʌʃ·ən) *adj*. & *n*. prusiano. —**Prussian blue**, azul de Prusia.

pry (prai) *n*. palanca. —*v.t*. [*pret*. & *p.p.* **pried**] **1**, (raise or force with a lever) levantar o forzar con una palanca. **2**, (remove with difficulty) arrancar. **3**, (secure by guile, as information) sonsacar; tirar de la lengua. —*v.i.* **1,** (snoop) espiar; huronear. **2,** (meddle) entremeterse. —*pryer,* n. fisgón; hurón.

prying ('prai·ıŋ) *n.* fisgoneo. —*adj.* fisgón [*fem.* -gona]; curioso.

psalm (saːm) *n.* salmo. —**psalmist,** *n.* salmista. —**psalmody** ('sa·mə·di) *n.* salmodia.

Psalter ('sɔl·tər) *n.* Salterio.

pseudo ('su·do) *adj.* seudo; pseudo; falso.

pseudonym ('su·də,nım) *n.* seudónimo.

pshaw (ʃɔ) *interj.* ¡fu!; ¡bah!; ¡vaya!

psittacosis (,sıt·ə'ko·sıs) *n.* psitacosis.

psoriasis (so'rai·ə·sıs) *n.* psoriasis.

psych (saik) *v.t., slang* **1,** (with **out**) ganar en astucia. **2,** (with **up**) prepararse; animarse. **3,** (decide oneself) decidirse; resolverse.

psyche ('sai·ki) *n.* psique; psiquis; *cap., myth.* Psique.

psychedelic (,sai·kə'dɛl·ık) *adj.* psicodélico.

psychiatry (sai'kai·ə·tri) *n.* psiquiatría. —**psychiatric** (,sai·ki'æt·rık) *adj.* psiquiátrico. —**psychiatrist,** *n.* psiquiatra.

psychic ('sai·kık) *adj.* psíquico. —*n.* médium.

psycho ('sai·ko) *n. & adj., slang* loco.

psychoanalysis (,sai·ko·ə'næl·ə·sıs) *n.* psicoanálisis. —**psychoanalyze,** *v.t.* psicoanalizar. —**psychoanalyst,** *n.* psicoanalista. —**psychoanalytic,** *adj.* psicoanalítico.

psychology (sai'kal·ə·dʒi) *n.* psicología; sicología. —**psychological** (,sai·kə'ladʒ·ə·kəl) *adj.* psicológico. —**psychologist,** *n.* psicólogo.

psychoneurosis (,sai·ko·nu'ro·sıs) *n.* [*pl.* **-ses** (-siz)] psiconeurosis.

psychopath ('sai·ko,pæθ) *n.* psicópata. —**psychopathic** (-'pæθ·ık) *adj.* psicopático.

psychopathology (,sai·ko·pə'θal·ə·dʒi) *n.* psicopatología.

psychopathy (sai'kap·ə·θi) *n.* psicopatía.

psychosis (sai'ko·sıs) *n.* [*pl.* **-ses** (siz)] psicosis.

psychotherapy (,sai·ko'θɛr·ə·pi) *n.* psicoterapia. —**psychotherapist,** *n.* psicoterapeuta.

psychotic (sai'kat·ık) *adj.* psicopático. —*n.* psicópata.

PT boat ('pi'ti) lancha torpedera.

pterodactyl (,tɛr·ə'dæk·təl) *n.* pterodáctilo.

Ptolemaic (,tal·ə'mei·ık) *adj.* de Tolomeo; tolemaico.

ptomaine ('to·mein) *n.* ptomaína.

pub (pʌb) *n., Brit.* taberna; cantina.

puberty ('pju·bər·ti) *n.* pubertad.

pubes ('pju·biz) *n.pl.* pubis.

pubescent (pju'bes·ənt) *adj.* pubescente; púber. —**pubescence,** *n.* pubescencia.

pubic ('pju·bık) *adj.* del pubis; púbico.

pubis ('pju·bis) *n.* pubis.

public ('pʌb·lık) *adj. & n.* público. —**public address system,** sistema de amplificación. —**public domain,** propiedad pública. —**public defender,** defensor de oficio. —**public enemy,** enemigo público. —**public relations,** relaciones públicas.

publican ('pʌb·lə·kən) *n.* **1,** *hist.* (tax collector) publicano. **2,** *Brit.* (tavern keeper) tabernero; posadero.

publication (,pʌb·lı'kei·ʃən) *n.* publicación.

public house *Brit.* taberna; cantina.

publicist ('pʌb·lı·sıst) *n.* publicista.

publicity (pʌb'lıs·ə·ti) *n.* publicidad. —*adj.* publicitario.

publicize ('pʌb·lı,saiz) *v.t.* publicar; hacer público.

public school escuela pública; *Brit.* colegio privado selecto.

public-spirited *adj.* patriótico.

public utility empresa de servicio público.

publish ('pʌb·lıʃ) *v.t.* **1,** (make publicly known) publicar; promulgar. **2,** (print and issue) imprimir; dar a luz; publicar.

publisher ('pʌb·lıʃ·ər) *n.* **1,** (proclaimer) promulgador. **2,** (bookseller) editor; librero.

puck (pʌk) *n.* **1,** *sports* (disk) disco de hockey; pelota. **2,** (sprite) duende.

pucker ('pʌk·ər) *v.t. & i.* **1,** (pleat) plegar. **2,** (wrinkle, as one's brows or lips) fruncir. —*n.* **1,** (pleat) pliegue. **2,** (wrinkle; wrinkling) frunce.

puckish ('pʌk·ıʃ) *adj.* **1,** (mischievous) travieso; juguetón. **2,** (elflike) de o como duende.

pudding ('pʊd·ɪŋ) *n.* budín; pudín.
puddle ('pʌd·əl) *n.* aguazal; charco; poza. —*v.t.* pudelar. —*v.i.* chapotear. —**puddler** (-lər) *n.* pudelador. —**puddling** (-lɪŋ) *n.* pudelación.
pudenda (pju'dɛn·də) *n.pl.* partes pudendas.
pudgy ('pʌdʒ·i) *adj.* regordete; gordiflón; rechoncho.
pueblo ('pwɛb·lo) *n.* pueblo.
puerile ('pju·ər·ɪl) *adj.* pueril. —**puerility** (-'ɪl·ə·ti) *n.* puerilidad.
puerperal (pju'ʌr·pər·əl) *adj.* puerperal.
Puerto Rican (‚pwɛr·tə'ri·kən) *adj. & n.* puertorriqueño; portorriqueño.
puff (pʌf) *n.* **1,** (blast, as of smoke, wind, or air) bocanada; vaharada; resoplido. **2,** (light pad) mota. **3,** *colloq.* (exaggerated praise) envanecimiento; alabanza. **4,** (pastry) bollo esponjado. —*v.t.* **1,** (emit forcibly) resoplar. **2,** (swell) inflar; dilatar; hinchar. **3,** (praise) engreír. —*v.i.* **1,** (swell) inflarse; hincharse. **2,** (boast) envanecerse; engreírse. **3,** (blow) soplar. **4,** (pant) jadear.
puffball ('pʌf‚bɔl) *n., bot.* bejín.
puff paste hojaldre.
puffy ('pʌf·i) *adj.* **1,** (swollen) inflado; hinchado. **2,** (self-satisfied) engreído; vano. **3,** (formed in puffs, as smoke or clouds) en bocanadas. **4,** (panting) jadeante.
pug (pʌg) *n.* **1,** (small dog) faldero; perrito de nariz respingada. **2,** = **pug nose. 3,** *slang* = **pugilist.**
pugilist ('pju·dʒə·lɪst) *n.* púgil. —**pugilism,** *n.* pugilismo; pugilato.
pugnacious (pʌg'nei·ʃəs) *adj.* pugnaz. —**pugnacity** (-'næs·ə·ti) *n.* pugnacidad.
pug nose nariz respingada. —**pug-nosed,** *adj.* braco.
puke (pjuk) *v.t. & i., vulg.* vomitar. —*n., vulg.* vómito.
pulchritude ('pʌl·krɪ‚tud) *n.* pulcritud.
pull (pʊl) *v.t. & i.* **1,** (tug; draw) tirar (de); halar. **2,** (take out or away; pluck) sacar; arrancar. **3,** (twist; sprain) torcer. **4,** (suck; draw in) chupar. **5,** (rip; tear) descoser. **6,** [*también*, **pull off**] *slang* (execute; carry out) llevar a cabo. —*n.* **1,** (tug; jerk) tirón. **2,** (device for opening a door, drawer, etc.) tirador. **3,** (cord or chain used for pulling or drawing) cuerda; cadeni-

lla. **4,** (strenuous effort) esfuerzo; pena. **5,** *slang* (influence) mano. —**pull ahead,** avanzar; adelantarse. —**pull apart,** romper(se); partir(se). —**pull at,** tirar de. —**pull away,** retirar(se); apartarse; alejarse. —**pull back,** retirar(se); recular. —**pull down, 1,** (demolish) derribar. **2,** (abase) degradar; humillar. —**pull in, 1,** (draw in) retraer; cobrar; tirar hacia sí. **2,** *colloq.* (arrive) llegar. —**pull on,** tirar de. —**pull oneself together,** componerse. —**pull out, 1,** (pluck; draw out) sacar; arrancar. **2,** (depart) salir; marcharse; decampar. —**pull through,** salir (o sacar a uno) de un aprieto, una enfermedad, etc. —**pull up, 1,** (raise) alzar; levantar; izar. **2,** (stop) parar; frenar.
pullet ·('pʊl·ɪt) *n.* pollita; polla. .
pulley ('pʊl·i) *n.* polea.
Pullman ('pʊl·mən) *n., T.N.* coche dormitorio; coche Pullman.
pullover ('pʊl‚o·vər) *n.* pulóver.
pulmonary ('pʊl·mə‚nɛr·i) *adj.* pulmonar.
pulmonate ('pʊl·mə‚neit) *adj.* pulmonado.
pulmotor ('pʊl‚mo·tər) *n., T.N.* pulmotor.
pulp (pʌlp) *n.* pulpa; médula. —**pulpy,** *adj.* pulposo; meduloso.
pulpit ('pʊl·pɪt) *n.* púlpito.
pulpwood ('pʌlp‚wʊd) *n.* madera de pulpa.
pulque ('pʊl·ki) *n.* pulque.
pulsate ('pʌl·set) *v.i.* pulsar. —**pulsation,** *n.* pulsación.
pulse (pʌls) *n.* pulso. —*v.i.* pulsar.
pulverize ('pʌl·və‚raiz) *v.t.* pulverizar. —*v.i.* pulverizarse. —**pulverization** (-rɪ'zei·ʃən) *n.* pulverización. —**pulverizer,** *n.* pulverizador.
puma ('pu·mə) *n.* puma.
pumice ('pʌm·ɪs) *n.* piedra pómez.
pummel ('pʌm·əl) *v.t.* golpear; caer encima a puñetazos. —**pummeling,** *n.* paliza.
pump (pʌmp) *n.* **1,** (machine) bomba; *naut.* pompa. **2,** (shoe) zapatilla. —*v.t.* **1,** (move with a pump) bombear. **2,** *colloq.* (draw information) sonsacar. —*v.i.* dar a la bomba. —**pumper,** *n.* bombero. —**pump up,** inflar.
pumpernickel ('pʌm·pər‚nɪk·əl) *n.* cierto pan de centeno, de origen alemán.
pumpkin ('pʌmp·kɪn) *n.* calabaza.

pun (pʌn) *n.* retruécano; equívoco; juego de palabras. —*v.i.* hacer juego(s) de palabras; decir equívocos.

punch (pʌntʃ) *n.* **1,** (blow) puñetazo. **2,** (tool) punzón. **3,** (beverage) ponche. —*v.t.* **1,** (strike) golpear; dar un puñetazo. **2,** (prod) punzar. **3,** (perforate) picar; perforar. —**punchy,** *adj.* aturdido. —**punch bowl,** ponchera. —**punch card,** tarjeta perforada. —**punchdrunk,** *adj.* aturdido, esp. a causa de numerosos golpes en la cabeza. —**punch line,** final de un chiste.

Punch (pʌntʃ) *n.* polichinela. *También,* **punchinello** (ˌpʌn·tʃə-'nɛl·o).

puncheon ('pʌn·tʃən) *n.* **1,** (large cask) tonel. **2,** (wooden post) madero; palo. **3,** (punching tool) punzón.

punctilious (pʌŋk'tɪl·i·əs) *adj.* puntilloso. —**punctilio** (-o) *n.* puntillo.

punctual ('pʌŋk·tʃu·əl) *adj.* puntual. —**punctuality** (-'æl·ə·ti) *n.* puntualidad.

punctuate ('pʌŋk·tʃu,eit) *v.t.* puntuar. —**punctuation,** *n.* puntuación.

puncture ('pʌŋk·tʃər) *v.t.* punzar; agujerar; perforar. —*n.* punzada; puntura; perforación.

pundit ('pʌn·dɪt) *n.* erudito.

pungent ('pʌn·dʒənt) *adj.* picante; mordaz. —**pungency,** *n.* picante; mordacidad.

punish ('pʌn·ɪʃ) *v.t.* castigar. —**punishable,** *adj.* punible; castigable. —**punishment,** *n.* castigo; punición.

punitive ('pju·nə·tɪv) *adj.* punitivo.

punk (pʌŋk) *n.* **1,** (tinder) yesca. **2,** *slang* (hoodlum) rufián; maleante. —*adj., slang* malo; bajo.

punster ('pʌn·stər) *n.* equivoquista.

punt (pʌnt) *n.* **1,** (flatbottomed boat) batea; barquichuelo chato que se impulsa con una vara. **2,** *football* puntapié que se da al balón al soltarlo de las manos. —*v.t. & i.* **1,** (propel with a pole) impeler (un barco) con una vara. **2,** *football* dar un puntapié (al balón) al soltarlo de las manos.

puny ('pju·ni) *adj.* **1,** (frail; sickly) débil; enfermizo. **2,** (insignificant) insignificante; de poca monta.

pup (pʌp) *n.* **1,** [*también,* **puppy** ('pʌp·i)] (young dog) perrito; cachorro. **2,** (young of various mammals) cachorro; cría. —**pup tent,** pequeña tienda de acampamento.

pupa ('pju·pə) *n.* [*pl.* **-pae** (-pi)] crisálida.

pupil ('pju·pəl) *n.* **1,** (student) alumno; pupilo; discípulo. **2,** *anat.* pupila.

puppet ('pʌp·ɪt) *n.* **1,** (doll) títere. **2,** (person or state controlled by another) monigote. —**puppeteer,** *n.* titiritero. —**puppetry,** arte de manejar los títeres. —**puppet show,** representación de títeres.

purblind ('pʌr·blaind) *adj.* **1,** (partly blind) cegato; corto de vista. **2,** (slow; dull) torpe; lerdo.

purchase ('pʌr·tʃəs) *v.t.* comprar. —*n.* **1,** (act of buying; thing bought) compra. **2,** *mech.* (grip; lever) aparato de fuerza; agarre.

pure (pjur) *adj.* puro.

purebred ('pjur,brɛd) *adj.* de pura raza.

purée (pju'rei) *n.* puré. —*v.t.* [-**réed, -réeing**] hacer un puré de.

purgation (pʌr'gei·ʃən) *n.* purgación.

purgative ('pʌr·gə·tɪv) *adj. & n.* purgante; purgativo.

purgatory ('pʌr·gə,tor·i) *n.* purgatorio.

purge (pʌrdʒ) *v.t.* purgar; depurar. —*n.* **1,** (purgative) purgante; catártico. **2,** (elimination of undesirables) purgación.

purify ('pjur·ɪ,fai) *v.t.* purificar. —*v.i.* purificarse. —**purification** (-fɪ'kei·ʃən) *n.* purificación.

purism ('pjur·ɪz·əm) *n.* purismo. —**purist,** *n.* purista. —**puristic,** *adj.* purista.

puritan ('pjur·ə·tən) *n. & adj.* puritano. —**puritanical** (-'tæn·ə·kəl) *adj.* puritano. —**puritanism,** *n.* puritanismo.

purity ('pjur·ɪ·ti) *n.* pureza.

purl (pʌrl) *n.* **1,** (knitting stitch) puntada invertida. **2,** (murmur, as of water) murmullo. **3,** (swirl; eddy) remolino. —*v.t. & i.* (in knitting) invertir (la puntada). —*v.i.* **1,** (murmur) murmurar. **2,** (swirl) arremolinarse.

purlieus ('pʌr·luz) *n.pl.* **1,** (bounds; limits) confines; límites. **2,** (environs) inmediaciones; alrededores.

purloin (pər'lɔin) *v.t.* robar; hurtar.

—**purloiner,** *n.* ladrón [*fem.* -drona].

purple ('pʌr·pəl) *n.* púrpura. —*adj.* purpúreo; púrpura.

purport (pər'port) *v.t.* **1,** (imply) significar. **2,** (pretend) pretender. —*n.* ('pʌr·port) **1,** (meaning; sense) significado; sentido. **2,** (purpose) intención; motivo.

purpose ('pʌr·pəs) *n.* **1,** (intention) propósito; intención. **2,** (intended effect; use) fin. —*v.t.* proponer. —**answer the purpose,** servir para el caso. —**on purpose,** adrede; a propósito. —**to little purpose,** con pocos resultados. —**to no purpose,** inútilmente.

purposeful ('pʌr·pəs·fəl) *adj.* **1,** (determined) determinado; intencional. **2,** (useful) útil; provechoso.

purposely ('pʌr·pəs·li) *adv.* adrede; expresamente.

purr (pʌr) *n.* ronroneo. —*v.i.* ronronear.

purse (pʌrs) *n.* **1,** (receptacle for money) bolsa. **2,** (finances) bolsa; recursos; finanzas. **3,** (public treasury) fisco. **4,** (money raised by collection) colecta. **5,** (prize money) premio. —*v.t.* plegar; fruncir (los labios). —**purse strings,** cordones de la bolsa.

purser ('pʌr·sər) *n.* contador de barco o navío.

purslane ('pʌrs·lein) *n.* verdolaga.

pursuance (pər'su·əns) *n.* prosecución.

pursuant (pər'su·ənt) *adj.* consiguiente. —**pursuant to,** conforme a.

pursue (pər'sur) *v.t.* **1,** (follow) seguir. **2,** (chase; try to catch) perseguir. **3,** (continue; carry on) proseguir.

pursuit (pər'sut) *n.* **1,** (act of following) persecución; seguimiento. **2,** (occupation) empleo; ocupación. **3,** (continuance; carrying on) prosecución. **4,** (search) busca; búsqueda. —**pursuit plane,** avión de caza.

purulent ('pjur·ə·lənt) *adj.* purulento. —**purulence,** *n.* purulencia.

purvey (pər'vei) *v.t. & i.* proveer; abastecer. —**purveyor,** *n.* proveedor [*fem.* -dora]; abastecedor [*fem.* -dora]. —**purveyor's shop,** proveeduría.

purview ('pʌr·vju) *n.* alcance; límite.

pus (pʌs) *n.* pus. —**pussy** ('pʌs·i) *adj.* purulento.

push (puʃ) *v.t.* **1,** (shove) empujar. **2,** (advance) pujar; avanzar. —*v.i.* empujar; dar empujones. —*n.* **1,** (shove) empujón. **2,** *colloq.* (vigor) empuje. **3,** (crowd) tropel; muchedumbre. —**push ahead,** avanzar; adelantarse. —**push away,** alejar; rechazar. —**push back,** echar atrás; retroceder. —**push down,** derribar. —**push in,** entremeterse. —**push on,** avanzar; apresurarse.

push button pulsador; botón de llamada. —**push-button,** *adj.* automático; por botón.

pushcart ('puʃ,kart) *n.* carretilla.

pusher ('puʃ·ər) *n.* **1,** (person or thing that pushes) empujador [*fem.* -dora]. **2,** *colloq.* (enterprising person) persona emprendedora o agresiva. **3,** *slang* (seller of drugs) vendedor [*fem.* -dora] de narcóticos.

pushover ('puʃ,o·vər) *n., slang* cosa muy fácil; persona de poca resistencia.

pusillanimous (,pju·sə'læn·ə·məs) *adj.* pusilánime. —**pusillanimity** (-lə'nɪm·ə·ti) *n.* pusilanimidad.

puss (pus) *n.* **1,** (cat) gato; gatito. **2,** *slang* (face) cara; rostro.

pussy ('pus·i) *n.* gato; gatito. *También,* **pussycat.**

pussyfoot ('pus·i,fut) *v.i., slang* tantear miedosamente; no declararse.

pussy willow ('pus·i) sauce de amentos muy sedosos.

pustule ('pʌs·tʃul) *n.* pústula. —**pustular** ('pʌs·tʃə·lər) *adj.* pustuloso.

put (put) *v.t.* [**put, putting**] **1,** (set; place) poner; meter; echar. **2,** (express) expresar. **3,** (propose) proponer. **4,** (ask, as a question) hacer. **5,** (impose) imponer. **6,** (send) enviar. **7,** (throw; cast) arrojar; lanzar; echar. **8,** (wage) apostar. —*n.* arrojada; lanza echada. —*adj., colloq.* fijo; fir —**put about,** virar; cambiar rumbo. —**put across,** *colloq* (transmit; impart) hacer compr o entender. **2,** (accomplish) re alcanzar; llevar a cabo. **3,** (put ceptance for) hacer aceptar. —**put aside, 1,** (reserve) ahorrar; asun- **2,** (discard) rechazar. —**p** **1,** (re der,** apartar. —**put awa**

serve) ahorrar. **2,** (store) guardar. **3,** (reject) rechazar; repudiar. **4,** *colloq.* (consume) comer o tomar. **5,** (confine) encerrar; recluir. **6,** (imprison) encarcelar. —**put back, 1,** (restore) devolver; restituir. **2,** (turn back) volver atrás; regresar. —**put by, 1,** (reserve) reservar; ahorrar; guardar. **2,** (reject) rechazar. —**put down, 1,** (record) apuntar; anotar. **2,** (repress) reprimir; sofocar. **3,** (lower) bajar; rebajar. **4,** (attribute) atribuir; imputar. **5,** (swallow) tragar. **6,** (put to death) matar. —**put forth, 1,** (grow; sprout) brotar; echar. **2,** (yield; produce) producir; dar. **3,** (propose) proponer. **4,** (publish) dar a luz; publicar. **5,** (exert) ejercer; emplear. —**put in, 1,** (insert) introducir; insertar; meter. **2,** (contribute) contribuir. **3,** (spend, as time) pasar o emplear (el tiempo). **4,** *naut.* arribar; llegar al puerto. —**put off, 1,** (postpone) aplazar; posponer. **2,** (discard) quitar; deshacerse de. **3,** (evade) eludir; evadir. **4,** (divert) apartar; desviar. —**put on, 1,** (clothe with) poner; ponerse; vestir. **2,** (pretend) fingir. **3,** (stage, as a play) presentar. **4,** (assume) pretender; darse: *put on airs,* darse ínfulas. **5,** (apply, as a brake) poner. —**put out, 1,** (emit) emitir; echar. **2,** (eject) despedir; sacar. **3,** (extinguish) apagar; extinguir. **4,** (gouge out, as an eye) sacar. **5,** (inconvenience; bother) molestar; incomodar. **6,** = **put forth.** —**put over, 1,** = **put across. 2,** (postpone) posponer; diferir. **3,** (perpetrate) perpetrar; ⸺meter. **4,** [*usu.* put it over (on ⸻meone)] engañar; estafar. ⸻nbaucar. —**put through, 1,** (carry t) llevar a cabo; realizar. **2,** (put ⸻contact) poner en comunicación. ⸻(cause to suffer or undergo) ⸻eter a; sujetar a; ocasionarle a ⸻ —**put together, 1,** (join; unite) ⸻ juntar. **2,** (amass) acumular; ⸻ntonar. —**put to shame,** ⸻onzar. —**put up, 1,** (set up) ⸻lish) establecer. **2,** (erect; o⸻ erigir; construir. **3,** (present) pa⸻proponer; presentar. **4,** (pack; alo⸻e) enlatar; envasar. **5,** (lodge) inci⸻hospedar. **6,** *colloq.* (incite) apos⸻alentar; provocar. **7,** (wager) conce⸻ **8,** *colloq.* (plan; scheme) l, (imp⸻r; proyectar. —**put upon,** ⸻e on) incomodar; molestar.

2, (victimize; dupe) engañar; estafar. —**put up with,** tolerar; aguantar; soportar. —**stay put,** no moverse; no ceder; quedarse firme.

putative ('pju·tə·tɪv) *adj.* putativo.

putdown ('pʊt,daun) *n., slang* desdén; desprecio; humillación.

put-on ('pʊt·an) *adj.* simulado; fingido. —*n., colloq.* engaño; embuste.

putrefy ('pju·trə,fai) *v.t.* podrir; pudrir. —*v.i.* podrirse; pudrirse. —**putrefaction** (-'fæk·ʃən) *n.* putrefacción; pudrición; pudrimiento.

putrescence (pju'trɛs·əns) *n.* putrefacción; pudrición; pudrimiento. —**putrescent,** *adj.* pútrido.

putrid ('pju·trɪd) *adj.* pútrido; podrido; putrefacto.

putt (pʌt) *n., golf* golpe con que se procura encajar la pelota en el agujero. —*v.t. & i.* dar (a la pelota) tal golpe.

puttee ('pʌt·i) *n.* polaina.

putter ('pʌt·ər) *n., golf* bastón que se emplea para encajar la pelota en el agujero. —*v.i.* trabajar sin sistema; malgastar el tiempo.

putty ('pʌt·i) *n.* masilla.

put-up *adj., colloq.* premeditado; concertado.

puzzle ('pʌz·əl) *n.* **1,** (perplexing thing) enigma. **2,** (test of ingenuity) acertijo; adivinanza; rompecabezas. —*v.t.* confundir; embrollar; enredar. —*v.i.* preguntarse; asombrarse. —**puzzlement,** *n.* confusión; perplejidad. —**puzzler** (-lər) *n.* enigma; rompecabezas. —**puzzling** (-lɪŋ) *adj.* enigmático.

pygmy ('pɪg·mi) *adj. & n.* pigmeo.

pyjamas (pə'dʒam·əz) *n.pl.* = **pajamas.**

pylon ('pai·lan) *n.* pilón.

pylorus (pai'lor·əs) *n.* piloro. —**pyloric,** *adj.* pilórico.

pyorrhea (,pai·ə'ri·ə) *n.* piorrea.

pyramid ('pɪr·ə·mɪd) *n.* pirámide. —*v.t. & i.* invertir ganancialmente. —**pyramidal** (pɪ'ræm·ə·dəl) *adj.* piramidal.

pyre (pair) *n.* pira.

pyrite ('pai·rait) *n.* pirita.

pyrites (pai'rai·tiz; pə-) *n.* pirita.

pyromania (,pai·ro'mei·ni·a) *n.* piromanía. —**pyromaniac,** *n.* pirómano; piromaníaco.

pyrotechnics (,pai·ro'tɛk·nɪks) *n.* pirotecnia. —**pyrotechnic,** *adj.* pirotécnico.

pyrrhic ('pɪr·ɪk) *adj.* pírrico.
Pyrrhic victory triunfo pírrico.

Pythagorean (pɪ,θæg·ə'ri·ən) *adj.* pitagórico.
python ('pai·θan) *n.* pitón.

Q

Q, q (kju) decimoséptima letra del alfabeto inglés.
quack (kwæk) *n.* **1,** (duck's cry) graznido. **2,** (false doctor) curandero; matasanos; medicastro. —*v.i.* parpar. —*adj.* falso. —**quackery,** *n.* curanderismo; curandería.
quad (kwaːd) *n.* **1,** (square court) patio cuadrangular, esp. en las universidades. **2,** *print.* cuadrado; cuadratín. **3,** *colloq.* = **quadruplet.**
Quadragesima (,kwad·rə'dʒes·ə·mə) *n.* cuadragésima.
quadrangle ('kwad,ræŋ·gəl) *n.* cuadrángulo. —**quadrangular** (kwad'ræŋ·gjə·lər) *adj.* cuadrangular; cuadrángulo.
quadrant ('kwad·rənt) *n.* cuadrante.
quadrat ('kwad·ræt) *n., print.* cuadrado; cuadratín.
quadrate ('kwad·reit) *adj. & n.* cuadrado. —*v.t. & i.* cuadrar.
quadratic (kwad'ræt·ɪk) *adj.* cuadrático. —**quadratic equation,** ecuación de segundo grado; cuadrática.
quadrennial (kwad'rɛn·i·əl) *adj. & n.* cuadrienal. —**quadrennium** (-əm) *n.* cuadrienio.
quadrilateral (,kwad·rə'læt·ər·əl) *adj. & n.* cuadrilátero.
quadrille (kwə'drɪl) *n.* cuadrilla.
quadrillion (kwad'rɪl·jən) *n. U.S.* mil billones; *Brit.* un millón de trillones; cuatrillón.
quadroon (kwad'ruːn) *n.* cuarterón.
quadruped ('kwad·ru,pɛd) *n. & adj.* cuadrúpedo.
quadruple ('kwad·ru·pəl) *adj.* cuádruple; cuádruplo. —*n.* cuádruplo. —*v.* (kwad'ru·pəl) —*v.t.* cuadruplicar. —*v.i.* cuadruplicarse.
quadruplet ('kwad·ru·plɪt; kwad'ru-) *n.* cuadrúpleto.
quadruplicate (kwad'rup·lɪ·kət) *adj. & n.* cuadruplicado. —*v.t.* (-,keit) cuadruplicar.
quaff (kwaf) *v.t. & i.* tragar; beber a grandes tragos. —*n.* trago.

quagmire ('kwæg,mair) *n.* cenagal; pantano fangoso.
quahog ('kwɔ·hag) *n.* almeja redonda de la costa del Atlántico.
quail (kweil) *v.i.* acobardarse; cejar; desanimarse. —*n., ornith.* codorniz.
quaint (kweint) *adj.* **1,** (unusual) curioso; raro. **2,** (eccentric) excéntrico. —**quaintness,** *n.* curiosidad.
quake (kweik) *v.i.* temblar; sacudirse; estremecerse. —*n.* **1,** (shake) agitación; temblor. **2,** (earthquake) terremoto. —**quaking,** *adj.* movedizo. —*n.* estremecimiento.
Quaker ('kwei·kər) *adj. & n.* cuáquero. —**Quakerism,** *n.* cuaquerismo.
qualification (,kwal·ɪ·fɪ'kei·ʃən) *n.* **1,** (limitation) calificación; modificación. **2,** (requirement) requisito. **3,** (fitness; competence) capacidad; competencia.
qualified ('kwal·ɪ,faid) *adj.* **1,** (limited) calificado. **2,** (fit; competent) competente; capaz.
qualify ('kwal·ɪ,fai) *v.t.* **1,** (modify) calificar; modificar; limitar. **2,** (authorize) autorizar. **3,** (enable) habilitar; capacitar. **4,** (mitigate) templar; suavizar. —*v.i.* llenar los requisitos; habilitarse; capacitarse.
qualitative ('kwal·ə,tei·tɪv) *adj.* cualitativo.
quality ('kwal·ə·ti) *n.* **1,** (trait) cualidad; propiedad. **2,** (essence) naturaleza; virtud. **3,** (high birth or rank) nobleza. **4,** (kind; class) calidad; clase. —*adj., colloq.* de calidad; superior.
qualm (kwaːm) *n.* **1,** (compunction) escrúpulo; remordimiento. **2,** (misgiving) duda. **3,** (sudden nausea) náusea; basca.
quandary ('kwan·də·ri) *n.* incertidumbre; perplejidad.
quantitative ('kwan·tɪ,tei·tɪv) *adj.* cuantitativo.
quantity ('kwan·tə·ti) *n.* cantidad.
quantum ('kwan·təm) *n.* [*pl.* **quanta** (-tə)] **1,** (amount) canti-

dad. 2, *physics* unidad cuántica; cuanto; quantum. —*adj.* cuántico.

quarantine ('kwar·ən,tin) *n.* cuarentena. —*v.t.* poner en cuarentena; aislar.

quarrel ('kwar·əl) *n.* riña; disputa; querella. —*v.i.* reñir; disputar. —**quarrelsome,** *adj.* reñidor; pendenciero.

quarry ('kwar·i) *n.* 1, (excavation) cantera. 2, (prey) presa; caza. —*v.t.* extraer; sacar de una cantera.

quart (kwort) *n.* cuarto de galón.

quarter ('kwor·tər) *n.* 1, (one-fourth) cuarta parte; cuarto. 2, (U.S. coin) cuarto de dólar; moneda de 25 centavos; *P.R.* peseta. 3, (period of three months) trimestre. 4, (one-fourth of a mile) cuadra. 5, (region) región; comarca. 6, (urban district) barrio. 7, (leg of an animal) pernil. 8, (mercy) merced; clemencia. 9, *naut.* cuadra. —*adj.* cuarto. —*v.t.* 1, (divide in four) dividir en cuatro; cuartear. 2, (carve; cut in pieces) descuartizar. 3, (lodge) alojar; hospedar. 4, *mil.* (billet) acantonar; acuartelar. —**quarters,** *n.pl.* vivienda; domicilio; *mil.* cuarteles. —**quarter note,** *mus.* negra.

quarterdeck ('kwor·tər,dɛk) *n.* alcázar.

quarterly ('kwor·tər·li) *adj.* trimestral. —*n.* revista o publicación trimestral. —*adv.* trimestralmente.

quartermaster ('kwor·tər,mæs·tər) *n.* 1, *mil.* comisario de guerra; comisario ordenador. 2, *naut.* cabo de brigadas. —**quartermaster corps,** intendencia militar. —**quartermaster general,** intendente de ejército.

quartet (kwor'tɛt) *n.* 1, (group of four) grupo de cuatro. 2, *mus.* cuarteto.

quarto ('kwor·to) *adj.* en cuarto. —*n.* [*pl.* **-tos**] libro en cuarto.

quartz (kworts) *n.* cuarzo.

quasar ('kwei·zar) *n.,* *astron.* cuásar.

quash (kwaʃ) *v.t.* 1, (suppress) reprimir; sofocar. 2, (annul) anular; invalidar.

quaternary (kwə'tar·nə·ri) *adj.* cuaternario; cuarto en orden; cuaterno. —*n.* cuaternario.

quatrain ('kwat,rein) *n.* cuarteto; redondilla.

quaver ('kwei·vər) *v.i.* 1, (tremble) temblar; vibrar. 2, (sing or speak tremulously) gorjear; trinar. —*n.* 1,

(tremor) temblor; vibración. 2, (trill; tremolo) trino; gorjeo; trémolo. 3, *mus.* (eighth note) corchea.

quay (kiː) *n.* muelle; desembarcadero.

queasy ('kwi·zi) *adj.* 1, (inclined to nausea) nauseabundo. 2, (squeamish) escrupuloso; quisquilloso. —**queasiness,** *n.* náusea.

queen (kwiːn) *n.* 1, (sovereign) reina. 2, *colloq.* (social leader) mujer preeminente. 3, *chess; cards* dama. —**queen bee,** abeja maestra; abeja reina. —**queen consort,** esposa del rey. —**queen dowager,** reina viuda. —**queen mother,** reina madre.

queenly ('kwin·li) *adj.* como o de reina; real. —**queenliness,** *n.* calidad o carácter de reina.

queer (kwir) *adj.* 1, (odd) raro; extraño; curioso; excéntrico. 2, *colloq.* (daft) chiflado. 3, *slang* (homosexual) invertido; maricón. —*v.t.,* *slang* dañar; comprometer. —**queerness,** *n.* rareza; extrañeza.

quell (kwel) *v.t.* 1, (suppress) reprimir; sofocar. 2, (calm) calmar; apaciguar.

quench (kwɛntʃ) *v.t.* 1, (satisfy) apagar. 2, (extinguish) extinguir. 3, (cool, as metal, by immersion) templar.

querulous ('kwer·ə·ləs) *adj.* querelloso; quejumbroso. —**querulousness,** *n.* quejumbre; mal genio.

query ('kwɪr·i) *n.* 1, (question) pregunta. 2, (doubt) duda. 3, (question mark) signo de interrogación. —*v.t. & i.* 1, (question) indagar; preguntar. 2, (doubt) dudar; poner en duda.

quest (kwɛst) *n.* búsqueda; indagación. —**in quest of,** en busca de.

question ('kwes·tʃən) *n.* 1, (inquiry) pregunta; interrogación. 2, (doubt) duda; disputa; pleito. 3, (subject of discussion) tema; cuestión; caso. —*v.i.* preguntar; informarse; examinar. —*v.t.* 1, (interrogate) interrogar. 2, (doubt) dudar. 3, (challenge) recusar. —**questionable,** *adj.* dudoso. —**questioning,** *n.* interrogatorio. —**beside the question,** que no viene al caso. —**out of the question,** imposible. —**it is a question of . . . ,** se trata de. . . . —**question mark,** signo o punto de interrogación. **—to ask a question,** hacer una pregunta.

questionnaire (ˌkwɛs·tʃəˈneɪr) n. cuestionario.

queue (kjuː) n. **1,** (tail) cola. **2,** (line of persons) hilera; cola. **3,** (pigtail) coleta. **—v.i.** [también, **queue up]** hacer cola.

quibble (ˈkwɪb·əl) n. subterfugio; sutileza; rodeo. **—v.i.** rodear; buscar escapatorias. **—quibbler** (-lər) n. rodeador [fem. -dora].

quiche (kiʃ) n. pastel de queso y huevos.

quick (kwɪk) adj. **1,** (fast) rápido; veloz; ligero. **2,** (alert) listo; alerto. **3,** (excitable) precipitado; irritable. **—adv.** pronto; rápidamente. **—n. 1,** (sensitivity) sensibilidad. **2,** (sensitive flesh) lo vivo; carne viva. **3,** (seat of emotions) lo más hondo del alma. **—be quick,** darse prisa.

quicken (ˈkwɪk·ən) v.t. acelerar; avivar; animar. **—v.i.** acelerarse; avivarse; animarse. **—quickening,** n. aceleración; avivamiento; animación.

quick-frozen adj. congelado al instante.

quickie (ˈkwɪk·i) n., slang cosa hecha a prisa.

quicklime (ˈkwɪkˌlaim) n. cal viva.

quickly (ˈkwɪk·li) adv. pronto; rápidamente.

quickness (ˈkwɪk·nəs) n. **1,** (rapidity) rapidez; velocidad. **2,** (alertness) agilidad; viveza.

quicksand (ˈkwɪkˌsænd) n. arena movediza.

quicksilver (ˈkwɪkˌsɪl·vər) n. azogue; mercurio.

quickstep (ˈkwɪkˌstɛp) n. **1,** mus. paso doble. **2,** mil. paso redoblado.

quick-tempered adj. colérico.

quick-witted adj. listo; astuto.

quid (kwɪd) n. **1,** (cud; chew of tobacco or gum) mascadura. **2,** Brit. slang (pound) libra esterlina.

quiescent (kwaiˈɛs·ənt) adj. tranquilo; quieto. **—quiescence,** n. quietud; reposo.

quiet (ˈkwai·ət) adj. **1,** (silent) callado; silencioso. **2,** (calm) tranquilo. **3,** (smooth) sosegado; manso. **4,** (unassuming) modesto. **5,** (subdued in color) bajo. **—v.t.** callar; calmar; sosegar. **—v.i.** callarse; calmarse. **—n.** reposo; tranquilidad; paz. **—quieting,** adj. cal-

mante. **—quietness,** n. tranquilidad; silencio.

quietude (ˈkwai·ə·tud) n. quietud; reposo.

quietus (kwaiˈi·təs) n. **1,** (release, as from debt) quita; quitanza; carta de pago. **2,** (death) fallecimiento; muerte.

quill (kwɪl) n. **1,** (feather) pluma. **2,** (feather pen) pluma para escribir. **3,** (sharp spine) púa.

quilt (kwɪlt) n. colcha. **—v.t.** colchar. **—quilting,** n. colchadura.

quince (kwɪns) n. **1,** (fruit) membrillo. **2,** (tree) membrillo; membrillero.

quinine (ˈkwai·nain) n. quinina.

quinquagenarian (ˌkwɪn·kwə·dʒəˈnɛr·i·ən) adj. & n. cincuentón [fem. -tona].

Quinquagesima (ˌkwɪn·kwə·ˈdʒɛs·ə·mə) n. quincuagésima.

quinquennium (kwɪnˈkwɛn·i·əm) n. quinquenio. **—quinquennial,** adj. quinquenal.

quinsy (ˈkwɪn·zi) n. angina.

quint (kwɪnt) n. **1,** (set of five) conjunto de cinco. **2,** mus. quinta. **3,** colloq. = **quintuplet. 4,** (in games of chance) quina.

quintal (ˈkwɪn·təl) n. quintal.

quintessence (kwɪnˈtɛs·əns) n. quintaesencia.

quintet (kwɪnˈtɛt) n. **1,** (group of five) grupo de cinco. **2,** mus. quinteto.

quintillion (kwɪnˈtɪl·jən) n. U.S. un millón de billones; trillón; Brit. un millón de cuatrillones; quintillón.

quintuple (ˈkwɪn·tju·pəl) adj. & n. quíntuplo. **—v.t.** multiplicar por cinco; quintuplicar. **—v.i.** quintuplicarse.

quintuplet (ˈkwɪn·tju·plit; kwɪnˈtʌp·lit) n. quintillizo; Amer. quíntuple.

quip (kwɪp) n. chiste. **—v.i.** [**quipped, quipping**] bromear; echar pullas.

quire (kwair) n. mano (de papel).

quirk (kwʌrk) n. **1,** (quick turn) giro; recodo; rodeo. **2,** (flourish, in writing) rasgo. **3,** (idiosyncrasy) peculiaridad; capricho; rareza.

quisling (ˈkwɪz·lɪŋ) n. traidor; quisling.

quit (kwɪt) v.t. abandonar; dejar; ceder. **—v.i.** desistir; cesar; parar. **—adj.** libre; absuelto.

quitclaim ('kwit,kleim) *n.* renuncia. —*v.t.* renunciar.

quite (kwait) *adv.* 1, (completely) completamente; totalmente. 2, *colloq.* (very) considerablemente; bastante.

quits (kwits) *adj., colloq.* en paz; corrientes. —**be quits,** estar corrientes; estar desquitados. —**cry quits,** darse por vencido; cesar la lucha.

quittance ('kwit·əns) *n.* 1, (discharge from obligation) quitanza. 2, (reward) recompensa.

quitter ('kwit·ər) *n.* desertor; cobarde.

quiver ('kwiv·ər) *v.i.* temblar; vibrar; estremecerse. —*n.* 1, (shake) temblor. 2, (arrow case) carcaj; aljaba. —**quivering,** *n.* tremor; estremecimiento.

quixotic (kwiks'at·ik) *adj.* quijotesco. —**quixotism** ('kwik·sə,tiz·əm) *n.* quijotismo.

quiz (kwiz) *n.* [*pl.* **quizzes**] 1, (examination) examen. 2, (radio or television program) programa de preguntas y respuestas. —*v.t.* [**quizzed, quizzing**] 1, (question) interrogar; examinar. 2, (chaff) burlarse de. 3, (peer at) mirar de hito en hito.

quizzical ('kwiz·ə·kəl) *adj.* 1, (chaffing) burlón; guasón. 2, (questioning) perplejo; curioso.

quoin (kɔin) *n.* 1, (corner of a building) rincón; ángulo; esquina. 2, (stone forming an angle) piedra angular. 3, (wedge) cuña. 4, *print.* cuña.

quoits (kwɔits) *n.sing.* juego de tejos. —**quoit,** *n.* tejo.

quondam ('kwan·dəm) *adj.* antiguo; de otro tiempo.

quonset hut ('kwan·sət) cobertizo de metal prefabricado.

quorum ('kwor·əm) *n.* quórum.

quota ('kwo·tə) *n.* cuota.

quotation (kwo'tei·ʃən) *n.* 1, (citation) cita. 2, *comm.* cotización. —**quotation marks,** comillas.

quote (kwot) *v.t.* 1, (cite) citar. 2, (state the price of) cotizar. —*n., colloq.* = **quotation.** —**quotes,** *n.pl., colloq.* = **quotation marks.**

quoth (kwoθ) *v.t., archaic* dije o dijo.

quotidian (kwo'tid·i·ən) *adj.* cotidiano; diario. —*n.* fiebre cotidiana.

quotient ('kwo·ʃənt) *n.* cuociente; cociente.

R

R, r (ar) décimoctava letra del alfabeto inglés.

rabbi ('ræb·ai) *n.* rabino; rabí. —**rabbinical** (rə'bin·i·kəl) *adj.* rabínico.

rabbit ('ræb·it) *n.* conejo. —**rabbit ears,** antena de televisión (*instalada encima del aparato*). —**Welsh rabbit** (o **rarebit**) queso derretido servido sobre pan tostado.

rabble ('ræb·əl) *n.* populacho; canalla. —**rabble rouser,** populachero. —**rabble rousing,** populachería. —**rabble-rousing,** *adj.* populachero.

rabid ('ræb·id) *adj.* 1, (furious) furioso. 2, (zealous) entusiasta; fanático. 3, (affected with rabies) rabioso. —**rabidity** (rə'bid·ə·ti) *n.* rabia.

rabies ('rei·biz) *n.* hidrofobia; rabia.

raccoon (ræ'kuːn) *n.* mapache.

race (reis) *n.* 1, (contest of speed) carrera; *naut.* regata. 2, (competition) lucha; contienda. 3, (ethnic group) raza. 4, (lineage) linaje; casta. 5, (current of water) corriente fuerte y rápida. 6, (channel for water) canal; caz. —*v.i.* 1, (run) correr. 2, (compete) competir. 3, (increase speed) acelerarse. 4, *mech.* marchar con velocidad excesiva. 5, *naut.* regatear. —*v.t.* 1, (run against) correr en competición con. 2, (rush) dar prisa a; acelerar. 3, *mech.* dar velocidad excesiva a. —**boat race,** regata. —**human race,** género humano. —**race course;** **race track,** pista de carreras; hipódromo.

raceme (re'siːm) *n.* racimo.

racer ('rei·sər) *n.* 1, (runner) corredor. 2, (horse) caballo de carreras. 3, (auto) auto de carrera.

raceway ('reis·wei) *n.* autódromo.

rachitis (rə'kai·tis) *n.* raquitismo; raquitis. —**rachitic** (-'kit·it) *adj.* raquítico.

racial ('rei·ʃəl) adj. racial.

racing ('rei·sɪŋ) n. carrera; carreras. —adj. de carrera.

racism ('reis·ɪz·əm) n. racismo. —**racist,** adj. & n. racista.

rack (ræk) n. 1, (frame) estante; percha. 2, mech. (toothed bar) cremallera. 3, (instrument of torture) potro (de tormento). 4, (pain) dolor; agonía. 5, (horse gait) trote. 6, (destruction) destrucción; ruina. —v.t. 1, (torture) torturar. 2, (worry) oprimir; atormentar. —v.i. 1, (worry) preocuparse. 2, (pace) andar a trote. —**rack one's brains,** devanarse los sesos.

racket ('ræk·ɪt) n. 1, (din) baraúnda; alboroto. 2, [también, **racquet**] sports (webbed bat) raqueta. 3, (dishonest enterprise) estafa. 4, pl. (game) trinquete. —**racketeer** (-ə'tɪɪr) n. trampeador; trapacero.

raconteur (,ræk·an'tʌr) n. cuentista.

racy ('reis·ɪ) adj. 1, (piquant) picante. 2, (vigorous) enérgico. 3, colloq. (risqué) sugestivo; atrevido.

radar ('rei·dar) n. radar.

radial ('rei·di·əl) adj. radial.

radian ('rei·di·ən) n. radián.

radiant ('rei·di·ənt) adj. 1, (emitting rays) radiante. 2, (beaming, as with joy) alegre; resplandeciente. —n. radiante. —**radiance,** n. resplandor.

radiate ('rei·di,eit) v.i. 1, (shine) brillar; resplandecer. 2, (emit rays) echar rayos. 3, (spread out) radiar. —v.t. radiar; fig. difundir. —adj. (·ət) radiado. —**radiation,** n. radiación.

radiator ('rei·di,ei·tər) n. radiador.

radical ('ræd·ɪ·kəl) adj. 1, math. radical. 2, (drastic) extremo. 3, (basic) fundamental. —n. 1, math; gram. raíz. 2, (fundamental) radical. 3, polit. radical; extremista. —**radicalism,** n. radicalismo.

radio ('rei·di·o) n. 1, (receiving set) radiorreceptor; radio. 2, (broadcasting medium) radiodifusión; radio. 3, (communication) radiocomunicación. —v.t. & i. radiodifundir; transmitir por radio. —adj. de radio; de radiodifusión. —**radio announcer,** radiolocutor [fem. -tora]. —**radio listener,** radioyente. —**radio monitor,** radioescucha. —**radio network,** red o cadena de emisoras. —**radio receiver,** radio-

rreceptor. —**radio repair,** radiotecnia. —**radio station,** emisora; radiodifusora; radioemisora. —**radio technician,** radiotécnico. —**radio technology,** radiotecnia. —**radio transmitter,** radioemisor; radiotransmisor.

radioactive (,rei·di·o'æk·tɪv) adj. radiactivo; radioactivo. —**radioactivity,** n. radiactividad; radioactividad.

radio-controlled adj. radiodirigido.

radiogram ('rei·di·o,græm) n. radiograma.

radiograph ('rei·di·o,græf) n. radiografía. —**radiography** (,rei·di'ag·rə·fi) n. radiografía.

radiology (,rei·di'al·ə·dʒi) n. radiología. —**radiological** (-ə'ladʒ·ɪ·kəl) adj. radiológico. —**radiologist,** n. radiólogo.

radioscopy (,rei·di'as·kə·pi) n. radioscopia.

radiosonde (-'sond) n. radiosonda.

radiotelegraph (,rei·di·o'tel·ə·græf) n. radiotelégrafo. —v.t. radiotelegrafiar. —**radiotelegraphy** (-o'leg·rə·fi) n. radiotelegrafía.

radiotelephone (,rei·di·o'tel·ə·fon) n. radioteléfono. —**radiotelephony** (-tə'lef·ə·ni) n. radiotelefonía.

radiotherapy (,rei·di·o'θer·ə·pi) n. radioterapia.

radish ('ræd·ɪʃ) n. rábano.

radium ('rei·di·əm) n. radio; rádium.

radius ('rei·di·əs) n. [pl. **radii** (-di·ai)] radio.

radon ('rei·dan) n. radón.

raffia ('ræf·i·ə) n. rafia.

raffish ('ræf·ɪʃ) adj. ruidoso; tunante; alborotoso. —**raffishness,** n. tunantería.

raffle ('ræf·əl) n. rifa. —v.t. rifar.

raft (ræft) n. 1, (float) balsa. 2, colloq. (large amount) montón; sinnúmero. —v.t. transportar en balsa.

rafter ('ræf·tər) n. viga; cabrio.

rag n. (ræg) 1, (piece of cloth) trapo. 2, pl. (shabby clothes) harapos; andrajos. 3, = **ragtime.** —v.t., slang molestar; burlarse de.

ragamuffin ('ræg·ə,mʌf·ɪn) n. golfo; pelagatos.

rage (reidʒ) n. 1, (anger) rabia; cólera; ira. 2, (violence) violencia; furia. 3, (fervor) entusiasmo. 4, slang (fad) moda; boga; novedad. —*v.i.* **1,** (be furious) rabiar; encolerizarse. **2,** (proceed with violence) arrebatarse. —**raging,** *adj.* furioso.

ragged ('ræg·id) *adj.* **1,** (shabby) harapiento; andrajoso. **2,** (slovenly) desaliñado. **3,** (uneven) desigual; escabroso.

raglan ('ræg·lən) *n.* raglán.

ragout (ræ'guǝ) *n.* estofado; guisado.

ragpicker ('ræg,pɪk·ər) *n.* andrajero; trapero.

ragtime ('ræg·taim) *n., mus.* tiempo sincopado.

ragweed ('ræg·wid) *n.* ambrosía.

rah (raǝ) *interj.* ¡viva!; ¡hurra!

raid (reid) *n.* **1,** (incursion) incursión. **2,** (attack) ataque. —*v.t. & i.* **1,** (invade) invadir; hacer incursión (en). **2,** (attack) atacar. **3,** (pillage; pilfer) pillar.

rail (reil) *n.* **1,** (barrier) barrera; baranda. **2,** (handrail) pasamano. **3,** (track) carril; riel. **4,** (rail system; railroads collectively) ferrocarril. **5,** *ornith.* rascón. —*adj.* ferroviario. —*v.t.* poner baranda a; cercar con barandas —*v.i.* quejarse. —**by rail,** por ferrocarril. —**rail at** o **against,** injuriar; ultrajar.

railing ('rei·lɪŋ) *n.* baranda; barandilla.

raillery ('rei·lə·ri) *n.* burla; zumba.

railroad ('reil·rod) *n.* ferrocarril; vía férrea. —*adj.* ferroviario. —*v.t., slang* **1,** (force through rapidly) ejecutar de prisa. **2,** (frame) fraguar; condenar falsamente. —**railroading,** *n.* trabajo o negocios de ferrocarril.

railway ('reil·wei) *adj. & n.* = **railroad.**

raiment ('rei·mənt) *n.* ropa; prendas de vestir.

rain (rein) *n.* lluvia. —*v.i.* llover. —*v.t.* llover; hacer llover. —**rainy,** *adj.* lluvioso. —**rain check,** billete válido para provecho en otra ocasión de un espectáculo cancelado a causa de la lluvia, o una venta especial, hasta reabastecimiento de las mercancías agotadas.

rainbow ('rein,bo) *n.* arco iris.

raincoat ('rein,kot) *n.* impermeable.

raindrop ('rein,drap) *n.* gota de lluvia.

rainfall ('rein,fɔl) *n.* lluvia; (promedio de la) precipitación.

rainstorm ('rein,storm) *n.* chubasco; aguacero.

raise (reiz) *v.t.* **1,** (lift) levantar; alzar. **2,** (build) erigir; edificar. **3,** (set upright) poner en pie. **4,** (rear) criar; cultivar. **5,** (exalt) ensalzar. **6,** (arouse) suscitar. **7,** (collect, as money) procurar. **8,** (produce) producir. —*n.* aumento de salario.

raised (reizd) *adj.* **1,** (leavened) fermentado. **2,** (in relief) en relieve; de realce.

raisin ('rei·zən) *n.* pasa; uva seca.

rajah ('ra·dʒə) *n.* rajá.

rake (reik) *n.* **1,** (garden tool) rastro; rastra; rastrillo. **2,** (dissolute man) libertino; calavera. **3,** *naut.* (slant) lanzamiento. —*v.t.* **1,** (gather or smooth with a rake) rastrear; rastrillar. **2,** (ransack) rebuscar. **3,** (scratch) rascar. **4,** *mil.* enfilar.

rakish ('reik·ɪʃ) *adj.* **1,** (slanted) inclinado. **2,** (jaunty) airoso. **3,** (dissolute) libertino.

rally ('ræl·i) *v.t.* **1,** (call together) reunir. **2,** (reassemble, as troops) reanimar; replegar. **3,** (tease) burlarse de; ridiculizar. —*v.i.* **1,** (get together) reunirse. **2,** (recover energy) reanimarse; recobrar sus fuerzas. —*n.* **1,** (mass meeting) reunión en masa. **2,** *tennis* ataque sostenido. **3,** *mil.* reunión de tropas. **4,** (renewal of energy) recuperación; recobro.

ram (ræm) *n.* **1,** (male sheep) carnero. **2,** *cap., astron.* Aries. **3,** (battering instrument) ariete. **4,** *naut.* espolón. —*v.t.* [**rammed, ramming**] **1,** (batter) empujar con violencia; chocar con o en. **2,** (drive down) apisonar; pisonear. **3,** (cram) henchir; amontonar.

RAM (ræm) *abr. de* **random access memory.**

ramble ('ræm·bəl) *v.i.* **1,** (wander) vagar; pasear. **2,** (deviate) divagar. —*n.* paseo.

rambler ('ræm·blər) *n.* **1,** (wanderer) paseador [*fem.* -dora]; divagador [*fem.* -dora]. **2,** (climbing rose) rosal trepador.

rambling ('ræm·blɪŋ) *adj.* **1,** (wandering) errante; divagador. **2,** (large; sprawling) grande; amplio; muy extendido.

rambunctious (ræm'bʌŋk·ʃəs) *adj., colloq.* ruidoso; alborotado. —**rambunctiousness,** *n.* alboroto.

ramify ('ræm·ɪ,fai) *v.i.* ramificarse. —*v.t.* dividir en ramas. —**ramifica-**

tion (-fɪ'kei·ʃən) *n.* ramificación; ramal.

ramp (ræmp) *n.* rampa.

rampage ('ræm·pedʒ) *n.* alboroto; rabia. —*v.i.* (*usu.* ræm'peidʒ) alborotar; rabiar.

rampant ('ræm·pənt) *adj.* **1,** (unchecked) desenfrenado. **2,** (luxuriant) abundante; extravagante. **3,** *heraldry* rampante.

rampart ('ræm·pərt) *n.* **1,** (fortification) muralla; terraplén. **2,** *fig.* (bulwark) baluarte; amparo; defensa.

ramrod ('ræm,rad) *n.* baqueta de fusil.

ramshackle ('ræm,ʃæk·əl) *adj.* destartalado.

ran (ræn) *v.,* *pret. de* **run.**

ranch (ræntʃ) *n.* rancho; hacienda. —**rancher; ranchman** (-mən) *n.* ranchero; hacendado.

rancid ('ræn·sɪd) *adj.* rancio. —**rancidity** (ræn'sɪd·ə·ti) *n.* rancidez.

rancor ('ræŋ·kər) *n.* rcncor. —**rancorous,** *adj.* rencoroso.

random ('ræn·dəm) *n.* azar; casualidad. —*adj.* casual; impensado. —**at random,** al azar. —**randomize** (-də,maiz) *v.t.* arreglar o disponer al azar. —**randomization** (-mə'zei·ʃən) *n.* arreglo o disposición al azar. —**random access memory,** *comput.* memoria de acceso casual.

randy ('ræn·di) *adj.,* *slang* cachondo.

ranee ('ra·ni) *n.* raní.

rang (ræŋ) *v.,* *pret. de* **ring.**

range (reindʒ) *v.t.* **1,** (arrange) colocar metódicamente; ordenar; clasificar. **2,** (oppose) alinear. **3,** (rove) recorrer. —*v.i.* **1,** (form a line) alinearse. **2,** (roam) vagar. **3,** (vary) fluctuar. —*n.* **1,** (row) serie; fila; hilera. **2,** (extent; scope) alcance. **3,** (distance) espacio; esfera. **4,** (series of mountains) cordillera. **5,** (grazing land) terreno de pasto. **6,** (shooting course) campo de tiro. **7,** (stove) hornillo; cocina. —**range finder,** telémetro.

ranger ('rein·dʒər) *n.* **1,** (forest guard) guardamayor de bosque. **2,** *cap.* (U.S. soldier) soldado especializado en hacer incursiones en el campo enemigo.

rangy ('rein·dʒi) *adj.* alto y flaco.

rani ('ra·ni) *n.* = **ranee.**

rank (ræŋk) *n.* **1,** (row) fila; hilera. **2,** (class; order) clase; distinción. **3,** (social position) esfera; posición. **4,** (relative position) rango; grado. **5,** *pl., mil.* soldados de fila; tropas. —*v.t.* **1,** (arrange in order) poner en fila. **2,** (classify) clasificar. **3,** (rate above) tener grado más alto que. —*v.i.* ocupar determinado grado o puesto. —*adj.* **1,** (luxuriant) exuberante; abundante. **2,** (thick; dense) espeso; denso. **3,** (coarse; gross) grosero. **4,** (fetid) maloliente. —**rank and file,** el pueblo; la gente común.

rankle ('ræŋ·kəl) *v.t.* enconar. —*v.i.* enconarse. —**rankling** (-klɪŋ) *adj.* enconoso. —*n.* encono.

ransack ('ræn·sæk) *v.t.* **1,** (search) escudriñar; rebuscar; registrar. **2,** (plunder) saquear; pillar.

ransom ('ræn·səm) *n.* rescate. —*v.t.* rescatar; redimir.

rant (rænt) *v.i.* delirar; disparatar. —*n.* [*también,* **ranting**] lenguaje extravagante; disparates.

rap (ræp) *n.* **1,** (quick, sharp blow) golpe seco; golpecito. **2,** *colloq.* (bit) bledo; ardite. **3,** *slang* (penalty) castigo; multa; consecuencias. **4,** *colloq.* (harsh criticism) crítica áspera; reprimenda. —*v.t. & i.* [**rapped, rapping**] (strike sharply) golpear vivamente; dar un golpe seco a. —*v.i.* (knock, as on a door) tocar; llamar. —*v.t., colloq.* (criticize harshly) criticar ásperamente; reprender. —**not to give (o care) a rap,** *colloq.* no darle (o importarle) a uno un bledo. —**rap session,** *colloq.* discusión informal. —**rap sheet,** *slang* expediente de contravenciones criminales. —**take (o pay) the rap,** *colloq.* sufrir las consecuencias; pagar los vidrios rotos.

rapacious (rə'pei·ʃəs) *adj.* rapaz. —**rapaciousness; rapacity** (rə'pæs·ə·ti) *n.* rapacidad.

rape (reip) *n.* **1,** (sexual violation) violación; estupro. **2,** (abduction) rapto. **3,** *bot.* colza. —*v.t.* **1,** (violate) violar; estuprar. **2,** (abduct) raptar. —**rapist,** *n.* estuprador.

rapid ('ræp·ɪd) *adj.* veloz; rápido. —**rapidity** (rə'pɪd·ə·ti); **rapidness,** *n.* rapidez. —**rapids,** *n.pl.* rápidos.

rapier ('rei·pi·ər) *n.* estoque.

rapine ('ræp·ɪn) *n.* rapiña.

rapport (ræ'pɔrr) *n.* acuerdo; armonía.

rapprochement (ˌræ·prɔʃ'maɴ) *n.* acercamiento.

rapscallion (ræp'skæl·jən) *n., colloq.* pícaro.

rapt (ræpt) *adj.* extasiado.

rapture ('ræp·tʃər) *n.* rapto; éxtasis. —**rapturous**, *adj.* extático; embelesado.

rare (reɪr) *adj.* **1**, (thin, as air) ralo. **2**, (uncommon) raro. **3**, (lightly cooked) poco cocido.

rarebit ('rɛr·bɪt) *n.* = **Welsh rabbit**.

rarefy ('rɛr·ə‚fai) *v.t.* enrarecer. —*v.t.* enrarecerse. —**rarefaction** (-'fæk·ʃən) *n.* rarefacción.

rarely ('rɛr·li) *adv.* raramente; rara vez; raras veces.

rareness ('rɛr·nəs) *n.* rareza.

rarity ('rɛr·ə·ti) *n.* rareza.

rascal ('ræs·kəl) *n.* tunante; bribón. —**rascality** (ræs'kæl·ə·ti) *n.* tunantería; bribonería.

rash (ræʃ) *adj.* imprudente; precipitado. —*n.* erupción de la piel; salpullido; sarpullido. —**rashness**, *n.* temeridad; arrojo.

rasher ('ræʃ·ər) *n.* magra; lonja de tocino.

rasp (ræsp) *v.t.* raspar; escofinar; rallar. —*v.i.* hacer chirrido. —*n.* raspa; escofina. —**rasping**, *adj.* raspante; ronco. —*n.* raspadura.

raspberry ('ræz‚bɛr·i) *n.* **1**, (fruit) frambuesa. **2**, (bush) frambueso. **3**, *slang* (expression of derision) pedorreta; *Amer.* trompetilla.

rat (ræt) *n.* **1**, (rodent) rata. **2**, *slang* (traitor) traidor; renegado. **3**, *slang* (informer) delator. **4**, *slang* (contemptible person) despreciable; mezquino. **5**, (roll of hair) bollo de pelo. —*v.i.* [**ratted, ratting**] **1**, (kill rats) cazar ratas. **2**, *slang* (inform) delatar. —**rat race**, ajetreo; competencia desenfrenada. —**smell a rat**, *colloq.* tener sospecha; desconfiar.

ratchet ('rætʃ·ɪt) *n.* rueda dentada; trinquete.

rate (reit) *n.* **1**, (measurement in relation to a standard) razón; proporción; medida. **2**, (price) tarifa. **3**, (speed) velocidad. **4**, (of interest or exchange) tipo. **5**, *pl., Brit.* (local tax) impuesto local. —*v.t.* **1**, (measure) estimar; tomar la medida de. **2**, (classify) clasificar. **3**, (appraise) valuar; tasar. **4**, (scold) regañar; reprender. —*v.i.* tener rango; tener valor. —**at any rate**, de todos modos; de cualquier modo. —**at that rate**, de ese modo; si es así. —**at the rate of**, a razón de.

ratepayer ('reit‚pei·ər) *n., Brit.* contribuyente.

rather ('ræð·ər) *adv.* **1**, (sooner) antes. **2**, (more correctly) mejor dicho; más bien. **3**, (on the contrary) al contrario; por el contrario. **4**, (somewhat) algo; bastante. **5**, (very) muy.

rathole ('ræt‚hol) *n.* ratonera.

rathskeller ('rats‚kɛl·ər) *n.* restaurante en un sótano.

ratify ('ræt·ə‚fai) *v.t.* ratificar. —**ratification** (-fɪ'kei·ʃən) *n.* ratificación.

rating ('rei·tɪŋ) *n.* **1**, (classification) clasificación. **2**, (appraisal) valuación. **3**, (rank) rango; grado. **4**, (scolding) regaño.

ratio ('rei·ʃo) *n.* proporción; *math.* razón; cociente.

ratiocinate (ˌræʃ·i'as·ə‚neit) *v.i.* raciocinar. —**ratiocination**, *n.* raciocinación; raciocinio.

ration ('rei·ʃən) *n.* ración. —*v.t.* proporcionar; racionar. —**rationing**, *n.* racionamiento. —**rations**, *n.pl.* comidas.

rational ('ræʃ·ən·əl) *adj.* racional. —**rationality** (-ə'næl·ə·ti) *n.* racionalidad.

rationale (ˌræʃ·ə'næl) *n.* racional.

rationalism ('ræʃ·ən·ə‚lɪz·əm) *n.* racionalismo. —**rationalist**, *n.* racionalista. —**rationalistic**, *adj.* racionalista.

rationalize ('ræʃ·ə·nə‚laiz) *v.t.* justificar; buscar razón para. —*v.i.* justificarse. —**rationalization** (-lɪ‚zei·ʃən) *n.* acto de justificar o justificarse.

rattan (ræ'tæn) *n.* **1**, (climbing palm) rotén; rota; junquillo. **2**, (cane) caña.

rattle ('ræt·əl) *v.t. & i.* (shake or move with quick sharp sounds) traquetear; golpetear. —*v.i.* (talk rapidly) parlotear. —*v.t.*, *colloq.* (confuse; upset) confundir; descomponer. —*n.* **1**, (noise; noisy movement) traqueteo; golpeteo; matraca. **2**, (noisemaker) matraca. **3**, (rattlesnake's tail) anillos córneos en la cola de la serpiente de cascabel. **4**, (noisy breathing; death rattle) estertor. —**rattle off**, enunciar rápidamente.

rattlebrain ('ræt·əl‚brein) *n.* ligero de cascos; casquivano.

rattler ('ræt·lər) n. **1,** = **rattlesnake. 2,** (freight train) tren de carga.

rattlesnake ('ræt·əl,sneik) n. serpiente de cascabel.

rattletrap ('ræt·əl,træp) n. objeto destartalado. —adj. destartalado.

rattrap ('ræt,træp) n. ratonera; fig. aprieto.

ratty ('ræt·i) adj. andrajoso. —**rattiness,** n. pobreza.

raucous ('rɔ·kəs) adj. ronco. —**raucousness,** n. ronquera.

raunchy ('rɔn·tʃi) adj., slang **1,** (indecent) sin vergüenza; descarado. **2,** (lustful) cachondo.

ravage ('ræv·ɪdʒ) v.t. **1,** (pillage) saquear; pillar. **2,** (ruin) estragar; arruinar. —n. **1,** (pillage) saque; pillaje. **2,** (ruin) estrago; ruina.

rave (reiv) v.i. delirar. —n., colloq. elogio delirante. —adj., colloq. entusiástico.

ravel ('ræv·əl) v.t. **1,** (unsew; fray) deshilar; deshebrar. **2,** (disentangle) desenredar. —n. hilacha.

raven ('rei·vən) n. cuervo. —adj. bien negro.

raven ('ræv·ən) v.t. devorar. —v.i. echarse sobre la presa. —**ravening,** adj. rapaz. —**ravenous,** adj. voraz; hambriento.

ravine (rə'viːn) n. hondonada; barranca.

ravioli (ræ·vi'o·li) n.pl. ravioles.

ravish ('ræv·ɪʃ) v.t. **1,** (abduct) raptar. **2,** (enrapture) extasiar; encantar. **3,** (rape) violar. —**ravishing,** adj. encantador.

ravishment ('ræv·ɪʃ·mənt) n. **1,** (abduction) rapto. **2,** (rapture) éxtasis; encanto. **3,** (rape) violación.

raw (rɔ) adj. **1,** (uncooked) crudo. **2,** (unripe) verde. **3,** (untreated) sin preparación; en bruto. **4,** (brutal) brutal. **5,** (cold and damp) frío y húmedo. **6,** (without cover) pelado. **7,** (untried) novato. **8,** (open, as a wound) descarnado. —n. [también, **rawness**] **1,** (crude state) crudeza. **2,** (sore) llaga. —**in the raw,** al natural. —**raw deal,** slang injusticia. —**raw material,** materia prima. —**raw spirits,** alcohol puro. —**raw sugar,** azúcar bruto.

rawboned ('rɔ,bond) adj. huesudo.

rawhide ('rɔ·haid) n. cuero crudo; cuero en verde.

ray (rei) n. **1,** (beam, as of light) rayo. **2,** (stripe) raya. **3,** (radius;

spoke) radio. **4,** ichthy. raya. **5,** zoöl. radio. —v.t. & i. radiar.

rayon ('rei·an) n. rayón.

raze (reiz) v.t. arrasar; demoler.

razor ('rei·zər) n. navaja de afeitar. —**razor blade,** hoja de afeitar. —**razor strop,** suavizador. —**safety razor,** máquina de afeitar.

razz (ræz) v.t. & i., slang escarnecer; mofarse (de). —n., slang (derision) crítica mordaz; mofa.

re (rei) n., mus. re.

re (riː) prep. acerca de; concerniente a. También, **in re.**

reach (ritʃ) v.t. **1,** (extend) tender; estirar; alargar. **2,** (attain) alcanzar. **3,** (establish communication with) establecer contacto con. **4,** (arrive at) llegar a; alcanzar. —v.i. **1,** (extend; stretch) extenderse; extender la mano o el brazo. **2,** (strive) esforzarse. —n. **1,** (act of reaching) estirón. **2,** (range; scope) alcance. **3,** (expanse; stretch) extensión. **4,** (distance) distancia. **5,** (capacity) facultad; capacidad.

react (ri'ækt) v.i. **1,** (act in response) reaccionar; responder. **2,** (interact) ejercer acción mutua; reaccionar entre sí.

reaction (ri'æk·ʃən) n. **1,** (response) reacción; respuesta. **2,** (interaction) interacción.

reactionary (ri'æk·ʃə,ner·i) adj. & n. reaccionario.

reactivate (ri,æk·tɪ·veit) v.t. reactivar.

reactive (ri'æk·tɪv) adj. reactivo.

reactor (ri'æk·tər) n. reactor.

read (riːd) v.t. & i. [pret. & p.p. **read** (rɛd)] **1,** (interpret written or printed matter) leer. **2,** (understand by observation) interpretar; entender. **3,** (guess, as someone's thoughts) adivinar (el pensamiento). —adj. (rɛd) leído; enterado. —n. (riːd) lectura. —**read only memory,** comput. memoria de sólo leer.

readable ('rid·ə·bəl) adj. **1,** (legible) legible. **2,** (easy to read) fácil de leer.

reader ('ri·dər) n. **1,** (person who reads) lector. **2,** (book) libro de lectura. **3,** (interpreter) intérprete. —**readership,** conjunto de lectores.

readily ('rɛd·ə·li) adv. **1,** (willingly) de buena gana. **2,** (easily) fácilmente.

readiness ('rɛd·i·nɪs) n. **1,** (preparedness) preparación. **2,** (willingness) disposición. **3,** (promptness) prontitud.

reading ('ri·dɪŋ) *n.* **1,** (act or content of reading) lectura. **2,** (recital) recitación. **3,** (interpretation) interpretación.

readjust (ˌri·ə'dʒʌst) *v.t.* reajustar. —**readjustment,** *n.* reajuste.

readout ('rid͵aut) *n. comput.* información impresa.

ready ('rɛd·i) *adj.* **1,** (prepared) preparado; listo. **2,** (willing) dispuesto. **3,** (about to) listo. **4,** (available) disponible; a la mano. **5,** (prompt) ligero. —*v.t.* preparar. —*v.i.* prepararse.

ready-made *adj.* hecho de antemano; ya hecho. —**ready-made clothes,** ropa hecha.

reaffirm (ˌri·ə'fʌrm) *v.t.* reafirmar.

reagent (ri'ei·dʒənt) *n.* reactivo.

real ('ri·əl) *adj.* **1,** (existing) real. **2,** (true) genuino; auténtico; verdadero. **3,** (immovable) inmueble. —*n.* (re'al) *(Spanish coin)* real. —**real estate; real property,** bienes raíces.

realism ('ri·ə·lɪz·əm) *n.* realismo. —**realist,** *n. & adj.* realista. —**realistic,** *adj.* realista. •

reality (ri'æl·ə·ti) *n.* **1,** (actuality) realidad. **2,** (truth) verdad.

realize ('ri·ə͵laiz) *v.t.* **1,** (acknowledge) reconocer; darse cuenta de. **2,** (understand) comprender. **3,** (achieve) efectuar; realizar. **4,** (earn) ganar. **5,** (exchange for cash) convertir en dinero contante. —**realization** (-lɪ'zei·ʃən) *n.* realización; comprensión.

really ('ri·ə·li) *adv.* **1,** (actually) en realidad; realmente. **2,** (truly) de veras. **3,** (indeed) efectivamente. —*interj.* ¡es verdad!; ¡de veras!

realm (rɛlm) *n.* **1,** (kingdom) reino. **2,** (scope) esfera.

realtor ('ri·əl͵tor) *n.* agente vendedor de casas; corredor de bienes raíces. —**realty,** *n.* bienes raíces.

ream (riːm) *n.* **1,** (quantity of paper) resma. **2,** *usu.pl., colloq.* (large amount) gran cantidad. —*v.t.* escariar.

reamer ('ri·mər) *n.* **1,** (reaming tool) escariador. **2,** (juice extractor) exprimidor.

reanimate (ri'æn·ə͵meit) *v.t.* reanimar. —*v.i.* reanimarse.

reap (rip) *v.t. & i.* segar; cosechar. —**reaping,** *n.* siega; cosecha.

reaper ('ri·pər) *n.* **1,** (one who reaps) segador. **2,** (reaping machine) segadora.

reappear (ˌri·ə'pɪr) *v.i.* reaparecer. —**reappearance,** *n.* reaparición.

reappoint (ˌri·ə'point) *v.t.* volver a nombrar. —**reappointment,** *n.* nuevo nombramiento.

rear (rɪr) *n.* **1,** (back part) parte de atrás; parte posterior. **2,** (innermost part) fondo. **3,** (tail end) cola. **4,** *mil.* retaguardia. —*adj.* posterior; trasero; de atrás; *mil.* de retaguardia. —*v.t.* **1,** (elevate) alzar; levantar. **2,** (erect) erigir; construir. **3,** (nurture; train) criar. —*v.i.* **1,** (rise on the hind legs) encabritarse. **2,** (feel resentment) resentirse. —**at** o **in the rear of, 1,** (behind) detrás de. **2,** (in the back part of) al fondo de. **3,** (at the tail end of) a la cola de. —**bring up the rear,** cerrar la marcha. —**rear admiral,** contraalmirante. —**rear back** (recoil), recular. —**rear end, 1,** (tail end) cola. **2,** (buttocks) nalga; trasero. —**rear guard,** retaguardia. —**rear sight,** alza.

rearm (ri'arm) *v.t.* rearmar. —*v.i.* rearmarse. —**rearmament** (ri'ar·mə·mənt) *n.* rearme.

rearmost ('rɪr͵most) *adj.* último; postrero.

rearrange (ˌri·ə'reindʒ) *v.t.* arreglar o disponer de nuevo. —**rearrangement,** *n.* nuevo arreglo; nueva disposición.

rearview mirror ('rɪr͵vju) retrovisor.

rearward ('rɪr·wərd) *adj.* de atrás. —*adv.* [*también,* **rearwards**] hacia atrás.

reason ('ri·zən) *n.* razón. —*v.t. & i.* razonar. —**reasonable,** *adj.* razonable. —**reasoning,** *n.* razonamiento; argumento. —*adj.* razonador.

reassemble (ˌri·ə'sɛm·bəl) *v.t.* volver a reunir; *mech.* volver a armar o a montar. —*v.i.* volver a reunirse.

reassert (ˌri·ə'sʌrt) *v.t.* afirmar de nuevo.

reassure (ˌri·ə'ʃur) *v.t.* asegurar; alentar. —**reassurance,** *n.* confianza restablecida; confianza.

rebate ('ri·beit) *n.* **1,** (discount) rebaja; descuento. **2,** (return of money) reembolso. —*v.t.* (rɪ'beit) **1,** (reduce; deduct) rebajar; descontar. **2,** (reimburse) devolver; reembolsar.

rebel (rɪ'bɛl) *v.t.* rebelarse. —*adj. &
n.* ('rɛb·əl) rebelde.
rebellion (rɪ'bɛl·jən) *n.* 1, (armed
revolt) insurrección. 2, (resistance
to authority) rebeldía. —**rebellious**,
adj. rebelde. —**rebelliousness**, *n.*
rebeldía.
rebirth ('ri·bʌrθ) *n.* renacimiento.
reborn (ri'born) *adj.* renacido.
rebound (rɪ'baʊnd) *v.i.* rebotar.
—*n.* ('ri-) 1, (return bounce) rebote.
2, *colloq.* (recovery from a love affair) recobro de mal de amores.
—**on the rebound**, de rebote.
rebuff (ri'bʌf) *v.t.* rechazar;
repulsar; desairar. —*n.* rechazo;
repulsa; desaire.
rebuild (ri'bɪld) *v.t.* [*pret. & p.p.*
-**built**] reconstruir; rehacer.
rebuke (rɪ'bjuk) *v.t.* regañar;
reprender; censurar. —*n.* censura;
reprensión.
rebus ('ri·bəs) *n.* jeroglífico.
rebut (rɪ'bʌt) *v.t.* rebatir; contradecir. —**rebuttal**, *n.* refutación.
recalcitrant (rɪ'kæl·sɪ·trənt) *adj.*
recalcitrante. —**recalcitrance**, *n.*
obstinación; terquedad.
recall (rɪ'kɔl) *v.t.* 1, (recollect)
recordar. 2, (call back) hacer volver.
3, (revoke) revocar. 4, (dismiss
from office) destituir; deponer. —*n.*
1, (recollection) recordación. 2,
(summons to return) llamada. 3,
(revocation) revocación. 4, (dismissal from office) destitución; deposición. 5, *mil.* llamada.
recant (rɪ'kænt) *v.t.* retractar. —*v.i.*
retractarse. —**recantation** (,ri·
kæn'tei·ʃən) *n.* retractación.
recap (ri'kæp) *v.t.* recauchar (*a
tire*); volver a tapar (*a container*).
—*n.* ('ri·kæp) 1, neumático
recauchado. 2, *colloq.* = **recapitulation.**
recapitulate (,ri·kə'pɪtʃ·ə,leit) *v.t.*
recapitular. —**recapitulation**, *n.*
recapitulación.
recapture (ri,kæp·tʃər) *v.t.* volver
a capturar; recobrar. —*n.* 1, (recovery) recobro. 2, (lawful confiscation) cobranza.
recast (ri'kæst) *v.t.* [*pret. & p.p.*
-**cast**] 1, (remold; remake) refundir.
2, (reconstruct) reconstruir.
recede (rɪ'sid) *v.i.* 1, (draw back)
retroceder. 2, (turn back) volverse
atrás. 3, (slope backward) inclinarse.
receipt (rɪ'sit) *n.* 1, (act of receiving) recepción. 2, (note acknowl-

edging payment) recibo; recibí. 3,
(recipe) receta. —*v.t.* dar un recibo
de; poner el recibí a. —**receipts**,
n.pl. ingresos. —**receipted**, *adj.*
pagado. —**acknowledge receipt
of**, acusar recibo de. —**receipt in
full**, recibo por saldo de cuenta.
receivable (rɪ'siv·ə·bəl) *adj.*
recibidero. —*n.* cuenta por cobrar.
receive (rɪ'siv) *v.t.* 1, (get; obtain)
recibir; tomar. 2, (accept) aprobar;
aceptar. 3, (hold) contener. 4,
(greet) recibir; acoger. 5, (deal in
unlawfully, as stolen goods)
receptar.
receiver (rɪ'siv·ər) *n.* 1, (one who
receives) recibidor; recipiente. 2,
(dealer in stolen goods) receptador
[*fem.* -dora]. 3, (custodian of a
bankrupt) síndico. 4, (instrument for
receiving signals) receptor. 5, (receptacle) receptáculo. —**receivership**, *n.* sindicatura.
recent ('ri·sənt) *adj.* 1, (of recent
time) reciente. 2, (modern)
moderno; fresco. —**recently**, *adv.*
recientemente; (*ante p.p.*) recién.
—**recency**, *n.* novedad.
receptacle (rɪ'sɛp·tə·kəl) *n.*
receptáculo; recipiente.
reception (rɪ'sɛp·ʃən) *n.* 1, (act of
receiving) recepción. 2, (welcome)
recibimiento; acogida. 3, (formal
gathering) recepción. —**receptionist**, *n.* recepcionista.
receptive (rɪ'sɛp·tɪv) *adj.*
receptivo. —**receptivity** (,ri·
sɛp'trɪv·ə·ti); **receptiveness**, *n.* receptividad.
recess ('ri·sɛs) *n.* 1, (rest period)
hora o tiempo de recreo. 2, (niche)
depresión; nicho. 3, (adjournment) receso. 4, *pl.* (place of seclusion) escondrijo; lugar apartado.
—*v.t.* (rɪ'sɛs) 1, (make a niche in)
hacer un nicho en. 2, (set in a
niche) poner en un nicho. 3, (set
back) retirar; apartar. —*v.i.*
suspenderse; descansar.
recession (rɪ'sɛʃ·ən) *n.* 1, (act of
receding) retroceso; retirada. 2,
archit. (recessed place) entrada. 3,
(renunciation) renuncia. 4, (economic relapse) depresión en
pequeña escala.
recessive (rɪ'sɛs·ɪv) *adj.* regresivo.
recharge (ri'tʃardʒ) *v.t.* recargar.
recherché (rə'ʃɛr·ʃei) *adj.* rebuscado.
recidivist (rɪ'sɪd·ə·vɪst) *n.* reincidente. —**recidivism**, *n.* reinci-

dencia. —**recidivous,** *adj.* reincidente.

recipe ('rɛs·ə·pi) *n.* receta.

recipient (rɪ'sɪp·i·ənt) *n.* & *adj.*
recibidor [*fem.* -dora]; recipiente.

reciprocal (rɪ'sɪp·rə·kəl) *adj.*
recíproco. —*n., math.* recíproca.

reciprocate (rɪ'sɪp·rə‚kəit) *v.t.* & *i.*
1, (return) reciprocar. **2,** (exchange)
intercambiar. **3,** *mech.* oscilar.
—**reciprocating engine,** motor a
movimiento oscilador.

reciprocation (rɪ‚sɪp·rə'kei·ʃən)
n. **1,** (return) reciprocación. **2,** (exchange) intercambio.

reciprocity (‚rɛs·ɪ'pras·ə·ti) *n.*
reciprocidad.

recital (rɪ'sai·təl) *n.* **1,** (narration)
relación; narración. **2,** *mus.* recital.

recitation (‚rɛs·ɪ'tei·ʃən) *n.* recitación.

recitative (‚rɛs·ɪ·tə'tiːv) *n., mus.*
recitado.

recite (rɪ'sait) *v.t.* **1,** (declaim)
recitar. **2,** (tell) relatar; narrar. **3,**
(enumerate) enumerar; contar. —*v.i.*
recitar.

reckless ('rɛk·ləs) *adj.* temerario;
imprudente. —**recklessness,** *n.*
temeridad; imprudencia.

reckon ('rɛk·ən) *v.t.* & *i.* **1,** (compute) contar; calcular. **2,** (regard)
estimar; apreciar. **3,** *colloq.* (guess)
creer; suponer. —**reckon on,** contar
con. —**reckon with,** tener en
cuenta.

reckoning ('rɛk·ən·ɪŋ) *n.* **1,** (computation) cálculo; cómputo. **2,** (accounting) cuenta; ajuste de cuentas.
3, *naut.* estima.

reclaim (rɪ'kleim) *v.t.* **1,** (assert
one's right to) reclamar. **2,** (redeem;
save) redimir. **3,** (recover) salvage)
recuperar; utilizar; sacar provecho
de.

reclamation (‚rɛk·lə'mei·ʃən) *n.*
1, (assertion of one's rights)
reclamación. **2,** (recovery; salvage)
recuperación; utilización.

recline (rɪ'klain) *v.t.* recostar;
reclinar. —*v.i.* recostarse; reclinarse.
—**reclining,** *adj.* reclinado; recostado. —**reclining seat,** asiento reclinable.

recluse (rɪ'klus) *n.* & *adj.* solitario;
apartadizo.

recognition (‚rɛk·əg'nɪʃ·ən) *n.*
reconocimiento.

recognizance (rɪ'kag·nə·zəns) *n.*
fianza.

recognize ('rɛk·əg‚naiz) *v.t.*

reconocer. —**recognizable,** *adj.*
reconocible.

recoil (rɪ'kɔil) *v.i.* recular. —*n.* **1,**
(backward move) reculada; retro-
ceso. **2,** (kick, as of a firearm) culatazo.

recollect (‚rɛk·ə'lɛkt) *v.t.* & *i.*
recordar. —**recollection** (-'lɛk·ʃən)
n. recuerdo; recordación.

recommence (‚ri·kə'mɛns) *v.t.* &
i. empezar de nuevo.

recommend (‚rɛk·ə'mɛnd) *v.t.*
recomendar. —**recommendation**
(-mɛn'dei·ʃən) *n.* recomendación.

recompense (‚rɛk·əm‚pɛns) *v.t.*
recompensar. —*n.* recompensa.

reconcile ('rɛk·ən‚sail) *v.t.* **1,** (restore) reconciliar. **2,** (adjust) ajustar;
adaptar; componer. **3,** (conciliate)
conciliar; concordar. —**reconcilable,** *adj.* reconciliable.
—**reconciliation** (-‚sɪl·i'ei·ʃən) *n.*
reconciliación.

recondite ('rɛk·ən‚dait) *adj.*
recóndito. —**reconditeness,** *n.*
reconditez.

recondition (‚ri·kən'dɪʃ·ən) *v.t.*
renovar.

reconnaissance (rɪ'kan·ə·səns)
n. reconocimiento; exploración.

reconnoiter (‚ri·kə'nɔi·tər) *v.t.*
reconocer. —*v.i.* practicar un
reconocimiento.

reconquer (ri'kaŋ·kər) *v.t.* reconquistar. —**reconquest** (ri'kan·
kwɛst) *n.* reconquista.

reconsider (‚ri·kən'sɪd·ər) *v.t.*
volver a considerar; repensar. —**reconsideration,** *n.* nueva consideración.

reconstitute (ri'kan·stə‚tjut) *v.t.*
reconstituir. —**reconstituent**
(‚ri·kən'stɪt·ju·ənt) *adj.* & *n.*
reconstituyente. —**reconstitution**
(ri‚kan·stɪ'tju·ʃən) *n.* reconstitución.

reconstruct (‚ri·kən'strʌkt) *v.t.* reconstruir. —**reconstruction,** *n.* reconstrucción.

record (rɪ'kord) *v.t.* **1,** (note)
apuntar; marcar; indicar. **2,** (enroll)
registrar; inscribir. **3,** (transcribe, as
sound) grabar. —*n.* ('rɛk·ərd) **1,** (act
of recording) registro; inscripción.
2, *usu.pl.* (data; information) datos
auténticos; anales; archivos. **3,**
(phonograph disk) disco. **4,** (highest
achievement) marca; *sports* récord.
5, *educ.* expediente académico. **6,**
(personal history) historial. —*adj.*
máximo; más alto. —**break a record,** batir un récord. —**make** o **set**

a record, establecer un récord. —**record cabinet,** discoteca. —**record changer,** cambiadiscos. —**record library,** discoteca. —**record player,** tocadiscos.

recorder (rɪ'kord·ər) n. 1, (registrar; archivist) registrador [fem. -dora]; archivero. 2, (registering instrument) indicador; contador. 3, (device for transcribing sound) grabadora. 3, (type of flute) caramillo. —**tape recorder,** grabadora de cinta; magnetófono.

recording (rɪ'kor·dɪŋ) n. 1, (register) registro. 2, (sound transcription) registro acústico; grabación. —adj. registrador.

recount (rɪ'kaunt) v.t. 1, (relate) relatar; contar. 2, (ri-) (count again) recontar. —n. (ri,kaunt) recuento.

recoup (rɪ'kup) v.t. recobrar. —v.i. recobrarse; desquitarse. —n. recobro.

recourse ('ri·kors) n. recurso; remedio. —**have recourse to,** recurrir a.

recover (rɪ'kʌv·ər) v.t. 1, (regain) recobrar; recuperar. 2, (save) rescatar. 3, law reivindicar. 4, (ri-) (cover again) recubrir. —v.i. 1, (regain health) restablecerse; reponerse. 2, law ganar un pleito. —**recovery,** n. recobro; recuperación; law reivindicación.

recreant ('rek·ri·ənt) adj. desleal; cobarde. —n. cobarde.

recreate ('rek·ri·eit) v.t. divertir. —v.r. divertirse.

re-create (,ri·kri'eit) v.t. recrear.

recreation (,rek·ri'ei·ʃən) n. recreación; recreo; diversión. —**recreational,** adj. de recreación. —**recreative** (-tɪv) adj. recreativo.

recriminate (rɪ'krɪm·ə,neit) v.t. & i. recriminar. —**recrimination,** n. recriminación.

recrudesce (,ri·kru'dɛs) v.i. 1, (become raw) recrudecer; recrudecerse. 2, (break out afresh) recaer. —**recrudescence,** n. recrudecimiento; recrudescencia. —**recrudescent,** adj. recrudescente.

recruit (rɪ'krut) v.t. 1, (enlist) reclutar. 2, (gather, as strength, provisions, etc.) acopiar; hacer acopio de. 3, (reinforce) reforzar. —n. 1, (new soldier) recluta. 2, (novice) novicio. —**recruiting; recruitment,** n. reclutamiento.

rectal ('rek·təl) adj. del recto; rectal.

rectangle ('rek,tæŋ·gəl) n. rectángulo. —**rectangular** (rek'tæŋ·gjə·lər) adj. rectangular.

rectify ('rek·tɪ,fai) v.t. rectificar. —**rectification** (-fɪ'kei·ʃən) n. rectificación. —**rectifier,** n. rectificador.

rectilinear (,rek·tə'lɪn·i·ər) adj. rectilíneo.

rectitude ('rek·tɪ,tjud) n. rectitud.

rector ('rek·tər) n. rector. —**rectorate** (-ət) n. rectorado. —**rectory,** n. rectoría.

rectum ('rek·təm) n. recto.

recumbent (rɪ'kʌm·bənt) adj. reclinado; recostado. —**recumbency,** n. reclinación.

recuperate (rɪ'kju·pə,reit) v.t. recobrar; recuperar. —v.i. restablecerse; reponerse. —**recuperation,** n. recuperación; recobro. —**recuperative** (-pər·ə·tɪv) adj. recuperativo.

recur (rɪ'kʌr) v.i. repetirse; volver; recurrir. —**recurrence,** n. repetición; retorno. —**recurrent,** adj. recurrente; periódico.

recusant ('rek·jə·zənt) n. & adj. recusante. —**recusancy,** n. recusación.

recycle (ri'sai·kəl) v.t. reciclar. —v.i. reciclarse. —**recycling,** n. reciclaje.

red (red) adj. rojo; colorado. —n. rojo; color rojo. —**in the red, 1,** (losing money) con pérdida; con déficit. 2, (in debt) endeudado. —**paint the town red,** slang echar una parranda; jaranear. —see **red,** colloq. encolerizarse.

redact (rɪ'dækt) v.t. redactar. —**redaction** (rɪ'dæk·ʃən) n. redacción. —**redactor,** n. redactor [fem. -tora].

redcap ('red,kæp) n. mozo de estación.

redden ('red·ən) v.t. enrojecer. —v.i. enrojecerse; sonrojarse.

reddish ('red·ɪʃ) adj. rojizo.

redeem (rɪ'dim) v.t. 1, (buy back; pay off) redimir. 2, (liberate) rescatar; libertar. 3, (fulfill, as a promise) cumplir. 4, (atone for) redimir; pagar. —**redeemable,** adj. redimible. —**redeemer,** n. redentor [fem. -tora].

redemption (rɪ'dɛmp·ʃən) n. redención. —**redemptive** (-tɪv) adj. redentor.

red-haired adj. pelirrojo.

redhanded (,rɛd'hæn·dɪd) *adj.* en flagrante.

redhead ('rɛd,hɛd) *n.* pelirrojo. —**redheaded**, *adj.* pelirrojo.

red herring pista falsa.

red-hot *adj.* **1,** (very hot) candente. **2,** *slang* (very new) muy nuevo; recentísimo. **3,** *slang* (fervid) ardiente; entusiasta; enérgico.

rediscover (,ri·dɪs'kʌv·ər) *v.t.* descubrir de nuevo.

redletter ('rɛd,lɛt·ər) *adj.* memorable.

red light luz roja; señal de paro. —**red-light district,** distrito de lupanares.

redneck ('rɛd,nɛk) *n.*, *slang; derog.* **1,** campesino, esp. en el sur de los EE.UU. **2,** persona intolerante en asuntos sociales y políticos.

redness ('rɛd·nəs) *n.* rojez.

redo (ri'duː) *v.t.* [*pret.* **redid** (-'dɪd) *p.p.* **redone** (-'dʌn)] rehacer; hacer de nuevo.

redolent ('rɛd·ə·lənt) *adj.* fragante; oloroso. —**redolence,** *n.* fragancia; olor. —**redolent of, 1,** (having the smell of) que huele a. **2,** (reminiscent or suggestive of) que recuerda.

redouble (rɪ'dʌb·əl) *v.t.* **1,** (double again) redoblar; reduplicar. **2,** (increase) aumentar. **3,** (echo) repetir. —*v.i.* redoblarse. —*n.* redoble.

redoubt (rɪ'daut) *n.* reducto.

redoubtable (rɪ'dau·tə·bəl) *adj.* formidable; tremendo.

redound (rɪ'daund) *v.i.* redundar.

redraft (rɪ'dræft) *v.t.* dibujar o diseñar de nuevo. —*n.* ('ri-) **1,** (new sketch or design) nuevo dibujo o diseño. **2,** *comm.* resaca.

redraw (rɪ'drɔ) *v.t.* **1,** (redesign) diseñar o planear de nuevo. **2,** *comm.* recambiar.

redress (rɪ'drɛs) *v.t.* remediar; reparar; corregir. —*n.* enmienda; remedio; compensación.

redskin ('rɛd,skɪn) *n.*, *derog.* piel roja.

red tape expedienteo; trámites.

reduce (rɪ'dus) *v.t.* **1,** (diminish) reducir; disminuir. **2,** (downgrade) degradar. **3,** (lower) rebajar. **4,** (subdue) subyugar. —*v.i., colloq.* rebajar de peso. —**reducible,** *adj.* reducible; reductible.

reduction (rɪ'dʌk·ʃən) *n.* reducción; disminución; rebaja.

redundant (rɪ'dʌn·dənt) *adj.*

superfluo; redundante. —**redundancy,** *n.* redundancia.

reduplicate (rɪ'dup·lə·keit) *v.t.* reduplicar. —**reduplication,** *n.* reduplicación.

redwood ('rɛd,wʊd) *n.* secoya.

reecho (ri'ɛk·o) *v.i.* resonar; repetir o responder el eco. —*n.* eco repetido.

reed (riːd) *n.* **1,** *bot.* caña; junquillo. **2,** (reed instrument) instrumento de lengüeta. **3,** *mus.* (vibrating piece) lengüeta.

reedy ('ri·di) *adj.* **1,** (of or like a reed) de o como caña. **2,** (full of reeds) lleno de cañas. **3,** (of thin, delicate tone) agudo y delgado.

reef (rif) *n.* **1,** (sand bar) arrecife; escollo. **2,** *naut.* rizo. **3,** *mining* veta; filón. —*v.t.*, *naut.* tomar rizos en.

reefer ('ri·fər) *n.* **1,** (short coat) chaqueta corta. **2,** *slang* cigarrillo de marijuana.

reek (rik) *v.i.* apestar; oler. —*v.t.* emitir; oler a. —*n.* vaho. —**reek of** o **with,** oler a; abundar en; tener o emitir en cantidad.

reel (riːl) *n.* **1,** (winding device) devanadera. **2,** (spool) carreta. **3,** (dance) baile vivo de origen escocés. **4,** (staggering motion) bamboleo; tambaleo. —*v.t.* (wind) devanar. —*v.i.* (stagger) bambolear; tambalear. —**off the reel,** rápidamente; sin vacilar. —**reel off,** enunciar rápidamente.

reelect (,ri·ɪ'lɛkt) *v.t.* reelegir. —**reelection,** *n.* reelección.

reembark (,ri·ɛm'bark) *v.i.* reembarcarse. —**reembarkation,** *n.* reembarque; reembarco.

reenforce (,ri·ɛn'fors) *v.t.* = **reinforce.**

reenter (ri'ɛn·tər) *v.i.* reentrar; reingresar. —*v.t.* reentrar en; reingresar en. —**reentry** (-tri) [*pl.* **-tries**] reingreso.

reestablish (,ri·ɛs'tæb·lɪʃ) *v.t.* restablecer. —**reestablishment,** *n.* restablecimiento.

reeve (riːv) *n.* **1,** (bird) hembra de la paloma moñuda. **2,** (town official) pedáneo; alcalde pedáneo. —*v.t.*, *naut.* pasar (un cabo) por un ojal; asegurar.

refection (rɪ'fɛk·ʃən) *n.* refacción; refección.

refectory (rɪ'fɛk·tə·ri); *n.* refectorio.

refer (rɪ'fʌr) *v.t.* **1,** (submit for consideration) referir. **2,** (direct) dirigir. **3,** (assign) asignar. **—referral,** *n.* recomendación. **—refer to, 1,** (relate to; be concerned with) tratar de; respectar. **2,** (have recourse to; appeal to) recurrir a; dirigirse a. **3,** (allude to) aludir a; referirse a.

referee (ˌrɛf·ə'riː) *n.* árbitro. **—***v.t.* & *i.* arbitrar.

reference ('rɛf·ə·rəns) *n.* **1,** (act of referring) referencia. **2,** (allusion) alusión. **3,** (recommendation) recomendación. **4,** (citation) mención. **—reference book,** libro de consulta. **—with reference to,** en cuanto a.

referendum (ˌrɛf·ə'rɛn·dəm) *n.* plebiscito; referéndum.

refill (ri'fɪl) *v.t.* rellenar. **—***n.* ('ri-) repuesto.

refine (ri'faɪn) *v.t.* **1,** (purify) refinar; purificar. **2,** (polish, as one's manners) pulir. **3,** (perfect) perfeccionar.

refined (ri'faɪnd) *adj.* **1,** (purified) refinado; purificado. **2,** (well-bred) cortés.

refinement (ri'faɪn·mənt) *n.* **1,** (act of refining) refinamiento. **2,** (good breeding) elegancia; cultura.

refiner (ri'faɪn·ər) *n.* refinador. **—refinery,** *n.* refinería. **—refining,** *n.* refinación.

refinish (ri'fɪn·ɪʃ) *v.t.* dar nuevo terminado o nueva capa; pintar de nuevo; revocar (paredes). **—refinishing,** *n.* nuevo terminado; nueva capa; nueva pintura; revocadura *(de paredes).*

refit (ri'fɪt) *v.t.* [**-fitted, -fitting**] reparar; restaurar.

reflect (ri'flɛkt) *v.t.* **1,** (throw back, as light) reflectar. **2,** (mirror) reflejar. **3,** (bring back as a consequence) causar; traer. **—***v.i.* **1,** (throw back rays) reflejar. **2,** (meditate) reflexionar. **—reflect on,** (discredit) desacreditar.

reflection (ri'flɛk·ʃən) *n.* **1,** (act of reflecting) reflexión. **2,** (image) reflejo. **3,** (meditation) meditación. **4,** (comment) comentario. **5,** (slur) reparo. **—reflective** (-tɪv) *adj.* reflexivo. **—reflector** (-tər) *n.* reflector.

reflex ('ri·flɛks) *n.* & *adj.* reflejo.

reflexive (ri'flɛk·sɪv) *adj.* reflexivo; reflejo.

reflux ('ri·flʌks) *n.* reflujo.

reforest (ri'fɔr·əst) *v.t.* repoblar con árboles. **—reforestation,** *n.*

repoblación de bosques; *(Amer.)* reforestación.

reform (ri'fɔrm) *v.t.* reformar. **—***v.i.* reformarse. **—***n.* reforma. reformista. **—reformer,** *n.* reformador [*fem.* -dora]; reformista.

re-form (ri'fɔrm) *v.t.* **1,** (form again) reformar; reconstituir. **2,** (make different) hacer diferente; dar otra forma a. **—***v.i.* **1,** (be formed anew) reformarse; reconstituirse. **2,** (change) volverse diferente; tomar otra forma.

reformation (ˌrɛf·ər'meɪ·ʃən) *n.* **1,** (change; reshaping) reformación; reforma. **2,** *cap., hist.* Reforma.

reformatory (ri'fɔr·mə·tor·i) *n.* reformatorio.

reformist (ri'fɔr·mɪst) *adj.* & *n.* reformista.

reform school reformatorio.

refract (ri'frækt) *v.t.* refractar; refringir. **—refracting; refractive,** *adj.* refringente. **—refraction** (ri'fræk·ʃən) *n.* refracción. **—refractor,** *n.* refractor.

refractory (ri'fræk·tə·ri) *adj.* refractario.

refrain (ri'freɪn) *v.i.* refrenarse; abstenerse. **—***n.* estribillo; refrán.

refresh (ri'frɛʃ) *v.t.* refrescar; renovar. **—***v.i.* refrescarse. **—refreshing,** *adj.* refrescante. **—refreshment,** *n.* refresco.

refrigerate (ri'frɪdʒ·ə·reit) *v.t.* refrigerar. **—refrigerant,** *n.* & *adj.* refrigerante. **—refrigeration,** *n.* refrigeración. **—refrigerator,** *n.* refrigerador; nevera.

refry (ri'fraɪ) *v.t.* refreír.

refuel (ri'fju·əl) *v.t.* repostar. **—***v.i.* repostarse.

refuge ('rɛf·judʒ) *n.* refugio; albergue; amparo. **—refugee,** *n.* refugiado. **—take refuge,** refugiarse.

refulgence (ri'fʌl·dʒəns) *n.* refulgencia; resplandor. **—refulgent,** *adj.* refulgente.

refund (ri'fʌnd) *v.t.* **1,** (pay back) reembolsar; devolver. **2,** (re-) (refinance) consolidar. **—***n.* ('ri·fʌnd) reembolso. **—refundable,** *adj.* restituible.

refurbish (ri'fʌr·bɪʃ) *v.t.* restaurar; reparar.

refusal (ri'fjuz·əl) *n.* **1,** (act of refusing) denegación; repulsa. **2,** (first option) opción exclusiva.

refuse (ri'fjuːz) *v.t.* **1,** (decline; deny) rehusar; denegar. **2,** (reject) rechazar. —*v.i.* no querer; no aceptar. —*n.* ('ref·jus) basura. —**refuse to,** negarse a.

refute (rɪ'fjut) *v.t.* refutar. —**refutation** (ˌrɛf·ju'tei·ʃən) *n.* refutación.

regain (rɪ'gein) *v.t.* **1,** (reach again) volver a; volver a alcanzar. **2,** (recover) recobrar; recuperar.

regal ('ri·gəl) *adj.* real; regio; majestuoso.

regale (rɪ'geil) *v.t.* regalar; festejar. —**regale oneself,** regalarse.

regalia (rɪ'gei·li·ə) *n.pl.* **1,** (emblems) insignias. **2,** (personal finery) galas; trajes de gala.

regard (rɪ'gard) *v.t.* **1,** (look upon) mirar; observar. **2,** (esteem) estimar; apreciar. **3,** (concern) concernir; referirse a. —*n.* **1,** (reference) relación; respecto. **2,** (respect) respeto; veneración. **3,** (scrutiny) mirada. **4,** (concern) interés; consideración. —**regardful,** *adj.* atento. —**regarding,** *prep.* tocante a; respecto a. —**as regards,** respecto a; en cuanto a. —**best regards to,** muchos recuerdos a; saludos cordiales a. —**in o with regard to,** respecto a; en cuanto a. —**without regard to,** sin considerar; sin tener en cuenta.

regardless (rɪ'gard·ləs) *adj.* descuidado; indiferente. —*adv.,* *colloq.* no obstante; en todo caso. —**regardless of,** no obstante; a pesar de; sin considerar.

regatta (rɪ'gæt·ə) *n.* regata.

regency ('ri·dʒən·si) *n.* regencia.

regenerate (ri'dʒən·ər͵eit) *v.t.* regenerar. —*v.i.* regenerarse. —*adj.* (-ət) regenerado. —**regeneration,** *n.* regeneración. —**regenerative** (-ə·tɪv) *adj.* regenerativo.

regent ('ri·dʒənt) *n.* **1,** (substitute ruler) regente. **2,** *educ.* director; miembro de la junta directiva. —*adj.* regente.

regicide ('rɛdʒ·ə͵said) *n.* **1,** (agent) regicida. **2,** (act) regicidio.

regime (re'ʒim) *n.* régimen; gobierno.

regimen ('rɛdʒ·ə·mən) *n.* régimen.

regiment ('rɛdʒ·ə·mənt) *n.* regimiento. —*v.t.* regimentar. —**regimental** (-'mɛn·təl) *adj.* regimental. —**regimentals,** *n.pl.* uniforme militar. —**regimentation** (-mɛn'tei·ʃən) *n.* regimentación.

region ('ri·dʒən) *n.* **1,** (area) región. **2,** (district) distrito; territorio. —**regional,** *adj.* regional. —**re-**gionalism,** *n.* regionalismo. —**regionalist,** *n.* regionalista. —**regionalistic,** *adj.* regionalista.

register ('rɛdʒ·ɪs·tər) *n.* **1,** (written record) archivo; registro. **2,** *mus.* (range) amplitud vocal o instrumental. **3,** (regulator, as for heat or air) regulador. **4,** (recording device) registrador. **5,** *print.* ajuste exacto; registro. **6,** (recording office) registro. **7,** (registrar) registrador [*fem.* -dora]. —*v.t.* **1,** (enroll) inscribir. **2,** (transcribe; record; copy) registrar. **3,** (indicate, as by a measuring device) registrar. **4,** (manifest; show) demostrar; manifestar. **5,** (insure delivery of, as a letter) certificar. **6,** *print.* registrar. —*v.i.* **1,** (enroll; record one's name) inscribir(se). **2,** *print.* estar en registro; registrarse. **3,** *colloq.* (make an impression) crear una impresión. —**registered nurse,** enfermero diplomado; enfermera diplomada.

registrar ('rɛdʒ·ɪs͵trar) *n.* registrador [*fem.* -dora].

registration (ˌrɛdʒ·ɪs'trei·ʃən) *n.* **1,** (act of registering) inscripción. **2,** (list of persons registered) registro; matrícula.

registry ('rɛdʒ·ɪs·tri) *n.* registro.

regnant ('rɛg·nənt) *adj.* reinante.

regress ('ri·grɛs) *n.* regreso; vuelta; retorno. —*v.i.* (rɪ'grɛs) regresar. —**regression** (rɪ'grɛʃ·ən) *n.* regresión. —**regressive** (rɪ'grɛs·ɪv) *adj.* regresivo; retrógrado.

regret (rɪ'grɛt) *v.i.* **1,** (lament) lamentar. **2,** (rue) sentir; arrepentirse de. —*n.* **1,** (grief) pena; pesadumbre. **2,** (remorse) compunción; remordimiento. **3,** *pl.* (excuses) excusas. —**regretful,** *adj.* triste; pesaroso. —**regrettable,** *adj.* lamentable.

regroup (ri'grup) *v.t.* reagrupar. —*v.i.* reagruparse.

regular ('rɛg·jə·lər) *adj.* **1,** (customary) regular; acostumbrado. **2,** (steady) uniforme. **3,** (normal) natural. **4,** *colloq.* (thorough) cabal. —*n.* regular. —**regularity** (-'lær·ə·ti) *n.* regularidad.

regularize ('rɛg·jə·lə͵raiz) *v.t.* regularizar. —*v.i.* regularizarse. —**regularization** (-rɪ'zei·ʃən) *n.* regularización.

regulate ('rɛg·jə͵leit) *v.t.* **1,** (direct) diciplinar. **2,** (keep in order) regular. **3,** (set rules for) reglamentar. **4,** (adjust) ajustar. **—regu-lator,** *n.* regulador. **—regulatory** (-lə,tor·i) *adj.* reglamentario; regulador.

regulation (,rɛg·jə'lei·ʃən) *n.* **1,** (rule) regla. **2,** (act or power of regulating) regulación. **3,** *usu. pl.* (set of rules) reglamento; reglamentación. **—adj.** de regla; regular.

regurgitate (ri'gʌr·dʒɪ,teit) *v.i.* regurgitar. **—v.t.** vomitar. **—regurgitation,** *n.* regurgitación.

rehabilitate (,ri·hə'bɪl·ə,teit) *v.t.* rehabilitar. **—rehabilitation,** *n.* rehabilitación.

rehash ('ri·hæʃ) *n., colloq.* refundición. **—v.t.** (ri'hæʃ) *colloq.* **1,** (make into another form) refundir; rehacer. **2,** (go over again) repasar; repetir.

rehearse (rɪ'hʌrs) *v.t.* **1,** (practice) ensayar. **2,** (repeat) repetir. **3,** (tell in detail) narrar. **—v.i.** practicar; ensayarse. **—rehearsal,** *n.* ensayo.

reheat (ri'hit) *v.t.* recalentar. **—reheating,** *n.* recalentamiento.

reign (rein) *n.* **1,** (rule; domain) reino. **2,** (period of rule) reinado. **—v.i.** reinar. **—reigning,** *adj.* reinante.

reimburse (,ri·ɪm'bʌrs) *v.t.* reembolsar. **—reimbursable,** *adj.* reembolsable. **—reimbursement,** *n.* reembolso.

rein (rein) *n.* rienda. **—v.t.** refrenar. **—free rein,** rienda suelta. **—throw off the reins,** soltar la rienda.

reincarnate (,ri·ɪn'kar·neit) *v.i.* encarnar de nuevo. **—reincarnation,** *n.* reencarnación.

reindeer ('rein,dɪr) *n.* reno.

reinforce (,ri·ɪn'fors) *v.t.* reforzar. **—reinforcement,** *n.* refuerzo. **—reinforced concrete,** hormigón armado.

reinstall (,ri·ɪn'stɔl) *v.t.* reinstalar. **—reinstallation** (,ri·ɪn·stə'lei·ʃən) *n.* reinstalación.

reinstate (,ri·ɪn'steit) *v.t.* reinstalar; reintegrar; restablecer. **—reinstatement,** *n.* reinstalación; reintegración.

reiterate (ri'ɪt·ə,reit) *v.t.* repetir; reiterar. **—reiteration,** *n.* repetición; reiteración.

reject (rɪ'dʒɛkt) *v.t.* **1,** (discard) descartar; desechar; rechazar. **2,** (refuse to accept) renunciar. **3,** (deny) negar. **—n.** ('ri-) cosa rechazada; desecho. **—rejection** (rɪ'dʒɛk·ʃən) *n.* rechazo.

rejoice (rɪ'dʒɔis) *v.t.* regocijar; alegrar. **—v.i.** regocijarse; alegrarse. **—rejoicing,** *n.* alegría; regocijo.

rejoin (ri'dʒɔin) *v.t.* **1,** (put back together) unir o juntar de nuevo. **2,** (resume membership in) reentrar en; unirse de nuevo a; volver a. **3,** (meet again) volver a encontrar. **—v.i.** volver; reentrar; reingresar.

rejoin (rɪ'dʒɔin) *v.i. & t.* contestar; replicar.

rejoinder (rɪ'dʒɔin·dər) *n.* respuesta; réplica.

rejuvenate (rɪ'dʒu·və,neit) *v.t.* rejuvenecer. **—v.i.** rejuvenecerse. **—rejuvenation,** *n.* rejuvenecimiento.

rekindle (ri'kɪn·dəl) *v.t.* volver a encender. **—v.i.** volver a encenderse.

relapse (rɪ'læps) *v.i.* recaer. **—n.** recaída; *med.* recidiva; retroceso.

relate (rɪ'leit) *v.t.* **1,** (connect) relacionar. **2,** (narrate) relatar; narrar; contar. **3,** (ally by kinship) emparentar. **—v.i.** relacionarse; referirse. **—related,** *adj.* afín; conexo; emparentado.

relation (rɪ'lei·ʃən) *n.* **1,** (narration) narración. **2,** (kin) pariente. **3,** (connection) relación; conexión. **4,** (reference) referencia. **—relations,** *n.pl.* **1,** (relatives) parentela. **2,** (connections) afinidad. **3,** (copulation) cópula; copulación.

relationship (rɪ'lei·ʃən·ʃɪp) *n.* **1,** (connection) relación. **2,** (kinship) parentesco.

relative ('rɛl·ə·tɪv) *adj.* relativo. **—n.** pariente. **—relativism,** *n.* relativismo. **—relativity** (-'tɪv·ə·ti) *n.* relatividad.

relax (rɪ'læks) *v.t.* relajar; laxar; ceder. **—v.i.** **1,** (slacken) relajarse; aflojarse. **2,** (amuse oneself) distraerse. **3,** (take one's ease) estar a sus anchas. **4,** (have peace of mind) estar tranquilo.

relaxation (,ri·læk'sei·ʃən) *n.* **1,** (slackening) aflojamiento; relajación; relajamiento. **2,** (recreation) distracción; recreo.

relay ('ri·lei) *n.* **1,** (fresh supply) relevo. **2,** (station; stopping point) posta. **3,** (shift) cambio; tanda; remuda. **—v.t.** **1,** [*pret. & p.p.* **-laid**] (replace) reemplazar. **2,** (send by a series of steps) mandar por remuda; retransmitir; reexpedir. **—relay race,** carrera de relevos.

release (rɪ'lis) *v.t.* **1,** (free) libertar.

2, (disengage; loose) soltar. 3, (exempt) eximir; aliviar. 4, (relinquish for display or sale) dar al público. —*n.* 1, (liberation) liberación. 2, (discharge) descargo. 3, (news item) publicación. 4, (surrender of claim) cesión.

relegate ('rɛl·ə,geit) *v.t.* relegar. —**relegation,** *n.* relegación.

relent (rɪ'lɛnt) *v.i.* ceder; aplacarse.

relentless (rɪ'lɛnt·ləs) *adj.* inexorable; implacable.

relevant ('rɛl·ə·vənt) *adj.* pertinente; apropiado. —**relevance,** *n.* pertinencia.

reliable (rɪ'lai·ə·bəl) *adj.* seguro; digno de confianza. —**reliability,** *n.* seguridad; confianza.

reliance (rɪ'lai·əns) *n.* confianza. —**reliant,** *adj.* confiado.

relic ('rɛl·ɪk) *n.* 1, (vestige) vestigio. 2, (religious memento) reliquia. 3, *pl.* (remains) residuo.

relict ('rɛl·ɪkt) *n.* viuda.

relief (rɪ'lif) *n.* 1, (mitigation) mitigación. 2, (release, as from pain) alivio. 3, (assistance to the poor) ayuda; asistencia. 4, (release by substitution) relevación. 5, (raised decoration) relieve. 6, (person or group that takes over another's duty) relevo.

relieve (rɪ'liːv) *v.t.* 1, (alleviate) aliviar. 2, (substitute) relevar. 3, (help) auxiliar; socorrer.

religion (rɪ'lɪdʒ·ən) *n.* religión.

religious (rɪ'lɪdʒ·əs) *adj. & n.* religioso [*fem.* religiosa]. —**religiosity** (-i'as·ə·ti) *n.* religiosidad.

relinquish (rɪ'lɪŋ·kwɪʃ) *v.t.* abandonar; renunciar. —**relinquishment,** *n.* renuncia.

reliquary ('rɛl·ə,kwɛr·i) *n.* relicario.

relish ('rɛl·ɪʃ) *v.t.* gustar de; saborear; paladear. —*n.* 1, (savor) sabor; gusto. 2, (appreciation) goce. 3, (appetizer) aperitivo; entremés. 4, (condiment) condimento.

relive (ri'lɪv) *v.t. & i.* volver a vivir.

reload (ri'loːd) *v.t.* recargar.

relocate (ri'lo·keit; ri·lo'keit) *v.t.* mudar; instalar en otra parte. —*v.i.* mudarse; instalarse en otra parte. —**relocation,** *n.* mudanza; instalación en otra parte.

reluctant (rɪ'lʌk·tənt) *adj.* renuente. —**reluctance,** *n.* renuencia; *elect.* reluctancia. —**reluctantly,** *adv.* de mala gana.

rely (rɪ'lai) *v.i.* confiar; fiarse. —**rely on** o **upon,** contar con; confiar en.

remain (rɪ'mein) *v.i.* 1, (stay) quedarse. 2, (continue in a state) permanecer. 3, (endure) persistir. 4, (be left over) restar. 5, (be held in reserve) quedarse en reserva. —**remains,** *n.pl.* restos. —**remaining,** *adj.* restante.

remainder (rɪ'mein·dər) *n.* 1, (what is left) resto; restante. 2, (surplus) remanente. 3, *math.* resta; residuo.

remake (rɪ'meik) *v.t.* [*pret. & p.p.* **-made**] rehacer. —*n.* ('ri-) cosa rehecha.

remand (rɪ'mænd) *v.t.* 1, (recall; send back) llamar. 2, *law* (send back to prison) volver a enviar a la cárcel. 3, *law* (transfer to another court) enviar a otro tribunal.

remark (rɪ'mark) *v.t.* 1, (observe) observar. 2, (comment; comment on) comentar. —*n.* observación; comentario. —**remarkable,** *adj.* notable; insigne.

remarry (rɪ'mær·i) *v.i.* volver a casarse.

remediable (rɪ'mi·di·ə·bəl) *adj.* remediable; reparable.

remedial (rɪ'mi·di·əl) *adj.* remediador; curativo.

remedy ('rɛm·ə·di) *n.* remedio. —*v.t.* remediar.

remember (rɪ'mɛm·bər) *v.t.* 1, (recall) recordar; acordarse de. 2, (observe, as an anniversary) observar. 3, *colloq.* (tip) dar propina. 4, (convey one's regards) presentar sus recuerdos (a). —*v.i.* acordarse; recordarse. —**remembrance** (-brəns) *n.* recuerdo.

remind (rɪ'maind) *v.t.* recordar; hacer presente. —**reminder,** *n.* recuerdo; recordatorio.

reminisce (,rɛm·ə'nɪs) *v.i.* recordar el pasado. —**reminiscence,** *n.* reminiscencia. —**reminiscent,** *adj.* recordativo.

remiss (rɪ'mɪs) *adj.* remiso; descuidado; negligente. —**remissness,** *n.* descuido; negligencia.

remission (rɪ'mɪʃ·ən) *n.* remisión.

remit (rɪ'mɪt) *v.t.* 1, (pardon) remitir; perdonar. 2, (refrain from exacting, as a tax or penalty) condonar. 3, (slacken) aflojar. 4, (restore) devolver; restituir. 5, (send, as payment) remesar; remitir. 6, *law* referir. —*v.i.* 1, (abate) aflojarse. **2,** (send payment) hacer remesa.

remittal (rɪ'mɪt·əl) *n.* renuncia; remesa.

remittance (rɪ'mɪt·əns) *n.* remesa. —**remittance man,** exiliado viviendo de remesas.

remnant ('rɛm·nənt) *n.* remanente; resto; retazo.

remodel (ri'mad·əl) *v.t.* reconstruir; convertir; renovar.

remonstrate (rɪ'man·streit) *v.i.* objetar; protestar. —**remonstrance,** *n.* protesta. —**remonstrant,** *adj.* & *n.* protestante.

remora ('rɛm·ə·rə) *n.* rémora.

remorse (rɪ'mɔrs) *n.* remordimiento. —**remorseful,** *adj.* arrepentido. —**remorseless,** *adj.* implacable.

remote (rɪ'mot) *adj.* remoto; apartado; ajeno. —**remoteness,** *n.* lejanía. —**remotely,** *adv.* a lo lejos. —**remote control,** mando a distancia.

remount (ri'maunt) *v.t.* & *i.* volver a montar o subir.

removable (rɪ'muv·ə·bəl) *adj.* **1,** (portable) transportable; portátil. **2,** (dismountable) desmontable. —*n.,* *usu.pl.* muebles; bienes muebles.

removal (rɪ'muv·əl) *n.* **1,** (taking away) remoción; removimiento; sacamiento. **2,** (change of location) traslado; mudanza. **3,** (dismissal) destitución; deposición. **4,** (obliteration) eliminación; aniquilación.

remove (rɪ'muːv) *v.t.* **1,** (take away) quitar; sacar. **2,** (change the location of) remover; trasladar; mudar. **3,** (dismiss) destituir; deponer. **4,** (obliterate) extirpar; eliminar; aniquilar. —*v.i.* mudarse; trasladarse. —*n.* **1,** (step; interval) paso. **2,** *Brit.* (change of location) traslado; mudanza.

remunerate (rɪ'mju·nə,reit) *v.t.* remunerar. —**remuneration,** *n.* remuneración. —**remunerative** (-rə·tɪv) *adj.* lucrativo; remuneratorio.

renaissance (,rɛn·ə'sans) *n.* renacimiento.

renascence (rɪ'næs·əns) *n.* renacimiento. —**renascent,** *adj.* renaciente.

renal ('ri·nəl) *adj.* renal.

rename (ri'neim) *v.t.* volver a nombrar; dar nuevo nombre a.

rend (rend) *v.t.* [*pret.* & *p.p.* **rent**] desgarrar; hender; hacer pedazos.

render ('rɛn·dər) *v.t.* **1,** (cause to be or become) volver; poner. **2,** (give; present) dar; rendir. **3,** (return) devolver. **4,** (translate) traducir. **5,** (interpret) interpretar. **6,** *cooking* derretir. **7,** (perform) ejecutar.

rendezvous ('ran·də,vu) *n.* [*pl.* -**vous** (-,vuːz)] cita; lugar de cita. —*v.i.* [-**voused** (-,vuːd), -**vousing** (-,vu·ɪŋ)] reunirse; acudir a una cita.

renegade ('rɛn·ə,geid) *adj.* & *n.* renegado.

renege (rɪ'nɪg) *v.i.* **1,** *cards* (revoke) renunciar. **2,** *colloq.* (back down) retirarse. —*n., cards* renuncio.

renew (rɪ'njuː) *v.t.* renovar. —**renewal,** *n.* renovación.

rennet ('rɛn·ɪt) *n.* cuajo.

renounce (rɪ'nauns) *v.t.* & *i.* renunciar. —**renouncement,** *n.* renunciación.

renovate ('rɛn·ə,veit) *v.t.* renovar. —**renovation,** *n.* renovación. —**renovator,** *n.* renovador.

renown (rɪ'naun) *n.* renombre; fama; reputación. —**renowned,** *adj.* célebre; famoso; renombrado.

rent (rent) *n.* **1,** (payment for use) alquiler; renta. **2,** (tear) desgarrón; rasgón; rotura. —*adj.* rasgado; desgarrado. —*v.t.* **1,** (lease) arrendar. **2,** (let; hire) alquilar. **3,** *pret.* & *p.p.* de **rend.** —*v.i.* **1,** (be leased) arrendarse. **2,** (be let or hired) alquilarse. —**for rent,** de alquiler; se alquila.

rental ('rɛn·təl) *n.* **1,** (money paid for use) alquiler; renta. **2,** (income from rented property) renta.

renter ('rɛn·tər) *n.* **1,** (tenant) inquilino; arrendatario. **2,** (owner) propietario; dueño; arrendador [*fem.* -dora].

renunciation (rɪ,nʌn·si'ei·ʃən) *n.* renunciación.

reopen (ri'o·pən) *v.t.* reabrir. —*v.i.* reabrirse.

reorganize (ri'or·gə,naiz) *v.t.* reorganizar. —*v.i.* reorganizarse. —**reorganization** (-nɪ'zei·ʃən) *n.* reorganización.

rep (rep) *n.* **1,** *slang* = **reputation.** **2,** *colloq.* = **representative. 3,**

colloq. = **repertory. 4,** *colloq.* = **repetition.**

repaint (ri'peint) *v.t.* pintar de nuevo; dar nueva mano. —**repainting,** *n.* nueva pintura; nueva mano de pintura.

repair (rɪ'peɪr) *v.i.* irse; dirigirse. —*v.t.* **1,** (mend) reparar; componer; arreglar. **2,** (make amends for) enmendar. —*n.* **1,** (act of repairing) reparación; arreglo. **2,** (restored condition) reparo. —**repairable,** *adj.* reparable. —**repairer,** *n.* reparador [*fem.* -dora].

repairman (rɪ'per,mæn) *n.* [*pl.* -men] reparador.

reparable ('rɛp·ə·rə·bəl) *adj.* reparable.

reparation (,rɛp·ə'rei·ʃən) *n.* **1,** (repair; amends) reparación. **2,** *usu.pl.* (compensation) indemnización; compensación.

repartee (,rɛp·ər'tiɹ) *n.* respuesta picante; réplica.

repast (rɪ'pæst) *n.* comida.

repatriate (ri'pei·tri,eit) *v.t.* repatriar. —**repatriation,** *n.* repatriación.

repay (ri'pei) *v.t.* **1,** (pay back) compensar. **2,** (reimburse) reembolsar. **3,** (return, as a visit) corresponder a. —**repayable,** reembolsable; compensable. —**repayment,** *n.* reembolso; compensación.

repeal (rɪ'piːl) *v.t.* revocar; abolir; anular. —*n.* revocación; abolición; anulación.

repeat (rɪ'pit) *v.t. & i.* **1,** (do again) repetir. **2,** (reiterate) reiterar. **3,** (recite) recitar de memoria. —*n., mus.* repetición. —**repeatedly,** *adv.* repetidamente; repetidas veces.

repeater (ri'pi·tər) *n.* **1,** (one who repeats) repetidor. **2,** (firearm) arma de repetición. **3,** (watch) reloj de repetición.

repel (rɪ'pɛl) *v.t.* **1,** (drive back) repeler; rechazar. **2,** (resist) resistir. **3,** (arouse repulsion in) repugnar; repulsar. —*v.i.* ser repulsivo.

repellent (rɪ'pɛl·ənt) *adj.* **1,** (resistant) impermeable. **2,** (repulsive) repulsivo. —*n.* remedio repercusivo.

repent (rɪ'pɛnt) *v.t. & i.* arrepentirse (de). —**repentance,** *n.* arrepentimiento. —**repentant,** *adj.* penitente; arrepentido.

repercussion (,ri·pər'kʌʃ·ən) *n.* **1,** (result of an action) repercusión. **2,** (echo) reverberación.

repertoire ('rɛp·ər,twar) *n.* repertorio.

repertory ('rɛp·ər·tor·i) *n.* **1,** (repertoire) repertorio. **2,** (inventory) inventario. —*adj.* de repertorio.

repetition (,rɛp·ə'tɪʃ·ən) *n.* repetición. —**repetitious,** *adj.* repetidor. —**repetitive** (rə'pɛt·ə·tɪv) *adj.* repetitivo.

repine (rɪ'pain) *v.i.* quejarse; afligirse. —**repining,** *n.* queja. —*adj.* descontento.

replace (rɪ'pleis) *v.t.* **1,** (put back) reponer. **2,** (take the place of) reemplazar. **3,** (substitute for) substituir.

replacement (rɪ'pleis·mənt) *n.* **1,** (act of replacing) reemplazo. **2,** (substitute) substituto. —**replacement part,** (pieza de) recambio.

replay (ri'plei) *v.t.* volver a jugar (un partido o un trozo); volver a tocar (una grabación). —*n.* ('ri·plei) repetición.

replenish (rɪ'plɛn·ɪʃ) *v.t.* rellenar; llenar; abastecer. —**replenishment,** *n.* abastecimiento.

replete (rɪ'plit) *adj.* repleto; lleno. —**repletion** (rɪ'pli·ʃən) *n.* plenitud; repleción.

replica ('rɛp·lɪ·kə) *n.* réplica; duplicado.

reply (rɪ'plai) *v.t. & i.* responder; contestar; replicar. —*n.* respuesta; contestación.

repopulate (ri'pap·jə,leit) *v.t.* repoblar. —**repopulation,** *n.* repoblación.

report (rɪ'port) *n.* **1,** (account) relato; informe. **2,** (rumor) rumor. **3,** (reputation) fama; reputación. **4,** *pl.* (record of court judgments) dictamen. **5,** (sound of explosion) estallido; detonación. —*v.i.* **1,** (serve as a reporter) ser reportero. **2,** (present oneself) comparecer. —*v.t.* **1,** (relate) relatar; reportar. **2,** (say) contar. —**report card,** calificación ecolar periódica.

reportage (rɪ'por·tɪdʒ) *n.* reportaje.

reporter (ri'por·tər) *n.* reportero; repórter; periodista.

repose (rɪ'poɹz) *n.* **1,** (rest) reposo; descanso. **2,** (tranquillity) paz. —*v.i.* **1,** (lie at rest) reposar. **2,** (be situated) situarse. **3,** (rely) fiarse. —*v.t.* **1,** (lay) tender. **2,** (set at rest) recostar. **3,** (place, as trust) confiar.

repository (rɪ'paz·ɪ·tor·i) *n.* repositorio; depósito.

repossess (ˌri·pəˈzɛs) v.t. recobrar; recuperar. —**repossession** (-ˈzɛʃ·ən) n. recobro.

repoussé (rə·puˈsei) adj. & n. repujado.

reprehend (ˌrep·riˈhɛnd) v.t. reprender; regañar; censurar. —**reprehensible** (-ˈhɛns·ə·bəl) adj. censurable; reprensible. —**reprehension** (-ˈhɛn·ʃən) n. regaño; reprensión. —**reprehensive** (-ˈhɛn·sɪv) adj. reprensor.

represent (ˌrep·riˈzɛnt) v.t. representar. —**representation** (-zɛnˈtei·ʃən) n. representación.

representative (ˌrep·riˈzɛn·tə·tɪv) adj. 1, (serving to represent) representativo. 2, (typical) típico. —n. representante; delegado.

repress (riˈprɛs) v.t. reprimir. —**repression** (riˈprɛʃ·ən) n. represión. —**repressive**, adj. represivo.

reprieve (riˈpriːv) v.t. 1, (grant a respite to) librar temporalmente; aliviar. 2, (delay the execution of) suspender la ejecución a. —n. 1, (respite) alivio; respiro. 2, (delay of execution) suspensión.

reprimand (ˈrep·rəˌmænd) v.t. reprender; censurar. —n. reprimenda.

reprint (riˈprɪnt) v.t. reimprimir. —n. (ˈri-) 1, (new impression) reimpresión. 2, (separately printed excerpt) tirada aparte.

reprisal (riˈprai·zəl) n. represalia.

reproach (riˈprotʃ) v.t. censurar; reprender; reprochar (algo a alguien). —n. reproche; censura. —**reproachful**, adj. reprensor.

reprobate (ˈrep·rəˌbeit) adj. & n. réprobo.

reproduce (ˌri·prəˈdus) v.t. reproducir. —v.i. reproducirse; procrear. —**reproduction** (-ˈdʌk·ʃən) n. reproducción. —**reproductive** (-ˈdʌk·tɪv) adj. reproductivo.

reproof (riˈpruf) n. reproche; censura.

reprove (riˈpruːv) v.t. reprobar; censurar. —**reproval**, n. censura.

reprovision (ˌri·proˈvɪʒ·ən) v.t. repostar; abastecer.

reptile (ˈrep·tɪl; -tail) n. reptil.

reptilian (repˈtɪl·jən) adj. reptil.

republic (riˈpʌb·lɪk) n. república.

republican (riˈpʌb·lɪk·ən) adj. & n. republicano. —**republicanism**, n. republicanismo.

republish (riˈpʌb·lɪʃ) v.t. volver a publicar. —**republication**, n. publicación repetida.

repudiate (riˈpju·di,eit) v.t. repudiar. —**repudiation**, n. repudio; repudiación.

repugnance (riˈpʌg·nəns) n. repugnancia. —**repugnant**, adj. repugnante. —**be repugnant to**, repugnar a.

repulse (riˈpʌls) v.t. 1, (repel) repeler; repulsar. 2, (reject) rechazar. —n. 1, (a driving back) repulsa; repulsión. 2, (rejection) rechazo.

repulsion (riˈpʌl·ʃən) n. repulsión.

repulsive (riˈpʌl·sɪv) adj. 1, (repelling) repulsivo. 2, (offensive) repugnante.

reputable (ˈrep·jə·tə·bəl) adj. estimable; respetable; honrado. —**reputability**, n. estima; respetabilidad; honradez.

reputation (ˌrep·jəˈtei·ʃən) n. reputación; fama; nombre.

repute (riˈpjut) n. reputación; estima; fama. —v.t. reputar; estimar. —**reputed**, adj. supuesto. —**reputedly**, adv. según la opinión común.

request (riˈkwɛst) n. 1, (petition) ruego; petición; solicitud. 2, (thing requested; order) pedido; encargo. —v.t. 1, (ask for) rogar; pedir; solicitar. 2, (order) pedir; encargar. —adj. pedido; a petición. —**on o upon request**, a pedido; a solicitud.

requiem (ˈri·kwi·əm; ˈrɛk·wi-) n. réquiem.

require (riˈkwair) v.t. 1, (demand) requerir. 2, (oblige; compel) exigir. 3, (need) necesitar.

requirement (riˈkwair·mənt) n. 1, (demand) requisito. 2, (exigency) exigencia. 3, (need) necesidad.

requisite (ˈrɛk·wə·zɪt) adj. necesario; esencial. —n. requisito.

requisition (ˌrɛk·wɪˈzɪʃ·ən) n. 1, (demand) demanda. 2, (written order) requisa; requisición. —v.t. 1, (demand) exigir. 2, (seize officially) requisar.

requital (riˈkwai·təl) n. 1, (return) compensación. 2, (retaliation) desquite.

requite (riˈkwait) v.t. 1, (return; repay) devolver; corresponder a. 2, (avenge) desquitarse de.

reread (riˈriːd) v.t. releer; leer otra vez. —**rereading**, n. nueva lectura.

rerun (riˈrʌn) v.t., TV; cinema volver a presentar. —n. (ˈri·rʌn) presentación repetida.

resale (ri'seil; 'ri-) *n.* reventa.
rescind (ri'sınd) *v.t.* rescindir.
rescission (ri'sıʒ·ən) *n.* rescisión.
rescript ('ri‚skrıpt) *n.* rescripto; edicto.
rescue ('res·kju) *v.t.* 1, (save from danger) salvar; librar; sacar de peligro. 2, (deliver) rescatar; redimir; libertar. —*n.* 1, (saving) salvamento; libramiento. 2, (deliverance) rescate; redención; liberación.
research (ri'sʌrtʃ) *n.* investigación. —*v.t.* & *i.* investigar. —**researcher,** *n.* investigador [*fem.* -dora].
resell (ri'sɛl) *v.t.* [*pret.* & *p.p.* -**sold**] revender.
resemble (ri'zɛm·bəl) *v.t.* asemejarse a; parecerse a. —**resemblance** (-bləns) *n.* semejanza.
resent (ri'zɛnt) *v.t.* resentirse de o por; agraviarse de o por. —**resentful,** *adj.* resentido; agraviado. —**resentment,** *n.* resentimiento.
reservation (‚rez·ər'vei·ʃən) *n.* 1, (act of withholding) reservación. 2, (thing withheld) reserva. 3, (limiting condition) reserva. 4, (restricted area) territorio reservado.
reserve (ri'zʌrv) *v.t.* reservar. —*n.* 1, (something kept for future use) reserva. 2, = **reservation.** 3, (self-restraint) reserva; discreción. 4, *mil.* reserva. —**reserved,** *adj.* reservado; discreto. —**reservist,** *n.* reservista.
reservoir ('rez·ər‚vwar) *n.* depósito; alberca.
reset (ri'sɛt) *v.t.* [-**set, -setting**] 1, encajar (una fractura). 2, volver a montar o a engastar (una joya). 3, *print.* recomponer.
reshape (ri'ʃeip) *v.t.* = **re-form.**
reship (ri'ʃıp) *v.t.* 1, (ship back or again) reembarcar. 2, (forward) reexpedir; reenviar.
reshipment (ri'ʃıp·mənt) *n.* 1, (shipping back or again) reembarque. 2, (forwarding) reexpedición; reenvío.
reside (ri'zaid) *v.i.* residir.
residence ('rez·ı·dəns) *n.* residencia. —**residency,** *n.* residencia. —**resident,** *n.* & *adj.* residente. —**residential** (-'dɛn·ʃəl) *adj.* residencial.
residue ('rez·ı‚dju) *n.* residuo; sobrante; resto. —**residual** (rə'zıdʒ·u·əl) *adj.* restante; residual.
resign (ri'zain) *v.t.* 1, (relinquish) renunciar. 2, (give up, as an office or position) dimitir. 3, (turn over to

another) resignar. —*v.i.* dimitir; darse de baja; *chess* abandonar. —**resign oneself,** resignarse; conformarse. —**resigned,** *adj.* resignado.
resignation (‚rez·ıg'nei·ʃən) *n.* 1, (relinquishment) renuncia. 2, (giving up, as of a position) dimisión. 3, (submission) resignación; conformidad.
resilience (ri'zıl·i·əns) *n.* 1, (elasticity) elasticidad. 2, (buoyancy) ánimo; viveza.
resilient (ri'zıl·i·ənt) *adj.* 1, (elastic) elástico. 2, (buoyancy) animoso; vivo.
resin ('rez·ın) *n.* resina. —**resinous,** *adj.* resinoso.
resist (ri'zıst) *v.t.* resistir; resistir a; impedir. —*v.i.* resistirse; oponerse.
resistance (ri'zıs·təns) *n.* resistencia. —**resistant,** *adj.* resistente.
resistible (ri'zıs·tə·bəl) *adj.* resistible.
resistor (ri'zıs·tər) *n.* resistor.
resold (ri'sold) *v.,* *pret.* & *p.p.* de **resell.**
resole (ri'sol) *v.t.* remontar; poner suela a.
resolute ('rez·ə·lut) *adj.* resuelto; determinado; firme.
resolution (‚rez·ə'lu·ʃən) *n.* resolución.
resolve (ri'zalv) *v.t.* resolver. —*v.i.* resolverse. —*n.* resolución. —**resolved,** *adj.* resuelto.
resonant ('rez·ə·nənt) *adj.* resonante. —**resonance,** *n.* resonancia.
resonate ('rez·ə‚neit) *v.i.* resonar. —**resonator,** *n.* resonador.
resort (ri'zort) *v.i.* frecuentar; concurrir. —*n.* 1, (vacation spot) sitio frecuentado; estación de veraneo, de esquí, etc. 2, (recourse) recurso. —**resort to; have resort to,** recurrir a.
resound (ri'zaund) *v.i.* 1, (reverberate) resonar. 2, (emit loud sounds) retumbar.
resounding (ri'zaun·dıŋ) *adj.* 1, (ringing) resonante. 2, (thorough) completo.
resource (ri'sors) *n.* recurso. —**resourceful,** *adj.* mañoso; hábil.
respect (ri'spɛkt) *v.t.* 1, (heed) respetar; acatar. 2, (honor) estimar; honrar. 3, (relate to) respectar; tocar. —*n.* 1, (high esteem) respeto; veneración. 2, (relation; aspect) respecto. 3, *pl.* (compliments)

saludos. —**in** o **with respect to,** (con) respecto a.

respectable (rɪ'spɛk·tə·bəl) *adj.* **1,** (highly regarded) respetable. **2,** (decent) honroso. **3,** (fairly good or large) considerable. —**respectability,** *n.* respetabilidad.

respectful (rɪ'spɛkt·fəl) *adj.* respetuoso. —**respectfully,** *adv.* respetuosamente. —**respectfully yours,** de Vd. atento y seguro servidor.

respecting (rɪ'spɛk·tɪŋ) *prep.* respecto a; tocante a.

respective (rɪ'spɛk·tɪv) *adj.* respectivo. —**respectively,** *adv.* respectivamente.

respiration (,rɛs·pə'rei·ʃən) *n.* respiración.

respirator ('rɛs·pə,rei·tər) *n.* **1,** (breathing device) respirador. **2,** (breathing mask) máscara respiradora.

respiratory (rə'spair·ə·tor·i) *adj.* respiratorio.

respire (rɪ'spair) *v.i. & t.* respirar.

respite ('rɛs·pɪt) *n.* **1,** (pause) respiro; reposo. **2,** (postponement) prórroga; suspensión.

resplendent (rɪ'splɛn·dənt) *adj.* resplandeciente. —**resplendence,** *n.* resplandor.

respond (rɪ'spand) *v.i.* **1,** (answer) responder; contestar. **2,** (react) reaccionar.

respondent (rɪ'span·dənt) *adj.* simpático; respondedor. —*n.* respondedor [*fem.* -dora]; *law* demandado.

response (rɪ'spans) *n.* **1,** (answer) respuesta; contestación; réplica. **2,** (reaction) reacción.

responsible (rɪ'span·sə·bəl) *adj.* **1,** (answerable) responsable. **2,** (entailing trust) de responsabilidad. —**responsibility,** *n.* responsabilidad.

responsive (rɪ'span·sɪv) *adj.* **1,** (answering) responsivo; respondedor. **2,** (consisting of responses) antifonal.

rest (rɛst) *n.* **1,** (repose) descanso; reposo. **2,** (support) soporte. **3,** *mus.* pausa. **4,** (remainder) resto; sobrante. —*v.i.* **1,** (cease action) parar; cesar; descansar. **2,** (be tranquil) reposar. **3,** (be supported) apoyarse. **4,** (remain) estar; quedar; permanecer. **5,** (trust) depender (de). —*v.t.* **1,** (place at rest) calmar. **2,** (place) poner; apoyar; descansar.

3, (allow to stand) colocar. **4,** *law* terminar. —**resting,** *n.* reposo. —**resting place,** descansadero. —**rest room,** excusado; retrete; baño.

restaurant ('rɛs·tə·rənt) *n.* restaurante. —**restaurateur** (-rə'tʌr) *n.* dueño de restaurante.

restful ('rɛst·fəl) *adj.* quieto; tranquilo; reposado.

restitution (,rɛs·tə'tju·ʃən) *n.* **1,** (act of returning) restitución. **2,** (act of making amends) indemnización. **3,** (restoration) restablecimiento.

restive ('rɛs·tɪv) *adj.* **1,** (uneasy) inquieto. **2,** (recalcitrant) terco; *(of a horse)* repropio.

restiveness ('rɛs·tɪv·nəs) *n.* **1,** (uneasiness) inquietud. **2,** (recalcitrance) terquedad.

restless ('rɛst·ləs) *adj.* desasosegado; inquieto. —**restlessness,** *n.* desasosiego; inquietud.

restock (ri'stak) *v.t.* **1,** (replenish) rellenar; abastecer. **2,** (restore fish and game to) repoblar.

restoration (,rɛs·tə'rei·ʃən) *n.* restauración.

restorative (rɪ'stor·ə·tɪv) *n. & adj.* restaurativo.

restore (rɪ'stor) *v.t.* **1,** (bring back) restaurar. **2,** (cure) curar. **3,** (renew) restablecer. **4,** (return to the owner) devolver; restituir.

restrain (rɪ'strein) *v.t.* **1,** (hinder) refrenar; impedir. **2,** (moderate; temper) cohibir. **3,** (limit) limitar; restringir.

restraint (rɪ'streint) *n.* **1,** (hindrance) refrenamiento. **2,** (self-control) cohibición; continencia. **3,** (limitation) limitación; restricción. —**restraint of trade,** impedimentos al libre comercio.

restrict (rɪ'strɪkt) *v.t.* restringir; limitar. —**restriction** (rɪ'strɪk·ʃən) *n.* restricción. —**restrictive,** *adj.* restrictivo.

result (rɪ'zʌlt) *v.i.* resultar. —*n.* resultado; resulta. —**resultant,** *adj. & n.* resultante. —**as a result (of),** de resultas (de).

resume (rɪ'zuːm) *v.t.* reasumir; reanudar. —*v.i.* seguir; continuar.

résumé (,rɛz·u'mei) *n.* resumen; sumario.

resumption (rɪ'zʌmp·ʃən) *n.* reasunción.

resurge (rɪ'sʌrdʒ) *v.i.* resurgir. —**resurgence,** *n.* resurgimiento.

resurrect (,rɛz·ə'rɛkt) *v.t.* **1,** (restore to life) resucitar. 2, (disinter) desenterrar.

resurrection (ˌrɛz·ə'rɛk·ʃən) *n.* 1, (returning to life) resurrección. 2, (disinterment) desentierro.

resuscitate (rɪ'sʌs·ə,teit) *v.t. & i.* resucitar. —**resuscitation**, *n.* resucitación.

retable (rɪ'tei·bəl) *n.* retablo.

retail ('ri·teil) *n.* venta al por menor; reventa. —*adj.* al por menor. —*v.t.* 1, (sell direct to consumer) vender al por menor; revender; detallar. 2, (tell in detail) contar en detalle; detallar. —*v.i.* venderse al por menor; revenderse; detallarse. —**retailer,** *n.* vendedor [*fem.* -dora] al por menor; revendedor [*fem.* -dora]; detallista.

retain (rɪ'tein) *v.t.* 1, (hold) retener. 2, (remember) recordar. 3, (hire) contratar.

retainer (rɪ'tei·nər) *n.* 1, (person or thing that retains) retenedor. 2, (servant) criado; dependiente. 3, (follower) adherente. 4, (fee) honorario. —**retaining wall,** pared de sostén o retención.

retake (ri'teik) *v.t.* volver a tomar; repetir (la toma). —*n.* ('ri-) nueva toma; toma repetida.

retaliate (rɪ'tæl·i,eit) *v.i.* vengarse; desquitarse. —*v.t.* devolver; pagar. —**retaliation,** *n.* venganza; desquite; represalia. —**retaliative** (-ə·tɪv); **retaliatory** (-ə·tor·i) *adj.* vengativo.

retard (rɪ'tard) *v.t.* 1, (slow down) retardar; retrasar. 2, (defer) aplazar. —**retardate** (rɪ'tar·deit) *n.* persona atrasada. —**retardation** (ˌri·tar·'dei·ʃən) *n.* retardo; atraso.

retch (rɛtʃ) *v.i.* esforzarse por vomitar; arquear. —**retching,** *n.* arqueada.

retell (ri'tɛl) *v.t.* [*pret. & p.p.* -**told**] recontar; volver a contar o decir.

retention (rɪ'tɛn·ʃən) *n.* retención. —**retentive** (-tɪv) *adj.* retentivo. —**retentiveness,** *n.* retentiva.

reticent ('rɛt·ə·sənt) *adj.* reticente; reservado. —**reticence,** *n.* reticencia; reserva.

retina ('rɛt·ɪ·nə) *n.* retina.

retinue ('rɛt·ə,nju) *n.* comitiva; séquito.

retire (rɪ'tair) *v.i.* 1, (retreat) retroceder. 2, (take refuge) refugiarse. 3, (withdraw) retirarse. 4, (be pensioned off) jubilarse. 5, (go to bed) acostarse. —*v.t.* 1,

(withdraw) retirar. 2, (relieve of duty) separar. 3, (pension off) jubilar. 4, (withdraw from circulation) recoger. —**retirement,** *n.* retiro; jubilación.

retired (rɪ'taird) *adj.* 1, (having discontinued work) retirado; jubilado. 2, (secluded) aislado; apartado.

retiring (rɪ'tair·ɪŋ) *adj.* retraído; recatado; recoleto.

retold (ri'told) *v.,* *pret. & p.p. de* **retell.**

retook (ri'tuk) *v.,* *pret. de* **retake.**

retort (rɪ'tort) *v.t.* 1, (return; turn back) devolver. 2, (reply sharply) contestar mordazmente. —*v.i.* replicar. —*n.* 1, (retaliatory remark) réplica. 2, (glass vessel) retorta.

retouch (ri'tʌtʃ) *v.t.* retocar. —*n.* retoque.

retrace (ri'treis) *v.t.* 1, (go back over) repasar. 2, (trace again) trazar de nuevo. —**retrace one's steps,** volver sobre sus pasos.

retract (rɪ'trækt) *v.t.* 1, (draw back) retraer. 2, (take back; recant) retractar. —*v.i.* 1, (shrink back) encogerse. 2, (recant) retractarse. —**retractable,** *adj.* retráctil.

retraction (rɪ'træk·ʃən) *n.* retracción.

retractor (rɪ'træk·tər) *n.* 1, *anat.* músculo retractor. 2, *surg.* retractor.

retransmit (ˌri·træns'mɪt) *v.t.* retransmitir.

retread (ri'trɛd) *v.t.* 1, (walk through again) caminar de nuevo; repasar; volver por. 2, (put new tread on, as a tire) recauchar; recauchutar. —*n.* ('ri-) 1, (act or result of retreading) recauchaje. 2, (a tire so treated) neumático recauchado.

retreat (rɪ'trit) *n.* 1, (withdrawal) retirada. 2, (seclusion; secluded place) retiro. 3, (asylum) asilo. 4, *mil.* retreta. —*v.i.* retirarse. —**beat a retreat,** retirarse.

retrench (rɪ'trɛntʃ) *v.t.* cercenar; disminuir. —*v.i.* economizar; reducirse. —**retrenchment,** *n.* rebaja; economía; cercenadura.

retrial (ri'trai·əl) *n.* nuevo proceso.

retribution (ˌrɛt·rə'bju·ʃən) *n.* retribución; justo castigo. —**retributive** (rɪ'trɪb·ju·tɪv) *adj.* retributivo.

retrieve (rɪ'triːv) *v.t.* recuperar; recobrar; restaurar. —*v.i.* cobrar la caza. —**retrieval,** *n.* recuperación; recobro.

retriever (rɪ'triv·ər) *n.* perro cobrador; perdiguero.

retroactive (,rɛt·ro'æk·tɪv) *adj.* retroactivo. —**retroactivity,** *n.* retroactividad.

retrogradation (,rɛt·ro·gre'dei·ʃən) *n.* **1,** (moving backward) retroceso. **2,** *astron.* retrogradación.

retrograde ('rɛt·rə,greid) *adj.* retrógrado. —*v.i.* **1,** (move backward) retroceder. **2,** *astron.* retrogradar.

retrogress ('rɛt·rə,grɛs) *v.i.* retrogradar. —**retrogression** (-'grɛʃ·ən) *n.* retrogresión. —**retrogressive** (-'grɛs·ɪv) *adj.* retrógrado.

retrospect ('rɛt·rə,spɛkt) *n.* mirada retrospectiva; retrospección. —**retrospective** (,rɛt·rə'spɛk·tɪv) *adj.* retrospectivo. —**retrospection** (-'spɛk·ʃən) *n.* retrospección. —**in retrospect,** retrospectivamente.

retry (ri'trai) *v.t.* procesar de nuevo.

return (rɪ'tʌrn) *v.i.* **1,** (go or come back) volver; retornar; regresar. **2,** (recur) recurrir. **3,** (reply) replicar. —*v.t.* **1,** (give back; restore) devolver; restituir. **2,** (repay, as a kindness) corresponder a. **3,** (repay) pagar. **4,** (report, as a verdict) dar (un fallo). **5,** (elect) elegir. **6,** (yield, as a profit) producir; rentar. —*n.* **1,** (giving back; restoring) devolución; restitución. **2,** (recurrence) repetición. **3,** (going or coming back) regreso; vuelta. **4,** (profit) rédito; ganancia. **5,** (reply) réplica; respuesta. **6,** (report) informe. —*adj.* de vuelta. —**returns,** *n.pl.* resultados; noticias. —**by return mail,** a vuelta de correo. —**in return,** en cambio. —**return match,** desquite. —**return ticket,** billete de ida y vuelta; billete de vuelta.

reunion (ri'jun·jən) *n.* reunión.

reunite (ri·ju'nait) *v.t.* reunir. —*v.i.* reunirse.

revamp (ri'væmp) *v.t.* renovar.

reveal (rɪ'viːl) *v.t.* revelar; divulgar; descubrir.

reveille ('rɛv·ə·li) *n.* diana.

revel ('rɛv·əl) *v.i.* **1,** (carouse) jaranear. **2,** (delight) deleitarse; gozarse. —*n.* jarana; bacanal; juerga. —**reveler,** *n.* calavera; juerguista. —**revelry,** *n.* jarana; juerga.

revelation (,rɛv·ə'lei·ʃən) *n.* **1,** (disclosure) revelación. **2,** *cap.,* *Bib.* Apocalipsis.

revenge (rɪ'vɛndʒ) *v.t.* vengar. —*n.* venganza. —**revengeful,** *adj.*

vengativo. —**take revenge,** vengarse.

revenue ('rɛv·ə,nju) *n.* **1,** (personal income) renta; rédito. **2,** (government income) rentas públicas. —**revenue officer,** agente fiscal.

reverberate (rɪ'vʌr·bə,reit) *v.i.* reverberar; retumbar; repercutir. —**reverberation,** *n.* retumbo; reverbero; reverberación.

revere (rɪ'vir) *v.t.* venerar; reverenciar.

reverence ('rɛv·ər·əns) *n.* **1,** (veneration) reverencia; veneración. **2,** *cap.* (title of clergy) Reverencia. **3,** (bow) reverencia. —*v.t.* venerar; reverenciar. —**do reverence,** rendir homenaje.

reverend ('rɛv·ər·ənd) *adj.* reverendo; venerable. —*n.,* *colloq.* reverendo; pastor.

reverent ('rɛv·ər·ənt) *adj.* **1,** (respectful) reverente. **2,** (devout) devoto. —**reverential** (-'rɛn·ʃəl) *adj.* reverencial.

reverie ('rɛv·ə·ri) *n.* ensueño.

reversal (rɪ'vʌr·səl) *n.* **1,** (turning about; changing to the opposite) inversión; cambio a lo contrario. **2,** *law* revocación.

reverse (rɪ'vʌrs) *adj.* invertido; opuesto. —*n.* **1,** (a change to the opposite) reversión; inversión. **2,** (setback) revés; descalabro; contratiempo. **3,** (opposite) lo opuesto; lo contrario. **4,** (other side; back) revés; reverso. **5,** (backward motion) marcha atrás. —*v.t.* **1,** (turn about) invertir. **2,** (cause to move backward) dar marcha atrás; poner en marcha atrás. **3,** *law* (set aside; annul) revocar; anular. —*v.i.* invertirse; cambiarse a lo contrario. —**reverse gear,** marcha atrás. —**reverse oneself,** cambiar de opinión.

reversible (rɪ'vʌr·sə·bəl) *adj.* **1,** (that can be turned or changed about) reversible. **2,** (two-sided) de dos caras. **3,** *law* revocable. —**reversibility,** *n.* reversibilidad.

reversion (rɪ'vʌr·ʒən) *n.* **1,** (act of reverting) reversión. **2,** (right of future possession) derecho de sucesión. —**reversionary,** *adj.* de o por reversión.

revert (rɪ'vʌrt) *v.i.* retroceder; revertir; recurrir.

review (rɪ'vjuː) *n.* **1,** (examination) examen. **2,** (survey of past events) repaso. **3,** (critical report) juicio crítico; reseña. **4,** *mil.* (parade) revista; parada. **5,** *law* (reconsideration) revisión. **6,** (journal) revista. —*v.t.* **1,** (look back on) ver de nuevo; recordar. **2,** (examine again) repasar; revisar. **3,** (write an evaluation of) reseñar; criticar. **4,** *mil.* pasar revista.

reviewer (rɪ'vju·ər) *n.* **1,** (examiner) examinador [*fem.* -dora]; revisor [*fem.* -sora]. **2,** (critic) crítico.

revile (rɪ'vail) *v.t.* vituperar; vilipendiar. —**revilement,** *n.* contumelia; oprobio; vilipendio.

revise (rɪ'vaiz) *v.t.* revisar; corregir; refundir. —**revision** (rɪ'vɪʒ·ən) *n.* revisión; corrección; refundición.

revisit (rɪ'vɪz·ɪt) *v.t.* volver a visitar.

revival (rɪ'vaiv·əl) *n.* **1,** (resuscitation) resucitación; reanimación. **2,** (restoration) restauración; restablecimiento. **3,** (renascence) renacimiento. **4,** *theat.* reposición. **5,** (religious awakening) despertamiento religioso.

revive (rɪ'vaiv) *v.t.* **1,** (resuscitate) resucitar; reanimar. **2,** (restore; renew) restaurar; restablecer. **3,** (reawaken) despertar. **4,** *theat.* reponer. —*v.i.* **1,** (come back to life or consciousness) resucitar; reanimarse. **2,** (be restored or renewed) restablecerse; renovarse; renacer. **3,** (reawaken) despertarse.

revocable ('rɛv·ə·kə·bəl) *adj.* revocable.

revocation (ˌrɛv·ə'kei·ʃən) *n.* revocación; derogación.

revoke (rɪ'vok) *v.t.* revocar. —*v.i.,* *cards* renunciar. —*n.,* *cards* renuncio.

revolt (rɪ'volt) *v.i.* **1,** (rebel) rebelarse. **2,** (feel revulsion) tener repugnancia; tener asco. —*v.t.* repugnar; dar asco a. —*n.* revuelta; sublevación; rebelión. —**revolting,** *adj.* repulsivo; repugnante; asqueroso.

revolution (ˌrɛv·ə'lu·ʃən) *n.* revolución. —**revolutionary,** *adj.* & *n.* revolucionario. —**revolutionist,** *n.* revolucionario. —**revolutionize,** *v.t.* revolucionar.

revolve (rɪ'valv) *v.i.* **1,** (rotate) rodar; revolverse. **2,** (move about a center) girar. **3,** (recur) suceder periódicamente. —*v.t.* **1,** (turn) voltear; hacer girar. **2,** (turn over in the mind) revolver. —**revolving,** *adj.* giratorio; rotativo. —**revolving**

door, puerta giratoria. —**revolving fund,** fondo rotativo.

revolver (rɪ'val·vər) *n.* revólver.

revue (rɪ'vjuː) *n.* revista musical.

revulsion (rɪ'vʌl·ʃən) *n.* revulsión; repugnancia.

reward (rɪ'word) *v.t.* **1,** (recompense) recompensar. **2,** (give in return for) premiar. —*n.* **1,** (recompense) recompensa. **2,** (prize) premio. **3,** (profit) remuneración. **4,** (cash award) gratificación. —**rewarding,** *adj.* provechoso.

reword (rɪ'wʌrd) *v.t.* decir o escribir en otras palabras.

rewrite (rɪ'rait) *v.t.* **1,** (write over) escribir de nuevo. **2,** (revise) corregir; refundir. —*n.* ('ri-) escrito corregido; refundición.

Rh factor ('ar'eitʃ) factor Rh (*de la sangre*).

rhapsodic (ræp'sad·ɪk) *adj.* rapsódico.

rhapsodize ('ræp·sə,daiz) *v.t.* decir o cantar extáticamente. —*v.i.* expresarse extáticamente.

rhapsody ('ræp·sə·di) *n.* rapsodia.

rhenium ('ri·ni·əm) *n.* renio.

rheostat ('ri·ə,stæt) *n.* reóstato.

rhesus ('ri·səs) *n.* macaco de la India. *También,* **rhesus monkey.**

rhetoric ('rɛt·ə·rɪk) *n.* retórica. —**rhetorical** (rə'tor·ɪ·kəl) *adj.* retórico. —**rhetorician** (-'rɪʃ·ən) *n.* retórico.

rheum (ruːm) *n.* legaña; catarro. —**rheumy,** *adj.* legañoso; catarroso.

rheumatic (ru'mæt·ɪk) *adj.* & *n.* reumático. —**rheumatism** ('ru·mə·tɪz·əm) *n.* reumatismo.

rhinestone ('rain,ston) *n.* diamante de imitación.

rhino ('rai·no) *n.* [*pl.* -**nos**] = **rhinoceros.**

rhinoceros (rai'nas·ər·əs) *n.* rinoceronte.

rhizome ('rai·zom) *n.* rizoma.

rhodium ('ro·di·əm) *n.* rodio.

rhododendron (ˌro·də'den·drən) *n.* rododendro.

rhomboid ('ram·bɔid) *n.* romboide.

rhombus ('ram·bəs) *n.* rombo.

rhubarb ('ru·barb) *n.* **1,** *bot.* ruibarbo. **2,** *slang* (noisy protest) barahúnda.

rhyme *también,* **rime** (raim) *n.* rima. —*v.t.* & *i.* rimar. —**rhymer,** *n.* rimador [*fem.* -dora]; versista. —**without rhyme or reason,** sin ton ni son.

rhythm ('rıð·əm) *n.* ritmo.
—**rhythmic** (-mık); **rhythmical**,
adj. rítmico.

rialto (ri'æl·to) *n.* **1,** (theatrical district) distrito teatral, esp. de Nueva York. **2,** (market place) mercado, esp. el Rialto de Venecia.

riata (ri'a·ta) *n.* reata.

rib (rıb) *n.* **1,** *anat.* costilla. **2,** *bot.* nervio grueso; costilla. **3,** (supporting beam) viga; listón. **4,** (thin rod, as of an umbrella frame) varilla. —*v.t.* **1,** (support with ribs) afianzar con vigas; listonear. **2,** (mark with lines or ridges) marcar con rayas; rayar. **3,** (flute; corrugate) acanalar. **4,** *colloq.* (tease) bromarse de; tomar el pelo a.

ribald ('rıb·əld) *adj.* lascivo; obsceno. —**ribaldry**, obscenidad; indecencia.

ribbed (rıbd) *adj.* **1,** (marked with lines or ridges) rayado. **2,** (fluted; corrugated) acanalado. **3,** (veined) nervudo.

ribbon ('rıb·ən) *n.* **1,** (band; tape) cinta. **2,** *pl.* (shreds) harapos; jirones. —*adj.* de o como cinta.

riboflavin (‚rai·bo'flei·vın) *n.* riboflavina.

rice (rais) *n.* arroz. —*v.t.* desmenuzar. —**ricer,** *n.* aparato para desmenuzar comestibles. —**rice field,** arrozal.

rich (rıtʃ) *adj.* **1,** (wealthy) rico; opulento. **2,** (abounding) abundante; copioso. **3,** (fertile) fértil. **4,** (luxurious) lujoso; elegante. **5,** (vivid) vivo. **6,** (succulent) suculento; rico. **7,** *colloq.* (preposterous) ridículo. **8,** *colloq.* (amusing) divertido.

riches ('rıtʃ·əz) *n.pl.* riqueza; opulencia.

richness ('rıtʃ·nəs) *n.* **1,** (wealth) riqueza. **2,** (luxury) lujo; elegancia. **3,** (vividness) viveza. **4,** (succulence) suculencia.

rick (rık) *n.* almiar; montón de paja, heno, etc.

rickets ('rık·ıts) *n.* raquitismo.

rickety ('rık·ə·ti) *adj.* **1,** (shaky) tambaleante; destartalado. **2,** (affected with rickets) raquítico.

rickey ('rık·i) *n.* coctel de ginebra.

ricochet (‚rık·ə'ʃei) *n.* rebote. —*v.i.* rebotar.

rid (rıd) *v.t.* [**rid, ridding**] desembarazar; librar. —*adj.* librado; libre; exento. —**riddance,** *n.* libramiento. —**be rid of,** estar libre de. —**get**

rid of, desembarazarse de; deshacerse de.

ridden ('rıd·ən) *v., p.p. de* ride.

riddle ('rıd·əl) *n.* **1,** (enigma) acertijo; adivinanza; enigma. **2,** (sieve) criba. —*v.t.* **1,** (fill with holes) acribillar. **2,** (sift) cribar.

ride (raid) *v.i.* [**rode, ridden, riding**] **1,** (be carried) montar; ir montado. **2,** (float, as a ship) flotar. **3,** (move on or about something) pasear; correr. **4,** (be a passenger) viajar. **5,** (function, as a vehicle) marchar; funcionar. —*v.t.* **1,** (be carried by; guide) montar. **2,** (float on) flotar sobre. **3,** (travel on or over) pasar por; recorrer. **4,** (oppress) tiranizar. **5,** (harass) acosar; perseguir. **6,** *colloq.* (tease) bromarse de; tomar el pelo a. —*n.* paseo. —**ride out,** aguantar; soportar.

rider ('raid·ər) *n.* **1,** (traveler on horseback) jinete. **2,** (passenger) pasajero. **3,** (clause added to a document) hojuela pegada a un documento.

ridge (rıdʒ) *n.* **1,** (crest) lomo. **2,** (hill) cerro. **3,** (mountain range) cordillera. **4,** (crease) arruga. **5,** *archit.* caballete. **6,** (mound of earth, as raised by a plow) caballón.

ridicule ('rıd·ə‚kjul) *n.* irrisión. —*v.t.* ridiculizar; poner en ridículo.

ridiculous (rı'dık·jə·ləs) *adj.* ridículo. —**ridiculousness**, *n.* ridiculez.

riding ('rai·dıŋ) *v., ger. de* ride. —*n.* **1,** (traveling) paseo; viaje. **2,** (horsemanship) equitación. —**riding boots,** botas de montar. —**riding coat,** redingote. —**riding habit,** vestido de montar.

rife (raif) *adj.* abundante; corriente; común.

riffle ('rıf·əl) *n.* **1,** (ripple) onda; rizo. **2,** *cards* cierta manera de barajar cartas. **3,** (set of grooves, as in a sluice) ranuras. —*v.t.* barajar.

riffraff ('rıf‚ræf) *n.* **1,** (rubbish) desperdicio. **2,** (rabble) gentuza; canalla.

rifle ('rai·fəl) *v.t.* **1,** (ransack) robar; pillar. **2,** (cut spiral grooves in) rayar. —*n.* fusil; rifle.

rifleman ('rai·fəl·mən) *n.* [*pl.* **-men**] fusilero; riflero.

rift (rıft) *n.* **1,** (crack) hendedura; grieta. **2,** (disagreement) desavenencia. —*v.t.* hender; partir. —*v.i.* partirse.

rig (rɪg) *v.t.* [**rigged, rigging**] 1, (equip) aparejar; equipar. 2, (dress) ataviar; vestir. 3, (fix arbitrarily) arreglar; manejar. —*n.* 1, (equipment) aparejo. 2, (attire) traje. 3, (carriage) carruaje; coche. 4, (oil derrick) torre de perforación. 5, (large truck) camión, esp. con acoplado. —**rigger**, *n.* aparejador [*fem.* -dora]. —**rigging**, *n.* aparejo; avíos.

right (rait) *adj.* 1, (just) recto; justo. 2, (correct) correcto. 3, (proper) propio; adecuado; conveniente. 4, (in good condition) en buen estado. 5, (well-ordered) bien arreglado. 6, (pert. to a certain side) derecho. 7, (conservative) conservador. 8, (direct) derecho; directo. 9, *geom.* recto; rectángulo. —*adv.* 1, (justly) justamente. 2, (correctly) correctamente. 3, (properly) propiamente; debidamente. 4, (exactly) exactamente. 5, (very) precisamente. 6, (toward the right) a o hacia la derecha. 7, (directly) directamente. —*n.* 1, (direction; side) derecha. 2, (conformity) conformidad. 3, (that which conforms to a rule) rectitud. 4, (just claim) derecho. 5, *polit.* derecha; partido conservador. —*v.t.* 1, (set straight) enderezar. 2, (correct) corregir; rectificar. 3, (vindicate) vindicar. —*v.i.* enderezarse. —*interj.* ¡bien!; ¡bueno! —**all right,** muy bien. —**be all right,** estar bien. —**be right; be in the right,** tener razón. —**by right** (o **rights**), debidamente; con justicia. —**put to right** (o **rights**), arreglar; rectificar; poner en orden. —**right away,** en seguida. —**right here,** aquí mismo. —**right now,** ahora mismo.

rightabout ('rait-ə,baut) *adv.* media vuelta.

right-angled *adj.* rectángulo.

righteous ('rai-tʃəs) *adj.* virtuoso; recto. —**righteousness**, *n.* virtud; rectitud.

rightful ('rait-fəl) *adj.* justo; legítimo. —**rightfulness**, *n.* justicia; legitimidad.

righthand ('rait,hænd) *adj.* derecho; de o a la derecha. —**righthand man,** brazo derecho.

righthanded ('rait,hæn·dɪd) *adj.* 1, (preferring the right hand) que

usa la mano derecha. 2, (done with the right hand) con la derecha. 3, (toward the right) a la derecha. —*adv.* con la derecha.

rightist ('rai-tɪst) *adj.* & *n.* derechista.

rightly ('rait-li) *adv.* 1, (correctly) correctamente; debidamente. 2, (justly) con razón; justamente; a justo título.

right-minded *adj.* justo; recto.

rightness ('rait-nəs) *n.* justicia; rectitud.

right of way 1, (precedence over another) precedencia; derecho de paso. 2, (legal passage across property) servidumbre de paso. 3, *R.R.* servidumbre de vía.

rightwing ('rait,wɪŋ) *adj.* derechista.

rigid ('rɪdʒ-ɪd) *adj.* 1, (stiff) rígido; tieso. 2, (strict) preciso; estricto. —**rigidity** (rɪ'dʒɪd-ə-ti) *n.* rigidez.

rigmarole ('rɪg-mə,rol) *n.* jerigonza.

rigor ('rɪg-ər) *n.* rigor. —**rigorous**, *adj.* riguroso. —**rigorousness**, *n.* rigurosidad.

rigor mortis (,rɪg·ər'mor·tɪs) rigidez de la muerte.

rile (rail) *v.t., colloq.* molestar; irritar.

rill (rɪl) *n.* riachuelo; regato.

rim (rɪm) *n.* 1, (edge) margen; borde; orilla. 2, (outer part of a wheel) llanta. 3, (mounting for a tire) aro. —*v.t.* [**rimmed, rimming**] bordear.

rime (raim) *n.* 1, = **rhyme**. 2, (hoarfrost) escarcha. —*v.t.* & *i.* = **rhyme**. —**rimy**, *adj.* escarchado.

rind (raind) *n.* corteza.

ring (rɪŋ) *v.i.* [**rang, rung, ringing**] 1, (sound, as a bell) sonar; tañer. 2, (resound; sound loudly) resonar; retumbar. 3, (signal with a bell) llamar; tocar. 4, (hum, as the ears) zumbar. 5, [*pret.* & *p.p.* **ringed**] (form or move in a circle) formar círculo; moverse en círculo. —*v.t.* 1, (cause to sound) sonar; tocar; tañer; repicar. 2, (proclaim, as with ringing of bells) proclamar; anunciar. 3, [*también,* **ring for**] (summon with a bell) llamar. 4, [*también, Brit.* **ring up**] (call on the telephone) llamar por teléfono. 5, [*pret.* & *p.p.* **ringed**] (encircle) cercar; rodear. —*n.* 1, (sound of a bell) toque; repique; tañido; sonido. 2, (telephone call) llamada;

timbrazo. **3,** (circle) círculo. **4,** (circular band) anillo; aro; argolla. **5,** (band worn on the finger) anillo; sortija. **6,** (arena) arena; circo. **7,** (bull ring) redondel. **8,** (boxing ring) cuadrilátero. **9,** (group) círculo; corro; cuadrilla. **10,** (gang) pandilla. **11,** pl. (puffiness under the eyes) ojeras. **12,** (characteristic impression or effect) tono; sonido. —adj. anular. —**ring familiar; have a familiar ring,** sonarle a uno. —**ring finger,** dedo anular. —**ring in,** substituir por otro; introducir fraudulentamente.

ringdove ('rɪŋ,dʌv) n. paloma torcaz.

ringer ('rɪŋ·ər) n. **1,** (person who rings a bell) campanero. **2,** slang (likeness) parecido; retrato. **3,** slang (fraudulent substitute) substituto; intruso.

ringing ('rɪŋ·ɪŋ) adj. resonante; sonoro; que suena. —n. **1,** (sound of a bell) campaneo; repique; retintín. **2,** (humming in the ears) zumbido.

ringleader ('rɪŋ,li·dər) n. cabecilla.

ringlet ('rɪŋ·lɪt) n. rizo; bucle.

ringmaster ('rɪŋ·mæs·tər) n. maestro de ceremonias (de un circo).

ringworm ('rɪŋ,wʌrm) n. tiña; empeine.

rink (rɪŋk) n. patinadero.

rinse (rɪns) v.t. enjuagar; aclarar. —n. enjuague.

riot ('rai·ət) n. **1,** (mob action) tumulto; alboroto; motín. **2,** (revelry) jarana. **3,** (confusion) confusión. —v.i. alborotar. —**rioter,** n. alborotador [fem. -dora]. —**riotous,** adj. alborotoso.

rip (rɪp) v.t. [**ripped, ripping**] **1,** (tear) rasgar; rajar. **2,** (saw with the grain) aserrar en la dirección de la fibra. **3,** colloq. (utter forcefully) explotar; soltar. **4,** sewing descoser. —v.i. **1,** (be torn) rasgarse. **2,** colloq. (rush) avanzar de cabeza. —n. **1,** (tear) rasgón. **2,** sewing descosido. **3,** colloq. (roué) pícaro. —**ripper,** n. rasgador [fem. -dora]. —**rip off,** slang estafar; engañar.

riparian (rɪ'pɛr·i·ən) adj. ribereño.

ripe (raip) adj. **1,** (mature) maduro. **2,** (in best condition) acabado; a punto. **3,** (ready) preparado. —**ripen,** v.t. & i. madurar. —**ripeness,** n. madurez.

rip-off ('rɪp,ɔf) n, slang estafa; engaño.

ripple ('rɪp·əl) n. **1,** (small wave) rizo. **2,** (murmur) murmullo. —v.t. rizar. —v.i. **1,** (undulate) rizarse. **2,** (murmur) murmurar.

riproaring ('rɪp,ror·ɪŋ) adj., slang bullicioso.

ripsaw ('rɪp,sɔ) n. sierra de hender.

riptide ('rɪp,taid) n. contracorriente fuerte.

rise (raiz) v.i. [**rose, risen** ('rɪz·ən)] **1,** (move upward) subir. **2,** (stand up) levantarse; ponerse en pie. **3,** (get out of bed) levantarse. **4,** (slope upward) ascender. **5,** (swell, as dough) fermentarse; crecer. **6,** (emerge) salir; nacer; asomar; surgir. **7,** (increase, as in value) mejorar. **8,** (rebel) rebelarse. **9,** (return to life) resucitar. —n. **1,** (ascent) ascención; subida. **2,** (degree of ascent) inclinación. **3,** (elevation) elevación; altura. **4,** (origin) origen. **5,** (increase) aumento. **6,** (advancement in position) ascenso —**early riser,** madrugador. —**get a rise out of,** despertar; animar. —**late riser,** dormilón. —**rise above,** sobreponerse a; vencer.

riser ('rai·zər) n. **1,** el o la que se levanta (temprano o tarde). **2,** (vertical part of a stair) contrahuella.

risible ('rɪz·ə·bəl) adj. risible. —**risibility,** n. risibilidad.

rising ('rai·zɪŋ) n. **1,** (ascent) subida. **2,** (insurrection) insurrección. **3,** (swelling, as of dough) fermento. **4,** (rebirth) renacimiento. **5,** (of the sun) salida. —adj. **1,** (ascendant) ascendiente. **2,** (growing) creciente. **3,** (coming up, as the sun) saliente.

risk (rɪsk) n. **1,** (peril) riesgo; peligro. **2,** (chance) albur. —v.t. **1,** (expose to loss) arriesgar. **2,** (take a chance of) aventurar. **3,** (try one's luck in) arriesgarse en. —**risky,** adj. arriesgado.

risqué (rɪs'kei) adj. escabroso; atrevido.

rite (rait) n. rito; ceremonia.

ritual ('rɪtʃ·u·əl) adj. ritual. —n. ritual; rito. —**ritualism,** n. ritualismo. —**ritualistic** (-ə'lɪs·tɪk) adj. ritualista.

rival ('rai·vəl) n. rival. —adj. rival; opuesto. —v.t. **1,** (compete with) rivalizar con. **2,** (emulate) emular. —**rivalry,** n. rivalidad.

river ('rɪv·ər) n. río. —**river bed,**

cauce o lecho de río. —**sell (some-one) down the river,** traicionar. —**up the river,** *slang* a la penitenciaría.

riverside ('rɪv·ər,said) *n.* ribera. —*adj.* ribereño.

rivet ('rɪv·ɪt) *n.* remache. —*v.t.* remachar. —**riveting,** *n.* remache; remachado. —**rivet one's eyes on,** clavar los ojos en.

rivulet ('rɪv·jə·lət) *n.* riachuelo.

roach (rotʃ) *n.* **1,** (fish) escarcho; rubio. **2,** (cockroach) cucaracha.

road (roːd) *n.* **1,** (highway) carretera. **2,** (means of approach) camino. **3,** (anchorage) rada.

roadbed ('rod,bɛd) *n.* base de carretera o ferrovía; firme; afirmado.

roadblock ('rod,blak) *n.* barricada; *fig.* obstáculo.

roadhouse ('rod,haus) *n.* restaurante o posada al lado de una carretera.

roadrunner ('rod,rʌn·ər) *n.* correcaminos.

roadside ('rod·said) *n.* borde del camino. —*adj.* al borde del camino.

roadstead ('rod·stɛd) *n.* rada.

roadster ('rod·stər) *n.* **1,** (small car) automóvil pequeño de turismo. **2,** (carriage horse) caballo de aguante.

roadway ('rod·wei) *n.* carretera; camino; vía.

roam (roːm) *v.i.* vagar. —*v.t.* vagar por; recorrer. —*n.* paseo.

roan (roːn) *adj.* ruano. —*n.* caballo ruano.

roar (roːr) *v.i.* rugir; bramar. —*v.t.* gritar. —*n.* rugido; bramido. —**roar with laughter,** reírse a carcajadas.

roaring ('ror·ɪŋ) *adj.* **1,** (noisy) rugiente. **2,** *slang* (outstanding) tremendo. —*n.* rugido.

roast (rost) *v.t.* **1,** (cook) asar. **2,** (dry by heat) tostar. **3,** *slang* (ridicule) ridiculizar. —*v.i.* asarse; tostarse. —*n.* **1,** (roasted meat) asado. **2,** (meat for roasting) carne para asar.

roast beef rosbif.

roaster ('ros·tər) *n.* asador.

rob (raːb) *v.t.* robar; hurtar. —**robber,** *n.* ladrón [*fem.* -drona].

robbery ('rab·ə·ri) *n.* robo; hurto.

robe (roːb) *n.* **1,** (gown) túnica. **2,** (blanket) manto. **3,** (dress) vestido; traje. **4,** (dressing gown) bata. —*v.t.* vestir. —*v.i.* vestirse.

robin ('rab·ɪn) *n.* petirrojo.

robot ('ro·bət) *n.* robot; autómata.

—*adj.* automático. —**robotics** (ro'bat·ɪks) *n.sing.* tecnología que utiliza autómatas.

robust ('ro·bʌst) *adj.* **1,** (strong) robusto; fuerte; recio. **2,** (rough) grosero; rudo. **3,** (arduous) arduo. —**robustness,** *n.* robustez; fuerza; vigor.

rock (rak) *n.* **1,** (large stone) roca; peña; peñasco. **2,** (any stone) piedra. **3,** *slang* (diamond) diamante. —*v.t.* mecer; balancear. —*v.i.* mecerse; oscilar. —**on the rocks, 1,** *colloq.* (of a drink) con hielo. **2,** (endangered) en peligro. —**rock candy,** azúcar candi. —**rock crusher,** triturador. —**rock crystal,** cuarzo; cristal de roca. —**rock garden,** jardín rocoso.

rock bottom el fondo; lo más profundo. —**rockbottom,** *adj.* mínimo; más bajo.

rockbound ('rak,baund) *adj.* **1,** (surrounded by rocks) rodeado de peñascos. **2,** (impenetrable) impenetrable.

rocker ('rak·ər) *n.* **1,** (chair that rocks) mecedora. **2,** (runner of a rocking chair) base curva de la mecedora. **3,** (cradle) cuna. **4,** *mech.* balancín.

rocket ('rak·ɪt) *n.* cohete. —*v.i.* ascender rápidamente. —**rocketry,** ciencia y técnica de los cohetes.

rocking chair ('rak·ɪŋ) mecedora.

rocking horse caballo mecedor.

rockribbed ('rak,rɪbd) *adj.* **1,** *lit.* rocoso. **2,** *fig.* inflexible; firme.

rocky ('rak·i) *adj.* **1,** (stony) rocoso. **2,** (shaky) tambaleante.

rococo (rə'ko·ko) *n. & adj.* rococó.

rod (raːd) *n.* **1,** (stick) vara. **2,** (scepter) cetro. **3,** (whip; switch) azote. **4,** (measure of length) medida de 16½ pies. **5,** *slang* (pistol) pistola; arma. **6,** *mech.* vástago. —**fishing rod,** caña de pescar.

rode (roːd) *v.,* *pret. de* ride.

rodent ('ro·dənt) *n. & adj.* roedor.

rodeo (ro'dei·o; 'ro·di·o) *n.* **1,** (cattle roundup) rodeo. **2,** (riding show) función de vaqueros.

roe (roː) *n.* **1,** (fish eggs) huevecillos de pescado. **2,** = roe deer.

roebuck ('ro,bʌk) *n.* macho del corzo.

roe deer corzo.

rogation (ro'gei·ʃən) *n.* rogativa; rogaciones.

roger ('radʒ·ər) *interj., slang* ¡muy bien!; ¡bueno!

rogue (roːg) *n.* **1,** (knave) bribón; pícaro; maleante. **2,** (ferocious animal) animal bravo. —**roguery,** *n.* picardía; bribonería. —**roguish,** *adj.* pícaro; picaresco. —**roguishness,** *n.* picardía.

roil (rɔil) *v.t.* **1,** (make turbid) enturbiar. **2,** (annoy) molestar; irritar.

roister ('rɔis·tər) *v.i.* fanfarronear. —**roisterer,** *n.* fanfarrón. —**roisterous,** *adj.* fanfarrón.

rôle (roːl) *n.* papel.

roll (roːl) *v.i.* **1,** (move by turning over and over) rodar. **2,** (turn about an axis) girar; dar vueltas; revolverse. **3,** (sway, as a ship) balancear. **4,** (reel; stagger) bambolear. **5,** (move in ripples) ondear. **6,** (sound, as a drum) redoblar. **7,** (make a full, deep sound) retumbar; resonar. **8,** (wallow) revolcarse. **9,** (curl up into a round or cylindrical shape) enrollarse. —*v.t.* **1,** (rotate) voltear; girar; revolver. **2,** (push or pull by means of wheels or rollers) hacer rodar; empujar o halar sobre ruedas o rodillos. **3,** (play, as a drum) redoblar. **4,** (curl or wrap up into a ball or cylinder) enrollar; envolver. **5,** (flatten with a roller) allanar con rodillo. **6,** (trill) vibrar. **7,** (move from side to side) menear; mover de un lado a otro. —*n.* **1,** (cylinder) rollo; cilindro. **2,** (small bread or biscuit) panecillo. **3,** (list of names) registro; lista; nómina. **4,** (swaying of a ship) balance. **5,** (reeling; staggering) bamboleo. **6,** (sound of a drum) redoble. **7,** (full, deep sound, as of thunder) retumbo. **8,** (swell, as of the sea) oleaje. **9,** (throw of the dice) echada de los dados. —**call the roll,** pasar lista. —**roll call,** acto de pasar lista. —**roll in money,** nadar en dinero. —**roll up, 1,** (wrap round) arrollar; envolver. **2,** (turn up, as the sleeves) arremangar. **3,** (accumulate; amass) amontonar.

rollback ('rol,bæk) *n.* rebaja (de precios, sueldos, etc.) hacia un nivel anterior.

rollbar ('rol,bar) *n.* barra de seguridad (instalada en la armazón de un automóvil).

roller ('rol·ər) *n.* **1,** (cylinder) rodillo; tambor; cilindro. **2,** (heavy wave) ola larga. **3,** (caster) ruedecilla; rueda. —**roller bearing,**

cojinete de rodillos. —**roller coaster,** montaña rusa. —**roller skate,** patín de ruedas.

rollick ('ral·ık) *v.i.* travesear; retozar; juguetear. —**rollicking,** *adj.* travieso; juguetón; retozón.

rolling ('rol·ıŋ) *n.* **1,** (rotating; revolving) rodadura. **2,** (swaying of a ship or vehicle) balanceo. **3,** (staggering; reeling) bamboleo. **4,** (wavy motion) undulación. —*adj.* **1,** (rotating; moving on wheels or rollers) rodante. **2,** (wavy) ondulado. —**rolling mill,** laminadero. —**rolling pin,** rodillo de pastelero. —**rolling stone,** piedra movediza. —**rolling stock,** material móvil.

rollover ('rol,o·vər) *n.* **1,** (overturn) vuelco. **2,** *fin.* extensión o renovación de un préstamo.

rolypoly ('ro·li·po·li) *adj.* rechoncho; gordiflón. —*n.* **1,** (pudding) pudín en forma de rollo. **2,** *colloq.* (fat person) gordiflón.

ROM (ram) *abr. de* **read only memory.**

Roman ('ro·mən) *adj.* **1,** (of or pert. to Rome) romano. **2,** *l.c.,* *typog.* redondo. —*n.* romano. —**Roman candle,** vela romana. —**Roman nose,** nariz aguileña.

Roman Catholic católico romano.

romance (ro'mæns) *n.* **1,** (novel) romance; novela. **2,** (fictitious talc) ficción; cuento. **3,** (love affair) aventura; amorío. **4,** (sentiment) romanticismo. —*adj., cap.* romance; neolatino. —*v.i.,* **1,** (tell stories) contar romances. **2,** *colloq.* (make love) amarse; tratarse cariñosamente. —*v.t., colloq.* cortejar.

Romanesque (,ro·mə'nɛsk) *adj.* & *n.* románico.

Romanian (ro'mei·ni·ən) *n.* & *adj.* rumano. *Tambien,* **Roumanian; Rumanian.**

Romanic (ro'mæn·ık) *adj.* románico.

Romanist ('ro·mən·ıst) *n.* romanista.

romantic (ro'mæn·tık) *adj.* **1,** (fanciful) fantástico. **2,** (amorous) romántico. **3,** (imaginative, as of literature) novelesco. —**romanticism** (-tı·sız·əm) *n.* romanticismo.

Romany ('ro·mə·ni) *n.* & *adj.* gitano.

romp (ramp) *v.i.* retozar; juguetear. —*n.* retozo.

rompers ('ramp·ərz) *n.pl.* traje de juego.

rondo ('ran·do) *n.* rondó.

rood (ruːd) *n.* **1,** (crucifix) crucifijo. **2,** (measure of length) pértica.

roof (ruf) *n.* **1,** (external covering) techo; tejado. **2,** *fig.* (house; home) hogar. **3,** (upper limit) máximo. —*v.t.* techar. —**roofer,** *n.* techador. —**roofing,** *n.* material de techar.

rook (rʊk) *n.* **1,** (crow) corneja; grajo. **2,** *chess* torre; roque. —*v.t.* *slang* estafar.

rookery ('rʊk·ə·ri) *n.* **1,** (abode of rooks) lugar frecuentado por cornejas. **2,** (breeding ground for certain animals) criadero de focas, aves marinas, grullas, etc. **3,** (hovel) casucha; cuchitril. **4,** (squalid quarter) barrio bajo.

rookie ('rʊk·i) *n.,* *slang* novato; bisoño.

room (ruːm) *n.* **1,** (space) lugar; sitio; espacio. **2,** (opportunity) ocasión; oportunidad. **3,** (apartment) cuarto; aposento; habitación; cámara. **4,** (one of a set of rooms) pieza. —*v.i.,* *colloq.* habitar; alojarse. —*v.t.,* *colloq.* alojar; hospedar. —**make** o **give room,** hacer lugar; abrir paso. —**rooming house,** casa de huéspedes.

roomer ('rum·ər) *n.* inquilino.

roommate ('rum,meit) *n.* compañero de cuarto o de departamento.

roomy ('rum·i) *adj.* espacioso; amplio. —**roominess,** *n.* espaciosidad.

roost (rust) *n.* **1,** (perch) percha. **2,** *colloq.* (resting place) lugar de descanso. —*v.i.* **1,** (sit on a perch) posar o descansar en la percha. **2,** (lodge; dwell) alojarse; habitar. —**rule the roost,** mandar; dominar; ser dueño.

rooster ('rus·tər) *n.* gallo.

root (rut) *n.* **1,** *bot.;* *gram.;* *math.* raíz. **2,** (of a tooth) raigón. **3,** (foundation) base. **4,** (origin) origen; causa; raíz. —*v.t.* **1,** (plant firmly) fijar. **2,** (dig up) hocicar; hozar. —*v.i.* **1,** (take root) arraigarse; echar raíces. **2,** (turn up the earth) hocicar. —**root beer,** bebida hecha de extractos de varias raíces. —**root for,** *slang* aplaudir. —**root up** o **out,** desarraigar; extirpar.

rooted ('rut·ɪd) *adj.* arraigado.

rooter ('rut·ər) *n.,* *slang* aplaudidor [*fem.* -dora]; animador [*fem.* -dora].

rope (rop) *n.* **1,** (cord) cuerda; soga; cabo. **2,** (string, as of pearls) fila; hilera. **3,** (stringy fiber) fibra; trenza. —*v.t.* **1,** (fasten) atar; amarrar. **2,** (catch with a rope) lazar. **3,** *slang,* usu. **rope in** (trick) engañar; embaucar. —**at the end of one's rope,** sin recursos. —**know the ropes,** *colloq.* ser experimentado; conocer a fondo (una cosa).

rorqual ('ror·kwəl) *n.* rorcual.

rosaceous (ro'zei·ʃəs) *adj.* rosáceo.

rosary ('ro·zə·ri) *n.* **1,** (prayer beads) rosario. **2,** (garland of roses) guirnalda de rosas. **3,** (rose garden) jardín de rosales.

rose (roːz) *n.* **1,** (flower) rosa. **2,** (color) color de rosa; rosa. —*adj.* de color de rosa; rosado. —**rose fever,** alergia nasal. —**rose window,** rosetón.

rose (roːz) *v.,* *pret. de* **rise.**

rosé (ro'zei) *adj.* rosado.

roseate ('ro·zi·ət) *adj.* rosado; rosáceo.

rosebud ('roz,bʌd) *n.* capullo de rosa.

rosebush ('roz,bʊʃ) *n.* rosal.

rosemary ('roz,mɛr·i) *n.* romero.

rosette (ro'zɛt) *n.* roseta; rosa.

rosewater ('roz,wɔ·tər) *n.* agua de rosas.

rosewood ('roz,wʊd) *n.* palo de rosa.

rosin ('raz·ɪn) *n.* resina.

roster ('ras·tər) *n.* **1,** (list of names) lista; nómina. **2,** (schedule) catálogo; itinerario; programa.

rostrum ('ras·trəm) *n.* tribuna.

rosy ('ro·zi) *adj.* **1,** (rose-colored) rosado. **2,** (favorable) favorable; optimista.

rot (rat) *v.t.* [**rotted, rotting**] **1,** (decompose) pudrir. **2,** (corrupt) corromper; deteriorar. —*v.i.* **1,** (decay) pudrirse. **2,** (become corrupt) corromperse. —*n.* **1,** (decay) podredumbre; pudrimiento; putrefacción. **2,** (parasitic disease) morriña. **3,** *slang* (nonsense) tontada; tontería; sandez.

rotary ('ro·tə·ri) *adj.* rotativo; giratorio. —*n.* glorieta.

rotate ('ro·teit) *v.i.* **1,** (turn) rodar; girar. **2,** (alternate) alternar. —*v.t.* **1,** (cause to turn) hacer girar; voltear. **2,** (alternate) alternar.

rotation (ro'tei·ʃən) *n.* rotación. —**by** o **in rotation,** por turno.

rotatory ('ro·tə,tor·i) *adj.* rotatorio.

rote (rot) *n.* repetición. —**learn by rote,** aprender de memoria.

rotisserie (ro'tɪs·ə·ri) *n.* asador.

rotor ('ro·tər) *n.* rotor; rueda móvil.

rotten ('rat·ən) *adj.* **1,** (decayed) podrido; putrefacto. **2,** (corrupt) corrompido. **3,** *colloq.* (very bad) malísimo; pésimo. —**rottenness,** *n.* podredumbre; putrefacción.

rotter ('rat·ər) *n.* pícaro; bribón; sinvergüenza.

rotund (ro'tʌnd) *adj.* **1,** (round; plump) redondo. **2,** (sonorous) rotundo.

rotunda (ro'tʌn·də) *n.* rotunda; rotonda.

rotundity (ro'tʌn·də·ti) *n.* **1,** (roundness; plumpness) redondez. **2,** (sonority) rotundidad.

roué (ru'ei) *n.* libertino.

rouge (ruʒ) *n.* **1,** (cosmetic) colorete. **2,** (jeweler's paste) rojo de joyero. —*v.t.* pintar; dar colorete a. —*v.i.* pintarse.

rough (rʌf) *adj.* **1,** (uneven; coarse) áspero; tosco; brusco. **2,** (natural; unfinished) bronco; bruto; cerril. **3,** (severe) severo; cruel; rudo. **4,** (uncouth) grosero; rústico. **5,** (stormy) tempestuoso; borrascoso. **6,** (approximate) aproximativo. —*n.* **1,** (roughness) crudeza; aspereza. **2,** (uneven terrain) terreno áspero. **3,** (rowdy) rufián. —*v.t.* **1,** (make rough) poner áspero. **2,** (work up in crude fashion) chapucear; labrar imperfectamente. **3,** (sketch) bosquejar; esbozar. **4,** (treat harshly) maltratar. —**in the rough,** en bruto. —**rough draft** o **sketch,** bosquejo; esbozo. —**rough it,** vivir en condiciones primitivas.

roughage ('rʌf·ɪdʒ) *n.* alimento áspero de poco valor nutritivo.

rough-and-ready *adj.* rudo pero eficaz.

rough-and-tumble *adj.* desordenado; violento.

roughen ('rʌf·ən) *v.t.* poner áspero. —*v.i.* ponerse áspero.

roughhouse ('rʌf,haus) *n., colloq.* pelotera; algazara; desorden. —*v.i., colloq.* portarse desordenadamente. —*v.t.* molestar; burlarse de.

roughly ('rʌf·li) *adv.* **1,** (not smoothly; not evenly) ásperamente; toscamente. **2,** (severely) severamente; cruelmente. **3,** (approximately) aproximadamente.

roughneck ('rʌf,nɛk) *n.* alborotador; rufián.

roughness ('rʌf·nəs) *n.* **1,** (unevenness; coarseness) aspereza; tosquedad. **2,** (severity) severidad; crueldad; rudeza. **3,** (agitation, as of the sea) turbulencia.

roughrider (rʌf'raid·ər) *n.* **1,** domador de caballos. **2,** *U.S. hist.* soldado de caballería.

roughshod (rʌf,ʃad) *adj.* **1,** *lit* herrado con púas o clavos. **2,** *fig.* (ruthless) despiadado. —**ride roughshod over,** pisotear; tratar con desprecio.

roulette (ru'lɛt) *n.* ruleta.

Roumanian (ru'mei·ni·ən) *n. & adj.* = **Romanian; Rumanian**

round (raund) *adj.* **1,** (circular) redondo. **2,** (curved) curvo. **3,** (light; brisk) ligero; veloz. **4,** (full) lleno; cabal. **5,** (sonorous) sonoro; rotundo. **6,** (clear; positive) rotundo. **7,** (without fractional part) redondo. —*n.* **1,** (round object) círculo; orbe; redondo. **2,** (roundness) redondez. **3,** *usu. pl.* (tour of duty) circuito; recorrido. **4,** (period of action) ronda. **5,** (song) canon. **6,** (rung of a ladder) peldaño; travesaño. **7,** (cut of meat) rodaja de carne. **8,** (of ammunition) munición para un solo tiro o salva. **9,** (salvo) andanada; salva; tiro. **10,** *boxing* asalto; suerte. —*v.t.* **1,** (make round) redondear. **2,** [*también,* **round out**] (complete) llenar; acabar; completar. **3,** (encircle) cercar. **4,** (go around) rondar; rodear. —*v.i.* **1,** (grow round) redondearse. **2,** (mature) desarrollarse. —*adv.* **1,** (on all sides) alrededor. **2,** (with a rotating movement) en redondo. **3,** (through a circuit) circularmente. **4,** (in circumference) de o por circunferencia. —*prep.* alrededor de; a la vuelta de. —**all year round,** todo el año. —**go** o **make the rounds,** ir de ronda; circular. —**round up,** recoger; rodear (el ganado).

roundabout ('raund·ə,baut) *adj.* indirecto; desviado. —*n., Brit.* glorieta.

rounder ('raun·dər) *n.* **1,** (one who travels a circuit) rondeador. **2,** *slang* (dissolute person) libertino; calavera.

roundhouse ('raund,haus) *n.* **1,** *naut.* toldilla. **2,** *R.R.* casa de máquinas.

roundish ('raund·ɪʃ) *adj.* casi redondo.

roundly ('raund·li) *adv.* redondamente.

roundness ('raund·nəs) *n.* redondez.

round robin 1, (petition) memorial firmado en rueda. **2,** (competition) concurso mutuo.

round-shouldered *adj.* cargado de espaldas.

round trip viaje de ida y vuelta.

roundup ('raund·ʌp) *n.* rodeo; recogida; reunión.

roundworm ('raund‚wʌrm) *n.* ascáride; lombriz intestinal.

rouse (rauz) *v.t.* **1,** (waken) despertar. **2,** (alert) animar. **3,** (excite) excitar. **4,** (stir up, as game) levantar. —*v.i.* **1,** (waken) despertarse. **2,** (become alert) animarse; moverse. —**rousing,** *adj.* vigoroso; fuerte.

roustabout ('raust‚ə‚baut) *n.* peón; trabajador.

rout (raut) *n.* **1,** (confused retreat) derrota; desbandada. **2,** (disorderly crowd) tumulto; chusma; populacho. —*v.t.* **1,** (disperse) derrotar. **2,** (cut away) cortar. —**rout out,** sacar; arrancar o arrojar fuera.

route (rut) *n.* **1,** (road) ruta; camino; vía. **2,** (course) curso; itinerario; vía. —*v.t.* encaminar; despachar.

routine (ru'tin) *n.* rutina. —*adj.* rutinario.

rove (rov) *v.i.* vagar. —*v.t.* vagar por; recorrer.

rover ('ro·vər) *n.* **1,** (wanderer) errante; vagamundo. **2,** (pirate) pirata; corsario. **3,** (pirate ship) buque de piratas; corsario.

row (ro) *v.i.* remar. —*v.t. & i.* remar; bogar. —**rower,** *n.* remero.

row (rau) *n.* pelea; camorra; lío; trifulca. —*v.i.* pelearse. —**raise a row,** armar camorra; armar lío.

rowboat ('ro‚bot) *n.* bote; bote de remos.

rowdy ('rau·di) *n.* rufián. —*adj.* ruidoso; bullicioso. —**rowdyish,** *adj.* alborotoso. —**rowdyism,** *n.* alboroto.

rowel ('rau·əl) *n.* **1,** (wheel of a spur) rodaja de espuela. **2,** (cutting wheel) rodaja de cortar.

rowlock ('ro‚lak) *n.* chumacera.

royal ('rɔi·əl) *adj.* **1,** (kingly) real. **2,** (majestic) majestuoso. —**royalism,** *n.* realismo. —**royalist,** *adj. & n.* realista.

royalty ('rɔi·əl·ti) *n.* **1,** (rank) realeza. **2,** (royal person) personaje real. **3,** *usu.pl.* (fees) derechos.

rub (rʌb) *v.t.* [**rubbed, rubbing**] **1,** (stroke hard) frotar; restregar. **2,** (graze) rozar. **3,** (polish) pulir; limpiar. **4,** *colloq.,* (annoy) fastidiar; molestar; incomodar. —*v.i.* frotarse; restregarse. —*n.* **1,** (act of rubbing) frote; fricción; roce. **2,** (massage) masaje. **3,** (annoyance) fastidio; estorbo; molestia. —**rub down, 1,** (massage) dar masaje. **2,** (scrub) limpiar. —**rub in,** hacer penetrar (por los poros); *slang* insistir en. —**rub off, 1,** (remove) quitar. **2,** (clean) limpiar frotando. —**rub up, 1,** (polish) repasar. **2,** (excite) excitar. —**rub out,** borrar.

rub-a-dub ('rʌb·ə‚dʌb) *n.* rataplán; tantarantán.

rubber ('rʌb·ər) *n.* **1,** (person or thing that rubs) frotador; borrador. **2,** (elastic substance) goma; caucho; hule. **3,** (eraser) goma de borrar; borrador. **4,** (overshoe) chanclo; galocha. **5,** (series of games) partida. **6,** (deciding game) jugada final. —*adj.* de goma; de caucho; elástico. —**rubberize,** *v.t.* encauchar; engomar. —**rubbery,** *adj.* gomoso; elástico. —**rubber band,** goma; liga de goma. —**rubber check,** *slang* cheque sin fondos.

rubberneck ('rʌb·ər‚nɛk) *n., slang* **1,** (inquisitive person) preguntón. **2,** (sightseer) turista. —*adj.* de turista. —*v.i.* estirar el cuello.

rubber stamp 1, (imprinting device) sello de goma; estampilla. **2,** *colloq.* (one who approves uncritically) persona que aprueba automáticamente. —**rubber-stamp,** *v.t.* **1,** (imprint) estampar. **2,** *colloq.* (approve uncritically) aprobar automáticamente.

rubbish ('rʌb·ɪʃ) *n.* **1,** (refuse) basura; desecho. **2,** (nonsense) disparate; tontería.

rubble ('rʌb·əl) *n.* **1,** (rough broken stones) ripio. **2,** (trash) desecho.

rubdown ('rʌb‚daun) *n.* masaje.

rube (rub) *n., slang* rústico; patán; *Amer.* jíbaro.

rubella (ru'bɛl·ə) *n.* rubéola.

rubicund ('ru·bə‚kʌnd) *adj.* rubicundo. —**rubicundity** (-'kʌn·də·ti) *n.* rubicundez.

rubidium (ru'bɪd·i·əm) *n.* rubidio.

ruble *también,* **rouble** ('ru·bəl) *n.* rublo.

rubric ('ru·brɪk) *n.* rúbrica.
ruby ('ru·bi) *n.* **1,** (gem) rubí. **2,** (color) color de rubí.
ruck (rʌk) *n.* **1,** (fold) arruga. **2,** (common crowd) multitud; vulgo. —*v.t.* arrugar. —*v.i.* arrugarse.
rucksack ('rʌk,sæk) *n.* mochila; alforja.
ruckus ('rʌk·əs) *n., colloq.* lío; jaleo.
ruction ('rʌk·ʃən) *n., colloq.* batahola; alboroto.
rudder ('rʌd·ər) *n.* timón.
ruddy ('rʌd·i) *adj.* rojizo; rubicundo. —**ruddiness,** *n.* rojez; rubicundez.
rude (ruːd) *adj.* **1,** (crude) rudo; crudo; primitivo. **2,** (illbred) malcriado; majadero. **3,** (discourteous) descortés. **4,** (rugged) fuerte; robusto; recio. —**rudeness,** *n.* rudeza.
rudiment ('ru·dɪ·mənt) *n.* rudimento.
rudimentary (ru·dɪˈmɛn·tə·ri) *adj.* rudimentario.
rue (ruː) *v.t.* **1,** (causing sorrow or pity) arrepentirse de; sentir; lamentar. —*v.i.* arrepentirse. —*n., bot.* ruda.
rueful ('ruː·fəl) *adj.* **1,** (causing sorrow or pity) lamentable; lastimoso. **2,** (feeling sorrow or pity) triste; lastimero.
ruff (rʌf) *n.* **1,** (frilled collar) lechuguilla. **2,** (fringe of fur or feathers) collar. **3,** (kind of pigeon) paloma moñuda. **4,** *cards* fallada. —*v.t., cards* fallar.
ruffian ('rʌf·i·ən) *n.* rufián; tunante. —**ruffianism,** *n.* rufianería; tunantería.
ruffle ('rʌf·əl) *v.t.* **1,** (draw up in folds) fruncir; rizar; arrugar. **2,** (disturb) molestar; enojar. **3,** (disarrange) desaliñar; descomponer. **4,** *mus.* redoblar (el tambor). —*n.* **1,** *sewing* volante fruncido. **2,** *mus.* redoble.
rug (rʌg) *n.* **1,** (floor covering) tapete; alfombra. **2,** (lap robe) manta de viaje.
rugged ('rʌg·ɪd) *adj.* **1,** (rough) arrugado; tosco; escabroso. **2,** (unpolished) sin pulir; inculto. **3,** (harsh) áspero; austero. **4,** (tempestuous) furioso; tempestuoso. **5,** (strong) robusto; fuerte.
ruin ('ru·ɪn) *n.* **1,** (collapse) ruina; caída; derrota. **2,** (destroyer) devastador [*fem.* -dora]; destructor [*fem.* -tora]. **3,** (devastation)

devastación; desastre. **4,** (corruption) corrupción; degradación. —*v.t.* **1,** (destroy) arruinar; destrozar. **2,** (spoil) estropear. **3,** (bankrupt) empobrecer.
ruination (,ru·ɪˈnei·ʃən) *n.* ruina; perdición.
ruinous ('ru·ɪn·əs) *adj.* ruinoso; desastroso; fatal.
rule (ruːl) *n.* **1,** (regulation) regla; ley. **2,** (custom) norma; método; precepto. **3,** (government) gobierno; mando. **4,** (measuring stick) escala; regla. **5,** (straight line) raya. —*v.t.* **1,** (decide) determinar; arreglar. **2,** (govern) gobernar; controlar; regir. **3,** (mark with lines) reglar; rayar. —*v.i.* **1,** (govern; command) mandar; regir. **2,** (prevail) prevalecer. —**rule of thumb,** metro empírico; regla empírica. —**rule out,** no admitir; excluir.
ruler ('ru·lər) *n.* **1,** (one who governs) gobernante. **2,** (measuring stick) regla.
ruling ('ru·lɪŋ) *n.* **1,** (decision) decisión; fallo. **2,** (set of lines) rayado; renglonadura. —*adj.* gobernante. —**ruling pen,** tiralíneas.
rum (rʌm) *n.* ron. —*adj., slang* **1,** (odd) extraño; raro. **2,** (bad) malo; desfavorable. —**rum runner,** *n.* contrabandista de licores.
Rumanian (ruˈmei·ni·ən) *n. & adj.* = Romanian; Roumanian
rumba ('rʌm·bə) *n.* rumba.
rumble ('rʌm·bəl) *v.i.* retumbar; rugir. —*v.t.* hacer retumbar; decir o hacer retumbando. —*n.* **1,** (thunderous sound) estruendo; retumbo. **2,** (low, murmuring sound) rugido. **3,** *slang* (gang fight) camorra; riña. —**rumble seat,** asiento trasero descubierto (de un coche).
ruminant ('ru·mɪ·nənt) *adj. & n.* rumiante.
ruminate ('ru·mə,neit) *v.t. & i.* rumiar. —**rumination,** *n.* rumia; rumiación. —**ruminative,** *adj.* meditativo.
rummage ('rʌm·ɪdʒ) *v.t. & i.* revolver; explorar; rebuscar. —*n.* rezagos. —**rummage sale,** venta de rezagos.
rummy ('rʌm·i) *n.* **1,** (card game) cierto juego de cartas. **2,** *slang* (alcoholic) alcohólico. —*adj., slang* extraño; singular.
rumor *también,* **rumour** ('ru·mər) *n.* rumor. —*v.t.* rumorear.

rump (rʌmp) *n.* **1,** (buttocks) ancas; nalgas; rabada. **2,** (remnant) remanente; residuo.

rumple ('rʌm·pəl) *v.t.* arrugar; ajar. —*v.i.* arrugarse; ajarse. —*n.* arruga.

rumpus ('rʌm·pəs) *n.* batahola; alboroto. —**rumpus room,** cuarto de juegos.

run (rʌn) *v.i.* [**ran, run, running**] **1,** (move swiftly) correr. **2,** (make haste) apresurarse. **3,** (flee) huir; escaparse. **4,** (travel) andar; marchar. **5,** (go regularly) recorrer. **6,** (flow) fluir. **7,** (discharge a fluid) chorrear. **8,** (spread) difundirse. **9,** (operate) funcionar; marchar. **10,** (compete) competir. **11,** (pass by) transcurrir. **12,** (tend; incline) inclinarse. **13,** (continue) continuar; seguir. **14,** (be a candidate) ser candidato. —*v.t.* **1,** (direct) dirigir; manejar. **2,** (travel through or past) correr; recorrer. **3,** (incur, as a risk) correr. **4,** (smuggle) pasar de contrabando. **5,** (exhibit, as a film) exhibir. **6,** (project, as a film) proyectar; pasar. **7,** (draw, as a line) trazar; tirar. —*n.* **1,** (rapid movement; race) carrera. **2,** (journey) excursión. **3,** (current) flujo. **4,** (course) curso. **5,** (tendency) tendencia. **6,** (extraordinary demand) asedio. **7,** *baseball* carrera. **8,** *cards* secuencia. **9,** (free access) libre uso. **10,** (animal range) terreno de pasto. **11,** (herd) rebaño. **12,** (brook) arroyo; riachuelo. **13,** (stocking ravel) carrera. **14,** (class; kind) clase; tipo; género. —**in the long run,** a la larga. —**on the run, 1,** (hurriedly) apresuradamente; de prisa. **2,** (in retreat) huyendo; en fuga. —**run across,** dar con; encontrar. —**run against, 1,** (oppose) oponerse a. **2,** (encounter) encontrar; dar con; chocar con. —**run down, 1,** (pursue and catch) alcanzar; llegar a coger. **2,** (trace) trazar. **3,** (crush by passing over) atropellar. **4,** (disparage) rebajar; desacreditar. **5,** (become exhausted or worn out) agotarse; acabarse; dejar de funcionar. —**run (a) fever,** tener calentura. —**run in, 1,** *print.* poner de seguido. **2,** *slang* (arrest) arrestar. —**run into,** encontrar; dar con; chocar con. —**run off, 1,** *print.* imprimir; tirar. **2,** (do or make quickly) hacer rápidamente; enunciar rápidamente. **3,** (flow out or away) escurrir; derramarse. **4,**

(turn away from) desviarse de. —**run on,** continuar; seguir. —**run out, 1,** (leave hurriedly) salir; huirse; escaparse. **2,** (expire) terminar; expirar. **3,** (become exhausted or worn out) agotarse; acabarse. —**run over, 1,** (overflow) rebosar. **2,** (go beyond) pasar; pasarse de; exceder. **3,** (pass over; crush) atropellar. **4,** (trample) pisotear; atropellar. —**run through, 1,** (impale) traspasar; empalar. **2,** (do or say quickly) hacer rápidamente; enunciar rápidamente.

runabout ('rʌn·ə·baut) *n.* **1,** (sports car) coche ligero. **2,** (light carriage) birlocho. **3,** (small boat) lancha. **4,** (wanderer) vagamundo.

runaround ('rʌn·ə·raund) *n.* **1,** *slang* (evasion) evasiva. **2,** (type set around an illustration) letras alrededor de un grabado.

runaway ('rʌn·ə·wei) *adj.* **1,** (escaping) fugitivo; *(of a horse)* desbocado. **2,** (easily won) fácil. —*n.* **1,** (escaped horse) caballo desbocado. **2,** (fugitive) prófugo; fugitivo. **3,** (flight) fuga. **4,** (easy victory) victoria fácil.

run-down *adj.* **1,** (in poor health) enfermizo. **2,** (broken down) destartalado; desvencijado. **3,** (exhausted; used up) agotado; acabado.

rune (ruːn) *n.* **1,** (magic) misterio; magia. **2,** (letter) runa.

rung (rʌŋ) *v., p.p. de* **ring.** —*n.* travesaño.

runnel ('rʌn·əl) *n.* arroyo.

runner ('rʌn·ər) *n.* **1,** (racer) corredor [*fem.* -dora]. **2,** (messenger) mensajero. **3,** (slide, as of a sled) corredera. **4,** *bot.; zoöl.* estolón. **5,** (narrow rug) alfombra estrecha. **6,** (stocking ravel) carrera.

runner-up *n.* contendiente que termina segundo.

running ('rʌn·ɪŋ) *n.* **1,** (act of running) carrera. **2,** (operation) marcha; funcionamiento. **3,** (suppuration) supuración. —*adj.* **1,** (moving) corriente; en marcha. **2,** (adapted for running) corredor. **3,** (suppurating) supurante. —*adv.* en sucesión. —**running hand,** letra cursiva. —**running headline,** título de página. —**running knot,** lazo corredizo. —**twice running,** dos veces seguidas. —**a week running,** una semana entera.

running board estribo.

runny ('rʌn·i) *adj.* **1,** (watery)

coladizo. **2,** (pussy) supurante. **3,** (sniffly) que gotea.

run-off *n.* **1,** (water spill) agua de desagüe. **2,** (deciding contest) carrera final.

run-of-the-mill *adj.* común; ordinario.

runt (rʌnt) *n.* enano.

run-through *n.* **1,** (review) repaso. **2,** (rehearsal) ensayo.

runway ('rʌn·wei) *n.* **1,** *R.R.* vía. **2,** *aero.* pista de aterrizaje. **3,** (channel) cauce.

rupee (ru'piː; 'ru-) *n.* rupia.

rupture ('rʌp·tʃər) *n.* **1,** (break) ruptura; rompimiento. **2,** (disagreement) desavenencia. **3,** (hernia) hernia. —*v.t.* **1,** (break) romper; reventar. **2,** *pathol.* quebrar. —*v.t.* romperse.

rural ('rʊr·əl) *adj.* rural.

ruse (ruːz) *n.* ardid; artimaña; recoveco.

rush (rʌʃ) *v.i.* **1,** (drive forward) lanzarse; abalanzarse. **2,** (hurry) precipitarse. —*v.t.* **1,** (hasten) acelerar. **2,** (push) empujar con violencia. **3,** *football* avanzar (el balón) **4,** *slang* inducir a unirse a una fraternidad. **5,** *slang* (court) galantear. —*n.* **1,** (forward surge) acometida; embestida. **2,** (dash) asedio. **3,** (haste) prisa. **4,** (urgency) urgencia. **5,** *bot.* junco. **6,** *football* lucha violenta; adelanto del balón. —*adj.* **1,** (urgent) urgente. **2,** (made of rush) de junco. —**rush hour,** hora de más tránsito. —**rush in,** entrar precipitadamente. —**rush in on,** entrar sin avisar. —**rush through,** hacer de prisa.

rusk (rʌsk) *n.* galleta; rosca.

russet ('rʌs·ɪt) *adj.* & *n.* (color) moreno rojizo.

Russian ('rʌʃ·ən) *adj.* & *n.* ruso.

rust (rʌst) *n.* **1,** (corrosive formation) moho; herrumbre. **2,** (reddish color) color rojizo. —*adj.* rojizo. —*v.t.* enmohecer. —*v.i.* enmohecerse.

rustic ('rʌs·tɪk) *adj.* **1,** (rural) rústico. **2,** (simple) sencillo. **3,** (rude) grosero. —*n.* rústico; campesino.

rusticity (rʌs'tɪs·ə·ti) *n.* rusticidad.

rustle ('rʌs·əl) *v.i.* **1,** (make a murmuring or rubbing sound) susurrar. **2,** *slang* (move vigorously) moverse; apresurarse. —*v.t.* **1,** (cause to murmur; rub softly) hacer susurrar; agitar levemente. **2,** *slang* (cause to move; hurry) apresurar; empujar. **3,** *slang* (gather or produce quickly) recoger; conseguir o preparar en seguida. **4,** *slang* (steal, as cattle) hurtar; robar; *Amer.* arrear. —*n.* susurro.

rustler ('rʌs·lər) *n.*, *U.S.* ladrón de ganado.

rusty ('rʌs·ti) *adj.* **1,** (covered with rust) mohoso; enmohecido. **2,** (reddish) rojizo. **3,** (hoarse) ronco. **4,** *colloq.* (out of practice) entorpecido.

rut (rʌt) *n.* **1,** (narrow track) bache; surco. **2,** (habit) rutina. **3,** (period of heat in animals) celo; brama. —**rutted,** *adj.* surcado. —**rutty,** *adj.* lleno de surcos.

rutabaga (ˌru·tə'bei·gə) *n.* nabo de Suecia.

ruthenium (ru'θi·ni·əm) *n.* rutenio.

ruthless ('ruθ·lɪs) *adj.* despiadado; cruel. —**ruthlessness,** *n.* crueldad.

rye (rai) *n.* **1,** (grain) centeno. **2,** (liquor) whisky de centeno.

S

S, s (ɛs) décimonona letra del alfabeto inglés.

sabbath ('sæb·əθ) *n.* **1,** (Jewish) sábado. **2,** (Christian) domingo. —*adj.* **1,** (Jewish) sabático. **2,** (Christian) dominical.

sabbatical (sə'bæt·ɪ·kəl) *adj.* sabático; dominical. —*n.* [*también,* **sabbatical year**] año sabático; año de licencia.

saber ('sei·bər) *n.* sable. —*v.t.* dar

un sablazo o sablazos a; herir o matar a sablazos.

sable ('sei·bəl) *n.* **1,** *zoöl.* marta cebellina. **2,** *heraldry* sable. **3,** *pl.* (mourning clothes) vestidos de luto. —*adj.* **1,** (of sable fur) de marta cebellina. **2,** (black) negro.

sabot (sæ'boʳ) *n.* zueco.

sabotage ('sæb·ɔˌtaʒ) *n.* sabotaje. —*v.i.* & *t.* sabotear. —**saboteur** (-'tʌːr) *n.* saboteador [*fem.* -dora].

sac (sæk) *n., anat.; bot.; zoöl.* saco.
saccharin ('sæk·ə·rın) *n.* sacarina.
—**saccharine**, *adj.* sacarino; de sacarina; *fig.* azucarado.
sacerdotal (,sæs·ər'do·təl) *adj.* sacerdotal.
sachet (sæ'ʃei) *n.* saquito perfumador.
sack (sæk) *n.* **1,** (bag) saco. **2,** (loose garment) saco; chaqueta. **3,** *slang* (dismissal) despido. **4,** (plunder) saqueo; pillaje. —*v.t.* **1,** (put in bags) ensacar; poner en sacos. **2,** *slang* (dismiss) echar; despedir. **3,** (plunder) saquear.
sackcloth ('sæk,klɔθ) *n.* brea; harpillera. —**in sackcloth and ashes,** en hábito de penitencia.
sacral ('sei·krəl) *adj., anat.; relig.* sacro.
sacrament ('sæk·rə·mənt) *n.* sacramento. —**sacramental** (-'mɛn·təl) *adj.* sacramental.
sacred ('sei·krıd) *adj.* sacro; sagrado.
sacrifice ('sæk·rə,fais) *n.* sacrificio. —*v.t.* sacrificar. —*v.i.* sacrificarse. —**sacrificial** (-'fıʃ·əl) *adj.* sacrificatorio; de sacrificio.
sacrilege ('sæk·rə·lıdʒ) *n.* sacrilegio. —**sacrilegious** (-'lıdʒ·əs) *adj.* sacrílego.
sacristan ('sæk·rıs·tən) *n.* sacristán. —**sacristy,** *n.* sacristía.
sacroiliac (,sæk·ro'ıl·ı·æk) *adj.* sacroilíaco. —*n.* región sacroilíaca.
sacrosanct ('sæk·rə,sæŋkt) *adj.* sacrosanto.
sacrum ('sei·krəm) *n.* [*pl.* -**cra** (-krə)] sacro; hueso sacro.
sad (sæd) *adj.* **1,** (sorrowful) triste. **2,** *colloq.* (bad; poor) malo; deplorable. —**sadden,** *v.t.* entristecer. —*v.i.* entristecerse. —**sad sack,** *slang* caso perdido.
saddle ('sæd·əl) *n.* **1,** (seat for a rider on a horse) silla; silla de montar. **2,** (bicycle seat) sillín. **3,** (padded part of a harness) cincha. **4,** (cut of meat) cuarto trasero. —*v.t.* **1,** (put a saddle on) ensillar. **2,** (burden) cargar; gravar.
saddlebag ('sæd·əl,bæg) *n.* alforja.
sadism ('sei·dız·əm) *n.* sadismo. —**sadist,** *n.* sadista. —**sadistic** (sə'dıs·tık) *adj.* sadista.
sadness ('sæd·nəs) *n.* tristeza.
sadomasochism (,sei·do'mæs·ə·kız·əm) *n.* sadomasoquismo. —**sadomasochist,** *n.* sadomasoquis-

ta. —**sadomasochistic,** *adj.* sadomasoquista.
safari (sə'far·i) *n.* safari.
safe (seif) *adj.* **1,** (free from danger) seguro; salvo. **2,** (unharmed) ileso; intacto. **3,** (trustworthy) digno de confianza. **4,** (harmless) innocuo. —*n.* caja fuerte; caja de caudales.
safe-conduct (seif'kan·dʌkt) *n.* salvoconducto; salvaguardia.
safe-cracker *n.* ladrón de cajas fuertes.
safe-deposit box caja de seguridad.
safeguard ('seif,gard) *n.* salvaguardia. —*v.t.* salvaguardar.
safekeeping (,seif'ki·pıŋ) *n.* custodia; cuidado; depósito.
safeness ('seif·nəs) *n.* seguridad.
safety ('seif·ti) *n.* **1,** (safeness) seguridad. **2,** (protection) protección. —*adj.* de seguridad. —**safety belt,** cinturón de seguridad; *naut.* cinturón salvavidas. —**safety glass,** vidrio o cristal de seguridad. —**safety match,** fósforo de seguridad. —**safety pin,** imperdible. —**safety razor,** máquina o maquinilla de afeitar. —**safety valve, 1,** (automatic escape valve) válvula de seguridad. **2,** *fig.* (emotional outlet) válvula de escape. —**safety zone,** zona de seguridad.
safflower ('sæ·flau·ər) *n.* cártamo; cártama.
saffron ('sæf·rən) *n.* azafrán.
sag (sæg) *n.* **1,** (bending) combadura; comba. **2,** *naut.* deriva. **3,** (decline in price) baja. —*v.i.* **1,** (bend) combarse; ceder. **2,** (droop) pender; colgar; aflojarse. **3,** (weaken) debilitarse; declinar. **4,** (decline in price) bajar.
saga ('sa·gə) *n.* saga.
sagacious (sə'gei·ʃəs) *adj.* sagaz; astuto.
sagacity (sə'gæs·ə·ti) *n.* sagacidad.
sage (seidʒ) *adj.* sabio; sagaz. —*n.* **1,** (wise man) sabio. **2,** *bot.* (herb) salvia. —**sagebrush** ('seidʒ,brʌʃ) *n.* artemisa.
Sagittarius (,sædʒ·ı'tɛr·ı·əs) *n.* Sagitario.
saguaro (sə'wa·ro) *n.* [*pl.* -**ros**] saguaro. *También,* **sahuaro.**
said (sɛd) *v., pret. & p.p. de* say.
sail (seil) *n.* **1,** (of a ship) vela. **2,** (arm of a windmill) brazo. **3,** (ride in a vessel) paseo o viaje en barco.

—*v.i.* **1,** (move along in a vessel) navegar. **2,** (begin a voyage) embarcarse; salir. **3,** (glide) navegar; flotar; deslizarse. —*v.t.* **1,** (handle; steer) gobernar; manejar. **2,** (travel on or over) navegar. —**set sail,** hacerse a la mar; hacerse a la vela.

sailboat ('seil,bot) *n.* barco de vela; velero.

sailcloth ('seil,klɔθ) *n.* lona.

sailfish ('seil,fıʃ) *n.* aguja de mar.

sailing ('sei·lıŋ) *n.* **1,** (navigation) navegación. **2,** (ride on a vessel) paseo en barco. **3,** (departure from port) salida. —*adj.* velero; de vela.

sailor ('sei·lər) *n.* **1,** (mariner; seaman) marino; marinero. **2,** (hat) canotié. —*adj.* marinero; marino.

saint (seint) *n. & adj.* santo [*fem.* santa]. —*v.t.* canonizar. —**sainthood,** *n.* santidad. —**saintliness,** *n.* santidad. —**saintly,** *adj.* santo.

Saint Bernard (bər'nard) perro de San Bernardo.

sainted ('sein·tıd) *adj.* **1,** (canonized) canonizado. **2,** (sacred) bendito; santificado. **3,** (saintly) santo.

Saint Elmo's fire ('ɛl·moɹz) *n.* fuego de San Telmo.

Saint Vitus's dance ('vai·təs) baile de San Vito.

sake (seik) *n.* **1,** (purpose) motivo; razón. **2,** (interest; benefit) interés; bien. —**for goodness' sake,** por el amor de Dios.

salaam (sə'laɹm) *n.* zalema. —*v.t.* hacer zalemas a. —*v.i.* hacer zalemas.

salable también, **saleable** ('seil·ə·bəl) *adj.* vendible.

salacious (sə'lei·ʃəs) *adj.* salaz; lascivo. —**salaciousness,** *n.* salacidad; lascivia.

salad ('sæl·əd) *n.* ensalada. —**salad bowl,** ensaladera. —**salad days,** ingenuidad juvenil. —**salad dressing,** aderezo; aliño.

salamander ('sæl·ə,mæn·dər) *n.* salamandra.

salami (sə'la·mi) *n.* embutido; salchichón.

salaried ('sæl·ə·rid) *adj.* **1,** (receiving a salary) asalariado. **2,** (yielding a salary) retribuido.

salary ('sæl·ə·ri) *n.* salario.

sale (seil) *n.* **1,** (selling) venta. **2,** (auction) subasta. —**for sale,** de venta; se vende. —**on sale,** en venta. —**sales manager,** gerente de ventas. —**salesroom,** *n.* salón de ventas o de exhibiciones. —**sales tax,** impuesto de o sobre ventas.

salesman ('seilz·mən) *n.* **1,** (traveling agent) vendedor; viajante. **2,** [*también,* **salesclerk**] (seller in a store) dependiente. —**salesgirl; saleslady; saleswoman,** *n.* dependienta; vendedora.

salesmanship ('seilz·mən·ʃıp) *n.* **1,** (work of a salesman) venta. **2,** (ability at selling) arte de vender.

salicylate ('sæl·ə,sıl·et; sə'lıs· ə,leit) *n.* salicilato. —**salicylic** ('sæl·ə,sıl·ık) *adj.* salicílico.

salient ('sei·li·ənt) *adj.* sobresaliente; destacado. —*n.* saliente. —**salience,** *n.* énfasis; lo que sobresale.

saline ('sei·lain; -lin) *adj.* salino. —**salinity** (sə'lın·ə·ti) *n.* salinidad.

saliva (sə'lai·və) *n.* saliva. —**salivary** ('sæl·ə·ver·i) *adj.* salival. —**salivate** ('sæl·ə,veit) *v.i.* salivar. —**salivation,** *n.* salivación.

sallow ('sæl·o) *adj.* pálido; lívido. —**sallowness,** *n.* palidez; lividez.

sally ('sæl·i) *n.* **1,** *mil.* salida; acometida. **2,** (sudden start) arranque; ímpetu. **3,** (bright retort) salida; ocurrencia. —*v.i.* acometer; hacer una salida.

salmagundi (,sæl·mə'gʌn·di) *n.* salpicón; mescolanza.

salmon ('sæm·ən) *n.* salmón.

salmonella (,sæl·mə'nɛl·ə) *n.* salmonela.

salon (sə'laɹn) *n.* salón.

saloon (sə'luɹn) *n.* **1,** (public bar) cantina; taberna. **2,** (public room of a ship) salón. **3,** (sedan) sedán.

salt (sɔlt) *n.* **1,** (mineral) sal. **2,** *colloq.* (sailor) marinero. —*adj.* salado; salino. —*v.t.* **1,** (season) echar o poner sal a. **2,** (give tang to) avivar; aguzar. **3,** (preserve with salt) salar. —**salted,** *adj.* salado. —**salt away,** guardar; ahorrar. —**not worth one's salt,** no valer un comino.

saltcellar ('sɔlt,sɛl·ər) *n.* salero. También, **salt shaker.**

saltine (,sɔl'tin) *n.* galleta salada.

salt lick lamedero.

saltpeter también, **saltpetre** (,sɔlt'pi·tər) *n.* salitre.

salt water agua salobre; agua salada. —**salt-water,** *adj.* de agua salada; marino.

saltwort ('sɔlt,wʌrt) *n.* barrilla.

salty ('sɔl·ti) *adj.* **1,** (containing

salt) salado. **2,** (witty; pungent) agudo; picante; saleroso.

salubrious (sə'lu·bri·əs) *adj.* salubre; saludable. —**salubriousness; salubrity,** *n.* salubridad.

salutary ('sæl·jə·tɛr·i) *adj.* saludable; beneficioso.

salutation (ˌsæl·ju'tei·ʃən) *n.* salutación; saludo.

salutatory (sə'lu·tə·tor·i) *adj.* saludador. —*n.* discurso; salutación. —**salutatorian** (-'tor·i·ən) *n.* saludador [*fem.* -dora].

salute (sə'lut) *v.t. & i.* saludar. —*n.* saludo.

Salvadoran (ˌsæl·və'dor·ən); **Salvadorean; Salvadorian** (-'dor·i·ən) *adj. & n.* salvadoreño.

salvage ('sæl·vɪdʒ) *n.* salvamento. —*v.t.* salvar.

salvation (sæl'vei·ʃən) *n.* salvación. —**Salvation Army,** Ejército de Salvación.

salve (sæv) *n.* **1,** (ointment) ungüento. **2,** *fig.* (consolation) alivio; consuelo. —*v.t.* **1,** (heal) curar con ungüentos. **2,** (soothe) aliviar.

salver ('sæl·vər) *n.* bandeja.

salvo ('sæl·vo) *n.* salva.

Samaritan (sə'mær·ə·tən) *adj. & n.* samaritano.

samarium (sə'mær·i·əm) *n.* samario.

samba ('sam·bə) *n.* samba.

same (seim) *adj. & pron.* mismo. —*adv.* igualmente. —**all the same,** a pesar de todo. —**just the same,** lo mismo; sin embargo.

sameness ('seim·nəs) *n.* **1,** (identity) igualdad; identidad. **2,** (monotony) monotonía.

samovar ('sæm·ə·var) *n.* samovar.

sampan ('sæm·pæn) *n.* sampán.

sample ('sæm·pəl) *n.* muestra; prueba. —*v.t.* probar; catar.

sampler ('sæm·plər) *n.* **1,** (piece of embroidery) dechado; marcador. **2,** (tester) probador; catador. **3,** (one who prepares samples) preparador [*fem.* -dora] de muestras.

samurai ('sæm·u·rai) *n.* samurai.

sanatorium (ˌsæn·ə'tor·i·əm) *n.* [*pl.* -a (-ə)] sanatorio.

sanctify ('sæŋk·tə·fai) *v.t.* santificar. —**sanctification** (-fɪ'kei·ʃən) *n.* santificación.

sanctimony ('sæŋk·tə·mo·ni) *n.* beatería; santurronería. —**sanctimonious** (-'mo·ni·əs) *adj.* beato; beaturrón; santurrón.

sanction ('sæŋk·ʃən) *n.* sanción. —*v.t.* sancionar.

sanctity ('sæŋk·tə·ti) *n.* santidad.

sanctuary ('sæŋk·tʃu,ɛr·i) *n.* **1,** (sacred place) santuario. **2,** (place of refuge) asilo; refugio.

sanctum ('sæŋk·təm) *n.* **1,** (sacred place) lugar sagrado. **2,** (refuge) retiro; refugio.

sand (sænd) *n.* **1,** (fine mineral particles) arena. **2,** *pl.* (desert; beach) arenal; playa; desierto. **3,** *slang* (courage) ánimo; resolución. —*v.t.* **1,** (sprinkle with sand) enarenar. **2,** (rub with sandpaper) lijar.

sandal ('sæn·dəl) *n.* sandalia.

sandalwood ('sæn·dəl,wʊd) *n.* sándalo.

sandbag ('sænd,bæg) *n.* saco de arena. —*v.t.* **1,** (block with sandbags) guarnecer con sacos de arena. **2,** *slang* (hit or betray unexpectedly) golpear o traicionar inesperadamente.

sandblast ('sænd,blæst) *v.t.* limpiar con arena a presión.

sand bar *n.* banco o arrecife de arena.

sandbox ('sænd,baks) *n.* cajón de arena. *También,* **sand box.**

sander ('sæn·dər) *n.* **1,** (person who sands) lijador. **2,** (device for spreading sand) arenadora. **3,** (machine for rubbing or smoothing) lijadora.

sandhog ('sænd,hag) *n.* trabajador de túnel.

sandman ('sænd,mæn) *n.* [*pl.* -men] genio del sueño.

sandpaper ('sænd,pei·pər) *n.* lija. —*v.t.* lijar.

sandpiper ('sænd,pai·pər) *n.* ave zancuda semejante a la agachadiza.

sandstone ('sænd,ston) *n.* arenisca.

sandwich ('sænd·wɪtʃ) *n.* emparedado; sandwich. —*v.t.* intercalar; insertar.

sandy ('sæn·di) *adj.* **1,** (of or like sand) arenoso; arenisco. **2,** (yellowish) rufo; de color de arena. **3,** *slang* (courageous) valeroso; valiente; animoso.

sane (sein) *adj.* cuerdo; sensato; juicioso. —**saneness,** *n.* cordura; sensatez.

sang (sæŋ) *v.,* *pret. de* **sing.**

sangría (sæŋ'gri·ə) *n.* (a drink made of wine and fruit juice) sangría.

sanguinary ('sæŋ·gwɪ,nɛr·i) *adj.* sanguinario.

sanguine ('sæŋ·gwɪn) *adj.* 1, (hopeful) confiado; optimista; esperanzado. 2, (ruddy) sanguino; sanguíneo; rubicundo. —**sanguinolent** (sæn'gwɪn·ə·lənt) *adj.* sanguinolento.

sanitarium (,sæn·ə'tɛr·i·əm) *n.* sanatorio.

sanitary ('sæn·ə,tɛr·i) *adj.* sanitario; higiénico. —**sanitize** ('sæn·ə·taiz) *v.t.* sanear. —**sanitary belt,** cinturón o cordón sanitario. —**sanitary napkin,** toallita o almohadilla higiénica; absorbente higiénico.

sanitation (,sæn·ə'tei·ʃən) *n.* 1, (science or practice of hygienics) saneamiento. 2, (disposal of refuse and sewage) sanidad.

sanity ('sæn·ə·ti) *n.* cordura; juicio; sensatez.

sank (sæŋk) *v., pret. de* **sink.**

Sanskrit también, **Sanscrit** ('sæn·skrɪt) *n. & adj.* sánscrito.

Santa Claus ('sæn·tə,klɔz) papá Noel.

sap (sæp) *n.* 1, (juice of a plant) savia. 2, *slang* (fool) tonto; necio. 3, *mil.* zanja; zapa. —*v.t.* [**sapped, sapping**] 1, (undermine) zapar; socavar. 2, (weaken) debilitar; agotar. —**sapper,** *n.* zapador.

sapid ('sæp·ɪd) *adj.* sápido. —**sapidity** (sə'pɪd·ə·ti) *n.* sapidez.

sapient (sei·pi·ənt) *adj.* sapiente. —**sapience,** *n.* sapiencia.

sapling ('sæp·lɪŋ) *n.* vástago; renuevo.

sapphire ('sæf·air) *n.* zafiro. —*adj.* zafirino; zafíreo. —**sapphirine** ('sæf·ər·ɪn) *adj.* zafirino; zafíreo.

sappy ('sæp·i) *adj.* 1, (juicy) jugoso; lleno de savia. 2, (vigorous) enérgico; vigoroso. 3, *slang* (foolish) necio; tonto.

saraband ('sær·ə,bænd) *n.* zarabanda.

Saracen ('sær·ə·sən) *n. & adj.* sarraceno.

sarcasm ('sar·kæz·əm) *n.* sarcasmo. —**sarcastic** (sar'kæs·tɪk) *adj.* sarcástico; mordaz.

sarcoma (sar'ko·mə) *n.* sarcoma.

sarcophagus (sar'kaf·ə·gəs) *n.* sarcófago.

sardine (sar'diːn) *n.* sardina.

sardonic (sar'dan·ɪk) *adj.* sardónico; mordaz; sarcástico.

sargasso (sar'gæs·o) *n.* sargazo.

sarge (sardʒ) *n., colloq.* = **sergeant.**

sarong (sə'rɔŋ) *n.* sarong.

sarsaparilla (,sæs·pə'rɪl·ə) *n.* zarzaparrilla.

sartorial (sar'tor·i·əl) *adj.* de sastre; de sastrería.

sash (sæʃ) *n.* 1, (window frame) marco o bastidor de ventana. 2, (band around the waist) banda; faja. —*v.t.* proveer de bastidores; poner marcos a.

sass (sæs) *v.t., slang* tratar con insolencia. —*n.* impertinencia; insolencia. —**sassy,** *adj.* impertinente; insolente. —**sassiness,** *n.* insolencia; descaro.

sassafras ('sæs·ə,fræs) *n.* sasafrás.

sat (sæt) *v., pret. & p.p. de* **sit.**

Satan ('sei·tən) *n.* Satán; el diablo. —**satanic** (sə'tæn·ɪk) *adj.* satánico.

satchel ('sætʃ·əl) *n.* maletín; cartapacio; mochila.

sate (seit) *v.t.* 1, (satisfy) saciar; satisfacer; llenar. 2, (surfeit; glut) hastiar; hartar.

sateen (sæ'tiːn) *n.* satén.

satellite ('sæt·ə,lait) *n.* satélite.

satiate ('sei·ʃi,eit) *v.t.* saciar; hartar; hastiar. —**satiable,** *adj.* saciable. —**satiation,** *n.* saciedad.

satiety (sə'tai·ə·ti) *n.* saciedad; hastío.

satin ('sæt·ən) *n.* raso. —*adj. de* raso; satinado. —**satiny,** *adj.* satinado.

satinwood ('sæt·ən,wʊd) *n.* aceitillo.

satire ('sæt·air) *n.* sátira. —**satiric** (sə'tɪr·ɪk); **satirical,** *adj.* satírico. —**satirist** (-ə·rɪst) *n.* satírico.

satirize ('sæt·ə·raiz) *v.t.* satirizar.

satisfaction (,sæt·ɪs'fæk·ʃən) *n.* satisfacción. —**satisfactory** (-tə·ri) *adj.* satisfactorio.

satisfy ('sæt·ɪs,fai) *v.t.* 1, (supply the needs of) satisfacer. 2, (pay fully) pagar; resarcir. 3, (convince) convencer. 4, (fulfill the conditions of) colmar; cumplir. 5, (atone for) contentar; dar satisfacción a. —*v.i.* satisfacer; dar satisfacción.

satrap ('sæt·ræp) *n.* sátrapa. —**satrapy,** *n.* satrapía.

saturate ('sætʃ·ə,reit) *v.t.* saturar; impregnar. —**saturation,** *n.* saturación. —**saturable,** *adj.* saturable.

Saturday ('sæt·ər·de) *n.* sábado. —*adj.* sabatino; del sábado.

Saturn ('sæt·ərn) *n.* Saturno.
saturnine ('sæt·ər,nain) *adj.* saturnino.
satyr ('sæt·ər) *n.* sátiro.
sauce (sɔs) *n.* 1, (dressing) salsa; crema. 2, (compote of fruit) jalea; compota. 3, *colloq.* (pertness) insolencia; descaro. 4, *fig.* (zest) salsa; sabor.
saucepan ('sɔs,pæn) *n.* cacerola; cazuela.
saucer ('sɔ·sər) *n.* platillo; platito.
saucy ('sɔ·si) *adj.* 1, (rude) descarado; insolente. 2, (pert) vivo; gracioso; simpático.
sauerkraut ('sau·ər,kraut) *n.* encurtido de col picada; chucruta.
saunter ('sɔn·tər) *v.i.* 1, (stroll) pasear; dar un paseo. 2, (walk with leisurely step) andar con paso tranquilo. —*n.* 1, (stroll) paseo. 2, (leisurely step) paso tranquilo.
sausage ('sɔ·sɪdʒ) *n.* salchicha; embutido; butifarra; longaniza.
sauté (so'tei) *v.t.* saltear. —*adj.* salteado.
sauterne (so'tʌrn) *n.* vino de Sauternes; vino blanco.
savage ('sæv·ɪdʒ) *n.* & *adj.* salvaje. —**savagery,** *n.* salvajismo.
savanna (sə'væn·ə) *n.* sabana.
savant (sæ'vant) *n.* erudito; sabio; letrado.
save (seiv) *v.t.* 1, (preserve) salvar; preservar. 2, (conserve) guardar; conservar. 3, (make safe) salvar; librar. 4, (keep safe) amparar; proteger. 5, (put aside for the future) ahorrar; guardar. 6, (gain) ganar; ahorrar; economizar. —*v.i.* economizar. —*prep.* salvo; excepto. —*conj.* a no ser que.
saving ('sei·vɪŋ) *n.* 1, (economy) ahorro; economía. 2, *law* (exception) salvedad; excepción. —*adj.* 1, (economical) ahorrativo; económico. 2, (redeeming) salvador. —*prep.* salvo; excepto. —*conj.* a no ser que. —**daylight saving time,** horario de verano. —**savings account,** cuenta de ahorros. —**savings bank,** caja de ahorros; banco de ahorros.
savior ('seiv·jər) *n.* salvador; *cap.* [*usu.* **Saviour**] el Salvador; Jesucristo.
savoir-faire (,sæv·war'feːr) *n.* maña; destreza.
savoir-vivre (,sæv·war'viː·vrə) *n.* buenos modales.
savor (,sei·vər) *n.* sabor; gusto.

—*v.t.* 1, (season) sazonar. 2, (taste) saborear; gustar. —*v.i.* oler. —**savor of,** saber a; oler a.
savory ('sei·və·ri) *adj.* sabroso; agradable. —*n.* 1, (appetizer) aperitivo. 2, *bot.* ajedrea.
savvy ('sæv·i) *v.t.* & *i., slang* comprender; entender. —*n., slang* comprensión; entendimiento.
saw (sɔː) *n.* 1, (cutting tool) sierra. 2, (proverb) refrán; dicho. —*v.i.* & *t.* serrar; aserrar. —*v., pret. de* **see.**
sawbones ('sɔ·bonz) *n.sing.* & *pl., slang* cirujano; médico.
sawbuck ('sɔ·bʌk) *n.* 1, (sawhorse) cabrilla. 2, *slang* billete de diez.
sawdust ('sɔ·dʌst) *n.* serrín; aserrín; aserraduras.
sawfish ('sɔ,fɪʃ) *n.* pez sierra.
sawhorse ('sɔ,hors) *n.* cabrilla; burro; borrico.
sawmill ('sɔ,mɪl) *n.* aserradero; serrería.
sawyer ('sɔ·jər) *n.* aserrador.
Saxon ('sæk·sən) *n.* & *adj.* sajón [*fem.* -jona].
saxophone ('sæk·sə,fon) *n.* saxófono; saxofón. —**saxophonist,** *n.* saxofonista.
say (sei) *v.t.* [*pret.* & *p.p.* **said**] decir. —*n.* 1, (what one has to say) decir; dicho. 2, (chance to speak) turno (de hablar). —**I should say so!,** ¡Ya lo creo! —**have a** *or* **one's say,** tener voz. —**it goes without saying,** cae de su peso. —**no sooner said than done,** dicho y hecho. —**that is to say,** es decir.
saying ('sei·ɪŋ) *n.* dicho; refrán.
say-so *n., colloq.* 1, (unsupported statement; rumor) rumor. 2, (right of decision) decisión; autoridad.
scab (skæb) *n.* 1, (crust over a sore) costra. 2, (mange) roña; sarna. 3, (strikebreaker) esquirol. 4, *slang* (scoundrel) truhán; truante; bribón.
scabbard ('skæb·ərd) *n.* vaina.
scabby ('skæb·i) *adj.* 1, (covered with scabs) costroso; roñoso. 2, (mean) vil; despreciable; bajo.
scabies ('skei·biz) *n.* escabiosis; sarna.
scabrous ('skei·brəs) *adj.* escabroso.
scads (skædz) *n.pl., slang* montañas; montones; puñados.
scaffold ('skæf·əld) *n.* 1, (temporary platform) tablado. 2, (supporting framework) andamio. 3, (platform for a gallows) patíbulo;

cadalso. —**scaffolding**, *n.* andamio; andamiaje.

scalawag ('skæl·ə‚wæg) *n.*, *colloq.* truhán; golfo.

scald (skɔld) *v.t.* escaldar. —*n.* escaldadura.

scale (skeil) *n.* **1**, (flake) escama. **2**, (ladder) escala. **3**, (instrument for weighing) balanza. **4**, (series of marks; system of proportion; gradation) escala. **5**, *mus.* escala. —*v.t.* **1**, (remove scales from) escamar; limpiar de escamas. **2**, (cover with scales) poner escamas a. **3**, (cause to skip) tirar al ras; hacer resbalar. **4**, (weigh) pesar. **5**, (climb) escalar. **6**, (project according to scale) poner a escala. **7**, (reduce to a scale) reducir a escala. **8**, (regulate) graduar a escala. —*v.i.* **1**, (climb) trepar; escalar. **2**, (flake) pelarse. **3**, (become covered with scales) cubrirse de escamas; formarse escamas.

scalene (skei'lin) *adj.* escaleno.

scallion ('skæl·jən) *n.* **1**, = **shallot**. **2**, = **leek**.

scallop ('skæl·əp) *n.* **1**, (mollusk) molusco bivalvo. **2**, (its shell) pechina; concha. **3**, (small decorative curve) festón. —*v.t.* **1**, (cut in scallops) festonear. **2**, (bake) cocer u hornear a la crema; cocer en concha.

scalp (skælp) *n.* cuero cabelludo; pericráneo. —*v.t.* **1**, (remove the scalp of) arrancar el pericráneo a; quitar el cuero cabelludo a. **2**, *colloq.* (buy and sell at inflated prices) revender a precios exorbitantes. —**scalper**, *n.* revendedor [*fem.* -dora]; desollador [*fem.* -dora].

scalpel ('skæl·pəl) *n.* escalpelo; bisturí.

scaly ('skei·li) *adj.* **1**, (covered with scales) escamoso. **2**, *slang* (despicable) vil; despreciable.

scamp (skæmp) *n.* bribón; truhán; pícaro. —*v.t.* chapucear.

scamper ('skæm·pər) *v.i.* escabullirse; escaparse.

scan (skæn) *v.t.* **1**, (scrutinize) escudriñar. **2**, (glance hastily) dar un vistazo a. **3**, escandir. **4**, *TV; comput.* explorar. —*v.i.* medir versos. —**scanner**, *n.* explorador.

scandal ('skæn·dəl) *n.* escándalo. —**scandalize**, *v.t.* escandalizar. —**scandalous**, *adj.* escandaloso.

scandalmonger ('skæn·dəl‚mʌŋ-

gər) *n.* propagador [*fem.* -dora] de escándalos; murmurador [*fem.* -dora].

Scandinavian (‚skæn·dɪ'nei·vi·ən) *n. & adj.* escandinavo.

scandium ('skæn·di·əm) *n.* escandio.

scansion ('skæn·ʃən) *n.* escansión.

scant (skænt) *adj.* escaso; insuficiente. —**scanty,** *adj.* limitado; corto.

scapegoat ('skeip‚got) *n.* cabeza de turco; víctima propiciatoria.

scapegrace ('skeip‚greis) *n.* truhán; pícaro; bribón.

scapula ('skæp·jə·lə) *n.* omóplato; escápula.

scapular ('skæp·jə·lər) *adj.* escapular. —*n.* **1**, (eccles. garment) escapulario. **2**, *surg.* vendaje para el omóplato.

scar (skɑɪr) *n.* cicatriz; marca; señal. —*v.t.* señalar; marcar. —*v.i.* cicatrizarse.

scarab ('skær·əb) *n.* escarabajo.

scarce (skɛrs) *adj.* **1**, (not abundant) escaso; insuficiente; limitado. **2**, (uncommon) raro; extraño. —**scarcely,** *adv.* apenas; escasamente; ciertamente no. —**scarcely ever,** raramente; casi nunca.

scarcity ('skɛr·sə·ti) *n.* **1**, (shortage; lack) escasez; insuficiencia; carestía. **2**, (uncommonness) rareza. *También*, **scarceness**.

scare (skɛɪr) *v.t.* **1**, (frighten) asustar; espantar. **2**, (intimidate) amedrentar; atemorizar. —*v.i.* amedrentarse; atemorizarse. —*n.* susto; alarma. —**scare away,** espantar; ahuyentar. —**scare up,** *colloq.* conseguir; obtener; recoger.

scarecrow ('sker‚kro) *n.* espantajo; espantapájaros.

scarf (skarf) *n.* **1**, (decorative strip) banda; faja. **2**, (muffler) bufanda. **3**, (shawl) chal. **4**, (cravat) chalina. **5**, *carp.* ensambladura francesa.

scarlet ('skar·lɪt) *n. & adj.* escarlata. —**scarlet fever,** escarlatina; escarlata.

scarp (skarp) *n.* escarpa; escarpadura; declive.

scary ('skɛr·i) *adj.,* *colloq.* **1**, (frightening) temible; pavoroso. **2**, (timid) tímido; asustadizo.

scat (skæt) *v.t.,* *colloq.* ahuyentar. —*interj.* ¡fuera!; ¡zape!

scathe (skeið) *v.t.* denunciar; acusar. —**scathing,** *n.* denuncia;

acusación; crítica. —*adj.* áspero;
duro; rudo.

scatology (skæ'tal·ə·dʒi) *n.*
escatología. —**scatological** (ˌskæt·
ə'ladʒ·ɪ·kəl) *adj.* escatológico.

scatter ('skæt·ər) *v.t.* diseminar;
esparcir; desparramar. —*v.i.* diseminarse; desparramarse. —*n.* esparcimiento; dispersión. —**scatter rug**,
alfombra pequeña.

scatterbrain ('skæt·ər,brein) *n.*
cabeza de chorlito. —**scatterbrained**, *adj.* ligero de cascos; casquivano.

scattering ('skæt·ər·ɪŋ) *n.* **1**, (dispersal) esparcimiento; dispersión. **2**,
(sparse distribution) pequeño
número; pequeña cantidad.

scavenger ('skæv·ɪn·dʒər) *n.* **1**,
(street cleaner) basurero; barrendero. **2**, (animal) animal de carroña.

scenario (sɪ'ner·i·o) *n.* libreto;
guión; argumento.

scene (siːn) *n.* **1**, *theat.* escena. **2**,
(view; picture) paisaje; vista. **3**,
(display of feeling) espectáculo;
arrebato; escena.

scenery ('sin·ə·ri) *n.* **1**, (landscape)
paisaje. **2**, *theat.* decoración.

scenic ('si·nɪk) *adj.* **1**, (pert. to scenery) escénico. **2**, (picturesque)
pintoresco; atractivo.

scent (sɛnt) *n.* **1**, (odor) olor;
aroma. **2**, (course of an animal)
pista; rastro. **3**, (perfume) perfume;
aroma. **4**, (sense of smell) olfato.
—*v.t.* **1**, (smell) oler; olfatear. **2**,
(suspect) sospechar. **3**, (perfume)
perfumar; aromatizar.

scepter *también,* **sceptre** ('sɛp·tər)
n. cetro.

sceptic ('skɛp·tɪk) *n. & adj.* =
skeptic. —**sceptical**, *adj.* = **skeptical**. —**scepticism** (-tɪ·sɪz·əm) *n.* =
skepticism.

schedule ('skedʒ·ʊl) *n.* **1**, (list;
catalogue) lista; catálogo; cuadro. **2**,
(agenda) plan; programa; agenda. **3**,
(timetable) horario. —*v.t.* **1**, (include in a schedule) proyectar;
planear; programar. **2**, (make a
schedule of) catalogar. **3**, (set the
time for) fijar la hora de.

scheme (skiːm) *n.* **1**, (system;
plan) esquema; proyecto; designio. **2**, (plot) confabulación; ardid;
treta. —*v.t. & i.* proyectar; planear;
urdir. —**schematic** (ski'mæt·ɪk)
adj. esquemático. —**scheming**, *adj.*
intrigante; urdidor.

schemer ('ski·mər) *n.* **1**, (one who

makes schemes) proyectista. **2**,
(plotter) intrigante; urdidor [*fem.*
-dora].

schism ('sɪz·əm) *n.* cisma.
—**schismatic** (sɪz'mæt·ɪk) *adj.*
cismático.

schist (ʃɪst) *n.* esquisto.

schizoid ('skɪz·ɔid; 'skɪt·sɔid) *adj.
& n.* esquizofrénico.

schizophrenia (ˌskɪz·ə'fri·ni·ə;
ˌskɪt·sə-) *n.* esquizofrenia. —**schizophrenic** (-'frɛn·ɪk) *adj. & n.* esquizofrénico.

schnapps (ʃnaps) *n.* aguardiente;
licor.

schnozzle ('ʃnaz·əl) *n., slang*
nariz.

scholar ('skal·ər) *n.* **1**, (student)
escolar; estudiante. **2**, (learned man)
erudito; intelectual. **3**, (student with
a scholarship) becario.

scholarly ('skal·ər·li) *adj.* erudito;
intelectual. —*adv.* eruditamente.

scholarship ('skal·ər·ʃɪp) *n.* **1**,
(learning) erudición. **2**, (monetary
assistance) beca.

scholastic (skə'læs·tɪk) *n. & adj.*
escolástico. —**scholasticism** (-tə·
sɪz·əm) *n.* escolasticismo.

school (skuːl) *n.* **1**, (educational establishment) escuela. **2**, (large body
of fish) banco; cardumen. —*v.t.*
instruir; enseñar; adiestrar.

school board junta de educación
o de instrucción pública.

schoolbook ('skul,bʊk) *n.* libro de
texto; libro escolar.

schoolboy ('skul,bɔi) *n.* alumno
(de escuela).

schoolgirl ('skul,gʌrl) *n.* alumna
(de escuela).

schoolhouse ('skul,haus) *n.* edificio escolar; escuela.

schooling ('skul·ɪŋ) *n.* instrucción; enseñanza.

schoolmaster ('skul,mæs·tər) *n.*
maestro de escuela.

schoolmate ('skul,meit) *n.* compañero o compañera de escuela.

schoolmistress ('skul,mɪs·trɪs)
n. maestra de escuela.

schoolroom ('skul,rum) *n.* aula;
clase; sala (de clase).

schoolteacher ('skul,titʃ·ər) *n.*
maestro o maestra de escuela.

schoolyard ('skul,jard) *n.* patio de
recreo.

schooner ('sku·nər) *n.* **1**, *naut.*
goleta; escuna. **2**, (beer glass) caña;
vaso grande.

sciatic (sai'æt·ɪk) *adj.* ciático.
—**sciatica** (-ɪ·kə) *n.* ciática.

science ('sai·əns) *n.* ciencia.

scientific (,sai·ən'tɪf·ɪk) *adj.* científico.

scientist ('sai·ən·tɪst) *n.* científico; hombre o mujer de ciencia.

scimitar ('sɪm·ə·tər) *n.* cimitarra.

scintilla (sɪn'tɪl·ə) *n.* huella; la menor partícula.

scintillate ('sɪn·tə,leit) *v.i.* centellar. —**scintillation**, *n.* centelleo.

scion ('sai·ən) *n.* vástago.

scissors ('sɪz·ɔrz) *n.sing.* o *pl.* tijeras. —**scissor**, *v.t.* cortar con tijeras.

sclerosis (sklɪ'ro·sɪs) *n.* [*pl.* -ses (-siz)] esclerosis.

sclerotic (sklɪ'rat·ɪk) *adj.* esclerótico.

scoff (skaf) *v.i.* mofarse; burlarse. —*n.* mofa; burla. —**scoff at**, mofarse de; burlarse de.

scold (skold) *v.t.* & *i.* regañar; reprender. —*n.* regañón (*fem.* regañona). —**scolding**, *n.* reprimenda; reprensión; regaño.

scone (skoɹn) *n.* bizcocho blando; galleta.

scoop (skup) *n.* **1,** (deep shovel for taking up sand, dirt, etc.) pala; cucharón de grúa. **2,** (kitchen utensil) cucharón; paleta. **3,** (bailing vessel) achicador. **4,** (act of scooping; amount taken) cucharada; paletada. **5,** (hollow) hueco; cavidad. **6,** *colloq.* (journalistic beat) primicia; primera publicación de una noticia. —*v.t.* **1,** (hollow out) ahuecar; vaciar. **2,** (bail out) achicar. **3,** (remove with a scoop) sacar (con pala, paleta, cucharón, etc.) **4,** *colloq., journalism* publicar antes que nadie.

scoot (skut) *v.i., colloq.* correr precipitadamente; volar. —*v.t., colloq.* arrojar. —*n., colloq.* carrera precipitada.

scooter ('skut·ər) *n.* **1,** (child's vehicle) patín; deslizador. **2,** (iceboat) deslizador; lancha rápida.

scope (skop) *n.* **1,** (outlook; range) alcance; campo. **2,** (room for free action or observation) campo o esfera de acción. **3,** (extent; length) extensión; alcance.

scopolamine (sko'pal·ə,min) *n.* escopolamina.

scorbutic (skor'bju·tɪk) *adj.* escorbútico.

scorch (skortʃ) *v.t.* **1,** (singe) chamuscar; socarrar. **2,** (parch) agostar; resecar; abrasar. **3,** (criticize harshly) reprochar; criticar duramente. —*v.i.* chamuscarse; resecarse. —*n.* chamusquina.

score (scoɹr) *n.* **1,** (in sports and games) tanteo; tantos. **2,** (reckoning) cuenta. **3,** (notch) muesca; mella. **4,** (scratch) señal; raya. **5,** (reason; ground) motivo; razón. **6,** (twenty) veintena; *pl.* muchos; montones. **7,** *mus.* partitura. **8,** (grade; rating) calificación. —*v.t.* **1,** (mark) rayar; marcar con muescas o rayas. **2,** (reckon) contar; anotar (tantos). **3,** (achieve) conseguir; ganar; lograr. **4,** (rate) calificar. **5,** *mus.* instrumentar. **6,** (berate) regañar; criticar duramente. —*v.i.* **1,** (in sports and games) apuntarse un tanto; ganar un punto. **2,** (make notches) hacer rayas; hacer muescas o señales. —**keep score**, tantear; apuntar los tantos.

scoria ('skɔr·i·ə) *n.* escoria.

scorn (skorn) *n.* desprecio; desdén. —*v.t.* desdeñar; despreciar. —**scornful**, *adj.* desdeñoso.

Scorpio ('skor·pi·o) *n., astron.* Escorpión.

scorpion ('skor·pi·ən) *n.* alacrán; escorpión.

Scot (skat) *n.* = Scotsman.

Scotch (skatʃ) *adj.* escocés. —*n.* **1,** (language) escocés. **2,** (whiskey) whisky escocés. **3,** *l.c.* (cut) corte; señal; marca. **4,** *l.c.* (block) obstáculo; impedimento. **5,** *l.c.* (wedge) cuña; calce. —*v.t., l.c.* **1,** (cut) cortar; marcar. **2,** (foil; quash) frustrar. **3,** (block) calzar; poner cuña a. —**Scotch tape**, (*T.N.*) cinta de celulosa. —**Scotch terrier**; **Scottie** ('skat·i) perro escocés.

Scotchman ('skatʃ·mən) *n.* [*pl.* -men] escocés.

scot-free (,skat'fri:) *adj.* **1,** (exempt; clear) exento; libre; limpio. **2,** (unpunished) impune.

Scots (skats) *adj.* escocés. —*n.* **1,** (language) escocés. **2,** *pl. de* Scot. —**Scotsman** (-mən) *n.* [*pl.* -men] escocés. —**Scotswoman**, *n.* [*pl.* -women] escocesa.

Scottish ('skat·ɪʃ) *adj.* & *n.* escocés.

scoundrel ('skaun·drəl) *n.* truhán; pícaro; canalla. —**scoundrelly** (-drə·li) *adj.* truhán; canallesco.

scour (skaur) *v.t.* **1,** (clean by friction) estregar; restregar. **2,** (flush) limpiar a chorro. **3,** (purge) purgar. **4,** (search through) reconocer; explorar detenidamente. —**scouring,** *n.* fregado; estregamiento. —**scourings,** *n.pl.* residuo; desecho.

scourge (skʌrdȝ) *n.* **1,** (whip) azote; flagelo. **2,** (affliction) calamidad; aflicción. —*v.t.* azotar; flagelar.

scout (skaut) *n.* **1,** *mil.* (soldier) batidor; explorador; escucha; (plane or ship) avión o barco de reconocimiento. **2,** *cap.* (Boy Scout) niño explorador; (Girl Scout) niña exploradora. **3,** *colloq.* (fellow) tipo; sujeto. —*v.t. & i.* (reconnoiter) explorar; reconocer. —*v.t.* (scoff at) mofarse de.

scoutmaster ('skaut,mæs·tər) *n.* [*fem.* **scoutmistress**] (-,mɪs·trɪs) jefe de escuchas.

scow (skau) *n.* lanchón; barcaza.

scowl (skaul) *v.i.* fruncir el ceño; poner mala cara. —*n.* ceño; mala cara.

scrabble ('skræb·əl) *v.i.* **1,** (scratch; scrape) raspar; arañar. **2,** (scrawl) garabatear; hacer garabatos. —*n.* **1,** (scrawl) garabato. **2,** *cap., T.N.* (word game) cierto juego basado en crucigramas.

scraggly ('skræg·li) *adj.* áspero; irregular; rudo.

scraggy ('skræg·i) *adj.* delgado; huesudo; anguloso.

scram (skræm) *v.i., slang* marcharse; largarse.

scramble ('skræm·bəl) *v.i.* **1,** (climb) trepar. **2,** (crawl) arrastrarse. **3,** (struggle) pelear; bregar; revolverse. —*v.t.* revolver; mezclar. —*n.* **1,** (fight) contienda; lucha. **2,** (climb) ascenso; trepa. —**scrambled eggs,** revoltillo de huevos; huevos revueltos.

scrap (skræp) *n.* **1,** (fragment) parte; trozo; fragmento. **2,** *pl.* (leftovers) sobras. **3,** (discarded iron or steel) chatarra; metal viejo. **4,** *slang* (quarrel) pelea; pendencia; camorra. —*v.t.* **1,** (break up) romper; destrozar; convertir en chatarra. **2,** (discard) desechar; descartar. —*v.i., slang* (quarrel) pelearse; reñir.

scrapbook ('skræp,bʊk) *n.* álbum de recortes.

scrape (skreip) *v.t.* **1,** (shave the surface of) raspar; rascar. **2,** (scratch; graze) arañar. —*v.i.* **1,** (scrape; grate) raspar; rascar.

2, (produce a harsh noise) desafinar. —*n.* **1,** (act of scraping) raspadura; arañazo. **2,** (sound of scraping) chirrido. **3,** (embarrassing situation) aprieto; apuro; lío. —**scrape along; scrape through,** ir tirando; arreglárselas. —**scrape out** o **off,** borrar; raer. —**scrape up; scrape together,** recoger penosamente; amontonar poco a poco.

scraper ('skrei·pər) *n.* **1,** (tool; person) raspador; rascador. **2,** *slang* (violinist) rascatripas. **3,** *slang* (barber) carnicero. **4,** (small rug) limpiabarros.

scraping ('skrei·pɪŋ) *n.* **1,** (scratching) raedura; raspadura. **2,** *pl.* (shavings) raspaduras. **3,** *pl.* (savings) ahorros.

scrappy ('skræp·i) *adj., slang* peleador.

scratch (skrætʃ) *v.t.* **1,** (mark or wound slightly) arañar; hacer rasguños a. **2,** (rub, as to relieve itching) rascar. **3,** (rub roughly) raer; raspar. **4,** (erase) borrar. **5,** (withdraw from a race) borrar. —*v.i.* **1,** (dig) escarbar; raspar. **2,** (rub, as to relieve itching) rascar. **3,** (scribble) garabatear. **4,** (get along with difficulty) ir tirando. —*n.* **1,** (act or result of scratching) rasguño; arañazo; rascadura; raya. **2,** (scribble) garabato. **3,** (starting point) línea de partida; principio. **4,** *slang* (money) dinero. —**scratch pad,** cuaderno de notas; libreta de apuntes.

scratchy ('skrætʃ·i) *adj.* **1,** (roughly done or made) irregular; a remiendos. **2,** (itchy; irritating) áspero; rudo; burdo. **3,** (making a scraping noise) chirriante.

scrawl (skrɔːl) *v.t.* garabatear. —*n.* garabato.

scrawny ('skrɔ·ni) *adj* magro; huesudo; delgado. —**scrawniness,** *n.* delgadez.

scream (skriːm) *v.t.* vociferar. —*v.i.* gritar; chillar; dar alaridos. —*n.* **1,** (shrill cry) grito; chillido; alarido. **2,** *colloq.* (highly amusing person or thing) cosa o persona divertida; tiro.

screamer ('skri·mər) *n.* **1,** *slang, journalism* titular escandaloso. **2,** (person who screams) gritón; chillón. **3,** (outstanding person or thing) persona o cosa sobresaliente.

screech (skritʃ) *v.i. & t.* chillar.

—*n.* chillido. —**screechy,** *adj.* chillón.

screen (skriːn) *n.* **1,** (covered frame or frames) biombo; mampara. **2,** (sifter) cedazo; tamiz. **3,** (protective wire mesh) alambrera; tela metálica; (for a fireplace or lamp) pantalla. **4,** (protective formation) cortina. **5,** (pretext) cortina; capa. **6,** (surface for projecting pictures) pantalla. **7,** *print.* retícula; trama. —*v.t.* **1,** (conceal) ocultar; tapar. **2,** (protect) defender; proteger. **3,** (sift) cerner; tamizar. **4,** (classify) separar; tamizar; examinar. **5,** (record on film) rodar; filmar. **6,** (exhibit) proyectar; exhibir.

screenplay ('skrin,plei) *n.* guión.

screw (skruː) *n.* **1,** (fastener) tornillo. **2,** (propeller) hélice. **3,** (coercion) coerción. **4,** *slang* (prison guard) celador. —*v.t.* **1,** (turn; attach) atornillar; enroscar. **2,** (contort) obligar; forzar. —*v.i.* atornillarse; enroscarse. —**have a screw loose,** tener flojos los tornillos; faltarle a uno un tornillo.

screwball ('skruː-bɔl) *n. & adj., slang* (eccentric) extravagante; excéntrico; estrafalario.

screwdriver ('skruː,drai·vər) *n.* atornillador; destornillador.

screw-eye ('skruː,ei) *n.* armella.

screwy ('skruː·i) *adj.* **1,** (twisted) torcido; tortuoso. **2,** *slang* (crazy) loco; chiflado.

scribble ('skrib·əl) *v.i. & t.* garabatear. —*n.* garabato. —**scribbler** (-lər) *n.* mal escritor.

scribe (skraib) *n.* **1,** (amanuensis) amanuense; escribiente. **2,** *Bib.* escriba. **3,** (author) autor; escritor. —*v.t.* trazar con punzón.

scrimmage ('skrim·idʒ) *n.* pelea; lucha; *football* encuentro; jugada. —*v.i.* encontrarse; pelear.

scrimp (skrimp) *v.t. & i.* escatimar. —**scrimpy,** *adj.* tacaño.

scrip (skrip) *n.* cédula; abonaré; pagaré.

script (skript) *n.* **1,** (handwriting) escritura. **2,** *print.* letra cursiva. **3,** *theat.* libreto; guión; manuscrito.

scripture ('skrip·tʃər) *n.* escritura; sagrada escritura. —**scriptural,** *adj.* bíblico.

scrivener ('skriv·nər) *n.* escribano.

scrofula ('skraf·jə·lə) *n.* escrófula. —**scrofulous,** *adj.* escrofuloso.

scroll (skroːl) *n.* **1,** (roll of paper or parchment) rollo de papel o pergamino. **2,** (list; schedule) lista; libro. **3,** *archit.* voluta.

scrollwork ('skrol,wʌrk) *n.* dibujo o adornos de volutas.

scrotum ('skro·təm) *n.* escroto.

scrounge (skraundʒ) *v.t. & i.* sonsacar.

scrub (skrʌb) *v.t. & i.* fregar; estregar; restregar. —*n.* **1,** (underbrush) maleza; matorral. **2,** (bushy terrain) monte bajo. **3,** (person or thing smaller than usual) chaparro; enano. **4,** *sports* (substitute player) suplente. **5,** (team made up of such players) segundo equipo. —*adj.* **1,** (makeshift) provisional. **2,** (inferior) inferior. **3,** (undersized) enano.

scrubby ('skrʌb·i) *adj.* **1,** (undersized) achaparrado; pequeño. **2,** (shabby) andrajoso.

scruff (skrʌf) *n.* nuca. —**scruffy,** *adj.* desaliñado.

scrumptious ('skrʌmp·ʃəs) *adj., colloq.* muy fino; elegante; de chupete.

scruple ('skruː·pəl) *n.* escrúpulo. —*v.i.* tener o sentir escrúpulos; escrupulizar. —**scrupulous** ('skrup-jə·ləs) *adj.* escrupuloso. —**scrupulousness,** *n.* escrupulosidad.

scrutinize ('skruː·tə·naiz) *v.t.* escudriñar; escrutar. —**scrutiny,** *n.* escrutinio; escudriñamiento.

scuba ('sku·bə) *n., abr. de* self-contained underwater breathing apparatus.

scud (skʌd) *v.i.* correr rápidamente; volar; deslizarse.

scuff (skʌf) *v.t.* **1,** (spoil by scraping) rayar; rascar. **2,** (scrape with the feet) desgastar con los pies. —*v.i.* arrastrar los pies. —*n.* **1,** (act of scuffing) rayado. **2,** (worn spot) desgaste. **3,** (slipper) zapatilla; chinela.

scuffle ('skʌf·əl) *v.i.* **1,** (brawl) forcejear; luchar; pelear. **2,** (drag the feet) arrastrar los pies. —*n.* **1,** (brawl) lucha; pelea. **2,** (dragging of feet) arrastre de los pies.

scull (skʌl) *n.* **1,** (oar) espadilla. **2,** (boat) bote. —*v.t.* impulsar o mover a remo. —*v.i.* remar.

scullery ('skʌl·ə·ri) *n.* trascocina; espetera.

scullion ('skʌl·jən) *n.* pinche; sollastre.

sculpture ('skʌlp·tʃər) *n.* escultura. —*v.t. & i.* esculpir. —**sculp-**

tural, *adj.* escultural. **—sculptor** (-tər) *n.* escultor [*fem.* -tora].

scum (skʌm) *n.* **1,** (layer of impurities) espuma; impureza; nata. **2,** (refuse) hez; escoria; desecho. **3,** (riffraff) canalla. **—scummy,** *adj.* espumoso.

scurf (skʌrf) *n.* costra; caspa.

scurrilous ('skʌr·ə·ləs) *adj.* grosero; insolente. **—scurrility** (skʌr'ɪl·ə·ti) *n.* grosería; insolencia.

scurry ('skʌr·i) *v.i.* [-ried; -rying] correr; escabullirse. **—n.** [*pl.* -ries] huída.

scurvy ('skʌr·vi) *n.* escorbuto. **—adj.** despreciable; vil; ruin.

scuttle ('skʌt·əl) *n.* **1,** (container) balde; cubo. **2,** (small opening) agujero; abertura. **3,** (trapdoor) escotillón. **4,** *naut.* (hatchway) escotilla. **5,** (hurried run) fuga; huída. **—v.t.** hundir; echar a pique. **—v.i.** huir; correr; escapar.

scythe (saið) *n.* guadaña. **—v.t.** cortar con guadaña; segar.

sea (siː) *n.* mar. **—at sea, 1,** (on the ocean) en el mar. **2,** *fig.* (confused) confuso; perplejo. **—follow the sea; go to sea,** hacerse marinero. **—put to sea,** hacerse a la mar.

sea bass (bæs) róbalo; cherna.

seaboard ('si,bord) *n.* costa; litoral.

sea bream (brim) besugo.

seacoast ('si,kost) *n.* litoral; costa.

sea cow manatí; vaca marina.

seafarer ('siː,fɛr·ər) *n.* navegante; marinero.

seafaring ('siː,fɛr·ɪŋ) *adj.* navegante; marinero. **—n. 1,** (profession) marinería. **2,** (travel by sea) navegación.

seafood ('si,fud) *n.* pescado y marisco.

seafowl ('si,faul) *n.* ave de mar.

seagoing ('si,go·ɪŋ) *adj.* de alta mar.

sea gull gaviota.

sea horse caballito de mar.

seal (siːl) *n.* **1,** (stamp; mark; tight closure) sello. **2,** (marine animal) foca. **—v.t.** sellar.

sea legs (lɛgz) pie marino.

sea level nivel del mar.

sea lion león marino.

sealskin ('sil,skɪn) *n.* piel de foca.

seam (siːm) *n.* **1,** (joint made by sewing) costura. **2,** (scar) costurón. **3,** (wrinkle) arruga. **4,** (fissure) grieta; raja. **5,** (stratum) filón; veta. **—v.t. 1,** (join by sewing) coser. **2,**

(mark with wrinkles) arrugar. **—v.i.** (crack) agrietarse.

seaman ('si·mən) *n.* [*pl.* -men] marino; marinero.

seamanship ('si·mən·ʃɪp) *n.* marinería; náutica.

seamless ('sim·ləs) *adj.* sin costura.

seamstress ('sim·strɪs) *n.* modista; costurera.

seamy ('si·mi) *adj.* **1,** (showing seams) con costuras. **2,** (rough; coarse) basto. **—the seamy side,** el aspecto menos atractivo.

seance ('sei·ans) *n.* sesión, esp. de espiritismo.

seaplane ('si,plein) *n.* hidroplano; hidroavión.

seaport ('si,port) *n.* puerto; puerto de mar.

sear (sɪr) *v.t.* **1,** (burn) chamuscar; socarrar. **2,** (cauterize) cauterizar. **3,** (make callous) endurecer; insensibilizar. **4,** (dry up) marchitar; secar; agostar.

search (sʌrtʃ) *v.t.* **1,** (explore) explorar; buscar. **2,** (examine) indagar; investigar; examinar. **3,** (frisk) cachear. **4,** (pierce) penetrar; taladrar. **—v.i.** buscar. **—n. 1,** (investigation) investigación; indagación. **2,** (seeking) busca; búsqueda. **3,** (frisking) cacheo. **—searching,** *adj.* agudo; penetrante. **—search warrant,** orden de registro.

searchlight ('sʌrtʃ,lait) *n.* reflector.

seascape ('si,skeip) *n.* marina.

seashell ('si,ʃel) *n.* concha; caracol marino.

seashore ('si,ʃor) *n.* orilla del mar; playa.

seasick ('si·sɪk) *adj.* mareado. **—seasickness,** *n.* mareo.

seaside ('si,said) *n.* playa; orilla del mar.

season ('si·zən) *n.* **1,** (quarter of the year) estación. **2,** (appropriate period of time) temporada; sazón. **—v.t. 1,** (ripen) madurar; sazonar. **2,** (cure) curar. **3,** (flavor) sazonar. **4,** (accustom) acostumbrar; habituar. **5,** (soften) moderar; templar. **—v.i.** madurarse; sazonarse; curarse. **—seasonable,** *adj.* conveniente; oportuno. **—seasonal,** *adj.* de temporada; estacional. **—seasoning,** *n.* aderezo; condimento; aliño. **—season ticket,** billete de abono.

seat (sit) *n.* **1,** (place to sit) asiento.

2, (back part of trousers) fondillos. **3,** (administrative center) sede. **4,** (center of learning) centro de enseñanza. **5,** (residence) residencia. **6,** (site) lugar; sitio. **7,** (membership) asiento; plaza. —*v.t.* **1,** (place on a seat; furnish with a seat) sentar; colocar; acomodar. **2,** (fix; locate) establecer; arraigar. **3,** (have seating capacity for) tener cabida para. **4,** (adjust in place) ajustar en su sitio. —**seat belt,** cinturón de seguridad. —**seat cover,** funda de asiento. —**seating capacity,** cabida; aforo.

sea urchin erizo de mar.

sea wall dique marítimo; malecón.

seaward ('si·wərd) *adj. & adv.* hacia el mar.

seaway ('si·we) *n.* ruta marítima.

seaweed ('si·wid) *n.* alga marina.

seaworthy ('si,wʌr·ði) *adj.* marinero; apto para navegar.

sebum ('si·bəm) *n.* sebo. —**sebaceous** (sɪ'bei·ʃəs) *adj.* sebáceo. —**seborrhea** (,sɛb·ə'ri·ə) *n.* seborrea.

secant ('si·kænt; -kənt) *n.* secante.

secede (sɪ'siːd) *v.i.* retirarse; separarse.

secession (sɪ'sɛʃ·ən) *n.* secesión. —**secessionism,** *n.* secesionismo. —**secessionist,** *adj. & n.* secesionista.

seclude (sɪ'kluːd) *v.t.* recluir; encerrar. —**seclusion** (-'kluː·ʒən) *n.* reclusión. —**seclusive** (-'kluː·sɪv) *adj.* solitario.

second ('sɛk·ənd) *adj.* segundo. —*n.* **1,** (person or thing after the first) segundo. **2,** (supporter) ayudante; partidario. **3,** (attendant in a duel) padrino; (in boxing) segundo. **4,** (imperfect product) artículo de segunda calidad. **5,** (unit of time) segundo. **6,** (in dates) dos. **7,** *mus.* segunda. —*v.t.* secundar; apoyar; apadrinar.

secondary ('sɛk·ən,dɛr·i) *adj.* secundario.

second-class *adj.* de segunda clase; inferior.

second fiddle papel secundario.

second-guess *v.t.* **1,** (anticipate) anticiparse a. **2,** (criticize) criticar, esp. con retrospección.

second hand segundero.

second-hand *adj.* de segunda mano.

second lieutenant alférez; subteniente.

second-rate *adj.* inferior.

second sight clarividencia.

secrecy ('si·krə·si) *n.* secreto.

secret ('si·krɪt) *adj.* secreto; oculto. —*n.* secreto. —**secret service,** policía secreta.

secretary ('sɛk·rə,tɛr·i) *n.* **1,** (assistant) secretario. **2,** (cabinet member) ministro. **3,** (desk) escritorio. —**secretarial** (-'tɛr·i·əl) *adj.* de o para secretarios. —**secretariat** (-'tɛr·i·ət) *n.* secretaría. —**secretaryship,** *n.* secretaría.

secrete (sɪ'krit) *v.t.* **1,** (hide) esconder; ocultar. **2,** *physiol.* secretar. —**secretion** (sɪ'kri·ʃən) *n.* secreción.

secretive (sɪ'kri·tɪv) *adj.* reservado; reticente; callado.

secretory (sɪ'kri·tə·ri) *adj.* secretor; secretorio.

sect (sɛkt) *n.* secta. —**sectarian** (sɛk'tɛr·i·ən) *n. & adj.* sectario. —**sectarianism,** *n.* sectarismo.

section ('sɛk·ʃən) *n.* **1,** (portion) sección. **2,** *geog.* región. **3,** *geom.; archit.; mil.* sección; *surg.* sección; operación. —*v.t.* seccionar.

sectional ('sɛk·ʃə·nəl) *adj.* **1,** (composed of several sections) seccional. **2,** (cut straight) transversal; seccional. **3,** (local) local; regional. —**sectionalism,** *n.* regionalismo; localismo.

sector ('sɛk·tər) *n.* sector.

secular ('sɛk·jə·lər) *adj.* secular; seglar. —**secularism,** *n.* secularismo; —**secularist,** *n.* secularista. —**secularistic,** *adj.* secularista.

secularize ('sɛk·jə·lə,raiz) *v.t.* secularizar. —**secularization** (-rɪ'zei·ʃən) *n.* secularización.

secure (sɪ'kjur) *adj.* seguro. —*v.t.* **1,** (make safe) asegurar; salvar; proteger. **2,** (make certain) asegurar; garantizar. **3,** (obtain) obtener; conseguir. **4,** (fasten) asegurar; afianzar. —*v.i.* asegurarse.

security (sɪ'kjur·ə·ti) *n.* **1,** (safety; certainty; safeguard) seguridad. **2,** (guarantee; surety) seguridad; garantía. **3,** (guarantor) garante; fiador. **5,** *usu.pl., comm.* obligaciones; valores; títulos.

sedan (sɪ'dæn) *n.* sedán. —**sedan chair,** silla de manos.

sedate (sɪ'deit) *adj.* tranquilo; sosegado; serio. —**sedateness,** *n.* sosiego; calma.

sedation (sɪ'dei·ʃən) *n.* sedación.

sedative ('sɛd·ə·tɪv) *n. & adj.* sedante; sedativo.

sedentary ('sɛd·ən·tɛr·i) *adj.* sedentario.

sedge (sɛdʒ) *n.* juncia.

sediment ('sɛd·ə·mənt) *n.* sedimento. —**sedimentary** (-'mɛn·tə·ri) *adj.* sedimentario. —**sedimentation** (-mən'tei·ʃən) *n.* sedimentación.

sedition (sɪ'dɪʃ·ən) *n.* sedición. —**seditious**, *adj.* sedicioso.

seduce (sɪ'dus) *v.t.* seducir. —**seducer**, *n.* seductor [*fem.* -tora] —**seduction** (-'dʌk·ʃən) *n.* seducción. —**seductive** (-'dʌk·tɪv) *adj.* seductivo; atractivo.

sedulous ('sɛdʒ·ə·ləs) *adj.* diligente; asiduo. —**sedulousness**; **sedulity** (sɪ'dʒu·lə·ti) *n.* diligencia; ahinco.

see (siː) *v.t. & i.* [saw, seen, seeing] 1, (perceive by the eye) ver; percibir. 2, (regard; consider) mirar. 3, (understand) comprender; entender. —*v.t.* 1, (witness) ver; presenciar. 2, (receive) recibir. 3, (consult) consultar. 4, (escort) acompañar. 5, (attend) ver; atender. 6, *cards* (meet or call, as a bet) ver; aceptar. —*n.* sede. —**see about, 1,** (inquire into) investigar; indagar. 2, (ascertain) averiguar. 3, (attend to) atender; cuidar de. —**see after**, cuidar; cuidar de. —**see into, 1,** (investigate) investigar; indagar. 2, (understand) penetrar; comprender; reconocer. —**see off**, despedir; acompañar hasta la despedida. —**see that; see to it that**, tener cuidado que. —**see through, 1,** (accomplish) llevar a cabo (una cosa). 2, (assist) ayudar; sostener (a una persona). 3, (penetrate) penetrar. —**see to**, atender a; pensar en.

seed (siːd) *n.* semilla; simiente. —*v.t. & i.* (sow with seed) sembrar. —*v.t.* (remove the seeds from) despepitar. —*adj.* seminal. —**go to seed**, deteriorarse; echarse a perder. —**seed pearl**, aljófar.

seedling ('sid·lɪŋ) *n.* 1, (young plant) plantón; planta de semilla. 2, (young tree) vástago; renuevo.

seedy ('si·di) *adj.* 1, (containing much seed) lleno de semillas; semilloso. 2, (shabby) desaseado; desastrado. 3, (gone to seed) deteriorado; inútil. —**seediness**, *n.* desaseo; calidad de desastrado.

seeing ('si·ɪŋ) *adj.* vidente. —*n.* vista; el ver. —*conj.* visto que; por

cuanto que. —**seeing-eye dog**, perro de ciego.

seek (sik) *v.t.* [*pret. & p.p.* sought] 1, (go in search of) buscar. 2, (search; explore) explorar; recorrer. 3, (resort to) dirigirse a. 4, (attempt; endeavor) intentar; esforzarse por; procurar. —*v.i.* buscar.

seem (siːm) *v.i.* parecer. —**seeming**, *adj.* aparente. —*n.* apariencia.

seemly ('sim·li) *adj.* adecuado; decoroso; decente. —**seemliness**, *n.* decencia; decoro.

seen (siːn) *v., p.p. de* see.

seep (sip) *v.i.* colarse; filtrarse; escurrirse. —**seepage**, *n.* escape; coladura; filtración.

seer (sɪr) *n.* 1, (clairvoyant) clarividente. 2, (prophet) profeta.

seeress ('sɪr·ɪs) *n.* 1, (clairvoyant) clarividente. 2, (prophetess) profetisa.

seersucker ('sɪr,sʌk·ər) *n.* sirsaca.

seesaw ('si,sɔ) *n.* 1, (balancing board) balancín; columpio de tabla. 2, (up-and-down movement) vaivén; balance. —*adj.* de vaivén; de balance. —*v.t.* columpiar; balancear. —*v.i.* columpiarse; balancearse.

seethe (siːð) *v.i.* 1, (boil) hervir; bullir. 2, (be agitated) agitarse.

segment ('sɛg·mənt) *n.* segmento; sección. —*v.t.* dividir en segmentos. —**segmental** (sɛg'mɛn·təl) *adj.* segmental. —**segmentation**, *n.* segmentación.

segregate ('sɛg·rə,geit) *v.t.* segregar; separar. —*v.i.* segregarse; separarse. —**segregation**, *n.* segregación; separación. —**segregationist**, *adj. & n.* segregacionista.

segue ('sɛg·wei) *n., radio; TV* breve interludio musical. —*v.i.* marcar con breve interludio musical el pasaje a la siguiente escena.

seine (sein) *n.* jábega. —*v.t. & i.* pescar con jábega.

seismic (saiz·mɪk) *adj.* sísmico.

seismograph ('saiz·mə·græf) *n.* sismógrafo. —**seismographic** (-'græf·ɪk) *adj.* sismográfico. —**seismogram** (-,græm) *n.* sismograma.

seismology (saiz'mal·ə·dʒi) *n.* sismología. —**seismological** (saiz·mə'ladʒ·ɪ·kəl) *adj.* sismológico. —**seismologist** (-'mal·ə·dʒɪst) *n.* sismólogo; sismologista.

seismometer (saiz'ma·mə·tər) *n.* sismómetro.

seize (siːz) *v.t.* **1**, (grasp) aferrar; agarrar; coger; asir. **2**, (take possession of) apoderarse de. **3**, (confiscate) secuestrar; requisar; embargar. **4**, (comprehend) entender; comprender. **5**, (take advantage of) aprovecharse de. **6**, (afflict) atacar.

seizure ('si·ʒər) *n.* **1**, (grasping) aferramiento; asimiento. **2**, (confiscation) secuestro; embargo; requisa. **3**, (fit; attack) acceso; ataque.

seldom ('sɛl·dəm) *adv.* raramente; pocas veces; rara vez.

select (sɪ'lɛkt) *v.t.* seleccionar; escoger. —*adj.* selecto; escogido. —**selection** (-'lɛk·ʃən) *n.* selección. —**selective,** *adj.* selectivo. —**selectivity** (,sɪ·lɛk'trv·ɔ·ti) *n.* selectividad. —**selective service,** conscripción; quintas; servicio militar.

selenium (sɪ'li·ni·əm) *n.* selenio.

self (sɛlf) *n.* [*pl.* **selves**] uno mismo. —*pron., colloq.* sí mismo. —*adj.* **1**, (same) mismo. **2**, (uniform) idéntico; propio; del mismo género. **3**, (unmixed) puro. —**the self,** el yo.

self-addressed *adj.* dirigido a sí mismo.

self-assurance *n.* confianza en sí mismo. —**self-assured,** *adj.* seguro de sí.

self-centered *adj.* egocéntrico.

self-command *n.* dominio propio; dominio de sí.

self-complacent *adj.* complacido de sí mismo. —**self-complacency; self-complacence,** *n.* complacencia en sí mismo.

self-conceit *n.* presunción; arrogancia. —**self-conceited,** *adj.* presumido; arrogante.

self-confidence *n.* confianza en sí. —**self-confident,** *adj.* seguro de sí.

self-conscious *adj.* cohibido; tímido; apocado. —**self-consciousness,** *n.* timidez; apocamiento.

self-contained *adj.* **1**, (reserved) reservado; callado. **2**, (complete in itself) completo en sí. **3**, (self-sufficient) independiente.

self-control *n.* dominio de sí.

self-controlled *adj.* **1**, (master over one's self) dueño de sí. **2**, (automatic) automático.

self-criticism *n.* autocrítica.

self-deception *n.* engaño de sí mismo.

self-defeating *adj.* contraproducente.

self-defense *n.* defensa propia.

self-denial *n.* abnegación.

self-destruction *n.* autodestrucción; suicidio.

self-determination *n.* autodeterminación.

self-discipline *n.* autodisciplina.

self-educated *adj.* autodidacto.

self-effacing *adj.* modesto. —**self-effacement,** *n.* modestia.

self-esteem *n.* estima propia; amor propio; respeto propio.

self-evident *adj.* obvio; claro; patente.

self-explanatory *adj.* que se explica por sí.

self-expression *n.* expresión de la propia personalidad.

self-governed *también,* **self-governing** *adj.* autónomo; independiente. —**self-government,** *n.* autonomía.

self-help *n.* ayuda propia.

self-important *adj.* arrogante; altivo. —**self-importance,** *n.* arrogancia; altivez.

self-imposed *adj.* voluntario.

self-improvement *n.* mejoramiento de sí mismo.

self-induced *adj.* inducido por sí mismo.

self-indulgent *adj.* desenfrenado; inmoderado. —**self-indulgence,** *n.* desenfreno; inmoderación.

self-inflicted *adj.* que uno mismo se ha infligido.

self-interest *n.* egoísmo; interés personal.

selfish ('sɛl·fɪʃ) *adj.* egoísta. —**selfishness,** *n.* egoísmo.

selfless ('sɛlf·ləs) *adj.* desinteresado; desprendido. —**selflessness,** *n.* desinterés; desprendimiento.

self-loading *adj.* autocargador.

self-love *n.* egoísmo; amor propio.

self-made *adj.* formado por sí mismo.

self-pity *n.* compasión de sí mismo.

self-portrait *n.* autorretrato.

self-possessed *adj.* sereno; dueño de sí. —**self-possession,** *n.* dominio de sí.

self-preservation *n.* propia conservación.

self-propelled *adj.* autopropulsado; automotor.

self-protection *n.* defensa o protección propia.

self-realization *n.* realización propia.

self-reliance *n.* confianza en sí mismo. —**self-reliant,** *adj.* confiado en sí mismo.

self-reproach *n.* represión de sí mismo.

self-respect *n.* pundonor; respeto de sí mismo; decoro.

self-restraint *n.* dominio de sí.

self-righteous *adj.* santurrón; beatón; hipócrita. —**self-righteousness,** *n.* santurronería; beatería; hipocresía.

self-sacrifice *n.* sacrificio de sí mismo.

selfsame ('sɛlf,seim) *adj.* idéntico; igual; mismísimo.

self-satisfied *adj.* satisfecho de sí mismo. —**self-satisfaction,** *n.* satisfacción de sí mismo.

self-seeking *adj.* egoísta. —*n.* egoísmo. —**self-seeker,** *n.* egoísta.

self-service *n.* autoservicio. —*adj.* de autoservicio.

self-starter *n.* arranque automático.

self-styled *adj.* que se llama a sí mismo; que se considera a sí mismo.

self-sufficient *adj.* **1,** (independent) suficiente a sí mismo; independiente. **2,** (conceited) presumido; vanidoso.

self-support *n.* mantenimiento propio; economía propia. —**self-supporting,** *adj.* que se mantiene a sí mismo.

self-sustaining *adj.* que se sostiene o mantiene a sí mismo.

self-taught *adj.* autodidacto.

self-willed *adj.* terco; obstinado.

self-winding *adj.* automático; de cuerda automática.

self-worship *n.* egolatría.

sell (sɛl) *v.t.* [*pret.* & *p.p.* **sold**] **1,** (transfer for money) vender. **2,** (keep for sale; deal in) vender; tener a la venta o en venta. **3,** (betray) traicionar; vender. **4,** (win acceptance of) hacer aceptar. **5,** *colloq.* (convince) convencer. **6,** *slang* (dupe) engañar; chasquear. —*v.i.* **1,** (engage in selling) vender. **2,** (be in demand) venderse; tener venta. **3,** (be sold; be for sale) venderse; estar en venta. **4,** (be accepted) tener aceptación. —**seller,** *n.* vendedor [*fem.* -dora]. —**selling,** *n.* venta; comercio.

sellout ('sɛl,aut) *n.* **1,** (liquidation)

saldo; realización; venta final. **2,** (complete disposal, as of theater seats) venta total. **3,** *slang* (betrayal) traición.

seltzer ('sɛl·tsər) *n.* seltz; agua de seltz; agua carbónica.

selvage ('sɛl·vɪdʒ) *n.* orillo.

selves (sɛlvz) *n., pl. de* **self.**

semantic (sɪ'mæn·tɪk) *adj.* semántico. —**semantics,** *n.* semántica.

semaphore ('sɛm·ə,for) *n.* semáforo.

semblance ('sɛm·bləns) *n.* **1,** (likeness) semblanza; parecido. **2,** (outward appearance) apariencia; exterior.

semen ('si·mən) *n.* semen.

semester (sɪ'mɛs·tər) *n.* semestre.

semiannual (,sɛm·i'æn·ju·əl) *adj.* semestral.

semibreve ('sɛm·ɪ,briv) *n.* semibreve.

semicircle ('sɛm·ɪ,sʌr·kəl) *n.* semicírculo. —**semicircular,** *adj.* semicircular.

semicolon ('sɛm·ɪ,ko·lən) *n.* punto y coma.

semifinal (,sɛm·ɪ'fai·nəl) *adj.* & *n.* semifinal. —**semifinalist,** *adj.* & *n.* semifinalista.

semimonthly (,sɛm·ɪ'mʌnθ·li) *adj.* bimensual.

seminal ('sɛm·ə·nəl) *adj.* seminal.

seminar ('sɛm·ə,nar) *n.* seminario.

seminary ('sɛm·ə,nɛr·i) *n.* seminario. —**seminarist,** *n.* seminarista.

semi-precious *adj.* semiprecioso.

semi-private *adj.* repartido entre dos o más personas.

semiquaver (,sɛm·i'kwei·vər) *n.* semicorchea.

Semite ('sɛm·ait) *n.* semita. —**Semitic** (sə'mɪt·ɪk) *adj.* & *n.* semítico.

semitone ('sɛm·ɪ,ton) *n., mus.* semitono.

semitrailer (,sɛm·i'trei·lər) *n.* semirremolque.

semiweekly (,sɛm·ɪ'wik·li) *adj.* bisemanal. —*n.* publicación bisemanal.

semolina (,sɛm·ə'li·nə) *n.* sémola.

senate ('sɛn·ɪt) *n.* senado.

senator ('sɛn·ə·tər) *n.* senador. —**senatorial** (-'tor·i·əl) *adj.* senatorial. —**senatorship,** *n.* senaduría.

send (sɛnd) *v.t.* **1,** (cause to go) mandar; enviar. **2,** (dispatch) despachar; remitir; expedir. **3,** (impel) lanzar; enviar. **4,** (emit) emitir.

5, (transmit) transmitir. **6,** *slang* (excite) estimular; excitar.

sender ('sɛn·dər) *n.* **1,** (one who sends) remitente. **2,** (transmitter) transmisor.

send-off *n.* **1,** (start) comienzo; empujón. **2,** *colloq.* (farewell demonstration) despedida afectuosa.

senescent (sə'nɛs·ənt) *adj.* **1,** (old) senil; que envejece. **2,** (of old age) de la vejez; de los ancianos. —**sénescence,** *n.* senectud; envejecimiento.

seneschal ('sɛn·ə·ʃəl) *n.* senescal.

senile ('si·naɪl) *adj.* senil. —**senility** (sə'nɪl·ə·ti) *n.* senilidad.

senior ('sin·jər) *adj.* **1,** (older; elder) mayor. **2,** (older in office or service) más antiguo; decano. **3,** (of or pert. to a graduating class) del último año. **4,** *usu. en la abr.* **Sr.,** denotando el padre del mismo nombre: *David Jones, Sr.,* David Jones, padre. —*n.* **1,** (older person; elder) mayor. **2,** (person of higher rank) persona más antigua; socio más antiguo. **3,** (member of the senior class) alumno del último año. —**senior citizen,** anciano.

seniority (sin'jar·ə·ti) *n.* **1,** (state or quality of being senior) antigüedad. **2,** (precedence) prioridad.

señor (sein'jor) *n.* señor. —**señora** (-'jo·rə) *n.* señora. —**señorita** (,sen·jə'ri·tə) *n.* señorita.

sensation (sɛn'sei·ʃən) *n.* sensación. —**sensational,** *adj.* sensacional. —**sensationalism,** *n.* sensacionalismo.

sense (sɛns) *n.* sentido; juicio. —*v.t.* sentir; percibir.

senseless ('sɛns·ləs) *adj.* **1,** (unconscious) inconsciente. **2,** (without meaning) sin sentido. **3,** (unreasoning; mad) insensato. **4,** (stupid) necio; estúpido.

senselessness ('sɛns·ləs·nəs) *n.* **1,** (unconsciousness) inconsciencia. **2,** (unreason; madness) insensatez. **3,** (stupidity) necedad; estupidez.

sensibility (,sɛn·sə'bɪl·ə·ti) *n.* **1,** (sensory or mental perception) sensibilidad; susceptibilidad. **2,** *usu. pl.* (refined feelings) sentimientos delicados.

sensible ('sɛn·sə·bəl) *adj.* **1,** (perceptible to the senses or the intellect) sensible. **2,** (aware; cognizant) susceptible; sabedor; conocedor. **3,**

(reasonable) razonable; sensato. **4,** (capable of sensation) sensitivo.

sensitive ('sɛn·sə·tɪv) *adj.* **1,** (pert. to the senses) sensitivo; sensorio. **2,** (capable of receiving sensations; responsive; easily hurt) sensitivo; sensible; susceptible. —**sensitiveness; sensitivity** (-'tɪv·ə·ti) *n.* sensibilidad; susceptibilidad.

sensitize ('sɛn·sə,taiz) *v.t.* sensibilizar.

sensor ('sɛn·sər) *n.* sensor.

sensory ('sɛn·sə·ri) *adj.* sensorio.

sensual ('sɛn·ʃu·əl) *adj.* sensual. —**sensualism,** *n.* sensualismo. —**sensualist,** *n.* sensualista. —**sensualistic,** *adj.* sensualista. —**sensuality** (-'æl·ə·ti) *n.* sensualidad.

sensuous ('sɛn·ʃu·əs) *adj.* sensual; voluptuoso. —**sensuousness,** *n.* sensualidad.

sentence ('sɛn·təns) *n.* **1,** (group of words) frase; oración. **2,** *law* sentencia. —*v.t.* sentenciar; condenar.

sententious (sɛn'tɛn·ʃəs) *adj.* sentencioso.

sentient ('sɛn·ʃənt) *adj.* consciente; sensible; sensitivo. —**sentience,** *n.* consciencia; sensibilidad.

sentiment ('sɛn·tə·mənt) *n.* sentimiento. —**sentimental** (-'mɛn·təl) *adj.* sentimental. —**sentimentalism,** *n.* sentimentalismo. —**sentimentalist,** *n.* sentimental. —**sentimentality** (-mɛn'tæl·ə·ti) *n.* sentimentalismo.

sentinel ('sɛn·tə·nəl) *n.* centinela.

sentry ('sɛn·tri) *n.* centinela. —**sentry box,** garita de centinela.

sepal ('si·pəl) *n.* sépalo.

separate ('sɛp·ə,reit) *v.t.* separar; dividir. —*v.i.* separarse; dividirse. —*adj.* (-ət) separado; suelto. —**separable** (-ər·ə·bəl) *adj.* separable. —**separation** (-'rei·ʃən) *n.* separación. —**separator** (-rei·tər) *n.* separador.

separatism ('sɛp·ə·rə,tɪz·əm) *n.* separatismo. —**separatist** (-,rə·tɪst) *adj. & n.* separatista.

sepia ('si·pi·ə) *n. & adj.* sepia.

sepoy ('si·pɔi) *n.* cipayo.

sepsis ('sɛp·sɪs) *n.* sepsis.

September (sɛp'tɛm·bər) *n.* septiembre; setiembre.

septet (sɛp'tɛt) *n.* **1,** (group of seven) grupo de siete. **2,** *mus.* septeto.

septic ('sɛp·tɪk) *adj.* séptico.

septillion (sɛp'tɪl·jən) *n. U.S.* un millón de trillones; cuatrillón; *Brit.* un millón de sextillones; septillón.

septuagenarian (,sɛp·tʃu·ə·dʒə'nɛr·i·ən) *adj. & n.* septuagenario.

Septuagesima (,sɛp·tʃu·ə'dʒɛs·ə·mə) *n.* septuagésima.

septum ('sɛp·təm) *n.* [*pl.* **-ta** (-tə)] septo.

septuple ('sɛp·tju·pəl) *adj. & n.* séptuplo. —*v.t.* septuplicar. —*v.i.* septuplicarse.

sepulcher *también,* **sepulchre** ('sɛp·əl·kər) *n.* sepulcro. —**sepulchral** (sə'pʌl·krəl) *adj.* sepulcral.

sequel ('si·kwəl) *n.* 1, (continuation) continuación; secuencia. 2, (aftermath) secuela; resultado; consecuencia.

sequence ('si·kwəns) *n.* 1, (succession) secuencia; sucesión. 2, (order of succession) orden; sucesión. 3, (series) serie; secuencia. 4, *cards* escalera. 5, *motion pictures; mus.; eccles.* secuencia. —**sequent**, *adj.* consecuente. —*n.* consecuencia. —**sequential** (sɪ'kwɛn·ʃəl) *adj.* consecutivo.

sequester (sɪ'kwɛs·tər) *v.t.* 1, (put aside) apartar; separar. 2, *law* (confiscate) secuestrar.

sequestration (,si·kwɛs'trei·ʃən) *n.* 1, (seclusion; separation) reclusión; separación; apartamiento. 2, *law* (confiscation) secuestro.

sequin ('si·kwɪn) *n.* lentejuela.

sequoia (sɪ'kwɔi·ə) *n.* secoya.

seraglio (sɪ'ræl·jo) *n.* serrallo.

serape (sɛ'ra·pi) *n.* sarape.

seraph ('sɛr·əf) *n.* [*pl.* **seraphim** (-ə·fɪm) o **seraphs**] serafín. —**seraphic** (sə'ræf·ɪk) *adj.* seráfico.

Serb (sʌrb) *n. & adj.* servio. *También,* **Serbian** ('sʌr·bi·ən).

Serbo-Croatian (,sʌr·bo·kro'ei·ʃən) *adj. & n.* servocroata.

sere (sɪr) *adj.* marchito; mustio; seco.

serenade (,sɛr·ə'neid) *n.* serenata. —*v.t. & i.* dar serenata (a).

serendipity (,sɛr·ən'dɪp·ə·ti) *n.* supuesta capacidad de hacer hallazgos fortuitos.

serene (sə'ri·n) *adj.* sereno. —**serenity** (sə'rɛn·ə·ti); **sereneness**, *n.* serenidad.

serf (sʌrf) *n.* siervo. —**serfdom**, *n.* servidumbre.

serge (sʌrdʒ) *n.* sarga.

sergeant ('sar·dʒənt) *n.* 1, (non-

commissioned officer) sargento. 2, (court officer) alguacil. —**sergeant-at-arms**, oficial del orden.

serial ('sɪr·i·əl) *adj.* por entregas. —*n.* serial; obra por series o entregas.

serialize ('sɪr·i·ə,laiz) *v.t.* publicar por entregas; *radio; TV* emitir por series.

serially ('sɪr·i·ə·li) *adv.* 1, (in series) en serie; por series. 2, (in installments) por entregas.

series ('sɪr·iz) *n. sing. & pl.* serie.

serious ('sɪr·i·əs) *adj.* serio; grave. —**seriously**, *adv.* en serio. —**seriousness**, *n.* seriedad; gravedad.

sermon ('sʌr·mən) *n.* sermón. —**sermonize**, *v.t. & i.* predicar; sermonear.

serous ('sɪr·əs) *adj.* seroso. —**serosity** (sɪ'ras·ə·ti) *n.* serosidad.

serpent ('sʌr·pənt) *n.* serpiente. —**serpentine** (-pən,tin; -,tain) *adj.* serpentino. —*n., mineral:* serpentina.

serrate ('sɛr·it) *adj.* serrado; dentado. *También,* **serrated** (-ei·tɪd) —**serration** (sɛ'rei·ʃən) *n.* endentadura.

serried ('sɛr·id) *adj.* apretado.

serum ('sɪr·əm) *n.* suero.

servant ('sʌr·vənt) *n.* sirviente; criado; *fem.* sirvienta; criada.

serve (sʌrv) *v.t.* 1, (do services for; aid; be sufficient for; avail) servir. 2, [*usu.* **serve for**] (be a substitute for) reemplazar; sustituir. 3, *law* (give a summons, writ, etc., to) notificar; citar; entregar viva citación a. 4, (go through or spend, as time in service, in prison, etc.) cumplir; servir. 5, *sports* servir. 6, (cover, as animals) cubrir. 7, (supply) abastecer; proveer; suplir. —*v.i.* 1, (act as a servant; perform service) servir. 2, (suffice) bastar; ser suficiente. 3, (be suitable or convenient) servir (de o para). 4, *sports* servir. —*n., sports* saque; servicio. —**serve one right**, estar uno bien servido; merecérselo uno: *(It) serves him right,* Se lo merece; (Está) bien servido.

server ('sʌr·vər) *n.* 1, (servant) criado; servidor. 2, (waiter) mozo. 3, (tray) bandeja.

service ('sʌr·vɪs) *n.* 1, (act or result of serving; duty performed; services supplied) servicio. 2, (religious devotions) servicios; oficios religiosos. 3, (set, as of dishes) juego; servicio. **4,** *law* entrega. —**serviceable,** *adj.* servible; útil; duradero. —**service station,** puesto de servicio.

serviceman *n.* [*pl.* **-men**] **1,** *mil.* militar. **2,** (repairman) mecánico. *También,* **service-man; service man.**

serviette (ˌsʌr·vi'ɛt) *n.* servilleta.

servile ('sʌr·vɪl) *adj.* servil. —**servility** (sʌr'vɪl·ə·ti) *n.* servilismo.

serving ('sʌr·vɪŋ) *n.* porción.

servitude ('sʌr·vɪˌtud) *n.* servidumbre; esclavitud.

sesame ('sɛs·ə·mi) *n.* sésamo; ajonjolí.

session ('sɛʃ·ən) *n.* **1,** (assembly) sesión. **2,** (school term) período escolar.

sestet (sɛs'tɛt) *n.* sexteto.

set (sɛt) *v.t.* [**set, setting**] **1,** (put; place) poner; colocar. **2,** (fix) fijar; armar; instalar. **3,** (establish) establecer. **4,** (determine) fijar; determinar. **5,** (adjust) ajustar; arreglar. **6,** (start) comenzar; introducir; establecer. **7,** (mount, as a gem) engastar; montar. **8,** (adapt to music) poner música a; poner letra a. **9,** *print.* componer. **10,** (cause to hatch) poner a empollar. —*v.i.* **1,** (sink; settle) hundirse; declinar. **2,** (disappear below the horizon) ponerse. **3,** (become firm or hard) cuajarse; endurecerse. **4,** (tend) inclinarse. **5,** (fit) sentar; caer. **6,** (brood, as a hen) empollar. —*n.* **1,** (collection) colección; juego. **2,** (group of persons) pandilla; camarilla; compañía. **3,** *theat.* (scenery) decorados; decoración. **4,** (hardening) endurecimiento. **5,** (tendency) inclinación; dirección. **6,** *mech.* (system of interrelated parts) tren. **7,** *sports* partida. **8,** (transmitting or receiving device) aparato. —*adj.* **1,** (placed) colocado; puesto. **2,** (fixed) fijo; firme. **3,** (adjusted) arreglado; ajustado. **4,** (determined; prescribed) determinado; decidido; resuelto. **5,** *colloq.* (ready) preparado; dispuesto. —**set about to,** ponerse a. —**set apart,** separar; apartar. —**set aside, 1,** (reserve; store) guardar; reservar. **2,** (annul) anular; abrogar. **3,** (reject) rechazar; desechar. —**set back, 1,** (retard) detener; retrasar. **2,** (reverse) hacer retroceder. **3,** *colloq.* (cost; cause the loss of) costar.

—**set down, 1,** (put in place) poner; colocar; instalar. **2,** (lay down; rest) acostar; descansar. **3,** (alight) aterrizar; bajar; apearse. **4,** (attribute) atribuir. **5,** (put in writing) poner por escrito. —**set fire to; set afire,** pegar fuego a. —**set forth, 1,** (state; express) exponer; expresar. **2,** (exhibit) disponer; exhibir. **3,** (start out) ponerse en camino. —**set in, 1,** (begin) empezar; comenzar; aparecer. **2,** (blow or flow toward shore) soplar o fluir hacia tierra. —**set off, 1,** (cause to start) dar ímpetu a; excitar; animar. **2,** (put in relief; accentuate) poner de relieve; realzar; destacar. **3,** (depart) salir; partir. **4,** (detonate) hacer estallar o saltar. **5,** (adorn; embellish) adornar; embellecer. **6,** (separate) separar; apartar. —**set on, 1,** (incite) azuzar; incitar. **2,** (attack) atacar; acometer; asaltar. —**set out, 1,** (limit; mark out) demarcar. **2,** (display; arrange) disponer. **3,** (start) ponerse en camino. —**set out to,** proponerse (hacer); ponerse a. —**set up, 1,** (raise) levantar; alzar. **2,** (elevate; exalt) ensalzar. **3,** (set in a vertical position) enderezar. **4,** (construct) erigir; construir. **5,** (establish) establecer; instituir. **6,** (install) instalar. **7,** (start; undertake) comenzar; emprender. **8,** (fit out) armar; montar. —**set up shop,** poner tienda. —**set upon, 1,** (attack) atacar; acometer; asaltar. **2,** (incite to attack, as a dog) azuzar.

setback ('sɛt·bæk) *n.* **1,** (reverse) revés; contrariedad. **2,** *archit.* retraqueo.

settee (sɛ'tiː) *n.* canapé; sofá pequeño.

setter ('sɛt·ər) *n.* **1,** (dog) perro perdiguero. **2,** *print.* compositor.

setting ('sɛt·ɪŋ) *n.* **1,** (environment) local; sitio; ambiente. **2,** (stage scenery) escena; decoración. **3,** (mounting for jewelry) montadura; engaste. **4,** (disappearance below the horizon) puesta; ocaso.

settle ('sɛt·əl) *v.t.* **1,** (put in order) arreglar; ordenar; componer. **2,** (establish; decide) decidir; fijar; determinar. **3,** (adjust, as a dispute) arreglar; moderar; calmar. **4,** (colonize) colonizar; poblar. **5,** (clear of dregs) aclarar; clarificar. **6,** (pay, as a bill) cancelar; saldar; pagar. —*v.i.* **1,** (become fixed) fijarse; asentarse; posarse. **2,** (establish a permanent residence) establecerse; fijar residencia; arraigar. **3,** (become clear) clarificarse; sedimentarse. **4,** (sink) hundirse; caer. **5,** (decide) determinarse; decidirse. **6,** (arrange) arreglarse; conformarse. —*n.* banco largo, usu. de madera. —**settle down to,** ponerse a. —**settle on,** decidirse en; escoger.

settlement ('sɛt·əl·mənt) *n.* **1,** (adjustment) arreglo; ajuste. **2,** (payment) cancelación; liquidación; pago. **3,** (small colony) colonia; poblado. **4,** *law* (conveyance of property) traspaso de bienes; (amount of property conveyed) asignación. **5,** (welfare establishment) centro benéfico.

settler ('sɛt·lər) *n.* colonizador.

set-to *n., colloq.* pelea; lucha; contienda.

setup *n.* **1,** (system) sistema; disposición. **2,** (bodily posture) porte; compostura. **3,** *slang* (contest easily won) triunfo fácil. **4,** (elements to be mixed with liquor) ingredientes.

seven ('sɛv·ən) *n. & adj.* siete.

sevenfold ('sɛv·ən,fold) *adj. & n.* séptuplo; siete veces (más). —*adv.* siete veces; en un séptuplo.

seven hundred setecientos. —**seven-hundredth,** *adj. & n.* septingentésimo.

seventeen ('sɛv·ən,tin) *n. & adj.* diecisiete; diez y siete. —**seventeenth,** *adj. & n.* decimoséptimo; diecisieteavo.

seventh ('sɛv·ənθ) *adj.* séptimo. —*n.* séptimo; séptima parte; *mus.* séptima.

seventy ('sɛv·ən·ti) *n. & adj.* setenta. —**seventieth,** *adj. & n.* septuagésimo; setentavo.

sever ('sɛv·ər) *v.t.* **1,** (separate) separar; dividir; desunir. **2,** (break off) cortar; romper.

several ('sɛv·ər·əl) *adj.* **1,** (a small number) varios. **2,** (distinct) distintos; diversos. —*n.* algunos; varios.

severance ('sɛv·ər·əns) *n.* separación; división; ruptura. —**severance pay,** indemnización por despido.

severe (sɪ'vɪr) *adj.* **1,** (stern) severo; austero; duro. **2,** (extreme; intense) riguroso; intenso; extremo; grave.

severity (sɪ'vɛr·ə·ti) *n.* **1,** (sternness) severidad; austeridad. **2,** (intensity) intensidad; fuerza.

sew (soɹ) *v.t. & i.* [*pret.* **sewed;** *p.p.* **sewed** o **sewn**] coser.

sewage ('su·ɪdʒ) *n.* aguas de albañal; aguas sucias.

sewer ('su·ər) *n.* albañal; cloaca. —**sewerage,** *n.* alcantarillado.

sewing ('so·ɪŋ) *n.* costura. —**sewing machine,** máquina de coser.

sewn (soɹn) *v., p.p. de* sew.

sex (sɛks) *n.* sexo. —*adj.* sexual; del sexo. —**sex appeal,** atracción sexual. —**sexless,** *adj.* asexual.

sexagenarian (,sɛk·sə·dʒə'nɛr·i·ən) *adj. & n.* sexagenario.

Sexagesima (,sɛk·sə'dʒɛs·ə·mə) *n.* sexagésima.

sexism ('sɛks·ɪz·əm) *n.* prejuicio contra el sexo opuesto. —**sexist,** *adj. & n.* sexista.

sexpot ('sɛks,pat) *n., colloq.* mujer atractiva y excitante.

sextant ('sɛks·tənt) *n.* **1,** *math.* sexta parte del círculo. **2,** *naut.* sextante.

sextet *también,* **sextette** (sɛks'tɛt) *n.* **1,** (group of six) grupo de seis. **2,** *mus.* sexteto.

sextillion (sɛks'tɪl·jən) *n. U.S.* mil trillones; *Brit.* un millón de quintillones; sextillón.

sexton ('sɛks·tən) *n.* sacristán.

sextuple ('sɛks·tju·pəl) *adj. & n.* séxtuplo. —*v.t.* sextuplicar. —*v.i.* sextuplicarse.

sexual ('sɛk·ʃu·əl) *adj.* sexual. —**sexuality** (-'æl·ə·ti) *n.* sexualidad. —**sexual intercourse,** coito.

sexy ('sɛks·i) *adj., slang* sexual; apetecible; incitante. —**sexiness,** *n.* atracción sexual.

shabbiness ('ʃæb·i·nəs) *n.* **1,** (seediness) desaseo; estado andrajoso. **2,** (meanness) ruindad.

shabby ('ʃæb·i) *adj.* **1,** (seedy) andrajoso; desastrado. **2,** (much worn) raído; usado. **3,** (mean) bajo; ruín.

shack (ʃæk) *n.* cabaña; choza. —**shack up** (with), *slang* cohabitar (con).

shackle ('ʃæk·əl) *n.* **1,** (fetter) grillo; grillete. **2,** (coupling device) traba. **3,** (bar of a padlock) barra; cadena. —*v.t.* **1,** (chain) poner grillos o grilletes a; encadenar. **2,** (hamper) impedir; poner trabas a; estorbar.

shad (ʃæd) *n.* sábalo.

shaddock ('ʃæd·ək) *n.* pamplemusa.

shade (ʃeid) *n.* **1,** (darkness; dark area) sombra. **2,** (trace; degree) matiz; sombra; grado. **3,** (ghost) fantasma; sombra. **4,** (screen, as for a lamp) pantalla. **5,** (covering for a window) visillo; cortina. **6,** (visor; eyeshade) visera. **7,** (gradation of color) matiz; rasgo; gradación. —*v.t.* **1,** (screen from light) resguardar; proteger. **2,** (obscure) obscurecer; sombrear. **3,** (add shading to) sombrear. —*v.i.* cambiar o variar gradualmente.

shading ('ʃei·dɪŋ) *n.* **1,** (slight difference) matiz; tinte; tono. **2,** (application of shade) sombreado.

shadow ('ʃæd·o) *n.* sombra. —*v.t.* **1,** (shade) obscurecer; sombrear. **2,** (cloud) ensombrecer; nublar. **3,** (trail) seguir como sombra. **4,** (add shading to) sombrear; dar sombreado a.

shadowy ('ʃæd·o·i) *adj.* **1,** (without reality) indefinido; vago. **2,** (shaded) sombreado; umbroso.

shady ('ʃei·di) *adj.* **1,** (giving shade; full of shade) sombrío; umbroso. **2,** (concealed; secret) obscuro; tenebroso. **3,** *colloq.* (of questionable character) sospechoso; dudoso. —**shadiness,** *n.* obscuridad; tenebrosidad.

shaft (ʃæft) *n.* **1,** (long cylindrical stem, as of an arrow) astil. **2,** (arrow; dart) flecha; dardo. **3,** (handle) mango. **4,** (bar transmitting motion) árbol; eje. **5,** (passage, as in a mine or for an elevator) pozo. **6,** (bolt; ray; beam) rayo. **7,** *archit.* (body of a column) fuste. **8,** (pole for attaching harness) limonera; vara. **9,** (flagpole) asta.

shag (ʃæg) *v.t.* poner o hacer áspero. —*n.* felpa; lana áspera.

shaggy ('ʃæg·i) *adj.* **1,** (having rough hair) hirsuto; velludo. **2,** (unkempt) tosco; rudo. —**shagginess,** *n.* aspereza; tosquedad.

Shah (ʃɑ) *n.* cha.

shake (ʃeik) *v.t.* [**shook, shaken, shaking**] **1,** (cause to vibrate; agitate) sacudir; estremecer; agitar. **2,** (weaken) debilitar; flaquear. **3,** (upset; disturb) perturbar; inquietar. **4,** (cause to doubt or waver) hacer vacilar. **5,** (clasp, as the hand, in greeting) estrechar; apretar. **6,** *slang* (get rid of) deshacerse de; zafarse de. —*v.i.* **1,** (be agitated) agitarse; sacudirse. **2,** (tremble) temblar; vibrar. **3,** (totter; toddle) titubear.

—*n.* **1,** (agitation) sacudida; sacudimiento; agitación. **2,** (vibration) vibración; temblor. **3,** (tottering) titubeo. **4,** *pl.* (chills) escalofrío de la fiebre intermitente. **5,** *colloq.* (instant) instante; momentito. **6,** (a shaken drink, as a milk shake) batido. —**no great shakes,** *colloq.* de poca monta. —**shake down, 1,** (bring down by shaking) sacudir; zafar; bajar sacudiendo. **2,** (cause to settle by shaking) hacer depositar. **3,** (put through performance trials) probar; poner a prueba. **4,** *slang* (extort money from) chantajear; extorsionar dinero a.

shakedown ('ʃeik,daun) *n.* **1,** (makeshift bed) cama improvisada. **2,** (performance trial) prueba. **3,** *slang* (extortion) concusión; extorsión; chantaje.

shaken ('ʃei·kən) *v., p.p. de* **shake.**

shaker ('ʃei·kər) *n.* **1,** (agitator) agitador. **2,** (container for sprinkling) espolvoreador. **3,** *cap., relig.* miembro de una secta religiosa.

shakeup ('ʃeik·ʌp) *n.* **1,** (reorganization) reorganización. **2,** (disturbance) conmoción; perturbación.

shako ('ʃei·ko) *n.* [*pl.* -os] chacó.

shaky ('ʃei·ki) *adj.* **1,** (trembling) tembloroso; trémulo. **2,** (wavering) vacilante. **3,** (doubtful) dudoso. **4,** (wobbly) cojo.

shale (ʃeil) *n.* pizarra.

shall (ʃæl) *v.aux.* [*pret.* **should**] **1,** *forma los tiempos futuros en la primera persona: I shall die,* moriré. **2,** *expresa determinación, obligación o necesidad en segunda y tercera personas: he shall die,* morirá; que muera; tiene que morir; *thou shalt not steal,* no hurtarás.

shallop ('ʃæl·əp) *n.* chalupa.

shallot (ʃə'lat) *n.* chalote; ascalonia.

shallow ('ʃæl·o) *adj.* bajo; poco profundo; *fig.* superficial. —*n.* bajío; bajo.

shalt (ʃælt) *v., arcaico, segunda pers. del sing. del pres. de ind. de* **shall.**

sham (ʃæm) *adj.* fingido; simulado; falso. —*n.* fingimiento; impostura; farsa. —*v.i. & t.* [**shammed, shamming**] simular; fingir.

shaman ('ʃa·mən) *n.* chamán. —**shamanism,** *n.* chamanismo.

shamble ('ʃæm·bəl) *v.i.* andar bamboleándose; andar arrastrando los pies; vacilar. —*n.* **1,** (shambling walk) bamboleo; paso vacilante. **2,** *pl.* (slaughterhouse) matadero; degolladero. **3,** (scene of destruction) tumulto; devastación.

shame (ʃeim) *n.* **1,** (remorseful consciousness of guilt) remordimiento de culpabilidad. **2,** (disgrace; dishonor) deshonra; ignominia; oprobio. **3,** (modesty; shyness) vergüenza; bochorno; modestia. **4,** (pity; lamentable condition) lástima. —*v.t.* **1,** (make ashamed) avergonzar. **2,** (disgrace) deshonrar; afrentar. **3,** (to embarrass) abochornar.

shamefaced (ˈʃeim,feist) *adj.* vergonzado; vergonzoso; tímido. —**shamefacedness** (-ˈfei·sɪd·nəs) *n.* pudor; timidez; vergüenza.

shameful (ˈʃeim-fəl) *adj.* **1,** (modest; shy) vergonzoso. **2,** (infamous; disgraceful) ignominioso; escandaloso. **3,** (indecent) indecente.

shameless (ˈʃeim·ləs) *adj.* desvergonzado; sin vergüenza; descarado. —**shamelessness,** *n.* desvergüenza; descaro.

shampoo (ʃæmˈpuː) *v.t.* dar (un) champú; lavar la cabeza a. —*n.* champú.

shamrock (ˈʃæm,rak) *n.* trébol irlandés.

shank (ʃæŋk) *n.* **1,** *anat.* caña o canilla de la pierna; zanca (de las aves). **2,** *mech.* (shaft) astil; mango; caña. —**ride on shank's mare** o **pony,** ir a pie; ir en coche de San Francisco.

shan't (ʃænt) *contr. de* shall not.

shanty (ˈʃæn·ti) *n.* [*pl.* **-ties**] cabaña; choza.

shape (ʃeip) *n.* **1,** (form; contour) forma; figura; contorno. **2,** (appearance) apariencia; aspecto. **3,** (condition) estado; condición. —*v.t.* **1,** (give form to) formar; dar forma a. **2,** (adapt) arreglar; ajustar. **3,** (express) modelar; tallar; hacer. —*v.i.* formarse; tomar forma; desarrollarse. —**be in bad shape,** *colloq.* estar mal. —**put into shape,** arreglar; poner en orden.

shapeless (ˈʃeip·ləs) *adj.* informe.

shapely (ˈʃeip·li) *adj.* bien formado; bien proporcionado. —**shapeliness,** *n.* buena proporción; belleza.

share (ʃeːr) *n.* **1,** (portion; allotted part) porción; parte. **2,** (unit of corporate stock) acción. **3,** (plow blade) reja. —*v.t.* **1,** (divide; apportion) distribuir; repartir; dividir. **2,** (have or use jointly) compartir; partir; participar de; tomar parte en. —*v.i.* **1,** (partake) participar; tener parte; gozar o disfrutar con otros. **2,** (give a portion to others) repartir; compartir; tener una parte. —**fall to the share of,** tocar a; caer en parte a. —**go shares,** entrar o ir a la parte. —**share alike,** repartir igualmente; tener una parte igual. —**share and share alike,** por igual; por partes iguales.

sharecropper (ˈʃer,krap·ər) *n.* aparcero. —**sharecropping,** *n.* aparcería.

shareholder (ˈʃer,hol·dər) *n.* accionista.

shark (ʃark) *n.* **1,** *ichthy.* tiburón. **2,** (predatory person) estafador. **3,** *slang* (expert) perito; experto. —**loan shark,** usurero.

sharkskin (ˈʃark·skɪn) *n.* tejido de algodón de apariencia sedosa, que se usa para trajes.

sharp (ʃarp) *adj.* **1,** (having a fine cutting edge) agudo; cortante; afilado. **2,** (pointed) puntiagudo. **3,** (clear; distinct) claro; distinto; bien marcado. **4,** (abrupt) repentino. **5,** (violent; forceful) violento; fuerte; rudo. **6,** (angular) anguloso. **7,** (pungent) picante; acre; mordaz. **8,** (acute; shrill) agudo; penetrante. **9,** (clever) astuto; listo; vivo. **10,** (barely honest) dudoso; sospechoso. **11,** *mus.* sostenido. —*adv.* **1,** (sharply) agudamente. **2,** (quickly) vivamente. **3,** (exactly) exactamente; precisamente; en punto. —*n.* **1,** *mus.* sostenido. **2,** (cheat) estafador; fullero. **3,** *colloq.* (expert) perito.

sharpen (ˈʃar·pən) *v.t. & i.* **1,** (put on a cutting edge) afilar; amolar. **2,** (put a point on) sacar punta a. **3,** (make more acute) aguzar; sutilizar.

sharpener (ˈʃar·pən·ər) *n.* amolador; afilador. —**pencil sharpener,** cortalápiz; sacapuntas.

sharper (ˈʃar·pər) *n.* **1,** (cheat) tahur; fullero. **2,** (swindler) estafador; trampista.

sharpness (ˈʃarp·nəs) *n.* **1,** (cutting or piercing quality; acuteness) agudeza. **2,** (clearness) claridad. **3,** (pungency) acritud; mordacidad. **4,** (cleverness) astucia; viveza. **5,** (violence) violencia.

sharpshooter (ˈʃarp,ʃu·tər) *n.* tirador certero; tirador experto.

shatter (ˈʃæt·ər) *v.t. & i.* **1,** (break in pieces) hacer(se) añicos; estrellar(se); astillar(se). **2,** (disorder; impair) quebrar(se); romper(se). —**shatters,** *n.pl.* pedazos; trozos; añicos; fragmentos.

shatterproof (ˈʃæt·ər,pruf) *adj.* inastillable.

shave (ʃeiv) *v.t.* **1,** (slice with a keen instrument) rasurar; afeitar; raer. **2,** (make bare) rapar. **3,** (cut down gradually, as with a plane) cepillar. **4,** (come very close to) raspar; rozar. —*v.i.* rasurarse; afeitarse. —*n.* rasura; *Amer.* afeitada. —**have a close shave,** *colloq.* **1,** por poco no escaparse. **2,** salvarse por milagro.

shaven (ˈʃei·vən) *adj.* afeitado; rasurado. —**clean-shaven,** bien afeitado.

shaver (ˈʃei·vər) *n.* **1,** (barber) barbero. **2,** (device or machine for shaving) máquina de afeitar. **3,** *colloq.* (youngster) jovencito; rapaz.

shaving (ˈʃei·vɪŋ) *n.* **1,** (cutting) afeitado; rasura. **2,** *pl.* (thin slices cut off) cepilladuras; virutas. —**shaving brush,** brocha de afeitar. —**shaving dish,** bacía. —**shaving knife,** navaja de afeitar.

shawl (ʃɔl) *n.* chal; mantón.

she (ʃiː) *pron.pers.* ella. —*adj. & n.* hembra.

sheaf (ʃif) *n.* [*pl.* **sheaves** (ʃiːvz)] **1,** (of grain, hay, etc.) gavilla; haz. **2,** (of papers, currency, etc.) lío; paquete.

shear (ʃir) *v.t.* [*p.p.* **shorn**] **1,** (clip or cut) tonsurar; rapar. **2,** (remove by clipping, as fleece) esquilar; trasquilar. —**shears,** *n.sing. & pl.* tijeras grandes.

she-ass *n.* borrica; burra.

sheath (ʃiθ) *n.* **1,** (case; covering) cubierta; envoltura; manguito; funda. **2,** (scabbard) vaina.

sheathe (ʃiːð) *v.t.* envainar; enfundar; poner vaina, funda o cubierta a.

she-cat *n.* gata.

shed (ʃɛd) *v.t.* **1,** (molt) mudar. **2,** (emit; throw off) echar; emitir; arrojar. **3,** (cause to flow off) verter; derramar. **4,** (disperse, as light) esparcir; difundir; dar; echar. **5,** (get rid of) deshacerse de; desprenderse de. —*v.i.* pelechar. —*n.* cobertizo; tinglado; colgadizo.

she'd (ʃid) *contr. de* **she would** o **she had.**

she-devil *n.* diabla.

sheen (ʃiːn) *n.* lustre; viso; resplandor.

sheep (ʃip) *n.sing. & pl.* **1,** (ewe) oveja. **2,** (ram) carnero. **3,** (timid person) papanatas; simplón.

sheep dog perro de pastor.

sheepfold (ˈʃip,fold) *n.* redil; aprisco. *También,* **sheepcote** (-,kot).

sheepish (ˈʃip·ɪʃ) *adj.* avergonzado; corrido; encogido.

sheepskin (ˈʃip·skɪn) *n.* **1,** (sheep's fur) zalea. **2,** (cured skin of a sheep) badana. **3,** (parchment) pergamino. **4,** *colloq.* (diploma) diploma (de pergamino).

sheer (ʃir) *adj.* **1,** (very thin; diaphanous) ligero; fino; delgado; diáfano; transparente. **2,** (unmixed; absolute) puro; claro; completo; cabal. **3,** (precipitous) escarpado. —*adv.* **1,** (absolutely; quite) puramente; claramente; cabalmente. **2,** (steeply) escarpadamente. —*v.i.* [*usu.,* **sheer off**] alargarse; desviarse. —*n.* **1,** (swerve; deviation) desviación. **2,** (thin, light material) tela fina y transparente.

sheet (ʃit) *n.* **1,** (cloth; bedding) sábana. **2,** (flat, thin piece) hoja. **3,** (newspaper) periódico; diario. **4,** (expanse or surface, as of ice or water) extensión. **5,** (rope fastened to a sail) escota.

sheeting (ˈʃit·ɪŋ) *n.* **1,** (material for bedsheets) lencería para sábanas. **2,** (thin plates, as of metal) laminado.

she-goat *n.* cabra.

sheik (ʃik) *n.* **1,** (Arab chief) jeque. **2,** *slang* (bold lover) tenorio; don Juan; galán.

shekel (ˈʃɛk·əl) *n.* siclo. —**shekels,** *n.pl., slang* dinero.

shelf (ʃɛlf) *n.* [*pl.* **shelves**] **1,** (horizontal support) anaquel; estante. **2,** (ledge) repisa. **3,** (outcropping of rock) escalón de roca; saliente de roca. **4,** (reef) arrecife; escollo. **5,** (sand bar) bajío; banco de arena.

shell (ʃɛl) *n.* **1,** (hard outer case or covering) casco; cubierta; corteza. **2,** (nutshell; eggshell) cáscara. **3,** (sea shell) concha; caracol. **4,** (covering of crustaceans and insects) caparazón. **5,** (turtle shell) carapacho; coraza. **6,** (vegetable pod) vaina; vainilla. **7,** (framework) armazón; esqueleto. **8,** (hull of a ship) casco. **9,** (projectile) bomba; proyectil. **10,** (cartridge) cápsula; cartucho. **11,** (long, narrow rowboat used for racing) bote largo y angosto que se usa para regatas. —*v.t.* **1,** (remove or take out of the shell) descascarar; descortezar; desvainar; desgranar. **2,** (bombard) bombardear. —**shell game,** estafa que se efectúa con tres cáscaras de nuez y un guisante escondido debajo de una de ellas. —**shell out,** *slang* entregar; sacar. —**shell shock,** neurosis de guerra.

she'll (ʃil) *contr. de* **she will** o **she shall.**

shellac (ʃəˈlæk) *n.* laca; goma laca. —*v.t.* barnizar con laca.

shellfish (ˈʃelˌfɪʃ) *n.* marisco; mariscos.

shelter (ˈʃel·tər) *n.* **1,** (covering; protection) abrigo; amparo; resguardo; protección. **2,** (refuge) refugio; asilo. **3,** (lodging) hospedaje; alojamiento; albergue. —*v.t.* **1,** (cover; protect) abrigar; amparar; resguardar; proteger. **2,** (house) hospedar; alojar.

shelve (ʃelv) *v.t.* **1,** (put on a shelf) poner o guardar en un estante. **2,** (put aside; put off) arrinconar; poner a un lado; diferir. —*v.i.* inclinarse.

shelves (ʃelvz) *n., pl. de* **shelf.**

shelving (ˈʃel·vɪŋ) *n.* **1,** (set of shelves) estantería; anaquelería. **2,** (material for shelves) material para estantes o anaqueles.

shenanigans (ʃəˈnæn·ə·gənz) *n.pl., colloq.* travesuras; bromas; tonterías.

shepherd (ˈʃep·ərd) *n.* pastor. —*adj.* pastoril; del pastor. —*v.t.* pastorear. —**shepherdess,** *n.* pastora. —**shepherd dog,** perro de pastor.

sherbet (ˈʃɑr·bət) *n.* sorbete.

sheriff (ˈʃer·ɪf) *n.* alguacil mayor; oficial de justicia de un condado inglés o norteamericano.

sherry (ˈʃer·i) *n.* jerez; vino de Jerez.

she's (ʃiːz) *contr. de* **she is** o **she has.**

shibboleth (ˈʃɪb·ə·lεθ) *n.* contraseña; palabra que sirve de santo y seña.

shield (ʃiːld) *n.* **1,** (armor) escudo; broquel. **2,** (protection) amparo; égida; patrocinio. **3,** (protector) protector; defensor. **4,** (for the armpit) sobaquera. **5,** (escutcheon) escudo de armas. —*v.t.* escudar; amparar; resguardar; proteger.

shield-bearer *n.* escudero.

shift (ʃɪft) *v.t.* **1,** (transfer) trasladar; transferir. **2,** (change) cambiar; mudar; desviar. —*v.i.* **1,** (change place, position, direction, etc.) desviarse; mudarse; trasladarse; transferirse. **2,** (alter) alterar; cambiar. **3,** [*también,* **make shift**] (get along) ingeniarse; darse maña; componérselas. —*n.* **1,** (change; turning) cambio; desviación. **2,** (group of workmen) tanda de obreros. **3,** (work period) tarea; turno. **4,** (expedient; resource) expediente; suplente. —**shiftless,** *adj.* negligente; descuidado. —**shifty,** *adj.* furtivo; falso.

shill (ʃɪl) *n., slang* cómplice.

shillelagh (ʃəˈlei·li) *n.* cachiporra irlandesa.

shilling (ˈʃɪl·ɪŋ) *n.* chelín.

shilly-shally (ˈʃɪl·iˈʃæl·i) *v.i.* estar irresoluto; vacilar; roncear. —*adj.* irresoluto; roncero. —*adv.* irresolutamente. —**shilly-shallying,** *n.* vacilación; irresolución; roncería.

shim (ʃɪm) *n.* calce. —*v.t.* calzar.

shimmer (ˈʃɪm·ər) *v.i.* brillar con luz trémula; resplandecer. —*n.* luz trémula; débil resplandor. —**shimmery,** *adj.* resplandeciente.

shimmy (ˈʃɪm·i) *n.* **1,** (abnormal vibration) vibración anormal. **2,** (jazz dance) baile norteamericano muy animado. **3,** *colloq.* (chemise) camisa de mujer.

shin (ʃɪn) *n.* espinilla. —*v.t. & i.* [**shinned, shinning**] trepar.

shinbone (ˈʃɪnˌbon) *n.* espinilla; tibia.

shindig (ˈʃɪn·dɪg) *n., slang* fiesta; juerga; parranda.

shine (ʃain) *v.t.* **1,** (polish; brighten) pulir; bruñir; dar brillo a. **2,** [*pret. & p.p.* **shone**] (point or direct, as a light) dirigir; echar (una luz). —*v.i.* [*pret. & p.p.* **shone**] **1,** (glow) lucir; brillar; resplandecer. **2,** (excel) sobresalir; destacarse; distinguirse. —*n.* **1,** (luster) resplandor; brillo; lustre. **2,** (fair weather) claridad; buen tiempo. **3,** (polishing, as of shoes) lustre; *Mex.* bola.

shiner (ˈʃai·nər) *n.* **1,** (minnow) pececillo de la familia de la carpa. **2,** *slang* (black eye) ojo morado.

shingle (ˈʃɪŋ·gəl) *n.* **1,** (roof covering) tablita de madera, pizarra, asbesto, etc., usada como teja. **2,** (closely bobbed hair) pelo corto. **3,** (small signboard) muestra; letrero; rótulo. **4,** (gravelly beach) playa guijarrosa.

shingles ('ʃɪŋ·gəlz) *n.sing. o pl., pathol.* zona.

shining ('ʃai·nɪŋ) *adj.* brillante; resplandeciente. —*n.* brillo; resplandor.

shinny ('ʃɪn·i) *n.* juego de niños parecido al hockey. —*v.i.* trepar.

Shinto ('ʃɪn·to) *n.* sintoísmo. —*adj.* sintoísta. —**Shintoism,** *n.* sintoísmo. —**Shintoist,** *adj. & n.* sintoísta.

shiny ('ʃai·ni) *adj.* brillante; resplandeciente.

ship (ʃɪp) *n.* **1,** (large vessel) barco; buque; bajel; nave; navío. **2,** (aircraft) aeronave; avión. —*v.t.* [**shipped, shipping**] **1,** (put or take on board) embarcar; poner a bordo. **2,** (send; transport) despachar; enviar; remesar; transportar. —*v.i.* **1,** (embark) embarcarse; ir a bordo. **2,** (enlist as a sailor) alistarse como marino; engancharse como marinero.

shipboard ('ʃɪp,bord) *n.* bordo. —**on shipboard,** a bordo.

shipbuilder ('ʃɪp,bɪl·dər) *n.* constructor de buques; ingeniero naval.

shipbuilding ('ʃɪp,bɪl·dɪŋ) *n.* construcción naval.

shipload ('ʃɪp,lod) *n.* cargamento; cargazón.

shipmaster ('ʃɪp,mæs·tər) *n.* patrón; capitán de buque.

shipmate ('ʃɪp,meit) *n.* camarada de a bordo.

shipment ('ʃɪp·mənt) *n.* **1,** (act or result of shipping) embarque; cargamento; expedición; partida. **2,** (quantity of goods shipped) despacho; envío; remesa.

shipowner ('ʃɪp,o·nər) *n.* naviero.

shipper ('ʃɪp·ər) *n.* exportador [*fem.* -dora]; expedidor [*fem.* -dora]; remitente.

shipping ('ʃɪp·ɪŋ) *n.* **1,** (the business of transporting goods) embarque; expedición. **2,** (ships collectively) barcos; buques; marina; flota. —**shipping agent,** consignatario de buques. —**shipping clerk,** dependiente encargado de embarques; dependiente de muelle.

ship's carpenter carpintero de ribera.

shipshape ('ʃɪp,ʃeip) *adj.* bien arreglado; en buen orden.

shipwreck ('ʃɪp,rɛk) *n.* **1,** (sinking or destruction of a ship) naufragio. **2,** *fig.* (ruin) desastre; desgracia; ruina. —*v.t.* echar a pique; hacer naufragar. —*v.i.* irse a pique; naufragar. —**be shipwrecked,** naufragar.

shipwright ('ʃɪp,rait) *n.* carpintero de ribera; constructor de buques.

shipyard ('ʃɪp,jard) *n.* astillero.

shire (ʃair) *n.* condado.

shirk (ʃʌrk) *v.t.* evadir; evitar; faltar a. —*v.i.* remolonear; faltar (a su deber, al trabajo, etc.). —**shirker,** *n.* el que se evade de hacer algo.

shirr (ʃʌr) *v.t.* **1,** *sewing* fruncir. **2,** *cooking* cocer (huevos) en el horno con pan rallado. —*n., sewing* frunce.

shirt (ʃʌrt) *n.* camisa. —**in shirt sleeves,** en camisa; en mangas de camisa. **keep one's shirt on,** *slang,* tener calma; tener paciencia.

shirting ('ʃʌr·tɪŋ) *n.* tela para camisas.

shirtmaker ('ʃʌrt,mei·kər) *n.* camisero.

shirttail ('ʃʌrt,teil) *n.* faldón; pañal.

shirtwaist ('ʃʌrt,weist) *n.* blusa de mujer.

shiver ('ʃɪv·ər) *v.i.* **1,** (tremble, as with cold or fear) temblar; estremecerse; tiritar. **2,** (shatter) estrellarse; hacerse añicos. —*v.t.* romper de un golpe; estrellar; hacer añicos. —*n.* **1,** (tremor) temblor; estremecimiento. **2,** (chill) escalofrío; tiritón. **3,** (fragment) añico; trozo; fragmento.

shivery ('ʃɪv·ə·ri) *adj.* **1,** (trembling with cold or fear) estremecido; trémulo. **2,** (susceptible to cold) friolento. **3,** (causing shivers) frío. **4,** (easily shattered) quebradizo.

shoal (ʃoːl) *n.* **1,** (sandbank) bajío; bajo; banco de arena. **2,** (large body of fish) cardumen; banco. **3,** (crowd) muchedumbre. —*adj.* bajo; poco profundo.

shoat (ʃot) *n.* cochinillo; lechón.

shock (ʃak) *n.* **1,** (violent impact) choque; golpe. **2,** (sudden fear) susto. **3,** (surprise) sorpresa; sobresalto. **4,** (prostration; stroke) choque; postración nerviosa. **5,** (jolt of electricity) sacudida eléctrica. **6,** (earth tremor) temblor de tierra. **7,** (sheaf of grain) gavilla; haz. **8,** (thick mass, as of hair) greña; mechón. —*v.t.* **1,** (affect violently) chocar; sacudir. **2,** (surprise) sorprender; asustar; sobresaltar. **3,** (outrage) ultrajar; afrentar; escandalizar. **4,** (stack, as grain) hacinar; hacer gavillas (de mieses). —**shock absorber,** amortiguador. —**shock therapy,** tratamiento por electrochoques. —**shock troops,** tropas de asalto. —**shock wave,** onda de choque.

shocking ('ʃak·ɪŋ) *adj.* chocante; espantoso; escandaloso.

shod (ʃad) *v., pret. & p.p. de* shoe.

shoddy ('ʃad·i) *n.* **1,** (low quality fabric; anything inferior) lana artificial o regenerada; material inferior. **2,** (sham) imitación; impostura; farsa. —*adj.* **1,** (inferior) de pacotilla; inferior. **2,** (sham; false) falso; fingido; simulado.

shoe (ʃuː) *n.* **1,** (footwear) zapato. **2,** (horseshoe) herradura. **3,** (outer covering) cubierta. **4,** (tire) llanta. **5,** (curved part of a brake, anchor, etc.) zapata. **6,** (runner, as of a sled) suela. —*v.t.* [*pret. & p.p.* shod] calzar; herrar (un caballo); enllantar (una rueda). —**be in someone's shoes,** hallarse en el pellejo de uno. —**shoe blacking,** betún para zapatos. —**shoe polish,** betún. —**shoe store,** zapatería; tienda de calzado.

shoehorn ('ʃu,horn) *n.* calzador.

shoelace ('ʃu,leis) *n.* cordón o lazo de zapato.

shoemaker ('ʃu,mei·kər) *n.* zapatero.

shoeshine ('ʃu,ʃain) *n.* brillo; lustre; *Mex.* bola.

shoestring ('ʃu,strɪŋ) *n.* **1,** = shoelace. **2,** (small amount of capital) muy poco dinero; poco capital.

shoetree ('ʃu,tri) *n.* horma para zapato.

shone (ʃoʊn) *v., pret. & p.p. de* shine.

shoo (ʃuː) *interj.* ¡fuera! —*v.t.* ahuyentar. —**shoo-in,** *n.* candidato o contendiente con máxima probabilidad de ganar.

shook (ʃuk) *v., pret. de* shake.

shoot (ʃut) *v.t.* [*pret. & p.p.* shot] **1,** (hit, kill or wound with a missile from a weapon) matar o herir con arma de fuego o arma arrojadiza. **2,**

(discharge, as a weapon) descargar; disparar; tirar; hacer fuego con. **3,** (execute by shooting) fusilar. **4,** (send out or forth) arrojar; echar; lanzar. **5,** (traverse rapidly) atravesar; pasar rápidamente. **6,** (take a picture of) fotografiar; tomar. **7,** (produce, as a motion picture) rodar; filmar. **8,** (throw, as dice) echar (los dados); jugar a (los dados). —*v.i.* **1,** (discharge a missile) tirar; hacer fuego. **2,** (hunt) cazar; ir de caza. **3,** (dart forth or along) arrojarse; abalanzarse; precipitarse. **4,** (be emitted) brotar; salir. **5,** (sprout) brotar; crecer. **6,** [*usu.* shoot up] (grow rapidly) crecer a palmos; espigarse. —*n.* **1,** (act of shooting; shooting competition) tiro; tiro al blanco. **2,** (shooting party) partida de caza. **3,** (sprout) botón; renuevo; retoño; vástago. —*interj., slang* ¡caramba!; ¡cuernos! —**shootout,** *n.* tiroteo.

shooting ('ʃu·tɪŋ) *n.* **1,** (firing of weapons) tiro; fuego; fusilería. **2,** (hunt) caza con escopeta. **3,** (filming) rodaje. —**shooting gallery,** galería de tiro. —**shooting iron,** *slang,* arma de fuego. —**shooting match,** certamen de tiradores. —**shooting pain,** punzada; dolor agudo. —**shooting star,** estrella fugaz.

shop (ʃap) *n.* **1,** (store) tienda. **2,** (workroom; factory) taller; fábrica. —*v.i.* [**shopped, shopping**] comprar; ir de compras; hacer compras. —**talk shop,** hablar de negocios.

shopkeeper ('ʃap,ki·pər) *n.* tendero.

shoplift ('ʃap,lɪft) *v.t. & i.* robar (mercancías). —**shoplifter,** *n.* ladrón de tiendas. —**shoplifting,** *n.* ratería en las tiendas.

shopper ('ʃap·ər) *n.* comprador [*fem.* -dora].

shopping ('ʃap·ɪŋ) *n.* **1,** (buying) acto de ir a las tiendas o de hacer compras. **2,** (collection of things bought) compras; recado. —**shopping district,** barrio comercial.

shopwindow ('ʃap,wɪn·do) *n.* aparador; escaparate; vitrina.

shopworn ('ʃap,worn) *adj.* deteriorado por haber estado expuesto en la tienda.

shore (ʃor) *n.* **1,** (land adjacent to water) costa; orilla; ribera. **2,** (beach) playa. **3,** (prop; support) puntal. —*v.t.* [*also,* shore up] apuntalar; poner puntales a. —**shoring**, *n.* apuntalamiento; puntales. —**shore leave**, permiso para ir a tierra.

shoreward ('ʃor·wərd) *adj. & adv.* hacia la costa.

shorn (ʃorn) *v., p.p. de* **shear**.

short (ʃort) *adj.* **1**, (not long; not tall) corto; bajo; pequeño; chico. **2**, (brief; concise) breve; conciso; sucinto. **3**, (deficient) inadecuado; escaso; limitado. **4**, (crumbling readily, as pastry) que se desmigaja fácilmente. **5**, (curt) áspero; brusco; seco; corto. —*adv.* **1**, (briefly) brevemente; en breve. **2**, (abruptly) bruscamente; rudamente. **3**, (insufficiently) insuficientemente; escasamente. —*n.* **1**, (short film) película de corto metraje. **2**, *pl.* (short trousers or drawers) calzoncillos; shorts. **3**, *elect.* corto circuito. —*v.t., elect.* poner en corto circuito. —**cut short**, interrumpir; cortarle (a uno) la palabra. —**fall short**, faltar; escasear. —**fall short of**, no alcanzar a; no llegar a. —**for short**, para abreviar. —**in short**, en suma; en resumen; brevemente. —**in short order**, en seguida. —**on short notice**, con poco aviso. —**run short of**, acabársele o írsele acabando a uno algo. —**short cut**, atajo. —**short of**, **1**, (inadequately supplied with) escaso de. **2**, (except for; but for) fuera de. **3**, (far from; removed from) lejos de. —**short shrift**, despedida brusca. —**stop short**, parar en seco. —**the long and short of it**, en resumen; en resumidas cuentas.

shortage ('ʃor·tɪdʒ) *n.* **1**, (scarcity) escasez; carestía. **2**, (lack) falta. **3**, (deficit) déficit.

short allowance media ración.

shortbread ('ʃort,brɛd) *n.* mantecado.

shortcake ('ʃort,keik) *n.* torta de frutas.

short-change *v.t., colloq.* **1**, (give inadequate change to) defraudar al dar el vuelto. **2**, *fig.* (cheat) engañar; estafar.

short circuit corto circuito. —**short-circuit**, *v.t.* poner en corto circuito. —*v.i.* ponerse en corto circuito.

shortcoming (ʃort'kʌm·ɪŋ) *n.* defecto; deficiencia.

shorten ('ʃor·tən) *v.t.* **1**, (reduce in length) acortar; recortar. **2**,

(abridge) abreviar; compendiar; resumir. **3**, (add shortening to) poner grasa o manteca a; hacer quebradiza (la pastelería).

shortening ('ʃor·tən·ɪŋ) *n.* **1**, (reduction in length) acortamiento. **2**, (abbreviation) abreviación. **3**, (fat or grease used in making pastry) grasa; manteca; mantequilla.

shortfall ('ʃort,fɔl) *n.* déficit.

shorthand ('ʃort,hænd) *n.* estenografía; taquigrafía. —*adj.* estenográfico; taquigráfico.

shorthanded (ʃort,hæn·dɪd) *adj.* escaso de mano de obra; escaso de obreros.

shortlived ('ʃort,laivd) *adj.* corto de vida; pasajero.

shortly ('ʃort·li) *adv.* **1**, (briefly) brevemente; en breve. **2**, (soon) pronto; luego. **3**, (abruptly) en seco; de repente. **4**, (curtly) bruscamente.

shortness ('ʃort·nəs) *n.* **1**, (brevity) cortedad; brevedad. **2**, (small stature) pequeñez. **3**, (scarcity; lack) escasez; falta.

shortsighted ('ʃort,sait·ɪd) *adj.* **1**, (nearsighted) miope; corto de vista. **2**, (lacking foresight; not provident) falto de perspicacia; impróvido.

shortsightedness (-nəs) *n.* **1**, (nearsightedness) miopía; cortedad de vista. **2**, (lack of foresight) falta de perspicacia; improvidencia.

shortstop ('ʃort·stap) *n.* beisbolero colocado entre las segunda y tercera bases.

short story cuento; historieta.

short-term *adj.* a corto plazo.

short ton tonelada corta o menor *(2,000 libras)*.

short wave onda corta. —**short-wave**, *adj.* de onda corta.

short-winded ('ʃort,wɪn·dɪd) *adj.* asmático; corto de respiración.

shorty ('ʃor·ti) *n., colloq.* bajete.

shot (ʃat) *n.* **1**, (act of shooting) tiro; disparo. **2**, (impact of a missile) balazo; cañonazo; escopetazo. **3**, (small pellets) balas; perdigones; munición. **4**, (range) alcance; tiro. **5**, (one who shoots) tirador. **6**, *games* (move; stroke) jugada; turno; tirada. **7**, *slang* (attempt) tentativa. **8**, *slang* (guess) conjetura. **9**, *slang* (drink; swallow) trago; *Amer.* palo. **10**, (snapshot) instantánea; foto. **11**, *sports* (weight used for throwing) peso. —*v., pret. & p.p. de* **shoot**. —**not by a long shot**, *colloq.* ni por asomo; ni con mucho; ni por pienso. —**put the shot,** tirar o lanzar el peso. —**shot through with,** lleno de; acribillado de. —**take a shot at,** *slang,* **1,** (fire at) disparar un tiro a. **2,** (attempt) hacer una tentativa de. **3,** (guess) adivinar; conjeturar.

shotgun (ˈʃatˌgʌn) *n.* escopeta.

shot-put *n.* tiro o lanzamiento del peso.

should (ʃud) *v. aux.* **1,** *pret. de* **shall. 2,** *forma los tiempos condicionales en la primera persona: I should buy it if I had enough money,* Lo compraría si tuviera bastante dinero. **3,** *expresa obligación, necesidad o expectación en todas las personas: We should help him,* Debiéramos ayudarlo.

shoulder (ˈʃol·dər) *n.* **1,** *anat.* hombro; espalda. **2,** (cut of meat) brazuelo; cuarto delantero. **3,** (ledge) borde; capa. **4,** (the unpaved side of a road) borde; saliente. —*v.t. & i.* **1,** (to carry on or as on the shoulder) echar(se) a la espalda; cargar al hombro; llevar a hombros. **2,** *fig.* (take responsibility for) asumir; cargar con; tomar sobre sí. **3,** (push with the shoulder) codear; meter el hombro; empujar con el hombro. —**give the cold shoulder,** tratar o recibir fríamente; no hacerle caso a uno; negarse a recibirle a uno. —**shoulder arms,** *mil.* armas al hombro. —**shoulder belt,** tahalí. —**shoulder bone** o **blade,** escápula; omóplato. —**straight from the shoulder,** con toda franqueza.

shout (ʃaut) *v.t. & i.* (cry out) gritar; vocear. —*n.* grito; alarido; voz. —**shout acclaim,** aclamar; dar vivas; vitorear. —**shout down,** silbar.

shouting (ˈʃau·tɪŋ) *n.* gritería; vocerío; aclamación.

shove (ʃʌv) *v.t. & i.* **1,** (push along) empujar; hacer avanzar; dar empellones. **2,** (jostle) codear. —*n.* empujón; empellón. —**shove off, 1,** (move away from the shore) alejar(se); hacerse a la mar. **2,** *slang* (leave) irse; marcharse; salir.

shovel (ˈʃʌv·əl) *n.* pala. —*v.t. & i.* palear.

show (ʃo) *v.t.* [*p.p.* **shown** o **showed**] **1,** (allow to be seen; exhibit) mostrar; enseñar; exhibir; exponer; descubrir. **2,** (point out; indicate) indicar; señalar. **3,** (instruct; explain) enseñar; explicar. **4,**

(guide; lead) guiar; conducir. **5,** (prove; demonstrate) probar; demostrar. **6,** (exhibit, as a film) exhibir. **7,** (project, as a film) proyectar; pasar. **8,** (perform, as a play) representar; actuar. —*v.i.* **1,** (be seen; appear) mostrarse; aparecer; asomar. **2,** (be revealed) descubrirse; dejarse ver; manifestarse. **3,** *racing* terminar tercero. **4,** (be exhibited, as a film) exhibirse. **5,** (be performed, as a play) representarse. —*n.* **1,** (spectacle) espectáculo. **2,** (theatrical performance) función; espectáculo; representación. **3,** (exhibition) exposición; exhibición. **4,** (ostentatious display) boato; gala; pompa; ostentación. **5,** *colloq.* (chance) suerte; oportunidad; lance. **6,** (indication; outward sign) indicación; manifestación; señal. **7,** (outward appearance) apariencia; exterior. —**in open show,** públicamente. —**make a good show,** hacer gran papel. —**make a show of,** hacer gala de. —**show off, 1,** (reveal; exhibit) dejar ver; descubrir; exhibir. **2,** (behave ostentatiously) lucirse; jactarse; pavonearse; darse ínfulas. —**show up, 1,** (expose) descubrir; exponer; desenmascarar. **2,** (appear) aparecer; presentarse; dejarse ver. **3,** *colloq.* (arrive) llegar. **4,** *colloq.* (outdo; excel over) superar; aventajar.

show bill cartel; cartelón.

showboat (ˈʃoˌbot) *n.* barco teatro.

showcase (ˈʃoˌkeis) *n.* vitrina; escaparate.

showdown (ˈʃo·daun) *n.* prueba decisiva.

shower (ˈʃau·ər) *n.* **1,** (light rain; spray) lluvia; rociada. **2,** (downpour) aguacero; chaparrón. **3,** (a large number) abundancia; copia; lluvia; rociada. **4,** (bestowal of gifts, as to a bride) tertulia para obsequiar a una novia. **5,** (shower bath) ducha. —*v.t.* **1,** (wet copiously) mojar; regar. **2,** (bestow or scatter abundantly) derramar con abundancia; rociar. —*v.i.* **1,** (rain) llover; caer un aguacero; chaparrear. **2,** (take a shower bath) bañarse en la ducha. —**showery,** *adj.* lluvioso.

showing (ˈʃo·ɪŋ) *n.* **1,** (display) exposición. **2,** (performance) presentación.

showman (ˈʃo·mən) *n.* [*pl.* **-men**] empresario; director de espectáculos. —**showmanship,** *n.* calidad o habilidad de empresario.

shown (ʃoːn) *v., p.p. de* **show.**

show-off *n.* fanfarrón; jactancioso.

showroom ('ʃoˌrum) *n.* sala de exhibición.

show window escaparate o ventana de tienda; vitrina.

showy ('ʃoˑi) *adj.* 1, (imposing) lujoso; suntuoso; magnífico. 2, (gaudy) ostentoso; aparatoso; vistoso; llamativo. —**showiness,** *n.* esplendor; ostentación; magnificencia.

shrank (ʃræŋk) *v., pret. de* **shrink.**

shrapnel ('ʃræp·nəl) *n.* granada de metralla.

shred (ʃred) *v.t.* [**shredded, -ding**] desmenuzar; hacer tiras o trizas. —*n.* 1, (small strip) tira; jirón; andrajo. 2, (particle) fragmento; partícula; pizca. —**in shreds,** andrajoso; raído.

shrew (ʃruː) *n.* 1, (a scolding woman) arpía; mujer regañona. 2, (animal) musaraña. —**shrewish,** *adj.* malhumorado; regañón; regañador.

shrewd (ʃruːd) *adj.* astuto; sutil; perspicaz; listo; vivo. —**shrewdness,** *n.* sutileza; perspicacia; astucia.

shriek (ʃrik) *n.* grito agudo; chillido. —*v.t. & i.* chillar; gritar.

shrift (ʃrɪft) *n.* confesión; absolución. —**make short shrift of,** terminar en seguida; acabar pronto con.

shrike (ʃraik) *n.* alcaudón.

shrill (ʃrɪl) *adj.* penetrante; agudo; chillón. —*v.t. & i.* chillar. —**shrillness,** *n.* agudeza.

shrimp (ʃrɪmp) *n.* 1, (crustacean) camarón. 2, *colloq.* (small person) hombrecillo; renacuajo; bajete.

shrine (ʃrain) *n.* altar; santuario; relicario; sepulcro de santo.

shrink (ʃrɪŋk) *v.i.* [**shrank, shrunk, shrinking**] 1, (contract; diminish; shrivel) contraerse; disminuir; estrecharse; encogerse. 2, (draw back; recoil) retirarse. —*v.t.* encoger; contraer. —*n., slang* psiquiatra. —**shrinkage,** *n.* contracción; disminución; encogimiento.

shrive (ʃraiv) *v.t.* [**shrived** o **shrove, shriven**] confesar. —*v.i.* confesarse.

shrivel ('ʃrɪv·əl) *v.t. & i.* arru-

gar(se); fruncir(se); encoger(se); marchitar(se).

shriven ('ʃrɪv·ən) *v., p.p. de* **shrive.**

shroud (ʃraud) *n.* 1, (burial cloth) mortaja; sudario. 2, (cover; screen; envelope) cubierta; velo. 3, *pl., naut.* (strong guy ropes) obenques. —*v.t.* 1, (wrap for burial) amortajar. 2, (cover; conceal) cubrir; ocultar.

shrove (ʃroːv) *v., pret. de* **shrive.**

Shrove Tuesday martes de carnaval.

shrub (ʃrʌb) *n.* arbusto; mata. —**shrubbery,** *n.* arbustos.

shrug (ʃrʌg) *v.t.* [**shrugged, shrugging**] encoger; contraer. —*v.i.* encogerse de hombros. —*n.* encogimiento de hombros.

shrunk (ʃrʌŋk) *v., p.p. de* **shrink.**

shrunken ('ʃrʌŋk·ən) *adj.* 1, (contracted in size) encogido. 2, (shriveled) marchito; seco.

shuck (ʃʌk) *n.* 1, (husk or pod, as of corn) hollejo; vaina; cáscara. 2, (oyster or clam shell) concha. —*v.t.* deshollejar; descascarar; descortezar; pelar; quitar la concha a. —**shucks!,** *interj.* ¡caramba!

shudder ('ʃʌd·ər) *n.* estremecimiento; temblor. —*v.i.* temblar de miedo o de horror; estremecerse.

shuffle ('ʃʌf·əl) *v.t. & i.* 1, (scrape, as the feet) arrastrar (los pies). 2, (mix, as cards) barajar; mezclar. 3, (shift; change about) cambiar; mudar; remover. —*n.* 1, (scraping of the feet) arrastre de los pies. 2, (mixing of cards) barajadura. 3, (shift; change) cambio; mudanza; movimiento. 4, (ruse) evasiva. —**shuffle off,** deshacerse de; zafarse de.

shuffleboard ('ʃʌf·əlˌbord) *n.* juego de tejo.

shun (ʃʌn) *v.t. & i.* [**shunned, shunning**] apartarse (de); evitar; esquivar; huir; rehuir.

shunt (ʃʌnt) *v.t.* 1, (turn aside) apartar; desviar. 2, *R.R.* (shift, as a train) desviar. 3, *elect.* derivar; poner en derivación. —*n.* 1, (turning aside; shifting) desviación. 2, *R.R.* aguja; cambio de vía; desvío. 3, *elect.* derivación; (device for shunting) derivador. —**shunt off,** eludir; evadir; echarle a uno el muerto.

shush! (ʃʌʃ) *interj.* ¡chito! —*v.t.* hacer callar.

shut (ʃʌt) *v.t.* 1, (close) cerrar. 2,

(cover; put a lid on) tapar. **3**, (fold up) plegar; doblar. —*v.i.* cerrarse. —*adj.* cerrado. —**shut down, 1**, (close) cerrar(se). **2**, (cease functioning) parar. —**shut in**, encerrar. —**shut off, 1**, (enclose) encerrar. **2**, (isolate) aislar. **3**, (cut the flow or supply of) cortar. —**shut out, 1**, (exclude) excluir; prohibir o impedir la entrada a. **2**, *sports* (prevent from scoring) no permitir (a un equipo) ganar tantos. —**shut up, 1**, (close) cerrar; tapar. **2**, (confine) encerrar. **3**, (imprison) aprisionar; encarcelar. **4**, (silence) hacer callar; callar la boca a. **5**, (be silent) callarse.

shut-down *n.* cesación de trabajo.

shut-eye *n.*, *colloq.* sueño; siesta.

shut-in *n.* inválido recluido.

shut-off *n.* **1**, (valve) válvula. **2**, (stoppage) cierre.

shut-out *n.* **1**, (lockout) paro. **2**, *sports* triunfo en que el equipo vencido no gana ningún tanto.

shutter ('ʃʌt·ər) *n.* **1**, (person or thing that closes) cerrador. **2**, (of a window) postigo; contraventana. **3**, (of a store) cierre de escaparate. **4**, *photog.* obturador.

shuttle ('ʃʌt·əl) *n.* **1**, *weaving* lanzadera. **2**, *R.R.* tren que hace viajes cortos de ida y vuelta. **3**, *(aerospace)* transbordador espacial. —*v.i.* ir y venir a cortos intervalos. —*v.t.* transportar a cortos intervalos.

shuttlecock ('ʃʌt·əl·kak) *n.* volante.

shy (ʃai) *adj.* **1**, (bashful; timid) vergonzoso; tímido. **2**, (easily frightened) asustadizo. **3**, (cautious; wary) cauteloso; prudente; recatado. **4**, (scant; short) escaso (de). —*v.i.* **1**, (start back in fear) asustarse; espantarse. **2**, (evade) esquivarse. **3**, (recoil) retroceder. **4**, (rear, as a horse) respingar. **5**, (veer off) desviarse; apartarse. —*v.t.* (throw) lanzar; arrojar. —*n.* **1**, (start; fright) salto; sobresalto. **2**, (rearing, as of a horse) respingo. **3**, (throw) lance; arrojada.

shylock ('ʃai·lak) *n.* usurero.

shyness ('ʃai·nəs) *n.* timidez; reserva; recato.

shyster ('ʃai·stər) *n.*, *colloq.* picapleitos; leguleyo; abogadillo tramposo.

si (si) *n.*, *mus.* si.

Siamese (ˌsai·ə'miːz) *adj.* & *n.* siamés.

sibilant ('sɪb·ə·lənt) *adj.* & *n.* sibilante.

sibling ('sɪb·lɪŋ) *n.* hermano o hermana. —*adj.* emparentado.

sibyl ('sɪb·ɪl) *n.* sibila.

sic (sɪk) *v.t.* [**sicked, sicking**] **1**, (attack) atacar; asaltar. **2**, (set upon, as a dog) azuzar. —*adv., print.* exactamente como está, aunque erróneo.

sick (sɪk) *adj.* **1**, (ill) enfermo; malo. **2**, (nauseated) nauseado. **3**, (depressed) alicaído; desanimado; deprimido. **4**, (disgusted) ultrajado; enfadado. —*n.* los enfermos. —*v.t.* = sic. —**sick of**, cansado de; harto de. —**take sick**, caer enfermo.

sick bay enfermería (de a bordo).

sickbed ('sɪk,bɛd) *n.* lecho de enfermo.

sicken ('sɪk·ən) *v.t.* **1**, (make ill) enfermar. **2**, (disgust) dar asco; nausear. **3**, (weaken) debilitar; extenuar. —*v.i.* **1**, (become ill) enfermarse; caer enfermo. **2**, (be disgusted) tener asco; tener repugnancia. **3**, (be surfeited) cansarse; hartarse. **4**, (weaken) debilitarse. —**sickening,** *adj.* asqueroso; nauseabundo; repugnante.

sickle ('sɪk·əl) *n.* hoz; segadera; segur.

sickly ('sɪk·li) *adj.* **1**, (unhealthy) achacoso; enfermizo. **2**, (mawkish) asqueroso; nauseabundo. **3**, (feeble) enclenque; débil; lánguido. —**sickliness,** *n.* achaque; malestar; enfermedad.

sickness ('sɪk·nəs) *n.* **1**, (illness) enfermedad; mal. **2**, (nausea) náusea; basca.

side (said) *n.* **1**, (terminal surface or line) lado; cara; faz. **2**, (either half, as of a body) costado; lado. **3**, (slope of a hill) falda; ladera. **4**, (point of view) parte; opinión. **5**, (faction) facción; partido. **6**, (water's edge) orilla; margen. **7**, (lateral surface of a ship) banda; bordo; costado. **8**, (point; place; direction) parte; lado. —*adj.* **1**, (lateral) de lado. **2**, (indirect) indirecto; oblicuo. **3**, (incidental) incidental; secundario. —*v.i.* tomar parte; tomar partido. —**by the side of,** al (o por el) lado de. —**on all sides,** por todos lados; por todas partes. —**right side,** *(of a garment, of material, etc.)* cara. —**side against,**

oponerse a; estar contra; declararse contra. —**side with,** estar por; ser partidario de; declararse por. —**split one's sides,** reventarse o desternillarse de risa. —**take sides,** tomar partido. —**wrong side,** *(of a garment, of material, etc.)* revés.

side arms armas de cinto.

sideboard ('said,bord) *n.* aparador.

sideburns ('said,bʌrnz) *n.pl.* patillas.

sidecar ('said,kar) *n.* **1,** (of a motorcycle) cochecillo de lado; sidecar. **2,** (cocktail) sidecar.

side dish plato de entrada.

side glance mirada de soslayo o de través.

side-kick *n., slang* compañero; socio.

sidelight ('said·lait) *n.* **1,** (incidental aspect) noticia o detalle incidental. **2,** (narrow window beside a door) luz lateral.

side line 1, (additional service or merchandise) negocio accesorio; ocupación secundaria. **2,** *sports* (boundary) línea lateral. *También,* **sideline,** *n.* —**sideline,** *v.t.* sacar del juego o de cualquier actividad. —**on the side lines,** fuera del juego o de cualquier actividad; sin participar.

sidelong ('said·lɒŋ) *adj.* de lado; lateral. —*adv.* lateralmente; de lado.

sidereal (sai'dɪr·i·əl) *adj.* estelar; sideral; sidéreo.

sidesaddle ('said,sæd·əl) *n.* silla de montar de mujer. —*adv.* a mujeriegas.

side show función, exhibición, diversión, etc., secundaria.

sideslip ('said,slɪp) *n.* deslizamiento o resbalamiento lateral. —*v.i.* [-slipped, -slipping] deslizar o resbalar lateralmente.

sidesplitting ('said,splɪt·ɪŋ) *adj.* desternillante.

side step 1, (step to the side) paso hacia un lado. **2,** (step or stair located at the side) escalón de lado. —**sidestep,** *v.i.* hacerse a un lado; apartarse; desviarse. —*v.t.* evitar; esquivar.

sidestroke ('said,strok) *n.* brazada de costado.

sideswipe ('said,swaip) *v.t.* golpear o rozar oblicuamente. —*n.* golpe o rozadura dada oblicuamente.

sidetrack ('said·træk) *n.* aparta-

dero; desviadero. —*v.t.* apartar; desviar.

sidewalk ('said·wɔk) *n.* acera; *Mex.* banqueta.

sidewall ('said,wɔl) *n.* flanco (de un neumático).

sideward ('said·wərd) *adj.* lateral; de lado. —*adv.* [*también,* **sidewards**] de lado; de costado.

sideways ('said,weiz) *adj.* oblicuo; sesgado. —*adv.* de lado; al través; oblicuamente. *También,* **sidewise** (-waiz).

side whiskers patillas.

sidewinder ('said,wain·dər) *n.* **1,** (snake) especie de serpiente de cascabel. **2,** *slang* (blow from the side) golpe lateral. **3,** (missile) cohete supersónico.

siding ('sai·dɪŋ) *n.* **1,** *R.R.* apartadero; desviadero. **2,** (of a house) entablado (de los costados).

sidle ('sai·dəl) *v.i.* ir de lado. —*n.* movimiento oblicuo. —**sidle up to** o **against,** acercarse de lado (a una persona o cosa).

siege (si:dʒ) *n.* **1,** *mil.* asedio; cerco; sitio. **2,** (long illness or suffering) enfermedad larga; sufrimiento largo.

sienna (si'ɛn·ə) *n.* tierra de siena; siena.

sierra (si'ɛr·ə) *n.* sierra; cordillera.

siesta (si'ɛs·tə) *n.* siesta. —*v.i.* dormir o echar la siesta; dormitar; sestear.

sieve (sɪv) *n.* tamiz; cedazo; criba.

sift (sɪft) *v.t.* **1,** (pass through a sieve) cerner; cribar; tamizar **2,** (scrutinize) examinar; escudriñar. —**sifter,** *n.* tamiz; cedazo; criba.

sigh (sai) *v.i.* suspirar. —*v.t.* decir suspirando; lamentar. —*n.* suspiro. —**sigh for** o **after,** anhelar; añorar; morirse por.

sight (sait) *n.* **1,** (faculty of vision) vista; visión. **2,** (point of view) concepto; parecer; modo de ver. **3,** (view; glimpse) mirada; vista; vistazo. **4,** (appearance; aspect) apariencia; aspecto. **5,** (something seen) vista; cuadro; espectáculo; escena. **6,** *colloq.* (horror) horror; espantajo; adefesio. **7,** (an aid to aiming) mira. **8,** (aim) puntería. —*v.t.* **1,** (see) avistar; ver con un instrumento. **2,** (aim at) apuntar (una arma) a. —**at sight,** a primera vista; *comm.* a la vista. —**catch sight of,** avistar; vislumbrar. —**come in** (o **into**) **sight,** asomar;

aparecer. —**keep out of sight,** no dejar(se) ver; ocultar(se). —**know by sight,** conocer de vista. —**lose sight of,** perder de vista. —**not by a long sight,** ni por mucho. —**on sight,** a primera vista. —**out of sight,** perdido de vista. —**sight unseen,** sin examinarlo; sin haberlo visto.

sighted ('sai·tɪd) *adj.* que tiene vista; que puede ver.

sightless ('sait·ləs) *adj.* **1,** (blind) ciego. **2,** (invisible) invisible.

sightly ('sait·li) *adj.* bello; hermoso; vistoso.

sightseeing ('sait,si·ɪŋ) *n.* paseo para ver puntos de interés; turismo. —**sightsee,** *v.i., colloq.* hacer turismo; visitar puntos de interés. —**sightseer** ('-'si·ər) *n.* turista.

sign (sain) *n.* **1,** (mark or symbol) marca; signo. **2,** (display board) cartel; tablero; muestra; letrero. **3,** (gesture) señal; indicación. **4,** (symptom) síntoma. **5,** (trace) vestigio; traza; huella; rastro. —*v.t.* **1,** (put one's name to) firmar. **2,** (indicate by a sign) señalar; indicar. **3,** (put under contract) contratar. —*v.i.* firmar. —**sign away** (o **over**), ceder; traspasar (mediante escritura). —**sign off, 1,** *radio; TV* terminar la transmisión. **2,** *slang* (stop talking) callarse. —**sign on,** contratar; contratarse. —**sign up,** inscribirse; alistarse.

signal ('sɪg·nəl) *n.* señal. —*adj.* **1,** (of or for signaling) de señal; de señales. **2,** (notable) insigne; notable; señalado. —*v.t.* señalar. —*v.i.* hacer señales. —**signal code,** código o sistema de señales. —**signal corps,** cuerpo de señales. —**signal light,** fanal; semáforo; faro.

signalize ('sɪg·nə·laiz) *v.t.* señalar; distinguir.

signalman ('sɪg·nəl·mən) *n.* [*pl.* -**men**] hombre encargado de comunicación por señales; *R.R.* guardavía; *mil.* soldado del cuerpo de señales.

signatory ('sɪg·nə·tor·i) *adj. & n.* firmante; signatario.

signature ('sɪg·nə·tjur) *n.* **1,** (name written by oneself) firma. **2,** (distinguishing mark or trait) rúbrica; signatura. **3,** *print.; mus.* signatura.

signboard ('sain,bord) *n.* letrero; muestra.

signer ('sai·nər) *n.* firmante; signatario.

signet ('sɪg·nət) *n.* sello. —**signet ring,** sortija de sello.

significance (sɪg'nɪf·ɪ·kəns) *n.* **1,** (real or implied meaning) significado; significación. **2,** (consequence) consecuencia; importancia. **3,** (expressiveness) expresión; fuerza de expresión; energía. —**significant,** *adj.* significante; significativo; importante.

signify ('sɪg·nɪ,fai) *v.t.* significar. —**signification** (-fɪ'kei·ʃən) *n.* significación; significado; sentido.

signor (si'njor) *n.* [*pl.* -**ri**] señor. *También,* **signore** [*pl.* -**ri**] (-'njo·re). —**signora** [*pl.* -**re**] (-'njo·ra) *n.* señora. —**signorina** [*pl.* -**ne**] (,si·njo'ri·na) *n.* señorita.

signpost ('sain,post) *n.* indicador de dirección; poste de guía.

silage ('sai·lɪdʒ) *n.* ensilaje.

silence ('sai·ləns) *n.* silencio. —*v.t.* silenciar; hacer (o mandar) callar; acallar. —*interj.* ¡chis!; ¡silencio! —**silencer,** *n.* silenciador.

silent ('sai·lənt) *adj.* **1,** (making no sound) silencioso; callado. **2,** (not pronounced) mudo. **3,** (tacit) tácito. —**be silent,** callarse. —**remain silent,** callar; guardar silencio; no chistar. —**silent partner,** socio comanditario.

silhouette (,sɪl·u'ɛt) *n.* silueta. —*v.t.* hacer aparecer en silueta; perfilar.

silica ('sɪl·ə·kə) *n.* sílice. —**silicate** (-ɪ·kət) *n.* silicato. —**siliceous;** **silicious** (sɪ'lɪʃ·əs) *adj.* silíceo.

silicon ('sɪl·ɪ·kən) *n.* silicio.

silicone ('sɪl·ə,kon) *n.* silicón.

silicosis (,sɪl·ɪ'ko·sɪs) *n.* silicosis.

silk (sɪlk) *n.* seda. —*adj.* de seda; sedeño. —**floss silk,** seda floja. —**raw silk,** seda en rama. —**shot silk,** seda tornasolada. —**silk cotton,** seda vegetal. —**waste silk,** borra de seda. —**watered silk,** muaré; seda ondeada.

silken ('sɪlk·ən) *adj.* **1,** (made of silk) de seda. **2,** (resembling silk) sedoso. **3,** (smooth) blando; suave.

silk-stocking *adj.* aristocrático. —*n.* aristócrata.

silkworm ('sɪlk,wʌrm) *n.* gusano de seda.

silky ('sɪlk·i) *adj.* sedoso.

sill (sɪl) *n.* **1,** (of a door) umbral. **2,** (of a window) antepecho.

silly ('sɪl·i) *adj.* **1,** (foolish; witless)

bobo; necio; tonto. **2,** (ridiculous) absurdo; disparatado; insensato. **—silliness,** *n.* bobería; tontería; necedad.

silo ('sai·lo) *n.* silo. —*v.t.* ensilar.

silt (sɪlt) *n.* cieno; aluvión. —*v.t. & i.* obstruir(se) con aluvión.

silver ('sɪl·vər) *n.* **1,** (metal) plata. **2,** (coin or coins; money) plata; moneda de plata. **3,** (color) color plateado; color argentino. **4,** (silverware) vajilla de plata. —*adj.* **1,** (made of silver) de plata. **2,** (silverplated) plateado. **3,** (sonorous, as the voice) argentino; sonoro. —*v.t.* **1,** (plate with silver) platear. **2,** (coat, as a mirror, with mercury) azogar.

silver foil hoja de plata.

silver fox zorro plateado.

silver lining aspecto prometedor en medio de desventuras.

silver plate 1, (coating of silver) plateadura. **2,** (silverware) vajilla de plata —**silver-plated,** *adj.* plateado.

silver screen pantalla cinematográfica.

silversmith ('sɪl·vər͵smɪθ) *n.* platero. —**silversmith's shop,** platería.

silver-tongued *adj.* elocuente.

silverware ('sɪl·vər·wer) *n.* **1,** (sterling silver) vajilla de plata. **2,** (silver plate) vajilla plateada. **3,** (wrought silver) plata labrada.

silvery ('sɪl·və·ri) *adj.* argentino; argénteo.

simian ('sɪm·i·ən) *n.* mono; simio. —*adj.* símico.

similar ('sɪm·ə·lər) *adj.* similar; semejante; parecido.

similarity (͵sɪm·ə'lær·ə·ti) *n.* semejanza.

simile ('sɪm·ə͵li) *n.* comparación; símil.

similitude (sɪ'mɪl·ɪ͵tud) *n.* **1,** (resemblance) similitud; semejanza. **2,** (comparison) comparación.

simmer ('sɪm·ər) *v.t. & i.* hervir o cocer a fuego lento. —*n.* ebullición o cocción lenta. —**simmer down,** *colloq.* tranquilizarse.

simon-pure (͵sai·mən'pjʊr) *adj.* auténtico; genuino; verdadero.

simony ('sai·mə·ni) *n.* simonía.

simoom (sɪ'muːm) *n.* simún. También, **simoon** (-'muːn).

simp (sɪmp) *n., slang* bobo; papamoscas; papanatas.

simper ('sɪm·pər) *v.t. & i.* sonreír afectadamente o bobamente. —*n.* sonrisa afectada.

simple ('sɪm·pəl) *adj.* **1,** (elementary) fácil. **2,** (plain) llano; simple. **3,** (pure; absolute) puro; mero. **4,** (unaffected; unassuming) sencillo; ingenuo; cándido. **5,** (humble) modesto; humilde. **6,** (easily deceived; silly) inocente; bobo; necio; mentecato.

simple-hearted *adj.* cándido; ingenuo.

simple-minded *adj.* **1,** (ingenuous) sencillo; cándido; ingenuo. **2,** (stupid) mentecato; necio; imbécil; estúpido. —**simple-mindedness,** *n.* estupidez; necedad.

simpleton ('sɪm·pəl·tən) *n.* simplón; bobalicón; papanatas.

simplicity (sɪm'plɪs·ə·ti) *n.* **1,** (lack of complexity) simplicidad. **2,** (ingenuousness) sencillez; candor; ingenuidad. **3,** (stupidity) estupidez; necedad.

simplify ('sɪm·plɪ͵fai) *v.t.* simplificar. —**simplification** (-fɪ'kci·ʃən) *n.* simplificación.

simplistic (sɪm'plɪs·tɪk) *adj.* ingenuo; que simplifica demasiado.

simply ('sɪm·pli) *adv.* **1,** (without complexity) simplemente; sencillamente. **2,** (merely; solely) meramente; solamente.

simulacrum (͵sɪm·jə'lei·krəm) *n.* [*pl.* **-cra** (-krə)] simulacro.

simulate ('sɪm·jə͵leit) *v.t.* simular; imitar. —**simulation,** *n.* simulación; imitación.

simultaneous (͵sai·məl'tei·ni·əs) *adj.* simultáneo. —**simultaneity** (-tə'nei·ə·ti); **simultaneousness,** *n.* simultaneidad.

sin (sɪn) *n.* pecado; culpa; transgresión. —*v.i.* [**sinned, sinning**] pecar; errar.

since (sɪns) *adv.* **1,** (from then until now) desde entonces. **2,** (subsequently) después. **3,** (before now; ago) hace; ha: *long since,* hace mucho tiempo; *three months since,* tres meses ha. —*prep.* desde; después de. —*conj.* **1,** (from the time when; during the time after) desde que; despues (de) que. **2,** (because) como; puesto que; ya que; pues; pues que.

sincere (sɪn'sɪr) *adj.* sincero; abierto; franco. —**yours sincerely,** su seguro servidor (*abr.* S.S.S.).

sincerity (sɪn'sɛr·ə·ti) *n.* sinceridad; franqueza.

sine (sain) *n., math.* seno.

sinecure ('sai·nə,kjur) *n.* sinecura.

sinew ('sɪn·ju) *n.* **1,** (tendon) tendón; fibra; nervio. **2,** (strength; vigor) fortaleza; vigor; fibra; nervio.

sinewy ('sɪn·ju·i) *adj.* **1,** (strong; vigorous) fuerte; robusto; vigoroso. **2,** (stringy; fibrous) fibroso; nervudo.

sinful ('sɪn·fəl) *adj.* **1,** (committing sin) pecador. **2,** (motivated by sin) pecaminoso.

sing (sɪŋ) *v.t. & i.* [**sang, sung, singing**] **1,** (utter musically) cantar. **2,** (murmur; whistle) murmurar; silbar. **3,** (warble) gorjear. **4,** (ring, as the ears) zumbar. —*n.* **1,** (singing sound) silbido; zumbido. **2,** (act of singing) canto. —**singable,** *adj.* cantable.

singe (sɪndʒ) *v.t.* [*ger.* **singeing**] chamuscar; socarrar. —*n.* chamusquina; socarra. —**singeing,** *n.* socarra.

singer ('sɪŋ·ər) *n.* cantor (*m.*); cantante (*m. & f.*); cantatriz (*f.*).

Singhalese (,sɪŋ·gə'liz) *adj. & n.* cingalés.

singing ('sɪŋ·ɪŋ) *n.* canto. —*adj.* cantante.

single ('sɪŋ·gəl) *adj.* **1,** (pert. to one; individual) simple; particular; individual. **2,** (alone; detached) distinto; solo; único. **3,** (unmarried) soltero. —*v.t.* [*usu.* **single out**] separar; escoger; singularizar. —*n.* **1,** (that which is single) simple; individuo. **2,** *baseball* batazo de una base. **3,** *pl., tennis* juego de simples. —**singleness,** *n.* unidad; sencillez. —**not a single word,** ni una (sola) palabra. —**single file,** fila india. —**single life,** celibato.

single-breasted *adj.* de un solo pecho; de una sola hilera de botones.

single-handed *adj. & adv.* **1,** (unaided) sin ayuda; solo. **2,** (done with one hand) de o para una mano.

singleminded ('sɪŋ·gəl,main·dɪd) *adj.* resuelto; que tiene un solo propósito —**singlemindedness,** *n.* determinación; resolución.

singleton ('sɪŋ·gəl·tən) *n., cards* única carta de un palo.

single-track *adj.* de una sola vía. —**single-track mind,** mente estrecha; punto de vista muy limitado.

singletree ('sɪŋ·gəl·tri) *n.* balancín.

singly ('sɪŋ·gli) *adv.* **1,** (separately; individually) individualmente; separadamente; a solas. **2,** (one at a time) uno a uno; de uno en uno.

singsong ('sɪŋ,sɒŋ) *adj.* monótono. —*n.* sonsonete; cadencia uniforme.

singular ('sɪŋ·gju·lər) *adj.* **1,** (unusual) raro; extraño; singular. **2,** *gram.* singular. —**singularity** (-'lær·ə·ti) *n.* singularidad; rareza.

sinister ('sɪn·ɪs·tər) *adj.* siniestro.

sink (sɪŋk) *v.i.* [**sank, sunk, sinking**] **1,** (fall; decline) caer; bajar; decaer. **2,** (settle) sentarse. **3,** (become submerged) sumergirse; hundirse; irse a pique o al fondo. **4,** (incline downward) bajar; descender. **5,** (decrease) rebajar; disminuir. —*v.t.* **1,** (force downward) sumergir; hundir. **2,** (cause to submerge) echar a pique. **3,** (place by excavation) excavar; cavar o abrir (un pozo). **4,** (diminish) disminuir; disipar. **5,** (suppress; overwhelm) abatir; sumir; deprimir. **6,** (invest) invertir. **7,** (drive into the ground) enterrar. —*n.* **1,** (basin) fregadero. **2,** (drain; sewer) sumidero; desaguadero. **3,** *fig.* (filthy or corrupt place) sentina. —**sink in; sink into one's mind,** grabarse en la memoria. —**sink one's teeth into,** clavar el diente en.

sinkable ('sɪŋk·ə·bəl) *adj.* hundible; sumergible.

sinker ('sɪŋk·ər) *n., fishing* plomada.

sinking fund fondo de amortización.

sinless ('sɪn·ləs) *adj.* impecable; puro. —**sinlessness,** *n.* impecabilidad.

sinner ('sɪn·ər) *n.* pecador [*fem.* -dora].

sinuous ('sɪn·ju·əs) *adj.* sinuoso. —**sinuosity** (-'ɑs·ə·ti); **sinuousness,** *n.* sinuosidad.

sinus ('sai·nəs) *n.* seno. —**sinusitis** (-nə'sai·tɪs) *n.* sinusitis.

sip (sɪp) *v.t. & i.* [**sipped, sipping**] sorber; chupar. —*n.* sorbo.

siphon ('sai·fən) *n.* sifón. —*v.t.* sacar con sifón.

sipper ('sɪp·ər) *n.* sorbedor.

sir (sʌr) *n.* **1,** (respectful term of address to a man) señor. **2,** *cap.* (title of a knight or baronet) caballero.

sire (sair) *n*. **1,** (father) padre; progenitor. **2,** (address to a sovereign) señor. —*v.t.* engendrar.

siren ('sai·rən) *n*. sirena.

Sirius ('sɪr·i·əs) *n., astron.* Sirio; Canícula.

sirloin ('sʌr·lɔin) *n*. solomillo; solomo.

sirocco (sə'rak·o) *n*. siroco.

sirup ('sɪr·əp) *n*. = **syrup.**

sisal ('sai·səl) *n*. sisal; henequén.

sissy ('sɪs·i) *n., colloq.* adamado; afeminado; maricón.

sister ('sɪs·tər) *n*. hermana. —*adj.* hermano; gemelo.

sisterhood ('sɪs·tər,hud) *n*. **1,** (state or relationship of a sister) hermandad. **2,** (association) cofradía de mujeres; hermandad.

sister-in-law *n*. [*pl.* **sisters-in-law**] cuñada; hermana política.

sisterly ('sɪs·tər·li) *adj.* como corresponde a hermanas; con hermandad; de hermana.

sit (sɪt) *v.i.* [**sat, sitting**] **1,** (be seated; take a seat) sentarse; estar sentado; tomar asiento. **2,** (perch) posarse; encaramarse. **3,** (remain) quedarse; detenerse. **4,** (be in session; convene) reunirse; celebrar junta o sesión. **5,** (be located) estar; quedarse; estar colocado. **6,** (pose, as for a portrait) posar; modelar; servir de modelo; hacerse retratar. —**sit down,** sentarse; estar sentado. —**sit in (on),** tomar parte (en). —**sit out, 1,** (decline to participate) no tomar parte; permanecer sentado. **2,** (stay to the end of) aguantar o quedarse hasta el fin (de). —**sit on** o **upon, 1,** (take part in) tomar parte en. **2,** *slang* (repress) hacer callar; reprimir; reprender. **3,** *slang* (retain; hold) guardar en su poder; no soltar. —**sit still,** estarse quieto; no levantarse. —**sit tight,** *colloq.* mantenerse firme; estar o seguir con sus trece. —**sit up, 1,** (come to a sitting position) levantarse; incorporarse. **2,** (stay awake) velar. —**sit well,** venir, caer, sentar o quedar bien.

sitcom ('sɪt,kam) *n., abr. de* **situation comedy.**

sit-down strike huelga de sentados o de brazos caídos.

site (sait) *n*. local; sitio; lugar.

sit-in *n*. ocupación de un edificio o un sitio en señal de protesta.

sitter ('sɪt·ər) *n*. cuidaniños.

sitting ('sɪt·ɪŋ) *n*. sesión; sentada.

—*adj.* sentado. —**sitting duck,** blanco muy fácil; víctima fácil. —**sitting room,** sala de descanso o de espera; sala de estar; antesala.

situate ('sɪtʃ·ju,eit) *v.t.* situar; colocar; poner. —**situated,** *adj.* situado; colocado; ubicado.

situation (,sɪtʃ·ju'ei·ʃən) *n*. **1,** (location) posición; situación; ubicación. **2,** (condition) situación; condición; estado. **3,** (employment; position) empleo; puesto; colocación; plaza. —**situation comedy,** *radio; TV* programa serial en que los personajes se encuentran en situaciones cómicas.

six (sɪks) *n*. & *adj.* seis. —**at sixes and sevens,** en desorden.

sixfold ('sɪks,fold) *adj.* & *n*. séxtuplo; seis veces (más). —*adv.* seis veces; en un séxtuplo.

six hundred seiscientos. —**six-hundredth,** *adj.* & *n*. sexcentésimo.

sixpence ('sɪks·pəns) *n., Brit.* medio chelín; seis peniques. —**sixpenny,** *adj.* de seis peniques, *fig.* miserable; mezquino.

six-shooter *n., colloq.* revólver de seis tiros.

sixteen (sɪks'tiːn) *n*. & *adj.* dieciséis; diez y seis. —**sixteenth** (-'tinθ) *adj.* & *n*. décimosexto; dieciseisavo.

sixth (sɪksθ) *adj.* sexto. —*n*. sexto; sexta parte; *mus.* sexta. —**sixth sense,** sexto sentido.

sixty ('sɪks·ti) *n*. & *adj.* sesenta. —**sixtieth,** *adj.* & *n*. sexagésimo; sesentavo.

size (saiz) *n*. **1,** (dimensions; bulk) tamaño; dimensiones; magnitud. **2,** (standard measure for shoes, clothes, etc.) número; tamaño; talla; medida. **3,** [*también,* **sizing**] (gluey substance for bonding or glazing) cola de retal o de retazo; apresto; aderezo. —*v.t.* **1,** (estimate) tomar las medidas a; medir. **2,** (apply glaze to) aderezar; sisar; aprestar. —**sizable; sizeable,** *adj.* bastante grande; considerable.

sizzle ('sɪz·əl) *v.i.* chisporrotear; sisear. —*n*. chisporroteo; siseo.

skate (skeit) *n*. **1,** (for gliding on ice) patín; patín de hielo o de cuchilla. **2,** (roller skate) patín de ruedas. **3,** (fish) raya. —*v.i.* patinar. —**skater,** *n*. patinador [*fem.* -dora]. —**skating,** *n*. patinaje.

skateboard ('skeit,bord) *n*. tabla de patinar sobre ruedas.

skedaddle (skɪ'dæd·əl) *v.i., slang* largarse; poner pies en polvorosa.

skein (skein) *n.* madeja.

skeletal ('skɛl·ə·təl) *adj.* 1, (of or pert. to a skeleton) de o del esqueleto. 2, (thin; emaciated) esquelético.

skeleton ('skɛl·ə·tən) *n.* 1, *anat.* esqueleto. 2, (inner framework) armadura; armazón. 3, (outline) esbozo; bosquejo. —*adj.* 1, = **skeletal.** 2, (greatly reduced) reducido. —**skeleton key,** llave maestra.

skeptic ('skɛp·tɪk) *n. & adj.* escéptico. —**skeptical,** *adj.* escéptico.

skepticism ('skɛp·tɪ·sɪz·əm) *n.* escepticismo.

sketch (skɛtʃ) *n.* 1, (rough drawing) croquis; esbozo; boceto; bosquejo; esquicio. 2, (outline; synopsis) esquema; plan; sinopsis; reseña. 3, (short humorous act; skit) burla; parodia; sátira; entremés. —*v.t.* esquiciar; bosquejar; dibujar. —**sketchy,** *adj.* abocetado; bosquejado; esquiciado.

skew (skjuː) *v.i.* andar o moverse oblicuamente; torcerse. —*v.t.* sesgar. —*adj.* sesgado; oblicuo. —*n.* desviación.

skewer ('skju·ər) *n.* brocheta; espetón. —*v.t.* espetar.

ski (skiː) *n.* esquí. —*v.i.* esquiar. —**skier,** *n.* esquiador [*fem.* -dora]. —**skiing,** *n.* equismo; esquí.

skid (skɪd) *n.* 1, (timber or metal band forming a track) rail; riel; carril. 2, (supporting runner) patín. 3, (friction brake) galga. 4, (wooden platform for supporting small loads) calzo. 5, (wooden support for the side of a ship at dock) varadera. 6, (act of skidding) patinaje; resbalón; deslizamiento. —*v.t. & i.* [**skidded,** -**ding**] 1, (slide without rotating) resbalar(se); deslizar(se); patinar. 2, (swerve) desviar(se). —**on the skids,** *slang* fracasado; desventurado. —**skid row** o **road,** barrio de vagabundos y alcohólicos.

skiddoo! (skɪ'duː) *interj., slang* ¡lárgate!

skiff (skɪf) *n.* esquife.

ski lift ascensor funicular para esquiadores.

skill (skɪl) *n.* habilidad; pericia; destreza; maña. —**skilled,** *adj.* experto; hábil; diestro. —**skillful, skilful,** *adj.* experto; de experto.

skillet ('skɪl·ɪt) *n.* 1, (frying pan)

sartén. 2, (long-handled saucepan) cacerola o cazuela pequeña, de mango largo.

skim (skɪm) *v.t.* [**skimmed, -ming**] 1, (lift or scrape off the top of a liquid) desnatar; espumar; rasar. 2, (read superficially) hojear (un libro); leer superficialmente. 3, (glide lightly over) rozar; rasar. —**skim milk,** leche desnatada.

skimmer ('skɪm·ər) *n.* espumadera.

skimp (skɪmp) *v.t. & i.* (scrimp; provide meagerly) escatimar. —*v.i.* 1, (be stingy) ser tacaño. 2, (do carelessly) chapucear. —**skimpy,** *adj.* tacaño; mezquino; escaso.

skin (skɪn) *n.* 1, *anat.* piel; cutis. 2, (pelt) pellejo; cuero. 3, (rind or peel) corteza; cáscara. 4, (container made of skin) pellejo; odre. —*v.t.* [**skinned, skinning**] 1, (remove the skin from; peel) desollar; despellejar; mondar; pelar. 2, *slang* (swindle) engañar; estafar; embaucar. —**be nothing but skin and bones,** estar en los huesos. —**be soaked to the skin,** calarse (o estar calado) hasta los huesos. —**save one's skin,** salvar el pellejo.

skin-deep *adj.* superficial.

skindiver ('skɪn,daɪ·vər) *n.* buzo sin escafandra. —**skindiving,** *n.* buceo sin escafandra.

skinflint ('skɪn·flɪnt) *n.* avaro; tacaño.

skin game fullería; estafa.

skinner ('skɪn·ər) *n.* 1, (one who skins) desollador. 2, (furrier) peletero. 3, (mule driver) mulero.

skinny ('skɪn·i) *adj.* flaco; descarnado. —**skinniness,** *n.* flaqueza.

skin-tight *adj.* ajustado al cuerpo.

skip (skɪp) *v.i.* [**skipped, skipping**] 1, (jump lightly) saltar; brincar. 2, (bounce; ricochet) rebotar. 3, *colloq.* (flee) escaparse. —*v.t.* 1, (jump over) saltar. 2, (pass over; omit) omitir; pasar por alto; saltar. —*n.* 1, (jump) salto; brinco. 2, (omission) omisión. —**skipping rope,** comba.

skipper ('skɪp·ər) *n.* jefe; capitán; patrón (de barco). —*v.t.* patronear (un barco).

skirmish ('skɑr·mɪʃ) *n.* escaramuza. —*v.i.* escaramuzar.

skirt (skɑrt) *n.* 1, (woman's garment) falda; saya. 2, (edge; border) orilla; borde; margen. 3, *slang* (woman) muchacha; mujer; hembra;

pl. faldas. —*v.t. & i.* bordear; ir o pasar por la orilla (de).

skit (skɪt) *n.* burla; sátira; parodia.

skitter ('skɪt·ər) *v.i. & t.* deslizarse saltando; saltar ligeramente.

skittish ('skɪt·ɪʃ) *adj.* 1, (apt to shy) asustadizo. 2, (restless) inconstante; caprichoso. 3, (coy) recatado; tímido.

skulduggery (skʌl'dʌg·ə·ri) *n.* fullería; chanchullo.

skulk (skʌlk) *v.i.* 1, (sneak away) huirse furtivamente; escurrirse; escabullirse. 2, (slink; lurk) rondar; andar a sombra de tejado; ocultarse; acechar. 3, (shirk) remolonear.

skull (skʌl) *n.* calavera; cráneo; casco. —**skull and crossbones**, calavera con dos huesos cruzados *(en la bandera de los piratas y en recipientes de sustancias tóxicas).*

skullcap ('skʌl,kæp) *n.* casquete.

skunk (skʌŋk) *n.* 1, *zoöl.* mofeta. 2, *colloq.* (contemptible person) sinvergüenza; canalla. —*v.t., slang* no permitir (a un equipo) ganar tantos.

sky (skai) *n.* cielo. —**out of a clear (blue) sky,** inesperadamente; de repente.

sky blue azul celeste; cerúleo. —**sky-blue,** *adj.* azul celeste; cerúleo.

skydiving ('skai,dai·vɪŋ) *n.* salto con paracaídas. —**skydive,** *v.i.* lanzarse con paracaídas.

sky-high *adj. & adv.* tan alto como el cielo; por las nubes.

skylark ('skai,lark) *n.* alondra; calandria. —*v.i., colloq.* chacotear; jaranear; calaverear.

skylight ('skai,lait) *n.* claraboya; tragaluz.

skyline ('skai,lain) *n.* 1, (tall buildings seen outlined against the sky) perspectiva (de una ciudad); línea de rascacielos. 2, (visible horizon) línea del horizonte.

sky pilot *slang,* clérigo; capellán.

skyrocket ('skai,rak·ɪt) *n.* cohete; volador. —*v.i.* subir como un cohete.

skyscraper ('skai,skrei·pər) *n.* rascacielos.

skyward ('skai·wərd) *adj. & adv.* hacia el cielo.

skywriting ('skai,rai·tɪŋ) *n.* escritura aérea.

slab (slæb) *n.* 1, (flat stone) losa. 2, (wooden plank) plancha; tabla. 3, (slice) tajada; lonja; loncha.

slack (slæk) *adj.* 1, (loose; lax) flojo; suelto; relajado. 2, (slow; sluggish) lento; tardo. 3, (negligent) descuidado. 4, (inactive) inactivo. —*n.* 1, (slack condition or part) flojedad. 2, (decrease in activity) inactividad.

slacken ('slæk·ən) *v.t.* 1, (loosen) aflojar; soltar; relajar. 2, (retard; check) retardar; detener. —*v.i.* 1, (become loose) aflojarse; soltarse; relajarse. 2, (abate) mermar; menguar. 3, (lessen; fall off) disminuir; rebajar; decaer.

slacker ('slæk·ər) *n.* 1, (lazy person) perezoso; haragán. 2, (shirker) el que esquiva su deber; *mil.* prófugo.

slacks (slæks) *n.pl.* pantalones holgados.

slag (slæg) *n.* escoria.

slain (slein) *v., p.p. de* **slay.**

slake (sleik) *v.t.* 1, (appease) apagar; aplacar; satisfacer. 2, (extinguish) extinguir; apagar. 3, (moderate) moderar; aflojar. 4, (treat with water, as lime) apagar.

slam (slæm) *v.t.* [**slammed, slamming**] 1, (shut noisily) cerrar de golpe. 2, (bang down) dejar caer de golpe. 3, (strike; collide with) chocar con; golpear; dar en. 4, (hurl violently) arrojar; tirar. 5, *slang* (criticize harshly) criticar ásperamente; poner frito. —*v.i.* 1, (shut noisily) cerrarse de golpe. 2, (strike; collide) chocar; dar; dar de golpe. —*n.* 1, (blow; stroke) golpe. 2, (loud closing of a door) portazo. 3, *slang* (criticism) crítica áspera. 4, *cards* bola; bolo; slam. —**slam-bang,** *adv., colloq.* repentinamente.

slander ('slæn·dər) *n.* calumnia; difamación; denigración. —*v.t.* calumniar; difamar; denigrar. —**slanderous,** *adj.* calumnioso; difamatorio.

slang (slæŋ) *n.* jerga; jerigonza; germanía; argot.

slant (slænt) *v.t.* inclinar; sesgar; poner sesgado; dar una dirección oblicua a. —*v.i.* inclinarse; sesgarse; estar o ponerse sesgado. —*n.* 1, (oblique direction or position) declive; inclinación. 2, (bias) sesgo. 3, (point of view) punto de vista; opinión; parecer.

slap (slæp) *v.t.* [**slapped, slapping**] 1, (strike with the open hand or something flat) dar una palmada, manotada o bofetada. 2, (strike;

beat) golpear; pegar; dar en (una cosa); darle a (una persona). 3, (rebuke) castigar; reprender; censurar. —n. 1, (blow with the open hand) palmada; manotada; bofetada. 2, (insult; rebuff) insulto; afrenta. 3, (rebuke) castigo; reprensión; censura. —adv., colloq. 1, (suddenly) de golpe; de repente. 2, (straight; directly) derecho.

slapdash ('slæp,dæʃ) adj. descuidado; chapucero. —adv. de prisa; a lo loco.

slapstick ('slæp,stık) n. comedia burlesca; comedia de payasadas. —adj. burlesco; grosero.

slash (slæʃ) v.t. 1, (hack violently) acuchillar; dar cuchilladas. 2, (make slits in) cortar; acuchillar. 3, (reduce drastically) rebajar fuertemente. —n. 1, (stroke or wound) tajo; tajada; corte; cuchillada. 2, (ornamental slit) corte; cortadura; cuchillada. 3, usu. pl. (swampy tract) fangal; pantano.

slat (slæt) n. tablilla.

slate (sleit) n. 1, (mineral) pizarra; esquisto. 2, (writing tablet) pizarra para escribir. 3, (color) color de pizarra. 4, (list of candidates) lista de candidatos. —v.t. 1, (cover with slate) cubrir de pizarra; empizarrar. 2, (enter as a candidate) poner en candidatura. 3, (destine; single out) destinar; señalar. —a clean slate, las manos limpias. —wipe off the slate; wipe the slate clean, borrar el pasado; empezar de nuevo.

slattern ('slæt·ərn) n. mujer desaliñada. —slatternly, adj. puerco; desaliñado.

slaty ('slei·ti) adj. pizarroso.

slaughter ('slɔ·tər) 1, (killing of animals for food) carnicería; matanza. 2, (massacre; carnage) mortandad; estrago. —v.t. matar.

slaughterhouse ('slɔ·tər,haus) n. matadero; degolladero.

Slav (slaːv) n. & adj. eslavo.

slave (sleiv) n. esclavo; siervo. —v.i. trabajar como esclavo. —slave driver, capataz de esclavos. —slave labor, trabajo de esclavos; trabajadores forzados. —slave trade o traffic, trata o tráfico de esclavos.

slaveholding ('sleiv,hol·dıŋ) n. posesión de esclavos. —adj. manteniendo esclavos. —slaveholder, n. dueño de esclavos.

slaver ('slei·vər) n. 1, (trader in slaves) negrero. 2, (slave ship) barco negrero.

slaver ('slæv·ər) v.i. babear; babosear. —n. baba.

slavery ('slei·və·ri) n. esclavitud; servidumbre.

Slavic ('slav·ık) adj. & n. eslavo.

slavish ('slei·vıʃ) adj. servil; esclavizado.

Slavonic (slə'van·ık) adj. & n. eslavo; esclavón; esclavonio.

slaw (slɔ) n. ensalada de col.

slay (slei) v.t. [slew, slain, slaying] 1, (kill) matar. 2, slang (affect powerfully) emocionar; conmover. —slayer, n. asesino; homicida.

sleazy ('sli·zi; 'slei-) adj. baladí; ligero; flojo.

sled (slɛd) n. trineo; narria. —v.t. [sledded, sledding] llevar en trineo. —v.i. ir o pasearse en trineo. —sledding, n., colloq. camino; paso; manera de llevarse una persona o una cosa.

sledge (slɛdʒ) n. 1, (large sled) trineo; narria. 2, = sledgehammer.

sledgehammer ('slɛdʒ,hæm·ər) n. acotillo.

sleek (slik) adj. 1, (smooth and glossy) liso; alisado. 2, (well groomed) nítido; aseado; acicalado. 3, (suave) artero; mañoso; zalamero. —v.t. alisar; pulir; suavizar. —sleekness, n. lisura; lustre.

sleep (slip) n. sueño. —v.i. [pret. & p.p. slept] dormir. —v.t. 1, (pass, as time, in sleep) pasar durmiendo; malgastar (el tiempo) durmiendo. 2, (accommodate for sleeping) acomodar; caber (para dormir). —fall asleep, dormirse. —go to sleep, dormirse. —last sleep, la muerte. —put to sleep, adormecer; dormir. —sleep in, alojarse (un criado) en casa del dueño. —sleep like a top, dormir como un lirón. —sleep off one's liquor, desollar la zorra; dormir la mona. —sleep on (a problem), consultar con la almohada. —sleep soundly, dormir a pierna suelta; dormir profundamente.

sleeper ('sli·pər) n. 1, (one who sleeps) durmiente. 2, R.R. (sleeping car) coche-cama; coche-dormitorio. 3, R.R. (tie) traviesa; Amer. durmiente. 4, colloq. (unexpected success) triunfo inesperado.

sleepiness ('sli·pi·nəs) n. sueño; modorra; somnolencia.

sleeping ('sli·pıŋ) adj. 1, (in a state of sleep) durmiente. 2, (of or for sleep) de dormir; para dormir. —**sleeping bag,** saco de dormir. —**sleeping car,** coche-cama; coche-dormitorio. —**sleeping pill,** píldora para dormir. —**sleeping sickness,** encefalitis letárgica; enfermedad del sueño.

sleepless ('slip·ləs) *adj.* **1,** (restless; wakeful) desvelado; insomne. **2,** (watchful) despierto; vigilante. —**spend a sleepless night,** pasar la noche en vela.

sleepwalker ('slip,wɔk·ər) *n.* sonámbulo. —**sleepwalk,** *v.i.* padecer sonambulismo. —**sleepwalking,** *n.* sonambulismo.

sleepy ('sli·pi) *adj.* **1,** (drowsy) soñoliento; amodorrado. **2,** (tranquil; quiet) tranquilo. —**be sleepy,** tener sueño.

sleepyhead ('sli·pi,hɛd) *n.* dormilón.

sleet (slit) *n.* cellisca. —*v.i.* cellisquear. —**sleety,** *adj.* cubierto de cellisca; lleno de cellisca.

sleeve (sliɪv) *n.* **1,** (part of a garment) manga. **2,** *mech.* dedal largo; manguito de enchufe.

sleigh (slei) *n.* trineo. —**sleigh bell,** cascabel. —**sleigh ride,** paseo en trineo.

sleight (slait) *n.* **1,** (trick) ardid; artificio; estratagema. **2,** (skill; dexterity) pericia; maña; astucia. —**sleight-of-hand,** *n.* escamoteo; prestidigitación.

slender ('slɛn·dər) *adj.* **1,** (thin) delgado; flaco; tenue. **2,** (scanty) escaso; insuficiente. **3,** (weak) débil; delicado. —**slenderness,** *n.* delgadez.

slenderize ('slɛn·dər,aiz) *v.t. & i.,* *colloq.* adelgazar.

slept (slɛpt) *v.,* *pret. & p.p.* de **sleep.**

sleuth (sluθ) *n.* **1,** *colloq.* (detective) detective. **2,** (bloodhound) sabueso.

slew (sluɹ) **1,** *v.,* *pret.* de **slay. 2,** *v.i.* (veer; twist) virár; torcerse. —*n.* [*también,* **slue**] **1,** (twist) torcimiento. **2,** *colloq.* (great number) multitud; montón.

slice (slais) *n.* **1,** (thin piece) rebanada; tajada; lonja. **2,** (act of cutting) tajada. **3,** *golf* (oblique stroke) golpe dado oblicuamente a la pelota. —*v.t. & i.* rebanar; hacer rebanadas; cortar en lonjas o tajadas. —**slicer,** *n.* rebanador.

slick (slɪk) *adj.* **1,** (sleek) liso;

lustroso. **2,** (ingenious; sly) astuto; mañoso. **3,** (slippery) resbaladizo. —*n.* **1,** (smooth patch) punto liso y lustroso. **2,** (magazine printed on coated paper) revista de papel liso. —*v.t.* alisar; pulir; acicalar.

slicker ('slɪk·ər) *n.* **1,** (oilskin coat) impermeable. **2,** *colloq.* (sly fellow; swindler) estafador; trampista.

slide (slaid) *v.i.* [*pret. & p.p.* **slid**] **1,** (slip over a smooth surface) resbalar; deslizar. **2,** (go smoothly) patinar. **3,** (lapse into error) errar; pecar; cometer un desliz. —*v.t.* hacer resbalar; introducir con cuidado o artificio. —*n.* **1,** (act of sliding) resbalón; desliz. **2,** (slippery place) resbaladero. **3,** (avalanche) derrumbe; derrumbamiento. **4,** (sliding part) cursor; pieza corrediza. **5,** (picture on glass for projection on a screen) diapositiva. **6,** (specimen holder) portaobjetos. —**let (something) slide,** dejar pasar; no hacer caso de. —**slide into,** meter(se) en; colarse en. —**slide out** o **away,** colarse; escabullirse. —**slide over,** pasar ligeramente.

slide fastener cierre cremallera.

slide rule regla de cálculo.

sliding ('slai·dɪŋ) *adj.* **1,** (moving by slipping) corredizo. **2,** (adjustable) móvil.

slight (slait) *adj.* **1,** (small) pequeño; escaso. **2,** (of little importance) insignificante; ligero; leve. **3,** (slender; frail) delgado; delicado. —*v.t.* **1,** (disdain; ignore) desairar; menospreciar; desdeñar. **2,** (do negligently) descuidar; desatender. —*n.* **1,** (discourtesy) desaire; menosprecio; desdén. **2,** (neglect) desatención; descuido.

slim (slɪm) *adj.* **1,** (slender; thin) delgado; esbelto. **2,** (meager) escaso; insuficiente. —*v.t. & i.* adelgazar.

slime (slaim) *n.* **1,** (mud; ooze) légamo; limo; cieno; fango. **2,** (mucous secretion) baba; babaza. **3,** (filth) suciedad; porquería. —**slimy,** *adj.* viscoso; legamoso; fangoso.

slimness ('slɪm·nəs) *n.* **1,** (slenderness) delgadez. **2,** (meagerness) escasez; insuficiencia.

sling (slɪŋ) *n.* **1,** (slingshot) honda; tirador. **2,** (bandage for suspending an injured limb) cabestrillo. **3,** (shoulder strap for a rifle) portafusil. **4,** (mixed drink) bebida de ginebra con azúcar y nuez

moscada. —*v.t.* [*pret.* & *p.p.* **slung**]
1, (hurl) tirar; arrojar; lanzar. 2,
(suspend) suspender; colgar.

slingshot ('slɪŋ‚ʃat) *n.* honda;
tirador. *También,* **sling shot.**

slink (slɪŋk) *v.i.* [*pret.* & *p.p.*
slunk] andar furtivamente; andar a
sombra de tejado. —**slink away,** escabullirse; escurrirse.

slip (slɪp) *v.i.* [**slipped, slipping**] 1,
(lose one's hold; slide) deslizarse;
resbalar; irse los pies. 2, (err)
cometer un desliz; equivocarse. 3,
(move quietly) pasar sin ser visto;
meterse furtivamente. 4, (become
loose or separated) zafarse; soltarse.
—*v.t.* 1, (put or move quietly) meter
o introducir secretamente; sacar a
hurtadillas. 2, *naut.* (cast off) largar o soltar (un cabo). —*n.* 1,
(act of slipping) resbalón; desliz;
deslizamiento; traspié. 2, (error)
falta; error; lapso. 3, (woman's undergarment) combinación de mujer.
4, (pillowcase) funda de almohada.
5, *naut.* (space between two
wharves) embarcadero. 6, (strip, as
of paper) tira; pedazo de papel;
papeleta. 7, (slender person) persona muy delgada. 8, (plant cutting)
vástago; sarmiento. —**give the slip
to,** escaparse de; zafarse de;
deshacerse de. —**let a chance slip,**
perder la ocasión. —**slip away,**
desaparecerse; huirse. —**slip in,**
introducirse; insinuarse; entremeterse. —**slip into,** ponerse (una
prenda de vestir). —**slip off,**
quitarse de encima; soltar. —**slip
one's mind,** olvidársele a uno una
cosa. —**slip on one's clothing,**
vestirse de prisa. —**slip out,** salir
sin ser observado. —**slip out of
joint,** dislocarse; *Amer.* zafarse (un
hueso). —**slip through,** colarse;
escurrirse; filtrarse.

slip cover funda.

slip knot nudo corredizo.

slip-on *adj.* & *n.* 1, (casual wear)
de quita y pon. 2, = **slipover.**

slipover ('slɪp‚o‚vər) *adj.* & *n.*
(suéter, chaqueta, etc.) que se pone
por la cabeza; pulóver.

slippage ('slɪp‚ɪdʒ) *n.* deslizamiento.

slipper ('slɪp‚ər) *n.* zapatilla;
babucha; chancleta; chinela;
pantufla.

slippery ('slɪp‚ə‚ri) *adj.* 1,
(smooth; slick) resbaladizo;

resbaloso. 2, (elusive) engañador;
furtivo.

slipshod ('slɪp‚ʃad) *adj.* abandonado; descuidado.

slip-up *n.* error; falta; desliz.

slit (slɪt) *v.t.* [**slitted** o **slit, slitting**]
1, (make a long narrow cut in)
hacer una incisión en; partir. 2, (cut
into strips) cortar en tiras. —*n.*
abertura; cortada; incisión.

slither ('slɪð‚ər) *v.i.* culebrear. —*n.*
culebreo.

sliver ('slɪv‚ər) *n.* 1, (splinter)
brizna; astilla. 2, (textile fiber)
fibra; hebra.

slob (slab) *n., slang* puerco.

slobber ('slab‚ər) *v.i.* babear;
babosear. —*n.* baba. —**slobbery,**
adj. baboso.

sloe (slo) *n.* 1, (fruit) endrina. 2,
(tree) endrino. —**sloe-colored,** *adj.*
endrino. —**sloe-eyed,** *adj.* de
ojos endrinos. —**sloe gin,** ginebra
de endrinas.

slog (slag) *v.i.* [**slogged, slogging**]
trabajar afanosamente; echar los
bofes. —*v.t.* dar; pegar; golpear.
—*n.* golpe; bofetón.

slogan ('slo‚gən) *n.* grito de
combate o de partido; lema; mote.

sloop (slup) *n.* balandra; balandro;
chalupa.

slop (slap) *n.* 1, (puddle) líquido
derramado en el suelo; mojadura. 2,
(unappetizing mess) suciedad;
gachas; té o café flojo. 3, *pl.* (waste
liquid; sewage) agua sucia; lavazas;
desperdicios. 4, *pl.* (seamen's gear)
equipaje de marineros. —*v.t.*
[**slopped, slopping**] 1, (spill)
splash) verter; derramar; salpicar. 2,
(soil) mojar; ensuciar. —*v.i.* 1,
(spill; splash) derramarse; salpicar.
2, *colloq.* (speak or act effusively)
hablar o actuar con sensiblería.

slope (slop) *n.* 1, (slanting surface)
cuesta; pendiente. 2, (degree of
slant) inclinación; declive; sesgo. 3,
(watershed) vertiente. —*v.i.* inclinarse; estar en declive. —*v.t.* inclinar; sesgar; cortar en sesgo; formar
en declive.

sloppy ('slap‚i) *adj.* 1, (untidy)
desaliñado; desaseado; cochino;
puerco; sucio. 2, (clumsy; bungling)
chapucero. 3, (muddy) lodoso;
cenagoso. 4, (wearisome; effusive)
empalagoso.

slosh (slaʃ) *n.* 1, (slush) nieve a
medio derretir; fango; cieno; lodo
blando. 2, (nonsense) tontería; dis-

parate. —*v.i.* chapotear. —*v.t.* menear (un líquido) haciendo ruido de chapaleteo.

slot (slat) *n.* abertura; ranura. —**slot machine**, máquina de vender; traganíqueles; tragamonedas.

sloth (slɔθ) *n.* **1,** (laziness) pereza. **2,** *zoöl.* perezoso. —**slothful,** *adj.* holgazán; perezoso.

slotted ('slat·ɪd) *adj.* con aberturas o ranuras.

slouch (slautʃ) *v.i.* ir o estar cabizbajo; agacharse; repantigarse. —*n.* **1,** (drooping posture) postura muy floja o relajada. **2,** (inept person) persona incompetente. —**slouch hat,** sombrero gacho.

slough (slau) *n.* lodazal; cenagal; fangal; *fig.* abismo.

slough (slʌf) *n.* **1,** (molted skin) pellejo suelto que se muda; *(of snakes)* camisa; *(of insects)* tela. **2,** *med.* (dead tissue) escara. —*v.t.* **1,** (molt; shed) mudar; echar de sí. **2,** (discard) descartar; desechar. —*v.i.* mudarse; echarse; caerse.

Slovak ('slo·væk) *adj.* & *n.* eslovaco.

sloven ('slʌv·ən) *n.* persona desaseada o desaliñada. —**slovenly,** *adj.* desaseado; desaliñado. —*adv.* desaliñadamente.

Slovene (slo'viːn) *adj.* & *n.* esloveno.

slow (sloː) *adj.* **1,** (taking a relatively long time) lento; pausado; detenido; tardo; tardío. **2,** (dull-witted) lerdo; estúpido; torpe. **3,** (tardy; sluggish) tardo; pesado; flojo. **4,** (slack) flojo; inactivo. **5,** (tedious) pesado; aburrido. **6,** (behind time or schedule) atrasado. —*adv.* despacio; lentamente; pausadamente. —*v.t.* retardar; atrasar. —*v.i.* retardarse; atrasarse; aflojar el paso; ir más despacio. —**slowly,** *adv.* despacio; lentamente; pausadamente. —**slow down; slow up,** retardar(se); detener(se).

slowdown ('slo·daun) *n.* atraso; detención.

slow motion movimiento lento. —**slow-motion,** *adj.* & *adv.* a cámara lenta.

slowness ('slo·nəs) *n.* **1,** (tardiness; delay) lentitud; tardanza; atraso; detención. **2,** (dullness) torpeza; estupidez.

slowpoke ('slo·pok) *n.* posma; haragán.

slow-witted *adj.* lerdo; torpe; estúpido.

sludge (slʌdʒ) *n.* lodo; cieno; fango.

slue (sluː) *n.* & *v.* = **slew.**

slug (slʌg) *n.* **1,** (metal bar; ingot) lingote. **2,** *zoöl.* babosa. **3,** (bullet) bala. **4,** *colloq.* (heavy blow) porrazo; puñetazo. **5,** *slang* (drink; swallow) trago. —*v.t.* & *i.* [**slugged, slugging**] aporrear; abofetear; dar puñetazos.

slugabed ('slʌg·ə,bɛd) *n.* dormilón; perezoso.

sluggard ('slʌg·ərd) *n.* holgazán; haragán; posma.

sluggish ('slʌg·ɪʃ) *adj.* tardo; perezoso; pesado; flojo. —**sluggishness,** *n.* pereza; pesadez; posma.

sluice (slus) *n.* **1,** (artificial channel) canal; acequia; presa. **2,** (sluice gate) compuerta; bocacaz. —*v.t.* **1,** (draw off through a sluice) soltar; dar paso a. **2,** (flush; wash) regar; lavar. —*v.i.* salir (el agua).

slum (slʌm) *n.* barrio bajo. —*v.i.* [**slummed, slumming**] visitar los barrios bajos.

slumber ('slʌm·bər) *v.i.* dormitar; dormir. —*n.* sueño. —**slumberous,** *adj.* soñoliento.

slump (slʌmp) *v.i.* **1,** (sink; collapse) desplomarse; hundirse. **2,** (decline; fall) bajar. **3,** (fail) fracasar; no tener éxito. **4,** (slouch) agacharse; repantigarse. —*n.* **1,** (collapse) desplome; hundimiento. **2,** (decline) baja. **3,** (failure) fracaso. **4,** (slouch) postura floja.

slung (slʌŋ) *v.,* *pret.* & *p.p.* de **sling.**

slunk (slʌŋk) *v.,* *pret.* & *p.p.* de **slink.**

slur (slʌr) *v.t.* [**slurred, slurring**] **1,** (run together; blur in speaking) comerse (sonidos o sílabas); farfullar. **2,** (treat slightingly; ignore) pasar por encima; suprimir; ocultar. **3,** (disparage; insult) menospreciar; rebajar; insultar. **4,** *mus.* ligar; marcar con una ligadura. —*n.* **1,** (indistinct pronunciation) farfulla; pronunciación indistinta. **2,** (disparaging remark or act) borrón o mancha en la reputación; reparo; afrenta. **3,** *mus.* ligadura.

slurp (slʌrp) *v.t.* & *i.* comer o beber burbujeando.

slush (slʌʃ) *n.* **1,** (watery snow) nieve a medio derretir. **2,** (watery mixture of mud, etc.) fango; cieno;

lodo blando. **3,** (drivel) sentimentalismo; sensiblería; ñoñería. **—slush fund,** fondos guardados en reserva para usos especiales.

slut (slʌt) *n.* **1,** (slovenly woman) mujer desaliñada. **2,** (loose woman) ramera; prostituta. **3,** (female dog) perra.

sly (slai) *adj.* **1,** (shrewd; clever) astuto; listo; sutil; mañoso. **2,** (stealthy; furtive) secreto; furtivo. **3,** (roguish) pícaro. **—on the sly,** furtivamente; a hurtadillas.

smack (smæk) *v.t.* **1,** (separate, as the lips, with a sharp sound) chuparse (los labios). **2,** (slap) dar una palmada, manotada o bofetada. **3,** (kiss noisily) besar ruidosamente; dar un beso ruidoso; hacer sonar un beso en. **—v.i.** (make a sharp sound; slap) chuparse los labios; saborearse; rechuparse; relamerse; chasquear (un látigo). **—n. 1,** (trace; suggestion) olor; sabor; dejo; gustillo. **2,** (slap; blow) manotada; palmada; golpe. **3,** (resounding kiss) beso ruidoso. **4,** (smacking noise) chasquido. **5,** (bit; small amount) pizca. **6,** (fishing vessel) esmaque. **—adv.** directamente; redondamente. **—smacker,** *n., slang* dólar; billete de dólar. **—smacking,** *adj.* fuerte; redondo. **—smack of,** oler a; saber a; tener olor o sabor de.

small (smɔl) *adj.* **1,** (little) pequeño; chico; menudo. **2,** (humble) bajo; insignificante; humilde; obscuro. **3,** (mean; petty) mezquino; miserable; ruin. **4,** *typog.* minúsculo. **—n.** parte más estrecha. **—small arms,** armas portátiles; armas ligeras. **—small change,** dinero menudo. **—small fry, 1,** (young fish) pececillos. **2,** (children) niños; chiquillos. **3,** (insignificant persons or things) personas o cosas de poca monta. **—small hours,** altas horas de la noche; primeras horas de la mañana. **—small potatoes,** *colloq.* persona o cosa de poca monta. **—small talk,** charla; plática; conversación sin importancia.

smallish ('smɔl·ɪʃ) *adj.* algo pequeño.

small-minded *adj.* **1,** (petty; mean) mezquino; miserable; ruin. **2,** (illiberal) iliberal; intolerante; estrecho de miras.

smallness ('smɔl·nəs) *n.* pequeñez.

smallpox ('smɔl·paks) *n.* viruelas.

smart (smart) *v.i.* **1,** (sting) escocer; picar; resquemar. **2,** (feel physical or mental distress) escocerse; dolerse; sentirse. **—v.t. 1,** (sting) picar; resquemar. **—n. 1,** (sting) escozor; picazón; comezón; resquemor. **2,** (mental distress) aflicción; dolor. **—adj. 1,** (keen; acute; severe) agudo; picante; punzante; mordaz. **2,** (brisk) vivo; enérgico; despejado. **3,** (vigorous; forceful) fuerte; rudo. **4,** (clever; shrewd) listo; astuto; inteligente. **5,** (vivacious; witty) vivaz; vivaracho. **6,** (neat; stylish) elegante; a la moda; de buen tono. **7,** (presumptuous) presuntuoso; sabihondo. **—smart aleck** ('æl·ɪk) *colloq.* presuntuoso; sabihondo. **—smart set,** gente de buen tono.

smarten ('smar·tən) *v.t.* **1,** (spruce up) hermosear; embellecer. **2,** (quicken) animar; avivar. **—v.i.** animarse; avivarse.

smartness ('smart·nəs) *n.* **1,** (keenness) agudeza. **2,** (briskness) viveza; energía. **3,** (force; vigor) fuerza; violencia. **4,** (cleverness) astucia; inteligencia. **5,** (vivacity) vivacidad. **6,** (elegance) elegancia.

smash (smæʃ) *v.t.* **1,** (break to pieces) romper; quebrar; hacer pedazos; estrellar. **2,** (defeat utterly) destrozar; arruinar; aplastar. **3,** (strike against) chocar con; topar con. **—v.i. 1,** (break to pieces) romperse; quebrarse; hacerse pedazos; estrellarse. **2,** (strike; collide) chocar; topar. **—n. 1,** (violent blow) choque o tope violento. **2,** (destruction) quebrazón; quiebra; fracaso; derrota completa. **3,** (sweet drink) refresco o bebida alcohólica hecha con menta, azúcar y agua. **—go to smash,** arruinarse; destrozarse. **—smash hit,** *colloq.* éxito magnífico.

smash-up *n.* ruina; quiebra; choque desastroso.

smattering ('smæt·ər·ɪŋ) *n.* conocimiento superficial; tintura.

smear (smɪr) *v.t.* **1,** (cover with something sticky, grease, etc.) untar. **2,** (soil; dirty) embarrar; manchar; tiznar. **3,** (daub; as with paint) pintorrear. **4,** (blot; blur) borrar; emborronar. **5,** (slander) calumniar; denigrar. **—v.i.** mancharse; borrarse. **—n. 1,** (spot; smudge) mancha; embarradura. **2,** (blot) borrón.

3, (slander) calumnia; denigración. **4,** *med.* frotis.

smell (smɛl) *v.t.* [*pret.* & *p.p.* **smelled** o **smelt**] **1,** (perceive through the nose) oler. **2,** (sniff) husmear; olfatear. **3,** (detect or discover as though by smell) oler; percibir; descubrir. —*v.i.* oler; heder; husmear. —*n.* **1,** (sense of smell) olfato. **2,** (odor; scent; aroma) olor; perfume; fragancia; aroma. **3,** (act of smelling) husmeo; acción de oler. **4,** (trace) traza; vestigio. —**smelly,** *adj.* hediondo. —**smelling salts,** sales aromáticas. —**smell of,** oler a; tener olor de. —**smell out,** descubrir.

smelt (smɛlt) *v.t.* (fuse; melt) fundir. —*v., pret.* & *p.p. de* **smell.** —*n., ichthy.* eperlano.

smelter ('smɛl·tər) *n.* fundidor.

smelting ('smɛl·tɪŋ) *n.* fundición.

smidgen ('smɪdʒ·ən) *n., colloq.* pizca.

smile (smail) *n.* sonrisa. —*v.i.* sonreír; sonreírse. —*v.t.* expresar con una sonrisa. —**smiling,** *adj.* risueño.

smirch (smʌrtʃ) *v.t.* **1,** (soil; dirty) manchar; ensuciar; tiznar. **2,** (defame) difamar; deshonrar; tiznar. —*n.* **1,** (stain; smear) mancha; tiznón. **2,** (dishonor) deshonra.

smirk (smʌrk) *n.* sonrisa boba o afectada. —*v.i.* sonreírse afectadamente o estúpidamente.

smite (smait) *v.t.* [**smote, smitten**] **1,** (strike; afflict) golpear; herir; afligir. **2,** (affect; captivate) conmover; encantar; tocar al alma.

smith (smɪθ) *n.* herrero; herrador. —**smithy,** *n.* herrería.

smithereens (ˌsmɪð·ər'iːnz) *n.pl.* añicos; pedazos.

smitten ('smɪt·ən) *v., p.p. de* **smite.** —*adj.* **1,** (impressed) impresionado. **2,** (in love) enamorado.

smock (smak) *n.* bata corta; camisa de mujer; blusa de obrero. —**smock frock,** blusa de campesino.

smog (smag) *n.* mezcla de niebla y humo.

smoke (smok) *n.* **1,** (visible vapor from a burning substance) humo. **2,** (something unsubstantial) humo; vapor; humareda. **3,** (cigar or cigarette) fumada; tabaco. —*v.i.* **1,** (emit smoke) humear; hacer humo. **2,** (burn tobacco) fumar. —*v.t.* **1,** (puff on, as tobacco, opium, etc.) fumar. **2,** (cure with smoke) ahumar. —**go**

up in smoke; end in smoke, volverse humo. —**no smoking,** se prohibe fumar; prohibido fumar. —**smoke out,** echar fuera con humo; *fig.* descubrir.

smoked (smokt) *adj.* ahumado.

smokehouse ('smok,haus) *n.* cuarto cerrado para ahumar carnes, pieles, etc.

smoker ('smo·kər) *n.* **1,** (one who smokes) fumador. **2,** = **smoking room. 3,** = **smoking car. 4,** (social function) tertulia en que se permite fumar.

smoke screen cortina de humo; humo de protección.

smokestack ('smok,stæk) *n.* chimenea.

smoking car vagón de fumar; coche fumador.

smoking jacket batín.

smoking room fumadero; salón de fumar.

smoky ('smo·ki) *adj.* humeante; humoso.

smolder *también,* **smoulder** ('smol·dər) *v.i.* **1,** (burn and smoke without flame) arder lentamente, sin llama o en rescoldo. **2,** *fig.* (lie suppressed) arder (una pasión); estar latente.

smooth (smuːð) *adj.* **1,** (flat; even) plano; llano. **2,** (soft to the touch; slick) liso; suave; alisado. **3,** (without sudden variation; uniform) igual; parejo; uniforme. **4,** (mild; bland) suave; blando; meloso; dulce. **5,** (pleasant; peaceful) tranquilo; agradable. **6,** (flowing; fluent) flúido; fácil. —*v.t.* **1,** (make even) allanar; alisar; suavizar. **2,** (calm; mollify) calmar; aliviar; ablandar.

smoothness ('smuð·nəs) *n.* **1,** (flatness; evenness) llanura. **2,** (softness) lisura; suavidad. **3,** (uniformity) igualdad; uniformidad. **4,** (mildness) blandura; dulzura. **5,** (pleasantness; peacefulness) tranquilidad. **6,** (flowing quality) fluidez; facilidad.

smorgasbord ('smor·gəs,bord) *n.* entremeses suecos.

smote (smot) *v., pret. de* **smite.**

smother ('smʌð·ər) *v.t.* **1,** (suffocate; deprive of air) ahogar; asfixiar; sofocar. **2,** (stifle; suppress) suprimir; disfrazar; ocultar. —*v.i.* ahogarse; asfixiarse.

smoulder ('smol·dər) *v.i.* = **smolder.**

smudge (smʌdʒ) *n.* **1,** (blot; smear) mancha; tiznón; borrón. **2,** (smoky fire) humareda; nube espesa de humo. —*v.t.* tiznar; manchar; ensuciar. —*v.i.* mancharse; borrarse. —**smudgy,** *adj.* ensuciado; tiznado.

smug (smʌg) *adj.* presumido; vanidoso; satisfecho de sí mismo. —**smugness,** *n.* presunción; vanidad; satisfacción de sí mismo.

smuggle ('smʌg·əl) *v.t.* meter o sacar de contrabando. —*v.i.* contrabandear; hacer contrabando. —**smuggler** (-lər) *n.* contrabandista. —**smuggling** (-lɪŋ) *n.* comercio de contrabando.

smut (smʌt) *n.* **1,** (sooty matter) tizne; tizón; mancha; suciedad. **2,** (obscenity) indecencia; obscenidad.

smutty ('smʌt·i) *adj.* **1,** (sooty) tiznado; manchado; sucio. **2,** (obscene) indecente; obsceno.

snack (snæk) *n.* bocado; bocadillo; refrigerio; merienda. —**snack bar,** puesto de refrescos; cantina. —**snack basket,** fiambrera.

snafu (ˌsnæˈfu) *adj., slang* desordenado; confuso; enredado. —*n., slang* desorden; confusión; enredo.

snag (snæg) *n.* **1,** (obstacle) obstáculo; tropiezo. **2,** (bump; lump) nudo (en la madera); protuberancia. —*v.t.* [snagged, snagging] **1,** (impede; entangle) impedir; enredar. **2,** (pull out) arrancar.

snail (sneil) *n.* **1,** *zoöl.* caracol; babosa. **2,** (slowpoke) posma. —**snail's pace,** paso de tortuga; paso de caracol.

snake (sneik) *n.* culebra; sierpe; serpiente; víbora. —*v.t.* arrastrar tirando de. —*v.i.* culebrear; serpentear. —**snake in the grass,** *colloq.* traidor; engañador; seductor.

snake charmer encantador de serpientes.

snaky ('snei·ki) *adj.* **1,** (of or like a snake) de culebra. **2,** (flexible; sinuous) culebrino; serpentino; tortuoso. **3,** (treacherous) traidor; pérfido.

snap (snæp) *v.i.* [snapped, snapping] **1,** (make a sudden sharp sound) chasquear; dar un chasquido. **2,** (break or loosen suddenly) estallar; quebrarse; soltarse. **3,** (move suddenly) sacudirse; apresurarse. **4,** (bite) echar una mordedura; procurar morder;

morder. **5,** (speak sharply) volverse áspero; hablar bruscamente. —*v.t.* **1,** (cause to make a sharp sound) chasquear. **2,** (break) romper; quebrar; hacer estallar. **3,** (loose suddenly) soltar; lanzar; tirar. **4,** (retort) contestar mordazmente. **5,** (grab) coger; agarrar; asir; lanzarse sobre. **6,** (take a snapshot of) sacar una instantánea de; tomar (una instantánea). —*n.* **1,** (sharp sound) estallido; chasquido; castañeta (hecha con los dedos). **2,** (quick motion) sacudida; lance. **3,** (closing or locking device) cierre de resorte; corchete. **4,** (sudden closing, as of a trap) mordedura. **5,** (thin, brittle cake) galletita. **6,** (briskness; vigor) vigor; energía; fuerza. **7,** (brief spell) período corto, esp. de frío. **8,** *slang* (easy task) ganga. **9,** = **snapshot.** —*adj.* **1,** (offhand) impensado; hecho de prisa o de repente. **2,** (easy) fácil. —**not to care a snap,** no importarle a uno un ardite. —**snap fastener,** broche de presión. —**snap judgment,** decisión atolondrada. —**snap lock,** cerradura de golpe. —**snap one's fingers,** tronar los dedos; castañetear con los dedos. —**snap one's fingers at,** burlarse de; mofarse de. —**snap out of it,** *slang* componerse. —**snap shut,** cerrar(se) de golpe. —**snap together,** apretar; abrochar. —**snap up,** agarrar; asir; aceptar en seguida.

snapdragon ('snæp,dræg·ən) *n.* becerra.

snapper ('snæp·ər) *n.* **1,** (person or thing that snaps) mordedor. **2,** (fish) pez comestible del Golfo de México. **3,** (snapping turtle) gran tortuga voraz de la América del Norte.

snappish ('snæp·ɪʃ) *adj.* irritable; mordaz.

snappy ('snæp·i) *adj.* **1,** (snapping; crackling) crepitante. **2,** (brisk; cold and stimulating) vivo; fresco. **3,** (tart; spicy) picante. **4,** *colloq.* (smart; stylish) elegante; de moda. **5,** *colloq.* (lively; quick) astuto; listo. **6,** = **snappish.**

snapshot ('snæp·ʃat) *n.* instantánea.

snare (sneːr) *n.* **1,** (trap) trampa; cepo; lazo. **2,** (cord, as of a drum) lazo; tirante. —*v.t.* **1,** (catch; trap) coger con una trampa. **2,** (catch; seize) agarrar; coger. **3,** (entangle) foul) enredar; enmarañar. —**snare drum**, tambor con tirantes de cuerda.

snarl (snarl) v.t. & i. 1, (growl) gruñir. 2, (entangle) enredar(se); enmarañar(se). —n. 1, (growl) gruñido. 2, (tangle) enredo; nudo.

snatch (snætʃ) v.t. arrebatar; agarrar. —v.i. tratar de agarrar o arrebatar. —n. 1, (act of snatching) arrebatamiento; agarrón. 2, slang (kidnaping) secuestro; Amer. plagio. 3, (fragment; bit) pedacito; trozo; fragmento. —by (o in) snatches, a ratos; poco a poco.

sneak (snik) v.i. venir o irse a hurtadillas; colarse; escurrirse. —v.t. 1, (do furtively) hacer a escondidas. 2, (put in or take out furtively) meter o sacar a hurtadillas. 3, colloq. (steal) robar; ratear. —adj. furtivo; traicionero. —n. 1, (furtive action) acción furtiva. 2, (one who sneaks) persona solapada. 3, pl. = sneakers.

sneakers ('sni·kərz) n.pl., colloq. zapatos de playa; zapatos de tela con suela de goma; Mex. tenis.

sneaking ('sni·kɪŋ) adj. 1, (fawning; obsequious) servil; bajo; vil. 2, (furtive) furtivo; oculto; secreto.

sneak thief ratero; ladrón de poca monta.

sneaky ('sni·ki) adj. 1, (furtive) furtivo; oculto; secreto. 2, (secretive) solapado. 3, (treacherous) traicionero.

sneer (snɪr) v.i. hablar o mirar con desprecio; burlarse; mofarse. —v.t. proferir con desprecio. —n. mirada de desprecio; risa falsa o burlona. —**sneering**, adj. burlador; despreciativo. —**sneer at**, mofarse de; burlarse de.

sneeze (sniːz) n. estornudo. —v.i. estornudar. —**not to be sneezed at**, colloq. considerable; digno de consideración.

snicker ('snɪk·ər) v.i. reírse tontamente. —n. risita; risa tonta. También, **snigger**.

snide (snaid) adj. socarrón y despreciativo.

sniff (snɪf) v.i. 1, (inhale audibly through the nose) olfatear; resoplar; resollar. 2, (show scorn or disdain) menospreciar; manifestar desprecio con resoplidos. —v.t. 1, (inhale sharply) husmear; ventear. 2, (perceive by smell) oler; percibir;

descubrir. —n. olfateo; husmeo; venteo.

sniffle ('snɪf·əl) v.i. sorber; resollar; resoplar. —n. sorbo; resuello; resoplido. —**sniffles**, n.pl. catarro; legaña; romadizo.

snifter ('snɪf·tər) n. 1, (brandy glass) vaso de pera. 2, slang (short drink) trago; W.I. palo.

snigger ('snɪg·ər) v.i. & n. = snicker.

snip (snɪp) v.t. & i. [snipped, snipping] tijeretear; dar tijeretadas; cortar o recortar con tijeras. —n. 1, (act or sound of snipping) tijeretada. 2, (piece cut off) retazo; pedacito. 3, pl. (tin shears) tijeras para metal. 4, colloq. (small or insignificant person) persona de poca monta; impertinente.

snipe (snaip) n. agachadiza. —v.i. 1, (hunt snipe) cazar agachadizas. 2, (shoot from hiding) tirar desde un acecho. —**sniper**, n. francotirador [fem. -dora].

snippet ('snɪp·ɪt) n. 1, (scrap; fragment) recorte; retazo. 2, colloq. (small or insignificant person) persona de poca monta; impertinente.

snippy ('snɪp·i) adj., colloq. 1, (snappish) irritable; mordaz. 2, (insolent) insolente; impertinente.

snitch (snɪtʃ) v.t., slang (steal) ratear; hurtar; robar. —v.i., slang (turn informer) soplar; hacerse delator. —**snitch on**, delatar; denunciar.

snivel ('snɪv·əl) v.i. gimotear; lloriquear. —n. gimoteo; lloriqueo.

snob (snaːb) n. snob; esnob. —**snobbish**, adj. snob; esnob. —**snobbishness**, **snobbery**, n. snobismo; esnobismo.

snood (snuːd) n. cintillo; redecilla.

snoop (snup) v.i., colloq. curiosear; fisgonear; espiar. —n., colloq. curioso; fisgón; espía; espión. —**snooping**, n. curioseo; fisgoneo. —**snoopy**, adj. curioso; entrometido.

snoot (snut) n., slang hocico; narices; cara.

snooty ('snu·ti) adj., slang esnob; altanero. —**snootiness**, n. esnobismo; altanería.

snooze (snuːz) v.i., colloq. dormitar; sestear. —n., colloq. siesta; siestecita; sueñito.

snore (snoːr) v.i. roncar. —n. ronquido. —**snorer**, n. roncador [fem. -dora].

snorkel ('snor·kəl) n. tubo de

respiración para submarinos; esnórquel.

snort (snort) *v.i.* **1,** (force air audibly through the nose) resoplar; bufar. **2,** (scoff) mofarse. —*n.* **1,** (snorting sound) resoplido; bufido. **2,** *slang* (short drink) trago; chispo; *W.I.* palo.

snot (snat) *n., vulg.* **1,** (mucus) moco. **2,** (impudent youngster) mocoso. —**snotty,** *adj., colloq.* mocoso.

snout (snaut) *n.* hocico.

snow (snoz) *n.* **1,** (white water crystals) nieve. **2,** *slang* (cocaine or heroin) cocaína; heroína. —*v.t.* nevar. —*v.t.* **1,** (let fall like snow) nevar. **2,** (cover with snow) cubrir con nieve. **3,** *slang* (hoax) engañar; burlar. —**snow job,** *slang* embaucamiento; embuste. —**snow under,** cubrir con nieve; *fig.* abrumar; aplastar.

snowball ('sno·bɔl) *n.* bola de nieve. —*v.t.* tirar bolas de nieve a. —*v.i.* crecer rápidamente.

snowbank ('sno,bæŋk) *n.* banco de nieve.

snowbird ('sno,bʌrd) *n.* **1,** *ornith.* pinzón de las nieves. **2,** *slang* (drug addict) narcómano. **3,** *colloq.* (winter visitor) turista invernal.

snow-blind *adj.* que padece obscurecida la vista a causa del reflejo de la nieve.

snowbound ('sno·baund) *adj.* sitiado o detenido por la nieve.

snowclad ('sno,klæd) *adj.* tapado de nieve.

snow cone granizado.

snowdrift ('sno,drift) *n.* montón de nieve; ventisquero.

snowfall ('sno·fɔl) *n.* nevada; nevasca; caída de nieve.

snowflake ('sno,fleik) *n.* copo de nieve.

snow flurry nevisca.

snowman ('sno·mæn) *n.* [*pl.* -men] **1,** (snow statue) hombre de nieve; figura de nieve. **2,** (supposed Tibetan beast) bestia de nieve.

snowmobile ('sno·mo,bil) *n.* vehículo automotor adaptado para recorrer la nieve.

snowplow ('sno,plau) *n.* limpianieves; quitanieves.

snowshoe ('sno,ʃu) *n.* raqueta; barajón.

snowslide ('sno,slaid) *n.* alud; avalancha de nieve.

snowstorm ('sno,storm) *n.* borrasca de nieve; nevasca; ventisca.

snowy ('sno·i) *adj.* nevado.

snub (snʌb) *v.t.* [**snubbed, snubbing**] **1,** (stop or check suddenly) parar de repente. **2,** (slight) menospreciar; desairar. —*n.* **1,** (sudden stop) parada en seco. **2,** (slight) desaire; menosprecio. —*adj.* chato.

snuff (snʌf) *v.i.* olfatear; resoplar. —*v.t.* **1,** (inhale sharply) husmear; ventear. **2,** (draw in through the nose) aspirar; sorber por la nariz. **3,** (extinguish, as a candle) apagar; despabilar. —*n.* **1,** (sniff) olfateo; resoplido. **2,** (powdered tobacco) tabaco en polvo; rapé. **3,** (charred end of a candle) pabilo; moco.

snuffbox ('snʌf,baks) *n.* tabaquera.

snuffle ('snʌf·əl) *v.i.* **1,** (sniff; sniffle) olfatear; resollar. **2,** (talk with a nasal twang) ganguear. —*n.* **1,** (sniffing) olfateo; resuello. **2,** (nasal twang) gangueo. —**snuffles,** *n.pl.* catarro nasal; romadizo.

snug (snʌg) *adj.* **1,** (comfortable) cómodo. **2,** (tight-fitting) ajustado. **3,** (compact) compacto; estrecho.

snuggle ('snʌg·əl) *v.i.* acurrucarse; anidarse. —*v.t.* apretar; arrimar. —**snuggle up to,** arrimarse a; apretarse contra.

so (soz) *adv.* **1,** (thus; in such a manner) así; de este modo; de esta manera. **2,** (in such a degree or amount) tan; tanto. **3,** (very; much) muy; mucho. **4,** (consequently) por tanto; por consiguiente. **5,** (also; likewise) también; igualmente. **6,** *colloq.* (indeed; really) de veras; ya. **7,** *colloq.* (well; then) pues; entonces. —*conj.* así que; de modo que; con tal (de) que; a condición (de) que. —*pron.* (*usu. reemplazando una palabra o frase ya mencionada*) lo; eso: *He did it, but I didn't think so,* Lo hizo, pero no lo creí; *I told you so,* Te lo dije; Te dije eso. —*interj.* ¡eh!; ¡pues!; ¡bien! —**and so,** pues; así pues. —**and so forth,** etcétera. —**so on,** y así sucesivamente. —**ever so much,** muchísimo. —**is that so?,** ¿de veras? —**just so, 1,** (exactly) ni más ni menos; precisamente. **2,** (perfect) perfecto; bien arreglado. —**or so,** poco más o menos; como: *ten dollars or so,* diez dólares poco más o menos; como diez dólares. —**so as to,** de manera de; para (+

inf.). **—so far,** hasta ahora; hasta aquí. **—so long,** hasta la vista; hasta luego. **—so many,** tantos. **—so much,** tanto. **—so much as,** nada más (que); siquiera; a lo menos. **—so much for,** basta con. **—so much the better (o worse),** tanto mejor (o peor). **—so that,** así que; de modo que; para que. **—so to speak,** por decirlo así. **—so what?,** ¿pues qué?

soak (sok) *v.i.* penetrar; calarse; filtrarse. —*v.t.* **1,** (drench; saturate) remojar; ensopar; empapar. **2,** (absorb) empapar; embeber; chupar; absorber. **3,** *slang* (beat) golpear; pegar; aporrear. **4,** *slang* (charge exorbitantly) robarle a uno (un vendedor); cobrarle a uno un precio desproporcionado. —*n.* **1,** (act or result of soaking) remojo; empapamiento. **2,** *slang* (hard blow) golpe; puñetazo; bofetón. **3,** *slang* (drunkard) borrachín; bebedor.

so-and-so *n.* fulano; fulano de tal.

soap (sop) *n.* jabón. —*v.t.* enjabonar; jabonar.

soapbox ('sop·baks) *n.* tribuna improvisada.

soap dish jabonera.

soaping ('so·pɪŋ) *n.* jabonadura.

soap opera novela; telenovela.

soapstone ('sop,ston) *n.* esteatita.

soapsuds ('sop·sʌdz) *n.pl.* jabonaduras.

soapwort ('sop·wʌrt) *n.* jabonera; saponaria.

soapy ('so·pi) *adj.* jabonoso; enjabonado.

soar (sor) *v.i.* **1,** (fly upward) remontarse; volar muy alto. **2,** (glide) planear; volar. **3,** (rise higher) elevarse; subir. —*n.* **1,** (flight) remonte; vuelo. **2,** (glide) planeo. —**soaring,** *adj.* elevado. —*n.* = **soar.**

sob (sɑːb) *v.i. & t.* [**sobbed, sobbing**] sollozar. —*n.* sollozo.

sober ('so·bər) *adj.* **1,** (not intoxicated) sobrio; no-embriagado. **2,** (sedate; serious; solemn) moderado; templado; cuerdo; sensato. **3,** (subdued, as in color) apagado. —*v.t.* **1,** (relieve of intoxication) desembriagar. **2,** (temper; moderate) templar; moderar; poner sobrio. —*v.i.* desembriagarse; volverse sobrio. —**soberness,** *n.* sobriedad.

sobriety (so'braɪ·ə·ti) *n.* sobriedad.

sobriquet ('so·brɪ,keɪ) *n.* apodo. *También,* **soubriquet.**

so-called *adj.* así llamado; supuesto.

soccer ('sak·ər) *n.* fútbol; balompié.

sociable ('so·ʃə·bəl) *adj.* sociable; amigable; comunicativo. —*n.* fiesta; tertulia; velada. —**sociability,** *n.* sociabilidad.

social ('so·ʃəl) *adj.* social. —*n.* reunión social. —**social register,** libro de la buena sociedad; libro de oro. —**social science,** ciencias sociales. —**social security,** seguro social; previsión social. —**social work,** servicio social; auxilio social.

socialism ('so·ʃəl·ɪz·əm) *n.* socialismo. —**socialist,** *n. & adj.* socialista. —**socialistic,** *adj.* socialista.

socialite ('so·ʃə,laɪt) *n., colloq.* persona de la buena sociedad.

socialize ('so·ʃə,laɪz) *v.t.* socializar. —*v.i.* socializarse. —**socialization** (-lɪ'zeɪ·ʃən) *n.* socialización.

society (sə'saɪ·ə·ti) *n.* **1,** (group; community) sociedad. **2,** (fashionable world) buena sociedad; mundo elegante. **3,** (company) compañía. —**societal** (-təl) *adj.* social.

sociology (,so·si'al·ə·dʒi) *n.* sociología. —**sociological** (-ə'ladʒ·ɪ·kəl) *adj.* sociológico. —**sociologist,** *n.* sociólogo.

sociopath ('so·si·o,pæθ) *n.* persona antisocial. —**sociopathic** (-'pæθ·ɪk) *adj.* antisocial.

sock (sak) *n.* **1,** (short stocking) calcetín. **2,** *slang* (hard blow) golpetazo; puñetazo; porrazo. —*v.t., slang* golpear; pegar. —**socked in,** *slang* cerrado (el tráfico aéreo) a causa de la neblina.

socket ('sak·ɪt) *n.* **1,** (hollow; groove) hueco; encaje. **2,** (of the eye) cuenca. **3,** (of a tooth) alvéolo. **4,** *elect.* enchufe. —*v.t.* encajar.

sod (sad) *n.* **1,** césped. **2,** *slang, Brit.* tipo; sujeto; sodomita. —*v.t.* cubrir de césped.

soda ('so·də) *n.* **1,** (sodium or sodium compound) soda; sosa. **2,** (carbonated water) agua de soda; agua gaseosa; agua de seltz. —**soda ash,** cenizas de sosa; barrilla. —**soda cracker,** galletita salada. —**soda fountain,** fuente de sodas. —**soda pop,** soda; gaseosa.

sodality (so'dæl·ə·ti) *n.* cofradía; hermandad.

sodden ('sad·ən) *adj.* empapado.

sodium ('so·di·əm) *n.* sodio.

sodomy ('sad·ə·mi) *n.* sodomía. —**sodomite** (-ˌmait) *n.* sodomita.

sofa ('so·fə) *n.* sofá. —**sofa bed,** sofá cama.

soft (sɔft) *adj.* **1,** (not hard) suave; blando. **2,** (mild) suave; dulce. **3,** (yielding easily) flojo; flexible. **4,** (not loud) suave. **5,** (kind; lenient) manso; tierno. **6,** (delicate; frail) delicado; delgado. **7,** *phonet.* sonoro; sibilante. **8,** *colloq.* (easy) fácil. —*adv.* suavemente; blandamente.

softball ('sɔftˌbɔl) *n.* sófbol.

soft-boiled *adj.* pasado por agua.

soft coal carbón bituminoso; hulla.

soft drink refresco.

soften ('sɔf·ən) *v.t.* ablandar; suavizar; templar. —*v.i.* ablandarse; suavizarse; templarse. —**softener,** *n.* ablandador; suavizador.

softhearted ('sɔft·harˌtɪd) *adj.* manso; bondadoso.

softly ('sɔft·li) *adv.* **1,** (gently) suavemente; blandamente. **2,** (quietly) suavemente; en voz baja.

softness ('sɔft·nəs) *n.* suavidad; blandura; dulzura; flojedad.

soft-pedal *v.t.* moderar; templar; bajar.

soft soap 1, *lit.* jabón blando o suave. **2,** *fig., colloq.* (flattery) adulación; lisonja. —**softsoap,** *v.t., colloq.* dar jabón; enjabonar; lamer el ojo.

soft-spoken *adj.* de voz suave.

software ('sɔft·wer) *n., comput.* logical.

soft water agua blanda; agua dulce.

softy ('sɔf·ti) *n., colloq.* persona pusilánime; persona débil.

soggy ('sag·i) *adj.* empapado; ensopado.

soil (sɔil) *n.* suelo; tierra. —*v.t.* manchar; ensuciar. —*v.i.* mancharse; ensuciarse.

soirée (swa'rei) *n.* tertulia; velada.

sojourn ('so·dʒʌrn) *v.i.* morar; estarse; permanecer. —*n.* morada; estancia; permanencia.

sol (sol) *n., mus.* sol.

Sol (sal) *n.* el Sol.

solace ('sal·ɪs) *n.* solaz; consuelo; alivio. —*v.t.* solazar; consolar; confortar.

solar ('so·lər) *adj.* solar. —**solar plexus,** plexo solar.

solarium (so'lɛr·i·əm) *n.* solana; solario.

sold (sold) *v., pret. & p.p. de* **sell.**

solder ('sad·ər) *n.* soldadura. —*v.t.*

soldar; estañar. —**soldering iron,** soldador.

soldier ('sol·dʒər) *n.* soldado; militar. —*v.i.* **1,** (perform military service) militar; servir como soldado. **2,** (goldbrick) zanganear. **3,** (malinger) fingirse enfermo. —**soldierly,** *adj.* soldadesco; militar. —**soldiery,** *n.* soldadesca; servicio militar. —**soldier of fortune,** aventurero.

sole (sol) *n.* **1,** (undersurface of a foot) planta. **2,** (undersurface of a shoe) suela. **3,** (fish) lenguado. —*adj.* solo; único; exclusivo. —*v.t.* poner suela a. —**solely,** *adv.* solamente; únicamente.

solecism ('sal·əˌsɪz·əm) *n.* solecismo.

solemn ('sal·əm) *adj.* solemne; grave; serio. —**solemnity** (sə'lɛm·nə·ti) *n.* solemnidad; pompa; gravedad; seriedad. —**solemnize** (-ˌnaiz) *v.t.* solemnizar; celebrar solemnemente.

solenoid ('so·ləˌnɔid) *n.* solenoide.

solicit (sə'lɪs·ɪt) *v.t. & i.* solicitar. —**solicitation,** *n.* solicitación.

solicitor (sə'lɪs·ə·tər) *n.* **1,** (one who solicits) solicitador. **2,** (lawyer) procurador.

solicitous (sə'lɪs·ə·təs) *adj.* solícito.

solicitude (sə'lɪs·ə·tud) *n.* solicitud.

solid ('sal·ɪd) *adj.* **1,** (three-dimensional) sólido. **2,** (compact; dense) compacto; denso. **3,** (firm; hard; strong) firme; duro; robusto; fuerte. **4,** (united; unanimous) unido; unánime. **5,** (entire) entero; todo. —*n.* sólido. —**solid geometry,** geometría del espacio. —**solid-state,** *adj., elect.* estado sólido.

solidarity (ˌsal·ɪ'dær·ə·ti) *n.* solidaridad.

solidary ('sal·ɪˌdɛr·i) *adj.* solidario.

solidify (sə'lɪd·əˌfai) *v.t.* solidificar. —*v.i.* solidificarse. —**solidification** (-fɪˈkei·ʃən) *n.* solidificación.

solidity (sə'lɪd·ə·ti) *n.* solidez.

soliloquy (sə'lɪl·ə·kwi) *n.* soliloquio; monólogo. —**soliloquize** (-ˌkwaiz) *v.i.* soliloquiar; monologar.

solitaire ('sal·əˌtɛr) *n.* solitario.

solitary ('sal·əˌtɛr·i) *adj.* **1,** (alone) solitario. **2,** (single; sole) solo; único. **3,** (isolated) aislado; poco frecuentado; desierto. —*n.* solitario; ermitaño. —**in solitary confinement,** incomunicado.

solitude ('sal·ə,tud) *n.* soledad.

solmization (,sal·mə'zei·ʃən) *n.* solfa; solfeo.

solo ('so·lo) *n.* [*pl.* -**los**] solo. —*adj.* a solas; hecho a solas. —**soloist,** *n.* solista.

solon ('so·lan) *n.* legislador.

solstice ('sal·stɪs) *n.* solsticio.

soluble ('sal·jə·bəl) *adj.* soluble. —**solubility,** *n.* solubilidad.

solution (sə'lu·ʃən) *n.* solución.

solve (salv) *v.t.* **1,** (find the answer to) resolver. **2,** (disentangle) desenredar; desenlazar. —**solvable,** *adj.* soluble.

solvency ('sal·vən·si) *n.* solvencia.

solvent ('sal·vənt) *adj.* solvente. —*n.* disolvente.

soma ('so·mə) *n.* [*pl.* -**mata** (-mə·tə)] soma. —**somatic** (-'mæt·ɪk) *adj.* somático.

somber *también,* **sombre** ('sam·bər) *adj.* sombrío.

sombrero (sam'brɛr·o) *n.* [*pl.* -**ros**] sombrero.

some (sʌm) *adj.indef.* **1,** (of an unspecified quantity) algo de; un poco de. *Muchas veces no se expresa en español: Give me some bread,* Deme pan o un poco de pan. **2,** (of an unspecified number) unos; algunos. **3,** (certain one or ones) algún (*pl.* algunos); cierto (*pl.* ciertos); cualquiera (*pl.* cualesquiera). **4,** *slang* (considerable; notable) bueno; famoso; menudo. —*pron. indef.* **1,** (an unspecified part) parte; una parte; algo. **2,** (an unspecified number) unos; algunos; unos cuantos. —*adv.* **1,** (approximately) como; unos: *some twenty persons,* como veinte personas; unas veinte personas. **2,** *colloq.* (somewhat) algo; un poco. **3,** *colloq.* (a great deal) bastante; mucho.

somebody ('sʌm,bad·i; -,bʌd·i; -bə·di) *pron.indef.* alguien. —*n.* personaje. —**somebody else,** algún otro; otra persona.

someday ('sʌm,dei) *adv.* algún día.

somehow ('sʌm,hau) *adv.* de algún modo; de alguna manera. —**somehow or other,** de una manera u otra.

someone ('sʌm·wʌn) *pron.indef.* alguien. —**someone else,** algún otro; otra persona.

someplace ('sʌm,pleis) *adv. & n.* = somewhere.

somersault ('sʌm·ər,sɔlt) *n.* salto mortal.

something ('sʌm,θɪŋ) *n.* algo; alguna cosa.

sometime ('sʌm,taim) *adv.* alguna vez; en algún tiempo. —*adj.* anterior; antiguo.

sometimes ('sʌm,taimz) *adv.* a veces; algunas veces.

someway ('sʌm,wei) *adv.* = somehow. *También,* **someways.**

somewhat ('sʌm,hwat) *adv.* algo; un tanto; un poco. —*n.* algo; alguna cosa; un poco.

somewhere ('sʌm,hwer) *adv.* a o en algún sitio o alguna parte. —**somewhere else,** a o en otra parte.

somnambulate (sam'næm·bjə·,leit) *v.i.* padecer sonambulismo.

somnambulism (sam'næm·bjə·lɪz·əm) *n.* sonambulismo. —**somnambulist,** *n.* sonámbulo.

somniferous (sam'nɪf·ər·əs) *adj.* somnífero.

somnolent ('sam·nə·lənt) *adj.* soñoliento. —**somnolence,** *n.* somnolencia.

son (sʌn) *n.* hijo.

sonar ('so·nar) *n.* sonar.

sonata (sə'na·tə) *n.* sonata.

song (sɔŋ) *n.* **1,** (short poem set to music) canción. **2,** (poetry) poesía. **3,** (act or sound of singing) canto; cantar. —**for a song,** muy barato.

songbird ('sɔŋ,bʌrd) *n.* cantor (*fem.* cantatriz; cantora); ave canora.

songbook ('sɔŋ,buk) *n.* cancionero.

songfest ('sɔŋ,fɛst) *n.* fiesta cantante.

songster ('sɔŋ·stər) *n.* cantor; cantante; cancionista. —**songstress** (-strəs) *n.* cantora; cantatriz; cancionista.

sonic ('san·ɪk) *adj.* sónico. —**sonic boom,** estampido supersónico.

son-in-law *n.* [*pl.* **sons-in-law**] yerno; hijo político.

sonnet ('san·ɪt) *n.* soneto. —**sonneteer** (-ə'tɪr) *n.* sonetista.

sonny ('sʌn·i) *n., colloq.* hijito.

sonorous (sə'nor·əs) *adj.* sonoro; resonante. —**sonority,** *n.* sonoridad.

soon (sun) *adv.* pronto. —**as soon as,** luego que; tan pronto como; apenas. —**how soon?,** ¿cuándo? —**soon after,** poco despues (de).

sooner ('su·nər) *adv., comp. de* **soon;** más pronto; antes; mejor. —**I**

would (o **had**) **sooner die,** antes la muerte; preferiría morir. **—no sooner said than done,** dicho y hecho. **—sooner or later,** tarde o temprano; a la corta o a la larga. **—the sooner the better,** cuanto antes mejor.

soonest ('sun·ıst) *adv.,superl. de* soon; lo más pronto. **—at the soonest,** cuanto antes.

soot (sut) *n.* hollín; tizne. **—sooty,** *adj.* hollimiento; tiznado.

sooth (suθ) *n., archaic* verdad.

soothe (su:ð) *v.t.* **1,** (calm; mollify) calmar; apaciguar. **2,** (allay; mitigate) aliviar; mitigar; sosegar.

soothsayer ('su:θ,sei·ər) *n.* adivino; adivinador [*fem.* -dora].

sop (sap) *n.* **1,** (something dipped in a liquid) sopa. **2,** (something given to appease) regalo; apaciguamiento. **—v.t.** [**sopped, sopping**] **1,** (dip; soak) empapar; ensopar. **2,** [*usu.* **sop up**] (absorb) embeber; absorber.

sophism ('saf·ız·əm) *n.* sofisma.

sophist ('saf·ıst) *n.* sofista. **—sophistic** (sə'fıs·tık) *adj.* sofista.

sophisticate (sə'fıs·tı·keit) *v.t.* hacer mundano. **—n.** (-kət) persona mundana. **—sophisticated** (-,kei·tıd) *adj.* mundano. **—sophistication** (-'kei·ʃən) *n.* mundanería.

sophistry ('saf·ıs·tri) *n.* sofistería.

sophomore ('saf·ə·mor) *n.* estudiante de segundo año. **—sophomoric** (-'mor·ık) *adj.* juvenil; inmaduro.

soporific (,sap·ə'rıf·ık) *adj. & n.* soporífero.

sopping ('sap·ıŋ) *adj.* empapado; ensopado. **—sopping wet,** empapado; ensopado; calado hasta los huesos.

soppy ('sap·i) *adj.* **1,** (soaked) empapado; ensopado. **2,** (rainy) lluvioso.

soprano (sə'præn·o) *n.* [*pl.* -os] soprano. **—adj.** de soprano.

sorcery ('sor·sə·ri) *n.* hechicería; brujería. **—sorcerer,** *n.* hechicero; brujo. **—sorceress,** *n.* hechicera; bruja.

sordid ('sor·dıd) *adj.* sórdido. **—sordidness,** *n.* sordidez.

sore (so:r) *adj.* **1,** (sensitive; painful) dolorido; inflamado; enconado; tierno. **2,** (suffering pain) afligido; apenado. **3,** *colloq.* (offended; angry) enojado; ofendido; picado. **—n.** herida; llaga; úlcera.

—soreness, *n.* dolor; dolencia; inflamación.

sorehead ('sor,hɛd) *n., colloq.* persona resentida; persona susceptible.

sorghum ('sor·gəm) *n.* sorgo; zahína.

sorority (sə'ror·ə·ti) *n.* hermandad de mujeres.

sorrel ('sar·əl) *n.* **1,** (plant) acedera. **2,** (color) rojizo; alazán. **3,** (horse) alazán. **—adj.** rojizo; alazán.

sorrow ('sar·o) *n.* pesar; tristeza; dolor; pena. **—v.i.** entristecerse; apenarse. **—sorrowful,** *adj.* triste; afligido; pesaroso.

sorry ('sar·i) *adj.* **1,** (feeling sorrow) triste; pesaroso; afligido. **2,** (feeling regret) arrepentido. **3,** (feeling pity) compasivo. **4,** (deplorable) triste; malo; lastimoso. **5,** (worthless; mean) vil; despreciable. **—be** o **feel sorry,** sentir; compadecer: *I am sorry,* Lo siento; *I am very sorry,* Lo siento mucho; *I am sorry for her,* La compadezco; *I am sorry to do this,* Siento hacer esto.

sort (sort) *n.* **1,** (class) clase; especie. **2,** (character) tipo. **3,** (way; fashion) estilo; manera; modo. **—v.t.** **1,** (classify) clasificar. **2,** (separate) separar; escoger; entresacar. **—after a sort,** de cierto modo; hasta cierto punto. **—all sorts of,** toda clase de. **—of sorts, 1,** (of various kinds) de varias clases. **2,** (mediocre) de poco valor. **—sort of,** *colloq.* algo; más o menos. **—out of sorts,** indispuesto; malhumorado.

sortie ('sor·ti) *n.* salida.

so-so *adj.* mediano; pasadero; regular. **—adv.** así así; medianamente; regularmente.

sot (sat) *n.* zaque; beodo; borrachín.

soubriquet ('so·brı,kei; 'su-) *n.* = **sobriquet.**

soufflé (su'flei) *n.* flan.

sought (sot) *v., pret. & p.p. de* seek.

soul (so:l) *n.* **1,** (spirit) alma; espíritu. **2,** (courage) ánimo; fuerza. **3,** (human being) ser humano. **—soulful,** *adj.* conmovedor; espiritual. **—soulless,** *adj.* desalmado; sin conciencia.

sound (saund) *n.* **1,** (vibration perceived by the ear) sonido. **2,** (noise) ruido. **3,** (inlet) brazo de mar. **4,** (strait) estrecho. **—adj.** **1,** (in good health or condition) sano. **2,** (unhurt) ileso. **3,** (whole; unimpaired) entero; perfecto. **4,** (firm; strong; solid) firme; fuerte; sólido. **5,** (financially solvent) solvente. **6,** (reliable) confiable; seguro. **7,** (honorable) honrado; recto. —*v.i.* **1,** (make a sound; be heard) sonar. **2,** (make a noise) hacer ruido. **3,** (seem; appear) parecer. **4,** (measure depth of water) sondar; sondear. —*v.t.* **1,** (cause to sound) tocar; sonar. **2,** (utter) proferir; enunciar; pronunciar. **3,** (measure the depth of) sondar; sondear. **4,** (probe) tentar; examinar; investigar. —*adv.* profundamente. —**of sound mind,** en su juicio cabal. —**sound effects,** efectos sonoros. —**sound film,** película sonora. —**sound off, 1,** (count) contar. **2,** *slang* (speak) hablar; parlotear. —**sound out,** tantear. —**sound sleep,** sueño profundo. —**sound track,** banda o guía sonora. —**sound wave,** onda sonora.

sounding ('saun·dɪŋ) *adj.* sonante; sonoro; resonante. —*n.* sondeo; sonda. —**sounding board, 1,** *mus.; elect.* caja de resonancia; tornavoz. **2,** (spokesperson) portavoz. **3,** persona o grupo que evalúa nuevas ideas. —**sounding line,** sonda.

soundless ('saund·ləs) *adj.* **1,** (silent) silencioso; mudo. **2,** (unfathomable) insondable.

soundly ('saund·li) *adv.* **1,** (solidly; firmly) fuertemente; firmemente. **2,** (completely) cabalmente; enteramente; profundamente.

soundness ('saund·nəs) *n.* **1,** (good health or condition) sanidad; salud. **2,** (firmness; strength) firmeza; fuerza; solidez. **3,** (wholeness) entereza; perfección. **4,** (solvency) solvencia. **5,** (reliability) seguridad.

soundproof ('saund,pruf) *adj.* a prueba de sonido.

soup (sup) *n.* **1,** (food) sopa. **2,** *slang* (nitroglycerin) nitroglicerina. —**in the soup,** *slang* en apuros; en aprietos. —**soup dish** o **plate,** plato sopero. —**soup ladle,** cucharón. —**soup spoon,** cuchara de sopa.

soupy ('su·pi) *adj.* **1,** (thin, as gruel) claro. **2,** (thick, as fog) pegajoso; espeso.

sour (saur) *adj.* **1,** (having an acid or tart taste) agrio; ácido; acre; áspero. **2,** (unpleasant) desagradable; enfadoso; malhumorado. —*v.t.* agriar; avinagrar; fermentar. —*v.i.*

agriarse; avinagrarse; cortarse; fermentar. —**sour grapes,** uvas verdes.

source (sors) *n.* fuente; origen.

sour cream crema cortada.

sourdough ('saur,do) *n.* **1,** (leaven) levadura. **2,** (prospector) buscador.

sourness ('saur·nəs) *n.* **1,** (sour or harsh taste) agrura; acidez; aspereza. **2,** (unpleasantness) mal humor; acrimonia.

sourpuss ('saur,pʊs) *n., slang* persona malhumorada.

souse (saus) *v.t.* **1,** (drench; soak) mojar; chapuzar. **2,** (pickle) escabechar; poner en escabeche; adobar. **3,** *slang* (intoxicate) embriagar. —*n., slang* (drunkard) borrachín; borracho.

south (sauθ) *n.* sur; sud; mediodía. —*adj.* sur; del sur; meridional. —*adv.* al sur; hacia el sur.

southeast (,sauθ'ist) *n.* sudeste; sureste. —*adj.* del o hacia el sudeste. —*adv.* al o hacia el sudeste.

southeaster (,sauθ'is·tər) *n.* viento (del) sudeste.

southeasterly (,sauθ'is·tər·li) *adj.* (del) sudeste. —*adv.* hacia el sudeste.

southeastern (,sauθ'is·tərn) *adj.* (del) sudeste.

southerly ('sʌð·ər·li) *adj.* sur; del sur; hacia el sur. —*adv.* hacia el sur.

southern ('sʌð·ərn) *adj.* sur; del sur; meridional; sureño. —**southerner,** *n.* sureño; habitante del sur. —**southern lights,** aurora austral.

southland ('sauθ·lənd) *n.* tierras del sur; sur; mediodía.

southpaw ('sauθ,pɔ) *n. & adj., slang* zurdo.

South Pole polo sur.

southward ('sauθ·wərd) *adj.* en o de dirección sur. —*adv.* hacia el sur.

southwest (,sauθ'wɛst) *n.* sudoeste; suroeste. —*adj.* del o hacia el sudoeste. —*adv.* al o hacia el sudoeste.

southwester (,sauθ'wɛs·tər) *n.* viento (del) sudeste.

southwesterly (,sauθ'wɛs·tər·li) *adj.* (del) sudoeste. —*adv.* hacia el sudoeste.

southwestern (,sauθ'wɛs·tərn) *adj.* (del) sudoeste.

souvenir (,su·və'nɪr) *n.* recuerdo.

sovereign ('sav·rɪn) *n.* **1,** (ruler) soberano. **2,** (Brit. coin) moneda inglesa de oro del valor de una libra esterlina. —*adj.* soberano; supremo. —**sovereignty,** soberanía.

soviet ('so·vi·ɛt) *n.* soviet; *pl.* soviets o soviéticos. —*adj.* soviético.

sow (soʊ) *v.t.* & *i.* [*p.p.* sowed o sown] sembrar. —**sow one's wild oats,** correr sus mocedades.

sow (sau) *n.* puerca; cochina.

sower ('so·ər) *n.* sembrador [*fem.* -dora].

sowing ('so·ɪŋ) *n.* siembra.

sox (saks) *n.pl.,var. de* socks.

soy (sɔi) *n.* soya; soja. *También,* soya ('sɔ·jə).

soybean ('sɔi,bin) *n.* semilla de soya.

spa (spaɹ) *n.* balneario de aguas minerales.

space (speis) *n.* espacio. —*v.t.* espaciar. —*adj.* espacial; del espacio. —**space bar,** espaciador. —**space heater,** calentador pequeño. —**space shuttle,** transbordador espacial. —**space station,** estación espacial. —**space suit,** traje espacial.

spacecraft ('speis,kræft) *n.* astronave.

spaceman ('speis,mæn) *n.* [*pl.* -men] astronauta.

spaceship ('speis,ʃɪp) *n.* astronave.

spacewalk ('speis,wɔk) *n.* paseo en el espacio.

spacious ('spei·ʃəs) *adj.* espacioso. —**spaciousness,** *n.* espaciosidad.

spade (speid) *n.* **1,** (garden tool) pala; laya. **2,** (sapper's tool) zapa. **3,** *cards* pique *(in the French deck);* espada *(in the Spanish deck).* —*v.t.* labrar con la pala; layar.

spadework ('speid·wʌrk) *n.* trabajo preliminar.

spaghetti (spə'gɛt·i) *n.* fideos.

spahi ('spa·hi) *n.* espahí.

span (spæn) *n.* **1,** (extent) extensión; espacio; alcance; distancia. **2,** (distance from thumb to forefinger) palmo. **3,** (bridge) puente. **4,** (distance traversed by a bridge) luz de puente. **5,** (opening of an arch) ojo. **6,** (pair of draft animals) par; pareja. **7,** (wing length) envergadura. —*v.t.* [**spanned, spanning**] **1,** (measure) medir a palmos; medir. **2,** (traverse) atravesar; cruzar. **3,** (comprise; include) abarcar; abrazar.

spangle ('spæŋ·gəl) *n.* lentejuela;

bricho. —*v.t.* adornar con lentejuelas; estrellar.

Spaniard ('spæn·jərd) *n.* español.

spaniel ('spæn·jəl) *n.* perro de aguas.

Spanish ('spæn·ɪʃ) *adj.* & *n.* español [*fem.* -ñola].

Spanish-American *adj.* & *n.* hispanoamericano.

Spanish Main el mar de las Antillas.

spank (spæŋk) *n.* nalgada. —*v.t.* dar nalgadas. —*v.i.* correr; ir de prisa.

spanker ('spæŋk·ər) *n.* **1,** *colloq.* (large or outstanding thing) cosa muy grande o hermosa o de mucho éxito. **2,** *naut.* cangreja de popa.

spanking ('spæŋk·ɪŋ) *n.* nalgada; tunda. —*adj., colloq.* **1,** (swift) veloz; ligero. **2,** (very large or outstanding) muy grande o hermoso. **3,** (strong) fuerte; robusto.

spanner ('spæn·er) *n., Brit.* desvolvedor; llave.

spar (spaɹ) *n.* **1,** *naut.* verga. **2,** *aero.* viga mayor. **3,** (mineral) espato. —*v.i.* [**sparred, sparring**] **1,** (box cautiously) boxear; atrancar. **2,** (dispute) disputar; reñir; pelear.

spare (speɹ) *v.t.* **1,** (show mercy to) perdonar; hacer gracia de; permitir vivir. **2,** (refrain from) abstenerse de; refrenarse de. **3,** (dispense with) pasarse sin. **4,** (have available) disponer de; tener disponible. **5,** (skimp; save) escatimar; ahorrar; economizar. —*v.i.* economizar. —*adj.* **1,** (in excess) de sobra; sobrante. **2,** (in reserve) de recambio; de repuesto. **3,** (available) disponible. **4,** (lean) flaco; delgado. **5,** (meager) escaso; mezquino. **6,** (frugal) ahorrativo. —*n.* pieza de recambio o de repuesto. —**have (time, money,** *etc.***) to spare,** tener (tiempo, dinero, etc.) de sobra. —**spare no expense,** no escatimar gastos. —**spare part,** pieza de recambio o de repuesto. —**spare time,** tiempo desocupado; ratos perdidos.

sparerib ('sper,rɪb) *n.* costilla de cerdo casi descarnada; costilla superior.

sparing ('sper·ɪŋ) *adj.* **1,** (scanty) escaso; poco; limitado. **2,** (economical) ahorrativo; frugal; económico.

spark (spark) *n.* **1,** (fiery particle) chispa. **2,** (glimmer) vislumbre; destello. **3,** *colloq.* (suitor) galán. **4,**

(dandy) petimetre; pisaverde. —*v.i.* chispear; echar chispas. —*v.t.* **1,** (kindle; motivate) animar; despertar; excitar. **2,** *colloq.* (court; woo) galantear; cortejar.

sparkle ('spar·kəl) *v.i.* **1,** (emit little sparks) chispear; centellear. **2,** (glitter) relucir. **3,** (effervesce) espumar; ser espumoso. **4,** (be vivacious) brillar; destellar; ser vivaz. —*n.* **1,** (small spark) chispita. **2,** (brilliance) esplendor; brillo. **3,** (vivacity) brillo; destello; vivacidad.

sparkler ('spar·klər) *n.* **1,** (something that sparkles) centelleador. **2,** (diamond) brillante; diamante.

sparkling ('spar·klɪŋ) *adj.* **1,** (emitting sparks) chispeante; centelleante. **2,** (effervescent) espumoso.

spark plug bujía.

sparrow ('spær·o) *n.* gorrión. —**sparrow hawk,** gavilán.

sparse (spars) *adj.* **1,** (thinly distributed) poco denso; esparcido. **2,** (thin; scanty) escaso. —**sparseness; sparsity,** *n.* escasez.

Spartan ('spar·tən) *adj.* & *n.* espartano.

spasm ('spæz·əm) *n.* espasmo.

spasmodic (spæz'mad·ɪk) *adj.* espasmódico.

spastic ('spæs·tɪk) *adj.* & *n.* espástico.

spat (spæt) *n.* **1,** (petty dispute) riña; disputa. **2,** (light blow) palmadita; manotada. **3,** (splash, as of rain) gota grande de lluvia. **4,** *usu.pl.* (short cloth gaiters) polainas. **5,** (young oyster) ostra joven. —*v.i.* [**spatted, spatting**] (quarrel) reñir; pelear. —*v.t.* (strike lightly) dar palmaditas o manotadas. —*v.,* *pret.* & *p.p.* de **spit.**

spate (speit) *n.* crecida; torrente.

spatial ('spei·ʃəl) *adj.* espacial.

spatter ('spæt·ər) *v.t.* & *i.* **1,** (scatter or sprinkle in small drops) rociar; regar. **2,** (splash) salpicar; manchar. —*n.* salpicadura; rociada.

spatula ('spætʃ·ə·lə) *n.* espátula.

spawn (spɔːn) *n.* **1,** (eggs or young of fishes, etc.) freza; huevos; pececillos. **2,** (offspring) cría; prole. **3,** *fig.* (result) resultado; fruto. —*v.i.* poner huevos; desovar; frezar. —*v.t.* producir en abundancia; engendrar; procrear.

spay (spei) *v.t.* castrar (hembras); sacar los ovarios a.

speak (spik) *v.t.* & *i.* [**spoke, spoken, speaking**] hablar. —*v.t.* **1,** (say) decir. **2,** (utter; pronounce) proferir; pronunciar. —**so to speak,** por decirlo así. —**speak for itself,** ser manifiesto; ser claro. —**speak one's mind,** decir lo que piensa; hablar sin rodeos. —**speak out,** hablar claro; elevar la voz. —**speak thickly,** hablar con media lengua. —**speak through the nose,** ganguear. —**speak to the point,** ir al grano. —**speak up,** hablar alto.

speakeasy ('spik·i·zi) *n., slang* taberna ilegal.

speaker ('spik·ər) *n.* **1,** (one who speaks) el que habla. **2,** (participant in a conversation) interlocutor. **3,** (orator) orador [*fem.* -dora]. **4,** (lecturer) conferenciante. **5,** (presiding officer) presidente. **6,** (loudspeaker) altavoz; *Amer.* altoparlante. —**speaker of Spanish, English,** *etc.,* persona de habla española, inglesa, etc.

speaking ('spi·kɪŋ) *adj.* hablante. —*n.* **1,** (speech) habla. **2,** (oratory) oratoria; elocuencia. —*interj. (in answering the telephone)* ¡al habla! —**English-speaking, Spanish-speaking,** *etc.,* *adj.* de habla inglesa, española, etc.

spear (spɪr) *n.* **1,** (weapon) lanza. **2,** *bot.* tallo. —*v.t.* lancear; dar lanzadas.

spearhead ('spɪr,hed) *n.* **1,** (point of a spear) punta de lanza. **2,** *fig.* (leader) lancero; líder.

spearmint ('spɪr·mɪnt) *n.* hierbabuena puntiaguda; menta verde.

special ('speʃ·əl) *adj.* especial; particular. —**special delivery,** correspondencia urgente.

specialist ('speʃ·ə·lɪst) *n.* especialista.

specialize ('speʃ·ə,laiz) *v.t.* especializar. —*v.i.* especializarse. —**specialization** (-lɪ'zei·ʃən) *n.* especialización.

specialty ('speʃ·əl·ti) *n.* especialidad.

specie ('spi·ʃi) *n.* dinero contante; efectivo; numerario.

species ('spi·ʃiz) *n.sing.* & *pl.* especie.

specific (spə'sɪf·ɪk) *adj.* & *n.* específico.

specify ('spes·ə,fai) *v.t.* especificar. —**specification** (-fɪ'kei·ʃən) *n.* especificación.

specimen ('spɛs·ə·mən) n. espécimen; muestra; ejemplar.

specious ('spi·ʃəs) adj. especioso; engañoso. —**speciousness,** n. especiosidad.

speck (spɛk) n. 1, (spot) mácula; manchita. 2, (small particle; bit) partícula; mota; pizca. —v.t. manchar; salpicar.

speckle ('spɛk·əl) n. punto; mota. —v.t. motear; puntear; salpicar.

specs (spɛks) n.pl., colloq. = spectacles.

spectacle ('spɛk·tə·kəl) n. 1, (sight; display) espectáculo. 2, pl. (eyeglasses) anteojos; espejuelos; lentes; gafas.

spectacular (spɛk'tæk·jə·lər) adj. espectacular; ostentoso; aparatoso. —n. programa espectacular.

spectator ('spɛk·tei·tər) n. espectador [fem. -dora].

specter también, **spectre** ('spɛk·tər) n. espectro; fantasma. —**spectral** (-trəl) adj. espectral.

spectrogram ('spɛk·trə,græm) n. espectrograma. —**spectrograph** (-græf) n. espectrógrafo.

spectrometer (spɛk'tram·ə·tər) n. espectrómetro.

spectroscope ('spɛk·trə·skop) n. espectroscopio. —**spectroscopic** (-'skap·ɪk) adj. espectroscópico. —**spectroscopy** (-'tras·kə·pi) n. espectroscopia.

spectrum ('spɛk·trəm) n. espectro.

speculate ('spɛk·jə,leit) v.i. especular. —**speculation,** n. especulación. —**speculative** (-lə·tɪv) adj. especulativo. —**speculator,** n. especulador [fem. -dora].

sped (spɛd) v., pret. & p.p. de speed.

speech (spitʃ) n. 1, (power of speaking) habla. 2, (address) discurso. 3, (language) habla; idioma; lenguaje. 4, (manner of speaking) lenguaje; manera de hablar. —**speechless,** adj. mudo; callado.

speed (spiːd) n. 1, (rapidity or rate of motion) velocidad; rapidez. 2, (haste) prisa. 3, (promptness) presteza; prontitud. —v.t. [pret. & p.p. **speeded** o **sped**] 1, (expedite) acelerar; apresurar; dar prisa; expedir. 2, [usu. **speed up**] (increase the speed of) acelerar; avivar. 3, (send) despedir; despachar. —v.i. 1, (move rapidly) correr; apresurarse; darse prisa. 2, [usu.

speed up] (increase speed) acelerar. 3, (go too fast) ir con exceso de velocidad. —**at full speed,** a carrera tendida; a toda velocidad; a todo correr. —**full speed,** galope; carrera tendida. —**make speed,** acelerarse; apresurarse. —**speed limit,** velocidad máxima.

speedboat ('spid,bot) n. lancha de carreras.

speeder ('spi·dər) n. 1, (person or thing that moves fast) persona o cosa que corre a gran velocidad. 2, (driver who exceeds the speed limit) automovilista que corre a velocidad excesiva.

speeding ('spi·dɪŋ) n. 1, (acceleration) aceleración. 2, (excessive speed) exceso de velocidad; extravelocidad.

speedometer (spi'dam·ə·tər) n. velocímetro; celerímetro.

speed-up n., colloq. aceleramiento; aceleración.

speedway ('spid·wei) n. carretera abierta.

speedy ('spid·i) adj. veloz; rápido; ligero.

spell (spɛl) v.t. [pret. & p.p. **spelled** o **spelt**] 1, (form or express by or in letters) deletrear; escribir. 2, (signify; mean) significar; indicar. 3, [pret. & p.p. **spelled**] (replace temporarily; relieve) revezar; reemplazar; relevar. —v.i. deletrear; saber deletrear; escribir con buena (o mala) ortografía. —n. 1, (charm; enchantment) hechizo; encanto. 2, (turn; shift) tanda; turno. 3, (short period) rato; corto período; tiempito. 4, colloq. (ailment) ataque (de una enfermedad). —**by spells,** a ratos; por turnos. —**put under a spell; cast a spell on,** hechizar; encantar. —**spell out,** 1, (write or pronounce by letters) deletrear. 2, (explain in detail) detallar; explicar.

spellbinder ('spɛl,bain·dər) n. orador hechizante.

spellbinding ('spɛl,bain·dɪŋ) adj. hechizante; encantador.

spellbound ('spɛl·baund) adj. encantado; hechizado.

speller ('spɛl·ər) n. 1, (one who spells) deletreador. 2, (textbook) silabario; abecedario.

spelling ('spɛl·ɪŋ) n. deletreo; ortografía. —**spelling bee,** concurso de ortografía. —**spelling book** o **primer** ('prɪm·ər) silabario; abecedario.

spelt (spɛlt) v., pret. & p.p. de
spell. —n., bot. espelta.
spend (spɛnd) v.t. & i. [pret. & p.p.
spent] **1,** (expend; consume) gastar.
2, (employ, as time) pasar.
—**spender,** n. gastador [fem. -dora].
spendthrift ('spɛnd·θrɪft) n. &
adj. pródigo; derrochador; manirroto; Amer. botarate.
spent (spɛnt) v., pret. & p.p. de
spend. —adj. **1,** (fatigued) cansado;
extenuado. **2,** (used up) gastado;
agotado; consumido.
sperm (spʌrm) n. esperma.
sperm whale cachalote.
spew (spjuː) v.t. & i. vomitar;
arrojar; escupir. —n. vómito.
sphere (sfɪr) n. esfera. —**spherical**
('sfɛr·ɪ·kəl) adj. esférico.
spheroid ('sfɪr·ɔɪd) n. esferoide.
—**spheroidal** (sfɪ'rɔɪ·dəl) adj.
esferoidal.
sphincter ('sfɪŋk·tər) n. esfínter.
sphinx (sfɪŋks) n. esfinge.
spice (spais) n. **1,** (seasoning)
especia; condimento. **2,** (zest; piquancy) picante; gusto; saborete. **3,**
(cream; choice part) nata; flor y
nata. —v.t. **1,** (season) especiar;
condimentar; sazonar. **2,** (add zest
to) dar picante o gusto a. —**spicy,**
adj. especiado; condimentado;
picante; sabroso.
spick-and-span ('spɪk·ən'spæn)
adj. limpio; puro; flamante.
spider ('spai·dər) n. araña.
—**spider web,** telaraña.
spiel (spiːl; ʃpiːl) n., slang discurso
persuasivo; arenga. —v.i. arengar.
—**spieler,** n. vociferador [fem.
-dora].
spigot ('spɪg·ət) n. llave; grifo;
espita.
spike (spaik) n. **1,** (large nail) clavo
largo; perno; alcayata. **2,** (sharp-
pointed projection) resalto; punta. **3,**
bot. espiga. —v.t. **1,** (pierce or fasten with spikes) empernar; clavar. **2,**
(frustrate) frustrar. **3,** (put an end to)
acabar; poner fin a. **4,** (add liquor
to) añadir licor a.
spikenard ('spaik·nərd) n. nardo;
espicanardo.
spill (spɪl) v.t. [pret. & p.p. **spilled**
o **spilt**] verter; derramar. —v.i.
derramarse; perderse; rebosar. —n.
1, (flowing or running out)
derrame; derramamiento. **2,** (upset)
vuelco. **3,** colloq. (fall, as from a
horse) caída. —**spill the beans,**
slang revelar el secreto.

spillway ('spɪl·wei) n. bocacaz;
vertedero.
spilt (spɪlt) v., pret. & p.p. de **spill.**
spin (spɪn) v.t. [**spun, spinning**] **1,**
(twist into threads) hilar. **2,** (make
with threads; weave) tejer. **3,** (cause
to revolve rapidly) hacer girar. **4,**
(narrate) contar, esp. cuentos largos
e increíbles. —v.i. **1,** (revolve rapidly) girar; dar vueltas. **2,** (move or
ride rapidly) rodar. —n. **1,** (spinning motion; spiral course) giro;
vuelta. **2,** (rapid ride) paseo. **3,**
aero. barrena. —**spin out,** alargar;
prolongar. —**take a spin; go for a
spin,** dar un paseo; dar una vuelta.
spinach ('spɪn·ɪtʃ) n. **1,** (plant)
espinaca. **2,** (leaves used as food)
espinacas.
spinal ('spai·nəl) adj. espinal.
—**spinal column,** columna vertebral; espina dorsal. —**spinal cord,**
médula espinal.
spindle ('spɪn·dəl) n. **1,** (for spinning) huso. **2,** (shaft; axle) eje;
árbol. —**spindling** (-dlɪŋ); **spindly**
(-dli) adj. largo y delgado; flaco.
spindle-legged adj. zanquilargo.
También, **spindle-shanked.**
spine (spain) n. **1,** (backbone) dorsal; espinazo. **2,** (quill; thorn)
espina; púa. **3,** (stiff backing, as of
a book) lomo. —**spineless,** adj.
pusilánime; cobarde.
spinet ('spɪn·ɪt) n. espineta.
spinner ('spɪn·ər) n. **1,** (person)
(masc.) hilador; (fem.) hilandera. **2,**
(machine) máquina hiladora;
máquina de hilar.
spinning ('spɪn·ɪŋ) n. hilandería.
—adj. hilador. —**spinning machine,** máquina hiladora; máquina
de hilar. —**spinning mill,** hilandería. —**spinning wheel,** torno de
hilar.
spin-off n. subproducto.
spinster ('spɪn·stər) n. soltera;
solterona. —**spinsterhood,** n.
soltería.
spiny ('spai·ni) adj. espinoso.
spiral ('spai·rəl) n. espiral. —adj.
enrollado; acaracolado; espiral.
—v.i. moverse o volar en espiral.
—**spiral staircase,** escalera espiral
o de caracol.
spire (spair) n. **1,** archit. aguja. **2,**
(coil) espira. **3,** (spike; stalk) tallo.
spirit ('spɪr·ɪt) n. **1,** (inspiring principle; soul) espíritu; alma. **2,** (nature) carácter; genio. **3,** (attitude;
disposition) humor; temple. **4,** usu.

pl. (vivacity; optimism) viveza; vivacidad; alegría. **5,** *usu. pl.* (courage) ánimo; valor. **6,** (ghost) espectro; fantasma. **7,** *pl.* (distillate) extracto; quintaesencia. **8,** *pl.* (alcoholic liquor) alcohol; licor. —*v.t.* [*usu.* **spirit away** o **off**] llevar o conducir secretamente; arrebatar. —**be in good** *or* **high spirits,** estar alegre; estar de buen humor. —**be in low spirits; be low in spirit,** estar desanimado o abatido. —**good** o **high spirits,** alegría; vivacidad; buen humor. —**keep up one's spirits,** mantener el valor; no desanimarse. —**lose (one's) spirit,** desanimarse. —**low spirits,** abatimiento; decaimiento. —**out of spirits,** triste; abatido. —**show spirit,** mostrar buen ánimo.

spirited ('spɪr·ɪt·ɪd) *adj.* vivo; fogoso; animoso.

spirit lamp lámpara de alcohol.

spiritless ('spɪr·ɪt·ləs) *adj.* exánime; apocado; sin ánimo.

spirit level nivel de aire.

spiritual ('spɪr·ɪ·tʃu·əl) *adj.* espiritual. —*n.* canción religiosa de los negros.

spiritualism ('spɪr·ɪ·tʃu·ə·lɪz·əm) *n.* espiritismo. —**spiritualist,** *n.* espiritista. —**spiritualistic,** *adj.* espiritista.

spirituous ('spɪr·ɪ·tʃu·əs) *adj.* espirituoso.

spit (spɪt) *v.i. & t.* [*pret. & p.p.* **spat** o **spit**; *ger.* **spitting**] (eject, as saliva from the mouth) escupir; expectorar; esputar. —*v.t.* **1,** (spew out) vomitar; arrojar. **2,** [*pret. & p.p.* **spitted**] (impale on a sharp point) espetar. —*n.* **1,** (saliva) saliva; escupo. **2,** (sharp bar or stick) asador; espetón; varilla. **3,** (narrow point of land) punta o lengua de tierra. —**the spit and image of,** el retrato de.

spite (spaɪt) *n.* despecho; rencor; inquina; malevolencia. —*v.t.* vejar; causar pesar; molestar. —**in spite of,** a pesar de; a despecho de; no obstante.

spiteful ('spaɪt·fəl) *adj.* rencoroso; malicioso.

spittle ('spɪt·əl) *n.* saliva; esputo; escupo.

spittoon (spɪ'tuːn) *n.* escupidera.

spitz (spɪts) *n.* perro de Pomerania.

splash (splæʃ) *v.t.* **1,** (spatter, as with mud or water) enlodar; manchar. **2,** (dash; scatter about)

salpicar; rociar. —*v.i.* chapotear; chapalear. —*n.* **1,** (act or sound of splashing) chapoteo; chapaleteo. **2,** (quantity splashed) salpicadura; rociada. **3,** (ostentatious display) ostentación; espectáculo.

splashy ('splæʃ·i) *adj.* **1,** (wet; muddy) fangoso; lodoso. **2,** (ostentatious) llamativo.

splatter ('splæt·ər) *v.t. & i. & n.* = **spatter.**

splay (spleɪ) *v.t.* **1,** (bevel) achaflanar; biselar. **2,** (spread out) desplegar; extender. —*v.i.* desplegarse; extenderse. —*adj.* desplegado; extendido. —*n.* bisel; chaflán.

splayfoot ('spleɪ.fʊt) *n.* pie aplastado y desplegado. —**splayfooted,** *adj.* que tiene los pies aplastados y desplegados.

spleen (spliːn) *n.* **1,** *anat.* bazo. **2,** (ill humor) mal humor; esplín; melancolía. **3,** (anger) ira; rencor. —**vent one's spleen,** descargar la bilis o el rencor.

splendid ('splen·dɪd) *adj.* espléndido. *También, colloq.,* **splendiferous** (-'dɪf·ə·rəs).

splendor *también,* **splendour** ('splen·dər) *n.* esplendor. —**splendorous,** *adj.* espléndido.

splenetic (splɪ'net·ɪk) *adj.* bilioso; rencoroso.

splice (splaɪs) *v.t.* empalmar; juntar. —*n.* empalme; juntura. —**get spliced,** *slang* casarse.

spline (splaɪn) *n.* **1,** (flexible strip of wood) astilla; varilla flexible de madera o de metal. **2,** (slot; groove) ranura.

splint (splɪnt) *n.* astilla; tablilla; *surg.* cabestrillo. —*v.t.* entablillar.

splinter ('splɪn·tər) *n.* astilla. —*v.t.* astillar. —*v.i.* astillarse.

splinterproof ('splɪn·tər.pruf) *adj.* inastillable.

split (splɪt) *v.t.* [**split, splitting**] hendir; partir; dividir. —*v.i.* hendirse; partirse; dividirse. —*n.* **1,** (crack; rent) hendidura; grieta. **2,** (division; schism) separación; cisma. **3,** (half-bottle) media botella; botella pequeña. —*adj.* hendido; partido; dividido. —**split hairs,** pararse en pelillos. —**split-level,** *adj.* de pisos construidos a desnivel. —**split one's sides with laughter,** desternillarse o reventar de risa.

splotch (splatʃ) *n.* mancha; borrón.

—*v.t.* manchar; emborronar; salpicar.

splurge (splʌrdʒ) *n.* ostentación; alarde. —*v.i.* alardear; hacer alarde.

splutter ('splʌt·ər) *v.t.* & *i.* farfullar. —*n.* farfulla.

spoil (spɔil) *v.t.* [*pret.* & *p.p.* **spoiled** o **spoilt**] **1,** (seriously impair) dañar; estropear; echar a perder. **2,** (overindulge, as a child) malcriar; mimar; corromper. **3,** (pervert) pervertir. **4,** (plunder; despoil) pillar; saquear; despojar. —*v.i.* podrirse; corromperse; echarse a perder. —**spoils,** *n.pl.* despojos; botín; presa. —**spoil for,** ansiar; anhelar.

spoilage ('spɔi·lidʒ) *n.* deterioro.

spoiled (spɔild) *adj.* consentido; mimado; engreído.

spoilsport ('spɔil,sport) *n.* aguafiestas.

spoke (spok) *n.* rayo de rueda. —*v., pret. de* **speak.**

spoken ('spo·kən) *v., p.p. de* **speak.** —*adj.* hablado.

spokesman ('spoks·mən) *n.* [*pl.* **-men**] [*fem.* **spokeswoman** (*pl.* **-women**)] portavoz. *También,* **spokesperson,** *n.m.* & *f.*

spoliation (,spo·li'ei·ʃən) *n.* despojo.

spondee ('span·di) *n.* espondeo.

sponge (spʌndʒ) *n.* esponja. —*v.t.* & *i.* **1,** (absorb; wipe up) esponjar; sorber. **2,** *colloq.* (live at another's expense) pegar la gorra; ir o andar de gorra. —**sponger,** *n., colloq.* gorrón; parásito. —**spongy,** *adj.* esponjoso; fofo.

sponge cake bizcocho ligero y esponjoso.

sponsor ('span·sər) *n.* **1,** (one who vouches or supports) patrocinador [*fem.* -dora]. **2,** (godfather; godmother) padrino; madrina. —*v.t.* **1,** (vouch for; support) patrocinar. **2,** (act as godparent for) apadrinar.

sponsorship ('span·sər·ʃip) *n.* **1,** (support; surety) patrocinio. **2,** (being a godparent) padrinazgo.

spontaneity (,span·tə'ni·ə·ti) *n.* espontaneidad.

spontaneous (span'tei·ni·əs) *adj.* espontáneo. —**spontaneousness,** *n.* espontaneidad.

spoof (spuf) *n., slang* engaño; broma; burla. —*v.t.* engañar; burlarse de. —*v.i.* bromear; burlar.

spook (spuk) *n., colloq.* fantasma; espectro. —*v.t.* espantar; horripilar.

—**spooky,** *adj.* espectral; misterioso; horripilante.

spool (spuːl) *n.* carrete; canilla. —*v.t.* devanar.

spoon (spuːn) *n.* cuchara; cucharita; cucharón. —*v.i.*, *colloq.* besuquearse; hocicarse.

spoonbill ('spun,bil) *n.* espátula.

spoonful ('spun,ful) *n.* cucharada; cucharadita.

spoony ('spu·ni) *adj.* & *n.*, *colloq.* besucón.

spoor (spur) *n.* huella; pista.

sporadic (spə'ræd·ik) *adj.* esporádico.

spore (spoːr) *n.* espora; simiente.

sport (sport) *n.* **1,** (game; athletic activity) deporte. **2,** (fun; diversion) pasatiempo; diversión; placer. **3,** (jesting) broma; burla. **4,** (plaything) juguete. **5,** (object of ridicule) hazmerreír. **6,** *colloq.* (gambler) jugador. **7,** *colloq.* (sportsmanlike person) jugador generoso; buen perdedor. **8,** (sportsman) deportista. **9,** *colloq.* (flashy person) guapo; petimetre. **10,** *colloq.* (good companion) compañero; compadre. **11,** *biol.* mutante. —*adj.* deportivo; de deporte. —*v.t. colloq.* vestir; lucir; ostentar. —*v.i.* **1,** (play) jugar; divertirse. **2,** (jest; trifle) burlar; bromear. **3,** *biol.* hacer o producir mutación. —**make sport of,** burlarse de.

sporting ('spor·tiŋ) *adj.* deportivo; de juego; de deporte. —**sporting house,** burdel; prostíbulo.

sportive ('spor·tiv) *adj.* festivo; juguetón.

sports *adj.* deportivo; de deporte.

sportscast ('sports,kæst) *n.* programa deportivo. —**sportscaster** *n.* locutor de programa deportivo.

sportsman ('sports·mən) *n.* [*pl.* **-men**] deportista.

sportsmanlike (-laik) *adj.* de deportista; de buen jugador.

sportsmanship (-ʃip) *n.* arte y pericia en el deporte; afición a los deportes.

sportswear ('sports,wɛr) *n.* traje (o trajes) de deporte.

sportswoman ('sports,wum·ən) *n.* [*pl.* **-women**] deportista.

sporty ('spor·ti) *adj.*, *colloq.* **1,** (sporting) deportivo. **2,** (flashy) guapo; llamativo.

spot (spat) *n.* **1,** (stain; blemish) mancha. **2,** (small mark or speck) marca; mota. **3,** (place) sitio; lugar. **4,** *colloq.* (small amount) poquito; pizca. **5,** *colloq.* = **spotlight.** —*v.t.* [**spotted, -ting**] **1,** (stain) manchar. **2,** (mark with specks) motear; salpicar. **3,** (place; locate) colocar; localizar; poner. **4,** (recognize; espy) reconocer; avistar. **5,** (scatter; distribute) esparcir; diseminar. **6,** (remove stains from) limpiar; quitar manchas de. **7,** *colloq.* (give a handicap of or to) dar una ventaja de o a. —*v.i.* **1,** (become spotted) mancharse. **2,** (cause spots) manchar; producir manchas. —*adj.* **1,** (at hand) a mano; disponible. **2,** (ready, as money) contante; efectivo. —**hit the spot,** *colloq.* **1,** (strike the mark) dar en el blanco. **2,** (satisfy) dar satisfacción. —**in a spot,** en apuro; en un aprieto. —**in spots,** aquí y allí. —**on the spot, 1,** (in a given place) allí mismo. **2,** (at once) al punto; en el acto. **3,** = **in a spot.** —**touch a sore spot,** dar en lo vivo.

spot check examen casual o al azar.

spotless ('spat·ləs) *adj.* inmaculado; limpio.

spotlight ('spat·lait) *n.* **1,** (light) foco; proyector; luz concentrada. **2,** (public notice) atención del público.

spotted ('spat·ɪd) *adj.* moteado; abigarrado.

spotter ('spat·ər) *n.* **1,** (cleaner) quitamanchas. **2,** *mil.* apuntador [*fem.* -dora].

spotty ('spat·i) *adj.* **1,** (covered with spots) manchado. **2,** (uneven) desigual; irregular.

spouse (spaus) *n.* cónyuge.

spout (spaut) *v.t.* **1,** (discharge in a stream) arrojar o echar en chorro. **2,** (declaim) declamar. —*v.i.* **1,** (flow in a stream) chorrear; salir en chorro. **2,** (speak pompously) declamar; perorar. —*n.* **1,** (stream) chorro. **2,** (tube for carrying off rain) canelón. **3,** (device for pouring or drawing a liquid) pitón; caño; (*of a coffee pot or teapot*) pico.

sprain (sprein) *n.* torcedura. —*v.t.* torcer.

sprang (spræŋ) *v., pret. de* **spring.**

sprat (spræt) *n.* pequeño arenque.

sprawl (sprɔːl) *v.i.* tenderse; arrellanarse; extenderse. —*n.* postura arrellanada; extensión (*de una ciudad*).

spray (sprei) *n.* **1,** (fine liquid particles) rociada; rocío; espuma del mar. **2,** (atomizer) rociadera; rociador. **3,** (branch) rama. —*v.t. & i.* rociar. —**sprayer,** *n.* rociadera. —**spray gun,** rociadera; pulverizadora.

spread (sprɛd) *v.t. & i.* [*pret. & p.p.* **spread**] **1,** (open or stretch out; unfold) tender(se); extender(se); desplegar(se). **2,** (scatter) esparcir(se); desparramar(se). **3,** (set out; display) exhibir; poner a la vista. **4,** (push apart) apartar(se); abrir(se). **5,** (smear) untar. **6,** (disseminate) propagar(se); difundir(se). **7,** (prepare, as a table) poner (la mesa). —*n.* **1,** (extension; expansion) extensión. **2,** (expanse) espacio; extensión. **3,** (feast) banquete; festín. **4,** (coverlet) colcha; cobertor (de cama). **5,** (difference) diferencia; discrepancia. **6,** (wingspread) envergadura. **7,** (something spread on) capa; jalea, mantequilla, queso, etc., que se unta al pan.

spreadsheet ('sprɛd·ʃit) *n.* hoja electrónica.

spree (spri) *n.* jarana; juerga; parranda; borrachera. —**go on a spree,** ir de juerga; echar una borrachera.

sprig (sprɪg) *n.* **1,** (branch) rama; ramita. **2,** (lad) joven; jovencito; mozuelo.

sprightly ('sprait·li) *adj.* vivo; vivaracho; animado. —*adv.* vivamente; con viveza. —**sprightliness,** *n.* viveza; vivacidad.

spring (sprɪŋ) *v.i.* [**sprang, sprung, springing**] **1,** (leap) saltar; brincar. **2,** (rise up; issue forth suddenly) salir; brotar; emanar; nacer. **3,** (warp) combarse; encorvarse. **4,** (be suddenly released) soltarse de golpe. —*v.t.* **1,** (release suddenly) soltar. **2,** (cause to leap) hacer saltar. **3,** (warp) torcer; combar; encorvar. **4,** (present or make known suddenly) dar (descubrir; echar, etc.) de sopetón. **5,** *slang* (provide bail for) poner fianza por. —*n.* **1,** (leap) salto; brinco. **2,** (season) primavera. **3,** (device for applying tension) muelle; resorte. **4,** (elasticity) elasticidad. **5,** (water rising from the ground) fuente; manantial. **6,** (source) fuente; origen. —*adj.* **1,** (motivated by tension) de muelle; de resorte. **2,** (of springtime) primaveral. **3,** (flowing up from the ground) de manantial. —**spring a leak,** hacer agua; abrirse una vía de agua en. —**spring chicken,** polluelo; mujercita. —**spring fever,** ataque primaveral. —**spring lock,** cerradura de golpe o de muelle. —**spring mattress,** colchón de muelles. —**spring tide,** marea fuerte; aguas vivas.

springboard ('sprɪŋ,bord) n. trampolín.

springer ('sprɪŋ·ər) n. perro de España; perro de caza.

springtime ('sprɪŋ,taim) n. primavera; época primaveral. También, **springtide.**

springy ('sprɪŋ·i) adj. elástico; ágil. —**springiness,** n. elasticidad.

sprinkle ('sprɪŋ·kəl) v.t. 1, (scatter in drops or particles) regar; rociar; esparcir. 2, (strew) salpicar. —v.i. lloviznar; caer en gotas. —n. 1, (light rain) llovizna. 2, (scattering in drops or particles) rociada. 3, (small amount) poquito; pizca.

sprinkler ('sprɪŋ·klər) n. regadera; rociadera.

sprinkling ('sprɪŋ·klɪŋ) n. 1, (scattering in drops) rociada; aspersión. 2, (small amount) poco; pizca. 3, (light rain) llovizna.

sprint (sprɪnt) n. carrera corta a toda velocidad. —v.i. correr a toda velocidad.

sprit (sprɪt) n., naut. botavara.

sprite (sprait) n. duende; hada.

sprocket ('sprak·ɪt) n. diente de rueda de cadena. —**sprocket wheel,** rueda de cadena.

sprout (spraut) v.i. brotar; retoñar. —v.t. hacer brotar; crecer. —n. brote; retoño; renuevo.

spruce (sprus) adj. pulido; pulcro; elegante. —v.t. & i. pulir(se); engalanar(se). —n. abeto rojo; picea.

sprung (sprʌŋ) v., p.p. de **spring.**

spry (sprai) adj. listo; vivo; ágil. —**spryness,** n. agilidad; viveza.

spud (spʌd) n. 1, (chisel) escoplo. 2, (weeding hoe) escarda. 3, colloq. (potato) patata; papa.

spume (spjuːm) v.t. & i. espumar. —n. espuma.

spun (spʌn) v., pret. & p.p. de **spin.**

spunk (spʌŋk) n., colloq. coraje; valor; ánimo. —**spunky,** adj. valiente; valeroso.

spur (spʌr) n. 1, (of a horseman) espuela. 2, (of a gamecock) espolón. 3, (of a mountain) estribo; espolón. 4, (branch line) ramal. 5,

fig. (stimulus) estímulo; espuela. —v.t. 1, (goad; urge on) espolear. 2, (incite) picar; incitar; estimular. —v.i. apretar el paso. —**on the spur of the moment,** de repente; sin reflexión. —**spur on,** espolear. —**win one's spurs,** ganar la dignidad de caballero; llevarse la palma.

spurious ('spjur·i·əs) adj. espurio; falso; ilegítimo. —**spuriousness,** n. falsedad.

spurn (spʌrn) v.t. rechazar; desdeñar; menospreciar.

spurt (spʌrt) n. 1, (gush of liquid) chorro. 2, (short, sudden effort) impulso; arranque; esfuerzo repentino. —v.i. 1, (gush) chorrear. 2, (make a sudden effort) esforzarse repentinamente; hacer un esfuerzo repentino. —v.t. echar en chorro; hacer salir en chorro.

sputnik ('spʌt·nɪk) n. satélite artificial, esp. soviético.

sputter ('spʌt·ər) v.i. 1, (sizzle) chisporrotear. 2, (speak rapidly and confusedly) farfullar. —v.t. farfullar; enunciar farfullando. —n. 1, (sizzling) chisporroteo. 2, (rapid, confused utterance) farfulla.

sputum ('spjuː·təm) n. [pl. -ta (tə)] esputo.

spy (spai) n. espía. —v.i. espiar. —v.t. 1, (watch furtively) espiar; atisbar. 2, (discover) divisar; columbrar. —**spy on,** espiar; observar; atisbar. —**spy out,** descubrir; reconocer.

spyglass ('spai,glæs) n. catalejo.

squab (skwab) n. pichón. —adj. 1, (newly hatched) acabado de nacer; implume. 2, (short and stout) regordete; rechoncho.

squabble ('skwab·əl) n. querella; riña; disputa. —v.i. reñir; disputar.

squad (skwad) n. escuadra. —**squad car,** coche patrullero.

squadron ('skwad·rən) n. 1, naval escuadra. 2, (of cavalry) escuadrón. 3, aero. escuadrilla.

squalid ('skwal·ɪd) adj. escuálido. —**squalidness; squalidity** (skwa·'lɪd·ə·ti) n. escualidez.

squall (skwɔl) n. 1, (yell) chillido. 2, (storm) borrasca; chubasco. 3, colloq. (disturbance) riña; reyerta. —v.t. & i. (yell) chillar. —v.i. (storm) estar o ponerse borrascoso. —**squally,** adj. borrascoso.

squalor ('skwal·ər) n. escualidez.

squander ('skwan·dər) v.t. disipar;

malgastar; despilfarrar; derrochar. —*n.* despilfarro; derroche.

square (skwe:r) *n.* **1,** (plane figure) cuadrado. **2,** (open area in city) plaza. **3,** (city block) manzana; *Amer.* cuadra. **4,** (carpenter's instrument) escuadra. **5,** *math.* cuadrado. —*adj.* **1,** (at right angles; of square shape) cuadrado; cuadriculado. **2,** (straight; even) derecho. **3,** (honest) honrado; justo. **4,** (unequivocal) exacto; preciso. **5,** (satisfying, as a meal) bueno; completo; suficiente. —*v.t.* **1,** (make square) cuadrar; cuadricular. **2,** (adjust) ajustar. **3,** (settle, as a debt) pagar. —*v.i.* concordar; conformarse. —*adv.* **1,** (fairly) justamente; honradamente. **2,** (at right angles) en ángulo recto. **3,** (directly) derecho. **4,** (exactly) exactamente; precisamente. —**square dance,** contradanza; danza de figuras. —**square deal,** juego limpio; trato honrado. —**square off,** ponerse en actitud de lucha. —**square root,** raíz cuadrada. —**square shooter,** *colloq.* persona honrada.

squash (skwaʃ) *v.t.* **1,** (crush) aplastar; apabullar. **2,** (cram; crowd) apiñar; apretar. **3,** (bruise; mangle) magullar. **4,** (put down; quell) reprimir; sofocar. **5,** (put an end to) poner fin a; acabar con. **6,** (refute) confutar. —*v.i.* **1,** (be crushed) aplastarse. **2,** (be crowded) apiñarse; apretarse. —*n.* **1,** (crushing) aplastamiento. **2,** (crowding) apiñamiento. **3,** (game) tenis de pared. **4,** *bot.* calabaza.

squat (skwat) *v.i.* [**squatted, -ting**] **1,** (sit; crouch) acuclillarse. **2,** (settle on land without right) establecerse sin derecho o para formar un derecho. —*adj.* **1,** (in a squatting position) en cuclillas. **2,** (short and heavy) rechoncho. —*n.* posición (de una persona) en cuclillas. —**squatter,** *n.* advenedizo; intruso; colono usurpador.

squaw (skwɔ:) *n.* india norteamericana.

squawk (skwɔk) *v.i.* **1,** (cry hoarsely) chillar; graznar. **2,** *slang* (complain) quejarse. **3,** *slang* (inform) delatar; soplar. —*v.t.* decir chillando. —*n.* **1,** (hoarse cry) chillido; graznido. **2,** *slang* (complaint) queja.

squeak (skwik) *v.i.* **1,** (make a shrill sound) chirriar. **2,** *slang* (inform) delatar; soplar. —*v.t.* **1,** (utter shrilly) decir chirriando. **2,** (cause to squeak) hacer chirriar. —*n.* chirrido. —**have a narrow squeak,** *colloq.* escaparse por un pelo.

squeal (skwi:l) *v.i.* **1,** (utter a loud, sharp sound) chillar; dar alaridos. **2,** *slang* (inform) delatar; soplar. —*v.t.* decir chillando. —*n.* **1,** (loud, sharp sound) chillido; alarido. **2,** *slang* (informing) soplo; soplido; denuncia. —**squealer,** *n.*, *slang* (informer) delator [*fem.* -tora]; soplón.

squeamish ('skwi·mɪʃ) *adj.* **1,** (queasy) nauseabundo. **2,** (easily offended) delicado; quisquilloso; remilgado. —**squeamish stomach,** estómago delicado.

squeegee ('skwi·dʒi) *n.* enjugador de goma. —*v.t.* secar con un enjugador.

squeeze (skwi:z) *v.t.* **1,** (compress) comprimir; apretar. **2,** (extract by squeezing) exprimir; estrujar. **3,** (cram; crowd) apiñar; tupir. **4,** (extort) extorsionar; sacar por fuerza. **5,** (oppress) oprimir; agobiar; acosar. **6,** (force; compel) obligar; forzar. **7,** (embrace) abrazar. **8,** (clasp) apretar; estrechar. —*v.i.* pasar, salir o entrar apretándose. —*n.* **1,** (pressure) apretón; estrechón. **2,** (extortion) extorsión; concusión. **3,** (cramming; crowding) apiñamiento. **4,** (compulsion) obligación; coerción. **5,** (embrace) abrazo. **6,** (clasp) apretón; estrechón. **7,** (tight situation) aprieto; apuro. —**put the squeeze on,** *colloq.* hacer la forzosa a.

squeezer ('skwi·zər) *n.* exprimidor; exprimidora.

squelch (skwɛltʃ) *v.t.* **1,** (crush) apabullar; despachurrar. **2,** (suppress) sofocar; sojuzgar. **3,** (silence) acallar; hacer callar. —*v.i.* chapalear; chapotear.

squib (skwɪb) *n.* **1,** (lampoon) pasquín; sátira. **2,** (firecracker) cohete crepitante.

squid (skwɪd) *n.* calamar.

squint (skwɪnt) *v.i.* bizcar. —*adj.* bizco; bisojo. —*n.* **1,** (squinting) mirada bizca; mirada de soslayo. **2,** (strabismus) estrabismo.

squint-eyed *adj.* bizco; bisojo.

squire (skwair) *n.* **1,** (knight's attendant; rural landholder; justice of the peace) escudero. **2,** (lady's escort) acompañante. —*v.t.* **1,** (serve as attendant) servir como escudero. 2, (escort) acompañar.

squirm (skwʌrm) *v.i.* torcerse; retorcerse. —*n.* torcimiento; retorcimiento. —**squirm out (of)**, escaparse de; salir con dificultad (de).

squirrel ('skwʌr·əl) *n.* ardilla.

squirt (skwʌrt) *v.i.* chorrear; salir a chorros. —*v.t.* arrojar a chorros. —*n.* **1,** (spurt; jet) chorro; chisguete. **2,** (device for squirting) jeringa. **3,** *colloq.* (insignificant person) mocoso.

stab (stæb) *v.t. & i.* apuñalar; dar de puñaladas. —*n.* **1,** (blow with a pointed weapon) puñalada. **2,** *colloq.* (attempt) tentativa.

stability (stə'bɪl·ə·ti) *n.* estabilidad; permanencia.

stabilization (,stei·bə·lai'zei·ʃən) *n.* estabilización.

stabilize ('stei·bə,laiz) *v.t.* estabilizar.

stabilizer ('stei·bə,laiz·ər) *n.* estabilizador.

stablo ('ɛtei·bəl) *n.* **1,** (shelter for horses) establo; cuadra; caballeriza. **2,** (group of horses; horse attendants) caballeriza. —*adj.* estable; firme. —*v.t.* poner en un establo. —*v.i.* estar colocado en un establo.

stableboy ('stei·bəl,bɔi) *n.* mozo de caballos.

stablegirl ('stei·bəl,gʌrl) *n.* moza de caballos.

staccato (stə'ka·to) *adj., mus.* staccato; picado.

stack (stæk) *n.* **1,** (orderly pile) pila; montón. **2,** (pile of hay or straw) almiar; montón de heno; parva de paja. **3,** (chimney) cañón de chimenea. **4,** (set of shelves) estantería. **5,** *colloq.* (large amount) gran número; montón. —*v.t.* amontonar; apilar; hacinar.

stadium ('stei·di·əm) *n.* [*pl.* **-ums** o **-a** (ə)] estadio.

staff (stæf) *n.* [*pl.* **staves**] **1,** (stick) palo; bastón. **2,** (pole; shaft) asta; astil. **3,** (support) apoyo; sostén. **4,** *mus.* pentagrama. **5,** [*pl.* **staffs**] (personnel) personal; *mil.* estado mayor; *naut.; aero.* tripulación. —*adj.* del personal; *mil.* del estado mayor. —*v.t.* proveer de personal; *mil.* proveer de estado mayor; *naut.; aero.* tripular. —**staffer,** *n.* miembro del personal; funcionario. —**staff of life,** sostén de la vida; alimento; pan. —**staff of office,** bastón de mando.

stag (stæg) *n.* **1,** *zoöl.* ciervo; venado. **2,** *colloq.* (man, esp. unaccompanied) varón solo. —*adj., colloq.* exclusivo para hombres. —*v.i., colloq.* ir solo (un hombre).

stage (steidʒ) *n.* **1,** (platform) andamio; cadalso. **2,** (dais) tribuna; estrado. **3,** (step; phase) etapa; punto; fase. **4,** (theater platform) escena; escenario. **5,** (theatrical profession) teatro. **6,** (relay station) posta. **7,** = **stagecoach.** —*v.t.* poner en escena; escenificar; representar. —*v.i.* viajar en diligencia. —**by easy stages,** por grados; gradualmente. —**by short stages,** a pequeñas etapas; a cortas jornadas.

stagecoach ('steidʒ,kotʃ) *n.* diligencia.

stage fright miedo al público.

stagehand ('steidʒ,hænd) *n.* tramoyista.

stage manager director de escena.

stage-struck *adj.* loco por el teatro.

stage whisper aparte; susurro en voz alta.

stagger ('stæg·ər) *v.i.* **1,** (reel) sway) bambolear; tambalear. **2,** (hesitate; waver) vacilar. —*v.t.* **1,** (cause to reel) hacer tambalear. **2,** (overwhelm) sorprender; asustar. **3,** (arrange in overlapping sequences) escalonar. —*n.* **1,** (unsteady movement) tambaleo; bamboleo. **2,** (hesitation) vacilación.

stagnant ('stæg·nənt) *adj.* estancado.

stagnate ('stæg·neit) *v.i.* estancarse. —**stagnation,** *n.* estancación; estancamiento.

staid (steid) *adj.* grave; serio; formal; sentado.

stain (stein) *n.* **1,** (discoloration) decoloración. **2,** (blot; taint) mancha; mácula; borrón. **3,** (coloring substance) tinte; tintura. **4,** *fig.* (dishonor) mancha; mancilla; deslustre; desdoro. —*v.t.* **1,** (discolor) descolorar; desteñir. **2,** (soil) manchar; ensuciar. **3,** (tint) colorar; teñir; tintar. **4,** *fig.* (besmirch) mancillar; desdorar; deslustrar. —*v.i.* **1,** (discolor) decolorarse; desteñirse. **2,** (become soiled) mancharse.

stained glass vidrio de color. —**stained-glass window,** vidriera de colores.

stainless ('stein·ləs) *adj.* **1,** (immune to rust) inoxidable. **2,** (spotless) inmaculado. —**stainless steel,** acero inoxidable.

stair (ste₁r) *n.* **1,** (step) escalón; peldaño. **2,** (staircase) escalera. —**stairs,** *n.pl.* escalera.

staircase ('ster,keis) *n.* escalera; caja de la escalera.

stairway ('ster·wei) *n.* escalera.

stairwell ('ster·wel) *n.* hueco de escalera. *También,* **stair well.**

stake (steik) *n.* **1,** (pointed stick) estaca. **2,** (pole; post) poste. **3,** (money wagered) apuesta. **4,** (risk) riesgo; peligro. **5,** (prize) premio. **6,** (interest; investment) interés. —*v.t.* **1,** (tie to a stake) estacar; atar a una estaca. **2,** (mark with stakes) estacar; señalar con estacas. **3,** (wager) apostar. **4,** (risk) arriesgar; aventurar. **5,** (provide with money or resources) financiar; apoyar; sostener. —**at stake,** en juego; arriesgado. —**die at the stake,** morir en la hoguera. —**pull up stakes,** *colloq.* irse; mudarse.

stake-out *n.* vigilancia.

stalactite (stə'læk·tait) *n.* estalactita.

stalagmite (stə'læg,mait) *n.* estalagmita.

stale (steil) *adj.* **1,** (rancid; spoiled) rancio; pasado. **2,** (old; aged) viejo; añejo. **3,** (exhausted, as air) viciado. **4,** (hackneyed) trillado; gastado. —*v.t.* **1,** (age) envejecer; añejar. **2,** (spoil) enranciar. —*v.i.* **1,** (age) envejecerse; añejarse. **2,** (spoil) enranciarse; picarse; pasarse.

stalemate ('steil,meit) *n.* **1,** (tie; draw) empate; tablas. **2,** (deadlock) punto muerto; estancamiento. —*v.t.* **1,** (tie) empatar; *chess* hacer tablas. **2,** (put in deadlock) estancar. —*v.i.* **1,** (tie) empatarse; *chess* quedar tablas. **2,** (be deadlocked) estancarse; llegar a un punto muerto.

stalk (stɔk) *n.* **1,** (stem) tallo; pedúnculo. **2,** (haughty gait) paso majestuoso. **3,** (hunting) caza a la espera; acecho. —*v.t.* **1,** (pursue stealthily) cazar a la espera; acechar. **2,** (walk boldly through) pasar con porte majestuoso por. —*v.i.* **1,** (walk stiffly) andar con paso majestuoso o airado. **2,** (hunt furtively) cazar a la espera; cazar al acecho.

stall (stɔːl) *n.* **1,** (stable) establo; cuadra. **2,** (compartment for an animal) pesebre; casilla de establo. **3,** (market booth) puesto; tenderete. **4,** *Brit.* (orchestra seat) butaca; luneta. **5,** (choir seat; pew) banco; asiento de iglesia o del coro. **6,** *colloq.* (pretext; evasion) pretexto; escapatoria; evasiva. **7,** (arrested motion) parada; atascamiento. —*v.t.* **1,** (stable, as an animal) poner en un establo. **2,** (stop; check) parar; estancar. **3,** *colloq.* (put off; evade) detener; evadir. —*v.i.* **1,** (stop) pararse; atascarse; atollarse. **2,** *colloq.* (act or speak evasively) hacer la pala.

stallion ('stæl·jən) *n.* caballo padre; caballo semental; *Amer.* garañón.

stalwart ('stɔl·wərt) *adj.* **1,** (sturdy; brave) fuerte; valiente. **2,** (loyal) constante; leal. —*n.* **1,** (brave person) bravo. **2,** (loyal supporter) partidario leal.

stamen ('stei·mən) *n.* estambre.

stamina ('stæm·ə·nə) *n.* vigor; fuerza vital; fibra.

stammer ('stæm·ər) *v.i.* tartamudear; *Amer.* gaguear. —*v.t.* decir tartamudeando. —*n.* tartamudeo; *Amer.* gagueo. —**stammerer,** *n.* tartamudo; *Amer.* gago. —**stammering,** *n.* tartamudeo; *Amer.* gagueo.

stamp (stæmp) *v.t.* **1,** (trample; crush) pisar; pisotear; hollar. **2,** (seal) sellar. **3,** (impress; imprint) estampar; imprimir; marcar. **4,** (cut out by stamping) troquelar; acuñar. **5,** (mark; characterize) marcar; señalar. —*v.i.* patalear. —*n.* **1,** (thrust of the foot) pataleo; patada. **2,** (seal) sello. **3,** (rubber marking device) estampilla. **4,** (token of payment of postage or tax) sello; timbre. **5,** (impress; imprint) estampa; marca; impresión. **6,** (cutting device; die) troquel. **7,** (kind; sort) tipo; clase; estampa. —**stamping ground,** sitio frecuentado por uno. —**stamp out,** extinguir; extirpar; borrar.

stampede (stæm'piːd) *n.* estampida; espantada. —*v.t.* ahuyentar; hacer huir en desorden. —*v.i.* ahuyentarse; precipitarse.

stance (stæns) *n.* postura; posición; actitud.

stanch (stæntʃ) *v.t.* estancar; restañar. —*adj.* **1,** (strong; firm) fuerte; firme. **2,** (loyal) fiel; leal. **3,** (watertight) estanco.

stanchion ('stæn·ʃən) *n.* puntal; montante; *naut.* candelero *(usu.pl.).*

stand (stænd) *v.i.* 1, (be in an upright position) estar de pie; estar derecho; *Amer.* estar parado. 2, (assume an upright position) ponerse de pie; levantarse; *Amer.* pararse. 3, (be stagnant; stop) quedarse; detenerse; pararse. 4, (be placed or situated) estar; estar situado. 5, (remain; continue) seguir; quedarse; persistir; mantenerse. 6, (hold firm) mantenerse firme; aguantar. 7, (be or remain in effect) valer; tener fuerza; tener valor; estar en vigor. 8, (be; hold a certain opinion or position) estar; ponerse. 9, (have a certain height) medir; tener (determinada altura). 10, *naut.* (bear; head) dirigirse; llevar rumbo o dirección. 11, *Brit.* (be a candidate) ser candidato; presentarse como candidato. —*v.t.* 1, (set upright) poner derecho. 2, (endure) tolerar; soportar; aguantar. 3, (undergo) sufrir; someterse a. 4, *colloq.* (pay for) pagar; sufragar. —*n.* 1, (position) posición; postura; actitud. 2, (stop) parada. 3, (platform) plataforma; tribuna; estrado. 4, (small table) mesita. 5, (support) pie; pedestal. 6, (market stall) puesto; quiosco. 7, (resistance) resistencia; oposición. 8, (location) puesto; sitio. 9, (music rack; lectern) atril. 10, (podium) podio. —**it stands to reason,** es lógico; es razonable. —**make a stand,** mantenerse; aguantar; resistir. —**stand a chance,** tener probabilidad; tener esperanza. —**stand against,** oponerse a; resistir. —**stand alone,** estar o mantenerse solo. —**stand aside,** apartarse; abrir paso. —**stand back,** retroceder; retirarse. —**stand back of,** apoyar; respaldar. —**stand by, 1,** (assist) asistir; atender. 2, (support; defend) apoyar; respaldar; defender. 3, (keep to) mantenerse a. 4, (wait) esperar; aguardar. —**stand for, 1,** (represent; signify) representar; denotar; significar. 2, (endure) tolerar; soportar; aguantar. 3, (favor; support) estar por; apoyar; sostener. —**stand forth,** destacarse; adelantarse. —**stand in awe of,** tener temor de. —**stand in good stead,** servir; ser útil; ser provechoso. —**stand in line,** hacer cola. —**stand in need (of),**

necesitar; tener necesidad (de). —**stand in someone's light,** quitarle la luz a uno. —**stand in the way (of),** impedir; estorbar; cerrar el paso (a). —**stand in (well) with,** tener mano con; tener buenas relaciones con. —**stand off, 1,** (withdraw) apartarse. 2, (withstand) resistir; negar. —**stand on, 1,** (depend on) depender de; basarse en. 2, (insist on; affirm) mantener; insistir en. —**stand on end, 1,** (set upright) poner derecho; poner de punta. 2, (bristle, as the hair) encresparse; erizarse. —**stand one's ground,** mantenerse firme; estar o seguir en sus trece. —**stand on tiptoe,** ponerse de puntillas. —**stand out, 1,** (be prominent) sobresalir; destacarse. 2, (show clearly) distinguirse; notarse; saltar a los ojos. 3, (resist) resistir; mantenerse firme; no ceder. —**stand pat,** mantenerse firme; quedarse; no cambiar. —**stand to, 1,** (work steadily at) seguir con; dedicarse a. 2, (stand by) atender; estar alerta. 3, (keep; abide by) cumplir con; mantenerse en. —**stand up, 1,** (rise) levantarse; *Amer.* pararse. 2, (set upright) poner derecho. 3, (endure) durar; persistir; aguantar. 4, *slang* (disappoint) dejar plantado. —**stand up for,** apoyar; defender. —**stand up to,** enfrentar; encararse a o con.

standard ('stæn·dərd) *n.* 1, (criterion) norma; regla; patrón. 2, (flag; banner) bandera; estandarte; pabellón. 3, (emblem) emblema; símbolo. 4, (something upright) algo parado; derecho. —*adj.* 1, (regular) normal; corriente; regular. 2, (prescribed by law) legal; de marca; de ley. 3, (classic) clásico. 4, (having authority) de autoridad; de categoría. —**standard time,** hora civil.

standardbearer ('stæn·dərd,ber·ər) *n.* abanderado.

standardize ('stæn·dər,daiz) *v.t.* normalizar; uniformar; regularizar; *Amer.* estandardizar. —**standardization** (-di'zei·ʃən) *n.* normalización; regularización; *Amer.* estandardización.

stand-by *n.* [*pl.* -bys] 1, (loyal supporter) adherente fiel. 2, (something reliable) recurso seguro.

standee (stæn'diː) *n.,* *colloq.*

espectador, viajero, etc. que no tiene asiento.

stand-in n. doble.

standing ('stæn·dɪŋ) n. 1, (rank; status) rango; posición; condición. 2, (duration) duración; permanencia. 3, (halt) parada. 4, (reputation) reputación; fama. —adj. 1, (upright; on the feet) derecho; en o de pie; Amer. parado. 2, (permanent) permanente; establecido. 3, (stagnant) estancado. 4, (stationary) inmóvil; estacionario; parado. —**standing order,** orden permanente. —**standing room,** sitio para estar de pie. —**standing room only,** no quedan asientos.

stand-off n. empate. —adj. reservado; indiferente. —**stand-offish,** adj. reservado; indiferente.

stand-out n., colloq. disidente; intransigente.

standpipe ('stænd,paip) n. tubo o columna de alimentación de agua.

standpoint ('stænd,pɔint) n. punto de vista.

standstill ('stænd,stɪl) n. alto; parada; pausa. —**be at a standstill,** quedar parado. —**come to a standstill,** pararse.

stanza ('stæn·zə) n. estrofa.

staphylococcus ('stæf·ə·lə,kak·əs) n. [pl. **cocci** (-,kak·sai)] estafilococo. También, colloq. **staph** (stæf).

staple ('stei·pəl) n. 1, (wire clamp) grapa. 2, (principal commodity) artículo, género o producto principal. 3, (raw material) materia prima. 4, (textile fiber) fibra textil. —adj. básico; principal. —v.t. engrapar. —**stapler** (-plər) n. engrapadora.

star (star) n. 1, (luminous body; five-pointed figure; leading performer) estrella. 2, (asterisk) asterisco. —v.t. [**starred, starring**] 1, (set or mark with stars) estrellar; adornar con estrellas. 2, (mark with an asterisk) marcar con asterisco. 3, (feature) presentar como estrella. —v.i. 1, (have a major role) ser estrella. 2, (be outstanding) sobresalir; destacarse. —adj. principal; brillante; sobresaliente. —**stardom,** n. condición o estado de estrella.

starboard ('star·bərd) n. estribor.

starch (startʃ) n. 1, (food substance) almidón; fécula. 2, (stiffening substance) almidón. 3, fig. (stiffness) formalidad; seriedad. 4,

slang (vigor) energía; vigor. —v.t. almidonar.

Star Chamber tribunal secreto y arbitrario.

starchy ('star·tʃi) adj. 1, (containing starch) feculento. 2, (stiffened with starch) almidonado. 3, fig. (formal) formal; tieso; serio.

stare (steɪr) v.i. mirar fijamente; mirar con asombro o insolencia. —v.t. clavar la vista en; mirar fijamente. —n. mirada fija. —**stare down,** apocar con la mirada. —**stare one in the face, 1,** (look fixedly at) encararse con uno; darle a uno en la cara. 2, (be conspicuous) saltar a los ojos.

starfish ('star·fɪʃ) n. estrellamar; estrella de mar.

stargaze ('star,geiz) v.i. 1, (watch the stars) mirar las estrellas. 2, (daydream) soñar despierto. —**stargazing,** n. sueño; distracción.

stargazer ('star,gei·zər) n. 1, (astronomer or astrologer) astrónomo; astrólogo. 2, (dreamer) soñador [fem. -dora].

stark (stark) adj. 1, (rigid) rígido; tieso. 2, (desolate) desolado. 3, (downright) completo; cabal; puro. —adv. 1, (utterly) completamente; cabalmente. 2, (rigidly) rígidamente. —**stark mad,** loco rematado.

stark-naked adj. completamente desnudo; en cueros.

starless ('star·ləs) adj. sin estrellas.

starlet ('star·lɪt) n. joven estrella; estrella principiante.

starlight ('star,lait) n. luz de las estrellas. —adj. estrellado; muy claro.

starling ('star·lɪŋ) n. estornino.

starlit ('star·lɪt) adj. estrellado; muy claro.

starred (stard) adj. 1, (marked with stars) estrellado. 2, (marked with an asterisk) marcado con asterisco. 3, fig. (lucky) afortunado. 4, (featured) presentado como estrella.

starry ('star·i) adj. 1, (filled with stars) estrellado. 2, (sparkling) centelleante; rutilante. 3, (of or from the stars) estelar; celestial.

Stars and Stripes bandera de los Estados Unidos de América.

star-spangled adj. estrellado; sembrado de estrellas. —**the Star-Spangled Banner,** bandera e himno nacional de los Estados Unidos de América.

start (start) *v.i.* **1,** (begin) empezar; comenzar; principiar. **2,** (begin to move) ponerse en marcha; *mech.* arrancar. **3,** (jump; leap) sobresaltar; respingar. **4,** (arise) nacer. —*v.t.* **1,** (begin) empezar; iniciar. **2,** (set in motion) poner en marcha. **3,** (send off) despedir. **4,** (flush; rouse, as game) levantar. —*n.* **1,** (beginning) comienzo; principio. **2,** (departure) salida; partida. **3,** (place of departure) punto de salida. **4,** (lead; handicap) ventaja. **5,** (sudden movement) sobresalto; respingo. **6,** (fright; shock) susto. **7,** *mech.* arranque. —**by fits and starts,** a saltos y corcovos; esporádicamente. —**start after,** salir en busca de. —**start in,** empezar; ponerse a. —**start off,** salir; ponerse en marcha. —**start out, 1,** (set forth) ponerse en camino; salir; partir. **2,** (begin) principiar; empezar. —**start up, 1,** (jump; leap suddenly) sobresaltar; levantarse de repente. **2,** (come into being) salir o brotar de golpe. **3,** (begin to move or function) ponerse en marcha; arrancar.

starter ('star·tər) *n.* **1,** (person or thing that starts) iniciador [*fem.* -dora]. **2,** *mech.* arranque. **3,** *elect.* encendedor. **4,** *sports* juez de salida.

starting point punto de partida; punto de salida.

startle ('star·təl) *v.t.* espantar; asustar; sobresaltar; sorprender. —*n.* susto; sobresalto. —**startling** ('start·lɪŋ) *adj.* sorprendente; asombroso.

starvation (star'vei·ʃən) *n.* inanición; hambre.

starve (starv) *v.i.* hambrear; pasar o sufrir hambre; morir de hambre. —*v.t.* matar de hambre; hambrear. —**starved,** *adj.* hambriento; famélico. —**starving,** *adj.* hambriento; famélico.

starveling ('starv·lɪŋ) *adj. & n.* hambriento.

state (steit) *n.* **1,** (condition) estado; condición. **2,** (political entity) estado. **3,** (ceremony; pomp) pompa; fausto; ceremonia. —*adj.* de o del estado; estatal; público. —*v.t.* **1,** (declare) declarar; enunciar; afirmar. **2,** (define; formulate) formular; exponer. —**in state,** con gran pompa o ceremonia. —**lie**

in state, estar expuesto en capilla ardiente.

statecraft ('steit,kræft) *n.* política; arte de gobernar.

stated ('stei·tɪd) *adj.* **1,** (declared) declarado; afirmado. **2,** (fixed) establecido; fijo; determinado.

statehood ('steit·hʊd) *n.* estatidad.

statehouse ('steit,haus) *n.* edificio del Estado.

stately ('steit·li) *adj.* majestuoso; augusto; noble; grande. —**stateliness,** *n.* majestuosidad; nobleza; grandeza.

statement ('steit·mənt) *n.* **1,** (declaration) declaración; exposición; informe; relato. **2,** *comm.* estado de cuenta.

stateroom ('steit,rum) *n.* **1,** *naut.* camarote. **2,** *R.R.* compartimiento particular.

state room gran salón; salón de recepción.

stateside ('steit,said) *adj. & adv.* en o hacia los EE.UU.

statesman ('steits·mən) *n.* [*pl.* -men (-mɛn)] estadista. —**stateswoman** (-,wʊm·ən) *n.fem.* [*pl.* -women (-,wɪm·ən)] estadista. —**statesmanship,** *n.* oficio de estadista.

static ('stæt·ɪk) *adj.* estático. —*n.* interferencia. —**statics,** *n.sing.* estática.

station ('stei·ʃən) *n.* **1,** (designated place) estación. **2,** (status; condition) estado; condición. **3,** (stopping place) puesto; paradero. **4,** *radio; TV* emisora; estación. **5,** *mil; naval* apostadero. —*v.t.* colocar; disponer; apostar.

stationary ('stei·ʃə·nɛr·i) *adj.* estacionario.

stationer ('stei·ʃə·nər) *n.* papelero.

stationery ('stei·ʃə·nɛr·i) *n.* papelería; efectos de escritorio o de oficina. —**stationery store,** papelería.

station house cuartel de policía.

stationmaster ('stei·ʃən,mæs·tər) *n.* jefe de estación.

station wagon camioneta.

statistician (,stæt·əs'tɪʃ·ən) *n.* estadístico.

statistics (stə'tɪs·tɪks) *n.sing.* estadística. —*n.pl.* estadísticas; datos estadísticos. —**statistical,** *adj.* estadístico.

stator ('stei·tər) *n.* estator.

statuary ('stætʃ·ʊ·ɛr·i) *n.* estatuaria; colección de estatuas; imaginería.

statue ('stætʃ·ʊ) *n.* estatua; imagen.

statuesque (ˌstætʃ·ʊ'ɛsk) *adj.* majestuoso; noble; imponente.

statuette (ˌstætʃ·ʊ'ɛt) *n.* estatuilla; estatuita.

stature ('stætʃ·ər) *n.* **1,** (height) estatura; altura; talla; tamaño. **2,** (quality) carácter; condición.

status ('stæt·əs; 'stei·təs) *n.* estado; condición; posición.

status quo (ˌstæt·əs'kwoɹ; ˌstei·təs-) condición actual o anterior (de las cosas).

statute ('stætʃ·ut) *n.* estatuto; ley; reglamento. —**statute law,** derecho escrito. —**statute mile,** milla terrestre. —**statute of limitations,** ley de prescripción.

statutory ('stætʃ·ʊ·tor·i) *adj.* estatutario; reglamentario.

staunch (stɔntʃ) *v. & adj.* = stanch.

stave (steiv) *n.* **1,** (part of a barrel) duela de barril. **2,** (stick; staff) palo; bastón. **3,** (stanza) estrofa; estancia. **4,** *mus.* (staff) pentagrama. **5,** (ladder rung) peldaño. —*v.t.* [*pret. & p.p.* **staved** o **stove**] **1,** (break; crush) romper; quebrar. **2,** (furnish with staves) poner duelas a. —**stave in,** romper; quebrar; desfondar. —**stave off,** evitar; impedir; parar.

staves (steivz) *n.* **1,** *pl. de* **staff. 2,** *pl. de* **stave.**

stay (stei) *v.i.* **1** (remain) quedarse; permanecer. **2,** (reside) habitar. **3,** (lodge temporarily) hospedarse; alojarse, **4,** (stop) pararse; detenerse. **5,** *colloq.* (hold out) perseverar; mantenerse; durar. —*v.t.* **1,** (halt) parar; detener; impedir. **2,** (delay) suspender; prorrogar. **3,** (support) apoyar; sostener. **4,** (satisfy; appease) apagar. **5,** (remain for the duration of) quedarse por; quedarse hasta el fin de. —*n.* **1,** (stop; pause) parada. **2,** (sojourn) permanencia; morada; estada; estancia. **3,** (delay) suspensión; prórroga. **4,** (support) apoyo; sostén. **5,** *naut.* (supporting cable) estay. **6,** (brace; wire support) varilla; ballena *(de corsé).*

stay-at-home *adj.* hogareño. —*n.* persona hogareña.

staysail ('stei,seil; -səl) *n.* vela de estay.

stead (stɛd) *n.* lugar; sitio. —**stand**

in good stead, servir; ser útil; ser provechoso.

steadfast ('stɛd·fæst) *adj.* firme; resuelto; constante. —**steadfastness,** *n.* constancia; resolución.

steady ('stɛd·i) *adj.* **1,** (firm; fixed) fijo; firme; estable. **2,** (constant) constante. **3,** (even; regular) regular; uniforme. **4,** (loyal) constante; leal. **5,** (sober) sobrio; serio; asentado. **6,** (resolute) resuelto. —*v.t.* **1,** (fix; settle) estabilizar; fijar; afirmar. **2,** (calm) calmar; asentar. —*v.i.* **1,** (become settled) estabilizarse; fijarse; afirmarse. **2,** (become calm) calmarse; asentarse —*n.*, *colloq.* novio [*fem.* novia]. —**go steady,** *colloq.* ser novios.

steak (steik) *n.* **1,** (cut of meat, fish, etc.) lonja; tajada; filete. **2,** (beefsteak) bistec.

steal (stiɹl) *v.t.* [*pret.* **stole;** *p.p.* **stolen**] robar; hurtar. —*v.i.* colarse; escabullirse; pasar furtivamente. —*n.*, *colloq.* **1,** (act of stealing) something stolen) robo; hurto. **2,** (bargain) baratillo.

stealth (stɛlθ) *n.* cautela; recato; astucia. —**stealthy,** *adj.* clandestino; furtivo; secreto. —**by stealth,** a hurtadillas; a escondidas; furtivamente.

steam (stiɹm) *n.* **1,** (vapor) vapor; vaho. **2,** *colloq.* (energy) energía; vigor; entusiasmo. —*v.t.* **1,** (treat with steam) saturar con vapor; dar un baño de vapor a. **2,** (cook with steam) cocer al vapor. **3,** (make cloudy or misty) empañar. —*v.i.* **1,** (emit vapor) echar vapor. **2,** (evaporate) evaporarse. **3,** (move or function by steam) marchar o funcionar a vapor; *naut.* navegar (por medio del vapor). —*adj.* de vapor.

steamboat ('stim,bot) *n.* vapor; buque de vapor.

steam engine máquina de vapor.

steamer ('stim·ər) *n.* **1,** (device for steam treating) vaporizador. **2,** (steamship) vapor; buque de vapor. —**steamer rug,** manta de viaje. —**steamer trunk,** baúl de camarote.

steamfitter ('stim,fit·ər) *n.* montador de calderas de vapor.

steam heat calefacción por vapor.

steam roller aplanadora.

steamship ('stim,ʃɪp) *n.* vapor; buque de vapor.

steam shovel excavadora de vapor.

steamy ('sti·mi) *adj.* **1,** (full of or emitting steam) vaporoso. **2,** (cloudy; misty) empañado.

steed (sti:d) *n.* corcel; caballo de combate o de carrera.

steel (sti:l) *n.* **1,** (metal) acero. **2,** (blade; weapon) cuchillo; arma blanca. **3,** (for striking fire with a flint) eslabón. —*adj.* **1,** (of steel) de acero. **2,** (like steel) acerado. **3,** (hard; tough) duro; firme; fuerte. **4,** (of or pert. to the steel industry) siderúrgico. —*v.t.* acerar; *fig.* fortalecer. —**alloy steel,** acero de aleación. —**carbon steel,** acero al carbono. —**stainless steel,** acero inoxidable. —**steel oneself,** fortalecerse; endurecerse. —**steel wool,** estropajo. —**tool steel,** acero de herramientas.

steel mill fábrica de acero.

steelwork ('stil·wʌrk) *n.* montaje de acero. —**steelworker,** *n.* obrero en una fábrica de acero. —**steelworks,** *n. sing.* & *pl.* fábrica de acero.

steely ('sti·li) *adj.* **1,** (of or like steel) de acero; acerado. **2,** *fig.* (hard; tough) duro; fuerte; firme.

steelyard ('sti:l,jard; -jərd) *n.* romana.

steep (stip) *adj.* **1,** (precipitous) escarpado; empinado. **2,** *colloq.* (high-priced) alto; excesivo. —*v.t.* saturar; empapar; remojar. —*v.i.* empaparse; remojarse. —**steepen,** *v.t.* poner más escarpado. —*v.i.* volverse más escarpado. —**steepness,** *n.* pendiente; inclinación.

steeple ('sti·pəl) *n.* aguja; campanario; espira.

steeplechase ('sti·pəl,tʃeis) *n.* carrera de obstáculos.

steeplejack ('sti·pəl,dʒæk) *n.* reparador de campanarios, chimeneas, torres, etc.

steer (stɪr) *v.t.* dirigir; guiar; conducir; *naut.* navegar; gobernar. —*v.i.* dirigirse; obedecer al timón; gobernarse. —*n.* buey. —**steer clear of,** evitar; huir de; mantenerse alejado de.

steerage ('stɪr·ɪdʒ) *n.* **1,** (part of a ship) antecámara de bajel; proa. **2,** (steering) gobierno; dirección.

steering wheel 1, *naut.* rueda del timón. **2,** *auto.* volante.

steersman ('stɪrz·mən) *n.* [*pl.* -men] timonero; timonel; piloto.

stein (stain) *n.* pichel, esp. para cerveza.

stellar ('stɛl·ər) *adj.* estelar; astral.

stem (stɛm) *n.* **1,** (of a plant) tallo; pedúnculo; tronco. **2,** (of a glass) pie. **3,** (of a pen or a smoking pipe) cañón. **4,** *mech.* varilla. **5,** *gram.* tema; base. **6,** *naut.* roda. —*v.t.* [**stemmed, stemming**] **1,** (stop; check) detener; refrenar. **2,** (dam) represar. **3,** (make headway against) navegar contra; oponerse a; resistir; embestir. —**from stem to stern,** de proa a popa. —**stem from,** nacer de; provenir de —**stem the tide,** rendir la marea.

stemware ('stɛm·wer) *n.* copas de pie.

stench (stɛntʃ) *n.* hedor; hediondez; peste.

stencil ('stɛn·səl) *n.* estarcido; marca; patrón para estarcir. —*v.t* estarcir.

stenography (stə'nag·rə·fi) *n.* estenografía; taquigrafía. —**stenographer,** estenógrafo; taquígrafo. —**stenographic** (,stɛn·ə'græf·ɪk) *adj.* estenográfico; taquigráfico.

stentorian (stɛn'tor·i·ən) *adj.* estentóreo.

step (stɛp) *n.* **1,** (movement of the foot; pace; gait; short distance) paso. **2,** (stair; rung of a ladder) peldaño; escalón. **3,** (footboard) estribo. **4,** (footprint) huella; pisada. **5,** *pl.* (flight of stairs) escalera. **6,** (degree; grade) grado. **7,** *mus.* intervalo. **8,** (measure; action toward a goal) medida. —*v.i.* [**stepped, stepping**] **1,** (move the feet) dar un paso; dar pasos. **2,** (walk) andar; caminar. **3,** (dance) bailar. **4,** (move briskly) ir de prisa. **5,** (put the foot on or in; press with the foot) pisar. —*v.t.* **1,** (set down, as the foot) plantar (el pie). **2,** (dance) bailar. **3,** (measure; pace off) medir a pasos. **4,** (arrange in steps) escalonar. —**break step,** romper paso. —**in step, 1,** (keeping rhythm) a compás; llevando el paso. **2,** (in accord) de acuerdo. —**keep (in) step,** llevar el paso. —**out of step, 1,** (not in rhythm) no llevando el paso. **2,** (in disagreement) en desacuerdo. —**step aside,** apartarse; hacerse a un lado; abrir paso. —**step back,** retroceder; volver hacia atrás. —**step by step,** paso a paso. —**step down, 1,** (resign) darse de baja; dimitir. **2,** (decrease) disminuir; reducir. **3,** (descend) bajar; descender. —**step forth,**

adelantarse; avanzar; presentarse.
—**step in, 1,** (enter) entrar. **2,** (inter-vene) meterse; intervenir. —**step on,** pisar; pisotear. —**step on it,** *colloq.* darse prisa; apresurarse; acelerar. —**step out, 1,** (leave) salir. **2,** (walk briskly) ir de prisa; acelerar el paso. **3,** *colloq.* (go out for a good time) ir de parranda; ir de juerga. —**step up, 1,** (move up-ward) subir. **2,** (approach; advance) acercarse; avanzar **3,** (increase) aumentar; levantar. **4,** (accelerate) acelerar; apretar (el paso). —**take steps, 1,** (move; walk) dar pasos. **2,** (take action) tomar medidas. —**watch one's step,** tener cuidado.

stepbrother ('stɛp,brʌð·ər) *n.* her-manastro; medio hermano.

stepchild ('stɛp,tʃaild) *n.* [*pl.* -**children**] hijastro o hijastra.

stepdaughter ('stɛp,dɔ·tər) *n.* hijastra.

stepfather ('stɛp,fa·ðər) *n.* pa-drastro.

step-ins *n.pl.* pantaloncitos de mujer.

stepladder ('stɛp,læd·ər) *n.* escala; escalera.

stepmother ('stɛp,mʌð·ər) *n.* madrastra.

stepparent ('stɛp,pɛr·ənt) *n.* pa-drastro o madrastra.

steppe (stɛp) *n.* estepa.

stepping stone pasadera; *fig.* escalón.

stepsister ('stɛp,sɪs·tər) *n.* herma-nastra; medio hermana.

stepson ('stɛp,sʌn) *n.* hijastro.

stere (stɪr) *n.* estéreo.

stereo ('stɛr·i·o) *n.* estéreo.

stereophonic (,stɛr·i·ə'fan·ɪk) *adj.* estereofónico.

stereoscope ('stɛr·i·ə,skop) *n.* estereoscopio. —**stereoscopic** (-'skap·ɪk) *adj.* estereoscópico. —**stereoscopy** (-'as·kə·pi) *n.* este-reoscopia.

stereotype ('stɛr·i·ə,taip) *n.* este-reotipo; clisé. —*adj.* estereotípico. —*v.t.* estereotipar. —**stereotyped,** *adj.* estereotipado. —**stereotypy,** *n.* estereotipia.

sterile ('stɛr·ɪl) *adj.* estéril. —**sterility** (stə'rɪl·ə·ti) *n.* esterili-dad.

sterilize ('stɛr·ə,laiz) *v.t.* esterili-zar. —**sterilization** (-lɪ'zei·ʃən) *n.* esterilización. —**sterilizer,** *n.* esteri-lizador.

sterling ('stʌr·lɪŋ) *adj.* **1,** (of

standard quality; as silver) esterlina. **2,** (pure; genuine) puro; genuino. **3,** (noble) noble; excelente. —*n.* **1,** (silver) plata de ley. **2,** (silverware) vajilla de plata. —**pound sterling,** libra esterlina.

stern (stʌrn) *adj.* **1,** (severe) severo; estricto; áspero; austero. **2,** (relentless) firme; inexorable. —*n.* popa. —**sternness,** *n.* severidad; aspereza.

sternum ('stʌr·nəm) *n.* [*pl.* **ster-nums** o **sterna** (-nə)] esternón.

sternway ('stʌrn·wei) *n.,* *naut.* cía.

stertorous ('stʌr·tə·rəs) *adj.* estertoroso.

stet (stɛt) reténgase.

stethoscope ('stɛθ·ə·skop) *n.* estetoscopio.

stevedore ('sti·və·dor) *n.* esti-bador.

stew (stu:) *n.* **1,** (food) estofado; guisado; *Amer.* sancocho. **2,** (anxi-ety) ansiedad; apuro. —*v.t.* & *i.* (cook) estofar; guisar. —*v.i.* (worry) inquietarse; preocuparse. —**stewed fruit,** compota de frutas.

steward ('stu·ərd) *n.* **1,** (manager of a household) mayordomo; senes-cal. **2,** (administrator) administra-dor; encargado. **3,** (kitchen man-ager) despensero. **4,** *aero; naut.* camarero.

stewardess ('stu·ər·dɪs) *n.* **1,** (manager of a household) mayor-doma; ama de llaves. **2,** (adminis-trator) administradora. **3,** *naut.* camarera. **4,** *aero.* camarera; aza-fata; *Amer.* aeromoza.

stewardship ('stu·ərd·ʃɪp) *n.* **1,** (household management) mayordo-mía. **2,** (administration) administra-ción; cargo.

stewpan ('stu:·pæn) *n.* cazuela; cacerola.

stick (stɪk) *n.* **1,** (piece of wood) palo; bastón. **2,** (club; cudgel) porra; macana. **3,** (wand; bar; rod) vara; barra. **4,** *aero.* palanca de mando. **5,** (stab) estocada; puñalada. **6,** *colloq.* (dull, stupid person) bobo; bodoque. **7,** (things arranged in a line or string) ristra. **8,** *pl., colloq.* (rural districts) campo; campiña. —*v.t.* [*pret & p.p.* **stuck**] **1,** (pierce) picar; punzar. **2,** (stab) apuñalar. **3,** (thrust) empu-jar. **4,** (put; place) poner; meter. **5,** (at-tach) pegar; juntar; adherir. **6,** *colloq.* (puzzle) coger de bobo;

confundir. **7,** *slang* (impose upon; deceive) engañar; embaucar. —*v.i.* **1,** (remain) quedarse. **2,** (extend) proyectarse. **3,** (scruple) escrupulizar. **4,** (adhere) pegarse; agarrarse. **5,** (stagnate) atascarse; estancarse. **6,** (persist) continuar; persistir. —**stick around,** *slang* quedarse. —**stick at,** persistir en; mantenerse a. —**stick by,** apoyar; sostener. —**stick in,** clavar; hincar; encajar. —**stick-in-the-mud,** *n.* persona muy conservadora. —**stick one's hands up,** alzar las manos. —**stick out, 1,** (project) sobresalir; proyectarse. **2,** (push out) sacar (la lengua); asomar (la cabeza). **3,** (be conspicuous) saltar a los ojos; ser muy evidente. —**stick them up!,** ¡manos arriba! —**stick to, 1,** (adhere to) adherirse a; mantenerse a o en. **2,** (persist in) persistir en; aferrarse a. —**stick together,** unirse; quedarse unidos; juntarse. —**stick up, 1,** (hold straight up) alzar; sacar hacia arriba **2,** (stand up) estar o ponerse de punta; levantarse; erizase. **3,** *slang* (rob) asaltar; atracar; robar. —**stick up for,** *colloq.* defender; secundar; declararse por.

sticker ('stɪk·ər) *n.* **1,** (persistent person) persona insistente; testarudo. **2,** (adhesive label) etiqueta; marbete engomado. **3,** (bur; barb) espina; púa; punta. **4,** *colloq.* (puzzler) enigma; rompecabezas.

stickle ('stɪk·əl) *v.i.* tener escrúpulos; escrupulizar.

stickler ('stɪk·lər) *n.* **1,** (scrupulous person) persona escrupulosa o quisquillosa. **2,** *colloq.* (puzzler) enigma; rompecabezas.

stick shift cambio manual.

stick-up *n., slang* robo; atraco a mano armada.

sticky ('stɪk·i) *adj.* **1,** (adhesive; gummy) pegajoso; viscoso. **2,** (humid) húmedo. **3,** *colloq.* (difficult) delicado; difícil.

stiff (stɪf) *adj.* **1,** (rigid) tieso; rígido; inflexible. **2,** (strong; harsh) fuerte. **3,** (difficult) difícil; arduo; riguroso. **4,** (formal) formal; tieso; serio. **5,** (awkward) desmañado; torpe. **6,** *colloq.* (high, as of prices) excesivo; alto. —*n., slang* **1,** (corpse) cadáver; muerto. **2,** (excessively formal person) persona tiesa y ceremoniosa. **3,** (awkward person) bodoque.

stiffen ('stɪf·ən) *v.t.* atiesar. —*v.i.* atiesarse.

stiff-necked ('stɪf,nɛkt) *adj.* terco; obstinado; testarudo.

stiffness ('stɪf·nəs) *n.* **1,** (rigidity) rigidez; inflexibilidad. **2,** (vigor) fuerza. **3,** (difficulty) dificultad; rigor. **4,** (formality) formalidad; ceremonia. **5,** (awkwardness) torpeza.

stifle ('stai·fəl) *v.t.* ahogar; sofocar. —*v.i.* ahogarse; sofocarse.

stigma ('stɪg·mə) *n.* [*pl.* **stigmas** o **stigmata** (-mə·tə)] estigma. —**stigmatize** (-taiz) *v.t.* estigmatizar.

stile (stail) *n.* portillo con escalones o molinete para pasar de un cercado a otro.

stiletto (stɪ'lɛt·o) *n.* estilete.

still (stɪl) *adj.* **1,** (motionless) inmóvil; fijo. **2,** (tranquil; quiet) tranquilo; quieto. **3,** (silent) mudo; callado; silencioso. **4,** (lifeless) muerte; inanimado. —*n.* **1,** (distilling apparatus) alambique; destiladera. **2,** (distillery) destilería. **3,** *poet.* (silence; quiet) silencio; calma. **4,** (still photograph) vista fija; afiche. —*adv.* **1,** (up to the time indicated) todavía; aún. **2,** (even; yet) aún. **3,** (nevertheless) sin embargo; no obstante. —*v.t.* **1,** (silence) silenciar; acallar. **2,** (calm) calmar; aplacar. **3,** (muffle) amortiguar. **4,** (stop; halt) parar; detener. —*conj.* sin embargo.

stillbirth ('stɪl,bʌrθ) *n.* parto muerto.

stillborn ('stɪl,born) *adj.* nacido muerto.

still life naturaleza muerta; bodegón.

stillness ('stɪl·nəs) *n.* **1,** (motionlessness) inmovilidad. **2,** (calm; quiet) calma; tranquilidad. **3,** (silence) silencio.

stilt (stɪlt) *n.* zanco. —**stilted,** *adj.* formal; afectado; pomposo; altisonante.

stimulant ('stɪm·jə·lənt) *adj. & n.* estimulante.

stimulate ('stɪm·jə,leit) *v.t.* estimular; excitar. —**stimulation,** *n.* estímulo; excitación.

stimulus ('stɪm·je·ləs) *n.* [*pl.* **-li** (-lai)] estímulo; aguijón.

sting (stɪŋ) *v.t.* [*pret. & p.p.* **stung**] **1,** (prick; puncture) picar; pinchar; punzar. **2,** (smart; itch) picar; resquemar. **3,** (distress) atormentar; remorder. **4,** (goad) estimular;

aguijonear; espolear. **5,** *slang* (dupe) embaucar; estafar. —*v.i.* escocer; picar. —*n.* **1,** (sharp-pointed organ) aguijón; púa. **2,** (thorn; spine) púa. **3,** (act of stinging; wound caused by stinging) picada; picadura; punzada. **4,** (goad) aguijón; estímulo. **5,** (distress) remordimiento. **6,** (sharp pain) escozor; picazón.

stinger ('stɪŋ·ər) *n.* **1,** (person or thing that stings) aguijador; pinchador. **2,** (stinging organ) aguijón; púa. **3,** (thorn; spine) púa. **4,** (drink) bebida alcohólica con crema de menta, aguardiente y hielo.

stingray ('stɪŋ,reɪ) *n.* pastinaca.

stingy ('stɪn·dʒi) *adj.* **1,** (niggardly) mezquino; miserable; tacaño. **2,** (scanty) escaso; limitado; poco. —**stinginess,** *n.* tacañería.

stink (stɪŋk) *v.i.* [*pret.* **stank** o **stunk;** *p.p.* **stunk**] heder; apestar. —*v.t.* dar mal olor a; apestar. —*n.* hedor; hediondez; peste; mal olor. —**raise a stink,** *slang* armar el lío padre. —**stink out,** ahuyentar con mal olor. —**stink up,** dar mal olor a; apestar.

stinker ('stɪŋk·ər) *n.* **1,** (person or thing that stinks) persona o cosa apestosa. **2,** *slang* (despicable person) persona despreciable; canalla.

stinking ('stɪŋk·ɪŋ) *adj.* apestoso; hediondo.

stint (stɪnt) *v.t.* limitar; restringir. —*v.i.* limitarse; ceñirse; ser económico. —*n.* **1** (limitation) límite; restricción. **2,** (fixed amount) cuota; porción. **3,** (allotted task) tarea; faena.

stipend ('staɪ·pənd) *n.* estipendio.

stipple ('stɪp·əl) *v.t.* puntear; picar. —*n.* picadura; punteado. —**stippling** (-lɪŋ) *n.* picadura; punteado.

stipulate ('stɪp·jə·leɪt) *v.t.* estipular. —**stipulation,** *n.* estipulación.

stir (stʌr) *v.t.* [**stirred, stirring**] **1,** (move; agitate) mover; agitar. **2,** (mix) revolver; menear. **3,** (rouse) despertar; conmover; excitar. **4,** (poke, as a fire) atizar. —*v.i.* **1,** (move) moverse. **2,** (awake) despertarse. **3,** (arise) levantarse. **4,** (take place; happen) tener lugar; suceder; pasar. —*n.* **1,** (movement) movimiento; actividad. **2,** (excitement) conmoción; agitación; alboroto. **3,** (poke; shove) empujón.

4, *slang* (prison) cárcel; prisión. —**stirrer,** *n.* agitador; palillo.

stirring ('stʌr·ɪŋ) *adj.* conmovedor; emocionante; estimulante.

stirrup ('stʌr·əp) *n.* estribo; *naut.* codillo. —**stirrup cup,** copa de despedida.

stitch (stɪtʃ) *n.* **1,** *sewing, knitting, etc.* punto; puntada. **2,** (sudden sharp pain) punzada; dolor punzante. **3,** *colloq.* (bit) pizca. —*v.t. & i.* coser; dar puntadas (en) —**be in stitches,** *colloq.* desternillarse de risa.

St. John's bread = carob.

stoat (stoʊt) *n.* armiño, esp. en piel de verano.

stock (stɒk) *n.* **1,** (trunk or stem) tronco; tallo. **2,** (race; lineage) cepa; estirpe. **3,** (related group) raza; familia. **4,** (handle of a tool) mango; manija. **5,** (of a firearm) culata; caja; encaro. **6,** (livestock) ganado. **7,** (supply of merchandise) surtido; existencias. **8,** (reserve supply) reserva. **9,** (raw materials) materias primas. **10,** (corporate shares) acciones; valores. **11,** (meat broth) caldo. **12,** *cards* baceta. **13,** *pl.* (instrument of punishment) cepo. **14,** *bot.* (gillyflower) alhelí. **15,** *theat.* repertorio. —*v.t.* **1,** (supply; furnish) surtir; proveer; abastecer; acopiar. **2,** (have on hand) tener a mano; tener en existencias. **3,** (provide with fish or wildlife) poblar. —*adj.* **1,** (kept on hand) a mano; de surtido. **2,** (ordinary) común; corriente. **3,** (of the stock market) bursátil. **4,** (of livestock) ganadero; del ganado. **5,** *theat.* de repertorio. —**in stock,** en existencias; disponible; a mano. —**out of stock,** agotado. —**take stock,** hacer inventario. —**take stock in, 1,** (buy shares in) comprar acciones de. **2,** *colloq.* (believe) creer; confiar en. **3,** *colloq.* (give importance to) dar importancia a. —**stock-in-trade,** existencias. —**stock up (on),** surtirse (de); proveerse (de).

stockade (stɒk'eɪd) *n.* empalizada; estacada; valla. —*v.t.* empalizar.

stockbroker ('stɒk,broʊ·kər) *n.* corredor de acciones; bolsista.

stock car 1, *R.R.* vagón para el ganado. **2,** *auto.* coche de serie.

stock company 1, *comm.* sociedad por acciones; sociedad anónima. **2,** *theat.* compañía de repertorio.

stock exchange bolsa.

stock farm hacienda de ganado; *Amer.* rancho; estancia.

stockfish ('stak,fɪʃ) *n.* bacalao seco; cualquier pescado partido y secado al aire.

stockholder ('stak,hol·dər) *n.* accionista.

stocking ('stak·ɪŋ) *n.* media; calceta.

stock market bolsa; mercado de valores.

stockpile ('stak,pail) *n.* surtido; reserva. —*v.t.* acumular; reunir.

stockroom ('stak·rum) *n.* almacén; depósito de mercancías.

stock-still *adj.* completamente inmóvil; rígido.

stocky ('stak·i) *adj.* rechoncho.

stockyard ('stak·jard) *n.* corral para ganados.

stodgy ('stadʒ·i) *adj.* pesado.

stogy *también,* **stogie** ('sto·gi) *n.* 1, (cigar) cigarro largo y delgado. 2, (shoe) zueco.

stoic ('sto·ɪk) *n. & adj.* estoico. —**stoical,** *adj.* estoico. —**stoicism** (-ɪ·sɪz·əm) *n.* estoicismo.

stoke (stok) *v.t. & i.* 1, (poke; stir, as a fire) atizar. 2, (feed fuel; tend) alimentar; palear.

stoker ('sto·kər) *n.* 1, (person) fogonero; paleador. 2, (machine) alimentador de hogar.

stole (stoːl) *n.* estola. —*v.,* *pret. de* **steal.**

stolen ('sto·lən) *v., p.p. de* **steal.**

stolid ('stal·ɪd) *adj.* impasible; insensible. —**stolidity** (stə'lɪd·ə·ti) *n.* impasibilidad; insensibilidad.

stomach ('stʌm·ək) *n.* 1, *anat.* (digestive organ) estómago. 2, (abdomen; belly) abdomen; vientre; barriga. 3, (appetite) apetito. 4, (inclination; liking) deseo; inclinación. —*v.t.* 1, (eat; digest) tragar; digerir. 2, (tolerate) aguantar; tolerar.

stomachache ('stʌm·ək,eik) *n.* indigestión; dolor de estómago; empacho.

stomachic (sto'mæk·ɪk) *adj.* estomacal. —*n.* tónico; medicamento estomacal.

stomp (stamp) *v.t. & i., dial.* pisotear; patalear. —*n.* pisoteo; pataleo.

stone (stoːn) *n.* 1, (rock) piedra. 2, (gem) gema; piedra preciosa. 3, (pit of fruits) hueso. 4, (gravestone) lápida. 5, *med.* piedra; cálculo. 6, [*pl.* **stone**] (British unit of weight)

peso de 14 libras. —*v.t.* 1, (throw stones at) apedrear; lapidar. 2, (cover with stone) revestir de piedra. 3, (pave with stone) adoquinar; pavimentar con piedras. 4, (remove the pit from) deshuesar. —*adj.* pétreo; de piedra. —**leave no stone unturned,** no dejar piedra por mover; hacer todo lo posible. —**within a stone's throw,** a tiro de piedra.

stone-blind *adj.* completamente ciego.

stonecutter ('ston,kʌt·ər) *n.* cantero. —**stonecutting,** *n.* cantería.

stone-dead *adj.* muerto como una piedra.

stone-deaf *adj.* completamente sordo; sordo como una tapia.

stonemason ('ston,mei·sən) *n.* albañil; picapedrero. —**stonemasonry,** *n.* albañilería.

stone quarry cantera.

stonewall ('ston·wɔl) *v.i., slang* negarse a contestar o a cooperar.

stonework ('ston·wʌrk) *n.* cantería. —**stoneworker,** *n.* cantero; picapedrero.

stony ('sto·ni) *adj.* 1, (of or like stone) pétreo. 2, (full of stones) pedregoso; petroso. 3, (hard; rigid) duro; fijo. 4, (unfeeling) insensible; empedernido; de corazón duro.

stony-hearted *adj.* empedernido; de corazón duro.

stood (stud) *v., pret. & p.p. de* **stand.**

stooge (stuːdʒ) *n., colloq.* 1, *theat.* compañero asistente de un cómico. 2, (henchman) lacayo; secuaz; sicario. —*v.i., colloq.* servir; atender servilmente.

stool (stuːl) *n.* 1, (seat) taburete; banquillo; banqueta. 2, (toilet) inodoro; excusado. 3, (evacuation) evacuación de vientre. 4, (excrement) excremento. 5, (decoy) señuelo; reclamo. 6, = **stool pigeon.** —*v.i.* 1, (evacuate the bowels) exonerar el vientre. 2, *colloq.* (inform) delatar; soplar. 3, *colloq.* (spy) espiar.

stool pigeon 1, (decoy) señuelo. 2, *colloq.* (informer) delator [*fem.* -tora]; soplón [*fem.* -plona]. 3, *colloq.* (spy) espía.

stoop (stup) *v.i.* 1, (bend the body) inclinarse; doblarse; encorvarse. 2, (lower oneself) rebajarse; humillarse. —*v.t.* inclinar; doblar; encorvar. —*n.* 1, (bending of the body) inclinación; encorvada. 2, (condescension) descenso; humillación. 3, (front steps) escalinata.

stoop-shouldered *adj.* cargado de espaldas.

stop (stap) *v.t.* [**stopped, stopping**] 1, (halt) parar; detener. 2, (cease) cesar; dejar. 3, (stanch) estancar; restañar. 4, (block; plug) tapar; cerrar. 5, (finish) acabar; terminar. 6, (intercept) interceptar. 7, (interrupt) interrumpir; suspender. 8, (prevent) impedir. —*v.i.* 1, (halt) parar(se); detenerse. 2, (cease) cesar (de); dejar (de) 3, (tarry; make a stay) quedarse; alojarse; hospedarse. —*n.* 1, (halt; cessation) parada; alto; pausa; detención; cesación. 2, (place where trains, buses, etc., stop) parada; estación. 3, (stay; sojourn) estada; estancia. 4, (pause in a journey) escala. 5, (obstruction) obstáculo; impedimento; obstrucción. 6, (check; curb) freno. 7, (plug; stopper) tapón. 8, (period; end of sentence) punto. 9, *phonet.* explosiva. 10, *photog.* abertura. 11, *mus.* (of a fretted instrument) traste; (of an organ) registro. —*interj.* ¡alto!; ¡basta! —**put a stop to,** poner fin a; acabar con. —**stop at nothing,** no pararse en escrúpulos. —**stop off,** pararse un rato. —**stop off at,** pasar por. —**stop over,** hacer alto; detenerse. —**stop short,** parar(se) en seco. —**stop up,** tapar; atorar; represar; obstruir.

stopcock ('stap,kak) *n.* llave; grifo; espita.

stopgap ('stap,gæp) *n.* expediente. —*adj.* provisional; interino.

stoplight ('stap,lait) *n.* 1, *R.R.* semáforo. 2, *auto.* (tail light) farol de cola. 3, (traffic light) señal o luz de parada.

stopover ('stap,o·vər) *n.* parada intermedia; escala.

stoppage ('stap·idʒ) *n.* 1, (halt) parada; alto; detención. 2, (obstruction) taponamiento; obstrucción. 3, (interruption) interrupción; suspensión. 4, (damming, as of water) represa. 5, (labor strike) huelga; paro.

stopper ('stap·ər) *n.* tapón; tarugo. —*v.t.* taponar.

stop sign señal de parada.

stop signal señal o luz de parada.

stopwatch ('stap,watʃ) *n.* cronómetro.

storage ('stor·idʒ) *n.* almacenaje. —**storage battery,** acumulador.

store (storr) *n.* 1, (shop; selling establishment) tienda; almacén. 2, (storage place) depósito; almacén. 3, (supply) provisión; acopio. 4, *pl.* (supplies, provisions, etc.) pertrechos; víveres; municiones. 5, (reserve) reserva; repuesto. 6, (abundance) abundancia; gran cantidad. —*v.t.* 1, (stock; accumulate) surtir; guardar; acumular. 2, (furnish; supply) proveer; abastecer. 3, (put in reserve) almacenar; depositar. —**be in store for,** esperarle a uno (una cosa). —**in store,** guardado; en reserva. —**set store by,** estimar o apreciar mucho; dar importancia a. —**store away,** guardar; ahorrar. —**store up,** acumular.

storehouse ('stor,haus) *n.* almacén; depósito.

storekeeper ('stor,ki·pər) *n.* 1, (shopkeeper) tendero. 2, (keeper of supplies) guardalmacén; *naut.* pañolero.

storeroom ('stor·rum) *n.* almacén; bodega; despensa; *naut.* pañol.

storied ('stor·id) *adj.* 1, (celebrated in story) historiado. 2, (having a specified number of floors or stories) de (tantos) pisos: *seven-storied,* de siete pisos.

stork (stork) *n.* cigüeña.

storm (storm) *n.* 1, (atmospheric disturbance) tempestad; temporal; tormenta; *naut.* borrasca. 2, (vehement outbreak; tumult) arrebato; explosión; alboroto; tumulto. 3, (violent assault) ataque; asalto. —*v.i.* 1, (blow; be stormy) haber tempestad; emborrascarse. 2, (fume; rage) estar enfurecido; estar encolerizado; rabiar. 3, (rush; move with violence) precipitarse. —*v.t.* asaltar; atacar; tomar por asalto; expugnar.

storm cloud nubarrón.

storm door contravidriera *(de puerta).*

storm troops tropas de asalto. *También,* **storm troopers.**

storm window contravidriera *(de ventana).*

stormy ('stor·mi) *adj.* tempestuoso; *naut.* borrascoso.

story ('stor·i) *n.* 1, (narrative) cuento; historia; relato. 2, (plot of a novel, play, etc.) argumento; trama. 3, *colloq.* (lie) mentira; embuste. 4, (floor of a building) alto; piso. 5, (gossip; rumor) chisme; rumor. —*v.t.* historiar.

storyteller ('stor·i,tɛl·ər) *n.* **1,** (narrator) cuentista; narrador. **2,** *colloq.* (fibber; liar) cuentón; embustero; mentiroso. **3,** *colloq.* (gossip) chismoso.

stoup (stup) *n.* pila de agua bendita.

stout (staut) *adj.* **1,** (corpulent) corpulento; gordo; fornido. **2,** (strong; sturdy) fuerte; robusto; sólido. **3,** (vigorous; forceful) fuerte; recio. **4,** (brave) resuelto; intrépido. —*n.* cerveza fuerte.

stouthearted (,staut'har·tɪd) *adj.* resuelto; valeroso; intrépido.

stove (stoːv) *n.* **1,** (for heating) estufa. **2,** (for cooking) hornillo; cocina. **3,** (furnace; oven) horno. —*v., pret. & p.p. de* **stave.**

stovepipe ('stov,paip) *n.* tubo de estufa o de hornillo. —**stovepipe hat,** sombrero de copa alta.

stow (stoː) *v.t.* **1,** (store; pack) meter; guardar; esconder; *naut.* estibar; arrumar. **2,** *slang* (stop; cease) cesar; dejar. —**stow away, 1,** (store) guardar; esconder. **2,** (hide aboard a ship, train, etc.) embarcarse clandestinamente; colarse.

stowaway ('sto·ə·wei) *n.* polizón.

strabismus (strə'bɪz·məs) *n.* estrabismo.

straddle ('stræd·əl) *v.t. & i.* **1,** (sit or stand astride) montar a horcajadas; ponerse a horcajadas (en). **2,** *colloq.* (favor both sides) favorecer a ambos lados. —*n.* posición del que se pone a horcajadas.

strafe (streif) *v.t. & i.* **1,** *mil.* bombardear intensamente. **2,** *aero.* ametrallar en vuelo bajo.

straggle ('stræg·əl) *v.i.* **1,** (wander away; stray) desviarse; extraviarse; andar perdido. **2,** (lag) rezagarse. **3,** (spread irregularly or untidily) desparramarse; esparcirse. —**straggly** (-li); **straggling** (-lɪŋ), *adj.* desordenado; esparcido; rezagado.

straggler ('stræg·lər) *n.* **1,** (of persons) rezagado; vagamundo; tunante. **2,** (of objects, as a branch, etc.) rama extendida; objeto aislado.

straight (streit) *adj.* **1,** (without bend or deviation) derecho; directo; en línea recta. **2,** (upright; honorable) recto; justo; honrado; íntegro. **3,** (regular; orderly) ordenado; en orden. **4,** (frank; outspoken) sincero; franco. **5,** (continuous) seguido; continuo. **6,** (exact) exacto; correcto. **7,** (unmodified;

undiluted) puro. —*adv.* **1,** (directly) derecho; directamente. **2,** (honorably) rectamente; justamente; honradamente. **3,** (frankly) sinceramente; francamente. **4,** (continuously) continuamente; sin interrupción. **5,** (exactly) exactamente. **6,** (immediately) en seguida; en el acto. —*n.* **1,** (straight part) recta. **2,** *poker* escalera. —**straight away; straight off,** en seguida. —**straight face,** cara seria. —**straight from the shoulder,** con toda franqueza.

straightaway ('streit·ə·wei) *adj.* derecho; recto; en línea recta. —*n.* recta.

straightedge ('streit,ɛdʒ) *n.* regla.

straighten ('streit·ən) *v.t.* **1,** (set straight) enderezar. **2,** (put in order) arreglar; poner en orden. —*v.i.* **1,** (become straight) enderezarse. **2,** (come to order) arreglarse.

straightforward (,streit'for·wərd) *adj.* **1,** (direct) derecho; directo; recto. **2,** (honest; sincere) honrado; franco; sincero. —*adv.* **1,** (directly) directamente; en línea recta. **2,** (honestly; sincerely) honradamente; francamente; sinceramente.

straightness ('streit·nəs) *n.* rectitud.

straightway ('streit·wei) *adv.* luego; en seguida; inmediatamente.

strain (strein) *v.t.* **1,** (stretch) estirar. **2,** (exert to the utmost) forzar. **3,** (injure; sprain) torcer. **4,** (filter) colar; tamizar. **5,** (distort) torcer; deformar. **6,** (press; squeeze) exprimir. —*v.i.* esforzarse. —*n.* **1,** (tension) tensión; tirantez. **2,** (great effort) esfuerzo. **3,** (sprain) torcedura. **4,** (force; stress) fuerza; carga; peso. **5,** *mus.* aire; melodía. **6,** (lineage; descent) raza; linaje; estirpe. **7,** (kind; species) forma; clase; especie. **8,** (inherited trait) rasgo racial; genio. **9,** (manner; style) estilo. **10,** (trace; streak) huella; traza.

strained (streind) *adj.* forzado.

strainer ('strei·nər) *n.* coladera; colador.

strait (streit) *n.* **1,** *geog.* (passage of water) estrecho. **2,** (difficulty) apuro; aprieto. —*adj.* angosto; estrecho; apretado.

straiten ('strei·tən) *v.t.* **1,** (limit; contract) acortar; angostar; contraer.

2, (distress; embarrass) estrechar; apretar. —**in straitened circumstances,** apurado; en un aprieto.
strait jacket camisa de fuerza.
strait-laced adj. austero; puritano; estricto.
strand (strænd) v.t. 1, (drive or run aground) hacer encallar; hacer embarrancar; varar. 2, (leave in a helpless position) dejar desamparado; dejar plantado. —v.i. encallar; embarrancar; varar. —n. 1, (fiber; filament) hebra; filamento. 2, (string) hilo. 3, (things arranged on a string) hilera. 4, (tress) trenza. 5, (lock of hair) guedeja; pelo. 6, (part forming a rope) ramal. 7, (shore) playa; costa; ribera.
stranded ('stræn·dɪd) adj. 1, (aground) encallado; varado. 2, (lost and helpless) desamparado; perdido. 3, (woven of strands) trenzado; retorcido.
strange (streindʒ) adj. 1, (unfamiliar; surprising) extraño; extraordinario; raro 2, (alien) ajeno; foráneo; forastero. 3, (reserved; distant) retraído; reservado; esquivo. —**strangeness,** n. extrañeza; rareza.
stranger ('strein·dʒər) n. 1, (person not known) extranjero; desconocido. 2, (outsider; foreigner) extranjero; forastero. 3, (newcomer) recién llegado. 4, (novice) novicio; principiante.
strangle ('stræŋ·gəl) v.t. estrangular; ahogar. —v.i. estrangularse; ahogarse.
strangulate ('stræŋ·gju·leit) v.t. estrangular; obstruir.
strangulation (stræŋ·gju'lei·ʃən) n. estrangulación.
strap (stræp) n. 1, (strip of leather) correa. 2, (strip of metal, cloth, etc.) tira; banda; tirante. 3, (razor strop) suavizador. —v.t. 1, (fasten with a strap) liar; atar con correa, tira, banda, etc. 2, (beat with a strap) azotar con una correa. 3, (strop) suavizar. 4, colloq. (oppress) apretar; apurar; acosar.
straphanger ('stræp,hæŋ·ər) n., colloq. pasajero sin asiento que se aguanta a los tirantes de un tren, ómnibus, etc.
strapped (stræpt) adj., colloq. 1, (harassed) apretado; acosado. 2, (broke; in financial distress) pelado.
strapper ('stræp·ər) n., colloq. persona (esp. un muchacho) fuerte y enérgica.

strapping ('stræp·ɪŋ) adj., colloq. 1, (robust) fuerte; robusto. 2, (enormous) enorme.
strata ('strei·tə; 'stræt·ə) n., pl. de **stratum.**
stratagem ('stræt·ə·dʒəm) n. estratagema; ardid; artimaña; treta.
strategic (strə'ti·dʒɪk) adj. estratégico.
strategy ('stræt·ə·dʒi) n. estrategia. —**strategist,** n. estratégico; estratega.
stratify ('stræt·ə·fai) v.t. estratificar. —v.i. estratificarse. —**stratification** (-fɪ'kei·ʃən) n. estratificación.
stratosphere ('stræt·ə,sfɪr) n. estratosfera.
stratum ('strei·təm) n. [pl. -ta] 1, (layer) estrato. 2, fig. (class; division) clase; categoría; nivel.
stratus ('strei·təs) n., meteorol. estrato.
straw (strɔː) n. paja. —adj. 1, (of or like straw) pajizo; de paja. 2, (false) falso; ficticio. 3, (worthless) de ningún valor; de bagatela. —**catch at a straw,** asirse de un cabello; tomar medidas desesperadas. —**I don't care a straw,** no me importa un pito (o un bledo). —**straw in the wind,** indicación; sugerencia. —**the last straw,** el acabóse; el colmo.
strawberry ('strɔ,ber·i) n. fresa.
straw-colored adj. pajizo; de color de paja.
straw hat sombrero de paja; canotié.
straw man 1, (straw figure) figura de paja. 2, (scarecrow) espantapájaros. 3, (false witness) testigo falso. 4, (figurehead) testaferro. 5, (person of no importance) nulidad.
straw vote escrutinio exploratorio; encuesta.
stray (strei) v.i. 1, (wander) vagar; errar. 2, (deviate) extraviarse; desviarse; descarriarse. —adj. 1, (wandering; lost) extraviado; perdido. 2, (isolated) suelto; aislado. 3, (casual) casual; de casualidad; fortuito. —n. animal perdido; persona perdida o extraviada; vagabundo.
streak (strik) n. 1, (line; stripe) raya; lista; línea. 2, (ray of light) rayo. 3, (stratum; vein) veta; vena. 4, (strain; tendency) rasgo. 5, colloq. (spell; period) período; rato;

racha (de fortuna). —*v.t.* rayar; *Amer.* listar. —*v.i.* **1,** (become streaked) rayarse. **2,** (move fast) correr como un rayo; volar; precipitarse. —**like a streak,** *colloq.* como un rayo.

streaky ('stri·ki) *adj.* **1,** (marked with streaks) rayado; veteado; abigarrado. **2,** (sporadic) esporádico; irregular. **3,** (uneven; variable) desigual; variado; diverso.

stream (stri:m) *n.* **1,** (body of water) río; arroyo. **2,** (current; flow) corriente; flujo; chorro. **3,** (course; trend) curso; corriente. **4,** (succession; line) fila; desfile. —*v.i.* **1,** (flow) correr; fluir; manar. **2,** (gush) chorrear. **3,** (move swiftly) correr; precipitarse.

streamer ('stri·mər) *n.* **1,** (pennant) gallardete; banderola. **2,** (narrow ribbon) cinta. **3,** (tail of a comet) cabellera; cola.

streamline ('strim·lain) *v.t.* **1,** (shape so as to offer little wind resistance) dar forma aerodinámica. **2,** (modernize; make more efficient) modernizar; adelgazar. —*adj.* aerodinámico. —*n.* línea o forma aerodinámica.

streamlined ('strim·laind) *adj.* **1,** (shaped so as to offer little wind resistance) de forma aerodinámica. **2,** (modernized; efficient) modernizado; adelgazado.

street (strit) *n.* calle.

street Arab pilluelo; golfillo. *También,* **street urchin.**

streetcar ('strit·kar) *n.* tranvía.

street cleaner basurero. —**street cleaning,** limpieza de calles; servicio de sanidad.

streetwalker ('strit,wɔk·ər) *n.* cantonera; ramera; mujer de la calle.

strength (streŋθ) *n.* **1,** (force; power) fuerza; poder; potencia; vigor. **2,** (intensity) intensidad. **3,** (potency) potencia. **4,** (number of personnel) número; fuerza; fuerzas. —**by main strength,** a pulso. —**on the strength of,** basado en; basándose en.

strengthen ('streŋ·θən) *v.t.* **1,** (make strong) fortalecer; fortificar; reforzar. **2,** (intensify) intensificar. **3,** (make more potent) aumentar la potencia de. **4,** (confirm) confirmar; corroborar. —*v.i.* fortalecerse; fortificarse; reforzarse.

strenuous ('stren·ju·əs) *adj.* **1,** (arduous) arduo; difícil. **2,** (vigorous) estrenuo; enérgico; vigoroso.

streptococcus (,strɛp·tə'kak·əs) *n.* [*pl.* **-cocci** (-sai)] estreptococo.

streptomycin (,strɛp·tə'mai·sɪn) *n.* estreptomicina.

stress (strɛs) *n.* **1,** (strain) tensión; esfuerzo. **2,** (emphasis) énfasis; realce. **3,** (accent) acento. **4,** (pressure; coercion) coerción; compulsión. **5,** (urgency) urgencia; apuro. —*v.t.* **1,** (subject to strain) someter a tensión. **2,** (emphasize) dar énfasis a; recalcar; subrayar; dar importancia a. **3,** (accent) acentuar. —**lay stress on,** insistir en; realzar; dar importancia a.

stretch (strɛtʃ) *v.t.* **1,** (extend) extender; alargar. **2,** (lay flat) tender. **3,** (pull) estirar. **4,** (exaggerate) exagerar. **5,** (strain) forzar —*v.i.* **1,** (extend) extenderse. **2,** (lie flat) tenderse. **3,** (be pulled or tightened) estirarse **4,** (relax) desperezarse; repantigarse. —*n.* **1,** (extent) extensión. **2,** (pulling; tightening) estirón. **3,** (distance) distancia. **4,** (period of time) período; tiempo; rato. **5,** (straightaway) recta. **6,** *slang* (prison term) condena.

stretcher ('strɛtʃ·ər) *n.* **1,** (litter) camilla; andas. **2,** (device for stretching) estirador; bastidor.

stretcher-bearer *n.* camillero.

strew (stru:) *v.t.* [*p.p.* **strewed** o **strewn** (stru:n)] **1,** (scatter) esparcir; derramar; desparramar. **2,** (overspread by scattering) salpicar; sembrar; polvorear.

striate ('strai·et) *adj.* estriado. —*v.t.* estriar. —**striated,** *adj.* estriado.

stricken ('strɪk·ən) *adj.* **1,** (afflicted) afligido. **2,** (wounded; struck) herido. **3,** (overwhelmed) agobiado. —*v., p.p.* de **strike.** —**stricken in years,** entrado en años.

strict (strɪkt) *adj.* **1,** (exact) exacto; puntual. **2,** (scrupulous) escrupuloso. **3,** (rigorous) estricto; riguroso; severo; austero.

strictness ('strɪkt·nəs) *n.* **1,** (exactness) exactitud; puntualidad **2,** (scrupulousness) escrupulosidad. **3,** (rigorousness) rigor; severidad; austeridad.

stricture ('strɪk·tʃər) *n.* **1,** (censure) censura; crítica. **2,** *med.* constricción.

stride (straid) *v.i.* [**strode** (stro:d),

stridden ('strɪd·ən)] ˋandar a trancos; dar zancadas. —*v.t.* **1,** (go along or through at a stride) pasar o cruzar a zancadas. **2,** (straddle) montar a horcajadas. —*n.* tranco; zancada; paso largo. —**at a stride,** a trancos. —**hit one's stride,** alcanzar su paso normal. —**make great strides,** progresar rápidamente. ▪

strident ('straɪ·dənt) *adj.* estridente; chillón; llamativo. —**stridency,** *n.* estridencia.

strife (straɪf) *n.* contienda; lucha; refriega.

strike (straɪk) *v.t.* [*pret.* **struck**; *p.p.* **struck** o **stricken**] **1,** (deal a blow; hit) golpear; pegar; dar un golpe. **2,** (attack) atacar; asaltar. **3,** (collide with) chocar con; dar en o con. **4,** (cause to ignite) encender; sacar fuego de. **5,** (stamp; mint) acuñar. **6,** (print; imprint) imprimir. **7,** (cause to sound by striking) tocar. **8,** (announce by striking, as the hour) dar. **9,** (discover suddenly) descubrir repentinamente; dar en o con; tropezar con. **10,** (impress) impresionar; conmover. **11,** (lower; pull down) arriar; derribar. **12,** (afflict) afligir. **13,** (occur to; come to the notice of) ocurrírsele a uno. **14,** (erase; cancel) borrar; tachar. **15,** (conclude; as an agreement) concluir; concertar. **16,** (appear to; seem to) parecerle a uno. **17,** (cause a work stoppage in) salir o estar en huelga contra. **18,** (assume, as a pose or attitude) asumir; afectar. —*v.i.* **1,** (inflict a blow) dar un golpe a golpes; golpear. **2,** (collide) chocar; dar. **3,** (attack) atacar; dar el asalto. **4,** (run aground) varar; encallar. **5,** (grab at bait) coger el anzuelo. **6,** *naut.* (surrender) arriar la bandera. **7,** (announce the hour) dar la hora. **8,** (produce a sound) sonar; tocar. **9,** (produce a flame) encenderse. **10,** (refuse to work) salir o estar en huelga. **11,** (proceed in a certain direction) dirigirse; avanzar. —*n.* **1,** (work stoppage) huelga. **2,** (blow) golpe. **3,** (discovery) descubrimiento. **4,** (sudden good fortune) golpe de fortuna. —**strike camp,** batir tiendas. —**strike down,** derribar; aterrar. —**strike dumb,** aturdir; pasmar; confundir; dejar mudo. —**strike home,** dar en el hito. —**strike it rich,** descubrir una bonanza; tener

un golpe de fortuna. —**strike off,** quitar; borrar; tachar. —**strike out, 1,** (set out) dirigirse; avanzar; ponerse en marcha. **2,** (cancel) borrar; tachar. **3,** (deal blows) dar golpes. **4,** *baseball* retirar al bateador; retirarse el bateador. **5,** *colloq.* (fail) fracasar. —**strike up, 1,** (start playing or singing) empezar a tocar o cantar. **2,** (initiate) trabar (una amistad); entablar (una discusión).

strikebreaker ('straɪk‚breɪk·ər) *n.* esquirol; rompehuelgas.

striker ('straɪ·kər) *n.* **1,** (person or thing that strikes) golpeador. **2,** (worker on strike) huelguista. **3,** (bell clapper) badajo. **4,** (hammer, as of a firearm) percusor.

striking ('straɪ·kɪŋ) *adj.* **1,** (remarkable) extraordinario; impresionante. **2,** (refusing to work) en huelga.·

string (strɪŋ) *n.* **1,** (line; cord) cordón; cuerda. **2,** *pl.* (musical instruments) instrumentos de cuerda. **3,** (chain) cadena. **4,** (things arranged on a string) sarta. **5,** (succession; series) serie; fila; hilera. **6,** *colloq.* (limitation) limitación; condición. —*v.t.* [*pret.* & *p.p.* **strung**] **1,** (provide with strings) encordar. **2,** (tie or bind with string) encordar; encordelar; atar con cuerdas. **3,** (arrange on a string) ensartar; enfilar; enhilar. **4,** (form in a line) enfilar; colocar en serie. **5,** (stretch like a string) tender. **6,** (hang by a string) colgar de una cuerda. **7,** *colloq.* (hoax) engañar; burlar. —*v.i.* **1,** (form into a string) colocarse en fila. **2,** (extend) extenderse. **3,** (move or progress in a string) marchar o avanzar en fila. —**on a string,** en poder de uno. —**pull strings,** ejercer uno clandestinamente su influencia. —**string along,** *colloq.* engañar; burlar; decepcionar. —**string along with,** *colloq.* estar o ponerse de acuerdo con; tener confianza en. —**stringed instrument,** instrumento de cuerda. —**string up,** *slang* ahorcar.

string bean habichuela verde; ejote; judía verde.

stringent ('strɪn·dʒənt) *adj.* estricto; riguroso; severo. —**stringency,** *n.* rigor; severidad.

stringy ('strɪŋ·i) *adj.* fibroso; correoso.

strip (strɪp) *v.t.* [**stripped, strip-**

ping] 1, (deprive; divest) despojar; robar. 2, (undress) desnudar; desvestir. 3, (remove the covering from) descortezar. 4, *mech.* (tear off) estropear. 5, (dismantle) desmantelar. 6, (remove; take off) quitar. —*v.i.* desnudarse; desvestirse. —*n.* 1, (narrow piece) tira; faja; lista; listón; jirón. 2, (continuous series) sucesión; serie. 3, *aero.* (runway) pista de aterrizaje.

stripe (straip) *n.* 1, (narrow band or mark) raya; lista; banda; franja. 2, (stroke or mark of a whip) latigazo; azotazo. 3, (insignia; chevron) galón. 4, (type; sort) tipo; índole; clase. —*v.t.* rayar; listar. —**striped**, *adj.* rayado; listado.

stripling ('strɪp·lɪŋ) *n.* mozalbete; mozuelo.

stripper ('strɪp·ər) *n.* artista de strip tease.

strip tease número de cabaret en que la artista se desnuda.

strive (straiv) *v.i.* [*pret.* **strove**; *p.p.* **striven** ('strɪv·ən)] esforzarse; luchar; empeñarse; competir. —**strive to**, esforzarse por.

stroboscope ('strab·ə·skop) *n.* estroboscopio.

strode (strod) *v.,* *pret. de* **stride**.

stroke (strok) *n.* 1, (blow) golpe. 2, (play; move) jugada. 3, (sounding of a bell or chime) campanada. 4, (movement or mark of a pen) plumada; (of a brush) pincelada; brochada. 5, (apoplectic seizure) apoplejía; ataque de parálisis. 6, (caress) caricia. 7, (line; streak) raya. 8, (lightning flash) rayo; relámpago. 9, (thunderclap) trueno. 10, (beat of the heart) latido. 11, (mechanical motion) embolada; carrera. 12, (movement of an oar) remada. 13, (blow of a whip) latigazo. 14, (movement of the arms) brazada. 15, (occurrence of fortune) golpe de fortuna. —*v.t.* acariciar; frotar suavemente. —**at one stroke**, de un golpe; de una vez. —**at the stroke of**, al dar las diez; a las diez precisas o en punto.

stroll (strol) *v.i.* dar un paseo; pasearse; callejear; vagar. —*v.t.* pasearse por. —*n.* paseo.

stroller ('stro·lər) *n.* 1, (person walking) paseante. 2, (wanderer) vagabundo. 3, (baby carriage) cochecillo de niño. 4, (itinerant entertainer) cómico ambulante.

strong (strɔŋ) *adj.* 1, (powerful)

fuerte; firme; robusto; poderoso. 2, (fullbodied, as a beverage) cargado. 3, (intense) intenso. 4, (spicy) picante. 5, (rancid) rancio. 6, (offensive, as language) feo; injurioso. 7, (amounting to; numbering) ascendiendo a: *six hundred strong,* ascendiendo a seiscientos. —*adv.* fuertemente.

strong-arm *adj.* violento. —*v.t.* coercer.

strongbox ('strɔŋ,baks) *n.* cofre fuerte; caja de caudales.

stronghold ('strɔŋ,hold) *n.* fortaleza; plaza fuerte.

strong-minded *adj.* decidido; de firmes creencias.

strong-willed *adj.* decidido; de voluntad firme.

strontium ('stran·ʃi·əm; -ti-) *n.* estroncio.

strop (strap) *n.* suavizador. —*v.t.* suavizar.

strophe ('stro·fi) *n.* estrofa.

strove ('stro:v) *v.,* *pret. de* **strive**.

struck (strʌk) *v.,* *pret. & p.p. de* **strike**. —*adj.* (affected by a labor strike) en huelga.

structure ('strʌk·tʃər) *n.* 1, (form) estructura. 2, (something built) construcción; edificio. —*v.t.* construir; componer. —**structural**, *adj.* estructural.

struggle ('strʌg·əl) *n.* 1, (conflict) lucha; pelea; conflicto. 2, (extreme effort) esfuerzo. —*v.i.* 1, (fight) luchar; pelear. 2, (strive) esforzarse.

strum (strʌm) *v.t. & i.* [**strummed**, **strumming**] rasguear. —*n.* rasgueo. —**strumming**, *n.* rasgueo.

strumpet ('strʌm·pət) *n.* ramera; prostituta.

strung (strʌŋ) *v.,* *pret. & p.p. de* **string**.

strut (strʌt) *v.i.* contonearse; pavonearse; farolear. —*n.* 1, (swagger) contoneo; pavoneo. 2, (brace) tornapunta; riostra; puntal.

strychnine ('strɪk·nɪn) *n.* estricnina.

stub (stʌb) *n.* 1, (fragment; end) trozo; fragmento. 2, (tree stump) tocón; cepa. 3, (cigarette or cigar end) colilla. 4, (short, thick piece) zoquete. 5, (short piece of a ticket or check; coupon) talón. —*adj.* romo; obtuso; embotado. —*v.t.* [**stubbed, stubbing**] 1, (pull out by the roots) desarraigar. 2, (clear of stumps) quitar los tocones de. 3, (strike by accident) chocar; tropezar.

stubble ('stʌb·əl) n. 1, (stubs of grain) rastrojo. 2, (rough growth, as of beard) cerda.

stubbly ('stʌb·li) adj. 1, (full of stubble) lleno de rastrojo. 2, (bristly) erizado; cerdoso.

stubborn ('stʌb·ərn) adj. 1, (obstinate) obstinado; terco; cabezudo; testarudo. 2, (unyielding) intratable; inflexible; intransigente.

stubbornness ('stʌb·ərn·nəs) n. 1, (obstinacy) obstinación; terquedad; testarudez. 2, (resoluteness) inflexibilidad; intransigencia.

stubby ('stʌb·i) adj. 1, (full of stubs) lleno de tocones. 2, (short and thick) romo; embotado. 3, (bristly) cerdoso. 4, (stocky) rechoncho; regordete.

stucco ('stʌk·o) n. estuco. —v.t. estucar. —**stuccowork**, n. estucado.

stuck (stʌk) v., pret. & p.p. de stick.

stuck-up adj., colloq. altanero; tieso; esquivo; reservado.

stud (stʌd) n. 1, (ornamental tack) tachón. 2, (shirt button) botón de camisa. 3, (post; support) poste; montante. 4, (pin; peg) clavija; estaquilla. 5, (breeding horse) caballo padre. 6, (herd of breeding horses) caballada; yeguada. 7, (breeding establishment) acaballadero. —adj. semental; de o para cría. —v.t. [studded, studding] 1, (decorate with studs) tachonar; clavetear. 2, (be scattered over; cover) salpicar.

studbook ('stʌd·buk) n. registro genealógico de caballos.

student ('stu·dənt) n. 1, (pupil) estudiante; discípulo; alumno. 2, (scholar; researcher) investigador.

stud farm acaballadero.

studhorse ('stʌd,hors) n. caballo padre.

studied ('stʌd·id) adj. estudiado; deliberado; premeditado.

studio ('stu·di·o) n. estudio; taller.

studious ('stu·di·əs) adj. estudioso; aplicado; diligente.

study ('stʌd·i) n. 1, (mental effort) estudio. 2, (research) investigación. 3, (branch of learning) estudio; disciplina. 4, (academic subject) asignatura. 5, (deep thought) meditación profunda. 6, (room reserved for study) escritorio;

gabinete; despacho; estudio. —v.t. & i. [pret. & p.p. **studied**] estudiar.

stuff ('stʌf) n. 1, (material) material. 2, (cloth) tela; género. 3, (things; effects) cosas; efectos; bienes. 4, (rubbish; junk) basura. 5, (nonsense) tontería. —v.t. 1, (fill; pack) rellenar. 2, (cram) atestar; colmar; henchir. 3, (plug; block) tapar; atascar; atarugar. 4, (glut with food) atracar; hartar. 5, (force in; thrust in) meter; clavar; apretar. —v.i. atracarse; hartarse.

stuffed shirt slang presumido; persona arrogante y altanera.

stuffing ('stʌf·iŋ) n. relleno.

stuffy ('stʌf·i) adj. 1, (poorly ventilated) mal ventilado; cerrado; sofocante. 2, (stopped up, as from a cold) tapado; catarroso. 3, colloq. (dull) aburrido. 4, colloq. (prudish) mojigato; remilgado. 5, colloq. (old-fashioned) chapado a la antigua.

stultify ('stʌl·tə·fai) v.t. 1, (make absurd) poner en ridículo. 2, (make ineffectual) anular; viciar. 3, (make stupid) embrutecer.

stumble ('stʌm·bəl) v.i. 1, (trip) tropezar. 2, (stagger) titubear; bambolear. 3, (falter in speech) titubear; vacilar. 4, (blunder) errar. —n. 1, (false step) traspié; tropezón; tropiezo. 2, (blunder) desliz; desatino. —**stumble on, upon** o **across,** tropezar con; dar con.

stumbling block ('stʌm·bliŋ) tropiezo; escollo.

stump (stʌmp) n. 1, (tree trunk) tocón; cepa. 2, (remaining part; end; butt) trozo; fragmento; (of an amputated limb) muñón; (of a cigar or cigarette) colilla; (of a tooth) raigón; (of a tail) rabo. 3, (political rostrum) tribuna para discursos políticos. 4, (heavy step) paso pesado. 5, slang (leg) pierna; pata. —v.t. 1, (lop) cortar; amputar. 2, (campaign politically in) recorrer haciendo discursos políticos; solicitar votos en o de. 3, colloq. (perplex) confundir; dejar perplejo. —v.i. 1, (campaign; electioneer) dar discursos políticos; solicitar votos. 2, (walk heavily) renquear; cojear. —**up a stump,** colloq. perplejo; confuso; en un aprieto.

stumpy ('stʌm·pi) adj. 1, (stocky) regordete; rechoncho; tozo. 2, (abounding in stumps) lleno de tocones.

stun (stʌn) *v.t.* [**stunned, stunning**] aturdir; pasmar.

stung (stʌŋ) *v., pret. & p.p. de* **sting.**

stunk (stʌŋk) *v., pret. & p.p. de* **stink.**

stunning ('stʌn·ɪŋ) *adj.* **1,** (that stuns) aturdidor. **2,** *colloq.* (remarkable) elegante; bellísimo; de chupete.

stunt (stʌnt) *n.* **1,** (exhibition of skill) ejercicio de habilidad; maniobra sensacional. **2,** (acrobatic feat) acrobacia; jugada acrobática; *aero.* vuelo acrobático. **3,** (dwarfed creature) engendro. —*v.t.* impedir (el desarrollo de). —*v.i.* hacer acrobacia; hacer maniobras sensacionales.

stupefaction (ˌstu·pə'fæk·ʃən) *n.* estupefacción; estupor.

stupefy ('stju·pə·fai) *v.t.* **1,** (induce stupor in) embrutecer; entorpecer. **2,** (amaze) pasmar; aturdir; atontar. —**stupefied,** *adj.* estupefacto; aletargado.

stupendous (stju'pɛn·dəs) *adj.* estupendo; maravilloso; enorme.

stupid ('stju·pɪd) *adj.* estúpido; torpe; necio. —**stupidity** (stju'pɪd·ə·ti) *n.* estupidez; torpeza; necedad.

stupor ('stu·pər) *n.* estupor. —**in a stupor,** estupefacto; aletargado.

sturdy ('stʌr·di) *adj.* **1,** (strong; stout) fuerte; robusto. **2,** (firm) firme; resuelto; determinado.

sturgeon ('stʌr·dʒən) *n.* esturión.

stutter ('stʌt·ər) *v.i.* tartamudear. —*v.t.* decir tartamudeando. —*n.* tartamudeo. —**stutterer,** *n.* tartamudo.

sty (stai) *n.* [*pl.* **sties** (staiz)] **1,** (pigpen) pocilga. **2,** (inflammation of the eyelid) orzuelo.

Stygian ('stɪdʒ·i·ən) *adj.* estigio; tenebroso.

style (stail) *n.* **1,** (fashion) moda. **2,** (manner) estilo; manera; forma. **3,** (elegance) elegancia. **4,** (stylus) estilo. **5,** (name; title) nombre; título. **6,** *bot.* estilo. — *v.t.* **1,** (design) diseñar. **2,** (name) nombrar; designar. —**stylish,** *adj.* elegante; de moda. —**stylist,** *n.* estilista.

stylistic (stai'lɪs·tɪk) *adj.* estilístico. —**stylistics,** *n.* estilística.

stylize ('stai·laiz) *v.t.* estilizar.

stylus ('stai·ləs) *n.* **1,** (pointed in-

strument) estilo. **2,** (phonograph needle) aguja.

stymie ('stai·mi) *n., golf* obstáculo producido por la pelota de un adversario encontrándose entre el agujero y la pelota del otro. —*v.t.* obstruir; *fig.* frustrar.

styptic ('stɪp·tɪk) *adj. & n.* estíptico.

styrene ('stai·rin) *n.* estireno.

Styrofoam ('stai·rə,fom) *n., T.N.* tipo de plástico esponjoso.

suave (swaːv) *adj.* afable; gentil; urbano. —**suavity,** *n.* afabilidad; gentileza; urbanidad.

sub (sʌb) *n., colloq., abr. de* **substitute, submarine.**

subaltern (sʌb'ɔl·tərn) *n. & adj.* subalterno.

subatomic *adj.* subatómico.

subcommittee *n.* subcomisión; subcomité.

subcompact *n. & adj.* automóvil pequeño.

subconscious (sʌb'kan·ʃəs) *adj.* subconsciente. —*n.* subconsciente; subconsciencia. —**subconsciousness,** *n.* subconsciencia.

subcontinent *n.* subcontinente.

subcontract (sʌb'kan·trækt) *n.* subcontrato. —*v.t. & i* (ˌsʌb·kən'trækt) subcontratar. —**subcontractor** (-'trækt·ər) *n.* subcontratista.

subcutaneous (ˌsʌb·kju'tei·ni·əs) *adj.* subcutáneo.

subdivide ('sʌb·dɪ·vaid) *v.t.* subdividir. —*v.i.* subdividirse. —**subdivision,** *n.* subdivisión.

subdue (səb'duː) *v.t.* **1,** (conquer; overcome) sojuzgar; subyugar; dominar. **2,** (diminish; soften) suavizar; disminuir; reducir. **3,** (repress) reprimir; dominar.

subject ('sʌb·dʒɪkt) *n.* **1,** (theme; topic) sujeto; asunto; tema. **2,** (recipient of treatment, examination, etc.) sujeto. **3,** (person under power of another) súbdito. **4,** (academic course) asignatura. **5,** *gram.* sujeto. —*adj.* **1,** (under power of another) súbdito; sujeto. **2,** (liable; disposed) sujeto; expuesto; propenso. **3,** [*en la expresión* **subject to**] (contingent upon) a condición de. —*v.t.* (səb'dʒɛkt) sujetar; someter. —**subject matter,** asunto; materia.

subjection (səb'dʒɛk·ʃən) *n.* sujeción; sometimiento.

subjective (səb'dʒɛk·tɪv) *adj.*

subjetivo. —**subjectivity.** (ˌsʌb·dʒɛkˈtɪv·ə·ti) n. subjetividad.

subjoin (səbˈdʒɔin) v.t. añadir; agregar.

subjugate (ˈsʌb·dʒə,geit) v.t. subyugar; sojuzgar. —**subjugation,** n. subyugación.

subjunctive (səbˈdʒʌŋk·tɪv) adj. subjuntivo.

sublease n. subarriendo. —v.t. [también, **sublet**] subarrendar.

sublimate (ˈsʌb·lə,meit) v.t. sublimar. —n. sublimado. —**sublimation,** n. sublimación.

sublime (səˈblaim) adj. sublime. —**sublimity** (səˈblɪm·ə·ti) n. sublimidad.

subliminal (sʌbˈlɪm·ə·nəl) adj. subconsciente.

submachine gun ametralladora portátil.

submarine (ˌsʌb·məˈriːn) adj. & n. submarino.

submerge (səbˈmʌrdʒ) v.t. sumergir. —v.i. sumergirse.

submersible (səbˈmʌr·sə·bəl) adj. sumergible. —n. sumergible; submarino.

submersion (səbˈmʌr·ʒən) n. sumersión.

submission (səbˈmɪʃ·ən) n. sumisión; sometimiento.

submissive (səbˈmɪs·ɪv) adj. sumiso.

submit (səbˈmɪt) v.t. someter. —v.i. someterse.

subnormal adj. subnormal.

suborbital adj. suborbital.

subordinate (səˈbor·dɪ·nət) adj. & n. subordinado; subalterno. —v.t. (-,neit) subordinar. —**subordination,** n. subordinación.

suborn (səˈborn) v.t. sobornar. —**subornation** (ˌsʌb·orˈnei·ʃən) n. soborno; sobornación.

subpoena (səbˈpi·nə; sə-) n. comparendo; citación. —v.t. citar; emplazar.

subrogate (ˈsʌb·ro,geit) v.t. subrogar. —**subrogation,** n. subrogación.

sub rosa (sʌbˈro·zə) adv. secretamente; en secreto.

subscribe (səbˈskraib) v.t. suscribir. —v.i. **1,** (sign) suscribirse; firmar. **2,** (promise; accept an obligation) suscribirse; abonarse. —**subscribe to, 1,** (promise to pay) suscribirse a; abonarse a. **2,** (endorse; consent to) suscribir; aceptar; consentir en.

subscriber (səbˈskrai·bər) n. suscriptor; abonado.

subscript adj. suscrito. —n. índice suscrito.

subscription (səbˈskrɪp·ʃən) n. **1,** (assent; agreement) suscripción. **2,** (signature) firma. **3,** (promise to pay) suscripción; abono.

subsequent (ˈsʌb·sə·kwənt) adj. subsecuente; subsiguiente; posterior. —**subsequence,** n. subsecuencia.

subserve (səbˈsʌɪrv) v.t. servir; ayudar.

subservience (səbˈsʌr·vi·əns) n. **1,** (subordinate status) subordinación. **2,** (servility) servilismo.

subservient (səbˈsʌr·vi·ənt) adj. **1,** (subordinate) subordinado; subalterno. **2,** (servile) servil.

subset n. conjunto contenido en otro.

subside (səbˈsaid) v.i. **1,** (sink; settle) hundirse. **2,** (fall to a lower level) bajar de nivel; menguar. **3,** (abate) apaciguarse; calmar.

subsidence (səbˈsai·dəns) n. **1,** (sinking; settling) hundimiento. **2,** (falling to a lower level) bajada. **3,** (abatement) apaciguamiento; calma.

subsidiary (səbˈsɪd·i·ɛr·i) adj. subsidiario; auxiliar; sucursal. —n. rama; filial; división; sucursal.

subsidize (ˈsʌb·sɪ·daiz) v.t. subvencionar.

subsidy (ˈsʌb·sə·di) n. subsidio; subvención.

subsist (səbˈsɪst) v.i. subsistir. —**subsistence,** n. subsistencia.

subsoil n. subsuelo.

subsonic (sʌbˈsan·ɪk) adj. subsónico.

substance (ˈsʌb·stəns) n. sustancia.

substandard adj. inferior a la norma.

substantial (səbˈstæn·ʃəl) adj. **1,** (of or having substance; real) sustancial; sustancioso. **2,** (strong) fuerte; sólido. **3,** (ample; important) considerable. **4,** (wealthy) rico; acomodado.

substantiate (səbˈstæn·ʃi·eit) v.t. comprobar; verificar; establecer. —**substantiation,** n. comprobación; verificación.

substantive (ˈsʌb·stən·tɪv) adj. & n. sustantivo.

substitute (ˈsʌb·stə,tjut) n. sustituto; suplente. —v.t. & i. sustituir. —**substitution,** n. sustitución.

substratum *n.* substrato.
subsume (səb'suːm) *v.t.* subsumir.
subterfuge ('sʌb·tər,fjudʒ) *n.* subterfugio; escapatoria; salida; evasión.
subterranean ('sʌb·tə'rei·ni·ən) *adj.* subterráneo.
subteen *n.* joven de menor de trece años. —*adj.* menor de trece años.
subtend (sʌb'tɛnd) *v.t.* subtender.
subtitle *n.* subtítulo.
subtle ('sʌt·əl) *adj.* **1,** (delicate; refined) sutil; delicado; tenue; refinado. **2,** (artful; crafty) artificioso. **3,** (discriminating; shrewd) perspicaz; agudo; astuto.
subtlety ('sʌt·əl·ti) *n.* **1,** (delicacy) sutileza; delicadeza. **2,** (artfulness) artificio; destreza. **3,** (shrewdness) agudeza; astucia.
subtract (səb'trækt) *v.t.* & *i.* sustraer.
subtraction (səb'træk·ʃən) *n.* sustracción.
subtrahend ('sʌb·trə·hɛnd) *n.* sustraendo.
subtropical *adj.* subtropical.
suburb ('sʌb·ʌrb) *n.* suburbio; arrabal; urbanización; *pl.* afueras; inmediaciones.
suburban (səb'ʌrb·ən) *adj.* suburbano. —**suburbanite,** *n.* suburbano.
suburbia (sə'bʌr·bi·ə) *n.* las afueras; los suburbios.
subvention (sʌb'vɛn·ʃən) *n.* subvención; subsidio.
subversion (səb'vʌr·ʒən) *n.* subversión. —**subversive** (-sɪv) *adj.* subversivo. —*n.* subversor. [*fem.* -sora].
subvert (səb,vʌrt) *v.t.* subvertir.
subway ('sʌb·wei) *n.* **1,** (underground railroad) tren subterráneo; metro. **2,** (underground passage) paso subterráneo; galería subterránea.
succeed (sək'siːd) *v.i.* **1,** (terminate well) triunfar; tener buen éxito; salir bien. **2,** (follow) suceder. —*v.t.* suceder a.
succeeding (sək'si·dɪŋ) *adj.* subsiguiente; posterior.
success (sək'sɛs) *n.* **1,** (favorable outcome) triunfo; éxito; fortuna; buen resultado. **2,** (person or thing that prospers) persona o cosa afortunada.
successful (sək'səs·fəl) *adj.* próspero; afortunado; que tiene buen éxito.

succession (sək'sɛʃ·ən) *n.* sucesión. —**in succession,** seguido; sucesivo; sucesivamente.
successive (sək'sɛs·ɪv) *adj.* sucesivo.
successor (sək'sɛs·ər) *n.* sucesor.
succinct (sək'sɪŋkt) *adj.* sucinto.
succor ('sʌk·ər) *n.* ayuda; socorro; auxilio. —*v.t.* ayudar; socorrer.
succotash ('sʌk·ə,tæʃ) *n.* guiso de maíz con habas.
succulent ('sʌk·jə·lənt) *adj.* suculento. —**succulence,** *n.* suculencia.
succumb (sə'kʌm) *v.i.* sucumbir; rendirse; morir.
such (sʌtʃ) *indef.adj.* tal; semejante. —*indef.pron.* tal; un tal; el, la, los o las (que). —**as such,** como tal. —**such a,** tal; semejante. —**such a large house,** una casa tan grande. —**such and such,** tal y tal; tal y tal cosa; fulano de tal. —**such as,** quien(es); el, la, los o las que. —**such that,** de tal modo que; de manera que; de suerte que.
suck (sʌk) *v.t.* & *i.* chupar; mamar; sorber. — *n.* chupada; mamada; sorbo.
sucker ('sʌk·ər) *n.* **1,** (person or thing that sucks) chupador. **2,** *bot.* mamón; chupón. **3,** *colloq.* (lollipop) pirulí; *Amer.* chupete. **4,** *colloq.* (dupe) primo; bobo.
suckle ('sʌk·əl) *v.t.* amamantar; lactar; dar el pecho. —*v.i.* mamar.
suckling ('sʌk·lɪŋ) *adj.* & *n.* mamón. —*n.* (young pig) lechón.
sucrose ('su·kros) *n.* sucrosa.
suction ('sʌk·ʃən) *n.* succión. —**suction pump,** bomba aspirante.
sudden ('sʌd·ən) *adj.* súbito; repentino; imprevisto. —**suddenly,** *adv.* súbitamente; de súbito; de repente. —**suddenness,** *n.* rapidez; precipitación.
suds (sʌdz) *n.pl.* **1,** (water foaming with soap) jabonaduras; espuma. **2,** *slang* (beer) cerveza.
sue (suː) *v.t.* demandar. —*v.i.* poner pleito; entablar juicio. —**sue for peace,** pedir la paz.
suede (sweid) *n.* piel curtida semejante a la de gamuza.
suet ('su·ɪt) *n.* sebo; grasa; gordo.
suffer ('sʌf·ər) *v.t.* **1,** (undergo; endure) sufrir; padecer. **2,** (tolerate) soportar; tolerar. **3,** (allow) permitir. —*v.i.* sufrir.
sufferance ('sʌf·ər·əns) *n.* **1,** (tacit consent) tolerancia; consenti-

miento. **2,** (endurance) sufrimiento; paciencia; resignación.

sufferer ('sʌf·ər·ər) *n.* paciente; sufridor [*fem.* -dora]; doliente; víctima.

suffering ('sʌf·ər·ɪŋ) *n.* sufrimiento; pena; dolor; padecimiento; tormento. —*adj.* doliente.

suffice (sə'fais) *v.i.* bastar; ser suficiente. —*v.t.* satisfacer. —**suffice it to say,** baste decir.

sufficiency (sə'fɪʃ·ən·si) *n.* suficiencia; lo suficiente.

sufficient (sə'fɪʃ·ənt) *adj.* suficiente; amplio; bastante.

suffix ('sʌf·ɪks) *n.* sufijo. —*v.t.* (*usu.* sə'fɪks) añadir.

suffocate ('sʌf·ə·keit) *v.t.* sofocar; asfixiar; ahogar. —*v.i.* sofocarse; asfixiarse; ahogarse. —**suffocation,** *n.* sofoco; asfixia; ahogo.

suffrage ('sʌf·rɪdʒ) *n.* sufragio; voto.

suffragette (ˌsʌf·rə'dʒɛt) *n.* sufragista.

suffragist ('sʌf·rə·dʒɪst) *n.* sufragista; votante.

suffuse (sə'fjuːz) *v.t.* difundir; bañar; cubrir.

suffusion (sə'fju·ʒən) *n.* sufusión.

sugar ('ʃʊg·ər) *n.* azúcar. —*v.t.* azucarar; endulzar. —*v.i.* formar azúcar; *Amer.* azucararse. —*adj.* azucarero; de azúcar.

sugar beet remolacha azucarera.

sugar bowl azucarera.

sugar candy azúcar piedra; azúcar cande.

sugar cane cañamiel; caña dulce; caña de azúcar.

sugar-coat *v.t.* acaramelar; almibarar; garapiñar; *fig.* endulzar. —**sugar coating,** garapiña; baño de azúcar.

sugar daddy *slang,* viejo rico que mantiene con lujo a una mujer joven.

sugar loaf pan de azúcar.

sugar maple arce del azúcar.

sugar mill trapiche; molino de azúcar; *Cuba* batey.

sugar plantation cañamelar.

sugarplum ('ʃʊg·ər͵plʌm) *n.* confite; dulce.

sugary ('ʃʊg·ə·ri) *adj.* **1,** (of or containing sugar) azucarado; acaramelado; dulce. **2,** *fig.* (flattering) meloso; melifluo.

suggest (səg'dʒɛst) *v.t.* sugerir; indicar; intimar.

suggestible (səg'dʒɛs·tə·bəl) *adj.* sugestionable.

suggestion (səg'dʒɛs·tʃən) *n.* sugestión; sugerencia; indicación; intimación.

suggestive (səg'dʒɛs·tɪv) *adj.* sugestivo; sugerente.

suicidal (ˌsu·ə'sai·dəl) *adj.* suicida; *fig.* ruinoso.

suicide ('su·ə·said) *n.* **1,** (agent) suicida. **2,** (act) suicidio; *fig.* ruina. —**commit suicide,** suicidarse.

suit (sut) *n.* **1,** (set; ensemble) juego. **2,** (set of clothes) traje. **3,** *law* pleito; proceso; demanda. **4,** (petition) petición; solicitación. **5,** (courtship) galanteo; cortejo. **6,** *cards* palo. —*v.t.* **1,** (be appropriate to) satisfacer; caer bien a. **2,** (adapt) adaptar; acomodar. **3,** (serve) servir; convenir a. **4,** (provide with clothes) vestir. —*v.i.* convenir; ser apropiado; caer bien. —**bring suit,** poner pleito; entablar juicio. —**follow suit, 1,** *cards* seguir el palo; servir del palo. **2,** *fig.* seguir la corriente; hacer lo mismo. —**suit oneself,** hacer lo que quiera.

suitable ('sut·ə·bəl) *adj.* apropiado; conforme; conveniente. —**suitability,** *n.* conformidad; conveniencia.

suitcase ('sut·keis) *n.* maleta.

suite (swit) *n.* **1,** (series; set) serie; juego. **2,** (retinue) séquito; tren; comitiva. —**suite of rooms,** juego de habitaciones; serie de piezas; apartamento.

suited ('sut·ɪd) *adj.* **1,** (conformable) conforme; adecuado. **2,** (adapted) apto; idóneo.

suiting ('sut·ɪŋ) *n.* tela para trajes.

suitor ('sut·ər) *n.* **1,** (one who courts a woman) pretendiente; galán; aspirante. **2,** (petitioner) postulante; suplicante. **3,** (litigant) demandante; pleiteador.

sulfa ('sʌl·fə) *n. & adj.* sulfa.

sulfate ('sʌl·fet) *n.* sulfato.

sulfide ('sʌl·faid) *n.* sulfuro.

sulfur ('sʌl·fər) *n.* azufre. —*v.t.* azufrar; sulfurar. —**sulfur mine,** azufrera.

sulfurate ('sʌl·fju͵reit) *v.t.* azufrar; sulfurar.

sulfuric (sʌl'fju·rɪk) *adj.* sulfúrico.

sulfurous ('sʌl·fər·əs) *adj.* sulfuroso; azufrado.

sulk (sʌlk) *v.i.* amorrarse; estar o ponerse ceñudo. —*n.* ceño; mal humor.

sulky ('sʌl·ki) *adj.* malcontento; resentido. —*n.* calesín de un solo asiento.

sullen ('sʌl·ən) *adj.* hosco; malhumorado; resentido. —**sullenness,** *n.* hosquedad; mal humor; resentimiento.

sully ('sʌl·i) *v.t.* manchar; desdorar; mancillar; desprestigiar.

sulphate ('sʌl·feit) *n.* = sulfate. —**sulphide** (-faid) *n.* = sulfide. —**sulphur** (-fər) *n.* = sulfur. —**sulphurate** (-fju·reit) *v.t.* = sulfurate. —**sulphuric** (-'fjur·ɪk) *adj.* = sulfuric. —**sulphurous** (-fər·əs) *adj.* = sulfurous.

sultan ('sʌl·tən) *n.* sultán.

sultana (sʌl'tæn·ə) *n.* sultana.

sultanate ('sʌl·tə,neit) *n.* sultanía; sultanato.

sultry ('sʌl·tri) *adj.* sofocante; bochornoso.

sum (sʌm) *n.* **1,** (amount; quantity) cantidad. **2,** (total) suma; monta; total. **3,** (gist; substance) suma; esencia; sustancia. —*v.t.* [**summed, summing**] sumar. —**sum to,** ascender a; montar a. —**sum up,** resumir; compendiar.

sumac ('ʃu·mæk; 'su-) *n.* zumaque.

summarize ('sʌm·ə,raiz) *v.t.* resumir; compendiar.

summary ('sʌm·ə·ri) *n.* resumen; sumario; compendio. —*adj.* sumario; breve; conciso.

summation (sə'mei·ʃən) *n.* total; gran total; suma.

summer ('sʌm·ər) *n.* verano. —*adj.* veraniego; de verano; estival. —*v.i.* veranear; pasar el verano.

summer camp campamento de veraneo.

summerhouse ('sʌm·ər,haus) *n.* glorieta; cenador; cenadero.

summer resort centro de veraneo.

summertime ('sʌm·ər,taim) *n.* verano; tiempo de verano.

summery ('sʌm·ə·ri) *adj.* veraniego; estival.

summit ('sʌm·ɪt) *n.* ápice; cima; cumbre; pináculo.

summon ('sʌm·ən) *v.t.* **1,** (call) llamar. **2,** (call together) convocar. **3,** *law* citar; emplazar. **4,** (command) mandar. **5,** (call forth; gather) reunir; hacer acopio de.

summons ('sʌm·ənz) *n.* **1,** (call) llamada; convocación; orden. **2,** *law* emplazamiento; citación. —*v.t., colloq.* emplazar; citar.

sumptuous ('sʌmp·tʃu·əs) *adj.* suntuoso. —**sumptuousness,** *n.* suntuosidad.

sun (sʌn) *n.* sol. —*v.t.* [**sunned, sunning**] asolear; solear. —*v.i.* asolearse; tomar el sol. —*adj.* de o del sol; solar. —**place in the sun,** un puesto en el mundo. —**under the sun,** debajo del sol; en este mundo.

sun bath baño de sol.

sunbathe ('sʌn,beið) *v.i.* tomar el sol; asolearse.

sunbeam ('sʌn·bim) *n.* rayo de sol.

sunbonnet ('sʌn,ban·ɪt) *n.* gorra de sol.

sunburn ('sʌn·bʌrn) *n.* quemadura de sol. —*v.t.* quemar al sol. —*v.i.* quemarse al sol. —**sunburnt** (-bʌrnt) *adj.* tostado por el sol.

sundae ('sʌn·di) *n.* helado con jarabe y frutas o nueces.

Sunday ('sʌn·de) *n.* domingo. —*adj.* dominical; del domingo. —**dress up in one's Sunday best,** endomingarse.

Sunday school escuela dominical; escuela bíblica.

sunder ('sʌn·dər) *v.t.* separar; romper; partir. —*v.i.* separarse; romperse; partirse. —**in sunder,** en partes; en pedazos.

sundial ('sʌn,dail) *n.* reloj de sol; cuadrante solar.

sundown ('sʌn·daun) *n.* puesta del sol; anochecer.

sundry ('sʌn·dri) *adj.* varios; diversos. —**sundries,** *n.pl.* artículos diversos.

sunfish ('sʌn·fɪʃ) *n.* rueda.

sunflower ('sʌn,flau·ər) *n.* girasol; mirasol.

sung ('sʌŋ) *v., p.p. de* **sing.**

sunglasses ('sʌn,glæs·ɪz) *n.pl.* lentes o gafas de sol.

sunk (sʌŋk) *v., p.p. de* **sink.**

sunken ('sʌŋk·ən) *adj.* sumido; hundido.

sunlamp ('sʌn,læmp) *n.* lámpara de rayos ultravioletas.

sunlight ('sʌn,lait) *n.* luz del sol; sol.

sunlit ('sʌn·lɪt) *adj.* iluminado por el sol; claro.

sunny ('sʌn·i) *adj.* **1,** (bright with sunshine) asoleado; claro. **2,** *fig.* (cheerful) alegre; risueño. —**be sunny,** hacer sol.

sun porch solana.

sunrise ('sʌn·raiz) *n.* amanecer;

salida del sol. —**from sunrise to sunset**, de sol a sol.

sunset ('sʌn·sɛt) *n.* puesta del sol; ocaso del sol; anochecer.

sunshade ('sʌn·ʃeid) *n.* **1,** (parasol) quitasol; parasol; sombrilla. **2,** (awning) toldo. **3,** (visor) visera.

sunshine ('sʌn·ʃain) *n.* **1,** (sunlight) sol; luz del sol; día. **2,** (sunny spot) solana. **3,** *fig.* (cheer) alegría.

sunspot ('sʌn·spat) *n.* mancha o mácula solar.

sunstroke ('sʌn·strok) *n.* insolación; tabardillo.

suntan ('sʌn·tæn) *n.* atezamiento; quemadura de sol. —*v.t.* broncear. —*v.i.* broncearse.

sunup ('sʌn·ʌp) *n.* = **sunrise.**

sup (sʌp) *v.i.* [**supped, supping**] **1,** (eat the evening meal) cenar. **2,** (sip) sorber. —*n.* sorbo.

super ('su·pər) *n., colloq.* = **superintendent, supernumerary,** *etc.* —*adj., colloq.* **1,** (extra fine) superfino. **2,** (extra large) grande; grandísimo.

superable ('su·pər·ə·bəl) *adj.* superable.

superabundant *adj.* superabundante; sobreabundante. —**superabundance,** *n.* superabundancia; sobreabundancia.

superannuated (ˌsu·pər'æn·ju·ei·tɪd) *adj.* **1,** (retired) jubilado; fuera de servico. **2,** (obsolete) anticuado.

superb (su'pʌrb) *adj.* soberbio; espléndido; magnífico.

supercargo *n.* sobrecargo.

supercharger *n.* superalimentador.

supercilious (ˌsu·pər'sɪl·i·əs) *adj.* altanero; desdeñoso.

superego *n.* super ego.

superficial (ˌsu·pər'fɪʃ·əl) *adj.* superficial. —**superficiality** (-i'æl·ə·ti) *n.* superficialidad.

superfine *adj.* superfino.

superfluous (su'pʌr·flu·əs) *adj.* superfluo; sobrado. —**superfluity** (ˌsu·pər'flu·ə·ti) *n.* superfluidad.

superfortress *n.* superfortaleza.

superheat *v.t.* recalentar. —*v.i.* recalentarse.

superheterodyne *adj.* superheterodino.

superhighway *n.* autopista.

superhuman *adj.* sobrehumano.

superimpose *v.t.* sobreponer; superponer. —**superimposition,** *n.* superposición.

superintend (ˌsu·pər·ɪn'tɛnd) *v.t.* superentender; dirigir; vigilar.

superintendent (ˌsu·pər·ɪn·'tɛn·dənt) *n.* superintendente. —**superintendency,** *n.* superintendencia.

superior (sə'pɪr·i·ər) *adj.* **1,** (higher; greater) superior. **2,** (better) superior; mejor. **3,** (haughty) arrogante; altanero. **4,** (indifferent) indiferente. —*n.* superior [*fem.* superiora].

superiority (sə,pɪr·i'ar·ə·ti) *n.* **1,** (quality of being higher, greater or better) superioridad. **2,** (haughtiness) arrogancia; altanería.

superlative (sə'pʌr·lə·tɪv) *adj.* & *n.* superlativo.

superman *n.* [*pl.* **-men**] superhombre.

supermarket *n.* supermercado.

supernal (su'pʌr·nəl) *adj.* **1,** (lofty) superno; supremo. **2,** (celestial) celeste; celestial.

supernatural *adj.* sobrenatural.

supernumerary (ˌsu·pər'nju·mə·rer·i) *adj.* & *n.* supernumerario. —*n., theat,* figurante; comparsa.

superpose *v.t.* sobreponer; superponer. —**superposition,** *n.* superposición.

superpower *n.* superpotencia.

superscribe (ˌsu·pər'skraib) *v.t.* sobrescribir.

superscript *adj.* sobrescrito. —*n.* índice sobrescrito.

superscription (ˌsu·pər'skrɪp·ʃən) *n.* sobrescrito.

supersede (ˌsu·pər'siːd) *v.t.* suplantar; reemplazar.

supersonic *adj.* supersónico.

superstition (ˌsu·pər'stɪʃ·ən) *n.* superstición. —**superstitious,** *adj.* supersticioso.

superstructure *n.* superestructura.

supervene (ˌsu·pər'viːn) *v.i.* sobrevenir; supervenir. —**supervention** (-'vɛn·ʃən) *n.* superveniencia.

supervise ('su·pər,vaiz) *v.t* superentender; vigilar; dirigir. —**supervision** (-'vɪʒ·ən) *n.* superintendencia; dirección; supervisión.

supervisor ('su·pər,vai·zər) *n.* **1,** (director) superintendente; jefe; director [*fem.* -tora]. **2,** (foreman) sobrestante; capataz.

supervisory (ˌsu·pər'vai·zə·ri) *adj.* de superintendencia.

supine (su'pain) *adj.* supino.

supper ('sʌp·ər) *n.* cena. —**eat o have supper,** cenar; tomar la cena.

suppertime ('sʌp·ər·taim) *n.* hora de cenar.

supplant (sə'plænt) *v.t.* suplantar; reemplazar; sustituir.

supple ('sʌp·əl) *adj.* **1,** (pliant) flexible; manejable. **2,** (lithe) ágil. **3,** (yielding) dócil; sumiso.

supplement ('sʌp·lə·mənt) *n.* suplemento. —*v.t.* suplementar. —**supplemental** (-'mɛn·təl); **supplementary** (-'mɛn·tə·ri) *adj.* suplementario.

suppliant ('sʌp·li·ənt) *adj. & n.* suplicante.

supplicant ('sʌp·lə·kənt) *adj. & n.* suplicante.

supplicate ('sʌp·lɪ·keit) *v.t. & i.* suplicar. —**supplication,** *n.* súplica.

supply (sə'plai) *v.t.* suministrar; proveer; abastecer; surtir; suplir. —*n.* suministro; provisión; abasto; abastecimiento; *pl.* provisiones; víveres; pertrechos. —**supplier,** *n.* abastecedor. —**supply and demand,** oferta y demanda.

support (sə'port) *v.t.* **1,** (bear; hold up) sostener; mantener; soportar. **2,** (uphold; aid) asistir; ayudar; amparar. **3,** (favor) respaldar; favorecer. **4,** (provide for; maintain) proveer; mantener; sustentar. **5,** (endure) soportar; tolerar. **6,** *theat.* (act, as a role) desempeñar; hacer (un papel). **7,** *theat.* (accompany a leading performer) acompañar. —*n.* **1,** (base; person or thing that bears or holds up) soporte; sostén; apoyo. **2,** (maintenance) sustento; manutención. —**supportable,** *adj.* soportable; tolerable.

supporter (sə'por·tər) *n.* **1,** (adherent) partidario. **2,** (base; holder) soporte; sostén; apoyo. **3,** (belt; truss) suspensorio. **4,** (suspender) tirante.

suppose (sə'poːz) *v.t.* suponer; presumir; imaginar. —**supposing that,** dado el caso que.

supposed (sə'poːzd) *adj.* supuesto; presunto. —**supposedly** (sə'poːzɪd·li) *adv.* según se supone.

supposition (,sʌp·ə'zɪʃ·ən) *n.* suposición; supuesto.

supposititious (sə,paz·ɪ'tɪʃ·əs) *adj.* supuesto; fingido.

suppository (sə'paz·ə,tor·i) *n.* supositorio.

suppress (sə'prɛs) *v.t.* suprimir. —**suppressant,** *n. & adj.* supresor. —**suppression** (sə'prɛʃ·ən) *n.* supresión.

suppurate ('sʌp·jə·reit) *v.i.* supurar. —**suppuration,** *n.* supuración.

supremacy (su'prɛm·ə·si) *n.* supremacía.

supreme (sə'priːm) *adj.* supremo.

surcease (sʌr'sis) *n.* cesación.

surcharge ('sʌr·tʃardʒ) *n.* sobrecarga. —*v.t.* sobrecargar.

surcingle ('sʌr·sɪŋ·gəl) *n.* sobrecincha.

surcoat ('sʌr·kot) *n.* sobretodo.

surd (sʌrd) *n.* sordo; *phonet.* sonido sordo; *math.* número sordo.

sure (ʃur) *adj.* **1,** (certain) seguro; cierto; indudable. **2,** (stable; firm) seguro; firme; estable. **3,** (infallible) infalible; efectivo. —*adv., colloq.* seguramente; sin duda. —*interj.* ¡seguro!; ¡claro! —**be sure,** asegurarse. —**be sure to,** no faltar de; no dejar de. —**be sure not to,** guardarse de; tener cuidado de. —**for sure,** seguramente; sin duda. —**make sure,** asegurar; asegurarse. —**make sure of,** asegurarse de. —**sure enough,** *colloq.* a buen seguro; con certeza. —**to be sure,** seguramente; sin duda.

surefire ('ʃur,fair) *adj., colloq.* seguro; de éxito seguro.

surely ('ʃur·li) *adv.* seguramente; sin duda.

sureness ('ʃur·nəs) *n.* seguridad; certeza.

surety ('ʃur·ə·ti) *n.* **1,** guarantee. seguridad; garantía; fianza. **2,** (guarantor) fiador [*fem.* -dora]; garante. —**of a surety,** de seguro. —**be surety for,** ser fiador de; salir garante de; responder de.

surf (sʌrf) *n.* oleaje; rompiente. —*v.i.* correr las olas.

surface ('sʌr·fɪs) *n.* superficie. —*adj.* superficial. —*v.t.* allanar; alisar; igualar. —*v.i.* emerger; salir a la superficie.

surfboard ('sʌrf,bord) *n.* tablón de mar.

surfeit ('sʌr·fɪt) *n.* exceso; empacho; empalago. —*v.t.* empachar; empalagar.

surge (sʌrdʒ) *n.* oleada; oleaje. —*v.i.* surgir; agitarse.

surgeon ('sʌr·dʒən) *n.* cirujano. —**Surgeon General** [*pl.* **Surgeons General**] médico mayor; jefe de sanidad militar o naval.

surgery ('sʌr·dʒə·ri) *n.* **1,** (operation) cirugía. **2,** (operating room) sala de operaciones. **3**, (doctor's office) consultorio; despacho.

surgical ('sʌr·dʒɪ·kəl) *adj.* quirúrgico.

surly ('sʌr·li) *adj.* malhumorado; rudo; hosco; arisco. —**surliness**, *n.* hosquedad; rudeza.

surmise (sʌr'maiz) *n.* conjetura; suposición. —*v.t. & i.* conjeturar; suponer.

surmount (sʌr'maunt) *v.t.* **1**, (overcome) superar; vencer. **2**, (pass over) pasar por encima de. **3**, (rise above) elevarse sobre. **4**, (place something on top of; crown) coronar. —**surmountable**, *adj.* superable; vencible.

surname ('sʌr·neim) *n.* **1**, (family name) apellido. **2**, (epithet) sobrenombre. —*v.t.* apellidar.

surpass (sʌr'pæs) *v.t.* sobrepujar; exceder; superar; sobrepasar. —**surpassable**, *adj.* superable. —**surpassing**, *adj.* sobresaliente; superior; incomparable.

surplice ('sʌr·plɪs) *n.* sobrepelliz.

surplus ('sʌr·plʌs) *n.* sobra; sobrante; exceso; *comm.* superávit. —*adj.* sobrante; de sobra; excedente.

surprise (sər'praiz) *v.t.* sorprender. —*n.* sorpresa. —*adj.* repentino; inesperado. —**surprising**, *adj.* sorprendente.

surrealism (sə'ri·ə·lɪz·əm) *n.* surrealismo. —**surrealist**, *n. & adj.* surrealista. —**surrealistic**, *adj.* surrealista.

surrender (sə'ren·dər) *v.t.* rendir; ceder; entregar. —*v.i.* rendirse; ceder; entregarse. —*n.* rendición; entrega; sumisión.

surreptitious (ˌsʌr·əp'tɪʃ·es) *adj.* subrepticio.

surrey ('sʌr·i) *n.* birlocho.

surrogate ('sʌr·ə·geit) *n.* **1**, (substitute) sustituto. **2**, *law* juez de testamentarías. **3**, *eccles.* vicario.

surround (sə'raund) *v.t.* rodear; cercar; circundar; *mil.* sitiar. —**surrounding**, *adj.* circundante; circunvecino. —**surroundings**, *n.pl.* alrededores; ambiente.

surtax ('sʌr·tæks) *n.* impuesto adicional.

surveillance (sʌr'vei·ləns) *n.* vigilancia.

survey (sʌr'vei) *v.t.* **1**, (examine) examinar; inspeccionar. **2**, (view) mirar; contemplar. **3**, (measure) medir. —*n.* ('sʌr·vei) **1**, (examina-

tion) examen; inspección. **2**, (measurement) agrimensura; medición. **3**, (general view) vista; panorama. —**surveying**, *n.* agrimensura. —**surveyor**, *n.* agrimensor.

survival (sʌr'vai·vəl) *n.* **1**, (act of surviving) supervivencia. **2**, (something that has survived) sobreviviente; resto.

survive (sʌr'vaiv) *v.i.* sobrevivir; quedar vivo; salvarse. —*v.t.* sobrevivir a. —**survivor**, *n.* sobreviviente. —**survivorship**, *n.* supervivencia.

susceptible (sə'sep·tə·bel) *adj.* susceptible; impresionable. —**susceptibility**, *n.* susceptibilidad; tendencia.

suspect (sə'spekt) *v.t.* **1**, (surmise) sospechar. **2**, (distrust) recelar; dudar de. —*v.i.* sospechar. —*n. & adj.* ('sʌs·pekt) sospechoso.

suspend (sə'spend) *v.t.* suspender. —*v.i.* cesar.

suspenders (sə'spend·ərz) *n.pl.* tirantes.

suspense (sə'spens) *n.* **1**, (indecision) suspenso **2**, (uncertainty) incertidumbre; duda. **3**, (anxiety) ansiedad. **4**, (delay) suspensión; detención.

suspension (sə'spen·ʃən) *n.* suspensión. —**suspension bridge**, puente colgante; puente de suspensión. —**suspension points**, puntos suspensivos.

suspensive (sə'spen·sɪv) *adj.* suspensivo.

suspensory (sə'spen·sə·ri) *adj. & n.* suspensorio.

suspicion (sə'spɪʃ·ən) *n.* **1**, (act of suspecting) sospecha; desconfianza. **2**, (inkling; trace) traza; huella.

suspicious (sə'spɪʃ·əs) *adj.* **1**, (arousing suspicion) sospechoso. **2**, (feeling suspicion) sospechoso; suspicaz; receloso. —**suspiciousness**, *n.* suspicacia; desconfianza; recelo.

suspire (sə'spair) *v.i.* suspirar.

sustain (sə'stein) *v.t.* **1**, (maintain; support) sostener; mantener; sustentar. **2**, (encourage) apoyar; alentar. **3**, (endure; undergo) aguantar; sufrir. **4**, (defend; uphold) apoyar; defender. **5**, (confirm; prove) confirmar; probar. **6**, *mus.* (prolong, as a tone) prolongar; sostener. —**sustaining program**, *radio; TV* programa sin patrocinador.

sustenance ('sʌs·tə·nəns) *n.* **1,** (act of sustaining) mantenimiento; sostenimiento. **2,** (nourishment; means of living) sustento; alimentos; víveres; subsistencia.

sutler ('sʌt·lər) *n.* vivandero.

suture ('su·tʃər) *n.* sutura. —*v.t.* coser; unir con suturas.

suzerain ('su·zə·rɪn) *adj. & n.* soberano. —**suzerainty,** *n.* soberanía.

svelte (svɛlt) *adj.* esbelto.

swab (swɑːb) *n.* **1,** (mop; rag) estropajo; bayeta; *naut.* lampazo. **2,** (absorbent cotton, sponge, etc.) algodoncillo; esponja; paño. **3,** *slang* (lout) patán; zafio. —*v.t.* [**swabbed, swabbing**] fregar; limpiar; *naut.* lampacear.

swaddle ('swad·əl) *v.t.* fajar; empañar; envolver con fajas. —**swaddling** (-lɪŋ) **cloth,** faja; pañal. —**swaddling clothes,** pañales; envoltura.

swag (swæg) *n., slang* botín; robo; despojo; hurto.

swagger ('swæg·ər) *v.i.* **1,** (strut) contonearse; pavonearse. **2,** (brag) fanfarronear. —*n.* **1,** (strut) contoneo; pavoneo. **2,** (boast) fanfarronada.

swain (swein) *n.* **1,** (lover) galán; enamorado; amante. **2,** (country boy) zagal.

swallow ('swal·o) *v.t. & i.* tragar; deglutir. —*n.* **1,** (act of swallowing) deglución. **2,** (something swallowed) trago. **3,** *ornith.* golondrina.

swallowtail ('swal·o,teil) *n.* frac. *También,* **swallow-tailed coat.**

swam (swæm) *v., pret. de* **swim.**

swamp (swamp) *n.* pantano; ciénaga. —*v.t.* **1,** (flood; sink) inundar; hundir; sumergir. **2,** (overwhelm) abrumar. —*v.i.* inundarse; hundirse.

swampland ('swamp,lænd) *n.* pantanal; cenagal.

swampy ('swam·pi) *adj.* pantanoso; cenagoso.

swan (swɑːn) *n.* cisne. —**swan song,** canto del cisne.

swank (swæŋk) *n., slang* pretensión; ostentación. —*adj., slang* pretencioso; ostentoso. —*v.i. slang* contonearse; pavonearse. —**swanky,** *adj., slang* elegante; vistoso.

swan's-down *n.* plumón de cisne.

swap (swap) *v.t. & i.* [**swapped, swapping**] *colloq.* cambalachear;

cambiar; intercambiar; trocar. —*n.* cambalache; trueque; cambio.

sward (sword) *n.* césped.

swarm (sworm) *n.* enjambre. —*v.i.* **1,** (form or move in a swarm) enjambrar; hormiguear. **2,** (climb) trepar.

swarthy ('swor·ði) *adj.* atezado; moreno; trigueño; prieto.

swash (swaʃ) *v.t. & i.* = **splash.**

swashbuckler ('swaʃ·bʌk·lər) *n.* espadachín; fanfarrón; valentón. —**swashbuckling,** *adj.* fanfarrón; valentón. —*n.* fanfarronada; valentonada.

swastika ('swas·tɪ·kə) *n.* svástica; cruz gamada.

swat (swat) *v.t.* [**swatted, swatting**] *colloq.* golpear. —*n., colloq.* golpe recio.

swatch (swatʃ) *n.* muestra de tela; tira.

swath (swaθ) *n.* **1,** (row of mown grass or grain) guadañada. **2,** (row; line) ringlera. **3,** (strip) tira; faja. —**cut a wide swath,** hacer gran papel.

swathe (sweið) *v.t.* envolver; fajar; vendar. —*n.* envoltura; faja; venda.

sway (swei) *v.i.* **1,** (bend) ladearse; inclinarse. **2,** (swing) oscilar; vacilar. **3,** (totter) bambolear; tambalear. **4,** (turn away) desviarse; apartarse. **5,** (have control or influence) tener dominio; tener influencia. —*v.t.* **1,** (cause to bend) ladear. **2,** (cause to swing) hacer oscilar. **3,** (influence; persuade) influir en; persuadir; convencer. **4,** (move; affect) conmover; impresionar. **5,** (divert) desviar; detener. **6,** (rule; control) gobernar; dominar. **7,** (wield; brandish) blandir; sacudir. —*n.* **1,** (swaying movement) oscilación; bamboleo; tambaleo. **2,** (inclination) inclinación; ladeo. **3,** (impetus; force) fuerza; influencia. **4,** (rule) mando; dominio; imperio. —**hold sway (over),** gobernar; dominar; regir.

swear (swerr) *v.t. & i.* [*pret.* **swore;** *p.p.* **sworn**] (vow) jurar. —*v.i.* (curse) maldecir; jurar; blasfemar; echar maldiciones. —*v.t.* (administer an oath to) juramentar. —**swear an oath,** juramentarse; prestar juramento; jurar. —**swear by,** jurar por; poner entera confianza en. —**swear in,** juramentar; hacer prestar juramento.

—**swear off,** renunciar; dejar.
—**swear out,** obtener por juramento.

swearing ('swɛr·ɪŋ) *n.* **1,** (taking an oath) jura; juramento. **2,** (cursing) maldición; el vicio de jurar.

swearword ('swɛr,wʌrd) *n.* blasfemia; maldición; palabra fea.

sweat (swɛt) *v.t. & i.* [*pret. & p.p.* **sweat** o **sweated**] (perspire) sudar —*v.t.* **1,** (cause to sweat) hacer sudar. **2,** (solder) soldar. —*n.* **1,** (perspiration; moisture) sudor. **2,** (anxiety) ansia; excitación. **3,** (hard work) fatiga; esfuerzo. —**in a sweat,** nadando en sudor. —**sweat blood,** esmerarse; echar la sangre. —**sweat out, 1,** (cure by sweating) curar por medio del sudor. **2,** *slang* (await; expect) aguardar; esperar.

sweater ('swɛt·ər) *n.* suéter; malla.

sweatshirt ('swɛt,ʃʌrt) *n.* malla; jersey.

sweatshop ('swɛt,ʃɑp) *n.* taller opresor; taller donde se trabaja mucho por poca paga.

sweaty ('swɛt·i) *adj.* sudoroso; sudoso.

Swedish ('swi·dɪʃ) *adj. & n.* sueco. —**Swede** (swi:d) *n.* sueco.

sweep (swip) *v.t.* [*pret. & p.p.* **swept**] **1,** (clean, as with a broom) barrer. **2,** (move or carry along) arrastrar; llevarse; arrebatar. **3,** (touch; brush lightly) rozar. **4,** (pass swiftly over) recorrer; pasar por. **5,** *colloq.* (win decisively) ganar todo; ganar enteramente. —*v.i.* **1,** (clean) barrer. **2,** (move swiftly) correr; lanzarse; precipitarse. **3,** (reach; extend) extenderse. **4,** (move proudly) marchar pomposamente. —*n.* **1,** (cleaning) barredura; barrido. **2,** (swift movement) arrastre; arrebato; carrera. **3,** (scope; extent) alcance; extensión. **4,** (sweeper) barrendero [*fem.* barrendera] **5,** (complete victory) triunfo total. —**sweeper,** *n.* barrendero [*fem.* barrendera].

sweeping ('swi·pɪŋ) *adj.* comprensivo; amplio. —*n.* barredura; barrido. —**sweepings,** *n.pl.* barreduras.

sweepstakes ('swip·steiks) *n. sing. & pl.* **1,** (contest) lotería; rifa de carreras de caballos. **2,** (prize) gran premio.

sweet (swit) *adj.* **1,** (pleasant-tasting) dulce. **2,** (pleasing) agradable; encantador. **3,** (amiable) amable; gentil. **4,** (gentle) suave. **5,** (dear; precious) querido; amado. **6,** (fresh) fresco. **7,** (fragrant) oloroso; de buen olor. —*n.* **1,** (sweetness) dulzura. **2,** (something sweet) dulce; confite. **3,** (beloved person) querido [*fem.* querida]. —*adv.* dulcemente; suavemente. —**be sweet on,** *colloq.* estar enamorado de.

sweet basil albahaca.

sweetbread ('swit,brɛd) *n.* molleja.

sweetbrier ('swit,brai·ər) *también,* **sweetbriar** *n.* eglantina.

sweet corn maíz tierno.

sweeten ('swi·tən) *v.t.* **1,** (add sugar to) endulzar; dulcificar; azucarar. **2,** (make pleasant) suavizar. —**sweetener,** *n.* dulcificante. —**sweetening,** *n.* endulzadura. —*adj.* dulcificante.

sweetheart ('swit,hart) *n.* novio; enamorado; querido; [*fem.* novia; enamorada; querida].

sweetie ('swit·i) *n.,* *colloq.* = **sweetheart.**

sweetmeat *n.* dulce; confite; golosina.

sweetness ('swit·nəs) *n.* dulzura.

sweet pea guisante de olor.

sweet potato batata; buniato.

sweet-talk *v.t.* lisonjear; engatusar. —*n.* lisonja(s); engatusamiento.

sweet tooth *colloq.* golosina. —**have a sweet tooth,** ser goloso; ser dulcero.

sweet-toothed ('swit,tuðd) *adj.* goloso; dulcero.

swell (swɛl) *v.t.* [*pret.* **swelled;** *p.p.* **swelled** o **swollen**] **1,** (expand; inflate) hinchar; inflar. **2,** (increase) aumentar. **3,** (make vain; flatter) engreír. —*v.i.* **1,** (expand) hincharse; inflarse. **2,** (increase) aumentarse; crecer. **3,** (rise in waves, as the sea) embravecerse. —*n.* **1,** (bulge) hinchazón. **2,** (large wave) oleada; oleaje. **3,** *mus.* crescendo. **4,** *colloq.* (stylish person) persona elegante; petimetre. —*adj.* **1,** *colloq.* (stylish) elegante. **2,** *slang* (excellent) excelente; magnífico. —**swelled head,** *colloq.* entono; engreimiento.

swelling ('swɛl·ɪŋ) *n.* **1,** (bulge) hinchazón; protuberancia. **2,** (increase) aumento.

swelter ('swɛl·tər) *v.t.* abrumar de calor; sofocar. —*v.i.* sofocarse. —*n.* calor excesivo.

swept (swɛpt) *v.,* *pret. & p.p. de* **sweep.**

swerve (swɅrv) v.t. desviar; apartar. —v.i. desviarse; apartarse. —n. desviación; desvío.

swift (swɪft) adj. 1, (rapid) veloz; rápido; vivo. 2, (sudden) repentino. 3, (prompt) pronto; presto. —adv. velozmente; rápidamente. —n., ornith. vencejo. —swiftness, n. velocidad; rapidez.

swig (swɪg) v.t. & i. [swigged, swigging] colloq. beber a grandes tragos. —n., colloq. trago.

swill (swɪl) n. 1, (garbage) basura; desperdicios. 2, (food for animals) bazofia. 3, (swig) trago. —v.t. 1, (wash) lavar; enjuagar. 2, (drink greedily) beber a grandes tragos. 3, (make drunk) emborrachar. —v.i. emborracharse.

swim (swɪm) v.i. [swam, swum, swimming] 1, (move through water) nadar. 2, (float) flotar. 3, (be dizzy) tener vértigo; estar desvanecido; írsele la cabeza. —v.t. pasar o recorrer nadando. —n. 1, (act of swimming) natación; Amer. nadada. 2, (dizziness) vahido; desmayo. —in the swim, andando con la corriente.

swim bladder nadadera.

swimmer ('swɪm·ər) n. nadador [fem. -dora].

swimming ('swɪm·ɪŋ) n. natación. —adj. 1, (that swims) nadador. 2, (of or for swimming) natatorio. 3, (dizzy) vertiginoso. 4, (teeming) lleno (de). —swimmingly, adv. sin dificultad; felizmente; lisamente.

swimming hole nadadero.

swimming pool piscina.

swim suit traje de baño. También, swimming suit.

swindle ('swɪn·dəl) v.t. & i. defraudar; estafar; embaucar. —n. fraude; estafa; petardo. —swindler (-dlər) n. estafador [fem. -dora]; embaucador [fem. -dora]; chupón [fem. -pona].

swine (swain) n.sing. & pl. cerdo; puerco; cochino; marrano.

swineherd ('swain,hɅrd) n. porquerizo.

swing (swɪŋ) v.i. [pret. & p.p. swung] 1, (move back and forth) oscilar; vacilar. 2, (ride and swing) columpiarse. 3, (sway) balancearse. 4, (hang) estar colgado. 5, (change direction) volverse; dar una vuelta; virar. 6, (revolve; rotate) volverse; dar vueltas; girar. —v.t. 1, (move back and forth) hacer oscilar;

mover; menear. 2, (brandish) blandir; sacudir. 3, (hang) colgar. 4, (cause to revolve) hacer girar; dar vueltas a. 5, (manage; bring about) manejar; llevar a cabo; efectuar. —n. 1, (movement back and forth) oscilación; balanceo; vaivén. 2, (act or manner of making a swinging stroke) golpe; manera de golpear. 3, (length of swing) alcance. 4, (turn) vuelta. 5, (freedom of action) libertad de acción; libre carrera. 6, (rhythm) ritmo; compás. 7, (playground device) columpio. 8, mus. variedad de jazz; swing. —in full swing, en plena operación; en plena marcha.

swingletree ('swɪŋ·gəl,triː) n. balancín.

swing shift colloq. turno de la tarde.

swinish ('swai·nɪʃ) adj. 1, (porcine) porcino. 2, (despicable) cochino; sucio; puerco.

swipe (swaip) v.t. & i. 1, colloq. (strike) golpear. 2, slang (steal) hurtar; sisar; ratear. —n., colloq. golpe fuerte.

swirl (swɅrl) v.i. arremolinarse; girar; dar vueltas. —v.t. hacer girar. —n. remolino; torbellino.

swish (swɪʃ) v.i. susurrar; silbar; sisear. —v.t. agitar; hacer susurrar. —n. susurro; silbido; siseo.

Swiss (swɪs) adj. & n. suizo.

switch (swɪtʃ) n. 1, (flexible rod) varilla; fusta. 2, elect. conmutador; interruptor. 3, (tress cf detached hair) moño. 4, R.R. agujas; Amer. cambiavía. 5, (change; shift) cambio; desviación. —v.t. 1, (whip) varear; fustigar. 2, (change; shift) cambiar; desviar. 3, elect. conmutar. 4, R.R. desviar. —v.i. cambiar; desviarse. —switch off, apagar; cortar; desconectar. —switch on, poner; encender; Amer. prender.

switchblade ('swɪtʃ,bleid) n. navaja de muelle.

switchboard ('swɪtʃ,bord) n. tablero de conmutadores; cuadro de distribución.

switchman ('swɪtʃ·mən) n. [pl. -men] guardagujas; Amer. cambiavía; cambiador.

swivel ('swɪv·əl) n. eslabón giratorio. —v.i. girar sobre un eje. —v.t. 1, (cause to turn) hacer girar sobre un eje. 2, (fasten with a swivel) enganchar con eslabón giratorio.

swivel chair silla giratoria.

swizzle stick palillo (*para menear bebidas*).

swollen ('swo·lən) *v.*, *p.p. de* swell. —*adj.* 1, (inflated) hinchado. 2, (increased) aumentado; crecido.

swoon (swuːn) *v.i.* desmayarse; desvanecerse. —*n.* desmayo; desvanecimiento.

swoop (swup) *v.t.* agarrar; arrebatar. —*v.i.* precipitarse; caer a plomo. —*n.* bajada repentina; calada.

sword (sord) *n.* espada. —**sword cane,** estoque.

swordfish ('sord,fɪʃ) *n.* pez espada.

swordplay ('sord,plei) *n.* esgrima.

swordsman ('sordz·mən) *n.* [*pl.* -men] espadachín; espada; esgrimidor. —**swordsmanship,** *n.* esgrima.

swore (swor) *v.*, *pret. de* swear.

sworn (sworn) *v.*, *p.p. de* swear.

swum (swʌm) *v.*, *p.p. de* swim.

swung (swʌŋ) *v.*, *pret. & p.p. de* swing.

Sybarite ('sɪb·ə·rait) *n.* sibarita. —**Sybaritic** (-'rɪt·ɪk) *adj.* sibarita; sibarítico.

sycamore ('sɪk·ə,mor) *n.* (fig-like Near Eastern tree) sicómoro. 2, (European maple) falso plátano; arce blanco. 3, (Amer. plane tree) plátano.

sycophant ('saik·ə·fənt) *n.* adulador [*fem.* -dora]; sicofante.

syllabic (sɪ'læb·ɪk) *adj.* silábico.

syllabicate (sɪ'læb·ɪ·keit) *v.t.* silabear. —**syllabication,** *n.* silabeo.

syllabify (sɪ'læb·ə,fai) *v.t.* silabear. —**syllabification** (-fɪ'kei·ʃən) *n.* silabeo.

syllable ('sɪl·ə·bəl) *n.* sílaba.

syllabus ('sɪl·ə·bəs) *n.* [*pl.* -bi (-bai)] sílabo; compendio.

syllogism ('sɪl·ə·dʒɪz·əm) *n.* silogismo.

sylph (sɪlf) *n.* silfo [*fem.* sílfide].

sylvan ('sɪl·vən) *adj.* silvestre; selvático.

symbiosis (sɪm·bi'o·sɪs) *n.* simbiosis. —**symbiotic** (-bi'at·ɪk) *adj.* simbiótica.

symbol ('sɪm·bəl) *n.* símbolo. —**symbolic** (sɪm'bal·ɪk) *adj.* simbólico.

symbolism ('sɪm·bə·lɪz·əm) *n.* simbolismo.

symbolize ('sɪm·bə·laiz) *v.t.* simbolizar.

symmetry ('sɪm·ə·tri) *n.* simetría.

symmetrical (sɪ'mɛt·rɪ·kəl) *adj.* simétrico.

sympathetic (,sɪm·pə'θɛt·ɪk) *adj.* simpático; compasivo.

sympathize ('sɪm·pə,θaiz) *v.i.* simpatizar; compadecer(se); condolerse. —**sympathize with,** compadecer(se) de; condolerse de.

sympathy ('sɪm·pə·θi) *n.* 1, (affinity) simpatía. 2, (compassion) compasión; conmiseración; condolencia.

symphony ('sɪm·fə·ni) *n.* sinfonía. —**symphonic** (sɪm'fan·ɪk) *adj.* sinfónico.

symposium (sɪm'po·zi·əm) *n.* 1, (meeting for discussion) coloquio. 2, (collection of writings) colección de artículos, comentarios, etc., sobre un mismo tema.

symptom ('sɪmp·təm) *n.* síntoma.

symptomatic (,sɪmp·tə'mæt·ɪk) *adj.* sintomático.

synagogue ('sɪn·ə·gag) *n.* sinagoga.

synapse ('sɪn·æps) *n.* sinapsis.

synchronize ('sɪŋ·krə,naiz) *v.t. & i.* sincronizar. —**synchronization** (-ni'zei·ʃən) *n.* sincronización. —**synchronous,** *adj.* sincrónico.

syncopate ('sɪŋ·kə,peit) *v.t.* sincopar. —**syncopation,** *n.* síncopa.

syncope ('sɪŋ·kə·pi) *n.* 1, *med.* síncope. 2, *gram.* síncopa; síncope.

syndicate ('sɪn·dɪ,keit) *v.t.* sindicar. —*v.i.* sindicarse. —*n.* (-kət) sindicato. —**syndication,** *n.* sindicación.

syndrome ('sɪn,droːm) *n.* síndrome.

synergism ('sɪn·ər·dʒɪz·əm) *n.* sinergia. *Also,* **synergy** ('sɪn·ər·dʒi).

synod ('sɪn·əd) *n.* sínodo. —**synodal,** *adj.* sínodal.

synonym ('sɪn·ə·nim) *n.* sinónimo.

synonymous (sɪ'nan·ə·məs) *adj.* sinónimo.

synopsis (sɪ'nap·sɪs) *n.* [*pl.* -ses (-siz)] sinopsis. —**synoptic** (-tɪk) *adj.* sinóptico.

syntax ('sɪn·tæks) *n.* sintaxis. —**syntactical** (sɪn'tæk·tɪ·kəl) *adj.* sintáctico.

synthesis ('sɪn·θə·sɪs) *n.* [*pl.* -ses (-siz)] síntesis.

synthesize ('sɪn·θə,saiz) *v.t.* sintetizar. —**synthesizer** (-,sai·zər) *n.* sintetizador.

synthetic (sɪn'θɛt·ɪk) *adj.* sintético.

syphilis ('sɪf·ə·lɪs) *n.* sífilis.
—**syphilitic** (-'lɪt·ɪk) *n.* & *adj.*
sifilítico.
syphon ('sai·fən) *n.* & *v.* = **siphon.**
syringe (sə'rɪndʒ) *n.* jeringa. —*v.t.*
jeringar.
syrup ('sɪr·əp) *n.* jarabe; almíbar.
system ('sɪs·təm) *n.* sistema.

systematic (ˌsɪs·tə'mæt·ɪk) *adj.*
sistemático.
systematize ('sɪs·tə·mə,taiz) *v.t.*
sistematizar.
systemic (sɪs'tɛm·ɪc) *adj., anat;
physiol.* del sistema.
systole ('sɪs·tə,li) *n.* sístole.
—**systolic** (sɪs'tal·ɪk) *adj.* sistólico.

T

T, t (ti) vigésima letra del alfabeto
inglés. —**to a T,** exactamente.
tab (tæb) *n.* **1,** (flap, strap)
lengüeta; correa. **2,** (tag; label)
etiqueta; rótulo. **3,** *colloq.* (account)
cuenta. —**keep tab** (o **tabs**) **on,**
colloq. velar; vigilar.
tabasco (tə'bæs·ko) *n.* tabasco.
tabby ('tæb·i) *n.* **1,** (striped cat)
gato atigrado. **2,** (female cat) gata.
3, (old maid) solterona. **4,** (female
gossip) chismosa. **5,** (fabric) seda
ondeada; muaré.
tabernacle ('tæb·ər·næk·əl) *n.* **1,**
(dwelling; temple) tabernáculo. **2,**
eccles. sagrario.
table ('tei·bəl) *n.* **1,** (furniture)
mesa **2,** (plateau) meseta. **3,** (food;
meal) mesa. **4,** (list) tabla. **5,** (index) índice. —*v.t.* **1,** (place on a table) colocar en la mesa. **2,** (postpone) entablar; dejar sobre la mesa.
3, (list) catalogar. —**table tennis,**
ping-pong. —**turn (the) tables,**
volver las tornas.
tableau ('tæb·lo) *n.* **1,** (picture)
cuadro. **2,** (series of pictures) retablo. **3,** (dramatic scene) representación teatral; espectáculo.
tablecloth ('tei·bəl,klɔθ) *n.* mantel.
table d'hôte ('tab·əl'dot) comida a
precio fijo; plato del día.
tableland ('tei·bəl,lænd) *n.* meseta.
tablespoon ('tei·bəl,spun) *n.* cuchara. —**tablespoonful** (-,fʊl) [*pl.*
-fuls] *n.* cucharada.
tablet ('tæb·lɪt) *n.* **1,** (plaque)
lápida; tarja; placa; losa **2,** (pill)
tableta; pastilla; comprimido;
píldora. **3,** (soap) pastilla. **4,** (writing pad) bloc de papel; cuader-
nillo.
tableware ('tei·bəl·wer) *n.*
servicio; cubierto.
tabloid ('tæb·lɔid) *n.* gaceta.

pequeño periódico muy ilustrado.
—*adj.* condensado.
taboo *also,* **tabu** (tæ'buː) *n.*
prohibición; exclusión; tabú. —*adj.*
prohibido; tabú. —*v.t.* prohibir.
tabor ('tei·bər) *n.* tamborín.
taboret (ˌtæb·ə'rɛt) *n.* **1,** (stool)
banquillo; taburete. **2,** (drum)
tamborín. **3,** (embroidery frame)
bastidor. **4,** (ornamental stand)
mesita.
tabular ('tæb·jə·lər) *adj.* tabular;
tabulado.
tabulate ('tæb·jə,leit) *v.t.* tabular;
catalogar. —**tabulation,** *n.* tabulación. —**tabulator,** *n.* tabulador.
tachometer (tə'kam·ə·tər) *n.*
tacómetro.
tacit ('tæs·ɪt) *adj.* tácito.
taciturn ('tæs·ə·tʌrn) *adj.* taciturno; silencioso. —**taciturnity**
(-tʌrn·ə·ti) *n.* taciturnidad.
tack (tæk) *n.* **1,** (nail) tachuela;
puntilla; clavillo. **2,** *sewing* hilván;
embaste. **3,** *naut.* bordada; virada.
4, (course of action) línea de conducta. —*v.t.* **1,** (nail) clavar. **2,** *sewing* hilvanar; embastar; puntear.
—*v.i., naut.* cambiar de rumbo;
bordear; dar bordadas.
tacking ('tæk·ɪŋ) *n.* **1,** *sewing*
hilván; embaste. **2,** *naut.* bordeo;
bordada.
tackle ('tæk·əl) *n.* **1,** (apparatus)
aparejo. **2,** (gear) avíos; equipo;
enseres. **3,** *football* **a.** (act)
agarrada; atajada. **b.** (player)
atajador. —*v.t.* **1,** (seize) asir;
agarrar; *football* atajar. **2,** (undertake) acometer; abordar.
tacky ('tæk·i) *adj.* **1,** (sticky)
pegajoso; viscoso. **2,** *colloq.*
(dowdy) desaliñado; descuidado.
taco ('ta·ko) *n.* a Mexican dish consisting of a tortilla filled with meat,
cheese, etc.; taco.
tact (tækt) *n.* tacto; tino; diploma-

cia; discreción. —**tactful,** *adj.* diplomático; discreto. —**tactless,** *adj.* indiscreto.

tactic ('tæk·tɪk) *n.* táctica; táctico. —**tactical,** *adj.* táctico. —**tactician** (tæk'tɪʃ·ən) *n.* táctico.

tactics ('tæk·tɪks) *n.* táctica.

tactile ('tæk·tɪl) *adj.* **1,** (of or pert. to touch) táctil. **2,** (tangible) tangible; palpable.

tadpole ('tæd·pol) *n.* renacuajo.

taffeta ('tæf·ɪ·tə) *n.* tafetán.

taffy ('tæf·i) *n.* melcocha; caramelo.

tag (tæg) *n.* **1,** (label) etiqueta; rótulo. **2,** (small card; slip) cartela. **3,** (appendage) cola; cosa atada al extremo. **4,** (rag; tatter) andrajo; pingajo. **5,** (saying; refrain) refrán; mote; frase hecha. **6,** (game) juego de niños. —*v.t.* [**tagged, tagging**] **1,** (label) poner etiqueta a. **2,** (mark; identify) marcar; señalar. **3,** (tap, as in the game of tag) tocar. **4,** *colloq.* (follow closely) seguir de cerca; pisar los talones a. —**tag after; tag along,** *colloq.* seguir de cerca; seguir pisando los talones. —**tag sale,** venta de artículos usados.

Tagalog (ta'ga·lag; 'tæg·ə‚lag) *adj.* & *n.* tagalo.

tail (teil) *n.* **1,** (appendage) cola; rabo. **2,** (end) extremo; extremidad; cola. **3,** (of a comet) cola; rastro. **4,** *pl.* (reverse side of a coin) reverso de una moneda; cruz. **5,** *pl., colloq.* = **tailcoat.** —*v.t.* & *i.* seguir de cerca; perseguir; pisar los talones (a). —**tail end,** extremo; cola.

tailcoat ('teil‚kot) *n.* frac.

tailgate ('teil‚geit) *n.* compuerta de cola. *También,* **tailboard** (-‚bord) —*v.t.* & *i.* seguir (a otro vehículo) muy cerca, de modo peligroso.

taillight ('teil‚lait) *n.* farol trasero; farol de cola.

tailor ('tei·lər) *n.* sastre. —*v.t.* **1,** (shape to fit the body) entallar; hacer (un traje) a medida. **2,** (outfit with clothing) proveer de ropa; vestir. —*v.i.* ser sastre.

tailoring ('tei·lər·ɪŋ) *n.* sastrería.

tailor-made *adj.* hecho a medida.

tailpipe ('teil‚paip) *n.* tubo de escape.

tailspin ('teil‚spɪn) *n., aero.* caída en barrena. *También,* **tail spin.**

tailwind ('teil‚wɪnd) *n., aero.* ‚ to de cola. *También,* **tail wind.**

‚ (teint) *n.* **1,** (stain; blemish) ‚ mancha; mácula. **2,** (contam-

ination) infección; corrupción. —*v.t.* **1,** (stain) manchar; ensuciar. **2,** (corrupt) corromper; inficionar. —*v.i.* inficionarse; corromperse; podrirse.

take (teik) *v.t.* [*pret.* **took;** *p.p.* **taken**] **1,** (get; get possession of) tomar. **2,** (seize) coger; asir. **3,** (carry) llevar. **4,** (lead; escort) llevar; conducir. **5,** (accept; receive) aceptar; recibir. **6,** (remove) quitar; sacar. **7,** (assume) tomar; asumir; suponer. **8,** (capture, in certain games) comer. **9,** *photog.* tomar; sacar. **10,** (endure) soportar; tolerar; aguantar. **11,** (understand; construe) percibir; conceptuar. **12,** (undergo) sufrir; someterse a. **13,** (keep) quedarse con. **14,** (subtract) sustraer. **15,** (win) ganar. **16,** (drink; ingest) tomar. **17,** *slang* (cheat; dupe) engañar; embaucar. **18,** (need; require) necesitar. **19,** (note; write down) apuntar. **20,** (do; perform, as a walk, ride, leap, etc.) dar (un paseo, un brinco, etc.). —*v.i.* **1,** (turn out well; have the desired effect) salir bien; tener buen éxito; resultar bien. **2,** (begin growing, as a plant) arraigarse. **3,** (engage; be hooked or joined) agarrarse; engancharse; engranar. **4,** (ignite) prender; encender. **5,** (go; proceed) encaminarse; dirigirse. —*n.* **1,** (act of taking; thing taken) toma. **2,** *slang* (receipts) taquilla; entrada. —**take after, 1,** (resemble) parecerse a. **2,** (pursue) perseguir. —**take apart,** desmontar; desmantelar; despedazar. —**take away,** quitar; sacar; llevarse. —**take back, 1,** (return) devolver. **2,** (regain) recibir devuelto; recobrar. **3,** (retract) retractar; desdecirse de. —**take down, 1,** (remove; lower) bajar; descolgar. **2,** (take apart) desmontar; desmantelar. **3,** (note) apuntar. **4,** (humiliate) humillar; rebajar. —**take ill o be taken ill,** *colloq.* enfermarse; caer enfermo. —**take in, 1,** (admit; receive) admitir; recibir; acoger. **2,** (make smaller) encoger; estrechar. **3,** (include; comprise) abarcar; comprender; englobar. **4,** (comprehend) entender; comprender. **5,** (cheat; trick) estafar; embaucar; engañar. **6,** (visit; tour) visitar. —**take it out on,** *colloq.* desahogarse en o contra. —**take off, 1,** (remove) quitar. **2,** (deduct) descontar; sustraer. **3,** (depart) irse;

marcharse; salir. **4,** *aero.* despegar. **5,** *colloq.* (mimic) imitar; remedar; parodiar. —**take on, 1,** (acquire) tomar. **2,** (employ) tomar; contratar. **3,** (undertake) cargar con; tomar sobre sí. **4,** (begin) empezar. **5,** (assume; affect) afectar. **6,** (challenge) desafiar; enfrentar. **7,** *colloq.* (be excited) excitarse; conmoverse. —**take out,** sacar. —**take over, 1,** (take possession of) apoderarse de; tomar posesión de. **2,** (take charge of) cargar con; hacerse cargo de. —**take sick** o **be taken sick,** *colloq.* enfermarse; caer enfermo. —**take to, 1,** (form the habit of) ponerse a; dedicarse a. **2,** (go to or toward) dirigirse a; marcharse hacia. **3,** (become fond of) aficionarse a; tomar cariño a. —**take up, 1,** (raise) levantar. **2,** (begin) empezar. **3,** (assume) cargar con. **4,** (resume) reasumir; reanudar. **5,** (occupy) ocupar. **6,** (fill) llenar. **7,** (shrink) encoger; estrechar. **8,** (remove the slack from) estirar. **9,** (absorb) absorber. **10,** (take possession of) tomar posesión de. **11,** (become interested in) aficionarse a; dedicarse a; aplicarse a. **12,** (seek advice about) consultar. **13,** (study) estudiar. —**take upon** (o **on**) **oneself,** cargar con; tomar sobre sí. —**take up with,** asociarse con; relacionarse con.

taken ('tei·kən) *v., p.p. de* **take.** —**taken aback,** confundido; pasmado. —**be taken aback,** quedarse mudo; asombrarse.

take-off *n.* **1,** *aero.* salida; despegue. **2,** (leap) salto. **3,** *colloq.* (imitation) imitación; caricatura; parodia.

taking ('tei·kɪŋ) *adj.* **1,** (attractive) atractivo; encantador. **2,** *colloq.* (contagious) contagioso. *n.* **1,** (act of taking; something taken) toma. **2,** *pl.* (receipts) ingresos; taquilla.

talc (tælk) *n.* talco.

talcum ('tæl·kəm) *n.* talco; polvos de talco.

tale (teil) *n.* **1,** (narrative) cuento. **2,** (falsehood) mentira; ficción. **3,** (gossip) chisme; rumor. **4,** (tally) cuenta.

talebearer ('teil,bɛr·ər) *n.* cuentón [*fem.* -tona]; soplón [*fem.* -plona] chismoso.

talent ('tæl·ənt) *n.* **1,** (skill) talento; ingenio; habilidad; capacidad. **2,** (old coin; measure of weight) talento. —**talented,** *adj.* talentoso.

talesman (teilz·mən) *n.* [*pl.* -**men**] jurado suplente.

talion ('tæl·i·ən) *n.* talión.

talisman ('tæl·ɪs·mən) *n.* talismán.

talk (tɔk) *v.t. & i.* (speak) hablar. —*v.i.* **1,** (chat) charlar; platicar. **2,** (converse) conversar. **3,** (gossip) chismear. —*v.t.* **1,** (speak about) hablar de. **2,** (convince) convencer hablando. —*n.* **1,** (conversation) conversación. **2,** (chat) charla; plática. **3,** (discourse) discurso; conferencia. **4,** (gossip) chisme; rumor. **5,** (language) habla. —**big talk,** *slang* fanfarronada; jactancia. —**make talk, 1,** (chat) charlar. **2,** (cause gossip) dar que hablar. —**small talk,** charla. —**talk away,** pasar (el tiempo) hablando; hablar incesantemente. —**talk back,** responder atrevidamente. —**talk big,** *slang* jactarse; fanfarronear. —**talk down,** hacer callar; tapar la boca a. —**talk down to,** hablarle a uno con menosprecio o condescendencia. —**talk into,** convencer; persuadir. —**talk one's head** (o **arm**) **off,** *slang* hablar hasta el cansancio. —**talk out of,** disuadirle a uno (de una cosa). —**talk over,** discutir; consultar. —**talk show,** *colloq.* programa de discusión. —**talk up, 1,** (promote) fomentar; promover. **2,** (speak loudly) hablar alto.

talkative ('tɔk·e·tɪv) *n.* hablador; locuaz; parlero. —**talkativeness,** *n.* locuacidad.

talker ('tɔk·ər) *n.* hablador [*fem.* -dora].

talkie ('tɔ·ki) *n., colloq.* = **talking picture.**

talking picture película hablada.

talking-to *n., colloq.* reprensión; reprimenda.

tall (tɔl) *adj.* **1,** (high in stature) alto; elevado. **2,** *colloq.* (unbelievable) increíble; exagerado. —**tallness,** *n* altura; estatura.

tallow ('tæl·ó) *n.* sebo.

tally ('tæl·i) *n.* **1,** (count) cuenta; enumeración. **2,** (label) etiqueta; rótulo. **3,** (score) tanteo. **4,** (counterpart) contraparte. **5,** (agreement) correspondencia; conformidad. —*v.t.* **1,** (count) contar; enumerar. **2,** (record) registrar; notar. **3,** (label) marcar. **4,** (make agree) ajustar; acomodar. —*v.i.* cuadrar; concordar; corresponder.

tallyho (,tæl·i'hoɪ) *n.* coche de

cuatro caballos. —*interj.* grito del cazador.

Talmud ('tæl·mʌd) *n.* talmud. —**Talmudic** (-'mju·dɪk) *adj.* talmúdico. —**Talmudist** (-'mju·dɪst) *n.* talmudista.

talon ('tæl·ən) *n.* **1,** (claw) garra; zarpa. **2,** *cards* (stock) baceta.

talus ('tei·ləs) *n.* **1,** *anat.* hueso del tobillo; tobillo. **2,** *geol.* talud; inclinación; pendiente.

tam (tæm) *n., abr. de* **tam-o'-shanter.**

tamable ('tei·mə·bəl) *adj.* domable; domesticable.

tamale (tə'mal·i) *n.* tamal.

tamarind ('tæm·ə·rɪnd) *n.* tamarindo.

tambourine (ˌtæm·bə'riːn) *n.* pandereta; tamboril; tamborín.

tame (teim) *adj.* **1,** (domesticated) domado; domesticado. **2,** (meek) manso; sumiso; dócil. **3,** (dull) aburrido; soso; insulso. —*v.t.* amansar; domar; domesticar. —**tameness,** *n.* docilidad; mansedumbre; sumisión.

tam-o'-shanter ('tæm·ə·ʃæn·tər) *n.* boina escocesa.

tamp (tæmp) *v.t.* apisonar; apelmazar; golpear.

tamper ('tæm·pər) *v.i.* entremeterse; meterse. —*n.* pisón. —**tamper with,** enredar; falsificar; adulterar.

tampon ('tæm·pan) *n.* tapón. —*v.t.* taponar.

tan (tæn) *v.t.* [**tanned, tanning**] **1,** (cure, as leather) curtir; zurrar. **2,** (burn in the sun) tostar; quemar. **3,** *colloq.* (flog) zurrar; azotar. —*v.i.* broncearse al sol. —*n.* **1,** (curing material) corteza; tanino. **2,** (color) moreno amarillento; color de canela. **3,** (suntan) atezamiento; quemadura de sol. —*adj.* **1,** (of tan color) de color de canela. **2,** (bronzed by the sun) bronceado; tostado al sol. —**tan one's hide,** zurrar; azotar.

tanager ('tæn·ə·dʒər) *n.* tángara.

tandem ('tæn·dəm) *n.* tándem. —*adj. & adv.* en tándem.

tang (tæŋ) *n.* **1,** (taste) sabor; gustillo. **2,** (noise) tañido. **3,** *mech.* espiga. —*v.i.* tañer; sonar; retiñir. —*v.t.* tañer.

tangency ('tæn·dʒən·si) *n.* tangencia.

tangent ('tæn·dʒənt) *n.* **1,** *geom.* tangente. **2,** (deviation) cambio de dirección. —*adj.* tocante; tangente.

—**go** (o **fly**) **off at** (o **on**) **a tangent,** cambiar rumbo súbitamente; desviarse.

tangential (tæn'dʒɛn·ʃəl) *adj.* tangencial.

tangerine (ˌtæn·dʒə'riːn) *n.* **1,** (fruit) mandarina. **2,** (color) anaranjado rojizo.

tangible ('tæn·dʒə·bəl) *adj.* tangible; palpable; corpóreo. —**tangibles,** *n.pl.* bienes materiales.

tangle ('tæŋ·gəl) *v.t.* enredar; enmarañar; confundir; embrollar. —*v.i.* enredarse. —*n.* enredo; maraña; confusión; embrollo.

tango ('tæŋ·go) *n.* tango.

tank (tæŋk) *n.* **1,** (container) tanque. **2,** (armored car) carro de combate; tanque —*v.t.* depositar en un tanque. —**tank up; get tanked up,** *slang* emborracharse.

tankage ('tæŋk·ɪdʒ) *n.* **1,** (capacity) cabida de un tanque. **2,** (storage; charge for storage) almacenaje.

tankard ('tæŋk·ərd) *n.* jarro con tapa; pichel.

tank car vagón cisterna; vagón tanque.

tanker ('tæŋk·ər) *n.* **1,** (ship) buque tanque; buque cisterna; petrolero. **2,** = **tank car. 3,** = **tank truck.**

tank truck camión petrolero.

tanner ('tæn·ər) *n.* curtidor. —**tannery,** *n.* tenería; curtiduría.

tannin ('tæn·ɪn) *n.* tanino. —**tannic,** *adj.* tánico.

tantalize ('tæn·tə·laiz) *v.t.* atormentar; exasperar; provocar.

tantalum ('tæn·tə·ləm) *n.* tantalio.

tantamount ('tæn·tə,maunt) *adj.* equivalente.

tantrum ('tæn·trəm) *n.* berrinche; pataleta; rabieta.

tap (tæp) *n.* **1,** (light blow) palmadita; golpecito. **2,** (faucet) llave; grifo; caño; espita. **3,** (plug; stopper) tapón. **4,** (connection) toma. **5,** = **taproom. 6,** *surg.* saja; sajadura. —*v.t.* [**tapped, tapping**] **1,** (strike lightly) dar palmaditas o golpecitos a o en; golpear levemente. **2,** (pierce; broach) taladrar; agujerear. **3,** (draw, as liquid) sacar. **4,** *surg.* sajar. **5,** (make a connection with) hacer o poner una toma en; intervenir (un teléfono). —*v.i.* **1,** (strike lightly) dar golpecitos; golpear levemente. **2,** (knock, as at a door) llamar. —**on tap, 1,** (served from a tap) de grifo; de barril. **2,** *colloq.* (ready) disponible; a mano.

tap dance zapateado. —**tap-dance,** *v.i.* zapatear; bailar el zapateado.

tape (teip) *n.* **1,** (ribbon) cinta. **2,** (adhesive) esparadrapo. —*v.t.* **1,** (bind) encintar; atar con cinta. **2,** (measure) medir *(con una cinta métrica).* **3,** *colloq.* (record) grabar.

tape measure cinta métrica; cinta de medir.

taper ('tei·pǝr) *n.* **1,** (candle) cerilla; vela larga y delgada. **2,** (gradual decrease) diminución gradual. —*v.t. & i.* disminuir(se) gradualmente; rematar(se) en punta. —**tapered,** *adj.* rematado en punta; de forma cónica. —**taper off,** disminuir(se) gradualmente; parar gradualmente.

tape-record ('teip·rǝ,kord) *v.t.* grabar (sobre cinta). —**tape recorder,** grabadora de cinta; magnetófono. —**tape recording,** grabación (sobre cinta).

tapestry ('tæp·ɪs·tri) *n.* tapiz; tapicería; colgadura. —*v.t.* entapizar.

tapeworm ('teip·wʌrm) *n.* tenia; solitaria.

tapioca (tæp·i'o·kǝ) *n.* tapioca.

tapir ('tei·pǝr) *n.* tapir; danta.

tappet ('tæp·ɪt) *n.* leva.

taproom ('tæp,rum) *n.* bar; cantina; taberna.

taproot ('tæp,rʊt; -,rut) *n.* raíz principal.

taps (tæps) *n.pl.* toque de queda.

tar (tɑːr) *n.* **1,** (viscid product) alquitrán; brea; pez. **2,** *colloq.* (sailor) marinero. —*v.t.* alquitranar; embrear; betunar. —*adj.* de alquitrán; alquitranado. —**tar and feather,** embrear y emplumar.

tarantella (,tær·ǝn'tel·ǝ) *n.* tarantela.

tarantula (tǝ'ræn·tʃǝ·lǝ) *n.* tarántula.

tardy ('tɑr·di) *adj.* **1,** (late) tardío; demorado. **2,** (slow) tardo; moroso; lento; rezagado. —**tardiness,** *n.* tardanza; demora.

tare (teɪr) *n.* **1,** *bot.* (vetch) arveja. **2,** *Bib.* (weed) cizaña. **3,** *comm.* tara.

target ('tɑr·gɪt) *n.* **1,** (mark in aiming) blanco. **2,** (object of attack) objeto. —**target practice,** tiro al blanco.

tariff ('tær·ɪf) *n.* **1,** (duties) tarifa; arancel. **2,** (price list) lista de precios. —*adj.* arancelario.

tarn (tɑrn) *n.* lago pequeño en las montañas.

tarnish ('tɑr·nɪʃ) *v.t. & i.* deslustrar(se); deslucir(se); empañar(se); manchar(se). —*n.* deslustre; mancha.

taro ('tɑ·ro) *n.* taro.

tarpaulin (tɑr'pɔ·lɪn) *n.* tela impermeable; empegado.

tarpon ('tɑr·pan) *n.* tarpón.

tarragon ('tær·ǝ·gan) *n.* estragón.

tarry ('tɑr·i) *adj.* alquitranado; embreado; semejante a la brea o al alquitrán.

tarry ('tær·i) *v.t.* [**tarried; tarrying**] **1,** (delay) demorarse; tardar. **2,** (stay) detenerse; quedarse. **3,** (wait) esperar.

tarsus ('tɑr·sǝs) *n.* tarso. —**tarsal** (-sǝl) *adj.* del tarso.

tart (tɑrt) *adj.* **1,** (sour) acre; ácido; agrio. **2,** *fig.* (trenchant) picante; mordaz. —*n.* **1,** (pastry) tarta; pastel de fruta. **2,** (loose woman) ramera.

tartan ('tɑr·tǝn) *n.* tartán.

Tartar ('tɑr·tǝr) *adj. & n.* tártaro.

tartar ('tɑr·tǝr) *n.* **1,** *chem.* tártaro. **2,** *dent.* sarro. —**cream of tartar,** crémor tártaro. —**tartar steak,** carne picada cruda.

tartaric (tɑr'tɑr·ɪk) *adj.* tártrico; tartárico.

task (tæsk) *n.* faena; tarea; labor. —*v.t.* **1,** (assign work to) atarear; poner tarea a. **2,** (burden) cargar; sobrecargar. —**take (someone) to task,** reprender; censurar.

task force grupo, esp. militar o naval, reunido para una misión especial.

taskmaster ('tæsk,mæs·tǝr) *n.* **1,** (overseer) capataz; supervisor. **2,** (disciplinarian) ordenancista.

tassel ('tæs·ǝl) *n.* borla. —*v.t.* poner borlas a; adornar con borlas.

taste (teist) *v.t.* gustar; probar; saborear. —*v.i.* saber; tener sabor o gusto. —*n.* **1,** (sense of taste) gusto. **2,** (flavor) gusto; sabor. **3,** (mouthful) bocado; sorbo; trago. **4,** (inclination; liking) gusto; predilección; preferencia. **5,** (sample) muestra; ejemplar. **6,** (discernment) gusto; buen gusto. —**in (good o bad) taste,** de (buen o mal) gusto. —**taste of; taste like,** saber a. —**to (one's) taste,** a gusto.

taste bud papila del gusto.

tasteful ('teist·fəl) *adj.* de buen gusto; elegante.

tasteless ('teist·ləs) *adj.* **1,** (lacking flavor) insípido; soso; desabrido. **2,** (in bad taste) de mal gusto.

taster ('teis·tər) *n.* catador [*fem.* -dora].

tasty ('teis·ti) *adj.* sabroso; apetitoso; gustoso.

tat (tæt) *v.t. & i.* hacer encaje de frivolité.

Tatar ('ta·tar) *adj. & n.* tártaro.

tatter ('tæt·ər) *n.* andrajo; harapo; guiñapo. —**tattered,** *adj.* andrajoso; harapiento.

tatterdemalion (,tæt·ər·dɪ·'meil·jən) *n.* guiñapo; golfo; pelagatos.

tatting ('tæt·ɪŋ) *n.* encaje de frivolité.

tattle ('tæt·əl) *v.i.* **1,** (talk idly) charlar; chacharear. **2,** (gossip) chismear. **3,** (tell tales) soplar; delatar; divulgar secretos. —*v.t.* divulgar (secretos). —*n.* **1,** (idle talk) charla; cháchara. **2,** (gossip) chisme; chismografía.

tattler ('tæt·lər) *n.* chismoso; soplón [*fem.* -plona]; acusón [*fem.* -sona].

tattletale ('tæt·əl,teil) *n.* = **tattler.**

tattoo (tæ'tuː) *n.* **1,** (drawing on the skin) tatuaje. **2,** (drum or bugle call) retreta. **3,** (drum roll) redoble. —*v.t.* tatuar. —*v.i.* tamborilear.

taught (tɔt) *v.,* *pret. & p.p.* de **teach.**

taunt (tɔnt) *v.t.* mofarse de; burlarse de; tirar pullas a. —*n.* mofa; burla; pulla.

taupe (top) *n. & adj.* gris pardo.

taurine ('tɔ·rain) *adj.* taurino.

Taurus ('tor·əs) *n.* Tauro.

taut (tɔt) *adj.* **1,** (stretched; tense) tenso; tieso; tirante. **2,** (tidy) limpio; pulido; aseado. —**tauten,** *v.t.* tensar. —**tautness,** *n.* tensión; tirantez.

tautology (tɔ'tal·ə·dʒi) *n.* tautología. —**tautological** (,tɔ·tə·'ladʒ·ɪ·kəl) *adj.* tautológico.

tavern ('tæv·ərn) *n.* **1,** (bar) taberna; cantina. **2,** (inn) mesón; posada; fonda. —**tavern keeper,** tabernero; posadero.

taw (tɔ) *n.* canica; bola.

tawdry ('tɔ·dri) *adj.* cursi; charro; chillón. —**tawdriness,** *n.* cursilería; charrería.

tawny ('tɔ·ni) *adj. & n.* leonado; amarillento.

tax (tæks) *n.* **1,** (compulsory payment) impuesto; contribución. **2,** (burden; task) esfuerzo; trabajo; obligación. —*v.t.* **1,** (exact payment of) poner impuestos a o sobre. **2,** (burden) abrumar; cargar; exigir demasiado de. **3,** (accuse) acusar; culpar. —**taxable,** *adj.* sujeto a impuestos; tributable.

taxation (tæk'sei·ʃən) *n.* **1,** (levying of taxes) imposición de contribuciones. **2,** (taxes collectively) impuestos; contribuciones.

tax bracket tarifa; escala.

tax collection recaudación; recaudamiento. —**tax collector,** recaudador [*fem.* -dora].

tax-exempt *adj.* exento de impuestos.

taxi ('tæk·si) *n.* taxímetro; taxi. —*v.i.* **1,** (travel by taxi) ir en taxi. **2,** *aero.* taxear.

taxicab ('tæk·si,kæb) *n.* taxímetro; taxi.

taxi dancer muchacha que cobra por bailar.

taxidermy ('tæk·sə,dʌr·mi) *n.* taxidermia. —**taxidermist,** *n.* taxidermista.

taxi driver taxista; cochero; chófer.

taximeter ('tæk·si,mi·tər; tæk·'sɪ·mə·tər) *n.* taxímetro.

taxonomy (tæks'an·ə·mi) *n.* taxonomía. —**taxonomic** (,tæks·ə'nam·ɪk); **taxonomical,** *adj.* taxonómico. —**taxonomist,** *n.* taxonomista.

taxpayer ('tæks·pei·ər) *n.* contribuyente.

tax shelter inversión que sirve para reducir los impuestos sobre ingresos.

tea (tiː) *n.* té.

tea ball bolsita para preparar el té.

teach (titʃ) *v.t. & i.* [*pret. & p.p.* **taught**] enseñar. —**teachable,** *adj.* dócil; educable.

teacher ('titʃ·ər) *n.* maestro [*fem.* maestra]; profesor [*fem.* -sora]; instructor [*fem.* -tora].

teaching ('titʃ·ɪŋ) *n.* **1,** (instruction) enseñanza. **2,** (precept) doctrina; precepto.

teacup ('ti·kʌp) *n.* taza para té. —**teacupful,** *n.* taza llena; cabida de una taza.

teahouse ('ti,haus) *n.* salón de té.

teak (tik) *n.* teca.

teakettle ('ti,kɛt·əl) *n.* tetera.

teal (tiːl) *n.* trullo.

team (tiːm) n. **1,** (group) equipo; partido; grupo. **2,** (group of draft animals) tiro. **3,** (pair of horses) tronco. **4,** (pair of oxen) yunta. —v.t. **1,** (harness together) uncir; enganchar; enyugar. **2,** (haul with a team) acarrear. —v.i. [también, **team up**] unirse; asociarse; colaborar.

teammate ('tim,meit) n. compañero o compañera de equipo.

teamster ('tim·stər) n. **1,** (driver of draft animals) conductor de un tiro de caballos o bueyes; arriero. **2,** (carter) carretero. **3,** (truck driver) camionero.

teamwork ('tim·wʌrk) n. cooperación; solidaridad; coordinación de esfuerzo.

teapot ('ti·pat) n. tetera.

tear (teːr) v.t. [pret. **tore**; p.p. **torn**] rasgar; desgarrar; romper. —v.i. **1,** (rip) rasgarse; romperse; dividirse. **2,** (move swiftly) correr; precipitarse. —n. **1,** (rip) rasgón; desgarro; desgarradura. **2,** (outburst) arrebato; furia. **3,** slang (spree) borrachera; parranda. —**tear away,** arrancar. —**tear down, 1,** (demolish) derribar; arrasar; asolar. **2,** (dismantle) desmantelar. **3,** (disprove) refutar. —**tear off, 1,** (rip away) arrancar; separar con violencia. **2,** (run) correr; precipitarse. —**tear out,** arrancar; sacar. —**tear up,** romper; hacer pedazos.

tear (tɪr) n. lágrima. —v.i. echar lágrimas.

teardrop ('tɪr,drap) n. lágrima.

tearful ('tɪr·fəl) adj. lloroso; lacrimoso; lagrimoso. —**tearfulness,** n. lloriqueo; llanto.

tear gas (tɪr) gas lacrimógeno.

tearoom ('ti,rum) n. salón de té; pequeño restaurante.

tea rose rosa de té.

teary ('tɪr·i) adj. lloroso.

tease (tiːz) v.t. **1,** (annoy) embromar; molestar; importunar. **2,** (card; comb) cardar. —n. **1,** (act of annoying) fastidio; burla; broma. **2,** (one who annoys) embromador. —**teaser,** n. **1,** (joker) bromista. **2,** (coquette) coqueta. **3,** (puzzle) adivinanza; rompecabezas.

teasel también, **teazel** ('ti·zəl) n. **1,** bot. cardencha. **2,** (instrument for carding) carda. —v.t. cardar.

teaspoon ('ti·spun) n. cucharita. —**teaspoonful** (-,ful) n. cucharadita.

teat (tit) n. teta; tetilla; pezón.

tea wagon mesita con ruedas para servir.

technetium (tɛk'niʃ·i·əm) n. tecnecio.

technical ('tɛk·nɪ·kəl) adj. técnico.

technicality (,tɛk·nɪ'kæl·ə·ti) n. **1,** (technical terms or procedure) tecnicismo. **2,** (subtlety) argucia; sutileza.

technician (tɛk'nɪʃ·ən) n. técnico.

technicolor ('tɛk·nə,kʌl·ər) n. tecnicolor.

technics ('tɛk·nɪks) n. técnica.

technique (tɛk'nik) n. técnica.

technocracy (tɛk'nak·rə·si) n. tecnocracia. —**technocrat** ('tɛk·nə,kræt) n. tecnócrata. —**technocratic** (-'kræt·ɪk) adj. tecnocrático.

technology (tɛk'nal·ə·dʒi) n. tecnología. —**technological** (,tɛk·nə'ladʒ·ɪ·k·əl) adj. tecnológico. —**technologist,** n. tecnólogo.

techy también, **tetchy** ('tɛtʃ·i) adj. malhumorado; enojadizo; quisquilloso.

tectonic (tɛk'tan·ɪk) adj. tectónico. —**tectonics,** n. tectónica.

ted (tɛd) v.t. esparcir (para secar).

teddy bear ('tɛd·i) oso de juguete.

tedious ('ti·di·əs) adj. tedioso; molesto; pesado; aburrido. —**tediousness,** n. tedio; aburrimiento; pesadez.

tedium ('ti·di·əm) n. aburrimiento; tedio; pesadez.

tee (tiː) n. **1,** (T-shaped object) algo en forma de T. **2,** golf tee. —v.t. colocar en el tee. —**tee off,** impulsar la bola de golf desde el tee. —**teed off,** slang irritado; enojado. —**to a tee,** precisamente; exactamente.

teem (tiːm) v.i. abundar; rebosar. —**teeming with,** abundante en; lleno de.

teenage ('tin·eidʒ) adj. adolescencia; de 13 a 19 años de edad. —**teenager,** n. adolescente; joven de 13 a 19 años de edad.

teens (tiːnz) n.pl. **1,** (age) edad de 13 a 19 años. **2,** (numerals) números cuyos nombres terminan en -teen.

teeny ('ti·ni) adj., colloq. = **tiny.**

teepee también, **tepee** ('ti·pi) n. cabaña de pieles de los indios.

teeter ('ti·tər) v.i. balancear; columpiarse; tambalear. —n. **1,** (swaying movement) balance;

vaivén; tambaleo. **2,** (seesaw) balancín; columpio.

teeth (tiθ) *n., pl. de* **tooth.**

teethe (ti:ð) *v.i.* echar los dientes; dentar.

teething ('ti·ðıŋ) *n.* dentición. —**teething ring,** chupador; chupete.

teetotal (ti'to·təl) *adj.* **1,** *colloq.* (entire) entero; completo; total. **2,** (abstaining entirely) abstemio. —**teetotaler,** *n.* abstemio. —**teetotalism,** *n.* abstinencia total.

tegument ('tɛg·jə·mənt) *n.* tegumento.

te-hee (ti'hi:) *v.i.* reírse entre dientes. —*n.* risita; risa tonta. —*interj.* ¡ji, ji!

telecast ('tɛl·ə·kæst) *n.* emisión por televisión. —*v.t. & i.* emitir por televisión.

telegram ('tɛl·ə,græm) *n.* telegrama.

telegraph ('tɛl·ə,græf) *n.* telégrafo. —*v.t. & i.* telegrafiar. —**telegraph operator,** telegrafista.

telegrapher (tə'lɛg·rə·fər) *n.* telegrafista.

telegraphic (,tɛl·ə'græf·ık) *adj.* telegráfico.

telegraphy (tə'lɛg·rə·fi) *n.* telegrafía.

telekinesis (,tɛl·ə·kə'ni·sıs) *n.* telequinesis.

telemeter (tə'lɛm·ə·tər) *n.* telémetro. —**telemetry** (-tri) *n.* telemetría.

teleology (,ti·li'al·ə·dʒi) *n.* teleología. —**teleological** (-ə'ladʒ·ı·kəl) *adj.* teleológico.

telepathy (tə'lɛp·ə·θi) *n.* telepatía. —**telepathic** (,tɛl·ə'pæθ·ık) *adj.* telepático.

telephone ('tɛl·ə·fon) *n.* teléfono. —*v.t. & i.* telefonear. —**telephone operator,** telefonista.

telephonic (,tɛl·ə'fan·ık) *adj.* telefónico.

telephony (tə'lɛf·ə·ni) *n.* telefonía.

telephoto (,tɛl·ə'fo·to) *n.* telefoto. —*adj.* telefotográfico. —**telephotographic,** *adj.* telefotográfico. —**telephotography** (-fə'tag·rə·fi) *n.* telefotografía.

telescope ('tɛl·ə·skop) *n.* telescopio. —*v.t.* **1,** (encase) enchufar; encajar. **2,** (condense) condensar; abreviar. —*v.i.* enchufarse; encajarse.

telescopic (,tɛl·ə'skap·ık) *adj.* telescópico.

teletype ('tɛl·ə,taip) *n.* teletipo.

televiewer ('tɛl·ə,vju·ər) *n.* televidente.

televise ('tɛl·ə·vaiz) *v.t* televisar.

television ('tɛl·ə·vıʒ·ən) *n.* televisión. —*adj.* televisor. —**television set,** televisor.

tell (tɛl) *v.t.* [*pret. & p.p.* **told**] **1,** (make known; express) decir. **2,** (command) decir; mandar. **3,** (narrate) decir; contar; relatar. **4,** (count) contar; enumerar. **5,** (discern) conocer; distinguir. **6,** (decide) decidir; determinar. **7,** (reveal) descubrir; revelar. —*v.i.* **1,** (speak) hablar. **2,** (have force or effect) tener efecto; producir efecto. **3,** (determine) decidir; determinar. —**tell off, 1,** (count) contar; enumerar. **2,** *colloq.* (rebuke) reprender; censurar. **3,** *colloq.* (confront; defy) arrostrar; dar cara a; enfrentar. —**tell on, 1,** (tire; wear out) agotar; extenuar. **2,** *colloq.* (inform on) delatar; denunciar. —**tell one's mind,** decir lo que piensa; hablar sin rodeos.

teller ('tɛl·ər) *n.* **1,** (informant) narrador [*fem.* -dora]; relator [*fem.* -tora]. **2,** (bank clerk) cajero. **3,** (one who counts votes) escrutador [*fem.* -dora]. —**paying teller,** pagador [*fem.* -dora]. —**receiving teller,** recibidor [*fem.* -dora].

telling ('tɛl·ıŋ) *adj.* eficaz; notable; fuerte. —*n.* narración.

telltale ('tɛl,teil) *n.* **1,** (tattler) chismoso; soplón [*fem.* -plona]; cuentón [*fem.* -tona]. **2,** (indicator; gauge) indicador; medidor; contador. **3,** (indication) indicio; señal. —*adj.* indicador; revelador.

tellurium (tɛ'lur·i·əm) *n.* telurio.

telly ('tɛl·i) *n., Brit.* televisión.

temblor (tɛm·blər; -'blo:r) *n.* terremoto; temblor de tierra.

temerarious (,tɛm·ə'rɛr·i·əs) *adj.* temerario.

temerity (tə'mɛr·ə·ti) *n.* temeridad.

temper ('tɛm·pər) *n.* **1,** (hardness of metals) temple. **2,** (disposition) genio; humor; temple; temperamento. **3,** (anger) ira; cólera; mal genio; enojo. —*v.t.* templar. —*v.i.* templarse. —**go** (o **fly**) **into a temper,** * encolerizarse; arrebatarse. —**keep one's temper,** dominarse; tener calma. —**lose one's temper,** encolerizarse; perder la paciencia.

tempera ('tɛm·pər·ə) *n.* templa. —**in tempera,** al temple.

temperament ('tɛm·pər·ə·mənt) *n.* temperamento.

temperamental (ˌtɛm·pər·ə·'mɛn·təl) *adj.* **1,** (innate) propio; original; característico. **2,** (excitable; moody) caprichoso; veleidoso; mudadizo.

temperance ('tɛm·pər·əns) *n.* **1,** (moderation) templanza; temperancia; moderación. **2,** (abstinence) abstinencia.

temperate ('tɛm·pər·ət) *adj.* **1,** (moderate) templado; moderado. **2,** (abstemious) abstemio. —**temperateness,** *n.* templanza; moderación.

temperature ('tɛm·pər·ə·tʃur) *n.* temperatura.

tempered ('tɛm·pərd) *adj.* templado.

tempest ('tɛm·pɪst) *n.* **1,** (windstorm) tempestad; temporal; tormenta. **2,** (excitement) tumulto; conmoción; alboroto.

tempestuous (tɛm'pɛs·tʃu·əs) *adj.* **1,** (stormy) tempestuoso. **2,** (violent; turbulent) impetuoso; violento; turbulento.

template ('tɛm·plɪt) *n.* = templet.

temple ('tɛm·pəl) *n.* **1,** (church) templo; iglesia. **2,** *anat.* sien.

templet *también,* **template** ('tɛm·plɪt) *n.* plantilla; patrón.

tempo ('tɛm·po) *n.* tiempo; ritmo; compás.

temporal ('tɛm·pə·rəl) *adj.* temporal.

temporary ('tɛm·pə·rɛr·i) *adj.* temporal; temporario; temporáneo. —**temporarily** (-'rɛr·ə·li) *adv.* temporalmente; por algún tiempo.

temporize ('tɛm·pə,raiz) *v.i.* temporizar; contemporizar.

tempt (tɛmpt) *v.t.* **1,** (lure; incite) tentar; incitar; inducir. **2,** (provoke) provocar. **3,** (attract) atraer. —**tempter,** *n.* tentador. —**temptress** ('tɛmp·trɪs) *n.* tentadora.

temptation (tɛmp'tei·ʃən) *n.* tentación.

ten (tɛn) *n. & adj.* diez.

tenable ('tɛn·ə·bəl) *adj.* defendible.

tenacious (tə'nei·ʃəs) *adj.* tenaz.

tenacity (tə'næs·ə·ti) *n.* tenacidad.

tenancy ('tɛn·ən·si) *n.* tenencia.

tenant ('tɛn·ənt) *n.* **1,** (one who rents or leases) inquilino; arrendatario. **2,** (owner) residente.

tenantry ('tɛn·ən·tri) *n.* **1,** (tenancy) tenencia. **2,** (tenants collectively) inquilinos; arrendatarios.

tench (tɛntʃ) *n.* tenca.

tend (tɛnd) *v.t.* **1,** (take care of) cuidar; velar; vigilar; guardar. **2,** (serve) servir. —*v.i.* tender; dirigirse; inclinarse. —**tend on,** atender; servir.

tendency ('tɛn·dən·si) *n.* tendencia; propensión.

tendentious (tɛn'dɛn·ʃəs) *adj.* tendencioso. —**tendentiousness,** *n.* tendencia.

tender ('tɛn·dər) *adj.* **1,** (soft) tierno; blando; delicado. **2,** (weak; frail) débil; endeble; delicado. **3,** (sensitive; difficult to handle) delicado; arduo; arriesgado. **4,** (affectionate) cariñoso; afectuoso. **5,** (painful) dolorido. **6,** (compassionate) compasivo; considerado. **7,** (scrupulous) delicado; escrupuloso. —*n.* **1,** (offer) oferta. **2,** (one who tends) guarda; guardián; vigilante. **3,** *R.R.* ténder. **4,** *naut.* falúa; lancha. —*v.t.* **1,** (make tender) enternecer; ablandar. **2,** (offer) ofrecer; tender; presentar.

tenderfoot ('tɛn·dər,fut) *n.* [*pl* -**foots** o -**feet**] novato; bisoño; pipiolo.

tenderhearted ('tɛn·dər,har·tɪd) *adj.* compasivo; tierno de corazón; bondadoso. —**tenderheartedness,** *n.* compasión; bondad.

tenderize ('tɛn·dər,aiz) *v.t.* enternecer; ablandar.

tenderloin ('tɛn·dər·lɔin) *n.* **1,** (cut of meat) filete. **2,** (city district) barrio de mala vida.

tenderness ('tɛn·dər·nəs) *n.* **1,** (softness; delicateness) ternura; blandura; delicadeza. **2,** (affection) cariño; afectuosidad.

tendon ('tɛn·dən) *n.* tendón.

tendril ('tɛn·drɪl) *n.* zarcillo.

tenebrous ('tɛn·ə·brəs) *adj.* tenebroso.

tenement ('tɛn·ə·mənt) *n.* vivienda; alojamiento; habitación. —**tenement house,** casa de vecindad.

tenet ('tɛn·ət) *n.* dogma; credo; principio.

tenfold ('tɛn·fold) *adj. & n.* décuplo; diez veces (más). —*adv.* diez veces; en un décuplo.

tennis ('tɛn·ɪs) *n.* tenis. —**tennis player,** tenista.

tenon ('tɛn·ən) *n.* espiga. —*v.t.* espigar; despatillar.

tenor ('tɛn·ər) *n.* **1,** (course) curso; tenor. **2,** (tendency) tendencia. **3,**

(nature) carácter. **4,** (meaning) significado. **5,** *mus.* tenor. —*adj.* de o para tenor. —**tenor clef,** clave de do.

tenpenny ('tɛn,pɛn·i; -pə·ni) *adj.* de diez peniques; que vale diez peniques. —**tenpenny nail,** clavo de tres pulgadas.

tenpins ('tɛn·pɪnz) *n.* bolos. —**tenpin.** *n.* bolo.

tense (tɛns) *adj.* tenso; tieso; estirado; tirante. —*v.t.* tensar; hacer tenso. —*v.i.* tensarse; ponerse tenso. —*n., gram.* tiempo. —**tenseness,** *n.* tirantez; tensión.

tensile ('tɛn·sɪl) *adj.* **1,** (undergoing or producing tension) tensor. **2,** (ductile) dúctil; maleable. —**tensile strength,** resistencia a la tensión.

tension ('tɛn·ʃən) *n.* **1,** (strain) tensión; tirantez. **2,** (anxiety) ansia; congoja. —**tensional,** *adj.* de tensión.

tensity ('tɛn·sə·ti) *n.* tensión.

tensor ('tɛn·sər) *n.* tensor.

tent (tɛnt) *n.* **1,** (shelter) tienda; tienda de campaña; pabellón **2,** *surg.* tapón. —*v.i.* acampar.

tentacle ('tɛn·tə·kəl) *n.* tentáculo.

tentative ('tɛn·tə·tɪv) *adj.* tentativo.

tenterhook ('tɛn·tər,hʊk) *n.* alcayata. —**on tenterhooks,** en suspenso; muy ansioso.

tenth (tɛnθ) *adj.* décimo. —*n.* décimo; décima parte; *mus.* décima.

tenuous ('tɛn·ju·əs) *adj.* tenue; delicado; fino. —**tenuousness,** *n.* tenuidad.

tenure ('tɛn·jər) *n.* tenencia.

tenure track camino hacia la tenencia. —**tenure-track,** *adj.* que lleva a la tenencia.

tepee ('ti·pi) *n.* = teepee.

tepid ('tɛp·ɪd) *adj.* tibio. —**tepidity** (tɛ'pɪd·ə·ti); **tepidness,** *n.* tibieza.

tequila (tə'ki·lə) *n.* tequila.

terbium ('tʌr·bi·əm) *n.* terbio.

tercentenary (tʌr'sɛn·tə·nɛr·i) *adj.* de trescientos años. —*n.* tricentenario.

term (tʌrm) *n.* **1,** (word or phrase) término. **2,** (time) período; plazo; término. **3,** *math.; logic* término. **4,** (semester) semestre. **5,** *pl.* (conditions) condiciones. —*v.t.* nombrar; llamar; denominar. —**be on good (o bad) terms,** tener buenas (o malas) relaciones; llevarse bien (o mal). —**bring to terms,** imponer

condiciones a; vencer. —**come to terms,** someterse; ceder; ponerse de acuerdo.

termagant ('tʌr·mə·gənt) *n.* mujer regañona; fiera. —*adj.* reñidor; pendenciero.

terminable ('tʌr·mə·nə·bəl) *adj.* terminable.

terminal ('tʌr·mə·nəl) *adj.* terminal; final; último. —*n.* **1,** (end) término; fin. **2,** *elect.* borne; terminal. **3,** *R.R.* estación terminal.

terminate ('tʌr·mə,neit) *v.t. & i.* terminar; acabar; concluir. —**termination,** *n.* terminación; fin; límite; *gram.* desinencia.

terminology (,tʌr·mə'nal·ə·dʒi) *n.* terminología.

term insurance seguro a tiempo fijo.

terminus ('tʌr·mə·nəs) *n.* [*pl.* **-ni** (-nai) o **-nuses**] término; final; fin; *R.R.* estación terminal.

termite ('tʌr·mait) *n.* termita; hormiga blanca.

tern (tʌrn) *n.* **1,** (sea bird) golondrina de mar. **2,** (set of three) terna; terno.

ternary ('tʌr·nə·ri) *adj. & n.* ternario.

terpsichorean (,tʌrp·si·kə'ri·ən) *adj.* del baile; perteneciente al baile. —*n.* bailarín (*fem.* bailarina).

terrace ('tɛr·əs) *n.* **1,** (embankment) terraplén. **2,** *agric.* terraza. **3,** (flat roof or balcony) terraza; terrado; azotea. —*v.t.* terraplenar; escalonar.

terra cotta ('tɛr·ə'kat·ə) *n.* terracota; barro cocido.

terra firma ('tɛr·ə'fʌr·mə) tierra firme.

terrain (tə'rein) *n.* terreno.

terramycin (,tɛr·ə'mai·sɪn) *n.* terramicina.

terrapin ('tɛr·ə·pɪn) *n.* tortuga del Atlántico.

terraqueous (tɛr'ei·kwi·əs) *adj.* terráqueo.

terrarium (tə'rɛr·i·əm) *n.* [*pl.* **-iums** o **-ia** (-i·ə)] terrario.

terrazzo (tɛr'rat·so) *n.* piso veneciano.

terrestrial (tə'rɛs·tri·əl) *adj.* terrestre; terreno.

terrible ('tɛr·ə·bəl) *adj.* **1,** (frightful) terrible; pavoroso; espantoso. **2,** *colloq.* (very bad) desagradable; muy malo. —**terribleness,** *n.* terribilidad. —**terribly,** *adv.* terriblemente; *colloq.* muy.

terrier ('tɛr·i·ər) n. terrier.
terrific (tə'rɪf·ɪk) adj. 1, (dreadful) terrífico; espantoso. 2, colloq. (extraordinary) extraordinario; maravilloso.
terrify ('tɛr·ɪ,fai) v.t. aterrar; espantar; horrorizar; aterrorizar. —**terrifying,** terrible; terrífico; espantoso.
territorial (,tɛr·ɪ'tor·i·əl) adj. territorial.
territory ('tɛr·ɪ·tor·i) n. territorio.
terror ('tɛr·ər) n. terror.
terrorist ('tɛr·ər·ɪst) n. terrorista. —**terrorism,** n. terrorismo. —**terroristic,** adj. terrorista.
terrorize ('tɛr·ər,aiz) v.t. aterrorizar.
terror-stricken adj. aterrorizado.
terry ('tɛr·i) n. albornoz. También, **terry cloth.**
terse (tʌrs) adj. conciso; breve; sucinto; terso. —**terseness,** n. brevedad; tersura.
tertian fever ('tʌr·ʃən) terciana; tercianas.
tertiary ('tʌr·ʃi·ɛr·i) adj. & n. terciario.
test (tɛst) n. 1, (examination) prueba; examen; educ.; psychol. test. 2, (experiment) ensayo; experimento. —v.t. probar; comprobar; examinar. —**test tube,** tubo de ensayo.
testament ('tɛs·tə·mənt) n. testamento. —**testamentary** (-'mɛn·tə·ri) adj. testamentario.
testate ('tɛs·teit) adj. testado.
testator ('tɛs·tei·tər) n. testador.
testatrix (tɛs'tei·trɪks) n. [pl. -trices (-trɪ·siz)] testadora.
testes ('tɛs·tiz) n.pl. testes; testículos. También, **testis** [pl. -tes (-tiz)].
testicle ('tɛs·tə·kəl) n. testículo; teste.
testify ('tɛs·tɪ·fai) v.t. & i. testificar.
testimonial (,tɛs·tə'mo·ni·əl) n. 1, (recommendation) certificado; certificación; recomendación. 2, (tribute) homenaje. —adj. 1, (certifying) testimonial; que hace fe. 2, (recommending) de recomendación. 3, (expressing esteem) de homenaje.
testimony ('tɛs·tə·mo·ni) n. testimonio.
testosterone (tɛs'tɑs·tə·ron) n. testosterona.
testy ('tɛs·ti) adj. enojadizo; quisquilloso; áspero. —**testiness,** n. enojo; enfado; aspereza.

tetanus ('tɛt·ə·nəs) n. tétano.
tetchy ('tɛtʃ·i) adj. = **techy.**
tête-à-tête ('tɛt·ə'tet) n. conversación cara a cara. —adj. confidencial. —adv. confidencialmente; en privado.
tether ('tɛð·ər) n. traba; maniota; atadura. —v.t. atar. —**at the end of one's tether,** al límite de la paciencia o de los recursos de uno.
tetragon ('tɛt·rə,gan) n. tetrágono. —**tetragonal** (tɛ'træg·ə·nəl) adj. tetragonal.
tetrahedron (,tɛt·rə'hi·drən) n. tetraedro. —**tetrahedral,** adj. tetraédrico.
tetrarch ('tɛt·rark) n. tetrarca. —**tetrarchy,** n. tetrarquía.
Teuton ('tu·tən) n. teutón; tudesco. —**Teutonic** (tu'tan·ɪk) adj. & n. teutónico; tudesco.
text (tɛkst) n. texto.
textbook ('tɛkst,bʊk) n. libro de texto; libro escolar.
textile ('tɛks·tɪl) adj. textil. —n. tejido; tela; textil.
textual ('tɛks·tʃʊ·əl) adj. textual.
texture ('tɛks·tʃər) n. textura.
thalamus ('θæl·ə·məs) n. tálamo. —**thalamic** (θə'læm·ɪk) adj. talámico.
thallium ('θæl·i·əm) n. talio.
than (ðæn) conj. que; (before numerals) de.
thank (θæŋk) v.t. agradecer; dar gracias a. —**thank God,** gracias a Dios. —**thank you,** gracias; muchas gracias.
thankful ('θæŋk·fəl) adj. agradecido; grato; reconocido. —**thankfulness,** n. agradecimiento; gratitud; reconocimiento.
thankless ('θæŋk·ləs) adj. desagradecido; ingrato. —**thanklessness,** n. ingratitud; desagradecimiento.
thanks (θæŋks) n.pl. gracias; agradecimiento. —interj. ¡gracias!
thanksgiving (,θæŋks'gɪv·ɪŋ) n. acción de gracias. —**Thanksgiving Day,** día de acción de gracias.
that (ðæt) adj. dem. [pl. **those**] ese (fem. esa); aquel (fem. aquella). —pron.dem. [pl. **those**] ése (fem. ésa; neut. eso); aquél (fem. aquélla; neut. aquello). —pron.rel. que; quien; cual; el que; la que; lo que. —conj. que; para que; a fin de que; de modo que. —adv. tan. —**at that,** con eso; con todo eso. —**in that,** porque. —**that is,** eso es; es

decir. —**that much,** tanto. —**that's that!,** ¡así es!; ¡punto! —**that which,** el, lo o la que. —**what of that?,** ¿qué importa eso?; ¿qué significa eso?

thatch (θætʃ) *n.* **1,** (straw) paja; bálago; caña. **2,** (straw roof) techo de paja. **3,** *colloq.* (hair) pelo. —*v.t.* cubrir de paja.

thaw (θɔː) *v.t.* deshelar; derretir. —*v.i.* **1,** (melt) deshelarse; derretirse. **2,** *fig.* (relent) aplacarse; ablandarse; ceder. —*n.* deshielo; derretimiento.

the (ðə; *ante vocal* ði) *art.def.* el; la; lo; los; las. —*adv.* cuanto. —**the more . . . the more,** cuanto más . . . tanto más.

theater *también,* **theatre** ('θiːəˑtər) *n.* teatro.

theatrical (θiˈætˑrɪˑkəl) *adj.* teatral. —**theatricals,** *n.pl.* funciones teatrales.

theatrics (θiˈætˑrɪks) *n.* arte teatral; teatro.

thee (ðiː) *pron.pers.,* arcaico y poético **1,** *como complemento de verbo* te; a ti. **2,** *como complemento de prep.* ti. **3,** *tras* than, *en comparaciones* tú. —**with thee,** contigo.

theft (θɛft) *n.* robo; hurto.

their (ðɛːr) *adj. pos.* su (*pl.* sus); de ellos; de ellas.

theirs (ðɛːrz) *pron. pos.* el suyo; la suya; lo suyo; los suyos; las suyas; el, la, lo, los o las de ellos (o ellas).

theism ('θiːˑɪzˑəm) *n.* teísmo. —**theist,** *n.* teísta. —**theistic** (θiˈɪsˑtɪk) *adj.* teísta.

them (ðɛm) *pron.pers.m. & f. pl.* **1,** *como complemento directo de verbo* los; las; les. **2,** *como complemento indirecto* les; a ellos; a ellas. **3,** *como complemento de prep.* ellos; ellas. **4,** *tras* than, *en comparaciones* ellos; ellas.

theme (θiːm) *n.* tema. —**thematic** (θiˈmætˑɪk) *adj.* temático.

themselves (ðɛmˈsɛlvz) *pron. pers.* ellos; ellas; ellos mismos; ellas mismas. —*pron.refl.* **1,** *como complemento de verbo se:* They washed themselves, Se lavaron; They put them on themselves, Se los pusieron. **2,** *como complemento de prep.* sí; sí mismos; sí mismas. —**with themselves,** consigo.

then (ðɛn) *adv.* **1,** (at that time) entonces; en aquel tiempo; en

aquellos tiempos. **2,** (afterward; next) después; luego. **3,** (in that case; therefore) pues. **4,** (besides; moreover) además. **5,** (at another time) en otro tiempo. —*adj.* de entonces; de aquel tiempo. —*n.* aquel tiempo; aquellos tiempos. —**then and there,** en seguida; en el acto.

thence (ðɛns) *adv.* **1,** (from there) de allí; desde allí; **2,** (from that time) desde entonces. **3,** (therefore) por eso; por esa razón.

thenceforth ('ðɛnsˑfɔrθ) *adv.* desde entonces; de allí en adelante.

theocracy (θiˈakˑrəˑsi) *n.* teocracia. —**theocratic** (ˌθiˑəˈkrætˑɪk) *adj.* teocrático.

theology (θiˈalˑəˑdʒi) *n.* teología. —**theological** (ˌθiˑəˈladʒˑɪˑkəl) *adj.* teológico; teologal. —**theologian** (ˌθiˑəˈloˑdʒiˑən) *n.* teólogo.

theorem ('θiˑəˑrəm) *n.* teorema.

theoretical (ˌθiˑəˈrɛtˑɪˑkəl) *adj.* teórico.

theoretics (ˌθiˑəˈrɛtˑɪks) *n.* teórica.

theorist ('θiˑəˑrɪst) *n.* teórico.

theorize ('θiˑəˌraiz) *v.i.* teorizar.

theory ('θiˑəˑri) *n.* teoría.

theosophy (θiˈasˑəˑfi) *n.* teosofía. —**theosophical** (ˌθiˑəˈsafˑɪˑkəl) *adj.* teosófico. —**theosophist** (θiˈasˑəˑfist) *n.* teósofo.

therapeutic (θɛrˑəˈpjuˑtɪk) *adj.* terapéutico. —**therapeutics,** *n.* terapéutica.

therapy ('θɛrˑəˑpi) *n.* terapéutica. —**therapist,** *n.* terapeuta.

there (ðɛːr) *adv.* **1,** allí; allá; ahí. —*interj.* ¡mira!; ¡toma!; ¡vaya! —**(be) all there,** (estar) en sus cabales. —**there is; there are,** hay.

thereabout ('ðɛrˑəˌbaut) *adv.* **1,** (near that place or time) por allí; por ahí; cerca. **2,** (approximately) aproximadamente. *También,* **thereabouts.**

thereafter (ðɛrˈæfˑtər) *adv.* después de eso; de allí en adelante.

thereat ('ðɛrˌæt) *adv.* **1,** (at that place) allí; en aquel lugar. **2,** (at that time) entonces; en eso **3,** (for that reason) por eso.

thereby ('ðɛrˌbai) *adv.* **1,** (by that means) así; de ese modo. **2,** (in that connection) con eso. **3,** (near that place) por ahí cerca.

therefor ('ðɛrˌfor) *adv.* para eso.

therefore ('ðɛrˌfor) *adv.* por eso;

por tanto; por lo tanto; por consiguiente.

therefrom (ðɛr'frʌm) *adv.* de eso; de allí.

therein (ðɛr'ın) *adv.* en eso; en ello; allí dentro.

thereinafter (,ðɛr·ın'æf·tər) *adv.* posteriormente; más adelante.

thereinto (ðɛr'ın·tu) *adv.* dentro de eso o de aquello.

thereof (ðɛr'ʌv) *adv.* de eso; de ello.

thereon ('ðɛr·an) *adv.* 1, (on that) en eso; sobre eso. 2, (following that) luego; en seguida.

thereto ('ðɛr·tu) *adv.* a eso; a ello.

theretofore ('ðɛr·tə,for) *adv.* hasta entonces.

thereunder (ðɛr'ʌn·dər) *adv.* bajo eso; debajo de eso.

thereunto (ðɛr'ʌn·tu) *adv.* a eso; a ello.

thereupon ('ðɛr·ə·pan) *adv.* 1, (upon that) en eso; sobre eso. 2, (concerning that) de eso; de ello. 3, (because of that) por eso. 4, (following that) luego; en seguida.

therewith ('ðɛr·wıθ) *adv.* 1, (with that) con eso. 2, (in addition to that) además de eso. 3, (following that) luego; en seguida.

therewithal ('ðɛr·wıð·ɔl) *adv.* a más; además.

thermal ('θʌr·məl) *adj.* termal; térmico.

thermic ('θʌr·mık) *adj.* térmico.

thermit ('θʌr·mıt) *n.* termita. *También,* **thermite** (-mait).

thermocouple ('θʌr·mo,kʌp·əl) *n.* par termoeléctrico.

thermodynamics (,θʌr·mo·dai'næm·ıks) *n.* termodinámica. —**thermodynamic,** *adj.* termodinámico.

thermoelectric (,θʌr·mo·ı'lɛk·trık) *adj.* termoeléctrico.

thermometer (θʌr'mam·ı·tər) *n.* termómetro. —**thermometric** (,θʌr·mə'mɛt·rık) *adj.* termométrico.

thermonuclear (,θʌr·mo'nuk·li·ər) *adj.* termonuclear.

thermos ('θʌr·məs) *n.,* termos.

thermostat ('θʌr·mə·stæt) *n.* termóstato. —**thermostatic** (-'stæt·ık) *adj.* termostático.

thesaurus (θi'sor·əs) *n.* [*pl.* **-ri** (-rai)] tesauro.

these (ðiːz) *adj.dem.* estos; estas. —*pron. dem.* éstos; éstas.

thesis ('θi·sıs) *n.* [*pl.* **-ses** (-siz)] tesis.

Thespian ('θɛs·pi·ən) *adj.* relativo a Tespis; trágico; dramático. —*n.* actor trágico.

thew (ðjuː) *n.* músculo.

they (ðei) *pron.pers.* ellos; ellas.

they'd (ðeid) *contr. de* they would o they had.

they'll (ðeil) *contr. de* they will o they shall.

they're (ðɛr) *contr. de* they are.

they've (ðeiv) *contr. de* they have.

thiamine ('θai·ə·miːn) *n.* tiamina. *También,* **thiamin** (-mın)

thick (θık) *adj.* 1, (heavy; massive) grueso; espeso; macizo. 2, (dense) denso; espeso; tupido. 3, (having a certain thickness) de espesor: *six inches thick,* de seis pulgadas de espesor. 4, (abundant) abundante. 5, (filled; crammed) lleno. 6, (murky) brumoso; nebuloso. 7, (mentally dull) torpe; estúpido; embotado 8, *colloq.* (unpleasant) desagradable; insoportable. 9, *colloq.* (intimate) íntimo. —*n.* 1, (thickness; thickest part) espesor, grueso. 2, (most active part) lo más fuerte; lo más reñido. —*adv.* 1, (thickly) espesamente; densamente. 2, (abundantly) abundantemente. —**lay it on thick,** *colloq.* exagerar. —**thick and fast,** abundantemente; frecuentemente. —**through thick and thin,** por las buenas y las malas.

thicken ('θık·ən) *v.t.* espesar. —*v.i.* 1, (become thick) espesarse. 2, (become complicated) complicarse; enredarse.

thicket ('θık·ıt) *n.* espesura; maleza; soto; boscaje.

thickheaded ('θık,hɛd·ıd) *adj.* torpe; estúpido; embotado.

thickness ('θık·nəs) *n.* 1, (massiveness) espesura. 2, (dimension) espesor. 3, (denseness) densidad. 4, (consistency) consistencia. 5, (thickest part) espesor; grueso. 6, (layer) capa; estrato.

thickset ('θık·sɛt) *adj.* fornido; rechoncho; grueso.

thick-skinned *adj.* 1, (having a thick skin) de pellejo espeso. 2, (insensitive) insensible.

thief (θif) *n.* [*pl.* **thieves** (θiːvz)] ladrón [*fem.* -drona].

thieve (θiːv) *v.i.* robar; hurtar. —**thievery,** *n.* latrocinio; hurto; robo. —**thieving; thievish,** *adj.* ladrón; rápaz.

thigh (θai) *n.* muslo.

thighbone ('θai·bon) *n.* fémur.
thimble ('θɪm·bəl) *n.* 1, (sewing dedal. 2, *mech.* manguito de enchufe;
abrazadera.
thimblerig ('θɪm·bəl‚rɪg) *n.* =
shell game.
thin (θɪn) *adj.* 1, (slender) delgado;
flaco. 2, (sparse) escaso; ralo. 3,
(watery) aguado; claro. 4, (flimsy)
débil; insubstancial. 5, (fine; light)
tenue; ligero; fino. —*v.t.* [thinned,
thinning] 1, (make slender) adelgazar. 2, (make sparse) enrarecer. 3,
(make watery) aguar; aclarar. —*v.i.*
1, (become sparse) enrarecerse. 2,
(become watery) aclararse. —*adv.*
delgadamente; ligeramente.
thine (ðain) *pron.poss., arcaico y
poético* tuyo; tuya; tuyos; tuyas.
—*adj.poss.* tu; tus.
thing (θɪŋ) *n.* cosa; objeto.
—**make a good thing of,** sacar
provecho de. —**no such thing,** no
(hay) tal cosa. —**not a thing,** nada.
—**poor thing,** pobrecito (*fem.*
pobrecita). —**see things,** *colloq.* ver
visiones; imaginarse (cosas). —**the
thing,** lo necesario; lo que se desea.
think (θɪŋk) *v.t. & i.* [*pret. & p.p.*
thought] 1, (conceive in the mind)
pensar. 2, (believe) creer. 3, (reflect) pensar; considerar; reflexionar. 4, (judge) juzgar. 5, (intend)
pensar; tener intención (de). —*n.,
colloq.* pensamiento; reflexión.
—**think about,** 1, (fix the mind on)
pensar en. 2, (have an opinion of)
pensar de. —**think better of,** repensar; volver a considerar. —**think
ill of,** tener mala opinión de.
—**think nothing of,** tener en poco.
—**think of,** 1, (consider) pensar en;
considerar. 2, (have an opinion of)
pensar de. 3, (recall) acordarse;
ocurrírsele a uno. —**think on,** pensar en; reflexionar en. —**think out
o through,** considerar en lo total;
decidir; determinar. —**think over,**
pensar en; reflexionar en. —**think
up,** inventar; imaginar. —**think
well of,** tener buena opinión de.
thinkable ('θɪŋk·ə·bəl) *adj.*
pensable; concebible.
thinker ('θɪŋk·ər) *n.* pensador
[*fem.* -dora].
thinking ('θɪŋk·ɪŋ) *adj.* pensador.
—*n.* 1, (thought) pensamiento. 2,
(opinion) parecer; opinión; juicio.
thinner ('θɪn·ər) *n.* solvente.
thinness ('θɪn·nəs) *n.* 1, (slender-

ness) delgadez; flacura. 2, (sparseness) escasez; raleza. 3, (fineness)
tenuidad; ligereza; fineza.
thinskinned ('θɪn‚skɪnd) *adj.* 1,
(having a thin skin) de pellejo delgado. 2, (sensitive) sensitivo; sensible; susceptible.
third (θʌrd) *adj.* tercero. —*n.* tercio; tercero; tercera parte; *mus.*
tercera. —**third degree,** interrogatorio (*de un preso*). —**third finger,**
(dedo) anular.
third-rate *adj.* de tercera clase;
inferior.
thirst (θʌrst) *n.* 1, (dryness) sed. 2,
(desire) anhelo; ansia; deseo
ardiente. —*v.i.* tener sed; estar
sediento. —**thirst for,** anhelar;
ansiar; desear vivamente.
thirsty ('θʌrs·ti) *adj.* sediento.
—**be thirsty,** tener sed.
thirteen (θʌr'tiːn) *n. & adj.* trece.
—**thirteenth,** *adj. & n.* decimotercio; trezavo.
thirty ('θʌr·ti) *n. & adj.* treinta.
—**thirtieth,** *adj. & n.* trigésimo;
treintavo.
this (ðɪs) *adj.dem* [*pl.* those] este;
esta. —*pron.dem.* [*pl.* those] éste;
ésta; esto. —*adv.* tan.
thistle ('θɪs·əl) *n.* cardo; abrojo.
thither ('θɪð·ər) *adv.* allá; hacia
allá; para allá. —*adj.* más lejano.
thitherto ('θɪð·ər·tu) *adv.* hasta
entonces; hasta allá.
tho (ðoɪ) *conj. & adv.* = **though.**
thong (θɔŋ) *n.* trasca; tira de cuero;
correa.
thorax ('θor·æks) *n.* tórax. —**thoracic** (θə'ræs·ɪk) *adj.* torácico.
thorium ('θor·i·əm) *n.* torio.
thorn (θorn) *n.* 1, (spine) espina;
púa; pincho. 2, (shrub) espino. 3,
fig. (annoyance) espina; pesadumbre; molestia.
thorny ('θor·ni) *adj.* 1, (prickly)
espinoso. 2, (annoying; difficult)
molesto; arduo; difícil.
thorough ('θʌr·o) *adj.* 1, (complete) acabado; completo; cabal;
cumplido. 2, (detailed; minute)
cuidadoso; minucioso; esmerado.
thoroughbred ('θʌr·ə·brəd) *adj.*
de casta; de pura sangre; de raza
pura. —*n.* animal o persona de
casta; caballo de raza.
thoroughfare ('θʌr·ə·fer) *n.* 1,
(highway) vía pública; carretera; camino. 2, (transit) paso; tránsito.
—**no thoroughfare,** calle cerrada;
prohibido el paso.

thoroughgoing ('θʌr·ə,go·ɪŋ) *adj.* 1, (complete) cabal; completo; perfecto. 2, (exhaustive) minucioso; detallado. 3, (painstaking) cuidadoso; esmerado. 4, (effective) eficaz.

thoroughness ('θʌr·o·nəs) *n.* 1, (completeness) entereza; perfección. 2, (minuteness) minuciosidad; esmero.

those (ðo:z) *adj.dem.* esos; esas; aquellos; aquellas. —*pron.dem.* ésos; ésas; aquéllos; aquéllas.

thou (ðau) *pron.pers., arcaico y poético* tú.

though (ðo:) *conj.* aunque; siquiera; bien que; no obstante; aun cuando. —*adv.* sin embargo. —**as though,** como si.

thought (θɔt) *n.* 1, (thinking) pensamiento; meditación. 2, (idea) concepto; propósito; idea. 3, (reasoning) reflexión; juicio; opinión. 4, (consideration) atención; consideración. 5, (intention) intención. —*v., pret. & p.p. de* think.

thoughtful ('θɔt·fəl) *adj.* 1, (pensive) pensativo; meditativo. 2, (heedful; mindful) precavido; previsor. 3, (considerate) atento; considerado; solícito. —**thoughtfulness,** *n.* atención; consideración; solicitud.

thoughtless ('θɔt·ləs) *adj.* 1, (unthinking) irreflexivo. 2, (careless) descuidado. 3, (rash) imprudente; indiscreto. 4, (inconsiderate) inconsiderado.

thoughtlessness ('θɔt·ləs·nəs) *n.* 1, (unthinking attitude or behavior) irreflexión; inadvertencia. 2, (carelessness) descuido. 3, (rashness) imprudencia; indiscreción. 4, (inconsiderateness) inconsideración.

thousand ('θau·zənd) *adj.* mil. —*n.* mil; millar.

thousandfold ('θau·zənd·fold) *adj. & n.* mil veces (más). —*adv.* mil veces.

thousandth ('θau·zəndθ) *adj.* milésimo. —*n.* milésimo; milésima parte.

thrall (θrɔ:l) *n.* 1, (captive) esclavo; siervo. 2, (bondage) esclavitud; servidumbre. —**thraldom; thralldom,** *n.* esclavitud; servidumbre.

thrash (θræʃ) *v.t.* 1, (beat) azotar; zurrar. 2, (thresh) trillar; desgranar. —*v.i.* arrojarse o tirarse violen-

tamente. —**thrash out,** discutir detalladamente; decidir; resolver.

thrasher ('θæʃ·ər) *n.* 1, (thresher) trillador; trilladora. 2, *ornith.* ave canora norteamericana semejante al tordo.

thrashing ('θræʃ·ɪŋ) *n.* paliza; zurra.

thread (θrɛd) *n.* 1, (thin cord; fiber) hilo; hebra; fibra; filamento. 2, *mech.* rosca; filete. 3, *fig.* (sequence) hilo. —*v.t.* 1, (pass through the eye of a needle). enhebrar; enhilar. 2, (string) ensartar. —*v.t. & i.* (pass through laboriously) colar (por); pasar (por).

threadbare ('θrɛd·beir) *adj.* 1, (shabby) raído. 2, (hackneyed) gastado; trillado.

threat (θrɛt) *n.* amenaza.

threaten ('θrɛt·ən) *v.t. & i.* amenazar.

three (θriː) *n. & adj.* tres.

three-cornered *adj.* tricornio. —**three-cornered hat,** sombrero de tres picos.

three-dimensional *adj.* tridimensional.

threefold ('θri·fold) *adj. & n.* triple; tres veces (más). —*adv.* tres veces; en un triple.

three hundred trescientos. —**three-hundredth,** *adj. & n.* tricentésimo.

thresh (θrɛʃ) *v.t.* 1, (beat, as grain) trillar; desgranar. 2, (discuss exhaustively) discutir detalladamente. 3, = thrash.

thresher ('θrɛʃ·ər) *n.* 1, (one who threshes) trillador. 2, (machine) trilladora. 3, [*también,* thresher shark] zorra marina; zorra de mar.

threshing ('θrɛʃ·ɪŋ) *n.* trilla; trilladura. —**threshing floor,** era.

threshold ('θrɛʃ·old) *n.* 1, (doorsill) umbral. 2, (beginning) entrada; comienzo; principio; umbrales.

threw (θru:) *v., pret. de* throw.

thrice (θrais) *adv.* tres veces.

thrift (θrift) *n.* ahorro; economía; frugalidad. —**thrifty,** *adj.* económico; frugal; ahorrativo.

thrill (θrɪl) *v.t.* emocionar; conmover; excitar. —*v.i.* emocionarse; conmoverse; excitarse. —*n.* emoción; estremecimiento; excitación. —**thriller,** *n.* representación excitante. —**thrilling,** *adj.* emocionante; vivo; espeluznante.

thrive (θraiv) *v.i.* [*pret.* **throve** o **thrived;** *p.p.* **thrived** o **thriven**

(θrɪv·ən)] medrar; florecer; prosperar.

throat (θrot) n. garganta. —**jump down one's throat,** reprender severamente.

throaty ('θro·ti) adj. gutural; ronco.

throb (θraːb) v.i. [**throbbed, throbbing**] latir; pulsar; palpitar. —n. latido; palpitación; pulsación. —**throbbing,** adj. palpitante. —n. palpitación; latido.

throe (θroː) n. dolor vivo; espasmo. —**throes,** n.pl. agonía; angustia.

thrombosis (θram'bo·sɪs) n. trombosis.

throne (θroːn) n. trono. —v.t. entronar.

throng (θrɔŋ) n. muchedumbre; multitud; gentío; tropel. —v.i. agolparse; apiñarse. —v.t. llenar; atestar; apretar.

throstle ('θras·əl) n. 1, (bird) tordo; malvís. 2, mech. máquina de torcer o devanar; telar continuo.

throttle ('θrat·əl) n. regulador; acelerador. —v.t. ahogar; estrangular; sofocar. —v.i. ahogarse.

through (θruː) prep. por; a través de; por medio de; por entre. —adv. de un lado a otro; de parte a parte; desde el principio hasta el fin; completamente; enteramente. —adj. directo; continuo. —**be through,** acabar; haber acabado. —**get through (with),** terminar; acabar (con).

throughout (θru'aut) adv. por todo; por todas partes; en todas partes; de un extremo a otro. —prep. en todo; por todo; durante todo; a lo largo de.

throve (θroːv) v., pret. de thrive.

throw (θroː) v.t. & i. [pret. **threw;** p.p. **thrown** (θroːn)] tirar; arrojar; lanzar; echar. —n. 1, (a throwing; distance thrown) tiro; tirada; lance. 2, (shawl) chal. 3, (coverlet) colcha. —**throw away, 1,** (discard) tirar; botar; rechazar. **2,** (waste) malgastar; desperdiciar. **3,** (lose; miss) perder. —**throw down,** derribar; echar por tierra. —**throw in, 1,** (engage, as a clutch) engranar. **2,** (add) añadir. —**throw off, 1,** (cast aside) desechar; deshacerse de. **2,** (elude) eludir; escaparse de. **3,** (emit) emitir; echar. —**throw open,** abrir de repente; abrir completamente. —**throw out, 1,** (reject) botar; desechar. **2,** (put

forth) proponer; tender. **3,** (disengage) desengranar. —**throw over,** abandonar. —**throw up, 1,** (renounce; resign) renunciar. **2,** (reproach with) echar en cara. **3,** (construct rapidly) construir rápidamente. **4,** (vomit) vomitar.

throwaway ('θro·ə·wei) n. volante; impreso.

throwback ('θro·bæk) n. retroceso.

thru (θruː) prep., adv. & adj. = through.

thrum (θrʌm) v.t. & i. [**thrummed, thrumming**] rasguear; tocar mal. —**thrumming,** n. rasgueo.

thrush (θrʌʃ) n. **1,** (bird) tordo; malvís. **2,** (disease) ubrera.

thrust (θrʌst) v.t. & p.p. [pret. & p.p. **thrust**] **1,** (push; shove) empujar. **2,** (drive; impel) impeler. **3,** (force in) meter; hincar; clavar; encajar. **4,** (force upon) imponer. —v.i. **1,** (rush forward) arrojarse; precipitarse. **2,** (attack; charge) acometer; embestir. **3,** (strike with a weapon) dar una estocada, puñalada, etc. —n. **1,** (push) empujón. **2,** (attack) acometida. **3,** (stab) puñalada; estocada; lanzada. **4,** mech. empuje.

thud (θʌd) n. ruido sordo; batacazo. —v.t. golpear con ruido sordo. —v.i. hacer un ruido sordo.

thug (θʌg) n. matón; asesino; rufián.

thulium ('θu·li·əm) n. tulio.

thumb (θʌm) n. pulgar. —v.t. **1,** (handle) manejar; manosear. **2,** (rifle, as pages of a book) hojear. —**all thumbs,** tosco; zafio; rudo. —**thumb a ride; thumb one's way = hitchhike.** —**under one's thumb,** bajo el poder de.

thumb index índice recortado.

thumbnail ('θʌm,neil) n. uña del pulgar. —adj. muy pequeño; mínimo.

thumbscrew ('θʌm,skru) n. **1,** (screw turned by hand) tornillo de mariposa. **2,** (instrument of torture) empulgueras.

thumbtack ('θʌm,tæk) n. chinche; tachuela.

thump (θʌmp) n. trastazo; porrazo. —v.t. golpear; aporrear. —v.i. **1,** (fall heavily) cascar. **2,** (stamp; pound) golpear; dar un porrazo. **3,** (walk noisily) andar pesadamente. —**thumping,** adj., colloq. muy grande.

thunder ('θʌn·dər) n. **1,** (natural

phenomenon) trueno. **2,** (loud noise) estruendo. **3,** (vehement utterance) fulminación; amenaza. —*v.i.* **1,** (make a loud noise) tronar. **2,** (utter denunciations) fulminar. **3,** (move noisily) pasar con estruendo. —*v.t.* fulminar; arrojar; proferir con estruendo. —**steal one's thunder,** anticiparse a uno; robarle a uno su idea.

thunderbolt ('θʌn·dər‚bolt) *n.* **1,** (flash of lightning) rayo. **2,** (surprise) censura o fulminación inesperada.

thunderclap ('θʌn·dər‚klæp) *n.* trueno; tronido.

thunderhead ('θʌn·dər‚hɛd) *n.* cúmulo; nubarrón.

thunderous ('θʌn·dər·əs) *adj.* tonante; tronante; atronador.

thundershower ('θʌn·dər‚ʃau·ər) *n.* tronada; chubasco con truenos.

thunderstorm ('θʌn·dər‚storm) *n.* tronada.

thunderstruck ('θʌn·dər‚strʌk) *adj.* atónito; estupefacto.

Thursday ('θɜrz·de) *n.* jueves.

thus (ðʌs) *adv.* **1,** (in this manner) así; de este modo; de esta manera. **2,** (to this extent) tan; tanto; a ese grado. **3,** (hence) en consecuencia.

thwack (θwæk) *v.t.* zurrar; pegar; golpear; aporrear. —*n.* golpe; porrazo; latigazo.

thwart (θwort) *v.t.* frustrar; contrariar; estorbar; impedir. —*n.* banco de remeros; banco de bogar.

thy (ðai) *adj.pos., arcaico y poético* tu; tus.

thyme (taim) *n.* tomillo.

thymus ('θai·məs) *n.* timo.

thyroid ('θai·rɔid) *n.* tiroides. —*adj.* tiroideo. —**thyroid gland,** tiroides.

thyself (ðai'sɛlf) *pron.pers., arcaico y poético* tú; tú mismo. —*pron.refl.* **1,** *como complemento de verbo* te. **2,** *como complemento de prep.* ti; ti mismo. —**with thyself,** contigo.

ti (tiz) *n., mus.* si.

tiara (ti'ɛr·ə) *n.* tiara; diadema.

tibia ('tɪb·i·ə) *n.* [*pl.* **tibiae** (-i) o **tibias** (-əz)] tibia.

tic (tɪk) *n.* tic.

tick (tɪk) *n.* **1,** (sound) tictac. **2,** (pillow slip) funda. **3,** (parasite) garrapata. **4,** (mark) punto; contraseña; contramarca. **5,** (instant) instante; momento. **6,** *colloq.* (credit) crédito; fiado. —*v.t.* marcar;

señalar; contramarcar. —*v.i.* hacer tictac (*un reloj*); latir (*el corazón*).

ticker ('tɪk·ər) *n.* **1,** (something that ticks) algo que hace tictac. **2,** (telegraphic device) receptor telegráfico que imprime una cinta. **3,** *slang* (watch) reloj. **4,** *slang* (heart) corazón.

ticket ('tɪk·ɪt) *n.* **1,** (token of admission) billete; boleto; entrada. **2,** (electoral slate) lista de candidatos. **3,** (label; tag) marbete; etiqueta. **4,** *colloq.* (summons) citación. —*v.t.* rotular; marcar; poner etiqueta a. —**that's the ticket!** *colloq.* ¡eso es! —**ticket office; ticket window,** taquilla.

ticking ('tɪk·ɪŋ) *n.* cutí.

tickle ('tɪk·əl) *v.t.* **1,** (excite by stroking) cosquillear; hacer cosquillas a. **2,** (please) gustar; halagar; divertir. —*v.i.* **1,** (produce tickling) hacer cosquillas. **2,** (feel ticklish) tener o sentir cosquillas. —*n.* cosquillas; cosquilleo. —**be tickled pink,** *slang* alegrarse mucho.

tickler ('tɪk·lər) *n.* **1,** (person or thing that tickles) persona o cosa que hace cosquillas. **2,** (memo pad) libro de apuntes. **3,** (puzzler) rompecabezas.

ticklish ('tɪk·lɪʃ) *adj.* **1,** (sensitive to tickling) cosquilloso. **2,** (delicate; tricky) delicado; difícil; enredoso. —**ticklishness,** *n.* cosquillas. —**be ticklish,** tener o sentir cosquillas.

ticktacktoe (‚tɪk·tæk'toz) *n.* juego de tres en raya.

ticktock ('tɪk‚tak) *n.* tictac.

tidal ('tai·dəl) *adj.* de marea. —**tidal wave,** ola de marea; oleada; marejada.

tidbit ('tɪd·bɪt) *n.* bocadillo; golosina. *También,* **titbit.**

tiddlywinks ('tɪd·li·wɪŋks) *n.* juego de la pulga.

tide (taid) *n.* **1,** (rise and fall of water) marea. **2,** (current; flow) corriente; flujo; torrente. **3,** (time; season) tiempo; estación; temporada. —*v.t.* llevar; hacer flotar. —*v.i.* flotar con la marea. —**go with the tide,** seguir la corriente. —**tide over,** **1,** (help momentarily) ayudar por un tiempo. **2,** (overcome) superar. —**turn the tide,** cambiar el curso (de); decidir.

tideland ('taid‚lænd) *n.* estero.

tidewater ('taid‚wɔ·tər) *n.* agua de marea. —*adj.* costanero.

tidings ('tai·dɪŋz) *n.pl.* noticias; nuevas.

tidy ('tai·di) *adj.* aseado; limpio; ordenado. —*v.t.* asear; limpiar; arreglar. —**tidiness,** *n.* aseo; limpieza; orden.

tie (tai) *v.t.* [**tied, tying**] **1,** (fasten) atar; amarrar; liar. **2,** *mus.* ligar. **3,** (score the same as in a contest) empatar. **4,** (limit, confine) restringir; limitar; confinar. —*v.i.* **1,** (join) atarse; unirse. **2,** (make the same score) empatarse. —*n.* **1,** (something that binds) lazo; atadura. **2,** (neckwear) corbata; *Amer.* chalina. **3,** (equal scores) empate. **4,** *mus.* ligadura. **5,** (crossbeam) travesaño. **6,** *R.R.* traviesa; *Amer.* durmiente. **7,** (affinity) lazo; vínculo; parentesco. —**tie down,** restringir; limitar; confinar. —**tie up, 1,** (fasten) atar; amarrar. **2,** (wrap) envolver. **3,** (obstruct) impedir; obstruir. **4,** (occupy) ocupar.

tier (tɪr) *n.* fila; hilera; ringlera.

tie-up *n.* **1,** (stoppage) parada; paralización. **2,** *colloq.* (connection) lazo; vínculo.

tiff (tɪf) *n.* riña; disgusto; pique. —*v.i.* reñir; enfadarse; disputarse.

tiger ('tai·gər) *n.* tigre.

tiger lily azucena atigrada.

tight (tait) *adj.* **1,** (firmly fixed; fast) firme; seguro; fuerte. **2,** (fitting closely) apretado; estrecho; ajustado. **3,** (compact; dense) compacto; denso. **4,** (taut; tense) tirante; tenso; tieso. **5,** (hard to obtain) escaso; limitado. **6,** (sealed; impermeable) estanco; hermético. **7,** *colloq.* (stingy) tacaño; agarrado. **8,** *colloq.* (drunk) borracho. —*adv.* fuertemente. —**sit tight, 1,** (refrain from moving) aguantarse; quedarse tranquilo. **2,** (hold firm) estar o seguir en sus trece.

tighten ('tai·tən) *v.t.* apretar; estirar. —*v.i.* apretarse; estirarse.

tightfisted ('tait,fɪs·tɪd) *adj.* tacaño; agarrado.

tightlipped ('tait,lɪpt) *adj.* discreto; callado; reservado.

tightrope ('tait,rop) *n.* cuerda de equilibrista o volatinero.

tights (taits) *n.pl.* calzón muy ajustado; traje de malla.

tightwad ('tait·wad) *n., slang* tacaño; avaro; cicatero.

tigress ('tai·grɪs) *n.* tigresa.

tilde ('tɪl·də) *n.* tilde.

tile (tail) *n.* **1,** (ceramic tile) azulejo. **2,** (floor tile) baldosa. **3,** (roof tile) teja. —*v.t.* azulejar; baldosar; embaldosar; tejar; enlosar.

tilework ('tail,wʌrk) *n.* enlosado; embaldosado; tejado.

tile works tejar.

tiling ('tai·lɪŋ) *n.* azulejos; baldosas; tejas.

till (tɪl) *prep.* hasta. —*conj.* hasta que; mientras que. —*n.* gaveta o cajón de mostrador. —*v.t.* cultivar; arar; labrar.

tillage ('tɪl·ɪdʒ) *n.* labranza; cultivo; labor.

tiller ('tɪl·ər) *n.* **1,** *agric.* labrador; cultivador; agricultor. **2,** *naut.* palanca o caña del timón **3,** *hortic.* pendón; serpollo.

tilt (tɪlt) *v.t.* **1,** (slant) ladear; inclinar. **2,** (attack, in a joust) acometer; dar una lanzada a. —*v.i.* **1,** (slant) inclinarse; ladearse. **2,** (joust) pelear; luchar en un torneo. —*n.* **1,** (slant) ladeo; declive; inclinación. **2,** (contest) justa; torneo. **3,** (awning) toldo; tendal. —**(at) full tilt,** a toda correr.

timber ('tɪm·bər) *n.* **1,** (wood) madera; maderaje; maderamen. **2,** (beam) madero; viga. **3,** (trees) árboles de monte. —*v.t.* construir de madera; enmaderar. —**timber line,** línea o límite de la vegetación arbórea.

timberwork *n.* enmaderamiento; maderamen.

timbre ('tɪm·bər) *n.* timbre; tono.

time (taim) *n.* **1,** (duration) tiempo. **2,** (hour) hora. **3,** (point in time) hora; momento. **4,** *mus.* tiempo; compás; ritmo. **5,** (prison sentence) término; condena. **6,** (working shift) horas trabajadas. **7,** (period) época; era; período. **8,** (turn; occasion) vez; oportunidad; turno. **9,** *pl.* (in multiplication) veces. —*v.t.* **1,** (measure the time of) calcular o medir el tiempo de. **2,** (choose the time for) hacer a tiempo oportuno. **3,** (regulate) regular; sincronizar. —*adj.* **1,** (of or pert. to time) del tiempo. **2,** (on installment) a plazos. **3,** (equipped with a timer) regulador; horario; de tiempos. —**all the time,** todo el tiempo. —**at all times,** en todo momento. —**at no time,** nunca; en ninguna ocasión. —**at the same time, 1,** (simultaneously) a la vez. **2,** (nevertheless) sin embargo. —**at times,** a veces; unas veces. —**behind the times,** fuera de moda; chapado a la antigua. —**behind time,** atrasado. —**do time,** *colloq.* cumplir una condena; estar encarcelado. —**for some time,** de un tiempo a esta parte. —**for the time being,** por el momento. —**from time to time,** de vez en cuando; una que otra vez. —**gain time,** adelantarse. —**have a good time,** divertirse; pasar un buen rato. —**in due time,** a su tiempo; con tiempo. —**in no time,** al instante; al momento. —**in time, 1,** (eventually) a su tiempo; con tiempo. **2,** (at the appropriate time) a tiempo; con tiempo. **3,** (in rhythm) a compás. —**keep time,** llevar el compás; andar bien (*un reloj*). —**lose time,** atrasarse. —**make time,** ganar tiempo; acelerarse; adelantarse. —**many a time,** muchas veces. —**on time, 1,** (punctual; punctually) puntual(mente); a la hora debida. **2,** (on installment) a plazos. —**out of time, 1,** (untimely) fuera de tiempo. **2,** (out of rhythm) fuera de compás. —**time after time; time and again,** repetidas veces. —**time out,** tiempo de descanso; tiempo descontado. —**time out of mind,** tiempo inmemorable. —**What time is it?,** ¿Qué hora es?

timecard ('taim,kard) *n.* tarjeta registradora.

time clock reloj registrador.

time exposure exposición de tiempo.

time-honored *adj.* anciano; venerable; tradicional.

timekeeper ('taim,ki·pər) *n.* alistador de tiempo; *sports* juez de tiempo.

timeless ('taim·ləs) *adj.* eterno. —**timelessness,** *n.* eternidad.

timely ('taim·li) *adj.* oportuno; a propósito; a tiempo. —**timeliness,** *n.* oportunidad.

timepiece ('taim,pis) *n.* reloj; cronómetro.

timer ('tai·mər) *n.* regulador o marcador de tiempo; *mech.* regulador del encendido.

timeserver ('taim,sʌr·vər) *n.* contemporizador [fem. -dora]. —**timeserving,** *adj.* contemporizador.

timetable ('taim,tei·bəl) *n.* itinerario; horario; guía.

timeworn ('taim,worn) *adj.* gastado por el tiempo; trillado.

time zone *n.* huso horario.

timid ('tim·id) *adj.* tímido; encogido; corto. —**timidity** (ti'mid·ə·ti); **timidness,** *n.* timidez; cortedad.

timing ('tai·miŋ) *n.* **1,** (synchronization) sincronización. **2,** (choice of time) elección de tiempo.

timorous ('tim·ə·rəs) *adj.* tímido; temeroso. —**timorousness,** *n.* timidez; temor.

timothy ('tim·ə·θi) *n., bot.* fleo. *También,* **timothy grass.**

timpani ('tim·pə·ni) *n.pl.* = **tympani.**

tin (tin) *n* **1,** (metal) estaño; lata. **2,** (sheet metal) hojalata; hoja de lata. **3,** (container) lata. —*adj.* **1,** (of tin) de lata. **2,** (valueless) sin valor; falso. —*v.t.* **1,** (cover with tin) estañar. **2,** (preserve in a can) enlatar; envasar.

tincture ('tiŋk·tʃər) *n.* tintura. —*v.t.* tinturar.

tinder ('tin·dər) *n.* yesca.

tine (tain) *n.* diente; púa.

tin foil hoja de estaño; hoja fina.

ting (tiŋ) *n.* retintín; tintineo; tilín. —*v.t.* repicar; sonar. —*v.i.* retiñir; tintinear.

ting-a-ling ('tiŋ·ə,liŋ) *n.* tilín.

tinge (tindʒ) *v.t.* [*ger.* **tingeing** o **tinging**] teñir; colorar; matizar. —*n.* tinte; color; matiz.

tingle ('tiŋ·gəl) *v.i.* hormiguear; picar; sentir hormigueo. —*v.t.* producir hormigueo a o en. —*n.* hormigueo; picazón; comezón.

tinker ('tiŋk·ər) *n.* **1,** (mender of pots and pans) calderero remendón. **2,** (bungler) chapucero. **3,** (bungling work) chapuz. **4,** (repairman) reparador. —*v.t.* chapucear; estropear. —*v.i.* hacer chapucerías. —**not worth a tinker's dam,** no vale un comino. —**tinker with,** entretenerse con; tontear con; enredar.

tinkle ('tiŋ·kəl) *v.i.* tintinear; retiñir; hacer retintín. —*v.t.* repicar; hacer retiñir. —*n.* tintineo; retintín; tilín.

tinny ('tin·i) *adj.* **1,** (of or like tin) de o como estaño. **2,** (flimsy) débil; endeble. **3,** (metallic in sound) que tintinea como el estaño. **4,** (metallic in taste) que sabe a estaño.

tin plate hojalata; hoja de lata. —**tin-plate,** *v.t.* estañar.

tinsel ('tin·səl) *n.* oropel; relumbrón. —*adj.* de oropel; de relumbrón —*v.t.* decorar; adornar.

tinsmith ('tin,smiθ) *n.* hojalatero.

tint (tɪnt) *n.* tinte; color; matiz. —*v.t.* teñir; colorar; matizar.

tintinnabulation (,tɪn·tɪ,næb·jə 'lei·ʃən) *n.* repiqueteo; tintineo.

tintype ('tɪn·taip) *n.* ferrotipo.

tinware ('tɪn·wer) *n.* hojalatería.

tiny ('tai·ni) *adj.* diminuto; menudo; chiquito.

tip (tɪp) *n.* 1, (point) punta. 2, (end) punta; extremo; extremidad. 3, (metal point) contera. 4, (gratuity) propina. 5, (tilt) inclinación. 6, (information) noticia o aviso confidencial. 7, (light blow) golpecito; toque ligero. —*v.t.* [**tipped, tipping**] 1, (tilt) ladear; inclinar. 2, (overturn) volcar. 3, (give a gratuity to) dar una propina a. 4, (provide with a point) poner punta a. 5, (strike lightly) golpear ligeramente; tocar. 6, *colloq.* (inform) informar; soplarle a uno. —*v.i.* inclinarse; ladearse. —**tip off**, *colloq.* informar; advertir. —**tip over**, volcar; volcarse.

tipoff ('tɪp·ɔf) *n., colloq.* advertencia; indirecta; sugerencia.

tippet ('tɪp·ɪt) *n.* bufanda.

tipple ('tɪp·əl) *v.t. & i.* beber mucho. —**tippler** (-lər) *n.* bebedor.

tipster ('tɪp·stər) *n., colloq.* informante confidencial.

tipsy ('tɪp·si) *adj.* chispo; achispado; alegre. —**tipsiness,** *n.* embriaguez; chispa.

tiptoe ('tɪp·to) *n.* punta del pie. —*adj. & adv.* de puntillas. —*v.i.* andar de puntillas.

tiptop ('tɪp·tap) *n.* cima; cumbre. —*adj.* espléndido; soberbio.

tirade ('tai·red) *n.* diatriba; invectiva; tirada.

tire (tair) *v.i.* cansarse; fatigarse; aburrirse. —*v.t.* cansar; fatigar; importunar; aburrir. —*n.* [*también, Brit.* **tyre**] llanta; neumático; goma.

tired (taird) *adj.* cansado; fatigado; aburrido.

tireless ('tair·ləs) *adj.* incansable; infatigable.

tiresome ('tair·səm) *adj.* cansado; aburrido; pesado; tedioso; molesto.

'tis (tɪs) *contr. de* it is.

tissue ('tɪʃ·ju) *n.* tejido. —**tissue paper,** papel de seda.

tit (tɪt) *n.* 1, (nag) jamelgo; jaco; jaca. 2, (bird) paro. 3, (teat) pezón; tetilla. 4, *vulg.* (breast) teta. —**tit for tat,** tal para cual; ojo por ojo.

titan ('tai·tən) *n.* titán. —**titanic**

titanic (tai'tæn·ɪk) *adj.* titánico; titanio; gigante.

titanium (tai'tei·ni·əm) *n.* titanio.

titbit ('tɪt·bɪt) *n.* = **tidbit.**

tithe (taið) *n.* 1, (tenth part) décimo; décima parte. 2, (contribution to the church) diezmo. 3, (small part) pizca. —*v.t. & i.* diezmar.

titi (ti'ti) *n.* 1, (monkey) titi. 2, ('ti·ti) (plant) cirila.

titian ('tɪʃ·ən) *n. & adj.* castaño rojizo.

titillate ('tɪt·ə,leit) *v.t.* cosquillear; hacer titilar; excitar; estimular. —**titillation,** *n.* titilación; cosquilleo; excitación.

titivate ('tɪt·ɪ,veit) *v.t. & i., colloq.* engalanar(se); emperifollar(se). —**titivation,** *n.* engalanamiento; perifollos.

title ('tai·təl) *n.* título; *sports* campeonato. —*v.t.* titular; intitular; nombrar. —**titled,** *adj.* noble; que tiene título de nobleza. —**title deed,** título de propiedad. —**title page,** portada; frontispicio. —**title role,** papel principal; papel que da título a una obra.

titmouse ('tɪt,maus) *n.* paro.

titter ('tɪt·ər) *v.i.* reír nerviosamente. —*n.* risita; risa contenida.

tittle ('tɪt·əl) *n.* pequeño signo; jota; ápice.

tittle-tattle ('tɪt·əl'tæt·əl) *n.* chisme; habladuría. —*v.i.* chismear.

titular ('tɪt·jə·lər) *adj.* titular; nominal.

tizzy ('tɪz·i) *n., slang* excitación sin motivo.

TNT ('ti·ɛn'ti) *n.* trinitrotolueno; TNT.

to (tu) 1, (toward) a; hacia. 2, (as far as; until) a; hasta. 3, (for; intended for) a; para. 4, (into) en. 5, (with relation to) con: *He is very kind to me,* Es muy amable conmigo. 6, (according to) según. 7, (in order to) para. 8, (before, in telling time) menos: *a quarter to three,* las tres menos cuarto. 9, (with necessity or obligation to) por; que: *many things to do,* muchas cosas que hacer; *we have to see it,* tenemos que verlo. 10, (belonging to) de: *the key to the house,* la llave de la casa. 11, *indicando el infinitivo:* to sing, cantar. —*adv.* 1, (forward) hacia adelante. 2, (closed; engaged) cerrado; encajado. 3, (to the matter at hand) a la obra. 4, (near) cerca:

We were close to when it happened, Estábamos muy cerca cuando sucedió. **—as to,** cuanto a. **—come to,** recobrarse; volver en sí. **—to and fro,** de acá para allá; alternativamente.

toad (to:d) *n.* sapo.

toadstool ('tod,stul) *n.* seta venenosa; hongo venenoso.

toady ('to·di) *n.* adulador; zalamero. **—***v.t.* & *i.* halagar; adular.

to-and-fro ('tu·ənd,froːr) *adj.* alternativo; de vaivén.

toast (tost) *n.* 1, (bread) tostada. 2, (compliment) brindis. **—***v.t.* 1, (expose to heat) tostar. 2, (compliment) brindar a o por; beber a la salud de. **—toaster,** *n.* tostador; tostadora.

toastmaster ('tost,mæs·tər) *n.* maestro de ceremonias.

tobacco (tə'bæk·o) *n.* tabaco. **—***adj.* de tabaco; tabacalero. **—tobacco grower,** tabacalero. **—tobacco plantation,** tabacal. **—tobacco pouch,** tabaquera.

tobacconist (tə'bæk·ə,nɪst) *n.* tabaquero.

toboggan (tə'bag·ən) *n.* tobogán. **—***v.i.* 1, (coast on snow) deslizarse en un tobogán. 2, *fig.* (fall rapidly) caer precipitadamente.

tocsin ('tak·sɪn) *n.* 1, (alarm) toque de campana; campanada de alarma. 2, (alarm bell) campana de alarma.

today (tə'dei) *n.* hoy. **—***adv.* hoy; hoy día; actualmente.

toddle ('tad·əl) *v.i.* hacer pinitos; titubear. **—***n.* pinitos; titubeo. **—toddler,** *n.* niño titubeador.

toddy ('tad·i) *n.* ponche.

to-do (tə'duː) *n.* bullicio; lío; conmoción; alharaca.

toe (toː) *n.* 1, (digit of the foot) dedo del pie. 2, (tip of a stocking or shoe) puntera. 3, (forepart of a hoof) pezuña. 4, (half of a cloven hoof) pesuño. 5, (projection; tip) punta; extremo; pie. **—***v.t.* & *i.* tocar, alcanzar o pegar con la punta del pie. **—on one's toes,** alerta. **—toe the line** (o mark), portarse como es debido.

toecap ('toː,kæp) *n.* puntera.

toe hold 1, (footing) agarre con los dedos del pie. 2, (advantage) ventaja. 3, (support for the toe) repisa. 4, (entry; penetration) arraigo; pie.

toenail ('toː,neil) *n.* uña del pie; uña del dedo del pie.

toffee también, **toffy** ('taf·i) *n.* melcocha.

tog (ta:g) *n.*, *colloq.* vestido; traje; *pl.* ropa. **—***v.t.* [**togged, togging**] vestir. **—***v.i.* vestirse.

toga ('to·gə) *n.* toga.

together (tu'geð·ər) *adv.* 1, (assembled) juntos. 2, (at the same time) a la vez; al mismo tiempo. 3, (in succession) sucesivos; sucesivamente; de seguida. 4, (in agreement) de acuerdo. 5, (in common) en común. **—together with,** junto con.

toggery ('tag·ə·ri) *n.*, *colloq.* 1, (clothes) ropa; vestido. 2, (clothing shop) ropería.

toggle ('tag·əl) *n.* 1, (transverse bar or pin) barra traviesa; fiador atravesado. 2, (linkage of levers) palanca acodillada. **—toggle joint,** junta de codillo. **—toggle switch,** interruptor a palanca.

toil (tɔil) *v.i.* afanarse; esforzarse; atarearse. **—***n.* 1, (work) faena; trabajo; esfuerzo; fatiga. 2, *pl.* (snare) trampa; red; lazo. **—toiler,** *n.* trabajador [*fem.* -dora].

toilet ('tɔi·lɪt) *n.* 1, (water closet) retrete; excusado; *Amer.* inodoro. 2, (dressing room) tocador. 3, (personal appearance) vestido; atavío. **—toilet bowl,** taza. **—toilet paper,** papel higiénico o sanitario. **—toilet set,** juego de tocador. **—toilet water,** loción.

toiletry ('tɔi·lɪt·ri) *n.* artículos de tocador.

toilsome ('tɔil·səm) *adj.* fatigoso; penoso.

toilworn ('tɔil·worn) *adj.* cansado; fatigado.

token ('to·kən) *n.* 1, (sign; symbol) señal; símbolo; marca. 2, (keepsake) recuerdo. 3, (coin; counter) ficha; tanto. **—***adj.* nominal; de poco valor. **—by the same token,** de la misma manera; en consecuencia. **—as a token of; in token of,** en señal de.

told (told) *v.*, *pret.* & *p.p. de* **tell.**

tolerable ('tal·ər·ə·bəl) *adj.* 1, (endurable) tolerable; soportable. 2, (passable) pasable; regular; mediano.

tolerance ('tal·ər·əns) *n.* tolerancia. **—tolerant,** *adj.* tolerante.

tolerate ('tal·ə,reit) *v.t.* tolerar; soportar. **—toleration,** *n.* tolerancia.

toll (toːl) *n.* 1, (tax) derecho; impuesto. 2, (fee for travel or transit) peaje; portazgo. **3,** (peal of a bell) doble; toque. **4,** (loss) pérdida. **5,** (mortality) baja; mortalidad. —*v.t. & i.* doblar; tocar; tañer. —**toll bridge,** puente de peaje. —**toll call,** llamada de larga distancia. —**toll collector,** peajero. —**toll gate,** puerta o barrera de peaje. —**toll road,** carretera de peaje.

Toltec ('tal·tɛk) *adj. & n.* tolteca.

toluene ('tal·ju·in) *n.* tolueno.

tom (taːm) *n.* macho de algunos animales.

tomahawk ('tam·ə·hɔk) *n.* hacha de guerra de los indios americanos. —**bury the tomahawk,** hacer las paces.

tomato (tə'mei·to; -'ma-) *n.* **1,** (fruit) tomate; jitomate. **2,** (plant) tomatera.

tomb (tuːm) *n.* tumba; sepulcro.

tomboy ('tam,bɔi) *n.* marimacho.

tombstone ('tum,ston) *n.* lápida funeraria.

tomcat ('tam·kæt) *n.* gato.

tome (toːm) *n.* tomo; libro grande.

tomfool ('tam'ful) *n. & adj.* necio; tonto.

tomfoolery (tam'ful·ə·ri) *n.* payasada; tontería; calaverada.

tommygun ('tam·i,gʌn) *n., colloq.* pistola ametralladora.

tommyrot ('tam·i,rat) *n., slang* disparate; tontería.

tomorrow (tə'mar·o) *n. & adv.* mañana. —**the day after tomorrow,** pasado mañana.

tomtit ('tam·tɪt) *n.* paro; pájaro pequeño.

tom-tom ('tam,tam) *n.* tam-tam.

ton (tʌn) *n.* tonelada.

tonal ('ton·əl) *adj.* tonal.

tonality (to'næl·ə·ti) *n.* tonalidad.

tone (toːn) *n.* tono. —*v.t.* entonar; —**tone arm,** fonocaptor. —**tone color,** timbre. —**tone deaf,** duro de oído. —**tone down,** suavizar el tono (de); moderar(se). —**tone in with,** armonizar con. —**tone poem,** poema sinfónico. —**tone up,** entonar(se); reforzar(se); elevar el tono (de).

tong (taŋ) *n.* sociedad china.

tongs (taŋz) *n.pl.* tenazas; pinzas; tenacillas.

tongue (tʌŋ) *n.* **1,** *anat.* lengua. **2,** (language) idioma; lengua. **3,** *mech.; carp.; mus., etc.* lengüeta; espiga. —*v.t.* **1,** (sound with the tongue) producir (sonidos) con la lengua. **2,** (put a tongue on) poner lengüeta a. **3,** *carp.* ensamblar a lengüeta y ranura. —**hold one's tongue,** morderse la lengua. —**tongue and groove,** lengüeta y ranura. —**tongue in cheek,** chistoso; chistosamente.

tongue-lashing *n.* reprensión; reprimenda.

tongue-tie *n.* impedimento en el habla. —*v.t.* dejar mudo; acallar. —**tongue-tied,** *adj.* que tiene impedimento en el habla; *fig.* mudo; aturdido.

tongue twister trabalenguas.

tonic ('tan·ɪk) *n.* **1,** (medicine; anything invigorating) tónico. **2,** *mus.; phonet.* tónica. —*adj.* tónico. —**tonicity** (to'nɪs·ə·ti) *n.* tonicidad.

tonight (tə'nait) *n. & adv.* esta noche.

tonnage ('tʌn·ɪdʒ) *n.* tonelaje.

tonneau (tə'nor) *n.* [*pl.* neaus o -neaux (-norz)] compartimiento posterior de un automóvil.

tonsil ('tan·səl) *n.* tonsila; amígdala.

tonsillectomy (,tɑn·sə'lɛk·tə·mi) *n.* tonsilectomía.

tonsillitis (,tan·sə'lai·tɪs) *n.* tonsilitis; amigdalitis.

tonsorial (tan'sor·i·əl) *adj.* barberil.

tonsure ('tan·ʃər) *n.* tonsura. —*v.t.* tonsurar.

tony ('ton·i) *adj., colloq.* elegante. —**toniness,** *n., colloq.* elegancia.

too (tuː) *adv.* **1,** (in addition) además; asimismo; también. **2,** (more than enough) demasiado. **3,** (exceedingly) extremadamente.

took (tuk) *v., pret. de* take.

tool (tuːl) *n.* herramienta; instrumento. —*v.t. & i.* **1,** (work with a tool) trabajar con herramienta. **2,** (install machine tools) instalar maquinaria (en).

toot (tut) *n.* **1,** (sound of a horn) toque de bocina, de pito, etc. **2,** *slang* (spree) parranda; juerga. —*v.t.* sonar; tocar. —*v.i.* bocinar; pitar; sonar (una bocina, un pito, etc.).

tooth (tuθ) *n.* [*pl.* **teeth**] diente. —**in the teeth of,** frente a; en desafío de; contra la fuerza de. —**throw (something) in one's teeth,** echar en cara. —**tooth and nail,** desesperadamente; encarnizadamente.

toothache ('tuθ,eik) *n.* dolor de muelas.

toothbrush ('tuθ,brʌʃ) *n.* cepillo de dientes.

toothed (tuːðd) *adj.* dentado; dentellado.

toothless ('tuθ·ləs) *adj.* desdentado; desmolado.

toothpaste ('tuθ,peist) *n.* pasta dentífrica.

toothpick ('tuθ,pɪk) *n.* mondadientes; escarbadientes; palillo.

tooth powder polvo dentífrico.

toothsome ('tuθ·səm) *adj.* sabroso; gustoso.

top (tap) *n.* **1,** (apex; summit) ápice; cima; cumbre; tope. **2,** (head) cabeza; jefe. **3,** (surface) superficie. **4,** (lid; cover) tapa. **5,** (roof) techo. **6,** (toy) trompo; peón; peonza. **7,** *auto.* capota. —*adj.* **1,** (highest) más alto; último; superior. **2,** (principal) principal; primero. **3,** (of or on the surface) superficial. —*v.t.* [**topped, topping**] **1,** (be the top of) coronar; estar encima de. **2,** (be at the top of; head) encabezar. **3,** (furnish with a top) cubrir; tapar. **4,** (reach the top of) alcanzar la cima de. **5,** (get over; vault) salvar; saltar. **6,** (rise above; surpass) aventajar; sobrepasar. **7,** (cut off the top of; lop) descabezar; desmochar. **8,** (complete; perfect) coronar; rematar. —**blow one's top,** *slang* **1,** (lose patience) arrebatarse en ira; enfurecerse. **2,** (become insane) volverse loco. —**from top to bottom,** de arriba abajo. —**from top to toe,** de pies a cabeza. —**on top,** triunfante; victorioso. —**on top of, 1,** (above) encima de. **2,** (besides) además de. **3,** (following upon) luego después de. **4,** (aware of) al corriente de; enterado de. —**on top of the world,** *colloq.* sumamente afortunado, próspero, etc.

topaz ('to·pæz) *n.* topacio. —*adj.* de color de topacio; amarillo.

topcoat ('tap,kot) *n.* abrigo; sobretodo; abrigo de entretiempo.

tope (top) *v.t. & i.* beber con exceso. —**toper,** *n.* bebedor [*fem.* -dora].

topflight ('tap,flait) *adj., colloq.* sobresaliente; superior.

topgallant ('tap,gæl·ənt) *n.* juanete. —**topgallant sail,** juanete.

top hat sombrero de copa.

top-heavy *adj.* demasiado pesado por arriba; inestable; inseguro.

topic ('tap·ɪk) *n.* tema; asunto; tópico.

topical ('tap·ɪ·kəl) *adj.* **1,** (local) tópico. **2,** (of current interest) de interés general; corriente. **3,** (pert. to the topic) temático.

topknot ('tap,nat) *n.* moño.

topless ('tap·ləs) *adj.* con el busto desnudo.

topmast ('tap,mæst) *n.* mastelero.

topmost ('tap·most) *adj.* (el) más alto.

topnotch ('tap,natʃ) *adj., colloq.* excelente; superior.

topography (tə'pag·rə·fi) *n.* topografía. —**topographical** (tap·ə'græf·ɪ·kəl) *adj.* topográfico. —**topographer,** *n.* topógrafo.

topper ('tap·ər) *n.* **1,** (top hat) sombrero de copa. **2,** (woman's topcoat) abrigo de mujer. **3,** *colloq.* (excellent person or thing) persona o cosa de primera clase.

topping ('tap·ɪŋ) *adj.* sobresaliente; superior; excelente. —*n.* **1,** (crest) cresta; copete. **2,** (covering) capa; revestimiento.

topple ('tap·əl) *v.i.* caerse; volcarse; derribarse. —*v.t.* volcar; derribar.

tops (taps) *adj., slang* mejor; de primera clase; superior.

topsail ('tap,seil) *n.* gavia.

top-secret *adj.* lo más secreto.

topsides ('tap·saidz) *n.pl., naut.* borda. —**topside,** *adv.* en o hacia la cubierta.

topsoil ('tap,sɔil) *n.* capa superior del suelo.

topsy-turvy (tap·si'tʌr·vi) *adj.* trastornado; desordenado. —*adv.* al revés. —*n.* desorden; trastorno. —**turn topsy-turvy,** trastornar; trasegar; desordenar.

toque (tok) *n.* toca.

Torah ('to·rə) *n.* Tora.

torch (tortʃ) *n.* **1,** (flaming light) tea; antorcha. **2,** (flashlight) linterna eléctrica. **3,** (blowtorch) soplete; antorcha a soplete. —*v.t., colloq.* pegar fuego a. —**carry a** (o **the**) **torch for,** *slang* estar enamorado de; morirse por.

torchbearer ('tortʃ,bɛr·ər) *n.* **1,** (leader) líder. **2,** *colloq.* (servile follower) secuaz.

torchlight ('tortʃ,lait) *n.* luz de tea o antorcha.

tore (tor) *v., pret. de* **tear.**

toreador ('tor·ɪ·ə,dor) *n.* toreador; torero.

torment (tor'mɛnt) *v.t.* atormentar;

torturar. —*n.* ('tor·mɛnt) tormento. —**tormentor,** *n.* atormentador [*fem.* -dora].

torn (toːrn) *v., p.p. de* tear.

tornado (tor'nei·do) *n.* manga o tromba de viento; tornado.

torpedo (tor'pi·do) *n.* torpedo. —*v.t.* torpedear. —**torpedo boat,** torpedero.

torpid ('tor·pɪd) *adj.* torpe; aletargado.

torpor ('tor·pər) *n.* 1, (sluggishness) torpor; torpeza; entorpecimiento. 2, (stupidity) estupidez. 3, (lethargy) letargo. *También,* **torpidity** (tor'pɪd·ə·ti).

torque (tork) *n.* esfuerzo de torsión o rotación.

torrent ('tor·ənt) *n.* torrente. —**torrential** (to'rɛn·ʃəl) *adj.* torrencial.

torrid ('tor·ɪd) *adj.* tórrido; ardiente.

torsion ('tor·ʃən) *n.* torsión. —**torsional,** *adj.* de torsión; torsional.

torso ('tor·so) *n.* tronco; torso.

tort (tort) *n., law* agravio indemnizable.

tortilla (tor'ti·jə) *n.* torta de harina de maíz; *Mex.* tortilla.

tortoise ('tor·təs) *n.* tortuga.

tortoise shell carey. —**tortoiseshell,** *adj.* de carey; de color carey.

tortuous ('tor·tʃu·əs) *adj.* tortuoso. —**tortuousness; tortuosity** (-'as·ə·ti) *n.* tortuosidad.

torture ('tor·tʃər) *n.* tortura; tormento. —*v.t.* 1, (put to torture) torturar. 2, (distort) torcer; deformar. —**torturer,** *n.* torturador [*fem.* -dora]. —**torturous,** *adj.* torturador.

tory ('tor·i) *n. & adj.* conservador; tory.

toss (tɔs) *v.t.* 1, (throw) arrojar; echar; tirar; lanzar. 2, (shake; tumble about) voltear; menear; agitar. 3, (jerk) sacudir. —*v.i.* 1, (sway) mecerse; ondear. 2, (move restlessly) agitarse; menearse. 3, (flip a coin) jugar cara y cruz. —*n.* 1, (throw) echada; tiro. 2, (shake; shaking) meneo; agitación. 3, (jerk) sacudida. —**toss off, 1,** (do offhandedly) hacer rápidamente o improvisadamente. 2, (gulp down) tragar de golpe. —**toss up,** jugar a cara y cruz.

tosspot ('tɔs,pat) *n.* bebedor [*fem.* -dora]; borrachín [*fem.* -china].

toss-up *n.* 1, (tossing of a coin) cara y cruz. 2, *colloq.* (even chance) probabilidad igual.

tot (tat) *n.* 1, (small child) nene; chiquito. 2, (small quantity) poco; pizca. —*v.t., colloq.* [**totted, totting**] sumar. —**tot up,** *colloq.* sumar.

total ('to·təl) *adj. & n.* total. —*v.t.* 1, (add) sumar. 2, (amount to) ascender a.

totalitarian (to,tæl·ɪ'tɛr·i·ən) *adj. & n.* totalitario. —**totalitarianism,** *n.* totalitarismo.

totality (to'tæl·ə·ti) *n.* totalidad.

tote (tot) *v.t., colloq.* llevar; cargar. —*n., colloq.* carga; acarreo. —**tote bag,** bolsa grande.

totem ('tot·əm) *n.* tótem. —*adj.* totémico. —**totemism,** *n.* totemismo. —**totem pole,** pilar totémico.

totter ('tat·ər) *v.i.* tambalearse. —*n.* tambaleo. —**tottery,** *adj.* tambaleante.

toucan (tu'kan) *n.* tucán; *Amer.* picofeo.

touch (tʌtʃ) *v.t.* 1, (come in contact with) tocar. 2, (reach; attain) alcanzar. 3, (move emotionally) conmover; impresionar 4, (affect) afectar. 5, (be equal to) igualar. 6, *slang* (borrow or beg from) dar un sablazo a. —*v.i.* tocar; tocarse. —*n.* 1, (sense of feeling) tacto. 2, (act of touching; detail of handiwork; skill or style) toque. 3, (small quantity or degree) poquito; pizca. 4, *slang* (cadging) sablazo. —**in touch with, 1,** (in communication with) en comunicación con; en contacto con. 2, (informed about) enterado de; al corriente de. —**touch at,** hacer escala en. —**touch off, 1,** (detonate) descargar. 2, (provoke) provocar; estimular. 3, (represent accurately) representar con precisión; acabar. —**touch on** o **upon, 1,** (approach) aproximarse a. 2, (refer to; treat) referirse a; tocar el tema de. —**touch up,** retocar.

touch and go ('tʌtʃ·ən,go) situación precaria o arriesgada. —**touch-and-go,** *adj.* arriesgado; difícil.

touchdown ('tʌtʃ·daun) *n.* jugada *(de fútbol)*; tanto.

touched (tʌtʃt) *adj.* 1, (demented) tocado. 2, (affected with emotion) emocionado.

touching ('tʌtʃ·ɪŋ) *prep.* referente

a; acerca de. —*adj.* conmovedor; impresionante.

touchstone ('tʌtʃ,ston) *n.* piedra de toque.

touchwood ('tʌtʃ,wud) *n.* yesca.

touchy ('tʌtʃ·i) *adj.* **1,** (irritable) quisquilloso; susceptible **2,** (risky) arriesgado; delicado. —**touchiness**, *n.* susceptibilidad.

tough (tʌf) *adj.* duro. —*n.* maleante; pendenciero; rufián. —**tough luck**, mala suerte; desgracia.

toughen ('tʌf·ən) *v.t.* endurecer. —*v.i.* endurecerse.

toughness ('tʌf·nəs) *n.* dureza.

toupee (tu'pei) *n.* tupé.

tour (tur) *n.* **1,** (travel) excursión; recorrido; jira. **2,** (shift) turno. —*v.i.* viajar. —*v.t.* recorrer; visitar.

touring (tur·ɪŋ) *n.* turismo. —*adj.* turístico.

tourist ('tur·ɪst) *n.* turista. —*adj.* turístico; de turista. —**tourism**, *n.* turismo.

tourmaline ('tur·mə,lin) *n.* turmalina.

tournament ('tur·nə·mənt) *n.* torneo; justa.

tourney ('tur·ni) *n.* torneo; justa. —*v.i.* tornear; justar.

tourniquet ('tur·nɪ·kɛt) *n.* torniquete.

tousle ('tau·zəl) *v.t.* despeinar; desgreñar. —*n.* enredo; maraña.

tout (taut) *v.i.* **1,** (in racing) vender información. **2,** (canvass) solicitar negocios o votos. **3,** (spy) espiar. —*v.t.* **1,** (praise) elogiar; dar bombo. **2,** (in racing) vender información a. —*n.* espía; solicitante.

tow (to) remolcar. —*n.* **1,** (act of towing) remolque. **2,** (fiber) estopa. —**towage**, *n.* remolque.

toward (tord; tword) *prep.* **1,** (in the direction of) hacia. **2,** (in furtherance of) en apoyo de. **3,** (with respect to) tocante a; para con. **4,** (near) cerca de. *También,* **towards.**

towboat ('to·bot) *n.* remolcador.

towel ('tau·əl) *n.* toalla. —*v.t.* secar con toalla. —**toweling**, *n.* género para toallas. —**towel rack**, toallero.

tower ('tau·ər) *n.* torre. —*v.i.* elevarse; sobresalir. —**towering**, *adj.* elevado; sobresaliente.

towheaded ('to,hɛd·ɪd) *adj.* de pelo rubio claro o pajizo.

towline ('to·lain) *n.* cable de remolque; sirga. *También,* **tow line.**

town (taun) *n.* ciudad; pueblo;

municipio. —**go to town,** *slang* **1,** (go on a spree) ir de parranda. **2,** (work diligently) aplicarse; esmerarse. **3,** (be successful) tener éxito. —**on the town,** en la calle. —**paint the town red,** *slang* ir de parranda.

town council concejo municipal.

town crier pregonero.

town hall casa de ayuntamiento.

town house casa de ciudad.

townhouse ('taun,haus) *n., Brit.* casa de ayuntamiento.

town meeting reunión de vecinos.

townsfolk ('taunz,fok) *n.pl.* vecinos.

township ('taun·ʃɪp) *n.* **1,** (unit of territory) municipio; término municipal. **2,** (town) ciudad.

townsman ('taunz·mən) *n.* [*pl.* -men] ciudadano; conciudadano; vecino.

townspeople ('taunz,pi·pəl) *n.pl.* vecinos.

towpath ('to,pæθ) *n.* camino de sirga.

towrope ('to,rop) *n.* cable de remolque; sirga. *También,* **tow rope.**

tow truck camión de remolque.

toxemia (tak'si·mi·ə) *n.* toxemia.

toxic ('tak·sɪk) *adj.* tóxico. —**toxicant**, *n.* tóxico. —**toxicity** (tak'sɪs·ə·ti) *n.* toxicidad.

toxicology (tak·sɪ'kal·ə·dʒi) *n.* toxicología. —**toxicological** (-kə·'ladʒ·ɪ·kəl) *adj.* toxicológico. —**toxicologist**, *n.* toxicólogo.

toxin ('tak·sɪn) *n.* toxina.

toy (tɔi) *n.* **1,** (plaything) juguete. **2,** (trifle) fruslería; bagatela. **3,** (dog) perrito; perrillo. —*adj.* **1,** (toylike) semejante a un juguete; de jugar. **2,** (decorative) de adorno. **3,** (diminutive) diminuto; pequeñito. —*v.i.* jugar; juguetear.

toyshop ('tɔi,ʃap) *n.* juguetería.

trace (treis) *n.* **1,** (mark) rastro; huella; señal. **2,** (small quantity) pizca. **3,** (line) trazo. **4,** (copy) calco. **5,** (harness) tirante. —*v.t.* **1,** (follow the track of) rastrear. **2,** (investigate) investigar; hallar el origen de. **3,** (copy) trazar; calcar. **4,** (plan) diseñar; planear. —**tracer**, *n.* & *adj.* trazador; rastreador. —**tracer bullet**, bala trazante.

tracery ('trei·sə·ri) *n.* tracería.

trachea ('trei·ki·ə) *n.* tráquea. —**tracheal**, *adj.* traqueal.

tracheotomy (ˌtrei·kiˈat·ə·mi) *n.* traqueotomía.

trachoma (trəˈko·mə) *n.* tracoma.

tracing ('trei·siŋ) *n.* calco; trazo.

track (træk) *n.* **1,** (trace; trail) huella; rastro; pisada. **2,** (rails) vía; carriles; rieles. **3,** (race course) pista de carreras. **4,** (running and jumping sports) carreras y saltos. **5,** (path) sendero; vereda. **6,** (sequence) sucesión; serie. **7,** (course of motion) trayectoria. **8,** *mech.* (rail; runner) corredera. **9,** (wake of a ship) estela. —*v.t.* **1,** (pursue; trace) perseguir; rastrear. **2,** (make a track on or with) dejar huellas en o de. **3,** (traverse) atravesar; cruzar. —**in one's tracks,** allí mismo; en el acto. —**keep track of,** mantener en orden; mantener comunicación con. —**lose track of,** perder de vista; alejarse de. —**make tracks,** *colloq.* marcharse; huirse. —**off the track,** desviado; descarrilado. —**on the (right) track,** en el rastro; en el buen camino. —**track down,** buscar; perseguir; capturar. —**track record,** *colloq.* expediente de éxitos y de fracasos.

track meet concurso de carreras y saltos.

tract (trækt) *n.* **1,** (region) región; comarca; terreno. **2,** *anat.* sistema; canal. **3,** (brief treatise) opúsculo; folleto.

tractable ('træk·tə·bəl) *adj.* dócil; tratable. —**tractability** (-ˈbɪl·ə·ti) *n.* docilidad.

tractile ('træk·tɪl) *adj.* dúctil.

traction ('træk·ʃən) *n.* tracción.

tractor ('træk·tər) *n.* tractor.

trade (treid) *n.* **1,** (commerce) comercio; tráfico; trato; negocio. **2,** (occupation) oficio. **3,** (exchange) trueque; canje. **4,** (customers) clientes; clientela. **5,** *pl.* = **trade winds.** —*v.t.* trocar; cambiar; dar en cambio. —*v.i.* comerciar; dedicarse al comercio. —**trade on,** explotar; aprovecharse de.

trade-in *n.* objeto dado en pago parcial de una compra.

trademark ('treid,mark) *n.* marca de fábrica; marca registrada.

trade name razón social; marca de fábrica; marca registrada.

trade-off *n.* trueque; cambio.

trader ('trei·dər) *n.* comerciante; negociante; tratante.

tradesman ('treidz·mən) *n.* [*pl.* -**men**] mercader; tendero.

trade union sindicato; gremio de obreros.

trade winds vientos alisios.

trading ('trei·diŋ) *n.* comercio; negocio. —*adj.* mercantil; comercial. —**trading post,** factoría.

tradition (trəˈdɪʃ·ən) *n.* tradición. —**traditional,** *adj.* tradicional. —**traditionalism,** *n.* tradicionalismo. —**traditionalist,** *n. & adj.* tradicionalista.

traduce (trəˈdjus) *v.t.* calumniar; difamar.

traffic ('træf·ɪk) *n.* **1,** (trade) tráfico; trato. **2,** (circulation) tráfico; tránsito. —*v.i.* [**trafficked, trafficking**] traficar. —**traffic circle,** glorieta de tráfico. —**traffic jam,** congestión; *W.I.* tapón; *S.A.* taco.

trafficker ('træf·ɪk·ər) *n.* traficante.

tragedy ('trædʒ·ə·di) *n.* tragedia. —**tragedian** (trəˈdʒi·di·ən) *n.* trágico. —**tragedienne** (trəˌdʒi·di'en) *n.f.* trágica.

tragic ('trædʒ·ɪk) *adj.* trágico. También, **tragical.**

tragicomedy (ˌtrædʒ·ɪˈkam·ə·di) *n.* tragicomedia. —**tragicomic,** *adj.* tragicómico.

trail (treil) *v.t.* **1,** (drag loosely) arrastrar. **2,** (track) rastrear; seguir la pista de. **3,** *colloq.* (follow) seguir; andar detrás de. **4,** (make a path through) abrir o marcar una senda por. **5,** (carry, as by the feet) llevar; pisar. —*v.i.* **1,** (be dragged) ser arrastrado; arrastrarse. **2,** (proceed idly; lag) proceder lentamente; rezagarse. **3,** (be dispersed) dispersarse. **4,** (creep, as plants) trepar. —*n.* **1,** (path) sendero; vereda. **2,** (track) rastro; huella; pista. **3,** (something that trails behind) cola; estela. —**trail off,** disminuir poco a poco.

trailblazer *n.* precursor [*fem.* -sora]; iniciador [*fem.* -dora]; pionero.

trailer ('trei·lər) *n.* **1,** (vehicle) remolque; camión acoplado. **2,** (mobile house) casa rodante; coche-habitación. **3,** (trailing plant) planta rastrera. **4,** *motion pictures* anuncio de próximas películas.

train (trein) *n.* **1,** *R.R.* tren. **2,** (persons, vehicles, etc. traveling together) procesión; cortejo. **3,** (retinue) comitiva; séquito. **4,** (something that trails behind) cola. **5,** (series) serie; sucesión; tren.

—*v.t.* **1,** (instruct) adiestrar; entrenar. **2,** (aim) apuntar. —*v.i.* adiestrarse; entrenarse. —**trainee,** *n.* persona que se adiestra; novicio; recluta. —**trainer,** *n.* entrenador [*fem.* -dora]; (*of animals*) amaestrador [*fem.* -dora].

training ('trei·nɪŋ) *n.* **1,** (instruction) instrucción; educación. **2,** (development of skills) adiestramiento; entrenamiento.

trainman ('trein·mən) *n.* [*pl.* -men] ferroviario.

traipse (traips) *v.i., colloq.* caminar.

trait (treit) *n.* rasgo; característica; cualidad.

traitor ('trei·tər) *n.* traidor. —**traitorous,** *adj.* traidor; traicionero. —**traitress** (-trɪs) *n.f.* traidora.

trajectory (trə'dʒɛk·tə·ri) *n.* trayectoria.

tram (træm) *n.* **1,** (wheeled car) corro; vagón; vagoneta. **2,** *Brit.* (streetcar) tranvía.

tramcar ('træm·kar) *n., Brit.* tranvía.

trammel ('træm·əl) *n.* **1,** (impediment) impedimento; obstáculo. **2,** (instrument for drawing ellipses) compás de vara. **3,** (shackle) grillete; maniota; traba. —*v.t.* trabar; impedir.

trammel net trasmallo.

tramp (træmp) *v.i.* **1,** (walk with a heavy step) pisar con fuerza; andar pesadamente. **2,** (walk resolutely) andar con resolución. **3,** (wander) vagar; vagabundear. —*v.t.* **1,** (traverse on foot) viajar a pie por; recorrer. **2,** (trample underfoot) hollar; pisotear. —*n.* **1,** (heavy tread) paso pesado; marcha pesada. **2,** (sound) ruido de pisadas. **3,** (long walk) caminata; paseo largo. **4,** (vagabond) vagabundo. **5,** (ship) buque de carga volandero. **6,** (prostitute) ramera.

trample ('træm·pəl) *v.t.* pisotear; hollar. —*n.* pisoteo.

trampoline (,træm·pə'lin) *n.* trampolín.

tramp steamer vapor volandero.

tramway ('træm·wei) *n., Brit.* tranvía.

trance (træns) *n.* **1,** (hypnotic state) estupor; catalepsia; estado hipnótico. **2,** (rapture) rapto; éxtasis; arrobamiento. **3,** (daze) reverie) ofuscación; ensimismamiento.

tranquil ('træŋ·kwɪl) *adj.*

tranquilo; sereno. —**tranquillity** (træŋ'kwɪl·ə·ti) *n.* tranquilidad. —**tranquilize,** *v.t.* tranquilizar. —**tranquilizer,** *n.* tranquilizante.

transact (træns'ækt) *v.t. & i.* tramitar; negociar; llevar a cabo.

transaction (træns'æk·ʃən) *n.* **1,** (negotiation; deal) transacción; tramitación; negocio. **2,** *pl.* (proceedings) actos; trabajos.

transatlantic (,træns·ət'læn·tɪk) *adj.* transatlántico.

transceiver (træn'si·vər) *n.* transceptor; aparato transmisor-receptor.

transcend (træn'sɛnd) *v.t.* trascender. —**transcendence,** *n.* trascendencia. —**transcendent,** *adj.* trascendente. —**transcendental** (,træn·sɛn'dɛn·təl) *adj.* trascendental. —**transcendentalism,** *n.* trascendentalismo.

transcontinental (,træns·kan·tɪ 'nɛn·təl) *adj.* transcontinental.

transcribe (træn'skraib) *v.t.* transcribir.

transcript ('træn·skrɪpt) *n.* trasunto; copia; *Amer.* transcrito; *educ.* certificado de estudios.

transcription (træn'skrɪp·ʃən) *n.* transcripción.

transept ('træn·sɛpt) *n.* crucero.

transfer (træns'fʌr) *v.t.* **1,** (make over possession of) transferir; traspasar. **2,** (convey) transportar; trasladar. **3,** (transship) transbordar. **4,** (relocate) trasladar. **5,** (copy) reproducir; reportar. **6,** (trace) calcar. —*v.i.* cambiar *(de tren, tranvía, etc.);* transbordar. —*n.* ('træns·fər) **1,** (taking over possession) transferencia; traspaso. **2,** (transport) transporte; traslado. **3,** (relocation) traslado. **4,** (copy) reproducción; copia. **5,** (tracing) calco. **6,** (ticket of transfer) billete de transferencia. **7,** (changing of vehicles) transbordo. —**transferable,** *adj.* transferible. —**transference** (-'fʌr·əns) *n.* transferencia.

transfigure (træns'fɪg·jər) *v.t.* transfigurar. —**transfiguration,** *n.* transfiguración. —**transfigurement,** *n.* transfiguración.

transfix (træns'fɪks) *v.t.* **1,** (pierce through) traspasar; atravesar. **2,** (impale) empalar; espetar. **3,** (astound) dejar atónito. —**transfixion** ('fɪk·ʃən) *n.* transfixión.

transfixed (træns'fɪkst) *adj.* **1,**

(pierced; impaled) transfijo. **2,** (astounded) atónito.

transform (træns'form) *v.t.* transformar. —**transformation** (ˌtrænsfər'mei·ʃən) *n.* transformación. —**transformer,** *n.* transformador.

transformism (træns'formɪz·əm) *n.* transformismo. —**transformist,** *n.* transformista.

transfuse (træns'fjuːz) *v.t.* transfundir. —**transfusion** (-'fjuːʒən) *n.* transfusión.

transgress (træns'grɛs) *v.t.* **1,** (go beyond) traspasar; exceder. **2,** (violate) transgredir; infringir. —*v.i.* propasarse; excederse; pecar. —**transgression** (-'grɛʃ·ən) *n.* transgresión; pecado. —**transgressor,** *n.* transgresor [*fem.* -sora]; pecador [*fem.* -dora].

transient ('træn·ʃənt) *adj.* transitorio; pasajero. —*n.* transeúnte. —**transience,** *n.* transitoriedad.

transistor (træn'sɪs·tər) *n.* transistor.

transit ('træn·sɪt) *n.* tránsito.

transition (træn'zɪʃ·ən) *n.* transición. —**transitional,** *adj.* transitorio; de transición.

transitive ('træn·sə·tɪv) *adj.* & *n.* transitivo.

transitory ('træn·sə·tor·i) *adj.* transitorio; pasajero. —**transitoriness,** *n.* transitoriedad.

translate (træns'leit) *v.t.* traducir. —**translator,** *n.* traductor.

translation (træns'lei·ʃən) *n.* **1,** (interpretation) traducción; versión. **2,** *mech.* traslación.

transliterate (træns'lɪt·ər·eit) *v.t.* transcribir. —**transliteration,** *n.* transcripción; transliteración.

translucent (træns'lu·sənt) *adj.* translúcido. —**translucence,** *n.* translucidez.

transmigration (ˌtrans·mai'grei·ʃən) *n.* transmigración. —**transmigrate.** *v.i.* transmigrar.

transmissible (træns'mɪs·ə·bəl) *adj.* transmisible. —**transmissibility,** *n.* transmisibilidad.

transmission (træns'mɪʃ·ən) *n.* transmisión.

transmit (træns'mɪt) *v.t.* transmitir. —**transmittal,** *n.* transmisión. —**transmitter,** *n.* transmisor.

transmute (træns'mjut) *v.t.* transmutar. —**transmutation** (ˌtræns·mju'tei·ʃən) *n.* transmutación.

transom ('træn·səm) *n.* **1,** (of a door or window) montante. **2,** (crossbeam) travesaño.

transparent (træns'pɛr·ənt) *adj.* transparente. —**transparence; transparency,** *n.* transparencia.

transpire (træn'spair) *v.i.* **1,** (exhale; perspire) transpirar. **2,** (become known) trascender; transpirar. **3,** (happen) acontecer; suceder. —**transpiration** (-spɪ'rei·ʃən) *n.* transpiración.

transplant (træns'plænt) *v.t.* trasplantar. —*n.* ('træns-) trasplante. —**transplantation** (ˌtrænsplæn'tei·ʃən) *n.* trasplante.

transponder (træn'span·dər) *n.* radiofaro de respuesta.

transport (træns'port) *v.t.* **1,** (convey; imbue with emotion) transportar. **2,** (banish) deportar. —*n.* ('træns·port) transporte.

transportation (ˌtræns·por'tei·ʃən) *n.* **1,** (act or means of transporting) transporte. **2,** (travel expenses) coste del transporte. **3,** (travel ticket) pasaje; billete de viaje.

transpose (træns'poz) *v.t.* transponer; *mus.* transportar. —**transposition** (-pə'zɪʃ·ən) *n.* transposición; *mus.* transportación.

transship (træn'ʃɪp) *v.t.* transbordar. —**transshipment,** *n.* transbordo.

transsonic (træn'sa·nɪk) *adj.* transónico.

transubstantiate (træn·səb'stæn·ʃi·eit) *v.t.* transubstanciar. —**transubstantiation,** *n.* transubstanciación.

transverse (træns'vʌrs) *adj.* transverso; transversal. —**transversal,** *n.* transversal.

transvestism (trænz'vɛs·tɪz·əm) *también,* **transvestitism** (-tɪtɪz·əm) *n.* transvestismo. —**transvestic,** *adj.* transvestista. —**transvestite** (-tait) *n.* transvestista.

trap (træp) *n.* **1,** (snare) trampa; cepo. **2,** (trapdoor) trampa; escotillón. **3,** (bend in a pipe) sifón. **4,** *pl.* (baggage) equipaje. **5,** *pl.* (percussion instrument) instrumentos de percusión; batería. **6,** (carriage) carruaje ligero de dos ruedas. **7,** *slang* (mouth) boca. —*v.t.* [**trapped, trapping**] **1,** (catch) entrampar; atrapar. **2,** (adorn) adornar; enjaezar. —*v.i.* entrampar.

trapdoor ('træp·dor) *n.* trampa; escotillón. *También,* **trap door.**

trapeze (trə'piːz) *n.* trapecio.
trapezium (trə'piːzi·əm) *n.* **1,** *geom.* trapezoide. **2,** *anat.* trapecio.
trapezoid ('træp·ɪ·zɔid) *n.* **1,** *geom.* trapecio. **2,** *anat.* trapezoide.
trapezoidal (ˌtræp·ə'zɔi·dəl) *adj.* trapezoidal.
trapper ('træp·ər) *n.* el que caza con trampas; trampero.
trappings ('træp·ɪŋz) *n. pl.* **1,** (harness) jaeces; arreos. **2,** (adornments) adornos.
Trappist ('træp·ɪst) *adj. & n.* trapense.
traprock ('træp,rak) *n.* roca ígnea, como el basalto.
trapshooting ('træp,ʃu·tɪŋ) *n.* tiro de pichón.
trash (træʃ) *n.* basura; desecho; desperdicio. —*v.t.,* *slang.* destrozar. —**trashy,** *adj.* fútil; despreciable. —**trash can,** basurero.
trauma ('trɔ·mə; 'trau-) *n.* trauma. —**traumatic** (-'mæt·ɪk) *adj.* traumático. —**traumatism** (-tɪz·əm) *n.* traumatismo. —**traumatize** (-taiz) *v.t.* traumatizar.
travail ('træv·eil) *n.* **1,** (hard work) afán; pena; labor penosa. **2,** (labor pains) parto; dolores de parto. —*v.i.* **1,** (toil) afanarse; esforzarse. **2,** (suffer labor pains) estar de parto.
travel ('træv·əl) *v.i.* **1,** (move; proceed) viajar. **2,** *colloq.* (move speedily) correr. —*v.t.* viajar por; recorrer. —*n.* **1,** (act of traveling; journey) viaje. **2,** (traffic) circulación; tráfico. **3,** *mech.* movimiento; carrera.
traveler ('træv·əl·ər) *n.* viajero; *comm.* viajante. —**traveler's check,** cheque de viajeros.
traveling ('træv·ə·lɪŋ) *adj.* **1,** (journeying) viajante. **2,** (of or for travel) de viaje; para viajar. **3,** *mech.* corredizo. —**traveling expenses,** gastos de viaje. —**traveling salesman,** viajante.
travelogue *también,* **travelog** ('træv·ə,lɔg; -,lag) *n.* conferencia ilustrada sobre viajes.
traverse (trə'vʌrs) *v.t.* **1,** (pass across) atravesar; cruzar; recorrer. **2,** (contradict; obstruct) contradecir; estorbar. **3,** (turn and aim a gun) volver y apuntar. —*n.* ('træv·ɜrs) **1,** (crosspiece) travesaño. **2,** (traversing) travesía. —*adj.* transversal.
travesty ('træv·ɪs·ti) *n.* parodia; farsa. —*v.t.* parodiar.

trawl (trɔl) *n.* red barredera. —*v.t. & i.* pescar rastreando. —**trawler,** *n.* barco rastreador.
tray (trei) *n.* **1,** (serving plate) bandeja; azafate. **2,** (trough) batea; cubeta. **3,** (case) cajón.
treachery ('tretʃ·ə·ri) *n.* traición; perfidia; deslealtad. —**treacherous,** *adj.* traidor; traicionero; alevoso. —**treacherousness,** *n.* traición; perfidia.
treacle ('triː·kəl) *n.* melaza.
tread (tred) *v.i.* [*pret.* **trod;** *p.p.* **trod** o **trodden**] andar; caminar; pisar. —*v.t.* **1,** (walk in, on or along; trample) hollar; pisar; pisotear. **2,** (execute by walking or dancing) andar; bailar. —*n.* **1,** (step; stepping) paso; pisada. **2,** (surface that touches the ground) superficie de rodadura; banda. **3,** (bearing surface) cara. **4,** (support for the foot) peldaño; escalón.
treadle ('tred·əl) *n.* pedal.
treadmill ('tred·mɪl) *n.* molino de rueda de andar.
treason ('triː·zən) *n.* traición. —**treasonable,** *adj.* traidor; desleal. —**treasonous,** *adj.* traidor; traicionero.
treasure ('treʒ·ər) *n.* tesoro. —*v.t.* **1,** (collect and save) atesorar. **2,** (prize) apreciar.
treasurer ('treʒ·ər·ər) *n.* tesorero.
treasure trove tesoro hallado.
treasury ('treʒ·ə·ri) *n.* **1,** (funds) erario; tesoro. **2,** (place) tesorería. **3,** (ministry) ministerio de hacienda.
treat (trit) *v.t.* **1,** (deal with; subject to a process) tratar. **2,** (entertain) agasajar; regalar. —*v.i.* **1,** (discuss; carry on negotiations) tratar. **2,** (bear the expense of regalement) convidar; regalar. —*n.* **1,** (regalement) convite. **2,** *colloq.* (anything enjoyable) solaz; deleite; placer. —**treat as,** tomar de. —**treat of,** tratar de.
treatise ('triː·tɪs) *n.* tratado.
treatment ('trit·mənt) *n.* tratamiento; trato.
treaty ('triː·ti) *n.* tratado; convenio; pacto.
treble ('treb·əl) *adj.* **1,** (threefold) triple. **2,** (high in pitch) sobreagudo; de tiple. —*n.* tiple; sobreagudo. —*v.t.* triplicar. —*v.i.* triplicarse. —**treble clef,** clave de sol.
trebly ('treb·li) *adv.* tres veces.
tree (triː) *n.* **1,** *bot.; mech.* árbol. **2,** (gallows) horca. **3,** (cross) cruz.

—*v.t.* obligar a refugiarse en un árbol; *fig.* apremiar; acosar.

treetop ('tri,tap) *n.* copa; cima de árbol.

trefoil ('tri·fɔil) *n.* trébol.

trek (trɛk) *v.i.* [**trekked, trekking**] emigrar; viajar. —*n.* emigración; viaje.

trellis ('trɛl·ɪs) *n.* enrejado; espaldera.

tremble ('trɛm·bəl) *v.i.* temblar; estremecerse. —*n.* temblor; estremecimiento. —**trembly** (-bli) *adj.* trémulo; tembloroso.

tremendous (trɪ'mɛn·dəs) *adj.* tremendo; enorme. —**tremendousness,** *n.* enormidad.

tremolo ('trɛm·ə·lo) *n.* trémolo.

tremor ('trɛm·ər) *n.* tremor; temblor; vibración.

tremulous ('trɛm·jə·ləs) *adj.* **1,** (trembling) trémulo. **2,** (timid; irresolute) tímido; indeciso. —**tremulousness,** *n.* temblor.

trench (trɛntʃ) *n.* **1,** (ditch) zanja. **2,** *mil.* trinchera. —*v.t.* zanjar; atrincherar. —*v.i.* hacer trincheras; atrincherarse.

trenchant ('trɛn·tʃənt) *adj.* **1,** (incisive) mordaz; punzante. **2,** (vigorous) eficaz; enérgico. **3,** (thoroughgoing) cabal; bien definido. —**trenchancy,** *n.* mordacidad; eficacia; energía.

trench coat abrigo impermeable; trinchera.

trencherman ('trɛn·tʃər·mən) *n.* [*pl.* -**men**] glotón; comilón.

trench mouth inflamación de las mucosas de la boca.

trend (trɛnd) *n.* tendencia; dirección; curso; inclinación. —*v.i.* tender; dirigirse. —**trendy,** *adj.,* *colloq.* de moda; a la moda.

trepan (trə'pæn) *n.* trépano. —*v.t.* [-**panned, -panning**] trepanar. —**trepanning,** *n.* trepanación.

trepidation (,trɛp·ə'dei·ʃən) *n.* trepidación; miedo.

trespass ('trɛs·pəs) *v.i.* **1,** (encroach) entrar sin directo; infringir. **2,** (sin) pecar. —*n.* **1,** (encroachment) infracción; violación. **2,** (sin) transgresión; pecado. —**no trespassing,** prohibida la entrada; prohibido el paso.

trespasser ('trɛs,pæs·ər) *n.* **1,** (intruder) intruso. **2,** (encroacher) violador [*fem.* -dora]; infractor [*fem.* -tora]. **3,** (sinner) pecador [*fem.* -dora].

tress (trɛs) *n.* **1,** (lock; braid of hair) rizo; bucle; trenza. **2,** *pl.* (hair of the head) cabellera.

trestle ('trɛs·əl) *n.* **1,** (sawhorse) caballete. **2,** (bridge) puente de caballetes.

trey (trei) *n.* tres.

triad ('trai·æd) *n.* terna; tríada.

trial ('trai·əl) *n.* **1,** *law* juicio; proceso. **2,** (test) prueba; examen. **3,** (attempt) ensayo; tentativa. **4,** (hardship) aflicción; tribulación. —*adj.* **1,** *law* judicial; probatorio. **2,** (experimental) experimental; de prueba. —**trial balance,** balance de comprobación. —**trial balloon,** medio de probar la opinión pública. —**trial and error,** tanteo; prueba.

triangle ('trai·æŋ·gəl) *n.* **1,** *geom.; mus.; fig.* triángulo. **2,** (drawing instrument) cartabón; escuadra. —**triangular** (trai'æŋ·gju·lər) *adj.* triangular; triángulo.

triangulate (trai'æŋ·gju·leit) *v.t.* triangular. —**triangulation,** *n.* triangulación.

tribe (traib) *n.* tribu. —**tribal,** *adj.* tribal; tribal.

tribesman ('traibz·mən) *n.* [*pl.* -**men**] miembro de una tribu.

tribulation (,trɪb·jə'lei·ʃən) *n.* tribulación.

tribunal (trai'bju·nəl) *n.* tribunal; juzgado.

tribune ('trɪb·jun) *n.* **1,** (Roman magistrate; defender of the people) tribuno; defensor del pueblo. **2,** (dais) tribuna.

tributary ('trɪb·jə·tɛr·i) *n. & adj.* tributario.

tribute ('trɪb·jut) *n.* tributo.

trice (trais) *n.* momento; instante. —**in a trice,** en un abrir y cerrar de ojos.

tricentennial (,trai·sɛn'tɛn·i·əl) *adj. & n.* = **tercentenary.**

triceps ('trai·sɛps) *n.* tríceps.

trichina (trɪ'kai·nə) *n.* triquina.

trichinosis (,trɪk·ə'no·sɪs) *n.* triquinosis.

trick (trɪk) *n.* **1,** (stunt; feat) juego; jugada; ejercicio de habilidad; acrobacia. **2,** (ruse; deception) treta; ardid; artificio. **3,** (hoax; swindle) trampa; estafa; engaño; truco. **4,** (prank; practical joke) chasco; broma; burla; travesura. **5,** (peculiar habit) costumbre; vicio. **6,** *cards* baza. **7,** *colloq.* (girl) chiquita; muchacha. **8,** (turn of work or duty) turno; tarea; tanda. —*adj.* **1,** (deceptive) fraudulento. **2,** (crafty) astuto; mañoso. **3,** (involving skill) ingenioso; acrobático; sensacional. —*v.t.* engañar; estafar; embaucar; embelecar. —**be up to one's tricks,** hacer de las suyas. —**do** (o **turn**) **the trick,** servir para el caso; tener el efecto deseado. —**learn the tricks of the trade,** adiestrarse; volverse experto. —**play tricks,** hacer burlas. —**trick out,** ataviar; vestir; adornar; engalanar.

trickery ('trɪk·ə·ri) *n.* tramparía; embeleco; estafa.

trickle ('trɪk·əl) *v.i.* **1,** (flow slowly) escurrir; gotear. **2,** (move in or out gradually) escurrirse; colar; colarse. —*v.t.* verter gota a gota. —*n.* **1,** (thin stream) goteo; chorro delgado. **2,** (gradual movement) escurrimiento.

trickster ('trɪk·stər) *n.* tramposo; embaucador [*fem.* -dora]; bromista.

tricksy ('trɪk·si) *adj.* **1,** (spruce; smart) elegante; pulcro. **2,** (playful) juguetón; travieso. **3,** (deceptive) engañoso; tramposo.

tricky ('trɪk·i) *adj.* **1,** (deceitful) engañoso; tramposo. **2,** (clever; sly) astuto; ingenioso; mañoso. **3,** (intricate) intrincado; arduo.

tricolor ('trai·kʌl·ər) *adj.* & *n.* tricolor.

tricorn ('trai·korn) *adj.* & *n.* tricornio.

tricot ('tri·ko) *n.* tricot; tejido de punto.

tricuspid (trai'kʌs·pɪd) *adj.* & *n.* tricúspide.

tricycle ('trai·sɪk·əl) *n.* triciclo.

trident ('trai·dənt) *n.* & *adj.* tridente.

tried (traid) *v., pret.* & *p.p. de* **try**.

trifle ('trai·fəl) *n.* pequeñez; fruslería; bagatela. —*v.i.* tratar o hablar sin seriedad; chancear. —*v.t.* malgastar; perder. —**trifler** (-flər) *n.* persona frívola; chancero. —**trifling** (-flɪŋ) *adj.* insignificante; frívolo; chancero. —**trifle away,** malgastar. —**trifle with,** chancearse con; burlarse con.

trifocal ('trai·fo·kəl) *adj.* trifocal. —**trifocals,** *n.pl.* lentes trifocales.

trifoliate (trai'fo·li·ɪt) *adj.* trifoliado.

trifurcate (trai'fʌr·ket) *v.t.* trifurcar. —*adj.* (-kət) trifurcado. —**trifurcation,** *n.* trifurcación.

trig (trɪg) *adj.* **1,** (neat) pulcro; elegante. **2,** (sound; firm) firme; fuerte.

trigger ('trɪg·ər) *n.* gatillo; disparador. —*v.t.* disparar.

trigonometry (,trɪg·ə'nam·ə·tri) *n.* trigonometría. —**trigonometric** (-nə'mɛt·rɪk) *adj.* trigonométrico.

trihedron (trai'hi·drən) *n.* triedro. —**trihedral,** *adj.* triedro.

trilateral (trai'læt·ər·əl) *adj.* trilátero.

trill (trɪl) *n.* trino; gorjeo. —*v.i.* trinar; gorjear.

trillion ('trɪl·jən) *n.* *U.S.* un millón de millones; billón; *Brit.* un millón de billones; trillón.

trilogy ('trɪl·ə·dʒi) *n.* trilogía.

trim (trɪm) *v.t.* [**trimmed, trimming**] **1,** (make neat or orderly) arreglar; ordenar. **2,** (adjust) ajustar; adaptar. **3,** (clip; prune) recortar; podar; despabilar (una vela). **4,** (adorn) adornar; guarnecer. **5,** *colloq.* (defeat) vencer. —*v.i.* **1,** (preserve balance) equilibrarse; igualarse; *naut.* orientarse. **2,** (vacillate) balancearse; vacilar. —*n.* **1,** (condition) condición; estado; disposición. **2,** (equipment) equipo; aparatos. **3,** (dress) traje; vestido. **4,** (adornment) adorno; decoración; guarnición. **5,** (molding) moldeado; moldura. **6,** (clipping) recorte. —*adj.* **1,** (neat) pulcro; elegante. **2,** (orderly) arreglado; ordenado.

trimester (trai'mɛs·tər) *n.* trimestre.

trimmer ('trɪm·ər) *n.* **1,** (decorator; dresser) guarnecedor [*fem.* -dora]. **2,** (machine) máquina de recortar o igualar. **3,** (timesaver) contemporizador [*fem* -dora].

trimming ('trɪm·ɪŋ) *n.* **1,** (decoration) guarnición; adorno. **2,** (fringe) orla; ribete. **3,** (garnish) aderezo. **4,** *pl.* (accessories) accesorios. **5,** *colloq.* (thrashing) paliza; zurra. **6,** *colloq.* (defeat) derrota.

trimness ('trɪm·nəs) *n.* **1,** (neatness) pulcritud; elegancia. **2,** (orderliness) arreglo; orden.

trimonthly (trai'mʌnθ·li) *adj.* trimestral

trinitrotoluene (,trai·nai·tro·'tal·ju·in) *n.* trinitrotolueno. =TNT

trinity ('trɪn·ə·ti) *n.* trinidad.

trinket ('trɪŋ·kɪt) *n.* dije; baratija.

trinomial (trai'no·mi·əl) *n.* trinomio.

trio ('tri·o) *n.* trío.

triode ('trai·od) *n.* tríodo.

trip (trɪp) *n.* **1,** (journey) viaje; excursión. **2,** (stumble) tropezón;

traspié; zancadilla. **3,** (slip; error) desliz; error. **4,** (step) paso ágil. **5,** *mech.* (catch; release mechanism) escape; trinquete. **6,** (act of releasing or firing) disparo. —*v.i.* [**tripped, tripping**] **1,** (stumble) tropezar. **2,** (make a mistake) equivocarse; errar. **3,** (run lightly; skip) correr ágilmente; brincar; saltar. **4,** (dance) bailar con agilidad. —*v.t.* **1,** (cause to stumble or err) trompicar; echar la zancadilla a; armar un lazo a. **2,** (perform with a tripping step) ejecutar con agilidad. **3,** (release suddenly) disparar; soltar. **4,** (overturn) volcar.

tripartite (trai'par·tait) *adj.* tripartito.

tripe (traip) *n.* **1,** (food) callos; tripas; mondongo. **2,** *slang* (rubbish) fruslería; disparate.

triphammer ('trɪp·hæm·ər) *n.* martinete de fragua; martillo pilón.

triphthong ('trɪf·θɔŋ) *n.* triptongo.

triplane ('trai,plein) *n.* triplano.

triple ('trɪp·əl) *adj. & n.* triple. —*v.t.* triplicar. —*v.i.* triplicarse.

triplet ('trɪp·lɪt) *n.* **1,** (one of a triple birth) trillizo. **2,** (group of three) terno. **3,** *mus.* tresillo.

triplex ('trɪp·lɛks) *adj.* triple; tríplice. —*n.* cosa triple; apartamento de tres pisos.

triplicate ('trɪp·lɪ·keit) *v.t.* triplicar. —*adj. & n.* (-kət) triplicado. —**triplication,** *n.* triplicación.

tripod ('trai·pad) *n.* trípode. —**tripodal** ('trɪp·ə·dəl) *adj.* en trípode; de forma de trípode.

tripper ('trɪp·ər) *n.* **1,** (runner) corredor. **2,** (jumper) saltador. **3,** (release mechanism) trinquete; escape; disparador.

tripping ('trɪp·ɪŋ) *adj.* **1,** (lively) ágil; veloz; ligero. **2,** *mech.* (releasing) disparador; de escape.

triptych ('trɪp·tɪk) *n.* tríptico.

trireme ('trai·rim) *n.* trirreme.

trisect (trai'sɛkt) *v.t.* trisecar. —**trisection** (-'sɛk·ʃən) *n.* trisección.

trisyllable (trai'sɪl·ə·bəl) *n.* trisílabo. —**trisyllabic** (,trai·sɪ'læb·ɪk) *adj.* trisílabo.

trite (trait) *adj.* gastado; trillado; vulgar.

tritium ('trɪʃ·jəm) *n.* tritio.

triton ('trai·tən) *n.* tritón.

triturate ('trɪtʃ·ə·reit) *v.t.* triturar. —**trituration,** *n.* trituración.

triumph ('trai·ʌmf) *n.* triunfo; victoria. —*v.i.* triunfar; vencer.

triumphal (trai'ʌm·fəl) *adj.* triunfal.

triumphant (trai'ʌm·fənt) *adj.* victorioso; triunfante.

triumvir (trai'ʌm·vər) *n.* triunviro. —**triumvirate** (-və·rɪt) *n.* triunvirato.

trivalent ('trai·vei·lənt) *adj.* trivalente.

trivet ('trɪv·ɪt) *n.* trébedes.

trivia ('trɪv·i·ə) *n.pl.* trivialidades; fruslerías.

trivial ('trɪv·i·əl) *adj.* trivial.

triviality (,trɪ·vi'æl·ə·ti) *n.* trivialidad.

troche ('tro·ki) *n.* tableta; pastilla.

trochee ('tro·ki) *n.* troqueo. —**trochaic** (tro'kei·ɪk) *adj. & n.* trocaico.

trod (trad) *v., pret. & p.p. de* tread.

trodden ('trad·ən) *v., p.p. de* tread.

troglodyte ('trag·lə,dait) *n.* **1,** (cave dweller) troglodita. **2,** (hermit) ermitaño; solitario. —**troglodytic** (-'dɪt·ɪk) *adj.* troglodítico.

troika ('trɔi·kə) *n.* troica.

Trojan horse ('tro·dʒən) caballo de Troya; señuelo.

troll (trol) *v.i. & t.* **1,** (sing) cantar en voz alta y alegre; cantar en sucesión. **2,** (fish) pescar arrastrando el anzuelo. **3,** (roll) voltear; rodar. —*n.* **1,** (song) canon. **2,** (fishing equipment) aparejo de pescar. **3,** (bait) cebo; anzuelo. **4,** (fairy dwarf) gnomo; enano.

trolley ('tral·i) *n.* **1,** (pulley) trole. **2,** (streetcar) tranvía. —**trolley bus,** trolebús.

trollop ('tral·əp) *n.* **1,** (slovenly woman) mujer desaseada. **2,** (prostitute) prostituta; ramera.

trombone (tram'bon) *n.* trombón. —**trombonist,** trombón.

troop (trup) *n.* tropa. —*v.t.* juntar; reunir. —*v.i.* marchar en orden; desfilar. —**trooper,** *n.* soldado; agente de policía.

trope (trop) *n.* tropo.

trophic ('traf·ɪk) *adj.* trófico.

trophy ('tro·fi) *n.* trofeo.

tropic ('tra·pɪk) *n.* trópico. —**tropical,** *adj.* tropical.

tropism ('tro·pɪz·əm) *n.* tropismo.

troposphere ('trop·ə,sfɪr) *n.* troposfera.

trot (trat) *v.i.* [**trotted, trotting**]

trotar. —v.t. hacer trotar. —n. 1,
(gait) trote. 2, colloq. (crib)
traducción ilícita que usan los
estudiantes. 3, = **trotline.** —**trot
out,** colloq. sacar para mostrar o
exhibir.

troth (troθ) n. 1, (promise to
marry) esponsales. 2, arcaico
(truth) fe; verdad. —**plight one's
troth,** contraer esponsales.

trotline ('trat·lain) n. palangre.

trotter ('trat·ər) n. trotón; pie de
cerdo o carnero.

troubadour ('tru·bə·dor) n.
trovador.

trouble ('trʌb·əl) n. 1, (distress)
pena; aflicción; congoja. 2, (misfortune) desgracia; calamidad. 3, (inconvenience) molestia. 4, (disturbance) estorbo; confusión; desorden; lío. 5, (bother; effort) pena;
esfuerzo. 6, (breakdown) avería;
defecto; falla. —v.t. 1, (afflict)
afligir; apenar. 2, (annoy; inconvenience) molestar; incomodar. 3,
(worry) preocupar; inquietar. 4,
(disturb) perturbar; confundir. —v.i.
molestarse; darse pena. —**be in
trouble,** estar en un apuro. —**be
worth the trouble,** valer la pena.
—**get into trouble,** meterse en líos.
—**look for trouble,** entremeterse;
buscar tres pies al gato.

troublemaker ('trʌb·əl,mei·kər)
n. buscarruidos; picapleitos; Amer.
buscapleitos.

troubleshooter ('trʌb·əl,ʃu·tər)
n. componedor [fem. -dora];
reparador [fem. -dora]; enderezador
[fem. -dora].

troublesome ('trʌb·əl·səm) adj.
molesto; penoso; importuno.

troublous ('trʌb·ləs) adj. inquieto;
turbulento; confuso.

trough (trɔf) n. 1, (container)
artesa. 2, (feeding trough) pesebre.
3, (ditch) zanja. 4, (gutter) canal. 5,
(hollow) abismo; hueco; seno.

trounce (trauns) v.t. 1, (thrash)
zurrar; azotar; castigar. 2, colloq.
(defeat) derrotar; vencer.

troupe (trup) n. compañía teatral;
troupe. —v.i. viajar como miembro
de una compañía.

trouper ('tru·pər) n. miembro de
una compañía teatral; actor viejo;
actriz vieja.

trousers ('trau·zərz) n.pl. pantalones; calzones. —**trouser,** adj.
relativo al pantalón; de pantalón.

trousseau (tru'soɹ) n. ajuar de
novia; trousseau.

trout (traut) n. trucha.

trow (troɹ) v.i., arcaico creer;
pensar.

trowel ('trau·əl) n. paleta; llana;
hortic. desplantador.

troy (troi) adj. relativo al sistema de
pesos troy. —**troy weight,** sistema
de pesos usado para el oro, la plata,
gemas, etc.; una libra (de doce
onzas) vale cerca 373 gramos.

truant ('tru·ənt) adj. haragán; que
hace novillos. —n. novillero.
—**truancy,** n. ausencia injustifi-
cada. —**play truant,** hacer novillos; hacerse la rabona.

truce (trus) n. tregua.

truck (trʌk) n. 1, (motor vehicle)
camión; carro. 2, (hand cart)
carretilla. 3, (frame on wheels)
juego de ruedas. 4, (top of a pole
or mast) remate de asta o mástil.
5, (vegetables) hortalizas para el
mercado. 6, (miscellaneous articles)
artículos varios. 7, (barter) trueque;
permuta; cambio; negocio. 8,
colloq. (dealings) negocio; relaciones. 9, colloq. (rubbish) desechos;
desperdicios. —v.t. 1, (transport)
transportar por camión; acarrear. 2,
(barter) trocar; cambalachear. —v.i.
1, (drive) conducir un camión. 2,
(deal) traficar; cambalachear.
—**truckage,** n. acarreo; camionaje.
—**trucker,** n. camionero. —**truck-
man** (-mən) n. dueño o conductor
de camiones. —**truck farm; truck
garden,** huerto de hortalizas.

truckle ('trʌk·əl) n. ruedecilla.
—v.t. mover sobre ruedecillas.
—v.i. 1, (roll) rodar sobre ruedecillas. 2, (submit) someterse servilmente. —**truckle bed,** carriola.

truculent ('trʌk·jə·lənt) adj.
truculento; cruel. —**truculence,** n.
truculencia; crueldad.

trudge (trʌdʒ) v.i. andar trabajosamente. —v.t. recorrer trabajosamente. —n. marcha penosa.

true (truɹ) adj. 1, (factual) verdadero. 2, (exact) exacto; correcto. 3,
(faithful) leal; constante; fiel. 4,
(genuine) genuino; auténtico;
propio. 5, (rightful) justo; legítimo.
6, (aligned) alineado. —adv. verdaderamente; exactamente. —n. 1,
(truth) verdad; lo verdadero. 2,
(alignment) alineamiento. —v.t.
alinear. —**come true,** realizarse.
—**in true,** alineado. —**out of true,**

desalineado. —**run true to form,** actuar según se esperaba. —**true to life,** verdadero; conforme con la realidad.

true-blue adj. leal; fiel; constante.

truebred ('tru·brɛd) adj. de casta legítima.

truehearted (tru'har·tɪd) adj. fiel; leal; sincero. —**trueheartedness,** n. fidelidad; lealtad; sinceridad.

trueness ('tru·nəs) n. verdad; sinceridad.

truffle ('trʌf·əl) n. trufa.

truism ('tru·ɪz·əm) n. axioma; verdad evidente; perogrullada.

trull (trʌl) n. prostituta; ramera.

truly ('tru·li) adv. verdaderamente; exactamente; sinceramente. —**truly yours; yours truly,** su seguro servidor.

trump (trʌmp) n. 1, cards triunfo. 2, colloq. (fine person) persona excelente; dije. —v.i., cards triunfar; fallar. —v.t. 1, cards jugar un triunfo sobre. 2, (surpass) sobrepujar; superar. —**trump up,** forjar; inventar.

trumpery ('trʌmp·ə·ri) adj. vistoso; de oropel. —n. 1, (something showy) oropel. 2, (rubbish) tontería; disparate.

trumpet ('trʌm·pɪt) n. 1, (musical instrument) trompeta. 2, (animal cry) berreo. 3, (hearing aid) audífono; trompetilla. —v.t. pregonar a son de trompeta. —v.i. trompetear. —**trumpeter,** n. trompetero; trompeta.

truncate ('trʌŋ·keit) v.t. truncar. —adj. truncado. —**truncation,** n. truncamiento.

truncheon ('trʌn·tʃən) n. 1, (cudgel) cachiporra. 2, (staff of authority) bastón de mando. —v.t. zurrar con cachiporra; aporrear.

trundle ('trʌn·dəl) n. rodillo; ruedecilla. —v.t. hacer rodar. —v.i. rodar; girar. —**trundle bed,** carriola.

trunk (trʌŋk) n. 1, anat.; bot. tronco. 2, (proboscis) trompa. 3, (container) baúl; cofre. 4, (main line) línea o tubería maestra. 6, pl. (short trousers) pantalones cortos; taparrabos; Amer. trusa. —adj. troncal; principal. —**trunkful** (-‚fʊl) n. baúl lleno. —**trunk line,** línea interurbana.

truss (trʌs) v.t. 1, (bind) atar; liar. 2, (support) armar; apuntalar. 3, (skewer) espetar. —n. 1, (frame-work) armadura. 2, (belt) braguero. 3, (bundle) haz; paquete; lío.

trust (trʌst) n. 1, (assured reliance; confidence) confianza; fe; expectación. 2, (credit) crédito. 3, (charge; obligation) cargo; obligación. 4, (that which is entrusted) depósito. 5, (monopoly) monopolio; cartel. —v.t. fiarse de; confiar en. —v.i. confiar; fiar. —**in trust, 1,** (in confidence) en confianza. 2, (in custody) en depósito. —**on trust, 1,** (on credit) a crédito; al fiado. 2, (on faith) de buena fe.

trust company banco de depósito; compañía fiduciaria.

trustee (trʌs'tiː) n. depositario; administrador [fem. -dora]. —**trusteeship,** n. cargo de administrador; administración fiduciaria.

trustful ('trʌst·fəl) adj. confiado.

trustworthy ('trʌst·wʌr·ði) adj. confiable; fidedigno. —**trustworthiness,** n. integridad; honradez.

trusty ('trʌs·ti) adj. leal; seguro. —n. preso que goza de ciertos privilegios.

truth (truθ) n. verdad; realidad. —**in truth,** en verdad; de veras. —**of a truth,** seguramente.

truthful ('truθ·fəl) adj. verídico; veraz; verdadero. —**truthfulness,** n. veracidad.

try (trai) v.t. [pret. & p.p. **tried**] 1, (attempt; essay) intentar; ensayar; probar; tratar. 2, (test) probar; examinar. 3, law procesar; ver (un litigio). 4, (subject to strain) exasperar; poner a prueba; irritar. 5, (refine) refinar; purificar. —v.i. tratar; hacer lo posible. —n. prueba; intento; ensayo. —**try out, 1,** (test; prove) probar(se); someter(se) a prueba. 2, (refine) refinar; purificar.

trying ('trai·ɪŋ) adj. molesto; penoso.

tryout ('trai·aut) n. experimento; prueba de competencia.

tryst (trɪst) n. cita, esp. de amantes.

tsar (zar) n. zar. —**tsarevitch** (-ə·vɪtʃ) n. zarevitz. —**tsarevna** (-'ɛv·nə) n. zarevna. —**tsarina** (-'i·nə) n. zarina.

tsetse (tsɛt·si) n. tsetsé.

T-shirt n. camiseta de mangas cortas.

T square regla en forma de T.

tub (tʌb) n. 1, (bathtub) bañera. 2, (vessel) cuba; tonel. 3, colloq. (boat) buque viejo y lento. 4, *colloq.* (bath) baño. —*v.t. & i.* bañar(se) en bañera.

tuba ('tu·bə) *n.* tuba.

tubby ('tʌb·i) *adj.* 1, (short and fat) rechoncho. 2, (dull, as of a sound) sordo. —*n., colloq.* cuba; gordiflón.

tube (tuːb) *n.* 1, (hollow cylinder) tubo; caño. 2, (tunnel) túnel. 3, (subway) tranvía subterráneo; metro. 4, (inner tube) cámara.

tuber ('tu·bər) *n.* tubérculo. —**tuberous,** *adj.* tuberoso.

tubercle ('tu·bər·kəl) *n.* tubérculo; protuberancia. —**tubercle bacillus,** bacilo tuberculoso.

tubercular (tu'bʌr·kjə·lər) *adj. & n.* tuberculoso.

tuberculin (tu'bʌr·kjə·lɪn) *n.* tuberculina.

tuberculosis (tu,bʌr·kjə'lo·sɪs) *n.* tuberculosis.

tuberculous (tu'bʌr·kjə·ləs) *adj.* tuberculoso.

tuberose ('tub·roz) *n.* tuberosa.

tubing ('tu·bɪŋ) *n.* tubería.

tubular ('tu·bju·lər) *adj.* tubular.

tuck (tʌk) *v.t.* 1, (cram) atestar; henchir. 2, (wrap) arropar. 3, (make tucks in) alforzar. 4, (draw up; gather) arremangar. 5, (fold) doblar. —*v.i.* fruncir; contraerse. —*n.* alforza. —**tuck away,** 1, (put away; hide) guardar; ocultar. 2, *slang* (eat or drink heartily) comer o beber mucho y con gusto. —**tuck up,** arremangar.

tucker ('tʌk·er) *n.* 1, (person or machine that tucks) alforzador. 2, (neckcloth) pañoleta. —*v.t., colloq.* cansar; fatigar. —**tuckered out,** *colloq.* cansado; extenuado.

Tuesday ('tuz·de) *n.* martes.

tuft (tʌft) *n.* 1, (bunch; cluster) copete; ramillete; manojo. 2, (topknot) moño. 3, (lock of hair) mechón. 4, (tassel) borla. 5, (plume) penacho. —*v.t.* poner borlas, penachos, etc., a. —**tufted,** *adj.* copetudo; penachudo.

tug (tʌg) *v.t.* **[tugged, tugging]** 1, (pull) tirar con fuerza de. 2, (drag) arrastrar. 3, (haul) halar. 4, (tow) remolcar. —*v.i.* 1, (pull) tirar con fuerza. 2, (strive) esforzarse. —*n.* 1, (strong pull) tirón. 2, (tugboat) remolcador. 3, (struggle) esfuerzo supremo. 4, (strap) tirante; correa; cuerda. —**tug of war,** lucha de la cuerda; *fig.* lucha por la supremacía.

tugboat ('tʌg,bot) *n.* remolcador.

tuition (tu'ɪʃ·ən) *n.* 1, (fee) costo

de la enseñanza. 2, (teaching) enseñanza.

tulip ('tu·lɪp) *n.* tulipán.

tulle (tuːl) *n.* tul.

tumble ('tʌm·bəl) *v.i.* 1, (fall down) caer; desplomarse. 2, (descend rapidly) venirse abajo; precipitarse. 3, (roll about) voltear; rodar. 4, (gymnastics) saltar; hacer acrobacia. 5, *slang* (become aware) caer en la cuenta. —*v.t.* 1, (upset) trastornar. 2, (throw; put in disorder) arrojar; desarreglar. 3, (rotate) voltear; hacer girar. —*n.* 1, (act of tumbling) tumbo; vuelco; voltereta; caída. 2, (state of confusion) confusión; desorden. 3, *slang* (sign of recognition) señal de reconocimiento.

tumble-down *adj.* destartalado.

tumbler ('tʌm·blər) *n.* 1, (glass) vaso sin pie. 2, (gymnast) acróbata; volatinero. 3, (part of a lock) fiador. 4, *mech.* (rotating part) tambor.

tumbleweed ('tʌm·bəl,wid) *n.* planta rodadora.

tumefaction (,tu·mə'fæk·ʃən) *n.* tumefacción.

tumescent (tu'mɛs·ənt) *adj.* tumescente. —**tumescence,** *n.* tumescencia.

tumid ('tu·mɪd) *adj.* hinchado; tumefacto; túmido. —**tumidity** (tu'mɪd·ə·ti) *n.* hinchazón; tumefacción.

tummy ('tʌm·i) *n., colloq.* barriga; pipa; panza.

tumor ('tu·mər) *n.* tumor.

tumult ('tu·mʌlt) *n.* tumulto; motín; agitación. —**tumultuous** (tu'mʌl·tʃu·əs) *adj.* tumultuoso; agitado.

tun (tʌn) *n.* cuba; tonel.

tuna ('tu·nə) *n.* 1, *ichthy.* atún. 2, *bot.* tuna.

tundra ('tʌn·drə) *n.* tundra.

tune (tuːn) *n.* 1, (air; melody) aire; melodía; tonada. 2, (adjustment to proper pitch) afinación. 3, (harmony; accord) armonía; acorde. 4, (good condition) buen estado. —*v.t.* 1, (put in tune) templar; afinar. 2, (harmonize) armonizar. 3, *radio; TV* sintonizar. —**change one's tune,** mudar de tono. —**in tune,** afinado. —**out of tune,** desafinado. —**tune in,** sintonizar. —**tune up,** 1, *mech.* ajustar. 2, *mus.* acordar.

tuneful ('tuːn·fəl) *adj.* armonioso; melodioso.

tuneless 1202 turn

tuneless ('tuːn·ləs) *adj.* discorde; disonante.

tuner ('tu·nər) *n.* afinador; *radio; TV* sintonizador.

tune-up *n.* reglaje; puesta a punto (de un motor).

tungsten ('tʌŋ·stən) *n.* tungsteno.

tunic ('tu·nɪk) *n.* túnica.

tuning ('tu·nɪŋ) *n.* **1,** (adjusting tune) afinación. **2,** (harmonization) armonización. **3,** *radio; TV* sintonización. —**tuning fork**, diapasón.

tunnel ('tʌn·əl) *n.* **1,** (passage) túnel. **2,** (burrow) madriguera. —*v.t.* horadar; construir un túnel en o por. —*v.i.* excavar.

tunny ('tʌn·i) *n.* tonina.

turban ('tʌr·bən) *n.* **1,** (headdress) turbante. **2,** (brimless hat) sombrero sin alas.

turbid ('tʌr·bɪd) *adj.* turbio. —**turbidity** (tər'bɪd·ə·ti) *n.* turbidez.

turbine ('tʌr·bɪn; -bain) *n.* turbina.

turbojet ('tʌr·bo,dʒɛt) *n.* turborreactor.

turboprop ('tʌr·bo,prap) *n.* turbopropulsor.

turbot ('tʌr·bət) *n.* rodaballo.

turbulent ('tʌr·bju·lənt) *adj.* turbulento. —**turbulence**, *n.* turbulencia.

tureen (tu'riːn) *n.* sopera.

turf (tʌrf) *n.* **1,** (grass) césped. **2,** (sod) tepe. **3,** (race track) hipódromo; carreras de caballos; turf. **4,** (peat) turba. —*v.t.* cubrir con césped.

turgid ('tʌr·dʒɪd) *adj.* turgente. —**turgidity** (tər'dʒɪd·ə·ti) *n.* turgencia.

Turk (tʌrk) *n.* turco.

turkey ('tʌr·ki) *n.* **1,** (bird) pavo. **2,** *slang* (failure) fracaso. —**talk turkey**, *colloq.* hablar francamente.

turkey buzzard aura; gallinazo; *Amer.* zopilote.

Turkish ('tʌr·kɪʃ) *adj. & n.* turco. —**Turkish bath**, baño turco. —**Turkish towel**, toalla gruesa y afelpada.

turmeric ('tʌr·mər·ɪk) *n.* cúrcuma.

turmoil ('tʌr·mɔil) *n.* disturbio; alboroto; tumulto.

turn (tʌrn) *v.t.* **1,** (shift; twist) volver; dar vuelta a. **2,** (change the course of) desviar. **3,** (reverse) dar vuelta a. **4,** (revolve; rotate) hacer girar; voltear. **5,** (shape in a lathe) tornear. **6,** (use; apply) emplear;

utilizar. **7,** (alter) modificar; adaptar. **8,** (cause to become) volver; tornar. **9,** (make sour) agriar. **10,** (meditate on) meditar sobre; revolver. **11,** (go around) doblar. **12,** (sprain) torcer. —*v.i.* **1,** (rotate) rodar; girar. **2,** (spin) dar vueltas. **3,** (assume a new direction) cambiar de curso; virar; volver. **4,** (change) volverse; modificarse. **5,** (become sour) agriarse. **6,** (become curved) encorvarse. —*n.* **1,** (rotation) giro; vuelta. **2,** (change of direction) desviación. **3,** (bend) curva; recodo. **4,** (coil) espira **5,** (occcasion to act) turno. **6,** (aspect; shape) forma; figura; aspecto. **7,** (change) mudanza. **8,** (tendency) tendencia. **9,** *colloq.* (shock) impresión violenta; susto. —**at every turn**, a cada momento. —**bad turn**, mala pasada; mala jugada. —**be one's turn**, tocarle a uno. —**good turn**, favor; servicio. —**in turn**, por turno; a su turno. —**out of turn**, fuera de orden. —**take a turn**, **1,** (change) volverse; cambiar. **2,** (go around) dar una vuelta. —**take turns**, alternar; turnar. —**to a turn**, exactamente; perfectamente. —**turn about**, dar vuelta; voltearse. —**turn and turn about**, uno tras otro. —**turn around**, dar vuelta. —**turn aside** desviar(se); apartar(se). —**turn away**, **1,** (send away) despedir. **2,** (divert) desviar. **3,** (alienate) alejar; enajenar. —**turn back**, **1,** (go back) volverse; volver atrás. **2,** (send back) devolver. **3,** (repel) rechazar; repulsar. **4,** (retreat) retroceder. —**turn down**, **1,** (fold down) plegar(se) o doblar(se) hacia abajo. **2,** (reject) rechazar. **3,** (lower) bajar. —**turn from**, desviar(se) de; apartar(se) de. —**turn in**, **1,** (enter) entrar. **2,** (point inward) doblar(se) hacia adentro. **3,** (deliver) entregar. **4,** (return) devolver. **5,** *colloq.* (retire) acostarse. —**turn in and out**, serpentear. —**turn off**, **1,** (change direction) desviar(se) de. **2,** (branch off) apartarse; bifurcarse. **3,** (extinguish) apagar. **4,** (cut off) cortar. **5,** (dismiss) despedir; despachar. **6,** *slang* (cease to excite; lose interest in) aburrir; aburrirse de. —**turn on**, **1,** (switch on) encender; poner. **2,** (start the flow of) abrir. **3,** (attack) volverse contra; caerle encima a uno. **4,** (depend on) depender de. **5,** *slang* (excite; stimulate) excitar; estimular. —**turn out, 1,** (extinguish) apagar. **2,** (put outside) sacar; echar fuera. **3,** (come or go out) salir. **4,** (be present) asistir; presentarse. **5,** (produce) hacer; fabricar; producir. **6,** (result) salir; quedar. **7,** (happen) acontecer; suceder. **8,** (become) volverse; ponerse. **9,** (equip; dress) ataviar; vestir; equipar. **10,** *colloq.* (arise) levantarse. —**turn over, 1,** (turn upside down) volcar(se); trastornar(se). **2,** (roll over) volver(se); voltear. **3,** (ponder) considerar; revolver. **4,** (hand over) entregar; pasar; ceder. **5,** (start running, as a motor) prender; hacer girar. **6,** (riffle, as pages) hojear. **7,** (buy and sell) mover (mercancías). —**turn tail,** huirse; poner pies en polvorosa. —**turn to, 1,** (refer to) recurrir a; consultar. **2,** (apply to) dirigirse a. **3,** (go to for help) pedir socorro a; acudir a. **4,** (get to work) poner manos a la obra —**turn up, 1,** (fold upward) plegar(se) al doblar(se) hacia arriba. **2,** (turn face upwards) volver(se). **3,** (discover) descubrir; desenterrar. **4,** (increase the volume of) dar más volumen a; poner más fuerte. **5,** (happen) acontecer; suceder. **6,** (arrive; appear) llegar; dejarse ver; aparecer. **7,** (be found) encontrarse; hallarse; venir a mano. —**turn upon, 1,** (attack) volverse contra. **2,** (depend on) depender de. —**turn upside down,** volcar(se); trastornar(se).

turnabout ('tʌrn·ə·baut) *n.* **1,** (turning) vuelta completa. **2,** (alternation of privileges) alternación de privilegios.

turnbuckle ('tʌrn,bʌk·əl) *n.* torniquete; eslabón giratorio.

turncoat ('tʌrn,kot) *n.* tránsfuga; renegado.

turner ('tʌr·nər) *n.* **1,** (woodworker) tornero. **2,** (gymnast) acróbata; volatinero.

turning ('tʌr·nɪŋ) *adj.* giratorio; rotatorio. —*n.* **1,** (act of turning) vuelta. **2,** (bend; curve) recodo; curva. **3,** (shaping in a lathe) torneo; torneado. —**turning point,** punto decisivo; punto crucial.

turnip ('tʌr·nəp) *n.* nabo.

turnkey ('tʌrn,ki) *n.* llavero; carcelero.

turnout ('tʌrn·aut) *n.* **1,** (gathering) concurrencia. **2,** (output) rendi-

miento; producción total. **3,** (outfit) ropa; equipo. **4,** *R.R.* (siding) apartadero.

turnover ('tʌrn,o·vər) *n.* **1,** (volume of business) monto de las transacciones comerciales. **2,** (change of personnel) cambio de personal; reorganización. **3,** (pastry) pastel con repulgo.

turnpike ('tʌrn·paik) *n.* carretera; autopista.

turnstile ('tʌrn·stail) *n.* molinete.

turntable ('tʌrn·tei·bəl) *n.* **1,** *R.R.* placa giratoria; tornavía. **2,** (of a phonograph) portadiscos.

turpentine ('tʌr·pən·tain) *n.* trementina; aguarrás.

turpitude ('tʌr·pɪ·tud) *n.* depravación; vileza; torpeza. —**turpitudinous** (-'tud·ɪ·nəs) *adj.* depravado; vil; torpe.

turquoise ('tʌr·kwɔiz) *n.* turquesa.

turret ('tʌr·ɪt) *n.* **1,** (small tower) torrecilla. **2,** (part of a lathe) torrecilla de torno; portaherramientas. **3,** (gun tower) torre blindada. —**turret lathe,** torno de torrecilla.

turtle ('tʌr·təl) *n.* tortuga; carey. —**turn turtle,** volcar; zozobrar.

turtledove ('tʌr·təl,dʌv) *n.* tórtola.

turtleneck ('tʌr·təl,nek) *n.* cuello vuelto o alto; suéter con tal cuello.

tush (tʌʃ) *interj.* ¡bah! —*n.* **1,** (tusk) colmillo. **2,** (tuʃ) *slang* (buttocks) nalgas.

tusk (tʌsk) *n.* **1,** (tooth) colmillo. **2,** (toothlike part) púa; diente.

tusker ('tʌs·kər) *n.* animal colmilludo.

tussle ('tʌs·əl) *n.* riña; pelea; agarrada. —*v.i.* reñir; pelear; agarrarse.

tut (tʌt) *interj.* ¡basta!; ¡bah!

tutelage ('tu·tə·lɪdʒ) *n.* tutela; instrucción.

tutelary ('tu·tə,lɛr·i) *adj.* tutelar.

tutor ('tu·tər) *n.* tutor; preceptor. —*v.t.* enseñar; instruir. —*v.i.* **1,** (teach) dar lecciones particulares. **2,** *colloq.* tomar lecciones particulares.

tutorage ('tu·tər·ɪdʒ) *n.* tutela.

tutorial (tu'tor·i·əl) *adj.* preceptoral.

tutti-frutti ('tu·ti'fru·ti) *n.* tutti-frutti; dulce de varias frutas.

tuwhit, tuwhoo (tʊ'hwɪt·tʊ·'hwuɾ) graznido del búho.

tux (tʌks) *n., colloq.* = **tuxedo.**

tuxedo (tʌk'si·do) *n.* smoking; esmoquin.

TV ('ti'vi) *n., colloq.* televisión.

—**TV dinner,** comida para televidentes.

twaddle ('twad·əl) *v.i.* disparatar; charlar; decir tonterías. —*n.* habladuría; charla; disparates; tonterías.

twain (twein) *adj. & n.,* arcaico y poético dos.

twang (twæŋ) *n.* **1,** (sound of a string) tañido; punteado. **2,** (nasal sound) gangueo. —*v.t.* tañer; puntear. —*v.i.* ganguear.

'twas (twʌz) *contr. de* **it was.**

tweak (twik) *v.t.* pellizcar retorciendo. —*n.* tirón; torcedura.

tweed (twi:d) *n.* paño de lana de varios colores. —**tweeds,** *n.pl.* vestidos hechos con ese paño.

tweet (twit) *v.i.* gorjeo; pío. —*v.i.* gorjear; piar.

tweezers ('twi·zərz) *n.pl.* tenacillas; pinzas.

twelve (twɛlv) *adj. & n.* doce. —**twelfth** (twɛlfθ) *adj. & n.* duodécimo; dozavo. —**Twelfth Night,** Vigilia de Reyes.

twenty ('twɛn·ti) *adj. & n.* veinte. —**twentieth,** *adj. & n.* vigésimo; veintavo.

'twere (twʌr) *contr. de* **it were.**

twerp (twʌrp) *n., slang* lelo; bobo.

twice (twais) *adv.* dos veces; el doble. —**twice-told,** *adj.* repetido.

twiddle ('twid·əl) *v.t.* menear; hacer girar (los pulgares). —*v.i.* entretenerse con tonterías.

twig (twig) *n.* ramito; vástago.

twilight ('twai·lait) *n.* crepúsculo. —*adj.* crepuscular. —**twilight sleep,** narcosis obstétrica.

twill (twil) *n.* tela cruzada.

'twill (twil) *contr. de* **it will.**

twin (twin) *adj. & n.* gemelo. —*v.t.* **1,** (give birth to twins) parir (gemelos). **2,** (pair; couple) emparejar. —*v.i.* **1,** (give birth to twins) parir gemelos. **2,** (be paired or coupled) emparejarse.

twine (twain) *n.* **1,** (strong cord) tramilla. **2,** (something twisted) trenza. —*v.t.* retorcer; enroscar; entrelazar. —*v.i.* retorcerse; enroscarse; entrelazarse.

twinge (twindʒ) *n.* dolor agudo; punzada. —*v.t.* causar un dolor agudo a. —*v.i.* sentir un dolor agudo. —**twinge of conscience,** pena del ánimo; remordimiento.

twinkle ('twiŋ·kəl) *v.i.* **1,** (shine) centellear. **2,** (sparkle, as the eyes) parpadear; pestañear. **3,** (flutter)

moverse rápidamente. —*v.t.* **1,** (cause to shine) hacer centellear. **2,** (wink) guiñar; abrir y cerrar rápidamente (los ojos). —*n.* **1,** (gleam) centelleo; destello. **2,** (wink) parpadeo; guiñada. **3,** (quick movement) movimiento rápido.

twinkling ('twiŋk·liŋ) *n.* **1,** (gleam) centelleo. **2,** (instant) instante. —**in the twinkling of an eye,** en un abrir y cerrar de ojos.

twirl (twʌrl) *v.t.* **1,** (spin) hacer girar. **2,** (throw) arrojar; lanzar. —*v.i.* **1,** (spin) girar; dar vueltas. **2,** (wind) enrollarse. —*n.* **1,** (gyration) vuelta; giro. **2,** (curl) enroscadura. —**twirler,** *n.* lanzador de béisbol.

twist (twist) *v.t.* **1,** (wrap) enrollar; arrollar. **2,** (warp; distort) torcer. **3,** (curl) enroscar. **4,** (twine) entrelazar. **5,** (cause to rotate) hacer girar. **6,** (bend) doblar; trenzar. **7,** (pervert in meaning) torcer el sentido de; interpretar mal. —*v.i.* **1,** (be bent or coiled) torcerse; envolverse; enrollarse. **2,** (rotate) girar; dar vueltas. **3,** (change direction) desviarse; virar. **4,** (be distorted in shape) deformarse. **5,** (follow a crooked course) serpentear. —*n.* **1,** (bend; curve) recodo; curva. **2,** (tangle; crook) enredo; torcedura. **3,** (twisting motion) contorsión; serpenteo. **4,** (inclination) inclinación; propensión; sesgo. **5,** (something formed by twisting) rollo; rosca. **6,** (pastry) trenza; torcido. **7,** (bread or roll) rosca. **8,** (cord) torzal; torcido.

twister ('twis·tər) *n.* **1,** (person or thing that twists) torcedor. **2,** = **tornado.**

twit (twit) *v.t.* [**twitted, twitting**] reprender; escarnecer. —*n.* reprensión; escarnio.

twitch (twitʃ) *v.t.* **1,** (pull) tirar bruscamente; sacudir. **2,** (pinch; squeeze) pellizcar; estrujar. —*v.i.* **1,** (writhe) crisparse. **2,** (quiver) temblar. —*n.* **1,** (muscular contraction) espasmo. **2,** (tremor) temblor. **3,** (tug) tirón; estirón.

twitter ('twit·ər) *v.i.* **1,** (chirp) gorjear. **2,** (giggle) reír nerviosamente. **3,** (be excited) estar agitado. **4,** (chatter) cotorrear. —*n.* **1,** (chirping) gorjeo. **2,** (excitement) agitación; conmoción.

'twixt (twikst) *prep., contr. de* **betwixt.**

two (tu:) *adj. & n.* dos.

two-by-four *n.* tabla de dos pulgadas de espesor y cuatro de ancho.

two-edged *adj.* de doble filo.

two-faced *adj.* falso; hipócrita.

two-fisted *adj., colloq.* vigoroso; valiente.

twofold ('tu·fold) *adj. & n.* doble; dos veces (más). —*adv.* dos veces; doblemente.

two-handed *adj.* **1,** (having or requiring two hands) de o para dos manos. **2,** (ambidextrous) ambidextro.

two hundred doscientos. —**two-hundredth,** *adj. & n.* ducentésimo.

twopence ('tʌp·əns) *n.* moneda de dos peniques.

twopenny ('tʌp·ə·ni) *adj.* **1,** (worth twopence) de dos peniques. **2,** (cheap) de poco valor; insignificante.

twosome ('tu·səm) *n.* pareja; dúo.

two-step *n.* paso doble.

two-time *v.t., slang* engañar. —**two-timer,** *n.* engañador [*fem.* -dora].

'twould (twʊd) *contr. de* **it would.**

two-way *adj.* **1,** (street) de doble dirección. **2,** *radio; TV* emisor y receptor. **3,** (mutual) mutuo; bilateral.

tycoon (tai'kuːn) *n., colloq.* magnate.

tying ('tai·iŋ) *v., ger. de* **tie.**

tyke (taik) *n.* **1,** (dog) perro. **2,** (child) niño; chiquillo.

tympani ('tɪm·pə·ni) *n.pl.* atabales; timbales. —**tympanist,** *n.* timbalero.

tympanum ('tɪm·pə·nəm) *n.* **1,** (stretched membrane; drum) membrana tensa; timbal. **2,** *anat.; archit.* tímpano. **3,** (diaphragm) diafragma.

type (taip) *n.* tipo. —*v.t.* **1,** (classify) clasificar. **2,** (symbolize) simbolizar; representar. —*v.t. & i.* (typewrite) mecanografiar; escribir a máquina.

typecast ('taip,kæst) *v.t.* encasillar (a un actor)

typeface ('taip,feis) *n.* carácter; tipo.

typescript ('taip,skrɪpt) *n.* material escrito a máquina.

typesetter ('taip,set·ər) *n.* tipógrafo; cajista.

typewrite ('taip,rait) *v.t. & i.* mecanografiar; escribir a máquina. —**typewriter,** *n.* máquina de escribir; tipiadora. —**typewriting,** *n.* mecanografía; dactilografía.

typhoid ('tai·fɔid) *adj.* tifoideo. —**typhoid fever,** fiebre tifoidea; tifoidea.

typhoon (tai'fuːn) *n.* tifón.

typhus ('tai·fəs) *n.* tifo; tifus.

typical ('tɪp·ɪ·kəl) *adj.* típico.

typify ('tɪp·ɪ·fai) *v.t.* **1,** (exemplify) ser ejemplo de. **2,** (symbolize) simbolizar.

typist ('taip·ɪst) *n.* mecanógrafo; dactilógrafo.

typo ('tai·po) *n., colloq.* error tipográfico.

typographer (tai'pag·rə·fər) *n.* tipógrafo.

typographical (,tai·pə'græf·ɪ·kəl) *adj.* tipográfico.

typography (tai'pag·rə·fi) *n.* tipografía.

tyrannical (tɪ'ræn·ɪ·kəl) *adj.* tiránico; tirano.

tyrannosaurus (tɪ'ræn·ə'sɔ·rəs) tiranosauro. *También,* **tyrannosaur.**

tyrannous ('tɪr·ə·nəs) *adj.* tirano; tiránico.

tyranny ('tɪr·ə·ni) *n.* tiranía. —**tyrannize,** *v.t. & i.* tiranizar.

tyrant ('tai·rənt) *n.* tirano.

tyre (tair) *n., Brit.* = **tire.**

tyro ('tai·ro) *n.* novicio; bisoño.

tzar (zar) *n.* = **tsar.** —**tzarevitch,** *n.* = **tsarevitch.** —**tzarevna,** *n.* = **tsarevna.** —**tzarina,** *n.* = **tsarina.**

tzetze ('tset·si) *n.* = **tsetse.**

U

U, u (ju) vigésima primera letra del alfabeto inglés.

ubiquitous (ju'bɪk·wə·təs) *adj.* ubicuo. —**ubiquitousness; ubiquity** (-wə·ti) *n.* ubicuidad.

U-boat *n.* submarino alemán.

udder ('ʌd·er) *n.* ubre.

UFO ('ju'ɛf'oɪ) *abr. de* **Unidentified Flying Object,** objeto volante no identificado.

ugh (ʌg) *interj.* ¡pu!; ¡puf!

ugly ('ʌg·li) *adj.* feo. —**ugliness,** *n.* fealdad.

UHF *abr. de* **ultra-high frequency.**

ukase ('ju·kes) *n.* ukase; ucase.

Ukrainian (ju'krei·ni·ən) *adj.* & *n.* ucranio.

ukulele (,ju·kə'lei·li) *n.* ukulele.

ulcer ('ʌl·sər) *n.* úlcera. —**ulcerous,** *adj.* ulceroso.

ulcerate ('ʌl·sər·eit) *v.t.* ulcerar. —*v.i.* ulcerarse. —**ulceration,** *n.* ulceración.

ulna ('ʌl·nə) *n.* cúbito.

ulster ('ʌl·stər) *n.* levitón.

ulterior (ʌl'tɪr·i·ər) *adj.* ulterior.

ultimate ('ʌl·tə·mət) *adj.* **1,** (farthest; last) último; final. **2,** (fundamental) fundamental; esencial. **3,** (maximum) sumo; máximo. —*n.* extremo.

ultimatum (,ʌl·tə'mei·təm) *n.* ultimátum.

ultimo ('ʌl·tɪ·mog) *adj.* del mes pasado o último.

ultra ('ʌl·trə) *adj.* extremado; excesivo; ultra. —*n.* extremista; ultra.

ultra-high frequency frecuencia ultraalta. *Abr.* **UHF.**

ultramarine (,ʌl·trə·mə'riːn) *n.* & *adj.* ultramarino.

ultrasonic (,ʌl·trə'sa·nɪk) *adj.* ultrasónico.

ultrasound ('ʌl·trə,saund) *n.* ultrasonido.

ultraviolet (,ʌl·trə'vai·ə·lɪt) *adj.* ultravioleta.

ululate ('jul·jə·leit) *v.i.* ulular. —**ululation,** *n.* ululación.

umber ('ʌm·bər) *n.* tierra de sombra. —*adj.* pardo; obscuro. —*v.t.* sombrear.

umbilical (ʌm'bɪl·ɪ·kəl) *adj.* umbilical. —**umbilical cord,** cordón umbilical.

umbilicus (ʌm'bɪl·ɪ·kəs) *n.* [*pl.* **-ci** (-sai)] ombligo.

umbra ('ʌm·brə) *n.* sombra.

umbrage ('ʌm·bridʒ) *n.* **1,** (resentment) resentimiento. **2,** (shade) sombra; umbría. —**take umbrage at,** resentirse por.

umbrageous (ʌm'brei·dʒəs) *adj.* **1,** (shady) sombroso; umbroso. **2,** (resentful) resentido.

umbrella (ʌm'brɛl·ə) *n.* paraguas; sombrilla. —**umbrella man,** paragüero. —**umbrella shop,** paragüería. —**umbrella stand,** paragüero.

umpire ('ʌm·pair) *n.* árbitro. —*v.t.* arbitrar. —*v.i.* arbitrar; ser árbitro.

umpteen (ʌmp'tin) *adj., colloq.* muchísimos. —**umpteenth,** *adj.* enésimo.

unabashed *adj.* descocado; desvergonzado.

unabated *adj.* cabal; completo; no disminuido.

unable *adj.* incapaz; inhábil.

unabridged *adj.* no abreviado; completo.

unaccented *adj.* inacentuado.

unacceptable *adj.* inaceptable.

unaccompanied *adj.* **1,** (alone) solo. **2,** *mus.* sin acompañamiento.

unaccountable *adj.* **1,** (inexplicable) inexplicable. **2,** (not responsible) irresponsable; no responsable.

unaccounted-for *adj.* **1,** (unexplained) inexplicado. **2,** (missing) ausente; no hallado.

unaccustomed *adj.* **1,** (unused) no acostumbrado. **2,** (unusual) desacostumbrado; insólito.

unacquainted *adj.* que no conoce. —**be unacquainted with,** no conocer; ignorar.

unadaptable *adj.* inadaptable.

unadoptable *adj.* inadaptable.

unadorned *adj.* sencillo; sin adorno.

unadulterated *adj.* genuino; puro; inadulterado.

unadvised *adj.* indiscreto; imprudente.

unaffected *adj.* **1,** (unmoved) impasible; no conmovido. **2,** (natural) sencillo; natural; inafectado.

unafraid *adj.* valiente; intrépido.

unaided *adj.* sin ayuda; solo.

unalienable *adj.* inalienable.

unalloyed *adj.* **1,** (pure) sin mezcla; puro. **2,** (utter; complete) cabal; completo; absoluto.

unalterable *adj.* inalterable.

unaltered *adj.* inalterado.

unambiguous *adj.* inequívoco; claro.

unambitious *adj.* no ambicioso; sin ambicíon.

un-American *adj.* antiamericano.

unanimity (,ju·nə'nim·ə·ti) *n.* unanimidad.

unanimous (ju'næn·ə·məs) *adj.* unánime.

unannounced *adj.* no anunciado.

unanswerable *adj.* incontrovertible; incontestable.

unanticipated *adj.* inesperado.

unappealable *adj.* inapelable.

unappealing *adj.* falto de atracción; poco atrayente.

unappetizing *adj.* poco apetitoso.

unappreciative *adj.* desagradecido; ingrato.

unapproachable *adj.* 1, (inaccessible) inaccesible; inasequible; inabordable. 2, (incomparable) incomparable; sin igual.

unapt *adj.* 1, (unskillful) inepto; inhábil. 2, (not inclined) poco inclinado; poco propenso. 3, (unsuitable) inadecuado.

unarm *v.t.* desarmar. —**unarmed**, *adj.* desarmado.

unascertainable *adj.* inaveriguable.

unashamed *adj.* desvergonzado.

unasked *adj.* 1, (unsolicited) insolicitado. 2, (not invited) no convidado.

unassailable *adj.* 1, (impregnable) inexpugnable; inatacable. 2, (incontrovertible) incontestable; incontrovertible.

unassembled *adj.* desmontado; sin montar.

unassimilable *adj.* inasimilable.

unassisted *adj.* sin ayuda; solo.

unassuming *adj.* modesto.

unattached *adj.* 1, (unconnected) suelto; libre. 2, (unmarried) soltero; célibe.

unattainable *adj.* inasequible; inalcanzable.

unattendance *n.* inasistencia.

unattended *adj.* 1, (alone) solitario; solo; sin séquito. 2, (neglected) desatendido.

unattractive *adj.* sin atractivo; feo.

unauthorized *adj.* desautorizado; sin autorización.

unavailable *adj.* indisponible.

unavailing *adj.* inútil; ineficaz; infructuoso.

unavoidable *adj.* inevitable; ineludible.

unaware *adj.* desatentido; inconsciente. —*adv.* = **unawares.** —**unawareness,** *n.* inconsciencia.

unawares *adv.* 1, (unknowingly) inadvertidamente; sin saberlo; sin pensar. 2, (unexpectedly) inesperadamente; de improviso.

unbalance *n.* desequilibrio. —*v.t.* desequilibrar. —**unbalanced,** *adj.* desequilibrado.

unbar *v.t.* [**unbarred, -barring**] desatrancar.

unbearable *adj.* insoportable; insufrible; inaguantable.

unbeaten *adj.* 1, (undefeated)

invicto; insuperado. 2, (untrod) no pisado; no frecuentado.

unbecoming *adj.* indecoroso; impropio.

unbeknown (ˌʌn·bi'noːn) *adj.* desconocido; inadvertido. *También,* **unbeknownst.** —**unbeknown to,** sin conocimiento de; sin saberlo (uno).

unbelief *n.* 1, (incredulity) incredulidad. 2, (lack of faith) descreimiento; irreligión.

unbelievable *adj.* increíble.

unbeliever *n.* 1, (doubter) incrédulo. 2, (infidel) descreído; infiel.

unbelieving *adj.* 1, (incredulous) incrédulo. 2, (faithless) descreído; infiel.

unbend *v.t.* [*pret. & p.p.* **unbent**] 1, (release) aflojar; soltar. 2, (straighten) enderezar. —*v.i.* 1, (relax) descansar; relajarse. 2, (straighten) enderezarse. —**unbending,** *adj.* inflexible; resoluto.

unbiased *adj.* imparcial; desinteresado.

unbidden *adj.* 1, (not commanded) espontáneo. 2, (not invited) no convidado.

unbind *v.t.* [*pret. & p.p.* **unbound**] desatar; soltar.

unbleached *adj.* crudo; sin blanquear.

unblessed (ʌn'blɛst) *adj.* 1, (without blessing) sin bendecir. 2, (wretched) desdichado. *También,* **unblest.**

unblinking *adj.* sin pestañear; (*fig.*) impasible.

unblushing *adj.* desvergonzado.

unbolt *v.t.* 1, (unbar) desatrancar. 2, (unscrew) desvolver; desenroscar.

unbolted *adj.* 1, (unfastened) desatrancado; no asegurado. 2, (not sifted) sin cerner.

unborn *adj.* no nacido.

unbosom (ʌn'buz·əm) *v.t.* revelar; confesar. —**unbosom oneself,** desahogarse; abrir el pecho.

unbound *adj.* 1, (without binding) no encuadernado. 2, (free) suelto; libre. —*v.,* *pret. & p.p. de* **unbind.**

unbounded *adj.* infinito; ilimitado.

unbowed (ʌn'baud) *adj.* 1, (not bent) no inclinado; no doblado. 2, (not subdued) no domado.

unbrace *v.t.* aflojar; soltar.

unbraid *v.t.* destrenzar.

unbreakable *adj.* irrompible.

unbridled *adj.* desenfrenado; irrefrenable. —**unbridle,** *v.t.* desenfrenar.

unbroken *adj.* **1,** (intact) intacto; entero. **2,** (not violated) inviolado. **3,** (continuous) continuo; sin interrupción. **4,** (not subdued) no domado.

unbuckle *v.t.* deshebillar.

unburden *v.t.* descargar. —**unburden oneself,** desahogarse.

unburied *adj.* insepulto.

unbusinesslike *adj.* poco práctico; poco metódico.

unbutton *v.t.* desabotonar; desabrochar.

uncalled-for *adj.* **1,** (not required) innecesario; no pedido. **2,** (gratuitous) gratuito; inmerecido.

uncanny (ʌn'kæn·i) *adj.* misterioso; extraño; raro.

uncap (ʌn'kæp) *v.t.* [**uncapped, -capping**] destapar.

uncared-for *adj.* desamparado; abandonado.

uncaused *adj.* sin motivo; sin razón.

unceasing *adj.* incesante.

unceremonious *adj.* **1,** (informal) informal; sin ceremonia. **2,** (curt) descortés; abrupto.

uncertain *adj.* incierto. —**uncertainty.** *n.* incertidumbre.

unchain *v.t.* desencadenar.

unchallenged *adj.* indisputable.

unchangeable *adj.* inmutable; incambiable; inalterable.

unchanged *adj.* inalterado; sin cambiar.

unchanging *adj.* inmutable; inalterable.

uncharitable *adj.* poco caritativo; duro.

uncharted *adj.* inexplorado.

unchaste *adj.* incasto.

unchecked *adj.* **1,** (unbridled) desenfrenado. **2,** (not verified) no verificado.

unchristian *adj.* anticristiano.

uncircumcised *adj.* incircunciso.

uncircumscribed *adj.* incircunscrito.

uncivil *adj.* incivil; descortés.

uncivilized *adj.* incivilizado; bárbaro.

unclad *adj.* desnudo; desvestido.

unclaimed *adj.* no reclamado; sin reclamar.

unclasp *v.t.* **1,** (unfasten) desabrochar. **2,** (release) librar; soltar.

unclassifiable *adj.* inclasificable.

unclassified *adj.* inclasificado.

uncle ('ʌŋ·kəl) *n.* tío. —**say** o **cry uncle,** rendirse; darse por vencido.

unclean *adj.* inmundo; sucio; impuro.

uncleanliness *n.* suciedad; inmundicia.

uncleanly (ʌn'klɛn·li) *adj.* inmundo; sucio. —*adv.* (ʌn'klin·li) suciamente.

unclench *v.t.* soltar; aflojar; desasir.

uncloak *v.t.* descubrir. —*v.i.* descubrirse.

unclog *v.t.* [**unclogged, -clogging**] desembarazar; desatrancar; desatascar.

unclose (ʌn'kloːz) *v.t.* **1,** (open) abrir. **2,** (disclose) descubrir; revelar.

unclothe *v.t.* desarropar; desvestir; desnudar. —*v.i.* desarroparse; desvestirse; desnudarse.

unclouded *adj.* despejado.

uncoil *v.t.* desenrollar. —*v.i.* desenrollarse.

uncollectible *adj.* incobrable.

uncomfortable *adj.* incómodo.

uncommitted *adj.* libre; no comprometido.

uncommon *adj.* raro; extraordinario; insólito.

uncommunicative *adj.* inconversable; reservado.

uncomplaining *adj.* no quejoso; paciente; sufrido.

uncompleted *adj.* inacabado; incompleto.

uncomplicated *adj.* no complicado; sencillo; incomplexo.

uncomplimentary *adj.* poco halagüeño.

uncompromising *adj.* intransigente; resoluto.

unconcern (ˌʌn·kən'sʌrn) *n.* indiferencia; despreocupación. —**unconcerned,** *adj.* indiferente; despreocupado.

unconditional *adj.* incondicional.

unconditioned *adj.* **1,** (natural) no condicionaado; natural. **2,** = **unconditional.**

unconfessed *adj.* inconfeso.

unconformity *n.* desconformidad.

uncongenial *adj.* **1,** (unfriendly) antipático. **2,** (incompatible) incompatible.

unconnected *adj.* inconexo; desconectado.

unconquerable *adj.* inconquistable.

unconscionable *adj.* **1,** (unscrupulous) inescrupuloso. **2,** (unreasonable) desrazonable. **3,** (excessive) excesivo.

unconscious (ʌn'kan·ʃəs) *adj. & n.* inconsciente. —**unconsciousness,** *n.* inconsciencia.

unconstitutional *adj.* anticonstitucional.

uncontaminated *adj.* incontaminado; puro.

uncontrollable *adj.* irrefrenable; ingobernable.

unconventional *adj.* informal; libre; despreocupado.

uncooked *adj.* crudo.

uncooperative *adj.* poco cooperativo; roncero.

uncork *v.t.* descorchar; destaponar.

uncorrupted *adj.* incorrupto.

uncountable *adj.* incontable; innumerable.

uncounted *adj.* **1,** (not counted) no contado. **2,** (countless) innumerable.

uncouple *v.t.* desacoplar; *R.R.* desenganchar.

uncouth (ʌn'kuθ) *adj.* **1,** (boorish) tosco; grosero. **2,** (strange) extraño; extraordinario.

uncover *v.t.* **1,** (remove the cover from) destapar; descubrir. **2,** (disclose) descubrir; revelar. **3,** (remove the clothing from) desarropar. —*v.i.* descubrirse.

uncritical *adj.* poco discerniente; inexperto.

uncrown *v.t.* destronar. —**uncrowned,** *adj.* sin corona.

unction ('ʌŋk·ʃən) *n.* unción.

unctuous ('ʌŋ·tʃu·əs) *adj.* untuoso. —**unctuousness,** *n.* untuosidad.

uncultivated *adj.* inculto.

uncultured *adj.* inculto.

uncured *adj.* no curado; crudo.

uncurl *v.t.* desrizar. —*v.i.* desrizarse.

uncut *adj.* no cortado; entero; completo.

undamaged *adj.* indemne; intacto.

undaunted *adj.* impávido; impertérrito.

undeceive *v.t.* desengañar.

undecided *adj.* indeciso.

undecipherable *adj.* indescifrable.

undefeated *adj.* invicto.

undefended *adj.* indefenso.

undefiled *adj.* impoluto.

undefinable *adj.* indefinible.

undefined *adj.* indefinido.

undemocratic *adj.* antidemocrático.

undemonstrative *adj.* reservado; poco expresivo.

undeniable *adj.* innegable.

undenominational *adj.* no sectario.

under ('ʌn·dər) *prep.* **1,** (below; beneath) bajo; debajo de. **2,** (less than) menos de; menos que. **3,** (inferior to) inferior a. **4,** (subject to) sujeto a; sometido a. **5,** (according to) conforme a; según. —*adj.* inferior. —*adv.* debajo; abajo; más abajo. —**bring under,** dominar. —**go under, 1,** (fail) fracasar. **2,** (sink) hundirse. —**keep under,** oprimir. —**under a cloud,** en apuros.

underact *v.t. & i.* actuar atenuadamente (un papel).

underage (ˌʌn·dər'eidʒ) *adj.* menor de edad.

underarm *adv.* de la axila. —**underarm perspiration,** sobaquina.

underarmed *adj.* sin suficientes armas.

underbid *v.t.* [**underbid, -bidding**] ofrecer menos que.

underbred *adj.* **1,** (ill-bred) malcriado; mal educado. **2,** (not of pure breed) de raza impura.

underbrush *n.* maleza.

undercarriage *n.* bastidor; *aero.* tren de aterrizaje.

undercharge *v.t.* cargar o cobrar menos (o de menos). —*n.* cargo insuficiente.

underclass *n.* clase baja o inferior.

underclassman (ˌʌn·dər'klæs·mən) *n.* [*pl.*-**men**] alumno universitario de los dos primeros años.

underclothes *n.pl.* ropa interior.

undercoat *n.* **1,** *paint.* primera capa o mano. **2,** *auto.* capa anticorrosiva.

undercook *v.t. & i.* cocer(se) poco.

undercover *adj.* secreto; clandestino.

undercurrent *n.* **1,** (lower current) corriente inferior. **2,** (hidden tendency) tendencia oculta.

undercut (ʌn·dər'kʌt) *v.t.* [**undercut, -cutting**] socavar. —*adj.* ('ʌn-) socavado. —*n.* ('ʌn-) socavación; socava.

underdevelop *v.t.* desarrollar

incompletamente. —**underdeveloped,** adj. subdesarrollado.

underdo v.t. [pret. **underdid;** p.p. **underdone**] **1,** (do too little) hacer poco; escatimar. **2,** = **undercook.**

underdog ('ʌn·dər·dɔg) n. perdedor; víctima.

underdone adj. a medio cocer; insuficientemente cocido.

underdrawers ('ʌn·dər,drɔrs) n.pl. calzoncillos.

underestimate (,ʌn·dər'ɛs·tɪ·meit) v.t. & i. **1,** (misjudge in cost or value) apreciar demasiado bajo; estimar en menos del valor. **2,** (hold in low esteem) desestimar; menospreciar. —n. (-mət) **1,** (too low a price or value) apreciación demasiado baja; presupuesto demasiado bajo. **2,** (low esteem) desestimación; menosprecio.

underexpose v.t. exponer insuficientemente. —**underexposure,** n. exposición insuficiente; poca exposición.

underfed adj. desnutrido.

underfeed v.t. [pret. & p.p. **underfed**] alimentar poco. —**underfeeding,** n. desnutrición.

underfoot adj. & adv. debajo de los pies; fig. molestando; estorbando.

undergarment n. prenda de vestir interior.

undergo v.t. [**underwent, -gone, -going**] **1,** (experience) pasar por; correr. **2,** (endure) sufrir; padecer. **3,** (be subjected to) estar sometido a; someterse a.

undergraduate adj. no graduado; de o para el bachillerato. —n. estudiante del bachillerato.

underground adj. **1,** (subterranean) subterráneo. **2,** (secret) secreto; clandestino. —adv. **1,** (beneath the surface) bajo tierra; debajo de la tierra. **2,** (secretly) clandestinamente. —n. **1,** (underground space or passage) subterráneo. **2,** (secret movement) movimiento oculto; resistencia. **3,** Brit. = **subway.**

undergrown adj. poco crecido; poco desarrollado; enano.

undergrowth n. **1,** (underbrush) maleza; chamarasca. **2,** (arrested development) pequeñez; desarrollo impedido.

underhand adj. (deceitful) taimado; clandestino; disimulado.

—adj. & adv., sports con la mano debajo del nivel de los hombros.

underhanded adj. taimado; clandestino; disimulado. —**underhandedly,** adv. bajo cuerda; a socapa; disimuladamente.

underhung adj. **1,** (suspended) suspendido. **2,** (jutting out, as the jaw) sobresaliente.

underlay (ʌn·dər'lei) v.t. [prep. & p.p. **underlaid**] **1,** (place under) poner debajo. **2,** (raise; reinforce) levantar; reforzar. **3,** (raise; reinforce) levantar; reforzar. **4,** v. pret. de. **underlie.** —n. ('ʌn·dər·lei) calzo.

underlie v.t. [**underlay, -lain, -lying**] **1,** (lie under) estar o extenderse debajo de. **2,** (support) sostener; sustentar; ser la base o fundamento de.

underline v.t. subrayar. —n. raya.

underling ('ʌn·dər·lɪŋ) n. inferior; subordinado; secuaz.

underlying adj. **1,** (placed beneath) subyacente. **2,** (basic) fundamental. **3,** (obscure) oculto. —v., p.r.p. de **underlie.**

undermine ('ʌn·dər,main) v.t. minar; socavar.

undermost adj. ínfimo; más bajo. —adv. a lo más bajo.

underneath (,ʌn·dər'niθ) adv. debajo. —prep. debajo de; bajo. —adj. inferior. —n. parte inferior.

undernourish v.t. alimentar poco. —**undernourished,** adj. desnutrido. —**undernourishment,** n. desnutrición.

underpants n.pl. calzoncillos.

underpass n. paso bajo; paso inferior.

underpay v.t. [pret. & p.p. **underpaid**] pagar mal; pagar insuficientemente. —n. pago insuficiente. —**underpaid,** adj. mal pagado. —**underpayment,** n. pago insuficiente.

underpin v.t. [**underpinned, -pinning**] apuntalar. —**underpinning,** n. apuntalamiento.

underplay v.t. & i. actuar atenuadamente (un papel).

underpopulated adj. poco poblado. —**underpopulation,** n. poca población; baja población.

underprice v.t. pedir insuficiente por; poner demasiado barato.

underprivileged adj. necesitado; desvalido.

underproduce v.t. & i. producir insuficientemente. —**underproduc-**

tion, *n.* producción insuficiente; baja producción.

underprop *v.t.* [**underpropped, -propping**] apuntalar.

underrate (,ʌn·dər'reit) *v.t.* desapreciar; menospreciar.

underripe *adj.* inmaduro; verde.

underrun *v.t.* [**underran, -run, -running**] correr por debajo.

underscore ('ʌn·dər·skor) *v.t.* subrayar. —*n.* raya.

undersea *adj.* submarino. —*adv.* bajo la superficie del mar.

undersecretary *n.* subsecretario.

undersell *v.t.* [*pret. & p.p.* **undersold**] vender más barato (que).

undershirt *n.* camiseta.

underside *n.* superficie inferior.

undersign *v.t.* subscribir. —**the undersigned,** el infrascrito; el abajo firmado.

undersized *adj.* de talla menor; de corta estatura.

underskirt *n.* enagua; enaguas.

underslung *adj.* colgante; suspendido debajo del eje.

undersoil *n.* subsuelo.

undersold *v., pret. & p.p. de* **undersell.**

understand (,ʌn·dər'stænd) *v.t. & i.* [*pret. & p.p.* **understood**] **1,** (comprehend) comprender; entender. **2,** (assume; supply mentally) sobrentender. —**understandable,** *adj.* comprensible.

understanding (,ʌn·dər'stæn·dɪŋ) *n.* **1,** (comprehension) entendimiento. **2,** (agreement) acuerdo. —*adj.* **1,** (comprehending) inteligente; entendedor. **2,** (sympathetic) comprensivo.

understate *v.t.* declarar o manifestar incompletamente; decir con poca fuerza. —**understatement,** *n.* expresión exageradamente moderada.

understock *v.t.* surtir poco (de).

understood (,ʌn·dər'stud) *adj.* **1,** (comprehended) entendido. **2,** (agreed) convenido. **3,** (assumed) sobrentendido. —*v., pret. & p.p. de* **understand.**

understudy ('ʌn·dər,stʌd·i) *n.* actor sustituto; sustituto; suplente. —*v.t.* aprender (un papel o empleo) para poder sustituir (a otro).

undertake *v.t.* [*pret.* **undertook;** *p.p.* **undertaken**] **1,** (take upon oneself) emprender; entrar en; tomar a su cargo. **2,** (commit oneself to) comprometerse a.

undertaker *n.* funerario; director de pompas fúnebres.

undertaking (ʌn·dər'tei·kɪŋ) *n.* **1,** (task; enterprise) empresa. **2,** ('ʌn·dər-) (business of an undertaker) empresa funeraria.

under-the-counter *adj.* bajo mano; ilícito.

underthings *n.pl.* ropa interior.

undertone *n.*, **1,** (low voice) voz baja. **2,** (subdued color) matiz suavizado. **3,** (background) fondo.

undertow ('ʌn·dər,to) *n.* resaca.

undervalue *v.t.* desapreciar; desestimar. —**undervaluation,** *n.* desaprecio; desestimación.

underwaist *n.* corpiño.

underwater *adj.* submarino; bajo agua.

underwear ('ʌn·dər·wɛr) *n.* ropa interior.

underweight *n.* peso escaso; flaqueza. —*adj.* de peso escaso; flaco.

underwent *v., pret. de* **undergo.**

underworld *n.* **1,** (criminal element) hampa; mundo de vicio. **2,** (hell) infierno; averno.

underwrite *v.t.* [*pret.* **underwrote;** *p.p.* **underwritten**] **1,** (subscribe) suscribir. **2,** (guarantee) asegurar.

underwriter *n.* asegurador [*fem.* -dora].

undeserved *adj.* inmerecido.

undeserving *adj.* desmerecedor; indigno.

undesigning *adj.* sincero; sencillo; sin malicia.

undesirable *adj.* indeseable.

undetermined *adj.* indeterminado.

undeterred *adj.* impávido; impertérrito.

undeveloped *adj.* sin desarrollo; subdesarrollado.

undeviating *adj.* **1,** (straight) directo. **2,** (unvarying) sin rodeo; siempre igual.

undies ('ʌn·diz) *n.pl., colloq.* = **underwear.**

undigested *adj.* indigesto.

undignified *adj.* indecoroso; indecente.

undiminished *adj.* entero; completo; íntegro.

undiplomatic *adj.* poco diplomático; indiscreto.

undirected *adj.* **1,** (without direction) sin dirección. **2,** (without address) sin señas.

undiscernible *adj.* imperceptible; indiscernible.

undiscerning *adj.* poco discerniente; inexperto.

undisciplined *adj.* indisciplinado.

undisclosed *adj.* no revelado; oculto; secreto.

undiscouraged *adj.* impávido; firme; resoluto.

undiscovered *adj.* no descubierto; oculto.

undiscriminating *adj.* poco discerniente; falto de buen gusto.

undisguised *adj.* cándido; franco; abierto; sin disfraz.

undismayed *adj.* impávido; firme; no desanimado.

undisposed *adj.* no dispuesto. —**undisposed of, 1,** (available) disponible. **2,** (unsold) no vendido. **3,** (unsettled) no decidido; no arreglado.

undisputed *adj.* incontestable; incontrovertible.

undistinguishable *adj.* indistinguible.

undistinguished *adj.* no distinguido; ordinario.

undisturbed *adj.* imperturbado; tranquilo.

undivided *adj.* indiviso; entero.

undo (ʌn'doɹ) *v.t.* [**undid, undone, undoing**] **1,** (cancel; annul) deshacer; anular. **2,** (unfasten) desatar; desliar. **3,** (ruin) arruinar; perder.

undoing (ʌn'do·ɪŋ) *n.* **1,** (canceling; annulling) anulación. **2,** (ruin) ruina; pérdida.

undone *v., p.p. de* undo. —*adj.* **1,** (not done) sin hacer; por hacer. **2,** (unfastened) desatado. **3,** (ruined) arruinado; perdido.

undoubted *adj.* indudable; fuera de duda. —**undoubtedly,** *adv.* indudablemente; sin duda.

undrape *v.t.* desvestir; desnudar. —**undraped,** *adj.* desnudo.

undress *v.t.* desvestir; desnudar. —*v.i.* desvestirse; desnudarse. —*n.* ropa de casa; *mil.* traje de cuartel; uniforme diario. —*adj.* informal.

undue (ʌn'dju; -'duɹ) *adj.* **1,** (improper) indebido. **2,** (excessive) excesivo. **3,** (not payable) no vencido; no debido.

undulant ('ʌn·djə·lənt) *adj.* ondulante.

undulate ('ʌn·djə,leit) *v.t. & i.* ondular. —**undulation,** *n.* ondulación.

unduly (ʌn'du·li) *adv.* **1,** (improperly) indebidamente. **2,** (excessively) excesivamente.

undying *adj.* imperecedero.

unearned *adj.* **1,** (not earned) no ganado. **2,** (not deserved) inmerecido.

unearth (ʌn'ʌrθ) *v.t.* **1,** (disinter) desenterrar. **2,** (discover) descubrir.

unearthly *adj.* **1,** (supernatural) sobrenatural. **2,** (ghostly) espectral. **3,** (frightful) horripilante. **4,** *colloq.* (strange) extraño; raro; fantástico.

uneasy (ʌn'i·zi) *adj.* **1,** (disturbed) inquieto; desasosegado. **2,** (awkward) desmañado; falto de gracia. —**uneasiness,** *n.* inquietud; desasosiego.

uneatable *adj.* incomible.

uneconomical *adj.* antieconómico.

uneducated *adj.* ineducado. —**uneducable,** *adj.* ineducable.

unembarrassed *adj.* desembarazado; aplomado.

unemotional *adj.* impasible; frío.

unemployed *adj.* **1,** (without work) desempleado; desocupado. **2,** (not in use) inutilizado; improductivo.

unemployment *n.* desempleo; desocupación; cesantía. —**unemployment compensation,** beneficios del seguro contra el desempleo. —**unemployment insurance,** seguro contra el desempleo.

unencompassable *adj.* inabarcable.

unencumbered *adj.* **1,** (unhampered) libre; sin trabas. **2,** (not crowded) desahogado. **3,** *law* libre de gravamen.

unending *adj.* infinito; interminable.

unendurable *adj.* inaguantable; insoportable.

unenforceable *adj.* incumplible.

unengaged *adj.* libre; desocupado; no comprometido.

unenlightened *adj.* no iluminado; ignorante.

unenviable *adj.* poco envidiable.

unenvied *adj.* no envidiado.

unequal *adj.* **1,** (of different measure; uneven) desigual. **2,** (inadequate) insuficiente; inadecuado. **3,** (unjust) injusto; parcial.

unequaled *adj.* inigualado; sin igual.

unequivocal *adj.* inequívoco.
unerring (ʌnˈɛr·ɪŋ) *adj.* infalible.
unessential *adj.* no esencial; superfluo.
unethical *adj.* poco ético.
uneven *adj.* **1,** (unequal) desigual. **2,** (rough) escabroso; quebrado. **3,** (irregular) irregular. **4,** (odd) impar.
uneventful *adj.* tranquilo; sin novedad.
unexampled (ˌʌn·ɛgˈzæm·pəld) *adj.* sin precedente; sin par; único.
unexcelled *adj.* insuperado.
unexceptionable *adj.* irrecusable; irreprensible.
unexceptional *adj.* ordinario; corriente.
unexchangeable *adj.* incambiable; impermutable.
unexcited *adj.* no excitado; tranquilo; sereno.
unexciting *adj.* no excitante; árido; aburrido.
unexpected *adj.* inesperado.
unexpended *adj.* no expendido.
unexpired *adj.* no expirado; no vencido.
unexplained *adj.* inexplicado. —**unexplainable,** *adj.* inexplicable.
unexploited *adj.* no explotado; desaprovechado.
unexplored *adj.* inexplorado.
unexposed *adj.* no expuesto.
unexpressed *adj.* inexpresado.
unexpressive *adj.* inexpresivo.
unexpurgated *adj.* no expurgado.
unfading *adj.* inmarchitable.
unfailing *adj.* **1,** (inexhaustible) inagotable. **2,** (infallible) indefectible; infalible.
unfair *adj.* **1,** (unjust) injusto. **2,** (dishonest) falso; deshonesto. **3,** *sports* sucio.
unfaithful *adj.* infiel.
unfaltering *adj.* sin vacilar; firme; resuelto.
unfamiliar *adj.* **1,** (not well known) poco familiar; poco conocido. **2,** (not well versed) no familiarizado.
unfamiliarity *n.* **1,** (strangeness) falta de familiaridad. **2,** (lack of knowledge) desconocimiento.
unfashionable *adj.* singular; raro; opuesto a la moda.
unfasten *v.t.* soltar; desatar; desabrochar; desenganchar.
unfathomable *adj.* insondable.
unfavorable *adj.* desfavorable.
unfeasible *adj.* impracticable.

unfeeling *adj.* **1,** (insensible) insensible. **2,** (hardhearted) duro de corazón; cruel.
unfeigned *adj.* genuino; verdadero; sincero.
unfenced *adj.* no cercado; abierto.
unfetter *v.t.* desencadenar.
unfettered *adj.* libre; suelto; liberado.
unfilial *adj.* que no conviene a un hijo; impropio de un hijo.
unfilled *adj.* no lleno; vacío; vacante.
unfinished *adj.* incompleto; inconcluso; inacabado.
unfit *adj.* **1,** (incapable) incapaz; inhábil. **2,** (unsuitable) impropio; desconveniente. —*v.t.* [**unfitted, -fitting**] inhabilitar.
unfitting *adj.* impropio; indecoroso.
unfix *v.t.* soltar; desatar.
unflappable (ʌnˈflæp·ə·bəl) *adj. slang* impasible.
unflagging *adj.* persistente; incansable.
unflattering *adj.* poco halagüeño; poco favorecedor.
unfledged *adj.* **1,** (without feathers) implume. **2,** (immature) inmaduro.
unflinching *adj.* resuelto; firme; sin retroceso.
unfold *v.t.* **1,** (spread out) desdoblar; desplegar. **2,** (unwrap) desenvolver. **3,** (reveal) revelar; descubrir. **4,** (develop) desarrollar.
unforbearing *adj.* intolerante; poco indulgente.
unforeseeable *adj.* imprevisible.
unforeseen *adj.* imprevisto.
unforgettable *adj.* inolvidable.
unforgivable *adj.* imperdonable. —**unforgiving,** *n.* inclemente; inexorable.
unforgotten *adj.* inolvidado.
unformed *adj.* informe; crudo; no desarrollado.
unfortunate *adj.* desgraciado; desafortunado; infeliz. —**unfortunately,** *adv.* por desgracia; desgraciadamente; infelizmente.
unfounded *adj.* infundado.
unfrequented *adj.* poco frecuentado; solitario.
unfriendly *adj.* poco amistoso; áspero; enemigo.
unfrock (ʌnˈfrak) *v.t.* expulsar (*a un sacerdote*).
unfruitful *adj.* infructuoso.
unfulfilled *adj.* incumplido.

unfurl (ʌn'fʌrl) v.t. desplegar; extender.

unfurnished adj. 1, (without furniture) desamueblado. 2, (unsupplied) desprovisto.

ungainly (ʌn'gein·li) adj. desmañado; desgarbado.

ungallant adj. poco galante; poco caballeroso; descortés.

ungenerous adj. poco generoso; tacaño.

ungentlemanly adj. poco caballeroso; descortés.

ungird v.t. desceñir.

unglue v.t. despegar.

ungodly adj. 1, (godless) impío; profano; ateo; sindiós. 2, colloq. (outrageous) atroz. —adv., colloq. muy; extremadamente.

ungovernable adj. indomable; ingobernable.

ungraceful adj. desgarbado; falto de gracia.

ungracious adj. 1, (unpleasant) desagradable. 2, (discourteous) descortés.

ungrammatical adj. ingramatical.

ungrateful adj. ingrato; desagradecido.

ungrounded adj. 1, (unfounded) infundado. 2, (unversed) poco instruído. 3, elect. sin conductor a tierra.

ungrudging adj. voluntario; de buena gana.

unguarded adj. 1, (unprotected) desguarnecido; indefenso. 2, (indiscreet) incauto; indiscreto.

unguent ('ʌŋ·gwənt) n. ungüento.

ungulate ('ʌŋ·gjə·let) adj. & n. ungulado.

unhallowed adj. profano; impío.

unhampered adj. libre; no impedido.

unhand v.t. desatar; soltar.

unhandsome adj. 1, (homely) feo. 2, (rude) descortés. 3, (stingy) poco generoso; tacaño.

unhandy adj. 1, (unskillful) inepto; desmañado. 2, (cumbersome) incómodo.

unhappy adj. infeliz; desdichado; triste. —**unhappiness**, n. desdicha; tristeza.

unharmed adj. ileso; incólume.

unharmful adj. inofensivo; innocuo.

unharness v.t. desenjaezar; desguarnecer; desarmar.

unhatched adj. no salido del cascarón; fig. no descubierto.

unhealthful adj. malsano; insalubre.

unhealthy adj. 1, (sickly) enfermizo; achacoso. 2, = **unhealthful**.

unheard adj. 1, (not heard) no oído. 2, (unknown) desconocido.

unheard-of adj. inaudito.

unheated adj. no calentado; sin calefacción.

unheeded adj. desatendido. —**unheedful**, adj. desatento. —**unheeding**, adj. descuidado; no haciendo caso.

unhesitating adj. decidido; resuelto; pronto.

unhindered adj. libre; no impedido.

unhinge (ʌn'hɪndʒ) v.t. desquiciar.

unhitch v.t. desenganchar.

unholy (ʌn'ho·li) adj. 1, (profane) impío; profano. 2, colloq. (dreadful) terrible; atroz.

unhook v.t. desenganchar; descolgar.

unhoped-for adj. inesperado.

unhorse (ʌn'hors) v.t. desmontar.

unhurried adj. sin prisa; pausado.

unhurt adj. ileso; incólume.

unhygienic adj. antihigiénico.

unhyphenated adj. sin guión; fig. cabal; entero; íntegro.

unicameral (ˌju·nə'kæm·ə·rel) adj. unicameral.

unicellular (ˌju·nə'sɛl·jə·lər) adj. unicelular.

unicorn ('ju·nə·korn) n. unicornio.

unicycle ('ju·nɪˌsai·kəl) n. monociclo.

unidentified adj. no identificado; desconocido.

uniform ('ju·nə·form) n. & adj. uniforme. —v.t. uniformar. —**uniformity** (-'for·mə·ti) n. uniformidad.

unify ('ju·nə·fai) v.t. unificar. —**unification** (-fɪ'kei·ʃən) n. unificación.

unilateral (ˌju·nə'læt·ər·əl) adj. unilateral.

unimaginable adj. inimaginable.

unimaginative adj. poco imaginativo.

unimpaired adj. inalterado; intacto.

unimpassioned adj. no apasionado; frío.

unimpeachable adj. irrecusable; intachable; incensurable.

unimpeded *adj.* libre; no impedido.

unimportant *adj.* insignificante; poco importante. —**unimportance,** *n.* poca importancia.

unimposing *adj.* poco imponente; poco impresionante.

unimpressed *adj.* poco impresionado; poco conmovido.

unimpressive *adj.* poco impresionante.

unimproved *adj.* **1,** (not improved) no mejorado; no adelantado. **2,** (undeveloped, as land) sin urbanizar.

unincorporated *adj.* no incorporado.

uninflammable *adj.* incombustible.

uninflected *adj.* sin inflexión.

uninfluential *adj.* poco influyente.

uninformed *adj.* ignorante; no informado.

uninhabitable *adj.* inhabitable.

uninhabited *adj.* deshabitado; inhabitado.

uninhibited *adj.* desenfrenado; desenvuelto; libre; abierto.

uninitiated *adj.* no iniciado; inexperto.

uninjured *adj.* ileso; incólume.

uninspired *adj.* no inspirado; sin inspiración.

uninspiring *adj.* que no inspira; árido; aburrido.

unintelligent *adj.* estúpido; torpe; bruto.

unintelligible *adj.* ininteligible.

unintentional *adj.* no intencional; hecho sin intención.

uninterested *adj.* no interesado.

uninteresting *adj.* sin interés; soso; aburrido.

uninterrupted *adj.* ininterrumpido; continuo. —**uninterruptedly,** *adv.* sin interrupción; continuamente.

uninvited *adj.* no convidado; insolicitado.

union ('jun·jən) *n.* **1,** (combination; joining; joint) unión. **2,** (labor organization) sindicato; gremio; *Amer.* unión. —*adj.* gremial; del sindicato.

unionism ('jun·jən·ɪz·əm) *n.* sindicalismo; unionismo. —**unionist,** *n.* sindicalista; unionista.

unionize ('jun·jən·aiz) *v.t.* sindicar; agremiar. —*v.i.* sindicarse; agremiarse. —**unionization** (-ɪ·

'zei·ʃən) *n.* sindicación; agremiación.

Union Jack pabellón de la Gran Bretaña.

union shop taller agremiado.

union suit prenda de ropa interior de una sola pieza.

unique (ju'nik) *adj.* único; singular. —**uniqueness,** *n.* singularidad; unicidad.

unirrigated *adj.* sin riego.

unisex ('ju·nɪˌsɛks) *adj.* unisexo.

unisexual (ˌju·nɪ'sɛk·ʃu·əl) *adj.* unisexual.

unison ('ju·nə·sən) *n.* **1,** *mus.* unisón. **2,** (agreement) concordancia; armonía. —*adj.* unísono. —**in unison,** unísono; al unísono.

unissued (ʌn'ɪʃˌud) *adj.* **1,** (not emitted) no emitido. **2,** (unpublished) no publicado; inédito.

unit ('ju·nɪt) *n.* unidad. —*adj.* unitario.

unitarian (ˌju·nə'tɛr·i·ən) *adj.* & *n.* unitario.

unitary ('ju·nə·tɛr·i) *adj.* unitario.

unite (ju'nait) *v.t.* unir. —*v.i.* unirse. —**united,** *adj.* unido.

United States Estados Unidos (de América). —*adj.* estadounidense.

unity ('ju·nə·ti) *n.* unidad.

univalent (ˌju·nə'vei·lənt) *adj.* univalente.

univalve *adj.* & *n.* univalvo.

universal (ˌju·nə'vʌr·səl) *adj.* universal. —**universality** (-vər'sæl·ə·ti) *n.* universalidad.

universalist (ju·nə'vʌr·səl·ɪst) *adj.* & *n.* universalista. —**universalism,** *n.* universalismo.

universalize (ˌju·nə'vʌr·səˌlaiz) *v.t.* universalizar.

universal joint articulación universal.

universe ('ju·nə·vʌrs) *n.* universo.

university (ju·nə'vʌr·sə·ti) *n.* universidad. —*adj.* universitario.

unjoin *v.t.* separar; desunir.

unjoint *v.t.* desencajar; descoyuntar.

unjust *adj.* injusto.

unjustifiable *adj.* injustificable.

unjustified *adj.* injustificado.

unkempt (ʌn'kɛmpt) *adj.* **1,** (disheveled) desgreñado; despeinado. **2,** (untidy) desaliñado; desaseado. **3,** (rough) rudo; tosco.

unkind *adj.* duro; severo; áspero. —**unkindness,** *n.* severidad; aspereza.

unknit v.t. [pret. & p.p. **unknitted** o **unknit**; ger. **unknitting**] destejer.

unknot v.t. [unknotted, -knotting] desatar; desligar.

unknowable adj. incognoscible; insabible.

unknowing adj. ignorante; inadvertido. —**unknowingly,** adv. inadvertidamente; sin saberlo.

unknown adj. desconocido; ignoto; incógnito. —n. desconocido; math. incógnita.

unlace v.t. desenlazar; desatar.

unladen adj. descargado.

unladylike adj. impropio de una dama; poco delicado.

unlamented adj. no lamentado; no llorado.

unlash v.t. desatar; desligar.

unlatch v.t. abrir soltando el pestillo; saltar el pestillo de.

unlawful adj. 1, (illegal) ilegal; ilícito. 2, (illegitimate) ilegítimo. —**unlawfulness,** n. ilegalidad.

unlearn v.t. desaprender.

unlearned (ʌn'lʌr·nɪd) adj. 1, (ignorant) ignorante; indocto. 2, (ʌn'lʌrnd) (not mastered) no aprendido; no estudiado. 3, (ʌn'lʌrnd) (innate) innato; natural; instintivo.

unleash v.t. desencadenar; soltar.

unleavened adj. ázimo; sin levadura.

unless (ʌn'lɛs) conj. a menos que; a no ser que; si no. —prep. excepto; si no es.

unlettered adj. 1, (uneducated) indocto; inculto. 2, (illiterate) analfabeto.

unlicensed adj. sin licencia; no autorizado.

unlighted adj. 1, (dark) oscuro; no iluminado. 2, (not burning) no encendido. También, **unlit.**

unlikable también, **unlikeable,** adj. poco agradable; desagradable.

unlike adj. diferente; desemejante; dispar. —prep. diferente a; a diferencia de. —**unlikeness,** n. diferencia; desemejanza.

unlikely adj. 1, (improbable) inverosímil; improbable. 2, (not inclined) poco inclinado; poco propenso. —adv. improbablemente. —**unlikelihood,** n. improbabilidad.

unlimited adj. 1, (boundless) ilimitado; infinito. 2, (unrestricted) sin restricción. 3, (indefinite) indefinido.

unlined adj. 1, (without lining) sin forro. 2, (unruled) sin rayar. 3, (unwrinkled) sin arrugas.

unlink v.t. deseslabonar.

unlisted adj. no registrado.

unlit adj. = **unlighted.**

unload v.t. 1, (discharge) descargar. 2, (get rid of) deshacerse de. —**unloading,** n. descarga; descargo.

unlock v.t. 1, (open) abrir. 2, (reveal) revelar; descubrir.

unloose (ʌn'lus) v.t. desatar; aflojar; soltar.

unloosen (ʌn'lu·sən) v.t. aflojar; soltar.

unloved adj. no amado.

unlovely adj. antipático; desagradable; feo.

unlucky adj. 1, (having bad luck) desgraciado; sin suerte; desafortunado. 2, (bringing bad luck) aciago; funesto; siniestro; de mal agüero.

unmake v.t. [pret. & p.p. **unmade**] 1, (undo) deshacer. 2, (depose) deponer.

unman (ʌn'mæn) v.t. [unmanned, -manning] 1, (unnerve) desanimar; privar de fuerza. 2, (emasculate) afeminar; castrar; capar. 3, (deprive of men) privar de hombres; desguarnecer.

unmanageable adj. inmanejable; intratable.

unmanful adj. indigno de un hombre; poco varonil.

unmanly adj. 1, (effeminate) afeminado. 2, (cowardly) cobarde; vil; ruin.

unmannerly adj. malcriado; descortés. —adv. descortésmente.

unmarked adj. no señalado.

unmarketable adj. invendible.

unmarried adj. soltero; célibe.

unmask v.t. desenmascarar. —v.i. desenmascararse.

unmatched adj. único; sin par; sin igual.

unmeaning (ʌn'mi·nɪŋ) adj. sin sentido; sin expresión.

unmeasured adj. ilimitado.

unmentionable adj. infando. —**unmentionables,** n.pl. ropa interior; prendas íntimas.

unmerciful adj. inclemente; despiadado.

unmerited adj. inmerecido.

unmethodical adj. poco metódico; desarreglado; irregular.

unmindful adj. olvidadizo; desatento; descuidado.

unmistakable adj. inequívoco.

unmitigated *adj.* **1,** (not lessened) no mitigado; no disminuido. **2,** (absolute) cabal; absoluto.

unmixed *adj.* puro; sencillo; sin mezcla.

unmolested *adj.* quieto; tranquilo.

unmoor *v.t.* desamarrar.

unmoral *adj.* amoral.

unmounted *adj.* desmontado; no montado.

unmoved *adj.* impasible; inmoto; no conmovido.

unmoving *adj.* **1,** (motionless) inmóvil. **2,** (lacking appeal) seco; árido.

unmusical *adj.* disonante; discorde.

unmuzzle *v.t.* quitar el bozal a; *fig.* dejar hablar.

unnamed *adj.* innominado; anónimo.

unnatural *adj.* **1,** (contrary to nature) innatural; desnaturalizado. **2,** (artificial; affected) artificial; afectado.

unnecessary *adj.* innecesario; superfluo; inútil. —**unnecessarily,** *adv.* sin necesidad, inútilmente.

unneeded *adj.* innecesario; no necesitado.

unneedful *adj.* **1,** (unnecessary) innecesario; inútil. **2,** (not needy) no necesitado; bien provisto.

unneighborly *adj.* adusto; poco sociable.

unnerve (ʌn'nʌrv) *v.t.* **1,** (weaken) enervar; debilitar. **2,** (dishearten) acobardar; desanimar.

unnoticeable *adj.* imperceptible; poco llamativo.

unnoticed *adj.* inadvertido; desapercibido; pasado por alto.

unnumbered *adj.* **1,** (innumerable) innumerable. **2,** (not numbered) sin número; no numerado.

unobjectionable *adj.* irrecusable; irreprensible.

unobliging *adj.* poco servicial; poco atento.

unobservable *adj.* inobservable.

unobservant *adj.* poco observador. —**unobservance,** *n.* inobservancia.

unobserved *adj.* desapercibido.

unobserving *adj.* desatento.

unobstructed *adj.* libre; no obstruido.

unobtainable *adj.* inasequible.

unobtrusive *adj.* discreto; modesto; no intruso.

unoccupied *adj.* **1,** (idle) desocupado; ocioso. **2,** (vacant) vacante; libre. **3,** (untenanted) desalquilado.

unoffending *adj.* inofensivo; innocuo; inocente.

unofficial *adj.* no oficial.

unopened *adj.* cerrado.

unopposed *adj.* sin oposición.

unorganized *adj.* inorganizado.

unorthodox *adj.* heterodoxo.

unostentatious *adj.* modesto; sencillo; no presumido.

unpack *v.t.* desempaquetar; desempacar; desembalar.

unpaid *adj.* no pagado; sin pagar.

unpalatable *adj.* desabrido.

unparalleled *adj.* sin par; sin igual; único.

unpardonable *adj.* imperdonable.

unparliamentary *adj.* no parlamentario.

unpatriotic *adj.* poco patriótico; antipatriótico.

unpaved *adj.* no empedrado; no asfaltado; sin pavimento.

unpayable *adj.* impagable.

unpen (ʌn'pɛn) *v.t.* [**unpenned, -penning**] libertar; soltar del redil.

unpeopled *adj.* despoblado.

unperceivable *adj.* imperceptible. —**unperceived,** *adj.* inadvertido; desapercibido. —**unperceiving,** *adj.* poco perceptivo.

unpersuadable *adj.* impersuasible.

unperturbable *adj.* imperturbable. —**unperturbed,** *adj.* imperturbado.

unpin *v.t.* [**unpinned, -pinning**] desprender.

unpitying *adj.* inclemente; despiadado; inconmovible.

unplanned *adj.* no planeado; sin planear.

unpleasant *adj.* desagradable; displicente. —**unpleasantness,** *n.* desagrado; disgusto; desazón.

unpleasing *adj.* desagradable; enfadoso.

unplowed *adj.* inculto; no arado.

unplug *v.t.* [**unplugged, -plugging**] desenchufar.

unplumbed (ʌn'plʌmd) *adj.* **1,** (not fathomed) no sondado; insondable. **2,** (without plumbing) sin cañerías.

unpolished *adj.* **1,** (crude) áspero; rudo; grosero. **2,** (not buffed) no pulido; sin bruñir.

unpolluted *adj.* impoluto.

unpopular *adj.* impopular.
—**unpopularity,** *n.* impopularidad.
unpracticed *adj.* **1,** (unskilled) inexperto; inepto. **2,** (not practiced) no practicado.
unprecedented (ʌn'prɛs·ə·dɛnt·ɪd) *adj.* inaudito; sin precedente.
unpredictable *adj.* que no se puede predecir; incierto.
unprejudiced *adj.* no prejuiciado; sin prejuicio; imparcial.
unpremeditated *adj.* impremeditado.
unprepared *adj.* desprevenido; desapercibido. —**unpreparedness,** *n.* desapercibimiento.
unprepossessing (ˌʌn·pri·pəˈzes·ɪŋ) *adj.* poco atrayente; feo.
unpresentable *adj.* impresentable.
unpretending *adj.* modesto.
unpretentious *adj.* modesto; sencillo.
unpreventable *adj.* inevitable; ineludible.
unprincipled *adj.* inescrupuloso.
unprintable *adj.* que no se puede imprimir.
unproductive *adj.* improductivo.
unprofessional *adj.* no profesional; impropio de un profesional.
unprofitable *adj.* **1,** (not gainful) no lucrativo; poco provechoso. **2,** (unavailing) inútil; vano.
unpromising *adj.* poco prometedor.
unpronounceable *adj.* impronunciable.
unpronounced *adj.* inarticulado; no pronunciado.
unpropitious *adj.* no favorable; poco propicio.
unprosperous *adj.* impróspero; desafortunado.
unprotected *adj.* desvalido; desamparado.
unproved *adj.* no probado. *También,* **unproven.**
unprovided *adj.* desprovisto; desapercibido; desprevenido.
unprovoked *adj.* sin motivo; sin provocación.
unpublished *adj.* inédito.
unpunished *adj.* impune.
unqualified *adj.* **1,** (incompetent) inhábil; incompetente. **2,** (absolute) absoluto; completo.
unquenchable *adj.* **1,** (inextinguishable) inextinguible. **2,** (insatiable) insaciable.

unquestionable *adj.* indudable; incuestionable; indiscutible.
unquestioned *adj.* indisputable; incontestable.
unquiet *adj.* inquieto; desasosegado.
unquote *v.t.* & *i.* cerrar la cita.
unravel *v.t.* desenredar; desenmarañar.
unread (ʌn'rɛd) *adj.* **1,** (unlearned) indocto. **2,** (not read) no leído; sin leer.
unreadable *adj.* ilegible.
unready *adj.* **1,** (unprepared) desprevenido. **2,** (not quick) lento; torpe; lerdo.
unreal *adj.* irreal.
unreality *n.* irrealidad.
unrealizable *adj.* irrealizable.
unrealized *adj.* no realizado.
unreason *n.* sinrazón; irracionalidad.
unreasonable *adj.* irrazonable; desrazonable.
unreasoning *adj.* irracional.
unreceptive *adj.* poco receptivo; indiferente.
unrecognizable *adj.* irreconocible.
unrecognized *adj.* irreconocido.
unrecorded *adj.* no registrado.
unredeemed *adj.* no redimido.
unreel *v.t.* desenrollar. —*v.i.* desenrollarse.
unrefined *adj.* **1,** (raw) impuro; no refinado. **2,** (lacking polish) tosco; grosero.
unreflecting *adj.* **1,** (opaque) opaco. **2,** (thoughtless) irreflexivo.
unregenerate *adj.* no regenerado; degenerado.
unrelated *adj.* no relacionado; sin conexión; sin parentesco.
unrelenting *adj.* incompasivo; inflexible; inexorable.
unreliable *adj.* indigno de confianza; incierto. —**unreliability,** *n.* incertidumbre.
unrelieved *adj.* **1,** (not alleviated) no aliviado. **2,** (not helped) no socorrido.
unreligious *adj.* irreligioso.
unremembered *adj.* olvidado.
unremitting *adj.* incansable; constante; incesante.
unremorseful *adj.* impenitente; sin remordimiento.
unremunerative *adj.* poco lucrativo.
unrepentant *adj.* impenitente. *También,* **unrepenting.**

unrepresentative *adj.* anormal; poco típico.

unrepresented *adj.* no representado; sin representación.

unrequited *adj.* no recompensado; no correspondido.

unresentful *adj.* no resentido; sin resentimiento.

unreserved *adj.* **1,** (candid) franco; libre; abierto. **2,** (not restricted) libre; no reservado.

unreservedly (ˌʌn·rɪˈzɑr·vɪd·li) *adv.* sin reserva; francamente; sin restricción.

unresisting *adj.* no resistente; sin resistencia. *También,* **unresistant.**

unresolved *adj.* indeciso; no resuelto.

unresponsive *adj.* poco responsivo; desinteresado.

unrest (ʌnˈrɛst) *n.* **1,** (restlessness) inquietud; desasosiego. **2,** (disorder) desorden.

unrestrained —*adj.* desenfrenado; libre; suelto. —**unrestraint,** *n.* desenfreno; libertad.

unrestricted *adj.* no restringido; sin restricción.

unrevealed *adj.* oculto; no revelado.

unrewarded *adj.* no recompensado; no premiado.

unrhythmical *adj.* poco rítmico; irregular.

unrig *v.t.* [**unrigged, -rigging**] desaparejar.

unrighteous *adj.* inicuo; perverso; malvado. —**unrighteousness,** *n.* iniquidad; perversidad; maldad.

unrightful *adj.* injusto; ilegítimo.

unripe *adj.* inmaduro; verde.

unrivaled *adj.* sin rival.

unrobe *v.t.* desarropar; desnudar. —*v.i.* desarroparse; desnudarse.

unroll *v.t.* desenrollar; desplegar. —*v.i.* desenrollarse; desplegarse.

unromantic *adj.* poco romántico.

unruffled *adj.* tranquilo; sereno; impertérrito.

unruled *adj.* **1,** (not governed) no gobernado; sin gobierno. **2,** (unlined) sin rayar.

unruly (ʌnˈru·li) *adj.* **1,** (unmanageable) indomable; intratable; indócil; inmanejable. **2,** (disorderly) desordenado. **3,** (mischievous) malmandado; revoltoso; desobediente.

unsaddle *v.t.* desensillar.

unsafe *adj.* peligroso; inseguro. —**unsafety,** *n.* peligro.

unsaid *adj.* no proferido; no dicho. —*v., pret. & p.p. de* **unsay.**

unsaleable (ʌnˈseil·ə·bəl) *también,* **unsalable** *adj.* invendible.

unsalted *adj.* no salado; sin sal.

unsanctioned *adj.* no sancionado; no autorizado.

unsanitary *adj.* insalubre; antihigiénico.

unsatisfactory *adj.* poco satisfactorio.

unsatisfied *adj.* insatisfecho.

unsatisfying *adj.* que no satisface; inadecuado.

unsaturated *adj.* no saturado.

unsavory *adj.* **1,** (tasteless) insípido; soso; desabrido. **2,** (unpleasant) desagradable; displicente. **3,** (disreputable) deshonroso; de mala conducta.

unsay *v.t.* [*pret. & p.p.* **unsaid**] retractar; desdecirse de.

unscathed *adj.* ileso; incólume.

unscheduled *adj.* sin horario fijo; fuera del programa.

unscholarly *adj.* **1,** (unbecoming a scholar) impropio de un erudito. **2,** (unschooled) indocto; ignorante.

unschooled *adj.* indocto; ignorante.

unscientific *adj.* poco científico.

unscramble *v.t.* desenredar.

unscratched *adj.* ileso; incólume; sin arañazo alguno.

unscrew *v.t.* destornillar; desenroscar; desvolver.

unscrupulous *adj.* inescrupuloso. —**unscrupulousness,** *n.* inescrupulosidad.

unseal *v.t.* desellar.

unseasonable *adj.* intempestivo; inoportuno; *(of weather)* desabrido.

unseasoned *adj.* **1,** (without condiment) soso; no sazonado. **2,** (inexperienced) no habituado; inexperto. **3,** (not dried or ripened) verde.

unseat *v.t.* **1,** (dislodge) quitar del asiento. **2,** (remove from office) destituir; echar abajo. **3,** (unhorse) desmontar.

unseaworthy *adj.* incapaz de navegar.

unsecured *adj.* no asegurado.

unseeing *adj.* ciego.

unseemly *adj.* indecoroso; impropio. —*adv.* indecorosamente; impropiamente.

unseen *adj.* inadvertido; no visto; invisible.

unselfish *adj.* desinteresado; no

egoísta; generoso. —**unselfishness,** *n.* desinterés; generosidad.

unserviceable *adj.* inútil; inservible.

unset *adj.* no puesto; no plantado.

unsettle *v.t.* **1,** (disarrange) desarreglar; poner en desorden. **2,** (disturb) inquietar; perturbar; trastornar.

unsettled *adj.* **1,** (disarranged) desarreglado. **2,** (unsteady) inconstante; inestable. **3,** (undecided) indeciso; indeterminado. **4,** (without settlers) deshabitado; despoblado. **5,** (unpaid) no pagado; no saldado.

unsew *v.t.* [*pret.* **unsewed;** *p.p.* **unsewed** o **unsewn**] descoser.

unsex *v.t.* quitarle a uno la sexualidad.

unshackle *v.t.* desencadenar; libertar.

unshaded *adj.* sin sombra.

unshakeable *adj.* inmutable; firme; resuelto.

unshaken *adj.* seguro; firme.

unshaped *adj.* informe; sin forma.

unshapely *adj.* desproporcionado; deforme.

unshaven *adj.* sin afeitar; barbudo. *También,* **unshaved.**

unsheathe *v.t.* desenvainar.

unsheltered *adj.* desamparado; desabrigado.

unship *v.t.* [**unshipped, -shipping**] **1,** (unload) desembarcar. **2,** (dismount) desmontar; desarmar.

unshod *adj.* descalzo; sin herraduras.

unshriven *adj.* inconfeso.

unsightly *adj.* feo; deforme. —**unsightliness,** *n.* fealdad; deformidad.

unsigned *adj.* no firmado; anónimo.

unsingable *adj.* no cantable.

unsinkable *adj.* insumergible.

unskilled *adj.* inhábil; inepto; imperito.

unskillful *adj.* inhábil; inepto; desmañado. —**unskillfulness,** *n.* inhabilidad; ineptitud; impericia.

unslaked *adj.* no apagado. —**unslaked lime,** cal viva.

unsling *v.t.* [*pret.* & *p.p.* **unslung**] descolgar.

unsmiling *adj.* serio; severo.

unsnap *v.t.* [**unsnapped, -snapping**] desabrochar.

unsnarl *v.t.* desenmarañar; desenredar.

unsociable *adj.* insociable; intratable; malavenido.

unsold *adj.* no vendido.

unsoldierly *adj.* indigno de un soldado.

unsolicited *adj.* insolicitado.

unsolvable *adj.* insoluble.

unsolved *adj.* sin resolver.

unsophisticated *adj.* natural; sencillo.

unsought *adj.* encontrado; aparecido; no buscado.

unsound *adj.* **1,** (defective) defectuoso; poco firme. **2,** (sickly) enfermizo; achacoso. **3,** (false) erróneo; falso; falaz. **4,** (rotten) podrido; corrompido.

unsparing *adj.* **1,** (lavish) pródigo; generoso; suntuoso. **2,** (unmerciful) cruel; despiadado.

unspeakable (ʌn'spi·kə·bəl) *adj.* **1,** (ineffable) inefable; indecible. **2,** (execrable) execrable; infando; incalificable.

unspecified *adj.* no especificado.

unspent *adj.* no gastado.

unspoiled *adj.* intacto; natural.

unspoken *adj.* no hablado; callado.

unsportsmanlike *adj.* indigno de un deportista.

unspotted *adj.* inmaculado; sin mancha.

unstable (ʌn'stei·bəl) *adj.* **1,** (not firm) inestable. **2,** (changeable) inconstante; mudadizo.

unstained *adj.* **1,** (without blemish) impoluto; inmaculado. **2,** (not tinted) no teñido; sin color.

unstated *adj.* **1,** (not declared) no declarado; no mencionado. **2,** (not fixed) indeterminado.

unstatesmanlike *adj.* indigno de un estadista.

unsteady *adj.* **1,** (unstable) inseguro; inestable. **2,** (shaky) vacilante; tembloroso. **3,** (wobbly) cojo; tembleque. **4,** (wavering) inconstante; irresoluto.

unstick *v.t.* [*pret.* & *p.p.* **unstuck**] despegar.

unstinted *adj.* no limitado; liberal.

unstinting *adj.* generoso; pródigo; liberal.

unstitch *v.t.* descoser.

unstop *v.t.* [**unstopped, -stopping**] **1,** (uncork) destaponar. **2,** (unclog) desatascar.

unstrained *adj.* natural; liso.

unstrap *v.t.* [unstrapped, -strapping] desceñir; soltar.

unstressed *adj.* **1,** (without emphasis) sin énfasis. **2,** (unaccented) inacentuado.

unstring *v.t.* [*pret.* & *p.p.* unstrung] **1,** (remove the strings from) desencordar; desencordelar. **2,** (remove from a string) desensartar. **3,** (unnerve) debilitar; enervar; trastornar.

unstrung *v., pret.* & *p.p. de* unstring. —*adj.* debilitado; trastornado.

unstuck *adj.* despegado. —*v., pret.* & *p.p. de* unstick. —come unstuck, despegarse.

unstudied *adj.* natural; espontáneo.

unsubdued *adj.* indomado; indómito.

unsubstantial *adj.* insubstancial.

unsubstantiated *adj.* no comprobado; no verificado.

unsuccessful *adj.* infructuoso; sin éxito; fracasado; impróspero.

unsuitable *adj.* **1,** (inappropriate) inadecuado; incongruente; inconveniente. **2,** (unbecoming) impropio. **3,** (incompetent) incompetente; inhábil.

unsuited *adj.* **1,** (inappropriate) inadecuado; impropio; incongruente. **2,** (incompetent) incompetente; ineficaz.

unsullied *adj.* inmaculado.

unsung *adj.* no celebrado; sin honores.

unsupported *adj.* sin sostén; sin apoyo.

unsure *adj.* inseguro; incierto.

unsurpassable *adj.* inmejorable; insuperable.

unsurpassed *adj.* insuperado; sin par.

unsusceptible *adj.* no susceptible; insensible.

unsuspected *adj.* insospechado.

unsuspecting *adj.* no sospechoso; no receloso; confiado. *También,* unsuspicious.

unsustained *adj.* sin apoyo; no sostenido.

unsweetened *adj.* no endulzado.

unswept *adj.* polvoriento; no barrido.

unswerving *adj.* fijo; firme; inmutable.

unsworn *adj.* no juramentado.

unsympathetic *adj.* antipático; indiferente.

unsystematic *adj.* sin sistema; poco metódico.

untack *v.t.* quitar las tachuelas a; *sewing* deshilvanar.

untactful *adj.* indiscreto; poco diplomático.

untainted *adj.* incorrupto; inmaculado.

untaken *adj.* no tomado; no cogido.

untamable *también,* untameable *adj.* indomable.

untamed *adj.* indómito; indomado.

untangle *adj.* desenredar; desenmarañar; desembarazar.

untapped *adj.* no explotado; no utilizado.

untarnished *adj.* lustroso; no deslucido; no deslustrado; sin mancha.

untasted *adj.* no probado.

untaught (ʌn'tɔt) *adj.* **1,** (uneducated) ineducado; indocto. **2,** (natural) natural; instintivo.

unteachable *adj.* ineducable; indócil.

untenable *adj.* insostenible.

untenanted (ʌn'ten-ənt·ɪd) *adj.* desalquilado; desocupado; vacante.

untended *adj.* desatendido.

untested *adj.* no probado.

untether *v.t.* desatar; soltar.

unthankful *adj.* ingrato; desagradecido.

unthinkable *adj.* inconcebible.

unthinking *adj.* descuidado; desatento; irreflexivo.

unthoughtful *adj.* **1,** (inconsiderate) desconsiderado. **2,** = unthinking.

unthought-of *adj.* **1,** (not occurring to one's mind) no soñado; no imaginado. **2,** (unforeseen) impensado; imprevisto. **3,** (forgotten) olvidado.

unthread *v.t.* **1,** (ravel) deshilar; deshilachar. **2,** (unstring) desensartar.

unthrifty *adj.* pródigo; manirroto.

unthrone *v.t.* destronar.

untidy *adj.* desaliñado; desaseado. —untidiness, *n.* desaliño; desaseo.

untie *v.t.* [untied, -tying] desatar; desligar; desamarrar.

until (ʌn'tɪl) *prep.* hasta. —*conj.* hasta que.

untillable *adj.* incultivable; no arable.

untilled *adj.* inculto; no cultivado.

untimely (ʌn'taim·li) *adj.* **1,** (premature) prematuro. **2,** (unseasonable) intempestivo; inoportuno. —*adv.* **1,** (prematurely) prematuramente. **2,** (unseasonably) intempestivamente; a deshora; a destiempo.

untiring *adj.* incansable; infatigable.

unto (ʌn·tu) *prep., arcaico y poético* a; para; hasta.

untold *adj.* **1,** (not told) no dicho; no narrado. **2,** (incalculable) incalculable.

untouchable *adj. & n.* intocable.

untouched *adj.* **1,** (intact) intacto; ileso. **2,** (unmoved) no conmovido; no afectado.

untoward (ʌn'tord) *adj.* **1,** (unfavorable) desfavorable; displicente. **2,** (unfortunate) desdichado. **3,** (unruly) indócil; intratable.

untrained *adj.* indisciplinado; no adiestrado; imperito.

untrammeled *adj.* sin trabas; libre; no impedido.

untranslatable *adj.* intraducible.

untranslated *adj.* no traducido; sin traducir.

untraveled *adj.* **1,** (unfrequented) no frecuentado; aislado; solitario. **2,** (not having traveled) que no ha viajado; hogareño.

untried *adj.* no probado.

untrimmed *adj.* **1,** (unadorned) no guarnecido; sin adorno. **2,** (uncut) no cortado; no afeitado.

untrod *adj.* no pisado; no frecuentado.

untroubled *adj.* **1,** (calm) quieto; tranquilo. **2,** (clear) claro; transparente.

untrue *adj.* **1,** (false) falso; mendaz. **2,** (incorrect) incorrecto; inexacto. **3,** (unfaithful) infiel.

untrustworthy *adj.* indigno de confianza.

untruth *n.* mentira; falsedad. —**untruthful,** *adj.* mentiroso; falso.

untutored *adj.* indocto; ignorante.

untwine *v.t.* **1,** (separate) destorcer; desenroscar. **2,** (disentangle) desenmarañar.

untwist *v.t.* **1,** (untwine) destorcer; desenroscar. **2,** (unravel) desenredar; desenmarañar.

unusable *adj.* inútil; inservible.

unused (ʌn'juːzd) *adj.* **1,** (not in use) inusitado; desusado. **2,** (unexploited) desaprovechado. **3,** (unaccustomed) no acostumbrado. **4,** (new) nuevo.

unusual *adj.* extraño; raro;

extraordinario; desacostumbrado; insólito.

unutterable *adj.* inefable; indecible.

unuttered *adj.* no proferido; callado.

unvanquished *adj.* invicto.

unvaried *adj.* no variado; constante; uniforme.

unvarnished *adj.* **1,** (not varnished) no barnizado; sin barnizar. **2,** (unadorned) sencillo; sin adorno.

unvarying *adj.* invariable.

unveil *v.t.* **1,** (remove the veil from) quitar el velo a. **2,** (reveal) descubrir; revelar. **3,** (inaugurate) inaugurar.

unventilated *adj.* sin ventilación.

unverifiable *adj.* no verificable.

unverified *adj.* no verificado; sin verificar.

unversed *adj.* no versado; poco instruido; inexperto.

unvexed *adj.* quieto; tranquilo; imperturbado.

unvisited *adj.* no visitado; solitario.

unvoiced *adj.* **1,** (unexpressed) inarticulado; inexpresado. **2,** *phonet.* sordo; insonoro.

unwanted *adj.* no deseado; despreciado; rechazado.

unwarrantable *adj.* **1,** (unjustifiable) inexcusable; injustificable. **2,** (untenable) insostenible.

unwarranted *adj.* **1,** (unjustified) injustificado. **2,** (improper) indebido. **3,** (unauthorized) desautorizado. **4,** (without guarantee) sin garantía.

unwary *adj.* incauto; imprudente; irreflexivo.

unwashed *adj.* sin lavar; sucio; puerco. —**the great unwashed,** la canalla; el populacho.

unwatched *adj.* no velado; no vigilado; desatendido.

unwavering *adj.* determinado; firme; resuelto.

unwearied *adj.* **1,** (not tired) no cansado. **2,** (tireless) infatigable; incansable.

unwearying *adj.* infatigable; incansable.

unweave *v.t.* [*pret.* **unwove;** *p.p.* **unwoven**] deshilar; destejer.

unwed *adj.* soltero; no casado.

unwelcome *adj.* **1,** (not well received) mal acogido. **2,** (bothersome) importuno; molesto.

unwell *adj.* indispuesto.

unwept *adj.* no llorado; no lamentado.

unwholesome *adj.* malsano; insalubre.

unwieldy (ʌn'wil·di) *adj.* pesado; ponderoso; inmanejable.

unwilling *adj.* desinclinado. —**unwillingly,** *adv.* de mala gana. —**unwillingness,** *n.* mala gana; repugnancia.

unwind (ʌn'waind) *v.t.* [*pret.* & *p.p.* **unwound**] devanar; desenrollar. —*v.i.* devanarse; desenrollarse.

unwise *adj.* **1,** (imprudent) indiscreto; imprudente. **2,** (foolish) tonto; ignorante.

unwitting (ʌn'wit·iŋ) *adj.* inadvertido; inconsciente. —**unwittingly,** *adv.* inadvertidamente; sin saberlo.

unwomanly *adj.* impropio de una mujer; poco mujeril.

unwonted (ʌn'wʌn·tid; -'wan-) *adj.* insólito; desacostumbrado.

unworkable *adj.* impracticable.

unworked *adj.* no trabajado; no labrado.

unworkmanlike *adj.* desmañado; chapucero.

unworldly *adj.* no mundano; espiritual.

unworn *adj.* no usado; no gastado; nuevo.

unworthy *adj.* indigno; desmerecedor. —**unworthiness,** *n.* desmerecimiento.

unwound (ʌn'waund) *v., pret.* & *p.p. de* **unwind.**

unwounded (ʌn'wun·did) *adj.* ileso.

unwove *v., pret. de* **unweave.**

unwoven *v., p.p. de* **unweave.** —*adj.* no tejido; sin tejer.

unwrap *v.t.* [**unwrapped, -wrapping**] desenvolver.

unwrinkle *v.t.* estirar; desarrugar. —*v.i.* desarrugarse. —**unwrinkled,** *adj.* sin arrugas; liso.

unwritten *adj.* **1,** (not in writing) no escrito; verbal. **2,** (blank) en blanco. **3,** (traditional) tradicional. —**unwritten law,** ley no escrita.

unyielding *adj.* **1,** (unrelenting) inflexible; inconmovible; inexorable. **2,** (stubborn) terco; reacio. **3,** (unsubdued) indómito; indomado.

unyoke *v.t.* **1,** (release from a yoke) desuncir. **2,** (separate) separar; desunir.

unyouthful *adj.* envejecido; desmejorado.

unzip *v.t.* abrir la cremallera de.

up (ʌp) *adv.* **1,** (higher) arriba; en lo alto. **2,** (at or to a point of importance) hacia arriba. **3,** (to an equally advanced point) hasta el mismo nivel. **4,** (thenceforth; from a certain time on) en adelante. **5,** (on one's feet) en pie; derecho; *Amer.* parado. **6,** (out of bed) levantado; fuera de cama. **7,** (completely) completamente; todo. **8,** (well prepared) informado; prevenido; informado; versado. **9,** (into activity) en marcha. **10,** (ended) terminado; vencido; cumplido. **11,** (together; close) junto (a). —*prep.* **1,** (to a higher position on or in) a o en lo alto de; hacia arriba de. **2,** (farther along) arriba de. **3,** (toward the interior of) en o hasta el interior de. —*adj.* **1,** (going up) ascendente. **2,** (in a higher position) alto; elevado. **3,** (standing) en pie; derecho; *Amer.* parado. **4,** (out of bed) levantado. **5,** (above the horizon) levantado. **6,** (increased; advanced) aumentado; subido. **7,** (ended) terminado; acabado. **8,** (due; payable) vencido. **9,** (in an excited state) airado; animado. **10,** *colloq.* (happening) pasando; sucediendo: *what's up?,* ¿qué pasa? —*n.* **1,** (upward movement or course) elevación; subida. **2,** (improvement) mejoría. —*v.t. colloq.* [**upped, upping**] **1,** (raise) elevar; alzar; subir. **2,** (increase) aumentar. **3,** (bet or bid more than) apostar o pujar más que. —*v.i., colloq.* levantarse. —**it's all up (with),** todo se acabó. —**on the up and up,** *slang* franco; sincero. —**up against,** *colloq.* cara a cara con; frente a. —**up against it,** en apuros. —**up and (+ *inf.*),** *colloq.* hacer (algo) de repente. —**up and about,** levantado. —**up and doing,** activo; ocupado. —**up and down,** arriba y abajo; por todas partes. —**up a tree,** *slang* en apuros. —**ups and downs,** altibajos; vaivenes. —**up there!** ¡alto ahí! —**up to, 1,** (as far as) hasta. **2,** (equal to; competent for) adecuado para; competente para. **3,** *colloq.* (occupied with) armando; planeando; proyectando. **4,** (dependent or incumbent upon) tocándole a uno; dependiendo a uno: *it's up to you,* a ti toca; depende de ti. —**up to date,** al día;

hasta la fecha. —**up to snuff,** listo; capaz.

up-and-coming ('ʌp-ən,kʌm-ɪŋ) *adj., colloq.* emprendedor y prometedor.

upbear ('ʌp-ber) *v.t.* [*pret.* **upbore;** *p.p.* **upborne**] sostener; levantar.

upbeat ('ʌp-bit) *n., mus.* nota por anticipado. —*adj., colloq.* optimista; contento.

upbraid (ʌp'breid) *v.t.* reprender; regañar. —**upbraiding,** *n.* reprensión.

upbringing ('ʌp-brɪŋ-ɪŋ) *n.* crianza; educación.

upcountry ('ʌp,kʌn-tri) *n.* interior; serranía. —*adj.* del interior. —*adv.* en o hacia el interior; tierra adentro.

update ('ʌp-deit) *n.* actualización, —*v.t.* poner al día; actualizar.

updraft ('ʌp-dræft) *n.* corriente ascendente.

upend (ʌp'ɛnd) *v.t.* poner de punta. —*v.i.* ponerse de punta.

upfront (ʌp'frʌnt) *adj.* 1, (sincere) franco; sincero. 2, (in advance) por adelantado.

upgrade ('ʌp-greid) *n.* subida. —*adj.* ascendente. —*adv.* cuesta arriba. —*v.t.* mejorar; adelantar; elevar.

upheaval (ʌp'hiv-əl) *n.* 1, (violent upward movement) solevantamiento. 2, (uprising) sublevación. 3, (sudden change; upset) trastorno.

upheave ('ʌp-hiːv) *v.t.* solevantar. —*v.i.* solevantarse.

uphill ('ʌp-hɪl) *adv.* cuesta arriba. —*adj.* 1, (rising) ascendente. 2, (arduous) difícil; penoso.

uphold (ʌp'hold) *v.t.* [*pret. & p.p.* **upheld**] apoyar; sostener.

upholster (əp'hol-stər) *v.t.* tapizar. —**upholsterer,** *n.* tapicero. —**upholstery,** *n.* tapicería.

upkeep ('ʌp-kip) *n.* mantenimiento.

upland ('ʌp-lənd) *adj.* elevado; alto. —*n.* terreno elevado.

uplift (ʌp'lɪft) *v.t.* 1, (raise) levantar. 2, (edify) edificar; mejorar. —*n.* ('ʌp-lɪft) 1, (raising) elevación; levantamiento. 2, (edification) edificación; mejora.

upmost ('ʌp-most) *adj. & adv.* = **uppermost.**

upon (ə'pɑn) *prep.* 1, (on) en; sobre; encima de. 2, (toward) sobre; hacia. 3, (against) contra. 4, (following) tras; después de. 5, (about; concerning) sobre; de; acerca de. 6, (at the time of) a; al (+ *inf.*). 7, (in

addition to) sobre. —**upon my honor,** a fe mía. —**upon my word,** por mi palabra.

upper ('ʌp-ər) *adj.* 1, (higher) superior; más alto; más elevado. 2, (further inland) interior. 3, (outer, esp. of garments) exterior. —*n.* 1, (upper part) parte superior. 2, (of a shoe) pala. —**on one's uppers,** *colloq.* andrajoso; desastrado; indigente.

upper berth litera alta.

upper case caja alta; (letra) mayúscula; letra de caja alta. —**upper-case,** *adj.* de caja alta; mayúscula; de o con mayúsculas.

upperclass *adj.* de clase superior; aristocrático.

upperclassman (,ʌp-ər'klæs-mən) *n.* [*pl.* **-men**] alumno universitario de los dos últimos años.

uppercut *n.* golpe en corto de abajo arriba.

upper deck cubierta alta.

upper hand maestría; dominio; ventaja.

upper house cámara alta.

upper middle class alta burguesía.

uppermost ('ʌp-ər-most) *adj.* 1, (highest) más alto; más elevado. 2, (foremost) preeminente; principal; primero. —*adv.* en lo más alto; en primer lugar.

uppish ('ʌp-ɪʃ) *adj., colloq.* altanero; altivo. *También,* **uppity** ('ʌp-ə-ti). —**uppishness,** *n.* altanería.

upraise (ʌp'reiz) *v.t.* levantar; elevar.

uprear (ʌp'rɪːr) *v.t.* 1, (raise) levantar; elevar. 2, (exalt) exaltar. 3, (bring up) criar; educar. —*v.i.* levantarse.

upright ('ʌp-rait) *adj.* 1, (vertical) recto; derecho; vertical. 2, (honest) recto; justo. —*adv.* verticalmente; recto. —*n.* montante; pieza vertical. —**uprightness,** *n.* rectitud; probidad. —**upright piano,** piano vertical.

uprise (ʌp'raiz) *v.i.* [*pret.* **uprose;** *p.p.* **uprisen** (-'rɪz-ən)] 1, (get up) levantarse. 2, (ascend) subir; elevarse. 3, (revolt) sublevarse. —*n.* ('ʌp-raiz) subida.

uprising (ʌp'raiz-ɪŋ) *n.* 1, (revolt) sublevación; solevantamiento. 2, (ascent) subida; cuesta.

uproar ('ʌp-ror) *n.* tumulto; alboroto.

uproarious (ʌp'ror·i·əs) *adj.* ruidoso; tumultuoso.

uproot (ʌp'ruːt) *v.t.* desarraigar; desplantar.

uprose (ʌp'roːz) *v.*, *pret de.* **uprise.**

upset (ʌp'sɛt) *v.t.* [*pret. & p.p.* **upset;** *ger.* **upsetting**] **1,** (tip over) volcar. **2,** (disturb) trastornar; desordenar. **3,** (defeat) derrotar. —*v.i.* volcarse. —*adj.* **1,** (overturned) volcado. **2,** (disturbed) trastornado; desordenado. **3,** (sick) indispuesto. —*n.* (ʌp'sɛt) **1,** (overturning) vuelco. **2,** (disturbance) trastorno; desorden. **3,** (illness) indisposición. **4,** (defeat) derrota. —**upsetting,** *adj.* inquietante; desconcertante.

upshot (ʌp'ʃat) *n.* **1,** (result) resultado; remate; conclusión. **2,** (gist) esencia; quid; suma total.

upside (ʌp'said) *n.* parte superior.

upside down 1, (turned over) al revés; lo de arriba abajo. **2,** (confused) trastornado; desordenado. —**turn upside down,** trastornar; desordenar.

upside-down *adj.* **1,** (overturned) al revés. **2,** (confused) trastornado; desordenado.

upstage (ʌp'steidʒ) *adj.* **1,** (at the rear of the stage) de fondo. **2,** *colloq.* (haughty) altanero; arrogante. —*adv.* en o hacia el fondo de la escena. —*v.t.* **1,** *theat.* ocultar de vista (un actor a otro). **2,** *colloq.* (snub) desdeñar; desairar.

upstairs (ʌp'stɛːrz) *adv.* arriba. —*adj.* de arriba. —*n.* piso(s) de arriba.

upstanding (ʌp'stæn·dɪŋ) *adj.* **1,** (erect) recto; derecho. **2,** (honorable) respetable; honroso.

upstart (ʌp'start) *n. & adj.* advenedizo; presuntuoso.

upstream (ʌp'striːm) *adv.* río arriba; aguas arriba. —*adj.* de río arriba; que va río arriba; ascendente.

uptake (ʌp'teik) *n.* **1,** (ventilating pipe or shaft) tubo o conducto de ventilación. **2,** (comprehension) realización; comprensión.

uptight (ʌp'tait) *adj.*, *slang* **1,** (uneasy) tenso; nervioso. **2,** (conventional) convencional.

up-to-date (ʌp'tə'deit) *adj.* al día; moderno; de última moda.

uptown (ʌp'taun) *adj.* de arriba; de lo alto de la ciudad. —*adv.* arriba; en o hacia lo alto de la ciudad. —*n.* lo alto de la ciudad.

upturn (ʌp'tʌrn) *n.* **1,** (upward turn) vuelta hacia arriba. **2,** (improvement) mejora. —*v.t. & i.* (ʌp'tʌrn) **1,** (turn up) volver(se) hacia arriba. **2,** (turn over) volcar(se).

upward (ʌp'wərd) *adv.* [*también,* **upwards**] hacia arriba. —*adj.* ascendente. —**upward(s) of,** más de.

uranium (ju'rei·ni·əm) *n.* uranio.

Uranus (jur'ə·nəs) *n.* Urano.

urban (ʌr'bən) *adj.* urbano.

urbane (ʌr'bein) *adj.* cortés; afable; urbano. —**urbanity** (ʌr'bæn·ə·ti) *n.* urbanidad.

urbanize (ʌr'bə,naiz) *v.t.* urbanizar. —**urbanization** (-nɪ'zei·ʃən) *n.* urbanización.

urchin (ʌr'tʃɪn) *n.* **1,** (gamin) pilluelo; golfillo. **2,** *zoöl.* erizo.

urea (ju'ri·ə) *n.* urea.

uremia (ju'ri·mi·ə) *n.* uremia. —**uremic,** *adj.* urémico.

ureter (ju'ri·tər) *n.* uretra.

urge (ʌrdʒ) *v.t.* **1,** (advocate strongly) abogar por; empujar. **2,** (drive) impeler; propulsar. **3,** (entreat) instar; solicitar. **4,** (incite) incitar; aguijonear; estimular. **5,** (harry) apremiar; acosar. —*n.* impulso.

urgency (ʌr·dʒən·si) *n.* **1,** (necessity) urgencia. **2,** (insistence) instancia; insistencia.

urgent (ʌr·dʒənt) *adj.* urgente. —**be urgent,** instar; urgir; ser urgente.

urgently (ʌr·dʒənt·li) *adv.* urgentemente; de urgencia; de emergencia.

urging (ʌr·dʒɪŋ) *n.* instancia; insistencia.

uric (ʌjur·ik) *adj.* úrico.

urinal (ʌjur·i·nəl) *n.* **1,** (receptacle) orinal. **2,** (place) urinario; urinal.

urinalysis (jur·i'næl·ə·sis) *n.* urinálisis; uranálisis.

urinary (ʌjur·i·nɛr·i) *adj.* urinario; urinal.

urinate (ʌjur·i,neit) *v.t. & i.* orinar.

urination (jur·i'nei·ʃən) *n.* urinación; micción.

urine (ʌjur·in) *n.* orina; orines.

urn (ʌrn) *n.* **1,** (vase) urna. **2,** (container for coffee or tea) cafetera o tetera con grifo.

urology (ju'ral·ə·dʒi) *n.* urología. —**urological** (-ə'ladʒ·ɪ·kəl) *adj.* urológico. —**urologist,** *n.* urólogo.

Ursa Major ('ʌr·sə) Osa Mayor. —**Ursa Minor,** Osa Menor.

ursine ('ʌr·sain) *adj.* ursino; úrsido; del oso.

urticaria (‚ʌr·tə'kɛr·i·ə) *n.* urticaria.

us (ʌs) *pron. pers. m. & f. pl.* **1,** *como complemento de verbo* nos. **2,** *como complemento de prep.* nosotros [*fem.* nosotras]. **3,** *tras* **than,** *en comparaciones* nosotros [*fem.* nosotras].

usable *también,* **useable** ('juz·ə·bəl) *adj.* útil; utilizable; servible. —**usability; useability,** *n.* utilidad.

usage ('ju·sidʒ) *n.* **1,** (use) uso; empleo. **2,** (custom) uso; usanza; costumbre. **3,** (treatment) trato; tratamiento.

use (juːz) *v.t.* **1,** (employ) usar; emplear. **2,** (behave toward; treat) tratar. **3,** (consume) agotar; consumir; gastar. —*v.i., con inf.* soler; acostumbrar; tener costumbre (de): *We used to visit them every week,* Solíamos visitarlos todas las semanas. —*n.* (jus) **1,** (act or result of using) uso. **2,** (employment) uso; empleo. **3,** (custom) uso; costumbre. **4,** (need) necesidad. **5,** (purpose) motivo. —**be of no use,** no servir para nada; ser inútil. —**have no use for, 1,** (have no need of) no necesitar; no servirse de. **2,** (have dislike or distaste for) tener en poco; no querer saber de. —**in use,** en uso; que se usa; ocupado. —**make use of,** servirse de; utilizar; hacer uso de. —**of use,** útil; que sirve. —**out of use,** fuera de uso; desusado; inusitado; fuera de moda. —**put to use,** servirse de; utilizar. —**used to,** acostumbrado a. —**get** (o **become**) **used to,** acostumbrarse a. —**use up, 1,** (use completely) usar todo; usar completamente; agotar. **2,** (fatigue) cansar; fatigar; rendir.

useful ('jus·fəl) *adj.* útil. —**usefulness,** *n.* utilidad.

useless ('jus·ləs) *adj.* inútil. —**uselessness,** *n.* inutilidad.

user ('juz·ər) *n.* **1,** (one who uses) usuario. **2,** (consumer) consumidor.

usher ('ʌʃ·ər) *n.* **1,** (doorkeeper) ujier; portero. **2,** (person who assists in seating) acomodador. —*v.t.* **1,** (show to a seat) acomodar. **2,** (introduce) introducir; anunciar.

usherette (‚ʌʃ·ər'ɛt) *n.* acomodadora.

usual ('ju·ʒu·əl) *adj.* usual; común; acostumbrado. —**as usual,** como de costumbre.

usually ('ju·ʒu·ə·li) *adv.* usualmente; comúnmente; por lo común.

usualness ('ju·ʒu·əl·nəs) *n.* costumbre; frecuencia.

usufruct ('ju·zju‚frʌkt) *n.* usufructo.

usurer ('ju·ʒər·ər) *n.* usurero.

usurious (ju'ʒur·i·əs) *adj.* usurario.

usurp (ju'sʌrp) *v.t.* usurpar. —**usurpation,** *n.* usurpación. —**usurper,** *n.* usurpador [*fem.* -dora].

usury ('ju·ʒə·ri) *n.* usura.

utensil (ju'ten·səl) *n.* utensilio.

uterus ('ju·tər·əs) *n.* [*pl.* **-i** (-ai)] útero. —**uterine** (-ɪn) *adj.* uterino.

utilitarian (ju‚tɪl·ə'ter·i·ən) *adj.* utilitario. —*adj. & n.* utilitarista. —**utilitarianism,** *n.* utilitarismo.

utility (ju'tɪl·ə·ti) *n.* **1,** (usefulness) utilidad. **2,** (public service) empresa de servicio público.

utilize ('ju·tə‚laiz) *v.t.* utilizar; usar. —**utilizable,** *adj.* utilizable. —**utilization** (-lɪ'zei·ʃən) *n.* uso; utilización.

utmost ('ʌt·most) *adj.* **1,** (extreme) sumo; extremo; supremo. **2,** (last) último. **3,** (farthest) más lejano. **4,** (greatest) mayor; más grande. —*n.* lo sumo; lo mayor. —**do one's utmost,** hacer todo lo posible; hacer cuanto pueda.

Utopia; utopia (ju'to·pi·ə) *n.* utopía; utopia. —**Utopian; utopian** *adj.* utópico. —*n. & adj.* utopista. —**utopianism,** *n.* utopismo.

utter ('ʌt·ər) *v.t.* proferir; pronunciar; expresar. —*adj.* cabal; completo; total; absoluto.

utterance ('ʌt·ər·əns) *n.* pronunciación; expresión; declaración.

utterly ('ʌt·ər·li) *adv.* cabalmente; totalmente; completamente.

uttermost ('ʌt·ər·most) *adj. & n.* = **utmost.**

uvula ('ju·vjə·lə) *n.* [*pl.* **-las** o **-lae** (-li)] úvula. —**uvular,** *adj.* uvular.

uxoricide (ʌk'sor·ɪ·said) *n.* **1,** (act) uxoricidio. **2,** (agent) uxoricida.

uxorious (ʌk'sor·i·əs) *adj.* gurrumino. —**uxoriousness,** *n.* gurrumina; condescendencia.

V

V, v (vi) vigésima segunda letra del alfabeto inglés.

vacancy ('vei·kən·si) *n.* 1, (emptiness) vacío. 2, (unfilled position) vacante; vacancia. 3, (untenanted quarters) apartamento o habitación vacante.

vacant ('vei·kənt) *adj.* 1, (empty) vacío. 2, (unoccupied) vacante. 3, (untenanted) desalquilado. 4, (free; devoid of activity) libre. 5, (empty of thought) vago; necio.

vacate ('vei·keit) *v.t.* 1, (leave unoccupied) vacar; vaciar; desocupar. 2, *law* anular; revocar. —*v.i., colloq.* irse; salir; marcharse.

vacation (ve'kei·ʃən) *n.* vacación; vacaciones. —*v.i.* pasar las vacaciones; estar de vacaciones. —**on vacation,** de vacaciones.

vaccine ('væk·sin) *n.* vacuna. —**vaccinate** (-sə·neit) *v.t.* vacunar. —**vaccination,** *n.* vacunación.

vacillate ('væs·ə·leit) *v.i.* vacilar. —**vacillation,** *n.* vaivén; vacilación.

vacuole ('væk·ju,ol) *n.* vacuola.

vacuous ('væk·ju·əs) *adj.* 1, (empty) vacuo; vacío. 2, (inane) necio; mentecato. —**vacuity** (væ'kju·ə·ti) *n.* vacuidad; vaciedad.

vacuum ('væk·jum) *n.* [*pl.* vacuums o vacua (-ə)] vacío. —**vacuum bottle,** termos. —**vacuum cleaner,** aspiradora. —**vacuum-packed,** envasado al vacío. —**vacuum tube,** tubo al vacío.

vagabond ('væg·ə,band) *adj. & n.* vagabundo. —**vagabondage,** *n.* vagabundeo.

vagary (və'gɛr·i) *n.* capricho.

vagina (və'dʒai·nə) *n.* vagina. —**vaginal** ('vædʒ·ɪ·nəl) *adj.* vaginal.

vaginate ('vædʒ·ɪ·neit) *adj.* envainado.

vagrant ('vei·grənt) *adj.* vagante; vagabundo. —*n.* vago; vagante; vagabundo.

vague (veig) *adj.* vago; indeterminado. —**vagueness,** *n.* vaguedad.

vain (vein) *adj.* 1, (empty; futile) vano; inútil. 2, (conceited) vano; vanidoso; presuntuoso. —**vainness,** *n.* vanidad. —**in vain,** inútilmente; en vano.

vainglory (vein'glo·ri) *n.*

vanagloria. —**vainglorious,** *adj.* vanaglorioso.

vainly ('vein·li) *adv.* 1, (in vain) inútilmente; en vano. 2, (conceitedly) vanidosamente; presuntuosamente.

valance ('væl·əns) *n.* cenefa.

vale (veil) *n.* valle.

valedictory (,væl·ə'dɪk·tə·ri) *adj.* de despedida. —*n.* discurso de despedida. —**valedictorian** (-'tɔr·i·ən) *n.* alumno [*fem.* -a] que da el discurso de despedida.

valence ('vei·ləns) *n.* valencia.

valentine ('væl·ən,tain) *n.* 1, (greeting) tarjeta de San Valentín. 2, (sweetheart) amado o amada del día de San Valentín. —**St. Valentine's Day,** día de los enamorados; día de San Valentín.

valerian (və'lɪr·i·ən) *n.* valeriana.

valet ('væl·ət; væ'lei) *n.* ayuda de cámara.

valiant ('væl·jənt) *adj.* valiente; valeroso. —**valiancy,** *n.* valentía; valor.

valid ('væl·ɪd) *adj.* válido.

validate ('væl·ə,deit) *v.t.* validar. —**validation,** *n.* validación.

validity (və'lɪd·ə·ti) *n.* validez.

valise (və'lis) *n.* valija; maleta; *Amer.* velís.

valley ('væl·i) *n.* valle.

valor ('væl·ər) *n.* valor.

valorous ('væl·ər·əs) *adj.* valeroso.

valuable ('væl·ju·ə·bəl) *adj.* valioso; de valor. —**valuables,** *n.pl.* objetos de valor. —**valuableness,** *n.* valor.

valuation (,væl·ju'ei·ʃən) *n.* 1, (appraisal) valuación; valoración. 2, (assessment) tasa; tasación.

value ('væl·ju) *n.* valor —*v.t.* 1, (estimate the value of) valuar; valorar. 2, (esteem) estimar; apreciar.

valued ('væl·jud) *adj.* 1, (estimated) valorado. 2, (esteemed) estimado; apreciado.

valueless ('væl·ju·ləs) *adj.* sin valor.

valve (vælv) *n.* 1, *anat.; mech.* válvula. 2, *bot.; zoöl.* valva. 3, *mus.* llave.

valvular ('væl·vjə·lər) *adj.* valvular.

vamoose (væ'mus) *v.i.*, *slang* largarse; marcharse.

vamp (væmp) *n.* **1,** (of a shoe) pala. **2,** (patch) remiendo; parche. **3,** *mus.* acompañamiento improvisado. **4,** (scheming woman) vampiresa. —*v.t.* & *i.* **1,** (patch) remendar; *Amer.* parchar. **2,** *mus.* improvisar. **3,** *slang* (flirt) coquetear (con).

vampire ('væm·pair) *n.* vampiro.

van (væn) *n.* **1,** (wagon; truck) carro de carga; camión. **2,** *Brit.* (baggage or freight car) furgón de equipajes. **3,** (vanguard) vanguardia.

vanadium (və'nei·di·əm) *n.* vanadio.

vandal ('væn·dəl) *n.* vándalo. —*adj.* vándalo; vandálico. —**vandalism,** *n.* vandalismo.

vandyke (væn'daik) *n.* barba puntiaguda. *También,* **Vandyke beard.**

vane (vein) *n.* **1,** (weathercock) veleta. **2,** (of a propeller) paleta. **3,** (of a windmill) aspa.

vanguard ('væn·gard) *n.* vanguardia.

vanilla (və'nɪl·ə) *n.* vainilla.

vanish ('væn·ɪʃ) *v.i.* desvanecerse; desaparecer.

vanity ('væn·ə·ti) *n.* **1,** (pride; emptiness; futility) vanidad. **2,** (cosmetic case) estuche de afeites; neceser. **3,** (dressing table) tocador.

vanquish ('væŋ·kwɪʃ) *v.t.* vencer; conquistar. —**vanquisher,** *n.* vencedor [*fem.* -dora]; conquistador [*fem.* -dora].

vantage ('væn·tɪdʒ) *n.* ventaja; superioridad. —**vantage point; vantage ground,** posición de ventaja.

vapid ('væp·ɪd) *adj.* soso; insípido.

vapidity (və'pɪd·ə·ti) *n.* insipidez.

vapor ('vei·pər) *n.* **1,** (mist; steam) vapor. **2,** (fog) niebla; bruma. **3,** (fumes) vaho; exhalación; humo. —**vapor trail,** estela de condensación.

vaporize ('vei·pər‚aiz) *v.t.* vaporizar. —*v.i.* vaporizarse. —**vaporization** (-ɪ'zei·ʃən) *n.* vaporización. —**vaporizer,** *n.* vaporizador.

vaporous ('vei·pər·əs) *adj.* **1,** (misty) vaporoso. **2,** (fleeting) fugaz. **3,** (fanciful) vano; quimérico. —**vaporousness,** *n.* vaporosidad.

variable ('vɛr·i·ə·bəl) *adj.* & *n.*

variable. —**variability,** *n.* variabilidad.

variance ('vɛr·i·əns) *n.* **1,** (change) variación. **2,** (difference) diferencia; discrepancia. **3,** (disagreement) desacuerdo; desavenencia. —**at variance,** en desacuerdo; reñido.

variant ('vɛr·i·ənt) *adj.* & *n.* variante.

variation (‚vɛr·i'ei·ʃən) *n.* variación.

varicella (‚vær·ə'sɛl·ə) *n.* varicela.

varicolored ('vær·i‚kʌl·ərd) *adj.* abigarrado.

varicose ('vær·ɪ‚kos) *adj.* varicoso. —**varicosity** (-'kas·ə·ti) *n.* varicosidad. —**varicose veins,** varicosis.

varied ('vɛr·id) *adj.* variado.

variegate ('vɛr·i·ə‚geit) *v.t.* jaspear; motear. —**variegated,** *adj.* jaspeado; moteado; abigarrado.

variety (və'rai·ə·ti) *n.* variedad.

variola (və'rai·ə·lə) *n.* viruela; variola.

various ('vɛr·i·əs) *adj.* vario; diferente; diverso. —**variousness,** *n.* diversidad.

varlet ('var·lɪt) *n.*, *archaic* **1,** (attendant) lacayo. **2,** (rascal) truhán; bribón. —**varletry,** *n.* chusma.

varmint ('var·mənt) *n.*, *dial.* **1,** (bug) bicho. **2,** (despicable person) pícaro; tunante.

varnish ('var·nɪʃ) *n.* barniz. —*v.t* barnizar.

varsity ('var·sə·ti) *n.* equipo universitario. —*adj.* universitario.

vary ('vɛr·i) *v.t.* & *i.* variar.

vascular ('væs·kjə·lər) *adj.* vascular.

vase (veis) *n.* vaso; jarrón.

vasectomy (væ'sɛk·tə·mi) *n.* vasectomía.

vasomotor (‚væs·o'mo·tər) *adj.* vasomotor.

vassal ('væs·əl) *n.* & *adj.* vasallo. —**vassalage,** *n.* vasallaje.

vast (væst) *adj.* vasto. —**vastly,** *adv.* en sumo grado; muy; mucho. —**vastness,** *n.* vastedad.

vat (væt) *n.* tina; cuba; tonel.

Vatican ('væt·ɪ·kən) *n.* Vaticano. —*adj.* vaticano.

vaudeville ('vod·vɪl) *n.* zarzuela; variedades; vodevil. —**vaudevillian** (vod'vɪl·jən) *n.* zarzuelista; comediante.

vault (vɔlt) *n.* **1,** (arched roof or chamber) bóveda. **2,** (storage cellar) cueva; bodega. **3,** (safe) caja de caudales. **4,** (leap) salto. —*v.t.* (arch) abovedar. —*v.t. & i.* (leap) saltar. —**vaulted,** *adj.* abovedado.

vaunt (vɔnt) *v.t.* ostentar; jactarse de. —*v.i.* jactarse. —*n.* jactancia. —**vaunting,** *adj.* jactancioso.

VCR *abr. de* **videocassette recorder** (o **player**).

V-Day día de la victoria.

veal (viːl) *n.* ternera; carne de ternera.

vector ('vɛk·tər) *n.* vector. —*adj.* vector; vectorial.

vedette (vəˈdɛt) *n.* **1,** *mil.* centinela avanzada de a caballo. **2,** *naval* buque escucha.

veep (vip) *n., slang* vicepresidente.

veer (vir) *v.t. & i.* **1,** (turn) virar. **2,** *naut.* (let out) soltar(se); aflojar(se). —*n.* virada.

vegetable ('vɛdʒ·tə·bəl) *n.* hortaliza; legumbre; vegetal. —*adj.* vegetal.

vegetal ('vɛdʒ·ə·təl) *adj.* vegetal.

vegetarian (ˌvɛdʒ·əˈtɛr·i·ən) *n. & adj.* vegetariano. —**vegetarianism,** *n.* vegetarianismo.

vegetate ('vɛdʒ·ə,teit) *v.i.* vegetar. —**vegetation,** *n.* vegetación. —**vegetative,** *adj.* vegetativo.

vehemence ('vi·ə·məns) *n.* vehemencia.

vehement ('vi·ə·mənt) *adj.* vehemente.

vehicle ('vi·ə·kəl) *n.* vehículo. —**vehicular** (viˈhɪk·jə·lər) *adj.* de o para vehículos; vehicular.

veil (veil) *n.* velo. —*v.t.* velar.

vein (vein) *n.* vena. —*v.t.* vetear; jaspear. —**veined,** *adj.* venoso; veteado. —**veiny,** *adj.* venoso; veteado.

velar ('vi·lər) *adj.* velar.

vellum ('vɛl·əm) *n.,* **1,** (skin) vitela. **2,** (paper) pergamino.

velocipede (vəˈlas·ə,pid) *n.* velocípedo.

velocity (vəˈlas·ə·ti) *n.* velocidad.

velodrome ('vɛl·ə,droːm) *n.* velódromo.

velours (vəˈlur) *n.* terciopelado.

velum ('vi·ləm) *n.* velo del paladar.

velure (vəˈlur) *n.* terciopelado.

velvet ('vɛl·vɪt) *n.* terciopelo. —*adj.* de terciopelo; aterciopelado. —**velvety,** *adj.* aterciopelado.

velveteen (ˌvɛl·vəˈtiːn) *n.* veludillo.

venal ('vi·nəl) *adj.* venal; mercenario.

venality (viˈnæl·ə·ti) *n.* venalidad.

vend (vend) *v.t. & i.* vender. —**vender,** *n.* vendedor [*fem.* -dora]. —**vendible,** *adj.* vendible. —**vending machine,** vendedora automática; *W.I.* vellonera.

vendetta (venˈdɛt·ə) *n.* vendetta.

vendor ('vɛn·dər) *n.* vendedor. [*fem.* -dora].

veneer (vəˈnɪr) *n.* **1,** (thin covering) chapa; enchapado. **2,** (appearance) apariencia. —*v.t.* **1,** (cover with a thin layer) enchapar. **2,** (disguise) disfrazar.

venerable ('vɛn·ər·ə·bel) *adj.* venerable. —**venerability; venerableness,** *n.* venerabilidad.

venerate ('vɛn·ə,reit) *v.t.* venerar. —**veneration,** *n.* veneración.

venereal (vəˈnɪr·i·əl) *adj.* venéreo.

Venetian (vəˈni·ʃən) *adj. & n.* veneciano.

Venetian blind veneciana; persiana.

vengeance ('vɛn·dʒəns) *n.* venganza. —**take vengeance,** vengarse. —**with a vengeance, 1,** (furiously) con violencia. **2,** (extremely) extremamente; con extremo.

vengeful ('vɛndʒ·fəl) *adj.* vengativo. —**vengefulness,** *n.* calidad de vengativo.

venial ('vi·ni·əl) *adj.* venial.

veniality (ˌvi·niˈæl·ə·ti) *n.* venialidad.

venire (vɪˈnai·ri) *n.* orden de convocación del jurado.

venireman (vɪˈnai·ri·mən) *n.* [*pl.* -men] jurado; persona llamada para jurado.

venison ('vɛn·ə·zən) *n.* venado; carne de venado.

venom ('vɛn·əm) *n.* veneno. —**venomous,** *adj.* venenoso.

venous ('vi·nəs) *adj.* venoso; venal.

vent (vent) *n.* **1,** (release) desahogo; expresión. **2,** (opening) orificio; agujero. **3,** (air hole) respiradero. **4,** (opening in a garment) abertura. **5,** *zoöl.* ano. —*v.t.* **1,** (make an opening in) proveer de abertura; abrir un respiradero en. **2,** (allow to escape) dar salida a; dejar escapar. **3,** (give release to) desahogar; expresar. —**give vent to,** desahogar. —**vent one's feelings,** desahogarse.

ventilate ('vɛn·tə,leit) *v.t.* ventilar. —**ventilation,** *n.* ventilación. —**ventilator,** *n.* ventilador.

ventral ('vɛn·trəl) *adj.* ventral.

ventricle ('vɛn·trɪ·kəl) *n.* ventrículo.

ventricular (vɛn'trɪk·ju·lər) *adj.* ventricular.

ventriloquism (vɛn'trɪl·ə·kwɪz·əm) *n.* ventriloquía. —**ventriloquist,** *n.* ventrílocuo.

venture ('vɛn·tʃər) *n.* empresa arriesgada; riesgo. —*v.t.* aventurar; arriesgar. —*v.i.* osar; aventurarse; arriesgarse. —**venturesome,** *adj.* atrevido; aventurado; emprendedor. —**venturous,** *adj.* osado; atrevido; aventurado. —**venturousness,** *n.* arrojo; osadía. —**at a venture,** a la ventura. —**venture capital,** capital especulativo.

venue ('vɛn·ju) *n.* jurisdicción en que se ha cometido un crimen o donde tiene lugar el proceso. —**change of venue,** cambio de tribunal en un pleito.

Venus ('vi·nəs) *n.* Venus.

veracious (və'rei·ʃəs) *adj.* verdadero; veraz; verídico. —**veraciousness; veracity** (və'ræs·ə·ti) *n.* veracidad.

veranda (və'ræn·də) *n.* pórtico; veranda.

verb (vʌrb) *n.* verbo. —*adj.* verbal. —**verbal,** *adj.* verbal.

verbalize ('vʌr·bəl·aiz) *v.t.* **1,** (express in words) expresar por medio de palabras. **2,** *gram.* (make into a verb) transformar en verbo. —*v.i.* ser verboso; expresarse con verbosidad.

verbatim (vʌr'bei·təm) *adj. & adv.* al pie de la letra; verbatim.

verbena (vʌr'bi·nə) *n.* verbena.

verbiage ('vʌr·bi·ɪdʒ) *n.* verbosidad; verborrea.

verbose (vər'bos) *adj.* verboso. —**verbosity** (-'bas·ə·ti) *n.* verbosidad; verborrea.

verdant ('vʌr·dənt) *adj.* **1,** (green) verdeante. **2,** (inexperienced) inexperto; verde. —**verdancy,** *n.* verdura; verdor.

verdict ('vʌr·dɪkt) *n.* veredicto; fallo; decisión.

verdigris ('vʌr·də,gris) *n.* verdete.

verdure ('vʌr·dʒər) *n.* verdura; verdor.

verge (vʌrdʒ) *n.* **1,** (edge; brink) borde; margen. **2,** (limit; boundary) linde; lindero; confín. **3,** (shaft of a column) fuste. **4,** (rod; staff) vara. —*v.i.* **1,** (tend) tender; inclinarse. **2,** (approach) acercarse; aproximarse.

—**on the verge of,** al borde de; a punto de; a dos dedos de. —**verge on** o **upon,** rayar en; acercarse a.

verger ('vʌr·dʒər) *n.* **1,** (staff bearer) macero. **2,** (church attendant) sacristán.

verify ('vɛr·ə·fai) *v.t.* verificar. —**verifiable,** *adj.* verificable. —**verification** (-fɪ'kei·ʃən) *n.* verificación.

verily ('vɛr·ə·li) *adv.* verdaderamente; de o en verdad.

verisimilitude (,vɛr·ɪ·sɪ'mɪl·ə·tjud) *n.* verosimilitud.

veritable ('vɛr·ɪ·tə·bəl) *adj.* verdadero. —**veritably** (-bli) *adv.* verdaderamente.

verity ('vɛr·ə·ti) *n.* verdad; realidad.

vermicelli (,vʌr·mə'sɛl·i; -tʃɛl·i) *n.* fideos.

vermicide ('vʌr·mɪ·said) *n.* vermicida. —**vermicidal** (-'sai·dəl) *adj.* vermicida.

vermicular (vʌr'mɪk·ju·lər) *adj.* vermicular.

vermiculate (vʌr'mɪk·ju·lət) *adj.* vermicular.

vermiform ('vʌr·mə·form) *adj.* vermiforme.

vermifuge ('vʌr·mə,fjudʒ) *adj. & n.* vermífugo.

vermillion (vər'mɪl·jən) *n.* bermellón. —*adj.* bermejo.

vermin ('vʌr·mɪn) *n.* sabandija; bicho; gusano. —**verminous,** *adj.* verminoso.

vermouth (vər'muθ) *n.* vermut.

vernacular (vər'næk·jə·lər) *adj. & n.* vernáculo.

vernal ('vʌr·nəl) *adj.* **1,** (of spring) vernal. **2,** (of youth) juvenil.

vernier ('vʌr·ni·ər) *n.* vernier.

veronica (və'ran·ə·kə) *n.* verónica.

versatile ('vʌr·sə·tɪl) *adj.* **1,** (adaptable) flexible; hábil para muchas cosas. **2,** *bot.; zoöl.* versátil.

versatility (vʌr·sə'tɪl·ə·ti) *n.* **1,** (adaptability) flexibilidad; habilidad para muchas cosas. **2,** *bot.; zoöl.* versatilidad.

verse (vʌrs) *n.* verso; *Bib.* versículo.

versed (vʌrst) *adj.* versado.

versify ('vʌr·sə·fai) *v.t. & i.* versificar. —**versification** (-fɪ'kei·ʃən) *n.* versificación.

version ('vʌr·ʒən) *n.* versión.

verso ('vʌr·so) *n.* **1,** (left-hand page) verso; vuelto. **2,** (reverse side) reverso; revés.

versus ('vʌr·səs) *prep.* versus; contra; en contra de.

vertebra ('vʌr·tə·brə) *n.* [*pl.* **-brae** (-bri) o **bras**] vértebra. —**vertebral,** *adj.* vertebral.

vertebrate ('vʌr·tə·breit) *adj.* & *n.* vertebrado.

vertex ('vʌr·tɛks) *n.* [*pl.* **-es** o **vertices** (-tə·siz)] **1,** (highest point) cima; cumbre; ápice. **2,** *anat.; math.* vértice. **3,** *astron.* cenit.

vertical ('vʌr·tə·kəl) *adj.* & *n.* vertical.

vertiginous (vər'tɪdʒ·ə·nəs) *adj.* vertiginoso.

vertigo ('vʌr·tə·go) *n.* vértigo.

verve (vʌrv) *n.* entusiasmo; viveza; vigor.

very ('vɛr·i) *adv.* muy; mucho. —*adj.* **1,** (true; genuine) verdadero. **2,** (self; same) mismo. **3,** (in the fullest sense) completo; cabal. **4,** (pure; simple) mero; puro. —**the very same,** el mismo; el mismísimo.

vesicle ('vɛs·ə·kəl) *n.* vesícula.

vesicular (vɛ'sɪk·ju·lər) *adj.* vesicular.

vesiculate (vɛ'sɪk·ju₁leit) *adj.* vesiculoso.

vesper ('vɛs·pər) *n.* **1,** (evening) tarde; anochecer; víspera. **2,** *pl.* (religious service) vísperas. —*adj.* vespertino.

vespertine ('vɛs·pər·tɪn; -tain) *adj.* vespertino.

vessel ('vɛs·əl) *n.* **1,** (ship) bajel; buque. **2,** (container) vasija. **3,** *anat.; bot.* vaso.

vest (vɛst) *n.* chaleco. —*v.t.* **1,** (clothe) vestir. **2,** (give possession of) investir; conceder; dar posesión de. **3,** (endow) investir (de); revestir (de).

vestal ('vɛs·təl) *adj.* & *n.* vestal.

vested ('vɛst·ɪd) *adj.* **1,** (clothed) vestido. **2,** (established) revestido; establecido. —**vested interests,** intereses creados.

vestibule ('vɛs·tə₁bjul) *n.* vestíbulo; zaguán.

vestige ('vɛs·tɪdʒ) *n.* vestigio.

vestigial (vɛs'tɪdʒ·i·əl) *adj.* vestigial; rudimentario.

vestment ('vɛst·mənt) *n.* vestimenta; vestidura.

vest-pocket *adj.* para el bolsillo del chaleco; de bolsillo; diminuto; en miniatura.

vestry ('vɛs·tri) *n.* **1,** (room) vestuario; sacristía. **2,** (chapel) capilla. **3,** (church council) junta parroquial.

vestryman ('vɛs·tri·mən) *n.* [*pl.* **-men**] miembro de la junta parroquial.

vet (vɛt) *n., colloq.* **1,** = **veteran. 2,** = **veterinary** o **veterinarian.** —*v.t., colloq.* examinar; revisar.

vetch (vɛtʃ) *n.* arveja.

veteran ('vɛt·ər·ən) *n.* & *adj.* veterano.

veterinarian (₁vɛt·ər·ə'nɛr·i·ən) *n.* veterinario.

veterinary ('vɛt·ər·ə·nɛr·i) *adj.* & *n.* veterinario. —**veterinary medicine,** veterinaria.

veto ('vi·to) *n.* veto. —*adj.* del veto. —*v.t.* vetar.

vex (vɛks) *v.t.* vejar; molestar; irritar.

vexation (vɛks'ei·ʃən) *n.* vejación; molestia.

vexatious (vɛks'ei·ʃəs) *adj.* vejatorio; penoso; enfadoso.

via ('vai·ə; 'vi·ə) *prep.* vía.

viability (₁vai·ə'brl·ə·ti) *n.* viabilidad.

viable ('vai·ə·bəl) *adj.* viable.

viaduct ('vai·ə·dʌkt) *n.* viaducto.

vial ('vai·əl) *n.* frasco; redoma; ampolleta.

viand ('vai·ənd) *n.* vianda. —**viands,** *n.pl.* manjares delicados; vitualla.

viaticum (vai'æt·ə·kəm) *n.* viático.

vibes (vaibz) *n.pl., slang* **1,** (vibrations) vibraciones. **2,** = **vibraharp.**

vibraharp ('vai·brə-) *n.* vibráfono. *También,* **vibraphone.**

vibrancy ('vai·brən·si) *n.* vibración; viveza.

vibrant ('vai·brənt) *adj.* vibrante.

vibrate ('vai·breit) *v.t.* & *i.* vibrar. —**vibratile** (-brə·tɪl) *adj.* vibrátil. —**vibration,** *n.* vibración. —**vibrator,** *n.* vibrador. —**vibratory** (-brə·tor·i) *adj.* vibratorio; vibrador.

viburnum (vɪ'bʌr·nəm) *n.* viburno.

vicar ('vɪk·ər) *n.* vicario. —**vicarage,** *n.* vicaría.

vicarial (vai'kɛr·i·əl) *adj.* vicario.

vicariate (vai'kɛr·i·ɪt) *n.* vicaría; vicariato.

vicarious (vai'kɛr·i·əs) *adj.* vicario. —**vicariousness,** *n.* calidad de vicario.

vicarship ('vɪk·ər·ʃɪp) *n.* vicaría; vicariato.

vice (vais) *n.* **1,** (evil; defect) vicio.

2, = **vise.** —*prep.* en lugar de; en vez de.

vice admiral vicealmirante.

vicegerent (ˌvais'dʒɛr·ənt) *n.* vicegerente.

vicennial (vai'sɛn·i·əl) *adj.* vicenal. —*n.* vicenio.

vice president vicepresidente. —**vice presidency,** vicepresidencia.

viceregal (vais'ri·gəl) *adj.* virreinal.

viceroy ('vais·rɔi) *n.* virrey. —**viceroyalty** (vais'rɔi·əl·ti) *n.* virreinato; virreino. —**viceroyship,** *n.* virreinato; virreino.

vice versa ('vai·si'vʌr·sə) viceversa.

vicinity (vɪ'sɪn·ə·ti) *n.* vecindad.

vicious ('vɪʃ·əs) *adj.* vicioso. —**viciousness,** *n.* vicio; depravación.

vicissitude (vɪ'sɪs·ɪ·tjud) *n.* vicisitud.

victim ('vɪk·tɪm) *n.* víctima.

victimize ('vɪk·tɪm·aiz) *v.t.* **1,** (sacrifice) hacer víctima; inmolar. **2,** (swindle) embaucar; estafar.

victor ('vɪk·tər) *n.* vencedor [*fem.* -dora].

victoria (vɪk'tor·i·ə) *n.* (carriage) victoria.

Victorian (vɪk'tor·i·ən) *adj.* victoriano.

victorious (vɪk'tor·i·əs) *adj.* victorioso; triunfante.

victory ('vɪk·tə·ri) *n.* victoria; triunfo; éxito.

victrola (vɪk'tro·lə) *n.* fonógrafo.

victual ('vɪt·əl) *v.t. & i.* abastecer(se); proveer(se). —**victuals,** *n.pl.* víveres; vituallas.

victualer ('vɪt·əl·ər) *n.* abastecedor [*fem.* -dora].

vicuña (vɪ'kun·jə) *n.* vicuña. *También,* **vicuna** (vɪ'kun·ə).

video ('vɪd·i·o) *n.* video. —*adj.* de video; perteneciente al video. —**videocassette,** *n.* videocasete. —**videodisc,** *n.* videodisco. —**videotape,** *n.* videocinta.

video camera videocámara.

videocassette recorder o **player** videocasetera.

vie (vai) *v.i.* [**vied, vying**] competir; rivalizar.

view (vju) *n.* **1,** (sight; vision) vista; visión. **2,** (inspection) examen; inspección. **3,** (scene) vista; panorama; paisaje. **4,** (appearance) apariencia; aspecto. **5,** (opinion) opinión; parecer. **6,** (aim) intento; propósito. **7,** (mental attitude) concepto.—*v.t.* **1,** (see) mirar; ver. **2,** (examine) examinar; inspeccionar. **3,** (consider) considerar; contemplar. —**come into view,** asomar; aparecer. —**in view,** a la vista. —**in view of,** a vista de. ┬**on view,** expuesto; en exhibición. —**with a view to,** con el propósito de.

viewer ('vju·ər) *n.* **1,** (one who sees) mirador; espectador. **2,** (examiner) inspector; veedor. **3,** *TV* televidente. **4,** = viewfinder.

viewfinder ('vju,fain·dər) *n.* visor.

viewless ('vju·ləs) *adj.* **1,** (offering no view) sin perspectiva, **2,** (invisible) invisible. **3,** (having no opinion) sin opinión.

viewpoint ('vju·pɔint) *n.* punto de vista.

vigesimal (vɪ'dʒes·ɪ·məl) *adj.* **1,** (twentieth) vigésimo. **2,** (counting by twenties) vigesimal.

vigil ('vɪdʒ·əl) *n.* vela; vigilia. —**keep vigil (over),** velar; vigilar.

vigilant ('vɪdʒ·ə·lənt) *adj.* vigilante. —**vigilance,** *n.* vigilancia.

vigilante (ˌvɪdʒ·ə'læn·ti) *n.* vigilante.

vignette (vɪn'jɛt) *n.* **1,** (ornamental design) viñeta. **2,** *print.* (headpiece) cabecera. **3,** (literary piece) ensayo; retrato literario.

vigor ('vɪg·ər) *n.* vigor; fuerza; energía. —**vigorous,** *adj.* vigoroso. —**vigorously,** *adv.* con energía; vigorosamente.

viking ('vai·kɪŋ) *n.* antiguo pirata escandinavo; viking.

vile (vail) *adj.* vil; bajo; despreciable. —**vileness,** *n.* vileza; bajeza.

vilify ('vɪl·ə·fai) *v.t.* vilipendiar; envilecer. —**vilification** (-fɪ'kei·ʃən) *n.* vilipendio; envilecimiento.

villa ('vɪl·ə) *n.* quinta; villa.

village ('vɪl·ɪdʒ) *n.* aldea; población. —**villager,** *n.* aldeano.

villain ('vɪl·ən) *n.* villano; malvado. —**villainous,** *adj.* villano; malvado; malo. —**villainy,** *n.* villanía; villanada; maldad.

vim (vɪm) *n.* energía; fuerza; vigor; enjundia.

vinaigrette (ˌvɪn·ə'grɛt) *n.* **1,** (container) vinagrera. **2,** (sauce) vinagreta.

vindicate ('vɪn·də,keit) *v.t.* vindicar. —**vindication,** *n.* vindicación. —**vindicatory** (-kə·tor·i) *adj.* vindicativo; vindicatorio.

vindictive (vɪn'dɪk·tɪv) *adj.*
vengativo. —**vindictiveness,** *n.*
calidad de vengativo; ansia de
venganza.

vine (vain) *n.* **1,** (climbing or trailing plant) enredadera. **2,** (grapevine) vid; parra.

vinegar ('vɪn·ə·gər) *n.* vinagre.
—**vinegary,** *adj.* avinagrado.
—**vinegar cruet,** vinagrera.
—**vinegar sauce,** vinagreta.

vineyard ('vɪn·jərd) *n.* viña;
viñedo.

viniculture ('vɪn·ə-) *n.* vinicultura.

vintage ('vɪn·tɪdʒ) *n.* vendimia.
—*adj.* clásico; antiguo; excelente.

vintner ('vɪnt·nər) *n.* vinatero.

vinyl ('vai·nɪl) *n.* vinilo.

viol ('vai·əl) *n.* viola.

viola (vi'o·lə; vai-) *n.* viola.

violate ('vai·ə͵leit) *v.t.* violar.
—**violation,** *n.* violación.

violent ('vai·ə·lənt) *adj.* violento.
—**violence,** *n.* violencia.

violet ('vai·ə·lɪt) *n.* & *adj.* violeta.

violin (vai·ə'lɪn) *n.* violín.
—**violinist,** *n.* violinista.

violist (vi'o·lɪst; vai-) *n.* viola.

violoncello (͵vai·ə·lən'tʃel·o) *n.*
violoncelo. —**violoncellist,** *n.*
violoncelista.

VIP (͵vi·ai'pi) *n., slang, abr. de*
very important person, dignatario;
alto personaje.

viper ('vai·pər) *n.* víbora. —**viperous, viperish,** *adj.* viperino.

viperine ('vai·pər·ɪn) *adj.* viperino.

virago (vɪ'rei·go) *n.* regañona; virago.

viral ('vai·rəl) *adj.* relacionado con
un virus; causado por un virus.

virgin ('vʌr·dʒɪn) *n.* & *adj.* virgen.
—**virginal,** *adj.* & *n.* virginal.

virgin birth 1, *theol.* parto
virginal. **2,** *zoöl.* partenogénesis.

Virginia reel (vʌr'dʒ·ɪn·jə) baile
de Virginia.

virginity (vʌr'dʒɪn·ə·ti) *n.*
virginidad.

virginium (vʌr'dʒɪn·i·əm) *n.* =
francium.

Virgo ('vʌr·go) *n., astron.* Virgo;
Virgen.

virgule ('vʌr·gjul) *n.* vírgula.

virile ('vɪr·əl) *adj.* viril. —**virility**
(və'rɪl·ə·ti) *n.* virilidad.

virtual ('vʌr·tʃu·əl) *adj.* virtual.

virtue ('vʌr·tʃu) *n.* virtud.
—**virtuous,** *adj.* virtuoso.

—**virtuousness,** *n.* virtuosidad.
—**by o in virtue of,** en virtud de.

virtuosity (͵vʌr·tʃu'as·ə·ti) *n.*
virtuosismo.

virtuoso (͵vʌr·tʃu'o·so) *n.* [*pl.* **-sos**
o **-si** (-si)] virtuoso.

virulence ('vɪr·jə·ləns) *n.* virulencia.

virulent ('vɪr·jə·lənt) *adj.* virulento.

virus ('vai·rəs) *n.* virus.

visa ('vi·zə) *n.* visado; *Amer.* visa.
—*v.t.* visar. *También,* **visé.**

visage ('vɪz·ɪdʒ) *n.* **1,** (face) rostro;
visaje; semblante. **2,** (appearance)
apariencia; aspecto.

vis-à-vis (vi·za'vi) *prep.* frente a;
enfrente de; comparado con.

viscera ('vɪs·ər·ə) *n.pl.* vísceras.
—**visceral,** *adj.* visceral.

viscid ('vɪs·ɪd) *adj.* viscoso.
—**viscidness; viscidity** (vɪs'ɪd·ə·ti)
n. viscosidad.

viscose ('vɪs·kos) *n.* viscosa.

viscosity (vɪs'kas·ə·ti) *n.*
viscosidad.

viscount ('vai·kaunt) *n.* vizconde.
—**viscountess,** *n.* vizcondesa.
—**viscountship,** *n.* vizcondado.

viscous ('vɪs·kəs) *adj.* viscoso.

vise (vais) *n.* torno; tornillo.

visé (vi'zei) *n.* & *v.t.* = **visa.**

visible ('vɪz·ə·bəl) *adj.* visible.
—**visibility,** *n.* visibilidad.

Visigoth ('vɪz·ɪ·gaθ) *n.* visigodo.

Visigothic (͵vɪz·ɪ'gaθ·ɪk) *adj.*
visigodo; visigótico. —*n.* visigodo.

vision ('vɪʒ·ən) *n.* visión.
—**visionary,** *adj.* & *n.* visionario.

visit ('vɪz·ɪt) *v.t.* **1,** (call upon; go
to see) visitar. **2,** (send, as a punishment) mandar. —*v.i.* visitar; hacer
visitas; visitarse. —*n.* visita.

visitant ('vɪz·ɪ·tənt) *adj.* & *n.*
visitante.

visitation (͵vɪz·ɪ'tei·ʃən) *n.* visitación.

visiting ('vɪz·ə·tɪŋ) *adj.* visitador;
visitante; de visita. —**visiting card,**
tarjeta de visita.

visitor ('vɪz·ɪ·tər) *n.* visitante;
visita. —**have a visitor** (o **visitors**),
tener visita.

visor *también,* **vizor** ('vai·zər) *n.*
visera.

vista ('vɪs·tə) vista; perspectiva;
panorama.

visual ('vɪʒ·u·əl) *adj.* visual.

visualize ('vɪʒ·u·ə·laiz) *v.t.* & *i.*
imaginarse; representarse; visualizar. —**visualization** (-ɪ'zei·ʃən) *n.*

imagen; representación; visualización.

vital ('vai·təl) *adj.* **1**, (of or pert. to life) vital. **2**, (fatal) fatal; mortal. **3**, (essential) esencial; indispensable. **4**, (of supreme importance) vital; de suma importancia. **5**, (energetic) enérgico; vivaz. —**vitals**, *n.pl.* vísceras; partes vitales. —**vital signs**, signos vitales.

vitalism ('vai·təl·ɪz·əm) *n.* vitalismo. —**vitalist**, *n.* vitalista. —**vitalistic**, *adj.* vitalista.

vitality (vai'tæl·ə·ti) *n.* vitalidad; vida.

vitalize ('vai·tə,laiz) *v.t.* vitalizar. —**vitalization** (-ɪ'zei·ʃən) *n.* vitalización.

vital statistics estadística; estadísticas.

vitamin ('vai·tə·mɪn) *n.* vitamina.

vitiate ('vɪʃ·i·eit) *v.t.* viciar. —**vitiation**, *n.* viciación.

viticulture ('vɪt·ə-) *n.* viticultura.

vitreous ('vɪt·ri·əs) *adj.* vítreo. —**vitreous humor**, humor vítreo.

vitrify ('vɪt·rɪ·fai) *v.t.* vitrificar. —**vitrification** (-fɪ'kei·ʃən); **vitrifaction** (-'fæk·ʃən) *n.* vitrificación.

vitriol ('vɪt·ri·əl) *n.* **1**, *chem.* vitriolo. **2**, (sarcasm) sarcasmo; mordacidad.

vitriolic (,vɪt·ri'al·ɪk) *adj.* **1**, (of or resembling vitriol) vitriólico. **2**, (sarcastic) sarcástico; cáustico; mordaz.

vituperate (vai'tju·pə,reit) *v.t.* vituperar. —**vituperation**, *n.* vituperación; vituperio. —**vituperative**, *adj.* vituperioso.

vivacious (vɪ'vei·ʃəs; vai-) *adj.* vivaz. —**vivaciousness; vivacity** (vɪ'væs·ə·ti) *n.* vivacidad.

vivid ('vɪv·ɪd) *adj.* vivo; vívido. —**vividness**, *n.* viveza.

vivify ('vɪv·ə·fai) *v.t.* vivificar; avivar. —**vivification** (-fɪ'kei·ʃən) *n.* vivificación.

viviparous (vai'vɪp·ə·rəs) *adj.* vivíparo.

vivisect ('vɪv·ə·sɛkt) *v.t.* disecar vivo.

vivisection ('vɪv·ə,sɛk·ʃən) *n.* vivisección.

vixen ('vɪk·sən) *n.* **1**, (female fox) zorra; hembra del zorro. **2**, (ill-tempered woman) mujer regañona. —**vixenish**, *adj.* regañona.

vizier (vɪ'zɪr) *n.* visir.

vizor ('vai·zər) *n.* = **visor**.

vocable ('vo·kə·bəl) *n.* vocablo; voz.

vocabulary (vo'kæb·ju·lɛr·i) *n.* vocabulario.

vocal ('vo·kəl) *adj.* **1**, (of or pert. to the voice) vocal. **2**, (vocalic) vocálico. **3**, (expressive) expresivo. —*n.* vocal. —**vocal cords**, cuerdas vocales.

vocalic (vo'kæl·ɪk) *adj.* vocálico.

vocalist ('vo·kəl·ɪst) *n.* cantor; cantante; vocalista.

vocalize ('vo·kəl·aiz) *v.t. & i.* vocalizar. —**vocalization** (-ɪ'zei·ʃən) *n.* vocalización.

vocation (vo'kei·ʃən) *n.* vocación. —**vocational**, *adj.* vocacional.

vocative ('vak·ə·tɪv) *adj. & n.* vocativo.

vociferate (vo'sɪf·ə·reit) *v.i. & t.* vociferar. —**vociferation**, *n.* vociferación.

vociferous (vo'sɪf·ə·rəs) *adj.* clamoroso; vociferador; vociferante. —**vociferously**, *adv.* a gritos; con viveza. —**vociferousness**, *n.* clamorosidad.

vodka ('vad·kə) *n.* vodka.

vogue (voːg) *n.* moda; boga. —**be in vogue**, estar en boga; ser de moda.

voice (vɔis) *n.* voz; *phonet.* sonoridad. —*v.i.* **1**, (express) expresar; proclamar. **2**, *phonet.* sonorizar. —*v.i.* sonorizarse. —**at the top of one's voice**, a voz en cuello; a voz en grito. —**with one voice**, a una voz.

voiced (vɔist) *adj.* **1**, (having a voice) que tiene voz. **2**, (expressed) expresado; proclamado. **3**, *phonet.* sonoro.

voiceless ('vɔis·ləs) *adj.* **1**, (dumb, silent) mudo. **2**, (unexpressed) inexpresado. **3**, *phonet.* sordo; insonoro; mudo. —**voicelessness**, *n.*, *phonet.* sordez.

voicing ('vɔis·ɪŋ) *n.*, *phonet.* sonorización.

void (vɔid) *adj.* **1**, (empty) vacío. **2**, (unoccupied) desocupado; vacante. **3**, (invalid) nulo; inválido. **4**, (useless) vano; inútil. **5**, (lacking) falto; privado; desprovisto. —*n.* **1**, (emptiness) vacío. **2**, (opening; gap) hueco. —*v.t.* **1**, (empty) vaciar; evacuar. **2**, (nullify) anular.

voidance ('vɔid·əns) *n.* **1**, (annulment) anulación. **2**, *eccles.* (vacancy) vacante.

voile (vɔil) *n.* espumilla.

volatile ('val·ə·tɪl) *adj.* volátil. —**volatility** (-'tɪl·ə·ti) *n.* volatilidad.

volatilize ('val·ə·tɪl,aiz) *v.t.* volatilizar. —*v.i.* volatilizarse.

volcano (val'kei·no) *n.* volcán. —**volcanic** (-'kæn·ɪk) *adj.* volcánico. —**volcanism** (-kən·ɪz·əm) *n.* volcanismo.

vole (voɹl) *n.* campañol.

volition (vo'lɪʃ·ən) *n.* volición. —**volitive** ('val·ə·tɪv); **volitional,** *adj.* volitivo.

volley ('val·i) *n.* **1,** (simultaneous discharge) descarga. **2,** (downpour) lluvia. **3,** *games* voleo. —*v.t.* **1,** (fire) descargar. **2,** *games* volear.

volleyball ('val·i,bɒl) *n.* volibol.

volt (volt) *n.* voltio. —**voltage,** *n.* voltaje.

voltaic (val'tei·ɪk) *adj.* voltaico.

voltaism ('val·tə·ɪz·əm) *n.* voltaísmo; galvanismo.

voltmeter ('volt,mi·tər) *n.* voltímetro.

volubility (,val·jə'bɪl·ə·ti) *n,* volubilidad.

voluble ('val·jə·bəl) *adj.* voluble.

volume ('val·jum) *n.* **1,** (mass) volumen. **2,** (book) tomo; volumen.

voluminous (və'lu·mɪ·nəs) *adj.* voluminoso. —**voluminousness,** *n.* voluminosidad.

voluntary ('val·ən·tɛr·i) *adj.* voluntario. —*n., mus.* solo de órgano. —**voluntariness,** *n.* voluntariedad.

volunteer (,val·ən'tɪr) *n.* & *adj.* voluntario. —*v.t.* ofrecer. —*v.i.* servir de voluntario; ofrecerse.

voluptuary (və'lʌp·tʃu·ɛr·i) *n.* voluptuoso.

voluptuous (və'lʌp·tʃu·əs) *adj.* voluptuoso. —**voluptuousness,** *n.* voluptuosidad.

volute (və'lut) *n.* voluta.

vomit ('vam·ɪt) *v.t.* & *i.* vomitar. —*n.* vómito. —**vomitive,** *adj.* & *n.* vomitivo.

voodoo ('vu·du) *n.* & *adj.* vodú. —**voodooism,** *n.* voduismo. —**voodooist,** *n.* voduista.

voracious (vo'rei·ʃəs) *adj.* voraz. —**voraciousness; voracity** (vo'ræs·ə·ti) *n.* voracidad.

vortex ('vor·tɛks) *n.* [*pl.* **-texes** o **-tices** (-tɪ·siz)] vórtice.

votary ('vo·tə·ri) *n.* **1,** (one bound by vows) religioso; monje; monja. **2,** (devotee) aficionado; devoto. **3,** (adherent) partidario. —*adj.* votivo.

vote (vot) *n.* voto. —*v.i.* & *t.* votar. —**voter,** *n.* votante; elector. —**voting,** *n.* votación.

votive ('vo·tɪv) *adj.* votivo.

vouch (vautʃ) *v.t.* & *i.* atestiguar; garantizar. —**vouch for,** responder de o por.

voucher ('vautʃ·ər) *n.* **1,** (one who vouches) fiador [*fem.* -dora]; garante. **2,** (receipt) comprobante.

vouchsafe (vautʃ'seif) *v.t.* otorgar; conceder; dignarse hacer o dar. —*v.i.* dignarse.

vow (vau) *n.* voto; promesa. —*v.t.* votar; prometer; jurar; hacer voto de. —*v.i.* hacer voto.

vowel ('vau·əl) *n.* vocal. —*adj.* vocálico.

voyage ('vɔi·ɪdʒ) *n.* viaje. —*v.i.* viajar. —*v.t.* viajar por; atravesar. —**voyager,** *n.* viajero.

vulcanite ('vʌl·kən·ait) *n.* vulcanita.

vulcanize ('vʌl·kə,naiz) *v.t.* vulcanizar. —**vulcanization** (-nɪ'zei·ʃən) *n.* vulcanización.

vulgar ('vʌl·gər) *adj.* vulgar; grosero.

vulgarian (vʌl'gɛr·i·ən) *n.* persona grosera; maleducado.

vulgarism ('vʌl·gər·ɪz·əm) *n.* vulgarismo.

vulgarity (vʌl'gɛr·ə·ti) *n.* vulgaridad; grosería.

vulgarize ('vʌl·gə,raiz) *v.t.* vulgarizar. —**vulgarization** (-rɪ'zei·ʃən) *n.* vulgarización.

Vulgate ('vʌl·geit) *n.* Vulgata.

vulnerable ('vʌl·nər·ə·bəl) *adj.* vulnerable. —**vulnerability** (-'bɪl·ə·ti) *n.* vulnerabilidad.

vulpine ('vʌl·pain) *adj.* vulpino; zorruno.

vulture ('vʌl·tʃər) *n.* **1,** (bird) buitre. **2,** (rapacious person) bárbaro; pícaro; rapaz. —**vulturine** (-tʃə·rain); **vulturous,** *adj.* buitrero.

vulva ('vʌl·və) *n.* vulva.

vying ('vai·ɪŋ) *v.,* *ger. de* **vie.**

W

W, w ('dʌb·əl·ju) vigésima tercera letra del alfabeto inglés.

wabble ('wab·əl) v.i. & n. = **wobble.** —**wabbly** (-li) adj. = **wobbly.**

wack (wæk) n., slang excéntrico; estrafalario.

wacky ('wæk·i) adj., slang excéntrico; loco. —**wackiness,** n., slang excentricidad; locura.

wad (waᵣd) n. **1,** (small, soft mass) bolita; masa. **2,** (packing; filling) guata; borra. **3,** (roll; bundle) lío; atado. —v.t. [**wadded, wadding**] **1,** (compress) apelmazar; apelotonar. **2,** (pack; fill) acolchar; henchir; rellenar. **3,** (form into a bundle) liar; atar; envolver.

wadding ('wad·ɪŋ) n. guata; entretela; bolitas de algodón.

waddle ('wad·əl) v.i. anadear. —n. anadeo.

wade (weid) v.t. vadear. —v.i. andar en el agua, el barro, etc.; proceder con dificultad. —n. **1,** (act of wading) vadeamiento. **2,** (ford) vado. —**wade into,** colloq. atacar; embestir; lanzarse a o en. —**wade through,** ir con dificultad por; hacer con dificultad.

wader ('weid·ər) n. **1,** (one who wades) vadeador [fem. -dora]. **2,** (bird) ave zancuda.

waders ('weid·ərz) n.pl. botas de vadear; botas altas impermeables.

wafer ('wei·fər) n. **1,** barquillo; caramelo. **2,** eccles. hostia. **3,** pharm. sello.

wafery ('wei·fə·ri) adj. acaramelado; delgado; fino; ligero.

waffle ('waf·əl) n. barquillo. —v.i., colloq. vacilar. —**waffle iron,** barquillero.

waft (waft) v.t. llevar por el aire o por encima del agua. —v.i. **1,** (float) llevarse por el aire; flotar. **2,** (blow gently) soplar levemente. —n. **1,** (floating) flotación; flotamiento. **2,** (breeze; gust) ráfaga. **3,** (odor) olor. **4,** (waving) movimiento trémolo.

wag (wæg) v.t. [**wagged, wagging**] hacer oscilar; menear. —v.i. oscilar; menearse. —n. **1,** (wagging motion) oscilación; meneo. **2,** (wit) bromista; burlón. —**wag the tongue,** charlar; hablar mucho.

wage (weidʒ) n. paga; salario.

—v.t. emprender; perseguir. —**wage war,** hacer guerra.

wage earner trabajador [fem. -dora]; asalariado.

wager ('wei·dʒər) n. apuesta. —v.t. & i. apostar.

wages ('wei·dʒɪz) n.pl. paga; salario; sueldo; recompensa.

waggish ('wæg·ɪʃ) adj. chocarrero; juguetón; retozón; bufón.

waggle ('wæg·əl) v.t. oscilar; menear. —v.i. oscilar; menearse. —n. oscilación; meneo.

wagon ('wæg·ən) n. **1,** (transport vehicle) carro; vagón. **2,** Brit. (freight car) furgón. —**be on the wagon,** slang abstenerse de tomar bebidas alcohólicas.

wagoner ('wæg·ən·ər) n. carretero.

wagonload ('wæg·ən,lod) n. carretada; vagonada.

wagon train tren de equipajes.

waif (weif) n. **1,** (abandoned child) expósito. **2,** (homeless child) niño vagabundo. **3,** (stray animal) animal perdido.

wail (weil) v.i. llorar; gemir; lamentarse. —n. gemido; lamento.

wainscot ('wein·skət) n. enmaderamiento; friso de madera. —v.t. enmaderar.

wainscoting ('wein·skət·ɪŋ) n. enmaderamiento.

wainwright ('wein·rait) n. carretero.

waist (weist) n. **1,** (part of the body or of a garment) cintura. **2,** (garment) blusa; corpiño.

waistband ('weist,bænd) n. pretina.

waistcoat ('weist·kot; 'wɛs·kət) n. chaleco.

waistline ('weist·lain) n. cintura; talle.

wait (weit) v.t. **1,** (expect) esperar; aguardar. **2,** (serve) servir. **3,** colloq. (delay; put off) posponer; diferir. —v.i. **1,** (remain) esperar; aguardar. **2,** (serve) servir. —n. espera. —**wait for,** esperar; aguardar. —**wait on** (o **upon**), **1,** (serve) servir; atender. **2,** (call on; visit) visitar; ir a ver. **3,** (result from) seguirse de; inferirse de. **4,** (pay

1236

one's respects to) presentar sus respetos a.

waiter ('weit·ər) *n.* camarero; mozo.

waiting ('weit·ıŋ) *n.* 1, (expectation) espera. 2, (service) servicio. —*adj.* 1, (that waits) que espera. 2, (of or for waiting) de espera. 3, (serving) de servicio. —**in waiting**, de honor; de servicio.

waiting room sala de espera.

waitress ('weit·rıs) *n.* camarera; moza.

waive (weiv) *v.t.* ceder; renunciar a; desistir de.

waiver ('weiv·ər) *n.* renuncia; desistimiento.

wake (weik) *v.t.* [*pret.* **waked** o **woke**; *p.p.* **waked**] despertar. —*v.i.* 1, (rouse oneself) despertar; despertarse. 2, (stay awake) velar. —*n.* 1, (vigil) vela; vigilia. 2, (for a dead person) velatorio. 3, (track, as of a ship) estela. 4, (trace; trail) huella. —**in the wake of**, de resultas de; a consecuencia de.

wakeful ('weik·fəl) *adj.* vigilante; desvelado. —**wakefulness**, *n.* vigilia; desvelo.

waken ('weik·ən) *v.t.* despertar. —*v.i.* despertar; despertarse.

waking ('weik·ıŋ) *n.* vela; vigilia. —*adj.* despierto. —**waking hours**, horas de vela.

wale (weil) *n.* 1, (mark of a whip or stick) roncha; raya; verdugón. 2, *naut.* cinta. 3, (ridge on the surface of cloth) relieve.

walk (wɔk) *v.i.* 1, (proceed on foot) andar; caminar. 2, (stroll) pasearse; dar un paseo. 3, (conduct oneself) portarse; conducirse. 4, *baseball* pasar (a primera base). —*v.t.* 1, (take out for a walk) pasear. 2, (traverse) andar por; atravesar; recorrer. 3, (cause to walk) hacer andar. 4, (accompany in walking) acompañar caminando. 5, *baseball* dejar pasar (a primera base). —*n.* 1, (act of walking; distance walked) paseo; caminata. 2, (gait) andar; paso. 3, (pacing, as of a horse) paso; andadura. 4, (path) paseo; vereda; senda; alameda. 5, (sidewalk) acera; *Mex.* banqueta. 6, (footwalk) andén. 7, (station in life) carrera; condición. 8, (occupation) oficio; empleo. 9, (easy victory) triunfo fácil. 10, (easy victory) triunfo fácil. —**go for a walk**, salir a pasear; dar un paseo. —**take a walk**, dar un paseo.

—**walk away**, marcharse; irse. —**walk away from**, alejarse de. —**walk in**, entrar; pasar adelante. —**walk in on (someone)**, sorprenderle a uno. —**walk off**, 1, (leave) marcharse; irse. 2, (get rid of by walking) deshacerse de (caminando). —**walk off with**, 1, (steal) robar. 2, (carry off) cargar con; llevarse. 3, (win) ganar. —**walk out**, 1, (leave) salir; marcharse. 2, *colloq.* (go on strike) salir en huelga. —**walk out on**, *colloq.* abandonar; renunciar a. —**walk up**, subir. —**walk up to**, acercarse a.

walkaway ('wɔk·ə·we) *n.*, *colloq.* triunfo fácil.

walker ('wɔk·ər) *n.* 1, (for a child) andaderas; andador. 2, (for an invalid) andador. 3, (one good at walking) andador [*fem.* -dora].

walkie-talkie ('wɔk·i'tɔk·i) *n.* radioteléfono portátil.

walk-in *adj.* 1, (closet) bastante grande para entrar en él. 2, (apartment; business) con puerta a la calle. 3, (services) que se puede(n) conseguir sin cita previa.

walking ('wɔk·ıŋ) *adj.* 1, (that walks) que anda; andante. 2, (itinerant) ambulante; errante. 3, (oscillating) oscilante; de vaivén. —*n.* 1, (act of walking) paseo. 2, (gait) andar; paso. —**walking papers**, *slang* despedida. —**walking stick**, bastón.

walkout ('wɔk·aut) *n.*, *colloq.* huelga.

walkup ('wɔk·ʌp) *n.*, *colloq.* apartamento de escaleras.

wall (wɔl) *n.* 1, (enclosure; partition) pared. 2, (supporting or outer wall) muro. 3, (rampart) muralla. —*v.t.* emparedar; tapiar; amurallar. —**drive to the wall**, poner entre la espada y la pared. —**go to the wall**, 1, (yield) rendirse; entregarse. 2, (fail) fracasar.

wallboard ('wɔl·bord) *n.* tabla de yeso.

wallet ('wal·ıt) *n.* cartera; *Amer.* billetera.

walleye ('wɔl·ai) *n.* ojo saltón; *ichthy.* pez de ojos saltones. —**walleyed**, *adj.* de ojos saltones.

wallflower ('wɔl,flau·ər) *n.* 1, *bot.* alhelí. 2, *colloq.* (girl without a partner at a dance) plantada; mujer sin pareja.

wallop ('wal·əp) *v.t.*, *colloq.* zurrar;

tundir; aporrear. —*n., colloq.* **1,** (blow) golpe fuerte. **2,** (force) fuerza; energía.

walloping ('wal·əp·ıŋ) *adj., colloq.* grande; enorme. —*n., colloq.* **1,** (thrashing) zurra; tunda; aporreo. **2,** (defeat) derrota.

wallow ('wal·o) *v.i.* revolcarse. —*n.* **1,** (act) revuelco; revolcón. **2,** (place) revolcadero.

wallpaper ('wal,pei·pər) *n.* empapelado. —*v.t.* empapelar.

walnut ('wɔl·nʌt) *n.* **1,** (tree; wood) nogal. **2,** (fruit) nuez.

walrus ('wal·rəs) *n.* morsa.

waltz ('wɔlts) *n.* vals. —*adj.* de vals. —*v.i.* valsar; bailar valses.

wampum ('wam·pəm) *n.* **1,** (shell money) cuentas de concha que servían como dinero a los indios americanos. **2,** *slang* (money) dinero.

wan (waːn) *adj.* **1,** (pale) pálido. **2,** (sickly) macilento; demacrado.

wand (wand) *n.* vara.

wander ('wan·dər) *v.i.* vagar; errar; extraviarse. —**wanderer,** *n.* vagamundo; vagabundo. —**wandering,** *n.* paseo; extravío. —*adj.* errante.

wanderlust ('wan·dər͵lʌst) *n.* ansia de vagar.

wane (wein) *v.i.* **1,** (lessen) menguar; disminuir. **2,** (decline) decaer; declinar. —*n.* **1,** (lessening) mengua; menguante; disminución. **2,** (decline) decadencia; decaimiento; declinación. —**wane of the moon,** menguante de la luna.

wangle ('wæŋ·gəl) *v.t., colloq.* **1,** (obtain by guile) conseguir por artimañas. **2,** (cajole) engatusar; embaucar. **3,** (manipulate) manipular; adulterar; falsificar. **4,** (wiggle) sacudir. —*v.i., colloq.* **1,** (contrive; scheme) urdir; ingeniarse; darse maña. **2,** (wiggle out; escape) sacudirse; extricarse. —*n., colloq.* ardid; treta; trampa.

wanness ('waːn·nəs) *n.* **1,** (paleness) palidez. **2,** (sickly appearance) demacración.

want (want) *v.t.* **1,** (desire) desear. **2,** (need) necesitar. **3,** (lack) carecer de. —*v.i.* carecer. —*n.* **1,** (desire) deseo. **2,** (need) necesidad. **3,** (lack) falta; carencia. —**for want of,** por falta de. —**in want,** pobre; necesitado. —**wanted** *adj. (úsase en anuncios)* **1,** (for employment) se necesita. **2,** (by the police) buscado; demandado.

want ad *colloq.* anuncio clasificado; anuncio de requerimiento.

wanting ('want·ıŋ) *adj.* **1,** (missing; lacking) que falta. **2,** (inadequate) falto (de); defectuoso; deficiente. —*prep.* sin; menos.

wanton ('wan·tən) *adj.* **1,** (immoral) lascivo; licencioso. **2,** (malicious) malicioso; perverso. **3,** (reckless) extravagante; irreflexivo. **4,** (playful) juguetón; travieso. —*n.* libertino; ramera. —*v.i.* retozar; juguetear. —*v.t.* malgastar.

wantonness ('wan·tən·nəs) *n.* **1,** (immorality) lascivia; libertinaje. **2,** (malice) malicia; perversidad. **3,** (recklessness) extravagancia; irreflexión. **4,** (playfulness) travesura.

war (wɔːr) *n.* guerra. —*v.i.* [**warred, warring**] guerrear. —*adj.* guerrero; de guerra. —**at war,** en guerra. —**go to war,** declarar la guerra; ir a la guerra. —**wage war,** hacer guerra.

warble ('wor·bəl) *v.i.* gorjear; trinar. —*v.t.* cantar. —*n.* gorjeo; trino.

warbler ('wor·blər) *n.* gorjeador; *ornith.* curruca.

war cry grito de guerra.

ward (word) *n.* **1,** (dependent) pupilo. **2,** (guardianship) tutela; custodia. **3,** (district) barrio; distrito. **4,** (of a hospital) cuadra. **5,** (of a lock) guarda. **6,** (defense) defensa; posición defensiva. —*v.t.* [*usu.* **ward off**] parar; desviar; evitar.

war dance danza guerrera; danza de guerra.

warden ('wor·dən) *n.* **1,** (custodian) custodio; guardián. **2,** (director of a prison) carcelero.

warder ('wor·dər) *n.* **1,** (guard; custodian) guardián. **2,** *Brit.* (prison warden) carcelero.

ward heeler ('hiː·lər) *colloq.* político subordinado; politicastro.

wardrobe ('word·rob) *n.* **1,** (storage place for clothing) guardarropa; guardarropía; *theat.* vestuario. **2,** (supply of clothing) vestuario; vestido.

wardroom ('word·rum) *n.* cuartel de oficiales.

wardship ('word·ʃıp) *n.* tutela; custodia.

ware (wɛːr) *n.* **1,** (merchandise) mercancía. **2,** (crockery) vajilla; loza.

warehouse ('wɛr·haus) *n.* almacén; depósito. —*v.t.* almacenar.

warehouseman ('wɛr,haus·mən) *n.* [*pl.* **-men**] **1,** (owner or manager) almacenista. **2,** (employee) guardalmacén.

wares (wɛrz) *n.pl.* mercadería; mercancías.

warfare ('wor·fɛr) *n.* guerra; arte de la guerra.

warhead ('wor·hɛd) *n.* cabeza de explosivo. *Also,* **war head.**

war horse caballo de guerra; *fig.* veterano.

warily ('wɛr·ɪ·li) *adv.* cautamente; cautelosamente.

wariness ('wɛr·i·nəs) *n.* cautela; precaución.

warlike ('wor·laik) *adj.* belicoso; guerrero.

war lord jefe militar.

warm (worm) *adj.* **1,** (having or giving heat) tibio; caliente. **2,** (of weather or climate) cálido; caluroso. **3,** (affectionate) humano; simpático; cariñoso. **4,** (impassioned) ardiente; acalorado. **5,** (lively) vivo; animado. **6,** (fresh) recién hecho; fresco. **7,** *colloq.* (close to discovering something) cercano. **8,** (protecting from cold) que abriga. —*v.t.* calentar; acalorar; entibiar. —*v.i.* calentarse. —**be warm, 1,** (of the weather) hacer calor. **2,** (of a person) tener calor. **3,** (of a thing) estar caliente. —**warm over,** recalentar. —**warm up, 1,** (make or become warm) calentar; calentarse. **2,** (reheat) recalentar. **3,** (become friendly) hacerse más amistoso. **4,** (become enthusiastic) entusiasmarse. **5,** (become mild, as the weather) templar.

warmblooded ('worm,blʌd·ɪd) *adj.* **1,** *zoöl.* de sangre caliente. **2,** *fig.* apasionado. —**warmbloodedness,** *n.* apasionamiento; frenesí.

warm front frente caliente.

warmhearted ('worm,har·tɪd) *adj.* afectuoso. —**warmheartedness,** *n.* afectuosidad.

warming pan calentador.

warmly ('worm·li) *adv.* **1,** (fervently) ardientemente; con ardor **2,** (cordially) cordialmente.

warmness ('worm·nəs) *n.* = **warmth.**

warmonger ('wor,mʌŋ·gər) *n.* incitador; instigador; fomentador de la guerra.

warmth (wormθ) *n.* **1,** (heat) calor. **2,** (passion) fervor; ardor; entusiasmo. **3,** (cordiality) cordialidad.

warn (worn) *v.t.* avisar; advertir; precaver.

warning ('worn·ɪŋ) *n.* aviso; amonestación; precaución. —*adj.* amonestador.

warp (worp) *v.t.* **1,** (twist; bend) torcer; combar. **2,** (pervert) pervertir. **3,** *naut.* mover con espía. —*v.i.* torcerse; combarse. —*n.* **1,** (distortion) comba; torcedura. **2,** (bias) sesgo; prejuicio. **3,** *weaving* urdimbre. **4,** *naut.* espía.

war paint pintura de guerra; camuflaje.

warpath ('wor·pæθ) *n.* sendo de la guerra; campaña guerrera. —**on the warpath,** en guerra; preparado para la guerra; *fig.* dispuesto a pelear.

warplane ('wor·plein) *n.* avión de combate; avión militar.

warrant ('war·ənt) *n.* **1,** (authorization) autorización; sanción. **2,** (guarantee) garantía. **3,** (decree) decreto; orden. **4,** (certificate) cédula; documento; escritura. **5,** (justification) justificación; razón. **6,** *law* citación. —*v.t.* **1,** (guarantee) garantizar. **2,** (authorize) autorizar. **3,** (justify) justificar. **4,** (assure) asegurar. **5,** (certify) certificar. —**warrantee,** *n.* afianzado. —**warrantor,** *n.* fiador; garante.

warrant officer suboficial; oficial subalterno.

warranty ('war·ən·ti) *n.* **1,** (authorization) autorización; sanción. **2,** (justification) justificación. **3,** (guarantee) garantía.

warren ('war·ən) *n.* conejera.

warrior ('wor·jər) *n.* guerrero.

warship ('wor·ʃɪp) *n.* buque de guerra.

wart (wort) *n.* verruga. —**warty,** *adj.* verrugoso.

warthog ('wort·hɔg) *n.* jabalí de verrugas. *También,* **wart hog.**

wartime ('wor·taim) *n.* tiempo de guerra.

war whoop grito de guerra.

wary ('wɛr·i) *adj.* cauto; cauteloso.

was (wʌz) *v.,* pret. de **be.**

wash (waʃ) *v.t.* **1,** (clean) lavar; limpiar. **2,** (wet; drench) mojar; bañar. **3,** (flow over; cover) lavar. **4,** (carry, as water) llevar. —*v.i.* **1,** (wash oneself; be washed) lavarse; limpiarse. **2,** (do laundry) lavar la ropa. **3,** (be carried, as by water) llevarse por el agua. **4,** (flow; beat) batir. **5,** *colloq.* (withstand examination) mantenerse; comprobarse. —*n.* **1,** (act of washing; things to be washed) lavado. **2,** (soapy water) lavazas. **3,** (liquid refuse) despojos; desperdicios. **4,** (rush of water or waves) el romper del agua. **5,** (lotion) loción. **6,** (silt; debris) aluvión. **7,** (ground covered by water) charco; pantano. —**washed out, 1,** (faded) desteñido. **2,** (exhausted) debilitado; agotado. **3,** (expelled after failure) eliminado. —**washed up,** *colloq.* gastado; terminado; fracasado.

washable ('waʃ·ə·bəl) *adj.* lavable.

wash and wear ('waʃ·ən‚wer) (ropa) de lavar y poner.

washbasin ('waʃ‚bei·sən) *n.* = **washbowl.**

washboard ('waʃ‚bord) *n.* tabla de lavar.

washbowl ('waʃ‚bol) *n.* jofaina; palangana; lavamanos.

washcloth ('waʃ‚klɔθ) 'n. trapo de lavar; paño para lavarse.

washer ('waʃ·ər) *n.* **1,** (person or thing that washes) lavador. **2,** (washing machine) lavadora. **3,** *mech.* arandela.

washerwoman ('waʃ·ər‚wʊm·ən) *n.* [*pl.* **-women**] lavandera.

washing ('waʃ·ɪŋ) *n.* lavado; ropa de lavar. —**washings,** *n.pl.* lavadura.

washing machine lavadora; lavarropas; máquina de lavar.

washing soda sosa de lavar.

washout ('waʃ‚aut) *n.* **1,** (erosion by water) derrubio; derrumbe. **2,** *slang* (failure) fracaso.

washrag ('waʃ‚ræg) *n.* = **washcloth.**

washroom ('waʃ‚rum) *n.* lavabo; *Amer.* lavatorio.

washstand ('waʃ‚stænd) *n.* lavabo; lavamanos.

washtub ('waʃ‚tʌb) *n.* tina o cuba de lavar.

wash water lavazas.

washwoman ('waʃ‚wʊm·ən) *n.* [*pl.* **-women**] lavandera.

washy ('waʃ·i) *adj.* **1,** (wet; soaked) húmedo; mojado. **2,** (watery) aguado; débil. **3,** (insipid) insulso; soso.

wasp (wasp) *n.* avispa.

waspish ('wasp·ɪʃ) *adj.* **1,** (slim-

waisted) delgado; de cintura delgada. **2,** (bad-tempered) enojadizo; áspero; malhumorado.

wassail ('was·əl) *n.* **1,** (toast) brindis. **2,** (drink) bebida especiada. **3,** (drinking party) jarana; parranda. —*v.i.* jaranear. —**wassailer,** *n.* brindador [*fem.* -dora]; juerguista; borrachón [*fem.* -chona]. —**wassail bowl,** copa.

wastage ('weis·tɪdʒ) *n.* derroche; pérdida; desgaste.

waste (weist) *adj.* **1,** (desolate) desierto; yermo. **2,** (untilled) inculto. **3,** (rejected) desechado. **4,** (superfluous) sobrante. —*v.t.* **1,** (squander) malgastar; derrochar; desperdiciar. **2,** (devastate) asolar; devastar. **3,** (wear away; use up) gastar; consumir. **4,** (lose) perder. —*v.i.* **1,** (lose vigor) decaer; perder la salud, el vigor, etc. **2,** (be used up) gastarse; consumirse. **3,** (pass, as time) pasar. —*n.* **1,** (misuse) derroche; despilfarro. **2,** (loss) pérdida. **3,** (barren land) yermo; desierto. **4,** (decline) decadencia; decaimiento. **5,** (discarded matter) basura; desperdicios; despojos. **6,** (excrement) excremento. **7,** (discarded textile fiber) hilacha; borra. —**go to waste,** perderse; desperdiciarse. —**lay waste,** asolar; devastar. —**waste away,** decaer; gastarse; consumirse.

wastebasket ('weist‚bæs·kɪt) *n.* canasto o cesto para papeles.

wasteful ('weist·fəl) *adj.* manirroto; pródigo; derrochador. —**wastefulness,** *n.* prodigalidad.

wasteland ('weist·lænd) *n.* yermo; despoblado; desierto.

waste pipe tubo de desagüe; desaguadero.

waster ('weis·tər) *n.* = **wastrel.**

wastrel ('weis·trəl) *n.* derrochador; pródigo.

watch (watʃ) *v.t.* **1,** (look at) mirar; ver. **2,** (guard) velar; vigilar; guardar. **3,** (observe closely) observar; espiar. **4,** (take care of) cuidar; guardar. **5,** (look out for) tener cuidado con. **6,** (be on the lookout for) estar a la mira de. —*v.i* **1,** (look; observe) mirar; ver. **2,** (stay awake or alert) velar. **3,** (be careful) tener cuidado. —*n.* **1,** (vigil) vela; vigilia. **2,** (tour of duty) guardia; vela; vigilia. **3,** (sentinel) guardia; centinela; vigilante. **4,** (group of guards; patrol) guardia;

ronda. **5,** (close observation) vigilancia. **6,** (timepiece) reloj. —**be on the watch for, 1,** (be on the lookout for) estar a la mira de. **2,** (be careful of) tener cuidado con. —**keep watch,** estar de guardia. —**keep watch over,** velar; vigilar; cuidar. —**watch for,** esperar; estar a la mira de. —**watch out (for),** tener cuidado (con). —**watch over,** velar; vigilar; guardar; cuidar.

watchcase ('watʃ,keis) *n.* relojera; caja de reloj.

watchdog ('watʃ,dɔg) *n.* perro de guarda; perro guardián.

watcher ('watʃ·ər) *n.* velador [*fem.* -dora]; observador [*fem.* -dora]; vigilante.

watchful ('watʃ·fəl) *adj.* alerto; vigilante; cuidadoso. —**watchfulness,** *n.* vigilancia; cuidado.

watchmaker ('watʃ,mei·kər) *n.* relojero. —**watchmaking,** *n.* relojería.

watchman ('watʃ·mən) *n.* [*pl.* -men] sereno; vigilante; velador.

watch pocket relojera.

watchtower ('watʃ,tau·ər) *n.* atalaya; vigía.

watchword ('watʃ·wʌrd) *n.* **1,** (password) contraseña; santo y seña. **2,** (slogan) lema; mote.

water ('wat·ər; 'wɔ·tər) *n.* agua. —*adj.* acuático; de o para agua. —*v.t.* **1,** (dilute) aguar. **2,** (irrigate) regar. **3,** (sprinkle) rociar. **4,** (moisten; wet) mojar; bañar; humedecer. **5,** (supply water to) proveer de agua. **6,** (give to drink, as animals) abrevar. **7,** *fin.* aumentar el valor nominal de (las acciones) sin aumento equivalente en el capital. —*v.i.* **1,** (fill with tears, as the eyes) llorar. **2,** (fill with water) llenarse de agua; aguarse. **3,** (take on water) tomar agua. **4,** (drink, as animals) abrevarse. **5,** (fill with saliva, as the mouth) hacérsele a uno agua la boca. —**above water,** flotante. —**be in deep water,** estar con el agua al cuello. —**be on the water wagon,** *slang* abstenerse de tomar bebidas alcohólicas. —**go by water,** ir por mar; ir por barco. —**hold water, 1,** (retain water) retener el agua. **2,** *fig.* (be sound or consistent) mantenerse firme; comprobarse. —**make one's mouth water,** hacerle a uno agua la boca. —**make water, 1,** (urinate) hacer aguas. **2,** *naut.* hacer agua. —**of the**

first water, de primera clase. —**pass water,** hacer aguas. —**pour (o throw) cold water on,** desanimar; desalentar.

water bearer aguador [*fem.* -dora]; *cap., astron.* Acuario.

waterbed ('wat·ər,bɛd) *n.* cama de agua.

waterborne ('wat·ər,born) *adj.* flotante; llevado por el agua.

water buffalo carabao.

water bug chinche de agua.

water carrier 1, (water bearer) aguador [*fem.* -dora]. **2,** (ship) buque cisterna.

water closet letrina; excusado; retrete.

water color acuarela. —**water-color,** *adj.* hecho a la acuarela. —**water-colorist,** *n.* acuarelista.

water-cooled *adj.* refrigerado por agua.

water cooler refrigerador de agua.

watercourse ('wat·ər,kors) *n.* corriente de agua.

watercress ('wat·ər,krɛs) *n.* berro. *También,* **water cress.**

water cure cura de aguas.

waterfall ('wat·ər,fɔl) *n.* cascada; catarata; caída o salto de agua.

waterfowl ('wat·ər,faul) *n.* ave acuática.

waterfront ('wat·ər,frʌnt) *n.* puerto; muelles.

water heater calentador de agua; termosifón.

waterhole ('wat·ər,hol) *n.* **1,** (pool) charco. **2, = watering place.**

water ice sorbete; helado.

wateriness ('wat·ər·i·nəs; 'wɔ·tər-) *n.* acuosidad.

watering ('wat·ər·ɪŋ; 'wɔ·tər-) *n.* riego. —*adj.* de riego.

watering can regadera.

watering place 1, (spa) balneario. **2,** (for animals) abrevadero; aguadero.

watering trough abrevadero; aguadero.

water level nivel de agua.

water lily lirio de agua; nenúfar.

waterline ('wat·ər,lain) *n.* línea de flotación.

waterlogged ('wat·ər,lɔgd) *adj.* **1,** (awash) anegado en agua; inundado. **2,** (soaked) empapado de agua.

water main cañería maestra.

watermark ('wat·ər,mark) *n.* filigrana. —*v.t.* marcar al agua.

watermelon ('wat·ər‚mɛl·ən) *n.* sandía.

water mill molino de agua.

water pipe cañería de agua.

water polo polo acuático.

water power fuerza hidráulica.

waterproof ('wat·ər·pruf) *adj.* a prueba de agua; impermeable. —*n.* impermeable. —*v.t.* impermeabilizar. —**waterproofing**, *n.* impermeabilización.

water rat 1, (European animal) rata de agua. 2, = **muskrat**.

watershed ('wat·ər·ʃɛd) *n.* 1, (dividing ridge) línea divisoria. 2, (river basin) cuenca. 3, (turning point) momento decisivo.

waterside ('wat·ər‚said) *n.* orilla; borde del agua.

water ski esquí acuático.

water-soak *v.t.* empapar de agua.

water spaniel perro de aguas.

water sports deportes acuáticos.

waterspout ('wat·ər‚spaut) *n.* 1, *meteorol.* tromba marina; manga de agua. 2, (duct) canelón. 3, (outlet for water) boquilla.

water spring manantial.

water supply abastecimiento de agua.

water table nivel superior del agua subterránea.

water tank aljibe; cisterna.

water tender aljibe; buque cisterna.

watertight ('wat·ər·tait) *adj.* 1, (impermeable) impermeable; estanco. 2, *fig.* (unassailable) seguro; inatacable.

water tower 1, (elevated water tank) arca de agua. 2, (firefighting apparatus) torre de agua para incendios.

waterway ('wat·ər·wei) *n.* 1, (channel) canal. 2, (navigable stream) río navegable; vía fluvial. 3, (current) corriente de agua.

water wheel 1, (for power) rueda hidráulica. 2, (for lifting water) rueda de agua.

water wings nadaderas.

waterworks ('wat·ər‚wʌrks) *n.sing. & pl.* obras hidráulicas.

waterworn ('wat·ər‚worn) *adj.* gastado por la acción del agua.

watery ('wat·ər·i) *adj.* 1, (of or pert. to water; containing water) acuoso; ácueo; de agua. 2, (moist; wet) mojado. 3, (thin; diluted) aguado; claro; ralo. 4, (tearful) lagrimoso; lloroso. 5, (weak; insipid)

insípido; evaporado. 6, (full of or secreting a morbid discharge) seroso.

watt (wat) *n.* vatio. —**wattage**, *n.* vatiaje.

wattle ('wat·əl) *n.* 1, (framework) zarzo. 2, *ornith.* barba. —*v.t.* 1, (intertwine) entrelazar; entretejer. 2, (construct with wattles) construir con zarzos.

wattmeter ('wat‚mi·tər) *n.* vatímetro.

wave (weiv) *v.t.* 1, (agitate) agitar; sacudir; hacer oscilar. 2, (brandish) blandir. 3, (form in waves) ondular. 4, (signal with) hacer señales con. —*v.i.* 1, (undulate) ondear; ondular. 2, (signal) hacer señales con la maño. —*n.* 1, (movement of water) ola; onda. 2, (spell, as of heat or cold) ola de calor, de frío, etc. 3, (undulation) onda. 4, (signal, as with the hand) señal. 5, (curves or curls in the hair) ondulación.

wave band banda de ondas.

wave length longitud de onda.

wavelet ('weiv·lit) *n.* oleadita; olita.

waver ('wei·vər) *v.i.* 1, (sway; flutter) ondear; oscilar; tremolar. 2, (vacillate) vacilar; dudar; estar indeciso. 3, (tremble) temblar; vibrar. 4, (fluctuate) fluctuar. —*n.* 1, (flutter) oscilación. 2, (vacillation) vacilación. 3, (trembling) temblor; vibración. 4, (fluctuation) fluctuación.

wavering ('wei·vər·iŋ) *adj.* ligero; inconstante; irresoluto. —*n.* irresolución; vacilación; fluctuación.

wavy ('weiv·i) *adj.* ondulado; ondulante.

wax (wæks) *n.* cera. —*v.t.* encerar; dar con cera. —*v.i.* 1, (grow; increase) crecer; aumentarse. 2, (become) hacerse; ponerse; volverse.

waxen ('wæk·sən) *adj.* ceroso; de o como cera.

wax match cerilla; *Amer.* cerillo.

wax museum museo de cera.

wax paper papel encerado.

waxworks ('wæks‚wʌrks) *n.pl.* obras de cera; figuras de cera.

waxy ('wæks·i) *adj.* ceroso; de o como cera.

way (wei) *n.* 1, (road; path) camino; vía. 2, (manner) modo; manera; *pl.* modales. 3, (means) medio. 4, (custom) uso; costumbre; hábito. 5, (direction) dirección; sentido. 6, (distance) distancia. **7,** (condition) condición; estado. **8,** *pl., naut.* anguilas. —*adv., colloq.* lejos. —**across the way,** al otro lado; en frente. —**across the way from,** enfrente de; frente a. —**all the way,** por todo el camino; hasta el fin; hasta lo extremo. —**any way,** de cualquier manera; de todas maneras. —**be in the way,** estorbar; incomodar. —**by the way, 1,** (in passing) de paso. **2,** (along the way) por el camino **3,** (incidentally) a propósito. —**by way of, 1,** (via) vía; por. **2,** (by means of) por vía de; por modo de. **3,** (in the capacity of) a título de. —**every way; every which way,** *colloq.* **1,** (in every direction) por todas partes; de todos lados. **2,** (in every manner or respect) de todas maneras. —**get in the way,** estorbar; incomodar; meterse. —**get out of the way,** quitar(se) de en medio; quitarse de encima (una tarea). —**get under way, 1,** (begin) iniciar(se); comenzar(se). **2,** *naut.* hacerse a la vela. —**give way, 1,** (yield) ceder; retroceder, **2,** (break) romperse. —**give way to,** entregarse a; echarse a. —**go one's way,** marcharse. —**go out of one's way, 1,** (detour) desviarse; dar rodeos. **2,** (inconvenience oneself) darse molestia; molestarse. —**have a way with,** entenderse con; llevarse bien con. —**have one's way,** salirse con la suya. —**in a bad way,** *colloq.* en mal estado. —**in a way,** de cierto modo; de cierta manera. —**in the way,** que estorba; que incomoda. —**in the way of,** como; a título de; a guisa de. —**keep out of the way,** apartar(se); echar(se) de un lado. —**lose one's way,** perderse. —**make one's way, 1,** (open a path) abrirse paso. **2,** (succeed) hacer carrera; tener éxito. —**make way,** abrir(se) paso; ceder el paso. —**mend one's ways,** mudar de vida. —**on the way, 1,** (in passing) de paso. **2,** (along the way) en el camino. —**out of the way, 1,** (aside) a un lado. **2,** (disposed of) acabado; despachado. **3,** (remote) lejano; apartado. **4,** (concealed) escondido; ocultado. **5,** (improper) impropio; fuera de orden. **6,** (unusual) fuera de lo común. **7,** (lost) perdido; descarriado. —**over the way,** al otro lado; en frente. —**pave**

the way (for), allanar el camino (a). —**put out of the way,** quitar de en medio. —**see one's way (clear) to,** ver el modo (de). —**take one's way,** marcharse. —**under way,** en marcha; en camino; *naut.* a la vela. —**way down,** bajada. —**way in,** entrada. —**way off,** *colloq.* lejos. —**way out,** salida. —**ways and means,** medios y arbitrios. —**way through,** pasaje. —**way up,** subida.

waybill ('wei·bɪl) *n.* hoja de ruta.

wayfarer ('wei·fer·ər) *n.* pasajero; viajante; caminante. —**wayfaring,** *adj.* caminante.

waylay ('wei·lei) *v.t.* [*pret. & p.p.* **waylaid** (-leid)] asechar; trasechar.

way-out *adj., slang* **1,** (unusual, strange) raro; extraño. **2,** (excellent) magnífico; fenomenal.

wayside ('wei·said) *n.* borde del camino.

way station estación secundaria; estación de paso.

wayward ('wei·wərd) *adj.* **1,** (erring; straying) descarriado; extraviado. **2,** (willful) díscolo; indócil; voluntarioso. **3,** (capricious) voluble; veleidoso.

waywardness ('wei·wərd·nəs) *n.* **1,** (straying) descarrío; extravío. **2,** (willfulness) indocilidad; voluntariedad. **3,** (capriciousness) volubilidad; veleidad.

we (wi) *pron.pers.* nosotros [*fem.* nosotras].

weak (wik) *adj.* débil; endeble; flojo.

weaken ('wik·ən) *v.t. & i.* **1,** (make or become weak) debilitar(se); enflaquecer. **2,** (diminish) disminuir(se); atenuar(se).

weakfish ('wik,fɪʃ) *n.* pez americano comestible.

weak-kneed *adj.* irresoluto; cobarde.

weakling ('wik·lɪŋ) *n.* **1,** (frail person) alfeñique. **2,** (coward) cobarde. —*adj.* débil.

weakly ('wik·li) *adj.* enclenque; enfermizo; achacoso. —*adv.* débilmente.

weak-minded *adj.* **1,** (feebleminded) imbécil; falto de seso. **2,** (irresolute) irresoluto.

weakness ('wik·nəs) *n.* **1,** (feebleness) debilidad. **2,** (liking; fondness) gusto; afición.

weal (wil) *n.* **1,** (mark of a whip or stick) roncha; raya; verdugón. **2,** *archaic* (welfare) bienestar.

1244

---

wealth (wɛlθ) *n.* riqueza.
wealthy ('wɛlθ·i) *adj.* rico;
opulento; adinerado. —**wealthiness,**
n. afluencia; opulencia.
wean (wiːn) *v.t.* destetar; *fig.*
apartar. —**weaning,** *n.* destete.
weanling ('wiːn·lɪŋ) *n.* niño o animal destetado.
weapon ('wɛp·ən) *n.* arma.
weaponed ('wɛp·ənd) *adj.* armado.
weaponless ('wɛp·ən·ləs) *adj.*
desarmado.
wear (wɛːr) *v.t.* [*pret.* **wore**; *p.p.*
worn] **1,** (carry on the body) llevar;
usar. **2,** (consume) gastar; consumir.
3, (weary) cansar; agotar. **4,** (show;
manifest) manifestar; exhibir. —*v.i.*
1, (be consumed) gastarse; consumirse. **2,** (last; hold up) durar;
ser duradero. **3,** (pass, as time) pasar; correr. —*n.* **1,** (deterioration)
desgaste; deterioro. **2,** (use) uso. **3,**
(clothing) ropa. **4,** (fashion) estilo;
moda **5,** (durability) durabilidad.
—**wear away,** gastar(se); con-
sumir(se). —**wear down, 1,** (deteriorate) gastar(se); consumir(se). **2,**
(tire) cansar(se); agotar(se). —**wear
off, 1,** (consume or be consumed)
gastar(se); consumir(se). **2,** (disappear gradually) pasar; desaparecer.
—**wear on,** pasar lentamente.
—**wear out, 1,** (deteriorate)
gastar(se); deteriorar(se). **2,** (fatigue) cansar(se); agotar(se).
wearable ('wɛr·ə·bəl) *adj.* que se
puede llevar. —**wearables,** *n.pl.*
ropa; prendas de vestir.
wear and tear desgaste; deterioro.
wearer ('wɛr·ər) *n.* usador [*fem.*
-dora]; quien lleva (una cosa).
weariness ('wɪr·i·nəs) *n.* **1,** (fatigue) cansancio; fatiga; lasitud. **2,**
(boredom) tedio; fastidio;
aburrimiento.
wearing ('wɛr·ɪŋ) *adj.* **1,** (for
wear) que se lleva. **2,** (causing deterioration) que consume; que
deteriora. **3,** (tiresome) tedioso;
fastidioso. —**wearing apparel,**
ropa; prendas de vestir.
wearisome ('wɪr·i·səm) *adj.*
tedioso; fastidioso; aburrido.
—**wearisomeness,** *n.* tedio; fastidio; aburrimiento.
weary ('wɪr·i) *adj.* **1,** (tired)
agotado; cansado. **2,** (causing fatigue) penoso; fastidioso. **3,** (dis-

contented) descontento; aburrido.
—*v.t. & i.* cansar(se).
weasel ('wi·zəl) *n.* comadreja.
weather ('wɛð·ər) *n.* **1,** (atmospheric condition) tiempo. **2,** (inclement conditions) intemperie.
—*v.t.* **1,** (expose to weather) airear;
solear. **2,** (impair by exposure)
desgastar; deteriorar *(por la
intemperie).* **3,** (resist; survive)
aguantar; superar; sobrevivir a.
—*v.i.* **1,** (deteriorate by exposure)
desgastarse por la intemperie. **2,**
(resist exposure) resistir a la
intemperie. —*adj.* **1,** (atmospheric)
atmosférico. **2,** (meteorological)
meteorológico. **3,** *naut.* de barlovento. —**keep one's weather eye
open,** *colloq.* velar; vigilar; estar a
la mira. —**under the weather,**
colloq. **1,** (ill) indispuesto; enfermo.
2, (drunk) borracho.
weatherbeaten ('wɛð·ər·bit·ən)
adj. curtido o gastado por la
intemperie.
weatherboard ('wɛð·ər,bord) *n.*
1, (clapboard) tabla(s) de chilla. **2,**
naut. lado del viento.
weathercock ('wɛð·ər,kak) *n.* veleta.
weatherglass ('wɛð·ər,glæs) *n.*
barómetro.
weathering ('wɛð·ər·ɪŋ) *n.*
desgaste *(por la acción atmosférica).*
weatherize ('wɛð·ə,raiz) *v.t.*
poner a prueba del tiempo.
weatherman ('wɛð·ər·mæn) *n.*
[*pl.* -**men**] meteorologista.
weatherproof ('wɛð·ər·pruf) *adj.*
a prueba del tiempo.
weather strip burlete.
weather vane veleta.
weather-wise *adj.* hábil en la
pronosticación del tiempo; *fig.*
perceptivo; perspicaz.
weave (wiːv) *v.t.* [*pret.* **wove**; *p.p.*
woven] **1,** (form into fabric) tejer.
2, (interlace) entretejer; entrelazar;
trenzar. **3,** (unite) unir; reunir. **4,**
(construct) construir. —*v.i.* **1,** (do
weaving) tejer. **2,** (become inter-
laced) entrelazarse. **3,** (move from
side to side) zigzaguear. —*n.* tejido.
weaver ('wi·vər) *n.* tejedor [*fem.*
-dora].
weaving ('wi·vɪŋ) *n.* **1,** (making
of fabric) tejido. **2,** (motion from
side to side) zigzagueo.
web (wɛb) *n.* **1,** (woven fabric)
tejido; tela. **2,** (tissue) tejido. **3,**

(network) red. **4,** (spider's web) telaraña. **5,** (membrane) membrana. **6,** (trap; snare) trampa; red; enredo.

webbed ('wɛbd) *adj.* **1,** (woven) tejido. **2,** (joined by a web) palmeado.

webbing ('wɛb·ɪŋ) *n.* **1,** (strip of woven cloth) tira de tela; cinta. **2,** (membrane) membrana.

webfooted ('wɛb,fʊt·ɪd) *adj.* palmípedo.

we'd (wiːd) *contr. de* we should, we would o we had.

wed (wɛd) *v.t.* [**wedded, wedding**] **1,** (join in matrimony) casar. **2,** (give in marriage) dar en casamiento; casar. **3,** (take as a spouse) casarse con. —*v.i.* casarse.

wedded ('wɛd·ɪd) *adj.* casado.

wedding ('wɛd·ɪŋ) *n.* boda; bodas; casamiento; nupcias. —*adj.* de boda; nupcial.

wedge (wɛdʒ) *n.* cuña. —*v.t.* acuñar; apretar; encajar. —*v.i.* forzarse; encajarse.

wedlock ('wɛd·lak) *n.* matrimonio.

Wednesday ('wɛnz·de) *n.* miércoles.

wee (wiː) *adj.* menudo; diminuto; chiquitico.

weed (wiːd) *n.* **1,** (undesired plant) mala hierba; yerbajo. **2,** *colloq.* (tobacco) tabaco; cigarro; cigarrillo. **3,** *pl.* (mourning clothes) ropa de luto. —*v.t. & i.* escardar; desherbar. —**weed out,** arrancar; extirpar; eliminar.

weeder ('wid·ər) *n.* **1,** (person) escardador; desherbador. **2,** (tool) escarda.

weeding ('wid·ɪŋ) *n.* escarda; deshierba. —**weeding hoe,** escarda.

weedy ('wid·i) *adj.* **1,** (full of weeds) lleno de malas hierbas. **2,** (lanky) flaco; larguirucho.

week (wik) *n.* semana.

weekday ('wik·dei) *n.* día laborable.

week end fin de semana. *También,* **weekend** ('wik,ɛnd) *n.* —*v.i.* pasar el fin de semana.

weekly ('wik·li) *adj.* semanal. —*adv.* semanalmente. —*n.* semanario.

ween (wiːn) *v.t. & i., archaic* pensar; creer; suponer.

weenie *también,* **weeny** ('wi·ni) *n., colloq.* = **wiener.**

weep (wip) *v.i.* [*pret. & p.p.* **wept**] **1,** (shed tears; emit moisture) llorar. **2,** (droop) languidecer. —*v.t.* **1,**

(shed) verter; derramar (lágrimas). **2,** (lament) lamentar; llorar. —**weeper,** *n.* llorón. [*fem.* -rona].

weeping ('wip·ɪŋ) *n.* lloro; lloriqueo. —*adj.* llorón; lloroso.

weeping willow sauce llorón.

weevil ('wi·vəl) *n.* gorgojo.

weft (wɛft) *n.* trama.

weigh (wei) *v.t. & i.* pesar. —**weigh anchor,** levar el ancla; levar anclas. —**weigh down,** sobrecargar; agobiar. —**weigh in,** *sports* pesarse. —**weigh on,** oprimir; agobiar. —**weigh out,** pesar *(en determinadas cantidades).*

weight (weit) *n.* **1,** (unit of weight; measure of weight; something heavy) peso. **2,** (heaviness) pesantez; pesadez. **3,** (load; burden) peso; carga; gravamen. **4,** (counterweight) pesa; contrapeso. **5,** (importance) importancia; significado. **6,** (influence) influencia. —*v.t.* **1,** (add weight to) poner (un) peso a. **2,** (load; burden) cargar; gravar. **3,** (give a certain value to) dar valor o importancia a. —**carry weight,** tener importancia, valor o influencia. —**lose weight,** rebajar de peso; adelgazar. —**pull one's weight,** hacer su parte. —**put on weight,** aumentar de peso; engordar.

weightless ('weit·ləs) *adj.* sin peso. —**weightlessness,** *n.* falta de peso.

weighty ('weit·i) *adj.* **1,** (heavy) pesado; ponderoso. **2,** (burdensome) gravoso. **3,** (important) importante. **4,** (influential) influyente. —**weightiness,** *n.* pesadez.

weir (wɪr) *n.* **1,** (sluice) compuerta. **2,** (low dam) presa. **3,** (fence for catching fish) cañal; cerco de cañas.

weird (wird) *adj.* **1,** (eerie) sobrenatural; espectral; misterioso. **2,** *colloq.* (odd) extraño; raro. —**weirdness,** *n.* **1,** misterio. **2,** extrañeza.

Weird Sisters Las Parcas.

welch (wɛltʃ) *v.t. & i.* = **welsh.**

welcome ('wɛl·kəm) *adj.* bienvenido. —*n.* bienvenida; recepción; acogida. —*v.t.* dar la bienvenida a; recibir; acoger. —*interj.* ¡bienvenido! —**you're welcome,** no hay de qué; de nada. —**you're welcome to it,** está a la disposición de Vd.; se lo regalo.

weld (wɛld) *v.t.* soldar; *fig.* juntar; unir. —*n.* soldadura; unión; juntura.

—**welder,** *n.* soldador [*fem.* -dora].
—**welding,** *n.* soldadura.

welfare ('wɛl,fɛr) *n.* **1,** (well-being) bienestar. **2,** (aid to the needy) asistencia pública.

we'll (wiːl) *contr. de* we shall o we will.

well (wɛl) *n.* **1,** (hole; shaft) pozo. **2,** (spring) fuente; manantial. **3,** (source) fuente. **4,** (stairwell) hueco de escalera. —*v.i.* manar; bullir; borbotar. —*v.t.* manar. —*adv.* [better, best] bien. —*adj.* [better, best] bien; bueno. —*interj.* ¡bien!; ¡bueno!; ¡vaya! —**as well,** también. —**as well as,** así como. —**well and good,** enhorabuena; bien está. —**well then,** pues bien.

well-accomplished *adj.* consumado; completo.

well-acquainted *adj.* **1,** = well-informed. **2,** (on familiar terms) familiar; íntimo; muy conocido.

well-advised *adj.* prudente; bien aconsejado.

well-aimed *adj.* certero.

well-appointed *adj.* bien amueblado; bien equipado.

well-attended *adj.* bien concurrido.

well-balanced *adj.* bien balanceado; bien ajustado; bien equilibrado.

well-behaved *adj.* de buena conducta.

well-being *n.* bienestar.

wellborn ('wɛl·born) *adj.* bien nacido.

wellbred ('wɛl·brɛd) *adj.* bien educado; bien criado; cortés.

well-chosen *adj.* selecto; escogido.

well-cooked *adj.* bien cocido.

well-defined *adj.* claro; evidente; manifiesto.

well-disposed *adj.* **1,** (well arranged) bien arreglado. **2,** (favorably inclined) bien dispuesto.

well-doer *n.* bienhechor [*fem.* -chora].

well-done *adj.* **1,** (well-cooked) bien cocido. **2,** (well-made) bien hecho. *También,* well done. —**well done!,** ¡ánimo!; ¡bien va!; ¡bravo!

well-favored *adj.* hermoso; guapo; bien parecido.

well-fed *adj.* rechoncho; regordete; *fig.* próspero.

well-fixed *adj., colloq.* rico; pertrechado; acomodado.

well-founded *adj.* bien fundado.

well-groomed *adj.* bien arreglado; acicalado.

well-grounded *adj.* **1,** = well-informed. **2,** = well-founded.

wellhead ('wɛl·hɛd) *n.* **1,** (source) fuente; origen. **2,** (spring) fuente; manantial.

well-heeled *adj., slang* rico; pertrechado; acomodado.

well-informed *adj.* bien informado.

well-intentioned *adj.* bien intencionado.

well-kept *adj.* bien cuidado; bien atendido.

well-known *adj.* bien conocido; familiar.

well-made *adj.* bien hecho; bien formado.

well-mannered *adj.* de buenos modales; cortés.

well-meaning *adj.* bienintencionado.

well-meant *adj.* bienintencionado.

well-nigh *adj.* casi.

well-off *adj.* afortunado; acomodado; adinerado.

well-ordered *adj.* bien ordenado; bien arreglado.

well-read (wɛl'rɛd) *adj.* muy leído; educado; erudito.

well-rounded *adj.* **1,** (shapely) redondeado; bien proporcionado. **2,** (complete) completo; cabal; íntegro.

well-spent *adj.* bien empleado; bien gastado.

well-spoken *adj.* bienhablado.

wellspring ('wɛl·sprɪŋ) *n.* fuente; manantial.

well-thought-of *adj.* bienquisto; de buena fama.

well-timed *adj.* oportuno.

well-to-do ('wɛl·tə,du) *adj.* acomodado; adinerado.

well-turned *adj.* simétrico; bien formado.

well-wisher *n.* amigo; partidario.

well-worded *adj.* bien expresado.

well-worn *adj.* gastado; trillado; vulgar.

well-wrought *adj.* bien trabajado.

welsh (wɛlʃ) *v.i., slang* defraudar; retirarse. —**welsh on,** retirarse de; dejar de cumplir.

Welsh (wɛlʃ) *adj. & n.* galés. —**Welshman** (-mən) *n.* [*pl.* -men] galés. —**Welsh woman,** galesa.

Welsh rabbit plato de queso derretido con cerveza que se sirve con tostadas. *También,* **Welsh rarebit.**

welt (wɛlt) *n.* **1,** (mark of a whip or stick) roncha; raya; verdugón. **2,** (part of a shoe) vira. **3,** (cord trimming) ribete.

welter ('wɛl·tər) *v.i.* **1,** (wallow) revolcarse. **2,** (be soaked) empaparse. **3,** (toss; tumbling) agitarse; menearse. —*n.* **1,** (tossing; tumbling) agitación; meneo. **2,** (turmoil) confusión; alboroto; tumulto.

welterweight ('wɛl·tər-) *n.* & *adj.* peso welter.

wen (wɛn) *n.* lobanillo.

wench (wɛntʃ) *n.* **1,** (girl) moza; muchacha. **2,** (lewd woman) ramera; puta. —*v.i.* putear.

wend (wɛnd) *v.i.* proceder; dirigirse. —*v.t.* dirigir; seguir (su camino).

went (wɛnt) *v.,* pret. de **go.**

wept (wɛpt) *v.,* pret. & p.p. de **weep.**

we're (wɪr) *contr.* de **we are.**

were (wʌr) *v.,* pret. de **be.** —**as it were,** por decirlo así; como si fuese.

werewolf ('wɪr·wʊlf; 'wʌr-) *n.* licántropo.

west (wɛst) *n.* oeste; poniente; occidente. —*adj.* oeste; del oeste; occidental. —*adv.* hacia el oeste; al oeste.

westerly ('wɛst·ər·li) *adj.* oeste; occidental; del oeste; hacia el oeste. —*adv.* hacia el oeste.

western ('wɛst·ərn) *adj.* occidental; al o del oeste. —*n.* película o cuento que trata del oeste de los EE.UU. —**westernize,** *v.t.* occidentalizar.

westerner ('wɛst·ərn·ər) *n.* occidental; habitante del oeste.

westward ('wɛst·wərd) *adj.* en o de dirección oeste. —*adv.* hacia el oeste.

wet (wɛt) *adj.* **1,** (covered with moisture) mojado; húmedo. **2,** (rainy) lluvioso. **3,** (not yet dry) fresco. **4,** *colloq.* (opposed to prohibition) antiprohibicionista. —*n.* **1,** (moisture) humedad. **2,** (water) agua. **3,** (rain) lluvia. **4,** *colloq.* (one opposed to prohibition) antiprohibicionista. —*v.t.* & *i.* [**wet** o **wetted, wetting**] **1,** (moisten) humedecer(se). **2,** (urinate) orinar(se). —**all wet,** *slang* equivocado. —**wet one's whistle,**

colloq. tomar una bebida; tomar un chispo.

wetback ('wɛt·bæk) *n.* bracero mexicano ilegalmente entrado en los EE.UU.

wet blanket *slang* aguafiestas.

wether ('wɛð·ər) *n.* carnero castrado.

wetness ('wɛt·nəs) *n.* humedad.

wet nurse ama de leche; ama de cría; nodriza. —**wet-nurse,** *v.t.* criar; dar de mamar.

we've (wiːv) *contr.* de **we have.**

whack (hwæk) *v.t.* & *i.* pegar; golpear; vapulear. —*n.* **1,** (blow) golpe. **2,** *slang* (attempt) prueba; lance; tentativa. **3,** *slang* (share) porción; parte. —**out of whack,** *slang* que no funciona bien. —**whack up,** *slang* dividir; repartir.

whacking ('hwæk·ɪŋ) *adj., slang* grande; enorme.

whacky ('hwæk·i) *adj., slang* = **wacky.**

whale (hweil) *n.* ballena. —*v.t., colloq.* azotar; vapulear; zurrar. —*v.i.* pescar ballenas. —**a whale of a. . . . ,** *colloq.* un. . . . enorme, extraordinario, etc.

whaleboat ('hweil·bot) *n.* ballenero.

whalebone ('hweil·bon) *n.* ballena.

whaler ('hweil·ər) *n.* ballenero.

whaling ('hweil·ɪŋ) *n.* **1,** (whale fishing) pesca de ballenas; industria ballenera. **2,** *colloq.* (thrashing) paliza; zurra.

wham (hwæm) *n.* **1,** (blow) golpe fuerte. **2,** (sound) ruido sordo. —*v.t.* [**whammed, whamming**] golpear con fuerza. —*v.i.* chocar con ruido. —*interj.* ¡pum!; ¡zas!

whammy ('hwæm·i) *n., slang* hechizo.

whang (hwæŋ) *v.t.* & *i.* golpear ruidosamente. —*n.* golpe.

wharf (hworf) *n.* [*pl.* **wharves** (hworvz) o **wharfs**] embarcadero; muelle.

wharfage ('hworf·ɪdʒ) *n.* muellaje.

what (hwat) *pron.rel.* lo que. —*pron.interr.* ¿qué?; ¿cuál? —*adj. rel.* el (la, los, las). . . . que. —*adj.interr.* ¿qué. . . . ? —*interj.* ¡qué! —**and what not,** y qué sé yo qué más. —**what a. . . . !,** ¡qué. . . . ! —**what about. . . . ?,** ¿y. . . . ?: *what about the children?,* ¿y los niños? —**what for, 1,** (why) ¿para qué?;

¿por qué? **2,** *slang* (punishment) castigo; paliza; zurra. —**what if,** ¿y si. . . . ?; ¿qué será si. . . . ? —**what it takes,** *colloq.* lo necesario. —**what of it** (o **that)?,** ¿qué importa eso? —**what though,** aun cuando; ¿qué importa que. . . . ? —**what's what,** *colloq.* las realidades; las cosas como están; cuántas son cinco.

whatever (hwat'ɛv·ər) *pron.* cualquier cosa que; todo lo que; no importa que. —*adj.* cualquier . . . que.

whatnot ('hwat·nat) *n.* **1,** (shelf for bric-a-brac) rinconera; estante. **2,** (anything) cualquier cosa.

whatsoever (,hwat·so'ɛv·ər) *pron. & adj.* = **whatever.**

wheal (hwiːl) *n.* roncha; raya; verdugón.

wheat (hwit) *n.* trigo. —**adj.** de trigo.

wheaten ('hwit·ən) *adj.* de trigo.

wheedle ('hwi·dəl) *v.t.* **1,** (cajole; coax) halagar; engatusar; hacer la rueda a. **2,** (get by cajolery) conseguir por halagos; sonsacar.

wheel (hwiːl) *n.* **1,** (circular frame) rueda. **2,** (bicycle) bicicleta. **3,** (steering device) volante. **4,** (helm) timón; gobierno. **5,** *slang* (important person) dignatario; alto personaje. —*v.t.* **1,** (move on wheels) mover o transportar por medio de ruedas. **2,** (turn; roll) hacer girar; hacer rodar. **3,** (provide with wheels) proveer de ruedas. —*v.i.* girar; rodar. —**fifth wheel,** persona o cosa superflua. —**wheel about, 1,** (turn) dar vuelta; virar. **2,** (change) cambiar (de opinión; de partido, etc.).

wheelbarrow ('hwil·bær·o) *n.* carretón; carretilla.

wheelbase ('hwil·beis) *n.* base de ejes; distancia entre ejes.

wheel chair silla de ruedas.

wheeled (hwiːld) *adj.* con ruedas.

wheeler-dealer *n., slang* persona emprendedora.

wheel horse caballo de varas; *fig.* trabajador; persona emprendedora.

wheelhouse ('hwil·haus) *n.* caseta del timón.

wheeling ('hwil·ɪŋ) *n.* **1,** (rolling; moving on wheels) rodadura. **2,** (road conditions) estado; condición (*de una carretera*). **3,** (cycling) paseo en bicicleta. **4,** (rotation) rotación.

wheelman ('hwil·mən) *n.* [*pl.* -men] **1,** (helmsman) timonel; timonero. **2,** (cyclist) ciclista.

wheelwork ('hwil·wʌrk) *n.* rodaje.

wheelwright ('hwil·rait) *n.* aperador; carretero.

wheeze (hwiːz) *v.i.* resollar; jadear. —*n.* **1,** (act or sound of wheezing) jadeo; resuello. **2,** (trite remark) cuento o chiste viejo; perogrullada.

whelk (hwelk) *n.* **1,** *zoöl.* buccino. **2,** (pimple) grano; barro.

whelm (hwɛlm) *v.t.* aplastar; abrumar; anonadar.

whelp (hwɛlp) *n.* cachorro. —*v.i. & t.* parir; dar a luz.

when (hwɛn) *adv., conj. & n.* cuando.

whence (hwɛns) *adv.* **1,** (from what place) de donde. **2,** (wherefore) por eso; por consiguiente. —*conj.* de donde.

whencesoever (,hwɛns·so'ɛv·ər) *adv.* de dondequiera. —*conj.* de dondequiera que.

whenever (hwɛn'ɛv·ər) *conj.* cuando quiera que; siempre que. —*adv.* cuando.

where (hwɛr) *adv. & conj.* **1,** (at or in what place) donde; en donde; por donde. **2,** (to or toward what place) adonde. **3,** (from what place) de donde.

whereabouts ('hwɛr·ə,bauts) *n.* paradero. —*adv. & conj.* donde; por donde.

whereas (hwɛr'æz) *conj.* **1,** (since) puesto que; ya que; en vista de que. **2,** (while on the contrary) mientras que; por el contrario.

whereat (hwɛr'æt) *conj.* a lo cual; con lo cual.

whereby (hwɛr'bai) *adv.* por lo cual; con lo cual; ¿cómo?; ¿de dónde?

wherefore ('hwɛr·for) *adv.* **1,** (why) porque; por qué. **2,** (for which) por lo que. —*conj.* por eso; por consiguiente. —*n.* el porqué.

wherefrom ('hwɛr·frʌm) *conj.* de donde.

wherein (hwɛr'ɪn) *adv.* donde; en donde; en que.

whereinto (hwɛr'ɪn·tu) *adv.* en donde; dentro de lo que.

whereof (hwɛr'ʌv) *conj.* de lo cual; de que.

whereon (hwɛr'an) *adv.* en que; sobre lo cual.

wheresoever (,hwɛr·so'ɛv·ər)

adv. dondequiera. —*conj.* dondequiera que.

whereto (hwɛr'tu) *adv.* adonde; a lo que.

whereupon ('hwɛr·ʌ,pan) *adv.* sobre que; en donde. —*conj.* con lo cual; después de lo cual.

wherever (hwɛr'ɛv·ər) *adv.* donde. —*conj.* dondequiera que.

wherewith (hwɛr'wɪθ) *adv.* con que; con lo cual. —*n.* lo necessario.

wherewithal ('hwɛr·wɪð·ɔl) *n.* los medios; lo necesario.

whet (hwɛt) *v.t.* [**whetted, whetting**] 1, (sharpen) afilar; aguzar. 2, (stimulate) estimular; abrir (el apetito).

whether ('hwɛð·ər) *conj.* si —**whether ... or,** sea (que) ... o; si ... o. —**whether or no,** en todo caso; de todas maneras.

whetstone ('hwɛt,ston) *n.* piedra de afilar; esmoladera.

whey (hwei) *n.* suero.

wheyey ('hwei·i) *adj.* seroso.

which (hwɪtʃ) *pron.rel.* que; el (la, lo, los, las) que. —*pron.interr.* ¿cuál?; ¿cuáles? —*adj.rel* el (la, los, las) que. —*adj.interr.* ¿qué ... ?; ¿cuál?; ¿cuáles?

whichever (hwɪtʃ'ɛv·ər) *pron. & adj.* cualquiera; *pl.* cualesquiera.

whiff (hwɪf) *n.* 1, (puff; breath) soplo; vaharada 2, (odor; reek) vaho. 3, (puff of smoke) fumada; fumarada. 4, (small amount) pizca. —*v.t.* 1, (waft) llevar por el aire; llevar con un soplo. 2, (blow out in puffs) echar en bocanadas. 3, (smoke) fumar. —*v.i.* 1, (blow) soplar. 2, (emit puffs) echar bocanadas.

whiffletree ('hwɪf·əl·tri) *n.* balancín.

whig (hwɪg) *n. & adj.* liberal; whig.

while (hwail) *n.* rato. —*conj.* mientras que; a la vez que. —*v.t.* pasar. —**all the while (that),** todo el tiempo (que). —**between whiles,** de vez en cuando. —**the while,** mientras tanto. —**while away,** pasar (divirtiéndose); engañar (el tiempo). —**worth the (o one's) while,** provechoso; que vale la pena.

whilst (hwailst) *conj.* mientras que.

whim (hwɪm) *n.* antojo; capricho; veleidad.

whimper ('hwɪm·pər) *v.i.* llori-

quear. —*v.t.* decir lloriqueando. —*n.* lloriqueo; quejido.

whimsical ('hwɪm·zɪ·kəl) *adj.* caprichoso; fantástico. —**whimsicality** (-'kæl·ə·ti) *n.* capricho; fantasía.

whimsy ('hwɪm·zi) *n.* 1, (whim) capricho; veleidad; fantasía. 2, (quaint humor) humorismo raro o anticuado.

whimwham ('hwɪm,hwæm) *n.* 1, (trinket) bagatela; baratija. 2, = whim. 3, *pl.* (jitters) nerviosidad.

whin (hwɪn) *n.* tojo.

whine (hwain) *v.i.* lloriquear; gimotear. —*v.t.* decir lloriqueando. —*n.* lloriqueo; gimoteo; llanto.

whinny ('hwɪn·i) *v.i.* relinchar. —*n.* relincho.

whip (hwɪp) *v.t.* [**whipped, whipping**] 1, (lash; beat) azotar. 2, (seize or move swiftly) coger, sacar, lanzar, etc. súbitamente. 3, (urge on; drive) empujar; estimular; aguijonear. 4, (beat, as eggs or cream) batir. 5, *colloq.* (defeat) derrotar; vencer. —*v.i.* 1, (move swiftly) lanzarse; arrojarse. 2, (thrash about) sacudirse; agitarse. —*n.* 1, (lash) azote; látigo. 2, (kind of dessert) batido. 3, *polit.* subjefe de partido (*en un cuerpo legislativo*). —**whip up,** 1, (arouse) excitar; estimular. 2, (prepare hastily) hacer o preparar de prisa.

whipcord ('hwɪp,kord) *n.* tela gruesa con canillas diagonales.

whip hand mano del látigo; *fig.* ventaja; dominio.

whiplash ('hwɪp·læʃ) *n.* 1, (point of a whip) tralla; punta de látigo. 2, (blow with a whip) latigazo.

whipped cream crema batida.

whipped potatoes puré de papas.

whipper ('hwɪp·ər) *n.* azotador.

whipper-snapper ('hwɪp·ər· snæp·ər) *n.* impertinente; mequetrefe; casquivano.

whippet ('hwɪp·ɪt) *n.* lebrel.

whipping ('hwɪp·ɪŋ) *n.* 1, (flogging) paliza; azotaina. 2, *colloq.* (defeat) derrota.

whipping boy cabeza de turco; víctima.

whippletree ('hwɪp·əl·tri) *n.* balancín.

whippoorwill ('hwɪp·ər,wɪl) *n.* chotacabras norteamericano.

whir (hwʌr) *v.i.* [**whirred, whirring**] girar dando zumbido. —*v.t.*

hacer girar con zumbido. —*n.* zumbido.

whirl ('hwʌrl) *v.i.* arremolinarse; girar; dar vueltas. —*v.t.* hacer girar. —*n.* **1,** (turn) vuelta; giro. **2,** (swirl) remolino; torbellino. **3,** (tumult) tumulto; alboroto. **4,** (giddiness) vahido; vértigo.

whirligig ('hwʌrl-ə-gɪg) *n.* **1,** (toy) molinete; molinillo. **2,** (merry-go-round) tiovivo. **3,** = **whirligig beetle.**

whirligig beetle escribano del agua.

whirlpool ('hwʌrl,pul) *n.* remolino.

whirlwind ('hwʌrl,wɪnd) *n.* torbellino; manga o tromba de viento.

whirlybird ('hwɪrl·i,bʌrd) *n., slang* helicóptero.

whish (hwɪʃ) *n.* zumbido; silbido. —*v.i.* zumbar; silbar.

whisk (hwɪsk) *n.* **1,** (brush) escobilla; cepillo. **2,** (swift movement) movimiento rápido. **3,** (bunch of straw) manojo. **4,** (wire beater) batidor. —*v.t.* **1,** (clean with a brush) cepillar. **2,** (move or remove swiftly) mover o llevar rápidamente. **3,** (beat) batir. —*v.i.* moverse rápidamente; marcharse de prisa. —**whisk away** (o **off**), quitar rápidamente; hacer desaparecer.

whisk broom escobilla.

whisker ('hwɪs·kər) *n.* pelo de la barba; *pl.* barba; barbas; (of a cat) bigotes. —**whiskered,** *adj.* barbado; barbudo.

whiskey *también,* **whisky** ('hwɪs·ki) *n.* whisky; licor.

whisper ('hwɪs·pər) *v.i.* **1,** (speak softly) cuchichear; susurrar. **2,** (rustle) susurrar. **3,** (gossip) chismear. —*v.t.* cuchichear; decir al oído; decir en voz baja. —*n.* **1,** (soft speech; something spoken softly) cuchicheo; susurro. **2,** (rustling sound) susurro. **3,** (gossip) chisme. —**in a whisper,** en voz baja.

whist (hwɪst) *n.* whist. —*interj.* ¡chito!; ¡chitón!

whistle ('hwɪs·əl) *v.t. & i.* silbar. —*n.* **1,** (sound) silbido; pitido. **2,** (device) silbato; pito. —**whistler,** *n.* silbador. —**whistle for, 1,** (call by whistling) silbar a. **2,** *colloq.* (expect in vain) buscar o esperar en vano. —**whistle stop,** apeadero.

whit (hwɪt) *n.* ápice; jota; pizca. —**every whit,** del todo; entera-

mente. —**not a whit,** de ninguna manera. —**not care a whit (for),** no importarle a uno un ardite o bledo.

white (hwait) *adj.* **1,** (color) blanco. **2,** (pale) pálido. **3,** *colloq.* (honorable; fair) justo; recto; generoso. —*n.* **1,** (color; person or thing of white color) blanco. **2,** (white of egg) clara de huevo. —*v.t.* blanquear; blanquecer. —**bleed (someone) white,** agotarle a uno el dinero, los recursos, etc.

white ant termita; hormiga blanca.

whitecap ('hwait,kæp) *n., usu.pl.* paloma; palomilla; cabrilla.

white-collar *adj.* de oficina. —**white-collar worker,** oficinista.

white elephant elefante blanco; posesión arruinadora.

white feather símbolo de cobardía. —**show the white feather,** mostrarse cobarde.

whitefish ('hwait,fɪʃ) *n.* corégono.

white heat calor blanco; *fig.* excitación; agitación. —**to a white heat,** al blanco.

white-hot *adj.* calentado al blanco; *fig.* excitado; muy agitado.

white lead albayalde.

white lie mentira oficiosa.

white-livered *adj.* cobarde.

whiten ('hwait-ən) *v.t.* blanquear; blanquecer. —*v.i.* blanquear; blanquecerse.

whiteness ('hwait-nəs) *n.* **1,** (white color) blancura. **2,** (paleness) palidez. **3,** (purity) pureza; candor.

whitening ('hwait-ən-ɪŋ) *n.* blanqueo.

whiteout ('hwait,aut) *n.* líquido borrador. —*v.t.* [*also,* **white out**] borrar; tachar.

white plague tuberculosis; tisis.

white slave prostituta involuntaria. —**white slavery,** trata de blancas.

whitewash ('hwait,waʃ) *n.* **1,** (paint) lechada. **2,** (concealment) encubrimiento (*de faltas, injusticias, etc.*). **3,** *sports, colloq.* = **shut-out.** —*v.t.* **1,** (paint) blanquear; enjalbegar; enyesar. **2,** (conceal; gloss over) encubrir (faltas, injusticias, etc.). **3,** *sports, colloq.* = **shut out.**

whitewashing ('hwait,waʃ·ɪŋ) *n.* blanqueo.

whither ('hwɪð·ər) *adv.* ¿adónde? —*conj.* adonde.

whithersoever (ˌhwɪð·ər·so'ɛv·ər) adv. adondequiera.

whiting ('hwait·ɪŋ) n. 1, (fish) merluza; pescada. 2, (powdered chalk) blanco de España; tiza.

whitish ('hwait·ɪʃ) adj. blancuzco; blanquecino. —**whitishness,** n. blancura.

whitlow ('hwɪt·lo) n. panadizo.

Whitsun ('hwɪt·sən) adj. de Pentecostés. —**Whitmonday,** n. lunes de Pentecostés. —**Whitsunday,** n. domingo de Pentecostés. —**Whitsuntide** (-sən·taid) n. semana de Pentecostés.

whittle ('hwɪt·əl) v.t. & i. 1, (carve) cortar o formar con un cuchillo. 2, (curtail; reduce) disminuir poco a poco; cercenar.

whity ('hwait·i) adj. = whitish. —n. [also, **whitey**] derog. blanco; los blancos.

whiz (hwɪz) v.i. [**whizzed, whizzing**] zumbar; silbar. —n. 1, (whirring sound) zumbido. 2, slang (outstanding person or thing) fenómeno.

who (huː) pron.rel. que; quien (pl. quienes); que (la, los, las) que. —pron.interr. ¿quién? (pl. ¿quiénes?).

whoa (hwo) interj. ¡so!

whodunit (huˈdʌn·ɪt) n., slang novela policíaca; drama policíaco.

whoever pron.rel. quienquiera que; cualquiera que; quien. —pron. interr. ¿quién? (pl. ¿quienes?)

whole (hoːl) adj. 1, (entire; complete) entero; completo. 2, (all) todo. 3, (sound) sano; en buena salud. —n. total; todo. —**as a whole,** en conjunto. —**made out of whole cloth,** enteramente ficticio. —**on the whole,** en el todo; en general.

wholehearted (hol'har·tɪd) adj. de todo corazón; sincero; entusiasta.

wholeness ('hol·nəs) n. totalidad; integridad.

whole note redonda.

wholesale ('hol·sel) n. venta al por mayor. —adj. 1, (in large quantities) en grande; al por mayor. 2, (widespread) general; extendido. —v.t. & i. vender(se) al por mayor. —**wholesaler,** n. mayorista.

wholesome ('hol·səm) adj. saludable; salubre. —**wholesomeness,** n. salubridad.

whole-wheat adj. de trigo entero.

wholly ('ho·li) adv. totalmente; enteramente; completamente.

whom (huːm) pron. rel. que; quien

(pl. quienes); a quien (pl. a quienes). —pron.interr. ¿a quién?

whoop (hwup) v.i. 1, (shout; cry) gritar; chillar; vocear. 2, (pant) jadear; respirar ruidosa y convulsivamente. —n. 1, (shout; cry) grito; alarido; chillido. 2, (panting) jadeo; inspiración ruidosa y convulsiva. —interj. ¡olé!; ¡upa! —**whoop (it) up,** slang 1, (celebrate noisily) alborotar; celebrar. 2, (create enthusiasm for) fomentar; promover.

whoopee ('hwup·i) n., slang hilaridad; alegría. —interj. ¡olé! —**make whoopee,** slang celebrar; jaranear.

whooping cough tos ferina.

whoops (hwups) interj. ¡ay!

whopper ('hwap·ər) n., colloq. enormidad. —**whopping,** adj., colloq. enorme.

whore (hoːr) n. prostituta; puta. —v.i. putear.

whorehouse ('hor,haus) n. burdel; prostíbulo.

whoreson ('hoːr·sən) n. bastardo; hijo de puta.

whoring ('hor·ɪŋ) n. putaísmo; putería.

whorish ('hor·ɪʃ) adj. putesco; lascivo.

whorl (hwʌrl; hworl) n. espiral.

whortleberry ('hwʌr·təl,bɛr·i) n. arándano.

whose (huːz) pron. & adj.rel. cuyo; de quien. —pron. & adj.interr. ¿de quién?

whosoever (ˌhu·so'ɛv·ər) pron.rel. quienquiera que.

why (hwai) adv.rel. por qué. —adv.interr. ¿por qué? —conj. por qué; por lo que; por el que. —n. el porqué. —interj. ¡pues!; ¡cómo!; ¡que!; ¡pero ...! —**the why(s) and wherefore(s),** los porqués y los cómos. —**why not?,** ¿cómo no?

wick (wɪk) n. pabilo; mecha.

wicked ('wɪk·ɪd) adj. 1, (evil) malo; inicuo; perverso. 2, (bad; grievous) malo; grave; penoso. 3, (naughty) travieso; juguetón; picaresco. —**wickedness,** n. maldad; iniquidad; perversidad.

wicker ('wɪk·ər) n. mimbre. —adj. de mimbre.

wicker basket cesto de mimbres.

wickerwork ('wɪk·ər·wʌrk) n. cestería.

wicket ('wɪk·ɪt) n. 1, (small door or gate) portillo; postigo. 2, (small window) ventanilla. **3,** (hoop, in croquet) aro.

wide (waid) *adj.* **1,** (broad) ancho. **2,** (of a certain width) de ancho: *three feet wide,* tres pies de ancho. **3,** (extensive) amplio; extenso. **4,** (loose-fitting) holgado. **5,** (fully open) del todo abierto. —*adv.* **1,** (far) lejos. **2,** (fully) de par en par. **3,** (astray) fuera. —**wide of,** lejos de; fuera de.

wide-awake *adj.* despabilado; vigilante.

wide-eyed *adj.* con los ojos abiertos de par en par.

widely ('waid·li) *adv.* mucho; extensamente.

widen ('waid·ən) *v.t.* ensanchar. —*v.i.* ensancharse.

wideness ('waid·nəs) *n.* anchura.

wide-open *adj., colloq.* **1,** (open) abierto de par en par. **2,** (permissive) exento de la ley.

widespread ('waid,sprɛd) *adj.* **1,** (opened wide) extendido. **2,** (far-flung) muy extenso; vasto.

widgeon ('wɪdʒ·ən) *n.* cerceta.

widow ('wɪd·o) *n.* **1,** (surviving wife) viuda. **2,** *cards* baceta. —*v.t.* privar de marido; dejar viuda.

widower ('wɪd·o·ər) *n.* viudo.

widowhood ('wɪd·o·hʊd) *n.* viudez.

width (wɪdθ) *n.* anchura; ancho; extensión.

wield (wild) *v.t.* **1,** (handle) manejar; usar. **2,** (exercise, as power) ejercer. —**wieldy,** *adj.* manejable.

wiener ('wi·nər) *n.* salchicha de carne de vaca y cerdo.

wife (waif) *n.* [*pl.* **wives**] esposa; mujer.

wifehood ('waif·hʊd) *n.* estado de casada.

wifely ('waif·li) *adj.* de o como esposa.

wig (wɪg) *n.* peluca.

wigged (wɪgd) *adj.* que lleva peluca.

wigging ('wɪg·ɪŋ) *n., Brit. colloq.* reprimenda; regaño.

wiggle ('wɪg·əl) *v.t.* menear. —*v.i.* menearse; culebrear. —*n.* meneo; culebreo.

wiggler ('wɪg·lər) *n.* persona o cosa que se menea; larva de mosquito.

wiggly ('wɪg·li) *adj.* **1,** (that wiggles) que se menea. **2,** (wavy) ondulado; ondulante.

wigmaker ('wɪg,mei·kər) *n.* peluquero; fabricante de pelucas.

wigwag ('wɪg·wæg) *v.t. & i.* [-**wagged, -wagging**] **1,** = **wag. 2,** (signal by waving) hacer (señales) con banderas, luces, etc. —*n.* **1,** (wagging) meneo; oscilación. **2,** (signaling) comunicación por banderas, luces, etc.

wigwam ('wɪg·wam) *n.* choza o jacal de forma cónica que usan algunos indios norteamericanos.

wild (waild) *adj.* **1,** (living in the natural state) salvaje; silvestre. **2,** (desolate) desierto; despoblado. **3,** (fierce) feroz; fiero; bravo. **4,** (unruly) travieso; desenfrenado. **5,** (violent) violento; impetuoso. **6,** (mad) loco. **7,** (excited) frenético. **8,** (preposterous) absurdo; descabellado. **9,** (disordered) desordenado; desarreglado. **10,** (badly aimed) errado. —*adv.* violentamente; frenéticamente; locamente. —*n.* yermo; desierto; monte. —**run wild,** crecer salvaje; andar a rienda suelta. —**wild about,** *colloq.* loco por.

wild boar jabalí.

wildcat ('waild·kæt) *n.* **1,** *zoöl.* gato montés. **2,** (violent person) luchador [*fem.* -**dora**]; persona colérica. **3,** (risky venture) empresa arriesgada. **4,** (oil strike) pozo que da en un depósito inesperado de petróleo. **5,** *R.R.* locomotora suelta. —*adj.* **1,** (risky) arriesgado; quimérico. **2,** (illicit) ilegal; ilícito. **3,** (harebrained) atolondrado; disparatado. —*v.t. & i.* [-**catted, -catting**] explorar o buscar en lugares improductivos. —**wildcat strike,** huelga sin autorización.

wilderness ('wɪl·dər·nəs) *n.* desierto; yermo.

wild-eyed *adj.* de mirada furiosa; *(fig.)* extremista.

wildfire ('waild,fair) *n.* fuego desatado; fuego griego. —**spread like wildfire,** esparcirse rápidamente.

wild fowl aves de caza.

wild goose ganso bravo. —**wild-goose chase,** empresa quimérica; búsqueda sin provecho.

wildness ('waild·nəs) *n.* **1,** (wild state) estado salvaje. **2,** (desolateness) desolación; soledad. **3,** (savagery) salvajismo. **4,** (fierceness) ferocidad; fiereza. **5,** (madness) locura.

wildwood ('waild·wʊd) *n.* bosque; selva.

wile (wail) *n.* 1, (trick) estratagema; ardid. 2, (deceit) engaño. —*v.t.* engañar; engatusar. —**wile away,** pasar (divirtiéndose); engañar (el tiempo).

will (wɪl) *n.* 1, (volition) voluntad; albedrío. 2, (wish; desire) deseo; voluntad. 3, (determination) determinación. 4, (testament) testamento. —*v.t. & i.* (wish; decree) querer; desear. —*v.t.* (bequeath) legar; dejar (en testamento). —*v.aux.* [*pret* **would**] denota 1, *el futuro en la segunda y tercera personas: he will go,* irá. 2, *determinación, coerción o necesidad, en la primera persona: we will go,* iremos; sí que iremos; tenemos que ir. 3, *deseo; voluntad: will you go?,* ¿quiere Vd. ir? 4, *capacidad: the elevator will hold ten persons,* el ascensor puede acomodar diez personas. 5, *costumbre; hábito: he will go for days without eating,* suele pasar días sin comer. 6, *probabilidad: that will be the doctor,* será el médico.

willful ('wɪl·fəl) *adj.* 1, (headstrong) obstinado; terco; testarudo; voluntarioso. 2, (intentional) voluntario; premeditado; con toda intención. —**willfulness,** *n.* terquedad; testarudez; voluntariedad.

willies ('wɪl·iz) *n.pl., colloq.* escalofrío; estremecimiento.

willing ('wɪl·ɪŋ) *adj.* 1, (inclined) inclinado; dispuesto. 2, (ready; obliging) solícito; atento; complaciente. 3, (voluntary) voluntario.

willingly ('wɪl·ɪŋ·li) *adv.* voluntariamente; de buena gana.

willingness ('wɪl·ɪŋ·nəs) *n.* 1, (inclination) inclinación; disposición. 2, (readiness) solicitud; complacencia. 3, (goodwill) buena voluntad; buena gana.

will-o'-the-wisp (ˌwɪl·ə·ðə·'wɪsp) *n.* 1, (fire caused by decaying matter) fuego fatuo. 2, (illusion) ilusión; quimera.

willow ('wɪl·o) *n.* sauce. —**willow grove,** sauzal.

willowy ('wɪl·o·i) *adj.* delgado; esbelto.

will power fuerza de voluntad.

willy-nilly ('wɪl·i'nɪl·i) *adv.* de todos modos; quieras o no quieras. —*adj.* indeciso; vacilante.

wilt (wɪlt) *v.t.* marchitar. —*v.i.* 1, (fade) marchitarse. 2, (languish)

languidecer. 3, (lose courage) desanimarse; acobardarse.

wilt (wɪlt) *v.* *arcaico, segunda persona del sing. del pres. de ind. de* **will.**

wily ('wai·li) *adj.* astuto; listo; mañoso.

wimble ('wɪm·bəl) *n.* barrena; taladro.

wimp (wɪmp) *n., colloq.* melindroso; persona pusilánima.

wimple ('wɪm·pəl) *n.* toca.

win (wɪn) *v.t.* [*pret. & p.p.* **won;** *ger.* **winning**] 1, (gain) ganar. 2, (reach; attain) alcanzar. 3, (prevail over) conquistar; persuadir. —*v.i.* ganar; triunfar; prevalecer; tener éxito. —*n., colloq.* triunfo; éxito. —**win out,** *colloq.* triunfar; prevalecer; tener éxito. —**win over,** conquistar.

wince (wɪns) *v.i.* retroceder; echarse atrás; respingar. —*n.* respingo.

winch (wɪntʃ) *n.* molinete; torno.

wind (wɪnd; *en poesía, también* waind) *n.* 1, (current of air) viento. 2, (breath) aliento; respiración. 3, (scent) viento; husmo; olor. —*adj.* de viento. —*v.t.* 1, (expose to the air) airear; ventilar. 2, (scent) husmear; olear. 3, (put out of breath) dejar sin aliento; agotar. —**break wind,** ventosear. —**get the wind up,** *colloq.* airarse; alterarse. —**get wind of,** descubrir; enterarse de. —**in the wind,** pendiente; inminente.

wind (waind) *v.t.* [*pret. & p.p.* **wound** (waund)] 1, (turn) dar vuelta a. 2, (wrap up or around) envolver; enrollar. 3, (twist) torcer. 4, (reel, as yarn) devanar. 5, (twine) entrelazar; enroscar. 6, (tighten the spring of) dar cuerda a. —*v.i.* 1, (move in a curving path) serpentear; dar vueltas. 2, (twine) entrelazarse; enroscarse. 3, (form a coil; wrap around) enrollarse; envolverse. —*n.* vuelta; recodo. —**wind off,** desenrollar; desenvolver. —**wind up,** 1, (roll up; coil) enrollar(se); envolver(se). 2, (finish) terminar; acabar(se); acabar por. 3, (tighten the spring of) dar cuerda a. 4, *baseball* tomar impulso.

windage ('wɪn·dɪdʒ) *n.* desvío de un proyectil por efecto del viento; corrección de ello.

windbag ('wɪnd,bæg) *n., slang* charlatán; fanfarrón.

windblown ('wɪnd,bloːn) *adj.* **1,** (carried by the wind) llevado por el viento. **2,** (of a certain type of coiffure) recortado y peinado hacia la frente.

windborne ('wɪnd,born) *adj.* llevado por el viento.

windbreak ('wɪnd,breik) *n.* seto, cercado o hilera de árboles que abriga contra el viento.

windbreaker ('wɪnd,brei·kər) *n.* chaqueta de cuero o lana con cintura y bocamangas de elástico.

winded ('wɪn·dɪd) *adj.* agotado; falto de aliento.

winder ('wain·dər) *n.* **1,** (one who winds) devanador [*fem.* -dora]. **2,** (reel) devanadera. **3,** (key for winding a spring) llave.

windfall ('wɪnd,fɔl) *n.* fruta caída del árbol; *fig.* provecho o ganancia inesperada.

windflower ('wind,flau·ər) *n.* anémona.

windgall ('wɪnd,gɔl) *n., vet.* aventadura; agalla.

wind gauge (wɪnd) anemómetro.

windiness ('wɪn·di·nəs) *n.* **1,** (abundance of wind) ventosidad. **2,** (talkativeness) verbosidad. **3,** (boastfulness) vanidad; jactancia. **4,** (flatulence) flatulencia.

winding ('wain·dɪŋ) *n.* **1,** (turn; bend) vuelta; rodeo; recodo. **2,** (wrapping) arrollamiento. **3,** (twisting) torcedura. —*adj.* **1,** (turning; bending) sinuoso; tortuoso. **2,** (of or for winding) que arrolla o envuelve. —**winding sheet,** mortaja; sudario. —**winding stairs,** escalera de caracol.

wind instrument (wɪnd) instrumento de viento.

windjammer ('wɪnd,dʒæm·ər) *n.* **1,** (sailing ship) velero; buque de vela. **2,** (sailor) marinero en un velero.

windlass ('wɪnd·ləs) *n.* torno; molinete.

windmill ('wɪnd,mɪl) *n.* **1,** (machine) molino de viento. **2,** (child's toy) molinete.

window ('wɪn·do) *n.* **1,** (opening) ventana. **2,** (show window) escaparate de tienda; vitrina. **3,** (of an auto or coach; of an envelope; for tickets) ventanilla.

window box tiesto de ventana.

window dressing adorno o arreglo de escaparates; *fig.* ostentación; fingimiento.

window envelope sobre de ventanilla.

window glass vidrio de ventana.

windowpane ('wɪn·do,pein) *n.* cristal de ventana.

window shade persiana; transparente; visillo.

windowshop ('wɪn·do,ʃap) *v.i.* [**-shopped, -shopping**] mirar mercancías en las vitrinas sin comprar.

window shutter contraventana.

window sill antepecho.

windpipe ('wɪnd,paip) *n.* tráquea.

windrow ('wɪnd,ro) *n.* hilera o montón de hierba o de heno arrollado por el viento o puesto a secar.

windshield ('wɪnd,ʃild) *n.* parabrisas. —**windshield wiper,** limpiaparabrisas.

windsock ('wɪnd,sak) *n.* manga de aire. *También,* **wind sleeve; wind cone.**

windstorm ('wɪnd,storm) *n.* ventarrón.

windup ('waind,ʌp) *n., colloq.* **1,** (conclusion) término; acción final; conclusión. **2,** *baseball* movimiento del lanzador tomando impulso.

windward ('wɪnd·wərd) *n.* barlovento. —*adj.* de barlovento. —*adv.* a barlovento.

windy ('wɪn·di) *adj.* **1,** (of or full of wind) ventoso. **2,** (exposed to the wind) expuesto al viento; a barlovento. **3,** (stormy) tempestuoso; borrascoso. **4,** (talkative) verboso; parlero. **5,** (boastful) vano; jactancioso. **6,** (flatulent) flatulento. —**it is windy,** hace viento.

wine (wain) *n.* vino. —*adj.* vinícola; vinatero. —*v.t.* obsequiar o regalar con vino. —*v.i.* beber vino.

winebibber ('wain,bɪb·ər) *n.* borrachón [*fem.* -chona]; bebedor [*fem.* -dora].

wine cellar bodega.

wineglass ('wain,glæs) *n.* copa para vino.

winegrower ('wain,gro·ər) *n.* vinicultor. —**winegrowing,** *n.* vinicultura.

wine merchant vinatero.

wine press lagar.

winery ('wain·ə·ri) *n.* lagar.

wineskin ('wain,skɪn) *n.* odre; pellejo de vino.

winetaster ('wain,teis·tər) *n.* catavinos.

wing (wɪŋ) *n.* **1,** (organ or device

for flying; projecting part) ala. **2,** (flight) vuelo. **3,** *mil.; archit.* ala. **4,** *theat.* bastidor. **5,** (faction) facción. **6,** *slang* (arm) brazo. —*v.i.* volar. —*v.t.* **1,** (traverse in flight) volar por. **2,** (provide with wings) proveer de alas. **3,** (send swiftly) arrojar; impeler. **4,** (wound in the wing or arm) herir en el ala o el brazo. —**on the wing,** volando. —**take wing,** volarse; irse volando.

winged ('wɪŋ·ɪd) *adj.* alado.

winglet ('wɪŋ·lɪt) *n.* aleta.

wingspread *n.* envergadura.

wink (wɪŋk) *v.t. & i.* guiñar. —*n.* guiño; guiñada. —**forty winks,** *colloq.* siesta; siestecita. —**not to sleep a wink,** no pegar o cerrar los ojos. —**wink at,** pasar por alto; dejar pasar.

winkle ('wɪŋk·əl) *n.* caracol marino; litorina.

winner ('wɪn·ər) *n.* ganador [*fem.* -dora]; premiado.

winning ('wɪn·ɪŋ) *adj.* **1,** (victorious) victorioso; triunfante; ganador. **2,** (charming) atrayente; encantador. **3,** (persuasive) persuasivo. —*n.* victoria; triunfo. —**winnings,** *n.pl.* ganancias.

winnow ('wɪn·o) *v.t.* **1,** (blow the chaff from) aventar. **2,** (sift; select) escudriñar; entresacar. **3,** (beat, as wings) batir. —*v.i.* **1,** (remove chaff) aventar. **2,** (beat the wings) aletear; batir (las alas).

wino ('wai·no) *n., slang* bebedor; borracho.

winsome ('wɪn·səm) *adj.* atrayente; simpático. —**winsomeness,** *n.* atracción; simpatía.

winter ('wɪn·tər) *n.* invierno. —*adj.* invernal; de o del invierno. —*v.t.* hacer invernar. —*v.i.* invernar.

wintergreen ('wɪn·tər‚grin) *n.* gaulteria.

winterize ('wɪn·tər‚aiz) *v.t.* preparar para el invierno.

winter quarters invernadero.

wintertime ('wɪn·tər·taim) *n.* invierno.

wintry ('wɪn·tri) *adj.* invernal; frío. *También,* **wintery** ('wɪn·tər·i).

winy ('wai·ni) *adj.* vinoso.

wipe (waip) *v.t.* **1,** (clean) limpiar. **2,** (rub) frotar. **3,** (dry) enjugar. —*n.* frotadura; limpiadura. —**wipe out, 1,** (erase) borrar. **2,** (destroy) aniquilar; destruir; matar. **3,** (settle, as a debt) enjugar.

wiper ('wai·pər) *n.* **1,** (cleaner) limpiador. **2,** (cloth) paño; trapo.

wire (wair) *n.* **1,** (metal; thread) alambre. **2,** = **telegraph. 3,** = **telegram.** —*adj.* de alambre. —*v.t.* **1,** (furnish with wire) proveer de alambre. **2,** (fasten with wire) atar con alambre. —*v.t. & i.* (telegraph) telegrafiar. —**get (in) under the wire,** llegar o terminar al último momento. —**pull wires,** ejercer uno su influencia, esp. en secreto.

wire cloth tela metálica.

wire gauge calibrador de alambre.

wireless ('wair·ləs) *adj.* inalámbrico; sin hilos. —*n.* radiotelefonía; radiotelegrafía; radio. —*v.t. & i.* comunicar(se) por radio.

wirephoto ('wair‚fo·to) *n.* [*pl.* **-tos**] *T.N.* telefotografía.

wirepulling ('wair‚pʊl·ɪŋ) *n.*, *colloq.* maquinaciones secretas; intrigas.

wire recorder magnetófono.

wire screen tela metálica.

wiretap ('wair‚tæp) *v.t.* [**-tapped, -tapping**] intervenir (un teléfono). —*n.* conexión secreta para interceptar mensajes telefónicos o telegráficas.

wiring ('wair·ɪŋ) *n.* alambrado; instalación de alambres.

wiry ('wair·i) *adj.* **1,** (of or like wire) de o como alambre. **2,** (lean and strong) delgado pero fuerte.

wisdom ('wɪz·dəm) *n.* **1,** (knowledge) sabiduría. **2,** (prudence) prudencia; juicio; cordura. —**wisdom tooth,** muela cordal; muela del juicio.

wise (waiz) *adj.* **1,** (knowing) sabio. **2,** (prudent) prudente; cuerdo. **3,** *colloq.* (informed) enterado; informado. **4,** *slang* (conceited) arrogante; altanero. **5,** *slang* (impudent) atrevido; descarado; fresco. —*n.* manera; modo; guisa. —**be wise (to),** *slang* estar al tanto (de). —**get wise (to),** *slang* caer en la cuenta; enterarse (de). —**put wise (to),** *slang* poner al tanto (de). —**wise up (to),** *slang* poner al tanto (de); caer en la cuenta (de).

wiseacre ('waiz‚ei·kər) *n.* sabihondo; chocarrero.

wisecrack ('waiz·kræk) *n.* dicharacho; broma; pulla. —*v.i.* bromear; echar pullas. —**wisecracker,** *n.* bromista.

wise guy *slang* **1,** (braggart)

fanfarrón. **2,** (know-it-all) sábelo-todo.

wish (wɪʃ) *n.* deseo. —*v.t. & i.* desear. —**wish for,** desear; anhelar. —**wish something on someone,** plantarle o pegarle a uno una cosa molesta.

wishbone ('wɪʃ·bon) *n.* espoleta; hueso de la suerte.

wishful ('wɪʃ·fəl) *adj.* deseoso; anheloso; ansioso. —**wishfully,** *adj.* ansiosamente; con anhelo. —**wishfulness,** *n.* deseo; anhelo; ansia. —**wishful thinking,** ilusión; optimismo.

wishy-washy ('wɪʃ·i·wɒʃ·i) *adj., colloq,* **1,** (watery) aguado. **2,** (insipid) soso; insulso. **3,** (feeble) débil; flojo.

wisp (wɪsp) *n.* **1,** (small bunch) manojo; puñado. **2,** (tuft of hair) mechón. **3,** (slender strip) tira; jirón. **4,** (fragment) fragmento; pizca; trozo. **5,** (curl of smoke) espiral; pluma. **6,** = **whisk broom.**

wispy ('wɪs·pi) *adj.* sutil; delicado.

wisteria (wɪs'tɪr·i·ə) *n.* vistaria. *También,* **wistaria** (wɪs'ter·i·ə).

wistful ('wɪst·fəl) *adj.* ansioso; anhelante; pensativo. —**wistfulness,** *n.* ansiedad; anhelo.

wit (wɪt) *n.* **1,** (reason) juicio. **2,** (cleverness) agudeza. **3,** (clever person) chistoso. **4,** (clever remark) dicho agudo; chiste. **5,** (ingenuity) ingenio. —**wits,** *n.pl.* juicio; razón. —**be at one's wits' end,** no saber que hacer o decir. —**keep (o have) one's wits about one,** tener calma. —**live by one's wits,** vivir de gorra. —**out of one's wits,** fuera de sí. —**to wit,** a saber.

witch (wɪtʃ) *n.* bruja; hechicera. —*v.t.* embrujar; hechizar.

witchcraft ('wɪtʃ·kræft) *n.* brujería.

witch doctor curandero; médico brujo.

witchery ('wɪtʃ·ə·ri) *n.* hechicería; brujería.

witch hazel hamamelis.

witching ('wɪtʃ·ɪŋ) *adj.* hechicero; encantador; mágico.

with (wɪð; wɪθ) *prep.* **1,** (in company of; by means of) con. **2,** (consisting of; characterized by; apart from) de. **3,** (against) contra.

withal (wɪð'ɔl) *adv.* **1,** (besides) además; también. **2,** (thereby) así; de este modo. **3,** (thereupon) luego;

en seguida. **4,** (still) por otro lado; a pesar de eso. —*prep.* con.

withdraw (wɪð'drɔ; wɪθ-) *v.t.* [-**drew,** -**drawn**] retirar; sacar. —*v.i.* retirarse.

withdrawal (wɪð'drɔ·əl; wɪθ-) *n.* retiro; retirada.

withe (waɪð) *n.* mimbre.

wither ('wɪð·ər) *v.i.* **1,** (shrivel; fade) marchitarse. **2,** (languish) languidecer. **3,** (quail; cower) acobardarse; desanimarse. —*v.t.* **1,** (cause to fade) marchitar. **2,** (cow; shame) avergonzar; amedrentar; desanimar.

withers ('wɪð·ərz) *n.pl.* cruz.

withhold (wɪð'hold; wɪθ-) *v.t.* [*pret. & p.p.* **withheld**] **1,** (hold back) retener; detener; contener. **2,** (refuse) negar.

withholding tax porción del impuesto sobre la renta retenido de antemano.

within (wɪð'ɪn; wɪθ-) *adv.* dentro; adentro. —*prep.* **1,** (in; inside of) dentro de. **2,** (in reach of) al alcance de. **3,** (less than) menos de.

without (wɪð'aut; wɪθ-) *adv.* fuera; afuera. —*prep.* **1,** (outside of) fuera de. **2,** (beyond) más allá de. **3,** (lacking; devoid of) sin. —**do (o go) without,** privarse de; pasar sin.

withstand (wɪð'stænd; wɪθ-) *v.t.* [*pret. & p.p.* **withstood** (-'stud)] resistir; aguantar; soportar.

withy ('wɪð·i) *n.* mimbre. —*adj.* flexible; ágil.

witless ('wɪt·ləs) *adj.* necio; tonto; insensato.

witness ('wɪt·nəs) *n.* **1,** (person) testigo. **2,** (testimony) testimonio. —*v.t.* **1,** (testify to) atestiguar. **2,** (be present at) presenciar; asistir a. **3,** (sign) firmar como testigo. **4,** (exhibit) mostrar; manifestar. —*v.i.* ser testigo; servir de testigo; dar testimonio.

witticism ('wɪt·ɪ·sɪz·əm) *n.* dicho agudo; agudeza; chiste; gracia.

wittiness ('wɪt·ɪ·nəs) *n.* agudeza; gracia.

wittingly ('wɪt·ɪŋ·li) *adv.* adrede; a propósito; a sabiendas.

witty ('wɪt·i) *adj.* agudo; gracioso; chistoso; ocurrente.

wive (waiv) *v.i.* casarse. —*v.t.* **1,** (take as a wife) casarse con; tomar por esposa. **2,** (provide with a wife) proveer de esposa; casar.

wives (waivz) *n., pl. de* **wife.**

wizard ('wɪz·ərd) *n.* **1,** (sorcerer)

brujo; hechicero. **2,** *colloq.* (expert) experto. —*adj.* hechicero; mágico.

wizardry ('wɪz·ərd·ri) *n.* hechicería; brujería.

wizen ('wɪz·ən) *v.t.* & *i.* marchitar(se). —**wizened,** *adj.* marchito.

woad (woːd) *n.* hierba pastel; glasto.

wobble ('wab·əl) *v.i.* **1,** (stagger) bambolear; tambalear. **2,** (tremble) temblequear. **3,** (waver) vacilar. —*n.* bamboleo; tambaleo. —**wobbly** (-li) *adj.* inestable; inseguro; temblequé.

woe (woː) *n.* desgracia; aflicción; pena; dolor. —*interj.* ¡ay! —**woe is me!,** ¡ay de mí!

woebegone ('wo·bi,gan) *adj.* triste; abatido; desgraciado.

woeful ('wo·fəl) *adj.* **1,** (sad) triste; abatido. **2,** (causing woe) lastimoso; funesto. **3,** (wretched) miserable; mezquino.

woke (wok) *v.,* *pret. de* **wake.**

wolf (wulf) *n.* [*pl.* **wolves** (wulvz)] lobo. —*v.t.* comer vorazmente; devorar. —**cry wolf,** gritar ¡al lobo!; dar falsa alarma. —**keep the wolf from the door,** cerrar la puerta al hambre.

wolfhound ('wulf·haund) *n.* galgo lobero.

wolfish ('wul·fɪʃ) *adj.* lobero; lupino.

wolfram ('wul·frəm) *n.* tungsteno; volframio.

wolfsbane ('wulfs,bein) *n.* matalobos; acónito.

wolverine (,wul·və'riːn) *n.* glotón.

woman ('wum·ən) *n.* [*pl.* **women**] mujer. —*adj.* femenino; de mujer.

woman-hater *n.* misógino.

womanhood ('wum·ən·hud) *n.* **1,** (condition) estado de mujer. **2,** = **womanliness. 3,** = **womankind.**

womanish ('wum·ən·ɪʃ) *adj.* mujeril; femenil; afeminado.

womanize ('wum·ə·naiz) *v.t.* afeminar. —*v.i.* ser mujeriego. —**womanizer,** *n.* hombre mujeriego.

womankind ('wum·ən,kaind) *n.* femineidad; las mujeres; el mundo femenino.

womanlike ('wum·ən,laik) *adj.* mujeril.

womanly ('wum·ən·li) *adj.* mujeril; femenil. —**womanliness,** *n.* femineidad.

womb (wuːm) *n.* útero; matriz; vientre.

women ('wɪm·ən) *n.,* *pl. de* **woman.**

won (wʌn) *v.,* *pret. & p.p. de* **win.**

wonder ('wʌn·dər) *n.* **1,** (admiration) admiración; asombro. **2,** (cause of admiration) maravilla; prodigio. —*v.i.* **1,** (marvel) maravillarse; admirarse; asombrarse. **2,** (doubt) dudar. —*v.t.* querer saber; preguntarse. —**for a wonder,** por milagro. —**no wonder,** no hay que extrañar; no es extraño.

wonderful ('wʌn·dər·fəl) *adj.* admirable; maravilloso.

wonderland ('wʌn·dər·lænd) *n.* tierra de maravillas.

wonderment ('wʌn·dər·mənt) *n.* maravilla; admiración; asombro.

wonder-struck *adj.* atónito; pasmado; asombrado. *También,* **wonder-stricken.**

wondrous ('wʌn·drəs) *adj.* maravilloso.

won't (wont) *contr. de* **will not.**

wont (want) *adj.* acostumbrado. —*n.* costumbre; uso. —**be wont to,** soler; acostumbrar.

wonted ('wan·tɪd; 'wʌn-) *adj.* usual; habitual; acostumbrado.

woo (wuː) *v.t.* & *i.* (court) cortejar; galantear. —*v.t.* (seek) buscar; solicitar.

wood (wud) *n.* **1,** (substance; timber) madera. **2,** (forest) bosque. **3,** (scrap wood; firewood) leña. **4,** = **woodwind.** —*adj.* **1,** (made of wood) de madera. **2,** (living in woods) silvestre; de los bosques.

wood alcohol alcohol metílico.

woodbine ('wud,bain) *n.* madreselva.

wood borer carcoma.

wood carving talla en madera.

woodchuck ('wud,tʃʌk) *n.* marmota de América.

woodcock ('wud·kak) *n.* chocha.

woodcraft ('wud·kræft) *n.* **1,** (wood lore) conocimiento de los bosques. **2,** = **woodworking.**

woodcut ('wud·kʌt) *n.* grabado en madera.

woodcutter ('wud·kʌt·ər) *n.* leñador.

wooded ('wud·ɪd) *adj.* arbolado.

wooden ('wud·ən) *adj.* **1,** (made of wood) de madera. **2,** (dull; stupid) torpe; lerdo; estúpido.

wood engraving grabado en madera.

woodenheaded ('wud·ən,hɛd·ɪd) *adj.* estúpido; zopenco.

woodland ('wʊd·lənd) *n.* arbolado; bosque.

wood louse cochinilla.

woodman ('wʊd·mən) *n.* [*pl.* -men] 1, (woodcutter) leñador. 2, *Brit.* (forester) guardabosque.

woodpecker ('wʊd·pɛk·ər) *n.* picaposte; picamaderos.

wood pigeon paloma torcaz.

wood pulp pulpa de madera.

woodruff ('wʊd,rʌf) *n.* asperilla.

woodshed ('wʊdʃɛd) *n.* leñera.

woodsman ('wʊdz·mən) *n.* [*pl.* -men] hombre que vive o trabaja en los bosques.

wood sorrel acedera menor.

woodwind ('wʊd,wɪnd) *n.* instrumento de viento de madera.

woodwork ('wʊd·wʌrk) *n.* maderamen; enmaderamiento. —**woodworker,** *n.* ebanista; carpintero. —**woodworking,** *n.* ebanistería; carpintería.

woody ('wʊd·i) *adj.* 1, (of or like wood) leñoso; de o como madera. 2, (wooded) arbolado.

wooer ('wu·ər) *n.* galán; pretendiente.

woof *n.* 1, (wuf) *weaving* trama. 2, (wʊf) (growl) gruñido. —*v.i.* (wʊf) gruñir.

wooing ('wu·ɪŋ) *n.* galanteo.

wool (wʊl) *n.* lana. —*adj.* de lana. —**all wool and a yard wide,** genuino; auténtico. —**pull the wool over someone's eyes,** engañarle a uno.

woolbearing ('wʊl,bɛr·ɪŋ) *adj.* lanar.

woolen *también,* **woollen** ('wʊl·ən) *adj.* de lana. —**woolens,** *n.pl.* géneros de lana; ropa de lana.

woolgathering ('wʌl,gæð·ər·ɪŋ) *n.* distracción. —*adj.* distraído.

woolly *también,* **wooly** ('wʊl·i) *adj.* lanudo; lanoso. —**woollies,** *n.pl.* ropa interior de lana.

woozy ('wu·zi) *adj., slang* aturdido.

word (wʌrd) *n.* 1, (unit of meaning) remark; advice) palabra. 2, (lexical unit) vocablo; voz. 3, (saying) dicho; sentencia. 4, *cap., Bib.* Verbo. 5, (password) santo y seña. 6, (order) orden. 7, (news) noticia; noticias. 8, (message) mensaje; recado. —*v.t.* frasear; expresar en palabras. —**be as good as one's word,** cumplir lo prometido. —**break one's word,** faltar a su palabra. —**by word of mouth,** de palabra; de boca. —**eat one's**

words, retractarse; retirar sus palabras. —**give one's word,** prometer; comprometerse. —**have a word with,** hablar cuatro palabras con. —**have words (with),** tener palabras mayores (con). —**leave word,** dejar dicho. —**mark my words,** atiéndame; atienda lo que digo. —**my word!,** ¡válgame Dios! —**put in a good word for,** recomendar. —**take at one's word,** tomarle a uno la palabra. —**take one's word for it,** fiarse de la palabra de uno. —**take the words out of one's mouth,** quitarle a uno la palabra de la boca. —**the last word,** la última moda. —**upon my word,** palabra de honor; ¡a fe mía! —**word for word,** al pie de la letra; verbatim. —**word processing,** procesamiento de palabras.

wordbook ('wʌrd·bʊk) *n.* 1, (dictionary) diccionario; vocabulario; léxico. 2, (libretto) libreto.

wording ('wʌr·dɪŋ) *n.* fraseología.

wordless ('wʌrd·ləs) *adj.* 1, (speechless) mudo; callado; falto de palabras. 2, (unexpressed) inexpresado. 3, (inexpressible) inexpresable.

wordy ('wʌr·di) *adj.* verboso; palabrero. —**wordiness,** *n.* verbosidad; palabrería.

wore (wɔr) *v., pret. de* **wear.**

work (wʌrk) *n.* 1, (effort; toil) trabajo; labor. 2, (employment) trabajo; empleo. 3, (occupation) trabajo; profesión; oficio. 4, (undertaking) empresa; proyecto. 5, (task) tarea. 6, (result of effort; creation) obra. —*v.t.* 1, (cause to work) hacer trabajar. 2, (shape; form) trabajar; elaborar. 3, (use; wield) manejar; emplear. 4, (cause; bring about) causar; producir. 5, (solve) resolver. 6, (till) labrar. 7, (exploit) explotar. 8, (persuade) persuadir. 9, (make or gain by effort) forjar; conseguir con esfuerzo. 10, (provoke) provocar. —*v.i.* 1, (do work) trabajar. 2, (function) trabajar; funcionar; marchar. 3, (proceed or change slowly) colarse; abrirse paso; volverse poco a poco. —**works,** *n.sing.* o *pl.* fábrica; taller. —*n.pl.* mecanismo; movimiento. —**at work,** trabajando. —**get the works,** *slang* ser víctima; sufrir un castigo. —**give one the works,** *slang* 1, (kill) matar. 2, (punish) castigar; maltratar; humillar. —**make short**

(o **quick**) **work of,** acabar pronto con. —**out of work,** desempleado. —**shoot the works,** *slang* arriesgar todo; esforzarse lo más posible. —**work force,** personal; fuerza de trabajo. —**work in,** meter(se); introducir(se). —**work off,** deshacerse de. —**work on** (o **upon**), influir en; persuadir. —**work out, 1,** (become loose) aflojarse. **2,** (exhaust) agotar. **3,** (bring about) producir. **4,** (develop) desarrollar; elaborar. **5,** (solve) resolver. **6,** (result) resultar. **7,** *sports* (train) entrenarse. **8,** (exercise) hacer ejercicios. —**work up, 1,** (advance) adelantarse. **2,** (prepare) preparar; elaborar. **3,** (excite) estimular; excitar.

workable ('wʌrk·ə·bəl) *adj.* **1,** (feasible) factible; practicable. **2,** (exploitable) explotable. **3,** (tillable) laborable.

workaday ('wʌrk·ə‚dei) *adj.* común; ordinario; de cada día.

workaholic (‚wʌrk·ə'hal·ɪk) *n.*, *slang* persona excesivamente dedicada al trabajo, como si fuera adicta.

workbench ('wʌrk‚bentʃ) *n.* mesa o banco de trabajo.

workbook ('wʌrk·bʊk) *n.* libro de ejercicios; libro de trabajo.

workday ('wʌrk·de) *n.* **1,** (day on which one works) día laborable; día de trabajo. **2,** (time worked in one day) jornada.

worker ('wʌr·kər) *n.* trabajador [*fem.* -dora]; obrero.

workhouse ('wʌrk·haus) *n.* **1,** (prison) taller penitenciario. **2,** *Brit.* = **poorhouse.**

working ('wʌrk·ɪŋ) *adj.* **1,** (that works) que trabaja; que funciona. **2,** (of or for work) de trabajo. —*n.* **1,** (functioning) funcionamiento. **2,** (exploiting) explotación. —**workings,** *n.pl.* labores.

working class clase obrera.

working day = **workday.**

working girl obrera; trabajadora.

workingman ('wʌrk·ɪŋ·mæn) *n.* [*pl.*-**men**] obrero; trabajador. —**working woman** obrera; trabajadora.

workman ('wʌrk·mən) *n.* [*pl.*-**men**] **1,** = **workingman. 2,** (craftsman) artífice; artesano.

workmanlike ('wʌrk·mən·laik) *adj.* hecho con pericia; bien ejecutado; digno de un artesano.

workmanship ('wʌrk·mən·ʃɪp) *n.* manera de ejecutar un trabajo; artesanía.

workout ('wʌrk·aut) *n.* ejercicio.

workroom ('wʌrk·rum) *n.* taller; gabinete de trabajo.

workshop ('wʌrk·ʃap) *n.* taller.

workstation ('wʌrk‚stei·ʃən) *n.* puesto de trabajo.

workweek ('wʌrk·wik) *n.* semana de trabajo.

world (wʌrld) *n.* mundo. —*adj.* mundial. —**bring into the world,** echar al mundo. —**for all the world,** exactamente. —**in the world, 1,** (on earth) en el mundo. **2,** (ever) jamás. —**not for all the world,** por nada del mundo. —**on top of the world,** *slang* en los cielos; regocijado. —**out of this world,** *slang* divino; excelente. —**think the world of,** poner en el cielo. —**world without end,** por los siglos de los siglos.

worldling ('wʌrld·lɪŋ) *n.* persona mundana.

worldly ('wʌrld·li) *adj.* mundano. —**worldliness,** *n.* mundanería; mundanalidad.

worldly-wise *adj.* experimentado; corrido; mundano.

world power potencia mundial.

worldwide ('wʌrld‚waid) *adj.* mundial.

worm (wʌrm) *n.* gusano; lombriz. —*v.t.* **1,** (rid of worms) limpiar de lombrices. **2,** (get by artifice) sonsacar; conseguir por artimañas. —*v.i.* arrastrarse; deslizarse; serpentear. —**worm oneself** (o **one's way**) **in** o **into,** insinuarse (en). —**worm something out of someone,** sonsacarle a uno una cosa.

worm-eaten *adj.* **1,** (eaten by worms) carcomido; apolillado. **2,** (worn-out) desgastado; consumido; trillado.

worm gear engranaje de tornillo sin fin.

wormhole ('wʌrm‚hol) *n.* agujero dejado por una carcoma o un gusano.

wormlike ('wʌrm·laik) *adj.* vermicular; vermiforme.

wormwood ('wʌrm·wʊd) *n.* **1,** (plant; absinthe) ajenjo. **2,** *fig.* (bitterness) amargura.

wormy ('wʌr·mi) *adj.* **1,** (infested with worms) gusaniento; gusanoso;

carcomido. **2,** = **wormlike. 3,** (debased) ruin; arrastrado.

worn (worn) *v., p.p. de* **wear.** —*adj.* **1,** (showing the effects of wear) gastado; consumido; raído. **2,** (exhausted) cansado; fatigado.

worn-out *adj.* **1,** (no longer serviceable) gastado; consumido; inservible. **2,** (spent) rendido; extenuado.

worriment ('wʌr·i·mənt) *n.* **1,** (anxiety) inquietud; preocupación. **2,** (cause of worry) molestia; enojo.

worrisome ('wʌr·i·səm) *adj.* **1,** (causing worry) inquietante; molesto; enojoso. **2,** (inclined to worry) inquieto; aprensivo.

worry ('wʌr·i) *v.t.* **1,** (harass) atormentar; acosar; molestar. **2,** (disturb) inquietar; preocupar. —*v.i.* inquietarse; preocuparse. —*n.* **1,** (anxiety) preocupación; inquietud. **2,** (cause of worry) molestia; enojo.

worrywart ('wʌr·i·wort) *n., colloq.* persona excesivamente preocupada.

worse (wʌrs) *adj. & adv. comp.* peor. —*n.* lo peor; la peor parte. —**for the worse,** en mal. —**little the worse for wear,** apenas usado; poco gastado. —**so much the worse; all the worse,** tanto peor. —**worse and worse,** de mal en peor; peor que peor; cada vez peor.

worsen ('wʌr·sən) *v.t. & i.* empeorar.

worship ('wʌr·ʃɪp) *n.* adoración; culto. —*v.t.* adorar; venerar. —*v.i.* dar culto. —**your worship,** vuestra merced.

worshiper ('wʌr·ʃɪp·ər) *n.* adorador [*fem.* -dora]; devoto.

worshipful ('wʌr·ʃɪp·fəl) *adj.* **1,** (worthy of worship) venerable; honorable; respetable. **2,** (offering worship) adorador.

worst (wʌrst) *adj. & adv. superl.* peor. —*n.* lo peor; la peor parte. —*v.t.* vencer; derrotar. —**at the worst,** a lo más. —**get the worst of it,** llevar la peor parte. —**give one the worst of it,** darle a uno la peor parte; derrotarle a uno. —**if worse comes to worst,** si pasa lo peor. —**in the worst way,** *slang* mucho; enormemente. —**make the worst of,** tomar en peor; tomar a mal.

worsted ('wus·tɪd) *n.* estambre. —*adj.* de estambre.

wort (wʌrt) *n.* **1,** (plant) planta;

hierba. **2,** (beverage) cerveza nueva; mosto de cerveza.

worth (wʌrθ) *n.* **1,** (value) valor; precio. **2,** (merit) mérito. —*adj.* **1,** (deserving of) digno de. **2,** (of the value of) del valor de; que vale; que tiene precio de. **3,** (having a certain wealth) que tiene; que posee. —**be worth,** valer; tener precio de; tener; poseer. —**be worth (the) while,** valer la pena (de). —**for all one is worth,** a más no poder.

worthiness ('wʌr·ði·nəs) *n.* dignidad; excelencia; mérito.

worthless ('wʌrθ·ləs) *adj.* **1,** (valueless) sin valor. **2,** (useless) inútil; inservible. **3,** (without merit) indigno; despreciable. —**be worthless,** no valer nada.

worthlessness ('wʌrθ·ləs·nəs) *n.* **1,** (lack of value) falta de valor. **2,** (uselessness) inutilidad. **3,** (lack of merit) indignidad.

worthwhile ('wʌrθ,hwail) *adj.* **1,** (important) de mérito; de importancia. **2,** (profitable) provechoso.

worthy ('wʌr·ði) *adj.* digno; benemérito. —*n.* benemérito; notable; héroe.

would (wud) *v., pret. de* **will.** —*v.aux.;* denota además. **1,** el condicional *(presente o pasado)* en la segunda y tercera personas: *he would go if he had the time,* iría si tuviera el tiempo; *he would have gone if he had had the time,* habría ido si hubiera tenido el tiempo. **2,** deseo; anhelo: *would that it were so!,* ¡ojalá que fuera verdad! **3,** pedido; súplica: *would you help me?,* ¿quisiera ayudarme?

would-be *adj.* supuesto; fingido.

wound (wund) *n.* herida. —*v.t. & i.* herir.

wound (waund) *v., pret. & p.p. de* **wind.** —**get wound up,** *colloq.,* excitarse.

wove (woːv) *v., pret. de* **weave.**

woven ('woˑvən) *v., p.p. de* **weave.**

wow (wau) *interj.* ¡ah!; ¡ay! —*v.t. slang* cautivar; encantar; pasmar. —*n., slang* maravilla; prodigio.

wrack (ræk) *n.* **1,** (destruction) destrucción; ruina. **2,** (wrecked ship) naufragio. **3,** (wreckage) despojos.

wraith (reiθ) *n.* fantasma; espectro.

wrangle ('ræŋ·gəl) *v.i.* reñir; disputar. —*v.t.* **1,** (get by argument) conseguir disputando. **2,** (round up, as livestock) rodear. —*n.* riña; disputa; contienda.

wrangler ('ræŋ·glər) *n.* **1,** (one who argues) disputador [*fem.* -dora]; pendenciero. **2,** (cowboy) vaquero que rodea el ganado. **3,** *Brit.* alumno que gana altos honores en matemáticas.

wrap (ræp) *v.t. & i.* [**wrapped, wrapping**] envolver(se); enrollar (se). —*n.* abrigo. —**under wraps,** oculto; secreto. —**wrap up,** envolver; arropar(se). —**wrapped up in,** absorto en; entregado a; envuelto en.

wraparound ('ræp·ə·raund) *adj.* que circunda el cuerpo antes de ceñirse. —*n.* capa; manto.

wrapper ('ræp·ər) *n.* **1,** (covering) cubierta; envoltura. **2,** (robe) bata; guardapolvo. **3,** (of a newspaper) faja. **4,** (of a cigar) capa.

wrapping ('ræp·ɪŋ) *n.* envoltura. —**wrapping paper,** papel de envolver.

wrap-up *n.* conclusión; resumen. —**wrap up, 1,** (conclude) concluir. **2,** (summarize) resumir.

wrath (ræθ) *n.* cólera; ira; furia. —**wrathful,** *adj.* colérico; iracundo; furioso.

wreak (rik) *v.t.* **1,** (inflict) infligir; visitar. **2,** (give vent to) descargar.

wreath (riθ) *n.* **1,** (garland; crown) guirnalda; corona. **2,** (puff, as of smoke) espiral.

wreathe (riːð) *v.t.* **1,** (adorn with a wreath) enguirnaldar. **2,** (entwine; wrap) envolver; enroscar. **3,** (twist; coil) tejer; entretejer; ensortijar. —*v.i.* enroscarse.

wreck (rɛk) *n.* **1,** (destruction) destrucción; ruina. **2,** (collision) choque; colisión. **3,** (something wrecked; ruin) ruina. **4,** (shipwreck) naufragio. —*v.t.* **1,** (destroy) destruir; arruinar; destrozar. **2,** (cause to be shipwrecked) hacer naufragar. **3,** (raze) arrasar; demoler. **4,** (dismantle) desmantelar; desmontar. —*v.i.* arruinarse; destrozarse.

wreckage ('rɛk·ɪdʒ) *n.* **1,** (destruction) destrucción; ruina. **2,** (wrecked ship) náufrago. **3,** (debris) despojos; restos.

wrecker ('rɛk·ər) *n.* **1,** (person or thing that wrecks) demoledor; destructor. **2,** *auto.* camión de auxilio. **3,** *R.R.* carro de auxilio.

wren (rɛn) *n.* reyezuelo.

wrench (rɛntʃ) *n.* **1,** (twist) arranque; torcedura. **2,** (anguish) dolor; angustia. **3,** (tool) llave; desvolvedor. —*v.t.* arrancar; torcer.

wrest (rɛst) *v.t.* arrebatar; arrancar.

wrestle ('rɛs·əl) *v.i.* luchar. —*v.t.* luchar con. —*n.* lucha. —**wrestler** (-lər) *n.* luchador [*fem.* -dora]. —**wrestling** (-lɪŋ) *n.* lucha.

wretch (rɛtʃ) *n.* infeliz; miserable; desgraciado.

wretched ('rɛtʃ·ɪd) *adj.* **1,** (miserable) desdichado; miserable; mezquino. **2,** (distressful) malo; doloroso; penoso. **3,** (poor) malo; malísimo. **4,** (despicable) vil; despreciable; ruin.

wretchedness ('rɛtʃ·ɪd·nəs) *n.* **1,** (misery) desdicha; miseria. **2,** (meanness) vileza; ruindad.

wriggle ('rɪg·əl) *v.t.* menear. —*v.i.* **1,** (move back and forth) menearse. **2,** (twist; writhe) culebrear; serpentear. **3,** (dodge; equivocate) regatear. —*n.* **1,** (motion back and forth) meneo. **2,** (twisting; writhing) culebreo; serpenteo. —**wriggle in** (o **into**), colarse (en). —**wriggle out** (o **away**), escaparse; escabullirse; sacar el cuerpo.

wriggler ('rɪg·lər) *n.* = **wiggler.**

wriggly ('rɪg·li) *adj.* **1,** (that writhes) que se menea o culebrea. **2,** (twisting; winding) tortuoso; serpentino.

wright (rait) *n.* artífice.

wring (rɪŋ) *v.t.* [*pret. & p.p.* **wrung**] **1,** (twist) torcer; retorcer. **2,** (squeeze out) exprimir. **3,** (extract forcibly) arrancar. **4,** (grieve; anguish) afligir; angustiar; acongojar. —*n.* **1,** (twist) torsión; torcedura. **2,** (squeeze) expresión.

wringer ('rɪŋ·ər) *n.* exprimidor; exprimidora.

wringing wet empapado.

wrinkle ('rɪŋ·kəl) *n.* **1,** (furrow) arruga. **2,** *colloq.* (clever idea) invento; novedad. —*v.t. & i.* arrugar(se). —**wrinkly** (-kli) *adj.* arrugado.

wrist (rɪst) *n.* muñeca.

wristband ('rɪst·bænd) *n.* puño de camisa; bocamanga.

wristlet ('rɪst·lɪt) *n.* elástico para la muñeca; brazalete.

wrist watch reloj de pulsera.

writ (rɪt) *n.* escrito; auto.

write (rait) *v.t. & i.* [*pret.* **wrote**; *p.p.* **written**] escribir. —**write down,** poner por escrito; apuntar.

—**write off**, cancelar; amortizar.
—**write out**, poner por escrito; escribir sin abreviar. —**write up, 1,** (set down in detail) describir o contar en detalle. **2,** (bring up to date) poner al día. **3,** (praise; ballyhoo) ensalzar; alabar; dar bombo a.

write-in *adj.* añadido por escrito. —*n.* candidato no oficial.

write-off *n* cancelación; amortización.

writer ('rai·tər) *n.* escritor [*fem.* -tora]. —**writer's cramp,** calambre de los escribientes.

write-up *n., colloq.* **1,** (report) relato. **2,** (praise) alharaca; bombo; publicidad.

writhe (raið) *v.t. & i.* (twist) torcer(se); contorcer(se); retorcer(se). —*v.i.* (suffer) acongojarse; agonizar.

writing ('rai·tɪŋ) *n.* **1,** (act of writing) escritura. **2,** (something written) escrito. **3,** (handwriting) escritura; letra. **4,** (literary work) obra. **5,** (literary profession) profesión de escritor; literatura; letras. —*adj.* de o para escribir. —**in writing,** por escrito.

writing desk escritorio.

written ('rɪt·ən) *v., p.p. de* **write.** —*adj.* escrito; por escrito.

wrong (rɔːŋ) *adj.* **1,** (unjust) injusto. **2,** (bad) malo. **3,** (incorrect) erróneo; incorrecto. **4,** (mistaken) equivocado. **5,** (false) falso; falaz. **6,** (inconvenient) inoportuno. **7,** (unsuitable) inadecuado; impropio. —*adv.* **1,** (badly) mal. **2,** (incorrectly) incorrectamente. **3,** (in the wrong direction) por el mal camino. **4,** (inside out) al revés. —*n.* **1,** (injustice) injusticia. **2,** (harm; injury) daño; perjuicio. **3,** (evil) mal. **4,** (error) error. **5,** (sin) pecado; transgresión. —*v.t.* **1,** (harm) agraviar; injuriar; ofender. **2,** (ma-

lign) calumniar; difamar. **3,** (seduce) engañar; abusar de. —**be in the wrong,** estar equivocado; tener culpa. —**be wrong,** no tener razón; estar equivocado; ser malo; no ser justo. —**be wrong with,** pasarle (algo) a: *something is wrong with my watch,* le pasa algo a mi reloj. —**do wrong,** obrar o hacer mal. —**get (someone) in wrong,** perjudicarle a uno; comprometerle a uno. — **go wrong,** salir mal; perderse; extraviarse. —**right or wrong,** a tuertas o a derechas. —**take (something) wrong,** tomar a mal. —**wrong side,** revés. —**wrong side out,** al revés.

wrongdoer ('rɔŋ,du·ər) *n.* malhechor [*fem.* -chora].

wrongdoing ('rɔŋ,du·ɪŋ) *n.* pecado; maldad.

wrongful ('rɔŋ·fəl) *adj.* **1,** (bad; evil) malo; injusto; inicuo. **2,** (erroneous) equivocado. **3,** (unlawful) ilegal; ilícito.

wrong-headed *adj.* terco; testarudo.

wrongly ('rɔŋ·li) *adv.* **1,** (badly) mal. **2,** (erroneously) por error; equivocadamente.

wrongness ('rɔŋ·nəs) *n.* **1,** (injustice) injusticia. **2,** (error) error; falacia. **3,** (incorrectness) inexactitud.

wrote (rot) *v., pret. de* **write.**

wroth (raθ) *adj.* encolerizado; iracundo.

wrought (rɔt) *adj.* **1,** (formed; made) hecho; forjado. **2,** (hammered) hecho al martillo.

wrought iron hierro dulce.

wrought up *adj.* excitado; conmovido.

wrung (rʌŋ) *v., pret. & p.p. de* **wring.**

wry (rai) *adj.* **1,** (twisted) torcido. **2,** (perverse) pervertido; terco. —**wry face,** mueca; mohín.

X

X, x (eks) vigésima cuarta letra del alfabeto inglés.

xanthein ('zæn·θi·ɪn) *n.* xanteína.

xanthin ('zæn·θɪn) *n.* xantina.

xanthous ('zæn·θəs) *adj.* amarillento.

X-chromosome *n.* cromosoma X.

xenon ('zi·nan) *n.* xenón.

xenophobe ('zɛn·ə,fob) *n.* xenófobo. —**xenophobia,** *n.* xenofobia. —**xenophobic,** *adj.* xenófobo.

xerography (zɪ'rag·rə·fi) *n.* xero-

grafía. —**xerographic** (-rə'græf·ɪk)
adj. xerográfico.
Xerox (zɪ'raks; 'zi-) *n., T.N.* **1,** (machine) máquina xerográfica. **2,** (copy)
xerografía. —*v.t. (l.c.)* xerografiar.
Xmas ('ɛks·məs) *n., contr. de*
Christmas.
X ray rayo X; radiografía.
x-ray *adj.* radiográfico. —*v.t.* someter a los rayos X.

xylem ('zai·lɛm) *n.* xilema.
xylophagous (zai'laf·ə·gəs) *adj.*
xilófago.
xylograph ('zai·lə·græf) *n.* xilografía. —**xylographic** (-'græf·ɪk)
adj. xilográfico. —**xylography**
(zai'lag·rə·fi) *n.* xilografía.
xylophone ('zai·lə,foːn) *n.* xilófono.

Y

Y, y (wai) vigésima quinta letra del
alfabeto inglés.
yacht (jat) *n.* yate. —*v.i.* pasear o
correr en yate.
yachting ('jat·ɪŋ) *n.* navegación o
paseo en yate; deporte del yate.
yachtsman ('jats·mən) *n.* [*pl.*
-men] aficionado a los yates; timón.
—**yachtswoman,** *n.fem.* [*pl.*
-women (-,wɪm·ən)] aficionada a
los yates.
yah! (ja) *interj.* ¡bah!; ¡puf!
yahoo ('ja·hu) *n.* hombre rudo;
patán.
Yahweh ('ja·we) *n.* Yahvé.
yak (jæk) *n.* yak.
yam (jæm) *n.* ñame; batata.
yammer ('jæm·ər) *v.i.* lloriquear;
lamentar. —*n.* lloriqueo; lamento.
yank (jæŋk) *v.t. & i., colloq.* halar;
arrancar; tirar. —*n.* tirón; arranque.
—*adj. & n., cap., slang* yanqui.
Yankee ('jæŋ·ki) *adj. & n.* yanqui.
yap ('jæp) *v.i.* [**yapped, yapping**] **1,**
(bark) ladrar. **2,** *slang* (chatter)
charlar; chacharear. —*n.***1,** (bark)
ladrido. **2,** *slang* (idle talk) charla;
palabrería. **3,** *slang* (mouth) boca.
yard (jard) *n.* **1,** (enclosure) patio;
corral. **2,** (measure) yarda. **3,** *naut.*
verga.
yardage ('jar·dɪdʒ) *n.* medida en
yardas.
yardarm ('jard,arm) *n.* penol;
singlón.
yardstick ('jard,stɪk) *n.* **1,** (measuring stick) yarda; vara de medir.
2, *fig.* (standard) norma; regla.
yarn (jarn) *n.* **1,** (spun fiber) hilado.
2, *colloq.* (story) cuento. —*v.i.,*
colloq. decir cuentos, esp. cuentos
largos e increíbles.
yarrow ('jær·o) *n.* milenrama;
milhojas.
yaw (jɔː) *v.i.* **1,** *naut.* guiñar. **2,**

aero. desviarse. —*n.* **1,** *naut.*
guiñada. **2,** *aero.* desvío.
yawl (jɔːl) *n.* yola.
yawn (jɔːn) *v.i.* **1,** (open the mouth)
bostezar. **2,** (gape) abrirse. —*n.* **1,**
(opening the mouth) bostezo. **2,**
(chasm) abertura; hendedura;
abismo.
yaws (jɔːz) *n.* frambesia.
ye (ji) *pron. pers., arcaico* vosotros.
—*art. def., arcaico* (ði) el; la.
yea (jei) *adv.* sí. —*n.* voto
afirmativo; sí.
year (jɪr) *n.* año. —**year in, year
out,** año tras año.
yearbook ('jɪr·bʊk) *n.* anuario.
yearling ('jɪr·lɪŋ) *n.* añojo.
yearlong ('jɪr·lɔŋ) *adj.* de un año
entero; que dura un año.
yearly ('jɪr·li) *adj.* anual. —*adv.*
anualmente.
yearn (jʌrn) *v.i.* anhelar; desear.
—**yearning,** *n.* deseo; anhelo.
yeast (jist) *n.* levadura. —**yeasty,**
adj. espumoso.
yegg (jeg) *n.* ladrón, esp. uno que
quiebra las cajas fuertes.
yell (jel) *v.i. & t.* gritar. —*n.* grito.
yellow ('jɛl·o) *n.* **1,** (color) amarillo. **2,** (egg yolk) yema de huevo.
—*adj.* **1,** (color) amarillo. **2,** *colloq.*
(cowardly) cobarde. **3,** (sensational,
as a newspaper) sensacional;
escandaloso. —*v.t.* poner amarillo.
—*v.i.* ponerse amarillo; marchitarse.
yellowbelly ('jɛl·o,bɛl·i) *n., slang*
cobarde.
yellowbird ('jɛl·o,bʌrd) *n.* oropéndola.
yellow fever fiebre amarilla.
yellowish ('jɛl·o·ɪʃ) *adj.* amarillento.
yellow jack 1, = yellow fever. **2,**
(quarantine flag) bandera amarilla.
3, *ichthy.* jurel.

yellow jacket variedad de avispa.
yellowness ('jɛl·o·nəs) *n.* amarillez.
yellow streak cobardía; rasgo de cobarde.
yelp (jɛlp) *v.i.* gañir. —*n.* gañido.
yen (jɛn) *n.* 1, (monetary unit) yen. 2, *colloq.* (yearning) deseo; anhelo. —*v.i.*, *colloq.* [**yenned, yenning**] desear; anhelar.
yeoman ('jo·mən) *n.* [*pl.* **-men**] *naut.* 1, (storekeeper) pañolero. 2, (clerk) oficinista de a bordo.
yeomanly ('jo·mən·li) *adj.* valiente; firme; leal. —*adv.* valerosamente.
yeoman service servicio efectivo y leal. También, **yeoman's service.**
yes (jɛs) *adv.* & *n.* sí. —*v.t.* & *i.* decir sí (a). —**say yes,** dar el sí.
yesman ('jɛs,mæn) *n.*, *slang* [*pl.* **-men**] conformista; hombre del sí.
yester ('jɛs·tɛr) *adj.* pasado.
yesterday ('jɛs·tər·dei) *n.* & *adv.* ayer. —**the day before yesterday,** anteayer.
yestereve ('jɛs·tər·iːv) *adv.* & *n.*, *arcaico y poético* ayer por la tarde.
yestermorn ('jɛs·tər·morn) *adv.* & *n.*, *arcaico y poético* ayer por la mañana.
yesternight ('jɛs·tər·nait) *adv.* & *n.*, *arcaico y poético* anoche.
yesteryear ('jɛs·tər·jɪr) *adv.* & *n.*, *arcaico y poético* antaño.
yet (jɛt) *adv.* aún; todavía. —*conj.* sin embargo; no obstante. —**as yet,** todavía; hasta ahora. —**not yet,** todavía no.
yew (juː) *n.* tejo.
Yiddish ('jɪd·ɪʃ) *n.* & *adj.* yiddish.
yield ('jiːld) *v.t.* 1, (produce) producir; dar. 2, (give in return) rendir; redituar. 3, (concede; grant) ceder; conceder. 4, (admit) admitir; reconocer. —*v.i.* 1, (produce) producir. 2, (surrender) rendirse; ceder; entregarse. 3, (submit) someterse. 4, (give way) ceder. 5, (accede) acceder; consentir. —*n.* 1, (production) producción. 2, (return) rédito; rendimiento. 3, (revenue) renta.
yielding ('jil·dɪŋ) *adj.* complaciente; condescendiente.
yodel ('jo·dəl) *v.t.* & *i.* cantar modulando rápidamente la voz desde el tono natural al falsete, y viceversa. —*n.* canto hecho de esta manera.

yoga ('jo·gə) *n.* yoga. —**yogi** (-gi) *n.* yogi.
yogurt ('jo·gurt) *n.* yogurt.
yoicks (jɔiks) *interj.* grito que usan los cazadores para excitar los perros.
yoke (jok) *n.* 1, (bond; servitude) yugo. 2, (pair of draft animals) yunta. —*v.t.* enyugar; uncir.
yokel ('jo·kəl) *n.* rústico; patán; *Amer.* jíbaro.
yolk (jok) *n.* yema.
yon (jan) *adj.* & *adv.*, *arcaico* = **yonder.**
yonder ('jan·dər) *adj.* aquel. —*adv.* allí; allá.
yore (jorr) *n.* tiempos pasados; otro tiempo. —**of yore,** antaño; antiguamente.
you (juː) *pron.pers.sing.* & *pl.* tú; usted; vosotros; ustedes.
you'd (juːd) *contr. de* **you should, you would** o **you had.**
you'll (juːl) *contr. de* **you will** o **you shall.**
young (jʌŋ) *adj.* joven. —*n.pl.* cría. —**with young,** encinta; preñada. —**young people,** jóvenes; juventud.
younger ('jʌŋ·gər) *adj.* *comp.* menor; más joven. —**youngest,** *adj.superl.* menor.
youngling ('jʌŋ·lɪŋ) *n.* jovenzuelo; jovencito.
youngster ('jʌŋ·stər) *n.* jovencito; mozalbete; chiquito.
your (jur) *adj.pos.* tu; vuestro; su; de usted; de ustedes.
you're (jur) *contr. de* **you are.**
yours (jurz) *pron.pos.* tuyo; vuestro; suyo; el (la, lo, los, las) de usted o ustedes.
yourself (jur'sɛlf) *pron.pers.* tú; usted; tú mismo; usted mismo. —*pron.refl.* 1, *como complemento de verbo* te; se: *did you hurt yourself?,* ¿te lastimaste?; ¿se lastimó Vd.? 2, *como complemento de prep.* ti; sí; usted; ti mismo; sí mismo; usted mismo.
yourselves (jur'sɛlvz) *pron.pers.* vosotros; ustedes; vosotros mismos; ustedes mismos. —*pron.refl.* 1, *como complemento de verbo* os; se. 2, *como complemento de prep.* vosotros; sí; ustedes; vosotros mismos; sí mismos; ustedes mismos.
youth (juθ) *n.* 1, [*pl.* **youths** (juðz)] (young man) joven. 2, (quality of

being young) juventud; mocedad. —*n.pl.* los jóvenes; la juventud.

youthful ('juθ·fəl) *adj.* joven; juvenil. —**youthfulness**, *n.* juventud; lozanía.

you've (juːv) *contr. de* you have.

yowl (jaul) *v.i.* aullar; dar alaridos; gritar. —*n.* aullido; alarido; grito.

yoyo ('jo·jo) *n.* **1,** (toy) yo-yo. **2,** *slang* (eccentric) loco; chiflado.

ytterbium (ɪ'tʌr·bi·əm) *n.* iterbio.

yttrium ('ɪt·ri·əm) *n.* itrio.

yuan ('ju·ən) *n.* yuan.

yucca ('jʌk·ə) *n.* yuca.

Yugoslav ('ju·go‚slav) *adj.* & *n.* yugoslavo; yugoeslavo.

Yule (juːl) *n.* Navidad.

yuletide ('jul·taid) *n,* Navidades.

yummy ('jʌm·i) *adj.,* *colloq.* delicioso; apetitoso.

yuppie ('jʌp·i) *n., colloq.* joven ambicioso.

Z

Z, z (ziː) vigésima sexta letra del alfabeto inglés.

zany ('zei·ni) *n.* gracioso; bufón; payaso. —*adj.* gracioso; cómico.

zap (zæp) *v.t., slang* matar; destruir; derrotar.

zeal (ziːl) *n.* celo.

zealot ('zɛl·ət) *n.* fanático. —**zealotry,** *n.* fanatismo.

zealous ('zɛl·əs) *adj.* celoso.

zebra ('zi·brə) *n.* cebra.

zebu ('zi·bju) *n.* cebú.

zed (zɛd) *n.* zeta; zeda.

zenith ('zi·nɪθ) *n.* cenit; zenit.

zephyr ('zɛf·ər) *n.* céfiro.

zero ('zɪr·o) *n.* cero. —*adj.* nulo. —**zero hour,** hora cero; hora final.

zest (zɛst) *n.* **1,** (enjoyment) entusiasmo; gusto. **2,** (flavor) gusto; sabor.

zestful ('zɛst·fəl) *adj.* **1,** (joyful) entusiasta; alegre. **2,** (flavorful) sabroso; rico.

zeta ('zei·tə) *n.* zeta.

zigzag ('zɪg‚zæg) *n.* zigzag; zigzagueo. —*adj.* en zigzag; tortuoso. —*adv.* en zigzag; zigzagueando. —*v.i.* [-**zagged,** -**zagging**] zigzaguear. —*v.t.* mover en zigzag.

zilch (zɪltʃ) *n., slang* nada; cero.

zillion ('zɪl·jən) *adj.* & *n., colloq.* número incontable.

zinc (zɪŋk) *n.* zinc.

zinnia ('zɪn·i·ə) *n.* zinia.

Zion ('zai·ən) *n.* Sion. —**Zionism,** *n.* sionismo. —**Zionist,** *adj.* & *n.* sionista.

zip (zɪp) *n.* **1,** (whizzing sound) zumbido; silbido. **2,** *colloq.* (energy) energía; vigor. —*v.i.* [**zipped,** **zipping**] **1,** (make a whizzing sound) zumbar; silbar. **2,** *colloq.*

(move swiftly) pasar o moverse rápidamente; volar. —*v.t.* cerrar o abrir (un cierre relámpago).

ZIP Code (zɪp) código postal.

zipper ('zɪp·ər) *n.* cremallera; cierre relámpago.

zippy ('zɪp·i) *adj., colloq.* vivo; enérgico.

zircon ('zʌr·kan) *n.* circón.

zirconium (zər'ko·ni·əm) *n.* circonio.

zit (zɪt) *n., slang* grano; *(pl.)* acné.

zither ('zɪθ·ər) *n.* cítara.

zodiac ('zo·di·æk) *n.* zodíaco. —**zodiacal** (zo'dai·ə·kəl) *adj.* zodiacal.

zombi ('zam·bi) *n.* zombi.

zone (zoːn) *n.* zona. —*v.t.* dividir en zonas.

zoning law ordenanza municipal sobre nueva construcción en un barrio determinado.

zoo (zuː) *n.* parque zoológico.

zoölogy (zo'al·ə·dʒi) *n.* zoología. —**zoölogical** (‚zo·ə'ladʒ·ɪ·kəl) *adj.* zoológico. —**zoölogist,** *n.* zoólogo.

zoom (zuːm) *n.* **1,** (buzzing sound) zumbido. **2,** *aero.* empinadura. —*v.i.* **1,** (make a buzzing sound) zumbar. **2,** *aero.* empinarse. —*v.t.,* *aero.* hacer empinar.

Zoroastrian (‚zor·o'æs·tri·ən) *adj.* zoroástrico. —**Zoroastrianism,** *n.* zoroastrismo.

Zouave (zu'aːrv) *n.* zuavo.

zounds (zaundz) *interj., arcaico* ¡válgame Dios!

Zulu ('zu·lu) *adj.* & *n.* zulú.

zygote ('zai·got) *n.* cigoto.

zymurgy ('zai·mər·dʒi) *n.* cimurgia; zimurgia.

RESUMEN DEL INGLÉS

I. El alfabeto

El alfabeto inglés contiene 26 letras.

Letra	Nombre (en pronunciación fonética)
A	ei
B	biː
C	siː
D	diː
E	iː
F	ɛf
G	dʒiː
H	eitʃ
I	ai
J	dʒei
K	kei
L	ɛl
M	ɛm
N	ɛn
O	oː
P	piː
Q	kjuː
R	ar
S	ɛs
T	tiː
U	juː
V	viː
W	'dʌ·bəl·juː
X	ɛks
Y	wai
Z	ziː

II. La pronunciación del inglés

VOCALES

Símbolo fonético	Sonido aproximado en el español	Ejemplos ortográficos
a	como la *a* de *calma*, pero más abierta	**father** ('fa·ðər) **slot** (slat)
æ	como la *a* de *gato*, pero mucho más cerrada	**cat** (kæt)
e	como la *e* de *seda;* en nuestro sistema se usa únicamente en sílaba inacentuada	**Friday** ('frai·de)
ɛ	como la *e* de *bello;* es más abierta que la (e) precedente	**met** (mɛt)

1266

Símbolo fonético	Sonido aproximado en el español	Ejemplos ortográficos
eɪr	Como la *er* de *merlo*, pero más larga y abierta	**dare** (deɪr) **lair** (leɪr)
i	como la *i* de *vino*; en sílaba acentuada es más larga y suena como diptongo (ij)	**sleep** (slip) **lobby** ('lab·i)
ɪ	como la *i* de *mitad*, pero más abierta y relajada	**skin** (skɪn)
ɪr	como la *ir* de *mirlo*, pero más larga y abierta	**fear** (fɪr)
ɔ	como la *o* de *bola*	**song** (sɔŋ)
o	como la *o* de *bola*, pero más cerrada	**lowly** ('lo·li)
oɪ	como la (o) precedente, pero más larga; suena a menudo como diptongo (oʊ)	**road** (roɪd)
or	como la *or* de *sordo*, pero más larga y abierta	**floor** (flor) **sort** (sort)
u	como la *u* de *luna*	**spook** (spuk)
ʊ	como la *u* de *bulto*, pero más abierta y relajada	**pull** (pʊl)
ʊr	como la *ur* de *surco*, pero más larga y abierta	**sure** (ʃʊr)
ʌ	una vocal relajada intermedia entre la *o* de *corro* y la *a* de *carro*	**but** (bʌt)
ʌr	como la (ʌ) precedente, seguida de (r); úsase únicamente en sílaba acentuada; en muchas regiones no suena la (r), sin embargo la vocal tiene siempre colorido de (r)	**burn** (bʌrn) **her** (hʌr)
ə	una vocal más relajada que la (ʌ); úsase únicamente en sílaba inacentuada	**comma** ('kam·ə) **label** ('lei·bəl) **censor** ('sɛn·sər) **focus** ('fo·kəs)

DIPTONGOS

ai	como la *ai* de *baile*, pero con (a) más abierta	**pine** (pain) **buy** (bai)
au	como la *au* de *causa*	**house** (haus) **owl** (aul)
ei	como la *ei* de *veinte*	**fate** (feit)
ɔi	como la *oy* de *doy*	**boil** (bɔil)
ju	como la *iu* de *viuda*	**beauty** ('bju·ti)
jʊ	como la (ju) precedente, pero con vocal más abierta	**bureau** ('bjʊr·o)

CONSONANTES

Símbolo fonético	*Sonido aproximado en el español*	*Ejemplos ortográficos*
b	como la *b* de *burro* o la *v* de *vaya*	**bin** (bɪn)
d	como la *d* de *día*, pero con la punta de la lengua colocada en el alvéolo superior y no, como en el español, detrás de los dientes superiores	**day** (dei)
f	como la *f* de *faja*	**fish** (fɪʃ)
g	como la *g* de *gala*	**go** (goɹ)
h	como la *j* de *conejo*, con articulación relajada	**hat** (hæt)
hw	como la *ju* de *juez*, con articulación relajada de la *j*	**where** (hweɹr)
j	como la *y* de *yerno* o la *i* de los diptongos *ia, ie, io, iu* (*viaje, bien, biombo, ciudad*)	**yet** (jɛt) **yard** (jard) **yoke** (jok) **beauty** ('bju·ti)
k	como la *c* de *cola* o la *qu* de *quedo*	**keep** (kip) **quay** (kiɹ)
kw	como la *cu* de *cuando*	**quick** (kwɪk)
ks	como la *x* de *sexto*	**six** (sɪks)
l	como la *l* de *lazo*	**late** (leit)
m	como la *m* de *masa*	**man** (mæn)
n	como la *n* de *negro*	**nod** (naɹd)
p	como la *p* de *pulso*	**pen** (pɛn)
r	un sonido muy distinto de la *r* del español; se pronuncia con la punta de la lengua elevada hacia el paladar y doblada hacia atrás. Es más prolongada que la *r* del español. En muchas regiones apenas se pronuncia ante consonante o al final de palabra.	**run** (rʌn) **carrot** ('kær·ət) **part** (part) *o* (paɹt) **upper** ('ʌp·ər) *o* ('ʌp·ə)
s	como la *s* de *sala*	**sing** (sɪŋ) **cent** (sɛnt) **ferocity** (fə'ra·sə·ti)
t	como la *t* de *tela*, pero con la punta de la lengua colocada en el alvéolo superior y no, como en el español, detrás de los dientes superiores	**talk** (tɔk) **bitter** ('bɪt·ər) **put** (pʊt)

Símbolo fonético	*Sonido aproximado en el español*	*Ejemplos ortográficos*
v	como la *b* de *deber* o la *v* de *uva*, pero con el labio inferior colocado entre los dientes superiores e inferiores y no, como en el español, con los dos labios juntos	**van** (væn) **give** (gɪv) **river** ('rɪv·ər)
w	como la *u* de los diptongos *ua, ue, ui, uo (cuando, bueno, cuidado, cuota)*	**want** (want) **wet** (wɛt) **win** (wɪn) **wove** (woːv)
z	como la pronunciación variante de la *s* ante consonante sonora *(desde, mismo)*	**zone** (zoːn) **rose** (roːz)
θ	como la *z* o la *c* ante *e* o *i* del ceceo *(zona, cero, cita)*	**thin** (θɪn)
ð	como la *d* entre vocales o al final de palabra *(cada, mitad)*	**then** (ðɛn)
ʃ	como la *ch* de *charla*, pero con omisión del elemento explosivo (t)	**shall** (ʃæl) **wish** (wɪʃ)
tʃ	como la *ch* de *charco*	**chin** (tʃɪn) **much** (mʌtʃ)
ʒ	como la pronunciación variante en ciertas regiones (Argentina, Uruguay, etc.) de la *y* de *yo* o la *ll* de *calle*	**azure** ('æʒ·ər)
dʒ	como la *y* de *yo* o la *ll* de *llama*, con articulación enfática	**joke** (dʒok)
ŋ	como la *n* ante *c* o *g (cinco, mango)*	**sing** (sɪŋ) **rank** (ræŋk) **finger** ('fɪŋ·gər)
N	indica nasalización de la vocal precedente	**denouement** (ˌde·nu'maN)

OTROS SÍMBOLOS

ː	indica vocal larga	**rod** (raːd) **steal** (stiːl) **low** (loː) **blue** (bluː)
'	acento principal ⎫ Se colocan al principio	**mother** ('mʌð·ər)
ˌ	acento secundario ⎬ de la sílaba acentuada	**delegation** (ˌdɛl·ə'gei·ʃən)
·	indica la separación de sílabas donde no haya señal de acento principal o secundario, o al final de línea	**education** (ˌɛd·ju'kei·ʃən)

III. Puntuación

La puntuación en el inglés tiene ciertos usos que difieren de los del español:

1. Los puntos de interrogación y de admiración nunca se usan en pareja. Cada oración interrogativa o admirativa del inglés lleva un solo punto al final:

Where are you going?

What an idea!

2. Las comillas (" ") se usan para denotar toda cita directa. Se repiten las comillas cuando viene interrumpida una cita al interior de una oración:

"What are you doing here," he asked, "at this time of night?"

En los diálogos se usan las comillas para indicar cambio de interlocutor:

"Well, there was a man there named Martin. . . ."

"Oh. So that's it. I suppose he didn't tell you anything?"

"No. He asked questions."

"What sort of questions?"

IV. Uso de las mayúsculas

El inglés se sirve más de las mayúsculas que el español. Se escriben generalmente con mayúscula los nombres y adjetivos que denotan nacionalidad, religión, idioma, etc., los días de la semana, los meses del año y el pronombre *I:* a Spaniard, the French nation, the English language, a Methodist, Tuesday, June, you and I.

V. Reglas para la división ortográfica de las sílabas en el inglés

Regla fundamental

En cuanto sea posible, la división ortográfica debe seguir la pronunciación, es decir, se dejan abiertas las sílabas largas (las que contienen una vocal larga o un diptongo) y las sílabas inacentuadas, mientras que se cierran las sílabas cortas (las que contienen una vocal corta seguida de consonante simple).

flo·rist (la primera sílaba es larga)
pero **for·eign** (la primera sílaba es corta)

Reglas específicas

1. ciertos sufijos nunca se dividen:

-tion, -sion, -cious, etc.

2. En los nombres que denotan un agente o actor, el sufijo **-er** debe separarse de la consonante que precede, mientras que el sufijo **-or** va incluido en la misma sílaba con la consonante:

ad·vis·er
pero **ad·vi·sor**

3. El sufijo **-ed** no forma una sílaba aparte cuando es muda la **e**. Cuando la **e** se pronuncia, el sufijo forma una sílaba:

> **ad·vised** (la **e** es muda)
> **wast·ed** (la **e** se pronuncia)

4. Cuando la consonante final de una palabra viene doblada por añadidura de una terminación que empieza con una vocal, las sílabas se dividen entre estas dos consonantes:

> **pad·ded**
> **sit·ter**

Si la terminación se añade a una palabra que ya termina en una consonante doble, las dos consonantes no se dividen:

> **add·er**
> **putt·er**

En los demás casos se dividen generalmente las consonantes dobles al interior de una palabra:

> **lad·der**
> **lit·tle**

VI. Los sustantivos

A. El género
Por lo general el inglés tiene unicamente el *género natural;* el género gramatical no existe. Son masculinos los nombres de varón o de animal macho, femeninos los nombres de mujer o de animal hembra y neutros los nombres de cosas inanimadas.

the man, the boy, Peter, the horse son masculinos.
the woman, the girl, Mary, the mare son femeninos.
the book, the country, the train, the house son neutros.

Ciertos nombres de cosas inanimadas suelen considerarse femeninos o masculinos sin dejar de ser neutros por lo general:

The ship has lost her (*o* its) mast.
The enemy is being attacked on his (*o* its) flank.

B. Plural de los sustantivos
1. Generalmente se forma el plural añadiendo s al singular. La s tiene el sonido sordo (s̀) cuando sigue una consonante sorda; tiene el sonido sonoro (z) cuando sigue una consonante sonora o un sonido vocálico:

s sorda		
laugh (læf), laughs (læfs)	risa, risas
hat (hæt), hats (hæts)	sombrero, sombreros
cup (kʌp), cups (kʌps)	taza, tazas
cake (keik), cakes (keiks)	bizcocho, bizcochos

s sonora	tub (tʌb), tubs (tʌbz)	cuba, cubas
	card (kard), cards (kardz)	naipe, naipes
	leg (lɛg), legs (lɛgz)	pierna, piernas
	dove (dʌv), doves (dʌvz)	paloma, palomas
	reel (riːl), reels (riːlz)	bobina, bobinas
s sonora	toe (toːr), toes (toːrz)	dedo, dedos
	sofa ('soˑfə), sofas ('soˑfəz)	sofá, sofás
	tie (tai), ties (taiz)	corbata, corbatas
	toy (toi), toys (toiz)	juguete, juguetes
	knee (niː), knees (niːz)	rodilla, rodillas

2. Añaden **es** los nombres terminados en sibilantes (s, z, ʃ, ʒ, tʃ, dʒ). Si la grafía termina en **e** muda, se añade **s**. De cualquier modo, la terminación **es** en estos casos se pronuncia (ɪz).

dress (drɛs), dresses ('drɛsˑɪz)	vestido, vestidos
buzz (bʌz), buzzes ('bʌzˑɪz)	zumbido, zumbidos
fish (fɪʃ), fishes ('fɪʃˑɪz)	pez, peces
garage (gəˈraːʒ), garages (gəˈraːʒˑɪz)	garage, garages
church (tʃʌrtʃ), churches ('tʃʌrˑtʃɪz)	iglesia, iglesias
judge (dʒʌdʒ), judges ('dʒʌdʒˑɪz)	juez, jueces

3. *Formas irregulares*

a. Muchos sustantivos que terminan en **f** o **fe** (f) forman el plural cambiando esta **f** o **fe** en **ve** (v) y añadiendo **s** (z):

knife (naif), knives (naivz)	cuchillo, cuchillos
leaf (lif), leaves (liːvz)	hoja, hojas

Ciertos nombres de esta clase forman el plural de manera regular así como irregular:

hoof (hʊf), hoofs (hʊfs) *o*	pata, patas
hooves (huːvz)	

b. Los sustantivos que terminan en **-y** precedida de consonante cambian la **-y** en **-i** cuando añaden **-es:**

lady ('leiˑdi), ladies ('leiˑdiz)	señora, señoras
lily ('lɪlˑi), lilies ('lɪlˑiz)	lirio, lirios

Ciertos sustantivos que terminan en **-y** precedida de vocal forman el plural cambiando la **-y** en **-i** y añadiendo **-es;** algunos de ellos tienen igualmente la forma regular:

money ('mʌnˑi), monies *o*	dinero, fondos
moneys ('mʌnˑiz)	

c. Algunos sustantivos forman el plural de manera enteramente irregular:

man (mæn), men (mɛn)	hombre, hombres
woman ('wʊm·ən), women ('wɪm·ən)	mujer, mujeres
child (tʃaild), children ('tʃɪl·drən)	niño, niños
foot (fʊt), feet (fit)	pie, pies
tooth (tuθ), teeth (tiθ)	diente, dientes
ox (aks), oxen ('ak·sən)	buey, bueyes
mouse (maus), mice (mais)	ratón, ratones

VII. *Los adjetivos*

A. Los adjetivos del inglés no tienen concordancia con los sustantivos. Son invariables en cuanto a género y número. Normalmente el adjetivo precede al sustantivo. En ciertos casos, puede seguir al sustantivo.

1. En la poesía:

A knight bold and true, un caballero valiente y fiel.

2. En ciertos modismos tradicionales:

A knight-errant, un caballero andante
A court-martial, un consejo de guerra
An heir presumptive, un heredero presuntivo

3. En los casos en que el adjetivo va seguido de una frase calificativa:

A sight wonderful to behold, una vista maravillosa para contemplar.
A man just in all his ways, un hombre completamente justo.

B. *Comparación de los adjetivos*

La comparación normal de los adjetivos consiste en añadir para el comparativo el sufijo **-er** (o **-r** cuando terminan en **-e** muda) y para el superlativo el sufijo **-est** (o **-st** cuando terminan en **-e** muda). Estas normas se aplican a los adjetivos de las clases siguientes:

1. Adjetivos monosílabos:

quick, rápido *quicker,* más rápido *quickest,* el más rápido
pure, puro *purer,* más puro *purest,* el más puro

2. Adjetivos bisílabos acentuados en la última sílaba:

forlorn, triste *forlorner,* más triste *forlornest,* el más triste
severe, severo *severer,* más severo *severest,* el más severo

3. Algunos adjetivos bisílabos que terminan en sílaba inacentuada, a condición que no resulten difíciles de pronunciar cuando se les añaden los sufijos **-er** y **-est**:

handsome, hermoso *handsomer,* más hermoso *handsomest,* el más hermoso
little, pequeño *littler,* más pequeño *littlest,* el más pequeño
yellow, amarillo *yellower,* más amarillo *yellowest,* el más amarillo

Los demás adjetivos bisílabos y todos los de más de dos sílabas forman el comparativo y el superlativo anteponiendo los adverbios **more** y **most**:

beautiful, bello *more beautiful,* más bello *most beautiful,* el más bello
prudent, prudente *more prudent,* más prudente *most prudent,* el más
prudente

Además, cualquier adjetivo, aunque admita la añadidura de los sufijos
-er y **-est,** puede formar el comparativo y el superlativo anteponiéndose
los adverbios **more** y **most:**

brave valiente *braver* o *more brave,* más valiente *bravest* o *most
brave,* el más valiente

Los adjetivos que terminan en consonante simple precedida de vocal
corta acentuada doblan la consonante final al añadir **-er** o **-est:**

fat, gordo *fatter,* más gordo *fattest,* el más gordo

Los adjetivos que terminan en **-y** precedida de consonante cambian la
-y en **-i** al añadir **-er** o **-est:**

happy, feliz *happier,* más feliz *happiest,* el más feliz

El superlativo absoluto de los adjetivos se forma anteponiendo **very** o
most:

a very (o *most*) *beautiful girl,* una muchacha muy linda (o lindísima)

El comparativo de igualdad se expresa con el adverbio **as** (a veces **so,**
especialmente en las oraciones negativas):

He is as tall as John, Él es tan alto como Juan.
We are not so rich as they, No somos tan ricos como ellos.

El comparativo y el superlativo de inferioridad se expresan con los
adverbios **less** o **least:**

He is less intelligent than Henry, Él es menos inteligente que Enrique.
She is the least attractive girl in the group, Ella es la muchacha menos
atrayente del grupo.

Comparativos y superlativos irregulares:

good, bueno	*better,* mejor	*best,* el mejor
well, bien	*better,* mejor	*best,* el mejor

bad } *ill* } malo	*worse,* peor	*worst,* el peor	

little { pequeño poco	*lesser,* menor *less,* menos	*least* { el menor el menos		

much, mucho *many,* muchos	*more,* más	*most* { el más los más	

far, lejano	*farther* *further* } más lejano

farthest
furthest } el más lejano

VIII. Los adverbios

A. *Formación de los adverbios*

Casi todos los adjetivos forman adverbios añadiendo el sufijo **-ly**:

strong, fuerte   *strongly,* fuertemente
graceful, gracioso   *gracefully,* graciosamente

En los casos siguientes se efectúan varios cambios en la forma:

1. Los adjetivos terminados en **-ble** forman adverbios con la terminacion **-bly**:

passable, pasable   *passably,* pasablemente
noble, noble   *nobly,* noblemente
sensible, sensible   *sensibly,* sensiblemente

2. Los adjetivos terminados en **-y** cambian la **-y** en **-i**:

lazy, perezoso   *lazily,* perezosamente

Hay unas excepciones, especialmente en los adjetivos monosílabos:

sly, furtivo   *slyly,* furtivamente
dry, seco   *drily* o *dryly,* secamente

3. Los adjetivos terminados en **-ic** añaden **-ally**:

poetic, poético   *poetically,* poéticamente

Hay unas excepciones:

public, público   *publicly,* públicamente

B. *Comparación de los adverbios*

1. Los adverbios monosílabos forman el comparativo y el superlativo añadiendo los sufijos **-er** o **-est**:

fast, rápidamente *faster,* más rápidamente *fastest,* lo más rápidamente
close, cerca *closer,* más cerca *closest,* lo más cerca

2. Los demás forman el comparativo y el superlativo anteponiendo los adverbios **more** o **most**:

bravely, valientemente *more bravely,* más valientemente *most bravely,* lo más valientemente
probably, probablemente *more probably,* más probablemente *most probably,* lo mas probablemente

3. El superlativo absoluto de los adverbios se forma anteponiendo **very** o **most**:

very (o *most*) *quickly,* muy rápidamente; rapidísimamente

4. El comparativo de igualdad y el comparativo y el superlativo de inferioridad de los adverbios siguen las mismas normas que rigen los adjetivos:

This room is as richly decorated as that one, Esta sala es tan ricamente adornada como aquélla.

This box is not so completely filled as yours, Esta caja no está tan completamente llena como la de Vd.

He arrived less promptly than I, Él llegó menos pronto que yo.

She sings the least agreeably of the whole group, Ella canta lo menos agradablemente de todo el grupo.

5. Comparativos y superlativos irregulares:

well, bien   *better,* mejor   *best,* lo mejor

$\left.\begin{array}{l} badly \\ ill \end{array}\right\}$ mal   *worse,* peor   *worst,* lo peor

little, poco   *less,* menos   *least,* lo menos

much, mucho   *more,* más   *most,* lo más

far, lejos $\left.\begin{array}{l} farther \\ further \end{array}\right\}$ más lejos $\left.\begin{array}{l} farthest \\ furthest \end{array}\right\}$ lo más lejos

IX. Los verbos

A. Verbos débiles

Son débiles o regulares los verbos que forman el pretérito y el participio pasivo añadiendo el sufijo **-ed** al infinitivo, es decir, la forma primitiva del verbo. Los infinitivos que terminan en **e** muda añaden **-d**.

La terminación **-ed** o **-d** se pronuncia (t) cuando el infinitivo termina en una consonante sorda (con excepción de **t**):

Infinitivo	Pretérito y participio pasivo	
look	looked	
laugh	laughed	
romp	romped	
miss	missed	con **-ed**
lash	lashed	
watch	watched	
chafe	chafed	
like	liked	con **-d**
hope	hoped	

La terminación **-ed** o **-d** se pronuncia (d) cuando el infinitivo termina en una consonante sonora (con excepción de **d**):

Infinitivo	Pretérito y participio pasivo	
rub	rubbed	
rig	rigged	
foil	foiled	
calm	calmed	
turn	turned	con **-ed**
roar	roared	
fizz	fizzed	
clang	clanged	

Infinitivo	Pretérito y participio pasivo
jibe	jibed
pile	piled
lure	lured
rhyme	rhymed
dine	dined } con -d
raze	razed
dive	dived
garage	garaged
edge	edged

La terminación **-ed** se pronuncia (ɪd) cuando el infinitivo termina en **d** o **t** o en una de éstas seguida de **e** muda:

Infinitivo	Pretérito y participio pasivo
land	landed } con -ed
suit	suited
chide	chided } con -d
mate	mated

La terminación **-ed** se pronuncia (d) cuando el infinitivo termina en vocal o diptongo:

Infinitivo	Pretérito y participio pasivo
row	rowed
lie	lied
coo	cooed
vow	vowed
relay	relayed
carry	carried

Los verbos que terminan en consonante simple precedida de una vocal corta acentuada doblan la consonante cuando añaden **-ed**:

Infinitivo	Pretérito y participio pasivo
pat	patted
sup	supped
jig	jigged
rub	rubbed
pad	padded
jam	jammed
pin	pinned
occur	occurred
rebel	rebelled

Los verbos que terminan en **-y** precedida de consonante cambian la **-y** en **-i** cuando añaden **-ed**:

Infinitivo	Pretérito y participio pasivo
marry	married
tidy	tidied
try	tried
qualify	qualified

Ciertos verbos débiles forman el pretérito y el participio pasivo añadiendo el sufijo **-t**. Algunos de ellos tienen además la forma regular en **-d** o **-ed**:

Infinitivo	Pretérito y participio pasivo
bend	bent
bless	blest *o* blessed
build	built
burn	burnt *o* burned
dwell	dwelt *o* dwelled
gild	gilt *o* gilded
gird	girt *o* girded
lean	leant *o* leaned
leap	leapt *o* leaped
learn	learnt *o* learned
rend	rent
send	sent
smell	smelt *o* smelled
speed	sped *o* speeded
spell	spelt *o* spelled
spend	spent
spill	spilt *o* spilled

Ciertos verbos débiles forman el participio pasivo con el sufijo **-n** o **-en**. Algunos de ellos tienen además la forma regular en **-d** o **-ed**:

Infinitivo	Participio pasivo
hew	hewn *o* hewed
mow	mown *o* mowed
prove	proven *o* proved
saw	sawn *o* sawed
show	shown *o* showed
sow	sown *o* sowed
strew	strewn *o* strewed

B. *Verbos fuertes*

Son fuertes los verbos que cambian la vocal de la raíz para formar el pretérito y el participio pasivo. Éste puede tener un sufijo **-en,** o **-n,** o puede carecer de sufijo:

Infinitivo	Pretérito	Participio pasivo
abide	abode	abode
arise	arose	arisen
awake	awoke *o* awaked	awaken *o* awaked
bear	bore	borne *o* born
become	became	become
befall	befell	befallen
beget	begat	begot *o* begotten
begin	began	begun
bid	bade	bidden
bide	bode *o* bided	bode *o* bided
bite	bit	bitten
blow	blew	blown
break	broke	broken
choose	chose	chosen
cleave	cleft *o* cleaved *o* clove	cleft *o* cleaved *o* cloven

Infinitivo	*Pretérito*	*Participio pasivo*
cling	clung	clung
come	came	come
crow	crew	crowed
dare	dared *o* durst	dared
dig	dug	dug
dive	dove *o* dived	dove *o* dived
draw	drew	drawn
drink	drank	drunk
drive	drove	driven
eat	ate	eaten
fall	fell	fallen
fling	flung	flung
fly	flew	flown
forbid	forbade *o* forbid	forbidden
forget	forgot	forgotten
forgive	forgave	forgiven
forsake	forsook	forsaken
freeze	froze	frozen
get	got	got *o* gotten
give	gave	given
grow	grew	grown
hang	hung *o* hanged	hung *o* hanged
heave	hove *o* heaved	hove *o* heaved
hide	hid	hidden
know	knew	known
lie	lay	lain
mistake	mistook	mistaken
ride	rode	ridden
ring	rang	rung
rise	rose	risen
run	ran	run
see	saw	seen
shake	shook	shaken
shine	shone *o* shined	shone *o* shined
shrink	shrank	shrunk
sing	sang	sung
sink	sank	sunk
slay	slew	slain
sling	slung	slung
slink	slinked *o* slunk	slinked *o* slunk
smite	smote	smitten
speak	spoke	spoken
spin	spun	spun
spring	sprang	sprung
stave	stove *o* staved	stove *o* staved
steal	stole	stolen
stick	stuck	stuck
sting	stung	stung
stink	stank *o* stunk	stunk
stride	strode	stridden
strike	struck	struck *o* stricken
string	strung	strung

Infinitivo	*Pretérito*	*Participio pasivo*
strive	strove *o* strived	striven *o* strived
swear	swore	sworn
swim	swam	swum
swing	swung	swung
take	took	taken
tear	tore	torn
thrive	throve *o* thrived	thriven *o* thrived
throw	threw	thrown
tread	trod *o* treaded	trod *o* trodden *o* treaded
wake	woke *o* waked	waked
wear	wore	worn
weave	wove *o* weaved	woven *o* weaved
win	won	won
write	wrote	written

C. *Verbos mixtos*

Son mixtos los verbos que cambian la vocal de la raíz para formar el pretérito y el participio pasivo, pero que añaden el sufijo **-d** o **-t**. Además son generalmente idénticos el pretérito y el participio pasivo:

Infinitivo	*Pretérito y participio pasivo*
behold	beheld
bereave	bereft *o* bereaved
beseech	besought *o* beseeched
bind	bound
bleed	bled
breed	bred
bring	brought
buy	bought
catch	caught
clothe	clad *o* clothed
creep	crept
deal	dealt
dream	dreamt *o* dreamed
feed	fed
feel	felt
fight	fought
find	found
flee	fled
grind	ground
hear	heard
hold	held
keep	kept
kneel	knelt *o* kneeled
lead	led
leave	left
lend	lent
light	lit *o* lighted
lose	lost
mean	meant
meet	met

Infinitivo	Pretérito y participio pasivo
say	said
seek	sought
sell	sold
shoe	shod
shoot	shot
sit	sat
sleep	slept
slide	slid
speed	sped
spit	spat o spit
stand	stood
sweep	swept
teach	taught
tell	told
think	thought
weep	wept
wind	wound

D. Ciertos verbos que terminan en **-d** o **-t** son invariables en el pretérito y el participio pasivo:

Infinitivo	Pretérito y participio pasivo
bet	bet
bid	bid
burst	burst
cast	cast
cost	cost
cut	cut
fit *(v.i.)*	fit
put	put
quit	quit o quitted
set	set
slit	slit
spread	spread
thrust	thrust
wet	wet o wetted

E. *Verbos irregulares*

Son irregulares los verbos que tienen pretéritos y participios pasivos que no se conforman con ninguna de las clases ya mencionadas:

Infinitivo	Pretérito	Participio pasivo
be	was, were	been
do	did	done
go	went	gone
have	had	had
make	made	made

N.B.: Formas irregulares del presente de indicativo: **be**: I *am*; he, she, it *is*; you, we, they *are*; **do**: he, she, it *does*; **go**: he, she, it *goes*; **have**: he, she, it *has*.

F. *Verbos defectivos*

Son defectivos los verbos que carecen de participio pasivo o de pretérito, o de los dos:

Infinitivo	Pretérito	Participio pasivo
can	could	————
may	might	————
must	————	————
ought	————	————
shall	should	————
will	would	————

G. *El presente de indicativo*

1. Con excepción del verbo **be**, el presente de indicativo de los verbos ingleses es idéntico al infinitivo en todas las personas menos la tercera persona del singular. Ésta se forma normalmente con el sufijo **-es** o **-s**. Se añade **-es** cuando el infinitivo termina en un sonido sibilante (s), (z), (ʃ), (ʒ), (tʃ), (dʒ):

Infinitivo	Tercera persona del singular
dress	dresses
race	races
fizz	fizzes
doze	dozes
push	pushes
garage	garages
watch	watches
judge	judges

En todos los demás casos se añade **-s**.

2. La terminación **-es** siempre se pronuncia (ız). La terminación **-s** es sorda (s) cuando va precedida de una consonante sorda (p, t, k, f, θ); es sonora (z) cuando va precedida de una consonante sonora (b, d, g, v, ð, r, l, m, n, ŋ), una vocal o un diptongo (a, ɛ, i, ɔ, o, u, ai, au, ɔi, etc.).

3. Los verbos que terminan en **-y** precedida de consonante cambian la **-y** en **-i** cuando añaden **-es**:

Infinitivo	Tercera persona del singular
marry	marries
tidy	tidies
try	tries
qualify	qualifies

4. Formas irregulares de la tercera persona del singular:

Infinitivo	Tercera persona del singular
do	does (dʌz)
go	goes (goːz)
have	has (hæz)
say	says (sɛz)

5. El presente de indicativo del verbo **be** es del todo irregular:

> I **am**
> you **are** (*sing. o pl.*)
> he, she *o* it **is**
> we **are**
> they **are**

H. *Formación del gerundio*

Todos los verbos del inglés forman el gerundio añadiendo el sufijo **-ing** al infinitivo.

Los verbos que terminan en consonante simple precedida de una vocal corta acentuada doblan la consonante cuando añaden **-ing**:

Infinitivo	*Gerundio*
dig	digging
put	putting
knit	knitting
begin	beginning
forget	forgetting
rebel	rebelling

Los verbos que terminan en **e** muda generalmente omiten la e cuando añaden **-ing**:

Infinitivo	*Gerundio*
bake	baking
ride	riding
note	noting

Ciertos verbos conservan la **e**:

dye	dyeing
shoe	shoeing
singe	singeing
canoe	canoeing

PREFIJOS INGLESES

	Equivalentes en español	Significados y usos	Ejemplos
a-	—	**1,** *contracción preposicional denotando* en; a; hacia:	*abed,* en cama; *aside,* al lado; *astern,* a popa
		2, *contr. de* **of**:	*akin,* afín
		3, *denota* intensidad:	*arouse,* animar
		4, *arcaico, indica* acción progresiva:	*agoing,* listo para marchar
		5, *indica* parte en la acción:	*awake,* despertar
		6, *var. de* **ab**-:	*avert,* apartar
		7, *var. de* **ad**-:	*ascribe,* adscribir
	a-	**8,** negación; carencia:	*acatholic,* acatólico; *amoral,* amoral
ab-	ab-	**1,** separación; cese; alejamiento:	*abduction,* abducción
			abjure, abjurar
		Se convierte en **a-** *ante* m, p, v:	*amentia,* demencia
		Frecuentemente en **abs-** *ante* c, t:	*abstract,* abstracto
		2, origen:	*aborigenes,* aborígenes
abs-	abs-	*Var. de* **ab-** *ante* c, t:	*abstract,* abstracto
ac-	—	*Var. de* **ad-** *ante* c, q, y a veces k:	*accept,* aceptar; *acquit,* absolver; *acknowledge,* reconocer
acro-	acro-	altura; cima; borde:	*acropolis,* acrópolis; *acrobatics,* acrobacia
ad-	ad-	adición; dirección; tendencia:	*adhere,* adherirse
aero-; aer-; aeri-	aero-; aer-; aeri-	*en, del o relacionado con* el aire:	*aeronaut,* aeronauta; *aeriform,* aeriforme
af-	—	*Var. de* **ad-** *ante* f:	*affirm,* afirmar
ag-	—	*Var. de* **ad-** *ante* g:	*aggregate,* agregado

	Equivalentes en español	Significados y usos	Ejemplos
al-	—	*Var. de* **ad-** *ante* l:	*alliteration,* aliteración
allo-	alo-	variación; alejamiento; diferencia:	*allopathy,* alopatía
alto-; alti-	alto-; alti-	alto; altura:	*alto-cumulus,* alto-cúmulo; *altimeter,* altímetro
ambi-	ambi-	1, ambos; por ambos lados: 2, alrededor:	*ambidextrous,* ambidiestro *ambient,* ambiente
amphi-	anfi-	1, ambos; doble: 2, alrededor de: 3, de ambas especies:	*amphibious,* anfibio *amphitheater,* anfiteatro *amphibology,* anfibología
an-	an-	1, negación; carencia; *var. de* **a-** *ante* vocal:	*anarchy,* anarquía; *anaphrodisiac,* anafrodisíaco
	—	2, *var. de* **ad-** *ante* n:	*annul,* anular
	an-.	3, *var. de* **ana-** *ante* vocal:	*anode,* ánodo
ana-	ana-	1, en alto; hacia arriba: 2, contra; hacia atrás: 3, de nuevo: 4, del todo; completo: 5, conforme; similar:	*anathema,* anatema *anagram,* anagrama *Anabaptist,* anabaptista *analysis,* análisis *analogy,* analogía
Anglo-	anglo-	inglés; de o referente a Inglaterra:	*Anglo-American,* angloamericano; *Anglophobe,* anglófobo
ant-	—	*Var. de* **anti-** *ante* vocal:	*antacid,* antiácido
ante-	ante-	antes *(en tiempo o en espacio)*:	*antediluvian,* antediluviano; *antechamber,* antecámara

	Equivalentes en español	Significados y usos	Ejemplos
antho	anto-	flor:	*anthology*, antología
anthropo-	antropo-	hombre:	*anthropology*, antropología
anti-	anti-	**1,** contra:	*antislavery*, antiesclavitud
		2, falso; rival:	*antipope*, antipapa
		3, opuesto; contrario:	*antigrammatical*, antigramatical; *antipode*, antípoda
		4, *med.* curativo; preventivo:	*antidote*, antídoto
ap-	—	**1,** *Var. de* **ad-** *ante* p:	*approve*, aprobar
		2, *Var. de* **apo-** *ante vocal o* h:	*aphelion*, afelio
apo-	apo-	**1,** separado de:	*apogee*, apogeo
		2, de:	*aponeurosis*, aponeurosis
		3, desde:	*apothem*, apotema
aqua-; **aque-**	acua-; acue-; agua-	agua; de o perteneciente al agua:	*aquatint*, acuatinta; *aqueduct*, acueducto; *aquamarine*, aguamarina
ar-	ar-	*Var. de* **ad-** *ante* r:	*arrest*, arrestar
arch(a)eo-	arqueo-	antigüedad:	*arch(a)eology*, arqueología
arch-; **arche-;** **archi-**	archi-; arqui-; arz-; arque-	preeminencia; prioridad:	*archduke*, archiduque; *architect*, arquitecto; *archbishop*, arzobispo; *archetype*, arquetipo
as-	—	*Var. de* **ad-** *ante* s:	*associate*, asociar
astro-	astro-	estrella:	*astrology*, astrología; *astronomy*, astronomía
at-	—	*Var. de* **ad-** *ante* t:	*attract*, atraer

	Equivalentes en español	Significados y usos	Ejemplos
audio-; **audi-**	audio-; audi-	oír; oído:	*audio-visual*, audiovisual; *audiphone*, audífono
auto-; **aut-**	auto-; aut-	mismo; propio;	*automobile*, automóvil; *autarchy*, autarquía
avi-	avi-	ave; pájaro:	*aviculture*, avicultura
batho-; **bathy-**	bato-; bati-	profundo; profundidad:	*bathometer*, batómetro; *bathyscaphe*, batiscafo
be-	—	**1,** *hállase en muchas palabras derivadas del anglosajón y apenas modifica el sentido:*	*belong*, pertenecer
		2, *forma verbos transitivos:*	*belittle*, rebajar
		3, *con algunos verbos expresa carácter pasivo o reflexivo:*	*bemused*, pasmado
		4, alrededor:	*becloud*, oscurecer; *beset*, sitiar
bene-	bene-; ben-	bueno; bien:	*beneficial*, benéfico; *benediction*, bendición
bi-	bi-	**1,** dos:	*biconvex*, biconvexo
		2, dos veces:	*biyearly*, semestral; dos veces al año
		3, una vez de cada dos:	*bimonthly*, bimestral
		4, doble:	*bicephalous*, bicéfalo
biblio-	biblio-	**1,** libro:	*bibliography*, bibliografía
		2, Biblia:	*bibliolatry*, adoración de la Biblia
bin-	bin-	*Var. de* **bi-**:	*binocular*, binocular
bio-	bio-	vida:	*biography*, biografía; *biology*, biología
bis-	—	*Var. de* **bi-** *ante vocal o* s:	*bisaxillary*, biaxilar; *bissextile*, bisiesto

	Equivalentes en español	Significados y usos	Ejemplos
brachy-	braqui-	corto:	*brachycephalic,* braquicéfalo
brevi-	brevi-	breve; corto:	*brevipennate,* brevipenne
cardi(o)-	cardi(o)-	corazón:	*cardiogram,* cardiograma; *cardialgia,* cardialgia
cata-	cata-	1, oposición: 2, abajo; hacia abajo: 3, disolución; destrucción:	*catapult,* catapulta *catabolism,* catabolismo *cataclysm,* cataclismo
ceno-; **coeno-**	ceno-	1, común: 2, nuevo; reciente:	*cenobite,* cenobita *Cenozoic,* cenozoico
cent(i)-	cent(i)-	ciento; centésima parte:	*centigrade,* centígrado; *centimeter,* centímetro; *centennial,* centenario
centro-; **centri-**	centro; centri-	centro; central:	*centrosome,* centrosoma; *centrifugal,* centrífugo
cerebro-	cerebro-	cerebro; mente:	*cerebrospinal,* cerebroespinal
chiro-	quiro-	mano:	*chiromancy,* quiromancia
chromato-	cromato-	1, color: 2, cromatina:	*chromatology,* cromatología *chromatolysis,* cromatólisis
chromo-; **chromi-;** **chrom-**	cromo-; cromi-; crom-	1, color: 2, cromo:	*chromolithography,* cromolitografía *chromo-arsenate,* cromo-arseniato
chrono-	crono-	tiempo:	*chronology,* cronología

	Equivalentes en español	Significados y usos	Ejemplos
circum-	circum-; circun-	alrededor:	*circumpolar,* circumpolar; *circumstance,* circunstancia
co-	co-	*Var. de* **com-**; 1, asociación: 2, acción conjunta: 3, *matemáticas,* complemento de:	*coadjutor,* coadjutor *cooperation,* cooperación *cosine,* coseno
col-	—	*Var. de* **com-** *ante* l:	*collateral,* colateral
com-	com-; con-	con; juntamente; por entero. *Tiene la forma* **com-** *ante* b, m, p *y a veces* f: *Por asimilación fonética, tiene la forma* **col-** *ante* l: **cor-** *ante* r: **con-** *ante toda consonante con excepción de* b, h, l, m, p, r, w. *Tiene la forma* **co-** *ante vocal, ante* h, w *y a veces otras consonantes:*	*combine,* combinar; *commit,* cometer; *compose,* componer; *comfort,* confortar *collaborate,* colaborar *correspond,* corresponder *coalition,* coalición; *cohabit,* cohabitar; *coworker,* colaborador
con-	con-	*Var. de* **com-** *ante* c, d, f, g, j, n, q, s, t, v:	*concave,* cóncavo; *condone,* condonar; *confide,* confiar; *congress,* congreso; *conjunct,* conjunto; *connote,* connotar; *conquest,* conquista; *consent,* consentir; *contact,* contacto; *convert,* convertir
contra-	contra-	contra; oposición:	*contravene,* contravenir
cor-	cor-	*Var. de* **com-** *ante* r:	*correspond,* corresponder
cosmo-	cosmo-	cosmos:	*cosmography,* cosmografía

	Equivalentes en español	Significados y usos	Ejemplos
counter-	contra-	contra; oposición:	*counterweight*, contrapeso
cross-	—	1, al través; transversalmente: 2, opuesto; oposición:	*crosscut*, corte transversal *cross-purposes*, objetivos opuestos
crypt(o)-	cripto-	oculto:	*cryptogram*, criptograma; *cryptanalysis*, criptoanálisis
cyclo-	ciclo-	círculo; circular:	*cyclorama*, ciclorama
cyto-	cito-	célula:	*cytology*, citología
de-	de-; des-	1, disminución: 2, privación: 3, sentido contrario: 4, negación: 5, intensificación:	*degrade*, degradar *dethrone*, destronar *decentralize*, descentralizar *demerit*, demérito *decompound*, volver a componer
deca-	deca-	diez; décuplo:	*decameter*, decámetro
deci-	deci-	1, diez: 2, décima parte:	*decipolar*, que tiene diez polos *decimeter*, decímetro
demi-	semi-	1, mitad: 2, inferior:	*demitasse*, tacita *demigod*, semidiós
dermo-; derm-	dermo-; derm-	piel:	*dermoblast*, dermoblasto; *dermalgia*, dermalgia
dermato-; dermat-	dermato-; dermat-	piel:	*dermatology*, dermatología; *dermathemia*, dermatemia
dextro-	dextro-	derecha; a la derecha:	*dextrogyrate*, dextrógiro
di-	di-	1, dos; dos veces; el doble: 2, *Var. de* **dis-**: 3, *Var. de* **dia-**:	*digraph*, dígrafo *divest*, despojar *diactinic*, diactínico

	Equivalentes en español	Significados y usos	Ejemplos
dia-	dia-	**1,** separación: **2,** oposición: **3,** a través:	*diacritical,* diacrítico *diamagnetic,* diamagnético *diagonal,* diagonal
dif-	—	*Var. de* **dis-** *ante* f:	*difference,* diferencia
dis-	dis-; des-; di-	**1,** negación: **2,** oposición; contraste: **3,** separación:	*discontinuous,* discontinuo, descontinuo *dissimilar,* disímil, desemejante *dissident,* disidente
duo-	duo-	dos:	*duodecimal,* duodecimal
dyna-	dina-	fuerza:	*dynatron,* dinatrón
dynamo-	dinamo-	fuerza:	*dynamometer,* dinamómetro
dys-	dis-	dificultad; mal:	*dyspepsia,* dispepsia
e-	e-	*Var. de* **ex-**:	*emanation,* emanación
ec-	ec-	*Var. de* **ex-**:	*eczema,* eczema
ecto-	ecto-	externo:	*ectoderm,* ectodermo
electro-; **electri-**	electro-; electri-	electricidad:	*electrotype,* electrotipo; *electrify,* electrificar.
em-	em-	*Var. de* **en-** *ante* b, p, m:	*embellish,* embellecer; *empiric,* empírico
en-	en-	**1,** en; dentro; *forma* *verbos indicando* colocación del objeto en un lugar, condición, etc.: **2,** *Intensifica la* *acción de ciertos* *verbos transitivos:* **3,** en; al interior; *especialmente en* *palabras de origen* *griego:*	*enclose,* encerrar; *enrich,* enriquecer *entangle,* enmarañar *endemic,* endémico

	Equivalentes en español	Significados y usos	Ejemplos
endo-	endo-	dentro; interno:	*endocrine,* endocrino
ento-	ento-	dentro; interior:	*entophyte,* entofita
entomo-	entomo-	insecto:	*entomology,* entomología
eo-	eo-	temprano; primitivo:	*eolithic,* eolítico
ep-	ep-	*Var. de* **epi-** *ante vocal:*	*eponym,* epónimo
epi-	epi-	sobre; entre; hasta:	*epicenter,* epicentro
equi-	equi-	igual:	*equivalent,* equivalente
eso-	eso-	en; interno; oculto:	*esoteric,* esotérico
ethno-	etno-	pueblo; raza:	*ethnography,* etnografía
eu-	eu-	bien; bueno:	*euphony,* eufonía
ex-	ex-	**1,** fuera; fuera de; más allá: **2,** antes; que ha sido:	*export,* exportar *ex-president,* expresidente
exo-	exo-	fuera; exterior:	*exogenous,* exógeno
extra-	extra-	más allá; fuera:	*extraterritorial,* extraterritorial
extro-	extro-	*Var. de* **extra-:**	*extrovert,* extrovertido
ferro-; ferri-	ferro-; ferri-	hierro:	*ferrochromium,* ferrocromo; *ferriferous,* ferrífero
for-	—	**1,** lejos; aparte: **2,** negación: **3,** intensidad:	*forget,* olvidar *forbid,* prohibir *forlorn,* abandonado
fore-	—	**1,** anterior *(en tiempo o lugar):* **2,** superior en rango:	*forenoon,* mañana; *forepaw,* pata delantera *foreman,* capataz

	Equivalentes en español	Significados y usos	Ejemplos
Franco-	franco-	francés:	*Franco-American,* francoamericano
Gallo-	galo-	francés; galo:	*Gallophile,* galófilo, francófilo
galvano-	galvano-	electricidad:	*galvanometer,* galvanómetro
gamo-	gamo-	*biol.,* unión:	*gamopetalous,* gamopétalo
gastro-	gastro-	estómago:	*gastronome,* gastrónomo
gene-	gene-	generación; descendencia:	*genealogy,* genealogía
geno-	geno-	pueblo; raza:	*genocide,* genocidio
geo-	geo-	tierra:	*geocentric,* geocéntrico
gono-	gono-	perteneciente al sexo *o* a la reproducción sexual:	*gonorrhea,* gonorrea
Graeco-	greco-	*Var. de* **Greco-***:*	*Graeco-Roman,* grecorromano
grand-	—	*Denota* relación de ascendencia o descendencia remontándose una generación:	*grandfather,* abuelo; *grandson,* nieto
grapho-	grafo-	escritura; dibujo:	*graphology,* grafología
great-	—	*Denota* relación de ascendencia o descendencia remontándose una generación; *úsase antepuesto al prefijo* **grand-** *o en vez de éste; se repite para indicar ascendencia o descendencia más remota:*	*great-uncle* o *granduncle,* tío abuelo; *great-grandfather,* bisabuelo; *great-great-grandfather,* tatarabuelo

	Equivalentes en español	Significados y usos	Ejemplos
Greco-	greco-	griego	*Greco-Roman,* grecorromano
gyn-	gin-	mujer; hembra:	*gynandrous,* ginandro
gyne-	gine-	*Var. de* **gyn-**:	*gyneolatry,* gineolatría
gyneco-	gineco-	mujer:	*gynecology,* ginecología
gyno-	gino-	*Var. de* **gyn-**:	*gynophore,* ginóforo
gyro-	giro-	círculo; giro; vuelta:	*gyroscope,* giróscopo
haema-; **haemo-**	hema-; hemo-	*Var. de* **hema-;** **hemo-**:	*haemachrome,* hemacroma; *haemorrhage;* hemorragia
halo-	halo-	sal:	*halogen,* halógeno
hecto-	hecto-	cien:	*hectogram,* hectogramo
helico-	helico-	espiral; hélice:	*helicopter,* helicóptero
helio-	helio-	sol:	*heliograph,* heliógrafo
hema-; **hemo-**	hema-; hemo-	sangre:	*hemachrome,* hemacroma; *hemorrhage,* hemorragia
hemat(o)-	hemat(o)-	sangre:	*hematolysis,* hematólisis; *hematemesis,* hematémesis
hemi-	hemi-	medio:	*hemicycle,* hemiciclo
hepta-	hepta-	siete:	*heptagon,* heptágono
hetero-	hetero-	diferente; disconforme:	*heterosexual,* heterosexual
hexa-	hexa-	seis:	*hexagon,* hexágono
hippo-	hipo-	caballo:	*hippodrome,* hipódromo

	Equivalentes en español	Significados y usos	Ejemplos
histo-	histo-	tejido:	*histology,* histología
holo-	holo-	entero; todo:	*holocaust,* holocausto
homeo-	homeo-	igual; semejante:	*homeopathy,* homeopatía
homo-	homo-	mismo; igual:	*homogeneous,* homogéneo
hydro-	hidro-	1, agua: 2, hidrógeno:	*hydroelectric,* hidroeléctrico *hydrocarbon,* hidrocarbono
hyper-	hiper-	sobre; superior; excesivo:	*hypersensitive,* hipersensitivo
hypo-	hipo-	1, bajo; inferior; escaso: 2, *química,* grado menor de oxidación:	*hypodermic,* hipodérmico; *hypotaxis,* hipotaxis; *hypoplasia,* hipoplasia *hyposulfite,* hiposulfuro
hystero-	histero-	1, útero; matriz: 2, histeria:	*hysterotomy,* histerotomía *hysterogenic,* histerogénico
ichthyo-	ictio-	pez:	*ichthyosaur,* ictiosauro
ideo-	ideo-	idea:	*ideology,* ideología
idio-	idio-	personalidad; peculiaridad:	*idiosyncrasy,* idiosincrasia
il-	—	*Var. de* **in-** *ante* l:	*illiterate,* analfabeto
ill-	mal-	mal:	*ill-treat,* maltratar; *ill-disposed,* maldispuesto
im-	—	*Var. de* **in-** *ante* m, b, p:	*immaculate,* inmaculado; *imbibe,* embeber; *impoverish,* empobrecer

	Equivalentes en español	Significados y usos	Ejemplos
in-	in-; en-	**1,** *Forma nombres y adjetivos denotando* privación; negación:	*incautious,* incauto
		2, en; dentro; hacia:	*inborn,* innato
		3, *Forma verbos expresando* existencia, movimiento *o* dirección hacia dentro:	*inclose,* incluir
		4, *A veces tiene una función puramente intensiva:*	*intrust,* confiar
infra-	infra-	bajo; inferior:	*infrared,* infrarrojo
inter-	inter-; entre-	entre; durante:	*international,* internacional; *interregnum,* interregno; *interview,* entrevista
intra-	intra-	dentro:	*intravenous,* intravenoso
intro-	intro-	dentro; hacia adentro:	*introduce,* introducir; *introvert,* introvertido
ir-	ir-	*Var. de* **in-** *ante* r:	*irrational,* irracional
iso-	iso-	igual:	*isotherm,* isoterma
juxta-	yuxta-	cerca; junto; cercano:	*juxtaposition,* yuxtaposición
kilo-	kilo-; quilo-	mil:	*kilogram,* kilogramo, quilogramo
lacto-; lacti-	lacto-; lacti-	leche:	*lactometer,* lactómetro; *lactiferous,* lactífero
levo-	levo-	izquierda:	*levogyrate,* levógiro
litho-	lito-	piedra:	*lithography,* litografía
loco-	loco-	lugar:	*locomotion,* locomoción
ogo-	logo-	palabra:	*logotype,* logotipo

	Equivalentes en español	Significados y usos	Ejemplos
luni-	luni-	luna:	*lunisolar,* lunisolar
macro-	macro-	largo; grande:	*macroscopic,* macroscópico
magni-	magni-	grande:	*magnificent,* magnífico
mal:	mal-	malo; mal; imperfecto:	*maladjusted,* desajustado; *maltreatment,* maltrato
male-	male-	*Var. de* **mal-**:	*malediction,* maledicencia
mani-; **manu-**	mani-; manu-	mano:	*manicure,* manicura; *manufacture,* manufactura
matri-	matri-	madre:	*matriarchate,* matriarcado
mega-	mega-	1, grande: 2, millón:	*megalith,* megalito *megacycle,* megaciclo
megalo-	megalo-	enorme; muy grande:	*megalocephalic,* megalocéfalo
melano-	melano-	negro:	*melanosis,* melanosis
melo-	melo-	canción; música:	*melomaniac,* melómano
meso-	meso-	medio:	*mesocarp,* mesocarpio
meta-	meta-	1, junto con; del *o* en el centro; más allá; después: 2, cambio; transformación:	*metacenter,* metacentro; *metaphysics,* metafísica *metathesis,* metátesis
metro-	metro-	1, medida: 2, útero; vientre: 3, matriz; madre:	*metrology,* metrología *metrorrhagia,* metrorragia; *metropolis,* metrópolis
micro-	micro-	muy pequeño:	*microcosm,* microcosmo

	Equivalentes en español	Significados y usos	Ejemplos
mid-	medio-	medio; centro; a mediados de:	*midday,* mediodía; *midweek,* a mediados de semana
mille-	mile-	mil:	*millepore,* milépora
milli-	mili-	milésima parte:	*millimeter,* milímetro
mis-	—	1, malo; equivocado:	*mispronunciation,* mala pronunciación
	—	2, sentido negativo u opuesto:	*mischance,* contratiempo
	mis-	3, *Var. de* **miso-**:	*misanthrope,* misántropo
miso-	miso-	odio; repulsión:	*misogynous,* misógino
mono-	mono-	uno; solo:	*monotheist,* monoteísta
morpho-	morfo-	forma:	*morphology,* morfología
muco-	muco-	membrana mucosa; moco:	*mucoprotein,* mucoproteína
multi-	multi-	muchos:	*multimillionaire,* multimillonario
myco-	mico-	hongo:	*mycology,* micología
myo-	mio-	músculo:	*myocardium,* miocardio
myria-	miria-	1, muchos; numerosos:	*myriapod,* miriápodo
		2, diez mil:	*myriameter,* miriámetro
naso-	naso-	nariz:	*nasofrontal,* nasofrontal
necro-	necro-	muerte; muerto:	*necrology,* necrología
nemato-	nemato-	hilo; filamento:	*nematocyst,* nematocisto

	Equivalentes en español	Significados y usos	Ejemplos
nephro-; **nephr-**	nefro-; nefr-	riñón:	*nephrotomy,* nefrotomía; *nephritis,* nefritis
neuro-; **neur-**	neuro-; neur-	nervio:	*neurology,* neurología; *neuritis,* neuritis
nitro-	nitro-	nitrógeno; compuesto de nitrógeno:	*nitrobenzene,* nitrobencina; *nitrocellulose,* nitrocelulosa
nocti-; **noct-**	nocti-; noct-	noche:	*noctiluca,* noctíluco; *noctambulism,* noctambulismo
non-	—	*Usado ante nombres, adjetivos y adverbios imprimiendo un matiz de* negación o carencia *mas sin expresar tanta fuerza o énfasis como* **un-, in-**:	*nonresident,* transcúntc; *nonsense,* tontería
o-	o-	*Var. de* **ob-** *ante* m:	*omit,* omitir
ob-	ob-	**1,** hacia; mirando hacia: **2,** en contra de; opuesto: **3,** sobre: **4,** al revés:	*oblique,* oblicuo *object,* objetar *observe,* observar *obovoid,* obovoide
oc-	—	*Var. de* **ob-** *ante* c:	*occur,* ocurrir
octa-	octa-	*Var. de* **octo-**:	*octagon,* octágono
octo-; oct-	octo-; oct-	ocho:	*octogenarian,* octogenario; *octillion,* octillón
oculo-	oculo-	ojo:	*oculomotor,* oculomotor
of-	—	*Var. de* **ob-** *ante* f:	*offend,* ofender

	Equivalentes en español	Significados y usos	Ejemplos
oleo-	oleo-	aceite:	*oleomargarine,* oleomargarina
oligo-; olig	oligo-; olig-	poco; escaso:	*oligopoly,* oligopolio; *oligarchy,* oligarquía
omni-	omni-	todo:	*omnipotent,* omnipotente
onoma-	onoma-	nombre:	*onomatopoeia,* onomatopeya
oö-	oo-	huevo:	*oögenesis,* oogénesis
op-	—	*Var de* **ob-** *ante* p:	*oppress,* oprimir
ornitho-	ornito-	pájaro:	*ornithology,* ornitología
ortho-	orto-	derecho; correcto:	*orthostatic,* ortostático; *orthodox,* ortodoxo
osteo-	osteo-	hueso:	*osteology,* osteología
oto-; ot-	oto-; ot-	oído: .	*otology,* otología; *otalgia,* otalgia
out-	—	**1,** sobre; que excede; que se destaca:	*outstanding,* sobresaliente; *outstrip,* sobrepasasr
		2, externo; exterior; afuera:	*outlet,* salida; *outskirts,* afueras
		3, alejado; que se aleja:	*out-of-the-way,* apartado; *outbound,* que sale; *outlaw,* proscrito, bandido
over-	—	**1,** sobre; encima:	*overseer,* supervisor; *overcoat,* sobretodo
		2, a través; por; al otro lado:	*overland,* por tierra; *overseas,* ultramar
		3, sobre-; exceso; con exceso:	*overflow,* sobreabundancia, exceso; *overburden,* sobrecargar
		4, superación; culminación:	*overpower,* dominar, subyugar; *overmatch,* sobrepujar
		5, alteración; trastorno:	*overturn,* volcar; *overthrow,* derribar

	Equivalentes en español	Significados y usos	Ejemplos
ovi-	ovi-	huevo:	*oviform*, oviforme
oxy-	oxi-	1, oxígeno: 2, agudo:	*oxysulfide*, oxisulfuro *oxycephalic*, oxicefálico
paedo-	—	*Var. de* **pedo-**:	*paediatrics*, pediatría
paleo-	paleo-	antiguo; primitivo:	*paleology*, paleología
pan-	pan-	total; completo; universal:	*Pan-American*, panamericano; *pandemic*, pandemia
panto-	panto-	*Var. de* **pan-**:	*pantograph*, pantógrafo
para-	para-	1, cerca; además de; más allá: 2, *patol.* anormal: 3, protección; resguardo:	*paramilitary*, paramilitar; *paraphrase*, paráfrasis *paranoia*, paranoia *parachute*, paracaídas
pari-	pari-	igual:	*paripinnate*, paripinado
patho-	pato-	enfermedad:	*pathology*, patología
patri-	patri-	padre:	*patriarchy*, patriarcado
pedi-	pedi-	1, pie: 2, niño:	*pedicure*, pedicura *pediatrics*, pediatría
pedo-	pedo-	niño:	*pedodontia*, pedodoncia
penni-	peni-	pluma:	*penniform*, peniforme
penta-	penta-	cinco:	*pentagon*, pentágono
per-	per-	1, a través: 2, completamente; del todo: 3, *química*, mayor valencia:	*perennial*, perenne *persuade*, persuadir *peroxide*, peróxido
peri-	peri-	alrededor:	*periphery*, periferia

	Equivalentes en español	Significados y usos	Ejemplos
petro-; **petri-**	petro-; petri-	piedra:	*petrography,* petrografía; *petrify,* petrificar
phago-	fago-	que come; que destruye:	*phagocyte,* fagocito
philo-; **phil-**	filo-; fil-	cariño; inclinación:	*philology,* filología; *philanthropy,* filantropía; *philharmonic,* filarmónico
phlebo-; **phleb-**	flebo-; fleb-	vena:	*phlebotomy,* flebotomía; *phlebitis,* flebitis
phono-; **phon-**	fono-; fon-	sonido:	*phonograph,* fonógrafo; *phonetic,* fonético
photo-	foto-	1, luz: 2, fotografía:	*photodynamics,* fotodinámica *photoengraving,* fotograbado
phyllo-	filo-	hoja:	*phylloxera,* filoxera
physio-	fisio-	naturaleza; natural:	*physiology,* fisiología
phyto-	fito-	planta; vegetal:	*phytogenesis,* fitogénesis
pisci-	pisci-	pez:	*pisciculture,* piscicultura
plasmo-	plasmo-	plasma; forma;	*plasmolysis,* plasmólisis
platy-	plati-	ancho:	*platyrrhine,* platirrino
plexi-	plexi-	tejido; entretejido:	*plexiform,* plexiforme
pluri-	pluri-	muchos; diversos:	*pluricellular,* pluricelular
pneumato-	neumato-	1, aire; vapor: 2, respiración; aliento:	*pneumatolysis,* neumatólisis *pneumatometer,* neumatómetro

	Equivalentes en español	Significados y usos	Ejemplos
pneumo-	neumo-	pulmón:	*pneumoconiosis,* neumoconiosis
pneumono-	neumono-	pulmón; pulmones:	*pneumonophore,* neumonóforo
podo-; podi-	podo-; podi-	pie:	*podometer,* podómetro; *podiatry,* podiatría
poly-	poli-	muchos:	*polygamy,* poligamia
post-	post-; pos-	después; trás; detrás:	*postlude,* postludio; *postpone,* posponer
pre-	pre-	antes de *(en tiempo, lugar o grado):*	*precedence,* precedencia; *predecessor,* predecesor; *preeminent,* preeminente
preter-	preter-	más allá de; más que:	*preternatural,* preternatural
pro-	pro-	**1,** en *o* a favor de:	*pro-French,* profrancés
		2, en vez *o* lugar de:	*proconsul,* procónsul
		3, hacia adelante:	*proceed,* proseguir
		4, hacia afuera:	*project,* proyectar
		5, delante *(en tiempo o lugar):*	*prologue,* prólogo; *proscenium,* proscenio
proto-	proto-	**1,** primero:	*protomartyr,* protomártir
		2, *química, indicando* proporción más baja que la de otros elementos:	*protochloride,* protocloruro
pseudo-	(p)seudo-	falso; engañoso:	*pseudomorph,* (p)seudomorfo
psycho-	(p)sico-	mente; proceso mental:	*psychology,* (p)sicología
ptero-	ptero-	ala:	*pterodactyl,* pterodáctilo
pyro-	piro-	fuego:	*pyrometer,* pirómetro

	Equivalentes en español	Significados y usos	Ejemplos
quadri-	cuadri-	cuatro:	*quadrinomial,* cuadrinomio
quasi-	cuasi-	casi:	*quasicontract,* cuasicontrato
radio-	radio-	1, comunicación por ondas: 2, radioactividad:	*radiotelegraphy,* radiotelegrafía *radiotherapy,* radioterapia
re-	re-	1, atrás; en dirección opuesta: 2, otra vez; de nuevo: 3, resistencia; oposición: 4, intensificación:	*reaction,* reacción *reelect,* reelegir *reject,* rechazar *reinforcement,* refuerzo
recti-; rect-	recti-; rect-	recto:	*rectilinear,* rectilíneo; *rectangle,* rectángulo
retro-	retro-	1, atrás *(en tiempo o espacio):* 2, anterior:	*retrospection,* retrospección *retroactive,* retroactivo
rheo-	reo-	corriente; flujo:	*rheometer,* reómetro
rhino-	rino-	nariz:	*rhinoplasty,* rinoplastia
rhizo-	rizo-	raíz:	*rhizopod,* rizópodo
sangui-	sangui-	sangre:	*sanguiferous,* sanguífero
sarco-	sarco-	carne:	*sarcophagus,* sarcófago
sauro-	sauro-	lagarto:	*sauropod,* saurópodo
schizo-	esquizo-	disociamiento:	*schizophrenia,* esquizofrenia
sclero-	esclero-	duro:	*scleroderma,* esclerodermia

	Equivalentes en español	Significados y usos	Ejemplos
seismo-	sismo-	terremoto; temblor de tierra:	*seismometer,* sismómetro
self-	—	1, *Denota* valor reflexivo *en el nombre o adjetivo al que va unido, generalmente con un guión:*	*self-control,* dominio de sí; *self-addressed,* dirigido a uno mismo
		2, acción autónoma *o* automática:	*self-styled,* con estilo propio; *self-adjusting,* de ajuste automático
semi-	semi-	1, mitad; medio:	*semicircle,* semicírculo
		2, en parte; a medias:	*semiofficial,* semioficial
sept-	sept-	siete (*var. de* **septi-**):	*septet,* septeto
septi-	septi-	1, siete:	*septilateral,* septilateral
		2, decomposición; putrefacción:	*septicemia,* septicemia
		3, septo; tabique:	*septifragal,* septífraga
sero-	sero-	sero:	*serology,* serología
sesqui-	sesqui-	uno y medio:	*sesquicentennial,* sesquicentenario
sex-	sex-	seis:	*sexennial,* sexenio
sinistr-; sinistro-	sinistro-	a la izquierda:	*sinistrorse,* sinistrorso; *sinistral,* siniestro
Sino-	sino-	chino:	*Sinology,* sinología
soli-	soli-	solo; a solas:	*soliloquy,* soliloquio
somato-	somato-	cuerpo:	*somatology,* somatología
sphero-	esfero-	esfera; relacionado con la esfera:	*spherometer,* esferómetro
spiro-	espiro-	1, respiración:	*spirometer,* espirómetro
		2, espiral:	*spirochete,* espiroqueta

	Equivalentes en español	Significados y usos	Ejemplos
sporo-	esporo-	espora:	*sporocarp*, esporocarpio
stato-	estato-	estabilidad:	*statocyst*, estatocisto
step-	—	*Denotando* parentesco o relación por nuevo matrimonio de los padres:	*stepson*, hijastro
stereo-	estereo-	sólido; de *o* con tres dimensiones:	*stereophonic*, estereofónico
stomato-	estomato-	boca:	*stomatology*, estomatología
strati-; strato-	estrati-; estrato-	estrato:	*stratification*, estratificación; *stratosphere*, estratosfera
sub-	sub-	1, bajo; debajo: 2, menor grado *o* intensidad: 3, inferior; de menor categoría: 4, resultado de división:.	*subsoil*, subsuelo *subtropical*, subtropical *subordinate*, subordinado *sublease*, subarrendar; *subgroup*, subgrupo
subter-	subter-	bajo; debajo:	*subterfuge*, subterfugio
suc-	—	*Var. de* **sub-** *ante* c:	*succumb*, sucumbir
suf-	—	*Var. de* **sub-** *ante* f:	*suffix*, sufijo
sup-	—	*Var. de* **sub-** *ante* p:	*suppress*, suprimir
super-	super-	sobre; encima de; superior:	*supereminence*, supereminencia
supra-	supra-	sobre:	*suprarenal*, suprarrenal
sur-	—	*Var. de* **sub-** *ante* r:	*surreptitious*, subrepticio
sus-	sus-	*Var. de* **sub-** *ante* c:	*susceptible*, susceptible

	Equivalentes en español	Significados y usos	Ejemplos
syl-	—	*Var. de* **syn-** *ante* l:	*syllogism,* silogismo
sym-	sim-	*Var. de* **syn-** *ante* b, p, m:	*symbiosis,* simbiosis; *symposium,* simposio; *symmetry,* simetría
syn-	sin-	junto; junto con:	*synchronic,* sincrónico
taxi-; taxo-	taxi-; taxo-	orden; colocación:	*taxidermy,* taxidermia; *taxonomy,* taxonomía
tele-	tele-	lejano; distante:	*telescope,* telescopio
tetra-	tetra-	cuatro:	*tetrahedron,* tetraedro
theo-	teo-	de Dios o dioses:	*theology,* teología
there-	—	*Combinado con preposiciones forma adverbios denotando* lugar; tiempo; dirección; procedencia:	*thereunder,* bajo eso; *thereafter,* después de eso; *therefrom,* de allí; *therefore,* por lo tanto
thermo-; therm-	termo-; term-	calor:	*thermonuclear,* termonuclear; *thermion,* termión
topo-	topo-	lugar:	*toponymy,* toponimia
toxico-	toxico-	veneno; tóxico:	*toxicogenic,* toxicógeno
toxo-; tox-	toxo-; tox-	venenoso; relacionado con tóxicos:	*toxoplasmosis,* toxoplasmosis; *toxemia,* toxemia
tracheo-; trache-	traqueo-; traque-	tráquea:	*tracheotomy,* traqueotomía; *tracheitis,* traqueítis
trans-	trans-	**1,** a través; sobre; más allá de; al, del *o* en el otro lado de: **2,** a través de: **3,** cambio:	*transatlantic,* transatlántico *translucent,* translúcido *transform,* transformar

	Equivalentes en español	Significados y usos	Ejemplos
tri-	tri-	**1,** tres; conteniendo tres *o* tres partes: **2,** tres veces: **3,** cada tres:	*tricycle,* triciclo; *triceps,* triceps *triplicate,* triplicar *triennial,* trienio
tropho-	trofo-	alimento; nutrición:	*trophoplasm,* trofoplasma
tropo-	tropo-	cambio; transformación:	*troposphere,* troposfera
typo-	tipo-	tipo; impresión:	*typography,* tipografía
ultra-	ultra-	**1,** más allá de: **2,** extremista:	*ultraviolet,* ultravioleta *ultranationalism,* ultranacionalismo
un-	—	**1,** in-; anti-; no; contrario: **2,** de-; des-; privación; reverso:	*unhappy,* infeliz; *un-American,* antiamericano *unarm,* desarmar; *unscrew,* destornillar; *unseal,* desellar
under-	sub-; so-	**1,** bajo; inferior: **2,** poco; menos: **3,** interior:	*underground,* subterráneo; *undersecretary,* subsecretario; *undermine,* socavar *undercook,* cocer poco; *undersell,* vender más barato *underclothes,* ropa interior
uni-	uni-	uno; uno solo:	*unison,* unísono; *unicorn,* unicornio
up-	—	**1,** arriba; hacia arriba; en lo alto: **2,** recto; derecho: **3,** hacia el interior:	*uphill,* cuesta arriba *upstanding,* recto, honroso; *upend,* poner de punta *upcountry,* tierra adentro
uro-	uro-	orina; sistema urinario:	*uroscopy,* uroscopia; *urology,* urología
vaso-	vaso-	vaso; tubo; canal:	*vasomotor,* vasomotor

	Equivalentes en español	Significados y usos	Ejemplos
vermi-	vermi-	gusano; lombriz:	*vermicide,* vermicida
vice-	vice-	**1,** substituto:	*vice-president,* vicepresidente
		2, del segundo grado *o* rango:	*viceconsul,* vicecónsul
vis-	viz-	*Var. de* **vice-**:	*viscount,* vizconde
where-	—	*Combinado con preposiciones forma adverbios denotando* que; lo que:	*whereby,* por lo que; *whereinto,* dentro de lo que
with-	—	**1,** contra: **2,** atrás:	*withstand,* resistir *withhold,* retener, retirar
xantho-	xanto-	amarillo:	*xanthophilia,* xantofilia
xeno-	xeno-	extraño; extranjero:	*xenophobia,* xenofobia
xero-	xero-	seco; sequedad:	*xerophthalmia,* xeroftalmia
xylo-	xilo-	madera:	*xylophone,* xilófono
zoö-	zoo-	animal:	*zoölogy,* zoología

SUFIJOS INGLESES

	Equivalentes en español	Significados y usos	Ejemplos
-able	-able; -ible	*Forma adjetivos denotando capacidad; habilidad:*	*excitable,* excitable; *punishable,* punible
-ably	-ablemente	*Forma adverbios de los adjetivos terminados en* **-able**:	*amicably,* amigablemente
-ac	-aco	*Forma adjetivos que denotan* **1,** característica: **2,** relación; pertenencia: *Generalmente estos adjetivos pueden usarse como nombres.*	*elegiac,* elegíaco *cardiac,* cardíaco
-acea; **-aceas**	-áceos -áceas	*zoöl.; bot.; forma nombres de* órdenes, familias y clases:	*crustacea,* crustáceos; *graminaceae,* *gramináceas*
-aceous	-áceo	*Forma adjetivos, especialmente con los nombres terminando en* **-acea** *o* **aceae**:	*cetaceous,* cetáceo; *orchidaceous,* orquidáceo
-acious	-az	*Forma adjetivos indicando característica; posesión:*	*audacious,* audaz
-acity	-acidad	*Forma nombres expresando cualidad:*	*pugnacity,* pugnacidad
-acy	-acia	*Forma nombres que indican* calidad; condición:	*fallacy,* falacia
-ad	—	**1,** *Forma nombres indicando un determinado grupo de unidades:* **2,** *Var. de* **-ade** (*def.* **3**):	*triad,* grupo de tres *Olympiad,* olimpíada

	Equivalentes en español	Significados y usos	Ejemplos
-ade	-ado; -ada	**1,** *Forma nombres indicando* acción; efecto *o* resultado de la acción:	*renegade,* renagado; *ambuscade,* emboscada
		2, *Compone nombres de bebidas:*	*lemonade,* limonada
		3, *Var. de* **-ad**:	*decade,* década
-ae	-as	*Terminación plural de algunos nombres femeninos derivados del latín:*	*alumnae,* alumnas
		A veces, es una alternativa para el plural regular:	*formulae* o *formulas,* fórmulas
-age	-aje	*Forma nombres denotando*	
		1, acción:	*pillage,* pillaje
		2, resultado:	*cartage,* carretaje
		3, colectividad:	*foliage,* follaje
		4, estado; condición	*bondage,* esclavitud
		5, domicilio; sitio:	*parsonage,* rectoría
		6, derechos; costo:	*wharfage,* muellaje
-al	-al	**1,** *Forma adjetivos denotando* relación; pertenencia; calidad:	*national,* nacional
		2, *Forma nombres expresando* acción *o* efecto:	*acquittal,* exoneración
-an	-ano; -ana	*Forma nombres y adjetivos denotando* relación; calidad; pertenencia:	*American,* americano; *Christian,* cristiano; *diocesan,* diocesano
-ance; -ancy	-ancia; -encia	*Forma nombres de adjetivos terminados en* **-ant**:	*abundance,* abundancia; *assistance,* asistencia; *occupancy,* ocupación
-androus	-andro	macho:	*monandrous,* monandro

	Equivalentes en español	Significados y usos	Ejemplos
-ane	-ano	1, *química,* *terminación de* hidrocarburos saturados: 2, *Var. de* **-an** *para diferenciarse de otro vocablo terminado en* **-an**:	*methane,* metano *urbane,* urban, urbano
-aneous	-áneo	*Forma adjetivos denotando* relación; pertenencia:	*instantaneous,* instantáneo
-ant	-ante; -ente	1, *Forma adjetivos equivalentes al participio en* **-ing**: 2, *Forma nombres indicando* ocupación; profesión:	*reliant,* confiado; *defiant,* desafiador *accountant,* contador; *servant,* sirviente
-anthous	-anto	*Forma adjetivos denotando* flor:	*monanthous,* monanto
-ar	-ar; -al	*Forma adjetivos y nombres que indican* modo; relación; pertenencia:	*linear,* lineal; *regular,* regular
-arch	-arca	gobernante:	*monarch,* monarca; *tetrarch,* tetrarca
-archy	-arquía	gobierno; mando:	*autarchy,* autarquía
-ard; -art	—	*Forma nombres, generalmente con sentido despectivo:*	*drunkard,* borrachón; *braggart,* fanfarrón
-aria	-aria	*Forma el plural de nombres que:* 1, *expresan* clasificación; género: 2, *terminan el singular en* **-arium**:	 *cineraria,* cineraria *honoraria,* honorarios
-arian	-ario	*Forma nombres y adjetivos denotando* 1, edad:	 *centenarian,* centenario

	Equivalentes en español	Significados y usos	Ejemplos
		2, doctrina; relación:	*sectarian,* sectario; *disciplinarian,* disciplinario
		3, profesión:	*antiquarian,* anticuario
-arious	-ario	*Forma adjetivos expresando* relación: pertenencia:	*precarious,* precario
-arium	-ario	*Forma nombres denotando* **1,** lugar especial: **2,** relación con otra cosa:	*aquarium,* acuario *honorarium,* honorario
-ary	-ario; -aria	**1,** *Forma adjetivos que denotan* relación; pertenencia: **2,** *Forma nombres que denotan* profesión: **3,** *Forma nombres indicando* cesión de algo:	*secondary,* secundario; *disciplinary,* disciplinario *notary,* notario *beneficiary,* beneficiario; *concessionary,* concesionario
-ase	-asa	*química,* enzima:	*diastase,* diastasa
-asis	-asis	*med.* enfermedad:	*elephantiasis,* elefantíasis
-asm	-asmo	*Forma nombres indicando* acción; tendencia; calidad:	*spasm,* espasmo; *enthusiasm,* entusiasmo
-ast	-asta	*Indica la persona o la cosa en nombres correspondiendo a nombres terminados en* **-asm:**	*enthusiast,* entusiasta
-aster	-astro; -astra	*Forma nombres diminutivos y despectivos:*	*poetaster,* poetastro
-atary	-atario	*Forma nombres que denotan* agencia; relación:	*mandatory,* mandatario

	Equivalentes en español	Significados y usos	Ejemplos
-ate	—	1, *Forma verbos:*	*accumulate,* acumular
	—	2, *Forma adjetivos:*	*innate,* innato
	—	3, *a veces, equivale al participio usado como adjetivo:*	*desolate,* desolado
	—	4, *Expresa la forma sustantiva del verbo:*	*precipitate,* precipitado; *mandate,* mandato
	-ato	5, *química, terminación de los nombres de* sales formadas por ácidos:	*acetate,* acetato
	-ado	6, *biol., indica* forma; tipo:	*vertebrate,* vertebrado
	-ato	7, *Forma nombres denotando* dignidad; cargo:	*cardinalate,* cardinalato
-atic; -atical	-ático	*Forma adjetivos que denotan* estado; relación:	*aquatic,* acuático; *sabbatical,* sabático
-ation	-ación	*Expresa acción o efecto en nombres verbales:*	*concentration,* concentración; *generation,* generación
-atious	—	*Forma adjetivos de nombres terminados en* **-ation**:	*vexatious,* vejatorio; *disputatious,* disputador
-ative	-ativo	*Forma adjetivos usados frecuentemente como sustantivos que expresan* relación; tendencia:	*demonstrative,* demostrativo; *operative,* agente
-atory	-atorio; -atario	*Forma adjetivos y nombres que denotan* pertenencia; sitio; agente:	*amatory,* amatorio; *laboratory,* laboratorio; *signatory,* signatario
-biosis	-biosis	*Forma nombres denotando* medio de vida *o* subsistencia:	*symbiosis,* simbiosis
-ble	-ble	*Var. de* **-able** *o* **-ible**:	*soluble,* soluble

	Equivalentes en español	Significados y usos	Ejemplos
-bund	-bundo	*Forma adjetivos expresando* tendencia; comienzo de una acción:	*moribund,* moribundo
-burger	—	*Sufijo extraído de* **hamburger,** *añadido a otros* bocadillos *de semejante composición:*	*cheeseburger,* albondigón con queso
-cene	-ceno	1, común: 2, nuevo; reciente:	*cenobite,* cenobita *Miocene,* mioceno
-chrome	-cromo	1, color: 2, *química,* cromo:	*polychrome,* polícromo *mercurochrome,* mercuro-cromo
-cidal	-cida	*Forma adjetivos de los nombres terminados en* **-cide**:	*suicidal,* suicida
-cide	-cida -cidio	1, que mata: 2, acción de matar:	*suicide,* suicida; *germicide,* germicida *homicide,* homicidio
-cle	—	*Var. de.* **-cule**:	*particle,* partícula; *article,* artículo
-cracy	-cracia	*Forma nombres indicando* 1, mando; autoridad: 2, clase gobernadora: 3, forma de gobierno:	*autocracy,* autocracia *aristocracy,* aristocracia *democracy,* democracia
-crat	-crata	*Forma nombres denotando personas, correspondiendo a los nombres terminados en* **-cracy**:	*autocrat,* autócrata; *aristocrat,* aristócrata; *democrat,* demócrata
-cratic	-crático	*Forma adjetivos de los nombres terminados en* **-crat** *o* **-cracy**:	*autocratic,* autocrático; *aristocratic,* aristocrático; *democratic,* democrático

	Equivalentes en español	Significados y usos	Ejemplos
-cule	-culo; -cula	*Forma diminutivos de nombres y adjetivos:*	minuscule, minúsculo; molecule, molécula
-cy	-cia	*Forma nombres denotando*	
		1, cualidad:	expediency, conveniencia
		2, entes abstractos:	autocracy, autocracia
		3, artes, profesiones:	necromancy, nigromancia
		4, empleo:	captaincy, capitanía
-cyte	-cito	célula:	thrombocyte, trombocito
-derm	-dermo	piel:	pachyderm, paquidermo
-dom	—	*Forma nombres indicando*	
		1, dominio; jurisdicción; dignidad:	kingdom, reino; earldom, marquesado
		2, condición; estado:	martyrdom, martirio
		3, colectividad:	Christendom, cristiandad
-dyne	-dino	fuerza:	superheterodyne, superheterodino
-ean	—	*Forma nombres y adjetivos denotando* relación; pertenencia:	Mediterranean, mediterráneo
-ectomy	-ectomía	*cirugía,* extirpación:	appendectomy, apendectomía
-ed	—	1, *Forma pretéritos de verbos:*	I wanted, quise
		2, *Forma participios pasivos:*	talked, hablado; rained, llovido
		3, *Forma adjetivos de nombres denotando* característica; formación; posesión:	bearded, barbudo; armored, blindado; armed, armado

	Equivalentes en español	Significados y usos	Ejemplos
-ee	—	1, *Forma nombres denotando* objeto *o* recipiente de una acción:	*lessee,* arrendatario; *payee,* portador, tenedor
		2, *Forma nombres con sentido diminutivo:*	*goatee,* perilla
-eer	-ero; -ario	1, *Forma nombres denotando* profesión; actividad:	*engineer,* ingeniero; *volunteer,* voluntario
	—	2, *Forma verbos derivados de nombres:*	*electioneer,* solicitar votos
-emia	-emia	*Forma nombres denotando* cierta condición de la sangre:	*anemia,* anemia
-en	—	1, *Forma verbos de adjetivos:*	*weaken,* debilitar(se);
		o *de nombres:*	*frighten,* atemorizar
		2, *Forma el participio pasivo de muchos verbos fuertes:*	*written,* escrito
		3, *Forma adjetivos denotando* sustancia: apariencia:	*golden,* dorado
		4, *Forma el plural de algunos nombres:*	*oxen,* bueyes; *children,* niños
		5, *Forma diminutivos:*	*maiden,* doncella
		6, *Forma ciertos nombres femeninos:*	*vixen,* zorra
		7, *Indica* persona; clase:	*citizen,* ciudadano
-ence; -ency	-encia	*Forma nombres indicando* acción; cualidad; condición, *que corresponden a adjetivos terminados en* **-ent**:	*violence,* violencia; *solvency,* solvencia
-ene	-eno	*química, forma los nombres de algunos* hidrocarburos:	*ethylene,* etileno

	Equivalentes en español	Significados y usos	Ejemplos
-ent	-ente; -iente	1, *Forma adjetivos equivalentes al participio activo:*	*different,* diferente; *ardent,* ardiente
		Algunos se usan como nombres:	*deterrent,* deterrente
		2, *Forma nombres indicando* agente; actor:	*regent,* regente
-er	—	1, *Añadido a verbos forma nombres de personas o cosas con sentido de* agente:	*driver,* conductor
		2, *Unido a nombres denota* ocupación; conexión:	*philosopher,* filósofo; *prisoner,* prisionero
		3, *Con nombres de lugar indica* habitante:	*Londoner,* londinense
		4, *Denota* característica:	*three-master,* velero de tres palos
		5, *Forma el comparativo de adjetivos y adverbios:*	*greener,* más verde; *slower,* más despacio
		6, *Forma nombres de acción, esp. en derecho:*	*waiver,* renuncia
		7, *Forma verbos frecuentativos:*	*patter,* golpetear
-ery	-ería	*Forma nombres denotando*	
		1, colectivad:	*pottery,* alfarería
		2, condición; estado:	*drudgery,* afán
		3, agregación:	*finery,* atavíos
		4, ocupación	*surgery,* cirugía
		5, utensilios; productos:	*cutlery,* cuchillería
		6, lugares de actividad mercantil:	*haberdashery,* camisería
		7, lugares donde se recoge o cría:	*piggery,* pocilga
-es	—	1, *En los verbos, forma la tercera persona singular del presente de indicativo tras sibilantes* (s, sh, ch, etc.):	*he wishes,* desea; *he passes,* él pasa

	Equivalentes en español	Significados y usos	Ejemplos
		2, *Forma el plural de nombres terminados en sibilantes* (s, sh, ch, *etc.*):	*dresses,* vestidos; *watches,* relojes
-esce	-ecer	*Terminación de verbos incoativos:*	*convalesce,* convalecer; *deliquesce,* derretirse
-escence	-ecencia	*Forma nombres de verbos terminados en* **-esce** *o de adjetivos terminados en* **-escent**:	*convalescence,* convalecencia
-escent	-ecente; -eciente	*Forma adjetivos, usados a veces como nombres, de verbos terminados en* **-esce** *o de nombres terminados en* **-escence**:	*convalescent,* convaleciente
-ese	-és; -esa	*Forma adjetivos y nombres expresando* relación geográfica; idioma; nacionalidad, *etc.*:	*Portuguese,* portugués (-esa)
-esque	-esco	*Forma adjetivos expresando* apariencia; forma; modo:	*picturesque,* pintoresco; *arabesque,* arabesco
-ess	—	*Forma nombres femeninos:*	*hostess,* anfitriona; *authoress,* autora; *princess,* princesa
-est	—	**1,** *Forma el superlativo de adjetivos y adverbios:*	*coldest,* el más frío; *latest,* lo más tarde
		2, *arcaico; poético, forma presente y pretérito de verbos con el pronombre* **thou**:	*thou goest,* tú vas; *thou madest,* tú hiciste
-et	—	*Forma nombres diminutivos:*	*islet,* islote; *fillet,* filete

	Equivalentes en español	Significados y usos	Ejemplos
-eth	—	1, *Forma números ordinales y fraccionarios:*	*twentieth,* vigésimo, veintavo
		2, *arcaico; poético, forma la tercera persona singular del presente:*	*he goeth,* él va
-ey	—	*Var de.* **-y,** *en las palabras terminadas en* **-y:**	*clayey,* arcilloso
-facient	-faciente	causante:	*stupefacient,* estupefaciente
-ferous	-fero	que tiene, lleva o produce:	*coniferous,* conífero
-fic	-fico	causante; que crea:	*terrific,* terrorífico
-fication	-ficación	*Forma nombres de los verbos terminados en* **-fy:**	*glorification,* glorificación
-florous	-floro	que tiene o produce cierta especie o número de flores:	*uniflorous,* unífloro
-fold	—	*Denota* multiplicación; veces:	*tenfold,* diez veces
-free	—	exento:	*taxfree,* exento de impuestos
-fugal	-fugo	*Forma adjetivos correspondiendo a nombres terminados en* **-fuge:**	*centrifugal,* centrífugo
-fuge	-fuga	*Forma nombres expresando* agente *o* instrumento que expulsa:	*centrifuge,* centrífuga
-ful	-oso	1, *Forma adjetivos expresando* lleno de; característico de; tendente a:	*beautiful,* hermoso; *careful,* cuidadoso; *harmful,* peligroso

	Equivalentes en español	Significados y usos	Ejemplos
	-ada	**2,** *Forma nombres expresando* contenido:	*spoonful,* cucharada
-fy	-ficar	hacer; hacerse:	*purify,* purificar; *intensify,* intensificar, intensificarse
-gamous	-gamo	*Forma adjetivos denotando* unión; matrimonio:	*monogamous,* monógamo
-gamy	-gamia	*Forma nombres denotando* unión; matrimonio:	*monogamy,* monogamia
-gen	-geno	*Forma nombres indicando* **1,** *química,* engendrador; generador: **2,** *biol.* lo engendrado o generado:	*hydrogen,* hidrógeno *exogen,* exógeno
-genic	-génico	*Forma adjetivos que corresponden a los nombres terminados en* -gen *o* -geny:	*photogenic,* fotogénico
-genous	-geno; -gena	*Forma adjetivos denotando* engendrado; generado:	*nitrogenous,* nitrógeno, nitrogenado; *indigenous,* indígena
-geny	-genia	*Forma nombres indicando* origen:	*ontogeny,* ontogenia
-glot	-glota	idioma; lengua:	*polyglot,* políglota
-gon	-gono	*Forma nombres denotando figuras planas geométricas con determinado número de ángulos:*	*polygon,* polígono
-gony	-gonía	génesis; origen:	*cosmogony,* cosmogonía

	Equivalentes en español	Significados y usos	Ejemplos
-grade	-grado	Forma adjetivos denotando	
		1, movimiento; andar:	digitigrade, digitígrado
		2, gradación:	centigrade, centígrado
-gram	-grama	1, escritura; dibujo:	telegram, telegrama; diagram, diagrama
	-gramo	2, unidad de peso del sistema métrico:	kilogram, kilogramo
-graph	-grafía	1, escrito; grabado:	monograph, monografía; lithograph, litografía
	-grafo	2, medio o instrumento para escribir, dibujar, grabar, etc.:	telegraph, telégrafo; phonograph, fonógrafo
-graphy	-grafía	1, ciencia; estudio:	geography, geografía
		2, arte; artesanía:	choreography, coreografía
		3, arte, facultad o medio de escribir, grabar, dibujar, etc.:	telegraphy, telegrafía; calligraphy, caligrafía
		4, escritura; representación por escrito:	orthography, ortografía
-gynous	-gino	Forma adjetivos expresando relación con mujer; hembra:	androgynous, andrógino
-gyny	-ginia	Forma nombres de los adjetivos terminados en -gynous:	androgyny, androginia
-handed	—	Forma adjetivos relacionados con mano:	left-handed zurdo; heavy-handed, de o con mano fuerte; four-handed game, partida de cuatro jugadores
-head	—	1, Forma nombres relacionados con cabeza:	redhead, pelirrojo; blockhead, zoquete
		2, Var. antigua de -hood:	godhead, divinidad

	Equivalentes en español	Significados y usos	Ejemplos
-hearted	—	*Forma adjetivos denotando* cierta calidad de carácter, disposición, etc.:	*halfhearted*, tímido; *bighearted*, magnánimo
-hedral	-édrico	*Forma adjetivos de los nombres terminados en* **-hedron**:	*polyhedral*, poliédrico
-hedron	-edro	*Forma nombres denotando* figuras sólidas geométricas con determinado número de caras:	*tetrahedron*, tetraedro
-hood	—	*Forma nombres indicando* **1,** cualidad; condición; estado:	*bachelorhood*, soltería; *knighthood*, caballería
		2, conjunto de personas:	*neighborhood*, vecindario
-ia		*Forma nombres indicando*	
	—	**1,** plurales latinos y colectivos:	*bacteria*, bacterias
	-ia	**2,** países y regiones:	*Australia*, Australia; *Dalmatia*, Dalmacia
-ial	-ial	*Forma adjetivos denotando* relacion; pertenencia:	*ministerial*, ministerial
-iasis	-íasis	enfermedad:	*elephantiasis*, elefantíasis
-iatric	-iátrico	*Forma adjetivos de los nombres terminados en* **-iatrics** *o* **-iatry**:	*psychiatric*, psiquiátrico
-iatrics; -iatry	-iatría	ciencia o tratamiento de enfermedades:	*pediatrics*, pediatría; *psychiatry*, psiquiatría
-ible	-ible	*Forma adjetivos expresando* capacidad; habilidad:	*legible*, legible

	Equivalentes en español	Significados y usos	Ejemplos
-ic	-ico	*Forma adjetivos indicando*	
		1, relación; cualidad; pertenencia; característica:	*poetic,* poético
		2, *química,* presencia de uno de los componentes en valencia mayor:	*nitric,* nítrico
-ice	-icio; -icia	*Forma nombres denotando* acción; cualidad; condición:	*sacrifice,* sacrificio; *justice,* justicia
-ician	—	*Forma nombres denotando* profesión:	*mortician,* director de funeraria
-icious	-icioso	*Forma adjetivos denotando* cualidad; relación:	*pernicious,* pernicioso
-ics	-ica	*Forma nombres denotando* arte; ciencia:	*athletics,* atlética; *physics,* física
-id	-ido	**1,** *Forma nombres y adjetivos denotando* cualidad; relación:	*torrid,* tórrido; *fluid,* flúido
		2, *zoöl.* miembro de una familia o grupo:	*arachnid,* arácnido
-ida; -idae	-idos	*zoöl.* miembros de una familia o grupo:	*Arachnida,* arácnidos; *Canidae,* cánidos
-ide	-uro	*química, forma nombres de* compuestos binarios:	*sulfide,* sulfuro
-ie	—	*Forma diminutivos:*	*kiddie,* nenito
-ier	-ero	*Forma nombres denotando* profesión:	*hotelier,* hotelero
-il; -ile	-il	*Forma adjetivos denotando* tendencia; relación:	*civil,* civil; *docile,* dócil

	Equivalentes en español	Significados y usos	Ejemplos
-in	-ina	*Forma nombres denotando compuestos y elementos químicos; preparaciones farmacéuticas; minerales: La mayoría de estos nombres aparecen hoy en la forma -ine.*	*glycerin,* glicerina; *lanolin,* lanolina
-ine	-ino	*1, Forma adjetivos denotando cualidad; relación:*	*canine,* canino; *opaline,* opalino
	-ina	*2, Forma nombres abstractos:*	*discipline,* disciplina; *medicine,* medicina
	-ina	*3, Forma nombres femeninos:*	*heroine,* heroína; *Christine,* Cristina
	—	*4, química, forma nombres denotando elementos químicos; preparaciones farmacéuticas; minerales:*	*chlorine,* cloro; *vaseline,* vaselina
-ing	—	*1, Forma gerundios:*	*teaching,* enseñanza; *reading,* lectura
		2, Forma el participio presente de los verbos:	*he is reading,* está leyendo
		Estos participios se usan también como adjetivos:	*a striking story,* una historia impresionante
-ion	-ión	*1, Forma nombres abstractos:*	*option,* opción; *fusion,* fusión
		2, Forma nombres concretos denotando personas o cosas:	*centurion,* centurión; *legion,* legión
-ious	-ioso	*Forma adjetivos denotando cualidad; relación:*	*religious,* religioso; *anxious,* ansioso
-ise	—	*1, Var. de -ice, formando nombres:*	*merchandise,* mercancías
		2, Var. de -ize, formando verbos:	*advertise,* anunciar

	Equivalentes en español	Significados y usos	Ejemplos
-ish	—	*Forma adjetivos*	
		1, perteneciente o relacionado con una nación o grupo:	*Spanish,* español; *Polish,* polonés
		2, parecido; característico:	*devilish,* endiablado; *boyish,* aniñado
		3, *perteneciente o relacionado con un idioma:*	*Danish,* danés
		4, más bien; bastante:	*tallish,* más bien alto;
		5, aproximadamente:	*bluish,* azulado; *thirtyish,* de unos treinta
-ism	-ismo	*Forma nombres indicando* doctrina; práctica; sistema:	*socialism,* socialismo
-ist	-ista	*Forma nombres de los verbos terminados en* **-ize** *y nombres en* **-ism,** *que definen a la persona que* estudia, tiene profesión, cree, propaga, etc.:	*anthropologist,* antropólogo; *physicist,* físico; *Methodist,* metodista
-istic; -istical	-ístico	*Forma adjetivos frecuentemente derivados de nombres terminando en* **-ist:**	*artistic,* artístico; *casuistical,* casuístico
-istics	-ística	*Forma nombres de adjetivos terminando en* **-istic** *y denota* práctica *o* ciencia de:	*ballistics,* balística
-ite		*Forma nombres indicando*	
	-ita	**1,** origen; procedencia:	*Israelite,* israelita
	-ita	**2,** seguidor; discípulo:	*Carmelite,* carmelita
	-ita; -ito	**3,** roca; mineral:	*dolomite,* dolomita; *graphite,* grafito
	-ito	**4,** *quím.* compuesto, esp. la sal de un ácido con la desinencia **-ous:**	*sulfite,* sulfito
	—	**5,** fósil:	*trilobite,* trilobites

	Equivalentes en español	Significados y usos	Ejemplos
	—	**6,** *Forma adjetivos y nombres derivados de adjetivos:*	*erudite,* erudito: *opposite,* opuesto
	—	**7,** *Forma verbos de acción:*	*ignite,* encender
-itic; itical	-ítico	*Forma adjetivos denotando* **1,** origen: **2,** semejante; perteneciente:	*Levitical,* levítico *granitic,* granítico; *political,* político
-ition	-ición	*Forma nombres verbales denotando* acción; efecto:	*composition,* composición; *definition,* definición
-itious	-icio; -icioso	*Forma adjetivos que frecuentemente corresponden a nombres terminados en* **-ition**:	*fictitious,* ficticio; *superstitious,* supersticioso
-itis	-itis	inflamación:	*bronchitis,* bronquitis
-itive	-itivo	*Forma adjetivos expresando* relación; tendencia:	*sensitive,* sensitivo
-ity	-idad	*Forma nombres denotando* cualidad; condición:	*activity,* actividad
-ium	-io	*Forma nombres de terminología científica:*	*actinium,* actinio
-ive	-ivo	*Forma adjetivos verbales denotando* función; tendencia; disposición:	*formative,* formativo; *passive,* pasivo
-ize	-izar	*Forma verbos de nombres y adjetivos denotando* **1,** *en verbos transitivos* hacer, rendir, suministrar, desempeñar *o* tratar en cierta forma:	*realize,* realizar; *civilize,* civilizar

	Equivalentes en español	Significados y usos	Ejemplos
		2, *en verbos intransitivos* actuar, funcionar *o* practicar en forma determinada:	*economize,* economizar; *theorize,* teorizar
-kin	—	*Forma diminutivos:*	*lambkin,* corderito
-later; -lator	-latra	adorador:	*idolater, idolator,* idólatra
-latry	-latría	adoración:	*idolatry,* idolatría
-less	—	*Forma adjetivos indicando* carencia; ausencia:	*restless,* inquieto; *sleeveless,* sin mangas
-let	—	*Forma nombres diminutivos:*	*booklet,* folleto
-like	—	*Forma adjetivos denotando* semejanza:	*birdlike,* como pájaro
-ling	—	**1,** *Forma nombres indicando* persona *o* cosa relacionada con, *generalmente con tono despectivo:*	*underling,* inferior, secuaz; *hireling,* mercenario
		2, *Forma diminutivos:*	*duckling,* patito
		3, *Forma adverbios de modo:*	*darkling,* a oscuras
-lite	-lita	*Forma nombres de* minerales:	*cryolite,* criolita
-lith	-lito	piedra:	*monolith,* monolito
-lithic	-lítico	*Forma adjetivos* **1,** *derivados de nombres terminados en* **-lith**:	*monolithic,* monolítico
		2, *denota* períodos arqueológicos:	*neolithic,* neolítico
-lived	—	*Forma adjetivos, generalmente unidos por guión, denotando* duración:	*long-lived,* longevo

	Equivalentes en español	Significados y usos	Ejemplos
-logic; **-logical**	-lógico	*Forma adjetivos de nombres terminados en* **-logy**:	*analogic, analogical,* analógico
-logue; **-log**	-logo	*Forma nombres denotando* conversación; escrito; descripción; diálogo:	*dialogue, dialog,* diálogo; *Decalogue,* decálogo; *catalogue, catalog,* catálogo
-logy	-logía	*Forma nombres denotando* **1,** ciencia; doctrina:	*cosmology,* cosmología
		2, colección; grupo:	*anthology,* antología
-long	—	*Forma adjetivos y adverbios denotando* extensión; dirección:	*sidelong,* de costado; *headlong,* de cabeza; *livelong,* todo, entero
-ly	—	*Forma* **1,** *adjetivos denotando* relación; pertenencia:	*manly,* varonil
		2, *adverbios de modo:*	*quickly,* de prisa; *slowly,* despacio
		3, *adverbios de tiempo:*	*weekly,* semanalmente, por semana
-lysis	-lisis	desintegración; destrucción:	*analysis,* análisis; *paralysis,* parálisis
-lyte	-lito	*Forma nombres denotando* resultado *o* producto de desintegración *o* destrucción:	*electrolyte,* electrolito
-lytic	-lítico	*Forma adjetivos de nombres terminados en* **-lysis**:	*analytic, analítico; paralytic,* paralítico
-lyze	-lizar	*Forma verbos de nombres terminados en* **-lysis**:	*analyze,* analizar; *paralyze,* paralizar
-mancy	-mancia	adivinación:	*necromancy,* nigromancia

	Equivalentes en español	Significados y usos	Ejemplos
-ment	-mento	*Forma nombres denotando* acción; resultado:	*experiment,* experimento
-meter	-metro	1, instrumento para medir: 2, metro: 3, medida poética:	*voltmeter,* voltímetro *kilometer,* kilómetro *hexameter,* hexámetro
-metry	-metría	ciencia o proceso de medir:	*anthropometry,* antropometría
-minded	—	*Forma adjetivos denotando* inclinación o disposición de la mente:	*like-minded,* del mismo parecer; *strong-minded,* testarudo
-mony	-monio; -monia	*Forma nombres denotando* cualidad; estado; condición:	*matrimony,* matrimonio; *acrimony,* acrimonia
-morph	-morfo	*Forma nombres denotando* semejanza en forma o aparencia:	*isomorph,* isomorfo
-morphic; -morphous	-morfo; -mórfico	*Forma adjetivos denotando* semejanza en forma o apariencia:	*isomorphic,* isomorfo; *anthropomorphous,* antropomorfo
-morphism	-morfismo	*Forma nombres de los adjetivos terminados en* **-morphic** o **-morphous**:	*anthropomorphism,* antropomorfismo
-most	—	*Forma superlativos:*	*uppermost,* más alto
-motive	-motriz; -motor	*Forma adjetivos denotando* movimiento; propulsión:	*automotive,* automotriz, automotor

	Equivalentes en español	Significados y usos	Ejemplos
-motor	-motor; -motriz	*Forma nombres y adjetivos denotando* movimiento; propulsión:	*vasomotor,* vasomotor *locomotor,* locomotriz
-ness	—	*Añadido a adjetivos forma nombres denotando* cualidad; condición:	*boldness,* audacia; *greatness,* grandeza
		Si el adjetivo termina en -y generalmente la cambia por -i antes de añadir el sufijo:	*dirtiness,* suciedad
-nomy	-nomía	*Forma nombres denotando* 1, conocimiento; ciencia; estudio: 2, distribución; administración; gobierno:	*astronomy,* astronomía *taxonomy,* taxonomía; *economy,* economía; *autonomy,* autonomía
-n't	—	*contr. de* **not:** *A veces, la contracción afecta también la forma del verbo:*	*hasn't* = **has not.** *shan't* = **shall not.**
-ock	—	*Forma diminutivos:*	*hillock,* montículo
-ode	-odo -oda	1, conducto; vía: 2, como; a la manera de:	*cathode,* cátodo *geode,* geoda; *hematode,* hematoda
-oid	-oide	parecido; semejante:	*celluloid,* celuloide
-ol	-ol	*Forma nombres denotando* alcohol *o* derivado de fenol:	*menthol,* mentol
-ole	-ole	*Forma nombres de ciertos compuestos orgánicos:*	*azole,* azole
-oma	-oma	tumor:	*fibroma,* fibroma

	Equivalentes en español	Significados y usos	Ejemplos
-on	-ón	*Forma nombres denotando* **1,** *física,* partículas subatómicas: **2,** *química,* gases inertes: **3,** *Var. de* **-one**:	 *proton,* protón *argon,* argón *silicon,* silicio
-one	-ona; -ón	*química, forma nombres de* cetonas:	*acetone,* acetona; *silicone,* silicón
-onym	-ónimo	*Forma nombres denotando* nombre; apelativo:	*synonym,* sinónimo
-onymous	-ónimo	*Forma adjetivos de los nombres terminados en* **-onym**:	*synonymous,* sinónimo
-onymy	-onimia	*Forma nombres de los adjetivos terminados en* **-onymous**:	*toponymy,* toponimia
-ope	-ope	*Denota* persona con determinado estado *o* defecto del ojo:	*myope,* miope
-opia	-opía	*Indica* estado *o* defecto del ojo:	*myopia,* miopía
-opic	-ope	*Forma adjetivos de los nombres terminados en* **-ope** *u* **-opia**:	*myopic,* miope
-or	-or	*Forma nombres denotando* **1,** agente: **2,** calidad; condición:	 *instructor,* instructor; *ejector,* eyector *horror,* horror; *languor,* langor
-orama	-orama	*Forma nombres denotando* vista; espectáculo:	*diorama,* diorama
-orium	-orio	*Forma nombres indicando* lugar:	*sanatorium,* sanatorio

	Equivalentes en español	Significados y usos	Ejemplos
-ory	-orio	**1,** *Forma adjetivos expresando* característica; relación; pertenencia:	*transitory,* transitorio; *compensatory,* compensatorio
		2, *Forma nombres indicando* lugar:	*refectory,* refectorio
	-orio; -oria	**3,** *Forma nombres indicando* acción; resultado:	*interrogatory,* interrogatorio; *trajectory,* trayectoria
-ose	-oso	**1,** *Forma adjetivos denotando* lleno de; caracterizado por:	*morbose,* morboso; *bellicose,* belicoso
	-osa	**2,** *química,* carbohidrato:	*cellulose,* celulosa
-osis	-osis	**1,** proceso:	*osmosis,* ósmosis
		2, enfermedad:	*neurosis,* neurosis
-osity	-osidad	*Forma nombres correspondientes a adjetivos terminados en* **-ose** *u* **-ous:**	*verbosity,* verbosidad; *generosity,* generosidad
-ous	-oso	*Forma adjetivos denotando* **1,** lleno de; caracterizado por:	*vicious,* vicioso
		2, *química, indicando menor valencia que la expresada por* **-ic:**	*sulfurous,* sulfuroso
-parous	-paro	*Forma adjetivos expresando* que produce; que da a luz:	*oviparous,* ovíparo
-path	-pata	*Forma nombres de personas que corresponden a nombres terminados en* **-pathy:**	*psychopath,* psicópata; *homeopath,* homeópata
-pathic	-pático	*Forma adjetivos de nombres terminados en* **-pathy:**	*psychopathic,* psicopático; *homeopathic,* homeopático

	Equivalentes en español	Significados y usos	Ejemplos
-pathy	-patía	1, sensación; afección; sufrimiento:	*antipathy,* antipatía
		2, enfermedad:	*psychopathy,* psicopatía
		3, tratamiento de enfermedades:	*homeopathy,* homeopatía
-ped; -pede	-pedo	pie; *con determinado número o género de pies o patas:*	*quadruped,* cuadrúpedo; *aliped,* alípedo; *centipede,* ciempiés
-pedia	-pedia	educación; enseñanza:	*encyclopedia,* enciclopedia
-pedic	-pédico	*Forma adjetivos de nombres terminados en* **-pedia**:	*encyclopedic,* enciclopédico
-pedics	-pedia	adiestramiento; corrección:	*orthopedics,* ortopedia
-penny	—	*Acompañando a un numeral indica* 1, precio; valor:	*sixpenny,* seis peniques
		2, tamaño, esp. de clavos:	*tenpenny nail,* clavo tamaño diez
-pepsia	-pepsia	digestión:	*dyspepsia,* dispepsia
-peptic	-péptico	*Forma adjetivos de nombres terminados en* **-pepsia**:	*dyspeptic,* dispéptico
-phage	-fago	devorador:	*xylophage,* xilófago
-phagous	-fago	*Forma adjetivos de nombres terminados en* **-phage** *o* **-phagy**:	*xylophagous,* xilófago; *anthropophagous,* antropófago
-phagy	-fagia	calidad de devorador:	*anthropophagy,* antropofagia
-phane	-fana	*Forma nombres denotando semejanza:*	*cymophane,* cimofana

	Equivalentes en español	Significados y usos	Ejemplos
-phasia	-fasia	*Forma nombres denotando* cierto defecto en el habla:	*aphasia*, afasia
-phile	-filo	que gusta de; que tiene afición por:	*Francophile*, francófilo; *bibliophile*, bibliófilo
-philia	-filia	1, afición; inclinación: 2, tendencia:	*chromatophilia*, cromatofilia *hemophilia*, hemofilia
-philism	-filia	*Forma nombres de los adjetivos terminados en* -phile *o* -philous:	*bibliophilism*, bibliofilia
-philous	-filo	que gusta de:	*photophilous*, fotófilo
-phobe	-fobo	que siente aversión *o* desagrado:	*Anglophobe*, anglófobo
-phobia	-fobia	aversión; desagrado:	*claustrophobia*, claustrofobia
-phone	-fono	sonido:	*audiphone*, audífono
-phonia	-fonía	1, *Forma nombres denotando* trastorno en habla o sonido: 2, *Var. de* -phony	*aphonia*, afonía
-phony	-fonía	*Forma nombres abstractos correspondientes a nombres terminados en* -phone:	*telephony*, telefonía
-phore	-foro	que lleva:	*electrophore*, electróforo
-phyl(l)-	-fila	hoja:	*chlorophyl(l)*, clorofila
-phyllous	-filo	con determinado número *o* clase de hojas:	*chlorophyllous*, clorófilo

	Equivalentes en español	Significados y usos	Ejemplos
-phyte	-fito	*Forma nombres denotando* planta o vegetal con determinado habitat o naturaleza:	*saprophyte*, saprófito
-plane	-plano	avión:	*hydroplane*, hidroplano
-plasia; -plasis	-plasia; -plasis	formación; desarrollo:	*hypoplasia*, hipoplasia; *metaplasis*, metaplasis
-plasm	-plasma	formación:	*protoplasm*, protoplasma
-plast	-plasto	*Forma nombres denotando* estructura de protoplasma:	*chromoplast*, cromoplasto
-plasty	-plastia	*Forma nombres denotando* 1, forma de desarrollo: 2, operación de cirugía plástica:	*dermatoplasty*, dermatoplastia *rhinoplasty*, rinoplastia
-plegy	-plejía	ataque; parálisis:	*hemiplegia*, hemiplejía
-ploid	-ploide	*Forma adjetivos denotando* determinado número de cromosomas:	*diploid*, diploide
-pod	-podo	pie:	*pseudopod*, seudópodo
-polis	-polis	ciudad:	*cosmopolis*, cosmópolis
-proof	—	*Forma nombres y adjetivos denotando* a prueba de:	*waterproof*, impermeable
-pter	-ptero	*Forma nombres denotando* miembro de un orden caracterizado por determinado número o especie de alas:	*hymenopter*, himenóptero

	Equivalentes en español	Significados y usos	Ejemplos
-pterous	-ptero	*Forma adjetivos denotando* determinado número *o* especie de alas:	*hymenopterous,* himenóptero
-'re	—	*Contr. de* **are**:	*they're = they are,* ellos son
-ric	—	*Forma nombres indicando* cargo; jurisdicción:	*bishopric,* obispado
-rrhage; -rhage	-rragia	anormalidad en flujo *o* emisión:	*hemorrhage,* hemorragia
-rrhea; -rrhoea	-rrea	flujo; emisión:	*diarrhea, diarrhoea,* diarrea
-rrhine	-rrino	nariz:	*platyrrhine,* platirrino
-ry	—	*Var. de* **-ery**:	*jewelry,* joyería; *mimicry,* mímica
-'s	—	**1,** *añadido a nombres* indica posesión; pertenencia:	*John's hat,* el sombrero de Juan
		2, *contr. de* **is** *o* **has**:	*He's here = He is here,* Está aquí; *He's finished = He has finished,* Ha terminado
		3, *contr. de* **us**:	*Let's go = Let us go,* Vamos
-s	—	**1,** *Forma la tercera persona singular del presente de indicativo de los verbos:*	*he looks,* él mira
		Tras sibilantes, y algunas veces tras vocal, se convierte en **-es**:	*he crushes,* él tritura; *she goes,* ella va
		2, *Forma el plural de los nombres:*	
		Tras sibilante, y algunas veces tras vocal, se convierte en **-es**:	*birds,* pájaros *fishes,* peces; *tomatoes,* tomates
-saur	-sauro	lagarto:	*dinosaur,* dinosauro

	Equivalentes en español	Significados y usos	Ejemplos
-scope	-scopio	*Forma nombres denotando* instrumento *o* sistema para observar *o* ver:	*fluoroscope,* fluoroscopio
-scopy	-scopia	observación *o* examen por medio de instrumentos ópticos:	*fluoroscopy,* fluoroscopia
-sect	—	cortar; dividir:	*vivisect,* disecar en vivo
-ship	—	*Forma nombres denotando* **1,** cualidad; condición:	*friendship,* amistad; *hardship,* contratiempo
		2, dignidad; oficio:	*governorship,* gobierno, oficio de gobernador
		3, habilidad; capacidad:	*seamanship,* marinería
-sion	-sión	*Forma nombres denotando* acción; resultado; calidad; condición:	*admission,* admisión; *confusion,* confusión
-some	—	**1,** *Forma adjetivos denotando* tendencia; inclinación:	*quarrelsome,* pendenciero
		2, *añadido a numerales indica* grupo:	*threesome,* trío
	-soma	**3,** cuerpo:	*chromosome,* cromosoma
-sophic; -sophical	-sófico	*Forma adjetivos de los nombres terminados en* -sophy:	*philosophic, philosophical,* filosófico
-sophy	-sofía	ciencia; conocimiento:	*philosophy,* filosofía
-sperm	-sperma	esperma:	*gymnosperm,* gimnosperma

	Equivalentes en español	Significados y usos	Ejemplos
-spore	-spora	espora:	*endospore,* endospora
-sporous	-sporo	que tiene esporas:	*gymnosporous,* gimnosporo
-stat	-stato	*Forma nombres denotando* **1,** equilibrio; posición o condición fija: **2,** instrumento que mantiene un sistema en posición o condición fija:	 *aerostat,* aeróstato *thermostat,* termóstato
-static	-stático	*Forma adjetivos que corresponden a nombres terminando en* **-stat** *o* **-statics**:	*photostatic,* fotostático; *hydrostatic,* hidrostático
-statics	-stática	*Forma nombres de* ciencias relacionadas con el equilibrio de fuerzas:	*hydrostatics,* hidrostática
-ster	—	*Forma nombres denotando* personas con determinada condición *o* actividad: *Frecuentemente tiene valor despectivo:*	*punster,* amigo de equívocos; *oldster,* viejo *rhymester,* poetastro
-stress	—	*Forma nombres femeninos denotando* actividad; profesión:	*songstress,* cantante; *seamstress,* costurera
't	—	*Contr. de* **it:**	*'twas not so = it was not so,* no fue así
-taxis	-taxis	colocación; orden:	*thermotaxis,* termotaxis
-technic; -technical	-técnico	*Forma adjetivos correspondientes a los nombres terminados en* **-technics**:	*electrotechnic, electrotechnical,* electrotécnico

	Equivalentes en español	Significados y usos	Ejemplos
-technics	-tecnia	*Forma nombres denotando* artes; ciencias; industrias:	*electrotechnics,* electrotecnia
-teen	—	*Forma los* números del 13 al 19:	*thirteen,* trece; *nineteen,* diez y nueve
-th	—	**1,** *Forma nombres abstractos denotando* estado; cualidad; acción:	*growth,* crecimiento; *warmth,* calor
		2, *Compone* números ordinales:	*fourth,* cuarto
		3, *arcaico; poét.; forma la tercera persona singular del presente:*	*he hath,* él tiene; *he hath spoken,* ha hablado
-therm	-terma	calor:	*isotherm,* isoterma
-thermy	-termia	*Forma nombres abstractos de los nombres terminados en* **-therm**:	*diathermy,* diatermia
-tion	-ción	*Forma nombres abstractos derivados de verbos denotando* acción; estado; resultado:	*conception,* concepción
-tious	-cioso	*Forma adjetivos correspondientes a los nombres terminando en* **-tion**:	*seditious,* sedicioso
-tome	-tomo	instrumento cortante:	*microtome,* micrótomo
-tomy	-tomía	*Forma nombres indicando* **1,** corte; división:	*dichotomy,* dicotomía
		2, operación quirúrgica:	*appendectomy,* apendectomía
-tor	-tor; -dor	*Forma nombres denotando* agente:	*director,* director; *dictator,* dictador

	Equivalentes en español	Significados y usos	Ejemplos
-trix	-triz; -dora; -tora	*Forma el femenino correspondiente a algunos nombres terminados en* **-tor**:	*aviatrix,* aviadora; *executrix,* ejecutora
-trophic	-trófico	*Forma adjetivos correspondientes a nombres terminando en* **-trophy**:	*hypertrophic,* hipertrófico
-trophy	-trofia	nutrición:	*atrophy,* atrofia
-tropic	-trópico	*Forma adjetivos correspondiendo a los nombres terminados en* **-tropismo**:	*heliotropic,* heliotrópico
-tropism	-tropismo	*Forma nombres denotando* tendencia a volverse hacia cierta meta:	*heliotropism,* heliotropismo
-tropy	-tropía	*Forma nombres denotando* cambio; transformación:	*entropy,* entropía
-tude	-tud	*Forma nombres abstractos denotando* cualidad; estado:	*aptitude,* aptitud
-ty	—	**1,** *Forma numerales, indicando* diez veces:	*sixty,* sesenta
	-dad; -tad	**2,** *Forma nombres abstractos denotando* cualidad; estado:	*liberty,* libertad; *beauty,* beldad
-type	-tipo	**1,** forma; tipo:	*prototype,* prototipo
	-tipo	**2,** impresión; reproducción:	*daguerrotype,* daguerrotipo
	-tipia	**3,** imprenta; sistema de imprimir:	*linotype,* linotipia
-typy	-tipia	imprenta; arte de imprimir:	*electrotypy,* electrotipia
-ule	-ula	*Forma diminutivos:*	*sporule,* espórula

	Equivalentes en español	Significados y usos	Ejemplos
-ulent	-ulento	lleno de:	*virulent,* virulento
-ulous	-ulo	*Forma adjetivos denotando* inclinación; tendencia:	*tremulous,* trémulo; *credulous,* crédulo
-ure	-ura	*Forma nombres denotando* 1, acción: 2, agencia; instrumento: 3, condición: 4, resultado: 5, organismo; colectividad:	*censure,* censura *ligature,* ligadura *composure,* compostura *discomfiture,* desconcierto *prefecture,* prefectura
-uria	-uria	orina; condición patológica de la orina:	*albuminuria,* albuminuria
-valent	-valente	*química, forma adjetivos denotando* valencia:	*monovalent,* monovalente
-vora	-voros	*zoöl.; forma nombres de* familias o grupos:	*Carnivora,* carnívoros
-vore	-voro	*Forma nombres de familias o grupos de animales indicando la manera de alimentarse:*	*carnivore,* carnívoro
-vorous	-voro	*Forma adjetivos correspondiendo a nombres terminados en* **-vore** *o* **-vora**:	*carnivorous,* carnívoro
-ward; -wards	—	en dirección de; hacia:	*backward(s),* hacia atrás, atrasado; *eastward(s),* hacia el este
-ways	—	*Forma adverbios denotando* dirección; manera; posición:	*endways,* derecho, de punta

	Equivalentes en español	Significados y usos	Ejemplos
-wise	—	*Forma adverbios denotando* dirección; manera; posición:	*sidewise,* lateralmente, de lado; *clockwise,* según las manillas del reloj
-y	—	**1,** *Forma adjetivos denotando:*	
		a. abundante en; caracterizado por:	*stony,* pedregoso; *juicy,* jugoso
		b. que sugiere o recuerda:	*a doggy smell,* olor a perro
		c. recalcando o intensificando una sensación:	*stilly,* callado, silencioso
		2, *Forma diminutivos cariñosos:*	*Johnny,* Juanito; *pussy,* gatito
		3, *Forma nombres denotando:*	
		a. condición; estado:	*jealousy,* celos; *infancy,* infancia
		b. acción:	*inquiry,* pregunta
-zoa	-zoos	*pl. de.* **-zoon**:	*Protozoa,* protozoos
-zoic	-zoico	*Forma adjetivos denotando*	
		1, animal; vida animal:	*phanerozoic,* fanerozoico
		2, *geol.* era *(de determinados fósiles):*	*Mesozoic,* mesozoico
-zoon	-zoo	animal:	*spermatozoon,* espermatozoo

NOMBRES GEOGRÁFICOS—
GEOGRAPHICAL NAMES

(L) = lengua (N) = habitante; ciudadano; indígena; residente

CONTINENTES	Derivados	CONTINENTS	Derivatives
África	africano	Africa	African
América	americano	America	American
América Central; Centroamérica	centroamericano	Central America	Central American
Antártica	antártico	Antarctica	Antarctic
Asia	asiático	Asia	Asian; Asiatic
Eurasia	Eurasiático	Eurasia	Eurasian
Europa	europeo	Europe	European
Norteamérica; América del Norte	norteamericano	North America	North American
Sudamérica; América del Sur	sudamericano	South America	South American

PAÍSES, REGIONES	Derivados	COUNTRIES, REGIONS	Derivatives
Adén		Aden	
Afganistán	afgano	Afghanistan	Afghan
África del Sur; República Sudafricana	sudafricano	South Africa	South African
Albania	albanés (-esa)	Albania	Albanian
Alemania	alemán (-ana)	Germany	German
Alemania Occidental		West Germany	
Alemania Oriental		East Germany	
Alto Volta (Burkina Faso)	voltense	Upper Volta (Burkina Faso)	Upper Voltan
América Latina; Latinoamérica	latinoamericano	Latin America	Latin American
Andalucía	andaluz	Andalusia	Andalusian
Andorra	andorrano	Andorra	Andorran
Angola	angoleño; angolés (-esa)	Angola	Angolan
Antigua		Antigua	
Arabia	árabe	Arabia	Arabian
Arabia Saudita	árabe saudita	Saudia Arabia	Saudi; Saudi Arabian
Argelia	argelino	Algeria	Algerian

PAÍSES, REGIONES	Derivados	COUNTRIES, REGIONS	Derivatives
Argentina	argentino	Argentina	Argentinian; Argentine
Armenia	armenio	Armenia	Armenian
Asia Menor		Asia Minor	
Australia	australiano	Australia	Australian
Austria	austríaco	Austria	Austrian
Austrolasia		Australasia	Australasian
Azerbaiján	azerbaijaní; azerbeyaní	Azerbaijan	Azerbaijani
Bahamas	bahamés (-esa)	Bahamas	Bahamian
Bahrein		Bahrain; Bahrein	
Bangladesh		Bangladesh	Bangladeshi
Barbados	barbadense	Barbados	Barbadian
Baviera		Bavaria	Bavarian
Bélgica	belga	Belgium	Belgian
Belice		Belize	Belizan
Benín		Benin	
Besarabia		Bessarabia	Bessarabian
Bielorusia	bielorruso	Belarus	Belorussian
Birmania	birmano	Burma (Myanmar)	Burman (N); Burmese (L)
Bohemia	boemio	Bohemia	Bohemian
Bolivia	boliviano	Bolivia	Bolivian
Borgoña	borgoñón (-ñona)	Burgundy	Burgundian
Bosnia		Bosnia	Bosnian
Botswana		Botswana	
Brasil	brasileño	Brazil	Brazilian
Bretaña	bretón (-ona)	Brittany	Breton
Brunei		Brunei	
Bulgaria	búlgaro	Bulgaria	Bulgarian
Burkina Faso		Burkina Faso	
Burundi	burundés (-esa)	Burundi	Burundian
Bután	butanés (-esa)	Bhutan	Bhutanese
Cachemira		Kashmir	
Camboya; Kampuchea	camboyano	Cambodia; Kampuchea	Cambodian
Camerún	camerunés (-esa); camerunense	Cameroon	Cameroonian
Canadá	canadiense	Canada	Canadian
Castilla	castellano	Castile	Castilian
Cataluña	catalán	Catalonia	Catalonian
Ceilán	cingalés (-esa)	Ceylon (Sri Lanka)	Ceylonese; Sin(g)halese
Cerdeña	sardo	Sardinia	Sardinian
Chad	chadiano	Chad	Chadian
Checoslovaquia	checoslovaco	Czechoslovakia	Czechoslovakian
Chile	chileno	Chile	Chilean
China	chino	China	Chinese

PAÍSES, REGIONES	Derivados	COUNTRIES, REGIONS	Derivatives
Chipre	chipriota	Cyprus	Cyprian; Cypriote
Colombia	colombiano	Colombia	Colombian
Congo	congolés (-esa); congoleño	Congo	Congolese
Córcega	corso	Corsica	Corsican
Corea	coreano	Korea	Korean
Corea del Norte	norcoreano	North Korea	North Korean
Corea del Sur	surcoreano	South Korea	South Korean
Cornualles	córnico	Cornwall	Cornish
Costa Rica	costarriqueño; costarricense	Costa Rica	Costa Rican
Crimea		Crimea	Crimean
Croacia	croata	Croatia	Croatian
Cuba	cubano	Cuba	Cuban
Dalmacia	dálmata	Dalmatia	Dalmatian
Dinamarca	danés (-esa)	Denmark	Danish (L); Dane (N)
Djibouti		Djibouti	
Dominica		Dominica	
Ecuador	ecuatoriano	Ecuador	Ecuadorian (-ean)
Egipto	egipcio	Egypt	Egyptian
El Salvador	salvadoreño	El Salvador	Salvadorian (-ean)
Emiratos Árabes Unidos		United Arab Emirates	
Eritrea		Eritrea	Eritrean
Escandinavia	escandinavo	Scandinavia	Scandinavian
Escocia	escocés (-esa)	Scotland	Scot (N); Scotch; Scottish (L)
Eslovaquia	eslovaco	Slovakia	Slovakian
Eslovenia	esloveno	Slovenia	Slovene; Slovenian
España	español (-ola)	Spain	Spaniard (N); Spanish (L)
Estados Unidos de América	norteamericano	United States of America	American
Estonia	estonio	Est(h)onia	Est(h)onian
Etiopía	etíope; etiope	Ethiopia	Ethiopian
Fenicia	fenicio	Phoenicia	Phoenician
Fidji		Fiji	Fijian
Filipinas	filipino	Philippines	Filipino; Filipine
Finlandia	finlandés (-esa)	Finland	Finn (N); Finnish (L)
Flandes	flamenco	Flanders	Fleming (N); Flemish (L)
Francia	francés (-esa)	France	French
Gabón	gabonés (-esa)	Gabon	Gabonese
Gales	galés (-esa)	Wales	Welsh

PAÍSES, REGIONES	Derivados	COUNTRIES, REGIONS	Derivatives
Galicia	gallego	Galicia	Galician
Gambia	gambiano	Gambia	Gambian
Georgia		Georgia	Georgian
Ghana	ganés (-esa)	Ghana	Ghanian; Ghanaian
Gibraltar		Gibraltar	
Gran Bretaña	británico	Great Britain	British
Grecia	griego	Greece	Greek; Grecian
Grenada; Granada		Grenada	Grenadian
Groenlandia	groenlandés (-esa)	Greenland	Greenlander (N)
Guatemala	guatemalteco	Guatemala	Guatemalan
Guinea	guineo; guineano	Guinea	Guinean
Guinea Ecuatorial	ecuatoguineano	Equatorial Guinea	
Guinea-Bissau		Guinea-Bissau	
Guyana	guyanés (-esa)	Guyana	Guyanian; Guyanese
Haití	haitiano	Haiti	Haitian
Holanda	holandés (-esa)	Holland	Dutch
Honduras	hondureño	Honduras	Honduran
Hong Kong		Hong Kong	
Hungría	húngaro	Hungary	Hungarian
Iberia	ibérico	Iberia	Iberian
India	indio; hindú	India	Indian
Indochina	indochino (N)	Indochina	Indochinese
Indonesia	indonesio; indonésico	Indonesia	Indonesian
Inglaterra	inglés (-esa)	England	English
Irán	iraní; iranio	Iran	Iranian
Iraq; Irak	iraquí; irakí	Iraq; Irak	Iraqi; Iraki
Irlanda	irlandés (-esa)	Ireland	Irish
Irlanda del Norte		Northern Ireland	
Islandia	islandés (-esa)	Iceland	Icelandic (L); Icelander (N)
Islas Británicas	británico	British Isles	British
Israel	israelí; israelita	Israel	Israeli
Italia	italiano	Italy	Italian
Jamaica	jamaiquino; jamaicano	Jamaica	Jamaican
Japón	japonés (-esa)	Japan	Japanese
Jordania	jordano	Jordan	Jordanian
Kenya; Kenia	keniano	Kenya	Kenyan
Kiribati		Kiribati	
Kuwait; Koweit	kuwaití; koweití	Kuwait	Kuwaiti
La Costa de Marfil		Ivory Coast	
Labrador	labradoresco	Labrador	Labradoran

PAÍSES, REGIONES	Derivados	COUNTRIES, REGIONS	Derivatives
Laos	laosiano	Laos	Laotian
Latvia	latvio; letón	Latvia	Latvian; Lett (N); Lettish (L)
Lesotho		Lesotho	
Líbano	libanés (-esa)	Lebanon	Lebanese
Liberia	liberiano	Liberia	Liberian
Libia	libio	Libya	Libyan
Liechtenstein		Liechtenstein	
Lituania	lituano	Lithuania	Lithuanian
Luxemburgo	luxemburgués (-esa)	Luxemb(o)urg	Luxemb(o)urgian
Macao		Macao	
Macedonia	macedón; macedonio; macedónico	Macedonia	Macedonian
Malasia	malasio	Malaysia	Malaysian
Malawi	malawiano	Malawi	Malawian
Maldivas	maldivo	Maldives	Maldive
Malí	maliense	Mali	Malian
Malta	maltés (-esa)	Malta	Maltese
Manchuria	manchú; manchuriano	Manchuria	Manchu; Manchurian
Marruecos	marroquí	Morocco	Moroccan
Mauricio	mauriciano	Mauritius	Mauritian
Mauritania	mauritano	Mauritania	Mauritanian
Mesopotamia	mesopotámico	Mesopotamia	Mesopotamian
México	mexicano	Mexico	Mexican
Micronesia	micronesio	Micronesia	Micronesian
Mónaco	monegasco	Monaco	Monacan
Mongolia	mongol	Mongolia	Mongol (N); Mongolian (L)
Mozambique	mozambiqueño	Mozambique	Mozambican
Namibia	namibio	Namibia	Namibian
Nauru	nauruano	Nauru	Nauruan
Nepal	nepalés (-esa); nepalí	Nepal	Nepalese
Nicaragua	nicaragüense	Nicaragua	Nicaraguan
Níger	nigerio; nigerino	Niger	
Nigeria	nigeriano; nigerio	Nigeria	Nigerian
Normandía	normando	Normandy	Norman
Noruega	noruego	Norway	Norwegian
Nueva Guinea		New Guinea	
Nueva Inglaterra		New England	New Englander (N)
Nueva Zelandia	neozelandés (-esa)	New Zealand	New Zealander (N)
Oceanía	oceánico	Oceania	Oceanian
Omán	omaní	Oman	Omani
Países Bajos		Benelux	

PAÍSES, REGIONES	Derivados	COUNTRIES, REGIONS	Derivatives
Países Bajos	neerlandés (-esa)	Netherlands	Netherlander (N)
Pakistán; Paquistán	pakistaní; paquistaní; pakistano; paquistano	Pakistan	Pakistani
Palestina	palestino	Palestine	Palestinian
Panamá	panameño	Panama	Panamanian
Papua-Nueva Guinea		Papua New Guinea	
Paraguay	paraguayo	Paraguay	Paraguayan
Patagonia		Patagonia	Patagonian
Pendjab	penjabo; penjabi	Punjab	Punjabi
Persia	persa (N,L); pérsico (L); persiano (N)	Persia	Persian
Perú	peruano	Peru	Peruvian
Polinesia	polinesio	Polynesia	Polynesian
Polonia	polonés (-esa); polaco	Poland	Pole (N); Polish (L)
Portugal	portugués (-esa)	Portugal	Portuguese
Prusia	prusiano	Prussia	Prussian
Puerto Rico	puertorriqueño	Puerto Rico	Puerto Rican
Qatar; Katar		Qatar	
Reino Unido	británico	United Kingdom	British
República Centroafricana		Central African Republic	
República de Cabo Verde		Cape Verde, Republic of	
República de los Comores		Comoros, Republic of the	
República de Seychelles		Seychelles	
República de Sierra Leona	sierraleonés (-esa)	Sierra Leone	
República Dominicana	dominicano	Dominican Republic	Dominican
República Malgache	malgache	Malgasy Republic	
Ruanda	ruandés (-esa)	Rwanda	Rwandan
Rumania	rumano	Romania; Rumania	Romanian; Rumanian
Rusia	ruso	Russia	Russian
Samoa	samoano	Samoa	Samoan
San Marino	sanmarinense	San Marino	San Marinese
Senegal	senegalés (-esa)	Senegal	Senegalese
Serbia; Servia	servio; servocroata (L)	Serbia	Serbian; Serbo-Croatian (L)
Siam	siamés (-esa)	Siam	Siamese
Siberia	siberiano	Siberia	Siberian
Sicilia	siciliano	Sicily	Sicilian

PAÍSES, REGIONES	Derivados	COUNTRIES, REGIONS	Derivatives
Singapur	singapurense	Singapore	Singaporean
Siria	sirio	Syria	Syrian
Somalia	somalí	Somalia	Somali; Somalian
Sri Lanka	cingalés (-esa); ceilandés (-esa)	Sri Lanka	Sri Lankan
Sudán	sudanés (-esa)	Sudan	Sudanese
Suecia	sueco	Sweden	Swede (N); Swedish (L)
Suiza	suizo	Switzerland	Swiss
Suriname	surinamés (-esa)	Surinam	Surinamese
Swazilandia	swazi; swazilandés (-esa)	Swaziland	Swazi
Tailandia	tailandés (-esa)	Thailand	Thai
Taiwán	taiwanés (-esa)	Taiwan	Taiwanese
Tanzanía	tanzaniano	Tanzania	Tanzanian
Terranova		Newfoundland	
Tibet	tibetano	Tibet	Tibetan
Tirol	tirolés (-esa)	Tyrol	Tyrolean
Togo	togolés (-esa)	Togo	Togolese
Tonga	tongano	Tonga	Tongan
Trinidad y Tobago		Trinidad and Tobago	
Túnez	tunecino	Tunisia	Tunisian
Turquía	turco	Turkey	Turk (N); Turkish (L)
Tuvalu	tuvaluano	Tuvalu	Tuvaluan
Ucrania	ucranio; ucraniano	Ukraine	Ukrainian
Uganda	ugandés (-esa)	Uganda	Ugandan
Unión Soviética	soviético	Soviet Union	Soviet
Uruguay	uruguayo	Uruguay	Uruguayan
Vanuatu		Vanuatu	
Vaticano		Vatican	
Venezuela	venezolano	Venezuela	Venezuelan
Viet Nam	vietnamita; vietnamés (-esa)	Vietnam	Vietnamese
Yemen	yemení; yemenita	Yemen	Yemeni; Yemenite
Yucatán		Yucatan	
Yugoslavia	yugoslavo	Yugoslavia	Yugoslav (N); Yugoslavian
Yukón		Yukon	
Zaire	zairense	Zaire	Zairean; Zairian
Zambia	zambiano; zambés (-esa)	Zambia	Zambian
Zimbabwe	simbabwense	Zimbabwe	Zimbabwean

CIUDADES	Derivados	CITIES	Derivatives
Addis Abeda		Addis Ababa, Ethiopia	
Ahmadabad		Ahmadabad, India	
Alejandría		Alexandria, Egypt	
Argel	argelino	Algiers	Algerian
Amsterdam		Amsterdam, Holland	
Ánkara		Ankara, Turkey	
Atenas		Athens, Greece	Athenian
Bagdad		Baghdad, Iraq	
Bangalore		Bangalore, India	
Bangkok		Bangkok, Thailand	
Barcelona		Barcelona, Spain	
Beijing (Pekín)		Beijing (Peking), China	
Beirut		Beirut, Lebanon	
Belgrado		Belgrade, Yugoslavia (Serbia)	
Belo Horizonte		Belo Horizonte, Brazil	
Berlín		Berlin, Germany	Berliner (N)
Belén		Bethlehem, Israel	
Bogotá	bogotano	Bogotá, Colombia	
Bombay		Bombay, India	
Boston		Boston, USA	Bostonian
Bruselas		Brussels, Belgium	
Bucarest		Bucharest, Romania	
Budapest		Budapest, Hungary	
Buenos Aires	porteño; bonairense	Buenos Aires, Argentina	
El Cairo		Cairo, Egypt	
Calcuta		Calcutta, India	
Cantón		Canton (Guangzhou), China	
Caracas		Caracas, Venezuela	
Casablanca		Casablanca, Morocco	
Chengdu		Chengdu, China	
Chicago		Chicago, USA	Chicagoan

CIUDADES	Derivados	CITIES	Derivatives
Chongqing		Chongqing; Chungking, China	
Copenhague		Copenhagen, Denmark	
Dallas		Dallas, USA	
Damasco		Damascus, Syria	
Delhi		Delhi, India	
Detroit		Detroit, USA	
Dacca		Dhaka, Bangladesh	
Edimburgo		Edinburgh, Scotland	
Essen		Essen, Germany	
Estocolmo		Stockholm, Sweden	
Filadelfia		Philadelphia, USA	
Florencia	florentino	Florence, Italy	Florentine
Ginebra		Geneva, Switzerland	
Guadalajara		Guadalajara, Spain; Mexico	
Guangzhou		Guangzhou (Canton), China	
La Haya		Hague (The), Holland	
Hamburgo (N)	hamburgués (-esa)	Hamburg, Germany	
Harbín; Jarbín		Harbin, China	
La Habana	habanero	Havana, Cuba	habanero
Ho Chi Minh		Ho Chi Minh City (Saigon), Vietnam	
Hongkong		Hong Kong	
Houston		Houston, USA	
Haiderabad		Hyderabad, India	
Islamabad		Islamabad, Pakistan	
Estambul		Istanbul, Turkey	
Jakarta		Jakarta, Indonesia	
Jerusalén		Jerusalem, Israel	
Karachi		Karachi, Pakistan	
Kiev		Kiev, Ukraine	
Kinshasa		Kinshasa, Zaire	
Kobe		Kobe, Japan	
Kyoto		Kyoto, Japan	
Lagos		Lagos, Nigeria	

CIUDADES	Derivados	CITIES	Derivatives
Lahore		Lahore, Pakistan	
Leningrado		Leningrad, Russia	
Lima		Lima, Peru	
Lisboa		Lisbon, Portugal	
Londres	londinense	London, England	Londoner (N)
Los Ángeles		Los Angeles, USA	Angeleno (N)
Madrás		Madras, India	
Madrid	madrileño	Madrid, Spain	Madrilene
Manchester		Manchester, England	
Manila		Manila, Philippines	
Marsella		Marseille(s), France	
La Meca		Mecca, Saudi Arabia	
Melbourne		Melbourne, Australia	
México, D.F.		Mexico City	
Milán	milanés	Milan, Italy	Milanese
Monterrey		Monterrey, Mexico	
Montreal		Montreal, Canada	
Moscú	moscovita	Moscow, Russia	Muscovite
Munich		Munich, Germany	
Nagoya		Nagoya, Japan	
Nankín		Nanking, China	
Nápoles	napolitano	Naples, Italy	Neapolitan
Nueva Delhi		New Delhi, India	
Nueva York	neoyorquino	New York, USA	New Yorker (N)
Odesa		Odessa, Ukraine	
Osaka		Osaka, Japan	
Oslo		Oslo, Norway	
Ottawa		Ottawa, Canada	
París	parisiense	Paris, France	Parisian
Pequín, Pekín		Peking (Beijing), China	
Petrogrado, Rusia		Petrograd, Russia	
Poona		Poona, India	
Puerto Príncipe		Port-au-Prince, Haiti	
Porto Alegre		Porto Alegre, Brazil	

CIUDADES	Derivados	CITIES	Derivatives
Praga		Prague, Czechoslovakia	
Pusan		Pusan, So. Korea	
Rangún		Rangoon (Yaugôn), Myanmar	
Río de Janeiro		Rio de Janeiro, Brazil	
Riyadh		Riyadh, Saudi Arabia	
Roma	romano	Rome, Italy	Roman
Saigón		Saigon (Ho Chi Minh), Vietnam	
Salvador		Salvador, Brazil	
San Francisco		San Francisco, USA	
San Petersburgo, Rusia		St. Petersburg, Russia	
Santiago de Chile		Santiago, Chile	
São Paulo		São Paulo, Brazil	
Sarajevo		Sarajevo, Bosnia	
Seúl		Seoul, So.Korea	
Sevilla	sevillano	Seville, Spain	
Shangai		Shanghai, China	
Shenyang		Shenyang, China	
Singapur		Singapore	
Sofía		Sofia, Bulgaria	
Surabaya		Surabaya, Indonesia	
Sidney		Sydney, Australia	
Taegu		Taegu, So.Korea	
Taipei		Taipei, Taiwan	
Tanger		Tangiers, Morocco	
Tashkent		Tashkent, Uzbekistan	
Teherán		Tehran, Iran	
Tianjin		Tianjin (Tientsin), China	
Tokio		Tokyo, Japan	
Toronto		Toronto, Canada	
Troya	troyano	Troy	Trojan
Túnez		Tunis, Tunisia	
Venecia	veneciano	Venice, Italy	Venetian
Viena	vienés (-esa)	Vienna, Austria	Viennese
Varsovia		Warsaw, Poland	

CIUDADES	Derivados	CITIES	Derivatives
Wáshington		Washington, USA	
Wuhan		Wuhan, China	
Yaugôn		Yaugôn, Myanmar	
Yokohama		Yokohama, Japan	
Zagreb		Zagreb, Serbia	

ISLAS

ISLANDS

Antigua	Antigua
Antillas	Antilles
Antillas Mayores	Greater Antilles
Antillas Menores	Lesser Antilles
Aruba	Aruba
Azores	Azores
Bali	Bali
Bermuda	Bermuda
Borneo	Bornco
Célebes	Celebes
Comores	Comoros
Corfú	Corfu
Creta	Crete
Curaçao	Curaçao
Groenlandia	Greenland
Guadalcanal	Guadalcanal
Guadalupe	Guadeloupe
Guam	Guam
Hispaniola	Hispaniola
Hokkaido	Hokkaido
Hondo	Honshu
I. De Pascua	Easter I.
I. de Victoria	Victoria I.
I. Príncipe Eduardo	Prince Edward I.
I. Vancouver	Vancouver I.
I. Zanzíbar	Zanzibar
Indias Occidentales (Antillas)	West Indies (Antilles)
Indias Orientales	East Indies
Is. Aleutianas	Aleutian Is.
Is. Baleares	Balearic Is.
Is. Cabo Verde	Cape Verde Is.
Is. Canarias	Canary Is.
Is. Carolinas	Caroline Is.
Is. de Barlovento	Windward Is.
Is. de la Mancha	Channel Is.
Is. de Sotavento	Leeward Is.
Is. Feroé	Faroe Is.
Is. Galápagos	Galapagos Is.
Is. Hébridas	Hebrides
Is. Maldivas	Maldive Is.

ISLAS	ISLANDS
Is. Malvinas	Falkland Is.
Is. Marianas	Mariana Is.
Is. Marquesas	Marquesas Is.
Is. Marshall	Marshall Is.
Is. Orcadas	Orkney Is.
Is. Ryukyu	Ryukyu Is.
Is. Salomón	Solomon Is.
Is. Shetland	Shetland Is.
Is. Vírgenes	Virgin Is.
Isla de Man	Man, Isle of
Islandia	Iceland
Iwo Jima	Iwo Jima
Java	Java
Kiushiu	Kyushu
Leyte	Leyte
Long Island	Long I.
Luzón	Luzon
Madagascar	Madagascar
Maderas	Made(i)ra Is.
Mallorca	Majorca
Martinica	Martinique
Menorca	Minorca
Mindanao	Mindanao
Okinawa-Jima	Okinawa
Reunión	Réunion
Rodas	Rhodes
Sajalín	Sakhalin
Shikoku	Shikoku
Sumatra	Sumatra
Tahití	Tahiti
Tasmania	Tasmania
Terranova	Newfoundland
Tierra de Baffín	Baffin I.
Tierra del Fuego	Tierra del Fuego
Timor	Timor

OCÉANOS	OCEANS
Océano Antártico	Antarctic Ocean
Océano Ártico	Arctic Ocean
Océano Atlántico	Atlantic Ocean
Océano Índico	Indian Ocean
Océano Pacífico	Pacific Ocean

MARES	SEAS
Lago Aral	Aral Sea
Mar Adriático	Adriatic Sea
Mar Amarillo	Yellow Sea
Mar Arábigo	Arabian Sea
Mar Báltico	Baltic Sea
Mar Blanco	White Sea

MARES	SEAS
Mar Caribe; Mar de las Antillas	Caribbean Sea
Mar Caspio	Caspian Sea
Mar de Azov	Azov, Sea of
Mar de Bering	Bering Sea
Mar de Irlanda	Irish Sea
Mar de los Sargazos	Sargasso Sea
Mar de Okhotsk	Okhotsk, Sea of
Mar del Japón	Japan, Sea of
Mar del Norte	North Sea
Mar Egeo	Aegean Sea
Mar Mediterráneo	Mediterranean Sea
Mar Meridional de la China	South China Sea
Mar Muerto	Dead Sea
Mar Negro	Black Sea
Mar Oriental de la China	East China Sea
Mar Rojo	Red Sea
Mar Tasmán; Mar de Tasmania	Tasman Sea

LAGOS	LAKES
Alberto Nyanza	Albert Nyanza
Baikal	Baikal
Chad	Chad
Erie	Erie
Gran Lago de los Esclavos	Great Slave
Gran Lago de los Osos	Great Bear
Gran Lago Salado	Great Salt
Hurón	Huron
Ladoga	Ladoga
Lago Léman; Lago de Ginebra	Geneva
Los Grandes Lagos	Great Lakes
Michigan	Michigan
Nyassa	Nyassa
Onega	Onega
Ontario	Ontario
Superior	Superior
Tanganika	Tanganyika
Titicaca	Titicaca
Victoria Nyanza	Victoria Nyanza

RÍOS	RIVERS
R. Amarillo	Yellow
R. Amazonas	Amazon
R. Amur	Amur
R. Columbia	Columbia
R. Congo	Congo
R. Danubio	Danube
R. Delaware	Delaware
R. Dniéper	Dnieper
R. Dniéster	Dniester
R. Don	Don

RÍOS	RIVERS
R. Elba	Elbe
R. Éufrates	Euphrates
R. Ganges	Ganges
R. Grande	Rio Grande
R. Huang Ho	Huang Ho
R. Hudson	Hudson
R. Indus *o* Singh	Indus
R. Irauadi	Irawaddy
R. Irtish	Irtysh
R. Jordán	Jordan
R. Lena	Lena
R. Loira	Loire
R. Mackenzie	Mackenzie
R. Mekong	Mekong
R. Misisipí	Mississippi
R. Misuri	Missouri
R. Níger	Niger
R. Nilo	Nile
R. Ob *u* Obi	Ob
R. Oder	Oder
R. Ohio	Ohio
R. Orinoco	Orinoco
R. Paraná	Paraná
R. Po	Po
R. Potomac	Potomac
R. Rin	Rhine
R. Ródano	Rhône
R. San Lorenzo	St. Lawrence
R. Sena	Seine
R. Susquehanna	Susquehanna
R. Támesis	Thames
R. Tigris	Tigris
R. Ural	Ural
R. Vístula	Vistula
R. Volga	Volga
R. Volta	Volta
R. Yang Tse Kiang *o* Azul	Yangtze
R. Yenisei	Yenisei
R. Yukón	Yukon
R. Zambeze	Zambezi; Zambesi

GOLFOS, BAHÍAS, ESTRECHOS, CANALES	GULFS, BAYS, STRAITS, CHANNELS, CANALS
Bahía *o* Mar de Hudson	Hudson Bay
Bósforo	Bosporus
Canal de Florida	Florida Strait
Canal de la Mancha	English Channel
Canal de Panamá	Panama Canal
Canal de Suez	Suez Canal
Estrecho de Bering	Bering Strait
Estrecho de Gibraltar	Gibraltar, Strait of

GOLFOS, BAHÍAS, ESTRECHOS, CANALES	GULFS, BAYS, STRAITS, CHANNELS, CANALS
Estrecho de Magallanes	Magellan, Strait of
Golfo de Adén	Aden, Gulf of
Golfo de Bengala	Bengal, Bay of
Golfo de California; Mar de Cortez	California, Gulf of
Golfo de México	Mexico, Gulf of
Golfo de San Lorenzo	St. Lawrence, Gulf of
Golfo de Vizcaya	Biscay, Bay of
Golfo Pérsico	Persian Gulf
Vía Marítima San Lorenzo	St. Lawrence Seaway

SIERRAS, CORDILLERAS	MOUNTAIN RANGES
Alpes	Alps Mts., Europe
Balcanes	Balkans, Europe
C. de las Cascadas	Cascade Range, USA-Canada
C. de los Andes	Andes Mts., South America
C. de los Himalaya	Himalaya Mts., Asia
Montañas Rocosas	Rocky Mts., USA
Mtes. Adirondacks	Adirondack Mts., USA
Mtes. Allegheny	Allegheny Mts., USA
Mtes. Apalaches	Appalachian Mts., USA
Mtes. Cárpatos	Carpathian Mts., Europe
Mtes. Catskills	Catskill Mts., USA
Mtes. Caucaso	Caucasus Mts., Europe
Mtes. Pirineos	Pyrenees Mts., Europe
Mtes. San Elías	St. Elias Mts., Alaska-Yukon
Mtes. Urales	Ural Mts., Russia-Siberia
Sierra Nevada	Sierra Nevada, USA

PICOS	MOUNTAIN PEAKS
Aconcagua	Aconcagua, Argentina (Andes)
Elbrus	Elbrus, Europe (Caucasus)
Etna	Etna, Sicily
Everest	Everest, Nepal-Tibet (Himalayas)
Fujiyama	Fujiyama, Japan
Kilimanjaro	Kilimanjaro, Tanzania
Logan	Logan, Canada (St. Elias Mts.)
Matterhorn; Cervino	Matterhorn, Switzerland (Alps)
Mauna Loa	Mauna Loa, Hawaii
McKinley	McKinley, Alaska
Monte Blanco	Mont Blanc, France-Italy (Alps)
Monte Rosa	Monte Rosa, Switzerland (Alps)
Orizaba	Orizaba, Mexico
Pikes Peak	Pikes Peak, USA (Rockies)
Popocatépetl	Popocatepetl, Mexico
Rainier	Rainier, USA (Cascades)
Shasta	Shasta, USA (Cascades)
Sinaí	Sinai, Egypt
Vesubio	Vesuvius, Italy
Whitney	Whitney, USA (Sierra Nevada)